National Security Law

ASPEN CASEBOOK SERIES

National Security Law

Fifth Edition

Stephen Dycus
Professor of Law
Vermont Law School

Arthur L. Berney
Professor Emeritus
Boston College

William C. Banks
Director, Institute for National Security and Counterterrorism (INSCT)
Board of Advisors Distinguished Professor
Syracuse University

Peter Raven-Hansen
Glen Earl Weston Research Professor of Law
Co-director, National Security and U.S. Foreign Relations Law Program
George Washington University

Wolters Kluwer
Law & Business

Published by Wolters Kluwer Law & Business in New York.

Wolters Kluwer Law & Business serves customers worldwide with CCH, Aspen Publishers, and Kluwer Law International products. (www.wolterskluwerlb.com)

To contact Customer Service, e-mail customer.service@wolterskluwer.com, call 1-800-234-1660, fax 1-800-901-9075, or mail correspondence to:

Wolters Kluwer Law & Business
Attn: Order Department
PO Box 990
Frederick, MD 21705

Printed in the United States of America.

1 2 3 4 5 6 7 8 9 0

ISBN 978-0-7355-9475-3

Library of Congress Cataloging-in-Publication Data

Dycus, Stephen.
    National security law / Stephen Dycus, Arthur L. Berney, William C. Banks. — 5th ed.
        p. cm.
    Rev. ed. of: National security law / Stephen Dycus . . . [et al.]. 4th ed. c2007.
    Includes bibliographical references and index.
    ISBN 978-0-7355-9475-3
    1. National security — Law and legislation — United States. I. Berney, Arthur L., 1930-
II. Banks, William C. III. National security law. IV. Title.
    KF4651.N377 2011
    343.73'01 — dc23

                                                                                    2011028319

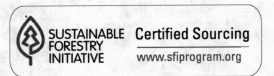

About Wolters Kluwer Law & Business

Wolters Kluwer Law & Business is a leading global provider of intelligent information and digital solutions for legal and business professionals in key specialty areas, and respected educational resources for professors and law students. Wolters Kluwer Law & Business connects legal and business professionals as well as those in the education market with timely, specialized authoritative content and information-enabled solutions to support success through productivity, accuracy and mobility.

Serving customers worldwide, Wolters Kluwer Law & Business products include those under the Aspen Publishers, CCH, Kluwer Law International, Loislaw, Best Case, ftwilliam.com and MediRegs family of products.

CCH products have been a trusted resource since 1913, and are highly regarded resources for legal, securities, antitrust and trade regulation, government contracting, banking, pension, payroll, employment and labor, and healthcare reimbursement and compliance professionals.

Aspen Publishers products provide essential information to attorneys, business professionals and law students. Written by preeminent authorities, the product line offers analytical and practical information in a range of specialty practice areas from securities law and intellectual property to mergers and acquisitions and pension/benefits. Aspen's trusted legal education resources provide professors and students with high-quality, up-to-date and effective resources for successful instruction and study in all areas of the law.

Kluwer Law International products provide the global business community with reliable international legal information in English. Legal practitioners, corporate counsel and business executives around the world rely on Kluwer Law journals, looseleafs, books, and electronic products for comprehensive information in many areas of international legal practice.

Loislaw is a comprehensive online legal research product providing legal content to law firm practitioners of various specializations. Loislaw provides attorneys with the ability to quickly and efficiently find the necessary legal information they need, when and where they need it, by facilitating access to primary law as well as state-specific law, records, forms and treatises.

Best Case Solutions is the leading bankruptcy software product to the bankruptcy industry. It provides software and workflow tools to flawlessly streamline petition preparation and the electronic filing process, while timely incorporating ever-changing court requirements.

ftwilliam.com offers employee benefits professionals the highest quality plan documents (retirement, welfare and non-qualified) and government forms (5500/PBGC, 1099 and IRS) software at highly competitive prices.

MediRegs products provide integrated health care compliance content and software solutions for professionals in healthcare, higher education and life sciences, including professionals in accounting, law and consulting.

Wolters Kluwer Law & Business, a division of Wolters Kluwer, is headquartered in New York. Wolters Kluwer is a market-leading global information services company focused on professionals.

To our teachers

Summary of Contents

Contents

CHAPTER 4. *The President's National Security Powers*   52

CHAPTER 5. *Congress's National Security Powers*   90

PART II.   INTERNATIONAL LAW AS "OUR LAW"   161

Preface

As we approach the tenth anniversary of the terrorist attacks on the World Trade Center and the Pentagon on September 11, 2001, the field of National Security Law continues to evolve rapidly. After an aggressive assertion of executive power by the Bush administration in the first few years after 9/11, we saw a push back by the courts (on surveillance, detention, and military commissions), to some extent by Congress (on coercive interrogation), and eventually by the voters. But the Obama administration has changed the rhetoric more than the content of counterterrorism policies — continuing to rely heavily on military force, indefinite detention, military commission trials, expansive electronic surveillance programs, and frequent use of the state secrets privilege to restrict access to national security information in litigation. Nevertheless, these judicial challenges, legislative initiatives, and executive reforms have produced more durable structures, processes, and institutions for counterterrorism, if not for the field generally. The Fifth Edition of National Security Law reflects these trends.

The Framework chapters in Part I remain the core of the book, with materials on the President, Congress, and the courts sharpened and updated. The chapter on the judicial role in national security features two new cases — one on the political question doctrine and a second on the state secrets privilege, an increasingly common basis for judicial avoidance.

Mindful of the growing importance of International Law as "our law" in the national security field, we have created a new Part II that addresses not only the processes for incorporation of international law into our own, but also the content of the law concerning resort to war (*jus ad bellum*) and law concerning the conduct of war (*jus in bello*). These new materials are referred to repeatedly in later chapters.

Part III, on the Use of Force Abroad, applies the core materials from the framework and international law chapters to studies of the Vietnam War, the War Powers Resolution, collective defense, self-defense and rescue, and humanitarian operations, with the addition of a new chapter on targeted killing. Included here are new materials on continuing U.S. military operations in Afghanistan and the northwest territories of Pakistan, as well as U.S. participation in NATO operations over Libya.

We have completely reorganized Part IV, Intelligence Operations and Collection, to make the structure and legal regulation of the intelligence community easier to teach and understand, while continuing to dissect critical developments in the law of surveillance. A new chapter on Programmatic Surveillance authorized by the 2008

FISA amendments rounds out a case study, begun in the Fourth Edition, of the Bush administration's warrantless surveillance program.

In Part V, Detaining Terrorist Suspects, we have significantly restructured chapters on habeas corpus and detention, reflecting the many developments in this area since the last edition. Likewise, in Part VI, Interrogating Terrorist Suspects, we have expanded our treatment of interrogation and extraordinary rendition, using old and new materials that we believe will be even more provocative than before.

Part VII, Prosecuting Threats to National Security, treats the evolving law and procedures in criminal trials for material support and terrorism-related offenses. And an expanded chapter on military commissions supplies a basis for examining the ongoing controversy over whether to try terrorist suspects in civilian or military courts.

Part VIII, on Homeland Security, details in two chapters the legal components of the homeland security apparatus that has grown rapidly in the years after 9/11, as well as the domestic role of the military.

Finally, Part IX updates our extensive treatment of legal issues in Protecting National Security Information — from citizens' access to government records to the punishment of leaks. The latter topic has taken on new importance with recent prosecutions of suspected leakers under the espionage laws.

But if the order and priority of topics within National Security Law have changed, the reasons for studying this subject remain the same. The subject matter is still complex and difficult, the political and legal issues are perennially contentious, and there are few settled answers. Yet it is hard to think of another topic as current and provocative. Long before the terrorist attacks on 9/11, it offered the opportunity to bring front-page news into the classroom and to better understand the special responsibility that comes with citizenship in a free and open democracy.

National Security Law helps advance other important educational goals as well. These materials examine the structure and functioning of the government by focusing on the pervasive issue of national defense. They explore every aspect of the domestic legal process, and they integrate experiences from other courses in a new setting. Finally, they offer important insights about the significance of law outside the courtroom and about the interaction of law and politics.

While this book is designed for a course utilizing the "case method" of study, it also serves well as a background reader for lecture courses. In addition to descriptive text, it includes many primary materials, such as judicial opinions, executive orders, statutes, and official correspondence. Because such materials tend to be episodic, disorganized, and incomplete, reading and integrating them places a premium on the student's initiative. Learning from such sources is not passive learning; it is hard but exciting work. This process resembles the work of lawyers and other decision makers in the national security field. To simulate their experience, and to help focus your study, we have posed many hypothetical questions of the sort faced by national security professionals. Few of the answers can be found in a treatise or secondary treatment of the matter; the questions outpace academic production of such reference works. Like national security professionals, we have to rely on an uneven variety of primary sources.

We have tried to fill in some of the blanks with relatively fulsome notes and questions, which are not intended as optional reading, but are of equal importance with the primary materials. They should be reviewed with equal care in preparing for class. We have tried to supply all the information you need to answer the questions — to the extent they are answerable at all.

If you wish to read more, or if you are using the book as an initial research source, the notes and questions also mention some of the most important authorities dealing with each topic. It is not necessary to go outside of these pages to get a well-rounded introduction to National Security Law, but an occasional excursion to the library will prove stimulating.

Even more stimulating — and central to a good National Security Law course — will be regular perusal of a national newspaper. National security issues are almost always front-page news, and it is inevitable that several important stories will play themselves out even as you read this book. Follow them and apply the analysis that you learn here. That application is, after all, the object of this study, not just a by-product.

Finally, we cannot claim in what follows that we have always been politically or ideologically neutral. But we have struggled to present a balanced view of every important issue, because we take seriously the persuasive power of the written word. National security is too important to be left to the "conservative" or the "liberal" alone; good legal analysis is neither.

The manuscript for this Fifth Edition was completed in June 2011. Given the incredibly dynamic nature of our field, important developments will require its augmentation almost immediately. Ours is truly a work in progress. We invite you to join this work, and we welcome your reactions, comments, and suggestions.

Stephen Dycus
William C. Banks
Peter Raven-Hansen

June 2011

Acknowledgments

Stephen Dycus owes a special debt of gratitude to Alan B. Sherr and the late Reverend William Sloane Coffin Jr., whose independent, nearly simultaneous suggestions provided the genesis for this book. I am also especially grateful to my wife Elizabeth for her many sacrifices during its preparation. Thanks are due to Dean Jesse H. Choper and the faculty at Boalt Hall and to the late William A. Brockett for their hospitality during a sabbatical leave, to Colonel Dennis R. Hunt and the faculty of the Law Department at the U.S. Military Academy, West Point, and to my colleagues at Vermont Law School. I also want to recognize the contributions of a succession of bright, energetic research assistants: Alexander W. Banks, Sara Baynard, Daniel Burke, Claude T. Buttrey, Kimberly Chehardy, Daronda Combs, Charles S. Conerly, Carole L. Conragon, Michael Cretella, Lewis M. Csedrik, Edward Demetriou, Abigail Doolittle, Matthew T. Einstein, Robin E. Eiseman, Sean C. Flynn, Thomas H. French, Gina M. Godfrey, Eric Goldwarg, A. Morgan Goodson, Barbara J. Grabowski, Daniel Patrick Greene, Eric Hutchens, Jessica E. Jay, Michael Kennedy, Byron W. Kirkpatrick, Rhona J. Kisch, Karl M. Kurt, Steven F. Lachman, David C. Lashway, Bernard M. Lewis, Robin Longe, Pamela I. Lundquist, William G. Madsen, Matthew Marks, William L. "Trey" Martin, David M. Meezan, Jesse Moorman, Caitlin Morgenstern, Daphne Moritz, Alexander Mullee, Taylor Neff, Sue Ann M. Orsini, Matthew C. Porterfield, Carole A. Powers, Catherine Rawson, Daniel Richardson, Heather Rider, Alan Roughton, Karen E. Russell, Sam Schneider, Elaine C. Schwartz, Alexandra Sherertz, Nathaniel Shoaff, Brooks M. Smith, Rebecca Turner, Charles J. Veith, Emily Wetherell, and Karen M. Willis. I particularly thank my executive assistant, Ginny Burnham, for her contributions to this edition. Finally, I am grateful for the opportunity to undertake this work with three wonderful coauthors, who have become best friends in the process.

William Banks dedicates this edition to the memory of Brady Howell, a former National Security Law student and victim of the September 11 attack on the Pentagon. I also thank the Syracuse University law and graduate students who tested these materials in draft form, reacted to them in the first three editions, and provided many useful suggestions for this revision. I am grateful to my Deans, Michael Hoeflich, Daan Bravemen, Hannah Arterian, and Mitchell Wallerstein, for their generous support of this project, and to my colleagues Spike Bowman and William Wiecek for their comments on draft chapters. My research assistants, Diane Exoo, Doug Steele, Charles Fox, Michael Johnson, Christina Zampas, Patricia Adams, Andrew Kanter, Jennifer

Morris, Margaret Lyons, Courtland Rae, Shivani Mehta, Ruben Saenz, Bill Dorry, Danielle Raymond, Laura Zuber, Andrea Masselli, Jessica Trombetta, and Ryan Cole were immensely helpful and supportive along the way. Finally, I want to thank my friends Steve Dycus, Peter Raven-Hansen, and Arthur Berney for involving me in this project. Their intelligence and commitment to exploring this remarkable field continue to be an invaluable source of inspiration to me.

Peter Raven-Hansen thanks Alexis Victoria Chapin, Lisa G. Fuller, Christopher T. Gailu Jr., Robyn D. Herman, Kristine Kassekert, Michael F. Kohler, Rachel Kramer, Douglas J. Lutz, Andrew G. Mergen, Stephan Rice, Kelly Rich, Jennifer Riddle, Justin T. Ryan, Anne Schwartz, David Silverband, Todd A. Sinkins, Kevin Stack, Jeremy Stein, Ian K. Sweedler, Caroline E. Turner, Earl R. Uehling, Paul C. Vitrano, and Walter L. Williams, all George Washington University Law School students whose energetic and conscientious assistance made prior editions of this book possible. For their enormous help in this edition, I'd like to thank Jennifer Healy and Josh Weiss. I would also like to thank M.E. (Spike) Bowman, William R. Cumming, Douglas Letter, and Daniel C. Schwartz for their comments and support. I am grateful to my wife Winnie for her patience through another edition, and to my friends and co-authors for keeping it fun. Finally, my special thanks and respect to Steve Dycus, whose leadership and occasional martial law delivered the fifth, as they did all prior editions. Without him, there would be no book.

This work would not have been started and could not have been completed without the efforts of our esteemed original coauthor, Arthur Berney. Arthur thinks and writes with piercing clarity. His brilliant case study on the *Pentagon Papers* case, which appears in a somewhat modified form at the end of the book, is a perennial favorite of students and of ours. Arthur has provided inspiration and moral leadership for the book. He is kind to a fault, yet stubborn when it comes to speaking the truth. In the Preface to the First Edition he wrote, "I did what little I could" to promote understanding of the work of lawyers as peacemakers. He was far too modest. We remain enormously grateful to Arthur for his original contributions and for his continuing friendship.

Together, the authors deeply appreciate the support and encouragement of the staff at Little, Brown and Aspen, especially Ruth Elvin, Susan Junkin, Mari Megias, Julie Nahil, Suzanne W.B. Rapcavage, and Barbara Rappaport, our copy editors, as well as Richard R. Heuser, Carol McGeehan, Michael Gregory, Jessica Barmack, Carmen Corral-Reid, Melody Davies, Sarah Hains, Jay Harward, Eric Holt, Kurt Hughes, Laurel Ibey, Darren Kelly, Elizabeth Kenny, Peggy Rehberger, Barbara Roth, Heather Shaff, Anne Starr, and Kathy Yoon.

The authors also gratefully acknowledge permission to reprint excerpts or to reproduce images from the following:

Abraham Lincoln Presidential Library and Museum. *President Lincoln in Spring 1861*. Photographer unknown.

Abrams, Floyd. Telegram from John Mitchell.

Borosage, Robert L., *Para-Legal Authority and Its Perils*, 40 Law & Contemp. Probs. 166 (1976). Copyright © 1976 by Duke University School of Law. Reprinted by permission of the author and Law and Contemporary Problems.

Carroll Publishing. Chart on organization of the intelligence community (2005). Reprinted by permission of Carroll Publishing.

Curator, Supreme Court of the United States. Images of Justices Jackson, O'Connor, and Powell.

Ken Heinen. *Associate Justice Lewis F. Powell Jr.* Copyright © 1986 by Ken Heinen.

Inglesby, Thomas, Rita Grossman & Tara O'Toole, *A Plague on Your City: Observations from TOPOFF*, 32 Clinical Infectious Diseases 436 (2001). Copyright © 2001 by The University of Chicago Press. Reprinted by permission of the authors and Oxford University Press.

Lewis, Anthony, *The Constitution and the Press* (unpublished course materials, Harvard Law School). Copyright © 1974 by Anthony Lewis. Reprinted by permission of the author.

Lowenthal, Mark M., Intelligence: *From Secrets to Policy* (3d ed. 2006). Reprinted by permission of the publisher, CQ Press. Copyright © 2006 CQ Press, a division of Congressional Quarterly Inc.

Monaghan, Henry P., *Presidential War-Making*, 50 B.U.L. Rev. 19 (1970) (special issue). Copyright © 1970 by The Boston University Law Review. Reprinted by permission of the author and The Boston University Law Review.

National Archives and Records Administration. *Japanese-American heads of families line up for relocation, San Francisco, 1942.*

National Security Archive. Image of Elvis Presley and President Nixon.

Toles, Tom, cartoon (*"Hello, Col. North?"*). Reproduced by permission of Mr. Toles and *The Buffalo News.*

United Nations, *U.N. Security Council.* UN Photo by Devra Berkowitz.

Virginia Museum of Fine Arts, Richmond. *Washington as Statesman at the Constitutional Convention,* by Junius Brutus Stearns, 1856. Gift of Edgar William and Bernice Chrysler Garbisch. Photo: Katherine Wetzel. Copyright © by Virginia Museum of Fine Arts.

WashingtonDCStockImages.com. *Vietnam Veterans Memorial Wall, Washington, DC.* Courtesy of dcphototours.com.

Worldatlas.com. CIA maps of Afghanistan, Iraq, and Libya.

Wormuth, Francis D. & Edwin B. Firmage, *To Chain the Dog of War* (2d ed. 1989). Copyright © 1989 by Southern Methodist University Press. Reprinted by permission of Southern Methodist University Press and Edwin Firmage.

Editors' Note

In general we have adhered to the rules for citation of authority followed by most lawyers and courts. They are set out in *The Bluebook: A Uniform System of Citation* (19th ed. 2010). For reasons of economy we have omitted without notation many citations within excerpted materials, and we have removed almost all parallel citations. We have, on the other hand, sought to provide citations that will enable readers to locate and review original sources. We have included URLs for many materials available online, but not for those easily located by a Google search.

To make it easier to refer back to materials where they were originally published, we have preserved original footnote numbers in all excerpted materials. Editors' footnotes are numbered consecutively throughout each chapter. Additions to quoted or excerpted materials are enclosed in brackets.

National Security Law

Introduction

> The law spoke too softly to be heard amidst the din
> of arms.
>
> *Plutarch, Lives: Caius Marius*[1]

A. PURPOSES

There is no field of legal study more critical to the well-being of our people or our republic than National Security Law. In a world that bristles with animosity and danger, an inadequate national defense would jeopardize our lives and ideals. Yet measures taken in the name of national security sometimes pose comparable threats to those same ideals of liberty and justice. This irony has not escaped the attention of the Supreme Court:

> [T]his concept of "national defense" cannot be deemed an end in itself, justifying any exercise of legislative power designed to promote such a goal. Implicit in the term "national defense" is the notion of defending those values and ideals which set this Nation apart. For almost two centuries, our country has taken singular pride in the democratic ideals enshrined in its Constitution. . . . It would indeed be ironic if, in the name of national defense, we would sanction the subversion of one of those liberties . . . which make the defense of the Nation worthwhile. [*United States v. Robel*, 389 U.S. 258, 264 (1968).]

The delicate balance of liberty and security must be appraised and learned, and learned again, by each generation of students of law and public policy. One purpose of this book is to promote the study of that balance.

It might appear that national security issues have only recently taken center stage in our national life. In fact, they have held that position periodically throughout our history. In the first 75 years of the republic, the federal courts unhesitatingly, though infrequently, grappled with core issues of national defense — the existence, legality, and scope of war and military authority. Congress and the executive closely debated questions of war power and foreign policy, not just because they were conscious of setting precedent, but also because each assumed an independent constitutional duty to consider the legality of executive conduct. No one called the resulting body of law — articulated in relatively few judicial opinions and laid bare in a larger number of congressional debates — "national security law." The makers of this law simply

---

1. John Langhorne & William Langhorne, trans. (n.d.).

applied their evolving understanding of the constitutional framework and their ordinary legal skills to the problems of security as these presented themselves.

Seven major wars in the last hundred years (including the first one ever lost — or at least not won — by American forces), the prolonged tension of the Cold War, the specter of a nuclear holocaust, and the unstable post-Cold War world have changed the way we approach national security law. So, tragically, have the terrorist attacks on the World Trade Center and the Pentagon on September 11, 2001. Today, the lines between foreign and domestic issues of national security, and even between peace and war, have seriously eroded: Every foreign issue has domestic ramifications, and the country lives in a seemingly permanent state of war. The front line — the battle zone — is no longer at a safe distance abroad; it is also in Oklahoma City, lower Manhattan, and Arlington, Virginia. And the rules of engagement now must be tailored for use at home as well as abroad.

This state of affairs has empowered and perhaps emboldened the Commander in Chief — the President — to stake out national security as executive domain. Justice Stewart noted as much when he said executive power "in the two related fields of national defense and international relations[,] . . . largely unchecked by the Legislative and Judicial branches, has been pressed to the very hilt since the advent of the nuclear missile age." *New York Times Co. v. United States*, 403 U.S. 713, 727 (1971) (concurring). A second purpose of our study is therefore to examine the constitutional distribution of decision-making authority among the branches of government in our democracy.

Despite these developments, or perhaps because of them, the judiciary has grown increasingly reluctant to answer questions involving national security claims, even some that it squarely addressed earlier in our nation's history. Congress, too, with but few exceptions, has often shied away from serious debate of the same questions in recent years. Ironically, it has sometimes done so by asserting that such questions are for the courts, not for Congress, to resolve. More often, it has simply avoided the questions by acquiescing in executive conduct. If it is true, as Justice Black said, that "[t]he word 'security' is a broad, vague generality," *id.* at 719 (concurring), it nonetheless has today assumed a talismanic quality that often mesmerizes the courts into inaction, quiets congressional debate, and sometimes persuades the executive to think of national security as an end in itself.

Another major purpose of this book is to demonstrate that national security is no talisman.

> [T]he concept of military necessity is seductively broad, and has a dangerous plasticity. Because they invariably have the visage of overriding importance, there is always a temptation to invoke security "necessities" to justify an encroachment upon civil liberties. For that reason, the military-security argument must be approached with a healthy skepticism . . . . [*Brown v. Glines*, 444 U.S. 348, 369 (1980) (Brennan, J., dissenting).]

We hope to encourage that skepticism by using ordinary legal skills to help find answers to questions about national security. Not all answers, of course; not always comforting answers either, because security concerns are always factors that weigh in legal analysis.

Relatively few of these answers are to be found in reported judicial opinions addressing national security. Such opinions are "rare, episodic, and afford little precedential value for subsequent cases," given their typically narrow and contextually limited holdings. *Dames & Moore v. Regan*, 453 U.S. 654, 661 (1980). We do try to demonstrate, however, that legal analysis is relevant and useful outside of the courtroom and appellate opinions, and that legal questions of national security do not lose their urgency just because courts will not answer them. These legal questions persist in dialogues both within and between the political branches. In that nonjudicial setting, they are not so much answered authoritatively as temporarily negotiated. But legal analysis, with an appreciation for the constitutional framework of our system, is crucial in formulating the negotiating positions, defining terms of the dialogue, and memorializing the bargains that are struck.

The failure of courts to give authoritative answers to many questions of national security law suggests to some that public opinion is what ultimately counts in this field.

> In the absence of governmental checks and balances present in other areas of our national life, the only effective restraint upon executive policy and power in the areas of national defense and international affairs may lie in an enlightened citizenry — in an informed and critical public opinion which alone can here protect the values of democratic government. [*New York Times Co. v. United States*, 403 U.S. 713, 728 (1971) (Stewart, J., concurring).]

Another facet of our study is therefore to explore the law governing access to the information that would enlighten citizens (and their representatives in Congress) about matters of national security. Again, ordinary legal skills and analysis, here applied by a sometimes less reluctant judiciary, are critical in weighing rights of access against the need to protect truly sensitive information.

Finally, we intend to demonstrate not only that legal skills and analysis *can* be brought to bear on questions of national security but that they *should* be. Our unabashed purpose here is to stimulate wider thought about the appropriate legal framework for national security decisions. Ultimately, the study of national security law is simply the study of how we should deal with danger by democratic means under the rule of law.

B. ORGANIZATION

In Part I we establish a legal and political framework for the study of particular national security subjects in later chapters. Starting with the text of the U.S. Constitution, we see that two centuries of interpretation have lent meaning to the often cryptic language of the founding document, but that questions still outnumber answers. We systematically examine the role that each branch of the government plays in national security matters. Separate chapters address the creation and application of international law to domestic national security law, as well as the content of international laws concerning resort to war and the conduct of war.

Part II of the book explores our use of force abroad. Beginning with a case study of the Vietnam War and an analysis of the resulting War Powers Resolution, this part of the book then successively considers collective self-defense, unilateral self-defense and rescue, targeted killings, and humanitarian interventions. Part III deals with intelligence operations and intelligence collection, related subjects that sometimes bring the President and Congress into conflict. Intelligence collection also presents difficult questions about how to balance privacy and security. Part IV addresses the detention of terrorist suspects, while Part V concerns the rules for interrogation of suspects in custody. In Part VI we consider criminal prosecution of terrorists in civilian and military courts. Part VII analyzes plans for responding to another major terrorist attack on the U.S. homeland. Finally, Part VIII addresses access to and protection of national security information, including the classification system, public access to such information by statute and other means, "leaks," and censorship.

Our hope is to provide you with a well-rounded, albeit far from comprehensive, introduction to this very dynamic field. For even after more than two centuries of experience, the field of national security law is still evolving rapidly. Patterns for controlling the nation's defense apparatus change from one presidential administration to the next, and sometimes *within* a single administration, while some of the most fundamental questions about allocation of authority remain unanswered. There are nevertheless some constant analytic approaches and underlying principles in the field. We believe that mastery of these will provide the knowledge, skills, and experience you need to play a role in the development of national security law and policy.

I

Framework

Providing for the "Common Defence": The Original Understanding

The purpose of this chapter is to plumb the original understanding of the Constitution's allocation of national security powers. Because the text alone furnishes an incomplete record, our search for the Framers' intent requires a brief review of English history and European political theory that probably influenced the Framers, the American experience with government prior to the Constitution, records of the 1787 Convention, and the subsequent ratification debates. *See* Louis Fisher, *Presidential War Power* 1-16 (2d ed. 2004). We nevertheless begin with the text, as we must in any quest for the meaning of a written constitution.

A. THE CONSTITUTIONAL TEXT

You should carefully review the excerpts from Articles I-IV of the Constitution found in the Appendix. Focus on the text. Try to suppress what you know about our nation's history since 1787. What are your first impressions? How is the responsibility to "provide for the common defence" allocated among the three branches of government?

Judging simply by the proportion of words, the extensive national security powers given Congress in Article I appear to overwhelm the meager listing for the President in Article II. Article I gives Congress authority to "declare War, grant Letters of Marque and Reprisal, and make Rules concerning Captures on Land and Water," which indicates some legislative role in the commitment of American armed forces to combat. Congress also is empowered to "raise and support" the armed forces and to "make Rules for the Government and Regulation of the land and naval Forces." In addition, Congress is authorized to "regulate Commerce with foreign Nations," to provide for the militia and for calling it forth "to execute the Laws of the Union, suppress Insurrections, and repel Invasions," and "to make all Laws which shall be necessary and proper" for executing any power conferred by the Constitution. Other provisions, particularly the one for impeachment of the President, also suggest legislative dominance. Congress escapes subservience to the executive by the guarantee of meeting "at least once in every Year," by the grant of immunity from arrest during a legislative session and from questioning in any other place about any speech or debate, and by the assignment to each House of control over its membership.

By contrast, the President is provided only one obvious national security power by being designated the "Commander in Chief." Moreover, the President is directed to command the armed forces only when they are "called into the actual Service of the United States." National security powers may be allocated to the President as part of the mandate to "take Care that the Laws be faithfully executed." The other Article II grants that may concern national security seem modest in comparison to powers conferred upon Congress: to appoint and receive ambassadors and ministers, and to make treaties (both powers shared with the Senate).

We now know that the judiciary may have a role in resolving disputes between the other two branches. However, aside from the reference in Article III, section 3, to the crime of treason, there is no indication in the constitutional text that the judiciary is to be involved in decisions about the national defense.

Yet both the executive and the courts have played powerful roles in providing for our national security over the last two centuries. How can this history be reconciled with the language of the Constitution? Closer examination of the text reveals the potential for the allocation of national security powers actually reflected in our history. It also demonstrates the futility of trying to divine the Framers' intent from the text alone.

First, Articles I and II assign overlapping functions. For example, the President becomes a legislator of sorts when recommending to Congress "such measures as he shall judge necessary and expedient" and when vetoing bills and resolutions, subject to a two-thirds override by each chamber of Congress. Further, although Congress may tax to "provide for the common Defence" and direct how monies are spent, the President may argue that the "take Care" Clause permits him to act alone in an emergency, using unappropriated or otherwise obligated funds from the Treasury. Similarly, because the President is required to give Congress information "from time to time," he must have been expected to obtain information of interest to Congress. He may obtain the opinion in writing of the principal officer in each of the executive departments, including the Department of Defense, concerning that department's duties. Finally, while the declaration of war is textually committed to Congress, the Commander-in-Chief power could be read to enable the President to use the military to defend against an attack on the United States. Because Article I, section 10, allows a state to "engage in War" if "actually invaded, or in such imminent Danger as will not admit of delay," it seems reasonable to claim as much power for the President if the nation is attacked, when consultation with Congress is not possible or practical.

Second, the text itself is anything but precise. Many of its words are general, not self-defining, and are capable of supporting multiple meanings. Consider the power to "declare War." While the language clearly allocates control over some important aspects of national security decision making to Congress, the text does not say what constitutes a "war" or, for that matter, what it means to "declare" one. Does "war" include small-scale skirmishes, purposefully limited in duration? Does the "Marque and Reprisal" power instead cover these limited hostilities? *See generally* Jules Lobel, *Covert War and Congressional Authority: Hidden War and Forgotten Power,* 134 U. Pa. L. Rev. 1035 (1986). Or should "Marque and Reprisal" be thought of as an anachronism, referring to long-abandoned state-sponsored private battles with pirates? *See* John C. Yoo, *The Continuation of Politics by Other Means: The Original Understanding of War Powers,* 84 Cal. L. Rev. 167, 251 (1996). Should "to declare" be read to give Congress merely a right to recognize an existing state of war? *Id.* at 242. Or is that language intended to confer the general control over initiating war? *See* Michael D. Ramsey,

Textualism and War Powers, 69 U. Chi. L. Rev. 1543 (2002). Or something in between these polar extremes? *See* Harold H. Koh, *The National Security Constitution: Sharing Power After the Iran-Contra Affair* 69, 79 (1990). What about uses of the military that do not create a state of war? *See* Ramsey, *supra*, at 1546-1547. To what extent does the clause giving Congress the power to "make Rules concerning Captures on Land and Water" enable Congress to control detention of persons and property during wartime? *See* Ingrid Weurth, *The Captures Clause*, 76 U. Chi. L. Rev. 1683 (2009). And what is the meaning of the text that empowers Congress "[t]o make Rules for the Government and Regulation" of the military? There is similar textual uncertainty about the reach of congressional fiscal powers. May Congress exercise its appropriation powers to limit executive powers? To what extent must Congress provide basic operating funds for the executive? May funding be conditioned on compliance with congressional wishes? *See generally* William C. Banks & Peter Raven-Hansen, *National Security Law and the Power of the Purse* (1994).

Concerning presidential authority, there is also vagueness in the language of Article II, most notably the Commander-in-Chief provision. A narrow reading of the Clause indicates no policy-making authority and relegates the President to the status of first general. *See* Louis Henkin, *Constitutionalism, Democracy, and Foreign Affairs* 26 (1990). A broad reading of Article II, on the other hand, combined with a restrictive reading of Article I — the Declaration, Marque and Reprisal, and Rules and Regulation Clauses — would expand the Commander-in-Chief power to include all military actions not unequivocally given to Congress. *See* Yoo, *supra*, at 252-255. A similar range of constructions may be afforded the "take Care" language, the power to "receive Ambassadors and other public Ministers," and the statement in Article II, section 1, vesting "[t]he executive Power" in the President. Because the parallel Article I language vests in Congress "[a]ll legislative Powers herein granted," the omission of the words "herein granted" from the text of Article II could be construed to allow the President to do virtually anything "executive" in nature so long as such action is not assigned exclusively to Congress by explicit Article I language. *See* Alexander Hamilton, *Pacificus No. 1*, Gazette of the United States (Philadelphia), June 29, 1793, *reprinted in* 15 *The Papers of Alexander Hamilton* 33-43 (Harold C. Syrett ed., 1969).

Third, the text fails altogether to prescribe or allocate power over some important areas of national security. For example, while Article I, section 9, forbids suspending the privilege of the writ of habeas corpus "unless when in Cases of Rebellion or Invasion the public Safety may require it," the text does not say who possesses the power to suspend the writ. In addition, the meager text is by itself inadequate for deciding the scope and locus of authority for deploying American troops abroad or in defense of the homeland, contracting for private or foreign fighting forces, engaging in covert paramilitary actions (or, for that matter, any intelligence activities), interdicting convoys, engaging in airlifts or blockades, or threatening or promising to do any of the above.

May Congress delegate power to the President? In part because there is no explicit rule in the text forbidding congressional delegations to the executive, such delegations are routinely upheld. But how far may Congress go in delegating its own powers? May the power to declare war be delegated, or would such a wholesale transfer violate the Constitution? The text itself provides little guidance, although the structure of the Constitution may be read to forbid such a sweeping delegation. When Congress merely remains silent while the President takes some national security initiative committed by the Constitution to Congress, is the President acting legally? The answer depends on the construction given to the vague text, since the Constitution fails to describe the effect of legislative inaction. What if the President acts unilaterally in an area not explicitly prescribed or allocated by the Constitution to any branch?

All these uncertainties provoke spirited debates at both ends of Pennsylvania Avenue and among academics. Most national security disputes are resolved in the political process. But when persuasion fails, and the political process will not yield a clear or generally acceptable answer, these disputes end up in court, where the Framers arguably meant for them to be resolved.

Fortunately, the three branches have usually cooperated in making and carrying out national security policy. The practical need for effective administration provides an incentive for Congress to nurture executive branch cooperation. Further, the President's participation in the legislative process is textually assured through his powers to call Congress into special session, to recommend legislation, to provide information about the state of the Union, and to veto any legislative measure. At the same time, any tendency of the President to seek autonomy in the wording of ambiguous text is confined by some explicit and crucial grants to Congress — appropriations and declaration of war to name just two.

Thus, the original understanding of the allocation of national security powers cannot be derived solely from the text of the Constitution. We must broaden our search and consider what is likely to have influenced the delegates to the Philadelphia Convention: British history and European political theory, as well as seminal American events such as the Revolutionary War and earlier efforts at self-government. While the effect of these influences cannot be measured precisely in the Constitution or in the views of any single delegate, it is generally accepted that a combination of theory and practical experience weighed heavily in the plan for a new government.

B.   PRE-CONSTITUTIONAL HISTORY AND POLITICAL THEORY IN EUROPE

Many of the Philadelphia delegates were well read in history and political philosophy — from ancient Greece and Rome to contemporary Continental Europe. As erstwhile Englishmen, however, the Framers turned to English ideas and experiences above all others.

It is nonetheless difficult to calculate the British influence on the Constitution and on its national security provisions in particular. The allocation of war-making and foreign affairs powers fluctuated widely in England between the fifteenth and eighteenth centuries, and the unwritten British constitution simply reflected rather than guided this changing relationship. In general, the Crown dominated all foreign and military affairs until the seventeenth century, when Parliament began successfully to assert its constitutional claims to power. Before the surge in parliamentary strength, the "prerogative" powers[1] of the Crown permitted it to exercise unilaterally, among other things, most national security powers — declaring wars, issuing letters of marque

---

1. The royal prerogative was described by John Locke:

Where the Legislative and Executive Power are in distinct hands, . . . there the good of the Society requires, that several things should be left to the discretion of him, that has the Executive Power. For the Legislators not being able to foresee, and provide, by Laws, for all, that may be useful and reprisal, making treaties and appointments, and raising armies and navies. The prerogative powers were generally accepted as being free from limitation by Parliament or the courts.

From the mid-seventeenth century onward, Parliament and the Crown alternately dominated decision making about national security matters. When Parliament asserted itself it often relied on its control of the purse and its ability to obtain information from the executive. The Parliament taxed for military programs, controlled the raising and keeping of standing armies in times of peace, and successfully placed restrictive conditions on military appropriations. If the Crown ignored legislation restricting a foreign affairs initiative, the Parliament could and on occasion did resort to impeachment, dismissal, or execution. *See* Banks & Raven-Hansen, *supra* p. 9, at 13-17.

On the other hand, if Parliament was uncooperative, the Crown might secure funding for its ventures from local governments or by borrowing, and it could dismiss Parliament for any reason — if Parliament had not acted first. Further, secret initiatives were sometimes undertaken, and information was often withheld from Parliament under a claim of executive discretion. *See* Abraham D. Sofaer, *War, Foreign Affairs and Constitutional Power: The Origins* 6-15 (1976); W. Taylor Reveley III, *War Powers of the President and Congress: Who Holds the Arrows and Olive Branch?* 53-55 (1981).

In addition to their legacy of shifting royal and parliamentary powers, which had so affected war-making and foreign affairs, the British brought with them theoretical principles central to their own constitutional development that greatly influenced the Americans. The most important intellectual contribution was the idea of separation of powers. The theory of separation assigned different powers to different institutions and persons in government in order to forestall tyranny, to promote the government's legitimacy, and to make government more efficient. *See generally* William Gwynn, *The Meaning of the Separation of Powers* (1965). John Locke, writing between 1679 and 1683, relied on his theory of separation to advance the argument for the Whig view of government. His ideas significantly influenced constitutional development in England and in America.

> In all Cases, whilst the Government subsists, *the Legislative is the Supream Power*. For what can give Laws to another, must needs be superior to him....
>
> But because the Laws, that are at once, and in a short time made, have a constant and lasting force, and need a *perpetual Execution*, or an attendance thereunto: Therefore

---

to the Community, the Executor of the Laws, having the power in his hands, has by the common Law of Nature, a right to make use of it, for the good of the Society, in many Cases, where the municipal Law has given no direction, till the Legislative can conveniently be Assembled to provide for it....

This Power to act according to discretion, for the publick good, without the prescription of the Law, and sometimes even against it, *is* that which is called *Prerogative*. For since in some Governments the Law-making Power is not always in being, and is usually too numerous, and so too slow, for the dispatch requisite to Execution... there is a latitude left to the Executive power, to do many things of choice, which the Laws do not prescribe....

The old Question will be asked in this matter of *Prerogative*, But *who shall be Judge* when this Power is made a right use of? I Answer: Between an Executive Power in being, with such a Prerogative, and a Legislative that depends upon his will for their convening, there can be no *Judge on Earth*: As there can be none, between the Legislative, and the People, should either the Executive, or the Legislative, when they have got the Power in their hands, design, or go about to enslave, or destroy them. The People have no other remedy in this, as in all other cases where they have no Judge on Earth, but to *appeal to Heaven*. [John Locke, *Two Treatises of Government* 392-393, 397 (Peter Laslett ed., 1967).]

'tis necessary there should be a *Power always in being*, which should see to the *Execution* of the Laws that are made, and remain in force. And thus the *Legislative* and *Executive Power* come often to be separated.

There is another *Power* in every Commonwealth, which one may call *natural*, because it is that which answers to the Power every Man naturally had before he entered into Society. For though in a Commonwealth the Members of it are distinct Persons still in reference to one another, and as such are governed by the Laws of Society; yet in reference to the rest of Mankind, they make one Body, which is, as every Member of it before was, still in the State of Nature with the rest of Mankind. Hence it is, that the Controversies that happen between any Man of the Society with those that are out of it, are managed by the publick; and an injury done to a Member of their Body, engages the whole in the reparation of it. So that under this Consideration, the whole Community is one Body in the State of Nature, in respect of all other States or Persons out of its Community.

This therefore contains the Power of War and Peace, Leagues and Alliances, and all the Transactions, with all Persons and Communities without the Commonwealth, and may be called *Federative*, if any one pleases. So the thing be understood, I am indifferent to the Name.

These two Powers, *Executive* and *Federative*, though they be really distinct in themselves, yet one comprehending the *Execution* of the Municipal Laws of the Society *within* its self, upon all that are parts of it; the other the management of the *security and interest of the publick without*, with all those that it may receive benefit or damage from, yet they are always almost united. And though this *federative Power* in the well or ill management of it be of great moment to the Commonwealth, yet it is much less capable to be directed by antecedent, standing, positive Laws, than the *Executive;* and so must necessarily be left to the Prudence and Wisdom of those whose hands it is in, to be managed for the publick good. For the *Laws* that concern Subjects one amongst another, being to direct their actions, may well enough *precede* them. But what is to be done in reference to *Foreigners*, depending much upon their actions, and the variation of designs and interests, must be *left* in great part *to* the *Prudence* of those who have this Power committed to them, to be managed by the best of their Skill, for the advantage of the Commonwealth.

Though, as I said, the *Executive* and *Federative Power* of every Community be really distinct in themselves, yet they are hardly to be separated, and placed, at the same time, in the hands of distinct Persons. For both of them requiring the force of the Society for their exercise, it is almost impracticable to place the Force of the Commonwealth in distinct, and not subordinate hands; or that the *Executive* and *Federative Power* should be *placed* in Persons that might act separately, whereby the Force of the Publick would be under different Commands: which would be apt sometime or other to cause disorder and ruine. [Locke, *supra*, at 382-386.]

The judicial power was born as the third real power in England when Parliament assured the independence of the judges from the King's previously unfettered control over their removal. Yet the judges still were viewed as executive officers while in office. It was Montesquieu in his *Spirit of Laws*, published in 1748, who provided the theoretical challenge to the distinct federative power of the executive described by Locke. Montesquieu's theory subdivided the federative and the law enforcement powers of the executive, treated the judiciary as a distinct branch, and offered the tripartite separation that is reflected in the American Constitution. For Montesquieu, the preservation of liberty required such a separation:

When the legislative and executive powers are united in the same person, or in the same body of magistracy, there can be no liberty; because apprehensions may arise, lest the same monarch or senate should enact tyrannical laws, to execute them in a tyrannical manner.

Again, there is no liberty, if the power of judging be not separated from the legislative and executive powers. Were it joined with the legislative, the life and liberty of the subject would be exposed to arbitrary control; for the judge would be then the legislator. Were it joined to the executive power, the judge might behave with all the violence of an oppressor. [Charles Louis de Secondat, Baron de Montesquieu, *The Spirit of Laws* 202 (David Wallace Carrithers ed., 1977).]

The problem with the separation of powers theory, however, was that it failed to account for the real class conflicts and overlapping authority that actually characterized the British system. A second theory, that of mixed government, helped to harmonize theory and practice. According to mixed government theory, balance in government could be maintained by mixing classes and institutions of society—kings, lords, and commoners—and combining various primary forms of government, namely monarchy, aristocracy, and democracy. A systematic attempt at creating "counterpoisal pressures... might keep the system stable and healthy." Bernard Bailyn, *The Origins of American Politics* 20 (1970). Thus, separated branches would share all the government's powers, checking against abuses by any single group in society or in government. For example, broad prerogative powers did not necessarily always belong to the King unchecked by the Parliament. The King or his ministers could be criticized or even impeached for their misuse of power. Moreover, either branch could initiate or exercise a prerogative power.

Locke recognized the importance of balancing and mixing powers when he conceded that many things must be left to executive discretion, subject to nullification or modification by legislation. For Locke, both separation of powers and mixed government served to make the King subject to the representative Parliament. Thus, assuming that both the separation and mixed government theories of Locke and Montesquieu influenced the U.S. Constitution, the ambiguities of the American text might be quite intentional reflections of the essential fluidity of these concepts.

General theories of government were not the only European notions to influence the text of the Constitution. The Framers' views of war and peace, in their declared and undeclared forms, seem to be derived especially from Grotius, Pufendorf, Vattel, and Burlamaqui. Charles A. Lofgren, *War-Making Under the Constitution: The Original Understanding*, 81 Yale L.J. 672, 689-697 (1972). For Grotius, declared wars were "perfect," involving committed nations in opposition. Undeclared wars were "imperfect," and occurred in situations where the sovereign authorized private reprisals aimed at claiming property held by subjects of another sovereign. Hugo Grotius, *The Rights of Wars and Peace* 538-549 (Jean Barbeyrac trans., 1738) (1625). Burlamaqui argued that imperfect war and reprisals were often one and the same, but that a sovereign might itself engage in reprisals using its own forces:

A perfect war is that, which entirely interrupts the tranquillity of the state, and lays a foundation for all possible acts of hostility. An imperfect war, on the contrary, is that, which does not entirely interrupt the peace, but only in certain particulars, the public tranquillity being in other respects undisturbed.

This last species of war is generally called reprisals, of the nature which we shall here give some account. By reprisals then we mean *that imperfect kind of war, or those acts of hostility, which sovereigns exercise against each other, or, with their consent, their subjects, by seizing the persons or effects of the subjects of a foreign commonwealth, that refuseth to do us justice.* . . . [II Jean Jacques Burlamaqui, *The Principles of Natural and Political Law* 180 (Thomas Nugent trans., 5th ed. 1807), *cited with approval in Miller v. The Resolution,* 2 U.S. (2 Dall.) 1, 21 (Ct. App. in Cases of Capture 1781).]

There was no consensus among the theorists about whether a declaration was necessary to initiate war, though no one argued that a declaration was required to wage a defensive war. Before the American Revolution, however, when such "declarations" were made, they were usually only formal, largely ceremonial announcements. Lofgren, *supra,* at 691-693.

Contemporaneous writings indicate that "a nation might 'declare' war, not only by a formal announcement, but also by an act of hostility." Ramsey, *supra* p. 8, at 1590. For example, Locke wrote:

The State of War is a State of Enmity and Destruction; And therefore declaring by Word or Action, not a passionate or hasty, but a sedate settled Design, upon another Mans Life, puts him in a State of War with him against whom he has declared such an intention. [Locke, *supra* p. 10 n.1, at 278.]

According to Professor Ramsey, Locke, Blackstone, and other international law scholars used "declare" to mean "an action (taking up arms) that itself makes a statement." Launching an attack could constitute "declaring" war. Ramsey, *supra,* at 1636.

War making without a formal declaration was common in the eighteenth century, some of it under the collective noses of the soon-to-be American convention delegates. Between 1754 and 1756 the undeclared beginnings of the Seven Years War between Britain and France occurred mostly on American soil, and Americans were exposed to the undeclared war between Britain and France during the Revolutionary War.

The long-standing European practice of state-sanctioned private reprisals to satisfy private claims during peacetime all but disappeared during the first half of the eighteenth century. Yet sovereign states continued to press their own claims by reprisal, either through use of public forces or private ships, or by the issuance of letters of marque and reprisal. Indeed, recent English history known to the Americans included examples of state reprisals that resulted in general war.

This history underscores the importance of the Declaration and the Marque and Reprisal Clauses in the U.S. Constitution. The Framers knew from the European experience that war might be limited or complete, that limited hostilities were often authorized through letters of marque and reprisal, and that minor skirmishes or even major ones could begin by "Word or Action," as Locke put it. Lofgren, *supra* p. 13, at 693-697. *See generally* Lobel, *supra* p. 8.

C.   THE AMERICAN EXPERIENCE PRIOR TO 1787

These British and European influences may have seemed secondary to the Framers compared with the lessons learned firsthand from state, colonial, and national governments prior to the Philadelphia Convention in 1787. Before the Revolution, the mood in the colonies was notoriously antiexecutive. While the structures of colonial governments varied, all but Connecticut and Rhode Island formally placed most of the important powers in their governors, including command of the military, a veto of legislation, authority to raise and spend funds on certain projects, and discretion to delay enforcement of legislation until approved in England. The colonial governors were mostly British agents and were widely disliked in the colonies, even though the colonists' complaints often were traceable to the actions of Parliament. Yet despite the theoretical preeminence of the governors, the legislatures dominated colonial government through fiscal initiatives, investigations, and various other measures, and they effectively controlled the governors, even in the exercise of war and foreign affairs powers. Sofaer, *supra* p. 11, at 15-17.

After the Revolution, constitutional theories of separation and mixed government seem to have been ignored, as seven of the eight state governments formed between 1776 and 1778 adopted constitutions that subordinated the executive to the legislature. A second wave of state constitution-making, however, including New York, Massachusetts, and New Hampshire, provided relatively greater authority for the governors. Yoo, *supra* p. 8, at 228-234. The new state legislatures responded early and often to popular local issues, sometimes restricting interstate commerce and undermining national stability. Eventually, as disorder and instability increased, many began to feel that a stronger national government was needed.

Again, early experiences with a national government had been marked by a pervasive antiexecutive mood. Beginning with the First Continental Congress in 1774, the national legislature was used by the states as a national executive, at first to conduct the Revolutionary War and later to manage other fiscal and national security tasks. But while Congress sought to carry out its policies through committees, boards, and appointed agents, it soon became apparent that the exigencies of the war were beyond the legislature's capacity to manage. Broad powers had to be delegated to the Board of War and to General George Washington. Nevertheless, Washington and other military leaders were often forced to choose between acting on the basis of ambiguous grants of authority or referring questions to Congress for decisions. This arrangement proved to be extremely inefficient.

> The subordination of the military to civilian control was a central axiom of the [English constitutional theory] that had led the colonists into rebellion. But broad agreement on this principle hardly provided Congress with useful guidelines for determining how direct and close its supervision of the army should be.... From 1775 to 1781, Congress was intimately concerned with the organization and administration of the army. It established rules of war and discipline, pay scales, terms of enlistment, and detailed regulations governing the procurement of supplies and provisions by the quartermaster and commissary departments; it also seemed to be regularly beset with the incessant complaints — sometimes petty, sometimes substantive, but never forgotten — of its officer corps. [Jack N. Rakove, *The Beginning of National Politics: An Interpretive History of the Continental Congress* 196-197 (1979).]

Congressional direction of the war even threatened the loyalty of its soldiers:

> Loyalty to the Congress was constantly strained but it never snapped; every soldier and officer may have cursed Congress fifty times for every word of praise, and most may have thought their hardships stemmed as much from congressional indifference, ineptness, and corruption as from unavoidable difficulties; but discontent rarely threatened to erupt into mutiny. [Forrest McDonald, *E Pluribus Unum: The Formation of the American Republic 1776-1790*, at 12 (1965).]

The Continental Congress's cumbersome executive structures and its inability to raise money for the national government led many influential Americans, including Washington and Hamilton, to urge a strengthened national executive.

One consequence of the Revolutionary War was the emergence of a decidedly American view concerning standing armies. On the one hand, the War served to remind the 1787 Convention delegates that a regular standing army was needed to enable the nation to defend itself against another nation. As Alexander Hamilton later argued, the part-time militia was not an adequate substitute for a regular army:

> These garrisons must either be furnished by occasional detachments from the militia, or by permanent corps in the pay of the government. The first is impracticable; and if practicable, would be pernicious. The militia would not long, if at all, submit to be dragged from their occupations and families to perform that most disagreeable duty in times of profound peace. And if they could be prevailed upon or compelled to do it, the increased expense of a frequent rotation of service, and the loss of labor and disconcertion of the industrious pursuits of individuals, would form conclusive objections to the scheme. It would be as burdensome and injurious to the public as ruinous to private citizens. [*The Federalist No. 24*, at 161 (Alexander Hamilton) (Clinton Rossiter ed., 1961).]

On the other hand, the Americans knew that a standing army could be dangerous if not adequately controlled. They had come to deplore the use of the British army to enforce unpopular policies. The post-Revolutionary War solution, then, was to place responsibility for control of the military in the hands of the legislature. Legislative dominance of the military could be accomplished, it was first thought, by strict control over appropriations. The state assemblies controlled the governors' use of the military by imposing conditions on supply bills and even by specifying the conduct of military operations. *See* Banks & Raven-Hansen, *supra* p. 9, at 18-22; Elias E. Huzar, *The Purse and the Sword: Control of the Army by Congress Through Military Appropriations 1933-1950*, at 18-23 (1950).

D.   THE FRAMERS' VIEW

The adoption of the Articles of Confederation in 1781 did little to satisfy the demand for a stronger executive. First, the states retained sovereignty except to the extent that powers were "expressly" granted to the United States. Second, while Congress was given significant powers, including "the sole and exclusive right and power of determining on peace and war," the national government had no enforcement power and no independent executive. The business of governing thus continued much as it had before, with increasing delegations over foreign and military affairs to agents such as General Washington. As the national debt grew and the states threatened the national economy by disrupting commerce and issuing paper money, the national government proved unable to maintain order in the fragile Union. By early 1787 the Continental Congress could no longer ignore the demand for change.

Congress called upon the states to send delegates to a convention for the purpose of reforming the government of the Union. The 55 delegates representing all states except Rhode Island ranged from 81-year-old Benjamin Franklin to John Dickinson, who had refused to sign the Declaration of Independence. Most of the delegates had served in the Continental Congress, and most were wealthy. So much a part of the American elite were the delegates that Thomas Jefferson, who was in Paris and did not attend, called the convention "really an assembly of demi-gods." Max Farrand, *The Framing of the Constitution of the United States* 39 (1913).

Widespread demand for a stronger executive forced the Philadelphia delegates to confront basic structural questions: Should the executive be one person or many? Should there be an executive veto? How should the executive be selected, and should the executive serve more than one term? An even bigger issue was how to resolve the federalism question. The federalists wanted a stronger executive than did the states' righters, later known as antifederalists. Compared to these questions, the nature and scope of specific powers for the executive, especially in relation to those of Congress, were peripheral issues in 1787. Indeed, most of the attention given by the Framers and Ratifiers to issues of national security was directed toward national survival and state responsibilities, state incitements of other states and Indians, and state diplomatic activity.

1.   The Convention

Unfortunately, records of deliberations at the Constitutional Convention are few and are unreliable. The meetings themselves were secret, and the Convention Journal recorded only formal motions and votes. Many delegates took notes. The most extensive of these were James Madison's, though his were revised 30 years after the Convention. The various sources are compiled in the four-volume Max Farrand, *The Records of the Federal Convention of 1787* (rev. ed. 1937) (hereinafter *Records*).

There was a general consensus among Convention delegates about the need for a strengthened national government. They approved the so-called Virginia Plan, drafted by Madison, to give Congress the rights vested in it by the earlier Articles

Washington at the Constitutional Convention of 1787.

Junius Brutus Stearns, 1856. Virginia Museum of Fine Arts, Richmond. Gift of Edgar William and Bernice Chrysler Garbisch. Photo: Katherine Wetzel © Virginia Museum of Fine Arts.

of Confederation. 3 *Records, supra,* at 593. They also agreed in principle to a single executive who would have explicit powers of execution and a conditional veto over legislation. It was clear from the start that the delegates wanted to create an executive who would be more than a mere agent of the legislature. They rejected a New Jersey Plan that would have provided for a relatively weak, plural, single-term executive, removable by a majority of the states, yet having the power "to direct all military operations." *Id.* at 611-613.

After additional debate the delegates instructed a Committee on Detail to prepare a draft Constitution. The resulting draft vested "The Executive Power of the United States . . . in a . . . President," who would be "Commander in Chief of the Army and Navy of the United States, and of the Militia of the several States." Congress was given the power to "make war," to appropriate funds, and "to call for the aid of the militia, in order to execute the laws of the Union, enforce treaties, suppress insurrections, and repel invasions." 2 *Records, supra,* at 167-172.

In the ensuing Convention debates on the draft, James Wilson of Pennsylvania opposed granting the House sole power to initiate revenue bills. Wilson's arguments and Edmund Randolph's prevailing response indicate a general understanding that the appropriations power would be employed to control the military. *Id.* at 273-274, 279.

Charles Pinckney of South Carolina complained that requiring the whole Congress to declare war would be cumbersome:

> Mr. Pinckney. . . . Its proceedings were too slow. It wd. meet but once a year. The Hs. of Reps. would be too numerous for such deliberations. The Senate would be the best depositary, being more acquainted with foreign affairs, and most capable of proper resolutions. If the States are equally represented in Senate, so as to give no advantage to large States, the power will notwithstanding be safe, as the small have their all at stake in such cases as well as the large States. It would be singular for one authority to make war, and another peace.
>
> Mr. Butler. The Objections agst the Legislature lie in a great degree agst the Senate. He was for vesting the power in the President, who will have all the requisite qualities, and will not make war but when the Nation will support it.
>
> Mr. M(adison) and Mr. Gerry moved to insert "*declare*," striking out "*make*" war; leaving to the Executive the power to repel sudden attacks.
>
> Mr. Sharman thought it stood very well. The Executive shd. be able to repel and not to commence war. "Make" better than "declare" the latter narrowing the power too much.
>
> Mr. Gerry never expected to hear in a republic a motion to empower the Executive alone to declare war.
>
> Mr. Elseworth. there is a material difference between the cases of making *war*, and making *peace*. It shd. be more easy to get out of war, than into it. War also is a simple and overt declaration. peace attended with intricate & secret negociations.
>
> Mr. Mason was agst giving the power of war to the Executive, because not (safely) to be trusted with it; or to the Senate, because not so constructed as to be entitled to it. He was for clogging rather than facilitating war; but for facilitating peace. He preferred "*declare*" to "*make*." [*Id.* at 318-319.]

In support of Madison's motion, Rufus King of Massachusetts argued "that 'make' war might be understood to 'conduct' it which was an Executive function." *Id.* at 319.

Eventually, Pinckney's motion to vest the war power solely in the Senate was overwhelmingly rejected and Madison's motion was approved. The Journal records and Madison's notes unfortunately report inconsistent tallies on the two votes taken on Madison's motion, one before and one after King's speech, making it impossible to be certain about the meaning of the change. Madison and Gerry probably wanted the President to be able to respond to "sudden attacks" without a declaration of war, which some delegates thought was intended by the original language. Others, including King, wanted to be certain it was understood that the conduct of a war after its initiation was for the executive. No better consensus from the debate can be safely stated, although nothing in the change suggests an intention to allow the President to "make" war without a declaration. *See* Sofaer, *supra* p. 11, at 31-32. Even Hamilton, ardent advocate of a strong executive, favored limiting the executive in war-making and would have given the Senate the declaration power, leaving to the President the "direction of war when authorized or begun," 1 *Records, supra,* at 292, though he knew that many contemporary wars were not technically declared. Lofgren, *supra* p. 13, at 680.

Viewing the larger debate and the process of drafting the Constitution does help place the war powers allocation question in some perspective. First, the draft presented to the Convention by the Committee on Detail assigned the power "to make war" to Congress, though the point had scarcely been debated. The same Committee named the President as Commander in Chief without any record of controversy. The President was to be first general, but was not to initiate hostilities. As for military action short of declared war, the Committee on Detail did not include in the list of powers given to the new legislature the power to issue letters of marque and reprisal, which the old Congress enjoyed under the Articles. At Pinckney's request such language was added and approved without discussion. 2 *Records, supra,* at 324, 326. We cannot ascertain from the Convention records whether this action was meant to ensure congressional primacy over undeclared hostilities. However, the contemporaneous understanding about the use of letters of marque and reprisal suggests that purpose.

Pinckney's motion to vest the war power in the Senate included granting to the Senate the power "to make treaties." 3 *Records, supra,* at 427. As in the debate on the War Declaration Clause, Madison and others eventually cautioned against unfettered Senate power over treaties. After floor discussion, in which Madison urged a role for the President out of fear of parochialism in the Senate, a committee was formed, which reported the following language: "The president, by and with the advice and consent of the Senate, shall have power to make treaties. . . . But no treaty shall be binding without the consent of two-thirds of the members present." 2 *Records, supra,* at 495. James Wilson proposed adding "and House of Representatives" after the word "Senate," on grounds that treaties should be fully sanctioned as laws if they were to operate as laws. Following objections from Robert Sherman and others that the secrecy that would necessarily attend some treaty negotiations made referral to the House impractical, Wilson's motion was defeated. *Id.* at 538. Among several other failed amendments was a proposal by Madison to permit the Senate alone to make peace treaties. Madison argued that the President "would necessarily derive so much power and importance from a state of war that he might be tempted, if authorized, to impede a treaty of peace." *Id.* at 540.

While the treaty-making powers were being shaped, the eventual Supremacy Clause was drafted to make "all treaties made and ratified under the authority of the United States," along with laws enacted by the Congress, "the supreme law." *Id.* at 28. Supported by Madison's admonition that federal dominance in foreign relations was necessary "to the efficacy and security of the general government," *id.* at 27, the Supremacy Clause became a part of the Constitution, along with the provision in Article I, section 10, restricting states from entering into treaties or entering into any "agreement or compact" with a foreign nation without the consent of Congress. Complaints from those who feared the loss of state sovereignty and from others who feared that omission of the House of Representatives from the treaty-making process could lead to abuse of the power, did not sway the delegates. Nor did the Framers prescribe any limits on the subject matter of treaties, or supply a rule for resolving a conflict between a treaty and the Constitution or the laws.

Meanwhile, the delegates were gradually constructing an executive branch that would be unitary and independent and vested with considerable authority. In keeping with their general interest in balancing the powers of government, the President's selection, vested in the Congress by the Committee on Detail, became an election by state electors for an unrestricted number of four-year terms. The President was also given a conditional veto over legislation. Once the independence of the office was established, the delegates broadened the grounds for impeachment by the legislature to provide a check in the other direction. But they voted down proposals to allow Congress to define the content of "executive power," and no general argument was advanced against Congress's ability to delegate powers to the executive. Sofaer, *supra* p. 11, at 36-38, 56; Reveley, *supra* p. 11, at 98-99. In the end, the delegates themselves did little to define the executive.

2.   Ratification

There remained the difficult task of persuading the state ratifying conventions to approve the new Constitution. The ensuing debates in the states, like those in Philadelphia, scarcely addressed the question of how and by which institution the new government would initiate war. Indeed, the Confederation government already had the war-making power, and the question of initiating war was eclipsed by the more immediately volatile issues of federal, state, or civilian-military sovereignty. At the same time, there was debate about supporting an existing war through taxation, about control of the military, and about the use of standing armies.

Despite the limited debates on war-making powers, there is indirect evidence from the ratification period that reveals more clearly how the war-making provisions were understood. Because the Philadelphia debates were secret, the ratifiers themselves had to rely on the words of the Constitution and on the propaganda of the time to establish the meaning of the document.

The Federalist Papers, written by Madison, Hamilton, and Jay to promote ratification, indicate that the new war declaration clause was practically the same as the earlier Articles' grant to Congress of "determining on" war. In *The Federalist No. 41*, Madison wrote: "The existing confederation establishes this power in the most ample form." *The Federalist No. 41*, at 256 (James Madison) (Clinton Rossiter ed., 1961). Delegate Wilson made the same point at the Pennsylvania convention. He rejected the notion of a unilateral presidential power over war-making, remarking that the new "system will not hurry us into war. . . . It will not be in the power of a single man, or a single body of men, to involve us in such distress; for the important power of declaring war is vested in the legislature at large." 1 *Debates in the Several State*

Conventions on the Adoption of the Federal Constitution 528 (Jonathan Elliot ed., 1888) (hereinafter *Elliot's Debates*).

There is similar evidence that the Commander-in-Chief power was viewed narrowly. In *The Federalist No. 69*, Hamilton compared the Commander in Chief's prerogative to that of the British Crown, finding the former "much inferior."

> It would amount to nothing more than the supreme command and direction of the military . . . while that of the British King extends to the *declaring* of war, and to the *raising and regulating* of fleets and armies — all which by the Constitution under consideration, would appertain to the legislature. [*The Federalist No. 69*, at 418 (Alexander Hamilton) (Clinton Rossiter ed., 1961).]

The fact that the authors of the *Federalist Papers* described the assignment of war powers in such terms suggests that they believed this view would be well received in the states.

Madison insisted in general argument that pure separation of the nation's powers was neither desirable nor intended by the theorists. Instead, mixed powers and checks and balances were essential:

> Ambition must be made to counteract ambition. . . . But what is government itself but the greatest of all reflections on human nature? If men were angels, no government would be necessary. If angels were to govern men, neither external nor internal controls on government would be necessary. In framing a government which is to be administered by men over men, the great difficulty lies in this: you must first enable the government to control the governed; and in the next place oblige it to control itself. A dependence on the people is, no doubt, the primary control on the government; but experience has taught mankind the necessity of auxiliary precautions. [*The Federalist No. 51*, at 322 (James Madison) (Clinton Rossiter ed., 1961).]

For Madison, the balance was completed by having a dominant bicameral legislature and a partial veto in the executive. The House retained the original appropriations power, while the Senate had a special role in treaties and appointments. Similarly, the strong and independent President would be able to prevent legislative tyranny. Thus, separation ensured independence while it divided responsibilities along functional lines.

To be sure, there were arguments during this period that a stronger executive would promote governmental efficiency and dispatch. For example, it might have been inferred from the proposed government's ability to raise and support armed forces, and thereby to deter a surprise attack on the United States, that the President was empowered to respond to such a sudden attack. However, the arguments based on efficiency and dispatch were not made in connection with initiating war. *See, e.g., The Federalist No. 64*, at 12-13 (John Jay) (Clinton Rossiter ed., 1961) (discussing the treaty power).

During the South Carolina debate on the Constitution, convention delegate Major Pierce Butler explained that, while the initial proposal to vest the treaty power solely in the Senate was defeated as "inimical to the genious of a republic, by destroying the necessary balance," a motion to give the power to the President was overcome as "throwing into his hands the influence of a monarch, having an opportunity of involving his country in a war whenever he wished. . . ." 4 *Elliot's Debates, supra,* at 262-263. Only when it was suggested that the House of Representatives join the Senate in approving treaties was it noted that "negotiations always required the greatest secrecy, which could not be expected in a large body." *Id.*

Throughout the ratification process, the objective of the federalists was to defend the entire proposed national government, not one branch of it at the expense of another. For example, Hamilton argued that the two-year limit on military appropriations would prevent the legislature from giving the executive power to build a large standing army. But his objective was to persuade ratifiers to support the proposed new government, not to aggrandize legislative power. Reveley, *supra* p. 11, at 105. In addition, to the extent that the vagueness in describing the President's powers caused fears among the ratifiers, they were substantially mollified by the comforting, though unspoken, assumption that Washington would become the first President, and that he would never abuse his powers.

The ratification debates tend to confirm that the "declare" language could not fairly be read to limit Congress to formal war-initiation. No ratifier argued that the President has unilateral power to engage in hostilities without congressional approval in the absence of a sudden attack. Undeclared wars were thought to be possible, but it is not altogether clear under what circumstances and by whom they could be initiated. *See* Lofgren, *supra* p. 13, at 694-700.

New Hampshire became the necessary ninth state to ratify the Constitution in June 1788, and the new government officially commenced in March 1789. In that year, Jefferson wrote to Madison that "[w]e have already given in example one effectual check to the Dog of War by transferring the power of letting him loose from the Executive to the Legislative body, from those who are to spend to those who are to pay." 15 *The Papers of Thomas Jefferson* 397 (Julian P. Boyd ed., 1958).

Still, careful analysis of the original understanding leaves much unsettled. No provision or argument was made against legislative delegations of military matters to the executive; nor were the required indicia of a valid delegation spelled out. Similarly, there is no evidence that Congress was barred from authorizing hostilities without a declaration of war. The President's authority to "repel sudden attacks" was not clarified; nor was there any indication of what constitutes an attack, or when an attack should be considered imminent. Yet *The Federalist* strongly suggests that the textual uncertainties and overlaps in function and power were intended as an integral part of the overall design. Sofaer, *supra* p. 11, at 58-59.

NOTES AND QUESTIONS

1. *The Preamble.* Does the language of the Preamble to the Constitution help to describe the locus or scope of authority for keeping the nation secure? Suppose that some government action demonstrably harmed the "common defence," or threatened to do so. Could the Preamble be invoked to stop it? *See* Arthur Selwyn Miller, *Nuclear Weapons and Constitutional Law,* in *Nuclear Weapons and Law* 235, 241-243 (Arthur Selwyn Miller & Martin Feinrider eds., 1984).

2. *Textual Conflicts and Silences in the National Security Constitution.* Can you say exactly what provisions of Articles I and II might bring the President and Congress into conflict in providing for the national security, and why?

Various national defense issues are not addressed at all in the text of the Constitution. For example, may the President solicit the financial support of foreign countries for military initiatives not authorized by Congress? May the Congress authorize and appropriate funds for the purchase of military hardware and then restrict its use by the President? May the courts direct the President to disclose sensitive information about foreign affairs to Congress? How should such questions be resolved?

3. *Anti-Executive Sentiments.* Are you clear on the reasons for the strong anti-executive sentiment in America before the 1787 Constitutional Convention? Can you see any of that sentiment reflected in the text of the Constitution or in the ratification debates? Do you see evidence of it in political debates today about national security issues?

4. *A Merely "Juridical" War Power?* Professor John Yoo maintains that the Declaration Clause reflects the Framers' understanding of eighteenth century practice that a declaration of war is not required to authorize combat. Instead, he argues, a declaration simply reflects Congress's "judgment of a current status of relations, not an authorization of war." Yoo, *supra* p. 8, at 248. According to Professor Yoo, in this role Congress performs a judicial function rather than its typical enactment of positive law. *Id.* at 248-249. How would you respond to Professor Yoo's assessment?

Professor Yoo argues further that the Constitution permits the President to initiate wars unless Congress acts through an appropriations restriction or impeachment to stop him. *Id.* at 174. Professor Yoo finds partial support for his conclusion in Article I, section 10, which states, "No State shall . . . engage in war." Thus, "if the Framers intended to require congressional consent before war, they . . . were perfectly capable of making their wishes known. . . . Had the Framers intended to prohibit the President from initiating wars, they easily could have incorporated a Section 10 analogue into Article II." *Id.* at 255. What are the strengths and weaknesses of this argument?

5. *Tactical War Powers.* There is ample evidence that the legislature was not meant to make tactical military decisions once war was initiated. But where exactly does the legislature's responsibility stop? Just how much autonomy should the President enjoy as Commander in Chief? If the Framers had addressed these questions, what basic political values would have shaped their debate?

6. *An Obsolete War Power?* "That was then; this is now," the saying goes. Why should we care what the Framers intended? Of what relevance today is the "original understanding" of the Constitution when, from a distance of two centuries, we have to decide whether the President can unilaterally send American warships into the Persian Gulf, or whether Congress can limit the President's ability to use nuclear weapons first, or whether the courts can help decide either question?

The Gloss of History: An Introduction to the Separation of National Security Powers

Almost 200 years after the Constitutional Convention, a leading student of the presidency flatly rejected the supposition that the Convention created a government of separated powers. "It did nothing of the sort. Rather, it created a government of separated institutions *sharing* powers." Richard E. Neustadt, *Presidential Power* 26 (2d ed. 1980). Even those who disagree that the branches share power would today have to agree that they share authority over the same subjects, although they usually exercise it in different forms.

The more astute observers of the proposed constitutional design recognized these truisms from the start. "How is the executive?" asked a delegate to the Virginia ratifying convention. "Contrary to the opinion of all the best writers, blended with the legislative. We have asked for bread, and they have given us a stone." Louis Fisher, *President and Congress* 24 (1972). Indeed, the blending was intended and foreseen by some of the Framers. In any event, the actual experience of government under the Constitution finally wore away any lingering doubts.

In this chapter we introduce the framework of separated institutions sharing national security authority, and its historical gloss, by analyzing *Youngstown Sheet & Tube Co. v. Sawyer*, 343 U.S. 579 (1952) (*The Steel Seizure Case*), and the grouping of presidential powers that Justice Jackson described in his concurring opinion. *The Steel Seizure Case* is memorable for the apparent simplicity and formalism of Justice Black's opinion for the Court. A careful reading and comparison of the several concurring and dissenting opinions, however, suggests that a majority of the Justices took an approach to the separation of powers that is very different from Justice Black's.

The opinions collectively considered several arguments for constitutional or statutory authority for the President to seize the steel plants in a wartime emergency. First, the Solicitor General argued for authority from the Commander-in-Chief Clause. Second, he also claimed constitutional authority for the President to act unilaterally in response to emergencies. Third, several Justices considered the theory that the President had acquired customary authority by his past conduct with Congress's acquiescence. Fourth, others considered whether, even absent specific statutory authority, the President had a kind of aggregate authority from his duty to enforce the entire mass of statutes. The last two theories might be called theories of "near-miss" statutory authority to the degree that both took into account statutes that were relevant to the plant seizure without specifically authorizing it.

How did each Justice respond (if he did) to each of these claims of authority, and how did the numbers add up for each claim? You may find it helpful to fill in a table with the Justices in rows and the arguments in columns to answer this question. The point of this exercise is to probe beyond Justice Black's somewhat formalistic opinion for the Court and to examine in greater depth the logic and support in the alternative arguments for authority in a case implicating the nation's national security in wartime.

A. *THE STEEL SEIZURE CASE* AND ITS THEORIES OF PRESIDENTIAL POWER

Youngstown Sheet & Tube Co. v. Sawyer
(*The Steel Seizure Case*)
United States Supreme Court, 1952
343 U.S. 579

Mr. Justice BLACK delivered the opinion of the Court. We are asked to decide whether the President was acting within his constitutional power when he issued an order directing the Secretary of Commerce to take possession of and operate most of the Nation's steel mills. The mill owners argue that the President's order amounts to lawmaking, a legislative function which the Constitution has expressly confided to the Congress and not to the President. The Government's position is that the order was made on findings of the President that his action was necessary to avert a national catastrophe which would inevitably result from a stoppage of steel production, and that in meeting this grave emergency the President was acting within the aggregate of his constitutional powers as the Nation's Chief Executive and the Commander in Chief of the Armed Forces of the United States....

[The facts are set forth in Exec. Order No. 10,340, 17 Fed. Reg. 3139 (1952), which was reproduced in an appendix to the Court's opinion, 343 U.S. at 583-589. A copy of the order as it was originally published is reproduced *infra* pp. 26-27.]

...The Secretary immediately issued his own possessory orders, calling upon the presidents of the various seized companies to serve as operating managers for the United States. They were directed to carry on their activities in accordance with regulations and directions of the Secretary. The next morning the President sent a message to Congress reporting his action.... Twelve days later he sent a second message.... Congress has taken no action.

Obeying the Secretary's orders under protest, the companies brought proceedings against him in the District Court.... Holding against the Government on all points, the District Court on April 30 issued a preliminary injunction restraining the Secretary from "continuing the seizure and possession of the plants...and from acting under the purported authority of Executive Order No. 10340."

The President's power, if any, to issue the order must stem either from an act of Congress or from the Constitution itself. There is no statute that expressly authorizes the President to take possession of property as he did here. Nor is there any act of Congress to which our attention has been directed from which such a power can fairly be implied. Indeed, we do not understand the Government to rely on statutory authorization for this seizure. There are two statutes which do authorize the President

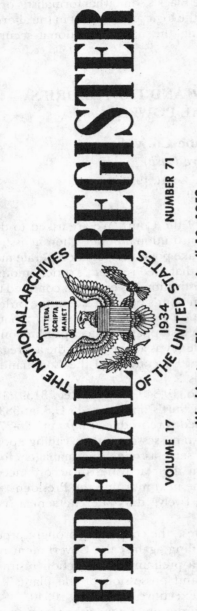

FEDERAL REGISTER

THE NATIONAL ARCHIVES

1934

LITTERA SCRIPTA MANET

OF THE UNITED STATES

VOLUME 17

NUMBER 71

Washington, Thursday, April 10, 1952

EXECUTIVE ORDER 10340

DIRECTING THE SECRETARY OF COMMERCE TO TAKE POSSESSION OF AND OPERATE THE PLANTS AND FACILITIES OF CERTAIN STEEL COMPANIES

WHEREAS on December 16, 1950, I proclaimed the existence of a national emergency which requires that the military, naval, air, and civilian defenses of this country be strengthened as speedily as possible to the end that we may be able to repel any and all threats against our national security and to fulfill our responsibilities in the efforts being made throughout the United Nations and otherwise to bring about a lasting peace; and

WHEREAS American fighting men

ber 22, 1951, pursuant to Executive Order No. 10233, and a strike has been called for 12:01 A. M., April 9, 1952; and

WHEREAS a work stoppage would immediately jeopardize and imperil our national defense and the defense of those joined with us in resisting aggression, and would add to the continuing danger of our soldiers, sailors, and airmen engaged in combat in the field; and

WHEREAS in order to assure the continued availability of steel and steel products during the existing emergency, it is necessary that the United States take possession of and operate the plants, facilities, and other property of the said companies as hereinafter provided:

that such activities do not interfere with the operation of such plants, facilities, and other properties.

4. Except so far as the Secretary of Commerce shall otherwise provide from time to time, the managements of the plants, facilities, and other properties possession of which is taken pursuant to this order shall continue their functions, including the collection and disbursement of funds in the usual and ordinary course of business in the names of their respective companies and by means of any instrumentalities used by such companies.

5. Except so far as the Secretary of Commerce may otherwise direct, existing rights and obligations of such companies shall remain in full force and

and fighting men of other nations of the United Nations are now engaged in deadly combat with the forces of aggression in Korea, and forces of the United States are stationed elsewhere overseas for the purpose of participating in the defense of the Atlantic Community against aggression; and

WHEREAS the weapons and other materials needed by our armed forces and by those joined with us in the defense of the free world are produced to a great extent in this country, and steel is an indispensable component of substantially all of such weapons and materials; and

WHEREAS steel is likewise indispensable to the carrying out of programs of the Atomic Energy Commission of vital importance to our defense efforts; and

WHEREAS a continuing and uninterrupted supply of steel is also indispensable to the maintenance of the economy of the United States, upon which our military strength depends; and

WHEREAS a controversy has arisen between certain companies in the United States producing and fabricating steel and the elements thereof and certain of their workers represented by the United Steel Workers of America, CIO, regarding terms and conditions of employment; and

WHEREAS the controversy has not been settled through the processes of collective bargaining or through the efforts of the Government, including those of the Wage Stabilization Board, to which the controversy was referred on Decem-

NOW, THEREFORE, by virtue of the authority vested in me by the Constitution and laws of the United States, and as President of the United States and Commander in Chief of the armed forces of the United States, it is hereby ordered as follows:

1. The Secretary of Commerce is hereby authorized and directed to take possession of all or such of the plants, facilities, and other property of the companies named in the list attached hereto, or any part thereof, as he may deem necessary in the interests of national defense; and to operate or to arrange for the operation thereof and to do all things necessary for, or incidental to, such operation.

2. In carrying out this order the Secretary of Commerce may act through or with the aid of such public or private instrumentalities or persons as he may designate; and all Federal agencies shall cooperate with the Secretary of Commerce to the fullest extent possible in carrying out the purposes of this order.

3. The Secretary of Commerce shall determine and prescribe terms and conditions of employment under which the plants, facilities, and other properties possession of which is taken pursuant to this order shall be operated. The Secretary of Commerce shall recognize the rights of workers to bargain collectively through representatives of their own choosing and to engage in concerted activities for the purpose of collective bargaining, adjustment of grievances, or other mutual aid or protection, provided

effect, and there may be made, in due course, payments of dividends on stock, and of principal, interest, sinking funds, and all other distributions upon bonds, debentures, and other obligations, and expenditures may be made for other ordinary corporate or business purposes.

6. Whenever in the judgment of the Secretary of Commerce further possession and operation by him of any plant, facility, or other property is no longer necessary or expedient in the interest of national defense, and the Secretary has reason to believe that effective future operation is assured, he shall return the possession and operation of such plant, facility, or other property to the company in possession and control thereof at the time possession was taken under this order.

7. The Secretary of Commerce is authorized to prescribe and issue such regulations and orders not inconsistent herewith as he may deem necessary or desirable for carrying out the purposes of this order; and he may delegate and authorize subdelegation of such of his functions under this order as he may deem desirable.

HARRY S. TRUMAN

THE WHITE HOUSE,
April 8th, 1952; 9:50 p. m. e. s. t.

to take both personal and real property under certain conditions. However, the Government admits that these conditions were not met and that the President's order was not rooted in either of the statutes. The Government refers to the seizure provisions of one of these statutes (§201(b) of the Defense Production Act) as "much too cumbersome, involved, and time-consuming for the crisis which was at hand."

Moreover, the use of the seizure technique to solve labor disputes in order to prevent work stoppages was not only unauthorized by any congressional enactment; prior to this controversy, Congress had refused to adopt that method of settling labor disputes. When the Taft-Hartley Act was under consideration in 1947, Congress rejected an amendment which would have authorized such governmental seizures in cases of emergency. Apparently it was thought that the technique of seizure, like that of compulsory arbitration, would interfere with the process of collective bargaining. Consequently, the plan Congress adopted in that Act did not provide for seizure under any circumstances. Instead, the plan sought to bring about settlements by use of the customary devices of mediation, conciliation, investigation by boards of inquiry, and public reports. In some instances temporary injunctions were authorized to provide cooling-off periods. All this failing, unions were left free to strike after a secret vote by employees as to whether they wished to accept their employers' final settlement offer.

It is clear that if the President had authority to issue the order he did, it must be found in some provision of the Constitution. And it is not claimed that express constitutional language grants this power to the President. The contention is that presidential power should be implied from the aggregate of his powers under the Constitution. Particular reliance is placed on provisions in Article II which say that "the executive Power shall be vested in a President..."; that "he shall take Care that the Laws be faithfully executed"; and that he "shall be Commander in Chief of the Army and Navy of the United States."

The order cannot properly be sustained as an exercise of the President's military power as Commander in Chief of the Armed Forces. The Government attempts to do so by citing a number of cases upholding broad powers in military commanders engaged in day-to-day fighting in a theater of war. Such cases need not concern us here. Even though "theater of war" be an expanding concept, we cannot with faithfulness to our constitutional system hold that the Commander in Chief of the Armed Forces has the ultimate power as such to take possession of private property in order to keep labor disputes from stopping production. This is a job for the Nation's lawmakers, not for its military authorities.

Nor can the seizure order be sustained because of the several constitutional provisions that grant executive power to the President. In the framework of our Constitution, the President's power to see that the laws are faithfully executed refutes the idea that he is to be a lawmaker. The Constitution limits his functions in the lawmaking process to the recommending of laws he thinks wise and the vetoing of laws he thinks bad. And the Constitution is neither silent nor equivocal about who shall make laws which the President is to execute. The first section of the first article says that "All legislative powers herein granted shall be vested in a Congress of the United States...." After granting many powers to the Congress, Article I goes on to provide that Congress may "make all laws which shall be necessary and proper for carrying into Execution the foregoing Powers, and all other Powers vested by this Constitution in the Government of the United States, or in any Department or Officer thereof."

The President's order does not direct that a congressional policy be executed in a manner prescribed by Congress — it directs that a presidential policy be executed in a manner prescribed by the President. The preamble of the order itself, like that of many statutes, sets out reasons why the President believes certain policies should be adopted, proclaims these policies as rules of conduct to be followed, and again, like a statute, authorizes a government official to promulgate additional rules and regulations consistent with the policy proclaimed and needed to carry that policy into execution. The power of Congress to adopt such public policies as those proclaimed by the order is beyond question. It can authorize the taking of private property for public use. It can make laws regulating the relationships between employers and employees, prescribing rules designed to settle labor disputes, and fixing wages and working conditions in certain fields of our economy. The Constitution does not subject this lawmaking power of Congress to presidential or military supervision or control.

It is said that other Presidents without congressional authority have taken possession of private business enterprises in order to settle labor disputes. But even if this be true, Congress has not thereby lost its exclusive constitutional authority to make laws necessary and proper to carry out the powers vested by the Constitution "in the Government of the United States, or in any Department or Officer thereof."

The Founders of this Nation entrusted the lawmaking power to the Congress alone in both good and bad times. It would do no good to recall the historical events, the fears of power and the hopes for freedom that lay behind their choice. Such a review would but confirm our holding that this seizure order cannot stand.

The judgment of the District Court is affirmed.

Mr. Justice FRANKFURTER, concurring. . . . The issue before us can be met, and therefore should be, without attempting to define the President's powers comprehensively. . . .

. . . We must therefore put to one side consideration of what powers the President would have had if there had been no legislation whatever bearing on the authority asserted by the seizure, or if the seizure had been only for a short, explicitly temporary period, to be terminated automatically unless Congressional approval were given. These and other questions, like or unlike, are not now here. . . .

. . . No room for doubt remains that the proponents as well as the opponents of the bill which became the Labor Management Relations Act of 1947 clearly understood that as a result of that legislation the only recourse for preventing a shutdown in any basic industry, after failure of mediation, was Congress. Authorization for seizure as an available remedy for potential dangers was unequivocally put aside. . . .

. . . Previous seizure legislation had subjected the powers granted to the President to restrictions of varying degrees of stringency. Instead of giving him even limited powers, Congress in 1947 deemed it wise to require the President, upon failure of attempts to reach a voluntary settlement, to report to Congress if he deemed the power of seizure a needed shot for his locker. The President could not ignore the specific limitations of prior seizure statutes. No more could he act in disregard of the limitation put upon seizure by the 1947 act.

It cannot be contended that the President would have had power to issue this order had Congress explicitly negated such authority in formal legislation. Congress has expressed its will to withhold this power from the President as though it had said so in so many words. The authoritatively expressed purpose of Congress to disallow such power to the President and to require him, when in his mind the occasion arose for such a seizure, to put the matter to Congress and ask for specific authority from it, could not be more decisive if it had been written into §§206-210 of the Labor Management Relations Act of 1947. . . .

. . . The utmost that the Korean conflict may imply is that it may have been desirable to have given the President further authority, a freer hand in these matters. Absence of authority in the President to deal with a crisis does not imply want of power in the Government. Conversely the fact that power exists in the Government does not vest it in the President. The need for new legislation does not enact it. Nor does it repeal or amend existing law. . . .

It is one thing to draw an intention of Congress from general language and to say that Congress would have explicitly written what is inferred, where Congress has not addressed itself to a specific situation. It is quite impossible, however, when Congress did specifically address itself to a problem, as Congress did to that of seizure, to find secreted in the interstices of legislation the very grant of power which Congress consciously withheld. To find authority so explicitly withheld is not merely to disregard in a particular instance the clear will of Congress. It is to disrespect the whole legislative process and the constitutional division of authority between President and Congress. . . .

To be sure, the content of the three authorities of Government is not to be derived from an abstract analysis. The areas are partly interacting, not wholly disjointed. The Constitution is a framework for Government. Therefore the way the framework has consistently operated fairly establishes that it has operated according to its true nature. Deeply embedded traditional ways of conducting government cannot supplant the Constitution or legislation, but they give meaning to the words of a text or supply them. It is an inadmissibly narrow conception of American constitutional law to confine it to the words of the Constitution and to disregard the gloss which life has written upon them. In short, a systematic, unbroken, executive practice, long pursued to the knowledge of the Congress and never before questioned, engaged in by presidents who have also sworn to uphold the Constitution, making as it were such exercise of power part of the structure of our Government, may be treated as a gloss on "executive Power" vested in the President by §1 of Art. II. . . .

. . . In [*United States v. Midwest Oil,* 236 U.S. 459 (1915)], lands which Congress had opened for entry were, over a period of 80 years and in 252 instances, and by Presidents learned and unlearned in the law, temporarily withdrawn from entry so as to enable Congress to deal with such withdrawals. No remotely comparable practice can be vouched for executive seizure of property at a time when this country was not at war, in the only constitutional way in which it can be at war. It would pursue the irrelevant to reopen the controversy over the constitutionality of some acts of Lincoln during the Civil War. . . . Suffice it to say that he seized railroads in territory where armed hostilities had already interrupted the movement of troops to the beleaguered Capital, and his order was ratified by the Congress.

The only other instances of seizures are those during the periods of the first and second world wars. In his eleven seizures of industrial facilities, President Wilson acted, or at least purported to act, under authority granted by Congress. Thus his seizures cannot be adduced as interpretations by a President of his own powers in the absence of statute.

Down to the World War II period, then, the record is barren of instances comparable to the one before us. Of twelve seizures by President Roosevelt prior to the enactment of the War Labor Disputes Act in June, 1943, three were sanctioned by existing law, and six others were effected after Congress, on December 8, 1941, had declared the existence of a state of war. In this case, reliance on the powers that flow from declared war has been commendably disclaimed by the Solicitor General. Thus the list of executive assertions of the power of seizure in circumstances comparable to the present reduces to three in the six-month period from June to December of 1941. We need not split hairs in comparing those actions to the one before us, though much might be said by way of differentiation. Without passing on their validity, as we are not called upon to do, it suffices to say that these three isolated instances do not add up, either in number, scope, duration or contemporaneous legal justification, to the kind of executive construction of the Constitution revealed in the *Midwest Oil* case. Nor do they come to us sanctioned by long-continued acquiescence of Congress giving decisive weight in a construction by the Executive of its powers....

Mr. Justice DOUGLAS, concurring.... The legislative nature of the action taken by the President seems clear to me. When the United States takes over an industrial plant to settle a labor controversy, it is condemning property. The seizure of the plant is a taking in the constitutional sense....

But there is a duty to pay for all property taken by the Government. The command of the Fifth Amendment is that no "private property be taken for public use, without just compensation."...

The President has no power to raise revenues. That power is in the Congress by Article I, Section 8 of the Constitution.... The branch of government that has the power to pay compensation for a seizure is the only one able to authorize a seizure or make lawful one that the President has effected....

Stalemates may occur when emergencies mount and the Nation suffers for lack of harmonious, reciprocal action between the White House and Capitol Hill. That is a risk inherent in our system of separation of powers. The tragedy of such stalemates might be avoided by allowing the President the use of some legislative authority. The Framers with memories of the tyrannies produced by a blending of executive and legislative power rejected that political arrangement. Some future generation may, however, deem it so urgent that the President have legislative authority that the Constitution will be amended. We could not sanction the seizures and condemnations of the steel plants in this case without reading Article II as giving the President not only the power to execute the laws but to make some....

Mr. Justice JACKSON, concurring in the judgment and opinion of the Court.... A judge, like an executive adviser, may be surprised at the poverty of really useful and unambiguous authority applicable to concrete problems of executive power as they actually present themselves. Just what our forefathers did envision, or would have envisioned had they foreseen modern conditions, must be divined from materials almost as enigmatic as the dreams Joseph was called upon to interpret for Pharaoh. A century and a half of partisan debate and scholarly speculation yields no net result but only supplies more or less apt quotations from respected sources on each side of any question. They largely cancel each other. And court decisions are indecisive because of the judicial practice of dealing with the largest questions in the most narrow way.

Associate Justice Robert H. Jackson.

Photograph by Harris Ewing. Collection of the
Supreme Court of the United States.

The actual art of governing under our Constitution does not and cannot conform to judicial definitions of the power of any of its branches based on isolated clauses or even single Articles torn from context. While the Constitution diffuses power the better to secure liberty, it also contemplates that practice will integrate the dispersed powers into a workable government. It enjoins upon its branches separateness but interdependence, autonomy but reciprocity. Presidential powers are not fixed but fluctuate, depending upon their disjunction or conjunction with those of Congress. We may well begin by a somewhat oversimplified grouping of practical situations in which a President may doubt, or others may challenge, his powers, and by distinguishing roughly the legal consequences of this factor of relativity.

1. When the President acts pursuant to an express or implied authorization of Congress, his authority is at its maximum, for it includes all that he possesses in his own right plus all that Congress can delegate.[2] In these circumstances, and in these only, may he be said (for what it may be worth) to personify the federal sovereignty. If his act is held unconstitutional under these circumstances, it usually means that the federal government as an undivided whole lacks power. A seizure executed by the President pursuant to an act of Congress would be supported by the strongest of presumptions and the widest latitude of judicial interpretation, and the burden of persuasion would rest heavily upon any who might attack it.

2. When the President acts in absence of either a congressional grant or denial of authority, he can only rely upon his own independent powers, but there is a zone of twilight in which he and Congress may have concurrent authority, or in which its distribution is uncertain. Therefore, congressional inertia, indifference or quiescence may sometimes, at least as a practical matter, enable, if not invite, measures on independent presidential responsibility. In this area, any actual test of power is likely to depend on the imperatives of events and contemporary imponderables rather than on abstract theories of law.

2. It is in this class of cases that we find the broadest recent statements of presidential power, including those relied on here. *United States v. Curtiss-Wright Corp.*, 299 U.S. 304, involved, not the question of the President's power to act without congressional authority, but the question of his right to act under and in accord with an Act of Congress....

That case does not solve the present controversy. It recognized internal and external affairs as being in separate categories, and held that the strict limitation upon congressional delegations of power to the President over internal affairs does not apply with respect to delegations of power in external affairs. It was intimated that the President might act in external affairs without congressional authority, but not that he might act contrary to an Act of Congress....

3. When the President takes measures incompatible with the expressed or implied will of Congress, his power is at its lowest ebb, for then he can rely only upon his own constitutional powers minus any constitutional powers of Congress over the matter. Courts can sustain exclusive presidential control in such a case only by disabling the Congress from acting upon the subject. Presidential claim to a power at once so conclusive and preclusive must be scrutinized with caution, for what is at stake is the equilibrium established by our constitutional system.

Into which of these classifications does this executive seizure of the steel industry fit? It is eliminated from the first by admission, for it is conceded that no congressional authorization exists for this seizure. That takes away also the support of the many precedents and declarations which were made in relation, and must be confined, to this category.

Can it then be defended under flexible tests available to the second category? It seems clearly eliminated from that class because Congress has not left seizure of private property an open field but has covered it by three statutory policies inconsistent with this seizure. . . .

This leaves the current seizure to be justified only by the severe tests under the third grouping, where it can be supported only by any remainder of executive power after subtraction of such powers as Congress may have over the subject. In short, we can sustain the President only by holding that seizure of such strike-bound industries is within his domain and beyond control by Congress. Thus, this Court's first review of such seizures occurs under circumstances which leave presidential power most vulnerable to attack and in the least favorable of possible constitutional postures.

I did not suppose, and I am not persuaded, that history leaves it open to question, at least in the courts, that the executive branch, like the Federal Government as a whole, possesses only delegated powers. The purpose of the Constitution was not only to grant power, but to keep it from getting out of hand. However, because the President does not enjoy unmentioned powers does not mean that the mentioned ones should be narrowed by a niggardly construction. Some clauses could be made almost unworkable, as well immutable, by refusal to indulge some latitude of interpretation for changing times. I have heretofore, and do now, give to the enumerated powers the scope and elasticity afforded by what seem to be reasonable practical implications instead of the rigidity dictated by a doctrinaire textualism.

The Solicitor General seeks the power of seizure in three clauses of the Executive Article, the first reading, "The executive Power shall be vested in a President of the United States of America." Lest I be thought to exaggerate, I quote the interpretation which his brief puts upon it: "In our view, this clause constitutes a grant of all the executive powers of which the Government is capable." If that be true, it is difficult to see why the forefathers bothered to add several specific items, including some trifling ones.[9] . . .

. . . I cannot accept the view that this clause is a grant in bulk of all conceivable executive power but regard it as an allocation to the presidential office of the generic powers thereafter stated.

---

9. ". . . He may require the Opinion, in writing, of the principal Officer in each of the executive Departments, upon any Subject relating to the Duties of their respective Offices. . . ." U.S. Const., Art. II, §2. He ". . . shall Commission all the Officers of the United States." U.S. Const., Art. II, §3. Matters such as those would seem to be inherent in the Executive if anything is.

The clause on which the Government next relies is that "The President shall be Commander in Chief of the Army and Navy of the United States. . . ." These cryptic words have given rise to some of the most persistent controversies in our constitutional history. Of course, they imply something more than an empty title. But just what authority goes with the name has plagued presidential advisors who would not waive or narrow it by nonassertion yet cannot say where it begins or ends. It undoubtedly puts the Nation's armed forces under presidential command. Hence, this loose appellation is sometimes advanced as support for any presidential action, internal or external, involving use of force, the idea being that it vests power to do anything, anywhere, that can be done with an army or navy.

That seems to be the logic of an argument tendered at our bar — that the President having, on his own responsibility, sent American troops abroad derives from that act "affirmative power" to seize the means of producing a supply of steel for them. To quote, "Perhaps the most forceful illustrations of the scope of presidential power in this connection is the fact that American troops in Korea, whose safety and effectiveness are so directly involved here, were sent to the field by an exercise of the President's constitutional powers." Thus, it is said he has invested himself with "war powers."

I cannot foresee all that it might entail if the Court should indorse this argument. Nothing in our Constitution is plainer than that declaration of a war is entrusted only to Congress. Of course, a state of war may in fact exist without a formal declaration. But no doctrine that the Court could promulgate would seem to me more sinister and alarming than that a President whose conduct of foreign affairs is so largely uncontrolled, and often even is unknown, can vastly enlarge his mastery over the internal affairs of the country by his own commitment of the Nation's armed forces to some foreign venture. I do not, however, find it necessary or appropriate to consider the legal status of the Korean enterprise to discountenance argument based on it.

Assuming that we are in a war *de facto*, whether it is or is not a war *de jure*, does that empower the Commander in Chief to seize industries he thinks necessary to supply our army? The Constitution expressly places in Congress power "to raise and *support* Armies" and "to *provide* and *maintain* a navy." (Emphasis supplied.) This certainly lays upon Congress primary responsibility for supplying the armed forces. Congress alone controls the raising of revenues and their appropriation and may determine in what manner and by what means they shall be spent for military and naval procurement. I suppose no one would doubt that Congress can take over war supply as a Government enterprise. On the other hand, if Congress sees fit to rely on free private enterprise collectively bargaining with free labor for support and maintenance of our armed forces, can the Executive, because of lawful disagreements incidental to that process, seize the facility for operation upon Government-imposed terms?

There are indications that the Constitution did not contemplate that the title Commander in Chief *of the Army and Navy* will constitute him also Commander in Chief of the country, its industries and its inhabitants. He has no monopoly of "war powers," whatever they are. While Congress cannot deprive the President of the command of the army and navy, only Congress can provide him an army or navy to command. It is also empowered to make rules for the "Government and Regulation of land and naval Forces," by which it may to some unknown extent impinge upon even command functions.

That military powers of the Commander in Chief were not to supersede representative government of internal affairs seems obvious from the Constitution and from elementary American history. Time out of mind, and even now in many parts of the world, a military commander can seize private housing to shelter his troops. Not so, however, in the United States, for the Third Amendment says, "No Soldier shall, in time of peace be quartered in any house, without the consent of the Owner, nor in time of war, but in a manner to be prescribed by law." Thus, even in war time, his seizure of needed military housing must be authorized by Congress. It also was expressly left to Congress to "provide for calling forth the Militia to execute the Laws of the Union, suppress Insurrections and repel Invasions. . . ." Such a limitation on the command power, written at a time when the militia rather than a standing army was contemplated as the military weapon of the Republic, underscores the Constitution's policy that Congress, not the Executive, should control utilization of the war power as an instrument of domestic policy. Congress, fulfilling that function, has authorized the President to use the army to enforce certain civil rights. On the other hand, Congress has forbidden him to use the army for the purpose of executing general laws except when *expressly* authorized by the Constitution or by act of Congress.

While broad claims under this rubric often have been made, advice to the President in specific matters usually has carried overtones that powers, even under this head, are measured by the command functions usual to the topmost officer of the army and navy. Even then, heed has been taken of any efforts of Congress to negate his authority.

We should not use this occasion to circumscribe, much less to contract, the lawful role of the President as Commander in Chief. I should indulge the widest latitude of interpretation to sustain his exclusive function to command the instruments of national force, at least when turned against the outside world for the security of our society. But, when it is turned inward, not because of rebellion but because of a lawful economic struggle between industry and labor, it should have no such indulgence. His command power is not such an absolute as might be implied from that office in a militaristic system but is subject to limitations consistent with a constitutional Republic whose law and policy-making branch is a representative Congress. The purpose of lodging dual titles in one man was to insure that the civilian would control the military, not to enable the military to subordinate the presidential office. No penance would ever expiate the sin against free government of holding that a President can escape control of executive powers by law through assuming his military role. What the power of command may include I do not try to envision, but I think it is not a military prerogative, without support of law, to seize persons or property because they are important or even essential for the military and naval establishment.

The third clause in which the Solicitor General finds seizure powers is that "he shall take Care that the Laws be faithfully executed. . . ." That authority must be matched against words of the Fifth Amendment that "No person shall be . . . deprived of life, liberty, or property, without due process of law. . . ." One gives a governmental authority that reaches so far as there is law, the other gives a private right that authority shall go no farther. These signify about all there is of the principle that ours is a government of laws, not of men, and that we submit ourselves to rulers only if under rules.

The Solicitor General lastly grounds support of the seizure upon nebulous, inherent powers never expressly granted but said to have accrued to the office from the customs and claims of preceding administrations. The plea is for a resulting power to deal with a crisis or an emergency according to the necessities of the case, the unarticulated assumption being that necessity knows no law. . . .

The appeal . . . that we declare the existence of inherent powers *ex necessitate* to meet an emergency asks us to do what many think would be wise, although it is something the forefathers omitted. They knew what emergencies were, knew the pressures they engender for authoritative action, knew, too, how they afford a ready pretext for usurpation. We may also suspect that they suspected that emergency powers would tend to kindle emergencies. Aside from suspension of the privilege of the writ of habeas corpus in time of rebellion or invasion, when the public safety may require it, they made no express provision for exercise of extraordinary authority because of a crisis.[19] I do not think we rightfully may so amend their work, and, if we could, I am not convinced it would be wise to do so, although many modern nations have forthrightly recognized that war and economic crisis may upset the normal balance between liberty and authority. . . .

In the practical working of our government we already have evolved a technique within the framework of the Constitution by which normal executive powers may be considerably expanded to meet an emergency. Congress may and has granted extra-ordinary authorities which lie dormant in normal times but may be called into play by the Executive in war or upon proclamation of a national emergency. . . .

In view of the ease, expedition and safety with which Congress can grant and has granted large emergency powers, certainly ample to embrace this crisis, I am quite unimpressed with the argument that we should affirm possession of them without statute. Such power either has no beginning or it has no end. If it exists, it need submit to no legal restraint. I am not alarmed that it would plunge us straightway into dictatorship, but it is at least a step in that wrong direction.

As to whether there is imperative necessity for such powers, it is relevant to note the gap that exists between the President's paper powers and his real powers. The Constitution does not disclose the measure of the actual controls wielded by the modern presidential office. That instrument must be understood as an Eighteenth-Century sketch of a government hoped for, not as a blueprint of the Government that is. Vast accretions of federal power, eroded from that reserved by the States, have magnified the scope of presidential activity. Subtle shifts take place in the centers of real power that do not show on the face of the Constitution.

Executive power has the advantage of concentration in a single head in whose choice the whole Nation has a part, making him the focus of public hopes and expectations. In drama, magnitude and finality his decisions so far overshadow any others that almost alone he fills the public eye and ear. No other personality in public life can begin to compete with him in access to the public mind through modern methods of communications. By his prestige as head of state and his influence upon public opinion he exerts a leverage upon those who are supposed to check and balance his power which often cancels their effectiveness.

Moreover, rise of the party system has made a significant extraconstitutional supplement to real executive power. No appraisal of his necessities is realistic which overlooks that he heads a political system as well as a legal system. Party loyalties and interests, sometimes more binding than law, extend his effective control into branches of government other than his own and he often may win, as a political leader, what he cannot command under the Constitution. Indeed, Woodrow Wilson,

---

19. I exclude, as in a very limited category by itself, the establishment of martial law. . . .

commenting on the President as leader both of his party and of the Nation, observed, "If he rightly interpret the national thought and boldly insist upon it, he is irresistible.... His office is anything he has the sagacity and force to make it." I cannot be brought to believe that this country will suffer if the Court refuses further to aggrandize the presidential office, already so potent and so relatively immune from judicial review, at the expense of Congress.

But I have no illusion that any decision by this Court can keep power in the hands of Congress if it is not wise and timely in meeting its problems. A crisis that challenges the President equally, or perhaps primarily, challenges Congress. If not good law, there was worldly wisdom in the maxim attributed to Napoleon that "The tools belong to the man who can use them." We may say that power to legislate for emergencies belongs in the hands of Congress, but only Congress itself can prevent power from slipping through its fingers....

... With all its defects, delays and inconveniences, men have discovered no technique for long preserving free government except that the Executive be under the law, and that the law be made by parliamentary deliberations.

Such institutions may be destined to pass away. But it is the duty of the Court to be last, not first, to give them up.

Mr. Justice BURTON, concurring in both the opinion and judgment of the Court.... In the case before us, Congress authorized a procedure which the President declined to follow. Instead, he followed another procedure which he hoped might eliminate the need for the first. Upon its failure, he issued an executive order to seize the steel properties in the face of the reserved right of Congress to adopt or reject that course as a matter of legislative policy.

This brings us to a further crucial question. Does the President, in such a situation, have inherent constitutional power to seize private property which makes congressional action in relation thereto unnecessary? We find no such power available to him under the present circumstances. The present situation is not comparable to that of an imminent invasion or threatened attack. We do not face the issue of what might be the President's constitutional power to meet such catastrophic situations. Nor is it claimed that the current seizure is in the nature of a military command addressed by the President, as Commander in Chief, to a mobilized nation waging, or imminently threatened with, total war.[7]...

Mr. Justice CLARK, concurring in the judgment of the Court.... The limits of presidential power are obscure. However, Article II, no less than Article I, is part of "a constitution intended to endure for ages to come, and, consequently, to be adapted to the various *crises* of human affairs." Some of our Presidents, such as Lincoln, "felt that measures otherwise unconstitutional might become lawful by becoming indispensable to the preservation of the Constitution through the preservation of the nation." Others, such as Theodore Roosevelt, thought the President to be capable, as a "steward" of the people, of exerting all power save that which is specifically prohibited by the Constitution or the Congress. In my view — taught me not only by the decision of Mr. Chief Justice Marshall in *Little v. Barreme* [*infra* p. 78], but also by a score of other pronouncements of distinguished members of this

---

7. The President and Congress have recognized the termination of the major hostilities in the total wars in which the nation has been engaged. Many wartime procedures have expired or been terminated.

bench — the Constitution does grant to the President extensive authority in times of grave and imperative national emergency. In fact, to my thinking, such a grant may well be necessary to the very existence of the Constitution itself. As Lincoln aptly said, "[is] it possible to lose the nation and yet preserve the Constitution?" In describing this authority I care not whether one calls it "residual," "inherent," "moral," "implied," "aggregate," "emergency," or otherwise. I am of the conviction that those who have had the gratifying experience of being the President's lawyer have used one or more of these adjectives only with the utmost of sincerity and the highest of purpose.

I conclude that where Congress has laid down specific procedures to deal with the type of crisis confronting the President, he must follow those procedures in meeting the crisis; but that in the absence of such action by Congress, the President's independent power to act depends upon the gravity of the situation confronting the nation. I cannot sustain the seizure in question because here, as in *Little v. Barreme,* Congress had prescribed methods to be followed by the President in meeting the emergency at hand.

Mr. Chief Justice VINSON, with whom Mr. Justice REED and Mr. Justice MINTON join, dissenting. . . . Those who suggest that this is a case involving extraordinary powers should be mindful that these are extraordinary times. A world not yet recovered from the devastation of World War II has been forced to face the threat of another and more terrifying global conflict. . . .

. . . For almost two full years, our armed forces have been fighting in Korea, suffering casualties of over 108,000 men. Hostilities have not abated. The "determination of the United Nations to continue its action in Korea to meet the aggression" has been reaffirmed. Congressional support of the action in Korea has been manifested by provisions for increased military manpower and equipment and for economic stabilization, as hereinafter described. . . .

. . . Even ignoring for the moment whatever confidential information the President may possess as "the Nation's organ for foreign affairs," the uncontroverted affidavits in this record amply support the finding that "a work stoppage would immediately jeopardize and imperil our national defense." . . .

Focusing now on the situation confronting the President on the night of April 8, 1952, we cannot but conclude that the President was performing his duty under the Constitution to "take Care that the Laws be faithfully executed" — a duty described by President Benjamin Harrison as "the central idea of the office."

The President reported to Congress the morning after the seizure that he acted because a work stoppage in steel production would immediately imperil the safety of the Nation by preventing execution of the legislative programs for procurement of military equipment. And, while a shutdown could be averted by granting the price concessions requested by plaintiffs, granting such concessions would disrupt the price stabilization program also enacted by Congress. Rather than fail to execute either legislative program, the President acted to execute both.

Much of the argument in this case has been directed at straw men. We do not now have before us the case of a president acting solely on the basis of his own notions of the public welfare. Nor is there any question of unlimited executive power in this case. The President himself closed the door to any such claim when he sent his Message to Congress stating his purpose to abide by any action of Congress, whether approving or disapproving his seizure action. Here, the President immediately made sure that

Congress was fully informed of the temporary action he had taken only to preserve the legislative programs from destruction until Congress could act.

The absence of a specific statute authorizing seizure of the steel mills as a mode of executing the laws — both the military procurement program and the anti-inflation program — has not until today been thought to prevent the President from executing the laws. Unlike an administrative commission confined to the enforcement of the statute under which it was created, or the head of a department when administering a particular statute, the President is a constitutional officer charged with taking care that a "mass of legislation" be executed. Flexibility as to mode of execution to meet critical situations is a matter of practical necessity....

Whatever the extent of presidential power on more tranquil occasions, and whatever the right of the President to execute legislative programs as he sees fit without reporting the mode of execution to Congress, the single Presidential purpose disclosed on this record is to faithfully execute the laws by acting in an emergency to maintain the status quo, thereby preventing collapse of the legislative programs until Congress could act. The President's action served the same purposes as a judicial stay entered to maintain the status quo in order to preserve the jurisdiction of a Court....

In *United States v. Midwest Oil Co.*, this Court approved executive action where, as here, the President acted to preserve an important matter until Congress could act — even though his action in that case was contrary to an express statute. In this case, there is no statute prohibiting the action taken by the President in a matter not merely important but threatening the very safety of the Nation. Executive inaction in such a situation, courting national disaster, is foreign to the concept of energy and initiative in the Executive as created by the Founding Fathers. The Constitution was itself "adopted in a period of grave emergency.... While emergency does not create power, emergency may furnish the occasion for the exercise of power." The Framers knew, as we should know in these times of peril, that there is real danger in Executive weakness. There is no cause to fear Executive tyranny so long as the laws of Congress are being faithfully executed. Certainly there is no basis for fear of dictatorship when the executive acts, as he did in this case, only to save the situation until Congress could act....

NOTES AND QUESTIONS

Counting Heads in Steel Seizure. What exactly is the holding of *The Steel Seizure Case*? Which Justices acknowledge the power of the Commander in Chief to act without statutory authority, and in what circumstances? Which Justices would endorse a narrower constitutional emergency power in the President, despite the absence of statutory or express constitutional authority? Which Justices find "near miss" authority either by virtue of a consistent executive practice or by virtue of the President's obligation to enforce all the laws, including inconsistent statutes? Do not proceed through the remaining notes and questions until you have answered these questions as best you can. *See generally* Edward S. Corwin, *The Steel Seizure Case: Judicial Brick Without Straw*, 53 Colum. L. Rev. 53 (1953); Paul G. Kauper, *The Steel Seizure Case: Congress, the President and the Supreme Court*, 51 Mich. L. Rev. 141 (1952).

a. The President's Claim of Lawmaking Authority

1. *May the President Ever Make Law?* If we take literally Justice Black's description of the separation of powers, can the President ever be a lawmaker? His words are consistent with the nondelegation doctrine noted by the Supreme Court in 1892: "That Congress cannot delegate legislative power to the President is a principle universally recognized as vital to the integrity and maintenance of the system of government ordained by the Constitution." *Field v. Clark*, 143 U.S. 649, 692 (1892).

However, as early as 1813, the Court declined to apply any such doctrine literally. In *The Brig Aurora*, 11 U.S. (7 Cranch) 382 (1813), the Court upheld a delegation of power to the President to lift an embargo on European trade if he found that the Europeans had "ceased to violate the neutral commerce of the United States." The Court reasoned that the delegation of legislative power was contingent solely on a finding of facts. In *Field v. Clark* itself, after paying lip service to the "universally recognized" nondelegation principle, the Court upheld a delegation of power to the President to impose tariffs whenever he was "satisfied" of a need for them. 143 U.S. at 691-692.

Subsequently, reasoning partly from "governmental necessity," the Court suggested that any delegation of legislative power that contains an "intelligible principle" to guide the delegate's discretion could be sustained against a nondelegation attack. *J.W. Hampton, Jr. & Co. v. United States*, 276 U.S. 394, 409-410 (1928). *See also Mistretta v. United States*, 488 U.S. 361, 371-379 (1989) (applying the foregoing standards in rejecting a nondelegation attack on statute creating Sentencing Commission). In only two cases has the Supreme Court applied the nondelegation doctrine to strike down statutory delegations of power to the executive: *Schechter Poultry Corp. v. United States*, 295 U.S. 495 (1935), and *Panama Refining Co. v. Ryan*, 293 U.S. 388 (1935). The Court has not done so since 1935.

Against this background, Justice Black's opinion cannot be taken literally. The President *may* exercise *delegated* lawmaking power. Indeed, when he does so, "his authority is at its maximum," *The Steel Seizure Case*, 343 U.S. at 635 (Jackson, J., concurring), for he acts not only with his own authority but with all that Congress can delegate. The difficulty in *The Steel Seizure Case* in the majority's view was that there was neither a statutory delegation nor constitutional power for the seizure.

2. *The Form of the President's Law.* When the President does act properly as lawmaker, what form does his "law" take? The executive order by which President Truman ordered the seizure of the steel plants indicates the usual form of presidential law. *See generally* Adam L. Warber, *Executive Orders and the Modern Presidency: Legislating from the Oval Office* (2006); Phillip J. Cooper, *By Order of the President* (2002); Kenneth R. Mayer, *With the Stroke of a Pen* (2001). Presidential proclamations have also been used as presidential law, *see, e.g.*, *United States v. Curtiss-Wright Exp. Corp.*, 299 U.S. 304 (1936) (*infra* p. 53), but today they are reserved chiefly for ceremonial announcements.

Presidential national security law also may take the form of a National Security Decision Directive (NSDD), National Security Directive (NSD), Presidential Decision Directive (PDD), National Security Presidential Directive (NSPD), Presidential Policy Directive, or Presidential Study Directive (the labels vary from administration to administration), or perhaps a Military Order. *See generally* Cooper, *supra*, at 143-197. One survey of presidential laws identifies no fewer than 14 different labels that Presidents have used. Harold C. Relyea, *Presidential Directives: Background and Overview* (Cong. Res. Serv. 98-611 GOV), Nov. 26, 2008.

One difference is that executive orders and proclamations must be published in the *Federal Register,* 44 U.S.C. §1505 (2000), while national security directives need not be. In fact, only 247 of at least 1,042 presidential directives issued through the National Security Council (NSC) between 1961 and 1988 were publicly released for either congressional or public scrutiny. General Accounting Office, *National Security: The Use of Presidential Directives to Make and Implement U.S. Policy* 2 (Dec. 1988). Legislation has been proposed that would require filing of such directives with the Office of the Federal Register and their disclosure to the Speaker of the House and President Pro Tempore of the Senate. H.R. 5092, 100th Cong. (1988).

Another difference is that executive orders are usually sent to the U.S. Attorney General "for his consideration as to both form and legality," 1 C.F.R. §19.2(b) (2005), while national security directives are not. No published regulation governs the legal vetting of such directives, although in the first Bush administration the Attorney General attended NSC "meetings pertaining to his jurisdiction, including covert actions." G. Hughes (Exec. Sec'y to NSC), *Memorandum re: Description of [NSC] Organization* 1 (Apr. 18, 1989) (unclassified summary of NSD-1 (Jan. 30, 1989)). It is likely today that many national security directives are reviewed by the NSC Legal Adviser or the White House Counsel.

Typically an executive order cites its promulgating authority in its preamble. Eighty-three percent of the executive orders issued from 1945 to 1965 were issued upon specific statutory authority. Ruth P. Morgan, *The President and Civil Rights* 286 n.2 (1970). These presidential laws were thus made with delegated legislative authority and carried the same force and effect as statutes. *See generally* Peter Raven-Hansen, *Making Agencies Follow Orders: Judicial Review of Agency Violations of Executive Order 12,291,* 1983 Duke L.J. 285, 297-301. The rest of the orders were either executive housekeeping orders directed solely at the internal workings of the executive branch or purported exercises of inherent constitutional lawmaking authority in the President. The difficulty of the steel seizure order is laid bare by its preamble. What lawmaking authority did President Truman cite?

3. *Legislative Rules.* Presidential "law" may also take the form of regulations promulgated by presidential subordinates in the executive branch or in the "independent" agencies. Usually these regulations, or "legislative rules" in the administrative lawyer's jargon, are promulgated as exercises of legislative authority delegated directly to the subordinates. The Supreme Court has declared that so "long as [a] regulation remains in force the Executive Branch is bound by it, and indeed the United States as the sovereign composed of the three branches is bound to respect and enforce it." *United States v. Nixon,* 418 U.S. 683, 696 (1974). Even some regulations issued by the President or his subordinates gratuitously — without statutory compulsion — carry this effect. *See, e.g., Service v. Dulles,* 354 U.S. 363 (1957). *See generally* Peter Raven-Hansen, *Regulatory Estoppel: When Agencies Break Their Own "Laws,"* 64 Tex. L. Rev. 1 (1985).

b.   The Claim of War Powers as Commander in Chief

1. *The Effect of Declaration and Location.* The Korean War was an undeclared war fought overseas. Does the Court's rejection of the Commander-in-Chief Clause as

authority for the steel seizure turn on the locus of the war? On the locus of the exercise of presidential power at issue? On the absence of a declared war? How did the different Justices answer these questions? On the legality of the Korean War, see *infra* pp. 324-328. Interestingly, Chief Justice Rehnquist, who was Justice Jackson's law clerk at the time of *The Steel Seizure Case*, believed that the "profound ambivalence" about the undeclared Korean War was a major factor in the decision, which he believes would have come out differently during declared World War II. William H. Rehnquist, *The Supreme Court* 96-97 (2001).

2. *Scope of Commander-in-Chief Power*. What is the scope of the Commander-in-Chief power that emerges by negative inference from these opinions? Where in the Constitution do the asserted limits of the scope of the Commander-in-Chief power appear? Consider President Truman's assessment of *The Steel Seizure Case:*

> Whatever the six justices of the Supreme Court meant by their differing opinions about the Constitutional powers of the President, he must always act in a national emergency. It is not very realistic for the justices to say that comprehensive powers shall be available to the President only when a war has been declared or when the country has been invaded. We live in an age when hostilities begin without polite exchanges of diplomatic notes. There are no longer sharp distinctions between combatants and non-combatants, between military targets and the sanctuary of civilian areas. Nor can we separate the economic facts from the problems of defense and security....
>
> The President, who is Commander in Chief and who represents the interest of all the people, must [be] able to act at all times to meet any sudden threat to the nation's security. A wise President will always work with Congress, but when Congress fails to act or is unable to act in a crisis, the President, under the Constitution, must use his powers to safeguard the nation. [2 Harry S. Truman, *Memoirs: Years of Trial and Hope* 478 (Doubleday ed. 1956).]

Do you agree?

c.   The Claim of Inherent Emergency Powers

1. *"Inherent Powers" Defined*. The Solicitor General's last resort in *The Steel Seizure Case* was the argument that the seizure was a constitutional exercise of "inherent" presidential powers. As Justice Jackson observed, "Loose and irresponsible use of adjectives colors all non-legal and much legal discussion of presidential powers." 343 U.S. at 646. "Inherent" is sometimes used interchangeably with "implied," "incidental," "plenary," "aggregate," or even "general executive powers" allegedly conferred by the Vestiture, Take Care, and presidential Oath of Office Clauses of Article II. Here we will loosely use "inherent powers" to differentiate those that are farthest removed from any express grant of constitutional or statutory authority from those that appear to be more closely tied to — "implied" in — express grants of such authority, recognizing that all these powers fall on a continuum.

2. *Constitutional Emergency Powers*. Does the Constitution confer emergency powers? Consider Article I, section 8, clauses 15 and 18; Article I, section 9, clause 2; Article I, section 10, clause 3; and Article IV, section 4. Does Justice Jackson deny the existence of constitutional emergency powers? How, in his view, can the Republic cope with national emergencies? We explore emergency powers of the President in Chapter 4 and of the Congress in Chapter 5.

3. *Inherent Emergency Power After Steel Seizure.* After *The Steel Seizure Case*, does the President have *any* inherent constitutional emergency authority? See *infra* pp. 67-72, 83-89. Recall the lineup of the Justices concerning emergency powers. If the existence of such authority turns on the "gravity of the situation confronting the nation," 343 U.S. at 662 (Clark, J., concurring), who decides that question? How did the dissenters decide the gravity of the situation?

d.   The Claim of Customary Authority

Power Through Practice? Some scholars have argued that the President makes law severed from any statutory mooring by simply seizing the initiative — going first. *See* Terry M. Moe & William G. Howell, *The Presidential Power of Unilateral Action*, 15 J.L. Econ. & Org. 132, 134 (1999):

> Because presidents are executives, and because of the discretion, opportunities, and resources executives have available to them in politics, presidents are particularly well suited to be first-movers and to reap the agenda powers that go along with it. If they want to shift the status quo by taking unilateral action on their own authority, whether or not that authority is clearly established in law, they can simply do it — quickly, forcefully, and (if they like) with no advance notice. The other branches are then presented with a *fait accompli*, and it is up to them to respond. If they are unable to respond effectively, or decide not to, the President wins by default. And even if they do respond, which could take years, he may still get much of what he wants anyway. [*Id.* at 137.]

Justice Frankfurter seemed to agree, at least if the President takes the same kind of initiative with sufficient frequency. Justice Frankfurter asserted that

> a systematic, unbroken, executive practice, long pursued to the knowledge of the Congress and never before questioned, engaged in by Presidents who have also sworn to uphold the Constitution, making as it were such an exercise of power part of the structure of government, may be treated as a gloss on "executive Power" vested in the President by §1 of Art. II. [343 U.S. at 610-611.]

Executive practice in which Congress has acquiesced may evidence an appropriate interpretation of the Constitution and thus ripen into a kind of constitutional common law or custom. "Deeply embedded traditional ways of conducting the government cannot supplant the Constitution or legislation, but they give meaning to the words of a text or supply them." *Id.* at 610. *See generally* William C. Banks & Peter Raven-Hansen, *National Security Law and the Power of the Purse* 114-118 (1994).

Why did the history of plant seizures described by Justice Frankfurter not establish an executive practice in which Congress had acquiesced, creating a constitutional common law or customary authority for the steel seizure? What history would have laid a sufficient predicate for congressional acquiescence in the steel plant seizure?

e.   The Claim of Aggregate Executive Authority to Execute *All* the Laws

Aggregated Authority? Does the President's responsibility for executing the "mass of legislation" vest him with a whole of executive power that is greater than the sum of the delegated parts, or at least power "to faithfully execute" *all* "the laws in an emergency to maintain the status quo, thereby preventing collapse of the legislative programs until Congress could act"? *See The Steel Seizure Case*, 343 U.S. at 702 (Vinson, C.J., dissenting). *Cf. Myers v. United States*, 272 U.S. 52, 135 (1926) (The President "may properly supervise and guide [executive officers'] construction of the statutes under which they act in order to secure that unitary and uniform execution of the laws which Article II of the Constitution evidently contemplated in vesting general executive power in the President alone."). Does this aggregate authority and duty to coordinate statutory commands permit a President to choose among conflicting commands? What were the conflicting statutory commands in *The Steel Seizure Case*?

B.   JUSTICE JACKSON'S GROUPING OF PRESIDENTIAL POWERS

Although Justice Black wrote the opinion for the Court in *The Steel Seizure Case*, Justice Jackson's famous grouping of presidential powers is better remembered in separation-of-powers analysis. Chief Justice Rehnquist said it "brings together as much combination of analysis and common sense as there is in this area." *Dames & Moore v. Regan*, 453 U.S. 654, 661 (1981). We therefore consider each of Justice Jackson's groups in turn.

1.   When the President Acts Pursuant to Delegated Authority

Justice Jackson's first group of presidential powers involves situations in which "the President acts pursuant to an express or implied authorization of Congress," and "his authority is [therefore] at its maximum. . . ." 343 U.S. at 635. In these situations, the President purports to act on authority delegated by Congress. One scholar reports that in 50 cases purporting to apply Justice Jackson's framework, *none* falling into this category has found the President's action unconstitutional, or "even suggested that such an outcome was possible." Edward T. Swaine, *The Political Economy of Youngstown*, 83 S. Cal. L. Rev. 263, 311 (2010).

As noted above, the Court has long since ruled that Congress may delegate at least some of its legislative powers to the executive, as long as Congress legislates "intelligible principles" — standards — by which the executive discretion can be channeled and measured. The legality of the President's exercise of delegated authority therefore turns on (a) whether Congress may delegate the specific authority to the executive, (b) whether the delegating statute contains standards for the exercise of the delegated discretion, (c) whether the executive follows the standards, and (d) whether the exercise of delegated authority otherwise violates the Constitution.

For example, a majority of the Supreme Court conditionally upheld the President's order for the military detention of a U.S. citizen captured on the battlefield in Afghanistan on the authority of the Authorization for the Use of Military Force that Congress passed after 9/11. *See Hamdi v. Rumsfeld*, 542 U.S. 507 (2004), *infra* p. 831. Although the Authorization, set forth *infra* p. 97, did not expressly delegate detention authority to the President, it impliedly did so by authorizing "all necessary and appropriate force" against "nations, organizations, or persons" associated with the 9/11 attacks. The Authorization thus also contained a standard limiting executive detention discretion just to individuals falling into this category. Moreover, the majority of the Court reasoned that the Constitution poses "no bar to this Nation's holding one of its own citizens as an enemy combatant." *Hamdi*, 542 U.S. at 519. Due process, however, entitled Hamdi to "notice of the factual basis for his classification, and a fair opportunity to rebut the Government's factual assertions before a neutral decision-maker." *Id.*, 542 U.S. at 533. The Court therefore remanded the case for further proceedings.

2. When the President Acts with Congressional Acquiescence

Justice Jackson's second group of presidential powers falls into a "zone of twilight in which [the President] and Congress may have concurrent authority, or in which its distribution is uncertain [and] congressional inertia, indifference or quiescence may sometimes, at least as a practical matter, enable, if not invite, measures on independent presidential responsibility." *The Steel Seizure Case*, 343 U.S. at 637-638. This twilight zone can be occupied by an executive practice of the sort Justice Frankfurter identified: long continued, consistent, and known to Congress, in effect providing the executive with a claim of authority on a theory like adverse possession. Justice Frankfurter pointed, for example, to 252 instances over 80 years when the President had temporarily barred public entry on certain public lands in order to allow Congress to decide whether they should be kept pristine, from which the Supreme Court found customary authority in *Midwest Oil*, 236 U.S. 459 (1919).

However, Justice Frankfurter found "[n]o remotely comparable practice . . . [of] executive seizure of property at a time when this country is not at war, in the only constitutional way in which it can be at war." 342 U.S. at 611. Although presidents had also seized private property before President Truman's seizure of the steel plants (as Justice Frankfurter illustrated with a 14-page pull-out chart in an appendix to his opinion, 343 U.S. at 615-628), some of these seizures were during declared wars, and others were pursuant to express statutory authority. "Thus [these] seizures cannot be adduced as interpretations by a President of his own powers in the absence of statute." *Id.* After distinguishing most of the prior seizures, Justice Frankfurter finally reduced the list of seizures comparable to Truman's to just three.

> [I]t suffices to say that these three isolated instances do not add up, either in number, scope, duration or contemporaneous legal justification, to the kind of executive construction of the Constitution revealed in the *Midwest Oil* case. Nor do they come to us sanctioned by long-continued acquiescence of Congress giving decisive weight in a construction by the Executive of its powers.

Id. at 613.

If the practice of plant seizures was insufficient to establish customary authority in the twilight zone, Justice Frankfurter's brief analysis nevertheless laid down some markers for claims of such authority. One scholar has proposed that the relevant factors to consider include the consistency, frequency, duration, "density" (the number of times an act is repeated over the course of its duration), continuity, and normalcy (nonattribution to presidential or congressional personality aberrations or unique historical circumstances) of the executive practice, congressional notice of the practice, and meaningful congressional acquiescence. Michael J. Glennon, *The Use of Custom in Resolving Separation of Powers Disputes*, 64 B.U. L. Rev. 109, 128-138 (1984). The last, in turn, is a function of the absence of objection, the institutional opportunity to object, the utility of objection (none for a *fait accompli*), and noninterference with protected freedoms (tantamount to a rule of clear statement for acquiescence in executive practices restricting individual freedoms). *Id.* at 139-144.

3.   When the President Takes Measures Incompatible with the Expressed or Implied Will of Congress

Justice Jackson's third group of presidential powers consists of those that the President asserts in conflict with the express or implied will of Congress. The Supreme Court has decided almost a dozen cases in this group, although none has yet involved national security per se (unless you categorize *The Steel Seizure Case* as such a case). In *Public Citizen v. United States Department of Justice*, 491 U.S. 440 (1989), Justice Kennedy asserted that these cases fall into two groups, each representing a different analytical approach:

> In some of our more recent cases involving the powers and prerogatives of the President, we have employed something of a balancing approach, asking whether the statute at issue prevents the President "'from accomplishing [his] constitutionally assigned functions,'" *Morrison v. Olson*, 487 U.S. 654, 695 (1988), quoting *Nixon v. Administrator of General Services*, 433 U.S. 425, 443 (1977), and whether the extent of the intrusion on the President's powers "is justified by an overriding need to promote objectives within the constitutional authority of Congress." Ibid. In each of these cases, the power at issue was not explicitly assigned by the text of the Constitution to be within the sole province of the President, but rather was thought to be encompassed within the general grant to the President of the "executive Power." U.S. Const., Art. II, §1, cl. 1. Thus, for example, the relevant aspect of our decision in *Morrison* involved the President's power to remove Executive officers, a power we had recognized is not conferred by any explicit provision in the text of the Constitution (as is the appointment power), but rather is inferred to be a necessary part of the grant of the "executive Power." See *Myers v. United States*, 272 U.S. 52, 115-116 (1926). Similarly, in *Administrator of General Services*, we were confronted with the question of the Executive Branch's power to control the disposition of Presidential materials, a matter which, though vital to the President's ability to perform his assigned functions, is not given to exclusive Presidential control by any explicit provision in the Constitution itself. We said there that "the proper inquiry focuses on the extent to which [the congressional restriction] prevents the Executive Branch from accomplishing its constitutionally assigned functions," and that we would invalidate the statute only if the potential for disruption of the President's constitutional functions were present and if "that impact [were not] justified by an overriding need to promote objectives within the constitutional authority of Congress." 433 U.S., at 443. See also *United States v. Nixon*, 418 U.S. 683, 703-707 (1974) (Executive privilege).
>
> In a line of cases of equal weight and authority, however, where the Constitution by explicit text commits the power at issue to the exclusive control of the President, we have refused to tolerate *any* intrusion by the Legislative Branch. For example, the Constitution confers upon the President the "Power to grant Reprieves and Pardons for Offenses against the United States, except in Cases of Impeachment." U.S. Const., Art. II, §2, cl. 1. In *United States v. Klein*, 13 Wall. 128 (1872), the Court considered a federal statute that

allowed citizens who had remained loyal to the Union during the Civil War to recover compensation for property abandoned to Union troops during the War. At issue was the validity of a provision in the statute that barred the admission of a Presidential pardon in such actions as proof of loyalty. Although this provision dd not impose direct restrictions on the President's power to pardon, the Court held that the Congress could not in any manner limit the full legal effect of the President's power. As we said there: "[I]t is clear that the legislature cannot change the effect of . . . a pardon any more than the executive can change a law." Id., at 148. . . .

The justification for our refusal to apply a balancing test in these cases, though not always made explicit, is clear enough. Where a power has been committed to a particular Branch of the Government in the text of the Constitution, the balance already has been struck by the Constitution itself. It is improper for this Court to arrogate to itself the power to adjust a balance settled by the explicit terms of the Constitution. To take an obvious example, it would be improper for us to hold that, although the Constitution sets 35 as the age below which one cannot be President, age 30 would in fact be a permissible construction of this term. See U.S. Const., Art. II, §1. And it would be equally improper for us to determine that the level of importance at which a jury trial in a common-law suit becomes available is $1,000 instead of $20, as the Constitution provides. See U.S. Const., Amdt. 7. These minor adjustments might be seen as desirable attempts to modernize the original constitutional provisions, but where the Constitution draws a clear line, we may not engage in such tinkering.

However improper would be these slight adjustments to the explicit and unambiguous balances that are struck in various provisions of the Constitution, all the more improper would it be for this Court, which is, after all, one of the three coequal Branches of the Federal Government, to rewrite the particular balance of power that the Constitution specifies among the Executive, Legislative, and Judicial Departments. This is not to say that each of the three Branches must be entirely separate and distinct, for that is not the governmental structure of checks and balances established by the Framers. See *Mistretta v. United States*, 488 U.S. 361, 380-381 (1989); *Humphrey's Executor v. United States*, 295 U.S. 602, 629 (1935). But as to the particular divisions of power that the Constitution does in fact draw, we are without authority to alter them, and indeed we are empowered to act in particular cases to prevent any other Branch from undertaking to alter them. [*Id.* at 484-485 (Kennedy, J., with whom the Chief Justice and Justice O'Connor join, concurring in the judgment).]

NOTES AND QUESTIONS

1. *Category 3 National Security Initiatives.* Although very few category 3 national security disputes reach the courts, they still arise outside the courts. A number of national security initiatives during the George W. Bush administration presented legal questions arguably falling into Justice Jackson's category 3, including the following:

a. Does the Commander in Chief's power to order military detention of U.S. citizens trump 18 U.S.C. §4001(a) (2006), which prohibits detention of U.S. citizens except pursuant to an act of Congress?

b. Does the Commander in Chief's power to order the use of "enhanced interrogation techniques" against enemy combatants trump 18 U.S.C. §2340A (2006), which prohibits torture outside the United States?

c. Does judicial review of petitions for the writ of habeas corpus from military detainees in Guantánamo unconstitutionally interfere with the Commander in Chief's conduct of the military campaign against Al Qaeda and its supporters?

d. Does the Commander in Chief's power to collect intelligence trump the Foreign Intelligence Surveillance Act, 50 U.S.C. §§1801-1881g (2006 & Supp. III 2009), as amended by Pub. L. No. 111-259, §801, 124 Stat. 2654, 2746 (2010)?

e. Would the Commander in Chief's power to conduct the military campaign in Iraq trump legislation that would require redeployment of troops from Iraq by a certain date? (President Bush vetoed such a bill on the ground that it "purports to direct the conduct of the operations of the war in a way that infringes upon the powers vested in the Presidency by the Constitution, including as Commander in Chief of the Armed Forces." *See Message to the House of Representatives Returning Without Approval the "U.S. Troop Readiness, Veterans' Care, Katrina Recovery, and Iraq Accountability Appropriations Act, 2007,"* 43 Weekly Comp. Pres. Doc. 560 (May 1, 2007)).

See David J. Barron & Martin S. Lederman, *The Commander in Chief at the Lowest Ebb — Framing the Problem, Doctrine, and Original Understanding,* 121 Harv. L. Rev. 689, 706-711 (2008). We return to each of these questions in later chapters.

2. *Ascertaining the Will of Congress.* We have spoken of congressional inaction as one possible manifestation of congressional acquiescence in the making of custom-ary executive authority. But, as Justice Frankfurter found in *The Steel Seizure Case,* inaction also may manifest Congress's implied will to *deny* the President authority. According to one view, in deciding whether a challenged executive action falls into Jackson's third group because it violates the will of Congress, a court "should assess strong indicia of this will, such as recent congressional denials of executive branch requests for legislation, and is not restricted to language of enacted statutes." Christopher Bryant & Carl Tobias, *Youngstown Revisited,* 29 Hastings Const. L.Q. 373, 425 (2002). Does this insight help reconcile the treatment of legislative silence or inaction in *The Steel Seizure Case? See also Matthew Baker, Comment, The Sound of Congressional Silence: Judicial Distortion of the Legislative-Executive Balance of Power,* 2009 BYU L. Rev. 225.

3. *Formalism vs. Functionalism or "Balancing."* One scholar paraphrases Justice Kennedy's distinction as follows:

At times, [constitutional] text will be sufficient, without necessarily developing an overarching vision of the structure, to decide major cases: thus, the Presentment Clause and the bicamerality requirement furnished the rule of decision in *INS v. Chadha*; ... and the Appointments Clause did the same for *Buckley v. Valeo, Morrison v. Olson,* and *Freytag v. Commissioner.* Sometimes, however, it will be necessary to extrapolate what amounts to a blueprint of organizational relationships from the fundamental structural postulates one sees as informing the Constitution as a whole.... [This] sort of extrapolation ... is ... appropriate where explicit constitutional text provides little help in deciding separation of powers issues, such as questions of presidential privilege or immunity.... [1 Laurence H. Tribe, *American Constitutional Law* 130-131 (3d. ed. 2000).]

Which approach do you think would most often be appropriate to decide national security law conflicts between Congress and the President? Does it depend on how the various national security powers are assigned by the Constitution's "explicit text"? How "explicit" does a textual assignment need to be? If the President orders the detention of enemy combatants in a war in violation of rules for detention set out by statute, how should a court decide the resulting conflict in a proper case? On the one hand, the President is surely within his implied (or "explicit"?) command authority as Commander in Chief in ordering his troops to detain combatants. On the other hand, Congress has explicit authority to "make Rules concerning Captures on Land and Water," U.S. Const. art. I, §8, cl. 11, and to "make Rules for the Government and Regulation of the land and naval Forces," *id.* cl. 14, as well as to "define . . . Offences against the Law of Nations." *Id.* cl. 10.

Unfortunately for predictable constitutional analysis (but perhaps fortunately for the Republic), the President's national security powers are mostly implied in the Commander-in-Chief Clause, and the text often provides little help. This suggests that most national security law conflicts will be subject to the balancing or structural extrapolation approach.

4. *Aggrandizement vs. Encroachment.* Another analytic cut at separation of powers disputes in Justice Jackson's third grouping distinguishes between legislation by which Congress attempts to aggrandize power for itself (by, for example, appointing one of its members to an executive commission) and legislation that merely "encroaches" on another branch by limiting its power in some fashion or by assigning that power to a third branch. *See, e.g.,* Jonathan T. Molot, *Principled Minimalism: Restriking the Balance Between Judicial Minimalism and Neutral Principles,* 90 Va. L. Rev. 1753, 1823 (2004). Because the Framers were especially concerned about congressional usurpation of executive branch functions, *see Mistretta v. United States,* 488 U.S. 361, 411 n.35 (1989), self-aggrandizing legislation calls for especially careful scrutiny, under which it will almost always fail. Legislation merely limiting another branch, on the other hand, is judged by the balancing test described by Justice Kennedy.

5. *Reconciling the Analyses.* The apparent divergence between these lines of authority can possibly be reconciled by treating the different tests as sequential rather than as alternative. *See, e.g.,* Harold J. Krent, *Separating the Strands in Separation of Powers Controversies,* 74 Va. L. Rev. 1253, 1257 (1988); *cf.* Lee C. Weingart, Note, *Who Keeps the Secrets?: A Framework and Analysis of the Separation of Powers Dispute in American Foreign Service Association v. Garfinkle,* 59 Geo. Wash. L. Rev. 193 (1990). Thus, when deciding a separation of powers challenge to the action of a branch, a court first decides whether the branch has "acted outside the constitutionally prescribed means of conduct," Krent, *supra,* at 1256-1257, or has aggrandized itself by wielding power that is demonstrably and uniquely committed to another branch. If so, then the action is unconstitutional; no further consideration of its particular effects on the other branches or of its justifications is necessary. If not, however, then the court must consider whether the acting branch has exercised power in such a way that it disrupts the functioning of one or both of the other branches, and weigh that disruption against the asserted need for such an exercise of power. How would the steel seizure order have fared by this mode of analysis?

6. *Avoidance of Category 3 Disputes.* One reason that few category 3 disputes reach the courts is that neither political branch risks pressing its claim. The President often

avoids the dispute by straining to construe statutes, or executive practice and any congressional response, to find implied statutory authority or customary authority. *See* Trevor W. Morrison, *Constitutional Avoidance in the Executive Branch*, 106 Colum. L. Rev. 1189 (2006). On other occasions, the President uses a presidential signing statement — a statement issued contemporaneously with the signing of a bill into law — to assert that some part of a statute is unconstitutional and that he will therefore disregard it. *See generally* T.J. Halstead, *Presidential Signing Statements: Constitutional and Institutional Implications* (Cong. Research Serv. RL33667), Sept. 17, 2007; Louis Fisher, *Signing Statements: Constitutional and Practical Limits*, 16 Wm. & Mary Bill of Rts. J. 183 (2007). While such a statement may declare a category 3 dispute, it does not place that dispute before a court unless and until a plaintiff with standing challenges the executive's refusal to enforce some part of the statute. *See* Peter Raven-Hansen & William C. Banks, *From Vietnam to Desert Shield: The Commander in Chief's Spending Power*, 81 Iowa L. Rev. 79, 117-126 (1995). Even if a category 3 dispute is litigated, courts have their own strong rule of avoidance that asks whether "a construction of the statute is fairly possible by which the question may be avoided." *Crowell v. Benson*, 285 U.S. 22, 62 (1932).

7. *Revisiting Justice Jackson's Groupings from a Political Economy Perspective.* In the chapters that follow, we will have many occasions to apply and to test the usefulness of Justice Jackson's groupings, but, for now, consider this assessment. Justice Jackson's groupings were partly descriptive and chiefly static: that is, they did not take into account how the President would dynamically interact with Congress and the courts to avoid falling into the third group (where he would likely lose) or to channel analysis into the first group (where he would likely win). *See* Swaine, *supra* p. 44. In other words, the Jackson framework itself created institutional incentives that encourage the President to try to undermine or blur the framework. Taking this "political economy" perspective, one scholar suggests the following hypotheses about how the President will actually interact with Congress:

> . . . (1) the president's reluctance to risk review at Justice Jackson's "lowest ebb" will tend to discourage seeking congressional authorization at all; (2) the sufficiency within the framework of implied legislative authorization [e.g., its acceptance of either explicit or implied legislative authorization] diminishes the president's incentive to seek explicit authorization; (3) the president will seek to defuse any adverse expressions of congressional will with interpretive techniques [e.g., reading a statute narrowly to avoid a constitutional question, disfavoring "implied repeal," or insisting on a "clear statement"] that may confound the framework; and (4) attributing categorical significance to congressional action (or inaction) tends to substitute judicial for congressional judgment [i.e., it empowers the courts]. [*Id.* at 273.]

C.   THE ROLE OF THE COURTS

Justice Jackson did not entirely leave the third branch out of his account of presidential power. At the end of his opinion he remarked on the importance of separated powers among the political branches: "Such institutions may be destined to pass away. But it is the duty of the Court to be last, not first, to give them up." 343 U.S. at 655. Yet his observation was hardly needed in view of the Supreme Court's disposition of *Steel Seizure.* Its affirmance of a preliminary injunction against the Secretary of Commerce enjoining the plant seizure was a powerful statement that the courts' national security powers include the power to decide whether the President has crossed constitutional lines in carrying out his national security initiatives. Indeed, a judicial role can be carved out under each of Justice Jackson's groupings.

In the first grouping, in which the President acts pursuant to authority granted by Congress, the courts' role is to decide whether Congress had the power to delegate that authority to the President (that is, whether the statute violates the nondelegation doctrine); if so, whether the President's action has complied with the standards of the delegation (that is, whether he has followed the statute); and finally, whether that action violates any constitutional limit or right. In other words, while Congress sets the parameters for the President's action by the terms of its statutory delegation, the courts interpret and enforce them by judicial review.

In the second grouping, the judicial role is less evident, but Justice Frankfurter's analysis of the claim of customary authority limns its contours. The courts may consider whether the executive practice is sufficiently long-standing, consistent, and notorious—in the sense that such practice provided sufficient notice and contemporaneous legal justification for Congress—to warrant an inference of congressional acquiescence. Of course, even this is not enough if the practice violates a constitutional limitation—which the courts will also decide.

Finally, if the President has acted in defiance of a statutory command, only the courts remain as a check on an executive abuse of power. (Well, that is an exaggeration; Congress can try to enforce one statute with another (by cutting off appropriations, for example), or even impeach the President, and, of course, the people can vote a first-term President out of office in the next election.) "Presidential claim to a power at once so conclusive and preclusive must be scrutinized with caution," Justice Jackson warned, "for what is at stake is the equilibrium established by our constitutional system." 343 U.S. at 638. Scrutinized by whom? Certainly by the courts on an appropriate challenge.

Nevertheless, one would go away with an overblown impression of the judicial role from reading *Steel Seizure* alone. When the "equilibrium of the constitutional system" is threatened, it should come as no surprise that even the courts may wobble. They have authored a collection of reasons *not* to decide national security disputes and found others in the case-or-controversy requirement of Article III, enabling them often to shy away from making what could be momentous decisions that could powerfully affect our national security. These reasons include the *standing* requirement, which goes to the qualifications of the claimant; the *ripeness* requirement, which implicates the readiness of a dispute for judicial resolution; and the *political question doctrine*, which goes to the suitability of the issues in a case for judicial resolution and implicates judicial competency to tackle them. We take these up in Chapter 6.

The President's National Security Powers

The constitutional text offers little help in tracing the President's national security powers. These powers are nebulously vested in broad and opaque phrases like "executive Power," "take Care that the Laws be faithfully executed," and "Commander in Chief," or secreted between the lines by implication or practical necessity. Building on this spare text, theorists and Presidents have reached sharply contrasting conclusions about the scope of presidential authority.

President Theodore Roosevelt espoused by words and by example the "stewardship" theory of presidential power. "[The President is] a steward of the people bound actively and affirmatively to do all he could for the people. [It is] not only his right but his duty to do anything that the needs of the Nation demand, unless such action [is] forbidden by the Constitution or by the law." Theodore Roosevelt, *Autobiography* 372 (1914). Alexander Hamilton drew support for the same theory from the difference between Article I's opening sentence, conferring only "[a]ll legislative Powers *herein granted*" (emphasis supplied), and Article II's opening sentence, vesting the President with "[t]he executive Power" without express limitation. 7 *The Works of Alexander Hamilton* 80 (John C. Hamilton ed., 1851).

By contrast, President William H. Taft asserted that "[t]he true view of the Executive function is . . . that the President can exercise no power which cannot be fairly and reasonably traced to some specific grant of power or justly implied and included within such express grant as proper and necessary to its exercise." William H. Taft, *Our Chief Magistrate and His Powers* 139-140 (1925).

As Justice Jackson stated in *The Steel Seizure Case*, "a century and a half of partisan debate and scholarly speculation yields no net result but only supplies more or less apt quotations from respected sources on each side of the equation. They largely cancel each other out." *Youngstown Sheet & Tube Co. v. Sawyer*, 343 U.S. 579, 634-635 (1952) (*The Steel Seizure Case*) (Jackson, J., concurring). Consequently, this chapter uses neither the constitutional text nor political theory to organize the analysis of the President's national security powers, but instead divides these powers into four broad and overlapping functional categories. We look in turn at the President's foreign relations, Commander-in-Chief, and emergency powers, and the power to protect information.

A. THE PRESIDENT'S FOREIGN RELATIONS POWERS

Article II is surprisingly sparse in vesting any express foreign relations power in the President. He is given the power, by and with the advice and consent of the Senate, to make treaties, provided that two-thirds of the Senate approves, and to nominate and appoint ambassadors, again by and with the advice and consent of the Senate. It would be imprecise to say that he shares these powers with the Senate, but he certainly cannot exercise them without the Senate. He is also empowered to receive foreign ambassadors and ministers, though read literally, this sounds strictly ceremonial. Finally, he is vested with "[t]he executive Power." Some scholars have argued that this grant includes a "'residual' foreign affairs power" under the "ordinary eighteenth-century meaning of executive power." Saikrishna B. Prakash & Michael D. Ramsey, *The Executive Power over Foreign Affairs*, 111 Yale L.J. 231, 234 (2001).

Article I seems far more generous. It gives Congress the power to make laws regulating foreign commerce, to establish naturalization rules, and to define and punish piracies and offenses against the law of nations, as well as powers involving war, letters of marque and reprisal, captures on land and water, and the armed forces. Even proponents of a "residual foreign affairs power" describe that power as residual because it is "limited by specific allocations of foreign affairs power" to Congress. Prakash & Ramsey, *supra*, at 235.

But a simple headcount of listed powers is misleading. In the first place, Congress has found it practically necessary to delegate many foreign relations powers to the President, thus placing many of his foreign policy initiatives in Justice Jackson's category 1. The following case, *United States v. Curtiss-Wright Export Corp.*, provides what is perhaps the most famous example. Second, the President has acquired foreign relations power by taking the initiative in the absence of statutory prohibitions. The second case in this chapter, *Dames & Moore v. Regan*, illustrates an application of the theory of customary authority to uphold an executive deal to settle claims by U.S. nationals against foreign states and, derivatively, to suspend claims pending in U.S. courts. Both *Curtiss-Wright* and *Dames & Moore* illustrate theories of authority that undergird many other foreign relations initiatives by the President, as reflected in the notes and questions that follow. Third, the courts tread cautiously and deferentially when reviewing a presidential exercise of foreign relations powers, sometimes giving a gloss to the powers that cannot be found in any express constitutional text. The *Curtiss-Wright* decision is today perhaps better known for its gloss (describing the "very delicate, plenary and exclusive power of the President as the sole organ of the federal government in the field of international relations," 299 U.S. 304, 320 (1936)) than for its actual, more modest holding approving a statutory delegation of power to the President.

United States v. Curtiss-Wright Export Corp.

United States Supreme Court, 1936
299 U.S. 304

Mr. Justice Sutherland delivered the opinion of the Court. On January 27, 1936, an indictment was returned in the court below, the first count of which charges that appellees, beginning with the 29th day of May, 1934, conspired to sell in the United

States certain arms of war, namely, fifteen machine guns, to Bolivia, a country then engaged in armed conflict in the Chaco, in violation of the Joint Resolution of Congress approved May 28, 1934, and the provisions of a proclamation issued on the same day by the President of the United States pursuant to authority conferred by §1 of the resolution. In pursuance of the conspiracy, the commission of certain overt acts was alleged, details of which need not be stated. The Joint Resolution follows:

> *Resolved by the Senate and House of Representatives of the United States of America in Congress assembled,* That if the President finds that the prohibition of the sale of arms and munitions of war in the United States to those countries now engaged in armed conflict in the Chaco may contribute to the reestablishment of peace between those countries, and if after consultation with the governments of other American Republics and with their cooperation, as well as that of such other governments as he may deem necessary, he makes proclamation to that effect, it shall be unlawful to sell, except under such limitations and exceptions as the President prescribes, any arms or munitions of war in any place in the United States to the countries now engaged in that armed conflict, or to any person, company, or association acting in the interest of either country, until otherwise ordered by the President or by Congress.
>
> Sec. 2. Whoever sells any arms or munitions of war in violation of section 1 shall, on conviction, be punished by a fine not exceeding $10,000 or by imprisonment not exceeding two years, or both.

The President's proclamation, after reciting the terms of the Joint Resolution, declares:

> Now, therefore, I, Franklin D. Roosevelt, President of the United States of America, acting under and by virtue of the authority conferred in me by the said joint resolution of Congress, do hereby declare and proclaim that I have found that the prohibition of the sale of arms and munitions of war in the United States to those countries now engaged in armed conflict in the Chaco may contribute to the reestablishment of peace between those countries, and that I have consulted with the governments of other American Republics and have been assured of the cooperation of such governments as I have deemed necessary as contemplated by the said joint resolution; and I do hereby admonish all citizens of the United States and every person to abstain from every violation of the provisions of the Joint Resolution above set forth, hereby made applicable to Bolivia and Paraguay, and I do hereby warn them that all violations of such provisions will be rigorously prosecuted.
>
> And I do hereby enjoin upon all officers of the United States charged with the execution of the laws thereof, the utmost diligence in preventing violations of the said joint resolution and this my proclamation issued thereunder, and in bringing to trial and punishment any offenders against the same.
>
> And I do hereby delegate to the Secretary of State the power of prescribing exceptions and limitations to the application of the said joint resolution of May 28, 1934, as made effective by this my proclamation issued thereunder. . . .

It is contended that by the Joint Resolution, the going into effect and continued operation of the resolution was conditioned (a) upon the President's judgment as to its beneficial effect upon the reestablishment of peace between the countries engaged in armed conflict in the Chaco; (b) upon the making of a proclamation, which was left to his unfettered discretion, thus constituting an attempted substitution of the President's will for that of Congress; (c) upon the making of a proclamation putting an end to the operation of the resolution, which again was left to the President's unfettered discretion; and (d) further, that the extent of its operation in particular cases was subject to limitation and exception by the President, controlled by no standard. In each of these particulars, appellees urge that Congress abdicated its essential functions and delegated them to the Executive.

Whether, if the Joint Resolution had related solely to internal affairs it would be open to the challenge that it constituted an unlawful delegation of legislative power to the Executive, we find it unnecessary to determine. The whole aim of the resolution is to affect a situation entirely external to the United States, and falling within the category of foreign affairs. The determination which we are called to make, therefore, is whether the Joint Resolution, as applied to that situation, is vulnerable to attack under the rule that forbids a delegation of the lawmaking power. In other words, assuming (but not deciding) that the challenged delegation, if it were confined to internal affairs, would be invalid, may it nevertheless be sustained on the ground that its exclusive aim is to afford a remedy for a hurtful condition within foreign territory?

It will contribute to the elucidation of the question if we first consider the differences between the powers of the federal government in respect of foreign or external affairs and those in respect of domestic or internal affairs. That there are differences between them, and that these differences are fundamental, may not be doubted.

The two classes of powers are different, both in respect of their origin and their nature. The broad statement that the federal government can exercise no powers except those specifically enumerated in the Constitution, and such implied powers as are necessary and proper to carry into effect the enumerated powers, is categorically true only in respect of our internal affairs. In that field, the primary purpose of the Constitution was to carve from the general mass of legislative powers *then possessed by the states* such portions as it was thought desirable to vest in the federal government, leaving those not included in the enumeration still in the states. *Carter v. Carter Coal Co.*, 298 U.S. 238, 294. That this doctrine applies only to powers which the states had, is self evident. And since the states severally never possessed international powers, such powers could not have been carved from the mass of state powers but obviously were transmitted to the United States from some other source. During the colonial period, those powers were possessed exclusively by and were entirely under the control of the Crown. By the Declaration of Independence, "the Representatives of the United States of America" declared the United (not the several) Colonies to be free and independent states, and as such to have "full Power to levy War, conclude Peace, contract Alliances, establish Commerce and to do all other Acts and Things which Independent States may of right do."

As a result of the separation from Great Britain by the colonies acting as a unit, the powers of external sovereignty passed from the Crown not to the colonies severally, but to the colonies in their collective and corporate capacity as the United States of America. Even before the Declaration, the colonies were a unit in foreign affairs, acting through a common agency — namely the Continental Congress, composed of delegates from the thirteen colonies. That agency exercised the powers of war and peace, raised an army, created a navy, and finally adopted the Declaration of Independence. Rulers come and go; governments end and forms of government change; but sovereignty survives. A political society cannot endure without a supreme will somewhere. Sovereignty is never held in suspense. When, therefore, the external sovereignty of Great Britain in respect of the colonies ceased, it immediately passed to the union. See *Penhallow v. Doane*, 3 Dall. 54, 80-81. That fact was given practical application almost at once. The treaty of peace, made on September 3, 1783, was concluded between his Britannic Majesty and the "United States of America."

The Union existed before the Constitution, which was ordained and established among other things to form "a more perfect Union." Prior to that event, it is clear that the Union, declared by the Articles of Confederation to be "perpetual," was the sole possessor of external sovereignty and in the Union it remained without change save in so far as the Constitution in express terms qualified its exercise. The Framer's Convention was called and exerted its powers upon the irrefutable postulate that though the states were several their people in respect of foreign affairs were one. . . .

It results that the investment of the federal government with the powers of external sovereignty did not depend upon the affirmative grants of the Constitution. The powers to declare and wage war, to conclude peace, to make treaties, to maintain diplomatic relations with other sovereignties, if they had never been mentioned in the Constitution, would have vested in the federal government as necessary concomitants of nationality. Neither the Constitution nor the laws passed in pursuance of it have any force in foreign territory unless in respect of our own citizens; and operations of the nation in such territory must be governed by treaties, international understandings and compacts, and the principles of international law. As a member of the family of nations, the right and power of the United States in that field are equal to the right and power of the other members of the international family. Otherwise, the United States is not completely sovereign. The power to acquire territory by discovery and occupation, the power to expel undesirable aliens, the power to make such international agreements as do not constitute treaties in the constitutional sense, none of which is expressly affirmed by the Constitution, nevertheless exist as inherently inseparable from the conception of nationality. This the court recognized, and in each of the cases cited found the warrant for its conclusions not in the provisions of the Constitution, but in the law of nations. . . .

Not only, as we have shown, is the federal power over external affairs in origin and essential character different from that over internal affairs, but participation in the exercise of the power is significantly limited. In this vast external realm, with its important, complicated, delicate and manifold problems, the President alone has the power to speak or listen as a representative of the nation. He *makes* treaties with the advice and consent of the Senate; but he alone negotiates. Into the field of negotiation the Senate cannot intrude; and Congress itself is powerless to invade it. As Marshall said in his great argument of March 7, 1800, in the House of Representatives, "the President is the sole organ of the nation in its external relations, and its sole representative with foreign nations." Annals, 6th Cong., col. 613. The Senate Committee on Foreign Relations at a very early day in our history (February 15, 1816), reported to the Senate, among other things, as follows:

> The President is the constitutional representative of the United States with regard to foreign nations. He manages our concerns with foreign nations and must necessarily be most competent to determine when, how, and upon what subjects negotiation may be urged with the greatest prospect of success. For his conduct he is responsible to the Constitution. The committee considers this responsibility the surest pledge for the faithful discharge of his duty. They think the interference of the Senate in the direction of foreign negotiations calculated to diminish that responsibility and thereby to impair the best security for the national safety. The nature of transactions with foreign nations, moreover, requires caution and unity of design, and their success frequently

depends on secrecy and dispatch. U.S. Senate, Reports, Committee on Foreign Relations, vol. 8, p. 24.

It is important to bear in mind that we are here dealing not alone with an authority vested in the President by an exertion of legislative power, but with such an authority plus the very delicate, plenary and exclusive power of the President as the sole organ of the federal government in the field of international relations — a power which does not require as a basis for its exercise an act of Congress, but which, of course, like every other governmental power, must be exercised in subordination to the applicable provisions of the Constitution. It is quite apparent that if, in the maintenance of our international relations, embarrassment — perhaps serious embarrassment — is to be avoided and success for our aims achieved, congressional legislation which is to be made effective through negotiation and inquiry within the international field must often accord to the President a degree of discretion and freedom from statutory restriction which would not be admissible were domestic affairs alone involved. Moreover, he, not Congress, has the better opportunity of knowing the conditions which prevail in foreign countries, and especially is this true in time of war. He has his confidential sources of information. He has his agents in the form of diplomatic, consular and other officials. Secrecy in respect of information gathered by them may be highly necessary, and the premature disclosure of it productive of harmful results. Indeed, so clearly is this true that the first President refused to accede to a request to lay before the House of Representatives the instructions, correspondence, and documents relating to the negotiation of the Jay treaty — a refusal the wisdom of which was recognized by the House itself and has never since been doubted. In his reply to the request, President Washington said:

> The nature of foreign negotiations requires caution, and their success must often depend on secrecy; and even when brought to a conclusion a full disclosure of all the measures, demands, or eventual concessions which may have been proposed or contemplated would be extremely impolitic; for this might have a pernicious influence on future negotiations, or produce immediate inconveniences, perhaps danger and mischief, in relation to other powers. The necessity of such caution and secrecy was one cogent reason for vesting the power of making treaties in the President, with the advice and consent of the Senate, the principle on which that body was formed confining it to a small number of members. To admit, then, a right in the House of Representatives to demand and to have as a matter of course all the papers respecting a negotiation with a foreign power would be to establish a dangerous precedent.

The marked difference between foreign affairs and domestic affairs in this respect is recognized by both houses of Congress in the very form of their requisitions for information from the executive departments. In the case of every department except the Department of State, the resolution *directs* the official to furnish the information. In the case of the State Department, dealing with foreign affairs, the President is *requested* to furnish the information "if not incompatible with the public interest." A statement that to furnish the information is not compatible with the public interest rarely, if ever, is questioned.

When the President is to be authorized by legislation to act in respect of a matter intended to affect a situation in foreign territory, the legislator properly bears in mind the important consideration that the form of the President's action — or, indeed, whether he shall act at all—may well depend, among other things, upon the nature of the confidential information which he has or may thereafter receive, or upon the effect which his action may have upon our foreign relations. This consideration, in connection with what we have already said on the subject, discloses the unwisdom of requiring Congress in this field of governmental power to lay down narrowly definite standards by which the President is to be governed....

In the light of the foregoing observations, it is evident that this court should not be in haste to apply a general rule which will have the effect of condemning legislation like that under review as constituting an unlawful delegation of legislative power. The principles which justify such legislation find overwhelming support in the unbroken legislative practice which has prevailed almost from the inception of the national government to the present day....

...A legislative practice such as we have here, evidenced not by only occasional instances, but marked by the movement of a steady stream for a century and a half of time, goes a long way in the direction of proving the presence of unassailable ground for the constitutionality of the practice, to be found in the origin and history of the power involved, or in its nature, or in both combined....

Mr. Justice McREYNOLDS does not agree....

Mr. Justice STONE took no part in the consideration or decision of this case.

NOTES AND QUESTIONS

1. *Holding or Dictum?* What did the Court in *Curtiss-Wright* hold and what is the rationale for the holding? Is the discussion of the President's "plenary and exclusive" foreign affairs power dictum or is it a necessary first principle supporting the holding? *Compare The Steel Seizure Case*, 343 U.S. at 635-636 n.2 (Jackson, J., concurring) ("Much of the Court's opinion [in *Curtiss-Wright*] is dictum...."), *with* Charles A. Lofgren, *United States v. Curtiss-Wright Export Corporation: An Historical Reassessment*, 83 Yale L.J. 1, 12 (1973) (necessary first principle), *and Report of the Congressional Committees Investigating the Iran-Contra Affair, The Minority Report*, H.R. Rep. No. 433, S. Rep. No. 216, 100th Cong. 472 (1987) (hereinafter *Minority Report*) ("The Court's statements about the President's inherent foreign policy powers...were crucial to its final decision.").

2. *Practical Differences Between Foreign and Domestic Powers.* Leaving aside for the moment their sources, what are the practical differences between the federal government's foreign or external powers and its domestic or internal powers? Consider, for example, the government's ability to forecast when and how the powers will come into play, the speed with which they may need to be exercised, the need for flexibility once they have been exercised, their immediate impact on our daily lives, their long-term impact on our daily lives, their relationship to state powers, and the need for secrecy. Do you agree that these considerations, as a practical matter, require broader and less precise delegations from Congress to the President of authority for foreign affairs than those appropriate for delegations of authority for domestic affairs? *See* Roy E. Brownell II, *The Coexistence of United States v. Curtiss-Wright and Youngstown Sheet & Tube v. Sawyer in National Security Jurisprudence*, 16 J.L. & Pol. 1, 33-34 (2000).

Do the same kinds of practical considerations also require that we recognize broader *constitutional* power in the President in foreign than in domestic affairs?

Can such broad foreign affairs power be implied from the spare text of Article II? *See id.* at 29 (asserting that the President draws power from his duty to execute laws in the "unique legal realm which comprises the Law of Nations"). Is such power inherent in the constitutional office of the presidency? Or has it been created by executive custom in which Congress has acquiesced? However created, is it limited? If so, how?

3. *Extra-Constitutional Foreign Relations Power?* Do the same considerations, reinforced by history, require that we recognize *extraconstitutional* power in the President in foreign affairs, as Justice Sutherland argues? Is his theory consistent with the historical account set out in Chapter 2 of the framing of the Constitution? With the itemization of foreign affairs powers vested in Congress by Article I, section 8? Does Sutherland's theory necessarily dictate the primacy of the President in foreign affairs, or instead the sovereignty of the federal government as a whole? Does it follow from his theory that the Constitution has no application outside our borders?

Justice Sutherland's reasoning and authorities have been sharply challenged by constitutional scholars. *See, e.g.,* Michael D. Ramsey, *The Myth of Extraconstitutional Foreign Affairs Power,* 42 Wm. & Mary L. Rev. 379, 381 (2000) (*Curtiss-Wright* "wrongly describes the understanding of the drafters and ratifiers of the Constitution. There was no theory of extraconstitutional power in foreign affairs at the time the Constitution was drafted and ratified."); Lofgren, *supra* Note 1, at 32 ("[T]he history on which [major] segments [of *Curtiss-Wright*] rest is 'shockingly inaccurate.' If good history is a requisite to good constitutional law, then *Curtiss-Wright* ought to be relegated to history.") (citation omitted); David M. Levitan, *The Foreign Relations Power: An Analysis of Justice Sutherland's Theory,* 55 Yale L.J. 467, 489 (1946) (Sutherland's theory "does not harmonize with the [historical] facts."). *But see* Sarah H. Cleveland, *The Plenary Power Background of Curtiss-Wright,* 70 U. Colo. L. Rev. 1127 (1999) (arguing that *Curtiss-Wright* evolved from nineteenth-century jurisprudence of inherent plenary power); *see also* H. Jefferson Powell, *The Founders and the President's Authority Over Foreign Affairs,* 40 Wm. & Mary L. Rev. 1471 (1999) (asserting that the founders reflected a "coherent pattern of thought that accorded the President central responsibility for the foreign policy of the United States").

4. *The "Sole Organ" Claim.* Sutherland quotes then-Congressman, later Chief Justice, John Marshall for the proposition that "[t]he President is the sole organ of the nation in its external relations, and its sole representative with foreign nations." 299 U.S. at 319. Does it logically follow that the President is solely responsible for the *formulation* of foreign policy? Or does Marshall's language suggest only that the President is the nation's sole spokesperson and agent for communicating and executing foreign policy made by Congress or by him and the Congress together? One answer is suggested by the rest of John Marshall's statement from which Sutherland quoted. Marshall was defending President John Adams's extradition of a British subject to England pursuant to the Jay Treaty of 1795. He observed:

> The treaty, which is a law, enjoins the performance of a particular object. The person who is to perform this object is marked out by the Constitution, since the person is named who conducts the foreign intercourse, and is to take care that the laws be faithfully executed. The means by which it is to be performed, the force of the nation, are in the hands of this person.... Congress, unquestionably, may prescribe the mode, and Congress may devolve on others the whole execution of the contract; but, till this be

done, it seems the duty of the Executive department to execute the contract by any means it possesses. [10 *Annals of Cong.* 613-614.]

5. *The President as Foreign Policymaker.* As a practical matter, the President cannot be a mere conduit for congressionally made foreign policy. Professor Henkin argues that "the distinction between making foreign policy and conducting foreign relations is essentially empty: the President makes foreign policy by conducting foreign relations, by the way he conducts them and the content and tone he gives them." Louis Henkin, *Foreign Affairs and the Constitution,* 66 Foreign Aff. 284, 294 (Winter 1987/1988). Does it follow that the President alone makes foreign policy or that he can make policy at odds with that set by Congress? Consider Justice Jackson's statement in *The Steel Seizure Case,* 343 U.S. at 635-636 n.2, that *Curtiss-Wright* "intimated that the President might act in external affairs without congressional authority, but not that he might act contrary to an Act of Congress."

6. *Curtiss-Wright, So I'm Right.* The foregoing notes raise serious historical and analytic questions about the accuracy of Justice Sutherland's famous reference to the "very delicate, plenary and exclusive power of the President as the sole organ of the federal government in the field of international relations." 299 U.S. at 320. But does its accuracy—or possible quality as dictum—make any difference 75 years later?

Sometimes a memorable phrase, especially one that may escape close examination at the time because it seems not central to the result, can take on a life of its own, almost transcending the case in which it first appeared. Sutherland's statement has been cited countless times by both the courts and the President's lawyers—usually with little analysis of its origin—to support presidential foreign relations authority. The most persuasive way to counter such deference to the President is probably not to fault the reasoning of *Curtiss-Wright,* but to point instead to the role assigned to Congress in the action under review, the collaborative character of the action, the terms of any relevant statutory delegation, and other constitutional limits on the President. Recall that Justice Sutherland concluded his famous line by asserting unequivocally that this power, "of course . . . must be exercised in subordination to the applicable provisions of the Constitution." *Id.*

Dames & Moore v. Regan

United States Supreme Court, 1981
453 U.S. 654

Justice REHNQUIST delivered the opinion of the Court. . . . On November 4, 1979, the American Embassy in Tehran was seized and our diplomatic personnel were captured and held hostage. In response to that crisis, President Carter, acting pursuant to the International Emergency Economic Powers Act, 50 U.S.C. §§1701-1706 (1976 ed., Supp. III) (hereinafter IEEPA), declared a national emergency on November 14, 1979,[1] and blocked the removal or transfer of [Iranian assets]. Exec. Order

---

1. Title 50 U.S.C. §1701(a) (1976 ed., Supp. III) states that the President's authority under the Act "may be exercised to deal with any unusual and extraordinary threat, which has its source in whole or

No. 12170, 3 C.F.R. 457 (1980), note following 50 U.S.C. §1701 (1976 ed., Supp. III).[2] . . .

[Pursuant to the Order, the Secretary of the Treasury promulgated regulations nullifying attachments of Iranian assets on or after November 14, 1979, unless licensed by the Treasury Department. The Department subsequently licensed pre-judgment attachments in judicial proceedings against Iran. Dames & Moore sued Iranian defendants for breach of contract and obtained a pre-judgment attachment of Iranian assets.

Thereafter, the American hostages were released pursuant to an agreement obligating the United States to terminate all legal proceedings in U.S. courts involving claims of U.S. nationals against Iran, to nullify all attachments and judgments therein, to terminate such claims through binding arbitration, and to transfer U.S.-held Iranian assets to foreign banks for the satisfaction of any arbitration awards rendered against Iran. President Carter issued a series of executive orders implementing this agreement and "nullif[ying]" all non-Iranian interests in Iranian assets acquired after his initial blocking order. President Reagan subsequently ratified the Carter orders.

Meanwhile, Dames & Moore was granted summary judgment on its claim against the Iranian defendants, but the district court vacated all pre-judgment attachments and stayed further proceedings in light of the executive orders discussed above. Dames & Moore then filed an action in the district court to prevent enforcement of the executive orders and Treasury Department regulations implementing the agreement with Iran on the grounds that they were beyond the statutory and constitutional powers of the executive.]

Although we have in the past found and do today find Justice Jackson's classification [in *The Steel Seizure Case*, 343 U.S. at 635-638] of executive actions into three general categories analytically useful, we should be mindful of Justice Holmes' admonition, quoted by Justice Frankfurter in [that case at 343 U.S. 597] that "[t]he great ordinances of the Constitution do not establish and divide fields of black and white." *Springer v. Philippine Islands*, 277 U.S. 189, 209 (1928) (dissenting opinion). Justice Jackson himself recognized that his three categories represented "a somewhat over-simplified grouping," and it is doubtless the case that executive action in any particular instance falls, not neatly in one of three pigeonholes, but rather at some point along a spectrum running from explicit congressional authorization to explicit congressional prohibition. This is particularly true as respects cases such as the one before us, involving responses to international crises the nature of which Congress can hardly have been expected to anticipate in any detail.

In nullifying post-November 14, 1979, attachments and directing those persons holding blocked Iranian funds and securities to transfer them to the Federal Reserve Bank of New York for ultimate transfer to Iran, President Carter cited five sources of express or inherent power. The Government, however, has principally relied on §203 of the IEEPA as authorization for these actions. [The Court concluded that this

---

substantial part outside the United States, to the national security, foreign policy, or economy of the United States, if the President declares a national emergency with respect to such threat." Petitioner does not challenge President Carter's declaration of a national emergency.

2. Title 50 U.S.C. §1702(a)(1)(B) (1976 ed., Supp. III) empowers the President to investigate, regulate, direct and compel, nullify, void, prevent or prohibit, any acquisition, holding, withholding, use, transfer, withdrawal, transportation, importation or exportation of, or dealing in, or exercising any right, power, or privilege with respect to, or transactions involving, any property in which any foreign country or a national thereof has any interest. . . .

statute expressly authorized the nullification of the attachments and the transfer of assets.] . . .

. . . [T]here remains the question of the President's authority to suspend claims pending in American courts. Such claims have, of course, an existence apart from the attachments which accompanied them. In terminating these claims through Executive Order No. 12294 the President purported to act under authority of both the IEEPA and 22 U.S.C. §1732, the so-called "Hostage Act."

We conclude that although the IEEPA authorized the nullification of the attachments, it cannot be read to authorize the suspension of the claims. The claims of American citizens against Iran are not in themselves transactions involving Iranian property or efforts to exercise any rights with respect to such property. An in personam lawsuit, although it might eventually be reduced to judgment and that judgment might be executed upon, is an effort to establish liability and fix damages and does not focus on any particular property within the jurisdiction. The terms of the IEEPA therefore do not authorize the President to suspend claims in American courts. This is the view of all the courts which have considered the question.

The Hostage Act, passed in 1868, provides:

> Whenever it is made known to the President that any citizen of the United States has been unjustly deprived of his liberty by or under the authority of any foreign government, it shall be the duty of the President forthwith to demand of that government the reasons of such imprisonment; and if it appears to be wrongful and in violation of the rights of American citizenship, the President shall forthwith demand the release of such citizen, and if the release so demanded is unreasonably delayed or refused, the President shall use such means, not amounting to acts of war, as he may think necessary and proper to obtain or effectuate the release; and all the facts and proceedings relative thereto shall as soon as practicable be communicated by the President to Congress. Rev. Stat. §2001, 22 U.S.C. §1732.

We are reluctant to conclude that this provision constitutes specific authorization to the President to suspend claims in American courts. Although the broad language of the Hostage Act suggests it may cover this case, there are several difficulties with such a view. The legislative history indicates that the Act was passed in response to a situation unlike the recent Iranian crisis. Congress in 1868 was concerned with the activity of certain countries refusing to recognize the citizenship of naturalized Americans traveling abroad, and repatriating such citizens against their will. These countries were not interested in returning the citizens in exchange for any sort of ransom. This also explains the reference in the Act to imprisonment "in violation of the rights of American citizenship." Although the Iranian hostage-taking violated international law and common decency, the hostages were not seized out of any refusal to recognize their American citizenship — they were seized precisely *because* of their American citizenship. The legislative history is also somewhat ambiguous on the question whether Congress contemplated Presidential action such as that involved here or rather simply reprisals directed against the offending foreign country and *its* citizens.

Concluding that neither the IEEPA nor the Hostage Act constitutes specific authorization of the President's action suspending claims, however, is not to say that these statutory provisions are entirely irrelevant to the question of the validity of the President's action. We think both statutes highly relevant in the looser sense of indicating congressional acceptance of a broad scope for executive action in circumstances such as those presented in this case.... [T]he IEEPA delegates broad authority to the President to act in times of national emergency with respect to property of a foreign country. The Hostage Act similarly indicates congressional willingness that the President have broad discretion when responding to the hostile acts of foreign sovereigns. As Senator Williams, draftsman of the language eventually enacted as the Hostage Act, put it:

> If you propose any remedy at all, you must invest the Executive with some discretion, so that he may apply the remedy to a case as it may arise. As to England or France he might adopt one policy to relieve a citizen imprisoned by either one of those countries; as to the Barbary powers, he might adopt another policy; as to the islands of the ocean, another. With different countries that have different systems of government he might adopt different means. Cong. Globe, 40th Cong., 2d Sess., 4359 (1868).

Proponents of the bill recognized that it placed a "loose discretion" in the President's hands, id., at 4238 (Sen. Stewart), but argued that "[s]omething must be intrusted to the Executive" and that "[t]he President ought to have the power to do what the exigencies of the case require to rescue [a] citizen from imprisonment." Id., at 4233, 4357 (Sen. Williams). An original version of the Act, which authorized the President to suspend trade with a foreign country and even arrest citizens of that country in the United States in retaliation, was rejected because "there may be a great variety of cases arising where other and different means would be equally effective, and where the end desired could be accomplished without resorting to such dangerous and violent measures." Id., at 4233 (Sen. Williams).

Although we have declined to conclude that the IEEPA or the Hostage Act directly authorizes the President's suspension of claims for the reasons noted, we cannot ignore the general tenor of Congress's legislation in this area in trying to determine whether the President is acting alone or at least with the acceptance of Congress. As we have noted, Congress cannot anticipate and legislate with regard to every possible action the President may find it necessary to take or every possible situation in which he might act. Such failure of Congress specifically to delegate authority does not, "especially . . . in the areas of foreign policy and national security," imply "congressional disapproval" of action taken by the Executive. *Haig v. Agee*, [453 U.S. 280 (1981)], at 291. On the contrary, the enactment of legislation closely related to the question of the President's authority in a particular case which evinces legislative intent to accord the President broad discretion may be considered to "invite" "measures on independent presidential responsibility," *Youngstown*, 343 U.S. at 637 (Jackson, J., concurring). At least this is so where there is no contrary indication of legislative intent and when, as here, there is a history of congressional acquiescence in conduct of the sort engaged in by the President. It is to that history which we now turn.

Not infrequently in affairs between nations, outstanding claims by nationals of one country against the government of another country are "sources of friction" between the two sovereigns. *United States v. Pink*, 315 U.S. 203, 225 (1942). To resolve these difficulties, nations have often entered into agreements settling the claims of their respective nationals. As one treatise writer puts it, international agreements settling claims by nationals of one state against the government of another "are established international practice reflecting traditional international theory." L. Henkin, *Foreign Affairs and the Constitution* 262 (1972). Consistent with that principle, the United States has repeatedly exercised its sovereign authority to settle the claims of its nationals against foreign countries. Though those settlements have sometimes been made by treaty, there has also been a longstanding practice of settling such claims by executive agreement without the advice and consent of the Senate.[8] ... It is clear that the practice of settling claims continues today. Since 1952, the President has entered into at least 10 binding settlements with foreign nations, including an $80 million settlement with the People's Republic of China.

Crucial to our decision today is the conclusion that Congress has implicitly approved the practice of claim settlement by executive agreement. This is best demonstrated by Congress' enactment of the International Claims Settlement Act of 1949, 22 U.S.C. §1621 et seq. (1976 ed. and Supp. IV). The Act had two purposes: (1) to allocate to United States nationals funds received in the course of an executive claims settlement with Yugoslavia, and (2) to provide a procedure whereby funds resulting from future settlements could be distributed. To achieve these ends Congress created the International Claims Commission, now the Foreign Claims Settlement Commission, and gave it jurisdiction to make final and binding decisions with respect to claims by United States nationals against settlement funds. By creating a procedure to implement future settlement agreements, Congress placed its stamp of approval on such agreements. Indeed, the legislative history of the Act observed that the United States was seeking settlements with countries other than Yugoslavia and that the bill contemplated settlements of a similar nature in the future.

Over the years Congress has frequently amended the International Claims Settlement Act to provide for particular problems arising out of settlement agreements, thus demonstrating Congress' continuing acceptance of the President's claim settlement authority. ... As with legislation involving other executive agreements, Congress did not question the fact of the settlement or the power of the President to have concluded it. ... Finally, the legislative history of the IEEPA further reveals that Congress has accepted the authority of the Executive to enter into settlement agreements. Though the IEEPA was enacted to provide for some limitation on the President's emergency powers, Congress stressed that "[n]othing in this act is intended ... to interfere with the authority of the President to [block assets], or to impede the settlement of claims of U.S. citizens against foreign countries." S. Rep. No. 95-466, p. 6 (1977), U.S. Code Cong. & Admin. News, 1977, pp. 4540, 4544; 50 U.S.C. §1706(a)(1) (1976 ed., Supp. III).[11]

In addition to congressional acquiescence in the President's power to settle claims, prior cases of this Court have also recognized that the President does have some measure of power to enter into executive agreements without obtaining the

8. At least since the case of the "Wilmington Packet" in 1799, Presidents have exercised the power to settle claims of United States nationals by executive agreement. In fact, during the period of 1817-1917, "no fewer than eighty executive agreements were entered into by the United States looking toward the liquidation of claims of its citizens." W. McClure, *International Executive Agreements* 53 (1941).

11. Indeed, Congress has consistently failed to object to this longstanding practice of claim settlement by executive agreement, even when it has had an opportunity to do so. In 1972, Congress entertained legislation relating to congressional oversight of such agreements. But Congress took only limited action, requiring that the text of significant executive agreements be transmitted to Congress. 1 U.S.C. §112b. In *Haig v. Agee,* [453 U.S. 280], we noted that "[d]espite the longstanding and officially promulgated view that the Executive has the power to withhold passports for reasons of national security and foreign policy, Congress in 1978, 'though it once again enacted legislation relating to passports, left completely untouched the broad rule-making authority granted in the earlier Act.'" Ante, at 301, quoting *Zemel v. Rusk,* 381 U.S. 1, 12 (1965). Likewise in this case, Congress, though legislating in the area, has left "untouched" the authority of the President to enter into settlement agreements. ...

advice and consent of the Senate. In *United States v. Pink*, 315 U.S. 203 (1942), for example, the Court upheld the validity of the Litvinov Assignment, which was part of an Executive Agreement whereby the Soviet Union assigned to the United States amounts owed to it by American nationals so that outstanding claims of other American nationals could be paid. The Court explained that the resolution of such claims was integrally connected with normalizing United States' relations with a foreign state:

> Power to remove such obstacles to full recognition as settlement of claims of our nationals...certainly is a modest implied power of the President....No such obstacle can be placed in the way of rehabilitation of relations between this country and another nation, unless the historic conception of the powers and responsibilities...is to be drastically revised. *Id.* at 229-230....

Just as importantly, Congress has not disapproved of the action taken here. Though Congress has held hearings on the Iranian Agreement itself, Congress has not enacted legislation, or even passed a resolution, indicating its displeasure with the Agreement. Quite the contrary, the relevant Senate Committee has stated that the establishment of the Tribunal is "of vital importance to the United States." S. Rep. No. 97-71, p. 5 (1981).[13] We are thus clearly not confronted with a situation in which Congress has in some way resisted the exercise of Presidential authority.

Finally, we re-emphasize the narrowness of our decision. We do not decide that the President possesses plenary power to settle claims, even as against foreign governmental entities. As the Court of Appeals for the First Circuit stressed, "[t]he sheer magnitude of such a power, considered against the background of the diversity and complexity of modern international trade, cautions against any broader construction of authority than is necessary." *Chas. T. Main Intl., Inc. v. Khuzestan Water & Power Authority,* 651 F.2d [800 (1st Cir. 1980)], at 814. But where, as here, the settlement of claims has been determined to be a necessary incident to the resolution of a major foreign policy dispute between our country and another, and where, as here, we can conclude that Congress acquiesced in the President's action, we are not prepared to say that the President lacks the power to settle such claims....

The judgment of the District Court is accordingly affirmed....

[The opinion of Justice POWELL, concurring in part and dissenting in part, is omitted.]

NOTES AND QUESTIONS

1. *The Sounds of Congressional Silence in Dames & Moore and Steel Seizure.* In both *Dames & Moore* and *The Steel Seizure Case*, the President's authority to take private property was challenged, and in both cases the statutes were silent about that authority. How much weight may properly be assigned to congressional silence or inaction?

---

13. Contrast congressional reaction to the Iranian Agreements with congressional reaction to a 1973 Executive Agreement with Czechoslovakia. There the President sought to settle over $105 million in claims against Czechoslovakia for $20.5 million. Congress quickly demonstrated its displeasure by enacting legislation requiring that the Agreement be renegotiated. Though Congress has shown itself capable of objecting to executive agreements, it has rarely done so and has not done so in this case.

The Court routinely considers legislative inaction in common law cases, *see* Robert F. Williams, *Statutes as Sources of Law Beyond Their Terms in Common Law Cases*, 50 Geo. Wash. L. Rev. 554 (1982), and in deciding the validity of executive action. *See generally* William N. Eskridge Jr., *Interpreting Legislative Inaction*, 87 Mich. L. Rev. 67 (1988). On the other hand, the Court has admitted in other contexts that "we walk on quicksand when we try to find in the absence of . . . legislation a controlling legal principle." *Helvering v. Hallock*, 309 U.S. 106, 121 (1940). Why did congressional inaction in *The Steel Seizure Case* have a different meaning than it did in *Dames & Moore*? Are the two cases consistent in their treatment of legislative silence or inaction?

2. *Article I or Article II Power?* Was it really an Article II rather than an Article I power that the President exercised in *Dames & Moore*? The hostage release agreement with Iran was an executive agreement rather than a treaty. Although the Constitution refers to agreements between states and foreign powers in Article I, section 10, it prescribes no procedure for their making by the national government. However, presidents have long assumed the sole power to make them. *See generally* Louis Henkin, *Foreign Affairs and the Constitution* 176-184 (1972). As noted in *Dames & Moore*, the practice of settling claims by executive agreements is long-standing. In *United States v. Belmont*, 301 U.S. 324, 330-331 (1937), Justice Sutherland, writing for the Court, upheld such an agreement incident to the recognition of the Soviet Union as well "within the competence of the President," citing his view of the President as "sole organ" of the nation in foreign relations. Does *Dames & Moore* support an inherent power in the President to make executive agreements? See generally Chapter 7.

3. *The Predicate for Acquiescence. Dames & Moore* is significant as an illustration in Justice Jackson's twilight zone of how what Justice Frankfurter called "constitutional common law" and what we have called "customary" authority is made by congressional acquiescence in an executive practice. How were the requirements for making law by acquiescence satisfied in *Dames & Moore*? What congressional action, if any, would have defeated the claim of executive power, according to the Court?

4. *Practice or Just Policy? Dames & Moore* finds that presidents had engaged in a long *practice* of claims settlement. That is, they had actually settled numerous claims over a lengthy period. But suppose the executive branch had merely declared as *policy* that it had the authority to negotiate claims settlements, without actually executing that policy very often? (We noted in Chapter 3 that presidents have sometimes claimed in signing statements to possess certain authorities.) Would a consistent *claim* of authority, as opposed to an actual practice, be sufficient to establish customary authority by congressional acquiescence?

The Supreme Court so held in *Haig v. Agee*, 453 U.S. 280 (1981), in which Agee challenged the President's authority to revoke his passport on national security grounds. (Agee had disclosed the names of CIA agents stationed abroad, placing them in peril.) "Although a pattern of actual enforcement is one indicator of Executive policy, it suffices that the Executive has 'openly asserted' the power at issue." 453 U.S. at 303. The Court noted that the Executive had long and consistently asserted the power of passport revocation, that no statute prohibited it, that Congress had delegated to the Executive the power to make rules and regulations regarding the issuance of passports, and that Congress had re-enacted general passport authority, leaving that rule-making authority intact, notwithstanding the Executive's publication of regulations regarding revocation of passports. *Id.* at 298-299.

Does it make any practical difference to the theory of customary authority by congressional acquiescence whether the Executive has exercised the claimed authority, or merely declared it? Justice Brennan, dissenting in *Haig*, thought so.

> [A] requirement . . . of evidence of the Executive's *exercise* of discretion as opposed to its possession of discretion may best be understood as a preference for the strongest proof that Congress knew of and acquiesced in that authority. The presence of sensitive constitutional questions in the passport revocation context cautions against applying the normal rule that administrative constructions in cases of statutory construction are to be given great weight. Only when Congress had maintained its silence in the face of a consistent and substantial pattern of actual passport denials or revocations — where the parties will presumably object loudly, perhaps through legal action, to the Secretary's exercise of discretion — can this Court be sure that Congress is aware of the Secretary's actions and has implicitly approved that exercise of discretion. Moreover, broad statements by the Executive Branch relating to its discretion in the passport area lack the precision of definition that would follow from concrete applications of that discretion in specific cases. Although Congress might register general approval of the Executive's overall policy, it still might disapprove of the Executive's pattern of applying that broad rule in specific categories of cases. [*Id.* at 315-316.]

He noted that the majority identified only 3 occasions over 33 years when the Executive had actually revoked passports for national security reasons and only one pursuant to the regulations that the majority cited.

5. *Presidential Power or Congressional Power?* We have excerpted *Curtiss-Wright* and *Dames & Moore* in a chapter on presidential power because both are frequently cited by the President's lawyers to support claims of executive authority. But is this placement of the opinions correct? *Curtiss-Wright* upheld an exercise of statutory authority, and *Dames & Moore* upheld a consistent executive practice because of substantial evidence of congressional acquiescence — including collateral facilitating legislation — and the absence of any disapproval by Congress. Neither found an inherent, let alone preclusive, power of the President to take the challenged actions.

B. THE COMMANDER IN CHIEF'S WAR POWERS

The President's war powers are nowhere spelled out in the Constitution; they must inhere in the Commander-in-Chief Clause and the judicial and executive glosses on it. First, we consider in this part of the chapter the President's power to defend the nation against attack or insurrection — which we will call "the defensive war power." Second, we address "customary war powers" he may have acquired by consistent practice with congressional acquiescence, said to be evidenced by more than 300 uses of armed force in our history. Third, we analyze what many consider to be the "core" command authority inherent in the title Commander in Chief. Finally, we introduce the question of statutory limits on the President's war power. We will return to each of these issues several times in the following chapters.

1.   Defensive War Power

The Prize Cases

United States Supreme Court, 1863
67 U.S. (2 Black) 635

Mr. Justice GRIER. . . . [At the beginning of the Civil War, during a congressional recess, President Lincoln issued a proclamation by which he "deemed it advisable to set on foot a blockade of the ports within [certain of the Confederate states], in pursuance of the laws of the United States and of the law of nations. . . . If, therefore, with a view to violate such blockade, a vessel shall approach or shall attempt to leave either of said ports, she will be duly warned by the commander of one of the blockading vessels, who will endorse on her register the fact and date of such warning, and if the same vessel shall again attempt to enter or leave the blockaded port, she will be captured and sent to the nearest convenient port for such proceedings against her and her cargo, as prize, as may be deemed advisable." The owners of vessels that were captured as prizes during the blockade brought this action challenging the legality of the President's proclamation.]

Had the President a right to institute a blockade of ports in possession of persons in armed rebellion against the Government, on the principles of international law, as known and acknowledged among civilized States? . . .

The right of prize and capture has its origin in the "*jus belli,*" and is governed and adjudged under the law of nations. To legitimate the capture of a neutral vessel or property on the high seas, a war must exist *de facto,* and the neutral must have a knowledge or notice of the intention of one of the parties belligerent to use this mode of coercion against a port, city, or territory, in possession of the other.

Let us enquire whether, at the time this blockade was instituted, a state of war existed which would justify a resort to these means of subduing the hostile force.

War has been well defined to be, "That state in which a nation prosecutes its right by force." . . .

By the Constitution, Congress alone has the power to declare a national or foreign war. It cannot declare war against a State, or any number of States, by virtue of any clause in the Constitution. The Constitution confers on the President the whole Executive power. He is bound to take care that the laws be faithfully executed. He is Commander-in-Chief of the Army and Navy of the United States, and of the militia of the several States when called into the actual service of the United States. He has no power to initiate or declare a war either against a foreign nation or a domestic State. But by the Acts of Congress of February 28th, 1795, and 3d of March, 1807, he is authorized to call out the militia and use the military and naval forces of the United States in case of invasion by foreign nations, and to suppress insurrection against the government of a State or of the United States.

If a war be made by invasion of a foreign nation, the President is not only authorized but bound to resist force by force. He does not initiate the war, but is bound to accept the challenge without waiting for any special legislative authority. And whether the hostile party be a foreign invader, or States organized in rebellion, it is none the less a war, although the declaration of it be "*unilateral.*" Lord Stowell (1 Dodson, 247) observes, "It is not the less a war on *that account,* for war may exist without a declaration on either side. It is so laid down by the best writers on the law of nations. A declaration of war by one country only, is not a mere challenge to be accepted or refused at pleasure by the other." . . .

This greatest of civil wars was not gradually developed by popular commotion, tumultuous assemblies, or local unorganized insurrections. However long may have been its previous conception, it nevertheless sprung forth suddenly from the parent brain, a Minerva in the full panoply of *war*. The President was bound to meet it in the shape it presented itself, without waiting for Congress to baptize it with a name; and no name given to it by him or them could change the fact....

Whether the President in fulfilling his duties, as Commander-in-Chief, in suppressing an insurrection, has met with such armed hostile resistance, and a civil war of such alarming proportions as will compel him to accord to them the character of belligerents, is a question to be decided *by him,* and this Court must be governed by the decisions and acts of the political department of the Government to which this power was entrusted. "He must determine what degree of force the crisis demands." The proclamation of blockade is itself official and conclusive evidence to the Court that a state of war existed which demanded and authorized a recourse to such a measure, under the circumstances peculiar to the case....

If it were necessary to the technical existence of a war, that it should have a legislative sanction, we find it in almost every act passed at the extraordinary session of the Legislature of 1861, which was wholly employed in enacting laws to enable the Government to prosecute the war with vigor and efficiency. And finally, in 1861, we find Congress "*ex majore cautela*" [out of caution] and in anticipation of such astute objections, passing an act "approving, legalizing, and making valid all the acts, proclamations, and orders of the President, &c., as if they had been *issued and done under the previous express authority* and direction of the Congress of the United States."

Without admitting that such an act was necessary under the circumstances, it is plain that if the President had in any manner assumed powers which it was necessary should have the authority or sanction of Congress, that on the well known principle of law, "*omnis ratihabitio retrotrahitur et mandato equiparatur*" [ratifications relate back and are the equivalent of prior authority] this ratification has operated to perfectly cure the defect....

The objection made to this act of ratification, that it is *ex post facto,* and therefore unconstitutional and void, might possibly have some weight on the trial of an indictment in a criminal Court. But precedents from that source cannot be received as authoritative in a tribunal administering public and international law.

On this first question therefore we are of the opinion that the President had a right, *jure belli,* to institute a blockade of ports in possession of the States in rebellion, which neutrals are bound to regard....

Mr. Justice NELSON, dissenting [in an opinion in which Chief Justice TANEY and Justices CATRON and CLIFFORD concurred]....It is not to be denied...that if a civil war existed between that portion of the people in organized insurrection to overthrow this Government at the time this vessel and cargo were seized, and if she was guilty of a violation of the blockade, she would be lawful prize of war. But before this insurrection against the established Government can be dealt with on the footing of a civil war, within the meaning of the law of nations and the Constitution of the United States, and which will draw after it belligerent rights, it must be recognized or declared by the war-making power of the Government. No power short of this can change the legal status of the Government or the relations of its citizens from that of peace to a state of war, or bring into existence all those duties and obligations of neutral third parties growing out of a state of war. The war power of the Government must be exercised before this changed condition of the Government and people and of neutral third parties can be admitted. . . .

. . . [W]e find there that to constitute a civil war in the sense in which we are speaking, before it can exist, in contemplation of law, it must be recognized or declared by the sovereign power of the State, and which sovereign power by our Constitution is lodged in the Congress of the United States—civil war, therefore, under our system of government, can exist only by an act of Congress, which requires the assent of two of the great departments of the Government, the Executive and Legislative. . . .

. . . But we are asked, what would become of the peace and integrity of the Union in case of an insurrection at home or invasion from abroad if this power could not be exercised by the President in the recess of Congress, and until that body could be assembled?

The framers of the Constitution fully comprehended this question, and provided for the contingency. Indeed, it would have been surprising if they had not, as a rebellion had occurred in the State of Massachusetts while the Convention was in session, and which had become so general that it was quelled only by calling upon the military power of the State. The Constitution declares that Congress shall have power "to provide for calling forth the militia to execute the laws of the Union, suppress insurrections, and repel invasions." Another clause, "that the President shall be Commander-in-chief of the Army and Navy of the United States, and of the Militia of the several States when called into the actual service of the United States;" and, again: "He shall take care that the laws shall be faithfully executed." Congress passed laws on this subject in 1792 and 1795. 1 United States Laws, pp. 264, 424. [It also passed a law on the subject in 1807. Act of Mar. 3, 1807, ch. 39, 2 Stat. 443.] . . .

The Acts of 1795 and 1807 did not, and could not under the Constitution, confer on the President the power of declaring war against a State of this Union, or of deciding that war existed, and upon that ground authorize the capture and confiscation of the property of every citizen of the State whenever it was found on the waters. The laws of war, whether the war be civil or *inter gentes,* as we have seen, convert every citizen of the hostile State into a public enemy, and treat him accordingly, whatever may have been his previous conduct. This great power over the business and property of the citizen is reserved to the legislative department by the express words of the Constitution. It cannot be delegated or surrendered to the Executive. Congress alone can determine whether war exists or should be declared; and until they have acted, no citizen of the State can be punished in his person or property, unless he has committed some offence against a law of Congress passed before the act was committed, which made it a crime, and defined the punishment. The penalty of confiscation for the acts of others with which he had no concern cannot lawfully be inflicted. . . .

. . . [C]onsequently, . . . the President had no power to set on foot a blockade under the law of nations, and . . . the capture of the vessel and cargo in this case, and in all cases before us in which the capture occurred before the 13th of July, 1861 [the date on which Congress first authorized a naval blockade of the Confederacy], for breach of blockade, or as enemies' property, are illegal and void, and . . . the decrees of condemnation should be reversed and the vessel and cargo restored.

NOTES AND QUESTIONS

1. *Delegated Defensive Power.* In *Martin v. Mott,* 25 U.S. (12 Wheat.) 19 (1813), the Court for the first time discussed the President's power to repel invasions. It found the President to be "the sole and exclusive judge whether the exigency has arisen" and implied the unsuitability of such a determination for judicial review. Yet *Mott* was decided under a statute that delegated to the President the power to call forth the militia "as he may judge necessary to repel such invasion [by a foreign nation or Indian tribe]." Act of Feb. 28, 1795, ch. 36, 1 Stat. 424. "Whenever a statute gives a discretionary power to any person, to be exercised by him upon his own opinion of certain facts," the Court explained, "it is a sound rule of construction, that the statute constitutes him the sole and exclusive judge of the existence of those facts." 25 U.S. at 31-32. Into which of Justice Jackson's categories in *The Steel Seizure Case* does the power exercised in *Mott* fall?

2. *Inherent Defensive War Power.* The legal challenge to the naval blockade of the South in *The Prize Cases* presented the Supreme Court for the first time with the question whether the President has the inherent power to repel attacks — to conduct defensive war — without prior congressional authorization. What answer did the Court give? Why did the Court in *The Prize Cases* take such pains to define "war"? On September 12, 2001, President George W. Bush declared that the terrorist attacks on the World Trade Center and the Pentagon were "acts of war." *Remarks by the President in Photo Opportunity with the National Security Team,* Sept. 12, 2001, *at* http://www.whitehouse.gov/news/releases/2001/09/20010912-4.html. Did the circumstances that day or since fit the Court's definition of "war"?

Is there any danger that a President might *create* the conditions said to warrant a military response? Abraham Lincoln offered this warning about the President's invocation of his "repel attack" authority to fight the undeclared Mexican War of 1846:

> Allow the President to invade a neighboring nation, whenever he shall deem it necessary to repel an invasion and you allow him to do so, whenever he may choose to say he deems it necessary for such purpose, and you allow him to make war at pleasure. Study to see if you can fix any limit to his power in this respect, after you have given him so much as you propose. [2 Abraham Lincoln, *The Writings of Abraham Lincoln* 51 (Arthur Brooks Lapsley ed., 1906).]

Do you think President Lincoln's caution was justified in the middle of the nineteenth century? Is it warranted today?

3. *The Grounds of Decision in The Prize Cases.* Was it necessary to the decision in *The Prize Cases* to find that the President has inherent constitutional authority to respond to an attack? Could the Court have upheld the President's actions on any narrower ground? Can you argue that it did so? *See generally* Ludwell H. Johnson III, *Abraham Lincoln and the Development of Presidential War-Making Powers: Prize Cases (1863) Revisited,* 35 Civil War Hist. 208 (1989).

The dissenters in *The Prize Cases* did not contest the proposition that a civil war places the nation *in extremis.* Why then did they find the blockade unlawful? Did they conclude that the President's actions were forbidden by Congress? That such actions exceeded a congressional grant of authority? That the President lacked any inherent authority to order the blockade?

4. *The Scope of the President's Defensive War Power.* What is the scope of the power that the Court recognized? By the logic of the Court, is the President constitutionally empowered to meet *any* threat of force as he determines, without awaiting congressional authorization? Would *The Prize Cases* Court have approved the 1983 invasion of Grenada without prior congressional approval? The deployment of U.S. peacekeeping troops in Lebanon in 1983? The sending of U.S. military advisors to El Salvador in the 1980s? *See generally* Peter Raven-Hansen, *Constitutional Constraints: The War Clause,* in *The U.S. Constitution and the Power to Go to War* 35-43 (Gary M. Stern & Morton H. Halperin eds., 1994). Would *The Prize Cases* Court have approved an extended U.S. military campaign against terrorists and their training facilities in Somalia, Sudan, and Yemen in response to the September 11, 2001, terrorist attacks on the United States? Or would such a campaign impermissibly cross some line between defensive and offensive operations? *Compare* Saikrishna Prakash, *Unleashing the Dogs of War: What the Constitution Means by "Declare War,"* 93 Cornell L. Rev. 45, 57 (2007) ("early Presidents repeatedly distinguished between purely defensive operations and offensive operations designed to take the war to the enemy," reflecting the view that the President's defensive power was strictly defensive), *with* Michael D. Ramsey, *The President's Power to Respond to Attacks,* 93 Cornell L. Rev. 169, 194 (2007) (war results from the attack, and "shifting from offense to defense would not affect its status").

2.   Customary War Powers

Although we have formally declared war only 11 times in our history, we had used armed force abroad on more than 300 occasions through 2004. Richard F. Grimmett, *Instances of Use of United States Armed Forces Abroad, 1798-2008* (Cong. Res. Serv. RL30172), Jan. 27, 2010. Does this history indicate that the President may use armed force whenever he thinks it necessary to protect national security? That argument was made to support the legality of U.S. participation in the Vietnam War. The Legal Adviser to the State Department inferred from 125 prior congressionally unauthorized uses of armed force abroad that the President has the "power to deploy American forces abroad and commit them to military operations when . . . [he] deems such action necessary to maintain the security and defense of the United States. . . ." Leonard C. Meeker, *The Legality of United States Participation in the Defense of Viet-Nam,* 75 Yale L.J. 1085, 1100-1101 (1966), *infra* p. 276. *See also* J. Terry Emerson, *War Powers Resolution,* 74 W. Va. L. Rev. 53, app. A (1971) (citing usage for same proposition). Or does history suggest a narrower claim of presidential war power: that he has acquired some customary war powers with congressional acquiescence?

The answers may turn on the particulars: what uses of armed force were made in what circumstances? In the following excerpt, Professors Wormuth and Firmage argue that the particulars matter, and that after the history is disaggregated, the pieces do not reassemble into an inherent war power in the President. Professor Monaghan disagrees. For him, it is not the particulars but the frequency of the uses of force that has settled the legitimacy of an inherent presidential power to commit the armed forces to hostilities.

Francis D. Wormuth & Edwin B. Firmage,
To Chain the Dog of War
pages 145-151 (2d ed. 1989)

The lists [of presidential uses of armed force] are not accurately characterized by their compilers. For the purpose of analysis, the latest official list, that prepared by the State Department in 1967, is used here. The proportions of cases remain fairly constant through all the lists. Sometimes a case might fall under more than one heading, but it is placed here under what appears to be the most appropriate title. The cases in the State Department list can be categorized thus:

1.	Actions for which congressional authorization was claimed	7
2.	Naval self-defense	1
3.	Enforcement of law against piracy, no trespass	1
4.	Enforcement of law against piracy, technical trespass	7
5.	Landings to protect citizens before 1862	13
6.	Landings to protect citizens, 1865-1967	56
7.	Invasion of foreign or disputed territory, no combat	10
8.	Invasion of foreign or disputed territory, combat	10
9.	Reprisals against aborigines	9
10.	Other reprisals not authorized by statute	4
11.	Minatory demonstrations without combat	6
12.	Intervention in Panama	1
13.	Protracted occupation of Caribbean states	6
14.	Actions anticipating World War II	1
15.	Bombing of Laos	1
16.	Korean and Vietnamese Wars	2
17.	Miscellaneous	2
	Total	137

The first category in the list contains three of the limited wars declared by Congress; it includes one of the four conditional declarations of war. It includes two forays into Spanish Florida, purportedly undertaken under statutory authorization, and Woodrow Wilson's seizure of Veracruz on April 21, 1914, said to have been ratified by the joint resolution of April 22, 1914.

A number of other cases can be justified in terms other than presidential initiative. As for category 2, naval vessels have the right of self-defense at international and municipal law. Category 3 is merely obedience to statute. Although his naval commanders did not share his views, President Monroe took the position that the landings in category 4 required statutory authorization. We have no contemporary discussion of the thirteen landings in category 5. As we shall see, some of the fifty-six landings in category 6 enjoy statutory authorization. The invasion of foreign territory in categories 7 and 8 was illegal, but if the United States claimed the territory, the President's action in sending troops was not an act of war. Reprisals, as we have seen, are acts of war, and today naval regulations forbid officers to undertake them. [See *infra* p. 350.] The minatory demonstrations at sea in category 11 were intended to make other states nervous but were not acts of war. Theodore Roosevelt's intervention in Panama was naked aggression, and the United States paid twenty-five million dollars as compensation to Colombia. Category 13 represents merely an aspect of the involvement of the American executive in the Caribbean area. American forces actually occupied and administered three Caribbean countries: Cuba from 1906 to 1909, Haiti from 1915 to 1934, and the Dominican Republic from 1916 to 1924. On other occasions, forces of marines were permanently stationed in a Caribbean country in order to influence local politics; the longest such interventions were those in Nicaragua from 1912 to 1925 and from 1926 to 1933. In addition, the customshouses of sovereign states were occupied now and again, with or without authorization by treaty, and their finances were administered by the United States for extended periods. On occasion, at the instance of the United States, Latin American countries agreed to put their import duties in the hands of a representative of foreign bankers in case of default on a loan. But in no case was the executive action said to be grounded on a presidential war-making power. . . .

As for category 14, illegal presidential acts of war, as well as a congressional declaration of limited war in the form of the Lend-Lease Act, occurred before the Second World War, as we have already seen. No one would allege that presidential bombing of Laos was authorized by the Constitution or by statute. President Truman's entry into the Korean War was defended by the State Department as authorized by treaty — that is, by the United Nations Charter — and by the executive precedents we have been considering. The Vietnam War was alleged to be authorized by the Southeast Asia Collective Defense Treaty, the Tonkin Gulf Resolution, and the executive precedents. . . .

One cannot be sure, but the number of cases in which Presidents have personally made the decisions, unconstitutionally, to engage in war or in acts of war probably lies between one and two dozen. And in all those cases the Presidents have made false claims of authorization, either by statute or by treaty or by international law. They have not relied on their powers as commander in chief or as chief executive.

In the case of executive wars, none of the conditions for the establishment of constitutional power by usage is present. The Constitution is not ambiguous. No contemporaneous congressional interpretation attributes a power of initiating war to the President. The early Presidents, and indeed everyone in the country until the year 1950, denied that the President possessed such a power. There is no sustained body of usage to support such a claim. It can only be audacity or desperation that leads the champions of recent presidential usurpations to state that "history had legitimated the practice of presidential war-making."

Henry P. Monaghan, Presidential War-Making

50 B.U. L. Rev. 19, 25-27, 30-31 (Special Issue 1970)

The occasions on which presidents have refused to take military action abroad because of a lack of prior congressional authorization are few in number and increasingly rare. From the beginning of our constitutional history, presidents have both deployed the armed forces abroad and committed them to actual hostilities without explicit congressional authorization. In excess of one hundred and twenty instances of such action exist. The precedents extend back to Washington and include that great "strict constructionist" Jefferson; they run through the nineteenth century; and with the emergence of the United States as a global power in this century, they become sharper and more spectacular. The presidencies of the two Roosevelts provide classic examples. Moreover, no recent president has refused to commit the armed forces to actual hostilities because of a lack of congressional approval, as the conduct of Truman in Korea, Johnson in the Dominican Republic, and Kennedy, Johnson and Nixon in Southeast Asia demonstrate. Thus, argues the state department, "practice and precedent have confirmed the constitutional authority of the president to commit the armed forces to battle without a declaration of war."

The strength of the "practice and precedent" has, however, not gone unchallenged. Most writers who seek constitutionally based restrictions on the president's war-making power argue that the precedents are not compelling. Indeed, it has been suggested that there is only one prior illustration of presidential commitment of armed forces to war without congressional authorization, namely, Korea. The other instances cited, it is argued, were simply presidential responses to reprisals, or "relatively minor and short-lived occurrences [that] do not establish precedent for the massive and long-lasting [Vietnam] war...": "minor" and "short-lived" from whose point of view? Certainly not from the perspective of those against whom the armed forces were employed; and certainly not from the presidents' view, since they generally brought about the results intended. To dismiss American interventions in Latin America as "minor" amounts to recognition of presidential power to wage war against weak opponents for limited purposes.

The validity of each of the precedents relied upon by the state department need not be separately defended. Taken as a whole, they seem to me to add up to the following: with ever-increasing frequency, presidents have employed that amount of force that they deemed necessary to accomplish their foreign policy objectives. When little force was needed (e.g., in our incursions in Latin America), little was used; when larger commitments were necessary, they too were forthcoming. Whatever the intention of the Framers, the military machine has become simply an instrument for the achievement of foreign policy goals, which, in turn, have become a central responsibility of the presidency. Congress has seldom objected on legal grounds, and so the only limitation upon presidential power has been that imposed by political considerations. That is the teaching of our history.

To be sure, various legal theories have been advanced in defense of presidential power. In good lawyer-like fashion these theories have been framed in terms no broader than necessary to justify the particular presidential action at issue. For example, in the late nineteenth century, American troop interventions in Latin America were rationalized in terms of "inherent" presidential power "neutrally" to protect the rights of American citizens abroad during foreign disorders — a fiction that did not survive the turn of the century. Since presidential use of armed forces abroad has assumed considerably enlarged dimension in this century, it is hardly surprising that the supporting rationales have been constantly broadened and adjusted. The rationales have, in a word, followed the practice....

In varying degrees the commentators present us with visibly strained efforts to minimize the long and ever-accumulating practice of presidential "war-making," if one prefers that term. For better or worse that practice seems to me clearly established, as I have indicated. To my mind, this historical development of our institutions has settled the legitimacy of "inherent" presidential power to commit the armed forces to hostilities. A practice so deeply embedded in our governmental structure should be treated as decisive of the constitutional issue. History and practice are not here being appealed to in order to freeze forever the scope of a constitutional guarantee framed in terms of individual liberty; rather, this issue deals with the distribution of political power between the legislative and executive branches. Matters of this character are, in the words of Chief Justice Marshall, best left "to the practice of government." . . .

NOTES AND QUESTIONS

1. *Usage and Denials of Authority.* If usage is significant, should the relevant list include instances in which the Congress *refused* presidential requests for delegations of authority to use force abroad or *denied funding* for the continued use of force abroad? *See* Wormuth & Firmage, *supra* p. 73, ch. 5 (discussing such instances). Do such instances refute the claim that usage consists of an unbroken line of precedents for unilateral presidential military initiatives? See *supra* pp. 43, 45-46 (executive custom and congressional acquiescence).

2. *Usage and Necessity.* Alexander Hamilton wrote in *The Federalist No. 23* that it was undesirable to impose "constitutional shackles" on "the power to which the care of [the safety of the nation] is committed," because "it is impossible to foresee or define the extent and variety of national exigencies, or the correspondent extent and variety of means that may be necessary to satisfy them." *The Federalist No. 23*, at 153 (Clinton Rossiter ed., 1961). James Madison also noted in *The Federalist No. 41*, at 257 (Clinton Rossiter ed., 1961), that

> [t]he means of security can only be regulated by the means and the danger of attack. They will, in fact, be ever determined by these rules and no others. It is in vain to oppose constitutional barriers to the impulse of self-preservation. It is worse than in vain; because it places in the Constitution itself necessary usurpations of power; every precedent of which is a germ of unnecessary and multiplied repetitions.

Both observations, however, go only to the necessity of a flexible war power in the government at large, without specifying a branch. Indeed, both Hamilton and Madison made their comments in defense of the *congressional* power to raise armies. *See* Charles A. Lofgren, *War Making Under the Constitution: The Original Understanding*, 81 Yale L.J. 672, 688 (1972). Nevertheless, they gave clear expression to the view that war powers are necessarily adaptive, depending on variable and unforeseeable threats to the national security. From this premise, it is a small step to find the shape of presidential war powers in usage: the accumulation of presidential military initiatives since 1789.

Does the very diversity of usage prove that Madison was right in warning that the "means of security" will be governed only by the rule of necessity "and no others"? Does the President alone not have the practical capacity to respond to that rule? In short, is unpredictability not inherent in the nature of the problem, justifying allocation of war powers to the branch that is able to respond most quickly and flexibly? *See* Eugene V. Rostow, *"Once More Into the Breach": The War Powers Resolution Revisited*, 21 Val. U. L. Rev. 1, 9 (1986).

On the other hand, does the rule of necessity operate with equal force in all instances? If the nation is not itself put at risk and there is time to consider a response to foreign threats, *should* the President be empowered to fashion that response without first going to Congress?

3. *Customary Law Redux.* Upon what constitutional theory does a historically based claim of inherent presidential power to commit troops to hostilities rest? See generally *supra* pp. 42-43; Raven-Hansen, *supra* p. 72, at 31-32. If the theory is customary law by congressional acquiescence, aren't the particular circumstances of each military initiative relevant to the constitutional theory? And does it matter whether a use of force was a "quick strike military mission" or secret? *See* Tung Yin, *Structural Objections to the Inherent Commander-in-Chief Thesis*, 16 Transnat'l L. & Contemp. Probs. 966 (2007) (yes, as both affect notice).

4. *Negotiated War Powers.* If Professor Monaghan's theory is that exercise of the war power is negotiated between the branches, what is the point of studying legal limits on war powers? Isn't what the political branches negotiate then constitutional per se and doesn't the President hold all the cards in the negotiations? *See* Harold H. Koh, *Why the President (Almost) Always Wins in Foreign Affairs: Lessons of the Iran-Contra Affair*, 97 Yale L.J. 1255 (1988). How do constitutional claims, international law doctrines, and past military precedents fit into the next negotiation? *See generally* David J. Barron & Martin S. Lederman, *The Commander in Chief at the Lowest Ebb — Framing the Problem, Doctrine, and Original Understanding*, 121 Harv. L. Rev. 689, 724-725 (2008) (arguing that the "politics is law" model of war powers "seriously underestimates the role of traditional constitutional analysis — especially historical exegesis — in war powers disputation outside the context of litigation. . . . The interdepartmental struggle for war powers supremacy itself, in other words, is precisely about the rules of engagement."); Abram Chayes, *The Cuban Missile Crisis* 6-7 (1974) (suggesting that law affects the decisional process by acting as a constraint, supplying justification or legitimation, and providing organizational structures, procedures, and forums).

5. *Jackson's Category 3 Again.* If the President has acquired customary war power by congressional acquiescence, does it follow that Congress cannot take it away? Whether or not history establishes that the President may order the use of armed force abroad without prior statutory authority, may he act inconsistently with limits contained in prior statutory authority?

3. "Core" Presidential War Powers and Statutory Limits

The majority in *The Prize Cases* asserted that when the nation is attacked, the President "must determine what degree of force the crisis demands." In another Civil War decision, Chief Justice Chase declared in a concurring opinion that Congress's war power

> necessarily extends to all legislation essential to the prosecution of war with vigor and success, *except such as interferes with the command of the forces and the conduct of campaigns. That power and duty belong to the President as commander-in-chief.* Both these powers are derived from the Constitution, but neither is defined by that instrument. Their extent must be determined by their nature, and by the principles of our institutions. [*Ex parte Milligan*, 71 U.S. (4 Wall) 2, 139 (1866) (emphasis added).]

Do these statements suggest that the President's authority as Commander in Chief contains some "core" command authority that is not shared with Congress and is beyond its statutory reach?

Little v. Barreme

United States Supreme Court, 1804
6 U.S. (2 Cranch) 170

MARSHALL, Chief Justice, now delivered the opinion of the Court.... During the hostilities between the United States and France, an act for the suspension of all intercourse between the two nations was annually passed. That under which the *Flying-Fish* was condemned, declared every vessel, owned, hired, or employed wholly or in part by an American, which should be employed in any traffic or commerce with or for any person resident within the jurisdiction or under the authority of the French republic, to be forfeited together with her cargo; the one half to accrue to the United States, and the other to any person or persons, citizens of the United States, who will inform and prosecute for the same.

The 5th section of this act authorizes the President of the United States, to instruct the commanders of armed vessels, "to stop and examine any ship or vessel of the United States on the high sea, which there may be reason to suspect to be engaged in any traffic or commerce contrary to the true tenor of the act, and if upon examination it should appear that such ship or vessel is bound or sailing *to* any port or place within the territory of the French republic or her dependencies, it is rendered lawful to seize such vessel, and send her into the United States for adjudication."

[By this authority, a U.S. frigate commanded by Captain Little intercepted and captured an ostensibly Danish vessel named the *Flying-Fish* as it was returning *from* a French port. The ship's owners subsequently sued Captain Little for trespass.]

It is by no means clear that the President of the United States, whose high duty it is to "take care that the laws be faithfully executed," and who is commander in chief of the armies and navies of the United States, might not, without any special authority for that purpose, in the then existing state of things, have empowered the officers commanding the armed vessels of the United States, to seize and send into port for adjudication, American vessels which were forfeited by being engaged in this illicit commerce. But when it is observed that the ... 5th section [of the act] gives a special authority to seize on the high seas, and limits that authority to the seizure of vessels bound or sailing *to* a French port, the legislature seem to have prescribed that the manner in which this law shall be carried into execution was to exclude a seizure of any vessel not bound *to* a French port. Of consequence, however strong the circumstances might be, which induced Captain Little to suspect the *Flying-Fish* to be an American vessel, they could not excuse the detention of her, since he would not have been authorised to detain her had she been really American.

It was so obvious, that if only vessels sailing to a French port could be seized on the high seas, that the law would be very often evaded, that this act of congress appears to have received a different construction from the executive of the United States; a construction much better calculated to give it effect.

A copy of his act was transmitted by the secretary of the navy to the captains of the armed vessels, who were ordered to consider the 5th section as a part of their instructions. The same letter contained the following clause.

A proper discharge of the important duties enjoined on you, arising out of this act, will require the exercise of a sound and an impartial judgment. You are not only to do all that in you lies, to prevent all intercourse, whether direct or circuitous, between the ports of the *United States* and those of *France* or her dependencies, where the vessels *are apparently as well as really American,* and protected by *American* papers only, but you are to be vigilant that vessels or cargoes really *American,* but covered by *Danish* or other foreign papers, and bound *to* or *from French* ports, do not escape you.

These orders, given by the executive under the construction of the act of congress made by the department to which its execution was assigned, enjoin the seizure of American vessels sailing from a French port. Is the officer who obeys them liable for damages sustained by this misconstruction of the act, or will his orders excuse him? If his instructions afford him no protection, then the law must take its course, and he must pay such damages as are legally awarded against him; if they excuse an act not otherwise excusable, it would then be necessary to inquire whether this is a case in which the probable cause which existed to induce a suspicion that the vessel was American, would excuse the captor from damages when the vessel appeared in fact to be neutral.

I confess the first bias of my mind was very strong in favor of the opinion that though the instructions of the executive could not give a right, they might yet excuse from damages. I was very much inclined to think that a distinction ought to be taken between acts of civil and those of military officers; and between proceedings within the body of the country and those on the high seas. That implicit obedience which military men usually pay to the orders of their superiors, which indeed is indispensably necessary to every military system, appeared to me strongly to imply the principle that those orders, if not to perform a prohibited act, ought to justify the person whose general duty it is to obey them, and who is placed by the laws of his country in a situation which in general requires that he should obey them. I was strongly inclined to think that where, in consequence of orders from the legitimate authority, a vessel is seized with pure intention, the claim of the injured party for damages would be against that government from which the orders proceeded, and would be a proper subject for negotiation. But I have been convinced that I was mistaken, and I have receded from this first opinion. I acquiesce in that of my brethren, which is, that the instructions cannot change the nature of the transaction, or legalize an act which without those instructions would have been a plain trespass. . . .

Captain Little then must be answerable in damages to the owner of this neutral vessel. . . .

NOTES AND QUESTIONS

1. *The Commander in Chief's Command Authority: First General and Admiral?* One possible interpretation of the Framers' intent is that designation of the President as Commander in Chief merely placed him at the top of the military chain of command, making him First General and Admiral — essentially the top military commander

without independent war policy-making authority. At least as late as 1851, the Supreme Court clearly took this position. A unanimous Court held that the military occupation of a Mexican port by order of the President during the congressionally declared Mexican War did not annex it to the United States. *Fleming v. Page*, 50 U.S. (9 How.) 603 (1851). It reasoned that the President's

> duty and power are purely military. As commander in chief, he is authorized to direct the movements of the naval and military forces *placed by law at his command,* and to employ them in the manner he may deem most effectual to harass and conquer and subdue the enemy. He may invade the hostile country, and subject it to the sovereignty and authority of the United States. But his conquests do not enlarge the boundaries of this Union, nor extend the operation of our institutions and laws *beyond the limits assigned to them by the legislative power.* . . . [50 U.S. at 614-615 (emphasis supplied).]

2. *Command, Tactics, and "Core" Presidential War Powers.* While *Fleming* assigns a relatively narrow command authority to the President, subject to limits set by Congress, the assertion in *The Prize Cases* and the dicta from *Milligan* quoted in the introduction to this section have anchored a broader view of that power. That view is that the President, as Commander in Chief, has inherent and *preclusive* authority to command the military in authorized armed conflicts — variously called the authority to conduct campaigns, to command the troops on the battlefield, and to decide on tactics. By "preclusive," adherents of this theory of presidential war powers mean that these "core" war powers cannot be interfered with or limited by statute; that exercises of core command authority fall into Justice Jackson's category 3, in which "[c]ourts sustain exclusive Presidential control . . . only by disabling the Congress from acting upon the subject." *The Steel Seizure Case*, 343 U.S. 579, 637-638 (1952). For example, the infamous 2002 Office of Legal Counsel memorandum on torture argued that

> Congress can no more interfere with the President's conduct of the interrogation of enemy combatants than it can dictate strategic or tactical decisions on the battlefield. Just as statutes that order the President to conduct warfare in a certain manner or for specific goals would be unconstitutional, so too are laws that seek to prevent the President from gaining the intelligence he believes necessary to prevent attacks upon the United States. [*Memorandum from Jay S. Bybee, Assistant Att'y Gen., Office of Legal Counsel, to Alberto R. Gonzales, Counsel to the President* (Aug. 1, 2002), in *The Torture Papers: The Road to Abu Ghraib* 172, 207 (Karen J. Greenberg & Joshua L. Dratel eds., 2005).]

Does the case law we have read support this argument? The constitutional understanding? Interestingly, the United States argued to the Court in *The Prize Cases* that

> [t]he function to use the army and navy being in the President, the mode of using them, within the rules of civilized warfare, and *subject to established laws of Congress,* must be subject to his discretion as a necessary incident to the use, *in the absence of any act of Congress controlling him.* [Brief for the United States and Captors at 22, *The Prize Cases,* 67 U.S. (2 Black) 635, in 3 *Landmark Briefs and Arguments of the Supreme Court of the United States: Constitutional Law* 495 (Philip B. Kurland & Gerhard Casper eds., 1978) (emphases added).]

3. *Ascertaining the Will of Congress (Again).* Is the claim of preclusive command authority consistent with *Little*? The capture at issue in *Little v. Barreme* took place

during the undeclared but congressionally authorized Quasi-War with France. See *infra* p. 93. Why do you think the President interpreted the statute as he did? Had Congress expressly prohibited this capture? Or had Congress simply decided not to authorize the capture? If the latter, why was the capture unlawful? Would it have been unlawful absent any statute on point? How would you define the scope of the Commander in Chief's command authority after *Little*?

4. *Precedential Value.* What is the precedential value of *Little*? Does the case address the scope of the Commander in Chief's powers or the scope of Congress's power to control the conduct of war? *Compare* Abraham D. Sofaer, *War, Foreign Affairs and Constitutional Power: The Origins* 163 (1976) (*Little* "rests on the notion . . . that declared war involved a delegation to the executive and all citizens of general authority to commit hostilities against the enemy, while the conduct of undeclared or 'imperfect' war was limited to those actions authorized by Congress."), *with* John C. Yoo, *The Continuation of Politics By Other Means: The Original Understanding of War Powers*, 84 Cal. L. Rev. 167, 294-295 n.584 (1996) (*Little* never reached the issue of "the President's inherent constitutional authority to order captures going beyond Congress's commands."), *and* J. Gregory Sidak, *The Quasi War Cases — And Their Relevance to Whether "Letters of Marque and Reprisal" Constrain Presidential War Powers*, 28 Harv. J.L. & Pub. Pol'y 465, 492 (2005) ("[The] negative implication [of Chief Justice Marshall's statements in *Little*] was that congressional silence leaves the President free to act"). Can *Little* be distinguished from other cases on the ground that the Constitution provides Congress with express authority to make rules for capture? *See* U.S. Const. art. I, §8, cl. 11. Even more narrowly, does *Little* address just the liability of military subordinates asserting the "I was only following orders" defense?

Or does *Little* stand for the intermediate proposition that when Congress has prescribed the manner in which its authorization for the use of armed force is to be executed, its prescription "occupies the field" and is binding even on the President?

5. *Command Authority Revisited.* Consider this summary of the President's powers as Commander in Chief in time of war:

> The President, not Congress, makes all day-to-day tactical decisions in the combat deployment of armed forces. Indeed, even when it ends a use of force by cutting off funds, Congress cannot constitutionally interfere with the Commander in Chief's tactical decisions for the safe withdrawal of the armed forces. But as powerful as the command authority is, the framers still intended that the Commander in Chief "would amount to nothing more than the supreme command and direction of the military and naval forces, as first General and Admiral of the Confederacy . . . ," as Alexander Hamilton explained in the *Federalist Papers.* By making the President the Commander in Chief in Article II, the framers addressed what they recognized as a defect in the conduct of the Revolutionary War. They did not compromise their insistence in Article I on collective judgment in the decision for war.
>
> Nor did they give the Commander in Chief any constitutional right to ignore the terms of a congressional authorization for the use of force. When Congress gives the President the authority to conduct war, he or she must conduct it within that authority, just as the President must follow any law that is constitutionally made. [*Deciding to Use Force Abroad: War Powers in a System of Checks and Balances* 15 (The Constitution Project, Peter Raven-Hansen rptr., 2005).]

Can you say what distinguishes uses of force that are tactical from those that are not? Do you think congressional constraints have the same force when the President is fighting a war thrust upon us by attack as when he is fighting one authorized by Congress? Put another way, are you clear about precisely which Commander-in-Chief powers are preclusive? *See generally* Louis Fisher, *Presidential War Power* (2d ed. 2004).

6. *Begging the Question of Core Presidential War Powers.* Recent scholarship asserts that the widely held view that Congress cannot intrude on the core command powers of the President—like the "day-to-day tactical decisions in the combat deployment" or for "safe withdrawal" mentioned above—begs the question: what *are* the core powers? Barron & Lederman, *supra* p. 77. An exhaustive review of historical evidence and case law found that

> there is surprisingly little Founding-era evidence supporting the notion that the conduct of military campaigns is beyond legislative control and a fair amount of evidence that affirmatively undermines it. Instead, the text and evidence of original understanding provide substantial support only for the recognition of some version of a very different sort of preclusive power of the Commander in Chief—namely, a prerogative of superintendence when it comes to the military chain of command itself. That is, the President must to some considerable extent retain control over the vast reservoirs of military discretion that exist in every armed conflict, even when bounded by important statutory limitations; and thus Congress may not assign such ultimate decisionmaking discretion to anyone else (including subordinate military officers). [*Id.* at 696.]

Although this "prerogative of superintendence" importantly protects civilian command of the armed forces, Barron and Lederman found little evidence that it includes substantive war powers that are beyond the reach of statute. *See also* David J. Luban, *On the Commander-in-Chief Power*, 81 S. Cal. L. Rev. 477-571 (2008). Indeed, they conclude, even historical practice shows that

> a repeated, though not unbroken, deferential executive branch stance . . . appears to be premised on the assumption that the constitutional plan requires the nation's chief commander to guard his supervisory powers over the military chain of command jealously, to be willing to act in times of exigency if Congress is not available for consultation, and to use the very powerful weapon of the veto to forestall unacceptable limits proposed in the midst of military conflict—but that otherwise, the Constitution compels the Commander in Chief to comply with legislative restrictions. . . .
> . . . [F]or more than a century, there has been a working, dynamic practice within the political departments in which neither the Executive nor the legislature acted as if the Constitution prohibited congressional regulation [of the President's exercise of war powers]. [Barron & Lederman, *supra*, 121 Harv. L. Rev. at 949, 1108.]

On the other hand, recognizing that the "law of presidential power is often made through accretion"—in part, what we have called customary authority—this scholarship also recognized that recent claims of preclusive war power in the "War on Terror" may "subtly but increasingly influence future Executives to eschew the harder work of accepting legislative constraints as legitimate and actively working to make them tolerable by building public support for modifications." *Id.* at 1111. As we turn to such claims in the following chapters, consider the degree to which they, even if not historically correct, may have enlarged presidential power by "accretion."

C. THE PRESIDENT'S EMERGENCY POWERS

In re Neagle

United States Supreme Court, 1890
135 U.S. 1

Mr. Justice MILLER, for the Court.... [When David S. Terry and his wife, disappointed litigants, threatened the life of Supreme Court Justice Field, the Attorney General assigned U.S. Marshall David Neagle to protect the Justice while he sat on the circuit court in California. There Neagle shot and killed Terry in the course of an assault on Justice Field. Neagle was then arrested by state authorities and charged with murder. He sought release under a federal habeas corpus statute.]

It is urged ... that there exists no statute authorizing any such protection as that which Neagle was instructed to give Judge Field in the present case, and indeed no protection whatever against a vindictive or malicious assault growing out of the faithful discharge of his official duties; and that the language of section 753 of the Revised Statutes, that the party seeking the benefit of the writ of *habeas corpus* must in this connection show that he is "in custody for an act done or omitted in pursuance of a law of the United States," makes it necessary that upon this occasion it should be shown that the act for which Neagle is imprisoned was done by virtue of an act of Congress. It is not supposed that any special act of Congress exists which authorizes the marshals or deputy-marshals of the United States in express terms to accompany the judges of the Supreme Court through their circuits, and act as a body-guard to them, to defend them against malicious assaults against their persons....

In the view we take of the Constitution of the United States, any obligation fairly and properly inferrible from that instrument, or any duty of the marshal to be derived from the general scope of his duties under the laws of the United States, is "a law" within the meaning of this phrase. It would be a great reproach to the system of government of the United States, declared to be within its sphere sovereign and supreme, if there is to be found within the domain of its powers no means of protecting the judges, in the conscientious and faithful discharge of their duties, from the malice and hatred of those upon whom their judgments may operate unfavorably....

Where, then, are we to look for the protection which we have shown Judge Field was entitled to when engaged in the discharge of his official duties? Not to the courts of the United States; because, as has been more than once said in this court, in the division of the powers of government between the three great departments, executive, legislative, and judicial, the judicial is the weakest for the purposes of self-protection and for the enforcement of the powers which it exercises....

The legislative branch of the government can only protect the judicial officers by the enactment of laws for that purpose, and the argument we are now combatting assumes that no such law has been passed by Congress.

If we turn to the executive department of the government, we find a very different condition of affairs. The Constitution, section 3, Article 2, declares that the President "shall take care that the laws be faithfully executed" ....

Is this duty limited to the enforcement of acts of Congress or of treaties of the United States according to their *express terms*, or does it include the rights, duties and obligations growing out of the Constitution itself, our international relations, and all the protection implied by the nature of the government under the Constitution?

One of the most remarkable episodes in the history of our foreign relations, and which has become an attractive historical incident, is the case of Martin Koszta, a native of Hungary, who, though not fully a naturalized citizen of the United States, had in due form of law made his declaration of intention to become a citizen. While in Smyrna he was seized by command of the Austrian consul general at that place, and carried on board the Hussar, an Austrian vessel, where he was held in close confinement. Captain Ingraham, in command of the American sloop of war St. Louis, arriving in port at that critical period, and ascertaining that Koszta had with him his naturalization papers, demanded his surrender to him, and was compelled to train his guns upon the Austrian vessel before his demands were complied with. It was, however, to prevent bloodshed, agreed that Koszta should be placed in the hands of the French consul subject to the result of diplomatic negotiations between Austria and the United States. The celebrated correspondence between Mr. Marcy, Secretary of State, and Chevalier Hulsemann, the Austrian minister at Washington, which arose out of this affair, and resulted in the release and restoration to liberty of Koszta, attracted a great deal of public attention, and the position assumed by Mr. Marcy met the approval of the country and of Congress, who voted a gold medal to Captain Ingraham for his conduct in the affair. Upon what act of Congress then existing can any one lay his finger in support of the action of our government in this matter?

So, if the President or the Postmaster General is advised that the mails of the United States, possibly carrying treasure, are liable to be robbed, and the mail carriers assaulted and murdered in any particular region of country, who can doubt the authority of the President or of one of the executive departments under him to make an order for the protection of the mail, and of the persons and lives of its carriers, by doing exactly what was done in the case of Mr. Justice Field, namely, providing a sufficient guard, whether it be by soldiers of the army or by marshals of the United States, with a *posse comitatus* [see *infra* p. 1147] properly armed and equipped, to secure the safe performance of the duty of carrying the mail wherever it may be intended to go? . . .

We cannot doubt the power of the President to take measures for the protection of a judge of one of the courts of the United States who, while in the discharge of the duties of his office, is threatened with a personal attack which may probably result in his death, and we think it clear that where this protection is to be afforded through the civil power, the Department of Justice is the proper one to set in motion the necessary means of protection. . . .

But there is positive law investing the marshals and their deputies with powers which not only justify what Marshal Neagle did in this matter, but which imposed it upon him as a duty. In chapter fourteen of the Revised Statutes of the United States, which is devoted to the appointment and duties of the district attorneys, marshals, and clerks of the courts of the United States, section 788 declares:

> The marshals and their deputies shall have, in each State, the same powers, in executing the laws of the United States, as the sheriffs and their deputies in such State may have, by law, in executing the laws thereof.

> If, therefore, a sheriff of the State of California was authorized to do in regard to the laws of California what Neagle did, that is, if he was authorized to keep the peace, to protect a judge from assault and murder, then Neagle was authorized to do the same thing in reference to the laws of the United States. . . .

... That it would be the duty of a sheriff, if one had been present at this assault by Terry upon Judge Field, to prevent this breach of the peace, to prevent this assault, to prevent the murder which was contemplated by it, cannot be doubted.... So the marshal of the United States, charged with the duty of protecting and guarding the judge of the United States court against this special assault upon his person and his life, being present at the critical moment, when prompt action was necessary, found it to be his duty, a duty which he had no liberty to refuse to perform, to take the steps which resulted in Terry's death....

We therefore affirm the judgment of the Circuit Court authorizing his discharge from the custody of the sheriff of San Joaquin County.

Mr. Justice LAMAR (with whom concurred Mr. Chief Justice FULLER) dissenting.... The ground on which we dissent, and which in and by itself seems to be fatal to the case of the appellee, is this: That, in treating section 753 of the Revised Statutes as an act of authority for this particular use of the writ a wholly inadmissible construction is placed on the word "law," as used in that statute, and a wholly inadmissible application is made of the clause "in custody in violation of the Constitution ... of the United States."...

[The Attorney General maintains]

> that the President ... by the very fact that he is made the chief executive of the nation, and is charged to protect, preserve, and defend the Constitution, and to take care that the laws are faithfully executed, is invested with necessary and implied executive powers which neither of the other branches of the government can either take away or abridge; that many of these powers, pertaining to each branch of the government are self-executing, and in no way dependent, except as to the ways and means, upon legislation....

The President is sworn to "preserve, protect, and defend the Constitution." That oath *has* great significance. The sections which follow that prescribing the oath (secs. 2 and 3 of Art. 2) prescribe the duties and fix the powers of the President. But one very prominent feature of the Constitution which he is sworn to preserve, and which the whole body of the judiciary are bound to enforce, is the closing paragraph of sec. 8, Art. 1, in which it is declared that "the Congress shall have power ... to make all laws which shall be necessary and proper for carrying into execution the foregoing powers, and all other powers vested by this Constitution in the government of the United States, or in any department or officer thereof."

This clause is that which contains the germ of all the implication of powers under the Constitution. It is that which has built up the Congress of the United States into the most august and imposing legislative assembly in the world; and which has secured vigor to the practical operations of the government, and at the same time tended largely to preserve the equilibrium of its various powers among its co-ordinate departments, as partitioned by that instrument. And that clause alone conclusively refutes the assertion of the Attorney General that it was "the duty of the executive department of the United States to guard and protect, at any hazard, the life of Mr. Justice Field in the discharge of his duty, because such protection is essential to the existence of the government." Waiving the question of the essentiality of any such protection to the existence of the government, the manifest answer is, that the protection needed and to be given must proceed not from the President, but primarily from Congress. Again, while it is the President's duty to take care that the laws be faithfully executed, it is not his duty to *make* laws or a law of the United States. The laws he is to see executed are manifestly those contained in the Constitution, and those enacted by Congress, whose duty it is to make all laws necessary and proper for carrying into execution the powers of those tribunals. In fact, for the President to have undertaken to make any law of the United States pertinent to this matter would have been to invade the domain of power expressly committed by the Constitution exclusively to Congress. That body was perfectly able to pass such laws as it should deem expedient in reference to such matter; indeed, it has passed such laws in reference to elections, expressly directing the United States marshals to attend places of election, to act as peace officers, to arrest with and without process, and to protect the supervisors of election in the discharge of their duties; and there was not the slightest legal necessity out of which to imply any such power in the President. . . .

. . . [The Martin Koszta incident] was justified because it pertained to the foreign relations of the United States, in respect to which the federal government is the exclusive representative and embodiment of the entire sovereignty of the nation, in its united character. . . .

NOTES AND QUESTIONS

1. *The Holding of Neagle.* What is the holding of *Neagle?* Was it necessary for the Court to find that the President had the right and duty to execute "a law" of his own making, at least to protect the officers (and functions) of government? Was it necessary to find that Neagle was executing implied law of any kind, in light of the Court's recognition that his act was justified under a statute incorporating California law? Why was Neagle not simply permitted to stand trial in California? Can you reconcile *Neagle* with *The Steel Seizure Case?*

2. *Neagle and Rescue Abroad.* The *Neagle* Court cited with approval the Koszta episode, in which an American naval captain threatened force to obtain the release of an applicant for U.S. citizenship who was imprisoned by Austria. Unlike Marshal Neagle, the naval captain apparently acted against the instructions of the President and the Secretary of the Navy. *See* Wormuth & Firmage, *supra* p. 73, at 152 ("[H]is action was illegal when undertaken but was later ratified by congressional commendation."). Is *Neagle* authority for military rescue operations without prior congressional authorization? See *infra* pp. 367-375.

3. *Neagle and Emergencies at Home.* The *Neagle* Court also posed the hypothetical case of armed military protection for U.S. mail carriers. Is *Neagle* authority for the domestic use of troops without prior congressional authorization? See *infra* p. 1153. Five years after *Neagle,* the President sued on his own authority to enjoin the Pullman Strike on the ground that it threatened the transportation of the mails. The Court upheld an injunction, despite the absence of any statutory authority for such a suit, stating that

> [t]he entire strength of the nation may be used to enforce in any part of the land the full and free exercise of all national powers and security of all rights entrusted by the Constitution to its care. The strong arm of the national government may be put forth to brush

away all obstructions to the freedom of interstate commerce or the transportation of the mails. If the emergency arises, the army of the Nation, and all its militia, are at the service of the Nation to compel obedience to its law....

... [I]t is more to the praise than to the blame of the government, that, instead of determining for itself questions of right or wrong on the part of these petitioners and their associates and enforcing that determination by the club of the policeman and the bayonet of the soldier, it submitted all those questions to the peaceful determination of judicial tribunals.... [*In re Debs*, 158 U.S. 564, 582-583 (1895).]

Both *Debs* and *The Steel Seizure Case* involved presidential actions called necessary to protect against the effects of labor strikes. Is *Debs* good law after *The Steel Seizure Case*?

4. *Lincoln's Extra-Constitutional Claims.* Consider President Lincoln's justification for his unilateral issuance of the Emancipation Proclamation:

[M]y oath to preserve the constitution to the best of my ability, imposed upon me the duty of preserving, by every indispensable means, that government — that nation — of which the constitution was the organic law. Was it possible to lose the nation, and yet preserve the constitution? By general law life *and* limb must be protected; yet often a limb must be amputated to save a life; but a life is never wisely given to save a limb. I felt that measures, otherwise unconstitutional, might become lawful, by becoming indispensable to the preservation of the constitution, through the preservation of the nation. [Letter to Albert G. Hodges (Apr. 4, 1864), in 7 *Collected Works* 281 (Roy P. Basler ed., 1953-1955).]

Did Lincoln claim constitutional authority for the Proclamation? If his authority is extra-constitutional, what is its source? If there is some emergency power of self-preservation in the government, does it necessarily follow that it is vested in the President when Congress can act? Note that Congress had previously enacted the Confiscation Act, freeing all slaves put to hostile use by the Confederate forces. Act of Aug. 6, 1861, ch. 60, 12 Stat. 319. *See also* Act of July 17, 1862, ch. 195, 12 Stat. 589.

Lincoln anticipated his defense of the Emancipation Proclamation when he earlier authorized his generals to suspend the writ of habeas corpus, asking, "are all the laws, *but one,* to go unexecuted, and the government itself go to pieces, lest the one be violated?" Message to Congress (July 4, 1861), in 4 *Collected Works* 429-430 (Roy P. Basler ed., 1953-1955). In that case, however, he claimed no extra-constitutional authority, citing instead the habeas corpus suspension clause of the Constitution. U.S. Const. art. I, §9.

5. *The Limits of Inherent Emergency Power.* If the inherent executive power recognized in *Neagle* and *Debs* is not unlimited, what is its scope? Can Congress limit such executive power by statute? If it exists only during emergencies, how is the word "emergencies" to be defined? See *infra* p. 113. What emergency was presented in *Debs* that could not have been addressed by legislation? Was the emergency in *Neagle* more acute?

Consider the Court's statement in *Home Building & Loan Ass'n v. Blaisdell*, 290 U.S. 398, 425-426 (1934):

Emergency does not create power. Emergency does not increase granted power or remove or diminish the restrictions imposed upon power granted or reserved. The

Constitution was adopted in a period of grave emergency. Its grants of power to the Federal Government and its limitations of the powers of the States were determined in the light of emergency and they were not altered by emergency. What power was thus granted and what limitations were thus imposed are questions which have always been, and always will be, the subject of close examination under our constitutional system.

In *Reid v. Covert*, 354 U.S. 1, 5-6 (1957), the Court added, "The United States is entirely a creature of the Constitution. Its power and authority have no other source. It can only act in accordance with all the limitations imposed by the Constitution."

Recall that in *The Steel Seizure Case* the Solicitor General argued that the "customs and claims of preceding administrations" had given rise to an inherent presidential power "to deal with a crisis or an emergency according to the necessities of the case...." 343 U.S. at 646. Justice Jackson responded this way:

> The appeal ... that we declare the existence of inherent powers *ex necessitate* to meet an emergency asks us to do what many think would be wise, although it is something the forefathers omitted.... I do not think we rightfully may so amend their work, and, if we could, I am not convinced it would be wise to do so, although many modern nations have forthrightly recognized that war and economic crisis may upset the normal balance between liberty and authority.... [*Id.* at 649-651.]

6. *Delegated Emergency Power.* Suppose the President did not have inherent power to order the protection of Justice Field. Would this mean that the Justice would have had to fend for himself? If the President lacks inherent power, in other words, is the country helpless before a grave emergency?

Justice Jackson gave an answer to this question, too. "Absence of authority in the President to deal with a crisis does not imply want of power in the Government," he wrote. 343 U.S. at 603-604. If Congress can anticipate the emergency, it can delegate power to the President to deal with it. If Congress cannot anticipate precisely, it can delegate generally, just as the Court held that it was permitted to do in *Curtiss-Wright*. (And so it had in *Neagle,* by authorizing marshals to exercise the same powers as sheriffs and their deputies could under state law.)

In fact, as *Dames & Moore* discussed, Congress has delegated a wide range of emergency powers to the President. See *supra* pp. 60-62 (discussing International Emergency Economic Powers Act and Hostage Act). If the President foresees the need for some kind of emergency authority, he can seek it from Congress in advance of the particular occasions for its use. In theory, then, the issue of inherent presidential emergency power should only arise when Congress has failed to anticipate the emergency and there is no time for the President to seek advance authorization. *See generally* Bruce Ackerman, *The Emergency Constitution*, 113 Yale L.J. 1029 (2004) (proposing an enhanced "framework statute" for delegating and limiting emergency power).

7. *Responding to Unconstitutional Emergency Initiatives.* What if Congress has not anticipated a particular emergency and there is no time for the President to seek authorization? Is the President's unilateral response to the emergency necessarily lawful? According to Professor Lobel, at least until the beginning of the twentieth century the exercise of emergency power by the President was widely believed to be unconstitutional, except to repel attacks or pursuant to congressional authorization.

Jules Lobel, *Emergency Power and the Decline of Liberalism*, 98 Yale L.J. 1385, 1388-1397 (1989). Nevertheless, he suggests, such power might be exercised when "universal rules and reasoned disclosure" failed to meet a particular emergency, when law had to be replaced by "discretion and politics." *Id.* at 1390. Thus, in the gravest crisis the President would act unilaterally at his peril, subject to the possibility of impeachment, removal from office, or perhaps ratification by Congress. In other words, emergency rule was separated from the normal constitutional order, "thereby preserving the Constitution in its pristine form while providing the executive with the power, but not legal authority, to act in an emergency." *Id. See also* Oren Gross, *Chaos and Rules: Should Responses to Violent Crises Always Be Constitutional?*, 112 Yale L.J. 1011 (2003).

When the President acts unconstitutionally in an emergency, Congress has the sanction of impeachment and the people have the sanction of the ballot. But as a practical matter, under what circumstances is either sanction likely to be imposed? Note that Congress also has the option of ratifying presidential acts that were statutorily unauthorized when taken. *See Ex Parte Endo*, 323 U.S. 283, 303 n.24 (1944) ("Congress may of course do by ratification what it might have authorized.") (citation omitted); *The Prize Cases*, 67 U.S. (2 Black) at 671. *See generally* Clinton Rossiter, *Constitutional Dictatorship* (1948).

Congress's National Security Powers

Congress, unlike the President, is vested by the Constitution with a host of specific foreign affairs and war powers. Apart from the declaration of war power, however, these powers are rarely considered in isolation. The courts typically review national security legislation from the perspective of the aggregate congressional war powers. *See, e.g., Lichter v. United States*, 334 U.S. 742 (1948), *infra* p. 99.

In this chapter we begin in Part A with the power to authorize war. In Part B we deal with the delegation of national security powers and with national security appropriations. We analyze statutory emergency powers in Part C. Finally, in Part D we consider substantive and procedural limits on Congress's national security powers.

A. CONGRESSIONAL AUTHORIZATIONS FOR WAR

John Locke wrote that a nation could "declare" war "by Word or Action." John Locke, *Two Treatises of Government* 278 (Peter Laslett ed., 1967). A nation could declare war, he wrote, "by Word" by issuing a formal declaration of war. It could declare war by "Action" by engaging in an act of war. In our system, of course, Congress may not engage in an act of war, but it can authorize the executive to do so.

The following materials provide an example of each method of "declaring" war: our last formal declaration of war and one of the first statutory authorizations for war (prior authorizations for the use of military force were directed at Indians and pirates). Consider how they differ in scope and whether they exhaust the ways in which Congress can authorize war.

1. Declaration of War

Joint Resolution Declaring That a State of War Exists Between the Government of Rumania and the Government and the People of the United States and Making Provisions to Prosecute the Same

ch. 325, 56 Stat. 307 (June 5, 1942)

Whereas the Government of Rumania has formally declared war against the Government and the people of the United States of America: Therefore be it

Resolved by the Senate and the House of Representatives of the United States of America in Congress assembled, that the state of war between the United States and the Government of Rumania which has thus been thrust upon the United States is hereby formally declared; and the President is authorized and directed to employ the entire naval and military forces of the United States and the resources of the Government to carry on war against the Government of Rumania; and, to bring the conflict to a successful termination, all of the resources of the country are hereby pledged by the Congress of the United States.

NOTES AND QUESTIONS

1. *Responding to a State of War.* A formal declaration may be used to start a war. As the declaration again Rumania shows, a declaration may also recognize that we are already in a "state of war" by virtue of an attack. Similarly, in response to a declaration of war against the United States by the Bey of Tripoli, Congress enacted a statute in 1802 authorizing the President to instruct American naval commanders to seize Tripolitan vessels "and also to cause to be done all such other acts of precaution or hostility as the *state of war* will justify...." Act approved Feb. 6, 1802, ch. 4, 2 Stat. 129, 130 (emphasis supplied). Moreover, as we have seen, the President need not await a formal declaration or any other authorization by Congress before responding militarily to an attack. *See The Prize Cases,* 67 U.S. (2 Black) 635 (1863), *supra* p. 68.

2. *The Obsolescent Declaration of War?* Increasing state sensitivity to public diplomacy and world opinion, as well as the decline of opportunities for the lawful use of force occasioned by the proliferation of treaties and the evolution of customary international law, have long made declarations of war impolitic. As a consequence, "[a]lthough conflicts between and among states continue, no state has issued a formal declaration of war [since the 1948 Arab-Israeli War]. Indeed, some argue that a declaration of war today would constitute prima facie evidence of illegal aggression." Robert F. Turner, *The War Powers Resolution: Its Implementation in Theory and Practice* 25 (1983).

In fact, there is evidence that the declaration of war was already obsolete in 1789, by which date the concept of "defensive war" had taken such firm root in the law of nations that it was widely understood that war could be started without the formality of declaration. *See, e.g., The Federalist No. 25,* at 165 (Alexander Hamilton) (Clinton Rossiter ed., 1961) ("the ceremony of a formal denunciation of war has of late fallen into disuse"); Turner, *supra,* at 16 nn.45-57 (citing sources). In this light, is it likely that the Framers intended to vest Congress with only the increasingly anachronistic formal declaration power, *see* J. Gregory Sidak, *To Declare War,* 41 Duke L.J. 27 (1991), and no other constitutional means to choose war? What answer did the members of the Court give in *Bas*? Regardless of the framing history or current geopolitical realities, does the advent of non-state enemies, such as non-state-sponsored terrorists, now make formal declarations of war obsolete?

3. *Declaring War on Terrorists?* Formal declarations of war have always named belligerents that were sovereign states. Following the September 11, 2001 terrorist attacks on the World Trade Center and the Pentagon, however, a newspaper columnist wrote, and some members of Congress reportedly agreed, that "Congress... should immediately declare war. It does not have to name a country. It can declare war against those who carried out [the] attack." Robert Kagan, Op-Ed., *We Must Fight This War*, Wash. Post, Sept. 12, 2001. May Congress declare war on a group of people? May it declare war without naming any enemy at all? What Congress did instead was to authorize the use of military force by statute — not a formal declaration — against certain persons, organizations, and nations connected to the 9/11 attacks. See *infra* p. 97. Supposing Congress could declare war against a group of terrorists, why didn't it?

4. *Limitations on Declared War?* Is there any limitation on declared war? In *Brown v. United States*, 12 U.S. (8 Cranch) 110 (1814), the issue was whether the declaration of the War of 1812 justified seizure of British-owned timber in Massachusetts. The libellant argued that the President had the authority as Commander in Chief to order confiscation of enemy property in execution of the rights of general war. Chief Justice Marshall, writing for the majority, rejected the argument, citing Congress's express constitutional power to make rules concerning capture. He concluded that "the power of confiscating enemy property is in the legislature, and...the legislature has not yet declared its will to confiscate property which was within our territory at the declaration of war." *Id.* at 129. Justice Story disagreed, arguing that the President had the power to order confiscation during a declared war unless Congress or the "rules of warfare established among civilized nations" forbade it. *Id.* at 153-154. Thus, the President may have to await specific congressional authorization to execute at least some of the general war powers recognized by the law of nations.

5. *The Legal Domino Effects of War.* A formal declaration of war by Congress gives notice to neutrals of the existence of hostilities and of the identity of the belligerents, and it activates certain rights and obligations of neutrals and belligerents alike under international law. Although *Brown v. United States* held that the declaration of war did not authorize domestic seizures of enemy property, Congress more commonly *has* authorized a broad range of authorities that become available to the Executive when we are in a declared war or even simply a state of war. A declaration of war triggers approximately 30 standby statutory authorities that would not otherwise be available to the President. *See generally* Jennifer K. Elsea & Richard F. Grimmett, *Declarations of War and Authorizations for the Use of Military Force: Historical Background and Legal Implications* (Cong. Res. Serv. RL31133), Mar. 8, 2007. (Some of them may be activated as well by the President's declaration of a national emergency. See *infra* p. 111.) For example, under the Alien Enemy Act, 50 U.S.C. §21 (2006), "whenever there is a declared war between the United States and any foreign nation or government," citizens of "the hostile nation or government" who are at least 14 years old and not naturalized are subject to summary arrest, internment, and deportation when

the President so proclaims. The Trading with the Enemy Act, 50 U.S.C. App. §§1-44 (2006), enables the President to regulate or prohibit commerce with an enemy state or its citizens after "Congress has declared war or the existence of a state of war." And the President may authorize electronic surveillance, physical searches, and the use of pen registers and trap and trace devices to acquire foreign intelligence without a court order for up to 15 days "following a declaration of war by Congress." 50 U.S.C. §§1811, 1829, 1844 (2006).

More than 170 other standby authorities are available "in time of war" or "when war is imminent" *without* requiring a declaration of war. *See generally* Elsea & Grimmett, *supra*; J. Gregory Sidak, *War, Liberty, and Enemy Aliens*, 67 N.Y.U. L. Rev. 1402, 1430 & nn.138-145 (1992). These authorize the President to take land for military purposes; commandeer private production lines for war manufacturing; take control of private transportation for war transport; and sequester, hold, and dispose of enemy property, among other powers.

6. *Is Congress's War-Declaring Role Strictly Judicial?* In light of the legal domino effect of a formal declaration of war, some scholars have argued that a declaration is strictly a juridical pronouncement and that Congress's war-declaring role is therefore judicial rather than legislative. *See* John C. Yoo, *The Continuation of Politics by Other Means: The Original Understanding of War Powers*, 84 Cal. L. Rev. 167 (1996). According to this theory, the President manages international relations and, when diplomacy fails, decides unilaterally whether to use military force. *Id.* at 291. Congress only enters into the equation to raise and supply the troops or to provide an "appropriations check" on disfavored military adventures by the President. In short, "the Framers created a framework designed to encourage presidential initiative in war. Congress was given a role in war-making decisions not by the Declare War Clause, but by its powers over funding and impeachment. The courts were given no role at all." *Id.* at 170. Does Yoo's theory square with what we learned in Chapter 2 about the history of the framing of the Constitution?

2. Statutory Authorization for Use of Military Force

Bas v. Tingy
United States Supreme Court, 1800
4 U.S. (4 Dall.) 37

[As relations between France and the United States deteriorated between 1798-1800, Congress enacted a succession of measures approving naval actions against France. Initially, it authorized U.S. armed vessels of the recently established navy to capture French vessels that had "committed depredations" on U.S.-owned vessels or that were "found hovering" off U.S. coasts for that purpose. Act of May 28, 1798, ch. 48, 1 Stat. 561. When this measure did not adequately protect U.S. merchants on the high seas, Congress next authorized such merchants to defend themselves against "any search, restraint or seizure" by vessels operating under French colors. Act of June 25, 1798, ch. 60, 1 Stat. 572. This act also provided for the recapture of U.S.-owned vessels from the French and their restoration to their former owners upon payment of salvage value. Three days later Congress passed another act that provided for the judicial condemnation of captured vessels and for the return of recaptured vessels to their owners for a salvage payment of one-eighth the full value. Act of June 28, 1798, ch. 62, 1 Stat. 574. Eventually, Congress authorized U.S. public and private armed vessels to take any French armed vessels found on the high seas. Act of July 9, 1798, ch. 68, 1 Stat. 578.

The next year Congress passed a set of rules and regulations for its infant navy. This act provided:

> That for the ships or goods belonging to the citizens of the United States, or to the citizens or subjects of any nation, in amity with the United States, if retaken from the enemy within twenty-four hours, the owners are to allow one eighth part of the whole value for salvage, if after twenty-four hours, and under forty-eight, one fifth thereof, if above that and under ninety-six hours, one third part thereof, and if above that, one half, all of which is to be paid without any deduction whatsoever.... [Act of March 2, 1799, ch. 24, §7, 1 Stat. 709, 716.]

On April 21, 1799, Captain Tingy, commander of the public armed ship *Ganges*, recaptured the *Eliza*, which belonged to John Bas and had been captured by a French privateer on the high seas on March 31, 1799. After he returned the vessel to Bas, Tingy brought an action in libel for salvage. The question in the case was whether Tingy was entitled to one-eighth the value of the *Eliza*, as provided by the 1798 act, or one-half as provided by the 1799 act. The lower courts ruled that Tingy was entitled to half the value. On appeal to the Supreme Court, the Justices delivered their opinions seriatim. The opinion of Justice Moore in favor of affirmance is omitted.]

WASHINGTON, Justice.... 1st. [The 1798 Act] relates to re-captures from *the French*, and [the 1799 Act] relates to re-captures from *the enemy;* and, it is said, that "the enemy" is not descriptive of France, or of her armed vessels, according to the correct and technical understanding of the word.

The decision of this question must depend upon another; which is, whether, at the time of passing the act of congress of the 2d of March 1799, there subsisted a state of war between the two nations? It may, I believe, be safely laid down, that every contention by force between two nations, in external matters, under the authority of their respective governments, is not only war, but public war. If it be declared in form, it is called *solemn,* and is of the perfect kind; because one whole nation is at war with another whole nation; and *all* the members of the nation declaring war, are authorised to commit hostilities against all the members of the other, in every place, and under every circumstance. In such a war all the members act under a general authority, and all the rights and consequences of war attach to their condition.

But hostilities may subsist between two nations more confined in its nature and extent; being limited as to places, persons, and things; and this is more properly termed *imperfect war*, because not solemn, and because those who are authorised to commit hostilities, act under special authority, and can go no farther than to the extent of their commission. Still, however, it is *public war*, because it is an external contention by force, between some of the members of the two nations, authorised by the legitimate powers. It is a war between the two nations, though all the members are not authorised to commit hostilities such as in a solemn war, where the government restrain the general power.

Now, if this be the true definition of war, let us see what was the situation of the United States in relation to France. In March 1799, congress had raised an army;

stopped all intercourse with France; dissolved our treaty; built and equipt ships of war; and commissioned private armed ships; enjoining the former, and authorising the latter, to defend themselves against the armed ships of France, to attack them on the high seas, to subdue and take them as prize, and to re-capture armed vessels found in their possession. Here, then, let me ask, what were the technical characters of an American and French armed vessel, combating on the high seas, with a view the one to subdue the other, and to make prize of his property? They certainly were not friends, because there was a contention by force; nor were they private enemies, because the contention was external, and authorised by the legitimate authority of the two governments. If they were not our enemies, I know not what constitutes an enemy.

2d. But, secondly, it is said, that a war of the imperfect kind, is more properly called acts of hostility, or reprizal, and that congress did not mean to consider the hostility subsisting between France and the United States, as constituting a state of war.

In support of this position, it has been observed, that in no law prior to March 1799, is France styled our enemy, nor are we said to be at war. This is true; but neither of these things were necessary to be done: because as to France, she was sufficiently described by the title of the French republic; and as to America, the degree of hostility meant to be carried on, was sufficiently described without declaring war, or declaring that we were at war. Such a declaration by congress, might have constituted a perfect state of war, which was not intended by the government. . . .

. . . [T]herefore, in my opinion, the decree of the Circuit Court ought to be affirmed.

CHASE, Justice. . . . Congress is empowered to declare a general war, or congress may wage a limited war; limited in place, in objects, and in time. If a general war is declared, its extent and operations are only restricted and regulated by the *jus belli*, forming a part of the law of nations; but if a partial war is waged, its extent and operation depend on our municipal laws.

What, then, is the nature of the contest subsisting between America and France? In my judgment, it is a limited, partial, war. Congress has not declared war in general terms; but congress has authorized hostilities on the high seas by certain persons in certain cases. There is no authority given to commit hostilities on land; to capture unarmed French vessels, nor even to capture French armed vessels lying in a French port; and the authority is not given, indiscriminately, to every citizen of America, against every citizen of France; but only to citizens appointed by commissions, or exposed to immediate outrage and violence. So far it is, unquestionably, a partial war; but, nevertheless, it is a public war, on account of the public authority from which it emanates.

There are four acts, authorised by our government, that are demonstrative of a state of war. A belligerent power has a right, by the law of nations, to search a neutral vessel; and, upon suspicion of a violation of her neutral obligations, to seize and carry her into port for further examination. But by the acts of congress, an American vessel is authorised: 1st. To resist the search of a French public vessel: 2d. To capture any vessel that should attempt, by force, to compel submission to a search: 3d. To re-capture any American vessel seized by a French vessel: and 4th. To capture any French armed vessel wherever found on the high seas. This suspension of the law of nations, this right of capture and re-capture, can only be authorized by an act of the government, which is, in itself, an act of hostility. But still it is a restrained, or limited, hostility; and there are, undoubtedly, many rights attached to a general war, which do not attach to this modification of the powers of defence and aggression. . . .

The acts of congress have been analyzed to show, that a war is not openly denounced against France, and that France is no where expressly called the enemy of America: but this only proves the circumspection and prudence of the legislature. Considering our national prepossessions in favour of the French republic, congress had an arduous task to perform, even in preparing for necessary defence, and just retaliation. As the temper of the people rose, however, in resentment of accumulated wrongs, the language and the measures of the government became more and more energetic and indignant; though hitherto the popular feeling may not have been *ripe* for a solemn declaration of war; and an active and powerful opposition in our public councils, has postponed, if not prevented that decisive event, which many thought would have best suited the interest, as well as the honour of the United States. The progress of our contest with France, indeed, resembles much the progress of our revolutionary contest; in which, watching the current of public sentiment, the patriots of that day proceeded, step by step, from the supplicatory language of petitions for a redress of grievances, to the bold and noble declaration of national independence.

Having, then, no hesitation in pronouncing, that a partial war exists between America and France, and that France was an enemy, within the meaning of the act of March 1799, my voice must be given for affirming the decree of the Circuit Court.

PATERSON, Justice. As the case appears on the record, and has been accurately stated by the counsel, and by the judges, who have delivered their opinions, it is not necessary to recapitulate the facts. My opinion shall be expressed in a few words. The United States and the French republic are in a qualified state of hostility. An imperfect war, or a war, as to certain objects, and to a certain extent, exists between the two nations; and this modified warfare is authorized by the constitutional authority of our country. It is a war *quoad hoc* [to this extent]. As far as congress tolerated and authorized the war on our part, so far may we proceed in hostile operations. It is a maritime war; a war at sea as to certain purposes. The national armed vessels of France attack and capture the national armed vessels of the United States; and the national armed vessels of the United States are expressly authorized and directed to attack, subdue, and take, the national armed vessels of France, and also to re-capture American vessels. It is therefore a public war between the two nations, qualified, on our part, in the manner prescribed by the constitutional organ of our country. In such a state of things, it is scarcely necessary to add, that the term "enemy," applies; it is the appropriate expression, to be limited in its signification, import, and use, by the qualified nature and operation of the war on our part. The word enemy proceeds the full length of the war, and no farther. . . .

By the COURT: Let the decree of the Circuit Court be affirmed.

NOTES AND QUESTIONS

1. *Authorizing War Expressly Without Declaring It.* How did Congress express its decision to make war on France at the end of the eighteenth century? How broad was the resulting authority in the President as Commander in Chief? Could the President have deployed land forces to invade France or French possessions? Could he

have deployed the Navy to take the war to French ports? What answers are suggested by *Little v. Barreme*, 6 U.S. (2 Cranch) 170 (1804), *supra* p. 78?

Less than a year after *Bas*, the Court was again called upon to decide rights of salvage during the naval war with France. Writing for the Court, Chief Justice Marshall concluded that "[t]he whole powers of war being, by the constitution of the United States, vested in congress, the acts of that body can alone be resorted to as our guides in this enquiry." *Talbot v. Seeman*, 5 U.S. (1 Cranch) 1, 28 (1801). The Court unanimously found that Congress had authorized "partial hostilities" against France.

Do the Quasi-War cases (*Bas, Talbot, Little*) tell us anything about whether the President could have ordered similar hostilities without any congressional authorization at all? *Compare* J. Gregory Sidak, *The Quasi-War Cases — and Their Relevance to Whether "Letters of Marque and Reprisal" Constrain Presidential War Powers*, 28 Harv. J.L. & Pub. Pol'y 465, 482, 486 (2005) (asserting that the answer is no, because the cases do not address "how the Constitution divides between Congress and the President the power to commit the nation to waging a limited war"), *with Campbell v. Clinton*, 203 F.3d 19 (D.C. Cir. 2000), at 30 n.7 (Randolph, J., concurring) (citing *Little* for the proposition that executive power in war "was constrained by an absence of legislation"), and 38 (Tatel, J., concurring) (citing *Talbot* for the proposition that Congress possesses the "whole powers of war").

2. *Authorizing War on Terrorists?* On September 14, 2001, in response to the 9/11 terrorist attacks, Congress passed a joint resolution authorizing the President to

> use all necessary and appropriate force against those nations, organizations, or persons he determines planned, authorized, committed, or aided the terrorist attacks that occurred on September 11, 2001, or harbored such organizations, or persons, in order to prevent any future acts of international terrorism against the United States by such nations, organizations or persons. [Pub. L. No. 107-40, §2(a), 115 Stat. 224 (2001).]

This Authorization for the Use of Military Force (AUMF) became law when President Bush signed it on September 18, 2001. Is there any important difference between this law and a formal declaration of war? Do these two different forms of legislative authority affect U.S. relations with other nations differently? Or the domestic powers of the President? Or the legal "dominos" discussed in above?

3. *Impliedly Authorizing War by Statute.* How direct must a statute be that authorizes the use of force? In *Orlando v. Laird*, 443 F.2d 1039 (2d Cir. 1971), *infra* p. 286, the court found congressional authorization for the Vietnam War in, *inter alia*, military appropriations and selective service statutes. It did not cite *Bas*. Is there a difference between the form of authorization found in *Bas* or the September 18, 2001, joint resolution, *supra*, and authorization by appropriation or selective service legislation? On the authorization for the Vietnam War generally, see Chapter 10. If Congress can indirectly authorize war by appropriating money for it, is there any constitutional or practical limit on the form of war authorization?

4. *Area and Use Limitations in War.* Some have argued that the President has plenary power to conduct a constitutionally authorized war and that congressional efforts to control the use of weapons or movement of troops are therefore

unconstitutional. See *infra* pp. 296-297. Is this view consistent with *Bas*? With *Little v. Barreme*? Is there any constitutional difference between defining the scope of a limited war in the initial authorization and doing so during the war? Is there a constitutional ratchet that prevents Congress from modifying or rescinding an authorization for war, once granted? If not, what is the difference between such a modification and a statute directing the conduct of the war—for example, by ordering Platoon *A* to attack Hill *B*? What about a legislative command *not* to attack Hill *B*? Might the answer turn on the location of Hill *B*?

3.   Authorizing the Use of Military Force by "Partial Congressional Declaration" or Congressional Silence

Does Congress even need to use a statute to authorize the use of military force? Congress, or either House, can and often does express itself about uses of armed force in ways that fall short of the Article I process of bicameral approval and presentment of a bill to the President for his signature. Can such an act or expression constitutionally authorize the use of force?

NOTES AND QUESTIONS

1. *Legislative Action Short of a Statutory Enactment.* Could Congress authorize war by separate and substantively different actions in each House? Single-chamber resolutions ("simple resolutions") do not have bicameral approval and are not presented to the President for his signature. See *infra* p. 119 (discussing these requirements for normal legislation that has the force and effect of law). Conceding that without the President's signature (or a veto override) such resolutions lack the force and effect of statutes, Charles Tiefer nonetheless argues that

> [a]ctions by Congress short of enactment may elucidate the intent of congressional appropriations. . . . Formal and express presidential requests for congressional approval [to use military force] . . . may [also] bestow or confirm the legal significance of the corresponding congressional "partial" positions. Finally, Congress may take legally significant positions, even apart from a presidential request. [Charles Tiefer, *War Decisions in the Late 1990s by Partial Congressional Declaration*, 36 San Diego L. Rev. 1, 105 (1999).]

Is this theory of "partial congressional declaration" supported by any constitutional text or framing history? If you are skeptical, is the theory strengthened if we require that *each* House pass a "partial declaration" voting to support military action, even though the resulting simple resolutions do not precisely match?

2. *Authorization by Silence?* Does either House need to do anything at all to approve war? May Congress authorize war silently by acquiescence in a conflict started by the Executive? See *supra* pp. 72-77.

3. *Domino Effects of "Partial Congressional Declaration" or Silence?* If you have concluded that any of the foregoing forms of indirect authorization is constitutionally sufficient in place of a declaration, what, if any, domino effects does this form of

authorization risk? The potential for domino effects, as well as the need for account-ability for war decisions, has caused some scholars to insist on the formality of a declaration as a predicate for war. *See* Sidak, *supra*. Tiefer, in response, notes that the interaction between a President who requests approval for the use of force and the Houses of Congress that respond separately but approvingly "cranks up an elaborate machinery for the democratic inclusion of the nation in the military commitment decision," including "[h]earings, news coverage, briefings, disputes over conditions or demands for assurances, and floor debate." *Id.* at 125. Does this machinery satisfy the need for accountability? Does it answer the concerns of the Framers who were determined to make it difficult to go to war? See Chapter 2.

B.   DELEGATIONS AND APPROPRIATIONS FOR NATIONAL SECURITY

Lichter v. United States

Supreme Court of the United States, 1948
334 U.S. 742

Mr. Justice BURTON delivered the opinion of the Court. . . . [The Renegotiation Act was enacted in 1942, 56 Stat. 226, 245-246, and subsequently amended several times during the war. It authorized the government to determine and recapture "excessive profits" by private contractors. Several contractors challenged the consti-tutionality of this legislation.]

The Renegotiation Act was developed as a major wartime policy of Congress comparable to that of the Selective Service Act. The authority of Congress to autho-rize each of them sprang from its war powers. Each was a part of a national policy adopted in time of crisis in the conduct of total global warfare by a nation dedicated to the preservation, practice, and development of the maximum measure of individual freedom consistent with the unity of effort essential to success.

With the advent of such warfare, mobilized property in the form of equipment and supplies became as essential as mobilized manpower. Mobilization of effort extended not only to the uniformed armed services but to the entire population. Both Acts were a form of mobilization. The language of the Constitution authorizing such measures is broad rather than restrictive. It says "The Congress shall have Power . . . To raise and support Armies, but no appropriation of Money to that Use shall be for a longer Term than two Years; . . ." Art. I, §8, cl. 12. This places emphasis upon the supporting as well as upon the raising of armies. The power of Congress as to both is inescapably express, not merely implied. The conscription of manpower is a more vital interference with the life, liberty and property of the individual than is the conscription of his property or his profits or any substitute for such conscription of them. For his hazardous, full-time service in the armed forces a soldier is paid what-ever the Government deems to be a fair but modest compensation. Comparatively speaking, the manufacturer of war goods undergoes no such hazard to his personal safety as does a front-line soldier and yet the Renegotiation Act gives him far better assurance of a reasonable return for his wartime services than the Selective Service Act and all its related legislation give to the men in the armed forces. The constitutionality of the conscription of manpower for military service is beyond question.

The constitutional power of Congress to support the armed forces with equipment and supplies is no less clear and sweeping.[4] It is valid, *a fortiori.*

In view of this power "To raise and support Armies, . . ." and the power granted in the same Article of the Constitution "To make all Laws which shall be necessary and proper for carrying into Execution the foregoing Powers, . . ." the only question remaining is whether the Renegotiation Act was a law "necessary and proper for carrying into Execution" the war powers of Congress and especially its power to support armies.

It is impossible here to picture adequately all that might have been "necessary and proper" in 1942-1944 to meet the unprecedented responsibility facing Congress in this field. We do, however, catch a glimpse of it in authoritative, contemporaneous descriptions of the situation. . . .

. . . [These] describe a demand for production of war supplies in proportions previously unimagined. They call for production in a volume never before approximated and at an undreamed of speed. The results amply demonstrated the infinite value of that production in winning the war. It proved to be a *sine qua non* condition of the survival of the nation. Not only was it "necessary and proper" for Congress to provide for such production in the successful conduct of the war, but it was well within the outer limits of the constitutional discretion of Congress and the President to do so under the terms of the Renegotiation Act. . . .

The petitioners contend that the Renegotiation Act unconstitutionally attempted to delegate legislative power to administrative officials. . . .

The constitutional argument is based upon the claim that the delegation of authority contained in the Act carried with it too slight a definition of legislative policy and standards. Accordingly, it is contended that the resulting determination of excessive profits which were claimed by the United States amounted to an unconstitutional exercise of legislative power by an administrative official instead of a mere exercise of administrative discretion under valid legislative authority. . . .

. . . On the basis of (a) the nature of the particular constitutional powers being employed, (b) the current administrative practices later incorporated into the Act and (c) the adequacy of the statutory term "excessive profits" as used in this context, we hold that the authority granted was a lawful delegation of administrative authority and not an unconstitutional delegation of legislative power.

(a) *A constitutional power implies a power of delegation of authority under it sufficient to effect its purposes.* — This power is especially significant in connection with constitutional war powers under which the exercise of broad discretion as to methods to be employed may be essential to an effective use of its war powers by Congress. The degree to which Congress must specify its policies and standards in order that the administrative authority granted may not be an unconstitutional delegation of its own legislative power is not capable of precise definition. In peace or in war it is essential that the Constitution be scrupulously obeyed, and particularly that the respective Branches of the Government keep within the powers assigned to each by the Constitution. On the other hand, it is of the highest importance that the fundamental purposes of the Constitution be kept in mind and given effect in

---

4. "The Constitution grants to Congress power 'to raise and support Armies,' 'to provide and maintain a Navy,' and to make all laws necessary and proper to carry these powers into execution. Under this authority Congress can draft men for battle service. *Selective Draft Law Cases,* 245 U.S. 366. Its power to draft business organizations to support the fighting men who risk their lives can be no less." *United States v. Bethlehem Steel Corp.,* 315 U.S. 289, 305. . . .

order that, through the Constitution, the people of the United States may in time of war as in peace bring to the support of those purposes the full force of their united action. In time of crisis nothing could be more tragic and less expressive of the intent of the people than so to construe their Constitution that by its own terms it would substantially hinder rather than help them in defending their national safety.

In an address by Honorable Charles E. Hughes, of New York, on "War Powers Under The Constitution," September 5, 1917, 42 A.B.A. Rep. 232, 238-239, 247-248, he said:

> The power to wage war is the power to wage war successfully. The framers of the Constitution were under no illusions as to war. They had emerged from a long struggle which had taught them the weakness of a mere confederation, and they had no hope that they could hold what they had won save as they established a Union which could fight with the strength of one people under one government entrusted with the common defence. In equipping the National Government with the needed authority in war, they tolerated no limitations inconsistent with that object, as they realized that the very existence of the Nation might be at stake and that every resource of the people must be at command. . . .
>
> In the words of the Supreme Court: "It is also settled beyond dispute that the Constitution is not self-destructive. In other words, that the power which it confers on the one hand it does not immediately take away on the other. . . ." This was said in relation to the taxing power. Having been granted in express terms, the Court held it had not been taken away by the due process clause of the Fifth Amendment. As the Supreme Court put it in another case: "the Constitution does not conflict with itself by conferring upon the one hand a taxing power and taking the same power away on the other by the limitations of the due process clause."
>
> Similarly, it may be said that the power has been expressly given to Congress to prosecute war, and to pass all laws which shall be necessary and proper for carrying that power into execution. That power explicitly conferred and absolutely essential to the safety of the Nation is not destroyed or impaired by any later provision of the Constitution or by any one of the amendments. These may all be construed so as to avoid making the constitution self-destructive, so as to preserve the rights of the citizen from unwarrantable attack, while assuring beyond all hazard the common defence and the perpetuity of our liberties. These rest upon the preservation of the nation.
>
> It has been said that the Constitution marches. That is, there are constantly new applications of unchanged powers, and it is ascertained that in novel and complex situations, the old grants contain, in their general words and true significance, needed and adequate authority. So, also, we have a *fighting* Constitution. We cannot at this time fail to appreciate the wisdom of the fathers, as under this charter, one hundred and thirty years old — the constitution of Washington — the people of the United States fight with the power of unity, — as we fight for the freedom of our children and that hereafter the sword of autocrats may never threaten the world.

The war powers of Congress and the President are only those which are to be derived from the Constitution but, in the light of the language just quoted, the primary implication of a war power is that it shall be an effective power to wage the war successfully. Thus, while the constitutional structure and controls of our Government are our guides equally in war and in peace, they must be read with the realistic purposes of the entire instrument fully in mind. . . .

. . . We believe that the administrative authority there granted was well within the constitutional war powers then being put to their predestined uses. . . .

Accordingly, in each of the cases before us, the judgment of the Circuit Court of Appeals [upholding the Renegotiation Act] is affirmed.

Mr. Justice MURPHY concurs in the result in these cases.

Mr. Justice JACKSON concurs in [one of the three cases consolidated for review, but dissents in two others, including *Lichter*].

Mr. Justice DOUGLAS dissenting in part. [Opinion omitted.]

Greene v. McElroy
United States Supreme Court, 1959
360 U.S. 474

Mr. Chief Justice WARREN delivered the opinion of the Court. This case involves the validity of the Government's revocation of security clearance granted to petitioner, an aeronautical engineer employed by a private manufacturer which produced goods for the armed services. Petitioner was discharged from his employment solely as a consequence of the revocation because his access to classified information was required by the nature of his job. After his discharge, petitioner was unable to secure employment as an aeronautical engineer and for all practical purposes that field of endeavor is now closed to him. . . .

Petitioner contends that the action of the Department of Defense in barring him from access to classified information on the basis of statements of confidential informants made to investigators was not authorized by either Congress or the President and has denied him "liberty" and "property" without "due process of law" in contravention of the Fifth Amendment. . . .

The issue, as we see it, is whether the Department of Defense has been authorized to create an industrial security clearance program under which affected persons may lose their jobs and may be restrained in following their chosen professions on the basis of fact determinations concerning their fitness for clearance made in proceedings in which they are denied the traditional procedural safeguards of confrontation and cross-examination. . . .

The first proffered statute is the National Security Act of 1947, as amended, 5 U.S.C. §171 et seq. That Act created the Department of Defense and gave to the Secretary of Defense and the Secretaries of the armed services the authority to administer their departments. Nowhere in the Act, or its amendments, is there found specific authority to create a clearance program similar to the one now in effect.

Another Act cited by respondents is the Armed Service Procurement Act of 1947, as amended. It provides in 10 U.S.C. §2304 that:

> (a) Purchases of and contracts for property or services covered by this chapter shall be made by formal advertising. However, the head of an agency may negotiate such a purchase or contract, if— . . .
> > (12) the purchase or contract is for property or services whose procurement he determines should not be publicly disclosed because of their character, ingredients, or components.

It further provides in 10 U.S.C. §2306:

> (a) The cost-plus-a-percentage-of-cost system of contracting may not be used. Subject to this limitation and subject to subsections (b)-(e), the head of an agency may, in negotiating contracts under section 2304 of this title, make any kind of contract that he considers will promote the best interests of the United States.

Respondents argue that these statutes, together with 18 U.S.C. §798, which makes it a crime willfully and knowingly to communicate to unauthorized persons information concerning cryptographic or intelligence activities, and 50 U.S.C. §783(b), which makes it a crime for an officer or employee of the United States to communicate classified information to agents of foreign governments or officers and members of "Communist organizations," reflect a recognition by Congress of the existence of military secrets and the necessity of keeping those secrets inviolate.

Although these statutes make it apparent that Congress recognizes the existence of military secrets, they hardly constitute an authorization to create an elaborate clearance program which embodies procedures traditionally believed to be inadequate to protect affected persons.[29]

Lastly, the Government urges that if we refuse to adopt its "inferred" authorization reasoning, nevertheless, congressional ratification is apparent by the continued appropriation of funds to finance aspects of the program fashioned by the Department of Defense. Respondents refer us to Hearings before the House Committee on Appropriations on Department of Defense Appropriations for 1956, 84th Cong., 1st Sess. 774-781. At those hearings, the Committee was asked to approve the appropriation of funds to finance a program under which reimbursement for lost wages would be made to employees of government contractors who were temporarily denied, but later granted, security clearance. Apparently, such reimbursements had been made prior to that time out of general appropriations. Although a specific appropriation was eventually made for this purpose, it could not conceivably constitute a ratification of the hearing procedures, for the procedures were in no way involved in the special reimbursement program.

Respondents' argument on delegation resolves itself into the following: The President, in general terms, has authorized the Department of Defense to create procedures to restrict the dissemination of classified information and has apparently acquiesced in the elaborate program established by the Secretary of Defense even where application of the program results in restraints on traditional freedoms without the use of long-required procedural protections. Similarly, Congress, although it has not enacted specific legislation relating to clearance procedures to be utilized for industrial workers, has acquiesced in the existing Department of Defense program and has ratified it by specifically appropriating funds to finance one aspect of it.

If acquiescence or implied ratification were enough to show delegation of authority to take actions within the area of questionable constitutionality, we might agree with respondents that delegation has been shown here. In many circumstances,

---

29. As far as appears, the most substantial official notice which Congress had of the non-confrontation procedures used in screening industrial workers was embodied in S. Doc. No. 40, 84th Cong., 1st Sess., a 354-page compilation of laws, executive orders, and regulations relating to internal security, printed at the request of a single Senator, which reproduced, among other documents and without specific comment, the Industrial Personnel Security Review Regulation [which established the summary hearing procedures by which Greene's security clearance was revoked].

where the Government's freedom to act is clear, and the Congress or the President has provided general standards of action and has acquiesced in administrative interpretation, delegation may be inferred. Thus, even in the absence of specific delegation, we have no difficulty in finding, as we do, that the Department of Defense has been authorized to fashion and apply an industrial clearance program which affords affected persons the safeguards of confrontation and cross-examination. But this case does not present that situation. We deal here with substantial restraints on employment opportunities of numerous persons imposed in a manner which is in conflict with our long-accepted notions of fair procedures. Before we are asked to judge whether, in the context of security clearance cases, a person may be deprived of the right to follow his chosen profession without full hearings where accusers may be confronted, it must be made clear that the President or Congress, within their respective constitutional powers, specifically has decided that the imposed procedures are necessary and warranted and has authorized their use. Such decisions cannot be assumed by acquiescence or nonaction. *Kent v. Dulles*, 357 U.S. 116; *Peters v. Hobby*, 349 U.S. 331; *Ex Parte Endo*, 323 U.S. 283, 301-302. They must be made explicitly not only to assure that individuals are not deprived of cherished rights under procedures not actually authorized, but also because explicit action, especially in areas of doubtful constitutionality, requires careful and purposeful consideration by those responsible for enacting and implementing our laws. Without explicit action by lawmakers, decisions of great constitutional import and effect would be relegated by default to administrators who, under our system of government, are not endowed with authority to decide them.

Where administrative action has raised serious constitutional problems, the Court has assumed that Congress or the President intended to afford those affected by the action the traditional safeguards of due process. These cases reflect the Court's concern that traditional forms of fair procedure not be restricted by implication or without the most explicit action by the Nation's lawmakers, even in areas where it is possible that the Constitution presents no inhibition.

In the instant case, petitioner's work opportunities have been severely limited on the basis of a fact determination rendered after a hearing which failed to comport with our traditional ideas of fair procedure. The type of hearing was the product of administrative decision not explicitly authorized by either Congress or the President. Whether those procedures under the circumstances comport with the Constitution we do not decide. Nor do we decide whether the President has inherent authority to create such a program, whether congressional action is necessary, or what the limits on executive or legislative authority may be. We decide only that in the absence of explicit authorization from either the President or Congress the respondents were not empowered to deprive petitioner of his job in a proceeding in which he was not afforded the safeguards of confrontation and cross-examination.

Accordingly, the judgment is reversed and the case is remanded to the district court for proceedings not inconsistent herewith. . . .

Mr. Justice FRANKFURTER, Mr. Justice HARLAN and Mr. Justice WHITTAKER concur in the judgment on the ground that it has not been shown that either Congress or the President authorized the procedures whereby petitioner's security clearance was revoked, intimating no views as to the validity of those procedures.

[The opinions of Justices HARLAN, concurring specially, and CLARK, dissenting, are omitted.]

NOTES AND QUESTIONS

a. Delegations of National Security Authority

1. *The Scope of Congressional War Powers.* The Supreme Court has approved the exercise of the defense appropriations power and related congressional war powers to

> control the price of every commodity bought and sold within the national boundaries; to fix the amount of rent to be charged for every room, home, or building and this even though to an individual landlord there may be less than a fair return; to construct extensive systems of public works; to operate railroads; to prohibit the sale of liquor; to restrict freedom of speech in a manner that would be unwarranted in time of peace; to ration and allocate the distribution of every commodity important to the war effort; to restrict the personal freedom of American citizens by curfew orders and the designation of areas of exclusion; and, finally, to demand of every citizen that he serve in the armed forces of the nation. [*Spaulding v. Douglas Aircraft Co.*, 154 F.2d 419, 422-423 (9th Cir. 1946) (citations from Supreme Court decisions omitted).]

These powers may continue after the cessation of hostilities. The Court has recognized that the congressional war power "is not limited to victories in the field.... It carries with it inherently the power to guard against the immediate renewal of the conflict, and to remedy the evils which have arisen from its rise and progress." *Stewart v. Kahn*, 78 U.S. (11 Wall.) 493, 507 (1871). Do these powers also exist before any conflict arises?

2. *The Clear Statement Requirement.* In light of the sweep of the congressional defense appropriations and the war-supporting authority just described, why did the Court decline to find authority for the security clearance procedures employed by the executive in *Greene*? What is the holding of *Greene*? *See also Kent v. Dulles*, 357 U.S. 116 (1958) (declining to find statutory authority for the Secretary of State to restrict the right of travel absent explicit delegation from Congress). *But see Haig v. Agee*, 453 U.S. 280 (1981) (inferring authority to restrict the right of travel from congressional acquiescence in State Department policy). *See generally* Cass R. Sunstein, *Clear Statement Principles and National Security: Hamdan and Beyond*, 2006 Sup. Ct. Rev. 1.

3. *Clear Statements for Appropriations: The Endo Rule.* The Supreme Court has also applied an especially strong version of the clear statement rule to appropriations, on which the Executive relied for authority. *Greene* cited *Ex parte Endo*, 323 U.S. 283, 303 n.24 (1944), in which the Court said that to authorize or ratify executive action an appropriation must "plainly show a purpose to bestow the precise authority which is claimed." There the Court found no authorization for the continued detention of loyal Japanese Americans during World War II "where a lump appropriation was made for the overall program of the [War Relocation] Authority and no sums were earmarked for the single phase of the total program [there] involved." *Id.*

4. *Standards of National Security Delegation.* National security authority has often been delegated by Congress to the executive branch with only the barest of standards. The inherent variability and unpredictability of national security problems have always placed practical limits on the detail with which Congress could delegate in these areas. Today, the speed of modern communications and executive monopolization of national security information have aggravated the problem. *See generally* Jason A. Rosenberg et al., Note, *Historical and Structural Limitations on Congressional Abilities to Make Foreign Policy,* 50 B.U. L. Rev. 51 (Spec. Issue 1970). As noted above, the Court has not struck down any congressional delegation of lawmaking authority to the executive since 1935. See *supra* p. 40.

Do *Greene* and *Lichter* establish different standards for congressional delegation of national security authority? Can you distinguish the locus and effect of the authorities recognized in those cases? What were the specific constitutional rights allegedly threatened by the government in each case? *Greene* was decided after World War II. Would it have been decided the same way during wartime?

5. *The Delegability of the War Power.* After *Lichter,* is there any limit to delegations of war powers to the executive that do not directly curtail individual constitutional rights? May Congress delegate the power to declare war? Does the impracticality of antecedent standard-setting for the declaration of war suggest that Congress has no choice? Or does it suggest just the opposite: that it cannot? Consider the following argument advanced during the height of the Vietnam War after Congress had, by the Gulf of Tonkin Resolution, allegedly delegated war-making power to the President.

[I]t seems to me clearly the case that the exclusive responsibility of Congress to resolve the necessity and appropriateness of war as an instrument of national policy at any given time is uniquely not delegable at all. The pursuit of national interest by sustained extra-territorial uses of direct force was textually reserved to Congress alone after alternative formulations were pressed on precisely the grounds that conventionally rationalize a limited power to delegate an interstitial lawmaking authority to the executive, viz., superior expertise in the executive, the need for flexibility in the face of rapidly changing circumstances, the cumbersomeness of parliamentary processes, and a residual power to check the executive in the event of displeasure with the manner in which he might make war. To the extent that such arguments were considered to have merit, they were accommodated by *other* means among the several war-related clauses. To the extent that they were not thus accommodated, the conclusion seems inescapable that they were rejected and correspondingly, that no further latitude of executive control was to be permitted than that already provided for.

To express the same matter less passionately, specific contingencies which give sense and shape to the general doctrine permitting limited delegations of legislative power in other areas of congressional responsibility are *already* provided for in respect to war, *so far as it was felt safe to do so.* Thus, it was contemplated and made possible that peacetime armies might be raised under presidential discretion though this might even increase the risk of war. Similarly, an interim executive capacity to respond to outright emergencies, authorizing the president to resist invasion or repel an attack when war might be thrust upon the nation too quickly for Congress to convene to authorize even such limited defensive measures, was provided. Additionally, executive discretion to make command decisions of tactics and strategy within the express war declaration by Congress was conceded. Further confidence was also reposed of necessity in the President in recognizing that the congressional power would be exercised or not substantially depending upon the information and advice the President would provide in his emergency message of exigent circumstances asking for *their* decision to initiate hostilities, sustain present emergency defensive war actions he had taken, enlarge upon them, or, by doing nothing, require that our extraterritorial forces be immediately disengaged and withdrawn. Finally, although there might have been much to be said for a different view (so to make going to war especially grave and therefore desirably difficult to accomplish), the Constitution does not require that the declaration of war be an all or nothing response. . . .

But precisely because of these various provisions and accommodations, it is even more clearly the case that there is no standing room left for a theory which would transfer to the executive the power to authorize war on his own initiation. When all the accommodations to shared authority otherwise provided by the several war-related clauses are thus aggregated, it becomes quite evident that the determination as to whether circumstances at any given time in fact make it necessary and appropriate to engage in war, however limited in scope or objectives, resides solely in Congress subject to no delegation whatever. [William Van Alstyne, *Congress, the President, and the Power to Declare War: A Requiem for Vietnam*, 121 U. Pa. L. Rev. 1, 16-18 (1972).]

Can Professor Van Alstyne's argument be squared with *Lichter*?

Professor Lobel suggested that some kinds of decisions, including engagement in military hostilities, are uniquely for the Congress to make because "important issues of public policy should be decided by a broadly representative deliberative body." Jules Lobel, *Covert War and Congressional Authority: Hidden War and Forgotten Power*, 134 U. Pa. L. Rev. 1035, 1097-1098 (1986). He found support for his conclusion by analogy in *National Cable Television Ass'n v. United States*, 415 U.S. 336 (1974), which implied that the taxing power was nondelegable. But in *Skinner v. Mid-America Pipeline Co.*, 490 U.S. 212 (1989), the Court declared:

We discern nothing in this placement of the Taxing clause that would distinguish Congress' power to tax from its other enumerated powers — such as its commerce power, its power to *"raise and support Armies,"* its power to borrow money, or *its power to "make Rules for the government"* — in terms of the scope and degree of discretionary authority that Congress may delegate to the Executive in order that the President may "take Care that the Laws be faithfully executed." [*Id.* at 220-221 (emphasis added).]

Indeed, the Court has never expressly held any Article I power to be nondelegable. Does this cast doubt on Professor Lobel's conclusion or on Professor Van Alstyne's analysis?

b. Authorization by Defense Appropriation

1. *Appropriation as Acquiescence. Greene* suggests that in some instances appropriations may be regarded as a form of congressional acquiescence in executive practice, discussed *supra* pp. 45-46. Recall that congressional acquiescence presupposes adequate notice of the executive practice to the Congress. Key appropriations hearings in *Greene* were "off the record," in executive session, presumably to protect classified information. *See* 360 U.S. at 521 (Clark, J., dissenting). Why did the Court refuse to infer that Congress received notice during these executive sessions?

2. *Appropriations as "Back-Door Law."* Congress has traditionally distinguished *authorizations*—statutes delegating authority to the executive branch—from *appropriations*—statutes that fund the execution of delegated authority. The former have generally emanated from congressional committees with jurisdiction to oversee the relevant government function or executive agency, while the latter usually come out of the appropriations committees. Academic and occasional judicial efforts to deny the characterization "legislation" to appropriations, *see, e.g., Sierra Club v. Andrus*, 581 F.2d 895, 910-911 (D.C. Cir. 1978) (MacKinnon, J., concurring in part and dissenting in part), *rev'd*, 442 U.S. 347 (1979), have foundered on the text of Article I, which does not make this distinction. As the product of the Article I legislative process, appropriations are as much legislation as authorizations. Moreover, appropriations "are not only legislative specifications of money *amounts*, but also legislative specifications of the *powers, activities*, and *purposes*—what we may call, simply, 'objects'—for which the appropriated funds may be used." Kate Stith, *Congress' Power of the Purse*, 97 Yale L.J. 1343, 1352 (1988). Both chambers recognize the legislative nature of appropriations by requiring explanation or identification of appropriations bills that change "existing law." *See* House R. XXI, cl. 3; Senate R. XVI, cl. 8.

Nevertheless, the incidental nature of many appropriations measures and the often summary deliberation that attends them properly makes courts more hesitant to infer authority from such "back-door legislation" than from other kinds of legislation, as *Greene* suggests. *See* Neal Devins, *Regulation of Government Agencies Through Limitations Riders*, 1987 Duke L.J. 456, 458, 481, 499. *Compare Tennessee Valley Auth. v. Hill*, 437 U.S. 153, 174-188 (1978) (doctrine that repeals by implication are disfavored applies with special force to repeals by appropriations), *with United States v. Dickerson*, 310 U.S. 554 (1940) (finding repeal by appropriation rider after exhaustive analysis of its legislative history). Moreover, because most appropriations are for a specific term, the purposes for which they are enacted and the limitations they impose are also time-limited and subject to variation. "Court interpretations of limitation riders as amendments to previously enacted legislation, therefore, are inherently unreliable; they may be accurate one day, inaccurate the next, and irrelevant at the end of the fiscal year." Devins, *supra*, at 458. *See also id.* at 465, 498-499. *See generally* Peter Raven-Hansen & William C. Banks, *Pulling the Pursestrings of the Commander in Chief*, 80 Va. L. Rev. 833, 839-848 (1994).

3. *Nullifying Appropriation by Impoundment?* If an appropriation can authorize, does it also mandate? Suppose the President disapproves of the activity for which Congress has appropriated funds? Of course, in such a case he could veto the appropriation. But if he does not, or if his veto is overridden, may he simply decline to spend—and thus *impound*—the funds? Selective impoundment could give the President the practical equivalent of an item veto. What constitutional theories support or refute presidential impoundment claims? *See generally* Ralph S. Abascal & John R. Kramer, *Presidential Impoundment Part I: Historical Genesis and Constitutional Framework*, 62 Geo. L.J. 1549 (1974). Does it matter whether the impounded funds are for military forces or for nonmilitary foreign relations activities? *See* Timothy R. Harner, *Presidential Power to Impound Appropriations for Defense and Foreign Relations*, 5 Harv. J.L. & Pub. Pol'y 131 (1982). The Supreme Court has not yet ruled on the constitutional questions, but it has held that a particular impoundment violated the intent of the relevant statute. *See Train v. City of New York*, 420 U.S. 35 (1975). Congress attempted to regulate impoundment by enacting the Congressional Budget and

Impoundment Control Act of 1974, Pub. L. No. 93-344, §§1001-1017, 88 Stat. 297, 332-337, only to have a court of appeals invalidate part of the Act as an unconstitutional, albeit severable, legislative veto. *City of New Haven v. United States,* 809 F.2d 900 (D.C. Cir. 1987).

c.   Limitation by Defense Appropriation

1. *Appropriations with "Strings Attached."* The flip side of appropriation as authorization or delegation is appropriation as limitation.

> All appropriations...may be conceived of as lump-sum grants with "strings" attached. These strings, or conditions of expenditure, constitute legislative prescriptions that bind the operating arm of the government. Occasionally, conditions may be stated in an appropriations statute itself. For instance, an appropriations act may provide that "[n]o part of any appropriation contained in this Act shall be used...for publicity or propaganda purposes...." Alternatively, the appropriations act may require that the recipient agency allocate the amount appropriated among certain activities or in accordance with certain conditions. Often, the appropriations act explicitly incorporates other legislation, notably substantive legislation creating particular federal agencies or programs or granting particular agency powers. Moreover, all appropriations legislation effectively incorporates the prescriptions of statutes of general applicability. [Stith, *supra,* at 1353.]

Federal agencies may not use nonappropriated funds because their activities are authorized only to the extent of their appropriations. *Id.* at 1356. *See* Anti-Deficiency Act, 31 U.S.C. §1341(a)(I)(A) (2006) (prohibiting expenditures or obligations in excess of appropriations); U.S. Const. art. I, §9, cl. 7 ("No money shall be drawn from the Treasury, but in Consequence of Appropriations made by Law.").

In *Spaulding v. Douglas Aircraft,* 60 F. Supp. 985, 988 (S.D. Cal. 1945), *aff'd,* 154 F.2d 419 (9th Cir. 1946), the court stated that

> Congress in making appropriations has the power and authority not only to designate the purpose of the appropriation, but also the terms and conditions under which the executive department...may expend such appropriations....
>
> The purpose of appropriations, the terms and conditions under which said appropriations were made, is a matter solely in the hands of Congress and it is the plain and explicit duty of the executive branch...to comply with the same.

See also 27 Op. Att'y Gen. 259 (1909) (approving constitutionality of bill that conditioned funding of the Marine Corps on the maintenance of a ratio of 8 percent Marines to Navy enlisted men on Navy battleships). Usually limitations in appropriations acts pertain to the particular appropriated funds, but Congress has also used an appropriations rider to limit the executive in ways unrelated to the use or purpose of the appropriation. The Constitution, after all, contains no rule restricting any piece of legislation to a single subject.[1]

---

1. Each house has imposed a limited version of the rule on itself, restricting the use of riders to modify substantive legislation, *see* Senate R. XVI(4) and House R. XXI(2), but a violation of the rule merely makes the rider subject to procedural objection within the Congress and does not invalidate it as law.

2. *The Political Utility of Appropriations Riders.* Why does Congress rely so much on limitations in appropriations bills instead of building them into other legislation? Surely one reason is their comparative effectiveness:

> [A]ppropriations oversight is effective precisely because the statutory controls are so direct, unambiguous, and virtually self-enforcing. While agencies are able to bend the more ambiguous language of authorizing legislation to their own purposes, the dollar figures in appropriations bills represent commands which cannot be bent or ignored except at extreme peril to agency officials. [S. Comm. on Governmental Operations, 95th Cong., *Study of Federal Regulation: Congressional Oversight of Regulatory Agencies* 31 (Comm. Print 1977).]

Another reason is that sponsors of limitations can sometimes avoid the jurisdiction of hostile committees by inserting the limitations in appropriations bills.[2] They can also make it difficult for the President to veto the limitations by embedding them in needed appropriations bills, especially omnibus bills that provide for funding of many different programs.

3. *The History of Defense Appropriations Riders.* Partly out of the foregoing considerations, Congress has often used its defense appropriations power to control national security policy, particularly since World War II. *See generally* Eli E. Nobleman, *Financial Aspects of Congressional Participation in Foreign Relations*, 289 Annals 145 (1953); Stith, *supra* p. 108, at 1360-1361 nn.83-86. For example, Congress used its appropriations power to attempt to control and ultimately to end the Vietnam War, see *infra* pp. 302-306, and to attempt to control military assistance to the Contras fighting in Nicaragua. See *infra* pp. 492-498.

The language and history of the defense appropriations power raise the possibility that these limitations have a specially protected constitutional status. While the power of Congress generally to appropriate monies is implied from the Common Defense Clause, Article I, section 8, appropriations for the Army and Navy are separately and expressly authorized in clause 12 of the same section. The Framers were aware of the English Parliament's successful use of the purse in its struggle with the King, *see* Francis L. Coolidge Jr. & Joel David Sharrow, Note, *The War-Making Powers: The Intentions of the Framers in Light of Parliamentary History*, 50 B.U. L. Rev. 5 (Spec. Issue 1970), and of the extensive use of the purse to control the scope and conduct of colonial military operations. *See, e.g.*, Elias Huzar, *The Purse and the Sword* 22-23 (1971). As noted in Chapter 2, the Framers deliberately vested Congress with detailed defense appropriations powers and simultaneously limited the duration of any blank check that Congress might draw to support a standing army. *See* Garry J. Wooters, Note, *The Appropriations Power as a Tool of Congressional Foreign Policy Making*, 50 B.U. L. Rev. 34, 40 (Spec. Issue 1970). Moreover, the difficulty of anticipating precisely and in detail the

---

2. In both the House and Senate, there are three committees with specific jurisdiction over national security matters: Armed Services, Foreign Relations (International Relations in the House), and Intelligence. The Joint Economic Committee, Governmental Affairs (Government Reform and Oversight in the House), Appropriations, and, to a more general degree, Budget committees all have some oversight responsibilities for national security expenditures. Jurisdictional overlaps are common, however, and many other committees have oversight responsibility for incidental — especially internal — security functions. See generally the current *Congressional Directory* for a description of the jurisdiction and membership of relevant committees.

occasions for exercise of military force arguably increased the practical importance of defense appropriations as at least a post hoc control. *See generally* William C. Banks & Peter Raven-Hansen, *National Security Law and the Power of the Purse* 9-42 (1994); Michael J. Glennon, *Strengthening the War Powers Resolution: The Case for Purse-Strings Restrictions*, 60 Minn. L. Rev. 1 (1975).

C.   STATUTORY EMERGENCY POWERS

Proclamation No. 7463, Declaration of National Emergency by Reason of Certain Terrorist Attacks

66 Fed. Reg. 48,199 (Sept. 14, 2001)

A PROCLAMATION

A national emergency exists by reason of the terrorist attacks at the World Trade Center, New York, New York, and the Pentagon, and the continuing and immediate threat of further attacks on the United States.

NOW, THEREFORE, I, GEORGE W. BUSH, President of the United States of America, by virtue of the authority vested in me as President by the Constitution and the laws of the United States, I [sic] hereby declare that the national emergency has existed since September 11, 2001, and, pursuant to the National Emergencies Act (50 U.S.C. 1601 et seq.), I intend to utilize the following statutes: sections 123, 123a, 527, 2201(c), 12006, and 12302 of title 10, United States Code, and sections 331, 359, and 367 of title 14, United States Code.

This proclamation immediately shall be published in the Federal Register or disseminated through the Emergency Federal Register, and transmitted to the Congress.

This proclamation is not intended to create any right or benefit, substantive or procedural, enforceable at law by a party against the United States, its agencies, its officers, or any person.

IN WITNESS WHEREOF, I have hereunto set my hand this fourteenth day of September, in the year of our Lord two thousand one, and of the Independence of the United States of America the two hundred and twenty-sixth.

George W. Bush

Congress has enacted at least 77 standby emergency statutes that permit the President to act in ways that would be impermissible in the absence of a crisis. *See* Elsea & Grimmett, *supra* p. 92, at 45-77 (listing emergency standby statutes). *See also* Harold C. Relyea, *National Emergency Powers* (Cong. Res. Serv. 98-505 GOV), Aug. 30, 2007. Some of these statutory authorities may be activated by a declaration of war, some by a state of war, and some by a declaration of a national emergency. In Proclamation No. 7463, above, the President invoked standby authorities to activate the Ready Reserve, retired officers, and enlisted members of the Coast Guard; to suspend separation (retirement) of officers from the armed services; and to suspend certain numerical limitations on numbers of officers at certain ranks. Among other emergency statutes available to the President is one that allows him to commit troops to assist "any other country that he considers it advisable to assist in the interest of national defense," 10 U.S.C. §712 (2006), and another that permits him to enter into defense contracts without following the usual procedures. 50 U.S.C. §§1431-1433 (2006).

During the Vietnam War, it was revealed that President Nixon had relied on one of these emergency statutes, the Feed and Forage Act of 1861, 41 U.S.C. §11 (2006) (intended to provide fodder for cavalry horses), to finance the secret invasion of Cambodia. Nixon based his action on national emergencies, one dating from 1933, that were earlier declared and never revoked. This discovery led to passage in 1976 of the National Emergencies Act, 50 U.S.C. §§1601-1651 (2006), canceling all existing national emergencies. If a President now wishes to activate standby legislation, she must declare a new national emergency, indicate the statutory authority she intends to exercise, and notify Congress. *Id.* §§1621(a), 1631, 1641. *See* Glenn E. Fuller, Note, *The National Emergency Dilemma: Balancing the Executive's Crisis Powers with the Need for Accountability*, 52 S. Cal. L. Rev. 1453 (1979); Relyea, *supra*.

NOTES AND QUESTIONS

1. *Invoking Standby Authorities.* After Hurricane Katrina hit the Gulf Coast in August 2005, President Bush declared a national emergency and invoked 40 U.S.C. §3147 to suspend the Davis-Bacon Act wage supports for workers in the affected area in order to facilitate recovery construction. Proc. No. 7924, *To Suspend Subchapter IV of Chapter 31 of Title 40, United States Code, Within a Limited Geographic Area in Response to the National Emergency Caused by Hurricane Katrina*, 70 Fed. Reg. 54,227 (Sept. 8, 2005). Oddly, however, he simply found that "the conditions caused by Hurricane Katrina constitute a 'national emergency' within the meaning of section 3147 of title 40, United States Code." *Id.* at 54,227. He appears not to have followed the National Emergencies Act on this occasion. Was the claimed standby authority lawfully invoked? *See* Relyea, *supra*, at 19 ("A more likely course of action seemingly would have been for the President to declare a national emergency pursuant to the National Emergencies Act and to specify that he was, accordingly, activating the suspension authority."). Should it matter whether the President follows the National Emergencies Act when he seeks to invoke standby statutory emergency authority?

2. *The IEEPA.* In 1917, during World War I, Congress passed the Trading with the Enemy Act, which gives the President authority to regulate a variety of domestic and international economic transactions in wartime. The Act was amended in 1933 to make it applicable during peacetime national emergencies as well. *See* 50 U.S.C. App. §§1-44 (2006), as amended. It has been invoked by a succession of Presidents to take extraordinary foreign and domestic executive actions. A criminal prosecution for violation of the Act is traced in *United States v. Plummer*, 221 F.3d 1298 (11th Cir. 2000) (defendant apprehended trying to smuggle $50,000 worth of Cuban cigars).

The International Emergency Economic Powers Act (IEEPA), 50 U.S.C. §§1701-1707 (2006), which was invoked by President Carter and analyzed by the Court in *Dames & Moore v. Regan*, 453 U.S. 654 (1981), *supra* p. 60, was enacted in 1977 to curb perceived presidential abuses of authority under the Trading with the Enemy Act. Without disturbing the President's wartime authority under the earlier legislation, the IEEPA gives the President the same peacetime emergency economic powers as previously, but those powers may only be exercised following a new national emergency declaration. *See* Mary Margaret Coughlin Bowman, Note, *Presidential Emergency Powers Related to International Economic Transactions: Congressional Recognition of Customary Authority*, 11 Vand. J. Transnat'l L. 515 (1978).

In addition to its use in the Iran hostage crisis, the IEEPA has been invoked by Presidents to limit trade with South Africa, Libya, Panama, Iraq, Haiti, and the Balkans, as well as to restrict activities that threaten the further proliferation of nuclear, chemical, and biological weapons. Executive orders declaring national emergencies invoking the IEEPA are set out in the United States Code following the text of the statute.

3. *Defining "National Emergency."* The President may exercise power under the National Emergencies Act only after declaring a "national emergency." Do you know what a "national emergency" is? According to one commentator, "[n]o statute defines a national emergency. . . . The test for when a national emergency exists is completely subjective — anything the President says is a national emergency is a national emergency." Fuller, *supra*, 52 S. Cal. L. Rev. at 1458. Should Congress try to provide a definition of the term? Can you suggest suitable language? In the absence of a statutory definition, can you say how and by whom a presidential declaration of a national emergency could be challenged?

In 1985, President Reagan issued Executive Order No. 12,513, 50 Fed. Reg. 18,629 (May 1, 1985), to cut off trade with Nicaragua. The executive order provoked a suit by two U.S. business concerns trading in Nicaragua to enjoin enforcement of the embargo. *Beacon Prods. Corp. v. Reagan*, 633 F. Supp. 1191 (D. Mass. 1986), *aff'd*, 814 F.2d 1 (1st Cir. 1987). The plaintiffs argued that the President was not empowered to impose the embargo because Nicaragua did not pose "an unusual and extraordinary threat" as required by §1701(b) of IEEPA. The court found this aspect of the case to be a nonjusticiable political question. The court in *United States v. Yoshida International, Inc.*, 526 F.2d 560, 579 (C.C.P.A. 1975), a case testing the President's actions under the Trading with the Enemy Act, observed that "courts will not normally review the essentially political questions surrounding the declaration or continuance of a national emergency."

But in a more recent case, the court found that its review of administrative orders implementing the ban on trading with the Federal Republic of Yugoslavia did not "hamper the executive's conduct of foreign policy by injecting unacceptable sweeping challenges to foreign policy choices." *Milena Ship Mgmt. Co. v. Newcomb*, 804 F. Supp. 846, 850 (E.D. La. 1992), *aff'd*, 995 F.2d 620 (5th Cir. 1993), *cert. denied*, 510 U.S. 1071 (1994). On the other hand, the court observed, before granting a preliminary injunction to suspend the President's blocking orders, it had to "take into account the effect [of its actions] on the executive's ability to conduct foreign affairs, on the congressional policy behind the authorization of blocking orders, and on this country's obligations with respect to the United Nations." 804 F. Supp. at 854.

By avoiding judicial scrutiny of the President's grounds for invoking either the IEEPA or the National Emergencies Act, would a court not effectively nullify the efforts of Congress to regulate the President's emergency powers? *See* Jules Lobel, *Emergency Power and the Decline of Liberalism*, 98 Yale L.J. 1385, 1416-1418 (1989).

4. *Banning Travel.* In 1963, President Kennedy approved a Treasury Department regulation promulgated under the Trading with the Enemy Act that cut off trade and prohibited all economic transactions with Cuba. President Carter relaxed that

regulation in early 1977 to allow U.S. citizens to pay ordinary expenses of traveling to Cuba. But in 1982, President Reagan reimposed the ban on most travel without declaring a new national emergency. When it enacted the IEEPA, Congress adopted a grandfather clause providing that "authorities conferred upon the President by section 5(b) of the Trading with the Enemy Act which were being exercised with respect to a country on July 1, 1977" could "continue to be exercised." 91 Stat. 1625, note following 50 U.S.C. App. §5. The Supreme Court decided that the grandfather clause permitted the newly expanded travel ban. *Regan v. Wald,* 468 U.S. 222 (1984).

The Court also found that the ban did not violate the right to travel guaranteed by the Fifth Amendment's Due Process Clause, because the ban was, in the Court's view, "justified by weighty concerns of foreign policy." Citing the *Curtiss-Wright* decision for a "traditional deference to executive judgment '[i]n this vast external realm,'" the Court said there was an "adequate basis...to sustain the President's decision to curtail the flow of hard currency to Cuba—currency that could then be used in support of Cuban adventurism—by restricting travel." *Id.* at 242-243. On similar grounds, the court in *Walsh v. Brady,* 927 F.2d 1229 (D.C. Cir. 1991), upheld the travel ban against a First Amendment challenge. *See also Freedom to Travel Campaign v. Newcomb,* 82 F.3d 1431 (9th Cir. 1996). Does your reading of earlier decisions reveal such a tradition of deference? If the stated premise of *Curtiss-Wright* is correct, could the Court have decided otherwise?

5. *Takings in Emergencies.* Must the government pay compensation to the owners of claims destroyed by a suspension of dealings under the IEEPA? The *Dames & Moore* Court avoided answering this question when it determined that the plaintiff had an alternative means of at least partial redress. 453 U.S. at 688. In a later case, a landlord found itself unable to sue for past-due rentals or to collect on a related letter of credit from Yugoslav Airlines when President Bush invoked the IEEPA to block "all assets and property interests of Serbia, Montenegro, and the Federal Republic of Yugoslavia...in the United States." Exec. Order No. 12,808, 57 Fed. Reg. 23,299 (May 30, 1992). The court found that no compensable taking had occurred, in part because the "President's ability to deal effectively with international events is critical to the safety and prosperity of the nation." *Rockefeller Ctr. Props. v. United States,* 32 Fed. Cl. 586, 591 (1995). *See also Paradissiotis v. United States,* 49 Fed. Cl. 16, 23 (2001) ("The preservation of the national security interest of the United States...greatly outweighs plaintiff's [total] loss."). *See generally* David Meezan, Note, *Forgotten Rights: Takings Claims and the International Emergency Economic Powers Act,* 21 Vt. L. Rev. 591 (1996).

D.   LIMITATIONS ON CONGRESSIONAL WAR POWERS

1.   Substantive Limits on Congressional National Security Powers

a.   The Nondelegation Principle

We have seen that Congress's power to delegate national security powers to the executive branch is, at least theoretically, constrained by the "nondelegation principle." See *supra* p. 40. That principle requires Congress to make fundamental legislative judgments by including "intelligible principles" in any statutory delegation, so that executive discretion can be channeled and, on judicial review, measured. See *supra* p. 44. *Lichter, supra* p. 99, and *United States v. Curtiss-Wright Export Corp.*, 299 U.S. 304 (1936), *supra* p. 53, showed, however, that if the nondelegation principle ever had any teeth, they hardly leave marks on national security and foreign relations delegations.

b. The *Lovett* Principle

The nondelegation principle is just one example of a broader substantive constraint: that a statutory delegation not violate any provision of the Constitution. *Lovett v. United States*, 66 F. Supp. 142 (Ct. Cl. 1945), *aff'd on other grounds*, 328 U.S. 303 (1946), provides an illustration. There Congress had enacted a rider to the Wartime Urgent Deficiency Appropriation of 1943 forbidding the executive branch to disburse salaries to certain identified "subversive" employees unless they were reappointed with the advice and consent of the Senate. Because the House would not approve any appropriation without this provision, the Senate agreed to it. The President reluctantly signed the bill into law, asserting that the rider was unconstitutional. When the employees sued the United States in the Court of Claims for their salaries, the court ruled in favor of the employees on contract grounds. But Judge Whitaker, concurring, found that the provision violated the Bill of Attainder Clause of the Constitution by inflicting punishment without a judicial trial. 66 F. Supp. at 148. He asserted that even an exercise of the appropriation power "is subject to the limitation that it must not be exercised in a way that would nullify another provision of the Constitution." *Id.* Judge Madden acknowledged that Congress has the absolute *power* to withhold appropriations, but not the lawful *authority*.

> I do not think, therefore, that the power of the purse may be constitutionally exercised to produce an unconstitutional result such as taking of a citizen's liberty or property without due process of law, a conviction and punishment of a citizen for wholly innocent conduct, or a trespass upon the constitutional functions of another branch of the Government. [*Id.* at 152.]

The Supreme Court affirmed the judgment for the employees on the ground that the rider constituted an unconstitutional bill of attainder. 328 U.S. at 313-315. "The fact that the punishment is inflicted through the instrumentality of an Act specifically cutting off the pay of certain named individuals found guilty of disloyalty, makes it no less galling or effective than if it had been done by an Act which designated the conduct as criminal." *Id.* at 316.

Lovett does not stand alone. *See also United States v. Will*, 449 U.S. 200, 225-226 (1980) (appropriations act that reduces compensation of federal judges violates the Compensation Clause of Article I); *Brown v. Califano*, 627 F.2d 1221 (D.C. Cir. 1980) (construing an appropriations prohibition of agency support for mandatory busing narrowly to avoid finding it an unconstitutional prohibition of agency enforcement of the constitutional right to equal protection); *Blitz v. Donovan*, 538 F. Supp. 1119 (D.D.C. 1982) (appropriations provision that denies funds to persons who advocate the overthrow of the government violates the First Amendment).

The limitation on the congressional appropriations power recognized in *Lovett* and its companion cases has found other national security applications as well. *See* 41 Op. Att'y Gen. 507 (1960); 41 Op. Att'y Gen. 230 (1955); 4 Op. Off. Legal Counsel 731 (1980) (all concluding that Congress may not constitutionally use its appropriations power in a manner that violates direct constitutional commands); *cf. United States v. Robel*, 389 U.S. 258, 263-264 (1967) (quoting *Home Bldg. & Loan Ass'n v. Blaisdell*, 290 U.S. 398, 426 (1934): "[T]he phrase 'war power' cannot be invoked as a talismanic incantation to support any exercise of congressional power which can be brought within its ambit. '[E]ven the war power does not remove constitutional limitations safeguarding individual liberties.' "). Presumably what we will call the *Lovett* principle applies with equal force to legislation enacted under Congress's Necessary and Proper lawmaking authority and is not confined just to appropriations measures.

NOTES AND QUESTIONS

1. *Lovett or Lichter?* How can the *Lovett* limitation be squared with *Lichter*'s approval of the assertion that the congressional war power "is not destroyed or impaired by any later provision of the Constitution or by any one of the amendments"? *Lichter*, 334 U.S. at 781, *supra* p. 101 (quoting Chief Justice Hughes). One answer — or dodge — may be to read an appropriations rider or other statutory limitation narrowly to avoid impairing the executive war power. This principle of avoidance is reflected in the canon of statutory construction that "[w]hen the validity of an act of the Congress is drawn in question, and even if a serious doubt of constitutionality is raised, it is a cardinal principle that this Court will first ascertain whether a construction of the statute is fairly possible by which the question may be avoided." *Crowell v. Benson*, 285 U.S. 22, 62 (1932). Why didn't this canon apply in *Lovett?*

2. *Lovett and War Powers.* Does *Lovett* also support the proposition that Congress may not use its national security powers to "micro-manage" the conduct of war or foreign policy? Various judicial dicta assert that "Congress cannot direct the conduct of campaigns," *Ex parte Milligan*, 71 U.S. (4 Wall.) 2, 139 (1866) (dictum) (opinion of Chase, C.J., and Wayne, Swayne, and Miller, JJ., concurring), and that "Congress can not in the disguise of 'rules for the government' of the Army impair the authority of the President as commander in chief." *Swaim v. United States*, 28 Ct. Cl. 173, 221 (1893) (dictum), *aff'd*, 165 U.S. 553 (1897). *See also Youngstown Sheet & Tube Co. v. Sawyer*, 343 U.S. 579, 644 (1952), *supra* p. 35 (Jackson, J., concurring) ("Congress cannot deprive the President of the command of the army and navy," although "only Congress can provide him an army and navy to command"); Louis Henkin, *Foreign Affairs and the Constitution* 113, 361-362 n.74 (1972) (quoting Senator Borah, 69 Cong. Rec. 6760 (1928), as saying that "Congress could not, through the power of appropriation . . . infringe upon the right of the President to command whatever army he might find.").

The Minority Report of the Iran-Contra Committees described its objection to the use of appropriations limitations to manage foreign policy in these terms:

> Congress may not use its control over appropriations, including salaries, to prevent the executive or the judiciary from fulfilling Constitutionally mandated obligations. . . .

Congress does not have to create a State Department or an intelligence agency. Once such departments are created, however, the Congress may not prevent the President from using his executive branch employees from serving as the country's "eyes and ears" in foreign policy. Even if Congress refuses to fund such departments, it may not prevent the President from doing what he can without funds to act as the nation's "sole organ" in foreign affairs. . . .

What Congress grants by statute may be taken away by statute. But Congress may not ask the President to give up a power he gets from the Constitution, as opposed to one he gets from Congress, as a condition for getting something, whether money or some other good or power from Congress. [*Report of the Congressional Committees Investigating the Iran-Contra Affair, The Minority Report,* H.R. Rep. No. 100-433, S. Rep. No. 100-216, at 476 (1987) (hereinafter *Minority Report*).]

See also Assignment of Ground Forces of the United States to Duty in European Areas, S. Rep. No. 93-220, at 92-93 (1973) (statement of former Secretary of State Dean Acheson) ("Not only has the President the authority to use Armed Forces in carrying out the broad foreign policy of the United States and implementing treaties, but it is equally clear that this authority may not be interfered with by the Congress in the exercise of powers which it has under the Constitution."); Robert F. Turner, *The Power of the Purse: Controlling National Security Policy by Conditional Appropriations,* Atlantic Community Q. 79, 84 (1998) (asserting that, because "the command of military forces, and the gathering of intelligence information" are "vest[ed] exclusively in the President, . . . for Congress to seek to seize control of these powers through conditional appropriations is a dangerous challenge to our constitutional system of government").

Is there any difference between the constitutional commands discussed in *Lovett* or its companion cases and the "Constitutionally mandated obligations" to which the *Minority Report* refers? Does the *Minority Report* critique adequately account for the history of the defense appropriations power? See *supra* p. 110. Or for the reach of the Necessary and Proper Clause? *See War Powers Legislation 1973: Hearings on S. 440 Before the S. Comm. on Foreign Rel.,* 93d Cong. 20 (1973) (statement of Alexander Bickel) ("Nothing in the Constitution does or can empower Congress to do something unconstitutional, but much in the Constitution needs to be clarified or implemented, and except in the limited number of instances where exclusive power is specifically vested elsewhere, the necessary and proper clause authorizes Congress to do so, with respect to its own functions as well as those of the other branches. . . ."). *See generally* Raven-Hansen & Banks, *supra* p. 108, at 884-899.

3. *Lovett and Appropriations Limitations.* On rare occasions, the Supreme Court has struck down legislation for intruding impermissibly on the President's inherent constitutional authority. *See, e.g., Myers v. United States,* 272 U.S. 52 (1926) (statute requiring Senate consent to removal of a purely executive officer); *Ex parte Garland,* 71 U.S. 333 (1867) (statute limiting the effect of a presidential pardon). Until 1988, however, no federal court had ever struck down an appropriations limitation on the President's exercise of national security powers. In *National Federation of Federal Employees v. United States,* 688 F. Supp. 671 (D.D.C. 1988), *vacated and remanded sub nom. American Foreign Service Assn. v. Garfinkel,* 490 U.S. 153 (1989), a district court held unconstitutional an appropriations limitation on portions of an executive order

regulating disclosure of national security information to Congress by executive branch employees. The court found that Congress's "tug on the purse strings" intruded dramatically and unconstitutionally on the President's constitutionally imposed duty, as Commander in Chief and chief executive, to oversee national security information. 688 F. Supp. at 685. The court noted that the congressional limitation "is merely an appropriations measure by which no substantive rights or causes of action are created. By such a measure, Congress cannot accomplish that which by direct legislative action would be beyond its constitutional authority." *Id.* at 684 n.17. Was the court right in suggesting that "mere" appropriations measures may not create or presumably limit rights?

The Supreme Court subsequently vacated and remanded, chastising the district court for reaching the constitutional question before exhausting nonconstitutional grounds for decision. 490 U.S. at 161. Congressional access to intelligence information is addressed *infra* pp. 1242-1249.

4. *A Mandatory Appropriations Power?* If Congress may not use appropriations to control certain executive activities, *must* it appropriate funds for such activities? Judge Madden thought not in *Lovett.* He thought the physical "power of Congress to control expenditures is absolute." 66 F. Supp. at 152. Yet if the President herself is disabled from raising necessary funds for the exercise of an inherent constitutional power, congressional failure to appropriate would carry the same effect as a more direct legislative prohibition. Professor Stith concludes:

> Congress is obliged to provide public funds for constitutionally mandated activities — both obligations imposed upon the government generally [citing the periodic census, U.S. Const. art. I, §2, cl. 3] and independent constitutional activities of the President. For instance, . . . Congress itself would violate the Constitution if it refused to appropriate funds for the President to receive foreign ambassadors or to make treaties. [Stith, *supra* p. 108, at 1350-1351.]

See also Henkin, *supra* Note 2, at 113. *See generally* Peter Raven-Hansen & William C. Banks, *From Viet Nam to Desert Shield: The Commander in Chief's Spending Power,* 81 Iowa L. Rev. 79, 127-128 (1995).

5. *A Presidential Spending Power?* If you agree that Congress must appropriate funds in some instances, where does a refusal to appropriate leave the executive? May the President transfer funds from other appropriations in disregard of their otherwise valid limitations? *See generally* Louis Fisher, *Presidential Spending Power* (1975); Lucius Wilmerding Jr., *The Spending Power: A History of the Efforts of Congress to Control Expenditures* 3-19 (1943). Logic may suggest an affirmative answer, but the Appropriations Clause seems to provide the opposite answer: "No money shall be drawn from the Treasury, but in Consequence of Appropriations made by law. . . ." U.S. Const. art. I, §9, cl. 7. When Congress refuses to appropriate for the President's independent constitutional functions, her constitutional options are seemingly political — to seek the electoral replacement of the recalcitrant Congress or to violate appropriations laws and the Constitution, hoping for congressional ratification after the fact and risking her own replacement or, worse, impeachment.

Yet in this matter, too, custom has overtaken formalism, and the executive has from time to time transferred some funds between accounts without explicit appropriations authority but with apparent congressional acquiescence. *See* Fisher, *supra*, at 99-122. For example, President Nixon financed the Cambodian "incursion," see *supra* p. 112 and *infra* p. 294, by transferring funds from foreign assistance accounts. Fisher, *supra*, at 107. Moreover, executive branch officials have purported to find a distinction

> between the condition subsequent in an appropriation not yet completely spent and new appropriations. . . . If [the President] has used up all the money appropriated and then Congress refuses to provide any more, I think the Congress has effectively stopped the President from continuing the military action. I don't know how he can go on. If, on the other hand, he still had moneys that were unexpended, he could continue to spend those until such time as there was a court challenge and the court found that he was acting illegally. [*War Powers: A Test of Compliance: Hearings Before the Subcomm. on Int'l Security and Scientific Affairs, H. Comm. on Int'l Relations*, 94th Cong. 92 (1975) (testimony of Monroe Leigh, Legal Adviser to State Dep't).]

On what theory of statutory or constitutional construction does this distinction rest? *See generally* Raven-Hansen & Banks, *supra* at 117-126.

2.   Procedural Limits on Congressional National Security Powers: *Chadha*

The *Lovett* line of cases highlights the substantive constitutional limitation on the congressional national security power. Almost as important are the procedural limitations established by Article I. In *Immigration & Naturalization Service v. Chadha*, 462 U.S. 919, 952, 958 (1983), the Supreme Court held that to take legislative action — "action that had the purpose and effect of altering the legal rights, duties and relations of persons . . . outside the legislative branch" — Congress must act "in conformity with the express procedures of the Constitution's prescription for legislative action: passage by a majority of both Houses and presentment to the President." Accordingly, the Court struck down a statutory provision for a "one-house veto" by which Congress reserved to either House the power to veto by resolution an exercise of delegated authority by the Attorney General that would have changed the legal status of an alien. The Court gave short shrift to the argument that the retention of veto authority would be more efficient because it permitted Congress to give the executive needed freedom while preserving needed congressional control of the executive:

> The choices we discern as having been made in the Constitutional Convention impose burdens on governmental processes that often seem clumsy, inefficient, even unworkable, but those hard choices were consciously made by men who had lived under a form of government that permitted arbitrary governmental acts to go unchecked. There is no support in the Constitution or decisions of this Court for the proposition that the cumbersomeness and delays often encountered in complying with explicit constitutional standards may be avoided, either by the Congress or by the President. *See Youngstown Sheet & Tube Co. v. Sawyer*, 343 U.S. 579 (1952). With all the obvious flaws of delay, untidiness, and potential for abuse, we have not yet found a better way

to preserve freedom than by making the exercise of power subject to the carefully crafted restraints spelled out in the Constitution. [462 U.S. at 959.]

Shortly after *Chadha,* the Court summarily affirmed a decision striking down a two-House veto by concurrent resolution (requiring both Houses to veto an executive action, but omitting presentment of the veto resolution to the President). *United States Senate v. Federal Trade Comm'n,* 463 U.S. 1216 (1983).

Before *Chadha,* legislative vetoes had been an increasingly popular device for legislative control of executive action, inserted into nearly 200 statutes. Dissenting in *Chadha,* Justice White explained why:

> Without the legislative veto, Congress is faced with a Hobson's choice: either to refrain from delegating the necessary authority, leaving itself with a hopeless task of writing laws with the requisite specificity to cover endless special circumstances across the entire policy landscape, or in the alternative, to abdicate its law-making function to the executive branch and independent agencies. To choose the former leaves major national problems unresolved; to opt for the latter risks unaccountable policymaking by those not elected to fill that role. [462 U.S. at 968.]

The special difficulty of writing specific national security laws made the veto particularly appealing. Justice White listed 12 examples of such legislation in an appendix to his opinion, including the War Powers Resolution, *infra* p. 307, various Department of Defense appropriation and authorization acts, the International Security Assistance and Arms Control Act of 1976, and the National Emergencies Act.

NOTES AND QUESTIONS

1. *Are National Security Laws an Exception?* Should the *Chadha* Court have distinguished national security laws from ordinary domestic legislation in declaring the veto unconstitutional? Consider this argument: "Use of the veto as an instrument of the continuing political dialogue between President and Congress, on matters having high and legitimate political interest to both, and calling for flexibility for government generally, does not present the same problems as its use to control, in random and arbitrary fashion, those matters customarily regarded as the domain of administrative law." Peter L. Strauss, *Was There a Baby in the Bathwater? A Comment on the Supreme Court's Legislative Veto Decision,* 1983 Duke L.J. 789, 791-792. Several pre-*Chadha* decisions appeared to leave room for this kind of distinction. *See Consumer Energy Council of America v. Federal Energy Regulatory Comm'n,* 673 F.2d 425, 459 (D.C. Cir. 1982) ("[T]he foreign affairs veto presents unique problems since in that context there is the additional question whether Congress or the President or both have inherent power to act."), *summarily aff'd,* 463 U.S. 1216 (1983); *American Fed'n of Gov't Employees v. Pierce,* 697 F.2d 303, 308 (D.C. Cir. 1982) (statement of Judges Wald and Mikva supporting rehearing en banc).

Do you think, based on the brief summary of *Chadha*'s reasoning supplied above, that the Court left room for this distinction? It literally struck down only the veto provision in the Immigration and Nationality Act affecting the domestic power of the Attorney General to suspend the deportation of aliens. But Justice White clearly identified the national security vetoes in his appendix, and the majority opinion made no exception for them, nor is any exception immediately visible in its account of the Article I bicameral/presentment formula for legislative action.

2. *The Special Need for Checks on National Security Delegations.* On the other hand, the majority opinion may rest on the absence of any need for legislative control by veto over the *domestic* executive action at issue there. *See generally* Charles Tiefer, *The FAS Proposal: Valid Check or Unconstitutional Veto?*, in *First Use of Nuclear Weapons: Under the Constitution, Who Decides?* 143 (Peter Raven-Hansen ed., 1987). Explaining why the Attorney General's exercise of legislative authority to change a legal status did not violate the Article I formula, the Court said that

> [e]xecutive action under legislatively delegated authority that might resemble "legislative" action in some respects is not subject to the approval of both houses of Congress and the President for the reason that the Constitution does not so require. *That* kind of executive action is always subject to check by the terms of the legislation that authorized it; and if that authority is exceeded it is open to judicial review. [*Chadha*, 462 U.S. at 953 n.16 (emphasis supplied).]

Curtiss-Wright, Lichter, and *Dames & Moore,* however, all suggest a difference between delegations of domestic power and delegations of foreign affairs and war powers, and suggest further that the latter are not effectively "subject to check by the terms of the legislation" and by "judicial review" because doctrines of nonjusticiability are often invoked to deny judicial enforcement of foreign affairs and war powers legislation. See generally Chapter 6. Moreover,

> *Chadha* allowed no congressional role in decisions after the [Immigration and Nationality Act's] enactment because the [Act] defined the standards for executive action — as it had to, pursuant to the nondelegation doctrine. The Court viewed the subsequent congressional role (the veto resolution) as amending or repealing these previously defined standards. . . . However, regarding foreign affairs and war powers, . . . delegation theory from *Curtiss-Wright* to *Dames & Moore* means that the President's sources of authority and funding lack defined standards. . . . Thus, a mechanism for a congressional role does not amend or repeal a previous standard or limit, because there was none. Rather, it establishes a political check, in place of the domestic-style standards and judicial review which do not apply. . . .
>
> . . . [I]n the foreign sphere, and particularly that of war powers, a more complex and subtle model of authorization applies than the domestic delegation model. Authorization consists of the balance between the claimed inherent presidential powers and any congressional powers of limitation, looking at the various shades of acquiescence and challenge by each branch in the respective claims and limits. . . .
>
> Many steps in foreign affairs and wartime occur on a level of responsive interaction and cue-following by the executive and Congress, not strict delegation. [Tiefer, *supra*, at 150-152.]

Is this view consistent with *The Steel Seizure Case?* Can an analytic distinction between the "domestic model of delegation" and the "foreign/war powers model of responsive interaction" withstand the changes in communications, markets, and transportation that have steadily shrunk the modern world?

3. *Other Legislative Controls.* Congress, of course, has other devices for legislative control besides the veto. These include durational limits on authorizations ("sunset" provisions), joint resolutions of approval or disapproval (requiring presentment, unlike concurrent resolutions), and report-and-wait rules that require reporting to Congress for some specified period before executive action becomes legally effective. Are these constitutional after *Chadha?* Why or why not? *See Chadha,* 462 U.S. at 955 n.19 ("Beyond the obvious fact that Congress ultimately controls administrative agencies in the legislation that creates them, other means of control, such as durational limits on authorizations and formal reporting requirements, lie well within Congress' constitutional power."). *See generally* Stephen G. Breyer, *The Legislative Veto After Chadha,* 72 Geo. L.J. 785 (1984); Elliot H. Levitas & Stanley M. Brand, *Congressional Review of Executive and Agency Actions After Chadha: "The Son of Legislative Veto" Lives On,* 72 Geo. L.J. 801 (1984); Jonathan B. Fellows, Note, *Congressional Oversight Through Legislative Veto After INS v. Chadha,* 69 Cornell L. Rev. 1244 (1984).

Congress can also set a "fast track" for legislation in response to certain uses of delegated power. In addition, a veto resolution after *Chadha,* if lacking in legal effect, may still have persuasive impact on a judicial construction of the scope of delegated authority. *See Chadha,* 462 U.S. at 976 n.11 (White, J., dissenting). Perhaps for the latter reason, Congress had enacted 57 new legislative vetoes into 18 statutes as of March 1985, during the first two years *after Chadha* was decided. Louis Fisher, *Legislative Vetoes Enacted After Chadha* 1 (Cong. Res. Serv. RS22132), May 2, 2005.

4. *The Line-Item Veto.* Notwithstanding the importance of the defense appropriations power as a check on the Executive, in 1996 Congress almost gave away part of the power of the purse in the Line-Item Veto Act, Pub. L. No. 104-130, 110 Stat. 1200. The act permitted the President to cancel, *inter alia,* any "dollar amount of discretionary budget authority." The President could exercise this veto power only if it would reduce the federal budget deficit and would not impair any essential governmental function or harm the national interest. The cancellation took effect upon notice to the House and Senate and could be reversed within 30 days thereafter by passage of a "disapproval bill," which is not subject to the line-item veto authority. Thus, Congress would have to muster two-thirds plus one to ensure that an item of national security spending to which the President objected (for example, spending for a risky peace-keeping operation) would become law.

In *Clinton v. City of New York,* 524 U.S. 417 (1998), the Court struck down the Line-Item Veto Act because, by its provisions, the President had effectively amended two statutes without following the lawmaking procedure prescribed by Article I. President Clinton, however, had wielded his veto—his "cancellation" authority—against ordinary domestic statutes for ordinary domestic political purposes. Suppose, instead, he had cancelled certain national security expenditures, perhaps because he thought they represented pork-barrel spending to keep open an obsolete military base. Would such a "national security rescission" have been constitutional? *See* Roy E. Brownell II, *The Unnecessary Demise of the Line Item Veto Act: The Clinton Administration's Costly Failure to Seek Acknowledgment of "National Security Rescission,"* 47 Am. U. L. Rev. 1273 (1998) (arguing yes, based on the President's "Olympian powers in the national security realm" and past practice of national security impoundment—that is, the occasional failure of the President to spend all that was appropriated for some national security functions).

The Courts' National Security Powers

6

More than a century and a half ago, a visitor to this country had this to say about the way we govern ourselves: "Scarcely any political question arises in the United States that is not resolved, sooner or later, into a judicial question." Alexis de Tocqueville, 1 *Democracy in America* 280 (1945). This chapter shows that in cases involving national security, many courts have turned his observation upside down by refusing to hear seemingly judicial questions on grounds that they present "political questions." Or they appear to have gone out of their way to refuse to hear such cases because plaintiffs lack standing to sue, or because the controversies are not yet "ripe" for hearing. In still other cases they have excluded critical evidence from trials — or prevented trials altogether — on grounds that the evidence might be helpful to our enemies. More generally, this chapter is about the role that courts play in the resolution of national security disputes.

The starting point for exploring the courts' role is Article III of the Constitution, establishing the limits of federal judicial power and authorizing Congress to create lower federal courts to exercise some or all of that power. We examine the text briefly in Part A, below. We then recall that an important job of courts is to "say what the law is." *Marbury v. Madison,* 5 U.S. (1 Cranch) 137, 177 (1803). But this places the federal courts in a position to define their own role, subject to limits that Article III and Congress set. In Part B we explore the self-defining role of the federal courts and the various impediments they have erected to justiciability. Finally, in Part C we consider an emerging barrier to justiciability growing out of the law of evidence: the state secrets privilege.

A. THE FEDERAL JUDICIAL POWER GENERALLY

Records of the 1787 Philadelphia Convention tell us little about the Framers' original intent regarding the federal courts' responsibility for national security. We necessarily begin instead with the text of Article III, which states generally that the judicial power is "vested in one supreme Court, and in such inferior Courts as the Congress may from time to time ordain and establish." The language suggests an independent judiciary designed to interpret the laws and decide cases. *See generally The Federalist Nos. 22, 78, 80* (Clinton Rossiter ed., 1961). The Supreme Court and the lower federal courts hear all cases "arising under this Constitution, the Laws of the United States, and Treaties made ...." The Supreme Court is also given original jurisdiction over "all Cases affecting Ambassadors, other public Ministers and Consuls," and over those "between a State, or the Citizens thereof, and foreign States, Citizens, or Subjects," while it is granted appellate jurisdiction over other types of cases, subject to Congress's power to make "Exceptions, and ... Regulations." Congress has conferred general federal question jurisdiction on the courts in 28 U.S.C. §1331 (2006). Thus, struggles over national security prerogatives — at least if they pose questions arising under federal law, the Constitution, or treaties (and possibly other international law) — seem to meet both constitutional and statutory jurisdictional requirements for resolution in the federal courts.

B.   A SELF-DEFINING ROLE FOR COURTS: THE JUSTICIABILITY DOCTRINES

We saw in Chapters 3-5 that courts have often been called on to decide important national security law questions and have decided them. Illustrative are *The Steel Seizure Case, supra* p. 25; *Little v. Barreme, supra* p. 78; *Bas v. Tingy, supra* p. 93; and *The Prize Cases, supra* p. 68. Recall Justice Jackson's admonition, in *The Steel Seizure Case*, that in preserving the institutions of free government, "it is the duty of the Court to be last, not first, to give them up." *Youngstown Sheet & Tube Co. v. Sawyer*, 343 U.S. 579, 655 (1952) (Jackson, J., concurring).

We can see the same determination to "say what the law is" in recent litigation involving the so-called global war on terrorism. In one prominent case, for example, American citizen Yaser Hamdi, who allegedly was captured on the battlefield in Afghanistan, challenged his designation by the President as an "enemy combatant" and his indefinite military detention without judicial process. The government argued that the court should not question the detention of Hamdi by the Commander in Chief during wartime. In *Hamdi v. Rumsfeld*, 316 F.3d 450, 463 (4th Cir. 2003) (analyzed *infra* p. 831), the court conceded that "Article III contains nothing analogous to the specific powers of war carefully enumerated in Articles I and II." Nonetheless, important countervailing interests persuaded the court to review Hamdi's detention:

> The duty of the judicial branch to protect our individual freedoms does not simply cease whenever military forces are committed by the political branches to armed conflict. The Founders "foresaw that troublous times would arise, when rulers and people would ... seek by sharp and decisive measures to accomplish ends deemed just and proper; and that the principles of constitutional liberty would be in peril, unless established by irrepealable law." *Ex Parte Milligan*, 71 U.S. (4 Wall.) 2, 120 (1866). While that recognition does not dispose of this case, it does indicate one thing: The detention of United States citizens must be subject to judicial review. [*Id.* at 464.]

Courts have nevertheless tended to avoid the decision of national security disputes and thus to defer to the political branches in what may be an increasing number of cases. First and perhaps foremost, the federal courts are keenly aware of their own practical limitations in deciding such disputes. Thus, in a case involving a court's de novo review of classified documents withheld from a Freedom of Information Act requester, the court declared, "In view of the knowledge, experience and positions held by the three [government] affiants regarding military secrets, military planning and national security, their affidavits were entitled to 'the utmost deference.'" *Taylor v. Department of the Army*, 684 F.2d 99, 109 (D.C. Cir. 1982). This deference also stems in part from the courts' concern about their proper function in our constitutional system of government. In litigation seeking to stop the onset of the war in Iraq, for example, the court remarked that "before courts adjudicate a case involving the war powers allocated to the two political branches, they must be presented with a case or controversy that clearly raises the specter of undermining the constitutional structure." *Doe v. Bush*, 323 F.3d 133, 135 (1st Cir. 2003). Both of these judicial concerns — competence and constitutional function — are reflected in the judicial invocation of the *political question doctrine* to dismiss some national security disputes.

Second, courts have insisted that plaintiffs have a personal stake in the outcome of cases brought before them for resolution. The *standing* requirement has both textual roots in the case-or-controversy language of Article III and a prudential root in the courts' self-limitation.

Third, the need for a clear conflict and a concrete record of underlying facts — and sometimes the hope that with the passage of time the political branches might resolve a dispute on their own — has prompted courts to invoke the *ripeness doctrine*, by which courts mean that a case is simply not yet ready for judicial review.

These three nonjusticiability doctrines are addressed below. They may seem frustrating to a lawyer who thinks that national security law disputes should, like others, be resolved "neutrally" by the "least dangerous branch," as Hamilton described the judiciary. *The Federalist No. 78*, at 465 (Clinton Rossiter ed., 1961). We must remember, however, that when pressed in a national security emergency, even that branch may make decisions based on contemporary political realities rather than on neutral principles of law. *Korematsu v. United States*, 323 U.S. 214 (1944) (analyzed *infra* p. 812), is a tragic example. The Supreme Court's decision early in World War II upholding the military trial and conviction of eight German saboteurs — "ordered by the President in the declared exercise of his powers as Commander in Chief of the Army in time of war and of grave public danger" — may be another such case. *Ex parte Quirin*, 317 U.S. 1, 25 (1942) (analyzed *infra* p. 823).

1.   The Political Question Doctrine

Consider the following hypotheticals. John Henry has been nominated by the President to the Supreme Court and confirmed by the Senate. The Secretary of State has signed and sealed Henry's commission to the office, pursuant to a federal statute that also provides that a U.S. marshal shall deliver the commission to Henry. But the U.S. marshal refuses. Henry sues for a writ of mandamus, compelling the marshal to deliver the commission.

Now assume, instead, that Henry was not nominated to the Court by the President, but is convinced that he should have been. He sues for a writ of mandamus compelling the President to nominate him to the Supreme Court.

How are these cases different? In the first case, a federal statute sets a standard for deciding whether the defendant marshal has acted lawfully. A court could decide whether the marshal has violated the statute and, if it finds that he has and it has mandamus jurisdiction, could issue a writ ordering the marshal to do his statutory duty. In the second case, neither a federal statute nor the Constitution supplies any standard for deciding whom the President should nominate to the Supreme Court. Article II, section 2, merely declares that "he shall nominate, and by and with the Advice and Consent of the Senate, shall appoint . . . Judges of the Supreme Court . . . ." It doesn't say who they have to be, whether they need a law degree, whether they must be male or female, Catholic or Jewish, old or young, white or black. The Constitution leaves the selection to the President, in his discretion, subject to the check of Senate confirmation. Whether he should nominate Henry or someone else is a "political question" and not a question for the courts.

As Chief Justice John Marshall explained in *Marbury v. Madison*, 5 U.S. (1 Cranch) 137 (1803), on related (though not the same) facts:

> By the constitution of the United States, the President is invested with certain important political powers, in the exercise of which he is to use his own discretion, and is account- able only to his country in his political character, and to his own conscience. To aid him in the performance of these duties, he is authorized to appoint certain officers, who act by his authority and in conformity with his orders. In such cases, their acts are his acts; and whatever opinion may be entertained of the manner in which executive discretion may be used, still there exists, and can exist, no power to control that discretion. The subjects are political. They respect the nation, not individual rights, and being entrusted to the executive, the decision of the executive is conclusive.

Id. at 165-166. The selection of nominees to the Supreme Court is similarly a political question, "in the exercise of which [the President] is to use his own discretion, and is accountable only to his country in his political character," and is not for the courts to decide.

El-Shifa Pharmaceutical Industries Co. v. United States

United States Court of Appeals, District of Columbia Circuit (en banc), 2010
607 F.3d 836

GRIFFITH, Circuit Judge: . . .

I.

On August 7, 1998, the terrorist network headed by Osama bin Laden bombed United States embassies in Kenya and Tanzania. Hundreds were killed and thousands injured. On August 20, the United States responded by launching nearly simulta- neous missile strikes against two targets: a terrorist training camp in Afghanistan and a factory in Sudan believed to be "associated with the bin Ladin network" and "involved in the production of materials for chemical weapons." President William J. Clinton, Address to the Nation on Military Action Against Terrorist Sites in Afghani- stan and Sudan, 2 Pub. Papers 1460, 1461 (Aug. 20, 1998). . . .

In a letter to the Congress "consistent with the War Powers Resolution," the President reported that the strikes "were a necessary and proportionate response to the imminent threat of further terrorist attacks against U.S. personnel and facilities" and "were intended to prevent and deter additional attacks by a clearly identified terrorist threat." President William J. Clinton, Letter to Congressional Leaders Reporting on Military Action Against Terrorist Sites in Afghanistan and Sudan,

2 Pub. Papers 1464, 1464 (Aug. 21, 1998). The following day, in a radio address to the nation, President Clinton explained his decision to take military action, stating, "Our goals were to disrupt bin Ladin's terrorist network and destroy elements of its infrastructure in Afghanistan and Sudan. And our goal was to destroy, in Sudan, the factory with which bin Ladin's network is associated, which was producing an ingredient essential for nerve gas." President William J. Clinton, The President's Radio Address, 2 Pub. Papers 1464, 1465 (Aug. 22, 1998). Citing "compelling evidence that the bin Ladin network was poised to strike at us again" and was seeking to acquire chemical weapons, the President declared that "we simply could not stand idly by." *Id.*

Other government officials elaborated upon the President's justifications for the attack on the plant. On the day of the strike, the Secretary of Defense stated that bin Laden "had some financial interest in contributing to this particular facility." An unnamed "senior intelligence official" asserted at a press briefing, "[W]e know that bin Laden has made financial contributions to the Sudanese Military Industrial Complex[,] of which, we believe, the Shifa pharmaceutical plant is part." And on August 23, the National Security Advisor maintained that "Osama bin Laden was providing key financial help for the plant."

The plaintiffs in this case are the El-Shifa Pharmaceutical Industries Company (El-Shifa), the owner of the plant, and Salah El Din Ahmed Mohammed Idris (Idris), the principal owner of El-Shifa. They allege that striking the plant was a mistake, that it "was not a chemical weapons facility, was not connected to bin Laden or to terrorism, and was not otherwise a danger to public health and safety." Instead, the plaintiffs contend, the plant was Sudan's largest manufacturer of medicinal products, responsible for producing over half the pharmaceuticals used in Sudan. Because the case comes to us on appeal from a dismissal for lack of subject-matter jurisdiction, we take the plaintiffs' allegations as true. *See Tri-State Hosp. Supply Corp. v. United States,* 341 F.3d 571, 572 n.1 (D.C. Cir. 2003).

According to the plaintiffs, within days of the attack, the press debunked the President's assertions that the plant was involved with chemical weapons and associated with bin Laden. Confronted with their error, senior administration and intelligence officials backpedaled, issuing what the plaintiffs characterize as "revised" or "new justifications" for the strike and conceding that any relationship between bin Laden and the plant was "indirect." Although the United States attacked the plant without knowing who owned it, officials learned within three days of the strike that Idris was the owner. After that point, "unidentified U.S. government officials" began telling reporters that Idris maintained direct or indirect financial relations with bin Laden, purchased the plant on bin Laden's behalf, acted as a front man or agent for bin Laden in Sudan, and had "ties" to bin Laden. The plaintiffs contend that neither the contemporaneous nor post-hoc justifications for the attack were true . . . .

This lawsuit is only one of several actions the plaintiffs pursued to recoup their losses. They also sued the United States in the Court of Federal Claims, seeking $50 million as just compensation under the Takings Clause of the Constitution. The court dismissed the suit on the ground that "the enemy target of military force" has no right to compensation for "the destruction of property designated by the President as enemy war-making property." *El-Shifa Pharm. Indus. Co. v. United States,* 55 Fed. Cl. 751, 774 (2003). The United States Court of Appeals for the Federal Circuit affirmed, holding that the plaintiffs' takings claim raised a nonjusticiable political question. *See El-Shifa Pharm. Indus. Co. v. United States,* 378 F.3d 1346, 1361-70 (Fed. Cir. 2004), *cert. denied,* 545 U.S. 1139 (2005). On the legislative front, one member of the House of Representatives introduced a bill to compensate those who suffered injuries or property damage in the missile strike, *see* H.R. 894, 107th Cong. (2001), and a resolution directing the claims court to investigate the matter and issue a report to the House, *see* H.R. Res. 81, 107th Cong. (2001) (citing 28 U.S.C. §§1492, 2509). Both the bill and the resolution died in committee.

The plaintiffs brought this action in the United States District Court for the District of Columbia after the CIA denied their requests for compensation for the plant's destruction and for a retraction of the allegations that the plaintiffs were involved with terrorism. The plaintiffs sought at least $50 million in damages... claiming negligence in the government's investigation of the plant's ties to chemical weapons and Osama bin Laden and trespass in its destruction of the plant "without consent or justification." Their complaint also included a claim under the law of nations seeking a judicial declaration that the United States violated international law by failing to compensate them for the unjustified destruction of their property. Finally, the plaintiffs claimed that the President and other senior officials defamed them by publishing false statements linking Idris and the plant to bin Laden, international terrorism, or chemical weapons, knowing those statements were false or making them with reckless disregard for their veracity....

The district court granted the government's motion to dismiss the complaint for lack of subject-matter jurisdiction, *see* Fed. R. Civ. P. 12(b)(1), concluding that sovereign immunity barred all of the plaintiffs' claims. *See* [*El-Shifa Pharm. Indus. Co. v. United States*, 402 F. Supp. 2d 267 (D.D.C. 2005),] at 270-73. The court also noted that the complaint "likely present[ed] a nonjusticiable political question." *Id.* at 276....

The plaintiffs appealed... abandon[ing] any request for monetary relief, but still seek[ing] a declaration that the government's failure to compensate them for the destruction of the plant violated customary international law, a declaration that statements government officials made about them were defamatory, and an injunction requiring the government to retract those statements. A divided panel of this court affirmed the district court, holding that these claims are barred by the political question doctrine. *See El-Shifa Pharm. Indus. Co. v. United States*, 559 F.3d 578 (D.C. Cir. 2009). We vacated the panel's judgment and ordered rehearing *en banc. See El-Shifa Pharm. Indus. Co. v. United States*, 330 F. App'x 200 (D.C. Cir. 2009).

II.

"It is emphatically the province and duty of the judicial department to say what the law is," *Marbury v. Madison*, 5 U.S. (1 Cranch) 137, 177 (1803), but some "[q]uestions, in their nature political," are beyond the power of the courts to resolve, *id.* at 170. The political question doctrine is "essentially a function of the separation of powers," *Baker v. Carr*, 369 U.S. 186, 217 (1962), and "excludes from judicial review those controversies which revolve around policy choices and value determinations constitutionally committed for resolution to the halls of Congress or the confines of the Executive Branch," *Japan Whaling Ass'n v. Am. Cetacean Soc'y*, 478 U.S. 221, 230 (1986). *See also United States v. Munoz-Flores*, 495 U.S. 385, 394 (1990) (explaining that the "doctrine is designed to restrain the Judiciary from inappropriate interference in the business of the other branches of Government").

That some governmental actions are beyond the reach of the courts reflects the Constitution's limitation of the "judicial power of the United States" to "cases" or "controversies." U.S. Const. art. III. "It is therefore familiar learning that no justiciable "controversy" exists when parties seek adjudication of a political question." *Massachusetts v. EPA*, 549 U.S. 497, 516 (2007).

In the seminal case of *Baker v. Carr*, the Supreme Court explained that a claim presents a political question if it involves:

> [1] a textually demonstrable constitutional commitment of the issue to a coordinate political department; or [2] a lack of judicially discoverable and manageable standards for resolving it; or [3] the impossibility of deciding without an initial policy determination of a kind clearly for nonjudicial discretion; or [4] the impossibility of a court's undertaking independent resolution without expressing lack of the respect due coordinate branches of government; or [5] an unusual need for unquestioning adherence to a political decision already made; or [6] the potentiality of embarrassment from multifarious pronouncements by various departments on one question.

369 U.S. at 217. "To find a political question, we need only conclude that one [of these] factor[s] is present, not all." *Schneider v. Kissinger*, 412 F.3d 190, 194 (D.C. Cir. 2005).

Disputes involving foreign relations, such as the one before us, are "quintessential sources of political questions." *Bancoult v. McNamara*, 445 F.3d 427, 433 (D.C. Cir. 2006). Because these cases raise issues that "frequently turn on standards that defy judicial application" or "involve the exercise of a discretion demonstrably committed to the executive or legislature," *Baker*, 369 U.S. at 211, "[m]atters intimately related to foreign policy and national security are rarely proper subjects for judicial intervention," *Haig v. Agee*, 453 U.S. 280, 292 (1981). "Yet it is error to suppose that every case or controversy which touches foreign relations lies beyond judicial cognizance." *Baker*, 369 U.S. at 211. Even in the context of military action, the courts may sometimes have a role. *See Gilligan v. Morgan*, 413 U.S. 1, 11-12 (1973). Therefore, we must conduct "a discriminating analysis of the particular question posed" in the "specific case" before the court to determine whether the political question doctrine prevents a claim from going forward. *Baker*, 369 U.S. at 211.

In undertaking this discriminating analysis, we note, for example, that the political question doctrine does not bar a claim that the government has violated the Constitution simply because the claim implicates foreign relations. *See I.N.S. v. Chadha*, 462 U.S. 919 (1983) (holding the one-House legislative veto unconstitutional despite its use in matters of foreign affairs and the war powers). Because the judiciary is the "ultimate interpreter of the Constitution," *Baker*, 369 U.S. at 211, in most instances claims alleging its violation will rightly be heard by the courts. Similarly, that a case may involve the conduct of the nation's foreign affairs does not necessarily prevent a court from determining whether the Executive has exceeded the scope of prescribed statutory authority or failed to obey the prohibition of a statute or treaty. *See Japan Whaling*, 478 U.S. at 230 ("[O]ne of the Judiciary's characteristic roles is to interpret statutes, and we cannot shirk this responsibility merely because" of the "interplay" between the statute and "the conduct of this Nation's foreign relations."); *see also* David J. Barron & Martin S. Lederman, *The Commander in Chief at the Lowest Ebb—Framing the Problem, Doctrine, and Original Understanding*, 121 Harv. L. Rev. 689, 723 (2008) ("If there is a party with constitutionally sufficient standing to demand judicial protection from a presidential refusal to obey a statute during war, it is not clear why there should be a general rule that courts must leave the question to the political branches.").

   We have consistently held, however, that courts are not a forum for reconsidering the wisdom of discretionary decisions made by the political branches in the realm of foreign policy or national security. In this vein, we have distinguished between claims requiring us to decide whether taking military action was wise — a "policy choice[ ] and value determination[ ] constitutionally committed for resolution to the halls of Congress or the confines of the Executive Branch" — and claims "[p]resenting purely legal issues" such as whether the government had legal authority to act. *Campbell v. Clinton,* 203 F.3d 19, 40 (D.C. Cir. 2000) (Tatel, J., concurring) (quoting *Japan Whaling,* 478 U.S. at 230). Accordingly, we have declined to adjudicate claims seeking only a "determination[ ] whether the alleged conduct *should* have occurred." *Harbury v. Hayden,* 522 F.3d 413, 420 (D.C. Cir. 2008). . . . [T]he presence of a political question in these cases turns not on the nature of the government conduct under review but more precisely on the question the plaintiff raises about the challenged action. *See Campbell,* 203 F.3d at 40 (Tatel, J., concurring).

   The political question doctrine bars our review of claims that, regardless of how they are styled, call into question the prudence of the political branches in matters of foreign policy or national security constitutionally committed to their discretion. A plaintiff may not, for instance, clear the political question bar simply by "recasting [such] foreign policy and national security questions in tort terms." *Schneider,* 412 F.3d at 197 (explaining the courts could not determine whether taking military action was "wrongful" as an element of a wrongful death claim). Likewise — and contrary to the position adopted by Judge Kavanaugh [concurring herein] — a statute providing for judicial review does not override Article III's requirement that federal courts refrain from deciding political questions. *See Sierra Club v. Morton,* 405 U.S. 727, 732 n.3 (1972) (Congress may not confer jurisdiction on Art. III federal courts . . . to resolve "political questions," because suits of this character are inconsistent with the judicial function under Art. III." (internal citation omitted)). For example, in reviewing the Secretary of State's designation of a group as a "foreign terrorist organization" under the Antiterrorism and Effective Death Penalty Act, 8 U.S.C. §1189 (2006), we may decide whether the government has followed the proper procedures, whether the organization is foreign, and whether it has engaged in terrorist activity, but we may not determine whether "the terrorist activity of the organization threatens the security of United States nationals or the national security of the United States," *id.* §1189(a)(1)(C). *See People's Mojahedin Org. of Iran v. U.S. Dep't of State (PMOI),* 182 F.3d 17, 22-24 (D.C. Cir. 1999). Whether this last criterion has been met presents a nonjusticiable political question because the Secretary's assessments of whether the terrorist activities of foreign organizations constitute threats to the United States "are political judgments, 'decisions of a kind for which the Judiciary has neither aptitude, facilities nor responsibility and [that] have long been held to belong in the domain of political power not subject to judicial intrusion or inquiry.'" *PMOI,* 182 F.3d at 23. Neither a common law nor statutory claim may require the court to reassess "policy choices and value determinations" the Constitution entrusts to the political branches alone. *Japan Whaling,* 478 U.S. at 230.

   The conclusion that the strategic choices directing the nation's foreign affairs are constitutionally committed to the political branches reflects the institutional limitations of the judiciary and the lack of manageable standards to channel any judicial inquiry into these matters. *See generally* [*Walter Nixon v. United States,* 506 U.S. 224 (1993)], at 228-29 ("[T]he concept of a textual commitment to a coordinate political department is not completely separate from the concept of a lack of judicially discoverable and manageable standards for resolving it; the lack of judicially manageable standards may strengthen the conclusion that there is a textually demonstrable commitment to a coordinate branch.")....In military matters in particular, the courts lack the competence to assess the strategic decision to deploy force or to create standards to determine whether the use of force was justified or well-founded.

> The complex, subtle, and professional decisions as to the . . . control of a military force are essentially professional military judgments, subject *always* to civilian control of the Legislative and Executive Branches. The ultimate responsibility for these decisions is appropriately vested in branches of the government which are periodically subject to electoral accountability.

Gilligan, 413 U.S. at 10. It is not the role of judges to second-guess, with the benefit of hindsight, another branch's determination that the interests of the United States call for military action.

The case at hand involves the decision to launch a military strike abroad. Conducting the "discriminating analysis of the particular question posed" by the claims the plaintiffs press on appeal, *Baker,* 369 U.S. at 211, we conclude that both raise nonjusticiable political questions. The law-of-nations claim asks the court to decide whether the United States' attack on the plant was "mistaken and not justified." The defamation claim similarly requires us to determine the factual validity of the government's stated reasons for the strike. If the political question doctrine means anything in the arena of national security and foreign relations, it means the courts cannot assess the merits of the President's decision to launch an attack on a foreign target, and the plaintiffs ask us to do just that. Therefore, we affirm the district court's dismissal of the plaintiffs' law-of-nations and defamation claims.

A.

. . . [C]ourts cannot reconsider the wisdom of discretionary foreign policy decisions. The plaintiffs' law-of-nations claim falls squarely within this prohibition because it would require us to declare that the bombing of the El-Shifa plant was "mistaken and not justified." Whether an attack on a foreign target is justified — that is whether it is warranted or well-grounded — is a quintessential "policy choice[ ] and value determination[ ] constitutionally committed for resolution to the halls of Congress or the confines of the Executive Branch." *Japan Whaling,* 478 U.S. at 230. The plaintiffs appear to recognize this. On appeal they imply that they need only prove the United States failed to compensate them for an attack that was "mistaken." By asserting the El-Shifa bombing was "mistaken," the plaintiffs apparently mean that the United States would not have launched the strike if the relevant decisionmakers knew at the time what they allegedly know now — that the plant was neither involved in producing chemical weapons nor associated with bin Laden. But the political question doctrine does not permit us to mimic the constitutional role of the political branches by guessing how they would have conducted the nation's foreign policy had they been better informed. Whether the circumstances warrant a military attack on a foreign target is a "substantive political judgment[ ] entrusted expressly to the coordinate branches of government," *Gilligan,* 413 U.S. at 11, and using a judicial forum to reconsider its wisdom would be anathema to the separation of powers. Undertaking a counterfactual inquiry into how the political branches would have exercised their discretion had they known the facts alleged in the plaintiffs' complaint would be to make a political judgment, not a legal one.

Moreover, *Baker*'s prudential considerations counsel judicial restraint as well. First, the court lacks judicially manageable standards to adjudicate whether the attack on the El-Shifa plant was "mistaken and not justified." *See Baker*, 369 U.S. at 217. We could not decide this question without first fashioning out of whole cloth some standard for when military action is justified. The judiciary lacks the capacity for such a task. . . . Second, the decision to take military action is a "policy determination of a kind clearly for nonjudicial discretion." *Baker*, 369 U.S. at 217. Such foreign policy decisions are "delicate, complex, and involve large elements of prophecy. . . . They are decisions of a kind for which the Judiciary has neither aptitude, facilities nor responsibility. . . . " [*Chicago & S. Air Lines, Inc. v. Waterman S.S. Corp.*, 333 U.S. 103 (1948),] at 111. In short, the decision to launch the military attack on the El-Shifa plant was constitutionally committed to the political branches, *see, e.g.*, U.S. Const. art. I, §8, cl. 11; *id.* art. II, §2, cl. 1; and this court is neither an effective nor appropriate forum for reweighing its merits. . . .

In refusing to declare the El-Shifa attack "mistaken and not justified," we do not mean to imply that the contrary is true. We simply decline to answer a question outside the scope of our authority. By requiring that we reserve judgment, the political question doctrine protects the Congress and the Executive from judicial "invasion of their sphere," *Antolok v. United States*, 873 F.2d 369, 383 (D.C. Cir. 1989) (opinion of Sentelle, J.), and guards against "the reputation of the Judicial Branch [being] "borrowed by the political Branches to cloak their work in the neutral colors of judicial action," *PMOI*, 182 F.3d at 25 (quoting *Mistretta v. United States*, 488 U.S. 361, 407 (1989)). . . .

IV.

Our concurring colleagues charge the court with "*sub silentio* expand[ing] executive power." To the contrary, it is they who would work a *sub silentio* expansion. By asserting the authority to decide questions the Constitution reserves to Congress and the Executive, some would expand judicial power at the expense of the democratically elected branches. . . .

GINSBURG, Circuit Judge, with whom Circuit Judge ROGERS joins, concurring in the judgment [omitted].

KAVANAUGH, Circuit Judge, with whom Chief Judge SENTELLE joins, and with whom Circuit Judges GINSBURG and ROGERS join as to Part I, concurring in the judgment: . . .

II.

The political question doctrine has occupied a more limited place in the Supreme Court's jurisprudence than is sometimes assumed.[3] The Court has relied on the doctrine only twice in the last 50 years. *See Walter Nixon v. United States*, 506 U.S. 224 (1993); *Gilligan v. Morgan*, 413 U.S. 1 (1973). The Court has invoked the doctrine

---

3. The Supreme Court does not decline to resolve a case on political question grounds simply because the dispute involves or would affect national security or foreign relations. Indeed, from the time of John Marshall to the present, the Court has decided many sensitive and controversial cases that had enormous national security or foreign policy ramifications. . . .

in cases in which (i) the Constitution textually and exclusively commits interpretation of the relevant constitutional provision to one or both of the political branches or (ii) the constitutional provision at issue supplies no judicially manageable or discoverable standards for resolving the case. *See Walter Nixon,* 506 U.S. at 228.

Importantly, the Supreme Court has invoked the political question doctrine only in cases alleging violations of the Constitution. This is a statutory case. The Supreme Court has never applied the political question doctrine in a case involving alleged *statutory* violations. Never. . . .

There is good reason the political question doctrine does not apply in cases alleging statutory violations. If a court refused to give effect to a statute that regulated Executive conduct, it necessarily would be holding that Congress is unable to constrain Executive conduct in the challenged sphere of action. As a result, the court would be ruling (at least implicitly) that the statute intrudes impermissibly on the Executive's prerogatives under Article II of the Constitution. In other words, the court would be establishing that the asserted Executive power is exclusive and preclusive, meaning that Congress cannot regulate or limit that power by creating a cause of action or otherwise.

Applying the political question doctrine in statutory cases thus would not reflect benign deference to the political branches. Rather, that approach would systematically favor the Executive Branch over the Legislative Branch — without the courts' acknowledging as much or grappling with the critical separation of powers and Article II issues. The fact that use of the political question doctrine in statutory cases loads the dice against the Legislative Branch presumably explains why there is no Supreme Court precedent applying the doctrine in statutory cases — and why the Executive Branch (sometimes wary, for a variety of reasons, of advancing a straight Article II argument) may want the courts to invoke the doctrine in statutory cases of this sort. . . .

The political branches, mindful of the need for Executive discretion and flexibility in national security and foreign affairs, are unlikely to unduly hamper the Executive's ability to protect the Nation's security and diplomatic objectives. *See United States v. Curtiss-Wright Export Corp.,* 299 U.S. 304, 320-22 (1936). Relatedly, it is well-established that courts must be cautious about interpreting an ambiguous statute to constrain or interfere with the Executive Branch's conduct of national security or foreign policy. *See Dep't of the Navy v. Egan,* 484 U.S. 518, 529-30 (1988). And apart from all that, if a statute were passed that clearly limited the kind of Executive national security or foreign policy activities at issue in these cases, such a statute as applied might well violate Article II. . . .

A statute regulating or creating a cause of action to challenge the President's short-term bombing of foreign targets in the Nation's self-defense (or contesting the Executive Branch's subsequent statements about it as defamatory) might well unconstitutionally encroach on the President's exclusive, preclusive Article II authority as Commander in Chief.

But we need not definitively answer the sensitive and weighty Article II question in this case. . . .

NOTES AND QUESTIONS

1. *The Issues Posed by El-Shifa.* To determine whether the political question doctrine applies in a case, start by precisely identifying the issues that the case poses.

In *El-Shifa*, the plaintiffs argued that the government's investigation of the plant's ties to terrorism was negligent and that the attack on the plant was a trespass "without justification." The plaintiffs also argued that the government's allegations of such ties were defamatory — either false or made with reckless disregard for their veracity. Thus, both claims essentially raised the same questions: whether the government's intelligence was mistaken and, arguably, whether the missile strike was wise. Finally, the plaintiffs also argued that the government violated the law of nations by refusing to compensate them for the unjustified destruction of their property.

Was it necessary for the plaintiffs to prevail on *each* of these issues to gain relief? Could partial relief have been provided without resolving all these issues?

2. *Applying the Political Question Doctrine in El-Shifa.* The *El-Shifa* court acknowledged that not every foreign relations or national security case presents a nonjusticiable political question. It then proceeded to declare that "courts are not a forum for reconsidering the wisdom of discretionary decisions made by the political branches in the realm of foreign policy or national security." 607 F.3d at 842.

Thus, the court reminds us that the doctrine is not the "political *case* doctrine"; it's the "political *question* doctrine." Deciding whether the doctrine applies in a given case should therefore always start with the precise identification of the question(s) posed by the case. In *El-Shifa*, if the plaintiffs asked the court to decide whether U.S. intelligence was mistaken or whether the decision to strike the plant was wise, it seems self-evident that the law furnished no standard for the court to apply.

But was this the correct characterization of the issues posed by the plaintiffs? What about the claim that the U.S. refusal to pay compensation violated international law? The latter claim was brought in part under the Alien Tort Statute, 28 U.S.C. §1350 (2006), which authorizes suits brought "by an alien for a tort only, committed in violation of the law of nations or a treaty of the United States." However, it was unclear whether there was any customary law of international law to which the plaintiffs could point. By dismissing on political question grounds the court avoided having to address either the content of the substantive law, its applicability in U.S. courts, or sovereign immunity as to this claim. See generally Chapter 7 *infra*.

Many of the judicial decisions we have read up to this point — notably *The Steel Seizure Case, Curtiss-Wright, Dames & Moore, Little v. Barreme, Bas v. Tingy,* and *Greene v. McElroy* — presented national security law disputes involving discretionary decisions by the elected branches. Yet the courts decided those cases on the merits. In each of them, why did the court reach the merits instead of dismissing on political question grounds? (Hint: identify the issue and consider whether the law supplied a standard for deciding the issue.) Can you now discern what factors are likely to lead a court to decide not to decide the merits of a lawsuit, based on the political question doctrine?

3. *Textual Commitment or Prudential Abstention?* The *El-Shifa* court indicates that "strategic choices directing the nation's foreign affairs are constitutionally committed to the political branches." Does the political question doctrine have its source in the text of the Constitution or somewhere else? In this regard, what is the significance of the court's quotation from *Walter Nixon v. United States,* 506 U.S. 224, 228 (1993), in which the Supreme Court declared that "the concept of a textual commitment to a coordinate political department is not completely separate from the concept of a lack of judicially discoverable and manageable standards for resolving it"? Does it matter?

4. *Fact-Finding Difficulties.* Should the size or scope of a military operation affect a court's willingness to adjudicate its legality? Is the difficulty in deciding about a smaller military operation one of judicially discoverable and manageable standards, or of judicial resources and expertise?

In 1999, 31 members of the House of Representatives sued for a declaration that President Clinton violated the Constitution and the War Powers Resolution when he conducted air strikes in the Federal Republic of Yugoslavia without congressional authorization. In the Court of Appeals, Judges Silberman and Tatel disagreed on the application of the political question doctrine. Judge Silberman maintained that "no one" could challenge the President's actions because of a lack of "judicially discoverable and manageable standards" and because "the War Powers Clause claim implicates the political question doctrine." *Campbell v. Clinton*, 203 F.3d 19, 24-25 (D.C. Cir. 2000). Judge Tatel opined that "[w]hether the military activity in Yugoslavia amounted to 'war' within the meaning of the Declare War Clause . . . is no more standardless than any other question regarding the constitutionality of government action. . . . Courts have proven no less capable of developing standards to resolve war power challenges [than Fourth or First Amendment actions]." *Id.* at 40. Should the "lack of standards" rationale carry more weight in war powers disputes than it does in individual rights litigation?

5. *A "Limited Place" in the Supreme Court's Jurisprudence.* Why did Judge Kavanaugh concur separately? He distinguishes cases in which the Constitution is said to furnish a standard for decision from cases in which there is a statutory standard. And because the plaintiffs can point to no statutory standard for negligence in intelligence collection and analysis or wisdom in counter-terrorism policy, he says, the case falls within the "limited place" the Court has carved out for political question dismissals.

Of course, this does not mean that *any* statutory standard would justify judicial resolution. The Constitution truly does vest certain decisions in the President's discretion. Thus, according to Judge Kavanaugh, "if a statute were passed that clearly limited the kind of national security or foreign policy activities at issue in these cases, such a statute might well violate Article II." Just how limited is the "place" described by Judge Kavanaugh? Should a federal judge, for example, decline to decide a lawsuit challenging the President's alleged violation of a statutory restriction on the use of appropriated funds to detain American citizens in military custody indefinitely without judicial process?

6. *Effect of Dismissal.* Is it correct to say that a determination that the plaintiffs' lawsuit presents a nonjusticiable political question is effectively a ruling for the President? Is judicial intervention a greater threat to the separation of powers than letting the President have his way through judicial abstention?

2. Standing to Sue

In *Northeastern Florida Chapter, General Contractors of America v. City of Jacksonville*, 508 U.S. 656, 663-664 (1993), the Court declared that

a party seeking to invoke a federal court's jurisdiction must demonstrate three things: (1) "injury in fact," by which we mean an invasion of a legally protected interest that is "(a) concrete and particularized, and (b) actual or imminent, not conjectural or hypothetical," (2) a causal relationship between the injury and the challenged conduct, by which we mean that the injury "fairly can be traced to the challenged action of the defendant," and has not resulted "from the independent action of some third party not before the court," and (3) a likelihood that the injury will be redressed by a favorable decision, by which we mean that the "prospect of obtaining relief from the injury as a result of a favorable ruling" is not "too speculative" (internal citations omitted).

These requirements can also stop a national security law dispute at the courthouse door.

NOTES AND QUESTIONS

1. *Constitutional vs. Prudential Concerns.* Do you see anything in the Article III case-or-controversy requirement, or in its purposes, that would restrict access to the federal courts on the basis of the status of the parties, as distinct from the fitness of the issues for judicial resolution? Are the two issues related?

The Supreme Court has emphasized that, while Congress may express its intention to allow citizens to sue to vindicate interests protected by statute, the doctrine of standing is "an essential and unchanging part of the case-or-controversy requirement of Article III," *Lujan v. Defenders of Wildlife*, 504 U.S. 555, 559 (1992), which "defines with respect to the Judicial Branch the idea of separation of powers on which the Federal Government is founded." *Allen v. Wright*, 468 U.S. 737, 750 (1984). Like the political question doctrine, the law of standing thus has constitutional and prudential components. Unlike the Article III requirements, the prudential limits may be modified or abrogated by Congress. *Warth v. Seldin*, 422 U.S. 490, 501 (1975).

Do you think Congress could, consistently with the Article III standing requirement, allow any citizen to mount a judicial challenge to the President's unilateral deployment of troops abroad on grounds that the deployment should have been approved by Congress? On grounds that the deployment was prohibited by Congress?

2. *Relationship of Standing to Merits and Political Question.* In theory, the focus in deciding standing is on the fitness of a particular plaintiff to present a case adverse to the defendant, not on the merits of the substantive issues presented in the complaint. The standing doctrine thus is a narrower and less radical basis for dismissal of a lawsuit than the political question doctrine. A dismissal on standing grounds may simply mean that the wrong plaintiff initiated the action, not that the merits may not be adjudicated in a suit by a different plaintiff.

a.   Citizen Plaintiffs

1. *Standing for Concerned Citizens.* Would a concerned citizen have standing to bring a lawsuit seeking to enjoin a prospective military operation by the United States? In *Pietsch v. Bush*, 755 F. Supp. 62 (E.D.N.Y. 1991), a citizen sought a court order preventing hostilities between the United States and Iraq before the 1991 Gulf War. In concluding that Pietsch was not injured in fact, the court distinguished the interest of a concerned citizen from that of members of Congress (who "plainly have an interest in protecting their right to vote in matters entrusted to their respective

chambers by the Constitution") or a member of the armed forces deployed to the potential combat area. According to the court, Pietsch's claim that he was being made "an accessory to murder against his will," a compulsion causing him emotional distress, was "too abstract" to meet Article III requirements. *Id.* at 65-66.

The court in *Pietsch* also rejected the argument that a citizen has standing to sue the government to enforce obedience to the Constitution:

> [T]he Plaintiff does not have standing merely because as a citizen of the United States he has an "interest" in seeing the Government act constitutionally. In *Schlesinger v. Reservists Committee to Stop the War*, 418 U.S. 208 (1974), a citizens' group challenged the membership in the National Reserve by United States Congressmen as violative of the Ineligibility Clause of the Constitution (Article I, Section 6, clause 2). The plaintiffs contended that they had standing because as United States citizens they had an interest in insuring "the faithful discharge by members of Congress who are members of the Reserves of their duties as members of Congress, to which all citizens and taxpayers are entitled." Id. at p. 212. The United States Supreme Court rejected this argument, and held: "standing to sue may not be predicated upon an interest of the kind alleged here which is held in common by all members of the public, because of the necessarily abstract nature of the injury all citizens share." Id. at p. 220. The Plaintiff in this case has suffered no more cognizable injury than did the citizens in *Schlesinger,* and, therefore, does not have standing to maintain this action....
>
> ...As the Supreme Court stated in *Schlesinger*: "Our system of government leaves many crucial decisions to the political processes. The assumption that if respondents have no standing to sue, no one would have standing, is not a reason to find standing." *Schlesinger v. Reservists Committee to Stop the War, supra,* 418 U.S. at 227. [755 F. Supp. at 67.]

Similarly, a plaintiff's status as taxpayer does not entitle her to litigate a case alleging the illegal expenditure of tax dollars to pay for a war. *See, e.g., Velvel v. Nixon,* 415 F.2d 236 (10th Cir. 1969).

2. *Proving Injury.* In 2007, the Sixth Circuit Court of Appeals ruled in *American Civil Liberties Union v. National Security Agency,* 493 F.3d 644 (6th Cir. 2007), that the ACLU and other plaintiffs, including journalists, academics, and lawyers who regularly communicated with individuals overseas, lacked standing to challenge the Bush administration's warrantless surveillance program conducted by the National Security Agency, known as the Terrorist Surveillance Program (TSP) (described *infra* p. 609). The plaintiffs could not demonstrate that they had been direct targets of the secret surveillance, although many of them had professional ties with persons and organizations apparently suspected of terrorist activities. Because the plaintiffs could not show that their communications had been intercepted, their alleged injuries were too speculative to confer standing. Under the Foreign Intelligence Surveillance Act (FISA) (excerpted and discussed *infra* pp. 581-632), individuals are not entitled to know that they have been subject to surveillance and, absent the introduction into evidence in a criminal prosecution of information derived from such surveillance, a court has no authority to require the government to say whether individuals were subjected to surveillance. If the plaintiffs have no way short of becoming defendants in a criminal prosecution to find out whether they were subject to what they claim as unlawful surveillance, should Article III stand in the way of judicial resolution of the legality of the TSP?

After Congress amended FISA to enable broad warrantless surveillance of the international communications of non-U.S. persons in 2008, public interest organizations, their lawyers, and other plaintiffs filed suit alleging First and Fourth Amendment violations and claiming that their international communications will be monitored under the new legislation. Although they could not show that their communications had been or would be monitored, they asserted that they had an "actual and well-founded" fear of surveillance, and that they incurred costs in taking measures to protect the confidentiality of their international communications, in light of their fear of surveillance. In *Amnesty International USA v. Clapper*, 638 F.3d 118 (2d Cir. 2011), the court overturned a district court's dismissal of the suit and found that standing may be based on a reasonable fear of future injury and costs incurred to avoid that injury.

Military personnel challenging the President's authority to deploy them to a war zone have generally been found to have standing to sue. *See, e.g., Ange v. Bush*, 752 F. Supp. 509 (D.D.C. 1990).

b.   Congressional Plaintiffs

1. *Origins of Congressional Standing.* Members of Congress have often turned to the courts and sought relief for alleged harm to them in their official roles, or, put another way, to protect what they see as interests central to Congress. In *Mitchell v. Laird*, 488 F.2d 611 (D.C. Cir. 1973), for example, 13 members of Congress sought to enjoin military action in Southeast Asia and requested a declaration that the war was unconstitutional. In rejecting the government's claim that the plaintiffs lacked standing, the court stated that, assuming unconstitutional action by the executive, "a declaration to that effect would bear upon the duties of plaintiffs to consider whether to impeach defendants, and upon plaintiffs' quite distinct and different duties to make appropriations to support the hostilities, or to take other legislative actions related to such hostilities. . . ." *Id.* at 614. While the plaintiffs were found to have standing, however, the court dismissed the suit as presenting a political question.

2. *Complete Nullification.* In 1997 the Supreme Court ruled that legislators may not sue in their institutional capacity unless their votes have been "completely nullified" by allegedly illegal action. *Raines v. Byrd*, 521 U.S. 811, 829 (1997). Four Senators and two Representatives sued after voting against the line-item veto statute. They asserted that before the statute was enacted, the expenditure of funds in an appropriations bill would either be approved in its entirety or not at all. Under the line-item veto statute, however, the President could excise a particular spending item after a bill had been enacted. Thus, the members argued that their votes on the appropriations bills would be "less 'effective' than before, and that the 'meaning' and 'integrity' of their vote has changed." *Id.* at 825.

According to Chief Justice Rehnquist's opinion for the Court, the plaintiffs' votes on the line-item veto bill "were given full effect. They simply lost. . . ." *Id.* at 824. The disgruntled members' votes in the future were not "completely nullified" by the Line-Item Veto Act because a majority "may repeal the Act or exempt appropriations bills from its reach." *Id.* at 829. Although the Court did not expressly disavow its only related precedent, *Coleman v. Miller*, 307 U.S. 433 (1939) (upholding standing for 20 of Kansas's 40 state senators who voted not to ratify a proposed constitutional amendment), it is unclear how and to what extent the concept of institutional representation survives beyond the limited context of *Coleman*.

3. *Impact of Raines.* After *Raines*, should the *degree* of a legislator's injury have any effect on a court's willingness to decide a claim that an executive official has injured the legislator in his official capacity? Is it possible any longer for members of Congress ever to obtain standing to sue as representatives of their institution?

In *Campbell v. Clinton*, 52 F. Supp. 2d 34 (D.D.C. 1999), *aff'd*, 203 F.3d 19 (D.C. Cir. 2000), 31 members of the House of Representatives sued President Clinton seeking a declaration that the President's use of U.S. forces against Yugoslavia was unlawful under the Constitution and the War Powers Resolution, 50 U.S.C. §§1541-1548 (2006) (described *infra* pp. 307-322). The lawsuit was filed after President Clinton announced the commencement of NATO air and cruise missile attacks on Yugoslav targets on March 24, 1999, and after House votes on April 28 defeating a declaration of war (427-2), defeating an authorization of the air strikes (213-213), defeating a resolution ordering an immediate end to U.S. participation in the NATO operation (290-139), and approving a restriction on Defense Department appropriations for the deployment of U.S. ground troops in Yugoslavia without specific authorization. On May 20, Congress approved a supplemental appropriations bill for the conflict in Yugoslavia.

The plaintiffs sought to distinguish *Raines* by arguing that President Clinton's commitment of the United States to the air strikes in Yugoslavia "completely nullified" their votes against authorizing the military operation. They further noted that their votes helped defeat an authorization for the air strikes and a declaration of war, and that President Clinton ignored the votes and carried on as if Congress had authorized his actions. According to Judge Friedman's opinion denying the plaintiffs standing, however, the two votes emphasized by the plaintiffs "do not provide the President with...an unambiguous directive; neither vote...required the President to do anything or prohibited him from doing anything.... Congressional reaction to the air strikes has sent distinctly mixed messages." 52 F. Supp. 2d at 43-44. Judge Friedman reasoned that if the President had "persisted with air strikes in the face of...votes" against the President's position, there might have been standing to sue, but under the circumstances "there is no confrontation or impasse between the...branches and thus no legislative standing." *Id.*

It was also significant for Judge Friedman that some of the 213 who voted not to authorize the air and missile campaign or declare war then voted in favor of funding the conflict and against ordering the removal of the U.S. forces. Thus, the plaintiffs' position "appears not to be shared by a number of their colleagues the nullification of whose votes they seek to vindicate. While the Court is not suggesting that all 213 representatives who voted to defeat the authorization resolution must join in this lawsuit in order to establish legislative standing, the absence of any indication" that the plaintiffs were authorized to represent "even a substantial number" of the 213 "compels the conclusion" that the plaintiffs lack standing. *Id.* Do you agree that 213 congressional plaintiffs or some "substantial number" would have had standing to sue the President?

The Court of Appeals affirmed on standing grounds and maintained that the nullification standard of *Raines* is not met "whenever the government does something Congress voted against." 203 F.3d at 22. Instead, the *Campbell* appeals court construed *Raines* to require that the plaintiffs have "no legislative remedy." *Id.* at 23. In this case, the court pointed out, Congress could have passed a prohibition on the use of U.S.

forces in the Yugoslavia campaign. Similarly, Congress could have restricted appropriations for the same end, or it could have sought to impeach the President. Concurring in the judgment, Judge Randolph added that the plaintiffs' votes "were not
for naught." *Id.* at 31. The defeat of the declaration of war deprived the President of
the authority to expand hostilities against Yugoslavia, and the defeat of the authorization resolution denied the President the right to say that he was prosecuting the
bombing campaign with the House's approval. Did the *Campbell* courts correctly apply
Raines?

In *Kucinich v. Bush*, 236 F. Supp. 2d 1 (D.D.C. 2002), 32 members of the House
sued the President and other executive branch officials, challenging President
Bush's unilateral withdrawal from the 1972 Anti-Ballistic Missile (ABM) Treaty
without the approval of Congress. These plaintiffs voted in the House to prevent
the treaty termination but lost the vote. The claim that the House plaintiffs were
deprived of a constitutional right and duty to participate in treaty termination was
viewed by the court as "like the dilution of legislative power alleged in *Raines*, an
institutional injury lacking a personal, particularized nature." 236 F. Supp. 2d at 7.
Can you now describe circumstances when members of Congress would have
standing to sue?

3.   Ripeness

The ripeness doctrine allows the judiciary to avoid present adjudication of a
dispute by determining that future events may affect its shape or even its existence.
Like the standing and political question doctrines, ripeness may at least temporarily
bar a lawsuit because of the Article III case-or-controversy requirement or for prudential reasons. *See Reno v. Catholic Soc. Servs., Inc.*, 509 U.S. 43, 57 n.18 (1993). The
doctrine maintains that "federal courts . . . do not render advisory opinions. For adjudication of constitutional issues 'concrete legal issues, presented in actual cases, not
abstractions' are requisite." *United Pub. Workers v. Mitchell*, 330 U.S. 75, 89 (1947)
(internal citations omitted). Concerning claims that the President's actions lack
needed congressional approval, or that the President is acting contrary to a congressional mandate, Justice Powell, concurring in *Goldwater v. Carter*, 444 U.S. 996 (1979),
put it this way: "The Judicial Branch should not decide issues affecting the allocation
of power between the President and Congress until the political branches reach a
constitutional impasse." *Id.* at 997.

NOTES AND QUESTIONS

1. *Ripeness and the First Gulf War.* In November 1990, during the run-up to the first
Gulf War, 53 members of the House and one Senator filed a suit to enjoin a U.S. attack
against some 430,000 Iraqi troops deployed in and around Kuwait. While the lawsuit
was pending, the United States and allied forces amassed a similar number of troops
in Saudi Arabia and the Persian Gulf. The legal claim in *Dellums v. Bush*, 752 F. Supp.
1141 (D.D.C. 1990), was that the President could not attack Iraq without first obtaining a declaration of war or other explicit statutory authorization. Applying the
"impasse" standard from Justice Powell's opinion in *Goldwater v. Carter*, the court

denied the plaintiffs' motion for a preliminary injunction, declaring that "it is only if the majority of the Congress seeks relief from an infringement on its war-declaration power that it may be entitled to receive it." *Id.* at 1151. The court also found that the executive branch had not yet clearly committed itself to war against Iraq. *Id.* at 1152. Can you articulate a standard for presidential commitment and congressional disapproval that would make a dispute between the political branches ripe for adjudication?

2. *The 2003 War Against Iraq.* In October 2002, Congress authorized the President to "use the Armed Forces of the United States as he determines to be necessary and appropriate in order to (1) defend the national security of the United States against the continuing threat posed by Iraq; and (2) enforce all relevant United Nations Security Council resolutions regarding Iraq." Authorization for Use of Military Force Against Iraq Resolution of 2002, Pub. L. No. 107-243, §3(a), 116 Stat. 1498 (considered *infra* p. 354). In February 2003, active-duty members of the military, parents of military personnel, and members of Congress sued to enjoin the President from initiating a war against Iraq. *Doe v. Bush,* 323 F.3d 133 (1st Cir. 2003). The plaintiffs argued that "Congress and the President are in collision — that the President is about to act in violation of the October Resolution" — and that "Congress and the President are in collusion — that Congress has handed over to the President its exclusive power to declare war." *Id.* at 134. The court responded:

> Ripeness doctrine involves more than simply the timing of the case. It mixes various mutually reinforcing constitutional and prudential considerations. One such consideration is the need "to prevent the courts, through avoidance of premature adjudication, from entangling themselves in abstract disagreements." Another is to avoid unnecessary constitutional decisions. A third is the recognition that, by waiting until a case is fully developed before deciding it, courts benefit from a focus sharpened by particular facts. The case before us raises all three of these concerns. [*Id.* at 138.]

Ruling that the lawsuit was not ripe, the court said it was unable to determine that the President would disregard conditions attached to the statutory authorization: "In the present posture of this case, we do not know whether there will ever be an actual confrontation between the Legislative and Executive Branches." *Id.* at 139 (quoting from *Goldwater, supra*). Regarding the allegation of collusion, the court emphasized the "shared nature of the powers in question here," declaring that "courts are rightly hesitant to second-guess the form or means by which the coequal political branches choose to exercise their textually committed constitutional powers." *Id.* at 142, 144 (citing *Orlando v. Laird,* 443 F.2d 1039, 1043 (2d Cir. 1971), a Vietnam-era political question decision set forth *infra* p. 286).

Do you agree with the court that this case did not "clearly raise[] the specter of undermining the constitutional structure"? *Id.* at 135. Can you articulate a test for determining when a national security activity so undermines the constitutional structure that courts ought to intervene?

The court's decision was announced on March 13, 2003. The war was launched seven days later. Would the plaintiffs have obtained a ruling on the merits if the court had delayed its decision by a few days?

C.   THE STATE SECRETS PRIVILEGE: A NEW NONJUSTICIABILITY?

An early draft of the Federal Rules of Evidence included this provision:

Rule 509. Secrets of State and Other Official Information

(a) Definitions. (1) Secret of state. A "secret of state" is a governmental secret relating to the national defense or the international relations of the United States....

(b) General rule of privilege. The government has a privilege to refuse to give evidence and to prevent any person from giving evidence upon a showing of reasonable likelihood of danger that the evidence will disclose a secret of state or official information, as defined in this rule.

26 Charles Alan Wright & Kenneth W. Graham, *Federal Practice and Procedure* 415-416 (1992). Rule 509 was never enacted, leaving recognition of a "state secrets privilege" to judicial application as common law. Some of this law long preceded September 11 and the "war on terror," but there were relatively few cases before then. The most important Supreme Court cases involving the protection of national security secrets in civil litigation — *Totten v. United States* and *Reynolds v. United States* — and the two lines of case law they spawned are discussed in the following opinion.

Mohamed v. Jeppesen Dataplan, Inc.

United States Court of Appeals, Ninth Circuit (en banc), 2010
614 F.3d 1070, *cert. denied*, 131 S. Ct. 2442 (2011)

FISHER, Circuit Judge. This case requires us to address the difficult balance the state secrets doctrine strikes between fundamental principles of our liberty, including justice, transparency, accountability and national security. Although as judges we strive to honor *all* of these principles, there are times when exceptional circumstances create an irreconcilable conflict between them. On those rare occasions, we are bound to follow the Supreme Court's admonition that "even the most compelling necessity cannot overcome the claim of privilege if the court is ultimately satisfied that [state] secrets are at stake." *United States v. Reynolds*, 345 U.S. 1, 11 (1953). After much deliberation, we reluctantly conclude this is such a case, and the plaintiffs' action must be dismissed....

I.   BACKGROUND

We ... emphasize that this factual background is based only on the *allegations* of plaintiffs' complaint, which at this stage in the litigation we construe "in the light most favorable to the plaintiff[s], taking all [their] allegations as true and drawing all reasonable inferences from the complaint in [their] favor." *Doe v. United States*, 419 F.3d 1058, 1062 (9th Cir. 2005)....

A. Factual Background

1. The Extraordinary Rendition Program

Plaintiffs allege that the Central Intelligence Agency ("CIA"), working in concert with other government agencies and officials of foreign governments, operated an extraordinary rendition program to gather intelligence by apprehending foreign nationals suspected of involvement in terrorist activities and transferring them in secret to foreign countries for detention and interrogation by United States or foreign officials. According to plaintiffs, this program has allowed agents of the U.S. government "to employ interrogation methods that would [otherwise have been] prohibited under federal or international law." Relying on documents in the public domain, plaintiffs, all foreign nationals, claim they were each processed through the extraordinary rendition program. They also make the following individual allegations....

Plaintiff Binyam Mohamed, a 28-year-old Ethiopian citizen and legal resident of the United Kingdom, was arrested in Pakistan on immigration charges. Mohamed was allegedly flown to Morocco .... Moroccan authorities allegedly subjected Mohamed to "severe physical and psychological torture," including routinely beating him and breaking his bones. He says they cut him with a scalpel all over his body, including on his penis, and poured "hot stinging liquid" into the open wounds. He was blindfolded and handcuffed while being made "to listen to extremely loud music day and night." After 18 months in Moroccan custody, Mohamed was allegedly transferred back to American custody and flown to Afghanistan. He claims he was detained there in a CIA "dark prison" where he was kept in "near permanent darkness" and subjected to loud noise, such as the recorded screams of women and children, 24 hours a day. Mohamed was fed sparingly and irregularly and in four months he lost between 40 and 60 pounds. Eventually, Mohamed was transferred to the U.S. military prison at Guantanamo Bay, Cuba, where he remained for nearly five years. He was released and returned to the United Kingdom during the pendency of this appeal.

[Omitted here are similar accounts from four other individual plaintiffs, who claim that they were transported to Egypt, Morocco, Afghanistan, and/or Guantánamo Bay, Cuba.]

2. Jeppesen's Alleged Involvement in the Rendition Program

Plaintiffs contend that publicly available information establishes that defendant Jeppesen Dataplan, Inc., a U.S. corporation, provided flight planning and logistical support services to the aircraft and crew on all of the flights transporting each of the five plaintiffs among the various locations where they were detained and allegedly subjected to torture. The complaint asserts "Jeppesen played an integral role in the forced" abductions and detentions and "provided direct and substantial services to the United States for its so-called "extraordinary rendition" program," thereby "enabling the clandestine and forcible transportation of terrorism suspects to secret overseas detention facilities." It also alleges that Jeppesen provided this assistance with actual or constructive "knowledge of the objectives of the rendition program," including knowledge that the plaintiffs "would be subjected to forced disappearance, detention, and torture" by U.S. and foreign government officials.

B. Summary of the Claims

Plaintiffs brought suit against Jeppesen under the Alien Tort Statute, 28 U.S.C. §350, alleging seven theories of liability marshaled under two claims, one for "forced disappearance" and another for "torture and other cruel, inhuman or degrading treatment."

With respect to the forced disappearance claim, plaintiffs assert four theories of liability: (1) direct liability for active participation, (2) conspiracy with agents of the United States, (3) aiding and abetting agents of the United States and (4) direct liability "because [Jeppesen] demonstrated a reckless disregard as to whether Plaintiffs would be subjected to forced disappearance through its participation in the extraordinary rendition program and specifically its provision of flight and logistical support services to aircraft and crew that it knew or reasonably should have known would be used to transport them to secret detention and interrogation."

On the torture and degrading treatment claim, plaintiffs [make similar allegations.] . . .

Regarding Jeppesen's alleged actual or constructive knowledge . . . plaintiffs allege that Jeppesen['s] . . . "knowledge of the objectives of the rendition program" may be inferred from the fact that [it] . . . "falsified flight plans submitted to European air traffic control authorities to avoid public scrutiny of CIA flights" and that . . . "the governments of the destination countries routinely subject detainees to torture and other forms of cruel, inhuman, or degrading treatment." They also rely on U.S. State Department country reports describing torture as "routine" in some of the countries to which plaintiffs were allegedly rendered . . . .

C. Procedural History

Before Jeppesen answered the complaint, the United States moved to intervene and to dismiss plaintiffs' complaint under the state secrets doctrine. The then-Director of the CIA, General Michael Hayden, filed two declarations in support of the motion to dismiss, one classified, the other redacted and unclassified. The public declaration states that "[d]isclosure of the information covered by this privilege assertion reasonably could be expected to cause serious — and in some instances, exceptionally grave — damage to the national security of the United States and, therefore, the information should be excluded from any use in this case." It further asserts that "because highly classified information is central to the allegations and issues in this case, the risk is great that further litigation will lead to disclosures harmful to U.S. national security and, accordingly, this case should be dismissed."

The district court granted the motions to intervene and dismiss and entered judgment in favor of Jeppesen, stating that "at the core of Plaintiffs' case against Defendant Jeppesen are 'allegations' of covert U.S. military or CIA operations in foreign countries against foreign nationals — clearly a subject matter which is a state secret." Plaintiffs appealed. A three-judge panel of this court reversed and remanded. . . .

. . . While the appeal was pending Barack Obama succeeded George W. Bush as President of the United States. On September 23, 2009, the Obama administration announced new policies for invoking the state secrets privilege, effective October 1, 2009, in a memorandum from the Attorney General. *See* Memorandum from the Attorney Gen. to the Heads of Executive Dep'ts and Agencies on Policies and Procedures

Governing Invocation of the State Secrets Privilege (Sept. 23, 2009) ("Holder Memo"), http://www.justice.gov/opa/documents/state-secret-privileges.pdf. The government certified both in its briefs and at oral argument before the en banc court that officials at the "highest levels of the Department of Justice" of the new administration had reviewed the assertion of privilege in this case and determined that it was appropriate under the newly announced policies. . . .

III.   THE STATE SECRETS DOCTRINE

The Supreme Court has long recognized that in exceptional circumstances courts must act in the interest of the country's national security to prevent disclosure of state secrets, even to the point of dismissing a case entirely. *See Totten v. United States,* 92 U.S. 105 (1876). The contemporary state secrets doctrine encompasses two applications of this principle. One completely bars adjudication of claims premised on state secrets (the "*Totten* bar"); the other is an evidentiary privilege ("the *Reynolds* privilege") that excludes privileged evidence from the case and *may* result in dismissal of the claims. *See United States v. Reynolds,* 345 U.S. 1 (1953). . . .

A.   The *Totten* Bar

In 1876 the Supreme Court stated "as a *general principle* [ ] that public policy forbids the maintenance of any suit in a court of justice, the trial of which would inevitably lead to the disclosure of matters which the law itself regards as confidential." *Totten,* 92 U.S. at 107 (emphasis added). The Court again invoked the principle in 1953, citing *Totten* for the proposition that "where the very subject matter of the action" is "a matter of state secret," an action may be "dismissed on the pleadings without ever reaching the question of evidence" because it is "so obvious that the action should never prevail over the privilege." *Reynolds,* 345 U.S. at 11 n.26. This application of *Totten*'s general principle — which we refer to as the *Totten* bar — is "designed not merely to defeat the asserted claims, but to preclude judicial inquiry" entirely. *Tenet v. Doe,* 544 U.S. 1, 7 n.4 (2005).

The Court first applied this bar in *Totten* itself, where the estate of a Civil War spy sued the United States for breaching an alleged agreement to compensate the spy for his wartime espionage services. Setting forth the "general principle" quoted above, the Court held that the action was barred because it was premised on the existence of a "contract for secret services with the government," which was "a fact not to be disclosed." *Totten,* 92 U.S. at 107.

A century later, the Court applied the *Totten* bar in *Weinberger v. Catholic Action of Hawaii/Peace Education Project,* 454 U.S. 139, 146-47 (1981). There, the plaintiffs sued under the National Environmental Policy Act of 1969, 42 U.S.C. §4321 *et seq.,* to compel the Navy to prepare an environmental impact statement regarding a military facility where the Navy allegedly proposed to store nuclear weapons. The Court held that the allegations were "beyond judicial scrutiny" because, "[d]ue to national security reasons, . . . the Navy can neither admit nor deny that it proposes to store nuclear weapons at [the facility]." *Id.* (citing *Totten,* 92 U.S. at 107).

The Court more recently reaffirmed and explained the *Totten* bar in a case involving two former Cold War spies who accused the CIA of reneging on a commitment to provide financial support in exchange for their espionage services. Relying on "*Totten*'s core concern" of "preventing the existence of the plaintiffs' relationship with the Government from being revealed," the Court held that the action was, like *Totten* and *Weinberger,* incapable of judicial review. *Tenet,* 544 U.S. at 8-10.

Plaintiffs contend that the *Totten* bar applies *only* to a narrow category of cases they say are not implicated here, namely claims premised on a plaintiff's espionage relationship with the government. We disagree. We read the Court's discussion of *Totten* in *Reynolds* to mean that the *Totten* bar applies to cases in which "the very subject matter of the action" is "a matter of state secret." *Reynolds,* 345 U.S. at 11. "[A] contract to perform espionage" is only an example. *Id.* . . . Thus, although the claims in both *Totten* and *Tenet* were premised on the existence of espionage agreements, and even though the plaintiffs in both *Totten* and *Tenet* were themselves parties to the espionage agreements, the *Totten* bar rests on a general principle that extends beyond that specific context. We therefore reject plaintiffs' unduly narrow view of the *Totten* bar and reaffirm our holding in *Al-Haramain* [*Islamic Found., Inc. v. Bush,* 507 F.3d 1190 (9th Cir. 2007),] that the bar "has evolved into the principle that where the very subject matter of a lawsuit is a matter of state secret, the action must be dismissed without reaching the question of evidence." *Al-Haramain,* 507 F.3d at 1197. As we explain below, the *Totten* bar is a narrow rule, but it is not as narrow as plaintiffs contend. . . .

B. The *Reynolds* Privilege

In addition to the *Totten* bar, the state secrets doctrine encompasses a "privilege against revealing military [or state] secrets, a privilege which is well established in the law of evidence." *Reynolds,* 345 U.S. at 6-7. A successful assertion of privilege under *Reynolds* will remove the privileged evidence from the litigation. Unlike the *Totten* bar, a valid claim of privilege under *Reynolds* does not automatically require dismissal of the case. In some instances, however, the assertion of privilege will require dismissal because it will become apparent during the *Reynolds* analysis that the case cannot proceed without privileged evidence, or that litigating the case to a judgment on the merits would present an unacceptable risk of disclosing state secrets.

Reynolds involved a military aircraft carrying secret electronic equipment. *Id.* at 3. After the plane crashed, the estates of three civilian observers killed in the accident brought tort claims against the government. In discovery, plaintiffs sought production of the Air Force's official accident investigation report and the statements of three surviving crew members. The Air Force refused to produce the materials, citing the need to protect national security and military secrets. *Id.* at 4-5. . . .

The Supreme Court . . . sustained the government's claim of privilege because "there was a reasonable danger that the accident investigation report would contain references to the secret electronic equipment which was the primary concern of the mission." *Id.* at 10. . . . The Court did not, however, dismiss the case outright. Rather, given that the secret electronic equipment was unrelated to the cause of the accident, it remanded to the district court, affording plaintiffs the opportunity to try to establish their claims without the privileged accident report and witness statements. *Id.* at 11.

Analyzing claims under the *Reynolds* privilege involves three steps:

First, we must "ascertain that the procedural requirements for invoking the state secrets privilege have been satisfied." Second, we must make an independent determination whether the information is privileged. . . . Finally, "the ultimate question to be resolved is how the matter should proceed in light of the successful privilege claim."

Al-Haramain, 507 F.3d at 1202 (citation omitted) (quoting *El-Masri v. United States,* 479 F.3d 296, 304 (4th Cir. 2007)). We discuss these steps in turn.

1.   Procedural Requirements

a. Assertion of the privilege. "The privilege belongs to the Government and must be asserted by it; it can neither be claimed nor waived by a private party." *Reynolds,* 345 U.S. at 7 (footnotes omitted). The privilege "is not to be lightly invoked." *Id.* ...

To ensure that the privilege is invoked no more often or extensively than neces- sary, *Reynolds* held that "[t]here must be a formal claim of privilege, lodged by the head of the department which has control over the matter, after actual personal consideration by that officer." *Id.* at 7-8 (footnote omitted). . . . The formal claim must reflect the certifying official's *personal* judgment; responsibility for this task may not be delegated to lesser-ranked officials. The claim also must be presented in sufficient detail for the court to make an independent determination of the validity of the claim of privilege and the scope of the evidence subject to the privilege.

In the present case, General Michael Hayden, then-Director of the CIA, asserted the initial, formal claim of privilege and submitted detailed public and classified declarations. . . .

b. Timing. . . . Plaintiffs contend that the government's assertion of privilege was premature, urging that the *Reynolds* privilege cannot be raised before an obligation to produce specific evidence subject to a claim of privilege has actually arisen. We dis- agree. The privilege may be asserted at any time, even at the pleading stage.

The privilege indisputably may be raised with respect to discovery requests seek- ing information the government contends is privileged. . . . In addition, the govern- ment may raise the privilege to prevent the disclosure of privileged information in a responsive pleading . . . .

We also conclude that the government may assert a *Reynolds* privilege claim prospectively, even at the pleading stage, rather than waiting for an evidentiary dis- pute to arise during discovery or trial. In some cases, the court may be able to deter- mine with certainty from the nature of the allegations and the government's declarations in support of its claim of secrecy that litigation must be limited or cut off in order to protect state secrets, even before any discovery or evidentiary requests have been made. In such cases, waiting for specific evidentiary disputes to arise would be both unnecessary and potentially dangerous. *See Sterling v. Tenet,* 416 F.3d 338, 344 (4th Cir. 2005) ("Courts are not required to play with fire and chance further disclosure — inadvertent, mistaken, or even intentional — that would defeat the very purpose for which the privilege exists."). . . .

2.   The Court's Independent Evaluation of the Claim of Privilege

When the privilege has been properly invoked, "we must make an independent determination whether the information is privileged." *Al-Haramain,* 507 F.3d at 1202. The court must sustain a claim of privilege when it is satisfied, "from all the circum- stances of the case, that there is a reasonable danger that compulsion of the evidence will expose . . . matters which, in the interest of national security, should not be divulged." *Reynolds,* 345 U.S. at 10. If this standard is met, the evidence is absolutely privileged, irrespective of the plaintiffs' countervailing need for it. *See id.* at 11

("[E]ven the most compelling necessity cannot overcome the claim of privilege if the court is ultimately satisfied that [state] secrets are at stake."); *Halkin* [*v. Helms*, 690 F.2d 977 (D.C. Cir. 1982),] at 990.

This step in the *Reynolds* analysis "places on the court a special burden to assure itself that an appropriate balance is struck between protecting national security matters and preserving an open court system." *Al-Haramain*, 507 F.3d at 1203. In evaluating the need for secrecy, "we acknowledge the need to defer to the Executive on matters of foreign policy and national security and surely cannot legitimately find ourselves second guessing the Executive in this arena." *Id.* But "the state secrets doctrine does not represent a surrender of judicial control over access to the courts." *El-Masri*, 479 F.3d at 312. Rather, "to ensure that the state secrets privilege is asserted no more frequently and sweepingly than necessary, it is essential that the courts continue critically to examine instances of its invocation." *Ellsberg* [*v. Mitchell*, 709 F.2d 51 (D.C. Cir. 1983),] at 58. "We take very seriously our obligation to review the [government's claims] with a very careful, indeed a skeptical, eye, and not to accept at face value the government's claim or justification of privilege," *Al-Haramain*, 507 F.3d at 1203, though we must "do so without forcing a disclosure of the very thing the privilege is designed to protect. . . . Too much judicial inquiry into the claim of privilege would force disclosure of the thing the privilege was meant to protect, while a complete abandonment of judicial control would lead to intolerable abuses." *Reynolds*, 345 U.S. at 8.

We do not offer a detailed definition of what constitutes a state secret. The Supreme Court in *Reynolds* found it sufficient to say that the privilege covers "matters which, in the interest of national security, should not be divulged." *Id.* at 10. We do note, however, that an executive decision to *classify* information is insufficient to establish that the information is privileged. Although classification may be an indication of the need for secrecy, treating it as conclusive would trivialize the court's role, which the Supreme Court has clearly admonished "cannot be abdicated to the caprice of executive officers." *Reynolds*, 345 U.S. at 9-10.

3.   How Should the Matter Proceed?

When a court sustains a claim of privilege, it must then resolve "how the matter should proceed in light of the successful privilege claim." *Al-Haramain*, 507 F.3d at 1202 (quoting *El-Masri*, 479 F.3d at 304). The court must assess whether it is feasible for the litigation to proceed without the protected evidence and, if so, how.

When the government successfully invokes the state secrets privilege, "the evidence is completely removed from the case." *Kasza* [*v. Browner*, 133 F.3d 1159, 1170 (9th Cir. 1998),] at 1166. "[W]henever possible, sensitive information must be disentangled from nonsensitive information to allow for the release of the latter." *Id.* (quoting *Ellsberg*, 709 F.2d at 57). However, there will be occasions when, as a practical matter, secret and nonsecret information cannot be separated. In some cases, therefore, "it is appropriate that the courts restrict the parties' access not only to evidence which itself risks the disclosure of a state secret, but also those pieces of evidence or areas of questioning which press so closely upon highly sensitive material that they create a high risk of inadvertent or indirect disclosures." *Bareford v. Gen. Dynamics Corp.*, 973 F.2d 1138, 1143-44 (5th Cir. 1992); *see also Kasza*, 133 F.3d at 1166 ("[I]f seemingly innocuous information is part of a . . . mosaic, the state secrets privilege may be invoked to bar its disclosure and the court cannot order the government to disentangle this information from other [i.e., secret] information.").

Ordinarily, simply excluding or otherwise walling off the privileged information may suffice to protect the state secrets and "the case will proceed accordingly, with no consequences save those resulting from the loss of evidence." *Al-Haramain*, 507 F.3d at 1204 (quoting *Ellsberg*, 709 F.2d at 64).

In some instances, however, application of the privilege may require dismissal of the action. When this point is reached, the *Reynolds* privilege converges with the *Totten* bar, because both require dismissal. There are three circumstances when the *Reynolds* privilege would justify terminating a case.

First, if "the plaintiff cannot prove the *prima facie* elements of her claim with nonprivileged evidence, then the court may dismiss her claim as it would with any plaintiff who cannot prove her case." *Kasza*, 133 F.3d at 1166. Second, "if the privilege deprives the defendant of information that would otherwise give the defendant a valid defense to the claim, then the court may grant summary judgment to the defendant." *Kasza*, 133 F.3d at 1166 (quoting *Bareford*, 973 F.2d at 1141).

Third, and relevant here, even if the claims and defenses might theoretically be established without relying on privileged evidence, it may be impossible to proceed with the litigation because — privileged evidence being inseparable from nonprivileged information that will be necessary to the claims or defenses — litigating the case to a judgment on the merits would present an unacceptable risk of disclosing state secrets. . . .

IV. APPLICATION

We therefore turn to the application of the state secrets doctrine in this case. The government contends that plaintiffs' lawsuit should be dismissed, whether under the *Totten* bar or the *Reynolds* privilege, because "state secrets are so central to this case that permitting further proceeding[s] would create an intolerable risk of disclosure that would jeopardize national security."[6] Plaintiffs argue that the *Totten* bar does not apply and that, even if the government is entitled to some protection under the *Reynolds* privilege, at least some claims survive. . . .

A. The *Totten* Bar

The categorical, "absolute protection [the Court] found necessary in enunciating the *Totten* rule" is appropriate only in narrow circumstances. *Tenet*, 544 U.S. at 11. The *Totten* bar applies only when the "very subject matter" of the action is a state secret — i.e., when it is "obvious" without conducting the detailed analysis required by *Reynolds* "that the action [c]ould never prevail over the privilege." *Reynolds*, 345 U.S. at 11 n.26. The Court has applied the *Totten* bar on just three occasions, involving two different kinds of state secrets: In *Tenet* and *Totten* the Court applied the *Totten* bar to "the distinct class of cases that depend upon clandestine spy relationships," *see Tenet*, 544 U.S. at 9-10; *Totten*, 92 U.S. at 107, and in *Weinberger* the Court applied the *Totten* bar to a case that depended on whether the Navy proposed to store nuclear weapons at a particular facility, *see Weinberger*, 454 U.S. at 146-47. Although the Court has not limited the *Totten* bar to cases premised on secret espionage agreements or

6. The government's classified briefing and supporting declarations provide more specific support for the government's state secrets contentions. This information is crucial to our decision. *See El-Masri*, 479 F.3d at 312.

the location of nuclear weapons, neither has it offered much guidance on when the *Totten* bar applies beyond these limited circumstances. Because the *Totten* bar is rarely applied and not clearly defined, because it is a judge-made doctrine with extremely harsh consequences, and because conducting a more detailed analysis will tend to improve the accuracy, transparency and legitimacy of the proceedings, district courts presented with disputes about state secrets should ordinarily undertake a detailed *Reynolds* analysis before deciding whether dismissal on the pleadings is justified.

Here, some of plaintiffs' claims might well fall within the *Totten* bar. In particular, their allegations that Jeppesen conspired with agents of the United States in plaintiffs' forced disappearance, torture and degrading treatment are premised on the existence of an alleged covert relationship between Jeppesen and the government — a matter that the Fourth Circuit has concluded is "practically indistinguishable from that categorically barred by *Totten* and *Tenet.*" *El-Masri*, 479 F.3d at 309.[7] On the other hand, allegations based on plaintiffs' theory that Jeppesen should be liable simply for what it "should have known" about the alleged unlawful extraordinary rendition program while participating in it are not so obviously tied to proof of a secret agreement between Jeppesen and the government.

We do not resolve the difficult question of precisely which claims may be barred under *Totten* because application of the *Reynolds* privilege leads us to conclude that this litigation cannot proceed further. We rely on the *Reynolds* privilege rather than the *Totten* bar for several reasons. First, the government has asserted the *Reynolds* privilege along with the *Totten* bar, inviting the further inquiry *Reynolds* requires and presenting a record that compels dismissal even on this alternate ground.... Third, resolving this case under *Reynolds* avoids difficult questions about the precise scope of the *Totten* bar and permits us to conduct a searching judicial review, fulfilling our obligation under *Reynolds* "to review the [government's claim] with a very careful, indeed a skeptical, eye, and not to accept at face value the government's claim or justification of privilege." *Al-Haramain*, 507 F.3d at 1203.[8]

B.   The *Reynolds* Privilege

There is no dispute that the government has complied with *Reynolds*' procedural requirements for invoking the state secrets privilege by filing General Hayden's formal claim of privilege in his public declaration. We therefore focus on the second and third steps in the *Reynolds* analysis: *First,* whether and to what extent the matters the government contends must be kept secret are in fact matters of state secret; and *second,* if they are, whether the action can be litigated without relying on evidence that would necessarily reveal those secrets or press so closely upon them as to create an unjustifiable risk that they would be revealed. In doing so, we explain our decision as much as we can without compromising the secrets we are required to protect.

---

7. We do not decide whether any of plaintiffs' claims are cognizable under the Alien Tort Statute ("ATS"). But assuming that the conspiracy claims are cognizable, they require proof of an agreement. Plaintiffs' allegations confirm that their conspiracy claims depend on proof of a covert relationship.

8. This skepticism is all the more justified in cases that allege serious government wrongdoing. Such allegations heighten the risk that government officials may be motivated to invoke the state secrets doctrine not only by their obligation to protect national security but also by a desire to protect themselves or their associates from scrutiny.

1. Whether and to What Extent the Evidence Is Privileged

The government asserts the state secrets privilege over four categories of evidence. In particular, the government contends that neither it nor Jeppesen should be compelled, through a responsive pleading, discovery responses or otherwise, to disclose: "[1] information that would tend to confirm or deny whether Jeppesen or any other private entity assisted the CIA with clandestine intelligence activities; [2] information about whether any foreign government cooperated with the CIA in clandestine intelligence activities; [3] information about the scope or operation of the CIA terrorist detention and interrogation program; [or 4] any other information concerning CIA clandestine intelligence operations that would tend to reveal intelligence activities, sources, or methods." These indisputably are matters that the state secrets privilege may cover. *See, e.g., Tenet,* 544 U.S. at 11 (emphasizing the "absolute protection" the state secrets doctrine affords against revealing espionage relationships); *CIA v. Sims,* 471 U.S. 159, 175 (1985) ("Even a small chance that some court will order disclosure of a source's identity could well impair intelligence gathering and cause sources to "close up like a clam.").

We have thoroughly and critically reviewed the government's public and classified declarations and are convinced that at least some of the matters it seeks to protect from disclosure in this litigation are valid state secrets, "which, in the interest of national security, should not be divulged." *Reynolds,* 345 U.S. at 10. The government's classified disclosures to the court are persuasive that compelled or inadvertent disclosure of such information in the course of litigation would seriously harm legitimate national security interests. In fact, every judge who has reviewed the government's formal, classified claim of privilege in this case agrees that in this sense the claim of privilege is proper, although we have different views as to the scope of the privilege and its impact on plaintiffs' case. The plaintiffs themselves "do not dispute that, during the course of litigation, there may well be relevant evidence that may be properly withheld pursuant to the privilege." *See El-Masri,* 479 F.3d at 308-13 (affirming the dismissal of a case involving essentially the same types of claims on the basis of the state[] secrets doctrine).

We are precluded from explaining precisely which matters the privilege covers lest we jeopardize the secrets we are bound to protect. We can say, however, that the secrets fall within one or more of the four categories identified by the government and that we have independently and critically confirmed that their disclosure could be expected to cause significant harm to national security.

2. Effect on the Proceedings

Having determined that the privilege applies, we next determine whether the case must be dismissed under the *Reynolds* privilege. We have thoroughly considered plaintiffs' claims, several possible defenses, and the prospective path of this litigation. We also have carefully and skeptically reviewed the government's classified submissions . . . . We rely heavily on these submissions, which describe the state secrets implicated here, the harm to national security that the government believes would result from explicit or implicit disclosure, and the reasons why, in the government's view, further litigation would risk that disclosure.

Given plaintiffs' extensive submission of public documents and the stage of the litigation, we do not rely on the first two circumstances in which the *Reynolds* privilege requires dismissal — that is, whether plaintiffs could prove a prima facie case without privileged evidence, or whether the privilege deprives Jeppesen of evidence that would otherwise give it a valid defense to plaintiffs' claims. Instead, we assume without deciding that plaintiffs' prima facie case and Jeppesen's defenses may not inevitably depend on privileged evidence. Proceeding on that assumption, we hold that dismissal is nonetheless required under *Reynolds* because there is no feasible way to litigate Jeppesen's alleged liability *without creating an unjustifiable risk of divulging state secrets.* See *El-Masri*, 479 F.3d at 312 (coming to the same conclusion in a related and comparable case), *cert. denied*, 552 U.S. 947 (2007).[12]

We reach this conclusion because all seven of plaintiffs' claims, even if taken as true, describe Jeppesen as providing logistical support in a broad, complex process, certain aspects of which, the government has persuaded us, are absolutely protected by the state secrets privilege. Notwithstanding that some information about that process has become public, Jeppesen's alleged role and its attendant liability cannot be isolated from aspects that are secret and protected. Because the facts underlying plaintiffs' claims are so infused with these secrets, *any* plausible effort by Jeppesen to defend against them would create an unjustifiable risk of revealing state secrets, even if plaintiffs could make a prima facie case on one or more claims with nonprivileged evidence. *See Bareford*, 973 F.2d at 1144 ("[T]he danger that witnesses might divulge some privileged material during cross-examination is great because the privileged and non-privileged material are inextricably linked. We are compelled to conclude that the trial of this case would inevitably lead to a significant risk that highly sensitive information concerning this defense system would be disclosed.").

Here, further litigation presents an unacceptable risk of disclosure of state secrets no matter what legal or factual theories Jeppesen would choose to advance during a defense. Whether or not Jeppesen provided logistical support in connection with the extraordinary rendition and interrogation programs, there is precious little Jeppesen could say about its relevant conduct and knowledge without revealing information about how the United States government does *or does not* conduct covert operations. Our conclusion holds no matter what protective procedures the district court might employ. Adversarial litigation, including pretrial discovery of documents and witnesses and the presentation of documents and testimony at trial, is inherently complex and unpredictable. Although district courts are well equipped to wall off isolated secrets from disclosure, the challenge is exponentially greater in exceptional cases like this one, where the relevant secrets are difficult or impossible to isolate and

---

12. As the dissent correctly notes, we have previously disapproved of *El-Masri* for conflating the *Totten* bar's "very subject matter" inquiry with the *Reynolds* privilege. *See Al-Haramain*, 507 F.3d at 1201. We adhere to that approach today by maintaining a distinction between the *Totten* bar on the one hand and the *Reynolds* privilege on the other. Maintaining that distinction, however, does not mean that the *Reynolds* privilege can never be raised prospectively or result in a dismissal at the pleading stage. As we explained in *Al-Haramain* (as do we in the text), the *Totten* bar and the *Reynolds* privilege form a "continuum of analysis." 507 F.3d at 1201. A case may fall outside the *Totten* bar because its "very subject matter" is not a state secret, and yet it may become clear in conducting a *Reynolds* analysis that plaintiffs cannot establish a prima facie case, that defendants are deprived of a valid defense, or that the case cannot be litigated without presenting either a certainty or an unacceptable risk of revealing state secrets. When that point is reached, including, if applicable, at the pleading stage, dismissal is appropriate under the *Reynolds* privilege. Notwithstanding its erroneous conflation of the *Totten* bar and the *Reynolds* privilege, we rely on *El-Masri* because it properly concluded — "with respect to allegations comparable to those here — " that "virtually any conceivable response to [plaintiffs'] allegations would disclose privileged information," and, therefore, that the action could not be litigated "without threatening the disclosure" of state secrets. *El-Masri*, 479 F.3d at 308, 310.

even efforts to define a boundary between privileged and unprivileged evidence would risk disclosure by implication. In these rare circumstances, the risk of disclosure that further proceedings would create cannot be averted through the use of devices such as protective orders or restrictions on testimony.

Dismissal at the pleading stage under *Reynolds* is a drastic result and should not be readily granted. We are not persuaded, however, by the dissent's views that the state secrets privilege can never be "asserted during the pleading stage to excise entire allegations," or that the government must be required "to make its claims of state secrets with regard to specific items of evidence or groups of such items as their use is sought in the lawsuit."

. . . Here, our detailed *Reynolds* analysis reveals that the claims and possible defenses are so infused with state secrets that the risk of disclosing them is both apparent and inevitable. Dismissal under these circumstances, like dismissal under the *Totten* bar, reflects the general principle that "public policy forbids the maintenance of any suit in a court of justice, the trial of which would inevitably lead to the disclosure of matters which the law itself regards as confidential, and respecting which it will not allow the confidence to be violated." *Totten*, 92 U.S. at 107.

* * *

Although we are necessarily precluded from explaining precisely why this case cannot be litigated without risking disclosure of state secrets, or the nature of the harm to national security that we are convinced would result from further litigation, we are able to offer a few observations.

First, we recognize that plaintiffs have proffered hundreds of pages of publicly available documents, many catalogued in the dissent's Appendix, that they say corroborate some of their allegations concerning Jeppesen's alleged participation in aspects of the extraordinary rendition program. As the government has acknowledged, its claim of privilege does not extend to public documents. Accordingly, we do not hold that any of the documents plaintiffs have submitted are subject to the privilege; rather, we conclude that even assuming plaintiffs could establish their entire case *solely* through nonprivileged evidence — unlikely as that may be — any effort by Jeppesen to defend would unjustifiably risk disclosure of state secrets.

Second, we do not hold that the existence of the extraordinary rendition program is itself a state secret. The program has been publicly acknowledged by numerous government officials including the President of the United States. Even if its mere existence may once have been a "matter[ ] which, in the interest of national security, should not be divulged," it is not a state secret now. *Reynolds*, 345 U.S. at 10. Nonetheless, partial disclosure of the existence and even some aspects of the extraordinary rendition program does not preclude other details from remaining state secrets if *their* disclosure would risk grave harm to national security.

Third, we acknowledge the government's certification at oral argument that its assertion of the state secrets privilege comports with the revised standards set forth in the current administration's September 23, 2009 memorandum, adopted several years after the government first invoked the privilege in this case. Those standards require the responsible agency to show that "assertion of the privilege is necessary to protect information the unauthorized disclosure of which reasonably could be expected to cause significant harm to the national defense or foreign relations." *Holder Memo, supra,* at 1. They also mandate that the Department of Justice "will not defend an invocation of the privilege in order to: (i) conceal violations of the law, inefficiency, or administrative error; (ii) prevent embarrassment to a person, organization, or agency of the United States government; (iii) restrain competition; or (iv) prevent or delay the release of information the release of which would not reasonably be expected to cause significant harm to national security." *Id.* at 2. That certification here is consistent with our independent conclusion, having reviewed the government's public and classified declarations, that the government is not invoking the privilege to avoid embarrassment or to escape scrutiny of its recent controversial transfer and interrogation policies, rather than to protect legitimate national security concerns. . . .

VI.   CONCLUSION

We, like the dissent, emphasize that it should be a rare case when the state secrets doctrine leads to dismissal at the outset of a case. Nonetheless, there are such cases — not just those subject to *Totten*'s per se rule, but those where the mandate for dismissal is apparent even under the more searching examination required by *Reynolds*. This is one of those rare cases.

For all the reasons the dissent articulates — including the impact on human rights, the importance of constitutional protections and the constraints of a judge-made doctrine — we do not reach our decision lightly or without close and skeptical scrutiny of the record and the government's case for secrecy and dismissal. We expect our decision today to inform district courts that *Totten* has its limits, that every effort should be made to parse claims to salvage a case like this using the *Reynolds* approach, that the standards for peremptory dismissal are very high, and [that] it is the district court's role to use its fact-finding and other tools to full advantage before it concludes that the rare step of dismissal is justified. We also acknowledge that this case presents a painful conflict between human rights and national security. As judges, we have tried our best to evaluate the competing claims of plaintiffs and the government and resolve that conflict according to the principles governing the state secrets doctrine set forth by the United States Supreme Court.

For the reasons stated, we hold that the government's valid assertion of the state secrets privilege warrants dismissal of the litigation, and affirm the judgment of the district court. The government shall bear all parties' costs on appeal.

Affirmed.

[The concurring opinion of BEA, Circuit Judge, urging dismissal based on the *Totten* bar alone, is omitted.]

HAWKINS, Circuit Judge, with whom Judges SCHROEDER, CANBY, THOMAS, and PAEZ, Circuit Judges, join, dissenting: . . . The majority dismisses the case in its entirety before Jeppesen has even filed an answer to Plaintiffs' complaint. Outside of the narrow *Totten* context, the state secrets privilege has never applied to prevent parties from litigating the truth or falsity of allegations, or facts, or information simply because the government regards the truth or falsity of the allegations to be secret. Within the *Reynolds* framework, dismissal is justified if and only if specific privileged evidence is itself indispensable to establishing either the truth of the plaintiffs' allegations or a valid defense that would otherwise be available to the defendant. *See, e.g., Kasza v. Browner,* 133 F.3d 1159, 1166 (9th Cir. 1998).

This is important, because an approach that focuses on specific evidence after issues are joined has the benefit of confining the operation of the state secrets doctrine so that it will sweep no more broadly than clearly necessary. The state secrets doctrine is a judicial construct without foundation in the Constitution, yet its application often trumps what we ordinarily consider to be due process of law. This case now presents a classic illustration. Plaintiffs have alleged facts, which must be taken as true for purposes of a motion to dismiss, that any reasonable person would agree to be gross violations of the norms of international law, remediable under the Alien Tort Statute. They have alleged in detail Jeppesen's complicity or recklessness in participating in these violations. The government intervened, and asserted that the suit would endanger state secrets. The majority opinion here accepts that threshold objection by the government, so Plaintiffs' attempt to prove their case in court is simply cut off. They are not even allowed to attempt to prove their case by the use of nonsecret evidence in their own hands or in the hands of third parties.

It is true that, judicial construct though it is, the state secrets doctrine has become embedded in our controlling decisional law. Government claims of state secrets therefore must be entertained by the judiciary. But the doctrine is so dangerous as a means of hiding governmental misbehavior under the guise of national security, and so violative of common rights to due process, that courts should confine its application to the narrowest circumstances that still protect the government's essential secrets. When, as here, the doctrine is successfully invoked at the threshold of litigation, the claims of secret are necessarily broad and hypothetical. The result is a maximum interference with the due processes of the courts, on the most general claims of state secret privilege. It is far better to require the government to make its claims of state secrets with regard to specific items of evidence or groups of such items as their use is sought in the lawsuit. An official certification that evidence is truly a state secret will be more focused if the head of a department must certify that specific evidence sought in the course of litigation is truly a secret and cannot be revealed without danger to overriding, essential government interests. And when responsive pleading is complete and discovery under way, judgments as to whether secret material is essential to Plaintiffs' case or Jeppesen's defense can be made more accurately....

This is an appeal from a Rule 12 dismissal, which means that the district court was required to assume that the well-pleaded allegations of the complaint are *true,* and that we "construe the complaint in the light most favorable to the plaintiff[s]." *Doe v. United States,* 419 F.3d 1058, 1062 (9th Cir. 2005).... But Jeppesen has yet to answer or even to otherwise plead, so we have no idea what those defenses or assertions might be. Making assumptions about the contours of future litigation involves mere speculation, and doing so flies straight in the face of long standing principles of Rule 12 law by extending the inquiry to what *might* be divulged in future litigation....

NOTES AND QUESTIONS

1. *Invoking the State Secrets Privilege.* Because application of the privilege may have the draconian effect of ending a case or making it impossible to prove or to defend, the common law has required that the privilege be asserted in writing by a senior government official who has personally examined the putatively privileged material. In this case, the then-Director of the CIA filed a declaration so stating, in two forms — one classified for the court's eyes only, and one redacted and unclassified for

Mohamed and the public. In the Obama administration, a proposed invocation of the privilege is reviewed by the "State Secrets Review Committee," composed of senior Department of Justice officials, who make a recommendation to the Deputy Attorney General. *See* Memorandum from the Attorney General for Heads of Executive Departments and Agencies, *Policies and Procedures Governing Invocation of the State Secrets Privilege* (Sept. 23, 2009), *available at* http://www.justice.gov/opa/documents/state-secret-privileges.pdf. Should the same procedure be followed when the government invokes the *Totten* doctrine?

2. *Consequences of Recognizing the State Secrets Privilege.* Once the government has properly invoked the state secrets privilege, how should a court proceed? A litigant will be denied discovery of information deemed subject to the privilege, or denied the ability to introduce it into evidence. The litigant's need for the information or its relevance to the case at hand has no bearing on its discovery or admissibility once the court has determined that the information is privileged. (Note that a party may already possess the contested information but be barred from using it.)

Such a denial may not affect the eventual outcome of the case. It may, on the other hand, deprive the plaintiff of information she needs to avoid dismissal for failure to state a claim upon which relief can be granted, under Federal Rule of Civil Procedure 12(b)(6), or it may prevent a defendant from properly defending itself. It also may prevent a plaintiff from showing that she has an individual interest that entitles her to standing to sue. In *Halkin v. Helms*, 690 F.2d 977 (D.C. Cir. 1982), for example, the plaintiffs were unable to obtain records that might have shown that they were individually targeted by illegal FBI, CIA, Secret Service, and NSA surveillance of U.S. citizens opposed to the Vietnam War. See *infra* p. 534. In *Jeppesen* the court found that the consequences of recognizing the privilege were even more draconian: dismissal before trial, before discovery, and even before the defendant's answer to the complaint, to avoid unacceptable risks of disclosure of state secrets.

3. *Totten Bar vs. Reynolds Privilege.* As a categorical bar, *Totten* applies at the front of a lawsuit, as soon as the court is able to identify its subject matter as "inherently secret." It does not turn on a proffer-by-proffer evaluation of the evidence. The state secrets privilege, on the other hand, like other evidentiary privileges, has until recently been invoked as evidence is sought or offered during the course of litigation. Insofar as its application turns on specific evidence, it would ordinarily be inappropriate to invoke in a motion to dismiss, before an answer is filed, discovery has been taken, and any specific evidence has been sought or offered. *Jeppesen* suggests, however, that this difference is obliterated if the court can decide from the complaint and the government's state secrets declaration alone that litigation presents a grave risk of revealing state secrets, no matter what specific evidence the parties proffer. Why do you suppose the *Jeppesen* court did not simply rely on *Totten* to dismiss this case at the outset?

The *Jeppesen* court indicated that the Supreme Court has applied the *Totten* bar in one case not involving an espionage contract, *Weinberger v. Catholic Action of Hawaii/Peace Education Project*, 454 U.S. 139 (1981). In *Catholic Action*, environmental plaintiffs were unable to gain access to possible nuclear weapons information they needed to show a violation of the National Environmental Policy Act. Rather than dismissing because of the plaintiffs' resulting inability to state a claim upon which relief could be granted, under Federal Rule of Civil Procedure 12(b)(6), the Court declared that "whether or not the Navy has complied with NEPA 'to the fullest extent possible' is beyond judicial scrutiny." *Id.* at 146 (citing *Totten*). Has the *Jeppesen* court mischaracterized *Catholic Action*? If *Catholic Action* was relevant here, how did it support the decision in *Jeppesen*?

In articulating what it called the "*Reynolds* privilege," the *Jeppesen* majority recalled that the *Reynolds* Court cited *Totten* as a case "where the very subject matter of the action, a contract to perform espionage, was a matter of state secret." 345 U.S. at 11 n.26. But the citation in *Reynolds* appears in support of a statement that "even the most compelling necessity cannot overcome the claim of privilege if the court is ultimately satisfied that military secrets are at stake." *Id.* at 11. And the *Reynolds* case was not dismissed before trial. Is the *Jeppesen* court guilty of "judicial activism"?

4. *The Need for Secure Adjudication.* Is *Jeppesen*'s dismissal at the pleading stage, before Jeppesen was even required to answer, fair or necessary? In *In re United States*, 872 F.2d 472, 477 (D.C. Cir. 1989), the court declared, "Dismissal of a suit, and the consequent denial of a forum without giving the plaintiff her day in court...is indeed draconian." The court ordered instead that the case "be tried to the bench, a circumstance that will reduce the threat of unauthorized disclosure of confidential material." *Id.* at 478. Other courts have sought to avoid the draconian effect of outright dismissal by employing a special master, *Loral Corp. v. McDonnell Douglas Corp.*, 558 F.2d 1130 (2d Cir. 1977); imposing protective orders, *In re Under Seal*, 945 F.2d 1285 (4th Cir. 1992); or even conducting a secret trial, *Halpern v. United States*, 258 F.2d 36 (2d Cir. 1958). *See generally* Frank Askin, *Secret Justice and the Adversary System*, 18 Hastings Const. L.Q. 745 (1991). A special court, organized along the lines of the Foreign Intelligence Surveillance Court (*infra* p. 583), might be created to deal with these difficult cases. Can you think of other ways to try such cases without undue risk? Should the *Jeppesen* court have considered one of these alternatives?

Reacting to an increasing number of decisions like *Jeppesen* involving matters other than espionage contracts, the American Bar Association adopted a resolution on August 13, 2007, declaring that it "supports procedures and standards designed to ensure that whenever possible, federal civil cases are not dismissed based solely on the state secrets privilege." A bill in the 110th Congress would have codified the state secrets privilege and made it more difficult to apply the *Totten* bar or the so-called *Reynolds* privilege. S. 417, 110th Cong. (2009). Would enactment of legislation like this raise constitutional concerns?

5. *Judicial Deference.* The *Jeppesen* court declared:

> In evaluating the need for secrecy, "we acknowledge the need to defer to the Executive on matters of foreign policy and national security and surely cannot legitimately find ourselves second guessing the Executive in this arena." But "the state secrets doctrine does not represent a surrender of judicial control over access to the courts." [614 F.3d at 1081-1082 (citations omitted).]

The *El-Masri* court seemed far more deferential, declaring that

> [i]n assessing the risk that such a disclosure might pose to national security, a court is obliged to accord the "utmost deference" to the responsibilities of the executive branch.

Such deference is appropriate not only for constitutional reasons, but also practical ones: the Executive and the intelligence agencies under his control occupy a position superior to that of the courts in evaluating the consequences of a release of sensitive information. [479 F.3d at 305-306 (citations omitted).]

In the *Reynolds* case, the Supreme Court expressed an additional concern: "When . . . the occasion for the privilege is appropriate, . . . the court should not jeopardize the security which the privilege is meant to protect by insisting upon an examination of the evidence, even by the judge alone, in chambers." 345 U.S. at 10.

But in a more recent case involving a warrantless wiretap of an alleged domestic terrorist, the Court observed,

We cannot accept the Government's argument that internal security matters are too subtle and complex for judicial evaluation. Courts regularly deal with the most difficult issues of our society. There is no reason to believe that federal judges will be insensitive to or uncomprehending of the issues involved in domestic security cases. . . .

. . . Judges may be counted upon to be especially conscious of security requirements in national security cases. . . . Whatever security dangers clerical and secretarial personnel may pose can be minimized by proper administrative measures, possibly to the point of allowing the Government itself to provide the necessary clerical assistance. [*United States v. United States District Court (Keith)*, 407 U.S. 297, 320-321 (1972).]

Do you think the *Jeppesen* court struck the right balance between deference and skepticism? Do you agree with the *Jeppesen* dissent that the court should not speculate about the risk of disclosure in advance of a fuller development of the information?

6. *Reynolds Revisited.* The Supreme Court's landmark 1953 decision in *United States v. Reynolds* grew out of the crash in 1948 of a B-29 bomber. Surviving family members of three civilian engineers who perished brought suit for damages under the Federal Tort Claims Act. When they sought access through discovery to the official accident report, the Supreme Court accepted without question the Air Force's assertion that disclosure of the report would "seriously hamper[] national security." 345 U.S. at 5. The Court refused even to order in camera review of the report. When the report was declassified many years later, it was found to contain nothing that could apparently have been helpful to the nation's enemies, but instead to show pilot error, a failure to carry out special safety orders, and a history of maintenance problems with the B-29.

Despite this showing of apparent government misconduct, the Supreme Court denied without comment a motion for leave to file a petition for a writ of error *coram nobis* on June 23, 2003. *In re Herring*, 539 U.S. 940 (2003). When the *Reynolds* survivors filed a new action in the federal district court where the case had been heard 54 years earlier, they were again denied relief because they were unable to show that government officials in 1953 had committed intentional fraud on the court. *Herring v. United States*, 424 F.3d 384 (3d Cir. 2005), *cert. denied*, 547 U.S. 1123 (2006). The *Reynolds* litigation is extensively analyzed in Louis Fisher, *In the Name of National Security: Unchecked Presidential Power and the Reynolds Case* (2006).

Do you think these developments should affect the way courts consider state secrets privilege claims?

7. *Political Questions or State Secrets?* *El-Shifa* involves dismissal on grounds that courts are not fit to try such a case and out of a concern for separation of powers. *Jeppesen* involves dismissal on grounds that are different but related, applying what it calls the "*Reynolds* privilege" to dismiss without a trial because "state secrets are so central to this case that permitting further proceeding[s] would create an intolerable risk of disclosure that would jeopardize national security." Can you say how the two cases are conceptually related?

II

International Law as "Our Law"

The Domestic Effect of International Law

Charging a grand jury in a 1793 national security case, our first Chief Justice asserted that "the laws of the United States admit of being classed under the three heads of descriptions. 1st. All treaties made under the authority of the United States. 2d. The laws of nations. 3dly. The constitution, and statutes of the United States." *Trial of Gideon Henfield* (C.C.D. Pa. 1793) (charge to the grand jury by Jay, C.J.), *reprinted in* Francis Wharton, *State Trials of the United States During the Administrations of Washington and Adams* 49, 52-53 (1849). John Jay thus implied that some international agreements and customary international laws are part of our domestic law. But what part? What is their effect in U.S. law?

A thorough study of the framework of national security law must necessarily consider these questions, because so many national security actions implicate international law. However, the developing law on these questions has generated its own law school course on U.S. Foreign Relations Law. Consequently, this chapter only provides an introduction to the making and interpretation of treaties and executive agreements under U.S. law, and the effect of such instruments and of customary international law on (and as) domestic national security law.

The Supremacy Clause seems to supply one answer to the question of the domestic effect of international law by providing that "all Treaties made, or which shall be made, under the Authority of the United States, shall be the supreme Law of the Land...." U.S. Const. art. VI. But this only restates Jay's assertion about treaties; it does not explain the effect of a treaty that requires domestic legislation for its execution or that is inconsistent with a statute, let alone the effect of executive agreements or customary international law.

As necessary background for studying the legal effect of treaties and executive agreements, in Part A, we look briefly at the treaty-making process and how treaties and agreements are interpreted under our law. In Part B, we consider the domestic legal effect of treaties and executive agreements. In Part C, we address the statutory incorporation of international law into our own. Finally, in Part D, we analyze the domestic legal effect of customary international law that has not been expressly codified as our own law.

A.   THE MAKING AND INTERPRETATION
OF TREATIES AND AGREEMENTS

Under international law, an agreement between two or more states is considered to be a treaty—also called convention, pact, protocol, or accord—if (1) the states intend the agreement to be legally binding under international law; (2) the agreement deals with significant matters; (3) it clearly describes the obligations of the parties; and (4) it takes a form consistent with the intent that it be legally binding. Congressional Research Service, *Treaties and Other International Agreements: The Role of the United States Senate, A Study Prepared for the S. Comm. on Foreign Relations*, 106th Cong., 25-28 (Comm. Print 2001) (hereinafter *CRS Treaty Study*).

But under our Constitution, "treaties" are only those international agreements approved by a two-thirds vote of the Senate. U.S. Const. art. II, §2. However, the President is not constitutionally required to make international agreements by treaties alone. He may also make executive agreements: congressional-executive agreements based on statutory authorization, executive agreements based on treaties, and sole executive agreements based on independent constitutional authority.

1.   Treaties[1]

In the usual case, the executive branch negotiates an international agreement with a foreign state. It then transmits the agreement and any documents it considers to be integral parts of the treaty to the Senate for its approval. Under Senate rules, the proposed treaty is referred to the Senate Foreign Relations Committee, which typically holds hearings on it. At the hearings, the Department of State ordinarily will send a witness to provide the Administration's view of the meaning and importance of the treaty.

If the Committee reports the treaty out favorably, the full Senate will vote on it. The Senate may approve it by a vote of at least two-thirds of the Senators present—with or without conditions ("understandings" concerning its meaning, or "reservations," or "amendments," which condition consent on amendment or limitation of the substantive obligations it imposes)—or disapprove it.

Approval by the Senate is not "ratification." It is the President who ratifies an approved treaty by transmitting instruments of ratification to the treaty partners. If the Senate conditions its approval, the President communicates the conditions to the treaty partners in the instruments of ratification exchanged with them. Once these have been exchanged, the President proclaims that the treaty is in force or will come into force according to its terms (for example, when some prescribed number of states have ratified it).

NOTES AND QUESTIONS

1. *Negotiations—A Presidential Monopoly?* The making of a treaty starts with the state parties' negotiation of its terms. Does the Senate have any role to play in the

---

1. This brief account of the treaty process is based upon *CRS Treaty Study, supra*; *Relevance of Senate Ratification History to Treaty Interpretation*, 11 Op. Off. Legal Counsel 28 (1987); and Phillip R. Trimble, *United States Foreign Relations Law* 109-191 (2002).

negotiations? According to one scholar, from the Framers' use of the phrase "Advice and Consent" to describe the Senate's constitutional role and from other evidence, "it is fair to say that the original understanding of the treaty Power envisioned Senate participation prior to the negotiation and conclusion of treaties." Trimble, *supra*, at 116.

What are the pros and cons of involving the Senate in treaty negotiations? This was John Jay's answer:

> It seldom happens in the negotiation of treaties, of whatever nature, but that perfect *secrecy* and immediate *dispatch* are sometimes requisite. There are cases where the most useful intelligence may be obtained, if the persons possessing it can be relieved from apprehensions of discovery.... [T]here doubtless are many...who would rely on the secrecy of the President, but who would not confide in that of the Senate, and still less in that of a large popular assembly. The [constitutional] convention have done well, there- fore, in so disposing of the power of making treaties that although the President must, in forming them, act by the advice and consent of the Senate, yet he will be able to manage the business of intelligence in such manner as prudence may suggest. [*The Federalist No. 64*, at 392-393 (John Jay) (Clinton Rossiter ed., 1961).]

By the end of the Washington administration, it became the President's custom merely to inform the Senate of proposed negotiations when it consented to his appointment of the negotiator and to submit to the Senate a copy of his instructions to the negotiator only with the completed treaty. *See* Ralston Hayden, *The Senate and Treaties, 1789-1817*, at 105-106 (1920). Since then, the President has usually domi- nated the negotiating process and has typically only consulted the Senate after com- pleting negotiations, when formally submitting the negotiated treaty to it, *CRS Treaty Study*, *supra*, at 87, although the Senate (and sometimes the House) has participated earlier from time to time.

In light of these arguments, may the Senate alone or the Congress direct the President (or his delegate, the Secretary of State) to, say, "initiate negotiations as soon as possible for the development of bilateral or multilateral agreements with other nations" for the protection of sea turtles? *See* Pub. L. No. 101-162, §609(a)(1), 103 Stat. 988, 1037 (1989). In an opinion refusing an injunction to order the President to comply with such a statutory mandate, the court ruled that it

> has not and cannot lawfully order the Executive to comply with the terms of a statute that impinges upon power exclusively granted to the Executive Branch under the Constitution.... Because "the Constitution plainly grants the President the initiative in matters directly involved in the conduct of diplomatic" affairs, we cannot enforce the statute. [*Earth Island Inst. v. Christopher*, 6 F.3d 648, 653 (9th Cir. 1993) (internal citation omitted).]

Should the Senate be prohibited from dictating terms to be negotiated? From naming the negotiators for the United States? From designating Senators to serve as observers at the negotiations? From insisting on progress reports on negotiations? From forbidding negotiations on certain subjects or with certain states? *See generally CRS Treaty Study*, *supra*, at 69-82. In *Curtiss-Wright*, *supra* p. 53, Justice Sutherland claimed that the President "alone negotiates. Into the field of negotiation the Senate cannot intrude; and Congress itself is powerless to invade it." 299 U.S. at 319 (dictum). Was he right? *See* Louis Fisher, *Congressional Participation in the Treaty Process*,

137 U. Pa. L. Rev. 1511, 1512 (1989) (asserting that a presidential monopoly of treaty negotiation is an "historical myth").

2. *Consent.* After a treaty has been negotiated and signed or initialed, it is submitted to the Senate for "advice and consent." *See generally CRS Treaty Study, supra,* at 87-93. Typically, the treaty is referred to the Senate Foreign Relations Committee for consideration. Should the Administration be required to submit the full negotiating record to the Committee to aid its consideration? Should the Committee hold hearings in secret? What implications, if any, do your answers have for subsequent interpretation of the treaty?

As we noted, Senate consent to a treaty is not an all-or-nothing proposition. *See, e.g.,* Curtis A. Bradley & Jack L. Goldsmith, *Treaties, Human Rights, and Conditional Consent,* 149 U. Pa. L. Rev. 399 (2000); Michael J. Glennon, *The Senate Role in Treaty Ratification,* 77 Am. J. Int'l L. 257, 263-266 (1983); *CRS Treaty Study, supra,* at 96-100.

3. *The ABM Treaty Reinterpretation Controversy.*[2] In 1972, President Nixon and Soviet General Secretary Brezhnev signed the Treaty on the Limitation of Anti-Ballistic Missile Systems (ABM Treaty), which limited strategic defense systems. It was credited with forestalling a costly and destabilizing arms race in ABM technology and even more offensive nuclear missiles. In 1983, however, President Reagan announced the Strategic Defense Initiative (SDI). Its purpose was to develop "Star Wars" technology to defend against nuclear missile attack. After critics argued that testing and eventual implementation of such technology would require amending the ABM Treaty, the Reagan administration announced a reinterpretation of the ABM Treaty that would permit SDI development and testing. When opponents pointed out that the ratification hearings on the Treaty did not support this reinterpretation, the Administration cited a record of secret negotiations to support its reinterpretation. The Legal Adviser to the Department of State, Abraham D. Sofaer, argued that it is "the treaty that was made, irrespective of the explanations [the Senate] is provided." *See The ABM Treaty and the Constitution: Joint Hearings Before the S. Comm. on Foreign Relations and S. Comm. on the Judiciary,* 100th Cong. 351, 375 (1987) (hereinafter *ABM Treaty Hearings*) (statement of State Dep't Legal Adviser Abraham D. Sofaer).

In response, Senator Joseph Biden introduced Senate Resolution 167, which purported to set forth the "constitutional principles" governing treaty interpretation. The resolution provided that "the meaning [of a treaty] is to be determined in light of what the Senate understands the treaty to mean when it gives its advice and consent." That understanding, the resolution stated, is manifested by what the Senate formally expressed and also by "Senate approval or acceptance of, or Senate acquiescence in, interpretations of the treaty by the executive branch communicated to the Senate," but never "by matter of which it is not aware," such as secret negotiations not communicated to it.

Eventually, the Senate added a variant of the Biden resolution as a condition to approval of the Intermediate Range Nuclear Forces (INF) Treaty, although the

---

2. Except where otherwise noted, the description here is drawn from Symposium, *Arms Control Treaty Reinterpretation,* 137 U. Pa. L. Rev. 1353 (1989); and Abram Chayes & Antonia Handler Chayes, *Testing and Development of "Exotic" Systems Under the ABM Treaty: The Great Reinterpretation Caper,* 99 Harv. L. Rev. 1956 (1986).

condition technically applied just to that treaty. 134 Cong. Rec. S6724 (May 26, 1988). After he exchanged instruments of ratification of the INF Treaty with the Soviet Union, President Reagan wrote to the Senate disavowing the legal effect of the so-called Biden Condition. Senator Sam Nunn replied, "The Treaty, including this Condition, is now the supreme law of the land. And the President can no more change it with a letter than he can change any other law with a letter." Smith, *President Disputes Hill on Treaties*, Wash. Post, June 11, 1988 (quoting Senator Nunn).

4. *To What Treaty Did the Senate Consent?* An uncontroversial paraphrase of the Treaty Clause is that the President may make a treaty if the Senate has consented to it. A necessary corollary of this proposition is that "the President can only make the treaty to which the Senate consented; he cannot make a treaty other than the one to which the Senate consented." *See ABM Treaty Hearings, supra*, at 318 (statement of Professor Louis Henkin).

What is the role of Administration testimony to the Senate Foreign Relations Committee about the treaty? The Reagan administration subsequently claimed that "the Executive is, as a matter of domestic law, required to adhere to the interpretation of a treaty authoritatively shared with, and clearly intended, generally understood and relied upon by the Senate at the time of its advice and consent to ratification." Letter from White House Counsel Arthur B. Culvahouse to Senator Richard D. Lugar (Mar. 17, 1988), *reprinted in The INF Treaty*, S. Exec. Rep. No. 100-15, at 443 (1988).

Which witnesses are "authoritative"? How do we know whether an interpretation in their testimony was "clearly intended"? How do we know whether it was "generally understood and relied upon by the Senate"? *See generally* Gary M. Buechler, *Constitutional Limits on the President's Power to Interpret Treaties: The Sofaer Doctrine, the Biden Condition, and the Doctrine of Binding Authoritative Representations*, 78 Geo. L.J. 1983 (1990) (proposing to entrench only "authoritative executive representations" that have not been challenged by the Senate or a significant number of senators). The Office of Legal Counsel (OLC) has opined that:

> The weight to be given to an interpretative statement made by an Executive Branch official to the Senate during the ratification process will likely depend upon such factors as the formality of the statement, the identity and position of the Executive Branch official making the statement, the level of attention and interest focused on the meaning of the relevant treaty provision, and the consistency with which members of the Executive Branch adhered at the time to the view of the treaty provision reflected in the statement. [11 Op. Off. Legal Counsel at 37.]

5. *The Biden Condition.* Is the statement of "constitutional principles" in the Biden Condition constitutionally correct? The supporters of the Biden Condition also argued that "[i]mplicit understandings represent informal—but equally significant—legislative history," including hearings, committee reports, and floor debates. *The INF Treaty, supra*, at 439. The Biden Condition even provided that the Senate's unenacted "acquiescence" in executive branch interpretations was controlling. Since the Senate knows how to formalize its interpretations in amendments and reservations, why should we look past them? According to the OLC,

> [a]bsent such conditions, the Senate does not participate in setting the terms of the agreement between the [treaty] parties, and therefore statements made by Senators,

whether individually in hearings and debates or collectively in committee reports, should be accorded little weight unless confirmed by the Executive. . . . [11 Op. Off. Legal Counsel at 34.]

6. *The Importance of the Negotiating Record.* The Reagan administration also contended that when a treaty is ambiguous, the Executive may resort to a secret negotiating record to resolve the ambiguity, even though the record has not been disclosed to the Senate. Supporters of the Biden Condition disagreed, asserting that legislative history unknown to the Senate "could not, logically, be part of the 'meeting of the minds' between the President and the Senate extant on the date of Senate consent." *The INF Treaty, supra,* at 439. Thus, Professor Laurence Tribe testified during the controversy,

the President cannot present one treaty to the Senate, accompanied by various formal submittals, obtain the consent of the Senate to that treaty based in part on those submittals, and then unveil a hitherto secret record of negotiations or understandings — either internal to the executive branch or between the executive and the foreign signatory to the treaty — to defend an interpretation of the treaty inconsistent with what the Senate had been led to believe it was accepting. [*ABM Treaty Hearings, supra,* at 417-418.]

A negotiating record is an ill-defined and uneven collection of plenary statements read and exchanged by the negotiators, draft treaty texts prepared in the negotiations, and often numerous "memoranda of conversations" written after the fact by individual negotiators to summarize discussions. *See* David A. Koplow, *Constitutional Bait and Switch: Executive Reinterpretation of Arms Control Treaties,* 137 U. Pa. L. Rev. 1353, 1385-1386 (1989). *See also* Glennon, *supra* p. 166, at 139 (asserting that the "negotiating record is a term of art used to describe an agreed negotiating record, since it is only the joint intent of the parties that has significance under international law"). If the Administration intends to resolve treaty ambiguities using a secret negotiating record, how would you, as Chief Counsel to the Senate Foreign Relations Committee, advise the Committee to proceed in future hearings on submitted treaties? *See* Koplow, *supra,* 137 U. Pa. L. Rev. at 1377; Michael J. Glennon, *Interpreting "Interpretation": The President, the Senate, and When Treaty Interpretation Becomes Treaty Making,* 20 U.C. Davis L. Rev. 913, 919 (1987). How might your advice affect negotiations? *See* Buechler, *supra* p. 167, 78 Geo. L.J. at 2000-2001.

7. *Necessary Executive Reinterpretation of Treaties?* No treaty can anticipate every circumstance to which it might apply or every problem that may arise in its execution. Must the President therefore return to the Senate every time she encounters an unforeseen circumstance or problem? Or does she have some necessary power of interpretation to fill in the interstices of the treaty and make it work? If so, but you reject the Reagan administration's assertion of the limits of this power, what would you substitute?

Professor Koplow suggests that the Executive's power of reinterpretation is a function of the following factors: (a) what the Senate said in providing its advice and consent; (b) what was said to the Senate prior to its consent; (c) the attitude of the treaty partner(s) toward competing treaty interpretations; (d) support in the treaty text and record for competing interpretations; (e) the record of "subsequent practice" by the treaty parties; (f) how different the new interpretation is from the old; (g) whether the new interpretation purports to create new obligations or to release old ones; and (h) whether there are changed circumstances that affect the treaty. Koplow, *supra*, at 1418-1425. Would these factors make it harder or easier for "resourceful lawyers to support a preferred result"? *See* Phillip R. Trimble, *The Constitutional Common Law of Treaty Interpretation: A Reply to the Formalists*, 137 U. Pa. L. Rev. 1461, 1465 (1989) (expressing doubt concerning the soundness of any analytic approach that would "entrench" the meaning of a treaty).

8. *Deference to the Executive?* Do the factors listed in the preceding note give sufficient weight to the President's role in negotiating and executing a treaty—in other words, sufficient deference to the executive interpretation? The Supreme Court has stated that "[w]hile courts interpret treaties for themselves, the meaning given them by the departments of government particularly charged with their negotiation and enforcement is given great weight." *Kolovrat v. Oregon*, 366 U.S. 187, 194 (1961).

In urging that the Geneva Conventions did not apply to the U.S. conflict in Afghanistan, see *infra* p. 940, Attorney General Ashcroft advised President Bush that "when a President determines that a treaty does not apply, his determination is fully discretionary and will not be reviewed by the federal courts." Letter of Att'y General John Ashcroft to President George W. Bush (Feb. 1, 2002), *available at* http://www.gwu.edu/~nsarchiv/NSAEBB/NSAEBB127/020201.pdf. Is this advice consistent with the weight suggested by the Supreme Court? Or the role assigned the courts by Article III? In support of his advice, Attorney General Ashcroft cited dicta from *Clark v. Allen*, 331 U.S. 503, 508-509 (1947), that during war "the Chief Executive *or* Congress may have formulated a national policy quite inconsistent with the enforcement of a treaty in whole or in part" (emphasis added). But the Supreme Court in *Clark* relied for this proposition on an earlier state court opinion in which Judge Cardozo asserted that

> the President and Senate may denounce the treaty, and thus terminate its life. Congress may enact an inconsistent rule, which will control the action of the courts. The treaty of peace itself may set up new relations, and terminate earlier compacts, either tacitly or expressly. . . . But until some one of these things is done, until some one of these events occurs, while war is still flagrant, and the will of the political departments of the government unrevealed, the courts, as I view their function, play a humbler and more cautious part. It is not for them to denounce treaties generally, en bloc. Their part it is, as one provision or another is involved in some actual controversy before them, to determine whether, alone, or by force of connection with an inseparable scheme, the provision is inconsistent with the policy or safety of the nation in the emergency of war, and hence presumably intended to be limited to times of peace. [*Id.* at 509 (quoting *Techt v. Hughes*, 229 N.Y. 222, 242-243 (1920)).]

Does this passage support Attorney General Ashcroft's advice?

In any case, is heavy judicial deference to an executive interpretation of a U.S. treaty appropriate when the interpretation imposes conditions on the exercise of executive power? *See* Derek Jinks & Neal Kumar Katyal, *Disregarding Foreign Relations Law*, 116 Yale L.J. 1230 (2007) (asserting that the answer is no).

9. *Terminating Treaties.* In *Goldwater v. Carter*, 617 F.2d 697 (D.C. Cir.), *vacated and remanded*, 444 U.S. 996 (1979), Senator Goldwater challenged the constitutionality of President Jimmy Carter's unilateral termination of the U.S. Mutual Defense Treaty with Taiwan. The Court of Appeals upheld the President, rejecting the argument that treaties must be terminated in the same way they are approved—with the advice and consent of the Senate—noting, *inter alia*, that the theory has not been applied to the removal of ambassadors and some other executive officials appointed by the President with the advice and consent of the Senate. The Supreme Court subsequently vacated the opinion on justiciability grounds, 444 U.S. 996 (1979), leaving the question of termination authority unsettled.

Dissenting in *Goldwater*, Circuit Court Judge MacKinnon argued that because a constitutional treaty is the "Supreme Law of the Land," it can only be terminated by another law enacted by Congress (absent a superseding treaty). Under his theory, could the Senate alone terminate a treaty? Judge MacKinnon's syllogism was based on the proposition that treaties are like statutes. *See* Michael J. Glennon, *Constitutional Diplomacy* 150 (1990). The per curiam opinion in *Goldwater* dismissed this argument by asserting that the laws designated supreme by the Supremacy Clause "are not necessarily the same in their other characteristics, any more than are the circumstances and terms of their creation the same." 617 F.2d at 704.

Furthermore, the per curiam opinion appealed to practicality and history to uphold the President's power to terminate a treaty unilaterally. The opinion asserted that the Constitution imposes the "special and extraordinary" condition of treaty approval by a supermajority of the Senate because treaties risk tying the nation to "entangling alliances." *Id.* The opinion then implied that the risk to the country from *terminating* an entangling alliance is lower. *Id. See also* Louis Henkin, *Foreign Affairs and the Constitution* 169 (1972) ("'disentangling' is less risky and may have to be done quickly, and is often done piecemeal, or *ad hoc*, by various means or acts"). Is this logic sound? What if terminating a treaty raised a substantial risk that the erstwhile treaty party would retaliate in some way against the United States?

The President *has* terminated treaties unilaterally from time to time. The President's lawyers in *Goldwater* identified 26 instances of treaty termination, in 13 of which the President was said to have acted without Congress. *See Goldwater*, 617 F.2d at 723 (quoting President's brief). Judge MacKinnon responded by asserting that in 5 of the 13, there was a putative legislative basis for termination, and in 4 the treaty was already abrogated by the action of the other party. *Id.* at 733. What sort of history would demonstrate constitutional power in the President to terminate treaties? See *supra* pp. 43-44, describing a theory of constitutional customary law with congressional acquiescence. *See generally* Louis Henkin, *Litigating the President's Power to Terminate Treaties*, 73 Am. J. Int'l L. 647 (1979); David J. Scheffer, *The Law of Treaty Termination as Applied to the United States De-Recognition of the Republic of China*, 19 Harv. Int'l L.J. 931 (1978).

The foregoing history has led one scholar to conclude that

[r]ather than thinking of treaties as an odd form of domestic statute, it is more compelling to view them as an instrument of foreign policy, and to view treaty termination as one facet of a broad spectrum of activities conducted in the life of a treaty, ranging from negotiation through interpretation and supervision, all of which are within the domain of the executive branch. [Trimble, *supra* p. 169, at 151.]

2. Executive and Other Agreements

Dames & Moore v. Regan

United States Supreme Court, 1981
453 U.S. 654

[The opinion is set forth *supra* p. 60.]

NOTES AND QUESTIONS

1. *The Explosion in Executive Agreements.* In the half-century before World War II, executive agreements outnumbered treaties by a factor of only two to one. In the next 60 years, the discrepancy rose to almost 12 to 1. By the 1980s, the United States was entering into 300-400 executive agreements per year, compared to 8-26 treaties per year. *CRS Treaty Study, supra* p. 164, at xxxv-xxxvi. The agreements cover such diverse national security subjects as collective security, arms control and disarmament, status of U.S. forces stationed abroad, extradition, human rights, ceasefires, armistices and peace terms, military cooperation, and presumably intelligence collection and sharing. How would you explain the trend in favor of executive agreements?

2. *Types of Executive Agreements.* Executive agreements can be categorized by legal authority. *See Restatement (Third) of the Foreign Relations Law of the United States* (1987), §303. The first category consists of *congressional-executive agreements.* Congress either expressly enacts such agreements or, more commonly, delegates the authority to make them to the President. *CRS Treaty Study, supra* at 52-59. We saw in Chapter 5 that the courts have routinely sustained such delegations. *See, e.g., Field v. Clark,* 143 U.S. 649 (1892) (sustaining a foreign affairs delegation under which reciprocal trade agreements were made by the executive). The second category consists of *agreements made pursuant to treaty,* either by express authorization or by reasonable inference. Although the legal authority for treaty agreements has not been fully explored in the cases, in *Wilson v. Girard,* 354 U.S. 524, 528-529 (1957), the Supreme Court suggested that the Senate's approval of a treaty impliedly authorized the agreements necessary to carry it out.

The 1981 Iranian Hostage Agreement fell into a third, sometimes more controversial category of executive agreements: *sole executive agreements.* What constitutional authority would you cite for that type of agreement? *See United States v. Belmont,* 301 U.S. 324, 330-331 (1937) (citing President's role as sole organ of foreign relations in finding executive agreement "within [his] competence"). Sole executive agreements are legally most controversial because neither the Senate nor the House participates in their making. But they are also said to be relatively rare and typically confined to routine matters like exchanging information, holding consultations, and facilitating specific kinds of cooperation. Trimble, *supra* p. 164 n.1, at 115.

3. *Agreements and the Constitutional Text.* The Constitution expressly mentions treaties and describes the procedure for their making as well as their force and effect. Does the Constitution identify any other kind of international agreement? *See Ntakirutimana v. Reno,* 184 F.3d 419, 426 (5th Cir. 1999) (endorsing the assertion that the Constitution apparently contemplates other kinds of international agreements), *cert. denied,* 528 U.S. 1135 (2000). What textual constitutional arguments

can you make for and against the constitutionality in general of executive agreements? *See* U.S. Const. art. I, §10, cl. 3. One scholar argues that sole executive "agreements were clearly part of Crown prerogative and the eighteenth century concept of executive power. Not having been removed from the executive, like participation in the treaty power [given partly to the Senate], they fall comfortably within the Vesting Clause." Trimble, *supra*, at 132. What Supreme Court authority could you cite for this view of their legitimacy? What counter-argument could you make?

4. *The Interchangeability of Sole Executive Agreements and Treaties.* Are there some putative sole executive agreements for which the treaty process is constitutionally required? If not, what becomes of the Treaty Clause? If so, what differentiates permissible sole executive agreements from agreements for which the treaty process is required? Professor Louis Henkin suggests that "[o]ne is compelled to conclude that there are agreements which the President can make on his sole authority and others which he can make only with the consent of the Senate, but neither Justice Sutherland nor any one else has told us which are which." Henkin, *supra* p. 170, at 179. *See also* Edward Borchard, *Shall the Executive Agreement Replace the Treaty?*, 53 Yale L.J. 664 (1944). Do you think the President has constitutional authority to make a sole executive agreement that would require us to use military force to protect an ally against attack?

5. *The Interchangeability of Congressional-Executive Agreements and Treaties.* Congressional-executive agreements require approval by a simple majority of each House, while treaties require approval by a supermajority of the Senate. Consequently, some multilateral or bilateral national security undertakings that could obtain the requisite approval as congressional-executive agreements might fail as treaties. Are there some putative congressional-executive agreements for which the treaty process is constitutionally required? If so, how do we differentiate those congressional-executive agreements that are permissible from those that are not? Is the differentiating factor their importance, in terms of scope and impact? By this standard, a multilateral trade agreement requiring harmonization of financial, commercial, labor, and environmental laws and regulations for an entire continent would arguably need to be approved by the treaty process, while an agreement regarding housing for a U.S. military base in a foreign country would not.

In *Made in USA Foundation v. United States*, 242 F.3d 1300 (11th Cir.), *cert. denied, United Steelworkers v. United States*, 534 U.S. 1039 (2000), however, the court found the "importance" standard unworkable in a challenge to just such a trade agreement (the North American Free Trade Agreement (NAFTA)). Noting that neither the constitutional text nor the case law tells us "what exactly constitutes and distinguishes 'treaties'" from other kinds of agreements, it rejected the "nebulous argument that 'major and significant' agreements require Art. II, §2 ratification," because appellants failed "to supply any analytical framework whatsoever" for classifying agreements as "major and significant." *Id.* at 1315. Furthermore, it asserted that for a court to "adjudicate the 'significance' of an international commercial agreement as the critical determinant of whether or not it constitutes a treaty requiring Senate ratification . . . would . . . unavoidably thrust [it] into making policy judgments of the sort unsuited for the judicial branch." *Id.* at 1317. At the same time, the court conceded that the Treaty Clause does not leave the political branches "unfettered discretion" in deciding whether a particular agreement is subject to the rigors of the

Article II treaty process, because otherwise that process would be a "dead letter." *Id.* at 1319. Back to square one.

The State Department lists the following "considerations for selecting among constitutionally authorized procedures": degree of commitment or risk involved, intent to override state laws, need for subsequent legislation, past practice for similar agreements, congressional preference, degree of formality desired, proposed duration, need for prompt conclusion, and general international practice. *Treaties and Other International Agreements*, in 2 *Foreign Affairs Manual* ch. 700 (rev. Feb. 25, 1985), reprinted in *CRS Treaty Study, supra* p. 164, at 301. Professor Steve Charnovitz has recommended that Congress enact a "framework statute" for approving congressional-executive agreements as "a substitute for the Article II procedure." Steve Charnovitz, *Using Framework Statutes to Facilitate U.S. Treaty Making*, 98 Am. J. Int'l L. 969, 702 (2004).

6. *Case-Zablocki Act: A Congressional Limit on Agreements*. Congress has long worried about erosion of the treaty power in light of the increasing number of executive agreements. In 1961, Congress enacted the Arms Control and Disarmament Act, which provides that "no action shall be taken under this chapter or any other law" to commit the United States to reduce or limit arms "except pursuant to the treaty making power of the President under the Constitution or unless authorized by further affirmative legislation by the Congress of the United States." Pub. L. No. 87-297, §33, 75 Stat. 634 (codified as amended at 22 U.S.C. §2573 (2006)). Is this provision constitutional in all its applications?

Concern during the Vietnam War about secret security commitments prompted the Senate to pass a nonbinding "National Commitments Resolution" expressing its sense that a U.S. national commitment for the use of U.S. armed forces or financial assistance to allies should result "only from affirmative action taken by the executive and legislative branches of the United States Government by means of a treaty, statute, or concurrent resolution of both Houses of Congress specifically providing for such commitment." S. 85, 91st Cong. (1969). Ultimately, however, Congress backed away from any generic challenge to sole executive agreements, settling instead in the Case-Zablocki Act for requiring the President to make a timely submission to Congress of "the text of any international agreement (including text of any oral international agreement, which shall be reduced to writing) other than a Treaty." 1 U.S.C. §112b (2006). The Act provides that the President may submit classified agreements to the Senate Committee on Foreign Relations and the House Committee on International Affairs with an injunction of secrecy. Does the Act validate sole executive agreements by implication? Presidents Nixon, Ford, and Carter made secret agreements regarding South Vietnam, the Sinai, and disarmament, respectively, which they labeled "arrangements" or "accords" to avoid reporting. Does such labeling avoid the Case-Zablocki Act?

B.   THE DOMESTIC LEGAL EFFECT OF TREATIES AND EXECUTIVE AGREEMENTS

The Supremacy Clause clearly elevates treaties as the Supreme Law of the Land over state laws. Less clearly, it has been consistently interpreted to give executive agreements that same status, either as a form of "treaty" or as "laws of the United States." But this means only that treaties and executive agreements are supreme over state law, not that they are necessarily equal to one another. William C. Banks, *Treaties and Treaty Power*, in *Oxford Companion to the Supreme Court of the United States* 878 (Kermit L. Hall ed., 1992). If the Constitution is first among equals, why does it differentiate "Laws of the United States which shall be made *in Pursuance thereof*" and "Treaties made, or which shall be made, under the *Authority of the United States*"? U.S. Const. art. VI (emphasis added). And how are we to choose between a statute and a treaty when they are inconsistent?

Reid v. Covert

United States Supreme Court, 1957
354 U.S. 1

[Mrs. Covert killed her husband, a U.S. Air Force sergeant, at an airbase in England. Pursuant to a "status-of-forces" executive agreement with that country, she was tried and convicted by U.S. court-martial without a jury trial under the Uniform Code of Military Justice (UCMJ). On a petition for a writ of habeas corpus, she attacked her conviction on the grounds that it violated her Fifth and Sixth Amendment rights to be tried by a jury after indictment by a grand jury. The District Court granted the petition, and this appeal followed. Mrs. Covert's appeal was consolidated with a like appeal by Mrs. Smith, who had been tried and convicted in similar fashion in Japan.]

Mr. Justice BLACK announced the judgment of the Court and delivered an opinion, in which the Chief Justice, Mr. Justice DOUGLAS, and Mr. Justice BRENNAN join. . . .

I.

[The Supreme Court first held that the Fifth and Sixth Amendments protect American citizens abroad from actions by their government.]

II.

At the time of Mrs. Covert's alleged offense, an executive agreement was in effect between the United States and Great Britain which permitted United States military courts to exercise exclusive jurisdiction over offenses committed in Great Britain by American servicemen or their dependents. For its part, the United States agreed that these military courts would be willing and able to try and to punish all offenses against the laws of Great Britain by such persons. In all material respects, the same situation existed in Japan when Mrs. Smith killed her husband. Even though a court-martial does not give an accused trial by jury and other Bill of Rights protections, the Government contends that Art. 2(11) of U.C.M.J., insofar as it provides for the military trial of dependents accompanying the armed forces in Great Britain and Japan, can be sustained as legislation which is necessary and proper to carry out the United States' obligations under the international agreements made with those countries. The obvious and decisive answer to this, of course, is that no agreement with a foreign nation can confer power on the Congress, or on any other branch of Government, which is free from the restraints of the Constitution.

Article VI, the Supremacy Clause of the Constitution, declares:

> This Constitution, and the Laws of the United States which shall be made in Pursuance thereof; and all Treaties made, or which shall be made, under the Authority of the United States, shall be the supreme Law of the Land; . . .

There is nothing in this language which intimates that treaties and laws enacted pursuant to them do not have to comply with the provisions of the Constitution. Nor is there anything in the debates which accompanied the drafting and ratification of the Constitution which even suggests such a result. These debates as well as the history that surrounds the adoption of the treaty provision in Article VI make it clear that the reason treaties were not limited to those made in "pursuance" of the Constitution was so that agreements made by the United States under the Articles of Confederation, including the important peace treaties which concluded the Revolutionary War, would remain in effect. It would be manifestly contrary to the objectives of those who created the Constitution, as well as those who were responsible for the Bill of Rights — let alone alien to our entire constitutional history and tradition — to construe Article VI as permitting the United States to exercise power under an international agreement without observing constitutional prohibitions. In effect, such construction would permit amendment of that document in a manner not sanctioned by Article V. The prohibitions of the Constitution were designed to apply to all branches of the National Government and they cannot be nullified by the Executive or by the Executive and the Senate combined.

There is nothing new or unique about what we say here. This Court has regularly and uniformly recognized the supremacy of the Constitution over a treaty.[33] For example, in *Geofroy v. Riggs*, 133 U.S. 258, 267, it declared:

> The treaty power, as expressed in the Constitution, is in terms unlimited except by those restraints which are found in that instrument against the action of the government or of its departments, and those arising from the nature of the government itself and of that of the States. It would not be contended that it extends so far as to authorize what the Constitution forbids, or a change in the character of the government or in that of one of the States, or a cession of any portion of the territory of the latter, without its consent.

This Court has also repeatedly taken the position that an Act of Congress, which must comply with the Constitution, is on a full parity with a treaty, and that when a statute which is subsequent in time is inconsistent with a treaty, the statute to the extent of conflict renders the treaty null.[34] It would be completely anomalous to say that a treaty need not comply with the Constitution when such an agreement can be overridden by a statute that must conform to that instrument.

There is nothing in *Missouri v. Holland*, 252 U.S. 416, which is contrary to the position taken here. There the Court carefully noted that the treaty involved was not inconsistent with any specific provision of the Constitution. The Court was concerned with the Tenth Amendment which reserves to the States or the people all power not delegated to the National Government. To the extent that the United States can

---

33. We recognize that executive agreements are involved here but it cannot be contended that such an agreement rises to greater stature than a treaty.

34. In *Whitney v. Robertson*, 124 U.S. 190, 194, the Court stated: "By the Constitution a treaty is placed on the same footing, and made of like obligation, with an act of legislation. Both are declared by that instrument to be the supreme law of the land, and no superior efficacy is given to either over the other. . . . [I]f the two are inconsistent, the one last in date will control the other. . . ."

validly make treaties, the people and the States have delegated their power to the National Government and the Tenth Amendment is no barrier.

In summary, we conclude that the Constitution in its entirety applied to the trials of Mrs. Smith and Mrs. Covert. Since their court-martial did not meet the requirements of Art. III, §2, or the Fifth and Sixth Amendments we are compelled to determine if there is anything *within* the Constitution which authorizes the military trial of dependents accompanying the armed forces overseas. . . .

[The Court concluded at length that the congressional power to make rules for the government and regulation of the armed forces, U.S. Const. art. I, §8, cl. 14, did not provide the requisite authority. It affirmed the district court judgment releasing Mrs. Covert from custody and reversed the district court judgment against Mrs. Smith, with directions that she also be released.]

[The opinions of Justices Harlan and Frankfurter, concurring in the result, and Justice Clark, dissenting, are omitted here. Justice Whittaker took no part in the consideration or decision of the case.]

[Other parts of this decision are reproduced *infra* p. 709.]

Committee of U.S. Citizens Living in Nicaragua v. Reagan

United States Court of Appeals, D.C. Circuit, 1988
859 F.2d 929

[In 1986, the International Court of Justice (ICJ) held that the U.S. financial support of paramilitary activities by the Contras against the Sandinista government in Nicaragua violated both a treaty between the countries and customary international law. It concluded that the United States had a duty to refrain from continuing such support. The United States, however, withdrew from the court's jurisdiction before the court's decision, and President Reagan requested and Congress appropriated continued aid after the ICJ decision.

Plaintiffs, organizations, and individuals who opposed this policy brought the instant action for injunctive and declaratory relief against continued U.S. financial support for the Contras contrary to the U.N. Charter and customary international law. The District Court dismissed plaintiffs' entire complaint on political question grounds. The Court of Appeals also expressed serious doubts about the justiciability of plaintiffs' claims but preferred to rest its decision on other grounds. The court's decision on plaintiffs' treaty claim follows.]

Mikva, Circuit Judge. . . .

B.   Appellants Have No Basis in Domestic Law for Enforcing the ICJ Judgment

1.   The Status of International Law in the United States'
Domestic Legal Order

Appellants argue that the United States' decision to disregard the ICJ judgment . . . violate[s] part of a United States treaty, namely Article 94 of the U.N. Charter. That article provides that "[e]ach Member of the United Nations undertakes to comply with the decision of the International Court of Justice in any case to which it is a party." . . .

For purposes of the present lawsuit, the key question is not simply whether the United States has violated any...legal norms but whether such violations can be remedied by an American court or whether they can only be redressed on an international level. In short, do violations of international law have domestic legal consequences? The answer largely depends on what form the "violation" takes. Here, the alleged violation is the law that Congress enacted and that the President signed, appropriating funds for the Contras. When our government's two political branches, acting together, contravene an international legal norm, does this court have any authority to remedy the violation? The answer is "no" if the type of international obligation that Congress and the President violate is either a treaty or a rule of customary international law....

2. The Effect of Subsequent Statutes upon Prior Inconsistent Treaties

Although appellants' complaint alleges that Congress' funding of the Contras violates Article 94 of the U.N. Charter, appellants seem to concede here that such a claim is unavailing. They acknowledge, as they must, that "[o]rdinarily, treaty obligations may be overridden by subsequent inconsistent statutes."...

In the *Head Money Cases*, 112 U.S. 580 (1884), shipping companies protested payment of a tax on immigrants they had transported to America, arguing that the tax violated treaties of friendship with the immigrants' nations of origin. The Court held that, even if the statute requiring the tax was inconsistent with prior treaties, it necessarily displaced any conflicting treaty provisions for purposes of domestic law.

> A treaty, then, is a law of the land as an act of Congress is, whenever its provisions prescribe a rule by which the rights of the private citizen or subject may be determined....
>
> But even [so]...there is nothing in [a treaty] which makes it irrepealable or unchangeable. The Constitution gives it no superiority over an act of Congress in this respect, which may be repealed or modified by an act of a later date....
>
> In short, we are of the opinion that, so far as a treaty made by the United States with any foreign nation can become the subject of judicial cognizance in the courts of this country, it is subject to such acts as Congress may pass for its enforcement, modification, or repeal. [*Id.* at 598-599.]

No American court has wavered from this view in the subsequent century. Indeed, in a comparatively recent case, our court reaffirmed the principle that treaties and statutes enjoy equal status and therefore that inconsistencies between the two must be resolved in favor of the *lex posterior*. In *Diggs v. Shultz*, 470 F.2d 461 (D.C. Cir. 1972), cert. denied, 411 U.S. 931 (1973), this court reviewed a claim by citizens of what was then Southern Rhodesia, assailing the United States' failure to abide by U.N. Security Council Resolution 232. That resolution directed U.N. members to impose a trade embargo against Rhodesia. The court found that America's contravention of Resolution 232 was required by Congress' adoption of the so-called Byrd Amendment "whose purpose and effect...was to detach this country from the U.N. boycott of Southern Rhodesia in blatant disregard of our treaty undertakings." *Id.* at 466. "Under our constitutional scheme," the court concluded, "Congress can denounce treaties if it sees fit to do so, and there is nothing the other branches of government can do about it...[; thus] the complaint [states] no tenable claim in law." *Id.* at 466-467.

These precedents dispose of any claim by appellants that the United States has violated its treaty obligation under Article 94. It is true, of course, that the facts here differ somewhat from the situation in *Diggs*. Congress has not clearly repudiated the requirement in Article 94 that every nation comply with an ICJ decision "in any case to which it is a party." U.N. Charter, art. 94. Rather, our government asserts that it never consented to ICJ jurisdiction in cases like the Nicaragua dispute. Thus, Congress may well believe that its support for the Contras, while contravening the ICJ judgment, does not violate its treaty obligation under Article 94. And, unless Congress makes clear its intent to abrogate a treaty, a court will not lightly infer such intent but will strive to harmonize the conflicting enactments.

At this stage of the present case, however, the key question is not whether Congress intended to abrogate Article 94. Since appellants *allege* that Congress has breached Article 94, we must determine whether such a claim could ever prevail. The claim could succeed only if appellants could prove that a prior treaty—the U.N. Charter—preempts a subsequent statute, namely the legislation that funds the Contras. It is precisely that argument that the precedents of the Supreme Court and of this court foreclose. We therefore hold that appellants' claims based on treaty violations must fail.

Our conclusion, of course, speaks not at all to whether the United States has upheld its treaty obligations under international law. As the Supreme Court said in the *Head Money Cases*, a treaty "depends for the enforcement of its provisions on the interest and honor of the governments which are parties to it. If these fail, its infraction becomes the subject of international negotiations and reclamations . . . [but] with all this the judicial courts have nothing to do and can give no redress." 112 U.S. at 598. This conclusion reflects the United States' adoption of a partly "dualist" — rather than strictly "monist" — view of international and domestic law. "[D]ualists view international law as a discrete legal system [which] . . . operates wholly on an inter-nation plane." Louis Henkin, *The Constitution and United States Sovereignty: A Century of Chinese Exclusion and Its Progeny*, 100 Harv. L. Rev. 853, 864 (1987) (hereinafter Henkin, *United States Sovereignty*).

It is uncertain whether either our republican form of government or our Constitution's supremacy clause requires this subordination of treaties to inconsistent domestic statutes. Nevertheless, the "[Supreme] Court's jurisprudence about treaties inevitably reflects certain assumptions about the relation between international law and United States law." Henkin, *United States Sovereignty*, 100 Harv. L. Rev. at 870. Given that dualist jurisprudence, we cannot find—as a matter of *domestic* law—that congressional enactments violate prior treaties.

Finally, we note that even if Congress' breach of a treaty were cognizable in domestic court, appellants would lack standing to rectify the particular breach that they allege here. Article 94 of the U.N. Charter simply does not confer rights on private individuals. Treaty clauses must confer such rights in order for individuals to assert a claim "arising under" them. See U.S. Const. art. III, §2, cl. 1; 28 U.S.C. §1331 (1982). Whether a treaty clause does create such enforcement rights is often described as part of the larger question of whether that clause is "self-executing."

This court has noted that, in "determining whether a treaty is self-executing" in the sense of its creating private enforcement rights, "courts look to the intent of the signatory parties as manifested by the language of the instrument." *Diggs v. Richardson*, 555 F.2d 848, 851 (D.C. Cir. 1976). The court in *Diggs v. Richardson* concluded that the U.N. Security Council Resolution that plaintiffs sought to enforce (which barred commercial relations between U.N. members and Namibia) was "not addressed to the judicial branch of our government." *Id.* The resolution's provisions did not "by their terms confer rights upon individual citizens [but] call[ed] upon governments to take certain actions." *Id.* Applying the same test to Article 94 of the U.N. Charter, we reach a similar conclusion.

The second paragraph of Article 94 provides that,

> [i]f any party to a case fails to perform the obligations incumbent upon it under a judgment rendered by the [ICJ], the other party may have recourse to the Security Council, which may, if it deems necessary, make recommendations or decide upon measures to be taken to give effect to the judgment. [U.N. Charter art. 94, ¶2.]

Because only nations can be parties before the ICJ, appellants are not "parties" within the meaning of this paragraph. Clearly, this clause does not contemplate that individuals having no relationship to the ICJ case should enjoy a private right to enforce the ICJ's decision. Our interpretation of Article 94 is buttressed by a related provision in the Statute of the ICJ, which is incorporated by reference in the U.N. Charter. See U.N. Charter art. 92. The Statute provides that "[t]he decision of the Court has no binding force except between the parties and in respect of th[e] particular case." Taken together, these Charter clauses make clear that the purpose of establishing the ICJ was to resolve disputes between national governments. We find in these clauses no intent to vest citizens who reside in a U.N. member nation with authority to enforce an ICJ decision against their own government. . . .

[The court's decision on plaintiffs' customary law claim is reproduced *infra* p. 185.]

NOTES AND QUESTIONS

1. *Missouri v. Holland.* In *Missouri v. Holland,* 252 U.S. 416 (1920), the Court upheld a statute enacted pursuant to the Migratory Bird Treaty against a Tenth Amendment challenge, even though a federal court had previously sustained such a challenge to an earlier statute that imposed similar restrictions. The Court asserted in dicta that "[i]t is obvious that there may be matters of the sharpest exigency for the national well being that an act of Congress could not deal with but that a treaty followed by such an act could. . . ." *Id.* at 433. Does this suggest that the government could by treaty take actions otherwise forbidden by the Constitution? For example, does it mean that the President and the Senate could approve a treaty committing the United States to war in support of an ally without approval by the House? Does *Reid* supply an answer? Is *Holland* distinguishable? *See* Nicholas Quinn Rosenkranz, *Executing the Treaty Power,* 118 Harv. L. Rev. 1868 (2005) (arguing that *Holland* was wrongly decided and that treaties cannot increase the legislative power of Congress).

2. *Self-Executing and Non-Self-Executing Treaties. Committee of U.S. Citizens* quotes *The Head Money Cases,* 112 U.S. 580, 598-599 (1884), for the proposition that a treaty is the legal equivalent of a statute "whenever its provisions prescribe a rule by which the rights of the private citizen or subject may be determined." Chief Justice John Marshall asserted the same proposition more fully:

> Our constitution declares a treaty to be the law of the land. It is, consequently, to be regarded in courts of justice as equivalent to an act of the legislature, whenever it

operates of itself, without the aid of any legislative provision. But when the terms of the stipulation import a contract, when either of the parties engages to perform a particular act, the treaty addresses itself to the political, not the judicial department; and the legislature must execute the contract before it can become the rule for the court. [*Foster v. Neilson*, 27 U.S. (2 Pet.) 253, 314 (1829).]

Whether a treaty or a provision thereof is "self-executing" or not is therefore significant not only for deciding its enforceability in U.S. courts without the need for independent action by the legislature or Executive, but also for deciding whether it authorizes the President to act alone, without further legislation. *See generally* Carlos Manuel Vazquez, *The Four Doctrines of Self-Executing Treaties*, 89 Am. J. Int'l L. 695 (1995). Indeed, some have argued that making a treaty non-self-executing is "[t]he normal way to accommodate the interests of the House or Congress as a whole during the exercise of the Treaty Power . . . ." Trimble, *supra*, at 120. A non-self-executing treaty would remain the law of the land even though not enforceable in the courts; the executive and legislative branches would still have the duty to carry it out in good faith, but "[t]heir accountability is political, not judicial . . . ." Trimble, *supra*, at 163. Such a treaty would also still establish an international duty which the United States would breach by failing in due course to execute it. *See Restatement (Third), supra* p. 171, §111 (stating that a finding that a treaty is non-self-executing, when some time has lapsed since the treaty went into force, is a finding that the United States is in default of its international treaty obligations "and should be avoided").

Although the courts admit the possibility that treaties can be self-executing or non-self-executing, scholars are divided. Some take a dim view of the latter and argue that "the tendency of the Executive branch and in the courts to interpret treaties and treaty provisions as non-self-executing runs counter to the language, and spirit, and history of . . . Constitution." Henkin, *supra* p. 170, at 201. What constitutional text would you cite in support of this view, and why? Others account for the case law recognizing non-self-executing treaties by viewing such treaties as the exception. *See, e.g.*, Vazquez, *supra*, 89 Am. J. Int'l L. at 695; Carlos Manuel Vazquez, *Laughing at Treaties*, 99 Colum. L. Rev. 2154, 2176 (1999). Thus, they assert that non-self-executing treaties are either unconstitutional treaties, nonjusticiable precatory or hortatory treaties, treaties that do not create private rights of action, or treaties that expressly require enabling legislation. *Id. See also* Carlos Manuel Vazquez, *Treaties as Law of the Land: The Supremacy Clause and the Judicial Enforcement of Treaties*, 122 Harv. L. Rev. 599, 600 (2008) (arguing that "the Supremacy Clause establishes a default rule that treaties are directly enforceable in the courts like other laws, rebuttable only by a clear statement that the obligations imposed by the treaty are subject to legislative implementation").

On the other hand, Professor Yoo has vigorously argued that the history of the framing of the Constitution suggests (albeit ambiguously) that, to avoid leaving the people's most direct representatives in the House out of the lawmaking process, no treaty should be construed as self-executing. *Compare* John C. Yoo, *Globalism and the Constitution: Treaties, Non-Self-Execution, and the Original Understanding*, 99 Colum. L. Rev. 1955, 1962 (1999), *with* Martin S. Flaherty, *History Right? Historical Scholarship, Original Understanding, and Treaties as "Supreme Law of the Land,"* 99 Colum. L. Rev. 2095 (1999) (offering rebuttal of Yoo's historical arguments). To give effect to this asserted original intent, Yoo urges the courts to follow "[a] presumption of non-self-execution," at least when the treaty itself is silent. Yoo, *supra*, at 2092-2093. So far, the courts have not yet definitively taken either side in this academic debate about the domestic legal effect of treaties; they instead continue to find constitutional room for both kinds of treaties.

3. *Subject Matter Limitations on Self-Executing Treaties?* Are there some subjects on which self-executing treaties cannot operate because they fall within the exclusive legislative power of Congress? *See Edwards v. Carter*, 580 F.2d 1055, 1059 (D.C. Cir.) (dictum) (asserting that the Revenue Bill and Appropriations Clauses, U.S. Const. art. I, §7, cl. 1 & §9, cl. 7, respectively, "operate to limit the treaty power because the language of these provisions clearly precludes any method of appropriating money or raising taxes other than through the enactment of laws by the full Congress"), *cert. denied*, 436 U.S. 907 (1978). Many collective defense treaties to which the United States is a party provide that, in the event of an armed attack on a treaty partner, each partner will "act to meet the common danger in accordance with its constitutional processes," or words to that effect. Is this provision self-executing? If it were, would it be constitutional? *See Restatement (Third), supra* p. 171, §111(4)(c) (asserting that an international agreement of the United States is non-self-executing "if implementing legislation is constitutionally required").

4. *Deciding Whether a Treaty Is or Is Not Self-Executing.* How does the court in *Committee of U.S. Citizens* decide whether U.N. Charter article 94 is self-executing? *See also Restatement (Third)* §111(4); Michael A. McKenzie, *Treaty Enforcement in U.S. Courts*, 34 Harv. Int'l L.J. 596, 603 (1993) (adding to factors applied in *Committee of U.S. Citizens*, "the availability and feasibility of alternative enforcement mechanisms, implications of implying self-execution versus non-self-execution, and the existence of appropriate domestic procedures and institutions for the direct implementation of the treaty").

5. *Standing to Enforce.* As *Committee of U.S. Citizens* shows, private litigants are usually held either to lack standing or to have failed to state a cause of action, or both, to enforce non-self-executing international agreements. Courts often reason that private rights are merely "derivative" through their states and that private parties therefore lack standing to invoke international agreements as either swords or shields in the absence of a protest by the signatory state itself. *See, e.g., Matta-Ballesteros v. Henman*, 896 F.2d 255, 259 (7th Cir.), *cert. denied*, 498 U.S. 878 (1990); *United States v. Noriega*, 746 F. Supp. 1506, 1533 (S.D. Fla. 1990), *aff'd*, 117 F.3d 1206 (11th Cir. 1997).

6. *Last-in-Time Rule.* If a particular international agreement is the legal equivalent of a statute, it is logical, as a matter of domestic law, that it can be modified or superseded by statute. *Lex posterior*—the last in time—controls. *Restatement (Third)* §115. *See, e.g., Whitney v. Robertson*, 124 U.S. 190, 193-194 (1888), quoted *supra* p. 175 n.34; *The Chinese Exclusion Case*, 130 U.S. 581, 600 (1889). *But see* Jordan J. Paust, *Rediscovering the Relationship Between Congressional Power and International Law: Exceptions to the Last in Time Rule and the Primacy of Custom*, 28 Va. J. Int'l L. 392 (1988) (noting case law exceptions to last-in-time rule). Does this mean that Congress can modify or repeal an international agreement? What is the international effect of a subsequent statutory repealer?

7. *Rule of Avoiding Conflict with International Law.* Does your answer to the last question suggest how courts should construe U.S. legislation in light of prior

international agreements? *See Murray v. The Schooner Charming Betsy*, 6 U.S. (2 Cranch) 64, 118 (1804) ("an Act of Congress ought never to be construed to violate the law of nations if any other possible construction remains. . . ."); *Restatement (Third)* §114 ("Where fairly possible, a United States statute is to be construed so as not to conflict with international law or with an international agreement of the United States."). Did the court in *Committee of U.S. Citizens* find that Congress intended to violate the U.N. Charter when it appropriated funds for the Contras?

8. *Force and Effect of Executive Agreements.* The Supremacy Clause explicitly equates only treaties with laws of the United States. Do executive agreements have the same domestic legal effect as treaties? In *United States v. Pink*, 315 U.S. 203, 230 (1942), the Supreme Court declared that a treaty is the law of the land, and that "international compacts and agreements . . . have a similar dignity." While the case law suggests that congressional-executive agreements and agreements made pursuant to treaties have the same legal effect as constitutional treaties, it is less clear about the effect of sole executive agreements on prior statutory or treaty law. *See CRS Treaty Study, supra* p. 164, at 65-68. In *United States v. Guy W. Capps, Inc.*, 204 F.2d 655, 659-660 (4th Cir. 1953), *aff'd on other grounds*, 348 U.S. 296 (1955), the court held that a sole executive agreement concerning import limitations does not supersede a prior statute, citing Congress's express authority to regulate foreign commerce. U.S. Const. art. I, §8, cl. 3. How would you explain the difference in the cases? *Cf. Seery v. United States*, 127 F. Supp. 601 (Ct. Cl. 1955) (asserting that it "would indeed be incongruous if the Executive Department alone, without even the limited participation by Congress which is present when a treaty is ratified, could not only nullify . . . [an Act of Congress], but, by nullifying that Act . . . , destroy the Constitutional right of a citizen.").

In *American Insurance Ass'n v. Garamendi*, 539 U.S. 396 (2003), however, the Supreme Court found that a sole executive agreement preempted state law, asserting as a general proposition that "valid executive agreements are fit to preempt state law, just as treaties are." *Id.* at 416. Some scholars have expressed concern that *Garamendi* was asserting that sole executive agreements can generally alter legal rights and duties of citizens just as treaties can, even though neither the Senate nor Congress as a whole has any role in their making. *See* Bradford R. Clark, *Domesticating Sole Executive Agreements*, 93 Va. L. Rev. 1573, 1661 (2007). Professor Clark argues that sole executive agreements should only be permitted "to override preexisting legal rights . . . when the President has independent authority to do so," *id.* at 1577, as he has to recognize foreign governments, to pardon a foreign national, or to conduct peaceful military exercises with a foreign power. *Id.* at 1660. *See also* Myres S. McDougal & Asher Lans, *Treaties and Congressional-Executive Agreements: Interchangeable Instruments of National Policy: I*, 54 Yale L.J. 181, 317 (1945) (asserting that when a subject is within the President's special competence, he might disregard a prior statute "as an unconstitutional invasion of his own power").

C. STATUTORY INCORPORATION OF INTERNATIONAL LAW

As we have seen, Congress can legislate to fulfill international obligations created by non-self-executing treaties. It can also incorporate customary international law into our own law by codifying the international law in statutes. Congress's role is described with examples in the following excerpt from a case to which we return more fully in the last part of this chapter and in Chapter 30.

Al-Bihani v. Obama

United States Court of Appeals, D.C. Circuit (en banc), 2010
619 F.3d 1, 9

KAVANAUGH, Circuit Judge, concurring in the denial of rehearing en banc: . . . The important role Congress plays in this sphere is apparent from the text of the Constitution, which specifically authorizes Congress to "define and punish . . . Offences against the Law of Nations." *Id.* art. I, §8, cl. 10. The delegates to the Constitutional Convention expressly assigned that power to Congress because, as Gouverneur Morris aptly noted at the Convention, international-law principles are "often too vague and deficient to be a rule" without implementing legislation. 2 The Records of the Federal Convention of 1787, at 615 (Max Farrand ed., rev. ed. 1937); *see also United States v. Smith*, 18 U.S. (5 Wheat.) 153, 159 (1820) (international law "cannot, with any accuracy, be said to be completely ascertained and defined in any public code recognised by the common consent of nations").

Consistent with that constitutionally assigned role, Congress sometimes enacts statutes to codify international-law norms derived from non-self-executing treaties or customary international law, or to fulfill international-law obligations. The Foreign Sovereign Immunities Act of 1976 is a good example of that kind of legislation. The Act governs federal courts' jurisdiction to entertain suits against foreign nations. *See* 28 U.S.C. §§1602-1611. As the Supreme Court has recognized, "one of the primary purposes of the FSIA was to codify . . . extant international law." *Samantar v. Yousuf*, 130 S. Ct. 2278, 2289 (2010). Likewise, the War Crimes Act criminalizes certain conduct—including torture, rape, and hostage-taking—committed in war by or against U.S. nationals or members of the U.S. Armed Forces. The Act provides that this conduct "constitutes a grave breach of common Article 3" of the 1949 Geneva Conventions. *See* 18 U.S.C. §2441(c)(3), (d)(1). Similarly, the Genocide Convention Implementation Act of 1987 criminalizes participation in genocide and thereby implements a non-self-executing treaty to which the United States is a party. *See id.* §§1091-1093; Convention on the Prevention and Punishment of the Crime of Genocide, *adopted* Dec. 9, 1948, S. Treaty Doc. No. 81-15; *see also Demjanjuk v. Meese*, 784 F.2d 1114, 1116 (D.C. Cir. 1986) (Bork, J., in chambers) (Genocide Convention is not self-executing).

Congress also has passed several laws designed to implement certain aspects of the international Convention Against Torture, a non-self-executing treaty to which the United States is a party. *See* Convention Against Torture and Other Cruel, Inhuman or Degrading Treatment or Punishment, *adopted* Dec. 10, 1984, S. Treaty Doc. No. 100-20; *Wang v. Ashcroft*, 320 F.3d 130, 140 (2d Cir. 2003). For example, the Torture Victim Protection Act of 1991 creates a civil cause of action to recover damages for torture committed by foreign officials, "in part to fulfill the Convention's mandate that ratifying nations take action to ensure that torturers are held legally accountable for their actions." *Price v. Socialist People's Libyan Arab Jamahiriya*, 294 F.3d 82, 92 (D.C. Cir. 2002); *see* 18 U.S.C. §1350 note. Likewise, the federal criminal torture statute establishes criminal penalties for U.S. nationals (and non-U.S. persons present in the United States) who commit or conspire to commit torture outside U.S. territory; that statute fulfills U.S. obligations under Articles 4 and 5 of the Convention. 18 U.S.C. §§2340-2340A; *see Renkel v. United States*, 456 F.3d 640, 644 (6th Cir. 2006).

When incorporating international-law norms into domestic U.S. law, Congress sometimes simply enacts statutes that refer generically to "international law" (or some variation thereof) without further defining what international law requires. For example, federal piracy statutes permit the capture and forfeiture of vessels used for, and the imprisonment of individuals who commit, acts of "piracy as defined by the law of nations." 18 U.S.C. §1651; 33 U.S.C. §§384-385; *see Ex parte Quirin*, 317 U.S. 1, 29 (1942). Similarly, Congress has authorized the President to use military force to detain foreign vessels at American ports when such action is permitted "by the law of nations or the treaties of the United States." 22 U.S.C. §462. It has also empowered the President to impose sanctions on foreign countries that use chemical or biological weapons "in violation of international law." *Id.* §§5604-5605. In addition, Article 21 of the Uniform Code of Military Justice allows military commissions to the extent permitted by statute or the "law of war." 10 U.S.C. §821; *see Hamdan v. Rumsfeld*, 548 U.S. 557, 593 (2006) (Congress "preserved what power, under the Constitution and the common law of war, the President had had before 1916 to convene military commissions—with the express condition that the President and those under his command comply with the law of war"). Congress likewise has repeatedly directed Executive agencies to comply with "general" or "generally recognized" "principles of international law" when administering statutes that involve activities in international waters. *See, e.g.*, 10 U.S.C. §113 note (Sunken Military Craft, §1406(b)) (protection of sunken military vessels); 16 U.S.C. §1435(a) (management of national marine sanctuaries); 30 U.S.C. §1421 (issuance of permits for deepwater mining operations); 42 U.S.C. §9119 (issuance of permits for ocean thermal energy conversion facilities)....

NOTES AND QUESTIONS

1. *The Scope of Congress's Power to Define and Punish Offenses Against the Law of Nations.* The Law of Nations Clause has received surprisingly little scholarly or judicial attention despite its express (and textually unique) reference to the Law of Nations. Existing scholarship is said to be divided between the view that it makes all customary international law self-executing against the U.S. government and the view that the Clause makes all such law non-self-executing until Congress has codified it. *See* J. Andrew Kent, *Congress's Under-Appreciated Power to Define and Punish Offenses Against the Law of Nations*, 85 Tex. L. Rev. 843, 848 (2007).

2. *Offenses by States or Just Persons?* Professor Kent argues that the Law of Nations Clause addresses offenses by both individuals and states and therefore gives Congress a "lesser war power" to decide how to respond coercively to violations of international law by other states. *Id.* at 854-855. He also concludes, however, that by vesting this power in Congress, the Clause suggests that courts lack independent authority to entertain suits to punish violators absent legislative action to define the Law of Nations. *Id.* at 856.

D.   THE DOMESTIC LEGAL EFFECT OF CUSTOMARY INTERNATIONAL LAW AND *JUS COGENS*

Committee of U.S. Citizens Living in Nicaragua v. Reagan

United States Court of Appeals, D.C. Circuit, 1988
859 F.2d 929

[The facts of this case are set forth *supra* p. 176.]

MIKVA, J. . . .

3.   Customary International Law and Subsequent Inconsistent Statutes

In addition to relying on Article 94 to challenge continued funding of the Contras, appellants also invoke the rule "of customary international law that nations must obey the rulings of an international court to whose jurisdiction they submit." We accept that some version of this rule describes a norm of customary international law. . . . For the moment, we assume *arguendo* that Congress' decision to disregard the ICJ judgment violates customary international law.

The question is whether such a violation is cognizable by domestic courts. Once again, the United States' rejection of a purely "monist" view of the international and domestic legal orders shapes our analysis. Statutes inconsistent with principles of customary international law may well lead to international law violations. But within the domestic legal realm, that inconsistent statute simply modifies or supersedes customary international law to the extent of the inconsistency. Although the Supreme Court has never articulated this principle as a firm holding, the Court's persuasive dictum in an important early case established the principle that this and other courts follow.

In *The Paquete Habana*, 175 U.S. 677 (1900), the owner of fishing vessels captured and condemned as prize during the Spanish-American War sought compensation from the United States on the ground that customary international law prohibited such seizures. After canvassing prior state practice and the opinions of commentators, the Court concluded that the prohibition against seizure of boats engaged in coastal fishing, which arose at first from considerations of comity between nations, had ripened into "an established rule of international law." Id. at 708. The Court therefore held that the condemnation was improper because "international law is part of our law, and must be ascertained and administered by the courts of justice of appropriate jurisdiction." Id. at 700.

Justice GRAY, writing for the Court, qualified this famous statement about the domestic effect of international law with dictum of no less significance: "[W]here there is no treaty, and no controlling executive *or legislative act* or judicial decision, resort must be had to the customs and usages of nations." Id. (emphasis added). Thus, so far as concerned domestic law, the rule was laid down that subsequently enacted statutes would preempt existing principles of customary international law — just as they displaced prior inconsistent treaties. . . .

Few other courts have had occasion to consider the principle that, under domestic law, statutes supersede customary international law. But the principle is implicit in decisions that uphold the statutory abrogation of treaties, "since violation of a treaty is essentially a violation of the principle of customary international law requiring that treaties be observed." Louis Henkin, Foreign Affairs and the Constitution 460 n.61 (1972). . . .

4. Peremptory Norms of International Law (*Jus Cogens*)

Appellants argue that the rule requiring parties who have submitted to an international court to abide by its judgment is not only a principle of customary international law but has become a form of *jus cogens*. Because such peremptory norms are nonderogable and enjoy the highest status within international law, appellants conclude that these norms are absolutely binding upon our government as a matter of domestic law as well. Indeed, appellants assert that "the obligation stemming from the ICJ judgment . . . is such that it rises to the level of a constitutional obligation, which *cannot* be overridden by statute."

Appellants cite no authority for this assertion that a peremptory norm of international law operates domestically as if it were a part of our Constitution. So far as we know, no federal court has ever considered the concept — much less the domestic effect — of *jus cogens*. The Vienna Convention on the Law of Treaties, which reflects the common understanding of the term, defines *jus cogens* only in relation to *international* law: "A treaty is void if, at the time of its conclusion, it conflicts with a peremptory norm of general international law . . . [which] is a norm accepted by the international community of States as a whole as a norm from which no derogation is permitted. . . ." Vienna Convention on the Law of Treaties, May 23, 1969, art. 53, U.N. Doc. A/Conf. 39/27, 8 I.L.M. 679 (hereinafter "Vienna Convention").

We need not decide whether an ICJ judgment would restrict Congress' foreign affairs power if that judgment were in fact a peremptory norm of international law. ICJ judgments simply do not meet the Vienna Convention's — or any other authority's — definition of *jus cogens*. To see why, it is useful to clarify the criteria that determine when a rule becomes not only a customary but also a peremptory norm of international law.

"Customary international law results from a general and consistent practice of states followed by them from a sense of legal obligation." Restatement (Third) of Foreign Relations Law §102(2) (1987) (hereinafter "*Restatement*"). Thus, customary international law is continually evolving. At a crucial stage of that process, "[w]ithin the relevant states, the will has to be formed that the rule will become law if the relevant number of states who share this will is reached." Meijers, *How Is International Law Made?*, 9 Netherlands Y.B. Intl. L. 3, 5 (1978). As to what constitutes the necessary number of "relevant states," the ICJ has said that "State practice . . . should have been both extensive and virtually uniform in the sense of the provision invoked." *The North Sea Continental Shelf Case (Judgment)*, 1969 I.C.J. 12, 43. Finally, in order for such a customary norm of international law to become a peremptory norm, there must be a further recognition by "the international community . . . *as a whole* [that this is] a norm from which no derogation is permitted." Vienna Convention art. 53 (emphasis added).

Given these standards, it is clear that an ICJ judgment of the sort that was rendered against the United States in the Nicaragua case does not rise to the level of *jus cogens*. . . .

Fewer than a third of the U.N.'s member nations have filed unilateral declarations consenting to compulsory jurisdiction, and many of these have imposed significant reservations on the scope of their consent. More to the point, "[i]n the 1970s and 1980s, the Court's compulsory jurisdiction cases have been beset with non-appearing defendants." One scholar concludes that "States do not yet seem to have reached a stage where they are prepared to submit their disputes to international adjudication." . . . We conclude there is no evidence that an ICJ judgment, in a case of general compulsory jurisdiction, represents "a norm accepted and recognized by the international community of States as a whole as a norm from which no derogation is permitted." Vienna Convention art. 53.

Our conclusion is strengthened when we consider those few norms that arguably do meet the stringent criteria for *jus cogens*. The recently revised *Restatement* acknowledges two categories of such norms: "the principles of the United Nations Charter prohibiting the use of force," *Restatement* §102 comment k, and fundamental human rights law that prohibits genocide, slavery, murder, torture, prolonged arbitrary detention, and racial discrimination. *Id.* §702 & comment n. But see *Restatement* §331 comment e (doctrine of *jus cogens* is of such "uncertain scope" that a "domestic court should not on its own authority refuse to give effect to an agreement on the ground that it violates a peremptory norm").

Such basic norms of international law as the proscription against murder and slavery may well have the domestic legal effect that appellants suggest. That is, they may well restrain our government in the same way that the Constitution restrains it. If Congress adopted a foreign policy that resulted in the enslavement of our citizens or of other individuals, that policy might well be subject to challenge in domestic court under international law. Such a conclusion was indeed implicit in the landmark decision in *Filartiga v.Pena-Irala*, 630 F.2d 876 (2d Cir. 1980), which upheld jurisdiction over a suit by a Paraguayan citizen against a Paraguayan police chief for the death by torture of the plaintiff's brother. The court concluded that "official torture is now prohibited by the law of nations." *Id.* at 884 (footnote omitted). The same point has been echoed in our own court. Judge Edwards observed in *Tel-Oren v. Libyan Arab Republic*, 726 F.2d 774 (D.C. Cir. 1984), *cert. denied*, 470 U.S. 1003 (1985), that "commentators have begun to identify a handful of heinous actions—each of which violates definable, universal and obligatory norms," *id.* at 781 (Edwards, J., concurring), and that these include, at a minimum, bans on governmental "torture, summary execution, genocide, and slavery." *Id.* at 791 n.20.

We think it clear, however, that the harm that results when a government disregards or contravenes an ICJ judgment does not generate the level of universal disapprobation aroused by torture, slavery, summary execution, or genocide. . . . The ICJ judgment does not represent . . . a peremptory norm. . . .

D. Claims Arising under the Fifth Amendment

Appellants' final argument for enforcing the ICJ judgment is that continued funding of the Contras violates appellants' fifth amendment rights. . . .

1. The Fifth Amendment Conjoined with Principles of International Law

Since the Contras' deprivation of appellants' liberty and property is partly funded by the United States government, appellants claim that the government itself has inflicted the deprivation. They further allege that this deprivation "is arbitrary and unreasonable in that it is in violation of Article 94 of the United Nations Charter and is in violation of customary international law as set forth by the ICJ." The allegation of "arbitrary" conduct is crucial to appellants' claim because the "touchstone of [fifth amendment] due process is protection of the individual against arbitrary action of government." *Wolff v. McDonnell*, 418 U.S. 539, 558 (1974).

This attempt to convert putative violations of international law into violations of the fifth amendment suffers several defects. To begin with, since we have already determined that Congress' violation of a treaty is not cognizable in domestic court, we cannot find that activities that Congress has funded are "arbitrary and unreasonable" (and thus proscribed under the fifth amendment) by virtue of being "in violation of Article 94 of the United Nations Charter." Similarly, we have already determined that (1) even if customary international law requires adherence to ICJ judgments, Congress' violation of that law is not domestically cognizable; [and] (2) an ICJ judgment, by its own terms, operates only between the national governments that are parties to that judgment. . . . For these very reasons, we must reject appellants' argument that Congress' funding of the Contras violates the fifth amendment solely because it "is in violation of customary international law as set forth by the ICJ." *Id.*

Even if Congress' contravention of the ICJ judgment were somehow cognizable under the due process clause, such a contravention could not — by itself — transform appellants' injuries into fifth amendment violations. In other words, we disagree with appellants' implicit view that, whenever the government violates a legal norm and that violation coincides with injury to liberty or property interests, a due process violation necessarily results. The standard for what constitutes arbitrary government action under the fifth amendment is by no means so formulaic. Substantive due process doctrine does not protect individuals from all actions that infringe liberty or injure property in violation of some law. Rather, substantive due process prevents "governmental power from being 'used for purposes of oppression,'" *Daniels v. Williams*, 474 U.S. 327, 331 (1986) (citation omitted), or "abuse of government power that shocks the conscience[,]" *Shillingford v. Holmes*, 634 F.2d 263, 265 (5th Cir. 1981), or action that is "legally irrational [in that] it is not sufficiently keyed to any legitimate state interests." *Kindem v. City of Alameda*, 502 F. Supp. 1108, 1113-14 (N.D. Cal. 1980). . . .

The circumstances surrounding Congress' decision to disregard the ICJ judgment foreclose any conclusion that Congress thus acted "arbitrarily" against appellants. The United States fully contested the ICJ's jurisdiction in the Nicaragua conflict, invoking applicable principles of international law. When the U.S. government withdrew from the ICJ proceedings in the merits phase of the case, it did so because of a firmly stated view that (1) Nicaragua had not itself consented to, and therefore could not invoke, ICJ jurisdiction; (2) the dispute with Nicaragua was one involving "armed conflict," collective self-defense and preservation of regional stability, and thus fell outside the ICJ's jurisdiction as set forth in the U.N. Charter and in the ICJ's own precedents; and (3) the United States itself had never consented to jurisdiction over this type of conflict since, by reservation, it had expressly excluded "disputes arising under multilateral treaty" from the scope of its consent. *See* Statement on the U.S. Withdrawal from the Proceedings Initiated by Nicaragua in The International Court of Justice, *reprinted in* 24 I.L.M. 246 (1985). This objection to the ICJ's jurisdiction was followed by the joint determination of Congress and the President that, notwithstanding the recent ICJ decision, continued funding of the Contras was essential to the national security interests of the United States. *See* Military Construction Appropriations Act for Fiscal Year 1987, Pub. L. No. 99-500, §101(k), 100 Stat. 1783, 1783-300 (1986).

The United States' justifications for disregarding the ICJ judgment may or may not pass muster under international law. But as a matter of domestic law, these justifications refute any claim that Congress and the President acted so arbitrarily as to transform the resulting harm to appellants into denials of due process. We do not say that, whenever Congress and the President jointly pursue a foreign policy, the impact on individual citizens will inevitably comport with due process. We merely reject appellants' claim that the government acted "arbitrarily" toward them, in violation of their fifth amendment rights, *solely* because it contravened the ICJ judgment.

Finally, appellants' bid to convert a violation of the ICJ judgment into a violation of the fifth amendment fails because the ICJ judgment involves legal principles entirely unrelated to the due process clause. Appellants allege that the United States has injured its own citizens, a claim that the ICJ never considered. Rather, the ICJ held that the United States breached legal duties running between our nation's government and the government of Nicaragua.... The discrepancy between these principles of international law and appellants' claims that their government has violated their personal rights underscores the defect in appellants' contention that a violation of the ICJ judgment necessarily constitutes "arbitrary" action that violates their fifth amendment rights. For all of these reasons, we hold that the alleged violation of the ICJ judgment is not a sufficient predicate for a fifth amendment violation....

Sosa v. Alvarez-Machain

United States Supreme Court, 2004
542 U.S. 692

Justice SOUTER delivered the opinion of the Court. The two issues are whether respondent Alvarez-Machain's allegation that the Drug Enforcement Administration instigated his abduction [by José Francisco Sosa and others] from Mexico for criminal trial in the United States supports a claim against the Government under the Federal Tort Claims Act (FTCA or Act), 28 U.S.C. §1346(b)(1), §§2671-2680, and whether he may recover under the Alien Tort Statute (ATS), 28 U.S.C. §1350....

[The Court ruled that Alvarez-Machain had no claim under the FTCA. Under the ATS, Alzarez-Machain asserted a cause of action for violation of international law prohibiting arbitrary arrest and detention. The Court held that the ATS only created subject matter jurisdiction, not a cause of action for violation of international law.]

III ...

A ...

But holding the ATS jurisdictional raises a new question, this one about the interaction between the ATS at the time of its enactment and the ambient law of the era. Sosa would have it that the ATS was stillborn because there could be no claim for relief without a further statute expressly authorizing adoption of causes of action. *Amici* professors of federal jurisdiction and legal history take a different tack, that federal courts could entertain claims once the jurisdictional grant was on the books, because torts in violation of the law of nations would have been recognized within the common law of the time. We think history and practice give the edge to this latter position....

2

Before there was any ATS, a distinctly American preoccupation with these hybrid international norms had taken shape owing to the distribution of political power from independence through the period of confederation. The Continental Congress was hamstrung by its inability to "cause infractions of treaties, or of the law of nations to be punished," J. Madison, Journal of the Constitutional Convention 60 (E. Scott ed., 1893)....

The Framers responded by vesting the Supreme Court with original jurisdiction over "all Cases affecting Ambassadors, other public ministers and Consuls." U.S. Const., Art. III, §2, and the First Congress followed through. The Judiciary Act reinforced this Court's original jurisdiction over suits brought by diplomats, see 1 Stat. 80, ch. 20, §13, created alienage jurisdiction, §11 and, of course, included the ATS, §9.

3 ...

The ... inference to be drawn from the history is that Congress intended the ATS to furnish jurisdiction for a relatively modest set of actions alleging violations of the law of nations. Uppermost in the legislative mind appears to have been offenses against ambassadors, see *id.*, at 118; violations of safe conduct were probably understood to be actionable, *ibid.*, and individual actions arising out of prize captures and piracy may well have also been contemplated. *Id.*, at 113-114. But the common law appears to have understood only those three of the hybrid variety as definite and actionable, or at any rate, to have assumed only a very limited set of claims....

IV

We think it is correct, then, to assume that the First Congress understood that the district courts would recognize private causes of action for certain torts in violation of the law of nations, though we have found no basis to suspect Congress had any examples in mind beyond those torts corresponding to Blackstone's three primary offenses: violation of safe conducts, infringement of the rights of ambassadors, and piracy. We assume, too, that no development in the two centuries from the enactment of §1350 to the birth of the modern line of cases beginning with *Filartiga v. Pena-Irala*, 630 F.2d 876 (C.A.2 1980), has categorically precluded federal courts from recognizing a claim under the law of nations as an element of common law; Congress has not in any relevant way amended §1350 or limited civil common law power by another statute. Still, there are good reasons for a restrained conception of the discretion a federal court should exercise in considering a new cause of action of this kind. Accordingly, we think courts should require any claim based on the present-day law of nations to rest on a norm of international character accepted by the civilized world and defined with a specificity comparable to the features of the 18th-century paradigms we have recognized. This requirement is fatal to Alvarez's claim.

A

A series of reasons argue for judicial caution when considering the kinds of individual claims that might implement the jurisdiction conferred by the early statute. First, the prevailing conception of the common law has changed since 1789 in a way that counsels restraint in judicially applying internationally generated norms. When §1350 was enacted, the accepted conception was of the common law as "a transcendental body of law outside of any particular State but obligatory within it unless and until changed by statute." *Black and White Taxicab & Transfer Co. v. Brown and Yellow Taxicab & Transfer Co.*, 276 U.S. 518, 533 (1928) (Holmes, J., dissenting). Now, however, in most cases where a court is asked to state or formulate a common law principle in a new context, there is a general understanding that the law is not so much found or discovered as it is either made or created. . . .

Second, along with, and in part driven by, that conceptual development in understanding common law has come an equally significant rethinking of the role of the federal courts in making it. *Erie R. Co. v. Tompkins*, 304 U.S. 64 (1938), was the watershed in which we denied the existence of any federal "general" common law, which largely withdrew to havens of specialty, some of them defined by express congressional authorization to devise a body of law directly. Elsewhere this Court has thought it was in order to create federal common law rules in interstitial areas of particular federal interest. And although we have even assumed competence to make judicial rules of decision of particular importance to foreign relations, such as the act of state doctrine, the general practice has been to look for legislative guidance before exercising innovative authority over substantive law. It would be remarkable to take a more aggressive role in exercising a jurisdiction that remained largely in shadow for much of the prior two centuries.

Third, this Court has recently and repeatedly said that a decision to create a private right of action is one better left to legislative judgment in the great majority of cases. . . .

Fourth, the subject of those collateral consequences is itself a reason for a high bar to new private causes of action for violating international law, for the potential implications for the foreign relations of the United States of recognizing such causes should make courts particularly wary of impinging on the discretion of the Legislative and Executive Branches in managing foreign affairs. . . . Since many attempts by federal courts to craft remedies for the violation of new norms of international law would raise risks of adverse foreign policy consequences, they should be undertaken, if at all, with great caution. Cf. *Tel-Oren v. Libyan Arab Republic*, 726 F.2d 774, 813 (C.A.D.C.1984) (Bork, J., concurring) (expressing doubt that §1350 should be read to require "our courts [to] sit in judgment of the conduct of foreign officials in their own countries with respect to their own citizens").

The fifth reason is particularly important in light of the first four. We have no congressional mandate to seek out and define new and debatable violations of the law of nations, and modern indications of congressional understanding of the judicial role in the field have not affirmatively encouraged greater judicial creativity. It is true that a clear mandate appears in the Torture Victim Protection Act of 1991, 106 Stat. 73, providing authority that "establish[es] an unambiguous and modern basis for" federal claims of torture and extrajudicial killing, H.R. Rep. No. 102-367, pt. 1, p. 3 (1991). But that affirmative authority is confined to specific subject matter, and although the legislative history includes the remark that §1350 should "remain intact to permit suits based on other norms that already exist or may ripen in the future into rules of customary international law," *id.*, at 4, Congress as a body has done nothing to promote such suits. Several times, indeed, the Senate has expressly declined to give the federal courts the task of interpreting and applying international human rights law, as when its ratification of the International Covenant on Civil and Political Rights declared that the substantive provisions of the document were not self-executing.

B

These reasons argue for great caution in adapting the law of nations to private rights.... Justice Scalia concludes, however, that two subsequent developments should be understood to preclude federal courts from recognizing any further international norms as judicially enforceable today, absent further congressional action. As described before, we now tend to understand common law not as a discoverable reflection of universal reason but, in a positivistic way, as a product of human choice. And we now adhere to a conception of limited judicial power first expressed in reorienting federal diversity jurisdiction, see *Erie R. Co. v. Tompkins*, 304 U.S. 64 (1938), that federal courts have no authority to derive "general" common law.

Whereas Justice Scalia sees these developments as sufficient to close the door to further independent judicial recognition of actionable international norms, other considerations persuade us that the judicial power should be exercised on the understanding that the door is still ajar subject to vigilant doorkeeping, and thus open to a narrow class of international norms today. *Erie* did not in terms bar any judicial recognition of new substantive rules, no matter what the circumstances, and post-*Erie* understanding has identified limited enclaves in which federal courts may derive some substantive law in a common law way. For two centuries we have affirmed that the domestic law of the United States recognizes the law of nations. See, *e.g.*, [*Banco National de Cuba v. Sabbatino*, 376 U.S. 398, 423 (1964)] ("[I]t is, of course, true that United States courts apply international law as a part of our own in appropriate circumstances"); *The Paquete Habana*, 175 U.S. [677, 700 (1900)] ("International law is part of our law, and must be ascertained and administered by the courts of justice of appropriate jurisdiction, as often as questions of right depending upon it are duly presented for their determination"); *The Nereide*, 9 Cranch 388, 423 (1815) (Marshall, C.J.) ("[T]he Court is bound by the law of nations which is a part of the law of the land"); see also *Texas Industries, Inc. v. Radcliff Materials, Inc.*, 451 U.S. 630, 641 (1981) (recognizing that "international disputes implicating ... our relations with foreign nations" are one of the "narrow areas" in which "federal common law" continues to exist). It would take some explaining to say now that federal courts must avert their gaze entirely from any international norm intended to protect individuals.

We think an attempt to justify such a position would be particularly unconvincing in light of what we know about congressional understanding bearing on this issue lying at the intersection of the judicial and legislative powers. The First Congress, which reflected the understanding of the framing generation and included some of the Framers, assumed that federal courts could properly identify some international norms as enforceable in the exercise of §1350 jurisdiction. We think it would be unreasonable to assume that the First Congress would have expected federal courts to lose all capacity to recognize enforceable international norms simply because the common law might lose some metaphysical cachet on the road to modern realism. Later Congresses seem to have shared our view. The position we take today has been assumed by some federal courts for 24 years, ever since the Second Circuit decided *Filartiga v. Pena-Irala*, 630 F.2d 876 (C.A.2 1980) .... Congress, however, has not only expressed no disagreement with our view of the proper exercise of the judicial power, but has responded to its most notable instance by enacting legislation supplementing the judicial determination in some detail. See *supra* (discussing the Torture Victim Protection Act).

While we agree with Justice SCALIA to the point that we would welcome any congressional guidance in exercising jurisdiction with such obvious potential to affect foreign relations, nothing Congress has done is a reason for us to shut the door to the law of nations entirely. It is enough to say that Congress may do that at any time (explicitly, or implicitly by treaties or statutes that occupy the field) just as it may modify or cancel any judicial decision so far as it rests on recognizing an international norm as such.[19]

C

We must still, however, derive a standard or set of standards for assessing the particular claim Alvarez raises, and for this case it suffices to look to the historical antecedents. Whatever the ultimate criteria for accepting a cause of action subject to jurisdiction under §1350, we are persuaded that federal courts should not recognize private claims under federal common law for violations of any international law norm with less definite content and acceptance among civilized nations than the historical paradigms familiar when §1350 was enacted. See, *e.g., United States v. Smith*, 5 Wheat. 153, 163-180 (1820) (illustrating the specificity with which the law of nations defined piracy). This limit upon judicial recognition is generally consistent with the reasoning of many of the courts and judges who faced the issue before it reached this Court. See *Filartiga, supra* at 890 ("[F]or purposes of civil liability, the torturer has become — like the pirate and slave trader before him — *hostis humani generis,* an enemy of all mankind"). And the determination whether a norm is sufficiently definite to support a cause of action should (and, indeed, inevitably must) involve an element of judgment about the practical consequences of making that cause available to litigants in the federal courts.[21]

Thus, Alvarez's detention claim must be gauged against the current state of international law, looking to those sources we have long, albeit cautiously, recognized. . . .

19. Our position does not, as Justice SCALIA suggests, imply that every grant of jurisdiction to a federal court carries with it an opportunity to develop common law (so that the grant of federal-question jurisdiction would be equally as good for our purposes as §1350). Section 1350 was enacted on the congressional understanding that courts would exercise jurisdiction by entertaining some common law claims derived from the law of nations; and we know of no reason to think that federal-question jurisdiction was extended subject to any comparable congressional assumption. Further, our holding today is consistent with the division of responsibilities between federal and state courts after *Erie,* as a more expansive common law power related to 28 U.S.C. §1331 might not be.

21. This requirement of clear definition is not meant to be the only principle limiting the availability of relief in the federal courts for violations of customary international law, though it disposes of this case. For example, the European Commission argues as *amicus curiae* that basic principles of international law require that before asserting a claim in a foreign forum, the claimant must have exhausted any remedies available in the domestic legal system, and perhaps in other fora such as international claims tribunals. We would certainly consider this requirement in an appropriate case.

Another possible limitation that we need not apply here is a policy of case-specific deference to the political branches. For example, there are now pending in federal district court several class actions seeking damages from various corporations alleged to have participated in, or abetted, the regime of apartheid that formerly controlled South Africa. See *In re South African Apartheid Litigation*, 238 F. Supp. 2d 1379 (JPML 2002) (granting a motion to transfer the cases to the Southern District of New York). The Government of South Africa has said that these cases interfere with the policy embodied by its Truth and Reconciliation Commission, which "deliberately avoided a 'victors' justice' approach to the crimes of apartheid and chose instead one based on confession and absolution, informed by the principles of reconciliation, reconstruction, reparation and goodwill." The United States has agreed. In such cases, there is a strong argument that federal courts should give serious weight to the Executive Branch's view of the case's impact on foreign policy.

To begin with, Alvarez cites two well-known international agreements that, despite their moral authority, have little utility under the standard set out in this opinion. He says that his abduction by Sosa was an "arbitrary arrest" within the meaning of the Universal Declaration of Human Rights (Declaration), G.A. Res. 217A (III), U.N. Doc. A/810 (1948). And he traces the rule against arbitrary arrest not only to the Declaration, but also to article nine of the International Covenant on Civil and Political Rights (Covenant), Dec. 19, 1996, 999 U.N.T.S. 171, to which the United States is a party, and to various other conventions to which it is not. But the Declaration does not of its own force impose obligations as a matter of international law. And, although the Covenant does bind the United States as a matter of international law, the United States ratified the Covenant on the express understanding that it was not self-executing and so did not itself create obligations enforceable in the federal courts. Accordingly, Alvarez cannot say that the Declaration and Covenant themselves establish the relevant and applicable rule of international law. He instead attempts to show that prohibition of arbitrary arrest has attained the status of binding customary international law. . . .

Alvarez . . . invokes a general prohibition of "arbitrary" detention defined as officially sanctioned action exceeding positive authorization to detain under the domestic law of some government, regardless of the circumstances. Whether or not this is an accurate reading of the Covenant, Alvarez cites little authority that a rule so broad has the status of a binding customary norm today. He certainly cites nothing to justify the federal courts in taking his broad rule as the predicate for a federal lawsuit, for its implications would be breathtaking. His rule would support a cause of action in federal court for any arrest, anywhere in the world, unauthorized by the law of the jurisdiction in which it took place, and would create a cause of action for any seizure of an alien in violation of the Fourth Amendment, supplanting the actions under Rev. Stat. §1979, 42 U.S.C. §1983 and *Bivens v. Six Unknown Fed. Narcotics Agents,* 403 U.S. 388 (1971), that now provide damages remedies for such violations. . . .

Whatever may be said for the broad principle Alvarez advances, in the present, imperfect world, it expresses an aspiration that exceeds any binding customary rule having the specificity we require. Creating a private cause of action to further that aspiration would go beyond any residual common law discretion we think it appropriate to exercise. It is enough to hold that a single illegal detention of less than a day, followed by the transfer of custody to lawful authorities and a prompt arraignment, violates no norm of customary international law so well defined as to support the creation of a federal remedy.

* * *

The judgment of the Court of Appeals is *Reversed.*

Justice SCALIA, with whom THE CHIEF JUSTICE and JUSTICE THOMAS join, concurring in part and concurring in the judgment. There is not much that I would add to the Court's detailed opinion, and only one thing that I would subtract: its reservation of a discretionary power in the Federal Judiciary to create causes of action for the enforcement of international-law-based norms. Accordingly, I join Parts I, II, and III of the Court's opinion in these consolidated cases. Although I agree with much in Part IV, I cannot join it because the judicial lawmaking role it invites would commit the Federal Judiciary to a task it is neither authorized nor suited to perform. . . .

III

The analysis in the Court's opinion departs from my own in this respect: After concluding in Part III that "the ATS is a jurisdictional statute creating no new causes of action," the Court addresses at length in Part IV the "good reasons for a restrained conception of the *discretion* a federal court should exercise in considering a new cause of action" under the ATS (emphasis added). By framing the issue as one of "discretion," the Court skips over the antecedent question of authority. This neglects the "lesson of *Erie*," that "grants of jurisdiction alone" (which the Court has acknowledged the ATS to be) "are not themselves grants of law-making authority." [Daniel J. Meltzer, *Customary International Law, Foreign Affairs, and Federal Common Law*, 42 Va. J. Int'l L. 513 (2002)], at 541. On this point, the Court observes only that no development between the enactment of the ATS (in 1789) and the birth of modern international human rights litigation under that statute (in 1980) "has categorically *precluded* federal courts from recognizing a claim under the law of nations as an element of common law" (emphasis added). This turns our jurisprudence regarding federal common law on its head. The question is not what case or congressional action *prevents* federal courts from applying the law of nations as part of the general common law; it is what *authorizes* that peculiar exception from *Erie*'s fundamental holding that a general common law *does not exist....*

Because today's federal common law is not our Framers' general common law, the question presented by the suggestion of discretionary authority to enforce the law of nations is not whether to extend old-school general-common-law adjudication. Rather, it is whether to create new federal common law. The Court masks the novelty of its approach when it suggests that the difference between us is that we would "close the door to further independent judicial recognition of actionable international norms," whereas the Court would permit the exercise of judicial power "on the understanding that the door is still ajar subject to vigilant doorkeeping." The general common law was the old door. We do not close that door today, for the deed was done in *Erie*. Federal common law is a *new* door. The question is not whether that door will be left ajar, but whether this Court will open it....

American law—the law made by the people's democratically elected representatives—does not recognize a category of activity that is so universally disapproved by other nations that it is automatically unlawful here, and automatically gives rise to a private action for money damages in federal court. That simple principle is what today's decision should have announced.

[Concurring opinions of GINSBURG and BREYER, JJ., are omitted.]

NOTES AND QUESTIONS

a.   The Making and Incorporation of Customary International Law

1. *The Making of Customary International Law.* How is customary international law made? *See Restatement (Third), supra* p. 171, §102(2) ("Customary international law results from a general and consistent practice of states followed by them from a sense of legal obligation.") (*opinio juris*). *See also* Jordan Paust, *International Law as Law of the*

United States 1-5 (1995); Anthony D'Amato, *The Concept of Custom in International Law* (1971). How does the process compare to the process for making common law? *See* Henkin, *supra* p. 178, at 878-886. To the process for establishing constitutional custom? How, once established, is customary international law changed? *See* Phillip R. Trimble, *A Revisionist View of Customary International Law*, 33 UCLA L. Rev. 665, 710-712 (1986). Notwithstanding the holding of *The Paquete Habana*, some scholars have complained that customary international law is so malleable that it is no more than "a matter of taste, . . . [and] [a]s such, . . . cannot function as a legitimate source of substantive legal norms. . . ." J. Patrick Kelly, *The Twilight of Customary International Law*, 40 Va. J. Int'l L. 449, 451 (2000). *See also* Jack L. Goldsmith & Eric A. Posner, *A Theory of Customary International Law*, 66 U. Chi. L. Rev. 1113 (1999).

2. *Incorporating Customary International Law as a Rule of Decision. The Paquete Habana* holds that "international law is part of our law" and indicates that it includes "the customs and usages of nations," *supra* p. 185. The statements have become virtually hornbook law, as reflected in the *Restatement (Third)* §111 cmt. d ("customary international law, while not mentioned explicitly in the Supremacy Clause, [is] also federal law. . . . Customary international law is considered to be like common law in the United States, but it is federal law."). Anticipating the *Erie* critique of incorporation (voiced by Justice Scalia in *Sosa*) — that federal courts lack the authority to "make" federal common law by incorporation — some scholars have argued that selective incorporation falls squarely within what the Supreme Court called an "enclave" of federal common law-making authority for matters dealing with foreign relations. *See* Michael P. Van Alstine, *Federal Common Law in an Age of Treaties*, 89 Cornell L. Rev. 892 (2004) (citing *Banco Nacional De Cuba v. Sabbatino*, 376 U.S. 398, 426-427 (1964)).

Sosa, of course, dealt strictly with the scope of the ATS — specifically, which international law claims were enforceable under the ATS. But does it cast doubt on the breadth, if not correctness, of the *Restatement*'s statement of the law? Does *Sosa* embrace the view that customary international law is a self-executing part of our law, *see, e.g.*, Ralph G. Steinhardt, *Laying One Bankrupt Critique to Rest: Sosa v. Alvarez-Machain and the Future of International Human Rights Litigation in U.S. Courts*, 57 Vand. L. Rev. 2241 (2004), or does it, more narrowly, address only whether and to what extent a particular statute (the ATS) authorizes application of customary international law as domestic law? *See* Curtis A. Bradley, Jack L. Goldsmith & David H. Moore, *Sosa, Customary International Law, and the Continuing Relevance of Erie*, 120 Harv. L. Rev. 869 (2007).

3. *Enforcing Customary International Law Under the ATS.* Is *Filartiga*, noted in both of the principal cases, still good law after *Sosa*? Would an alien have a claim under the ATS for murder by terrorist attack? For unlawful military detention or abusive military interrogation? For transnational trafficking in women for the purpose of prostitution? If you are not sure, what changes in international law would it take to make these claims actionable under the ATS according to the reasoning of *Sosa*?

b. "Controlling" Executive and Legislative Acts and Judicial Decisions

1. *Controlling Legislative Acts and Customary Law.* As the Supreme Court said in *Murray v. The Schooner Charming Betsy*, 6 U.S. (2 Cranch) 64, 118 (1804), and as

Committee of U.S. Citizens reaffirms, *supra* p. 182, our laws should be construed, where fairly possible, to avoid violating customary, no less than conventional, international law. But if reconciliation proves impossible, which prevails? If the conflict cannot be fairly avoided and customary international law is incorporated into our federal common law, does it necessarily follow that Congress can override it by statute? *See* Henkin, *supra* p. 178, at 876-877 (no). And if Congress can, will any statute do? Did the Court's reference in *The Paquete Habana* to "*controlling . . . legislative act*" (emphasis added) imply that there are some statutes that do not override customary international law? What is the implication of the last-in-time rule, *supra* p. 181, for the domestic effect of customary international law? Because "custom is either constantly reenacted through a process of recognition and behavior involving patterns of expectation and practice or it loses its validity and force as law," is customary law "necessarily 'last in time' "? *See* Paust, *supra* p. 181, at 418, 436-437.

   2. *Controlling Judicial Decisions and Customary Law.* The dictum in *The Paquete Habana* also suggests that controlling judicial decisions can override customary international law. By what theory? Is *Sosa* consistent with this dictum?

   3. *Controlling Executive Acts and Customary Law.* The most controversial implication of the *Paquete Habana* dictum is that a controlling executive act may override customary international law. Consider, first, arguments against this proposition. Can you make one based on the *Charming Betsy* rule of avoidance? If you recast this rule as a presumption of congressional intent that the United States abide by international law, what is the implication for presidential power under Justice Jackson's typology, *supra* p. 44? *See* Jules Lobel, *The Limits of Constitutional Power: Conflicts Between Foreign Policy and International Law*, 71 Va. L. Rev. 1071, 1120 (1985).
   Another argument against the executive power to override customary international law flows from its asserted selective incorporation into the federal common law.

   Federal common law is binding on every executive branch official, including the President. Congress can by statute create a different rule, however, because federal common law is interstitial; it fills in gaps between the statutes and gives way when an inconsistent law is enacted. Consequently, with congressional authorization, the Chief Executive can disregard any norm of customary international law. But in the face of congressional silence, he is required to respect a clearly defined and widely accepted norm of customary international law. [Michael J. Glennon, *Can the President Do No Wrong?*, 80 Am. J. Int'l L. 923 (1986).]

See also Jordan J. Paust, *The President Is Bound by International Law*, 81 Am. J. Int'l L. 377, 388-389 (1987); Michael J. Glennon, *Raising the Paquete Habana: Is Violation of Customary International Law by the Executive Unconstitutional?*, 80 Nw. U. L. Rev. 321 (1986); Lobel, *supra*, at 1078-1090 (tracing historical relationship between common law, natural law, and the law of nations). *Sosa* stresses the very limited common lawmaking authority of the courts. Does the President have any? *See* Henkin, *supra* p. 178, at 879 (no general lawmaking authority). Finally, consider the potential consequences of a U.S. violation of international law. Do they suggest any practical allocation of the power to violate among the three branches? *See* Glennon, *supra*, 80 Nw. U. L. Rev. at 360-361.

The chief argument for executive power to override customary international law is grounded in the process by which new consensus is forged in the international community.

> If a nation or a group of nations seeks to alter an established rule of customary international law, it must forge a new state practice and *opinio juris.* This development does not take place instantaneously; rather it takes time. In order to effect that change, states interested in a new rule of customary law must take action that violates existing law and they must encourage others to do the same....
>
> If customary international law were static, or there were an international legislature capable of changing the law, a required congressional authorization whenever the United States sought to violate international law would be manageable. But in the present system, required congressional approval would place unacceptable obstacles in the way of U.S. participation in the international legal system. The evolution of the community law system would not be amenable to case-by-case authorization by Congress. Just as the international system requires that the President be able to enter into executive agreements and, apparently, to terminate treaties unilaterally, so must the President have the unilateral power to enter into the international lawmaking process. [Jonathan I. Charney, *The Power of the Executive Branch of the United States Government to Violate Customary International Law,* 80 Am. J. Int'l L. 913, 914, 916-917 (1986).]

See also Henkin, *supra* p. 178, at 881-883 (arguing that the President may unilaterally terminate or modify customary international law, and, more problematically, violate such law when his act is "within the confines of his role as sole organ or as commander-in-chief").

Perhaps the debate is beside the point. One scholar observes that the courts "have not yet 'found' a [customary international law] norm contrary to the position of the political branches. When the courts 'find' or apply customary international law, they have normally only done so when one or more of the political branches had clearly endorsed the result." Trimble, *supra,* at 188.

4.   *Who Performs the Controlling Executive Act?* Assuming that a controlling executive act can supersede customary international law, what officer must perform that act? Does *The Paquete Habana* give an answer? *See* Glennon, *supra,* 80 Nw. U. L. Rev. at 338-339. Does Professor Charney's argument for the overriding effect of controlling presidential acts, *supra,* suggest an answer? In *Garcia-Mir v. Meese,* 788 F.2d 1446 (11th Cir.), *cert. denied sub nom. Ferrer-Mazorra v. Meese,* 479 U.S. 889 (1986), the court held that an act of the Attorney General overrode presumed international customary law prohibiting prolonged arbitrary detention, although the court acknowledged that *The Paquete Habana* "suggests that lower level officials cannot by their acts render international law inapplicable." 788 F.2d at 1454.

Recall that courts will not lightly infer a congressional intent to abrogate a treaty. *See Committee of U.S. Citizens, supra* p. 176, 859 F.2d at 936-937. How clear must the *executive* intent be to override customary law? *See* Ralph G. Steinhardt, *Human Rights Litigation and the "One-Voice" Orthodoxy in Foreign Affairs,* in *World Justice? U.S. Courts and International Human Rights* 23, 39 (Mark Gibney ed., 1991) (suggesting that the executive is "oblige[d] at least to overrule a prior position of [international] law specifically and explicitly"). What could be the disadvantages of requiring a clear statement? *See* Charney, *supra,* at 919 ("In the present international system, a state seeking a new rule of customary law justifies its actions by arguing that they are within the law. . . . [N]o state assert[s] that it [is] violating existing law.").

c.   *Jus Cogens*

1.   *Jus Cogens.* What is the difference between customary international law and *jus cogens*? In *Siderman de Blake v. Republic of Argentina*, 965 F.2d 699, 715 (9th Cir. 1992), *cert. denied*, 507 U.S. 1017 (1993), the court explained it as follows:

> Customary international law, like international law defined by treaties and other international agreements, rests on the consent of states. A state that persistently objects to a norm of customary international law . . . is not bound. . . .
>   In contrast, *jus cogens* "embraces customary laws considered binding on all nations" and is "derived from values taken to be fundamental by the international community, rather than from the fortuitous or self-interested choices of nations". . . . [T]he fundamental and universal norms constituting *jus cogens* transcend such consent, as exemplified by the theories underlying the judgments of the Nuremberg tribunals following World War II. [Citation omitted.]

Does this basis for *jus cogens* suggest an answer to the question of primacy in our own law that was reserved in *Committee of U.S. Citizens*? Or does *Sosa*, by implication (emphasizing that Congress intended to authorize claims for piracy under the ATS)?

2.   *Jus Cogens as a Guide to Construction of Constitutional Law.* Even if *jus cogens* is not controlling by its own force, its possible overlap with constitutionally based human rights may give it indirect force as a guide to construction of constitutional law — what might be called "interpretative incorporation." *Cf.* Melissa A. Waters, *Creeping Monism: The Judicial Trend Toward Interpretive Incorporation of Human Rights Treaties*, 107 Colum. L. Rev. 628 (2007) (discussing this effect of non-self-executing human rights treaties like the International Covenant on Civil and Political Rights). Why was the court in *Committee of U.S. Citizens* not persuaded by the customary international law in determining whether the government's action violated due process?

What are the advantages, if any, of using international law in this fashion? *See* Harold Hongju Koh, *Is International Law Really State Law?*, 111 Harv. L. Rev. 1824, 1853 (1998) ("When construing customary international law, federal courts arguably exercise less judicial discretion than when making other kinds of federal common law, as their task is not to create rules willy-nilly, but rather to discern rules of decision from an existing corpus of customary international law rules."); Tamela R. Hughlett, *International Law: The Use of International Law as a Guide to Interpretation of the United States Constitution*, 45 Okla. L. Rev. 169, 180-183 (1992) ("The use of international law is even more compelling than most interpretive methods because it is not the subjective decision of a single judge, but a product of years of distillation of principles formed through international consensus.").

What are the disadvantages? *See* Jonathan Turley, *Dualistic Values in the Age of International Jurisprudence*, 44 Hastings L.J. 185, 185 (1993) (arguing that U.S. rejection of monism reflects a distrust of laws that have not undergone the test of a balanced and checked deliberative process); Trimble, *supra* p. 196, at 708-709, 713-714, 716-725 (arguing that courts lack the institutional capacity to participate fully in the development of customary international law and that application of that law by U.S. courts is illegitimate because it is irreconcilable with American political tradition). *See also* Curtis A. Bradley & Jack L. Goldsmith, *Customary International Law as Federal Common Law: A Critique of the Modern Position*, 110 Harv. L. Rev. 815, 857 (1997) ("the modern position that [customary international law] is federal common law is in tension with basic notions of American representative democracy").

d. The Continuing Incorporation Debate

Some of the questions addressed above were raised again in the following case growing out of the U.S. combat against Al Qaeda and the Taliban in Afghanistan. The case asks whether customary international laws of armed conflict limit or otherwise inform the President's authority under the Authorization for Use of Military Force (AUMF) that authorized the combat.

Al-Bihani v. Obama

United States Court of Appeals, D.C. Circuit (en banc), 2010
619 F.3d 1

[Ghaleb Nassar Al-Bihani is a detainee in the U.S. detention facility at Guantánamo Bay, who served as a brigade cook for a Taliban brigade in combat with U.S.-led coalition forces in Afghanistan during fall 2001. He filed a petition for habeas corpus in the U.S. District Court for the District of Columbia. The court denied his petition, finding that the government had legal authority to detain anyone who was part of or who supported Taliban or Al Qaeda forces or associated forces in hostilities against the United States or its coalition partners.

Al-Bihani appealed, in part on the theory that relying solely on "support" for Al Qaeda or the Taliban as an independent basis for detention violates international law. A panel of the Court of Appeals rejected this argument, asserting that "[t]here is no indication in the AUMF [authorizing combat against Al Qaeda and the Taliban, see *supra* p. 97] that Congress intended the international laws of war to act as extra-textual limiting principles for the President's war powers under the AUMF." *Al-Bihani v. Obama*, 590 F.3d 866, 871 (D.C. Cir. 2010). Unless such laws have been "implemented domestically," it reasoned, international laws of war "are not a source of authority for U.S. Courts." *Id.* Judge Stephen Williams concurred only in part, stating that because the AUMF clearly authorized Al Bihani's detention, there was no need for the panel to pronounce "dictum" about the role of law-of-war limitations in limning the President's authority, which went beyond even the government's arguments in the case.

The panel opinion in *Al-Bihani* is discussed *infra* regarding military detention after 9/11. See Chapter 30. But the panel opinion and Judge Williams's concurring opinion brought new attention to a recent debate among scholars about the incorporation of international law into our law. The debate blossomed in a subsequent decision denying Al-Bihani's petition for rehearing *en banc*. It prompted a 44-page article-length statement by Judge Kavanaugh, concurring in the denial, and a partial rebuttal by Judge Williams. Excerpts follow.]

SENTELLE, Chief Judge, and GINSBURG, HENDERSON, ROGERS, TATEL, GARLAND, and GRIFFITH, Circuit Judges, concurring in the denial of rehearing en banc: We decline to en banc this case to determine the role of international law-of-war principles in interpreting the AUMF because, as the various opinions issued in the case indicate, the panel's discussion of that question is not necessary to the disposition of the merits. *See also* Gov't's Resp. to Pet. for Reh'g and Reh'g En Banc at 1-2 (stating that the dispute over the role of the law of war does not "change[ ] the outcome").

BROWN, Circuit Judge, concurring in the denial of rehearing en banc:...I sense...something more significant than a narrow concern over dictum or deference at work in the seven-member concurrence. There is in the scholarly community an intuition that domestic statutes do not stand on their own authority, but rather rest against the backdrop of international norms. This intuition has taken many argumentative forms, some more emphatic than others. For instance, there are those scholars who believe domestic statutes are merely suggestive wordings to which courts can and should append international legal norms, regardless of congressional intent. Others are more shy, imparting to Congress a general intent to legislate in conformity with international law and therefore reasoning that all statutes, unless containing a clear statement otherwise, should be read by courts to incorporate international legal norms. However this intuition is phrased, perhaps the majority of judges on this court are apprehensive about unambiguously rejecting it. So, even though the panel decision foreclosed the idea, the short concurrence may represent a wish to leave open a possibility — however slight — that domestic statutes are in fact subordinate to an overarching international legal order.

If that is their wish, it is a curious one. The idea that international norms hang over domestic law as a corrective force to be implemented by courts is not only alien to our caselaw, but an aggrandizement of the judicial role beyond the Constitution's conception of the separation of powers. *See United States v. Yunis*, 924 F.2d 1086, 1091 (D.C. Cir.1991) ("[T]he role of judges...is to enforce the Constitution, laws, and treaties of the United States, not to conform the law of the land to norms of customary international law."). That aggrandizement is clear in the more extreme scholarly opinions calling for courts to ignore congressional intent in favor of international norms. And it is only slightly better disguised in the superficially restrained claims that Congress intends to conform its actions with global ideals, and that a clear statement is required if courts are to be prevented from reading international law into statutory text. Traditional clear statement rules are justified on the basis of preserving statutes against possible nullification by a constitutional value, keeping both Congress and the judiciary within their constitutional capacities. However, a demand that Congress clearly enunciate the inapplicability of international norms is not premised on any constitutional value; nothing in the Constitution compels the domestic incorporation of international law. Instead, what such a demand protects is a *policy* preference, imputing to Congress a general posture toward international restrictions and erecting the highest interpretive hurdle to the legitimate prerogative of Congress to legislate apart from them. This is a restrained search for legislative "intent" only in the most Orwellian sense — one that grants judges license to usurp the legislative role and dictate to Congress what it is supposed to think. Surprisingly, proponents of this idea actually claim it guards the separation of powers. But if that is the case, then the cure is truly worse than the disease....

I see much of this scholarly idea in Judge Williams' separate opinion....

This sprint into judicial immodesty cannot be redeemed by Judge Williams' argument that international law parallels traditional tools of statutory interpretation, and that by turning to it for substantive meaning courts are only divining the intent of Congress. I am unaware of *any* federal judicial opinion — and Judge Williams cites none — that has ever before characterized international discourse as a traditional tool of statutory interpretation on par with legislative history, usage in other domestic statutes and cases, or dictionary definitions. The varied process by which international law is made — through treaty, tribunal decision, and the constant churn of state practice and *opinio juris* — shares few, if any, of the qualities that give the traditional sources of interpretation their authority. Courts turn to legislative history because it comes from the mouths of legislators and therefore arguably sheds light on their intentions and understandings. Courts examine the usage of terms in other statutes and judicial decisions because our law is a closed and coherent system that strives for internal consistency. And courts consult dictionaries for the same reason most people do: our law, like the rest of our society, is dependent on language's technical meaning among American English speakers. On none of these grounds can the use of international law be justified. . . .

There is no indication that the AUMF placed any international legal limits on the President's discretion to prosecute the war and, in light of the challenge our nation faced after September 11, 2001, that makes eminent sense. Confronted with a shadowy, non-traditional foe that succeeded in bringing a war to our doorstep by asymmetric means, it was (and still is) unclear how international law applies in all respects to this new context. The prospect is very real that some tradeoffs traditionally struck by the laws of war no longer make sense. That Congress wished the President to retain the discretion to recalibrate the military's strategy and tactics in light of circumstances not contemplated by our international obligations is therefore sensible, and reflects the traditional sovereign prerogative to violate international law or terminate international agreements.

The only way a court could reach the opposite conclusion is to go beyond the AUMF's text, freeing it — as Judge Williams suggests — to appeal to an international meta-narrative, one activated whenever a legal issue touches on matters that strike the judge as transnational in flavor. Judges act prudently when they consciously forego opportunities for policymaking. Therefore, ignoring the text and plain meaning of a statute to privilege a more creative interpretation is the antithesis of prudence. And, in a time of war, it has the inconvenient effect of upending more than a century of our jurisprudence based on an understanding as old as the Republic: that the "conduct of foreign relations of our government is committed by the Constitution to the executive and legislative . . . departments," not to the judiciary. *Oetjen v. Cent. Leather Co.*, 246 U.S. 297, 302 (1918).

The only proper judicial role in this case is the truly modest route taken by the panel opinion in *Al-Bihani*. We read [the AUMF words] "necessary and appropriate" in its traditional sense, taking Congress at its word that the President is to have wide discretion. This is a modest course because the President retains the leeway to implement his authority as broadly or narrowly as he believes appropriate — consistent with international law or not — and the legislature, in turn, may add whatever limits or constraints it deems wise as the war progresses. This ensures that wartime decisions will be informed by the expertise of the political branches, stated in a clear fashion, and that the decisionmakers will be accountable to the electorate.

None of those benefits accrue if the conduct of the military is subject to judicial correction based on norms of international discourse. Such an approach would place ultimate control of the war in the one branch insulated from both the battlefield and the ballot box. That would add further illegitimacy to the unpredictable and ad hoc rules judges would draw from the primordial stew of treaties, state practice, tribunal decisions, scholarly opinion, and foreign law that swirls beyond our borders. It is no comfort to the military to say, as Judge Williams does, that courts will only apply international rules they deem to possess the qualities of serious reason, evenhanded-ness, and practicality. Those are not judicially manageable standards. Those are buzz-words, the pleasing sound of which nearly lulls the mind into missing the vision of judicial supremacy at the heart of Judge Williams' opinion.

KAVANAUGH, Circuit Judge, concurring in the denial of rehearing en banc: ... Al-Bihani's invocation of international law raises two fundamental questions. First, are international-law norms automatically part of domestic U.S. law? Second, even if international-law norms are not automatically part of domestic U.S. law, does the 2001 AUMF incorporate international-law principles as judicially enforceable limits on the President's wartime authority under the AUMF? The answer to both questions is no.

First, international-law norms are not domestic U.S. law in the absence of action by the political branches to codify those norms. Congress and the President can and often do incorporate international-law principles into domestic U.S. law by way of a statute (or executive regulations issued pursuant to statutory authority) or a self-executing treaty. When that happens, the relevant international-law principles become part of the domestic U.S. law that federal courts must enforce, assuming there is a cognizable cause of action and the prerequisites for federal jurisdiction are satisfied. But in light of the Supreme Court's 1938 decision in *Erie Railroad Co. v. Tompkins*, 304 U.S. 64 (1938), which established that there is no federal general common law, international-law norms are not enforceable in federal courts unless the political branches have incor-porated the norms into domestic U.S. law. None of the international-law norms cited by Al-Bihani has been so incorporated into domestic U.S. law.

Second, the 2001 AUMF does not expressly or impliedly incorporate judicially enforceable international-law limits on the President's direction of the war against al Qaeda and the Taliban. In authorizing the President to employ force, the AUMF authorizes the President to command the U.S. military to kill, capture, and detain the enemy, as Commanders in Chief traditionally have done in waging wars throughout American history. Congress enacted the AUMF with knowledge that the U.S. Consti-tution and other federal statutes would limit the President's conduct of the war. But neither the AUMF's text nor contemporaneous statements by Members of Congress suggest that Congress intended to impose judicially enforceable *international-law* limits on the President's authority under the AUMF. . . .

Before proceeding to the analysis of these issues, I emphasize three overarching points about the position advanced in this separate opinion.

First, this opinion recognizes and reinforces the traditional roles of Congress, the President, and the Judiciary in national-security-related matters — roles enduringly articulated in Justice Jackson's separate opinion in *Youngstown Sheet & Tube Co. v. Sawyer*, 343 U.S. 579 (1952). Courts enforce constitutionally permissible constraints imposed *by Congress* on the President's war powers. So, too, courts enforce judicially manageable limits imposed *by the U.S. Constitution* on the President's war powers. But courts may not interfere with the President's exercise of war powers based on international-law norms that the political branches have not seen fit to enact into domestic U.S. law.

Second, the limited authority of *the Judiciary* to rely on international law to restrict the American war effort does not imply that *the political branches* should ignore or disregard international-law norms. The principles of the international laws of war (and of international law more generally) deserve the respect of the United States. Violating international-law norms and breaching international obligations may trigger serious consequences, such as subjecting the United States to sanctions, undermining U.S. standing in the world community, or encouraging retaliation against U.S. personnel abroad. Therefore, Congress and the President are often well-advised to take account of international-law principles when considering potential legislation or treaties. And even when international-law norms have not been incorporated into domestic U.S. law, the Executive Branch, to the extent permissible under its constitutional and statutory authority, is often wise to pay close attention to those norms as a matter of sound policy, international obligation, or effective foreign relations.

But in our constitutional system of separated powers, it is for Congress and the President — not the courts — to determine in the first instance whether and how the United States will meet its international obligations. When Congress and the President have chosen not to incorporate international-law norms into domestic U.S. law, bedrock principles of judicial restraint and separation of powers counsel that courts respect that decision.

Third, consistent with that constitutional division of authority, Congress has enacted a significant body of legislation to prohibit certain wartime actions by the Executive and military that contravene American values. For example, Congress has adopted a detailed and extensive Uniform Code of Military Justice, which governs many aspects of military conduct. *See* 10 U.S.C. §§801-946. Congress also has passed separate laws banning genocide and war crimes, including laws criminalizing grave breaches of the Geneva Conventions (such as rape, torture, and murder). *See, e.g.,* 18 U.S.C. §§1091, 2441. In addition, acting pursuant to congressional authorization, the Executive Branch has promulgated numerous legally binding rules that regulate wartime conduct of the military. *See, e.g.,* Enemy Prisoners of War, Retained Personnel, Civilian Internees and Other Detainees, Army Reg. 190-8, §1-1(b) (Oct. 1, 1997). Those laws, along with many other statutes and regulations, together constitute a comprehensive body of domestic U.S. laws of war.

In his thoughtful opinion in connection with the denial of rehearing, Judge Williams says that it "would be an odd member of Congress who supposed that in authorizing the use of military force he was embracing uses equivalent to *all* such uses that have ever occurred: think Nanking 1937-38; Katyn 1940; Lidice 1942; My Lai 1968." Williams Op. at 54. I agree entirely with Judge Williams on that point, but not because I believe Congress intended for U.S. courts to enforce international-law norms against the Executive. Rather, when Congress authorized war in 2001, it did so knowing that domestic U.S. law already prohibited a variety of improper wartime conduct. Judge Williams' worrisome hypotheticals are thus already taken care of — by the domestic U.S. laws of war — and do not support his suggestion that the AUMF incorporates international-law norms. Notably, Judge Williams points to no examples of violations of international law that would be contrary to fundamental American values but that are not already independently prohibited by domestic U.S. law. There is a good deal of overlap between the international laws of war and domestic U.S. laws regulating war. When there is divergence, however, Congress and the President — not the courts — have the authority in the first instance to decide whether and how to conform U.S. law to international law. . . .

I

Four categories of law are relevant to this case: federal statutes; self-executing treaties made by the President with the concurrence of two-thirds of the Senate; non-self-executing treaties made by the President with the concurrence of two-thirds of the Senate; and customary international law.

Those four categories do not share the same status in U.S. law. As I will explain, statutes and self-executing treaties are domestic U.S. law and thus enforceable in U.S. courts. By contrast, non-self-executing treaties and customary international law are not domestic U.S. law. *See Medellín v. Texas*, 552 U.S. 491 (2008); *Sosa v. Alvarez-Machain*, 542 U.S. 692 (2004). Only when international-law principles are incorporated into a statute or a self-executing treaty do they become domestic U.S. law enforceable in U.S. courts.

In this case, none of the purported international-law principles cited by Al-Bihani has been incorporated into a statute or self-executing treaty. Those principles are therefore not part of the domestic law of the United States and, on their own, do not authorize a U.S. court to order Al-Bihani's release from U.S. military detention.

A...

First, international-law norms may be incorporated into legislation approved by a majority in both Houses of Congress and signed by the President (or enacted over a presidential veto, or by operation of the Constitution's ten-day rule). *See* U.S. Const. art. I, §7....

Second, in addition to being incorporated into a statute (or executive regulation adopted pursuant thereto), international-law principles may become part of domestic U.S. law by means of a self-executing treaty that is made by the President with the concurrence of two-thirds of the Senate. A self-executing treaty is one that "reflect[s] a determination by the President who negotiated it and the Senate that confirmed it that the treaty has domestic effect." *Medellín*, 552 U.S. at 521. By contrast, a treaty is non-self-executing when it "reads like a compact between independent nations that depends for the enforcement of its provisions on the interest and the honor of the governments which are parties to it." *Id.* at 508-09 (quoting *Head Money Cases*, 112 U.S. 580, 598 (1884)) (internal quotation marks omitted)....

B

By contrast, international-law principles found in non-self-executing treaties and customary international law, but not incorporated into statutes or self-executing treaties, are not part of domestic U.S. law.

The Supreme Court has squarely held that non-self-executing treaties "are not domestic law." *Medellín*, 552 U.S. at 505 (quotation omitted). Therefore, "responsibility for transforming an international obligation arising from a non-self-executing treaty into domestic law falls to Congress." *Id.* at 525-26.

The Supreme Court has likewise indicated that customary international law is not automatically part of domestic U.S. law. *See Sosa*, 542 U.S. 692. Customary international law is said to arise from the "general and consistent practice of states followed by them from a sense of legal obligation." Restatement (Third) of Foreign Relations Law of the United States §102(2) (1987). It is a kind of international common law.

It does not result from any of the mechanisms specified in the U.S. Constitution for the creation of U.S. law. For that reason, although norms of customary international law may obligate the United States internationally, they are not part of domestic U.S. law. Customary-international-law norms become part of domestic U.S. law only if the norms are incorporated into a statute or self-executing treaty.

To be sure, there was a time when U.S. courts stated that customary international law was "part of our law" so that "where there is no treaty, and no controlling executive or legislative act or judicial decision, resort must be had to the customs and usages of civilized nations; and, as evidence of these, to the works of jurists and commentators." *The Paquete Habana*, 175 U.S. 677, 700 (1900). But that oft-quoted statement reflected the notion, common in the early years of the Nation but now discredited, that international law was part of the general common law that federal courts could apply. *See Sosa*, 542 U.S. at 714-15; *Erie R.R. Co. v. Tompkins*, 304 U.S. 64, 79 (1938) (historically, the common law was viewed as "a transcendental body of law outside of any particular State but obligatory within it unless and until changed by statute") (quotation omitted).

But as decided by the Supreme Court in its landmark *Erie* decision in 1938, the view that federal courts may ascertain and enforce international-law norms as part of the general common law is fundamentally inconsistent with a proper understanding of the role of the Federal Judiciary in our constitutional system. In *Erie*, the Supreme Court famously held that there is no general common law enforceable by federal courts. *Erie*, 304 U.S. at 78. The Court said that "law in the sense in which courts speak of it today does not exist without some definite authority behind it." *Id.* at 79 (quotation omitted).

Erie means that, in our constitutional system of separated powers, federal courts may not enforce law that lacks a domestic sovereign source. *Erie* "requires federal courts to identify the sovereign source for every rule of decision," and the "appropriate "sovereigns' under the U.S. Constitution are the federal government and the states." [Curtis A. Bradley & Jack L. Goldsmith, *Customary International Law*, 110 Harv. L. Rev. 815, 852 (1997).] . . . .

II

Even though none of the international-law sources Al-Bihani relies on is part of domestic U.S. law, Al-Bihani and amici alternatively argue that courts must nonetheless apply international-law principles in resolving cases under the 2001 Authorization for Use of Military Force, Pub. L. No. 107-40, 115 Stat. 224. In particular, Al-Bihani and amici contend that we should interpret the AUMF as incorporating international-law principles that limit the President's authority under the AUMF to wage war against al Qaeda and the Taliban.

On its face, this is a radical argument. Al-Bihani and amici would have the Federal Judiciary limit the scope of the President's war-making authority — *not* based on the Constitution and *not* based on express language in a statute or self-executing treaty, but rather based on international-law norms that have never been enacted into domestic U.S. law by American lawmakers.

For the reasons set forth at length below, the argument advanced by Al-Bihani and amici lacks merit: Congress has broadly authorized the President to wage war against al Qaeda and the Taliban. Neither the AUMF's text nor its legislative history suggests that Congress intended international-law principles to limit the scope of that congressional authorization. Congress often incorporates international-law princi-ples into federal law; it did not do so here. Courts must respect that decision. Congress has also enacted a vast body of domestic U.S. laws of war. But Congress has provided no indication that it wants courts to freelance and go beyond Congress's direction by imposing international-law limits on the Executive. Moreover, the *Charming Betsy* canon of statutory construction does not authorize courts to read international-law limitations into the authority granted to the President by the AUMF. The Supreme Court's decision in *Hamdi v. Rumsfeld*, 542 U.S. 507 (2004), similarly does not support Al-Bihani's submission....

* * *

To sum up on *Charming Betsy*: The canon exists to the extent it supports applying the presumption against extraterritorial application of federal statutes. Beyond that, after *Erie* and particularly after *Sosa* and *Medellín*, it is not appropriate for courts to use the *Charming Betsy* canon to alter interpretation of federal statutes to conform them to norms found in non-self-executing treaties and customary international law, which Congress has not chosen to incorporate into domestic U.S. law. In the alternative, even if one disagrees with that broader proposition and concludes that use of the *Charming Betsy* canon is appropriate in some such cases, it should not be invoked against the Executive Branch, which has the authority to weigh international-law considerations when interpreting the scope of ambiguous statutes. And even if one also disagrees with that, it is not appropriate for courts to narrow a congressional authorization of war based on international-law norms that are not part of domestic U.S. law....

Williams, Senior Circuit Judge:...Judge Kavanaugh, I think, fails to adequately distinguish between treatment of international law norms as "judicially enforceable limits" on Presidential authority, or as "domestic U.S. law," and use of such norms as a "basis for courts to alter their interpretation of federal statutes." By "alter their interpretation," I take Judge Kavanaugh to mean (as I said above) for a court to allow international law to persuade it to adopt a *narrower* interpretation of the President's authority than it would otherwise have chosen. I will assume that Judge Kavanaugh is correct as to the impropriety of the stronger use of international law (treating it as "domestic law"), but I believe him incorrect on the weaker (allowing it to affect a court's statutory interpretation).

Courts use a wide range of information outside the words of a statute to find those words' meaning. This reflects the simple truth that the question of a word's meaning is an empirical one: what have persons in the relevant community actually meant when using the words that appear in a statute? Among the most obvious out-side sources to resolve that question are legislative history, usage in other laws and in judicial decisions, and dictionaries. Courts use all three incessantly. Dictionaries, of course, are only scholars' claims as to how people have historically used the words in question. Because military conflict is commonly an international phenomenon, words relating to such conflict are used in international discourse, of which interna-tional law is a subset. That international law has a normative element is nothing special; virtually all laws do — yet laws represent widely known public uses of language that legislatures often repackage in novel combinations and contexts. It would be an odd member of Congress who supposed that in authorizing the use of military force he was embracing uses equivalent to *all* such uses that have ever occurred: think Nanking 1937-38; Katyn 1940; Lidice 1942; My Lai 1968. More generally, it seems improbable that in authorizing the use of all "necessary and appropriate force" Congress could have contemplated employment of methods clearly and unequivocally condemned by international law.

Judge Kavanaugh agrees with that conclusion, but argues that we infer such limits on Congress's grant of power simply from penalties or prohibitions in *domestic* law. He is surely correct that this is *one* source for finding limits on an authorization of military force, but that does not make it the only legitimate source of such limits. In some circumstances, Judge Kavanaugh's "domestic U.S. law of war" may have relatively little to say on a question that international practice has addressed for centuries. It obviously seemed so to the Supreme Court in *Hamdi v. Rumsfeld*, 542 U.S. 507, 518-21 (2004), where the plurality looked to international norms on the question of whom the President may detain pursuant to the AUMF, and for how long.

Before *Erie R.R. Co. v. Tompkins*, 304 U.S. 64 1188 (1938), U.S. courts undoubtedly used international law to help resolve cases. It appears to have been uncontroversial for international law to serve not only as a species of federal general common law, binding absent contrary domestic law, but also as a source of interpretive guidance regarding statutes passed by Congress, see, e.g., *Brown v. United States*, 8 Cranch 110, 124-28 (1814) (Marshall, C.J.) (interpreting the domestic legal effects of a U.S. declaration of war in part by reference to international norms, along with constitutional principles and domestic statutes). To dispute that commonsensical understanding, after all, requires defending the unlikely view that international law—unlike other known binding laws—offered no useful information whatsoever regarding the meaning of new laws on similar subjects. In Judge Kavanaugh's view, *Erie* effectively proscribed use of international law as "enforceable" U.S. law. But that landmark case left intact the pre-existing alternative role of international law as a store of information regarding the sense of words Congress enacts into laws governing international matters—a role that never depended on international law's being a form of federal general common law (which *Erie* famously banished). *Erie* hardly requires that every last source of information regarding the meaning of words in statutes be an enacted law; if it does, federal courts have been disobeying its command for more than seven decades.

Even Judge Kavanaugh appears to acknowledge that international law may in some circumstances properly shape a court's interpretation of a federal statute. If I understand him correctly, though, he accepts reliance on international law to *expand* the meaning of a statutory grant of executive authority but never to *contract* it (the benchmark being the reading the court would otherwise have reached). Use of international law as a one-way ratchet seems to me illogical. As Curtis Bradley and Jack Goldsmith put it in *Congressional Authorization and the War on Terrorism*, if the international laws of war "can inform the powers that Congress has implicitly granted to the President in the AUMF, they logically can inform the boundaries of such powers." 118 Harv. L. Rev. 2047, 2094 (2005). To whatever extent the international laws of war shed light on what the AUMF lets the President do, they shed light in all directions, not just one. If international law supports finding a grant of the "X" power (a power that by hypothesis the court would not otherwise have found), it must support some inquiry into what "X" means. . . .

NOTES AND QUESTIONS

1. *Dictum?* Did the AUMF incorporate the customary international laws of armed conflict? If not, do they operate of their own force to limit the President? Or do they

have any other influence on the construction of the scope of the authority vested by the AUMF? How does Judge Kavanaugh answer, and why? How does Judge Williams answer? If the AUMF itself confers all the necessary detention authority, why does it matter what the international law is? Are the statements in *Al-Bihani* about international law dicta or necessary to the judgment?

2. *Changing Perspectives on International Law.* At the start of this chapter, we quoted Chief Justice Jay's charge to a jury that "the laws of the United States admit of being classed under the three heads of descriptions," treaties, statutes, and "the law of nations." Is Judge Kavanaugh's view of the incorporation of international law as our own consistent with this charge?

One explanation for the Framers' apparent greater tolerance for accepting the law of nations as part of our law was practical necessity. The fledgling United States of America, without either a standing army or a navy in the beginning, and surrounded by hostile Indians, the British (with whom we had just had a war and were to have another in 1812), the French (with whom we fought the Naval War), and the Spanish (with whom we eventually went to war a century later), looked to the law of nations as a kind of security—a possible limit on acts against us. More than 200 years later, many say that a robust United States of America, with the world's largest economy and largest military (and the third largest population), no longer needs the law of nations, which is now, irritatingly, often deployed to try to limit *us.*

Might this American exceptionalist view account for hostility to incorporation in our age? If so, is it likely to be a lasting foundation for rejecting "unexecuted" international law? Should it take into account the claim that there are certain moral precepts that are universal? Is it relevant to the incorporation debate that the Declaration of Independence not only started by declaring certain "truths to be self-evident," but also stated that "a decent respect to the opinions of mankind" required them to be declared? Or is what might be called an "internationalist" view both unrealistic and unnecessary, insofar as the United States can formally and democratically incorporate such international laws as are still necessary or desirable?

3. *Just Say No?* In alarmed response to the declared willingness of some Justices of the Supreme Court to consider international law in deciding domestic law issues, a bill was introduced in the House in 2003 declaring that "[t]he Supreme Court should base its decisions on the Constitution and the Laws of the United States, and not on the law of any foreign country or any international law." H.R. 446, 108th Cong. (2003). Do you see any legal issues that would be raised by such a measure? Legal issues aside, would it be a good idea?

4. *Just Say Yes, But.* An alternative to forbidding the consideration of international law in deciding domestic law issues is to discipline the project. Thus, one scholar suggests four guidelines. First, there must be a neutral theory as to which international law materials are relevant and how they are used. Second, we must take the "bitter with the sweet," using the materials evenhandedly to constrict as well as enlarge domestic rights. Third, we must "get the facts right" by rigorously identifying actual international practices. Fourth, we must eschew "shortcuts" by reliance on "unrepresentative proxies such as United Nations agencies." Michael D. Ramsey, *International Materials and Domestic Rights: Reflections on Atkins and Lawrence*, 98 Am. J. Int'l L. 69, 69-70 (2004). Isn't the first guideline the whole game?

8

The Right to Wage War (jus ad bellum)

On June 26, 1945, world leaders gathered in San Francisco to sign the Charter of the United Nations. The agony of the world's greatest armed conflict was fresh in their minds. The fighting in Europe had just ended, but the U.S. atomic bombings of Hiroshima and Nagasaki, as well as a peace treaty with Japan, still lay in the future. This searing experience inspired a declaration that the first purpose of the newly formed organization was

> [t]o maintain international peace and security, and to that end: to take effective control measures for the prevention and removal of threats to the peace, and for the suppression of acts of aggression or other breaches of the peace, and to bring about by peaceful means, and in conformity with the principles of justice and international law, adjustment or settlement of international disputes or situations which might lead to a breach of the peace. [U.N. Charter art. 1, para. 1.]

The core principle for implementation of this resolution was set forth in Article 2, paragraph 4, of the Charter, which declares: "All Members shall refrain in their international relations from the threat or use of force against the territorial integrity or political independence of any state, or in any other manner inconsistent with the Purposes of the United Nations."

The U.N. Charter is only the latest in a long series of efforts to avoid the scourge of war, extending at least as far back as Biblical times. In between, theologians and jurists from St. Augustine to Hugo Grotius, among many others, developed a theory of a "just war." In 1919, Article 10 of the Covenant of the League of Nations called for states to "respect and preserve as against external aggression the territorial integrity and political independence of all Members of the League." Then in the General Treaty for the Renunciation of War as an Instrument of National Policy (Kellogg-Briand Pact), Aug. 27, 1928, 94 L.N.T.S. 57, the parties declared that they "condemn recourse to war for the solution to international controversies," and agreed that settlement of disputes "shall never be sought except by pacific means." *See generally* Ian Brownlie, *International Law and the Use of Force by States* 3-111 (1963); Yoram Dinstein, *War, Aggression, and Self-Defense* 63-85 (4th ed. 2005).

The tragic history of the world shows, however, that these efforts to preserve the peace have so far achieved only limited success. Yet they have profoundly affected the development of a part of the international law of armed conflict that we refer to as *jus ad bellum*— Latin for "the right to wage war." That law was codified to some degree by the U.N. Charter in 1945, and it has since been shaped by the Charter, as we see in this chapter.

A related, parallel body of law, *jus in bello*, is concerned with the conduct of war once it has begun. Also referred to as the law of war, the law of armed conflict, or international humanitarian law, its purpose is to limit the suffering of combatants and noncombatants alike to what is necessary to achieve the legitimate political goals of a conflict. Principles of *jus in bello* are introduced in the next chapter.

In Part A of this chapter we look at some of the main structural elements of the modern *jus ad bellum*, as spelled out in the U.N. Charter. Then in Part B we review a historic 1986 World Court decision, the *Nicaragua Case*, that supplies content not only to the law of the Charter, but also to customary norms that both inspired and were inspired by the Charter. The principles introduced and analyzed here play a central role in the relations of the United States with the rest of the world, and they strongly inform much of national security law, as we see in later chapters.

A. LAW REGARDING RESORT TO THE USE OF FORCE: THE BASIC ELEMENTS

1. The United Nations Charter: Making War to Preserve or Restore Peace

The central tenet of the U.N. Charter is Article 2(4), which forbids the "threat or use of force against the territorial integrity or political independence of any state." It reflects the highest ideal of the signing states. It is mirrored in Article 2(3) by a commitment that "[a]ll Members shall settle their international disputes by peaceful means in such a manner that international peace and security, and justice, are not endangered." But the signers of the Charter were students of history, and they understood that despite such high-minded declarations conflicts would erupt into violence in the future. They therefore adopted two carefully tailored, narrow exceptions to this foundational prohibition. These exceptions are designed to ward off breaches of the peace or to restore peace if fighting breaks out.

One exception concerns the Security Council, to which the Charter gives "primary responsibility for the maintenance of international peace and security." Art. 42(1). The Security Council is a political body with five permanent members, each of which has veto power (China, France, Russia, the United Kingdom, and the United States), and ten non-permanent, elected members. Acting entirely on its own initiative, the Security Council may approve the use of force when it determines the existence of a threat to the peace, a breach of the peace, or an act of aggression. Member states have agreed in Article 25 to "accept and carry out the decisions of the Security Council."

U.N. Security Council.

U.N. photo by Devra Berkowitz.

The other recognized exception to the Article 2(4) ban on the use of force allows one nation to defend itself from an armed attack by another, or to come to the aid of another state that is attacked — at least for a time. But the Security Council also has an important role to play in the exercise of this "inherent right of individual or collective self-defense." Both exceptions are outlined in the Charter provisions set forth below.

Charter of the United Nations

June 26, 1945, 59 Stat. 1031, T.S. No. 993

CHAPTER VII. ACTION WITH RESPECT TO THREATS TO THE PEACE, BREACHES OF THE PEACE, AND ACTS OF AGGRESSION

Article 39

The Security Council shall determine the existence of any threat to the peace, breach of the peace, or act of aggression and shall make recommendations, or decide what measures shall be taken in accordance with Articles 41 and 42, to maintain and restore international peace and security.

Article 40

In order to prevent an aggravation of the situation, the Security Council may, before making the recommendations or deciding upon the measures provided for in Article 39, call upon the parties concerned to comply with such provisional measures as it deems necessary or desirable. Such provisional measures shall be without prejudice to the rights, claims, or position of the parties concerned. The Security Council shall duly take account of failure to comply with such provisional measures.

Article 41

The Security Council may decide what measures not involving the use of armed force are to be employed to give effect to its decisions, and it may call upon the Members of the United Nations to apply such measures. These may include complete or partial interruption of economic relations and of rail, sea, air, postal, telegraphic, radio, and other means of communication, and the severance of diplomatic relations.

Article 42

Should the Security Council consider that measures provided for in Article 41 would be inadequate or have proved to be inadequate, it may take such action by air, sea, or land forces as may be necessary to maintain or restore international peace and security. Such actions may include demonstrations, blockade, and other operations by air, sea, or land forces of Members of the United Nations.

Article 43

1. All Members of the United Nations, in order to contribute to the maintenance of international peace and security, undertake to make available to the Security Council, on its call and in accordance with a special agreement or agreements, armed forces, assistance, and facilities, including rights of passage, necessary for the purpose of maintaining international peace and security.

2. Such agreement or agreements shall govern the numbers and types of forces, their degree of readiness and general location, and the nature of the facilities and assistance to be provided.

3. The agreement or agreements shall be negotiated as soon as possible on the initiative of the Security Council. They shall be concluded between the Security Council and Members or between the Security Council and groups of Members and shall be subject to ratification by the signatory states in accordance with their respective constitutional processes. . . .

Article 51

Nothing in the present charter shall impair the inherent right of individual and collective self-defense if an armed attack occurs against a Member of the United Nations, until the Security Council has taken measures necessary to maintain international peace and security. Measures taken by Members in the exercise of this right of self-defense shall be immediately reported to the Security Council and shall not in any way affect the authority and responsibility of the Security Council under the present Charter to take at any time such action as it deems necessary in order to maintain or restore international peace and security.

NOTES AND QUESTIONS

1. *The Need for Security Council Approval.* Recognizing the provisions of Chapter VII of the U.N. Charter as exceptional, can you describe the sequence of events that might provoke the invocation of each respective article, from Article 39 to Article 42, leading to eventual authorization for the use of military force? Do you think an individual state or group of states might find it extremely inconvenient, even dangerous, to have to persuade a majority of the U.N. Security Council members to authorize such use (and to persuade all of the permanent members not to veto it)? Can you imagine why every member state agreed to abide by these provisions?

The Security Council has invoked Chapter VII to approve the use of force a number of times. Chapter 12 includes case studies involving reliance on such approval in the Korean War, the 1991 Persian Gulf War, and the ongoing war in Afghanistan. In Chapter 13, we analyze the war in Iraq that began in 2003, for which clear Security Council approval was not obtained. And in Chapter 15 we consider the effect of Security Council approval for humanitarian missions in Somalia in 1992 and Libya in 2011.

   2. *Article 42: Actions "It May Take."* Since the signing of the U.N. Charter in 1945, not a single Article 43 agreement has been signed.

> The tensions of the Cold War soon eclipsed efforts to negotiate any special agreements, leaving the Security Council dependent on the willingness of member states to provide troops on an ad hoc basis. Moreover, with the notable exception of Korea, superpower disagreement essentially barred the United Nations from authorizing collective military action in response to acts of aggression — until the Persian Gulf War following Iraq's invasion of Kuwait in August 1990. Instead, during the Cold War, the United Nations developed a more limited capacity for responding to conflict, namely, consensual deployment of "peacekeeping" forces to perform tasks such as monitoring ceasefires and observing the demobilization of opposing forces. [Jane E. Stromseth, *Rethinking War Powers: Congress, the President, and the United Nations*, 81 Geo. L.J. 597, 598-599 (1993).]

Indeed, until 1990 the Security Council determined the existence of a breach of the peace on only three occasions — the Korean War in 1950, the Falkland Islands War in 1982, and the Iran-Iraq War in 1987 — and threats to the peace another three times. And it approved the use of force in response only once, in Korea, when the Soviets were boycotting the Security Council, and then only to "recommend" that member states assist South Korea in repelling the attack from the North. (Excluded from consideration here is approval of numerous so-called "peacekeeping" deployments, analyzed in Chapter 15.) Otherwise, the exercise or threat of a veto by one of the permanent members, often for reasons having nothing to do with collective security, prevented the Security Council from playing the peacemaking role envisioned for it by the signers of the U.N. Charter. The same political tensions that paralyzed the Security Council prevented the conclusion of any Article 43 agreements. *See* Dinstein, *supra* p. 210, at 292-294; *see also* Frederic L. Kirgis Jr., *The Security Council's First Fifty Years*, 89 Am. J. Int'l L. 506, 512 (1995).

   According to one view, "the central idea of a globally sanctioned police action was never abandoned; . . . the failure to implement Article 43 merely led to organic growth and the alternative creation of police action through Article 42, which does not require special agreements." Thomas M. Franck & Faiza Patel, *UN Police Action in Lieu of War: "The Old Order Changeth,"* 85 Am. J. Int'l L. 63, 66 (1991). Does the language of Article 42 support this reading of it? Or is the Article 42 provision for the use of force by the Security Council necessarily qualified by Article 43? *See* Michael J. Glennon, *The Constitution and Article VII of the United Nations Charter*, 85 Am. J. Int'l L. 74, 77-80 (1991) (citing extensive evidence that the use of force under Article 42 was understood to be dependent on the existence of an Article 43 agreement); Stromseth, *supra*, at 612-614 (same); Dinstein, *supra*, at 304-305 (same).

   A different reading of history holds that in the absence of Article 43 agreements to create a standby military force for deployment under Article 42, the Security Council has come to rely instead on voluntary contributions of forces by member states in response to "recommendations" or "authorizations" under Article 39 — or more generally under Chapter VII. *See* Dinstein, *supra*, at 310.

   Recall that Article 25 obliges member states to "accept and carry out the decisions of the Security Council in accordance with the present Charter." Article 48(1) also provides: "The action required to carry out the decisions of the Security Council for the maintenance of international peace and security shall be taken by all the Members of the United Nations or by some of them, as the Security Council may determine." Article 49 directs states to provide mutual assistance in carrying out "measures decided upon by the Security Council." Does it matter under which provision of the Charter the Security Council acts?

3. *Individual and Collective Self-Defense.* The use of force may be permissible without Security Council approval, at least for a time, as an exercise of every state's inherent right of individual or collective self-defense, as set forth in Article 51. Some commentators argue that Article 51 was meant to replace traditional self-help measures, providing for an immediate response to aggression until — but only until — the Security Council has had time to act. *See* Franck & Patel, *supra*, at 64. Others maintain that Article 51 simply restates the right of individual and collective self-defense that is inherent in sovereignty, and that this right remains intact until the Security Council has dealt *successfully* with an international conflict. Eugene V. Rostow, *Until What? Enforcement Action or Collective Self-Defense?*, 85 Am. J. Int'l L. 506, 511 (1991). Can you tell from the text what was intended? Can you see practical difficulties with each claimed meaning?

Article 51 conditions the use of force in self-defense without Security Council approval on the existence of an "armed attack," whereas the Security Council may authorize the use of force if it determines the existence of "any threat to the peace, breach of the peace, or act of aggression," a potentially much lower standard. What accounts for the difference? *See* Dinstein, *supra*, at 283-289.

4. *Military Actions Without Security Council Approval.* Suppose a state or group of states decides that a development somewhere in the world requires the use of military force. Suppose further that efforts to secure the approval of the U.N. Security Council are unsuccessful or that the Security Council's response is ambiguous. Does the U.N. Charter permit such use of force without clear approval from the Security Council? These questions are squarely presented by NATO's bombing of the Federal Republic of Yugoslavia in 1999, noted *infra* p. 342, *see* Sean D. Murphy, *Legal Regulation of the Use of Force*, 93 Am J. Int'l L. 628 (1999); and by the March 2003 invasion of Iraq by the United States and its coalition partners. See *infra* pp. 354-367.

2. The Role of the United States Under Chapter VII

In 1945, during debate on the United Nations Charter, some Senators argued for a reservation to the Charter that would have allowed Congress to approve or reject each use of American armed forces under an Article 43 special agreement. Otherwise, they insisted, the Charter represented an unconstitutional delegation of war-making authority to the U.N. Security Council. But two-thirds of the Senate were persuaded to approve the Charter without reservation, partly on grounds that (1) Congress would have an opportunity to approve the terms of any special agreement, and (2) the United States could veto any Security Council resolution invoking the special agreement. *See* Stromseth, *supra*, at 604-612.

Within months of ratification of the Charter, however, Congress undertook to spell out more clearly the respective roles of the executive and legislative branches in fulfilling U.S. obligations under Chapter VII. The United Nations Participation Act, 22 U.S.C. §§287 to 287e-3 (2006), as amended by Pub. L. No. 111-195, §107(a)(1), 124 Stat. 1312, 1337 (2010), instructs U.S. representatives at the United Nations to vote in accordance with instructions from the President, and it directs the President to report any Security Council enforcement actions to the Congress. It also authorizes the President to implement any economic sanctions approved by the Security Council. Concerning the deployment of U.S. military forces pursuant to a resolution of the Security Council under Article 42, the Act provides as follows:

United Nations Participation Act
22 U.S.C. §§287 to 287e-2 (2006)

§287D. USE OF ARMED FORCES; LIMITATIONS

The President is authorized to negotiate a special agreement or agreements with the Security Council which shall be subject to the approval of the Congress by appropriate Act or joint resolution, providing for the numbers and types of armed forces, their degree of readiness and general location, and the nature of facilities and assistance, including rights of passage, to be made available to the Security Council on its call for the purpose of maintaining international peace and security in accordance with article 43 of said Charter. The President shall not be deemed to require the authorization of the Congress to make available to the Security Council on its call in order to take action under article 42 of said Charter and pursuant to such special agreement or agreements the armed forces, facilities, or assistance provided for therein: Provided, That, except as authorized in section 287d-1 of this title [referring to noncombatant assistance to the United Nations, see *infra* p. 419], nothing herein contained shall be construed as an authorization to the President by the Congress to make available to the Security Council for such purpose armed forces, facilities, or assistance in addition to the forces, facilities, and assistance provided for in such special agreement or agreements.

NOTES AND QUESTIONS

1. *The U.N. Charter as U.S. Law?* Article 2(5) of the United Nations Charter provides that "[a]ll Members shall give the United Nations every assistance in any action it takes in accordance with the present Charter." Article 25 provides that "Members of the United Nations agree to accept and carry out the decisions of the Security Council. . . ." Articles 48 and 49 contain similar commitments, as noted above. As a treaty approved by the Senate, the U.N. Charter is part of the "Law of the Land" under Article VI of the U.S. Constitution. Is the President not therefore empowered — indeed obliged — to "execute" the terms of the Charter, just as he would any other law under the Take Care Clause, by enforcing resolutions of the Security Council? How do you think the Framers of the Constitution would have answered? *See generally* Chapter 2; James A.R. Nafziger & Edward M. Wise, *The Status in United States Law of Security Council Resolutions Under Chapter VII of the United Nations*

Charter, 46 Am. J. Comp. L. 421 (1998). One leading scholar responded this way: "The President and the Senate cannot use the treaty procedure to strip the House of Representatives of its prerogatives over the use of military force." Louis Fisher, *Side-stepping Congress: Presidents Acting Under the U.N. and NATO*, 47 Case W. Res. L. Rev. 1237, 1256 (1997).

2. *Effect of the United Nations Participation Act.* What was the effect, if any, of the United Nations Participation Act on the President's domestic authority to send U.S. military forces into battle pursuant to a Security Council mandate, but without the approval of Congress? What does the timing of its passage suggest? Would your answer be affected by the provisions of the Charter under which the Security Council purported to act? According to one commentator, "the President could not, by an affirmative vote in the Security Council, confer upon himself power to use armed force that he would not otherwise possess. The text of the UNPA [United Nations Participation Act] makes that clear, as does a review of its legislative history." Glennon, *supra* p. 214, at 78. *See also* Fisher, *supra*, 47 Case W. Res. L. Rev. at 1249-1254. A dramatically different reading of the same history may be found in Robert F. Turner, *Truman, Korea, and the Constitution: Debunking the "Imperial President" Myth*, 19 Harv. J.L. & Pub. Pol'y 533 (1996).

3. *Categorizing Uses of U.S. Troops.* During debate on approval of the U.N. Charter, the Senate was persuaded that special agreement forces would be used only in a "police action" of such limited scope and duration that it would not constitute a "war" in either an international or constitutional sense. Secretary of State John Foster Dulles testified that Congress's war powers would not be implicated if "we are talking about a little bit of force to be used as a police demonstration. . . . [But] if this is going to be a large volume of force which is going to put a big drain on the resources of the United States or commit us to great and costly adventures, then the Congress ought to have a voice in this matter." *The Charter of the United Nations: Hearings Before the Senate Committee on Foreign Relations*, 79th Cong. 655 (1945), *quoted in* Stromseth, *supra*, at 609. Can this explanation be squared with the text of the Constitution or with your understanding of the Framers' intent? Others argued that a police action would not be war for constitutional purposes because small-scale forces had historically been deployed by U.S. presidents without congressional authorization "to protect American citizens abroad, to prevent an invasion of the territory, or to suppress insurrection." Memorandum by John W. Davis, Phillip C. Jessup & Quincy Wright, *reprinted in* 91 Cong. Rec. 8065, 8066, 79th Cong. (1945). Do such deployments furnish a precedent for U.N.-mounted police actions?

Can you define "police action"? If your answer is that it is "not a war," are you prepared to say what a "war" is? Is the Supreme Court's definition of war in *The Prize Cases*, *supra* p. 68 ("that state in which a nation prosecutes its right by force"), hopelessly outdated for this purpose? *See generally* Peter Raven-Hansen, *Constitutional Constraints: The War Clause*, in *The U.S. Constitution and the Power to Go to War* 40-41 (Gary M. Stern & Morton H. Halperin eds., 1993). However the terms are defined, would Congress need to be consulted if a conflict in which U.S. forces were deployed escalated from "police action" to "war"? If the labels are important, who should be able to make an authoritative pronouncement about the character of a particular conflict?

B.   CONTENT OF *JUS AD BELLUM*

The historic 1986 decision of the International Court of Justice (World Court) excerpted below offers valuable insights into both the meaning of the United Nations Charter and the content of customary international law concerning the aggressive use of force by states. Because the decision is very long and complex, we have edited it extensively here, occasionally summarizing detailed explanations. We have also inserted section headings in outline form, lacking in the original, to help keep the issues straight.

Case Concerning Military and Paramilitary Activities in and Against Nicaragua (Nicaragua v. United States of America)

International Court of Justice, 1986
1986 I.C.J. 14

[In 1984 Nicaragua filed an application with the Court asserting that the United States was engaged in aggression against it, in violation of Article 2(4) of the United Nations Charter, other treaty obligations, and customary international norms. Specifically, it alleged (1) that U.S. forces had carried out direct armed attacks against Nicaragua by air, land, and sea; and (2) that the United States had recruited, trained, armed, equipped, financed, and directed paramilitary actions in and against Nicaragua by a group known as Contras. Nicaragua sought an order from the Court to stop the aggression and pay compensation.

The dispute between Nicaragua and the United States began with the fall of President Anastasio Somoza Debayle in Nicaragua in July 1979. A junta led by the Frente Sandinista de Liberacion Nacional (Sandinistas) took over the government. Opponents of the new regime, mainly former supporters of Somoza, in particular ex-members of the National Guard, formed themselves into irregular military forces and began an armed opposition.

In 1981, partly in response to reports that the Sandinistas were supplying arms and other logistical support to guerrillas in El Salvador, the Reagan administration began covert aid to the Contras. This aid was later publicly acknowledged in official statements by the President and high United States officials, and in a 1983 budget resolution Congress provided funds for U.S. intelligence agencies to support "directly or indirectly, military or paramilitary operations in Nicaragua." (The Reagan administration's efforts to oust the Sandinista regime in Nicaragua led to the Iran-Contra Affair, analyzed *infra* pp. 488-503.)]

MERITS...

[I.   THE COURT'S JURISDICTION]

[The United States asserted that the Court lacked jurisdiction to act on Nicaragua's application. The United States had earlier consented to the compulsory adjudication of disputes by the Court under Article 36(2) of the Statute of the International Court of Justice. But the U.S consent included a reservation providing that the Court's compulsory jurisdiction would not extend to "disputes arising under a multilateral treaty, unless (1) all parties to the treaty affected by the decision are also parties to the case before the Court, or (2) the United States of America specially agrees to jurisdiction." Because neither of those conditions was satisfied, the Court decided in a separate, preliminary ruling that it was indeed barred from deciding on U.S. compliance with the Charter of the United Nations, a multilateral treaty. But it decided that it was authorized to rule on questions of customary international law. 1984 I.C.J. 392 (Nov. 26). The United States then announced that it would not participate further in the case. The United States had, however, already addressed many of Nicaragua's assertions in its pleadings on jurisdiction. The U.S. arguments are referred to in the opinion below.]

[II. ESTABLISHED FACTS]

106. . . . [I]t is in the Court's view established that the support of the United States authorities for the activities of the contras took various forms over the years, such as logistic support, the supply of information on the location and movements of the Sandinista troops, the use of sophisticated methods of communication, the deployment of field broadcasting networks, radar coverage, etc. The Court finds it clear that a number of military and paramilitary operations by this force were decided and planned, if not actually by United States advisers, then at least in close collaboration with them, and on the basis of the intelligence and logistic support which the United States was able to offer, particularly the supply aircraft provided to the contras by the United States. . . .

108. . . . [T[he evidence [does not, however,] warrant a finding that the United States gave "direct and critical combat support," at least if that form of words is taken to mean that this support was tantamount to direct intervention by the United States combat forces, or that all contra operations reflected strategy and tactics wholly devised by the United States. . . .

109. . . . [D]espite the heavy subsidies and other support provided to them by the United States, there is no clear evidence of the United States having actually exercised such a degree of control in all fields as to justify treating the contras as acting on its behalf.

110. . . . The Court [is] unable to determine that the contra force may be equated for legal purposes with the forces of the United States. This conclusion, however, does not of course suffice to resolve the entire question of the responsibility incurred by the United States through its assistance to the contras.

111. In the view of the Court it is established that the contra force has, at least at one period, been so dependent on the United States that it could not conduct its crucial or most significant military and paramilitary activities without the multi-faceted support of the United States. This finding is fundamental in the present case. . . .

126. The Court has before it, in the Counter-Memorial on jurisdiction and admissibility filed by the United States, the assertion that the United States, pursuant to the inherent right of individual and collective self-defence, . . . has responded to requests from El Salvador . . . for assistance in [its] self-defence against aggression by Nicaragua. . . .

127. Nicaragua claims that the references made by the United States to the justification of collective self-defence are merely "pretexts" for the activities of the

United States. It has alleged that the true motive for the conduct of the United States is unrelated to the support which it accuses Nicaragua of giving to the armed opposition in El Salvador, and that the real objectives of United States policy are to impose its will upon Nicaragua and force it to comply with United States demands. In the Court's view, however, if Nicaragua has been giving support to the armed opposition in El Salvador, and if this constitutes an armed attack on El Salvador and the other appropriate conditions are met, collective self-defence could be legally invoked by the United States, even though there may be the possibility of an additional motive, one perhaps even more decisive for the United States, drawn from the political orientation of the present Nicaraguan Government. The existence of an additional motive, other than that officially proclaimed by the United States, could not deprive the latter of its right to resort to collective self-defence....

160. ... [T]he Court is satisfied that, between July 1979, the date of the fall of the Somoza regime in Nicaragua, and the early months of 1981, an intermittent flow of arms was routed via the territory of Nicaragua to the armed opposition in El Salvador. On the other hand, the evidence is insufficient to satisfy the Court that, since the early months of 1981, assistance has continued to reach the Salvadorian armed opposition from the territory of Nicaragua on any significant scale, or that the Government of Nicaragua was responsible for any flow of arms at either period....

[III.   APPLICABLE LAW]

[A.   U.N. Charter vs. Customary International Law]

173. ... The United States contends that the only general and customary international law on which Nicaragua can base its claims is that of the Charter: in particular, the Court could not, it is said, consider the lawfulness of an alleged use of armed force without referring to the "principal source of the relevant international law," namely, Article 2, paragraph 4, of the United Nations Charter. In brief, in a more general sense "the provisions of the United Nations Charter relevant here subsume and supervene related principles of customary and general international law." The United States concludes that "since the multilateral treaty reservation bars adjudication of claims based on those treaties, it bars all of Nicaragua's claims." Thus the effect of the reservation in question is not, it is said, merely to prevent the Court from deciding upon Nicaragua's claims by applying the multilateral treaties in question; it further prevents it from applying in its decision any rule of customary international law the content of which is also the subject of a provision in those multilateral treaties.

174. ... The United States apparently takes the view that the existence of principles in the United Nations Charter precludes the possibility that similar rules might exist independently in customary international law, either because existing customary rules had been incorporated into the Charter, or because the Charter influenced the later adoption of customary rules with a corresponding content....

176. As regards the suggestion that the areas covered by the two sources of law are identical, the Court observes that the United Nations Charter, the convention to which most of the United States argument is directed, by no means covers the whole area of the regulation of the use of force in international relations. On one essential point, this treaty itself refers to pre-existing customary international law; this reference to customary law is contained in the actual text of Article 51, which mentions the "inherent right" (in the French text the "droit naturel") of individual or collective self-defence, which "nothing in the present Charter shall impair" and which applies in the event of an armed attack. The Court therefore finds that Article 51 of the Charter is only meaningful on the basis that there is a "natural" or "inherent" right of self-defence, and it is hard to see how this can be other than of a customary nature, even if its present content has been confirmed and influenced by the Charter. Moreover the Charter, having itself recognized the existence of this right, does not go on to regulate directly all aspects of its content. For example, it does not contain any specific rule whereby self-defence would warrant only measures which are proportional to the armed attack and necessary to respond to it, a rule well established in customary international law. Moreover, a definition of the "armed attack" which, if found to exist, authorizes the exercise of the "inherent right" of self-defence, is not provided in the Charter, and is not part of treaty law. It cannot therefore be held that Article 51 is a provision which "subsumes and supervenes" customary international law. It rather demonstrates that in the field in question, the importance of which for the present dispute need hardly be stressed, customary international law continues to exist alongside treaty law. The areas governed by the two sources of law thus do not overlap exactly, and the rules do not have the same content. This could also be demonstrated for other subjects, in particular for the principle of non-intervention. . . .

178. There are a number of reasons for considering that, even if two norms belonging to two sources of international law appear identical in content, and even if the States in question are bound by these rules both on the level of treaty-law and on that of customary international law, these norms retain a separate existence. . . . [I]f the two rules in question also exist as rules of customary international law, the failure of the one State to apply the one rule does not justify the other State in declining to apply the other rule. Rules which are identical in treaty law and in customary international law are also distinguishable by reference to the methods of interpretation and application. A State may accept a rule contained in a treaty not simply because it favours the application of the rule itself, but also because the treaty establishes what that State regards as desirable institutions or mechanisms to ensure implementation of the rule. Thus, if that rule parallels a rule of customary international law, two rules of the same content are subject to separate treatment as regards the organs competent to verify their implementation, depending on whether they are customary rules or treaty rules. The present dispute illustrates this point. . . .

181. . . . [Concerning the opposite argument, that the Charter] constituted a marked departure from a customary international law which still exists unmodified, the Charter gave expression in this field to principles already present in customary international law, and that law has in the subsequent four decades developed under the influence of the Charter, to such an extent that a number of rules contained in the Charter have acquired a status independent of it. The essential consideration is that both the Charter and the customary international law flow from a common fundamental principle outlawing the use of force in international relations. . . .

182. The Court concludes that it should exercise the jurisdiction conferred upon it by the United States declaration of acceptance under Article 36, paragraph 2, of the Statute [of the International Court of Justice], to determine the claims of Nicaragua based upon customary international law notwithstanding the exclusion from its jurisdiction of disputes "arising under" the United Nations . . . Charter[].

[B.   Content of Customary International Law]

[1.   Prohibition on the Threat or Use of Force]

183. In view of this conclusion, the Court has next to consider what are the rules of customary international law applicable to the present dispute. For this purpose, it has to direct its attention to the practice and opinio juris of States; as the Court recently observed,

> It is of course axiomatic that the material of customary international law is to be looked for primarily in the actual practice and opinio juris of States, even though multilateral conventions may have an important role to play in recording and defining rules deriving from custom, or indeed in developing them. (*Continental Shelf (Libyan Arab Jamahiriya/ Malta)*, I.C.J. Reports 1985, pp. 29-30, para. 27.)

In this respect the Court must not lose sight of the Charter of the United Nations . . . , notwithstanding the operation of the multilateral treaty reservation. Although the Court has no jurisdiction to determine whether the conduct of the United States constitutes a breach of [that] convention[], it can and must take them into account in ascertaining the content of the customary international law which the United States is also alleged to have infringed. . . .

186. It is not to be expected that in the practice of States the application of the rules in question should have been perfect, in the sense that States should have refrained, with complete consistency, from the use of force or from intervention in each other's internal affairs. The Court does not consider that, for a rule to be established as customary, the corresponding practice must be in absolutely rigorous conformity with the rule. In order to deduce the existence of customary rules, the Court deems it sufficient that the conduct of States should, in general, be consistent with such rules, and that instances of State conduct inconsistent with a given rule should generally have been treated as breaches of that rule, not as indications of the recognition of a new rule. If a State acts in a way prima facie incompatible with a recognized rule, but defends its conduct by appealing to exceptions or justifications contained within the rule itself, then whether or not the State's conduct is in fact justifiable on that basis, the significance of that attitude is to confirm rather than to weaken the rule. . . .

188. The Court . . . finds that both Parties take the view that the principles as to the use of force incorporated in the United Nations Charter correspond, in essentials, to those found in customary international law. The Parties thus both take the view that the fundamental principle in this area is expressed in the terms employed in Article 2, paragraph 4, of the United Nations Charter. They therefore accept a treaty-law obligation to refrain in their international relations from the threat or use of force against the territorial integrity or political independence of any State, or in any other manner inconsistent with the purposes of the United Nations. The Court has however to be satisfied that there exists in customary international law an opinio juris as to the binding character of such abstention. This opinio juris may, though with all due caution, be deduced from, inter alia, the attitude of the Parties and the attitude of States towards certain General Assembly resolutions, and particularly resolution 2625 (XXV) entitled "Declaration on Principles of International Law concerning Friendly Relations and Co-operation among States in accordance with the Charter of the

United Nations [G.A. Res. 2625 (XXV), U.N. Doc. A/2625 (Oct. 24, 1970)]."
The . . . attitude referred to expresses an opinio juris respecting such rule (or set of
rules), to be thenceforth treated separately from the provisions . . . of the Charter. . . .

190. A further confirmation of the validity as customary international law of the
principle of the prohibition of the use of force expressed in Article 2, paragraph 4, of
the Charter of the United Nations may be found in the fact that it is frequently
referred to in statements by State representatives as being not only a principle of
customary international law but also a fundamental or cardinal principle of such law.
The International Law Commission, in the course of its work on the codification of
the law of treaties, expressed the view that "the law of the Charter concerning the
prohibition of the use of force in itself constitutes a conspicuous example of a rule in
international law having the character of jus cogens" (paragraph (1) of the commentary of the Commission to Article 50 of its draft Articles on the Law of Treaties, ILC
Yearbook, 1966-II, p. 247). . . . The United States, in its Counter-Memorial on the
questions of jurisdiction and admissibility, found it material to quote the views of
scholars that this principle is a "universal norm," a "universal international law," a
"universally recognized principle of international law," and a "principle of jus
cogens." . . .

[2.   Exception to the Prohibition for Self-Defense]

193. The general rule prohibiting force allows for certain exceptions. In view of
the arguments advanced by the United States to justify the acts of which it is accused
by Nicaragua, the Court must express a view on the content of the right of self-
defence, and more particularly the right of collective self-defence. First, with regard
to the existence of this right, it notes that in the language of Article 51 of the United
Nations Charter, the inherent right (or "droit naturel") which any State possesses in
the event of an armed attack, covers both collective and individual self-defence. Thus,
the Charter itself testifies to the existence of the right of collective self-defence in
customary international law. [So also, the Court concludes,] the wording of certain
General Assembly declarations adopted by States demonstrates [that they] regard the
exception to the prohibition of force constituted by the right of individual or collective self-defence as already a matter of customary international law.

194. With regard to the characteristics governing the right of self-defence, since
the Parties consider the existence of this right to be established as a matter of customary international law, they have concentrated on the conditions governing its
use. . . . The Parties also agree in holding that whether the response to the attack is
lawful depends on observance of the criteria of the necessity and the proportionality
of the measures taken in self-defence. . . .

195. In the case of individual self-defence, the exercise of this right is subject to
the State concerned having been the victim of an armed attack. Reliance on collective
self-defence of course does not remove the need for this. There appears now to be
general agreement on the nature of the acts which can be treated as constituting
armed attacks. . . . [I]n customary law, the prohibition of armed attacks may apply to
the sending by a State of armed bands to the territory of another State, if such an
operation, because of its scale and effects, would have been classified as an armed
attack rather than as a mere frontier incident had it been carried out by regular armed
forces. But the Court does not believe that the concept of "armed attack" includes not
only acts by armed bands where such acts occur on a significant scale but also

assistance to rebels in the form of the provision of weapons or logistical or other support. Such assistance may be regarded as a threat or use of force, or amount to intervention in the internal or external affairs of other States. It is also clear that it is the State which is the victim of an armed attack which must form and declare the view that it has been so attacked. There is no rule in customary international law permitting another State to exercise the right of collective self-defence on the basis of its own assessment of the situation. Where collective self-defence is invoked, it is to be expected that the State for whose benefit this right is used will have declared itself to be the victim of an armed attack. . . .

199. . . . [T]he Court finds that in customary international law, . . . there is no rule permitting the exercise of collective self-defence in the absence of a request by the State which regards itself as the victim of an armed attack. The Court concludes that the requirement of a request by the State which is the victim of the alleged attack is additional to the requirement that such a State should have declared itself to have been attacked.

200. . . . Article 51 of the United Nations Charter requires that measures taken by States in exercise of this right of self-defence must be "immediately reported" to the Security Council. . . . Whatever influence the Charter may have had on customary international law in these matters, it is clear that in customary international law it is not a condition of the lawfulness of the use of force in self-defence that a procedure so closely dependent on the content of a treaty commitment and of the institutions established by it, should have been followed. On the other hand, if self-defence is advanced as a justification for measures which would otherwise be in breach both of the principle of customary international law and of that contained in the Charter, it is to be expected that the conditions of the Charter should be respected. Thus for the purpose of enquiry into the customary law position, the absence of a report may be one of the factors indicating whether the State in question was itself convinced that it was acting in self-defence. . . .

[3.   Intervention]

202. The principle of non-intervention involves the right of every sovereign State to conduct its affairs without outside interference; though examples of trespass against this principle are not infrequent, the Court considers that it is part and parcel of customary international law. As the Court has observed: "Between independent States, respect for territorial sovereignty is an essential foundation of international relations" (I.C.J. Reports 1949, p. 35), and international law requires political integrity also to be respected. Expressions of an opinio juris regarding the existence of the principle of non-intervention in customary international law are numerous and not difficult to find. Of course, statements whereby States avow their recognition of the principles of international law set forth in the United Nations Charter cannot strictly be interpreted as applying to the principle of non-intervention by States in the internal and external affairs of other States, since this principle is not, as such, spelt out in the Charter. But it was never intended that the Charter should embody written confirmation of every essential principle of international law in force. The existence in the opinio juris of States of the principle of non-intervention is backed by established and substantial practice. . . .

205. . . . As regards . . . the content of the principle of non-intervention — the Court will define only those aspects of the principle which appear to be relevant to the

resolution of the dispute. In this respect it notes that, in view of the generally accepted formulations, the principle forbids all States or groups of States to intervene directly or indirectly in internal or external affairs of other States. A prohibited intervention must accordingly be one bearing on matters in which each State is permitted, by the principle of State sovereignty, to decide freely. One of these is the choice of a political, economic, social and cultural system, and the formulation of foreign policy. Intervention is wrongful when it uses methods of coercion in regard to such choices, which must remain free ones. The element of coercion, which defines, and indeed forms the very essence of, prohibited intervention, is particularly obvious in the case of an intervention which uses force, either in the direct form of military action, or in the indirect form of support for subversive or terrorist armed activities within another State. . . .

206. However, before reaching a conclusion on the nature of prohibited intervention, the Court . . . has to consider whether there might be indications of a practice illustrative of belief in a kind of general right for States to intervene, directly or indirectly, with or without armed force, in support of an internal opposition in another State, whose cause appeared particularly worthy by reason of the political and moral values with which it was identified. For such a general right to come into existence would involve a fundamental modification of the customary law principle of non-intervention. . . .

209. The Court . . . finds that no such general right of intervention, in support of an opposition within another State, exists in contemporary international law. The Court concludes that acts constituting a breach of the customary principle of non-intervention will also, if they directly or indirectly involve the use of force, constitute a breach of the principle of non-use of force in international relations.

210. . . . [I]f one State acts towards another State in breach of the principle of non-intervention, may a third State lawfully take such action by way of counter-measures against the first State as would otherwise constitute an intervention in its internal affairs? A right to act in this way in the case of intervention would be analogous to the right of collective self-defence in the case of an armed attack, but both the act which gives rise to the reaction, and that reaction itself, would in principle be less grave. Since the Court is here dealing with a dispute in which a wrongful use of force is alleged, it has primarily to consider whether a State has a right to respond to intervention with intervention going so far as to justify a use of force in reaction to measures which do not constitute an armed attack but may nevertheless involve a use of force. . . .

211. The Court has recalled above (paragraphs 193 to 195) that for one State to use force against another, on the ground that that State has committed a wrongful act of force against a third State, is regarded as lawful, by way of exception, only when the wrongful act provoking the response was an armed attack. Thus the lawfulness of the use of force by a State in response to a wrongful act of which it has not itself been the victim is not admitted when this wrongful act is not an armed attack. In the view of the Court, under international law in force today — whether customary international law or that of the United Nations system — States do not have a right of "collective" armed response to acts which do not constitute an "armed attack." . . .

[4.   Respect for State Sovereignty]

212. The Court should now mention the principle of respect for State sovereignty, which in international law is of course closely linked with the principles of the prohibition of the use of force and of non-intervention. The basic legal concept of

State sovereignty in customary international law, expressed in, inter alia, Article 2, paragraph 1, of the United Nations Charter ["The Organization is based on the principle of the sovereign equality of all its Members."], extends to the internal waters and territorial sea of every State and to the air space above its territory....

[IV.   APPLICATION OF LAW TO THE FACTS]

[A.   Direct and Indirect Uses of Force]

227.... For the most part, the complaints by Nicaragua are of the actual use of force against it by the United States. Of the acts which the Court has found imputable to the Government of the United States, the following are relevant in this respect:

—the laying of mines in Nicaraguan internal or territorial waters in early 1984;

—certain attacks on Nicaraguan ports, oil installations and a naval base.

These activities constitute infringements of the principle of the prohibition of the use of force, defined earlier, unless they are justified by circumstances which exclude their unlawfulness, a question now to be examined....

228.... As to the claim that United States activities in relation to the contras constitute a breach of the customary international law principle of the non-use of force, the Court finds that, subject to the question whether the action of the United States might be justified as an exercise of the right of self-defence, the United States has committed a prima facie violation of that principle by its assistance to the contras in Nicaragua, by "organizing or encouraging the organization of irregular forces or armed bands ... for incursion into the territory of another State," and "participating in acts of civil strife ... in another State," in the terms of General Assembly resolution 2625 (XXV). According to that resolution, participation of this kind is contrary to the principle of the prohibition of the use of force when the acts of civil strife referred to "involve a threat or use of force." In the view of the Court, while the arming and training of the contras can certainly be said to involve the threat or use of force against Nicaragua, this is not necessarily so in respect of all the assistance given by the United States Government. In particular, the Court considers that the mere supply of funds to the contras, while undoubtedly an act of intervention in the internal affairs of Nicaragua, as will be explained below, does not in itself amount to a use of force.

[B.   Collective Self-Defense]

229. The Court must thus consider whether, as the Respondent claims, the acts in question of the United States are justified by the exercise of its right of collective self-defence against an armed attack.... For the Court to conclude that the United States was lawfully exercising its right of collective self-defence, it must first find that Nicaragua engaged in an armed attack against El Salvador....

230.... Even assuming that the supply of arms to the opposition in El Salvador could be treated as imputable to the Government of Nicaragua, to justify invocation of the right of collective self-defence in customary international law, it would have to be equated with an armed attack by Nicaragua on El Salvador. As stated above, the Court is unable to consider that, in customary international law, the provision of arms to the opposition in another State constitutes an armed attack on that State....

232. The exercise of the right of collective self-defence presupposes that an armed attack has occurred; and it is evident that it is the victim State, being the most directly aware of that fact, which is likely to draw general attention to its plight. It is also evident that if the victim State wishes another State to come to its help in the exercise of the right of collective self-defence, it will normally make an express request to that effect. . . .

233. . . . So far as El Salvador is concerned, it appears to the Court that while El Salvador did in fact officially declare itself the victim of an armed attack, and did ask for the United States to exercise its right of collective self-defence, this occurred only on a date much later than the commencement of the United States activities which were allegedly justified by this request. . . .

235. There is also an aspect of the conduct of the United States which the Court is entitled to take into account as indicative of the view of that State on the question of the existence of an armed attack. At no time, up to the present, has the United States Government addressed to the Security Council, in connection with the matters the subject of the present case, the report which is required by Article 51 of the United Nations Charter in respect of measures which a State believes itself bound to take when it exercises the right of individual or collective self-defence. The Court, whose decision has to be made on the basis of customary international law, has already observed that in the context of that law, the reporting obligation enshrined in Article 51 of the Charter of the United Nations does not exist. It does not therefore treat the absence of a report on the part of the United States as the breach of an undertaking forming part of the customary international law applicable to the present dispute. But the Court is justified in observing that this conduct of the United States hardly conforms with the latter's avowed conviction that it was acting in the context of collective self-defence as consecrated by Article 51 of the Charter. . . .

237. Since the Court has found that the condition sine qua non required for the exercise of the right of collective self-defence by the United States is not fulfilled in this case, the appraisal of the United States activities in relation to the criteria of necessity and proportionality takes on a different significance. As a result of this conclusion of the Court, even if the United States activities in question had been carried on in strict compliance with the canons of necessity and proportionality, they would not thereby become lawful. If however they were not, this may constitute an additional ground of wrongfulness. On the question of necessity, the Court observes that the United States measures taken in December 1981 (or, at the earliest, March of that year) cannot be said to correspond to a "necessity" justifying the United States action against Nicaragua on the basis of assistance given by Nicaragua to the armed opposition in El Salvador. First, these measures were only taken, and began to produce their effects, several months after the major offensive of the armed opposition against the Government of El Salvador had been completely repulsed (January 1981), and the actions of the opposition considerably reduced in consequence. Thus it was possible to eliminate the main danger to the Salvadorian Government without the United States embarking on activities in and against Nicaragua. Accordingly, it cannot be held that these activities were undertaken in the light of necessity. Whether or not the assistance to the contras might meet the criterion of proportionality, the Court cannot regard the United States activities . . . relating to the mining of the Nicaraguan ports and the attacks on ports, oil installations, etc., as satisfying that criterion. Whatever uncertainty may exist as to the exact scale of the aid received by the Salvadorian armed opposition from Nicaragua, it is clear that these latter United States activities in question could not have been proportionate to that aid. Finally on this point, the Court must also observe that the reaction of the United States in the context of what it regarded as self-defence was continued long after the period in which any presumed armed attack by Nicaragua could reasonably be contemplated.

238. Accordingly, the Court concludes that the plea of collective self-defence against an alleged armed attack on El Salvador . . . advanced by the United States to justify its conduct toward Nicaragua, cannot be upheld; and accordingly that the United States has violated the principle prohibiting recourse to the threat or use of force by the acts listed in paragraph 227 above, and by its assistance to the contras to the extent that this assistance "involve[s] a threat or use of force" (paragraph 228 above). . . .

[C.   Intervention]

241. . . . It appears to the Court to be clearly established first, that the United States intended, by its support of the contras, to coerce the Government of Nicaragua in respect of matters in which each State is permitted, by the principle of State sovereignty, to decide freely; and secondly that the intention of the contras them- selves was to overthrow the present Government of Nicaragua. . . . Even if it be accepted, for the sake of argument, that the objective of the United States in assisting the contras was solely to interdict the supply of arms to the armed opposition in El Salvador, it strains belief to suppose that a body formed in armed opposition to the Government of Nicaragua, and calling itself the "Nicaraguan Democratic Force," intended only to check Nicaraguan interference in El Salvador and did not intend to achieve violent change of government in Nicaragua. The Court considers that in international law, if one State, with a view to the coercion of another State, supports and assists armed bands in that State whose purpose is to overthrow the government of that State, that amounts to an intervention by the one State in the internal affairs of the other, whether or not the political objective of the State giving such support and assistance is equally far reaching. . . .

242. The Court therefore finds that the support given by the United States, up to the end of September 1984, to the military and paramilitary activities of the contras in Nicaragua, by financial support, training, supply of weapons, intelligence and logistic support, constitutes a clear breach of the principle of non-intervention. . . .

246. . . . [T]he principle of non-intervention derives from customary interna- tional law. It would certainly lose its effectiveness as a principle of law if intervention were to be justified by a mere request for assistance made by an opposition group in another State — supposing such a request to have actually been made by an opposi- tion to the regime in Nicaragua in this instance. . . .

247. . . . [W]hile the concept of an armed attack includes the despatch by one State of armed bands into the territory of another State, the supply of arms and other support to such bands cannot be equated with armed attack. Nevertheless, such activities may well constitute a breach of the principle of the non-use of force and an intervention in the internal affairs of a State, that is, a form of conduct which is certainly wrongful, but is of lesser gravity than an armed attack. . . .

249. . . . While an armed attack would give rise to an entitlement to collective self- defence, a use of force of a lesser degree of gravity cannot, as the Court has already observed, produce any entitlement to take collective counter-measures involving the use of force. The acts of which Nicaragua is accused, even assuming them to have been established and imputable to that State, could only have justified proportionate counter-measures on the part of the State which had been the victim of these acts, namely El Salvador. . . . They could not justify counter-measures taken by a third State, the United States, and particularly could not justify intervention involving the use of force. . . .

[D.   Respect for State Sovereignty]

251. The effects of the principle of respect for territorial sovereignty inevitably overlap with those of the principles of the prohibition of the use of force and of non-intervention. Thus the assistance to the contras, as well as the direct attacks on Nicaraguan ports, oil installations, etc. . . . not only amount to an unlawful use of force, but also constitute infringements of the territorial sovereignty of Nicaragua, and incursions into its territorial and internal waters. Similarly, the mining operations in the Nicaraguan ports not only constitute breaches of the principle of the non-use of force, but also affect Nicaragua's sovereignty over certain maritime expanses. . . .

252. These violations cannot be justified either by collective self-defence, for which, as the Court has recognized, the necessary circumstances are lacking, nor by any right of the United States to take counter-measures involving the use of force in the event of intervention by Nicaragua in El Salvador, since no such right exists under the applicable international law. They cannot be justified by the activities in El Salvador attributed to the Government of Nicaragua. The latter activities, assuming that they did in fact occur, do not bring into effect any right belonging to the United States which would justify the actions in question. Accordingly, such actions constitute violations of Nicaragua's sovereignty under customary international law. . . .

263. The finding of the United States Congress also expressed the view that the Nicaraguan Government had taken "significant steps towards establishing a totalitarian Communist dictatorship." However the regime in Nicaragua be defined, adherence by a State to any particular doctrine does not constitute a violation of customary international law; to hold otherwise would make nonsense of the fundamental principle of State sovereignty, on which the whole of international law rests, and the freedom of choice of the political, social, economic and cultural system of a State. Consequently, Nicaragua's domestic policy options, even assuming that they correspond to the description given of them by the Congress finding, cannot justify on the legal plane the various actions of the Respondent complained of. The Court cannot contemplate the creation of a new rule opening up a right of intervention by one State against another on the ground that the latter has opted for some particular ideology or political system. . . .

292. For these reasons,

THE COURT . . . [by 12 votes to 3],

- Rejects the justification of collective self-defence maintained by the United States of America in connection with the military and paramilitary activities in and against Nicaragua the subject of this case;

- Decides that the United States of America, by training, arming, equipping, financing and supplying the contra forces or otherwise encouraging, supporting and aiding military and paramilitary activities in and against Nicaragua, has acted, against the Republic of Nicaragua, in breach of its obligation under customary international law not to intervene in the affairs of another State;

- Decides that the United States of America, by certain attacks on Nicaraguan territory . . . ; and further by those acts of intervention . . . which involve the use of force, has acted, against the Republic of Nicaragua, in breach of its obligation under customary international law not to use force against another State;

- Decides that the United States of America, by directing or authorizing overflights of Nicaraguan territory, and by the acts imputable to the United States . . . has acted, against the Republic of Nicaragua, in breach of its obligation under customary international law not to violate the sovereignty of another State;

- Decides that, by laying mines in the internal or territorial waters of the Republic of Nicaragua during the first months of 1984, the United States of America has acted, against the Republic of Nicaragua, in breach of its obligations under customary international law not to use force against another State, not to intervene in its affairs, not to violate its sovereignty and not to interrupt peaceful maritime commerce;

- Decides that the United States of America is under a duty immediately to cease and to refrain from all such acts as may constitute breaches of the foregoing legal obligations;

- Decides that the United States of America is under an obligation to make reparation to the Republic of Nicaragua for all injury caused to Nicaragua by the breaches of obligations under customary international law enumerated above.

[Judge Stephen Schwebel, a U.S. citizen, voted "against" on each of these decisions. Other decisions by sometimes different votes are omitted here.]

(Signed) *Nagendra Singh*, President.

[Separate concurring and dissenting opinions of various judges are omitted.]

NOTES AND QUESTIONS

1. *The Political Decision to Engage in Aggression.* Can you guess why the Reagan administration decided, in early 1981, to take the actions that led to this suit in the World Court? How do you think the President assessed the legality under the U.N. Charter of direct military attacks on Nicaragua or of support for the Contras? Might the U.S. role on the Security Council have affected his judgment about the practical outcome? Do you suppose he considered the likelihood that these actions would be called into question before the World Court? Why do you think that many of these actions were carried out covertly? For sometimes sharply contrasting answers to these questions, *compare* Theodore Draper, *A Very Thin Line: The Iran-Contra Affairs* 15-50, 558-579 (1991), *with* John Norton Moore, *The Secret War in Central America: Sandinista Assault on World Order* 5-73 (1987).

How likely is it that the experience recounted here will dissuade states from resorting to force in resolving future disputes? What politically viable legal reforms can you suggest that would further deter aggression?

2. *World Court vs. Security Council.* In contesting the subject matter jurisdiction of the Court, the United States argued that questions about the unlawful use of force

were committed exclusively to the political organs of the United Nations, in particular to the Security Council, and that the Court's involvement would improperly interfere with an exercise of the inherent right of individual and collective self-defense under Article 51. It noted further that only a few days before filing its application with the Court, Nicaragua had submitted a draft resolution containing the same allegations to the Security Council, and that the resolution had not been adopted. The Court ruled that the "Council has functions of a political nature assigned to it, whereas the Court exercises purely judicial functions. Both organs can therefore perform their separate but complementary functions with respect to the same events." 1984 I.C.J. 392, 431-436 (Nov. 26). Do the two bodies — the Court and the Security Council — differ in their competence to address the issues raised in the *Nicaragua Case*? What would be the practical effect of a contrary ruling?

The Court in the principal case observed that it was "not asked to say that the Security Council was wrong." *Id.* at 436. But should we worry that the two might someday come into conflict? *See* Dinstein, *supra* p. 210, at 318-325.

3. *Treaty Law vs. Customary International Law.* The refusal of the United States to submit to the jurisdiction of the Court in a dispute involving a multilateral treaty obligation reflects one of the most hallowed aspects of sovereignty in our international system: a state may not be compelled to do anything it has not voluntarily agreed to do. Why did the United States insist that the Court also lacked jurisdiction to rule on U.S. compliance with customary norms governing the use of force? Did the United States argue that the U.N. Charter codified existing customary international norms, or that the norms are the product of international agreement in the Charter? Does it matter?

Is it relevant to the question of jurisdiction that the content of the two sources of law is or is not precisely the same? What differences in the two sources are recognized by the Court? How did those differences arise?

4. *Formation of Customary International Law.* In the view of one authority, the formation of customary international law "results from a general and consistent practice of states followed by them from a sense of legal obligation." Restatement (Third) of Foreign Relations Law §102(2) (1987). Regarding the consistent practice of states, in another case the Court remarked, "State practice . . . should have been both extensive and virtually uniform in the sense of the provision invoked." *The North Sea Continental Shelf Case* (Judgment), 1969 I.C.J. 12, 43. Unfortunately, history is replete with examples, many of them very recent, of states resorting to violence without the approval of the U.N. Security Council and for reasons having nothing to do with self-defense. How then did the Court determine that the practice of states was sufficiently consistent to form a customary norm prohibiting the use of force? Do you think the degree of consistency required in this case might be different from that in the formation of a customary norm concerned with, say, welcoming ceremonies for visiting heads of state? Should it be different?

The development of customary international law also requires state practice to be based on a sense of legal obligation, or *opinio juris*. Where does the Court find expressions of that sense of legal obligation independent of the requirements of the Charter? What, if any, was the effect of characterizations of the prohibition on the use of force as peremptory law — *jus cogens*? *See* Dinstein, *supra*, at 99-104.

5. *Scope of the Customary Prohibition on the Threat or Use of Force.* A substantial, direct, armed attack by one state against another violates the customary prohibition on the

use of force, unless it is excused by some recognized exception to the prohibition. The Court found that the United States committed such an attack when U.S. personnel mined Nicaraguan harbors and carried out aerial strikes against ports, a military base, and oil installations in that country. But both the United States and Nicaragua also engaged in various lesser, indirect uses of force. How did the Court determine that some of these lesser actions violated the prohibition, while others did not? Were its distinctions based on the instrumentalities employed in the actions — for example, training of rebel forces as opposed to, say, merely providing financial support for them? Were they influenced by the severity of the effects of those actions — for example, loss of life versus economic damage? Other factors? Some combination of these? What is the source of the factors?

A definition of aggression was adopted by the U.N. General Assembly in Resolution 3314, G.A. Res. 3314 (XXIX), U.N. Doc. A/3314 (Dec. 14, 1974). In addition to acts condemned by the Court in the *Nicaragua Case*, it includes blockades and permission by a state for use of its territory to attack other states. It also describes the *first* use of force in contravention of the Charter as prima facie evidence of aggression.

6. *Self-Defense.* Because of the U.S. multilateral treaty reservation, the Court was asked to identify not only a customary general ban on the use of force in international relations, but also customary exceptions to that ban. Where did it find a customary exception for self-defense?

The threat or use of force in self-defense can only be justified, under either Article 51 or customary law, by the existence of an "armed attack." What, according to the Court, constitutes an armed attack, and what does not? Why do you suppose the Court drew the line where it did?

The right of self-defense is also generally agreed to be qualified by a requirement that it be based on "a necessity of self-defense, instant, overwhelming, leaving no choice of means, no moment for deliberation." Secretary of State Daniel Webster penned this formula in connection with an 1837 dispute between the United States and Great Britain — the *Caroline* affair. 6 *The Works of Daniel Webster* 261 (1851). What purpose is served by each of these criteria? Did the actions of the United States in the principal case satisfy each one?

In another case the Court declared that the burden of proving facts showing the existence of an armed attack rests on the state claiming to act in self-defense. *Case Concerning Oil Platforms (Iran v. United States)*, 2003 I.C.J. 161, 189 (Nov. 6). Why place the burden there?

Why does the Court insist that before one state comes to the aid of another as an act of collective self-defense, the second state must (a) declare that it has come under attack and (b) request assistance? Even with these safeguards, of course, one can see a potential for collusion between assisting and assisted states to create a pretext for aggression against a third state. How could this potential be reduced?

Article 51 provides that any exercise of the inherent right of self-defense "shall be immediately reported to the Security Council." What is the purpose of this requirement? How does it bear on the outcome of the *Nicaragua Case*?

Only those illegal uses of force amounting to armed attacks can justify forceful responses in self-defense. What recourse is available to victims of lesser uses of force?

7. *Non-Intervention.* In paragraphs 202-211 of its opinion, the Court describes the principle of non-intervention. What is that principle? Why does the Court address it,

instead of disposing of the case solely on the basis of the customary norm prohibiting the use of force? Can you say what forms of coercion are forbidden by this principle? How about promises of financial aid or threats to withhold such aid? Trade sanctions? Support for one's external enemies?

Might an intervention in support of an internal opposition ever be permissible? What about intervention against a state with a corrupt, tyrannical, non-democratic government? Suppose the state were engaged in genocide against some of its people? *See* Dinstein, *supra*, at 90-91 (asserting that use of force "unilaterally in order to overthrow a despotic (even genocidal) regime" would run afoul of Article 2(4)).

What if military intervention is invited by one of several factions within a state, when none of the factions can establish a clearly legitimate claim to leadership of the government? U.S. military involvement in Vietnam from 1954-1975 (see Chapter 10), in Grenada in 1983, and in Panama in 1989 might be characterized this way. Intervention in Libya in 2011, authorized by the U.N. Security Council, ostensibly on humanitarian grounds, is examined *infra* pp. 430-439.

If one state commits a prohibited intervention against another, but not an armed attack, why should a third state not be entitled to employ forceful "counter-measures" to assist the first state, by way of analogy to the inherent right of collective self-defense? How about counter-measures not amounting to a use of force?

8. *Respect for Sovereignty.* What is protected by the principle of respect for state sovereignty? How is this principle related to the customary prohibition on the use of force and to the principle of non-intervention?

9. *Necessity and Proportionality.* The Court declares that if the use of force is ever justified as a matter of customary international law, it must satisfy the criteria of necessity and proportionality. In its 1996 Advisory Opinion on the *Legality of the Threat or Use of Nuclear Weapons*, 1996 I.C.J. 226, 245 (July 8), the Court indicated that the same requirements exist under Article 51. What policy is served by these requirements? Which U.S. actions toward Nicaragua failed to meet the criteria, and why?

10. *War as a Crime.* At the end of World War II, the tribunal established to punish Nazi criminals described the initiation of a war of aggression as "not only an international crime; it is the supreme international crime differing only from other war crimes in that it contains within itself the accumulated evil of the whole." *International Military Tribunal (Nuremberg)*, Judgment, 1 I.M.T. 171, 186 (Oct. 1, 1946). U.N. General Assembly Resolution 3314, *supra*, Annex art. 5(2), also states that a "war of aggression is a crime against international peace. Aggression gives rise to international responsibility." The resolution also sets out a fairly detailed definition of aggression, as noted above.

The International Criminal Court, established by the Rome Treaty of the International Criminal Court, July 17, 1998, 2187 U.N.T.S. 90, was originally declared to have jurisdiction to prosecute the crime of aggression. But its authority to act was delayed until a definition of the crime, based on General Assembly Resolution 3314, was agreed upon in 2010. Resolution RC/Res. 6 (June 11, 2010). *See U.S. Delegation Active in ICC Negotiations to Define Crime of Aggression*, 104 Am. J. Int'l L. 511 (2010); *see generally The International Criminal Court: Challenges to Achieving Justice and Accountability in the 21st Century* 215-245 (Mark S. Ellis & Richard J. Goldstone eds., 2008); Dinstein, *supra*, at 117-150. Under the terms of the agreement, however, no prosecution can take place before 2017 at the earliest.

International
Humanitarian Law
(jus in bello)

9

The international law concerning the right to wage war, or *jus ad bellum*, examined in the last chapter is aimed at deterring the use of armed force by states against each other. It is also supposed to regulate states' uses of force against terrorists and other non-state actors. A related, parallel body of law, *jus in bello*, is concerned with the conduct of war once it has begun. Also referred to as international humanitarian law (IHL) or the law of armed conflict (LOAC),[1] its purpose is to limit the suffering of combatants and noncombatants alike to what is necessary to achieve the legitimate political goals of a conflict.

Several framework principles constitute IHL, including requirements that any use of military force be based on *distinction* (distinguishing carefully between military targets and civilians in order to protect the latter), and *proportionality* (forbidding any use of force that causes incidental civilian casualties that are disproportionate to the military advantage from the operation). IHL has been extensively codified, most prominently in a series of Hague Conventions, which address permissible targets and weaponry, and Geneva Conventions, which are concerned with the treatment of prisoners and other noncombatants and the conduct of occupying forces. Other such conventions deal with poison gas, anti-personnel land mines, blinding lasers, the protection of cultural objects, and other matters relating to the effects of war. Humanitarian law principles are also found in a robust, rapidly evolving body of customary international law. In addition, some IHL violations are criminalized by the Rome Statute of the International Court, July 17, 1998, 2187 U.N.T.S. 90, an international agreement to which the United States is not yet a party. *See generally The International Criminal Court: Challenges to Achieving Justice and Accountability in the 21st Century* (Mark S. Ellis & Richard J. Goldstone eds., 2008).

IHL is a subset of international law, partially incorporated as U.S. law. Another subset of international law, international human rights law (HRL), applies in peacetime and, some would say, during armed conflicts as well. The view of the United States is that, during armed conflicts, HRL gives way to IHL and its *jus in bello* principles. *Operational Law Handbook* 40 (Marie Anderson & Emily Zukauskas eds., 2008). (The relationship between IHL and HRL is considered *infra* Chapter 14.)

---

1. We use the term international humanitarian law (IHL) because of its international currency and its growing use in academic discourse. The terms law of armed conflict and laws of war are synonymous.

For reasons of national interests, as well as military strategy and tactics, limits on what soldiers may do in war have existed throughout history. From religious precepts to chivalry to customs and then rules, nations and their armies eventually developed military codes for conflict that included penalties for their violation. In the United States in 1862, Professor Francis Lieber persuaded the Union War Department to assign him to write a compilation of the customary rules of warfare — the Lieber Code. Then came the Hague and the 1949 Geneva Conventions and, eventually, 1977 Protocols that have expanded the reach and protections of the basic instruments.

The extensive provisions of the Geneva Conventions of 1949 apply only to armed conflicts of an international (inter-state) character, not to non-international armed conflicts (most other armed conflicts, including at least some insurrections) (*see* Geneva III, art. 4, *infra* p. 237), except for baseline, general humanitarian protections for victims of all armed conflicts found in Common Article 3. The Protocols, adopted 28 years later, sought to extend the basic Geneva principles to a wider range of conflicts, especially to national liberation movements then battling colonial powers, and to describe emerging customs and new principles. Additional Protocol I (AP I) is concerned with international armed conflicts, while Additional Protocol II (AP II) is applicable to non-international armed conflicts, but neither has been ratified by the United States. Still, as explained below, the United States follows some of their principles as customary international law.

The resulting law leaves much to be desired. Because armed conflicts today frequently involve violent clashes between states and non-state actors — terrorists, insurgents, guerrilla groups, even pirates — the Geneva Conventions and their Protocols often fail to provide clear guidance for belligerents. *See* John B. Bellinger III & Vijay M. Padmanabhan, *Detention Operations in Contemporary Conflicts: Four Challenges for the Geneva Conventions and Other Existing Law*, 105 Am. J. Int'l L. 201, 205-213 (2011). Even when the Conventions apply to such conflicts, they may not adapt easily to the weaponry, tactics, and personnel employed in modern irregular warfare.

Some argue that HRL, supplemented by domestic laws, can govern all such conflicts. But the relationship of these laws to IHL is complex, and the patchwork of rules that would result from this approach might be more bewildering than helpful. *Id.* at 209-212. As things now stand, states and lawyers struggle to apply IHL to these conflicts, and state militaries may in practice simply treat all armed conflicts the same. *See* Michael N. Schmitt, *Targeting and International Humanitarian Law in Afghanistan*, 39 Israel Y.B. on Hum. Rts. 307, 308 (2009) (IHL norms in international and non-international armed conflicts "have become nearly indistinguishable.")

This chapter offers an introduction to IHL — just enough to understand the basics and the significance of *jus in bello* for national security law. Three sets of materials provide the framework. In Part A, we review excerpts of the Geneva Conventions, one of their two Protocols, and the Rome Statute of the International Criminal Court (ICC), focusing chiefly on provisions intended to protect the victims of war. In Part B, we consider IHL rules for selecting targets and protecting civilians during armed conflict, applying them to the 2011 U.S. and NATO military operation against Libya. Finally, in Part C, we examine a judicial decision arising from the conflict in the Balkans in the 1990s to examine the *in bello* rules for detention and treatment of prisoners in war. Our broader objective here is to lay the foundation for a more extensive application of these principles when we consider targeted killings, detention and interrogation of terrorist suspects, and military commissions in later chapters.

A. AUTHORITIES FOR *JUS IN BELLO*

1. IHL for the Victims of War — The 1949 Geneva Conventions

The 1863 Lieber Code and a first Geneva Convention adopted at a meeting of the International Committee of the Red Cross (ICRC) in 1864 established the practice of codifying customary law for the conduct of armed conflicts. Despite continuing efforts to institutionalize humane wartime practices before and after World War I, the horrific casualties and brutal atrocities of World War II brought renewed determination to protect the victims of war. Meanwhile, regulation of the means of waging war was partly addressed by Hague treaties and partly left to customary law. The 1949 Geneva Conventions continued to deal with the victims of war, leaving regulation of battlefield conduct to the earlier Hague rules and custom. Additional Protocols to the Geneva Conventions in 1977 combined elements of the earlier conventions and customs to create a more nearly comprehensive set of *in bello* rules.

There are four separate 1949 Geneva Conventions. The Convention for the Amelioration of the Condition of the Wounded and Sick in Armed Forces in the Field (Geneva I) and the Convention for the Amelioration of the Condition of Wounded, Sick and Shipwrecked Members of the Armed Forces at Sea (Geneva II) provide similar protections for, respectively, land and seaborne forces. Several provisions of Geneva III and Geneva IV, excerpted next, contain central components of contemporary *in bello* safeguards. Note that Common Articles 1-3 are identical throughout the four Conventions. Provisions of Geneva III and IV and Additional Protocol I set out below fall roughly into three categories: (1) those stating broad ideals or describing procedural requirements, (2) those regulating the means for waging warfare, and (3) those dealing in greater detail with the treatment of prisoners. See if you can place each provision into one of these categories, recognizing that there may be some overlap in a few instances. The Rome Statute subsequently drew on IHL in listing prosecutable war crimes.

Geneva Convention Relative to the Treatment of Prisoners of War, August 12, 1949 (Geneva III)
T.I.A.S. 3362, 75 U.N.T.S. 135

Article 1

The High Contracting Parties undertake to respect and to ensure respect for the present Convention in all circumstances.

Article 2

In addition to the provisions which shall be implemented in peace time, the present Convention shall apply to all cases of declared war or of any other armed conflict which may arise between two or more of the High Contracting Parties, even if the state of war is not recognized by one of them.

The Convention shall also apply to all cases of partial or total occupation of the territory of a High Contracting Party, even if the said occupation meets with no armed resistance.

Although one of the Powers in conflict may not be a party to the present Convention, the Powers who are parties thereto shall remain bound by it in their mutual relations. They shall furthermore be bound by the Convention in relation to the said Power, if the latter accepts and applies the provisions thereof.

Article 3

In the case of armed conflict not of an international character occurring in the territory of one of the High Contracting Parties, each party to the conflict shall be bound to apply, as a minimum, the following provisions:

1. Persons taking no active part in the hostilities, including members of armed forces who have laid down their arms and those placed hors de combat by sickness, wounds, detention, or any other cause, shall in all circumstances be treated humanely, without any adverse distinction founded on race, colour, religion or faith, sex, birth or wealth, or any other similar criteria.

To this end the following acts are and shall remain prohibited at any time and in any place whatsoever with respect to the above-mentioned persons:

(a) Violence to life and person, in particular murder of all kinds, mutilation, cruel treatment and torture;

(b) Taking of hostages;

(c) Outrages upon personal dignity, in particular, humiliating and degrading treatment;

(d) The passing of sentences and the carrying out of executions without previous judgment pronounced by a regularly constituted court affording all the judicial guarantees which are recognized as indispensable by civilized peoples. . . .

Article 4

A. Prisoners of war, in the sense of the present Convention, are persons belonging to one of the following categories, who have fallen into the power of the enemy:

1. Members of the armed forces of a Party to the conflict as well as members of militias or volunteer corps forming part of such armed forces.

2. Members of other militias and members of other volunteer corps, including those of organized resistance movements, belonging to a Party to the conflict and operating in or outside their own territory, even if this territory is occupied, provided that such militias or volunteer corps, including such organized resistance movements, fulfil the following conditions:

(a) That of being commanded by a person responsible for his subordinates;

(b) That of having a fixed distinctive sign recognizable at a distance;

(c) That of carrying arms openly;

(d) That of conducting their operations in accordance with the laws and customs of war.

3. Members of regular armed forces who profess allegiance to a government or an authority not recognized by the Detaining Power.

4. Persons who accompany the armed forces without actually being members thereof, such as civilian members of military aircraft crews, war correspondents,

supply contractors, members of labour units or of services responsible for the welfare of the armed forces, provided that they have received authorization from the armed forces which they accompany, who shall provide them for that purpose with an identity card similar to the annexed model.

5. Members of crews, including masters, pilots and apprentices, of the merchant marine and the crews of civil aircraft of the Parties to the conflict, who do not benefit by more favourable treatment under any other provisions of international law.

6. Inhabitants of a non-occupied territory, who on the approach of the enemy spontaneously take up arms to resist the invading forces, without having had time to form themselves into regular armed units, provided they carry arms openly and respect the laws and customs of war....

Article 5

The present Convention shall apply to the persons referred to in Article 4 from the time they fall into the power of the enemy and until their final release and repatriation.

Should any doubt arise as to whether persons, having committed a belligerent act and having fallen into the hands of the enemy, belong to any of the categories enumerated in Article 4, such persons shall enjoy the protection of the present Convention until such time as their status has been determined by a competent tribunal....

Article 17

Every prisoner of war, when questioned on the subject, is bound to give only his surname, first names and rank, date of birth, and army, regimental, personal or serial number, or failing this, equivalent information.

If he wilfully infringes this rule, he may render himself liable to a restriction of the privileges accorded to his rank or status.... [Most of the remaining provisions of this Convention spell out conditions of confinement of prisoners of war, including rights to health care, exercise, mail, food, etc.] ...

Article 87

Prisoners of war may not be sentenced by the military authorities and courts of the Detaining Power to any penalties except those provided for in respect of members of the armed forces of the said Power who have committed the same acts.

When fixing the penalty, the courts or authorities of the Detaining Power shall take into consideration, to the widest extent possible, the fact that the accused, not being a national of the Detaining Power, is not bound to it by any duty of allegiance, and that he is in its power as the result of circumstances independent of his own will....

Collective punishment for individual acts, corporal punishments, imprisonment in premises without daylight and, in general, any form of torture or cruelty, are forbidden....

Geneva Convention Relative to the Protection of Civilian Persons in Time of War, August 12, 1949 (Geneva IV)

T.I.A.S. 3362, 75 U.N.T.S. 287

Article 1 [see Geneva Convention III] . . .

Article 2 [see Geneva Convention III] . . .

Article 3 [see Geneva Convention III] . . .

Article 4

Persons protected by the Convention are those who, at a given moment and in any manner whatsoever, find themselves, in case of a conflict or occupation, in the hands of a Party to the conflict or Occupying Power of which they are not nationals.

Nationals of a State which is not bound by the Convention are not protected by it. Nationals of a neutral State who find themselves in the territory of a belligerent State, and nationals of a co-belligerent State, shall not be regarded as protected persons while the State of which they are nationals has normal diplomatic representation in the State in whose hands they are.

The provisions of Part II are, however, wider in application, as defined in Article 13. . . .

Article 5

Where, in the territory of a Party to the conflict, the latter is satisfied that an individual protected person is definitely suspected of or engaged in activities hostile to the security of the State, such individual person shall not be entitled to claim such rights and privileges under the present Convention as would, if exercised in the favour of such individual person, be prejudicial to the security of such State.

Where in occupied territory an individual protected person is detained as a spy or saboteur, or as a person under definite suspicion of activity hostile to the security of the Occupying Power, such person shall, in those cases where absolute military security so requires, be regarded as having forfeited rights of communication under the present Convention.

In each case, such persons shall nevertheless be treated with humanity, and in case of trial, shall not be deprived of the rights of fair and regular trial prescribed by the present Convention. They shall also be granted the full rights and privileges of a protected person under the present Convention at the earliest date consistent with the security of the State or Occupying Power, as the case may be. . . .

Article 31

No physical or moral coercion shall be exercised against protected persons, in particular to obtain information from them or from third parties. . . .

Article 49

Individual or mass forcible transfers, as well as deportations of protected persons from occupied territory to the territory of the Occupying Power or to that of any other country, occupied or not, are prohibited, regardless of their motive.

Nevertheless, the Occupying Power may undertake total or partial evacuation of a given area if the security of the population or imperative military reasons do demand. Such evacuations may not involve the displacement of protected persons outside the bounds of the occupied territory except when for material reasons it is impossible to avoid such displacement. Persons thus evacuated shall be transferred back to their homes as soon as hostilities in the area in question have ceased. . . .

Article 146

The High Contracting Parties undertake to enact any legislation necessary to provide effective penal sanctions for persons committing, or ordering to be committed, any of the grave breaches of the present Convention defined in the following Article.

Each High Contracting Party shall be under the obligation to search for persons alleged to have committed, or to have ordered to be committed, such grave breaches, and shall bring such persons, regardless of their nationality, before its own courts. It may also, if it prefers, and in accordance with the provisions of its own legislation, hand such persons over for trial to another

High Contracting Party concerned, provided such High Contracting Party has made out a *prima facie* case.

Each High Contracting Party shall take measures necessary for the suppression of all acts contrary to the provisions of the present Convention other than the grave breaches defined in the following Article.

In all circumstances, the accused persons shall benefit by safeguards of proper trial and defence, which shall not be less favourable than those provided by Article 105 and those following of the Geneva Convention relative to the Treatment of Prisoners of War of August 12, 1949.

Article 147

Grave breaches to which the preceding Article relates shall be those involving any of the following acts, if committed against persons or property protected by the present Convention: wilful killing, torture or inhuman treatment, including biological experiments, wilfully causing great suffering or serious injury to body or health, unlawful deportation or transfer or unlawful confinement of a protected person, compelling a protected person to serve in the forces of a hostile Power, or wilfully depriving a protected person of the rights of fair and regular trial prescribed in the present Convention, taking of hostages and extensive destruction and appropriation of property, not justified by military necessity and carried out unlawfully and wantonly.

2.   IHL Revised: The Protocols Additional and the Rome Statute

After the Korean War, the world's wars began to evolve from large, state-against-state conflicts involving competing armies into smaller, more episodic conflicts, often involving states fighting non-state entities, such as insurgents, guerrillas, revolutionaries, or terrorists. At the same time, a growing body of HRL called into question certain IHL assumptions. In 1977, with the encouragement of national liberation groups, and despite strong opposition from the United States and some of its allies, delegates from a majority of states approved significant amendments to the Geneva Conventions. The Protocols supplement rather than replace the Conventions. Protocol I, excerpted below, covers international armed conflicts—defined more broadly than before—and it effectively codifies the *in bello* regulation of the battlefield. Protocol II, not excerpted here, expands upon the protections in Common Article 3 for individuals in armed conflicts that are not of an international (interstate) character.

A continuing determination to provide a forum for international criminal prosecution of the worst offenders of *in bello* rules came to fruition in 1998, with adoption of the Rome Statute and creation of the International Criminal Court. Its central provision conferring jurisdiction over war crimes is also excerpted below.

The United States has not ratified Protocol I or Protocol II to the Geneva Conventions. In AP I, the United States particularly objected to detailed rules about discrimination during attacks, a prohibition on reprisals that could deter IHL violations, modifications to prisoner-of-war (POW) categories, and changes in the definition of international armed conflicts to include indigenous armed struggles against colonial or racist regimes. However, in 1987 the Deputy Legal Adviser to the Department of State indicated that the United States recognizes nearly two-thirds of the articles in Protocol I as customary international law. Michael J. Matheson, *Additional Protocol I as Expressions of Customary International Law*, 2 Am. U. J. Int'l L. & Pol'y 415 (1987). Such recognition is indicated by annotations to some of the provisions below. Almost 20 years later, Matheson affirmed his earlier position. Michael J. Matheson, *Continuity and Change in the Law of War: 1975-2005: Detainees and POWs*, 38 Geo. Wash. Int'l L. Rev. 543 (2006). Some have asserted that the Matheson statement is not authoritative, *see* W. Hays Parks, *"Special Forces" Wear of Non-Standard Uniforms*, 4 Chi. J. Int'l L. 519 n.55 (2003), but no office of the U.S. government has disavowed his statement. In March 2011, President Obama announced that he would urge the Senate to ratify AP II, and that the United States would apply Article 75 of AP I (below) to individuals detained in international armed conflicts. Office of the Press Secretary, The White House, *Fact Sheet: New Actions on Guantanamo and Detainee Policy*, Mar. 7, 2011.

Protocol Additional to the Geneva Conventions of August 12, 1949, and Relating to the Protection of Victims of International Armed Conflicts, June 8, 1977 (Protocol I)

1125 U.N.T.S. 3, 16 I.L.M. 1391

PART I — GENERAL PROVISIONS

Article 1 — General principles and scope of application

1. The High Contracting Parties undertake to respect and to ensure respect for this Protocol in all circumstances.

2. In cases not covered by this Protocol or by other international agreements, civilians and combatants remain under the protection and authority of the principles of international law derived from established custom, from the principles of humanity and from dictates of public conscience.

3. This Protocol, which supplements the Geneva Conventions of 12 August 1949 for the protection of war victims, shall apply in the situations referred to in Article 2 common to those Conventions.

4. The situations referred to in the preceding paragraph include armed conflicts in which peoples are fighting against colonial domination and alien occupation and against racist regimes in the exercise of their right of self-determination, as enshrined in the Charter of the United Nations and the Declaration on Principles of International Law concerning Friendly Relations and Co-operation among States in accordance with the Charter of the United Nations....

PART III — METHODS AND MEANS OF WARFARE, COMBATANT AND PRISONER-OF-WAR STATUS

Article 35 — Basic rules[2]

1. In any armed conflict, the right of the Parties to the conflict to choose methods or means of warfare is not unlimited.

2. It is prohibited to employ weapons, projectiles and material and methods of warfare of a nature to cause superfluous injury or unnecessary suffering.

3. It is prohibited to employ methods or means of warfare which are intended, or may be expected, to cause widespread, long-term and severe damage to the natural environment....

Article 41 — Safeguard of an enemy hors de combat

1. A person who is recognized or who, in the circumstances should be recognized to be *hors de combat* shall not be made the object of attack.

2. A person is *hors de combat* if:
    (a) he is in the power of an adverse Party;
    (b) he clearly expresses an intention to surrender; or
    (c) he has been rendered unconscious or is otherwise incapacitated by wounds or sickness, and therefore is incapable of defending himself;
provided that in any of these cases he abstains from any hostile act and does not attempt to escape.

3. When persons entitled to protection as prisoners of war have fallen into the power of an adverse Party under unusual conditions of combat which prevent their evacuation as provided for in Part III, Section I, of the Third Convention, they shall be released and all feasible precautions shall be taken to ensure their safety....

Article 43 — Armed forces

1. The armed forces of a Party to a conflict consist of all organized armed forces, groups and units which are under a command responsible to that Party for the

[2. Recognized as customary international law by the United States. — Eds.]

conduct of its subordinates, even if that Party is represented by a government or an authority not recognized by an adverse Party. Such armed forces shall be subject to an internal disciplinary system which, inter alia, shall enforce compliance with the rules of international law applicable in armed conflict.

2. Members of the armed forces of a Party to a conflict (other than medical personnel and chaplains covered by Article 33 of the Third Convention) are combatants, that is to say, they have the right to participate directly in hostilities.

3. Whenever a Party to a conflict incorporates a paramilitary or armed law enforcement agency into its armed forces it shall so notify the other Parties to the conflict.

Article 44 — Combatants and prisoners of war

1. Any combatant, as defined in Article 43, who falls into the power of an adverse Party shall be a prisoner of war.

2. While all combatants are obliged to comply with the rules of international law applicable in armed conflict, violations of these rules shall not deprive a combatant of his right to be a combatant or, if he falls into the power of an adverse Party, of his right to be a prisoner of war, except as provided in paragraphs 3 and 4.

3. In order to promote the protection of the civilian population from the effects of hostilities, combatants are obliged to distinguish themselves from the civilian population while they are engaged in an attack or in a military operation preparatory to an attack. Recognizing, however, that there are situations in armed conflicts where, owing to the nature of the hostilities an armed combatant cannot so distinguish himself, he shall retain his status as a combatant, provided that, in such situations, he carries his arms openly:

(a) during each military engagement, and

(b) during such time as he is visible to the adversary while he is engaged in a military deployment preceding the launching of an attack in which he is to participate. Acts which comply with the requirements of this paragraph shall not be considered as perfidious within the meaning of Article 37, paragraph 1 (c).

4. A combatant who falls into the power of an adverse Party while failing to meet the requirements set forth in the second sentence of paragraph 3 shall forfeit his right to be a prisoner of war, but he shall, nevertheless, be given protections equivalent in all respects to those accorded to prisoners of war by the Third Convention and by this Protocol. This protection includes protections equivalent to those accorded to prisoners of war by the Third Convention in the case where such a person is tried and punished for any offences he has committed.

5. Any combatant who falls into the power of an adverse Party while not engaged in an attack or in a military operation preparatory to an attack shall not forfeit his rights to be a combatant and a prisoner of war by virtue of his prior activities.

6. This Article is without prejudice to the right of any person to be a prisoner of war pursuant to Article 4 of the Third Convention.

7. This Article is not intended to change the generally accepted practice of States with respect to the wearing of the uniform by combatants assigned to the regular, uniformed armed units of a Party to the conflict. . . .

Article 45 — Protection of persons who have taken part in hostilities

1. A person who takes part in hostilities and falls into the power of an adverse Party shall be presumed to be a prisoner of war, and therefore shall be protected by

the Third Convention, if he claims the status of prisoner of war, or if he appears to be entitled to such status, or if the Party on which he depends claims such status on his behalf by notification to the detaining Power or to the Protecting Power. Should any doubt arise as to whether any such person is entitled to the status of prisoner of war, he shall continue to have such status and, therefore, to be protected by the Third Convention and this Protocol until such time as his status has been determined by a competent tribunal.

2. If a person who has fallen into the power of an adverse Party is not held as a prisoner of war and is to be tried by that Party for an offence arising out of the hostilities, he shall have the right to assert his entitlement to prisoner-of-war status before a judicial tribunal and to have that question adjudicated. Whenever possible under the applicable procedure, this adjudication shall occur before the trial for the offence. The representatives of the Protecting Power shall be entitled to attend the proceedings in which that question is adjudicated, unless, exceptionally, the proceedings are held in camera in the interest of State security. In such a case the detaining Power shall advise the Protecting Power accordingly.

3. Any person who has taken part in hostilities, who is not entitled to prisoner-of-war status and who does not benefit from more favourable treatment in accordance with the Fourth Convention shall have the right at all times to the protection of Article 75 of this Protocol. In occupied territory, any such person, unless he is held as a spy, shall also be entitled, notwithstanding Article 5 of the Fourth Convention, to his rights of communication under that Convention. . . .

PART IV — CIVILIAN POPULATION

Article 48 — Basic rule

In order to ensure respect for and protection of the civilian population and civilian objects, the Parties to the conflict shall at all times distinguish between the civilian population and combatants and between civilian objects and military objectives and accordingly shall direct their operations only against military objectives.

Article 49 — Definition of attacks and scope of application

1. "Attacks" means acts of violence against the adversary, whether in offence or in defence.

2. The provisions of this Protocol with respect to attacks apply to all attacks in whatever territory conducted, including the national territory belonging to a Party to the conflict but under the control of an adverse Party.

3. The provisions of this section apply to any land, air or sea warfare which may affect the civilian population, individual civilians or civilian objects on land. They further apply to all attacks from the sea or from the air against objectives on land but do not otherwise affect the rules of international law applicable in armed conflict at sea or in the air.

4. The provisions of this section are additional to the rules concerning humanitarian protection contained in the Fourth Convention, particularly in part II thereof, and in other international agreements binding upon the High Contracting Parties, as well as to other rules of international law relating to the protection of civilians and civilian objects on land, at sea or in the air against the effects of hostilities.

Article 50 — Definition of civilians and civilian population

1. A civilian is any person who does not belong to one of the categories of persons referred to in Article 4 (A) (1), (2), (3) and (6) of the Third Convention and in Article 43 of this Protocol. In case of doubt whether a person is a civilian, that person shall be considered to be a civilian.

2. The civilian population comprises all persons who are civilians.

3. The presence within the civilian population of individuals who do not come within the definition of civilians does not deprive the population of its civilian character.

Article 51 — Protection of the civilian population[3]

1. The civilian population and individual civilians shall enjoy general protection against dangers arising from military operations. To give effect to this protection, the following rules, which are additional to other applicable rules of international law, shall be observed in all circumstances.

2. The civilian population as such, as well as individual civilians, shall not be the object of attack. Acts or threats of violence the primary purpose of which is to spread terror among the civilian population are prohibited.

3. Civilians shall enjoy the protection afforded by this section, unless and for such time as they take a direct part in hostilities.

4. Indiscriminate attacks are prohibited. Indiscriminate attacks are:

   (a) those which are not directed at a specific military objective;

   (b) those which employ a method or means of combat which cannot be directed at a specific military objective; or

   (c) those which employ a method or means of combat the effects of which cannot be limited as required by this Protocol;

and consequently, in each such case, are of a nature to strike military objectives and civilians or civilian objects without distinction.

5. Among others, the following types of attacks are to be considered as indiscriminate:

   (a) an attack by bombardment by any methods or means which treats as a single military objective a number of clearly separated and distinct military objectives located in a city, town, village or other area containing a similar concentration of civilians or civilian objects; and

   (b) an attack which may be expected to cause incidental loss of civilian life, injury to civilians, damage to civilian objects, or a combination thereof, which would be excessive in relation to the concrete and direct military advantage anticipated.

6. Attacks against the civilian population or civilians by way of reprisals are prohibited.

7. The presence or movements of the civilian population or individual civilians shall not be used to render certain points or areas immune from military operations, in particular in attempts to shield military objectives from attacks or to shield, favour or impede military operations. The Parties to the conflict shall not direct the

[3. Recognized in part as customary law by the United States. — Eds.]

movement of the civilian population or individual civilians in order to attempt to shield military objectives from attacks or to shield military operations.

8. Any violation of these prohibitions shall not release the Parties to the conflict from their legal obligations with respect to the civilian population and civilians, including the obligation to take the precautionary measures provided for in Article 57....

Article 57 — Precautions in attack[4]

1. In the conduct of military operations, constant care shall be taken to spare the civilian population, civilians and civilian objects.

2. With respect to attacks, the following precautions shall be taken:
   (a) those who plan or decide upon an attack shall:
      (i) do everything feasible to verify that the objectives to be attacked are neither civilians nor civilian objects and are not subject to special protection but are military objectives within the meaning of paragraph 2 of Article 52 and that it is not prohibited by the provisions of this Protocol to attack them;
      (ii) take all feasible precautions in the choice of means and methods of attack with a view to avoiding, and in any event to minimizing, incidental loss of civilian life, injury to civilians and damage to civilian objects;
      (iii) refrain from deciding to launch any attack which may be expected to cause incidental loss of civilian life, injury to civilians, damage to civilian objects, or a combination thereof, which would be excessive in relation to the concrete and direct military advantage anticipated;
   (b) an attack shall be cancelled or suspended if it becomes apparent that the objective is not a military one or is subject to special protection or that the attack may be expected to cause incidental loss of civilian life, injury to civilians, damage to civilian objects, or a combination thereof, which would be excessive in relation to the concrete and direct military advantage anticipated;
   (c) effective advance warning shall be given of attacks which may affect the civilian population, unless circumstances do not permit.

3. When a choice is possible between several military objectives for obtaining a similar military advantage, the objective to be selected shall be that the attack on which may be expected to cause the least danger to civilian lives and to civilian objects.

4. In the conduct of military operations at sea or in the air, each Party to the conflict shall, in conformity with its rights and duties under the rules of international law applicable in armed conflict, take all reasonable precautions to avoid losses of civilian lives and damage to civilian objects.

5. No provision of this article may be construed as authorizing any attacks against the civilian population, civilians or civilian objects....

Article 72 — Field of application

The provisions of this Section are additional to the rules concerning humanitarian protection of civilians and civilian objects in the power of a Party to the conflict contained in the Fourth Convention, particularly Parts I and III thereof, as well as to

---

[4. Recognized as customary law by the United States. — Eds.]

other applicable rules of international law relating to the protection of fundamental human rights during international armed conflict. . . .

Article 75 — Fundamental guarantees[5]

1. In so far as they are affected by a situation referred to in Article 1 of this Protocol, persons who are in the power of a Party to the conflict and who do not benefit from more favourable treatment under the Conventions or under this Protocol shall be treated humanely in all circumstances and shall enjoy, as a minimum, the protection provided by this Article without any adverse distinction based upon race, colour, sex, language, religion or belief, political or other opinion, national or social origin, wealth, birth or other status, or on any other similar criteria. Each Party shall respect the person, honour, convictions and religious practices of all such persons.

2. The following acts are and shall remain prohibited at any time and in any place whatsoever, whether committed by civilian or by military agents:

(a) violence to the life, health, or physical or mental well-being of persons, in particular:

(i) murder;

(ii) torture of all kinds, whether physical or mental;

(iii) corporal punishment; and

(iv) mutilation;

(b) outrages upon personal dignity, in particular humiliating and degrading treatment, enforced prostitution and any form of indecent assault;

(c) the taking of hostages;

(d) collective punishments; and

(e) threats to commit any of the foregoing acts.

3. Any person arrested, detained or interned for actions related to the armed conflict shall be informed promptly, in a language he understands, of the reasons why these measures have been taken. Except in cases of arrest or detention for penal offences, such persons shall be released with the minimum delay possible and in any event as soon as the circumstances justifying the arrest, detention or internment have ceased to exist.

4. No sentence may be passed and no penalty may be executed on a person found guilty of a penal offence related to the armed conflict except pursuant to a conviction pronounced by an impartial and regularly constituted court respecting the generally recognized principles of regular judicial procedure, which include the following:

(a) the procedure shall provide for an accused to be informed without delay of the particulars of the offence alleged against him and shall afford the accused before and during his trial all necessary rights and means of defence;

(b) no one shall be convicted of an offence except on the basis of individual penal responsibility;

(c) no one shall be accused or convicted of a criminal offence on account of any act or omission which did not constitute a criminal offence under the national or international law to which he was subject at the time when it was committed; nor shall a heavier penalty be imposed than that which was applicable at the time when the criminal offence was committed; if, after the commission of the offence,

[5. Recognized as customary law by the United States. — Eds.]

provision is made by law for the imposition of a lighter penalty, the offender shall benefit thereby;

(d) anyone charged with an offence is presumed innocent until proved guilty according to law;

(e) anyone charged with an offence shall have the right to be tried in his presence;

(f) no one shall be compelled to testify against himself or to confess guilt;

(g) anyone charged with an offence shall have the right to examine, or have examined, the witnesses against him and to obtain the attendance and examination of witnesses on his behalf under the same conditions as witnesses against him;

(h) no one shall be prosecuted or punished by the same Party for an offence in respect of which a final judgement acquitting or convicting that person has been previously pronounced under the same law and judicial procedure;

(i) anyone prosecuted for an offence shall have the right to have the judgement pronounced publicly; and

(j) a convicted person shall be advised on conviction of his judicial and other remedies and of the time-limits within which they may be exercised. . . .

6. Persons who are arrested, detained or interned for reasons related to the armed conflict shall enjoy the protection provided by this Article until their final release, repatriation or re-establishment, even after the end of the armed conflict.

7. In order to avoid any doubt concerning the prosecution and trial of persons accused of war crimes or crimes against humanity, the following principles shall apply:

(a) persons who are accused of such crimes should be submitted for the purpose of prosecution and trial in accordance with the applicable rules of international law; and

(b) any such persons who do not benefit from more favourable treatment under the Conventions or this Protocol shall be accorded the treatment provided by this Article, whether or not the crimes of which they are accused constitute grave breaches of the Conventions or of this Protocol.

8. No provision of this Article may be construed as limiting or infringing any other more favourable provision granting greater protection, under any applicable rules of international law, to persons covered by paragraph 1. . . .

Article 85 — Repression of breaches of this Protocol[6]

1. The provisions of the Conventions relating to the repression of breaches and grave breaches, supplemented by this Section, shall apply to the repression of breaches and grave breaches of this Protocol.

2. Acts described as grave breaches in the Conventions are grave breaches of this Protocol if committed against persons in the power of an adverse Party protected by Articles 44, 45 and 73 of this Protocol, or against the wounded, sick and shipwrecked of the adverse Party who are protected by this Protocol, or against those medical or religious personnel, medical units or medical transports which are under the control of the adverse Party and are protected by this Protocol.

3. In addition to the grave breaches defined in Article 11, the following acts shall be regarded as grave breaches of this Protocol, when committed wilfully, in violation

[6. Recognized as customary law by the United States. — Eds.]

of the relevant provisions of this Protocol, and causing death or serious injury to body or health:

>   (a) making the civilian population or individual civilians the object of attack;

>   (b) launching an indiscriminate attack affecting the civilian population or civilian objects in the knowledge that such attack will cause excessive loss of life, injury to civilians or damage to civilian objects, as defined in Article 57, paragraph 2 (a)(iii);

>   (c) launching an attack against works or installations containing dangerous forces in the knowledge that such attack will cause excessive loss of life, injury to civilians or damage to civilian objects, as defined in Article 57, paragraph 2 (a)(iii);

>   (d) making non-defended localities and demilitarized zones the object of attack;

>   (e) making a person the object of attack in the knowledge that he is hors de combat;

>   (f) the perfidious use, in violation of Article 37, of the distinctive emblem of the red cross, red crescent or red lion and sun or of other protective signs recognized by the Conventions or this Protocol.

4. In addition to the grave breaches defined in the preceding paragraphs and in the Conventions, the following shall be regarded as grave breaches of this Protocol, when committed wilfully and in violation of the Conventions or the Protocol:

>   (a) the transfer by the occupying Power of parts of its own civilian population into the territory it occupies, or the deportation or transfer of all or parts of the population of the occupied territory within or outside this territory, in violation of Article 49 of the Fourth Convention;

>   (b) unjustifiable delay in the repatriation of prisoners of war or civilians;

>   (c) practices of apartheid and other inhuman and degrading practices involving outrages upon personal dignity, based on racial discrimination;

>   (d) making the clearly-recognized historic monuments, works of art or places of worship which constitute the cultural or spiritual heritage of peoples and to which special protection has been given by special arrangement, for example, within the framework of a competent international organization, the object of attack, causing as a result extensive destruction thereof, where there is no evidence of the violation by the adverse Party of Article 53, subparagraph (b), and when such historic monuments, works of art and places of worship are not located in the immediate proximity of military objectives;

>   (e) depriving a person protected by the Conventions or referred to in paragraph 2 of this Article of the rights of fair and regular trial.

5. Without prejudice to the application of the Conventions and of this Protocol, grave breaches of these instruments shall be regarded as war crimes.

Article 86 — Failure to act[7]

1. The High Contracting Parties and the Parties to the conflict shall repress grave breaches, and take measures necessary to suppress all other breaches, of the Conventions or of this Protocol which result from a failure to act when under a duty to do so.

[7. Recognized as customary law by the United States. — Eds.]

2. The fact that a breach of the Conventions or of this Protocol was committed by a subordinate does not absolve his superiors from penal disciplinary responsibility, as the case may be, if they knew, or had information which should have enabled them to conclude in the circumstances at the time, that he was committing or was going to commit such a breach and if they did not take all feasible measures within their power to prevent or repress the breach. . . .

Rome Statute of the International Criminal Court
2187 U.N.T.S. 90, July 17, 1998

Article 8: War crimes

1. The Court shall have jurisdiction in respect of war crimes in particular when committed as part of a plan or policy or as part of a large-scale commission of such crimes.

2. For the purpose of this Statute, "war crimes" means:

(a) Grave breaches of the Geneva Conventions of 12 August 1949, namely, any of the following acts against persons or property protected under the provisions of the relevant Geneva Convention:

(i) Wilful killing;

(ii) Torture or inhuman treatment, including biological experiments;

(iii) Wilfully causing great suffering, or serious injury to body or health;

(iv) Extensive destruction and appropriation of property, not justified by military necessity and carried out unlawfully and wantonly;

(v) Compelling a prisoner of war or other protected person to serve in the forces of a hostile Power;

(vi) Wilfully depriving a prisoner of war or other protected person of the rights of fair and regular trial;

(vii) Unlawful deportation or transfer or unlawful confinement;

(viii) Taking of hostages.

(b) Other serious violations of the laws and customs applicable in international armed conflict, within the established framework of international law, namely, any of the following acts:

(i) Intentionally directing attacks against the civilian population as such or against individual civilians not taking direct part in hostilities;

(ii) Intentionally directing attacks against civilian objects, that is, objects which are not military objectives;

(iii) Intentionally directing attacks against personnel, installations, material, units or vehicles involved in a humanitarian assistance or peacekeeping mission in accordance with the Charter of the United Nations, as long as they are entitled to the protection given to civilians or civilian objects under the international law of armed conflict;

(iv) Intentionally launching an attack in the knowledge that such attack will cause incidental loss of life or injury to civilians or damage to civilian objects or widespread, long-term and severe damage to the natural environment which would be clearly excessive in relation to the concrete and direct overall military advantage anticipated;

(v) Attacking or bombarding, by whatever means, towns, villages, dwellings or buildings which are undefended and which are not military objectives; . . .

(xiv) Declaring abolished, suspended or inadmissible in a court of law the rights and actions of the nationals of the hostile party; . . .

(xxi) Committing outrages upon personal dignity, in particular humiliating and degrading treatment; . . . .

(c) In the case of an armed conflict not of an international character, serious violations of article 3 common to the four Geneva Conventions of 12 August 1949, namely, any of the following acts committed against persons taking no active part in the hostilities, including members of armed forces who have laid down their arms and those placed hors de combat by sickness, wounds, detention or any other cause:

(i) Violence to life and person, in particular murder of all kinds, mutilation, cruel treatment and torture;

(ii) Committing outrages upon personal dignity, in particular humiliating and degrading treatment;

(iii) Taking of hostages;

(iv) The passing of sentences and the carrying out of executions without previous judgement pronounced by a regularly constituted court, affording all judicial guarantees which are generally recognized as indispensable.

(d) Paragraph 2 (c) applies to armed conflicts not of an international character and thus does not apply to situations of internal disturbances and tensions, such as riots, isolated and sporadic acts of violence or other acts of a similar nature.

(e) Other serious violations of the laws and customs applicable in armed conflicts not of an international character, within the established framework of international law, namely, any of the following acts:

(i) Intentionally directing attacks against the civilian population as such or against individual civilians not taking direct part in hostilities; . . .

(f) Paragraph 2 (e) applies to armed conflicts not of an international character and thus does not apply to situations of internal disturbances and tensions, such as riots, isolated and sporadic acts of violence or other acts of a similar nature. It applies to armed conflicts that take place in the territory of a State when there is protracted armed conflict between governmental authorities and organized armed groups or between such groups.

3. Nothing in paragraph 2 (c) and (e) shall affect the responsibility of a Government to maintain or re-establish law and order in the State or to defend the unity and territorial integrity of the State, by all legitimate means.

NOTES AND QUESTIONS

1. *Architecture and Stature of the Conventions.* Every nation in the world has ratified the four 1949 Geneva Conventions. Like the earlier Geneva Conventions, the overarching purpose of the 1949 Conventions is to protect the victims of armed conflict, including the wounded, prisoners of war, and civilians. Accordingly, the regulation of battlefield tactics is left to other treaties, such as the 1907 Hague Regulation IV, and to customary law. Can you see the basic orientation of the Conventions toward victim protection in the provisions of Geneva III and IV excerpted above?

Articles 1-3 are "Common Articles," in that they are repeated verbatim in all four Conventions. Other common articles deal with execution of the Conventions or with procedural matters. What are the cornerstone protections of Articles 1-3? What is their likely practical effect?

2. *Grave Breaches.* Each of the four Geneva Conventions requires the enactment of domestic legislation to punish grave breaches. *See, e.g.,* Geneva IV, art. 146. Exactly what constitutes a "grave breach"? What is the difference between a grave breach and a war crime, and where would you expect to find a list of war crimes? What are the scope and content of each state's obligation to seek redress for grave breaches? *See id.* art. 147.

What domestic criminal provisions would you expect to find in U.S. laws that reflect the obligations of Geneva IV? Consider, for example, the Torture Act, 18 U.S.C. §§2340-2340B (2006), assessed *infra* Chapter 31. What do you suppose is the measure of compliance with Article 146? In the United States, the Uniform Code of Military Justice (UCMJ) has since 1951 provided the mechanism for trying our own soldiers for alleged grave breaches. *See infra* p. 924. Civilians may now also be tried for grave breaches pursuant to the War Crimes Act of 1996, 18 U.S.C. §2441 (2006), and the Military Extraterritorial Jurisdiction Act, 18 U.S.C. §§3261-3267 (2006). *See infra* p. 948. Historically, enemy soldiers have been tried for grave breaches before military commissions, "juries" of military officers. *See infra* Chapter 36.

What is the jurisdiction of the International Criminal Court (ICC)? Could it try alleged grave breaches? What about war crimes? Genocide? Crimes against humanity?

3. *International and Non-International Armed Conflicts.* A wholly indigenous rebellion within a single state is one kind of non-international armed conflict. Before 9/11, the Taliban were the de facto government of parts of Afghanistan, in armed conflict with the Northern Alliance, an indigenous group of war lords. Was that conflict of a non-international character? Did its character change when the United States deployed forces in Afghanistan against the Taliban and Al Qaeda after 9/11? Which type is the U.S. conflict with Al Qaeda and the Taliban today? See *infra* p. 400. With reference to the Geneva Conventions, what is the legal and practical significance of the distinction?

Apart from the difficulty in distinguishing international from non-international armed conflicts, how would you distinguish an internal armed conflict from a domestic riot or rebellion? AP II states that it does not apply to "situations of internal disturbances and tensions, such as riots, isolated and sporadic acts of violence and other acts of a similar nature, as not being armed conflicts." AP II, art. 2. What is the dividing line? *See Commentary, Convention (I) for the Amelioration of the Condition of the Wounded and Sick in Armed Forces in the Field. Geneva, 12 August 1949* (Jean S. Pictet ed., 1952), at 49, *available at* http://www.icrc.org/ihl.nsf/com/365-570006?opendocument (suggesting criteria, including "an organized military force, an authority responsible for its acts...having the means of respecting...the Convention...[and a] *de jure* Government [that] has recognized the insurgents as belligerents."). Who decides, and what legal difference, if any, does it make?

4. *Common Article 3.* Until Additional Protocol II was adopted in 1977, Common Article 3 was the only provision in the Geneva Conventions dealing explicitly with

conflicts "not of an international character." What protections are provided in Common Article 3, and which persons are entitled to them? What is the measure of "humane treatment"? *See infra* p. 940. Are these protections different from those afforded to victims of an international conflict?

5. *Jus in Bello as Custom and the Protocols.* As indicated above, the 1949 Geneva Conventions did not address issues of targeting, including the core principles of distinction, military necessity, unnecessary suffering, and proportionality. Yet those principles were part of customary law and were, to some extent, codified separately in the Hague and other treaties. What difference does it make whether IHL is customary or enshrined in a treaty provision? Can you figure out why the United States has recognized some of the AP I provisions as customary law but not others? Why not sign on lock, stock, and barrel?

Reviewing the excerpted provisions of AP I, which ones articulate the principles of distinction, necessity, unnecessary suffering, and proportionality? See if you can extract from those articles a workable set of rules to guide soldiers in the field.

6. *Are the Geneva Conventions Obsolete?* Fresh from the horrors of World War II, the delegates to the 1949 conference in Geneva were determined to codify an extensive set of protections for the victims of state-on-state wars. They were not thinking about terrorism, insurgencies, guerrilla movements, or armed revolutions. The 1977 Protocols made only modest progress toward explicitly addressing such asymmetric warfare.

Even before the September 11 attacks, however, it was clear that conflicts between states and non-state entities were becoming increasingly common. In 2002, then-White House Counsel Alberto Gonzales wrote that the war on terrorism "renders obsolete Geneva's strict limitations on questioning of enemy prisoners and renders quaint some of its provisions." Alberto R. Gonzales, *Memorandum to the President, Decision re Application of the Geneva Convention on Prisoners of War to the Conflict with Al Qaeda and the Taliban*, Jan. 25, 2002. Do you agree?

Do the Geneva Conventions and their Protocols apply to an armed conflict between a state and a terrorist organization? Between a state and an insurgent group? Soldiers in an armed conflict of an international character are entitled to "combatant immunity" for uses of force that otherwise comply with IHL. They can be detained as POWs, but not tried for shooting at enemy soldiers, which is lawful combat. Could individuals fighting for a terrorist group or an insurgency be similarly entitled to combatant immunity? Are they be entitled to *any* of the protections of the Conventions or Protocols? *See* Common Article 3. If not, should the Conventions be amended? What specific amendments would you recommend?

There may soon be greater clarity about IHL, at least from the perspective of the United States. The Pentagon's Law of War Working Group has worked off and on for 14 years on a new *Department of Defense Law of War Manual*, the first comprehensive compilation of U.S. understandings of the treaties and state practice that make up IHL. The new *Manual* is expected to be released in 2011. *See* W. Hays Parks, *National Security Law in Practice: The Department of Defense Law of War Manual*, Nov. 8, 2010, *available at* http://www.americanbar.org/content/dam/aba/migrated/natsecurity/ hays_parks_speech11082010.authcheckdam.pdf.

B. TARGETING AND PROTECTING CIVILIANS IN ARMED CONFLICT

Authority to Use Military Force in Libya

U.S. Department of Justice, Office of Legal Counsel, Apr. 1, 2011
35 Op. O.L.C. ___

Memorandum opinion for: The Attorney General

From: Caroline D. Krass, Prin. Dep. Asst. Att'y General

... In mid-February 2011, amid widespread popular demonstrations seeking governmental reform in the neighboring countries of Tunisia and Egypt, as well as elsewhere in the Middle East and North Africa, protests began in Libya against the autocratic government of Colonel Muammar Qadhafi, who has ruled Libya since taking power in a 1969 coup. Qadhafi moved swiftly in an attempt to end the protests using military force. Some Libyan government officials and elements of the Libyan military left the Qadhafi regime, and by early March, Qadhafi had lost control over much of the eastern part of the country, including the city of Benghazi. The Libyan government's operations against its opponents reportedly included strafing of protesters and shelling, bombing, and other violence deliberately targeting civilians. Many refugees fled to Egypt and other neighboring countries to escape the violence, creating a serious crisis in the region.

On February 26, 2011, the United Nations Security Council ("UNSC") unanimously adopted Resolution 1970, which "[e]xpress[ed] grave concern at the situation in the Libyan Arab Jamahiriya," "condemn[ed] the violence and use of force against civilians," and "[d]eplor[ed] the gross and systematic violation of human rights" in Libya. S.C. Res. 1970, U.N. Doc. S/RES/1970 (Feb. 26, 2011); Press Release, Security Council, In Swift, Decisive Action, Security Council Imposes Tough Measures on Libyan Regime, Adopting Resolution 1970 in Wake of Crackdown on Protesters, U.N. Press Release SC/10187/Rev. 1 (Feb. 26, 2011). The resolution called upon member states, among other things, to take "the necessary measures" to prevent arms transfers "from or through their territories or by their nationals, or using their flag vessels or aircraft"; to freeze the assets of Qadhafi and certain other close associates of the regime; and to "facilitate and support the return of humanitarian agencies and make available humanitarian and related assistance" in Libya. S.C. Res. 1970, ¶¶9, 17, 26. The resolution did not, however, authorize members of the United Nations to use military force in Libya.

The Libyan government's violence against civilians continued, and even escalated, despite condemnation by the UNSC and strong expressions of disapproval from other regional and international bodies. See, e.g., African Union, Communique of the 265th Meeting of the Peace and Security Council, PSC/PR/COMM.2(CCLXV) (Mar. 10, 2011) (describing the "prevailing situation in Libya" as "pos[ing] a serious threat to peace and security in that country and in the region as a whole" and "[r]eiterat[ing] AU's strong and unequivocal condemnation of the indiscriminate use of force and lethal weapons"); News Release, Organization of the Islamic Conference, OIC General Secretariat Condemns Strongly the Excessive Use of Force

Against Civilians in the Libyan Jamahiriya (Feb. 22, 2011), *available at* http://www.oic-oci. org/topic_detail.asp?t_id=4947&x_key= (reporting that "the General Secretariat of the Organization of the Islamic Conference (OIC) voiced its strong condemnation of the excessive use of force against civilians in the Arab Libyan Jamahiriya")....

By March 17, 2011, Qadhafi's forces were preparing to retake the city of Benghazi. Pledging that his forces would begin an assault on the city that night and show "no mercy and no pity" to those who would not give up resistance, Qadhafi stated in a radio address: "We will come house by house, room by room. It's over. The issue has been decided." See Dan Bilefsky & Mark Landler, *Military Action Against Qaddafi Is Backed by U.N.*, N.Y. Times, Mar. 18, 2011, at A1. Qadhafi, President Obama later noted, "compared [his people] to rats, and threatened to go door to door to inflict punishment.... We knew that if we... waited one more day, Benghazi, a city nearly the size of Charlotte, could suffer a massacre that would have reverberated across the region and stained the conscience of the world." Press Release, Office of the Press Secretary, The White House, Remarks by the President in Address to the Nation on Libya (Mar. 28, 2011) ("Obama March 28, 2011 Address"), *available at* http://www. whitehouse.gov/the-press-office/2011/03/28/remarks-president-address-nation-libya.

Later the same day, the UNSC addressed the situation in Libya again by adopting, by a vote of 10-0 (with five members abstaining), Resolution 1973, which imposed a no-fly zone and authorized the use of military force to protect civilians. See S.C. Res. 1973, U.N. Doc. S/RES/1973 (Mar. 17, 2011) [*infra* p. 435]; Press Release, Security Council, Security Council Approves 'No-Fly Zone' Over Libya, Authorizing 'All Necessary Measures' to Protect Civilians, by Vote of 10 in Favour with 5 Abstentions, U.N. Press Release SC/10200 (Mar. 17, 2011). In this resolution, the UNSC determined that the "situation" in Libya "continues to constitute a threat to international peace and security" and "demand[ed] the immediate establishment of a cease-fire and a complete end to violence and all attacks against, and abuses of, civilians." S.C. Res. 1973. Resolution 1973 authorized member states, acting individually or through regional organizations, "to take all necessary measures... to protect civilians and civilian populated areas under threat of attack in the Libyan Arab Jamahiriya, including Benghazi, while excluding a foreign occupation force of any form on any part of Libyan territory." *Id.* ¶4. The resolution also specifically authorized member states to enforce "a ban on all [unauthorized] flights in the airspace of the Libyan Arab Jamahiriya in order to help protect civilians" and to take "all measures commensurate to the specific circumstances" to inspect vessels on the high seas suspected of violating the arms embargo imposed on Libya by Resolution 1970. *Id.* ¶¶6-8, 13.

In remarks on March 18, 2011, President Obama stated that, to avoid military intervention to enforce Resolution 1973, Qadhafi needed to: implement an immediate ceasefire, including by ending all attacks on civilians; halt his troops' advance on Benghazi; pull his troops back from three other cities; and establish water, electricity, and gas supplies to all areas. Press Release, Office of the Press Secretary, The White House, Remarks by the President on the Situation in Libya (Mar. 18, 2011) ("Obama March 18, 2011 Remarks"), *available at* http://www.whitehouse.gov/the-press-office/ 2011/03/18/remarks-president-situation-libya.... Despite a statement from Libya's Foreign Minister that Libya would honor the requested ceasefire, the Libyan government continued to conduct offensive operations, including attacks on civilians and civilian-populated areas. See Press Release, Office of the Press Secretary, The White House, Letter from the President Regarding Commencement of Operations in Libya:

Text of a Letter from the President to the Speaker of the House of Representatives and the President Pro Tempore of the Senate (Mar. 21, 2011) ("Obama March 21, 2011 Report to Congress"), *available at* http://www.whitehouse.gov/the-press-office/2011/03/21/letter-president-regardingcommencement-operations-libya. In response, on March 19, 2011, the United States, with the support of a number of its coalition partners, launched airstrikes against Libyan targets to enforce Resolution 1973. Consistent with the reporting provisions of the War Powers Resolution, 50 U.S.C. §1543(a) (2006) [*infra* p. 307], President Obama provided a report to Congress less than forty-eight hours later, on March 21, 2011. The President explained:

> At approximately 3:00 p.m. Eastern Daylight Time, on March 19, 2011, at my direction, U.S. military forces commenced operations to assist an international effort authorized by the United Nations (U.N.) Security Council and undertaken with the support of European allies and Arab partners, to prevent a humanitarian catastrophe and address the threat posed to international peace and security by the crisis in Libya. As part of the multilateral response authorized under U.N. Security Council Resolution 1973, U.S. military forces, under the command of Commander, U.S. Africa Command, began a series of strikes against air defense systems and military airfields for the purposes of preparing a no-fly zone. These strikes will be limited in their nature, duration, and scope. Their purpose is to support an international coalition as it takes all necessary measures to enforce the terms of U.N. Security Council Resolution 1973. These limited U.S. actions will set the stage for further action by other coalition partners.

Obama March 21, 2011 Report to Congress. . . .

. . . [T]he President explained that "United States forces are conducting a limited and well-defined mission in support of international efforts to protect civilians and prevent a humanitarian disaster" and thus had targeted only "the Qadhafi regime's air defense systems, command and control structures, and other capabilities of Qadhafi's armed forces used to attack civilians and civilian populated areas." *Id.* The President also indicated that "[w]e will seek a rapid, but responsible, transition of operations to coalition, regional, or international organizations that are postured to continue activities as may be necessary to realize the objectives of U.N. Security Council Resolutions 1970 and 1973." *Id.* As authority for the military operations in Libya, President Obama invoked his "constitutional authority to conduct U.S. foreign relations" and his authority "as Commander in Chief and Chief Executive." *Id.* . . .

On March 28, 2011, President Obama addressed the nation regarding the situation in Libya. The President stated that the coalition had succeeded in averting a massacre in Libya and that the United States was now transferring "the lead in enforcing the no-fly zone and protecting civilians on the ground . . . to our allies and partners." Obama March 28, 2011 Address. In future coalition operations in Libya, the President continued, "the United States will play a supporting role — including intelligence, logistical support, search and rescue assistance, and capabilities to jam regime communications." *Id.* The President also reiterated the national interests supporting military action by the United States. "[G]iven the costs and risks of intervention," he explained, "we must always measure our interests against the need for action." *Id.* But, "[i]n this particular country — Libya — at this particular moment, we were faced with the prospect of violence on a horrific scale," and "[w]e had a unique ability to stop that violence." *Id.* Failure to prevent a slaughter would have disregarded

America's "important strategic interest in preventing Qaddafi from overrunning those who oppose him":

> A massacre would have driven thousands of additional refugees across Libya's borders, putting enormous strains on the peaceful — yet fragile — transitions in Egypt and Tunisia. The democratic impulses that are dawning across the region would be eclipsed by the darkest form of dictatorship, as repressive leaders concluded that violence is the best strategy to cling to power. The writ of the United Nations Security Council would have been shown to be little more than empty words, crippling that institution's future credibility to uphold global peace and security. So while I will never minimize the costs involved in military action, I am convinced that a failure to act in Libya would have carried a far greater price for America.

Id. As of March 31, 2011, the United States had transferred responsibility for all ongoing coalition military operations in Libya to the North Atlantic Treaty Alliance ("NATO")....

NOTES AND QUESTIONS

1. *Status of the Conflict.* What defines an "armed" conflict? Is it the level of violence? Number of casualties? Duration of the fighting? Nature of the warfare? Do the Conventions provide a clear definition? *See* Common Articles 2 and 3; AP I art. 1. Is there any doubt that the fighting in Libya in early 2011 was an armed conflict?

There is, as we have seen, more than one kind of armed conflict. A declared war between two or more states is easy to characterize: it is an international armed conflict, and all of the protections of the Geneva Conventions are applicable. By contrast, the uprising in Libya that began in early 2011 was, at least initially, a wholly indigenous armed insurrection bordering on civil war, giving it the appearance of a conflict not of an international character. Did that character change when NATO, the United States, and other states became involved militarily?

Who is entitled to label an armed conflict as international or non-international? How did the label or labels affect the rules for conducting military operations in Libya?

2. *Effect of the Security Council Resolutions on Jus in Bello.* Do you think the Security Council's establishment of a no-fly zone over Libya affected the applicability of IHL there? Did Security Council Resolution 1973 authorize military action beyond the maintenance of a no-fly zone? If it did, what was the scope of the authorization? How much discretion was conferred on NATO to protect civilians and civilian "populated areas"? Could NATO forces have undertaken ground or naval operations against Libyan armed forces? Could they have attacked members of the Libyan security forces who were not directly engaged in attacks on civilians but were supporting those attacks in some way, far from the field of battle? *See* Michael N. Schmitt, *Wings Over Libya: The No-Fly Zone in Legal Perspective,* 36 Yale J. Int'l L. Online 45 (2011) (arguing that the resolution creates broad authority to attack Libyan air and ground forces that is nevertheless limited by IHL).

A Secretary-General Bulletin and an International Committee of the Red Cross (ICRC) commentary agree that IHL applies in enforcing a Security Council action.

See U.N. Secretariat, *Secretary-General's Bulletin: Observance by United Nations Forces of International Humanitarian Law*, U.N. Doc. ST/SGB/1999/13 (Aug. 6, 1999), *reprinted in* 38 I.L.M. 1656; International Comm. of the Red Cross, *Commentary to the Third Geneva Convention Relative to the Treatment of Prisoners of War* 23 (Jean S. Pictet ed., 1960). *See also* Schmitt, *supra*, at 50-51, 54.

3. *Individual Battlefield Status.* One important qualifier to the principle noted just above is that IHL rules are "tempered by the scope of the authorization." Schmitt, *supra*, at 54. Review the Geneva Convention provisions on individual status alongside Security Council Resolution 1973. What is the geographic extent of the zone that may be targeted? Who may be attacked while enforcing the no-fly zone? Must the targets be inside the zone? If Qaddafi forces are captured by NATO personnel enforcing the no-fly zone, what provisions govern their detention and return? Do the same provisions apply to any NATO troops captured by the Libyan armed forces?

Can you describe the categories of persons who may be found on a battlefield? Why do you suppose it has become so hard to reliably distinguish combatants from civilians? We explore more fully the post-September 11 problems of labeling prisoners as combatants, unlawful combatants, or something else, *infra* p. 830.

In the Libya conflict, as in many other contemporary armed conflicts both international and not of an international character, government forces did not always wear uniforms or otherwise distinguish themselves as members of the state's military. How can we determine whether an apparently protected civilian is taking a "direct part in hostilities"? *See* AP I art. 51.3. What does it mean to end civilian protection from attack "for such time" as they directly participate? Must there be specific hostile acts, or would hostile intent suffice? Is a bomb maker or military accountant taking "direct part"? A driver? A chef? Does the civilian who takes direct part regain his immunity when he goes home at night?

What was the battlefield status of persons fighting for the Libyan rebels against Libyan government forces? Did the rebels constitute "armed forces" as understood in Common Article 3? Did the status of an individual rebel fighter turn on whether she was taking a "direct part in hostilities," or were members of such non-state armed groups equivalent to state soldiers? According to an influential 2009 study by the ICRC, membership in an organized armed group depends on the individual's function. A member is a combatant if he engages in a "continuous combat function . . . rather than a spontaneous, sporadic, or temporary role." ICRC, *Interpretive Guidance on the Notion of Direct Participation in Hostilities under International Humanitarian Law* 1007-1008, *reprinted in* 872 Int'l Rev. Red Cross 991 (Dec. 2008). Does the "continuous combat function" criterion make it easier to determine who directly participates in hostilities?

Today, Common Article 3 is customary international law applicable to all armed conflicts. What is the measure of the humane treatment required by that article? *See infra* Chapter 31. What other *jus in bello* protections are due captured persons in any kind of conflict? What additional protections are required for detainees in an international armed conflict?

4. *Distinction.* Many feel that the principle of distinction is the most important *jus in bello* rule. An ICRC study begins its list of customary norms this way: "Rule 1.

The parties to the conflict must at all times distinguish between civilians and combatants. . . . Attacks must not be directed against civilians." Jean-Marie Henckaerts, *Study on Customary International Humanitarian Law: A Contribution to the Understanding and Respect for the Rule of Law in Armed Conflict*, 87 Int'l Rev. Red Cross 175, 198 (Mar. 2005). Civilian objects are subject to the same principle. *Id.*; AP I art. 52.

Distinction was not mentioned as such in the Conventions until the Additional Protocols were adopted in 1977. If you advised the NATO forces enforcing the Security Council resolution, how would you translate AP I art. 48 into operational rules? If Libyan armed forces purposefully wore civilian clothing, with no insignias or other identifying features, how would U.S. and NATO commanders and pilots in the air know who their lawful targets were?

Applying the principle of distinction, civilian aircraft should not be attacked. But Security Council Resolution 1973 established a ban on all flights in Libyan air space. Did that mean a civilian aircraft entering the no-fly zone forfeited its civilian status and became a lawful target? *See* AP I art. 50(1), *supra*; art. 52(2) (Military objectives are objects "which by their nature, location, purpose or use make an effective contribution to military action and whose total or partial destruction, capture or neutralization, in the circumstances ruling at the time, offers a definite military advantage."). *See also* Schmitt, *supra*, at 51 (concluding that the resolution and the AP I provisions permit targeting of civilian aircraft).

At this writing, rebel forces remained pinned down in eastern Libya and continued to suffer heavy casualties. Witnesses, survivors, and some physical evidence showed that Qaddafi forces had repeatedly fired into residential neighborhoods with cluster bombs and ground-to-ground rockets, both anti-personnel weapons that are difficult to aim precisely but are designed to cause casualties over a wide area. C.J. Chivers, *Qaddafi Troops Fire Cluster Bombs into Civilian Areas*, N.Y. Times, Apr. 15, 2011. Does use of these weapons violate IHL?

5. *Necessity*. If distinction is the most humanitarian principle in IHL, the principle of necessity permits only "those measures which are indispensable for securing the ends of war, and which are lawful." U.S. War Dep't, *Instructions for the Government of Armies of the United States in the Field* (*General Orders No. 100: The Lieber Code*) art. 14 (Apr. 24, 1863). Which GC provisions reflect the principle of necessity? How should legal advisers give the concept practical meaning?

6. *Unnecessary Suffering*. The AP I provision in Article 35 makes it clear that the principle of unnecessary suffering limits the means for waging war. How would you define the key terms "of a nature," "superfluous injury," and "unnecessary suffering"? Does the U.S. use of cruise missiles fail the test? How about the use of cluster bombs in residential neighborhoods by Libyan armed forces? How is the principle of unnecessary suffering different from the principle of distinction?

7. *Proportionality*. Review AP I arts. 51.5(b) and 57.2(b), *supra*. The focus is clearly on civilians, not combatants. How do the two sets of protections differ? What do you suppose is the measure of "excessive" harm to civilians? Could you draft a more precise rule? Why do you think the drafters employed such open-ended terms? Is the 1956 U.S. Army field manual provision better: "[L]oss of life and damage to property incidental to attacks must not be excessive in relation to the concrete and

direct military advantage expected to be gained"? Department of the Army, *The Law of Land Warfare* (FM 27-10) ¶41 (1956). Under the Army rule, could a military operation that is anticipated to cause extensive civilian casualties ever be lawful?

Do proportionality requirements apply in non-international armed conflicts? If attacks on civilian aircraft violating the Libyan no-fly zone would not violate the principle of distinction and related AP I articles (see Note 5, *supra*), might they nonetheless have violated the principle of proportionality? Does the answer depend on whether those aircraft were determined to be directly participating in hostilities at the time of targeting? *See* Schmitt, *supra*, at 52 (yes to both questions). Would the presence of clearly innocent civilians on the civilian aircraft in such circumstances alter the calculus and preclude an attack? *See id.* (maybe).

How does the principle of proportionality differ from the principles of distinction and unnecessary suffering?

8. *War Crimes.* What, according to the Rome Statute of the International Criminal Court, must be shown to prove a war crime? How do the requirements differ in international and non-international armed conflicts? What is the differences between war crimes and grave breaches?

Because no definition can capture all possible violations of IHL, there is no fixed catalog of offenses. May civilians commit war crimes? How about members of organized armed groups? Taliban or Al Qaeda members? Where would prosecutions against such persons be brought? Should a greater effort be made to try to define all war crimes?

C.   TREATMENT OF PRISONERS IN WAR

In 1992, during the conflict in the Balkans that accompanied the breakup of Yugoslavia, Bosnian Muslim and Croat forces took control of villages with mostly Bosnian Serb populations in and around Konjic in central Bosnia and Herzegovina. Persons detained in a prison camp in the village of Celebici were tortured, sexually assaulted, subjected to cruel and inhuman treatment, and killed by camp guards and their commanders. In 1993, following mass atrocities in Croatia and Bosnia and Herzegovina, the United Nations Security Council created its first international criminal tribunal, the International Criminal Tribunal for the former Yugoslavia (ICTY). *See* Statute of the International Criminal Tribunal for the Former Yugoslavia (ICTY), as amended, *available at* http://www.un.org/icty/legaldoc-e/index.htm, established by S.C. Res. 827, U.N. Doc. S/RES/827 (May 25, 1993). Later that same year three Bosnian Muslims and one Bosnian Croat connected to the abuses at Celebici were indicted. They were arrested in 1996 and brought to the Hague in 1997 for a trial before the ICTY. The judgment of the trial chamber in *Prosecutor v. Delalic*, IT-96-T (ICTY Nov. 1998), found three of the four defendants guilty of multiple grave breaches of the Geneva Conventions for acts of willful killing, torture, sexual abuse, and inhuman treatment of detainees at the Celebici prison camp. In the Appeals Chamber of the ICTY, the four defendants and the prosecution challenged the Trial Chamber's legal standard for determining what constitutes the unlawful confinement of civilians, and its decision that some of the civilians in the camp were unlawfully detained. Excerpts from the Appeals Chamber decision follow:

Prosecutor v. Delalic (Celebici Case)

International Criminal Tribunal for the Former Yugoslavia, 2001
Appeals Chamber, Case No. IT-96-21-A
http://www.icty.org/x/cases/mucic/acjug/en/cel-aj010220.pdf

V.   UNLAWFUL CONFINEMENT OF CIVILIANS...

(i)   The unlawful confinement of civilians

320. The offence of unlawful confinement of a civilian ... [is] a grave breach of the Geneva Conventions.... The Trial Chamber found that the confinement of civilians during armed conflict may be permissible in limited cases, but will be unlawful if the detaining party does not comply with the provisions of Article 42 of Geneva Convention IV, which states:

> The internment or placing in assigned residence of protected persons may be ordered only if the security of the Detaining Power makes it absolutely necessary.
> If any person, acting through the representatives of the Protecting Power, voluntarily demands internment, and if his situation renders this step necessary, he shall be interned by the Power in whose hands he may be.

Thus the involuntary confinement of a civilian where the security of the Detaining Power does not make this absolutely necessary will be unlawful. Further, an initially lawful internment clearly becomes unlawful if the detaining party does not respect the basic procedural rights of the detained persons and does not establish an appropriate court or administrative board as prescribed in Article 43 of Geneva Convention IV. That article provides:

> Any protected person who has been interned or placed in assigned residence shall be entitled to have such action reconsidered as soon as possible by an appropriate court or administrative board designated by the Detaining Power for that purpose. If the internment or placing in assigned residence is maintained, the court or administrative board shall periodically, and at least twice yearly, give consideration to his or her case, with a view to the favourable amendment of the initial decision, if circumstances permit.
> Unless the protected persons concerned object, the Detaining Power shall, as rapidly as possible, give the Protecting Power the names of any protected persons who have been interned or subjected to assigned residence, or have been released from internment or assigned residence. The decisions of the courts or boards mentioned in the first paragraph of the present Article shall also, subject to the same conditions, be notified as rapidly as possible to the Protecting Power.

321. In its consideration of the law relating to the offence of unlawful confinement, the Trial Chamber also referred to Article 5 of Geneva Convention IV [*supra* p. 239].... This provision reinforces the principle behind Article 42, that restrictions on the rights of civilian protected persons, such as deprivation of their liberty by confinement, are permissible only where there are reasonable grounds to believe that the security of the State is at risk.

322. The Appeals Chamber agrees with the Trial Chamber that the exceptional measure of confinement of a civilian will be lawful only in the conditions prescribed by Article 42, and where the provisions of Article 43 are complied with. Thus the detention or confinement of civilians will be unlawful in the following two circumstances:

> (i) when a civilian or civilians have been detained in contravention of Article 42 of Geneva Convention IV, i.e., they are detained without reasonable grounds to believe that the security of the Detaining Power makes it absolutely necessary; and
> (ii) where the procedural safeguards required by Article 43 of Geneva Convention IV are not complied with in respect of detained civilians, even where their initial detention may have been justified.

(ii)   Was the confinement of the Celebici camp detainees unlawful?

323. As stated above, the Trial Chamber found that the persons detained in the Celebici camp were civilian protected persons for the purposes of Article 4 of Geneva Convention IV [*supra* p. 239]. The Trial Chamber accepted evidence that indicated that a number of the civilians in the camp were in possession of weapons at the time of their capture, but refrained from making any finding as to whether the detaining power could legitimately have formed the view that the detention of this category of persons was necessary for the security of that power. However, the Trial Chamber also found that the confinement of a significant number of civilians in the camp could not be justified by any means. Even taking into account the measure of discretion which should be afforded to the detaining power in assessing what may be detrimental to its own security, several of the detained civilians could not reasonably have been considered to pose any sufficiently serious danger as to warrant their detention. The Trial Chamber specifically accepted the evidence of a number of witnesses who had testified that they had not participated in any military activity or even been politically active, including a 42-year old mother of two children. It concluded that at least this category of people were detained in the camp although there existed no serious and legitimate reason to conclude that they seriously prejudiced the security of the detaining party, which indicated that the detention was a collective measure aimed at a specific group of persons, based mainly on their ethnic background. . . .

326. [One of the defendants] contends that since "the Trial Chamber, in determining that they [the civilians] were protected persons, found that they were not loyal to [. . .] Bosnia and Herzegovina, then they are virtually ipso facto security risks to the Government in that they are supporting the rebel forces." He explains the detention of persons who may not have borne arms on the basis that "if not engaged in actual fighting, then they are certainly in a position to provide food, clothing, shelter and information to those who are."

327. In the Appeals Chamber's view, there is no necessary inconsistency between the Trial Chamber's finding that the Bosnian Serbs were regarded by the Bosnian authorities as belonging to the opposing party in an armed conflict and the finding that some of them could not reasonably be regarded as presenting a threat to the detaining power's security. To hold the contrary would suggest that, whenever the armed forces of a State are engaged in armed conflict, the entire civilian population of that State is necessarily a threat to security and therefore may be detained. It is perfectly clear from the provisions of Geneva Convention IV referred to above that there is no such blanket power to detain the entire civilian population of a party to the conflict in such circumstances, but that there must be an assessment that each civilian taken into detention poses a particular risk to the security of the State. This is reflected in the ICRC Commentary to Article 42 of Geneva Convention IV:

> [. . .] the mere fact that a person is a subject of an enemy Power cannot be considered as threatening the security of the country where he is living; it is not therefore a valid reason for interning him or placing him in assigned residence.

Thus the Appeals Chamber agrees with the conclusion reached by the Trial Chamber that "the mere fact that a person is a national of, or aligned with, an enemy party cannot be considered as threatening the security of the opposing party where he is living, and is not, therefore, a valid reason for interning him."

328. It was contended by [one defendant] that detention in the present case was justified under international law because "[t]he government is clearly entitled to some reasonable time to determine which of the detainees is a danger to the State's security." Although the Appeals Chamber accepts this proposition, it does not share the view apparently taken by [this defendant] as to what is a "reasonable time" for this purpose. The reasonableness of this period is not a matter solely to be assessed by the detaining power. The Appeals Chamber recalls that Article 43 of Geneva Convention IV provides that the decision to take measures of detention against civilians must be "reconsidered as soon as possible by an appropriate court or administrative board." Read in this light, the reasonable time which is to be afforded to a detaining power to ascertain whether detained civilians pose a security risk must be the minimum time necessary to make enquiries to determine whether a view that they pose a security risk has any objective foundation such that it would found a "definite suspicion" of the nature referred to in Article 5 of Geneva Convention IV. Although the Trial Chamber made no express finding upon this issue, the Appeals Chamber is satisfied that the only reasonable finding upon the evidence is that the civilians detained in the Celebici camp had been detained for longer than such a minimum time.

329. The Trial Chamber found that a Military Investigative Commission for the crimes allegedly committed by the persons confined in the Celebici camp was established, but that this Commission did not meet the requirements of Article 43 of Geneva Convention IV as it did not have the necessary power to decide finally on the release of prisoners whose detention could not be considered as justified for any serious reason. There is therefore nothing in the activities of the Commission which could justify the continued detention of detainees in respect of whom there was no reason to categorise as a security risk. Indeed, it appears to have recommended the release of several of the Celebici camp detainees, albeit without result. Delic submits that "the government had the right to continue the confinement until it determined that the State's security would not be harmed by release of the detainees." This submission, which carries the implication that civilian detainees may be considered a risk to security which makes their detention absolutely necessary until proved otherwise, completely reverses the onus of justifying detention of civilians. It is upon the detaining power to establish that the particular civilian does pose such a risk to its security that he must be detained, and the obligation lies on it to release the civilian if there is inadequate foundation for such a view.

330. The Trial Chamber, as the trier of facts, is in the best position to assess and weigh the evidence before it, and the Appeals Chamber gives a margin of deference to a Trial Chamber's evaluation of the evidence and findings of facts. Nothing put to the Appeals Chamber indicates that there is anything unreasonable in the relevant sense in the Trial Chamber's findings as to the unlawful nature of the confinement of a number of civilians in the Celebici camp. As observed in the ICRC Commentary, the measure of confinement of civilians is an "exceptionally severe" measure, and it is for that reason that the threshold for its imposition is high—it must, on the express terms of Article 42, be "absolutely necessary." It was open to the Trial Chamber to accept the evidence of a number of witnesses that they had not borne arms, nor been active in political or any other activity which would give rise to a legitimate concern that they posed a security risk. The Appeals Chamber is also not satisfied that the Trial Chamber erred in its conclusion that, even if it were to accept that the initial confinement of the individuals detained in the Celebici prison-camp was lawful, the continuing confinement of these civilians was in violation of international humanitarian law, as the detainees were not granted the procedural rights required by article 43 of Geneva Convention IV.

NOTES AND QUESTIONS

1. *Confining Civilians.* Under what circumstances are civilians *not* protected persons according to the Geneva Conventions? When would it be permissible to confine civilians during an armed conflict? Reading Articles 5, 42, and 43 of Geneva Convention IV together, what grounds would justify civilian detention? What procedures must attend such confinement?

2. *Loyalty to the Host State as a Measure of Who May Be Detained?* If some of the civilians detained were not loyal to Bosnia and Herzegovina, why wasn't it lawful for the Bosnian authorities to presume that they were not protected? Do you think the requirement that the detaining authority have a "reasonable time" to determine whether detainees are a danger to the state strikes the right balance between liberty and security? Did the Appeals Chamber correctly weigh the competing interests? Could the Military Investigative Commission have made definitive judgements about loyalty if it had met the requirements of Article 43?

3. *Other Protections for Protected Persons.* The excerpt of the *Delalic* case provided here concerns the unlawful confinement of civilians. Reviewing the provisions of Geneva Conventions II and IV and AP I set out above, can you say what other protections exist for persons *while* they are confined? How and why do these protections differ from those considered in Part B of this chapter, which are designed to protect persons *before* they are taken into custody?

4. *Redress for Violations of IHL?* The ICTY is an extraordinary court, one created by the U.N. Security Council after worldwide condemnation of the atrocities in the Balkans. If there were no ICTY, how could the victims of Celebici gain redress? What courts would conceivably hear their cases? *See generally* Mark S. Ellis, *Combating Impunity and Enforcing Accountability as a Way to Promote Peace and Stability—The Role of International War Crimes Tribunals*, 2 J. Nat'l Security L. & Pol'y 111 (2006).

5. *POWs and Combatants.* Who qualifies as a POW in an armed conflict? How would you apply the Geneva Convention criteria for POW status to insurgents? To members of terrorist groups? To rebels fighting to liberate a nation from colonial rule? What is the significance, in each instance, of the fact that a person did or did not take a direct part in hostilities?

Whatever the status of detainees, can the detaining authority employ torture or cruel and inhuman methods to obtain information from them? We address this question in connection with the interrogation of Taliban and Al Qaeda prisoners after 9/11, in Chapters 31-32.

6. *Custom and Human Rights Law.* In addition to the protections embedded in the Geneva Conventions, there is a large and growing body of related customary law and HRL. Where would you look to find these supplemental norms? How would they be interpreted alongside the Geneva provisions?

III

Using Force Abroad

How We Go to War: Lessons from Vietnam   **10**

> Perhaps it would not be impossible to write a systematic theory of war, full of intelligence and substance; but the theories we presently possess are very different. Quite apart from their unscientific spirit, they try so hard to make their systems coherent and complete that they are stuffed with commonplaces, truisms, and nonsense of every kind.
>
> *Carl von Clausewitz, c. 1816-1818*[1]

> We are living in a pre-war and not a post-war world.
>
> *Eugene V. Rostow, 1976*[2]

In *Bas v. Tingy*, 4 U.S. (4 Dall.) 37, 43 (1800), *supra* p. 93, Justice Chase used the label "general war" to describe an armed conflict that is not "limited in place, in objects, and in time" and is restricted and regulated only by the *jus belli*, the law of war. The Vietnam War, which we analyze in this chapter, fits that definition in some respects. The U.S. government poured some $738 billion (in 2011 constant dollars) into that conflict over a period of more than two decades, and 58,000 Americans and more than a million Vietnamese lost their lives in the process. On the other hand, the use of U.S. forces was confined to one fairly small geographical area; there was no general mobilization of military and civilian resources during the Vietnam War, as there had been in the two world wars; no new national emergency was declared, as in the Korean War; and Congress did not formally declare war against another sovereign state.

The commitments of human resources and matériel may be less in "imperfect wars" (again borrowing the term from early cases like *Bas v. Tingy*), or what are sometimes termed "low-intensity conflicts," and in secret wars, when the United States uses force abroad without disclosing its actions. Still, for various reasons the stakes may be just as high.

The labels attached to particular conflicts are important, because they affect the sources and scope of authority and the decision-making process for sending military forces into battle. Yet the same basic legal principles apply in both large wars and small

---

1. Author's preface to an unpublished manuscript on the theory of war, in Carl von Clausewitz, *On War* 61 (Michael Howard & Peter Paret eds., 1976).
2. Quoted in Robert Scheer, *With Enough Shovels: Reagan, Bush and Nuclear War* 5 (1982), *reprinted in* Thomas Powers & Ruthven Tremain, *Total War: What It Is, How It Got That Way* 136 (1988).

ones, perfect and imperfect wars, and covert uses of force. More important is the process by which we decide to wage war and to attach the appropriate labels.

In this chapter we explore both the process for going to war and the process for ending it. Part A traces the history of the Vietnam War, arguments for its legality, and how these arguments fared in courts. Part B then takes up legislative efforts to limit the scope of the war. Finally, Part C treats the end game, especially appropriations measures designed to bring the war to a close. These materials reveal the motivation for enactment of the War Powers Resolution in 1973 (addressed in the next chapter), and they show why the "Vietnam syndrome" has influenced every subsequent congressional debate about uses of armed force.

A.   GOING TO WAR IN VIETNAM

The Vietnam War was — and remains — extremely controversial. You must not underestimate the complexity of the legal and political issues surrounding America's longest foreign war, nor the depth of feeling in those touched by it. You should also bear in mind that the record is still fragmentary, still being written. Much of what is set out in the following brief report was not known to the American people until long after the events described, and was not known even to members of Congress charged by the Constitution with initiating and supporting the continuation of war.

1.   How the War Began: A Brief History[3]

The Viet people have a national identity dating back at least to the third century B.C., when they occupied an area comprising much of what came to be known as North Vietnam. Despite a number of interruptions (including occupation by the Chinese at intervals spanning more than a thousand years), Vietnam expanded southward until, at the beginning of the nineteenth century, it included roughly the same geographical area that it does today. Before the end of the century, however, Vietnam, like its neighbors Laos and Cambodia, became a part of French Indochina. It was then taken over by the Japanese at the beginning of World War II.

Before the French returned to power in 1945, the Viet Minh, a coalition of nationalist groups led by Ho Chi Minh, declared the independent Democratic Republic of Vietnam with its headquarters in Hanoi. The French refused to recognize this indigenous government, however, and repeated appeals by Ho Chi Minh during 1945-1946 for U.S. assistance were ignored. France then became locked in a guerilla war that continued for more than seven years, with the Viet Minh receiving critical support from the Communist Chinese beginning in 1950.

Alarmed at the prospect of a Communist takeover in Vietnam, the U.S. government provided escalating economic and military aid to the French — from $10 million in 1950 to $1.1 billion in 1954 — and even drew up contingency plans for U.S.

---

3. This account is drawn from a variety of original and secondary sources, among them *The Pentagon Papers: The Defense Department History of United States Decision-making on Vietnam* (Mike Gravel ed., 1971) (4 vols.); S. Comm. on Foreign Relations, *Hearings on the Causes, Origins, and Lessons of the Vietnam War*, 92d Cong. (1972); and a multivolume report prepared by the Congressional Research Service for the Senate Committee on Foreign Relations, *The U.S. Government and the Vietnam War: Part I, 1945-1961*, and *Part II, 1961-1964*, S. Prt. No. 98-185 (1984); *Part III, January-July 1965*, S. Prt. No. 100-163 (1988).

military intervention that included the use of atomic weapons. Despite French requests, only a small number of U.S. military advisors were sent to Vietnam before the disastrous defeat of French forces at Dienbienphu in May 1954. In July of that year the French, with no realistic military or political alternatives, signed the Geneva Accords, in which they agreed to a cease-fire and withdrawal to the south of a demilitarized zone along the seventeenth parallel. It was understood that no additional troops or equipment would be introduced into either the North or the South except to maintain the status quo. The signatories also agreed that the country would be reunified following elections in 1956. Although neither the United States nor the newly formed State of Vietnam, based in Saigon and supported by the United States as a non-Communist alternative to Ho Chi Minh's government, signed the Accords, the United States pledged that it would not interfere with the agreement.

Yet U.S. leaders were dismayed, fearing (probably correctly) a Communist electoral victory in 1956. Even before the Accords were signed, President Eisenhower dispatched a secret military mission led by Colonel Edward G. Lansdale, a CIA operative, to conduct paramilitary operations and psychological warfare against the North. Soon thereafter, the U.S. began sending direct military aid to the South Vietnamese government of President Ngo Dinh Diem, in violation of the Geneva Accords. Diem was urged by the U.S. government not to participate in the elections contemplated by the Accords, and the elections were never held. In September 1954, the United States signed the Southeast Asia Collective Defense Treaty (SEATO Treaty) and persuaded other SEATO members to extend the treaty's protection to South Vietnam, which was not a signatory. The treaty called for each signer to "act to meet the common danger" posed by an attack on any area covered by the treaty.

As the United States assumed an ever larger role in South Vietnamese affairs, its goals included a strong, stable, constitutional government in the South, the weakening of Communist influence throughout Vietnam, and eventually free elections to reunify the country under non-Communist leadership. However, widespread corruption and nepotism in the Diem regime, the failure of land reform, imprisonment of political opponents, and forced resettlements helped to create an estranged populace and pave the way for a growing insurgency in the South led by the Viet Cong. When Hanoi began to take control of Viet Cong operations in 1959 and infiltrate its own forces into the South in violation of the Geneva Accords, full-scale war began once more. In July 1959 two American servicemen in uniform, the first of many following the French withdrawal, were killed by guerillas at Bien Hoa.

In the spring of 1961, President Kennedy broadened the American commitment by secretly dispatching 400 Special Forces troops and 100 other military advisors to the South, again clearly violating the Geneva agreement. The President also directed clandestine attacks on North Vietnamese and Laotian targets using U.S.-trained South Vietnamese forces. Despite continuing concerns about the ineffectiveness of the Diem government and suggestions from some of his advisors that the United States withdraw entirely, the President was persuaded, like Presidents Truman and Eisenhower before him, that the fall of South Vietnam would quickly result in the Communist domination of all Southeast Asia—the so-called "domino" theory. In November 1961, President Kennedy accepted the recommendations of his Secretaries of State and Defense to send additional support forces, including helicopters and other airlift equipment, naval patrols, and intelligence units. By the end of 1962 there were some 11,000 U.S. troops in South Vietnam, most of them in advisory or

From S. Comm. on Foreign Relations, The U.S. Government and the Vietnam War (Part I), S. Prt. No. 98-185, at XIII (1984).

support roles, and within another year the number had grown to 16,000. But President Kennedy resisted growing pressure from his advisors to send in large numbers of ground combat forces.

While control of the countryside slipped more and more from the hands of the Saigon government, Buddhist-led protests in the cities during 1963 were brutally suppressed. Later the same year, the United States encouraged and assisted a coup in which President Diem was killed. The government then changed hands nine times over the next 18 months, before Air Vice Marshall Nguyen Cao Ky assumed control and, in 1967, General Nguyen Van Thieu was elected President. Ky became Vice

President, and their government was able to remain in power until a few days before Communist forces entered Saigon in 1975.

After President Kennedy was assassinated in November 1963, President Johnson quickly authorized stepped-up clandestine operations by U.S. and South Vietnamese forces, including commando raids against northern rail and highway targets and bombardment of North Vietnamese coastal installations by PT boats. These operations were approved in Washington and supervised by the chief of the U.S. Military Assistance Command in Saigon. Elaborate secret plans for increased American military involvement, including full-scale bombing of the North in an effort to cut off support for the Viet Cong, were also drawn up, while the deteriorating military situation in the South and in Laos was reportedly concealed from Congress and the public as much as possible. In the early summer of 1964, the President's advisors even drafted a standby congressional resolution intended to be the equivalent of a declaration of war. Privately, President Johnson called the war "the biggest damn mess I ever saw" and lamented that "I don't think it's worth fighting for, and I don't think we can get out."[4]

On July 30, 1964, South Vietnamese commandos at the direction of General William Westmoreland, the U.S. commander in Saigon, launched raids against two North Vietnamese islands in the Gulf of Tonkin. Three days later, on August 2, several North Vietnamese PT boats attacked the U.S. destroyer *Maddox*, which was on an intelligence-gathering mission in the Gulf. One PT boat was sunk by gunfire from the *Maddox*, while two others were damaged by aircraft from the carrier *Ticonderoga*, which was stationed nearby. The next day, the *Maddox* was ordered back into the Gulf accompanied by the destroyer *C. Turner Joy* at the same time that South Vietnamese naval forces carried out two more attacks on the North. The day after that, on August 4, North Vietnamese torpedo boats reportedly attacked both U.S. destroyers in what came to be called the "Tonkin Gulf incident." However, there were no confirmed visual sightings of any North Vietnamese craft, and it now seems certain that there was no second attack.[5] Indeed, President Johnson remarked to Under Secretary of State George W. Ball a few days later, "Hell, those dumb, stupid sailors were just shooting at flying fish!"

Nevertheless, later on August 4, without waiting for further confirmation, the President briefed congressional leaders on the supposed incident and described his plan for a military response. There is no indication that he told them about U.S. responsibility for the earlier clandestine actions against the North or about recent air strikes against North Vietnamese targets inside Laos. Before the day was over, retaliatory raids were launched against targets selected months earlier — four North Vietnamese PT boat bases and an oil depot holding about 10 percent of the North's petroleum supply. Just before midnight, President Johnson went on television to describe these events to the nation, calling the U.S. response "limited and fitting." "We still seek no wider war," he declared.[6] With a presidential election just 90 days

---

4. *Tapes Show Johnson Saw Vietnam War As Pointless in 1964*, N.Y. Times, Feb. 15, 1997.

5. A study by a National Security Agency (NSA) historian released in late 2005, supported by newly declassified signals intelligence (SIGINT) reports, indicates that there was no attack on U.S. ships in the Tonkin Gulf on August 4, 1964, and that evidence pointing to an attack was "deliberately skewed" by NSA officials. *See* National Security Archive, *Tonkin Gulf Intelligence "Skewed" According to Official History and Intercepts*, Dec. 1, 2005, *at* http://www.gwu.edu/~nsarchiv/NSAEBB/NSAEBB132/press20051201.htm (with links to relevant documents).

6. 2 Pub. Papers 927 (Aug. 4, 1964).

away, the President apparently was eager to appear firmly anti-Communist but not reckless. According to one observer, "the Gulf of Tonkin affair presented itself as the perfect vehicle for Johnson to ride from August through election day."[7]

The next day, August 5, a revised draft resolution prepared by the Johnson administration was introduced in Congress by Senator Fulbright and Representative Morgan. In the ensuing brief debate, the Administration acknowledged the July 30 raids (but apparently not the raids on August 3), while it disavowed any connection whatsoever between the raids and the movements of the *Maddox*. The Tonkin Gulf Resolution, as it is now known, was passed on August 7, 1964, with only two dissenting votes in the Senate and none in the House. The resolution provided in part:

Tonkin Gulf Resolution
Pub. L. No. 88-408, 78 Stat. 384 (1964)

Whereas naval units of the Communist regime in Vietnam, in violation of the principles of the Charter of the United Nations and of international law, have deliberately and repeatedly attacked United States naval vessels lawfully present in international waters, and have thereby created a serious threat to international peace; and

Whereas these attacks are part of a deliberate and systematic campaign of aggression that the Communist regime in North Vietnam has been waging against its neighbors and the nations joined with them in the collective defense of their freedom; and

Whereas the United States is assisting the peoples of southeast Asia to protect their freedom and has no territorial, military or political ambitions in the area, but desires only that these peoples should be left in peace to work out their own destinies in their own way: Now, therefore, be it

Resolved . . . That the Congress approves and supports the determination of the President, as Commander in Chief, to take all necessary measures to repel any armed attack against the forces of the United States and to prevent further aggression.

Sec. 2. . . . Consonant with the Constitution of the United States and the Charter of the United Nations and in accordance with its obligations under the Southeast Asia Collective Defense Treaty, the United States is, therefore, prepared, as the President determines, to take all necessary steps, including the use of armed force, to assist any member or protocol state of the Southeast Asia Collective Defense Treaty requesting assistance in defense of its freedom.

Sec. 3. This resolution shall expire when the President shall determine that the peace and security of the area is reasonably assured . . . except that it may be terminated earlier by concurrent resolution of the Congress.

It is surely no accident that the resolution was drawn in such broad terms. President Johnson is said to have remarked that it was "like grandma's nightshirt — it covered everything."[8]

Within weeks after passage of the Tonkin Gulf Resolution, a consensus was reached at the White House to initiate a bombing campaign against the North in an effort to prevent the collapse of the Saigon government and to persuade Hanoi to suspend aid to the Viet Cong. But in the midst of a presidential election campaign against Senator Barry Goldwater, who was portrayed by the Democrats as

7. Gordon M. Goldstein, *Lessons in Disaster: McGeorge Bundy and the Path to War in Vietnam* 133 (2008).
8. Stanley Karnow, *Vietnam: A History* 374 (1983).

trigger-happy, President Johnson delayed the bombing and instead quietly ordered a resumption of coastal raids, destroyer patrols, and South Vietnamese air strikes on Laotian infiltration routes. Then, in February 1965, following Viet Cong attacks on U.S. forces at Bien Hoa, Pleiku, and Qui Nhon, the President gave the order for a sustained air war against the North, code-named Operation Rolling Thunder. The bombing campaign continued, with only short interruptions, for more than three years.

As the U.S. commitment in Vietnam grew, members of the public and Congress, especially Senator Fulbright, grew increasingly uneasy about the apparent lack of clear military and political objectives there. On April 7, 1965, President Johnson offered this rationale in a speech to the nation:

Why are we in South Viet-Nam? We are there because we have a promise to keep. Since 1954 every American President has offered support to the people of South Viet-Nam. We have helped to build, and we have helped to defend. Thus, over many years, we have made a national pledge to help South Viet-Nam defend its independence. And I intend to keep that promise. To dishonor that pledge, to abandon this small and brave nation to its enemies, and to the terror that must follow, would be an unforgivable wrong.

We are also there to strengthen world order. Around the globe from Berlin to Thailand are people whose well-being rests in part on the belief that they can count on us if they are attacked. To leave Viet-Nam to its fate would be to shake the confidence of all these people in the value of an American commitment and in the value of America's word. The result would be increased unrest and instability, and even wider war.

We are also there because there are great stakes in the balance. Let no one think for a moment that retreat from Viet-Nam would bring an end to conflict. The battle would be renewed in one country and then another. The central lesson of our time is that the appetite of aggression is never satisfied. . . .

In recent months attacks on South Viet-Nam were stepped up. Thus, it became necessary for us to increase our response and to make attacks by air. This is not a change of purpose. It is a change in what we believe that purpose requires.

We do this in order to slow down aggression. We do this to increase the confidence of the brave people of South Viet-Nam who have bravely borne this brutal battle for so many years with so many casualties. And we do this to convince the leaders of North Viet-Nam — and all who seek to share their conquest — of a simple fact: We will not be defeated. We will not grow tired. We will not withdraw, either openly or under the cloak of a meaningless agreement. . . . [3 Pub. Papers 395 (Apr. 7, 1965).]

Soon after the air strikes began, it became apparent that they would not materially disrupt North Vietnam's largely agrarian economy and flexible transportation system. Indeed, the bombing only seemed to stiffen Hanoi's resolve to fight on. The day before his April 7 address, the President approved an 18,000–20,000-man increase in U.S. forces in the South. More important, he ordered Marine battalions to leave their coastal enclaves for the first time and go on the offensive against Communist forces. However, these orders were kept secret to avoid the appearance of a change in policy.

In May, the President asked for and Congress approved a $700 million supplemental appropriation to help finance the expanding war effort. Pub. L. No. 89-18, 79 Stat. 109 (1965). Almost immediately thereafter, General Westmoreland began to request large increases in ground forces to carry out the new search-and-destroy strategy and to offset a rapid buildup in Viet Cong recruitment and infiltration by North Vietnamese Army troops from the North. These requests were not made public, but by the end of 1965 there were 184,000 U.S. troops in Vietnam. Approval was given for another 207,000 troops during 1966, and by early 1968 U.S. combat forces there totaled 510,000. It was not enough. Then-Defense Secretary Robert S. McNamara lamented much later that the United States had undertaken "a guerrilla war with conventional military tactics against a foe willing to absorb enormous casualties in a country without the fundamental political stability necessary to conduct effective military and pacification operations. It could not be done, and it was not done."[9]

A major turning point in the war occurred on January 31, 1968, during the Lunar New Year holiday, when Viet Cong and North Vietnamese forces launched the so-called "Tet offensive" against more than 100 cities and bases and the U.S. embassy in Saigon. The attack took U.S. forces completely by surprise. Tactically, the offensive failed, as the Viet Cong suffered devastating losses. Strategically, however, it arguably succeeded, because the massive scale and ferocity of the attacks caused Pentagon planners to rethink their goals and strategies. More important, its initial local successes — such as the siege of the U.S. embassy and the occupation of the historic city of Hue — were prominently featured on television news reports back in the United States, thereby focusing public attention even more closely on the conflict and raising for the first time the specter of defeat.

President Johnson relieved General Westmoreland of his command not long after, and on March 31 he announced a cutback in the bombing of the North to the twentieth parallel. In the same speech, the President declared that he would not be a candidate for reelection later that year.

Three days later, North Vietnam agreed to peace talks in Paris. When the bombing of the North was halted altogether in November, the peace talks were expanded to include representatives of the Viet Cong and the Saigon government. The negotiations continued for four more years before bearing fruit.

2.   Legal Foundations for the Commitment of U.S. Forces

The following memorandum from Leonard C. Meeker, who was Legal Adviser to the Department of State during the Johnson administration, contains the clearest and most succinct legal rationale for escalating and continuing the Vietnam war effort. It lays out three arguments for why the war was legal without a formal declaration of war, each based on theories surveyed in Chapters 3-8.

Leonard C. Meeker, The Legality of United States Participation in the Defense of Viet-Nam

54 Dep't St. Bull. 474 (1966), *reprinted in* 75 Yale L.J. 1085 (1966)

. . . There can be no question in present circumstances of the President's authority to commit United States forces to the defense of South Viet-Nam. The grant of authority to the President in article II of the Constitution extends to the actions of the United States currently undertaken in Viet-Nam. In fact, however, it is unnecessary to determine whether this grant standing alone is sufficient to authorize the actions

9. Robert S. McNamara, *In Retrospect: The Tragedy and Lessons of Vietnam* 212 (1995).

taken in Viet-Nam. These actions rest not only on the exercise of Presidential powers under article II but on the SEATO treaty — a treaty advised and consented to by the Senate — and on actions of the Congress, particularly the joint resolution of August 10, 1964. . . .

A. THE PRESIDENT'S POWER UNDER ARTICLE II OF THE CONSTITUTION EXTENDS TO THE ACTIONS CURRENTLY UNDERTAKEN IN VIET-NAM

Under the Constitution, the President, in addition to being Chief Executive, is Commander in Chief of the Army and Navy. He holds the prime responsibility for the conduct of United States foreign relations. These duties carry very broad powers, including the power to deploy American forces abroad and commit them to military operations when the President deems such action necessary to maintain the security and defense of the United States. . . .

In 1787 the world was a far larger place, and the framers probably had in mind attacks upon the United States. In the 20th century, the world has grown much smaller. An attack on a country far from our shores can impinge directly on the nation's security. In the SEATO treaty, for example, it is formally declared that an armed attack against Viet-Nam would endanger the peace and safety of the United States.

Since the Constitution was adopted there have been at least 125 instances in which the President has ordered the armed forces to take action or maintain positions abroad without obtaining prior congressional authorization, starting with the "undeclared war" with France (1798-1800). For example, President Truman ordered 250,000 troops to Korea during the Korean War of the early 1950's. President Eisenhower dispatched 14,000 troops to Lebanon in 1958.

The Constitution leaves to the President the judgment to determine whether the circumstances of a particular armed attack are so urgent and the potential consequences so threatening to the security of the United States that he should act without formally consulting the Congress.

B. THE SOUTHEAST ASIA COLLECTIVE DEFENSE TREATY AUTHORIZES THE PRESIDENT'S ACTIONS

Under article VI of the United States Constitution, "all Treaties made, or which shall be made, under the Authority of the United States, shall be the supreme Law of the Land." Article IV, paragraph 1, of the SEATO treaty establishes as a matter of law that a Communist armed attack against South Viet-Nam endangers the peace and safety of the United States. In this same provision the United States has undertaken a commitment in the SEATO treaty to "act to meet the common danger in accordance with its constitutional processes" in the event of such an attack.

Under our Constitution it is the President who must decide when an armed attack has occurred. He has also the constitutional responsibility for determining what measures of defense are required when the peace and safety of the United States are endangered. If he considers that deployment of U.S. forces to South Viet-Nam is required, and that military measures against the source of Communist aggression in North Viet-Nam are necessary, he is constitutionally empowered to take those measures. . . .

It has recently been argued that the use of land forces in Asia is not authorized under the treaty because their use to deter armed attack was not contemplated at the time the treaty was considered by the Senate. Secretary Dulles testified at that time that we did not intend to establish (1) a land army in Southeast Asia capable of deterring Communist aggression, or (2) an integrated headquarters and military organization like that of NATO; instead, the United States would rely on "mobile striking power" against the sources of aggression. However, the treaty obligation in article IV, paragraph 1, to meet the common danger in the event of armed aggression, is not limited to particular modes of military action. What constitutes an adequate deterrent or an appropriate response, in terms of military strategy, may change; but the essence of our commitment to act to meet the common danger, as necessary at the time of an armed aggression, remains. In 1954 the forecast of military judgment might have been against the use of substantial United States ground forces in Viet-Nam. But that does not preclude the President from reaching a different military judgment in different circumstances, 12 years later.

C.   THE JOINT RESOLUTION OF CONGRESS OF AUGUST 10, 1964, AUTHORIZES UNITED STATES PARTICIPATION IN THE COLLECTIVE DEFENSE OF SOUTH VIET-NAM . . .

Following the North Vietnamese attacks in the Gulf of Tonkin against United States destroyers, Congress adopted, by a Senate vote of 88-2 and a House vote of 416-0, a joint resolution containing a series of important declarations and provisions of law.

Section 1 resolved that "the Congress approves and supports the determination of the President, as Commander in Chief, to take all necessary measures to repel any armed attack against the forces of the United States and to prevent further aggression." Thus, the Congress gave its sanction to specific actions by the President to repel attacks against United States naval vessels in the Gulf of Tonkin and elsewhere in the western Pacific. Congress further approved the taking of "all necessary measures . . . to prevent further aggression." This authorization extended to those measures the President might consider necessary to ward off further attacks and to prevent further aggression by North Viet-Nam in Southeast Asia. . . .

Section 2 . . . constitutes an authorization to the President, in his discretion, to act — using armed force if he determines that is required — to assist South Viet-Nam at its request in defense of its freedom. The identification of South Viet-Nam through the reference to "protocol state" in this section is unmistakable, and the grant of authority "as the President determines" is unequivocal. . . .

Congressional realization of the scope of authority being conferred by the joint resolution is shown by the legislative history of the measure as a whole. The following exchange between Senators Cooper and Fulbright is illuminating:

Mr. Cooper [John Sherman Cooper]: . . .   The Senator will remember that the SEATO Treaty, in article IV, provides that in the event an armed attack is made upon a party to the Southeast Asia Collective Defense Treaty, or upon one of the protocol states such as South Vietnam, the parties to the treaty, one of whom is the United States, would then take such action as might be appropriate, after resorting to their constitutional processes. I assume that would mean, in the case of the United States, that Congress would be asked to grant the authority to act.

Does the Senator consider that in enacting this resolution we are satisfying that requirement of article IV of the Southeast Asia Collective Defense Treaty? In other words, are we now giving the President advance authority to take whatever action he may deem necessary respecting South Vietnam and its defense or with respect to the defense of any other country included in the treaty?

Mr. Fulbright: I think that is correct.

Mr. Cooper: Then, looking ahead, if the President decided that it was necessary to use such force as could lead into war, we will give the authority by this resolution?

Mr. Fulbright: That is the way I would interpret it. If a situation later developed in which we thought the approval should be withdrawn it could be withdrawn by concurrent resolution.

The August 1964 joint resolution continues in force today [1966]. Section [3] of the resolution provides that it shall expire "when the President shall determine that the peace and security of the area is reasonably assured by international conditions created by action of the United Nations or otherwise, except that it may be terminated earlier by concurrent resolution of the Congress." The President has made no such determination, nor has Congress terminated the joint resolution.

Instead, Congress in May 1965 approved an appropriation of $700 million to meet the expense of mounting military requirements in Viet-Nam. (Public Law 89-18, 79 Stat. 109.) The President's message asking for this appropriation stated that this was "not a routine appropriation. For each Member of Congress who supports this request is also voting to persist in our efforts to halt Communist aggression in South Vietnam." The appropriation act constitutes a clear congressional endorsement and approval of the actions taken by the President.

On March 1, 1966, the Congress continued to express its support of the President's policy by approving a $4.8 billion supplemental military authorization by votes of 392-4 and 93-2. An amendment that would have limited the President's authority to commit forces to Viet-Nam was rejected in the Senate by a vote of 94-2.

D. NO DECLARATION OF WAR BY THE CONGRESS IS REQUIRED TO AUTHORIZE UNITED STATES PARTICIPATION IN THE COLLECTIVE DEFENSE OF SOUTH VIET-NAM

No declaration of war is needed to authorize American actions in Viet-Nam. As shown in the preceding sections, the President has ample authority to order the participation of United States armed forces in the defense of South Viet-Nam.

Over a very long period in our history, practice and precedent have confirmed the constitutional authority to engage United States forces in hostilities without a declaration of war. This history extends from the undeclared war with France and the war against the Barbary pirates at the end of the 18th century to the Korean war of 1950-53.

James Madison, one of the leading framers of the Constitution, and Presidents John Adams and Jefferson all construed the Constitution, in their official actions during the early years of the Republic, as authorizing the United States to employ its armed forces abroad in hostilities in the absence of any congressional declaration of war. Their views and actions constitute highly persuasive evidence as to the meaning and effect of the Constitution. History has accepted the interpretation that was placed on the Constitution by the early Presidents and Congresses in regard to the lawfulness of hostilities without a declaration of war. The instances of such action in our history are numerous.

In the Korean conflict, where large-scale hostilities were conducted with an American troop participation of a quarter of a million men, no declaration of war was made by the Congress. The President acted on the basis of his constitutional responsibilities. While the Security Council, under a treaty of this country—the United Nations Charter—recommended assistance to the Republic of Korea against the Communist armed attack, the United States had no treaty commitment at that time obligating us to join in the defense of South Korea. In the case of South Viet-Nam we have the obligation of the SEATO treaty and clear expressions of congressional support. If the President could act in Korea without a declaration of war, a fortiori he is empowered to do so now in Viet-Nam.

It may be suggested that a declaration of war is the only available constitutional process by which congressional support can be made effective for the use of United States armed forces in combat abroad. But the Constitution does not insist on any rigid formalism. It gives Congress a choice of ways in which to exercise its powers. In the case of Viet-Nam the Congress has supported the determination of the President by the Senate's approval of the SEATO treaty, the adoption of the joint resolution of August 10, 1964, and the enactment of the necessary authorizations and appropriations. . . .

NOTES AND QUESTIONS

1. *Meeker's Article II Argument: Inherent Presidential Authority.* Leonard Meeker described the President's foreign relations powers in very broad terms, insisting that the Article II designation as Executive and Commander in Chief enabled the President to commit American forces to military operations "when the President deems such actions necessary to maintain the security and defense of the United States." The same broad claims have been made for the President more recently in connection with what was for a time called the "global war on terrorism." See *infra* p. 1172. Can you briefly marshal, from your earlier reading, arguments for and against such an expansive reading of the President's powers?

2. *Changing Circumstances and War-Making Authority.* As Mr. Meeker pointed out, strategic considerations in defending the nation today are quite different from those that faced the Framers two centuries ago. Do they require, however, an interpretation of the Constitution that gives greater independence to the President than in the past? Professor Velvel argued that the President's war powers have instead been diminished:

[I]n the world of today and tomorrow, even small wars can cause a chain of events which could bring mass destruction to the human race. . . . Such wars have a way of escalating, as has the struggle in Vietnam. They thus carry with them the ultimate risk of nuclear war. If the nation is to run this risk, the decision to do so should be as widely dispersed as the Constitution permits—the decision should be made by 535 federal legislators rather than a tiny handful of executive officials. [Lawrence R. Velvel, *The War in Viet Nam: Unconstitutional, Justiciable, and Jurisdictionally Attackable*, 16 U. Kan. L. Rev. 449, 470-471 (1968).]

How would you compare Professor Velvel's assumptions about the strategic implications of American involvement in Southeast Asia with those of Mr. Meeker?

With the terrorist attacks on the World Trade Center and the Pentagon on September 11, 2001, the world seems smaller still. Extensive media coverage gave an immediate face to the violence and provided an unprecedented intimacy with the suffering of the victims. Americans were left feeling vulnerable at home in a way that they never had during the Cold War. How should a court respond to these developments in interpreting the President's Article II powers today?

3. *The Power to Repel Sudden Attacks.* Is there any doubt that North Vietnamese military operations in South Vietnam created a "state of war" as that term was defined in *The Prize Cases, supra* p. 68? Did the President have the authority as Commander in Chief to treat an attack on any ally as if it were an attack on the United States? Has the President's implied "repel attack" authority expanded over time because of advances in military technology? Has his authority changed because of the emergence of stateless terrorists who rely on weapons of mass destruction to threaten the nation?

4. *Usage and Presidential War Making.* The spare language of Article II was said by Mr. Meeker to be augmented by usage. He recalled 125 earlier instances when troops were deployed by the President without the approval of Congress. Look closely at the historical examples he cites. Is his history sound?

Professor Moore observed that while these incidents represent "a substantial gloss which experience has placed on the Constitution," most of them involved short commitments and few losses; the ones that did not were highly controversial, such as the Korean War and the Mexican War of 1846. John Norton Moore, *Law and the Indo-China War* 542-543 (1972). How do you think Justice Frankfurter would have responded to this "usage" argument based on his opinion in *The Steel Seizure Case, supra* p. 25?

5. *Meeker's Treaty Authorization Argument.* The SEATO Treaty was, as Mr. Meeker pointed out, the "supreme Law of the Land," according to Article VI of the Constitution. Was the President therefore obliged as part of his Article II duties to "faithfully execute" the treaty as law by sending U.S. troops and equipment to Southeast Asia? How would you make that argument from the language of the treaty?

Southeast Asia Collective Defense (SEATO) Treaty

Sept. 28, 1954, 6 U.S.T. 81, 209 U.N.T.S. 28

ARTICLE IV

1. Each Party recognizes that aggression by means of armed attack in the treaty area against any of the Parties or against any State or territory which the Parties by unanimous agreement may hereafter designate, would endanger its own peace and safety, and agrees that it will in that event act to meet the common danger in accordance with its constitutional processes. Measures taken under this paragraph shall be immediately reported to the Security Council of the United Nations.

2. If, in the opinion of any of the Parties, the inviolability or the integrity of the territory or the sovereignty or political independence of any Party in the treaty area or of any other State or territory to which the provisions of paragraph 1 of this Article from time to time apply is threatened in any way other than by armed attack or is affected or threatened by any fact or situation which might endanger the peace of the area, the Parties shall consult immediately in order to agree on the measures which should be taken for the common defense. . . .

ARTICLE IX . . .

2. The Treaty shall be ratified and its provisions carried out by the Parties in accordance with their respective constitutional processes. . . .

Could the treaty itself be taken to satisfy U.S. constitutional processes—to authorize presidential action without additional debate and approval? Recall that the Framers rejected a proposal by Charles Pinckney to give the Senate alone the power to commit the nation to a state of war. See *supra* p. 18. Did Mr. Meeker not seek to achieve the same result indirectly, since the power to enter into treaties is given in Article II, section 2, to the President, with the advice and consent of two-thirds of the Senators present but without the concurrence of the House of Representatives? *See* John Hart Ely, *War and Responsibility: Constitutional Lessons of Vietnam and Its Aftermath* 13-15 (1993); *see also* William Van Alstyne, *Congress, the President, and the Power to Declare War: A Requiem for Vietnam*, 121 U. Pa. L. Rev. 1, 14 (1972) (arguing that the treaty was merely "an international contractual obligation—obliging Congress to make the declaration of war if it intends to fulfill the treaty commitment"; Louis Fisher, *Sidestepping Congress: Presidents Acting Under the U.N. and NATO*, 47 Case W. Res. L. Rev. 1237, 1256-1257 (1997) (Congress's approval required).

Can doubts about the internal authority of the treaty be resolved by reference to the President's independent powers of self-defense? How are those two authorities related in Mr. Meeker's argument? *See generally* Michael Glennon, *United States Mutual Security Treaties: The Commitment Myth*, 24 Colum. J. Transnat'l L. 509 (1986).

6. *Collective Self-Defense and International Law.* Aside from any obligations under the SEATO Treaty, did U.S. involvement in the Vietnam conflict violate either the U.N. Charter prohibition on the use of force or customary international norms? Mr. Meeker argued that the Republic of Viet Nam (R.V.N.) was subjected to armed attack by Communist North Vietnam, and that the United States was engaged in a lawful collective defense of its ally. 75 Yale L.J. at 1085. The R.V.N. certainly declared publicly that it was the victim of an armed attack, and it requested the military assistance of the United States—prerequisites to collective self-defense noted by the World Court in the *Nicaragua Case, supra* p. 218.

Some scholars contended, however, that the Republic of Viet Nam was not a separate sovereign state, and that Vietnam was embroiled in a civil, rather than an international war, making foreign intervention impermissible. They noted also that the 1954 Geneva Accords called for elections and unification of the country in 1956, a scant two years later. Yet when Mr. Meeker wrote his article, the Saigon and Hanoi governments had functioned as separate political and ideological entities for more than a decade, and each had been recognized by a number of other nations. Moreover, neither the Saigon government nor the United States signed the Accords, and each claimed not to be bound by their terms, especially the elections provision.

Defenders of U.S. involvement maintained that the cease-fire line established by the Geneva Accords along the seventeenth parallel was intended to permanently divide Vietnam into two states, even though the Accords provided that "the military demarcation line is provisional and should not in any way be interpreted as constituting a political or territorial boundary." Whatever the intent of the parties to the Accords, they argued further, the movement of North Vietnamese troops and matériel across the cease-fire line, in an effort to disrupt the political and territorial integrity of the Republic of Viet Nam, violated international norms and justified U.S. bombing of the North in response. Earlier U.S. and R.V.N. actions crossing the cease-fire line in the other direction were ignored in the debate or simply were not known until publication of the *Pentagon Papers* in 1971. Finally, it was claimed that even if the conflict in the South could be regarded as entirely indigenous, U.S. support for the Saigon government was warranted because the Viet Cong were materially aided by another state — namely, North Vietnam.

Supposing U.S. intervention to be justified as an act of collective self-defense, it was also circumscribed by Article 51 of the U.N. Charter, which permits such acts only "until the Security Council has taken measures necessary to maintain international peace and security," and requires such acts to be "immediately reported" to the Security Council. Why didn't the United States seek Security Council approval of its intervention? How long do you think the intervention could legitimately continue without such approval? See *infra* p. 361.

7. *Meeker's Third Argument: Tonkin Gulf Resolution as a Declaration of War?* Undersecretary of State Nicholas Katzenbach called the Tonkin Gulf Resolution "not a declaration of war" but "the functional equivalent" of such a declaration. *U.S. Commitments to Foreign Powers: Hearings Before the S. Comm. on Foreign Relations on S. Res. No. 151*, 90th Cong. 82, 145 (1967). Recall that in *Bas v. Tingy, supra* p. 93, the Supreme Court decided that Congress could authorize the President to engage in what Justice Washington called an "imperfect war" without a formal declaration. *See also Talbot v. Seeman*, 5 U.S. (1 Cranch) 1, 28 (1801). Indeed, the United States has been engaged in only five "declared" wars. Can you suggest why Congress did not formally declare war if it intended to authorize hostilities on such a large scale?

In the immediate aftermath of the 2001 terrorist attacks on the World Trade Center and the Pentagon, several members of Congress introduced resolutions that would have formally declared war on an unnamed enemy. Why do you suppose that Congress did not adopt such a resolution?

8. *Scope of the Tonkin Gulf Resolution.* Was the Tonkin Gulf Resolution intended by Congress to vest the President with the broad powers claimed by him? If the language of the resolution was sufficient to authorize the bombing of North Vietnam and the introduction of several hundred thousand American ground troops into the South, would it also have permitted the use of nuclear weapons to halt the spread of Communism in Southeast Asia, as some military leaders recommended? *See* Velvel, *supra* Note 2, at 473.

Are any doubts about the scope of the resolution dispelled by Mr. Meeker's reference to the debate between Senators Fulbright and Cooper at the time of passage? Other exchanges during consideration of the measure indicate a very different understanding. *See id.* at 473-476. Five years later it was recalled:

> The prevailing attitude was not so much that Congress was granting or acknowledging the executive's authority to take certain actions but that it was expressing unity and support for the President in a moment of national crisis and, therefore, that the exact words in which it expressed those sentiments were not of primary importance.
>   ...Although the language of the resolution lends itself to the interpretation that Congress was consenting in advance to a full-scale war in Asia should the President think it necessary, that was not the expectation of Congress at the time. In adopting the resolution Congress was closer to believing that it was helping to *prevent* a large-scale war by taking a firm stand than it was laying the legal basis for the conduct of such a war. [S. Comm. on Foreign Relations, S. Rep. No. 91-129, at 22-23 (1969).]

But does the Committee's statement reflect more than just congressional sour grapes? What should we make of the fact that the Committee then failed to take decisive action to repudiate the President's interpretation of the resolution?

Referring not only to the Tonkin Gulf Resolution but also to the appropriations and draft legislation that followed it, Professor Ely argued that Congress did approve U.S. military activities in Vietnam, although it "invariably did so with enormous ambiguity.... [Congress] lacks the will and/or courage to stop the President from involving us in military ventures, but at the same time has no wish to be held accountable for the wars he gets us into." John Hart Ely, *The American War in Indochina, Part I: The (Troubled) Constitutionality of the War They Told Us About*, 42 Stan. L. Rev. 876, 922 (1990). Professor Ely wanted to devise a "bright-line test of authorization as a way of forcing our representatives in Congress to take a clear stand, up front, on questions of war and peace." *Id.* at 924. Do you think such a bright-line test would be a good idea? Can you articulate such a test?

9. *Authorization of Force Against Terrorism.* Just three days after the September 11, 2001, terrorist attacks on the World Trade Center and the Pentagon, Congress approved, with only one dissenting vote in the House, a joint resolution authorizing the President to

> use all necessary and appropriate force against those nations, organizations, or persons he determines planned, authorized, committed, or aided the terrorist attacks that occurred on September 11, 2001, or harbored such organizations or persons, in order to prevent any future acts of international terrorism against the United States by such nations, organizations, or persons. [Pub. L. No. 107-40, §2(a), 115 Stat. 224 (2001).]

Do you think this resolution differs from the Tonkin Gulf Resolution in the scope of the authority it grants to the President? Can Congress have intended to give President George W. Bush as much discretion in the selection of targets and the use of military force as Presidents Johnson and Nixon claimed for themselves during the Vietnam War? How long do you think the authority provided by this resolution was meant to continue? Taking into account as well as you can the popular clamor for an immediate, strong response to the 9/11 attack, can you suggest amending language for the resolution excerpted above that might have preserved for Congress a larger role in formulating an appropriate response?

10. *Sharing Responsibility for the War.* As the Supreme Court noted in *The Prize Cases, supra* p. 68, *Martin v. Mott,* noted *supra* p. 71, and *Curtiss-Wright, supra* p. 53, the executive is uniquely well-equipped to gather and analyze information relevant to the decision to commit the nation to a state of war. But if the President fails or refuses to share that information with Congress, can the legislative branch fairly judge what laws will be "necessary and proper for carrying into Execution" Congress's enumerated powers under Article I, section 8?

Not until 1971 was it disclosed that President Johnson and his advisors had kept a great deal from Congress that might have affected its vote on the Gulf of Tonkin Resolution. In that year the *New York Times* and the *Washington Post* published parts of a 7,000-page top-secret Pentagon history of the Vietnam conflict, the so-called *Pentagon Papers,* covering the period from World War II to August 1968. (The leaking of the history and government efforts to prevent its publication are recounted in Chapter 43.)

Of course, Congress might have voted the same way if it had been told about other U.S. activities in the Tonkin Gulf or about Administration plans for possible escalation of the war effort. Should the withholding of such information affect the force of the resolution as law? Senator Fulbright, who was floor manager of the Tonkin Gulf Resolution in the Senate, suggested this analysis: "Now in contract law, a contract induced by fraud or mistake is voidable. Perhaps some analogous doctrine in constitutional law should apply when statutory authority is given a president on the basis of fraudulent or mistaken representations." J. William Fulbright, *Foreword,* in Michael J. Glennon, *Constitutional Diplomacy* at xiii (1990). Is Senator Fulbright's analogy fair or useful?

11. *Delegating War Power.* Assuming that Congress is empowered to delegate at least some of its war powers to the President, is it a legal problem, a practical problem, or both, that in the Gulf of Tonkin Resolution the delegation is described in very broad terms? What about the September 14, 2001, resolution excerpted *supra* Note 9? See generally *supra* pp. 106-107. Or is any risk of executive overreaching minimized by Congress's ability to modify or repeal its authorization at any subsequent time?

12. *Legal Opinion or Advocacy?* More than four decades after Mr. Meeker, the State Department's Legal Adviser, wrote the memorandum set out above, he offered this observation:

> I know you understand the situation in which we found ourselves when asked to write the 1966 memorandum. It had to be, and indeed was intended to be, an advocate's piece. Senator Joseph Sill Clark, of Pennsylvania, observed sympathetically three years later when I was being questioned by the Senate Foreign Relations Committee, "As lawyers we have all had the experience of being given a bad brief to argue; we just do the best we can with it." An unbiased memorandum meant to be objective would naturally have been different — giving both sides of the arguments about Presidential power and recognizing that justification of U.S. actions under international law was open to much dispute.
>
> Back in the 1960s we in the Office of the Legal Adviser spent much time on the necessity of constructing the Viet Nam memorandum. What we cared about a good deal

more was trying to assure that U.S. conduct in the Viet Nam war be compatible with the requirements of the Geneva Conventions, and making the case to Secretary of State Dean Rusk that the U.S. should seek at once a cease-fire in place to stop the hostilities. It should be said that he always gave us a fair hearing. He simply disagreed, for reasons we understood, and the up-shot was a failure of our efforts.

Today the American public and the rest of the world are confronted with a U.S. Administration that acts on the principle of unilateral decision and with disregard of treaty and other international obligations. I continue to hope that change for the better lies ahead. As Thomas Hardy is reported to have said, "if way to the Better there be, it exacts a full look at the Worst." [Letter from Leonard Meeker to Stephen Dycus (Mar. 25, 2007).]

Do you think most readers in 1966 would have regarded the memorandum as merely an "advocate's piece"? Who, in any event, was the Legal Adviser's client?

3.   Testing the Legitimacy of the War in Court

United States involvement in the military conflict in Southeast Asia was challenged in court by a number of plaintiffs on various grounds. All but a few of the suits were dismissed with the statement that the plaintiffs lacked standing to sue or that the issues presented to the court were political and therefore nonjusticiable. In the case that follows, the court had to assess its own role in the governance process while examining the separation of powers between the political branches. It declined to find all the issues nonjusticiable, but which did it reach?

Orlando v. Laird

United States Court of Appeals, Second Circuit, 1971
443 F.2d 1039, *cert. denied*, 404 U.S. 869 (1971)

ANDERSON, J. Shortly after receiving orders to report for transfer to Vietnam, Pfc. Malcolm A. Berk and Sp. E5 Salvatore Orlando, enlistees in the United States Army, commenced separate actions in June, 1970, seeking to enjoin the Secretary of Defense, the Secretary of the Army and the commanding officers, who signed their deployment orders, from enforcing them. The plaintiffs-appellants contended that these executive officers exceeded their constitutional authority by ordering them to participate in a war not properly authorized by Congress.

. . . [I]n *Berk v. Laird*, 429 F.2d 302 (2nd Cir. 1970) . . . [w]e held that the war declaring power of Congress, enumerated in Article I, section 8, of the Constitution, contains a "discoverable standard calling for *some* mutual participation by Congress," and directed that Berk be given an opportunity "to provide a method for resolving the question of when specified joint legislative-executive action is sufficient to authorize various levels of military activity," and thereby escape application of the political question doctrine to his claim that congressional participation has been in this instance, insufficient. . . .

It is the appellants' position that the sufficiency of congressional authorization is a matter within judicial competence because that question can be resolved by "judicially discoverable and manageable standards" dictated by the congressional power "to declare War." See *Baker v. Carr*, 369 U.S. 186 (1962); *Powell v. McCormack*, 395 U.S.

486 (1969). They interpret the constitutional provision to require an express and explicit congressional authorization of the Vietnam hostilities though not necessarily in the words, "We declare that the United States of America is at war with North Vietnam." In support of this construction they point out that the original intent of the clause was to place responsibility for the initiation of war upon the body most responsive to popular will and argue that historical developments have not altered the need for significant congressional participation in such commitments of national resources. They further assert that, without a requirement of express and explicit congressional authorization, developments committing the nation to war, as a *fait accompli*, became the inevitable adjuncts of presidential direction of foreign policy, and, because military appropriations and other war-implementing enactments lack an explicit authorization of particular hostilities, they cannot, as a matter of law, be considered sufficient.

Alternatively, appellants would have this court find that, because the President requested accelerating defense appropriations and extensions of the conscription laws after the war was well under way, Congress was, in effect, placed in a straitjacket and could not freely decide whether or not to enact this legislation, but rather was compelled to do so. For this reason appellants claim that such enactments cannot, as a factual matter, be considered sufficient congressional approval or ratification.

The Government on the other hand takes the position that the suits concern a non-justiciable political question; that the military action in South Vietnam was authorized by Congress in [the Tonkin Gulf Resolution] considered in connection with the SEATO Treaty; and that the military action was authorized and ratified by congressional appropriations expressly designated for use in support of the military operations in Vietnam.

We held in the first *Berk* opinion that the constitutional delegation of the war-declaring power to the Congress contains a discoverable and manageable standard imposing on the Congress a duty of mutual participation in the prosecution of war. Judicial scrutiny of that duty, therefore, is not foreclosed by the political question doctrine. *Baker v. Carr, supra; Powell v. McCormack, supra.* As we see it, the test is whether there is any action by the Congress sufficient to authorize or ratify the military activity in question. The evidentiary materials produced at the hearings in the district court clearly disclose that this test is satisfied.

The Congress and the Executive have taken mutual and joint action in the prosecution and support of military operations in Southeast Asia from the beginning of those operations. The Tonkin Gulf Resolution, enacted August 10, 1964 (repealed December 31, 1970) was passed at the request of President Johnson and, though occasioned by specific naval incidents in the Gulf of Tonkin, was expressed in broad language which clearly showed the state of mind of the Congress and its intention fully to implement and support the military and naval actions taken by and planned to be taken by the President at that time in Southeast Asia, and as might be required in the future "to prevent further aggression." Congress has ratified the executive's initiatives by appropriating billions of dollars to carry out military operations in Southeast Asia[2] and by extending the Military Selective Service Act with full

---

2. In response to the demands of the military operations the executive during the 1960s ordered more and more men and material into the war zone; and congressional appropriations have been commensurate with each new level of fighting. Until 1965, defense appropriations had not earmarked funds for Vietnam. In May of that year President Johnson asked Congress for an emergency supplemental appropriation "to provide our forces [then numbering 35,000] with the best and most modern supplies

knowledge that persons conscripted under that Act had been, and would continue to be, sent to Vietnam. Moreover, it specifically conscripted manpower to fill "the substantial induction calls necessitated by the current Vietnam buildup."[3]

There is, therefore, no lack of clear evidence to support a conclusion that there was an abundance of continuing mutual participation in the prosecution of the war. Both branches collaborated in the endeavor, and neither could long maintain such a war without the concurrence and cooperation of the other.

Although appellants do not contend that Congress can exercise its war-declaring power only through a formal declaration, they argue that congressional authorization cannot, as a matter of law, be inferred from military appropriations or other war-implementing legislation that does not contain an express and explicit authorization for the making of war by the President. Putting aside for a moment the explicit authorization of the Tonkin Gulf Resolution, we disagree with appellants' interpretation of the declaration clause for neither the language nor the purpose underlying that provision prohibits an inference of the fact of authorization from such legislative action as we have in this instance. The framers' intent to vest the war power in Congress is in no way defeated by permitting an inference of authorization from legislative action furnishing the manpower and materials of war for the protracted military operation in Southeast Asia.

The choice, for example, between an explicit declaration on the one hand and a resolution and war-implementing legislation, on the other, as the medium for expression of congressional consent involves "the exercise of a discretion demonstrably committed to the . . . legislature," *Baker v. Carr, supra* at 211, and therefore, invokes the political question doctrine.

Such a choice involves an important area of decision making in which, through mutual influence and reciprocal action between the President and the Congress, policies governing the relationship between this country and other parts of the world are formulated in the best interests of the United States. If there can be nothing more than minor military operations conducted under any circumstances, short of an express and explicit declaration of war by Congress, then extended military operations could not be conducted even though both the Congress and the President were agreed that they were necessary and were also agreed that a formal declaration of war would place the nation in a posture in its international relations which would be against its best interests. For the judicial branch to enunciate and enforce such a standard would be not only extremely unwise but also would constitute a deep invasion of the political question domain. As the Government says, ". . . decisions regarding the form and substance of congressional enactments authorizing hostilities are determined by highly complex considerations of

---

and equipment." 111 Cong. Rec. 9283 (May 4, 1965). Congress appropriated $700 million for use "upon determination by the President that such action is necessary in connection with military activities in Southeast Asia." Pub. L. 89-18, 79 Stat. 109 (1965). Appropriation acts in each subsequent year explicitly authorized expenditures for men and material sent to Vietnam. The 1967 appropriations act, for example, declared Congress' "firm intention to provide all necessary support for members of the Armed Forces of the United States fighting in Vietnam" and supported "the efforts being made by the President of the United States . . . to prevent an expansion of the war in Vietnam and to bring that conflict to an end through a negotiated settlement. . . ." Pub. L. 90-5, 81 Stat. 5 (1967). . . .

3. In H. Rep. No. 267, 90th Cong., 1st Sess. 38 (1967), in addition to extending the conscription mechanism, Congress continued a suspension of the permanent ceiling on the active duty strength of the Armed Forces, fixed at 2 million men, and replaced it with a secondary ceiling of 5 million. . . .

diplomacy, foreign policy and military strategy inappropriate to judicial inquiry." It would, indeed, destroy the flexibility of action which the executive and legislative branches must have in dealing with other sovereigns. What has been said and done by both the President and the Congress in their collaborative conduct of the military operations in Vietnam implies a consensus on the advisability of *not* making a formal declaration of war because it would be contrary to the interests of the United States to do so. The making of a policy decision of that kind is clearly within the constitutional domain of those two branches and is just as clearly not within the competency or power of the judiciary.

Beyond determining that there has been *some* mutual participation between the Congress and the President, which unquestionably exists here, with action by the Congress sufficient to authorize or ratify the military activity at issue, it is clear that the constitutional propriety of the means by which Congress has chosen to ratify and approve the protracted military operations in Southeast Asia is a political question. The form which congressional authorization should take is one of policy, committed to the discretion of the Congress and outside the power and competency of the judiciary, because there are no intelligible and objectively manageable standards by which to judge such actions. *Baker v. Carr, supra*, 369 U.S. at 217; *Powell v. McCormack, supra*, 395 U.S. at 518. . . .

[The concurring opinion of KAUFMAN, J., is omitted.]

NOTES AND QUESTIONS

1. *The Importance of Being First.* What is the practical political importance of the plaintiffs' "straitjacket" argument that after the President put U.S. resources — and honor — on the line, Congress was hard put to pull them back? Should that argument have affected the court's judgment about compliance with the Declare War Clause in Article I? Do you think Congress felt so constrained when it voted for the Gulf of Tonkin Resolution? *See* Van Alstyne, *supra* p. 282, at 23.

2. *The Importance of Collaboration.* In a companion case, *Berk v. Laird*, 429 F.2d 302, 304 (2d Cir. 1970), the government insisted that "the President's authority as Commander in Chief, in the absence of a declared war, is co-extensive with his broad and unitary power in the field of foreign affairs," citing *Curtiss-Wright.* The *Berk* court rejected this contention because "the congressional power to 'declare' a war would be reduced to an antique formality, leaving no executive 'duty' to follow constitutional steps which can be judicially identified." *Id.* at 305.

The *Berk* court went on to say, "Since orders to fight must be issued in accordance with proper authorization from both branches under some circumstances, executive officers are under a threshold constitutional 'duty [that] can be judicially identified and its breach judicially determined,'" *id.*, quoting *Baker v. Carr*, 369 U.S. 186, 198 (1962). Can you describe the "threshold constitutional duty" that the courts must be prepared to identify? Can you say under what "circumstances" proper authorization from both political branches would *not* be required to fight?

3. *The Adequacy of Collaboration.* What is the source of the *Orlando* court's "mutual participation" standard for prosecution of the war? What is the source of the court's

test for determining when there has been "sufficient" mutual participation? Do you see an element of circularity in the test? Does that circularity make this case look "political" and therefore nonjusticiable?

If the standard of "some mutual participation" is discoverable by the courts, will the "highly complex considerations of diplomacy, foreign policy and military strategy" be compromised less than if a single clear act—a declaration of war—were required?

4. *Different Approaches to Collaboration.* In *Massachusetts v. Laird,* 451 F.2d 26 (1st Cir. 1971), on facts substantially identical to those in *Orlando,* the court focused on the first decisional factor in *Baker v. Carr, supra*—"whether there is a 'textually demonstrable commitment of the issue to a coordinate political department' of government." *Id.* at 31.

> [T]he war power of the country is an amalgam of powers, some distinct and others less sharply limned. In certain respects, the executive and the Congress may act independently. The Congress may without executive cooperation declare war, thus triggering treaty obligations and domestic emergency powers. The executive may without Congressional participation repel attack, perhaps catapulting the country into a major conflict. But beyond these independent powers, each of which has its own rationale, the Constitutional scheme envisages the joint participation of the Congress and the executive in determining the scale and duration of hostilities. . . .
>
> As to the power to conduct undeclared hostilities beyond emergency defense, then, we are inclined to believe that the Constitution, in giving some essential powers to Congress and others to the executive, committed the matter to both branches, whose joint concord precludes the judiciary from measuring a specific executive action against any specific clause in isolation. In arriving at this conclusion we are aware that while we have addressed the problem of justiciability in the light of the textual commitment criterion, we have also addressed the merits of the constitutional issue. [*Id.* at 31-33.]

The court found the requisite joint concord in Congress's appropriation of billions of dollars over a number of years to support the war effort. In short, *Massachusetts v. Laird* found a constitutional requirement for collaboration between the political branches in a "textually demonstrable commitment" to those two branches, while the *Orlando* court found it in a judicially "discoverable and manageable standard" in the Declaration Clause.

With the tests in *Orlando* and *Massachusetts v. Laird* compare this suggested alternative:

> Congressional authorization need not be by formal declaration of war. . . . A joint resolution, signed by the President, is the most tenable method of authorizing the use of force today. To be meaningful, the resolution should be passed only after Congress is aware of the basic elements of the situation, and has had reasonable time to consider their implications. The resolution should not, as a rule, be a blank check leaving the place, purpose and duration of hostilities to the President's sole discretion. To be realistic, however, the resolution must leave the Executive wide discretion to respond to changing circumstances. [W. Taylor Reveley III, *Presidential War-Making: Constitutional Prerogative or Usurpation?* 55 Va. L. Rev. 1243, 1289-1290 (1969).]

Is Reveley's test constitutionally sound? How difficult would it be for the court to apply in a given case? Would the test be satisfied by the Tonkin Gulf Resolution or the subsequent appropriations and selective service legislation or both? By the September 14, 2001, resolution approving the use of military force against terrorists?

5. *Collaboration by Appropriation.* An important aspect of Congress's collaboration, according to both the First and Second Circuit Courts, was that it approved the expenditure of very large sums of money for the conduct of the war. Is the courts' analysis consistent with *Greene v. McElroy, supra* p. 102? Could the appropriations be said to have ratified the executive's actions? Did they meet the requirements for congressional acquiescence? See *supra* pp. 45-46. *See also* Ely, *supra* p. 282, at 27-30.

On the same day in September 2001 that Congress adopted its resolution approving the use of military force against terrorists and their sponsors, it appropriated $40 billion for "assistance to victims of the attacks, and to deal with other consequences of the attacks . . . including for the costs of . . . (2) providing support to counter, investigate, or prosecute domestic or international terrorism; . . . and (5) supporting national security." Pub. L. No. 107-38, 115 Stat. 220 (2001). Do you think this appropriation would bolster a possible presidential claim of authority to act without consulting Congress further?

6. *Political Question?* Invocation of the political question doctrine in many of the Vietnam cases caused great consternation among some commentators. For example, "If the judiciary, the organ of government most fundamentally committed to the vindication of constitutional principle, decides it cannot play its accustomed role in the Vietnam controversy, our basic institutional alternative to lawlessness is lost." Warren F. Schwartz & Wayne McCormack, *The Justiciability of Legal Objections to the American Military Effort in Vietnam,* 46 Tex. L. Rev. 1033, 1036 (1968). *See also* Velvel, *supra* p. 280, at 479-485; Louis Henkin, *Is There a Political Question Doctrine?* 85 Yale L.J. 597, 623-624 (1976). Professor Moore, on the other hand, while noting the importance of judicial candor in abstaining in these cases, cautioned against what he called an oversimplification of difficulties inherent in the judicial resolution of such major claims. Moore, *supra* p. 281, at 573.

The nation's highest court maintained sphinx-like silence on the justiciability of the Vietnam War cases. Dissenting from the refusal to rule in *Massachusetts v. Laird,* Justice Douglas complained, "The question of an unconstitutional war is neither academic nor 'political.' This case has raised the question in an adversary setting. It should be settled here and now." 400 U.S. 886, 900 (1970). *See also Mitchell v. United States,* 386 U.S. 972 (1967) (Douglas, J., dissenting from denial of certiorari); *Mora v. McNamara,* 389 U.S. 934 (1967) (Douglas and Stewart, JJ., dissenting); and *Atlee v. Richardson,* 411 U.S. 911 (1973) (Brennan, Douglas, and Stewart, JJ., voting to note probable jurisdiction). Only in *Atlee* did the Court affirm (without opinion) a lower court ruling that a test of the constitutionality of the war presented a nonjusticiable political question. *Atlee v. Laird,* 347 F. Supp. 689 (E.D. Pa. 1972). Can you guess why the Court decided not even to hear arguments in any of these cases? *See* Rodric B. Schoen, *A Strange Silence: Vietnam and the Supreme Court,* 33 Washburn L.J. 275 (1994).

7. *Standing to Sue?* Despite some uncertainty early on, it seems to have been settled that military personnel with orders for duty in Vietnam had standing to test

the legitimacy of the war. *See, e.g., Berk v. Laird,* 429 F.2d 302, 306 (2d Cir. 1970); *see also* Moore, *supra* p. 281, at 575.

In *Massachusetts v. Laird,* noted *supra* p. 290, the Commonwealth brought suit alleging impairment of its interest as a sovereign state under the Constitution, since "one branch, the executive, has exercised war-making powers, which the Commonwealth and its sister states had agreed would be exercised only by Congress." 451 F.2d at 28. Massachusetts also sued as *parens patriae,* citing the deaths and injuries of its inhabitants, consequential loss of their prospective civic and tax contributions, increased claims of dependents, additional burdens on its economy, disadvantage to its absentee voters, mass demonstrations, and damage to its public's morale. *Id.* Without deciding the issue of standing, the court expressed doubt about the status of the Commonwealth as protector of the rights of its citizens, since the "federal government is the ultimate *parens patriae* of every American citizen." *Id.* at 29. When the Supreme Court earlier denied leave for the state to file a bill of complaint in the same case, 400 U.S. 886 (1970), Justice Douglas dissented, arguing that only the executive, not the "federal government," represented the citizens in the prosecution of the war. *Id.* at 888.

Standing for members of Congress who brought suit challenging the legitimacy of the war was recognized in one case, *Mitchell v. Laird,* 488 F.2d 611, 613-614 (D.C. Cir. 1973), but denied in another, *Holtzman v. Schlesinger,* 484 F.2d 1307, 1315 (2d Cir. 1973), *infra* p. 303. Recent refinements in the law of standing for members of Congress are described *supra* pp. 138-140.

A law professor's suit to test the constitutionality of the war was dismissed on grounds that he had standing neither as an individual citizen nor as a taxpayer. *Velvel v. Nixon,* 415 F.2d 236 (10th Cir. 1969). Other cases with similar results are analyzed *supra* pp. 136-138.

8. *Challenges Based on International Law.* What result, on a motion to dismiss, if Orlando had asserted that his orders to Vietnam were unlawful because the United States was waging an aggressive war in violation of international law? In *United States v. Sisson,* 294 F. Supp. 515, 517 (D. Mass. 1968), the court noted that "[f]or argument's sake one may assume that a conscript has a standing to object to induction in a war declared contrary to a binding international obligation." But the court refused to rule on a charge that U.S. operations in Vietnam violated such an obligation, calling the case political and therefore nonjusticiable on grounds that the court (especially a court of the state accused of the violation) was "incapable of eliciting the facts during a war." *Id.* at 517-518. Similarly, in *United States v. Berrigan,* 283 F. Supp. 336, 342-343 (D. Md. 1968), *aff'd,* 417 F.2d 1009 (4th Cir. 1969), *cert. denied,* 397 U.S. 909 (1970), the court declared in dicta that "'[t]he Nurnberg defense' is premised on a finding that the government is acting in violation of international law in waging an aggressive war, and, as such, cannot be raised here because the question of violations of international law by the government is uniquely a 'political question.'"

More recently, however, in *Committee of U.S. Citizens Living in Nicaragua v. Reagan,* 859 F.2d 929, 941 (D.C. Cir. 1988), *supra* p. 176, the court indicated that if Congress adopted a foreign policy that violated a peremptory norm of international law, "that policy might well be subject to challenge in domestic court." The court mentioned as examples of such norms the prohibitions on slavery, torture, summary execution, and genocide. And in *Nicaragua v. United States,* 1986 I.C.J. 14, 100 [para. 190], the World

Court declared that "the prohibition of the use of force . . . constitutes a conspicuous example of a rule in international law having the character of *jus cojens*."

Taking an altogether different tack, an even more recent decision by a different D.C. Circuit panel included the remarkable and much remarked-upon statement that "[t]he international laws of war as a whole have not been implemented domestically by Congress and are therefore not a source of authority for U.S. courts." *Al-Bihani v. Obama*, 590 F.3d 866, 871 (D.C. Cir. 2010) (see *infra* p. 200).

How do you think these rulings might affect the willingness of a domestic court today to adjudicate a claim that the United States was engaging in unprovoked aggression? That the United States had done so?

B.   LIMITING THE SCOPE OF THE VIETNAM WAR

Following the Tet offensive in early 1968, public controversy over U.S. involvement in Indochina grew dramatically. Antiwar demonstrations at the Democratic National Convention in Chicago that year turned violent when police and National Guard troops clashed with protesters, while military intelligence units infiltrated dissident groups for the stated purpose of preventing domestic disorder. *See Laird v. Tatum*, 408 U.S. 1 (1972) (see *infra* p. 1161). Massive demonstrations in cities around the country followed later in the year. Vice President Hubert Humphrey became the Democratic Party nominee for President, first supporting and then renouncing the Johnson administration's policies in Southeast Asia, but not in time to save his candidacy, leaving Richard Nixon to win the election in November by a narrow margin. During the election campaign, candidate Nixon pledged to bring the Vietnam War to an end as quickly as possible. President Nixon described his progress in fulfilling that promise in a speech to the nation on April 7, 1971:

> When I left Washington in January of 1961 after serving 8 years as Vice President under President Eisenhower, there were no American combat forces in Vietnam. No Americans had died in combat in Vietnam.
>
> When I returned to Washington as President 8 years later, there were 540,000 American troops in Vietnam. Thirty-one thousand had died there. Three hundred Americans were being lost every week and there was no comprehensive plan to end the United States involvement in the war.
>
> . . . In June of 1969, I announced a withdrawal of 25,000 men; in September, 40,000; December, 50,000; April of 1970, 150,000. By the first of next month, May 1, I will have brought home more than 265,000 Americans — almost half of the troops in Vietnam when I took office. [3 Pub. Papers 523.]

The President then announced that he would pull out an additional 100,000 American troops before the end of 1971. *Id.* at 524.

The pace of withdrawal was not quick enough for many. Questions about the moral basis for the war multiplied with the revelation that U.S. troops had massacred 347 civilians in the village of My Lai in 1968. Pressure for ending the war reached a crescendo with the publication of the *Pentagon Papers* in June 1971.

Key to President Nixon's plans for winding down the war was a process called "Vietnamization." It was hoped that after U.S. troops were withdrawn, U.S. political objectives in Vietnam still might be achieved if only South Vietnamese forces were better able to defend themselves, so in 1969 large quantities of modern military supplies were shipped to the Saigon government for that purpose. However, direct U.S. military support was still to be provided on two new fronts.

1.   Cambodia[10]

Like Vietnam, Cambodia was a French colony until 1954, when it achieved independence under the leadership of Prince Norodom Sihanouk. During the Vietnam War, North Vietnamese units used the jungles of Cambodia as a sanctuary and base from which to conduct operations across the border into Vietnam. Some of their bases in the "fish hook" area of Cambodia (see map *supra* p. 272) were within easy striking distance of Saigon.

Almost as soon as President Nixon took office, he decided to launch air strikes across the Cambodian border against a massing of North Vietnamese troops there. The extension of U.S. might into new territory was necessary, he reasoned, to ensure the safety of U.S. forces in South Vietnam and to signal his resolve to the North Vietnamese. But the bombing was kept secret from the American people, from all but a few members of Congress, and even from many in the Pentagon.

Prince Sihanouk was overthrown by his prime minister, Lon Nol, in March 1970, some say with CIA complicity, and as the Cambodian army came under increasing pressure from Viet Cong, North Vietnamese, and local Communist Khmer Rouge forces, Lon Nol appealed to the United States for help. On April 30, President Nixon announced to the nation that 20,000 U.S. and South Vietnamese troops supported by U.S. aircraft had attacked Viet Cong and North Vietnamese bases inside Cambodia.

The President's announcement caused a spasm of protest in this country. Demonstrators at Kent State University were met by National Guard troops called out by the Ohio governor, and in the ensuing clash four students were shot and killed. In the days following, hundreds of other universities were forced by student and faculty strikes to close down, and 100,000 protestors marched on government buildings in Washington.

After U.S. combat forces were pulled out of Cambodia in the late summer, the Senate, but not the House, passed the Cooper-Church Amendment to the Foreign Military Sales Act. *See* S. Rep. No. 91-865, at 15 (1970), *reprinted in* 1970 U.S.C.C.A.N. 6054. It would have prohibited expenditures from any source for "retaining United States forces in Cambodia" or "conducting any combat activity in the air above Cambodia in support of Cambodian forces." Then, in January 1971, Congress passed and the President agreed to the following amendment to the Supplemental Foreign Assistance Authorization of 1971:

> In line with the expressed intention of the President . . . , none of the funds authorized or appropriated pursuant to this or any other Act may be used to finance the introduction of United States ground combat troops into Cambodia, or to provide United States advisers to or for Cambodian military forces in Cambodia. [Pub. L. No. 91-652, §7, 85 Stat. 1942, 1943 (1971).]

10. United States military action in Cambodia is described in William Shawcross, *Sideshow: Kissinger, Nixon and the Destruction of Cambodia* (1979). *See also* John Hart Ely, *War and Responsibility, supra* p. 282, at 30-32, 34-46, 98-104; Ely, *The American War in Indochina, Part I, supra* p. 284, at 902-905, 908-922; and Ely, *The American War in Indochina, Part II: The Unconstitutionality of the War They Didn't Tell Us About*, 42 Stan. L. Rev. 1093, 1137-1148 (1990).

2. Laos[11]

Like its neighbors, Vietnam and Cambodia, Laos became an independent state in 1954. The Communist Pathet Lao insurgency in that country, with support from North Vietnam, prompted President Kennedy to send a small covert force to Laos in 1961 in an effort to prevent further Communist advances. A second Geneva Agreement the following year called for withdrawal of foreign troops and establishment of a neutral coalition government headed by Prince Souvanna Phouma. Nonetheless, many North Vietnamese forces remained. While the United States withdrew its uniformed military personnel, it continued to support a "secret" army of some 70,000 Hmong tribesmen and as many as 21,000 Thai "volunteers." This large force was financed, trained, supplied, transported, and sometimes accompanied into battle by CIA operatives, many of whom were former U.S. Army Green Berets. See *supra* p. 271. In addition, between 1967 and 1972, U.S. military units based in South Vietnam apparently crossed the border more than 1,000 times to fight in Laos.

In June 1964, the United States began bombing operations in northern Laos to support the Laotian "secret" army. The following year the United States commenced bombing of the Ho Chi Minh Trail in the Laotian panhandle. By the time the attacks stopped nine years later, U.S. planes had dropped between 1.6 and 2 million tons of bombs in Laos, more than were released over Germany and Japan during all of World War II.

Although the Laotians, North Vietnamese, Soviets, and Chinese were perfectly aware of what was going on, Congress and the American public were kept in substantial ignorance of these developments. President Johnson explained privately that while Souvanna Phouma needed U.S. support to ward off the Pathet Lao, the Laotian leader preferred to maintain the appearance of neutrality. Without revealing the full extent of U.S. military actions in Laos, President Nixon announced that he had ordered U.S. forces to cut off the flow of troops and matériel down the Ho Chi Minh Trail and to force North Vietnamese compliance with the second Geneva Agreement. Richard M. Nixon, *Scope of U.S. Involvement in Laos*, 62 Dep't St. Bull. 405 (1970).

Anxious about apparently increasing U.S. military involvement in Southeast Asia and skeptical about President Nixon's assurances to the contrary, Congress passed this amendment to the Department of Defense Appropriation Act, 1970:

> In line with the expressed intention of the President of the United States, none of the funds appropriated by this Act shall be used to finance the introduction of American ground combat troops into Laos or Thailand. [Pub. L. No. 91-171, §643, 83 Stat. 469, 487 (1969).]

In February 1971, President Nixon, observing the strict language of the amendment, approved the invasion of northern Laos by a 30,000-troop South Vietnamese force supported by U.S. helicopters and bombers. Viewed as a major test of the Vietnamization program, this attempt to cut off troops and matériel from the Ho

---

11. United States military operations in Laos are recounted in Ely, *War and Responsibility, supra* p. 282, at 68-97; Ely, *The American War in Indochina, Part II, supra* p. 294, at 1094-1137; John M. Orman, *Presidential Secrecy and Deception: Beyond the Power to Persuade* 99-122 (1980); and Christopher Robbins, *The Ravens: The Men Who Flew in America's Secret War in Laos* (1987).

Chi Minh Trail ended in failure, and there was the predictable outcry that the war had been expanded without authorization from Congress.

NOTES AND QUESTIONS

1. *Mutual Participation in a Secret War?* What was the source of the President's authority to extend U.S. military might into Cambodia and Laos? Can it be found in the language of the Gulf of Tonkin Resolution, *supra* p. 274? Did other congressional acts constitute "some mutual participation" or "joint concord" between the political branches to authorize these incursions without full knowledge on the part of Congress?

The bombing of Cambodia between March 1969 and April 1970 was conducted almost entirely in secret. Flight records were destroyed. The State Department, the Secretary of the Air Force, and even the Air Force Chief of Staff were kept in the dark, and only a handful of members of Congress were told about the operations. U.S. military involvement in Laos was also concealed from Congress until at least 1969. Does this concealment have any bearing on the question of authority? *See* Ely, *War and Responsibility, supra* p. 282, at 68-104; Ely, *The American War in Indochina, Part II, supra* p. 294, at 1105-1148.

2. *Inherent Tactical Authority?* Did the President's Article II powers alone furnish the needed authority? Assistant Attorney General (later Chief Justice) William Rehnquist offered this legal rationale for the introduction of U.S. ground forces into Cambodia:

> The President's determination to authorize incursion into these Cambodian border areas is precisely the sort of tactical decision traditionally confided to the Commander-in-Chief in the conduct of armed conflict. . . . Faced with a substantial troop commitment to such hostilities made by the previous Chief Executive, and approved by successive Congresses, President Nixon had an obligation as Commander-in-Chief of the Armed Forces to take what steps he deemed necessary to assure their safety in the field. . . . It is a decision made during the course of an armed conflict already commenced as to how that conflict will be conducted, rather than a determination that some new and previously unauthorized military venture will be taken. [William H. Rehnquist, *The Constitutional Issues — Administration Position*, 45 N.Y.U. L. Rev. 628, 638-639 (1970).]

Do you agree with Rehnquist's analysis? Does it contain a standard for distinguishing between tactical decisions and those that need advance approval from Congress?

3. *Area and Use Limitations.* May Congress properly approve the induction of troops and the purchase of military supplies, then restrict the President's use of those forces in certain areas? Could it limit the President's use of some weaponry? Congress has occasionally adopted such limitations — for example, in the Selective Service Act of 1940, Pub. L. No. 76-783, 54 Stat. 885 (1940), which prohibited the assignment of U.S. conscriptees to duty outside the Western Hemisphere, except in U.S. possessions.

Professor Moore indicates that in authorizing the use of force Congress "might include limitations as to area of belligerent activities, kinds of activities authorized, and duration of the authorization." Moore, *supra* p. 281, at 560. He also suggests that

Congress might appropriately restrict the President's use of internationally prohibited chemical or biological weapons, which could involve "profound effects on international relations and the grave risk of escalation and unnecessary suffering." *Id.* at 566. But he warns that such additional requirements "should not be such as to limit needed flexibility of the President to respond to changed circumstances or to interfere with the President's power to make command decisions incident to successful prosecution of the war." *Id.* at 560-561.

Drawing on your readings in Chapters 4 and 5, can you make the cases for and against the constitutionality of congressional prohibitions on the deployment of U.S. forces in Laos or Cambodia? Military leaders repeatedly urged Presidents Kennedy and Johnson to authorize the use of nuclear weapons in Vietnam, even though such use was thought to present the risk that China would be drawn into the conflict. Might Congress have barred such use? Can you describe the boundary between proper and inappropriate congressional limitations? Do you think a court would ever be prepared to recognize such a boundary?

4. *Appropriations Limitations.* Is it important that the legislation that cut off funds for Cambodian operations omitted the language of the Cooper-Church Amendment, *supra* p. 294, which would have explicitly prohibited the aerial bombardment of Cambodia? Do you see any practical difference between the language of the respective funding restrictions for Cambodia and for Laos-Thailand?

5. *Border "Incursions" and International Law.* Were U.S. and South Vietnamese military activities in Laos and Cambodia permissible defensive measures incident to the defense of South Vietnam according to international law principles? Or did they represent naked aggression against the territories of two neutral sovereign states? On the one hand, Cambodia was accused of violating its duty as a neutral to expel Viet Cong and North Vietnamese forces operating from its territory, although as a practical matter it hardly seemed capable of doing so. On the other hand, Cambodia was said to be justified by Article 51 of the U.N. Charter in requesting U.S. assistance to defend against attack from those same forces. For their part, North Vietnam and the Viet Cong were charged with violating Cambodian and Laotian neutrality and with ignoring the requirements of the second Geneva Agreement concerning withdrawal of foreign troops from Laos. These violations, as well as the need to defend South Vietnamese territory, were said to justify the actions in question. The arguments on both sides are rehearsed, for example, in Richard A. Falk, *The Cambodian Operation and International Law*, 65 Am. J. Int'l L. 1 (1971); John Norton Moore, *Legal Dimensions of the Decision to Intercede in Cambodia*, 65 Am. J. Int'l L. 38 (1971).

Vietnam Veterans Memorial Wall, Washington, DC.

Photo courtesy of dcphototours.com.

C. ENDING THE VIETNAM WAR

1. Repeal of the Gulf of Tonkin Resolution

At the end of 1970, spurred by public dissent and frustrated by President Nixon's decision to invade Cambodia, Congress voted to repeal the Gulf of Tonkin Resolution by a single sentence attached to an unrelated measure. Pub. L. No. 91-672, §12, 84 Stat. 2053 (1971). In a case challenging the President's orders for deployment to Vietnam, an Army draftee argued that the repeal eliminated the congressional "mutual participation" on which the *Orlando* court based its finding of presidential authority. *DaCosta v. Laird* (*DaCosta I*), 448 F.2d 1368 (2d Cir. 1971). The *DaCosta I* court concluded, however, that "there was sufficient legislative action in extending the Selective Service Act and in appropriating billions of dollars to carry on military and naval operations in Vietnam to ratify and approve the measures taken by the Executive, even in the absence of the Gulf of Tonkin Resolution." *Id.* at 1369.

The court went on to declare:

It was not the intent of Congress in passing the repeal amendment to bring all military operations in Vietnam to an abrupt halt. The Executive was then endeavoring to unwind the conflict as rapidly as it was feasible to do so. It has steadily pursued that objective up to the present time and has declared it to be its intention to continue the withdrawals of combat forces. If the Executive were now escalating the prolonged struggle instead of decreasing it, additional supporting action by the Legislative Branch over what is presently afforded, might well be required. But that is not the case before us. . . .

As the constitutional propriety of the means by which the Executive and the Legislative branches engaged in mutual participation in prosecuting the military operations in Southeast Asia, is, as we held in *Orlando*, a political question, so the constitutional propriety of the method and means by which they mutually participate in winding down the conflict and disengaging the nation from it, is also a political question and outside of the power and competency of the judiciary. [*Id.* at 1369-1370.]

NOTES AND QUESTIONS

1. *Unwinding the Conflict?* How did the court know that it was not the intent of Congress to halt all military operations? Why was the Gulf of Tonkin Resolution repealed if not to remove that legislative authority for U.S. involvement in Vietnam? Was the repealer a nullity? Why do you think Congress did not express itself more clearly on this issue one way or the other? *Compare* Van Alstyne, *supra* p. 282, at 20-21, 27-28 (authority for war revoked), *with* Ely, *supra* p. 282, at 33 ("just more of Congress's playing Pontius Pilate").

Suppose Congress had wanted to bring the conflict to a prompt halt. Adopting the court's logic, would anything short of a "declaration of peace," a direct order to remove the troops, or a cutoff of funding galvanize the court to intervene?

How did the court know that the executive was endeavoring to unwind the conflict as rapidly as possible? Was it because the President publicly said so? Should the court have decided a case of such moment simply on the assurance of one of the parties to the controversy? In *Mitchell v. Laird*, 488 F.2d 611, 615-616 (D.C. Cir. 1973), the court observed:

> When on January 20, 1969 President Nixon took office, and when on the same or even later dates the other individual defendants took their present offices, they were faced with a belligerent situation not of their creation. Obviously, the President could not properly execute the duties of his office or his responsibility as Commander-in-Chief by ordering hostilities to cease on the very day he took office. Even if his predecessors had exceeded their constitutional authority, President Nixon's duty did not go beyond trying, in good faith and to the best of his ability, to bring the war to an end as promptly as was consistent with the safety of those fighting and with a profound concern for the durable interests of the nation — its defense, its honor, its morality.
>
> Whether President Nixon did so proceed is a question which at this stage in history a court is incompetent to answer. A court cannot procure the relevant evidence: some is in the hands of foreign governments, some is privileged. Even if the necessary facts were to be laid before it, a court would not substitute its judgment for that of the President, who has an unusually wide measure of discretion in this area, and who should not be judicially condemned except in a case of clear abuse amounting to bad faith. Otherwise a court would be ignoring the delicacies of diplomatic negotiation, the inevitable bargaining for the best solution of an international conflict, and the scope which in foreign affairs must be allowed to the President if this country is to play a responsible role in the council of the nations.
>
> In short, we are faced with what has traditionally been called a "political question" which is beyond the judicial power conferred by Article III of the United States Constitution. . . .

What if it could have been demonstrated that the President's statement did not reveal the whole truth, or even that he had deliberately lied? Do you think the court would then have been willing to declare the war effort unconstitutional, since the legitimacy of the war depended on "joint concord" or "some mutual participation" between the President and Congress? Would Congress have ordered the withdrawal of troops from hostilities?

2. *Political Options.* According to one commentator, the court should have been reluctant to intervene because Congress, if it chose to do so, could have cut off funding, censured the President, or even instituted impeachment proceedings against him. *See* Moore, *supra* p. 281, at 583. On the other hand, Justice Douglas observed in his dissent from the Supreme Court's refusal to hear one Vietnam case, "If we determine that the Indochina conflict is unconstitutional because it lacks a congressional declaration of war, the Chief Executive is free to seek one, as was President Truman free to seek congressional approval after our *Steel Seizure* decision." *Massachusetts v. Laird*, 400 U.S. 886, 899 (1970). How should the *DaCosta I* court have weighed these contrasting political possibilities? Was the court justified in waiting for a clearer expression of congressional intent to end the war more quickly?

3. *The Straightjacket Redux.* Unlike the *DaCosta I* court, the court in *Mitchell v. Laird, supra*, refused to characterize other legislation as "approval or ratification of a war already being waged at the direction of the President alone." 488 F.2d at 615.

> This court cannot be unmindful of what every schoolboy knows: that in voting to appropriate money or to draft men a Congressman is not necessarily approving of the

continuation of a war no matter how specifically the appropriation or draft act refers to that war. A Congressman wholly opposed to the war's commencement and continuation might vote for the military appropriations and for the draft measures because he was unwilling to abandon without support men already fighting. An honorable, decent, compassionate act of aiding those already in peril is no proof of consent to the actions that placed and continued them in that dangerous posture. We should not construe votes cast in pity and piety as though they were votes freely given to express consent. [*Id.*]

Does the *Mitchell* court's theory help to explain why Congress continued to pour troops and matériel into the war effort year after year? Is Congress powerless, as a practical matter, to stop the process once it is begun by the President? Does the phenomenon described by the court raise doubts about the feasibility of inferring congressional authorization or ratification from "mere" appropriations? See *supra* p. 105.

4. *Winding Up to Wind Down?* Like the war itself, peace talks that began in Paris in 1968 seemed to drag on interminably as first one side and then the other hoped to gain some advantage at the bargaining table from success on the battlefield. In February 1970, direct, secret talks began between National Security Adviser Henry Kissinger and North Vietnamese envoy Le Duc Tho, but those negotiations, too, moved slowly. At the end of March 1972, North Vietnamese regulars and the Viet Cong launched a new coordinated offensive in the South. Only 6,000 Americans remaining in the country were equipped for combat, and, while more than a million South Vietnamese were under arms, the future of the Vietnamization program seemed to be in jeopardy. President Nixon decided that the only way to conclude peace talks on favorable terms was to finally cut off the flow of war matériel from the Soviet Union and China to North Vietnam — not by a diplomatic initiative but by forcibly closing the northern seaports. To that end, in May the President ordered the mining of the ports and harbors of North Vietnam and the continuation of air and naval strikes against military targets north of the seventeenth parallel.

The expanded use of force produced yet another challenge in court. Recalling the language of *DaCosta I* that "[i]f the Executive were now escalating the prolonged struggle instead of decreasing it, additional supporting action by the Legislative Branch . . . might well be required," 448 F.2d at 1370, the plaintiff argued that "the President's conduct has so altered the course of hostilities in Vietnam as to make the war as it is currently pursued different from the war . . . held in *Orlando* and *DaCosta [I]* to have been constitutionally ratified and authorized by Congress." *DaCosta v. Laird (DaCosta III)*, 471 F.2d 1146, 1154 (2d Cir. 1973). The court again dismissed on political question grounds, this time citing a lack of discoverable and manageable judicial standards:

Judges, deficient in military knowledge, lacking vital information upon which to assess the nature of battlefield decisions, and sitting thousands of miles from the field of action, cannot reasonably or appropriately determine whether a specific military operation constitutes an "escalation" of the war or is merely a new tactical approach within a continuing strategic plan. . . . Are the courts required to oversee the conduct of the war on a daily basis . . . ? [*Id.* at 1155.]

Did the court reverse itself in its assessment of its own fitness to rule on a complicated fact situation — namely, whether the President was trying to wind down the war?

Once the President declared that it was necessary to intensify the war effort in order to wind it down, was there any way for the court to avoid characterizing the

President's action as "tactical"? How do you think the *DaCosta III* court would have ruled on a presidential decision to use nuclear weapons in North Vietnam? How about a decision to bomb Beijing?

2. Another Congressional Step Back

The debate about the war was transformed dramatically in June 1971 with publication of the *Pentagon Papers*, which revealed more than two decades of executive concealment and duplicity about U.S. involvement in Southeast Asia. See *supra* p. 271 and Chapter 43. In the late fall of 1971, Congress passed and the President signed a defense appropriations measure, to which was attached the Mansfield Amendment, so called for its Senate sponsor:

Mansfield Amendment

Pub. L. No. 92-156, §601(a), 85 Stat. 423, 430 (1971)

It is hereby declared to be the policy of the United States to terminate at the earliest possible date all military operations of the United States in Indochina, and to provide for the prompt and orderly withdrawal of all United States military forces at a date certain, subject to the release of all American prisoners of war held by the government of North Vietnam and forces allied with such Government and an accounting for all Americans missing in action who have been held by or known to such Government or such forces. . . .

The amendment went on to "urge and request" the President to implement this policy by negotiating for an immediate cease-fire in Indochina and to set a date certain for the withdrawal of all U.S. forces from the area, contingent on the return of prisoners of war and an accounting for Americans missing in action. Nearly identical language appeared in an earlier measure amending the Military Selective Service Act, Pub. L. No. 92-129, §401, 85 Stat. 348, 360 (1971).

NOTES AND QUESTIONS

1. *A Congressional Commitment?* Why do you think the Mansfield Amendment was not cast in more forceful terms? Should we conclude from the merely aspirational tone of the measure that a majority in Congress still approved of the President's actions in Southeast Asia, albeit grudgingly? Did the amendment serve to diminish the President's authority in any way?

2. *Effect of a Signing Statement.* In a statement on signing the military appropriations bill containing the Mansfield Amendment, President Nixon had this to say:

Section 601 expresses a judgment about the manner in which the American involvement in the war should be ended. However, it is without binding force or effect, and it does not reflect my judgment about the way in which the war should be brought to a conclusion. My signing of the bill that contains this section, therefore, will not change the policies I have pursued and that I will continue to pursue toward this end. [3 Pub. Papers 1114 (Nov. 17, 1971).]

Should a court testing the continued legitimacy of the war have been influenced by President Nixon's statement? If so, how? *See* T.J. Halstead, *Presidential Signing Statements: Constitutional and Institutional Implications* (Cong. Res. Serv. RL33667), Sept. 17, 2007.

3.   Cutting Off Funding for the War

The Hanoi government was outraged at President Nixon's renewed bombing and mining of its ports, but in the summer of 1972 Le Duc Tho met again in Paris with Dr. Kissinger. In October the two men reached a tentative agreement calling for a cease-fire, withdrawal of all remaining U.S. forces, and an exchange of prisoners. Political matters would be worked out among the various Vietnamese parties utilizing an interim "council of reconciliation." But the Saigon government balked at the agreement, and a number of details proved impossible to resolve quickly. In an effort to break the impasse, President Nixon ordered yet another round of bombing in the North, and in late December U.S. B-52s and other aircraft dropped 40,000 tons of bombs on the area between Hanoi and Haiphong. Then on January 27, 1973, a formal peace agreement was signed in Paris that closely resembled the one agreed to in October. The last U.S. troops left South Vietnam on March 29, 1973, and the last U.S. prisoners of war were allegedly released in Hanoi on April 1.

In Cambodia, air support for the Lon Nol regime had continued after all U.S. ground forces were withdrawn in 1970. When an effort to end fighting between Phnom Penh and Khmer Rouge forces in early 1973 ended in failure, U.S. forces began saturation bombing of Communist positions in that country. But a majority in Congress had finally had enough, and on May 31 a bill was passed containing the following amendment by Senator Thomas Eagleton:

> None of the funds herein appropriated under this act or heretofore appropriated under any other act may be expended to support directly or indirectly combat activities in, over or from off the shores of Cambodia or in or over Laos by United States forces. [29 Cong. Q. Almanac 102 (1973).]

President Nixon vetoed the bill on June 27, however, complaining that it would interfere with chances for a negotiated settlement in Cambodia, and the House failed to override his veto. Then on June 29, in a compromise, Congress approved and the President signed a measure to end all further U.S. military involvement in Southeast Asia:

Joint Resolution Making Continuing Appropriations for Fiscal Year 1974

Pub. L. No. 93-52, §108, 87 Stat. 130 (July 1, 1973)

Sec. 108. Notwithstanding any other provision of law, on or after August 15, 1973, no funds herein or heretofore appropriated may be obligated or expended to finance directly or indirectly combat activities by United States military forces in or over or from off the shores of North Vietnam, South Vietnam, Laos, or Cambodia.

The result is described in the following decision.

Holtzman v. Schlesinger

United States Court of Appeals, Second Circuit, 1973
484 F.2d 1307

MULLIGAN, J. This is an appeal from a judgment of the United States District Court [declaring] . . . that "there is no existing Congressional authority to order military forces into combat in Cambodia or to release bombs over Cambodia, and that military activities in Cambodia by American armed forces are unauthorized and unlawful. . . ." The order further enjoined and restrained the named defendants and their officers, agents, servants, employees and attorneys "from participating in any way in military activities in or over Cambodia or releasing any bombs which may fall in Cambodia." . . .

At the outset . . . we should emphasize that we are not deciding the wisdom, the propriety or the morality of the war in Indo-China and particularly the on-going bombing in Cambodia. This is the responsibility of the Executive and the Legislative branches of the government. The role of the Judiciary is to determine the legality of the challenged action and the threshold question is whether under the "political question" doctrine we should decline even to do that. . . .

We fail to see how the present challenge involving the bombing in Cambodia is in any significant manner distinguishable from the situation discussed by Judge Kaufman in *Da Costa v. Laird* [*DaCosta III*]. . . . If we were incompetent to judge the significance of the mining and bombing of North Vietnam's harbors and territories, we fail to see our competence to determine that the bombing of Cambodia is a "basic change" in the situation and that it is not a "tactical decision" within the competence of the President. . . . While we as men may well agonize and bewail the horror of this or any war, the sharing of Presidential and Congressional responsibility particularly at this juncture is a bluntly political and not a judicial question. . . .

The court below and our dissenting Brother assume that since American ground forces and prisoners have been removed and accounted for, Congressional authorization has ceased as determined by virtue of the so-called Mansfield Amendment, P.L. 92-156, 85 Stat. 430, §601. The fallacy of this position is that we have no way of knowing whether the Cambodian bombing furthers or hinders the goals of the Mansfield Amendment. That is precisely the holding of *Da Costa v. Laird* [*DaCosta III*]. Moreover, although §601(a)(1) of the Amendment urges the President to remove all military forces contingent upon release of American prisoners, it also in §601(a)(2) urges him to negotiate for an immediate cease fire by all parties in the hostilities in *Indo-China*. (Emphasis added.) In our view, the return and repatriation of American troops only represents the beginning and not the end of the inquiry as to whether such a basic change has occurred that the Executive at this stage is suddenly bereft of power and authority. That inquiry involves diplomatic and military intelligence which is totally absent in the record before us, and its digestion in any event is beyond judicial management. . . .

Since the argument that continuing Congressional approval was necessary, was predicated upon a determination that the Cambodian bombing constituted a basic change in the war not within the tactical discretion of the President and since that is a determination we have found to be a political question, we have not found it necessary to dwell at length upon Congressional participation. . . . We cannot resist however commenting [on] the most recent expression of Congressional approval by appropriation, [Section 108 of] the Joint Resolution Continuing Appropriations for Fiscal 1974 (P.L. 93-52), enacted into law July 1, 1973. . . .

Assuming arguendo that the military and diplomatic issues were manageable and that we were obliged to find some participation by Congress, we cannot see how this provision does not support the proposition that the Congress has approved the Cambodian bombing. The statute is facially clear. . . . It is [nevertheless] urged that since the Constitution entrusts the power to declare war to a majority of the Congress, the veto exercised makes it possible for the President to thwart the will of Congress by holding one-third plus one of the members of either House. . . .

We cannot agree that the Congress was "coerced" by the President's veto. There was unquestionably a Congressional impasse resulting from the desire of a majority of Congress to stop bombing immediately and the desire of the President that his discretion be unfettered by an arbitrarily selected date. Instead of an acute constitutional confrontation, as Senator Javits noted, an "agreement" was reached. (119 Cong. Rec. S12561 (daily ed. June 29, 1973)). . . .

While the Constitution vests the war declaring authority in the Congress, the Founding Fathers also conferred the veto power upon the President. (Art. I, §7, cl. 2). The suggestion that the veto power is impotent with respect to an authority vested solely in Congress by the Constitution is unsupported by any citation of authority and is hardly persuasive. It of course assumes here that the Cambodian bombing constitutes a new war requiring a new declaration and that it is not part of the extrication of a long suffering nation from an Indo-China war lasting for several years. This again in our view is the nucleus of the issue and we have no way of resolving that question particularly here on a motion for summary judgment. . . .

The judgment is reversed and the case is remanded with instructions to dismiss the complaint. The mandate shall issue forthwith.

OAKES, J. (dissenting). . . . Has Congress ratified or authorized the bombing in Cambodia by appropriations acts or otherwise? . . .

. . . [A]n argument could be made that congressional authorization of appropriations with knowledge of our "presence" in Cambodia was ratification. But for authorization on the part of Congress by way of an appropriation to be effective, the congressional action must be based on a knowledge of the facts. *Greene v. McElroy*, 360 U.S. 474, 506-507 (1959) (appropriation to Defense Department for security program did not ratify procedure denying right of an individual to confront witnesses). I am aware of only one instance in which it has previously been argued that a war was illegal as a result of Congress being misinformed as to the underlying facts surrounding American participation in that war. While the argument was unique and unsuccessful to boot, however, time has vindicated it, I believe. Furthermore, it was advanced by one whose views are worth consideration, even if they were expressed in "dissent," so to speak. I refer of course to Abraham Lincoln and his argument as a lone Congressman on January 12, 1848, in opposition to our "incursion" into Mexico and what later was called the Mexican War. *See* Cong. Globe, 30th Cong. 1st Sess. 93 et seq. (Appendix 1848).

And here, incredibly enough, it appears that neither the American people nor the Congress, at the time it was voting appropriations in aid of the war in Vietnam, were given the facts pertaining to our bombing in Cambodia. Recent disclosures have indicated that Air Force B-52 bombers were secretly attacking Cambodia in 1969, 1970 and even later while the United States was publicly proclaiming respect for Cambodian neutrality. . . .

. . . But the Congress whose ratification by way of appropriations acts is contended for here did not become aware of these covert bombings until July of 1973. And meanwhile the Congress had declared in the so-called Mansfield Amendment that it was "the policy of the United States to terminate at the earliest practicable date all military operations of the United States in Indochina. . . ." Appropriations Authorization-Military Procurement Act of 1972, Pub. L. No. 92-156, §601, 85 Stat. 423 (92nd Cong., 1st Sess. 1971). . . .

We come then to the effect of the legislation, following upon a presidential veto of an immediate prohibition against the use of funds to bomb in Cambodia, adopted as a compromise this July 1st: the Continuing Appropriations Act for Fiscal Year 1974, Pub. L. No. 93-52, 93rd Cong. 2nd Sess. (July 1, 1973) which expressly provided that ". . . on or after August 15, 1973, no funds herein or heretofore appropriated may be obligated or expended to finance directly or indirectly combat activities by United States military forces in or over or from off the shores of North Vietnam, South Vietnam, Laos or Cambodia." §108. . . .

It can be argued that Congress could, if it had so desired, cut off the funds for bombing Cambodia immediately by overriding the Presidential veto. This was indeed championed by those voting against the ultimate compromise Resolution. But it does not follow that those who voted in favor of the Resolution were thereby putting the Congressional stamp of approval on the bombing continuation. While the Resolution constituted a recognition that executive *power* was being exercised, it did not constitute a concession that such exercise was rightful, lawful or constitutional. . . .

. . . Congress, as I see it, took the only practical way out. It acknowledged the reality of the Executive's exercise of power even while it disputed the Executive's authority for that exercise. It agreed to a final cut-off date as the best practical result but never conceded the legality or constitutionality of interim exercise.

Thus the Resolution of July 1, 1973 cannot be the basis for legalization of otherwise unlawful Executive action. We are talking here about the separate branches of government, and in doing so we must distinguish between the exercise of power on the one hand and authorization for such exercise on the other. That the Executive Branch had the power to bomb in Cambodia, there can be no doubt; it did so, and indeed is continuing to do so. Whether it had the constitutional authority for its action is another question. . . .

NOTES AND QUESTIONS

1. *Vetoing Peace?* Is there any reason to suspect that the presidential veto process described in Article I, section 7, of the Constitution does not apply to congressional war making, as it does to other congressional acts? Should it matter that a particular act of Congress could be viewed not as war making, but as peacemaking — that it might take two-thirds of Congress to stop a war already begun? See *supra* p. 18 (remarks of George Mason); Ely, *supra* p. 282, at 43-46.

2. *Informed Participation.* Judge Oakes suggested that congressional consent is dependent on knowledge, citing *Greene v. McElroy,* 360 U.S. 474 (1959), *supra* p. 102. Is *Greene* distinguishable? Do you think the court should have taken account

of the fact that information about the bombing of Cambodia was not widely available
at the time Congress was voting on military appropriations? Can you imagine some
mechanism for Congress to keep itself informed about such developments?

3. *Judicial Realpolitik? Holtzman v. Schlesinger* was heard in a highly charged political atmosphere, as suggested by the series of stays and countermands by members of
the Supreme Court during the pendency of the case. *See* 414 U.S. 1316 (1973), 414
U.S. 1321 (1973). Newspaper headlines were filled with the story of secret bombings,
and the threat of impeachment proceedings was in the air. Indeed, it was suggested
that the Cambodia bombing be one of the impeachment counts. *See Hearings Before the
Comm. on the Judiciary Pursuant to H. Res. 803, Resolution Authorizing and Directing the
Comm. on the Judiciary to Investigate Whether Sufficient Grounds Exist for the House of Representatives to Exercise Its Constitutional Power to Impeach Richard M. Nixon, Book XI: Bombing
of Cambodia*, 93d Cong. (1974). Although the executive protested that Congress had
no right to fetter the executive's use of force, the Secretary of State submitted an
affidavit to the court committing the government to a termination of the bombing on
August 15, only seven days after the *Holtzman* case was decided. Do you think these
circumstances influenced the court's decision? Should they have? Do they affect the
value of the *Holtzman* decision as precedent for future cases?

United States bombing in Cambodia was halted on August 14, 1973, in accordance with the congressional mandate. In spite of the cease-fire prescribed in the
Paris peace agreement, forces on both sides moved quickly to consolidate their holdings in the South, but by the summer of 1974 Viet Cong and North Vietnamese troops
had recaptured all of the ground they had lost earlier. With the withdrawal of U.S.
forces, the South Vietnamese economy began to crumble, and the Thieu regime's
hold on the population grew more and more tenuous. United States support was
reduced sharply after President Nixon resigned in August 1974, while the North
Vietnamese poured new troops and supplies into the South for a climactic assault.
Finally, Communist troops entered Saigon on April 30, 1975, bringing the war to an
end.

The War Powers Resolution 11

The War Powers Resolution (WPR), enacted in 1973, was a legislative response to the Vietnam War. Congress hoped the measure would establish a consensual inter-branch procedure that would prevent the President alone or both political branches together from taking the country to war by stealth or inadvertence. But any hope of consent or cooperation was dashed when President Nixon vetoed the bill, and Congress overrode his veto. *See* Pat M. Holt, *The War Powers Resolution* 1-2 (1978). No President has conceded the constitutionality of the WPR or, many would say, fully complied with it, and its legal and practical effect today is unclear.

After reviewing the provisions of the WPR and President Nixon's veto message, we will analyze the resolution section by section in notes and questions. Several case studies in which the WPR was invoked for specific deployments of U.S. armed forces are presented in the following chapters.

War Powers Resolution
50 U.S.C. §§1541-1548 (2006)

SECTION 1. SHORT TITLE

This joint resolution may be cited as the "War Powers Resolution."

SECTION 2 [§1541]. PURPOSE AND POLICY

(a) It is the purpose of this chapter to fulfill the intent of the framers of the Constitution of the United States and insure that the collective judgment of both the Congress and the President will apply to the introduction of United States Armed Forces into hostilities, or into situations where imminent involvement in hostilities is clearly indicated by the circumstances, and to the continued use of such forces in hostilities or in such situations.

(b) Under article I, section 8, of the Constitution, it is specifically provided that the Congress shall have the power to make all laws necessary and proper for carrying into execution, not only its own powers but also all other powers vested by the Constitution in the Government of the United States, or in any department or officer thereof.

(c) The constitutional powers of the President as Commander-in-Chief to introduce United States Armed Forces into hostilities, or into situations where imminent involvement in hostilities is clearly indicated by the circumstances, are exercised only pursuant to (1) a declaration of war, (2) specific statutory authorization, or (3) a national emergency created by attack upon the United States, its territories or possessions, or its armed forces.

SECTION 3 [§1542]. CONSULTATION

The President in every possible instance shall consult with Congress before introducing United States Armed Forces into hostilities or into situations where imminent involvement in hostilities is clearly indicated by the circumstances, and after every such introduction shall consult regularly with the Congress until United States Armed Forces are no longer engaged in hostilities or have been removed from such situations.

SECTION 4 [§1543]. REPORTING REQUIREMENT

(a) In the absence of a declaration of war, in any case in which United States Armed Forces are introduced—

(1) into hostilities or into situations where imminent involvement in hostilities is clearly indicated by the circumstances;

(2) into the territory, airspace or waters of a foreign nation, while equipped for combat, except for deployments which relate solely to supply, replacement, repair, or training of such forces; or

(3) in numbers which substantially enlarge United States Armed Forces equipped for combat already located in a foreign nation;

the President shall submit within 48 hours to the Speaker of the House of Representatives and to the President pro tempore of the Senate a report, in writing, setting forth—

(A) the circumstances necessitating the introduction of United States Armed Forces;

(B) the constitutional and legislative authority under which such introduction took place; and

(C) the estimated scope and duration of the hostilities or involvement.

(b) The President shall provide such other information as the Congress may request in the fulfillment of its constitutional responsibilities with respect to committing the Nation to war and to the use of United States Armed Forces abroad.

(c) Whenever United States Armed Forces are introduced into hostilities or into any situation described in subsection (a) of this section, the President shall, so long as such Armed Forces continue to be engaged in such hostilities or situation, report to the Congress periodically on the status of such hostilities or situation as well as on the scope and duration of such hostilities or situation, but in no event shall he report to the Congress less often than once every six months.

SECTION 5 [§1544]. CONGRESSIONAL ACTION

(a) Each report submitted pursuant to section 1543(a)(1) of this title shall be transmitted to the Speaker of the House of Representatives and to the President pro tempore of the Senate on the same calendar day. Each report so transmitted shall be referred to the Committee on Foreign Affairs of the House of Representatives and to the Committee on Foreign Relations of the Senate for appropriate action. If, when the report is transmitted, the Congress has adjourned sine die or has adjourned for any period in excess of three calendar days, the Speaker of the House of Representatives and the President pro tempore of the Senate, if they deem it advisable (or if petitioned by at least 30 percent of the membership of their respective Houses) shall jointly request the President to convene Congress in order that it may consider the report and take appropriate action pursuant to this section.

(b) Within sixty calendar days after a report is submitted or is required to be submitted pursuant to section 1543(a)(1) of this title, whichever is earlier, the President shall terminate any use of United States Armed Forces with respect to which such report was submitted (or required to be submitted), unless the Congress (1) has declared war or has enacted a specific authorization for such use of United States Armed Forces, (2) has extended by law such sixty-day period, or (3) is physically unable to meet as a result of an armed attack upon the United States. Such sixty-day period shall be extended for not more than an additional thirty days if the President determines and certifies to the Congress in writing that unavoidable military necessity respecting the safety of United States Armed Forces requires the continued use of such Armed Forces in the course of bringing about a prompt removal of such forces.

(c) Notwithstanding subsection (b) of this section, at any time that United States Armed Forces are engaged in hostilities outside the territory of the United States, its possessions and territories without a declaration of war or specific statutory authorization, such forces shall be removed by the President if the Congress so directs by concurrent resolution.

[Sections 6 & 7, §§1545-1546, Congressional Priority Procedures for Joint Resolution or Bill, and for Concurrent Resolution, respectively, provide for expedited consideration of measures to approve the President's actions under §1544(b) or disapprove them under §1544(c).]

SECTION 8 [§1547]. INTERPRETATION OF JOINT RESOLUTION

(a) Authority to introduce United States Armed Forces into hostilities or into situations wherein involvement in hostilities is clearly indicated by the circumstances shall not be inferred—

(1) from any provision of law (whether or not in effect before November 7, 1973), including any provision contained in any Appropriation Act, unless such provision specifically authorizes the introduction of United States Armed Forces into hostilities or into such situations and states that it is intended to constitute specific statutory authorization within the meaning of this chapter; or

(2) from any treaty heretofore or hereafter ratified unless such treaty is implemented by legislation specifically authorizing the introduction of United States

Armed Forces into hostilities or into such situations and stating that it is intended to constitute specific statutory authorization within the meaning of this chapter. . . .

(c) For purposes of this chapter, the term "introduction of United States Armed Forces" includes the assignment of members of such Armed Forces to command, coordinate, participate in the movement of, or accompany the regular or irregular military forces of any foreign country or government when such military forces are engaged, or there exists an imminent threat that such forces will become engaged, in hostilities.

(d) Nothing in this chapter —

(1) is intended to alter the constitutional authority of the Congress or of the President, or the provisions of existing treaties; or

(2) shall be construed as granting any authority to the President with respect to the introduction of United States Armed Forces into hostilities or into situations wherein involvement in hostilities is clearly indicated by the circumstances which authority he would not have had in the absence of this chapter.

SECTION 9 [§1548]. SEPARABILITY OF PROVISIONS

If any provision of this chapter or the application thereof to any person or circumstance is held invalid, the remainder of the chapter and the application of such provision to any other person or circumstance shall not be affected thereby.

Richard M. Nixon, Veto of the War Powers Resolution
5 Pub. Papers 893 (Oct. 24, 1973)

To the House of Representatives:

I hereby return without my approval House Joint Resolution 542 — the War Powers Resolution. While I am in accord with the desire of the Congress to assert its proper role in the conduct of our foreign affairs, the restrictions which this resolution would impose upon the authority of the President are both unconstitutional and dangerous to the best interests of our Nation. . . .

CLEARLY UNCONSTITUTIONAL

House Joint Resolution 542 would attempt to take away, by a mere legislative act, authorities which the President has properly exercised under the Constitution for almost 200 years. One of its provisions would automatically cut off certain authorities after sixty days unless the Congress extended them. Another would allow the Congress to eliminate certain authorities merely by the passage of a concurrent resolution — an action which does not normally have the force of law, since it denies the President his constitutional role in approving legislation.

I believe that both these provisions are unconstitutional. The only way in which the constitutional powers of a branch of the Government can be altered is by amending the Constitution — and any attempt to make such alterations by legislation alone is clearly without force.

UNDERMINING OUR FOREIGN POLICY

While I firmly believe that a veto of House Joint Resolution 542 is warranted solely on constitutional grounds, I am also deeply disturbed by the practical consequences of this resolution. For it would seriously undermine this Nation's ability to act decisively and convincingly in times of international crisis. As a result, the confidence of our allies in our ability to assist them could be diminished and the respect of our adversaries for our deterrent posture could decline. A permanent and substantial element of unpredictability would be injected into the world's assessment of American behavior, further increasing the likelihood of miscalculation and war.

If this resolution had been in operation, America's effective response to a variety of challenges in recent years would have been vastly complicated or even made impossible. We may well have been unable to respond in the way we did during the Berlin crisis of 1961, the Cuban missile crisis of 1962, the Congo rescue operation in 1964, and the Jordanian crisis of 1970—to mention just a few examples. In addition, our recent actions to bring about a peaceful settlement of the hostilities in the Middle East would have been seriously impaired if this resolution had been in force.

While all the specific consequences of House Joint Resolution 542 cannot yet be predicted, it is clear that it would undercut the ability of the United States to act as an effective influence for peace. For example, the provision automatically cutting off certain authorities after 60 days unless they are extended by the Congress could work to prolong or intensify a crisis. Until the Congress suspended the deadline, there would be at least a chance of United States withdrawal and an adversary would be tempted therefore to postpone serious negotiations until the 60 days were up. Only after the Congress acted would there be a strong incentive for an adversary to negotiate. In addition, the very existence of a deadline could lead to an escalation of hostilities in order to achieve certain objectives before the 60 days expired.

The measure would jeopardize our role as a force for peace in other ways as well. It would, for example, strike from the President's hand a wide range of important peace-keeping tools by eliminating his ability to exercise quiet diplomacy backed by subtle shifts in our military deployments. It would also cast into doubt authorities which Presidents have used to undertake certain humanitarian relief missions in conflict areas, to protect fishing boats from seizure, to deal with ship or aircraft hijackings, and to respond to threats of attack. Not the least of the adverse consequences of this resolution would be the prohibition contained in section 8 against fulfilling our obligations under the NATO treaty as ratified by the Senate. Finally, since the bill is somewhat vague as to when the 60 day rule would apply, it could lead to extreme confusion and dangerous disagreements concerning the prerogatives of the two branches, seriously damaging our ability to respond to international crises.

FAILURE TO REQUIRE POSITIVE CONGRESSIONAL ACTION

I am particularly disturbed by the fact that certain of the President's constitutional powers as Commander in Chief of the Armed Forces would terminate automatically under this resolution 60 days after they were invoked. No overt Congressional action would be required to cut off these powers — they would disappear automatically unless the Congress extended them. In effect, the Congress is here attempting to increase its policymaking role through a provision which requires it to take absolutely no action at all.

In my view, the proper way for the Congress to make known its will on such foreign policy questions is through a positive action, with full debate on the merits of the issue and with each member taking the responsibility of casting a yes or no vote after considering those merits. The authorization and appropriations process represents one of the ways in which such influence can be exercised. I do not, however, believe that the Congress can responsibly contribute its considered, collective judgment on such grave questions without full debate and without a yes or no vote. Yet this is precisely what the joint resolution would allow. It would give every future Congress the ability to handcuff every future President merely by doing nothing and sitting still. In my view, one cannot become a responsible partner unless one is prepared to take responsible action.

STRENGTHENING COOPERATION BETWEEN THE CONGRESS AND THE EXECUTIVE BRANCHES

The responsible and effective exercise of the war powers requires the fullest cooperation between the Congress and the Executive and the prudent fulfillment by each branch of its constitutional responsibilities. House Joint Resolution 542 includes certain constructive measures which would foster this process by enhancing the flow of information from the executive branch to the Congress. Section 3, for example, calls for consultation with the Congress before and during the involvement of the United States forces in hostilities abroad. This provision is consistent with the desire of this Administration for regularized consultations with the Congress in an even wider range of circumstances. . . .

Richard Nixon
The White House

NOTES AND QUESTIONS

a.   The "Substantive" Provisions of Section 2

Under-Inclusiveness of the WPR? The Senate originally took a substantially more specific approach to itemizing the President's constitutional war powers than WPR §2(c). The Senate included the powers "to take necessary and appropriate retaliatory actions in the event of [an armed attack upon the U.S., its territories or possessions]," "to forestall the direct and imminent threat of [an attack against the armed forces of the United States located outside the United States, its territories, and possessions]," and "to protect while evacuating citizens and nationals of the United States, as rapidly as possible, from [certain situations] involving a direct and imminent threat to [their] lives." S. 440, 93d Cong. §3 (1973). Which version more faithfully tracks the constitutional war and emergency powers of the executive recognized in such cases as *The Prize Cases, supra* p. 68, and *Neagle, supra* p. 83? Is even the Senate version complete? Could *any* list be complete? If not, can you think of any other way to frame the "substantive" provision of the WPR that is not under-inclusive? *See* John Hart Ely, *Suppose Congress Wanted a War Powers Act That Worked,* 88 Colum. L. Rev. 1379, 1394 (1988).

In light of the rescue and other war powers asserted by the President, is the WPR unconstitutional? What bearing does WPR §8(d) have on your answer? If these *are* inherent constitutional powers of the President, does Congress have any authority to define them? *See* Stephen L. Carter, *The Constitutionality of the War Powers Resolution*, 70 Va. L. Rev. 101, 117 (1984). To limit them? See *supra* p. 115 (discussing the *Lovett* principle and Congress's appropriations and necessary and proper powers).

Critics of the WPR argue that it unconstitutionally attempts to overturn 200 years of history, during which the President established his claim to war-making authority by usage. *See, e.g.,* J. Terry Emerson, *The War Powers Resolution Tested: The President's Independent Defense Power*, 51 Notre Dame Law. 187, 195-201 (1975); Eugene V. Rostow, *"Once More Unto the Breach": The War Powers Resolution Revisited*, 21 Val. U. L. Rev. 1, 5-18 (1986); Eugene V. Rostow, *Great Cases Make Bad Law: The War Powers Act*, 50 Tex. L. Rev. 833 (1972) (criticizing an early Senate version of the WPR). Defenders of the WPR note that past congressional acquiescence in executive war powers at most establishes that the President may exercise them "*if Congress does not try to stop him. If Congress does* try to stop him, then by definition it is no longer acquiescing." Carter, *supra*, at 124 (emphasis in original). Moreover, presidential claims of inherent and exclusive war-making power were first made openly in 1950, and defenders argue that "23 years of deviance" from the pre-1950 understanding of war powers "hardly seem sufficient so definitely to have redefined the constitutional arrangement as to render unconstitutional the [WPR's] attempt to return to the prior understanding." Ely, *supra*, at 1392.

The Senate itemization of these powers was contained not in the "purpose and policy" section of its bill, but in an operational section entitled "Emergency Use of the Armed Forces." This section stated that U.S. troops could be introduced only in certain enumerated instances, the last of which was prior specific congressional authorization. The Conference Committee deliberately moved its itemization to WPR §2 and explained that subsequent sections were not dependent on the language of §2(c). H.R. Rep. No. 93-547, at 8 (1973) (Conf. Rep.). Why do you suppose the Committee made this change? Does this affect your judgment of the constitutionality of the WPR?

b.   Consultation

1. *With Whom?* When does the WPR require the President to consult Congress before introducing U.S. armed forces? Is it satisfied by consultation with a few selected members of Congress? With the relevant congressional leadership? With the leadership plus the membership of relevant committees? With all the members of Congress? What are the practical problems attending each alternative? The WPR's failure to answer these questions has prompted numerous proposed amendments. *See, e.g.,* S.J. Res. 323 & H.R.J. Res. 601, 100th Cong. (1988) (specifying both a small leadership group composed of the Speaker of the House, President pro tempore of the Senate, and the majority and minority leaders of each body, and a larger "permanent consultative group" of these 6 plus 12 committee leaders).

2. *For What?* Does the WPR require advance consultation about exercises of inherent presidential war-making authority? If so, by what authority? *See* Rostow, *supra*, at 41 (Congress may not command the President to "consult" with any of its members because "[a]ny such attempt would interfere with the President's most sensitive executive discretion, that of political leadership.").

3. *How?* What does "consult" mean? The House report on the WPR expressly rejected

the notion that consultation should be synonymous with merely being informed. Rather, consultation in this provision means that a decision is pending on a problem and that Members of Congress are being asked by the President for their advice and opinions and, in appropriate circumstances, their approval of action contemplated. Furthermore, for consultation to be meaningful, the President must himself participate and all information relevant to the situation must be made available. [H.R. Rep. No. 93-287, at 6-7 (1973).]

Former Secretary of State Cyrus Vance has written that "consultation" means not only advance transmittal of all relevant information to the congressional leadership in sufficient time "to permit a reasonable opportunity to absorb the information, consider its implications, and form a judgment before irrevocable decisions are made by the President," but also "that the congressional leadership should have a real opportunity to communicate its views to the President or at least to his closest advisors." Cyrus R. Vance, *Striking the Balance: Congress and the President Under the War Powers Resolution*, 133 U. Pa. L. Rev. 79, 87-91 (1984).

4. *Why?* Other critics ask what good it would do to consult with Congress about most questions of national security or foreign relations: its members are allegedly parochial, partisan, poorly informed, preoccupied with re-election, and, in a word, collectively unwise about national security and foreign affairs. Indeed, involving them may effectively amount only to involving their staffs, with a substantially increased risk of leaks that will compromise national security. *See, e.g.,* Robert F. Turner, *Repealing the War Powers Resolution* 110 (1991).

If this critique is correct, does it bear on the constitutionality of the WPR? The Senate Foreign Relations Committee's answer was that the Framers vested the war power in Congress "not primarily because they felt confident that the legislature would necessarily exercise it more wisely but because they expected the legislature to exercise it more *sparingly* than it had been exercised by the Crown, or would be likely to be exercised by the President as successor to the Crown." S. Rep. No. 93-220, at 86 (1973) (emphasis in original). *See also* Carter, *supra* p. 313, at 128 ("policy is not unconstitutional *merely* because it is unwise").

c.   The "Hostilities" Trigger and the Reporting Requirements

1. *The Textual Trigger and Its Legislative History.* What is the trigger for application of the WPR's §4(a)(1) reporting and §5(b) 60-day clock provisions? The House Report explained that

[i]n addition to a situation in which fighting actually has begun, *hostilities* also encompasses a state of confrontation in which no shots have been fired but where there is a clear and present danger of armed conflict. "*Imminent hostilities*" denotes a situation in which there is a clear potential either for such a state of confrontation or for actual armed conflict. [H.R. Rep. No. 93-287, at 7 (1973) (emphasis in original).]

Does this explanation help? What is a "clear potential" for a "clear and present danger"? What does WPR §8(c) add? *See generally* William H. Hardy Jr., Note, *A Tug of War: The War Powers Resolution and the Meaning of "Hostilities,"* 15 Pac. L.J.

265 (1984) (urging broad definition of "hostilities" to prevent presidential *fait accomplis* in committing troops).

2. *Defining "Hostilities" or "War" in the "Tanker War."* In 1987, Iranian attacks on oil tankers in the Persian Gulf prompted President Reagan to deploy U.S. naval vessels as escorts. *See generally* Ely, *supra* p. 312, at 1381-1383 (from which most of the following narrative is drawn). By mid-1988, 31 U.S. vessels were patrolling the Gulf. On April 14, a mine seriously damaged a U.S. frigate, injuring ten members of the crew. Blaming Iran, U.S. forces destroyed two Iranian oil platforms. Two Iranian jets approached an American cruiser but were driven off by anti-aircraft missiles. An Iranian missile boat fired on the cruiser and missed but was then destroyed by return fire from U.S. boats and planes. Meanwhile, in response to attacks by armed Iranian speedboats on a U.S.-flagged supply boat, U.S. planes sank one speedboat and damaged two others. Later the same day, the United States responded to an attack by Iranian frigates on U.S. vessels by sinking one and crippling the other with missiles and aerial bombs. On July 3, 1988, a U.S. cruiser in the Persian Gulf mistook a civilian Iranian airliner for a warplane and downed it with a missile, killing 290 people. The Chairman of the Joint Chiefs of Staff explained that the cruiser's action differed from the Soviet downing of a Korean airliner because the latter did not occur in "a war zone, there was not combat in progress, there was not combat there normally." *Statement by Joint Chiefs' Chairman: "U.S. Deeply Regrets This Incident"... but Commanders on the Scene Believed "Their Units Were in Jeopardy,"* N.Y. Times, July 4, 1988. Vice President Bush echoed this explanation: "The Iranians shouldn't be sending an airliner over a combat zone.... A captain is under fire in combat." Richard Halloran, *U.S. Aides Cautious on Airbus Inquiry,* N.Y. Times, Aug. 4, 1988. Notwithstanding these developments, President Reagan never filed a WPR §4(a)(1) report. Should he have? The Administration's "position seemed to be that we were at war but there was no danger of hostilities." Ely, *supra,* at 1383.

This "Tanker War" in the Persian Gulf generated litigation that produced two strikingly different opinions about the nature of the hostilities. In *Lowry v. Reagan,* 676 F. Supp. 333 (D.D.C. 1987), the court declined to decide whether the hostilities required the President to file an "imminent hostilities report," partly on grounds that the case presented a political question. In response to the congressional plaintiff's argument that the WPR's legislative history indicated a clear intent to involve Congress in the decision-making process at a relatively early stage of U.S. military involvement abroad, the court said:

> If one were to take this discussion at face value, it might be possible to make a common-sense determination regarding the existence of hostilities. However, two considerations compel the Court to question this approach. First, and most importantly, the very absence of a definitional section in the Resolution, coupled with debate suggesting that determinations of "hostilities" were intended to be political decisions made by the President and Congress, suggest to this Court that fixed legal standards were deliberately omitted from this statutory scheme. Second, the factual evaluation of "hostilities [and] ... situations where imminent involvement in hostilities is clearly indicated by the circumstances" is always hampered, to some degree, by a Court's lack of access to intelligence information and other pertinent expertise. This is exacerbated by the ever-changing intensity of "hostilities," especially when they are in their early stages. The President must have flexibility in executing military and foreign policy on a day to day basis. Thus, this Court is inclined to conclude that this case does not present judicially manageable standards. [*Id.* at 340-341 n.53.]

In *Koohi v. United States*, 976 F.2d 1328 (9th Cir. 1992), the heirs of deceased passengers and crew of the Iranian airliner shot down by the U.S. cruiser *Vincennes* in the Persian Gulf sued the United States and certain defense contractors for damages under the Federal Tort Claims Act (FTCA), 28 U.S.C. §§1346(b), 2671-2680 (2000). The court had to decide whether the claim fell within the FTCA exception for "[a]ny claim arising out of combatant activities of the military or naval forces, or the Coast Guard during time of war." After noting that the events surrounding the "tanker war" in the Persian Gulf "are a matter of historical record, are supported by documentation in the district court record, and are — to the extent that they are relevant to the outcome of the case before us — beyond reasonable dispute," the court reached the issue whether the hostilities constituted a "time of war."

We do not express any view concerning the constitutionality of acts of war by American armed forces in the absence of a formal declaration of war. We simply note that such acts have occurred with regularity in recent years, and that from a practical standpoint "time of war" has come to mean periods of significant armed conflict rather than times governed by formal declarations of war. Since neither the text nor the legislative history of the FTCA expressly states whether Congress intended the combatant activities exception to apply to undeclared conflicts, we must arrive at our conclusion primarily through the use of those techniques to which we have previously adverted — reason and judgment. Here, that process leads us, inexorably, to construe the exception in light of contemporary realities. By giving the term "time of war" its full current meaning rather than a crabbed, artificial, or technical reading we make common sense out of unclear words and best effectuate the purposes of the statute: we shield the government from the type of liability it never intended to assume.

It seems clear that the purpose of the exception we are construing is to ensure that the government will not be liable for negligent conduct by our armed forces in times of combat. Whether that combat is formally authorized by the Congress or follows less formal actions of the Executive and Legislative branches would seem to be irrelevant to Congress's objectives....

In sum, we have no difficulty in concluding that when, as a result of a deliberate decision by the executive branch, United States armed forces engage in an organized series of hostile encounters on a significant scale with the military forces of another nation, the FTCA exception applies. Under those circumstances, a "time of war" exists, at least for purposes of domestic tort law.

There can be no doubt that during the "tanker war" a "time of war" existed. The United States' involvement in naval combat while the Iran-Iraq war was in progress was the result of a deliberate decision on the part of the executive branch to engage in hostile military activities vis-a-vis Iran in order to protect Gulf shipping.... Under the circumstances, we believe that the shooting down of the Airbus by the *Vincennes* falls within the FTCA's exception for combatant activities during time of war. Accordingly, the plaintiffs' FTCA action against the *Vincennes* is barred by the doctrine of sovereign immunity. [976 F.2d at 1334-1335.]

Are these opinions, concerning the same hostilities, reconcilable?

3. *Proposed Substitute Triggers.* One scholar has proposed linking the WPR trigger with the rules of engagement governing our armed forces in a deployment. He would substitute "significant armed conflict" for "imminent hostilities" using this definition:

For purposes of this Act, "significant armed conflict" means (i) any conflict expressly authorized by Congress, or (ii) any mission conducted by the U.S. armed forces pursuant to Rules of Engagement authorizing the use of force beyond the scope of authority provided by the inherent right of self-defense permitting those forces to initiate hostilities with any state or non-state opponent. [Geoffrey Corn, *Triggering Congressional War Powers Notification: A Proposal to Reconcile Constitutional Practice with Operational Reality*, 14 Lewis & Clark L. Rev. 687, 738 (2010).]

The standing rules of engagement "establish fundamental policies and procedures governing the actions to be taken by US commanders during all military operations and contingencies and routine Military Department functions." Chairman of the Joint Chiefs of Staff Instruction 3121.01B: *Standing Rules of Engagement/Standing Rules for the Use of Force for US Forces* §6 (June 13, 2005), *reprinted in* Int'l & Operational Law Dep't, Judge Advocate General's Legal Ctr. & Sch., U.S. Army, *Operational Law Handbook* 95, 96-97 (2007), *available at* http://www.fas.org/irp/doddir/army/law2007.pdf. Do you see any problems in using this definition?

4. *Triggering Reporting.* When does the trigger for reporting to Congress differ from the trigger for consulting with Congress and from the trigger for the 60-day clock under §5(b)? What problems do you foresee arising from any differences? If the President wanted to evade the 60-day clock without openly defying the WPR reporting requirement, what could he do?

Of 127 WPR reports submitted by presidents through 2009, only one cited §4(a)(1). Richard F. Grimmett, *The War Powers Resolution After Thirty-Six Years* 10 (Cong. Res. Serv. R41199), Apr. 22, 2010 (reporting deployment of forces for armed rescue of crew taken hostage on Cambodian seizure of the *Mayaguez*). Instead, the reporting formulas have been calculatingly vague, "taking note of Section 4" of the WPR or reporting "[b]ecause of my desire that Congress be informed on this matter and consistent with the reporting provisions of the War Powers Resolution." Subcomm. on Int'l Security and Scientific Affairs, H. Comm. on Foreign Affairs, 98th Cong., *War Powers Resolution: Relevant Documents, Correspondence, Reports* 40-47 (Comm. Print 1983). For an update of WPR reports through early 2011, *see* Richard F. Grimmett, *War Powers Resolution: Presidential Compliance* (Cong. Res. Serv. RL33532), Feb. 23, 2011.

5. *The Content of WPR Reports.* One student asserts that the intended purposes of a WPR report are triggering the 60-day clock, prompting a dialogue between the branches about the use of force, promoting accountability for the decision to use force, disciplining the decision-making process within the executive branch, and providing Congress with information sufficient for it to legislate concerning the use of force. *See* Daniel L. Richards, *Reporting Under the War Powers Resolution: Section 4*, in George Washington University Law School War Powers Project (GWU Project), *The War Powers Resolution: Origins, History, Criticism and Reform*, 2 J. Nat'l Security L. 59 (1998).

How would you change the reporting requirements to better fulfill the purposes of the WPR? In light of the continued refusal of courts to decide WPR questions, what is the significance of a WPR report's description of the legal authority for a deployment?

d.   The 60-Day Clock

1. *A Self-Executing Clock?* Section 5(b) establishes a 60-day (plus 30-day extension) limit on the commitment of troops without congressional authorization. What

happens under the WPR if the President refuses to file a §4(a)(1) report or files under the wrong provision? Is §5(b) self-enforcing, or must Congress pull a "second trigger" by declaring that a report is "required to be submitted" within the meaning of the provision? In *Crockett v. Reagan*, 558 F. Supp. 893, 901 (D.D.C. 1982), *aff'd*, 720 F.2d 1355 (D.C. Cir. 1983), the court found that

> the legislative scheme did not contemplate court-ordered withdrawal when no report has been filed, but rather, it leaves open the possibility for a court to order that a report be filed or, alternatively, withdrawal 60 days after a report was filed or required to be filed by a court or Congress.... [W]here no report has been filed, and the priority procedures would not be invoked, the majority of Congress might not be of the opinion that a specific authorization is necessary for continued involvement and take no action, unaware that this course could result in mandatory withdrawal. In that instance court-ordered withdrawal could thwart the will of the majority of Congress. Therefore, when a report has not been filed, it is consistent with the purposes and structure of the WPR to require further congressional action before the automatic termination provision operates.

But see Steven V. Roberts, *War Powers? What War Powers?* N.Y. Times, Oct. 6, 1987 (quoting Richard P. Conlon, executive director of the Democratic Study Group, who protested that "Congress should not have to pass a new law in order to enforce a law already on the books.").

2. *Constitutionality of 60-Day Clock.* Why did President Nixon oppose WPR §5(b)? If §2(c) itemizes the President's inherent *constitutional* powers to introduce U.S. armed forces into hostilities, how can Congress subject those powers to the statutory limitations of §5(b)? What practical impact could §5(b) have on the President's decision to arm U.S. forces? On the degree to which a President might escalate U.S. involvement? On the safety with which a required withdrawal of troops could be carried out? *See* Turner, *supra* p. 314, at 129-155; Bradley Larschan, *The War Powers Resolution: Conflicting Constitutional Powers, the War Powers and U.S. Foreign Policy*, 16 Den. J. Int'l L. & Pol'y 33, 71 (1987). Are these consequences of the WPR alone or of any reading of the Constitution that requires congressional approval for nondefensive hostilities abroad? *See* Ely, *supra* p. 312, at 1400. *See also* Walter L. Williams, *The Sixty-Day Rule of the War Powers Resolution: Section 5(b)*, in GWU Project, *supra*, at 98-99 (attributing practical problems of warfare under the WPR to the Constitution, not the WPR's 60-day rule, and noting that the President retains the option of obtaining congressional approval for longer deployments).

3. *A Free Pass?* In any case, *within* the 60- (or 90-) day time limit, has not the WPR given the President a free pass to use armed force abroad? Consider the following assessment:

> [T]he defect at the heart of the WPR is that it has given *both* the President and Congress a putative free pass. In the actual contemporary exercise of war powers, perception has become reality as both the media and many members of Congress overlook the WPR's disclaimer of authority [§8(d)(2), 50 U.S.C. §1547(c)(2) (2006).] Thus, some proponents of unilateral presidential action invoke the putative sixty-day free pass as license to use force abroad without constitutionally required advance authorization from Congress. Congress, for its part, takes false comfort that it has somehow fulfilled its

constitutional duty to decide on uses of force abroad by doing nothing. [*Deciding to Use Force Abroad: War Powers in a System of Checks and Balances* 33-34 (The Constitution Project, Peter Raven-Hansen rptr., 2005).]

See also Louis Fisher & David Gray Adler, *The War Powers Resolution: Time to Say Goodbye,* 113 Pol. Sci. Q. 1, 11 (1998) (urging repeal of the WPR to "eliminate the concession of 1973 that presidents may use military force anywhere in the world, for whatever reason, for up to ninety days, if not longer"). Although some might quarrel about triggering events, prior to the Operation Allied Force bombing campaign against the Federal Republic of Yugoslavia in 1999, see *infra* p. 342, no combat operation had ever "run the sixty-day clock" without statutory authorization. *See* Geoffrey S. Corn, *Clinton, Kosovo, and the Final Destruction of the War Powers Resolution,* 42 Wm. & Mary L. Rev. 1149, 1154 (2001). Does this history prove that the WPR has become a "free pass"?

e.   The Concurrent Resolution

The WPR was a *joint resolution*, which must be presented to the President before becoming law. A *concurrent resolution* is not presented to the President for his signature and, according to *Chadha,* is therefore not law. See *supra* p. 120. WPR §5(c) authorizes Congress by concurrent resolution to direct the removal of troops from abroad within the 60-day period. Is WPR §5(c) constitutional after *Chadha*? *Compare* Carter, *supra* p. 313, at 129-132 (yes, by analogy to a congressionally proposed constitutional amendment, which the Supreme Court declared exempt from presentment in *Hollingsworth v. Virginia,* 3 U.S. (3 Dall.) 378 (1798)), *with* Clarence A. Berdahl, *War Powers of the Executive in the United States* 95-96 (1921) (presentment of a bill declaring war is necessary), *and* Daniel E. Lungren & Mark L. Krotoski, *The War Powers Resolution After the Chadha Decision,* 17 Loy. L.A. L. Rev. 767, 786 n.84 (1984) (every declaration of war has been signed by the President). Or is a concurrent resolution of disapproval merely a constitutional expression of congressional will that moves the presidential action into the "twilight zone," where authority depends partly on congruence with the "expressed *or implied* will of Congress"? *See* Martin Wald, Note, *The Future of the War Powers Resolution,* 36 Stan. L. Rev. 1407, 1433 (1984) (quoting *The Steel Seizure Case,* 343 U.S. at 637 (Jackson, J., concurring), *supra* p. 33); Vance, *supra,* at 85 (WPR creates a procedure by which Congress expresses "its institutional judgment" on the question of whether the President has constitutional authority to act).

f.   The Rule of Construction

1. *Inferences of Authorization from Statutes.* WPR §8(a)(1) supplies a rule of construction intended to prevent inferences of authority for the use of armed forces such as those the courts made in *Orlando v. Laird, supra* p. 286, and *Holtzman v. Schlesinger, supra* p. 303. Suppose that Congress passed and the President signed into law a supplemental appropriation providing $2 billion for "the use and support of U.S. armed forces to protect citizens of Darfur, a region of Sudan, from military and paramilitary aggression." How, if at all, would the rule of construction apply to such an appropriation? If the new statute would not satisfy the WPR, which

statute would control? *Compare* William C. Banks & Peter Raven-Hansen, *National Security Law and the Power of the Purse* 130-131 (1994) (asserting that the WPR does not, because when two statutes clash, the clearly expressed intent — if discernible — of the last in time controls), *with* Michael J. Glennon, *Mr. Sofaer's War Powers Partnership*, 80 Am. J. Int'l L. 584, 586 (1986) (asserting a "first-in-time" rule of construction by which all post-WPR legislation must be read *in pari materia* with and subordinate to WPR §8), *and* Ely, *supra* p. 312, at 1418 (asserting that the WPR creates "a strong rule of construction . . . telling us how to read the intent of a later Congress").

2. *Inferences of Authorization from Treaties.* WPR §8(a)(2) prohibits the inference of authorization from treaties such as the Southeast Asia Collective Defense Treaty (SEATO). Does it make all mutual defense treaties non-self-executing, regardless of their language? Does it prevent deployment of U.S. armed forces in U.N. operations without a specific authorization from Congress? *See* WPR §§8(b), 9(d). *See generally* Andrew K. Schiff, Note, *The War Powers Resolution: From the Halls of Congress to the Hills of Bosnia, Inertia Should Give Way to Post-Cold War Reality*, 11 Am. U. J. Int'l L. & Pol'y 877 (1996).

g. Replacing the WPR

A study commission recently recommended that

> Congress should replace the War Powers Resolution with legislation that fairly acknowledges the President's defensive war powers, omits any arbitrary general time limit on deployments of force, reasserts the constitutionally-derived clear statement rule for use-of-force bills, and prescribes rules for their privileged and expedited consideration. [*Deciding to Use Force Abroad, supra*, at 40.]

Do you agree? What bill language would you propose? What would be the likely practical consequence of simply rescinding the WPR? What benefits do you see from leaving it as is?

h. The WPR in Practice

Consider this March 21, 2011, WPR report:

Letter from the President to the Speaker of the House of Representatives and the President Pro Tempore of the Senate (March 21, 2011)

http://www.whitehouse.gov/the-press-office/2011/03/21/letter-president-regarding-commencement-operations-libya

At approximately 3:00 P.M. Eastern Daylight Time, on March 19, 2011, at my direction, U.S. military forces commenced operations to assist an international effort authorized by the United Nations (U.N.) Security Council and undertaken with the support of European allies and Arab partners, to prevent a humanitarian catastrophe and address the threat posed to international peace and security by the crisis in Libya. As part of the multilateral response authorized under U.N. Security Council Resolution 1973, U.S. military forces, under the command of Commander, U.S. Africa Command, began a series of strikes against air defense systems and military airfields for the purposes of preparing a no-fly zone. These strikes will be limited in their nature, duration, and scope. Their purpose is to support an international coalition as it takes all necessary measures to enforce the terms of U.N. Security Council Resolution 1973. These limited U.S. actions will set the stage for further action by other coalition partners.

United Nations Security Council Resolution 1973 authorized Member States, under Chapter VII of the U.N. Charter, to take all necessary measures to protect civilians and civilian populated areas under threat of attack in Libya, including the establishment and enforcement of a "no-fly zone" in the airspace of Libya. United States military efforts are discrete and focused on employing unique U.S. military capabilities to set the conditions for our European allies and Arab partners to carry out the measures authorized by the U.N. Security Council Resolution.

Muammar Qadhafi was provided a very clear message that a cease-fire must be implemented immediately. The international community made clear that all attacks against civilians had to stop; Qadhafi had to stop his forces from advancing on Benghazi; pull them back from Ajdabiya, Misrata, and Zawiya; and establish water, electricity, and gas supplies to all areas. Finally, humanitarian assistance had to be allowed to reach the people of Libya.

Although Qadhafi's Foreign Minister announced an immediate cease-fire, Qadhafi and his forces made no attempt to implement such a cease-fire, and instead continued attacks on Misrata and advanced on Benghazi. Qadhafi's continued attacks and threats against civilians and civilian populated areas are of grave concern to neighboring Arab nations and, as expressly stated in U.N. Security Council Resolution 1973, constitute a threat to the region and to international peace and security. His illegitimate use of force not only is causing the deaths of substantial numbers of civilians among his own people, but also is forcing many others to flee to neighboring countries, thereby destabilizing the peace and security of the region. Left unaddressed, the growing instability in Libya could ignite wider instability in the Middle East, with dangerous consequences to the national security interests of the United States. Qadhafi's defiance of the Arab League, as well as the broader international community moreover, represents a lawless challenge to the authority of the Security Council and its efforts to preserve stability in the region. Qadhafi has forfeited his responsibility to protect his own citizens and created a serious need for immediate humanitarian assistance and protection, with any delay only putting more civilians at risk.

The United States has not deployed ground forces into Libya. United States forces are conducting a limited and well-defined mission in support of international efforts to protect civilians and prevent a humanitarian disaster. Accordingly, U.S. forces have targeted the Qadhafi regime's air defense systems, command and control structures, and other capabilities of Qadhafi's armed forces used to attack civilians and civilian populated areas. We will seek a rapid, but responsible, transition of operations to coalition, regional, or international organizations that are postured to continue activities as may be necessary to realize the objectives of U.N. Security Council Resolutions 1970 and 1973.

For these purposes, I have directed these actions, which are in the national security and foreign policy interests of the United States, pursuant to my constitutional authority to conduct U.S. foreign relations and as Commander in Chief and Chief Executive.

I am providing this report as part of my efforts to keep the Congress fully informed, consistent with the War Powers Resolution. I appreciate the support of the Congress in this action.

Barack Obama
The White House

Why didn't President Obama cite WPR §4(a)(1) when he had deployed aircraft to conduct "a series of strikes against air defense systems and military airfields. . . ."? Weren't these "imminent hostilities," if anything is? Did the report and its timing comply with the letter of the WPR? Its spirit?

What legal and political difference would it have made if the President had submitted a WPR report a week *before* the air strikes, instead of two days *after*? Would the answer depend on whether the earlier report expressly cited §4(a)(1)? *See* WPR §5(b) (triggering the 60-day clock, discussed *supra*).

The President's order to deploy U.S. air assets in the no-fly campaign against Qadhafi's forces set off a spirited public debate about the legality of the action, implications for U.S. interests, and an apparent lack of clarity in the campaign's objectives. The President consulted informally with various members of Congress beforehand, but there was no formal consultation under WPR §3. Might a more structured consultation process or an earlier report have triggered a congressional debate on these topics that could have aired any conflicting objectives, required the Administration to sharpen its focus, and possibly prompted legislation to address the matter? Or would the inevitably partisan debate only have delayed or undercut what the Administration said was a necessary foreign policy initiative? Should such political considerations, if they existed, have influenced the President's decisions about whether and how to comply with the WPR?

On March 31, 2011, it was reported that President Obama had signed a secret order (a "finding") for the deployment of CIA operatives in Libya to gather intelligence and to supply arms and other support to rebel forces opposed to Qadhafi. *See* Mark Mazzetti & Eric Schmitt, *C.I.A. Agents in Libya Aid Air Strikes and Meet Rebels*, N.Y. Times, Mar. 31, 2011. Was this development covered by the WPR?

In mid-June 2011, three months after the President's WPR letter to Congress (reproduced above), President Obama reportedly decided that he had legal authority to continue U.S. involvement in the air war in Libya without congressional approval. *See* Charlie Savage, *2 Top Lawyers Lose Argument on War Power*, N.Y. Times, June 18, 2011. The 2011 U.S. military mission in Libya is analyzed further *infra* pp. 430-439.

Collective Self-Defense

The transcendent purpose of the United Nations Charter is to make war less likely. It seeks to do so primarily by expressing the signing states' shared commitment to "refrain in their international relations from the threat or use of force against the territorial integrity or political independence of any state." U.N. Charter art. 2(4). It also sets out mechanisms for the peaceful resolution of disputes. For example, Article 33(1) declares:

> The parties to any dispute, the continuance of which is likely to endanger the mainte-nance of international peace and security, shall, first of all, seek a solution by negotiation, enquiry, mediation, conciliation, arbitration, judicial settlement, resort to regional agen-cies or arrangements, or other peaceful means of their own choice.

In addition, the Charter provides for an array of organizations and activities designed to fight disease, hunger, and illiteracy; promote social justice; encourage participatory government; and foster development and self-reliance — all with a view to alleviating conditions that nurture unrest and conflict among states.

Still, the signers of the Charter were acutely aware that peace was a work in pro-gress. They knew that some institutional mechanism was needed to abate the threat or use of coercion, violence, or force, and to help restore order if armed conflict erupted. They also recognized that military force might be necessary to preserve or bring about peace. They understood, as well, that a decision to employ force in this way ought to be undertaken deliberately and only as a last resort, and that the resulting violence would likely be more limited and purposeful if it required the agreement of many nations acting together. Thus, Articles 39-43 of the Charter spell out standards and procedures for the use of force under the authority of the United Nations, as we saw in Chapter 8. In this chapter we consider the application of these provisions in several conflicts in which the United States played (and in one instance still plays) a leading role.

The U.N. Charter would not have been signed without an understanding that in some instances states would not have to wait for the deliberative mechanism spelled out in Article 39 of the Charter to respond militarily to an emerging threat or an act of aggression. Accordingly, Article 51 preserves the universally recognized right of every state, or of states in collaboration, to act in self-defense. This right, also introduced in Chapter 8, is addressed here, as well as in the next chapter.

Here we consider three large-scale conflicts — the Korean War, the Persian Gulf War, and the ongoing war in Afghanistan — as examples of collective self-defense, by which we mean the use of force by one or more states to assist another state that is the victim of unprovoked aggression. In all three conflicts the President relied in part on the U.N. Charter and U.N. Security Council resolutions as authority for commitments of U.S. troops. In Afghanistan we introduce the North Atlantic Treaty Organization (NATO) as an example of a regional organization operating under the auspices of the Security Council. Each of these case studies raises important questions of legitimacy under international as well as domestic law. All three offer important lessons about the interactions of these two sources of law, and about the correlative roles of the President, Congress, and U.S. courts in deciding to use military force abroad.

A. THE KOREAN "POLICE ACTION"[1]

In 1966, early in the Vietnam War, the State Department Legal Adviser cited the Korean War as precedent for the President's exercise of inherent Article II power to send U.S. forces into battle without formally consulting Congress. See *supra* p. 277. Professor Moore called it "a poor precedent." John Norton Moore, *Law and the Indo-China War* 557 (1972). The Korean War was cited again in 1990 by members of the first Bush administration, who argued that the President did not need Congress's approval for offensive military action in the Persian Gulf War.

In this part of the chapter we consider domestic and international law justifications for U.S. involvement in the Korean War, and, in the process, the importance of that war as a precedent for future uses of force abroad.

1. The Outbreak of War

In 1943, while Korea was still occupied by the Japanese, President Roosevelt, Prime Minister Churchill, and Generalissimo Chiang Kai-shek announced in the Cairo Declaration that Korea would "in due course" be free and independent. Two years later, at the Potsdam Conference in July 1945, it was agreed that at war's end the United States would occupy the Korean peninsula south of the thirty-eighth parallel, while the Soviets would take over the area north to Korea's border with China. United Nations-sponsored efforts to establish a unified democratic government soon broke down, leaving the two major powers to sponsor their own politically sympathetic governments led, respectively, by Syngman Rhee in the South and Kim Il Sung in the North. Each one eventually claimed to represent all of Korea.

Early on the morning of Sunday, June 25, 1950 (local time), without any warning, North Korean forces launched a massive invasion of the South. A 500-man U.S.

---

1. Except where otherwise noted, background for this study is drawn from Max Hastings, *The Korean War* (1987); Burton I. Kaufman, *The Korean War: Challenge in Crisis, Credibility, and Command* (1986); Callum A. MacDonald, *Korea: The War Before Vietnam* (1986); Glenn D. Paige, *The Korean Decision, June 24-30, 1950* (1968); David Rees, *Korea: The Limited War* (1964); James L. Stokesbury, *A Short History of the Korean War* (1988); Jane E. Stromseth, *Rethinking War Powers: Congress, the President, and the United Nations*, 81 Geo. L.J. 597, 621-640 (1993); A. Kenneth Pye, *The Legal Status of the Korean Hostilities*, 45 Geo. L.J. 45 (1956); and Dean Acheson, *Review of U.N. and U.S. Action to Restore Peace*, 23 Dep't St. Bull. 43 (1950).

military assistance group was stationed in South Korea at the time. Later the same day, the United States presented a resolution to the U.N. Security Council calling on North Korea to stop its aggression and asking member states to "render every assistance to the United Nations in the execution of this resolution." S.C. Res. 82, U.N. Doc. S/INF/4/Rev. 1 (1950). The Soviet Union, which presumably would have vetoed the resolution, was boycotting the Security Council at the time to protest Nationalist Chinese representation of China at the United Nations. The vote was 9-0 in favor of the resolution, with one abstention.

2. The President's Response

Before the day ended, President Truman ordered U.S. air and naval forces to assist in the evacuation of American dependents and noncombatants from Korea. The next day, June 26, as the military situation quickly deteriorated, the President directed U.S. forces to provide support for South Korean troops. He announced his decision to the American people the day after that. It was not until later on June 27, however, that the U.N. Security Council adopted a second resolution in which it "recommended" that member states "furnish such assistance to the Republic of Korea as may be necessary to repel the armed attack and to restore international peace and security in the area." S.C. Res. 83, U.N. Doc. S/INF/4/Rev. 1 (1950).

Although Congress was in session at the time of the North Korean invasion, President Truman waited until June 27 to brief congressional leaders on the conflict—after he had ordered U.S. forces into combat. On June 29 and 30, the President approved U.S. air strikes against North Korea and directed the deployment of U.S. ground combat forces. But he elected not to ask Congress to approve any of these actions, fearing that an extended public debate might weaken the American effort to blunt this first major Communist aggression in the Far East.

Almost every member of Congress publicly supported the substance of the President's decision to act promptly to repel the North Korean attack. Still, some worried about Congress's exclusion from the process of deciding to enter the conflict. Responding to that concern, a July 3 State Department memorandum declared:

> The President, as Commander in Chief of the Armed Forces of the United States, has full control over the use thereof. He also has authority to conduct the foreign relations of the United States. Since the beginning of United States history, he has, upon numerous occasions, utilized these powers in sending armed forces abroad. The preservation of the United Nations for the maintenance of peace is a cardinal interest of the United States. Both traditional international law and Article 39 of the United Nations Charter and the resolution pursuant thereto authorize the United States to repel the armed aggression against the Republic of Korea. [23 Dep't St. Bull. 173 (1950).]

The memorandum called North Korean defiance of the Security Council resolutions "a threat to the peace and security of the United States and to the security of United States forces in the Pacific." The memorandum also cited 85 earlier instances in which presidents had used military force abroad without a declaration of war. The President's supporters referred to the Korean conflict as a "police action" rather than a war, to suggest that congressional approval was not required.

Despite some members' misgivings, in the days and weeks that followed, Congress tacitly approved President Truman's actions. On June 27, it voted overwhelmingly to approve an extension of the draft, a matter on which it earlier had been sharply divided. Congress also lifted the ceiling on the size of the armed forces, and it increased taxes to help pay for the war. In early September it gave the President extensive new powers to manage the wartime economy in the Defense Production Act of 1950, Act of Sept. 8, 1950, 64 Stat. 798, codified as amended at 50 App. U.S.C.A. §§2061-2172 (2006 & Supp. III 2009), stating, for example, that "[t]he President is authorized . . . to allocate materials, services, and facilities in such manner . . . as he shall deem necessary or appropriate to promote the national defense." *Id.* §2071(a).

United States warplanes were sent into the battle on June 26. The first U.S. ground forces arrived in Korea on July 1. One week later, the Security Council adopted a third resolution placing all forces defending South Korea under the unified command of the United States. The fighting ended three years later where it had started, with a cease-fire along the thirty-eighth parallel. The United States had suffered 33,629 killed and more than 100,000 wounded. Some 50,000 South Korean troops were killed. The exact extent of North Korean losses is still unknown.

NOTES AND QUESTIONS

1. *Korean and Vietnam Wars Compared.* The Korean conflict was different from the one in Indochina, see *supra* Chapter 10, in several ways that might bear on the legality of President Truman's actions. Can you say how?

2. *Source of Presidential Authority?* If you had written the July 3, 1950, State Department memorandum excerpted above, what authority would you have cited for the President's claim to have "full control" over the use of the armed forces? Could you argue that Congress lacked authority to stop him from sending U.S. troops to Korea? *See* John Hart Ely, *War and Responsibility: Constitutional Lessons of Vietnam and Its Aftermath* 10-11 (1993) (recalling contemporary discussion of this issue).

If the "preservation of the United Nations for the maintenance of peace" was really at stake in Korea, did characterizing it as a "cardinal interest of the United States" provide the President with authority that he otherwise lacked? How could that characterization have been tested?

3. *A Role for Congress or the Courts?* What is the significance of President Truman's decision not to ask Congress for its approval of his actions, even retrospectively? How, if at all, was the President's authority affected by the United Nations Participation Act, discussed *supra* pp. 216-217? *See* Louis Fisher, *The Korean War: On What Legal Basis Did Truman Act?*, 89 Am. J. Int'l L. 21, 33 (1995) (arguing that "Truman's legal authority was nonexistent").

Did subsequent legislation extending the draft and financing the war effort cure any constitutional deficiency? Is there any doubt in your mind that there was "some mutual participation" between the President and Congress, as that term was used in *Orlando v. Laird, supra* p. 286?

Do you think any court would have entertained a challenge to the legitimacy of the war? If not, can you describe the probable reason or reasons for judicial abstention? If the answer is yes, can you say who would have had standing to sue?

4. *A Paradigm Shift?* Professor Ely suggested that the "position taken by the Truman administration respecting Korea ruptured [a] long-standing consensus"

about Congress's proper role in foreign affairs. Ely, *supra*, at 62. Can you point to evidence of such a "long-standing consensus"? How might Ely's argument bear on future assertions of Korea as a precedent for the unilateral executive use of force? What effect, if any, do you think enactment of the War Powers Resolution, *supra* p. 307, had on this precedent?

5. *The U.N. Security Council's Role.* Recall the exceptions in Chapter VII of the U.N. Charter to the general prohibition in Article 2(4) of the threat or use of force by one state against another. *Supra* p. 211. Which provisions of Chapter VII do you think authorized the U.N. Security Council resolutions responding to the North Korean invasion?

The June 27, 1950, Security Council resolution "recommended" that member states furnish military assistance to South Korea. Why do you suppose the resolution took the form of a recommendation rather than an "authorization" or an "order"? Do you think the choice of words had any legal significance? *Compare* Stromseth, *supra* p. 324, at 602 n.20 (indicating that member states would be obligated if the Security Council "'decides' to take action" rather than simply "recommending"); Michael J. Glennon, *The Constitution and Article VII of the United Nations Charter*, 85 Am. J. Int'l L. 74, 75 (1991) (arguing that use of the term "authorizes" in Security Council Resolution 678 in advance of the 1991 Persian Gulf War imposed "no obligation on the United States to use armed force"); *and* Yoram Dinstein, *War, Aggression, and Self-Defense* 281 (4th ed. 2005) ("Member States can make up their own minds whether to follow or to ignore non-compulsory calls for action issued by the Council."); *with* Thomas M. Franck & Faiza Patel, *UN Police Action in Lieu of War: "The Old Order Changeth,"* 85 Am. J. Int'l L. 63, 65 (1991) (arguing that in case of aggression, a recommendation becomes "an *obligation* which none can shirk").

What did the Security Council authorize when, in Resolution 83, it recommended that member states "furnish such assistance to the Republic of Korea as may be necessary to repel the armed attack and to restore international peace and security in the area"? Did it mean, for example, that forces coming to the aid of South Korea could push north of the 38th parallel? *See* Jules Lobel & Michael Ratner, *Bypassing the Security Council: Ambiguous Authorizations to Use Force, Cease-Fires, and the Iraqi Inspection Regime*, 93 Am. J. Int'l L. 124, 138-139 (1999) (recalling debate within the Truman administration about this point).

Does it matter that President Truman ordered U.S. military forces into action *before* the Security Council adopted its June 27 resolution? *Compare* Fisher, *supra*, at 22-33 (arguing that Truman administration did not act pursuant to U.N. authority), *with* Robert F. Turner, *Truman, Korea, and the Constitution: Debunking the "Imperial President" Myth*, 19 Harv. J.L. & Pub. Pol'y 533, 564 (1996) ("so what?").

6. *Collective Self-Defense?* Did President Truman get the authority he needed from Article 51, which approves acts of collective self-defense "until" the Security Council can act? See *supra* p. 213. Might Article 51 have provided justification for President Truman's deployment of troops to Korea even *after* the June 27 Security Council resolution? Professor Rostow argued that "the forces which finally prevailed in Korea were national forces carrying out a mission of collective self-defense under American direction, not a Security Council enforcement action." Eugene V. Rostow, *Until What? Enforcement Action or Collective Self-Defense?*, 85 Am. J. Int'l L. 506, 508 (1991). *Contra* Glennon, *supra*, at 81.

7. *Police Action?* While the conflict raged in Korea, it was referred to by many as a "police action" rather than a war. *See* Fisher, *supra*, at 33-34; Stromseth, *supra*, at 630-631. Do you think this characterization of the conflict had any legal significance? *Compare* Franck & Patel, *supra*, at 71 (reporting that a majority in Congress approved the President's unilateral use of force in Korea on the basis that it was a "police action"), *with* Stromseth, *supra*, at 604 ("Congress expected U.N. 'police actions' to be limited in size; if a conflict escalated and required a large-scale commitment of U.S. troops, it would be 'war' under the U.S. Constitution even if it was authorized by the U.N. Security Council."). Recall our discussion of police actions *supra* p. 217.

B.   THE PERSIAN GULF WAR[2]

1.   The Invasion of Kuwait

In 1990, Iraq boasted the world's second largest oil reserves and fourth largest army, which had been battle-tested in a multiyear war with Iran. Iraq and Kuwait had long disputed drilling rights to the large oil fields that lie near their common border. Asserting that Kuwait was extracting oil from fields that lay partly in Iraq, that Kuwait was not paying its fair share of the costs of defending the area from Iran, and that some Kuwaiti territory belonged to Iraq, Iraq invaded Kuwait on August 2, 1990. More than 100,000 Iraqi troops quickly occupied Kuwait and detained many foreigners, including some 2,500 Americans. Eventually, the Iraqi troop level in the Kuwait theater reached 450,000, substantially more than were needed to garrison Kuwait, posing a serious threat to the adjacent kingdom of Saudi Arabia, a long-time U.S. ally in the Middle East.

2.   Operation Desert Shield

"For forty years after the United Nations authorized the use of force in Korea, Cold War tensions rendered the collective security machinery of the U.N. Charter largely unusable. On August 2, 1990, however, . . . the Security Council took united action." Stromseth, *supra*, at 640. The Security Council, acting expressly under Articles 39 and 40, promptly adopted Resolution 660, which declared a breach of international peace and security, condemned the invasion, and demanded Iraq's immediate and unconditional withdrawal. S.C. Res. 660, U.N. Doc. S/RES/660 (Aug. 2, 1990). Four days later, the Security Council approved Resolution 661, which imposed a trade embargo on Iraq. S.C. Res. 661, U.N. Doc. S/RES/661 (Aug. 6, 1990). Over the next several months additional resolutions declared the purported Iraqi annexation of Kuwait null and void, demanded release of third-state nationals, approved a maritime blockade, and cut off air transport in and out of Iraq and Kuwait.

Determined not to appease Saddam Hussein, who was Iraq's military leader, President George H.W. Bush acted quickly to enforce the embargo imposed by Resolution 661. He dispatched elements of the 82nd Airborne Division and the U.S. Air

---

2. The facts in this study are drawn in part from Rick Atkinson, *Crusade* (1993); Bob Woodward, *The Commanders* (1991); Lawrence Freedman & Efraim Karsh, *The Gulf Conflict, 1990-1991: Diplomacy and War in the New World Order* (1993); *Gulf War Legal and Diplomatic Documents*, 13 Hous. J. Int'l L. 281 (1991); and *Iraqi Symposium*, 15 S. Ill. U. L.J. 411 (1991).

Force to Saudi Arabia on August 8, commencing what became known as Operation Desert Shield. Although he asserted that the mission of the U.S. forces was "wholly defensive," he declared that the United States sought "the immediate and unconditional withdrawal of all Iraqi forces from Kuwait," restoration of the legitimate Kuwaiti government, security in the Gulf, and protection of Americans in Kuwait. He also advised that "to assume that Iraq will not attack again would be unwise and unrealistic."

Congress was not in session at the time, and the President did not call it back. On August 10, however, he sent a letter to the Speaker of the House and the President Pro Tempore of the Senate "in accordance with my desire that Congress be fully informed and consistent with the War Powers Resolution." The letter stated that he had dispatched U.S. forces "equipped for combat" to respond to the Iraqi "threat" along the Kuwaiti-Saudi Arabian border, "pursuant to my constitutional authority to conduct our foreign relations and as Commander in Chief." He added that he did "not believe that involvement in hostilities is imminent." 26 Weekly Comp. Pres. Docs. 1225 (Aug. 9, 1990).

On August 28, President Bush briefed selected members of Congress at the White House about Operation Desert Shield. By that time, U.S. military operations in Saudi Arabia had expanded, as American commanders nervously eyed the growing number of Iraqi troops poised at the Saudi border and expressed open concern about the consequences if they crossed. On October 1, the House of Representatives passed a simple resolution condemning Iraq, reaffirming the objectives asserted by President Bush, affirming its support for the Security Council resolutions, and noting the requirements of the War Powers Resolution. The House also expressed support for

the President's emphasis on diplomatic efforts, international sanctions, and negotiations under the auspices of the United Nations to achieve the United States objectives. . . . The United States shall continue to emphasize the use of diplomatic and other nonmilitary means in order to achieve those objectives and policies, while maintaining credible United States and multinational deterrent military force. [H.R.J. Res. 658, §3, 101st Cong. (1990).]

Representative Dante Fascell, Chairman of the House Foreign Affairs Committee, explained that the House resolution was "not a declaration of war," but was intended "to show that the Congress has acted affirmatively." 136 Cong. Rec. H8441 (Oct. 1, 1990). The Senate passed its own resolution the following day, "strongly approv[ing] the leadership of the President," and supporting

continued action by the President in accordance with the decisions of the United Nations Security Council and in accordance with United States constitutional and statutory processes, including authorization and appropriation of funds by the Congress, to deter Iraqi aggression and to protect American lives and vital interests in the region. [S. Con. Res. 147, 101st Cong. (1990).]

Neither resolution was voted on by both Houses.

On October 1, 1990, Congress voted supplemental appropriations for Operation Desert Shield, which included lines for "military personnel" and "operation and maintenance," without further detail. Pub. L. No. 101-403, 104 Stat. 867 (1990). Five weeks later, on November 5, Congress passed the Iraq Sanctions Act of 1990.

Pub. L. No. 101-513, 104 Stat. 1979 (1990). In the act, Congress declared its support for "the actions that have been taken by the President in response to . . . [the] invasion," required continued consultation with Congress, and approved economic and trade sanctions against Iraq.

3. The Buildup

United States and Saudi forces were augmented by forces of other U.N. members who were persuaded (chiefly by U.S. diplomatic efforts) to join the "coalition." United States naval forces patrolled the Persian Gulf, intercepting vessels bound to or from Iraq and Kuwait, in order to enforce the trade embargo. By early November, President Bush had deployed approximately 230,000 U.S. armed forces in Saudi Arabia and the Persian Gulf. Although Iraq had by that time released Americans and other foreigners it had earlier detained, and the threat of further invasion had apparently receded, on November 8 the Administration announced its intention to deploy an additional 150,000 U.S. troops to provide the United States and its allies with what President Bush called an "adequate offensive military option" to oust Iraq from Kuwait. The decision was reportedly made a week earlier, on October 30, just before the mid-term congressional elections. Secretary of Defense Richard Cheney also rationalized the buildup by emphasizing the coalition forces' ability "to conduct offensive military operations."

On November 29, in a vote widely attributed to the diplomatic efforts of the Bush administration, the Security Council passed the following resolution:

United Nations Security Council, Resolution 678
S.C. Res. 678, U.N. Doc. S/RES/678 (Nov. 29, 1990)

The Security Council, . . .

Noting that, despite all efforts by the United Nations, Iraq refuses to comply with its obligations to implement resolution 660 (1990) and [ten] subsequent relevant resolutions, in flagrant contempt of the Security Council, . . .

Determined to secure full compliance with its decisions,

Acting under Chapter VII of the Charter,

1. *Demands* that Iraq comply fully with resolution 660 (1990) and all subsequent relevant resolutions and decides, while maintaining all its decisions, to allow Iraq one final opportunity, as a pause of good will, to do so;

2. *Authorizes* Member States cooperating with the Government of Kuwait, unless Iraq on or before 15 January 1991 fully implements, as set forth in paragraph 1 above, the above-mentioned resolutions, to use all necessary means to uphold and implement resolution 660 (1990) and all subsequent relevant resolutions and to restore international peace and security in the area;

3. *Requests* all States to provide appropriate support for the actions undertaken in pursuance of paragraph 2 of this resolution. . . .

In short, Resolution 678 established a deadline for Iraqi compliance with Resolution 660 and "all subsequent relevant resolutions," and authorized the use of "all necessary means" to enforce those resolutions thereafter.

During this period, the President did not request any authorization for the use of force from Congress. Asked at a press conference on January 9, 1991, whether he thought he needed such authorization, he replied, "No, I don't think I need it. . . . I feel that I have the authority to fully implement the United Nations resolutions." 27 Weekly Comp. Pres. Docs. 17-18 (Jan. 14, 1991). The following year President Bush remarked, "I didn't have to get permission from some old goat in the United States Congress to kick Saddam Hussein out of Kuwait." 28 Weekly Comp. Pres. Docs. 1120-1121 (June 29, 1992).

4.   Operation Desert Storm

Notwithstanding his repeated insistence that he already possessed all the authority he needed to send U.S. troops into battle against Saddam Hussein, in early January the President sent the following letter to congressional leaders:

Letter to Congressional Leaders on the Persian Gulf Crisis
27 Weekly Comp. Pres. Doc. 17 (Jan. 8, 1991)

Dear Mr. Speaker:

The current situation in the Persian Gulf, brought about by Iraq's unprovoked invasion and subsequent brutal occupation of Kuwait, threatens vital U.S. interests. The situation also threatens the peace. It would, however, greatly enhance the chances for peace if Congress were now to go on record supporting the position adopted by the UN Security Council on twelve separate occasions. Such an action would underline that the United States stands with the international community and on the side of law and decency; it also would help dispel any belief that may exist in the minds of Iraq's leaders that the United States lacks the necessary unity to act decisively in response to Iraq's continued aggression against Kuwait.

Secretary of State Baker is meeting with Iraq's Foreign Minister on January 9. It would have been most constructive if he could have presented the Iraqi government a Resolution passed by both houses of Congress supporting the UN position and in particular Security Council Resolution 678. As you know, I have frequently stated my desire for such a Resolution. Nevertheless, there is still opportunity for Congress to act to strengthen the prospects for peace and safeguard this country's vital interests.

I therefore request that the House of Representatives and the Senate adopt a Resolution stating that Congress supports the use of all necessary means to implement UN Security Council Resolution 678. Such action would send the clearest possible message to Saddam Hussein that he must withdraw without condition or delay from Kuwait. Anything less would only encourage Iraqi intransigence; anything else would risk detracting from the international coalition arrayed against Iraq's aggression.

Mr. Speaker, I am determined to do whatever is necessary to protect America's security. I ask Congress to join with me in this task. I can think of no better way than for Congress to express its support for the President at this critical time. This truly is the last best chance for peace.

Sincerely,
George Bush

After a dramatic debate four days later, Congress responded by passing the following joint resolution, by a vote of 52-47 in the Senate and 250-183 in the House:

Authorization for Use of Military Force Against Iraq
Pub. L. No. 102-1, 105 Stat. 3 (Jan. 14, 1991)

Joint Resolution to authorize the use of United States Armed Forces pursuant to United Nations Security Council Resolution 678.

Whereas the Government of Iraq without provocation invaded and occupied the territory of Kuwait on August 2, 1990;

Whereas both the House of Representatives (in H.J. Res. 658 of the 101st Congress) and the Senate (in S. Con. Res. 147 of the 101st Congress) have condemned Iraq's invasion of Kuwait and declared their support for international action to reverse Iraq's aggression;

Whereas, Iraq's conventional, chemical, biological, and nuclear weapons and ballistic missile programs and its demonstrated willingness to use weapons of mass destruction pose a grave threat to world peace;

Whereas the international community has demanded that Iraq withdraw unconditionally and immediately from Kuwait and that Kuwait's independence and legitimate government be restored;

Whereas the United Nations Security Council repeatedly affirmed the inherent right of individual or collective self-defense in response to the armed attack by Iraq against Kuwait in accordance with Article 51 of the United Nations Charter;

Whereas, in the absence of full compliance by Iraq with its resolutions, the United Nations Security Council in Resolution 678 has authorized member states of the United Nations to use all necessary means, after January 15, 1991, to uphold and implement all relevant Security Council resolutions and to restore international peace and security in the area; and

Whereas Iraq has persisted in its illegal occupation of, and brutal aggression against Kuwait:

Now, therefore, be it

Resolved by the Senate and House of Representatives of the United States of America in Congress assembled, . . .

SECTION 2. AUTHORIZATION FOR USE OF UNITED STATES ARMED FORCES

(a) **Authorization.** The President is authorized, subject to subsection (b), to use United States Armed Forces pursuant to United Nations Security Council Resolution 678 (1990) in order to achieve implementation of Security Council Resolutions 660, 661, 662, 664, 665, 666, 667, 669, 670, 674, and 677.

(b) **Requirement for Determination That Use of Military Force Is Necessary.** Before exercising the authority granted in subsection (a), the President shall make available to the Speaker of the House of Representatives and the President pro tempore of the Senate his determination that—

(1) the United States has used all appropriate diplomatic and other peaceful means to obtain compliance by Iraq with the United Nations Security Council resolutions cited in subsection (a); and

(2) that those efforts have not been and would not be successful in obtaining such compliance. . . .

On January 16, 1991, President Bush reported to Congress that the United Nations had exhausted diplomatic and other peaceful means of obtaining Iraqi compliance with the Security Council's resolutions. The next day, at 2:38 A.M. local time, Army Apache helicopters carrying rockets, missiles, and extra fuel tanks commenced Operation Desert Storm by hitting Iraqi radar sites to help clear the way for more massive coalition air attacks. For the next six weeks, coalition air forces bombed Iraqi military targets and infrastructure, until February 24, when coalition forces launched a ground attack into southern Iraq and Kuwait. By February 26, Iraqi forces were fleeing Kuwait City under fire, and the city was liberated the next day. On February 28, President Bush ordered a halt in the fighting. The war officially ended a month later with Iraqi acceptance of cease-fire terms in U.N. Security Council Resolution 687, S.C. Res. 687, U.N. Doc. S/RES/687 (Apr. 3, 1991).

NOTES AND QUESTIONS

1. *Role of the U.N. Security Council.* U.N. Security Council Resolution 660, adopted on the day Iraqi forces invaded Kuwait, relied expressly on the authority of Articles 39 and 40 of the Charter. All the subsequent resolutions dealing with the crisis either were silent on the source of their authority or simply claimed to be based on Chapter VII, rather than on a specific article. Can you say what provisions of the Charter authorized each resolution? Why do you suppose the Security Council was not more specific in describing its authority in each instance?

Might the coalition forces led by the United States have been justified, as a matter of international law, in using force to evict Saddam Hussein from Kuwait without any action on the part of the Security Council? By one view,

> Considering that the military operations of the Coalition in 1991 were a manifestation of collective self-defense — rather than collective security — there was technically no need for the specific mandate of Resolution 678 to legally validate the launching of strikes against Iraq. Article 51 *per se* ought to have sufficed.... [Dinstein, *supra* p. 327, at 276.]

If so, why did the Security Council get involved?

Could Resolution 678 have been interpreted to authorize coalition forces to fight all the way to Baghdad, in order to remove the Saddam Hussein regime? Or perhaps beyond? *See Lobel & Ratner,* supra p. 327, at 139 (the language to "restore international peace and security in the area" could mean "Iraq or the entire Middle East").

2. *Authority for Operation Desert Shield.* Upon what authority did President Bush deploy U.S. military forces equipped for combat to the Gulf beginning on August 8, 1990? Did that deployment start the 60-day clock ticking under War Powers Resolution §5(b) (*supra* p. 309)? Do you think the President complied with the War Powers Resolution? What authorization, if any, did either congressional actions or the U.N. Security Council resolutions give the President during the fall of 1990?

3. *Authority for Operation Desert Storm.* Would President Bush have had constitutional authority to launch Operation Desert Storm unilaterally, as he contended? How would you compare his powers with those of President Truman at the beginning of the Korean War? Consider not only each President's inherent war powers, but also the effect, if any, of various U.N. Security Council resolutions.

Why do you suppose President Bush, after maintaining so emphatically that he needed no congressional approval to order U.S. troops into battle in Iraq, finally decided to send the January 8, 1991, letter to Congress set out above? What exactly did the letter request? Did the President get what he asked for?

Why do you think Congress did not formally declare war on Iraq? What, precisely, did it authorize instead? Did it give President Bush the authority to annihilate the Iraqi Republican Guards? To carpet-bomb Baghdad? Did that authority change after the Iraqis were driven out of Kuwait?

Section 2(c)(1) of the Authorization for Use of Military Force Against Iraq provided, "Consistent with section 8(a)(1) of the War Powers Resolution, the Congress declares that this section is intended to constitute specific statutory authorization within the meaning of section 5(b) of the War Powers Resolution." How, if at all, do you think this provision might have affected the precedent set in Korea for unilateral presidential war power? For presidential authority based on U.N. Security Council resolutions?

C.   AFGHANISTAN

1.   The U.S. Response to 9/11 in Afghanistan

In the immediate aftermath of the terrorist attacks on September 11, 2001, the United States reached out to other nations around the globe for assistance in gathering intelligence about terrorist suspects, apprehending persons believed to be connected with the attacks, freezing their financial assets, and mounting a military response against Osama bin Laden's sponsors in Afghanistan. It also asked for help from international organizations.

On the evening of the 11th, the NATO Council announced:

> The NATO nations unanimously condemn these barbaric acts committed against a NATO member state. The mindless slaughter of so many innocent civilians is an unacceptable act of violence without precedent in the modern era. It underscores the urgency of intensifying the battle against terrorism, a battle that the NATO countries — indeed all civilised nations — must win. All Allies stand united in their determination to combat this scourge. [NATO Press Release PR/CP (2001) 122, Sept. 12, 2001.]

The next day, the U.N. Security Council passed a resolution calling on "all States to work together urgently to bring to justice the perpetrators, organizers, and sponsors of these terrorist attacks." S.C. Res. 1368, U.N. Doc. S/RES/1368 (Sept. 12, 2001). In both Resolution 1368 and Resolution 1373, U.N. Doc. S/RES 1373 (Sept. 28, 2001), which likewise condemned the 9/11 attacks, the Security Council expressly recognized "the inherent right of individual or collective self-defence in accordance with the Charter."

On September 20, the United States issued an ultimatum to the Taliban-led government of Afghanistan to turn over Al Qaeda leaders. When its ultimatum was rejected, the United States wrote to the Security Council on October 7, 2001, to say that it had clear and compelling evidence that Al Qaeda played a central role in the 9/11 attacks. Furthermore, it said, in the exercise of its Article 51 right of self-defense to prevent and deter further attacks, it was initiating military action — Operation Enduring Freedom (OEF) — against Al Qaeda terrorist training camps and Taliban military bases in Afghanistan. Letter from the Permanent Representative of the United States of America to the President of the Security Council, Oct. 7,

CIA map of Afghanistan.

Courtesy worldatlas.com.

2001, 40 I.L.M. 1281 (2001). The letter presumably satisfied Article 51's requirement to immediately report to the Security Council any resort to self-defense.

Operation Enduring Freedom eventually drew support from 70 nations. Fighting against Taliban militants continued throughout the country as of early 2011. Nearly 1,500 U.S. troops had been killed and another 10,500 wounded.

2. The United Nations Role

Two years before the terrorist attacks of 9/11, the Security Council had determined that the Taliban's provision of sanctuary and training for terrorists inside Afghanistan, as well as its refusal to turn over Osama bin Laden and others for criminal prosecution, posed a threat to international peace and security. It directed member states to bar most Taliban air traffic and to freeze all Taliban financial resources. S.C. Res. 1267, U.N. Doc. S/RES 1267 (Oct. 15, 1999). In December 2000, the Security Council expanded its injunction to halt all non-humanitarian flights in or out of Afghanistan and cut off shipments of arms into the country. S.C. Res. 1333, U.N. Doc. S/RES 1333 (Dec. 19, 2000). Unfortunately, these measures failed to dislodge bin Laden. One scholar was prompted to write that

> where urgent action against entities like Al Qaeda and its affiliates is required, the responses which may, at the most, be expected from the Security Council . . . will not be sufficient in real time; in these circumstances, unilateral and, by its nature, anticipatory military action may be the only meaningful action. [W. Michael Reisman, *International Legal Dynamics and the Design of Feasible Missions: The Case of Afghanistan*, in *The War in Afghanistan: A Legal Analysis* 59, 67 (Michael N. Schmitt ed., 2009).][3]

3. The legality of "anticipatory" or "preemptive" self-defense is explored in the next chapter.

By early December 2001, the Taliban had been routed from Afghanistan by U.S. and indigenous Afghan forces. The Security Council endorsed the Agreement on Provisional Arrangements in Afghanistan Pending the Re-establishment of Permanent Government Institutions (Bonn Agreement), Dec. 5, 2001, *available at* http:// www.afghangovernment.com/AfghanAgreementBonn.htm, to create a new interim government in Kabul led by Hamid Karzai. S.C. Res. 1383, U.N. Doc. S/RES 1383 (Dec. 6, 2001).

Independently of the OEF military deployment led by the United States, the Security Council then authorized the creation of an International Security Assistance Force (ISAF) in Afghanistan, with responsibility for supporting the interim Afghan government in and around Kabul. S.C. Res. 1386, U.N. Doc. S/RES 1386 (Dec. 20, 2001). ISAF's mission is security and stabilization — to disarm the insurgents, train the Afghan police and military, establish the rule of law, help with elections, and combat drug production and trafficking — while that of OEF is counterterrorism. The Security Council called on member states to contribute personnel and equipment to ISAF, which was organized and led initially by Great Britain, then by a succession of other states. ISAF's mandate was later extended to cover all of Afghanistan. The initial resolution also authorized member states participating in ISAF to "take all necessary measures to fulfil its mandate." By early 2011, ISAF included more than 130,000 troops from 48 countries, including the United States. A description and updates on ISAF's mission may be found at NATO/OTAN, *Afghanistan: International Security Assistance Force* (updated regularly), *at* http://www.nato.int/isaf/. *See also* Alan Cole, *Legal Issues in Forming the Coalition*, in *The War in Afghanistan: A Legal Analysis*, *supra*, at 141.

The Security Council has also taken a number of non-military measures in an effort to restore and preserve the peace in Afghanistan. In January 2002, for example, it directed U.N. member states to freeze all financial assets of Osama bin Laden and various members of Al Qaeda and the Taliban, to block international travel by these individuals, and to prevent their acquisition of weapons. S.C. Res. 1390, U.N. Doc. S/RES 1390 (Jan. 28, 2002). The following March the Security Council endorsed the establishment of the United Nations Assistance Mission in Afghanistan (UNAMA), whose job is to coordinate international donor activity in the recovery and reconstruction of the country. S.C. Res. 1401, U.N. Doc. S/RES 1401 (Mar. 28, 2002). *See* Rhoda Margesson, *United Nations Assistance Mission in Afghanistan: Background and Policy Issues* (Cong. Res. Serv. R40747), Dec. 27, 2010. Other resolutions have dealt variously with human rights (especially the rights of women and children), the rule of law, elections, corruption, and the drug trade.

The U.N. Secretary General delivers an extensive report to the Security Council every three months on conditions in Afghanistan, most recently at this writing U.N. Secretary-General, *The Situation in Afghanistan and Its Implications for International Peace and Security*, U.N. Doc. A/65/612-S/2010/630 (Dec. 10, 2010).

3.   A New Role for NATO

The North Atlantic Treaty Organization (NATO) was created in 1949 by the North Atlantic Treaty, Apr. 4, 1949, 63 Stat. 2241, 34 U.N.T.S. 243. It originally consisted of five European states, plus Canada and the United States. Greece and Turkey joined two years later. NATO's original mission was the defense of Western Europe against the Soviet Union. Since the end of the Cold War, NATO has grown to include 28 states, a number of them former Soviet bloc countries. *See generally North Atlantic Treaty Organization* (updated Aug. 25, 2008), *at* http://www.nato.int/cps/en/natolive/what_is_nato.htm; NATO/OTAN, *NATO Handbook* (updated June 17, 2004), *at* http://www.nato.int/docu/handbook/2001/index.htm.

The signers of the U.N. Charter anticipated the creation of regional organizations like NATO:

Charter of the United Nations
June 26, 1945, 59 Stat. 1031, T.S. No. 993

CHAPTER VIII. REGIONAL ARRANGEMENTS

Article 52

1. Nothing in the present Charter precludes the existence of regional arrangements or agencies for dealing with such matters relating to the maintenance of international peace and security as are appropriate for regional action, provided that such arrangements or agencies and their activities are consistent with the Purposes and Principles of the United Nations.

2. The Members of the United Nations entering into such arrangements or constituting such agencies shall make every effort to achieve pacific settlement of local disputes through such regional arrangements or by such regional agencies before referring them to the Security Council.

3. The Security Council shall encourage the development of pacific settlement of local disputes through such regional arrangements or by such regional agencies either on the initiative of the states concerned or by reference from the Security Council. . . .

Article 53

1. The Security Council shall, where appropriate, utilize such regional arrangements or agencies for enforcement action under its authority. But no enforcement action shall be taken under regional arrangements or by regional agencies without the authorization of the Security Council. . . .

Because NATO's goals are relatively limited, its founding document is much shorter and simpler than the U.N. Charter. Its governing body, the NATO Council, based in Brussels, makes decisions by consensus. Unlike the Security Council, NATO has a military command structure, headed in early 2011 by a U.S. Navy Admiral. Like the Security Council, however, it has no military force of its own, but depends on contributions of troops and matériel from member states.[4]

---

4. A number of other regional alliances around the world have also been organized to address breaches or threatened breaches of the peace. For example, in the Western Hemisphere the Organization of American States was used to enforce a quarantine of Cuba during the missile crisis there in 1962 and to send peacekeeping forces into the Dominican Republic in 1965. The Organization of Eastern Carribean States was said to have requested the U.S. invasion of Grenada in 1983. Elsewhere, the Organization of African Unity has deployed peacekeeping forces a number of times, including in the Darfur region of Sudan.

The day after the terrorist attacks on the World Trade Center and the Pentagon, the NATO Council decided that if "this attack was directed from abroad against the United States, it shall be regarded as an action covered by Article 5 of the [North Atlantic] Treaty, which states that an armed attack against one or more of the Allies in Europe or North America shall be considered an attack against them all." NATO Press Release (2001) 124, Sept. 12, 2001. *See NATO in Afghanistan* (updated Feb. 7, 2011), *at* http://www.nato.int/cps/en/natolive/topics_69349.htm. On October 2, the Council determined that the attack had come from abroad.

Article 5 goes on to say that when one or more member states comes under attack, each of the other states,

> in exercise of the right of individual or collective self-defence recognised by Article 51 of the Charter of the United Nations, will assist the Party or Parties so attacked by taking forthwith, individually and in concert with the other Parties, such action as it deems necessary, including the use of armed force, to restore and maintain the security of the North Atlantic area.

Each NATO member state thus had to decide for itself whether to come to the aid of the United States. Some immediately did by contributing forces to OEF, as an act of collective self-defense under Article 51 of the U.N. Charter, upon the assumption that the terrorist attacks of 9/11 constituted an armed attack.

On August 11, 2003, NATO became directly involved as an institution by taking command of ISAF. This was NATO's first-ever deployment of forces outside of Europe. Since that time, NATO member states have all contributed personnel to ISAF, although not all have been combat-equipped or permitted by their governments to engage in combat, and there has been persistent disagreement about the scope of ISAF's mission. Nevertheless, despite the different missions of ISAF and OEF, NATO nations agreed in 2009 that the ISAF commander would also be "dual-hatted" as commander of U.S. forces in OEF. These developments are extensively described in Steve Bowman & Catherine Dale, *War in Afghanistan: Strategy, Military Operations, and Issues for Congress* (Cong. Res. Serv. R40156), June 8, 2010; and Vincent Morelli & Paul Belkin, *NATO in Afghanistan: A Test of the Transatlantic Alliance* (Cong. Res. Serv. RL33627), Dec. 3, 2009.

In early 2006, the Afghan government and members of the international community, including the United Nations and NATO, agreed in the Afghanistan Compact, Feb. 1, 2006, *at* http://www.nato.int/isaf/docu/epub/pdf/afghanistan_compact.pdf, that through the end of 2010

> the NATO-led International Security Assistance Force (ISAF), the US-led Operation Enduring Freedom (OEF) and partner nations involved in security sector reform will continue to provide strong support to the Afghan Government in establishing and sustaining security and stability in Afghanistan, subject to participating states' national approval procedures.

The Security Council endorsed the Compact in S.C. Res. 1659, U.N. Doc. S/RES/ 1659 (Feb. 15, 2006).

In various resolutions the Security Council has declared its appreciation and support for OEF and for NATO's leadership of ISAF. It even declared that OEF "operates... in accordance with the applicable rules of international law." S.C.

Res. 1943, U.N. Doc. S/RES/1943 (Oct. 13, 2010). Yet the Security Council has not expressly authorized OEF. Neither has it explicitly approved NATO's institutional role as leader of ISAF, despite the requirement in Article 53(1) for authorization of enforcement actions by regional organizations.

4. A Plan for Transition to Peace

In 2010, the Afghan government, NATO, and ISAF foreign ministers agreed on a plan for a "phased transition" in which Afghans will gradually "take full responsibility for security, governance and development." By the end of 2014, Afghan National Security Forces are to develop the capability to address existing and new security challenges, with continued support from ISAF. Meanwhile, the Afghan government will further develop the rule of law, manage public administration at all levels, and promote sustained socio-economic development. *See Declaration by the North Atlantic Treaty Organisation (NATO) and the Government of the Islamic Republic of Afghanistan on an Enduring Partnership*, Nov. 20, 2010, *at* http://www.nato.int/cps/en/natolive/official_texts_68724.htm. *See also* Peter Baker & Rod Nordland, *U.S. Envisions Path to Ending Afghan Combat*, N.Y. Times, Nov. 14, 2010. Past and possible future developments for both ISAF and OEF are surveyed in Kenneth Katzman, *Afghanistan: Post-Taliban Governance, Security, and U.S. Policy* (Cong. Res. Serv. RL30588), Jan. 26, 2011.

NOTES AND QUESTIONS

1. *The President's Domestic Authority.* What domestic authority was President Bush exercising when he ordered the launch of Operation Enduring Freedom on October 7, 2001? It is commonly thought that the Authorization for Use of Military Force (AUMF), enacted three weeks earlier on September 18 (see *supra* p. 97), provided authority to invade Afghanistan. Can you tell from the language of the measure precisely what Congress intended to authorize the President to do, with how many troops and what kind of weaponry, where, and for how long?

2. *9/11 as Armed Attack?* Any exercise of the inherent right of collective self-defense under Article 51 must be premised on the existence of a significant "armed attack," as we learned in the *Nicaragua Case, supra* p. 218. Otherwise, the use of force must be approved by the Security Council. Article 51 says nothing, however, about the source of an attack. If the attack comes from another sovereign state, as it did when Iraq invaded Kuwait in 1990, military force may be used against the attacking state. But on 9/11 the attack came from a non-state entity, Al Qaeda. Does such an attack justify a military response, or is a criminal prosecution the only permissible recourse? *Compare* Louis Henkin, *International Law: Politics and Values* 126 (1995) ("It is difficult to make an 'armed attack' out of a limited, isolated terrorist attack or even a few sporadic ones."), *with* Adam Roberts, *Afghanistan and International Security*, in *The War in Afghanistan: A Legal Analysis, supra* p. 335, at 4, 15 (arguing that in Resolution 1368 "the Council accepted that a right of self-defense could apply to a State when it was attacked by a non-State entity"), *and* Dinstein, *supra* p. 327, at 208 ("terrorist attacks qualify as armed attacks").

Should the answer turn on the size or destructive effect of the terrorist action? How do you think the World Court would answer this question, based on its decision in the *Nicaragua Case, supra* p. 218? *See* Mary Ellen O'Connell, *Lawful Self-Defense to Terrorism*, 63 U. Pitt. L. Rev. 889, 890-893 (2002) (arguing that a forceful response was justified, based on the scale and gravity of the attacks).

3. *Criteria for Self-Defense.* The World Court has declared that any use of force in self-defense must be necessary and proportional. See *supra* p. 221. The following criteria were articulated by Daniel Webster in a mid-nineteenth century dispute called the *Caroline* affair: a violent response to an attack must reflect "a necessity of self-defense, instant, overwhelming, leaving no choice of means, no moment for deliberation." See *supra* p. 232. Were these criteria satisfied when the United States launched Operation Enduring Freedom?

4. *Attacking the Terrorists Where They Live.* Following the terrorist attacks of 9/11, in order to abate the threat of another attack it clearly was reasonably necessary to deny Al Qaeda the safe haven from which it operated, that is, to use force to kill, capture, or displace its members wherever they could be found. If the de facto Taliban government of Afghanistan had consented to U.S. military actions inside its borders to root out Al Qaeda, of course, Operation Enduring Freedom would not have violated either Afghanistan's sovereignty or the Article 2(4) ban on the use of force. Without such an invitation from the Taliban, did OEF violate international law? According to one authority, if the host state cannot or will not deal with its resident terrorist threat, the victim state may use force to do what the host state should have done. Dinstein, *supra*, at 244-245.

5. *State Responsibility for a Terrorist Attack?* In a 1949 decision, the World Court declared that it is "every State's obligation not to allow knowingly its territory to be used for acts contrary to the rights of other States." *Corfu Channel* (U.K. v. Alb.), 1949 I.C.J. 4, 22 (Apr. 9). Were OEF forces justified by a breach of this obligation in attacking the state of Afghanistan and its Taliban government?

Non-state attackers like Al Qaeda may be based in a failed state, like Somalia, or in one where the government is not in full control of its territory, like Yemen. The state from which an attack is launched may be a willing host — perhaps because its political goals are aligned with the non-state entity. Or the host state may actually sponsor the attacker. Should it matter to the victim of a terrorist attack whether the non-state attacker was controlled by, sponsored by, merely tolerated by, or even known to the host state? Should the state under attack have to wait for the International Court of Justice to characterize the relationship between a non-state attacker and its host state before using force against the host state if it is necessary to prevent another attack?

In the *Nicaragua Case* the World Court said that before holding the United States responsible for attacks by the Contras on Nicaragua, it had to determine "whether or not the relationship of the contras to the United States Government was so much one of dependence on the one side and control on the other that it would be right to equate the contras, for legal purposes, with an organ of the United States Government, or as acting on behalf of that Government." *Nicaragua Case, supra* p. 218, ¶109. On September 11, 2001, it appeared that the Taliban government of Afghanistan was not only a knowing, willing host to Al Qaeda, but also controlled by Al Qaeda to some degree, rather than the other way around. According to one observer, "the Taliban,

Afghanistan's de facto government, developed such close links to the known terrorist organization al Qaeda that it became responsible for the acts of al Qaeda." O'Connell, *supra*, 63 U. Pitt. L. Rev. at 901. *See also* Sean D. Murphy, *Terrorism and the Concept of "Armed Attack" in Article 51 of the U.N. Charter*, 43 Harv. Int'l L.J. 41, 50 (2002) (suggesting that the incidents of September 11 might be imputable to the de facto, Taliban government of Afghanistan). Was the OEF thus entitled to remove the Taliban from its control of the Afghan government? *Compare* O'Connell, *supra*, 63 U. Pitt. L. Rev. at 904 ("Eliminating the whole government structure created by the Taliban, as a war aim was beyond necessary self-defense.), *with* Roberts, *supra*, at 31 ("The Council's acceptance of regime change in Afghanistan was justified once the Taliban had refused to remove Al-Qaeda . . . .").

6. *Duration of the Response.* The inherent right of self-defense presumably continues as long as the threat of another armed attack persists. Article 51 permits the use of force in self-defense "until the Security Council has taken measures necessary to maintain international peace and security." As of early 2011, international peace and security clearly had not been restored in Afghanistan. Moreover, the terrorist threat that was said to justify the exercise of self-defense in the first place was still very significant. To make matters worse, the threat appeared to have metastasized, as off-shoots of Al Qaeda sprang up in Yemen, East Africa, and elsewhere. How long will the United States and its OEF partners be justified in using force to abate this threat?

7. *Acts of Self-Defense Outside of Afghanistan.* U.S. military forces involved in OEF have repeatedly carried out military actions in Pakistan. Some of these have involved targeted attacks on individuals or groups using unmanned drone aircraft. See Chapter 14. The Pakistani government apparently has tacitly consented to these strikes, so long as they target only "foreign fighters," although there has been much controversy surrounding the collateral deaths of many civilians. U.S. forces have occasionally chased militants across the border in "hot pursuit." They have also conducted covert actions against militant targets in the northwest tribal areas.

Are any of these OEF actions outside of Afghanistan justified as exercises of the Article 51 right of self-defense? *See generally* Sean D. Murphy, *The International Legality of US Cross-Border Operations from Afghanistan into Pakistan*, in *The War in Afghanistan: A Legal Analysis*, *supra* p. 335, at 109, and sources cited therein. What about U.S. military attacks on suspected terrorist targets in Yemen? See *infra* p. 377.

8. *The Roles of International Organizations.* Why do you suppose the Security Council did not expressly authorize OEF? What did it do instead? Recall that the right to use force in self-defense is recognized under Article 51 only "until the Security Council has taken measures necessary to maintain international peace and security." Were the United States and its allies entitled to continue OEF even after the Security Council authorized the creation of ISAF in December 2001? If so, for how long? See *supra* p. 341, Note 6.

Why didn't NATO as an institution join OEF? Why did NATO wait so long (two years) to take over the leadership of ISAF? Some possible answers are offered in Roberts, *supra*.

In 1993 the Security Council authorized member states, "acting nationally or through regional organizations," to use force in Bosnia-Herzegovina. S.C. Res. 816, U.N. Doc. S/RES/816 (Mar. 31, 1993). Why didn't the Security Council adopt a similar resolution to approve NATO's intervention as an enforcement action under Article 53(1)? According to one authority, "there is a difference between the exercise of collective self-defense and an enforcement undertaking stemming from Article 53(1).... When exercising collective self-defense, NATO does not require the advance authorization of the Security Council." Dinstein, *supra*, at 313. Once the Security Council has approved the use of force, however, as it did when it authorized the creation of ISAF, can we distinguish between self-defense under Article 51 and an enforcement action by a regional organization under Article 53(1)? Does the distinction have any legal significance?

The situation in Afghanistan stands in sharp contrast to one in former Yugoslavia in 1999. NATO forces engaged in a 78-day bombing campaign there aimed at stopping massive human rights violations by Serbian security forces and the Yugoslav army against ethnic Albanians in the breakaway province of Kosovo. NATO characterized its action not as a response to an attack on one of its members under Article 3 of the North Atlantic Treaty, but as "necessary to avert a humanitarian catastrophe," to "prevent instability spreading in the region," and to "support the political aims of the international community." Press Statement by Dr. Javier Solana, Secretary General of NATO, Mar. 23, 1999, *at* http://www.nato.int/docu/pr/1999/p99-040e.htm. For its part, the Security Council repeatedly described the violence in Kosovo as a "threat to peace and security in the region," called for a cease-fire, imposed an arms embargo, and adopted other measures to try to bring about a peaceful solution. But it did not approve the use of force. (Presumably, it could not have done so because of a certain veto by Russia.) Moreover, NATO's intervention could not be justified as an exercise of collective self-defense under Article 51, because Kosovo was not a state, but an integral part of Yugoslavia. Thus, NATO's military action fit neither of the textual exceptions to the Article 2(4) ban on resort to force. *See* Dinstein, *supra*, at 313-315; Louis Henkin, *Kosovo and the Law of "Humanitarian Intervention,"* 93 Am. J. Int'l L. 824 (1999); Ruth Wedgwood, *NATO's Campaign in Yugoslavia*, 93 Am. J. Int'l L. 828 (1999). Whether it might have been justified as a humanitarian intervention is a matter of considerable controversy that we address in Chapter 15.

9. *Comparing the Conflicts.* Consider the factual differences in the three case studies in this chapter. How do the conflicts in Korea, Kuwait, and Afghanistan compare in terms of

(a) Contemporary economic and geopolitical conditions?

(b) Contemporary U.S. domestic politics?

(c) The magnitude of the violence and destruction resulting from the initial outbreak of hostilities?

(d) The legal character of the entity initiating the conflict — whether the entity was a sovereign state, a non-state actor, or some combination of the two?

(e) The responses of international organizations?

(f) The responses of individual states, including the United States?

(g) The duration of the conflict?

How, if at all, did these facts influence the legal rights and obligations of parties in each of these conflicts?

Unilateral Self-Defense and Rescue —13

If the Framers changed the proposed constitutional text to accommodate a presidential power "to repel sudden attacks," see *supra* p. 18, they were at once prescient and naïve. They were prescient because after more than two centuries the United States has fought only five declared wars[1] and five undeclared large foreign wars.[2] By contrast, the President has unilaterally deployed armed forces on a lesser scale more than 300 times, often asserting inherent defensive authority. Many of these involved the alleged protection of U.S. nationals or, more recently, peacekeeping, stabilization, or humanitarian operations (see Chapter 14). *See* Richard F. Grimmett, *Instances of Use of United States Armed Forces Abroad, 1798-2009* (Cong. Res. Serv. RL30172), Mar. 10, 2011; *see also* Louis Fisher, *Presidential War Power* (2d ed. 2004).

The Framers were also naïve if they thought that any implied presidential "sudden attack" power could be confined literally to repelling sudden attacks. That power has been invoked repeatedly by presidents not only to justify an immediate use of defensive force to repel attacks, but also to rescue Americans and their property, to retaliate against foreign states and persons, and, in recent years, to strike first in anticipatory self-defense.

What is the constitutional authority for such use of military force without congressional approval? One theory is that it is subsumed within the President's defensive war power. Another is that it is supported by customary authority with congressional acquiescence. (Recall the requirements for such authority, discussed *supra* pp. 45-46.) The broadest theory is simply that the President has constitutional authority to use force abroad, subject only to Congress's spending power and its power to decide the juridical consequences of using force. As you read this chapter, consider which of these theories is most convincing.

The term "unilateral" has a second aspect explored in this chapter, that is, the use of military force by this nation acting alone. In the previous chapter we saw that

---

1. The War of 1812, the 1846-1848 Mexican War, the Spanish-American War, and the two World Wars.

2. The Korean War, the Vietnam War, the 1991 Persian Gulf War, the Iraq War, and the ongoing war in Afghanistan. *See generally* Francis D. Wormuth & Edwin B. Firmage, *To Chain the Dog of War* 55, 59 (2d ed. 1989) (noting also several authorizations of limited war).

the United States may join with other states, formally or informally, to act in self-defense against attacks or threats from sovereign states or terrorists or both. It may do so within the framework of the United Nations or another international organization. Or it may use force to preserve or restore order under the mandate of the U.N. Security Council. Here we consider the international law implications when the United States employs military force abroad on its own initiative — without the collaboration of other states and without the imprimatur of any international group.

In Part A, we revisit *The Prize Cases* and the President's power of immediate self-defense. In Part B, we consider the President's power to strike first or to strike back, and whether it matters which is which. In Part C, we analyze the theory of preemptive self-defense, asserted by the United States in connection with its invasion of Iraq in 2003. And in Part D, we explore the relatively uncontroversial extension of the President's unilateral power to the rescue of Americans abroad.

A. REPELLING SUDDEN ATTACKS

1. Authority to Repel Sudden Attacks: The Basic Understanding

The Prize Cases

United States Supreme Court, 1863
67 U.S. (2 Black) 635

[The opinion is set forth *supra* p. 68.]

2. The Gulf of Sidra Incident: Repelling (Or Provoking?) Attack[3]

In 1973, Libya claimed as its territorial waters the entire Gulf of Sidra, a body of water that extends roughly 90 to 150 miles north of the Libyan coast and measures about 275 miles across. The United States has generally refused to recognize claims of territorial waters running more than 12 miles offshore. Accordingly, it formally rejected Libya's claim to the Gulf of Sidra in February 1974. 1974 Dig. U.S. Prac. Int'l L. 293-294.

Libyan leader Muammar el-Qaddafi declared a "line of death" across the northern boundary of the Gulf, and two Libyan fighters fired at American planes operating inside it in 1981. Both Libyan aircraft were shot down in return fire. After the 1981 incident, U.S. naval forces conducted exercises inside the line drawn by Qaddafi on seven or eight occasions through January 1986.

In March 1986, the United States began an unusual buildup of carrier forces in the area of the line. U.S. carrier-based planes flew 375 flights south of the line, and a

---

3. Except where otherwise noted, the background for this account is drawn from *War Powers, Libya, and State-Sponsored Terrorism: Hearing Before the Subcomm. on Arms Control, International Security and Science of the H. Comm. on Foreign Affairs*, 99th Cong. (1986) (hereinafter *Libya Hearings*); Pat Towell, *Military Strikes Against Libya Receive Capitol Hill Support*, 44 Cong. Q. 699-702 (Mar. 29, 1986); and Stephen R. Ratner, *The Gulf of Sidra Incident of 1981: The Lawfulness of Peacetime Aerial Engagements*, in *International Incidents* 181 (W. Michael Reisman & Andrew R. Willard eds., 1988).

naval task force crossed it for 75 hours. On March 24, Libyan shore-based batteries fired on U.S. planes inside the line.

News of these events prompted Chairman Dante Fascell of the House Committee on Foreign Affairs to complain that the Reagan administration had failed to comply with the War Powers Resolution. Chairman Fascell wrote to the President:

> [T]hese deployments constituted from the outset a situation where imminent involvement in hostilities was a distinct possibility clearly indicated by the circumstances even prior to today's development.
>
> Under the circumstances, prior consultation with Congress was required under the War Powers Act.
>
> In view of these circumstances, I respectfully urge you to comply fully with the provisions of the War Powers Resolution before the situation evolves further. [Letter from Chairman Fascell to President Reagan (Mar. 24, 1986), *reprinted in Libya Hearings, supra,* at 207-208.]

On the afternoon of March 24, U.S. carrier-based aircraft returned the Libyan shore-based fire with missiles designed to home in on anti-aircraft radar. The missiles apparently struck home. At the same time, U.S. planes and ships attacked five and sank at least two Libyan missile-armed ships that had approached the U.S. fleet too closely. Two days later, the Pentagon announced the end of the naval exercise.

As these events unfolded, the Administration made the following reply to Chairman Fascell:

> First, our maneuvers in the Gulf have long been planned, as part of a global freedom-of-navigation program by which the United States preserves its rights to use international waters and airspace. Numerous similar prior operations did not provoke a response. We obviously cannot be deterred from exercising our rights by Qadhafi's legally baseless claims or by his threats.
>
> We disagree with your claim that our "actions in the Gulf of Sidra have failed to adequately satisfy the requirements of the War Powers Resolution." Nor do we believe that the Resolution was intended to require consultation before conducting naval maneuvers in international waters or airspace. We considered this question carefully and concluded that conducting the operations did not place U.S. forces into hostilities or into a situation in which imminent hostilities were clearly indicated by the circumstances. Contrary to your letter's suggestion, it is not enough under the statute that an operation create "a distinct possibility" of hostilities. After Libya attacked our forces, we notified congressional leaders.
>
> Our plans in this instance have been known to all, including Qadhafi himself. The very purpose of the present operation has been to exercise our rights, openly and unambiguously. [Letter from William L. Ball III (Assistant to President Reagan) to Chairman Fascell (Mar. 26, 1986), *reprinted in Libya Hearings, supra,* at 209.]

Newspaper reports asserted that the naval maneuvers were intended to provoke Libyan attacks and thus justify U.S. counterattacks, apparently planned at least as early as March 14. Responding to these reports in part and to Chairman Fascell's complaint, the Legal Adviser to the State Department gave the following testimony in congressional hearings.

Statement of Abraham D. Sofaer, Legal Adviser to the Department of State, The War Powers Resolution and Antiterrorist Operations (April 29, 1986)

reprinted in Libya Hearings, supra, at 22-26

Issues under the War Powers Resolution have also been raised where U.S. forces have engaged in a military exercise in conformity with international law. The incident in the Gulf of Sidra in late March illustrates the situation. Does the resolution require the President to consult and report in this kind of case? ...

The War Powers Resolution was not intended to require consultation before conducting maneuvers in international waters or airspace in the context of this global freedom of navigation program. We are aware of no previous suggestion that the resolution would require consultation in such situations. This question was carefully considered in connection with the Sidra exercise in March, and the decision was made that the conduct of those operations did not place U.S. forces into hostilities or into a situation in which imminent involvement in hostilities was "clearly indicated by the circumstances." The United States has conducted its exercises not only in Sidra but around the world, not only in March but for years — and, in most instances, without hostile response. We have, in fact, been in the Gulf of Sidra area 16 times since 1981, and we have crossed Qadhafi's so-called line of death seven times before the operation last March. Only once before did Qadhafi respond with military action, and, in that instance, he was singularly unsuccessful. While we must always be aware of the risks and be prepared to deal with all contingencies, we have every right to expect that neither Libya nor any other country will take hostile action against U.S. forces while they are lawfully in and over areas of the high seas. The threat of a possible hostile response is not sufficient to trigger the consultation requirement of section 3, which refers only to actual hostilities and to situations in which imminent involvement in hostilities is "clearly indicated" by the circumstances.

Where a peaceful, lawful exercise does, in fact, result in hostile action to which U.S. forces must respond in immediate self-defense, such an isolated engagement should not normally be construed as constituting the introduction of U.S. Armed Forces into a situation of actual or imminent hostilities for the purpose of the reporting requirement of section 4 of the resolution. No report was submitted in the case of the 1981 Sidra incident, in which two Libyan aircraft were shot down after they fired at U.S. aircraft. Similarly, during the period in which U.S. peacekeeping forces were deployed in the Beirut area in 1983, many incidents occurred in which hostile forces attacked and U.S. peacekeeping forces responded in immediate self-defense. Yet, *no* separate war powers report was submitted for each of these incidents. Of course, a different situation might be presented if U.S. forces withdrew from an area and subsequently returned for the purpose of undertaking further military action. ...

NOTES AND QUESTIONS

1. *Immediate Self-Defense. The Prize Cases* involved the President's authority to respond to force with force in a war. Does it support the same authority to respond immediately to attacks on U.S. military forces abroad, even when the exchange is not

part of any larger scale conflict? What answer is suggested by the "sudden attack" language in the fragmentary record of the Philadelphia Convention, *supra* p. 18?

2. *Authority for Minatory Exercises.* In general principle, freedom of navigation and overflight is a well-established customary international norm. The craft of any state are entitled to pass through, over, or under bodies of water considered critical to international commerce and security. The right of passage free from interference by riparian states has been codified and clarified to some extent by the United Nations Convention on the Law of the Sea, Dec. 10, 1982, 1833 U.N.T.S. 397. While the United States is not yet a party, it regards the Convention as an accurate reflection of customary norms concerning maritime navigation and overflights. Nevertheless, some states object to certain of its terms regarding maritime boundaries and conditions of passage. Since 1979, the Defense Department's U.S. Freedom of Navigation program has repeatedly challenged what it regards as excessive coastal state claims, for example in the Straits of Gibraltar, Hormuz, and Malacca. *See* William J. Aceves, *The Freedom of Navigation Program: A Study of the Relationship Between Law and Politics,* 19 Hastings Int'l & Comp. L. Rev. 259 (1996); John W. Rolph, *Freedom of Navigation and the Black Sea Bumping Incident,* 135 Mil. L. Rev. 137 (1992); Department of Defense, *Freedom of Navigation* (n.d.), *at* http://www.dod.gov/execsec/adr1999/apdx_i.html.

Establishing freedom of navigation is one, but not the only, purpose of minatory exercises, which generally are intended to demonstrate national strength and resolve. Such exercises are often classified, however, to avoid international political friction. Rolph, *supra,* 135 Mil. L. Rev. at 150. To what extent may Congress be said to have tacitly approved by acquiescence this tactic for pursuing U.S. foreign policy interests? Is its approval needed?

3. *Applying the WPR.* In the 1981 Gulf of Sidra incident fire was exchanged and two Libyan fighters were shot down. In the five succeeding years, seven or eight comparable freedom of navigation exercises did not draw fire. Given this history, was the 1986 exercise a situation "where imminent involvement in hostilities is clearly indicated by the circumstances," requiring consultation with and notice to Congress under War Powers Resolution §4(a)(1), *supra* p. 308? Legal Adviser Sofaer asserted that the situation "should not normally be construed as" a triggering event under the WPR. *See also* Robert F. Turner, *The War Powers Resolution: Its Implementation in Theory and Practice* 79-80 (1983) (noting that the United States did not initiate fire). Do you agree? In the alternative, does the constitutional savings clause of WPR §2(c) place the Gulf of Sidra deployment outside the Resolution, whether or not it involved "imminent hostilities"?

4. *Provoking Attack?* If our forces were lawfully deployed over the "line of death," then surely their return of Libyan fire fits even the narrowest definition of a presidential power to repel sudden attacks. Or does it? Some experts have written that the 1981 Libyan attack had no chance of success because of the great margin of technological superiority enjoyed by the American F-14s over the export version Soviet SU-22s used by the Libyans. Letter to the Editor from J. McFaul, Proc. U.S. Naval Inst. 42 (May 1982). Was the 1981 U.S. response defensive or retaliatory?

In 1986, U.S. forces attacked Libyan vessels for approaching too closely, even though the Libyans had not attacked. Was this later U.S. action defensive or retaliatory? *See* David Blundy & Andrew Lycett, *Qaddafi and the Libyan Revolution* 7 (1986) (alleging that in the 1986 incident American planes crossed the 12-mile limit and flew over Libyan land to provoke a Libyan military response). *See also* George P. Politakis, *From Action Stations to Action: U.S. Naval Deployment, "Non-Belligerency," and "Defensive Reprisals" in the Final Year of the Iran-Iraq War*, 25 Ocean Dev. & Int'l L. 31 (1994) (arguing that U.S. attacks against Iranian oil platforms and patrol boats during the Tanker War, *supra* p. 315, went beyond internationally permissible self-defense to constitute unlawful armed reprisals). If either action was not defensive, what was the source of presidential authority to order it?

B.   STRIKING FIRST (OR STRIKING BACK?): ANTICIPATORY SELF-DEFENSE

Customary international law has long recognized that no requirement exists for states to "absorb the first hit." The doctrine of anticipatory or preemptive self-defense, as developed historically, is applicable only when there is a clear and imminent danger of attack. The means used for preemptive response must be strictly limited to those required for the elimination of the danger, and must be reasonably proportional to that objective. [James P. Terry, *Countering State-Sponsored Terrorism: a Law-Policy Analysis*, 36 Naval L. Rev. 159, 171 (1986).]

This statement echoes a general understanding that Article 51 of the U.N. Charter, which describes an "inherent right of individual and collective self-defense if an armed attack occurs," does not mean that an attack must be completed before a targeted state may employ force to protect itself. A practical, flexible reading of the term "armed attack" suggests instead that a forceful response is also justified once an attack is under way. *See* Mary Ellen O'Connell, *Lawful Self-Defense to Terrorism*, 63 U. Pitt. L. Rev. 889, 894 (2002) ("[W]here one state is in the process of launching an attack on another, self-defense may begin. There must be a plan for the attack, and the plan must be in the course of implementation.); Yoram Dinstein, *War, Aggression and Self-Defence* 187 (4th ed. 2005) ("the right to self-defence can be invoked in response to an armed attack as soon as . . . it is morally certain that the armed attack is under way (however incipient the stage of the attack is)."). The trouble, as always, comes in the details, both in deciding precisely the point in time at which a growing threat warrants a resort to force and in determining what force to use and how. Two case studies, both involving responses to terrorist attacks, illustrate the difficulty of applying the relevant law.

1.   The 1986 U.S. Attack on Libya

On April 5, 1986, just two weeks after the violent confrontation between U.S. and Libyan military forces in the Gulf of Sidra, a terrorist bomb exploded in a Berlin nightclub, killing a U.S. soldier and injuring 64 other Americans. Administration officials immediately linked the Libyan People's Bureau in East Berlin to the bombing. News accounts quickly spread that the United States was planning a retaliatory raid using carrier-based aircraft and F-111s based in Britain. The attack came on April 14, with U.S. planes dropping bombs on Libyan coastal targets, suspected terrorist training facilities, and Qaddafi's residential compound.

Although Congress was in session at the time, President Reagan contacted congressional leaders just three hours before the first bombs fell. That evening he announced to the American people in a televised address:

> ... I warned Colonel Qaddafi we would hold his regime accountable for any new terrorist attacks launched against American citizens. More recently, I made it clear we would respond as soon as we determined conclusively who was responsible for such attacks....
>
> This monstrous brutality is but the latest act in Colonel Qaddafi's reign of terror. The evidence is now conclusive that the terrorist bombing of La Belle discotheque was planned and executed under the direct orders of the Libyan regime....
>
> ... When our citizens are abused or attacked anywhere in the world, on the direct orders of a hostile regime, we will respond, so long as I'm in this Oval Office. Self-defense is not only our right, it is our duty. It is the purpose behind the mission undertaken tonight—a mission fully consistent with Article 51 of the United Nations Charter.
>
> We believe that this pre-emptive action against his terrorist installations will not only diminish Colonel Qaddafi's capacity to export terror—it will provide him with incentives and reasons to alter his criminal behavior. [*Address by President Reagan on Libya,* Apr. 14, 1986, *reprinted in Libya Hearings, supra* p. 344, at 214.]

Responding to criticism from members of Congress that the President had failed to engage in the advance consultation required by §3 of the War Powers Resolution, *supra* p. 308, the State Department Legal Adviser insisted that

> extensive consultations occurred with congressional leaders. They were advised of the President's intention after the operational deployments had commenced, but hours before military action occurred. This satisfied the resolution's requirement that consultation occur "before" the "introduction" of troops into hostilities or a situation of imminent hostilities. Congressional leaders had ample opportunity to convey their views to the President before any irrevocable actions were taken (in fact, no one who was consulted objected to the actions undertaken). [Statement of Abraham D. Sofaer, Legal Adviser to the Department of State, *The War Powers Resolution and Antiterrorist Operations* (Apr. 29, 1986), *reprinted in Libya Hearings, supra* p. 344, at 26-31.]

He went on to declare that Congress had effectively given its approval in advance by voting appropriations for "the creation and maintenance of the forces whose function, at least in part, is to defend Americans from terrorism through the measured use of force." *Id.*

NOTES AND QUESTIONS

1. *State of War?* After years of uncertainty about who was actually behind the terrorist bombing of the West Berlin nightclub, it now seems clear that Qaddafi was responsible. Even before the confrontation between U.S. and Libyan forces in the Gulf of Sidra, however, Qaddafi had advocated a "people's war" against the United States: "We must force America to fight on one hundred fronts all over the earth.... Every Libyan must take up guns, bombs, and with their guns and bombs they will teach a lesson to America." *State-Sponsored Terrorism: Hearing Before the S. Comm. on Armed Services,* 99th Cong. 5-6 (1986) (statement of J. Kirkpatrick, quoting March 2, 1984, Qaddafi speech). Was the United States thereby placed in a state of *de facto* general war, triggering the Commander in Chief's general defensive war powers?

2. *Anticipatory Self-Defense?* In his address to the nation on April 14, 1986, President Reagan declared that "this pre-emptive action against his terrorist installations will not only diminish Colonel Qaddafi's capacity to export terror — it will provide him with incentives and reasons to alter his criminal behavior." He also invoked Article 51. In light of Qaddafi's threats of armed action against Americans wherever they could be found, and the execution of that threat in the nightclub bombing, could the U.S. attack on Libya not be viewed as anticipatory self-defense — repelling a reasonably anticipated future attack? Or was it a punitive act of retaliation — a reprisal? Could it have been both punitive and defensive?

Any use of military force, including a justified act of anticipatory self-defense, must be necessary, discriminatory, and proportional. *See supra* p. 348; Terry, *supra*, 36 Naval L. Rev. at 177-178. Did the U.S. attack satisfy these criteria? It was reported that only military facilities were targeted, although Qaddafi's residential compound was apparently inadvertently bombed. 36 Naval L. Rev. at 181-184. But was an attack on Libyan military facilities proportional to an ongoing threat of terrorist attacks? *See* Jordan Paust, *Responding Lawfully to International Terrorism: the Use of Force Abroad*, 8 Whittier L. Rev. 711, 731 (1986).

According to one scholar, "Unilateralism sits uncomfortably in a multilateral world. At the most general level, unilateral determinations can evoke concern that one state has taken on the role of judge, jury and policeman." Ruth Wedgwood, *The Enforcement of Security Council Resolution 687: The Threat of Force Against Iraq's Weapons of Mass Destruction*, 92 Am. J. Int'l L. 724, 726 (1998). Should a state that invokes its right of anticipatory self-defense be required to explain its factual predicate for doing so? *Compare* O'Connell, *supra*, 63 U. Pitt. L. Rev. at 895 ("The defending state need only show by clear and convincing evidence that future attacks are planned."), *with* Terry, *supra*, 36 Naval L. Rev. at 176 ("Unfortunately, to publicly establish the linkage necessary to justify a response to terrorism can require that we reveal the source of our information."). Can you think of a way to avoid the perception that a purported act of anticipatory self-defense is really just naked aggression?

3. *Reprisal?* In the view of one eminent scholar, "few propositions about international law have enjoyed more support than the proposition that, under the Charter of the United Nations, the use of force by way of reprisals is illegal." Derek Bowett, *Reprisals Involving Recourse to Armed Force*, 66 Am. J. Int'l L. 1, 1 (1972). *See also* Ian Brownlie, *International Law and the Use of Force by States* 281 (1963). Generally speaking, a reprisal is the use of force by one state in response to an earlier violation of international law by another state. Professor Bowett goes on to point out that

> reprisals are punitive in character: they seek to impose reparation for the harm done, or to compel a satisfactory settlement of the dispute created by the initial illegal act, or to compel the delinquent state to abide by the law in the future. But, coming after the event and when the harm has already been inflicted, reprisals cannot be characterized as a means of protection. [Bowett, *supra*, 66 Am. J. Int'l L. at 3.]

Such unilateral acts by aggrieved states also present the very risk of provoking wider violence that Article 2(4) is supposed to prevent.

Bowett's emphatic declaration does not, however, reflect a uniform practice of states; many examples can be cited of states' taking matters into their own hands.

Moreover, as he acknowledges, the difference between illegal reprisal and legal self-defense lies chiefly in the aim or purpose of the responding state. And in a given case, it may be exceptionally difficult to discern the actual motives of the responding state. *Id. See also* Dinstein, *supra*, at 221-230; William V. O'Brien, *Reprisals, Deterrence and Self-defense in Counterterror Operations*, 30 Va. J. Int'l L. 421 (1990).

Was the U.S. attack on Libya a reprisal? If so, was it illegal as a violation of Article 2(4)? *See* Dinstein, *supra*, at 229 ("In substance, these were acts of defensive armed reprisals."). Was the legitimacy of the bombing raid diminished by the fact that it occurred nine days after the nightclub bombing? *See* Paust, *supra*, 8 Whittier L. Rev. at 730. Might the delay be excused by the difficulty in attribution of responsibility for the terrorist attack in Berlin, or by the need for reflection to decide on a proper response? *See* David Turndorf, *The U.S. Raid on Libya: A Forceful Response to Terrorism*, 14 Brook. J. Int'l L. 187, 216 (1988).

Professor Bowett suggests that "reprisals have proved to be productive of greater violence rather than a deterrent to violence." Bowett, *supra*, 66 Am. J. Int'l L. at 16, 32. The 1986 air raid on Libya, for example, was followed in 1988 by the bombing of Pan Am Flight 103 over Lockerbie, Scotland, with more than 200 Americans on board. A Libyan intelligence officer was eventually convicted of planting the bomb. How might the potential for such unintended consequences be reduced?

4. *A Role for Congress?* The State Department Legal Adviser argued that the "need for swiftness and secrecy" justified delaying notice to congressional leaders until just hours before the bombing. However, more than a week passed between the nightclub bombing and the U.S. attack on April 14. Were members of Congress really given time to convey their disapproval — indeed, even to decide whether they approved or not? One purpose of the consultation requirement in WPR §3 is to improve the quality of executive branch decision making by seeking outside advice. Could that purpose have been served by the President's briefings?

Recall that the Framers reserved for Congress the authority to "Grant Letters of Marque and Reprisal." U.S. Const. art. I, §8. Should Congress play a greater role in deciding upon reprisals?

2.   The 1998 Attacks on Sudan and Afghanistan

On August 7, 1998, truck bombs exploded at the U.S. embassies in Kenya and Tanzania, killing nearly 300 people, including 12 Americans. Two weeks later, on August 20, the United States launched 79 Tomahawk cruise missiles against terrorist training camps in Afghanistan and a Sudanese pharmaceutical plant that the United States alleged to be a chemical weapons facility. President Clinton explained that he ordered the attacks because "we have convincing evidence that [Islamic terrorist groups, including that of Osama bin Laden] . . . played the key role in the Embassy bombings . . . and compelling information that they were planning additional terrorist attacks against our citizens. . . ." He had notified certain congressional leaders on August 19 that the attacks were coming and had sent Congress a letter the day after the attacks reporting, "consistent with the War Powers Resolution," that

[t]he United States acted in exercise of our inherent right of self-defense consistent with Article 51 of the United Nations Charter. These strikes were a necessary and

proportionate response to the imminent threat of further terrorist attacks against U.S. personnel and facilities. These strikes were intended to prevent and deter additional attacks by a clearly identified terrorist threat. [Letter to Congressional Leaders Reporting on Military Action Against Terrorist Sites in Afghanistan and Sudan, 34 Weekly Comp. Pres. Doc. 1650 (Aug. 21, 1998).]

The President's National Security Adviser explained that the responses were "appropriate" not only under Article 51, but also "under a 1996 statute in Congress, for us to try to disrupt and destroy those kinds of military terrorist targets." The statute was apparently the Antiterrorism and Effective Death Penalty Act of 1996 (AEDPA). Pub. L. No. 104-132, 110 Stat. 1255 (1996). In the AEDPA, Congress prohibited various kinds of assistance to countries that sponsor or harbor terrorists. In the preamble to these prohibitions, it made the following "finding," among others: "the President should use all necessary means, including covert action and military force, to disrupt, dismantle, and destroy international infrastructure used by international terrorists, including overseas terrorist training facilities and safe havens." *Id.* §324(4). The finding was not codified, but it appears instead in the annotations to a codified prohibition on assistance to countries that aid terrorist states. 22 U.S.C. §2377 (2006).

Reports on the results of the attacks varied. A spokesman for bin Laden reported that 28 people were killed in the attacks on the camps. Sudan reported that ten were injured in the attack on the pharmaceutical plant. The U.S. government subsequently asserted that a soil sample from the plant revealed the presence of a precursor chemical for the production of VX, a nerve agent. Other evidence suggested that the plant was an unguarded pharmaceutical producer, which had often been visited by foreign dignitaries, and that the soil sample contained a chemical structure resembling an agricultural insecticide. A civil suit growing out of the attack in Sudan is set forth *supra* p. 126.

NOTES AND QUESTIONS

1. *Congressional Authorization for the Attacks.* Did either law cited by the Administration supply authority for the attacks? Would they authorize an attack against bin Laden himself? See *infra* pp. 403-410 for a discussion of assassination.

2. *Striking First or Striking Back?* The 1998 attacks (like the 1986 air strike on Libya) might be characterized either as striking first (in anticipatory self-defense) or striking back (in reprisal). Were they clearly one or the other? Recall our discussion in Notes 2 and 3 above. Should the two cases bear different labels because of facts unique to each?

How should the Reagan administration have responded to any uncertainty it might have felt in characterizing its reaction to the East Africa embassy bombings? Should it have sought clearer guidance from Congress before launching the attacks in Sudan and Afghanistan? Should it have asked for approval from the U.N. Security Council? What part do you suppose domestic politics might have played in its decision?

3. *Compliance with the WPR?* Was the 1998 attack on bin Laden's terrorist training camps in Afghanistan subject to the War Powers Resolution? Does the text of the WPR, *supra* p. 307, suggest an answer?

Suppose the U.S. attack had been carried out by CIA operatives or military special forces, rather than by cruise missiles launched from the Indian Ocean. Would that change the applicability of the WPR? Again, look carefully at the text of the statute. According to the State Department Legal Adviser:

> We have substantial doubt that the Resolution should, in general, be construed to apply to the deployment of . . . antiterrorist units, where operations of a traditional military character are not contemplated and where no confrontation is expected between our units and forces of another state. To be sure, the language of the resolution makes no explicit exception for activities of this kind, but such units can reasonably be distinguished from "forces equipped for combat" and their actions against terrorists differ greatly from the "hostilities" contemplated by the Resolution.
>
> Nothing in the legislative history indicated, moreover, that the Congress intended the Resolution to cover deployments of such antiterrorist units. These units are not conventional military forces. A rescue effort or an effort to capture or otherwise deal with terrorists, where the forces of a foreign nation are not involved, is not a typical military mission, and our *antiterrorist forces are not equipped to conduct sustained combat with foreign armed forces*. Rather, these units operate in secrecy to carry out precise and limited tasks designed to liberate U.S. citizens from captivity or to attack terrorist kidnappers and killers. *When used, these units are not expected to confront the military forces of a sovereign state.* In a real sense, therefore, action by an antiterrorist unit constitutes a use of force that is more analogous to law enforcement activity by police in the domestic context than it is to the "hostilities" between states contemplated by the War Powers Resolution. [*Libya Hearings, supra* p. 344, at 20-21 (statement of Abraham D. Sofaer, Legal Adviser to the Department of State) (emphasis in original).]

Do you agree? Can you find these distinctions in the Constitution? In the War Powers Resolution?

It turned out, as we saw in the last chapter, that bin Laden and the Al Qaeda network were intertwined with the Taliban (which ruled most of Afghanistan before the September 11 attacks), sharing resources and engaging in joint planning and defense. Does this fact affect your answer to the applicability of the WPR to the 1998 missile strikes? More generally, should the President's domestic legal authority for attacks in anticipatory self-defense turn on nice distinctions about the sponsorship of the terrorists?

4. *The Evidentiary Standard for Anticipatory Self-Defense.* When a state defends itself against ongoing attack, "the factual predicate for self-defense is clear and observable." Jules Lobel, *The Use of Force to Respond to Terrorist Attacks: The Bombing of Sudan and Afghanistan,* 24 Yale J. Int'l L. 537, 543 (1999). But when a state uses force in anticipatory self-defense against a stateless terrorist group operating abroad or against a state that gives such a group sanctuary, the factual predicate may be quite ambiguous. What sort of proof must be supplied by the state purporting to act in self-defense, and to whom?

Some have argued that, because death may ensue from such attacks, the appropriate evidentiary standard is a criminal one — beyond a reasonable doubt. *Id.* at 551; Sara N. Scheideman, *Standards of Proof in Forcible Responses to Terrorism,* 50 Syracuse L. Rev. 249 (2000). That is, the preemptively attacking state must make public for international scrutiny evidence that shows beyond a reasonable doubt that the terrorist group was responsible for terrorist attacks or that the state attacked knowingly harbored the group. Another scholar suggests instead that responsible decision makers must consider a host of "prudential considerations," including

> whether [the use of force] will make a martyr of the leader of the target organization, or deeply offend good relations with affected countries, or waste military assets that are not limitless . . . [;] whether the use of force will save the lives of innocent victims and prevent future attacks; whether it is the only realistic way to achieve deterrence by signaling that the responsible country will strike back hard; or whether a leader who has come to power by brutal means is likely to scoff at words and remonstrations that are not backed by force. [Ruth Wedgwood, *Responding to Terrorism: The Strikes Against bin Laden*, 24 Yale J. Int'l L. 559, 563 (1999).]

How would these possibly conflicting standards apply to the 1998 attacks on Sudan and Afghanistan? How should they be weighed against the need to abate a serious threat to national security?

Bin Laden and several of his associates were eventually indicted for the embassy bombings. The indictment alleged that these defendants, "together with other members and associates of al Qaeda and others known and unknown to the Grand Jury, unlawfully, willfully, and knowingly combined, conspired, confederated and agreed to kill nationals of the United States," including those who served in the U.S. embassies in Tanzania and Kenya. *See* Sean Murphy, *Contemporary Practice of the United States Relating to International Law*, 93 Am. J. Int'l L. 161, 166 (1999). Although bin Laden was not apprehended, the defendants who were tried were all convicted of various crimes and sentenced to life in prison without the possibility of parole. The convictions came, however, after lengthy trials and almost three years after the embassy bombings. On the other hand, the evidence of a terrorist link to the Sudanese pharmaceutical plant was apparently incorrect.

5. *Authority for the 2001 Military Campaign Against Al Qaeda and the Taliban in Afghanistan.* After the 9/11 terrorist attacks, Congress quickly took up and passed a measure that authorized the President to "use all necessary and appropriate force against those nations, organizations, or persons he determines planned, authorized, committed, or aided the terrorist attacks that occurred on September 11, 2001, or harbored such organizations, or persons, in order to prevent any future acts of international terrorism against the United States." Pub. L. No. 107-40, §2(a), 115 Stat. 224 (2001). The White House reportedly first proposed a joint resolution that would have added this language: "and to deter and pre-empt any future acts of terrorism and aggression against the United States." David Abramowitz, *The President, the Congress and Use of Force: Legal and Political Considerations in Authorizing Use of Force Against International Terrorism*, 43 Harv. Int'l L.J. 71, 73 (2002). Why do you suppose Congress did not include the additional language in the measure it passed? Should it have? Did its failure to do so limit the President's options to pursue terrorists?

C.   PREEMPTIVE WAR

1.   Planning for Another War in Iraq

The Persian Gulf War of 1991, analyzed *supra* pp. 328-334, ended with a formal cease-fire when Iraq accepted the terms of U.N. Security Council Resolution 687, S.C.

Res. 687, U.N. Doc. S/RES/687 (Apr. 3, 1991). Iraq agreed that it would allow a U.N. Special Commission (UNSCOM) to destroy and remove all of its chemical and biological weapons, as well as longer-range missiles, together with any facilities for research, development, and production of such weapons. *Id.* ¶¶8, 9. *See United Nations Special Commission (UNSCOM)* (n.d.), *at* http://www.un.org/Depts/unscom/General/basicfacts.html. A similar commitment was made concerning nuclear weapons, to be carried out by the Director General of the International Atomic Energy Agency with the assistance of UNSCOM. S.C. Res. 687, ¶¶9(b)(iii), 12, 13. Iraq also promised not to develop or acquire any such weapons in the future and to submit to monitoring to assure compliance. *Id.* ¶¶10, 12. In addition, it agreed that it would "not commit or support any act of international terrorism or allow any organization directed towards commission of such acts to operate within its territory." *Id.* ¶32.

CIA map of Iraq.

Courtesy worldatlas.com.

With the withdrawal of coalition forces from Iraq in 1991, the Iraqi government reacted to internal rebellions by attacking Kurdish dissidents in the North and Shias in the southern part of the country. The U.N. Security Council responded by adopting Resolution 688, S.C. Res. 688, U.N. Doc. S/RES/688 (Apr. 5, 1991), which demanded that Iraq end its repression of its own population and allow immediate access by humanitarian organizations. *Id.* ¶¶1-3. *See* Mary Ellen O'Connell, *Continuing Limits on UN Intervention in Civil War*, 67 Ind. L.J. 903, 904-909 (1992). Relying principally on this resolution, the United States, Great Britain, and France established "no-fly" zones in the North and South to prevent Iraqi attacks on civilian populations from the air, and the three countries carried out repeated air strikes on anti-aircraft installations and other targets within these zones over the next ten years. *See* Sean D. Murphy, *Assessing the Legality of Invading Iraq*, 92 Geo. L.J. 173, 215-216 (2004).

In late 1991, Congress approved "sense of the Congress" resolutions supporting the use of "all necessary means" to achieve the goals of Security Council Resolutions 687 and 688. National Defense Authorization Act for Fiscal Years 1992 and 1993, Pub. L. No. 102-190, §§1095, 1096, 105 Stat. 1290, 1488-1489 (1991).

A year and a half later, when the United States uncovered an Iraqi plot to assassinate former President Bush in Kuwait, President Clinton authorized a retaliatory response that targeted Iraq's intelligence headquarters in Baghdad with 23 cruise missiles. *See* Gwen Ifill, *U.S. Fires Missiles at Baghdad, Citing April Plot to Kill Bush*, N.Y. Times, June 27, 1993.

During the next seven years UNSCOM destroyed large quantities of chemical weapons and precursors, chemical and biological weapons facilities, and missile components. But Iraq violated its obligations repeatedly by interfering with UNSCOM inspectors and by failing to disclose information about its weapons programs.

See UNSCOM: Chronology of Main Events, Dec. 1999, *at* http://www.un.org/Depts/unscom/Chronology/chronologyframe.htm.

In August 1998, Congress adopted a measure declaring that Iraq was in "material and unacceptable breach" of various U.N. Security Council resolutions and urging the President to "take appropriate action, in accordance with the Constitution and relevant laws of the United States, to bring Iraq into compliance with its international obligations." Pub. L. No. 105-235, 112 Stat. 1538, 1541 (1998). Two months later, in response to Saddam Hussein's threat to terminate weapons-monitoring activities of the International Atomic Energy Agency (IAEA) and UNSCOM, Congress passed the Iraq Liberation Act of 1998, Pub. L. No. 105-338, 112 Stat. 3178. Included was a "sense of Congress" provision declaring, "It should be the policy of the United States to support efforts to remove the regime headed by Saddam Hussein from power in Iraq and to promote the emergence of a democratic government to replace that regime." *Id.* §3, 112 Stat. 3179. The measure also provided cash and military assistance for "Iraqi democratic opposition organizations." *Id.* §4, 112 Stat. 3179.

Matters finally came to a head in late 1998, when Iraq formally ended all cooperation with UNSCOM on October 31, and UNSCOM withdrew its staff from Iraq on December 16. The following day, U.S. and British forces launched a three-day air and missile attack code-named "Operation Desert Fox" against more than 100 military and industrial targets throughout Iraq. *See* Steven Lee Myers, *U.S. and Britain End Raids on Iraq, Calling Mission a Success*, N.Y. Times, Dec. 20, 1998.

Members of the George W. Bush administration began in early 2001 to plan for "regime change" in Iraq. They provided support for Iraqi opposition groups, and they leaked information about a supposed Iraqi nuclear weapons program that was discredited by Energy Department officials. Defense Secretary Donald Rumsfeld wrote in July, "If Saddam's regime were ousted, we would have a much-improved position in the region and elsewhere." Joyce Battle, *The Iraq War — Part I: The U.S. Prepares for Conflict, 2001*, Sept. 22, 2010, *at* http://www.gwu.edu/~nsarchiv/NSAEBB/NSAEBB326/index.htm.

Immediately after 9/11, President Bush pushed hard to identify a link between Saddam Hussein and the terrorist attacks on the World Trade Center and the Pentagon. Within days he asked for plans for an attack on Iraq. The Administration's planning before and after 9/11 is extensively documented in Battle, *supra*.

In the late summer of 2002, the Bush administration launched a campaign to generate public support for an invasion, describing Iraq as a threat to the United States. Vice President Dick Cheney declared on August 26, for example, "Simply stated, there is no doubt that Saddam Hussein now has weapons of mass destruction." *In Cheney's Words: The Administration Case for Removing Saddam Hussein*, N.Y. Times, Aug. 27, 2002. National Security Adviser Condoleezza Rice warned, "We don't want the smoking gun to be a mushroom cloud." *Top Bush Officials Push Case Against Saddam*, CNN.com, Sept. 8, 2002. And in a speech to the United Nations General Assembly President Bush stated,

> Saddam Hussein's regime is a grave and gathering danger. To suggest otherwise is to hope against the evidence. To assume this regime's good faith is to bet the lives of millions and the peace of the world in a reckless gamble. And this is a risk we must not take. [President's Remarks at the United Nations General Assembly (Sept. 12, 2002).]

In October 2002, the CIA completed its *National Intelligence Estimate, Iraq's Continuing Programs for Weapons of Mass Destruction Programs*, *available at* http://www.gwu.edu/~nsarchiv/NSAEBB/NSAEBB129/index.htm, along with an unclassified version, replete with maps and photos, *available at* http://www.gwu.edu/~nsarchiv/NSAEBB/NSAEBB129/nie_first release.pdf, stating that

> Iraq has continued its weapons of mass destruction (WMD) programs in defiance of UN resolutions and restrictions. Baghdad has chemical and biological weapons as well as missiles with ranges in excess of UN restrictions; if left unchecked, it probably will have a nuclear weapon during this decade.

Much of the information in the NIE turned out to be wrong.

2. Authority for a New War in Iraq

Just three weeks before the mid-term congressional elections in 2002, Congress approved the invasion of Iraq.

Authorization for Use of Military Force Against Iraq Resolution of 2002
Pub. L. No. 107-243, 116 Stat. 1498 (Oct. 16, 2002)

Whereas Iraq both poses a continuing threat to the national security of the United States and international peace and security in the Persian Gulf region and remains in material and unacceptable breach of its international obligations by, among other things, continuing to possess and develop a significant chemical and biological weapons capability, actively seeking a nuclear weapons capability, and supporting and harboring terrorist organizations; . . .

Whereas members of al Qaida, an organization bearing responsibility for attacks on the United States, its citizens, and interests, including the attacks that occurred on September 11, 2001, are known to be in Iraq;

Whereas Iraq continues to aid and harbor other international terrorist organizations, including organizations that threaten the lives and safety of United States citizens; . . .

Whereas Iraq's demonstrated capability and willingness to use weapons of mass destruction, the risk that the current Iraqi regime will either employ those weapons to launch a surprise attack against the United States or its Armed Forces or provide them to international terrorists who would do so, and the extreme magnitude of harm that would result to the United States and its citizens from such an attack, combine to justify action by the United States to defend itself; . . .

Whereas the President has authority under the Constitution to take action in order to deter and prevent acts of international terrorism against the United States, as Congress recognized in the joint resolution on Authorization for Use of Military Force (Public Law 107–40); and

Whereas it is in the national security interests of the United States to restore international peace and security to the Persian Gulf region: Now, therefore, be it

Resolved by the Senate and House of Representatives of the United States of America in Congress assembled . . .

SEC. 3. AUTHORIZATION FOR USE OF UNITED STATES ARMED FORCES

(a) Authorization — The President is authorized to use the Armed Forces of the United States as he determines to be necessary and appropriate in order to —

(1) defend the national security of the United States against the continuing threat posed by Iraq; and

(2) enforce all relevant United Nations Security Council resolutions regarding Iraq.

(b) Presidential Determination — In connection with the exercise of the authority granted in subsection (a) to use force the President shall, prior to such exercise or as soon thereafter as may be feasible, but no later than 48 hours after exercising such authority, make available to the Speaker of the House of Representatives and the President pro tempore of the Senate his determination that —

(1) reliance by the United States on further diplomatic or other peaceful means alone either (A) will not adequately protect the national security of the United States against the continuing threat posed by Iraq or (B) is not likely to lead to enforcement of all relevant United Nations Security Council resolutions regarding Iraq; and

(2) acting pursuant to this joint resolution is consistent with the United States and other countries continuing to take the necessary actions against international terrorist and terrorist organizations, including those nations, organizations, or persons who planned, authorized, committed or aided the terrorist attacks that occurred on September 11, 2001....

The U.S. government worked hard to obtain a resolution from the U.N. Security Council approving an invasion of Iraq — one at least as clear as Resolution 678, which on November 29, 1990, authorized the expulsion of Iraqi forces from Kuwait. See *supra* p. 330. On November 8, 2002, the Security Council adopted the following resolution:

United Nations Security Council, Resolution 1441

U.N. Doc. S/RES/1441 (Nov. 8, 2002)

The Security Council, ...

Recognizing the threat Iraq's non-compliance with Council resolutions and proliferation of weapons of mass destruction and long-range missiles poses to international peace and security,

Recalling that its resolution 678 (1990) authorized Member States to use all necessary means to uphold and implement its resolution 660 (1990) of 2 August 1990 and all relevant resolutions subsequent to resolution 660 (1990) and to restore international peace and security in the area,

Deploring the fact that Iraq has not provided an accurate, full, final, and complete disclosure, as required by resolution 687 (1991), of all aspects of its programmes to develop weapons of mass destruction and ballistic missiles with a range greater than one hundred and fifty kilometres ...

Deploring further that Iraq repeatedly ... failed to cooperate fully and unconditionally with UNSCOM and IAEA weapons inspectors, as required by resolution 687 (1991) ...

Deploring also that the Government of Iraq has failed to comply with its commitments pursuant to resolution 687 (1991) with regard to terrorism ...

Recalling that in its resolution 687 (1991) the Council declared that a ceasefire would be based on acceptance by Iraq of the provisions of that resolution, including the obligations on Iraq contained therein . . .

Acting under Chapter VII of the Charter of the United Nations,

1. *Decides* that Iraq has been and remains in material breach of its obligations under relevant resolutions, including resolution 687 (1991), in particular through Iraq's failure to cooperate with United Nations inspectors and the IAEA . . . ;

2. *Decides*, while acknowledging paragraph 1 above, to afford Iraq, by this resolution, a final opportunity to comply with its disarmament obligations under relevant resolutions of the Council; and accordingly decides to set up an enhanced inspection regime with the aim of bringing to full and verified completion the disarmament process established by resolution 687 (1991) . . . ;

3. *Decides* that . . . the Government of Iraq shall provide to [U.N. weapons inspectors] and the Council, not later than 30 days from the date of this resolution, a currently accurate, full, and complete declaration of all aspects of its programmes to develop chemical, biological, and nuclear weapons, ballistic missiles, and other delivery systems . . .

12. *Decides* to convene immediately upon receipt of a report [of noncompliance by Iraq with this resolution], in order to consider the situation and the need for full compliance with all of the relevant Council resolutions in order to secure international peace and security;

13. *Recalls*, in that context, that the Council has repeatedly warned Iraq that it will face serious consequences as a result of its continued violations of its obligations. . . .

On December 7, 2002, Iraq submitted a 12,000-page declaration stating that it had no weapons of mass destruction. But the declaration was deemed inadequate by the head of a new U.N. inspection team, Hans Blix, and others. Saddam Hussein later told FBI interrogators he worried that full disclosure might make him appear weak and invite attack from Iran. *See* Scott Shane, *Iraqi Dictator Told of Fearing Iran More Than He Did U.S.*, N.Y. Times, July 3, 2009. Meanwhile, U.N. weapons inspectors had resumed their search for weapons of mass destruction (WMD) in Iraq on November 27, 2002. *See* Sean D. Murphy, *Use of Military Force to Disarm Iraq*, 97 Am. J. Int'l L. 419, 419-421 (2003). Aside from some intermediate range missiles, however, which were destroyed, no such weapons were found before inspectors were forced to leave on March 17, 2003, in the face of the impending invasion.

On the home front, President Bush and members of his administration continued to press the case for war. In his State of the Union address, the President declared, "Saddam Hussein has gone to elaborate lengths, spent enormous sums, taken great risks to build and keep weapons of mass destruction." *State of the Union Address*, Jan. 28, 2003. "If Saddam Hussein does not fully disarm," he continued, "for the safety of our people and for the peace of the world, we will lead a coalition to disarm him." *Id.*

On February 5, 2003, Secretary of State Colin Powell delivered an address to the U.N. Security Council, punctuated by photographic exhibits, insisting, "There can be no doubt that Saddam Hussein has biological weapons and the capability to rapidly produce more, many more. . . . If biological weapons seem too terrible to contemplate, chemical weapons are equally chilling." *Powell's Address, Presenting "Deeply Troubling" Evidence on Iraq*, N.Y. Times, Feb. 6, 2003. Powell added, "These are not assertions. What we're giving you are facts and conclusions based on solid evidence." *Id.* Nevertheless, faced with opposition from France, Germany, and Russia, the United States was unable to procure a more forceful resolution than the one set out above.

Members of a U.S.-led coalition asserted that even without waiting for the inspection process to be completed and without further action by the Security Council, Resolution 1441 had cleared the way for coalition forces to "take their own steps" to secure Iraq's disarmament. These developments are traced in UN News Service stories, *at* http://www.un.org/news/dh/infocus/iraq/chronology-02-04.htm.

On March 18, 2003, President Bush sent the "determination" required by §3(b) of the October 16, 2002, joint resolution to congressional leaders. The next day, Operation Iraqi Freedom was launched with missile and aircraft attacks on Iraqi targets. The President addressed the nation in these words: "My fellow citizens, at this hour, American and coalition forces are in the early stages of military operations to disarm Iraq, to free its people, and to defend the world from grave danger." *President Bush Addresses the Nation,* Mar. 19, 2003. "Our nation enters this conflict reluctantly—yet, our purpose is sure," he declared. "The people of the United States and our friends and allies will not live at the mercy of an outlaw regime that threatens the peace with weapons of mass murder. We will meet that threat now . . . so that we do not have to meet it later with armies of firefighters and police and doctors on the streets of our cities." *Id.*

Less than a month later, with 135,000 U.S. troops deployed in Iraq, the last stronghold of forces loyal to Saddam Hussein was captured. On May 1, 2003, President Bush, standing in front of a banner proclaiming "Mission Accomplished," declared that "[m]ajor combat operations in Iraq have ended." *President Bush Announces Major Combat Operations in Iraq Have Ended* (May 1, 2003). For official news releases and press briefings, see the Web site of the Defense Department's Central Command, *at* http://www.centcom.mil/.

NOTES AND QUESTIONS

1. *War Without the 2002 Joint Resolution?* Prior to Congress's approval of the October 16, 2002, joint resolution, some maintained that the President already had the domestic authority needed to send troops into battle. *See* Mike Allen & Juliet Eilperin, *Bush Aides Say Iraq War Needs No Hill Vote; Some See Such Support as Politically Helpful,* Wash. Post, Aug. 26, 2002. What theories might support this argument? For an aggressive assertion of plenary presidential authority to wage war, *see* John C. Yoo's opinion for the Justice Department's Office of Legal Counsel, *The President's Constitutional Authority to Conduct Military Operations Against Terrorists and Nations Supporting Them* (Sept. 25, 2001), *at* http://www.usdoj.gov/olc/warpowers925.htm.

Did the President already have Congress's approval to go to war? Could he have relied, for example, on the 1991 Authorization for Use of Military Force Against Iraq, *supra* p. 332? Would such reliance have been dependent on the continued viability of U.N. Security Council Resolution 678, *supra* p. 330? Did either the Iraq Liberation Act of 1998 or Pub. L. No. 105-235, described *supra* p. 356, provide the needed authority? What about the resolution approved by Congress three days after the September 11, 2001, terrorist attack, *supra* p. 97?

Could the President have taken the country to war solely on the strength of his implied "repel attack" authority, based on the imminence and gravity of an Iraqi threat? If so, what facts would have justified the unilateral use of force? What legal procedures, if any, should have been followed before the President gave the order to attack?

2. *Compliance with Jus ad Bellum.* The United States asserted that no subsequent Security Council resolution was necessary to make war with Iraq legal under international law. On March 27, 2003, for example, the U.S. Permanent Representative to the United Nations, John Negroponte, declared that

> Resolution 687 (1991) imposed a series of obligations on Iraq that were the conditions of the ceasefire. It has long been recognized and understood that a material breach of those obligations removes the basis of the ceasefire and revives the authority to use force under resolution 678 (1990). Resolution 1441 (2002) explicitly found Iraq in continuing material breach. In view of Iraq's additional material breaches, the basis for the existing ceasefire has been removed and the use of force is authorized under resolution 678 (1990). [U.N. SCOR, 58th Sess., 4726th mtg. at 25, U.N. Doc. S/PV.4726 (Resumption 1).]

Does it seem likely that in 1990 (or 1991) the Security Council intended to approve military action more than a decade hence to enforce future resolutions of indeterminate content under circumstances impossible to predict? *See* Murphy, *supra* p. 355, at 178-229 (arguing that Negroponte was wrong); Jules Lobel & Michael Ratner, *Bypassing the Security Council: Ambiguous Authorizations to Use Force, Cease-Fires, and the Iraqi Inspection Regime*, 93 Am. J. Int'l L. 124, 125 (1999) (Security Council "authorizations should clearly articulate and limit the objectives for which force may be employed, and ambiguous authorizations should be narrowly construed; and . . . the authorization to use force should cease with the establishment of a permanent cease-fire unless explicitly extended by the Security Council.").

Coming at the question of legality from a different direction, one scholar claims, "A cease-fire, which merely suspends hostilities without terminating the war, does not extinguish the right of collective self-defense that remains legally intact for the duration of the war." Yoram Dinstein, *War, Aggression, and Self-Defence* 277 (4th ed. 2005). If you believe, like Professor Dinstein, that both the 1991 Gulf War and the 2003 invasion of Iraq were justified by Article 51, *id.* at 298-300, were the actions of the Security Council irrelevant?

If contemporaneous Security Council approval was needed to make the invasion comply with international law, did Resolution 1441 fill that need? According to the State Department Legal Adviser at the time,

> Just last November, in resolution 1441, the Council unanimously decided that Iraq has been and remains in material breach of its obligation. 1441 then gave Iraq a "final opportunity" to comply, but stated specifically that violations of the obligations, including the obligation to cooperate fully, under 1441 would constitute a further material breach. Iraq has clearly committed such violations and, accordingly, the authority to use force to address Iraq's material breaches is clear. [William H. Taft IV, Remarks Before National Association of Attorneys General (Mar. 20, 2003), *at* http://usinfo.org/wf-archive/2003/030321/epf515.htm.]

But did Resolution 1441 leave it to individual states to determine Iraqi compliance with the Security Council's various resolutions, or to decide how to respond to any perceived violations? Professor Stromseth suggests:

> While a full public account of the understandings among Security Council members regarding Resolution 1441 has yet to be disclosed, the text of Resolution 1441 can fairly

be read as an agreement to disagree over whether an additional Security Council resolution authorizing force was needed in the event of Iraqi noncompliance. [Jane E. Stromseth, *Law and Force After Iraq: A Transitional Moment*, 97 Am. J. Int'l L. 628, 630 (2003).]

How do you think the United States should have responded to such indeterminacy? *Compare* John Yoo, *International Law and the War in Iraq*, 97 Am. J. Int'l L. 563, 567 (2003) (arguing that the findings of Resolution 1441 "triggered Resolution 678's authorization to use force in Iraq"), *and* Ruth Wedgwood, *The Fall of Saddam Hussein: Security Council Mandates and Preemptive Self-Defense*, 97 Am. J. Int'l L. 576, 580 (2003) (noting that the resolution did not "constrain any Member State from acting to defend itself against the threat posed by Iraq or to enforce relevant United Nations resolutions"), *with* Sean D. Murphy, *Assessing the Legality of Invading Iraq*, 92 Geo. L.J. 173, 224 (2004) (pointing out that the United States sought, but was unable to obtain, a second resolution).

3. *Preemptive War.* In September 2002, on the eve of Congress's vote to authorize the attack on Iraq, the White House issued its *National Security Strategy of the United States of America, available at* http://georgewbush-whitehouse.archives.gov/nsc/nss/2002/, embracing for the first time as a public policy "the option of *preemptive actions* to counter a sufficient threat to our national security." "We must be prepared," it said, "to stop rogue states and their terrorist clients before they are able to threaten or use weapons of mass destruction against the United States and our allies and friends." *Id.* at 9-10 (emphasis added). It pointed to international law recognizing that "nations need not suffer an attack before they can lawfully take action to defend themselves against forces that present an imminent danger of attack," *id.* at 9, an apparent reference to Article 51 of the U.N. Charter, *supra* p. 213.

There was speculation that a U.S. invasion of Iraq would represent the first application of the newly announced preemption policy. Almost two months before coalition forces invaded Iraq, President Bush declared:

Some have said we must not act until the threat is imminent. Since when have terrorists and tyrants announced their intentions, politely putting us on notice before they strike? If this threat is permitted to fully and suddenly emerge, all actions, all words, and all recriminations would come too late. [State of the Union Address, Jan. 28, 2003.]

The President did not "explicitly characterize his military action as an implementation of the expansive concept of preemptive use of military force against rogue states with WMD." Richard F. Grimmett, *U.S. Use of Preemptive Military Force* 6 (Cong. Res. Serv. RS21311), Apr. 11, 2003. It was nevertheless widely viewed that way.

The practical downside of preemptive resort to self-defense has been described this way:

As one moves from an actual armed attack as the requisite threshold of reactive self-defense, to the palpable and imminent threat of attack, which is the threshold of anticipatory self-defense, and from there to the conjectural and contingent threat of the mere possibility of an attack at some future time, which is the threshold of preemptive self-defense, the self-assigned interpretive latitude of the unilateralist becomes wider, yet the nature and quantum of evidence that can satisfy the burden of proof resting on the unilateralist becomes less and less defined and is often, by the very nature of the exercise, extrapolative and speculative.... [U]ltimately the central issue is assessment by the risk-averse security specialists of one international actor of the intentions of another actor.... [O]ne actor's self-perceived good faith conviction, will often look like serious or hysterical misjudgment to some actors and like either cynical or self-deluded, naked aggression to others. [W. Michael Reisman & Andrea Armstrong, *The Past and Future of the Claim of Preemptive Self-Defense*, 100 Am. J. Int'l L. 525, 526 (2006).]

See also Jules Lobel, *Preventive War and the Lessons of History*, 67 U. Pitt. L. Rev. 307 (2006) (offering evidence that preventive wars are often "unnecessary and disastrous").

What factual predicates must be satisfied before Article 51 can be invoked pre-emptively on the basis of a single state's perception of a growing threat? Were those predicates satisfied in the run-up to Operation Iraqi Freedom? Is your answer affected by the U.N. Security Council's refusal to explicitly authorize the invasion of Iraq? By the fact that no weapons of mass destruction or significant terrorist connections were ever found?

Was the U.S. preemption policy consistent with Article 51 and other require-ments of the U.N. Charter? *Compare* David M. Ackerman, *International Law and the Preemptive Use of Force Against Iraq* 6 (Cong. Res. Serv. RS21314), Apr. 11, 2003 ("[I]t seems doubtful that the use of force against Iraq could be deemed to meet the traditional legal tests justifying preemptive attack."), *and* Thomas M. Franck, *What Happens Now? The United Nations After Iraq*, 97 Am. J. Int'l L. 607 (2003) (invasion not justified under Article 51), *with* John Yoo, *International Law and the War in Iraq*, 97 Am. J. Int'l L. 563 (2003) (invasion warranted as act of anticipatory self-defense).

If a preemptive attack was justified, might the U.S. use of nuclear weapons also have been warranted? *See* William M. Arkin, *The Nuclear Option in Iraq; The U.S. Has Lowered the Bar for Using the Ultimate Weapon*, L.A. Times, Jan. 26, 2003.

3.   Justifications for the War

The preamble to the October 16, 2002, resolution set out above declared that the United States faced a threat posed by a "significant" chemical, biological, and nuclear weapons capability, by the risk that the current Iraqi regime would "employ those weapons to launch a surprise attack against the United States or its Armed Forces," and by "the extreme gravity of harm that would result to the United States and its citizens from such an attack." After coalition forces invaded Iraq, however, no chem-ical, biological, or nuclear weapons were ever found. A detailed account of the fruit-less search for WMD appears in *Comprehensive Report of the Special Advisor to the DCI on Iraq's WMD (Duelfer Report)*, Sept. 30, 2004, *available at* https://www.cia.gov/library/reports/general-reports-1/iraq_wmd_2004/index.html.

Concerning the ongoing threat of terrorism, President Bush asserted before the war that "Saddam Hussein aids and protects terrorists, including members of al Qaeda." State of the Union Address, *supra*. The independent 9/11 Commission, however, found "no evidence [of] a collaborative operational relationship" between Iraq and al Qaeda, National Commission on Terrorist Attacks Upon the United States, *The 9/11 Commission Report* 66 (July 22, 2004), while the Senate Select Com-mittee on Intelligence found no "established formal relationship" between the two.

Report on the U.S. Intelligence Community's Prewar Intelligence Assessments on Iraq, July 9, 2004, at Conclusion 93, *available at* http://intelligence.senate.gov/iraqreport2.pdf. The Senate committee also cited a CIA assessment that there was "no evidence proving Iraqi complicity or assistance in an al-Qaida attack." *Id.* at 347.

How could the factual predicate for the war have been so totally, tragically wrong? According to the Senate Select Committee on Intelligence, most of the information available in the CIA's October 2002 *National Intelligence Estimate* concerning Iraq's WMD program was either "overstated" or "not supported by" the underlying intelligence reporting. *Id.* at 14. *See also* Commission on the Intelligence Capabilities of the United States Regarding Weapons of Mass Destruction (Silberman/Robb Commission), *Report to the President of the United States* (Mar. 31, 2005). An Iraqi exile appropriately code-named Curveball apparently provided fabricated information about Iraqi mobile bioweapons labs. *See* David Barstow, *Doubts on Source for Key Piece of Data Were Suppressed, Report Says,* N.Y. Times, Apr. 1, 2005. And a key piece of intelligence about Iraq's training of Al Qaeda members in the use of WMD reportedly came from Ibn al-Shaykh al-Libi. Libi was captured in Pakistan, then "rendered" to Egypt, where he says he was tortured to compel statements that he later recanted. *See* Douglas Jehl, *Qaeda-Iraq Link U.S. Cited Is Tied to Coercion Claim,* N.Y. Times, Dec. 9, 2005. See Chapter 33. Both of these sources were widely discredited within the intelligence community, yet the information they supplied found its way into speeches given by the President and others.

New concerns were raised in 2005 by the report of a meeting of top British officials, including Prime Minister Tony Blair, some three months before Congress voted to authorize the use of force in Iraq. Memorandum from Matthew Rycroft to David Manning, *Iraq: Prime Minister's Meeting, 23 July,* July 23, 2002, *reprinted in The Secret Downing Street Memo,* Sunday Times (London), May 1, 2005, *available at* http://www.timesonline.co.uk/article/0,,2087-1593607,00.html. The head of the British Secret Intelligence Service (MI6), just returned from talks with Director of Central Intelligence George Tenet and other Washington officials, reported that "[m]ilitary action was now seen as inevitable. Bush wanted to remove Saddam, through military action, justified by the conjunction of terrorism and WMD. But the intelligence and facts were being fixed around the policy." *Id. See also* Mark Danner, *The Secret Way to War,* N.Y. Rev. Books, June 9, 2005, at 70. For an elaborately documented argument that little consideration was given to alternatives to war, see John Prados & Christopher Ames, *The Iraq War—Part II: Was There Even a Decision?* (Oct. 1, 2010), *at* http://www.gwu.edu/~nsarchiv/NSAEBB/NSAEBB328/index.htm. And for evidence that the Bush and Blair administrations collaborated in making the case for war, see John Prados & Christopher Ames, *The Iraq War—Part III: Shaping the Debate* (Oct. 4, 2010), *at* http://www.gwu.edu/~nsarchiv/NSAEBB/NSAEBB330/index.htm.

Some suggested that the 2002 *National Intelligence Estimate* was crafted to support the President's determination to attack Iraq, while others concluded that the Bush administration had simply misled Congress and the American people, as well as the international community, about the existence of WMD. *See, e.g.,* John Prados, *Hood-winked: The Documents That Reveal How Bush Sold Us a War* (2004); Joseph Cirincionne, Jessica T. Matthews & George Perkovich, *WMD in Iraq: Evidence and Implications* (Carnegie Endowment for Int'l Peace 2004); Spencer Ackerman & John B. Judis, *The First Casualty,* New Republic, June 30, 2003, at 14. President Bush reacted angrily to charges from some in Congress that his administration's use of that intelligence was deliberately misleading. *See, e.g.,* Walter Pincus, *Newly Released Data Undercut Prewar*

Claims; Source Tying Bagdhad, Al Qaeda Doubted, Wash. Post, Nov. 6, 2005. "It is irresponsible," he countered, "for Democrats to now claim that we misled them and the American people. Leaders in my administration and members of the United States Congress from both political parties looked at the same intelligence on Iraq, and reached the same conclusion: Saddam Hussein was a threat." *President Delivers Remarks at Elmendorf AFB on War on Terror*, Nov. 14, 2005.

A final Senate Intelligence Committee study, *Report on Whether Public Statements Regarding Iraq by U.S. Government Officials Were Substantiated by Intelligence Information*, S. Rep. No. 110-345 (2008), *available at* http://intelligence.senate.gov/pdfs/110345. pdf, surely failed to satisfy either the President or his critics. "Statements by the President, Vice President, Secretary of State and the National Security Advisor regarding a possible Iraqi nuclear weapons program," it said, "were generally substantiated by intelligence community estimates, but did not convey the substantial disagreements that existed in the intelligence community." *Id.* at 15. It reached similar conclusions about other purported weapons programs and about links to terrorists.

NOTES AND QUESTIONS

1. *War Based on False Premises?* How important do you suppose the perceived WMD threat was in justifying the war? The terrorist connection? Did the fact that both of these factual predicates for the war were false affect the legal authority conferred by the 2002 joint resolution? Did it have any bearing on the President's exercise of his inherent "repel attack" power? Did it matter how the mistakes arose? Compare the debate about the Tonkin Gulf Resolution, *supra* p. 284. Senator Fulbright, one of the 1964 resolution's sponsors, later remarked, "I was hoodwinked." *Quoted in* John Hart Ely, *The American War in Indochina, Part I: The (Troubled) Constitutionality of the War They Told Us About*, 42 Stan. L. Rev. 877, 889 (1990).

2. *What Members of Congress Knew and When They Knew It.* Do you think members of Congress had access to the same intelligence that the President did when they voted to authorize the use of force in Iraq? What bearing, if any, does your answer have on the legitimacy of the October 16 resolution?

3. *Setting the Record Straight.* What could Congress do (if it chose to) to obtain information about the origins of the war that the President did not wish to disclose? What role or roles of Congress would be implicated by such an inquiry? What justifications would you expect the President to offer in withholding the requested data? How would you expect the dispute to be resolved? See *infra* p. 1248.

4. Victory in Iraq?

In October 2003, the U.N. Security Council, acting under Chapter VII of the U.N. Charter, authorized the deployment of a Multi-National Force Iraq (MNF-I) to assist in rebuilding the country's infrastructure, restoring order, and training Iraqi police and military personnel. The resolution also called for steps to establish a new representative government in Iraq. *See* S.C. Res. 1511, U.N. Doc. S/RES/1511 (Oct. 16, 2003). Two years later, U.S. military personnel represented some 160,000 of the nearly 180,000 MNF-I troops in Iraq. But despite the huge commitment, organized attacks by "insurgent" forces on MNF-I and Iraqi military forces, as well as on civilian targets, made the goal of lasting security and stability elusive.

As U.S. combat deaths mounted and questions about justifications for the war multiplied, public support for continued U.S. military involvement in Iraq began to erode. President Bush, however, expressed his determination to continue the fight. In November 2005, the National Security Council published *Victory in Iraq*. It called Iraq "the central front in our war on terror," and it noted a continuing U.S. commitment to make Iraq "peaceful, united, stable, democratic, and secure." *Id.* at 3-4.

The U.N. Security Council mandate for MNF-I expired at the end of 2008. An agreement between the United States and Iraq provided that U.S. military forces would remain in Iraq only through 2011, but that they would withdraw from Iraqi cities by mid-2009. *Agreement Between the United States of America and the Republic of Iraq on the Withdrawal of United States Forces from Iraq and the Organization of Their Activities During Their Temporary Presence in Iraq* 19-20 (Nov. 17, 2008), *available at* http://www.usf-iraq.com/images/CGs_Messages/security_agreement.pdf.

A year and a half later, President Obama announced that the U.S. combat mission in Iraq had ended, turning over to the Iraqi people "lead responsibility for the security of their country." A transitional force of U.S. troops was to remain in Iraq with a different mission: "advising and assisting Iraq's Security Forces, supporting Iraqi troops in targeted counterterrorism missions, and protecting our civilians." *Address to the Nation on the End of Combat Operations in Iraq*, Aug. 31, 2010.

By early 2011, as this was written, nearly 4,500 U.S. military personnel had been killed, and some 32,000 were wounded. Perhaps 100,000 Iraqis, some say more, had also died, the majority at the hands of other Iraqis; many of the Iraqi dead were civilians. Background and current information about U.S. military forces in Iraq are available at U.S. Forces—Iraq, *Operation New Dawn* (updated regularly), *at* http://www.usf-iraq.com/.

NOTES AND QUESTIONS

1. *Continuing Authority for the War?* If the reasons for military action changed over time, was the President's mandate under the October 16, 2002, resolution still good? Was the continued deployment merely a tactical decision properly entrusted to the President? See *supra* p. 80. Was the earlier mandate extended by Congress's recurring votes of appropriations for the war? See *supra* p. 97. Or should the President have sought new authority from Congress?

2. *War Without End?* In August 2005, President Bush declared:

> An immediate withdrawal of our troops in Iraq, or the broader Middle East, as some have called for, would only embolden the terrorists and create a staging ground to launch more attacks against America and free nations. So long as I'm the President, we will stay, we will fight, and we will win the war on terror. [*President Addresses Military Families, Discusses War on Terror*, Aug. 24, 2005.]

Congress nevertheless passed an appropriations measure in 2007 calling for the withdrawal of U.S. forces from Iraq by the end of March 2008, leaving behind only enough troops to protect U.S. citizens and diplomatic facilities, train and equip Iraqi security forces, and engage in "targeted special actions limited in duration and scope to killing or capturing members of al-Qaeda and other terrorist organizations with global reach." H.R. 1591, 110th Cong. §1904(c), (e) (2007). But the bill was vetoed by President Bush, who complained that it infringed on his powers as Commander in Chief. 43 Weekly Comp. Pres. Doc. 560 (May 1, 2007). May Congress cut off funding for the war, either in whole or in part, without violating separation-of-powers principles? *See* Jennifer K. Elsea, Michael John Garcia & Thomas J. Nicola, *Congressional Authority to Limit U.S. Military Operations in Iraq* (Cong. Res. Serv. RL33837), Feb. 27, 2008 (indicating that, while "not beyond debate," it may). Does this successful exercise of the veto power cast any doubt on the constitutional theory that the President can unilaterally use force, subject to the check of an appropriations cut-off? *See* John C. Yoo, *The Continuation of Politics by Other Means: The Original Understanding of War Powers*, 84 Cal. L. Rev. 167, 170 (1996) ("The Framers established a system which was designed to encourage presidential initiative in war, but which granted Congress an ultimate check on executive actions. Congress could express its opposition to executive war decisions only by exercising its powers over funding and impeachment.").

Would a simple "declaration of peace" — a joint resolution approved by a veto-proof majority in both Houses — be constitutional? *See id.* at 18-19. During confirmation hearings for Chief Justice John Roberts, the following colloquy took place between the nominee and Vermont Senator Patrick Leahy:

Senator Leahy: We [Congress] have the power to declare war. Do we have the power to terminate a war?

Judge Roberts: Senator, that's a question that I don't think can be answered in the abstract. You need to know the particular circumstances and exactly what the facts are and what the legislation would be like....

U.S. Senate Judiciary Committee Holds a Hearing on the Nomination of John Roberts to Be Chief Justice of the Supreme Court, Wash. Post Online, Sept. 13, 2005. Do you agree with the Chief Justice?

One scholar has suggested a solution to the conundrum of an armed conflict that Congress authorizes but may not stop: attach a fixed time limit to the original authorization, so that the President must return to Congress at intervals for approval to continue fighting. Stephen I. Vladeck, *Ludecke's Lengthening Shadow: The Disturbing Prospect of War Without End*, 2 J. Nat'l Security L. & Pol'y 53 (2006). Can you think of a constitutional objection to his scheme? A practical objection? Recall the critique of the "sixty-day clock" in the War Powers Resolution, *supra* p. 318.

D. RESCUE

1. Domestic Authority for Rescue: Basic Doctrine

In re Neagle

United States Supreme Court, 1890
135 U.S. 1

[The opinion is set forth *supra* p. 83.]

Durand v. Hollins

United States Circuit Court, Southern District of New York, 1860
8 F. Cas. 111 (No. 4186)

[In 1852, a group of adventurers seeking to corner the business of conducting travelers over the Central American isthmus established the "state" of Greytown in what is now Nicaragua. The United States backed a rival transit company partly owned by Nicaraguans. Wormuth & Firmage, *supra* p. 73, at 38. In the ensuing friction between the companies, a Greytown mob threatened the American minister to Central America and hit him with a bottle. The U.S. Secretary of the Navy then sent Captain Hollins of the U.S.S. *Cyane* to Greytown to obtain redress for damages done to property of the U.S.-backed company and an apology for the attack on the minister. When Greytown authorities did not comply with his demands, Hollins shelled the town and then burned what remained. An American owner of property destroyed by Hollins's actions subsequently sued him, and Hollins asserted in his defense that he was merely following orders.]

NELSON, Circuit Justice. . . . The executive power, under the constitution, is vested in the president of the United States (article 2, §1). He is commander-in-chief of the army and navy, (*Id.* §2), and has imposed upon him the duty to "take care that the laws be faithfully executed" (*Id.* §3). . . . There was also established another executive department, denominated the "Department of the Navy," the chief officer of which is called the "Secretary of the Navy," "whose duty it shall be to execute such orders as he shall receive from the president of the United States. . . ." Act Cong. April 30, 1798, §1 (1 Stat. 553).

As the executive head of the nation, the president is made the only legitimate organ of the general government, to open and carry on correspondence or negotiations with foreign nations, in matters concerning the interests of the country or of its citizens. It is to him, also, the citizens abroad must look for protection of person and of property, and for the faithful execution of the laws existing and intended for their protection. For this purpose, the whole executive power of the country is placed in his hands, under the constitution, and the laws passed in pursuance thereof; and different departments of government have been organized, through which this power may be most conveniently executed, whether by negotiation or by force. . . .

Now, as it respects the interposition of the executive abroad, for the protection of the lives or property of the citizen, the duty must, of necessity, rest in the discretion of the president. Acts of lawless violence, or of threatened violence to the citizen or his property, cannot be anticipated and provided for; and the protection, to be effectual or of any avail, may, not unfrequently, require the most prompt and decided action. Under our system of government, the citizen abroad is as much entitled to protection as the citizen at home. The great object and duty of government is the protection of the lives, liberty, and property of the people composing it, whether abroad or at home; and any government failing in the accomplishment of the object, or the performance of the duty, is not worth preserving.

I have said, that the interposition of the president abroad, for the protection of the citizen, must necessarily rest in his discretion; and it is quite clear that, in all cases where a public act or order rests in executive discretion neither he nor his authorized agent is personally civilly responsible for the consequences. As was observed by Chief

Justice Marshall, in *Marbury v. Madison*, 1 Cranch [5 U.S.] 165: "By the constitution of the United States, the president is invested with certain important political powers, in the exercise of which he is to use his own discretion, and is accountable only to his country in his political character, and to his own conscience. To aid him in the performance of these duties, he is authorized to appoint certain officers, who act by his authority, and in conformity with his orders. In such cases, their acts are his acts, and, whatever opinion may be entertained of the manner in which executive discretion may be used, still there exists, and can exist, no power to control that discretion. The subjects are political. They respect the nation, not individual rights, and, being intrusted to the executive, the decision of the executive is conclusive." This is a sound principle, and governs the present case. The question whether it was the duty of the president to interpose for the protection of the citizens at Greytown against an irresponsible and marauding community that had established itself there, was a public political question, in which the government, as well as the citizens whose interests were involved, was concerned, and which belonged to the executive to determine; and his decision is final and conclusive, and justified the defendant in the execution of his orders given through the secretary of the navy.

Judgment for defendant.

Hostage Act

22 U.S.C. §1732 (2006)

Whenever it is made known to the President that any citizen of the United States has been unjustly deprived of his liberty by or under the authority of any foreign government, it shall be the duty of the President forthwith to demand of that government the reasons of such imprisonment; and if it appears to be wrongful and in violation of the rights of American citizenship, the President shall forthwith demand the release of such citizen, and if the release so demanded is unreasonably delayed or refused, the President shall use such means, not amounting to acts of war, as he may think necessary and proper to obtain or effectuate the release; and all the facts and proceedings relative thereto shall as soon as practicable be communicated by the President to Congress.

---

2. The Iran Hostage Rescue Mission[4]

In November 1979, Iranian militants stormed the American Embassy in Teheran and took the Americans inside it hostage. By March 1980, diplomatic initiatives to gain their release had failed, and the Carter administration considered its military options. The Chairman of the Joint Chiefs of Staff outlined the details of a proposed rescue mission, contemplating a series of discrete and reversible but incredibly complex and difficult steps.

First, troops and materials would be pre-positioned in the Middle East and the Indian Ocean under cover of routinely scheduled activities. Second, eight helicopters and eight C-130 aircraft were to fly below Iranian radar coverage across 500 miles of desert at night to a rendezvous inside Iran, "Desert One," for refueling and reloading

---

4. Except where otherwise noted, this background is based upon Gary Sick, *All Fall Down* (1985); *American Hostages in Iran: The Conduct of a Crisis* (Warren Christopher ed., 1985); and Cyrus R. Vance, *Hard Choices* (1983).

of the helicopters. Third, the helicopters would proceed to a second mountain rendezvous, where they would remain concealed throughout the following day. Fourth, the rescue team would proceed to Teheran by local vehicles on the second night to undertake the actual rescue. Fifth, the helicopters would reappear just long enough to pick up the team and the hostages, and then fly to an abandoned airfield near Teheran to rendezvous again with the transport aircraft. Finally, helicopters abandoned, the group would fly to safety under an umbrella of heavy U.S. air power.

Secretary of State Cyrus Vance opposed any military initiative at that time. He reasoned that

> the hostages would be freed only when Khomeini was certain that all the institutions of the Islamic republic were in place.... Our only realistic course was to keep up the pressure on Iran while we waited for Khomeini to determine that the revolution had accomplished its purpose, and that the hostages were of no further value.

President Carter did not immediately approve the mission, preferring instead to exhaust all peaceful means for obtaining release of the hostages. But United States allies refused to adopt meaningful sanctions against Iran, and by April hopes of a negotiated release had dimmed even further. On April 9, National Security Adviser Brzezinski advised the President that, in his view, "a carefully planned and boldly executed rescue operation represents the only realistic prospect that the hostages — any of them — will be freed in the foreseeable future.... It is time for us to act now."

On April 11, during a National Security Council (NSC) meeting from which Secretary of State Vance was absent, President Carter decided that a rescue mission should be launched on April 24. On his return, Vance objected vociferously and was permitted to present his case at another NSC meeting. He noted that intelligence reports indicated that the hostages were in no physical danger and in satisfactory health, and that any rescue was almost certain to lead to deaths among them, as well as among the rescuers and the Iranians. He also noted that the Iranians could simply react by taking American journalists hostage and turning toward the Soviet Union. He reaffirmed his belief that time would lead to the release of the hostages. No one else supported his position, however, and the President reaffirmed his decision to go ahead. On April 17, Vance advised President Carter that he would have to resign if the mission went forward. He subsequently did resign after the mission was made public.

On the night of April 23, President Carter met with Senate Majority Leader Robert Byrd to develop a short list for congressional notification concerning "possible military action." He did not inform Byrd that the rescue mission would be launched just hours later, at 10:30 A.M. on April 24, 1980, Washington time.

The mission ran into difficulty when several of the helicopters failed. Advised that there were too few helicopters to carry out the remainder of the mission, President Carter ordered it aborted. In the ensuing rush to evacuate Desert One, a helicopter and a C-130 transport collided, killing eight persons, and the dead were abandoned with their equipment and sundry documents bearing on the mission.

Only after the mission was aborted were other congressional leaders informed by telephone late on April 24th and during the following morning. Within 48 hours of the time that U.S. units first entered Iranian air space, but well after the mission was aborted, President Carter sent the following message to Congress.

Letter of President Jimmy Carter to the Speaker of the House and President Pro Tempore of the Senate (April 26, 1980)

reprinted in 4 Pub. Papers 777

Because of my desire that Congress be informed on this matter and consistent with the reporting provisions of the War Powers Resolution of 1973 (Public Law 93-148), I submit this report.

On April 24, 1980, elements of the United States Armed Forces under my direction commenced the positioning stage of a rescue operation which was designed, if the subsequent stages had been executed, to effect the rescue of the American hostages who have been held captive in Iran since November 4, 1979, in clear violation of international law and the norms of civilized conduct among nations. The subsequent phases of the operation were not executed. Instead, for the reasons described below, all these elements were withdrawn from Iran and no hostilities occurred.

The sole objective of the operation that actually occurred was to position the rescue team for the subsequent effort to withdraw the American hostages. The rescue team was under my overall command and control and required my approval before executing the subsequent phases of the operation designed to effect the rescue itself. . . .

The remote desert area was selected to conceal this phase of the mission from discovery. At no time during the temporary presence of United States Armed Forces in Iran did they encounter Iranian forces of any type. . . .

At one point during the period in which United States Armed Forces elements were on the ground at the desert landing site a bus containing forty-four Iranian civilians happened to pass along a nearby road. The bus was stopped and then disabled. Its occupants were detained by United States Armed Forces elements until their departure, and then released unharmed. One truck closely followed by a second vehicle also passed by while United States Armed Forces elements were on the ground. These elements stopped the truck by a shot into its headlights. The driver ran to the second vehicle which then escaped across the desert. Neither of these incidents affected the subsequent decision to terminate the mission.

Our rescue team knew, and I knew, that the operation was certain to be dangerous. We were all convinced that if and when the rescue phase of the operation had been commenced, it had an excellent chance of success. . . .

The mission on which they were embarked was a humanitarian mission. It was not directed against Iran. It was not directed against the people of Iran. It caused no Iranian casualties.

This operation was ordered and conducted pursuant to the President's powers under the Constitution as Chief Executive and as Commander-in-Chief of the United States Armed Forces, expressly recognized in Section 8(d)(1) of the War Powers Resolution. In carrying out this operation, the United States was acting wholly within its rights, in accordance with Article 51 of the United Nations Charter, to protect and rescue its citizens where the government of the territory in which they are located is unable or unwilling to protect them.

Sincerely,
Jimmy Carter

Legal Opinion by Lloyd Cutler, President's Counsel, on War Powers Consultation Relative to the Iran Rescue Mission (May 9, 1980)

reprinted in War Powers Resolution: Relevant Documents, Correspondence, Reports: Hearing Before the Subcomm. on Int'l Security and Scientific Aff. of the H. Comm. on Foreign Aff., 98th Cong. 50 (1983)

1. In my opinion, the President's decision to use the armed forces in an attempt to rescue the American hostages in Iran, without consulting Congress before taking this action, was a lawful exercise of his constitutional powers as President and Commander-in-Chief, and did not violate the War Powers Resolution of 1973.

2. The President's constitutional power to use the armed forces to rescue Americans illegally detained abroad is clearly established. *In re Neagle*, 135 U.S. 1, *Durand v. Hollins*, 8 Fed. Cases 111. This power was expressly recognized in the Senate version of the War Powers Resolution, and is not negated by the final version of the Resolution, especially where, as here, those to be rescued include United States Marines.

3. His inherent constitutional power to conduct this kind of rescue operation, which depends on total surprise, includes the power to act before consulting Congress, if the President concludes, as he did in this case, that to do so would unreasonably endanger the success of the operation and the safety of those to be rescued.

4. Section 3 of the War Powers Resolution does require consulting with Congress "in every possible instance" before introducing United States Armed Forces into "hostilities or into situations where imminent involvement in hostilities is clearly indicated by the circumstances." In this case, the first stage of the operation — introducing the rescue team into Iran during the night of April 24 — did not involve any hostilities. The rescue effort itself was not to be initiated before the following night, and could have been aborted before any involvement in hostilities was "clearly indicated," and this is in fact what occurred.

5. In any event, Section 8(d)(1) of the War Powers Resolution provides that nothing in it "is intended to alter the constitutional authority of the Congress or of the President." If Section 3 were read to require prior consultation in these precise circumstances — where the President has inherent constitutional authority to conduct a rescue operation dependent on surprise and reasonable ground to believe that prior consultation would unreasonably endanger the success of the operation and the safety of those to be rescued — this would raise grave issues as to the constitutionality of Section 3. Since statutes and joint resolutions are to be read where possible in a manner that does not raise such grave constitutional issues, Section 3 and Section 8(d)(1), read together, should not be construed to require prior consultation under the precise circumstances of this case.

NOTES AND QUESTIONS

1. *Protecting Government Functions. Neagle* plainly holds that, under the Supremacy Clause, a United States employee "cannot be guilty" of a state law crime for performing a task within the general scope of his employment. 135 U.S. at 75. *See* Peter M. Shane & Harold H. Bruff, *The Law of Presidential Power* 460 (1988). Does it mean more than that? *See* Henry P. Monaghan, *The Protective Powers of the President*, 93 Colum. L. Rev. 1, 66 (1993) (arguing that *Neagle* suggests that the President may use force

without express statutory authority not only to defend the United States against sudden attack, but also to protect the personnel and property interests of the United States). In its opinion the Court noted with approval an intervention — without congressional authorization — by an American naval captain on behalf of a Hungarian applicant for U.S. citizenship who had been illegally detained abroad. 135 U.S. at 64 (the case of Martin Koszta). Can we assume from this reference and the facts of *Neagle* that the President is inherently empowered to do only what is immediately necessary to repel attacks on Americans or those waiting to become Americans? If the holding is not limited at least in this respect, then what limit is there on inherent presidential power to repel attacks and protect Americans? *See* Monaghan, *supra*, 93 Colum. L. Rev. at 70 (distinguishing between protection of U.S. government personnel and private Americans).

2. *Durand's Holding. Durand* has been cited for the proposition that rescue and reprisal are powers vested exclusively in the President. Did the court address, or need to address, the exclusivity of the President's rescue power? What is the actual holding? Some observers have found *Durand*'s reliance on the rescue power ironic. The property protected by the American intervention was that of a Nicaraguan corporation, and the U.S. citizen Durand's property was destroyed by the shelling.

Mr. Cutler's opinion cites *Neagle* and *Durand* as judicial authority for the President's constitutional authority to order rescue missions. Are they really apposite? Would you agree with the Iran-Contra Committee minority, who claimed, "the *Durand* case stands for the proposition that the President has the discretion to take whatever steps may be necessary, short of a full-scale war, to protect American citizens"? *Report of the Congressional Committees Investigating the Iran-Contra Affair, Minority Report*, H.R. Rep. No. 100-433, S. Rep. No. 100-216, at 474 (1987).

3. *Effect of the Hostage Act.* Does either case address the scope of the President's authority when Congress *has* enacted legislation on this point? Is the Hostage Act such legislation?

In the wake of the agreement by which the hostages were released, the Supreme Court held the Hostage Act inapplicable because the "hostages were not seized out of any refusal to recognize their American citizenship — they were seized precisely *because* of their American citizenship." *Dames & Moore v. Regan*, 453 U.S. 654, 677 (1981), *supra* p. 60 (emphasis in original). Analysis of the legislative history of the Act suggests that the Court was wrong; the Act was intended to include *any* "unfounded" or pretextual arrest of American citizens abroad. *See* Abner J. Mikva & Gerald L. Neuman, *The Hostage Crisis and the "Hostage Act,"* 49 U. Chi. L. Rev. 292, 330-332 (1982). Congress apparently agreed; it amended the Hostage Act in 1989 to insert "and otherwise not prohibited by law" after "acts of war" in response to administration initiatives to free American hostages during the Iran-Contra Affair, reflecting Congress's assumption that the Act applied to such hostages. *See* Anti-Terrorism and Arms Export Control Act Amendments of 1989, Pub. L. No. 101-222, 103 Stat. 1892 (codified at 22 U.S.C. §1732 (2006)).

The bill that became the Hostage Act originally would have authorized a President to take hostages in reprisal, but this provision was dropped as an improper delegation of the war-making power. Mikva & Neuman, *supra*, at 319-327. Even the restricted delegation of authority in the final bill was criticized by legislators who were concerned that it "would permit the President to perform further preliminary acts of hostility whose inevitable tendency would be to precipitate war, even if those acts did not technically come into the ban of the proviso." *Id.* at 335.

Given this history and the Act's careful circumscription of delegated authority to use "means not amounting to acts of war," what exactly is the lawful scope of a President's authority to rescue hostages? Is the Act constitutional? What is the relationship, if any, between the President's authority under the Hostage Act and international law? If, for example, customary international law allows armed intervention to rescue citizens held hostage abroad and does not treat such intervention as an act of war, what is the President's authority under the Act?

4. *Rescue and the War Powers Resolution.* The original Senate version of the War Powers Resolution authorized the President to make a carefully limited use of military force to "protect while evacuating" American citizens and nationals. S. 440, 93d Cong., §3(3) (1973). See *supra* p. 312. Does the omission of this provision from the final War Powers Resolution suggest that Congress intended to deny the President rescue authority? Could Congress constitutionally do so?

Was President Carter required to consult with Congress or to report the rescue mission under §4(a)(1) of the War Powers Resolution, *supra* p. 308? Mr. Cutler cited concerns about possible leaks as one reason for not informing Congress of the mission in advance. *See generally Minority Report, supra* p. 373, at 575. Is this a sufficient reason for failing to report to Congress under the WPR? For failing to obtain prior congressional authorization for a military initiative?

What good might it have done to consult congressional leaders? What advice could members of Congress have contributed to the hostage rescue decision that Secretary of State Vance had not already argued without success? President Carter wrote of his failure to inform Senator Byrd during their talk on April 23 that "[a]fter he left the White House, I wondered if it would have been better to involve him more directly in our exact plans for the mission. His advice would have been valuable to me then — and also twenty-four hours later." Jimmy Carter, *Keeping Faith: Memoirs of a President* 513-514 (1982). Political scientists have since argued that classic "groupthink" — in which "pressures internal to the group result in an overriding concern with maintaining a sense of an amiable in-group, at the cost of individual members ignoring or suppressing their doubts over policy options" — contributed significantly to the rescue mission fiasco. *See* Steve Smith, *Groupthink and the Hostage Rescue Mission,* 15 Brit. J. Pol. Sci. 117 (1984); Steve Smith, *Policy Preferences and Bureaucratic Position: The Case of the American Hostage Rescue Mission,* 61 Intl'l Aff. 9 (1984-1985).

5. *Differentiating Rescue and Repelling Attack.* The only authority cited by the Senate Foreign Relations Committee for the "protection" provision in its version of the War Powers Resolution was Madison's notation about the power to repel sudden attacks. S. Rep. No. 93-220, at 2-3 (1975). If the rescue authority is predicated on the implied power to repel sudden attacks, consider the following argument:

With respect to sudden attacks, there is a textual constitutional presumption that Congress will not be able [as an institution to address the unanticipated emergency]. Such a general presumption is not applicable to rescue operations. These operations involve emerging crises or they may involve relatively static and predictable situations. Once it is conceded in a particular context that there is or has been a substantial opportunity to contemplate action, the authority to decide whether to proceed devolves back to

Congress. Congress may then delegate authority to the President, but the President is without authority, under such circumstances, to act in the absence of some action by Congress. [Allan Ides, *Congress, Constitutional Responsibility and the War Power*, 17 Loy. L.A. L. Rev. 599, 636-637 (1984).]

What constitutional *text* creates this presumption? Do you agree with Professor Ides's conclusion? How would the Iran hostage rescue mission fare under his proposed analysis?

Is the capture of American citizens by itself a sufficient legal predicate for exercise of any implied presidential rescue power? If *Neagle* is legal authority for rescue missions, does it presuppose at least the threat of *imminent* harm to Americans? *Cf.* Jeffrey A. McCredie, *The April 14, 1986 Bombing of Libya: Act of Self-Defense or Reprisal?*, 19 Case W. Res. J. Int'l L. 215, 235 (1987) (noting that the right of rescue at international law is predicated upon "an imminent threat of injury to nationals").

6. *Rights of Nations to Rescue Their Nationals.* Iran complained that the hostage rescue effort was an act of naked aggression, in violation of Article 2(4) of the U.N. Charter. Nevertheless, it is generally agreed that each state is entitled to protect its nationals from harm abroad. If nationals of State A are unjustly held against their will or are in peril in State B, and State B is unable or unwilling to assist them, State A may intervene without waiting for an invitation from State B, as an exercise of its inherent right of self-defense under Article 51, as President Carter noted. Yoram Dinstein, *War, Aggression and Self-Defense* 231-234 (4th ed. 2005). The requirements of necessity, immediacy, and proportionality apply in this context as to other acts of self-defense. See *supra* p. 348. Did the U.S. rescue effort meet these criteria?

Targeting Terrorists 14

"Targeted killing" was not a term of art in human rights law or international humanitarian law prior to the 9/11 attacks. It has been used with increasing frequency since then to refer to U.S. attacks by unmanned aerial vehicles (UAVs) or "drones" on alleged Al Qaeda or Taliban targets. The U.N. Special Rapporteur for Human Rights asserts:

> The common element in all these contexts is that lethal force is intentionally and deliberately used, with a degree of pre-meditation, against an individual or individuals specifically identified in advance by the perpetrator. In a targeted killing, the specific goal of the operation is to use lethal force. This distinguishes targeted killings from unintentional, accidental, or reckless killings, or killings made without conscious choice. It also distinguishes them from law enforcement operations, e.g., against a suspected suicide bomber. Under such circumstances, it may be legal for law enforcement personnel to shoot to kill based on the imminence of the threat, but the goal of the operation, from its inception, should not be to kill. [Special Rapporteur on Extrajudicial, Summary or Arbitrary Executions, *Addendum: Study on Targeted Killings* at 5, U.N. Doc. A/HRC/14/24/Add.6 (May 28, 2010) (by Philip Alston).]

In Part A of this chapter, we begin with several brief accounts of U.S. targeted killing operations. The legality of each operation depends in part on the legal paradigm under which it is analyzed and in part on how it is conducted. In Part B, we apply the paradigm of international human rights law. In Part C, we shift to the paradigm of international humanitarian law. Finally, in Part D, we consider the effects of domestic law and an executive ban on "assassination."

A. TARGETED KILLING BY THE UNITED STATES AFTER 9/11[1]

In October 2001, on the first night of the campaign against Al Qaeda and the Taliban authorized by Congress after the September 11 attacks, a 27-foot-long,

---

1. This report is drawn from William C. Banks, *The Predator* (Maxwell Sch. of Citizenship & Pub. Affairs, Syracuse Univ., CS 0603-32, 2003); Kristen Eichensehr, *On the Offensive: Assassination Policy Under International Law*, 25 Harv. Int'l Rev. 1 (Fall 2003), *available at* http://hir.harvard.edu/articles/1149/3/; Seymour Hersh, *Manhunt*, New Yorker, Dec. 23, 2002, at 66, 74; Eblen Kaplan, *Targeted Killings* (Council on Foreign Rel. Mar. 2, 2006); Scott Shane, Mark Mazzetti & Robert F. Worth, *Secret Assault on Terrorism*

unmanned aerial vehicle (or drone) with a 49-foot wingspan called the Predator deployed over southern Afghanistan apparently identified Taliban leader Mullah Mohammed Omar in a convoy of cars fleeing Kabul. Following its agreement with military commanders, the CIA operators sought approval from the United States Central Command in Tampa to launch a Hellfire missile at Omar, who by then had sought cover in a building with an estimated 100 guards. General Tommy Franks reportedly declined to give approval based upon on-the-spot advice of his military lawyer. Other reports suggest that, in light of the number of possible casualties, he sought approval from the President, who personally approved the strike. But the resulting delay apparently allowed Omar to escape.

In February 2002, another Predator filmed a very tall man being greeted effusively by villagers. Osama bin Laden was said to be about six feet five inches tall. The order was quickly given to fire, but by that time the group had disbanded, and the Predator captured another image of a tall man and two others emerging from a wooded area. The Hellfire was launched, killing all three. Journalists later reported that they were locals who had been scavenging for wood. Bin Laden was not among them.

On November 3, 2002, video feeds from television cameras on a Predator, flying slowly 10,000-15,000 feet above Marib Province in Yemen, showed an RV speeding through the desert. A joint Yemeni and American intelligence team had for days been tracing cell phone calls by an Al Qaeda leader named Qaed Salim Sinan al-Harethi, and it determined that he was in the car. Al-Harethi was a prime suspect in the 2000 suicide bombing of the USS *Cole*, which had killed 17 U.S. sailors. Using a joystick to control the Predator remotely, a U.S. operator fired a Hellfire missile from the plane, striking the RV dead center and killing all five of its passengers. Yemeni security officials later took the bodies to a hospital in Yemen's capital, where U.S. officials obtained DNA samples. They confirmed that the Predator attack had "taken out" al-Harethi. They also identified one of the other victims as Kamal Derwish, a U.S. citizen who grew up near Buffalo and who reportedly recruited American Muslims for training in Al Qaeda camps.

MQ-1 Predator (armed with an AGM-114 Hellfire missile).

U.S. Air Force photo.

The United States employed drones in the Iraq war, but the pace of their use quickened and the geographic expanse of their deployment widened after 2006 intelligence findings by President Bush and revisions of them by President Obama in 2009 and 2010 authorized targeting Osama bin Laden and other top terrorist targets. Rather than "the hammer," according to White House counterterrorism adviser John O. Brennan, the United States would use "the scalpel." Indeed, in the first year of the Obama administration, more drone strikes were carried out than in the entire Bush presidency.

Widens on Two Continents, N.Y. Times, Aug. 14, 2010; Mark Mazzetti, Helene Cooper & Peter Baker, *Behind the Hunt for Bin Laden*, N.Y. Times, May 2, 2011; Michael D. Shear, *White House Corrects Bin Laden Narrative*, N.Y. Times, May 3, 2011.

Taliban and Al Qaeda insurgents in Afghanistan took advantage of the porous border and difficult terrain to maintain encampments in Pakistan as staging areas for cross-border raids on U.S. and NATO forces in Afghanistan. Drone strikes were, to some, an effective counter to these tactics. In an August 2009 strike, Hellfire missiles fired from a drone killed Baitullah Mehsud, head of the Pakistan Taliban. Mehsud had been a thorn in the side of the government of Pakistan for years, while he ordered abductions and killings on the streets of Pakistan, sabotaged Pakistani government officials and installations, and likely masterminded the assassination of former Prime Minister Benazir Bhutto. When he was killed, Mehsud was in Pakistan, either resting or receiving medical care on the roof of his father-in-law's house. To U.S. officials, killing Mehsud was an important tactical victory in the war against Taliban and Al Qaeda terrorists and insurgents. Yet Mehsud had commanded his extremists inside Pakistan, not Afghanistan, and the missile strike killed family members, bodyguards, and bystanders as well as Mehsud.

On May 25, 2010, another drone strike in remote Marib Province in Yemen targeted a small group of Al Qaeda operatives meeting in a desert location. The missile killed its targets, but it also killed the Deputy Governor of Marib Province who, unknown to U.S. officials, was meeting the Al Qaeda operatives to persuade them to lay down their arms (according to Yemen government sources). The Yemen strikes were neither confirmed nor denied by U.S. officials, and it was not clear whether the strikes were carried out by military or CIA personnel. Later the same year, the United States reportedly approved the targeting in Yemen of U.S. citizen Anwar al-Aulaqi on grounds that he was taking an active part in planning terrorist activities directed at the United States. At this writing, he had not yet been killed.

Finally, after months of careful intelligence gathering and extensive planning, on May 1, 2011, 79 American special forces personnel in 4 helicopters descended on a walled compound in Abbottabad, Pakistan, and, near the end of a 40-minute firefight, shot and killed Osama bin Laden. President Obama settled on a commando raid rather than a drone strike to avoid collateral damage (incidental civilian casualties) in a residential area and to permit verification of bin Laden's identity once he was captured or killed. When the Navy Seals located bin Laden on the top floor of the dwelling, he reportedly resisted arrest and was shot in the head. Bin Laden was not armed at the time, however. Several couriers and a woman were killed, but others in the compound (reportedly including one of bin Laden's wives) were uninjured, and apparently no damage was caused outside the compound.

Since September 11, 2001, Predators and other drones have reportedly been used hundreds of times to fire on targets in Afghanistan, Pakistan, Yemen, Iraq, and elsewhere. Apart from Osama bin Laden, a number of senior Taliban and Al Qaeda operatives have been killed in these attacks, including Al Qaeda's reputed chief of military operations, Mohammed Atef. But some number of innocent civilians have also been killed, sometimes deliberately as unavoidable collateral damage and sometimes simply by mistake.

B. TARGETED KILLING AND HUMAN RIGHTS LAW

Human rights law — international law that constrains governments in their treatment of civilians during peacetime — generally requires some kind of judicial procedure before anyone is executed (hence, the oft-stated concern about "*extra-judicial* killing or imprisonment"). The law enforcement model under human rights law rests on a presumption of innocence, a preference for arrest and detention by due process, and an insistence on credible evidence and fair trial before judicial punishment. *See generally* David Kretzmer, *Targeted Killing of Suspected Terrorists: Extra-Judicial Executions or Legitimate Means of Defence?*, 16 Eur. J. Int'l L. 171 (2005).

The International Covenant on Civil and Political Rights art. 6, Mar. 23, 1976, 999 U.N.T.S. 171, provides: "Every human being has the inherent right to life. This right shall be protected by law. No one shall be arbitrarily deprived of his life." This language resembles the text of the Fifth Amendment to the United States Constitution, which states: "No person shall . . . be deprived of life, liberty, or property, without due process of law. . . ."

The European Convention on Human Rights is similar:

Convention for the Protection of Human Rights and Fundamental Freedoms

Nov. 4, 1950, 213 U.N.T.S. 222

ARTICLE 2 – RIGHT TO LIFE

1. Everyone's right to life shall be protected by law. No one shall be deprived of his life intentionally save in the execution of a sentence of a court following his conviction of a crime for which this penalty is provided by law.

2. Deprivation of life shall not be regarded as inflicted in contravention of this Article when it results from the use of force which is no more than absolutely necessary:

(a) in defence of any person from unlawful violence;

(b) in order to effect a lawful arrest or to prevent the escape of a person lawfully detained;

(c) in action lawfully taken for the purpose of quelling a riot or insurrection.

The United Nations Basic Principles on the Use of Force and Firearms by Law Enforcement Officials (Sept. 7, 1990), *available at* http://www2.ohchr.org/english/law/pdf/firearms.pdf, address the subject in detail. Article 9 provides that "intentional lethal use of firearms may only be made when strictly unavoidable in order to protect life." Article 10 further provides that

> law enforcement officials shall identify themselves as such and shall give a clear warning of their intent to use firearms, with sufficient time for the warnings to be observed, unless to do so would unduly place the law enforcement officials at risk or would create a risk of death or serious harm to other persons, or would be clearly inappropriate or pointless in the circumstances of the incident.

In effect, the imminence of the threat provides the evidence needed to justify the use of lethal force and obviates any need to prove the target's intention. Kretzmer, *supra*, at 182. But unless the strict requirements of imminence and necessity through unavailability of other means are satisfied, the use of lethal force by law enforcement officers or, except in combat, military personnel would deny a suspected terrorist basic due process, "preventing the target from contesting the determination that he or she is a terrorist, and imposing a unilateral death penalty." Vincent-Joel Proulx, *If the Hat Fits, Wear it, If the Turban Fits, Run for Your Life: Reflections on the Indefinite Detention and Targeted Killing of Suspected Terrorists*, 56 Hastings L.J. 801, 889 (2005). Thus, "the very purpose of international human rights is defeated, whether through the violation of the right to a fair trial, the absolute circumvention of the right to liberty, or the disregard of the inherent right to life." *Id.* at 889-890.

Human rights law (HRL) is to be contrasted with international humanitarian law (IHL), addressed at length in Chapter 9, which governs the conduct of states in the midst of an armed conflict. There is overlap between the two sets of principles, and some resulting confusion. Indeed, as we see below, there is a growing tendency to apply HRL in armed conflicts, expanding the protections otherwise available to civilians and disarmed combatants. *See* Theodor Meron, *The Humanization of Humanitarian Law*, 94 Am. J. Int'l L. 239 (2000).

McCann v. United Kingdom

European Court of Human Rights, 1996
21 E.H.R.R. 97

[Authorities in the United Kingdom learned that Daniel McCann, Sean Savage, and Mairead Farrell of the Provisional IRA were planning to detonate a car bomb at a changing of the guard ceremony in Gibraltar on March 8, 1988. The authorities believed that the suspects would use a radio controlled detonation device. On March 6, 1988, the suspects were allowed to enter Gibraltar and were clandestinely followed by soldiers in the Special Air Service (SAS). The soldiers were wearing plain clothes and carrying concealed weapons.

The suspects parked a car and began to walk away. McCann appeared to notice Soldier A and then both McCann and Farrell made sudden movements. Fearing that they were going to detonate a bomb, Soldiers A and B shot and killed both McCann and Farrell. Soldier C ordered Savage to stop. Savage turned around and reached toward his hip. Soldier C, also fearing that Savage was going to detonate a bomb, shot and killed Savage. McCann, Savage, and Farrell were unarmed and did not have any detonating devices. Authorities later found keys to the parked car in Farrell's handbag. A subsequent search of the parked car turned up keys to a second car. The second car contained 64 kilograms of Semtex explosives, around which were packed 200 rounds of ammunition.

A coroner's inquest determined that the killings were lawful and justified. Relatives of the deceased disagreed. They first sued the United Kingdom's Ministry of Defence in Northern Ireland, but their suits were dismissed on grounds of sovereign immunity. They then complained to the European Commission on Human Rights, asserting that the killings violated Article 2 of the European Convention on Human Rights. The Commission concluded by a vote of 11 to 6 that no violation had occurred. The European Court of Human Rights reviewed the Commission's report, and issued the following judgment, adopted by a vote of 10 to 9.] . . .

200. The Court accepts that the soldiers honestly believed, in the light of the information that they had been given, as set out above, that it was necessary to shoot the suspects in order to prevent them from detonating a bomb and causing serious loss of life. The actions which they took, in obedience to superior orders, were thus perceived by them as absolutely necessary in order to safeguard innocent lives.

It considers that the use of force by agents of the State in pursuit of one of the aims delineated in Article 2(2) of the Convention may be justified under this provision where it is based on an honest belief which is perceived, for good reasons, to be valid at the time but which subsequently turns out to be mistaken. To hold otherwise would be to impose an unrealistic burden on the State and its law enforcement personnel in the execution of their duty, perhaps to the detriment of their lives and those of others.

It follows that, having regard to the dilemma confronting the authorities in the circumstances of the case, the actions of the soldiers do not, in themselves, give rise to a violation of this provision.

201. The question arises, however, whether the anti-terrorist operation as a whole was controlled and organised in a manner which respected the requirements of Article 2 and whether the information and instructions given to the soldiers which, in effect, rendered inevitable the use of lethal force, took adequately into consideration the right to life of the three suspects.

CONTROL AND ORGANISATION OF THE OPERATION

202. The Court first observes that, as appears from the Operational Order of the Commissioner, it had been the intention of the authorities to arrest the suspects at an appropriate stage. Indeed evidence was given at the Inquest that arrest procedures had been practised by the soldiers before 6 March and that efforts had been made to find a suitable place in Gibraltar to detain the suspects after their arrest.

203. It may be questioned why the three suspects were not arrested at the border immediately on their arrival in Gibraltar and why, as emerged from the evidence given by Inspector Ullger, the decision was taken not to prevent them from entering Gibraltar if they were believed to be on a bombing mission. Having had advance warning of the terrorists' intentions it would certainly have been possible for the authorities to have mounted an arrest operation. Although surprised at the early arrival of the three suspects, they had a surveillance team at the border and an arrest group nearby. In addition, the security services and the Spanish authorities had photographs of the three suspects, knew their names as well as their aliases and would have known what passports to look for.

204. On this issue, the Government submitted that at that moment there might not have been sufficient evidence to warrant the detention and trial of the suspects. Moreover, to release them, having alerted them to the authorities' state of awareness but leaving them or others free to try again, would obviously increase the risks. Nor could the authorities be sure that those three were the only terrorists they had to deal with or of the manner in which it was proposed to carry out the bombing.

205. The Court confines itself to observing in this respect that the danger to the population of Gibraltar — which is at the heart of the Government's submissions in the case — in not preventing their entry must be considered to outweigh the possible consequences of having insufficient evidence to warrant their detention and trial.

In its view, either the authorities knew that there was no bomb in the car — which the Court has already discounted — or there was a serious miscalculation by those responsible for controlling the operation. As a result, the scene was set in which the fatal shooting, given the intelligence assessments which had been made, was a foreseeable possibility if not a likelihood.

The decision not to stop the three terrorists from entering Gibraltar is thus a relevant factor to take into account under this head.

206. The Court notes that at the briefing on 5 March attended by Soldiers A, B, C and D it was considered likely that the attack would be by way of a large car bomb. A number of key assessments were made. In particular, it was thought that the terrorists would not use a blocking car; that the bomb would be detonated by a radio-control device; that the detonation could be effected by the pressing of a button; that it was likely that the suspects would detonate the bomb if challenged; that they would be armed and would be likely to use their arms if confronted.

207. In the event, all of these crucial assumptions, apart from the terrorists' intentions to carry out an attack, turned out to be erroneous. Nevertheless, as has been demonstrated by the Government, on the basis of their experience in dealing with the IRA, they were all possible hypotheses in a situation where the true facts were unknown and where the authorities operated on the basis of limited intelligence information.

208. In fact, insufficient allowances appear to have been made for other assumptions. For example, since the bombing was not expected until 8 March when the changing of the guard ceremony was to take place, there was equally the possibility that the three terrorists were on a reconnaissance mission. While this was a factor which was briefly considered, it does not appear to have been regarded as a serious possibility.

In addition, at the briefings or after the suspects had been spotted, it might have been thought unlikely that they would have been prepared to explode the bomb, thereby killing many civilians, as Mr McCann and Ms Farrell strolled towards the border area since this would have increased the risk of detection and capture. It might also have been thought improbable that at that point they would set up the transmitter in anticipation to enable them to detonate the supposed bomb immediately if confronted.

Moreover, even if allowances are made for the technological skills of the IRA, the description of the detonation device as a "button job" without the qualifications subsequently described by the experts at the Inquest, of which the competent authorities must have been aware, over-simplifies the true nature of these devices.

209. It is further disquieting in this context that the assessment made by Soldier G, after a cursory external examination of the car, that there was a "suspect car bomb" was conveyed to the soldiers, according to their own testimony, as a definite identification that there was such a bomb. It is recalled that while Soldier G had experience in car bombs, it transpired that he was not an expert in radio communications or explosives; and that his assessment that there was a suspect car bomb, based on his observation that the car aerial was out of place, was more in the nature of a report that a bomb could not be ruled out.

210. In the absence of sufficient allowances being made for alternative possibilities, and the definite reporting of the existence of a car bomb which, according to the assessments that had been made, could be detonated at the press of a button, a series of working hypotheses were conveyed to Soldiers A, B, C and D as certainties, thereby making the use of lethal force almost unavoidable.

211. However, the failure to make provision for a margin of error must also be considered in combination with the training of the soldiers to continue shooting once they opened fire until the suspect was dead. As noted by the Coroner in his summing up to the jury at the Inquest, all four soldiers shot to kill the suspects. Soldier E testified that it had been discussed with the soldiers that there was an increased chance that they would have to shoot to kill since there would be less time where there was a "button" device. Against this background, the authorities were bound by their obligation to respect the right to life of the suspects to exercise the greatest of care in evaluating the information at their disposal before transmitting it to soldiers whose use of firearms automatically involved shooting to kill.

212. Although detailed investigation at the Inquest into the training received by the soldiers was prevented by the public interest certificates which had been used, it is not clear whether they had been trained or instructed to assess whether the use of firearms to wound their targets may have been warranted by the specific circumstances that confronted them at the moment of arrest.

Their reflex action in this vital respect lacks the degree of caution in the use of firearms to be expected from law enforcement personnel in a democratic society, even when dealing with dangerous terrorist suspects, and stands in marked contrast to the standard of care reflected in the instructions in the use of firearms by the police which had been drawn to their attention and which emphasised the legal responsibilities of the individual officer in the light of conditions prevailing at the moment of engagement.

This failure by the authorities also suggests a lack of appropriate care in the control and organisation of the arrest operation.

213. In sum, having regard to the decision not to prevent the suspects from travelling into Gibraltar, to the failure of the authorities to make sufficient allowances for the possibility that their intelligence assessments might, in some respects at least, be erroneous and to the automatic recourse to lethal force when the soldiers opened fire, the Court is not persuaded that the killing of the three terrorists constituted the use of force which was no more than absolutely necessary in defence of persons from unlawful violence within the meaning of Article 2(2)(a) of the Convention.

214. Accordingly, it finds that there has been a breach of Article 2 of the Convention. . . .

Joint Dissenting Opinion of Judges Ryssdal, Bernhardt, Thór Vilhjálmsson, Gölcüklü, Palm, Pekkanen, Freeland, Baka and Jambrek.

1. We are unable to subscribe to the opinion of a majority of our colleagues that there has been a violation of Article 2 of the Convention in this case. . . .

8. First, in undertaking any evaluation of the way in which the operation was organised and controlled, the Court should studiously resist the temptations offered by the benefit of hindsight. The authorities had at the time to plan and make decisions on the basis of incomplete information. Only the suspects knew at all precisely what they intended; and it was part of the purpose, as it had no doubt been part of their training, to ensure that as little as possible of their intentions was revealed. It would be wrong to conclude in retrospect that a particular course would, as things later transpired, have been better than one adopted at the time under the pressures of an ongoing anti-terrorist operation and that the latter course must therefore be regarded as culpably mistaken. It should not be so regarded unless it is established that in the circumstances as they were known at the time another course should have been preferred.

9. Secondly, the need for the authorities to act within the constraints of the law, while the suspects were operating in a state of mind in which members of the security forces were regarded as legitimate targets and incidental death or injury to civilians as of little consequence, would inevitably give the suspects a tactical advantage which should not be allowed to prevail. The consequences of the explosion of a large bomb in the centre of Gibraltar might well be so devastating that the authorities could not responsibly risk giving the suspects the opportunity to set in train the detonation of such a bomb. Of course the obligation of the United Kingdom under Article 2(1) of the Convention extended to the lives of the suspects as well as to the lives of all the many others, civilian and military, who were present in Gibraltar at the time. But, quite unlike those others, the purpose of the presence of the suspects in Gibraltar was the furtherance of a criminal enterprise which could be expected to have resulted in the loss of many innocent lives if it had been successful. They had chosen to place themselves in a situation where there was a grave danger that an irreconcilable conflict between the two duties might arise.

10. Thirdly, the Court's evaluation of the conduct of the authorities should throughout take full account of (a) the information which had been received earlier about IRA intentions to mount a major terrorist attack in Gibraltar by an active service unit of three individuals; and (b) the discovery which (according to evidence given to the Inquest by Witness O) had been made in Brussels on 21 January 1988 of a car containing a large amount of Semtex explosive and four detonators, with a radio-controlled system — equipment which, taken together, constituted a device familiar in Northern Ireland.

In the light of (a), the decision that members of the SAS should be sent to take part in the operation in response of the request of the Gibraltar Commissioner of Police for military assistance was wholly justifiable. Troops trained in a counter-terrorist role and to operate successfully in small groups would clearly be a suitable choice to meet the threat of an IRA active service unit at large in a densely populated area such as Gibraltar, where there would be an imperative need to limit as far as possible the risk of accidental harm to passers-by.

The detailed operational briefing on 5 March 1988 shows the reasonableness, in the circumstances as known at the time, of the assessments then made. The Operational Order of the Gibraltar Commissioner of Police, which was drawn up on the same day, expressly proscribed the use of more force than necessary and required any recourse to firearms to be had with care for the safety of persons in the vicinity. It described the intention of the operation as being to protect life; to foil the attempt; to arrest the offenders; and the securing and safe custody of the prisoners.

All of this is indicative of appropriate care on the part of the authorities. So, too, is the cautious approach to the eventual passing of control to the military on 6 March 1988.

11. As regards the particular criticisms of the conduct of the operation which are made in the judgment, foremost among them is the questioning of the decision not to prevent the three suspects from entering Gibraltar. It is pointed out in paragraph 203 that, with the advance information which the authorities possessed and with the resources of personnel at their disposal, it would have been possible for them "to have mounted an arrest operation" at the border.

The judgment does not, however, go on to say that it would have been practicable for the authorities to have arrested and detained the suspects at that stage. Rightly so, in our view, because at that stage there might not be sufficient evidence to warrant their detention and trial. To release them, after having alerted them to the state of readiness of the authorities, would be to increase the risk that they or other IRA members could successfully mount a renewed terrorist attack on Gibraltar. In the circumstances as then known, it was accordingly not "a serious miscalculation" for the authorities to defer the arrest rather than merely stop the suspects at the border and turn them back into Spain. . . .

25. The accusation of a breach by a State of its obligation under Article 2 of the Convention to protect the right to life is of the utmost seriousness. For the reasons given above, the evaluation in paragraphs 203 to 213 of the judgment seems to us to fall well short of substantiating the finding that there has been a breach of the Article in this case. We would ourselves follow the reasoning and conclusion of the Commission in its comprehensive, painstaking and notably realistic report. Like the Commission, we are satisfied that no failings have been shown in the organisation and control of the operation by the authorities which could justify a conclusion that force was used against the suspects disproportionately to the purpose of defending innocent persons from unlawful violence. We consider that the use of lethal force in this case, however regrettable the need to resort to such force may be, did not exceed what was, in the circumstances as known as the time, "absolutely necessary" for that purpose and did not amount to a breach by the United Kingdom of its obligations under the Convention.

NOTES AND QUESTIONS

1. *Weighing the Alternative Outcomes in McCann.* The European Court of Human Rights sits like a court of appeals in cases like *McCann*, reviewing the fact and law conclusions of the European Commission on Human Rights. In this closely divided decision, on what basis did the majority of the Court reject the findings of the Commission? Was it failure of the UK security forces in not stopping the suspects from traveling into Gibraltar, or in using lethal force against them once there? Which opinion more faithfully applies Article 2 of the European Convention?

2. *Were the Predator Attacks in Pakistan and Yemen Extrajudicial Killings?* Applying HRL, the U.N. Special Rapporteur to the Commission on Human Rights expressed the opinion that the 2002 U.S. "attack in Yemen constitutes a clear case of extrajudicial killing." U.N. Econ. & Soc. Council, *Civil and Political Rights, Including the Questions of Disappearances and Summary Executions, Submitted to Comm'n on Human Rights,* U.N. Doc. E/CN.4/2003/3 (Jan. 13, 2003). The Swedish Foreign Minister reached a similar conclusion, calling the attack "a summary execution that violates human rights. Terrorists must be treated according to international law. Otherwise, any country can start executing those whom they consider terrorists." *Quoted in* Hersh, *supra* p. 376, at 4.

Do you agree? Does it matter legally whether the targeted killing is in the border region of Pakistan, in remote provinces of Yemen, in Somalia — or in Germany? Note that although Yemeni officials apparently cooperated in the targeted killing of al-Harethi, they had previously failed to apprehend him and may have been reluctant to do so because of a perceived debt owed to Osama bin Laden, who had assisted the Yemeni president in putting down a separatist movement in 1994. Should the availability of "normal judicial channels" make a difference in the law enforcement analysis? Should it matter legally that one of the persons traveling with al-Harethi in 2002 in Yemen was an American? Would a strike at American citizen al-Aulaqi in Yemen be lawful under HRL?

3. *Human Rights Law in Times of War or Armed Conflict?* If the incident that gave rise to the *McCann* litigation had occurred in Northern Ireland in the 1970s, or in Afghanistan in 2010, with the UK personnel deployed as part of the NATO force there, would HRL apply? The view of the United States is that, during armed conflicts, HRL gives way to IHL and its *jus in bello* principles. *Operational Law Handbook* 40 (Marie Anderson & Emily Zukauskas eds., 2008). Yet the ICJ and other international courts have applied HRL in armed-conflict settings. *See Legality of the Threat or Use of Nuclear Weapons, Advisory Opinion,* 1996 I.C.J. 226 (July 8). In the event of a conflict between HRL and IHL on the battlefield, the traditional U.S. view has been that the *in bello* rules are *lex specialis,* trumping HRL. Anderson & Zukauskas, *supra,* at 40. The European view is that HRL always applies, even alongside IHL on the battlefield. Marco Sassoli & Laura M. Olson, *The Relationship Between Human Rights and Humanitarian Law Where It Matters: Admissible Killing and Internment of Fighters in Non-International Armed Conflicts,* 90 Int'l Rev. Red Cross 599, 603 (Sept. 2008).

Can you think of situations in which the choice of law makes a practical difference? In an international armed conflict, a member of an armed group may be attacked so long as he has not surrendered or been rendered *hors de combat* (disabled from continuing to fight) by injury. See *supra* p. 242. But does the same presumption of lawful targeting apply in a non-international armed conflict? *See id.*

4. *Killing bin Laden.* Was the killing of Osama bin Laden by U.S. special forces lawful? Applying HRL, was the killing a permitted law enforcement operation or an extrajudicial killing? *See* Nils Melzer, *Targeted Killing in International Law* 423 (2008) (targeted killing must have a legal basis in domestic law, be preventative rather than punitive, have protection of human life from unlawful attack by the target as its exclusive purpose, "be absolutely necessary in qualitative, quantitative and temporal terms for the achievement of this purpose," and be the undesired outcome of an operation planned and conducted to minimize resource to lethal force"). Apparently, bin Laden was not armed when he was shot. Would that fact make the operation unlawful from an HRL perspective? Is it important that the Navy Seals feared that bin Laden might have prepared for the threat of capture by rigging himself as a "human IED" (improvised explosive device)?

C.   TARGETED KILLING AND INTERNATIONAL HUMANITARIAN LAW

In the following case, the Israeli Supreme Court applies IHL to Israel's targeted killing of Hamas operatives on the West Bank and in Gaza. But IHL does not make these areas free-fire zones. What are its requirements? For references to that law in Protocol I to the Geneva Convention, see *supra* p. 241.

Public Committee Against Torture in Israel v. Israel

Supreme Court of Israel, sitting as the High Court of Justice, 2006
46 I.L.M 375

President (Emeritus) A. BARAK: The Government of Israel employs a policy of preventative strikes which cause the death of terrorists in Judea, Samaria, or the Gaza Strip. It fatally strikes these terrorists, who plan, launch, or commit terrorist attacks in Israel and in the area of Judea, Samaria, and the Gaza Strip, against both civilians and soldiers. These strikes at times also harm innocent civilians. Does the State thus act illegally? That is the question posed before us.

1.   FACTUAL BACKGROUND

In February 2000, the second intifada began. A massive assault of terrorism was directed against the State of Israel, and against Israelis, merely because they are Israelis. This assault of terrorism differentiates neither between combatants and civilians, nor between women, men, and children. The terrorist attacks take place both in the territory of Judea, Samaria, and the Gaza Strip, and within the borders of the State of Israel. They are directed against civilian centers, shopping centers and markets, coffee houses and restaurants. Over the last five years, thousands of acts of terrorism have been committed against Israel. In the attacks, more than one thousand Israeli citizens have been killed. Thousands of Israeli citizens have been wounded. Thousands of Palestinians have been killed and wounded during this period as well.

2. In its war against terrorism, the State of Israel employs various means. As part of the security activity intended to confront the terrorist attacks, the State employs what it calls "the policy of targeted frustration" of terrorism. Under this policy, the security forces act in order to kill members of terrorist organizations involved in the planning, launching, or execution of terrorist attacks against Israel. During the second intifada, such preventative strikes have been performed across Judea, Samaria, and the Gaza Strip. According to the data relayed by petitioners, since the commencement of these acts, and up until the end of 2005, close to three hundred members of terrorist organizations have been killed by them. More than thirty targeted killing attempts have failed. Approximately one hundred and fifty civilians who were proximate to the location of the targeted persons have been killed during those acts. Hundreds of others have been wounded. The policy of targeted killings is the focus of this petition....

5.   THE GENERAL NORMATIVE FRAMEWORK

A.   International Armed Conflict

16. The general, principled starting point is that between Israel and the various terrorist organizations active in Judea, Samaria, and the Gaza Strip (hereinafter "the area") a continuous situation of armed conflict has existed since the first intifada.... [T]he situation was described in the supplement to the summary on behalf of the State Attorney (on January 26 2004):

> For more than three years now, the State of Israel is under a constant, continual, and murderous wave of terrorist attacks, directed at Israelis — because they are Israelis — without any discrimination between combatants and civilians or between men, women, and children. In the framework of the current campaign of terrorism, more than 900 Israelis have been killed, and thousands of other Israelis have been wounded to date, since late September 2000. In addition, thousands of Palestinians have been killed and wounded during that period. For the sake of comparison we note that the number of Israeli casualties in proportion to the population of the State of Israel, is a number of times greater than the percentage of casualties in the US in the events of September 11 in proportion to the US population. As is well known, and as we have already noted, the events of 9/11 were defined by the states of the world and by international organizations, with no hesitation whatsoever, as an "armed conflict" justifying the use of counterforce....

23. ... Are terrorist organizations and their members combatants, in regard[] to their rights in the armed conflict? Are they civilians taking an active part in the armed conflict? Are they possibly neither combatants nor civilians? What, then, is the status of those terrorists?

B.   Combatants

24. What makes a person a combatant? This category includes, of course, the armed forces. It also includes people who fulfill the following conditions: [see Geneva Convention III, art. 4, *supra* p. 237] ... In one case, I wrote:

> "The Lebanese detainees are not to be seen as prisoners of war. It is sufficient, in order to reach that conclusion, that they do not fulfill the provisions of article 4a(2)(d) of The Third Geneva Convention, which provides that one of the conditions which must be fulfilled in order to fit the definition of 'a prisoner of war' is 'that of conducting their operations in accordance with the laws and customs of war.' The organizations to which the Lebanese detainees belonged are terrorist organizations acting contrary to the laws and customs of war. Thus, for example, these organizations intentionally harm civilians, and shoot from within the civilian population, which serves them as a shield. Each of these is an act contrary to international law. Indeed, Israel's constant stance throughout the years has been to view the various organizations, like the Hizbollah, as organizations to which The Third Geneva Convention does not apply. We found no cause to intervene in that stance."

25. The terrorists and their organizations, with which the State of Israel has an armed conflict of international character, do not fall into the category of combatants.

They do not belong to the armed forces, and they do not belong to units to which international law grants status similar to that of combatants. Indeed, the terrorists and the organizations which send them to carry out attacks are unlawful combatants. They do not enjoy the status of prisoners of war. They can be tried for their participation in hostilities, judged, and punished. The Chief Justice of the Supreme Court of the United States, Stone C.J. discussed that, writing:

> "By universal agreement and practice, the law of war draws a distinction between the armed forces and the peaceful population of belligerent nations and also between those who are lawful and unlawful combatants. Lawful combatants are subject to capture and detention as prisoners of war by opposing military forces. Unlawful combatant are likewise subject to capture and detention, but in addition they are subject to trial and punishment by military tribunals for acts which render their belligerency unlawful" (*Ex Parte Quirin* 317 U.S. 1, 30 (1942); see also *Hamdi v. Rumsfeld*, 542 U.S. 507 (2004)).

. . . Needless to say, unlawful combatants are not beyond the law. They are not "outlaws." God created them as well in his image; their human dignity as well is to be honored; they as well enjoy and are entitled to protection, even if most minimal, by customary international law. That is certainly the case when they are in detention or brought to justice (see §75 of The First Protocol [Additional Protocol I, *supra* p. 247], which reflects customary international law). Does it follow that in Israel's conduct of combat against the terrorist organizations, Israel is not entitled to harm them, and Israel is not entitled to kill them even if they are planning, launching, or committing terrorist attacks? If they were seen as (legal) combatants, the answer would of course be that Israel is entitled to harm them. Just as it is permissible to harm a soldier of an enemy country, so can terrorists be harmed. Accordingly, they would also enjoy the status of prisoners of war, and the rest of the protections granted to legal combatants. However, as we have seen, the terrorists acting against Israel are not combatants according to the definition of that term in international law; they are not entitled to the status of prisoners of war; they can be put on trial for their membership in terrorist organizations and for their operations against the army. Are they seen as civilians under the law? It is to the examination of that question which we now turn.

C.   Civilians

26. Customary international law regarding armed conflicts protects "civilians" from harm as a result of the hostilities. . . . From that follows also the duty to do everything possible to minimize collateral damage to the civilian population during the attacks on "combatants." Against the background of that protection granted to "civilians," the question what constitutes a "civilian" for the purposes of that law arises. The approach of customary international law is that "civilians" are those who are not "combatants" (see §50(1) of The First Protocol). In the *Blaskic* case, the International Criminal Tribunal for the former Yugoslavia ruled that civilians are —

> "Persons who are not, or no longer, members of the armed forces."

That definition is "negative" in nature. It defines the concept of "civilian" as the opposite of "combatant." It thus views unlawful combatants — who, as we have seen, are not "combatants" — as civilians. Does that mean that the unlawful combatants are entitled to the same protection to which civilians who are not unlawful combatants are entitled? The answer is, no. Customary international law regarding armed conflicts determines that a civilian taking a direct part in the hostilities does not, at such time, enjoy the protection granted to a civilian who is not taking a direct part in the hostilities (see §51(3) of The First Protocol). The result is that an unlawful combatant is not a combatant, rather a "civilian." However, he is a civilian who is not protected from attack as long as he is taking a direct part in the hostilities. . . .

D. A Third Category: Unlawful combatants?

27. In the oral and written arguments before us, the State asked us to recognize a third category of persons, that of unlawful combatants. These are people who take active and continuous part in an armed conflict, and therefore should be treated as combatants, in the sense that they are legitimate targets of attack, and they do not enjoy the protections granted to civilians. However, they are not entitled to the rights and privileges of combatants, since they do not differentiate themselves from the civilian population, and since they do not obey the laws of war. Thus, for example, they are not entitled to the status of prisoners of war. The State's position is that the terrorists who participate in the armed conflict between Israel and the terrorist organizations fall under this category of unlawful combatants.

28. . . . We shall take no stance regarding the question whether it is desirable to recognize this third category. The question before us is not one of desirable law, rather one of existing law. In our opinion, as far as existing law goes, the data before us are not sufficient to recognize this third category. . . .

6.   CIVILIANS WHO ARE UNLAWFUL COMBATANTS

A. The Basic Principle: Civilians Taking a Direct Part in Hostilities are not Protected at Such Time they are Doing So

29. Civilians enjoy comprehensive protection of their lives, liberty, and property. "The protection of the lives of the civilian population is a central value in humanitarian law." "The right to life and bodily integrity is the basic right standing at the center of the humanitarian law intended to protect the local population." As opposed to combatants, whom one can harm due to their status as combatants, civilians are not to be harmed, due to their status as civilians. A provision in this spirit is determined in article 51(2) of The First Protocol, which constitutes customary international law:

> "The civilian population as such, as well as individual civilians, shall not be the object of attack. . . ."

Article 8(2)(b)(i)-(ii) of the Rome Statute of the International Criminal Court determines, in the same spirit, in defining a war crime, that if an order to attack civilians is given intentionally, that is a crime. That crime applies to those civilians who are "not taking direct part in hostilities." In addition, civilians are not to be harmed in an indiscriminate attack; in other words, in an attack which, inter alia, is not directed against a particular military objective (see §51(4) of The First Protocol, which constitutes customary international law). That protection is granted to all civilians, excepting those civilians taking a direct part in hostilities. . . .

B.   The Source of the Basic Principle and its Customary Character

30. The basic principle is that the civilians taking a direct part in hostilities are not protected from attack upon them at such time as they are doing so. This principle is manifest in §51(3) of The First Protocol, which determines:

> "Civilians shall enjoy the protection afforded by this section, unless and for such time as they take a direct part in hostilities."

As is well known, Israel is not party to The First Protocol. Thus, it clearly was not enacted in domestic Israeli legislation. Does the basic principle express customary international law? The position of The Red Cross is that it is a principle of customary international law. That position is acceptable to us.... In military manuals of many states, including England, France, Holland, Australia, Italy, Canada, Germany, the United States (Air Force), and New Zealand, the provision has been copied verbatim, or by adopting its essence, according to which civilians are not to be attacked, unless they are taking a (direct) part in the hostilities. The legal literature sees that provision as an expression of customary international law....

C.   The Essence of the Basic Principle...

32. ... [T]he basic principle is that the civilian population, and single civilians, are protected from the dangers of military activity and are not targets for attack. That protection is granted to civilians "unless and for such time as they take a direct part in hostilities" (§51(3) of The First Protocol). That provision is composed of three main parts. The first part is the requirement that civilians take part in "hostilities"; the second part is the requirement that civilians take a "direct" part in hostilities; the third part is the provision by which civilians are not protected from attack "for such time" as they take a direct part in hostilities. We shall discuss each of those parts separately.

D.   The First Part: "Taking ... part in hostilities"

33. Civilians lose the protection of customary international law dealing with hostilities of international character if they "take ... part in hostilities." What is the meaning of that provision? The accepted view is that "hostilities" are acts which by nature and objective are intended to cause damage to the army. Thus determines *Commentary on the Additional Protocols*, published by the Red Cross in 1987:

> "Hostile acts should be understood to be acts which by their nature and purpose are intended to cause actual harm to the personnel and equipment of the armed forces."

... It seems that acts which by nature and objective are intended to cause damage to civilians should be added to that definition. According to the accepted definition, a civilian is taking part in hostilities when using weapons in an armed conflict, while gathering intelligence, or while preparing himself for the hostilities. Regarding taking part in hostilities, there is no condition that the civilian use his weapon, nor is [there] a condition that he bear arms (openly or concealed). It is possible to take part in hostilities without using weapons at all. *Commentary on the Additional Protocols* discussed that issue:

"It seems that the word 'hostilities' covers not only the time that the civilian actually makes use of a weapon, but also, for example, the time that he is carrying it, as well as situations in which he undertakes hostile acts without using a weapon."

As we have seen, that approach is not limited merely to the issue of "hostilities" toward the army or the state. It applies also to hostilities against the civilian population of the state.

E.   Second Part: "Takes a Direct Part"

34. Civilians lose the protection against military attack, granted to them by customary international law dealing with international armed conflict (as adopted in The First Protocol, §51(3)), if "they take a direct part in hostilities." That provision differentiates between civilians taking a direct part in hostilities (from whom the protection from attack is removed) and civilians taking an indirect part in hostilities (who continue to enjoy protection from attack). What is that differentiation? A similar provision appears in Common Article 3 of The Geneva Conventions, which uses the wording "active part in hostilities." The judgment of the International Criminal Tribunal for Rwanda determined that these two terms are of identical content. What is that content? It seems accepted in the international literature that an agreed upon definition of the term "direct" in the context under discussion does not exist.

In that state of affairs, and without a comprehensive and agreed upon customary standard, there is no escaping going case by case, while narrowing the area of disagreement.... On this issue, the following passage from *Commentary on the Additional Protocols* is worth quoting:

"Undoubtedly there is room here for some margin of judgment: to restrict this concept to combat and active military operations would be too narrow, while extending it to the entire war effort would be too broad, as in modern warfare the whole population participates in the war effort to some extent, albeit indirectly."

Indeed, a civilian bearing arms (openly or concealed) who is on his way to the place where he will use them against the army, at such place, or on his way back from it, is a civilian taking "an active part" in the hostilities. However, a civilian who generally supports the hostilities against the army is not taking a direct part in the hostilities. Similarly, a civilian who sells food or medicine to unlawful combatants is also taking an indirect part in the hostilities. The third report of the Inter-American Commission on Human Rights states:

"Civilians whose activities merely support the adverse party's war or military effort or otherwise only indirectly participate in hostilities cannot on these grounds alone be considered combatants. This is because indirect participation, such as selling goods to one or more of the armed parties, expressing sympathy for the cause of one of the parties or, even more clearly, failing to act to prevent an incursion by one of the armed parties, does not involve acts of violence which pose an immediate threat of actual harm to the adverse party."

And what is the law in the space between these two extremes? On the one hand, the desire to protect innocent civilians leads, in the hard cases, to a narrow interpretation of the term "direct" part in hostilities. Professor Cassese writes:

"The rationale behind the prohibition against targeting a civilian who does not take a direct part in hostilities, despite his possible (previous or future) involvement in fighting, is linked to the need to avoid killing innocent civilians."

On the other hand, it can be said that the desire to protect combatants and the desire to protect innocent civilians leads, in the hard cases, to a wide interpretation of the "direct" character of the hostilities, as thus civilians are encouraged to stay away from the hostilities to the extent possible. Schmitt writes:

"Gray areas should be interpreted liberally, i.e., in favor of finding direct participation. One of the seminal purposes of the law is to make possible a clear distinction between civilians and combatants. Suggesting that civilians retain their immunity even when they are intricately involved in a conflict is to engender disrespect for the law by combatants endangered by their activities. Moreover, a liberal approach creates an incentive for civilians to remain as distant from the conflict as possible — in doing so they can better avoid being charged with participation in the conflict and are less liable to being directly targeted."

35. Against the background of these considerations, the following cases should also be included in the definition of taking a "direct part" in hostilities: a person who collects intelligence on the army, whether on issues regarding the hostilities or beyond those issues; a person who transports unlawful combatants to or from the place where the hostilities are taking place; a person who operates weapons which unlawful combatants use, or supervises their operation, or provides service to them, be the distance from the battlefield as it may. All those persons are performing the function of combatants. The function determines the directness of the part taken in the hostilities. However, a person who sells food or medicine to an unlawful combatant is not taking a direct part, rather an indirect part in the hostilities. The same is the case regarding a person who aids the unlawful combatants by general strategic analysis, and grants them logistical, general support, including monetary aid. The same is the case regarding a person who distributes propaganda supporting those unlawful combatants. If such persons are injured, the State is likely not to be liable for it, if it falls into the framework of collateral or incidental damage....

36. What is the law regarding civilians serving as a "human shield" for terrorists taking a direct part in the hostilities? Certainly, if they are doing so because they were forced to do so by terrorists, those innocent civilians are not to be seen as taking a direct part in the hostilities. They themselves are victims of terrorism. However, if they do so of their own free will, out of support for the terrorist organization, they should be seen as persons taking a direct part in the hostilities.

37. We have seen that a civilian causing harm to the army is taking "a direct part" in hostilities. What says the law about those who enlist him to take a direct part in the hostilities, and those who send him to commit hostilities? Is there a difference between his direct commanders and those responsible for them? Is the "direct" part taken only by the last terrorist in the chain of command, or by the entire chain? In our opinion, the "direct" character of the part taken should not be narrowed merely to the person committing the physical act of attack. Those who have sent him, as well, take "a direct part." The same goes for the person who decided upon the act, and the person who planned it. It is not to be said about them that they are taking an indirect part in the hostilities. Their contribution is direct (and active).

F.   The Third Part: "For Such Time"

38. Article 51(3) of The First Protocol states that civilians enjoy protection from the dangers stemming from military acts, and that they are not targets for attack, unless "and for such time" as they are taking a direct part in hostilities. The provisions of article 51(3) of The First Protocol present a time requirement. A civilian taking a part in hostilities loses the protection from attack "for such time" as he is taking part in those hostilities. If "such time" has passed — the protection granted to the civilian returns....

39. As regarding the scope of the wording "takes a direct part" in hostilities, so too regarding the scope of the wording "and for such time" there is no consensus in the international literature. Indeed, both these concepts are close to each other. However, they are not identical. With no consensus regarding the interpretation of the wording "for such time," there is no choice but to proceed from case to case. Again, it is helpful to examine the extreme cases. On the one hand, a civilian taking a direct part in hostilities one single time, or sporadically, who later detaches himself from that activity, is a civilian who, starting from the time he detached himself from that activity, is entitled to protection from attack. He is not to be attacked for the hostilities which he committed in the past. On the other hand, a civilian who has joined a terrorist organization which has become his "home," and in the framework of his role in that organization he commits a chain of hostilities, with short periods of rest between them, loses his immunity from attack "for such time" as he is committing the chain of acts. Indeed, regarding such a civilian, the rest between hostilities is nothing other than preparation for the next hostility.

40. These examples point out the dilemma which the "for such time" requirement presents before us. On the one hand, a civilian who took a direct part in hostilities once, or sporadically, but detached himself from them (entirely, or for a long period) is not to be harmed. On the other hand, the "revolving door" phenomenon, by which each terrorist has "horns of the alter" (1 Kings 1:50) to grasp or a "city of refuge" (Numbers 35:11) to flee to, to which he turns in order to rest and prepare while they grant him immunity from attack, is to be avoided. In the wide area between those two possibilities, one finds the "gray" cases, about which customary international law has not yet crystallized. There is thus no escaping examination of each and every case. In that context, the following four things should be said: first, well based information is needed before categorizing a civilian as falling into one of the discussed categories. Innocent civilians are not to be harmed. Information which has been most thoroughly verified is needed regarding the identity and activity of the civilian who is allegedly taking part in the hostilities. Cassese rightly stated that —

> "[I]f a belligerent were allowed to fire at enemy civilians simply suspected of somehow planning or conspiring to plan military attacks, or of having planned or directed hostile actions, the basic foundations of international humanitarian law would be seriously undermined. The basic distinction between civilians and combatants would be called into question and the whole body of law relating to armed conflict would eventually be eroded."

The burden of proof on the attacking army is heavy. In the case of doubt, careful verification is needed before an attack is made. Henckaerts & Doswald-Beck made this point:

"[W]hen there is a situation of doubt, a careful assessment has to be made under the conditions and restraints governing a particular situation as to whether there are sufficient indications to warrant an attack. One cannot automatically attack anyone who might appear dubious."

Second, a civilian taking a direct part in hostilities cannot be attacked at such time as he is doing so, if a less harmful means can be employed. In our domestic law, that rule is called for by the principle of proportionality. Indeed, among the military means, one must choose the means whose harm to the human rights of the harmed person is smallest. Thus, if a terrorist taking a direct part in hostilities can be arrested, interrogated, and tried, those are the means which should be employed. Trial is preferable to use of force. A rule-of-law state employs, to the extent possible, procedures of law and not procedures of force. That question arose in *McCann v. United Kingdom*, 21 E.H.R.R. 97 (1995)....In that state of affairs, [lethal force] should not be used. Third, after an attack on a civilian suspected of taking an active part, at such time, in hostilities, a thorough investigation regarding the precision of the identification of the target and the circumstances of the attack upon him is to be performed (retroactively). That investigation must be independent. In appropriate cases it is appropriate to pay compensation as a result of harm caused to an innocent civilian (see §3 of The Hague Regulations; §91 of The First Protocol). Last, if the harm is not only to a civilian directly participating in the hostilities, rather also to innocent civilians nearby, the harm to them is collateral damage. That damage must withstand the proportionality test. We shall now proceed to the examination of that question.

7. PROPORTIONALITY...

B. Proportionality in an International Armed Conflict

42. The principle of proportionality is a substantial part of international law regarding armed conflict (compare §51(5)(b) and 57 of The First Protocol). That law is of customary character. The principle of proportionality arises when the military operation is directed toward combatants and military objectives, or against civilians at such time as they are taking a direct part in hostilities, yet civilians are also harmed. The rule is that the harm to innocent civilians caused by collateral damage during combat operations must be proportionate. Civilians might be harmed due to their presence inside of a military target, such as civilians working in an army base; civilians might be harmed when they live or work in, or pass by, military targets; at times, due to a mistake, civilians are harmed even if they are far from military targets; at times civilians are forced to serve as "human shields" from attack upon a military target, and they are harmed as a result. In all those situations, and in other similar ones, the rule is that the harm to the innocent civilians must fulfill, inter alia, the requirements of the principle of proportionality....

44. The requirement of proportionality in the laws of armed conflict focuses primarily upon what our constitutional law calls proportionality "stricto senso," that is, the requirement that there be a proper proportionate relationship between the military objective and the civilian damage. However, the laws of armed conflict include additional components....

C. Proper Proportion between Benefit and Damage

45. The proportionality test determines that attack upon innocent civilians is not permitted if the collateral damage caused to them is not proportionate to the military advantage (in protecting combatants and civilians). In other words, attack is proportionate if the benefit stemming from the attainment of the proper military objective is proportionate to the damage caused to innocent civilians harmed by it. That is a values based test. It is based upon a balancing between conflicting values and interests. It is accepted in the national law of various countries. It constitutes a central normative test for examining the activity of the government in general, and of the military specifically, in Israel. In one case I stated:

> "Basically, this subtest carries on its shoulders the constitutional view that the ends do not justify the means. It is a manifestation of the idea that there is a barrier of values which democracy cannot surpass, even if the purpose whose attainment is being attempted is worthy." . . .

46. That aspect of proportionality is not required regarding harm to a combatant, or to a civilian taking a direct part in the hostilities at such time as the harm is caused. Indeed, a civilian taking part in hostilities is endangering his life, and he might — like a combatant — be the objective of a fatal attack. That killing is permitted. However, that proportionality is required in any case in which an innocent civilian is harmed. Thus, the requirements of proportionality stricto senso must be fulfilled in a case in which the harm to the terrorist carries with it collateral damage caused to nearby innocent civilians. The proportionality rule applies in regards to harm to those innocent civilians (see §51(5)(b) of The First Protocol). The rule is that combatants and terrorists are not to be harmed if the damage expected to be caused to nearby innocent civilians is not proportionate to the military advantage in harming the combatants and terrorists. Performing that balance is difficult. Here as well, one must proceed case by case, while narrowing the area of disagreement. Take the usual case of a combatant, or of a terrorist sniper shooting at soldiers or civilians from his porch. Shooting at him is proportionate even if as a result, an innocent civilian neighbor or passerby is harmed. That is not the case if the building is bombed from the air and scores of its residents and passersby are harmed. The hard cases are those which are in the space between the extreme examples. There, a meticulous examination of every case is required; it is required that the military advantage be direct and anticipated (see §57(2)(iii) of The First Protocol). Indeed, in international law, as in internal law, the ends do not justify the means. . . .

IMPLEMENTATION OF THE GENERAL PRINCIPLES IN THIS CASE

60. . . . The examination of the "targeted killing" — and in our terms, the preventative strike causing the deaths of terrorists, and at times also of innocent civilians — has shown that the question of the legality of the preventative strike according to customary international law is complex. The result of that examination is not that such strikes are always permissible or that they are always forbidden. The approach of customary international law applying to armed conflicts of an international nature is that civilians are protected from attacks by the army. However, that protection does not exist regarding those civilians "for such time as they take a direct part in hostilities" (§51(3) of The First Protocol). Harming such civilians, even if the result is death, is permitted, on the condition that there is no other less harmful means, and on the condition that innocent civilians nearby are not harmed. Harm to the latter must be proportionate. That proportionality is determined according to a values based test, intended to balance between the military advantage and the civilian damage. As we have seen, we cannot determine that a preventative strike is always legal, just as we cannot determine that it is always illegal. All depends upon the question whether the standards of customary international law regarding international armed conflict allow that preventative strike or not.

CONCLUSION

61. The State of Israel is fighting against severe terrorism, which plagues it from the area. The means at Israel's disposal are limited. The State determined that preventative strikes upon terrorists in the area which cause their deaths are a necessary means from the military standpoint. These strikes at times cause harm and even death to innocent civilians. These preventative strikes, with all the military importance they entail, must be made within the framework of the law. The saying "when the cannons roar, the muses are silent" is well known. A similar idea was expressed by Cicero, who said: "during war, the laws are silent" (silent enim legis inter arma). Those sayings are regrettable. They reflect neither the existing law nor the desirable law. It is when the cannons roar that we especially need the laws. Every struggle of the state — against terrorism or any other enemy — is conducted according to rules and law. There is always law which the state must comply with. There are no "black holes." In this case, the law was determined by customary international law regarding conflicts of an international character. Indeed, the State's struggle against terrorism is not conducted "outside" of the law. It is conducted "inside" the law, with tools that the law places at the disposal of democratic states. . . .

Harold Koh, The Obama Administration and International Law

Remarks to the Annual Meeting of the American Society of International Law, Mar. 25, 2010 *transcript available at* http://www.state.gov/s/l/releases/remarks/139119.htm

B.   USE OF FORCE

. . . [I]n all of our operations involving the use of force, including those in the armed conflict with al-Qaeda, the Taliban and associated forces, the Obama Administration is committed by word and deed to conducting ourselves in accordance with all applicable law. With respect to the subject of targeting, which has been much commented upon in the media and international legal circles, there are obviously limits to what I can say publicly. What I can say is that it is the considered view of this Administration — and it has certainly been my experience during my time as Legal Adviser — that U.S. targeting practices, including lethal operations conducted with the use of unmanned aerial vehicles, comply with all applicable law, including the laws of war.

The United States agrees that it must conform its actions to all applicable law. As I have explained, as a matter of international law, the United States is in an armed conflict with al-Qaeda, as well as the Taliban and associated forces, in response to the horrific 9/11 attacks, and may use force consistent with its inherent right to self-defense under international law. As a matter of domestic law, Congress author-ized the use of all necessary and appropriate force through the 2001 Authorization for Use of Military Force (AUMF). These domestic and international legal authorities continue to this day.

As recent events have shown, al-Qaeda has not abandoned its intent to attack the United States, and indeed continues to attack us. Thus, in this ongoing armed con-flict, the United States has the authority under international law, and the responsi-bility to its citizens, to use force, including lethal force, to defend itself, including by targeting persons such as high-level al-Qaeda leaders who are planning attacks. As you know, this is a conflict with an organized terrorist enemy that does not have conven-tional forces, but that plans and executes its attacks against us and our allies while hiding among civilian populations. That behavior simultaneously makes the applica-tion of international law more difficult and more critical for the protection of inno-cent civilians. Of course, whether a particular individual will be targeted in a particular location will depend upon considerations specific to each case, including those related to the imminence of the threat, the sovereignty of the other states involved, and the willingness and ability of those states to suppress the threat the target poses. In particular, this Administration has carefully reviewed the rules gov-erning targeting operations to ensure that these operations are conducted consis-tently with law of war principles, including:

- First, the principle of distinction, which requires that attacks be limited to military objectives and that civilians or civilian objects shall not be the object of the attack; and

- Second, the principle of proportionality, which prohibits attacks that may be expected to cause incidental loss of civilian life, injury to civilians, damage to civilian objects, or a combination thereof, that would be excessive in relation to the concrete and direct military advantage anticipated.

In U.S. operations against al-Qaeda and its associated forces — including lethal operations conducted with the use of unmanned aerial vehicles — great care is taken to adhere to these principles in both planning and execution, to ensure that only legitimate objectives are targeted and that collateral damage is kept to a minimum.

Recently, a number of legal objections have been raised against U.S. targeting practices. While today is obviously not the occasion for a detailed legal opinion responding to each of these objections, let me briefly address four:

First, some have suggested that the very act of targeting a particular leader of an enemy force in an armed conflict must violate the laws of war. But individuals who are part of such an armed group are belligerents and, therefore, lawful targets under international law. During World War II, for example, American aviators tracked and shot down the airplane carrying the architect of the Japanese attack on Pearl Harbor, who was also the leader of enemy forces in the Battle of Midway. This was a lawful operation then, and would be if conducted today. Indeed, targeting particular indi-viduals serves to narrow the focus when force is employed and to avoid broader harm to civilians and civilian objects.

Second, some have challenged the very use of advanced weapons systems, such as unmanned aerial vehicles, for lethal operations. But the rules that govern targeting do not turn on the type of weapon system used, and there is no prohibition under the laws of war on the use of technologically advanced weapons systems in armed conflict — such as pilotless aircraft or so-called smart bombs — so long as they are employed in conformity with applicable laws of war. Indeed, using such advanced technologies can ensure both that the best intelligence is available for planning operations, and that civilian casualties are minimized in carrying out such operations.

Third, some have argued that the use of lethal force against specific individuals fails to provide adequate process and thus constitutes unlawful extrajudicial killing. But a state that is engaged in an armed conflict or in legitimate self-defense is not required to provide targets with legal process before the state may use lethal force. Our procedures and practices for identifying lawful targets are extremely robust, and advanced technologies have helped to make our targeting even more precise. In my experience, the principles of distinction and proportionality that the United States applies are not just recited at meetings. They are implemented rigorously throughout the planning and execution of lethal operations to ensure that such operations are conducted in accordance with all applicable law. . . .

In sum, let me repeat: as in the area of detention operations, this Administration is committed to ensuring that the targeting practices that I have described are lawful.

NOTES AND QUESTIONS

1. *Interpreting IHL.* Based on your understanding of the basic principles of IHL reviewed in Chapter 9, is the Israeli government policy of preventative strikes lawful? Why didn't the Court say whether the policy of preventative strikes is always lawful or always unlawful?

2. *Classifying the Conflict.* Was the Second Intifada an international armed conflict? If the Geneva Conventions do not clearly answer the classification question in Israel, what other sources of law should be consulted? Of what legal and practical importance is the answer to the classification question?

The Special Rapporteur for the Human Rights Committee of the United Nations provided this assessment of what constitutes a non-international armed conflict:

> The tests for the existence of a non-international armed conflict are not as categorical as those for international armed conflict. This recognizes the fact that there may be various types of non-international armed conflicts. The applicable test may also depend on whether a State is party to Additional Protocol II to the Geneva Conventions. [Recall from Chapter 9 that the United States is not a party to AP II.] Under treaty and customary international law, the elements which would point to the existence of a non-international armed conflict against a non-state armed group are:
>
> (i) The non-state armed group must be identifiable as such, based on criteria that are objective and verifiable. This is necessary for IHL to apply meaningfully, and so that States may comply with their obligation to distinguish between lawful targets and civilians. The criteria include:
>   * Minimal level of organization
>   * Capability of the group to apply the Geneva Conventions (i.e., adequate command structure, and separation of military and political command)
>   * Engagement of the group in collective, armed, anti-government action
>   * For a conflict involving a State, the State uses its regular military forces against the group

- Admission of the conflict against the group to the agenda of the UN Security Council or the General Assembly

(ii) There must be a minimal threshold of intensity and duration. The threshold of violence is higher than required for the existence of an international armed conflict. To meet the minimum threshold, violence must be:
- "Beyond the level of intensity of internal disturbances and tensions, such as riots, isolated and sporadic acts of violence and other acts of a similar nature" (AP II).
- "[P]rotracted armed violence" among non-state armed groups or between a non-state armed group and a State;
- If an isolated incident, the incident itself should be of a high degree of intensity, with a high level of organization on the part of the non-state armed group;

(iii) The territorial confines can be:
- Restricted to the territory of a State and between the State's own armed forces and the non-state group (AP II); or
- A transnational conflict, i.e., one that crosses State borders (GC Art. 3). This does not mean, however, that there is no territorial nexus requirement.

Addendum: Study on Targeted Killings, supra p. 400.

Applying the Special Rapporteur's analysis, is the United States engaged in an armed conflict with Al Qaeda, the Taliban, and associated forces outside Iraq and Afghanistan? How important are the duration and intensity of the attacks, the closeness of ties among the attackers? Does this analysis account for changing conditions, say, in Pakistan or Yemen? If the United States is not engaged in an armed conflict in those places, is the only lawful means for countering those groups the use of law enforcement methods? What legal theories might then support the U.S. targeting operations? *See* Michael N. Schmitt, *21st Century Conflict: Can the Law Survive?*, 8 Melbourne J. Int'l L. 443, 458-468 (2007) (asymmetric warfare with non-state actors stresses IHL *in bello* rules); Eyal Benvinisti, *The Legal Battle to Define the Law on Transnational Asymmetric Warfare*, 20 Duke J. Comp. & Int'l L. 339 (2010) (same).

In what respects does State Department Legal Adviser Harold Koh disagree with the Special Rapporteur concerning the nature of the conflict the United States is fighting? Do his "considerations specific to each case," along with commitments to follow IHL principles of distinction and proportionality, satisfactorily respond to the Special Rapporteur's concerns? Are his historical examples on point? If not, what more is needed?

3. *Self-Defense?* The international law right of self-defense that Koh relies on to support U.S. actions is described in Chapter 12. Is the self-defense argument persuasive in relation to the terrorist and insurgent groups? How does the international law of self-defense fit, if at all, alongside IHL? (Domestic law authorities are considered in the next part of this chapter.)

4. *Status of Individuals Involved in the Conflict.* On what basis did the Israeli Supreme Court determine the status of the terrorist organizations and their members? Does Article 4 of the Third Geneva Convention (*supra* p. 237) answer the question? Is the netherworld between combatants and civilians unregulated by IHL? Are you persuaded that IHL should not regulate the third category of unlawful combatants? If so, is it because the IHL principle that permits targeting civilians taking direct part in hostilities provides the necessary authority? Taking into account

the Court's opinion in *Committee Against Torture* and the materials in Chapter 9, can you offer guidance to Israeli Defense Force (IDF) officials on when civilians may be targeted?

Is HRL clearer? Should it apply in this context? Did the Israeli Court apply HRL? Do you think the *McCann* precedent and the principle of proportionality require the IDF to try to arrest and detain rather than target the suspect individuals? Or does proportionality justify targeting individuals so long as the harm to innocent civilians is proportionate to the military gains? What is meant by what the Court called the "central normative test" for proportionality?

The U.N. Special Rapporteur offered the following perspective on targeting civilians who directly participate in hostilities:

There are three key controversies over DPH [direct participation in hostilities]. First, there is dispute over the kind of conduct that constitutes "direct participation" and makes an individual subject to attack. Second, there is disagreement over the extent to which "membership" in an organized armed group may be used as a factor in determining whether a person is directly participating in hostilities. Third, there is controversy over how long direct participation lasts.

It is not easy to arrive at a definition of direct participation that protects civilians and at the same time does not "reward" an enemy that may fail to distinguish between civilians and lawful military targets, that may deliberately hide among civilian populations and put them at risk, or that may force civilians to engage in hostilities. The key, however, is to recognize that regardless of the enemy's tactics, in order to protect the vast majority of civilians, direct participation may only include conduct close to that of a fighter, or conduct that directly supports combat. More attenuated acts, such as providing financial support, advocacy, or other non-combat aid, does not constitute direct participation.

Some types of conduct have long been understood to constitute direct participation, such as civilians who shoot at State forces or commit acts of violence in the context of hostilities that would cause death or injury to civilians. Other conduct has traditionally been excluded from direct participation, even if it supports the general war effort; such conduct includes political advocacy, supplying food or shelter, or economic support and propaganda (all also protected under other human rights standards). Even if these activities ultimately impact hostilities, they are not considered "direct participation." But there is a middle ground, such as for the proverbial "farmer by day, fighter by night," that has remained unclear and subject to uncertainty.

In 2009, the ICRC issued its Interpretive Guidance on DPH, which provides a useful starting point for discussion. In non-international armed conflict, according to the ICRC Guidance, civilians who participate directly in hostilities and are members of an armed group who have a "continuous combat function" may be targeted at all times and in all places. With respect to the temporal duration of DPH for all other civilians, the ICRC Guidance takes the view that direct participation for civilians is limited to each single act: the earliest point of direct participation would be the concrete preparatory measures for that specific act (e.g., loading bombs onto a plane), and participation terminates when the activity ends.

Under the ICRC's Guidance, each specific act by the civilian must meet three cumulative requirements to constitute DPH:

(i)   There must be a "threshold of harm" that is objectively likely to result from the act, either by adversely impacting the military operations or capacity of the opposing

party, or by causing the loss of life or property of protected civilian persons or
objects; and

(ii)   The act must cause the expected harm directly, in one step, for example, as an
integral part of a specific and coordinated combat operation (as opposed to harm
caused in unspecified future operations); and

(iii) The act must have a "belligerent nexus" — i.e., it must be specifically designed to
support the military operations of one party to the detriment of another.

Addendum: Study on Targeted Killings, supra. How do the criteria suggested by the
Special Rapporteur and the ICRC differ from those employed by the Israeli Supreme
Court? From the approach of the United States explained by Legal Adviser Koh? If the
direct participation test is not met, what legal authorities govern targeting? Does the
"continuous combat function" designator provide needed flexibility or unbridled
discretion for the targeting personnel?

If U.S. military personnel determine that a U.S. citizen is taking a direct part in
hostilities in Afghanistan or Yemen against the United States, do you see any IHL
principles that would stand in the way of carrying out the operation?

5. *Who May Conduct a Targeted Killing?* Assuming the existence of an armed conflict, may targeted killings lawfully be committed by agents of a state who are not
members of its armed forces? Consider the views of the Special Rapporteur:

Under IHL, civilians, including intelligence agents, are not prohibited from participating in hostilities. Rather, the consequence of participation is two-fold. First, because they
are "directly participating in hostilities" by conducting targeted killings, intelligence
personnel may themselves be targeted and killed. Second, intelligence personnel do
not have immunity from prosecution under domestic law for their conduct. They are
thus unlike State armed forces which would generally be immune from prosecution for
the same conduct (assuming they complied with IHL requirements). Thus,
CIA personnel could be prosecuted for murder under the domestic law of any country
in which they conduct targeted drone killings, and could also be prosecuted for violations of applicable US law.

It is important to note that if a targeted killing violates IHL (by, for example,
targeting civilians who were not "directly participating in hostilities"), then regardless
of who conducts it — intelligence personnel or State armed forces — the author, as well
as those who authorized it, can be prosecuted for war crimes.

Additionally, unlike a State's armed forces, its intelligence agents do not generally
operate within a framework which places appropriate emphasis upon ensuring compliance with IHL, rendering violations more likely and causing a higher risk of prosecution
both for war crimes and for violations of the laws of the State in which any killing occurs.
To the extent a State uses intelligence agents for targeted killing to shield its operations
from IHL and human rights law transparency and accountability requirements, it could
also incur State responsibility for violating those requirements. . . .

Addendum: Study on Targeted Killings, supra. Does it make sense legally to authorize the
CIA to engage in targeted killings but not to immunize them from prosecution? In the
ongoing counterterrorism campaign against Al Qaeda, the Taliban, and associated
groups, who would prosecute CIA or contract personnel for war crimes? Do you think
that the CIA could earn immunity from prosecution by demonstrating that its agents

are trained in IHL? That they or contract personnel are subject to accountability mechanisms that approximate a chain of command?

6. *Targeting bin Laden Redux.* Was the killing of Osama bin Laden by U.S. Navy Seals in Abbottabad, Pakistan, on May 1, 2011, lawful under IHL and other parts of international law? Review the *in bello* rules applied by the Israeli Supreme Court. *See also* Melzer, *supra* p. 386, at 426-427 (during armed conflict, a targeted killing must be "likely to contribute effectively to the achievement of a concrete and direct military advantage without there being an equivalent non-lethal alternative," and abide by principles of distinction and proportionality and any other precautionary measures required by IHL.) If there was no armed conflict in Abbottabad, is there *any* legal justification at international law for using lethal force against bin Laden? If so, what is it? *Compare* Koh, *supra* p. 397, *with* Thomas Darnstadt, *Was Bin Laden's Killing Legal?*, Spiegel Online, May 3, 2011, *at* http://www.spiegel.de/international/world/0,1518,druck-760358,00.html (suggesting that it is not clear that, at the time of his death, bin Laden commanded an organization that was conducting an armed conflict in or from Pakistan).

7. *Targeting Qadhafi.* If U.S. or NATO forces execute a similar operation to kill Colonel Muammar Qadhafi in Libya as part of operations to implement U.N. Security Council Resolution 1973, *supra* p. 255, how would the legal analysis of the targeting differ from the legal framework that applied to killing bin Laden?

D. U.S. LAW AND EXECUTIVE ORDER NO. 12,333

In 1976, a congressional committee found evidence of CIA involvement in assassination plots against foreign leaders (including President Ngo Dinh Diem of South Vietnam, who was murdered in a coup, and General René Schneider of Chile, who died in a kidnapping attempt), but it was unable to determine whether such involvement had been approved by senior officials. *See* Select Comm. to Study Governmental Operations with Respect to Intelligence Activities (Church Comm.), *Alleged Assassination Plots Involving Foreign Leaders*, S. Rep. No. 94-465 (1975) (*Church Comm. Report*). The CIA acknowledged, however, that it subsequently made payments to the Schneider kidnappers. *See* Central Intelligence Agency, *CIA Activities in Chile*, Sept. 18, 2000, *at* https://www.cia.gov/cia/reports/chile/index.html#15. When the Church Committee proposed legislation to forbid political assassination, the Ford administration preemptively promulgated its own prohibition by executive order. The prohibition was carried forward, with slight modifications, in Executive Order No. 12,333, 46 Fed. Reg. 59,941 (Dec. 4, 1981), which remains in effect at this writing (see *infra* p. 451):

> 2.11 Prohibition on Assassination. No person employed by or acting on behalf of the United States Government shall engage in, or conspire to engage in, assassination.
> 2.12 Indirect Participation. No agency of the Intelligence Community shall participate in or request any person to undertake activities forbidden by this Order....

Partly owing to this prohibition, military actions against terrorists or their supporters have usually been planned so as to avoid any appearance of targeting specific persons.

W. Hays Parks, Memorandum of Law:
Executive Order 12333 and Assassination

Dep't of the Army Pamphlet 27-50-204, *reprinted in* Army Law. 4 (Dec. 1989)

1. *Summary.* Executive Order 12333 prohibits assassination as a matter of national policy, but does not expound on its meaning or application. This memorandum explores the term and analyzes application of the ban to military operations at three levels: (a) conventional military operations; (b) counterinsurgency operations; and (c) peacetime counterterrorist operations. It concludes that the clandestine, low visibility, or overt use of military force against legitimate targets in time of war, or against similar targets in time of peace where such individuals or groups pose an immediate threat to United States citizens or the national security of the United States, as determined by competent authority, does not constitute assassination or conspiracy to engage in assassination, and would not be prohibited by the proscription in EO 12333 or by international law. . . .

3. a. *Assassination in General.* . . . While assassination generally is regarded as an act of murder for political reasons, its victims are not necessarily limited to persons of public office or prominence. The murder of a private person, if carried out for political purposes, may constitute an act of assassination. For example, the 1978 "poisoned-tip umbrella" killing of Bulgarian defector Georgi Markov by Bulgarian State Security agents on the streets of London falls into the category of an act of murder carried out for political purposes, and constitutes an assassination. In contrast, the murder of Leon Klinghoffer, a private citizen, by the terrorist Abu el Abbas during the 1985 hijacking of the Italian cruise ship *Achille Lauro*, though an act of murder for political purposes, would not constitute an assassination. The distinction lies not merely in the purpose of the act and/or its intended victim, but also under certain circumstances in its covert nature.[1] Finally, the killings of Martin Luther King and Presidents Abraham Lincoln, James A. Garfield, William McKinley and John F. Kennedy generally are regarded as assassination because each involved the murder of a public figure or national leader for political purposes accomplished through a surprise attack.

b. *Assassination in Peacetime.* In peacetime, the citizens of a nation — whether private individuals or public figures — are entitled to immunity from intentional acts of violence by citizens, agents, or military forces of another nation. . . .

Peacetime assassination, then, would seem to encompass the murder of a private individual or public figure for political purposes, and in some cases also require that the act constitute a covert activity, particularly when the individual is a private citizen. Assassination is unlawful killing, and would be prohibited by international law even if there were no executive order proscribing it.

c. *Assassination in Wartime.* . . . In wartime the role of the military includes the legalized killing (as opposed to murder) of the enemy, whether lawful combatants

---

1. *Covert operations* are defined as "operations which are planned and executed so as to conceal the identity of or permit plausible denial by the sponsor. They differ from clandestine operations in that emphasis is placed on concealment of identity of [the] sponsor rather than on concealment of the operation." In contrast, low visibility operations are . . . undertaken with the knowledge that the action and or sponsorship of the operation may preclude plausible denial by the initiating power. JCS Pub. 1, *Dictionary of Military and Associated Terms* (1 June 1987).

or unprivileged belligerents, and may include in either category civilians who take part in the hostilities.

The term *assassination* when applied to wartime military activities against enemy combatants or military objectives does not preclude acts of violence involving the element of surprise. Combatants are liable to attack at any time or place, regardless of their activity when attacked.... An individual combatant's vulnerability to lawful targeting (as opposed to assassination) is not dependent upon his or her military duties, or proximity to combat as such. Nor does the prohibition on assassination limit means that otherwise would be lawful; no distinction is made between an attack accomplished by aircraft, missile, naval gunfire, artillery, mortar, infantry assault, ambush, land mine or boobytrap, a single shot by a sniper, a commando attack, or other, similar means. All are lawful means for attacking the enemy and the choice of one vis-a-vis another has no bearing on the legality of the attack. If the person attacked is a combatant, the use of a particular lawful means for attack (as opposed to another) cannot make an otherwise lawful attack either unlawful or an assassination.

Likewise, the death of noncombatants ancillary to the lawful attack of a military objective is neither assassination nor otherwise unlawful. Civilians and other noncombatants who are within or in close proximity to a military objective assume a certain risk through their presence in or in proximity to such targets....

The scope of assassination in the U.S. military was first outlined in U.S. Army General Orders No. 100 (1863). Paragraph 148 states

> *Assassination.* The law of war does not allow proclaiming either an individual belonging to the hostile army, or a citizen, or a subject of the hostile government, an outlaw, who may be slain without trial by any captor, any more than the modern law of peace allows such international outlawry; on the contrary, it abhors such outrage....

This provision, consistent with the earlier writings of Hugo Grotius (Cf. Bk, III, Sec. XXXVIII(4)), has been continued in U.S. Army Field Manual 27-10, *The Law of Land Warfare* (1956), which provides (paragraph 31):

> Article 23b, Annex to Hague Convention IV, 1907) is construed as prohibiting assassination, proscription, or outlawry of an enemy, or putting a price upon an enemy's head, as well as offering reward for an enemy "dead or alive."...

[4]. *Conventional War.* . . . [An] unresolved issue concerns which civilians may be regarded as combatants, and therefore subject to lawful attack. While there is general agreement among the law of war experts that civilians who participate in hostilities may be regarded as combatants, there is no agreement as to the degree of participation necessary to make an individual civilian a combatant.... There is a lack of agreement on this matter, and no existing law of war treaty provides clarification or assistance. Historically, however, the decision as to the level at which civilians may be regarded as combatants or "quasi-combatants" and thereby subject to attack generally has been a policy rather than legal matter....

[5]. *Counterinsurgency.* Guerrilla warfare is particularly difficult to address because a guerrilla organization generally is divided into political and guerrilla (military) cadre, each garbed in civilian attire in order to conceal their presence or movement from the enemy....

Just as members of conventional military units have an obligation to wear uniforms in order to distinguish themselves from the civilian population, civilians have an obligation to refrain from actions that might place the civilian population at risk. A civilian who undertakes military activities assumes a risk of attack, and efforts by military forces to capture or kill that individual would not constitute assassination.

The wearing of civilian attire does not make a guerrilla immune from lawful attack, and does not make a lawful attack on a guerrilla an act of assassination. As with the attack of civilians who have combatant responsibilities in conventional war, the difficulty lies in determining where the line should be drawn between guerrillas/combatants and the civilian population in order to provide maximum protection from intentional attack to innocent civilians. The law provides no precise answer to this problem, and one of the most heated debates arising during and after the U.S. war in Vietnam surrounded this issue.however, ultimately the issue is settled along policy rather than legal lines. If a member of a guerrilla organization falls above the line established by competent authority for combatants, a military operation to capture or kill an individual designated as a combatant would not be assassination.

[6]. *Peacetime operations.* The use of force in peacetime is limited by . . . article 2(4) of the Charter of the United Nations [*supra* p. 211]. However, article 51 of the Charter of the United Nations recognizes the inherent right of self defense of nations. Historically the United States has resorted to the use of military force in peacetime where another nation has failed to discharge its international responsibilities in protecting U.S. citizens from acts of violence originating in or launched from its sovereign territory, or has been culpable in aiding and abetting international criminal activities. For example:

— 1804-1805: Marine First Lieutenant Presley O'Bannon led an expedition into Libya to capture or kill[6] the Barbary pirates.

— 1916: General "Blackjack" Pershing led a year-long campaign into Mexico to capture or kill the Mexican bandit Pancho Villa following Villa's attack on Columbus, New Mexico.

— 1928-1932: U.S. Marines conducted a successful campaign to capture or kill the Nicaraguan bandit leader Augusto Cesar Sandino.

— 1967: U.S. Army personnel assisted the Bolovian Army in its campaign to capture or kill Ernesto "Che" Guevara.

— 1985: U.S. naval forces were used to force an Egypt Air airliner to land at Sigonella, Sicily, in an attempt to prevent the escape of the *Achille Lauro* hijackers.

— 1986: U.S. naval and air forces attacked terrorist-related targets in Libya in response to the Libyan government's continued employment of terrorism as a foreign policy means.

6. In the employment of military force, the phrase "capture or kill" carries the same meaning or connotation in peacetime as it does in wartime. There is no obligation to capture rather than attack an enemy. In some cases, it may be preferable to utilize ground forces to capture (*e.g.*) a known terrorist. However, where the risk to U.S. forces is deemed too great, if the President has determined that the individual(s) pose such a threat to U.S. citizens as to require the use of military force, it would be legally permissible to employ (*e.g.*) an air strike against that individual or group rather than attempt his, her, or their capture, and would not constitute assassination.

Hence there is historical precedent for the use of military force to capture or kill individuals whose peacetime actions constitute a direct threat to U.S. citizens or national security.

The Charter of the United Nations recognizes the inherent right of self defense and does not preclude unilateral action against an immediate threat.

In general terms, the United States recognizes three forms of self defense:

a. Against an actual use of force, or hostile act.

b. Preemptive self defense against an imminent use of force.

c. Self defense against a continuing threat.[8]

A national decision to employ military force in self defense against a legitimate terrorist or related threat would not be unlike the employment of force in response to a threat by conventional forces; only the nature of the threat has changed, rather than the international legal right of self defense. The terrorist organizations envisaged as appropriate to necessitate or warrant an armed response by U.S. military forces are well-financed, highly-organized paramilitary structures engaged in the illegal use of force.[9]. . . .

NOTES AND QUESTIONS

1. *The Origins of the Executive Order Ban on Assassination.* As noted above, in 1976 the Church Committee proposed to criminalize the assassination or attempted assassination of "any foreign official because of such official's political views, actions, or statements, while such official is outside the United States." *Church Committee Report, supra* p. 403, at App. A. "Foreign official" was defined as "Chief of State or the political equivalent . . . of a foreign government . . . or of a foreign political group, party, military force, movement or other association with which the United States is not at war pursuant to a declaration of war or against which the United States Armed Forces have not been introduced into hostilities or situations pursuant to the provisions of the War Powers Resolution." *Id.*

However, President Ford headed off such legislation by adopting Executive Order No. 11,905, 41 Fed. Reg. 7703 (Feb. 19, 1976), prohibiting U.S. employees from engaging in "political assassination." In 1978, President Carter replaced this order with Executive Order No. 12,036, 43 Fed. Reg. 3674 (Jan. 26, 1978), which expanded the prohibition to include agents of the United States, and which dropped, without explanation, the modifier "political." President Reagan retained Carter's language as sections 2.11 and 2.12 in the still-current Executive Order No. 12,333, set out above. *See generally* William C. Banks & Peter Raven-Hansen, *Targeted Killing and*

---

8. . . . This right of self defense would be appropriate to the attack of terrorist leaders where their actions pose a continuing threat to U.S. citizens or the national security of the United States. As with an attack on a guerrilla infrastructure, the level to which attacks could be carried out against individuals within a terrorist infrastructure would be a policy rather than a legal decision.

9. In a conventional armed conflict, such individuals would be regarded as unprivileged belligerents, subject to attack, but not entitled to prisoner of war protection or exemption from prosecution for their crimes. Employment of military force against terrorists does not bestow prisoner of war protection upon members of the terrorist organization.

Assassination: The U.S. Legal Framework, 37 U. Rich. L. Rev. 667, 717-726 (2003); Jonathan M. Fredman, *Covert Action, Loss of Life, and the Prohibition on Assassination*, 1 Stud. Intelligence 15 (1997 unclassified ed.).

The Legal Adviser to the Department of State has argued that "the use of lawful weapons systems — consistent with the applicable laws of war — for precision targeting of specific high-level belligerent leaders when acting in self-defense or during an armed conflict is not unlawful, and hence does not constitute 'assassination'" under the executive order. Koh, *supra* p. 397. Is that argument consistent with the history of the order?

2. *Who May Be Targeted?*

a. *Saddam Hussein?* Would the executive order have barred the killing of Saddam Hussein, leader of Iraq, in 1991 during the first Gulf War, or in 2003, during the invasion of Iraq? *See* Stuart Taylor Jr., *Should We Just Kill Saddam?*, Legal Times, Feb. 4, 1991.

b. *Manuel Noriega?* Would the prohibition have applied to General Manuel Antonio Noriega, leader of Panama? In 1989 the CIA was approached for help by Panamanian military officers who proposed a coup against Noriega after he nullified a national election that he had lost. The officers sought nonlethal assistance in the form of money and equipment, but they admitted that Noriega might be killed in the coup. Could the U.S. have legally furnished assistance? *See* David B. Ottaway & Don Oberdorfer, *Administration Alters Assassination Ban*, Wash. Post, Nov. 4, 1989; David B. Ottaway, *CIA Aides Call Hill Rules No Hindrance*, Wash. Post, Oct. 18, 1989.

c. *Pablo Escobar?* How about targeting Colombian drug trafficker Pablo Escobar, who reportedly conducted a campaign of narco-terror and assassination against the government of Colombia, and who was indicted in the United States for drug trafficking and multiple drug-related murders? *See* Mark Bowden, *Killing Pablo* (2001) (asserting that U.S. Special Forces were actively involved in his death).

d. *The "Gucci Guys" Who Finance Terror?* After the September 11 terrorist attacks, some argued that the United States should go beyond targeting terrorist leaders. Consider the following recommendation:

> The United States should adopt a[n assassination] program aimed not only at the heads of the [terrorist] networks, but also at the arms and the fingers. It should locate and assassinate the killers, the planners, and the trainers. It should go beyond the organizations to target those who finance them and those who tend to communications and logistics. The program should target officials of the governments that give terrorists shelter. None should feel safe who knowingly aid these organizations — whether they launder their money or their clothes. [Lawrence J. Siskind, *Our Killer Instinct*, Legal Times, Oct. 8, 2001.]

Would such a program be lawful under the executive order? Would it be wise, now that we have learned that the "arms and fingers" of the group that executed the September 11 attacks apparently made significant preparations in Germany and that they had financing from institutions in Switzerland and Saudi Arabia? *See* Barton Gellman, *CIA Weighs "Targeted Killing" Missions*, Wash. Post, Oct. 28, 2001 (reporting that senior managers in CIA's Directorate of Operations urged targeting not just Al Qaeda's commanders, but also its financiers — "the Gucci guys, the guys who write the checks," because they are easier to find and because "it would have a tremendously chilling effect"). *See* Daniel Byman, *Do Targeted Killings Work?* 85 For. Aff. 95 (2006).

3. *Force and Effect of the Executive Order Ban.* How do you think the legal force of the executive order ban was affected by President Reagan's 1984 secret intelligence findings authorizing lethal operations against Libyan leader Muammar al-Qadhafi (*see* Bob Woodward & Walter Pincus, *1984 Order Gave CIA Latitude; Reagan's Secret Move to Counter Terrorists Called "License to Kill,"* Wash. Post, Oct. 5, 1988)? How about orders to kill bin Laden from President Clinton (*see* James Risen, *Bin Laden Was Target of Afghan Raid, U.S. Confirms,* N.Y. Times, Nov. 14, 1998), President George W. Bush, and President Obama? How would you assess President Obama's order for lethal operations against Anwar al-Aulaqi? *See* David Johnston & David E. Sanger, *Fatal Strike in Yemen Was Based on Rules Set Out by Bush,* N.Y. Times, Nov. 6, 2002; Scott Shane, *U.S. Approves Targeted Killing of American Cleric,* N.Y. Times, Apr. 6, 2010. *See* Memorandum from Acting Asst. Attorney General Randolph D. Moss to the President, *Legal Effectiveness of a Presidential Directive as Compared to an Executive Order,* Jan. 29, 2000 (concluding that presidential directives — and, by implication, findings — can have the same substantive legal effect as an executive order, and that any such presidential decision, however it is memorialized, remains effective upon a change in administration and until subsequent presidential action is taken). *See also* Banks & Raven-Hansen, *supra* p. 408, 37 U. Rich. L. Rev. at 725-726.

In the wake of the September 11 attacks, Rep. Bob Barr introduced the Terrorist Elimination Act of 2001, which provided that sections 2.11 and 2.12 of Executive Order No. 12,333 "shall have no further force or effect." H.R. 19, 107th Cong. (2001). Is such a law necessary to permit the military to use military strikes to remove a terrorist leader, as the bill's proposed findings indicate? Would it be constitutional? *See* Banks & Raven-Hansen, *supra,* 37 U. Rich. L. Rev. at 745-747.

4. *Targeted Killing at Home?* All the discussions about the executive order contemplate targeted killings or assassinations of foreign persons *abroad.* But is the order so restricted geographically?

A variety of domestic laws, in addition to ordinary criminal laws, seemingly prohibit the use of such tools against any person in the United States. *See, e.g.,* U.S. Const. amend. V (providing that "no person" shall be deprived of life "without due process of law"); Posse Comitatus Act, 18 U.S.C. §1385 (2006), *infra* p. 1147 (prohibiting the Army or Air Force from executing the laws without express constitutional or statutory authority); National Security Act of 1947, 50 U.S.C. §403-4a(d)(1) (2006) (prohibiting the CIA from performing "internal security functions"); *Idaho v. Horiuchi,* 253 F.3d 359, 377 (9th Cir.) (asserting, in a suit growing out of the Ruby Ridge killing by an FBI sharpshooter, that "wartime rules" of engagement permitting the targeting of suspects who pose no "immediate threat... [are] patently unconstitutional for a police action"), *vacated as moot,* 266 F.3d 986 (9th Cir. 2001).

Even assuming that the President could disregard these authorities, would a targeted killing of Ayman al-Zawahiri, the presumptive head of Al Qaeda after bin Laden's death, as he stepped off a civilian airline flight at O'Hare Airport in Chicago meet *any* of the other standards discussed in these notes?

5. *Costs and Benefits of Targeted Killing.* In 2009, CIA Director Leon Panetta claimed that drone strikes have been very effective because they have been very

precise in their targeting and involved a minimum amount of collateral damage. Charles Cooper, *No Longer a Debate About Targeted Killing*, CBSnews.com, July 21, 2010, http://www.cbsnews.com/stories/2009/07/21/opinion/main5176876.shtml. Targeted killing of the leaders of a terrorist group can change the group's organizational behavior. Elimination of its leaders may cause confusion and disarray; successors may become paranoid and secretive, impeding their ability to communicate with members; and members may become fearful about communicating even with one another. The terrorists may spend more and more of their time protecting themselves, with correspondingly less time to attack others. *See, e.g.,* Byman, *supra* p. 409, at 102-104 (reporting significant drop-off in Israeli civilian deaths from terrorist attacks "partly because Israel's targeted killings have shattered Palestinian terrorist groups and made it difficult for them to conduct effective operations"); Gal Luft, *The Logic of Israel's Targeted Killing*, 10 Middle East Q. 1 (Winter 2003). Lives are saved by attacks averted. In addition, the targeted killing of a suspected terrorist may cause fewer casualties (and lower costs) among counterterrorist forces than seeking to arrest him in hostile territory, let alone invading to destroy his group. Eichensehr, *supra* p. 376, at 4. Furthermore, extradition and prosecution may not be viable alternatives to the use of force when the terrorists take refuge in failed or sympathetic states. Finally, targeted killing satisfies domestic demands for the government to "do something" after a society has suffered terrorist attacks. *See* Byman, *supra*, at 102. Can you identify other benefits from targeted killing?

On the other hand, targeted killings carry significant costs as well. Terrorist groups adjust to decapitation; their decentralization largely negates the disruptive effect by creating many, or no, leaders. Successful targeted killing requires a heavy investment in real-time continuing intelligence and surveillance, as well as rapid response capability. Byman, *supra*, at 100 (quoting a former Israeli intelligence director as saying, "When a Palestinian child draws a picture of the sky, he doesn't draw it without a helicopter."). Even a successful killing may create a martyr for the terrorists, and perversely help them to recruit others, and it will often prompt retaliation. Finally, as the discussion of international law should suggest and the tense relationship between the United States and Pakistan after U.S. targeted killings inside Pakistani territory proves, targeted killing carries serious diplomatic costs, not just for negotiations to end the terrorism or to coordinate allies in the counterterrorist effort, but also for diplomatic efforts to condemn targeted killing by other states. Can you think of other costs of targeted killing? Should we include a moral cost in the calculus?

How would you balance costs and benefits of targeted killings by the United States in Afghanistan? In Northern Pakistan? In Yemen?

Humanitarian and Peace Operations 15

An increasingly frequent and important use of U.S. armed forces abroad is their deployment in circumstances where engagement in armed conflict is not the objective, or at least is not the primary objective. Some of these missions, including those responding to famines and other natural disasters, are strictly humanitarian. Others are mainly concerned with establishing or preserving peace or stability. In others, the mission is both humanitarian and strategic, as in military interventions to stop a government from engaging in genocide or ethnic cleansing of its own people, when the internal conflict threatens to spill across national borders. In a growing number of such missions the Defense Department works with other federal agencies (such as the U.S. Agency for International Development), indigenous militaries, international organizations (such as the United Nations), foreign partners, nongovernmental organizations (NGOs) (such as the International Committee of the Red Cross), and contractors to provide noncombat foreign assistance. It also conducts extensive training of foreign forces. These operations are variously described as relief efforts, peacekeeping, nation-building, or stabilization and reconstruction, among other terms. But the labels are sometimes imprecise, they may overlap, and they may change in the midst of a given operation.[1]

Congress has declared that "prompt United States assistance to alleviate human suffering caused by natural and manmade disasters is an important expression of the humanitarian concern and tradition of the people of the United States." 22 U.S.C. §2292(a) (2006). Disaster relief may also serve U.S. strategic needs by restoring stability and fostering good will in the affected areas. U.S. military forces have often played a key role in providing humanitarian assistance abroad, because they uniquely possess the transport capacity, personnel, and equipment to respond quickly where needed. When monsoon-triggered floods submerged almost one-fifth of Pakistan in 2010, for example, U.S. military fixed-wing aircraft and helicopters, as well as ground forces, delivered 25 million pounds of food, water, and other relief supplies to victims, built bridges, rescued thousands of people, and evacuated many more. Also in 2010, some 22,000 U.S. service members ferried supplies, provided medical assistance, and performed engineering and construction work in Haiti after a devastating earthquake there.

---

1. *See generally* Nina M. Serafino et al., *The Department of Defense Role in Foreign Assistance: Background, Major Issues, and Options for Congress* (Cong. Res. Serv. RL34639), Dec. 9, 2008; Nina M. Serafino, *Peacekeeping and Related Stability Operations: Issues of U.S. Military Involvement* (Cong. Res. Serv. RL33557), Jan. 24, 2007.

The Defense Department also sends its personnel abroad to help maintain or restore the peace, many under the auspices of the United Nations Security Council or NATO. In principle, "peacekeeping" forces are deployed in "transition situations where a state lacks capacity to manage affairs to assure domestic or international tranquility, yet the use of force in the traditional sense of armed conflict is not contemplated."[2] Such deployments often come at the end of armed hostilities and usually involve the use of unarmed or lightly armed personnel to police or "observe" cease-fires or armistices with the consent of the parties involved. Unfortunately, they may meet armed opposition from remnants of defeated armies or groups, or from insurgents.

"Peacemaking" interventions — in "situation[s] where the use of force in the traditional sense of armed conflict may be employed to restore tranquility"[3] — pose greater risks. These involve the deployment of armed forces into hostilities with the mission of using force to halt or limit the fighting, usually without the consent of all the contending parties.

U.S. Navy sailor carries a young earthquake victim in Haiti, Jan. 23, 2010.

DOD photo by Jim Garamone.

2. *See* George K. Walker, *United States National Security Law and United Nations Peacekeeping or Peacemaking Operations*, 29 Wake Forest L. Rev. 435, 445-446 (1994) (making the distinction and citing examples); Rajendra Ramlogan, *Towards a Vision of World Security: The United Nations Security Council and the Lessons of Somalia*, 16 Hous. J. Int'l L. 213, 248-250 (1993) (making the distinction).

3. Walker, *supra*, 29 Wake Forest L. Rev. at 445-446. Professor Walker acknowledges that "there is an elusive sliding scale between peacekeeping and peacemaking." *Id.* at 446. *See also* Michael O'Hanlon, *Saving Lives with Force: Military Criteria for Humanitarian Intervention* 7 (Brookings Inst. Press 1997) ("[I]t is probably better to leave the modifier 'peace' entirely out of the terminology and describe it as intervention to restore order."); Jon E. Fink, *From Peacekeeping to Peace Enforcement: The Blurring of the Mandate for the Use of Force in Maintaining International Peace and Security*, 19 Md. J. Int'l L. & Trade 1, 42 (1995) (noting that the distinction is "fading" as peacekeeping missions evolve into peace enforcement).

Toward the end of the twentieth century a new threat emerged that portends human suffering and conflict on a scale unprecedented in human history—climate change. This development will profoundly influence efforts to defend the United States. According to the Director of National Intelligence, "We continue to assess that global climate change will have wide-ranging implications for US national security interests over the next 20 years because it will aggravate existing world problems—such as poverty, social tensions, environmental degradation, ineffectual leadership, and weak political institutions—that threaten state stability."[4] This assessment is shared by the Pentagon: "While climate change alone does not cause conflict, it may act as an accelerant of instability or conflict, placing a burden to respond on civilian institutions and militaries around the world."[5]

The effects of a warming planet are already beginning to be felt. These include coastal flooding, extreme drought and regional water shortages, increased storm events, mass migrations, and the spread of disease. The poverty that accompanies deteriorating economic conditions will foster the growth of terrorism and extremism. Competition for arable land and water supplies will become acute both within and among some states. And some already fragile governments may simply fail.[6]

In response to these developments, the United States almost surely will send military forces abroad more and more often to furnish humanitarian assistance. It is also likely to deploy more troops than in the past on peacekeeping and peace-making missions. These forces will need to be specially trained and equipped, and they must, of course, be prepared to defend themselves from attack. They will also want clear, authoritative guidance in carrying out their missions.

In this chapter we consider various uses of U.S. military forces abroad in which combat is not the primary purpose. In Part A we examine existing international and domestic authorities for such operations. Then in Part B we look closely at one operation in Somalia in 1992 that began as a humanitarian mission and quickly "crossed the Mogadishu line" into something else. In Part C we introduce and briefly analyze the U.S. humanitarian intervention in Libya in early 2011, an operation that had only just begun as this edition of the casebook was completed.

A. AUTHORITY FOR PEACEFUL DEPLOYMENTS

1. International Authorities

Most U.S. noncombat military operations are carried out in conjunction with the United Nations or regional organizations. Since 1948, the U.N. Security Council has launched at least 64 humanitarian, peacekeeping, and stabilization missions. As of early 2011, some 99,000 military and police personnel from 114 countries were deployed in 17 such missions around the world. *See* United Nations Peacekeeping,

---

4. Dennis C. Blair, *Annual Threat Assessment of the US Intelligence Community for the Senate Select Committee on Intelligence*, Feb. 2, 2010, *available at* http://www.dni.gov/testimonies/20100202_testimony.pdf.

5. Department of Defense, *Quadrennial Defense Review Report*, Feb. 2010, at 84, *available at* http://www.defense.gov/qdr/images/QDR_as_of_12Feb10_1000.pdf.

6. Some strategic implications of the effects of climate change are described in U.N. Secretary-General, *Climate Change and Its Possible Security Implications: Rep. of the Secretary-General*, U.N. Doc. A/64/350 (Sept. 11, 2009); James Stuhltrager, *Global Climate Change and National Security*, 22 Nat. Resources & Env't 36 (2008).

Troop and Police Contributors (n.d.), *at* http://www.un.org/en/peacekeeping/ resources/statistics/contributors.shtml.

The U.N. Charter includes no express provision for the use of military forces in humanitarian or other kinds of noncombat missions. Chapter VI, entitled Peaceful Settlement of Disputes, nevertheless declares that

> [t]he Security Council may investigate any dispute, or any situation which might lead to international friction or give rise to a dispute, in order to determine whether the continuance of the dispute or situation is likely to endanger the maintenance of international peace and security. [U.N. Charter art. 34.]

Chapter VII of the Charter authorizes the Security Council to determine the existence of breaches or threats to the peace, and to "decide what measures shall be taken," including "such action by air, sea, or land forces as may be necessary to maintain or restore international peace and security." *Id.* arts. 39, 42. (See *supra* p. 212.) "Dag Hammarskjöld, the second U.N. Secretary-General, referred to peacekeeping as belonging to 'Chapter Six and a Half' of the Charter, placing it between traditional methods of resolving disputes peacefully, such as negotiation and mediation under Chapter VI, and more forceful action as authorized under Chapter VII." *United Nations Peacekeeping* (2010), *at* http://www.un.org/en/peacekeeping/. Procedures and authorities for U.N. peacekeeping operations, with links to relevant documents, are described at United Nations Documentation: Research Guide, *Peacekeeping, at* http://www.un.org/depts/dhl/resguide/specpk.htm#intro (updated Mar. 31, 2011).

According to the United Nations Secretariat, the Security Council authorizes the deployment of peacekeepers only when three principles are satisfied:

1. Consent of the parties. United Nations peacekeeping operations are deployed with the consent of the main parties to the conflict. This requires a commitment by the parties to a political process and their acceptance of a peacekeeping operation mandated to support that process. . . . In the absence of such consent, a United Nations peacekeeping operation risks becoming a party to the conflict; and being drawn towards enforcement action, and away from its intrinsic role of keeping the peace. . . .

2. Impartiality. United Nations peacekeeping operations must implement their mandate without favour or prejudice to any party. Impartiality is crucial to maintaining the consent and cooperation of the main parties, but should not be confused with neutrality or inactivity. United Nations peacekeepers should be impartial in their dealings with the parties to the conflict, but not neutral in the execution of their mandate. . . .

3. Non-use of force except in self-defense and defense of the mandate. . . . The environments into which United Nations peacekeeping operations are deployed are often characterized by the presence of militias, criminal gangs, and other spoilers who may actively seek to undermine the peace process or pose a threat to the civilian population. In such situations, the Security Council has given United Nations peacekeeping operations "robust" mandates authorizing them to "use all necessary means" to deter forceful attempts to disrupt the political process, protect civilians under imminent threat of physical attack, and/or assist the national authorities in maintaining law and order. . . .

Although on the ground they may sometimes appear similar, robust peacekeeping should not be confused with peace enforcement, as envisaged under Chapter VII of the Charter. Robust peacekeeping involves the use of force at the tactical level with the authorization of the Security Council and consent of the host nation and/or the main parties to the conflict. By contrast, peace enforcement does not require the consent of the main parties and may involve the use of military force at the strategic or international level, which is normally prohibited for Member States under Article 2(4) of the Charter, unless authorized by the Security Council.

A United Nations peacekeeping operation should only use force as a measure of last resort, when other methods of persuasion have been exhausted. . . . [*United Nations Peacekeeping Operations: Principles and Guidelines* 32-35 (2008), *available at* http://www. peacekeepingbestpractices.unlb.org/Pbps/Library/Capstone_Doctrine_ENG.pdf.]

The United States has adopted additional criteria for lending its troops to peace operations under either Chapter VI or Chapter VII:

A.   Participation advances U.S. interests and both the unique and general risks to American personnel have been weighed and are considered acceptable.
B.   Funds, personnel, and other resources are available for U.S. participation.
C.   U.S. participation is necessary for the success of the mission or to persuade other nations or organizations to participate.
D.   The role of U.S. forces is tied to clear objectives and an endpoint for U.S. participation can be identified.
E.   There is domestic political and congressional support for U.S. participation, or such support can be marshalled.
F.   Command and control arrangements governing the participation of American and foreign forces are acceptable to the U.S.

[Presidential Decision Directive/NSC-25, *U.S. Policy on Reforming Multilateral Peace Operations*, May 3, 1994, at Annex II, *available at* http://www.clintonlibrary.gov/_previous/Documents/2010 FOIA/Presidential Directives/PDD-25.pdf.]

Significant U.S. involvement in Chapter VII peace enforcement operations additionally requires the commitment of "sufficient forces to achieve our clearly defined political and military objectives," and a "clear intention of decisively achieving these objectives." *Id.*

NOTES AND QUESTIONS

1. *Authority for Peace Operations.* Are humanitarian and other deployments of military forces on noncombat missions authorized by Chapter VI or Chapter VII of the U.N. Charter? Both? Neither? Does it matter?

2. *The Importance of Labels.* What is the difference between "peacekeeping" and "peace enforcement" operations? Of what legal significance, if any, is the nomenclature? Who is entitled to designate a given operation as one or the other?

3. *Consent of the Parties.* Why is it important that the "main parties" to a conflict consent to the introduction of peacekeeping forces? Who are the main parties? What if the territory into which troops would be introduced has no functioning government?

4. *United States Involvement in Peace Operations.* The U.N. Security Council has always requested — never ordered — contributions of troops by individual member

states to humanitarian and other peace operations. Contributions of U.S. military forces are therefore always voluntary. *United Nations Peacekeeping Operations, supra,* at 52. Given the expense and danger, not to mention possible diplomatic complications, why would the United States ever want to commit its personnel to such an operation?

What is the significance of the policy that U.S. participation be "tied to clear objectives" and have an identifiable "endpoint"? Who must approve the objectives? How should "domestic political and congressional support" be determined?

5. *United States Troops Under Foreign Command.* When U.S. troops join peacekeeping forces operating under a U.N. Security Council mandate, they often report to foreign military commanders. President Clinton described U.S. practice:

> As President, I retain and will not relinquish command authority over U.S. forces. On a case-by-case basis, I will consider placing appropriate U.S. forces and personnel under the operational control of a competent UN commander for specific UN operations authorized by the Security Council. . . . The greater the U.S. military role, the less likely it will be that I will agree to have a UN commander exercise overall operational control over U.S. forces. Any large scale participation of U.S. forces in a major peace enforcement mission that is likely to involve combat should ordinarily be conducted under U.S. command and operational control or through competent regional organizations such as NATO or ad hoc coalitions. [Presidential Decision Directive/NSC-25, *supra,* at 3.]

"American forces have served under the operational control of foreign commanders since the Revolutionary War, including in World War I, World War II, Operation Desert Storm and in NATO since its inception." *The Clinton Administration's Policy on Reforming Multilateral Peace Operations,* May 1994, at 9, *available at* http://www.fas.org/irp/offdocs/pdd25.htm. *See generally* Edward F. Bruner & Nina M. Serafino, *Peacekeeping: Military Command and Control Issues* (Cong. Res. Serv. RL31120), Nov. 1, 2001.

Despite this history, some argue that the practice poses constitutional problems by ignoring constitutional limits on delegations of federal power outside the national government and by undermining accountability both to the President as Commander in Chief and, indirectly, to Congress. *See, e.g.,* John C. Yoo, *UN Wars, US War Powers,* 1 Chi. J. Int'l L. 355, 367-368 (2000). Others disagree. *See, e.g.,* Andrew J. Bacevich, *The Use of Force in the Clinton Era: Continuity or Discontinuity?* 1 Chi. J. Int'l L. 375, 377-378 (2000) (asserting, with examples, that "the notion that American troops as a matter of principle do not serve under foreign command is simply ahistorical"); Walker, *supra* p. 412, 29 Wake Forest L. Rev. at 441 n.53; David Kaye, *Are There Limits to Military Alliance? Presidential Power to Place American Troops Under Non-American Commanders,* 5 Transnat'l L. & Contemp. Probs. 399, 447 (1995) (President has "historical and constitutional authority to delegate command to non-American partners in military operations."). But could the President's deployment of U.S. troops under foreign command ever surrender his power to call them back or to override foreign commands? *See* Kaye, *supra,* 5 Transnat'l L. & Contemp. Probs. at 447 ("policy command, right of appeal, and the right to discipline" are nondelegable).

Section 8151(b)(2)(B) of the Department of Defense Appropriations Act, 1994, Pub. L. No. 103-139, 107 Stat. 1418 (1993), required that any U.S. forces deployed with a U.N. peacekeeping force in Somalia serve only under U.S. command and control. The proposed Peace Powers Act of 1995, S. 5, 104th Cong. (1995), would have prohibited the President from "subordinat[ing] to the command or operational control of any foreign national" any U.S. forces participating in U.N. peacekeeping activity unless Congress enacts legislation specifically approving such subordination, or the President first submits to designated congressional committees documents showing that U.S. unit commanders retain certain identified command prerogatives. Do these provisions violate the Constitution? *See* Office of Legal Counsel, *Placing of United States Armed Forces Under United Nations Operational or Tactical Control*, 20 Op. O.L.C. 182 (1996) (finding any such restrictions unconstitutional).

2. Domestic Authorities

As of early 2011, approximately 91 members of the U.S. armed forces were serving in six humanitarian or peacekeeping operations under the auspices of the U.N. Security Council, plus an additional number of U.S. contractors performing police duties. They were deployed in Chad, Congo, Haiti, Liberia, Sudan, and the Middle East. *See generally* Marjorie Ann Browne, *United Nations Peacekeeping: Issues for Congress* (Cong. Res. Serv. RL33700), Aug. 13, 2010. A much larger number were deployed as stabilization forces in Iraq and Afghanistan. In early 2011, additional U.S. forces were engaged in a military campaign in Libya. See *infra* pp. 320-322. At least some of these deployments were ordered pursuant to one or more of the following statutory authorities:

International Disaster Assistance
22 U.S.C. §2292 (2006)

(a) Congressional policy. The Congress, recognizing that prompt United States assistance to alleviate human suffering caused by natural and manmade disasters is an important expression of the humanitarian concern and tradition of the people of the United States, affirms the willingness of the United States to provide assistance for the relief and rehabilitation of people and countries affected by such disasters.

(b) General authority. Subject to the limitations in section 2292a of this title [relating to appropriations], and notwithstanding any other provision of this chapter or any other Act, the President is authorized to furnish assistance to any foreign country, international organization, or private voluntary organization, on such terms and conditions as he may determine, for international disaster relief and rehabilitation, including assistance relating to disaster preparedness, and to the prediction of, and contingency planning for, natural disasters abroad. . . .

Humanitarian and Other Assistance
10 U.S.C. §§401-405 (2006)

§401. HUMANITARIAN AND CIVIC ASSISTANCE PROVIDED IN CONJUNCTION WITH MILITARY OPERATIONS

(a) (1) Under regulations prescribed by the Secretary of Defense, the Secretary of a military department may carry out humanitarian and civic assistance activities in conjunction with authorized military operations of the armed forces in a country if the Secretary concerned determines that the activities will promote —

(A) the security interests of both the United States and the country in which the activities are to be carried out. . . .

(e) In this section, the term "humanitarian and civic assistance" means any of the following:

(1) Medical, surgical, dental, and veterinary care provided in areas of a country that are rural or are underserved by medical, surgical, dental, and veterinary professionals, respectively, including education, training, and technical assistance related to the care provided.

(2) Construction of rudimentary surface transportation systems.

(3) Well drilling and construction of basic sanitation facilities.

(4) Rudimentary construction and repair of public facilities.

§402.   TRANSPORTATION OF HUMANITARIAN RELIEF SUPPLIES TO FOREIGN COUNTRIES

(a) Notwithstanding any other provision of law . . . the Secretary of Defense may transport to any country, without charge, supplies which have been furnished by a nongovernmental source and which are intended for humanitarian assistance. Such supplies may be transported only on a space available basis. . . .

§404.   FOREIGN DISASTER ASSISTANCE

(a) In general. — The President may direct the Secretary of Defense to provide disaster assistance outside the United States to respond to manmade or natural disasters when necessary to prevent loss of lives or serious harm to the environment.

(b) Forms of assistance. — Assistance provided under this section may include transportation, supplies, services, and equipment.

(c) Notification required. — Not later than 48 hours after the commencement of disaster assistance activities to provide assistance under this section, the President shall transmit to Congress a report containing notification of the assistance provided, and proposed to be provided, under this section and a description of so much of the following as is then available:

(1) The manmade or natural disaster for which disaster assistance is necessary.

(2) The threat to human lives or the environment presented by the disaster.

(3) The United States military personnel and material resources that are involved or expected to be involved.

(4) The disaster assistance that is being provided or is expected to be provided by other nations or public or private relief organizations.

(5) The anticipated duration of the disaster assistance activities. . . .

Detail of Personnel to International Organizations
22 U.S.C. §2388 (2006)

Whenever the President determines it to be consistent with and in furtherance of the purposes of this chapter [relating to foreign assistance], the head of any agency of the United States Government is authorized to detail, assign, or otherwise make available to any international organization any officer or employee of his agency to serve with, or as a member of, the international staff of such organization, or to render any technical, scientific, or professional advice or service to, or in cooperation with, such organization.

United Nations Participation Act

22 U.S.C. §§287-287e-2 (2006), as amended by
Pub. L. No. 111-195, §107(a)(1), 124 Stat. 1312, 1337 (2010)

§287D-1. NONCOMBATANT ASSISTANCE TO UNITED NATIONS

(a) Armed forces details; supplies and equipment; obligation of funds; procurement and replacement of requested items. Notwithstanding the provisions of any other law, the President, upon the request by the United Nations for cooperative action, and to the extent that he finds that it is consistent with the national interest to comply with such request, may authorize, in support of such activities of the United Nations as are specifically directed to the peaceful settlement of disputes and not involving the employment of armed forces contemplated by chapter VII of the United Nations Charter—

(1) the detail to the United Nations, under such terms and conditions as the President shall determine, of personnel of the armed forces of the United States to serve as observers, guards, or in any non-combatant capacity, but in no event shall more than a total of one thousand of such personnel be so detailed at any one time. . . .

Also relevant are 10 U.S.C. §2561(a)(1) (2006), which allows the Defense Department to use appropriated funds for "transportation of humanitarian relief and for other humanitarian purposes worldwide," and 10 U.S.C. §2557 (2006), which authorizes the Secretary of Defense to make nonlethal excess military supplies available for humanitarian relief.

NOTES AND QUESTIONS

1. *Making Peace, Not War?* Does either a humanitarian or a peace operation involve the war power? If not, does Congress have to approve it? May Congress restrict such operations? *See* Matthew D. Berger, Note, *Implementing a United Nations Security Council Resolution: The President's Power to Use Force Without Authorization of Congress*, 15 Hastings Int'l & Comp. L. Rev. 83, 100 (1991) (asserting that "the President has exclusive control over all peacetime deployments which do not threaten war") (citation omitted). If the critical test is whether a particular deployment "threatens war," who should make that determination?

Should it make any difference whether the government (if there is one) of the country to which troops are deployed invites their intervention? Can an invited intervention be a war? *See* Jane E. Stromseth, *Collective Force and Constitutional Responsibility: War Powers in the Post-Cold War Era*, 50 U. Miami L. Rev. 145, 161 (1995) (arguing that the President does not require Congress's authorization if "all the parties to a conflict (not just some of them) consent to and support" a peacekeeping operation, because the chances of significant combat risks are then low).

2. *Labeling the Mission.* The primary purpose of any humanitarian mission is to "alleviate human suffering." 22 U.S.C. §2292(a). U.S. troops are deployed on "peacekeeping" or "stability" missions when there is a peace to keep, but that peace is threatened. "Peacemaking" involves the restoration of peace, employing force if necessary. Is it important to characterize a mission initially as one or another of these? Who should be able to make an authoritative pronouncement about the character of a particular mission?

According to the Defense Department,

> stability operations is defined as an overarching term encompassing various military missions, tasks, and activities conducted outside the United States in coordination with other instruments of national power to maintain or reestablish a safe and secure environment, provide essential governmental services, emergency infrastructure reconstruction, and humanitarian relief. [DOD Instr. 3000.05, *Stability Operations*, Sept. 16, 2009.]

> "Foreign Disaster Relief." Prompt aid that can be used to alleviate the suffering of foreign disaster victims. (Normally, it includes humanitarian services and transportation; the provision of food, clothing, medicines, beds and bedding, temporary shelter and housing; the furnishing of medical materiel, medical and technical personnel; and making repairs to essential services.) [DOD Dir. 5100.46, *Foreign Disaster Relief*, Dec. 4, 1975.]

> Peace Operations encompass multiagency and multinational crisis response and limited contingency operations involving all instruments of national power with military missions to contain conflict, redress the peace, and shape the environment to support reconciliation and rebuilding and facilitate the transition to legitimate governance. PO include peacekeeping, peace enforcement, peacemaking, peace building, and conflict prevention efforts. [Department of Defense, Jt. Pub. 3-29, *Foreign Humanitarian Assistance*, Mar. 17, 2009, at I-9.]

Are these definitions helpful? What is their legal significance?

3. *Congressional Authority for Humanitarian or Peace Operations.* How important do you think it is for the President to be confident about the scope of her authority in deploying U.S. troops abroad? Can you say precisely what is authorized by each of the foregoing statutes? What prerequisites must be satisfied before they are invoked? Should Congress provide definitions for the terms "disaster," "humanitarian," and "civic assistance"? How about "peacekeeping," "peacemaking," and "stability"?

In a given instance it may be necessary to act promptly, perhaps before there is time to seek the approval of Congress for a particular deployment. Should Congress give its approval in advance for such deployments? If so, how much flexibility should the President be given? What is the effect of the language "notwithstanding any other provision of this chapter or any other Act" in 22 U.S.C. §2292(b)? To what extent do you think Congress may constitutionally delegate or withhold such authority?

What if a purely humanitarian mission cannot prudently be carried out without the support of troops equipped for combat? Do these statutes authorize the deployment of such supporting forces? If so, might the President have to comply with the consultation, reporting, and other requirements of the War Powers Resolution, *supra* p. 307?

4. *Mission Creep or Mission Shift.* Suppose a mission begins peacefully, then turns violent. Under what circumstances, if any, must the President then seek congressional approval to stay and fight — to do more than simply use whatever force is necessary to safely withdraw the troops? Does the onset of hostilities trigger a requirement for the President to consult, report, or take any other action under the War Powers Resolution? Should it?

B. INTERVENTION IN SOMALIA: CROSSING THE MOGADISHU LINE[7]

With the fall of the Siad Barre government in 1991, Somalia plunged into a civil war among rival clans. The war not only directly threatened the population, it also disrupted food production and transportation in the midst of an extended drought and resulting famine. As the Secretary-General of the United Nations reportedly said, "There are more arms than food in Somalia." Over the next two years, some 350,000 Somalians would die from hunger and civil strife, and more than a million others would flee into refugee camps.

Alarmed at the heavy loss of life and the associated threat to international peace and security, the U.N. Security Council adopted a series of resolutions, beginning in January 1992, that urged the clans to cease hostilities, installed an arms embargo, and approved the dispatch of a small contingent of member state troops to help restore government institutions and provide security for humanitarian relief operations.

Congress got involved in April 1992 by passing the Horn of Africa Recovery and Food Security Act, Pub. L. No. 102-274, 106 Stat. 115 (1992). Noting that armed groups in Somalia were eroding "food security," it expressed the "sense of the Congress" that the President should, *inter alia*, "ensure, to the maximum extent possible and in conjunction with other donors, that emergency humanitarian assistance is being made available to those in need...." *Id.* §3(b)(3). It also stated that it should be U.S. policy

> to redouble its commendable efforts to secure safe corridors of passage for emergency food and relief supplies in affected areas ... [and] to lend the full support of the United States to all aspects of relief operations in the Horn of Africa, and to work in support of

---

7. Background for this case study is drawn in part from Terrence Lyons & Ahmed I. Samatar, *Somalia* (1995); Sean Murphy, *Humanitarian Intervention: The United Nations in an Evolving World* 217-243 (1996); Office of U.S. Foreign Disaster Assistance, Agency for Int'l Dev., *Situation Report No. 19* (Mar. 12, 1993); John R. Bolton, *Wrong Turn in Somalia*, 73 Foreign Aff. 266 (Jan./Feb. 1994); Ramlogan, *supra* p. 412; and Charles Ernest Edgar, *United States Use of Armed Force Under the United Nations... Who's in Charge?*, 10 J.L. & Pol. 299, 329-333 (1994).

[the] United Nations . . . in breaking the barriers currently threatening the lives of millions of refugees. . . . [*Id.* §4(b)(1), (4).]

Beginning in August 1992, U.S. planes helped airlift humanitarian relief supplies to Somalia. In the same month, the Senate urged the President to work with the U.N. Security Council "to deploy security guards [to protect relief shipments and workers], with or without the consent of the Somalia factions, in order to assure that humanitarian relief gets to those most in need. . . ." S. Con. Res. 132, 102d Cong. (1992). The House followed suit in October 1992 by expressing "the willingness of the United States to participate, consistent with applicable United States legal requirements, in the deployment of armed United Nations security guards, as authorized by the Security Council, in order to secure emergency relief activities," and emphasizing that the deployment should proceed "even in the event that an invitation by the various warring Somali factions cannot be obtained." H.R. Con. Res. 370, 102d Cong. (1992).

    The full Congress then declared that

[i]nternational peacekeeping activities take many forms and include observer missions, ceasefire monitoring, human rights monitoring, refugee and humanitarian assistance, monitoring and conducting elections, monitoring of police in the demobilization of former combatants, and reforming judicial and other civil and administrative systems of government. [Pub. L. No. 102-484, §1342(a)(2), 106 Stat. 2315, 2556 (1992).]

It also authorized the transfer of funds from Department of Defense appropriations to meet "unexpected and urgent" budget shortfalls for "international peacekeeping activities of the United Nations." 10 U.S.C. §403, *repealed* Pub. L. No. 104-106, §1061(g)(1), 110 Stat. 443 (1996).

    But clan militias continued to imperil relief workers and intercept relief convoys. In December 1992, the Security Council condemned continued "violations of international humanitarian law" in Somalia. It called for the deployment of 3,500 U.N. personnel there to coordinate humanitarian relief and to provide a secure environment for relief operations, and, pursuant to Chapter VII, authorized member states to use "all necessary means" to achieve these ends. S.C. Res. 794, U.N. Doc. S/RES/794 (Dec. 3, 1992). President George Bush responded on December 4, 1992, by ordering U.S. military forces to secure the airfield and port facility of Mogadishu and to provide a secure environment for the relief effort. The troops were deployed on December 8 and 9, and the President reported the deployment to Congress two days later. See *infra* p. 426. Within a month, 28,000 U.S. troops were deployed on and off the shores of Somalia. The legal advice given the President, his report to Congress, and Congress's response are reproduced below.

Authority of the President to Use United States Military Forces for the Protection of Relief Efforts in Somalia
16 Op. O.L.C. 8 (1992)

MEMORANDUM FOR THE ATTORNEY GENERAL

    You have asked for our opinion whether the President has the legal authority to commit United States Armed Forces to assist the United Nations in ensuring the safe delivery of food, medicine and other relief to the population in affected regions of Somalia. We understand that the mission of those troops will be to restore as quickly as possible the flow of humanitarian relief to those areas of Somalia most affected by famine and disease, and to facilitate the safe and orderly deployment of United Nations peacekeeping forces in Somalia in the near future. We also understand that private United States nationals are currently involved in relief operations in Somalia and United States military personnel are engaged in humanitarian supply flights into Somalia. We further understand that the efforts of the United States and other nations and of private organizations to deliver humanitarian relief to those areas of Somalia are being severely hampered by the breakdown of governmental authority in Somalia and, in particular, by armed bands who steal relief commodities for their own use.[1]

In our opinion, the President's role under our Constitution as Commander in Chief and Chief Executive vests him with the constitutional authority to order United States troops abroad to further national interests such as protecting the lives of Americans overseas. Accordingly, where, as here, United States government personnel and private citizens are participating in a lawful relief effort in a foreign nation, we conclude that the President may commit United States troops to protect those involved in the relief effort. In addition, we believe that long-standing precedent supports the use of the Armed Forces to protect Somalians and other foreign nationals in Somalia. We also believe that the President, in determining to commit the Armed Forces to this operation, may lawfully look to the importance to the national interests of the United States of upholding the recent United Nations resolutions regarding Somalia. Finally, we note that Congress has expressed its tacit approval for the President's exercise of his constitutional authority in this matter.

I

From the instructions of President Jefferson's Administration to Commodore Richard Dale in 1801 to "chastise" Algiers and Tripoli if they continued to attack American shipping, to the present, Presidents have taken military initiatives abroad on the basis of their constitutional authority. Against the background of this repeated past practice under many Presidents, this Department and this Office have concluded that the President has the power to commit United States troops abroad for the purpose of protecting important national interests. *See, e.g., Training of British Flying Students in the United States*, 40 Op. Atty. Gen. 58, 62 (1941) ("the President's authority has long been recognized as extending to the dispatch of armed forces outside of the United States, either on missions of good will or rescue, or for the purpose of protecting American lives or property or American interests") (Jackson, A.G.). As the

---

1. We note at the outset that the deployment of troops to Somalia appears primarily aimed at providing humanitarian assistance, and will only involve combat as an incident to that humanitarian mission. Thus, the current situation poses two questions: is there legal authority for United States Armed Forces to perform humanitarian tasks, and if so, may the President authorize those troops to engage in more purely military actions, such as self-defense and the creation of safe corridors for the provision of aid. We understand from the General Counsel of the Department of Defense that there is clear statutory authority for the use of the Armed Forces to support and to perform humanitarian tasks in Somalia. *E.g.*, 10 U.S.C. [§2561]; *see also* 22 U.S.C. §§2292, 2292*l*. We conclude in this opinion that in these circumstances the President's constitutional authority to authorize the troops to engage in various related military actions is also clear. We do not address issues raised by the proposed operation under the War Powers Resolution.

Supreme Court noted in *United States v. Verdugo-Urquidez*, 494 U.S. 259, 273 (1990), "[t]he United States frequently employs armed forces outside this country — over 200 times in our history — for the protection of American citizens or national security."

At the core of this power is the President's authority to take military action to protect American citizens, property, and interests from foreign threats. *See, e.g., Presidential Powers Relating to the Situation in Iran*, 4A Op. OLC 115, 121 (1979) ("It is well established that the President has the constitutional power as Chief Executive and Commander-in-Chief to protect the lives and property of Americans abroad."); *Presidential Power to Use the Armed Forces Abroad Without Statutory Authorization*, 4A Op. OLC 185, 187 (1980) ("Presidents have repeatedly employed troops abroad in defense of American lives and property."); *see also* Memorandum of William H. Rehnquist, Assistant Attorney General, Office of Legal Counsel, *Re: The President and the War Power: South Vietnam and the Cambodian Sanctuaries*, 8 (May 22, 1970) (President as Commander in Chief has authority "to commit military forces of the United States to armed conflict . . . to protect the lives of American troops in the field"). In *Durand v. Hollins*, 8 F. Cas. 111 (No. 4186) (C.C.S.D.N.Y. 1860) [*supra* p. 368], an American naval officer, under orders of the President and the Secretary of the Navy, bombarded Greytown, Nicaragua in retaliation for the Nicaraguan government's refusal to make reparations for attacks against United States citizens and property. In a suit brought against the naval officer, Justice Nelson held that the officer properly took this action, observing that such an attack on American citizens and property required the sort of swift and effective response that only the Executive could make.

> Acts of lawless violence, or of threatened violence to the citizen or his property, cannot be anticipated and provided for; and the protection, to be effectual or of any avail, may, not unfrequently, require the most prompt and decided action.

Id. at 112. Justice Nelson also stated that whether the President had a duty to act to protect the citizens involved "was a public political question . . . which belonged to the executive to determine." *Id. See also Youngstown Sheet & Tube Co. v. Sawyer*, 343 U.S. 579, 645 (1952) [*supra* p. 35] (Jackson, J., concurring) ("I should indulge the widest latitude of interpretation to sustain [the President's] exclusive function to command the instruments of national force, at least when turned against the outside world for the security of our society.").

Applying these principles to the present case, we conclude that the President can reasonably determine that the proposed mission is necessary to protect the American citizens already in Somalia. We understand that these include private United States citizens engaged in relief operations, and United States military personnel conducting humanitarian supply flights. The United Nations has determined that existing conditions in Somalia pose a threat to the lives and safety of these individuals and of non-Americans also engaged in efforts to deliver food, medicine and other relief to over two million Somalians. *See* Security Council Resolution No. 794 (December 3, 1992) (determining that the Somali situation "constitutes a threat to international peace and security," and expressing alarm at "reports of violence and threats of violence against personnel participating lawfully in impartial humanitarian relief activities").

It is also essential to consider the safety of the troops to be dispatched as requested by Resolution 794. The President may provide those troops with sufficient military protection to insure that they are able to carry out their humanitarian tasks safely and efficiently. He may also decide to send sufficient numbers of troops so that those who are primarily engaged in assisting the United Nations in noncombatant roles are defended by others who perform a protective function. *See, e.g.,* Memorandum of William H. Rehnquist [*supra*].

Nor is the President's power strictly limited to the protection of American citizens in Somalia. Past military interventions that extended to the protection of foreign nationals provide precedent for action to protect endangered Somalians and other non-United States citizens. For example, in 1965, President Lyndon Johnson explained that he had ordered United States military intervention in the Dominican Republic to protect both Americans and the citizens of other nations. *"An Assessment of the Situation in the Dominican Republic,"* 53 Dept. State Bull. 19, 20 (1965) ("to preserve the lives of American citizens and citizens of a good many other nations — 46 to be exact, 46 nations"). During the 1900–01 Boxer Rebellion in China, President McKinley, without prior congressional authorization, sent about 5,000 United States troops as part of a multi-national contingent to lift the siege of the foreign quarters in Peking after the Chinese government proved unable to control rebels. *Compilation of the Messages and Papers of the Presidents 1789-1902* at 113, 120 (James D. Richardson ed., Supp. 1904).[3]

The United States has an additional important national interest arising from the involvement of the United Nations in the Somalian situation. In a 1950 opinion supporting President Truman's decision to support the United Nations in repelling the invasion of South Korea, the State Department concluded that "[t]he continued existence of the United Nations as an effective international organization is a paramount United States interest." *Authority of the President to Repel the Attack on Korea,* 23 Dept. State Bull. 173, 177 (1950). We adopt that conclusion. Here, too, maintaining the credibility of United Nations Security Council decisions, protecting the security of United Nations and related relief efforts, and ensuring the effectiveness of United Nations peacekeeping operations can be considered a vital national interest, and will promote the United States' conception of a "new world order."

In Resolution 794, which was adopted pursuant to Chapter VII of the United Nations Charter, the Security Council has authorized the United States and other member States to use "all necessary means" to establish a secure environment for the delivery of essential humanitarian aid in Somalia. The President is entitled to rely on this Resolution, and on its finding that the situation in Somalia "constitutes a threat to international peace and security," in making his determination that the interests of the United States justify providing the military assistance that Resolution 794 calls for. Moreover, American assistance in giving effect to this and other Security Council resolutions pertaining to Somalia would in itself strengthen the prestige, credibility and effectiveness of the United Nations — which the President can legitimately find to be a substantial national foreign policy objective, and which will tend further to guarantee the lives and property of Americans abroad. . . .

---

3. A case of intervention on behalf of a foreign national, one Martin Koszta, was cited approvingly by the Supreme Court in *In re Neagle*, 135 U.S. 1, 64 (1890) [*supra* p. 83], as an example of the legitimate exercise of Executive power "growing out of the Constitution itself, our international relations, and all the protection implied by the nature of the government under the Constitution." *Id.* Although Koszta had expressed his intention of becoming naturalized, at the time of the events in question he was not an American citizen. . . . The Court noted that no Act of Congress sanctioned this armed intervention.

II

Finally, we note that the available evidence strongly suggests that Congress believes that the President's use of military force to assist United Nations relief and peacekeeping efforts in Somalia does not exceed his constitutional powers. In recent legislation, Congress appears to have recognized the President's authority to make use of military personnel, should he deem it necessary to carry out or protect humanitarian missions in Somalia. Section 3(b)(3) of the Horn of Africa Recovery and Food Security Act, Pub. L. No. 102-274, 106 Stat. 115 (1992) [noted *supra* p. 421], states that "[i]t is the sense of the Congress that the President should . . . ensure, to the maximum extent possible and in conjunction with other donors, that emergency humanitarian assistance is being made available to those in need. . . ." Section 4(a)(1) of the Act states in part that U.S. policy should be "to assure noncombatants . . . equal and ready access to all food, emergency, and relief assistance," and section 4(b)(1) states that pursuant to the United States policy of "seeking to maximize relief efforts" the United States should "redouble its commendable efforts to secure safe corridors of passage for emergency food and relief supplies in affected areas." Moreover, in section 2(3), Congress explicitly found that the actions of the government and armed opposition groups in Somalia "erode[d] food security" in that country.

Thus, Congress appears to have contemplated that the President might find it necessary to make use of military forces to ensure the safe delivery of humanitarian relief in Somalia, and to have assumed in such circumstances that the President possessed constitutional authority to do so.[6] *See also Dames & Moore* [*v. Regan*, 453 U.S. 654 (1981),] at 678-79 [*supra* p. 60].

Please let us know if we may be of further assistance.

Timothy E. Flanigan
Assistant Attorney General

Letter from President George Bush to Congressional Leaders

28 Weekly Comp. Pres. Doc. 2338 (Dec. 10, 1992)

Dear Mr. [Speaker/President]: . . .

On November 29, 1992, the Secretary General of the U.N. reported to the Security Council that the deteriorating security conditions in Somalia had severely disrupted international relief efforts and that an immediate military operation under U.N. authority was urgently required. On December 3, the Security Council adopted Resolution 794, which determined that the situation in Somalia constituted a threat to international peace and security, and, invoking Chapter VII of the U.N. Charter, authorized Member States to use all necessary means to establish a secure environment for humanitarian relief operations in Somalia. In my judgment, the deployment of U.S. Armed Forces under U.S. command to Somalia as part of this multilateral response to the Resolution is necessary to address a major humanitarian calamity,

---

6. As noted above, the quoted provisions of the Act are part of a "sense of Congress" resolution. A "sense of Congress" resolution does not, of course, give the President authority he does not otherwise possess. Nonetheless, we believe that the Congressional views expressed in the quoted portions of the Act are evidence that Congress recognized that the President has authority to use military force to accomplish the goals of the Act.

avert related threats to international peace and security, and protect the safety of Americans and others engaged in relief operations.

In the evening, Eastern Standard Time, on December 8, 1992, U.S. Armed Forces entered Somalia to secure the airfield and port facility of Mogadishu. Other elements of the U.S. Armed Forces and the Armed Forces of other Members of the United Nations are being introduced into Somalia to achieve the objectives of U.N. Security Council Resolution 794. No organized resistance has been encountered to date.

U.S. Army Forces will remain in Somalia only as long as necessary to establish a secure environment for humanitarian relief operations and will then turn over the responsibility of maintaining this environment to a U.N. peacekeeping force assigned to Somalia. Over 15 nations have already offered to deploy troops. While it is not possible to estimate precisely how long the transfer of responsibility may take, we believe that prolonged operations will not be necessary.

We do not intend that U.S. Armed Forces deployed to Somalia become involved in hostilities. Nonetheless, these forces are equipped and ready to take such measures as may be needed to accomplish their humanitarian mission and defend themselves, if necessary; they also will have the support of any additional U.S. Armed Forces necessary to ensure their safety and the accomplishment of their mission.

I have taken these actions pursuant to my constitutional authority to conduct our foreign relations and as Commander in Chief and Chief Executive, and in accordance with applicable treaties and laws. In doing so, I have taken into account the views expressed in H. Con. Res. 370, S. Con. Res. 132, and the Horn of Africa Recovery and Food Security Act, Public Law 102-274, on the urgent need for action in Somalia.

I am providing this report in accordance with my desire that Congress be fully informed and consistent with the War Powers Resolution. I look forward to cooperating with Congress in the effort to relieve human suffering and to restore peace and stability to the region.

Sincerely,
George Bush

On February 4, 1993, the Senate approved Senate Joint Resolution 45, noting President Bush's letter and asserting that he was "authorized to use United States armed forces pursuant to United Nations Security Council Resolution 794 in order to implement the resolution . . . within the meaning of section 5(b) of the War Powers Resolution." S.J. Res. 45, 103d Cong. (1993). The House, however, did not immediately follow suit.

In March 1993, the Security Council noted the continuing threat to peace and security in Somalia and called for a "prompt, smooth, and phased transition" from a U.S.-led task force to the U.N. Operation in Somalia (UNOSOM II). S.C. Res. 814, U.N. Doc. S/RES/814 (Mar. 26, 1993). The United States turned over command of the operation in May, although it continued to support U.N. efforts by providing approximately 3,000 U.S. logistics and other support personnel under UNOSOM II control. In addition, approximately 1,100 U.S. troops remained in the area as part of a Quick Reaction Force (QRF) for emergency operations under the operational control of U.S. commanders. By then, however, Congress had begun to have second thoughts. When the House finally approved a modified version of Senate Joint

Resolution 45 on May 25, 1993, it added a 12-month time limit on the authorization. S.J. Res. 45, 103d Cong., §4(c)(1) (1993) (as modified and approved by the House).

On June 5, 1993, forces of Somali warlord Mohammed Farah Hassan Aidid ambushed a U.N. convoy, killing 24 Pakistani troops and injuring three U.S. soldiers. The following day the Security Council adopted Resolution 837, which authorized UNOSOM II to take "all necessary measures against all those responsible" for the attack and to secure "their arrest and detention for prosecution, trial, and punishment." S.C. Res. 837, U.N. Doc. S/RES/837 (June 6, 1993).

On June 10, 1993, President Clinton reported these events to Congress and reaffirmed the deployment of U.S. armed forces to Somalia to accomplish their humanitarian mission "and to defend themselves." Approximately one week later, elements of the QRF launched air and ground strikes against Aidid's headquarters in a search for Aidid. This phase of the operations concluded in a bloody firefight with Aidid's forces on October 3-4, 1993, in which 17 U.S. soldiers were killed and 84 wounded. The name of a popular book and movie, *Black Hawk Down*, is based on the destruction of two U.S. helicopters during the attack. The disaster prompted speculation that the Administration had under-equipped the QRF to avoid inflaming congressional and public opinion. The press subsequently popularized the phrase "crossing the Mogadishu line" to describe a change in mission from peacekeeping to peacemaking.

President Clinton then reported to Congress that he would withdraw the troops by March 31, 1994. *Report on Military Operations in Somalia — Message from the President*, 139 Cong. Rec. H7796 (daily ed. Oct. 13, 1993). But a majority in Congress were not satisfied by these assurances. In the defense appropriation for 1994, Congress found that

> neither the expanded United Nations mission of national reconciliation, nor the broad mission of disarming the clans, nor any other mission not essential to the performance of the humanitarian mission has been endorsed or approved by the Senate; [and] the expanded mission of the United Nations was, subsequent to an attack on the United Nations force, diverted into a mission aimed primarily at capturing certain persons. . . . [Department of Defense Appropriations Act, 1994, Pub. L. No. 103-139, §8151(a)(4)-(5), 107 Stat. 1418, 1476 (1993).]

Accordingly, Congress authorized appropriations for U.S. forces in Somalia only through March 31, 1994, and required that they be placed under U.S. command and control. *Id.* §8151(b)(2)(B), 107 Stat. 1476-1477. Beyond that date, it authorized the obligation of funds for forces "sufficient only to protect American diplomatic facilities and American citizens, and noncombat personnel to advise the United Nations commander in Somalia," and to protect themselves. *Id.*, 107 Stat. 1476.

More generally, in the same Act, Congress expressed its sense that no funds appropriated by the Act should be spent for costs incurred by U.S. forces in "international peacekeeping or peace-enforcement operations" under the authority of Chapters VI or VII of the U.N. Charter or of a U.N. Security Council Resolution, or in "any significant . . . peacekeeping, or peace-enforcement operations," unless the President consulted with Congress prior to the operation, whenever possible, regarding the goals, mission, cost, funding, and anticipated duration and scope of the operation. *Id.* §8153(1)(a), 107 Stat. 1477. Taking another swipe at the United Nations, Congress found that the United Nations had not acquired the expertise or infrastructure to manage "peace enforcement" operations effectively. *Id.* §9001(5), 107 Stat. 1479. Congress expressed the sense that the President should consult with it before placing U.S. combat forces under the operational control of foreign commanders, and that he should describe the justification for foreign command, command and control arrangements, rules of engagement, and other details. *Id.* §9002, 107 Stat. 1479-1480.

Three weeks later, Congress revisited the Somalia issue in the National Defense Authorization Act for Fiscal Year 1994, Pub. L. No. 103-160, 107 Stat. 1547 (1993). That Act required the President to submit detailed reports about operations in Somalia, and it expressed the sense that he "should by November 15, 1993, seek and receive Congressional authorization in order for the deployment of United States Forces to Somalia to continue." *Id.* §1512(b)(3)-(4), 107 Stat. 1841. The President signed this measure into law on November 30, 1993. Less than three months later, on February 26, 1994, all U.S. forces were withdrawn from Somalia. The remaining UNOSOM II forces followed shortly thereafter.

NOTES AND QUESTIONS

1. *Statutory Authority for the Somalia Mission?* By what statutory authority, if any, did President George Bush initially deploy U.S. armed forces in Somalia? If there was statutory authority for the initial deployment of U.S. forces, did it also authorize subsequent deployments and mission changes? If the troops were lawfully deployed at the outset, did the President *need* any further authority to order them to find warlord Aidid? To put it differently, is "mission creep" inherently within the tactical discretion of the Commander in Chief? *See* Mark T. Uyeda, *Presidential Prerogative Under the Constitution to Deploy U.S. Military Forces in Low-Intensity Conflict*, 44 Duke L.J. 777, 813 n.187 (1995).

2. *Other Presidential Authority?* Statutes aside, what constitutional authority did the President claim in deploying U.S. armed forces in Somalia? How, if at all, is that authority limited? *See* Jane E. Stromseth, *Rethinking War Powers: Congress, the President, and the United Nations*, 81 Geo. L.J. 597, 660-664 (1993).

One commentator has speculated that "[s]ince the United Nations approached the United States requesting assistance in Somalia where there was no defined 'enemy' or 'aggression,' the subsequent commitment might be viewed as falling fully within Presidential police powers and not requiring Congressional authorization." Edgar, *supra* p. 421, 10 J.L. & Pol. at 331. Do you agree?

3. *Characterizing the Mission.* Does it matter whether the deployment is primarily for humanitarian purposes, or whether its goal is either peacekeeping or peacemaking? Is there a meaningful distinction among these missions? Consider this response:

When U.S. troops intervened in December 1992 to stop theft of food, they disrupted the political economy and stepped deep into the muck of Somali politics. By reestablishing some order, the U.S. operation inevitably affected the direction of Somali politics and became nation-building because the most basic component of nation-building is an end to anarchy. The current conventional wisdom that draws the distinctions between different types of intervention and stresses the desire to avoid nation-building may be analytically attractive, but it is not particularly helpful. How could anyone believe that landing 30,000 troops in a country was anything but a gross interference in its politics? The Mogadishu line was crossed as soon as troops were sent in. [Walter Clarke & Jeffrey Herbst, *Somalia and the Future of Humanitarian Intervention*, 75 Foreign Aff. 70, 74 (Mar./Apr. 1996).]

They conclude that "there is no such thing as a humanitarian surgical strike." *Id.* at 82. If they are right, what implication, if any, does this conclusion carry for the President's authority to order a humanitarian intervention into a politically unstable area?

4. *Operation Restore Hope and the War Powers Resolution.* Did the deployments of U.S. armed forces in Somalia satisfy the War Powers Resolution, *supra* p. 307? Is 22 U.S.C. §287d-1, part of the U.N. Participation Act, *supra* p. 216, pertinent to this question? *See* Walker, *supra* p. 412, 29 Wake Forest L. Rev. at 483. Congress has authorized the President to give up to $5 million of assistance to friendly countries and international organizations "for peacekeeping operations and other programs carried out in furtherance of the national security interests of the United States," including noncombatant assistance to the United Nations under the U.N. Participation Act. 22 U.S.C. §2348 (2006). But further assistance presumably requires additional legislation, unless the President has the constitutional authority to order assistance without prior congressional approval. Does this authorization satisfy the War Powers Resolution?

5. *Required Consultation.* Section 8153(1)(a) of the Defense Appropriations Act, 1994, *supra* p. 428, states the sense of Congress to forbid any use of the funds it appropriates for peacekeeping or peace-enforcing operations unless the President consults with Congress before the deployment, if possible, or immediately after. Is this provision constitutional? If you conclude that it is, does it necessarily follow that the consultation provision of the War Powers Resolution is also constitutional?

C. HUMANITARIAN INTERVENTION IN LIBYA—2011[8]

The U.S. military deployment in Somalia in 1992 was carried out with the invitation of—or at least without the objection of—the Somali government,

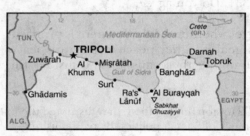

CIA map of Libya.

Courtesy worldatlas.com.

such as it was. U.S. intentions were purely humanitarian, and early on there was no expectation that U.S. troops would engage in any fighting. Even when violence erupted, there was no suggestion that the U.S. military presence in the Horn of Africa might violate the sovereignty of Somalia or basic principles of international law.

The U.S. use of military force in Libya in 2011 was very different in this sense.

8. This study is based on contemporary news accounts.

It presented a much clearer case of humanitarian intervention, defined by one scholar as "the threat or use of force by a state, group of states, or international organization primarily for the purpose of protecting the nationals of the target state from widespread deprivations of internationally recognized human rights." Murphy, *supra* p. 421, at 11-12. In Libya, the very purpose of the intervention by the United States and other states was to protect Libyan citizens from their own government, which was engaged in a concerted campaign to deny them basic human rights, including the right to life. Thus, the target state was very much opposed to the intervention.

There is widespread skepticism that a single state or group of states, or even a regional organization like NATO, may legally use force on humanitarian grounds in the absence of approval by the U.N. Security Council. In the *Nicaragua Case*, *supra* p. 218, for example, the World Court declared that "while the United States might form its own appraisal of the situation as to respect for human rights in Nicaragua, the use of force could not be the appropriate method to monitor or ensure such respect." *Id.* ¶268. NATO air attacks against Serbian forces engaged in shocking atrocities against ethnic Albanians in Kosovo in the spring of 1999 were criticized as a violation of U.N. Charter Article 2(4), although carried out with the best of intentions. *See, e.g.* Louis Henkin, *Kosovo and the Law of "Humanitarian Intervention"*, 93 Am. J. Int'l L. 824 (1999). According to one view, "By the law of the Charter, only the Security Council is empowered to take forcible action against a state which is in breach of its international undertakings to respect human rights." Yoram Dinstein, *War, Aggression and Self-Defence* 71-72 (4th ed. 2005).

But even authorization by the Security Council for intervention in a purely internal conflict is illegal, some say, as well as unwise. The Charter makes no clear provision for such actions, although the United Nations is variously concerned with the protection and promotion of human rights and the rule of law. More important, according to critics, is the seeming inconsistency with Article 2(7) of the Charter, which states,

> Nothing contained in the present Charter shall authorize the United Nations to intervene in matters which are essentially within the domestic jurisdiction of any state or shall require the Members to submit such matters to settlement under the present Charter; but this principle shall not prejudice the application of enforcement measures under Chapter VII.

The World Court has declared, moreover, that

> the principle of non-intervention . . . forbids all States or groups of States to intervene directly or indirectly in internal or external affairs of other States . . . bearing on matters in which each State is permitted, by the principle of State sovereignty, to decide freely. One of these is the choice of a political, economic, social and cultural system, and the formulation of foreign policy. [*Nicaragua Case, supra* p. 218, ¶205.]

No "general right of intervention, in support of an opposition within another State, exists in contemporary international law," the Court said, even when the cause espoused by that opposition "appear[s] particularly worthy by reason of the political and moral values with which it [i]s identified." *Id.* ¶¶206, 209. *See* Murphy, *supra*, at 290-294 (rehearsing arguments on both sides).

Even if a right of humanitarian intervention is recognized, problems abound in the enforcement of that right. With but few exceptions — genocide being one — there is no consensus among states about which human rights are inviolable, or which ones rise to a level of importance that excuses interference from foreign states. Equally troublesome is the question who should be entitled to make an authoritative determination that such rights are being violated. Even more, who is entitled to decide that a particular remedy — peaceful or forceful — is justified in a given case? *See, e.g.,* John N. Moore, *Toward an Applied Theory for the Regulation of Intervention,* in *Law and Civil War in the Modern World* 3, 24-25 (John Norton Moore ed., 1974) (suggesting criteria). All these difficulties are present in the case study that follows.

The story of the U.S. military mission in Libya in 2011 really began elsewhere — in Tunisia, Libya's neighbor to the west, and Egypt, on Libya's eastern border. A December 2010 uprising in Tunisia by citizens demanding democratic reforms led quickly to the overthrow of that country's despotic ruler of 23 years, and sent shock waves throughout the Arab world. On February 11, 2011, nearly three weeks of massive, widely televised street protests in Egypt forced the resignation of President Hosni Mubarak, who had imposed emergency rule there for 30 years. Meanwhile, demonstrators demanding democratic reforms also took to the streets in Jordan, Yemen, Algeria, Syria, Bahrain, Saudi Arabia, Libya, Iraq, and non-Arab Iran. As in Tunisia and Egypt, these protestors were often brutally suppressed by government forces.

Nowhere was the government response more violent than in Libya, where beginning in mid-February hundreds of demonstrators were killed by police, military forces, and mercenary soldiers loyal to Colonel Muammar el-Qaddafi, who had ruled that country with an iron hand for more than 40 years. Protesters nevertheless managed to seize control of Benghazi, Libya's second largest city, and other areas in the East. Although Western media lacked the ready access they enjoyed earlier in Egypt, accounts and images of government atrocities raised grave concerns in Europe and North America, and produced calls for measures to stop Qaddafi's slaughter of his own people. Moreover, there was widespread support for democratic reform in Libya, especially given Qaddafi's long and well-documented history of sponsoring international terrorism.

A number of states, including the United States, immediately took non-forceful steps to put pressure on Qaddafi to stop the violence. Here is an example:

Executive Order No. 13,566, Blocking Property and Prohibiting Certain Transactions Related to Libya
76 Fed. Reg. 11,315 (Feb. 25, 2011)

By the authority vested in me as President by the Constitution and the laws of the United States of America, including the International Emergency Economic Powers Act (50 U.S.C. 1701 et seq.) (IEEPA), the National Emergencies Act (50 U.S.C. 1601 et seq.) (NEA), and section 301 of title 3, United States Code,

I, BARACK OBAMA, President of the United States of America, find that Colonel Muammar Qadhafi, his government, and close associates have taken extreme measures against the people of Libya, including by using weapons of war, mercenaries, and wanton violence against unarmed civilians. I further find that there is a serious risk that Libyan state assets will be misappropriated by Qadhafi, members of his government, members of his family, or his close associates if those assets are not protected. The foregoing circumstances, the prolonged attacks, and the increased numbers of Libyans seeking refuge in other countries from the attacks, have caused a deterioration in the security of Libya and pose a serious risk to its stability, thereby constituting an unusual and extraordinary threat to the national security and foreign policy of the United States, and I hereby declare a national emergency to deal with that threat.

I hereby order:

Section 1. All property and interests in property that are in the United States, that hereafter come within the United States, or that are or hereafter come within the possession or control of any United States person, including any overseas branch, of the following persons are blocked and may not be transferred, paid, exported, withdrawn, or otherwise dealt in:

(a) the persons listed in the Annex to this order [several children of Muammar Qaddafi]; and

(b) any person determined by the Secretary of the Treasury, in consultation with the Secretary of State:

(i) to be a senior official of the Government of Libya;

(ii) to be a child of Colonel Muammar Qadhafi;

(iii) to be responsible for or complicit in, or responsible for ordering, controlling, or otherwise directing, or to have participated in, the commission of human rights abuses related to political repression in Libya;

(iv) to have materially assisted, sponsored, or provided financial, material, logistical, or technical support for, or goods or services in support of the activities described in subsection (b)(iii) of this section or any person whose property and interests in property are blocked pursuant to this order;

(v) to be owned or controlled by, or to have acted or purported to act for or on behalf of, any person whose property and interests in property are blocked pursuant to this order; or

(vi) to be a spouse or dependent child of any person whose property and interests in property are blocked pursuant to this order.

Sec. 2. All property and interests in property that are in the United States, that hereafter come within the United States, or that are or hereafter come within the possession or control of any United States person, including any overseas branch, of the Government of Libya, its agencies, instrumentalities, and controlled entities, and the Central Bank of Libya, are blocked and may not be transferred, paid, exported, withdrawn, or otherwise dealt in. . . .

Barack Obama

Libyan assets in the United States were estimated to be worth some $30 billion. The President's authority under the IEEPA is described *supra* p. 112.

The United Nations Security Council got involved the next day, when it adopted the following resolution:

United Nations Security Council, Resolution 1970

S.C. Res. 1970, U.N. Doc. S/RES/1970 (Feb. 26, 2011)

The Security Council,

Expressing grave concern at the situation in the Libyan Arab Jamahiriya and condemning the violence and use of force against civilians,

Deploring the gross and systematic violation of human rights, including the repression of peaceful demonstrators, expressing deep concern at the deaths of civilians, and rejecting unequivocally the incitement to hostility and violence against the civilian population made from the highest level of the Libyan government, . . .

Considering that the widespread and systematic attacks currently taking place in the Libyan Arab Jamahiriya against the civilian population may amount to crimes against humanity,

Expressing concern at the plight of refugees forced to flee the violence in the Libyan Arab Jamahiriya,

Recalling the Libyan authorities' responsibility to protect its population,

Underlining the need to respect the freedoms of peaceful assembly and of expression, including freedom of the media,

Stressing the need to hold to account those responsible for attacks, including by forces under their control, on civilians, . . .

Reaffirming its strong commitment to the sovereignty, independence, territorial integrity and national unity of the Libyan Arab Jamahiriya. . . .

Acting under Chapter VII of the Charter of the United Nations, and taking measures under its Article 41,

1. *Demands* an immediate end to the violence and calls for steps to fulfil the legitimate demands of the population;

2. *Urges* the Libyan authorities to:

   (a) Act with the utmost restraint, respect human rights and international humanitarian law, and allow immediate access for international human rights monitors; . . .

4. *Decides* to refer the situation in the Libyan Arab Jamahiriya since 15 February 2011 to the Prosecutor of the International Criminal Court; . . .

9. *Decides* that all Member States shall immediately take the necessary measures to prevent the direct or indirect supply, sale or transfer to the Libyan Arab Jamahiriya, from or through their territories or by their nationals, or using their flag vessels or aircraft, of arms and related materiel of all types, including weapons and ammunition, military vehicles and equipment, paramilitary equipment, and spare parts for the aforementioned, and technical assistance, training, financial or other assistance, related to military activities. . . .

15. *Decides* that all Member States shall take the necessary measures to prevent the entry into or transit through their territories of individuals listed in Annex I of this resolution or designated [by a committee established for that purpose by the resolution]. . . .

17. *Decides* that all Member States shall freeze without delay all funds, other financial assets and economic resources which are on their territories, which are owned or controlled, directly or indirectly, by the individuals or entities listed in Annex II of this resolution or designated by [the committee referred to above]. . . .

28. *Decides* to remain actively seized of the matter.

The travel ban applied to Qaddafi, certain members of his family, and several high government officials. The asset freeze applied to Qaddafi and to several of his sons and a daughter. Unfortunately, these measures only seemed to strengthen Qaddafi's resolve to hold onto power.

As the country descended toward civil war, the government turned its considerable military power against the protestors. "We will come house by house, room by room," Qaddafi declared. "We will have no mercy and no pity." Dan Bilefsky & Mark Landler, *Military Action Against Qaddafi Is Backed by U.N.*, N.Y. Times, Mar. 18, 2011. Many outside Libya described a moral imperative to intervene quickly to stop the slaughter of innocents, citing the tragic consequences of delay in responding to earlier internal conflicts in Bosnia, Rwanda, and Darfur.

An intense debate erupted within the Obama administration and in Congress about how the United States should respond to these developments. Some argued that the United States should immediately provide military assistance to the Libyan rebels. Others urged caution, stressing that no action be taken without clearly articulated goals and an exit strategy. Still others insisted that no important U.S. interests would be served by any involvement. In the midst of this debate, the Senate approved a measure on March 1

> strongly condemn[ing] the gross and systematic violations of human rights in Libya, including violent attacks on protesters demanding democratic reforms; . . . urg[ing] the United Nations Security Council to take such further action as may be necessary to protect civilians in Libya from attack, including the possible imposition of a no-fly zone over Libyan territory; . . . [and] support[ing] an orderly, irreversible transition to a legitimate democratic government in Libya. [S. Res. 85, 112th Cong. (2011).]

Illustrating the wide divergence of opinion, other measures introduced in Congress but not acted upon (as of this writing) called for the U.S. military to establish a no-fly zone in Libya — to prevent Qaddafi from attacking rebel forces from the air — and for the recognition of a new government there, while still others expressed the sense of Congress that the President should obtain specific statutory authorization for the use of U.S. armed forces in Libya. Another sought to cut off any funding for such use.

As the fighting continued, and rebel fighters began to be overmatched by Qaddafi forces, on March 12 the Arab League asked the U.N. Security Council to impose a no-fly zone over Libya. An opinion poll in the United States indicated that a majority of Americans favored air support for the rebels but not the commitment of U.S. ground troops. The Security Council, with Russia, China, India, and Brazil abstaining, then approved the following additional resolution:

United Nations Security Council, Resolution 1973

S.C. Res. 1973, U.N. Doc. S/RES/1973 (Mar. 17, 2011)

The Security Council, . . .

Deploring the failure of the Libyan authorities to comply with resolution 1970 (2011),

Expressing grave concern at the deteriorating situation, the escalation of violence, and the heavy civilian casualties, . . .

> *Condemning* the gross and systematic violation of human rights, including arbitrary detentions, enforced disappearances, torture and summary executions,...
>
> *Acting* under Chapter VII of the Charter of the United Nations,
>
> 1. *Demands* the immediate establishment of a cease-fire and a complete end to violence and all attacks against, and abuses of, civilians;...
>
> 4. *Authorizes* Member States that have notified the Secretary-General, acting nationally or through regional organizations or arrangements, and acting in cooperation with the Secretary-General, to take all necessary measures, notwithstanding paragraph 9 of resolution 1970 (2011), to protect civilians and civilian populated areas under threat of attack in the Libyan Arab Jamahiriya, including Benghazi, while excluding a foreign occupation force of any form on any part of Libyan territory,...
>
> 6. *Decides* to establish a ban on all flights in the airspace of the Libyan Arab Jamahiriya in order to help protect civilians;
>
> 7. *Decides further* that the ban imposed by paragraph 6 shall not apply to flights whose sole purpose is humanitarian, such as delivering or facilitating the delivery of assistance, including medical supplies, food, humanitarian workers and related assistance, or evacuating foreign nationals...
>
> 8. *Authorizes* Member States that have notified the Secretary-General and the Secretary-General of the League of Arab States, acting nationally or through regional organizations or arrangements, to take all necessary measures to enforce compliance with the ban on flights imposed by paragraph 6 above, as necessary...
>
> 29. *Decides* to remain actively seized of the matter.

Questions immediately arose about precisely what the Security Council resolution authorized, how it would be implemented, and by whom. On March 21, President Obama reported to Congress that he had ordered

> strikes against Libyan air defense systems and military airfields for the purposes of preparing a no-fly zone. These strikes will be limited in their nature, duration, and scope. Their purpose is to support an international coalition as it takes all necessary measures to enforce the terms of U.N. Security Council Resolution 1973. These limited U.S. actions will set the stage for further action by other coalition partners.
>
> The United States has not deployed ground forces into Libya....
>
> ...I have directed these actions, which are in the national security and foreign policy interests of the United States, pursuant to my constitutional authority to conduct U.S. foreign relations and as Commander in Chief and Chief Executive. [Letter from the President to the Speaker of the House of Representatives and the President Pro Tempore of the Senate (Mar. 21, 2011), *at* http://www.whitehouse.gov/the-press-office/2011/03/21/letter-president-regarding-commencement-operations-libya.]

The President described the report as "part of my efforts to keep the Congress fully informed, consistent with the War Powers Resolution." *Id.* (The full text of the letter is set out *supra* p. 320.) Separately, he stressed that Great Britain, France, and Arab states would take the lead in implementing the resolution. He and other Administration officials also insisted that the goal of U.S. involvement was not to remove Colonel Qaddafi from power.

Over the next several days, U.S. forces launched a large number of Tomahawk cruise missiles at Libyan air defenses, to enable U.S., British, and French aircraft to enforce the no-fly zone prescribed in Resolution 1973. These same aircraft also began attacking not only Iraqi airfields, but also Qaddafi's tanks and heavy artillery, expanding the no-fly zone into a no-drive zone, ostensibly in support of the broader humanitarian mission authorized by the Security Council. NATO began to enforce the arms embargo called for in Resolution 1970 on March 23. On March 27, NATO agreed to take on the entire military operation in Libya under Security Council Resolution 1973, with the United States handing over to its NATO allies all but support functions — supplies, aerial refueling, intelligence, and the like. *See* NATO/ OTAN, *NATO and Libya* (updated regularly), *at* http://www.nato.int/cps/en/nato live/71679.htm.

At the end of March, it was reported that President Obama had signed a secret finding authorizing CIA agents to enter Libya covertly to collect intelligence for military air strikes and meet with rebel forces. The finding also approved the supply of weapons and other support to the rebels. Mark Mazzetti & Eric Schmitt, *C.I.A. Spies Aiding Airstrikes and Assessing Rebel Leaders*, N.Y. Times, Mar. 31, 2011.

NOTES AND QUESTIONS

1. *The President's Authority?* In his report to Congress on March 21, 2011, *supra* p. 320, President Obama noted that he was acting "to assist an international effort authorized by the United Nations (U.N.) Security Council and undertaken with the support of European allies and Arab partners, to prevent a humanitarian catastrophe and address the threat posed to international peace and security by the crisis in Libya." Lacking specific congressional approval, he claimed that he had directed U.S. military intervention "pursuant to my constitutional authority to conduct U.S. foreign relations and as Commander in Chief and Chief Executive."

In a similar vein, the Justice Department's Office of Legal Counsel issued an opinion on April 1 concluding that "President Obama could rely on his constitutional power to safeguard the national interest by directing the anticipated military operations in Libya . . . without prior congressional authorization." *Authority to Use Military Force in Libya*, 35 Op. O.L.C. ___ (2011). Rehearsing all the arguments in its opinion on Somalia, *supra* p. 422, the new opinion stressed that two national interests in particular — "preserving regional stability and supporting the UNSC's credibility and effectiveness — provided a sufficient basis for the President's exercise of his constitutional authority to order the use of military force." Moreover, the opinion argued, the deployment in Libya was "limited in nature, scope, and duration," and "the risk of substantial casualties for U.S. forces would be low." The conflict was not a " 'war' within the meaning of the Declaration of War Clause," furthermore, because it did not concern a "prolonged and substantial military engagement[] . . . involving exposure of U.S. military personnel to significant risk over a substantial period."

Are you convinced by these arguments that specific congressional approval was not needed for U.S. involvement? Applying the criteria set out in the OLC opinion, is the case for unilateral presidential action stronger or weaker in Libya than it was in Somalia? Does this experience suggest that Congress ought to provide clearer guidance for future uses of military force?

Did the President's letter to Congress on March 19 satisfy the requirements of the War Power Resolution? Despite the President's failure to cite WPR §4(a)(1), which requires notice to Congress of the introduction of U.S. armed forces into hostilities or imminent hostilities, did the 60-day clock in WPR §5(b) begin to run? If so, precisely when? See *supra* p. 314.

Whether or not the President possessed domestic authority to send U.S. military forces into Libya, was his instruction to send covert CIA operatives into the country legal? See *infra* Chapter 17.

2. *The Scope of Security Council Resolution 1973.* How would you describe the objective or objectives of U.N. Security Council Resolution 1973? Why do you suppose five member states abstained from voting on it?

Did the protection of "civilians and civilian populated areas" include the defense of Libyan rebels seeking to overthrow the Qaddafi regime? Did it permit an alliance with the rebels?

What military actions were authorized by the term "all necessary measures"? In addition to a no-fly zone, did it approve air strikes on Qaddafi ground forces? Could member states have introduced ground troops to fight alongside Libyan rebels? Section 9 of Resolution 1970 established an arms embargo on Libya. Did this provision bar shipment of weapons to the beleaguered rebels? Humanitarian aid? Funds from the assets frozen by President Obama's executive order on February 25? What about sharing of battlefield intelligence from radio intercepts, Internet surveillance, or satellite imagery?

Some worried that pro-Qaddafi and rebel forces would fight to a stalemate. How long was the authority created by the resolution meant to continue?

3. *Grounds for Humanitarian Intervention?* Should the conflict in Libya be regarded as a civil war — a matter to be settled internally, for better or for worse? If so, could Resolution 1973 be squared with the principle of non-intervention in Article 2(7), set forth *supra* p. 431? With what the World Court declared in the *Nicaragua Case* about customary international law concerning interventions on humanitarian grounds, *supra* p. 218? Does it matter that the conflict in this case apparently was purely political, and not primarily ethnic, as in Rwanda, religious, as in Bosnia, or racial, as in Darfur? Would your answer be different if the conflict were instead fundamentally tribal? *See* David D. Kirkpatrick, *A Struggle for Democracy, or Just a Tribal Civil War?*, N.Y. Times, Mar. 22, 2011. Are you clear about which basic human rights the intervening states sought to vindicate? Are these rights so important that they justify what would otherwise be considered an inexcusable violation of Libya's sovereignty? Could the answer to the questions turn on possible effects of the conflict outside Libya's borders — for example, the creation of large numbers of refugees, who might threaten the peace and stability of neighboring states?

4. *Authority for "Regime Change"?* Was Resolution 1973 in fact authority for "regime change" in Libya? Many believed that the humanitarian goals of the resolution could not be achieved unless Qaddafi were forced to step down. If the resolution could be read to have that practical effect, did it exceed the scope of the Security Council's authority under the U.N. Charter? If not, what are the implications for the concept of sovereignty, always the touchstone of international relations?

5. *NATO's Role.* What was the legal basis for NATO's military involvement in Libya? If, as a regional organization, it needed the approval of the U.N. Security Council under Article 53(1), see *supra* p. 337, did it get it?

6. *Planning for Future Libyas.* As this was written, in Spring 2011, the outcome of fighting between government and rebel forces in Libya could not be predicted, while political upheaval continued throughout the Middle East and North Africa. It seemed quite possible, perhaps even likely, that over the near term we would continue to see civilian protestors seeking democratic reforms in a number of states. In some of those states the protestors might continue to be suppressed violently. And some of those states could be longtime allies of the United States — important because of their assistance in the fight against terrorists, their strategic location in an unstable part of the world, and/or our reliance on them to supply us with oil and gas. Should Congress try to anticipate such developments by adopting policies to govern U.S. military responses? What should those policies be, and how should they be expressed?

IV
Intelligence Operations and Collection

Organization and Authority of the Intelligence Community

16

The intelligence community is really two communities with distinctly different roles in protecting national security. This dual character has been the source of much confusion. Both roles are sometimes played by a single government agency, sometimes acting under the same statutory authority. The two roles are usually unrelated, although one may sometimes support the other.

One role of the intelligence community is the collection, analysis, and dissemination of information about threats to national security. The end of the Cold War and the emergence of asymmetric attacks on the United States have presented unprecedented challenges in this regard. Instead of a single-minded focus on the Soviet Union, intelligence agents now must target a wide range of potential enemies across the globe, including both states and potentially lethal non-state actors intent on doing harm to the United States. With the introduction of new technology, the cloak-and-dagger excitement of spy novels has given way somewhat to a tedious, mechanical sifting through masses of electronic data. Information is now easier to come by, harder to digest, and less trustworthy. Meanwhile, counterespionage efforts have become much more sophisticated. All these collection activities have raised new concerns about constitutional guarantees of privacy, free expression, and free association.

The other major role of the intelligence community is the conduct of covert actions. For most of our post-World War II history, the CIA (and occasionally other agencies) carried out such actions against the former Soviet Union or perceived communist threats around the world — in Southeast Asia, the Middle East, Latin America, and the Caribbean. U.S. agents generated propaganda and took part in political actions in an effort to influence other governments. They helped to overthrow governments in, for example, Iran, Guatemala, Cuba, and Chile. They were even involved in political assassinations, and they employed unsavory assets and groups, who were later revealed to be engaged in drug-trafficking and human rights abuses. Increasingly today, covert actions seek to attack and disrupt terrorist groups and ward off their planned attacks, to foil narcotics shipments, and to thwart financial transactions of black market weapons traders. As a former CIA lawyer once put it,

"CIA officers break the law every day." A. John Radsan, Remarks at a Conference at Duke University (Apr. 15, 2011).

Revelations about secret aspects of the Vietnam War and related disruptions of domestic protest groups, along with congressional investigations into intelligence excesses around the world through the early 1970s, began a reform process that truly took root only after the collapse of the Soviet Union. Congress has enacted a number of measures designed to give it a much larger oversight role than previously in both intelligence collection and covert actions, while the Executive has generally resisted these legislative initiatives, preferring to act independently. The courts, meanwhile, have become involved in the resulting disputes between the two political branches only rarely and reluctantly.

In this chapter, we examine the organization and legal authorities of the intelligence community. In Part A, we explore both statutory and executive authorities. In Part B, we focus on the post-9/11 reorganization of the community and identify some continuing problems and ambiguities.

In the chapters that follow, we see how these authorities apply in practice. In Chapter 17, we examine covert actions, with a particular emphasis on the Iran-Contra Affair and congressional oversight. In Chapter 18, we focus on dirty assets, military special operations, and the use of contractors. And in Chapters 19-25, we examine domestic intelligence collection before and after 9/11 — including privacy issues raised by government access to third-party records, data mining, security screening, and profiling — as well as surveillance abroad.

A.   AUTHORITY FOR INTELLIGENCE ACTIVITIES

1.   Statutory Authorities

General George Washington employed a cadre of spies and saboteurs during the Revolutionary War. Indeed, his intelligence agents played an important role in winning U.S. independence. Likewise, President Abraham Lincoln relied heavily on secret intelligence collection during the Civil War. Until World War II, intelligence was chiefly the responsibility of the military services (augmented by the FBI domestically). Caught by surprise when the Japanese bombed Pearl Harbor, wartime intelligence slowly developed a civilian capacity in the Office of Strategic Services (OSS) and, at war's end, the Central Intelligence Group (CIG). Tim Weiner, *Legacy of Ashes: The History of the CIA* 3-19 (2007). But at the end of the war there still was no coherent national intelligence service and no statutory authority for one. That changed in 1947 with the passage of legislation that, much amended, still forms the charter for the defense and intelligence communities.

The National Security Act of 1947, Pub. L. No. 80-253, 61 Stat. 495 (codified as amended in scattered sections of 10 & 50 U.S.C.), was slightly amended and recodified in 1992, 1993, 1996, and 2001. More significant changes, including the creation of the Director of National Intelligence (DNI), were made in the Intelligence Reform and Terrorism Prevention Act of 2004, Pub. L. No. 108-458, 118 Stat. 3638. References to the Act in the following text are to its current codification.

a. The DNI

The Act describes the authority of the DNI and of the CIA only in the most general terms. Regarding the DNI, the Act provides:

50 U.S.C. §403-1. Responsibilities and Authorities of the Director of National Intelligence

(a) Provision of intelligence

(1) The Director of National Intelligence shall be responsible for ensuring that national intelligence is provided—

(A) to the President;

(B) to the heads of departments and agencies of the executive branch;

(C) to the Chairman of the Joint Chiefs of Staff and senior military commanders;

(D) to the Senate and House of Representatives and the committees thereof; and

(E) to such other persons as the Director of National Intelligence determines to be appropriate.

(2) Such national intelligence should be timely, objective, independent of political considerations, and based upon all sources available to the intelligence community and other appropriate entities....

(b) Access to intelligence. Unless otherwise directed by the President, the Director of National Intelligence shall have access to all national intelligence and intelligence related to the national security which is collected by any Federal department, agency, or other entity, except as otherwise provided by law or, as appropriate, under guidelines agreed upon by the Attorney General and the Director of National Intelligence....

(f) Tasking and other authorities

(1) (A) The Director of National Intelligence shall—

(i) establish objectives, priorities, and guidance for the intelligence community to ensure timely and effective collection, processing, analysis, and dissemination (including access by users to collected data consistent with applicable law and, as appropriate, the guidelines referred to in subsection (b) and analytic products generated by or within the intelligence community) of national intelligence;

(ii) determine requirements and priorities for, and manage and direct the tasking of, collection, analysis, production, and dissemination of national intelligence by elements of the intelligence community, including—

(I) approving requirements (including those requirements responding to needs provided by consumers) for collection and analysis; and

(II) resolving conflicts in collection requirements and in the tasking of national collection assets of the elements of the intelligence community; and

(iii) provide advisory tasking to intelligence elements of those agencies and departments not within the National Intelligence Program. [See *infra* p. 461.]...

(4) The Director of National Intelligence shall ensure compliance with the Constitution and laws of the United States by the Central Intelligence Agency and shall ensure such compliance by other elements of the intelligence community through the host executive departments that manage the programs and activities that are part of the National Intelligence Program....

(6) The Director of National Intelligence shall establish requirements and priorities for foreign intelligence information to be collected under the Foreign Intelligence Surveillance Act of 1978 (50 U.S.C. 1801 et seq.), and provide assistance to the Attorney General to ensure that information derived from electronic surveillance or physical searches under that Act is disseminated so it may be used efficiently and effectively for national intelligence purposes, except that the Director shall have no authority to direct or undertake electronic surveillance or physical search operations pursuant to that Act unless authorized by statute or Executive order.

(7) The Director of National Intelligence shall perform such other functions as the President may direct. . . .

(h) Analysis. To ensure the most accurate analysis of intelligence is derived from all sources to support national security needs, the Director of National Intelligence shall—

(1) implement policies and procedures—

(A) to encourage sound analytic methods and tradecraft throughout the elements of the intelligence community;

(B) to ensure that analysis is based upon all sources available; and

(C) to ensure that the elements of the intelligence community regularly conduct competitive analysis of analytic products, whether such products are produced by or disseminated to such elements; . . .

(i) Protection of intelligence sources and methods

(1) The Director of National Intelligence shall protect intelligence sources and methods from unauthorized disclosure. . . .

b.   The CIA

Concerning the Central Intelligence Agency, the Act provides:

50 U.S.C. §403-4a. Director of Central Intelligence Agency

(a) Director of Central Intelligence Agency. There is a Director of the Central Intelligence Agency who shall be appointed by the President, by and with the advice and consent of the Senate.

(b) Supervision. The Director of the Central Intelligence Agency shall report to the Director of National Intelligence regarding the activities of the Central Intelligence Agency.

(c) Duties. The Director of the Central Intelligence Agency shall—

(1) serve as the head of the Central Intelligence Agency; and

(2) carry out the responsibilities specified in subsection (d) of this section.

(d) Responsibilities. The Director of the Central Intelligence Agency shall—

(1) collect intelligence through human sources and by other appropriate means, except that the Director of the Central Intelligence Agency shall have no police, subpoena, or law enforcement powers or internal security functions;

(2) correlate and evaluate intelligence related to the national security and provide appropriate dissemination of such intelligence;

(3) provide overall direction for and coordination of the collection of national intelligence outside the United States through human sources by elements of the intelligence community authorized to undertake such collection and, in coordination with other departments, agencies, or elements of the United States Government which

are authorized to undertake such collection, ensure that the most effective use is made of resources and that appropriate account is taken of the risks to the United States and those involved in such collection; and

(4) perform such other functions and duties related to intelligence affecting the national security as the President or the Director of National Intelligence may direct....

c. The National Security Council

The National Security Council (NSC) was created in the 1947 Act "to advise the President with respect to the integration of domestic, foreign, and military policies relating to the national security." National Security Act of 1947, Pub. L. No. 80-253, §101, 61 Stat. 495, 496. Its statutory members were the President, the Vice President, the Secretary of State, and the Secretary of Defense. 50 U.S.C. §402(a) (2006). The Secretary of Energy was added as a statutory member in 2007. Pub. L. No. 110-140, §932, 121 Stat. 1740. Other cabinet members and executive officials have been authorized by Congress to attend and participate in NSC meetings, subject to the President's direction (e.g., U.S. Coordinator for the Prevention of Weapons of Mass Destruction Proliferation and Terrorism, created by the Implementing Recommendations of the 9/11 Commission Act of 2007, Pub. L. No. 110-53, §1841(g), 121 Stat. 500 (2007)), or have simply been invited by Presidents to attend pursuant to each President's preferred management of the NSC system. *See* Cody M. Brown, *The National Security Council: A Legal History of the President's Most Powerful Advisers* 71-72 (2008).

The statutory functions of the NSC include the following:

(b) ... In addition to performing such other functions as the President may direct, for the purpose of more effectively coordinating the policies and functions of the departments and agencies of the Government relating to the national security, it shall ... be the duty of the Council—

(1) to assess and appraise the objectives, commitments, and risks of the United States in relation to our actual and potential military power, in the interest of national security, for the purpose of making recommendations to the President in connection therewith; and

(2) to consider policies on matters of common interest to the departments and agencies of the Government concerned with the national security, and to make recommendations to the President in connection therewith.... [50 U.S.C. §402(b).]

Originally, the 1947 Act authorized an executive secretariat to serve as staff to the NSC. In 1953, however, President Eisenhower created the position of Assistant to the President for National Security Affairs, now known as National Security Adviser, pursuant to a statute that authorized the appointment of "employees in the White House Office." 3 U.S.C. §105(a)(1), (2) (2006). The position was created to supervise the NSC staff and to brief the President on national security affairs. *See generally* Brown, *supra.* Nevertheless, the National Security Adviser's role has varied widely since then. *See* Office of the Historian, Bureau of Pub. Affairs, United States Dep't of State, *History of the National Security Council 1947–1997* (1997), *available at* http://www.fas.org/irp/offdocs/NSChistory.htm

NOTES AND QUESTIONS

1. *Why a Statute?* During World War II, some covert operations were directed by an agency called the Office of Strategic Services. Weiner, *supra*, at 7. When the war ended, the Administration debated whether to continue this practice based on executive authority or to seek statutory approval for it. Why would President Truman have sought legislative authority for intelligence operations? What impact did passage of the National Security Act have on claims of inherent executive power to conduct intelligence operations?

2. *The "Fifth Function": Covert Collection or Covert Action?* Early on the CIA relied on what is now codified as §403-4a(d)(4) of the 1947 Act (authority to "perform such other functions and duties related to intelligence affecting the national security as the President...may direct") as authority both to engage in the direct collection of intelligence and to conduct covert actions. *See* Select Comm. to Study Governmental Operations with Respect to Intelligence Activities (Church Comm.), *Foreign and Military Intelligence*, S. Rep. No. 94-755, bk. I, at 128-131 (1976) (*Church Comm. Report*); *Statement of Mitchell Rogovin, Special Counsel to the Director of Central Intelligence*, Hearings Before the House Select Comm. on Intelligence, 94th Cong., pt. 5, at 1729, 1734-1735 (1976); Robert Borosage, *Para-Legal Authority and Its Problems*, 40 Law & Contemp. Probs. 166, 175-177 (1976). This provision was referred to as "the fifth function" because of its original numbering in the National Security Act and the ambiguity surrounding the actual operations that it authorized. CIA Special Counsel Rogovin argued that the fifth function permitted the CIA "to conduct a broad range of operational assignments," including what are today called covert actions. Scholar Borosage and others disagreed, asserting that the fifth function included only intelligence collection, citing the absence from the legislative history of explicit references to covert or paramilitary actions. Does the language of §403-4a(d)(4) indicate which interpretation is correct? If Rogovin is right, can you explain why no one in public debate mentioned covert actions? Is it always possible to distinguish between the two types of CIA activities, particularly when the methods employed are similar?

3. *Military Intelligence.* The role for military intelligence agencies was not clearly spelled out in the 1947 Act:

> The 1947 Act provided no explicit charter for military intelligence. The charter and mission of military intelligence activities [were] established either by executive orders...or various National Security Council directives. These National Security Council Intelligence Directives (NSCIDs) were the principal means of establishing the roles and functions of all the various entities in the intelligence community. They composed the so-called "secret charter" for the CIA. However, most of them also permitted "departmental" intelligence activities, and in this way also provided the executive charter for the intelligence activities of the State Department and the Pentagon. However, the intelligence activities of the Department of Defense remained with the military rather than with the new Defense Department civilians. [*Church Comm. Rep.*, *supra*, bk. I, at 21.]

The military regularly collected intelligence for its own operations long before the enactment of the National Security Act. In light of this historical fact, can you explain why Congress omitted any explicit reference to military intelligence activities in the National Security Act? Could Congress have subjected the intelligence activities of the Department of Defense to the control of the CIA Director, or, more recently, of the DNI? Should it have done so? Do the executive orders and/or NSC directives establish sufficient legal authority for military intelligence activities? The principal executive order that speaks to military intelligence is considered in the next subsection. The activities of military intelligence agencies are examined *infra* pp. 519, 1160.

4. *Who Makes Intelligence Policy?* It is clear from the 1947 Act that the NSC was created neither to make national security decisions nor to carry them out. The same may be said of the later-created National Security Adviser. In fact, however, both the NSC staff and the National Security Adviser have engaged in operations, although these instances may be aberrations. See *infra* p. 495. Consider this assessment of the evolving role of the NSC:

> Since passage of the original National Security Act of 1947, Congress has left unchanged the fundamental purpose, function, and duties of the NSC. Each President has made an independent determination of the type of NSC that would best serve the nation. But over time, it is clear that the NSC has evolved from a limited advisory council to a vast network of interagency groups that are deeply involved in integrating national security policy development, oversight of implementation, and crisis management. This evolution has not been the result of congressional action, but rather presidential determination, rooted in the increasingly complex task of managing and optimizing U.S. national security. [Brown, *supra*, at 81.]

See also Richard A. Best, *The National Security Council: An Organizational Assessment* (Cong. Res. Serv. RL30840), Sept. 23, 2010.

It is equally clear from the 1947 Act that the CIA was not meant to make intelligence policy, especially given the requirement that the CIA act at the direction of the NSC. However, the CIA has on occasion been the driving force in intelligence operations policy-making, notwithstanding the 1947 Act. If the NSC and the CIA are strictly confined to executive roles, who does establish intelligence policy?

2.   Presidential Authority

After extensive media reports describing rogue CIA operations in Chile, Southeast Asia (during the Vietnam War), and scattered other locations across the globe through the early 1970s (see *infra* pp. 511-513), in 1975 the Senate created the Select Committee to Study Governmental Operations (later known as the Church Committee after its Chair, Senator Frank Church of Idaho). The Committee was charged with determining "the extent, if any, to which illegal, improper, or unethical activities were engaged in by the intelligence agencies." S. Res. 21, 94th Cong. (1975). The Church Committee found that the procedures for executive branch

Adapted from: Carroll Publishing, Bethesda, Md (2005), used by permission.

review of covert operations were inadequate and had on occasion been entirely circumvented. *See Church Comm. Report, supra,* bk. I, at 159. As part of an ambitious bill to regulate the intelligence community, the Committee recommended that a group consisting of the Secretaries of State and Defense, the National Security Adviser, the Director of the Central Intelligence Agency, the Attorney General, the Chairman of the Joint Chiefs of Staff, and the Director of the OMB (as an observer) be required to approve each covert action proposal and review all covert projects at least annually. *Id.* at 159-161.

Partly to avoid legislative interference in intelligence activities, President Ford responded by promulgating Executive Order No. 11,905, 41 Fed. Reg. 7707 (Feb. 18, 1976). The order created an Operations Advisory Group (OAG) with the membership recommended by the Church Committee, except that the Attorney General was made an observer rather than a member of the group. *Id.* §3(c). The OAG was charged with making a recommendation for each "special activity" and forwarding it, along with any dissents, to the President. *Id.* An Intelligence Oversight Board (IOB) was also created. *Id.* §6. The three-member Board would review, at the instance of members of the intelligence community, "activities that raise questions of legality or propriety." *Id.* The order also prohibited government employees from participating in assassination. It thus provided for at least some of what intelligence legislation might have regulated, with this crucial difference: the President could secretly change or waive self-imposed limitations on intelligence activities.

President Carter's Executive Order No. 12,036, 43 Fed. Reg. 3675 (Jan. 24, 1978), replaced the OAG with the Special Coordination Committee (SCC). The Carter order incorporated most of the provisions for high-level review of operational proposals from President Ford's order. However, the Attorney General became a full member of the SCC, *id.* §1-302, and her oversight role grew to include the responsibility to receive reports from intelligence agency heads and forward to the President information about possible unlawful activity by subordinate agency officials. *Id.* §§1-706, 3-302. The order also for the first time included requirements that the Director of the Central Intelligence Agency keep the congressional intelligence committees "fully and currently" informed of ongoing activities, as well as "any significant anticipated activities," *id.* §3-401, creating an oversight template that is still used today.

The Carter order was replaced in 1981 by another signed by President Reagan that, as amended, continues to set out presidential direction for intelligence operations and collection. Executive Order No. 12,333 remains today the most nearly comprehensive regulatory framework for U.S. intelligence activities.

Executive Order No. 12,333
United States Intelligence Activities

(as amended by Executive Order Nos. 13,284 (2003),
13,355 (2004), and 13,470 (2008))
73 Fed. Reg. 45,325 (July 30, 2008)

Timely, accurate, and insightful information about the activities, capabilities, plans, and intentions of foreign powers, organizations, and persons and their agents, is essential to the national security of the United States. All reasonable and lawful means must be used to ensure that the United States will receive the best intelligence possible. For that purpose, by virtue of the authority vested in me by the Constitution and the laws of the United States of America, including the National Security Act of 1947 (Act), as amended, and as President of the United States of America, in order to provide for the effective conduct of United States intelligence activities and the protection of constitutional rights, it is hereby ordered as follows:

PART 1. *GOALS, DIRECTIONS, DUTIES, AND RESPONSIBILITIES WITH RESPECT TO UNITED STATES INTELLIGENCE EFFORTS*

1.1 *Goals.* The United States intelligence effort shall provide the President, the National Security Council, and the Homeland Security Council with the necessary information on which to base decisions concerning the development and conduct of foreign, defense, and economic policies, and the protection of United States national interests from foreign security threats. All departments and agencies shall cooperate fully to fulfill this goal.

(a) All means, consistent with applicable Federal law and this order, and with full consideration of the rights of United States persons, shall be used to obtain reliable intelligence information to protect the United States and its interests. . . .

(g) All departments and agencies have a responsibility to prepare and to provide intelligence in a manner that allows the full and free exchange of information, consistent with applicable law and presidential guidance.

1.2 *The National Security Council.*

(a) *Purpose.* The National Security Council (NSC) shall act as the highest ranking executive branch entity that provides support to the President for review of, guidance for, and direction to the conduct of all foreign intelligence, counterintelligence, and covert action, and attendant policies and programs.

(b) *Covert Action and Other Sensitive Intelligence Operations.* The NSC shall consider and submit to the President a policy recommendation, including all dissents, on each proposed covert action and conduct a periodic review of ongoing covert action activities, including an evaluation of the effectiveness and consistency with current national policy of such activities and consistency with applicable legal requirements. The NSC shall perform such other functions related to covert action as the President may direct, but shall not undertake the conduct of covert actions. The NSC shall also review proposals for other sensitive intelligence operations.

1.3 *Director of National Intelligence.* Subject to the authority, direction, and control of the President, the Director of National Intelligence (Director) shall serve as the head of the Intelligence Community, act as the principal adviser to the President, to the NSC, and to the Homeland Security Council for intelligence matters related to national security, and shall oversee and direct the implementation of the National Intelligence Program and execution of the National Intelligence Program budget. The Director will lead a unified, coordinated, and effective intelligence effort. In addition, the Director shall, in carrying out the duties and responsibilities under this section, take into account the views of the heads of departments containing an element of the Intelligence Community and of the Director of the Central Intelligence Agency.

(a) Except as otherwise directed by the President or prohibited by law, the Director shall have access to all information and intelligence described in section

1.5(a) of this order. For the purpose of access to and sharing of information and intelligence, the Director: . . .

(2) Shall develop guidelines for how information or intelligence is provided to or accessed by the Intelligence Community in accordance with section 1.5(a) of this order, and for how the information or intelligence may be used and shared by the Intelligence Community. All guidelines developed in accordance with this section shall be approved by the Attorney General and, where applicable, shall be consistent with guidelines issued pursuant to section 1016 of the Intelligence Reform and Terrorism Protection Act of 2004 (Public Law 108-458) (IRTPA) [*infra* p. 551].

(b) In addition to fulfilling the obligations and responsibilities prescribed by the Act, the Director:

(1) Shall establish objectives, priorities, and guidance for the Intelligence Community to ensure timely and effective collection, processing, analysis, and dissemination of intelligence, of whatever nature and from whatever source derived; . . .

(3) Shall oversee and provide advice to the President and the NSC with respect to all ongoing and proposed covert action programs;

(4) In regard to the establishment and conduct of intelligence arrangements and agreements with foreign governments and international organizations:

(A) May enter into intelligence and counterintelligence arrangements and agreements with foreign governments and international organizations;

(B) Shall formulate policies concerning intelligence and counterintelligence arrangements and agreements with foreign governments and international organizations; and

(C) Shall align and synchronize intelligence and counterintelligence foreign relationships among the elements of the Intelligence Community to further United States national security, policy, and intelligence objectives; . . .

(6) Shall establish common security and access standards for managing and handling intelligence systems, information, and products, with special emphasis on facilitating:

(A) The fullest and most prompt access to and dissemination of information and intelligence practicable, assigning the highest priority to detecting, preventing, preempting, and disrupting terrorist threats and activities against the United States, its interests, and allies; and

(B) The establishment of standards for an interoperable information sharing enterprise that facilitates the sharing of intelligence information among elements of the Intelligence Community;

(7) Shall ensure that appropriate departments and agencies have access to intelligence and receive the support needed to perform independent analysis;

(8) Shall protect, and ensure that programs are developed to protect, intelligence sources, methods, and activities from unauthorized disclosure;

(9) Shall, after consultation with the heads of affected departments and agencies, establish guidelines for Intelligence Community elements for:

(A) Classification and declassification of all intelligence and intelligence-related information classified under the authority of the Director or the authority of the head of a department or Intelligence Community element; . . .

(14) Shall have ultimate responsibility for production and dissemination of intelligence produced by the Intelligence Community and authority to levy analytic tasks on intelligence production organizations within the Intelligence Community, in consultation with the heads of the Intelligence Community elements concerned; . . .

(16) Shall ensure the timely exploitation and dissemination of data gathered by national intelligence collection means, and ensure that the resulting intelligence is disseminated immediately to appropriate government elements, including military commands;

(17) Shall determine requirements and priorities for, and manage and direct the tasking, collection, analysis, production, and dissemination of, national intelligence by elements of the Intelligence Community, including approving requirements for collection and analysis and resolving conflicts in collection requirements and in the tasking of national collection assets of Intelligence Community elements (except when otherwise directed by the President or when the Secretary of Defense exercises collection tasking authority under plans and arrangements approved by the Secretary of Defense and the Director); . . .

(20) Shall ensure, through appropriate policies and procedures, the deconfliction, coordination, and integration of all intelligence activities conducted by an Intelligence Community element or funded by the National Intelligence Program. In accordance with these policies and procedures:

(A) The Director of the Federal Bureau of Investigation shall coordinate the clandestine collection of foreign intelligence collected through human sources or through human-enabled means and counterintelligence activities inside the United States;

(B) The Director of the Central Intelligence Agency shall coordinate the clandestine collection of foreign intelligence collected through human sources or through human-enabled means and counterintelligence activities outside the United States;

(C) All policies and procedures for the coordination of counterintelligence activities and the clandestine collection of foreign intelligence inside the United States shall be subject to the approval of the Attorney General; and

(D) All policies and procedures developed under this section shall be coordinated with the heads of affected departments and Intelligence Community elements; . . .

(c) The Director's exercise of authorities in the Act and this order shall not abrogate the statutory or other responsibilities of the heads of departments of the United States Government or the Director of the Central Intelligence Agency. . . .

1.4. *The Intelligence Community.* Consistent with applicable Federal law and with the other provisions of this order, and under the leadership of the Director, as specified in such law and this order, the Intelligence Community shall:

(a) Collect and provide information needed by the President and, in the performance of executive functions, the Vice President, the NSC, the Homeland Security Council, the Chairman of the Joint Chiefs of Staff, senior military commanders, and other executive branch officials and, as appropriate, the Congress of the United States;

(b) In accordance with priorities set by the President, collect information concerning, and conduct activities to protect against, international terrorism, proliferation of weapons of mass destruction, intelligence activities directed against the United States, international criminal drug activities, and other hostile activities directed against the United States by foreign powers, organizations, persons, and their agents;

(c) Analyze, produce, and disseminate intelligence; . . .

(f) Protect the security of intelligence related activities, information, installations, property, and employees by appropriate means, including such investigations of applicants, employees, contractors, and other persons with similar associations with the Intelligence Community elements as are necessary; . . .

(i) Perform such other functions and duties related to intelligence activities as the President may direct. . . .

1.5. *Duties and Responsibilities of the Heads of Executive Departments and Agencies.* The heads of all departments and agencies shall:

(a) Provide the Director access to all information and intelligence relevant to the national security or that otherwise is required for the performance of the Director's duties . . . except such information excluded by law, by the President, or by the Attorney General acting under this order at the direction of the President. . . .

1.6. *Heads of Elements of the Intelligence Community.* The heads of elements of the Intelligence Community shall:

(a) Provide the Director access to all information and intelligence relevant to the national security or that otherwise is required for the performance of the Director's duties, to include administrative and other appropriate management information, except such information excluded by law, by the President, or by the Attorney General acting under this order at the direction of the President;

(b) Report to the Attorney General possible violations of Federal criminal laws by employees and of specified Federal criminal laws by any other person as provided in procedures agreed upon by the Attorney General and the head of the department, agency, or establishment concerned, in a manner consistent with the protection of intelligence sources and methods, as specified in those procedures;

(c) Report to the Intelligence Oversight Board, consistent with Executive Order 13462 of February 29, 2008, and provide copies of all such reports to the Director, concerning any intelligence activities of their elements that they have reason to believe may be unlawful or contrary to executive order or presidential directive;

(d) Protect intelligence and intelligence sources, methods, and activities from unauthorized disclosure in accordance with guidance from the Director;

(e) Facilitate, as appropriate, the sharing of information or intelligence, as directed by law or the President, to State, local, tribal, and private sector entities;

(f) Disseminate information or intelligence to foreign governments and international organizations under intelligence or counterintelligence arrangements or agreements established in accordance with section 1.3(b)(4) of this order; . . .

(h) Ensure that the inspectors general, general counsels, and agency officials responsible for privacy or civil liberties protection for their respective organizations have access to any information or intelligence necessary to perform their official duties.

1.7. *Intelligence Community Elements.* Each element of the Intelligence Community shall have the duties and responsibilities specified below, in addition to those specified by law or elsewhere in this order. Intelligence Community elements within executive departments shall serve the information and intelligence needs of their respective heads of departments and also shall operate as part of an integrated Intelligence Community, as provided in law or this order.

(a) *The Central Intelligence Agency.* The Director of the Central Intelligence Agency shall:

(1) Collect (including through clandestine means), analyze, produce, and disseminate foreign intelligence and counterintelligence;

(2) Conduct counterintelligence activities without assuming or performing any internal security functions within the United States;

(3) Conduct administrative and technical support activities within and outside the United States as necessary for cover and proprietary arrangements;

(4) Conduct covert action activities approved by the President. No agency except the Central Intelligence Agency (or the Armed Forces of the United States in time of war declared by the Congress or during any period covered by a report from the President to the Congress consistent with the War Powers Resolution, Public Law 93-148) may conduct any covert action activity unless the President determines that another agency is more likely to achieve a particular objective;

(5) Conduct foreign intelligence liaison relationships with intelligence or security services of foreign governments or international organizations consistent with section 1.3(b)(4) of this order;

(6) Under the direction and guidance of the Director, and in accordance with section 1.3(b)(4) of this order, coordinate the implementation of intelligence and counterintelligence relationships between elements of the Intelligence Community and the intelligence or security services of foreign governments or international organizations; and

(7) Perform such other functions and duties related to intelligence as the Director may direct....

(c) *The National Security Agency.* The Director of the National Security Agency shall:

(1) Collect (including through clandestine means), process, analyze, produce, and disseminate signals intelligence information and data for foreign intelligence and counterintelligence purposes to support national and departmental missions;

(2) Establish and operate an effective unified organization for signals intelligence activities, except for the delegation of operational control over certain operations that are conducted through other elements of the Intelligence Community. No other department or agency may engage in signals intelligence activities except pursuant to a delegation by the Secretary of Defense, after coordination with the Director;

(3) Control signals intelligence collection and processing activities, including assignment of resources to an appropriate agent for such periods and tasks as required for the direct support of military commanders;

(4) Conduct administrative and technical support activities within and outside the United States as necessary for cover arrangements;

(5) Provide signals intelligence support for national and departmental requirements and for the conduct of military operations; ...

(g) *Intelligence Elements of the Federal Bureau of Investigation.* Under the supervision of the Attorney General and pursuant to such regulations as the Attorney

General may establish, the intelligence elements of the Federal Bureau of Investigation shall:

(1) Collect (including through clandestine means), analyze, produce, and disseminate foreign intelligence and counterintelligence to support national and departmental missions, in accordance with procedural guidelines approved by the Attorney General, after consultation with the Director;

(2) Conduct counterintelligence activities; and

(3) Conduct foreign intelligence and counterintelligence liaison relationships with intelligence, security, and law enforcement services of foreign governments or international organizations in accordance with sections 1.3(b)(4) and 1.7(a)(6) of this order....

(j) *The Office of the Director of National Intelligence.* The Director shall collect (overtly or through publicly available sources), analyze, produce, and disseminate information, intelligence, and counterintelligence to support the missions of the Office of the Director of National Intelligence, including the National Counterterrorism Center, and to support other national missions....

1.10. *The Department of Defense.* The Secretary of Defense shall:

(a) Collect (including through clandestine means), analyze, produce, and disseminate information and intelligence and be responsive to collection tasking and advisory tasking by the Director;

(b) Collect (including through clandestine means), analyze, produce, and disseminate defense and defense related intelligence and counterintelligence, as required for execution of the Secretary's responsibilities;

(c) Conduct programs and missions necessary to fulfill national, departmental, and tactical intelligence requirements;

(d) Conduct counterintelligence activities in support of Department of Defense components and coordinate counterintelligence activities in accordance with section 1.3(b)(20) and (21) of this order;

(e) Act, in coordination with the Director, as the executive agent of the United States Government for signals intelligence activities; ...

PART 2. *CONDUCT OF INTELLIGENCE ACTIVITIES...*

2.2. *Purpose.* ... Set forth below are certain general principles that, in addition to and consistent with applicable laws, are intended to achieve the proper balance between the acquisition of essential information and protection of individual interests. Nothing in this Order shall be construed to apply to or interfere with any authorized civil or criminal law enforcement responsibility of any department or agency.

2.3. *Collection of Information.* Elements of the Intelligence Community are authorized to collect, retain or disseminate information concerning United States persons only in accordance with procedures established by the head of the Intelligence Community element concerned ... and approved by the Attorney General ... after consultation with the Director. Those procedures shall permit collection, retention, and dissemination of the following types of information: ...

(b) Information constituting foreign intelligence or counterintelligence, including such information concerning corporations or other commercial organizations. Collection within the United States of foreign intelligence not otherwise obtainable shall be undertaken by the Federal Bureau of Investigation (FBI) or, when significant foreign intelligence is sought, by other authorized elements of the

Intelligence Community, provided that no foreign intelligence collection by such elements may be undertaken for the purpose of acquiring information concerning the domestic activities of United States persons; . . .

(e) Information needed to protect foreign intelligence or counterintelligence sources, methods, and activities from unauthorized disclosure. Collection within the United States shall be undertaken by the FBI except that other elements of the Intelligence Community may also collect such information concerning present or former employees, present or former intelligence element contractors or their present or former employees, or applicants for such employment or contracting; . . .

2.4. *Collection Techniques.* Elements of the Intelligence Community shall use the least intrusive collection techniques feasible within the United States or directed against United States persons abroad. Elements of the Intelligence Community are not authorized to use such techniques as electronic surveillance, unconsented physical searches, mail surveillance, physical surveillance, or monitoring devices unless they are in accordance with procedures established by the head of the Intelligence Community element concerned or the head of a department containing such element and approved by the Attorney General, after consultation with the Director. Such procedures shall protect constitutional and other legal rights and limit use of such information to lawful governmental purposes. These procedures shall not authorize:

(a) The Central Intelligence Agency (CIA) to engage in electronic surveillance within the United States except for the purpose of training, testing, or conducting countermeasures to hostile electronic surveillance;

(b) Unconsented physical searches in the United States by elements of the Intelligence Community other than the FBI, except for:

(1) Searches by counterintelligence elements of the military services directed against military personnel within the United States or abroad for intelligence purposes, when authorized by a military commander empowered to approve physical searches for law enforcement purposes, based upon a finding of probable cause to believe that such persons are acting as agents of foreign powers; and

(2) Searches by CIA of personal property of non-United States persons lawfully in its possession;

(c) Physical surveillance of a United States person in the United States by elements of the Intelligence Community other than the FBI, except for:

(1) Physical surveillance of present or former employees, present or former intelligence element contractors or their present or former employees, or applicants for any such employment or contracting; and

(2) Physical surveillance of a military person employed by a non-intelligence element of a military service; and

(d) Physical surveillance of a United States person abroad to collect foreign intelligence, except to obtain significant information that cannot reasonably be acquired by other means.

2.5. *Attorney General Approval.* The Attorney General hereby is delegated the power to approve the use for intelligence purposes, within the United States or against a United States person abroad, of any technique for which a warrant would be required if undertaken for law enforcement purposes, provided that such techniques shall not be undertaken unless the Attorney General has determined in each case that there is probable cause to believe that the technique is directed against a foreign power or an agent of a foreign power. The authority delegated pursuant to this paragraph, including the authority to approve the use of electronic surveillance as defined in the Foreign Intelligence Surveillance Act of 1978, as amended, shall be exercised in accordance with that Act.

2.6. *Assistance to Law Enforcement and Other Civil Authorities.* Elements of the Intelligence Community are authorized to: ...

    (b) Unless otherwise precluded by law or this Order, participate in law enforcement activities to investigate or prevent clandestine intelligence activities by foreign powers, or international terrorist or narcotics activities; ...

2.7. *Contracting.* Elements of the Intelligence Community are authorized to enter into contracts or arrangements for the provision of goods or services with private companies or institutions in the United States and need not reveal the sponsorship of such contracts or arrangements for authorized intelligence purposes. Contracts or arrangements with academic institutions may be undertaken only with the consent of appropriate officials of the institution.

2.8. *Consistency With Other Laws.* Nothing in this Order shall be construed to authorize any activity in violation of the Constitution or statutes of the United States.

2.9. *Undisclosed Participation in Organizations Within the United States.* No one acting on behalf of elements of the Intelligence Community may join or otherwise participate in any organization in the United States on behalf of any element within the Intelligence Community without disclosing such person's intelligence affiliation to appropriate officials of the organization, except in accordance with procedures established by the head of the Intelligence Community element concerned or the head of a department containing such element and approved by the Attorney General, after consultation with the Director. Such participation shall be authorized only if it is essential to achieving lawful purposes as determined by the Intelligence Community element head or designee. No such participation may be undertaken for the purpose of influencing the activity of the organization or its members except in cases where:

    (a) The participation is undertaken on behalf of the FBI in the course of a lawful investigation; or

    (b) The organization concerned is composed primarily of individuals who are not United States persons and is reasonably believed to be acting on behalf of a foreign power....

2.11. *Prohibition on Assassination.* No person employed by or acting on behalf of the United States Government shall engage in, or conspire to engage in, assassination.

2.12. *Indirect Participation.* No element of the Intelligence Community shall participate in or request any person to undertake activities forbidden by this Order.

2.13. *Limitation on Covert Action.* No covert action may be conducted which is intended to influence United States political processes, public opinion, policies, or media.

PART 3. *GENERAL PROVISIONS*

3.1. *Congressional Oversight.* The duties and responsibilities of the Director and the heads of other departments, agencies, elements, and entities engaged in intelligence activities to cooperate with the Congress in the conduct of its responsibilities for oversight of intelligence activities shall be implemented in accordance with applicable law, including title V of the [National Security Act of 1947, as amended]. The requirements of applicable law, including title V of the [National Security Act of 1947, as amended], shall apply to all covert action activities as defined in this Order. . . .

3.5. *Definitions.* For the purposes of this Order, the following terms shall have these meanings:

(a) *Counterintelligence* means information gathered and activities conducted to identify, deceive, exploit, disrupt, or protect against espionage, other intelligence activities, sabotage, or assassinations conducted for or on behalf of foreign powers, organizations, or persons, or their agents, or international terrorist organizations or activities.

(b) *Covert action* means an activity or activities of the United States Government to influence political, economic, or military conditions abroad, where it is intended that the role of the United States Government will not be apparent or acknowledged publicly, but does not include:

(1) Activities the primary purpose of which is to acquire intelligence, traditional counterintelligence activities, traditional activities to improve or maintain the operational security of United States Government programs, or administrative activities;

(2) Traditional diplomatic or military activities or routine support to such activities;

(3) Traditional law enforcement activities conducted by United States Government law enforcement agencies or routine support to such activities; or

(4) Activities to provide routine support to the overt activities (other than activities described in paragraph (1), (2), or (3)) of other United States Government agencies abroad.

(c) *Electronic surveillance* means acquisition of a nonpublic communication by electronic means without the consent of a person who is a party to an electronic communication or, in the case of a nonelectronic communication, without the consent of a person who is visibly present at the place of communication, but not including the use of radio direction-finding equipment solely to determine the location of a transmitter. . . .

(e) *Foreign intelligence* means information relating to the capabilities, intentions, or activities of foreign governments or elements thereof, foreign organizations, foreign persons, or international terrorists.

(f) *Intelligence* includes foreign intelligence and counter-intelligence.

(g) *Intelligence activities* means all activities that elements of the Intelligence Community are authorized to conduct pursuant to this order.

(h) *Intelligence Community* and agencies within the Intelligence Community refers to:

(1) The Office of the Director of National Intelligence;

(2) The Central Intelligence Agency;

(3) The National Security Agency;

(4) The Defense Intelligence Agency;

(5) The National Geospatial-Intelligence Agency;

(6) The National Reconnaissance Office;

(7) The other offices within the Department of Defense for the collection of specialized national foreign intelligence through reconnaissance programs;

(8) The intelligence and counterintelligence elements of the Army, the Navy, the Air Force, and the Marine Corps;

(9) The intelligence elements of the Federal Bureau of Investigation;

(10) The Office of National Security Intelligence of the Drug Enforcement Administration;

(11) The Office of Intelligence and Counterintelligence of the Department of Energy;

(12) The Bureau of Intelligence and Research of the Department of State;

(13) The Office of Intelligence and Analysis of the Department of the Treasury;

(14) The Office of Intelligence and Analysis of the Department of Homeland Security;

(15) The intelligence and counterintelligence elements of the Coast Guard; and

(16) Such other elements of any department or agency as may be designated by the President, or designated jointly by the Director and the head of the department or agency concerned, as an element of the Intelligence Community.

(i) *National Intelligence and Intelligence Related to National Security* means all intelligence, regardless of the source from which derived and including information gathered within or outside the United States, that pertains, as determined consistent with any guidance issued by the President, or that is determined for the purpose of access to information by the Director in accordance with section 1.3(a)(1) of this order, to pertain to more than one United States Government agency; and that involves threats to the United States, its people, property, or interests; the development, proliferation, or use of weapons of mass destruction; or any other matter bearing on United States national or homeland security.

(j) *The National Intelligence Program* means all programs, projects, and activities of the Intelligence Community, as well as any other programs of the Intelligence Community designated jointly by the Director and the head of a United States department or agency or by the President. Such term does not include programs, projects, or activities of the military departments to acquire intelligence solely for the planning and conduct of tactical military operations by United States Armed Forces.

(k) United States person means a United States citizen, an alien known by the intelligence element concerned to be a permanent resident alien, an unincorporated association substantially composed of United States citizens or permanent resident aliens, or a corporation incorporated in the United States, except for a corporation directed and controlled by a foreign government or governments. . . .

NOTES AND QUESTIONS

The preamble to Executive Order No. 12,333 is directed at intelligence information and its importance to the national security. Preamble language typically sets forth the presumed authority for the prescriptions that follow. Precisely what constitutional or statutory authority empowered the President to promulgate this executive order?

a.   Deciding on Intelligence Operations

1. *Who Initiates and Who Approves?* According to the executive order, which official or entity must approve an intelligence operation? Which officials or entities may originate proposals for covert action?

2. *Role of the NSC.* Consider the role of the NSC, as described in §1.2. As the "highest executive branch entity" involved in various intelligence activities, the NSC appears to be the primary link between the intelligence community and the President in deciding on intelligence policy and individual operations. According to the executive order, how does the NSC obtain the information it needs to fulfill its statutory role? What advantages and disadvantages do you see in NSC review and approval of covert actions? According to the executive order, is such review limited to the policies or criteria that inform decisions about individual operations, or is each proposal subject to the NSC review process? Does the NSC role include the conduct of intelligence actions?

3. *Military Intelligence Activities.* Which official approves intelligence collection by military agencies? What do you suppose constitute the "programs and missions" that the Secretary of Defense may conduct in meeting intelligence requirements? Does the executive order provide adequate legal authority to carry out those activities?

4. *Role of the DNI.* Section 1.3 of the order makes the DNI the "head" of the "intelligence community," a term defined at §3.5(h). Can you say how the "head" of the "community" is like or unlike the Secretary of a cabinet-level department, such as Homeland Security or Justice?

5. *Collection Assignments.* Section 1.3(b)(20) of the order assigns collection responsibilities. How are collections inside and outside the United States treated differently?

b.   The Internal Executive Branch Process for Approving Intelligence Operations

1. *Changing Internal Review.* What are the prescribed roles of the President, the Attorney General, and the NSC in the structure and process for making intelligence operations decisions? Can you tell who is now in charge of operational controls? How do you think these rules affect the speed with which decisions are made about intelligence operations? The quality of those decisions?

2. *Sorting Out the Players and Their Roles.* Can you describe the respective roles of the DNI, Director of the Central Intelligence Agency, National Security Adviser, and Attorney General, as well as their relationships to each other and to the President and NSC? What duties are exclusively assigned the CIA? *See* §1.7. You may wish to consult the organization chart on p. 450, *supra.*

3. *A Changed Definition.* President Carter's Executive Order No. 12,036, 43 Fed. Reg. 3675 (Jan. 24, 1978), defined "covert activities" as secret "activities conducted in support of national foreign policy objectives abroad *which are designed to further official United States programs and policies abroad.*" *Id.* §3-212. The italicized part of this

language was omitted from Executive Order No. 12,333, §3.5(b). Is the difference legally significant?

4. *The Role of Lawyers.* The Ford and Carter executive orders, unlike the original Reagan order, formally included the Justice Department in the covert action decision-making process. What role, if any, is assigned the Attorney General in covert action approval by the amended order? What other provisions does it make for lawyers to participate in the intelligence activities it addresses? Does their involvement really matter if the President is free to ignore their advice?

5. *President's Intelligence Advisory Board (PIAB).* The President's Intelligence Advisory Board (PIAB) is maintained within the Executive Office of the President and is charged to

> assess the quality, quantity, and adequacy of intelligence collection, of analysis and estimates, and of counterintelligence and other intelligence activities, assess the adequacy of management, personnel and organization in the intelligence community, and review the performance of all agencies of the Federal Government that are engaged in the collection, evaluation, or production of intelligence or the execution of intelligence policy and report the results of such assessments or reviews [to the President and DNI and heads of concerned departments]. [Executive Order No. 13,462, 73 Fed. Reg. 11,805 (Feb. 29, 2008), *as amended by* Executive Order No. 13,516, 74 Fed. Reg. 56,521 (Nov. 2, 2009).]

Its several members (up to 16) serve at the pleasure of the President and are appointed from among citizens outside government. The PIAB is specifically charged with making appropriate recommendations for actions to improve and enhance the performance of the intelligence efforts of the United States.

In 2008 President George W. Bush removed a requirement that the PIAB alert the Attorney General to intelligence activities that might violate federal criminal laws, and added a requirement that intelligence agencies provide information to the PIAB. Can you think of a reason he would do so? President Obama restored the requirement that the PIAB alert the Attorney General whenever it learns of "intelligence activities that involve possible violations of Federal criminal laws." Executive Order No. 13,516, §1(d), 74 Fed. Reg. 56,521. The Obama order also restored the requirement that the DNI and other agencies "shall provide such information and assistance as the PIAB and IOB [Intelligence Oversight Board] determine is needed to perform their functions." *Id.* §1(e).

c. Conducting Intelligence Operations

1. *Assigning Functions Among Agencies.* How can the intelligence functions of the CIA, National Security Agency (NSA), FBI, and Defense Department, addressed in §§1.7 and 1.10 of the executive order, be distinguished? Why do you suppose their responsibilities are assigned as they are? Do you see any grounds for possible confusion or conflict?

2. *Restrictions on Collection.* What kind of information may be collected by members of the intelligence community? Does it include information about, say, drug smuggling? Industrial espionage? The order distinguishes among collection

techniques by kind, location, and target. We examine these techniques in detail in later chapters, but here consider *why* the order treats them differently.

How is collection against U.S. persons more restricted than it is against others? Why do you think it is so restricted? *See* §2.3.

Why do you think collection inside the United States is generally limited to the FBI? What purpose is served by a requirement that the Attorney General approve collections for "intelligence purposes" inside the United States or against U.S. persons abroad when a judicial warrant would be needed if undertaken for law enforcement purposes? Why must the Attorney General find probable cause to believe that the target is a foreign power or agent of a foreign power?

Why are infiltration and participation in domestic organizations limited by §2.9 of the executive order?

3. *Political Impacts.* Why does §2.13 of the executive order prohibit covert actions intended to influence U.S. "political processes, public opinion, policies, or media"? Should the order address such influence if it is unintended—commonly referred to as "blowback"?

d.   Overseeing Intelligence Operation Decisions

1. *Making a Record.* Does the executive order require that intelligence operation decisions be made in writing? What considerations would enter into deciding whether to impose such a requirement within the executive branch? If such decisions are made in writing, should or must the writing be done before the operation is carried out?

2. *Reporting to Congress.* Section 3.1 of the order refers to oversight legislation that Congress has from time to time amended in response to its concerns about executive self-regulation. What intelligence activities does the order say must be reported to Congress? Do such requirements apply to the NSC or its staff?

3. *Intelligence Oversight Board (IOB).* In September 1993, President Clinton established the IOB as a standing committee of the PIAB, with the Chair of the IOB reporting through the Chair of the PIAB, changing the structure that had existed since President Ford established the IOB as a separate entity in 1976. Executive Order No. 12,863, 58 Fed. Reg. 58,441 (Sept. 13, 1993). As amended most recently by President George W. Bush, the functions of the IOB include informing the President of intelligence activities that the IOB believes "may be unlawful or contrary to Executive Order or presidential directive," and reviewing and assessing "the effectiveness, efficiency, and sufficiency of the processes by which the DNI and the heads of departments concerned perform their respective functions." Executive Order No. 13,462, §§6(b), (c), 73 Fed. Reg. 11,805 (Mar. 4, 2008). Will the IOB provide an effective check on violations of either statutory or executive order restrictions?

4. *Defining "Covert Action."* The fifth function provision of the original National Security Act was ambiguous about whether "covert action" was authorized. Does Executive Order No. 12,333 leave any doubt?

B.   INTELLIGENCE REORGANIZATION AFTER 9/11

The September 11, 2001, attacks on the World Trade Center and the Pentagon prompted numerous critiques of what some regarded as massive failures of intelligence. *See, e.g.,* S. Select Comm. on Intelligence & H. Permanent Select Comm. on Intelligence, *Joint Inquiry into Intelligence Community Activities Before and After the Terrorist Attacks of September 11, 2001,* S. Rep. No. 107-351, H.R. Rep. No. 107-792 (2002); *9/11 Commission Report: Final Report of the National Commission on Terrorist Attacks Upon the United States* (2004). How could such a devastating attack have been planned and carried out under our collective noses? Why did our intelligence agencies not know the attack was coming?

At that point in time it was the job of the Director of Central Intelligence (DCI), who was also the Director of the Central Intelligence Agency, to "provide overall direction for the collection of national intelligence through human sources by elements of the intelligence community." 50 U.S.C. §403-3(d)(2) (2000) (repealed 2004). The two congressional intelligence committees and the 9/11 Commission found that inadequate organization and management of the intelligence community prevented the DCI from ensuring that information about the hijackers' plans was shared with agency analysts, who could have "connected the dots" and uncovered the plot in advance. The 9/11 Commission also noted that limited legal authority forced the DCI to "direct agencies without controlling them." *9/11 Commission Report, supra,* at 357. The Commission pointed out that, especially for intelligence elements within the Department of Defense (DOD), the DCI "does not receive an appropriation for their activities, and therefore does not control their purse strings." *Id.* Similarly, the congressional joint inquiry found that even after DCI George J. Tenet ordered the intelligence community to give the Osama bin Laden network its highest priority, his words had little effect beyond the CIA. *Joint Inquiry, supra,* at 236.

Meanwhile, the Bush administration case for the 2003 Iraq war relied heavily on intelligence-based assertions that the Saddam Hussein regime had stockpiles of weapons of mass destruction (WMD) that would imminently be used against the United States and its allies. After President Bush declared an end to major combat operations in Iraq and investigators cleared the battlefield rubble, no WMD were found. In March 2005, a presidentially appointed commission found "that the Intelligence Community was dead wrong in almost all of its pre-war judgments about Iraq's weapons of mass destruction." Commission on the Intelligence Capabilities of the United States Regarding Weapons of Mass Destruction (Silberman/Robb Commission), *Report to the President of the United States* (transmittal letter) (Mar. 31, 2005). The commission found an "inability to collect good information," "serious errors in analyzing" the information collected, and a failure to distinguish assumptions from evidence in its analysis. *Id.* But the commission reached no conclusions about how the flawed intelligence was actually used in deciding to invade Iraq. See *supra* p. 354.

The intelligence failures of September 11 and in Iraq appeared to many observers as symptomatic of a larger struggle by our nation's intelligence agencies to confront the post-Cold War environment. Instead of focusing on the Soviet Union as the dominant threat, as it had since the origins of the CIA in 1947, the intelligence community today faces dozens of high-priority targets that include not only states but also highly diffuse transnational terrorism, crime, and weapons proliferation networks. Worse yet, advances in technology and potential dual uses of goods have made detection of weapons and facilities harder and made their concealment easier.

In its July 2004 report, the 9/11 Commission recommended several changes in the structure of the intelligence community:

- unifying strategic intelligence and operational planning against Islamist terrorists across the foreign-domestic divide with a National Counterterrorism Center;

- unifying the intelligence community with a National Intelligence Director;

- unifying the many participants in the counterterrorism effort and their knowledge in a network-based information-sharing system that transcends traditional governmental boundaries;

- unifying and strengthening congressional oversight to improve quality and accountability; and

- strengthening the FBI and homeland defenders.

See 9/11 Commission Report, supra, at 399-400.

1.   The Director of National Intelligence (DNI) — An Intelligence Czar?

Partly in response to the recommendations of the 9/11 Commission, in December 2004, Congress approved the most extensive reorganization of U.S. intelligence in more than half a century. Intelligence Reform and Terrorism Prevention Act of 2004, Pub. L. No. 108-458, 118 Stat. 3638 (hereinafter IRTPA). (Unless otherwise noted, references in the following description are to sections of the National Security Act of 1947 as amended by the IRTPA and as currently codified.) The 2004 Act responded — at least in part — to those who sought the creation of a cabinet-level intelligence czar. The Act created the position of DNI, appointed by the President and confirmed by the Senate and subject to the "authority, direction, and control of the President." 50 U.S.C. §403(b). The DNI serves as "head of the intelligence community" and as principal advisor to the President, National Security Council, and Homeland Security Council "for intelligence matters related to the national security." Id. §403(b)(1), (2). She also oversees and directs implementation of the National Intelligence Program. Id. §403(b)(3). The DNI may not simultaneously serve as Director of the CIA or as head of any other component of the intelligence community. Id. §403(c).

The DNI has direct authority over a Senate-confirmed Principal Deputy and up to four additional deputy directors appointed by the DNI, a National Counterterrorism Center, a National Counterproliferation Center, a General Counsel, a Director of Science and Technology, and a National Intelligence Council. Id. §403-3a(b), (c), (e). The former DCI post was eliminated, and the job of running the CIA was given to a Director of the CIA. Id. §403-4a.

2.   Budget Authority

An old inside-the-beltway adage says to "follow the money" if you want to find out where the power lies. The National Intelligence Program (NIP) includes all programs conducted by the intelligence community, other than programs to acquire intelligence "solely for planning and conduct of tactical military operations by the United States Armed Forces." Exec. Order No. 12,333 §3.5(j). The DNI must "develop and determine" the annual consolidated NIP budget. National Security Act §403-1(c)(1). She also directs the allocation of appropriations through the heads of departments containing agencies or organizations within the intelligence community and through the Director of the CIA. *Id.* §403-1(c)(5)(A). (Component intelligence agencies and lines of reporting are shown in the chart on p. 450.) Consequently, although the DNI's authority has thus been buttressed by budget authority over much of the intelligence community, the DNI has no direct prescriptive authority over intelligence support to military operations through the Department of Defense programs. *Id.* §403-1(c)(3)(A). Put differently, the DNI's budgetary authority does not include vast parts of the DOD budget, and DOD largely escapes the organizational structure and control mechanisms created by the reform legislation.

Despite the DNI's lack of control over the DOD intelligence budget, after consultation with the Secretary of Defense, the DNI must ensure that National Intelligence Program budgets for components of the intelligence community within DOD are adequate for the intelligence needs of DOD, including the intelligence needs of the service branches. *Id.* §403-1(c). In addition, the DNI, after consulting with the Secretary of Defense and Director of the CIA, must develop joint procedures to "improve the coordination and deconfliction" of operations that involve the U.S. armed forces and the CIA. *Id.* §403-1 note.

The DNI is responsible for establishing "objectives, priorities, and guidance" for elements of the intelligence community. *Id.* §403-1(f)(1)(A). She also must "determine requirements and priorities for, and manage and direct the tasking of" intelligence collection, analysis, production, and dissemination by entities of the intelligence community. *Id.* These authorities do not extend to the DNI if the President so directs or if the DNI and Secretary of Defense agree otherwise, or to dissemination of information to state and local governments and the private sector under the Homeland Security Act. *Id.* §403-1(f)(1)(B).

3. The New Structure for National Intelligence

Within the Office of the Director of National Intelligence (ODNI), a National Intelligence Council (NIC), composed of senior analysts and other experts appointed by the DNI, is charged with producing national intelligence estimates, evaluating intelligence collection and production performance, and otherwise assisting the DNI. *Id.* §403-3b. A Senate-confirmed General Counsel was created, as was a Civil Liberties Protection Officer and a Director of Science and Technology, both appointed by the DNI. *Id.* §§403-3c, 3d, 3e.

The Director of the CIA reports to the DNI, and the DNI remains responsible for intelligence collection, evaluation, and dissemination by the CIA, as well as for performing "such other functions and duties related to intelligence affecting the national security" as the President or DNI may direct. *Id.* §403-4a(d)(4). Thus, the original "fifth function," which was the putative statutory basis for covert operations by the CIA, has been retained.

The DNI oversees the National Counterterrorism Center (NCTC), created by the Act, and any other national intelligence centers determined necessary by the Director. *Id.* §404o. The Director of the NCTC is a Senate-confirmed presidential appointee who reports to the DNI generally but to the President on the planning and implementation of joint counterterrorism operations. *Id.*

A Privacy and Civil Liberties Oversight Board, appointed by the President, was established within the Executive Office of the President and charged with ensuring that privacy and civil liberties concerns are appropriately considered in the implementation of policies designed to protect against terrorism. The Board provides oversight of regulations and policies, advises the President and agencies in the executive branch, and reports to Congress. The Board has no power to compel production of information, but it may request such assistance from the Attorney General. 5 U.S.C. §601 note. Initial appointments to the Board were forwarded by President Obama to the Senate for confirmation in late 2010. *See* White House Office of the Press Secretary, *Nominations Sent to the Senate* (Dec. 17, 2010), *at* http://www.whitehouse.gov/the-press-office/2010/12/17/nominations-sent-senate.

NOTES AND QUESTIONS

1. *Authorities of the DNI in relation to the CIA.* Several authorities and responsibilities given to the DNI by IRTPA previously belonged to the DCI, who was also Director of the CIA. For example, the DNI must "ensure compliance with the Constitution and laws of the United States" by the CIA and other elements of the intelligence community. 50 U.S.C. §403-1(f)(4). Why would Congress and the President have determined to create an intelligence official superior to the Director of the CIA? Comparing the authorities of the Director of the CIA, *supra* p. 446, with those for the DNI, would you say that IRTPA makes the DNI the boss of the CIA Director? If the answer is not clear, what are the practical implications?

2. *The DNI and the Intelligence Community.* According to IRTPA §1073, 118 Stat. 3693, the "intelligence community," now headed by the DNI, consists of all the entities depicted in the chart on p. 450, except the President and the six listed cabinet departments. Given this definition, despite the incomplete budgetary authority now vested in the DNI, is the DNI effectively a "Secretary of Intelligence"? If not, how does the new post fall short of the Secretary model? Does IRTPA, provisions of which are reflected in the excerpt of the National Security Act of 1947 on p. 445, give the DNI the authority she needs to be effective? May she hire or fire agency heads? Does IRTPA tell the CIA or other agencies within the National Intelligence Program what to do?

3. *Military Intelligence.* If the NIP does not include military intelligence collected solely in support of tactical military operations, can you say which military intelligence activities are subject to IRTPA? Reading the pertinent provisions of Exec. Order No. 12,333 (§§1.3, 1.4, 1.5, 1.7, 1.10, and 3.5) alongside IRTPA, can you stitch together a complete picture of how military intelligence is controlled? What would you need to know to complete the picture?

4. *Defining the Scope of the Mission.* The terms "national intelligence" and "intelligence related to national security" are defined to include

all intelligence, regardless of the source from which derived and including information gathered within or outside the United States, that pertains...to more than one . . . agency; and that involves threats to the United States, its people, property, or interests; the development, proliferation, or use of weapons of mass destruction; or any other matter bearing on United States national or homeland security. [50 U.S.C. §401a(5).]

Are these definitions useful to the DNI in understanding the scope of her responsibilities? What categories of intelligence are outside the definition? How does this expansive definition affect the geographical boundaries of intelligence activities of the CIA? Of the FBI? Of DOD?

5. *The Fifth Function.* Under IRTPA, the DNI "shall perform such other functions as the President may direct." *Id.* §403-1(f)(7). The new Director of the CIA continues to "perform such other functions and duties related to intelligence affecting the national security as the President or National Security Council may direct." *Id.* §403-4a(d)(4), 118 Stat. 3661. Do you suppose the differences in what used to be referred to as the fifth function (for its original codification at 50 U.S.C. §403(d)(5)) are purposeful? If so, how do the authorities of the two offices differ in this regard? Parallel authorities for the DNI and Director of the CIA extend to "protect[ing] intelligence sources and methods from unauthorized disclosure." *Id.* §403-1(i)(1); 50 U.S.C. §403-3(c)(7).

6. *The Budget and Its Control.* In October 2010, DNI James R. Clapper reported that the fiscal year 2010 budget figure for the NIP was $53.1 billion. For the first time, General Clapper also disclosed the budget figures for the Military Intelligence Program (MIP) — $27 billion for 2010. Office of the Director of National Intelligence, News Release (Oct. 28, 2010), *at* http://www.fas.org/irp/news/2010/10/dni 102810.pdf. Within the NIP budget, about three-fourths of the total is for various DOD agencies, most for NSA and the National Reconnaissance Office (NRO). The rest is shared among the CIA, the FBI, and other agencies. *Media Conference Call with the Director of National Intelligence Mr. Dennis C. Blair* (Sept. 15, 2009), *available at* http://www.fas.org/irp/news/2009/09/dni091509-m.pdf.

Although intelligence budgets will continue to be developed in various individual agencies, the DNI has discretion under the Act to reject or revise items or programs and to direct that funds be spent or withheld. 50 U.S.C. §403-1c. Can you see how this budget and spending authority could make the DNI the final decision maker in the agencies of the NIP?

7. *The NCTC.* The Director of the NCTC reports to the DNI regarding intelligence operations, while the Director of the NCTC reports to the President regarding the "planning and progress of joint counterterrorism operations (other than intelligence operations)." 50 U.S.C. §404o(c)(3). What kinds of operations do you think are included among those that require direct reports to the President by the Director of the NCTC? Why would someone other than the DNI make those reports to the President? (The relationship of the NCTC to other information-sharing and terrorism assessment entities is considered in Chapter 19.)

The NCTC mission is to serve "as the primary organization in the United States Government for integrating and analyzing all intelligence pertaining to counterterrorism (except for information pertaining exclusively to domestic terrorism)." The center also serves as a "shared knowledge bank on terrorism information" and provides "USG agencies with the terrorism intelligence analysis and other information they need to fulfill their mission." *About the National Counterterrosim Center,* http://www.nctc.gov/about_us/about_nctc.html. *See* Richard A. Best Jr., *The National Counterterrorism Center (NCTC) — Responsibilities and Potential Congressional Concerns* (Cong. Res. Serv. RL41022), Jan. 15, 2010.

The Fort Hood attack by Major Nidal Hassan in November 2009 and the Abdulmutallab "underwear bomber" incident of December 25, 2009, prompted substantial criticisms of inadequate intelligence analysis by NCTC and other agencies, and served as reminders that NCTC lacks legal authority to require the cooperation of other agencies and departments in its efforts to integrate intelligence. A 2010 study concluded that the NCTC suffers from a lack of coordination and communication among the participating agencies, including the CIA and State Department. Project on National Security Reform, *Toward Integrating Complex National Missions: Lessons from the National Counterterrorism Center's Directorate of Strategic Operational Planning* (Feb. 2010), *available at* http://www.pnsr.org. What reforms would make the NCTC more effective?

8. *Reconsidering Intelligence Reorganization?* The recommendations of the 9/11 Commission and enactment of IRTPA quieted the intelligence reorganization debate only temporarily. In June 2010 the Congressional Research Service reported that

> Observers are divided over the success of the DNI position and the ODNI. Three DNIs have been successively appointed and confirmed; none served more than two years. A number of innovations have been undertaken in the intelligence community to encourage coordination and information sharing. However, some observers remain skeptical of the need for a DNI or ODNI. A widespread perception is that coordinative mechanisms and authorities as currently established are inadequate to the goal of creating a more flexible and agile intelligence effort. Still others see cooperative efforts in the intelligence community as a test-case of the extent to which independent federal agencies can work closely together without being merged under a single leader. [Richard A. Best Jr., *Intelligence Reform After Five Years: The Role of the Director of National Intelligence (DNI)* (Cong. Res. Serv. R41295), June 22, 2010, at Summary.]

An unreleased 2009 report from the ODNI concluded that "the IC continues its struggle to keep up with technological innovations in collection. Other challenges include transforming analysis [and] anticipating future threats." Laurie West Van Hook, *Reforming Intelligence: The Passage of the Intelligence Reform and Terrorism Prevention Act* 25 (ODNI) (Feb. 2009), *available at* http://www.fas.org/irp/dni/reform.pdf. Another unreleased report, this one from the PIAB to President Obama in June 2010, concluded that the DNI has been sidetracked in assuming leadership of the intelligence community by bitter disputes over authority and other distractions from the core mission. The PIAB found that ambiguities in IRTPA and the different approaches of the three directors to date have led to confusion about the director's authority. Josh Gerstein, *Panel Found "Distracted" DNI,* Politico, June 2, 2010, *available at* http://www.politico.com/news/stories/0610/38061.html. *See also* Patrick C. Neary, *Intelligence Reform, 2001-2009: Requiscat in Pace?,* 54 Stud. in Intelligence 1 (2010). Can you outline the statutory reforms that would eliminate the ambiguities in IRTPA and thus make the DNI the true head of intelligence? Do you agree that such reforms would be a good idea?

9. *The National Intelligence Strategy.* In 2009, DNI Dennis C. Blair issued a new strategy document, *The National Intelligence Strategy of the United States of America* (Aug. 2009), *available at* http://www.dni.gov/reports/2009_nis.pdf. The six "mission objectives" identified in the *Strategy* are combating violent extremism, countering WMD proliferation, providing strategic intelligence and warning, integrating counterintelligence capabilities, enhancing cybersecurity, and supporting current diplomatic, military, and law enforcement operations. In the foreword to the *Strategy* document, DNI Blair stated that the *Strategy* "reflects a more refined understanding of the threats we face and how we'll combat them." *Id.* at 1. Do you find support for all these roles in the legal authorities assessed in this chapter? Would you add or subtract from the list?

Covert Actions in Principle and Practice —17

Covert action is intended to influence people and events without revealing the source, or perhaps even the existence, of the influence.

> The history of covert action might be loosely grouped into three categories. *Propaganda* can be no more than a little money distributed secretly to a few journalists in country *X* to get them to write articles favorable to the United States — a "project," in CIA practice, but one that might have a budget of only a few thousand dollars. At the other extreme are covert *paramilitary operations*, secret military aid and training. Most though not all of these are large; the "secret" war in Laos, for instance, was not so much secret as unacknowledged, consuming several million dollars a day as a second front to the war in Vietnam but one managed by the CIA. In between, *political action* attempts to change the balance of political forces in a particular country, most often by secretly providing money to particular groups. [Gregory F. Treverton, *Covert Action: The CIA and the Limits of American Intervention in the Postwar World* 13 (1987).]

Propaganda operations can produce "blowback" — when a false story planted overseas by the CIA is reported in the United States. With worldwide 24-hour news outlets, blowback is inevitable. When it happens, must the CIA inform the media that the story is false? What if doing so would compromise the overseas operation?

Political action can also pose problems. If the CIA supports a foreign group for particular purposes — say, the Guatemalan military in a fight with Central American radicals — is the CIA legally responsible if its support is used instead to abuse the human rights of Guatemalan citizens?

Paramilitary covert actions have always been controversial. Such actions take a variety of forms:

> At one extreme, paramilitary operations have been tantamount to full-scale wars — "covert" only in the sense that the United States wanted to be able to deny that it was directly involved. Witness the "secret war" in Laos, an unadmitted war on the cheap, with CIA paramilitary specialists providing the advice and Laotian hill tribesmen doing the fighting. . . . Like earlier CIA paramilitary campaigns in Korea, Laos was part of an open American war; if the campaigns were meant to be secret, neither the war nor its purposes were.

At the other end of the spectrum, some paramilitary operations have amounted to little more than the clandestine transfer of a few weapons or of small amounts of training — for instance, for "palace guards" to protect friendly heads of state who would prefer not to be widely known as protected by the United States. . . .

All these paramilitary operations involved the same elements: money and weaponry for groups and movements the United States was supporting, plus clandestine ways to transfer both, plus CIA officers and others to provide training and advice. The weaponry was "sterile" — that is, not easy to identify as coming from the United States. . . .

To backstop these paramilitary operations, the CIA has developed networks of air carriers, some CIA "fronts," and some contractors to move arms and supplies — if not secretly, then at least as less visibly "American." During the Vietnam war, that network, centered on Air America, amounted to a large air force. After Vietnam, the CIA divested itself of these "proprietaries" but retained contacts with those companies; in many cases, the "new" private managers were the "old" CIA managers, now retired. Nor did even the names change: Southern Air Transport, a CIA company during the Vietnam war, shipped supplies to the CIA-sponsored Contras in Nicaragua two decades later as a "private" company. [*Id.* at 26-28.]

More recently, the CIA has assumed a growing role in a shadow war against Al Qaeda and its allies in countries distant from the recognized battlefields in Afghanistan and Iraq. In an increasingly stepped-up campaign against Al Qaeda during the first two years of the Obama administration, the CIA became "a paramilitary organization as much as a spying agency." Scott Shane, Mark Mazzetti & Robert F. Worth, *Secret Assault on Terrorism Widens on Two Continents,* N.Y. Times, Aug. 15, 2010, at A1. The CIA activities, including drone strikes in Pakistan, have not been publicly acknowledged, and many of its paramilitary and other intelligence operations have been outsourced to private contractors, whose accountability remains in question. *Id.*

This chapter explores the evolution of attempts to regulate U.S. covert actions. Part A starts by introducing an early congressional control on the use of private military forces, the Neutrality Act. In Part B, we look briefly at the early U.S. history of covert actions and secret agents. In Part C, we return to the "fifth function" in the National Security Act of 1947, debatably the first U.S. statutory authorization of covert activities. In Part D, we trace the evolution of congressional oversight of covert action. In Part E, we examine a case study of covert action — the Iran-Contra Affair — which tested the limits of statutory controls and criminal accountability. The experience of the Iran-Contra Affair resulted in a reform of congressional oversight, embodied in the Intelligence Authorization Act of 1991 and its amendments, with which we close the chapter in Part F.

A.   THE FIRST PUBLIC CONTROL — THE NEUTRALITY ACT

The original understanding of the use of private armies or contract agents to meet sovereign objectives is considered in Chapters 2 and 13. The Marque and Reprisal Clause may have been intended to vest in Congress all control over privateers. See *supra* p. 8. The Neutrality Act was passed in 1794, arguably to cement congressional control over private armies. In its current form, the Neutrality Act provides:

Whoever, within the United States, knowingly begins or sets on foot or provides or prepares a means for or furnishes the money for, or takes part in, any military or naval expedition or enterprise to be carried on from thence against the territory or dominion of any foreign prince or state, or of any colony, district, or people with whom the United States is at peace, shall be fined under this title or imprisoned not more than three years, or both. [18 U.S.C. §960 (2006).]

The original purpose of the Neutrality Act has been described this way:

One of the aims of the Neutrality Act was to protect the sovereignty of the United States by keeping United States citizens aloof from the intrigues of foreign government. Moreover, strict laws preventing U.S. citizens from encroaching on foreign disputes were seen as the quid pro quo for the non-interference by foreign governments in our affairs. . . .

The fundamental purpose of the Neutrality Act, however, lay not in asserting state sovereignty with respect to other states but in strengthening the authority of the central government vis-à-vis its citizens, particularly with respect to warfare. Thus Jefferson noted that:

If one citizen has a right to go to war of his own authority, every citizen has the same. If every citizen has that right, then the nation (which is composed of all its citizens) has a right to go to war, by the authority of its individual citizens. But this is not true either on the general principles of society, or by our Constitution, which gives that power to Congress alone and not to the citizens individually.[134]

Congress passed the Act, then, to help secure government control over the power to make war. In order to ensure that control Congress enacted a statute which had as its object "to repress and punish all enterprises of private war, one of the last relics of medieval barbarism." By outlawing private warfare, the Act would insure that national policy would be made by the government acting through Congress, and not by the acts of individuals. [Jules Lobel, *The Rise and Decline of the Neutrality Act: Sovereign and Congressional War Powers in United States Foreign Policy*, 24 Harv. Int'l L.J. 1, 24-25 (1983).]

See also United States v. Smith, 27 F. Cas. 1192 (C.C.D.N.Y. 1806) (Neutrality Act prosecution).

The courts have had few occasions to consider the application of the Neutrality Act in modern times. *See, e.g., United States v. Terrell*, 731 F. Supp. 473, 477 (S.D. Fla. 1989) (finding that "the history of American involvement in Nicaragua conclusively demonstrates that the United States was not 'at peace' with Nicaragua during the time frame charged in the indictment," despite U.S. funding of paramilitary operations by the Contras against the Nicaraguan government); *Dellums v. Smith*, 797 F.2d 817 (9th Cir. 1986) (finding that plaintiffs lacked standing to complain of the government's failure to prosecute alleged violations of Act). Would U.S. companies violate the Neutrality Act by training foreign military forces that are fighting governments abroad? See *infra* p. 522.

In a similar vein, Congress passed the Logan Act in 1799 to criminalize unauthorized efforts by any U.S. citizen who "directly or indirectly commences or carries on

---

134. Letter from Thomas Jefferson, Secretary of State, to Gouverneur Morris, U.S. Minister to France (Aug. 16, 1793), *reprinted in* 6 J. Moore, *A Digest of International Law* 917 (1906). *See also* Jefferson's Third Annual Message to Congress (Oct. 17, 1803), *reprinted in* 1 Richardson, *Messages & Papers of the Presidents* 357, 361 (1896). Similarly, Congressman Ames, in considering the Neutrality Act legislation, observed that the general authority of the United States was very weak, and that a purpose of the bill was thus to prevent being "driven into war by the licentious behavior of some individuals." 1 Annals of Cong. 743 (1794). *See also id.* at 744, 746 (remarks of Reps. Wadsworth and Hillhouse).

any correspondence or intercourse with any foreign government or of any officer or agent thereof, in relation to any disputes or controversies with the United States. . . ." 18 U.S.C. §953 (2006). *See* Michael V. Seitzinger, *Conducting Foreign Relations Without Authority: The Logan Act* (Cong. Res. Serv. RL33265), Jan. 20, 2010. Although never enforced by criminal prosecution, the Logan Act has been "used as a political tool to threaten citizens engaged in private diplomacy and to solidify the President's foreign relations power." Christiaan Highsmith, *The Liberty-Speech Framework: Resolving the Tension Between Foreign Affairs Power and First Amendment Freedoms*, 88 B.U. L. Rev. 745, 753 (2008). Like the Neutrality Act, the Logan Act was designed to strengthen the government's control over its foreign relations. Unlike the Neutrality Act, the Logan Act is presumably not enforced because of potential First and Fifth Amendment problems with any prosecution. *See generally* Seitzinger, *supra*; Drew Tedford, *Silent No More: The Logan Act as a Constitutionally Enforceable Tool in Foreign Policy*, 32 Hous. J. Int'l 733 (2010) (arguing that constitutional vagueness problems may be overcome by a narrowing construction). Those criticized by political opponents as having violated the Logan Act include Ross Perot, for his efforts to find missing American service personnel in Southeast Asia; former House Speaker Jim Wright, for his friendly relations with the Sandinista government in Nicaragua; and former Senator George McGovern, Reverend Jesse Jackson, and activist Jane Fonda, for their private trips as self-declared unofficial envoys of the United States. Seitzinger, *supra*, at 9.

NOTES AND QUESTIONS

1. *Elements of the Neutrality Act.* What are the critical terms of the Neutrality Act? Does it criminalize gifts to Hamas that are intended to fund attacks against Israel? How about joining the Taliban to fight against the government in Afghanistan? Would these actions violate the purposes of the Act?

Could the Act ever limit the actions of U.S. government officials acting in an official capacity? Might enforcement of the Act ever be related to the foreign policy goals of a particular administration?

2. *Logan Act Policy.* How important is the Logan Act in preserving the President's role as "sole organ" in U.S. foreign relations? Can you describe constitutional objections to its enforcement? Can you think of other ways to achieve its goals?

B.   COVERT ACTIONS: ORIGINS AND PRACTICE

Statement of Mitchell Rogovin, Special Counsel to the Director of Central Intelligence

Hearings Before the H. Select Comm. on Intelligence,
94th Cong., pt. 5, at 1729, 1732-1733 (1976)
[hereinafter Rogovin Memorandum]

. . . Beginning with George Washington, almost every President has appointed special agents to engage in certain activities with, or against, foreign countries. . . .

In the first century of the Nation's existence alone, more than 400 such agents were appointed by the President.

Early examples of covert action performed by these agents are legion. The following three are typical: One, in 1843, President Tyler secretly dispatched an agent to Great Britain to meet privately with individual government and opposition leaders and to attempt to influence public opinion with respect to matters affecting the two countries, without ever disclosing that he was a representative of the U.S. Government; two, in 1845, when President Polk feared that Mexico was on the verge of ceding California to Great Britain, he secretly dispatched an agent to California for the purpose of "defeating any attempt which may be made by foreign governments to acquire a control over that country"; and three, in 1869, when the United States had territorial designs on central and western Canada, President Grant sent an agent to that area to foment sentiment for separation from Canada and union with the United States. These examples show that the practice of appointment of special agents by the President for the purpose of conducting covert action in foreign countries is deeply rooted in our national history....

... Consequently, when the CIA was established in 1947, and when, shortly thereafter, it was delegated the responsibility for covert action, there was no attempt by the President to assert or exercise any new or theretofore unrecognized executive authority; he was merely delegating to the CIA various executive functions which were previously assigned to ad hoc special agents and other executive agencies....

Robert Borosage, Para-Legal Authority and Its Perils

40 Law & Contemp. Probs. 166, 173-174 (Summer 1976)

What of the 400 agents in the first hundred years or the "legion" of precedents cited in the [Rogovin] Memorandum? These refer to special agents selected by Presidents to represent them abroad.... [T]hey are agents of the President rather than officials of the government— "They have an employment, not an office"; their duties are generally special and temporary.

The "characteristic situations" in which special agents have been used include: "ceremonial occasions"; to speak for the President personally; international conferences and delegations; ... contacts with unrecognized states; technical matters requiring a high degree of expertness. In effect, then, the Rogovin Memorandum would have us consider the dispatch of Chief Justice Warren to DeGaulle's funeral as a precedent for covert action....

This is the longstanding practice from which the Rogovin Memorandum would derive a constitutional power for the President to employ a secret agency in widespread covert operations abroad. More than a difference of degree reaching a difference in kind, it is rather a simple form of sophistry to justify this dangerous agency on the basis of an inapposite tradition. The tortured logic of the Memorandum was not forwarded without reason, however. The CIA traces its birth back to an executive order issued by President Roosevelt in 1941, establishing the Office of Coordination and Information in the White House. Roosevelt issued the order four months before Pearl Harbor on the basis of "the authority vested in me as President of the United States...." Eleven months later, OCI became the Office of Strategic Services, a transformation directed by "military order," and OSS undertook both clandestine intelligence collection and para-military operations (covert action) throughout the war.

In 1945, OSS was disbanded by executive order, but four months later President Truman established the National Intelligence Authority and the Central Intelligence Group by a "Presidential Directive" issued without any proclaimed basis in law. The directive authorized the CIG to plan, develop and coordinate "such other functions and duties related to intelligence affecting the national security as the President . . . may from time to time direct." Thus, the CIA's immediate forebears were established by executive orders issued in peacetime. Although the CIG reportedly had no covert action arm, the Rogovin Memorandum claims . . . that it did engage in such activities. Only some notion of inherent power can legitimate this activity *post facto*. The Rogovin Memorandum seeks to legitimate this ancestry by inventing a birthright in inherent power.

NOTES AND QUESTIONS

1. *Secrecy and Inherent Power.* General claims for inherent presidential power in national security affairs are reviewed in Chapters 3 and 4. Arguments to support the more specific claim that the President may unilaterally engage the nation in covert intelligence operations, including paramilitary warfare, typically rely on the perceived need for secrecy. *See* Rogovin Memorandum, *supra*, at 1731-1733. Is there an inherent executive power to act secretly? *See In re Sealed Case*, 310 F.3d 717, 742 (FISA Ct. Rev. 2002) (President presumed to have inherent authority to conduct warrantless surveillance to obtain foreign intelligence information). Does the Declare War Clause represent a check on that power? *See* Charles Lofgren, *War-Making Under the Constitution: The Original Understanding*, 81 Yale L.J. 672, 689-697 (1972); Jules Lobel, *Covert War and Congressional Authority: Hidden War and Forgotten Power*, 134 U. Pa. L. Rev. 1035, 1078-1085 (1986); Louis Fisher, *Presidential War Power* 236-239 (2d ed. 2004).

2. *Secrecy and Delegated Power.* Recall the theories of congressional acquiescence and executive usage from Chapters 3-5. Can Congress be said to have tacitly approved the Executive's covert actions before 1947?

3. *A Variable Power?* To what extent does the authority to act secretly depend on the nature of the intelligence activity at issue? Is there constitutional authority to collect intelligence? If so, what is the source of that authority?

C. COVERT ACTIONS DURING THE COLD WAR

1. Interpreting the 1947 Act

In Chapter 16 we saw that the National Security Act provides especially open-ended authority for the CIA to engage in intelligence operations. The public legislative history of the 1947 Act indicates that the issue of covert action was not raised during enactment, and the text did not detail the CIA's functions or its relationship with the rest of the executive branch. *See* Thomas F. Troy, *Donovan and the CIA: A History of the Establishment of the Central Intelligence Agency* 377-410 (1981); John Ranelagh, *The Agency: The Rise and Decline of the CIA* 104-111 (1986). Nevertheless, several nagging questions about Congress's intent persist. First, some statements in the record suggest that witnesses and legislators did not always engage in a full and frank discussion of intelligence needs, apparently out of fear that the national security might be compromised by such a discussion. *See, e.g.,* 93 Cong. Rec. 9605 (1947) (statement of Rep. Manasco). Second, it has been argued that the ambiguous language of the so-called fifth function—authorizing the CIA to "perform such other functions and duties related to intelligence affecting the national security as the President or the Director of National Intelligence may direct," 50 U.S.C. §403-4a(d)(4)—was chosen so as not to advertise to the world that the nation was planning to conduct covert operations. S. Select Comm. to Study Governmental Operations with Respect to Intelligence Activities (Church Committee), *Foreign and Military Intelligence,* S. Rep. No 94-755, bk. I, at 485-486 (1976). Finally, the contemporary term "covert action" had no clearly understood forebear in 1947. While the terms "operational activities," "special operations," and "direct activities" were all used, they were employed to refer to secret collection of intelligence as well as to covert action. *Id.* at 486-487.

On the other hand, a 1947 memorandum from the CIA General Counsel to the Director offered this opinion of the new CIA authority:

> Taken out of context and without knowledge of its history, these Sections [50 U.S.C. §403-4a(d)(4)] could bear almost unlimited interpretation, provided that the services performed could be shown to be of benefit to an intelligence agency or related to national intelligence.... Even certain forms of S.O. [special operations] work could be held to benefit intelligence by establishment of W/T [wireless telegraph] teams in accessible areas, and by opening penetration points in confusion following sabotage or riot. *In our opinion, however, either activity would be an unwarranted extension of the functions authorized in Sections* [403-4a(d)(4)]. This is based on our understanding of the intent of Congress at the time these provisions were enacted. [*Quoted in id.* at 478.]

Similar conclusions about the 1947 Act were reached by the General Counsel in a 1962 memorandum to the Director. *Id.* at 478-479.

How should we interpret the "fifth function"? We know that activities authorized by §403-4a(d)(4) must be "related to intelligence affecting the national security." Does the language require that the *purpose* of the operation be to gather intelligence or simply that there be *a relationship* between intelligence and the operation, such as the use of similar sources or methods? For example, in 1948 the National Security Council (NSC) relied on an earlier version of §403-4a(d)(4) and this similarity of operational methods to instruct the Director of Central Intelligence (DCI) to conduct covert psychological operations designed to counteract similar Soviet actions. *Id.* at 490-491. If §403-4a(d)(4) requires a purpose to collect intelligence, many covert paramilitary actions undertaken in pursuit of military objectives would not be authorized by this section. If only a connection to intelligence must exist, even assassination of foreign leaders would be permitted if, for example, the agent-assassins previously supplied intelligence to the CIA. *See id.* at 131-132.

2.   Executive Branch Implementation

Post-enactment events quickly converted the National Security Act of 1947 from an academic debate about legislative intent into a real instrument of foreign policy. As the Church Committee reported:

At its first meeting in December, 1947, the National Security Council approved NSC-4 [/]A, which empowered the Secretary of State to coordinate information activities designed to counter communism. A top secret annex took cognizance of the "vicious psychological efforts of the USSR, its satellite countries, and Communist groups to discredit and defeat the activities of the U.S. and other Western powers." The NSC determined that "in the interests of world peace and U.S. national security the foreign information activities of the U.S. government must be supplemented by covert psychological operations."

The CIA was already engaged in clandestine collection of intelligence and, as the NSC put it, "The similarity of operational methods involved in covert psychological and intelligence activities and the need to ensure their secrecy and obviate costly duplication renders the CIA the logical agency to conduct such operations." Therefore, acting under the authority of section [403-4a(d)(4)] of the National Security Act of 1947, the NSC instructed the Director of Central Intelligence to initiate and conduct covert psychological operations that would counteract Soviet and Soviet-inspired covert actions and which would be consistent with U.S. foreign policy and overt foreign information activities.

In the following months, the CIA was involved in a number of covert actions. As the Soviet threat loomed larger and larger, the need for covert action, beyond psychological operations, seemed more pressing. On June 18, 1948, the NSC issued NSC-10/2 which superseded NSC-4[/]A, and vastly expanded the range of covert activities. The CIA was authorized to undertake economic warfare, sabotage, subversion against hostile states (including assistance to guerrilla and refugee liberation groups), and support of indigenous anti-communist elements in threatened countries.... [U]nder the authority of 50 U.S.C. §[403-4a(d)(4)], the NSC ordered the establishment in CIA of the Office of Special Projects (OSP), to conduct covert action. The Chief of OSP was to receive policy guidance from the Secretary of State and the Secretary of Defense. OSP (later, OPC) [Office of Policy Coordination] was to operate independently of all components of the CIA to the maximum degree consistent with efficiency.... [*Church Comm. Rep.*, *supra* p. 478, bk. I, at 490-491.]

According to John Prados, NSC-10/2 had three distinct features that were important in shaping the post-war evolution of American covert operations:

For the first time in a government decisional document, there appeared a mechanism designated by the President to approve and manage secret operations, and make them responsible to him. Second, and also for the first time, there appeared a comprehensive definition of covert operations. Finally, the CIA was again given primary responsibility for the mission, confirming the arrangement begun with NSC-4/A. [John Prados, *Presidents' Secret Wars* 29 (1986).]

Management of covert operations during the Truman administration is also reviewed in XII *Foreign Relations of the United States, 1964-1968, Western Europe*, at XXXI-XXXV (2001), *available at* http://www.state.gov/r/pa/ho/frus/johnson/b/xii/2961.htm.

NOTES AND QUESTIONS

1. *Authorities for Covert Actions.* Consider the range of covert actions permitted by NSC-10/2. Which of these are authorized by statute? Which by the Constitution? Which, if any, are prohibited by the Constitution?

2. *Could the CIA Authorize Operations That Violate U.S. Law?* In *United States v. Lopez-Lima*, 738 F. Supp. 1404 (S.D. Fla. 1990), Reinaldo Juan Lopez-Lima was charged with aircraft piracy in violation of a federal statute after he allegedly forced a Florida pilot at gunpoint to fly him and a co-defendant to Cuba in 1964. The outstanding indictment against Lopez-Lima was discovered only in 1989, when Lopez-Lima returned to the United States, was approached by the State Department as a possible source of information about Cuba, and was then arrested for hijacking the plane.

Lopez-Lima successfully defended the air piracy charge by arguing that the CIA authorized the hijacking as part of its effort to destabilize the Castro regime in Cuba. The court reasoned that because in 1981, Executive Order No. 12,333 ¶2.8 (*supra* p. 451) expressly disclaimed any authority "in this Order" to violate the Constitution or laws, and the CIA, pursuant to the fifth function, had conducted a range of rogue CIA operations detailed by the Church Committee, there was no requirement that the CIA comply with the law *before* 1981! The Court thus ordered a hearing in which Lopez-Lima would have an opportunity to persuade a jury that he reasonably relied on the authorization of CIA agents to sanction the hijacking.

Does it follow logically or legally that in 1964 the CIA could authorize Lopez-Lima to hijack a plane to Cuba? Consider ¶2.8 again. What other plausible interpretation can it bear? In *United States v. Rosenthal*, 793 F.2d 1214 (11th Cir. 1986), the court rejected a defense that the CIA could have authorized drug violations, based on the corrective language in Executive Order No. 12,333.

3. *Evolving Covert Action Policies.* The justification for covert operations shifted sharply between the immediate post-war years and the early 1970s, from containing international communism to serving more broadly as an instrument of U.S. foreign policy. While the rationale for covert operations evolved, attempts to harmonize the rationale with public policy were halting and controversial. Center for National Security Studies (CNSS), *Covert Operations and the Democratic Process: The Implications of the Iran/Contra Affair* 9 (1987) (hereinafter *CNSS*). Many officials argued that a range of covert activities seemed to be at odds with American principles. A 1954 report on CIA activities reflected this view:

> It is now clear that we are facing an implacable enemy whose avowed objective is world domination by whatever means and at whatever cost. There are no rules in such a game. Hitherto acceptable norms of human conduct do not apply. If the U.S. is to survive, long-standing American concepts of "fair play" must be reconsidered. We must develop effective espionage and counterespionage services and must learn to subvert, sabotage, and destroy our enemies by more clever, more sophisticated, and more effective methods than those used against us. It may become necessary that the American people be made acquainted with, understand and support this fundamentally repugnant philosophy. [*Quoted in Church Comm. Rep., supra* p. 478, bk. I, at 50.]

One alternative strategy would be to require that covert operations form some part of a larger overt program. *CNSS, supra,* at 9. Even more broadly, "consistency with American principles" has been suggested as a test for covert operations, requiring that both the aims and methods of particular operations be capable of winning public support if the operations were overt. *Id.* Do you think the early CIA initiatives would have met this test? Would political assassinations? Efforts to subvert democratic governments? Support for internal security forces that engage in the systematic violation of human rights?

How could a policy to require consistency with American principles be implemented? How could such a policy be enforced?

D. CONGRESSIONAL OVERSIGHT

1. From the Cold War Through Vietnam

For the first thirty years of its existence the agency's relationship with Congress was very informal indeed. In essence, the DCI and his close colleagues dealt personally and informally with the chairmen of the important and relevant Senate and House committees . . . and other senators and congressmen who were "friends" or who had significant political influence in areas important to the agency in Washington. This worked because the agency was trusted, its directors were respected, and it was seen as being America's principal defense against the subterranean machinations of world communism. . . .

The reluctance of the legislators to press the CIA for information about operations . . . was entirely understandable. . . . They preferred to be able to plead ignorance of specific information so that they would not find themselves compromised politically. CIA officials were content with this arrangement; they made it clear that they would provide the information asked of them, and if it was not asked, so be it. For over twenty-five years the system worked. [John Ranelagh, *The Agency: The Rise and Decline of the CIA* 281-285 (1988).]

CIA covert actions in Chile during the 1960s and early 1970s, designed to discredit left-leaning political leaders and to prevent them from assuming power (*see* Central Intelligence Agency, *CIA Activities in Chile* (Sept. 18, 2000), http://www.cia.gov/library/reports/general-reports-1/chile/index.html), along with Watergate and the Southeast Asia war, all served to focus public attention on the CIA and crystalize congressional determination to investigate intelligence abuses.

2. Budget Oversight

The importance of the defense appropriations power as a means of ensuring congressional participation in national security decision making was established in Chapters 5 and 10. Once funds are appropriated for covert actions, however, the open-ended authority given to the CIA in the National Security Act, along with the secret nature of intelligence operations, may make oversight of the expenditure of those funds especially difficult.

An adage from the Watergate era — "follow the money" — reminds us of one way for Congress and citizens to learn about covert action and other intelligence operations, albeit after the fact. The Statement and Account Clause of the Constitution, Article I, Section 9, Clause 7, states that "a regular Statement and Account of the Receipts and Expenditures of all public Money shall be published from time to time." Does the Constitution thus require that spending for intelligence programs, including covert action, be made public? If the "from time to time" qualifier affords some discretion to delay disclosure, is permanent budget secrecy foreclosed by the Constitution? If publication of budget details for intelligence programs, such as covert action, could compromise security, upon what legal basis may publication be avoided? Is there a lawful middle ground, such as required publication of the aggregate spending for intelligence programs without any detail?

Beginning in 1967, U.S. citizen-taxpayer William B. Richardson wrote a series of letters to the Treasury Department seeking information concerning detailed expenditures of the CIA. Richardson was provided copies of the "Combined Statement of Receipts, Expenditures, and Balances of the United States Government." But in accordance with the Central Intelligence Agency Act of 1949, which permits the Agency to account for its expenditures "solely on the certificate of the Director," 50 U.S.C. §403j(b) (2006), the Combined Statement did not provide information on the budget of the CIA. Richardson sued, claiming that §403j(b) violates the Statement and Account Clause. The Supreme Court eventually found that Richardson lacked standing as a citizen because his grievance was "generalized" and "common to all members of the public," while his claim as a taxpayer failed because there was no challenge to an enactment under the Taxing and Spending Clause and no claim based on a "specific constitutional limitation" on the taxing and spending power. *United States v. Richardson*, 418 U.S. 166, 175-177 (1974).

The Third Circuit Court of Appeals, sitting en banc, had found standing in *Richardson v. United States*, 465 F.2d 844 (3d Cir. 1972), and had this to say about the Statement and Account Clause:

> A responsible and intelligent taxpayer and citizen, of course, wants to know how his tax money is being spent. Without this information he cannot intelligently follow the actions of the Congress or of the Executive. Nor can he properly fulfill his obligations as a member of the electorate. The Framers of the Constitution deemed fiscal information essential if the electorate was to exercise any control over its representatives and meet their new responsibilities as citizens of the Republic. [*Id.* at 853.]

The framing history was reviewed by Judge Adams, dissenting:

> The debates regarding Article I, Section 9, Clause 7 . . . that occurred during the Constitutional Convention, shed light on the relative importance of that stipulation. . . . Farrand indicates that the discussion began with a statement by George Mason that "he did not conceive that the receipts and expenditures of the public money ought ever to be concealed. The people, he affirmed, had a right to know the expenditures of their money." 3 Farrand, *The Records of the Federal Convention of 1787*, at 326 (rev. ed. 1966). James Madison disagreed only with Mason's proposal of a fixed reporting period, stating that reports based on short periods:
>
>> would not be so full and connected as would be necessary for a thorough comprehension of them and detection of any errors. But by giving [the reporting officials] an opportunity of publishing them from time to time, as might be found easy and

convenient, they would be more full and satisfactory to the public, and would be sufficiently frequent. *Id.*

Rufus King objected to a full accounting on the ground that it would be "impracticable" to report "every minute shilling." 2 Farrand 618.

The argument that the duty to report the accounting runs to the public is based on a comparison of Article I, Section 9, Clause 7 with Article II, Section 3.... [T]he impact of the distinction between "shall be published" and "shall from time to time give to the Congress" becomes apparent. Furthermore, the Articles of Confederation, drafted by many of the same persons as the Constitution, required only that Congress inform the states of its indebtedness, as opposed to the requirement of publication of the receipt and expenditures of all public money. *Compare* U.S. Const. Art. I, §9, cl. 7 *with* Articles of Confederation, Art. IX, ¶5 (requiring Congress to account to the states for "sums of money...borrowed or emitted")....

Nevertheless, without denigrating the importance of Article I, Section 9, Clause 7, it would appear fair to conclude that it does not rise to the paramount stature of other constitutional provisions, such as those contained in the Bill of Rights. [465 F.2d at 871-872.]

NOTES AND QUESTIONS

1. *Congressional Authority to Limit Disclosure.* The Supreme Court stated in *Richardson* that "Congress has plenary power to exact any reporting and accounting requirement it considers appropriate." 418 U.S. at 178 n.11. Indeed, "[t]here has been no judicial enforcement of the Constitution's appropriations requirement against Congress itself." Kate Stith, *Congress' Power of the Purse*, 97 Yale L.J. 1343, 1392 (1988). Does the grant of the appropriations power to Congress necessarily include the power to interpret Article I, Section 9? *Cf. Powell v. McCormack*, 395 U.S. 486 (1969), holding that Congress's power to construe Article I, Section 5 (making each House "the Judge of the...Qualifications of its own Members) is limited. Is Congress's grant in the Central Intelligence Agency Act of 1949, *supra* p. 482, of discretion to withhold details of the CIA budget constitutional? Would a statutory requirement to publish the CIA budget be constitutional? Or *must* the Congress keep the CIA budget secret in the interest of national security? Do you think a federal court would decide this issue? *See generally* Stith, *supra*; William C. Banks & Peter Raven-Hansen, *National Security Law and the Power of the Purse* 105 (1994) (arguing that a requirement to disclose would be constitutional).

2. *Merits of the Richardson Suit.* If the merits had been reached in *Richardson,* what should have been the holding? That "all public Money" means what it says and applies to the CIA? That the CIA budget is one of those matters that the Framers understood might require secrecy? That whatever the Framers' intentions, the "from time to time" language provides Congress with discretion to shield CIA funds from public view indefinitely? In the No-Transfer Act of 1811, Congress secretly empowered the President to seize any part of Florida if any foreign power attempted to occupy the area, but the Act was not published until 1818. Act of Jan. 15, 1811, 3 Stat. 471 (1818). *See* Louis Fisher, *Presidential Spending Power* 214 (1975). Does the existence of an implied executive privilege in Article II, in addition to whatever discretion Congress enjoys under Article I, Section 9, provide authority for the government to keep any financial information from the public?

In the Virginia ratification debate, George Mason conceded that while "some matters, such as ongoing diplomatic negotiations and military operations, might require secrecy, he did not conceive that the receipts and expenditures of the public money ought ever to be concealed." 3 Jonathan Elliot, *Debates on the Federal Constitution* 459 (1836). Does the CIA budget simply reflect a situation not contemplated by the Framers — that disclosing expenses could undermine an ongoing secret collection or covert paramilitary operation?

3. *Secret Journal Clause.* Does the Secret Journal Clause of Article I, Section 5, lend support to the argument that a plain meaning construction of the Statement and Account Clause requires publication of intelligence spending? Or does the express recognition of the need for secrecy for the congressional journal reflect a more general acknowledgment that national security concerns might justify keeping information from the people?

4. *How the Money Game Works.* The 1949 Central Intelligence Agency Act grants expansive authority to the CIA concerning the transfer and use of public funds. The Act states that sums made available to the CIA "may be expended without regard to the provisions of law and regulations relating to the expenditure of Government funds." 50 U.S.C. §403j(b). Moreover, instead of direct appropriations to the CIA, the 1949 Act authorizes the Agency to transfer to and receive from other government agencies "such sums as may be approved" by the Office of Management and Budget (OMB) for any of the functions or activities authorized by the National Security Act of 1947. 50 U.S.C. §403f(a)(1). Other agencies are also permitted to transfer or receive from the CIA such sums "without regard to any provisions of law limiting or prohibiting transfers between appropriations." *Id.* Thus, funds for the intelligence community are first concealed in various inflated appropriation bills and then secretly transferred by OMB to the intelligence agencies after the bills are enacted.

In the formulation of the president's budget, the requests of the intelligence agencies are first coordinated by representatives of sponsoring agencies before being submitted to OMB for careful review of justifications and further coordination within the intelligence community. Once the president's budget is submitted to Congress, the portion for the intelligence agencies is segregated from the rest and discussed by members of the House and Senate Intelligence Committees and the relevant defense appropriations subcommittees meeting in executive session. The committees hold closed hearings at which agency staff answer questions and supply additional detail for the written budget justifications.

Once an NFIP [National Foreign Intelligence Program, now NIP] budget is approved by the intelligence and defense appropriation committees, a classified schedule of the authorizations and an explanation of the budget issues considered by the intelligence committees is made available to the executive branch and to the appropriations and armed services committees. This classified schedule lists the recommended allocation for all intelligence programs. When floor debate on the larger appropriation bills begins, the [NIP] budget is hidden within the recommended appropriations for other agencies, recently DOD. These appropriation accounts are inflated to reflect the pending budget transfers, but the members of Congress who are debating the budget and voting on appropriations do not know which figures are inflated or by how much. Congress is thus only mechanically involved in approving the budget . . . and its action in approving the remainder of the budget is clouded with the shell game of hiding the intelligence figures within other accounts.

　　After a budget is approved by Congress and the president, OMB receives instructions from the chair of the House Appropriations Committee as to the amounts and sources of budget transfers to be made to the intelligence agencies. OMB then carries out the transfers through its own highly secretive process. [Banks & Raven-Hansen, *supra*, at 52 (footnotes omitted)].

　　5. *Steps Toward Openness.* The budget for the intelligence community remains officially secret. However, beginning in 1991 all members of Congress were granted access to the classified annex to the defense appropriations bill that contains detailed information about appropriations for the intelligence community. Pub. L. No. 102-172, §6035, 105 Stat. 1150 (1991). In 2007, Congress required that the DNI disclose the aggregate amount of funds appropriated by Congress to the NIP for the fiscal year within 30 days of the end of the fiscal year unless the President files a written statement with Congress declaring that revealing the number "would damage national security." Implementing Recommendations of the 9/11 Commission Act of 2007, Pub. L. No. 110-53, §601, 121 Stat. 266 (codified at 50 U.S.C. §415(b)). In October 2010, DNI James R. Clapper reported that the fiscal year 2010 budget figure for the NIP was $53.1 billion. For the first time, General Clapper also disclosed the budget figures for the Military Intelligence Program (MIP) — $27 billion for 2010. Office of the Director of National Intelligence, News Release, *DNI Releases Budget Figure for 2010 National Intelligence Program* (Oct. 28, 2010), *at* http://www.fas.org/irp/news/2010/10/dni102810.pdf. For fiscal year 2010, the aggregate intelligence budget was thus $80.1 billion. *Id.* In February 2011, General Clapper revealed that the aggregate budget request for the NIP for fiscal year 2012 was $55 billion. Office of the Dir. of Nat'l Intelligence, Media Release, *DNI Releases Budget Figure for FY 2012 Appropriations Requested for the National Intelligence Program* Feb. 14, 2011), *at* http://www.fas.org/irp/news/2011/02/dni021411.pdf.

3. Congressional Oversight Reforms

a. The War Powers Resolution and Covert Action

　　The War Powers Resolution, 50 U.S.C. §§1541-1548 (2006), a product of the Vietnam War, was meant to limit unilateral executive war making. Yet it appears that Congress failed to address one of the most important forms of military action in modern times. As we saw in Chapter 11, many short-term military operations escape the time limits of the resolution or are arguably not subject to its strictures for other reasons. More important for our immediate purposes, the resolution applies only to "United States Armed Forces," 50 U.S.C. §§1542-1543, and so appears to exempt covert paramilitary operations conducted by U.S. agents other than members of the armed forces. Indeed, the legislative history seems to confirm that exemption. An amendment proposed by Senator Eagleton that would have extended the measure to private armies "employed by, under contract to, or under the direction of" the government failed to pass. 119 Cong. Rec. 25,079-25,092 (1973). *See* Newell L. Highsmith, *Policing Executive Adventurism: Congressional Oversight of Military and Paramilitary Operations,* 19 Harv. J. Legis. 327, 353-354 (1982). Thus, the War Powers Resolution may have inadvertently driven war making even farther underground. *See* Harold

Hongju Koh, *Why the President (Almost) Always Wins in Foreign Affairs: Lessons of the Iran-Contra Affair,* 97 Yale L.J. 1255, 1273 (1988); Douglas Steele, Note, *Covert Action and the War Powers Resolution: Preserving the Constitutional Balance,* 39 Syracuse L. Rev. 1139 (1988).

b. The Hughes-Ryan Amendment of 1974 and the Intelligence Oversight Act of 1980

Any remaining doubt that Congress had by legislation recognized the CIA's covert action function ended in 1974, when Congress passed the Hughes-Ryan Amendment to the Foreign Assistance Act, Pub. L. No. 93-559, §32, 88 Stat. 1795, 1804, which provided in part:

> Limitation on Intelligence Activities. (a) No funds appropriated under the authority of this or any other Act may be expended by or on behalf of the Central Intelligence Agency for operations in foreign countries, other than activities intended solely for obtaining necessary intelligence, unless and until the President finds that each such operation is important to the national security of the United States and reports, in a timely fashion, a description and scope of such operation to the appropriate committees of the Congress, including the Committee on Foreign Relations of the United States Senate and the Committee on Foreign Affairs of the United States House of Representatives.

Hughes-Ryan thus enforced some measure of accountability for certain "operations" not intended solely for obtaining intelligence by requiring a presidential finding for each operation, as well as a report of the operation to congressional committees. At the same time, subsection (b) of the Hughes-Ryan Amendment exempted from the law's requirements military actions in a declared war or "an exercise of powers by the President under the War Powers Resolution." Pub. L. No. 93-559, 88 Stat. 1804, *repealed,* Pub. L. No. 96-450, §407(a)(3), 94 Stat. 1981 (1980). The upshot seemed to be alternative oversight controls: a Hughes-Ryan finding and report for covert operations, or a War Powers resolution report for authorized military actions.

Soon after Hughes-Ryan was passed, CIA General Counsel Rogovin maintained that the amendment "clearly implies that the CIA is authorized to plan and conduct covert action." Rogovin Memorandum, *supra* p. 475, at 1737. The same conclusion was reached by two committees of the Association of the Bar of the City of New York. Committee on Civil Rights & Comm. on Int'l Human Relations, Association of the Bar of the City of New York, *The Central Intelligence Agency: Oversight and Accountability* 15 (1975). During floor debates, Representative Holtzman argued that the amendment would permit the CIA to "subvert or undermine foreign governments." 120 Cong. Rec. 39,165 (1974). On the other hand, Senator Hughes and others viewed the amendment as the beginning of a reform process. Information about the CIA's activities generated by the reporting requirement would inform Congress, so that Congress could determine what permanent controls to impose. 120 Cong. Rec. 39,488-39,490 (1974) (Sen. Hughes); *id.* at 39,491 (Sen. Baker and Sen. Symington). *See generally* Americo R. Cinquegrana, *Dancing in the Dark: Accepting the Invitation to Struggle in the Context of "Covert Action," the Iran-Contra Affair and the Intelligence Oversight Process,* 11 Hous. J. Int'l L. 177, 182-187 (1988).

Before Hughes-Ryan, the CIA reported to the Armed Services Committees and the Appropriations Committees of both Houses. Hughes-Ryan added the House Foreign Affairs and the Senate Foreign Relations Committees. The seventh and eighth oversight committees were added following the Church Committee investigations in 1975-1976, when each House established a special committee for oversight of intelligence. Scott Breckenridge, *The CIA and the U.S. Intelligence System* 266 (1986).

One clear purpose of Hughes-Ryan was to end the practice of "plausible deniability" for the President, at least in his relations with Congress. *See Church Comm. Rep., supra* p. 478, bk. I, at 58 ("The concept of plausible denial . . . is dead."). In addition to enhancing accountability for covert operations, requiring the President's approval was supposed to assure the President's careful review of proposals and promote effective internal debate in the executive branch. *CNSS, supra* p. 480, at 37-41.

In the Intelligence Oversight Act of 1980, Pub. L. No. 96-450, §407(b)(1), 94 Stat. 1975 (1981), Congress required that the heads of entities involved in intelligence activities "keep [the intelligence committees] fully and currently informed of all intelligence activities" for which the United States is responsible, "including any significant anticipated intelligence activity." *Id.* (adding 50 U.S.C. §413(a)(1)). The Act provided that the notice requirements do not constitute a prior approval requirement for covert actions, and it permitted the President to limit notice to eight selected members of Congress when necessary "to meet extraordinary circumstances affecting vital interests of the United States." *Id.* The Act also required intelligence agencies to report to the intelligence committees "in a timely fashion . . . any illegal intelligence activity or significant intelligence failure and any corrective action" taken or planned in connection with illegal activity or intelligence failure. *Id.*

NOTES AND QUESTIONS

1. *Authorization of Covert Actions?* Did the Hughes-Ryan Amendment provide statutory authority for covert actions? If so, was it wise to do so? Was it preferable to the cryptic provisions of the 1947 Act?

2. *Implementing Hughes-Ryan.* Consider the threshold for invoking Hughes-Ryan, that an operation be "important to the national security." What showing must the President have made to satisfy this standard? Should Congress have substituted "essential" or "grave threats" for "important"? What, if any, practical difference would it have made?

Could Congress have required the reports to be in writing prior to implementing a covert operation? Could it have required that each project be approved by Congress in advance? Note that Hughes-Ryan was an exercise of Congress's defense appropriations power. How, if at all, does that fact affect your answer to these questions?

3. *Modest Additional Reform Efforts.* When the American embassy in Teheran was seized and 52 American hostages were imprisoned by Iranian militants on November 4, 1979, there was widespread feeling that there had been an "intelligence failure" — that we should have detected signs of the revolution and anti-American unrest in Iran. Then, when the Soviet Union invaded Afghanistan on December 27, 1979, the tide effectively swung away from regulation and toward an enhanced intelligence capability.

The Intelligence Oversight Act of 1980, adding §501 of the National Security Act of 1947, Pub. L. No. 96-450, §407(b), 94 Stat. 1975, 1981 (1980), represented what the Senate Intelligence Committee was able to salvage of a more ambitious proposed statutory charter for the intelligence community. The 1980 Act was an especially modest product, considering that its provisions largely repeated oversight measures in President Carter's Executive Order No. 12,036, §§3-4, 43 Fed. Reg. 3678 (Jan. 24, 1978). What practical importance can be ascribed to the measure?

Shortcomings in the 1980 Act became apparent with the public disclosure six years later of the Iran-Contra Affair, which is analyzed below. Intelligence community abuses and criminal activity associated with that scandal provoked new oversight measures in 1991, as described in the next chapter.

E.   CASE STUDY: THE IRAN-CONTRA AFFAIR[1]

On November 3, 1986, Al-Shiraa, a Beirut weekly, reported that the United States had secretly sold arms to Iran, using Israel as an intermediary. Reports soon followed that linked the arms sales to a desire to gain the release of American hostages in Lebanon. After a brief investigation by the Justice Department, it was also revealed that some proceeds from the arms sales to Iran had been diverted to the Administration-supported Contras fighting the Sandinista government of Nicaragua, at a time when U.S. military aid to the Contras had been prohibited by Congress. A major scandal suddenly burst upon the scene: the Iran-Contra Affair. A member of the staff of the NSC, Lieutenant Colonel Oliver L. North, was effectively in charge of both operations. He was supported by National Security Advisers Robert McFarlane and Vice Admiral John Poindexter and by CIA Director William Casey.

The principal congressional and executive branch investigations of the Iran-Contra Affair shared a basic conclusion — that the scandal was not due to the patch-work legal controls of the national security system. The Tower Commission, appointed by President Reagan and made up of former Senator John Tower, former Senator/Secretary of State Edmund Muskie, and former National Security Adviser Brent Scowcroft, emphasized human failings, criticized the President's lax "management style," and concluded that, while systemic problems were found, "their solution does not lie in revamping the National Security Council system." President's Special Review Bd., *The Tower Commission Report* 1-4 (Feb. 26, 1987). The congressional committees looking into the affair, formed in January 1987 in the Senate and House, merged to conduct a ten-month investigation that included 40 days of public hearings, review of more than 300,000 documents, and examination or interview of more than 500 witnesses. Their final report concluded "that the Iran-Contra Affair resulted from the failure of individuals to observe the law, not from deficiencies in existing law or in our system of governance." H. Select Comm. to Investigate Covert Arms Transactions with Iran and S. Select Comm. on Secret Military Assistance to Iran and the Nicaraguan Opposition, *Report of the Congressional Committees Investigating the Iran-Contra Affair (Iran-Contra Report)*, S. Rep. No. 100-216/H.R. Rep. No. 100-433, at 423 (1987).

---

1. This account is drawn in part from Scott Armstrong, Malcolm Byrne, Tom Blanton & The National Security Archive, *The Chronology: The Documented Day-By-Day Account of Secret Military Assistance to Iran and the Contras* (1987); Theodore Draper, *A Very Thin Line: The Iran-Contra Affairs* (1991).

1. The Legality of the Arms Sales

A central issue in the Iran-Contra Affair is whether the President had authority to transfer arms to Iran. There are three possible sources of presidential authority for the transfer of arms to a foreign country. First, the President may seek to rely on Article II or on inherent constitutional powers. President Reagan's incentive to send arms to Iran was at least in part humanitarian in nature — he wanted to secure the return of the American hostages held in Lebanon. Thus, the arms transactions were something more than merely arms sales. Each was calculated to be a trade: arms for hostages. The President may therefore have been acting pursuant to implied constitutional powers to rescue Americans held abroad (see Chapter 13). In addition, the President's constitutional authority may have been enhanced by the Hostage Act, *supra* p. 369, if the Act is read as "necessary and proper for carrying into execution" the President's Article II powers.

If the President cannot find authority in the Constitution, it must come from Congress. The Arms Export Control Act, codified as amended at 22 U.S.C. §§2751-2796 (2006) (hereinafter AECA), allows the President to sell arms to foreign countries under certain conditions, including advance notice to Congress, but it gives Congress the opportunity to veto sales over certain dollar amounts. When Israel sent missiles to Iran in 1985, the Administration promised to replenish Israel's stockpile. Israel had obtained the missiles from the United States pursuant to the AECA, which also required an agreement between Israel and the United States that the United States give its written consent to any retransfer of the missiles. *Iran-Contra Report, supra,* at 418. Yet, according to the Iran-Contra Report,

> The President's authorization of the 1985 transfers to Iran [was] made without even a pretense of compliance with the AECA or Israel's written agreements with the United States. No written consent was sought or given; and even if Israel had sought a written consent, this government could not have given it without changing its own regulations. This is so because Iran, which was considered a terrorist nation by the United States and which was the subject of a U.S. arms embargo, was not eligible for direct sales. [*Id.*]

Furthermore, Iran never agreed not to retransfer the missiles, as the AECA required, and the President never reported the sales to Congress.

The President also may have had the power to transfer arms as part of a covert intelligence operation, subject to the finding and reporting requirements of §501 of the National Security Act, added by the Intelligence Oversight Act of 1980, *supra.* Could characterizing the sales this way excuse compliance with the AECA? Events leading up to the sales were described by the congressional committees as follows:

> In 1981, Attorney General William French Smith had taken the position — based on an analysis by the State Department Legal Adviser — that the restrictions of [the arms export] statutes applied only to transfers undertaken pursuant to them; the President, however, could approve a transfer "outside the context of those statutes" by utilizing the Economy Act and the National Security Act. Nonetheless, the Smith opinion recognized the Congressional reporting requirements applicable in any event, and specifically concluded that "the House and Senate Intelligence Committees should be informed of this proposal and the President's determinations."

When the Smith opinion was considered in the context of the Iran Finding in January 1986, its requirement of at least some form of prior Congressional notification was ignored. Instead, a memorandum from Poindexter to the President describing the Finding characterized that opinion as concluding "that under an appropriate finding you could authorize the CIA to sell arms to countries outside of the provisions of laws and reporting requirements for foreign military sales." Poindexter's memorandum recommended to the President "that you exercise your statutory prerogative to withhold notification...to the Congressional oversight committees until such time as you deem it to be appropriate." [*Iran-Contra Report*, *supra*, at 380.]

NOTES AND QUESTIONS

1. *Applying the Rescue Power.* Does the rescue power, like the repel power, require some immediate threat of harm? Or is rescue a longer-term power? The *Minority Report* of the congressional investigators of the Iran-Contra Affair maintained that "the *Durand* case [*supra* p. 368] stands for the proposition that the President has the discretion to take whatever steps may be necessary, short of a full scale war, to protect American citizens." *Iran-Contra Report, supra,* at 474 (*Minority Report*). Does this statement accurately reflect the holding of *Durand?* More generally, does it correctly state the scope of the President's constitutional rescue powers?

2. *Applying the Hostage Act.* Did the Hostage Act, *supra* p. 369, apply to the arms-for-hostages deals? If the Hostage Act did apply, did its terms permit the activities undertaken by the President on behalf of the hostages? There was apparently no effort to comply with the Hostage Act's requirement that "all facts and proceedings relative thereto shall as soon as practicable be communicated by the President to Congress."

3. *Arms for Hostages as a Covert Operation?* The *Minority Report* argues that the National Security Act provided an "alternative legal route" for the 1985 arms shipments to Iran:

> Like the AECA and FAA [Foreign Assistance Act], the National Security Act presupposes some kind of Presidential determination. Specifically, the determination must be that an action — in this case a retransfer — would "affect" the national security. If the CIA is involved, the so-called Hughes-Ryan Amendment requires a more emphatic Presidential determination. Instead of saying an activity must "affect" national security, Hughes-Ryan says it must be "important." More significantly, this determination must be made personally by the President, and reported in a "timely fashion" to Congress.
>
> We believe that the terms under which the President may use the National Security Act in fact meet all underlying purposes of the AECA and FAA, and that is why Congress has been satisfied to let the one approach be a substitute or alternative route to the other. The fact is that the 1985 Israeli transactions essentially — and legally — were equivalent to ones in which the United States sold the weapons directly to Iran. [*Iran-Contra Report, supra,* at 540.]

Do you find this analysis persuasive?

When Attorney General Meese was asked by the Tower Commission whether the CIA's activities in arranging the November 1985 shipment by the Israelis should have been preceded by a finding, he replied in a letter that "a finding under the Hughes-Ryan amendment would be required." *Tower Commission Report, supra* p. 488, at Appendix H. How would you answer?

4. *Using the Economy Act.* On January 17, 1986, President Reagan signed a finding that was a slight revision of one executed ten days earlier. The earlier finding, authorizing more shipments of missiles through Israel, was abandoned at CIA General Counsel Sporkin's urging, when he advised that the approval of Israeli sales would violate the AECA. The new finding, based on the National Security Act, would, according to Sporkin, permit the CIA to take Defense Department weapons and sell them to Israel or Iran directly under the Economy Act, Pub. L. No. 314-212, 47 Stat. 382 (1932). The Economy Act permits the President to transfer functions and property from one executive agency to another. *Id.*, 47 Stat. 413. But may the President avoid the AECA simply by labeling an arms transfer as a covert action? If so, did the revised finding comply with the National Security Act?

5. *Oral Findings?* Were findings for the arms sales to Iran required by Hughes-Ryan or §501 of the 1980 Intelligence Oversight Act, *supra* pp. 486-488? If so, what form should those findings have taken? Attorney General Meese testified that President Reagan's tacit oral approval of the early Israeli shipments established legal authorization for the covert direct sales. *Iran-Contra Report, supra,* at 488. Was the Meese opinion sound in light of §501? In light of the Hughes-Ryan Amendment?

6. *Constitutional Limits on Oversight?* Section 501 stated that its notice requirements applied "to the extent consistent with all applicable authorities and duties, including those conferred by the Constitution upon the executive and legislative branches of the government." CIA General Counsel Sporkin testified to the congressional committees that the alleged failures to comply with Hughes-Ryan and §501 could be defended as an exercise of constitutional power:

[*Sporkin:*]   The argument I'm making is . . . that §501 specifically recognizes that there are constitutional prerogatives which are not going to be dealt with by the notification. . . . I'm saying it is both a statutory matter as well as a constitutional matter because if the statute recognizes it, then the statute must mean that there are times when there will be non-notification. . . .

Representative Louis Stokes: . . . Do you believe that if covert action involves possible risk to life, but also involves significant policy changes, that such an operation still can be kept from the Congress for months, and perhaps years?

A: I think it would be wrong to do so, but I, again, I'm not going to say it would be illegal.

Q: Judge Sporkin, during the Jan. 16, 1986, meeting that you attended in the White House, when was it suggested by those attending there that Congress would be told about the Iran initiative?

A: It was suggested, my recollection as soon as the hostages were out.

Q: Did someone at the meeting advance the suggestion that Congress might not be told until the President left office, that is, if all the hostages had not been freed by that time?

A: I don't think it was put that way. It was put a different way. It was saying this President is
        going to have to make a report to this Congress to justify what he did even if it means the
        last day in office. That's the way it was put, not the other way. [*Joint Hearings Before the H.
        Select Comm. to Investigate Covert Arms Transactions with Iran and the S. Select Comm. on Secret
        Military Assistance to Iran and the Nicaraguan Opposition,* 100th Cong. 194-199 (1987) (tes-
        timony of Stanley Sporkin).]

Do you agree with Judge Sporkin's interpretation of §501? *See generally* Lawrence L.
Block & David B. Rivkin Jr., *The Battle to Control the Conduct of Foreign Intelligence and
Covert Operations: The Ultra-Whig Counterrevolution Revisited,* 12 Harv. J.L. & Pub. Pol'y
303, 342 (1989) (supporting that interpretation). How could Hughes-Ryan or §501
have been rewritten to remove any apparent ambiguities regarding the timing of
congressional notification?

    7. *Delayed Reporting.* The President's January 17, 1986, finding that authorized
direct arms sales to Iran was never reported to Congress. Like the rest of us, Congress
learned of the sales through the November 1986 Beirut newspaper story. At a news
conference shortly after the story broke, President Reagan said, "I have the right
under the law to defer reporting to Congress . . . and defer it until such time as
I believe it can safely be done with no risk to others." *See* Ruth Marcus, *Intelligence
Law: What Notice Does It Require?,* Wash. Post, Dec. 21, 1986, at A21. Do you agree with
the President's interpretation?

2.   Covert Support for the Contras and the Boland Amendments

    We have seen that many of our nation's most important national security dis-
putes are aired in the appropriations process. Indeed, because of Congress's reluctance to exercise its war declaration and marque and reprisal powers, the
appropriations power has become the primary congressional lever for checking
the national security initiatives of the executive branch. *See* Louis Fisher, *Constitutional
Conflicts Between Congress and the President* 192-219 (2007); Michael J. Glennon, *Strengthening the War Powers Resolution: The Case for Purse-Strings Restrictions,* 60 Minn. L. Rev. 1
(1975). At the same time, there has been ongoing statutory support for activities of
the intelligence community. Thus, appropriations legislation has served at different
times either to ratify national security actions (e.g., the 1949 Central Intelligence
Agency Act) or to control them (e.g., the 1973 and 1974 funding restrictions on
the Southeast Asia War). See *supra* p. 294.
    U.S. aid to the Nicaraguan Contra rebels and CIA involvement in their fight
became two of the most contentious issues in American politics in the early 1980s.
On December 1, 1981, President Reagan signed a finding that authorized the CIA to
"[s]upport and conduct . . . paramilitary operations against the Cuban presence and
Cuban Sandinista support infrastructure in Nicaragua and elsewhere in Central
America." *Iran-Contra Report, supra,* at 386 n.41. The finding was presented to the
intelligence committees. The stated purpose of this early covert program was the
interdiction of arms shipments from Nicaragua to the leftist insurgents in El Salvador.
However, the CIA relied on this finding to assist Contra rebels throughout Nicaragua.
Id. at 32.

Beginning in 1982, Congress enacted a series of measures, dubbed Boland Amendments for their sponsor, Representative Edward P. Boland, designed to limit that assistance. However, Congress was anything but steadfast in its opposition to supporting the Contras. On the one hand, chastened by its failure to assert its powers during the Vietnam War until very late, Congress was eager to act assertively to forestall a repeat of the Southeast Asia tragedy. On the other hand, many members of Congress felt that Central America presented a different kind of political and strategic situation, and that it might be imprudent to tie the President's hands. *See Iran-Contra Report, supra*, at 395-407; *id.* at 489-499 (*Minority Report*).

The most restrictive of these Contra aid measures, commonly referred to as "Boland II," was part of a continuing appropriations measure for fiscal year 1985 and was in place during the most critical period of clandestine support by the Reagan administration.

Boland II
Pub. L. No. 98-473, §8066(a), 98 Stat. 1837, 1935 (1984)

[N]o funds available to the Central Intelligence Agency, the Department of Defense, or any other agency or entity of the United States involved in intelligence activities may be obligated or expended for the purpose or which would have the effect of supporting, directly or indirectly, military or paramilitary operations in Nicaragua by any nation, group, organization, movement, or individual.

This prohibition came after it was revealed that the CIA had participated in the mining of Nicaraguan harbors and in military attacks on Nicaraguan oil facilities, with only scant notice to the intelligence committees. *See* John Prados, *Presidents' Secret Wars* 392-397 (1986); *see also* 1984 Cong. Q. Almanac 89. However, in spite of a growing congressional determination to terminate covert war making in Nicaragua, Senate conferees agreed to the House prohibition only by coupling it with a promise to consider the aid issue again four months later. Remarking on the successful conference compromise, Representative Boland stated that "[t]he compromise . . . clearly ends United States support for the war in Nicaragua. . . . [It] can only be renewed if the President can convince the Congress that this very strict prohibition should be overturned." 130 Cong. Rec. H11974 (daily ed. Oct. 10, 1984).

Boland II presents three discrete problems of interpretation. *First*, does the language "any other agency or entity" cover only agencies traditionally involved in intelligence operations, or does it also apply to any entity that is actually so involved? It was Lieutenant Colonel North and other members of the NSC staff, after all, not CIA officials (except for DCI Casey) or others traditionally active in covert operations, who were principally responsible for managing the resupply operation, including the diversion to the Contras of the proceeds of arms sales to Iran, as well as the solicitation of donations for the Contras from private citizens and officials of foreign nations. In this connection, reread Executive Order No. 12,333 §1.2, *supra* p. 452.

Second, does "involved" encompass indirect support? North and other NSC staffers helped arrange and coordinate the diversion of funds for the Contras, but they did not directly contribute money or weapons.

BY TOLES FOR THE BUFFALO NEWS

Third, did the phrase "no funds available" apply only to the appropriations bill for fiscal year 1985 of which Boland II was a part, or did it apply more broadly to funds available from any government account?

Finally, apart from the formal statutory construction, consider two more basic questions. Was there ever any serious doubt of the spirit, if not the articulated intent, of Boland II, given its origins? If not, are the President's lawyers nevertheless permitted, if not obliged, to read such legislation narrowly and legalistically on the theory that legislation in derogation of the President's national security authority must be construed strictly? *See* Banks & Raven-Hansen, *supra* p. 483, at 137-157.

NOTES AND QUESTIONS

1. *Was the Language Clear?* The congressional investigators found Boland II "clear on its face" and applicable to the diversion of funds to the Contras. *Iran Contra Report, supra,* at 399. Do you agree? In other years the various Boland amendments were sometimes more, and sometimes less, restrictive, but always controversial, prompting arguments that Boland II was so vague that its requirements could not be determined. Indeed, "[s]ome claimed that the Boland amendments were convenient fig leaves for Congressmen who wanted to be against 'another Vietnam' in Central America and at the same time did not want to be accused of allowing another country

to fall under Soviet control." Eugene V. Rostow, *President, Prime Minister, or Constitutional Monarch?* 22-23 (Institute for Nat'l Strategic Studies 1989).

Is Congress's vacillation evidence of its institutional incompetency on the part of Congress to make policy for covert operations? Of a congressional failure of nerve? Or was the variability Congress's response to successive executive branch evasions of the funding limitations? Is it important that Congress appears generally to have tightened the Boland restrictions in the belief that earlier versions were being disregarded by the executive branch? *See Iran-Contra Report, supra,* at 396. How do you think the executive branch should have responded to any uncertainty about Congress's intent?

2. *Application of Boland II to the NSC and Its Staff.* While the NSC and its staff were established in the National Security Act of 1947 to advise the President and to provide coordination of national security policies, see *supra* p. 449, the President's actual use of the NSC and its staff has varied considerably over time. President Reagan's Executive Order No. 12,333 directed the NSC to provide "review of, guidance for, and direction to the conduct of" covert operations, *id.* §1.2, while the CIA was to "conduct special activities approved by the President." *Id.* §1.8(e).

Notwithstanding details of the NSC charter in the National Security Act of 1947, how should the actual historical use of the NSC affect our interpretation of the language in Boland II? Can that question be answered without knowing what Congress, or at least the intelligence committees, knew about that historical practice? *See* Ed Jenkins & Robert H. Brink, *The National Security Council and the Iran-Contra Affair,* 18 Ga. J. Int'l & Comp. L. 19, 22-27 (1988).

3. *NSC Staff and the National Security Act.* In the period covered by Boland II, the NSC staff raised money and organized a private resupply operation for the Contras. President Reagan told the Tower Board that he did not know that the NSC staff was directly helping the Contras, and there was no presidential finding explicitly authorizing these activities. Did any or all of these activities violate Hughes-Ryan, as revised by the Intelligence Oversight Act of 1980 (p. 487)? The National Security Act?

4. *"No funds available."* In 1987, the Reagan administration asserted that Boland II restricted only funds appropriated under the appropriations measure to which it was attached, and that because none of those funds were earmarked for the NSC, the NSC was unaffected by Boland. *See* Gerald F. Seib, *White House Case Against Boland Amendment Attempts End Run Around Charges of Violation,* Wall St. J., May 18, 1987, at 56. According to the congressional committees, however, the "prohibition against employment of CIA funds 'available' to it precluded that agency from using its contingency reserve or any funds at its disposal." *Iran-Contra Report, supra,* at 401. Consider this General Accounting Office (GAO) assessment of general appropriations act provisions:

> Appropriation acts, in addition to making appropriations, frequently contain a variety of provisions either restricting the availability of the appropriations or making them available for some particular use. Such provisions come in two forms: (a) "provisos" attached directly to the appropriating language, and (b) general provisions. A general provision may apply solely to the act in which it is contained ("No part of any appropriation contained in this Act shall be used"), . . . or it may have general applicability ("No part of any appropriation contained in this or any other Act shall be

used").... Provisions of this type are no less effective merely because they are contained in appropriation acts. General provisions may be phrased in the form of restrictions or positive authority. [Office of Gen. Counsel, General Accounting Office, 1 *Principles of Federal Appropriations Law* 2-33 (3d ed. 2004).]

Boland II contains neither form of restriction described by the GAO. Does the "no funds available" language nonetheless imply a prohibition of general application? With respect to CIA support for the Contras, does the secret nature of CIA funding, see *supra* p. 481, help to explain why Boland II says "no funds available," instead of "no appropriations contained in this or any other Act"? Or could the CIA have legally assisted the Contras with funds available to it from sources other than the Defense Department?

5. *CIA Contingency Fund.* The Reagan administration's decision to provide assistance to the Nicaraguan Contras through a covert CIA program was made and carried out without public or congressional debate and without a specific appropriation for that purpose. The CIA contingency fund, a secret fund within the secret CIA budget, financed the Contras early on. In line with the CIA's 1949 statutory authority, the only "publication" of the costs of the operation came when President Reagan submitted a report to Congress and thus complied with the Hughes-Ryan reporting requirements. Thus, "there was no public accounting or even notice to most members of Congress of the actual investment in the Contras' cause." Banks & Raven-Hansen, *supra* p. 483, at 104.

In 1983, Congress explicitly prohibited the use of the CIA contingency fund to augment the appropriation in support of the Contras. *Iran-Contra Report, supra,* at 397. Nonetheless, the congressional investigators found that the Administration continued to rely on the contingency fund even after the cutoff of appropriated funds in 1984. *Id.* at 399-401.

Like the Central Intelligence Agency Act of 1949, the DOD appropriation measure each year permits certain spending solely on the certificate of the Secretary of Defense. "Special forces" is one type of military operation for which funds are permitted to be spent in this way. When appropriations for the Contras ran out in 1984, the Administration relied on DOD special forces budget authority to purchase equipment, which was then made available to the NSC and CIA staff who were supplying the Contras. *See* Kenneth Sharpe, *The Post-Vietnam Formula Under Siege: The Imperial Presidency and Central America,* 102 Pol. Sci. Q. 549, 561-562 (1987).

6. *Congressional Limits on Solicitation of Unappropriated Funds.* One of the most contentious issues surrounding Boland II concerns its application to the executive branch solicitation of funds from other countries. According to the congressional committees, it was understood that such solicitation was forbidden, even though Boland did not specifically address the matter. *Iran-Contra Report, supra,* at 403-404.

In spite of this understanding, between June 1984 and the beginning of 1986, $34 million was raised from foreign countries by Reagan administration officials for the Contras. Although the earliest third-country contributions went directly to the Contras, beginning in July 1985 Oliver North and others effectively ran an "off-the-shelf" covert operation with unappropriated funds. At the subsequent criminal trial of North, it was revealed that at least ten countries were solicited for contributions to the Contras and that several of the countries were later rewarded with increased U.S.

foreign aid. Stipulation of Facts, *United States v. North*, No. 88-0080-02 (D.D.C. Apr. 6, 1989); *Iran-Contra Report, supra*, at 16, 19-27.

The contributions given to the United States were not "funds available" from an appropriation or budget transfer. Do you understand why some officials of the State Department, CIA, and NSC nevertheless took the position internally that Boland II prohibited solicitation and use of such contributions to support the Contras?

7. *Congressional Limits on Spending Third-Party Contributions.* Whether or not the Boland Amendment applied, use of third-party contributions to support the Contras may have been restricted by other statutes:

> The Government may, of course, receive gifts. However, consistent with Congress' constitutionally exclusive power of the purse, gifts, like all other "miscellaneous receipts," must by statute (31 U.S.C. Section 484) be placed directly into the Treasury of the United States, and may be spent only pursuant to a Congressional appropriation. . . .
>
> The Constitutional process that lodges control of Government expenditures exclusively in Congress is further enforced by the Anti-Deficiency Act (31 U.S.C. Section 1341), which prohibits an officer of the United States from authorizing an expenditure that has not been the subject of a Congressional appropriation, or that exceeds the amount of any applicable appropriation. Thus it provides: "An officer or employee of the United States government may not make or authorize an expenditure or obligation exceeding an amount available in an appropriation or fund for the expenditure or obligation; or involve [the] government in a contract or obligation for the payment of money before an appropriation is made unless authorized by law." Violations of the Anti-Deficiency Act are made crimes by 31 U.S.C. Section 1350. [*Iran-Contra Report, supra* p. 488, at 412.]

A 1954 measure authorized the Secretary of the Treasury or the Administrator of General Services to accept gifts for "particular defense purposes," then to transfer such gifts into such "appropriation accounts" as will "best effectuate the intent of the donors," and to treat such amounts as appropriated. Pub. L. No. 83-537, 68 Stat. 566. Did this measure make the solicitation of third-country support for the Contra rebels legal? The 1954 statute was repealed in 1990. Pub. L. No. 101-403, §2608(b), 104 Stat. 874.

At least as early as June 25, 1984, months before Boland II was enacted, at a National Security Planning Group meeting attended by President Reagan, Secretary of State George Schultz reported an opinion of White House Chief of Staff James Baker that it would be an "impeachable offense" if the United States served as a conduit for third-country funding to the Contras. *Iran-Contra Report, supra*, at 39. Regarding U.S. solicitation of third-country support for the Contras, President Reagan remarked: "If such a story gets out, we'll all be hanging by our thumbs in front of the White House until we find out who did it." National Security Council, *National Security Planning Group Meeting, June 25, 1984, Minutes*, at 14.

8. *The President's Foreign Relations Power.* Does the President have implied power, incident to his power of diplomatic communication, to encourage third parties to pursue the policies he favors? Could Congress prohibit the President from exercising this power by talking with King Fahd or the President of Honduras about the Contras? Professor Rostow insists that "Presidents have used unorthodox channels in

diplomacy, usually for important reasons of policy, since Washington's day.... A diplomatic exploration conducted under the direction of the President can never be 'outside the normal government framework' and Congress has no power to regulate such Presidential activities." Rostow, *supra* p. 495, at 18. See also *supra* pp. 52-67.

Professor Stith, on the other hand, argues that a denial of appropriated funds forecloses the executive from

> all means of engaging in the prohibited activity because employees' salaries and other overhead costs are almost invariably paid out of appropriated funds.... In principle, a government employee acting in an official capacity — including the President — may not spend one minute to make one phone call to solicit private funds (for use of the government or directly for a third party) for an activity explicitly denied appropriated funds. [Stith, *supra*, 97 Yale L.J. at 1361-1362 (1988).]

Which conclusion best reflects your understanding of the constitutional powers in dispute?

9. *The President's Commander-in-Chief Power.* Does the Commander in Chief Clause empower the President to conduct covert operations without regard for the strictures of Boland II? To what extent do the terms of Boland II determine an answer to this question? Of what relevance is Justice Jackson's dictum in *The Steel Seizure Case* that, while the President's power of command is plenary, "only Congress can provide him an army or navy to command"? *Youngstown Sheet & Tube Co. v. Sawyer,* 343 U.S. 579, 644 (1952). Does Justice Jackson's proposition apply as much to proxy armies as to public armies?

3.   The Iran-Contra Affair in the Courts

Soon after the public disclosure of the Iran-Contra Affair, Attorney General Edwin Meese requested the appointment of an Independent Counsel pursuant to the Ethics in Government Act of 1978, Pub. L. No. 95-521, 92 Stat. 1824. A panel of judges appointed former federal judge Lawrence E. Walsh as Independent Counsel. Walsh and his staff conducted a 15-month investigation, and on March 16, 1988, a grand jury returned a 101-page, 23-count indictment against National Security Adviser John Poindexter, Lieutenant Colonel Oliver North, and two co-conspirators. The indictment charged the defendants with three categories of crimes: so-called political or foreign affairs crimes (conspiracy to violate the Boland Amendment and Executive Order No. 12,333), information crimes (obstruction of inquiries and proceedings, false statements, and falsification, destruction, and removal of documents), and garden-variety money crimes (illegal gratuities, embezzlement, and diversion of funds).

After the original four-defendant case was assigned, the defense filed more than 100 pretrial motions. The defendants challenged the validity of the indictment itself and the application of the Classified Information Procedures Act (CIPA) (discussed *infra* p. 1098), which governs the disclosure of classified information in trials, while they made demands for the discovery of hundreds of thousands of documents. Perhaps the most vexing problem for the prosecution was the fact that some defendants had been granted immunity from prosecution based on their testimony at congressional hearings. Rules restricting the use of such testimony are set out in *Kastigar v. United States*, 406 U.S. 331 (1972). After a motion and argument, Judge Gerhard A. Gesell agreed in June 1988 to sever the four trials, based on the defendants' contention that their planned use of the immunized testimony of their codefendants in their own defenses prevented a fair joint trial.

Independent Counsel Walsh elected to try North first. Going first permitted North to present himself as a patriotic fall guy and to blame his superiors and others for his law breaking. The severed trials also delayed by a year the completion of the questioning and other investigative steps in the remaining cases.

United States v. North

United States District Court, District of Columbia (1988)
708 F. Supp. 375

GESELL, District Judge. . . . In 1924, the Supreme Court described defrauding the United States in terms that clearly encompass North's conduct as alleged. Chief Justice Taft said:

> To conspire to defraud the United States means primarily to cheat the Government out of property or money, but it also means to interfere with or obstruct one of its lawful government functions by deceit, craft or trickery, or at least by means that are dishonest. It is not necessary that the Government shall be subjected to property or pecuniary loss by the fraud, but only that its legitimate official action and purpose shall be defeated by misrepresentation, chicane or the overreaching of those charged with carrying out governmental intention. *Hammerschmidt v. United States*, 265 U.S. 182, 188 (1924).

See also United States v. Haldeman, 559 F.2d 31 (D.C. Cir. 1976) (en banc), *cert. denied*, 431 U.S. 933 (1977); *United States v. Lewis*, 716 F.2d 16, 23 (D.C. Cir. 1983).

. . . The indictment clearly alleges a conspiracy which involved concealing the very existence of the profits of the enterprise from the start and hiding from Congress information relating to the conspirators' assistance for the contras. Its purpose depended on deceit from the start, and acts of concealment were actually part of the commission of the substantive crime. The cover-up elements of the conspiracy were not improperly added to stretch the statute of limitations to cover the conspiracy. . . .

References to the Boland Amendments will not be stricken from these counts of the indictment. Contrary to North's assertions . . . the references are appropriate to the charges in both counts 1 and 2, as well as to later counts in the indictment. Moreover, nothing has been presented to date that requires the Court to address the constitutional claim regarding the Boland Amendments or to question the legality of determinations made by the President in his working arrangements with the National Security Council.

North contends, in effect, that even if he was engaged in conduct that was inconsistent with the intent of the Boland Amendments, as the indictment recites, he still has not interfered with or obstructed a "lawful governmental function" by his effort to misrepresent what he was doing. The Boland Amendments are unconstitutional, he contends, because they attempt to regulate how the President should conduct foreign policy and, in any event, they were never meant to apply to the National Security Council. Thus according to North's view, his misrepresentations and evasions did not interfere with a lawful governmental function.

The difficulty with this argument is that the President and the White House staff, whatever their doubts as to the constitutional propriety of some aspects of the Boland Amendments as they applied to the NSC, were functioning in respect to pertinent aspects of this case as if they were in compliance with Boland.[2] While any White House uncertainty may bear on North's intent under certain counts, his understanding as to the constitutionality of Boland in no way affords an excuse for his alleged misconduct or entitled him to obstruct the way the government was, in fact, functioning. The President signed the laws containing the Boland Amendments and he apparently decided to comply with relevant aspects of the Boland Amendments, and was willing to respond to Congressional committee inquiries relating to compliance with the Boland Amendments. . . . North did not refuse to answer Congressional inquiries on the grounds that Congress had no constitutional right to query National Security Council officials with respect to covert acts being conducted through employees of the NSC. In fact, he is alleged to have asserted his, and the NSC's full compliance with the Boland Amendment.

The President was free within the prerogatives of his office to comply with the prohibitions of the Boland Amendments or to resist them in whole or in part if compliance would have unduly infringed on his responsibilities in the realm of foreign relations and national security. The language of the Boland Amendments is not precise in some pertinent respects and it has many aspects, but these ambiguities are of no consequence where the Executive and the Legislative branches act in harmony. If, as Independent Counsel contends he is prepared to prove, the President, both previous and subsequent to the enactment of Boland, chose to limit the activities of the National Security Council by directives and Executive Orders that were consistent with the Boland Amendments, North's alleged unauthorized deviation from such limitations must be viewed as contrary to lawful government functions. Thus he is alleged to have defrauded the United States. Similarly, if the President in some respect took, for example, a narrow view of the words "supporting" or "support" in the texts of the Amendments and authorized certain types of diplomatic contact with other nations vis-a-vis Nicaragua, North cannot be held to a higher standard if an aspect of his own conduct in this regard was so authorized. Thus, under all these circumstances, a facial attack on the constitutionality of the Boland Amendments is misplaced. As in most criminal cases, there are facts to be resolved, and separation of powers theories — over which much dispute exists — do not come under consideration if the facts show the affected Branches have accommodated to each other's interest to establish the manner in which government will function.

---

2. Another difficulty with North's motion to dismiss is that the conspiracy alleged involves more than just a conspiracy to circumvent Boland's restrictions. The conspiracy to defraud the United States has three parts, only the first of which hinges in large part on Boland. The second part involves conflicts of interest and self-dealing with respect to creation and disposition of surplus funds from the arms sales to Iran. The third part involves the corruption of the arms deals with Iran, and departures from its specified functions as stated in the President's written authorization. In addition to the three parts of the conspiracy to defraud the United States, the indictment also alleges a conspiracy to violate five separate substantive offenses.

The Court also refuses to strike references to Executive Order 12333 and National Security Decision Directive 159 and to preclude evidence relating to these provisions, as North urges. . . .[3] These orders form part of the framework of laws and regulations which North is alleged to have conspired to circumvent and impair. That they themselves do not carry criminal penalties is of no consequence. These are counts alleging conspiracy to defraud the United States and defeat its lawful governmental functions.

Moreover, the political question doctrine does not require dismissal. . . .

NOTES AND QUESTIONS

1. *United States v. North.* In subsequent preliminary rulings, Judge Gesell dismissed charges of theft and conspiracy to defraud the government when the White House refused to allow the disclosure of classified documents that were viewed by North's lawyers as essential to their defense.

As a policy matter, should we compel faithful execution of national security policy by using criminal sanctions? Does such a conspiracy charge simply constitute "the criminalization of policy differences," as later charged by President Bush in his statement pardoning several Iran-Contra figures?

2. *Following Orders.* In his defense, North claimed that his superiors in the White House authorized his acts. Does a criminal defendant have a duty to ascertain the authority of the authorizer? Does *Curtiss-Wright, supra* p. 53, support North's claim of his superiors' authority? Does the decision in *Durand v. Hollins, supra* p. 368, purportedly recognizing an inherent presidential rescue power, support North in this instance? Should it matter that the President claimed not to have authorized the diversion that underlay the indictment against North? Is *Little v. Barreme, supra* p. 78, relevant to the resolution of these questions?

The district court in North's case refused to instruct the jury that authorization was a complete defense, and the court of appeals affirmed. The latter concluded that North's suggested instruction

> goes so far as to conjure up the notion of a "Nuremberg" defense, a notion from which our criminal justice system, one based on individual accountability and responsibility, has historically recoiled. In the absence of clear and comprehensible Circuit authority that we must do so, we refuse to hold that following orders, without more, can transform an illegal act into a legal one. [*United States v. North*, 910 F.2d 843, 881 (D.C. Cir. 1990).]

3. Executive Order 12333, promulgated by the President in December of 1981, prohibits any United States intelligence agency, with the exception of the Central Intelligence Agency, from conducting covert actions with a Presidential finding that the agency was more likely than the CIA to achieve a particular objective. In early 1985, the President signed NSDD 159, which required the President to specifically approve by a written finding all covert actions undertaken by any United States Government agency or entity. NSDD [159] also states that each covert action is also considered a significant anticipated intelligence activity under Section 501 of the National Security Act and is subject to certain Congressional reporting requirements.

However, the court of appeals also found that a defendant's belief in authorization might relieve him of criminal liability if the statutory scienter standard requires knowledge that the act is unlawful, and not merely specific intent to do the act. *Id.* at 884. Is "I was only following orders" therefore still a backdoor defense in the D.C. Circuit?

3. *The Neutrality Act.* In *United States v. Terrell*, 731 F. Supp. 473 (S.D. Fla. 1989), Terrell and his companions were charged with supplying weapons to the Contras between October 1984 and mid-March 1985, thereby violating the Neutrality Act by providing the means for "a military . . . enterprise against a country with whom the United States is at peace." 18 U.S.C. §960 (2006). *See supra* p. 473. The defendants argued successfully that the United States was not "at peace" with Nicaragua during the relevant period. The charges were dismissed. The court found that the "at peace" inquiry was factual, not dependent on the existence of formal or declared war.

> The facts demonstrate the unceasing efforts of the executive branch to support the Contra cause, as well as Congressional support immediately before and also after Boland II. That the executive and legislative branches came into conflict regarding foreign policy is indisputable. That such conflict, and Congress' initial response to such conflict (Boland II), means that the United States was "at peace" with Nicaragua for the six months in the indictment after October 12, 1984, is absurd. [731 F. Supp. at 477.]

Because declarations of war have become anachronistic, what should the measure be of a state of peace or war for purposes of the Neutrality Act? Should Boland II be relevant in construing the critical text of the Neutrality Act? Should the prior or subsequent history of congressional support for the Contras be taken into account? Does the holding in *Terrell* suggest that the President can simply avoid criminal liability under the Neutrality Act by committing the very acts that the statute forbids?

4. *Conviction and Reversal.* Between his December 1986 appointment and the termination of the investigation in 1993, Independent Counsel Walsh charged 14 persons with criminal offenses. Eleven persons were convicted. One case was dismissed when the Bush administration refused to declassify information necessary for trial. See *infra* Chapter 35.

North was convicted of accepting an illegal gratuity, aiding and abetting in the obstruction of a congressional inquiry, and destruction of documents. Poindexter was convicted of five charges related to obstruction of inquiries, false statements, and destruction of documents. A court of appeals panel vacated both convictions and ordered proceedings to determine whether North's or Poindexter's immunized testimony before the congressional committees influenced witnesses in their trials. On remand, the obligation of the Independent Counsel was to prove by a preponderance of the evidence that each witness's testimony was independently derived. If it was not possible to separate out "unspoiled memory" from that influenced by the congressional testimony, evidence presented by the witness would be excluded. *United States v. North*, 910 F.2d at 862; *United States v. Poindexter*, 951 F.2d 369, 389-390 (D.C. Cir. 1991). The cases were subsequently dismissed on the motion of the Independent Counsel, who concluded that the required proofs would be impossible to make.

F. CONTINUING OVERSIGHT REFORMS

The congressional committees investigating the Iran-Contra Affair determined that the "Administration's conduct in the Iran-Contra Affair was inconsistent" with §501 of the 1980 Oversight Act because the Intelligence Committees were never informed by the President of the arms sales to Iran. *Iran-Contra Report, supra* p. 488, at 415. House and Senate Intelligence Committees introduced several bills seeking generally to strengthen the oversight process. *See* William Cohen, *Congressional Oversight of Covert Actions: The Public's Stake in the Forty-Eight Hour Rule,* 12 Harv. J.L. & Pub. Pol'y 285 (1989).

Congressional advocates of oversight reform differed sharply with Administration officials concerning the timing for notification of congressional leaders of a presidential finding authorizing a covert action. Instead of the "in a timely fashion" language first incorporated into the Hughes-Ryan Amendment, *supra* p. 486, the congressional reformers wanted presidential notification within 48 hours of a finding.

In a 1986 opinion, Assistant Attorney General Charles J. Cooper took the position that the President enjoys "unfettered discretion" in interpreting the "timely" notification requirement. President Bush sought to mollify members of the intelligence committees in an October 30, 1989, letter:

> Dear Mr. Chairman:
>
>   I am aware of your concerns regarding the provision of notice to Congress of covert action and the December 17, 1986 opinion of the Office of Legal Counsel of the Department of Justice, with which you strongly disagree primarily because of the statement that "a number of factors combine to support the conclusion that 'timely notice' language should be read to leave the President with virtually unfettered discretion to choose the right moment for making the required notification."
>
>   I can assure you that I intend to provide notice in a fashion sensitive to congressional concerns. The statute requires prior notice or, when no prior notice is given, timely notice. I anticipate that in almost all instances where prior notice is not provided, notice will be provided within a few days. Any withholding beyond this period would be based upon my assertion of the authorities granted this office by the Constitution. [Letter from President Bush to Intelligence Committees (Oct. 30, 1989), *reprinted in* H.R. Rep. No. 102-166, at 27 (1991).]

A major intelligence oversight reform bill, without the 48-hour notice requirement, was passed by both houses of Congress in 1990. But the President withheld his signature, and a pocket veto was recorded on November 30, 1990. *Memorandum of Disapproval for the Intelligence Authorization Act, Fiscal Year 1991,* Pub. Papers 1729 (1990). *See* William E. Conner, *Reforming Oversight of Covert Actions After the Iran-Contra Affair: A Legislative History of the Intelligence Authorization Act for FY 1991,* 32 Va. J. Int'l L. 871, 910-912 (1992).

In 1991, the intelligence committees agreed to revise the bill in light of the President's objections and concerns. After repealing the Hughes-Ryan Amendment, they substituted the following provisions for the Intelligence Oversight Act of 1980, *supra* p. 487:

Intelligence Authorization Act, Fiscal Year 1991[2]

Pub. L. No. 102-88, §§601-603, 105 Stat. 429, 441-445 (1991), as amended
(codified or to be codified at 50 U.S.C. §§413-414)
(U.S. Code section numbering used here)

§413.   GENERAL CONGRESSIONAL OVERSIGHT PROVISIONS

(a) (1) The President shall ensure that the congressional intelligence committees are kept fully and currently informed of the intelligence activities of the United States, including any significant anticipated intelligence activity as required by this title.

(2) Nothing in this title shall be construed as requiring the approval of the congressional intelligence committees as a condition precedent to the initiation of any significant anticipated intelligence activity.

(b) The President shall ensure that any illegal intelligence activity is reported promptly to the intelligence committees, as well as any corrective action that has been taken or is planned in connection with such illegal activity.

(c) The President and the congressional intelligence committees shall each establish such written procedures as may be necessary to carry out the provisions of this title.

(d) The House of Representatives and the Senate shall each establish, by rule or resolution of such House, procedures to protect from unauthorized disclosure all classified information, and all information relating to intelligence sources and methods, that is furnished to the congressional intelligence committees or to Members of Congress under this title. Such procedures shall be established in consultation with the Director of National Intelligence. In accordance with such procedures, each of the congressional intelligence committees shall promptly call to the attention of its respective House, or to any appropriate committee or committees of its respective House, any matter relating to intelligence activities requiring the attention of such House or such committee or committees.

(e) Nothing in this Act shall be construed as authority to withhold information from the congressional intelligence committees on the grounds that providing the information to the congressional intelligence committees would constitute the unauthorized disclosure of classified information or information relating to intelligence sources and methods.

(f) As used in this section, the term "intelligence activities" includes covert actions as defined in section [413b(e)], and includes financial intelligence activities.

§413a.   REPORTING OF INTELLIGENCE ACTIVITIES OTHER THAN COVERT ACTIONS

(a) To the extent consistent with due regard for the protection from unauthorized disclosure of classified information relating to sensitive intelligence sources and

---

2. The italicized subsections were added by the Intelligence Authorization Act for Fiscal Year 2010, Pub. L. No. 111-259, 124 Stat. 2654 (2010). *See infra* p. 509-510, Notes 2, 4.

methods or other exceptionally sensitive matters, the Director of National Intelligence and the heads of all departments, agencies, and other entities of the United States Government involved in intelligence activities shall —

(1) keep the congressional intelligence committees fully and currently informed of all intelligence activities, other than a covert action (as defined in section [413b(e)]), which are the responsibility of, are engaged in by, or are carried out for or on behalf of, any department, agency, or entity of the United States Government, including any significant anticipated intelligence activity and any significant intelligence failure; and

(2) furnish the congressional intelligence committees any information or material concerning intelligence activities *(including the legal basis under which the intelligence activity is being or was conducted)*, other than covert actions, which is within their custody or control, and which is requested by either of the congressional intelligence committees in order to carry out its authorized responsibilities. . . .

§413b. PRESIDENTIAL APPROVAL AND REPORTING OF COVERT ACTIONS

(a) The President may not authorize the conduct of a covert action by departments, agencies, or entities of the United States Government unless the President determines such an action is necessary to support identifiable foreign policy objectives of the United States and is important to the national security of the United States, which determination shall be set forth in a finding that shall meet each of the following conditions:

(1) Each finding shall be in writing, unless immediate action by the United States is required and time does not permit the preparation of a written finding, in which case a written record of the President's decision shall be contemporaneously made and shall be reduced to a written finding as soon as possible but in no event more than 48 hours after the decision is made.

(2) Except as permitted by paragraph (1), a finding may not authorize or sanction a covert action, or any aspect of any such action, which already has occurred.

(3) Each finding shall specify each department, agency, or entity of the United States Government authorized to fund or otherwise participate in any significant way in such action. Any employee, contractor, or contract agent of a department, agency, or entity of the United States Government other than the Central Intelligence Agency directed to participate in any way in a covert action shall be subject either to the policies and regulations of the Central Intelligence Agency, or to written policies or regulations adopted by such department, agency, or entity, to govern such participation.

(4) Each finding shall specify whether it is contemplated that any third party which is not an element of, or a contractor or contract agent of, the United States Government, or is not otherwise subject to United States Government policies and regulations, will be used to fund or otherwise participate in any significant way in the covert action concerned, or be used to undertake the covert action concerned on behalf of the United States.

(5) A finding may not authorize any action that would violate the Constitution or any statute of the United States.

(b) To the extent consistent with due regard for the protection from unauthorized disclosure of classified information relating to sensitive intelligence sources and methods or other exceptionally sensitive matters, the Director of National Intelligence and the heads of all departments, agencies, and entities of the United States Government involved in a covert action —

(1) shall keep the congressional intelligence committees fully and currently informed of all covert actions which are the responsibility of, are engaged in by, or are carried out for or on behalf of, any department, agency, or entity of the United States Government, including significant failures; and

(2) shall furnish to the congressional intelligence committees any information or material concerning covert actions *(including the legal basis under which the covert action is being or was conducted)* which is in the possession, custody, or control of any department, agency, or entity of the United States Government and which is requested by either of the congressional intelligence committees in order to carry out its authorized responsibilities.

(c) (1) The President shall ensure that any finding approved pursuant to subsection (a) shall be reported in writing to the congressional intelligence committees as soon as possible after such approval and before the initiation of the covert action authorized by the finding, except as otherwise provided in paragraph (2) and paragraph (3).

(2) If the President determines that it is essential to limit access to the finding to meet extraordinary circumstances affecting vital interests of the United States, the finding may be reported to the chairmen and ranking minority members of the congressional intelligence committees, the Speaker and minority leader of the House of Representatives, the majority and minority leaders of the Senate, and such other member or members of the congressional leadership as may be included by the President.

(3) Whenever a finding is not reported pursuant to paragraph (1) or (2) of this [sub]section, the President shall fully inform the congressional intelligence committees in a timely fashion and shall provide a statement of the reasons for not giving prior notice.

(4) In a case under paragraph (1), (2), or (3), a copy of the finding, signed by the President, shall be provided to the chairman of each congressional intelligence committee.

(5) (A) When access to a finding, or a notification provided under subsection (d)(1), is limited to the Members of Congress specified in paragraph (2), a written statement of the reasons for limiting such access shall also be provided.

(B) Not later than 180 days after a statement of reasons is submitted in accordance with subparagraph (A) or this subparagraph, the President shall ensure that—

(i) all members of the congressional intelligence committees are provided access to the finding or notification; or

(ii) a statement of reasons that it is essential to continue to limit access to such finding or such notification to meet extraordinary circumstances affecting vital interests of the United States is submitted to the Members of Congress specified in paragraph (2).

(d) (1) The President shall ensure that the congressional intelligence committees, or, if applicable, the Members of Congress specified in subsection (c)(2), are notified in writing of any significant change in a previously approved covert action, or any significant undertaking pursuant to a previously approved finding, in the same manner as findings are reported pursuant to subsection (c).

(2) In determining whether an activity constitutes a significant undertaking for purposes of paragraph (1), the President shall consider whether the activity —

(A) involves significant risk of loss of life;

(B) requires an expansion of existing authorities, including authorities relating to research, development, or operations;

(C) results in the expenditure of significant funds or other resources;

(D) requires notification under section [414(d)];

(E) gives rise to a significant risk of disclosing intelligence sources or methods; or

(F) presents a reasonably foreseeable risk of serious damage to the diplomatic relations of the United States if such activity were disclosed without authorization.

(e) As used in this title, the term "covert action" means an activity or activities of the United States Government to influence political, economic, or military conditions abroad, where it is intended that the role of the United States Government will not be apparent or acknowledged publicly, but does not include —

(1) activities the primary purpose of which is to acquire intelligence, traditional counterintelligence activities, traditional activities to improve or maintain the operational security of United States Government programs, or administrative activities;

(2) traditional diplomatic or military activities or routine support to such activities;

(3) traditional law enforcement activities conducted by United States Government law enforcement agencies or routine support to such activities; or

(4) activities to provide routine support to the overt activities (other than activities described in paragraph (1), (2), or (3)) of other United States Government agencies abroad.

(f) No covert action may be conducted which is intended to influence United States political processes, public opinion, policies, or media.

(g) (1) In any case where access to a finding reported under subsection (c) or notification provided under subsection (d)(1) is not made available to all members of a congressional intelligence committee in accordance with subsection (c)(2), the President shall notify all members of such committee that such finding or such notification has been provided only to the members specified in subsection (c)(2).

(2) In any case where access to a finding reported under subsection (c) or notification provided under subsection (d)(1) is not made available to all members of a congressional intelligence committee in accordance with subsection (c)(2), the President shall provide to all members of such committee a general description regarding the finding or notification, as applicable, consistent with the reasons for not yet fully informing all members of such committee.

(3) The President shall maintain —

(A) a record of the members of Congress to whom a finding is reported under subsection (c) or notification is provided under subsection (d)(1) and the date on which each member of Congress receives such finding or notification; and

(B) each written statement provided under subsection (c)(5)....

§414.   FUNDING OF INTELLIGENCE ACTIVITIES...

(c) No funds appropriated for, or otherwise available to, any department, agency, or entity of the United States Government may be expended, or may be directed to be expended, for any covert action, as defined in section [413b(e)], unless and until a Presidential finding required by subsection (a) of section [413b] has been signed or otherwise issued in accordance with that subsection.

(d) (1) Except as otherwise specifically provided by law, funds available to an intelligence agency that are not appropriated funds may be obligated or expended for an intelligence or intelligence-related activity only if those funds are used for activities reported to the appropriate congressional committees pursuant to procedures which identify—

(A) the types of activities for which non-appropriated funds may be expended; and

(B) the circumstances under which an activity must be reported as a significant anticipated intelligence activity before such funds can be expended.

(2) Procedures for purposes of paragraph (1) shall be jointly agreed upon by the congressional intelligence committees and, as appropriate, the Director of National Intelligence or the Secretary of Defense....

Statement on Signing the Intelligence Authorization Act, Fiscal Year 1991
27 Wkly. Comp. Pres. Docs. 1127, Aug. 14, 1991

Today I have signed H.R. 1455, the "Intelligence Authorization Act, Fiscal Year 1991."

I am pleased that the Congress has eliminated the most serious problems identified in my Memorandum of Disapproval of November 30, 1990, regarding its predecessor, S. 2834 (101st Congress). In particular, I am pleased that the Act, as revised, omits any suggestion that a "request" by the United States to third parties may constitute "covert action" as defined by the Act. In addition, I am pleased that the revised provision concerning "timely" notice to the Congress of covert actions incorporates without substantive change the requirement found in existing law. I reiterate my intention to proceed in this area as outlined in my letters to Senators Boren and Cohen of October 30, 1989; I am glad that the Congress has accepted that statement of intention and, in the spirit of comity in which it was offered, has not added any restrictions beyond those that the executive and legislative branches have agreed are found in existing law.

I remain concerned about legislatively directed policy determinations in the Act and provisions that are without effect because they are unconstitutional under the Supreme Court decisions in *INS v. Chadha*, 462 U.S. 919 (1983). I reiterate that the inclusion of such provisions is inappropriate.

Several provisions in the Act requiring the disclosure of certain information to the Congress raise constitutional concerns. These provisions cannot be construed to detract from the President's constitutional authority to withhold information the disclosure of which could significantly impair foreign relations, the national security, the deliberative processes of the Executive, or the performance of the Executive's constitutional duties.

I believe that the Act's definition of "covert action" is unnecessary. In determining whether particular military activities constitute covert actions, I shall continue to bear in mind the historic missions of the Armed Forces to protect the United States and its interests, influence foreign capabilities and intentions, and conduct activities preparatory to the execution of operations.

I am confident that this Act will lay to rest disputes that in the past have arisen between some Members of Congress and the executive branch, and I look forward to continued cooperation with the Intelligence Committees.

George Bush

NOTES AND QUESTIONS

1. *Definitions.* Consider the definition of "covert action." Is the revised definition clear and unambiguous? Is it an improvement over no definition at all? Does it contain all the relevant categories of activities? *See* W. Michael Reisman & James E. Baker, *Regulating Covert Action: Practices, Contexts, and Policies of Covert Coercion Abroad in International and American Law* 124 (1992). Is this definition an improvement over that contained in Executive Order No. 12,333?

2. *Gang-of-Eight Notice.* One contentious provision of the Intelligence Authorization Act for Fiscal Year 2010, Pub. L. No. 111-259, 124 Stat. 2654 (2010), modified the President's option in §413b(c)(2) to limit distribution of a covert action finding in exceptional cases to the so-called Gang of Eight. The President now must alert other members of the intelligence committees and provide them with a "general description" of the finding. §413b(g)(1), (2). The 2010 legislation also requires all heads of intelligence community agencies to certify annually to the intelligence committees that every required notice has been given or to state a reason why it has not been given. 50 U.S.C. §415d. Do you think this change significantly improves the oversight process? What about new provisions that require every procedure, statement, report, and notice to be in writing?

A few weeks after enactment of the 2010 Act, the House Intelligence Committee found in a classified report that in 16 cases since the 1990s agencies of the intelligence community failed to provide Congress with "complete, timely and accurate information" about their activities. Scott Shane, *Intelligence Bodies Faulted on Disclosure*, N.Y. Times, Nov. 18, 2010. The lapses included a CIA targeted killing program, the destruction of interrogation videotapes made in secret CIA prisons, CIA involvement in shooting down a missionary flight in Peru, NSA compliance with surveillance laws, and FBI surveillance of a Russian spy ring. *Id.* Do you think that the 2010 reforms will close the loop on oversight lapses?

3. *Legislative Veto?* President George H.W. Bush had objected to any provision that required prior approval of the intelligence committees before the President

could take certain actions, on the grounds that it would violate *INS v. Chadha*, noted *supra* p. 119. Is the 1991 Act constitutionally suspect for that reason?

4. *Legal Rationale for Activities.* In the FY 2010 Intelligence Authorization Act, Congress changed §§413a(a)(2) and 413b(b)(2), as shown by the italicized material in the excerpt above, to require the furnishing of information about "the legal basis" for a reported intelligence activity or covert action when requested by either of the intelligence committees. However, a letter from the ODNI General Counsel approving the compromise legislation stated that the Administration understands that the new provision "would not require disclosure of any privileged information or disclosure of information in any particular form." Letter from Robert Litt, ODNI General Counsel, to Dianne Feinstein, Chair, S. Select Comm. on Intelligence & Christopher Bond, Vice Chairman, S. Select Comm. on Intelligence, U.S. Senate (Sept. 27, 2010), *available at* http://www.fas.org/irp/congress/2010_cr/sen-fy10auth.html. The "legal basis" for a particular intelligence activity typically (although not always) may be found in an Office of Legal Counsel opinion. Could Congress constitutionally amend the statute to make it clearer that such an opinion must be furnished to the committees upon request? *See Constitutionality of Statute Requiring Executive Agency to Report Directly to Congress*, 6 Op. O.L.C. 632, 638-639 (1982).

5. *Findings and Deniability.* Presidential findings in support of covert action must be in writing, and they must be reported to the congressional intelligence committees. Can you tell from reading the Act how much detail the findings must provide about a planned covert action? Are the procedural requirements fashioned by Congress more about form than substance? May the President still deny U.S. involvement in a particular covert operation while complying with the statutory requirements? *See* A. John Radsan, *An Overt Turn on Covert Action*, 53 St. Louis U. L.J. 485, 539 (2009) (so arguing).

6. *Inspectors General.* In 1989, Congress amended the Central Intelligence Agency Act of 1949 to create a presidentially appointed Inspector General subject to Senate confirmation who initiates and conducts independent audits, investigations, and inspections of the CIA, and keeps the DCI (and now the DNI) and the Intelligence Committees "fully and currently informed about problems and deficiencies." Intelligence Authorization Act, Fiscal Year 1990, Pub. L. No. 101-193, §17(a)(3), (4), 103 Stat. 1701, 1711-1712 (1989) (codified as amended at 50 U.S.C. §403q(a)(3), (4)). The CIA IG is not given the power to issue subpoenas to other federal government agencies, but she is given her own staff and statutory access to CIA employees, who must cooperate on penalty of dismissal. 50 U.S.C. §403q(e)(2), (5). The FY 2010 Intelligence Authorization Act created a comparable Inspector General of the Intelligence Community within the Office of the Director of National Intelligence. Pub. L. No. 11-259, §405, 124 Stat. 2654, 2709-2719 (2010).

7. *The Continuing Importance of Executive Order No. 12,333.* Compare the reforms enacted by Congress with the executive branch oversight provided by the Executive Order. See if you can identify provisions of the Executive Order that have practical and legal significance beyond the requirements imposed by statute.

Defying Oversight? Dirty Assets, Special Military Operations, and Contractors

In the two preceding chapters, we established the basic legal authority for intelligence activities and the model of oversight of covert actions developed in response to the Iran-Contra Affair. We saw that, *on paper*, Executive Order No. 12,333 §1.7(a)(4) assigns to the CIA a virtual monopoly over covert actions (absent a presidential order to the contrary). We also saw that the 1991 Intelligence Authorization Act regulates covert actions by requiring written presidential findings that are reported to the intelligence committees. In this chapter, we survey three developments that challenge this neat model of CIA control, presidential finding, and reporting to Congress. The first is the CIA's employment of "dirty assets," whose activities the CIA may be unable to control, as discussed in Part A. The second is the growth of military special operations and attendant intelligence support activities, neither subject to CIA control nor, perhaps, to the congressional oversight regime for CIA covert operations. These are addressed in Part B. The last, considered in Part C, is the growing use of contractors by both the CIA and the military, blurring lines of accountability and control in the "shadow war" now being carried on against Al Qaeda and its affiliates in scattered locations across the globe.

A. PARAMILITARY AND DIRTY ASSETS

1. The Armée Clandestine in Laos[1]

After the 1962 Geneva agreements "neutralized" Laos and required all "foreign military personnel" to leave the country (see *supra* p. 295), the CIA took over a U.S. paramilitary operation for control of northern and central Laos in support of the government and against Communist Pathet Lao and North Vietnamese forces. Director of Central Intelligence (DCI) William Colby organized L'Armée Clandestine with a handful of CIA case officers and ran what became the largest paramilitary operation in U.S. history from across the border in Thailand. Tens of thousands of Hmong and other tribesmen were recruited for the CIA's private army. Upwards of 20,000 of them

---

1. Background and sources on U.S. involvement in Laos are supplied *supra* p. 295. In addition, *see* John Prados, *Presidents' Secret Wars* 261-296 (1986).

were U.S.-paid "volunteers" who had resigned from the Thai army. Colby and other case officers (substantially made up of Army Special Forces troops who joined the CIA payroll after the 1962 accords) trained and supplied these volunteers, transported and directed and sometimes participated in battles with them against the Pathet Lao, and supported them with bombing raids.

Nearly all of the equipment for the Armée Clandestine was supplied by the United States, typically delivered under the cover of the Agency for International Development (AID). The CIA also engaged in food drops and various other nation-building activities in Laos, in pursuit of Laotian support for American policies. As the costs of the program mounted, CIA briefs to subcommittees of the appropriations committees in Congress persuaded members to support ever-increasing spending for the covert program.

By the mid-1960s, about 250 Americans were either in Laos or commuting to assignments there. Air America pilots flew in support of the Laos program during time off from their regular flight routes. The pilots were paid bonuses, given tax breaks, and could earn $40,000 or more. Flying out of its Thailand bases, the 1969 Air America fleet had 29 helicopters, 20 light planes, and 19 medium transport planes. Ironically, the demand for transport in support of the Laos operation led to competition for the USAID contracts from a rival company, Continental Air Services. To avoid revealing the real nature of Air America, Continental Air was given some of the Laotian contract work. The air combat task was carried out by Air Force planes and pilots, not Air America. The U.S. Air Force role eventually grew to 100 fighter-bombers and supporting gunships.

By the late 1960s, CIA veterans grew tired and leery of the Laos operation, not due to the growing dissatisfaction with the larger war, but because the program was cumbersome and mostly overt rather than smoothly run and secret. Still, until the *New York Times* reported on the U.S. role in Laos in 1969, most Americans and members of Congress were unaware of the paramilitary program there.

2.   The Military Coup in Chile

Central Intelligence Agency, CIA Activities in Chile

September 18, 2000
http://www.cia.gov/cia/publications/chile

In the 1960s and the early 1970s, as part of the US Government policy to try to influence events in Chile, the CIA undertook specific covert action projects in Chile.... The overwhelming objective—firmly rooted in the policy of the period—was to discredit Marxist-leaning political leaders, especially Dr. Salvador Allende, and to strengthen and encourage their civilian and military opponents to prevent them from assuming power.

Overview of Covert Actions. At the direction of the White House and interagency policy coordination committees, CIA undertook...sustained propaganda efforts, including financial support for major news media, against Allende and other Marxists. Political action projects supported selected parties before and after the 1964 elections and after Allende's 1970 election....

Support for Coup in 1970.... CIA sought to instigate a coup to prevent Allende from taking office after he won a plurality in the 4 September election and before, as

Constitutionally required because he did not win an absolute majority, the Chilean Congress reaffirmed his victory. CIA was working with three different groups of plotters. All three groups made it clear that any coup would require the kidnapping of Army Commander Rene Schneider, who felt deeply that the Constitution required that the Army allow Allende to assume power. CIA agreed with that assessment. Although CIA provided weapons to one of the groups, we have found no information that the plotters' or CIA's intention was for the general to be killed. Contact with one group of plotters was dropped early on because of its extremist tendencies. CIA provided tear gas, submachine-guns and ammunition to the second group. The third group attempted to kidnap Schneider, mortally wounding him in the attack. CIA had previously encouraged this group to launch a coup but withdrew support four days before the attack because, in CIA's assessment, the group could not carry it out successfully.

Awareness of Coup Plotting in 1973. Although CIA did not instigate the coup that ended Allende's government on 11 September 1973, it was aware of coup-plotting by the military, had ongoing intelligence collection relationships with some plotters, and — because CIA did not discourage the takeover and had sought to instigate a coup in 1970 — probably appeared to condone it. There was no way that anyone, including CIA, could have known that Allende would refuse the putchists' offer of safe passage out of the country and that instead — with *La Moneda* Palace under bombardment from tanks and airplanes and in flames — would take his own life.

Knowledge of Human Rights Violations. CIA officers were aware of and reported to analysts and policymakers in 1973 that General Pinochet and the forces that overthrew the Allende Government were conducting a severe campaign against leftists and perceived political enemies in the early months after the coup. Activities of some security services portended a long-term effort to suppress opponents. In January 1974, CIA officers and assets were tasked to report on human rights violations by the Chilean government.

3. Other Dirty Asserts

The CIA has admitted that its clandestine assets in Chile were deeply involved in human rights abuses. One of the risks of employing private intelligence operatives (assets) is the relative inability to control an asset's behavior through the employment relationship or through thorough vetting prior to employment. The intelligence asset typically is sought out by U.S. intelligence officials because of the asset's potential ability to fulfill an intelligence objective. Suppose such an asset behaves unlawfully in the extreme and causes serious injury to the rights of a U.S. citizen or others. How should Congress or the executive branch regulate contractors and other assets to assure that they operate within a prescribed range of activities? What remedies should exist when abuses occur?

Before answering, consider these examples:

- In 2010, Mohammed Zia Salehi was the chief of administration of the Afghan National Security Council. During a U.S.-led corruption investigation, Salehi was overheard on a wiretap soliciting a bribe to intervene in an investigation into the role of a politically connected company in exporting large sums of money from the country. Salehi was arrested and jailed in July 2010, but after intervention by Afghan President Hamid Karzai, he was released and the charges against him were dismissed. At the time of his arrest, Afghan and U.S. officials confirmed that Salehi had been on the CIA payroll for years. It remains unclear what Salehi does or did for the Agency. A U.S. official defended the practice of paying foreign government officials, even if they engage in corrupt practices: "If you want intelligence in a war zone, you're not going to get it from Mother Theresa or Mary Poppins." Dexter Filkins & Mark Mazzetti, *Karzai Aide in Corruption Inquiry Is Tied to CIA*, N.Y. Times, Aug. 25, 2010; Rod Norland, *Afghans Drop All Corruption Charges Against Karzai Aide*, N.Y. Times, Nov. 8, 2010.

- David Headley was born in the United States and grew up in Pakistan with his parents, a Pakistani diplomat and a Philadelphia socialite. Before he finished high school, his parents divorced, and Headley moved to Philadelphia to help his mother run a bar and video rental stores. He was arrested on drug trafficking charges in 1987 and again in 1998, and each time he was given a lighter sentence in return for his cooperation with the Drug Enforcement Agency (DEA). Headley moved freely between the United States, Pakistan, and India as an informant for the DEA, despite warnings to government officials in October 2001 by a former girlfriend that Headley was sympathetic to extremist groups in Pakistan. Headley was married at least three times, perhaps simultaneously, and an American wife filed domestic abuse charges against him in 2005 and reported that he had ties to the terrorist group Lashkar-e-Taiba. The tip was passed on to the FBI Joint Terrorism Task Force. In 2007, his Moroccan wife told U.S. Embassy officials in Islamabad that she believed that her husband was planning a terrorist attack. The warnings were apparently not shared with DEA. Meanwhile, Headley began terrorist training with Lashkar-e-Taiba on at least four occasions between 2002 and 2005. Headley was apparently thought by Lashkar-e-Taiba to be an especially valuable asset because he could blend into settings where others might raise suspicion, and because his U.S. passport and American surname likewise enabled easy transit inside India and European nations. In 2007, Headley began scouting targets in Mumbai for a Lashkar-e-Taiba attack, where he stayed in the Taj Mahal Palace and hired fishing boats for tours of the port that helped him determine where a sea-based attack could land. In the November 2008 attacks in Mumbai by Lashkar-e-Taiba, 163 people were killed in a two-day seige on targets selected with Headley's help, including the Taj Mahal hotel. Shortly thereafter Headley contacted an Al Qaeda operative in Europe and began plotting to attack the Danish newspaper that had published cartoons of the Prophet Mohammad. Headley was arrested on October 3, 2009, as he was about to travel to Pakistan to deliver surveillance videos he had taken in Copenhagen. Ginger Thompson, Eric Schmitt & Souad Mekhennet, *DEA Deployed Mumbai Plotter Despite Warning*, N.Y. Times, Nov. 7, 2010.

- Humam Khalil Abu-Mulal al-Balawi, a young Jordanian medical doctor with a foreign wife and two children, was picked up in 2009 by Jordanian intelligence officials for questioning after his pseudonymous postings on extremist Web sites became especially strident. Sensing an intelligence opportunity, the Jordanians told Balawi that if he traveled to Pakistan and infiltrated extremist groups, he and his family would be left alone. Balawi agreed, and he began working for Jordanian and, later, American intelligence handlers after Balawi promised to lead them to Ayman al-Zawahiri, the deputy leader of Al Qaeda. Balawi produced credible information about extremists inside Pakistan, and the CIA relied on his information in conducting operations there. Then, on December 30, 2009, Balawi drove a red station wagon from Pakistan to a CIA installation in Afghanistan, where he was greeted by a CIA expert on Al Qaeda, who hoped to learn how the Americans could kill or capture al-Zawahiri. When an American security guard approached Balawi to conduct a pat-down search, Balawi triggered a switch and the ensuing blast killed everyone in the immediate area, including the CIA Al Qaeda expert, an analyst, and three other CIA officers, in addition to two American security guards on contract to the Agency, a Jordanian intelligence officer, and the car's driver. R. Jeffrey Smith, Joby Warwick & Ellen Nakashima, *CIA Bomber Struck Just Before Search*, Wash. Post, Jan. 10, 2010; Joby Warwick & Peter Finn, *Suicide Bomber Who Attacked CIA Post in Afghanistan Was Trusted Informant from Jordan*, Wash. Post, Jan. 5, 2010.

- In the early 1970s, the CIA managed to penetrate what was then the most feared terrorist organization that had targeted the United States and U.S. citizens in the Middle East—the Palestine Liberation Organization (PLO). Through a secret arrangement with Ali Hassan Salameh, the PLO's chief of intelligence, the CIA obtained extensive information about terrorist activities and groups, and Salameh himself intervened to stop planned attacks. Part of Salameh's motivation was his belief that working for the CIA could help the PLO achieve its political goals in the Middle East. Salameh was a terrorist, a member of Yasir Arafat's "Black September" organization, and he may have helped plan the slaughter of Israeli athletes at the Munich Olympics in 1972. Although the CIA targeted Salameh for assassination, agents continued to work with him until the Israelis killed him in 1979. *See* David Ignatius, *Penetrating Terrorist Networks*, Wash. Post, Sept. 16, 2001.

NOTES AND QUESTIONS

1. *The CIA in Laos.* In Laos, the CIA supported a "secret" army of tens of thousands of Hmong tribesmen and Thai "volunteers." This force was financed, trained, supplied, transported, and sometimes accompanied into battle by CIA operatives, many of whom were former U.S. Army Green Berets. Pursuant to what legal authority was this operation conducted? See *supra* pp. 295-297. *See also* John Hart Ely, *War and Responsibility: Constitutional Lessons of Vietnam and Its Aftermath* 68-97 (1993) (concluding that the "secret war" in Laos was unconstitutional). What purpose was served by keeping this operation secret from members of Congress and from the American people?

2. *The CIA in Chile.* The report, *CIA Activities in Chile*, was created in response to §311 of the Intelligence Authorization Act for Fiscal Year 2000, Pub. L. No. 106-120, 113 Stat. 1606, 1614 (1999), to answer lingering questions about the U.S. role in the coup that brought General Pinochet to power in Chile, and in human rights violations committed during the Pinochet rule. *See generally* National Security Archive, *Chile Documentation Project* (Nov. 13, 2000), *at* http://www.gwu.edu/~nsarchiv/latin_america/chile.htm.

According to the CIA report, "Efforts by the United States to support anti-Communist forces in Chile date back to the late 1950s and reflect the rivalry between the United States and the Soviet Union for influence throughout the Third World." *CIA Activities in Chile, supra,* at 5. The Church Committee reported that at a September 15, 1970, meeting between President Nixon, National Security Adviser Henry Kissinger, and DCI Richard Helms, Nixon and Kissinger directed the CIA to prevent Allende from taking power. According to Helms's notes, they were "not concerned [about the] risks involved," and they wanted Helms to "make the economy scream." *Id.* President Nixon instructed Helms and the CIA not to inform the 40 Committee, the State or Defense Departments, or the ambassador in Santiago. Staff of the S. Select Comm. to Study Governmental Operations with Respect to Intelligence Activities, 94th Cong., *Covert Action in Chile 1963-1973,* at 41 (1975). Were the instructions to Helms lawful? Do you think Congress would have approved of the CIA's involvement there if it had been informed? Would the American people have approved?

3. *The CIA and Constitutional War Powers.* Does the fact that the CIA, rather than the uniformed military, conducted the operation in Laos mean that it should not count as a "war" under the Constitution? *See* Ely, *supra,* at 73-75 (no).

4. *The CIA and the Drug Trade.* It was widely known that the CIA and Air America were passive participants in the lucrative and pervasive drug trade in Laos and Thailand. It was passive only in the sense that intelligence officials reported on the movement of drugs, sometimes by CIA-paid assets and on proprietary aircraft, but did nothing to stop it. Reporting about these linkages to unsavory elements helped spur congressional hearings and the eventual end of the Laotian secret war. *See* John Prados, *Safe for Democracy: The Secret Wars of the CIA* 344-357 (2006).

5. *Inverting the Fear of Terrorists Penetrating the United States.* David Headley grew up in the United States, with an American surname, and used his passport and surname to make it easier to travel and check out potential targets for his terrorist allies. He exported terrorism from the United States. Was the mistake in handling Headley a simple failure of information sharing? Was there a more basic failure in not paying close attention to the warnings of his extremist beliefs and associations? What could Congress or the executive branch do to make it less likely that another David Headley will penetrate U.S. intelligence agencies?

6. *Cooperating with Foreign Intelligence Agencies.* Was it the Jordanians' fault that al-Balawi successfully duped the CIA? What, if any, legal rules should govern cooperation with foreign governments' intelligence agencies?

7. *CIA Activities in Guatemala.* In 1991, Jennifer Harbury, an American citizen, married Efrain Bamaca-Velasquez, a Guatemalan citizen and high-ranking member of a Guatemalan rebel group. After returning to Guatemala in March 1992, Bamaca disappeared. Although the Guatemalan Army reported that Bamaca committed suicide during a skirmish between Army and rebel forces, in fact Bamaca had been captured and detained by the Guatemalan military for between 12 and 18 months. He was allegedly abused and tortured and, eventually, executed. Harbury learned of her husband's detention and torture from an escaped prisoner in early 1993, whereupon she contacted State Department officials, seeking information about her husband's status. They never provided her with any information.

After several failed attempts to learn more about Bamaca's fate, in 1995 Representative Robert Toricelli announced publicly that years earlier Bamaca had been killed on the orders of a paid CIA asset. Harbury then sued the CIA and other government officials, alleging that CIA officials collaborated in her husband's secret detention, torture, and murder. She asserted that some Guatemalan military officers who carried out the actions were paid CIA assets. Harbury sought injunctive relief and damages. *Harbury v. Deutch*, 233 F.3d 596 (D.C. Cir. 2000). Although the Court of Appeals refused to recognize a Fifth Amendment violation for the torture of Bamaca because the torture occurred in Guatemala, relying on *United States v. Verdugo-Urquidez*, 494 U.S. 259 (1990) (*infra* p. 712), the court agreed with Harbury that NSC and State Department officials deprived her of adequate access to the courts by giving her false and deceptive information about Bamaca. The Supreme Court unanimously reversed, *Christopher v. Harbury*, 536 U.S. 403 (2002), and found that her access-to-courts claim did not state a claim upon which relief could be granted. Although the Court preserved undecided tort counts naming CIA defendants for her emotional distress, problems of proof presented formidable hurdles, and no such suit could save Bamaca.

During the litigation, the government alleged that cover-ups of the type alleged by Harbury are sometimes "necessary in order to protect the national security or to maintain secrecy of classified intelligence sources or methods." Appellees' Petition for Reh'g at 2, *quoted in Harbury v. Deutch*, 244 F.3d at 957. Upon what authority would such a cover-up be permitted?

In 1995 President Clinton directed the Intelligence Oversight Board (IOB) to review allegations regarding the torture, disappearance, or death of U.S. citizens in Guatemala since 1984. The IOB *Report on the Guatemala Review* (June 28, 1996), *available at* http://www.ciponline.org/iob.htm, found that intelligence officials in Guatemala had laudable goals and that "achieving them and maintaining influence in Guatemala required that the CIA deal with some unsavory groups and individuals. The human rights records of the Guatemala security services were widely known to be reprehensible." *Id.* at 4. The IOB found two areas where the CIA's "performance was unacceptable. . . . [U]ntil late 1994, insufficient attention was given to allegations of serious human rights abuses made against several station assets or liaison contacts. Second, the CIA failed to provide enough information on this subject to policymakers and the Congress to permit proper policy and Congressional oversight." *Id.* What legal reforms might make these mistakes less likely to occur in the future?

8. *Mother Theresa or Mary Poppins?* Is the U.S. official's reference to these icons apt? Should recruiting of an asset for our intelligence agencies be predicated upon a finding of good moral character? If not, should Congress impose by statute a requirement that the asset not break local or U.S. laws? Would such a requirement be lawful? Apart from the embarrassment of having the CIA asset "outed" by what was for practical purposes a U.S. anti-corruption investigation, was there any harm caused by Salehi's soliciting bribes?

What lesson should we take from the Salameh experience? Does law have any role to play in deciding what to do with dirty assets in counterterrorism? Do you think the answer to this question has changed in the wake of the 9/11 terrorist attacks? Would any guidelines for intelligence assets like Salameh be constrained by the provisions of Executive Order No. 12,333, *supra* p. 451? If so, which provisions?

9. *The Value of Vetting.* After U.S. and coalition forces failed to find the weapons of mass destruction (WMD) that were part of the justification for the invasion of Iraq in 2003, see *supra* p. 363, President Bush appointed a commission to investigate the failure. Silberman/Robb Commission, *supra* p. 364. The commission reported in 2005 that "the Intelligence Community was dead wrong in almost all of its pre-war judgments about Iraq's weapons of mass destruction. This was a major intelligence failure. Its principal causes [included] the Intelligence Community's inability to collect good information about Iraq's WMD programs. . . ." *Id.* at 2.

The commission found that the story of a "pivotal source" code-named "Curveball," who lied to intelligence officials about Iraq's biological weapons program, was "an all-too-familiar one." *Id.* at 27, 367. The commission recommended that the CIA "take the lead in systematizing and standardizing the Intelligence Community's asset validation procedures . . . ways in which intelligence collectors ensure that the information provided to them is truthful and accurate." *Id.* at 372. Should lawyers play any role in such a system for vetting? Would dirty assets plausibly survive the vetting?

In response to headlines generated by accusations that the CIA conspired with Guatemalan military officers in torture and murder and in other atrocities in Guatemala, the CIA issued guidelines in June 1995 to make case officers more selective in their recruiting. Apparently the guidelines required case officers to obtain a waiver from CIA headquarters before employing any asset whose background included assassinations, torture, or other serious criminal activities. The guidelines did not prevent the CIA from employing dirty assets, but it established greater internal accountability and managerial control, making it less likely that a "cowboy" field agent would use a dirty asset without appropriately balancing risks and benefits.

The June 2000 report of the National Commission on Terrorism, *Countering the Changing Threat of International Terrorism, available at* http://www.fas.org/irp/threat/commission.html, maintained that the guidelines "have deterred and delayed vigorous efforts to recruit potentially useful informants. The CIA has created a climate that is overly risk averse." *Id.* at 10. The Commission recommended that the DCI "issue a directive that the 1995 guidelines will no longer apply to recruiting terrorist informants." *Id.* On June 4, 2000, however, a CIA spokesperson defended the guidelines and said that they had not impeded investigations of potential terrorism:

> No one knows better than we do that when combating terrorism it is often necessary to deal with unsavory individuals. But we do so with eyes wide open and with appropriate notification to senior officials. . . . [The CIA] has never . . . turned down a request to use someone, even someone with a record of human rights abuses, if we thought that person could be valuable in our overall counterterrorism program. [*Quoted in* Secrecy News, Sept. 14, 2001, *at* http://www.fas.org/sgp/news/secrecy/2001/09/091401.html.]

In the wake of the September 11, 2001, terrorist attacks on the World Trade Center and the Pentagon, Congress enacted legislation directing the DCI to rescind the portions of the 1995 guidelines pertaining to recruitment of counterterrorism assets. Intelligence Authorization Act for Fiscal Year 2002, Pub. L. No. 107-108, §403, 115 Stat. 1394, 1402 (2001). Would you have advised Congress to pass the rescission instruction? Former CIA Inspector General Frederick Hitz wrote that new guidelines issued since the legislation have "retained the requirement of an audit trail in . . . recognition of a need for some explanation to headquarters why a dirty asset ought to be on the payroll." Frederick P. Hitz, *Unleashing the Rogue Elephant: September 11 and Letting the CIA Be the CIA*, 25 Harv. J.L. & Pub. Pol'y 765, 769 (2002). Does this assurance compensate for whatever was lost in the rescission?

B.   MILITARY SPECIAL OPERATIONS AS INTELLIGENCE ACTIVITIES

As we saw in our survey of intelligence activities and responsibilities in Chapter 16, the Department of Defense (DOD) exercises effective control over much of the intelligence that is collected, analyzed, and distributed throughout the government. Under Executive Order No. 12,333, *supra* p. 451, the Defense Department is given responsibility for signals intelligence (SIGINT) and communications security activities (COMINT), "except as otherwise directed by the NSC." *Id.* §1.11(e). The Secretary of Defense must also "[d]irect, operate, control, and provide fiscal management for the National Security Agency and for defense and military intelligence and national reconnaissance entities." *Id.* §1.11(j). DOD's Defense Intelligence Agency (DIA) collects and provides military and military-related intelligence for the Secretary and for other agencies, *id.* §1.12(a), while the NSA is given exclusive authority to engage in SIGINT activities, subject to express exceptions granted by the Secretary, *id.* §1.12(b)(1). The Secretary is also given responsibility for "Offices for the collection of specialized intelligence through reconnaissance programs," *id.* §1.12(c), more recently identified publicly as the National Reconnaissance Office (NRO). Finally, the Secretary oversees collection and dissemination of military and military-related foreign intelligence and counterintelligence by the intelligence elements of the U.S. Army, Navy, Air Force, and Marine Corps. *Id.* §1.12(d).

In recent years, intelligence support for so-called special military operations, or SMO, has generated continuing controversy and legal problems. After the 1979 revolution in Iran and the seizure that year of American hostages in Tehran, military planners for an eventual hostage rescue operation needed human intelligence on the ground—to learn about the embassy compound where the hostages were held and to provide assistance before and during a rescue operation. The CIA had no agents who could provide the necessary intelligence. The Pentagon responded by creating an Intelligence Support Activity (ISA) to collect intelligence and also conduct secret military operations. The ISA consisted of Army Special Forces personnel and intelligence case officers. Although the hostage rescue operation ended in failure, *supra* p. 369, the Army decided to retain the ISA. *See* William E. Odom, *Fixing Intelligence for a More Secure America* 145 (2d ed. 2003).

During the 1980s, cooperation between the Army and the CIA increased, and the ISA became a permanent entity within DOD. After September 11, the ISA, code-named Gray Fox, invigorated by Defense Secretary Donald Rumsfeld to participate in the war on terrorism, began reporting to a new Under Secretary of Defense for Intelligence. But Gray Fox operated independently of the rest of the intelligence community. *See* William M. Arkin, *The Secret War: Frustrated by Intelligence Failures, the Defense Department Is Dramatically Expanding Its "Black World" of Covert Operations*, L.A. Times, Oct. 27, 2002.

More recently, DOD intelligence capabilities have been tasked with providing intelligence support to the counterinsurgency (COIN) in Afghanistan. Despite the best efforts of DOD to provide intelligence support in an environment where counter-terrorism, contingency operations, and COIN occur simultaneously, a Defense Science Board study found that DOD lacks a common understanding of COIN, and that no agreed upon set of intelligence requirements for COIN has been prescribed. *Report of the Defense Science Board Task Force on Defense Intelligence: Counterinsurgency (COIN) Intelligence, Surveillance, and Reconnaissance (ISR) Operations*, Feb. 2011, *available at* http://www.carlisle.army.mil/dime/documents/Defense%20Science%20Board%20-%20Coin%202011-05-COIN%5B1%5D.pdf.

NOTES AND QUESTIONS

1. *Legal Wiggle Room?* Is DOD subject to the same requirements as other members of the intelligence community for reporting its *intelligence activities* to the congressional intelligence committees under the Intelligence Authorization Act of 1991 (as amended), *supra* p. 504? Can you see any legal wiggle room that would permit DOD to avoid congressional oversight of its *intelligence collection*?

Is there any legal prohibition on DOD's engaging in *special operations* — either paramilitary actions or other secret measures — that previously were the exclusive domain of CIA? *See infra* p. 522. Must the Defense Department report such operations to the congressional intelligence committees as *covert actions*? Consider this assessment:

[C]ongressional oversight [of special operations] could be hampered by the military's reported practice of labeling its clandestine activities — those that are intended to be secret, but that can be publicly acknowledged if discovered or inadvertently revealed — as "operational preparation of the environment," rather than intelligence activities, even though they may pose the same diplomatic and national security risks.[40] So characterized, these activities might not be reported to the intelligence committees.[41] Any oversight that occurred would be conducted instead by the House and Senate Armed Services Committees.[42] Such a division of responsibilities might create a dangerous confusion.

Congressional involvement also might be frustrated by the statutory exclusion of "traditional . . . military activities or routine support to such activities" from the definition of "covert action."[43] If secret military preparations . . . are regarded as "traditional military activities," they might escape both the presidential findings requirement for covert actions and any reporting to the intelligence committees, under the rationale outlined above. [Stephen Dycus, *Congress's Role in Cyber Warfare*, 4 J. Nat'l Security L. & Pol'y 155, 161-162 (2010).]

40. *See* Alfred Cumming, *Covert Action: Legislative Background and Possible Policy Questions* (Cong. Res. Serv. RL33715), July 6, 2009, at 8.
41. According to one knowledgeable source, all such activities probably are reported as "intelligence activities" under §413, although the military regards these reports as voluntary.
42. In a report accompanying the FY 2010 Intelligence Authorization bill, the House Intelligence Committee complained that "[c]landestine military intelligence-gathering operations . . . often escape the scrutiny of the intelligence committees, and the congressional defense committees cannot be expected to exercise oversight outside of their jurisdiction." H.R. Rep. No. 110-186 (2009).
43. 50 U.S.C. §413b(e)(2).

What are the practical implications of not labeling a secret military operation a "covert action"?

Do the tasking requirements for covert actions in Executive Order No. 12,333 apply to DOD operations? If so, which provisions apply to which different kinds of military operations?

2. *Paramilitary or Military?* If Army Special Forces participate in covert actions under the direction of the CIA, are its personnel bound by Army regulations? Is a Special Forces covert operation an intelligence activity or a military operation? Does the distinction matter? Are the military covert operations subject to the War Powers Resolution? Other than covert action reporting, do any provisions of Executive Order No. 12,333 limit these military operations?

3. *An Iraq SAP.* One SAP reportedly was diverted from its original purpose of interrogating Taliban and Al Qaeda detainees to staffing detention and interrogation operations at the Abu Ghraib prison in Iraq. Seymour Hersh, *The Gray Zone: How a Secret Pentagon Program Came to Abu Ghraib,* New Yorker, May 24, 2004, at 38. When the prisoner abuse scandal broke in the spring of 2004, the commander of the 800th Military Police Brigade, the unit ostensibly in charge of the Abu Ghraib facility, stated that she could not always be sure who was who among the persons in civilian clothes managing interrogations. *Id.* The interrogation and treatment of detainees for investigative purposes is considered further in Chapters 31-32. Do you think it matters whether those in charge of investigative interrogations are DOD, rather than CIA, officials?

4. *Two Paramilitary Organizations or One?* Are there good reasons for the United States to have two paramilitary organizations — one managed by the CIA and one run by DOD? Is there a legal problem with this redundancy? Consider this view:

> The military's strength is in military skills and operations. These are not the strength of the [CIA] DO [Directorate of Operations]. Not surprisingly, DO paramilitary operations have generally been looked on by army officers as amateurish at best, usually designed to fail. A close comparative look at the record of army and . . . DO paramilitary operations would, in all likelihood, show that the [DOD] has more justification for disdaining DO paramilitary capabilities than the DO has. . . . This raises the question of whether or not the DO should drop its paramilitary capabilities and depend largely on those of the Department of Defense. . . . [T]he experience with Special Forces teams in Afghanistan seems to have convinced the secretary of defense that such a change is now desirable. [Odom, *supra* p. 519, at 148-149.]

Is this proposal workable? Lawful? Would the legal basis change between peacetime and wartime operations? In the war in Afghanistan after September 11, Special Forces teams were able to cooperate with anti-Taliban Afghan groups, but not through the efforts of the CIA, because initially the CIA had no contacts there. Instead, Russian intelligence services provided the sources that put the U.S. military in contact with the Afghans. In many cases, the Special Forces teams struck out on their own and formed alliances with Afghan groups without intelligence support. *Id.* at 25-26. Are there legal problems with Special Forces conducting such covert operations? In coordinating operations with Russian intelligence personnel?

C.   THE CIA, CONTRACTORS, AND THE "SHADOW WAR"

In the post-Cold War environment for intelligence operations, privatization has taken on new meaning. For example, U.S. participation in Plan Colombia and related anti-drug efforts in several Andean nations during the 1990s were contracted out in part to DynCorp, a private company that supplied pilots and mechanics for U.S.-owned aircraft sponsored by the State Department's International Narcotics and Law Enforcement Bureau. Media attention focused on the program in April 2001, when innocent civilians flying in a private plane were mistakenly shot down and killed by anti-drug surveillance aircraft operating over Peru. Although the attacking aircraft was Peruvian and was piloted by Peruvians, the program they were participating in was underwritten by the United States.

In Colombia, DynCorp and other contractors flew drug-crop fumigation missions, ferried battalions into combat, served as mechanics and logistical personnel, performed reviews of local armed forces, and gathered intelligence. DynCorp contract personnel also engaged in at least one firefight with Colombian Revolutionary Armed Forces (FARC) guerillas during a search and rescue mission. *See Drug Policy and Human Resources: Hearing Before the Subcomm. on Crim. Justice of the H. Government Reform Comm.*, 107th Cong. (2001) (statement of Adam Isacson), *available at* http://www. ciponline.org/colombia/050103.htm.

After 9/11, the CIA and contractors took on a range of new assignments, including engaging in or sponsoring paramilitary campaigns as an integral component of the U.S. counterterrorism response to the Taliban, Al Qaeda, and associated groups. In August 2010, the *New York Times* described a "shadow war against Al Qaeda and its allies":

> In roughly a dozen countries — from the deserts of North Africa, to the mountains of Pakistan, to former Soviet republics crippled by ethnic and religious strife — the United States has significantly increased military and intelligence operations, pursuing the enemy using robotic drones and commando teams, paying contractors to spy and training local operatives to chase terrorists. [Scott Shane, Mark Mazzetti & Robert F. Worth, *Secret Assault on Terrorism Widens on Two Continents*, N.Y. Times, Aug. 14, 2010.]

See also Lauren Ploch, *Countering Terrorism in East Africa: The U.S. Response* (Cong. Res. Serv. R41473), Nov. 3, 2010. At the direction of President Obama, the CIA intensified a campaign to target Al Qaeda and Taliban targets with missile-armed drones in Pakistan. In tandem with military raids against suspected Al Qaeda operatives in Yemen, Somalia, Kenya, and various locations in North Africa, private contractors have been hired to gather intelligence about insurgent activities in Pakistan. *Id.* Reports suggest that the Obama administration initiatives "accelerated a transformation of the CIA into a paramilitary organization as much as a spying agency." *Id.* At the same time, U.S. incursions beyond the traditional battlefields in Afghanistan and Iraq have been increasingly outsourced to private armies.

Journalist Bob Woodward wrote in 2010 that in Afghanistan the CIA created, controls, and funds a secret 3,000-man paramilitary force of local Afghans, known as Counterterrorism Pursuit Teams, trained to conduct covert paramilitary operations in Pakistan against Al Qaeda and Taliban targets. Bob Woodward, *Obama's Wars* 8, 52, 367 (2010).

In Yemen, an Al Qaeda offshoot was viewed by Obama administration officials as such an urgent threat in 2010 that officials added armed CIA drones to the existing U.S. military arsenal there. Greg Miller, *Military Drones Aid CIA's Mission*, Wash. Post, Oct. 3, 2010. The drones supplement CIA case officers collecting intelligence inside Yemen. Meanwhile, the U.S. military expanded its clandestine activities in the same region, pursuant to a secret directive, the Joint Unconventional Warfare Task Force Execute Order, signed in September 2009 by General David Patraeus. Mark Mazzetti, *U.S. Is Said to Expand Secret Actions in Mideast*, N.Y. Times, May 24, 2010. In part, the military has "sought in recent years to break its dependence" on the CIA and other intelligence agencies in areas without a significant U.S. troop presence. *Id.* The secret activities authorized by the 2009 order do not require the President's approval or reports to Congress. *Id.*

NOTES AND QUESTIONS

1. *Are the Paramilitary Forces Lawful?* News reports have not identified exactly which forces fighting the shadow war are U.S. military and which are sponsored by the CIA or contractors of the United States, and there is no public acknowledgment of these aspects of the military and paramilitary campaigns in the nations where the activities reportedly take place. Assuming that the news reports and Woodward book are accurate, which laws authorize these military and paramilitary operations? To what extent does their lawfulness depend on the constitutional powers of the Commander in Chief? Does the National Security Act (*supra* p. 444) authorize the 3,000-man CIA force described by Woodward in *Obama's Wars*? What laws govern the use of contractors that use armed force on behalf of the United States? For openers, review Executive Order No. 12,333 §2.7.

Are these paramilitary operations constrained in any way by the Neutrality Act, *supra* p. 473?

2. *Accountability and Congressional Oversight.* Review the oversight requirements imposed on the CIA in 1991, and the amendments added in 2010. Can you describe the likely involvement of the congressional intelligence committees in the covert operations that are integral parts of the shadow war? What knowledge would make the committees "fully and currently informed" (*supra* p. 487) about the operations? Should those committees be formally notified about the Counterterrorism Pursuit Teams in Afghanistan? About the drones program in Pakistan? Should the rules be rewritten to better account for these paramilitary operations? If so, what should the rules include?

3. *CIA or Military?* Who should run the shadow war? As a matter of international law, under what circumstances may one state conduct a paramilitary operation inside the sovereign borders of another state without the consent of the latter? Does your answer turn on whether the operation is conducted by CIA or by military forces? See *supra* p. 402.

If the CIA carries out a paramilitary campaign in Yemen, the operation would require presidential authorization and notice to the intelligence committees. Do these requirements apply to secret military operations? If captured, CIA operatives likely do not enjoy the protections of the Geneva Conventions, including prisoner-of-war status. *See* Gary D. Solis, *The Law of Armed Conflict: International Humanitarian Law in War* 220-224 (2010) (fighting without distinguishing as a combatant by wearing a uniform likely causes loss of combatant status). Military personnel do benefit from such protections, although the Geneva Conventions may not be in force in areas remote from a traditional battlefield. Would providing uniforms to the CIA operatives, with insignia or some other way to identify them as working for the CIA, solve the Geneva Conventions gap?

4. *Privatization of Intelligence.* The majority of personnel in the CIA's National Clandestine Service, the Defense Intelligence Agency (DIA), the National Counterterrorism Center (NCTC), and many overseas CIA stations are contractors. Simon Chesterman, *We Can't Spy . . . If We Can't Buy!: The Privatization of Intelligence and the Limits of Outsourcing "Inherently Governmental Functions"*, 19 Eur. J. Int'l L. 1055, 1056 (2008). What are the legal risks when private contractors engage in intelligence collection? If the contract collectors engage in unlawful conduct, what accountability mechanisms are available to redress their wrongdoing? If contractors engage in faulty intelligence analysis and thus skew U.S. policy, how may their mistakes be accounted for in congressional and executive oversight? *See id.* at 1065-1073 (arguing that contractors should be forbidden from engaging in inherently governmental functions).

Organizing for Intelligence Collection ——19

In this chapter we lay the foundation for a systematic consideration of the rules governing intelligence collection. How does the United States organize its intelligence collection missions? Which agencies are in charge of collection? What are the permissible collection techniques? How is surveillance, a critical subset of intelligence collection, managed and overseen? What legal arrangements facilitate the sharing of intelligence information, and which ones help ensure that the collection and dissemination of that information do not threaten personal freedoms?

The chart on p. 450 depicting the organization of the intelligence community serves as an important reminder that we have no single "Department of National Security." Instead, intelligence collection is overseen by the Office of the Director of National Intelligence and collected by several component agencies within the Department of Defense, the Department of State, the Department of Homeland Security, the Department of Justice (the FBI), the CIA, and other entities in scattered parts of our federal bureaucracy.

In Part A, we first introduce the intelligence cycle. In Part B, we survey briefly the range of intelligence collection disciplines and their evolution from 1947 to the present. In Part C, we examine the legal bases for intelligence collection and particular collection techniques, although we explore those techniques further in subsequent chapters. Finally, in Part D, we consider problems of information sharing and reform of the governance of intelligence collection.

A. THE INTELLIGENCE CYCLE

**Select Committee to Study Governmental Operations
with Respect to Intelligence Activities (Church Committee),
Foreign and Military Intelligence**
S. Rep. No. 94-755, bk. I, at 17-19 (1976)

In theory at least [intelligence] operations can be described in simple terms by the following cycle:

—Those who use intelligence, the "consumers," indicate the kind of information needed.

— These needs are translated into concrete "requirements" by senior intelligence managers.

— The requirements are used to allocate resources to the "collectors" and serve to guide their efforts.

— The collectors obtain the required information or "raw intelligence."

— The "raw intelligence" is collated and turned into "finished intelligence" by the "analysts."

— The finished intelligence is distributed to the consumer and the intelligence managers who state new needs, define new requirements, and make necessary adjustments in the intelligence programs to improve effectiveness and efficiency.

In reality this pattern is barely recognizable.

There are many different consumers, from the President to the weapons designer. Their needs can conflict. Consumers rarely take the time to define their intelligence needs and even if they do so there is no effective and systematic mechanism for translating them into intelligence requirements.

Therefore, intelligence requirements reflect what intelligence managers think the consumers need, and equally important, what they think their organizations can produce. Since there are many managers and little central control, each is relatively free to set his own requirements.

Resources therefore tend to be allocated according to the priorities and concerns of the various intelligence bureaucracies. Most intelligence collection operations are part of other organizations — the Department of Defense, the Department of State — and so their requirements and their consumers are often the first to be served.

Collecting intelligence is not an automatic process. There are many different kinds of intelligence, from a radar return to an indiscreet remark, and the problems in acquiring it vary greatly. Information that is wanted may not be available, or years may be required to develop an agency or a technical device to get it. Meanwhile intelligence agencies collect what they can.

In the world of bureaucracy, budgets, programs, procurement, and managers, the needs of the analyst can be lost in the shuffle. There has been an explosion in the volume and quality of raw intelligence but no equivalent increase in the capacity of analytical capabilities. As a result, "raw" intelligence increasingly dominates "finished" intelligence; analysts find themselves on a treadmill where it is difficult to do more than summarize and put in context the intelligence flowing in. There is little time or reward for the task of providing insight.

In the end the consumer, particularly at the highest levels of the government, finds that his most important questions are not only unanswered, but sometimes not even addressed.

To some extent, all this is in the nature of things. Many questions cannot be answered. The world of intelligence is dominated by uncertainty and chance, and those in the intelligence bureaucracy, as elsewhere in the Government, try to defend themselves against uncertainties in ways which militate against efficient management and accountability.

Beyond this is the fact that the organizations of the intelligence community must operate in peace but be prepared for war. This has an enormous impact on the kind of intelligence that is sought, the way resources are allocated, and the way the intelligence community is organized and managed.

The Idealized Intelligence Cycle

NOTES AND QUESTIONS

1. *Setting Requirements.* Intelligence serves policymakers and helps to shape policy. That policy in turn determines the need for additional intelligence and guides intelligence operations. There is, however, no formal mechanism for translating policy into intelligence requirements. Who should set intelligence objectives? How should those objectives be communicated to intelligence officials, following what kind of process?

2. *Collection.* Technical means offer tremendous advantages in collecting large volumes of information. Technical collection is, however, very expensive. Human intelligence is cheaper and may be more narrowly focused. How should these collection trade-offs be made, and by whom? If the mass of data collected through technical means cannot realistically be processed and analyzed, how should collection priorities be modified?

3. *Analysis, Delivery, and Consumption.* Some intelligence products are widely known — the President's Daily Briefings (PDBs), for example, and National Intelligence Estimates (NIEs). Analysis of intelligence and other, less well-known products are discussed in this and the next two chapters. How do you suppose it is decided which material collected is important enough to report, in whatever form? Who should receive intelligence reports — in the executive branch and in Congress? How rapidly should the information be provided, in how much detail, and in what form?

4. *Changing Requirements.* The Cold War and a preoccupation with the Soviet Union dominated the intelligence agenda until the fall of the Berlin Wall in 1989. From 1989 until the September 11 terrorist attacks in 2001, there was no comparably focused intelligence mission. September 11 provided a mission. The dominant role and most important legal questions concerning intelligence collection now revolve around countering the ongoing threat of terrorism.

B.   HOW IS INTELLIGENCE COLLECTED? — THE "INTS"

Intelligence collection is engaged in by people — human intelligence or espionage (HUMINT) — and by machines — geospatial intelligence (GEOINT), signals intelligence (SIGINT), and measurement and signatures intelligence (MASINT). Except for open-source intelligence (OSINT), each of the INTs has a self-contained process, from collection to delivery. This tendency toward "stovepipes" is exacerbated by an intentional redundancy among the separate INTs. By deploying different collection systems in pursuit of the same intelligence we hope to learn from the shared perspectives they offer — "all-source intelligence." We also compensate in one INT for a shortcoming in another.

Mark M. Lowenthal, Intelligence: From Secrets to Policy
pp. 82-105 (4th ed. 2009)

GEOINT

... is a direct descendant of the brief practice of sending soldiers up in balloons during the U.S. Civil War. In World War I and World War II, both sides used airplanes to obtain photos. Airplanes are still employed, but several nations now utilize imagery satellites. In the United States, the National Reconnaissance Office (NRO) develops these satellites. The National Geospatial-Intelligence Agency (which was the National Imagery and Mapping Agency, NIMA, until 2003) is responsible for processing and exploiting imagery. Some imagery also comes via the Defense Department's airborne systems, such as unmanned aerial vehicles (UAVs), or drones....

Imagery offers a number of advantages over other collection means. First, it is sometimes graphic and compelling. When shown to policymakers, an easily interpreted image can be worth a thousand words. Second, imagery is easily understood much of the time by policymakers. Even though few of them, if any, are trained imagery analysts, all are accustomed to seeing and interpreting images....

Imagery also suffers from a number of problems. The very graphic quality that is an advantage is also a disadvantage. An image can be too compelling, leading to hasty or ill-formed decisions or to the exclusion of other, more subtle intelligence that is contradictory. Also, the intelligence on an image may not be self-evident; it may require interpretation by trained photo interpreters who can see things that the untrained person cannot. At times, the policymakers must take on faith that the skilled analysts are correct.

Another disadvantage of imagery is that it is a snapshot, a picture of a particular place at a particular time.... Imagery is a static piece of intelligence, revealing something about where and when it was taken but nothing about what happened before or after....

SIGNALS INTELLIGENCE

SIGINT is a twentieth-century phenomenon. British intelligence pioneered the field during World War I, successfully intercepting German communications by tapping underwater cables. The most famous product of this work was the Zimmermann Telegram, a German offer to Mexico of an anti-U.S. alliance that Britain made available to the United States without revealing how it was obtained. With the advent of radio communications, cable taps were augmented by the ability to pluck signals from the air. The United States also developed a successful signals intercept capability that survived World War I. Prior to World War II the United States broke Japan's Purple code; Britain, via ULTRA, read German codes.

Today signals intelligence can be gathered by Earth-based collectors — ships, planes, ground sites or satellites. Again, U.S. SIGINT satellites are built by the NRO. The National Security Agency is responsible for both carrying out U.S. signals intelligence activities and protecting the United States against hostile SIGINT....

SIGINT consists of several different types of intercepts. The term is often used to refer to the interception of communications between two parties, which is also known as communications intelligence (COMINT). SIGINT can also refer to the pickup of data relayed by weapons during tests which is sometimes called telemetry intelligence (TELINT). Finally, SIGINT can refer to the pickup of electronic emissions from modern weapons and tracking systems (military and civil), which are useful means of gauging their capabilities, such as range and frequencies on which systems operate. This is sometimes referred to as electronic intelligence (ELINT)....

The ability to intercept communications is highly important, since it gives insight into what is being said, planned, and considered. It comes as close as one can, from a distance, to reading the other side's mind, a goal that cannot be achieved by imagery. Reading the actual messages and analyzing what they mean is called *content analysis*. Tracking communications also gives a good *indication and warning*....

COMINT has some weaknesses. First and foremost, it depends on the presence of communications that can be intercepted. If the target goes silent or opts to communicate via secure landlines instead of through the air, then the ability to undertake COMINT ceases to exist. Perhaps the landlines can be tapped, but doing so is a more difficult task than remote interception from a ground site or satellite. The target can also begin to *encrypt* — or code — its communications. Within the offensive/defensive struggle over SIGINT is a second struggle, that between encoders and codebreakers, or *cryptographers*.... Computers greatly increase the ability to construct complex, one-time use codes. Meanwhile, computers also make it more possible to attack these codes. Finally, the target can use false transmissions as a means of creating less compromising patterns or of subsuming important communications amid a flood of meaningless ones — in effect, increasing the ratio of noise to signals.

Another issue is the vast quantity of communications now available: telephones of all sorts, faxes, e-mails, and so on.... Even a focused collection plan collects more COMINT than can be processed and exploited. One means of coping with this is the *key-word search*, in which the collected data are fed into computers that look out for specific words or phrases. The words are used as indicators of the likely value of an intercept.... The war against terrorism has underscored a growing concern for SIGINT. As with the other collection disciplines, SIGINT was developed to collect intelligence on the Soviet Union and other nations. Terrorist cells offer much smaller signatures, which may not be susceptible to interception by remote SIGINT sensors. Therefore, a growing view is that future SIGINT will have to rely on sensors that have been physically placed close to the target by humans. In effect, HUMINT will become the enabler for SIGINT....

HUMAN INTELLIGENCE

HUMINT is espionage — spying — and is sometimes referred to as the world's second-oldest profession. It is as old as the Bible. Joshua sent two spies into Canaan before leading the Jewish people across the Jordan River. Spying is what most people think about when they hear the word "intelligence," whether they conjure up famous spies from history such as Nathan Hale or Mata Hari (both failures) or the many fictional spies such as James Bond. In the United States HUMINT is largely the responsibility of the CIA, through its Directorate of Operations (DO). DIA [Defense Intelligence Agency] also has a HUMINT capability with the Defense Humint Service, which it has sought to expand since the war in Afghanistan. . . .

HUMINT largely involves sending agents to foreign countries, where they attempt to recruit foreign nationals to spy. . . . [Agents must] identif[y] individuals who have access to the information that the United States may desire . . . gain[] their confidence and assess[] their weaknesses and susceptibility to being recruited . . . [and] mak[e] a *pitch* to them, suggesting a relationship. A source may accept a pitch for a variety of reasons: money, disaffection with their own government, blackmail, or thrills. Once the pitch has been accepted, the agent must meet with his sources [assets] regularly to receive information, holding meetings in a manner and in places that will reduce the risk of being caught and then transmitting the information back home. . . .

In addition to gaining the skills required for this activity, agents have to maintain their cover stories — the overt lives that give them a plausible reason for being in that foreign nation. . . .

In addition to recruiting foreign nationals, HUMINT agents may undertake more direct spying, such as stealing documents or planting sensors. Some of their information may come through direct observation of activity. . . .

An important adjunct to one's own HUMINT capabilities are those of allied or friendly services. Known as foreign liaison relationships, they offer several important advantages. First, the friendly service has greater familiarity with its own region. Second, its government may maintain a different pattern of relations with other states, more friendly in some cases or even having diplomatic relations where one's own government does not. These HUMINT-to-HUMINT relationships are somewhat formal in nature and tend to be symbiotic. They also entail risks, as one can never be entirely sure of the liaison partner's security procedures. . . . Furthermore, some liaison relationships may be with intelligence services that do not have the same standards in terms of operational limits, acceptable activities, and other criteria. A choice therefore has to be made between the value of the information being sought or exchanged and the larger question of the propriety of a relationship with this service. . . .

Espionage provides a very small part of the intelligence that is collected. IMINT [imagery intelligence] and SIGINT produce a greater volume of intelligence. But HUMINT, like SIGINT, has the major advantage of affording access to what is being said, planned, and thought. Moreover, clandestine human access to another government also may offer opportunities to influence that government by feeding it false or deceptive information. For intelligence targets where the technical infrastructure may be irrelevant as a fruitful target — such as terrorism, narcotics, or international crime, where the "signature" of activities is rather small — HUMINT may be the only available source.

HUMINT also has disadvantages. First, it cannot be done remotely, as is the case with various types of technical collection. It requires proximity and access and therefore must contend with the counterintelligence capabilities of the other side. It is also far riskier, as it jeopardizes individuals, and, if they are caught, could have political ramifications that are less likely to occur with technical collectors. . . .

Like all the other collection INTs, HUMINT is susceptible to deception. . . .

OPEN-SOURCE INTELLIGENCE

To some, OSINT may seem like a contradiction in terms. How can information that is openly available be considered intelligence? . . . OSINT includes a wide variety of information and sources:

- Media: newspapers, magazines, radio, television, and computer-based information.

- Public data: government reports, official data such as budgets, demographics, hearings, legislative debates, press conference speeches.

- Professional and academic: conferences, symposia, professional associations, academic papers, and experts. . . .

The major advantage of OSINT is its accessibility, although it still requires collection. . . .

The main disadvantage of OSINT is its volume. In many ways, it represents the worst wheat and chaff problem. Some argue that the so-called information revolution has made OSINT more difficult without a corresponding increase in usable intelligence. Computers have increased the ability to manipulate information; however, the amount of derived intelligence has not increased apace. . . .

NOTES AND QUESTIONS

1. *The Players.* An intelligence community organization chart showing the various member agencies as they existed in mid-2011 is set forth *supra* p. 450. You may find it helpful in relating the INTs to the agencies that conduct them and in understanding the relationships among the agencies.

2. *Redundancy.* Recall that one aim of intelligence collection is redundancy: send as many INTs as possible to pursue the same issue, resulting in all-source intelligence. Can you see the value in this purposeful overkill? Do you see particular strengths or weaknesses in any of the INTs that would cause you to emphasize or reduce its role in collection?

3. *Wheat vs. Chaff.* Technical collection systems are like vacuum cleaners. They sweep up lots of information, some of which may be useful for intelligence purposes. The National Security Agency (NSA) records 650 million events each day, and produces ten thousand daily reports. Lowenthal, *supra*, at 73. Can you see downside risks in relying on these technical systems? How may the risks be ameliorated?

4. *Diplomats as Spies?* Following the Wikileaks dissemination of State Department diplomatic cables in November 2010, attention was drawn to a few cables from 2008 and 2009 that instruct State Department personnel about how to fulfill the demands of a CIA National HUMINT Collection Directive. One such cable asked embassy staff abroad to gather information about foreign officials, including telephone numbers, e-mail addresses, credit card account numbers, frequent flier account numbers, work schedules, and other biographical and biometric information. Mark Mazzetti, *U.S.*

Expands Role of Diplomats in Spying, N.Y. Times, Nov. 28, 2010. Do you see any legal or practical objections to using diplomats to gather intelligence information? *See* Executive Order No. 12,333 §§1.4, 3.4(f), *supra* p. 451.

C.   WHO DOES THE COLLECTING?

Following creation of the Office of the Director of National Intelligence (ODNI) in 2004, the Director of National Intelligence (DNI) sits at the top of the 16 agencies considered part of the Intelligence Community. (See the chart on p. 450). Here we focus on the agencies whose collection activities are at once most central to the intelligence mission and most controversial legally.

Executive Order No. 12,333
United States Intelligence Activities
(as amended by Executive Order Nos. 13,284 (2003),
13,355 (2004), and 13,470 (2008))
73 Fed. Reg. 45,325 (July 30, 2008)

[The executive order is reproduced *supra* p. 451.]

1.   The CIA

National Security Act of 1947
Pub. L. No. 80-253, 61 Stat. 495 (as amended)

50 U.S.C. §403-4a. DIRECTOR OF CENTRAL INTELLIGENCE AGENCY...

(d) Responsibilities. The Director of the Central Intelligence Agency shall—
(1) collect intelligence through human sources and by other appropriate means, except that the Director of the Central Intelligence Agency shall have no police, subpoena, or law enforcement powers or internal security functions;
(2) correlate and evaluate intelligence related to the national security and provide appropriate dissemination of such intelligence;
(3) provide overall direction for and coordination of the collection of national intelligence outside the United States through human sources by elements of the intelligence community authorized to undertake such collection and, in coordination with other departments, agencies, or elements of the United States Government which are authorized to undertake such collection, ensure that the most effective use is made of resources and that appropriate account is taken of the risks to the United States and those involved in such collection; and
(4) perform such other functions and duties related to intelligence affecting the national security as the President or the Director of National Intelligence may direct....

Clearly, the CIA is assigned HUMINT collection tasks outside the United States. No less clearly, at first glance, the National Security Act draws the line at the border and forbids "internal" security functions. Yet the 1947 Act, as amended, calls on the

DNI to take any actions necessary to "protect intelligence sources and methods from unauthorized disclosure." 50 U.S.C. §403-1(i)(1). Such actions are not geographically limited or defined. Protecting sources and methods also means protecting its own facilities, including those in the United States. In addition, the CIA is to "perform such other functions and duties related to intelligence affecting the national security as the President or the National Security Council may direct." According to Mark Reibling, this language originally provided "a pair of operational baggy pants," while CIA Counsel Scott Breckinridge called the "other functions" language a "banana-peel clause." Mark Riebling, *Wedge: The Secret War Between the FBI and CIA* 79 (1994). In fact, Executive Order No. 12,333 §1.7(a)(2)-(3) directs the CIA also to perform "counterintelligence activities without assuming or performing internal security within the United States," as well as "administrative and technical support activities within . . . the United States as necessary for cover and proprietary activities." The following materials show that these openings to activities inside the United States have created some tension with the "internal security" prohibition.

Select Committee to Study Governmental Operations with Respect to Intelligence Activities (Church Committee), Foreign and Military Intelligence
S. Rep. No. 94-755, bk. I, at 136-139 (1976)

The National Security Act of 1947 defines the duties of the CIA in terms of "intelligence" or "intelligence relating to the national security." The legislative history of the Act clearly shows that Congress intended the activities authorized by this language to be related to foreign intelligence. This construction is aided by the statute's provision that "the Agency shall have no police, subpoena, law enforcement power, or internal-security functions," 50 U.S.C. [§403-4a(d)(1), *supra*]. . . .

The legislative history of the Act shows that in establishing the CIA Congress contemplated an agency which not only would be limited to foreign intelligence operations but one which would conduct very few of its operations within the United States. It was contemplated that the Agency would have its headquarters here, and in House Committee hearings in executive session the possibility of seeking foreign intelligence information from private American citizens who traveled abroad was discussed with approval. But in public and in private it was generally agreed among legislators and representatives of the Executive that the CIA would be "confined out of the continental limits of the United States and in foreign fields," that it should have no "police power or anything else within the confines of this country," and that it was "supposed to operate only abroad." . . .

The CIA . . . has interpreted the internal security prohibition narrowly to exclude investigations of domestic activities of American groups for the purpose of determining foreign associations. But history indicates that at the time of enactment of the National Security Act, threats to "internal security" were widely understood to include domestic groups with foreign connections. Investigations by the FBI of American groups with no such connections, in fact, have been a recent phenomenon. The original order from President Roosevelt to J. Edgar Hoover to begin internal security operations was to investigate foreign communist and fascist influence within the United States. There is no evidence that by 1947 these investigations were considered foreign intelligence. . . .

. . . As authority for some of its operations within the United States, the Agency has relied upon Section 102(d)(3) of the National Security Act, [50 U.S.C. §403-1(i)(1)], which charges the Director of Central Intelligence [now the Director of National Intelligence] with responsibility to protect intelligence sources and methods from unauthorized disclosure.

The CIA has construed the sources and methods language broadly to authorize investigation of domestic groups whose activities, including demonstrations, have potential, however remote, for creating threats to CIA installations, recruiters or contractors. In the course of carrying out these investigations the Agency has collected general information about the leadership, funding activities, and policies of targeted groups. . . .

The sources and methods language was discussed only briefly in the recorded legislative history of the National Security Act. . . . Despite congressional concern, expressed again and again during hearings and floor debates on the bill, that the CIA was to have no potential for infringing upon the rights of American citizens and that it was to be virtually excluded from acting within the United States, no one questioned whether the sources and methods language would raise problems in this area. The lack of interest in the provision suggests that it was not viewed as conveying new authority to investigate; rather it charged the Director of the Central Intelligence Agency with responsibility to use the authority which he already had to protect sensitive intelligence information. . . .

Halkin v. Helms

United States Court of Appeals, District of Columbia Circuit, 1982
690 F.2d 977

MacKinnon, J. Plaintiffs appeal several orders of the district court which resulted in the dismissal of their complaint for legal and equitable relief on claims arising out of certain activities of the Central Intelligence Agency (CIA) in the period from 1967 to 1974. The complaint alleged violations of plaintiffs' first, fourth, fifth and ninth amendment rights, and of section 102(d)(3) of the National Security Act of 1947, 50 U.S.C. [§403-4a(d)(1)]. For the reasons set forth below, the judgment of the district court is affirmed.

Appellants are 21 individuals and 5 organizations who in the late 1960's and early 1970's were involved in various activities seeking to protest and secure an end to the involvement of the United States in the Vietnam War. The individual appellees are seven named persons and an unspecified number of John Does who at the time plaintiffs' claims arose were officials of the CIA or were otherwise agents or employees of the United States government. The seven appellees referred to hereinafter as the "individual appellees"[1] were sued for damages in their individual capacities. The appellees also include the heads of the CIA, FBI, Department of Defense and Secret Service, who were sued in their official capacities and with respect to whom plaintiffs sought injunctive and declaratory relief only.

---

1. The individual appellees are Richard Helms (former Director of Central Intelligence), William E. Colby (same), James R. Schlesinger (same and also former Secretary of Defense), Cord Meyer, Jr. (Assistant Director for Plans of the CIA), James J. Angleton (Chief of CIA Counterintelligence Staff), Richard Ober (CIA Counterintelligence Staff), and Howard Osborn (Director of Security of the CIA).

Plaintiffs filed suit in October 1975, after disclosures by the press and by the President's Commission on CIA Activities Within the United States[6] (the Rockefeller Commission) revealed that government agencies, including the FBI and the CIA, had conducted intelligence operations that resulted in surveillance of United States citizens who opposed the war in Vietnam. These operations included intelligence gathering activities both within and without the United States. Two such intelligence gathering programs are the focus of the present litigation.

A. OPERATION CHAOS

The first program, designated by the CIA as Operation CHAOS, was an intelligence-gathering activity conducted by the CIA originally at the request of President Johnson which sought to determine the extent to which foreign governments or political organizations[8] exerted influence on or provided support to domestic critics of the government's Vietnam policies.[9] CHAOS was begun in 1967 by appellee Helms, who at the time was Director of Central Intelligence.[10] ...

Over the course of several years, Operation CHAOS produced six reports for the White House and some thirty-four reports for cabinet-level officials, dealing with the subject of foreign influence on the domestic antiwar movement. In the normal course of its operations, CHAOS also produced a steady stream of reports to the FBI and other agencies detailing the results of its various intelligence activities with respect to the antiwar movement.

Discovery conducted by plaintiffs in the district court revealed that among the several thousand computerized files it maintained on Americans involved in various aspects of the antiwar movement,[12] Operation CHAOS ultimately developed files on 15 of the individual appellants and the five appellant organizations. The gravamen of plaintiffs' claims with respect to Operation CHAOS concerned the several known methods whereby the CIA compiled information on plaintiffs' activities....

... [B]eginning in late 1969, the CHAOS office developed its own network of informants for the purposes of infiltrating various foreign antiwar groups located in foreign countries that might have had ties to domestic antiwar activity. Although the principal focus of such infiltration was foreign groups, it is now known that informants destined for such assignments were directed to infiltrate antiwar circles within the United States for the purpose of gaining knowledge of their operations and credibility as antiwar activists. In the course of these preliminary associations,

---

6. The Commission was established by Executive Order of President Ford on January 4, 1975, Executive Order No. 11828 (1975) and filed its final Report in June 1975.

8. Early CHAOS documents indicate the program's concern with the influence of "Soviets, Chicoms [Chinese Communists], Cubans and other Communist countries. ... Of particular interest is any evidence of foreign direction, control, training or funding."

9. According to early CHAOS documents, the domestic groups suspected of receiving such support included "radical students, anti-Vietnam war activists, draft resisters and deserters, black nationalists, anarchists, and assorted 'New Leftists.' "

10. Helms testified before the Rockefeller Commission that although the President never specifically directed the CIA to institute a program devoted to gathering this information, "the setting up of this unit [CHAOS] was what I conceived to be a proper action" to respond to "almost daily and weekly" requests of the President.

12. In addition to files containing information on the subject individual or group, the CIA's computer system indexed over 100,000 names of persons upon whom separate files were not maintained.

CHAOS agents apparently supplied information on the activities of domestic antiwar groups, and this information was placed in the general CHAOS data base.[16]

...Operation CHAOS made use of the facilities of other ongoing CIA surveillance programs. These included: (1) the CIA letter-opening program, which was directed at letters passing between the United States and the Soviet Union, and involved the examination of correspondence to and from individuals or organizations placed on a "watchlist";[17] (2) the Domestic Contact Service, a CIA office which solicits foreign intelligence information overtly from willing sources within the United States; (3) the CIA's "Project 2," which was directed at the infiltration of foreign intelligence targets by agents posing as dissident sympathizers and which, like CHAOS, had placed agents within domestic radical organizations for the purposes of training and establishment of dissident credentials; (4) the CIA's Project MERRIMAC, operated by the Office of Security, which was designed to infiltrate domestic antiwar and radical organizations thought to pose a threat to the security of CIA property and personnel; and (5) Project RESISTANCE, also a creature of the Office of Security, which gathered information on domestic groups without any actual infiltration.

From its inception, CHAOS also regularly received information from the FBI on that agency's investigations of the domestic antiwar movement.

B.　INTERNATIONAL ELECTRONIC COMMUNICATIONS

In addition to the surveillance activities carried out under the aegis of Operation CHAOS, plaintiffs complained of the CIA's practice of obtaining the contents of international communications (telephone, telegraph and radio transmissions) by submitting subjects' names on "watchlists" to the National Security Agency (NSA). NSA possesses the technology to scan the mass of signals transmitted through various communications systems and then to select out by computer those messages in which certain words or phrases occur. It is thereby possible for that agency to acquire all communications over a monitored system in which, for example, a person's name is mentioned. Between 1967 and 1973, the FBI, the Secret Service, and military intelligence agencies, as well as the CIA, submitted the names of domestic individuals and organizations on watchlists to NSA, and ultimately acquired through NSA the international communications of over a thousand American citizens....

C.　HISTORY OF THE LITIGATION

1. Discovery

Since this action was filed in October 1976, the parties have fought the bulk of their dispute on the battlefield of discovery. Shortly after filing their complaint,

---

16. The CIA admitted that CHAOS agents associated with at least one plaintiff within the United States and with an unspecified number of plaintiffs traveling in foreign countries; however, it refused to identify these plaintiffs.

17. In addition to the mail of persons who had been "watchlisted," the letter-opening program also examined randomly-selected letters moving between the United States and the Soviet Union.

plaintiffs sought the production of documents concerning (1) the conduct of Operation CHAOS in general, and (2) CHAOS surveillance of plaintiff individuals and organizations in particular. A large number of documents responsive to plaintiffs' request were produced, but with portions claimed to disclose sensitive information redacted. Approximately 200 responsive documents were withheld in their entirety.[27] Subsequently, as public reports further disclosed the extent of CIA domestic activities, plaintiffs in July 1977 sought additional discovery in the form of (3) requests for admissions that the CIA or foreign "liaison services" had conducted various types of surveillance against each plaintiff or against nonparty organizations to which plaintiffs belonged; (4) further interrogatories seeking more detailed justification of the redaction and withholding of documents previously requested; (5) a request for the production of [other] documents. . . .

The CIA declined to supply all of the information requested by plaintiffs. With respect to the identification of plaintiffs who had been the subjects of surveillance under the CHAOS program or by virtue of watchlists submitted by the CIA to NSA, the CIA claimed that more than the limited disclosure already given[28] would reveal the identities of covert sources and disclose the existence of liaison relationships with foreign intelligence services, and that therefore this information was privileged from discovery. The CIA declined . . . to answer plaintiffs' interrogatories seeking more detailed explanations of the redactions in the documents it had produced. . . . Finally, it refused to disclose whether any plaintiffs' names had been submitted on watchlists to NSA by the Special Operations Group.

In January 1978, plaintiffs pursuant to Fed. R. Civ. P. 37 filed a motion to compel the Director of the CIA to respond to plaintiffs' interrogatories and requests for production of documents. The CIA responded with two affidavits by then-Director Stansfield Turner formally claiming that the requested information was protected from discovery by the state secrets privilege. . . .

In a memorandum opinion filed August 30, 1978, the district court upheld the CIA's claim of the state secrets privilege and denied plaintiffs' motion to compel. . . .

Plaintiffs explicitly conceded in the district court that the successful invocation of the state secrets privilege by the Director of Central Intelligence made it impossible for them to go forward with their claims for *damages* based on statutory and constitutional violations occurring as a result of Operation CHAOS. Without access to the facts about the identities of particular plaintiffs who were subjected to CIA surveillance (or to NSA interception at the instance of the CIA), direct injury in fact to any of the plaintiffs would not have been susceptible of proof. . . .

---

27. The CIA furnished brief descriptions of documents that were entirely withheld (e.g., "Dispatch dated 1 August 1968, information on dissident activity abroad, mentions [plaintiff] in passing").

28. The CIA had admitted in the course of discovery that various identified and unidentified plaintiffs were on several occasions the targets of CHAOS surveillance or were subjected to surveillance in the course of CHAOS operations directed at other subjects. Specifically, it appears that under Operation CHAOS, the CIA (1) opened and copied the mail of three identified plaintiffs within the United States; (2) targeted the mail of at least two identified plaintiffs for opening; (3) had CHAOS agents attend private meetings of unidentified plaintiff organizations; (4) collected nonpublic information on nine other identified plaintiffs; (5) electronically surveilled two unidentified plaintiffs abroad in the course of operations directed at other persons; (6) had two agents who "were associated" with at least one unidentified plaintiff within the United States; and (7) had agents who "associated" with an undisclosed number of unidentified plaintiffs abroad, in the course of operations directed at other persons.

... The district court was on solid ground in refusing to compel production of documents on the basis of the Director's claim as asserted in the public affidavit without resort to any more detailed justification. . . . [The court also refused to compel the defendants to answer interrogatories or appear for oral depositions. Additional discussion of the state secrets privilege is presented *supra* p. 142.]

NOTES AND QUESTIONS

1. *Interpreting the 1947 Act.* What does it mean to say that "the Agency shall have no police, subpoena, or law enforcement powers or internal security functions"? There is no other express geographic limitation in the Act. To what extent may the CIA act within the United States? Are CIA authorities greater when operating abroad? Absent definitions in the Act, how should the CIA interpret the key terms "police," "law enforcement," and "internal security"?

2. *Authority for Operation CHAOS?* Did the domestic activities of Operation CHAOS exceed the statutory authority of the CIA? If the mission was to ascertain foreign influence on domestic dissident activities, was CIA accumulation of information on Americans needed to assess fairly whether the activities had foreign connections? Was CHAOS a legitimate program to protect CIA "sources and methods"? If you believe the operation exceeded statutory limits, does the Constitution supply the needed authority?

If you were responsible for approving staff requests to engage in surveillance of Americans, what criteria would you apply in deciding?

3. *Executive Order No. 12,333 and the National Security Act of 1947.* Compare §§1.7(a) and 2.3(b) of Executive Order No. 12,333, *supra*, to the National Security Act of 1947. Do you see any significant differences in the "such other functions and duties" authorizations in the Act and the Executive Order? What are they? How may the CIA "conduct counterintelligence activities" without performing any "internal security functions" within the United States? What do you suppose constitutes "foreign intelligence information not otherwise obtainable," and how may the CIA or NSA collect "significant" foreign intelligence within the United States without violating the proscription against collecting information on the domestic activities of United States persons? Executive Order No. 12,333 also anticipates that the CIA will engage in the "collection of foreign intelligence or counterintelligence within the United States," *id.* §1.8(a), and "participate in law enforcement activities to investigate or prevent clandestine intelligence activities by foreign powers or international terrorist or narcotics activities," *id.* §2.6(b). Can you reconcile these authorities with the "no police . . . or internal security" proviso in the 1947 Act?

4. *Weighing Government Misconduct and National Security Concerns.* In *Halkin*, the court's ruling against disclosure of the disputed evidence apparently made it impossible for individual plaintiffs to demonstrate any personal injury from government misconduct, resulting in dismissal of their claims for damages. Moreover, while several plaintiffs identified as subjects of CHAOS surveillance could establish standing to sue, they could not demonstrate such a cognizable danger of recurrent violation

of their rights as to entitle them to injunctive or declaratory relief. *Halkin*, 690 F.2d at 1003-1009.

Has the court concluded, in effect, that foreign policy considerations may excuse violations of the plaintiffs' statutory or constitutional rights? If the plaintiffs would otherwise have been entitled to damages under the Federal Tort Claims Act, is this an instance of uncompensated injury by the government without due process, in violation of the Fifth Amendment to the Constitution? *See Logan v. Zimmerman Brush Co.*, 455 U.S. 422, 428-431 (1982). The *Halkin* court observed:

> As in the other cases in which the need to protect sensitive information affecting the national security clashes with fundamental constitutional rights of individuals, we believe that "[t]he responsibility must be where the power is." *New York Times Co. v. United States*, 403 U.S. 713, 728 (1971) (Stewart, J., concurring). In the present context, where the Constitution compels the subordination of appellants' interest in the pursuit of their claims to the executive's duty to preserve our national security, this means that remedies for constitutional violations which cannot be proven under existing legal standards, if there are to be such remedies, must be provided by Congress. That is where the government's power to remedy wrongs is ultimately reposed. Consequently, that is where the responsibility for compensating those injured in the course of pursuing the ends of state must lie. [690 F.2d at 1001.]

If responsibility lies where the power is, what authority did the Executive have to launch Operation CHAOS without congressional authority? See *The Steel Seizure Case* (*supra* p. 25), 343 U.S. at 630-632 (Douglas, J., concurring).

Is it clear, as the court suggests, that the Constitution "compels" subordination of individual constitutional claims in cases like this one, or that the court in enforcing the organic law must prefer one part of it over another? In *United States Department of Justice v. Julian*, 486 U.S. 1, 13 (1988), the Supreme Court indicated that the state secrets privilege arises "as a result of judicial decision."

5. *Redefining the Scope of the Mission?* When Congress enacted the 2004 Intelligence Reform Act, *supra* p. 466, the terms "national intelligence" and "intelligence related to national security" were defined to include "all intelligence, regardless of the source from which derived and including information gathered within or outside the United States, that pertains . . . to more than one . . . agency; and that involves threats to the United States, its people, property, or interests; the development, proliferation, or use of weapons of mass destruction; or any other matter bearing on United States national or homeland security." Intelligence Reform and Terrorism Prevention Act of 2004, Pub. L. No. 108-458, §1012, 118 Stat. 3638, 3662. How does this expansive definition affect the geographical boundaries of intelligence activities by the CIA?

Note that the CIA tasking quoted *supra* p. 532 refers only to human intelligence collection. Is the implication of the amended Act that the CIA may lawfully collect intelligence through technical means inside the United States?

6. *The Director of National Intelligence and Internal Security.* Although the CIA internal security proviso remains after the enactment of the 2004 Intelligence Reform Act, no such constraint was imposed on the DNI by the Act. What are the legal and practical implications of omitting the internal security prohibition for the DNI?

Does the expanded definition of "national intelligence" noted above undercut the internal security prohibition for the CIA?

7. *Is Further Reform Needed?* Do the continuing ambiguities in the law concerning the domestic role of the CIA and its relationship to the FBI suggest a need for further statutory reform? Would it be preferable to list activities that the CIA may lawfully perform inside the United States, rather than to maintain a blanket prohibition of uncertain scope? Reviewing the 1947 Act and its 2004 amendments, along with Executive Order No. 12,333, can you come up with such a list? How would you describe the justifications for CIA collection activities inside the United States? Which methods of collection should be authorized and which ones prohibited, if any? Can you add language that would ensure coordination of CIA activities with those of the FBI and provide a mechanism for ensuring respect for the rights of U.S. persons? Should the "no internal security" proviso be amended to say "except as otherwise permitted by law"? *See* Grant T. Harris, *The CIA Mandate and the War on Terror*, 23 Yale L. & Pol'y Rev. 529, 571-576 (2005) (suggesting such changes).

2.   The FBI

The Attorney General is expressly vested with "primary investigative authority for all Federal crimes of terrorism." 18 U.S.C. §2332b(f) (2006). The FBI, in contrast, has scant statutory authority to carry out its mission. Lacking a legislative charter, the FBI operates on the basis of the Attorney General's authority found in 28 U.S.C. §533 (2006) to appoint officials:

(1) to detect and prosecute crimes against the United States;

(2) to assist in the protection of the person of the President; and . . .

(4) to conduct such other investigations regarding official matters under the control of the Department of Justice and the Department of State as may be directed by the Attorney General.

The FBI also draws investigative authority from statutes authorizing specific methods or purposes for collection, such as the Foreign Intelligence Surveillance Act (FISA), analyzed in Chapter 21.

All FBI investigations are conducted according to guidelines promulgated by the Attorney General and Executive Order No. 12,333. On September 29, 2008, Attorney General Michael Mukasey announced the issuance of the *Attorney General's Guidelines for Domestic FBI Operations, available at* http://www.usdoj.gov/ag/readingroom/guidelines.pdf, to take effect on December 1, 2008. The consolidated guidelines combine nearly uniform standards for all FBI domestic investigations and replace five sets of previously discrete guidance on crimes investigation, national security investigations, and foreign intelligence investigations.

Unlike the CIA or any other intelligence collector, the FBI therefore operates under the direction of the nation's highest law enforcement officer and within a culture of law enforcement. Nevertheless, the FBI has also sometimes strayed from its lawful domestic role and has undertaken efforts to disrupt domestic groups.

Select Committee to Study Governmental Operations
with Respect to Intelligence Activities (Church Committee),
Intelligence Activities and the Rights of Americans
S. Rep. No. 94-755, bk. II, at 86-89 (1976)

The FBI's initiation of COINTELPRO operations against the Ku Klux Klan, "Black Nationalists" and the "New Left" brought to bear upon a wide range of domestic groups the techniques previously developed to combat Communists and persons who happened to associate with them.

The start of each program coincided with significant national events. The Klan program followed the widely-publicized disappearance in 1964 of three civil rights workers in Mississippi. The "Black Nationalist" program was authorized in the aftermath of the Newark and Detroit riots in 1967. The "New Left" program developed shortly after student disruption of the Columbia University campus in the spring of 1968. While the initiating memoranda approved by Director Hoover do not refer to these specific events, it is clear that they shaped the context for the Bureau's decisions.

These programs were not directed at obtaining evidence for use in possible criminal prosecutions arising out of those events. Rather, they were secret programs— "under no circumstances" to be "made known outside the Bureau"—which used unlawful or improper acts to "disrupt" or "neutralize" the activities of groups and individuals targeted on the basis of imprecise criteria.

(1) *Klan and "White Hate" COINTELPRO.* — The expansion of Klan investigations, in response to pressure from President Johnson and Attorney General Kennedy, was accompanied by an internal Bureau decision to shift their supervision from the General Investigative Division to the Domestic Intelligence Division. One internal FBI argument for the transfer was that the Intelligence Division was "in a position to launch a disruptive counterintelligence program" against the Klan with the "same effectiveness" it had against the Communist Party.

Accordingly, in September 1964 a directive was sent to seventeen field offices instituting a COINTELPRO against the Klan and what the FBI considered to be other "White Hate" organizations (e.g., American Nazi Party, National States Rights Party) "to expose, disrupt, and otherwise neutralize" the activities of the groups, "their leaders, and adherents."

During the 1964-1971 period, when the program was in operation, 287 proposals for COINTELPRO actions against Klan and "White Hate" groups were authorized by FBI headquarters. Covert techniques used in this COINTELPRO included creating new Klan chapters to be controlled by Bureau informants and sending an anonymous letter designed to break up a marriage.

(2) *"Black Nationalist" COINTELPRO.* — The stated strategy of the "Black Nationalist" COINTELPRO instituted in 1967 was "to expose, disrupt, misdirect, discredit, or otherwise neutralize" such groups and their "leadership, spokesmen, members, and supporters." The larger objectives were to "counter" their "propensity for violence" and to "frustrate" their efforts to "consolidate their forces" or to "recruit new or youthful adherents." Field offices were instructed to exploit conflicts within and between groups; to use news media contacts to ridicule and otherwise discredit groups; to prevent "rabble rousers" from spreading their "philosophy" publicly; and to gather information on the "unsavory backgrounds" of group leaders.

In March 1968, the program was expanded from twenty-three to forty-one field offices and the following long-range goals were set forth:

(1)   prevent the "coalition of militant black nationalist groups";
(2)   prevent the rise of a "messiah" who could "unify and electrify" the movement, naming specifically Dr. Martin Luther King, Jr., Stokely Carmichael, and Elijah Muhammed;
(3)   prevent violence by pinpointing "potential troublemakers" and "neutralizing" them before they "exercise their potential for violence";
(4)   prevent groups and leaders from gaining "respectability" by discrediting them to the "responsible" Negro community, the "responsible" white community, "liberals" with "vestiges of sympathy" for militant black nationalist and "Negro radicals"; and
(5)   "prevent these groups from recruiting young people."

After the Black Panther Party emerged as a group of national stature, FBI field offices were instructed to develop "imaginative and hard-hitting counterintelligence measures aimed at crippling the BPP." Particular attention was to be given to aggravating conflicts between the Black Panthers and rival groups in a number of cities where such conflict had already taken on the character of "gang warfare with attendant threats of murder and reprisals."

During 1967-1971, FBI headquarters approved 379 proposals for COINTELPRO actions against "black nationalists." These operations utilized dangerous and unsavory techniques which gave rise to the risk of death and often disregarded the personal rights and dignity of the victims.

(3) *"New Left" COINTELPRO.* — The most vaguely defined and haphazard of the COINTELPRO operations was that initiated against the "New Left" in May 1968. It was justified to the FBI Director by his subordinates on the basis of the following considerations:

The nation was "undergoing an era of disruption and violence" which was "caused to a large extent" by individuals "generally connected with the New Left."

Some of these "activists" were urging "revolution" and calling for "the defeat of the United States in Vietnam."

The problem was not just that they committed "unlawful acts," but also that they "falsely" alleged police brutality, and that they "scurrilously attacked the Director and the Bureau" in an attempt to "hamper" FBI investigations and to "drive us off the college campuses."

Consequently, the COINTELPRO was intended to "expose, disrupt, and otherwise neutralize" the activities of "this group" and "persons connected with it." The lack of any clear definition of "New Left" meant, as an FBI supervisor testified, that "legitimate" and nonviolent antiwar groups were targeted because they were "lending aid and comfort" to more disruptive groups.

Further directives issued soon after initiation of the program urged field offices to "vigorously and enthusiastically" explore "every avenue of possible embarrassment" of New Left adherents. Agents were instructed to gather information on the "immorality" and the "scurrilous and depraved" behavior, "habits, and living conditions" of the members of targeted groups. This message was reiterated several months later, when the offices were taken to task for their failure to remain alert for and seek specific data depicting the "depraved nature and moral looseness of the

New Left" and to "use this material in a vigorous and enthusiastic approach to neu-tralizing them."

In July 1968, the field offices were further prodded by FBI headquarters to:

(1) prepare leaflets using "the most obnoxious pictures" of New Left leaders at various universities;

(2) instigate "personal conflicts or animosities" between New Left leaders;

(3) create the impression that leaders are "informants for the Bureau or other law enforcement agencies" (the "snitch jacket" technique);

(4) send articles from student or "underground" newspapers which show "depravity" ("use of narcotics and free sex") of New Left leaders to university officials, donors, legislators, and parents;

(5) have members arrested on marijuana charges;

(6) send anonymous letters about a student's activities to parents, neighbors and the parents' employers;

(7) send anonymous letters about New Left faculty members (signed "A Concerned Alumni" or "A Concerned Taxpayer") to university officials, legislators, Board of Regents, and the press;

(8) use "cooperative press contacts";

(9) exploit the "hostility" between New Left and Old Left groups;

(10) disrupt New Left coffee houses near military bases which are attempting to "influ-ence members of the Armed forces";

(11) use cartoons, photographs, and anonymous letters to "ridicule" the New Left;

(12) use "misinformation" to "confuse and disrupt" New Left activities, such as by notifying members that events have been cancelled.

During the period 1968-1971, 291 COINTELPRO actions against the "New Left" were approved by headquarters. Particular emphasis was placed upon preventing the targeted individuals from public speaking or teaching and providing "misinforma-tion" to confuse demonstrators.

NOTES AND QUESTIONS

1. *Suing the FBI over COINTELPRO.* In 1976, several Washington area residents who had been politically active in anti-war and civil rights activities in the 1960s and early 1970s brought suit against the FBI and District of Columbia officials for alleged violations of constitutional rights related to the FBI COINTELPRO program. In *Hobson v. Wilson*, 737 F.2d 1, 10 (D.C. Cir. 1984), *cert. denied sub nom. Brennan v. Hobson*, 470 U.S. 1084 (1985), the plaintiffs prevailed against most of the defendants. The Court of Appeals stated, "Government action taken with the intent to disrupt or destroy lawful organizations, or to deter membership in those groups, is absolutely unconstitutional." 737 F.2d at 29. What likely explains the different outcomes in *Halkin* and *Hobson*?

2. *Investigatory Authorizations Under Executive Order No. 12,333.* What constitutes a "lawful" FBI investigation within the meaning of Executive Order No. 12,333? What are the likely elements of a probable cause determination under §2.5? Review §2.4. Does any agency other than the FBI have authority to conduct physical searches inside

the United States? Is the answer the same for physical surveillance of U.S. persons within the United States? Under what circumstances may the FBI engage in physical surveillance of a U.S. person abroad?

3. *Authority for FBI Guidelines.* Do you think Congress should provide more explicit statutory authority for the FBI to conduct national security investigations? *See* Tom Lininger, *Sects, Lies, and Videotape: The Surveillance and Infiltration of Religious Groups,* 89 Iowa L. Rev. 1201 (2004) (so arguing).

4. *Relationship to Other Guidelines and Policies.* The 2008 *Attorney General's Guidelines for Domestic FBI Operations* repealed and replaced several existing sets of guidelines, including separate sets for criminal investigation, national security investigation, and foreign intelligence collection. Other Department of Justice guidelines affecting FBI activities remain in effect, including the *Attorney General's Guidelines on Federal Bureau of Investigation Undercover Operations* (May 2002), *available at* http://www.usdoj. gov/olp/fbiundercover.pdf; the *Attorney General's Guidelines Regarding the Use of FBI Confidential Human Sources* (Dec. 13, 2006), *available at* http://www.fas.org/irp/ agency/doj/fbi/chs-guidelines.pdf; and *Guidance Regarding the Use of Race by Federal Law Enforcement Agencies* (June 2003, updated July 2008), *available at* http://www. usdoj.gov/crt/split/documents/guidance_on_race.php. The 2008 *Guidelines for Domestic FBI Operations* do not apply to extraterritorial operations carried out by FBI agents or human sources in foreign countries. Attorney General Mukasey announced in September 2008 that he would be issuing new *Attorney General's Guidelines for Extraterritorial FBI Operations. See Memorandum from the Attorney General to Heads of Department Components* (Sept. 29, 2008), *available at* http://www.usdoj.gov/ag/readingroom/ guidelines-memo.pdf. Notwithstanding the general repeal of the earlier guidelines, the Attorney General directed that existing guidelines remain in effect in their application to extraterritorial operations until the new guidelines are issued. *Id.*

5. *Predicated Investigations.* The Guidelines state that predicated investigations are generally based on "allegations, reports, facts or circumstances indicative of possible criminal or national security-threatening activity, or the potential for acquiring information responsive to foreign intelligence requirements... [where] supervisory approval must be obtained." *Guidelines for Domestic FBI Operations* §II. Does the Constitution require some predicate activity before the FBI may launch an investigation? Would you infer such a requirement from statutes, or from Executive Order No. 12,333? What is the value of supervisory approval in predicated investigations?

6. *Infiltration.* Is CIA or FBI infiltration of domestic organizations permitted by Executive Order No. 12,333? On the basis of what information will the "agency head or designee" determine that infiltration is "essential to achieving lawful purposes"? If infiltration is authorized outside the limits of the order, what redress would be available to aggrieved persons? *See* Seth Kreimer, *Watching the Watchers: Surveillance, Transparency, and Political Freedom in the War on Terror,* 7 U. Pa. J. Const. L. 133 (2004).

7. *Assessments of the Guidelines.* The FBI's interpretation of the 2008 *Guidelines* was made public when it released, in response to a Freedom of Information Act (FOIA) lawsuit, its *Domestic Investigations and Operations Guide* (Dec. 16, 2008), *available at*

http://s3.amazonaws.com/nytdocs/docs/264/264.pdf. Prior to the opening of a formal investigation, FBI "assessments" may be undertaken without any predicate suspicion or threat. According to the *Domestic Investigations and Operations Guide*, the basis for opening an assessment "cannot be arbitrary or groundless suspicion," but the standard is "difficult to define." What is their value? Does the FBI have statutory authority to conduct these assessments? A former FBI agent stated that the *Guide* "raises fundamental questions about whether a domestic intelligence agency can protect civil liberties if they feel they have a right to collect broad personal information about people they don't even suspect of wrongdoing." Charlie Savage, *Loosening of F.B.I. Rules Stirs Privacy Concerns*, N.Y. Times, Oct. 29, 2009. According to a document released pursuant to a Freedom of Information Act request, the FBI initiated 11,667 assessments of people and groups in the four months between December 2008 and March 2009. Charlie Savage, *F.B.I. Casts Wide Net Under Relaxed Rules for Terror Inquiries, Data Show*, N.Y. Times, Mar. 26, 2011.

Note that the FBI may recruit human sources or task existing ones in an assessment. The *Attorney General's Guidelines Regarding the Use of FBI Confidential Human Sources* (Dec. 13, 2006), *supra*, provide detailed guidance on the use of human sources. Do you see any potential legal problems with the use of human sources in conducting an assessment?

In addition, the FBI may engage in physical surveillance in an assessment. Physical surveillance had been available to the Bureau in general crimes investigations at the assessment level. Do you see any legal issues in extending physical surveillance to this broader set of guidelines? Might these rules encourage the FBI to engage in fishing expeditions that waste resources and damage the reputations of innocent people?

8. *The Use of Race or Religion.* Section II of the 2003 *Guidance Regarding the Use of Race by Federal Law Enforcement Agencies*, *supra* p. 544, states that "federal law enforcement officers who are protecting national security . . . may consider race, ethnicity and other relevant factors to the extent permitted by our laws and the Constitution." When engaged in traditional law enforcement activities, officers may not use race or ethnicity to any degree, except that officers may rely on race or ethnicity in a specific suspect description. Is there any reason not to apply the same direction to national security investigations? To foreign intelligence investigations? Do you suppose that the assessments engaged in by the FBI might focus on members of a racial group? A religious group? Following the outing of an FBI informant who had infiltrated a California mosque in November 2010, Muslim organizations complained that overreaching FBI investigative tactics have damaged the relationship between the Muslim groups and the Bureau. Jerry Markon, *Mosque Infiltration Feeds Muslims' Distrust of FBI*, Wash. Post, Dec. 5, 2010. Should investigations be limited to circumstances where possible criminal or national security-threatening activity has been received by the FBI?

9. *Creation of a U.S. MI5?* MI5 (Military Intelligence, Section 5) is charged with counterintelligence and counterterrorism activities within the United Kingdom. It is headed by a permanent civil service employee (the Director General) answerable to the Home Secretary, and it does not have general law enforcement responsibilities. In recent years, some have suggested that the United States should create a domestic intelligence service patterned after MI5. *See, e.g.*, William E. Odom, *Fixing Intelligence*

for a More Secure America 180-182 (2d ed. 2003). Creating an American MI5 would avoid the conflict or competition between counterterrorism or counterintelligence and law enforcement, it is asserted, and thus make the FBI more effective at its counter-tasks. Instead of relying on the FBI to perform domestic intelligence gathering, an MI5-type agency might be separate from both the FBI and CIA (although, like them, it would report to the DNI). The FBI would then revert to what it has historically done best — fighting crime by building cases against criminals. The domestic intelligence agency, in contrast, would collect intelligence in the United States to guard against ongoing and future espionage or terrorist plots. The potential targets of the new agency could be wholly homegrown, like the Ku Klux Klan or domestic terrorists, or those with foreign origins or connections, such as Al Qaeda.

Would creation of a such a new agency be a good idea? If our MI5 reported to the DNI instead of directly to the President, and was no longer supervised by the chief law enforcement officer of the United States, are you satisfied that the agency would avoid the politically driven operations that bedeviled the nation in the Nixon years?

3. The NSA

The NSA is the largest agency within the intelligence community. It is devoted to communications security and to collecting and disseminating SIGINT. See *supra* p. 528. NSA's predecessor, the Armed Forces Security Agency (AFSA), was established within the Department of Defense in 1949, but because each military service branch continued to collect SIGINT for its own use, AFSA proved ineffectual in coordinating SIGINT activities. In October 1952, President Truman signed a secret directive to create the NSA in order to provide an effective structure for coordinating SIGINT activities for civilian and military consumers. Richard A. Best Jr., *The National Security Agency: Issues for Congress* (Cong. Res. Serv. RL30740) 16, Jan. 16, 2001; *see* Jeffrey T. Richelson, *The U.S. Intelligence Community* 30-37 (5th ed. 2008). Apart from annual appropriations for the NSA based on secret briefings about SIGINT activities before the appropriations committees, the first major legislation dealing with NSA was the National Security Agency Act of 1959, Pub. L. No. 86-36, 73 Stat. 63. It authorized the Secretary of Defense to "establish such positions, and to appoint . . . such officers and employees, in the National Security Agency, as may be necessary to carry out the functions of such agency." *Id.* §2. However, this measure dealt mostly with housekeeping matters inside the Agency and did not describe the functions of NSA.

Until it was revealed that U.S. intelligence agencies were spying on domestic groups opposed to the Vietnam War, there was little interest in the NSA among members of Congress or the public and little knowledge about the secretive agency. During the Church Committee hearings in 1976, NSA Director Lieutenant General Lew Allen Jr. provided the first open-session congressional testimony about NSA SIGINT activities and the NSA practice of establishing "watch lists," discussed in *Halkin, supra* p. 534. Although the Church Committee and its House counterpart, known as the Pike Committee, acknowledged the continuing importance of NSA's foreign intelligence collection activities, both committees also recommended specific authorizing legislation for NSA that would include strict limits on the monitoring of communications by U.S. citizens. *See* Church Committee, *supra* p. 525, bk. I, at 464; *Recommendations of the Final Report of the House Select Comm. on Intelligence*, H.R. Rep. No. 94-833, at 3 (1976). The congressional initiative toward a "legislative charter" for the intelligence agencies, including NSA, died in the 1979-1980 congressional session amidst partisan disputes, when the Soviet invasion of Afghanistan caught the United States by surprise and provoked new efforts to invigorate intelligence capabilities. See *supra* p. 487.

Congress did, however, enact FISA in 1978, authorizing and regulating electronic surveillance in the United States to obtain foreign intelligence. Because the NSA conducts electronic surveillance, FISA became an important part of the NSA's regulatory framework. We address FISA in detail in Chapters 21 and 22.

In 1992, the National Security Act of 1947 was amended to state that

> the Secretary of Defense shall ensure . . . through the National Security Agency (except as otherwise directed by the President or the National Security Council), the continued operation of an effective unified organization for the conduct of signals intelligence activities and shall ensure that the product is disseminated in a timely manner to authorized recipients. [Intelligence Authorization Act for Fiscal Year 1993, Pub. L. No. 102-496, §706, 106 Stat. 3180, 3194-3195 (1992) (codified as amended at 50 U.S.C. §403-5(b)(1) (2006).]

Additional guidance for the NSA has been provided by executive order.

Executive Order No. 12,333, United States Intelligence Activities
(as amended by Executive Order Nos. 13,284 (2003), 13,355 (2004), and 13,470 (2008)) 73 Fed. Reg. 45,325 (July 30, 2008)

1.12. Intelligence Components Utilized by the Secretary of Defense. . . . [T]he Secretary of Defense is authorized to utilize the following: . . .

(b) National Security Agency, whose responsibilities shall include:

(1) Establishment and operation of an effective unified organization for signals intelligence activities, except for the delegation of operational control over certain operations that are conducted through other elements of the Intelligence Community. No other department or agency may engage in signals intelligence activities except pursuant to a delegation by the Secretary of Defense;

(2) Control of signals intelligence collection and processing activities, including assignment of resources to an appropriate agent for such periods and tasks as required for the direct support of military commanders;

(3) Collection of signals intelligence information for national foreign intelligence purposes in accordance with guidance from the Director of Central Intelligence;

(4) Processing of signals intelligence data for national foreign intelligence purposes in accordance with guidance from the Director of Central Intelligence;

(5) Dissemination of signals intelligence information for national foreign intelligence purposes to authorized elements of the Government, including the military services, in accordance with guidance from the Director of Central Intelligence;

(6) Collection, processing and dissemination of signals intelligence information for counterintelligence purposes;

(7) Provision of signals intelligence support for the conduct of military operations in accordance with tasking, priorities, and standards of timeliness assigned by

the Secretary of Defense. If provision of such support requires use of national collection systems, these systems will be tasked within existing guidance from the Director of Central Intelligence;

(8) Executing the responsibilities of the Secretary of Defense as executive agent for the communications security of the United States Government; . . .

(10) Protection of the security of its installations, activities, property, information, and employees by appropriate means, including such investigations of applicants, employees, contractors, and other persons with similar associations with the NSA as are necessary. . . .

The power of NSA computers to collect massive amounts of data is staggering. NSA "employs more mathematicians than any other organization in the world and [its facilities contain] the densest concentration of computer power on the planet." Patrick Radden Keefe, *Chatter: Dispatches from the Secret World of Global Eavesdropping* 8 (2005). It uses sophisticated key-word searching and other techniques (often lumped together and referred to as "data mining") to perform some analysis on large amounts of material before it is delivered to other agencies. Its technical capacity actually far outstrips the human capacity to evaluate or use all the information it collects.

The Agency does not act upon the intelligence it collects. Instead, NSA passes that intelligence along to other civilian and military agencies and officials. *Id.* In its communications security role, NSA uses its SIGINT capabilities to detect espionage and other intelligence activities directed against the United States. For example, early in the Cold War NSA conducted a program code-named VENONA that used signal intercepts to detect Soviet espionage in the United States. Between 1943 and 1957, VENONA helped identify Alger Hiss, Julius Rosenberg, Klaus Fuchs, and others who served as Soviet agents. *See* Robert L. Benson, *The Venona Story* (National Security Agency/Central Security Service) (n.d.), *available at* http://www.nsa.gov/publications/publi00039.cfm. Many of the released intercepts may be viewed at http://www.nsa.gov/venona/. Additional background on the NSA may be found in three books by James Bamford, *The Shadow Factor: The Ultra-Secret NSA from 9/11 to the Eavesdropping on America* (2008); *Body of Secrets: Anatomy of the Ultra-Secret National Security Agency* (2001); and *Puzzle Palace* (1982).

NOTES AND QUESTIONS

1. *Authority to Create the NSA?* What authority did President Truman have to establish the NSA in 1952? The National Security Act of 1947, *supra* p. 444, created a Secretary of Defense and states that "[u]nder the direction of the President and subject to the provisions of this Act he shall . . . [e]stablish general policies and programs for the National Military Establishment and for all the departments and agencies therein." Pub. L. No. 80-253, §202(a)(1), 61 Stat. 495, 500. If this provision is insufficient, does the President possess constitutional authority to create an agency to collect SIGINT for foreign intelligence purposes? To collect SIGINT in the United States? What was the legal effect of annual appropriations for the NSA on its authority to perform SIGINT activities before the 1992 amendment to the National Security Act? See *supra* pp. 107-109.

2. *Watch Lists.* If the *Halkin* court had reached the merits, how should it have ruled on the plaintiffs' complaints concerning the NSA's use of watch lists? Watch lists were developed by identifying individual names, subjects, locations, and the like within a mass of communications to separate useful intelligence from background "noise." Watch lists were thus precursors to contemporary data-mining techniques, including those at issue in the post–September 11 NSA domestic eavesdropping program. See *infra* pp. 609-619.

During the Vietnam War period, congressional investigators learned of an NSA project known as Shamrock in which copies of international telegrams were provided on a daily basis to NSA by three telegraph companies. Church Committee, *supra* p. 525, bk. III, at 765-776. Pursuant to what legal authority would this project have been conducted? The congressional desire to bring practices such as these under legislative control helped assure the 1978 enactment of FISA, examined *infra* p. 581.

3. *Contemporary Authorities.* To what extent, if at all, does the 1959 National Security Agency Act, *supra* p. 549, authorize the activities of the NSA? Does the 1992 amendment to the National Security Act of 1947 constitute an adequate legislative charter for the NSA's activities? If not, what changes or additions would you recommend? To what extent do the provisions of Executive Order No. 12,333 supply the necessary details? What questions do you have about what the NSA may and may not do after reading these two measures?

4. *ECHELON.* An NSA program called ECHELON allegedly used data-mining techniques aimed at telecommunications from Europe for economic espionage. *Keefe, supra,* at 194-208. Sophisticated listening stations in the United States and Great Britain reportedly tracked these communications. *Id.* at 52-54. European leaders claimed that ECHELON was employed to steal secrets from European countries and pass them on to U.S. competitors. European Parliament, *Report of the Existence of a Global System for the Interception of Private and Commercial Communications (ECHELON Interception System),* July 11, 2001, *available at* http://www.fas.org/irp/program/process/rapport_echelon_en.pdf.

Does the NSA have the authority to conduct a program like ECHELON? Some in the United States countered the European complaints by maintaining that ECHELON was used to observe bribes by European companies of government officials in furtherance of their commercial interests. Keefe, *supra,* at 194-198. Do you see any legal problems with these techniques or with their objectives?

D. SHARING COLLECTED INTELLIGENCE

Some of the September 11 hijackers lived openly in the United States when their names or names of their close associates were on intelligence "watch lists." The watch-list information was not shared in a timely fashion among federal agencies, which might have been able to detect the hijackers' plot before it was implemented. Because intelligence about would-be terrorists might be obtained by the FBI, CIA, NSA, or agencies inside the Defense Department, or by a state or local law enforcement agency, the challenges of sharing intelligence are staggering. Moreover, the FBI, long embedded in its role as the federal government's chief law enforcement agency, has struggled to reshape its mission to incorporate a vigorous counterterrorism component. How should information classified by one agency be shared with another agency? How should a federal agency share with a state or local agency? How can information be shared in a secure way without jeopardizing the privacy interests of those identified in the intelligence?

Some coordination is required by Executive Order No. 12,333, and ODNI provides guidance to federal, state, and local agencies on sharing information through its Information Sharing Environment. *See Information Sharing Environment* (updated regularly), *at* http://www.ise.gov/. The FBI leads and coordinates foreign intelligence and counterintelligence activities in the United States, and the CIA, Department of Defense, and military intelligence entities must coordinate with the FBI. Executive Order No. 12,333 §§1.8(a), 1.11(d), 1.14, 1.12(d)(1). Outside the United States, all the intelligence agencies are required to coordinate with the CIA. *Id.* §§1.8(d), 1.11(d), 1.12(d)(1), 1.14(a). In practice, coordination has sometimes been difficult to achieve.

1.   Bridging the Law Enforcement/Intelligence Collection Divide

The National Security Act of 1947 declares that the CIA shall have no "internal security" functions. It was thus determined by Congress that the already functioning FBI would continue to serve as the nation's domestic security agency. At the same time, it was understood early on that the "internal security" prohibition in the 1947 Act would not forbid the CIA from coordinating or collecting *foreign* intelligence information in the United States. However, there was nothing in the Act to provide for CIA and FBI coordination, and no rules to say when the CIA could play a counterintelligence role in the United States. In theory, law enforcement and intelligence collection roles, activities, and methods had been legally and functionally separated to protect the integrity of their tasks and to protect the civil liberties of those targeted for investigation by the government. *See* Jonathan M. Fredman, *Intelligence Agencies, Law Enforcement, and the Prosecution Team*, 16 Yale L. & Pol'y Rev. 331, 336-337 (1998). Thus, the 1947 Act "cut the man down the middle . . . between domestic and foreign counterespionage." Mark Riebling, *Wedge: The Secret War Between the FBI and CIA* 78 (1994).

While the FBI has expanded its extraterritorial role to acquire information about transnational threats, the CIA and agencies inside the Departments of Homeland Security and Defense have also stepped up their efforts in support of counterterrorism. Intelligence gathering for counterterrorism must anticipate threats before they are carried out, while law enforcement typically reacts after the event. However, because terrorism and international crime pose national security threats that transcend both national borders *and* the borders between law enforcement and intelligence collection, coordination and cooperation are required among intelligence agencies and between the intelligence and law enforcement arms of the FBI.

As amended in 1996, the National Security Act permits agencies of the intelligence community, upon the request of a law enforcement agency, to "collect information outside the United States about individuals who are not United States persons." 50 U.S.C. §403-5a. Executive Order No. 12,333 establishes a legal presumption that agencies of the Intelligence Community may "participate in law enforcement activities to investigate or prevent clandestine intelligence activities by foreign powers, or inter-national terrorist or narcotics activities" unless "otherwise precluded by law or this Order." *Id.* §2.6. The order also explicitly charges the DNI with developing guidelines for sharing of intelligence information by the intelligence community, subject to approval by the Attorney General. §1.3(a)(2). The DNI also "shall ensure, through appropriate policies and procedures, the deconfliction, coordination, and integration of all intelligence activities conducted by an Intelligence Community element or funded by the National Intelligence Program." *Id.* §1.3(b)(20).

A USA Patriot Act provision authorizes a greater degree of interagency coopera-tion and sharing of information than was permitted previously. The Act permits, "[n]otwithstanding any other provision of law . . . foreign or counterintelligence . . . information obtained as part of a criminal investigation to be disclosed to any Federal law enforcement, intelligence, protective, immigration, national defense, or national security official in order to assist the official receiving that information in the perfor-mance of his official duties." Pub. L. No. 107-56, §203(d)(1), 115 Stat. 272, 281 (2001), amending 50 U.S.C. §403-5(d). The same discretion is given for the sharing of grand jury information. *Id.* §203(a)(1), 115 Stat. 278-279, amending 18 U.S.C. §6(e)(3)(C).

In the Intelligence Reform and Terrorism Prevention Act of 2004 (IRTPA), Pub. L. No. 108-458, 118 Stat. 3638, Congress created a National Counterterrorism Center (NCTC). *Id.* §1021m, 118 Stat. 3672. The Senate-confirmed Director of the NCTC reports to the DNI generally, but to the President on the planning and implementa-tion of joint counterterrorism operations. *Id.* The IRTPA vests in the DNI the "princi-pal authority to ensure maximum availability of and access to intelligence information within the intelligence community consistent with national security." *Id.* §1011(a), 118 Stat. 3650. IRTPA also requires a "coordinated environment" in which intelligence information can be "provided in its more shareable form." *Id.* §1016(b)(2), (d)(1), 118 Stat. 3665-3666. Information sharing is also addressed *infra* p. 692.

2. Coordinating the FBI

Owing at least in part to the FBI's long-standing tradition of performing the federal law enforcement role, intelligence collection and analysis efforts were long regarded inside the Bureau as of secondary importance. Even as additional resources and staff were devoted to intelligence collection and analysis inside the FBI during the 1990s, the intelligence function was still not central to the FBI mission. In addition to the perception among many that engaging heavily in intelligence work would only compromise the effectiveness of FBI law enforcement, the Bureau's reluctance to embrace an intelligence mission wholeheartedly was also due in part to our nation's cultural and historical antipathy to a domestic intelligence service. Images of the sinister omnipresence of the German Gestapo and the Soviet KGB were firmly etched into the public consciousness.

A few months after Congress created a revised intelligence community structure in December 2004, President Bush issued an order creating a new National Security Division (NSD) within the FBI that is subject to the overall direction of the DNI. *See* Douglas Jehl, *Bush to Create New Unit in F.B.I. for Intelligence*, N.Y. Times, June 30, 2005. The restructuring was designed to break down historic barriers between the FBI and CIA, while elevating the relative importance of the intelligence mission inside the FBI.

Id. The new division, called the National Security Service, includes counterterrorism and counterintelligence divisions and an intelligence directorate. A new position of Assistant Attorney General for National Security, in charge of counterterrorism, counterintelligence, and the Office of Intelligence Policy Review, was approved by Congress in the USA Patriot Improvement and Reauthorization Act of 2005, Pub. L. No. 109-177, §506(a), 120 Stat. 192, 247 (2006).

NOTES AND QUESTIONS

1. *Intelligence Reform and the FBI.* The restructuring accomplished by Congress in the IRTPA and later in the Patriot Reauthorization Act was "intended to break down old walls between foreign and domestic intelligence activities." Douglas Jehl, *Bush to Create New Unit in F.B.I. for Intelligence*, N.Y. Times, June 30, 2005. Do you see any downside risk in tearing down the wall between foreign and domestic intelligence? In lowering the historic barrier between the FBI and the CIA? To what extent will the FBI now be subject to the authority of the DNI? Whose job is it to ensure that the National Security Service not undertake activities that violate U.S. laws?

2. *Utility of the Information-Sharing Requirements.* Are the USA Patriot Act and IRTPA information-sharing provisions clearly advisable? Do these provisions raise the possibility that the CIA will collect information in the United States about Americans? In light of the complexities of mounting an effective counterterrorism strategy, can you think of any good alternatives to these information-sharing mechanisms? Can you think of ways to create greater accountability for their use?

What legal measures might improve information sharing across these jurisdictional lines? Between agencies? *See* Peter P. Swire, *Privacy and Information Sharing in the War on Terrorism*, 51 Vill. L. Rev. 951 (2006) (suggesting a due diligence checklist for information-sharing projects).

3. *Checks and Balances vs. Efficiency.* Is competition between the CIA and the FBI inevitable? If the coordination and competition problems *can* be solved, *should* they be solved? Or is it part of our nation's character "to chafe at bureaucratic inefficiency... [but] to distrust the centralization of power needed to correct it"? Riebling, *supra*, at 460. Are the agencies' missions so different that their work cannot be coordinated? Is the reluctance to vest one agency with both foreign and domestic security responsibility a sign of healthy skepticism about the dangers of the accumulation of power in one entity? In the end, is the foreign/domestic dichotomy that continues to dominate the law of internal security workable? Is it constitutionally defensible? Is the better dividing line one between intelligence collection and law enforcement?

The Fourth Amendment and National Security

20

Since the birth of our nation, Americans have worried about espionage committed by hostile foreign agents. In recent times, we have also become the targets of violent terrorist acts at home and abroad. To gather information about these threats to national security, we have employed many of the same techniques that are used in ordinary criminal investigations, including wiretaps, undercover agents and informants, physical searches of persons and places, and, more recently, sophisticated computer technologies, including e-mail intercepts and data mining.

In almost every instance, these measures have succeeded in protecting the American people from harm. In the process, however, government officials have occasionally lost sight of their mission, or strayed from it, and have violated individual privacy rights, just as in any criminal investigation gone awry. Where the subject of a probe is a possible terrorist act, which may be politically motivated, First Amendment freedoms of assembly and expression may be implicated as well. Special care is thus required in sorting out protected activities from those that could lead to violence or serious disruption of society and in selecting appropriate investigative techniques for each.

This sorting-out process is often complicated by a lack of information about the exact nature of suspected threats. While no one argues that a mere hunch about anticipated violent acts or subversion will justify surveillance of potential targets, something less than a completed illegal act must suffice. Thus, the development of standards for approval of investigations into national security threats is a critical legal issue.

In this and the succeeding five chapters we focus on intelligence collection within the United States and abroad — electronic surveillance; physical searches; the collection of tangible and electronic transactional records, such as travel records, telephone dialing and billing information, bank records, and library records; data mining of the resulting data bases; and watch list and screening measures for mass transit and other public places.

In this chapter, we start in Part A with a short primer on the Fourth Amendment and the "special needs" exceptions. In Part B, we examine the Supreme Court's seminal analysis of the President's claim of inherent authority to conduct warrantless electronic surveillance in domestic security investigations. In Part C, we consider whether subsequent lower court case law recognized a "foreign intelligence exception" to the warrant requirement of the Fourth Amendment.

In Chapter 21, we turn to statutory authority for electronic foreign intelligence surveillance in the Foreign Intelligence Surveillance Act (FISA) and related legislation. Chapter 22 examines the most recent extension of FISA procedures to permit programmatic surveillance without regard to particularized targets. In Chapter 23, we take up statutory authority for investigatory collection of tangible and electronic transactional records held by third parties, using court orders, national security letters, and subpoenas. In Chapter 24, we consider a range of other surveillance and collection techniques used to profile and "watchlist" terrorist suspects and to screen access to transportation systems, critical infrastructure, and other possible targets for terrorism. Finally, in Chapter 25, we shift our focus from domestic intelligence collection to the U.S. law governing national security surveillance abroad.

A.   THE FOURTH AMENDMENT FRAMEWORK

An introduction to the Fourth Amendment necessarily starts in colonial America. The British used a "general warrant" to conduct searches without probable cause — essentially fishing expeditions.

> The British general warrant was a search tool employed without limitation on location, and without any necessity to precisely describe the object or person sought. British authorities were simply given license to "break into any shop or place suspected" wherever they chose. With that kind of unfettered discretion, the general warrant could be, and often was, used to intimidate. General warrants executed during the reign of Charles I sought to intimidate dissidents, authors, and printers of seditious material by ransacking homes and seizing personal papers. In 1765, the courts declared general warrants illegal, and Parliament followed a year later.
>
> In the colonies, complaints that royal officials were violating the privacy of colonists through the use of writs of assistance, equivalent to general warrants, grew. Because English law did not, as yet, recognize a right of personal privacy, the crown's abuses in the colonies were not remediable at law. It was thus no surprise that the new American Constitution and the government it created would respect a series of individual freedoms.... [William C. Banks & M.E. Bowman, *Executive Authority for National Security Surveillance*, 50 Am. U. L. Rev. 1, 92-94 (2001).]

In reaction to the general warrant, the Framers adopted the Fourth Amendment to the U.S. Constitution. It provides:

> The right of the people to be secure in their persons, houses, papers, and effects, against unreasonable searches and seizures shall not be violated, and no Warrants shall issue, but upon probable cause, supported by Oath or affirmation, and particularly describing the place to be searched, and the persons or things to be seized.

The Amendment presents several threshold issues. First, federal agents can "search" a property just by looking at it from the street, as any member of the public can. Does the Fourth Amendment apply to such a search? In *Katz v. United States*, 389 U.S. 347 (1967), FBI agents placed an electronic listening device on the roof of a public telephone booth in Los Angeles. They did not seek a warrant. The agents recorded the voice of Charles Katz as he engaged in illegal gambling with contacts in other cities. Repudiating earlier Supreme Court precedents that limited Fourth Amendment coverage to situations in which a physical penetration of a constitutionally protected place occurred, the *Katz* Court ruled that "the Fourth Amendment protects people, not places." 389 U.S. at 351. But if the applicability of Fourth Amendment privacy focuses on people rather than places, what circumstances determine whether personal privacy concerns trigger the protection of the Constitution? Concurring, Justice Harlan suggested that Fourth Amendment coverage turns on the subjective existence of "a reasonable expectation of privacy." 389 U.S. at 360. The Harlan formulation thus supplies an answer to the question about a "search" of property in the public view. The Fourth Amendment does not bar such a search because the property owners have no reasonable expectation of privacy from public scrutiny. The "reasonable expectation of privacy" also guides courts in deciding whether a "search" has occurred. *See United States v. Jacobsen*, 466 U.S. 109 (1984); *Skinner v. Railway Labor Executives' Ass'n*, 489 U.S. 602 (1989).

Second, how does the warrant requirement in the Fourth Amendment relate to the reasonableness requirement? Is a warrantless search unreasonable *per se*? In 1967, the Supreme Court held that warrantless searches "are *per se* unreasonable — subject only to a few specifically established and well-delineated exceptions." *Katz, supra*, 389 U.S. at 357. It is the neutral determination of probable cause to issue a warrant that makes the warranted search reasonable; without a warrant, a search is presumptively unreasonable, unless it fits an exception.

Warrants, however, are now "more the exception than the rule." Joshua Dressler & Alan C. Michaels, *Understanding Criminal Procedure, Volume I: Investigation* 311 (4th ed. 2006). Some exceptions, said to be grounded in necessity, have been declared even in criminal investigations:

- searches incident to arrest, *United States v. Robinson*, 414 U.S. 218 (1973)

- automobile searches, *Michigan v. Long*, 463 U.S. 1032 (1983)

- "hot pursuit" or exigent circumstance searches, *Michigan v. Tyler*, 436 U.S. 499 (1978)

- "stop and frisk" searches, *Terry v. Ohio*, 392 U.S. 1 (1968)

Other exceptions have been recognized for searches conducted for purposes other than criminal investigation, such as accident prevention, protection of public health, or administrative compliance:

- the use of pen register devices, *Smith v. Maryland*, 442 U.S. 735 (1979)

- the contents of banking records, *United States v. Miller*, 425 U.S. 435 (1976)

- searches to prevent railroad accidents that cause "great human loss," *Skinner v. Railway Labor Executives' Ass'n*, 489 U.S. 602, 628 (1989)

- searches to help prevent the spread of disease or contamination during a public health crisis. *Camara v. Municipal Court*, 387 U.S. 523, 539 (1967)

Finally, some warrantless searches are permitted at borders and on the high sea on theories of traditional border control and/or public safety:

- searches of persons and things entering and leaving the United States, *United States v. Montoya de Hernandez*, 473 U.S. 531 (1985)

- searches of boats on navigable waters, *United States v. Villamonte-Marquez*, 462 U.S. 579 (1983)

- searches of airplanes. *United States v. Nigro*, 727 F.2d 100 (6th Cir. 1984) (en banc)

The last two groups of exceptions are sometimes labeled "special needs exceptions," because "special needs, beyond the normal need for [criminal] law enforcement, make the warrant and probable-cause requirement impracticable." *Griffin v. Wisconsin*, 483 U.S. 868, 872 (1987) (quoting *New Jersey v. T.L.O.*, 469 U.S. 325, 351 (1985) (Blackmun, J., concurring in judgment)). Although "special needs" may be "no more than a label that indicates a lax standard will apply," William J. Stuntz, *Implicit Bargains, Government Power, and the Fourth Amendment*, 44 Stan. L. Rev. 553, 554 (1992), that standard is still the reasonableness balancing standard. Dressler & Michaels, *supra*, at 327.

   In view of the devastation wrought by the airline hijackings on September 11, 2001, it is not hard to find a special need for warrantless preboarding airplane searches:

> When the risk is the jeopardy to hundreds of human lives and millions of dollars of property inherent in the pirating or blowing up of a large airplane, that danger alone meets the test of reasonableness, so long as the search is conducted in good faith for the purpose of preventing hijacking or like damage and with reasonable scope, and the passenger has been given notice of his liability to such a search so that he can avoid it by choosing not to travel by air. [*United States v. Edwards*, 498 F.2d 496, 500 (2d Cir. 1974).]

See also John Rogers, *Bombs, Borders, and Boarding: Combating International Terrorism at United States Airports and the Fourth Amendment*, 20 Suffolk Transnat'l L. Rev. 501 (1997); Chapter 22.

   What about a search prompted by nothing more than an anonymous tip of a planned bombing? In one case the Supreme Court remarked that it did not need to

> speculate about the circumstances under which the danger alleged in an anonymous tip might be so great as to justify a search even without a showing of reliability. We do not say, for example, that a report of a person carrying a bomb need bear the indicia of reliability we demand for a report of a person carrying a firearm before the police can constitutionally conduct a frisk. [*Florida v. J.L.*, 529 U.S. 266, 273-274 (2000).]

How does the anonymous tip case compare to the exceptional cases just mentioned? What additional facts about the bomb threat or the government's proposal concerning who or what was searched would you want to know before authorizing the search?

   Should concern for national security justify warrantless electronic surveillance of Americans suspected in some way of being connected to terrorist threats? Should it provide the basis for video surveillance of streets, parks, and other public places? If there is a national security exception to the warrant requirement, what is the scope of the exception, and what procedures should substitute for the warrant process? Consider the following assessment.

William C. Banks & M.E. Bowman, Executive
Authority for National Security Surveillance

50 Am. U. L. Rev. 1, 92-94 (2001)

Although the Fourth Amendment eliminated the abuses of general warrants, its commands remain unclear, especially in the face of technological progress. Moreover, the Fourth Amendment was designed to protect against overreaching in investigations of criminal enterprises. Investigations of politically motivated threats to our national security, such as terrorism or espionage, were simply not contemplated....

Terrorism presents a unique set of challenges in the United States. First, current criminal laws and traditional law enforcement processes cannot provide absolute protection against terrorist acts. While arrest, prosecution, and incarceration serve well to help prevent most crimes from occurring, the risk of catastrophic harm from terrorist attacks forces us to consider other means of prevention. Moreover, traditional Fourth Amendment requirements may thwart many investigations of terrorism, which depend on stealth to prevent terrorist plans before they are carried out.

Second, while terrorism is at its core a national security problem, it represents an unusual confluence of phenomena for the investigative community—the primary purpose of the investigation may be simultaneously and in equal measure law enforcement and national security. With few exceptions, the rules for gathering intelligence about terrorism in the United States are no different from the rules for ordinary criminal investigations.

Third, most prognostications are for more threats of terrorism in the United States in coming years, largely due to the perception that our defenses against conventional attacks are so formidable. Greater threats thus place an additional premium on greater intelligence resources and successes.

The tradition of liberty in the United States casts a shadow over all national security surveillance, and is an overriding problem in addressing terrorism concerns. The core openness of our society permits all of us, including the potential terrorist, considerable freedom to move about, to associate with others, and to act in furtherance of political aims. As recent terrorist incidents in the United States have created a sense of urgency among citizens and government officials to find better preventive strategies, reflection has also reminded us that hasty actions to thwart terrorism may threaten the freedoms that permit an open society. Thus, in seeking ways to investigate potential terrorist activity, just as in fashioning better responses to terrorist incidents, the measures adopted must not undermine our basic freedoms.

B.   A NATIONAL SECURITY EXCEPTION?

Foreign Intelligence Surveillance Act of 1977

S. Rep. No. 95-604, at 9-12 (1977)
[hereinafter *Senate Report No. 604*]

...In 1928, the Supreme Court in *Olmstead v. United States* [277 U.S. 468] held that wiretapping was not within the coverage of the Fourth Amendment. Three years later, Attorney General William D. Mitchell authorized telephone wiretapping, upon the personal approval of bureau chiefs, of syndicated bootleggers and in "exceptional cases where the crimes are substantial and serious, and the necessity is great and [the bureau chief and the Assistant Attorney General] are satisfied that the persons whose wires are to be tapped are of the criminal type." These general guidelines governed the Department's practice through the thirties and telephone wiretapping was considered to be an important law enforcement tool.

Congress placed the first restrictions on wiretapping in the Federal Communications Act of 1934, which made it a crime for any person "to intercept and divulge or publish the contents of wire and radio communications." [48 Stat. 1103.] The Supreme Court construed this section to apply to Federal agents and held that evidence obtained from the interception of wire and radio communications and the fruits of the evidence, were inadmissible in court. [*Nardone v. United States*, 302 U.S. 379 (1937); 308 U.S. 338 (1939).] However, the Justice Department did not interpret the Federal Communications Act or the *Nardone* decision as prohibiting the interception of wire communications per se; rather only the interception and divulgence of their contents outside the Federal establishment was considered to be unlawful. Thus, the Justice Department found continued authority for its national security wiretaps.

In 1940, President Roosevelt issued a memorandum to the Attorney General stating his view that electronic surveillance would be proper under the Constitution where "grave matters involving defense of the nation" were involved. The President authorized and directed the Attorney General "to secure information by listening devices [directed at] the conversation or other communications of persons suspected of subversive activities against the Government of the United States, including suspected spies." The Attorney General was requested "to limit these investigations so conducted to a minimum and to limit them insofar as possible to aliens."

This practice was continued in successive administrations....

In the early fifties, however, Attorney General J. Howard McGrath took the position that he would not approve or authorize the installation of microphone surveillances by means of trespass. This policy was quickly reversed by Attorney General Herbert Brownell in 1954 in a sweeping memorandum to FBI Director Hoover instructing him that the Bureau was indeed authorized to conduct such trespassory surveillances regardless of the fact of surreptitious entry, and without the need to first acquire the Attorney General's authorization. Such surveillance was simply authorized whenever the Bureau concluded that the "national interest" so required....

In *Katz v. United States*, 389 U.S. 347 (1967), the Supreme Court finally discarded the *Olmstead* doctrine and held that the Fourth Amendment's warrant provision did apply to electronic surveillance. The Court explicitly declined, however, to extend its holding to cases "involving the national security." 389 U.S. at 358 n.23. The next year, Congress followed suit: responding to the *Katz* case, Congress enacted the Omnibus Crime Control and Safe Streets Act (18 U.S.C. §§2510-2520). Title III of that Act established a procedure for the judicial authorization of electronic surveillance for the investigation and prevention of specified types of serious crimes and the use of the product of such surveillance in court proceedings. It prohibited wiretapping and electronic surveillance by persons other than duly authorized law enforcement officers, personnel of the Federal Communications Commission, or communication common carriers monitoring communications in the normal course of their employment.

Title III, however, disclaimed any intention of legislating in the national security area....

United States v. United States District Court (*Keith*)[1]

United States Supreme Court, 1972
407 U.S. 297

Associate Justice Lewis F. Powell Jr.

Copyright © 1986, Ken Heinen.

Mr. JUSTICE POWELL delivered the opinion of the Court. The issue before us is an important one for the people of our country and their Government. It involves the delicate question of the President's power, acting through the Attorney General, to authorize electronic surveillance in internal security matters without prior judicial approval.... This case brings the issue here for the first time. Its resolution is a matter of national concern, requiring sensitivity both to the Government's right to protect itself from unlawful subversion and attack and to the citizen's right to be secure in his privacy against unreasonable Government intrusion.

This case arises from a criminal proceeding in the United States District Court for the Eastern District of Michigan, in which the United States charged three defendants with conspiracy to destroy Government property in violation of 18 U.S.C. §371. One of the defendants, Plamondon, was charged with the dynamite bombing of an office of the Central Intelligence Agency in Ann Arbor, Michigan.

During pretrial proceedings, the defendants moved to compel the United States to disclose certain electronic surveillance information and to conduct a hearing to determine whether this information "tainted" the evidence on which the indictment was based or which the Government intended to offer at trial. In response, the Government filed an affidavit of the Attorney General, acknowledging that its agents had overheard conversations in which Plamondon had participated. The affidavit also stated that the Attorney General approved the wiretaps "to gather intelligence information deemed necessary to protect the nation from attempts of domestic organizations to attack and subvert the existing structure of the Government." The logs of the surveillance were filed in a sealed exhibit for in camera inspection by the District Court.

On the basis of the Attorney General's affidavit and the sealed exhibit, the Government asserted that the surveillance was lawful, though conducted without prior judicial approval, as a reasonable exercise of the President's power (exercised through the Attorney General) to protect the national security. The District Court held that the surveillance violated the Fourth Amendment, and ordered the Government to make full disclosure to Plamondon of his overheard conversations.

[1. This case is commonly referred to by the name of the federal district court judge who first heard it, Damon J. Keith. — Eds.]

... [T]he Court of Appeals for the Sixth Circuit ... held that the surveillance was unlawful and that the District Court had properly required disclosure of the overheard conversations....

I

Title III of the Omnibus Crime Control and Safe Streets Act, 18 U.S.C. §§2510-2520, authorizes the use of electronic surveillance for classes of crimes carefully specified in 18 U.S.C. §2516. Such surveillance is subject to prior court order. Section 2518 sets forth the detailed and particularized application necessary to obtain such an order as well as carefully circumscribed conditions for its use. The Act represents a comprehensive attempt by Congress to promote more effective control of crime while protecting the privacy of individual thought and expression. Much of Title III was drawn to meet the constitutional requirements for electronic surveillance enunciated by this Court in *Berger v. New York*, 388 U.S. 41 (1967), and *Katz v. United States*, 389 U.S. 347 (1967).

Together with the elaborate surveillance requirements in Title III, there is the following proviso, 18 U.S.C. §2511(3):

> Nothing contained in this chapter or in section 605 of the Communications Act of 1934 (48 Stat. 1143; 47 U.S.C. 605) shall limit the constitutional power of the President to take such measures as he deems necessary to protect the Nation against actual or potential attack or other hostile acts of a foreign power, to obtain foreign intelligence information deemed essential to the security of the United States, or to protect national security information against foreign intelligence activities. *Nor shall anything contained in this chapter be deemed to limit the constitutional power of the President to take such measures as he deems necessary to protect the United States against the overthrow of the Government by force or other unlawful means, or against any other clear and present danger to the structure or existence of the Government.* The contents of any wire or oral communication intercepted by authority of the President in the exercise of the foregoing powers may be received in evidence in any trial hearing, or other proceeding only where such interception was reasonable, and shall not be otherwise used or disclosed except as is necessary to implement that power. (Emphasis supplied.)

The Government relies on §2511(3). It argues that "in excepting national security surveillances from the Act's warrant requirement Congress recognized the President's authority to conduct such surveillances without prior judicial approval." The section thus is viewed as a recognition or affirmance of a constitutional authority in the President to conduct warrantless domestic security surveillance such as that involved in this case.

We think the language of §2511(3), as well as the legislative history of the statute, refutes this interpretation. The relevant language is that: "Nothing contained in this chapter ... shall limit the constitutional power of the President to take such measures as he deems necessary to protect ..." against the dangers specified. At most, this is an implicit recognition that the President does have certain powers in the specified areas. Few would doubt this, as the section refers — among other things — to protection "against actual or potential attack or other hostile acts of a foreign power." But so far as the use of the President's electronic surveillance power is concerned, the language is essentially neutral.

Section 2511(3) certainly confers no power, as the language is wholly inappropriate for such a purpose. It merely provides that the Act shall not be interpreted to limit or disturb such power as the President may have under the Constitution. In short, Congress simply left presidential powers where it found them. . . .

. . . [I]t would have been incongruous for Congress to have legislated with respect to the important and complex area of national security in a single brief and nebulous paragraph. This would not comport with the sensitivity of the problem involved or with the extraordinary care Congress exercised in drafting other sections of the Act. We therefore think the conclusion inescapable that Congress only intended to make clear that the Act simply did not legislate with respect to national security surveillances. . . .

. . . [V]iewing §2511(3) as a congressional disclaimer and expression of neutrality, we hold that the statute is not the measure of the executive authority asserted in this case. Rather, we must look to the constitutional powers of the President.

II

It is important at the outset to emphasize the limited nature of the question before the Court. This case raises no constitutional challenge to electronic surveillance as specifically authorized by Title III of the Omnibus Crime Control and Safe Streets Act of 1968. Nor is there any question or doubt as to the necessity of obtaining a warrant in the surveillance of crimes unrelated to the national security interest. Further, the instant case requires no judgment on the scope of the President's surveillance power with respect to the activities of foreign powers, within or without this country. The Attorney General's affidavit in this case states that the surveillances were "deemed necessary to protect the nation from attempts of *domestic organizations* to attack and subvert the existing structure of Government" (emphasis supplied). There is no evidence of any involvement, directly or indirectly, of a foreign power.[8]

Our present inquiry, though important, is therefore a narrow one. It addresses a question left open by *Katz*: "Whether safeguards other than prior authorization by a magistrate would satisfy the Fourth Amendment in a situation involving the national security. . . ." The determination of this question requires the essential Fourth Amendment inquiry into the "reasonableness" of the search and seizure in question, and the way in which that "reasonableness" derives content and meaning through reference to the warrant clause.

. . . [T]he President of the United States has the fundamental duty, under Art. II, §1, of the Constitution, to "preserve, protect and defend the Constitution of the United States." Implicit in that duty is the power to protect our Government against those who would subvert or overthrow it by unlawful means. In the discharge of this

---

8. Section 2511(3) refers to "the constitutional power of the President" in two types of situations: (i) where necessary to protect against attack, other hostile acts or intelligence activities of a "foreign power"; or (ii) where necessary to protect against the overthrow of the Government or other clear and present danger to the structure or existence of the Government. Although both of the specified situations are sometimes referred to as "national security" threats, the term "national security" is used only in the first sentence of §2511(3) with respect to the activities of foreign powers. This case involves only the second sentence of §2511(3), with the threat emanating — according to the Attorney General's affidavit — from "domestic organizations." Although we attempt no precise definition, we use the term "domestic organization" in this opinion to mean a group or organization (whether formally or informally constituted) composed of citizens of the United States and which has no significant connection with a foreign power, its agents or agencies. No doubt there are cases where it will be difficult to distinguish between "domestic" and "foreign" unlawful activities directed against the Government of the United States where there is collaboration in varying degrees between domestic groups or organizations and agents or agencies of foreign powers. But this is not such a case.

duty, the President — through the Attorney General — may find it necessary to employ electronic surveillance to obtain intelligence information on the plans of those who plot unlawful acts against the Government. The use of such surveillance in internal security cases has been sanctioned more or less continuously by various Presidents and Attorneys General since July 1946. . . .

Though the Government and respondents debate their seriousness and magnitude, threats and acts of sabotage against the Government exist in sufficient number to justify investigative powers with respect to them. The covertness and complexity of potential unlawful conduct against the Government and the necessary dependency of many conspirators upon the telephone make electronic surveillance an effective investigatory instrument in certain circumstances. The marked acceleration in technological developments and sophistication in their use have resulted in new techniques for the planning, commission, and concealment of criminal activities. It would be contrary to the public interest for Government to deny to itself the prudent and lawful employment of those very techniques which are employed against the Government and its law-abiding citizens. . . .

But a recognition of these elementary truths does not make the employment by Government of electronic surveillance a welcome development — even when employed with restraint and under judicial supervision. There is, understandably, a deep-seated uneasiness and apprehension that this capability will be used to intrude upon cherished privacy of law-abiding citizens. We look to the Bill of Rights to safeguard this privacy. Though physical entry of the home is the chief evil against which the wording of the Fourth Amendment is directed, its broader spirit now shields private speech from unreasonable surveillance. Our decision in *Katz* refused to lock the Fourth Amendment into instances of actual physical trespass. Rather, the Amendment governs "not only the seizure of tangible items, but extends as well to the recording of oral statements . . . without any 'technical trespass under . . . local property law.'" . . . *Katz, supra,* at 353. . . .

National security cases, moreover, often reflect a convergence of First and Fourth Amendment values not present in cases of "ordinary" crime. Though the investigative duty of the executive may be stronger in such cases, so also is there greater jeopardy to constitutionally protected speech. "Historically the struggle for freedom of speech and press in England was bound up with the issue of the scope of the search and seizure power," *Marcus v. Search Warrant,* 367 U.S. 717, 724 (1961). History abundantly documents the tendency of Government — however benevolent and benign its motives — to view with suspicion those who most fervently dispute its policies. Fourth Amendment protections become the more necessary when the targets of official surveillance may be those suspected of unorthodoxy in their political beliefs. The danger to political dissent is acute where the Government attempts to act under so vague a concept as the power to protect "domestic security." Given the difficulty of defining the domestic security interest, the danger of abuse in acting to protect that interest becomes apparent. . . .

III

As the Fourth Amendment is not absolute in its terms, our task is to examine and balance the basic values at stake in this case: the duty of Government to protect the domestic security, and the potential danger posed by unreasonable surveillance to individual privacy and free expression. If the legitimate need of Government to safeguard domestic security requires the use of electronic surveillance, the question is whether the needs of citizens for privacy and free expression may not be better protected by requiring a warrant before such surveillance is undertaken. We must also ask whether a warrant requirement would unduly frustrate the efforts of Government to protect itself from acts of subversion and overthrow directed against it.

Though the Fourth Amendment speaks broadly of "unreasonable searches and seizures," the definition of "reasonableness" turns, at least in part, on the more specific commands of the warrant clause....

... [W]here practical, a governmental search and seizure should represent both the efforts of the officer to gather evidence of wrongful acts and the judgment of the magistrate that the collected evidence is sufficient to justify invasion of a citizen's private premises or conversation. Inherent in the concept of a warrant is its issuance by a "neutral and detached magistrate." The further requirement of "probable cause" instructs the magistrate that baseless searches shall not proceed.

These Fourth Amendment freedoms cannot properly be guaranteed if domestic security surveillances may be conducted solely within the discretion of the Executive Branch.... The historical judgment, which the Fourth Amendment accepts, is that unreviewed executive discretion may yield too readily to pressures to obtain incriminating evidence and overlook potential invasions of privacy and protected speech.

It may well be that, in the instant case, the Government's surveillance of Plamondon's conversations was a reasonable one which readily would have gained prior judicial approval. But this Court "has never sustained a search upon the sole ground that officers reasonably expected to find evidence of a particular crime and voluntarily confined their activities to the least intrusive means consistent with that end." *Katz, supra*, at 356-357. The Fourth Amendment contemplates a prior judicial judgment, not the risk that executive discretion may be reasonably exercised. This judicial role accords with our basic constitutional doctrine that individual freedoms will best be preserved through a separation of powers and division of functions among the different branches and levels of Government. The independent check upon executive discretion is not satisfied, as the Government argues, by "extremely limited" post-surveillance judicial review. Indeed, post-surveillance review would never reach the surveillances which failed to result in prosecutions....

It is true that there have been some exceptions to the warrant requirement. But those exceptions are few in number and carefully delineated; in general, they serve the legitimate needs of law enforcement officers to protect their own wellbeing and preserve evidence from destruction. Even while carving out those exceptions, the Court has reaffirmed the principle that the "police must, whenever practicable, obtain advance judicial approval of searches and seizures through the warrant procedure," *Terry v. Ohio*, [392 U.S. 1, 20 (1968)].

The Government argues that the special circumstances applicable to domestic security surveillances necessitate a further exception to the warrant requirement. It is urged that the requirement of prior judicial review would obstruct the President in the discharge of his constitutional duty to protect domestic security. We are told further that these surveillances are directed primarily to the collecting and maintaining of intelligence with respect to subversive forces, and are not an attempt to gather evidence for specific criminal prosecutions. It is said that this type of surveillance should not be subject to traditional warrant requirements which were established to govern investigation of criminal activity, not ongoing intelligence gathering.

The Government further insists that courts "as a practical matter would have neither the knowledge nor the techniques necessary to determine whether there was probable cause to believe that surveillance was necessary to protect national security." These security problems, the Government contends, involve "a large number of complex and subtle factors" beyond the competence of courts to evaluate.

As a final reason for exemption from a warrant requirement, the Government believes that disclosure to a magistrate of all or even a significant portion of the information involved in domestic security surveillances "would create serious potential dangers to the national security and to the lives of informants and agents. . . . Secrecy is the essential ingredient in intelligence gathering; requiring prior judicial authorization would create a greater 'danger of leaks . . . because in addition to the judge, you have the clerk, the stenographer and some other officer like a law assistant or bailiff who may be apprised of the nature' of the surveillance." . . .

. . . There is, no doubt, pragmatic force to the Government's position.

But we do not think a case has been made for the requested departure from Fourth Amendment standards. . . . Security surveillances are especially sensitive because of the inherent vagueness of the domestic security concept, the necessarily broad and continuing nature of intelligence gathering, and the temptation to utilize such surveillances to oversee political dissent. We recognize, as we have before, the constitutional basis of the President's domestic security role, but we think it must be exercised in a manner compatible with the Fourth Amendment. In this case we hold that this requires an appropriate prior warrant procedure.

We cannot accept the Government's argument that internal security matters are too subtle and complex for judicial evaluation. Courts regularly deal with the most difficult issues of our society. There is no reason to believe that federal judges will be insensitive to or uncomprehending of the issues involved in domestic security cases. . . . If the threat is too subtle or complex for our senior law enforcement officers to convey its significance to a court, one may question whether there is probable cause for surveillance.

Nor do we believe prior judicial approval will fracture the secrecy essential to official intelligence gathering. The investigation of criminal activity has long involved imparting sensitive information to judicial officers who have respected the confidentialities involved. Judges may be counted upon to be especially conscious of security requirements in national security cases. Title III of the Omnibus Crime Control and Safe Streets Act already has imposed this responsibility on the judiciary in connection with such crimes as espionage, sabotage, and treason, §2516(1)(a) and (c), each of which may involve domestic as well as foreign security threats. Moreover, a warrant application involves no public or adversary proceedings: it is an *ex parte* request before a magistrate or judge. Whatever security dangers clerical and secretarial personnel may pose can be minimized by proper administrative measures, possibly to the point of allowing the Government itself to provide the necessary clerical assistance.

Thus, we conclude that the Government's concerns do not justify departure in this case from the customary Fourth Amendment requirement of judicial approval prior to initiation of a search or surveillance. Although some added burden will be imposed upon the Attorney General, this inconvenience is justified in a free society to protect constitutional values. Nor do we think the Government's domestic surveillance powers will be impaired to any significant degree. A prior warrant establishes presumptive validity of the surveillance and will minimize the burden of justification in post-surveillance judicial review. By no means of least importance will be the reassurance of the public generally that indiscriminate wiretapping and bugging of law-abiding citizens cannot occur.

IV

. . . [W]e do not hold that the same type of standards and procedures prescribed by Title III are necessarily applicable to this case. We recognize that domestic security surveillance may involve different policy and practical considerations from the surveillance of "ordinary crime." The gathering of security intelligence is often long range and involves the interrelation of various sources and types of information. The exact targets of such surveillance may be more difficult to identify than in surveillance operations against many types of crime specified in Title III. Often, too, the emphasis of domestic intelligence gathering is on the prevention of unlawful activity or the enhancement of the Government's preparedness for some possible future crisis or emergency. Thus, the focus of domestic surveillance may be less precise than that directed against more conventional types of crime.

Given these potential distinctions between Title III criminal surveillances and those involving the domestic security, Congress may wish to consider protective standards for the latter which differ from those already prescribed for specified crimes in Title III. Different standards may be compatible with the Fourth Amendment if they are reasonable both in relation to the legitimate need of Government for intelligence information and the protected rights of our citizens. For the warrant application may vary according to the governmental interest to be enforced and the nature of citizen rights deserving protection. . . .

. . . We . . . hold . . . that prior judicial approval is required for the type of domestic security surveillance involved in this case and that such approval may be made in accordance with such reasonable standards as the Congress may prescribe.

V

As the surveillance of Plamondon's conversations was unlawful, because conducted without prior judicial approval, the courts below correctly held that *Alderman v. United States*, 394 U.S. 165 (1969), is controlling and that it requires disclosure to the accused of his own impermissibly intercepted conversations. As stated in *Alderman*, "the trial court can and should, where appropriate, place a defendant and his counsel under enforceable orders against unwarranted disclosure of the materials which they may be entitled to inspect." 394 U.S. at 185.

The judgment of the Court of Appeals is hereby affirmed.

The CHIEF JUSTICE concurs in the result.

[The concurring opinions of DOUGLAS and WHITE, JJ., are omitted.]

NOTES AND QUESTIONS

1. *The Nature of the Privacy Interest.* Has your phone ever been tapped, or have you suspected that it was? Ever had your mail opened? Your e-mail or the history of your Internet use read by others without your permission? How did you feel (or how do you

think you would feel) upon discovering such an intrusion? Would you feel better knowing that a judge had issued a warrant to authorize it?

While acknowledging that "physical entry of the home is the chief evil" addressed by the Fourth Amendment, the Court found in *Keith*, as it had in *Katz*, that the "broader spirit" of the Amendment protects telephone conversations as well. But what is it about electronic surveillance that the Court found objectionable? Is it that a "search" of private conversations is being conducted, or is it the "convergence of First and Fourth Amendment values"? Does the privacy protected by the Court cover just governmental acquisition of personal or intimate information? By analogy, should the protection extend to information we reveal to others? *See* Chapter 23.

Arguably, a physical search may be less intrusive than a wiretap, especially if the electronic surveillance continues for weeks or months after the initial intrusion. *See Olmstead v. United States*, 277 U.S. 438, 473 (1928) (Brandeis, J., dissenting); *Berger v. New York*, 388 U.S. 41, 60 (1967).

Why is this freedom from unreasonable searches important to individuals? What purpose does it serve in society? *See generally* Alan Westin, *Privacy and Freedom* (1967).

2. *Inherent Surveillance Authority?* Does Article II, Section 1, implicitly authorize the President to conduct electronic surveillance? *See In re Neagle*, 135 U.S. 1 (1890), *supra* p. 83. Does Article II distinguish between domestic and foreign national security threats?

If the President possesses some independent constitutional authority to engage in domestic electronic surveillance, why, according to the *Keith* Court, is an exception to the warrant requirement not appropriate?

3. *The Baseline for Comparison: Ordinary Criminal (Title III) Electronic Surveillance.* Title III requires that an application for authorization to conduct electronic surveillance contain detailed information about the alleged criminal offense, the facilities and communication sought to be intercepted, the identity of the target (if known), the period of time sought for surveillance, and an explanation of whether other investigative methods have failed or why they are unlikely to succeed or are too dangerous. 18 U.S.C. §2518(1)(b)-(d) (2006). A court may issue an order for electronic surveillance only if it finds probable cause that communications related to the commission of a crime will be obtained through the surveillance. *Id.* §2518(3)(b). Can you see why intelligence agencies would seek to avoid the strictures of Title III in conducting electronic surveillance for intelligence purposes?

Title III also requires a warrant before the government may obtain access to stored communications, such as e-mail, during the first 180 days of storage. 18 U.S.C. §2703(a) (2006 & Supp. III 2009). After 180 days, the government may obtain access to stored communications pursuant to a search warrant or, after notice to the subscriber, pursuant to an administrative or grand jury subpoena or a court order. *Id.* §2703. See Chapter 23. Likewise, cell phones, display pagers, and voice pagers are protected by Title III. 18 U.S.C. §2510(1), (12) (2006).

4. *Deciding Whether a Warrant Should Issue.* Is probable cause the sole criterion for authorizing a warrant? Might it be appropriate for a magistrate to consider the extent to which the information sought is of an intimate nature? Or what uses the government intends for the information? *See* Russell D. Covey, *Pervasive Surveillance and the Future of the Fourth Amendment*, 80 Miss. L.J. 1289 (2011) (so arguing).

5. *Balancing Away the Warrant Requirement.* Does the Warrant Clause of the Fourth Amendment adequately protect privacy interests? What is the function of a "neutral and detached magistrate" in a warrant proceeding? Why did the government object to the warrant procedure for electronic surveillance in *Keith*?

Orin Kerr argues that the Warrant Clause plays only a modest role in national security investigations because courts are poorly equipped to decide whether a warrant requirement would be reasonable in the national security setting. Orin S. Kerr, *The Modest Role of the Warrant Clause in National Security Investigations*, 88 Tex. L. Rev. 1669 (2010). Professor Kerr explains that, unlike the usual Fourth Amendment case, in which police conduct a search and the court then decides whether the already executed, judicially warranted search met Fourth Amendment requirements, judges in national security investigations must decide in advance about hypothetical facts concerning hypothetical investigations, based on an unclear standard:

> Under . . . *Keith* . . . whether a warrant is required is based on whether requiring a warrant is workable, but that depends on what standard is required for obtaining a warrant. . . . [W]hat standard is required for obtaining a warrant depends on what kind of standard would make a warrant standard workable. [*Id.* at 1675-1676.]

Does Professor Kerr accurately describe the way the Warrant Clause was applied in *Keith*? Would you expect the Warrant Clause to diminish in importance in national security investigations? If so, what would take its place?

How did the *Keith* Court balance the President's Article II powers against the Fourth Amendment warrant requirement for domestic subjects? Did the Court fairly reconcile "the Government's right to protect itself from unlawful subversion and attack" with "the citizen's right to be secure in his privacy against unreasonable Government intrusion"? Should the Court have attached more importance to the fact that a magistrate's role could be performed more efficiently by after-the-fact judicial review where surveillance abuses are alleged?

6. *Warrantless Surveillance "To Save American Lives."* In December 2005, the *New York Times* revealed the existence of a four-year, large-scale warrantless electronic surveillance program that intercepted communications of some U.S. citizens. James Risen & Eric Lichtblau, *Bush Lets U.S. Spy on Callers Without Courts*, N.Y. Times, Dec. 16, 2005. At a White House press conference, President Bush offered this explanation for the warrantless surveillance:

> . . . We know that a two-minute phone conversation between somebody linked to al Qaeda here and an operative overseas could lead directly to the loss of thousands of lives. To save American lives, we must be able to act fast and to detect these conversations so that we can prevent new attacks.
>
> So, consistent with U.S. law and the Constitution, I authorized the interception of international communications of people with known links to al Qaeda and related terrorist organizations. . . .
>
> . . . I've reauthorized this program more than 30 times since the September 11th attacks, and I intend to do so for so long as our nation . . . faces the continuing threat of an enemy that wants to kill American citizens. [Press Conference of the President (Dec. 19, 2005).]

Assuming, arguendo, that Congress has enacted no applicable statute, would you agree, based on *Keith*, that the program described by the President is constitutional? Other aspects of this program are considered in Chapter 22.

7. *Domestic vs. Foreign Threats.* Justice Powell's interpretation of §2511(3) may have been crucial to the outcome of the case. His willingness to draw a sharp distinction between a "domestic organization" and "foreign" activities in the United States became the predicate for establishing the Fourth Amendment warrant requirement for "domestic" national security investigations. Why is the power to protect "domestic security" viewed with greater skepticism by the Court than the power to protect against foreign perils? Are the two concepts really different? Are foreign threats to national security necessarily greater than domestic ones? Does §2511(3) clearly reflect such a sharp distinction in the origin of national security threats?

Justice Powell also concluded that §2511(3) "is essentially neutral" regarding presidential power. Do you agree? Consider the provision's last sentence.

C.   A FOREIGN INTELLIGENCE EXCEPTION?

In *Keith*, Justice Powell suggested that national security wiretaps may not have to meet all the Fourth Amendment requirements applicable in criminal investigations, but he did not specify what alternative processes might be appropriate in such cases. Nor did the Court refer to the constitutional requirements for other forms of surveillance, such as searches of the home and person. The Court also emphasized that *Keith* did not involve any foreign power, but was strictly a case involving "domestic security."

Meanwhile, the agencies within the intelligence community had, since their inception after World War II, been developing their own guidelines for national security surveillance. After *Keith*, several lower courts considered the applicability of the Fourth Amendment to surveillance to obtain foreign intelligence.

. . . The Fifth Circuit in *United States v. Brown*, 484 F.2d 418 (5th Cir. 1973), *cert. denied*, 415 U.S. 960 (1974), upheld the legality of a surveillance in which the defendant, an American citizen, was incidentally overheard as a result of a warrantless wiretap authorized by the Attorney General for foreign intelligence purposes. The court found that on the basis of "the President's constitutional duty to act for the United States in the field of foreign affairs, and his inherent power to protect national security in the conduct of foreign affairs . . . the President may constitutionally authorize warrantless wiretaps for the purpose of gathering foreign intelligence." [484 F.2d at 426.]

In *United States v. Butenko*, 494 F.2d 593 (3d Cir. 1974) (en banc), *cert. denied sub nom. Ivanov v. United States*, 419 U.S. 881 (1974), the Third Circuit similarly held that electronic surveillance conducted without a warrant would be lawful so long as the primary purpose was to obtain foreign intelligence information. The court found that such surveillance would be reasonable under the Fourth Amendment without a warrant even though it might involve the overhearing of conversations.

However, in *Zweibon v. Mitchell*, 516 F.2d 594 (D.C. Cir. 1975), *cert. denied*, 425 U.S. 944 (1976), the Circuit Court of Appeals for the District of Columbia, in the course of an opinion requiring that a warrant must be obtained before a wiretap is installed on a domestic organization that is neither the agent of, nor acting in collaboration with, a foreign power, questioned whether any national security exception to the warrant requirement would be constitutionally permissible.

Although the holding of *Zweibon* was limited to the case of a domestic organization without ties to a foreign power, the plurality opinion of the court—in legal analysis closely patterned on *Keith*—concluded "that an analysis of the policies implicated by foreign security surveillance indicates that, absent exigent circumstances, all warrantless electronic surveillance is unreasonable and therefore unconstitutional." [*Senate Report No. 604, supra* p. 557, at 14, 15.]

Note that the Supreme Court declined to hear the appeals in each of these cases.

Zweibon was a suit for damages by members of the Jewish Defense League (JDL) for unlawful electronic surveillance. Although the JDL is a U.S. organization, JDL protest actions directed against Soviet facilities inside the United States risked a significant foreign relations problem with the Soviet Union. Despite the fact that "Soviet officials vigorously and continuously protested these activities, for which they held the United States Government responsible," 516 F.2d at 608, 609, the D.C. Circuit refused to rule that this foreign affairs tension was cause to waive the Fourth Amendment warrant requirement. *Id.* at 614. A similar result was reached in *Berlin Democratic Club v. Rumsfeld*, 410 F. Supp. 144 (D.D.C. 1976), where a warrant was required to wiretap Americans living in West Germany despite Department of Defense arguments about dangers to United States forces and to American foreign policy. *Id.* at 157.

While these lower court decisions about a possible foreign intelligence exception to the warrant requirement concerned wiretaps to collect foreign intelligence, the FBI also conducted warrantless physical searches. The Church Committee found that

[b]efore 1966, the FBI conducted over two hundred "black bag jobs." These warrantless surreptitious entries were carried out for intelligence purposes *other than* microphone installation, such as physical search and photographing or seizing documents.

. . . [T]here is no indication that the FBI informed any Attorney General about its use of "black bag jobs."

Surreptitious entries were performed by teams of FBI agents with special training in subjects such as "lock studies." Their missions were authorized in writing by FBI Director Hoover or his deputy, Clyde Tolson. A "Do Not File" procedure was utilized, under which most records of surreptitious entries were destroyed soon after an entry was accomplished.

The use of surreptitious entries against domestic targets dropped drastically after J. Edgar Hoover banned "black bag jobs" in 1966. . . . [S. Select Comm. to Study Governmental Operations with Respect to Intelligence Activities (Church Committee), *Intelligence Activities and the Rights of Americans*, S. Rep. No. 94-755, bk. III, at 355 (1976).]

One such black bag job was challenged in the following case, in which the government raised the defense of a foreign intelligence exception to the warrant requirement.

United States v. Ehrlichman

United States District Court, District of Columbia, 1974
376 F. Supp. 29, *aff'd*, 546 F.2d 910 (D.C. Cir. 1976),
cert. denied, 429 U.S. 1120 (1977)

GESELL, J. Five defendants stand indicted for conspiring to injure a Los Angeles psychiatrist [Dr. Lewis Fielding] in the enjoyment of his Fourth Amendment rights by entering his offices without a warrant for the purpose of obtaining the doctor's medical records relating to one of his patients, a Daniel Ellsberg, then under Federal indictment for revealing top secret documents. They now claim that broad pretrial discovery into the alleged national security aspects of this case is essential to the presentation of their defense, in that it will establish (1) that the break-in was legal under the Fourth Amendment because the President authorized it for reasons of national security, and (2) that even in the absence of such authorization the national security information available to the defendants at that time led them to the good-faith, reasonable belief that the break-in was legal and justified in the national interest. The Court has carefully considered these assertions, which have been fully briefed and argued over a two-day period, and finds them to be unpersuasive as a matter of law. . . .

The Fourth Amendment protects the privacy of citizens against unreasonable and unrestrained intrusion by Government officials and their agents. It is not theoretical. It lies at the heart of our free society. As the Supreme Court recently remarked, "no right is held more sacred." *Terry v. Ohio*, 392 U.S. 1, 9 (1968). Indeed, the American Revolution was sparked in part by the complaints of the colonists against the issuance of writs of assistance, pursuant to which the King's revenue officers conducted unrestricted, indiscriminate searches of persons and homes to uncover contraband. James Otis' famous argument in Lechmere's Case, challenging the writ as a "monster of oppression" and a "remnant of Star Chamber tyranny," sowed one of the seeds of the coming rebellion. The Fourth Amendment was framed against this background; and every state in the Union, by its own constitution, has since reinforced the protections and the security which that Amendment was designed to achieve.

Thus the security of one's privacy against arbitrary intrusion by governmental authorities has proven essential to our concept of ordered liberty. When officials have attempted to justify law enforcement methods that ignore the strictures of this Amendment on grounds of necessity, such excuses have proven fruitless, for the Constitution brands such conduct as lawless, irrespective of the end to be served. Throughout the years the Supreme Court of the United States, regardless of changes in its composition or contemporary issues, has steadfastly applied the Amendment to protect a citizen against the warrantless invasion of his home or office, except under carefully delineated emergency circumstances. No right so fundamental should now, after the long struggle against governmental trespass, be diluted to accommodate conduct of the very type the Amendment was designed to outlaw.

The break-in charged in this indictment involved an unauthorized entry and search by agents of the Executive branch of the Federal Government. It is undisputed that no warrant was obtained and no Magistrate gave his approval. Moreover, none of the traditional exceptions to the warrant requirement are claimed and none existed; however desirable the break-in may have appeared to its instigators, there is no indication that it had to be carried out quickly, before a warrant could have been obtained. On the contrary, it had been meticulously planned over a period of more than a month. The search of Dr. Fielding's office was therefore clearly illegal under the unambiguous mandate of the Fourth Amendment.

Defendants contend that even though the Fourth Amendment would ordinarily prohibit break-ins of this nature, the President has the authority, by reason of his special responsibilities over foreign relations and national defense, to suspend its requirements, and that he did so in this case. Neither assertion is accurate. Many of the landmark Fourth Amendment cases in this country and in England concerned citizens accused of disloyal or treasonous conduct, for history teaches that such suspicions foster attitudes within a government that generate conduct inimical to individual rights. See *United States v. United States District Court*, 407 U.S. 297, 314 (1972). The judicial response to such Executive overreaching has been consistent and emphatic: the Government must comply with the strict constitutional and statutory limitations on trespassory searches and arrests even when known foreign agents are involved. To hold otherwise, except under the most exigent circumstances, would be to abandon the Fourth Amendment to the whim of the Executive in total disregard of the Amendment's history and purpose.

Defendants contend that, over the last few years, the courts have begun to carve out an exception to this traditional rule for purely intelligence-gathering searches deemed necessary for the conduct of foreign affairs. However, the cases cited are carefully limited to the issue of wiretapping, a relatively nonintrusive search, *United States v. Butenko*, 494 F.2d 593 (3d Cir. 1974); *United States v. Brown*, 484 F.2d 418 (5th Cir. 1973); *Zweibon v. Mitchell*, 363 F. Supp. 936 (D.D.C. 1973), and the Supreme Court has reserved judgment in this unsettled area. *United States v. United States District Court*, 407 U.S. 297, 322 n.20 (1972). The Court cannot find that this recent, controversial judicial response to the special problem of national security wiretaps indicates an intention to obviate the entire Fourth Amendment whenever the President determines that an American citizen, personally innocent of wrongdoing, has in his possession information that may touch upon foreign policy concerns.[4] Such a doctrine, even in the context of purely information-gathering searches, would give the Executive a blank check to disregard the very heart and core of the Fourth Amendment and the vital privacy interests that it protects. . . .

The facts presented pretrial lead the Court to conclude as a matter of law that the President not only lacked the authority to authorize the Fielding break-in but also that he did not in fact give any specific directive permitting national security break-ins, let alone this particular intrusion. The President has repeatedly and publicly denied prior knowledge or authorization of the Fielding break-in, and the available transcripts of the confidential tape recordings support that claim. . . . [The evidence reflected] intense Presidential concern with the need to plug the national security leaks and a belief that Dr. Ellsberg might be involved, but no specific reference either to Dr. Fielding or to trespassory searches. . . .

Defendants adopt the fall-back position that even if the President did not specifically authorize the Fielding break-in, he properly delegated to one or more of the defendants or unindicted co-conspirators the authority to approve national security break-ins. Of course, since the President had no such authority in the first place, he could not have delegated it to others. Beyond this, however, the Court rejects the contention that the President could delegate his alleged power to suspend constitutional rights to non-law enforcement officers in the vague, informal, inexact terms noted above. Even in the wiretap cases the courts have stressed the fact that the

---

4. The doctrine of the President's inherent authority as "the sole organ of the nation in its external relations," 10 Annals of Cong. 613 (1800) (remarks of John Marshall), has been developed by a series of Supreme Court decisions dealing with the President's power to enter into international agreements and to prohibit commercial contracts which impede American foreign policy. *United States v. Curtiss-Wright Export Corp.*, 299 U.S. 304 (1936). None of these cases purport to deal with the constitutional rights of American citizens or with Presidential action in defiance of congressional legislation. When such issues have arisen, Executive assertions of inherent authority have been soundly rejected. See *Kent v. Dulles*, 357 U.S. 116 (1958); *Youngstown Sheet & Tube Co. v. Sawyer*, 343 U.S. 579 (1952).

President had specifically delegated the authority over "national security" wiretaps to his chief legal officer, the Attorney General, who approved each such tap. *See, e.g., Katz v. United States,* 389 U.S. 347, 364 (1967) (White, J., concurring). Whatever accommodation is required between the guarantees of the Fourth Amendment and the conduct of foreign affairs, it cannot justify a casual, ill-defined assignment to White House aides and part-time employees granting them an uncontrolled discretion to select, enter and search the homes and offices of innocent American citizens without a warrant. *Cf. Ex parte Milligan,* 71 U.S. (4 Wall.) 2 (1866); *Ex parte Merryman,* 17 Fed. Cas. p. 144, 151 (No. 9,487) (C.C. Md. 1861)....

Defendants' motions for discovery are granted to the extent set forth above and are denied in all other respects. The motion for dismissal because of the danger of exposing national security information is denied.

NOTES AND QUESTIONS

1. *Comparing Searches and Electronic Surveillance.* Is physical entry of the home more threatening to civil liberties than a wiretap? Microphone surveillance at one time required entry to install the device, which would, like a wiretap, transmit all conversations, including those not subject to the investigation. If a physical search is controlled, it will take less time and may focus only on material relevant to the investigation. Yet for many of us, invasion of our physical space is more threatening than the prospect of electronic surveillance. Why is that so?

2. *Accountability for the Exception.* While the D.C. Circuit Court affirmed the conviction in *United States v. Ehrlichman,* 546 F.2d 910 (D.C. Cir. 1976), *cert. denied,* 429 U.S. 1120 (1977), the panel was more circumspect than Judge Gesell. The court merely held that no "national security" exception to the warrant requirement could be invoked without specific authorization by the President or Attorney General. *Id.* at 925. Judge Wilkey elaborated:

The danger of leaving delicate decisions of propriety and probable cause to those actually assigned to ferret out "national security" information is patent, and is indeed illustrated by the intrusion undertaken in this case, without any more specific Presidential direction than that ascribed to Henry II vexed with Becket.[68] As a constitutional matter, if Presidential approval is to replace judicial approval for foreign intelligence gathering, the personal authorization of the President — or his alter ego for these matters, the Attorney General — is necessary to fix accountability and centralize responsibility for insuring the least intrusive surveillance necessary and preventing zealous officials from misusing the President's prerogative. [*Id.* at 926.]

3. *Executive (or Congressional) Approval as a Warrant Substitute?* Would the substitution of the President's or Attorney General's approval for a search compensate for the loss of the warrant procedure? The Attorney General at the time of the Fielding break-in was John N. Mitchell, who was subsequently sent to prison for perjury and conspiracy in connection with efforts to cover up the burglary of the Democratic National

---

68. Attributed as "Who will free me from this turbulent priest?" [Thomas Becket, the Archbishop of Canterbury, was murdered in 1170 by followers of Henry II, who are said to have interpreted Henry's remarks as a royal command. — Eds.]

Committee headquarters at the Watergate in Washington. The President was Richard M. Nixon, who was named an unindicted co-conspirator in the same affair. *See United States v. Haldeman*, 559 F.2d 31, 51 (D.C. Cir. 1976). Would presidential or attorney general approval of a search be a lawful substitute for probable cause if Congress approved such a regime by statute? *See* Chapter 21.

4. *A Domestic Intelligence Exception?* At the time of the break-in, Ellsberg had been indicted for disclosing the *Pentagon Papers* (a classified account of American involvement in the Vietnam War) to reporters. See *supra* p. 269 and *infra* p. 1280. Ehrlichman and his co-defendants argued that "the search was legal because [it was] undertaken pursuant to a delegated Presidential power to authorize such a search in the field of foreign affairs." *Ehrlichman*, 546 F.2d at 913. However, there was no accusation that Ellsberg or his psychiatrist had any relationship to a foreign power. What does Judge Wilkey's dictum, *supra* Note 2, suggest about the parameters of any such "national security" exception to the warrant requirement?

Consider again the warrantless surveillance program described by President Bush, *supra* p. 567. Does the *Ehrlichman* decision change your view about the constitutionality of the more recent surveillance program, again assuming no controlling legislative authority?

5. *Applying the Exception to Other Searches.* If there is some "national security" exception to the warrant requirement, is there a principled basis for limiting the exception to electronic surveillance? *See United States v. Ehrlichman*, 546 F.2d at 938 (Leventhal, J., concurring); David S. Eggert, Note, *Executive Order 12,333: An Assessment of the Validity of Warrantless National Security Searches*, 1983 Duke L.J. 611, 627-628. *See also* Banks & Bowman, *supra* p. 554, at 67 ("In light of the potentially greater intrusiveness of electronic surveillance, it may be reasonable to expect greater executive discretion to conduct warrantless searches than warrantless wiretaps."). In addition to the degree of intrusion, what factors should be taken into account in deciding whether the warrant requirement applies? *See Id.* at 67-68.

Should place matter? Although the Supreme Court in *Katz* famously proclaimed that the Fourth Amendment protects people, not places, even in *Katz* the defendant's use of a telephone booth became a "temporarily private place whose momentary occupants' expectations of freedom from intrusion are recognized as reasonable." 389 U.S. at 361 (Harlan, J., concurring). The distinction between people and places may thus be blurry, perpetuated by Justice Harlan's reasonable expectation of privacy test. Can you think of a better test that takes into account the nature of the intrusion, the type of privacy at risk, and the government's interests in acquiring and perhaps using the information?

Unlike a physical search, most computer searches involve the remote collection of digital electronic data. Is a computer search therefore a "search" under the Fourth Amendment? Under what circumstances are computer data "seized," and when would such a search or seizure be "reasonable"? Computer searches "challenge several of the basic assumptions underlying Fourth Amendment doctrine. Computers are like containers in a physical sense, homes in a virtual sense, and vast warehouses in an informational sense." Orin S. Kerr, *Searches and Seizures in a Digital World*, 119 Harv. L. Rev. 531, 533 (2005). Which perspective do you find most helpful in thinking about application of the Fourth Amendment to Internet and computer searches?

United States v. Truong Dinh Hung

United States Court of Appeals, Fourth Circuit, 1980
629 F.2d 908, *cert. denied,* 454 U.S. 1144 (1982)

WINTER, J. Truong Dinh Hung, more familiarly known as David Truong, and Ronald Humphrey were convicted of espionage, conspiracy to commit espionage and several espionage-related offenses for transmitting classified United States government information to representatives of the government of the Socialist Republic of Vietnam. In these appeals, they seek reversal of their convictions because of warrantless surveillance and searches....

We hold that the warrantless searches and surveillance did not violate the Fourth Amendment....

David Truong, a Vietnamese citizen and son of a prominent Vietnamese political figure, came to the United States in 1965. At least since his arrival in the United States, Truong has pursued an active scholarly and political interest in Vietnam and the relationship between Vietnam and the United States. In 1976, Truong met Dung Krall, a Vietnamese-American, the wife of an American Naval Officer, who had extensive contacts among the Vietnamese community in Paris. Truong persuaded Krall to carry packages for him to Vietnamese in Paris. The recipients were representatives of the Socialist Republic of Vietnam at the time of the 1977 Paris negotiations between that country and the United States. The packages contained copies of diplomatic cables and other classified papers of the United States government dealing with Southeast Asia. Truong procured the copies from Ronald Humphrey, an employee of the United States Information Agency, who obtained the documents surreptitiously, copied them, removed their classification markings and furnished the copies to Truong. In a statement given after his arrest, Humphrey said that his motive was to improve relations between the North Vietnamese government and the United States so that he could be reunited with a woman whom he loved who was a prisoner of the North Vietnamese government.

Unknown to Truong, Krall was a confidential informant employed by the CIA and the FBI. Krall kept these agencies fully informed of Truong's activities and presented the packages Truong had given her to the FBI for inspection, copying and approval before she carried the documents to Paris. The FBI permitted this operation to continue, while monitoring it closely, from approximately September, 1976, until January 31, 1978.

When the intelligence agencies first learned that Truong was transmitting classified documents to Paris, they were understandably extremely anxious to locate Truong's source for his data. Toward that end, the government conducted a massive surveillance of Truong. Truong's phone was tapped and his apartment was bugged from May, 1977 to January, 1978. The telephone interception continued for 268 days and every conversation, with possibly one exception, was monitored and virtually all were taped. The eavesdropping device was operative for approximately 255 days and it ran continuously. No court authorization was ever sought or obtained for the installation and maintenance of the telephone tap or the bug. The government thus ascertained that Humphrey was providing Truong with the copies of secret documents. This leak of sensitive information of course ceased when Truong and Humphrey were arrested on January 31, 1978....

The defendants raise a substantial challenge to their convictions by urging that the surveillance conducted by the FBI violated the Fourth Amendment and that all the evidence uncovered through that surveillance must consequently be suppressed. As has been stated, the government did not seek a warrant for the eavesdropping on Truong's phone conversations or the bugging of his apartment. Instead, it relied upon a "foreign intelligence" exception to the Fourth Amendment's warrant requirement. In the area of foreign intelligence, the government contends, the President may authorize surveillance without seeking a judicial warrant because of his constitutional prerogatives in the area of foreign affairs. On this basis, the FBI sought and received approval for the surveillance from the President's delegate, the Attorney General. This approval alone, according to the government, is constitutionally sufficient to authorize foreign intelligence surveillance such as the surveillance of Truong. . . .

. . . Although the Supreme Court has never decided the issue which is presented to us, it formulated the analytical approach which we employ here in an analogous case, *United States v. United States District Court* (*Keith*), 407 U.S. 297 (1972). . . .

For several reasons, the needs of the executive are so compelling in the area of foreign intelligence, unlike the area of domestic security, that a uniform warrant requirement would, following *Keith,* "unduly frustrate" the President in carrying out his foreign affairs responsibilities. First of all, attempts to counter foreign threats to the national security require the utmost stealth, speed, and secrecy. A warrant requirement would add a procedural hurdle that would reduce the flexibility of executive foreign intelligence initiatives, in some cases delay executive response to foreign intelligence threats, and increase the chance of leaks regarding sensitive executive operations.

More importantly, the executive possesses unparalleled expertise to make the decision whether to conduct foreign intelligence surveillance, whereas the judiciary is largely inexperienced in making the delicate and complex decisions that lie behind foreign intelligence surveillance. The executive branch, containing the State Department, the intelligence agencies, and the military, is constantly aware of the nation's security needs and the magnitude of external threats posed by a panoply of foreign nations and organizations. On the other hand, while the courts possess expertise in making the probable cause determination involved in surveillance of suspected criminals, the courts are unschooled in diplomacy and military affairs, a mastery of which would be essential to passing upon an executive branch request that a foreign intelligence wiretap be authorized. Few, if any, district courts would be truly competent to judge the importance of particular information to the security of the United States or the "probable cause" to demonstrate that the government in fact needs to recover that information from one particular source.

Perhaps most crucially, the executive branch not only has superior expertise in the area of foreign intelligence, it is also constitutionally designated as the preeminent authority in foreign affairs. The President and his deputies are charged by the constitution with the conduct of the foreign policy of the United States in times of war and peace. See *United States v. Curtiss-Wright Corp.*, 299 U.S. 304 (1936). Just as the separation of powers in *Keith* forced the executive to recognize a judicial role when the President conducts domestic security surveillance, so the separation of powers requires us to acknowledge the principal responsibility of the President for foreign affairs and concomitantly for foreign intelligence surveillance.

In sum, because of the need of the executive branch for flexibility, its practical experience, and its constitutional competence, the courts should not require the executive to secure a warrant each time it conducts foreign intelligence surveillance.[4]

However, because individual privacy interests are severely compromised any time the government conducts surveillance without prior judicial approval, this foreign intelligence exception to the Fourth Amendment warrant requirement must be carefully limited to those situations in which the interests of the executive are paramount. First, the government should be relieved of seeking a warrant only when the object of the search or the surveillance is a foreign power, its agent or collaborators. In such cases, the government has the greatest need for speed, stealth, and secrecy, and the surveillance in such cases is most likely to call into play difficult and subtle judgments about foreign and military affairs. When there is no foreign connection, the executive's needs become less compelling; and the surveillance more closely resembles the surveillance of suspected criminals, which must be authorized by warrant. Thus, if the government wishes to wiretap the phone of a government employee who is stealing sensitive documents for his personal reading or to leak to a newspaper, for instance, the absence of a foreign connection and the importance of individual privacy concerns contained within the Fourth Amendment lead to a requirement that the executive secure advance judicial approval for surveillance....

Second . . . the executive should be excused from securing a warrant only when the surveillance is conducted "primarily" for foreign intelligence reasons. We think that the district court adopted the proper test, because once surveillance becomes primarily a criminal investigation, the courts are entirely competent to make the usual probable cause determination, and because, importantly, individual privacy interests come to the fore and government foreign policy concerns recede when the government is primarily attempting to form the basis for a criminal prosecution. We thus reject the government's assertion that, if surveillance is to any degree directed at gathering foreign intelligence, the executive may ignore the warrant requirement of the Fourth Amendment.

The defendants urge that the "primarily" test does not go far enough to protect privacy interests. They argue that the government should be able to avoid the warrant requirement only when the surveillance is conducted "solely" for foreign policy reasons. The proposed "solely" test is unacceptable, however, because almost all foreign intelligence investigations are in part criminal investigations. Although espionage prosecutions are rare, there is always the possibility that the targets of the investigation will be prosecuted for criminal violations. Thus, if the defendants' "solely" test were adopted, the executive would be required to obtain a warrant almost every time it undertakes foreign intelligence surveillance, and, as indicated above, such a

---

4. Since the surveillance was conducted in this case, Congress has enacted the Foreign Intelligence Surveillance Act of 1978, 50 U.S.C. §1801 et seq. . . . While the Act suggests that it is possible for the executive branch to conduct at least some types of foreign intelligence surveillance while being subject to a warrant requirement, the complexity of the statute also suggests that the imposition of a warrant requirement, beyond the constitutional minimum described in this opinion, should be left to the intricate balancing performed in the course of the legislative process by Congress and the President. The elaborate structure of the statute demonstrates that the political branches need great flexibility to reach the compromises and formulate the standards which will govern foreign intelligence surveillance. Thus, the Act teaches that it would be unwise for the judiciary, inexpert in foreign intelligence, to attempt to enunciate an equally elaborate structure for core foreign intelligence surveillance under the guise of a constitutional decision. Such an attempt would be particularly ill-advised because it would not be easily subject to adjustment as the political branches gain experience in working with a warrant requirement in the foreign intelligence area.

requirement would fail to give adequate consideration to the needs and responsibilities of the executive in the foreign intelligence area.

In this case, the district court concluded that on July 20, 1977, the investigation of Truong had become primarily a criminal investigation. Although the Criminal Division of the Justice Department had been aware of the investigation from its inception, until summer the Criminal Division had not taken a central role in the investigation. On July 19 and July 20, however, several memoranda circulated between the Justice Department and the various intelligence and national security agencies indicating that the government had begun to assemble a criminal prosecution. . . .

Therefore, because there was more than enough evidence to indicate that Truong had collaborated with the Vietnamese government and because the district court did not err in choosing July 20 as the date when the investigation became primarily a criminal investigation, we do not disturb the decision of the district court to exclude all evidence obtained through the surveillance after July 20 but to permit the government to introduce evidence secured through the surveillance before July 20.

Because the Fourth Amendment warrant requirement is a critical constitutional protection of individual privacy, this discussion should conclude by underscoring the limited nature of this foreign intelligence exception to the warrant requirement which we recognize in the instant case. The exception applies only to foreign powers, their agents, and their collaborators. Moreover, even these actors receive the protection of the warrant requirement if the government is primarily attempting to put together a criminal prosecution. . . .

NOTES AND QUESTIONS

1. *The "Primary Purpose" Doctrine.* The court in *Truong* concluded that the standard for deciding the constitutionality of warrantless foreign intelligence surveillance that eventually became a criminal investigation was whether the "primary purpose" of the search was in fact to obtain foreign intelligence information. At what point does an investigation change from "primarily" foreign intelligence collection to "primarily" law enforcement? Does the "primary purpose" rule adequately accommodate the competing interests? Although FISA had been enacted by the time of the *Truong* decision, the surveillance of Truong was conducted before FISA and therefore not governed by its terms. However, the "primary purpose" standard became influential in construing the FISA authorization for intelligence surveillance. See Chapter 21.

2. *Deciding Reasonableness.* The court also found that intercepting Truong's phone calls and listening to conversations with visitors to Truong's apartment were "reasonable" efforts to locate the source of the purloined documents. 629 F.2d at 916-917. In light of the court's conclusion that no warrant was required for at least part of the surveillance, does it necessarily follow that the surveillance was reasonable? According to what criteria should reasonableness be determined?

3. *Package Searches.* Although the discussion of surveillance in *Truong* is not specifically directed to either electronic or non-electronic surveillance as such, the court did independently consider the constitutionality of the searches of packages Truong sent to Paris with Krall. The search of a letter and package conducted with executive

authorization but without a warrant before the July 20 date at which the surveillance became, in the court's view, criminal in nature, was treated as governed by a foreign intelligence exception to the warrant requirement. *Id.* at 916-917. Another package searched without either the authorization of the Attorney General or a warrant was not covered by a foreign intelligence exception to the warrant requirement but was nonetheless constitutional, according to the court, because Truong had no reasonable expectation of privacy in the package. *Id.*

4. *Reconciling the Cases?* Is there any way to square the reasoning of the court in *Truong* with the holding of the Supreme Court in *Keith?* With the holding by Judge Gesell in *Ehrlichman?* Does the *Truong* court's reasoning apply equally to inspection of sealed parcels and to installation of surveillance cameras in a target's workplace or home?

5. *Less Intrusive Surveillance.* First and Fourth Amendment interests have not always received such extensive judicial protection where arguably less intrusive information collection techniques are employed. For example, in an area that is open to visual surveillance, the monitoring of beeper signals from a radio transmitter placed in contraband material and picked up by a police radio receiver does not trigger Fourth Amendment protections, because the target has no legitimate expectation of privacy. *United States v. Knotts*, 460 U.S. 276, 284-285 (1983). The same result applies when the police use the beeper signal to monitor movements, so long as visual surveillance could have performed the monitoring. *Id.* at 285.

What are the implications of this extension of *Katz*—that someone who "knowingly exposes" her movements to others in a public place has no reasonable expectation of privacy—when others, including police or intelligence officials, take note of or record those movements? *Katz v. United States*, 389 U.S. 347, 351 (1967). Does this reduced expectation insulate from constitutional challenge the use of evolving technologies such as video cameras, video tracking devices, radio transmitting devices, visual magnification, and biometrics and face recognition for surveillance in public places? *See* Marc Jonathan Blitz, *Video Surveillance and the Constitution of Public Space: Fitting the Fourth Amendment to a World That Tracks Image and Identity*, 82 Tex. L. Rev. 1349, 1375-1398 (2004). Can you say which places are public and which are private? Is it conceivable that the growing use of evolving technologies to provide physical, or visual surveillance of individuals may become so pervasive and intense that it will constitute a Fourth Amendment search? *See* Afsheen John Radsan, *The Case for Stewart over Harlan on 24/7 Physical Surveillance*, 88 Tex. L. Rev. 1475, 1480 (2010) (so arguing).

In *Laird v. Tatum*, 408 U.S. 1, 10 (1972), the Supreme Court dismissed on standing grounds a complaint against an Army program that investigated civil disturbances by collecting personal information about individuals and organizations. See *infra* p. 1161. *See also Socialist Workers Party v. Attorney Gen.*, 510 F.2d 253 (2d Cir. 1974) (approving undercover FBI surveillance of convention of Young Socialists of America). *But see Philadelphia Yearly Meeting of the Religious Soc'y of Friends v. Tate*, 519 F.2d 1335 (3d Cir. 1975) (approving photography and compilation of records on political demonstrators but not the sharing of information with private employers or broadcasters). Constitutional protections generally have not been extended to investigations based on the use of informants and the examination of financial records held by third parties. *See* John Elliff, *The Attorney General's Guidelines for*

FBI Investigations, 69 Cornell L. Rev. 785, 788-789 (1984). Should the courts be more solicitous of individual rights in these cases?

6. *Effect of New Technologies on Fourth Amendment Law.* Does changing technology affect what privacy deserves constitutional protection? In *Kyllo v. United States,* 533 U.S. 27 (2001), decided a few months before 9/11, the police used thermal imaging technology to measure the heat radiating from the exterior walls of a private home to verify suspicions that high-intensity lamps were being used to grow marijuana indoors. Because the sense-enhancing technology permitted intrusion into the home that would not otherwise have been possible without physical intrusion, and because the thermal imaging technique is not in general public use, the Court found that the homeowner had a reasonable expectation of privacy that was violated. *Id.* at 34-35. What are the implications of the holding of *Kyllo* today, when weapons of mass destruction (WMD) terrorism threats may be monitored by nanotech sensors and scanning devices not yet in general use that may help prevent deployment of a WMD in a major city? *See* Covey, *supra* p. 566.

In 2010, the Supreme Court explained that the *Katz* Court "relied on its own knowledge and experience" in finding a reasonable expectation of privacy in a telephone booth, *City of Ontario v. Quon,* 130 S. Ct. 2619 (2010), but cautioned that "[i]t is not so clear that courts at present are on so sure a ground." *Id.* at 2629. The Court noted that

> Rapid changes in the dynamics of communication and information transmission are evident not just in the technology itself but in what society accepts as proper behavior. . . .
> . . . Cell phone and text message communications are so pervasive that some persons may consider them to be essential means or necessary instruments for self-expression, even self-identification. [*Id.* at 2629-2630.]

In the 1980s, the Supreme Court decided two cases involving the use of a government-installed locating device — a beeper — to monitor a suspect's location. In *United States v. Knotts,* 460 U.S. 276 (1983), no warrant was required when the surveillance revealed the location of the beeper in a public place, while in *United States v. Karo,* 468 U.S. 705 (1984), a warrant was required when the beeper was traced to the inside of a home. As we write, the equivalent issue is the use of global positioning system (GPS) devices for surveillance. GPS "is a satellite-based technology that reveals information about the location, speed, and direction of a targeted subject." Renee McDonald Hutchins, *Tied Up in Knotts? GPS Technology and the Fourth Amendment,* 55 UCLA L. Rev. 409, 414 (2007). Law enforcement authorities may use GPS technology for real-time tracking of targets in a range of settings. Are GPS devices sufficiently different from beepers that their use should require a traditional warrant? *See* Alison M. Smith, *Law Enforcement Use of Global Positioning (GPS) Devices to Monitor Motor Vehicles: Fourth Amendment Considerations* (Cong. Res. Serv. R41663), Feb. 28, 2011.

In many cities today, public cameras are ubiquitous, and video surveillance in stores, banks, mass transit facilities, and other places where crowds gather is now commonplace. Do individuals have important privacy interests in these public places that are threatened by the new surveillance systems? What predictions can you make about constitutional challenges to these new surveillance technologies? *See* Radsan, *supra,* 88 Tex. L. Rev. at 1490-1493; Covey, *supra.*

Congressional Authority for Foreign Intelligence Surveillance

21

Communications and surveillance technologies have undergone explosive growth since the digital and dot-com revolutions of the 1980s and 1990s. Both ordinary and Internet communications can be intercepted, and cell phone calls can be traced to the phone's location. Hidden recorders may preserve conversations, while parabolic microphones capture voices at long distances. Video surveillance cameras permit government officials to monitor public areas by closed-circuit television. Global positioning system (GPS) devices and electronic toll systems permit remote, 24/7 tracing of an individual's movements. Computer-driven scanners can search through millions of e-mail messages in a heartbeat. Emerging nanotechnology and bio-engineering will expand further the horizons of the government's capabilities for surveillance.

By providing the means to watch and listen to people and to trace their movements, electronic surveillance can help to detect and prevent terrorism and other security threats. It also may help to find those responsible for security-related crimes after the fact.

Yet unlike physical searches for particular information or things, electronic surveillance records everything a target says or does. Especially when undertaken over a long period on a continual basis, electronic surveillance casts a wide and open-ended net, capturing data that may be at best irrelevant and at worst deeply personal.

The Constitution contains two provisions that can guard against government abuses of such advanced technology. The Fourth Amendment was included in the Bill of Rights to counter any tendency toward the kind of intimidation practiced by the English Crown against its citizens. The First Amendment was added as a bulwark against government intrusions that could dampen political expression.

This chapter turns from the evolution of Fourth Amendment and national security surveillance law in the courts, discussed in Chapter 20, to statutory authorization for foreign intelligence surveillance in the Foreign Intelligence Surveillance Act (FISA), 50 U.S.C. §§1801-1881g (2006 & Supp. III 2009), as amended by Pub. L. No. 111-259, §801, 124 Stat. 2654, 2746 (2010). In Part A, we introduce the core FISA requirements and procedures for electronic surveillance and physical searches. (We separately examine FISA authorizations for pen registers, trap and trace devices, and the collection of business records in Chapter 23.) In Part B, we consider the tension — and, for a time, the "wall" — between surveillance to collect evidence for criminal law enforcement and surveillance to collect foreign intelligence. Finally, in Part C, we briefly assess trends in FISA electronic and physical surveillance.

A.   THE FOREIGN INTELLIGENCE SURVEILLANCE ACT (FISA): CORE REQUIREMENTS AND PROCEDURES

Two events prompted congressional enactment of FISA in 1978. First, the Supreme Court decision in *Keith* ended by asserting that "Congress may wish to consider protective standards for [domestic security surveillance]...which differ from those already prescribed for specified crimes in Title III." *United States v. United States District Court (Keith)*, 407 U.S. 297, 322 (1972), *supra* p. 559. Second, in addition to the Watergate scandal in 1973, the early 1970s saw startling revelations of illegal spying and other activities by U.S. intelligence agencies, including the FBI and CIA, and by the IRS and the military. These agencies sought to target and disrupt politically active domestic groups (principally civil rights and anti-war organizations), see *supra* pp. 534-559, and they engaged in widespread warrantless surveillance. The Senate Select Committee to Study Government Operations with Respect to Intelligence Activities, known as the Church Committee, for its chairman Senator Frank Church, summarized the effects of these domestic intelligence abuses in a 1976 report:

> ...FBI headquarters alone has developed over 500,000 domestic intelligence files, and these have been augmented by additional files at FBI Field Offices. The FBI opened 65,000 of these domestic intelligence files in 1972 alone. In fact, substantially more individuals and groups are subject to intelligence scrutiny than the number of files would appear to indicate, since typically, each domestic intelligence file contains information on more than one individual or group, and this information is readily retrievable through the FBI General Name Index.
>
> The number of Americans and domestic groups caught in the domestic intelligence net is further illustrated by the following statistics:
>
> - Nearly a quarter of a million first class letters were opened and photographed in the United States by the CIA between 1953-1973, producing a CIA computerized index of nearly one and one-half million names.
> - At least 130,000 first class letters were opened and photographed by the FBI between 1940-1966 in eight U.S. cities.
> - Some 300,000 individuals were indexed in a CIA computer system and separate files were created on approximately 7,200 Americans and over 100 domestic groups during the course of CIA's Operation CHAOS (1967-1973).
> - Millions of private telegrams sent from, to, or through the United States were obtained by the National Security Agency from 1947 to 1975 under a secret arrangement with three United States telegraph companies.
> - An estimated 100,000 Americans were the subjects of United States Army intelligence files created between the mid-1960's and 1971.
> - Intelligence files on more than 11,000 individuals and groups were created by the Internal Revenue Service between 1969 and 1973 and tax investigations were started on the basis of political rather than tax criteria.
> - At least 26,000 individuals were at one point catalogued on an FBI list of persons to be rounded up in the event of a "national emergency."

[S. Select Comm. to Study Government Operations with Respect to Intelligence Activities (Church Committee), *Intelligence Activities and the Rights of Americans*, S. Rep. No. 94-755, bk. II, at 6-7 (1976).]

Most of these surveillance and collection abuses were rationalized as foreign intelligence gathering. When Congress finally responded to the Supreme Court's invitation in *Keith*, therefore, it enacted standards for *foreign intelligence surveillance* inside the United States, not domestic security surveillance. In *United States v. Duggan*, 743 F.2d 59 (2d Cir. 1984), the court opined that

> Congress passed FISA to settle what it believed to be the unresolved question of the applicability of the Fourth Amendment warrant requirement to electronic surveillance for foreign intelligence purposes, and to "remove any doubt as to the lawfulness of such surveillance." H.R. Rep. 1283, pt. I, 95th Cong., 2d Sess. 25 (1978) ("House Report"). FISA reflects both Congress's "legislative judgment" that the court orders and other procedural safeguards laid out in the Act "are necessary to insure that electronic surveillance by the U.S. Government within this country conforms to the fundamental principles of the fourth amendment," S. Rep. No. 701, 95th Cong., 2d Sess. 13, *reprinted in* 1978 U.S. Code Cong. & Ad. News 3973, 3982 ("Senate Report 95-701"), and its attempt to fashion a "secure framework by which the Executive Branch may conduct legitimate electronic surveillance for foreign intelligence purposes within the context of this Nation's commitment to privacy and individual rights." S. Rep. No. 604, 95th Cong., 1st Sess. 15, *reprinted in* 1978 U.S. Code Cong. & Ad. News 3904, 3916 ("Senate Report 95-604"). [743 F.2d at 73.]

Domestic security surveillance, on the other hand, was by default left subject to the existing Title III criminal law enforcement framework.

Consider how FISA applied to the defendants in the following case.

United States v. Rosen

United States District Court, Eastern District of Virginia, 2006
447 F. Supp. 2d 538

ELLIS, District Judge. Defendants, Steven J. Rosen and Keith Weissman, are charged . . . with one count of conspiring to communicate national defense information to persons not entitled to receive it, in violation of 18 U.S.C. §793(d), (e) and (g). More specifically, Count One . . . alleges that between April 1999 and continuing until August 2004, Rosen and Weissman along with alleged co-conspirator Lawrence Franklin, then an employee of the Department of Defense ("DOD"), were engaged in a conspiracy to communicate information relating to the national defense to those not entitled to receive it. According to the superseding indictment, Franklin and certain other unnamed government officials with authorized possession of classified national defense information communicated that information to Rosen and Weissman, who were employed at the time as lobbyists for the American-Israel Public Affairs Committee (AIPAC). It is further alleged that Rosen and Weissman then communicated the information received from their government sources to members of the media, other foreign policy analysts, and certain foreign officials, none of whom were authorized to receive this information. . . .

In the course of its investigation of the alleged conspiracy, the government sought and obtained orders issued by the Foreign Intelligence Surveillance Court ("FISC") pursuant to the Foreign Intelligence Surveillance Act ("FISA"), 50 U.S.C. §1801 *et seq.*, authorizing certain physical searches and electronic surveillance. As the investigation pertained to national security, these applications and orders were classified. Because the government intends to offer evidence obtained or derived from physical searches and electronic surveillance authorized by these orders, defendants seek by motion (1) to obtain disclosure of the classified applications submitted to the FISC, the FISC's orders, and related materials, and/or (2) to suppress the evidence obtained or derived from any searches or surveillance conducted pursuant to the issued FISA orders. . . .

I.

FISA, enacted in 1978, was Congress's response to three related concerns: (1) the judicial confusion over the existence, nature and scope of a foreign intelligence exception to the Fourth Amendment's warrant requirement that arose in the wake of the Supreme Court's 1972 decision in *United States v. United States District Court*, 407 U.S. 297 (1972); (2) the Congressional concern over perceived Executive Branch abuses of such an exception;[2] and (3) the felt need to provide the Executive Branch with an appropriate means to investigate and counter foreign intelligence threats.[3] FISA accommodates these concerns by establishing a detailed process the Executive Branch must follow to obtain orders allowing it to collect foreign intelligence information "without violating the rights of citizens of the United States." *United States v. Hammoud*, 381 F.3d 316, 332 (4th Cir. 2004) (en banc), *vacated on other grounds*, 543 U.S. 1097 (2005), *reinstated in pertinent part*, 405 F.3d 1034 (2005). Although originally limited to electronic surveillance, FISA's coverage has now been expanded to include physical searches, as well. . . .[4]

FISA's detailed procedure for obtaining orders authorizing electronic surveillance or physical searches of a foreign power or an agent of a foreign power begins with the government's filing of an *ex parte*, under seal application with the FISC.[5] Such an application must be approved by the Attorney General and must include certain specified information. *See* 50 U.S.C. §§1804(a) and 1823(a). A FISC judge considering the application may also require the submission of additional information necessary to make the requisite findings under §§1805(a) and 1824(a).

---

2. *See* S. Rep. No. 95-604(I), at 7, 1978 U.S.C.C.A.N. 3904, 3908 [hereinafter S. Judiciary Comm. Rep.] ("This legislation is in large measure a response to the revelations that warrantless electronic surveillance in the name of national security has been seriously abused.").

3. *See generally* William C. Banks and M.E. Bowman, *Executive Authority for National Security Surveillance,* 50 Am. U. L. Rev. 1, 75-76 (2000) (describing the impetus for FISA).

4. *See* Intelligence Authorization Act for Fiscal Year 1995, Pub. L. No. 103-359, 108 Stat. 3443 (1994) (codified as amended at 50 U.S.C. §1821 *et seq.*). And, in 1998, Congress further amended FISA to create slightly different procedures for authorizing the use of pen registers and trap and trace devices for foreign intelligence information, *see* Intelligence Authorization Act for Fiscal Year 1999, Pub. L. No. 105-272, 112 Stat. 2405 (1998) (codified as amended at 50 U.S.C. §1841 *et seq.*), and to allow the executive branch access to business records for foreign intelligence and international terrorism investigations. *See* 18 U.S.C. §§1861-63. The parties' dispute involves only electronic surveillance and physical searches conducted pursuant to FISA.

5. The FISC consists of eleven district court judges selected by the Chief Justice from at least seven judicial circuits and serving staggered seven year terms. *See* 50 U.S.C. §1803(a). At least three of the FISC's judges must reside within twenty miles of Washington, D.C. *Id.* In the unlikely event that a FISA application is denied by a judge of the FISC, the government may seek review of such denial in the Foreign Intelligence Surveillance Court of Review (FISCR), and if necessary, in the Supreme Court of the United States. *See* 50 U.S.C. §1803(b).

After review of the application, a single judge of the FISC must enter an *ex parte* Order granting the government's application for electronic surveillance or a physical search of a foreign power or an agent of a foreign power provided the judge makes certain specific findings, including most importantly, that on the basis of the facts submitted by the applicant there is probable cause to believe that—

(1) the target of the electronic surveillance or physical search is a foreign power or an agent of a foreign power, except that no United States person may be considered a foreign power or an agent of a foreign power solely upon the basis of activities protected by the First Amendment to the Constitution of the United States; and

(2) for electronic surveillance, each of the facilities or places at which the electronic surveillance is directed is being used, or is about to be used, by a foreign power or an agent of a foreign power; or

(3) for physical searches, the premises or property to be searched is owned, used, possessed by, or is in transit to or from an agent of a foreign power or a foreign power.

See 50 U.S.C. §§1805(a) and 1823(a).[6] If the FISC judge's findings reflect that the government has satisfied the statute's requirements, the judge must issue an order approving the surveillance or search. Such an order must describe the target, the information sought, and the means of acquiring such information. *See* 50 U.S.C. §§1805(c)(1) and 1824(c)(1). The order must also set forth the period of time during which the electronic surveillance or physical searches are approved, which is generally ninety days or until the objective of the electronic surveillance or physical search has been achieved. *See* 50 U.S.C. §§1805(e)(1) and 1824(d)(1). Applications for a renewal of the order must generally be made upon the same basis as the original application and require the same findings by the FISC. *See* 50 U.S.C. §§1805(e)(2) and 1824(d)(2).

Although FISA is chiefly directed to obtaining "foreign intelligence information,"[7] the Act specifically contemplates cooperation between federal authorities conducting electronic surveillance and physical searches pursuant to FISA and federal law enforcement officers investigating clandestine intelligence activities. In this respect,

---

6. In addition to these probable cause findings, the FISC judge must also find that: (1) the President has authorized the Attorney General to approve applications for electronic surveillance or physical searches for foreign intelligence information; (2) that the application has been made by a Federal officer and approved by the Attorney General; (3) that the proposed minimization procedures meet the respective definitions of minimization procedures for electronic surveillance and physical searches; and (4) that the application contains all statements and certifications required by 50 U.S.C. §1804 for electronic surveillance and 50 U.S.C. §1823 for physical searches and, if the target is a United States person, the certification or certifications are not clearly erroneous on the basis of the statement made under sections 1804(a)(7)(E) and 1823(a)(7)(E) of title 18 and any other information furnished under sections 1804(d) and 1823(c) of this title. *See* 50 U.S.C. §§1805(a) and 1823(a).

7. FISA defines "foreign intelligence information" as—

(1) information that relates to, and if concerning a United States person is necessary to, the ability of the United States to protect against—

(A) actual or potential attack or other grave hostile acts of a foreign power or an agent of a foreign power;

(B) sabotage or international terrorism by a foreign power or an agent of a foreign power; or

(C) clandestine intelligence activities by an intelligence service or network of a foreign power or by an agent of a foreign power; or

(2) information with respect to a foreign power or foreign territory that relates to, and if concerning a United States person is necessary to—

(A) the national defense or the security of the United States; or

(B) the conduct of the foreign affairs of the United States.

50 U.S.C. §1801(e).

FISA explicitly allows the use of evidence derived from FISA surveillance and searches in criminal prosecutions. *See* 50 U.S.C. §§1806(k) and 1825(k).

If the Attorney General approves the use of evidence collected pursuant to FISA in a criminal prosecution, and the government intends to use or disclose FISA evidence at the trial of an "aggrieved person,"[8] the government must first notify the aggrieved person and the district court that the government intends to disclose or use the FISA evidence. *See* 50 U.S.C. §§1806(c) and 1825(d). On receiving such notification, an aggrieved person may seek to suppress any evidence derived from FISA surveillance or searches on the grounds that: (1) the evidence was unlawfully acquired; or (2) the electronic surveillance or physical search was not conducted in conformity with the Order of authorization or approval. *See* 50 U.S.C. §§1806(e) and 1825(f). And, if an aggrieved person moves to suppress FISA evidence or to obtain FISA material, then upon the filing of an affidavit by the Attorney General stating under oath that disclosure of such material would harm national security, the district court must review the FISA warrant applications and related materials *in camera* and *ex parte* to determine whether the surveillance or search "of the aggrieved person was lawfully authorized and conducted." 50 U.S.C. §§1806(f) and 1825(g).

This review is properly *de novo,* especially given that the review is *ex parte* and thus unaided by the adversarial process. Thus, the government's contention here that a reviewing district court must accord the FISC's probable cause determination "substantial deference" cannot be sustained in light of the Fourth Circuit's clear contrary statement on the issue. But the government is correct that the certifications contained in the applications should be "presumed valid." *See* 50 U.S.C. §1805(a)(5) (applying "clearly erroneous" standard to factual averments contained in certification when the target is a United States person)....

II.

At the threshold, defendants seek disclosure of the FISA applications, orders, and related materials at issue in this case so they may effectively participate in the review process. On this point FISA is clear: It allows a reviewing court to disclose such materials "only where such disclosure is necessary to make an accurate determination of the legality of the surveillance." 50 U.S.C. §1806(f). Defendants claim this condition is met, by arguing (1) that the FISC's determination that they were agents of a foreign power was surely wrong; and (2) that evidence of the government's evident failure to comply with FISA's minimization procedures requires disclosure. Neither argument is persuasive....

Review of the FISA applications, orders and other materials in this case presented none of the concerns that might warrant disclosure to defendants. The FISA dockets contained no facial inconsistencies, nor did they disclose any reason to doubt any of the representations made by the government in its applications.

---

8. FISA defines an "aggrieved person" with respect to electronic surveillance as "a person who is the target of an electronic surveillance or any other person whose communications or activities were subject to electronic surveillance." 50 U.S.C. §1801(k). With respect to physical searches, FISA similarly defines an "aggrieved person" as a "person whose premises, property, information, or material is the target of physical search or any other person whose premises, property, information, or material was subject to physical search." 50 U.S.C. §1821(2).

Likewise, the targets of the surveillance are precisely defined. Finally, although defendants claim that the discovery obtained from the government contains a significant amount of non-foreign intelligence information, this contention relies upon an inordinately narrow view of what constitutes foreign intelligence information, and therefore is unavailing. For these reasons, and given the government's legitimate national security interest in maintaining the secrecy of the information contained in the FISA applications, disclosure of the FISA materials to defendants is not warranted in this case.

III. . . .

Defendants' attack on the lawfulness of the FISA surveillance in this case focuses chiefly on two issues: (1) whether the FISC had probable cause to believe that the targets of the sanctioned surveillance were "agents of a foreign power," as required by FISA, and (2) whether there was proper compliance with the minimization procedures subsequent to the surveillance. Review of the FISA material confirms that both of these issues must be resolved in favor of the lawfulness of the surveillance.

Defendants' necessarily speculative contention that the FISC must have erred when it found probable cause to believe that the targets are agents of a foreign power is without merit. An agent of a foreign power is defined by the statute, in pertinent part, as any person who —

(A) knowingly engages in clandestine intelligence gathering activities for or on behalf of a foreign power, which activities involve or may involve a violation of the criminal statutes of the United States;

(B) pursuant to the direction of an intelligence service or network of a foreign power, knowingly engages in any other clandestine intelligence activities for or on behalf of such power, which activities involve or are about to involve a violation of the criminal statutes of the United States; . . . or

(E) knowingly aids or abets any person in the conduct of activities described in [the subparagraphs above] or knowingly conspires with any person to engage in activities described in [the subparagraphs above].

50 U.S.C. §1801(b)(2). Although the phrase "clandestine intelligence gathering activities" is not defined in FISA, the legislative history demonstrates that the drafters viewed these "activities" in light of the criminal espionage laws, including 18 U.S.C. §§793 and 794, and considered that such "activities" would include, for example, "collection or transmission of information or material that is not generally available to the public." *See* S. Rep. No. 95-701, at 21-22 (1978), 1978 U.S.C.C.A.N. 3973, 3990-91 [hereinafter S. Intelligence Rep.]. . . .

Importantly, FISA is clear that in determining whether there is probable cause to believe that a potential target of FISA surveillance or a FISA search is an agent of a foreign power, the FISC judge may not consider a United States person an agent of a foreign power "*solely* upon the basis of activities protected by the First Amendment." 305(a) (emphasis added). From this plain language, it follows that the determination may rely in part on activities protected by the First provided the determination also relies on activities not protected by the ment. This issue received extensive treatment in the legislative history, ent with the statute's plain language, makes clear that First Amendment activities cannot form the *sole* basis for concluding a U.S. person is an agent of a foreign power. The following excerpt from the legislative history illustrates this point:

> The Bill is not intended to authorize electronic surveillance when a United States person's activities, even though secret and conducted for a foreign power, consist entirely of lawful acts such as lobbying or the use of confidential contacts to influence public officials, directly or indirectly, through the dissemination of information. Individuals exercising their right to lobby public officials or to engage in political dissent from official policy may well be in contact with representatives of foreign governments and groups when the issues concern foreign affairs or international economic matters.
>
> They must continue to be free to communicate about such issues and to obtain information or exchange views with representatives of foreign governments or with foreign groups, free from any fear that such contact might be the basis for probable cause to believe they are acting at the direction of a foreign power thus triggering the government's power to conduct electronic surveillance.

See S. Intelligence Rep. at 29.

The legislative history makes equally clear, however, that this protection extends only to the "*lawful* exercise of First Amendment rights of speech, petition, assembly and association." *Id.* (emphasis added). Similarly, the House Report (Intelligence Committee) emphasized that FISA "would not authorize surveillance of ethnic Americans who *lawfully* gather political information and perhaps even *lawfully* share it with the foreign government of their national origin." *See In re Sealed Case,* 310 F.3d 717, 739 (FISCR 2002) (emphasis added) (quoting H. Rep. No. 95-1283, at 40). For example, electronic surveillance might be appropriate if there is probable cause to believe that—

> foreign intelligence services [are] hid[ing] behind the cover of some person or organization in order to influence American political events and deceive Americans into believing that the opinions or influence are of domestic origin and initiative and such deception is willfully maintained in violation of the Foreign Agents Registration Act.

S. Intelligence Rep. at 29. Thus, if the FISC judge has probable cause to believe that the potential target is engaged in *unlawful* activities in addition to those protected by the First Amendment, the FISC may authorize surveillance of a U.S. person.

In this respect, it is important to emphasize the significant difference between FISA's probable cause requirement and the government's ultimate burden to prove the existence of criminal activity beyond a reasonable doubt. Indeed, the Fourth Circuit has described probable cause in this context as "a fluid concept—turning on the assessment of probabilities in particular factual contexts—not readily, or even usefully, reduced to a neat set of rules." *United States v. Hammoud,* 381 F.3d [316 (4th Cir. 2004),] at 332 (upholding probable cause finding that Hammoud was an agent of Hizballah). Furthermore, "[i]n evaluating whether probable cause exists, it is the task of the issuing judge 'to make a practical, common-sense decision, whether, given all the circumstances set forth in the affidavit, there is a fair probability' that the search will be fruitful." *Id.* (quoting *Illinois v. Gates,* 462 U.S. 213, 238 (1983)); *see also Mason v. Godinez,* 47 F.3d 852, 855 (7th Cir. 1995) ("Probable cause means more than bare suspicion but less than absolute certainty that a search will be fruitful."). And, in making the probable cause determination, FISA permits a judge to "consider past activities of the target, as well as facts and circumstances relating to current or future activities of the target." 50 U.S.C. §1805(b). Furthermore, with respect to those U.S. persons suspected of involvement in clandestine intelligence activities, the probable cause determination "does not necessarily require a showing of an imminent violation of criminal law" because "Congress clearly intended a lesser showing of probable cause for these activities than that applicable to ordinary cases." *In re Sealed Case,* 310 F.3d at 738. Illustrative of this intent is FISA's description of clandestine intelligence activities as those that "involve or *may* involve a violation of the criminal statutes of the United States." 50 U.S.C. §1801(b)(2)(A); *see In re Sealed Case,* 310 F.3d at 738. As FISA's drafters made clear: "The term 'may involve' not only requires less information regarding the crime involved, but also permits electronic surveillance at some point prior to the time when a crime sought to be prevented, as for example, the transfer of classified documents, actually occurs." *In re Sealed Case,* 310 F.3d at 738 (quoting H. Rep. No. 95-1283, at 40). Thus, while the statute is intended to avoid permitting electronic surveillance solely on the basis of First Amendment activities, it plainly allows a FISC judge to issue an order allowing the surveillance or physical search if there is probable cause to believe that the target, even if engaged in First Amendment activities, may also be involved in unlawful clandestine intelligence activities, or in knowingly aiding and abetting such activities. In these circumstances, the fact that a target is also involved in protected First Amendment activities is no bar to electronic surveillance pursuant to FISA.

A thorough review of the FISA dockets in issue confirms that the FISC had ample probable cause to believe that the targets were agents of a foreign power quite apart from their First Amendment lobbying activities. While the defendants' lobbying activities are generally protected by the First Amendment, willful violations of §793 are not, and as is demonstrated by the allegations contained in the superseding indictment, the FISC had probable cause to believe that such violations had occurred in this case.

Defendants' second argument in support of their motion is that the government failed to follow the applicable minimization procedures. In this regard, it is true that once the electronic surveillance or the physical search has been approved, the government must apply the specific minimization procedures contained in the application to the FISC. These minimization procedures are "designed to protect, as far as reasonable, against the acquisition, retention, and dissemination of nonpublic information which is not foreign intelligence information." *In re Sealed Case,* 310 F.3d 717, 731 (FISCR 2002). While the specific minimization procedures for each application are classified, they must meet the definition of minimization procedures under §1801(h) for electronic surveillance and §1821(4) for physical searches. FISA minimization procedures include, in pertinent part—

> (1) specific procedures adopted by the Attorney General that are reasonably designed in light of the purpose and technique of the particular surveillance or search, to minimize the acquisition and retention, and prohibit the dissemination, of nonpublicly available information concerning unconsenting United States persons consistent with the need of the United States to obtain, produce, and disseminate foreign intelligence information;
>
> (2) procedures that require that nonpublicly available information, which is not foreign intelligence information, shall not be disseminated in a manner that identifies any United States person, without such person's consent, unless such person's identity is necessary to understand foreign intelligence information or assess its importance;

(3) notwithstanding paragraphs (1) and (2), procedures that allow for the retention and dissemination of information that is evidence of a crime which has been, is
being, or is about to be committed and that is to be retained or disseminated for law
enforcement purposes.

See 50 U.S.C. §§1801(h) and 1821(4). Congress intended these minimization procedures to act as a safeguard for U.S. persons at the acquisition, retention and dissemination phases of electronic surveillance and searches. *See* S. Intelligence Rep. at 39.
Thus, for example, minimization at the acquisition stage is designed to insure that the
communications of non-target U.S. persons who happen to be using a FISA target's
telephone, or who happen to converse with the target about non-foreign intelligence
information, are not improperly disseminated. *See id.* Similarly, minimization at the
retention stage is intended to ensure that "information acquired, which is not necessary for obtaining, producing, or disseminating foreign intelligence information, be
destroyed where feasible." *See In re Sealed Case,* 310 F.3d at 731 (quoting H. Rep.
No. 95-1283, at 56). Finally, the dissemination of foreign intelligence information
"needed for an approved purpose . . . should be restricted to those officials with a
need for such information." *Id.* As the Foreign Intelligence Surveillance Court of
Review has recently made clear, these procedures do not prohibit the sharing of
foreign intelligence information between FBI intelligence officials and criminal prosecutors when there is evidence of a crime. *Id.*

FISA's minimization procedures are meant to parallel the minimization procedures of Title III, which courts have sensibly construed as not requiring the
total elimination of innocent conversation. *See* S. Intelligence Rep. at 39 (citing *United
States v. Bynum,* 485 F.2d 490, 500 (2d Cir. 1973), *cert. denied,* 423 U.S. 952 (1975)).[15]
On the contrary, "[i]n assessing the minimization effort, the Court's role is to determine whether 'on the whole the agents have shown a high regard for the right of
privacy and have done all they reasonably could to avoid unnecessary intrusion.'"
Id. at 39-40 (quoting *United States v. Tortorello,* 480 F.2d 764 (2d Cir.), *cert. denied,* 414
U.S. 866 (1973)). Thus, "[a]bsent a charge that the minimization procedures have
been disregarded completely, the test of compliance is 'whether a good faith effort to
minimize was attempted.'" *Id.* (quoting *United States v. Armocida,* 515 F.2d 29, 44 (3d
Cir. 1975)).

Obviously, the extent of the government's minimization will depend largely on
its construction of the term "foreign intelligence information." And in this respect,
"foreign intelligence information" includes, among other things, "information that
relates to, and if concerning a United States person is necessary to, the ability of the
United States to protect against . . . clandestine intelligence activities by an intelligence service or network of a foreign power or by an agent of a foreign power." 50
U.S.C. §1801(e). Acknowledging the inherent difficulty in determining whether
something is related to clandestine activity, courts have construed "foreign intelligence information" broadly and sensibly allowed the government some latitude in its

---

15. Title III's minimization procedures provide, in pertinent part, that:

Every order and extension thereof shall contain a provision that the authorization to intercept shall
be executed as soon as practicable, shall be conducted in such a way as to minimize the interception
of communications not otherwise subject to interception under this chapter, and must terminate
upon attainment of the authorized objective, or in any event in thirty days.

See 18 U.S.C. §2518(5).

determination of what is foreign intelligence information. As the Fourth Circuit pointed out, "[i]t is not always immediately clear" whether a particular conversation must be minimized because "[a] conversation that seems innocuous on one day may later turn out to be of great significance, particularly if the individuals involved are talking in code." *Hammoud*, 381 F.3d at 334. For this reason, "when the government eavesdrops on clandestine groups . . . investigators often find it necessary to intercept all calls in order to record possible code language or oblique references to the illegal scheme." *United States v. Truong*, 629 F.2d 908, 917 (4th Cir. 1980). This latitude was intended by FISA's drafters who understood that it may be necessary to "acquire, retain and disseminate information concerning . . . the known contacts" of a U.S. person engaged in clandestine intelligence activities even though some of those contacts will invariably be innocent of any wrong-doing. H. Rep. No. 95-1283, at 58.

Given the breadth of the term "foreign intelligence information" in the context of investigating clandestine intelligence activities and the rule of reason that applies to the government's obligation to minimize non-pertinent information, defendants' motion to suppress for failure to properly minimize must be denied. The *ex parte, in camera* review of the FISA dockets discloses that any failures to minimize properly the electronic surveillance of the defendants were (i) inadvertent, (ii) disclosed to the FISC on discovery, and (iii) promptly rectified. . . .

NOTES AND QUESTIONS

a.   Title III Warrants for Ordinary Criminal Investigations

The general standard for searches in criminal investigations is set out in Federal Rule of Criminal Procedure 41. Among other things, Rule 41 permits warrants for a search and seizure of property that constitutes evidence of or is related to the commission of a crime. Rule 41 also requires that the target receive a copy of the warrant and an inventory of seized property, and that the investigator show "reasonable cause" for serving the warrant at night rather than in daylight.

As you read the following Notes and Questions, consider how FISA orders for electronic surveillance or physical searches are different, and why. After reading *Rosen*, would you say that FISA supplies a constitutionally adequate substitute for the traditional law enforcement warrant? What advantages does FISA provide for intelligence officials? What drawbacks are there to the FISA process, from the investigators' point of view? If FISA had not been enacted, how and pursuant to what authority would investigators have learned about the alleged criminal activities of the co-conspirators charged in *Rosen*? To what extent does the legality of FISA surveillance turn on whether the objective of the investigation is a criminal prosecution?

b.   The Scope of FISA Electronic Surveillance and Physical Searches

1. *Foreign Intelligence Information.* Review the definition of "foreign intelligence information" quoted in *Rosen, supra* p. 584. "International terrorism," which forms part of that definition, is itself defined in FISA to include activities that—

(1) involve violent acts or acts dangerous to human life that . . . would be a criminal violation if committed within the jurisdiction of the United States or any State;

(2) appear to be intended
   (A) to intimidate or coerce a civilian population;
   (B) to influence the policy of a government by intimidation or coercion; or
   (C) to affect the conduct of a government by assassination or kidnapping; and
(3) occur totally outside the United States, or transcend national boundaries in terms of the means by which they are accomplished, the persons they appear intended to coerce or intimidate, or the locale in which their perpetrators operate or seek asylum. [50 U.S.C. §1801(c).]

Can you think of some kinds of information that investigators of possible terrorism would be interested in having that could not be collected pursuant to FISA?

2. *Electronic Surveillance.* The form of the electronic surveillance used in *Rosen* was not specified. However, FISA defines four categories of electronic surveillance, some of which go beyond conventional telephone wiretaps and hidden microphones:

(f) "Electronic surveillance" means—
   (1) the acquisition by an electronic, mechanical, or other surveillance device of the contents of any wire or radio communication sent by or intended to be received by a particular, known United States person who is in the United States, if the contents are acquired by intentionally targeting that United States person, under circumstances in which a person has a reasonable expectation of privacy and a warrant would be required for law enforcement purposes;
   (2) the acquisition by an electronic, mechanical, or other surveillance device of the contents of any wire communication to or from a person in the United States, without the consent of any party thereto, if such acquisition occurs in the United States...;
   (3) the intentional acquisition by an electronic, mechanical, or other surveillance device of the contents of any radio communication, under circumstances in which a person has a reasonable expectation of privacy and a warrant would be required for law enforcement purposes, and if both the sender and all intended recipients are located within the United States; or
   (4) the installation or use of an electronic, mechanical, or other surveillance device in the United States for monitoring to acquire information, other than from a wire or radio communication, under circumstances in which a person has a reasonable expectation of privacy and a warrant would be required for law enforcement purposes. [50 U.S.C. §1801(f)(1)-(4).]

Does this definition cover surveillance by hidden microphones installed in a person's home or office? What about a listening device in a person's car? Is video surveillance covered? *See United States v. Koyomejian,* 946 F.2d 1450, 1451 (9th Cir. 1991), *aff'd in part, rev'd in part,* 970 F.2d 536 (9th Cir. 1992) (en banc), *cert. denied,* 506 U.S. 1005 (1992) (technique is covered).

3. *The Geographical Scope of FISA Electronic Surveillance.* Are there geographical limits to the communications subject to FISA electronic surveillance? Does FISA cover the surveillance of communications from Afghanistan to the United States? From the United States to Afghanistan? From one city to another within Afghanistan? If not the last, why do you think Congress did not require FISA authorization for such communications? Upon what authority would such surveillance be conducted?

4. *Physical Searches.* A "physical search" under FISA involves a "physical intrusion within the United States into premises or property . . . under circumstances in which a person has a reasonable expectation of privacy and a warrant would be required for law enforcement purposes." 50 U.S.C. §1821(5). What do you suppose counts as a "physical intrusion"? See *supra* p. 579, discussing *Kyllo v. United States*, 533 U.S. 27 (2001). The substantive provisions for physical searches track those for electronic surveillance. The procedures are somewhat different. A physical search may be approved "for the period necessary to achieve its purpose, or for ninety days, whichever is less." 50 U.S.C. §1824(d)(1). But a search may continue for up to one year if it is directed against a foreign power," or up to 120 days if the target is an agent of a foreign power. *Id.* §1824(d)(1)(A) and (B). Unlike the usual procedure for a search pursuant to a warrant, FISA does not require that agents knock before entry, supply notice of the search, particularize the object of the search, or inventory what is found for the target. The difference is based on practical considerations:

> Physical searches to gather foreign intelligence information depend upon stealth. If the targets of such searches discover that the United States Government had obtained significant information about their activities, those activities would likely be altered, rendering the information useless. [William F. Brown & Americo R. Cinquegrana, *Warrantless Physical Searches for Foreign Intelligence Purposes: Executive Order 12,333 and the Fourth Amendment,* 35 Cath. L. Rev. 97, 131 (1985).]

Does this explanation provide constitutional justification for either the FISA procedure or a wholly untethered warrantless search? *See* Daniel J. Malooly, *Physical Searches Under FISA: A Constitutional Analysis,* 35 Am. Crim. L. Rev. 411, 420-423 (1998).

5. *Who May Be Targeted?* In an espionage prosecution, it may be easy to see how the target of FISA surveillance falls within the definition of "agent of a foreign power." How do you suppose these determinations are made in national security or counterterrorism investigations? In addition to the portions of definitions reproduced in *Rosen,* FISA sets out two kinds of potential targets:

§1801. Definitions.

As used in this subchapter:
(a) "Foreign power" means—
(1) a foreign government or any component thereof, whether or not recognized by the United States;
(2) a faction of a foreign nation or nations, not substantially composed of United States persons;
(3) an entity that is openly acknowledged by a foreign government or governments to be directed and controlled by such foreign government or governments;
(4) a group engaged in international terrorism or activities in preparation therefor;
(5) a foreign-based political organization, not substantially composed of United States persons; or
(6) an entity that is directed and controlled by a foreign government or governments.
(b) "Agent of a foreign power" means—
(1) any person other than a United States person, who—
(A) acts in the United States as an officer or employee of a foreign power, or as a member of a foreign power as defined in subsection (a)(4) of this section;

(B) acts for or on behalf of a foreign power which engages in clandestine intelligence activities in the United States contrary to the interests of the United States, when the circumstances of such person's presence in the United States indicate that such person may engage in such activities in the United States, or when such person knowingly aids or abets any person in the conduct of such activities or knowingly conspires with any person to engage in such activities; or

(C) engages in international terrorism or activities in preparation therefore [*sic*]; or

(2) any person who— . . .

(C) knowingly engages in sabotage or international terrorism, or activities that are in preparation therefore [*sic*], or on behalf of a foreign power;

(D) knowingly enters the United States under a false or fraudulent identity for or on behalf of a foreign power or, while in the United States, knowingly assumes a false or fraudulent identity for or on behalf of a foreign power. . . .

Can you now describe the categories of targets that may be subjected to electronic surveillance or a physical search pursuant to FISA? Taking into account that to be an "agent of a foreign power" requires that the target work for or act on behalf of a "foreign power" (except for the "lone wolf" category described below) can you think of examples of a "foreign power" or "agent of foreign power"? Under what circumstances could a "United States person" be treated as an agent of a foreign power? How did these definitions apply to the subjects of surveillance in *Rosen*?

The so-called "lone wolf" provision, 50 U.S.C. §1801(b)(1)(C), was added by §6001 of the Intelligence Reform and Terrorism Prevention Act of 2004, Pub. L. No. 108-458, 118 Stat. 3638, 3742. If the lone wolf need not be linked in any way to a foreign power, has the "foreign agent" requirement effectively been eliminated for foreign intelligence surveillance? Can you identify any downside risks to the expanded definition? *See* Patricia L. Bellia, *The "Lone Wolf" Amendment and the Future of Foreign Intelligence Surveillance Law*, 50 Vill. L. Rev. 425, 428-429, 455-456 (2005); Elizabeth B. Bazan, *Intelligence Reform and Terrorism Prevention Act of 2004: "Lone Wolf" Amendment to the Foreign Intelligence Surveillance Act* (Cong. Res. Serv. RS22011), Dec. 29, 2004. Although the lone wolf provision has been subject to periodic sunsets since enactment, its authority was recently extended to June 1, 2015. Pub. L. No. 112-14, §2(b), 125 Stat. 216 (2011).

On the basis of what information would investigators make a "foreign agency" determination before seeking FISA surveillance? Can the FBI make such a determination without the surveillance permitted by FISA? See *infra* pp. 608-632.

c.   The FISA Application Process for Electronic Surveillance or a Physical Search

1. *The Special Court.* Congress relied on its Article III power to "ordain and establish" the lower federal courts when it created the Foreign Intelligence Surveillance Court (FISC). For background on the FISC and its procedures, *see* Elizabeth B. Bazan, *The U.S. Foreign Intelligence Surveillance Court and the U.S. Foreign Intelligence Surveillance Court of Review: An Overview* (Cong. Res. Serv. RL 33833), Jan. 24, 2007; *United States Foreign Intelligence Surveillance Court, Rules of Procedure*, Nov. 1, 2010, *available at* http://www.uscourts.gov/uscourts/RulesAndPolicies/rules/FISC_Rules_of_Procedure.pdf.

2. *An Overview of the Process for Obtaining a FISA Order for Electronic Surveillance or a Physical Search.* As shown by the flow chart below, after an investigation indicates a need for foreign intelligence, an application is prepared (by lawyers in the Department of Justice, typically supported by one or more affidavits from investigating agencies) and submitted to the FISC. The FISC considers the application in camera and ex parte; the targets of the proposed surveillance are not informed. If the FISC approves the order, it is executed by the NSA or the FBI in most cases. If the government subsequently seeks to introduce information obtained from the FISA surveillance as evidence in a criminal prosecution, the government must inform the defendant of that intent, as it did in *Rosen.* The defendant may then seek to suppress the materials on the grounds that the evidence was unlawfully acquired or that the surveillance or search was not conducted in conformity with the FISC order. In *Rosen*, the defendant sought disclosure of the FISA application and supporting materials in connection with its motion to suppress. If the Attorney General avers that such disclosure would harm national security, the criminal court will review the materials in camera and ex parte to decide de novo whether the FISC order and its execution by the government were lawful. The *Rosen* court was thus taking a "second look" at the FISA order, but its nominally de novo review standard considers only, for U.S. persons, whether the certifications contained in the original FISA application were "clearly erroneous" (which *Rosen* construes to make such certifications "presum[ptively] valid," or, for all other targets, whether the certifications were complete.

3. *What Must an Application Contain?* What are the essential components of an application for FISA surveillance? How do they differ from the elements of an application for a traditional warrant for law enforcement purposes?

In addition to the requirements summarized in *Rosen*, the Attorney General must find that the information sought "cannot reasonably be obtained by normal investigative techniques." 50 U.S.C. §1804(a)(7)(C). The application also must describe any past surveillance involving the target, the surveillance devices to be employed, the means of installation (including whether physical entry will be required), and the period of time for conducting the surveillance. *Id.* §1804(a)(8), (9), (10).

Due to the growing complexity of FISA applications, in 2001 the FBI developed FISA verification procedures (the so-called Woods Procedures, named for their author, FBI lawyer Michael J. Woods) to better ensure the accuracy of the facts in each FISA application, particularly concerning what FISA calls "probable cause," and the existence and nature of any parallel criminal processes or prior or ongoing asset relationship involving the target. The procedures include FBI computer database searches and requirements to check the status of the proposed target with the Asset and Informant Unit and Criminal Division. The Woods Procedures were declassified in 2002 and are available at http://www.fas.org/irp/agency/doj/fisa/woods/pdf. Are these likely to improve the accuracy of the FISA process? How will Congress or the public know of their success or failure?

4. *The FISA Order for Electronic Surveillance or a Physical Search.*

a. *Foreign Power or Agent Target.* FISA "probable cause" is fundamentally different from Title III probable cause. Under FISA, the FISC must find probable cause to believe what? Is the FISA probable cause standard quoted in *Rosen* more or less onerous than the general criminal probable cause standard?

Both FISA and federal criminal laws require something like the probability of a certain fact. But unlike Title III warrants, FISA orders are based "upon the probability of a possibility; the probability to believe that the foreign target of the order *may* engage in spying, or the probability to believe that the American target of the order *may* engage in criminal spying activities." Charles Doyle, *Memorandum to Senate Select Committee on Intelligence: Probable Cause, Reasonable Suspicion, and Reasonableness Standards in the Context of the Fourth Amendment and the Foreign Intelligence Surveillance Act* (Cong. Res. Serv.), Jan. 30, 2006, *available at* http://www.fas.org/sgp/crs/intel/m013006.pdf. Under what circumstances and according to what standard may the FISC question the determinations made in the application for surveillance? *See* William C. Banks & M.E. Bowman, *Executive Authority for National Security Surveillance*, 50 Am. U. L. Rev. 1, 83 (2001); Brown & Cinquegrana, *supra* p. 592, at 129-131.

What justifies the lesser probable cause requirement in FISA? The purpose of law enforcement is to prosecute those guilty of committing a crime, while intelligence investigations have a broader scope and seek to protect the nation from foreign enemies. Foreign intelligence investigations are often more open-ended. What are the legal implications if law enforcement and intelligence surveillance objectives blur or even merge, when intelligence information produces evidence that is used in a criminal prosecution? What answer does *Rosen* suggest?

b. *Foreign Power or Agent Locus.* The FISC must also find that there is probable cause to believe that the locus of the surveillance is being used or about to be used by, or, for physical searches, owned, used, or possessed by or in transit to or from, a foreign power or agent of a foreign power. This seemingly simple requirement was complicated by the increasing use of cell phones instead of the geographically fixed landlines that existed when FISA was adopted in 1978.

To cope with this change in technology, Federal Rule of Criminal Procedure 41(a) was amended in 2001 to permit a single law enforcement warrant to be used "in any district in which activities related to the terrorism may have occurred" in conducting "an investigation of domestic terrorism or international terrorism." USA Patriot Act §219, 115 Stat. 291. FISA was also amended in 2001 to permit the FISC to order these so-called "roving wiretaps." A roving wiretap permits investigators to listen in on any phone a target might use. If the judge "finds that the actions of the target of the application may have the effect of thwarting" the ability of the investigators to identify a specific communications carrier, Internet service provider, or other person needed to assist in the effective and secret execution of the surveillance, the order may authorize such assistance from multiple parties. USA Patriot Act §206, 115 Stat. 282 (amending 50 U.S.C. §1805(c)(2)(B)).

To complete the authorization for roving wiretaps, the FISA requirement that the FISC "specify . . . the nature and location of each of the facilities or places at which the electronic surveillance will be directed" was also amended by adding "if known" at the end. Intelligence Authorization Act for Fiscal Year 2002, Pub. L. No. 107-108, §314(a)(2)(A), 115 Stat. 1394, 1402 (amending 50 U.S.C. §1805(c)(1)(B)).

These provisions do not require that investigators first determine that the target is using the phone to be tapped. Does this authority permit investigators to tap a homeowner's phone if the target enters the home? Could they monitor the Internet use at the public library if the target enters the library?

In the 2006 USA Patriot Improvement and Reauthorization Act, Congress added a provision for orders when the "nature and location of . . . the facilities or places at which the surveillance will be directed is unknown." Within ten days after surveillance begins, investigators must provide the FISC with a description of the facility or place brought under surveillance, the reasons to believe that it is being used by the target, and any necessary minimization procedures. Pub. L. No. 109-177, §108, 120 Stat. 192, 203 (2006) (amending 50 U.S.C. §1805(c)(1)(B). The roving wiretap authorities, originally sunsetted, were recently extended to June 1, 2015. Pub. L. No. 112-14, §2(a), 125 Stat. 216 (2011).

c. *Minimization.* The FISC must also find that proposed minimization procedures meet statutory requirements. What is minimization, and why is it required? Do you agree with the *Rosen* court that the potential minimization breach in the *Rosen* investigation did not justify suppressing the FISA-derived evidence? Does the "rule of reason" standard adopted by the court adequately safeguard personal information?

The minimization procedures are classified, "although the internal review mechanisms include standard goals for all applications, as well as for situation-specific assessments for individual applications." Banks & Bowman, *supra* p. 595, at 89. Minimization plays an especially important role in protecting privacy when FISA processes are utilized to collect large quantities of personal information through data-mining techniques. The role of minimization in programmatic surveillance is considered in Chapter 22.

5. *Provisions for Emergency Surveillance.* FISA authorizes electronic surveillance without a court order in certain emergency circumstances. Such surveillance is permitted for up to a year when directed solely at communications between or among foreign powers or focused on their property, when there is "no substantial likelihood" that a communication involving a U.S. person will be acquired. 50 U.S.C. §1802.

More importantly, FISA states that when the Attorney General reasonably determines that "an emergency situation exists" regarding the employment of electronic surveillance to obtain foreign intelligence information "before an order authorizing such surveillance can with due diligence be obtained" and that there is a "factual basis for issuance of an order," the Attorney General may authorize the surveillance if a FISC judge is simultaneously informed and if an application is made to that judge "as soon as practicable, but not more than 72 hours" after the Attorney General authorization. 50 U.S.C. §1805(f). If the FISC does not issue a judicial order, the surveillance must stop "when the information sought is obtained, when the application for the order is denied, or after the expiration of 72 hours from the time of authorization by the Attorney General, whichever is earliest." *Id.* If no order is obtained, the information collected may not be used without consent "except with the approval of the Attorney General if the information indicates a threat of death or serious bodily harm to any person." *Id.*

Provision for physical searches in emergency circumstances is made on a basis parallel to that for electronic surveillance; the authority lasts for up to 72 hours, by which time an application for approval must be made to the FISC. 50 U.S.C. §§1822(a), 1824(e), (f). *See also* 50 U.S.C. §§1843(a), (b) (parallel emergency authorities for pen register and trap and trace devices).

Between FISA's enactment in 1978 and September 11, 2001, Attorneys General issued 47 emergency authorizations under FISA. In the 18 months after September 11, 2001, the Attorney General authorized more than 170 emergency wiretaps and/or physical searches under FISA. Dan Eggen & Robert O'Harrow Jr., *U.S. Steps Up Secret Surveillance*, Wash. Post, Mar. 23, 2003. Under 50 U.S.C. §1808(a)(2), the Attorney General must report annually to the intelligence committees the total number of emergency employments of electronic surveillance. The reports are not publicly available.

Are you troubled by the absence of a prior judicial check on these executive decisions? How can responsible officials be certain that these decisions satisfy statutory and constitutional norms? Given the availability of these FISA emergency provisions, can you envision any emergency that would justify foreign intelligence surveillance in the United States without complying with FISA? This question is addressed *infra* p. 615.

6. *Judicial Review of FISA Surveillance.* If no criminal prosecution is initiated following FISA surveillance, how would an individual subjected to unlawful surveillance under FISA be able to challenge the illegal conduct in court? The FISC does not publish its decisions, and its orders are sealed. Proceedings are ex parte and are thus normally not known to the targets of surveillance. 50 U.S.C. §§1802(a)(3), 1806(f)-(g).

As the *Rosen* defendants learned, even if targets of surveillance do find out, they may not be able to examine materials related to the surveillance as part of the criminal court's "second look" if the Attorney General files a claim of privilege under FISA §1806(f). Can you see why FISA permits the government to withhold the applications and accompanying affidavits and certifications from discovery in an adversarial proceeding? If the reviewing judge exercises his statutory discretion not to disclose portions of the documents, how will the targets of surveillance be able to appeal the judge's decision? On what basis could a court of appeals overturn the nondisclosure decision? *See ACLU v. Barr*, 952 F.2d 457 (D.C. Cir. 1991) (reviewing court may overturn a nondisclosure decision if the certifications of compliance with FISA requirements are clearly erroneous); *see also United States v. Rahman*, 189 F.3d 88 (2d Cir. 1999), *cert. denied*, 528 U.S. 982 (2000).

d. Constitutional Concerns

1. *Article III Case or Controversy?* The FISC receives applications and issues orders solely on an ex parte basis without any adversarial proceedings. Do such matters meet the Article III "case or controversy" requirements? *United States v. Megahey*, 553 F. Supp. 1180 (E.D.N.Y. 1982), held that FISA proceedings before the FISC "involve

concrete questions respecting the application of the Act and are in a form such that a judge is capable of acting on them." 553 F. Supp. at 1197. *See also United States v. Johnson*, 952 F.2d 565 (2d Cir. 1991), *cert. denied*, 506 U.S. 816 (1992); *United States v. Cavanaugh*, 807 F.2d 787 (9th Cir. 1987); *In re Kevork*, 788 F.2d 566 (9th Cir. 1986); *United States v. Falvey*, 540 F. Supp. 1306, 1313 (E.D.N.Y. 1982).

2. *Political Question Doctrine.* The courts that have heard challenges to FISA surveillance orders have ruled that their review itself is not barred by the political question doctrine. *See, e.g., United States v. Duggan*, 743 F.2d 59, 74-75 (2d Cir. 1984) (limited judicial role in determining whether the target of a warrant is properly subject to the prescribed procedure does not threaten political question values and does not inject courts into the making of foreign policy).

3. *Fourth Amendment.* In *United States v. Duggan*, 743 F.2d 59 (2d Cir. 1984), alleged members of the Provisional Irish Republican Army (PIRA) faced a number of charges relating to export, transportation, and delivery of explosives and firearms. Some of the evidence against them was derived from electronic surveillance pursuant to FISA. Defendants contended that FISA is unconstitutional on grounds that it violates the probable cause requirement of the Fourth Amendment. The court rejected their argument:

> We regard the procedures fashioned in FISA as a constitutionally adequate balancing of the individual's Fourth Amendment rights against the nation's need to obtain foreign intelligence information. The governmental concerns . . . make reasonable the adoption of prerequisites to surveillance that are less stringent than those precedent to the issuance of a warrant for a criminal investigation. . . .
>
> We conclude that these requirements provide an appropriate balance between the individual's interest in privacy and the government's need to obtain foreign intelligence information, and that FISA does not violate the probable cause requirement of the Fourth Amendment. . . . [*Id.* at 73-74.]

Although the Supreme Court has not considered the constitutionality of FISA, the lower courts have uniformly followed *Duggan* in upholding the FISA procedures. *See, e.g., Johnson, supra*, 952 F.2d at 575 (FISA satisfies Fourth Amendment requirements); *United States v. Pelton*, 835 F.2d 1067, 1075 (4th Cir. 1987) (same); *United States v. Ott*, 827 F.2d 473, 475-477 (9th Cir. 1987) (ex parte review procedures do not violate Fourth or Fifth Amendments); *Cavanaugh, supra*, 807 F.2d at 790 (FISA satisfies the Fourth Amendment).

One of us has written that "FISA was the product of a set of compromises unique to their time. . . . While . . . suspicion of criminal activity was an essential part of . . . FISA, . . . Congress did not intend for FISA to authorize surveillance for the purpose of enforcing the criminal laws." William C. Banks, *The Death of FISA*, 91 U. Minn. L. Rev. 1209, 1228 (2007). How does this "FISA as compromise" view compare with your understanding of the constitutionality of FISA?

4. *Confrontation.* Did the *Rosen* court's refusal to disclose the FISA materials to the defendants violate their due process confrontation rights? Although the Supreme Court has never decided a FISA appeal, the Court did deny review in a challenge to the government's refusal to disclose materials that supported an application for

FISA surveillance. In *United States v. Squillicote*, 221 F.3d 542 (4th Cir. 2000), *cert. denied*, 532 U.S. 971 (2001), a married couple were convicted of conspiring to commit espionage on behalf of East Germany, the Soviet Union, Russia, and South Africa. The FBI obtained 20 separate FISA orders for surveillance that lasted 550 days. Based almost exclusively on the FISA-derived evidence, the parties were sentenced to 22 and 17 years in prison, respectively. Although FISA and the Due Process Clause entitled the accused to question the basis for the government's surveillance, counsel for the accused spies were never permitted to see the underlying documentation that supported the applications for surveillance because the government invoked §1806(f) and filed a claim of privilege. Does §1806(f) comply with the Due Process Clause? Why do you think that the Supreme Court has declined to review a conviction on this basis?

5. *First Amendment.* What protections does FISA provide against surveillance that would burden expressive freedoms? What is meant by the prohibition against finding a U.S. person to be an agent of a foreign power "solely upon the basis of activities protected by the first amendment"? 50 U.S.C. §1805(a)(3)(A). The 1978 Senate Judiciary Committee report on FISA stated that activities protected by the First Amendment may not "form *any part* of the basis" for identifying a FISA target. *See Foreign Intelligence Surveillance Act of 1978: Hearing Before the Subcomm. on Criminal Laws and Procedures of the S. Comm. on the Judiciary*, 95th Cong. 13, 23 (1977) (emphasis added). Did the *Rosen* court take this legislative history into account in evaluating the rules for identifying a potential FISA target?

Did the court in *Rosen* fairly separate the defendants' activities that might be protected from those that are not so protected? What other information could be available to investigators that would permit the application to go forward without being "solely" based on protected First Amendment activities?

Review the definition of "agent of a foreign power" set out *supra* p. 586. Could the FISC grant a surveillance order based on an investigators' assessment that advocacy or fund raising on the part of a potential target constitutes "activities that are in preparation" for terrorism? Problems of profiling targets on the basis of their expressive activities are considered *infra* p. 694.

6. *Reprise: FISA and the Constitution.* After September 11, the Department of Justice maintained that "FISA . . . is not required by the Constitution." Letter from Daniel J. Bryant, Assistant Attorney General, to Senator Bob Graham, Chairman, S. Select Comm. on Intelligence (Aug. 6, 2002) (copy on file with authors). Do you agree?

B. FISA, LAW ENFORCEMENT, AND "THE WALL"

Some defendants in criminal cases have moved to suppress FISA-acquired evidence on the ground that the FISA surveillance was unlawful, because the evidence was originally sought as part of a criminal investigation. They maintain that the government has thus misused FISA to do an end run around Title III and the ordinary warrant and probable cause requirements of the Fourth Amendment. The government usually replies that the investigators sought only foreign intelligence information. Is it possible, indeed likely, that both sides are correct? In *Duggan, supra*, 743 F.2d at 78, the court concluded that an "otherwise valid FISA surveillance is not tainted" simply because the government anticipates that its fruits *may* be used in a criminal prosecution. But how can a judge determine that the government has not used FISA simply to avoid having to comply with Rule 41? *See United States v. Rahman*, 861 F. Supp. 247 (S.D.N.Y. 1994), *aff'd*, 189 F.2d 88 (2d Cir. 1999) (refusing to find an end run).

Before 2002, courts followed *United States v. Truong Dinh Hung*, 629 F.2d 908 (4th Cir. 1980), *supra* p. 574, and allowed evidence gathered during FISA surveillance to support a criminal conviction only after finding that intelligence collection was the "primary" purpose of the surveillance, *United States v. Johnson*, 952 F.2d 565 (1st Cir. 1991), *cert. denied*, 506 U.S. 816 (1992), or at least *a* purpose (not necessarily primary), *United States v. Sarkissian*, 841 F.2d 959, 964 (9th Cir. 1988). The assumption seemed to be that if the original purpose of the surveillance was intelligence gathering, there was no reason not to use the collected information in a criminal prosecution.

In the days and weeks after the September 11, 2001, terrorist attacks, it was widely reported that an investigative failure may have permitted a twentieth hijacker to escape pre-attack detection because of a concern based on "primary purpose." Zacarias Moussaoui was arrested on immigration charges a few weeks before the attacks. Officials at a private flight-training school had grown suspicious when Moussaoui said that he wanted to learn to fly large jet aircraft, but that he had no interest in becoming a commercial pilot. At about the same time, a French intelligence agency warned the FBI in a classified cable that Moussaoui had "Islamic extremist beliefs." David Johnston & Philip Shenon, *F.B.I. Curbed Scrutiny of Man Now a Suspect in Attacks*, N.Y. Times, Oct. 6, 2001. When FBI field agents in Minneapolis sought headquarters approval for a FISA search, they were turned down, apparently because there was insufficient indication that Moussaoui was an agent of a foreign power. The field agents then also failed to persuade headquarters to open a criminal investigation that would have employed grand jury subpoenas and law enforcement warrants to examine Moussaoui's computer and telephone records. Apparently, this request was denied because senior FBI officials worried that an open criminal investigation might thwart a later FISA application by defeating the primary purpose requirement. They were concerned in part because FISC Chief Judge Royce Lamberth had recently questioned the candor of Justice Department officials who sought FISA orders for targets who were already the subjects of criminal investigations. A criminal case was eventually opened and a FISA order was obtained, but only after the September 11 attacks. *Id.*

The belief that a full investigation of Moussaoui before September 11 might have led to exposure of the hijackers' plot helped spur enactment of the USA Patriot Act and, three years later, the lone-wolf provision in the Intelligence Reform and Terrorism Prevention Act of 2004. See *supra* p. 593. The criminal prosecution of Moussaoui is considered *infra* p. 1043.

Concerns about the primary purpose requirement produced an amendment to FISA in the USA Patriot Act. The meaning and constitutionality of the amendment are addressed in the following case.

In re: Sealed Case Nos. 02-001, 02-002

Foreign Intelligence Surveillance Court of Review, 2002
310 F.3d 717

Guy, Senior Circuit Judge, presiding; SILBERMAN and LEAVY, Senior Circuit Judges.

PER CURIAM: This is the first appeal from the Foreign Intelligence Surveillance Court to the Court of Review since the passage of the Foreign Intelligence

Surveillance Act (FISA), 50 U.S.C. §§1801-1862 (West 1991 and Supp. 2002), in 1978. The appeal is brought by the United States from a FISA court surveillance order which imposed certain restrictions on the government. . . .

I.

. . . [T]he court ordered that

> law enforcement officials shall not make recommendations to intelligence officials concerning the initiation, operation, continuation or expansion of FISA searches or surveillances. Additionally, the FBI and the Criminal Division [of the Department of Justice] shall ensure that law enforcement officials do not direct or control the use of the FISA procedures to enhance criminal prosecution, and that advice intended to preserve the option of a criminal prosecution does not inadvertently result in the Criminal Division's directing or controlling the investigation using FISA searches and surveillances toward law enforcement objectives.

To ensure the Justice Department followed these strictures the court also fashioned what the government refers to as a "chaperone requirement"; that a unit of the Justice Department, the Office of Intelligence Policy and Review (OIPR) (composed of 31 lawyers and 25 support staff), "be invited" to all meetings between the FBI and the Criminal Division involving consultations for the purpose of coordinating efforts "to investigate or protect against foreign attack or other grave hostile acts, sabotage, international terrorism, or clandestine intelligence activities by foreign powers or their agents." If representatives of OIPR are unable to attend such meetings, "OIPR shall be appri[s]ed of the substance of the meetings forthwith in writing so that the Court may be notified at the earliest opportunity."

These restrictions are not original to the order appealed. They were actually set forth in an opinion written by the former Presiding Judge of the FISA court on May 17 of this year. [*See In re All Matters Submitted to the Foreign Intelligence Surveillance Court*, 218 F. Supp. 2d 611 (2002).] . . .

. . . [T]he May 17 opinion of the FISA court . . . appears to proceed from the assumption that FISA constructed a barrier between counterintelligence/intelligence officials and law enforcement officers in the Executive Branch — indeed, it uses the word "wall" popularized by certain commentators (and journalists) to describe that supposed barrier.

The "wall" emerges from the court's implicit interpretation of FISA. The court apparently believes it can approve applications for electronic surveillance only if the government's objective is *not* primarily directed toward criminal prosecution of the foreign agents for their foreign intelligence activity. But the court neither refers to any FISA language supporting that view, nor does it reference the Patriot Act amendments, which the government contends specifically altered FISA to make clear that an application could be obtained even if criminal prosecution is the primary counter mechanism. . . .

II.

The government makes two main arguments. The first . . . is that the supposed pre-Patriot Act limitation in FISA that restricts the government's intention to use foreign intelligence information in criminal prosecutions is an illusion; it finds no support in either the language of FISA or its legislative history. The government does recognize that several courts of appeals, while upholding the use of FISA surveillances, have opined that FISA may be used only if the government's primary purpose in pursuing foreign intelligence information is not criminal prosecution, but the government argues that those decisions, which did not carefully analyze the statute, were incorrect in their statements, if not incorrect in their holdings.

Alternatively, the government contends that even if the primary purpose test was a legitimate construction of FISA prior to the passage of the Patriot Act, that Act's amendments to FISA eliminate that concept. . . .

The 1978 FISA

We turn first to the statute as enacted in 1978. . . . [The court reviewed the definitions of "foreign intelligence information" and "agent of a foreign power" and noted that each is concerned with national security crimes.]

In light of these definitions, it is quite puzzling that the Justice Department, at some point during the 1980s, began to read the statute as limiting the Department's ability to obtain FISA orders if it intended to prosecute the targeted agents — even for foreign intelligence crimes. To be sure, section 1804, which sets forth the elements of an application for an order, required a national security official in the Executive Branch — typically the Director of the FBI — to certify that "the purpose" of the surveillance is to obtain foreign intelligence information (amended by the Patriot Act to read "a significant purpose"). But as the government now argues, the definition of foreign intelligence information includes evidence of crimes such as espionage, sabotage or terrorism. Indeed, it is virtually impossible to read the 1978 FISA to exclude from its purpose the prosecution of foreign intelligence crimes, most importantly because, as we have noted, the definition of an agent of a foreign power — if he or she is a U.S. person — is grounded on criminal conduct. . . .

The origin of what the government refers to as the false dichotomy between foreign intelligence information that is evidence of foreign intelligence crimes and that which is not appears to have been a Fourth Circuit case decided in 1980. *United States v. Truong Dinh Hung*, 629 F.2d 908 (4th Cir. 1980). That case, however, involved an electronic surveillance carried out prior to the passage of FISA and predicated on the President's executive power. In approving the district court's exclusion of evidence obtained through a warrantless surveillance subsequent to the point in time when the government's investigation became "primarily" driven by law enforcement objectives, the court held that the Executive Branch should be excused from securing a warrant only when "the object of the search or the surveillance is a foreign power, its agents or collaborators," and "the surveillance is conducted 'primarily' for foreign intelligence reasons." *Id.* at 915. . . .

. . . [S]ome time in the 1980s — the exact moment is shrouded in historical mist — the Department [of Justice] applied the *Truong* analysis to an interpretation of the FISA statute. What is clear is that in 1995 the Attorney General adopted "Procedures for Contacts Between the FBI and the Criminal Division Concerning Foreign Intelligence and Foreign Counterintelligence Investigations."

Apparently to avoid running afoul of the primary purpose test used by some courts, the 1995 Procedures limited contacts between the FBI and the Criminal Division in cases where FISA surveillance or searches were being conducted by the FBI for foreign intelligence (FI) or foreign counterintelligence (FCI) purposes.

The procedures state that "the FBI and Criminal Division should ensure that advice intended to preserve the option of a criminal prosecution does not inadvertently result in either the fact or the appearance of the Criminal Division's *directing or controlling* the FI or FCI investigation toward law enforcement objectives." 1995 Procedures at 2, ¶6 (emphasis added). Although these procedures provided for significant information sharing and coordination between criminal and FI or FCI investigations, based at least in part on the "directing or controlling" language, they eventually came to be narrowly interpreted within the Department of Justice, and most particularly by OIPR, as requiring OIPR to act as a "wall" to prevent the FBI intelligence officials from communicating with the Criminal Division regarding ongoing FI or FCI investigations. . . .

The Patriot Act and the FISA Court's Decision

The passage of the Patriot Act altered and to some degree muddied the landscape. In October 2001, Congress amended FISA to change "the purpose" language in 1804(a)(7)(B) to "a significant purpose." It also added a provision allowing "Federal officers who conduct electronic surveillance to acquire foreign intelligence information" to "consult with Federal law enforcement officers to coordinate efforts to investigate or protect against" attack or other grave hostile acts, sabotage or international terrorism, or clandestine intelligence activities, by foreign powers or their agents. 50 U.S.C. §1806(k)(1). And such coordination "shall not preclude" the government's certification that a significant purpose of the surveillance is to obtain foreign intelligence information, or the issuance of an order authorizing the surveillance. *Id.* §1806(k)(2). Although the Patriot Act amendments to FISA expressly sanctioned consultation and coordination between intelligence and law enforcement officials, in response to the first applications filed by OIPR under those amendments, in November 2001, the FISA court for the first time adopted the 1995 Procedures, as augmented by the January 2000 and August 2001 Procedures, as "minimization procedures" to apply in all cases before the court.

The Attorney General interpreted the Patriot Act quite differently. On March 6, 2002, the Attorney General approved new "Intelligence Sharing Procedures" to implement the Act's amendments to FISA. The 2002 Procedures supersede prior procedures and were designed to permit the complete exchange of information and advice between intelligence and law enforcement officials. They eliminated the "direction and control" test and allowed the exchange of advice between the FBI, OIPR, and the Criminal Division regarding "the initiation, operation, continuation, or expansion of FISA searches or surveillance." On March 7, 2002, the government filed a motion with the FISA court, noting that the Department of Justice had adopted the 2002 Procedures and proposing to follow those procedures in all matters before the court. The government also asked the FISA court to vacate its orders adopting the prior procedures as minimization procedures in all cases and imposing special "wall" procedures in certain cases.

Unpersuaded by the Attorney General's interpretation of the Patriot Act, the court ordered that the 2002 Procedures be adopted, *with modifications*, as minimization procedures to apply in all cases. The court emphasized that the definition of minimization procedures had not been amended by the Patriot Act, and reasoned that the 2002 Procedures "cannot be used by the government to amend the Act in ways Congress has not." . . .

Undeterred, the government submitted the application at issue in this appeal on July 19, 2002, and expressly proposed using the 2002 Procedures *without modification*. In an order issued the same day, the FISA judge hearing the application granted an order for surveillance of the target but modified the 2002 Procedures consistent with the court's May 17, 2002 *en banc* order. It is the July 19, 2002 order that the government appeals....

... [T]he Patriot Act amendments clearly disapprove the primary purpose test. And as a matter of straightforward logic, if a FISA application can be granted even if "foreign intelligence" is only a significant—not a primary—purpose, another purpose can be primary. One other legitimate purpose that could exist is to prosecute a target for a foreign intelligence crime....

... [I]t is our task to do our best to read the statute to honor congressional intent. The better reading, it seems to us, excludes from the purpose of gaining foreign intelligence information a sole objective of criminal prosecution. We therefore reject the government's argument to the contrary. Yet this may not make much practical difference. Because, as the government points out, when it commences an electronic surveillance of a foreign agent, typically it will not have decided whether to prosecute the agent (whatever may be the subjective intent of the investigators or lawyers who initiate an investigation). So long as the government entertains a realistic option of dealing with the agent other than through criminal prosecution, it satisfies the significant purpose test.

The important point is—and here we agree with the government—the Patriot Act amendment, by using the word "significant," eliminated any justification for the FISA court to balance the relative weight the government places on criminal prosecution as compared to other counterintelligence responses. If the certification of the application's purpose articulates a broader objective than criminal prosecution—such as stopping an ongoing conspiracy—and includes other potential non-prosecutorial responses, the government meets the statutory test. Of course, if the court concluded that the government's sole objective was merely to gain evidence of past criminal conduct—even foreign intelligence crimes—to punish the agent rather than halt ongoing espionage or terrorist activity, the application should be denied.

... It can be argued, however, that by providing that an application is to be granted if the government has only a "significant purpose" of gaining foreign intelligence information, the Patriot Act allows the government to have a primary objective of prosecuting an agent for a non-foreign intelligence crime. Yet we think that would be an anomalous reading of the amendment. For we see not the slightest indication that Congress meant to give that power to the Executive Branch. Accordingly, the manifestation of such a purpose, it seems to us, would continue to disqualify an application. That is not to deny that ordinary crimes might be inextricably intertwined with foreign intelligence crimes. For example, if a group of international terrorists were to engage in bank robberies in order to finance the manufacture of a bomb, evidence of the bank robbery should be treated just as evidence of the terrorist act itself. But the FISA process cannot be used as a device to investigate wholly unrelated ordinary crimes....

III. ...

The FISA court expressed concern that unless FISA were "construed" in the fashion that it did, the government could use a FISA order as an improper substitute for an ordinary criminal warrant under Title III. That concern seems to suggest that the FISA court thought Title III procedures are constitutionally mandated if the government has a prosecutorial objective regarding an agent of a foreign power. But in *United States v. United States District Court* (*Keith*), 407 U.S. 297, 322 (1972)—in which the Supreme Court explicitly declined to consider foreign intelligence surveillance— the Court indicated that, even with respect to domestic national security intelligence gathering for prosecutorial purposes where a warrant was mandated, Title III procedures were not constitutionally required: "[W]e do not hold that the same type of standards and procedures prescribed by Title III are necessarily applicable to this case. We recognize that domestic security surveillance may involve different policy and practical considerations from the surveillance of 'ordinary crime.'" Nevertheless, in asking whether FISA procedures can be regarded as reasonable under the Fourth Amendment, we think it is instructive to compare those procedures and requirements with their Title III counterparts. Obviously, the closer those FISA procedures are to Title III procedures, the lesser are our constitutional concerns....

... [W]hile Title III contains some protections that are not in FISA, in many significant respects the two statutes are equivalent, and in some, FISA contains additional protections. Still, to the extent the two statutes diverge in constitutionally relevant areas—in particular, in their probable cause and particularity showings—a FISA order may not be a "warrant" contemplated by the Fourth Amendment.... We do not decide the issue but note that to the extent a FISA order comes close to meeting Title III, that certainly bears on its reasonableness under the Fourth Amendment....

Ultimately, the question becomes whether FISA, as amended by the Patriot Act, is a reasonable response based on a balance of the legitimate need of the government for foreign intelligence information to protect against national security threats with the protected rights of citizens....

It will be recalled that the case that set forth the primary purpose test as constitutionally required was *Truong*. The Fourth Circuit thought that *Keith*'s balancing standard implied the adoption of the primary purpose test. We reiterate that *Truong* dealt with a pre-FISA surveillance based on the President's constitutional responsibility to conduct the foreign affairs of the United States. 629 F.2d at 914. Although *Truong* suggested the line it drew was a constitutional minimum that would apply to a FISA surveillance, *see id.* at 914 n.4, it had no occasion to consider the application of the statute carefully. The *Truong* court, as did all the other courts to have decided the issue, held that the President did have inherent authority to conduct warrantless searches to obtain foreign intelligence information.... We take for granted that the President does have that authority and, assuming that is so, FISA could not encroach on the President's constitutional power. The question before us is the reverse, does FISA amplify the President's power by providing a mechanism that at least approaches a classic warrant and which therefore supports the government's contention that FISA searches are constitutionally reasonable....

... [The *Truong*] analysis, in our view, rested on a false premise and the line the court sought to draw was inherently unstable, unrealistic, and confusing. The false premise was the assertion that once the government moves to criminal prosecution, its "foreign policy concerns" recede. As we have discussed in the first part of the opinion, that is simply not true as it relates to counterintelligence. In that field the government's primary purpose is to halt the espionage or terrorism efforts, and criminal prosecutions can be, and usually are, interrelated with other techniques used to frustrate a foreign power's efforts....

CONCLUSION

...Even without taking into account the President's inherent constitutional authority to conduct warrantless foreign intelligence surveillance, we think the procedures and government showings required under FISA, if they do not meet the minimum Fourth Amendment warrant standards, certainly come close. We, therefore, believe firmly, applying the balancing test drawn from *Keith*, that FISA as amended is constitutional because the surveillances it authorizes are reasonable....

NOTES AND QUESTIONS

1. *The Holding.* What is the holding of *In re Sealed Case?* Is the holding based on FISA, on the Constitution, or both? Can you reconcile the holding with *Keith?* Does *Truong* have any continuing relevance to the law of national security surveillance?

2. *Purpose vs. Use.* The *Sealed Case* decision emphasized the importance of preserving the foreign intelligence objectives of FISA. In view of those objectives, on what basis did the FISCR object to barring the Criminal Division from directing or controlling the use of FISA procedures? Was the FISC order found defective because of the Patriot Act amendments to FISA, or would it have been reversed even if FISA had not been amended?

Is the FBI now permitted to conduct a secret search or wiretap for the primary purpose of investigating possible criminal activity even though there is no probable cause to suspect the commission of a crime? Although terrorism itself is criminal, terrorists may also engage in common criminal activities — credit card fraud, for example. If the Patriot Act amendment makes it easier for the FBI to manage parallel criminal and intelligence investigations, is the gain in effectiveness worth the risk of misuse of the process?

3. *"Special Needs."* In an omitted portion of the opinion, the FISCR analogized its support of the lowered wall to the Supreme Court's approval of warrantless and sometimes suspicionless searches that are designed to serve the government's "special needs, beyond the normal need for law enforcement." *In re Sealed Case,* 310 F.3d at 743, quoting *Vernonia School Dist. 47J v. Acton,* 515 U.S. 646, 653 (1995) (quoting *Griffin v. Wisconsin,* 483 U.S. 868, 873 (1987) (internal quotation marks omitted)). As noted in Chapter 20, the Court has upheld searches that do not satisfy conventional Fourth Amendment standards for suspicionless drug-testing of student athletes, government employees, and railroad workers, along with administrative searches of residences and certain highly regulated businesses. Are you persuaded that the Supreme Court's "special needs" cases are based on considerations analogous to the Justice Department procedures at issue in the principal case? The special needs doctrine is discussed by the FISCR in a second decision *infra* p. 620.

4. *The Aftermath.* In 2003, the FBI issued a classified field directive to further dismantle the wall between law enforcement and intelligence investigations. The directive spelled out the Model Counterterrorism Investigations Strategy (MCIS) and requirements that criminal and intelligence investigators physically work as part of the same teams investigating terrorism. Dan Eggen, *FBI Applies New Rules to*

Surveillance, Wash. Post, Dec. 13, 2003. In 2006 a National Security Division (NSD) was created at the Department of Justice by the USA Patriot Reauthorization and Improvement Act, *supra* p. 596. Creation of the NSD consolidated the former Office of Intelligence Policy and Review (OIPR) (now the Office of Intelligence) and the Counterterrorism and Counterespionage sections of the Criminal Division to ensure full coordination between intelligence investigators and criminal prosecutors. *See* http://www.justice.gov/nsd/about-nsd.html. Do the revised structures satisfy the requirements outlined in the FISCR decision? Is the new strategy constitutional?

C.   FISA TRENDS

The FISC has been active. More than 20,000 applications for surveillance or searches have been approved by the FISC since 1979. Brief annual FISA reports from the Attorney General, including the volume of applications approved for the year, are posted at http://www.fas.org/irp/agency/doj/fisa/#rept. During calendar year 2010, 1,579 applications were made to conduct electronic surveillance and physical searches (1,511 included requests to conduct electronic surveillance). Five applications were withdrawn by the government prior to a FISC ruling. The FISC did not deny any applications in whole or in part, and it made modifications to the proposed orders in 14 applications submitted by the government in 2010. *See* Letter from Ronald Weich, Assistant Attorney General, to Senator Harry Reid. (Apr. 29, 2011), *available at* http://www.fas.org/irp/agency/doj/fisa/2010rept.pdf. Although the most recent data show a reduction in the aggregate number of FISA applications for electronic surveillance since peaking at more than 2,000 annually in 2005, the lower number reflects congressional approval of programmatic surveillance in 2007 and 2008 (see Chapter 22), not an actual reduction in surveillance or in the workload of the FISC or DOJ. Spencer S. Hsu, *As Approvals Drop, Work on Secret Wiretaps Grows, U.S. Government Sources Say,* Wash. Post, Dec. 24, 2010. By comparison, an average of about 600-700 requests for electronic surveillance are submitted to federal courts by law enforcement officials under 18 U.S.C. §2518 annually. What do the numbers suggest?

Notwithstanding the ever-increasing use of FISA and the FISC, foreign intelligence surveillance of suspected terrorists under the terms and conditions of FISA has not been a panacea. In part, this is because

> experience demonstrates three harsh realities: first, it is often difficult to isolate U.S. persons from one or more foreign surveillance targets in a place or through electronic monitoring; second, it is often impossible to determine the relationship of a potential terrorist to a foreign power early in an investigation; and third . . . U.S. persons are as capable as any other of wreaking catastrophic havoc. [Banks & Bowman, *supra* p. 595, at 95.]

The lone-wolf provision, *supra* p. 593, is supposed to address the second of these concerns.

Programmatic Electronic Surveillance for Foreign Intelligence

With the ongoing revolution in digital communications, the idea of a geographic border has become an increasingly less viable marker for legal authorities and their limits. So has the citizenship or status of a target of electronic surveillance. Using the Internet, packets of data that constitute messages travel in disparate ways through global networks, many of which come through or end up in the United States. Those packets and countless Skype calls and instant and text messages originate from the United States in growing numbers, although the senders or recipients may be in the United States or abroad. Moreover, it may or may not be possible to identify senders or recipients by the e-mail addresses or phone numbers they use to communicate.

Do we think of our international communications as being somehow less private than our domestic calls? When FISA was enacted in 1978, Congress apparently exempted surveillance conducted abroad because in that era most Americans' communications did not travel along international wires. Now our message packets may travel abroad, even if we are in the United States corresponding by e-mail with a friend who is in the same city.

Because FISA was written to apply to broadly defined categories of "electronic surveillance" inside the United States, these recent developments in technology have brought the interception of many previously unregulated communications—e-mail is the most prominent example—inside the FISA scheme. Thus, with FISA's traditional focus on domestic collection, even a foreign-to-foreign text message intercepted from a server inside the United States requires compliance with FISA procedures.

Evolving technologies have also turned the traditional sequence of FISA processes on its head. We discovered after 9/11 that investigators could enter transactional data about potential terrorists and come up with a list that included four of the hijackers—a sort of reverse of a typical FISA investigation. Now data mining—the application of algorithms or other database techniques to reveal hidden characteristics or relationships—may be used to develop a list of targets for traditional FISA surveillance. In order to collect foreign intelligence data to mine, officials claim that they need access to telecom switches inside the United States, or that they need records of Internet traffic residing on servers in the United States. In either instance, of course, the collected data would almost certainly include information about U.S. persons.

In this chapter we first examine programmatic surveillance — collection of data without court orders identifying individual targets — conducted by the George W. Bush administration. The so-called Terrorist Surveillance Program (TSP) was hidden from public view for more than four years, in part at least because it was so controversial. We then explore congressional responses to technological change and to the TSP. In 2008 Congress codified programmatic surveillance as a new subtitle of FISA and, in doing so, ushered in a new era of warrantless surveillance, the legal parameters of which are still being formed. The second published decision of the Foreign Intelligence Surveillance Court of Review (FISCR), reproduced below, provides an early test of the legal efficacy of programmatic surveillance.

A. CASE STUDY: THE TERRORIST SURVEILLANCE PROGRAM

On December 16, 2005, the *New York Times* reported that, according to government officials, "President Bush secretly authorized the National Security Agency to eavesdrop on Americans and others inside the United States to search for evidence of terrorist activity without the court-approved warrants ordinarily required for domestic spying." James Risen & Eric Lichtblau, *Bush Lets U.S. Spy on Callers Without Courts*, N.Y. Times, Dec. 16, 2005. Pursuant to a still-secret executive order signed by the President in October 2001, the NSA had without warrants monitored the telephone and e-mail communications of thousands of persons inside the United States, where one end of the communication was outside the United States, in an effort to learn more about possible terrorist plots. *Id.* Later called the Terrorist Surveillance Program (TSP) by the Administration, the NSA surveillance created a major controversy, drawing out prominent critics and proponents alike, provoking hearings in Congress, prompting lawsuits by civil liberties organizations and by defendants who challenged their previous pleas or convictions, and generating countless op-ed pieces, blog debates, and commentary.

The Bush administration vigorously defended the TSP. President Bush first authorized the program for about 45 days and then renewed the authorization at the end of each succeeding 45-day period. *President's Radio Address* (Dec. 17, 2005), *at* http://georgewbush-whitehouse.archives.gov/news/releases//2005/12/20051217. html. According to the President, the program had to be approved "by our nation's top legal officials, including the Attorney General and the Counsel to the President." *Id.* Shortly after the story broke in the *New York Times*, the Justice Department's Office of Legislative Affairs immediately prepared a letter for congressional leaders summarizing its legal rationale for the NSA surveillance. Excerpts from that letter follow:

Letter from William E. Moschella, Assistant Attorney General, to The Honorable Pat Roberts, Chairman, Senate Select Committee on Intelligence et al.

Dec. 22, 2005
available at http://www.fas.org/irp/agency/doj/fisa/doj122205.pdf

As you know, in response to unauthorized disclosures in the media, the President has described certain activities of the National Security Agency ("NSA") that he has authorized since shortly after September 11, 2001. As described by the President, the

NSA intercepts certain international communications into and out of the United States of people linked to al Qaeda or an affiliated terrorist organization. The purpose of these intercepts is to establish an early warning system to detect and prevent another catastrophic terrorist attack on the United States. The President has made clear that he will use his constitutional and statutory authorities to protect the American people from further terrorist attacks, and the NSA activities the President described are part of that effort. Leaders of the Congress were briefed on these activities more than a dozen times.

The purpose of this letter is to provide an additional brief summary of the legal authority supporting the NSA activities described by the President.

As an initial matter, I emphasize a few points. The President stated that these activities are "crucial to our national security." The President further explained that "the unauthorized disclosure of this effort damages our national security and puts our citizens at risk. Revealing classified information is illegal, alerts our enemies, and endangers our country." These critical national security activities remain classified. All United States laws and policies governing the protection and nondisclosure of national security information, including the information relating to the activities described by the President, remain in full force and effect. The unauthorized disclosure of classified information violates federal criminal law. The Government may provide further classified briefings to the Congress on these activities in an appropriate manner. Any such briefings will be conducted in a manner that will not endanger national security.

Under Article II of the Constitution, including in his capacity as Commander in Chief, the President has the responsibility to protect the Nation from further attacks, and the Constitution gives him all necessary authority to fulfill that duty. *See, e.g., Prize Cases*, 67 U.S. (2 Black) 635, 668 (1863) (stressing that if the Nation is invaded, "the President is not only authorized but bound to resist by force . . . without waiting for any special legislative authority"); *Campbell v. Clinton*, 203 F.3d 19, 27 (D.C. Cir. 2000) (Silberman, J., concurring) ("[T]he *Prize Cases* . . . stand for the proposition that the President has independent authority to repel aggressive acts by third parties even without specific congressional authorization, and courts may not review the level of force selected."); *id.* at 40 (Tatel, J., concurring). The Congress recognized this constitutional authority in the preamble to the Authorization for the Use of Military Force ("AUMF") of September 18, 2001, 115 Stat. 224 (2001) ("[T]he President has authority under the Constitution to take action to deter and prevent acts of international terrorism against the United States."), and in the War Powers Resolution, *see* 50 U.S.C. §1541(c) ("The constitutional powers of the President as Commander in Chief to introduce United States Armed Forces into hostilities [] . . . [extend to] a national emergency created by attack upon the United States, its territories or possessions, or its armed forces.").

This constitutional authority includes the authority to order warrantless foreign intelligence surveillance within the United States, as all federal appellate courts, including at least four circuits, to have addressed the issue have concluded. *See, e.g., In re Sealed Case*, 310 F.3d 717, 742 (FISA Ct. of Rev. 2002) ("[A]ll the other courts to have decided the issue [have] held that the President did have inherent authority to conduct warrantless searches to obtain foreign intelligence information. . . . We take for granted that the President does have that authority. . . ."). The Supreme Court has said that warrants are generally required in the context of purely *domestic* threats, but it expressly distinguished *foreign* threats. *See United States v. United States*

District Court, 407 U.S. 297, 308 (1972). As Justice Byron White recognized almost 40 years ago, Presidents have long exercised the authority to conduct warrantless surveillance for national security purposes, and a warrant is unnecessary "if the President of the United States or his chief legal officer, the Attorney General, has considered the requirements of national security and authorized electronic surveillance as reasonable." *Katz v. United States*, 389 U.S. 347, 363-364 (1967) (White, J., concurring).

The President's constitutional authority to direct the NSA to conduct the activities he described is supplemented by statutory authority under the AUMF. The AUMF authorizes the President "to use all necessary and appropriate force against those nations, organizations, or persons he determines planned, authorized, committed, or aided the terrorists attacks of September 11, 2001, ... in order to prevent any future acts of international terrorism against the United States." §2(a). The AUMF clearly contemplates action within the United States, *see also id.* pmbl. (the attacks of September 11 "render it both necessary and appropriate that the United States exercise its rights to self-defense and to protect United States citizens both at home and abroad"). The AUMF cannot be read as limited to authorizing the use of force against Afghanistan, as some have argued. Indeed, those who directly "committed" the attacks of September 11 resided in the United States for months before those attacks. The reality of the September 11 plot demonstrates that the authorization of force covers activities both on foreign soil and in America.

In *Hamdi v. Rumsfeld*, 542 U.S. 507 (2004), the Supreme Court addressed the scope of the AUMF. At least five Justices concluded that the AUMF authorized the President to detain a U.S. citizen in the United States because "detention to prevent a combatant's return to the battlefield is a fundamental incident of waging war" and is therefore included in the "necessary and appropriate force" authorized by the Congress. *Id.* at 518-519 (plurality opinion of O'Connor, J.); *see id.* 587 (Thomas, J., dissenting). These five Justices concluded that the AUMF "clearly and unmistakably authorize[s]" the "fundamental incident[s] of waging war." *Id.* at 518-19 (plurality opinion); *see id.* at 587 (Thomas, J., dissenting).

Communications intelligence targeted at the enemy is a fundamental incident of the use of military force. Indeed, throughout history, signals intelligence has formed a critical part of waging war. In the Civil War, each side tapped the telegraph lines of the other. In the World Wars, the United States intercepted telegrams into and out of the country. The AUMF cannot be read to exclude this long-recognized and essential authority to conduct communications intelligence targeted at the enemy. We cannot fight a war blind. Because communications intelligence activities constitute, to use the language of *Hamdi*, a fundamental incident of waging war, the AUMF *clearly and unmistakably authorizes* such activities directed against the communications of our enemy. Accordingly, the President's "authority is at its maximum." *Youngstown Sheet & Tube Co. v. Sawyer*, 343 U.S. 579, 635 (1952) (Jackson, J., concurring); *see Dames & Moore v. Regan*, 453 U.S. 654, 668 (1981); *cf. Youngstown*, 343 U.S. at 585 (noting the absence of a statute "from which [the asserted authority] c[ould] be fairly implied").

The President's authorization of targeted electronic surveillance by the NSA is also consistent with the Foreign Intelligence Surveillance Act ("FISA"). Section 2511(2)(f) of title 18 provides, as relevant here, that the procedures of FISA and two chapters of title 18 "shall be the exclusive means by which electronic surveillance ... may be conducted." Section 109 of FISA, in turn, makes it unlawful to conduct electronic surveillance, "except as authorized by statute." 50 U.S.C. §1809(a)(1). Importantly, section 109's exception for electronic surveillance "authorized by statute" is broad, especially considered in the context of surrounding provisions. *See* 18 U.S.C. §2511(1) ("Except as otherwise specifically provided *in this chapter* any person who — (a) intentionally intercepts ... any wire, oral or electronic communication [] ... shall be punished ....") (emphasis added); *id.* §2511(2)(e) (providing a defense to liability to individuals "conduct[ing] electronic surveillance, ... as authorized by *that Act [FISA]*") (emphasis added).

By expressly and broadly excepting from its prohibition electronic surveillance undertaken "as authorized by statute," section 109 of FISA permits an exception to the "procedures" of FISA referred to in U.S.C. §2511(2)(f) where authorized by another statute, even if the other authorizing statute does not specifically amend section 2511(2)(f). The AUMF satisfies section 109's requirement for statutory authorization of electronic surveillance, just as a majority of the Court in *Hamdi* concluded that it satisfies the requirement in 18 U.S.C. §4001(a) that no U.S. citizen be detained by the United States "except pursuant to an Act of Congress." *See Hamdi*, 542 U.S. at 519 (explaining that "it is of no moment that the AUMF does not use specific language of detention"); *see id.* at 587 (Thomas, J., dissenting).

Some might suggest that FISA could be read to require that a subsequent statutory authorization must come in the form of an amendment to FISA itself. But under established principles of statutory construction, the AUMF and FISA must be construed in harmony to avoid any potential conflict between FISA and the President's Article II authority as Commander in Chief. *See, e.g., Zadvydas v. Davis*, 533 U.S. 678, 689 (2001); *INS v. St. Cyr*, 533 U.S. 289, 300 (2001). Accordingly, any ambiguity as to whether the AUMF is a statute that satisfies the requirements of FISA and allows electronic surveillance in the conflict with al Qaeda without complying with FISA procedures must be resolved in favor of an interpretation that is consistent with the President's long-recognized authority.

The NSA activities described by the President are also consistent with the Fourth Amendment and the protection of civil liberties. The Fourth Amendment's "central requirement is one of reasonableness." *Illinois v. McArthur*, 531 U.S. 326, 330 (2001) (internal quotation marks omitted). For searches conducted in the course of ordinary criminal law enforcement, reasonableness generally requires securing a warrant. *See Bd. of Educ. v. Earls*, 536 U.S. 822, 828 (2002). Outside the ordinary criminal law enforcement context, however, the Supreme Court has, at times, dispensed with the warrant, instead adjudging the reasonableness of a search under the totality of circumstances. *See United States v. Knights*, 534 U.S. 112, 118 (2001). In particular, the Supreme Court has long recognized that "special needs, beyond the normal need for law enforcement," can justify departure from the usual warrant requirement. *Vernonia School Dist. 47J v. Acton*, 515 U.S. 646, 653 (1995); *see also City of Indianapolis v. Edmond*, 531 U.S. 32, 41-42 (2000) (striking down checkpoint where "primary purpose was to detect evidence of ordinary criminal wrongdoing").

Foreign intelligence collection, especially in the midst of an armed conflict in which the adversary has already launched catastrophic attacks within the United States, fits squarely within the "special needs" exception to the warrant requirement. Foreign intelligence collection undertaken to prevent further devastating attacks on our Nation serves the highest purpose through means other than traditional law enforcement. *See In re Sealed Case*, 310 F.3d at 745; *United States v. Duggan*, 743 F.2d 59, 72 (2d Cir. 1984) (recognizing that the Fourth Amendment implications of foreign intelligence surveillance are far different from ordinary wiretapping, because they are not principally used for criminal prosecution).

Intercepting communications into and out of the United States of persons linked to al Qaeda in order to detect and prevent a catastrophic attack is clearly *reasonable*. Reasonableness is generally determined by "balancing the nature of the intrusion on the individual's privacy against the promotion of legitimate governmental interests." *Earls*, 536 U.S. at 829. There is undeniably an important and legitimate privacy interest at stake with respect to the activities described by the President. That must be balanced, however, against the Government's compelling interest in the security of the Nation, *see, e.g., Haig v. Agee*, 453 U.S. 280, 307 (1981) ("It is obvious and unarguable that no governmental interest is more compelling than the security of the Nation.") (citation and quotation marks omitted). The fact that the NSA activities are reviewed and reauthorized approximately every 45 days to ensure that they continue to be necessary and appropriate further demonstrates the reasonableness of these activities.

As explained above, the President determined that it was necessary following September 11 to create an early warning detection system. FISA could not have provided the speed and agility required for the early warning detection system. In addition, any legislative change, other than the AUMF, that the President might have sought specifically to create such an early warning system would have been public and would have tipped off our enemies concerning our intelligence limitations and capabilities. Nevertheless, I want to stress that the United States makes full use of FISA to address the terrorist threat, and FISA has proven to be a very important tool, especially in longer-term investigations. In addition, the United States is constantly assessing all available legal options, taking full advantage of any developments in the law.

We hope this information is helpful.

Sincerely,
William E. Moschella
Assistant Attorney General

NOTES AND QUESTIONS

1. *Nature of the Terrorist Surveillance Program.* What did the NSA actually do, as best you can tell from the Department of Justice (DOJ) letter? Were there any internal procedural controls? If so, what were they? Did they adequately safeguard any privacy rights that might have been implicated?

2. *The Predicate Legal Standard for Surveillance.* As indicated in the Justice Department letter, the TSP conducted surveillance of persons "linked to al Qaeda or an affiliated terrorist organization." How do you suppose it was determined whether a person fit that description? What legal standard would govern such a determination? In written answers to questions raised by Senators at a July 26, 2006, Senate Judiciary Committee hearing, NSA Director Keith B. Alexander stated that

> professional intelligence officers at [NSA], with the assistance of other elements of the Intelligence Community and subject to appropriate and vigorous oversight by the NSA Inspector General and General Counsel, among others, would rely on the best available intelligence information to determine whether there are reasonable grounds

to believe that a party to an international communication is affiliated with al Qaeda. [Senator Edward M. Kennedy, *FISA for the 21st Century: Questions for Lt. General Keith B. Alexander* (July 26, 2006), *available at* http://www.fas.org/irp/congress/2006_hr/alexander-qfr.pdf.]

Do you see any legal shortcomings in this description of the decision process and the legal standard for implementing TSP surveillance?

3. *Applicability of FISA.* Although FISA's scope is summarized in *United States v. Rosen* and the Notes and Questions following that case in Chapter 21, in considering the applicability of FISA to the TSP you will want to look in particular at the language of §1801(f), quoted *supra* p. 591. Consider also the complete text of 18 U.S.C. §2511(2)(e) and (f), governing ordinary criminal warrants:

(e) Notwithstanding any other provision of this title or section 705 or 706 of the Communications Act of 1934, it shall not be unlawful for an officer, employee, or agent of the United States in the normal course of his official duty to conduct electronic surveillance, as defined in section 101 of the Foreign Intelligence Surveillance Act of 1978, as authorized by that Act.

(f) Nothing contained in this chapter or chapter 121 or 206 of this title, or section 705 of the Communications Act of 1934, shall be deemed to affect the acquisition by the United States Government of foreign intelligence information from international or foreign communications, or foreign intelligence activities conducted in accordance with otherwise applicable Federal law involving a foreign electronic communications system, utilizing a means other than electronic surveillance as defined in section 101 [50 U.S.C. section 1801] of the Foreign Intelligence Surveillance Act of 1978, and procedures in this chapter or chapter 121 and the Foreign Intelligence Surveillance Act of 1978 shall be the exclusive means by which electronic surveillance, as defined in section 101 of such Act, and the interception of domestic wire, oral, and electronic communications may be conducted.

In addition, consider §1809(a)(1) of FISA (making unauthorized electronic surveillance a criminal offense):

A person is guilty of an offense if he intentionally—
(1) engages in electronic surveillance under color of law except as authorized by statute; or
(2) discloses or uses information obtained under color of law by electronic surveillance, knowing or having reason to know that the information was obtained through electronic surveillance not authorized by statute. [50 U.S.C. §1809(a)(1).]

Are you persuaded by the DOJ analysis that FISA is inapplicable to the TSP?

Does it affect your answer that on January 17, 2007, Attorney General Gonzales wrote to Senators Leahy and Specter of the Senate Judiciary Committee and advised them that on January 10, a FISC judge "issued orders authorizing the Government to target for collection international communications into or out of the United States where there is probable cause to believe that one of the communicants is a member or agent of al Qaeda or an associated terrorist organization"? Letter from Attorney General Alberto R. Gonzales to Sens. Leahy and Specter (Jan. 17, 2007), *available at* http://www.fas.org/irp/congress/2007_cr/fisa011707.html. According to the

Attorney General, these orders would "allow the necessary speed and agility" and, accordingly, all surveillance previously occurring under the TSP would thereafter be conducted with the approval of the FISC.

4. *Why Not FISA?* The government has an enviable track record in the FISC. See *supra* p. 607. Why did it not seek a FISA order for the TSP? In a January 2006 address, Attorney General Alberto R. Gonzales defended the decision not to rely on FISA:

> We have to remember that we're talking about a wartime foreign intelligence program. It is an "early warning system" with only one purpose: To detect and prevent the next attack on the United States from foreign agents hiding in our midst. It is imperative for national security that we can detect RELIABLY, IMMEDIATELY, and WITHOUT DELAY whenever communications associated with al Qaeda enter or leave the United States. That may be the only way to alert us to the presence of an al Qaeda agent in our country and to the existence of an unfolding plot.
>
> Consistent with the wartime intelligence nature of this program, the optimal way to achieve the necessary speed and agility is to leave the decisions about particular intercepts to the judgment of professional intelligence officers, based on the best available intelligence information. They can make that call quickly. If, however, those same intelligence officers had to navigate through the FISA process for each of these intercepts, that would necessarily introduce a significant factor of DELAY, and there would be critical holes in our early warning system.
>
> Some have pointed to the provision in FISA that allows for so-called "emergency authorizations" of surveillance for 72 hours without a court order. There's a serious misconception about these emergency authorizations. People should know that we do not approve emergency authorizations without knowing that we will receive court approval within 72 hours. FISA requires the Attorney General to determine IN ADVANCE that a FISA application for that particular intercept will be fully supported and will be approved by the court before an emergency authorization may be granted. That review process can take precious time. Thus, to initiate surveillance under a FISA emergency authorization, it is not enough to rely on the best judgment of our intelligence officers alone. Those intelligence officers would have to get the sign-off of lawyers at the NSA that all provisions of FISA have been satisfied, then lawyers in the Department of Justice would have to be similarly satisfied, and finally as Attorney General, I would have to be satisfied that the search meets the requirements of FISA. And we would have to be prepared to follow up with a full FISA application within the 72 hours. [Prepared Remarks for Attorney General Alberto R. Gonzales, Georgetown University Law Center, Jan. 24, 2006, *available at* http://www.usdoj.gov/ag/speeches/2006/ag_speech_0601241.html.]

In evaluating the Attorney General's statement, consider FISA's emergency surveillance provisions, quoted *supra* p. 596. Do you believe he was justified in bypassing the FISA procedures?

5. *The AUMF as Authority for the TSP?* Recall that the September 18, 2001, Authorization for the Use of Military Force (AUMF), *supra* p. 97, authorizes the President to

> use all necessary and appropriate force against those nations, organizations, or persons he determines planned, authorized, committed, or aided the terrorist attacks that occurred on September 11, 2001, or harbored such organizations, or persons, in order to prevent any future acts of international terrorism against the United States by such nations, organizations or persons. [Pub. L. No. 107-40, §2(a), 115 Stat. 224 (2001).]

Did it thereby authorize the TSP? (The Supreme Court's construction of the AUMF appears in the *Hamdi* case, *infra* p. 831.) Is it relevant to your answer that in the USA Patriot Act, enacted in October 2001, *after* enacting the AUMF, Congress amended FISA by, *inter alia*, extending the period of emergency surveillance from 24 hours to 72 hours, or that it left in place the following FISA provision?

> Notwithstanding any other law, the President, through the Attorney General, may authorize electronic surveillance without a court order under this subchapter to acquire foreign intelligence information for a period not to exceed fifteen calendar days following a declaration of war by the Congress. [50 U.S.C. §1811 (2006 & Supp. III 2009).]

In light of the comprehensive scheme detailed in FISA, should the more open-ended grant of authority in the AUMF be read to authorize the TSP?

In *Greene v. McElroy*, 360 U.S. 474 (1959), the Supreme Court declined to find authority for security clearance procedures employed by the Executive in the absence of explicit approval by either the President or Congress. *See also Kent v. Dulles*, 357 U.S. 116 (1958) (declining to find authority for the Secretary of State to restrict the right of travel absent explicit delegation from Congress). *But see Haig v. Agee*, 453 U.S. 280 (1981) (inferring authority to restrict the right of travel from congressional acquiescence in State Department policy). The *Greene* Court cited *Ex parte Endo*, 323 U.S. 283, 303 n.24 (1944), in which the Court declared that under the circumstances of that case a claim of Executive authority based on an appropriation would have to "plainly show a purpose to bestow the precise authority which is claimed." There the Court found no authorization for the continued imprisonment of loyal Japanese-Americans during World War II "where a lump appropriation was made for the overall program of the [War Relocation] Authority and no sums were earmarked for the single phase of the total program [there] involved." *Id.* Should a "clear statement" requirement apply to prevent reliance on the AUMF as authority for the TSP?

6. *Inherent Constitutional Authority?* In light of all the foregoing, did President Bush have inherent constitutional authority to order the TSP? Consider the President's exchange with a reporter at a December 19, 2005, press conference:

Q . . . [W]hy did you skip the basic safeguards of asking courts for permission for the intercepts?

THE PRESIDENT: First of all, I — right after September the 11th, I knew we were fighting a different kind of war. And so I asked people in my administration to analyze how best for me and our government to do the job people expect us to do, which is to detect and prevent a possible attack. That's what the American people want. We looked at the possible scenarios. And the people responsible for helping us protect and defend came forth with the current program, because it enables us to move faster and quicker. And that's important. We've got to be fast on our feet, quick to detect and prevent.

We use FISA still — you're referring to the FISA court in your question — of course, we use FISA. But FISA is for long-term monitoring. What is needed in order to protect the American people is the ability to move quickly to detect.

Now, having suggested this idea, I then, obviously, went to the question, is it legal to do so? I am — I swore to uphold the laws. Do I have the legal authority to do this? And the answer is, absolutely. As I mentioned in my remarks, the legal authority is derived from the Constitution, as well as the authorization of force by the United States Congress.

Are you persuaded by the President's statement? Consider the arguments made in the Justice Department letter. If you think there is a clash between the President's claim of authority and the statutes — placing the TSP in Justice Jackson's third category — how should we resolve it?

7. *The Fourth Amendment.* If the President has inherent constitutional authority for the TSP, notwithstanding any statute, does he also escape the strictures of the Fourth Amendment? If not, is the program constitutional? A few weeks after the September 11 attacks, Office of Legal Counsel (OLC) lawyers John Yoo and Robert Delahunty prepared a memorandum for White House Counsel Gonzales and DOD General Counsel William J. Haynes II, offering advice on the authority for the use of military force to prevent or deter terrorist activity inside the United States. *Memorandum for Alberto R. Gonzales & William J. Haynes, II, Authority for Use of Military Force to Combat Terrorist Activities Within the United States* (Oct. 23, 2001, *available at* http://www.fas.org/irp/agency/doj/olc/milforce.pdf. The authors argued that the President has expanded wartime powers that trump Fourth Amendment requirements:

> [H]owever well suited the warrant and probable cause requirements may be as applied to criminal investigations or to other law enforcement activities, they are unsuited to the demands of wartime and the military necessity to successfully prosecute a war against an enemy. In the circumstances of September 11, the Constitution provides the Government with expanded powers to prosecute the war effort. . . . In light of the well-settled understanding that constitutional constraints must give way in some respects to the exigencies of war, we think that the better view is that the Fourth Amendment does *not* apply to domestic military operations designed to deter and prevent further terrorist attacks. [*Id.* at 24-25 (emphasis in original).]

Are you persuaded?

8. *The End of TSP?* In his January 2007 letter to Senators Leahy and Specter, *supra* Note 3, Attorney General Gonzales concluded by stating that the President would not reauthorize the TSP when its current authorization expired. *Id.* Why would the President have chosen to discontinue the TSP? Did he do it because he was able to obtain the functional equivalent of the TSP through orders from the FISC? Review §§1804 and 1805 of FISA, described in *United States v. Rosen, supra* p. 582, and in the Notes and Questions that follow it. Can you imagine what the FISC orders say? At least one FISC judge may have agreed to treat the international telecom switches inside the United States as FISA "facilities." Assuming that communications involving Al Qaeda passed through telecom switches in the United States, obtaining such orders from the FISC gave the government access to nearly all international telecom traffic coming and going from the United States. *See* William C. Banks, *Programmatic Surveillance and FISA: Of Needles in Haystacks*, 88 Tex. L. Rev. 1633, 1643 (2010). How should a FISC judge have responded to the inevitable fact that the rest of America was using those switches at the same time? Whatever the content of the orders, do you think they ended the legal controversy over the TSP?

9. *The Lawsuits Challenging TSP.* Private plaintiffs filed lawsuits against agencies and/or officials of the government allegedly involved in the TSP. In *American Civil Liberties Union v. National Security Agency*, 438 F. Supp. 2d 754 (E.D. Mich. 2006),

a district court actually declared the TSP unlawful for violating both FISA and the Fourth Amendment. The Court of Appeals reversed, 493 F.3d 644 (6th Cir. 2007), ruling that the plaintiffs lacked standing because they could not prove that they had been subjected to the surveillance. In addition, the plaintiffs could not rely on discovery to develop their proof of injury because of the state secrets doctrine. *Id.* at 683, 687-688. The state secrets privilege is considered in Chapter 6.

In *Al-Haramain Islamic Foundation v. Bush*, 451 F. Supp. 2d 1215 (D. Or. 2006), *rev'd*, 507 F.3d 1190 (9th Cir. 2007), the plaintiff Foundation had, through government error in the discovery process in different litigation involving the Foundation and the Treasury Department, obtained documents showing that the government had recorded telephone conversations between one of its Saudi Arabia-based officers and two of its U.S.-based lawyers. Although the federal District Court in Oregon allowed the plaintiffs to rely on the documents as evidence that they were subjected to the TSP, 451 F. Supp. at 1227, 1229, the Ninth Circuit Court of Appeals reversed, but remanded the case to determine whether FISA preempts the state secrets privilege. 507 F.3d at 1193. Eventually all the remaining TSP lawsuits were transferred to the Northern District of California, where in 2008 Judge Vaughn Walker ruled that, in some circumstances, FISA preempts the state secrets privilege. *In re Telecommunications Records Litig.*, 564 F. Supp. 2d 1109, 1119 (N.D. Cal. 2008). But he dismissed the Foundation's case without prejudice after ruling that the accidentally disclosed documents remained subject to the state secrets privilege and thus could not provide the necessary proof of injury to establish standing. 564 F. Supp. 2d at 1137. In January 2011, Judge Walker dismissed the lawsuit after concluding that the plaintiffs lack standing to assert their claims. *In re National Security Agency Telecommunications Records Litig.*, Case No. 3:07-cv-01115-vrw (N.D. Cal. 2011), *available at* http://www.court housenews.com/2011/02/01/Government wiretaps.pdf.

If the courts are not likely to determine the lawfulness of TSP, can you think of other mechanisms that could provide some accountability for the TSP under FISA and the Constitution? *See* Kathleen Clark, *The Architecture of Accountability: A Case Study of the Warrantless Surveillance Program*, 2010 BYU L. Rev. 357, 390-404 (suggesting transparency mechanisms).

10. *Investigating the DOJ Lawyers?* In March 2004, Deputy Attorney General James B. Comey, acting for a hospitalized Attorney General John Ashcroft, refused to sign off on a reauthorization of the TSP. The expiring TSP was reauthorized the next day without DOJ approval. Comey considered resigning, and he learned that Ashcroft, FBI Director Mueller, and OLC head Jack Goldsmith would join him. Harold H. Bruff, *Bad Advice: Bush's Lawyers in the War on Terror* 152-154 (2009). In a later speech to the staff at NSA, Comey said that the lawyer is

> the custodian of our Constitution and the rule of law. It is the job of a good lawyer to say "yes." It is as much the job of a good lawyer to say "no." "No" is much, much harder. "No" must be spoken into a storm of crisis, with loud voices all around, with lives hanging in the balance. . . . It takes an understanding that, in the long run, intelligence under law is the only sustainable intelligence in this country. [James B. Comey, *Intelligence Under the Law*, 10 Green Bag 2d 439, 444 (2007).]

In 2006 more than 40 members of Congress requested that the Department of Justice Office of Professional Responsibility (OPR) investigate whether DOJ lawyers acted properly early on in approving the TSP. After OPR opened an investigation, the head of OPR requested that he and six OPR employees be given security clearances so that they could start their work. Apparently on the advice of Attorney General Alberto Gonzales, President Bush denied the clearances, blocking the investigation. Clark, *supra*, 2010 BYU L. Rev. at 402. What standards would have determined whether the DOJ lawyers acted properly?

11. *Amending FISA.* After one FISC judge reportedly approved some version of the TSP, a different FISC judge decided in May 2007 not to continue its approval. The Bush administration immediately urged Congress to pass statutory authorization for the program. In August 2007, Congress enacted the Protect America Act, Pub. L. No. 110-55, 121 Stat. 552, which permitted the DNI and the Attorney General to authorize collection of foreign intelligence concerning persons reasonably believed to be outside the United States, without obtaining an order from the FISC, even if one party to the communication was a U.S. citizen inside the United States. The Protect America Act expired by its own terms in February 2008, leading to the enactment on July 10, 2008, of the FISA Amendments Act.

B. THE FISA AMENDMENTS ACT AND THE FUTURE OF PROGRAMMATIC SURVEILLANCE

In July 2008, Congress enacted the FISA Amendments Act (FAA), Pub. L. No. 110-261, 122 Stat. 2436, 50 U.S.C. §§1881a et seq., which authorized until December 31, 2012, sweeping and suspicionless programmatic surveillance targeting individuals outside the United States. The core of the new subtitle of FISA contains this broad authorization:

§1881a. Procedures for Targeting Certain Persons Outside the United States Other than United States Persons.

(a) Authorization — Notwithstanding any other provision of law, upon the issuance of an order in accordance with subsection (i)(3) or a determination under subsection (c)(2), the Attorney General and the Director of National Intelligence may authorize jointly, for a period of up to 1 year from the effective date of the authorization, the targeting of persons reasonably believed to be located outside the United States to acquire foreign intelligence information.

(b) Limitations — An acquisition authorized under subsection (a) —

(1) may not intentionally target any person known at the time of acquisition to be located in the United States;

(2) may not intentionally target a person reasonably believed to be located outside the United States if the purpose of such acquisition is to target a particular, known person reasonably believed to be in the United States;

(3) may not intentionally target a United States person reasonably believed to be located outside the United States;

(4) may not intentionally acquire any communication as to which the sender and all intended recipients are known at the time of the acquisition to be located in the United States; and

(5) shall be conducted in a manner consistent with the fourth amendment to the Constitution of the United States. . . .

The FISC need not find probable cause of foreign agency or otherwise review individualized surveillance applications under the FAA. *Id.* §1881a(c)(4). Instead, the Attorney General and DNI merely certify to the FISC that acquisitions under the program will meet the targeting objectives and limitations set out above, and that they will satisfy traditional FISA minimization procedures. *Id.* §1881a(g). The certification also must state that the Attorney General had adopted guidelines to ensure that statutory procedures are complied with, that the targeting and minimization procedures and guidelines are consistent with the Fourth Amendment, and that a significant purpose of the programmatic collection is to obtain foreign intelligence information. *Id.*

Judicial review of the certifications, as well as targeting and minimization procedures, must be conducted prior to implementation of an authorization for surveillance, §1881a(i), unless the Attorney General and the DNI determine that "time does not permit" the prior review, in which case the authorization must be sought as soon as practicable, but not more than seven days after the determination is made. §1881a(g)(1)(B). In any event, the judicial review role of the FISC is quite limited:

> **§1881a(I). Judicial Review of Certifications and Procedures — . . .**
>
> (3) Orders —
>   (A) Approval — If the Court finds that a certification submitted in accordance with subsection (g) contains all the required elements and that the targeting and minimization procedures adopted in accordance with subsections (d) and (e) are consistent with the requirements of those subsections and with the fourth amendment to the Constitution of the United States, the Court shall enter an order approving the certification and the use . . . of the procedures for the acquisition. . . .

After a FISC judge approves the program features, the Attorney General and DNI authorize the surveillance program — without the need to obtain judicial orders for individual targets — and issue directives requesting (or compelling) communications carriers to assist. *Id.* §1881a(h). Such a directive was the basis for the following heavily redacted decision of the FISCR, only the second one issued in its 30-year history.

In re Directives [Redacted Text]* Pursuant to Section 105B of the Foreign Intelligence Surveillance Act

Foreign Intelligence Surveillance Court of Review, 2008
551 F.3d 1004

[This decision was based on the temporary Protect America Act, but it concerned some of the core provisions retained in the FISA Amendments Act. It was rendered on August 22, 2008, but only published in redacted form on January 12, 2009.]

---

*The text and footnotes that have been redacted from this opinion contain classified information.

SELYA, Chief Judge. This petition for review stems from directives issued to the petitioner [redacted text] pursuant to a now-expired set of amendments to the Foreign Intelligence Surveillance Act of 1978 (FISA), [50 U.S.C.A. §§1801-1871 (West 2003 & Supp. 2008)]. Among other things, those amendments, known as the Protect America Act of 2007 (PAA), Pub. L. No. 110-55, 121 Stat. 552, authorized the United States to direct communications service providers to assist it in acquiring foreign intelligence when those acquisitions targeted third persons (such as the service provider's customers) reasonably believed to be located outside the United States. Having received [redacted text] such directives, the petitioner challenged their legality before the Foreign Intelligence Surveillance Court (FISC). When that court found the directives lawful and compelled obedience to them, the petitioner brought this petition for review....

I. THE STATUTORY FRAMEWORK

On August 5, 2007, Congress enacted the PAA, codified in pertinent part at 50 U.S.C. §§1805a to 1805c, as a measured expansion of FISA's scope. Subject to certain conditions, the PAA allowed the government to conduct warrantless foreign intelligence surveillance on targets (including United States persons) "reasonably believed" to be located outside the United States. 50 U.S.C. §1805b(a). This proviso is of critical importance here.

Under the new statute, the Director of National Intelligence (DNI) and the Attorney General (AG) were permitted to authorize, for periods of up to one year, "the acquisition of foreign intelligence information concerning persons reasonably believed to be outside the United States" if they determined that the acquisition met five specified criteria. [They are set out in §1881a(b) above.]...Pursuant to this authorization, the DNI and the AG were allowed to issue directives to "person[s]"— a term that includes agents of communications service providers—delineating the assistance needed to acquire the information. *Id.* §1805b(e); *see id.* §1805b(a)(3).

The PAA was a stopgap measure. By its terms, it sunset[ted] on February 16, 2008. Following a lengthy interregnum, the lapsed provisions were repealed on July 10, 2008, through the instrumentality of the FISA Amendments Act of 2008, Pub. L. No. 110-261, §403, 122 Stat. 2436, 2473 (2008). But because the certifications and directives involved in the instant case were issued during the short shelf life of the PAA, they remained in effect. *See* FISA Amendments Act of 2008 §404(a)(1). We therefore assess the validity of the actions at issue here through the prism of the PAA. [redacted text]

II. BACKGROUND

Beginning in [redacted text] 2007, the government issued directives to the petitioner commanding it to assist in warrantless surveillance of certain customers [redacted text and footnote]. These directives were issued pursuant to certifications that purported to contain all the information required by the PAA.

The certifications require certain protections above and beyond those specified by the PAA. For example, they require the AG and the National Security Agency (NSA) to follow the procedures set out under Executive Order 12333 §2.5, 46 Fed. Reg. 59,941, 59,951 (Dec. 4, 1981), before any surveillance is undertaken. Moreover, affidavits supporting the certifications spell out additional safeguards to be employed in effecting the acquisitions. This last set of classified procedures has not been included in the information transmitted to the petitioner. In essence, as implemented, the certifications permit surveillances conducted to obtain foreign intelligence for national security purposes when those surveillances are directed against foreign powers or agents of foreign powers reasonably believed to be located outside the United States.

The . . . petitioner . . . refused to comply with the directives. On [redacted text], the government moved to compel compliance. Following amplitudinous briefing, the FISC handed down a meticulous opinion validating the directives and granting the motion to compel. . . .

III.   ANALYSIS . . .

B.   The Fourth Amendment Challenge. . . .

The petitioner's remonstrance has two main branches. First, it asserts that the government, in issuing the directives, had to abide by the requirements attendant to the Warrant Clause of the Fourth Amendment. Second, it argues that even if a foreign intelligence exception to the warrant requirements exists and excuses compliance with the Warrant Clause, the surveillances mandated by the directives are unreasonable and, therefore, violate the Fourth Amendment. The petitioner limits each of its claims to the harm that may be inflicted upon United States persons. . . .

2.   The Foreign Intelligence Exception.

The recurrent theme permeating the petitioner's arguments is the notion that there is no foreign intelligence exception to the Fourth Amendment's Warrant Clause. The FISC rejected this notion, positing that our decision in *In re Sealed Case* [310 F.3d 717, 721 (FISA Ct. Rev. 2002)] confirmed the existence of a foreign intelligence exception to the warrant requirement.

While the *Sealed Case* court avoided an express holding that a foreign intelligence exception exists by assuming arguendo that whether or not the warrant requirements were met, the statute could survive on reasonableness grounds, *see* 310 F.3d at 741-42, we believe that the FISC's reading of that decision is plausible.

The petitioner argues correctly that the Supreme Court has not explicitly recognized such an exception; indeed, the Court reserved that question in *United States v. United States District Court* (*Keith*), 407 U.S. 297, 308-09 (1972). But the Court has recognized a comparable exception, outside the foreign intelligence context, in so-called "special needs" cases. In those cases, the Court excused compliance with the Warrant Clause when the purpose behind the governmental action went beyond routine law enforcement and insisting upon a warrant would materially interfere with the accomplishment of that purpose. *See, e.g., Vernonia Sch. Dist. 47J v. Acton*, 515 U.S. 646, 653 (1995) (upholding drug testing of high-school athletes and explaining that the exception to the warrant requirement applied "when special needs, beyond the normal need for law enforcement, make the warrant and probable-cause requirement[s] impracticable" (quoting *Griffin v. Wisconsin*, 483 U.S. 868, 873 (1987))); *Skinner v. Ry. Labor Execs. Ass'n*, 489 U.S. 602, 620 (1989) (upholding regulations instituting drug and alcohol testing of railroad workers for safety reasons);

cf. Terry v. Ohio, 392 U.S. 1, 23-24 (1968) (upholding pat-frisk for weapons to protect officer safety during investigatory stop).

The question, then, is whether the reasoning of the special needs cases applies by analogy to justify a foreign intelligence exception to the warrant requirement for surveillance undertaken for national security purposes and directed at a foreign power or an agent of a foreign power reasonably believed to be located outside the United States. Applying principles derived from the special needs cases, we conclude that this type of foreign intelligence surveillance possesses characteristics that qualify it for such an exception.

For one thing, the purpose behind the surveillances ordered pursuant to the directives goes well beyond any garden-variety law enforcement objective. It involves the acquisition from overseas foreign agents of foreign intelligence to help protect national security. Moreover, this is the sort of situation in which the government's interest is particularly intense.

The petitioner has a fallback position. Even if there is a narrow foreign intelligence exception, it asseverates, a definition of that exception should require the foreign intelligence purpose to be the primary purpose of the surveillance. For that proposition, it cites the Fourth Circuit's decision in *United States v. Truong Dinh Hung*, 629 F.2d 908, 915 (4th Cir. 1980). That dog will not hunt.

This court previously has upheld as reasonable under the Fourth Amendment the Patriot Act's substitution of "a significant purpose" for the talismanic phrase "primary purpose." . . . In our view the more appropriate consideration is the programmatic purpose of the surveillances and whether — as in the special needs cases — that programmatic purpose involves some legitimate objective beyond ordinary crime control.

Under this analysis, the surveillances authorized by the directives easily pass muster. Their stated purpose centers on garnering foreign intelligence. There is no indication that the collections of information are primarily related to ordinary criminal-law enforcement purposes. Without something more than a purely speculative set of imaginings, we cannot infer that the purpose of the directives (and, thus, of the surveillances) is other than their stated purpose.

We add, moreover, that there is a high degree of probability that requiring a warrant would hinder the government's ability to collect time-sensitive information and, thus, would impede the vital national security interests that are at stake. *See, e.g., Truong Dinh Hung*, 629 F.2d at 915 (explaining that when the object of a surveillance is a foreign power or its collaborators, "the government has the greatest need for speed, stealth, and secrecy"). [redacted text] Compulsory compliance with the warrant requirement would introduce an element of delay, thus frustrating the government's ability to collect information in a timely manner. [redacted text]

For these reasons, we hold that a foreign intelligence exception to the Fourth Amendment's warrant requirement exists when surveillance is conducted to obtain foreign intelligence for national security purposes and is directed against foreign powers or agents of foreign powers reasonably believed to be located outside the United States.

3. Reasonableness.

This holding does not grant the government carte blanche: even though the foreign intelligence exception applies in a given case, governmental action intruding on individual privacy interests must comport with the Fourth Amendment's reasonableness requirement. Thus, the question here reduces to whether the PAA, as applied through the directives, constitutes a sufficiently reasonable exercise of governmental power to satisfy the Fourth Amendment.

. . . To determine the reasonableness of a particular governmental action, an inquiring court must consider the totality of the circumstances. *Samson v. California,* 547 U.S. 843, 848 (2006); *Tennessee v. Garner,* 471 U.S. 1, 8-9 (1985). This mode of approach takes into account the nature of the government intrusion and how the intrusion is implemented. The more important the government's interest, the greater the intrusion that may be constitutionally tolerated.

The totality of the circumstances model requires the court to balance the interests at stake. If the protections that are in place for individual privacy interests are sufficient in light of the governmental interest at stake, the constitutional scales will tilt in favor of upholding the government's actions. If, however, those protections are insufficient to alleviate the risks of government error and abuse, the scales will tip toward a finding of unconstitutionality.

Here, the relevant governmental interest — the interest in national security — is of the highest order of magnitude. *See Haig v. Agee,* 453 U.S. 280, 307 (1981); *In re Sealed Case,* 310 F.3d at 746. Consequently, we must determine whether the protections afforded to the privacy rights of targeted persons are reasonable in light of this important interest.

At the outset, we dispose of two straw men — arguments based on a misreading of our prior decision in *Sealed Case.* First, the petitioner notes that we found relevant six factors contributing to the protection of individual privacy in the face of a governmental intrusion for national security purposes. *See In re Sealed Case,* 310 F.3d at 737-41 (contemplating prior judicial review, presence or absence of probable cause, particularity, necessity, duration, and minimization). On that exiguous basis, it reasons that our decision there requires a more rigorous standard for gauging reasonableness.

This is a mistaken judgment. In *Sealed Case,* we did not formulate a rigid six-factor test for reasonableness. That would be at odds with the totality of the circumstances test that must guide an analysis in the precincts patrolled by the Fourth Amendment. We merely indicated that the six enumerated factors were relevant under the circumstances of that case.

Second, the petitioner asserts that our *Sealed Case* decision stands for the proposition that, in order to gain constitutional approval, the PAA procedures must contain protections equivalent to the three principal warrant requirements: prior judicial review, probable cause, and particularity. That is incorrect. What we said there — and reiterate today — is that the more a set of procedures resembles those associated with the traditional warrant requirements, the more easily it can be determined that those procedures are within constitutional bounds. We therefore decline the petitioner's invitation to reincorporate into the foreign intelligence exception the same warrant requirements that we already have held inapplicable.

Having placed *Sealed Case* into perspective, we turn to the petitioner's contention that the totality of the circumstances demands a finding of unreasonableness here. That contention boils down to the idea that the protections afforded under the PAA are insufficiently analogous to the protections deemed adequate in *Sealed Case* because the PAA lacks (i) a particularity requirement, (ii) a prior judicial review requirement for determining probable cause that a target is a foreign power or an agent of a foreign power, and (iii) any plausible proxies for the omitted protections. For good measure, the petitioner suggests that the PAA's lack of either a necessity requirement or a reasonable durational limit diminishes the overall reasonableness of surveillances conducted pursuant thereto.

The government rejoins that the PAA, as applied here, constitutes reasonable governmental action. It emphasizes both the protections spelled out in the PAA itself and those mandated under the certifications and directives. This matrix of safeguards comprises at least five components: targeting procedures, minimization procedures, a procedure to ensure that a significant purpose of a surveillance is to obtain foreign intelligence information, procedures incorporated through Executive Order 12333 §2.5, and [redacted text] procedures [redacted text] outlined in an affidavit supporting the certifications.

The record supports the government. Notwithstanding the parade of horribles trotted out by the petitioner, it has presented no evidence of any actual harm, any egregious risk of error, or any broad potential for abuse in the circumstances of the instant case. Thus, assessing the intrusions at issue in light of the governmental interest at stake and the panoply of protections that are in place, we discern no principled basis for invalidating the PAA as applied here. In the pages that follow, we explain our reasoning.

The petitioner's arguments about particularity and prior judicial review are defeated by the way in which the statute has been applied. When combined with the PAA's other protections, the [redacted text] procedures and the procedures incorporated through the Executive Order are constitutionally sufficient compensation for any encroachments.

The [redacted text] procedures [redacted text] are delineated in an ex parte appendix filed by the government. They also are described, albeit with greater generality, in the government's brief. [redacted text] Although the PAA itself does not mandate a showing of particularity, *see* 50 U.S.C. §1805b(b), this pre-surveillance procedure strikes us as analogous to and in conformity with the particularity showing contemplated by *Sealed Case*. 310 F.3d at 740. [redacted text]

The procedures incorporated through section 2.5 of Executive Order 12333, made applicable to the surveillances through the certifications and directives, serve to allay the probable cause concern. That section states in relevant part:

> The Attorney General hereby is delegated the power to approve the use for intelligence purposes, within the United States or against a United States person abroad, of any technique for which a warrant would be required if undertaken for law enforcement purposes, provided that such techniques shall not be undertaken unless the Attorney General has determined in each case that there is *probable cause* to believe that the technique is directed against *a foreign power or an agent of a foreign power*.

46 Fed. Reg. at 59,951 (emphasis supplied). Thus, in order for the government to act upon the certifications, the AG first had to make a determination that probable cause existed to believe that the targeted person is a foreign power or an agent of a foreign power. Moreover, this determination was not made in a vacuum. The AG's decision was informed by the contents of an application made pursuant to Department of

Defense (DOD) regulations. *See* DOD, Procedures Governing the Activities of DOD Intelligence Components that Affect United States Persons, DOD 5240.1-R, Proc. 5, Pt. 2.C (Dec.1982). Those regulations required that the application include a statement of facts demonstrating both probable cause and necessity. *See id.* They also required a statement of the period—not to exceed 90 days—during which the surveillance was thought to be required.[7] *See id.*

[redacted text and footnote]

The petitioner's additional criticisms about the surveillances can be grouped into concerns about potential abuse of executive discretion and concerns about the risk of government error (including inadvertent or incidental collection of information from non-targeted United States persons). We address these groups of criticisms sequentially.

The petitioner suggests that, by placing discretion entirely in the hands of the Executive Branch without prior judicial involvement, the procedures cede to that Branch overly broad power that invites abuse. But this is little more than a lament about the risk that government officials will not operate in good faith. That sort of risk exists even when a warrant is required. In the absence of a showing of fraud or other misconduct by the affiant, the prosecutor, or the judge, a presumption of regularity traditionally attaches to the obtaining of a warrant.

Here—where an exception affords relief from the warrant requirement—common sense suggests that we import the same presumption. Once we have determined that protections sufficient to meet the Fourth Amendment's reasonableness requirement are in place, there is no justification for assuming, in the absence of evidence to that effect, that those prophylactic procedures have been implemented in bad faith.

Similarly, the fact that there is some potential for error is not a sufficient reason to invalidate the surveillances. [redacted text]

Equally as important, some risk of error exists under the original FISA procedures—procedures that received our imprimatur in *Sealed Case*, 310 F.3d at 746. A prior judicial review process does not ensure that the types of errors complained of here [redacted text] would have been prevented.

It is also significant that effective minimization procedures are in place. These procedures serve as an additional backstop against identification errors as well as a means of reducing the impact of incidental intrusions into the privacy of non-targeted United States persons. The minimization procedures implemented here are almost identical to those used under FISA to ensure the curtailment of both mistaken and incidental acquisitions. These minimization procedures were upheld by the FISC in this case, and the petitioner stated at oral argument that it is not quarreling about minimization but, rather, about particularity. Thus, we see no reason to question the adequacy of the minimization protocol.

The petitioner's concern with incidental collections is overblown. It is settled beyond peradventure that incidental collections occurring as a result of constitutionally permissible acquisitions do not render those acquisitions unlawful. *See, e.g., United*

---

7. At oral argument, the government augmented this description, stating that, under the DOD procedure, the NSA typically provides the AG with a two-to-three-page submission articulating the facts underlying the determination that the person in question is an agent of a foreign power; that the National Security Division of the Department of Justice writes its own memorandum to the AG; and that an oral briefing of the AG ensues.

States v. Kahn, 415 U.S. 143, 157-58 (1974). The government assures us that it does not maintain a database of incidentally collected information from non-targeted United States persons, and there is no evidence to the contrary. On these facts, incidentally collected communications of non-targeted United States persons do not violate the Fourth Amendment.

To the extent that the petitioner may be concerned about the adequacy of the targeting procedures, it is worth noting that those procedures include provisions designed to prevent errors. [redacted text] Furthermore, a PAA provision codified at 50 U.S.C. §1805b(d) requires the AG and the DNI to assess compliance with those procedures and to report to Congress semi-annually. . . .

5.   Recapitulation.

After assessing the prophylactic procedures applicable here, including the provisions of the PAA, the affidavits supporting the certifications, section 2.5 of Executive Order 12333, and the declaration mentioned above, we conclude that they are very much in tune with the considerations discussed in *Sealed Case.* Collectively, these procedures require a showing of particularity, a meaningful probable cause determination, and a showing of necessity. They also require a durational limit not to exceed 90 days—an interval that we previously found reasonable.[11] *See In re Sealed Case,* 310 F.3d at 740. Finally, the risks of error and abuse are within acceptable limits and effective minimization procedures are in place.

Balancing these findings against the vital nature of the government's national security interest and the manner of the intrusion, we hold that the surveillances at issue satisfy the Fourth Amendment's reasonableness requirement.

IV.   CONCLUSION

Our government is tasked with protecting an interest of utmost significance to the nation—the safety and security of its people. But the Constitution is the cornerstone of our freedoms, and government cannot unilaterally sacrifice constitutional rights on the altar of national security. Thus, in carrying out its national security mission, the government must simultaneously fulfill its constitutional responsibility to provide reasonable protections for the privacy of United States persons. The judiciary's duty is to hold that delicate balance steady and true.

We believe that our decision to uphold the PAA as applied in this case comports with that solemn obligation. In that regard, we caution that our decision does not constitute an endorsement of broad-based, indiscriminate executive power. Rather, our decision recognizes that where the government has instituted several layers of serviceable safeguards to protect individuals against unwarranted harms and to minimize incidental intrusions, its efforts to protect national security should not be frustrated by the courts. This is such a case.

---

11. This time period was deemed acceptable because of the use of continuing minimization procedures. *In re Sealed Case,* 310 F.3d at 740. Those minimization procedures are nearly identical to the minimization procedures employed in this case. *See* text *supra.*

We need go no further. The decision granting the government's motion to compel is affirmed; the petition for review is denied and dismissed; and the motion for a stay is denied as moot.

So ordered.

ORDER

Whereas,

1. An opinion that addresses and resolves issues of statutory and constitutional significance has been filed under seal;

2. It would serve the public interest and the orderly administration of justice to publish this opinion;

3. Publication of an unredacted opinion would disclose materials that have been properly classified by the Executive Branch;

4. Redactions, after consultation with the Executive Branch, can be made to exclude such classified materials without distorting the content of the discussion of the statutory and constitutional issues;

5. Such redactions have been made by the Court;

It Is Hereby Ordered that:

1. The redacted opinion shall be published . . . .

2. Notwithstanding the publication of the redacted opinion, the parties and their counsel, and any agent of, or other person(s) working in concert with, any party or counsel, shall continue to handle and safeguard all classified information pertaining to this case in accordance with applicable security requirements and regulations and applicable orders issued by this Court or the FISC. . . .

NOTES AND QUESTIONS

a.   The FISA Amendments Act

1. *Changing Technologies.* The original 1978 definition of "electronic surveil-lance" excluded from FISA coverage the collection of foreign-to-foreign and foreign-to-domestic communications by tapping analog lines outside the United States or by intercepting satellite signals. With digitization and related technological changes, new collection techniques brought interceptions that had been conducted outside FISA within the definition of "electronic surveillance" and thus within FISA. A substantial share of the world's Internet traffic now passes through U.S.-based servers on its way from origins to destinations, allowing government agencies to gain access to communications from virtually everywhere from telecom facilities inside the United States. Thus, changing technologies have forced statutory reform in multiple ways. Are you persuaded that these changes in technology justify the programmatic surveillance authorized by the FAA?

2. *How Does the FAA Operate in Practice?* The FAA preserves the long-term FISA principle of relying on the location of the potential target of surveillance and then her U.S. person/non-U.S. person status as bases for regulation. Just how reliable a marker

is location in the digital age? How would the government know that an e-mail message sent from gmail.com or any similar provider originates from outside the United States? Or that a cell phone call placed from a phone with a New York City area code is actually being made by a terrorist suspect who is planning a terrorist attack from inside his home in Yemen? Can you see how over- and under-collection occurs under the FAA, using the assumptions embedded in the Act?

As was apparently the case with the TSP, the FAA does not limit the government to surveillance of particular, known persons reasonably believed to be outside the United States, but instead authorizes what are sometimes characterized as "basket warrants" for surveillance and eventual data mining. 50 U.S.C. §1881a(a). Non-U.S. person targets do not have to be suspected of being an agent of a foreign power, nor, for that matter, must they be suspected of involvement in terrorism or any national security or other crime. *Id.* Does it matter under the FAA that potential targets may be communicating with innocent persons inside the United States?

Presumably, once a specific target for further surveillance is identified through the FAA processes, the government applies to the FISC for an order to conduct traditional FISA electronic surveillance. Are you satisfied that this sequential use of FISA assures that collection objectives are met while protecting the Fourth and First Amendment rights of innocent persons who may be overheard?

3. *Targeting Under the FAA.* The programmatic collection provisions of FAA treat geography as a proxy for U.S. person status, and thus for targeting. Unlike the practice with traditional FISA applications, the government is not required to obtain an FISC order identifying the facilities, telephone lines, e-mail addresses, places, or property where any surveillance will be directed. Given the breadth of the authorization for programmatic surveillance in the FAA, what do you suppose are the targeting criteria? Who decides? Might targets include a terrorist organization? A large set of telephone numbers or e-mail addresses? An entire area code or ISP? Although details of the implementation of the program authorized by the FAA remain classified, experts guess that the government uses a broad vacuum-cleaner-like first stage of collection, focusing on transactional data, in which wholesale collection occurs after some filtering criteria are developed. A more particularized identification of content follows by mining the collected data. *See* Richard A. Posner, *Privacy, Surveillance, and Law,* 75 U. Chi. L. Rev. 254, 253 (2008).

Because of the difficulty of ascertaining a target's location, and because the location and identity of targets' correspondents are impossible to predict, over-collection seems unavoidable. For example, despite the statutory prohibition on deliberately targeting U.S. persons, incidental acquisition of U.S. person communications will occur whenever such a person uses any foreign telecommunications services, including the Internet. *Id.* at 252. Can you describe some protocol that would prevent, or at least reduce, such over-collection? Should the probable cause standard applicable in traditional FISA surveillance be imported into the FAA? Some flexible approach, with higher standards for relatively minor threats and lower standards for more serious threats?

Can you see how under-collection is also likely under the FAA? Consider a Saudi Al Qaeda operative who is located in Pakistan using a cell phone with a Washington, D.C., area code. Although subject to warrantless surveillance under the FAA, government officials might assume, on the basis of his cell phone information, that he is a U.S. person. Can you think of a statutory solution to the under-collection problem?

4. *FAA Minimization.* The minimization requirements for collection undertaken pursuant to the FAA are identical to those for traditional FISA surveillance described *supra* p. 589. 50 U.S.C. §1881a(e). The FISC does not review the implementation of minimization procedures or practices for the programmatic surveillance it approves, and the Act permits the government to retain and disseminate information relating to U.S. persons so long as the government determines that it is "foreign intelligence information." *Id.* §1801(h)(1). Do you see any potential for abuse of discretion in the retention and dissemination of information under the FAA that does not exist in traditional FISA collection? What could be done to reduce any such potential?

As an alternative to relying on minimization practices, some experts have proposed that collection limitations be relaxed in return for robust restrictions on the ability of government officials to access or use the information collected. Proposals include using automated filters to segregate communications involving U.S. persons from others, allowing the latter to be handled without much restriction; setting limits on the use of data that has been collected (e.g., for foreign intelligence purposes, not for unrelated criminal prosecution); requiring judicial approval before disseminating collected data; and using audit trails to hold officials accountable if they use data for impermissible purposes. *See* Markle Found., *Mobilizing Information to Prevent Terrorism* 65-71 (2006). Do you think that some version of the proposed authorized-use rules would be preferable to minimization?

5. *Extending FISA to U.S. Persons Abroad.* For the first time, FAA subjects surveillance intentionally targeting a U.S. person reasonably believed to be abroad to traditional FISA foreign agency/probable cause procedures. 50 U.S.C. §§1881b,1881c. Congress has thus undertaken to regulate a critical national security activity of the President outside the United States. Do you suppose the President was constrained in any way in such surveillance before FAA? Might the extension of FAA abroad raise constitutional questions that would not exist in its domestic application? Could, or should, the individual targeting requirement be applied to non-U.S. persons abroad? Some answers to these questions may be found in Chapter 25.

6. *Privacy in the Digital Age.* Should our conceptions of privacy be updated for the digital/social networking era? Is privacy now more about keeping information secret from the government than in the past? Is it about retaining control over how our personal information is made available to others, including the government? Or is privacy needed as a shield from excessive government power?

7. *Congressional Oversight.* The FAA requires that

> not less frequently than once every 6 months, the Attorney General shall fully inform, in a manner consistent with national security, the congressional intelligence committees and the Committees on the Judiciary of the Senate and the House of Representatives, consistent with the Rules of the House of Representatives, [and] the . . . Rules of the Senate . . . concerning the implementation of this title. . . . [50 U.S.C. §1881f.]

Similar assessments must be provided to the FISC, and the DOJ Inspector General and other IG offices of agencies authorized to collect information under the FAA may review compliance with FAA targeting and minimization procedures and guidelines.

The first semiannual assessments provided by the Attorney General and DNI found violations of the targeting and minimization procedures. The assessments state that the number of violations is small when compared to the volume of activity. *Semiannual Assessment of Compliance with Procedures and Guidelines Issued Pursuant to Section 702 of the Foreign Intelligence Surveillance Act, Submitted by the Attorney General and the Director of National Intelligence* (Dec. 2009), *available at* http://www.aclu.org/files/pdfs/natsec/faafoia20101129/FAAODNI0001.pdf.

8. *Fine-Tuning the FAA?* In view of the indeterminacy of target location and the lack of other targeting criteria in the FAA, should or *must* Congress revise the authorization for programmatic surveillance to satisfy Fourth Amendment requirements? According to one commentator, Congress should authorize automated monitoring under the FAA to identify potential threats, so long as there is

> a circumscribed but authorized procedure for follow-up monitoring or investigation of initial suspicion derived from automated monitoring. . . . [W]hat is needed, in my view, is the electronic surveillance equivalent of a *Terry* stop. [Kim Taipale, *The Ear of Dionysus: Rethinking Foreign Intelligence Surveillance*, 9 Yale J.L. & Tech. 128, 160 (2007).]

The initial automated monitoring presumably would consist of collecting telephone numbers and analyzing patterns of their use. Neither it nor the follow-up investigation would, according to Taipale's proposal, be subject to FISA procedures or would collect "content" for Fourth Amendment purposes. *Terry v. Ohio*, 392 U.S. 1 (1968), held that police may detain a suspect ("stop and frisk") for a brief period based on reasonable suspicion that a crime has been committed. Do you think the *Terry* case is analogous? Could officials collect, say, fragments of phone calls or e-mail messages, then check some database to learn whether the fragments lead to suspicion about a potential target? Presumably then officials would follow traditional FISA processes to conduct a full-blown collection. Can you see the value of granting officials discretion to make the follow-up monitoring Taipale advocates? What downside risks could you imagine?

9. *Exclusivity Redux.* The FAA includes this language regarding exclusivity:

> (a) Except as provided in subsection (b), the procedures of chapters 119, 121, and 206 of title 18, United States Code, and this Act shall be the exclusive means by which electronic surveillance and the interception of domestic wire, oral, or electronic communications may be conducted.
>
> (b) Only an express statutory authorization for electronic surveillance or the interception of domestic wire, oral, or electronic communications, other than as an amendment to this Act or chapters 119, 121, or 206 of title 18, United States Code, shall constitute an additional exclusive means for the purpose of subsection (a). [50 U.S.C. §1812]

Does this provision adequately express congressional determination to provide the exclusive rules for conducting electronic surveillance for foreign intelligence purposes? Could the President ever have a legal justification for circumventing the FAA?

10. *Testing the Constitutionality of the FAA in Court?* A mix of individuals and groups involved in human rights, media, law, and labor challenged the constitutionality of the core provision of the FAA that authorizes targeting non-U.S. persons outside the

United States for purposes of collecting foreign intelligence. The plaintiffs demonstrated that they incurred costs to adjust their means of communicating out of fear that the government would intercept their communications under the FAA. In *Amnesty International USA v. Clapper*, 638 F.3d 118 (2d Cir. 2011), a panel of the Second Circuit reversed a dismissal of the lawsuit and concluded that the plaintiffs have standing to sue because "the plaintiffs have established that they have a reasonable fear of injury and have incurred costs to avoid it." *Id.* at 122. On the merits, the plaintiffs claim that the FAA procedures violate the Fourth and First Amendments, Article III, and the principles of separation of powers. If the federal courts reach the merits in this lawsuit, how should the plaintiffs' claims be decided?

b.   The *In re Directives* Decision

1. *Comparing Procedural Protections in FISA and the PAA.* The petitioning telecom relied on the FISCR's *In re Sealed Case* decision in arguing that the procedural protections provided by the PAA were insufficient, including requirements of particularity and prior judicial review for probable cause of foreign agency. Are you satisfied that the protections in the PAA (which are practically the same in the FAA) satisfy the Fourth Amendment?

2. *Special Needs Redux.* Recall that in its first decision the FISCR relied in part on the special needs doctrine to uphold DOJ guidelines in 2002 that tore down the wall between intelligence officials and criminal and prosecutors. See *supra* p. 600. There the "special need" was foreign intelligence collection. Is the special needs doctrine better suited to programmatic surveillance than to traditional FISA collection? Are you persuaded that the special needs doctrine justifies a foreign intelligence exception to the Warrant Clause?

3. *Reasonableness Redux.* According to the FISCR, Fourth Amendment reasonableness was satisfied in part by a variety of safeguards found within and outside the PAA. How did the FISCR make its decision about reasonableness? Why did the court not inquire into the government's compliance with minimization requirements as an aspect of reasonableness? In addition, the FISCR relied on Executive Order No. 12,333 and a secret affidavit spelling out safeguards in deciding that there were adequate protections for the telecom. Do you agree with the court that redactions "can be made to exclude such classified materials without distorting the content of the discussion of the statutory and constitutional issues"?

Third-Party Records and Data Mining

The conventional wisdom after 9/11 was that U.S. national security agencies failed to "connect the dots" before the attacks. But some experts have noted that while there "certainly was a lack of dot-connecting before September 11," the more critical failure was that "[t]here were too few useful dots." Robert Bryant et al., *America Needs More Spies*, The Economist, July 12, 2003, at 30. In this chapter, we explore both parts of this insight.

In Part A we revisit privacy themes addressed in earlier chapters to test their portability to third-party records—personal information voluntarily turned over to others. Next, in Part B, we consider how so-called national security letters (NSLs) and Foreign Intelligence Surveillance Act (FISA) §215 orders are used to collect dots in quantity—transactional data—from third-party record holders like banks, telephone companies, Internet service providers, and travel agencies. Finally, in Part C, we look at how dots are connected by computer "data mining" to perform link analysis or pattern recognition.

A. FINDING THE DOTS — THIRD-PARTY RECORDS

1. Expectations of Privacy Regarding Third-Party Records

Smith v. Maryland
United States Supreme Court, 1979
442 U.S. 735

Mr. Justice BLACKMUN delivered the opinion of the Court. This case presents the question whether the installation and use of a pen register[1] constitutes a "search"

---

1. "A pen register is a mechanical device that records the numbers dialed on a telephone by monitoring the electrical impulses caused when the dial on the telephone is released. It does not overhear oral communications and does not indicate whether calls are actually completed." *United States v. New York Tel. Co.*, 434 U.S. 159, 161 n.1 [(1977)]. A pen register is "usually installed at a central telephone facility [and] records on a paper tape all numbers dialed from [the] line" to which it is attached. *United States v. Giordano*, 416 U.S. 505, 549 n.1 (1974).

within the meaning of the Fourth Amendment, made applicable to the States through the Fourteenth Amendment.

On March 5, 1976, in Baltimore, Md., Patricia McDonough was robbed. She gave the police a description of the robber and of a 1975 Monte Carlo automobile she had observed near the scene of the crime. After the robbery, McDonough began receiving threatening and obscene phone calls from a man identifying himself as the robber. On one occasion, the caller asked that she step out on her front porch; she did so, and saw the 1975 Monte Carlo she had earlier described to police moving slowly past her home. On March 16, police spotted a man who met McDonough's description driving a 1975 Monte Carlo in her neighborhood. By tracing the license plate number, police learned that the car was registered in the name of petitioner, Michael Lee Smith.

The next day, the telephone company, at police request, installed a pen register at its central offices to record the numbers dialed from the telephone at petitioner's home. The police did not get a warrant or court order before having the pen register installed. The register revealed that on March 17 a call was placed from petitioner's home to McDonough's phone. On the basis of this and other evidence, the police obtained a warrant to search petitioner's residence. The search revealed that a page in petitioner's phone book was turned down to the name and number of Patricia McDonough; the phone book was seized. Petitioner was arrested, [convicted, and sentenced to six years' imprisonment.] . . .

. . . In determining whether a particular form of government-initiated electronic surveillance is a "search" within the meaning of the Fourth Amendment, our lodestar is *Katz v. United States*, 389 U.S. 347 (1967)[5]. . . .

In applying the *Katz* analysis to this case, it is important to begin by specifying precisely the nature of the state activity that is challenged. The activity here took the form of installing and using a pen register. Since the pen register was installed on telephone company property at the telephone company's central offices, petitioner obviously cannot claim that his "property" was invaded or that police intruded into a "constitutionally protected area." Petitioner's claim, rather, is that, notwithstanding the absence of a trespass, the State, as did the Government in *Katz,* infringed a "legitimate expectation of privacy" that petitioner held. Yet a pen register differs significantly from the listening device employed in *Katz,* for pen registers do not acquire the *contents* of communications. This Court recently noted:

> "Indeed, a law enforcement official could not even determine from the use of a pen register whether a communication existed. These devices do not hear sound. They disclose only the telephone numbers that have been dialed—a means of establishing communication. Neither the purport of any communication between the caller and the recipient of the call, their identities, nor whether the call was even completed is disclosed by pen registers." *United States v. New York Tel. Co.,* 434 U.S. 159, 167 (1977).

5. Situations can be imagined, of course, in which *Katz*'s two-pronged inquiry would provide an inadequate index of Fourth Amendment protection. For example, if the Government were suddenly to announce on nationwide television that all homes henceforth would be subject to warrantless entry, individuals thereafter might not in fact entertain any actual expectation of privacy regarding their homes, papers, and effects. Similarly, if a refugee from a totalitarian country, unaware of this Nation's traditions, erroneously assumed that police were continuously monitoring his telephone conversations, a subjective expectation of privacy regarding the contents of his calls might be lacking as well. In such circumstances, where an individual's subjective expectations had been "conditioned" by influences alien to well-recognized Fourth Amendment freedoms, those subjective expectations obviously could play no meaningful role in ascertaining what the scope of Fourth Amendment protection was. In determining whether a "legitimate expectation of privacy" existed in such cases, a normative inquiry would be proper.

Given a pen register's limited capabilities, therefore, petitioner's argument that its installation and use constituted a "search" necessarily rests upon a claim that he had a "legitimate expectation of privacy" regarding the numbers he dialed on his phone.

This claim must be rejected. First, we doubt that people in general entertain any actual expectation of privacy in the numbers they dial. All telephone users realize that they must "convey" phone numbers to the telephone company, since it is through telephone company switching equipment that their calls are completed. All subscribers realize, moreover, that the phone company has facilities for making permanent records of the numbers they dial, for they see a list of their long-distance (toll) calls on their monthly bills. In fact, pen registers and similar devices are routinely used by telephone companies "for the purposes of checking billing operations, detecting fraud and preventing violations of law." *United States v. New York Tel. Co.*, 434 U.S., at 174-175. . . .

. . . Most phone books tell subscribers, on a page entitled "Consumer Information," that the company "can frequently help in identifying to the authorities the origin of unwelcome and troublesome calls." Telephone users, in sum, typically know that they must convey numerical information to the phone company; that the phone company has facilities for recording this information; and that the phone company does in fact record this information for a variety of legitimate business purposes. Although subjective expectations cannot be scientifically gauged, it is too much to believe that telephone subscribers, under these circumstances, harbor any general expectation that the numbers they dial will remain secret. . . .

. . . [E]ven if petitioner did harbor some subjective expectation that the phone numbers he dialed would remain private, this expectation is not "one that society is prepared to recognize as 'reasonable.' " This Court consistently has held that a person has no legitimate expectation of privacy in information he voluntarily turns over to third parties. E.g., *United States v. Miller*, 425 U.S. [435] at 442-444 [1976]. In *Miller,* for example, the Court held that a bank depositor has no "legitimate 'expectation of privacy' " in financial information "voluntarily conveyed to . . . banks and exposed to their employees in the ordinary course of business." 425 U.S. at 442. The Court explained:

> "The depositor takes the risk, in revealing his affairs to another, that the information will be conveyed by that person to the Government. . . . This Court has held repeatedly that the Fourth Amendment does not prohibit the obtaining of information revealed to a third party and conveyed by him to Government authorities, even if the information is revealed on the assumption that it will be used only for a limited purpose and the confidence placed in the third party will not be betrayed." *Id.* at 443.

Because the depositor "assumed the risk" of disclosure, the Court held that it would be unreasonable for him to expect his financial records to remain private.

This analysis dictates that petitioner can claim no legitimate expectation of privacy here. When he used his phone, petitioner voluntarily conveyed numerical information to the telephone company and "exposed" that information to its equipment in the ordinary course of business. In so doing, petitioner assumed the risk that the company would reveal to police the numbers he dialed. The switching equipment that processed those numbers is merely the modern counterpart of the operator who, in an earlier day, personally completed calls for the subscriber. Petitioner concedes that if he had placed his calls through an operator, he could claim no legitimate expectation of privacy. We are not inclined to hold that a different constitutional result is required because the telephone company has decided to automate. . . .

. . . We therefore conclude that petitioner in all probability entertained no actual expectation of privacy in the phone numbers he dialed, and that, even if he did, his expectation was not "legitimate." The installation and use of a pen register, consequently, was not a "search," and no warrant was required. . . .

Mr. Justice POWELL took no part in the consideration or decision of this case.

Mr. Justice STEWART, with whom Mr. Justice BRENNAN joins, dissenting. . . . The numbers dialed from a private telephone — although certainly more prosaic than the conversation itself — are not without "content." Most private telephone subscribers may have their own numbers listed in a publicly distributed directory, but I doubt there are any who would be happy to have broadcast to the world a list of the local or long distance numbers they have called. This is not because such a list might in some sense be incriminating, but because it easily could reveal the identities of the persons and the places called, and thus reveal the most intimate details of a person's life. . . .

Mr. Justice MARSHALL, with whom Mr. Justice BRENNAN joins, dissenting. . . . [E]ven assuming . . . that individuals "typically know" that a phone company monitors calls for internal reasons, it does not follow that they expect this information to be made available to the public in general or the government in particular. Privacy is not a discrete commodity, possessed absolutely or not at all. Those who disclose certain facts to a bank or phone company for a limited business purpose need not assume that this information will be released to other persons for other purposes.

The crux of the Court's holding, however, is that whatever expectation of privacy petitioner may in fact have entertained regarding his calls, it is not one "society is prepared to recognize as 'reasonable.'" In so ruling, the Court determines that individuals who convey information to third parties have "assumed the risk" of disclosure to the government. This analysis is misconceived in two critical respects.

Implicit in the concept of assumption of risk is some notion of choice. At least in the third-party consensual surveillance cases, which first incorporated risk analysis into Fourth Amendment doctrine, the defendant presumably had exercised some discretion in deciding who should enjoy his confidential communications. By contrast here, unless a person is prepared to forgo use of what for many has become a personal or professional necessity, he cannot help but accept the risk of surveillance. It is idle to speak of "assuming" risks in contexts where, as a practical matter, individuals have no realistic alternative.

More fundamentally, to make risk analysis dispositive in assessing the reasonableness of privacy expectations would allow the government to define the scope of Fourth Amendment protections. For example, law enforcement officials, simply by announcing their intent to monitor the content of random samples of first-class mail or private phone conversations, could put the public on notice of the risks they would thereafter assume in such communications. Yet, although acknowledging this implication of its analysis, the Court is willing to concede only that, in some circumstances, a further "normative inquiry would be proper." No meaningful effort is made to explain what those circumstances might be, or why this case is not among them.

In my view, whether privacy expectations are legitimate within the meaning of *Katz* depends not on the risks an individual can be presumed to accept when imparting information to third parties, but on the risks he should be forced to assume in a free and open society. . . .

The use of pen registers, I believe, constitutes such an extensive intrusion. To hold otherwise ignores the vital role telephonic communication plays in our personal and professional relationships, as well as the First and Fourth Amendment interests implicated by unfettered official surveillance. Privacy in placing calls is of value not only to those engaged in criminal activity. The prospect of unregulated governmental monitoring will undoubtedly prove disturbing even to those with nothing illicit to hide. Many individuals, including members of unpopular political organizations or journalists with confidential sources, may legitimately wish to avoid disclosure of their personal contacts. Permitting governmental access to telephone records on less than probable cause may thus impede certain forms of political affiliation and journalistic endeavor that are the hallmark of a truly free society. Particularly given the Government's previous reliance on warrantless telephonic surveillance to trace reporters' sources and monitor protected political activity, I am unwilling to insulate use of pen registers from independent judicial review. . . .

NOTES AND QUESTIONS

1. *Pen Registers and Trap and Trace vs. Wiretaps.* What is it about a pen register or trap and trace device that makes it so different from a wiretap? Should the differences have such constitutional significance? Consider the analogy to a mailed letter. The letter contains protected content, while the envelope contains only the mailing and return addresses and postage information. Thus, the contents of the letter are afforded protection, but the envelope is not. *See* Orin S. Kerr, *Internet Surveillance Law After the USA Patriot Act: The Big Brother That Isn't*, 97 Nw. U. L. Rev. 607, 611-616 (2003). Does the same contents/envelope distinction fit the pen register/trap and trace scenarios? Consider the views of Justices Stewart and Marshall. What "content" is arguably revealed by a pen register? *See* Daniel J. Solove, *Reconstructing Electronic Surveillance Law*, 72 Geo. Wash. L. Rev. 1264, 1286-1287 (2004).

2. *Comparing Katz.* Is the privacy interest recognized by the Court in *Katz* different in any appreciable way from the interest asserted in *Smith*? If the telephone company had the technical means to listen in on the phone calls in both cases, why protect one caller but not the other? Are the phone numbers dialed private? Should they be? *See* Patricia Bellia, *Surveillance Law Through Cyberlaw's Lens*, 72 Geo. Wash. L. Rev. 1375, 1405 (2004). Why should providing that information to a private third party matter so much in deciding what information the government can acquire? When you provide phone numbers to the phone company, do you expect that it will turn them over to Big Brother? Have you knowingly and willingly "assumed the risk" of such disclosure?

Alternatively, is the outcome in *Smith* best understood as reflecting a judgment that it doesn't really matter much, because the phone numbers were not of much value to the individual? *See* Daniel J. Solove, *Digital Dossiers and the Dissipation of Fourth Amendment Privacy*, 75 S. Cal. L. Rev. 1083 (2002).

3. *Extending Smith to the Internet.* Is *Smith* authority for searching e-mail subject lines and URLs without a warrant? See *infra* p. 648.

4. *A Statutory Remedy?* After *Smith*, Congress enacted the Pen Register Act, 18 U.S.C. §§3121-3127 (2006). The Act imposes a warrant requirement before the government may obtain a pen register. *Id.* §3121(a). However, in contrast to a traditional Fourth Amendment warrant based on probable cause, the government may obtain an order for a pen register simply by showing that its use is "relevant to an ongoing investigation." *Id.* §3123(a). The USA Patriot Act extended the pen register and trap and trace authorities to include addressing information on e-mail and to ISP and URL addresses. Pub. L. No. 107-56, §216, 115 Stat. 272, 288-290 (2001) (amending 18 U.S.C. §3127(3), (4)). See *infra* p. 666. Are these statutory provisions constitutional?

5. *The Implications of Smith. Smith* laid the foundation for more than just pen registers. If people have no legitimate expectation of privacy in information they voluntarily convey to the phone company in the normal course of business, then they also arguably have no such expectation in the transactional information they convey to hundreds of other third parties in the ordinary course of business. Congress therefore authorized the Foreign Intelligence Surveillance Court (FISC) to issue orders for transactional records pursuant to FISA §215 and enacted several other statutes authorizing the FBI to obtain transactional data by issuing NSLs without prior court order. These are described in the table on the next page. In calendar year 2005, the government reported that it had obtained 155 §215 orders and issued 9,254 NSLs related to U.S. persons (excluding NSLs for subscriber information). Letter from William E. Moschella (Assistant Attorney General, Dep't of Justice) to J. Dennis Hastert (Speaker, House of Representatives) (Apr. 28, 2006). Aggregate FBI use of NSLs increased from 8,500 requests in 2000 to 47,000 in 2005, while the percentage of NSLs used to investigate U.S. persons increased from 39 percent in 2003 to 57 percent in 2006. Charles Doyle, *National Security Letters in Foreign Intelligence Investigations: Legal Background and Recent Amendments* 13, 15 (Cong. Res. Serv. RL33320), Sept. 8, 2009.

6. *Some of the Dots: Transactional Data.* "'Transactional' information broadly describes information that documents financial or communications transactions without necessarily revealing the substance of those transactions." Michael J. Woods, *Counterintelligence and Access to Transactional Records: A Practical History of USA PATRIOT Act Section 215*, 1 J. Nat'l Security L. & Pol'y 37, 41 (2005). Such information includes telephone billing records that list numbers dialed, an Internet service provider's records showing a customer's Internet use, records of banking transactions and money transfers, credit card records, and travel records. It has reportedly proven invaluable in counterterrorist investigations. Terrorists can try to encrypt or otherwise disguise the substance of their communications, but "[i]t is far more difficult for them to cover their transactional footsteps." *Id.* at 41-42. Counter-terrorist analysts can use transactional information to perform "link analysis" to tie suspects together and thus help identify terror cells. *See* McCormick Tribune Found., *Counterterrorism Technology and Privacy* (Cantigny Conf. Rep.) 53 (Patrick J. McMahon

Profile of the Current NSL Statutes

NSL Statute	18 U.S.C. 2709	12 U.S.C. 3414	15 U.S.C. 1681u	15 U.S.C. 1681v	50 U.S.C. 436
Addressee	communications providers	financial institutions	consumer credit agencies	consumer credit agencies	financial institutions, consumer credit agencies, travel agencies
Certifying officials	senior FBI officials and SACs	senior FBI officials and SACs	senior FBI officials and SACs	supervisory official of an agency investigating, conducting intelligence activities relating to or analyzing int'l terrorism	senior officials no lower than Ass't Secretary or Ass't Director of agency w/employees w/access to classified material
Information covered	identified customer's name, address, length of service, and billing info	identified customer financial records	identified consumer's name, address, former address, place and former place of employment	all information relating to an identified consumer	all financial information relating to consenting, identified employee
Standard/ purpose	relevant to an investigation to protect against int'l terrorism or clandestine intelligence activities	sought for foreign counter-intelligence purposes to protect against int'l terrorism or clandestine intelligence activities	sought for an investigation to protect against int'l terrorism or clandestine intelligence activities	necessary for the agency's investigation, activities, or analysis relating to int'l terrorism	necessary to conduct a law enforcement investigation, counter-intelligence inquiry or security determination
Dissemination	only per Att'y Gen. guidelines	only per Att'y Gen. guidelines	w/ FBI, to secure approval for intell. investigation, to military investigators when inform. relates to military member	no statutory provision	only to agency of employee under investigation, DoJ for law enforcement or intell. purposes, or fed. agency when clearly relevant to mission
Immunity/fees	no provisions	no provisions	fees; immunity for good faith compliance with an NSL	immunity for good faith compliance with an NSL	reimbursement; immunity for good faith compliance with an NSL

apporteur, 2005). An example is the retrospective link analysis of the 9/11 hijackers. Woods, *supra*, at 42. It can also be used for pattern recognition and data matching to identify suspects. See *infra* pp. 671.

7. *The Expectation of Privacy in Transactional Records.* Do you, subjectively, have any expectation of privacy when you convey data to a bank or commercial vendor, dial a telephone number, or transmit an e-mail message? Of course, you do not expect to keep the information private from the bank, vendor, phone company, or Internet service provider. The entities with which you deal directly need the data to complete the transaction that you initiate. But do you also expect those entities to share the information with others? In fact, don't some vendors promise you just the opposite, and sometimes even provide a box to check or button to indicate whether you want such data to be shared?

Have the dramatic changes in patterns of commercial activity and communications in the decades since *Smith* and *Miller* made such an expectation reasonable? *See* Christopher Slobogin & Joseph E. Schumacher, *Reasonable Expectations of Privacy and Autonomy in Fourth Amendment Cases: An Empirical Look at "Understandings Recognized and Permitted by Society,"* 42 Duke L.J. 727 (1993) (reporting a survey suggesting that the public finds government perusal of bank records highly invasive). Was the reasonableness of such an expectation altered by the events of September 11, 2001? Consider the following case.

United States v. Warshak

United States Court of Appeals, Sixth Circuit, 2010
631 F.3d 266

BOGGS, Circuit Judge. Berkeley Premium Nutraceuticals, Inc., was an incredibly profitable company that served as the distributor of Enzyte, an herbal supplement purported to enhance male sexual performance. In this appeal, defendants Steven Warshak ("Warshak"), Harriet Warshak ("Harriet"), and TCI Media, Inc. ("TCI"), challenge their convictions stemming from a massive scheme to defraud Berkeley's customers. . . .

I. STATEMENT OF THE FACTS . . .

[During a criminal investigation of Steven Warshak for mail and wire fraud, money laundering, and related federal offenses, the government obtained an order from a United States Magistrate Judge directing an internet service provider, NuVox Communications, ("ISP") to turn over to government agents information pertaining to Warshak's e-mail account, including (1) customer account information, such as application information, "account identifiers," "[b]illing information to include bank account numbers," contact information, and "[any] other information pertaining to the customer, including set up, synchronization, etc."; (2) "[t]he contents of wire or electronic communications (not in electronic storage unless greater than 181 days old) that were placed or stored in directories or files owned or controlled" by the ISP; and (3) "[a]ll Log files and backup tapes." At a later date, Warshak was informed of the order and sought unsuccessfully to suppress evidence derived from his e-mails in his criminal trial.]

II. ANALYSIS

A. The Search & Seizure of Warshak's Emails

Warshak argues that the government's warrantless, *ex parte* seizure of approximately 27,000 of his private emails constituted a violation of the Fourth Amendment's prohibition on unreasonable searches and seizures.[12] The government counters that, even if government agents violated the Fourth Amendment in obtaining the emails, they relied in good faith on the Stored Communications Act ("SCA"), 18 U.S.C. §§2701 et seq., a statute that allows the government to obtain certain electronic communications without procuring a warrant. The government also argues that any hypothetical Fourth Amendment violation was harmless. We find that the government *did* violate Warshak's Fourth Amendment rights by compelling his Internet Service Provider ("ISP") to turn over the contents of his emails. However, we agree that agents relied on the SCA in good faith, and therefore hold that reversal is unwarranted.

1. The Stored Communications Act

The Stored Communications Act ("SCA"), 18 U.S.C. §§2701 et seq., "permits a 'governmental entity' to compel a service provider to disclose the contents of [electronic] communications in certain circumstances." *Warshak II*, 532 F.3d at 523. As this court explained in *Warshak II*:

> Three relevant definitions bear on the meaning of the compelled-disclosure provisions of the Act. "[E]lectronic communication service[s]" permit "users . . . to send or receive wire or electronic communications," [18 U.S.C.] §2510(15), a definition that covers basic e-mail services, *see* Patricia L. Bellia et al., *Cyberlaw: Problems of Policy and Jurisprudence in the Information Age* 584 (2d ed. 2004). "[E]lectronic storage" is "any temporary, intermediate storage of a wire or electronic communication . . . and . . . any storage of such communication by an electronic communication service for purposes of backup protection of such communication." 18 U.S.C. §2510(17). "[R]emote computing service[s]" provide "computer storage or processing services" to customers, *id.* §2711(2), and are designed for longer-term storage, *see* Orin S. Kerr, *A User's Guide to the Stored Communications Act, and a Legislator's Guide to Amending It,* 72 Geo. Wash. L. Rev. 1208, 1216 (2004).
>
> The compelled-disclosure provisions give different levels of privacy protection based on whether the e-mail is held with an electronic communication service or a remote computing service and based on how long the e-mail has been in electronic storage. The government may obtain the contents of e-mails that are "in electronic storage" with an electronic communication service for 180 days or less "only pursuant to a warrant." 18 U.S.C. §2703(a). The government has three options for obtaining communications stored with a remote computing service and communications that have been in electronic storage with an electronic service provider for more than 180 days: (1) obtain a warrant; [(2) use a generic form of authorization issued by the investigating agency;] or (3) obtain a court order under §2703(d). *Id.* §2703(a), (b).

532 F.3d at 523-24 (some alterations in original).

---

12. This is not the first time Warshak has raised this argument. In *Warshak v. United States,* 490 F.3d 455 (6th Cir. 2007) ("*Warshak I*"), a panel of this court determined that Warshak did indeed have a privacy interest in the contents of his emails. That decision was vacated on ripeness grounds. *See Warshak v. United States,* 532 F.3d 521 (6th Cir. 2008) (en banc) ("*Warshak II*"). In the present case, Warshak's claim is ripe for review.

2. Factual Background

Email was a critical form of communication among Berkeley personnel. As a consequence, Warshak had a number of email accounts with various ISPs, including an account with NuVox Communications. In October 2004, the government formally requested that NuVox prospectively preserve the contents of any emails to or from Warshak's email account. The request was made pursuant to [statute] and it instructed NuVox to preserve all future messages. NuVox acceded to the government's request and began preserving copies of Warshak's incoming and outgoing emails — copies that would not have existed absent the prospective preservation request. Per the government's instructions, Warshak was not informed that his messages were being archived. In January 2005, the government obtained a subpoena [authorized by statute] and compelled NuVox to turn over the emails that it had begun preserving the previous year. In May 2005, the government served NuVox with an *ex parte* court order under §2703(d) that required NuVox to surrender any additional email messages in Warshak's account. In all, the government compelled NuVox to reveal the contents of approximately 27,000 emails. Warshak did not receive notice of either the subpoena or the order until May 2006.

3. The Fourth Amendment . . .

Not all government actions are invasive enough to implicate the Fourth Amendment. "The Fourth Amendment's protections hinge on the occurrence of a "search," a legal term of art whose history is riddled with complexity." *Widgren v. Maple Grove Twp.*, 429 F.3d 575, 578 (6th Cir. 2005). A "search" occurs when the government infringes upon "an expectation of privacy that society is prepared to consider reasonable." *United States v. Jacobsen,* 466 U.S. 109, 113 (1984). This standard breaks down into two discrete inquiries: "first, has the [target of the investigation] manifested a subjective expectation of privacy in the object of the challenged search? Second, is society willing to recognize that expectation as reasonable?" *California v. Ciraolo,* 476 U.S. 207, 211 (1986) (citing *Smith v. Maryland,* 442 U.S. 735, 740 (1979)).

Turning first to the subjective component of the test, we find that Warshak plainly manifested an expectation that his emails would be shielded from outside scrutiny. As he notes in his brief, his "entire business and personal life was contained within the . . . emails seized." Appellant's Br. at 39-40. Given the often sensitive and sometimes damning substance of his emails, we think it highly unlikely that Warshak expected them to be made public, for people seldom unfurl their dirty laundry in plain view. *See, e.g., United States v. Maxwell,* 45 M.J. 406, 417 (C.A.A.F.1996) ("[T]he tenor and content of e-mail conversations between appellant and his correspondent, 'Launchboy,' reveal a[n] . . . expectation that the conversations were private."). Therefore, we conclude that Warshak had a subjective expectation of privacy in the contents of his emails.

The next question is whether society is prepared to recognize that expectation as reasonable. *See Smith,* 442 U.S. at 740. This question is one of grave import and enduring consequence, given the prominent role that email has assumed in modern communication. *Cf. Katz,* 389 U.S. at 352 (suggesting that the Constitution must be read to account for "the vital role that the public telephone has come to play in private communication"). Since the advent of email, the telephone call and the letter have waned in importance, and an explosion of Internet-based communication has taken place. People are now able to send sensitive and intimate information, instantaneously, to friends, family, and colleagues half a world away. Lovers exchange sweet nothings, and businessmen swap ambitious plans, all with the click of a mouse button. Commerce has also taken hold in email. Online purchases are often documented in email accounts, and email is frequently used to remind patients and clients of imminent appointments. In short, "account" is an apt word for the conglomeration of stored messages that comprises an email account, as it provides an account of its owner's life. By obtaining access to someone's email, government agents gain the ability to peer deeply into his activities. Much hinges, therefore, on whether the government is permitted to request that a commercial ISP turn over the contents of a subscriber's emails without triggering the machinery of the Fourth Amendment.

In confronting this question, we take note of two bedrock principles. First, the very fact that information is being passed through a communications network is a paramount Fourth Amendment consideration. *See ibid.*; *United States v. U.S. Dist. Court,* 407 U.S. 297, 313 (1972) ("[T]he broad and unsuspected governmental incursions into conversational privacy which electronic surveillance entails necessitate the application of Fourth Amendment safeguards."). Second, the Fourth Amendment must keep pace with the inexorable march of technological progress, or its guarantees will wither and perish. *See Kyllo v. United States,* 533 U.S. 27 (2001) (noting that evolving technology must not be permitted to "erode the privacy guaranteed by the Fourth Amendment"); *see also* Orin S. Kerr, *Applying the Fourth Amendment to the Internet: A General Approach,* 62 Stan. L. Rev. 1005, 1007 (2010) (arguing that "the differences between the facts of physical space and the facts of the Internet require courts to identify new Fourth Amendment distinctions to maintain the function of Fourth Amendment rules in an online environment").

With those principles in mind, we begin our analysis by considering the manner in which the Fourth Amendment protects traditional forms of communication. In *Katz,* the Supreme Court was asked to determine how the Fourth Amendment applied in the context of the telephone. There, government agents had affixed an electronic listening device to the exterior of a public phone booth, and had used the device to intercept and record several phone conversations. *See* 389 U.S. at 348. The Supreme Court held that this constituted a search under the Fourth Amendment, *see id.* at 353, notwithstanding the fact that the telephone company had the capacity to monitor and record the calls, *see Smith,* 442 U.S. at 746-47 (Stewart, J., dissenting). In the eyes of the Court, the caller was "surely entitled to assume that the words he utter[ed] into the mouthpiece w[ould] not be broadcast to the world." *Katz,* 389 U.S. at 352. The Court's holding in *Katz* has since come to stand for the broad proposition that, in many contexts, the government infringes a reasonable expectation of privacy when it surreptitiously intercepts a telephone call through electronic means. *Smith,* 442 U.S. at 746 (Stewart, J., dissenting) ("[S]ince *Katz,* it has been abundantly clear that telephone conversations are fully protected by the Fourth and Fourteenth Amendments.").

Letters receive similar protection. *See Jacobsen,* 466 U.S. at 114 ("Letters and other sealed packages are in the general class of effects in which the public at large has a legitimate expectation of privacy[.]"); *Ex Parte Jackson,* 96 U.S. 727, 733 (1877). While a letter is in the mail, the police may not intercept it and examine its contents unless they first obtain a warrant based on probable cause. *Ibid.* This is true despite the fact that sealed letters are handed over to perhaps dozens of mail carriers, any one of whom could tear open the thin paper envelopes that separate the private words from the world outside. Put another way, trusting a letter to an intermediary does not necessarily defeat a reasonable expectation that the letter will remain private.

See Katz, 389 U.S. at 351 ("[W]hat [a person] seeks to preserve as private, even in an area accessible to the public, may be constitutionally protected.").

Given the fundamental similarities between email and traditional forms of communication, it would defy common sense to afford emails lesser Fourth Amendment protection. *See* Patricia L. Bellia & Susan Freiwald, *Fourth Amendment Protection for Stored E-Mail,* 2008 U. Chi. Legal F. 121, 135 (2008) (recognizing the need to "eliminate the strangely disparate treatment of mailed and telephonic communications on the one hand and electronic communications on the other"); *City of Ontario v. Quon,* 130 S. Ct. 2619, 2631 (2010) (implying that "a search of [an individual's] personal e-mail account" would be just as intrusive as "a wiretap on his home phone line"); *United States v. Forrester,* 512 F.3d 500, 511 (9th Cir. 2008) (holding that "[t]he privacy interests in [mail and e-mail] are identical"). Email is the technological scion of tangible mail, and it plays an indispensable part in the Information Age. Over the last decade, email has become "so pervasive that some persons may consider [it] to be [an] essential means or necessary instrument[ ] for self-expression, even self-identification." *Quon,* 130 S. Ct. at 2630. It follows that email requires strong protection under the Fourth Amendment; otherwise, the Fourth Amendment would prove an ineffective guardian of private communication, an essential purpose it has long been recognized to serve. *See U.S. Dist. Court,* 407 U.S. at 313; *United States v. Waller,* 581 F.2d 585, 587 (6th Cir. 1978) (noting the Fourth Amendment's role in protecting "private communications"). As some forms of communication begin to diminish, the Fourth Amendment must recognize and protect nascent ones that arise. *See Warshak I,* 490 F.3d at 473 ("It goes without saying that like the telephone earlier in our history, e-mail is an ever-increasing mode of private communication, and protecting shared communications through this medium is as important to Fourth Amendment principles today as protecting telephone conversations has been in the past.").

If we accept that an email is analogous to a letter or a phone call, it is manifest that agents of the government cannot compel a commercial ISP to turn over the contents of an email without triggering the Fourth Amendment. An ISP is the intermediary that makes email communication possible. Emails must pass through an ISP's servers to reach their intended recipient. Thus, the ISP is the functional equivalent of a post office or a telephone company. As we have discussed above, the police may not storm the post office and intercept a letter, and they are likewise forbidden from using the phone system to make a clandestine recording of a telephone call — unless they get a warrant, that is. *See Jacobsen,* 466 U.S. at 114; *Katz,* 389 U.S. at 353. It only stands to reason that, if government agents compel an ISP to surrender the contents of a subscriber's emails, those agents have thereby conducted a Fourth Amendment search, which necessitates compliance with the warrant requirement absent some exception.

In *Warshak I,* the government argued that this conclusion was improper, pointing to the fact that NuVox contractually reserved the right to access Warshak's emails for certain purposes. While we acknowledge that a subscriber agreement might, in some cases, be sweeping enough to defeat a reasonable expectation of privacy in the contents of an email account, *see Warshak I,* 490 F.3d at 473; *Warshak II,* 532 F.3d at 526-27, we doubt that will be the case in most situations, and it is certainly not the case here.

As an initial matter, it must be observed that the mere *ability* of a third-party intermediary to access the contents of a communication cannot be sufficient to extinguish a reasonable expectation of privacy. In *Katz,* the Supreme Court found it reasonable to expect privacy during a telephone call despite the ability of an operator to listen in. *See Smith,* 442 U.S. at 746-47 (Stewart, J., dissenting). Similarly, the ability of a rogue mail handler to rip open a letter does not make it unreasonable to assume that sealed mail will remain private on its journey across the country. Therefore, the threat or possibility of access is not decisive when it comes to the reasonableness of an expectation of privacy.

Nor is the *right* of access. As the Electronic Frontier Foundation points out in its *amicus* brief, at the time *Katz* was decided, telephone companies had a right to monitor calls in certain situations. Specifically, telephone companies could listen in when reasonably necessary to "protect themselves and their properties against the improper and illegal use of their facilities." *Bubis v. United States*, 384 F.2d 643, 648 (9th Cir. 1967). In this case, the NuVox subscriber agreement tracks that language, indicating that "NuVox *may* access and use individual Subscriber information in the operation of the Service and as necessary to protect the Service." Acceptable Use Policy, *available at* http://business.windstream.com/Legal/acceptableUse.htm (last visited Aug. 12, 2010). Thus, under *Katz*, the degree of access granted to NuVox does not diminish the reasonableness of Warshak's trust in the privacy of his emails.

Our conclusion finds additional support in the application of Fourth Amendment doctrine to rented space. Hotel guests, for example, have a reasonable expectation of privacy in their rooms. *See United States v. Allen*, 106 F.3d 695, 699 (6th Cir. 1997). This is so even though maids routinely enter hotel rooms to replace the towels and tidy the furniture. Similarly, tenants have a legitimate expectation of privacy in their apartments. *See United States v. Washington*, 573 F.3d 279, 284 (6th Cir. 2009). That expectation persists, regardless of the incursions of handymen to fix leaky faucets. Consequently, we are convinced that some degree of routine access is hardly dispositive with respect to the privacy question.

Again, however, we are unwilling to hold that a subscriber agreement will *never* be broad enough to snuff out a reasonable expectation of privacy. As the panel noted in *Warshak I*, if the ISP expresses an intention to "audit, inspect, and monitor" its subscriber's emails, that might be enough to render an expectation of privacy unreasonable. *See* 490 F.3d at 472-73 (quoting *United States v. Simons*, 206 F.3d 392, 398 (4th Cir. 2000)). But where, as here, there is no such statement, the ISP's "control over the [e-mails] and ability to access them under certain limited circumstances will not be enough to overcome an expectation of privacy." *Id.* at 473.

We recognize that our conclusion may be attacked in light of the Supreme Court's decision in *United States v. Miller*, 425 U.S. 435 (1976). In *Miller,* the Supreme Court held that a bank depositor does not have a reasonable expectation of privacy in the contents of bank records, checks, and deposit slips. *Id.* at 442. The Court's holding in *Miller* was based on the fact that bank documents, "including financial statements and deposit slips, contain only information voluntarily conveyed to the banks and exposed to their employees in the ordinary course of business." *Ibid.* The Court noted,

> The depositor takes the risk, in revealing his affairs to another, that the information will be conveyed by that person to the Government.... [T]he Fourth Amendment does not prohibit the obtaining of information revealed to a third party and conveyed by him to Government authorities, even if the information is revealed on the assumption that it will be used only for a limited purpose and the confidence placed in the third party will not be betrayed.

Id. at 443 (citations omitted).

But *Miller* is distinguishable. First, *Miller* involved simple business records, as opposed to the potentially unlimited variety of "confidential communications" at issue here. *See ibid.* Second, the bank depositor in *Miller* conveyed information to the bank so that the bank could put the information to use "in the ordinary course of business." *Ibid.* By contrast, Warshak received his emails through NuVox. NuVox was an *intermediary,* not the intended recipient of the emails. *See* Bellia & Freiwald, *Stored E-Mail,* 2008 U. Chi. Legal F. at 165 ("[W]e view the best analogy for this scenario as the cases in which a third party carries, transports, or stores property for another. In these cases, as in the stored e-mail case, the customer grants access to the ISP because it is essential to the customer's interests."). Thus, *Miller* is not controlling.

Accordingly, we hold that a subscriber enjoys a reasonable expectation of privacy in the contents of emails "that are stored with, or sent or received through, a commercial ISP." *Warshak I,* 490 F.3d at 473; *see Forrester,* 512 F.3d at 511 (suggesting that "[t]he contents [of e-mail messages] may deserve Fourth Amendment protection"). The government may not compel a commercial ISP to turn over the contents of a subscriber's emails without first obtaining a warrant based on probable cause. Therefore, because they did not obtain a warrant, the government agents violated the Fourth Amendment when they obtained the contents of Warshak's emails. Moreover, to the extent that the SCA purports to permit the government to obtain such emails warrantlessly, the SCA is unconstitutional. . . .

[The court held that the government violated Warshak's Fourth Amendment rights by compelling the ISP to turn over e-mail without first obtaining a warrant based on probable cause. However, because the agents relied in good faith on provisions in the Stored Communications Act, the exclusionary rule did not apply.]

KEITH, Circuit Judge, concurring. Although I concur in the result the majority reaches, I write separately to provide clarification concerning whether Warshak's emails, obtained in violation of the Fourth Amendment, should have been excluded from trial under the exclusionary rule. . . .

Here, we are presented with a unique situation. As the majority notes, because the government requested a secret subpoena to confiscate Warshak's personal emails without his knowledge pursuant to §2703(b) and (d) of the Stored Communications Act ("SCA"), there is no need to exclude the evidence. The officers took these actions in good faith reliance upon these statutes. They requested the emails from NuVox via a §2703(b) subpoena and a §2703(d) order. Though the government failed to give notice within ninety days after the initial request, it did so only after the emails had been obtained and after an initial showing that notice should be delayed. While we today declare these statutes unconstitutional insofar as they permit the government to obtain such emails without a warrant, it does not follow that the evidence should have been excluded from Warshak's trial. Such an exclusion would not have a substantial deterrent effect on future Fourth Amendment violations enacted by the legislature. *See Herring v. United States,* 555 U.S. 135 (2009) (focusing on "the efficacy of the rule in deterring Fourth Amendment violations in the future"). Therefore, the majority rightfully affirms the district court's refusal to suppress Warshak's emails. With this I agree.

However, there is a further wrongdoing that troubles me today. Specifically, the government's request that NuVox preserve Warshak's stored and future email communications without Warshak's knowledge and without a warrant pursuant to §2703(f). Under §2703(f), "[a] provider of wire or electronic communication services or a remote computing service, upon the request of a governmental entity, shall take all necessary steps to *preserve* records and other evidence *in its possession* pending the issuance of a court order or other process." 18 U.S.C. §2703(f) (emphasis added). This subsection was added to the SCA in 1996 in an effort to supplement law enforcement resources and security. The Antiterrorism Act of 1996, Pub. L. 104-132, 110 Stat. 1305. While added in a completely different context from the creation of the statute, it is worthwhile to review the purpose of the statute as a whole when considering the meaning of this subsection.

Section 2703, as part of the Electronic Communications Privacy Act ("ECPA"), was enacted in 1986 as part of Congress's effort to maintain "a fair balance between the privacy expectations of American citizens and the legitimate needs of law enforcement agencies." S. Rep. 99-541, at 4, 1986 U.S.C.C.A.N. 3555, 3559. Moreover, the advent of the ECPA was precipitated by concerns about advancements in technology and the desire to protect personal and business information which individuals can no longer "lock away" with ease. The plain language of §2703(f) permits only the preservation of emails in the service provider's possession at the time of the request, not the preservation of future emails. Moreover, the Department of Justice, along with some theorists, emphasize that these requests "have no prospective effect." *See, e.g.,* Deirdre K. Mulligan, *Reasonable Expectations in Electronic Communications: A Critical Perspective on the Electronic Communications Privacy Act,* 72 Geo. Wash. L. Rev. 1557, 1565 (2004); U.S. Dep't of Justice, Searching and Seizing Computers and Obtaining Electronic Evidence in Criminal Investigations, Chapter III, §G(1) (2009), *available at* http://www.cybercrime.gov/ssmanual/03ssma.html ("[Section] 2703(f) letters should not be used prospectively to order providers to preserve records not yet created. If agents want providers to record information about future electronic communications, they should comply with the [Wiretap Act and the Pen/Trap statute].").
I find this statutory interpretation persuasive.

Following NuVox's policy, the provider would have destroyed Warshak's old emails but for the government's request that they maintain all current and prospective emails for almost a year without Warshak's knowledge. In practice, the government used the statute as a means to monitor Warshak after the investigation started without his knowledge and without a warrant. Such a practice is no more than backdoor wiretapping. I doubt that such actions, if contested directly in court, would withstand the muster of the Fourth Amendment. Email, much like telephone, provides individuals with a means to communicate in private. *See Warshak v. United States,* 490 F.3d 455, 469-70 (6th Cir. 2007), *vacated,* 532 F.3d 521 (6th Cir. 2008) (en banc). The government cannot use email collection as a means to monitor citizens without a warrant anymore than they can tap a telephone line to monitor citizens without a warrant. The purpose of §2703, along with the Stored Communications Act as a whole, is to maintain the boundaries between a citizen's reasonable expectation of privacy and crime prevention in light of quickly advancing technology. S. Rep. 99-541, at 4, 1986 U.S.C.C.A.N. 3555, 3559. To interpret §2703(f) as having both a retroactive and prospective effect would be contrary to the purpose of the statute as a whole.

While it was not the issue in today's decision, a policy whereby the government requests emails prospectively without a warrant deeply concerns me. I am furthermore troubled by the majority's willingness to disregard the current reading of §2703(f) without concern for future analysis of this statute. Nevertheless, because the government's violation of the Fourth Amendment stems from the order and/ or subpoena to obtain Warshak's email communications pursuant to §2703(b) and (d), the government acted in good faith upon the statute. The fact that their policy likely exceeded the parameters of §2703(f) is irrelevant to this analysis as they did not rely upon §2703 as a whole in requesting the secret subpoena and order to obtain these emails. Accordingly, the majority was correct in holding that the evidence falls within the good faith exception to the exclusionary rule. . . .

NOTES AND QUESTIONS

1. *E-mail Privacy.* Is the expansion of privacy protections to e-mail a reasonable and predictable extension of the line of cases from *Katz* to *Smith* and *Miller*? Are you persuaded by the court's analogies to telephones and letters? Is a search of a personal e-mail account as intrusive as a wiretap on a land line or cell phone? Is surveillance of the Internet significantly different from surveillance of the physical world? *See* Orin S. Kerr, *Applying the Fourth Amendment to the Internet: A General Approach,* 62 Stan. L. Rev. 1005, 1032 (2010) (no); Christopher Slobogin, *Privacy at Risk: The New Government Surveillance and the Fourth Amendment* (2007) (yes).

2. *Content vs. Non-Content.* In *United States v. Forrester,* 512 F. 3d 500 (9th Cir. 2008), the Ninth Circuit ruled, based on *Smith,* that the government did not trigger Fourth Amendment requirements when it asked an ISP to install a monitoring device that recorded the target's IP addresses, to/from addresses for e-mails, and the volume of messages sent from the account. How closely analogous are the pen register in *Smith* and Internet surveillance approved in *Forrester*? Do most Internet users expect privacy in both their content and non-content information? Does the assumption that a person does not retain a reasonable expectation of privacy in information disclosed to a third party apply equally to the Internet and the physical world? Should it matter legally whether the third party is merely an intermediary that does not need to access or analyze the electronic communications — a phone company, for example — as opposed to a bank that receives electronic deposits and withdrawals?

In a suit brought by a city police officer against city and police officials for violating the Fourth Amendment when police supervisors reviewed the contents of stored text messages sent and received on the officer's city-issued alphanumeric pager, the Supreme Court was willing to assume for the sake of argument that the police officer had a reasonable expectation of privacy in the messages. It held that the assumed search was nevertheless reasonable on the strength of the "special needs" exception. *City of Ontario v. Quon,* 130 S. Ct. 2619 (2010). The Court explained its reluctance to find an express privacy right:

> The Court must proceed with care when considering the whole concept of privacy expectations in communications made on electronic equipment owned by a government employer. The judiciary risks error by elaborating too fully on the Fourth Amendment implications of emerging technology before its role in society has become clear. In *Katz,* the Court relied on its own knowledge and experience to conclude that there is a reasonable expectation of privacy in a telephone booth. See [*Katz, supra,*] at 360-361 (Harlan, J., concurring). It is not so clear that courts at present are on so sure a ground. Prudence counsels caution before the facts in the instant case are used to establish far-reaching premises that define the existence, and extent, of privacy expectations enjoyed by employees when using employer-provided communication devices.

Rapid changes in the dynamics of communication and information transmission are evident not just in the technology itself but in what society accepts as proper behavior. . . .

Id. at 2629.

3. *The Role of the ISP and Privacy Policies.* Do you understand why the subscriber agreement between Warshak and NuVox did not defeat Warshak's reasonable expectation of privacy? Can you draft the language of an agreement that *would* extinguish the privacy expectation? Does the analogy to rented hotel rooms hold up in the world of the Internet and ISPs? In *Quon, supra,* the police department policy in effect stated that the city "reserves the right to monitor and log all network activity including e-mail and Internet use, with or without notice. Users should have no expectation of privacy or confidentiality when using these resources." *Id.* at 2625. The policy statement did not apply, on its face, to text messaging, although the city made clear to employees that the city would treat text messages the same way it treated e-mails. *Id.* However, unlike an e-mail sent on a city computer and transmitted through the city's own servers, a text message sent from a city pager was transmitted using wireless radio frequencies to a receiving station owned by a private ISP, where it was in turn routed from the ISP's transmitting station nearest to the recipient's pager or cell phone. *Id.* The holding in *Quon* is thus limited to stored text messages held by a third-party provider. According to the Court in *Quon,* "employer policies concerning communications will . . . shape the reasonable expectations of their employees, especially to the extent that such policies are clearly communicated." *Id.* at 2630. Is this assertion harmonious with what the *Katz* Court said about expectations of privacy?

4. *Comparing Business Records.* Is the contrast to bank records in *Miller* as starkly different from confidential e-mail communications as portrayed by the court? Does the fact that NuVox was an intermediary place the ISP in a fundamentally different legal posture from the bank in *Miller? See* Orin S. Kerr, *The Case for the Third-Party Doctrine,* 107 Mich. L. Rev. 561 (2009). Do you think that *Miller* would be decided the same way today?

5. *Repairing the Stored Communications Act?* Do you agree with Judge Keith that the government's warrantless request that NuVox preserve future as well as currently stored e-mails amounts to backdoor wiretapping in violation of the Fourth Amendment? How should Congress repair these shortcomings of the SCA? Would the imposition of traditional warrant procedures satisfy the objections? Would such a procedure be workable? If not, what kind of substitute would satisfy the government and the Fourth Amendment? *See* Orin S. Kerr, *A User's Guide to the Stored Communications Act, and a Legislator's Guide to Amending It,* 72 Geo. Wash. L. Rev. 1208 (2004).

2. Techniques and Authorities for Collection of Transactional Data

Building on the privacy theory of *Smith,* Congress enacted several statutes that authorized the FBI to use NSLs — issued without any prior judicial order — to obtain transactional records from third-party record holders. Here is a redacted example of such a letter, followed by a judicial decision in a case testing its legitimacy.

SECRET

ALL INFORMATION CONTAINED
HEREIN IS UNCLASSIFIED EXCEPT
WHERE SHOWN OTHERWISE

U.S. Department of Justice

Federal Bureau of Investigation

In Reply, Please Refer to
File No

[Drafting] Field Division
[Street Address]
[City, State, Zip]

[Month Date, Year]

[Mr /Mrs.] [COMPANY POINT OF CONTACT]
[TITLE]
[COMPANY]
[STREET ADDRESS]
[CITY, STATE No Zip Code]

Dear [Mr /Mrs] [LAST NAME]:

        Under the authority of Executive Order 12333, dated
December 4, 1981, and pursuant to Title 18, United States Code
(U.S.C.), Section 2709 (as amended, October 26, 2001), you are
hereby directed to provide the Federal Bureau of Investigation
██   b2-2
███   b7E-1
██

        In accordance with Title 18, U.S.C., Section 2709(b), I
certify that the information sought is relevant to an authorized
investigation to protect against international terrorism or
clandestine intelligence activities, and that such an
investigation of a United States person is not conducted solely
on the basis of activities protected by the first amendment of
the Constitution of the United States

        You are further advised that Title 18, U.S.C., Section
2709(c), prohibits any officer, employee or agent of yours from
disclosing to any person that the FBI has sought or obtained
access to information or records under these provisions.
██
███   b2-2
██   b7E-1

CLASSIFIED DECISIONS FINALIZED BY   CLASSIFIED BY 65179 dmk/bce/asw   6/5/2004
DEPARTMENT REVIEW COMMITTEE (DRC)   REASON: 1.4 (c)
DATE: 07-21-2004   DECLASSIFY ON: X 6/5/2029
CA# 03-2522   Patriot Act II-828

SECRET

DECLASSIFIED BY 65179 dmk/bce/asw
ON 8/3/2004

SECRET

[Mr /Mrs] [COMPANY POINT OF CONTACT]

Your cooperation in this matter is greatly appreciated

Sincerely,

[ADIC/SAC Name]
Assistant Director/Special

Agent in Charge

CLASSIFIED DECISIONS FINALIZED BY
DEPARTMENT REVIEW COMMITTEE (DRC)
DATE: ET-01-2004

CA# 03-2522

ALL INFORMATION CONTAINED
HEREIN IS UNCLASSIFIED EXCEPT
WHERE SHOWN OTHERWISE

CLASSIFIED BY 65/79 dmh/bcs/smw   6/30/2004
REASON: 1.5 (c)
DECLASSIFY ON: X 6/30/2029

2

SECRET   Patriot Act II-829

DECLASSIFIED BY 65/79 dmh/bcs/smw
ON 8/3/2004

Doe v. Ashcroft (*Doe I*)

United States District Court, Southern District of New York, 2004
334 F. Supp. 2d 471
vacated and remanded sub nom. Doe v. Gonzales,
449 F.3d 415 (2d Cir. 2006)

MARRERO, J. . . .

I. INTRODUCTION

Plaintiffs in this case challenge the constitutionality of 18 U.S.C. §2709 ("§2709").[1] That statute authorizes the Federal Bureau of Investigation ("FBI") to compel communications firms, such as internet service providers ("ISPs") or telephone companies, to produce certain customer records whenever the FBI certifies that those records are "relevant to an authorized investigation to protect against international terrorism or clandestine intelligence activities." [*Id.*] The FBI's demands under §2709 *are* issued in the form of national security letters ("NSLs"), which constitute a unique form of administrative subpoena cloaked in secrecy and pertaining to national security issues. The statute bars all NSL recipients from ever disclosing that the FBI has issued an NSL.

The lead plaintiff, called "John Doe" ("Doe") for purposes of this litigation, is described in the complaint as an internet access firm that received an NSL. . . .

II. BACKGROUND . . .

A. Doe's Receipt of an NSL

After receiving a call from an FBI agent informing him that he would be served with an NSL, Doe received a document, printed on FBI letterhead, which stated that, "pursuant to Title 18, United States Code (U.S.C.), Section 2709" Doe was "directed" to provide certain information to the Government. As required by the terms of §2709, in the NSL the FBI "certif[ied] that the information sought [was] relevant to an authorized investigation to protect against international terrorism or clandestine intelligence activities." Doe was "further advised" that §2709(c) prohibited him, or his officers, agents, or employees, "from disclosing to *any person* that the FBI has sought or obtained access to information or records under these provisions." Doe was "requested to provide records responsive to [the] request *personally*" to a designated individual, and to not transmit the records by mail or even mention the NSL in *any* telephone conversation. . . .

. . . Doe has not complied with the NSL request, and has instead engaged counsel to bring the present lawsuit.

B. §2709 in General

As stated above, §2709 authorizes the FBI to issue NSLs to compel communications firms to produce certain customer records whenever the FBI certifies that those

---

[1. This section was amended by the Patriot Improvement Act in 2006, *infra* p. 668, as explained in the following Notes and Questions. — Eds.]

records are relevant to an authorized international terrorism or counterintelligence investigation, and the statute also categorically bars NSL recipients from disclosing the inquiry. In relevant part, it states:

> (a) Duty to provide. — A wire or electronic communication service provider shall comply with a request for subscriber information and toll billing records information, or electronic communication transactional records in its custody or possession made by the Director of the Federal Bureau of Investigation under subsection (b) of this section.
>
> (b) Required certification. — The Director of the Federal Bureau of Investigation, or his designee in a position not lower than Deputy Assistant Director at Bureau headquarters or a Special Agent in Charge in a Bureau field office designated by the Director, may — (1) request the name, address, length of service, and local and long distance toll billing records of a person or entity if the Director (or his designee) certifies in writing to the wire or electronic communication service provider to which the request is made that the name, address, length of service, and toll billing records sought are relevant to an authorized investigation to protect against international terrorism or clandestine intelligence activities, provided that such an investigation of a United States person is not conducted solely on the basis of activities protected by the first amendment to the Constitution of the United States....
>
> (c) Prohibition of certain disclosure. — No wire or electronic communication service provider, or officer, employee, or agent thereof, shall disclose to any person that the Federal Bureau of Investigation has sought or obtained access to information or records under this section....

Section 2709 is one of only a handful of statutes authorizing the Government to issue NSLs. The other NSL statutes authorize the Government to compel disclosure of certain financial and credit records which it certifies are relevant to international terrorism or counter-intelligence investigations, and to compel disclosure of certain records of current or former government employees who have (or have had) access to classified information.[17]

C. Legislative History

Section 2709 was enacted as part of Title II of the Electronic Communications Privacy Act of 1986 ("ECPA"),[19] which sought to "protect privacy interests" in "stored wire and electronic communications" while also "protecting the Government's legitimate law enforcement needs."[20] ...

... As first enacted, §2709 required electronic communication service providers to produce subscriber information," "toll billing records information," or "electronic communication transactional records," upon the FBI's internal certification that (1) the information was "relevant to an authorized foreign counterintelligence investigation" and that (2) there were "specific and articulable facts giving reason to believe that the person or entity to whom the information sought pertains [was] a foreign power or an agent of a foreign power." ...

---

17. See 12 U.S.C. §3414 (financial records); 15 U.S.C. §§1681u, 1681v (credit records); 50 U.S.C. §436 (government employee records).

19. Pub. L. No. 99-508, §201, 100 Stat. 1848, 1867 (1986).

20. S. Rep. No. 99-541, at 3 (1986), *reprinted in* 1986 U.S.C.C.A.N. 3555, 3557.

The . . . most recent major revision to §2709 occurred in October 2001,[2] as part of the USA PATRIOT Act of 2001 ("Patriot Act").[39] In short, the Patriot Act removed the previous requirement that §2709 inquiries have a nexus to a foreign power, replacing that prerequisite with a broad standard of relevance to investigations of terrorism or clandestine intelligence activities. In hearings before the House Judiciary Committee on September 24, 2001, the Administration submitted the following explanation for the proposed change:

> NSL authority requires both a showing of relevance and a showing of links to an "agent of a foreign power." In this respect, [it is] substantially more demanding than the analogous criminal authorities, which require only a certification of relevance. Because the NSLs require documentation of the facts supporting the "agent of a foreign power" predicate and because they require the signature of a high-ranking official at FBI headquarters, they often take months to be issued. This is in stark contrast to criminal subpoenas, which can be used to obtain the same information, and are issued rapidly at the local level. In many cases, counter-intelligence and counterterrorism investigations suffer substantial delays while waiting for NSLs to be prepared, returned from headquarters, and served. The section would streamline the process of obtaining NSL authority. . . .

The House Judiciary Committee agreed that "[s]uch delays are unacceptable" and stated in its October 11, 2001, report that the Patriot Act would "harmonize[]" §2709 "with existing criminal law where an Assistant United States Attorney may issue a grand jury subpoena for all such records in a criminal case."

D. NSLs and Other Information-Gathering Authority

It is instructive to place the Government's NSL authority in the context of other means by which the Government gathers information of the type covered by §2709 because Congress (in passing and amending the NSL statutes) and the parties here (in contesting §2709's constitutionality) have drawn analogies to those other authorities as grounds for or against its validity. The relationship of §2709 to other related statutes supplies a backdrop for assessing congressional intent and judging the validity of the law on its face and as applied. In addition, an analysis of these analogous information-gathering methods indicates that NSLs such as the ones authorized by §2709 provide fewer procedural protections to the recipient than any other information-gathering technique the Government employs to procure information similar to that which it obtains pursuant to §2709.

1. Administrative Subpoenas

The most important set of statutes relevant to this case are those authorizing federal agencies to issue administrative subpoenas for the purpose of executing the particular agency's function. Ordinary administrative subpoenas, which are far more common than NSLs, may be issued by most federal agencies, as authorized by the hundreds of applicable statutes in federal law. For example, the Internal Revenue

---

[2. The statute was amended again in 2006 by the Patriot Improvement Act, *infra* p. 668, as explained in the following Notes and Questions. — Eds.]

39. *See* Pub. L. No. 107-56, §505, 115 Stat. 272, 365 (2001). . . .

Service (IRS) may issue subpoenas to investigate possible violations of the tax code, and the Securities Exchange Commission (SEC) may issue subpoenas to investigate possible violations of the securities laws....

There is a wide body of law which pertains to administrative subpoenas generally. According to the Government's central theory in this case, those standing rules would presumably also apply to NSLs, even if not so explicitly stated in the text of the statute. Where an agency seeks a court order to enforce a subpoena against a resisting subpoena recipient, courts will enforce the subpoena as long as: (1) the agency's investigation is being conducted pursuant to a legitimate purpose, (2) the inquiry is relevant to that purpose, (3) the information is not already within the agency's possession, and (4) the proper procedures have been followed. The Second Circuit has described these standards as "minimal." Even if an administrative subpoena meets these initial criteria to be enforceable, its recipient may nevertheless affirmatively challenge the subpoena on other grounds, such as an allegation that it was issued with an improper purpose or that the information sought is privileged.

Unlike the NSL statutes, most administrative subpoena laws either contain no provision requiring secrecy, or allow for only limited secrecy in special cases. For example, some administrative subpoena statutes permit the investigating agency to apply for a court order to temporarily bar disclosure of the inquiry, generally during specific renewable increments or for an appropriate period of time fixed by the court, where such disclosure could jeopardize the investigation....

2. Subpoena Authority in the Criminal Context

In its role as a party to a federal criminal proceeding (including a grand jury proceeding), the Government has broad authority to issue a subpoena to obtain witness testimony or "*any* books, papers, documents, data, or other objects the subpoena designates."[52] Although such subpoenas "are issued in the name of the district court over the signature of the clerk, they are issued pro forma and in blank to anyone requesting them," and the "court exercises no prior control whatsoever upon their use."[53]

The court becomes involved in the subpoena process only if the subpoenaed party moves to quash the request as "unreasonable or oppressive,"[54] or if the Government seeks to compel compliance with the subpoena. The reasonableness of a subpoena depends on the context. For example, to survive a motion to quash, a subpoena issued in connection with a criminal trial "must make a reasonably specific request for information that would be both relevant and admissible at trial."[55] By contrast, a grand jury subpoena is generally enforced as long as there is a "reasonable possibility that the category of materials the Government seeks will produce information relevant to the general subject of the grand jury's investigation."[56] Considering the grand jury's broad investigatory power and minimal court supervision, it is accurate to observe, as the Second Circuit did long ago, that "[b]asically the grand jury is a law enforcement agency."[57]

---

52. Fed. R. Crim. P. 17(a), (c)(1) (emphasis added).
53. *In re Grand Jury Proceedings*, 486 F.2d 85, 90 (3d Cir. 1973).
54. Fed. R. Crim. P. 17(c)(2).
55. *United States v. R. Enters., Inc.*, 498 U.S. 292, 299 (1991) (*citing United States v. Nixon*, 418 U.S. 683, 700 (1974)).
56. *Id.* at 301.
57. *United States v. Cleary*, 265 F.2d 459, 461 (2d Cir. 1959).

While materials presented in a criminal trial setting are generally public, the federal rules impose stringent secrecy requirements on certain grand jury participants, including the attorneys, court reporters, and grand jurors.[59] . . .

In certain contexts, the Government may issue subpoenas related to criminal investigations even without initiating a formal criminal proceeding. For example, the United States Attorney General is authorized to issue administrative subpoenas, without convening a grand jury, to investigate federal narcotics crimes, racketeering crimes, health care related crimes, and crimes involving the exploitation of children. In each of these instances, the administrative process is governed by the general rules described above, providing safeguards of judicial review.

3.   Background Rules Governing Disclosure of Stored Electronic Communications

Title II of the ECPA [also called the Stored Communications Act], in which §2709 was enacted, sets forth an intricate framework by which electronic communications providers, such as ISPs and phone companies, may be compelled to disclose stored electronic information to the Government. The framework described below operates independently of the rules governing NSLs issued pursuant to §2709, but may aid with interpretation of §2709.

The Government may obtain basic subscriber information[69] merely by issuing an authorized administrative subpoena, trial subpoena, or grand jury subpoena, and the Government need not notify the subscriber of the request.

If the Government gives prior notice to the subscriber, or otherwise complies with certain delayed notice procedures, the Government may also subpoena the *contents* of electronic communications which are either (1) retained on a system for storage purposes (*e.g.*, opened email which remains on an ISP's server), or (2) retained, for more than 180 days, in intermediate or temporary storage (*e.g.*, unopened email on an ISP's server). For the Government to obtain the contents of electronic communications kept for 180 days or less in intermediate or temporary storage (e.g., unopened email on an ISP's server), it must obtain a search warrant under Federal Rule of Criminal Procedure 41, or the state equivalent. In other words, the Government would have to appear before a neutral magistrate and make a showing of probable cause. The Government may also obtain a court order requiring an electronic communications service provider to turn over transactional and content information by setting forth "specific and articulable facts showing that there are reasonable grounds to believe that" the information sought is "relevant and material to an ongoing criminal investigation."[75]

The ECPA permits the Government to seek a court order prohibiting the communications provider from revealing the Government's inquiry "for such period as the court deems appropriate" if the court determines that such disclosure, among

---

59. *See* Fed. R. Crim. P. 6(e).

69. Basic subscriber information includes: (1) a subscriber's name and (2) address; (3) the subscriber's local and long distance telephone connection records, or records of session times and durations; (4) the subscriber's length of service and types of service he has utilized; (5) any telephone or instrument number or other subscriber number or identity, including any temporarily assigned network address; and (6) the subscriber's means and source of payment for the service. *See* 18 U.S.C. §2703(c)(2).

75. 18 U.S.C. §2703(d).

other things, would result in "destruction of or tampering with evidence" or "seriously jeopardizing an investigation or unduly delaying a trial."[76]

4.   Mail

Government law enforcement agencies are authorized to request the Postal Inspector to initiate a so-called "mail cover" to obtain any information appearing on the outside of a particular piece of mail.[77] Among other grounds, the law enforcement agency can obtain a mail cover by "specify[ing] the reasonable grounds to demonstrate the mail cover is necessary" to "[p]rotect the national security" or to "[o]btain information regarding the commission or attempted commission of a crime." There is no requirement that the mail sender or recipient be notified of the mail cover.

The Government must obtain a warrant based upon probable cause to open and inspect sealed mail because the contents of mail are protected by the Fourth Amendment. As the Supreme Court established long ago: "Whilst in the mail, [a person's papers] can only be opened and examined under like warrant, issued upon similar oath or affirmation, particularly describing the thing to be seized, as is required when papers are subjected to search in one's own household."[80]

5.   Pen Registers and Trap and Trace Devices

Pen registers and trap and trace devices record certain electronic communications data indicating the origins and destinations of various "dialing, routing, addressing, or signaling information," *e.g.*, the phone numbers dialed to and from a telephone.[81] In criminal investigations, the Government must apply for a court order, renewable in 60-day increments, to install or collect data from such devices, though the standard for issuing such an order is relatively low. The Government need only show that "the information likely to be obtained by such installation and use is relevant to an ongoing criminal investigation."[83]

The person owning the communications device is prohibited, unless otherwise directed by court order, from disclosing the fact that a pen register or trap and trace device is in effect.

6.   Wiretaps and Electronic Eavesdropping

The Fourth Amendment protects against warrantless Government wiretapping. Federal legislation specifies the procedures by which law enforcement officials may obtain a court order to conduct wiretaps and other forms of electronic eavesdropping. The requirements are rigorous. Among other things, the Government must show that: (1) "there is probable cause for belief that an individual is committing, has committed, or is about to commit" one of a list of enumerated crimes; (2) "there is probable cause for belief that particular communications concerning that offense will be obtained through such interception"; and (3) "normal investigative procedures

---

76. *Id.* §2705(b).
77. *See* 39 C.F.R. §233.3.
80. *See Ex parte Jackson*, 96 U.S. 727, 733 (1877).
81. *See* 18 U.S.C. §3127(3)-(4).
83. *Id.* §3123(a).

have been tried and have failed or reasonably appear to be unlikely to succeed if tried or to be too dangerous."[87] Such orders are not available "for any period longer than is necessary to achieve the objective of the authorization," subject to a renewable maximum of 30 days.[88] The communications provider is prohibited from disclosing that a wiretap or electronic surveillance is in place, "except as may otherwise be required by legal process and then only after prior notification" to the appropriate law enforcement authorities.[89]

7. Foreign Intelligence Surveillance Act . . .

[The court summarized the procedures for obtaining an order from the Foreign Intelligence Surveillance Court for electronic surveillance under FISA.]

The FISA also authorizes the Government to apply to the FISA court "for an order requiring the production of any tangible things (including books, records, papers, documents, and other items) for an investigation to obtain foreign intelligence information not concerning a United States person or to protect against international terrorism or clandestine intelligence activities. . . ."[99] Such an application need only specify that the inquiry is part of an authorized investigation and in accordance with the appropriate guidelines. Recipients of such an order are prohibited from disclosing to anyone (except those whose assistance is necessary to comply with the subpoena) that the inquiry was made.

Finally, FISA authorizes the Government to apply to the FISA court for an order, renewable in 90-day increments, to install a pen register or trap and trace device as part of "any investigation to obtain foreign intelligence information not concerning a United States person or to protect against international terrorism or clandestine intelligence activities." The Government need only certify to the court that it will likely obtain information relevant to a proper inquiry. Just as in the criminal context, the person owning the communications device is prohibited, unless otherwise directed by court order, from disclosing the fact that a pen register or trap and trace device is in effect. . . .

IV. DISCUSSION . . .

B. As Applied Here, Section 2709 Lacks Procedural Protections Necessary to Vindicate Constitutional Rights

1. Section 2709 and The Fourth Amendment[118] . . .

. . . The Fourth Amendment's protection against unreasonable searches applies to administrative subpoenas, even though issuing a subpoena does not involve a literal

---

87. *Id.* §2518(3).
88. *Id.* §2518(5).
89. *Id.* §2511(2)(a)(ii).
99. 50 U.S.C. §1861(a). [This authority was added by §215 of the USA Patriot Act, Pub. L. No. 107-108, §215, 115 Stat. 272, 287-288 (2001), and is therefore sometimes called a "Section 215 Order." It was amended by the Patriot Improvement Act, as explained in the Notes and Questions that follow this decision. — Eds.]
118. To be clear, the Fourth Amendment rights at issue here belong to the person or entity receiving the NSL, not to the person or entity to whom the subpoenaed records pertain. Individuals possess a limited Fourth Amendment interest in records which they voluntarily convey to a third party. *See* [Smith v.

physical intrusion or search. In so doing, the Supreme Court explained that the Fourth Amendment is not "confined literally to searches and seizures as such, but extends as well to the orderly taking under compulsion of process."[122]

However, because administrative subpoenas are "at best, constructive searches," there is no requirement that they be issued pursuant to a warrant or that they be supported by probable cause. Instead, an administrative subpoena needs only to be "reasonable," which the Supreme Court has interpreted to mean that (1) the administrative subpoena is "within the authority of the agency;" (2) that the demand is "not too indefinite;" and (3) that the information sought is "reasonably relevant" to a proper inquiry.[124]

While the Fourth Amendment reasonableness standard is permissive in the context of administrative subpoenas, the constitutionality of the administrative subpoena is predicated on the availability of a neutral tribunal to determine, after a subpoena is issued, whether the subpoena actually complies with the Fourth Amendment's demands. In contrast to an actual physical search, which must be justified by the warrant and probable cause requirements occurring *before* the search, an administrative subpoena "is regulated by, and its justification derives from, [judicial] process" available *after* the subpoena is issued.[125]

Accordingly, the Supreme Court has held that an administrative subpoena "may not be made and enforced" by the administrative agency; rather, the subpoenaed party must be able to "obtain judicial review of the reasonableness of the demand prior to suffering penalties for refusing to comply."[126] In sum, longstanding Supreme Court doctrine makes clear that an administrative subpoena statute is consistent with the Fourth Amendment when it is subject to "judicial supervision" and "surrounded by every safeguard of judicial restraint."[127]

Plaintiffs contend that §2709 violates this Fourth Amendment process-based guarantee because it gives the FBI alone the power to issue as well as enforce its own NSLs, instead of contemplating some form of judicial review. Although Plaintiffs appear to concede that the statute does not authorize the FBI to literally enforce the terms of an NSL by, for example, unilaterally seizing documents or imposing fines, Plaintiffs contend that §2709 has the *practical* effect of coercing compliance....

The crux of the problem is that the form NSL, like the one issued in this case, which is preceded by a personal call from an FBI agent, is framed in imposing language on FBI letterhead and which, citing the authorizing statute, orders a combination of disclosure in person and in complete secrecy, essentially coerces the

---

Maryland, 442 U.S. 735, 742-746 (1979), *supra* p. 633]; United States v. Miller, 425 U.S. 435, 440-443 (1976).] Nevertheless, as discussed below, many potential NSL recipients may have particular interests in resisting an NSL, *e.g.*, because they have contractually obligated themselves to protect the anonymity of their subscribers or because their own rights are uniquely implicated by what they regard as an intrusive and secretive NSL regime. For example, since the definition of "wire or electronic communication service provider," 18 U.S.C. §2709(a), is so vague, the statute could (and may currently) be used to seek subscriber lists or other information from an association that also provides electronic communication services (e.g., email addresses) to its members, or to seek records from libraries that many, including the *amici* appearing in this proceeding, fear will chill speech and use of these invaluable public institutions....

122. [*See United States v. Morton Salt Co.*, 338 U.S. 632, 651-652 (1950).]

124. *Id.* at 652.

125. *United States v. Bailey (In re Subpoena Duces Tecum)*, 228 F.3d 341, 348 (4th Cir. 2000).

126. *See v. City of Seattle*, 387 U.S. 541, 544-45 (1967); *see also Oklahoma Press Publishing Co. v. Walling*, 327 U.S. 186, 217 (1946).

127. *Oklahoma Press*, 327 U.S. at 217.

reasonable recipient into immediate compliance. Objectively viewed, it is improbable that an FBI summons invoking the authority of a certified "investigation to protect against international terrorism or clandestine intelligence activities," and phrased in tones sounding virtually as biblical commandment, would not be perceived with some apprehension by an ordinary person and therefore elicit passive obedience from a reasonable NSL recipient. The full weight of this ominous writ is especially felt when the NSL's plain language, in a measure that enhances its aura as an expression of public will, prohibits disclosing the issuance of the NSL to "any person." Reading such strictures, it is also highly unlikely that an NSL recipient reasonably would know that he may have a right to contest the NSL, and that a process to do so may exist through a judicial proceeding.

Because neither the statute, nor an NSL, nor the FBI agents dealing with the recipient say as much, all but the most mettlesome and undaunted NSL recipients would consider themselves effectively barred from consulting an attorney or anyone else who might advise them otherwise, as well as bound to absolute silence about the very existence of the NSL....

The evidence in this case bears out the hypothesis that NSLs work coercively in this way. The ACLU obtained, via the Freedom of Information Act ("FOIA"), and presented to the Court in this proceeding, a document listing all the NSLs the Government issued from October 2001 through January 2003. Although the entire substance of the document is redacted, it is apparent that hundreds of NSL requests were made during that period. Because §2709 has been available to the FBI since 1986 (and its financial records counterpart in RFPA since 1978), the Court concludes that there must have been hundreds more NSLs issued in that long time span. The evidence suggests that, until now, none of those NSLs was ever challenged in any court....

... The Court thus concludes that in practice NSLs are essentially unreviewable because, as explained, given the language and tone of the statute as carried into the NSL by the FBI, the recipient would consider himself, in virtually every case, obliged to comply, with no other option but to immediately obey and stay quiet....

Accordingly, the Court concludes that §2709, as applied here, must be invalidated because in all but the exceptional case it has the effect of authorizing coercive searches effectively immune from any judicial process, in violation of the Fourth Amendment....

2. NSLs May Violate ISP Subscribers' Rights

Plaintiffs have focused on the possibility that §2709 could be used to infringe subscribers' First Amendment rights of anonymous speech and association. Though it is not necessary to precisely define the scope of ISP subscribers' First Amendment rights, the Court concludes that §2709 may, in a given case, violate a subscriber's First Amendment privacy rights, as well as other legal rights, if judicial review is not readily available to an ISP that receives an NSL....

The Supreme Court has recognized the First Amendment right to anonymous speech at least since *Talley v. California*,[161] which invalidated a California law requiring that handbills distributed to the public contain certain identifying information about the source of the handbills. The Court stated that the "identification requirement would tend to restrict freedom to distribute information and thereby freedom of

---

161. 362 U.S. 60 (1960).

expression."[162] The Supreme Court has also invalidated identification requirements pertaining to persons distributing campaign literature, persons circulating petitions for state ballot initiatives, and persons engaging in door-to-door religious advocacy.

In a related doctrine, the Supreme Court has held that "compelled disclosure of affiliation with groups engaged in advocacy" amounts to a "restraint on freedom of association" where disclosure could expose the members to "public hostility."[166] Laws mandating such disclosures will be upheld only where the Government interest is compelling.

The Court concludes that such First Amendment rights may be infringed by application of §2709 in a given case. For example, the FBI theoretically could issue to a political campaign's computer systems operator a §2709 NSL compelling production of the names of all persons who have email addresses through the campaign's computer systems. The FBI theoretically could also issue an NSL under §2709 to discern the identity of someone whose anonymous online web log, or "blog," is critical of the Government. Such inquiries might be beyond the permissible scope of the FBI's power under §2709 because the targeted information might not be relevant to an authorized investigation to protect against international terrorism or clandestine intelligence activities, or because the inquiry might be conducted solely on the basis of activities protected by the First Amendment. These prospects only highlight the potential danger of the FBI's self-certification process and the absence of judicial oversight.

Other rights may also be violated by the disclosure contemplated by the statute; the statute's reference to "transactional records" creates ambiguity regarding the scope of the information required to be produced by the NSL recipient. If the recipient—who in the NSL is called upon to exercise judgment in determining the extent to which complying materials constitute transactional records rather than content—interprets the NSL broadly as requiring production of all e-mail header information, including subject lines, for example, some disclosures conceivably may reveal information protected by the subscriber's attorney-client privilege, *e.g.*, a communication with an attorney where the subject line conveys privileged or possibly incriminating information. Indeed, the practical absence of judicial review may lead ISPs to disclose information that is protected from disclosure by the NSL statute itself, such as in a case where the NSL was initiated solely in retaliation for the subscriber's exercise of his First Amendment rights, as prohibited by §2709(b)(1)-(b)(2). Only a court would be able to definitively construe the statutory and First Amendment rights at issue in the "First Amendment retaliation" provision of the statute, and to strike a proper balance among those interests.

The Government asserts that disclosure of the information sought under §2709 could not violate a subscriber's rights (and thus demands no judicial process) because the information which a §2709 NSL seeks has been voluntarily conveyed to the ISP who receives the NSL. According to the Government, an internet speaker relinquishes any interest in any anonymity, and any protected claim to that information, as soon as he releases his identity and other information to his ISP. In support of its position, the Government cites the Supreme Court's holding [in *Smith* and *Miller*] that, at least in the Fourth Amendment context involving the Government installing a pen register or obtaining bank records, when a person voluntarily conveys

162. *Id.* at 64.
166. *NAACP v. State of Alabama ex rel. Patterson*, 357 U.S. 449, 462 (1958).

information to third parties, he assumes the risk that the information will be turned over to the Government. . . .

The evidence on the record now before this Court demonstrates that the information available through a §2709 NSL served upon an ISP could easily be used to disclose vast amounts of anonymous speech and associational activity. For instance, §2709 imposes a duty to provide "electronic communication transactional records," a phrase which, though undefined in the statute, certainly encompasses a log of email addresses with whom a subscriber has corresponded and the web pages that a subscriber visits. Those transactional records can reveal, among other things, the anonymous message boards to which a person logs on or posts, the electronic newsletters to which he subscribes, and the advocacy websites he visits. Moreover, §2709 imposes a duty on ISPs to provide the names and addresses of subscribers, thus enabling the Government to specifically identify someone who has written anonymously on the internet.[175] As discussed above, given that an NSL recipient is directed by the FBI to turn over all information "*which you consider to be* an electronic communication transactional record," the §2709 NSL could also reasonably be interpreted by an ISP to require, at minimum, disclosure of all e-mail header information, including subject lines.

In stark contrast to this potential to compile elaborate dossiers on internet users, the information obtainable by a pen register is far more limited. As the Supreme Court in *Smith* was careful to note:

> [Pen registers] disclose only the telephone numbers that have been dialed — a means of establishing communication. Neither the purport of any communication between the caller and the recipient of the call, their identities, nor whether the call was even completed is disclosed by pen registers.[177]

The Court doubts that the result in *Smith* would have been the same if a pen register operated as a key to the most intimate details and passions of a person's private life.

The more apt Supreme Court case for evaluating the assumption of risk argument at issue here is *Katz v. United States*,[178] the seminal decision underlying both *Smith* and *Miller*. *Katz* held that the Fourth Amendment's privacy protections applied where the Government wiretapped a telephone call placed from a public phone booth. Especially noteworthy and pertinent to this case is the Supreme Court's remark that: "The Government's activities in electronically listening to and recording the petitioner's words violated the privacy upon which he justifiably relied while using the telephone booth and thus constituted a 'search and seizure' within the meaning of the Fourth Amendment."[180] The Supreme Court also stated that a person entering a phone booth who "shuts the door behind him" is "surely entitled to assume that the words he utters into the mouthpiece will not be broadcast to the world," and held

---

175. NSLs can potentially reveal far more than constitutionally-protected associational activity or anonymous speech. By revealing the websites one visits, the Government can learn, among many other potential examples, what books the subscriber enjoys reading or where a subscriber shops. As one commentator has observed, the records compiled by ISPs can "enable the government to assemble a profile of an individual's finances, health, psychology, beliefs, politics, interests, and lifestyle." Daniel J. Solove, *Digital Dossiers and the Dissipation of Fourth Amendment Privacy*, 75 S. Cal. L. Rev. 1083, 1084 (2002).

177. *Smith*, 442 U.S. at 741 (citation omitted).

178. 389 U.S. 347 (1967).

180. *Id.* at 353.

that, "[t]o read the Constitution more narrowly is to ignore the vital role that the public telephone has come to play in private communication."[181]

Applying that reasoning to anonymous internet speech and associational activity is relatively straightforward. A person who signs onto an anonymous forum under a pseudonym, for example, is essentially "shut[ting] the door behind him," and is surely entitled to a reasonable expectation that his speech, whatever form the expression assumes, will not be accessible to the Government to be broadcast to the world absent appropriate legal process. To hold otherwise would ignore the role of the internet as a remarkably powerful forum for private communication and association. Even the Government concedes here that the internet is an "important vehicle for the free exchange of ideas and facilitates associations."

To be sure, the Court is keenly mindful of the Government's reminder that the internet may also serve as a vehicle for crime. The Court equally recognizes that circumstances exist in which the First Amendment rights of association and anonymity must yield to a more compelling Government interest in obtaining records from internet firms. To this end, the Court re-emphasizes that it does not here purport to set forth the scope of these First Amendment rights in general, or define them in this or any other case. The Court holds only that such fundamental rights are certainly implicated in some cases in which the Government may employ §2709 broadly to gather information, thus requiring that the process incorporate the safeguards of some judicial review to ensure that if an infringement of those rights is asserted, they are adequately protected through fair process in an independent neutral tribunal. Because the necessary procedural protections are wholly absent here, the Court finds on this ground additional cause for invalidating §2709 as applied.

C. Constitutionality of the Non-Disclosure Provision

Finally, the Court turns to the issue of whether the Government may properly enforce §2709(c), the non-disclosure provision, against Doe or any other person who has previously received an NSL. Section 2709(c) states: "No wire or electronic communication service provider, or officer, employee, or agent thereof, shall disclose to any person that the Federal Bureau of Investigation has sought or obtained access to information or records under this section."

A threshold question concerning this issue is whether, as Plaintiffs contend, §2709(c) is subject to strict scrutiny as either a prior restraint on speech or a content-based speech restriction, or whether, as the Government responds, §2709(c) is subject to the more relaxed judicial review of intermediate scrutiny. The difference is crucial. A speech restriction which is either content-based or which imposes a prior restraint on speech is presumed invalid and may be upheld only if it is "narrowly tailored to promote a compelling Government interest." If "less restrictive alternatives would be at least as effective in achieving the legitimate purpose that the statute was enacted to serve," then the speech restriction is not narrowly tailored and may be invalidated. Under intermediate scrutiny, a speech restriction may be upheld as long as "it advances important governmental interests unrelated to the suppression of free speech and does not burden substantially more speech than necessary to further those interests."

---

181. *Id.* at 352.

The Court agrees with Plaintiffs that §2709(c) works as both a prior restraint on speech and as a content-based restriction, and hence, is subject to strict scrutiny. First, axiomatically the categorical non-disclosure mandate embodied in §2709(c) functions as prior restraint because of the straightforward observation that it prohibits speech before the speech occurs. As the Supreme Court articulated the threshold inquiry: "The relevant question is whether the challenged regulation authorizes suppression of speech in advance of its expression."[189] . . .

Second, the Court considers §2709(c) to be a content-based speech restriction. . . .

The Government . . . argues that §2709(c) is content-neutral because it prohibits certain disclosures irrespective of any particular speaker's views on NSLs, terrorism, or anything else. . . .

The Government's argument is unpersuasive. It fails to recognize that even a *viewpoint*-neutral restriction can be *content*-based, if the restriction pertains to an entire category of speech. . . .

The Government's claim to perpetual secrecy surrounding the FBI's issuance of NSLs, by its theory as advanced here an authority neither restrained by the FBI's own internal discretion nor reviewable by any form of judicial process, presupposes a category of information, and thus a class of speech, that, for reasons not satisfactorily explained, must forever be kept from public view, cloaked by an official seal that will always overshadow the public's right to know. In general, as our sunshine laws and judicial doctrine attest, democracy abhors undue secrecy, in recognition that public knowledge secures freedom. Hence, an unlimited government warrant to conceal, effectively a form of secrecy *per se,* has no place in our open society. Such a claim is especially inimical to democratic values for reasons borne out by painful experience. Under the mantle of secrecy, the self-preservation that ordinarily impels our government to censorship and secrecy may potentially be turned on ourselves as a weapon of self-destruction. When withholding information from disclosure is no longer justified, when it ceases to foster the proper aims that initially may have supported confidentiality, a categorical and uncritical extension of non-disclosure may become the cover for spurious ends that government may then deem too inconvenient, inexpedient, merely embarrassing, or even illicit to ever expose to the light of day. At that point, secrecy's protective shield may serve not as much to secure a safe country as simply to save face. . . .

. . . Section 2709(c) does not countenance the possibility that the FBI could permit modification of the NSL's no-disclosure order even in those or any other similar situations no longer implicating legitimate national security interests and presenting factual or legal issues that any court could reasonably adjudicate. Bluntly stated, the statute simply does not allow for that balancing of competing public interests to be made by an independent tribunal at any point. In this regard, it is conceivable that "less restrictive alternatives would be at least as effective in achieving the legitimate purpose that the statute was enacted to serve." For instance, Congress could require the FBI to make at least *some* determination concerning need before requiring secrecy, and ultimately it could provide a forum and define at least *some* circumstances in which an NSL recipient could ask the FBI or a court for a subsequent determination whether continuing secrecy was still warranted. . . .

189. *Ward v. Rock Against Racism,* 491 U.S. 781, 795 n.5 (1989) (emphasis omitted).

In this Court's judgment, . . . authorities persuasively confirm that the Government should be accorded a due measure of deference when it asserts that secrecy is necessary for national security purposes in a *particular situation* involving *particular persons* at a *particular time.* Here, however, the Government cites no authority supporting the open-ended proposition that it may universally apply these general principles to impose perpetual secrecy upon an entire category of future cases whose details are unknown and whose particular twists and turns may not justify, for all time and all places, demanding unremitting concealment and imposing a disproportionate burden on free speech. . . .

VI. CONCLUSION

To summarize, the Court concludes that the compulsory, secret, and unreviewable production of information required by the FBI's application of 18 U.S.C. §2709 violates the Fourth Amendment, and that the non-disclosure provision of 18 U.S.C. §2709(c) violates the First Amendment. The Government is therefore enjoined from issuing NSLs under §2709 or from enforcing the non-disclosure provision in this or any other case, but enforcement of the Court's judgment will be stayed pending appeal, or if no appeal is filed, for 90 days. . . .

A different district court also found that the nondisclosure provisions of the NSL legislation violated the First Amendment. *Doe v. Gonzales*, 386 F. Supp. 2d 66 (D. Conn. 2005) (*Doe II*). The two cases were consolidated on appeal.

NOTES AND QUESTIONS

1. *Matching Legal Thresholds and Processes with Government Surveillance and Collection Techniques.* Professor Orin Kerr identifies the following legal thresholds (standards for obtaining the information) and attendant processes (administrative or judicial or both) for government surveillance, in ascending order of strictness:

a. No standard or legal process. The government just gets the information it seeks.
b. Internal administrative process. There is no bifurcation between the issuing and enforcing authority.
c. Grand jury or administrative subpoena. The issuing and enforcing authority are bifurcated.
d. Certification court order. The government needs a court order, but gets it simply by certifying relevancy. The court does not decide whether the certification is justified.
e. Articulable facts court order. The government needs a court order and must offer specific and articulable facts to establish relevancy.
f. Probable cause search warrant. The traditional criminal law standard and the predicate preferred by the Fourth Amendment.
g. "Super" search warrant. Same, but government must first exhaust all other investigatory techniques or meet some other "plus" requirement beyond showing probable cause.
h. Prohibition. The government is forbidden from getting the information.

Adapted from Orin Kerr, *Internet Surveillance Law After the USA Patriot Act: The Big Brother That Isn't*, 97 Nw. U. L. Rev. 607, 620-621 (2003). Match one of these thresholds to each of the surveillance and collection techniques catalogued in *Doe v. Ashcroft.*

Recall that FISA electronic surveillance has its own unique threshold. See *supra* p. 566. Where would you place it in the hierarchy of thresholds? What about the threshold for national security surveillance ordered by the President on the basis of his own claimed unilateral authority? See *supra* p. 569. You may need to prepare a table of techniques and standards to do this exercise. Is there any logic or pattern to the matches reflected in your table?

Should one have to make a table to figure all this out? Looking just at electronic surveillance techniques, Professor Daniel Solove remarks, "The intricacy of electronic surveillance law is remarkable because it is supposed to apply not just to the FBI, but to state and local police — and even to private citizens. Given its complexity, however, it is unfair to expect these varying groups to comprehend what they can and cannot do." Daniel J. Solove, *Reconstructing Electronic Surveillance Law,* 72 Geo. Wash. L. Rev. 1264, 1293 (2004). If you agree, and if you believe that inclusion of nonelectronic surveillance techniques only compounds the complexity, should the law be simplified? How?

2. *Pen Registers and Trap and Trace Devices.* Before 1998, pen register and trap and trace devices were presumed to be included within the definition of "electronic surveillance," so that orders could be obtained using FISA processes subject to the requirements for gaining FISC approval to conduct electronic surveillance. Beginning in 1998, Congress amended FISA to enable the government to obtain pen register and trap and trace orders under less demanding standards. The authorities were amended again in the USA Patriot Act, Pub. L. No. 107-56, §214, 115 Stat. 272, 286 (2001).

First, the definitions of "pen register" and "trap and trace device" were changed to include "dialing, routing, addressing, or signaling information transmitted by an instrument or facility from which a wire or electronic communication is transmitted, provided . . . that such information shall not include the contents of any communication." *Id.* §216(c), 115 Stat. 290 (amending 18 U.S.C. §3127(3), (4)). In Internet or e-mail communications, does FISA's "contents" restriction really protect the substantive content of these communications? If the FBI can record search terms used at a given Web site visited by the target, how will it sort "addressing" information from contents? Is government access to e-mail and Web addresses any more threatening to privacy interests than access to telephone numbers? How so?

Second, nothing approaching "probable cause" is required for an order for pen registers or trap and trace devices. Instead, the 2001 amendments to FISA require only a certification by the applicant

> that the information likely to be obtained is foreign intelligence information not concerning a United States person or is relevant to an ongoing investigation to protect against international terrorism or clandestine intelligence activities, provided that such investigation of a United States person is not conducted solely upon the basis of activities protected by the first amendment. . . ." [USA Patriot Act §214(a)(2), 115 Stat. 286.]

The amendment was made at the same time that language was deleted that had required an investigation to be in pursuit of "foreign intelligence information or information concerning international terrorism," substituting a requirement that the investigation serve instead "to obtain foreign intelligence information not concerning a United States person or to protect against international terrorism or clandestine intelligence activities." *Id.* §214(a)(1). Can you see what operational effect the changed targeting language will have? Who may be targeted by pen register or trap and trace devices now?

In 2006 the authorities were further amended to permit the government to obtain records of past calls and e-mail use. 50 U.S.C. §1842(d)(2)(c). Pursuant to FBI Guidelines (described in Chapter 19), a FISA pen register or trap and trace order may issue if "the information likely to be obtained is foreign intelligence information not concerning a United States person or is relevant to an ongoing investigation to protect against international terrorism or clandestine intelligence activities." 50 U.S.C. §1842(c)(2). When may FISA pen register/trap and trace authorities be used to investigate a U.S. person?

3. *Access to Business Records.* As enacted in 1978, FISA did not specifically authorize the government to obtain "documents" or other "tangible things." In 1998, FISA was amended to permit the government to apply to the FISC for an order to obtain "records" from "a common carrier, public accommodation facility, physical storage facility or vehicle rental facility." 50 U.S.C. §1862(a). The 2001 USA Patriot Act provided authorization under FISA for orders for the production of "any tangible things (including books, records, papers, documents, and other items)." USA Patriot Act §215, 115 Stat. 287 (codified at 50 U.S.C. §1861(a)(1) (2006)). Can you see why investigators sought the business records authorities? Further amendments followed in 2006 and 2008, partly due to sunset provisions. In 2011, the business records provision was extended to June 1, 2015. Pub. L. No. 112-14, §2(a), 125 Stat. 216.

4. *The Relevancy Standard.* Prior to the USA Patriot Act, FISA orders for selected business records required a showing of a counterintelligence purpose and of "specific and articulable facts giving reason to believe that the person to whom the records pertain is a foreign power or agent of a foreign power." Pub. L. No. 105-272, §602, 112 Stat. 2396, 2411. The USA Patriot Act broadened eligible information to "tangible things," and it substituted a showing that the production was for an authorized investigation to protect against international terrorism, and that such an investigation of a U.S. person was not based solely upon activities protected by the First Amendment. USA Patriot Act, Pub. L. No. 107-56, §215, 115 Stat. 287. See *supra* p. 638. This was effectively a relevancy standard. The same criteria were adopted for NSLs. *Id.* §214, 112 Stat. 286. See *supra* p. 638.

How did the substitution of the relevancy standard for the FISA probable cause standard affect the scope of government surveillance authority? Consider the following assessment.

Previously, the FBI could get the credit card records of anyone suspected of being a foreign agent. Under the PATRIOT Act, broadly read, the FBI can get the entire database of the credit card company. Under prior law, the FBI could get library borrowing records only with a subpoena in a criminal investigation, and generally had to ask for the records of a specific patron. Under the PATRIOT Act, broadly read, the FBI can go into a public library and ask for the records on everybody who ever used the library, or who used it on a certain day, or who checked out certain kinds of books. It can do the same at any bank, telephone company, hotel or motel, hospital, or university—merely upon the claim that the information is...sought for...an investigation to protect against international terrorism or clandestine intelligence activities. [*Terrorism Investigations and the Constitution: Hearing Before the Subcomm. on the Constitution of the H. Comm. on the Judiciary*, 108th Cong. (2003) (statement of James X. Dempsey, Executive Director, Center for Democracy & Technology), *available at* 2003 WL 21153545.]

The relevancy standard has been defended on the basis of the Supreme Court's reasoning in *Smith* and *Miller* that a person who voluntarily conveys information to a third party to consummate a transaction has no legitimate privacy interest in the information. Section 215, however, is not on its face limited to transactional information; it applies to "any tangible things (including books, records, papers, documents, and other items)...." 50 U.S.C. §1861(a)(1). Does the Court's reasoning, even if correct, support the full breadth of §215? Suppose you entrust your personal diary to your brother. Would a §215 order to your brother be supported by the Court's reasoning?

   5. *Tightening the Relevancy Standard?* Although USA Patriot Act §215 requires a prior FISC order for FBI access to "tangible things," its relevancy standard is so low that the order is arguably boilerplate. The government itself has suggested that the FISC's role is simply to ascertain that the government has made the required certification of relevancy, not to determine that the certification is justified. *See* Letter from Jamie E. Brown, Acting Assistant Attorney General, Office of Legislative Affairs, U.S. Dep't of Justice, to F. James Sensenbrenner Jr., Chair, House Comm. on the Judiciary (May 13, 2003).
   In the USA Patriot Improvement and Reauthorization Act of 2005, Pub. L. No. 109-177, 120 Stat. 192 (2006) (hereinafter Patriot Improvement Act), §106, Congress amended FISA §215 to clarify the relevancy standard. The government must now supply a "statement of facts" demonstrating that there are "reasonable grounds" to believe that the order is relevant to a counterterrorist investigation, although a requested order is deemed "presumptively relevant" to an authorized foreign intelligence or counterterrorist investigation if the government can show that the tangible things pertain to a foreign power or agent or suspected agent of a foreign power under FISA, or to "an individual in contact with, or known to, a suspected agent of a foreign power who is the subject of such authorized investigation." *Id.* The request must also provide a particularized description of the records sought. *Id.* Does this amendment make it easier or harder for the government to obtain a §215 order?

   6. *Judicial Review of NSLs.* NSLs have been described as "the intelligence corollary to... administrative subpoena[s]." Lee S. Strickland, *New Information-Related Laws and the Impact on Civil Liberties*, Bull. Am. Soc'y for Info. Sci. & Tech., Feb./Mar. 2002, *available at* http://www.asis.org/Bulletin/Mar-02/strickland2. html. Neither administrative subpoenas nor NSLs require a prior court order. *See* Charles Doyle, *Administrative Subpoenas in Criminal Investigations: A Brief Legal Analysis* (Cong. Res. Serv. RL33321), Mar. 17, 2006; Charles Doyle, *Administrative Subpoenas and National Security Letters in Criminal and Foreign Intelligence Investigations: Background and Proposed Adjustments* (Cong. Res. Serv. RL 32880), Apr. 15, 2005. Why are the former lawful under the Fourth Amendment but not the latter, according to the court in *Doe v. Ashcroft?* How, if at all, can the infirmity of NSLs be cured without compromising national security?

In the Patriot Improvement Act, *supra*, §115, Congress for the first time authorized reciprocal means (described further in the next Note) for a recipient and the government to obtain judicial review after issuance of an NSL. A recipient of an NSL may petition a federal court to modify or set aside the letter "if compliance would be unreasonable, oppressive, or otherwise unlawful." (It also authorized the government to seek enforcement of an NSL from a federal court.) Does the opportunity for judicial review now afforded the NSL recipient satisfy the Fourth Amendment concern identified in the principal case?

7. *First Amendment Issues.* In *Doe v. Ashcroft*, the court found that NSLs for electronic communications records may impermissibly infringe First Amendment rights. Whose rights? (Hint: more than one category of person.) How are they infringed? How is this infringement different from that resulting from pen registers? How, if at all, could this infirmity be cured without compromising national security?

A former chief of the FBI's National Security Law Unit writes that the pre-9/11 "regulatory scheme governing counterintelligence, the higher legal standards for counterintelligence authorities, and even the 'wall' separating intelligence and criminal law enforcement have all functioned to counter-balance and contain a tendency toward excessive secrecy in this area." Woods, *supra* p. 638, at 67. Does the post-9/11 lowering of the legal standards and dismantling of the wall, see *supra* p. 599, upset that balance, supporting the conclusion that the nondisclosure provisions of the NSL statutes fail strict scrutiny? What answer does Judge Cardamone suggest?

In partial response to *Doe I* and *II*, in §§115-116 of the Patriot Improvement Act Congress enacted a sort of reciprocal notice procedure as a means of initiating judicial review. The Act authorized a recipient of an NSL to disclose the letter for the purpose of obtaining legal advice regarding her response and to petition a court to challenge the NSL, as noted above. A recipient also may seek a judicial order setting aside the nondisclosure requirement by showing "that there is no reason to believe that disclosure may endanger the national security of the United States, interfere with a criminal, counterterrorism, or counterintelligence investigation, interfere with diplomatic relations, or endanger the life or physical safety of any person." The government's certification to the contrary is conclusive, however. If, on the other hand, the petition is filed more than a year after the NSL is delivered, then the government must permit disclosure within 90 days unless it recertifies that disclosure would so endanger or interfere. A recertification is also treated as conclusive.

The *Doe I* plaintiffs did not think that this amendment laid the First Amendment issues to rest, and the Court of Appeals remanded for further consideration in light of the Patriot Improvement Act. What First Amendment arguments would you make for the plaintiffs on remand? Does the "conclusive" treatment of government certifications render this First Amendment protection toothless? See *infra* p. 671.

8. *Library Records.* You have to tell the library what book you are borrowing. Do you intend that the library, in turn, will tell the government? Although as of April 2005, the government denied having yet used NSLs for library records, *see Attorney General Defends Patriot Act*, CNN.com, Apr. 5, 2005, *at* http://www.cnn. com/2005/ POLITICS/04/05/patriot.act/, "John Doe II" turned out to be four Connecticut librarians who had received an NSL demanding library records. American Library Ass'n, *Library Connection Is "John Doe" — Board Speaks About NSL Order for Library Records*

(May 30, 2006), *available at* http://www.ala.org/Printer Template.cfm?Template=/ContentManagement/HTMLDisplay.cfm&Content ID=128280.

No potential application of §215 has drawn more criticism than its possible use to obtain library records. Can you guess why? Do you think the Fourth Amendment and/or the First Amendment is implicated? If library records enjoy a distinct First Amendment protection, should they be excluded from §215 authority?

In the USA Patriot Act Additional Reauthorizing Amendments Act of 2006, Congress excluded libraries from the definition of "wire or electronic communication service provider" for purposes of NSLs issued to obtain subscriber information and toll billing records information or electronic communication transactional records. Pub. L. No. 109-178, §§4(b) and 5, 120 Stat. 280, 281 (2006), *codified at* 18 U.S.C. §2709(f). *See* Yeh, *supra,* at 14-15 (describing dispute over construction of library exemption from "ISP" definition). It left libraries subject to §215 orders, however, although it also limited the number of FBI officials who could approve §215 applications for library records, as well as "book sales records, book customer lists, firearms sales records, tax return records, educational records, or medical records containing information that would identify a person." Patriot Improvement Act, *supra* p. 668, §106. Do all of these different kinds of information present the same constitutional issues?

9. *Inspector General's Reports and "Exigent Letters."* In the Patriot Improvement Act, Congress instructed the DOJ Inspector General (IG) to report on the FBI's use of NSLs. In a series of reports, the IG found a dramatic increase in the use of NSLs, as well as a significant number of violations of statutory authority, the *Attorney General Guidelines,* and internal FBI policies. Office of the Inspector Gen., U.S. Dep't of Justice, *A Review of the FBI's Use of National Security Letters* 121-124 (Mar. 2007), *available at* http://www.usdoj.gov/oig/special/s0703b.final.pdf. The IG also found that the FBI had sometimes obtained telephone billing records and subscriber information prior to serving NSLs or grand jury subpoenas by use of "exigent letters" and other informal methods outside the authorities for NSLs. *Id.* at 90. The exigent letters were premised on long-standing exceptions to Fourth Amendment requirements in the face of exigent circumstances, such as the destruction of evidence or danger to the officers. *See Richards v. Wisconsin,* 520 U.S. 385, 391 (1997). The Report indicated that the dominant use of NSLs was to develop evidence to support applications for FISA orders. *A Review of the FBI's Use of National Security Letters, supra,* at 65. A later report found that "the FBI's use of exigent letters became so casual, routine, and unsupervised that employees of all three communications providers sometimes generated exigent letters for FBI personnel to sign and return to them." *Report by the Office of the Inspector General of the Department of Justice on the Federal Bureau of Investigation's Use of Exigent Letters and Other Informal Requests for Telephone Records: Hearing Before the Subcomm. on the Constitution, Civil Rights, and Civil Liberties of the H. Comm. on the Judiciary,* 111th Cong. 14 (2010). Communication carriers assigned employees to FBI offices, where relaxed practices included offering sneak peeks—providing the FBI with a preview of the information available for a selected phone number before preparing documentation to justify a request. One FBI official observed that "it [was] like having the ATM in your living room." *Id.* at 15. The IG Reports indicated that corrective action was being taken.

10. *Continuing Litigation.* While consolidated appeals from the two district court cases were pending in the Second Circuit, Congress passed the Patriot Improvement Act,

and the government inadvertently revealed the names of the plaintiffs in *Doe II*. The Court of Appeals, in a per curiam opinion, dismissed *Doe II* as moot and vacated *Doe I* in part as moot, remanding the remainder for reconsideration in light of the Patriot Improvement Act. *Doe v. Gonzales*, 449 F.3d 415, 419 (2d Cir. 2006) (*Doe III*). On remand, the district court ruled that the amended statute still violated the First Amendment, because the nondisclosure requirement constituted a prior restraint and failed strict scrutiny under the First Amendment. *Doe v. Gonzales*, 500 F. Supp. 2d 379 (S.D.N.Y. 2007) (*Doe IV*). Although the government had a compelling national security interest, the Act vested executive officials with too much discretion without necessary procedural safeguards. The court also found that the judicial review standard and procedures violated separation of powers and failed the narrow tailoring required to meet First Amendment requirements. The Court of Appeals agreed for the most part, *John Doe, Inc. v. Mukasey*, 549 F.3d 861 (2d Cir. 2008) (*Doe V*), ruling that because judicial review must "place on the Government the burden to show a good reason to believe that disclosure may result in an enumerated harm, i.e., a harm related to an authorized investigation to protect against international terrorism or clandestine intelligence activities," *id.* at 881, such review may not be bound by a conclusive certification of harm as permitted in the statute. Yet if the government uses the reciprocal notice procedure as a means of initiating judicial review, it may include notice of a recipient's opportunity to contest the nondisclosure requirement in an NSL. *Id.* at 883.

On further remand, under the procedure suggested by the Court of Appeals, the district court held that the government had met its burden. *Doe v. Holder*, 665 F. Supp. 2d 426 (S.D.N.Y. 2009) (*Doe VI*). Subsequently, the court granted partial disclosure of material the FBI had requested, including the name, address, telephone number, account number, e-mail address, and billing information of a subscriber, but found that the government had met its burden to show harm from disclosure of the remaining information. *Doe v. Holder*, 703 F. Supp. 2d 313 (S.D.N.Y. 2010) (*Doe VII*).

Would you say that Congress, the executive branch, and the courts have worked out a reasonable and constitutionally adequate scheme for using NSLs?

B. CONNECTING THE DOTS — DATA MINING

In May 2006, a news article asserted that the National Security Agency had, with the cooperation of three telecommunication companies, been secretly collecting telephone call data (external or "envelope" data, but not internal or "content" data) on "tens of millions of Americans" in order (in the words of an anonymous source) to "create a database of every call ever made" within the nation's borders. Leslie Cauley, *NSA Has Massive Database of Americans' Phone Calls*, USA Today, May 11, 2006. Similar revelations of an alleged NSA program code-named "Stellar Wind" were reported in December 2008. Michael Isikoff, *The Fed Who Blew the Whistle*, Newsweek, Dec. 22, 2008. The information collected may include calling and called phone numbers, dates, times, and perhaps lengths of completed calls. The data may be used in programs that identify patterns of calling that could indicate particular activity of interest to investigators. For example, a computer using these programs to search phone calls by members of the Yemeni immigrant community in Buffalo might identify several phone numbers of interest. The calling records of these numbers would then be searched, yielding perhaps 100 other numbers with which each phone number of interest had repeated contact.

If we began with 100 interesting phone numbers from the community under inspection, we now have 10,000 active phone taps. Everything is computer-driven so far, and a single workday at Fort Meade is not yet over....

Social nets of people whom the computers think make "interesting phone calls" to each other are defined and stored, presumably forever, as persons of interest. Computers compare these government lists to others....

Establishing the social networks within communities and among individuals requires tapping phones without probable cause. Computers must be free to crawl through their databases and open every phone line along the way. Of necessity, many phone taps are brief and will be discarded. After all, only four "degrees of separation" will get you to all 100 million households in the United States when each phone has 100 contacts, all of them available in phone bill records.

Finding groups is a good way to find conspiracies. Unfortunately and despite attempts to be selective, a system with geometrical expansion will yield many false positives. At some point, therefore, human analysts inspect the computer harvest we have been discussing. It is possible that a court might be asked for a paper-based search warrant.... [J.I. Nelson, *How the NSA Warrantless Wiretap System Works: An Educated Guess* (rev. June 9, 2006), *available at* http://wiretapfacts. notlong.com/.]

This outline of a massive domestic intelligence program, including warrantless wiretaps, is, of course, simply an educated guess, as its author acknowledges. The government has not yet admitted the existence of the program, much less its details.

The use of pen registers and trap and trace devices contemplated in *Smith v. Maryland* represents a relatively limited, "retail" form of surveillance. The NSA call data program, by contrast, apparently involves a "wholesale" collection effort to create a megadatabase of domestic calls by everyone in the United States. Such a database can be analyzed or "mined" to create new, more useful sets of information.

Data mining involves the use of sophisticated data analysis tools to discover previously unknown, valid patterns and relationships in large data sets....

Data mining applications can use a variety of parameters to examine the data. They include association (patterns where one event is connected to another event, such as purchasing a pen and purchasing paper), sequence or path analysis (patterns where one event leads to another event, such as the birth of a child and purchasing diapers), classification (identification of new patterns, such as coincidences between duct tape purchases and plastic sheeting purchases), clustering (finding and visually documenting groups of previously unknown facts, such as geographic location and brand preferences), and forecasting (discovering patterns from which one can make reasonable predictions regarding future activities, such as the prediction that people who join an athletic club may take exercise classes). [Jeffrey W. Seifert, *Data Mining and Homeland Security: An Overview* (Cong. Res. Serv. RL 31798), Aug. 27, 2008.]

According to the Department of Homeland Security,

Data mining uses mathematical algorithms to construct statistical models that estimate the value of an unobserved variable — for example, the probability that an individual will engage in illegal activity. Data mining is best understood as an iterative process consisting of two separate stages: machine learning, where algorithms are applied against known data; and probabilistic inference, where the models built from algorithms are applied against unknown data to make predictions. [DHS Privacy Office, *Data Mining: Technology and Policy: 2008 Report to Congress* 31-32 (Dec. 2008).]

In a counterterrorism effort, "data mining can be a potential means to identify terrorist activities, such as money transfers and communications, and to identify and track individual terrorists themselves, such as through travel and immigration records." Seifert, *supra*, summary. *See generally* K.A. Taipale, *Data Mining and Domestic Security: Connecting the Dots to Make Sense of Data*, 5 Colum. Sci. & Tech. L. Rev. 2 (2003) (describing and assessing the technology). The NSA call data program is only the latest example of data mining for counterterrorism purposes. The following data-mining programs have also come to light:

- *The Total (Later Terrorist) Information Awareness Program (TIA).* This was a research project of the Defense Advanced Research Projects Agency (DARPA) in 2002 to develop technology programs to "counter asymmetric threats by achieving *total information awareness* useful for preemption, national security warning, and national security decision making." Department of Def., *Report to Congress Regarding the Terrorism Information Awareness Program, Detailed Information* 1 (May 20, 2003) (emphasis added). Serious public relations mistakes (placing TIA under the direction of a principal in the Iran-Contra scandal and adopting a logo with an all-seeing eye atop a pyramid over the globe with the motto "*scientia est potentia*" (knowledge is power)), *see* http://www.richardgingras. com/tia/, contributed to Congress's decision to cut off funding for TIA in its original form. *See generally* Seifert, *supra*, at 5-7; Gina Marie Stevens, *Privacy: Total Information Awareness Programs and Related Information Access* (Cong. Res. Serv. RL31730), Mar. 21, 2003.

- *Computer-Assisted Passenger Prescreening System (CAPPS II).* CAPPS II was an airline passenger prescreening program that used computer-generated profiles to select passengers for additional security screening — technically data-matching. It would have relied on commercial data to calculate "scores" for passengers. In fact, the Transportation Security Administration obtained such data from at least four airlines and two travel companies. But litigation made airlines wary of voluntarily sharing such data, the European Union objected, and Congress became concerned about false positives and a lack of procedures for correcting errors. In 2005, Congress prohibited the use of appropriated funds for CAPPS II or its successor, Secure Flight, until the Government Accountability Office certified that the system met certain privacy requirements. Seifert, *supra*, at 7-11. TSA put the Secure Flight requirements into effect in 2009, and airlines fully implemented the program in November 2010. *See* TSA, *Secure Flight — Frequently Asked Questions* (n.d.), *at* http://www.tsa.gov/what_we_do/layers/secureflight/faqs.shtm.

- *Investigative Data Warehouse (IDW).* The IDW serves as a centralized data access point for FBI agents nationwide. Apart from its utility in investigations, critics have accused the FBI of using IDW with data exploitation tools to predict future crimes from past behavior. Electronic Frontier Found., *Report on the Investigative Data Warehouse* (Apr. 2009), *at* http://www.eff.org/issues/foia/investigative-data-warehouse.report.

Several other new tools for data search, analysis, and fusion are described in a report to Congress from the ODNI, Office of the Director of National Intelligence, *2010 Data Mining Report*, 2010, *available at* http://www.fas.org/irp/dni/datamining11.pdf.

NOTES AND QUESTIONS

1. *Just Finding Clues?* Police investigators have always conducted "link analysis" when they interview witnesses who saw a crime committed or who know the victim, then looked for connections in the information obtained in the interviews. "Data mining is no more than the computational automation of traditional investigative skills — that is, the intelligent analysis of myriad 'clues' in order to develop a theory of the case." Taipale, *supra*, at 21. Does it follow that "using computers to analyze data is similar to a police officer examining the same information and does not violate personal privacy"? *Counterterrorism Technology and Privacy, supra* p. 638, at 27. Do the two processes have different implications for personal privacy or expectations of privacy? Should we distinguish, for example, between subject-specific searches and generalized undirected data mining to derive or to match patterns? If so, how is computerized pattern matching different, from a privacy perspective, from a police officer's observation of a masked individual running on a public street? *See* Taipale, *supra*, at 64.

2. *The Question Smith and Miller Did Not Ask.* Attorney General Alberto R. Gonzales defended the NSA call data program, without admitting its existence, by arguing that "[t]here is no reasonable expectation of privacy in those kinds of records," citing *Smith.* Walter Pincus, *Gonzales Defends Phone-Data Collection*, Wash. Post, May 24, 2006. But the Supreme Court focused in *Smith* and *Miller* on the surveillance and collection techniques (pen registers recording dialed numbers and subpoenas for bank records), not on what became of the information they yielded. The Court's focus was understandable from the perspective of traditionally reactive "retail" criminal law enforcement, which builds one case at a time.

But in the fight against terrorism, reactive law enforcement has given way to proactive and preventive law enforcement. *See* Peter Raven-Hansen, *Security's Conquest of Law Enforcement*, in *In Democracy's Shadow* ch. 12 (Marcus G. Raskin & A. Carl LeVan eds., 2005); Daniel J. Steinbock, *Data Matching, Data Mining, and Due Process*, 40 Ga. L. Rev. 1, 16-17 (2005). Data are collected and stored in databases, perhaps indefinitely, for the continuing "wholesale" preventive effort. Even if they are not immediately archived with other data, they can be "virtually aggregated" at any moment to create a dynamic megadatabase. *See* Taipale, *supra*, at 42.

Does the prospect of such indefinite retention and aggregation have any bearing on the expectation of privacy? Do you have a greater expectation of privacy in your aggregated data than in their parts? For example, are you willing to risk that airlines will disclose your travel plans to the government, yet not want those data linked to your other consumer and credit information? Should courts gauge the legitimacy of privacy expectations in each collected item of personal information by the possibility that it will be aggregated for data mining to establish personal behavior patterns and profiles?

> [W]hen combined together, bits and pieces of data begin to form a portrait of a person. The whole becomes greater than the parts. This occurs because combining information creates synergies. When analyzed, aggregated information can reveal new facts about a person that she did not expect would be known about her when the original, isolated data was collected. [Daniel J. Solove, *A Taxonomy of Privacy*, 154 U. Pa. L. Rev. 477, 507 (2006).]

Does your answer depend on the length of time that information may be maintained by a government agency? On the purpose for which the information was originally collected? *See* Laurence H. Tribe, Op-Ed., *Bush Stomps on Fourth Amendment,* Boston Globe, May 16, 2006, at A15 ("Even if one trusts the president's promise not to connect all the dots to the degree the technology permits, the act of collecting all those dots in a form that *permits* their complete connection at his whim is a 'search,'" and "[d]oing it to all Americans . . . is an 'unreasonable search' if those Fourth Amendment words have any meaning at all.").

In *United States Department of Justice v. Reporters Committee for Freedom of the Press,* 489 U.S. 749 (1989), Justice Stevens, writing for the Court, acknowledged that even public personal data enjoy a certain "practical obscurity" that may be altered by its aggregation into an easily searched database. Posing the issue as "whether the compilation of otherwise hard-to-obtain information alters the privacy interest implicated by disclosure of that information," he asserted that "there is a vast difference between the public records" accessible by diligent effort in sundry locations throughout the country and "a computerized summary located in a single clearinghouse of information." *Id.* at 764. But today many public records exist in easily searchable computer databases. Are any computerized records still "practically obscure," in the same sense that hard-copy records at the courthouse or land office once were? Does the ever-increasing use of data mining — in both the public and private sectors — suggest a diminishing expectation of privacy in data? *See Kyllo v. United States,* 533 U.S. 27, 34 (2001) (finding that the use of heat-sensing technology was an unreasonable search, "*at least where (as here) the technology in question is not in general public use*") (emphasis added)). *See also City of Ontario v. Quon,* 130 S. Ct. 2619, 2623 (2010) ("[r]apid changes in the dynamics of communication and information transmission" are causing privacy expectations to evolve).

3. *False Positives.* Credit card data have several attributes that contribute to the success of data mining: a large number of valid transactions, a large number of fraudulent transactions, repetitive fraudulent use that generates common data patterns, and a relatively low cost to "false positives" — valid purchases that are incorrectly flagged as fraudulent — since they usually simply trigger a confirming phone call to the credit card holder. *See* Peter P. Swire, *Privacy and Information Sharing in the War on Terrorism,* 51 Vill. L. Rev. 951 (2006). In contrast, the number of terrorist attacks is extremely low, terrorist attacks are far less likely to be repetitive, rather than one of a kind, and the cost of false positives is far higher, both to the falsely identified innocent person and to the government, which must use substantial resources to investigate that person. *Id. But see* Paul Rosenzweig, *Proposals for Implementing the Terrorist Information Awareness System* (Heritage Found. Legal Memorandum) 4 (Aug. 7, 2003) (suggesting that costs of false positives are "relatively modest"). These differences do not rule out data mining for counterterrorism purposes, but they might suggest the need for special rules for dealing with false positives. *See* Rosenzweig, *supra* (suggesting that "robust" mechanisms to correct false positives from counterterrorist data mining would make the high false positive rate acceptable in light of the consequences of failing to data mine); Steinbock, *supra* p. 674 (suggesting due process protections for persons against whom government action will be taken because of data matching, such as persons denied boarding because of a match on a terrorist watch list). Can you think of special rules to address these differences?

4. *Statutory Protection?* In *Whalen v. Roe,* 429 U.S. 589 (1977), the Court upheld a state law requiring disclosure of certain prescription information to the state, which could enter it into an electronic database. The Court stated, however,

> We are not unaware of the threat to privacy implicit in the accumulation of vast amounts of personal information in computerized data banks or other massive government files.... The right to collect and use such data for public purposes is typically accompanied by a concomitant statutory or regulatory duty to avoid unwarranted disclosures. Recognizing that in some circumstances that duty arguably has its roots in the Constitution, nevertheless New York's statutory scheme, and its implementing administrative procedures, evidence a proper concern with, and protection of, the individual's interest in privacy. [*Id.* at 605.]

Congress has required inter-agency agreements for computer-matching among federal agencies, *see* Computer Matching and Privacy Protection Act of 1988, Pub. L. No. 100-153, §1, 102 Stat. 2507 (1988), but it has also enacted Privacy Act exemptions for computer-matching and inter-agency data sharing for national security and law enforcement purposes. *See* 5 U.S.C. §§552a(a)(8)(B)(vi), 552a(b)(7), 552a(j) (2006). Numerous other statutes regulate particular databases, usually with broad exemptions for law enforcement. *See* Taipale, *supra,* at 53 n.223.

In 2006, Congress deferred regulating data mining and instead required the Attorney General to provide a report on any initiatives to "develop pattern-based data-mining technology." Patriot Improvement Act, *supra* p. 668, §126(b)(1), 120 Stat. 228. It defined "data mining" as

> a query or search or other analysis of one or more electronic databases, where (A) at least one of the databases was obtained from or remains under the control of a non-Federal entity, or the information was acquired initially by another department or agency of the Federal Government for purposes other than intelligence or law enforcement; (B) the search does not use personal identifiers of a specific individual or does not utilize inputs that appear on their face to identify or be associated with a specified individual to acquire information; and (C) a department or agency of the Federal Government is conducting the query or search or other analysis to find a pattern indicating terrorist or other criminal activity. [*Id.*]

How much counterterrorist data mining falls outside this definition? The definition expressly excludes "telephone directories, information publicly available via the Internet or available by any other means to any member of the public, any databases maintained, operated, or controlled by a State, local, or tribal government (such as a State motor vehicle database), or databases of judicial and administrative opinions." Even for what remains within the definition, however, Congress merely required the executive branch to give it a report.

What protections, if any, should Congress enact with respect to data mining by the government for counterterrorism purposes? *See* Report of the Technology and Privacy Advisory Comm., *supra* (recommending, *inter alia,* that Congress authorize the FISC to oversee government data mining but excluding data mining not involving U.S. persons or based on particularized suspicion); Rosenzweig, *supra.*

5. *The Inevitability of Data Mining in Counterterrorism?* In 2008, a committee of the National Research Council found that "automated identification of terrorists

through data mining is neither feasible as an objective nor desireable as a goal of technology development efforts." Committee on Technical & Privacy Dimensions of Info. for Terrorism Prevention & Other Nat'l Goals et al., National Research Council of the Nat'l Academies, *Protecting Individual Privacy in the Struggle Against Terrorists: A Framework for Program Assessment* 3-4 (2008), *available at* http://epic.org/misc/nrc_rept_100708.pdf. The committee noted the serious privacy intrusions that are an incident of data mining, but it also noted that much of the data collected in countering terrorism leads to false positives, that data mining is vulnerable to countermeasures, and, at most, data-mining techniques should be used as a "preliminary screening method for identifying individuals who merit additional follow-up investigation." *Id.* at 4. *See generally* The Constitution Project, *Principles for Government Data Mining: Preserving Civil Liberties in the Information Age* (Nov. 20, 2010), *available at* http://www.constitutionproject.org/pdf/DataMiningPublication.pdf. For surveillance conducted pursuant to FISA, presumably the preliminary screening would be subject to minimization requirements, supervised by the FISC. See *supra* p. 596. In light of the opaqueness of minimization procedures for FISA surveillance, can you imagine how supervision and oversight of a preliminary screening program to counter terrorism based on data-mining techniques could be structured and implemented? *See* William C. Banks, *Programmatic Surveillance and FISA: Of Needles and Haystacks*, 88 Tex. L. Rev. 1633, 1658-1666 (2010).

Screening for Security

On September 11, 2001, Mohamed Atta and Abdul Aziz al Omari boarded a 6 A.M. flight from Portland, Maine, to Boston's Logan International Airport.[1] A program called Computer Assisted Passenger Prescreening System (CAPPS) (see *supra* p. 673) selected Atta for special security measures, which consisted at the time of holding his checked bags until he was on board the airplane. At Logan, Atta and al Omari, and eight colleagues who joined them, went through security checkpoints to board two different planes, both bound for Los Angeles. They were screened by metal detectors calibrated to detect items with the metal content of at least a .22-caliber handgun. Some of these men are now thought to have carried box cutters or pocket utility knives (defined as having blades less than four inches long and permitted on flights at the time).

In the meantime, four out of five more colleagues were flagged by CAPPS at Dulles International Airport en route to board another flight bound for Los Angeles. Two of them — brothers — were selected for extra scrutiny by the airline customer representative at the check-in counter because one of the brothers lacked a photo identification and could not speak English, and they seemed suspicious. Both brothers had dark hair and swarthy complexions, and one had a dark mustache. Again the consequence was that their bags were held until they were on board the airplane. Several of the men at Dulles set off the metal detectors at the security checkpoint and were hand-wanded before being passed. One had his carry-on bag swiped by an explosive trace detector. All were videotaped at the checkpoint. Four additional colleagues boarded yet another Los Angeles–bound plane in Newark at about the same time.

Of the 19 men who eventually boarded the fateful flights in this fashion on September 11, 7 used Virginia driver's licenses as their identification at check-in.

---

1. These and other details in this introduction are drawn from *Final Report of the National Commission on Terrorist Attacks Upon the United States* (*9/11 Report*) (2004) (*9/11 Commission Report*) and *Protecting Our National Security from Terrorist Attacks: A Review of Criminal Terrorism Investigations and Prosecutions: Hearing Before the S. Comm. on the Judiciary*, 108th Cong. (2003) (statement of Paul McNulty, U.S. Attorney, E.D. Va.).

None of them lived in Virginia. They had obtained the licenses there because they learned that one could get a genuine driver's license in Virginia in one day for approximately $100 cash, with no questions asked.

The *9/11 Commission Report* tells the rest of the story.

> The 19 men were aboard four transcontinental flights. They were planning to hijack these planes and turn them into large guided missiles, loaded with up to 11,400 gallons of jet fuel. By 8:00 A.M. on the morning of Tuesday, September 11, 2001, they had defeated all the security layers that America's civil aviation system then had in place to prevent a hijacking. [*9/11 Commission Report* at 4.]

This chapter explores some of the legal issues raised by this defeat of what was and still is essentially a system designed to screen terrorists from entry to transportation systems and other high-risk targets. In Part A we explore issues of checkpoint searches. In Part B we consider the narrower concerns of identification and watch-list screening. Finally, in Part C we examine the difficult question of profiling.

A. CHECKPOINT SEARCHES

The government has been screening persons seeking entry into the country since the first Congress passed a customs statute exempting border searches from probable cause requirements. *See* 5 Wayne R. LaFave, *Search and Seizure* §10.5(a) (4th ed. 2004), *citing* Act of July 31, 1789, ch. 5, 1 Stat. 29, 43 (1789). Border searches without a warrant or probable cause have consistently been held reasonable as tools of national self-protection that are justified by "considerations specifically related to the need to police the border." *City of Indianapolis v. Edmond*, 531 U.S. 32, 38 (2000) (dictum).

Such searches are often conducted at airports where international flights land. At first, fear of airplane hijacking — "skyjacking" — in the 1960s, and then fear of bombs led to screening of air travelers. Such screening was upheld partly as a border search, and partly as an administrative or "regulatory" search:

> [S]creening searches of airline passengers are conducted as part of a general regulatory scheme in furtherance of an administrative purpose, namely, to prevent the carrying of weapons or explosives aboard aircraft, and thereby to prevent hijackings. The essential purpose of the scheme is not to detect weapons or explosives or to apprehend those who carry them, but to deter persons carrying such material from seeking to board at all. [*United States v. Davis*, 482 F.2d 893, 908 (9th Cir. 1973).]

The intrusiveness of the screening program had to match the "special need," leading to the conclusion that there was no justification for the compelled search of a person who elected not to board a plane. *Id. See generally* LaFave, *supra*, §10.6(c).

We have all grown accustomed to — if sometimes still annoyed by — security lines and checks at airports and to booting up our laptops as we go through the checkpoint. But have you had TSA agents or other security personnel look through the files on your computer? Does this process "prevent the carrying of weapons or explosives aboard aircraft," the ostensible special need for regulatory searches at airports. If it does not, is it lawful?

United States v. Arnold

United States Court of Appeals, Ninth Circuit, 2008
533 F.3d 1003, *cert. denied*, 129 S. Ct. 1312 (2009)

O'Scannlain, Circuit Judge: We must decide whether customs officers at Los Angeles International Airport may examine the electronic contents of a passenger's laptop computer without reasonable suspicion.

I...

[Michael Arnold arrived at Los Angeles International Airport from the Philippines and proceeded to customs, where he was selected by a U.S. Customs and Border Patrol (CBP) officer for secondary questioning. His laptop was booted up and an inspection of the files revealed several nude photographs. Special agents with the United States Department of Homeland Security, Immigration and Customs Enforcement (ICE) were then called in to question Arnold and to examine his computer. They found numerous images depicting what they believed to be child pornography. Arnold was released but later arrested on various child pornography charges.

The district court granted Arnold's motion to suppress, finding that: (1) reasonable suspicion was indeed necessary to search the laptop; and (2) the government had failed to meet the burden of showing that the CBP officers had reasonable suspicion to search. This appeal by the government followed.]

II

Arnold argues that the district court was correct in concluding that reasonable suspicion was required to search his laptop at the border because it is distinguishable from other containers of documents based on its ability to store greater amounts of information and its unique role in modern life.

Arnold argues that "laptop computers are fundamentally different from traditional closed containers," and analogizes them to "homes" and the "human mind." Arnold's analogy of a laptop to a home is based on his conclusion that a laptop's capacity allows for the storage of personal documents in an amount equivalent to that stored in one's home. He argues that a laptop is like the "human mind" because of its ability to record ideas, e-mail, internet chats and web-surfing habits....

III

A

The Fourth Amendment states that "[t]he right of the people to be secure in their persons, houses, papers, and effects, against unreasonable searches and seizures, shall not be violated...." U.S. Const. amend. IV. Searches of international passengers at American airports are considered border searches because they occur at the "functional equivalent of a border." *Almeida-Sanchez v. United States*, 413 U.S. 266, 273 (1973) ("For...example, a search of the passengers and cargo of an airplane arriving at a St. Louis airport after a non-stop flight from Mexico

City would clearly be the functional equivalent of a border search."). "It is axiomatic that the United States, as sovereign, has the inherent authority to protect, and a paramount interest in protecting, its territorial integrity." *United States v. Flores-Montano*, 541 U.S. 149, 153 (2004). Generally, "searches made at the border . . . are reasonable simply by virtue of the fact that they occur at the border. . . ." *United States v. Ramsey*, 431 U.S. 606, 616 (1977).

The Supreme Court has stated that:

> The authority of the United States to search the baggage of arriving international travelers is based on its inherent sovereign authority to protect its territorial integrity. By reason of that authority, it is entitled to require that whoever seeks entry must establish the right to enter and to bring into the country whatever he may carry.

Torres v. Puerto Rico, 442 U.S. 465, 472-73 (1979). In other words, the "Government's interest in preventing the entry of unwanted persons and effects is at its zenith at the international border." *Flores-Montano*, 541 U.S. at 152. Therefore, "[t]he luggage carried by a traveler entering the country may be searched at random by a customs officer . . . no matter how great the traveler's desire to conceal the contents may be." *United States v. Ross*, 456 U.S. 798, 823 (1982). . . .

B

Courts have long held that searches of closed containers and their contents can be conducted at the border without particularized suspicion under the Fourth Amendment. Searches of the following specific items have been upheld without particularized suspicion: (1) the contents of a traveler's briefcase and luggage, *United States v. Tsai*, 282 F.3d 690, 696 (9th Cir. 2002); (2) a traveler's "purse, wallet, or pockets," *Henderson v. United States*, 390 F.2d 805, 808 (9th Cir. 1967); (3) papers found in containers such as pockets, see *United States v. Grayson*, 597 F.2d 1225, 1228-29 (9th Cir. 1979) (allowing search without particularized suspicion of papers found in a shirt pocket); and (4) pictures, films and other graphic materials. *See United States v. Thirty-Seven Photographs*, 402 U.S. 363, 376 (1971); *see also United States v. 12,200-Ft. Reels of Super 8MM. Film*, 413 U.S. 123, 124-25 (1973) ("Import restrictions and searches of persons or packages at the national borders rest on different considerations and different rules of constitutional law from domestic regulations.").

Nevertheless, the Supreme Court has drawn some limits on the border search power. Specifically, the Supreme Court has held that reasonable suspicion is required to search a traveler's "alimentary canal," *United States v. Montoya de Hernandez*, 473 U.S. 531, 541 (1985), because "[t]he interests in human dignity and privacy which the Fourth Amendment protects forbid any such intrusion [beyond the body's surface] on the mere chance that desired evidence might be obtained." *Id.* at 540 n.3 (quoting *Schmerber v. California*, 384 U.S. 757, 769 (1966)). However, it has expressly declined to decide "what level of suspicion, *if any*, is required for non-routine border searches such as strip, body cavity, or involuntary x-ray searches." *Id.* at 541 n.4 (emphasis added). Furthermore, the Supreme Court has rejected creating a balancing test based on a "routine" and "non-routine" search framework, and has treated the terms as purely descriptive. *See United States v. Cortez-Rocha*, 394 F.3d 1115, 1122 (9th Cir. 2005).

Other than when "intrusive searches of *the person*" are at issue, *Flores-Montano*, 541 U.S. at 152 (emphasis added), the Supreme Court has held open the possibility, "that some searches of *property* are so destructive as to require" particularized suspicion. *Id.* at 155-56 (emphasis added) (holding that complete disassembly and reassembly of a car gas tank did not require particularized suspicion). Indeed, the Supreme Court has left open the question of "'whether, and under what circumstances, a border search might be deemed "unreasonable" because of the particularly offensive manner in which it is carried out.'" *Id.* at 155 n.2 (quoting *Ramsey*, 431 U.S. at 618 n.13).

C

In any event, the district court's holding that particularized suspicion is required to search a laptop, based on cases involving the search of the person, was erroneous. . . .

The Supreme Court has stated that "[c]omplex balancing tests to determine what is a 'routine' search of a vehicle, as opposed to a more 'intrusive' search of a person, have no place in border searches of vehicles." *Flores-Montano*, 541 U.S. at 152. Arnold argues that the district court was correct to apply an intrusiveness analysis to a laptop search despite the Supreme Court's holding in *Flores-Montano*, by distinguishing between one's privacy interest in a vehicle compared to a laptop. However, this attempt to distinguish *Flores-Montano* is off the mark. The Supreme Court's analysis determining what protection to give a vehicle was not based on the unique characteristics of vehicles with respect to other property, but was based on the fact that a vehicle, as a piece of property, simply does not implicate the same "dignity and privacy" concerns as "highly intrusive searches of the person." *Flores-Montano*, 541 U.S. at 152.

Furthermore, we have expressly repudiated this type of "least restrictive means test" in the border search context. *See Cortez-Rocha*, 394 F.3d at 1123 (refusing to fashion a "least restrictive means test for border control vehicular searches, and . . . refus[ing] to tie the hands of border control inspectors in such a fashion"). Moreover, in both *United States v. Chaudhry*, 424 F.3d 1051, 1054 (9th Cir. 2005) (finding the distinction between "routine" and "non-routine" inapplicable to searches of property) and *Cortez-Rocha*, 394 F.3d at 1122-23, we have recognized that *Flores-Montano* rejected our prior approach of using an intrusiveness analysis to determine the reasonableness of property searches at the international border.

Therefore, we are satisfied that reasonable suspicion is not needed for customs officials to search a laptop or other personal electronic storage devices at the border.

IV

While the Supreme Court left open the possibility of requiring reasonable suspicion for certain border searches of property in *Flores-Montano*, 541 U.S. at 155-56, the district court did not base its holding on the two narrow grounds left open by the Supreme Court in that case.

Arnold has never claimed that the government's search of his laptop damaged it in any way; therefore, we need not consider whether "exceptional damage to property" applies. Arnold does raise the "particularly offensive manner" exception to the government's broad border search powers. But, there is nothing in the record to indicate that the manner in which the CBP officers conducted the search was "particularly offensive" in comparison with other lawful border searches. According to Arnold, the CBP officers simply "had me boot [the laptop] up, and looked at what I had inside. . . ."

Whatever "particularly offensive manner" might mean, this search certainly does not meet that test. Arnold has failed to distinguish how the search of his laptop and its electronic contents is logically any different from the suspicionless border searches of travelers' luggage that the Supreme Court and we have allowed. *See Ross*, 456 U.S. at 823; *see also Vance*, 62 F.3d at 1156 ("In a border search, a person is subject to search of luggage, contents of pockets and purse without any suspicion at all.").

With respect to these searches, the Supreme Court has refused to draw distinctions between containers of information and contraband with respect to their quality or nature for purposes of determining the appropriate level of Fourth Amendment protection. Arnold's analogy to a search of a home based on a laptop's storage capacity is without merit. The Supreme Court has expressly rejected applying the Fourth Amendment protections afforded to homes to property which is "*capable of functioning as a home*" simply due to its size, or, distinguishing between "'worthy' and 'unworthy' containers." *California v. Carney*, 471 U.S. 386, 393-94 (1985).

In *Carney*, the Supreme Court rejected the argument that evidence obtained from a warrantless search of a mobile home should be suppressed because it was "*capable of functioning as a home.*" *Id.* at 387-88, 393-94. The Supreme Court refused to treat a mobile home differently from other vehicles just because it could be used as a home. *Id.* at 394-95. The two main reasons that the Court gave in support of its holding, were: (1) that a mobile home is "readily movable," and (2) that "the expectation [of privacy] with respect to one's automobile is significantly less than that relating to one's home or office." *Id.* at 391 (quotation marks omitted).

Here, beyond the simple fact that one cannot live in a laptop, *Carney* militates against the proposition that a laptop is a home. First, as Arnold himself admits, a laptop goes with the person, and, therefore is "readily mobile." *Carney*, 471 U.S. at 391. Second, one's "expectation of privacy [at the border] . . . is significantly less than that relating to one's home or office." *Id.*

Moreover, case law does not support a finding that a search which occurs in an otherwise ordinary manner, is "particularly offensive" simply due to the storage capacity of the object being searched. *See California v. Acevedo*, 500 U.S. 565, 576 (1991) (refusing to find that "looking inside a closed container" when already properly searching a car was unreasonable when the Court had previously found "destroying the interior of an automobile" to be reasonable in *Carroll v. United States*, 267 U.S. 132 (1925)).

Because there is no basis in the record to support the contention that the manner in which the search occurred was "particularly offensive" in light of other searches allowed by the Supreme Court and our precedents, the district court's judgment cannot be sustained. . . .

VI

For the foregoing reasons, the district court's decision to grant Arnold's motion to suppress must be

Reversed.

NOTES AND QUESTIONS

1. *Regulatory or Special Needs Search?* Requiring the air traveler to boot up her laptop may serve the special need of keeping explosives off planes because it presumably helps show that the laptop is a laptop, and not a box for carrying explosives,

like the dummy printers that Al Qaeda in the Arabian Peninsula reportedly tried to ship to the United States as air freight. But searching through your files and images, or address books and calendars on other electronic devices such as cell phones, cannot be similarly justified. Such searches may be justified, if at all, only as border searches. There the rationale is simply the sovereign's authority to control its borders. Note that this justification is not anchored in the legislative power to enact immigration laws; it extends even to traveling U.S. citizens who cross our borders.

2. *Consent.* Some of the airport screening cases argue that with notice of the screening programs, a passenger who elects travel by air impliedly consents to the screening. LaFave, *supra* p. 680, §10.6(g). If she consents, she waives her privacy interest. Is this logic compelling for air travelers? *See United States v. Davis*, 482 F.2d 893, 905 (9th Cir. 1973) (asserting that it would violate the principle that government cannot "avoid the restrictions of the Fourth Amendment by notifying the public that all telephone lines would be tapped or that all homes would be searched"); LaFave, *supra*, §10.6(g) (theory of implied consent "diverts attention from the more fundamental question of whether the nature of the regulation undertaken by the government is in fact reasonable under the Fourth Amendment").

3. *The Walk-Away Option.* Closely related to the consent theory is one that travelers have notice of the inspection and therefore can always refuse inspection and take alternative transportation. A few courts condition their finding that a screening program is reasonable upon the program's inclusion of this option. *See Davis, supra,* 482 F.2d at 910. Does this logic take into account the impact of the walk-away option on the government's security interest? A few courts have reasoned that "such an option would constitute a one-way street for the benefit of a party planning airplane mischief, since there is no guarantee that if he were allowed to leave he might not return and be more successful," and that "the very fact that a safe exit is available if apprehension is threatened would, by diminishing risk, encourage attempts." *United States v. Skipwith,* 482 F.2d 1272, 1282 (5th Cir. 1973) (Aldrich, J., dissenting, but this discussion adopted by majority). Does the apparently heightened risk of terrorism to transportation systems after 9/11 now justify finding that a screening system without this option can still be reasonable? Then-Circuit Judge Alito, writing for the Third Circuit Court of Appeals, thought so in *United States v. Hartwell,* 436 F.3d 174, 179 (3d Cir. 2006) (upholding a nonconsensual hand-wanding of Hartwell after he set off the metal detector at an airport).

4. *Laptop Searches.* A 2008 letter from Congressman Bernie Thompson to the CBP described such searches:

These practices include opening individual laptops; reading documents saved on the devices; accessing email accounts and reading through emails that have been sent and received; examining photographs; looking through personal calendars; and going through telephone numbers saved in cellular phones. Further, individuals have raised claims that these searches can sometimes last for hours and cause significant delay, while the subject of the search — often a U.S. citizen — is delayed entering the country and must sit by as the information contained in their personal devices [is] copied, confiscated or compromised. [Letter from Bennie G. Thompson, Chairman, U.S. House of Representatives, Committee on Homeland Security, to W. Ralph Basham, Commissioner, U.S. Customs and Border Protection (July 1, 2008).]

Arnold poses several limits on border searches? What are they? Why do they not apply to laptop searches for files and images? Should it make a difference if the laptop is removed from the border and searched elsewhere? If it is kept for months? *See* Constitution Project, *Suspicionless Border Searches of Electronic Devices: Legal and Privacy Concerns with the Department of Homeland Security's Policy* 5 (2011) (describing six-month retention of laptop seized at border and DHS policy permitting off-site retention for a "reasonable period"). One study concluded that even if laptop border searches are lawful, DHS policies permitting detention of electronic devices at a location and a time remote from the original border crossing "may impermissibly invade expectations of privacy and contravene well-settled Fourth Amendment principles." *Id.* at 6. *But see United States v. Cotterman,* 637 F.3d 1068 (9th Cir. 2011) ("travelers [do not] somehow have a constitutionally protected expectation that their property will not be removed from the border for search and, therefore, the Government must either staff every POE [point of entry] with the equipment and personnel needed to fully search all incoming property or otherwise be forced to blindly shut its eyes and hope for the best absent some particularized suspicion").

5. *Whole Body Imaging.* In 2010, TSA introduced whole body imaging (WBI) systems at airport checkpoints, and they are now the primary screening method at the busiest airports. Bart Elias, *Changes in Airport Passenger Screening Technologies and Procedures: Frequently Asked Questions* 1 (Cong. Res. Serv. R41502), Jan. 26, 2011. WBI systems notoriously capture a crude image of a passenger's body, causing some critics to call a WBI scan a "virtual strip search." *Id.* But TSA gives passengers the option of submitting to a pat-down search instead.

Does *Arnold* provide authority for the legality of WBI searches? Or are they "non-routine" and intrusive searches that require particularized suspicion? What arguments would you make based on the case law set out in *Arnold* to decide the legality of WBI searches? Does the pat-down option affect your answer?

6. *Subway and Train Searches.* After terrorist bombings of trains killed more than 200 in Madrid in 2004, and subway bombings killed 52 in London in 2005, the New York subway system instituted a random container inspection program, whereby subway passengers were randomly selected for inspection of knapsacks, parcels, and purses (confined to "what is minimally necessary to ensure that the . . . item does not contain an explosive device."). Selected passengers were afforded the option of leaving rather than submitting to inspection.

Arnold supplies no precedent for upholding the legality of this inspection program. Can you see why? On the other hand, the regulatory or special need rationale does apply. In a challenge to the program, a court described the rationale as follows:

> First, as a threshold matter, the search must "serve as [its] immediate purpose an objective distinct from the ordinary evidence gathering associated with crime investigation." *Nicholas v. Goord,* 430 F.3d 652, 663 (2d Cir. 2005). Second, once the government satisfies that threshold requirement, the court determines whether the search is reasonable by balancing several competing considerations. These balancing factors include (1) the weight and immediacy of the government interest, *Earls,* 536 U.S. at 834; (2) "the nature of the privacy interest allegedly compromised by" the search, *id.* at 830; (3) "the character of the intrusion imposed" by the search, *id.* at 832; and (4) the efficacy of the search in advancing the government interest. [*MacWade v. Kelly,* 460 F.3d 260, 268-269 (2d Cir. 2006).]

The court then found that the New York subway container inspection program served the immediate and substantial "special need of preventing a terrorist attack on the subway." While it acknowledged the subway rider's full expectation of privacy in his containers, it also found the search "minimally intrusive" and "reasonably effective" (a question given the walk-away option), and therefore, that the program was, on balance, constitutional. *Id.* at 270, 273-275. Will any inspection program intended to prevent a terrorist attack *ever* be, on balance, unconstitutional? What kind of subway security check would fail the special needs test?

7. *Building Entry Screening.* The balancing test articulated in the airport screening cases and adapted for the container-inspection program in *MacWade* is fact-sensitive. Do the factors carry the same weight when the government screens entry into a building? How is that different? In *Barrett v. Kunzig*, 331 F. Supp. 266, 274 (M.D. Tenn. 1971), the court found that "[w]hen the interest in protection of the government property and personnel from destruction is balanced against any invasion to the entrant's personal dignity, privacy, and constitutional rights, the government's substantial interest in conducting the cursory [article] inspection [at building entry] outweighs the personal inconvenience suffered by the individual." But there the court also emphasized the relatively unobtrusive nature of the article inspection and its neutral application to all entrants. Suppose the screening includes frisks? Body searches? Suppose, using a watch list, the security personnel select particular entrants for a second search? Does it matter whether the search is conducted at the Pentagon or the Smithsonian Museum of Natural History? Professor LaFave's answer is that "what is required is a judicial assessment of the magnitude of the danger and a judicial determination of what screening procedures will suffice to meet it." LaFave, *supra*, §10.7(a). How would you perform this requirement for these building searches?

B.   IDENTIFICATION AND WATCH-LISTING

Two of the 9/11 hijackers had been identified by the CIA as possible terrorist suspects and added to a State Department watch list of such suspects called "TIPOFF" on August 24, 2001. *9/11 Commission Report, supra* p. 679, at 270. TIPOFF was intended primarily to keep terrorists from getting visas to the United States. It was not shared with the FAA, which maintained a separate "no-fly list" of persons banned for air travel because of the threat they were thought to pose to civil aviation, as well as a "selectee list" of persons selected for further screening, such as hand-wanding and questioning. None of the hijackers were on either FAA list. *The 9/11 Investigations* 27 (Steve Strasser ed., 2004).

In 2003, President George W. Bush issued Homeland Security Presidential Directive 6 (HSPD-6) (Sept. 16, 2003), establishing a Terrorist Screening Center to consolidate the government's watch listing and screening. *See generally* William J. Krouse & Bart Elias, *Terrorist Watchlist Checks and Air Passenger Prescreening* 2 (Cong. Res. Serv. RL33645), Dec. 30, 2009. Subsequently, based partly on TIPOFF data, the National Counterterrorism Center (NCTC), under the Office of the Director of National Intelligence, created the Terrorist Identities Datamart Environment (TIDE) as the master repository for international terrorism data. TIDE "includes . . . all information the U.S. government possesses related to identities of individuals known or appropriately suspected to be or have been involved in activities constituting, in preparation for, in aid of, or related to [international] terrorism." National Counter-terrorism Center, *Terrorist Identities Datamart Environment (TIDE)* (n.d.), *available at* http://www.nctc.gov/docs/Tide_Fact_Sheet.pdf. By 2008, it had more than 540,000 names (though only 450,000 identities, because of aliases and name variants), fewer than 5 percent of which were for U.S. persons. *Id.*

In theory, the watch-list process begins when a member of the intelligence com-munity shares newly acquired information about suspected terrorists or their sup-porters with NCTC's TIDE. See the chart below. The standards applied are not public, although some anecdotal evidence suggests that they are at least partly subjective, that they may rest on indirect and possibly innocent connections to suspected terrorists as well as informant information of doubtful reliability, and that they err on the side of inclusion. Daniel J. Steinbock, *Designating the Dangerous: from Blacklists to Watch Lists*, 30 Seattle U. L. Rev. 65 (2006). NCTC nominates some of these persons, and the FBI-administered inter-agency Terrorist Screening Center (TSC) decides whether to accept the nomination for inclusion in the Consolidated Terrorist Screening Data-base (TSDB). Krouse & Elias, *supra*, at 203. The FBI also provides data about domestic terrorist suspects to the TSDB. As of 2009, it was reported that the TSDB contained more than one million records for more than 400,000 individuals.

The TSC then distributes TSDB-generated watch lists to end users — including all frontline screening agencies — such as the Transportation Security Administration (administering the no-fly and selectee lists), U.S. Customs and Border Protection, and the State Department's Bureau of Consular Affairs, as well the FBI, and state and local governments through the National Crime Information Center. A 2007 study identi-fied nine different end users, although the number and names of users has changed since then. *See* Peter M. Shane, *The Bureaucratic Due Process of Government Watch Lists*, 75 Geo. Wash. L. Rev. 804 (2007).

Terrorist Watch Listing and Screening Under HSPD-6

From William J. Krouse & Bart Elias, *Terrorist Watchlist Checks and Air Passenger Prescreening* 2 (Cong. Res. Serv. RL33645), Dec. 30, 2009.

The 9/11 Commission expressly recommended expanding traveler intelligence and traveler screening, with priority given to screening airline passengers for explosives. *9/11 Commission Report, supra,* at 385, 393. After a number of false starts, TSA has adopted the Secure Flight program for screening air travelers based in part on the collection of pre-flight information from passengers. No-fly and selectee watch lists were consolidated into the TSDB sometime in 2004, although they form only a small subset of the TSDB. In 2007, the head of TSA testified to efforts by TSA and TSC to reduce the number of persons on the no-fly list by as much as 50 percent, partly in response to the DHS Privacy Office's criticism of the quality of the list. Krouse & Elias, *supra,* at 12-13. It was reported then that the no-fly list includes about 4,000 individuals, while the selectee list includes some 14,000 names.

Before boarding a plane, a passenger must first supply some identification. What authority does the government have to require identification in the screening process? The following case provides some answers, and subsequent notes and questions address the related question of whether we should require a national identifier.

Gilmore v. Gonzales

United States Court of Appeals, Ninth Circuit, 2006
435 F.3d 1125, *cert. denied,* 549 U.S. 1110 (2007)

PAEZ, Circuit Judge. John Gilmore ("Gilmore") sued Southwest Airlines and the United States Attorney General, Alberto R. Gonzales, among other defendants, alleging that the enactment and enforcement of the Government's civilian airline passenger identification policy is unconstitutional. The identification policy requires airline passengers to present identification to airline personnel before boarding or be subjected to a search that is more exacting than the routine search that passengers who present identification encounter. Gilmore alleges that when he refused to present identification or be subjected to a more thorough search, he was not allowed to board his flights to Washington, D.C. Gilmore asserts that because the Government refuses to disclose the content of the identification policy, it is vague and uncertain and therefore violated his right to due process. He also alleges that when he was not allowed to board the airplanes, Defendants violated his right to travel, right to be free from unreasonable searches and seizures, right to freely associate, and right to petition the government for redress of grievances. . . .

[The government contended that the Security Directive authorizing the Transportation Security Administration to require passenger identification as a condition of boarding was "sensitive security information" that could not be shown to Gilmore or disclosed to the public. The court accepted this claim, but reviewed the Directive in camera.]

III. RIGHT TO TRAVEL

Gilmore alleges that the identification policy violates his constitutional right to travel because he cannot travel by commercial airlines without presenting identification, which is an impermissible federal condition. We reject Gilmore's right to travel argument because the Constitution does not guarantee the right to travel by any particular form of transportation. . . .

...Gilmore does not possess a fundamental right to travel by airplane even though it is the most convenient mode of travel for him. Moreover, the identification policy's "burden" is not unreasonable. The identification policy requires that airline passengers either present identification or be subjected to a more extensive search. The more extensive search is similar to searches that we have determined were reasonable and "consistent with a full recognition of appellant's constitutional right to travel." *United States v. Davis*, 482 F.2d 893, 912-13 (9th Cir. 1973).

...Additionally, Gilmore was free to decline both options and use a different mode of transportation. In sum, by requiring Gilmore to comply with the identification policy, Defendants did not violate his right to travel.

IV. FOURTH AMENDMENT

Gilmore next alleges that both options under the identification policy — presenting identification or undergoing a more intrusive search — are subject to Fourth Amendment limitations and violated his right to be free from unreasonable searches and seizures.

Request for Identification

Gilmore argues that the request for identification implicates the Fourth Amendment because "the government imposes a severe penalty on citizens who do not comply." Gilmore highlights the fact that he was once arrested at an airport for refusing to show identification and argues that the request for identification "[i]mposes the severe penalty of arrest." Gilmore further argues that the request for identification violates the Fourth Amendment because it constitutes "a warrantless general search for identification" that is unrelated to the goals of detecting weapons or explosives.

The request for identification, however, does not implicate the Fourth Amendment. "[A] request for identification by the police does not, by itself, constitute a Fourth Amendment seizure." *INS v. Delgado*, 466 U.S. 210, 216 (1984). Rather, "[a]n individual is seized within the meaning of the fourth amendment only if, in view of all of the circumstances surrounding the incident, a reasonable person would have believed that he was not free to leave." *United States v. $25,000 U.S. Currency*, 853 F.2d 1501, 1504 (9th Cir. 1988) (internal quotation marks omitted). In *Delgado*, the Supreme Court held that INS agents' questioning of factory workers about their citizenship status did not constitute a Fourth Amendment seizure. In *$25,000 U.S. Currency*, we held that a DEA agent's request for identification from a person waiting to board a flight was not a Fourth Amendment seizure.

Similarly, an airline personnel's request for Gilmore's identification was not a seizure within the meaning of the Fourth Amendment. Gilmore's experiences at the Oakland and San Francisco airports provide the best rebuttal to his argument that the requests for identification imposed a risk of arrest and were therefore seizures. Gilmore twice tried to board a plane without presenting identification, and twice left the airport when he was unsuccessful. He was not threatened with arrest or some other form of punishment; rather he simply was told that unless he complied with the policy, he would not be permitted to board the plane. There was no penalty for noncompliance.

Request to Search

[The Court rejected the Fourth Amendment challenge to the selectee search option, relying on the balancing analysis of *United States v. Davis*, 482 F.2d 893 (9th Cir. 1973), noted *supra* p. 680.]

CONCLUSION

In sum, we conclude that Defendants did not violate Gilmore's constitutional rights by adopting and implementing the airline identification policy. Therefore, his claims fail on the merits and we deny his petition for review. . . .

NOTES AND QUESTIONS

a.   Identification Requirements

1. *Identification for Screening Purposes and the Fourth Amendment.* "Effective checking of names against watch lists . . . requires that every person carry an accurate and secure form of identification." Steinbock, *Designating the Dangerous, supra*, at 113. Watch-listing is thus linked closely to the asserted need for more secure identification and to more frequent identification stops or checkpoints. *Id.*

Identification is mandatory for boarding flights. As *Gilmore* suggests, the Fourth Amendment poses no barrier to suspicionless government requests for identification at check-in or the security checkpoint, provided that a reasonable requested person would feel free to terminate the encounter. David J. Steinbock, *National Identity Cards: Fourth and Fifth Amendment Issues*, 56 Fla. L. Rev. 697, 711-714 (2004). Furthermore, the *MacWade* analysis suggests that "regulatory" (administrative) demands for identification at airport, transit system, and many building checkpoints would pass Fourth Amendment muster as well. *Id.* at 725-743. How would you apply that analysis to mandatory identification at the entrance to a federal building? What about a random demand for "your papers, please" made by police in a public street?

Of course, good identification serves not just a governmental interest, but also an individual interest in avoiding wrong matching. *See* Paul Rosenzweig & Jeff Jonas, *Correcting False Positives: Redress and the Watch List Conundrum*, 17 Legal Mem. (Heritage Found.) 10-11 (June 17, 2005), *available at* http://www.heritage.org/Research/HomelandDefense/lm17.cfm. For this reason in part but, more important, as a personal convenience, most persons voluntarily provide identification. That is, we voluntarily show our government-issued identification — usually a driver's license — to cash checks, to register for classes, and to obtain other privileges. Such voluntary disclosure presents no Fourth Amendment concern. Why not?

2. *A National Identity Card or Other Identifier?* Some have argued that after 9/11, we need a national identity card system. *See* Alan Dershowitz, *Why Fear National ID Cards?*, N.Y. Times, Oct. 13, 2001. *See generally* Steinbock, *Designating the Dangerous, supra* (citing proponents). An effective system "necessitates mandatory participation, both in the sense of having an identity within the system and in presenting identification when required." Steinbock, *National Identity Cards, supra*, 56 Fla. L. Rev. at 708.

A mandatory national identifier requirement would pose at least three kinds of legal issues. First, there may be a Fourth Amendment question if identification is demanded randomly in some places, such as public streets, as suggested above. "[O]ne of the primary reasons that governments created passports and identity cards was to restrict movement, alter patterns of migration, and control the movements of poor people and others viewed as undesirable." Daniel J. Solove, *A Taxonomy of Privacy*, 154 U. Pa. L. Rev. 477, 514 n.183 (2006).

Second, the "main point of identity checking is to make a connection between the identified individual and collection of data." Steinbock, *National Identity Cards*, *supra*, 56 Fla. L. Rev. at 700. A national identifier "would likely be but one component of a large and complex nationwide identity system, the core of which could be a database of personal information on the U.S. population." Computer Sci. & Telecomms. Bd., National Research Council, *IDs — Not That Easy: Questions About Nationwide Identity Systems* 7 (Stephen T. Kent & Lynette I. Millet eds., 2002). The legality of a national identifier system thus turns in part on the legality of the associated database or watch list. *See infra* pp. 693-695.

Third, identity checking may also generate data that can be used to track movements and purchases (e.g., subject was identified at 11:06 A.M. on June 20, 2006, at Constitution Ave. entrance to Department of Justice). The use of such data in a computer database raises some of the same privacy concerns created by government access to and use of third-party records. See Chapter 23. By providing identification on demand, does a person waive her privacy interest in the data? *See* Steinbock, *National Identity Cards*, *supra*, 56 Fla. L. Rev. at 748-752 (no, because identification is different from providing telephone numbers or banking information). Even if a single identification encounter does not offend privacy, does its aggregation into a database do so?

3. *The REAL ID Act — A Step in the Direction of a National ID Card?* In 2005, Congress enacted the REAL ID Act. Emergency Supplemental Appropriations Act for Defense, the Global War on Terror, and Tsunami Relief, Pub. L. No. 109-13, div. B, 119 Stat. 231, 302, *codified at* 49 U.S.C. §30301 note (2006). *See* Office of the Press Secretary, *Statement by Deputy Press Secretary Matt Chandler on DHS' Efforts to Enhance Driver's License Security* (Dec. 18, 2009), *available at* http://www.dhs.gov/ynews/releases/pr_1261170524591.shtm (extending deadline for material compliance). The REAL ID Act forbids any federal agency, three years after the Act's enactment, from accepting for any official purpose a state-issued driver's license or identification card unless it meets certain requirements. The identification must include name, address, date of birth, gender, a digital photo, signature, anti-tampering security features, and "[a] common machine-readable technology, with defined minimum data elements." 119 Stat. at 312. In addition, the state must insist on and verify certain identifying information and evidence of lawful status to issue such an identification. Finally, each state must "provide electronic access to all other States to information contained in the motor vehicle database of the States," which must include, at a minimum, "all data fields printed on drivers' licenses and identification cards issued by the State." *Id.* at 316. How is the REAL ID different from a national identity card? Which poses the larger privacy concern, the REAL ID or the database the Act requires? In *Whalen v. Roe*, 429 U.S. 589 (1977), noted *supra* p. 676, the Supreme Court found reasonable a mandatory prescription-reporting system tied to a centralized database, but only because the system limited access to the database

and criminalized unauthorized disclosures. What protections, if any, are necessary to make the motor vehicle database contemplated by the REAL ID Act reasonable?

b.   Watch Lists and Other Identification-Related Databases

1. *Blacklists and Watch Lists.* Watch lists are automated databases used to identify individuals or entities for consequences (such as denial of entry or boarding) based solely on their inclusion ("listing") in the database. *See* Government Accounting Office, *Terrorist Watch Lists Should Be Consolidated to Promote Better Integration and Sharing* 3 (GAO-03-322), Apr. 15, 2003, *available at* http://www.gao.gov/new.items/d03322.pdf; Steinbock, *Designating the Dangerous, supra.* Their use did not start with the counterterrorist efforts of the 1990s and later. The infamous "blacklists" of the McCarthy Era — listing "known" Communists and their "fellow travelers" — are a disturbing antecedent. Professor Steinbock summarizes the blacklists and the loyalty screening programs with which they were associated, as follows:

> Little or no effort was made to identify particular workers whose presence would actually pose some realistic threat to national security. Because Communist Party membership or "sympathetic association" with "subversive organizations," even long in the past, were [*sic*] deemed to be adequate proxies for dangerousness, large numbers of people were labeled disloyal or security threats who factually were not. In practice these programs often amounted, instead, to widespread punishment for the exercise of rights of belief, speech, and association. More broadly, they were also about public shaming and enforcing ideological conformity. [*Id.*]

Some procedural protections were eventually required by the courts or by Congress to protect victims of blacklisting and loyalty screening programs. Remarkably, "even [these] are wholly absent from twenty-first century listing. The result [today], in all likelihood, is a glut of both false positives and false negatives." *Id.* See *infra* Note 3.

2. *Mission Creep?* Watch lists are already used to control visa eligibility, entry, and departure, to screen airline passengers, to screen employees for sensitive jobs, and to trigger surveillance. *See id.* "Mission creep" — using lists for more and more purposes, including ordinary criminal and regulatory purposes, such as denial of firearms purchases — is a continuing risk. The Japanese-American internment experience suggests a more frightening mission — preventive detention in a perceived emergency. Indeed, the Japanese Americans who were detained in World War II were selected from a "custodial detention list" prepared by the FBI. *Id.* The FBI also prepared lists for use under the Emergency Detention Act of 1950, Pub. L. No. 81-831, 64 Stat. 1019. See *infra* pp. 737-738. By 1966, the FBI's "Security Index" had grown to 26,000 names. Steinbock, *Designating the Dangerous, supra.* Does the reasonableness of a watch list turn in part on some statutory control of the purposes for which it may be used? *See Whalen v. Roe*, 429 U.S. 589 (1977), noted *supra* p. 676; Solove, *supra* p. 692, at 520-522.

3. *False Positives and Protected Interests.* When an innocent person is erroneously included on a watch list or has the same name as someone on the list, the listing generates a "false positive." With approximately 8 percent of all air travelers being stopped each day and an estimated 70 million secondary screening searches being

conducted annually, even a small rate of false positives will snare many innocent travelers. *See* Rosenzweig & Jonas, *supra* p. 691, at 2 n.3.

Does a person have a right to due process in the no-fly decision, or, more plausibly, in the making or correction of the no-fly list? To establish a claim to due process, a person must first show that the challenged government action deprives her of life or a constitutionally protected liberty or property interest. *See American Mfrs. Mut. Ins. Co. v. Sullivan*, 526 U.S. 40, 59 (1999). The Supreme Court has held that something more than a mere reputational injury or "stigma" from the government action is required to make out a liberty interest. It requires "stigma-plus," the plus being some tangible burden such as loss of employment or of the opportunity to purchase alcohol. *See Wisconsin v. Constantineau*, 400 U.S. 433 (1971); *Paul v. Davis*, 424 U.S. 693 (1976). Does a person who is singled out for further screening or barred from boarding by his identification on a no-fly list meet the requirement? The court in *Green v. Transportation Security Administration*, 351 F. Supp. 2d 1119 (W.D. Wash. 2005), held no.

> As Plaintiffs point out, there can be little doubt that association with a government terrorist watch-list "might seriously damage [Plaintiffs'] standing and associations in [their] community," *Vanelli* [*v. Reynolds Sch. Dist. No. 7*, 667 F.2d 773, 777 n.5 (9th Cir. 1982) (citation omitted)], and Defendants have not argued otherwise.
>
> However, Plaintiffs fail to satisfy the "plus" prong of the stigma-plus doctrine....
>
> Plaintiffs, in the present matter, argue that their status has been altered because they are no longer able to travel like other airline passengers because of their alleged association with the No-Fly List. While Plaintiffs have a right to travel throughout the United States "uninhibited by statutes, rules, and regulations which unreasonably burden or restrict movement," *Saenz v. Roe*, 526 U.S. 489, 499 (1999), it is also true that "burdens on a single mode of transportation do not implicate the right to interstate travel." *Miller v. Reed*, 176 F.3d 1202, 1205 [(9th Cir. 1999)]. Thus, Plaintiffs do not have a right to travel without any impediments whatsoever. Indeed, Plaintiffs do not allege that they have suffered impediments different than the general traveling public.
>
> Plaintiffs also argue that their status has been altered because they have been publicly associated with the No-Fly List in full view of co-workers and the general traveling public. However, "injury to reputation alone is insufficient to establish a deprivation of a liberty interest protected by the Constitution." *Ulrich* [*v. City & County of San Francisco*, 308 F.3d 968, 982 (9th Cir. 2002)]. Plaintiffs have not alleged any tangible harm to their personal or professional lives that is attributable to their association with the No-Fly List, and which would rise to the level of a Constitutional deprivation of a liberty right. Furthermore, Plaintiffs have not alleged any injury to a property interest as a result of the disclosure of allegedly stigmatizing statements. Plaintiffs have not plead[ed] any tangible harm that satisfies the "plus" prong. Therefore, Plaintiffs have failed to state a stigma-plus Fifth Amendment claim. [*Green*, 351 F. Supp. 2d at 1129-1130.]

Do you agree? If you are denied boarding on a transcontinental flight because of your misidentification on a no-fly list, have you suffered any tangible burden? Suppose you have to get to the other coast as quickly as possible to see a dying relative? Is the court confusing the right to travel with the burden constituting a "plus factor"? *See* Shane, *supra* p. 688 ("court's analysis seems flatly wrong"); Justin Florence, Note, *Making the No Fly List: A Due Process Model for Terrorist Watchlists*, 115 Yale L.J. 2148, 2161 (2006) (asserting that the right to travel by plane is a liberty interest).

4. *Process Due in Watch List Making or Correction.* If, notwithstanding the *Green* decision, you think a watch-listed traveler has a constitutionally protected liberty

interest, what process is due her? *See Matthews v. Eldridge*, 424 U.S. 319 (1976) (which is discussed so often in national security cases, see *infra* pp. 835-838, that we do not repeat it here.)

Critics of watch lists have suggested several procedural fixes for false positives and misidentification. A "front-end" fix is to institute more careful vetting procedures for placing a name on the list and tighter, more transparent standards. *See* Shane, *supra*, at 19-26. Professor Steinbock, however, raises the question whether the cost of such additional procedure and/or higher evidentiary standards for watch-listing may be too high for effective prevention of terrorist entry. Given the magnitude of the risk, shouldn't doubts be resolved in favor of inclusion? *See* Steinbock, *Designating the Dangerous*, *supra* p. 688.

Another fix is "back-end": providing some procedure for the victim of misidentification or other false positive to clear his name from the list. *See* Rosenzweig & Jonas, *supra* (suggesting administrative procedures for deciding passenger complaints, with a right of appeal to federal court, as well as "wrong matching" procedures for full attribution of list entries and for a wrongly matched person to supply additional information to correct an error); Shane, *supra*, at 31; Florence, *supra*, at 2166-2178 (suggesting that passengers be given "advance notice" of watch-listing on inquiry and a right to an administrative hearing about the alleged listing error through a government-appointed and security-cleared "compensatory counsel"). Professor Steinbock suggests a different and simpler kind of back-end protection: restricting the consequences of being listed just to selection for further investigation, thus "putting the *watch* back in watch lists." Steinbock, *Designating the Dangerous, supra*.

The Intelligence Reform and Terrorism Prevention Act of 2004, Pub. L. No. 108-458, §4012(a)(1), 118 Stat. 3638, 3714-3715 (codified at 49 U.S.C. §44903(j)(2)(C)(iii)(I) (2006)), required TSA and DHS to create appeals procedures for listed persons to challenge their listings. DHS therefore established a Traveler Redress Inquiry Program (TRIP) for taking complaints. Congress also conditioned implementation of "Secure Flight"—the program for collecting preflight information on passengers for watch-list screening—on development of procedures for protecting privacy and providing redress for victims of false positives. Department of Homeland Security Appropriations Act of 2006, Pub. L. No. 109-90, §518, 119 Stat. 2064, 2085. *See generally* Office of Inspector Gen., Dep't of Justice, *Review of the Terrorist Screening Center's Efforts to Support the Secure Flight Program* (Aug. 2005), *available at* http://www.usdoj.gov/oig/reports/FBI/a0534/index.htm.

C.   PROFILING

Farag v. United States

United States District Court, Eastern District of New York, 2008
587 F. Supp. 2d 436

BLOCK, Senior District Judge: . . . On August 22, 2004, weeks away from the third anniversary of 9/11, plaintiffs Tarik Farag ("Farag") and Amro Elmasry ("Elmasry"), both Arabs, flew from San Diego to New York's John F. Kennedy Airport ("JFK") on American Airlines Flight 236. [Farag and Elmasry, longtime friends, were flying to JFK after vacationing in California. Both were born in Egypt, but Farag, 36, had moved to the United States in 1971 at age five and later became an American citizen. He was a retired New York City police officer, and was then employed by the United States Bureau of Prisons as a corrections officer. Elmasry, 37, was an Egyptian citizen; he was employed in Egypt by General Electric as an area sales manager for its Africa-East Mediterranean region and had a valid U.S. visa.] They claim that when they deplaned they were met by at least ten armed police officers in SWAT gear with shotguns and police dogs, ordered to raise their hands, frisked, handcuffed and taken to a police station, where they were placed in jail cells; they were not released until about four hours later, after having been interrogated at length during their imprisonment regarding suspected terrorist surveillance activity aboard the plane. The investigation yielded absolutely no evidence of wrongdoing.

Alleging that they were unlawfully seized and imprisoned, Farag and Elmasry have each brought an action under *Bivens v. Six Unknown Named Agents of Federal Bureau of Narcotics*, 403 U.S. 388 (1971), against defendants FBI Special Agent William Ryan Plunkett ("Plunkett") and New York City Police Department Detective Thomas P. Smith ("Smith"), two counterterrorism agents responsible for plaintiffs' seizures, detentions and interrogations. . . . Plunkett and Smith seek summary judgment as to plaintiffs' *Bivens* claims on the ground of qualified immunity. . . .

THE GOVERNMENT'S JUSTIFICATION FOR ITS CONDUCT

The Government lists the following actions of Farag and Elmasry on the aircraft, which, they argue, supported the agents' "concern that [plaintiffs] may [have been] conducting [terrorist] surveillance or probing operations," Gov't Br. at 5,[20] and justified the agents' seizures, detentions, and interrogations of plaintiffs:

— At the beginning of the flight, despite sitting on opposite sides of the aisle, plaintiffs spoke to each other over the heads of other passengers in a mixture of Arabic and English;

— Elmasry made an allegedly "unusual" initial seat change "from a window seat . . . to a middle seat . . . between two other male passengers";

— After Elmasry changed seats, he and Farag talked to each other "loudly" over the heads of other passengers in a mixture of Arabic and English;

— Elmasry looked at his watch when the plane took off, when the plane landed, and at other points during the flight;

— After the meal service, Elmasry "got out of his seat . . . , went into the aisle, leaned over to Farag, and spoke a 'very short sentence' to Farag in a mixture of Arabic and English";

— Immediately thereafter, plaintiffs moved together to the back of the plane, and did not take their carry-on luggage with them;

— Plaintiffs got up to return to the front of the cabin at the very end of the flight, after the "fasten seatbelt" indicator was lit;

20. In particular, the Government argues that "there was probable cause to believe that Plaintiffs were violating the Destruction of Aircraft Act, 18 U.S.C. §32, and the federal conspiracy statute, 18 U.S.C. §371, both of which have been upheld by the Second Circuit as providing legitimate grounds for prosecuting potential terrorist plots against United States-flag aircraft." Gov't Br. at 25 (citing *United States v. Yousef,* 327 F.3d 56, 86-88 (2d Cir. 2003)).

— Upon returning to the front of the plane, Farag did not sit in his original seat (17E), but rather, in Elmasry's original seat (18A), which was located directly behind Smith;

— After the plane landed, Elmasry took out his cellular phone and deleted five or six numbers;

— While the plane was taxiing to the gate, Elmasry told Smith that "he is from Egypt, that he works for GE, and that '[his] work is always traveling.'"

See Gov't Br. at 14-16.

The Government lists the following events that took place in the terminal at JFK, after plaintiffs were first detained, as further support for the agents' actions:

— Farag told Smith that "after 9/11, when the CIA had c[o]me into the Federal Bureau of Prisons, my supervisors had asked me to translate documents, to translate tapes, [and] in fact I did translate tapes";

— Farag told Smith that "I had guns pointed at me as a police officer";

— While Farag was telling these things to Smith, Farag was "jittery" and "shaking" and "[his] speech was not calm." He appeared "nervous" and seemed "jumpy and agitated," and he raised his voice.

See Gov't Br. at 25-26....

II. ANALYSIS

A. Were Plaintiffs Arrested?

[The court held that the plaintiffs were arrested.] ...

B. Was There Probable Cause for the Arrests?

Probable cause to arrest exists "where the arresting officer has 'knowledge or reasonably trustworthy information of facts and circumstances that are sufficient to warrant a person of reasonable caution in the belief that the person to be arrested has committed or is committing a crime.'" [*United States v. Delossantos*, 536 F.3d 155, 158 (2d Cir. 2008) (quoting *Walczyk v. Rio*, 496 F.3d 139, 156 (2d Cir. 2007))]. Only "those facts available to the officer at the time of the arrest and immediately before it" may be considered. *Lowth v. Town of Cheektowaga*, 82 F.3d 563, 569 (2d Cir. 1996) (citation omitted). Moreover, "[p]robable cause is to be assessed on an objective basis[,]" *Zellner v. Summerlin*, 494 F.3d 344, 369 (2d Cir. 2007); thus, "[a]n arresting officer's state of mind (*except for the facts that he knows*) is irrelevant...." *Id*. The standard is a "fluid and contextual" one, requiring "examin[ation of] the totality of the circumstances of a given arrest." *Delossantos*, 536 F.3d at 159 (citations omitted)....

1. Was There Probable Cause Based on Non-Ethnic Factors Alone?

The Government contends that even if the Court does not consider that plaintiffs were Arabs and that they were at times conversing in Arabic, the other factors relied upon by the Government constitute probable cause. The Court disagrees. The Government tacks together a number of benign circumstances in the apparent belief that their numerosity will carry the day. The Court acknowledges that the Second Circuit has cautioned district courts not to "engage[ ] in erroneous 'divide-and-conquer analysis'" by "declining to give weight to [individual] observation[s] 'that [were] by [themselves] readily susceptible to . . . innocent explanation[s.]'" *Id.* at 161 (quoting *United States v. Arvizu*, 534 U.S. 266, 274 (2002)); *accord* [*United States v. Sokolow*, 490 U.S. 1, 9 (1989)] ("Any one of these factors is . . . quite consistent with innocent travel. But we think taken together they amount to reasonable suspicion."). Yet, even viewing all of these circumstances as a whole, it cannot rationally be held that if, hypothetically, the plaintiffs were two Caucasian traveling companions speaking French, or another non-Arabic language which the agents did not understand, "a person of reasonable caution" would have believed that they were engaged in terrorist surveillance. *Delossantos*, 536 F.3d at 158.

Principally, the Government relies on the agents' observations of plaintiffs' seat-changing and Elmasry's "timing" events with his watch. But the agents acknowledged in their incident report that they knew the plaintiffs were friends; quite logically, friends would want to sit as close to each other as possible, and they would also logically return to the vicinity of their original seats when the plane was landing to retrieve their carry-on luggage. As for Elmasry looking at his watch upon takeoff, landing, and at various other times during the flight, the proportion of airline passengers who do this is probably higher than the proportion who do not. *See United States v. Jones*, 149 F.3d 364, 369 (5th Cir. 1998) ("A factual condition which is consistent with [criminal activity] will not predicate reasonable suspicion, if that factual condition occurs even more frequently among the law abiding public. . . . ").

The Government also argues that Elmasry's deletion of five or six telephone numbers from his cellular phone while he waited for the plane to reach the gate "could have been interpreted as destroying evidence[,]" Gov't Br. at 16. This conclusion, however, is utter speculation; the Government's Rule 56.1 Statement does not assert that Elmasry made any telephone calls during or after the flight, and the record gives no indication that Elmasry suspected he was about to be caught sufficient to imbue his acts with a suggestion of guilt.

Most troubling, the heavy reliance which the Government places on the plaintiffs' speaking "loudly" to each other over the heads of other passengers and otherwise drawing attention to themselves is counterintuitive: it simply makes no sense that if Elmasry were a terrorist on a surveillance mission, he would speak "loudly" across the aisle to his companion before takeoff, seek out and converse with the flight attendant, relocate to a seat "between two large men," or volunteer to one of those "large men" that he was from Egypt. What terrorist engaged in surveillance activity would behave so conspicuously? One would expect that such activity would be characterized by secrecy.

Nor could plaintiffs' conduct in the terminal be reasonably viewed as an escalation of events that would then have given rise to probable cause. The Court fails to grasp the significance of Farag telling Smith that because he spoke Arabic he had been asked by the Bureau of Prisons to translate tapes, and that guns had been pointed at him as a police officer — both logical consequences of his past and present employments.

Reliance on Farag's nervousness and raised voice is also problematic. *See, e.g., United States v. Ten Thousand Seven Hundred Dollars and No Cents in U.S. Currency*, 258 F.3d 215, 226-27 (3d Cir. 2001) ("[C]laimants' apparent nervousness is of minimal probative value, given that many, if not most, individuals can become nervous or agitated when detained by police officers." (citation omitted)). Moreover, Farag's "nervous" response to an unlawful show of force could not retroactively justify plaintiffs' arrests.

In sum, viewed in the light most favorable to plaintiffs, the non-ethnic factors cited by the Government do not constitute probable cause.

2. Would Consideration of Plaintiffs' Ethnicity Warrant a Finding of Probable Cause?

Allowing consideration of the plaintiffs' ethnicity and their use of Arabic would still not warrant a finding, in the context of the defendants' summary-judgment motion, that there was probable cause to arrest them. In other words, if the plaintiffs' view of events holds up at trial, their conduct was so benign that the ethnicity factor — even if it could be considered — would not change the outcome.

Nonetheless, the Court will address the ethnicity issue since the Government, given the importance it ascribes to the issue, would otherwise undoubtedly raise it at trial; moreover, the issue would probably surface if Smith and Plunkett were to take an interlocutory appeal from the Court's denial of that aspect of their motion seeking qualified immunity.

3. Can Plaintiffs' Arab Ethnicity Serve as a Probable Cause Factor?

The Government argues that plaintiffs' Arab ethnicity and use of the Arabic language are relevant factors in the probable-cause, as well as the reasonable-suspicion, calculus because "all of the persons who participated in the 9/11 terrorist attacks were Middle Eastern males[,]" Tr. of Oral Argument, July 18, 2008, at 18, and "the United States continues to face a very real threat of domestic terrorism from Islamic terrorists." Gov't Br. at 17.

The Government's position has some superficial appeal. After all, probable cause, and undoubtedly reasonable suspicion as well, is, once again, "a practical, nontechnical conception that deals with the factual and practical considerations of everyday life," *Delossantos*, 536 F.3d at 159 (internal quotation marks and citation omitted), and what American would not acknowledge that everyday life has changed in myriad ways, both great and small, since 9/11? Indeed, earlier this fall, the Second Circuit upheld a government program "that singled out male immigrants from two dozen predominantly Arab and Muslim countries for accelerated deportation after the Sept. 11, 2001, terrorist attacks[,]" Mark Hamblett, *Circuit Upholds Post-9/11 Effort That Singled Out Muslim Men*, N.Y.L.J., Sept. 25, 2008 at 1, finding it a "plainly rational attempt to enhance national security." *Rajah v. Mukasey*, 544 F.3d 427, [439 (2d Cir. 2008)].

Rajah, however, did not deal with ethnicity in the context of probable cause or reasonable suspicion. Indeed, the Government recognizes that "[t]here is no single precedent that resolves this case," Tr. of Oral Argument, July 18, 2008, at 17, which presumably accounts for its view of the case as one of first impression. Nevertheless, the interplay between race[33] and the Fourth Amendment is not a recent

---

33. For present purposes, the Court treats the "technically" distinct concepts of race and ethnicity as legal equivalents. *Iqbal v. Hasty*, 490 F.3d 143, 148 n.2 (2d Cir. 2007), *cert. granted sub nom. Ashcroft v. Iqbal*, — U.S. ——, 128 S. Ct. 2931 (2008). Moreover, the Court considers the fact that the plaintiffs spoke their native tongue, Arabic — as opposed to some other language equally unfamiliar to the agents — as inextricably related to, and legally indistinguishable from, plaintiffs' ethnicity per se.

phenomenon; courts and commentators have long struggled with the issue of whether and to what extent race can be a relevant consideration in the decision to detain an individual. *See, e.g.,* Samuel R. Gross & Katherine Y. Barnes, *Road Work: Racial Profiling and Drug Interdiction on the Highway,* 101 Mich. L. Rev. 651 (2002); Anthony C. Thompson, *Stopping the Usual Suspects: Race and the Fourth Amendment,* 74 N.Y.U. L. Rev. 956 (1999); Tracey Maclin, *Race and the Fourth Amendment,* 51 Vanderbilt L. Rev. 333 (1998); Sheri Lynn Johnson, *Race and the Decision to Detain a Suspect,* 93 Yale L.J. 214, 237 (1983). That legal backdrop obviously bears on the Court's analysis here.

At the outset, it should be understood that the Fourth Amendment — unlike the Equal Protection Clause — imposes no *a priori* restriction on race-based governmental action. As the Supreme Court noted in *Whren v. United States,* 517 U.S. 806 (1996):

> [T]he Constitution prohibits selective enforcement of the law based on considerations such as race. But the constitutional basis for objecting to intentionally discriminatory application of laws is the Equal Protection Clause, not the Fourth Amendment. Subjective intentions play no role in ordinary, probable-cause Fourth Amendment analysis.

Id. at 813; *see also United States v. Scopo,* 19 F.3d 777, 786 (2d Cir. 1994) (Newman, J., concurring) ("Though the Fourth Amendment permits a pretext arrest, if otherwise supported by probable cause, the Equal Protection Clause still imposes restraint on impermissibly class-based discriminations.").

In *Whren,* the existence of probable cause based on non-racial factors was conceded. *See* 517 U.S. at 810 ("Petitioners accept that Officer Soto had probable cause to believe that various provisions of the District of Columbia traffic code had been violated."). Thus, the Court opined only that an officer's subjective, potentially race-based motivations were irrelevant to the Fourth Amendment *once probable cause is established*; it was not called upon to address whether race might be relevant to the probable-cause analysis itself.

Although the Fourth Amendment does not single out race as a matter of special concern, it does impose a general requirement that *any* factor considered in a decision to detain must contribute to "a particularized and objective basis for suspecting the particular person stopped of criminal activity." *United States v. Cortez,* 449 U.S. 411, 417-18 (1981). Thus, as one commentator has observed, "race cannot affect probable cause or reasonable suspicion calculations unless it is statistically related to suspected criminal activity." Johnson, 93 Yale L.J. at 237. Whether such a relationship exists in a given case is necessarily a fact-specific inquiry; nevertheless, the case law reveals some recurring themes.

Perhaps the least controversial use of race in the context of the Fourth Amendment is its use as an *identifying* factor. If the victim of, or witness to, a crime describes the perpetrator as a young white male wearing a white shirt and black pants, there can be little doubt that law enforcement officials may consider that description in deciding whom to detain, even though the description is based, in part, on race.

Courts have also confronted the so-called "racial incongruity" argument — i.e., that race is indicative of criminality when members of a particular race seem "out of place" in a particular location. Some courts — including the Second Circuit — have sidestepped the issue by finding probable cause or reasonable suspicion based on other, non-racial factors. For example, in *United States v. Magda,* 409 F. Supp. 734 (S.D.N.Y. 1976), the district court found reasonable suspicion lacking where "[t]he reason for the stop was primarily because of an observed exchange...between a young black man and a young white man in an area of the city defined as 'narcotics prone.'" *Id.* at 740. The Second Circuit reversed, concluding that the circumstances and location of the transaction were sufficient to create reasonable suspicion; the circuit court made no mention of the race of the participants. *See United States v. Magda*, 547 F.2d 756, 758-59 (2d Cir. 1976); *see also United States v. Richard*, 535 F.2d 246, 248-249 (3d Cir. 1976) (noting that "the presence of two black males cruising in a car in a predominately white neighborhood is, by itself, insufficient cause for a belief that those persons have participated in a recent crime in the neighborhood," but reversing suppression order based on other factors); *State v. Wilson*, 775 So. 2d 1051, 1052 (La. 2000) ("[T]he officer made clear...that while racial incongruity 'did factor in,' he considered other circumstances more important in his decision to make an investigatory stop.").

Those courts that have squarely addressed the incongruity argument have uniformly rejected it. *See People v. Bower*, 24 Cal. 3d 638 (1979) ("[T]he presence of an individual of one race in an area inhabited primarily by members of another race is not a sufficient basis to suggest that crime is afoot."); *State v. Barber*, 118 Wash. 2d 335 (1992) ("It is the law that racial incongruity, i.e., a person of any race being allegedly 'out of place' in a particular geographic area, should never constitute a finding of reasonable suspicion of criminal activity"); *Phillips v. State*, 781 So. 2d 477, 479 (Fla. Dist. Ct. App. 2001) ("Clearly, the fact that a black person is merely walking in a predominantly white neighborhood does not indicate that he has committed, is committing, or is about to commit a crime.")....

But this case involves neither identification nor racial incongruity. Rather, defendants' argument that plaintiffs' Arab ethnicity is a relevant consideration is premised on the notion that Arabs have a greater *propensity* than non-Arabs toward criminal activity—namely, terrorism.

In support of this argument, defendants rely principally on language from the Supreme Court's opinion in *United States v. Brignoni-Ponce*, 422 U.S. 873 (1975). There, a roving border patrol agent had made a traffic stop based on nothing more than "the apparent Mexican ancestry" of the car's occupants. *Id.* at 885. The Supreme Court held that "this factor alone would [not] justify...a reasonable [suspicion]" of an immigration violation. *Id.* at 886. But it stated—in dictum—that "[t]he likelihood that any given person of Mexican ancestry is an alien is high enough to make Mexican appearance *a relevant factor*" in the Fourth Amendment calculus, if it were not *the only* basis for suspicion. *Id.* at 886-87 (emphasis added).[34]

Brignoni-Ponce's dictum was predicated on 1970 census figures establishing that in the border states between 8.5% and 20.4% of the ethnic-Mexican population self-registered as aliens. *Id.* at 886-87 & n.12. To the Court's knowledge, no court has ever marshaled statistics to conclude that racial or ethnic appearance is correlated with, and thus probative of, any type of criminal conduct *other than* immigration violations.

---

34. A year after *Brignoni-Ponce*, the Supreme Court held that officials at a border-control checkpoint could constitutionally single out motorists for inspection "even if it be assumed that such referrals are made largely on the basis of apparent Mexican ancestry." *United States v. Martinez-Fuerte*, 428 U.S. 543, 563 (1976). The Court recognized that such a criterion "would not sustain a roving-patrol stop," *id.*, but concluded that border-control checkpoints were exempt from the usual Fourth Amendment requirement of individualized suspicion. *See id.* at 562 ("[W]e hold that the stops and questioning at issue may be made in the absence of any individualized suspicion at reasonably located checkpoints."). Since there is obviously no contention that a traditional arrest or *Terry* stop is similarly exempt from that requirement, *Martinez-Fuerte* cannot support plaintiffs' detention.

See, e.g., United States v. Avery, 137 F.3d 343, 354 (6th Cir. 1997) ("[A]lthough the Court in *Brignoni-Ponce* stated 'the likelihood that any given person of Mexican ancestry is an alien is high enough to make Mexican appearance a relevant factor,' we refuse to adopt, by analogy, the concept that 'the likelihood that any given person of African ancestry is involved in drug trafficking is high enough to make African ancestry a relevant fact' in investigating drug trafficking . . . ." (citation omitted)).

Moreover, the statistical rationale behind the *Brignoni-Ponce* dictum does not translate to the present case: Even granting that all of the participants in the 9/11 attacks were Arabs, and even assuming *arguendo* that a large proportion of would-be anti-American terrorists are Arabs, the likelihood that *any given airline passenger* of Arab ethnicity is a terrorist is so negligible that Arab ethnicity has no probative value in a particularized reasonable-suspicion or probable-cause determination. *Accord United States v. Ramos*, [591 F. Supp. 2d 93, 104 (D. Mass. 2008)] (considering, in dicta, the applicability of *Brignoni-Ponce* to Arabs suspected of terrorist activity post-9/11, and noting that "[a]mong other things, the type of statistics relied upon in *Brignoni-Ponce* . . . have not been presented here.") [, *aff'd*, 629 F.3d 60 (1st Cir. 2010)].

Indeed, the Ninth Circuit, whose judgment the Supreme Court upheld in *Brignoni-Ponce*, revisited *Brignoni-Ponce*'s dictum 25 years later and held, albeit also in dicta, that the statistical inference on which it was based was no longer valid, even in its original illegal-immigration context:

> *Brignoni-Ponce* was handed down in 1975, some twenty-five years ago. Current demographic data demonstrate that the statistical premises on which its dictum relies are no longer applicable. The Hispanic population of this nation, and of the Southwest and Far West in particular, has grown enormously. . . . Accordingly, Hispanic appearance is of little or no use in determining which particular individuals among the vast Hispanic populace should be stopped by law enforcement officials on the lookout for illegal aliens. Reasonable suspicion requires *particularized* suspicion, and in an area in which a large number of people share a specific characteristic, that characteristic casts too wide a net to play any part in a particularized reasonable suspicion determination.

[*United States v. Montero-Camargo*, 208 F.3d 1122 (9th Cir. 2000),] at 1133-34 (emphasis in original). Notably, the Supreme Court has never revisited its dictum in *Brignoni-Ponce*, nor has it ever addressed whether, *absent* compelling statistical evidence, race or ethnicity may be used as a factor in the Fourth Amendment calculus to indicate criminal propensity. Accordingly, the Court finds that *Brignoni-Ponce* offers no support for the Government's position. . . .

There is no doubt that the specter of 9/11 looms large over this case. Although this is the first post-9/11 case to address whether race may be used to establish criminal propensity under the Fourth Amendment, the Court cannot subscribe to the notion that in the wake of 9/11 this may now be permissible. As the Second Circuit recently admonished, "the strength of our system of constitutional rights derives from the steadfast protection of those rights in both normal and unusual times." *Iqbal v. Hasty*, 490 F.3d 143, 159 (2d Cir. 2007) [, *rev'd on other grounds and remanded sub nom. Ashcroft v. Iqbal*, 129 S. Ct. 1937, 1954 (2009), *cert. granted and remanded*, 129 S. Ct. 2430 (2009), *cert. granted and remanded sub nom. Sawyer v. Iqbal*, 129 S. Ct. 2431 (2009)].

History teaches much the same lesson: The Supreme Court's approval of the internment of large numbers of Japanese-Americans during World War II, *see Korematsu v. United States*, 323 U.S. 214 (1945), is now widely regarded as a black

mark on our constitutional jurisprudence. The daughter of two such internees —
Kiyo Matsumoto — recently became the third Asian-American woman to be elevated
to the federal bench. At her induction ceremony, Judge Matsumoto recalled the
closing words of Justice Murphy's dissent in *Korematsu*; they are equally apt here:

> All residents of this nation are kin in some way by blood or culture to a foreign land. Yet
> they are primarily and necessarily a part of the new and distinct civilization of the United
> States. They must accordingly be treated at all times as the heirs of the American experi-
> ment and as entitled to all the rights and freedoms guaranteed by the Constitution.

323 U.S. at 206.

The Court "fully recognize[s] the gravity of the situation that confront[s] investigative officials of the United States as a consequence of the 9/11 attack[,]" *Iqbal*, 490
F.3d at 159 (2d Cir. 2007), and that the mindset of airline travelers has understandably been altered by 9/11. This justifiable apprehension must be assuaged by ensuring that security is strictly enforced, and by the passage of time without, hopefully,
other episodic affronts to our country; but fear cannot be a factor to allow for the
evisceration of the bedrock principle of our Constitution that no one can be arrested
without probable cause that a crime has been committed. . . .

CONCLUSION

For the reasons described above, the Court grants summary judgment in the Government's favor with respect to plaintiffs' conspiracy claims, plaintiffs' common-law
claims against Smith, and plaintiffs' §1981 claims. The Court denies summary judgment
with respect to plaintiffs' *Bivens* claims against Smith and Plunkett, plaintiffs' FTCA claims
against the United States, and Smith and Plunkett's qualified-immunity defense.

So ordered.

NOTES AND QUESTIONS

a.   Legal Analysis of Profiling

1. *The Easy Case: Individualized Description.* The Department of Justice has issued
guidance for federal law enforcement agencies on the use of race or ethnicity in conducting investigations. Civil Rights Div., U.S. Dep't of Justice, *Guidance Regarding the Use
of Race by Federal Law Enforcement Agencies* (June 2003) (*"DOJ Guidance"*). It asserts:

> In conducting activities in connection with a specific investigation, Federal law enforce-
> ment officers may consider race and ethnicity only to the extent that there is trustworthy
> information, relevant to the locality or time frame, that links persons of a particular race
> or ethnicity to an identified criminal incident, scheme, or organization. This standard
> applies even where the use of race or ethnicity might otherwise be lawful . . . .

This guidance reflects the generally accepted principle that law enforcement agents
may use race or an ethnic characteristic when it is part of the description of a particular suspect. *See* Sharon L. Davies, *Profiling Terror*, 1 Ohio St. J. Crim. L. 45, 54 & n.38

(2003) (citing decisions). "To act on the basis of a particular suspect's description as belonging to a given race is certainly to take race into account," Professor Ellmann explains, "but it is not to take *generalizations* about race into account." Stephen J. Ellmann, *Racial Profiling and Terrorism*, 46 N.Y.U. L. Rev. 675, 676 n.4 (2003). But the *DOJ Guidance*'s approval of profiling in some counterterrorism investigations may suggest how easily "the identification of a group of offenders by race tends to transform the physical description into a negative predictor and then into a mark of social status." Albert W. Alshuler, *Racial Profiling and the Constitution*, 2002 U. Chi. Legal F. 163, 265-266. Is being on the lookout for "Middle Eastern men" in their early 20s merely taking into account the fact that the original Al Qaeda membership seemed overwhelmingly to have included such men, or does it assume that they are more likely to commit future terrorist acts than Swedish grandmothers? Does the "lookout" profile stigmatize all young Middle Eastern men?

2. *Fourth Amendment Analysis: Mere "Relevance"?* The Fourth Amendment "special needs" (administrative search) analysis of racial profiling in security screening asks whether the race or ethnic factor in the profile is "clearly . . . relevant to the law enforcement need to be served." *United States v. Martinez-Fuerte*, 428 U.S. 543, 564 n.17 (1976). That it may constitute purposeful discrimination does not make the search or seizure unreasonable under the Fourth Amendment. *Whren v. United States*, 517 U.S. 806, 813 (1996). Thus, the Supreme Court has upheld secondary screening of persons at a border checkpoint made largely on the basis of apparent Mexican ancestry. *United States v. Martinez-Fuerte*, 428 U.S. 543, 563 (1976), relying in part on its earlier decision in *United States v. Brignoni-Ponce*, 422 U.S. 873 (1975), discussed in *Farag*.

The *DOJ Guidance* excerpted above permits the consideration of ethnicity in some law enforcement encounters. Did it permit such consideration in the encounter described in *Farag*? Was what the court called the "Arab ethnicity" of Farag and Elmasry relevant to a law enforcement need?

3. *Equal Protection Analysis: Stricter Scrutiny and Necessity?* Even if the arrest of Farag and Elmasry had survived a Fourth Amendment challenge, it would have raised questions under the Equal Protection Clause. At least as early as 1944, the Supreme Court declared that "all legal restrictions which curtail the rights of a single racial group are immediately suspect" and therefore subject to the "most rigid scrutiny." *Korematsu v. United States*, 323 U.S. 214, 216 (1944), *infra* p. 812. The scrutiny actually applied by the Court, however, did not overturn the government's program to intern 120,000 Japanese-Americans following the attack on Pearl Harbor. Although the Court acknowledged that "[n]othing short of apprehension by the proper military authorities of the gravest imminent danger to the public safety can constitutionally justify" such race-based discrimination, the Court deferred to the judgment of military authorities and found that exclusion of Japanese-Americans from certain areas "has a definite and close relationship to the prevention of crime and sabotage." 323 U.S. at 218.

Since *Korematsu*, the Court has refined equal protection analysis. When government action is challenged on equal protection grounds, "the issue is whether the government can identify a sufficiently important objective for its discrimination. What is a sufficient justification depends entirely on the type of discrimination." Erwin Chemerinsky, *Constitutional Law* 669-670 (3d ed. 2006). When the government discriminates on the basis of race, national origin, or, for some actions, alienage, its justification will be subject to "strict scrutiny" and upheld only "if it is proven necessary to achieve a compelling government purpose." *Id.* at 529 (footnote omitted). Other classifications may require only "rational basis" review, under which the law need only be rationally related to a legitimate government purpose, or "intermediate scrutiny." *Id.*

Can you formulate an argument for the legality of ethnic profiling of Farag and Elmasry under modern equal protection analysis?

4. *Ethnic Profiling at the Airport.* The *DOJ Guidance* also provides this example of appropriate increased scrutiny of certain ethnic groups to protect the nation's borders:

> Example: U.S. intelligence sources report that terrorists from a particular ethnic group are planning to use commercial jetliners as weapons by hijacking them at an airport in California during the next week. Before allowing men of that ethnic group to board commercial airplanes in California airports during the next week, Transportation Security Administration personnel, and other federal and state authorities, may subject them to heightened scrutiny.... [*DOJ Guidance, supra*, at 703.]

Would this guideline have justified the selection of Mohamed Atta or his colleagues for further screening at Logan Airport on September 11? What about the selection of persons like them for scrutiny *after* 9/11?

Could you justify their selection if it had been based only on the gate agent's suspicion of their "Middle Eastern" appearance? See *supra* p. 704. Consider the *DOJ Guidance*'s conclusion that "reliance solely upon generalized stereotypes is forbidden," for which it offers the following example:

> Example: At the security entrance to a Federal courthouse, a man who appears to be of a particular ethnicity properly submits his briefcase for x-ray screening and passes through the metal detector. The inspection of the briefcase reveals nothing amiss, the man does not activate the metal detector, and there is nothing suspicious about his activities or appearance. In the absence of any threat warning, the federal security screener may not order the man to undergo a further inspection solely because he appears to be of a particular ethnicity.

Reasonable suspicion is not required for border searches, as *Arnold* indicated. Indeed, a border officer need not give a reason for a search. What then is to prevent otherwise "forbidden" profiling by airport and border personnel? One study concludes that "the absence of any requisite level of suspicion to conduct border searches opens the door to racial or religious profiling." Constitution Project, *supra* p. 686, at 6. *See also* Yule Kim, *Border Searches of Laptops and Other Electronic Storage Devices* (Cong. Res. Serv. RL 34404), Nov. 16, 2009.

Might the screening be based on a *combination* of racial or ethnic characteristics *and* behavioral factors? Would it then satisfy the equal protection analysis and meet the standard set out in the *DOJ Guidance? See* Davies, *supra*, at 60-61 (noting that courts have required profiles to be based on more than racial or ethnic elements alone to withstand equal protection challenge).

b.   Practical Problems and Assessment of Profiling

1. *Problems of Applying Racial and Ethnic Classifications in Screening.* The *DOJ Guidance* is (deliberately?) vague about classification for profiling in counterterrorism

cases: it refers just to "ethnic groups." But "defenses of racial and ethnic profiling depend upon the ability of law enforcement officers to do it — to distinguish racial and ethnic groups from one another." Alschuler, *supra*, at 224. Does the legality not therefore depend partly on how the "ethnic group" is described and how much discretion that leaves checkpoint screeners or law enforcement officers?

One journalist characterized the New York subway system's random container inspection in *MacWade v. Kelly*, *supra* p. 686, as an "obvious absurdity" and an "appalling waste of effort." Charles Krauthammer, *Give Grandma a Pass: Politically Correct Screening Won't Catch Jihadists*, Wash. Post, July 29, 2005. Since "jihadist terrorism has been carried out . . . by young Muslim men," he reasoned, we should give "special scrutiny to young Islamic men." *Id. See also* Milton Hirsch & David O. Markus, *Fourth Amendment Forum*, 27 Champion 34 (Mar. 2003) ("since 9/11 attacks were perpetrated by "Arab Muslim men," there "exists a demonstrable, verifiable nexus between" such characteristics when used to select travelers for high-level screening "and conduct that American officials have a public duty to interdict").

Could you explain to subway security officers how to identify "Islamic men"? What about persons "of Middle Eastern appearance"? *See* John Derbyshire, *At First Glance: Racial Profiling, Burning Hotter*, Nat'l Rev. Online (Oct. 5, 2001), *at* http://www.nationalreview.com/derbyshire/derbyshire100501.shtml. What about "Arab-looking"? *See* Stuart Taylor Jr., *D.C. Dispatch: Politically Incorrect Profiling: A Matter of Life or Death*, Nat'l J., Nov. 6, 2001; Davies, *supra*, at 51 n.29 ("It is a common misconception that all Arabs are racially identifiable by their darker skin. In fact, Arabs may have white skin and blue eyes, olive or dark skin and brown eyes, and hair in a variety of textures.").

One danger of vague classifications is that they leave the screeners too much discretion, creating space for conscious or unconscious application of the screeners' own prejudices. The same may be true even of profiling that includes behavioral factors, such as unusual passenger nervousness or sweating or failure to make eye contact, in a profile together with racial or ethnic factors. After 9/11, for example, the American Civil Liberties Union reported that 67 percent of airline passengers subjected to personal searches upon entering the United States were people of color; black and Latino Americans were four to nine times as likely as white Americans to be x-rayed after being frisked or patted down; and black women were more likely than any other U.S. citizens to be strip-searched. *See* R. Spencer McDonald, Note, *Rational Profiling in America's Airports*, 17 BYU J. Pub. L. 113, 136 (2002) (citing American Civil Liberties Union press release (Mar. 26, 2002)).

In light of these considerations, were the "non-ethnic" factors that caused agents to "arrest" Farag and Elmasry objective or subjective — reasonable intuitions or masked discrimination? Consider this view:

> To insist that an experienced bomb-dog handler or baggage screener ignore any hunches while mindlessly sticking to random passenger screening is, at best, a waste of limited resources. Sky marshals, Transportation Security Administration screeners, and others on the front lines of counterterrorism should be afforded sufficient discretion to draw upon their common sense and experience regarding people who exhibit nonbehavioral risk factors. [John Winn, *The Legitimacy of Profiling*, Wash. Times, Dec. 30, 2009.]

Should the court in *Farag* have paid more deference to the "common sense and experience" of security professionals?

2. *Empirical Nexus?* In *United States v. Lopez*, 328 F. Supp. 1077 (E.D.N.Y. 1971), the court initially upheld the use of a passenger profile in the pre-1973 selective anti-skyjacking screening program and follow-up frisk. But when discovery revealed that the airline had unilaterally eliminated one element of the FAA-established profile and added "an ethnic element for which there was no experimental basis, thus raising serious equal protection problems," the court suppressed the evidence from the frisk. *Id.* at 1101. "The approved [FAA] system survives constitutional scrutiny only by its careful adherence to absolute objectivity and neutrality," the court explained. "When elements of discretion and prejudice are interjected it becomes constitutionally impermissible." *Id.*

Does this mean that any ethnic, religious, or national origin element of a screening profile must have at least "an experimental basis" to find a nexus between the element and the probability of a terrorist act? If so, does "Islamic men" or "Middle Eastern appearance" have such a nexus to terrorism, in light of the fact that all of the 9/11 hijackers were apparently Muslims from the Middle East? *Compare* Thomas W. Joo, *Presumed Disloyal: Executive Power, Judicial Deference, and the Construction of Race Before and After September 11*, 34 Colum. Hum. Rts. L. Rev. 1, 41-42 (2002) (the "categories of 'Arab' and 'Muslim' are simply too broad"; "even if a man of Arab descent is relatively more likely to be a terrorist than a non-Arab, the likelihood that any given Arab man is a terrorist remains negligible"), *with* Ellmann, *supra* p. 704, at 698 ("People sharing all of Al Qaeda's background characteristics still seem more likely to be our adversaries than most of the people who share none of them — even though the great majority of people sharing all of these characteristics have no connection to terrorism whatsoever.").

Professor Alshuler suggests that "when a police practice systematically subjects the members of a race to searches and seizures at a higher rate than their rate of offending, a court should hold the practice unconstitutional unless it is appropriately tailored to advance a significant state interest." Alshuler, *supra* p. 704, at 223. Would profiling of "Middle Eastern men" satisfy this test? *See id.* at 265 ("special screening of people of Arab ethnicity at airports . . . should be impermissible"). How would we measure their "rate of offending"?

Professor Harcourt suggests that the success and justification of profiling depend on more than "identifying a stable group trait that correlates with higher offending." It also depends on "how responsive different groups are to the targeted policing and whether they engage in forms of substitution" by recruiting from nonprofiled groups or substituting different types of attacks that are more immune to profiling. *See* Bernard E. Harcourt, *Muslim Profiles Post 9/11: Is Racial Profiling an Effective Counterterrorist Measure and Does It Violate the Right to Be Free from Discrimination?* (Univ. of Chi. Law Sch., John M. Olin Law & Econ. Working Paper No. 288 (2d Series), at 9-10, Mar. 2006), *available at* http://ssrn.com/abstract=893905.

> The central question [is] whether racial profiling of young Muslim men in the New York subways will likely detect a terrorist attack or instead lead to the recruitment of non-profiled persons and the substitution of other acts for subway attacks — in other words, whether profiling will detect or increase terrorist attacks. The answer to this question is pure speculation. In the end, then, there is no need or reason to engage in a rights trade-off by racial profiling as part of any subway screening. [*Id.* at 27-28.]

That is, without empirical evidence that racial profiling works, there is no need for it. Do you agree?

3. *Costs and Benefits of Profiling.* Proponents of counterterrorism profiling have argued that the cost to a victim of frequent false positives "is minuscule," while the cost to society of a false negative (letting a terrorist through) could be enormous. They conclude that racial profiling is justified by a cost-benefit analysis. *See* LaFave, *supra* p. 680 (summarizing arguments of some proponents); Ellman, *supra*, at 698-707. Does this analysis consider all the costs? What about the risk that Al Qaeda will respond to the profile by selecting terrorists who do not look "Islamic" or "Middle Eastern" (if you can figure out what this means), including Americans like Jose Padilla (see *infra* p. 855), thus increasing the rate of false negatives? What about the cost of creating hostility and anxiety in the U.S. community of persons from the Middle East, and discouraging its members from voluntary cooperation? *See generally* Ellman, *supra*, at 705-707; Davies, *supra* p. 703, at 73-74. How would you inventory and balance all the benefits and costs of racial profiling in security screening and counterterrorism investigations?

c. National Origin and Religious Profiling

1. *National Origin Profiling of Post-9/11 Detainees and Interviewees.* Following the September 11 attacks, law enforcement and immigration authorities detained more than 1,100 persons as part of their investigation. See generally Chapter 26. On November 27, 2001, the Bush administration provided a breakdown of some 600 persons still being held. According to the report, 548 detained on immigration charges hailed from 47 countries, including more than 200 from Pakistan, and smaller numbers from Egypt, Turkey, Yemen, and India. Dan Eggen, *About 600 Still Held in Connection with Attacks, Ashcroft Says*, Wash. Post, Nov. 28, 2001. An earlier newspaper investigation of 235 detainees found that the largest numbers were from Saudi Arabia, Egypt, and Pakistan, and that almost all of them were men in their 20s and 30s. Amy Goldstein, *A Deliberate Strategy of Disruption*, Wash. Post, Nov. 4, 2001. When these figures were reported, none of the detainees had been charged with any terrorist activity. Subsequently, the Administration conducted "voluntary" interviews targeting 5,000 mostly Middle Eastern aliens holding tourist, student, or business visas. *See* Allan Lengel, *Arab Men in Detroit to Be Asked to See U.S. Attorney*, Wash. Post, Nov. 27, 2001.

Did these actions constitute constitutionally suspect profiling? Did they violate the *DOJ Guidance? Compare* Davies, *supra*, at 80-81, *and* Ellmann, *supra*, at 726-727 (because mass interviews were based on stigmatizing racial generalization that promoted public stereotypes, created great resentment in the targeted community, and probably generated few, if any leads, they were "unjustifiable discrimination"), *with* Samuel R. Gross & Debra Livingston, *Racial Profiling Under Attack*, 102 Colum. L. Rev. 1413, 1436 (2002) (concluding that the interview campaign was profiling to the extent that the FBI assumed that Middle Eastern men were more likely than others to commit acts of terror but was not profiling to the extent that FBI agents were "pursuing case-specific information about the September 11 attacks, albeit in dragnet fashion"). Does it matter? Professors Gross and Livingston suggest that how the FBI selects its interviewees matters less than how they carry out the interviews. *Id.* at 1436-1437 ("Are the interviews conducted respectfully...?"). Do you agree?

The Second Circuit Court of Appeals rejected a claim by Muslim men who were detained for immigration violations after they had been identified as persons of "high interest" in the investigation following 9/11, that they had been impermissibly selected on the basis of their national origin. See *infra* pp. 746-750.

[P]laintiffs point to no authority clearly establishing an equal protection right to be free of selective enforcement of the immigration laws based on national origin, race, or religion at the time of plaintiffs' detentions. *See Reno v. American-Arab Anti-Discrimination Comm.*, 525 U.S. 471, 490-91 (1999) ("What will be involved in deportation cases is not merely the disclosure of normal domestic law enforcement priorities and techniques, but often the disclosure of foreign-policy objectives and (as in this case) foreign-intelligence products and techniques. The Executive should not have to disclose its 'real' reasons for deeming nationals of a particular country a special threat — or indeed for simply wishing to antagonize a particular foreign country by focusing on that country's nationals — and even if it did disclose them a court would be ill equipped to determine their authenticity and utterly unable to assess their adequacy"); *see also Zadvydas* [*v. Davis*, 533 U.S. 678, 696 (2001)] ("terrorism" might warrant "special arguments" for "heightened deference to the judgments of the political branches with respect to matters of national security"); *Mathews v. Diaz*, 426 U.S. 67, 81-82 (1976) ("The reasons that preclude judicial review of political questions also dictate a narrow standard of review of decisions made by the Congress or the President in the area of immigration and naturalization."); *but see Iqbal v. Hasty*, 490 F.3d 143, 175 (2d Cir.2007) (determining that *Reno* "does not stand for the proposition that the Government may subject members of a particular race, ethnicity, or religion to more restrictive conditions of confinement than members of other races, ethnic backgrounds, or religions"), rev'd on other grounds and remanded, *Ashcroft v. Iqbal*, 129 S.Ct. 1937, 1954 (2009). [*Turkmen v. Ashcroft*, 589 F.3d 542, 550 (2d Cir. 2009).]

2. *Religious Profiling?* In *Tabbaa v. Chertoff*, 509 F.3d 89 (2d Cir. 2007), the CBP had received classified information giving them reason to believe that terrorists or persons with terrorist ties would be attending a Muslim religious conference in Canada, which drew 13,000 individuals from across North America. They therefore, without particularizied suspicion, stopped a group of Muslim U.S. citizens at the border on their return from the conference and frisked, fingerprinted, photographed, questioned, and detained them for four to six hours, without telling them why they had been pulled aside. When these citizens challenged these actions in court, the court of appeals ultimately ruled that, as "routine" border searches, the actions did not violate the Fourth Amendment. It also held that the actions did not violate the plaintiffs' First Amendment rights of association or religious freedom under a strict scrutiny test, because they served a compelling counterterrorism need, and, *at the border*, this need could not have been satisfied by any significantly less restrictive means. *Id.* at 102-105.

3. *Profiling and National Identity Cards.* One commentator has argued that "[a] national identity card could facilitate greater civil liberties for groups targeted by racial and ethnic stereotyping and profiling. Membership would alleviate harassment because presentation of the card would result in an immediate check of one's identity with the national computerized data system." John Dwight Ingram, *Racial and Ethnic Profiling*, 29 T. Marshall L. Rev. 55, 83 (2003). Do you agree?

Surveillance Abroad ————25

The United States has long conducted law enforcement and intelligence investigations overseas. Such investigations are critical in detecting threats to national security. In this chapter we examine the question whether, when U.S. investigators go abroad, the Constitution travels with them to limit their activities and, if so, to what extent. In particular, we consider whether the protections of the Fourth Amendment apply outside the United States and, if they do, whether they apply to aliens the same way they do to U.S. citizens. And we ask how such protections might be influenced by practical considerations.

Reid v. Covert
United States Supreme Court, 1957
354 U.S. 1

[The facts and a portion of the opinion in this case are set out *supra* p. 174.]

Mr. Justice BLACK announced the opinion of the Court and delivered an opinion, in which the Chief Justice, Mr. Justice DOUGLAS, and Mr. Justice BRENNAN join. . . . At the beginning we reject the idea that when the United States acts against citizens abroad it can do so free of the Bill of Rights. The United States is entirely a creature of the Constitution. Its power and authority have no other source. It can only act in accordance with all the limitations imposed by the Constitution. When the Government reaches out to punish a citizen who is abroad, the shield which the Bill of Rights and other parts of the Constitution provide to protect his life and liberty should not be stripped away just because he happens to be in another land. . . .

The rights and liberties which citizens of our country enjoy are not protected by custom and tradition alone, they have been jealously preserved from the encroachments of Government by express provisions of our written Constitution.

Among those provisions, Art. III, §2 and the Fifth and Sixth Amendments are directly relevant to these cases. Article III, §2 lays down the rule that:

"The Trial of all Crimes, except in Cases of Impeachment, shall be by Jury; and such Trial shall be held in the State where the said Crimes shall have been committed; but when not committed within any State, the Trial shall be at such Place or Places as the Congress may by Law have directed."

The Fifth Amendment declares:

"No person shall be held to answer for a capital, or otherwise infamous crime, unless on a presentment or indictment of a Grand Jury, except in cases arising in the land or naval forces, or in the Militia, when in actual service in time of War or public danger; . . . ."

And the Sixth Amendment provides:

"In all criminal prosecutions, the accused shall enjoy the right to a speedy and public trial, by an impartial jury of the State and district wherein the crime shall have been committed. . . ."

The language of Art. III, §2 manifests that constitutional protections for the individual were designed to restrict the United States Government when it acts outside of this country, as well as here at home. After declaring that all criminal trials must be by jury, the section states that when a crime is "not committed within any State, the Trial shall be at such Place or Places as the Congress may by Law have directed." If this language is permitted to have its obvious meaning, §2 is applicable to criminal trials outside of the States as a group without regard to where the offense is committed or the trial held. From the very first Congress, federal statutes have implemented the provisions of §2 by providing for trial of murder and other crimes committed outside the jurisdiction of any State "in the district where the offender is apprehended, or into which he may first be brought." The Fifth and Sixth Amendments, like Art. III, §2, are also all inclusive with their sweeping references to "no person" and to "all criminal prosecutions."

This Court and other federal courts have held or asserted that various constitutional limitations apply to the Government when it acts outside the continental United States. While it has been suggested that only those constitutional rights which are "fundamental" protect Americans abroad, we can find no warrant, in logic or otherwise, for picking and choosing among the remarkable collection of "Thou shalt nots" which were explicitly fastened on all departments and agencies of the Federal Government by the Constitution and its Amendments. Moreover, in view of our heritage and the history of the adoption of the Constitution and the Bill of Rights, it seems peculiarly anomalous to say that trial before a civilian judge and by an independent jury picked from the common citizenry is not a fundamental right. . . . Trial by jury in a court of law and in accordance with traditional modes of procedure after an indictment by grand jury has served and remains one of our most vital barriers to governmental arbitrariness. These elemental procedural safeguards were embedded in our Constitution to secure their inviolateness and sanctity against the passing demands of expediency or convenience. . . .

The [holding in *In re Ross*, 140 U.S. 453 (1891),] that the Constitution has no applicability abroad has long since been directly repudiated by numerous cases. That approach is obviously erroneous if the United States Government, which has no power except that granted by the Constitution, can and does try citizens for crimes committed abroad. . . . At best, the *Ross* case should be left as a relic from a different era.

[Last term the Court] relied on the *"Insular Cases"* to support its conclusion that Article III and the Fifth and Sixth Amendments were not applicable to the trial of Mrs. Smith and Mrs. Covert.[22] We believe that reliance was misplaced. The *"Insular Cases,"* which arose at the turn of the [twentieth] century, involved territories which had only recently been conquered or acquired by the United States. These territories, governed and regulated by Congress under Art. IV, §3, had entirely different cultures and customs from those of this country....

Moreover, it is our judgment that neither the cases nor their reasoning should be given any further expansion. The concept that the Bill of Rights and other constitutional protections against arbitrary government are inoperative when they become inconvenient or when expediency dictates otherwise is a very dangerous doctrine and if allowed to flourish would destroy the benefit of a written Constitution and undermine the basis of our government. If our foreign commitments become of such nature that the Government can no longer satisfactorily operate within the bounds laid down by the Constitution, that instrument can be amended by the method which it prescribes. But we have no authority, or inclination, to read exceptions into it which are not there....

Mr. Justice HARLAN, concurring in the result.... As I have already stated, I do not think that it can be said that these safeguards of the Constitution are never operative without the United States, regardless of the particular circumstances. On the other hand, I cannot agree with the suggestion that every provision of the Constitution must always be deemed automatically applicable to American citizens in every part of the world. For *Ross* and the *Insular Cases* do stand for an important proposition, one which seems to me a wise and necessary gloss on our Constitution. The proposition is, of course, not that the Constitution "does not apply" overseas, but that there are provisions in the Constitution which do not *necessarily* apply in all circumstances in every foreign place.... In other words, what *Ross* and the *Insular Cases* hold is that the particular local setting, the practical necessities, and the possible alternatives are relevant to a question of judgment, namely, whether jury trial should be deemed a necessary condition of the exercise of Congress' power to provide for the trial of Americans overseas....

And so I agree with my brother Frankfurter that, in view of *Ross* and the *Insular Cases*, we have before us a question analogous, ultimately, to issues of due process; one can say, in fact, that the question of which specific safeguards of the Constitution are appropriately to be applied in a particular context overseas can be reduced to the issue of what process is "due" a defendant in the particular circumstances of a particular case.

On this basis, I cannot agree with the sweeping proposition that a full Article III trial, with indictment and trial by jury, is required in every case for the trial of a civilian dependent of a serviceman overseas. The Government, it seems to me, has made an impressive showing that at least for the run-of-the-mill offenses committed by dependents overseas, such a requirement would be as impractical and anomalous as it would have been to require jury trial for Balzac in Porto Rico....

So far as capital cases are concerned, I think they stand on quite a different footing than other offenses. In such cases the law is especially sensitive to demands

---

22. *Downes v. Bidwell,* 182 U.S. 244; *Territory of Hawaii v. Mankichi,* 190 U.S. 197; *Dorr v. United States,* 195 U.S. 138; *Balzac v. Porto Rico,* 258 U.S. 298.

for that procedural fairness which inheres in a civilian trial where the judge and trier of fact are not responsive to the command of the convening authority. I do not concede that whatever process is "due" an offender faced with a fine or a prison sentence necessarily satisfies the requirements of the Constitution in a capital case. . . . The number of such cases would appear to be so negligible that the practical problems of affording the defendant a civilian trial would not present insuperable problems.

On this narrow ground I concur in the result in these cases.

[The opinions of FRANKFURTER, J., concurring, and of CLARK, J., dissenting, are omitted.]

United States v. Verdugo-Urquidez
United States Supreme Court, 1990
494 U.S. 259

Chief Justice REHNQUIST delivered the opinion of the Court. The question presented by this case is whether the Fourth Amendment applies to the search and seizure by United States agents of property that is owned by a nonresident alien and located in a foreign country. We hold that it does not.

[Respondent René Martin Verdugo-Urquidez was a citizen and resident of Mexico who was apprehended by Mexican police and delivered to U.S. border authorities in response to a U.S. warrant for his arrest on drug-smuggling charges. Following his arrest, and while he was incarcerated in the United States, DEA agents searched Verdugo-Urquidez's property in Mexico with the approval of Mexican authorities, but without a U.S. warrant, and seized certain documents that were subsequently offered as evidence against him. The defendant sought to have that evidence excluded.]

The Fourth Amendment provides:

"The right of the people to be secure in their persons, houses, papers, and effects, against unreasonable searches and seizures, shall not be violated, and no Warrants shall issue, but upon probable cause, supported by Oath or affirmation, and particularly describing the place to be searched, and the persons or things to be seized."

That text, by contrast with the Fifth and Sixth Amendments, extends its reach only to "the people." Contrary to the suggestion of *amici curiae* that the Framers used this phrase "simply to avoid [an] awkward rhetorical redundancy," "the people" seems to have been a term of art employed in select parts of the Constitution. The Preamble declares that the Constitution is ordained and established by "the People of the United States." The Second Amendment protects "the right of the people to keep and bear Arms," and the Ninth and Tenth Amendments provide that certain rights and powers are retained by and reserved to "the people." See also U.S. Const., Amdt. 1 ("Congress shall make no law . . . abridging . . . *the right of the people* peaceably to assemble") (emphasis added); Art. I, §2, cl. 1 ("The House of Representatives shall be composed of Members chosen every second Year *by the People of the several States*") (emphasis added). While this textual exegesis is by no means conclusive, it suggests that "the people" protected by the Fourth Amendment, and by the First and

Second Amendments, and to whom rights and powers are reserved in the Ninth and Tenth Amendments, refers to a class of persons who are part of a national community or who have otherwise developed sufficient connection with this country to be considered part of that community. The language of these Amendments contrasts with the words "person" and "accused" used in the Fifth and Sixth Amendments regulating procedure in criminal cases.

What we know of the history of the drafting of the Fourth Amendment also suggests that its purpose was to restrict searches and seizures which might be conducted by the United States in domestic matters.... The available historical data show, therefore, that the purpose of the Fourth Amendment was to protect the people of the United States against arbitrary action by their own Government; it was never suggested that the provision was intended to restrain the actions of the Federal Government against aliens outside of the United States territory.

There is likewise no indication that the Fourth Amendment was understood by contemporaries of the Framers to apply to activities of the United States directed against aliens in foreign territory or in international waters. Only seven years after the ratification of the Amendment, French interference with American commercial vessels engaged in neutral trade triggered what came to be known as the "undeclared war" with France. In an Act to "protect the Commerce of the United States" in 1798, Congress authorized President Adams to "instruct the commanders of the public armed vessels which are, or which shall be employed in the service of the United States, to subdue, seize and take any armed French vessel, which shall be found within the jurisdictional limits of the United States, or elsewhere, on the high seas." §1 of An Act Further to Protect the Commerce of the United States, ch. 68, 1 Stat. 578.... Some commanders were held liable by this Court for unlawful seizures because their actions were beyond the scope of the congressional grant of authority, *see, e.g.*, *Little v. Barreme*, 2 Cranch 170, 177-178 (1804); *cf. Talbot v. Seeman*, 1 Cranch 1, 31 (1801) (seizure of neutral ship lawful where American captain had probable cause to believe vessel was French), but it was never suggested that the Fourth Amendment restrained the authority of congress or of United States agents to conduct operations such as this.

The global view taken by the Court of Appeals of the application of the Constitution is also contrary to this Court's decisions in the *Insular Cases*, which held that not every constitutional provision applies to governmental activity even where the United States has sovereign power. In *Dorr v. United States*, 195 U.S. 138 (1904), we declared the general rule that in an unincorporated territory—one not clearly destined for statehood—Congress was not required to adopt "a system of laws which shall include the right of trial by jury, and that *the Constitution does not, without legislation and of its own force, carry such right to territory so situated.*" 195 U.S. at 149 (emphasis added). Only "fundamental" constitutional rights are guaranteed to inhabitants of those territories.... [C]ertainly, it is not open to us in light of the *Insular Cases* to endorse the view that every constitutional provision applies wherever the United States Government exercises its power.

Indeed, we have rejected the claim that aliens are entitled to Fifth Amendment rights outside the sovereign territory of the United States. In *Johnson v. Eisentrager*, 339 U.S. 763 (1950), the Court held that enemy aliens arrested in China and imprisoned in Germany after World War II could not obtain writs of habeas corpus in our federal courts on the ground that their convictions for war crimes had violated the Fifth Amendment and other constitutional provisions. The *Eisentrager* opinion acknowledged that in some cases constitutional provisions extend beyond the citizenry;

"[t]he alien...has been accorded a generous and ascending scale of rights as he increases his identity with our society." *Id.*, at 770. But our rejection of extraterritorial application of the Fifth Amendment was emphatic:

> "Such extraterritorial application of organic law would have been so significant an innovation in the practice of governments that, if intended or apprehended, it could scarcely have failed to excite contemporary comment. Not one word can be cited. No decision of this Court supports such a view. *Cf. Downes v. Bidwell*, 182 U.S. 244 [(1901)]. None of the learned commentators on our Constitution has even hinted at it. The practice of every modern government is opposed to it." *Id.*, at 784.

If such is true of the Fifth Amendment, which speaks in the relatively universal term of "person," it would seem even more true with respect to the Fourth Amendment, which applies only to "the people."

To support his all-encompassing view of the Fourth Amendment, respondent points to language from the plurality opinion in *Reid v. Covert*, 354 U.S. 1 (1957)....Four Justices "reject[ed] the idea that when the United States acts *against citizens* abroad it can do so free of the Bill of Rights." *Id.*, at 5 (emphasis added). The plurality went on to say:

> "The United States is entirely a creature of the Constitution. Its power and authority have no other source. It can only act in accordance with all the limitations imposed by the Constitution. When the Government reaches out to punish *a citizen* who is abroad, the shield which the Bill of Rights and other parts of the Constitution provide to protect his life and liberty should not be stripped away just because he happens to be in another land." *Id.*, at 5-6 (emphasis added; footnote omitted).

Respondent urges that we interpret this discussion to mean that federal officials are constrained by the Fourth Amendment wherever and against whomever they act. But the holding of *Reid* stands for no such sweeping proposition: it decided that United States citizens stationed abroad could invoke the protection of the Fifth and Sixth Amendments. The concurring opinions by Justices Frankfurter and Harlan in *Reid* resolved the case on much narrower grounds than the plurality and declined even to hold that United States citizens were entitled to the full range of constitutional protections in all overseas criminal prosecutions. *See id.*, at 75 (Harlan, J., concurring in result) ("I agree with my brother Frankfurter that...we have before us a question analogous, ultimately, to issues of due process; one can say, in fact, that the question of which specific safeguards of the Constitution are appropriately to be applied in a particular context overseas can be reduced to the issue of what process is 'due' a defendant in the particular circumstances of a particular case"). Since respondent is not a United States citizen, he can derive no comfort from the *Reid* holding.

Verdugo-Urquidez also relies on a series of cases in which we have held that aliens enjoy certain constitutional rights. *See, e.g., Plyler v. Doe*, 457 U.S. 202, 211-212 (1982) (illegal aliens protected by Equal Protection Clause); *Kwong Hai Chew v. Colding*, 344 U.S. 590, 596 (1953) (resident alien is a "person" within the meaning of the Fifth Amendment); *Bridges v. Wixon*, 326 U.S. 135, 148 (1945) (resident aliens have First Amendment rights); *Russian Volunteer Fleet v. United States*, 282 U.S. 481 (1931) (Just Compensation Clause of Fifth Amendment); *Wong Wing v. United States*, 163 U.S. 228, 238 (1896) (resident aliens entitled to Fifth and Sixth Amendment rights);

Yick Wo v. Hopkins, 118 U.S. 356, 369 (1886) (Fourteenth Amendment protects resident aliens). These cases, however, establish only that aliens receive constitutional protections when they have come within the territory of the United States and developed substantial connections with this country. Respondent is an alien who has had no previous significant voluntary connection with the United States, so these cases avail him not. . . .

Not only are history and case law against respondent, but as pointed out in *Johnson v. Eisentrager,* 339 U.S. 763 (1950), the result of accepting his claim would have significant and deleterious consequences for the United States in conducting activities beyond its boundaries. The rule adopted by the Court of Appeals would apply not only to law enforcement operations abroad, but also to other foreign policy operations which might result in "searches or seizures." The United States frequently employs armed forces outside this country — over 200 times in our history — for the protection of American citizens or national security. Congressional Research Service, *Instances of Use of United States Armed Forces Abroad, 1798-1989* (E. Collier ed. 1989). Application of the Fourth Amendment to those circumstances could significantly disrupt the ability of the political branches to respond to foreign situations involving our national interest. Were respondent to prevail, aliens with no attachment to this country might well bring actions for damages to remedy claimed violations of the Fourth Amendment in foreign countries or in international waters. *See Bivens v. Six Unknown Federal Narcotics Agents,* 403 U.S. 388 (1971). . . . The Members of the Executive and Legislative Branches are sworn to uphold the Constitution, and they presumably desire to follow its commands. But the Court of Appeals' global view of its applicability would plunge them into a sea of uncertainty as to what might be reasonable in the way of searches and seizures conducted abroad. Indeed, the Court of Appeals held that absent exigent circumstances, United States agents could not effect a "search or seizure" for law enforcement purposes in a foreign country without first obtaining a warrant — which would be a dead letter outside the United States — from a magistrate in this country. Even if no warrant were required, American agents would have to articulate specific facts giving them probable cause to undertake a search or seizure if they wished to comply with the Fourth Amendment as conceived by the Court of Appeals. . . .

For better or for worse, we live in a world of nation-states in which our Government must be able to "function effectively in the company of sovereign nations." *Perez v. Brownell,* 356 U.S. 44, 57 (1958). Some who violate our laws may live outside our borders under a regime quite different from that which obtains in this country. Situations threatening to important American interests may arise halfway around the globe, situations which in the view of the political branches of our Government require an American response with armed force. If there are to be restrictions on searches and seizures which occur incident to such American action, they must be imposed by the political branches through diplomatic understanding, treaty, or legislation.

The judgment of the Court of Appeals is accordingly

Reversed.

Justice KENNEDY, concurring. . . . I take it to be correct, as the plurality opinion in *Reid v. Covert* sets forth, that the Government may act only as the Constitution authorizes, whether the actions in question are foreign or domestic. *See* 354 U.S., at 6. But this principle is only a first step in resolving this case. The question before us then becomes what constitutional standards apply when the Government acts, in reference to an alien, within its sphere of foreign operations. . . . [Various cases], as well as *United States v. Curtiss-Wright Export Corp.*, 299 U.S. 304, 318 (1936), stand for the proposition that we must interpret constitutional protections in light of the undoubted power of the United States to take actions to assert its legitimate power and authority abroad. Justice Harlan made this observation in his opinion concurring in the judgment in *Reid v. Covert*:

> "I cannot agree with the suggestion that every provision of the Constitution must always be deemed automatically applicable to American citizens in every part of the world. For *Ross* and the *Insular Cases* do stand for an important proposition, one which seems to me a wise and necessary gloss on our Constitution. The proposition is, of course, not that the Constitution 'does not apply' overseas, but that there are provisions in the Constitution which do not *necessarily* apply in all circumstances in every foreign place. In other words, it seems to me that the basic teaching of *Ross* and the *Insular Cases* is that there is no rigid and abstract rule that Congress, as a condition precedent to exercising power over Americans overseas, must exercise it subject to all the guarantees of the Constitution, no matter what the conditions and considerations are that would make adherence to a specific guarantee altogether impracticable and anomalous." 354 U.S., at 74.

The conditions and considerations of this case would make adherence to the Fourth Amendment's warrant requirement impracticable and anomalous. . . . The absence of local judges or magistrates available to issue warrants, the differing and perhaps unascertainable conceptions of reasonableness and privacy that prevail abroad, and the need to cooperate with foreign officials all indicate that the Fourth Amendment's warrant requirement should not apply in Mexico as it does in this country. For this reason, in addition to the other persuasive justifications stated by the Court, I agree that no violation of the Fourth Amendment has occurred in the case before us. The rights of a citizen, as to whom the United States has continuing obligations, are not presented by this case.

I do not mean to imply, and the Court has not decided, that persons in the position of the respondent have no constitutional protection. The United States is prosecuting a foreign national in a court established under Article III, and all of the trial proceedings are governed by the Constitution. All would agree, for instance, that the dictates of the Due Process Clause of the Fifth Amendment protect the defendant. Indeed, as Justice Harlan put it, "the question of which specific safeguards . . . are appropriately to be applied in a particular context . . . can be reduced to the issue of what process is 'due' a defendant in the particular circumstances of a particular case." *Reid, supra*, at 75. Nothing approaching a violation of due process has occurred in this case.

[The opinion of Justice STEVENS, concurring in the judgment on the grounds that, although the Fourth Amendment applied, the search was reasonable, is omitted.]

Justice BRENNAN, with whom Justice MARSHALL joins, dissenting. . . . The Court today creates an antilogy: the Constitution authorizes our Government to enforce our criminal laws abroad, but when Government agents exercise this authority, the Fourth Amendment does not travel with them. This cannot be. At the very least, the

Fourth Amendment is an unavoidable correlative of the Government's power to enforce the criminal law. . . .

When we tell the world that we expect all people, wherever they may be, to abide by our laws, we cannot in the same breath tell the world that our law enforcement officers need not do the same. Because we cannot expect others to respect our laws until we respect our Constitution, I respectfully dissent.

Justice BLACKMUN, dissenting. I cannot accept the Court of Appeals' conclusion, echoed in some portions of Justice Brennan's dissent, that the Fourth Amendment governs every action by an American official that can be characterized as a search or seizure. American agents acting abroad generally do not purport to exercise sovereign authority over the foreign nationals with whom they come in contact. The relationship between these agents and foreign nationals is therefore fundamentally different from the relationship between United States officials and individuals residing within this country.

I am inclined to agree with Justice Brennan, however, that when a foreign national is held accountable for purported violations of United States criminal laws, he has effectively been treated as one of "the governed" and therefore is entitled to Fourth Amendment protections. Although the Government's exercise of *power* abroad does not ordinarily implicate the Fourth Amendment, the enforcement of domestic criminal law seems to me to be the paradigmatic exercise of sovereignty over those who are compelled to obey. In any event, as Justice Stevens notes, respondent was lawfully (though involuntarily) within this country at the time the search occurred. Under these circumstances I believe that respondent is entitled to invoke protections of the Fourth Amendment. I agree with the Government, however, that an American magistrate's lack of power to authorize a search abroad renders the Warrant Clause inapplicable to the search of a noncitizen's residence outside this country.

The Fourth Amendment nevertheless requires that the search be "reasonable." And when the purpose of a search is the procurement of evidence for a criminal prosecution, we have consistently held that the search, to be reasonable, must be based upon probable cause. Neither the District Court nor the Court of Appeals addressed the issue of probable cause, and I do not believe that a reliable determination could be made on the basis of the record before us. I therefore would vacate the judgment of the Court of Appeals and remand the case for further proceedings.

NOTES AND QUESTIONS

1. *Does the Constitution Follow the Flag?* At the beginning of his opinion for the Court in *Reid v. Covert,* Justice Black famously declared that "[t]he United States is entirely a creature of the Constitution. Its power and authority have no other source." 354 U.S. at 5-6. Given the context of the case, he was clearly referring to the extraterritorial authority of the federal government. This statement stands in sharp contrast to Justice Sutherland's opinion for the majority in *United States v. Curtiss-Wright Corp.,* 299 U.S. 304, 315-316 (1936) (*supra* p. 53), in which he remarked, "The broad statement that the federal government can exercise no powers except those specifically enumerated in the Constitution, and such implied powers as are necessary

and proper to carry into effect the enumerated powers, is categorically true only in respect of our internal affairs."

Whatever the source of the foreign affairs power, both decisions recognize that the power is limited. *Reid* stated that the government "can only act in accordance with all the limitations imposed by the Constitution," 345 U.S. at 6, while *Curtiss-Wright* indicated that even its powers in international relations must be exercised "in subordination to the applicable provisions of the Constitution." 299 U.S. at 320. Such statements might suggest that the Bill of Rights is more of a structural limit on government power than a recital of individual protections. *See* Akhil Reed Amar, *The Bill of Rights as a Constitution*, 100 Yale L.J. 1131 (1991). Can these statements be squared with the *Verdugo-Urquidez* majority's declaration that not "every constitutional provision applies wherever the United States Government exercises its power"? *See generally* Kal Raustiala, *Does the Constitution Follow the Flag? The Evolution of Territoriality in American Law* (2009).

2. *Citizens vs. Aliens.* How did the citizenship of the defendants affect the outcomes in *Reid* and *Verdugo-Urquidez*? Chief Justice Rehnquist pointed out in *Verdugo-Urquidez* that aliens inside this country generally enjoy the same constitutional protections that U.S. citizens do. Can that equal treatment of citizens and aliens inside the United States be reconciled with his "textual exegesis" of the various Amendments — distinguishing between "persons" and "the people" — to make them apply differently to citizens and aliens abroad?

The majority in *Verdugo-Urquidez* indicated that in drafting the Fourth Amendment "it was never suggested that the provision was intended to restrain the actions of the Federal Government against aliens outside of the United States territory." 454 U.S. at 266. The Court also found no evidence that the Framers intended for the Amendment to constrain wartime military operations against enemies. Does it follow logically that the Framers therefore intended that the Fourth Amendment *not* apply to aliens abroad? Should we assume that they considered the matter at all? Can you think of any reason why the Framers might have wanted to guarantee freedom from unreasonable searches abroad to citizens but not aliens? *See generally* J. Andrew Kent, *A Textual and Historical Case Against a Global Constitution*, 95 Geo. L.J. 463, 465 (2007) (arguing, based on extensive analysis of the record, that "noncitizens outside the United States are to be protected only by diplomacy, treaties, the law of nations . . . , and nonconstitutional policy choices of the political branches").

3. *Sufficient Connection.* The *Verdugo-Urquidez* Court declared that the Fourth Amendment is inapplicable to aliens abroad who lack a "sufficient connection" to the United States. Can this limitation be found in the text of the Constitution?

What is a sufficient connection? The Court said only that Verdugo-Urquidez's connection was not sufficient to extend the protection of the Fourth Amendment to him, even though he was issued a green card in 1970 that he insisted was still valid, and even though the government claimed that he was engaged in trade (drug-trafficking) within the United States. Subsequent lower court decisions are inconsistent. *See, e.g., United States v. Defreitas*, 701 F. Supp. 2d 297 (E.D.N.Y. 2010) (alleged conspiracy to commit terrorist attack in the United States not a sufficient "voluntary connection"); *Martinez-Aguero v. Gonzalez*, 459 F.3d 618 (5th Cir. 2006) (regular and lawful entry into the United States sufficient). *See generally* Douglas I. Koff, *Post-Verdugo-Urquidez: The Sufficient Connection Test — Substantially Ambiguous, Substantially Unworkable*, 25 Colum. Hum. Rts. L. Rev. 435, 455-465 (1994). The resulting ambiguity makes it difficult for

U.S. officials engaged in overseas surveillance of aliens to know how to proceed. The differentiation among aliens also means that disparate standards may apply to co-defendants engaged in the same conduct, suspected of the same crimes, and subjected to the same search. What kind of connection did Justice Blackmun, dissenting, say makes the Fourth Amendment applicable to Verdugo-Urquidez?

Should courts draw a bright line? If so, what should it be? *Compare* Randall K. Miller, *The Limits of U.S. International Law Enforcement After Verdugo-Urquidez: Resurrecting Rochin*, 58 U. Pitt. L. Rev. 867, 885 n.88 (1997) (drawing the line at the border, thus denying Fourth Amendment protections to all aliens searched abroad, regardless of their connection to the United States), *with* Koff, *supra*, at 485 (extending Fourth Amendment protections to all persons except nonresident enemy aliens searched incident to a military confrontation).

4. *Justice Harlan's "Practical Necessities."* Justice Harlan, concurring in *Reid*, argued that some "provisions of the Constitution . . . do not *necessarily* apply in all circumstances in every foreign place." 354 U.S. at 74 (emphasis in original). Whether they apply, he wrote, depends on the "particular circumstances of a particular case." *Id.* at 75. Justice Black emphatically disagreed, warning that it would be "very dangerous" to allow "the Bill of Rights and other constitutional protections against arbitrary government [to become] inoperative when they become inconvenient or when expediency dictates otherwise." *Id.* at 14.

Is Harlan's theory of conditional applicability based in the Constitution? If not, what is its source? Is it "very dangerous"? How is that theory reflected in Justice Kennedy's concurring opinion in *Verdugo-Urquidez*? Does it provide an answer to the majority's worry that application of the Fourth Amendment abroad would plunge government officials into a "sea of uncertainty"?

5. *Conditional Applicability of Verdugo-Urquidez?* The *Verdugo-Urquidez* majority stated that in *Johnson v. Eisentrager*, its 1950 habeas corpus case, "our rejection of extraterritorial application of the Fifth Amendment was emphatic." 494 U.S. at 269. But that rejection was also conditional. The 1950 Court noted that "[i]f the Fifth Amendment confers its rights on all the world . . . the same must be true of the companion civil-rights Amendments, for none of them is limited by its express terms, territorially or as to persons." 339 U.S. at 784. Whether at home or abroad, the Court then pointed out, the "disabilities this country lays upon the alien who becomes also an enemy are imposed temporarily as an incident of war and not as an incident of alienage." 494 U.S. at 272. The petitioners for a writ of habeas corpus in *Eisentrager* admittedly were German soldiers in a declared war. The defendant in *Verdugo-Urquidez* was not, of course, a wartime enemy alien.

In a 2008 case involving aliens held at Guantánamo as "enemy combatants," the Supreme Court, relying heavily on Harlan's practical necessities theory, indicated that the *Eisentrager* Court's refusal to extend the Fifth Amendment to aliens abroad was conditional in another way. *Boumediene v. Bush*, 553 U.S. 723 (2008) (*infra* p. 787). Justice Kennedy wrote the opinion for the majority, declaring that

> if the Government's reading of *Eisentrager* were correct, the opinion would have marked not only a change in, but a complete repudiation of, the *Insular Cases'* (and later *Reid's*) functional approach to questions of extraterritoriality. We cannot accept the Government's view. Nothing in *Eisentrager* says that *de jure* sovereignty is or has ever been the only

relevant consideration in determining the geographic reach of the Constitution or of habeas corpus. Were that the case, there would be considerable tension between *Eisentrager,* on the one hand, and the *Insular Cases* and *Reid,* on the other. Our cases need not be read to conflict in this manner. A constricted reading of *Eisentrager* overlooks what we see as a common thread uniting the *Insular Cases, Eisentrager,* and *Reid:* the idea that questions of extraterritoriality turn on objective factors and practical concerns, not formalism. [*Id.* at 726-727.]

So saying, the Court ruled that the Guantánamo prisoners could apply for a writ of habeas corpus, although it expressly withheld any opinion about their substantive rights. Justice Scalia, dissenting, warned that the decision paved the way for "the extraterritorial reach of other constitutional protections as well." *Id.* at 850.

Is *Verdugo-Urquidez* still good law after *Boumediene?* Can you make the argument that application of the Fourth Amendment to aliens abroad now requires consideration of the practical necessities of each case, as urged by Justices Harlan and Kennedy? How would such a requirement affect the day-to-day work of law enforcement agents abroad?

In re Terrorist Bombings of U.S. Embassies in East Africa (Fourth Amendment Challenges)

United States Court of Appeals, Second Circuit, 2008
552 F.3d 157

[Two other opinions in the same case were filed the same day, dealing with, respectively, the admissibility, sufficiency, and alleged withholding of evidence, and sentencing, 552 F.3d 93; and Fifth and Sixth Amendment challenges, 552 F.3d 177.]

JOSÉ A. CABRANES, Circuit Judge. Defendant-appellant Wadih El-Hage, a citizen of the United States, challenges his conviction in the United States District Court for the Southern District of New York (Leonard B. Sand, Judge) on numerous charges arising from his involvement in the August 7, 1998 bombings of the American Embassies in Nairobi, Kenya and Dar es Salaam, Tanzania . . . .

El-Hage contends that the District Court erred by (1) recognizing a foreign intelligence exception to the Fourth Amendment's warrant requirement, (2) concluding that the search of El-Hage's home and surveillance of his telephone lines qualified for inclusion in that exception . . . . Because we hold that the Fourth Amendment's requirement of reasonableness—and not the Warrant Clause—governs extraterritorial searches of U.S. citizens and that the searches challenged on this appeal were reasonable, we find no error in the District Court's denial of El-Hage's [motion to suppress illegally obtained evidence]. . . . El-Hage's challenge to his conviction is therefore without merit.

I. BACKGROUND

A. Factual Overview

American intelligence became aware of al Qaeda's presence in Kenya by mid-1996 and identified five telephone numbers used by suspected al Qaeda associates.

United States v. Bin Laden, 126 F. Supp. 2d 264, 269 (S.D.N.Y. 2000). From August 1996 through August 1997, American intelligence officials monitored these telephone lines, including two El-Hage used: a phone line in the building where El-Hage lived and his cell phone. *See id.* The Attorney General of the United States then authorized intelligence operatives to target El-Hage in particular. *Id.* This authorization, first issued on April 4, 1997, was renewed in July 1997. *Id.* Working with Kenyan authorities, U.S. officials searched El-Hage's home in Nairobi on August 21, 1997, pursuant to a document shown to El-Hage's wife that was "identified as a Kenyan warrant authorizing a search for 'stolen property.'" *Id.* At the completion of the search, one of the Kenyan officers gave El-Hage's wife an inventory listing the items seized during the search. *Id.* El-Hage was not present during the search of his home. *Id.* It is uncontested that the agents did not apply for or obtain a warrant from a U.S. court....

II. DISCUSSION ...

B. The District Court's Denial of El-Hage's Motion to Suppress Evidence ...

2. Extraterritorial Application of the Fourth Amendment

In order to determine whether El-Hage's suppression motion was properly denied by the District Court, we must first determine whether and to what extent the Fourth Amendment's safeguards apply to overseas searches involving U.S. citizens. In *United States v. Toscanino,* a case involving a Fourth Amendment challenge to overseas wiretapping of a non-U.S. citizen, we observed that it was "well settled" that "the Bill of Rights has extraterritorial application to the conduct abroad of federal agents directed against United States citizens." 500 F.2d 267, 280-81 (2d Cir. 1974); *see also United States v. Verdugo-Urquidez,* 494 U.S. 259, 283 n.7 (1990) (Brennan, J., dissenting) (recognizing "the rule, accepted by every Court of Appeals to have considered the question, that the Fourth Amendment applies to searches conducted by the United States Government against United States citizens abroad"). Nevertheless, we have not yet determined the specific question of the applicability of the Fourth Amendment's Warrant Clause to overseas searches. Faced with that question now, we hold that the Fourth Amendment's warrant requirement does not govern searches conducted abroad by U.S. agents; such searches of U.S. citizens need only satisfy the Fourth Amendment's requirement of reasonableness....

... While never addressing the question directly, the Supreme Court provided some guidance on the issue in *United States v. Verdugo-Urquidez* .... [That guidance] and the following reasons weigh against imposing a warrant requirement on overseas searches.

First, there is nothing in our history or our precedents suggesting that U.S. officials must first obtain a warrant before conducting an overseas search. El-Hage has pointed to no authority—and we are aware of none—directly supporting the proposition that warrants are necessary for searches conducted abroad by U.S. law enforcement officers or local agents acting in collaboration with them; nor has El-Hage identified any instances in our history where a foreign search was conducted pursuant to an American search warrant. This dearth of authority is not surprising in light of the history of the Fourth Amendment and its Warrant Clause as well as the history of international affairs.... [Here the court reviews the *Verdugo-Urquidez*

Court's analysis of the history of the drafting of the Fourth Amendment.] Accordingly, we agree with the Ninth Circuit's observation that "foreign searches have neither been historically subject to the warrant procedure, nor could they be as a practical matter." *United States v. Barona*, 56 F.3d 1087, 1092 n.1 (9th Cir. 1995).[7]

Second, nothing in the history of the foreign relations of the United States would require that U.S. officials obtain warrants from foreign magistrates before conducting searches overseas or, indeed, [lead us] to suppose that all other states have search and investigation rules akin to our own. As the Supreme Court explained in *Verdugo-Urquidez:*

> For better or for worse, we live in a world of nation-states in which our Government must be able to function effectively in the company of sovereign nations. Some who violate our laws may live outside our borders under a regime quite different from that which obtains in this country. Situations threatening to important American interests may arise halfway around the globe, situations which in the view of the political branches of our Government require an American response with armed force. If there are to be restrictions on searches and seizures which occur incident to such American action, they must be imposed by the political branches through diplomatic understanding, treaty, or legislation.

494 U.S. at 275 (internal citation, quotation marks, and brackets omitted). The American procedure of issuing search warrants on a showing of probable cause simply does not extend throughout the globe and, pursuant to the Supreme Court's instructions, the Constitution does not condition our government's investigative powers on the practices of foreign legal regimes "quite different from that which obtains in this country." *Id.*

Third, if U.S. judicial officers were to issue search warrants intended to have extraterritorial effect, such warrants would have dubious legal significance, if any, in a foreign nation. *Cf. The Schooner Exchange v. M'Faddon*, 11 U.S. 116, 135 (1812) ("The jurisdiction of the nation within its own territory is necessarily exclusive and absolute. It is susceptible of no limitation not imposed by itself."). As a District Court in this Circuit recently observed, "it takes little to imagine the diplomatic and legal complications that would arise if American government officials traveled to another sovereign country and attempted to carry out a search of any kind, professing the authority to do so based on an American-issued search warrant." *United States v. Vilar*, No. 05-CR-621, 2007 WL 1075041, at *52 (S.D.N.Y. Apr. 4, 2007). We agree with that observation. A warrant issued by a U.S. court would neither empower a U.S. agent to

---

7. A U.S. citizen who is a target of a search by our government executed in a foreign country is not without constitutional protection—namely, the Fourth Amendment's guarantee of reasonableness which protects a citizen from unwarranted government intrusions. Indeed, in many instances, as appears to have been the case here, searches targeting U.S. citizens on foreign soil will be supported by probable cause.

The interest served by the warrant requirement in having a "neutral and detached magistrate" evaluate the reasonableness of a search is, in part, based on separation of powers concerns—namely, the need to interpose a judicial officer between the zealous police officer ferreting out crime and the subject of the search. These interests are lessened in the circumstances presented here for two reasons. First, a domestic judicial officer's ability to determine the reasonableness of a search is diminished where the search occurs on foreign soil. Second, the acknowledged wide discretion afforded the executive branch in foreign affairs ought to be respected in these circumstances.

A warrant serves a further purpose in limiting the scope of the search to places described with particularity or "the persons or things to be seized" in the warrant. U.S. Const. amend. IV. In the instant case, we are satisfied that the scope of the searches at issue was not unreasonable. *See* Parts II.B.3, *post.*

conduct a search nor would it necessarily compel the intended target to comply. It would be a nullity, or in the words of the Supreme Court, "a dead letter." *Verdugo-Urquidez,* 494 U.S. at 274.

Fourth and finally, it is by no means clear that U.S. judicial officers could be authorized to issue warrants for overseas searches, *cf. Weinberg v. United States,* 126 F.2d 1004, 1006 (2d Cir. 1942) (statute authorizing district court to issue search warrants construed to limit authority to the court's territorial jurisdiction), although we need not resolve that issue here.

For these reasons, we hold that the Fourth Amendment's Warrant Clause has no extraterritorial application and that foreign searches of U.S. citizens conducted by U.S. agents are subject only to the Fourth Amendment's requirement of reasonableness.

The District Court's recognition of an exception to the warrant requirement for foreign intelligence searches finds support in the pre-FISA law of other circuits. *See United States v. Truong Dinh Hung,* 629 F.2d 908, 913 (4th Cir. 1980); *United States v. Buck,* 548 F.2d 871, 875 (9th Cir. 1977); *United States v. Butenko,* 494 F.2d 593, 605 (3d Cir. 1974); *United States v. Brown,* 484 F.2d 418, 426 (5th Cir. 1973). We decline to adopt this view, however, because the exception requires an inquiry into whether the "primary purpose" of the search is foreign intelligence collection. *See Bin Laden,* 126 F. Supp. 2d at 277. This distinction between a "primary purpose" and other purposes is inapt. As the U.S. Foreign Intelligence Surveillance Court of Review has explained:

> [The primary purpose] analysis, in our view, rested on a false premise and the line the court sought to draw was inherently unstable, unrealistic, and confusing. The false premise was the assertion that once the government moves to criminal prosecution, its "foreign policy concerns" recede.... [T]hat is simply not true as it relates to counter-intelligence. In that field the government's primary purpose is to halt the espionage or terrorism efforts, and criminal prosecutions can be, and usually are, interrelated with other techniques used to frustrate a foreign power's efforts.

In re Sealed Case No. 02-001, 310 F.3d 717, 743 (Foreign Int. Surv. Ct. Rev. 2002).

In addition, the purpose of the search has no bearing on the factors making a warrant requirement inapplicable to foreign searches—namely, (1) the complete absence of any precedent in our history for doing so, (2) the inadvisability of conditioning our government's surveillance on the practices of foreign states, (3) a U.S. warrant's lack of authority overseas, and (4) the absence of a mechanism for obtaining a U.S. warrant. Accordingly, we cannot endorse the view that the normal course is to obtain a warrant for overseas searches involving U.S. citizens unless the search is "primarily" targeting foreign powers.

3. The Kenyan Searches Were Reasonable and Therefore Did Not Violate the Fourth Amendment.

...First, El-Hage insists that his Nairobi home deserves special consideration in light of the home's status as "the most fundamental bastion of privacy protected by the Fourth Amendment." Second, he contends that the electronic surveillance was far broader than necessary because it encompassed "[m]any calls, if not the predominant amount, [that] were related solely to legitimate commercial purposes, and/or purely family and social matters."

To determine whether a search is reasonable under the Fourth Amendment, we examine the "totality of the circumstances" to balance "on the one hand, the degree to which it intrudes upon an individual's privacy and, on the other, the degree to which it is needed for the promotion of legitimate governmental interests." *Samson v. California*, 547 U.S. 843, 848 (2006) (quoting *United States v. Knights*, 534 U.S. 112, 118-19 (2001)) (internal quotation marks omitted)....

a. The Search of El-Hage's Home in Nairobi Was Reasonable....

Applying that test to the facts of this case, we first examine the extent to which the search of El-Hage's Nairobi home intruded upon his privacy. The intrusion was minimized by the fact that the search was not covert; indeed, U.S. agents searched El-Hage's home with the assistance of Kenyan authorities, pursuant to what was identified as a "Kenyan warrant authorizing [a search]." *Bin Laden*, 126 F. Supp. 2d at 269. The search occurred during the daytime, *id.* at 285, and in the presence of El-Hage's wife, *id.* at 269. At the conclusion of the search, an inventory listing the items seized during the search was prepared and given to El-Hage's wife. *Id.* at 269. In addition, the District Court found that "[t]he scope of the search was limited to those items which were believed to have foreign intelligence value[,] and retention and dissemination of the evidence acquired during the search were minimized." *Id.* at 285.

As described above, U.S. intelligence officers became aware of al Qaeda's presence in Kenya in the spring of 1996. *Id.* at 268-69. At about that time, they identified five telephone lines used by suspected al Qaeda associates, one of which was located in the same building as El-Hage's Nairobi home; another was a cellular phone used by El-Hage. *Id.* After these telephone lines had been monitored for several months, the Attorney General of the United States authorized surveillance specifically targeting El-Hage. *Id.* That authorization was renewed four months later, and, one month after that, U.S. agents searched El-Hage's home in Nairobi. *Id.* This sequence of events is indicative of a disciplined approach to gathering indisputably vital intelligence on the activities of a foreign terrorist organization. U.S. agents did not breach the privacy of El-Hage's home on a whim or on the basis of an unsubstantiated tip; rather, they monitored telephonic communications involving him for nearly a year and conducted surveillance of his activities for five months before concluding that it was necessary to search his home. In light of these findings of fact, which El-Hage has not contested as clearly erroneous, we conclude that the search, while undoubtedly intrusive on El-Hage's privacy, was restrained in execution and narrow in focus.

Balanced against this restrained and limited intrusion on El-Hage's privacy, we have the government's manifest need to investigate possible threats to national security. As the District Court noted, al Qaeda "declared a war of terrorism against all members of the United States military worldwide" in 1996 and later against American civilians. *Id.* at 269. The government had evidence establishing that El-Hage was working with al Qaeda in Kenya. *Id.* On the basis of these findings of fact, we agree with the District Court that, at the time of the search of El-Hage's home, the government had a powerful need to gather additional intelligence on al Qaeda's activities in Kenya, which it had linked to El-Hage.

Balancing the search's limited intrusion on El-Hage's privacy against the manifest need of the government to monitor the activities of al Qaeda, which had been connected to El-Hage through a year of surveillance, we hold that the search of El-Hage's Nairobi residence was reasonable under the Fourth Amendment.

b. The Surveillance of El-Hage's Kenyan Telephone Lines Was Also Reasonable.

El-Hage appears to challenge the reasonableness of the electronic surveillance of the Kenyan telephone lines on the grounds that (1) they were overbroad, encompassing calls made for commercial, family or social purposes and (2) the government failed to follow procedures to "minimize" surveillance. Indeed, pursuant to defense counsel's analysis, "as many as 25 percent of the calls were either made by, or to" a Nairobi businessman not alleged to have been associated with al Qaeda. El-Hage also criticizes the government for retaining transcripts of irrelevant calls — such as conversations between El-Hage and his wife about their children — despite the government's assurance to the District Court that the surveillance had been properly "minimized." *See United States v. Ruggiero*, 928 F.2d 1289, 1302 (2d Cir. 1991) ("[A]ny [electronic] interception 'shall be conducted in such a way as to minimize the interception of communications not otherwise subject to interception.'" (quoting 18 U.S.C. §2518(5))).

It cannot be denied that El-Hage suffered, while abroad, a significant invasion of privacy by virtue of the government's year-long surveillance of his telephonic communications. The Supreme Court has recognized that, like a physical search, electronic monitoring intrudes on "the innermost secrets of one's home or office" and that "[f]ew threats to liberty exist which are greater than that posed by the use of eavesdropping devices." *Berger v. New York*, 388 U.S. 41, 63 (1967); *cf. Katz v. United States*, 389 U.S. 347, 352-54 (1967). For its part, the government does not contradict El-Hage's claims that the surveillance was broad and loosely "minimized." Instead, the government sets forth a variety of reasons justifying the breadth of the surveillance. These justifications, regardless of their merit, do not lessen the intrusion El-Hage suffered while abroad, and we accord this intrusion substantial weight in our balancing analysis.

Turning to the government's interest, we encounter again the self-evident need to investigate threats to national security presented by foreign terrorist organizations. When U.S. intelligence learned that five telephone lines were being used by suspected al Qaeda operatives, the need to monitor communications traveling on those lines was paramount, and we are loath to discount — much less disparage — the government's decision to do so.

Our balancing of these compelling, and competing, interests turns on whether the scope of the intrusion here was justified by the government's surveillance needs. We conclude that it was, for at least the following four reasons.

First, complex, wide-ranging, and decentralized organizations, such as al Qaeda, warrant sustained and intense monitoring in order to understand their features and identify their members. *See In re Sealed Case No. 02-001*, 310 F.3d 717, 740-41 (Foreign Int. Surv. Ct. Rev. 2002) ("Less minimization in the acquisition stage may well be justified to the extent . . . 'the investigation is focusing on what is thought to be a widespread conspiracy[,] [where] more extensive surveillance may be justified in an attempt to determine the precise scope of the enterprise.'" (quoting *Scott v. United States*, 436 U.S. 128, 140 (1978) (alteration in original))).

Second, foreign intelligence gathering of the sort considered here must delve into the superficially mundane because it is not always readily apparent what information is relevant. *Cf. United States v. Rahman*, 861 F. Supp. 2d 247, 252-53 (S.D.N.Y. 1994) (recognizing the "argument that when the purpose of surveillance is to gather intelligence about international terrorism, greater flexibility in acquiring and storing information is necessary, because innocent-sounding conversations may later prove to be highly significant, and because individual items of information, not apparently significant when taken in isolation, may become highly significant when considered together over time").

Third, members of covert terrorist organizations, as with other sophisticated criminal enterprises, often communicate in code, or at least through ambiguous language. *See, e.g., United States v. Salameh*, 152 F.3d 88, 108 (2d Cir. 1998) ("Because Ajaj was in jail and his telephone calls were monitored, Ajaj and Yousef spoke in code when discussing the bomb plot."). Hence, more extensive and careful monitoring of these communications may be necessary.

Fourth, because the monitored conversations were conducted in foreign languages, the task of determining relevance and identifying coded language was further complicated.

Because the surveillance of suspected al Qaeda operatives must be sustained and thorough in order to be effective, we cannot conclude that the scope of the government's electronic surveillance was overbroad. While the intrusion on El-Hage's privacy was great, the need for the government to so intrude was even greater. Accordingly, the electronic surveillance, like the search of El-Hage's Nairobi residence, was reasonable under the Fourth Amendment.

In sum, because the searches at issue on this appeal were reasonable, they comport with the applicable requirement of the Fourth Amendment and, therefore, El-Hage's motion to suppress the evidence resulting from those searches was properly denied by the District Court.

III. CONCLUSION . . .

For these reasons, and for those set forth in *In re Terrorist Bombings of U.S. Embassies in East Africa*, [552 F.3d 177] (2d Cir. 2008), the judgment of conviction entered by the District Court against El-Hage is **AFFIRMED** in all respects except that the sentence is **VACATED**, and the case is **REMANDED** to the District Court for the sole purpose of resentencing El-Hage as directed in *In re Terrorist Bombings of U.S. Embassies in East Africa*, [552 F.3d 93] (2d Cir. 2008).

NOTES AND QUESTIONS

1. *Foreign Intelligence Exception?* The District Court in El-Hage's case found a foreign intelligence exception to the Fourth Amendment's warrant requirement. Why did the Court of Appeals not base its decision on such an exception? Isn't foreign intelligence collection always a "significant purpose" of any overseas surveillance of suspected terrorists, as that term was used in *In re Sealed Case, supra* p. 600? Suppose several of El-Hage's at-large associates were secretly indicted with him, and surveillance of them continued until they were apprehended. Would the fruits of that surveillance also fall within the foreign intelligence exception?

2. *Warrants for Searches Abroad?* The court in *In re Terrorist Bombings* recalled its own declaration in an earlier case that it was "well settled" that "the Bill of Rights has extraterritorial application to the conduct abroad of federal agents directed against

United States citizens." *United States v. Toscanino*, 500 F.2d 267, 280-81 (2d Cir. 1974). Yet its application of the Fourth Amendment, omitting the warrant requirement, reflects Justice Harlan's pragmatism more than Justice Black's absolutism in *Reid v. Covert*. What practical considerations prompted the court to suspend this requirement?

Do you think a judicial warrant should be required for a foreign search? If so, how would you address the practical concerns described by the court? *See* Justin M. Sandberg, Comment, *The Need for Warrants Authorizing Foreign Intelligence Searches of American Citizens Abroad: A Call for Formalism*, 69 U. Chi. L. Rev. 403 (2002) (urging judicial creation of warrant requirement); Carrie Truehart, Comment, *United States v. Bin Laden and the Foreign Intelligence Exception to the Warrant Requirement for Searches of "United States Persons" Abroad*, 82 B.U. L. Rev. 555 (2002) (urging statutory implementation of asserted constitutional warrant requirement).

The USA Patriot Act, enacted shortly after the September 11, 2001, terrorist attacks, authorizes a federal magistrate "in any district in which activities related to terrorism may have occurred" to issue a warrant for a search of property or a person "within or outside the district." Pub. L. No. 107-56, §219, 115 Stat. 272, 291 (2001). Should this provision be interpreted to require judicial authorization for searches abroad?

3. *Reasonableness of Searches Abroad.* The *In re Terrorist Bombings* court held that even though the warrant requirement is inapplicable, searches of U.S. citizens conducted abroad still must be reasonable. How does the court test for reasonableness? Was its test for the physical search of El-Hage's home different from that for the tap on his telephone? Can you derive a general test from its analysis?

In *United States v. Barona*, 56 F.3d 1087 (9th Cir. 1995), a divided court came up with different tests for reasonableness of warrantless surveillance of U.S. citizens abroad in a drug-smuggling investigation. The majority looked to good faith compliance with the law of the foreign country where the surveillance was conducted, absent conduct that shocks the conscience. *Id.* at 1103. In fact, the United States has entered into a growing number of bilateral mutual legal assistance treaties (MLATs), which independently require U.S. officials operating abroad to comply with the law of the foreign state. *See, e.g.,* Treaty Between the United States and the Government of Mexico on Mutual Legal Assistance in Criminal Matters, Dec. 9, 1987, U.S.-Mex., art. 12, 1987 U.S.T. LEXIS 208 ("A request for search, seizure, and delivery of any object acquired thereby to the requesting State shall be executed if it includes the information justifying such action *under the laws of the requested Party*.") (emphasis supplied). Such treaties confer no private rights, but their very existence may support the *Barona* court's incorporation of a compliance-with-foreign-law requirement into the Fourth Amendment's reasonableness standard. (They also create formal methods for U.S. law enforcement authorities to obtain help with investigations abroad.)

Judge Reinhardt dissented vigorously. Under the majority's reasoning, he argued, Americans are not only relegated to the "vagaries of foreign law," they are given

> *even less* protection than foreign law since . . . the Constitution does not even require foreign officials to comply with their own law; all that is required is that American officials have a good faith belief that they did so. . . . [W]hen Americans enter Iraq, Iran, Singapore, Kuwait, China, or other similarly inclined foreign lands, they can be treated by the

United States government exactly the way those foreign nations treat their own citizens—at least for Fourth Amendment purposes. [56 F.3d at 1101.]

Instead, Judge Reinhardt argued, the government still must have probable cause for a foreign search, even if a warrant is impractical. On a motion to suppress, a court would make a post hoc determination of probable cause based on the government's explanation of why it initiated the search. "Because judicial scrutiny of the search will always take place *after* it has been conducted, there is no conceivable way that imposing such a requirement would hinder law enforcement efforts abroad—except to the extent that those efforts violate our own Constitution." *Id.* at 1102.

In determining the reasonableness of requiring a judicial warrant in domestic terrorism investigations, the Supreme Court in *United States v. United States District Court (Keith)*, 407 U.S. 297 (1972), *supra* p. 559, expressed concern that "unreviewed executive discretion may yield too readily to pressures to obtain incriminating evidence and overlook potential invasions of privacy and protected speech." 407 U.S. at 317. How did the *In re Terrorist Bombings* court address this concern? The *Barona* court?

4. *The Silver Platter Doctrine.* Suppose the Kenyan police *alone* had conducted the warrantless surveillance of El-Hage without probable cause and in flagrant violation of their own laws. Should a U.S. court suppress the fruits of such a foreign police surveillance? With two exceptions noted below, the courts have uniformly held no. *See, e.g., United States v. Defreitas*, 701 F. Supp. 2d 297, 304-305 (E.D.N.Y. 2010). Because the Bill of Rights does not protect Americans from the acts of foreign sovereigns and because applying the exclusionary rule to such acts would not deter them, such evidence can be turned over to U.S. law enforcement officials on a "silver platter" and admitted in U.S. criminal prosecutions. *See generally* Eric Bentley, *Toward an International Fourth Amendment: Rethinking Searches and Seizures After Verdugo-Urquidez*, 27 Vand. J. Transnat'l L. 329, 374-375 (1994); Robert L. King, *The International Silver Platter and the "Shocks the Conscience" Test: U.S. Law Enforcement Overseas*, 67 Wash. U. L.Q. 489, 511 (1989).

5. *The Joint Venture Exception.* Courts have recognized an exception to the silver platter doctrine for searches that are "joint ventures" between U.S. and foreign officials. Unfortunately, the courts have not reached a consensus on what constitutes a joint venture. Most agree that merely providing a tip to foreign police will not trigger the protections of the Fourth Amendment, and many hold that U.S. agents may request, be present during, or even participate in a search as long as they did not initiate and control it. *See* Bentley, *supra*, at 400 nn.297-314; Koff, *supra* p. 718, at 492 n.19. The *Restatement* declares, unhelpfully, that the exclusionary rule applies only when "the participation of United States law enforcement officers in the investigation, arrest, search, or interrogation through which the evidence was obtained was so substantial as to render the action that of the United States." *Restatement (Third) of Foreign Relations Law of the United States* §433(3) (1987). The Second Circuit has cut its own path by asking whether foreign police are acting as agents of the United States or whether U.S. law enforcement agents are evading our law by using foreign police. *See United States v. Maturo*, 982 F.2d 57, 61 (2d Cir. 1992). Apparently, U.S. participation in the Kenyan search was so substantial that the government did not contest responsibility.

6. *The Shocks-the-Conscience Exception.* A second exception to the silver platter doctrine exists for conduct that shocks the judicial conscience. It was articulated in *United States v. Toscanino*, 500 F.2d 267 (2d Cir. 1974), a forcible abduction case, and applied in *United States v. Fernandez-Caro*, 677 F. Supp. 893 (S.D. Tex. 1987), in which Mexican authorities "threatened to kill [the defendant], beat him about the face and body, poured water through his nostrils while he was stripped, bound, and gagged, and applied electrical shocks to his wet body, among other things." *Id.* at 894. Exclusion of a forced confession is "not based on our Fourth Amendment jurisprudence," said the majority in *Barona*, "but rather on the recognition that we may employ our supervisory powers when absolutely necessary to preserve the integrity of the criminal justice system." 56 F.3d at 1091. Such evidence may be excluded even when obtained by foreign officials not acting as agents of the United States. *Maturo, supra,* 982 F.2d at 60-61.

The joint venture and shocks-the-conscience exceptions to the silver platter doctrine are explored further in Chapter 33, where we consider the U.S. practice of rendering terrorist suspects to a third country for interrogation (and likely harsh treatment) by that country's police or intelligence officials.

7. *Statutory Authorization of Collection Abroad.* Six years after *Verdugo,* Congress authorized elements of the intelligence community (excluding the military service branches) to collect information outside the United States against non-U.S. persons at the request of law enforcement agencies, "notwithstanding that the law enforcement agency intends to use the information collected for purposes of a law enforcement investigation or counterintelligence investigation." 50 U.S.C. §403-5a(a) (2006).

In the FISA Amendments Act of 2008, Pub. L. No. 110-261, 122 Stat. 2436 (adding 50 U.S.C. §§1881-1885c (Supp. III 2009)), Congress authorized the Attorney General and the Director of National Intelligence, acting jointly, to approve the programmatic targeting of "persons reasonably believed to be located outside the United States to acquire foreign intelligence information." 50 U.S.C. §1881a. The measure responds to a dramatic increase in communications using the Internet and fiber-optic cable and to greater concern about the threat of international terrorism after 9/11. Once the Foreign Intelligence Surveillance Court approves a program for collection, based on assurances that a "significant purpose" of any acquisition is to obtain foreign intelligence information and that the usual FISA minimization procedures will be followed, intelligence agencies like the NSA may monitor and collect electronic data—e-mail and telephone calls, for example—on a wholesale basis, without an individualized judicial order normally required for the targeting of any particular person. The collected data are then apparently mined, using key-word and pattern-recognition algorithms, for whatever information might be of interest. The FISA Amendments Act also authorized for the first time collections inside the United States of electronic data about U.S. persons located abroad, 50 U.S.C. §1881b, and collections abroad against U.S. persons. *Id.* §1881c. In these latter two instances the FISC must approve the collection on an individualized basis, applying generally the same standards that it does for domestic targets. The 2008 legislation is analyzed in greater detail *supra* pp. 619-632. *See* William C. Banks, *Programmatic Surveillance and FISA: Of Needles and Haystacks,* 88 Tex. L. Rev. 1633 (2010).

Applying the lessons learned in this chapter, do you think these two measures satisfy the requirements of the Fourth Amendment? Specifically, will information collected following the statutory procedures described here be admissible as evidence in a criminal trial? Will a targeted individual be successful in a *Bivens* claim asserting that the collection violated her privacy rights?

V
Detaining Terrorist Suspects

Preventive Detention by Civil Authorities

The FBI began investigating the September 11 terrorist attacks (dubbed the PENTTBOM investigation) even before the last plane crashed.[1] But it was not only trying to identify, apprehend, and convict the perpetrators in the time-honored fashion of criminal investigations. Assistant Attorney General Michael Chertoff explained:

> In past terrorist investigations, you usually had a defined event and you're investigating it after the fact. That's not what we had here.... From the start, there was every reason to believe that there is more to come.... So we thought that we were getting information to prevent more attacks, which was even more important than trying any case that came out of the attacks. [*Quoted in* Toobin, *infra* n.1.]

The FBI immediately checked passenger manifests, airport terminal and parking garage videotapes, car rental agreements, credit card receipts, telephone records, and numerous other data sources to help identify the hijackers. It then extended its investigation to persons who lived or worked with the hijackers or otherwise crossed paths with them. Most of those interviewed were foreign nationals.

The FBI itself detained some or had state and local authorities detain them on suspicion of committing a variety of minor crimes. In addition, the FBI detained a few persons as "material witnesses." The Bureau asked the INS to detain many others who were in technical violation of their immigration status (out-of-status immigrants). In January 2002, the government initiated the "Absconder Apprehension Initiative" to locate and deport 6,000 Arabs and Muslims with outstanding deportation orders (among more than 300,000 foreign nationals subject to similar orders). By May 2003,

---

1. Background for this brief history was drawn from The Constitution Project, *Report on Post-9/11 Detentions* (June 2, 2004); Amnesty Int'l, *United States of America: Amnesty International's Concerns Regarding Post September 11 Detentions in the USA* (AMR 51/044/2002), Mar. 14, 2002; Jeffrey Rosen, *Holding Pattern,* New Republic, Dec. 10, 2001; *Hearing on DOJ Oversight: Preserving Our Freedom While Defending Against Terrorism, Before the S. Comm. on the Judiciary,* 107th Cong. (2001) (statements of John Ashcroft, Attorney General, and Michael Chertoff, Assistant Attorney General); Dan Eggen, *Many Held on Tenuous Ties to Sept. 11,* Wash. Post, Nov. 29, 2001; Department of Justice, *Attorney General Ashcroft Provides Total Number of Federal Criminal Charges and INS Detainees* (Nov. 27, 2001); Jeffrey Toobin, *Crackdown,* New Yorker, Nov. 5, 2001, at 56; Amy Goldstein, *A Deliberate Strategy of Disruption; Massive, Secretive Detention Effort Aimed Mainly at Preventing More Terror,* Wash. Post, Nov. 4, 2001.

another 2,747 noncitizens had been detained as part of a special registration program directed at Arabs and Muslims.

"We're clearly not standing on ceremony, and if there is a basis to hold them we're going to hold them," Chertoff said in reference to the detentions. *Id.* Attorney General John Ashcroft was even more blunt: "We have waged a deliberate campaign of arrest and detention to remove suspected terrorists who violate the law from our streets." *Hearing on DOJ Oversight, supra* note 1.

Within weeks of the 9/11 attacks, the media reported that more than 1,100 persons had been or were being detained by law enforcement authorities. Although the government declined to release a breakdown of this number, a newspaper investigation of 235 detainees whom it could identify indicated that the largest number were from Egypt, Saudi Arabia, and Pakistan. By the end of November, federal criminal charges had been brought against 104 individuals (most relating to possession of false identification or other fraud), of whom 55 were then in custody, while the INS had detained 548 persons for immigration violations.

This chapter explores the legality of detentions by civil authorities of suspected terrorists and persons with possible knowledge about terrorists in the wake of 9/11. We start in Part A by exploring the constitutional framework for arrest and detention, and the absence in U.S. law of a general statutory authority for preventive detention—detention to prevent a future harm or minimize the risk of harm. In Part B, we consider essentially pretextual criminal arrests and detention for "spitting on the sidewalk"—minor crimes—of persons suspected of some connection to or having information about terrorism. In Part C, we turn to the detention and removal of "high interest" (also called "special interest") immigrants, those suspected of being involved in terrorism or having information about terrorism. In Part D, we explore statutory authority for "investigatory detention" of "material witnesses" and how it was used or abused in the PENTTBOM investigation. Succeeding chapters deal with detention by the military before and after 9/11 of persons viewed as threatening national security.

A. CONSTITUTIONAL BASIS FOR PREVENTIVE DETENTION

One scholar has described circumstances in which the government might want to detain a suspected terrorist but is not ready "to file charges in open court as required for a criminal prosecution."

> The government may have learned of the individual from a confidential or foreign-government source that it cannot publicly disclose, or from an ongoing investigation. It may lack sufficient evidence to convict beyond a reasonable doubt, but have substantial grounds to believe that the individual was actively engaged in armed conflict for al Qaeda. The disclosures necessary for a public trial might seriously compromise the military struggle against the Taliban and al Qaeda. U.S. law has no formal statutory mechanism by which the government could detain such a person. [David Cole, *Out of the Shadows: Preventive Detention, Suspected Terrorists, and War*, 97 Cal. L. Rev. 693 (2009).]

Civil detention of persons who have not been convicted of a crime has been found reasonable for criminal arrestees who are flight risks or dangers to the community, aliens facing deportation, the mentally ill when they pose a danger, sexual offenders even after they have completed their sentences, people with communicable diseases (see Chapter 37), and various persons (drunks, addicts, and the homeless) for their own protection. *See* Adam Klein & Benjamin Wittes, *Preventive Detention in American Theory and Practice*, 2 Harv. Nat'l Sec. J. 85 (2011) (exploring each kind of existing detention authority). Some scholars have therefore argued that the presumption against preventive detention is a "civic myth," *id.* at 87, and others agree that "[p]reventive detention is in fact an established part of U.S. law." Cole, *supra*, at 695.

The relevant law is largely framed by the Fourth Amendment, which insists on "[t]he right of the people to be secure in their persons . . . against unreasonable . . . seizures," and which provides that no arrest warrants shall issue except upon probable cause. Since there is no probable cause (as that term is used in the Fourth Amendment) to believe that a preventive detainee has committed or is committing a crime, the detention must be reasonable in the circumstances. If the detainee is a U.S. citizen, the "Non-Detention Act," 18 U.S.C. §4001(a) (2006), provides, "No citizen shall be imprisoned or otherwise detained by the United States except pursuant to an Act of Congress." Civil detention of U.S. citizens thus appears to require explicit statutory authority.

In fact, none of the preventive detentions described here was said to be based on a naked exercise of executive power. *See* Stephanie Cooper Blum, *Preventive Detention in the War on Terror: A Comparison of How the United States, Britain, and Israel Detain and Incapacitate Terrorist Suspects*, Homeland Sec. Aff., Oct. 2008, at 1 (contrasting Israel's and Britain's preventive detention laws enacted by Parliament and "not just executive usurpations of power").

Moreover, there are strong reasons to be skeptical of preventive detention.

> First, preventive detention rests on a prediction about future behavior, and no one can predict the future. Decision makers all too often fall back on stereotypes and prejudices as proxies for dangerousness. . . . Second, the risk of unnecessarily detaining innocent people is high, because decision makers are likely to err on the side of detention. . . . Third, preventive detention is inconsistent with basic notions of human autonomy and free will. We generally presume that individuals have a choice to conform their conduct to the law. Thus, we do not criminalize thought or intentions, but only actions. . . . Thus, . . . [w]hile it is not always explicitly rationalized in such terms, constitutional doctrine governing preventive detention is best understood as reflecting a strong presumption that the criminal process is the preferred means for addressing socially dangerous behavior. [Cole, *supra*, at 696-697.]

NOTES AND QUESTIONS

1. *The Constitutional Standards for Detention.* Generally, the Fourth Amendment requires that police, before making an arrest, have probable cause to believe that a suspect has committed a crime. However, they are allowed to stop a person when there is an "articulable suspicion that the person has been, is, or is about to be engaged in criminal activity." *United States v. Place*, 462 U.S. 696, 702 (1983). *See Terry v. Ohio*, 392 U.S. 1, 9 (1968). Nevertheless, "reasonable suspicion of criminal activity," short of probable cause, only "warrants a temporary seizure for the purpose of questioning limited to the purpose of the stop." *Florida v. Royer*, 460 U.S. 491, 498 (1983).

The INS may stop and detain persons for questioning about their citizenship upon a *reasonable suspicion* that they are illegal aliens. *United States v. Brignoni-Ponce*, 422 U.S. 873, 882-883 (1975). Congress has authorized the arrest and detention of such aliens pending a decision about their removal. 8 U.S.C. §1226 (2006). But the Supreme Court has ruled that after a decision to remove, continued indefinite detention would present a serious due process issue, at least as to aliens already in the country, who enjoy Fifth Amendment protection. *Zadvydas v. Davis*, 533 U.S. 678 (2001).

Zadvydas, however, did not involve an alien suspected of terrorism. The Court emphasized that the detention there at issue "d[id] not apply narrowly to 'a small segment of particularly dangerous individuals,' say suspected terrorists." *Id.* at 691 (quoting *Kansas v. Hendricks*, 521 U.S. 346, 368 (1997) (involving preventive detention of convicted sexual predator until he is no longer dangerous)). "Neither do we consider terrorism or other special circumstances," it added, "where special arguments might be made for forms of preventive detention and for heightened deference to the judgments of the political branches with respect to matters of national security." *Zadvydas, supra*, 533 U.S. at 696.

Is the Court suggesting a "national security exception" to the Fifth Amendment guarantee of due process? In the same vein, could there be such an exception to the Fourth Amendment's protection against unreasonable seizure? (Recall that, before enactment of the Foreign Intelligence Surveillance Act (FISA) in 1978, some lower courts found a national security exception to the warrant requirement for some kinds of searches and electronic surveillance. See *supra* pp. 568-579.) How would you define such an exception? What limitations, if any, would the Fourth or Fifth Amendment place on the preventive detention of suspected alien terrorists in the United States?

2. *Due Process Requirements for Statutory Detention.* In *Denmore v. Hyung Joon Kim*, 538 U.S. 510 (2003), Justice Souter summarized the due process requirements for preventive detention as follows:

> [D]ue process requires a "special justification" for physical detention that "outweighs the individual's constitutionally protected interest in avoiding physical restraint" as well as "adequate procedural protections." "There must be a 'sufficiently compelling' governmental interest to justify such an action, usually a punitive interest in imprisoning the convicted criminal or a regulatory interest in forestalling danger to the community." The class of persons subject to confinement must be commensurately narrow and the duration of confinement limited accordingly. . . . Finally, procedural due process requires, at a minimum, that a detainee have the benefit of an impartial decisionmaker able to consider particular circumstances on the issue of necessity. [*Id.* at 557 (Souter, J., concurring in part and dissenting in part).]

Compare Klein & Wittes, *supra*, at 89 (arguing for "a relatively simply test" for counterterrorism detention: "Does America really need to do it, and if so, how can it do it in a fashion that minimizes erroneous incarcerations?"); Ian S. Speir, *Detention as Seizure: Deriving a Constitutional Infrastructure for U.S. Detention Policy* (Oct. 16, 2009), *available at* http://ssrn.com/abstract=1444928 (arguing that Fourth Amendment "constitutional infrastructure" consists of reasonableness, proportionality, and judicial review).

Applying similar standards in *United States v. Salerno*, 481 U.S. 739 (1987), a divided Supreme Court upheld the provisions of §3142(e) of the Bail Reform Act of 1984, 18 U.S.C. §§3141-3150, 3156 (2006 & Supp. III 2009), which authorized preventive detention (denial of bail) of arrestees on the grounds of flight risk or future dangerousness. The majority found that the Act authorized a "regulatory," rather than punitive, detention that was reasonably related to compelling government interests. The Court noted that regulatory interests in community safety can outweigh an individual's liberty interest, "[f]or example, in times of war and insurrection." *Salerno*, 481 U.S. at 748. But the Court emphasized that the Bail Reform Act authorized detention of an arrestee only when: (a) he has been arrested and indicted on probable cause of having committed one or more specified extremely dangerous offenses, (b) a court conducts a full-blown adversary hearing on the denial of bail, at which the arrestee is entitled to be represented by his own counsel, (c) the government persuades the court by clear and convincing evidence that no conditions of release can assure the presence of the arrestee or the safety of the community, and (d) the arrestee is given a right of appeal from the court's decision.

Did the post–September 11 detentions described above satisfy the Court's due process standards? Even if they did, does the Bail Reform Act occupy the field of preventive detention (leaving aside immigration detentions)?

3. *Cold War Detentions and the Non-Detention Act.* In 1950, Congress passed, over President Truman's veto, the Emergency Detention Act. Pub. L. No. 81-831, 64 Stat. 1019. Following a lengthy litany of the dangers of a "world communist movement," it authorized the President to declare an "Internal Security Emergency" in the event of an invasion, declaration of war by Congress, or "Insurrection within the United States in aid of a foreign enemy." *Id.* §102(a). In such an emergency, the President, acting through the Attorney General, was empowered to "apprehend and by order detain . . . each person as to whom there is reasonable ground to believe that such person probably will engage in, or probably will conspire with others to engage in, acts of espionage or of sabotage." *Id.* §103(a). The Justice Department constructed a half-dozen detention "camps" around the country pursuant to the Act, and during the Vietnam era it was suggested that war protests might be regarded for purposes of the Act as an "Insurrection within the United States in aid of a foreign enemy." *See* Alan M. Dershowitz, *The Role of Law During Times of Crisis: Would Liberty Be Suspended?*, in *Civil Disorder and Violence* 140-141 (Harry M. Cloor ed., 1972).

The Act was repealed unused by Pub. L. No. 92-129, 85 Stat. 348 (1971). The legislative history of the repealer cites First and Fifth Amendment violations and declares that "the concentration camp implications of the legislation render it abhorrent." H.R. Rep. No. 92-116, at 4 (1971), *reprinted in* 1971 U.S.C.C.A.N. 1438. But does the threat of further terrorist attacks after September 11, 2001, justify reenactment of the measure or one like it, permitting preventive detention of citizens and noncitizens alike as a counterterrorist measure? *See* Thomas F. Powers, *When to Hold 'Em*, Legal Aff. (Sept./Oct. 2004) (yes).

At the same time that it repealed the Emergency Detention Act, Congress adopted the Non-Detention Act, 18 U.S.C. §4001(a) (2006), set forth above. Does this Act apply to the detention of suspected terrorists? *See* Louis Fisher, *Detention of U.S. Citizens* (Cong. Res. Serv. RS22130), Apr. 28, 2005 (concluding from legislative history of the Non-Detention Act that Congress "intended the statutory language to restrict all detentions by the executive branch, not merely those by the Attorney General"). *See also Howe v. Smith*, 452 U.S. 473, 479 n.3 (1981) (the Act proscribes "detention of *any kind* by the United States, absent a congressional grant of authority to detain") (emphasis in original). Application of the Non-Detention Act was considered in *Hamdi v. Rumsfeld*, 542 U.S. 507 (2004) (*infra* p. 831).

B. "SPITTING ON THE SIDEWALK" — PRETEXTUAL(?) CRIMINAL DETENTION

Explaining the PENTTBOM detentions, Attorney General Ashcroft likened some of the arrests for minor crimes to Attorney General Robert Kennedy's policy of "arrest[ing] mobsters [for] spitting on the sidewalk if it would help in the battle against organized crime." Goldstein, *supra* p. 733 n.1. Identity fraud, credit card fraud, forgery, and larceny were among the criminal charges brought against some of the detainees. Prosecution of suspected terrorists for crimes directly related to acts of terrorism is addressed in Chapters 35 and 36.

NOTES AND QUESTIONS

1. *Pretextual?* A terror suspect who is arrested for "spitting on the sidewalk" has been arrested on a pretext: the government's real reason for the arrest is that it suspects he will commit a terrorist act or knows information about a planned future act. Is a pretextual arrest lawful? The Supreme Court said yes in *Whren v. United States*, 517 U.S. 806, 813 (1996), as long as there is objective probable cause for the actual arrest: "[s]ubjective intent [to detain the arrestee for terrorism-related conduct or information] . . . does not make otherwise lawful conduct [the arrest] unlawful or unconstitutional."

2. *The Practical Problem.* One difficulty with the spitting-on-the-sidewalk policy is that persons charged with such minor offenses are usually released on bail. Indeed, even *conviction* on such a charge often yields no term of imprisonment. Rising to the occasion, however, one federal magistrate denied bail for an immigrant from El Salvador who had allegedly helped some of the September 11 hijackers obtain false identity papers (apparently without knowing that they were terrorists), explaining that "[o]ne of the unspoken issues today is, after the events of September 11, is it going to be business as usual? I suspect not. The defendant, either wittingly or unwittingly, certainly contributed [to the attacks]." T.R. Reid & Allen Lengel, *Scotland Yard Says Hijackers May Have Trained in Britain; Terror Suspects Arrested in Spain, Holland*, Wash. Post, Sept. 27, 2001.

3. *PENTTBOM Convictions.* In mid-2005, the Bush administration asserted that terrorism investigations had resulted in charges against more than 400 suspects, half of whom were convicted. A *Washington Post* study of the Department of Justice's own list of prosecutions, however, indicated that only 39 of these convictions were for crimes related to terrorism or national security. Dan Eggen & Julie Tate, *U.S. Campaign Produces Few Convictions on Terrorism Charges*, Wash. Post, June 12, 2005. The majority were for minor crimes such as fraud, making false statements, and passport violations, for which the median sentence was just 11 months.

The Justice Department defended the numbers by arguing that many defendants were prosecuted for such crimes in exchange for nonpublic information that was valuable in other terrorism probes. *Id.* The former Associate Attorney General who headed the Office of Legal Policy had an additional explanation: "You're talking about a violation of law that may or may not rise to the level of what might usually be called a federal case. But the calculation does not happen in isolation; you are not just talking about the [minor] crime itself, but the suspicion of terrorism.... That skews the calculation in favor of prosecution." *Id.* (quoting Viet D. Dinh). In other words, the *Post* paraphrased, "the primary strategy is to use 'prosecutorial discretion' to detain suspicious individuals by charging them with minor crimes." *Id.* Replied a defense attorney, "That's fine if you take it as a given that you have the devil here," citing Al Capone (who was eventually prosecuted for income tax evasion) as an example, but "[t]he problem is . . . that you're going to make mistakes and you're going to hurt innocent people." *Id.*

C.   DETENTION OF "HIGH INTEREST" OR "SPECIAL INTEREST" IMMIGRANTS

The largest number of persons detained in the PENTTBOM investigation were immigrants arrested for visa violations. The Department of Justice adopted a "hold until cleared" policy for such detainees. An affidavit of an FBI agent opposing an immigrant detainee's bond request helps explain the process. Following the affidavit, a report of the Inspector General (IG) of the Department of Justice describes the "hold until cleared" policy and the conditions of detention for many of those detained. Detainees eventually challenged the policy and conditions of confinement in the case that follows the IG Report.

Affidavit of Michael E. Rolince, U.S. Dep't of Justice, Exec. Office for Immigration Review, Immigration Court

reprinted in Human Rights Watch, *Presumption of Guilt: Human Rights Abuses of Post-September 11 Detainees* app. B (Aug. 2002) *available at* http://www.hrw.org/reports/2002/us911/USA0802.pdf

In Bond Proceedings
RE: ALI ABUBAKR ALI AL-MAQTARI

Pursuant to 28 U.S.C. §1736, I, Michael E. Rolince, hereby declare as follows:

1. I have been employed by the Federal Bureau of Investigation (FBI) since September 1974 as a Special Agent, and since August 1998, I have been the Section Chief of the Counterterrorism Division's International Terrorism Operations Section (ITOS) at FBI Headquarters in Washington D.C....

3. As the ITOS Section Chief, I am personally involved in and have significant supervisory responsibilities for the nationwide FBI investigation initiated in response to a series of deadly terrorist attacks which occurred on September 11,

2001. As such, I am privy both to the broad scope of and to particular details from the investigation. . . .

5. The FBI has identified nineteen suspected hijackers, some of whose legal immigration status had expired. Based on a review of intelligence and other source information, the FBI has reason to believe that the hijackers were associated with al Qaeda, aka "the Base," an international network of terrorist cells controlled by Osama bin Laden, which has been formally designated by the Department of State as a foreign terrorist organization since October 8, 1999. Prior to the September 11, 2001 attacks, Osama bin Laden was being sought by the FBI in connection with the August 7, 1998 bombings of the United States embassies in Dar es Salaam, Tanzania, and Nairobi, Kenya, which killed over 200 individuals.

6. At the direction of President George W. Bush and Attorney General John Ashcroft, the FBI has initiated a nationwide investigation to identify and apprehend individuals involved in the hijackings and to prevent future acts of terrorism within the United States. To date the FBI has received or generated more than 250,000 leads from its web site, special hot line, a toll-free WATTS line, and in the FBI field offices, and additional leads are coming in every day. The investigation has yielded over 300 searches, and more than 100 court orders and 3000 subpoenas. There is still a great deal of information to be collected before the FBI will be in a position to determine the full scope of the terrorist conspiracy and to determine the full extent of damage that the terrorists intended to cause.

7. The FBI has come to believe that associates of the hijackers with connections to foreign terrorist organizations may still be in the United States. The tips received and the leads developed in our field offices have enabled the FBI to identify individuals who may have information about these associates, or, in fact, be among the participants. As explained below, the number of people of interest to the FBI is constantly changing as leads are followed and more information is obtained.

8. Information available to the FBI indicates a potential for additional terrorist incidents. As a result, the FBI has requested that all law enforcement agencies nationwide be on heightened alert. When there is threat information about a specific target, the FBI shares that information with appropriate state and local authorities. Several city and state officials have been contacted over the last few weeks to alert them to potential threats.

9. On September 23, 2001, the FBI issued a nationwide alert based on information indicating the possibility of attacks using crop-dusting aircraft. The FBI assesses the uses of this type of aircraft to distribute chemical or biological weapons of mass destruction as potential threats to Americans. At this point, there is no clear indication of the intended time or place of any such attack. The FBI has confirmed that Mohammed Atta, one of the suspected hijackers, was acquiring knowledge of crop-dusting aircraft prior to the attacks on September 11th. . . .

10. The investigation has also uncovered several individuals, including individuals who may have links to the hijackers, who fraudulently have obtained, or attempted to obtain, licenses to transport hazardous material.

11. In the context of this terrorism investigation, the FBI identified individuals whose activities warranted further inquiry. When such individuals were identified as aliens who were believed to have violated their immigration status, the FBI notified the Immigration and Naturalization Service (INS). The INS detained such aliens under the authority of the Immigration and Nationality Act. At this point, the FBI must consider the possibility that these aliens are somehow linked to, or may possess knowledge useful to the investigation of, the terrorist attacks on the World Trade Center and the Pentagon. The respondent, Ali Abubakr Ali Al-Maqtari (AL-MAQTARI), is one such individual.

12. As a result of a search previously described to the court, the FBI continues to download the hard drive of a computer. (The computer was found in a car belonging to Al-Maqtari's wife.) When interviewed by the FBI, Al-Maqtari said he had not used the laptop but purchased it used for $250 from a customer at the convenience store where he works. Al-Maqtari said that the customer obtained the computer from a third party. At present, the download of the hard drive is still running. Once this process is completed, the FBI will need several days to review the information obtained.

13. The FBI continues to actively pursue this investigation.

14. The business of counterterrorism intelligence gathering in the United States is akin to the construction of a mosaic. At this stage of the investigation, the FBI is gathering and processing thousands of bits and pieces of information that may seem innocuous at first glance. We must analyze all that information, however, to see if it can be fit into a picture that will reveal how the unseen whole operates. The significance of one item of information may frequently depend upon knowledge of many other items of information. What may seem trivial to some may appear of great moment to those within the FBI or the intelligence community who have a broader context within which to consider a questioned item or isolated piece of information. At the present stage of this vast investigation, the FBI is gathering and culling information that may corroborate or diminish our current suspicions of the individuals that have been detained. The Bureau is approaching that task with unprecedented resources and a nationwide urgency. In the meantime, the FBI has been unable to rule out the possibility that respondent is somehow linked to, or possesses knowledge of, the terrorist attacks on the World Trade Center and the Pentagon. To protect the public, the FBI must exhaust all avenues of investigation while ensuring that critical information does not evaporate pending further investigation.

I declare under penalty of perjury that the foregoing is true and correct. Executed on October 11, 2001, in Washington, D.C.

Michael E. Rolince
Federal Bureau of Investigation

Office of the Inspector General, Department of Justice, Press Release, The September 11 Detainees: A Review of theTreatment of Aliens Held on Immigration Charges in Connection with the Investigation of the September 11 Attacks

June 2, 2003, *available at* http://www.usdoj.gov/oig/special/0306/press.pdf

After the September 11 terrorist attacks, the Department of Justice (Department) used federal immigration laws to detain aliens in the United States who were suspected of having ties to the attacks or connections to terrorism, or who were encountered during the course of the Federal Bureau of Investigation's (FBI) investigation into the attacks. In the 11 months after the attacks, 762 aliens were detained in connection with the FBI terrorism investigation for various immigration offenses, including overstaying their visas and entering the country illegally.

The Office of the Inspector General (OIG) examined the treatment of these detainees, including their processing, bond decisions related to them, the timing of their removal from the United States or their release from custody, their access to counsel, and their conditions of confinement. . . .

Among the specific findings in the OIG's report:

Arrest, Charging & Assignment to a Detention Facility

The FBI in New York City made little attempt to distinguish between aliens who were subjects of the FBI terrorism investigation (called "PENTTBOM") and those encountered coincidentally to a PENTTBOM lead. The OIG report concluded that, even in the chaotic aftermath of the September 11 attacks, the FBI should have expended more effort attempting to distinguish between aliens who it actually suspected of having a connection to terrorism from [*sic*] those aliens who, while possibly guilty of violating federal immigration law, had no connection to terrorism but simply were encountered in connection with a PENTTBOM lead.

The INS did not consistently serve the September 11 detainees with notice of the charges under which they were being held within the INS's stated goal of 72 hours. The review found that some detainees did not receive these charging documents (called a "Notice to Appear" or NTA) for more than a month after being arrested. This delay affected the detainees' ability to understand why they were being held, obtain legal counsel, and request a bond hearing. . . .

The Department instituted a policy that all aliens in whom the FBI had an interest in connection with the PENTTBOM investigation required clearance by the FBI of any connection to terrorism before they could be removed or released. Although not communicated in writing, this "hold until cleared" policy was clearly understood and applied throughout the Department. The policy was based on the belief — which turned out to be erroneous — that the FBI's clearance process would proceed quickly. FBI agents responsible for clearance investigations often were assigned other duties and were not able to focus on the detainee cases. The result was that detainees remained in custody — many in extremely restrictive conditions of confinement — for weeks and months with no clearance investigations being conducted. The OIG review found that, instead of taking a few days as anticipated, the FBI clearance process took an average of 80 days, primarily because it was understaffed and not given sufficient priority by the FBI.

Bond and Removal Issues

The Department instituted a "no bond" policy for all September 11 detainees as part of its effort to keep the detainees confined until the FBI could complete its clearance investigations. The OIG review found that the INS raised concerns about this blanket "no bond" policy, particularly when it became clear that the FBI's clearance process was much slower than anticipated and the INS had little information in many individual cases on which to base its continued opposition to bond in immigration hearings. INS officials also were concerned about continuing to hold detainees while the FBI conducted clearance investigations where detainees had received a final removal or voluntary departure order. The OIG review found that the INS and the Department did not timely address conflicting interpretations of federal immigration law about detaining aliens with final orders of removal who wanted and were able to leave the country, but who had not been cleared by the FBI.

In January 2002, when the FBI brought the issue of the extent of the INS's detention authority to the Department's attention, the Department abruptly changed its position as to whether the INS should continue to hold aliens after they had received a final departure or removal order until the FBI had completed the clearance process. After this time, the Department allowed the INS to remove aliens with final orders without FBI clearance. In addition, in many cases the INS failed to review the detainees' custody determination as required by federal regulations.

The FBI's initial assessment of the September 11 detainees' possible connections to terrorism and the slow pace of the clearance process had significant ramifications on the detainees' conditions of confinement. Our review found that 84 September 11 detainees were housed at the MDC [Metropolitan Detention Center] in Brooklyn under highly restrictive conditions. These conditions included "lock down" for at least 23 hours per day; escort procedures that included a "4-man hold" with handcuffs, leg irons, and heavy chains any time the detainees were moved outside their cells; and a limit of one legal telephone call per week and one social call per month.

Among the OIG review's findings regarding the treatment of detainees held at the MDC and Passaic are:

Conditions of Confinement

BOP officials imposed a communications blackout for September 11 detainees immediately after the terrorist attacks that lasted several weeks. After the blackout period ended, the MDC's designation of the September 11 detainees as "Witness Security" inmates frustrated efforts by detainees' attorneys, families, and even law enforcement officials, to determine where the detainees were being held. We found that MDC staff frequently — and mistakenly — told people who inquired about a specific September 11 detainee that the detainee was not held at the facility when, in fact, the opposite was true.

The MDC's restrictive and inconsistent policies on telephone access for detainees prevented some detainees from obtaining legal counsel in a timely manner. Most of the September 11 detainees did not have legal representation prior to their detention at the MDC. Consequently, the policy developed by the MDC that permitted detainees one legal call per week — while complying with broad BOP national standards — severely limited the detainees' ability to obtain and consult with legal counsel. In addition, we found that in many instances MDC staff did not ask detainees if they wanted their one legal call each week. We also found that the list of pro bono attorneys provided to the detainees contained inaccurate and outdated information.

With regard to allegations of abuse at the MDC, the evidence indicates a pattern of physical and verbal abuse by some correctional officers at the MDC against some September 11 detainees, particularly during the first months after the attacks and during intake and movement of prisoners. Although the allegations of abuse have been declined for criminal prosecution, the OIG is continuing to investigate these matters administratively.

The OIG review found that certain conditions of confinement at the MDC were unduly harsh, such as subjecting the September 11 detainees to having two lights illuminated in their cells 24 hours a day for several months longer than necessary, even after electricians rewired the cellblock to allow the lights to be turned off individually. We also found that MDC staff failed to inform MDC detainees in a timely manner about the process for filing formal complaints about their treatment.

By contrast, the OIG review found that the detainees confined at Passaic had much different, and significantly less harsh, experiences than the MDC detainees. According to INS data, Passaic housed 400 September 11 detainees from the date of the terrorist attacks through May 30, 2002, the largest number of September 11 detainees held at any single U.S. detention facility. Passaic detainees housed in the general population were treated like "regular" INS detainees who also were held at the facility. Although we received some allegations of physical and verbal abuse, we did not find the evidence indicated a pattern of abuse at Passaic. However, the INS did not conduct sufficient and regular visits to Passaic to ensure the September 11 detainees' conditions of confinement were appropriate.

"The Justice Department faced enormous challenges as a result of the September 11 terrorist attacks, and its employees worked with dedication to meet these challenges," [Inspector General] Fine said. "The findings of our review should in no way diminish their work. However, while the chaotic situation and the uncertainties surrounding the detainees' connections to terrorism explain some of the problems we found in our review, they do not explain them all," Fine said. . . .

Iqbal v. Hasty

United States Court of Appeals, Second Circuit, 2007
490 F.3d 143
rev'd and remanded on other grounds, 129 S. Ct. 1937 (2009)

JON O. NEWMAN, Circuit Judge. . . .

[Javaid Iqbal is a Muslim Pakistani who was arrested by agents of the FBI and the Immigration and Naturalization Service on November 2, 2001, and charged with conspiracy to defraud and identity fraud. Following his arrest, he was detained in the MDC's (Metropolitan Detention Center in Brooklyn) general prison population until January 8, 2002, when he was removed from the general prison population and assigned to a special section of the MDC known as the Administrative Maximum Special Housing Unit ("ADMAX SHU"), where he remained until he was reassigned to the general prison population at the end of July 2002. He alleged that he was arrested and detained as a person "of high interest" solely because of his race, religion, and national origin, and not because of any involvement in terrorism. The complaint also alleged that Attorney General John Ashcroft and FBI Director Robert Mueller approved a policy of holding detainees "of high interest" in highly restrictive conditions until they were "cleared" by the FBI. Iqbal further alleged that he was kept in solitary confinement, mistreated in detention, handcuffed, shackled, beaten, and denied adequate food, and that the MDC staff called him, among other things, a "terrorist" and a "Muslim killer."

Iqbal pled guilty to non-terrorism charges, was sentenced, and eventually was removed to Pakistan. He brought this suit against his jailers, the Director of the FBI, and the Attorney General for damages based on violations of his constitutional and statutory rights as a result of the conditions of his confinement. Defendants moved to dismiss on grounds of qualified immunity. The lower court denied the motion, and this interlocutory appeal followed.] . . .

I. GENERAL PRINCIPLES OF QUALIFIED IMMUNITY . . .

. . . A defendant will be entitled to qualified immunity if either (1) his actions did not violate clearly established law or (2) it was objectively reasonable for him to believe that his actions did not violate clearly established law. . . .

. . . Several Defendants contend that even if the Plaintiff's complaint would survive a motion to dismiss in the face of a qualified immunity defense under normal circumstances, the post-9/11 context requires a different outcome. This argument is advanced on three fronts. First, some Defendants contend that the Government was entitled to take certain actions that might not have been lawful before 9/11 because the Government's interests assumed special weight in the post-9/11 context. Second, some Defendants contend that, even if the law was clearly established as to the existence of a right claimed to have been violated, it was not clearly established in the extraordinary circumstances of the 9/11 attack and its aftermath. Third, some Defendants contend that the post-9/11 context renders their actions objectively reasonable, an argument we do not reach in view of our disposition of their second contention.

We fully recognize the gravity of the situation that confronted investigative officials of the United States as a consequence of the 9/11 attack. We also recognize that some forms of governmental action are permitted in emergency situations that would exceed constitutional limits in normal times. *See Home Building & Loan Association v. Blaisdell,* 290 U.S. 398, 425-26 (1934) ("While emergency does not create power, emergency may furnish the occasion for the exercise of power."). But most of the rights that the Plaintiff contends were violated do not vary with surrounding circumstances, such as the right not to be subjected to needlessly harsh conditions of confinement, the right to be free from the use of excessive force, and the right not to be subjected to ethnic or religious discrimination. The strength of our system of constitutional rights derives from the steadfast protection of those rights in both normal and unusual times.

With some rights, for example, the right to be free from unreasonable searches, the existence of exigent circumstances might justify governmental action that would not otherwise be permitted. But, as we discuss below, the exigent circumstances of the post-9/11 context do not diminish the Plaintiff's right not to be needlessly harassed and mistreated in the confines of a prison cell by repeated strip and body-cavity searches. This and other rights, such as the right to be free from use of excessive force and not to be subjected to ethnic or religious discrimination, were all clearly established prior to 9/11, and they remained clearly established even in the aftermath of that horrific event. To whatever extent exigent circumstances might affect the lawfulness of the Defendants' actions or might have justified an objectively reasonable belief that their actions did not violate clearly established law, we consider the argument in connection with a particular claim.

With these general principles in mind, we turn to the Plaintiff's specific claims. . . .

III. CONDITIONS OF CONFINEMENT . . .

Because the Plaintiff was a pretrial detainee during his detention in the ADMAX SHU, his challenge to the conditions of his confinement arises from the substantive component of the Due Process Clause of the Fifth Amendment and not from the cruel and unusual punishment standards of the Eighth Amendment. *See Benjamin v. Fraser*, 343 F.3d 35, 49 (2d Cir. 2003). Pretrial detainees have not been convicted of a crime and thus "may not be punished in any manner — neither cruelly and unusually nor otherwise." *Id.* at 49-50. Courts considering challenges to confinement brought by pretrial detainees must first consider whether the circumstances of the particular confinement render the confinement punitive; since some restraint is necessary to confine a pretrial detainee, not all uncomfortable conditions or restrictions are necessarily punitive. *Id.* at 50. In *Bell v. Wolfish*, [441 U.S. 520 (1979)], the seminal case on the substantive due process claims of pretrial detainees, the Supreme Court recognized the following factors as relevant to the determination of whether a condition of confinement is punitive:

> "Whether the sanction involves an affirmative disability or restraint, whether it has historically been regarded as a punishment, whether it comes into play only on a finding of *scienter,* whether its operation will promote the traditional aims of punishment — retribution and deterrence, whether the behavior to which it applies is already a crime, whether an alternative purpose to which it may rationally be connected is assignable for it, and whether it appears excessive in relation to the alternative purpose assigned. . . ."

441 U.S. at 537-38 (quoting [*Kennedy v. Mendoza-Martinez*, 372 U.S. 144, 168-169 (1963)]). A court may infer that a condition of confinement is intended as punishment if it is not reasonably related to a legitimate government objective.

The complaint alleges, among other things, that MDC staff placed the Plaintiff in solitary confinement, deliberately subjected him to extreme hot and cold temperatures, shackled him every time he left his cell, and repeatedly subjected him to strip and body-cavity searches, and that these conditions were intended to be, and were in fact, punitive. Applying *Wolfish*, Judge Gleeson found these allegations sufficient to state a substantive due process claim, observing that whether the conditions were reasonably related to legitimate government objectives could not be determined on a motion to dismiss. . . .

The Plaintiff has alleged the purposeful infliction of restraints that were punitive in nature. Accordingly, the District Court need not have considered whether a Defendant was "deliberately indifferent" in inflicting the restraints or whether the restraints constituted cruel and unusual punishment. The right of pretrial detainees to be free from punitive restraints was clearly established at the time of the events in question, and no reasonable officer could have thought that he could punish a pretrial detainee by subjecting him to the practices and conditions alleged by the Plaintiff. . . .

VIII. RACIAL AND RELIGIOUS DISCRIMINATION

The Defendants argue that they are entitled to qualified immunity on the Plaintiff's First Amendment claim of religious discrimination and Fifth Amendment claim of racial or ethnic discrimination on three grounds: (1) the Plaintiff has failed to state a violation of clearly established rights, (2) the Plaintiff's allegations of discriminatory intent are too conclusory, and (3) the Plaintiff has not alleged the personal involvement of Ashcroft and Mueller.

The arguments of Ashcroft and Mueller challenging the sufficiency of the Plaintiff's race, ethnic, and religious discrimination claims misunderstand his complaint. They contend that his "complaint amounts to an objection that most of those persons determined to be of high interest to the 9/11 investigation were Muslim or from certain Arab countries," which they justify by pointing out that the 9/11 hijackers were Muslims from Arab countries. However, what the Plaintiff is alleging is that he was deemed to be "of high interest," and accordingly was kept in the ADMAX SHU under harsh conditions, solely because of his race, ethnicity, and religion. The Plaintiff also alleges that "Defendants specifically targeted [him] for mistreatment because of [his] race, religion, and national origin." These allegations are sufficient to state a claim of animus-based discrimination that any "reasonably competent officer" would understand to have been illegal under prior case law. *See Malley* [*v. Briggs*, 475 U.S. 335 (1986)], at 341. Accordingly, the Plaintiff's racial, ethnic, and religious discrimination claims cannot be dismissed on qualified immunity grounds at this stage of the litigation.

Hasty [former Warden of the MDC] also argues that the Plaintiff has failed to state a claim of discrimination. Citing *Reno v. American-Arab Anti-Discrimination Committee*, 525 U.S. 471 (1999) (*"AAADC"*), he argues that the Equal Protection Clause does not apply in the context of proceedings to remove illegal aliens and that the Government can permissibly deem nationals of a particular country to be a special threat. In *AAADC*, the Supreme Court concluded that a provision of the Illegal Immigration Reform and Immigrant Responsibility Act of 1996, 8 U.S.C. §1252(g), deprived the federal courts of jurisdiction to consider an illegal alien's selective enforcement challenge to deportation. *See* 525 U.S. at 487. The Court rejected the argument that it nevertheless had jurisdiction to consider an alien's constitutional arguments, holding that "an alien unlawfully in this country has no constitutional right to assert selective enforcement as a defense against his deportation," *see id.* at 488, even when the Government deports the alien "for the additional reason that it believes him to be a member of an organization that supports terrorist activity," *id.* at 492. *AAADC* affords the Defendants no relief. The Plaintiff is not challenging his deportation or even his arrest on criminal charges. Moreover, *AAADC* does not stand for the proposition that the Government may subject members of a particular race, ethnicity, or religion to more restrictive conditions of confinement than members of other races, ethnic backgrounds, or religions. . . .

The Plaintiff's allegations suffice to state claims of racial, ethnic, and religious discrimination. He alleges in particular that the FBI Defendants classified him "of high interest" solely because of his race, ethnic background, and religion and not because of any evidence of involvement in terrorism. He offers additional factual support for this allegation, stating that "within the New York area, all Arab Muslim men arrested on criminal or immigration charges while the FBI was following an investigative lead into the September 11th attacks — however unrelated the arrestee was to the investigation — were immediately classified as "of interest" to the post-September 11th investigation." We need not consider at this stage of the litigation whether these allegations are alone sufficient to state a clearly established constitutional violation under the circumstances presented because they are sufficient to state a violation when combined with the Plaintiff's allegation that, under the policy created and implemented by the Defendants, he was singled out for unnecessarily punitive conditions of confinement based on his racial, ethnic, and religious characteristics. . . .

CONCLUSION . . .

In sum, the serious allegations of gross mistreatment set forth in the complaint suffice, except as noted in this opinion, to defeat the Defendants' attempt to terminate the lawsuit at a preliminary stage, but, consistent with the important policies that justify the defense of qualified immunity, the defense may be reasserted in advance of trial after the carefully controlled and limited discovery that the District Court expects to supervise.

Affirmed in part, reversed in part, and remanded.

[Concurring opinion of JOSÉ A. CABRANES, J., omitted.]

Ashcroft v. Iqbal
United States Supreme Court, 2009
129 S. Ct. 1937

Justice KENNEDY delivered the opinion of the Court. . . . Respondent's account of his prison ordeal could, if proved, demonstrate unconstitutional misconduct by some governmental actors. But the allegations and pleadings with respect to these actors are not before us here. This case instead turns on a narrower question: Did respondent, as the plaintiff in the District Court, plead factual matter that, if taken as true, states a claim that petitioners deprived him of his clearly established constitutional rights. We hold respondent's pleadings are insufficient. . . .

IV. . . .

[The Court applied the federal "plausibility pleading" standard first announced in *Bell Atlantic Corp. v. Twombly*, 550 U.S. 544 (2007) (asking whether the "well-pleaded" — non-conclusory — allegations of the complaint "plausibly" state a claim) to the claims that Attorney General Ashcroft and FBI Director Mueller adopted a policy of discriminatory detention and treatment in detention.]

The September 11 attacks were perpetrated by 19 Arab Muslim hijackers who counted themselves members in good standing of al Qaeda, an Islamic fundamentalist group. Al Qaeda was headed by another Arab Muslim—Osama bin Laden—and composed in large part of his Arab Muslim disciples. It should come as no surprise that a legitimate policy directing law enforcement to arrest and detain individuals because of their suspected link to the attacks would produce a disparate, incidental impact on Arab Muslims, even though the purpose of the policy was to target neither Arabs nor Muslims. On the facts respondent alleges the arrests Mueller oversaw were likely lawful and justified by his nondiscriminatory intent to detain aliens who were illegally present in the United States and who had potential connections to those who committed terrorist acts. As between that "obvious alternative explanation" for the arrests, and the purposeful, invidious discrimination respondent asks us to infer, discrimination is not a plausible conclusion.

But even if the complaint's well-pleaded facts give rise to a plausible inference that respondent's arrest was the result of unconstitutional discrimination, that inference alone would not entitle respondent to relief. It is important to recall that respondent's complaint challenges neither the constitutionality of his arrest nor his initial detention in the MDC. Respondent's constitutional claims against petitioners rest solely on their ostensible "policy of holding post-September-11th detainees" in the ADMAX SHU once they were categorized as "of high interest." To prevail on that theory, the complaint must contain facts plausibly showing that petitioners purposefully adopted a policy of classifying post-September-11 detainees as "of high interest" because of their race, religion, or national origin.

This the complaint fails to do. Though respondent alleges that various other defendants, who are not before us, may have labeled him a person of "of high interest" for impermissible reasons, his only factual allegation against petitioners accuses them of adopting a policy approving "restrictive conditions of confinement" for post-September-11 detainees until they were "'cleared' by the FBI." Accepting the truth of that allegation, the complaint does not show, or even intimate, that petitioners purposefully housed detainees in the ADMAX SHU due to their race, religion, or national origin. All it plausibly suggests is that the Nation's top law enforcement officers, in the aftermath of a devastating terrorist attack, sought to keep suspected terrorists in the most secure conditions available until the suspects could be cleared of terrorist activity. Respondent does not argue, nor can he, that such a motive would violate petitioners' constitutional obligations. He would need to allege more by way of factual content to "nudg[e]" his claim of purposeful discrimination "across the line from conceivable to plausible." *Twombly*, 550 U.S. at 570. . . .

It is important to note, however, that we express no opinion concerning the sufficiency of respondent's complaint against the defendants who are not before us. Respondent's account of his prison ordeal alleges serious official misconduct that we need not address here. Our decision is limited to the determination that respondent's complaint does not entitle him to relief from [Ashcroft and Mueller.] . . .

V

We hold that respondent's complaint fails to plead sufficient facts to state a claim for purposeful and unlawful discrimination against petitioners. The Court of Appeals should decide in the first instance whether to remand to the District Court so that respondent can seek leave to amend his deficient complaint.

The judgment of the Court of Appeals is reversed, and the case is remanded for further proceedings consistent with this opinion.

It is so ordered.

[The dissenting opinion of Justice SOUTER, with whom Justice STEVENS, Justice GINSBURG, and Justice BREYER join, and separate dissenting opinion of Justice BREYER are omitted.]

NOTES AND QUESTIONS

1. *Immigration Detentions.* Aliens who have been found either inadmissible or removable for terrorist activity are subject to mandatory detention under the immigration laws until their removal can be effected. 8 U.S.C. §§1182(a)(3)(B), 1227(a)(4)(B) (2006 & Supp. 2009). *See generally* 8 Charles Gordon et al., *Immigration Law and Procedure* §108.02[2][b] (2005). Most of the September 11 detainees, however, were not charged with terrorist activity. For example, as the Rolince affidavit, *supra* p. 739, ¶11, suggests, Al-Maqtari was arrested for a minor immigration violation: overstaying his visa. *See* Goldstein, *supra* p. 733 n.1.

Prolonged detention for minor "overstays" is highly unusual, according to immigration lawyers. *See* Pat Leisner, *Detention After Attacks Challenged*, AP Online, Dec. 1, 2001. INS regulations before the September 11 attacks provided that persons suspected of immigration violations could be held for 24 hours before being charged. After the attacks, the Department of Justice lengthened the period to 48 hours, then authorized the Attorney General to stay for ten days the release of immigrants granted bond in order to allow the government to appeal. *Review of Custody Determinations*, 66 Fed. Reg. 54,909 (Oct. 31, 2001). Asked to explain what standard he used for staying releases ordered by immigration judges, Attorney General Ashcroft testified that "if the attorney general develops an understanding that it's against the national interest and would in some way potentially violate or jeopardize the national security, then those orders are overruled." *Hearing on DOJ Oversight*, *supra* p. 733. *See also Continued Detention of Aliens Subject to Final Orders of Removal*, 66 Fed. Reg. 56,967 (Nov. 14, 2001) (providing for indefinite detention of suspected terrorist aliens after expiration of removal period); Jess Bravin, *U.S. Issues Rules to Indefinitely Detain Illegal Aliens Who Are Potentially Terrorists*, Wall St. J., Nov. 15, 2001. Authorities explained that immigration charges are a good way to detain persons suspected of terrorist connections when the government lacks sufficient evidence to prove the connections. *Id.*

After March 2003, the government filed immigration charges against more than 500 people who were under scrutiny in terrorism investigations. Mary Beth Sheridan, *Immigration Law as an Anti-Terrorism Tool*, Wash. Post, June 13, 2005. The *Washington Post* reported in 2005 that 768 suspects were "secretly processed on immigration charges" in the 9/11 investigations, and most were deported after being cleared of terrorism connections. *Id.*

2. *The Burden of Proof.* In the final analysis, the FBI affidavit sought to justify the detention of Al-Maqtari on the basis that the Bureau was "unable to rule out the possibility that respondent is somehow linked to, or possesses knowledge of,

the terrorist attacks on the World Trade Center and the Pentagon." Rolince Aff. ¶14. Is this rationale consistent with the Fourth Amendment? With a presumption of innocence? Or was the FBI suggesting a new standard or presumption for detentions intended to prevent terrorist attacks?

3. *Pretextual Immigration Detention.* In *Turkmen v. Ashcroft*, No. 02 CV 2307(JG), 2006 WL 1662663 (E.D.N.Y. June 14, 2006), *aff'd in part and vacated in part*, 589 F.3d 542 (2d Cir. 2009), a group of post-9/11 immigration detainees, all but one of whom were Muslims of Middle Eastern origin, challenged their detention in part on the Fourth Amendment ground that they were really detained for criminal investigation without probable cause. The court rejected the challenge:

> [P]laintiffs' entire detention was authorized by the post-removal period [immigration] detention statute. [8 U.S.C. §1231(a)(2).] That the government may have been motivated by a desire to keep terrorism suspects in jail pending further investigation does not alter the legality of the detention. It is well-established that the government's "[s]ubjective intent . . . does not make otherwise lawful conduct illegal or unconstitutional." *Whren v. United States*, 517 U.S. 806, 813 (1996) (internal quotation marks omitted). Accordingly, even accepting as true plaintiffs' allegations regarding defendants' motives, the detention of plaintiffs was authorized pursuant to the post-removal detention statute and thus did not violate the Fourth Amendment. [*Turkmen, supra*, 2006 WL 1662663, *41.]

Can the statute invoked here have overcome limits imposed by the Fourth Amendment on government action?

4. *Profiling? Discriminatory Immigration Detention?* The overwhelming majority of the immigrants detained in the PENTTBOM investigation were Arab men. Moreover, they were detained for visa violations for which other nationalities were often released or bonded. "The approach is basically to target the Muslim and Arab community with a kind of zero-tolerance immigration policy. No other community is treated to zero-tolerance enforcement," said Professor David Cole. Sheridan, *supra*.

In *Turkmen*, the plaintiffs challenged the legality of selective enforcement of the immigration laws. On appeal, a two-judge panel (the third panel member, Judge Sotomayor, was elevated to the Supreme Court before the panel decision) found that there was no clearly established right to non-selective enforcement.

> [P]laintiffs point to no authority clearly establishing an equal protection right to be free of selective enforcement of the immigration laws based on national origin, race, or religion at the time of plaintiffs' detentions. *See Reno v. American-Arab Anti-Discrimination Comm.*, 525 U.S. 471, 490-91, (1999) ("What will be involved in deportation cases is not merely the disclosure of normal domestic law enforcement priorities and techniques, but often the disclosure of foreign-policy objectives and (as in this case) foreign-intelligence products and techniques. The Executive should not have to disclose its 'real' reasons for deeming nationals of a particular country a special threat — or indeed for simply wishing to antagonize a particular foreign country by focusing on that country's nationals — and even if it did disclose them a court would be ill equipped to determine their authenticity and utterly unable to assess their adequacy."); *see also Zadvydas*, 533 U.S. at 696 ("terrorism" might warrant "special arguments" for "heightened deference to the judgments of the political branches with respect to matters of national

security"); *Matthews v. Diaz*, 426 U.S. 67, 81-82 (1976) ("The reasons that preclude judicial review of political questions also dictate a narrow standard of review of decisions made by the Congress or the President in the area of immigration and naturalization."). [*Turkmen v. Ashcroft*, 589 F.3d 542, 550 (2d Cir. 2009).]

Is this two-judge panel's decision consistent with the panel decision in *Iqbal*? After the Supreme Court reversed and remanded *Iqbal*, what discrimination theory should the lower court apply to plaintiffs' remaining claims?

    5. *The USA Patriot Act Preventive Detention Provision.* Immediately after the 9/11 attacks, Attorney General Ashcroft asked Congress for authority to hold suspected alien terrorists indefinitely. Bravin, *supra.* Would such legislation be constitutional? Congress rebuffed this request, providing instead in the USA Patriot Act that the INS could hold immigrants for up to seven days before charging them and then hold them while immigration proceedings were pending if the Attorney General certified, at least every six months, that their release would threaten national security. Pub. L. No. 107-56, §412, 115 Stat. 272, 350-351 (2001). How, if at all, might you argue that this legislation affected the legality of subsequent immigration detentions in the PENTTBOM investigation?

    6. *The Ethics of Immigration Bond Hearings.* As the OIG report suggests, immigration laws, like the Bail Reform Act, *supra* p. 737, authorize immigration judges to deny bond for a detained immigrant if the government provides evidence of flight risk or dangerousness. The FBI, however, provided no information to sustain such determinations in many cases. Nevertheless, INS lawyers were apparently ordered to argue the "no bond" position in court without any evidence, using "boilerplate" language like that in the Rolince affidavit, *supra* p. 739. *See* Office of the Inspector Gen., U.S. Dep't of Justice, *The September 11 Detainees: A Review of the Treatment of Aliens Held on Immigration Charges in Connection with the Investigation of the September 11 Attacks* 78-80 (Apr. 2003), *available at* http://www.justice.gov/oig/special/0306/full.pdf. Was this ethical? *See id.* at 79, 81. In some cases, the alien succeeded in obtaining a bond order and in posting bond, but the INS, without appealing the order, continued to hold him anyway. Was this lawful? *See id.* at 87 (reporting that one INS official admitted not knowing what to tell the immigrant's lawyer, "because I cannot bring myself to say that the INS no longer feels compelled to obey the law"). How far may a government lawyer go in defending preventive detention if she is instructed that it is essential to a terrorism investigation?

    7. *The Length of Immigration Detentions.* In *Denmore v. Hyung Joon Kim*, 538 U.S. 510 (2003), the Supreme Court revisited the issue of immigration detention, this time considering a statutory provision for mandatory detention of criminal aliens pending their removal hearings. Admitting that individualized bond hearings might be feasible, the majority nevertheless concluded that "when the Government deals with deportable aliens, the Due Process Clause does not require it to employ the least burdensome means to accomplish its goal." *Id.* at 528. It therefore upheld the mandatory detention law but emphasized that such detentions pending removal were for less than 90 days in the majority of cases. Joining in the opinion, Justice Kennedy noted that if the removal proceedings were unreasonably delayed, "it could become necessary then to inquire whether the detention is not to facilitate

deportation, or to protect against risk of flight or dangerousness, but to incarcerate for other reasons." *Id.* at 532-533 (Kennedy, J., concurring). How would the post–September 11 immigration detentions described in the OIG report fare by these standards?

8. *Rights of Detainees.* Ordinarily, immigrant detainees have a due process right to counsel at their own expense. *See generally* Gordon, *supra*, §108.04[2][b]. The Department of Justice said it afforded the September 11 detainees that right, although some detainees reportedly found it difficult to exercise it. *See, e.g., Hearing on DOJ Oversight, supra* p. 733 n.1 (questions by Senator Feingold to Attorney General Ashcroft); Amnesty Int'l, *supra* p. 733 n.1, at 4-6 (reporting that many detainees were effectively denied access to a lawyer for substantial periods). Shortly after publication of the OIG report, a divided panel of the D.C. Circuit Court of Appeals found that various public interest groups had no right under the Freedom of Information Act or the First Amendment to assorted information about the post–September 11 detentions, which they sought in part to ascertain the legality of the detentions and conditions of confinement. *Center for Nat'l Sec. Studies v. United States Dep't of Justice,* 331 F.3d 918 (D.C. Cir. 2003), *cert. denied,* 540 U.S. 1104 (2004). Based presumably on the government's representations, a majority of the panel assumed that the immigrant detainees "have had access to counsel, and the INS has provided detainees with lists of attorneys willing to represent them. . . . They have also been free to disclose their names to the public." *Id.* at 921. In light of the OIG report, were these assumptions warranted? *See* The Constitution Project, *Recommendations for Reforming our Immigration Detention System and Promoting Access to Counsel in Immigration Proceedings* 2 (2009) (recommending improved access for immigrants in detention because "the laws governing removal are complex and may prove overwhelming for individuals with little or no knowledge of English, especially when held far from their families and other support networks.").

9. *International Legal Rights of Alien Detainees.* Detainees also have rights under international law. The Vienna Convention on Consular Relations, Apr. 24, 1963, 21 U.S.T. 77, 596 U.N.T.S. 261, which the United States has ratified, gives a foreign arrestee the right to have his government notified of his arrest. *Id.* art. 361(b). *See Sanchez-Llamas v. Oregon,* 548 U.S. 331 (2006) (assuming, without deciding, that the Convention grants individuals enforceable rights, violations will not be enforced by applying an exclusionary rule, and enforceability is conditioned on compliance with state procedural rules). What purpose do you think this right serves? State law enforcement authorities have notoriously disregarded this right, *see* Sean D. Murphy, *United States Practice in International Law 1999-2000,* at 39 & n.1 (2002), despite the primacy of the Convention under the Supremacy Clause. Apart from the Supremacy Clause, can you think of any policy reason why the United States should honor the Convention's notification requirement?

The International Covenant on Civil and Political Rights art. 9, Dec. 16, 1966, 999 U.N.T.S. 171, ratified by the United States in 1992, states that "[n]o one shall be subjected to arbitrary arrest or detention," and that "[a]nyone who is deprived of his liberty by arrest or detention shall be entitled to take proceedings before a court, in order that that court may decide without delay on the lawfulness of his detention." Were these provisions violated by the PENTTBOM detentions?

D. MATERIAL WITNESS DETENTIONS

The material witness statute, 18 U.S.C. §3144 (2006), provides as follows:

> If it appears from an affidavit filed by a party that the testimony of a person is material in a criminal proceeding, and if it is shown that it may become impracticable to secure the presence of the person by subpoena, a judicial officer may order the arrest of the person and treat the person in accordance with the provisions of section 3142 of this title [governing release on bond and requiring a judicial hearing]. No material witness may be detained because of inability to comply with any condition of release if the testimony of such witness can adequately be secured by deposition, and if further detention is not necessary to prevent a failure of justice. Release of a material witness may be delayed for a reasonable period of time until the deposition of the witness can be taken pursuant to the Federal Rules of Criminal Procedure.

The statute apparently was first used in a terrorism investigation to detain Terry Nichols, who was eventually convicted in connection with the Oklahoma City bombing. *See United States v. McVeigh*, 940 F. Supp. 1541, 1562 (D. Colo. 1996) (finding that Nichols's renunciation of U.S. citizenship and his association with Timothy McVeigh sufficiently showed probable cause to believe that it "may become impracticable" to rely on a subpoena to secure his testimony). After 9/11, it was used for the first time on a broader scale to detain persons suspected of having a connection with or information about terrorism. Although the government has not disclosed exactly how many persons it held as material witnesses in the PENTTBOM and subsequent counterterrorist investigations, Human Rights Watch reported that its research identified 70 such individuals as of June 2005. Human Rights Watch, *Witness to Abuse: Human Rights Abuses Under the Material Witness Law Since September 11*, 17 Hum. Rts. Watch 1 (June 2005). The plaintiff in the following case may be typical.

Ashcroft v. al-Kidd

United States Supreme Court, 2011
2011 WL 2119110

[Abdullah al-Kidd was born in Kansas and converted to Islam while attending the University of Idaho. In the spring of 2003, Al-Kidd was arrested at the airport on "a material witness warrant" as he prepared to fly to Saudi Arabia to study Arabic and Islamic law on a scholarship. The warrant had been issued on the strength of an FBI affidavit asserting that al-Kidd was believed to have information crucial to the criminal prosecution of Sami Omar Al-Hussayen for visa fraud and false statements. Al-Kidd was handcuffed, interrogated, and then detained for 16 days, during which he was strip-searched on multiple occasions, handcuffed and shackled, confined in a high-security unit, and allowed to leave his continuously lit cell for only one to two hours each day.

He was released under supervision after he surrendered his passport. These conditions were only lifted 15 months later, after Al-Hussayen's trial was completed. (Al-Hussayen, a suspected webmaster of an allegedly jihadist Web site, was not convicted of any charges against him but was deported to Saudi Arabia for visa violations.) Al-Kidd was never called as a witness, and no evidence of any criminal activity by him was ever discovered. He was fired from his job, separated from his wife, deprived of his scholarship for study in Saudi Arabia, and unable afterward to find steady employment.

Al-Kidd then sued Attorney General Ashcroft and others for injuries resulting from the alleged misuse of material witness detention and for the conditions of his confinement. After the district court denied the defendants' motion to dismiss, they appealed. A divided panel of the United States Court of Appeals for the Ninth Circuit affirmed, holding that the Fourth Amendment prohibits pretextual arrests absent probable cause of criminal wrongdoing, and that Ashcroft could not claim qualified or absolute immunity. A divided court then denied rehearing en banc, with eight judges voting to rehear the case. Defendants then petitioned for certiorari, and the Supreme Court granted their petition.]

Justice SCALIA delivered the opinion of the Court. . . .

II

Qualified immunity shields federal and state officials from money damages unless a plaintiff pleads facts showing (1) that the official violated a statutory or constitutional right, and (2) that the right was "clearly established" at the time of the challenged conduct. *Harlow v. Fitzgerald*, 457 U.S. 800, 818 (1982). . . . In this case, the Court of Appeals' analysis at both steps of the qualified-immunity inquiry needs correction.

A

The Fourth Amendment protects "[t]he right of the people to be secure in their persons, houses, papers, and effects, against unreasonable searches and seizures." An arrest, of course, qualifies as a "seizure" of a "person" under this provision, *Dunaway v. New York*, 442 U.S. 200, 207-208 (1979), and so must be reasonable under the circumstances. Al-Kidd does not assert that Government officials would have acted unreasonably if they had used a material-witness warrant to arrest him for the purpose of securing his testimony for trial. He contests, however (and the Court of Appeals here rejected), the reasonableness of using the warrant to detain him as a suspected criminal.

Fourth Amendment reasonableness "is predominantly an objective inquiry." [*Indianapolis v. Edmond*, 531 U.S. 32, 47 (2000).] We ask whether "the circumstances, viewed objectively, justify [the challenged] action." *Scott v. United States*, 436 U.S. 128, 138 (1978). If so, that action was reasonable "*whatever* the subjective intent" motivating the relevant officials. *Whren v. United States*, 517 U.S. 806, 814 (1996). This approach recognizes that the Fourth Amendment regulates conduct rather than thoughts, *Bond v. United States*, 529 U.S. 334, 338, n.2 (2000); and it promotes even-handed, uniform enforcement of the law, *Devenpeck v. Alford*, 543 U.S. 146, 153-154 (2004).

Two "limited exception[s]" to this rule are our special-needs and administrative-search cases, where "actual motivations" do matter. *United States v. Knights*, 534 U.S. 112, 122 (2001) (internal quotation marks omitted). A judicial warrant and probable cause are not needed where the search or seizure is justified by "special needs, beyond the normal need for law enforcement," such as the need to deter drug use in public schools, *Vernonia School Dist. 47J v. Acton*, 515 U.S. 646, 653 (1995) (internal quotation marks omitted), or the need to assure that railroad employees engaged in train operations are not under the influence of drugs or alcohol, *Skinner v. Railway Labor Executives' Assn.*, 489 U.S. 602 (1989); and where the search or seizure is in execution of an administrative warrant authorizing, for example, an inspection of fire-damaged premises to determine the cause, *Michigan v. Clifford*, 464 U.S. 287, 294 (1984) (plurality opinion), or an inspection of residential premises to assure compliance with a housing code, *Camara v. Municipal Court of City and County of San Francisco*, 387 U.S. 523, 535-538 (1967). But those exceptions do not apply where the officer's purpose is not to attend to the special needs or to the investigation for which the administrative inspection is justified. The Government seeks to justify the present arrest on the basis of a properly issued judicial warrant — so that the special-needs and administrative-inspection cases cannot be the basis for a purpose inquiry here.

Apart from those cases, we have almost uniformly rejected invitations to probe subjective intent. See *Brigham City v. Stuart*, 547 U.S. 398, 404 (2006). There is one category of exception, upon which the Court of Appeals principally relied. In *Edmond*, 531 U.S. 32, we held that the Fourth Amendment could not condone suspicionless vehicle checkpoints set up for the purpose of detecting illegal narcotics. Although we had previously approved vehicle checkpoints set up for the purpose of keeping off the road unlicensed drivers, *Delaware v. Prouse*, 440 U.S. 648, 663 (1979), or alcohol-impaired drivers, *Michigan Dept. of State Police v. Sitz*, 496 U.S. 444 (1990); and for the purpose of interdicting those who illegally cross the border, *United States v. Martinez-Fuerte*, 428 U.S. 543 (1976); we found the drug-detection purpose in *Edmond* invalidating because it was "ultimately indistinguishable from the general interest in crime control," 531 U.S., at 44. In the Court of Appeals' view, *Edmond* established that "'programmatic purpose' is relevant to Fourth Amendment analysis of programs of seizures without probable cause." 580 F.3d, at 968.

That was mistaken. It was not the absence of probable cause that triggered the invalidating-purpose inquiry in *Edmond*. To the contrary, *Edmond* explicitly said that it would approve checkpoint stops for "general crime control purposes" that were based upon merely "some quantum of individualized suspicion." 531 U.S., at 47. Purpose was relevant in *Edmond* because "programmatic purposes may be relevant to the validity of Fourth Amendment intrusions undertaken *pursuant to a general scheme without individualized suspicion*," *id.*, at 45-46 (emphasis added).

Needless to say, warrantless, "suspicionless intrusions pursuant to a general scheme," *id.*, at 47, are far removed from the facts of this case. A warrant issued by a neutral Magistrate Judge authorized al-Kidd's arrest. The affidavit accompanying the warrant application (as al-Kidd concedes) gave individualized reasons to believe that he was a material witness and that he would soon disappear. The existence of a judicial warrant based on individualized suspicion takes this case outside the domain of not only our special-needs and administrative-search cases, but of *Edmond* as well.

A warrant based on individualized suspicion in fact grants more protection against the malevolent and the incompetent than existed in most of our cases eschewing inquiries into intent. In *Whren* and *Devenpeck*, we declined to probe the motives behind seizures supported by probable cause but lacking a warrant approved by a detached magistrate. *Terry v. Ohio*, 392 U.S. 1, 21-22 (1968), and *Knights*, 534 U.S., at 121-122, applied an objective standard to warrantless searches justified by a lesser showing of reasonable suspicion. We review even some suspicionless searches for objective reasonableness. See *Bond,* 529 U.S., at 335-336, 338, n.2. If concerns about improper motives and pretext do not justify subjective inquiries in those less protective contexts, we see no reason to adopt that inquiry here.

Al-Kidd would read our cases more narrowly. He asserts that *Whren* establishes that we ignore subjective intent only when there exists "probable cause to believe that a violation of law has occurred," 517 U.S., at 811 — which was not the case here. That is a distortion of *Whren.* Our unanimous opinion held that we would not look behind an objectively reasonable traffic stop to determine whether racial profiling or a desire to investigate other potential crimes was the real motive. In the course of our analysis, we dismissed Whren's reliance on our inventory-search and administrative-inspection cases by explaining that those cases do not "endors[e] the principle that ulterior motives can invalidate police conduct that is justifiable on the basis of probable cause to believe that a violation of law has occurred," *id.,* at 811. But to say that ulterior motives do *not* invalidate a search that is legitimate because of probable cause to believe a crime has occurred is not to say that it *does* invalidate all searches that are legitimate for other reasons.

"[O]nly an undiscerning reader," *ibid.,* would think otherwise. We referred to probable cause to believe that a violation of law had occurred because that was the legitimating factor in the case at hand. But the analysis of our opinion swept broadly to reject inquiries into motive generally. See *id.,* at 812-815. We remarked that our special-needs and administrative-inspection cases are unusual in their concern for pretext, and do nothing more than "explain that the exemption from the need for probable cause (and warrant), which is accorded to searches made for the purpose of inventory or administrative regulation, is not accorded to searches that are *not* made for those purposes," *id.,* at 811-812. And our opinion emphasized that we had at that time (prior to *Edmond*) rejected every request to examine subjective intent outside the narrow context of special needs and administrative inspections. Thus, al-Kidd's approach adds an "only" to a sentence plucked from the *Whren* opinion, and then elevates that sentence (as so revised) over the remainder of the opinion, and over the consistent holdings of our other cases.

Because al-Kidd concedes that individualized suspicion supported the issuance of the material-witness arrest warrant; and does not assert that his arrest would have been unconstitutional absent the alleged pretextual use of the warrant; we find no Fourth Amendment violation.[3] Efficient and evenhanded application of the law demands that we look to whether the arrest is objectively justified, rather than to the motive of the arresting officer.

B

A Government official's conduct violates clearly established law when, at the time of the challenged conduct, "[t]he contours of [a] right [are] sufficiently clear" that every "reasonable official would have understood that what he is doing violates that

---

3. The concerns of Justices Ginsburg and Sotomayor about the validity of the warrant in this case are beside the point. The validity of the warrant is not our "opening assumption," it is the premise of al-Kidd's argument. Al-Kidd does not claim that Ashcroft is liable because the FBI agents failed to obtain a valid warrant. He takes the validity of the warrant as a given, and argues that his arrest nevertheless violated the Constitution because it was motivated by an illegitimate purpose. His separate Fourth Amendment and statutory claims against the FBI agents who sought the material-witness warrant, which are the focus of both concurrences, are not before us.

right." *Anderson v. Creighton*, 483 U.S. 635, 640 (1987). We do not require a case directly on point, but existing precedent must have placed the statutory or constitutional question beyond debate. See *ibid.*; *Malley v. Briggs*, 475 U.S. 335, 341 (1986). The constitutional question in this case falls far short of that threshold.

At the time of al-Kidd's arrest, not a single judicial opinion had held that pretext could render an objectively reasonable arrest pursuant to a material-witness warrant unconstitutional. . . .

The Court of Appeals also found clearly established law lurking in the broad "history and purposes of the Fourth Amendment." 580 F.3d, at 971. We have repeatedly told courts — and the Ninth Circuit in particular, see *Brosseau v. Haugen*, 543 U.S. 194, 198-199 (2004) (*per curiam*) — not to define clearly established law at a high level of generality. The general proposition, for example, that an unreasonable search or seizure violates the Fourth Amendment is of little help in determining whether the violative nature of particular conduct is clearly established.

The same is true of the Court of Appeals' broad historical assertions. The Fourth Amendment was a response to the English Crown's use of general warrants, which often allowed royal officials to search and seize whatever and whomever they pleased while investigating crimes or affronts to the Crown. According to the Court of Appeals, Ashcroft should have seen that a pretextual warrant similarly "gut[s] the substantive protections of the Fourth Amendmen[t]" and allows the State "to arrest upon the executive's mere suspicion." 580 F.3d, at 972.

Ashcroft must be forgiven for missing the parallel, which escapes us as well. The principal evil of the general warrant was addressed by the Fourth Amendment's particularity requirement which Ashcroft's alleged policy made no effort to evade. The warrant authorizing al-Kidd's arrest named al-Kidd and only al-Kidd. It might be argued, perhaps, that when, in response to the English abuses, the Fourth Amendment said that warrants could only issue "on probable cause" it meant only probable cause to suspect a violation of law, and not probable cause to believe that the individual named in the warrant was a material witness. But that would make *all* arrests pursuant to material-witness warrants unconstitutional, whether pretextual or not — and that is not the position taken by al-Kidd in this case. . . .

Qualified immunity gives government officials breathing room to make reasonable but mistaken judgments about open legal questions. When properly applied, it protects "all but the plainly incompetent or those who knowingly violate the law." *Malley*, 475 U.S., at 341. Ashcroft deserves neither label, not least because eight Court of Appeals judges agreed with his judgment in a case of first impression. He deserves qualified immunity even assuming — contrafactually — that his alleged detention policy violated the Fourth Amendment.

* * *

We hold that an objectively reasonable arrest and detention of a material witness pursuant to a validly obtained warrant cannot be challenged as unconstitutional on the basis of allegations that the arresting authority had an improper motive. Because Ashcroft did not violate clearly established law, we need not address the more difficult question whether he enjoys absolute immunity. The judgment of the Court of Appeals is reversed, and the case is remanded for further proceedings consistent with this opinion.

It is so ordered.

Justice KAGAN took no part in the consideration or decision of this case.

Justice KENNEDY, with whom Justice GINSBURG, Justice BREYER, and Justice SOTO-MAYOR join as to Part I, concurring. I join the opinion of the Court in full. In holding that the Attorney General could be liable for damages based on an unprecedented constitutional rule, the Court of Appeals for the Ninth Circuit disregarded the purposes of the doctrine of qualified immunity. This concurring opinion makes two additional observations.

I

The Court's holding is limited to the arguments presented by the parties and leaves unresolved whether the Government's use of the Material Witness Statute in this case was lawful. See *ante*, at ____ (noting that al-Kidd "does not assert that his arrest would have been unconstitutional absent the alleged pretextual use of the warrant"). Under the statute, a Magistrate Judge may issue a warrant to arrest someone as a material witness upon a showing by affidavit that "the testimony of a person is material in a criminal proceeding" and "that it may become impracticable to secure the presence of the person by subpoena." 18 U.S.C. §3144. The scope of the statute's lawful authorization is uncertain. For example, a law-abiding citizen might observe a crime during the days or weeks before a scheduled flight abroad. It is unclear whether those facts alone might allow police to obtain a material witness warrant on the ground that it "may become impracticable" to secure the person's presence by subpoena. *Ibid.* The question becomes more difficult if one further assumes the traveler would be willing to testify if asked; and more difficult still if one supposes that authorities delay obtaining or executing the warrant until the traveler has arrived at the airport. These possibilities resemble the facts in this case.

In considering these issues, it is important to bear in mind that the Material Witness Statute might not provide for the issuance of warrants within the meaning of the Fourth Amendment's Warrant Clause. The typical arrest warrant is based on probable cause that the arrestee has committed a crime; but that is not the standard for the issuance of warrants under the Material Witness Statute. See *ante*, at 11 (reserving the possibility that probable cause for purposes of the Fourth Amendment's Warrant Clause means "only probable cause to suspect a violation of law"). If material witness warrants do not qualify as "Warrants" under the Fourth Amendment, then material witness arrests might still be governed by the Fourth Amendment's separate reasonableness requirement for seizures of the person. Given the difficulty of these issues, the Court is correct to address only the legal theory put before it, without further exploring when material witness arrests might be consistent with statutory and constitutional requirements. . . .

Justice GINSBURG, with whom Justice BREYER and Justice SOTOMAYOR join, concurring in the judgment. Is a former U.S. Attorney General subject to a suit for damages on a claim that he instructed subordinates to use the Material Witness Statute as a pretext to detain terrorist suspects preventively? Given *Whren v. United States*, 517 U.S. 806 (1996), I agree with the Court that no "clearly established law" renders Ashcroft answerable in damages for the abuse of authority al-Kidd charged. But I join Justice Sotomayor in objecting to the Court's disposition of al-Kidd's Fourth Amendment claim on the merits; as she observes, *post*, at 1 (opinion concurring in judgment), that claim involves novel and trying questions that will "have no effect on the outcome of th[is] case." *Pearson v. Callahan*, 555 U.S. 223, 236-237 (2009).

In addressing al-Kidd's Fourth Amendment claim against Ashcroft, the Court assumes at the outset the existence of a *validly obtained* material witness warrant. That characterization is puzzling. See *post*, at 2 (opinion of Sotomayor, J.).[1] Is a warrant "validly obtained" when the affidavit on which it is based fails to inform the issuing Magistrate Judge that "the Government has no intention of using [al-Kidd as a witness] at [another's] trial," *post*, at 1, and does not disclose that al-Kidd had cooperated with FBI agents each of the several times they had asked to interview him . . . ?

Casting further doubt on the assumption that the warrant was validly obtained, the Magistrate Judge was not told that al-Kidd's parents, wife, and children were all citizens and residents of the United States. In addition, the affidavit misrepresented that al-Kidd was about to take a one-way flight to Saudi Arabia, with a first-class ticket costing approximately $5,000; in fact, al-Kidd had a round-trip, coach-class ticket that cost $1,700. Given these omissions and misrepresentations, there is strong cause to question the Court's opening assumption—a valid material-witness warrant—and equally strong reason to conclude that a merits determination was neither necessary nor proper.

I also agree with Justice Kennedy that al-Kidd's treatment presents serious questions, unaddressed by the Court, concerning "the [legality of] the Government's use of the Material Witness Statute in this case." In addition to the questions Justice Kennedy poses, and even if the initial material witness classification had been proper, what even arguably legitimate basis could there be for the harsh custodial conditions to which al-Kidd was subjected: Ostensibly held only to secure his testimony, al-Kidd was confined in three different detention centers during his 16 days' incarceration, kept in high-security cells lit 24 hours a day, strip-searched and subjected to body-cavity inspections on more than one occasion, and handcuffed and shackled about his wrists, legs, and waist. App. 29_36; cf. *Bell v. Wolfish,* 441 U.S. 520, 539, n.20 (1979) ("[L]oading a detainee with chains and shackles and throwing him in a dungeon may ensure his presence at trial and preserve the security of the institution. But it would be difficult to conceive of a situation where conditions so harsh, employed to achieve objectives that could be accomplished in so many alternative and less harsh methods, would not support a conclusion that the purpose for which they were imposed was to punish.").

However circumscribed al-Kidd's *Bivens* claim against Ashcroft may have been, see *Bivens v. Six Unknown Fed. Narcotics Agents,* 403 U.S. 388 (1971), his remaining claims against the FBI agents who apprehended him invite consideration of the issues Justice Kennedy identified. His challenges to the brutal conditions of his confinement have been settled. But his ordeal is a grim reminder of the need to install safeguards against disrespect for human dignity, constraints that will control officialdom even in perilous times.

Justice SOTOMAYOR, with whom Justice GINSBURG and Justice BREYER join, concurring in the judgment. I concur in the Court's judgment reversing the Court of Appeals because I agree with the majority's conclusion that Ashcroft did not violate clearly

---

1. Nowhere in al-Kidd's complaint is there any concession that the warrant gained by the FBI agents was validly obtained.

established law. I cannot join the majority's opinion, however, because it unnecessarily "resolve[s] [a] difficult and novel questio[n] of constitutional . . . interpretation that will 'have no effect on the outcome of the case.'" *Ante*, at 3 (quoting *Pearson v. Callahan*, 555 U.S. 223, 237 (2009)).

Whether the Fourth Amendment permits the pretextual use of a material witness warrant for preventive detention of an individual whom the Government has no intention of using at trial is, in my view, a closer question than the majority's opinion suggests. Although the majority is correct that a government official's subjective intent is generally "irrelevant in determining whether that officer's actions violate the Fourth Amendment," *Bond v. United States*, 529 U.S. 334, 338, n.2 (2000), none of our prior cases recognizing that principle involved prolonged detention of an individual without probable cause to believe he had committed any criminal offense. We have never considered whether an official's subjective intent matters for purposes of the Fourth Amendment in that novel context, and we need not and should not resolve that question in this case. All Members of the Court agree that, whatever the merits of the underlying Fourth Amendment question, Ashcroft did not violate clearly established law. . . .

NOTES AND QUESTIONS

1. *Material Witness Detentions in PENTTBOM.* Review the material witness statute, *supra* p. 754. What aspect of the procedure for detaining material witnesses might deter the government from making wider use of this legal basis for detention? Under what circumstances might material witness detention appeal to the government?

2. *Obtaining Testimony?* Human Rights Watch found that fewer than half of the 9/11 material witnesses were ever brought before a grand jury or court to testify; many were apparently held as suspects rather than as witnesses. *Witness to Abuse, supra* p. 754, at 2. The government has not been shy about explaining this use of the statute. For example, after acknowledging that the United States has no general preventive detention law, one architect of the post-9/11 detention policy said that "the material witness statute *gives the government effectively the same power*. . . . To the extent that it is a suspect involved in terror, you hold them on a material witness warrant, and you get the information until you find out what's going on." *Id.* at 19 (quoting Mary Jo White, former U.S. Attorney for the Southern District of New York) (emphasis added). In another case in which the material witness's lawyer argued that the government was holding his client as a criminal suspect, not as a witness, the government responded, "Based on evidence collected to date, the government cannot exclude the possibility that [the detainee] was criminally, rather than innocently, involved in how his fingerprint got to Spain." *Quoted in* Ricardo J. Bascuas, *The Unconstitutionality of "Hold Until Clear": Reexamining Material Witness Detentions in the Wake of the September 11th Dragnet*, 58 Vand. L. Rev. 677, 679 (2005) (citation omitted).

Here is what the Court of Appeals said about the government's motives in detaining al-Kidd:

— Al-Kidd's arrest was sought a month *after* Al-Hussayen was indicted, and more than a year *before* trial began, temporally distant from the time any testimony would have been needed.

— The FBI had previously investigated and interviewed al-Kidd, but had never suggested, let alone demanded, that he appear as a witness.

— The FBI conducted lengthy interrogations with al-Kidd while in custody, including about matters apparently unrelated to Al-Hussayen's alleged visa violations.

— Al-Kidd *never actually testified* for the prosecution in Al-Hussayen's or any other case, despite his assurances that he would be willing to do so.

— Ashcroft's immediate subordinate, FBI Director Mueller, testified before Congress that al-Kidd's *arrest* (rather than, say, the obtaining of the evidence he was supposedly going to provide against Al-Hussayen) constituted a "major success[ ]" in "identifying and dismantling terrorist networks." [*Al-Kidd v. Ashcroft*, 580 F.3d 949, 963-964 (9th Cir. 2009).]

Is there any doubt that al-Kidd was not detained primarily (or at all) to obtain his testimony for the Al-Hussayen case?

3. *Testimony: A Key to the Material Witness's Jail Cell?* The material witness statute makes a deposition an alternative to detention for obtaining grand jury testimony, effectively giving the detainee a key to his jail cell. Human Rights Watch reports, however, that the government has consistently opposed depositions or stalled taking them, citing national security reasons. *Witness to Abuse, supra*, at 79. Moreover, the government reportedly failed to advise many detainees of the reasons for their arrests, of their right to an attorney and to have an attorney present at their interrogations, and of their right to remain silent. *Id.* at 4.

4. *Probable Cause.* The Ninth Circuit had distinguished *Whren* on the grounds that it presupposes "ordinary" probable cause to believe that the arrestee has committed a crime, and that material witness arrests are based neither on ordinary probable cause nor even reasonable suspicion to believe that the arrestee has committed or is committing a crime. What was the Supreme Court's answer? It asserted that al-Kidd conceded that "individualized suspicion" justified his search, but individualized suspicion of what?

Has the Court definitively decided the legality of material witness detentions? If not, what is left open? Under what circumstances would a material witness arrest be unlawful, either under the statute or under the Constitution? Consider this assessment:

[I]t is quite possible that section 3144 going forward will turn out to be problematic under the Fourth Amendment quite apart from the question of pretext, at least when applied in some settings that appear particularly harsh. Second, the lingering prospect of *Bivens* liability for FBI agents who misstate or misrepresent facts in the underlying 3144 warrant application to some degree will check the prextual use of 3144.... Where the case can actually be made that the person's testimony is needed and at risk, however, this decision should pave the way for reliance on 3144 even if the underlying motivation is primarily to incapacitate a potentially dangerous person .... [Robert Chesney, *Supreme Court Rejects Fourth Amendment Challenge to Material Witness Detention in Al-Kidd v. Ashcroft* (May 31, 2011), *at* http://www.lawfareblog.com/2011/05/supreme-court-rejects-fourth-amendment-challenge-to-material-witness-detention-in-al-kidd-v-ashcroft/.]

5. *An Alternative Holding?* Should the majority have considered whether using the material witness statute for preventive detention fits under some national security exception to the Fourth Amendment's protection against unreasonable seizures? *See United States v. United States District Court (Keith)*, 407 U.S. 297 (1972), *supra* p. 559. How would you define such an exception?

6. *Clearly Established?* The Court unanimously held (with Justice Kagan recused) that Ashcroft did not violate clearly established law. Was the rest of the majority opinion necessary to the result?

The Great Writ: Habeas Corpus Before 9/11

27

The common law writ of habeas corpus is a guard against arbitrary, indefinite executive imprisonment that predates the Constitution by centuries. Blackstone sang its praises in 1759:

> Of great importance to the public is the preservation of this personal liberty: for if once it were left in the power of any, the highest, magistrate to imprison arbitrarily whomever he or his officers thought proper . . . there would soon be an end of all other rights and immunities. . . . To bereave a man of life, or by violence to confiscate his estate, without accusation or trial, would be so gross and notorious an act of despotism, as must at once convey the alarm of tyranny throughout the whole kingdom. But confinement of the person, by secretly hurrying him to gaol, where his sufferings are unknown or forgotten; is a less public, a less striking, and therefore a more dangerous engine of arbitrary government. . . .
>
> To make imprisonment lawful, it must either be, by process from the courts of judicature, or by warrant from some legal officer, having authority to commit to prison; which warrant must be in writing, under the hand and seal of the magistrate, and express the causes of the commitment, in order to be examined into (if necessary) upon a *habeas corpus*. If there be no cause expressed, the gaoler is not bound to detain the prisoner. For the law judges in this respect, . . . that it is unreasonable to send a prisoner, and not to signify withal the crimes alleged against him. [1 William Blackstone, *Commentaries* *132-133.]

Alexander Hamilton quoted from this same passage in The *Federalist No. 84*, at 444 (George Carey & James McClellan eds., 2001). And, as Justice Scalia has said, "The two ideas central to Blackstone's understanding—due process as the right secured, and habeas corpus as the instrument by which due process could be insisted upon by a citizen illegally imprisoned—found expression in the Constitution's Due Process and Suspension Clauses. *See* Amdt. 5; Art. I, §9, cl. 2." *Hamdi v. Rumsfeld*, 542 U.S. 507, 554-556 (2004) (Scalia, J., dissenting), *infra* p. 844. The Suspension Clause did not create the privilege of the writ; that privilege already existed as part of our common law heritage from England. Instead, the Clause forbids suspension of "[t]he Privilege of the Writ of Habeas Corpus . . . unless when in Cases of Rebellion or Invasion the public Safety may require it." Art. I, §9, cl. 2.

Congress has recognized the privilege by statute, as noted below. "The habeas statute clearly has expanded habeas corpus 'beyond the limits that obtained during the 17th and 18th centuries,'" the Supreme Court has observed, "[b]ut '[a]t its historical core, the writ of habeas corpus has served as a means of reviewing the legality of Executive detention, and it is in that context that its protections have been strongest.'" *Rasul v. Bush*, 524 U.S. 466, 474 (2004) (internal citations omitted).

We begin this chapter in Part A with a look at the current statutory basis for habeas corpus jurisdiction in federal courts. In Part B we consider when and how the writ may be suspended or restricted, and by whom. Finally, in Part C we inquire whether the writ was available to nonresident aliens before 9/11.

A. STATUTORY BASIS FOR HABEAS CORPUS

The current habeas corpus statute describes the qualifications of persons entitled to seek the writ, as well as basic procedures for a court to follow in considering a petition for a writ. What kind of hearing does the statute prescribe?

Habeas Corpus
28 U.S.C. §§2241-2255 (2006 & Supp. III 2009)

§2241. Power to Grant Writ

(a) Writs of habeas corpus may be granted by the Supreme Court, any justice thereof, the district courts and any circuit judge within their respective jurisdictions. . . .

(c) The writ of habeas corpus shall not extend to a prisoner unless —

(1) He is in custody under or by color of the authority of the United States or is committed for trial before some court thereof; or

(2) He is in custody for an act done or omitted in pursuance of an Act of Congress, or an order, process, judgment or decree of a court or judge of the United States; or

(3) He is in custody in violation of the Constitution or laws or treaties of the United States; or

(4) He, being a citizen of a foreign state and domiciled therein is in custody for an act done or omitted under any alleged right, title, authority, privilege, protection, or exemption claimed under the commission, order or sanction of any foreign state, or under color thereof, the validity and effect of which depend upon the law of nations; or

(5) It is necessary to bring him into court to testify or for trial. . . .

§2243. Issuance of Writ; Return; Hearing; Decision

A court, justice or judge entertaining an application for a writ of habeas corpus shall forthwith award the writ or issue an order directing the respondent to show cause why the writ should not be granted, unless it appears from the application that the applicant or person detained is not entitled thereto.

The writ, or order to show cause shall be directed to the person having custody of the person detained. It shall be returned within three days unless for good cause additional time, not exceeding twenty days, is allowed.

The person to whom the writ or order is directed shall make a return certifying the true cause of the detention.

When the writ or order is returned a day shall be set for hearing, not more than five days after the return unless for good cause additional time is allowed.

Unless the application for the writ and the return present only issues of law the person to whom the writ is directed shall be required to produce at the hearing the body of the person detained.

The applicant or the person detained may, under oath, deny any of the facts set forth in the return or allege any other material facts. . . .

The court shall summarily hear and determine the facts, and dispose of the matter as law and justice require.

B.   SUSPENDING THE WRIT

Although the Suspension Clause appears in that part of the Constitution devoted to an enumeration of legislative powers, there is no other textual clue about who possesses the power to suspend the writ. The question arose in an early Civil War era case, *Ex parte Merryman*, 17 F. Cas. 144 (C.C.D. Md. 1861) (No. 9487), when Chief Justice Taney ordered the release of a Southern sympathizer imprisoned at Fort McHenry. Merryman had been seized after President Lincoln signed an order authorizing suspension of the writ of habeas corpus. Said the Chief Justice, "I had supposed it to be one of those points in constitutional law upon which there was no difference of Opinion . . . that the privilege of the writ could not be suspended, except by act of congress." *Id.* at 148. However, Taney's decree was ignored by the President, and Merryman remained in prison for a time. A month later, in a message to a special session of Congress, Lincoln remarked that Taney's interpretation of the constitutional requirement would allow

President Lincoln in Spring 1861.

Photographer unknown. Courtesy of the Abraham Lincoln Presidential Library and Museum.

all the laws, but one, to go unexecuted, and the government itself go to pieces, lest that one be violated. . . . [T]he Constitution itself, is silent as to which, or who, is to exercise the power; and as the provision was plainly made for a dangerous emergency, it cannot be believed the framers of the instrument intended, that in every case, the danger should run its course, until Congress could be called together; the very assembling of which might be prevented, as was intended in this case, by the rebellion. [4 *The Collected Works of Abraham Lincoln* 430-431 (Roy P. Basler ed., 1953).]

Five years later, the full Supreme Court made it clear that under some circumstances the writ can properly be suspended.

Ex parte Milligan

United States Supreme Court, 1866
71 U.S. (4 Wall.) 2

[During the Civil War, Congress passed a statute in 1863 authorizing President Abraham Lincoln to suspend the writ of habeas corpus subject to certain limitations. The statute was summarized in the headnotes to this case as follows:

> The first section authorizes the suspension, during the Rebellion, of the writ of habeas corpus, throughout the United States, by the President.
>
> Two following sections limited the authority in certain respects.
>
> The second section required that lists of all persons, being citizens of States in which the administration of the laws had continued unimpaired in the Federal courts, who were then held, or might thereafter be held, as prisoners of the United States, under the authority of the President, otherwise than as prisoners of war, should be furnished by the Secretary of State and Secretary of War to the judges of the Circuit and District Courts. These lists were to contain the names of all persons, residing within their respective jurisdictions, charged with violation of national law. And it was required, in cases where the grand jury in attendance upon any of these courts should terminate its session without proceeding by indictment or otherwise against any prisoner named in the list, that the judge of the court should forthwith make an order that such prisoner, desiring a discharge, should be brought before him or the court to be discharged, on entering into recognizance, if required, to keep the peace and for good behavior, or to appear, as the court might direct, to be further dealt with according to law. Every officer of the United States having custody of such prisoners was required to obey and execute the judge's order, under penalty, for refusal or delay, of fine and imprisonment.
>
> The third section enacts, in case lists of persons other than prisoners of war then held in confinement, or thereafter arrested, should not be furnished within twenty days after the passage of the act, or, in cases of subsequent arrest, within twenty days after the time of arrest, that any citizen, after the termination of a session of the grand jury without indictment or presentment, might, by petition alleging the facts and verified by oath, obtain the judge's order of discharge in favor of any person so imprisoned, on the terms and conditions prescribed in the second section. [*Ex parte Milligan*, 71 U.S. 2, 4-5 (1866).]

Lambdin P. Milligan, a resident of Indiana, was arrested at his home in October 1864 by order of General Alvin P. Hovey, commander of the military district of Indiana, and held in close confinement "otherwise than as [a] prisoner[] of war." He was then brought before a military tribunal in Indianapolis, tried on charges ranging from conspiracy against the government to inciting insurrection, found guilty, and sentenced to be hanged.

In the meantime, on January 2, 1865, the United States Circuit Court for Indiana had met at Indianapolis and empanelled a grand jury to inquire whether any laws of the United States had been broken by anyone and to make presentments. The grand jury did not find any bill of indictment or make any presentment against Milligan, and on January 27 the court adjourned after discharging the grand jury from further service.

Milligan then petitioned the Circuit Court for his release, citing the foregoing statute and arguing that the military tribunal had no jurisdiction to try him. Although only the first part of the resulting opinion treats the suspension of the writ of habeas corpus, we provide an excerpt here of the full majority and concurring opinions in order to convey accurately the Court's view of the importance of the issues it presented. We take up later parts of the majority opinion *infra* pp. 822 and 1064.]

Mr. Justice DAVIS delivered the opinion of the court. . . . The importance of the main question presented by this record cannot be overstated; for it involves the very framework of the government and the fundamental principles of American liberty.

During the late wicked Rebellion, the temper of the times did not allow that calmness in deliberation and discussion so necessary to a correct conclusion of a purely judicial question. *Then*, considerations of safety were mingled with the exercise of power; and feelings and interests prevailed which are happily terminated. *Now* that the public safety is assured, this question, as well as all others, can be discussed and decided without passion or the admixture of any element not required to form a legal judgment. . . .

Milligan claimed his discharge from custody by virtue of the act of Congress "relating to *habeas corpus* and regulating judicial proceedings in certain cases," approved March 3d, 1863. Did that act confer jurisdiction on the Circuit Court of Indiana to hear this case?

In interpreting a law, the motives which must have operated with the legislature in passing it are proper to be considered. This law was passed in a time of great national peril, when our heritage of free government was in danger. An armed rebellion against the national authority, of greater proportions than history affords an example of, was raging; and the public safety required that the privilege of the writ of *habeas corpus* should be suspended. The President had practically suspended it, and detained suspected persons in custody without trial; but his authority to do this was questioned. It was claimed that Congress alone could exercise this power; and that the legislature, and not the President, should judge of the political considerations on which the right to suspend it rested. The privilege of this great writ had never before been withheld from the citizen; and as the exigence of the times demanded immediate action, it was of the highest importance that the lawfulness of the suspension should be fully established. It was under these circumstances, which were such as to arrest the attention of the country, that this law was passed. The President was authorized by it to suspend the privilege of the writ of *habeas corpus,* whenever, in his judgment, the public safety required; and he did, by proclamation, bearing date the 15th of September, 1863, reciting, among other things, the authority of this statute, suspend it. The suspension of the writ does not authorize the arrest of any one, but simply denies to one arrested the privilege of this writ in order to obtain his liberty.

It is proper, therefore, to inquire under what circumstances the courts could rightfully refuse to grant this writ, and when the citizen was at liberty to invoke its aid.

The second and third sections of the law are explicit on these points. The language used is plain and direct, and the meaning of the Congress cannot be mistaken. The public safety demanded, if the President thought proper to arrest a suspected person, that he should not be required to give the cause of his detention on return to a writ of *habeas corpus.* But it was not contemplated that such person should be detained in custody beyond a certain fixed period, unless certain judicial proceedings, known to the common law, were commenced against him. . . .

Milligan, in his application to be released from imprisonment, averred the existence of every fact necessary under the terms of this law to give the Circuit Court of Indiana jurisdiction. If he was detained in custody by the order of the President, otherwise than as a prisoner of war; if he was a citizen of Indiana and had never been in the military or naval service, and the grand jury of the district had met, after he had been arrested, for a period of twenty days, and adjourned without taking any proceedings against him, *then* the court had the right to entertain his petition and determine the lawfulness of his imprisonment. . . .

The controlling question in the case is this: Upon the *facts* stated in Milligan's petition, and the exhibits filed, had the military commission mentioned in it *jurisdiction*, legally, to try and sentence him? . . .

No graver question was ever considered by this court, nor one which more nearly concerns the rights of the whole people; for it is the birthright of every American citizen when charged with crime, to be tried and punished according to law. The power of punishment is, alone through the means which the laws have provided for that purpose, and if they are ineffectual, there is an immunity from punishment, no matter how great an offender the individual may be, or how much his crimes may have shocked the sense of justice of the country, or endangered its safety. By the protection of the law human rights are secured; withdraw that protection, and they are at the mercy of wicked rulers, or the clamor of an excited people. If there was law to justify this military trial, it is not our province to interfere; if there was not, it is our duty to declare the nullity of the whole proceedings. The decision of this question does not depend on argument or judicial precedents, numerous and highly illustrative as they are. These precedents inform us of the extent of the struggle to preserve liberty and to relieve those in civil life from military trials. The founders of our government were familiar with the history of that struggle; and secured in a written constitution every right which the people had wrested from power during a contest of ages. By that Constitution and the laws authorized by it this question must be determined. The provisions of that instrument on the administration of criminal justice are too plain and direct, to leave room for misconstruction or doubt of their true meaning. Those applicable to this case are found in that clause of the original Constitution which says, "That the trial of all crimes, except in case of impeachment, shall be by jury;" and in the fourth, fifth, and sixth articles of the amendments. The fourth proclaims the right to be secure in person and effects against unreasonable search and seizure; and directs that a judicial warrant shall not issue "without proof of probable cause supported by oath or affirmation." The fifth declares "that no person shall be held to answer for a capital or otherwise infamous crime unless on presentment by a grand jury, except in cases arising in the land or naval forces, or in the militia, when in actual service in time of war or public danger, nor be deprived of life, liberty, or property, without due process of law." And the sixth guarantees the right of trial by jury, in such manner and with such regulations that with upright judges, impartial juries, and an able bar, the innocent will be saved and the guilty punished. . . .

Time has proven the discernment of our ancestors; for even these provisions, expressed in such plain English words, that it would seem the ingenuity of man could not evade them, are *now*, after the lapse of more than seventy years, sought to be avoided. Those great and good men foresaw that troublous times would arise, when rulers and people would become restive under restraint, and seek by sharp and decisive measures to accomplish ends deemed just and proper; and that the principles of constitutional liberty would be in peril, unless established by irrepealable law. The history of the world had taught them that what was done in the past might be attempted in the future. The Constitution of the United States is a law for rulers and people, equally in war and in peace, and covers with the shield of its protection all classes of men, at all times, and under all circumstances. No doctrine, involving more pernicious consequences, was ever invented by the wit of man than that any of its provisions can be suspended during any of the great exigencies of government. Such a doctrine leads directly to anarchy and despotism, but the theory of necessity on which it is based is false; for the government, within the Constitution, has all the powers granted to it, which are necessary to preserve its existence; as has been happily proved by the result of the great effort to throw off its just authority.

Have any of the rights guaranteed by the Constitution been violated in the case of Milligan? and if so, what are they?

Every trial involves the exercise of judicial power; and from what source did the military commission that tried him derive their authority? Certainly no part of the judicial power of the country was conferred on them; because the Constitution expressly vests it "in one supreme court and such inferior courts as the Congress may from time to time ordain and establish," and it is not pretended that the commission was a court ordained and established by Congress. They cannot justify on the mandate of the President; because he is controlled by law, and has his appropriate sphere of duty, which is to execute, not to make, the laws; and there is "no unwritten criminal code to which resort can be had as a source of jurisdiction."

But it is said that the jurisdiction is complete under the "laws and usages of war."

It can serve no useful purpose to inquire what those laws and usages are, whence they originated, where found, and on whom they operate; they can never be applied to citizens in states which have upheld the authority of the government, and where the courts are open and their process unobstructed. This court has judicial knowledge that in Indiana the Federal authority was always unopposed, and its courts always open to hear criminal accusations and redress grievances; and no usage of war could sanction a military trial there for any offence whatever of a citizen in civil life, in nowise connected with the military service. Congress could grant no such power; and to the honor of our national legislature be it said, it has never been provoked by the state of the country even to attempt its exercise. One of the plainest constitutional provisions was, therefore, infringed when Milligan was tried by a court not ordained and established by Congress, and not composed of judges appointed during good behavior.

Why was he not delivered to the Circuit Court of Indiana to be proceeded against according to law? No reason of necessity could be urged against it; because Congress had declared penalties against the offences charged, provided for their punishment, and directed that court to hear and determine them. And soon after this military tribunal was ended, the Circuit Court met, peacefully transacted its business, and adjourned. It needed no bayonets to protect it, and required no military aid to execute its judgments. It was held in a state, eminently distinguished for patriotism, by judges commissioned during the Rebellion, who were provided with juries, upright, intelligent, and selected by a marshal appointed by the President. The government had no right to conclude that Milligan, if guilty, would not receive in that court merited punishment; for its records disclose that it was constantly engaged in the trial of similar offences, and was never interrupted in its administration of criminal justice. If it was dangerous, in the distracted condition of affairs, to leave Milligan unrestrained of his liberty because he "conspired against the government, afforded aid and comfort to rebels, and incited the people to insurrection," the *law* said arrest him, confine him closely, render him powerless to do further mischief; and then present his case to the grand jury of the district, with proofs of his guilt, and, if indicted, try him according to the course of the common law. If this had been done, the Constitution would have been vindicated, the law of 1863 enforced, and the securities for personal liberty preserved and defended....

When peace prevails, and the authority of the government is undisputed, there is no difficulty of preserving the safeguards of liberty; for the ordinary modes of trial are never neglected, and no one wishes it otherwise; but if society is disturbed by civil commotion — if the passions of men are aroused and the restraints of law weakened, if not disregarded — these safeguards need, and should receive, the watchful care of those intrusted with the guardianship of the Constitution and laws. In no other way can we transmit to posterity unimpaired the blessings of liberty, consecrated by the sacrifices of the Revolution.

It is claimed that martial law covers with its broad mantle the proceedings of this military commission. The proposition is this: that in a time of war the commander of an armed force (if in his opinion the exigencies of the country demand it, and of which he is to judge), has the power, within the lines of the military district, to suspend all civil rights and their remedies, and subject citizens as well as soldiers to the *rule* of his will; and in the exercise of his lawful authority cannot be restrained, except by his superior officer or the President of the United States.

If this position is sound to the extent claimed, then when war exists, foreign or domestic, and the country is subdivided into military departments for mere convenience, the commander of one of them can, if he chooses, within his limits, on the plea of necessity, with the approval of the Executive, substitute military force for and to the exclusion of the laws, and punish all persons, as he thinks right and proper, without fixed or certain rules.

The statement of this proposition shows its importance; for, if true, republican government is a failure, and there is an end of liberty regulated by law. Martial law, established on such a basis, destroys every guarantee of the Constitution, and effectually renders the "military independent of and superior to the civil power" — the attempt to do which by the King of Great Britain was deemed by our fathers such an offence, that they assigned it to the world as one of the causes which impelled them to declare their independence. Civil liberty and this kind of martial law cannot endure together; the antagonism is irreconcilable; and, in the conflict, one or the other must perish.

This nation, as experience has proved, cannot always remain at peace, and has no right to expect that it will always have wise and humane rulers, sincerely attached to the principles of the Constitution. Wicked men, ambitious of power, with hatred of liberty and contempt of law, may fill the place once occupied by Washington and Lincoln; and if this right is conceded, and the calamities of war again befall us, the dangers to human liberty are frightful to contemplate. If our fathers had failed to provide for just such a contingency, they would have been false to the trust reposed in them. They knew — the history of the world told them — the nation they were founding, be its existence short or long, would be involved in war; how often or how long continued, human foresight could not tell; and that unlimited power, wherever lodged at such a time, was especially hazardous to freemen. For this, and other equally weighty reasons, they secured the inheritance they had fought to maintain, by incorporating in a written constitution the safeguards which *time* had proved were essential to its preservation. Not one of these safeguards can the President, or Congress, or the Judiciary disturb, except the one concerning the writ of *habeas corpus*.

It is essential to the safety of every government that, in a great crisis, like the one we have just passed through, there should be a power somewhere of suspending the writ of *habeas corpus*. In every war, there are men of previously good character, wicked enough to counsel their fellow-citizens to resist the measures deemed necessary by a good government to sustain its just authority and overthrow its enemies; and their influence may lead to dangerous combinations. In the emergency of the times, an immediate public investigation according to law may not be possible; and yet, the peril to the country may be too imminent to suffer such persons to go at large. Unquestionably, there is then an exigency which demands that the government, if it should see fit in the exercise of a proper discretion to make arrests, should not be required to produce the persons arrested in answer to a writ of *habeas corpus*. The Constitution goes no further. It does not say after a writ of *habeas corpus* is denied a citizen, that he shall be tried otherwise than by the course of the common law....

It will be borne in mind that this is not a question of the power to proclaim martial law, when war exists in a community and the courts and civil authorities are overthrown. Nor is it a question what rule a military commander, at the head of his army, can impose on states in rebellion to cripple their resources and quell the insurrection. The jurisdiction claimed is much more extensive. The necessities of the service, during the late Rebellion, required that the loyal states should be placed within the limits of certain military districts and commanders appointed in them; and, it is urged, that this, in a military sense, constituted them the theatre of military operations; and, as in this case, Indiana had been and was again threatened with invasion by the enemy, the occasion was furnished to establish martial law. The conclusion does not follow from the premises. If armies were collected in Indiana, they were to be employed in another locality, where the laws were obstructed and the national authority disputed. On *her* soil there was no hostile foot; if once invaded, that invasion was at an end, and with it all pretext for martial law. Martial law cannot arise from a *threatened* invasion. The necessity must be actual and present; the invasion real, such as effectually closes the courts and deposes the civil administration.

It is difficult to see how the *safety* for the country required martial law in Indiana. If any of her citizens were plotting treason, the power of arrest could secure them, until the government was prepared for their trial, when the courts were open and ready to try them. It was as easy to protect witnesses before a civil as a military tribunal; and as there could be no wish to convict, except on sufficient legal evidence, surely an ordained and established court was better able to judge of this than a military tribunal composed of gentlemen not trained to the profession of the law.

It follows, from what has been said on this subject, that there are occasions when martial rule can be properly applied. If, in foreign invasion or civil war, the courts are actually closed, and it is impossible to administer criminal justice according to law, *then*, on the theatre of active military operations, where war really prevails, there is a necessity to furnish a substitute for the civil authority, thus overthrown, to preserve the safety of the army and society; and as no power is left but the military, it is allowed to govern by martial rule until the laws can have their free course. As necessity creates the rule, so it limits its duration; for, if this government is continued *after* the courts are reinstated, it is a gross usurpation of power. Martial rule can never exist where the courts are open, and in the proper and unobstructed exercise of their jurisdiction. It is also confined to the locality of actual war. Because, during the late Rebellion it could have been enforced in Virginia, where the national authority was overturned and the courts driven out, it does not follow that it should obtain in Indiana, where that authority was never disputed, and justice was always administered. And so in the case of a foreign invasion, martial rule may become a necessity in one state, when, in another, it would be "mere lawless violence."...

If the military trial of Milligan was contrary to law, then he was entitled, on the facts stated in his petition, to be discharged from custody by the terms of the act of Congress of March 3d, 1863....

The CHIEF JUSTICE delivered the following opinion [in which WAYNE, SWAYNE, and MILLER, JJ., concurred]. . . . [The Chief Justice agreed that the military commission was without lawful jurisdiction to try Milligan.] But the opinion which has just been read goes further; and as we understand it, asserts not only that the military commission held in Indiana was not authorized by Congress, but that it was not in the power of Congress to authorize it. . . .

We think that Congress had power, though not exercised, to authorize the Military Commission which was held in Indiana. . . .

Congress cannot direct the conduct of campaigns, nor can the President, or any commander under him, without the sanction of Congress, institute tribunals for the trial and punishment of offences, either of soldiers or civilians, unless in cases of a controlling necessity, which justifies what it compels, or at least insures acts of indemnity from the justice of the legislature.

We by no means assert that Congress can establish and apply the laws of war where no war has been declared or exists.

Where peace exists the laws of peace must prevail. What we do maintain is, that when the nation is involved in war, and some portions of the country are invaded, and all are exposed to invasion, it is within the power of Congress to determine in what states or district such great and imminent public danger exists as justifies the authorization of military tribunals for the trial of crimes and offences against the discipline or security of the army or against the public safety. . . .

NOTES AND QUESTIONS

1. *Presidential Authority to Suspend the Writ?* Although the privilege of the writ has been suspended on a number of other occasions, the question raised by *Merryman* has not yet reached the full Supreme Court. *But see Ex parte Bollman*, 8 U.S. (4 Cranch) 75, 101 (1807) ("If at any time the public safety should require the suspension of the powers vested by this act in the courts of the United States, it is for the legislature to say so. That question depends on political considerations, on which the legislature is to decide."). Do you see any danger in allowing the President, acting alone, to suspend the writ, as Lincoln did? *See* Michael Stokes Paulsen, *The Merryman Power and the Dilemma of Autonomous Executive Branch Interpretation*, 15 Cardozo L. Rev. 81, 88-99 (1993); (Chief Justice) William H. Rehnquist, *All the Laws But One: Civil Liberties in Wartime* 11-45 (1998) (criticizing Chief Justice Taney); Harold C. Relyea, *National Emergency Powers: A Brief Overview of Presidential Suspensions of the Habeas Corpus Privilege and Invocations of Martial Law* (Cong. Res. Serv.), Sept. 20, 1976; John T. Sharer, *Power, Idealism, and Compromise: The Coordinate Branches and the Writ of Habeas Corpus*, 26 Emory L.J. 149 (1977); and Martin S. Sheffer, *Presidential Power to Suspend Habeas Corpus: The Taney-Bates Dialogue and Ex parte Merryman*, 11 Okla. City U. L. Rev. 1 (1986).

What about a danger in not allowing the President, acting alone, to suspend? How, if at all, could the Suspension Clause be interpreted to balance the dangers?

2. *The Effect of Suspension.* What was the effect of President Lincoln's suspension of the privilege of the writ of habeas corpus? You should be clear that suspension provides no legal authority for either arrest or detention; it only prevents a court from requiring the Executive to justify its act. *See* Jared A. Goldstein, *Habeas Without Rights*,

2007 Wis. L. Rev. 1165, 1169 ("As Chief Justice John Marshall framed the habeas inquiry: 'The question is, what authority has the jailor to detain him?'") (footnotes omitted). Without the judicial safeguard of habeas review, the Executive has the *power* to detain, but its *legal authority to do so* must derive from something other than the fact of suspension. Much of the *Milligan* decision after the discussion of the suspension statute is devoted to exploring the question of authority for military detention, to which we return in depth in Chapter 29.

3. *Congress's Authority to Restrict Suspension by the President?* How had Congress limited the suspension authority it vested in President Lincoln? How did the arrest and military trial of Milligan violate the statutory limits Congress had established?

Is there any limit on Congress's ability to regulate the President's authority to suspend the writ? Did the *Milligan* decision shed any light on this question?

4. *Construing to Avoid the Constitutional Question.* By the usual rules of statutory construction, courts should construe legislation or executive orders, when "fairly possible," to avoid significant constitutional questions. *See Immigration & Naturalization Service v. St. Cyr,* 533 U.S. 289, 299-300 (2001). It may be especially desirable to avoid having to decide whether the executive alone may cut off access to the courts, because, "[a]t its historical core, the writ of habeas corpus has served as a means of reviewing the legality of executive detention, and it is in that context that its protections have been the strongest." *Id.* at 301. Thus, in *St. Cyr,* the Court construed a statute to allow habeas access to the courts, even though the statute was entitled "Elimination of Custody Review by Habeas Corpus." The Court insisted that any effort to restrict the privilege of seeking the writ must be clearly stated! *Id.* at 308-309 (finding that the title was not controlling, where the actual statutory text never mentioned habeas review).

5. *Congressional Limits on Routes to Review.* Could Congress, exercising its authority under Article III, Section 2, of the Constitution, limit judicial scrutiny of a suspension of the writ either by Congress or by the President? After the *Milligan* decision, Congress expressly provided for appeals to the Supreme Court from lower federal court decisions in habeas corpus proceedings. Act of Feb. 5, 1867, 14 Stat. 385. When a Southern newspaper editor was arrested and held for trial by a military commission on charges of libel and inciting insurrection, he applied for a writ of habeas corpus first to a federal circuit court and then to the Supreme Court. During the pendency of his appeal, Congress repealed the appellate jurisdiction of the Supreme Court under the 1867 Act. 15 Stat. 44 (1868). This apparent end run around *Milligan* was upheld in *Ex parte McCardle,* 74 U.S. (7 Wall.) 506 (1868), although the Court noted an alternate route to Supreme Court review. The Court then granted a petition for a *writ of certiorari* in another case involving the trial of a civilian in a military court. *Ex parte Yerger,* 75 U.S. (8 Wall.) 85 (1868). It based its decision on the appellate jurisdiction conferred on the Supreme Court by the Judicial Act of 1789 and by the Constitution to hear petitions for writs of habeas corpus. *Id.* at 96-106. Uncertainty about the constitutional necessity for an avenue of appeal to the Supreme Court is explored in William W. Van Alstyne, *A Critical Guide to Ex Parte McCardle,* 15 Ariz. L. Rev. 229 (1973); and Leonard G. Ratner, *Congressional Power Over the Appellate Jurisdiction of the Supreme Court,* 109 U. Pa. L. Rev. 157 (1960).

6. *Habeas Corpus After September 11.* In the massive PENTTBOM investigation that followed the terrorist attacks on September 11, 2001, the Justice Department extended by regulation from 24 to 48 hours the time that an alien suspected of an immigration violation could be held without criminal charges, and it provided for indefinite detention of suspected terrorist aliens. See *supra* p. 750. Do you think any of the several hundred persons detained for questioning for an extended period was entitled to a writ of habeas corpus?

C.   AVAILABILITY OF THE WRIT TO NONRESIDENT ALIENS BEFORE 9/11

Johnson v. Eisentrager

United States Supreme Court, 1950
339 U.S. 763

Mr. Justice JACKSON delivered the opinion of the Court. The ultimate question in this case is one of jurisdiction of civil courts of the United States *vis-à-vis* military authorities in dealing with enemy aliens overseas....

[U.S. armed forces captured 21 German nationals in service of German armed forces in China. A U.S. military commission sitting in China tried and convicted them of violating laws of war, namely, engaging in, permitting, or ordering continued military activity against the United States after the surrender of Germany and before the surrender of Japan. After conviction, their sentences were reviewed and approved by military reviewing authority. They were then repatriated to the U.S.-run Landsberg Prison in Germany to serve their sentences.

They filed a petition for a writ of habeas corpus in the District of Columbia, naming the Secretary of Defense, among others, and asserting that their trial, conviction, and imprisonment violated Articles I and III of the Constitution, the Fifth Amendment, and provisions of the Geneva Convention governing the treatment of prisoners of war.]

We are cited to no instance where a court, in this or any other country where the writ is known, has issued it on behalf of an alien enemy who, at no relevant time and in no stage of his captivity, has been within its territorial jurisdiction. Nothing in the text of the Constitution extends such a right, nor does anything in our statutes....

I.

Modern American law has come a long way since the time when outbreak of war made every enemy national an outlaw, subject to both public and private slaughter, cruelty and plunder. But even by the most magnanimous view, our law does not abolish inherent distinctions recognized throughout the civilized world between citizens and aliens, nor between aliens of friendly and of enemy allegiance, nor between resident enemy aliens who have submitted themselves to our laws and nonresident enemy aliens who at all times have remained with, and adhered to, enemy governments.

With the citizen we are now little concerned, except to set his case apart as untouched by this decision and to take measure of the difference between his status and that of all categories of aliens....

The alien, to whom the United States has been traditionally hospitable, has been accorded a generous and ascending scale of rights as he increases his identity with our society. Mere lawful presence in the country creates an implied assurance of safe conduct and gives him certain rights. . . .

But, in extending constitutional protections beyond the citizenry, the Court has been at pains to point out that it was the alien's presence within its territorial jurisdiction that gave the Judiciary power to act. In the pioneer case of *Yick Wo v. Hopkins*, the Court said of the Fourteenth Amendment, "These provisions are universal in their application, to all persons within the territorial jurisdiction, without regard to any differences of race, of color, or of nationality; * * *." 118 U.S. 356, 369. . . .

Since most cases involving aliens afford this ground of jurisdiction, and the civil and property rights of immigrants or transients of foreign nationality so nearly approach equivalence to those of citizens, courts in peace time have little occasion to inquire whether litigants before them are alien or citizen.

It is war that exposes the relative vulnerability of the alien's status. The security and protection enjoyed while the nation of his allegiance remains in amity with the United States are greatly impaired when his nation takes up arms against us. While his lot is far more humane and endurable than the experience of our citizens in some enemy lands, it is still not a happy one. But disabilities this country lays upon the alien who becomes also an enemy are imposed temporarily as an incident of war and not as an incident of alienage. . . .

. . . [T]he nonresident enemy alien, especially one who has remained in the service of the enemy, does not have even this qualified access to our courts, for he neither has comparable claims upon our institutions nor could his use of them fail to be helpful to the enemy. Our law on this subject first emerged about 1813 when the Supreme Court of the State of New York had occasion, in a series of cases, to examine the foremost authorities of the Continent and of England. It concluded the rule of the common law and the law of nations to be that alien enemies resident in the country of the enemy could not maintain an action in its courts during the period of hostilities. This Court has recognized that rule, and it continues to be the law throughout this country and in England.

II.

The foregoing demonstrates how much further we must go if we are to invest these enemy aliens, resident, captured and imprisoned abroad, with standing to demand access to our courts.

We are here confronted with a decision whose basic premise is that these prisoners are entitled, as a constitutional right, to sue in some court of the United States for a writ of *habeas corpus*. To support that assumption we must hold that a prisoner of our military authorities is constitutionally entitled to the writ, even though he (a) is an enemy alien; (b) has never been or resided in the United States; (c) was captured outside of our territory and there held in military custody as a prisoner of war; (d) was tried and convicted by a Military Commission sitting outside the United States; (e) for offenses against laws of war committed outside the United States; (f) and is at all times imprisoned outside the United States.

We have pointed out that the privilege of litigation has been extended to aliens, whether friendly or enemy, only because permitting their presence in the country implied protection. No such basis can be invoked here, for these prisoners at no relevant time were within any territory over which the United States is sovereign, and the scenes of their offense, their capture, their trial and their punishment were all beyond the territorial jurisdiction of any court of the United States.

Another reason for a limited opening of our courts to resident aliens is that among them are many of friendly personal disposition to whom the status of enemy is only one imputed by law. But these prisoners were actual enemies, active in the hostile service of an enemy power....

A basic consideration in *habeas corpus* practice is that the prisoner will be produced before the court. This is the crux of the statutory scheme established by the Congress; indeed, it is inherent in the very term "*habeas corpus.*"... To grant the writ to these prisoners might mean that our army must transport them across the seas for hearing. This would require allocation of shipping space, guarding personnel, billeting and rations. It might also require transportation for whatever witnesses the prisoners desired to call as well as transportation for those necessary to defend legality of the sentence. The writ, since it is held to be a matter of right, would be equally available to enemies during active hostilities as in the present twilight between war and peace. Such trials would hamper the war effort and bring aid and comfort to the enemy. They would diminish the prestige of our commanders, not only with enemies but with wavering neutrals. It would be difficult to devise more effective fettering of a field commander than to allow the very enemies he is ordered to reduce to submission to call him to account in his own civil courts and divert his efforts and attention from the military offensive abroad to the legal defensive at home. Nor is it unlikely that the result of such enemy litigiousness would be a conflict between judicial and military opinion highly comforting to enemies of the United States....

III.

The Court of Appeals dispensed with all requirement of territorial jurisdiction based on place of residence, captivity, trial, offense, or confinement. It could not predicate relief upon any intraterritorial contact of these prisoners with our laws or institutions. Instead, it gave our Constitution an extraterritorial application to embrace our enemies in arms. Right to the writ, it reasoned, is a subsidiary procedural right that follows from possession of substantive constitutional rights. These prisoners, it considered, are invested with a right of personal liberty by our Constitution and therefore must have the right to the remedial writ. The court stated the steps in its own reasoning as follows: "*First.* The Fifth Amendment, by its terms, applies to 'any person.' *Second.* Action of Government officials in violation of the Constitution is void. This is the ultimate essence of the present controversy. *Third.* A basic and inherent function of the judicial branch of a government built upon a constitution is to set aside void action by government officials, and so to restrict executive action to the confines of the constitution. In our jurisprudence, no Government action which is void under the Constitution is exempt from judicial power. *Fourth.* The writ of habeas corpus is the established, time-honored process in our law for testing the authority of one who deprives another of his liberty, — 'the best and only sufficient defense of personal freedom.' * * *" 174 F.2d 961, 963-964....

When we analyze the claim prisoners are asserting and the court below sustained, it amounts to a right not to be tried at all for an offense against our armed forces. If the Fifth Amendment protects them from military trial, the Sixth Amendment as clearly prohibits their trial by civil courts. The latter requires in all criminal prosecutions that "the accused" be tried "by an impartial jury of the State and district wherein the crime shall have been committed, which district shall have been previously ascertained by law." And if the Fifth be held to embrace these prisoners because it uses the inclusive term "no person," the Sixth must, for it applies to all "accused." No suggestion is advanced by the court below or by prisoners of any constitutional method by which any violations of the laws of war endangering the United States forces could be reached or punished, if it were not by a Military Commission in the theatre where the offense was committed. . . .

If this Amendment invests enemy aliens in unlawful hostile action against us with immunity from military trial, it puts them in a more protected position than our own soldiers. American citizens conscripted into the military service are thereby stripped of their Fifth Amendment rights and as members of the military establishment are subject to its discipline, including military trials for offenses against aliens or Americans. . . .

The decision below would extend coverage of our Constitution to nonresident alien enemies denied to resident alien enemies. The latter are entitled only to judicial hearing to determine what the petition of these prisoners admits: that they are really alien enemies. When that appears, those resident here may be deprived of liberty by Executive action without hearing. While this is preventive rather than punitive detention, no reason is apparent why an alien enemy charged with having committed a crime should have greater immunities from Executive action than one who it is only feared might at some future time commit a hostile act.

If the Fifth Amendment confers its rights on all the world except Americans engaged in defending it, the same must be true of the companion civil-rights Amendments, for none of them is limited by its express terms, territorially or as to persons. Such a construction would mean that during military occupation irreconcilable enemy elements, guerrilla fighters, and "were-wolves" [German nationals trained to conduct terrorist activities in postwar Germany] could require the American Judiciary to assure them freedoms of speech, press, and assembly as in the First Amendment, right to bear arms as in the Second, security against "unreasonable" searches and seizures as in the Fourth, as well as rights to jury trial as in the Fifth and Sixth Amendments.

Such extraterritorial application of organic law would have been so significant an innovation in the practice of governments that, if intended or apprehended, it could scarcely have failed to excite contemporary comment. Not one word can be cited. No decision of this Court supports such a view. None of the learned commentators on our Constitution has ever hinted at it. The practice of every modern government is opposed to it.

We hold that the Constitution does not confer a right of personal security or an immunity from military trial and punishment upon an alien enemy engaged in the hostile service of a government at war with the United States. . . .

IV. . . .

These prisoners do not assert, and could not, that anything in the Geneva Convention makes them immune from prosecution or punishment for war crimes.[14]

---

14. We are not holding that these prisoners have no right which the military authorities are bound to respect. The United States, by the Geneva Convention of July 27, 1929, 47 Stat. 2021, concluded with forty-six other countries, including the German Reich, an agreement upon the treatment to be accorded

Article 75 thereof expressly provides that a prisoner of war may be detained until the end of such proceedings and, if necessary, until the expiration of the punishment. . . .

V. . . .

Since in the present application we find no basis for invoking federal judicial power in any district, we need not debate as to where, if the case were otherwise, the petition should be filed.

For reasons stated, the judgment of the Court of Appeals is reversed and the judgment of the District Court dismissing the petition is affirmed.

Reversed.

Mr. Justice BLACK, with whom Mr. Justice DOUGLAS and Mr. Justice BURTON concur, dissenting. . . . In Parts I, II, and III of its opinion, the Court apparently holds that no American court can even consider the jurisdiction of the military tribunal to convict and sentence these prisoners for the alleged crime. . . . [T]his holding . . . is based on the facts that (1) they were enemy aliens who were belligerents when captured, and (2) they were captured, tried, and imprisoned outside our realm, never having been in the United States.

The contention that enemy alien belligerents have no standing whatever to contest conviction for war crimes by habeas corpus proceedings has twice been emphatically rejected by a unanimous Court [citing *Ex parte Quirin*, 317 U.S. 1 (1942), and *In re Yamashita*, 327 U.S. 1 (1946)]. . . . That we went on to deny the requested writ [in both cases] in no way detracts from the clear holding that habeas corpus jurisdiction is available even to belligerent aliens convicted by a military tribunal for an offense committed in actual acts of warfare.

. . . Does a prisoner's right to test legality of a sentence then depend on where the Government chooses to imprison him? Certainly the *Quirin* and *Yamashita* opinions lend no support to that conclusion, for in upholding jurisdiction they place no reliance whatever on territorial location. The Court is fashioning wholly indefensible doctrine if it permits the executive branch, by deciding where its prisoners will be tried and imprisoned, to deprive all federal courts of their power to protect against a federal executive's illegal incarcerations.

If the opinion thus means, and it apparently does, that these petitioners are deprived of the privilege of habeas corpus solely because they were convicted and imprisoned overseas, the Court is adopting a broad and dangerous principle. . . .

. . . It has always been recognized that actual warfare can be conducted successfully only if those in command are left the most ample independence in the theatre of operations. Our Constitution is not so impractical or inflexible that it unduly restricts such necessary independence. It would be fantastic to suggest that alien enemies could hail our military leaders into judicial tribunals to account for their day to day activities on the battlefront. Active fighting forces must be free to fight while hostilities are in progress. But that undisputable axiom has no bearing on this case or the general problem from which it arises. . . .

---

captives. These prisoners claim to be and are entitled to its protection. It is, however, the obvious scheme of the Agreement that responsibility for observance and enforcement of these rights is upon political and military authorities. . . .

The question here involves a far narrower issue. Springing from recognition that our government is composed of three separate and independent branches, it is whether the judiciary has power in habeas corpus proceedings to test the legality of criminal sentences imposed by the executive through military tribunals in a country which we have occupied for years. . . .

Though the scope of habeas corpus review of military tribunal sentences is narrow, I think it should not be denied to these petitioners and others like them. We control that part of Germany we occupy. These prisoners were convicted by our own military tribunals under our own Articles of War, years after hostilities had ceased. However illegal their sentences might be, they can expect no relief from German courts or any other branch of the German Government we permit to function. Only our own courts can inquire into the legality of their imprisonment. Perhaps, as some nations believe, there is merit in leaving the administration of criminal laws to executive and military agencies completely free from judicial scrutiny. Our Constitution has emphatically expressed a contrary policy. . . .

. . . Our nation proclaims a belief in the dignity of human beings as such, no matter what their nationality or where they happen to live. Habeas corpus, as an instrument to protect against illegal imprisonment, is written into the Constitution. Its use by courts cannot in my judgment be constitutionally abridged by Executive or by Congress. I would hold that our courts can exercise it whenever any United States official illegally imprisons any person in any land we govern. Courts should not for any reason abdicate this, the loftiest power with which the Constitution has endowed them.

NOTES AND QUESTIONS

1. *Comparing Milligan and Eisentrager.* How were *Milligan* and *Eisentrager* different factually in ways that might have affected the availability of the writ to the petitioners? Which of those ways, if any, were reflected in the text of the Constitution? In the respective extant habeas statutes? In concerns about separation of powers? In U.S. history? In practical considerations relating to the competence of courts? How did each Court weigh these factors?

2. *Substantive Constitutional Rights?* The Court of Appeals in *Eisentrager* was said to have reasoned that "[r]ight to the writ . . . is a subsidiary procedural right that follows from possession of substantive constitutional rights." 339 U.S. at 781. Was the Court justified in regarding the "procedural" right to the writ of habeas corpus as "subsidiary"?

Forty years on, in *United States v. Verdugo-Urquidez,* 494 U.S. 259 (1990), *supra* p. 712, the Court declared categorically that in *Eisentrager* it had emphatically "rejected the claim that aliens are entitled to Fifth Amendment rights outside the sovereign territory of the United States." *Id.* at 269. Is this an accurate characterization of the Court's 1950 decision? If not, did the Court have some other basis for rejecting the *Eisentrager* petitioners' application for the writ?

Did the *Eisentrager* Court necessarily have to determine the existence of substantive rights before deciding on the availability of the writ to vindicate such rights? In other words, does the Suspension Clause confer some substantive as well as procedural rights?

3. *Other Factors Influencing the Outcome?* In Part II of its opinion, the Court listed six factors that differentiated the petitioners from other prisoners. How important do you think each factor was in determining the availability of the writ? Were they all necessary to deny access to habeas? How did these factors interact?

4. *Alienage.* How important a role did the citizenship of the petitioners play in *Eisentrager?* What is the constitutional basis for the "inherent distinctions . . . between citizens and aliens" mentioned by the Court? Between friendly and enemy aliens? The Court referred to "a generous and ascending scale of rights" accorded to aliens by the courts. Can you describe the scale and name the rights? *See United States v. Verdugo-Urquidez, supra,* 494 U.S. at 270-273. Where did the *Eisentrager* petitioners fall on that scale?

5. *Impracticality of Giving Prisoners of War Habeas Access.* Suppose the Court had found that Eisentrager and other enemy soldiers with the same status *did have* the right to petition for a writ of habeas corpus. What practical difficulties might such a decision have raised for courts? What would have been the implications for national defense efforts in 1950? How about today?

6. *An Incident of War?* The *Eisentrager* Court explained that "[i]t is war that exposes the relative vulnerability of the alien's status." Was the United States still at war in 1950, when the case came to the Court? If the President's authority to imprison the petitioners depended on the existence of a war, in the same way that President Lincoln's authority to capture depended on the existence of a war in the *Prize Cases, supra* p. 68, was the United States engaged in a war as defined in that 1863 case? *See generally* Stephen I. Vladeck, *Ludecke's Lengthening Shadow: The Disturbing Prospect of War Without End,* 2 J. Nat'l Security L. & Pol'y 53 (2006).

7. *Soldiers' Rights and Human Rights in 1950.* The Court expressed concern that extending Fifth Amendment due process protections to Eisentrager and his fellow prisoners would "put them in a more protected position than our own soldiers." 339 U.S. at 783. This was a backhanded reference to the still primitive state of military justice at the time. The Uniform Code of Military Justice only became effective in 1951, a year after *Eisentrager,* and it took many years for it to evolve into the robust and procedurally fair system that it is today. International humanitarian law and international human rights also developed significantly after *Eisentrager.* See Chapter 9. Do these developments undercut the majority's treatment of the *Eisentrager* petitioner's right to personal freedom? If so, do they justify reinterpreting the holding, or does *Eisentrager* remain controlling precedent until it is expressly discarded by the Supreme Court?

8. *Availability of the Writ After 9/11.* It is often stated that "everything changed" after the terrorist attacks of 9/11. Did the events of that fateful day, with the resulting heightened awareness of our vulnerability to highly unpredictable attacks from elusive enemies, require us to rethink the meaning of the Suspension Clause? If they did, how is the meaning now different, and how can any such difference be put into practice?

The Great Writ: Habeas Corpus After 9/11

As the last chapter suggests, by 1950 it seemed reasonably clear that a U.S. citizen detained by her government was entitled to petition a federal court for a writ of habeas corpus (e.g., *Ex parte Milligan*), while an alien detained abroad for acts committed abroad could not (e.g., *Johnson v. Eisentrager*).

What then of aliens detained inside the United States? During the Second World War, the government had to decide what to do with eight German saboteurs who were caught in the United States. President Roosevelt opted to try them by military commission (a court composed of military officers) in Washington, D.C., because a commission could impose death sentences, unlike the civilian courts at the time. *See* David J. Danelski, *The Saboteurs' Case*, 1 J. S. Ct. Hist. 61 (1996). But the President also told his Attorney General, "I won't hand them over to any United States marshal armed with a writ of habeas corpus. Understand?" *Id.* The presidential proclamation establishing the military commission dealt with this eventuality by providing that defendants "shall not be privileged to seek any remedy or maintain any proceeding directly or indirectly, or to have any such remedy or proceeding brought on their behalf, in the courts of the United States," except under such regulations as the Attorney General might issue. Proclamation No. 2561, 7 Fed. Reg. 5101 (July 2, 1942). This transparent attempt to suspend the writ ultimately fared poorly in court, however. The Supreme Court concluded that nothing in the proclamation "foreclose[d] consideration by the courts of petitioners' contentions that the Constitution and the laws of the United States constitutionally enacted forbid their trial by military commission." *Ex parte Quirin*, 317 U.S. 1, 25 (1942), *infra* p. 823. Thus, even aliens had a right to petition for habeas when they were detained inside the United States.

A later World War II case involved an enemy soldier who petitioned for a writ of habeas corpus after being tried by a military commission in the then-unincorporated U.S. territory of the Phillipines. The Court declared that Congress "has not withdrawn, and the Executive branch of the government could not, unless there was suspension of the writ, withdraw from the courts the duty and power to make such inquiry into the authority of the commission as may be made by habeas corpus." *Application of Yamashita*, 327 U.S. 1, 9 (1946). Indeed, Justice Murphy characterized the claim that courts could not make such inquiries as an "obnoxious doctrine," which he said the Court "rejected fully and unquestionably." *Id.* at 30. Thus, it seemed that aliens in unincorporated U.S. territories had the right to petition for habeas.

After the 9/11 attacks, President George W. Bush issued a military order in November 2001 providing for the military detention and trial by military commission of noncitizens he designated as members of Al Qaeda or persons involved in acts of international terrorism. The language of the order closely resembled that used in the order issued by President Roosevelt in 1942. The order included the following provision:

Military Order of November 13, 2001, Detention, Treatment, and Trial of Certain Non-Citizens in the War Against Terrorism

66 Fed. Reg. 57,833 (Nov. 13, 2001)

SEC. 7. RELATIONSHIP TO OTHER LAW AND FORUMS...

(b) With respect to any individual subject to this order —
(1) military tribunals shall have exclusive jurisdiction with respect to offenses by the individual; and
(2) the individual shall not be privileged to seek any remedy or maintain any proceeding, directly or indirectly, or to have any such remedy or proceeding sought on the individual's behalf, in
(i) any court of the United States, or any State thereof,
(ii) any court of any foreign nation, or
(iii) any international tribunal....

Within a short time, persons captured by (or rendered to) U.S. forces in Afghanistan began to be imprisoned at the Guantánamo Bay Naval Station in Cuba, raising the question whether *they* were entitled to petition for habeas.

This chapter is devoted to an examination of the privilege of the writ of habeas corpus since the terrorist attacks of 9/11. In Part A, we review two Supreme Court decisions involving the availability of the writ to Guantánamo detainees. In Part B, we consider whether the writ is available to noncitizens imprisoned by the United States abroad. These materials present difficult but profoundly important questions of constitutional interpretation and statutory construction. They also test, once again, the role of courts in providing for national security.

One final introductory note concerns language. Some of the jargon used here is freighted with technical meaning, so it must be employed with care. Other terms may be chosen for their political or emotional content. An example of the latter is the word "detainee," which has come into vogue since 9/11 as a kinder, gentler euphemism for "prisoner." We use the two words here interchangeably.

A.   EXTENDING THE STATUTORY WRIT TO GUANTÁNAMO BAY DETAINEES

Soon after U.S. military operations against Al Qaeda and the Taliban commenced in Afghanistan in fall 2001, U.S. troops captured a number of individuals on the battlefield. Following a period of detention (and sometimes interrogation) in Afghanistan, many of these individuals were transferred to Guantánamo Bay, as noted

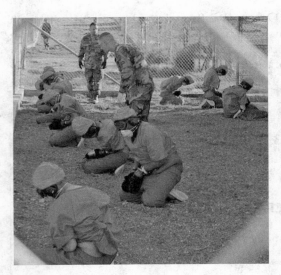

Detainees at Camp X-Ray, Guantánamo Bay Naval Base, Cuba.

DOD photo by Petty Officer 1st Class Shane T. McCoy, U.S. Navy.

above. Eventually, some Al Qaeda suspects captured or rendered to U.S. custody in other countries were also transferred to Guantánamo.

In 2002, two Australian citizens and twelve Kuwaiti citizens who were detained at Guantánamo filed habeas petitions in the U.S. District Court for the District of Columbia (on the theory that their custodian or jailor was located there), invoking the Habeas Corpus Act, 28 U.S.C. §§2241-2255 (2006 & Supp. III 2009), *supra* p. 765. The lower courts rejected their petitions, citing *Johnson v. Eisentrager,* 339 U.S. 763 (1950), for the proposition that "aliens detained outside the sovereign territory of the United States [may not] invok[e] a petition for a writ of habeas corpus." *Rasul v. Bush,* 215 F. Supp. 2d 55, 68 (D.D.C. 2002), *aff'd sub nom. Al Odah v. Bush,* 321 F.3d 1134 (D.C. Cir. 2003).

The Supreme Court reversed. It found the Guantánamo petitioners different from the *Eisentrager* detainees in important respects:

> They are not nationals of countries at war with the United States, and they deny that they have engaged in or plotted acts of aggression against the United States; they have never been afforded access to any tribunal, much less charged with and convicted of wrongdoing; and for more than two years they have been imprisoned in territory over which the United States exercises exclusive jurisdiction and control. [*Rasul v. Bush,* 542 U.S. 466, 467 (2004).]

It also held that *Eisentrager* dealt only with "the question of the prisoners' *constitutional* entitlement to habeas corpus," and made no more than "a passing reference" to the absence of "*statutory* authorization." *Id.* (emphasis in original). It then found that intervening case law had extended statutory habeas jurisdiction to encompass the petitioners' claims against a custodian in the District of Columbia. *Id.*

> In the end, the answer to the question presented is clear. Petitioners contend that they are being held in federal custody in violation of the laws of the United States.[15] No party questions the District Court's jurisdiction over petitioners' custodians. Cf. *Braden* [*v. 30th Judicial Circuit Court of Ky.,* 410 U.S. 484 (1973)], at 495. Section 2241, by its terms,

---

15. Petitioners' allegations — that, although they have engaged neither in combat nor in acts of terrorism against the United States, they have been held in Executive detention for more than two years in territory subject to the long-term, exclusive jurisdiction and control of the United States, without access to counsel and without being charged with any wrongdoing — unquestionably describe "custody in violation of the Constitution or laws or treaties of the United States." 28 U.S.C. §2241(c)(3).

requires nothing more. We therefore hold that §2241 confers on the District Court jurisdiction to hear petitioners' habeas corpus challenges to the legality of their detention at the Guantanamo Bay Naval Base. [*Rasul*, 542 U.S. at 483.]

NOTES AND QUESTIONS

1. *The Military Order's "Suspension" of the Writ.* Assuming that some of the petitioners in *Rasul* were detained pursuant to the Military Order of November 13, 2001, why did §7 of the order not cut off their access to the courts? First, consider whether, in light of §7's pedigree, it was intended to suspend the writ. Next, consider whether, in light of the "clear statement" rule declared in *Immigration & Naturalization Service v. St. Cyr*, 533 U.S. 289 (2001), *supra* p. 774, any such intent was stated with the required clarity.

2. *Eisentrager's "Dire Warning."* Sharply dissenting in *Rasul*, Justice Scalia quoted the "dire warning" in *Johnson v. Eisentrager*, 339 U.S. 763 (1950), to suggest that the Court's ruling would open the floodgates to habeas petitions by enemy aliens after we captured large numbers in battle. Indeed, alien detainees at Guantánamo quickly pressed habeas petitions in U.S. courts. *See In re Guantanamo Detainee Cases*, 355 F. Supp. 2d 443 (D.D.C. 2005) (reporting that 13 cases involving more than 60 detainees had been filed by July 2004). Can you think of an answer to this concern? *Ex parte Milligan* and the statute it applied in 1866 suggest one answer. What is it? See the Detainee Treatment Act of 2005, *infra* Note 6.

In an apparent effort to close, or at least control, the floodgates, the Pentagon announced shortly after the Supreme Court's decision in *Rasul* that it was creating a Combatant Status Review Tribunal (CSRT), to be staffed by military officers, before whom detainees could contest their combatant status. Memorandum for the Secretary of the Navy from Deputy Secretary of Defense Paul Wolfowitz, *Order Establishing Combatant Status Review Tribunal* (July 7, 2004), *available at* http://www.defense.gov/news/jul2004/d20040707review.pdf. Detainees would have the assistance of a "personal representative" assigned by the government, but not a lawyer, and they would have to overcome a "rebuttable presumption in favor of the government's evidence." *Id.* ¶¶c. and g.(12). Do you think this program could stem the tide of habeas petitions to federal courts? If you represented one of the Guantánamo prisoners, could you think of a way to challenge the CSRT program? *See* Mark Denbeaux & Joshua W. Denbeaux, *No-Hearing Hearings — CSRT: The Modern Habeas Corpus?* (Seton Hall Pub. Law Research Paper No. 951245, 2006), *available at* http://ssrn.com/abstract=951245.

3. *The Inner Realm of Military Affairs: What's Left of Eisentrager?* Justice Kennedy joined in the *Rasul* judgment by preserving part of *Eisentrager*. He found that *Eisentrager* approved of "a realm of political authority over military affairs where the judicial power may not enter," but also that the Guantánamo Bay detentions, far removed from hostilities and attended by no status-determining procedures, even by the military, fell outside that realm. If the *Rasul* majority had embraced those qualifications, what would be left of *Eisentrager?*

4. *The Detainees' Constitutional Rights. Rasul* was strictly a jurisdictional decision, finding that the Guantánamo detainees had the right to petition for habeas. It did not reach the next question, which is whether they could assert any constitutional rights

that were violated by their detention. But consider footnote 15, above, from the majority opinion. What answer to that question does the footnote suggest? Is the answer holding or dictum?

5. *Contextual Influences.* Speculation about the Court's motives is always treacherous. Yet between the oral arguments in *Rasul*, in which the government assured the Court that the detainees were being treated in compliance with basic international human rights principles, and the Court's decision, the press broke the scandal about abuse of prisoners in Iraq and possible use of torture by the United States in the interrogation of detainees. See *infra* pp. 926-939. Might the reports of mistreatment and of possible violations of international laws against torture have influenced the Court's decision on opening access to Article III courts?

6. *"Statutory Entitlement" and the Detainee Treatment Act of 2005. Rasul* ruled that the Guantánamo detainees had a "statutory entitlement" to petition for habeas. Congress responded quickly to *Rasul* by amending the relevant habeas statute in an effort to narrow that entitlement:

Detainee Treatment Act of 2005 (DTA)

Pub. L. No. 109-148, §1001-1006, 119 Stat. 2680, 2739-2744 (2005)

§1005. PROCEDURES FOR STATUS REVIEW OF DETAINEES OUTSIDE THE UNITED STATES . . .

(e) Judicial Review of Detention of Enemy Combatants. —
(1) In General. — Section 2241 of title 28, United States Code, is amended by adding at the end the following:

"(e) Except as provided in section 1005 of the Detainee Treatment Act of 2005, no court, justice, or judge shall have jurisdiction to hear or consider —
(1) an application for a writ of habeas corpus filed by or on behalf of an alien detained by the Department of Defense at Guantanamo Bay, Cuba; or
(2) any other action against the United States or its agents relating to any aspect of the detention by the Department of Defense of an alien at Guantanamo Bay, Cuba, who —
(A) is currently in military custody; or
(B) has been determined by the United States Court of Appeals for the District of Columbia Circuit in accordance with the procedures set forth in section 1005(e) of the Detainee Treatment Act of 2005 to have been properly detained as an enemy combatant.".

Section 1005(e)(2) and (e)(3) of the Act provided limited judicial review in the D.C. Circuit of the procedural validity of final decisions of CSRTs and of Military Commissions, but not review of the merits of such decisions.

Within months, however, a divided Supreme Court decided in *Hamdan v. Rumsfeld*, 548 U.S. 557 (2006), that federal courts *still* had statutory jurisdiction to hear a Guantánamo detainee's petition for the writ in a challenge to his prospective trial by military commission. Concerning military commissions, see generally Chapter 36.

The *Hamdan* majority reasoned that Congress had not clearly expressed an intent to withdraw habeas jurisdiction from pending cases like Hamdan's. *Id.* at 575-584.

B. EXTENDING THE CONSTITUTIONAL WRIT TO GUANTÁNAMO BAY DETAINEES (AND OTHERS?)

After extended negotiations with the Bush administration in which, according to most observers, the Administration prevailed, Congress responded to *Hamdan v. Rumsfeld* by enacting the Military Commissions Act of 2006 (MCA 2006), Pub. L. No. 109-366, 120 Stat. 2600. Section 7 of MCA 2006 was intended to further amend the habeas statute by cutting off all access to the courts for "an alien detained by the United States who has been determined by the United States to have been properly detained as an enemy combatant or is awaiting such determination," except for the limited review provided by DTA §1005(2) and (3), as noted above. Detainees promptly challenged the new act, as described in the following case.

Boumediene v. Bush
United States Supreme Court, 2008
553 U.S. 723

JUSTICE KENNEDY delivered the opinion of the Court. Petitioners are aliens designated as enemy combatants and detained at the United States Naval Station at Guantanamo Bay, Cuba. There are others detained there, also aliens, who are not parties to this suit.

Petitioners present a question not resolved by our earlier cases relating to the detention of aliens at Guantanamo: whether they have the constitutional privilege of habeas corpus, a privilege not to be withdrawn except in conformance with the Suspension Clause, Art. I, §9, cl. 2. We hold these petitioners do have the habeas corpus privilege. Congress has enacted a statute, the Detainee Treatment Act of 2005 (DTA), 119 Stat. 2739, that provides certain procedures for review of the detainees' status. We hold that those procedures are not an adequate and effective substitute for habeas corpus. Therefore, §7 of the Military Commissions Act of 2006 (MCA), 28 U.S.C.A. §2241(e) (Supp. 2007), operates as an unconstitutional suspension of the writ. We do not address whether the President has authority to detain these petitioners nor do we hold that the writ must issue. These and other questions regarding the legality of the detention are to be resolved in the first instance by the District Court.

I...

Interpreting the AUMF [Authorization for Use of Military Force, Pub. L. No. 107-40 (2001), *supra* p. 97], the Department of Defense ordered the detention of these petitioners, and they were transferred to Guantanamo. Some of these individuals were apprehended on the battlefield in Afghanistan, others in places as far away from there as Bosnia and Gambia. All are foreign nationals, but none is a citizen of a nation now at war with the United States. Each denies he is a member of the al Qaeda terrorist network that carried out the September 11 attacks or of the Taliban regime that provided sanctuary for al Qaeda. Each petitioner appeared before a separate CSRT [Combatant Status Review Tribunal]; was determined to be an enemy combatant; and has sought a writ of habeas corpus in the United States District Court for the District of Columbia.

[These initial petitions culminated in the Supreme Court's decision in *Rasul v. Bush*, 524 U.S. 466 (2004), extending *statutory* habeas corpus jurisdiction to Guantanamo. The Court there did not reach the question of *constitutional* habeas corpus jurisdiction, which is presented in the instant cases.] . . .

II

As a threshold matter, we must decide whether MCA §7 denies the federal courts jurisdiction to hear habeas corpus actions pending at the time of its enactment. We hold the statute does deny that jurisdiction, so that, if the statute is valid, petitioners' cases must be dismissed.

As amended by the terms of the MCA, §2241(e) now provides:

(1) No court, justice, or judge shall have jurisdiction to hear or consider an application for a writ of habeas corpus filed by or on behalf of an alien detained by the United States who has been determined by the United States to have been properly detained as an enemy combatant or is awaiting such determination.

(2) Except as provided in [§1005(e)(2) and (e)(3) of the DTA] no court, justice, or judge shall have jurisdiction to hear or consider any other action against the United States or its agents relating to any aspect of the detention, transfer, treatment, trial, or conditions of confinement of an alien who is or was detained by the United States and has been determined by the United States to have been properly detained as an enemy combatant or is awaiting such determination. . . .

III . . .

We begin with a brief account of the history and origins of the writ. Our account proceeds from two propositions. First, protection for the privilege of habeas corpus was one of the few safeguards of liberty specified in a Constitution that, at the outset, had no Bill of Rights. In the system conceived by the Framers the writ had a centrality that must inform proper interpretation of the Suspension Clause. Second, to the extent there were settled precedents or legal commentaries in 1789 regarding the extraterritorial scope of the writ or its application to enemy aliens, those authorities can be instructive for the present cases.

A

The Framers viewed freedom from unlawful restraint as a fundamental precept of liberty, and they understood the writ of habeas corpus as a vital instrument to secure that freedom. Experience taught, however, that the common-law writ all too often had been insufficient to guard against the abuse of monarchial power. That history counseled the necessity for specific language in the Constitution to secure the writ and ensure its place in our legal system. . . .

This history was known to the Framers. It no doubt confirmed their view that pendular swings to and away from individual liberty were endemic to undivided, uncontrolled power. The Framers' inherent distrust of governmental power was the driving force behind the constitutional plan that allocated powers among three independent branches. This design serves not only to make Government accountable but also to secure individual liberty. Because the Constitution's separation-of-powers structure, like the substantive guarantees of the Fifth and Fourteenth Amendments, *see Yick Wo v. Hopkins*, 118 U.S. 356, 374 (1886), protects persons as well as citizens, foreign nationals who have the privilege of litigating in our courts can seek to enforce separation-of-powers principles, see, *e.g., INS v. Chadha*, 462 U.S. 919, 958-959 (1983).

That the Framers considered the writ a vital instrument for the protection of individual liberty is evident from the care taken to specify the limited grounds for its suspension: "The Privilege of the Writ of Habeas Corpus shall not be suspended, unless when in Cases of Rebellion or Invasion the public Safety may require it." Art. I, §9, cl. 2; *see* Amar, *Of Sovereignty and Federalism*, 96 Yale L.J. 1425, 1509 n.329 (1987) ("[T]he non-suspension clause is the original Constitution's most explicit reference to remedies")....

In our own system the Suspension Clause is designed to protect against these cyclical abuses. The Clause protects the rights of the detained by a means consistent with the essential design of the Constitution. It ensures that, except during periods of formal suspension, the Judiciary will have a time-tested device, the writ, to maintain the "delicate balance of governance" that is itself the surest safeguard of liberty. *See Hamdi* [*v. Rumsfeld*, 542 U.S. 507 (2004)], at 536 (plurality opinion). The Clause protects the rights of the detained by affirming the duty and authority of the Judiciary to call the jailer to account. The separation-of-powers doctrine, and the history that influenced its design, therefore must inform the reach and purpose of the Suspension Clause.

B ...

To support their arguments, the parties in these cases have examined historical sources to construct a view of the common-law writ as it existed in 1789 — as have *amici* whose expertise in legal history the Court has relied upon in the past. The Government argues the common-law writ ran only to those territories over which the Crown was sovereign. Petitioners argue that jurisdiction followed the King's officers. Diligent search by all parties reveals no certain conclusions....

... We decline, therefore, to infer too much, one way or the other, from the lack of historical evidence on point.

IV

Drawing from its position that at common law the writ ran only to territories over which the Crown was sovereign, the Government says the Suspension Clause affords petitioners no rights because the United States does not claim sovereignty over the place of detention.

Guantanamo Bay is not formally part of the United States. *See* DTA §1005(g), 119 Stat. 2743. And under the terms of the lease between the United States and Cuba, Cuba retains "ultimate sovereignty" over the territory while the United States exercises "complete jurisdiction and control." *See* Lease of Lands for Coaling and Naval Stations, Feb. 23, 1903, U.S.-Cuba, Art. III, T.S. No. 418 (hereinafter 1903 Lease Agreement); *Rasul*, 542 U.S., at 471. Under the terms of the 1934 Treaty, however, Cuba effectively has no rights as a sovereign until the parties agree to modification of the 1903 Lease Agreement or the United States abandons the base. *See* Treaty Defining Relations with Cuba, May 29, 1934, U.S.-Cuba, Art. III, 48 Stat. 1683, T.S. No. 866.

The United States contends, nevertheless, that Guantanamo is not within its sovereign control. This was the Government's position well before the events of September 11, 2001. And in other contexts the Court has held that questions of sovereignty are for the political branches to decide. Even if this were a treaty interpretation case that did not involve a political question, the President's construction of the lease agreement would be entitled to great respect.

We therefore do not question the Government's position that Cuba, not the United States, maintains sovereignty, in the legal and technical sense of the term, over Guantanamo Bay. But this does not end the analysis. Our cases do not hold it is improper for us to inquire into the objective degree of control the Nation asserts over foreign territory....

A

The Court has discussed the issue of the Constitution's extraterritorial application on many occasions. These decisions undermine the Government's argument that, at least as applied to noncitizens, the Constitution necessarily stops where *de jure* sovereignty ends.

[The Court reviewed cases, including the *Insular Cases* and *Reid v. Covert*, 345 U.S. 1 (1957), as standing for the proposition that "whether a constitutional provision has extraterritorial effect depends upon the 'particular circumstances, the practical necessities, and the possible alternatives which Congress had before it' and, in particular, whether judicial enforcement of the provision would be 'impracticable and anomalous.'" (quoting Justice Harlan in *Reid*).] ...

Practical considerations weighed heavily as well in *Johnson v. Eisentrager*, 339 U.S. 763 (1950), where the Court addressed whether habeas corpus jurisdiction extended to enemy aliens who had been convicted of violating the laws of war. The prisoners were detained at Landsberg Prison in Germany during the Allied Powers' postwar occupation. The Court stressed the difficulties of ordering the Government to produce the prisoners in a habeas corpus proceeding. It "would require allocation of shipping space, guarding personnel, billeting and rations" and would damage the prestige of military commanders at a sensitive time. *Id.*, at 779. In considering these factors the Court sought to balance the constraints of military occupation with constitutional necessities. *Id.*, at 769-779; *see Rasul*, 542 U.S., at 475-476 (discussing the factors relevant to *Eisentrager*'s constitutional holding); 542 U.S., at 486 (Kennedy, J., concurring in judgment) (same).

True, the Court in *Eisentrager* denied access to the writ, and it noted the prisoners "at no relevant time were within any territory over which the United States is sovereign, and [that] the scenes of their offense, their capture, their trial and their punishment were all beyond the territorial jurisdiction of any court of the United States." 339 U.S., at 778. The Government seizes upon this language as proof positive that the *Eisentrager* Court adopted a formalistic, sovereignty-based test for determining the reach of the Suspension Clause. We reject this reading for three reasons.

First, we do not accept the idea that the above-quoted passage from *Eisentrager* is the only authoritative language in the opinion and that all the rest is dicta.

The Court's further determinations, based on practical considerations, were integral to Part II of its opinion and came before the decision announced its holding. *See* 339 U.S., at 781.

. . . Even if we assume the *Eisentrager* Court considered the United States' lack of formal legal sovereignty over Landsberg Prison as the decisive factor in that case, its holding is not inconsistent with a functional approach to questions of extraterritoriality. The formal legal status of a given territory affects, at least to some extent, the political branches' control over that territory. *De jure* sovereignty is a factor that bears upon which constitutional guarantees apply there.

Third, if the Government's reading of *Eisentrager* were correct, the opinion would have marked not only a change in, but a complete repudiation of, the *Insular Cases'* (and later *Reid*'s) functional approach to questions of extraterritoriality. We cannot accept the Government's view. Nothing in *Eisentrager* says that *de jure* sovereignty is or has ever been the only relevant consideration in determining the geographic reach of the Constitution or of habeas corpus. Were that the case, there would be considerable tension between *Eisentrager,* on the one hand, and the *Insular Cases* and *Reid,* on the other. Our cases need not be read to conflict in this manner. A constricted reading of *Eisentrager* overlooks what we see as a common thread uniting the *Insular Cases, Eisentrager,* and *Reid:* the idea that questions of extraterritoriality turn on objective factors and practical concerns, not formalism.

B

The Government's formal sovereignty-based test raises troubling separation-of-powers concerns as well. The political history of Guantanamo illustrates the deficiencies of this approach. The United States has maintained complete and uninterrupted control of the bay for over 100 years. . . . The necessary implication of the argument is that by surrendering formal sovereignty over any unincorporated territory to a third party, while at the same time entering into a lease that grants total control over the territory back to the United States, it would be possible for the political branches to govern without legal constraint.

Our basic charter cannot be contracted away like this. The Constitution grants Congress and the President the power to acquire, dispose of, and govern territory, not the power to decide when and where its terms apply. Even when the United States acts outside its borders, its powers are not "absolute and unlimited" but are subject "to such restrictions as are expressed in the Constitution." *Murphy v. Ramsey*, 114 U.S. 15, 44 (1885). Abstaining from questions involving formal sovereignty and territorial governance is one thing. To hold the political branches have the power to switch the Constitution on or off at will is quite another. The former position reflects this Court's recognition that certain matters requiring political judgments are best left to the political branches. The latter would permit a striking anomaly in our tripartite system of government, leading to a regime in which Congress and the President, not this Court, say "what the law is." *Marbury v. Madison*, 1 Cranch 137, 177 (1803).

These concerns have particular bearing upon the Suspension Clause question in the cases now before us, for the writ of habeas corpus is itself an indispensable mechanism for monitoring the separation of powers. The test for determining the scope of this provision must not be subject to manipulation by those whose power it is designed to restrain.

C

As we recognized in *Rasul,* 542 U.S., at 476; *id.,* at 487 (Kennedy, J., concurring in judgment), the outlines of a framework for determining the reach of the Suspension Clause are suggested by the factors the Court relied upon in *Eisentrager.* In addition to the practical concerns discussed above, the *Eisentrager* Court found relevant that each petitioner:

> "(a) is an enemy alien; (b) has never been or resided in the United States; (c) was captured outside of our territory and there held in military custody as a prisoner of war; (d) was tried and convicted by a Military Commission sitting outside the United States; (e) for offenses against laws of war committed outside the United States; (f) and is at all times imprisoned outside the United States." 339 U.S., at 777.

Based on this language from *Eisentrager,* and the reasoning in our other extraterritoriality opinions, we conclude that at least three factors are relevant in determining the reach of the Suspension Clause: (1) the citizenship and status of the detainee and the adequacy of the process through which that status determination was made; (2) the nature of the sites where apprehension and then detention took place; and (3) the practical obstacles inherent in resolving the prisoner's entitlement to the writ.

Applying this framework, we note at the onset that the status of these detainees is a matter of dispute. The petitioners, like those in *Eisentrager,* are not American citizens. But the petitioners in *Eisentrager* did not contest, it seems, the Court's assertion that they were "enemy alien[s]." In the instant cases, by contrast, the detainees deny they are enemy combatants. They have been afforded some process in CSRT proceedings to determine their status; but, unlike in *Eisentrager,* there has been no trial by military commission for violations of the laws of war. The difference is not trivial. The records from the *Eisentrager* trials suggest that, well before the petitioners brought their case to this Court, there had been a rigorous adversarial process to test the legality of their detention. The *Eisentrager* petitioners were charged by a bill of particulars that made detailed factual allegations against them. To rebut the accusations, they were entitled to representation by counsel, allowed to introduce evidence on their own behalf, and permitted to cross-examine the prosecution's witnesses.

In comparison, the procedural protections afforded to the detainees in the CSRT hearings are far more limited, and, we conclude, fall well short of the procedures and adversarial mechanisms that would eliminate the need for habeas corpus review. Although the detainee is assigned a "Personal Representative" to assist him during CSRT proceedings, the Secretary of the Navy's memorandum makes clear that person is not the detainee's lawyer or even his "advocate." The Government's evidence is accorded a presumption of validity. The detainee is allowed to present "reasonably available" evidence, but his ability to rebut the Government's evidence against him is limited by the circumstances of his confinement and his lack of counsel at this stage. And although the detainee can seek review of his status determination in the Court of Appeals, that review process cannot cure all defects in the earlier proceedings. *See* Part V, *infra.*

As to the second factor relevant to this analysis, the detainees here are similarly situated to the *Eisentrager* petitioners in that the sites of their apprehension and detention are technically outside the sovereign territory of the United States. As noted earlier, this is a factor that weighs against finding they have rights under the Suspension Clause. But there are critical differences between Landsberg Prison, circa

1950, and the United States Naval Station at Guantanamo Bay in 2008. Unlike its present control over the naval station, the United States' control over the prison in Germany was neither absolute nor indefinite. Like all parts of occupied Germany, the prison was under the jurisdiction of the combined Allied Forces. The United States was therefore answerable to its Allies for all activities occurring there. The Court's holding in *Eisentrager* was thus consistent with the *Insular Cases*, where it had held there was no need to extend full constitutional protections to territories the United States did not intend to govern indefinitely. Guantanamo Bay, on the other hand, is no transient possession. In every practical sense Guantanamo is not abroad; it is within the constant jurisdiction of the United States.

As to the third factor, we recognize, as the Court did in *Eisentrager,* that there are costs to holding the Suspension Clause applicable in a case of military detention abroad. Habeas corpus proceedings may require expenditure of funds by the Government and may divert the attention of military personnel from other pressing tasks. While we are sensitive to these concerns, we do not find them dispositive. Compliance with any judicial process requires some incremental expenditure of resources. Yet civilian courts and the Armed Forces have functioned along sideeach other at various points in our history. *See, e.g., Duncan v. Kahanamoku*, 327 U.S. 304 (1946); *Ex parte Milligan*, 4 Wall. 2 (1866). The Government presents no credible arguments that the military mission at Guantanamo would be compromised if habeas corpus courts had jurisdiction to hear the detainees' claims. And in light of the plenary control the United States asserts over the base, none are apparent to us.

The situation in *Eisentrager* was far different, given the historical context and nature of the military's mission in post-War Germany. When hostilities in the European Theater came to an end, the United States became responsible for an occupation zone encompassing over 57,000 square miles with a population of 18 million. In addition to supervising massive reconstruction and aid efforts the American forces stationed in Germany faced potential security threats from a defeated enemy. In retrospect the post-War occupation may seem uneventful. But at the time *Eisentrager* was decided, the Court was right to be concerned about judicial interference with the military's efforts to contain "enemy elements, guerilla fighters, and 'werewolves.'" 339 U.S., at 784.

Similar threats are not apparent here; nor does the Government argue that they are. The United States Naval Station at Guantanamo Bay consists of 45 square miles of land and water. The base has been used, at various points, to house migrants and refugees temporarily. At present, however, other than the detainees themselves, the only long-term residents are American military personnel, their families, and a small number of workers. The detainees have been deemed enemies of the United States. At present, dangerous as they may be if released, they are contained in a secure prison facility located on an isolated and heavily fortified military base.

There is no indication, furthermore, that adjudicating a habeas corpus petition would cause friction with the host government. No Cuban court has jurisdiction over American military personnel at Guantanamo or the enemy combatants detained there. While obligated to abide by the terms of the lease, the United States is, for all practical purposes, answerable to no other sovereign for its acts on the base. Were that not the case, or if the detention facility were located in an active theater of war, arguments that issuing the writ would be "impracticable or anomalous" would have more weight. *See Reid*, 354 U.S., at 74 (Harlan, J., concurring in result). Under the facts presented here, however, there are few practical barriers to the running of the writ.

To the extent barriers arise, habeas corpus procedures likely can be modified to address them.

It is true that before today the Court has never held that noncitizens detained by our Government in territory over which another country maintains *de jure* sovereignty have any rights under our Constitution. But the cases before us lack any precise historical parallel. They involve individuals detained by executive order for the duration of a conflict that, if measured from September 11, 2001, to the present, is already among the longest wars in American history. The detainees, moreover, are held in a territory that, while technically not part of the United States, is under the complete and total control of our Government. Under these circumstances the lack of a precedent on point is no barrier to our holding.

We hold that Art. I, §9, cl. 2, of the Constitution has full effect at Guantanamo Bay. If the privilege of habeas corpus is to be denied to the detainees now before us, Congress must act in accordance with the requirements of the Suspension Clause. *Cf. Hamdi,* 542 U.S., at 564 (Scalia, J., dissenting) ("[I]ndefinite imprisonment on reasonable suspicion is not an available option of treatment for those accused of aiding the enemy, absent a suspension of the writ"). This Court may not impose a *de facto* suspension by abstaining from these controversies. The MCA does not purport to be a formal suspension of the writ; and the Government, in its submissions to us, has not argued that it is. Petitioners, therefore, are entitled to the privilege of habeas corpus to challenge the legality of their detention.

V

In light of this holding the question becomes whether the statute stripping jurisdiction to issue the writ avoids the Suspension Clause mandate because Congress has provided adequate substitute procedures for habeas corpus. The Government submits there has been compliance with the Suspension Clause because the DTA review process in the Court of Appeals, *see* DTA §1005(e), provides an adequate substitute. Congress has granted that court jurisdiction to consider

> "(i) whether the status determination of the [CSRT] . . . was consistent with the standards and procedures specified by the Secretary of Defense . . . and (ii) to the extent the Constitution and laws of the United States are applicable, whether the use of such standards and procedures to make the determination is consistent with the Constitution and laws of the United States." §1005(e)(2)(C), 119 Stat. 2742. . . .

A

Our case law does not contain extensive discussion of standards defining suspension of the writ or of circumstances under which suspension has occurred. This simply confirms the care Congress has taken throughout our Nation's history to preserve the writ and its function. Indeed, most of the major legislative enactments pertaining to habeas corpus have acted not to contract the writ's protection but to expand it or to hasten resolution of prisoners' claims. . . .

. . . [Unlike those statutes], here we confront statutes, the DTA and the MCA, that were intended to circumscribe habeas review. Congress' purpose is evident not only from the unequivocal nature of MCA §7's jurisdiction-stripping language, 28 U.S.C.A. §2241(e)(1) (Supp. 2007) ("No court, justice, or judge shall have jurisdiction to hear or consider an application for a writ of habeas corpus . . ."), but also from a comparison of the DTA to the statutes at issue in [cases construing habeas-strengthening statutes]. . . . When Congress has intended to replace traditional habeas corpus with habeas-like substitutes, . . . it has granted to the courts broad remedial powers to secure the historic office of the writ. . . .

In contrast, the DTA's jurisdictional grant is quite limited. The Court of Appeals has jurisdiction not to inquire into the legality of the detention generally but only to assess whether the CSRT complied with the "standards and procedures specified by the Secretary of Defense" and whether those standards and procedures are lawful. DTA §1005(e)(2)(C), 119 Stat. 2742. If Congress had envisioned DTA review as coextensive with traditional habeas corpus, it would not have drafted the statute in this manner. . . . [M]oreover, there has been no effort to preserve habeas corpus review as an avenue of last resort. No saving clause exists in either the MCA or the DTA. And MCA §7 eliminates habeas review for these petitioners. . . .

To the extent any doubt remains about Congress' intent, the legislative history confirms what the plain text strongly suggests. . . .

It is against this background that we must interpret the DTA and assess its adequacy as a substitute for habeas corpus. . . .

B

We do not endeavor to offer a comprehensive summary of the requisites for an adequate substitute for habeas corpus. We do consider it uncontroversial, however, that the privilege of habeas corpus entitles the prisoner to a meaningful opportunity to demonstrate that he is being held pursuant to "the erroneous application or interpretation" of relevant law. *St. Cyr*, 533 U.S. at 302. And the habeas court must have the power to order the conditional release of an individual unlawfully detained — though release need not be the exclusive remedy and is not the appropriate one in every case in which the writ is granted. These are the easily identified attributes of any constitutionally adequate habeas corpus proceeding. But, depending on the circumstances, more may be required.

Indeed, common-law habeas corpus was, above all, an adaptable remedy. Its precise application and scope changed depending upon the circumstances. It appears the common-law habeas court's role was most extensive in cases of pretrial and noncriminal detention, where there had been little or no previous judicial review of the cause for detention. . . .

The idea that the necessary scope of habeas review in part depends upon the rigor of any earlier proceedings accords with our test for procedural adequacy in the due process context. *See Mathews v. Eldridge*, 424 U.S. 319, 335 (1976) (noting that the Due Process Clause requires an assessment of, *inter alia*, "the risk of an erroneous deprivation of [a liberty interest;] and the probable value, if any, of additional or substitute procedural safeguards"). . . .

Accordingly, where relief is sought from a sentence that resulted from the judgment of a court of record, . . . considerable deference is owed to the court that ordered confinement. Likewise in those cases the prisoner should exhaust adequate alternative remedies before filing for the writ in federal court. Both aspects of federal habeas corpus review are justified because it can be assumed that, in the usual course, a court of record provides defendants with a fair, adversary proceeding. . . . The present cases fall outside these categories, however; for here the detention is by executive order.

Where a person is detained by executive order, rather than, say, after being tried and convicted in a court, the need for collateral review is most pressing. A criminal conviction in the usual course occurs after a judicial hearing before a tribunal disinterested in the outcome and committed to procedures designed to ensure its own independence. These dynamics are not inherent in executive detention orders or executive review procedures. In this context the need for habeas corpus is more urgent. The intended duration of the detention and the reasons for it bear upon the precise scope of the inquiry. Habeas corpus proceedings need not resemble a criminal trial, even when the detention is by executive order. But the writ must be effective. The habeas court must have sufficient authority to conduct a meaningful review of both the cause for detention and the Executive's power to detain.

To determine the necessary scope of habeas corpus review, therefore, we must assess the CSRT process, the mechanism through which petitioners' designation as enemy combatants became final. Whether one characterizes the CSRT process as direct review of the Executive's battlefield determination that the detainee is an enemy combatant—as the parties have and as we do—or as the first step in the collateral review of a battlefield determination makes no difference in a proper analysis of whether the procedures Congress put in place are an adequate substitute for habeas corpus. What matters is the sum total of procedural protections afforded to the detainee at all stages, direct and collateral.

Petitioners identify what they see as myriad deficiencies in the CSRTs. The most relevant for our purposes are the constraints upon the detainee's ability to rebut the factual basis for the Government's assertion that he is an enemy combatant. As already noted, at the CSRT stage the detainee has limited means to find or present evidence to challenge the Government's case against him. He does not have the assistance of counsel and may not be aware of the most critical allegations that the Government relied upon to order his detention. *See* App. to Pet. for Cert. in No. 06-1196, at 156, ¶F(8) (noting that the detainee can access only the "unclassified portion of the Government Information"). The detainee can confront witnesses that testify during the CSRT proceedings. *Id.,* at 144, ¶g(8). But given that there are in effect no limits on the admission of hearsay evidence—the only requirement is that the tribunal deem the evidence "relevant and helpful," *ibid.,* ¶g(9) — the detainee's opportunity to question witnesses is likely to be more theoretical than real....

Even if we were to assume that the CSRTs satisfy due process standards, it would not end our inquiry. Habeas corpus is a collateral process that exists, in Justice Holmes' words, to "cu[t] through all forms and g[o] to the very tissue of the structure. It comes in from the outside, not in subordination to the proceedings, and although every form may have been preserved opens the inquiry whether they have been more than an empty shell." *Frank v. Mangum,* 237 U.S. 309, 346 (1915) (dissenting opinion). Even when the procedures authorizing detention are structurally sound, the Suspension Clause remains applicable and the writ relevant. *See* 2 Chambers, Course of Lectures on English Law 1767-1773, at 6 ("Liberty may be violated either by arbitrary *imprisonment* without law or the appearance of law, or by a lawful magistrate for an unlawful reason")....

Although we make no judgment as to whether the CSRTs, as currently constituted, satisfy due process standards, we agree with petitioners that, even when all the parties involved in this process act with diligence and in good faith, there is considerable risk of error in the tribunal's findings of fact. This is a risk inherent in any process that, in the words of the former Chief Judge of the Court of Appeals, is "closed and accusatorial." *See* [*Bismullah v. Gates*, 514 F.3d 1291, 1296 (D.C. Cir. 2008)] (Ginsburg, C.J., concurring in denial of rehearing en banc). And given that the consequence of error may be detention of persons for the duration of hostilities that may last a generation or more, this is a risk too significant to ignore.

For the writ of habeas corpus, or its substitute, to function as an effective and proper remedy in this context, the court that conducts the habeas proceeding must have the means to correct errors that occurred during the CSRT proceedings. This includes some authority to assess the sufficiency of the Government's evidence against the detainee. It also must have the authority to admit and consider relevant exculpatory evidence that was not introduced during the earlier proceeding....

The extent of the showing required of the Government in these cases is a matter to be determined. We need not explore it further at this stage. We do hold that when the judicial power to issue habeas corpus properly is invoked the judicial officer must have adequate authority to make a determination in light of the relevant law and facts and to formulate and issue appropriate orders for relief, including, if necessary, an order directing the prisoner's release.

C

We now consider whether the DTA allows the Court of Appeals to conduct a proceeding meeting these standards. "[W]e are obligated to construe the statute to avoid [constitutional] problems" if it is "'fairly possible'" to do so. *St. Cyr*, 533 U.S., at 299-300 (quoting *Crowell v. Benson*, 285 U.S. 22, 62 (1932))....

The DTA does not explicitly empower the Court of Appeals to order the applicant in a DTA review proceeding released should the court find that the standards and procedures used at his CSRT hearing were insufficient to justify detention. This is troubling. Yet, for present purposes, we can assume congressional silence permits a constitutionally required remedy....

The absence of a release remedy and specific language allowing AUMF challenges are not the only constitutional infirmities from which the statute potentially suffers, however. The more difficult question is whether the DTA permits the Court of Appeals to make requisite findings of fact. The DTA enables petitioners to request "review" of their CSRT determination in the Court of Appeals, DTA §1005(e)(2)(B)(i), 119 Stat. 2742; but the "Scope of Review" provision confines the Court of Appeals' role to reviewing whether the CSRT followed the "standards and procedures" issued by the Department of Defense and assessing whether those "standards and procedures" are lawful. §1005(e)(C), *ibid.* Among these standards is "the requirement that the conclusion of the Tribunal be supported by a preponderance of the evidence...allowing a rebuttable presumption in favor of the Government's evidence." §1005(e)(C)(i), *ibid.*

Assuming the DTA can be construed to allow the Court of Appeals to review or correct the CSRT's factual determinations, as opposed to merely certifying that the tribunal applied the correct standard of proof, we see no way to construe the statute to allow what is also constitutionally required in this context: an opportunity for the detainee to present relevant exculpatory evidence that was not made part of the record in the earlier proceedings.

On its face the statute allows the Court of Appeals to consider no evidence outside the CSRT record....

By foreclosing consideration of evidence not presented or reasonably available to the detainee at the CSRT proceedings, the DTA disadvantages the detainee by limiting the scope of collateral review to a record that may not be accurate or complete. In other contexts, *e.g.*, in post-trial habeas cases where the prisoner already has had a full and fair opportunity to develop the factual predicate of his claims, similar limitations on the scope of habeas review may be appropriate. In this context, however, where the underlying detention proceedings lack the necessary adversarial character, the detainee cannot be held responsible for all deficiencies in the record. . . .

Although we do not hold that an adequate substitute must duplicate §2241 in all respects, it suffices that the Government has not established that the detainees' access to the statutory review provisions at issue is an adequate substitute for the writ of habeas corpus. MCA §7 thus effects an unconstitutional suspension of the writ. In view of our holding we need not discuss the reach of the writ with respect to claims of unlawful conditions of treatment or confinement.

VI

A

In light of our conclusion that there is no jurisdictional bar to the District Court's entertaining petitioners' claims the question remains whether there are prudential barriers to habeas corpus review under these circumstances. . . .

In cases involving foreign citizens detained abroad by the Executive, it likely would be both an impractical and unprecedented extension of judicial power to assume that habeas corpus would be available at the moment the prisoner is taken into custody. If and when habeas corpus jurisdiction applies, as it does in these cases, then proper deference can be accorded to reasonable procedures for screening and initial detention under lawful and proper conditions of confinement and treatment for a reasonable period of time. Domestic exigencies, furthermore, might also impose such onerous burdens on the Government that here, too, the Judicial Branch would be required to devise sensible rules for staying habeas corpus proceedings until the Government can comply with its requirements in a responsible way. *Cf. Ex parte Milligan*, 4 Wall., at 127 ("If, in foreign invasion or civil war, the courts are actually closed, and it is impossible to administer criminal justice according to law, *then,* on the theatre of active military operations, where war really prevails, there is a necessity to furnish a substitute for the civil authority, thus overthrown, to preserve the safety of the army and society; and as no power is left but the military, it is allowed to govern by martial rule until the laws can have their free course"). Here, as is true with detainees apprehended abroad, a relevant consideration in determining the courts' role is whether there are suitable alternative processes in place to protect against the arbitrary exercise of governmental power.

The cases before us, however, do not involve detainees who have been held for a short period of time while awaiting their CSRT determinations. Were that the case, or were it probable that the Court of Appeals could complete a prompt review of their applications, the case for requiring temporary abstention or exhaustion of alternative remedies would be much stronger. These qualifications no longer pertain here. In some of these cases six years have elapsed without the judicial oversight that habeas corpus or an adequate substitute demands. And there has been no showing that the Executive faces such onerous burdens that it cannot respond to habeas corpus actions. To require these detainees to complete DTA review before proceeding with their habeas corpus actions would be to require additional months, if not years, of delay. The first DTA review applications were filed over a year ago, but no decisions on the merits have been issued. While some delay in fashioning new procedures is unavoidable, the costs of delay can no longer be borne by those who are held in custody. The detainees in these cases are entitled to a prompt habeas corpus hearing.

Our decision today holds only that the petitioners before us are entitled to seek the writ; that the DTA review procedures are an inadequate substitute for habeas corpus; and that the petitioners in these cases need not exhaust the review procedures in the Court of Appeals before proceeding with their habeas actions in the District Court. The only law we identify as unconstitutional is MCA §7, 28 U.S.C.A. §2241(e) (Supp. 2007). Accordingly, both the DTA and the CSRT process remain intact. Our holding with regard to exhaustion should not be read to imply that a habeas court should intervene the moment an enemy combatant steps foot in a territory where the writ runs. The Executive is entitled to a reasonable period of time to determine a detainee's status before a court entertains that detainee's habeas corpus petition. The CSRT process is the mechanism Congress and the President set up to deal with these issues. Except in cases of undue delay, federal courts should refrain from entertaining an enemy combatant's habeas corpus petition at least until after the Department, acting via the CSRT, has had a chance to review his status.

B

Although we hold that the DTA is not an adequate and effective substitute for habeas corpus, it does not follow that a habeas corpus court may disregard the dangers the detention in these cases was intended to prevent.... [T]he Suspension Clause does not resist innovation in the field of habeas corpus. Certain accommodations can be made to reduce the burden habeas corpus proceedings will place on the military without impermissibly diluting the protections of the writ.

In the DTA Congress sought to consolidate review of petitioners' claims in the Court of Appeals. Channeling future cases to one district court would no doubt reduce administrative burdens on the Government. This is a legitimate objective that might be advanced even without an amendment to §2241....

Another of Congress' reasons for vesting exclusive jurisdiction in the Court of Appeals, perhaps, was to avoid the widespread dissemination of classified information. The Government has raised similar concerns here and elsewhere. We make no attempt to anticipate all of the evidentiary and access-to-counsel issues that will arise during the course of the detainees' habeas corpus proceedings. We recognize, however, that the Government has a legitimate interest in protecting sources and methods of intelligence gathering; and we expect that the District Court will use its discretion to accommodate this interest to the greatest extent possible. *Cf. United States v. Reynolds*, 345 U.S. 1, 10 (1953) (recognizing an evidentiary privilege in a civil damages case where "there is a reasonable danger that compulsion of the evidence will expose military matters which, in the interest of national security, should not be divulged").

These and the other remaining questions are within the expertise and competence of the District Court to address in the first instance.

* * *

In considering both the procedural and substantive standards used to impose detention to prevent acts of terrorism, proper deference must be accorded to the political branches. *See United States v. Curtiss-Wright Export Corp.*, 299 U.S. 304, 320 (1936). Unlike the President and some designated Members of Congress, neither the Members of this Court nor most federal judges begin the day with briefings that may describe new and serious threats to our Nation and its people. The law must accord the Executive substantial authority to apprehend and detain those who pose a real danger to our security.

Officials charged with daily operational responsibility for our security may consider a judicial discourse on the history of the Habeas Corpus Act of 1679 and like matters to be far removed from the Nation's present, urgent concerns. Established legal doctrine, however, must be consulted for its teaching. Remote in time it may be; irrelevant to the present it is not. Security depends upon a sophisticated intelligence apparatus and the ability of our Armed Forces to act and to interdict. There are further considerations, however. Security subsists, too, in fidelity to freedom's first principles. Chief among these are freedom from arbitrary and unlawful restraint and the personal liberty that is secured by adherence to the separation of powers. It is from these principles that the judicial authority to consider petitions for habeas corpus relief derives.

Our opinion does not undermine the Executive's powers as Commander in Chief. On the contrary, the exercise of those powers is vindicated, not eroded, when confirmed by the Judicial Branch. Within the Constitution's separation-of-powers structure, few exercises of judicial power are as legitimate or as necessary as the responsibility to hear challenges to the authority of the Executive to imprison a person. Some of these petitioners have been in custody for six years with no definitive judicial determination as to the legality of their detention. Their access to the writ is a necessity to determine the lawfulness of their status, even if, in the end, they do not obtain the relief they seek.

Because our Nation's past military conflicts have been of limited duration, it has been possible to leave the outer boundaries of war powers undefined. If, as some fear, terrorism continues to pose dangerous threats to us for years to come, the Court might not have this luxury. This result is not inevitable, however. The political branches, consistent with their independent obligations to interpret and uphold the Constitution, can engage in a genuine debate about how best to preserve constitutional values while protecting the Nation from terrorism. *Cf. Hamdan* [*v. Rumsfeld*, 548 U.S. 557 (2006)], at 636 (Breyer, J., concurring) ("[J]udicial insistence upon that consultation does not weaken our Nation's ability to deal with danger. To the contrary, that insistence strengthens the Nation's ability to determine — through democratic means — how best to do so").

It bears repeating that our opinion does not address the content of the law that governs petitioners' detention. That is a matter yet to be determined. We hold that petitioners may invoke the fundamental procedural protections of habeas corpus. The laws and Constitution are designed to survive, and remain in force, in extraordinary times. Liberty and security can be reconciled; and in our system they are reconciled within the framework of the law. The Framers decided that habeas corpus, a right of first importance, must be a part of that framework, a part of that law.

The determination by the Court of Appeals that the Suspension Clause and its protections are inapplicable to petitioners was in error. The judgment of the Court of Appeals is reversed. The cases are remanded to the Court of Appeals with instructions that it remand the cases to the District Court for proceedings consistent with this opinion.

It is so ordered.

[Concurring opinion of Justice SOUTER, with whom Justice GINSBURG and Justice BREYER join, is omitted.]

Chief Justice ROBERTS, with whom Justice SCALIA, Justice THOMAS, and Justice ALITO join, dissenting. Today the Court strikes down as inadequate the most generous set of procedural protections ever afforded aliens detained by this country as enemy combatants. The political branches crafted these procedures amidst an ongoing military conflict, after much careful investigation and thorough debate. The Court rejects them today out of hand, without bothering to say what due process rights the detainees possess, without explaining how the statute fails to vindicate those rights, and before a single petitioner has even attempted to avail himself of the law's operation. And to what effect? The majority merely replaces a review system designed by the people's representatives with a set of shapeless procedures to be defined by federal courts at some future date. One cannot help but think, after surveying the modest practical results of the majority's ambitious opinion, that this decision is not really about the detainees at all, but about control of federal policy regarding enemy combatants. . . .

. . . The important point for me, however, is that the Court should have resolved these cases on other grounds. Habeas is most fundamentally a procedural right, a mechanism for contesting the legality of executive detention. The critical threshold question in these cases, prior to any inquiry about the writ's scope, is whether the system the political branches designed protects whatever rights the detainees may possess. If so, there is no need for any additional process, whether called "habeas" or something else. . . .

II . . .

. . . After much hemming and hawing, the majority appears to concede that the DTA provides an Article III court competent to order release. The only issue in dispute is the process the Guantanamo prisoners are entitled to use to test the legality of their detention. . . .

A . . .

Hamdi merits scant attention from the Court—a remarkable omission, as *Hamdi* bears directly on the issues before us. The majority attempts to dismiss *Hamdi's* relevance by arguing that because the availability of §2241 federal habeas was never in doubt in that case, "the Court had no occasion to define the necessary scope of habeas review . . . in the context of enemy combatant detentions." Hardly. *Hamdi* was all about the scope of habeas review in the context of enemy combatant detentions. The petitioner, an American citizen held within the United States as an enemy combatant, invoked the writ to challenge his detention. After "a careful examination both of the writ . . . and of the Due Process Clause," this Court enunciated the "basic process" the Constitution entitled Hamdi to expect from a habeas court under §2241.

That process consisted of the right to "receive notice of the factual basis for his classification, and a fair opportunity to rebut the Government's factual assertions before a neutral decisionmaker." In light of the Government's national security responsibilities, the plurality found the process could be "tailored to alleviate [the] uncommon potential to burden the Executive at a time of ongoing military conflict." For example, the Government could rely on hearsay and could claim a presumption in favor of its own evidence.

Hamdi further suggested that this "basic process" on collateral review could be provided by a military tribunal. It pointed to prisoner-of-war tribunals as a model that would satisfy the Constitution's requirements. Only "[i]n the *absence* of such process" before a military tribunal, the Court held, would Article III courts need to conduct full-dress habeas proceedings to "ensure that the minimum requirements of due process are achieved." *Ibid.* (emphasis added). And even then, the petitioner would be entitled to no more process than he would have received from a properly constituted military review panel, given his limited due process rights and the Government's weighty interests.

Contrary to the majority, *Hamdi* is of pressing relevance because it establishes the procedures American *citizens* detained as enemy combatants can expect from a habeas court proceeding under §2241. The DTA system of military tribunal hearings followed by Article III review looks a lot like the procedure *Hamdi* blessed. If nothing else, it is plain from the design of the DTA that Congress, the President, and this Nation's military leaders have made a good-faith effort to follow our precedent.

The Court, however, will not take "yes" for an answer....

III...

The majority rests its decision on abstract and hypothetical concerns. Step back and consider what, in the real world, Congress and the Executive have actually granted aliens captured by our Armed Forces overseas and found to be enemy combatants:

- The right to hear the bases of the charges against them, including a summary of any classified evidence.

- The ability to challenge the bases of their detention before military tribunals modeled after Geneva Convention procedures. Some 38 detainees have been released as a result of this process.

- The right, before the CSRT, to testify, introduce evidence, call witnesses, question those the Government calls, and secure release, if and when appropriate.

- The right to the aid of a personal representative in arranging and presenting their cases before a CSRT.

- Before the D.C. Circuit, the right to employ counsel, challenge the factual record, contest the lower tribunal's legal determinations, ensure compliance with the Constitution and laws, and secure release, if any errors below establish their entitlement to such relief.

In sum, the DTA satisfies the majority's own criteria for assessing adequacy. This statutory scheme provides the combatants held at Guantanamo greater procedural protections than have ever been afforded alleged enemy detainees—whether citizens or aliens—in our national history....

I respectfully dissent.

Justice SCALIA, with whom THE CHIEF JUSTICE, Justice THOMAS, and Justice ALITO join, dissenting.... Contrary to my usual practice,...I think it appropriate to begin with a description of the disastrous consequences of what the Court has done today.

I

America is at war with radical Islamists....

The game of bait-and-switch that today's opinion plays upon the Nation's Commander in Chief will make the war harder on us. It will almost certainly cause more Americans to be killed. That consequence would be tolerable if necessary to preserve a time-honored legal principle vital to our constitutional Republic. But it is this Court's blatant *abandonment* of such a principle that produces the decision today. The President relied on our settled precedent in *Johnson v. Eisentrager*, 339 U.S. 763 (1950), when he established the prison at Guantanamo Bay for enemy aliens. Citing that case, the President's Office of Legal Counsel advised him "that the great weight of legal authority indicates that a federal district court could not properly exercise habeas jurisdiction over an alien detained at [Guantanamo Bay]." Memorandum from Patrick F. Philbin and John C. Yoo, Deputy Assistant Attorneys General, Office of Legal Counsel, to William J. Haynes II, General Counsel, Dept. of Defense (Dec. 28, 2001). Had the law been otherwise, the military surely would not have transported prisoners there, but would have kept them in Afghanistan, transferred them to another of our foreign military bases, or turned them over to allies for detention. Those other facilities might well have been worse for the detainees themselves.

In the long term, then, the Court's decision today accomplishes little, except perhaps to reduce the well-being of enemy combatants that the Court ostensibly seeks to protect. In the short term, however, the decision is devastating. At least 30 of those prisoners hitherto released from Guantanamo Bay have returned to the battlefield. Some have been captured or killed. But others have succeeded in carrying on their atrocities against innocent civilians....

These, mind you, were detainees whom *the military* had concluded were not enemy combatants. Their return to the kill illustrates the incredible difficulty of assessing who is and who is not an enemy combatant in a foreign theater of operations where the environment does not lend itself to rigorous evidence collection. Astoundingly, the Court today raises the bar, requiring military officials to appear before civilian courts and defend their decisions under procedural and evidentiary rules that go beyond what Congress has specified. As the Chief Justice's dissent makes clear, we have no idea what those procedural and evidentiary rules are, but they will be determined by civil courts and (in the Court's contemplation at least) will be more detainee-friendly than those now applied, since otherwise there would no reason to hold the congressionally prescribed procedures unconstitutional. If they impose a higher standard of proof (from foreign battlefields) than the current procedures require, the number of the enemy returned to combat will obviously increase.

But even when the military has evidence that it can bring forward, it is often foolhardy to release that evidence to the attorneys representing our enemies. And one escalation of procedures that the Court *is* clear about is affording the detainees increased access to witnesses (perhaps troops serving in Afghanistan?) and to classified information. During the 1995 prosecution of Omar Abdel Rahman, federal prosecutors gave the names of 200 unindicted co-conspirators to the "Blind Sheik's" defense lawyers; that information was in the hands of Osama Bin Laden within two weeks. In another case, trial testimony revealed to the enemy that the United States had been monitoring their cellular network, whereupon they promptly stopped using it, enabling more of them to evade capture and continue their atrocities....

... The Court today decrees that no good reason to accept the judgment of the other two branches is "apparent." "The Government," it declares, "presents no credible arguments that the military mission at Guantanamo would be compromised if habeas corpus courts had jurisdiction to hear the detainees' claims." What competence does the Court have to second-guess the judgment of Congress and the President on such a point? None whatever. But the Court blunders in nonetheless. Henceforth, as today's opinion makes unnervingly clear, how to handle enemy prisoners in this war will ultimately lie with the branch that knows least about the national security concerns that the subject entails.

II

A...

... The Court admits that it cannot determine whether the writ historically extended to aliens held abroad, and it concedes (necessarily) that Guantanamo Bay lies outside the sovereign territory of the United States. Together, these two concessions establish that it is (in the Court's view) perfectly ambiguous whether the common-law writ would have provided a remedy for these petitioners. If that is so, the Court has no basis to strike down the Military Commissions Act, and must leave undisturbed the considered judgment of the coequal branches.

How, then, does the Court weave a clear constitutional prohibition out of pure interpretive equipoise? The Court resorts to "fundamental separation-of-powers principles" to interpret the Suspension Clause. According to the Court, because "the writ of habeas corpus is itself an indispensable mechanism for monitoring the separation of powers," the test of its extraterritorial reach "must not be subject to manipulation by those whose power it is designed to restrain."

That approach distorts the nature of the separation of powers and its role in the constitutional structure. The "fundamental separation-of-powers principles" that the Constitution embodies are to be derived not from some judicially imagined matrix, but from the sum total of the individual separation-of-powers provisions that the Constitution sets forth. Only by considering them one-by-one does the full shape of the *Constitution's* separation-of-powers principles emerge. It is nonsensical to interpret those provisions themselves in light of some general "separation-of-powers principles" dreamed up by the Court. Rather, they must be interpreted to mean what they were understood to mean when the people ratified them. And if the understood scope of the writ of habeas corpus was "designed to restrain" (as the Court says) the actions of the Executive, the understood *limits* upon that scope were (as the Court seems not to grasp) just as much "designed to restrain" the incursions of the Third Branch. "Manipulation" of the territorial reach of the writ by the Judiciary poses just as much a threat to the proper separation of powers as "manipulation" by the

Executive. As I will show below, manipulation is what is afoot here. The understood limits upon the writ deny our jurisdiction over the habeas petitions brought by these enemy aliens, and entrust the President with the crucial wartime determinations about their status and continued confinement.

B

The Court purports to derive from our precedents a "functional" test for the extraterritorial reach of the writ, which shows that the Military Commissions Act unconstitutionally restricts the scope of habeas. That is remarkable because the most pertinent of those precedents, *Johnson v. Eisentrager*, 339 U.S. 763, conclusively establishes the opposite. . . .

. . . *Eisentrager* nowhere mentions a "functional" test, and the notion that it is based upon such a principle is patently false . . . .

The category of prisoner comparable to these detainees are not the *Eisentrager* criminal defendants, but the more than 400,000 prisoners of war detained in the United States alone during World War II. Not a single one was accorded the right to have his detention validated by a habeas corpus action in federal court — and that despite the fact that they were present on U.S. soil. The Court's analysis produces a crazy result: Whereas those convicted and sentenced to death for war crimes are without judicial remedy, all enemy combatants detained during a war, at least insofar as they are confined in an area away from the battlefield over which the United States exercises "absolute and indefinite" control, may seek a writ of habeas corpus in federal court. And, as an even more bizarre implication from the Court's reasoning, those prisoners whom the military plans to try by full-dress Commission at a future date may file habeas petitions and secure release before their trials take place. . . .

III

Putting aside the conclusive precedent of *Eisentrager*, it is clear that the original understanding of the Suspension Clause was that habeas corpus was not available to aliens abroad, as Judge Randolph's thorough opinion for the court below detailed. . . .

. . . [A]ll available historical evidence points to the conclusion that the writ would not have been available at common law for aliens captured and held outside the sovereign territory of the Crown. Despite three opening briefs, three reply briefs, and support from a legion of *amici*, petitioners have failed to identify a single case in the history of Anglo-American law that supports their claim to jurisdiction. The Court finds it significant that there is no recorded case *denying* jurisdiction to such prisoners either. But a case standing for the remarkable proposition that the writ could issue to a foreign land would surely have been reported, whereas a case denying such a writ for lack of jurisdiction would likely not. At a minimum, the absence of a reported case either way leaves unrefuted the voluminous commentary stating that habeas was confined to the dominions of the Crown.

What history teaches is confirmed by the nature of the limitations that the Constitution places upon suspension of the common-law writ. It can be suspended only "in Cases of Rebellion or Invasion." Art. I, §9, cl. 2. The latter case (invasion) is plainly limited to the territory of the United States; and while it is conceivable that a rebellion could be mounted by American citizens abroad, surely the overwhelming majority of its occurrences would be domestic. If the extraterritorial scope of habeas turned on flexible, "functional" considerations, as the Court holds, why would the Constitution limit its suspension almost entirely to instances of domestic crisis? Surely there is an even greater justification for suspension in foreign lands where the United States might hold prisoners of war during an ongoing conflict. And correspondingly, there is less threat to liberty when the Government suspends the writ's (supposed) application in foreign lands, where even on the most extreme view prisoners are entitled to fewer constitutional rights. It makes no sense, therefore, for the Constitution generally to forbid suspension of the writ abroad if indeed the writ has application there. . . .

The Nation will live to regret what the Court has done today. I dissent.

NOTES AND QUESTIONS

1. *A Right to Habeas?* Although the Court treated *Boumediene* as a Suspension Clause case, there is nothing for Congress to suspend unless the detainees have a right to petition for habeas in the first place. The government, citing *Eisentrager*, argued that there is no right to habeas for noncitizen prisoners held abroad in a place, like the Landsberg prison, where the United States lacks "formal legal sovereignty." The Guantánamo prisoners thus had no habeas right, the government insisted, because Cuba retains "ultimate sovereignty" under its lease agreement with the United States.

How did the Court respond? How is the Guantánamo Bay Naval Station different from the Landsberg prison in Germany? Why did the Court say that the "Government's formal legal sovereignty test raises troubling separation-of-powers concerns"?

Ultimately, the Court chose function over form, suggesting a multifactor functional test for habeas. What is the functional framework it adopts, and how does it apply to the detainees? How is its application to them different from its application to the *Eisentrager* petitioners? For a vigorous argument that the majority's history was flatly wrong, *see* Raymond Randolph, *Originalism and History: the Case of Boumediene v. Bush*, 34 Harv. J.L. & Pub. Pol'y 89 (2010).

2. *Suspension?* Once the Court found that the detainees had a right to constitutional habeas, it immediately faced other questions. "If the privilege of habeas corpus is to be denied to the detainees," the Court observed, "Congress must act in accordance with the requirements of the Suspension Clause." 553 U.S. at 771. What does the Suspension Clause require? Did Congress seek to suspend the right when it enacted MCA 2006? If so, did it satisfy the requirements? What must Congress now do if it wants to suspend habeas for the Guantánamo detainees?

3. *Adequate Substitute?* The Court found that, without formally suspending the privilege of the writ, Congress could nevertheless restrict prisoners' access to the courts so long as it provided an "adequate substitute" for habeas corpus — one that preserves the "function" of habeas review. *Id.* at 773. In what respects did the processes established by MCA 2006 and the DTA fall short of preserving the writ's function?

Can you identify the baseline procedures for constitutional habeas? To put if differently, if you were a district court judge in the District of Columbia, could you determine from *Boumediene* what procedures you should use in entertaining habeas petitions from detainees in Guantánamo?

4. *Paying Deference to the Political Branches.* Isn't Justice Scalia clearly correct in asserting that the *Boumediene* majority's treatment of *Eisentrager* worked a "bait and switch" on the Bush administration? Note that *Eisentrager* was decided in 1950, just a year after the Geneva Conventions were signed and the same year that basic reforms were adopted in the U.S. system of military justice. Should the Administration have taken the "bait" without regard for the evolved and evolving regime of human rights, both at home and abroad?

If *Boumediene* worked a "switch," does it leave any room for practical necessity? For example, does it require habeas to be made available at the moment a prisoner is detained abroad? Do the same rules apply at home? What other accommodations does the Court make, or say that the district courts can make, to practical exigencies and administrative burdens?

5. *Does the Constitutional Writ Extend Beyond Guantánamo Bay?* While *Boumediene* dealt only with detainees held at Guantánamo, its functional test for extraterritorial application of habeas may apply elsewhere. In *Al Maqaleh v. Gates,* 605 F.3d 84 (D.C. Cir. 2010), the petitioners were three prisoners at Bagram Air Force Base in Afghanistan. The Court of Appeals rejected their argument that U.S. "control of Bagram under the lease of the military base is sufficient to trigger the extraterritorial application of the Suspension Clause.... Such an interpretation would seem to create the potential for the extraterritorial extension of the Suspension Clause to noncitizens held in any United States military facility in the world, and perhaps to an undeterminable number of other United States-leased facilities as well." *Id.* at 95.

Instead, it applied the multifaceted *Boumediene* functional test to decide the case. Regarding citizenship, the court found these petitioners (two Yemenis and a Tunisian) no different from those in *Boumediene.* The relatively scant process they received from an "Unlawful Enemy Combatant Review Board" (UECRB) weighed in their favor. But the location of their detention weighed the other way: "While it is certainly realistic to assert that the United States has *de facto* sovereignty over Guantánamo, the same simply is not true with respect to Bagram." *Id.* at 97. The tie-breaker was the third factor, "the practical obstacles inherent in resolving the prisoner's entitlement to the writ." Bagram was, the court noted, located in an active theater of war. "The United States asserts, and petitioners cannot credibly dispute, that all of the attributes of a facility exposed to the vagaries of war are present in Bagram." Accordingly, the court held "[w]e cannot, consistent with *Eisentrager* as elucidated by *Boumediene,* hold that the right to the writ of habeas corpus and the constitutional protections of the Suspension Clause extend to Bagram detention facility in Afghanistan." *Id.* at 97-98.

Did *Al Maqaleh* allow the Administration to create a new "black hole" for detainees? *See* Kal Raustiala, *Al Maqaleh v. Gates, 605 F.3d 84. U.S. Court of Appeals for the D.C. Circuit, May 21, 2010,* 104 Am. J. Int'l L. 647, 653 (2010) (wondering "whether the Obama administration's victory in *Al Maqaleh* will inevitably lead to charges that Bagram is simply a new Guantánamo—only even harsher and more remote."). Based on the analysis in *Al Maqaleh,* how would you decide the extraterritorial application of constitutional habeas to noncitizen detainees at a CIA detention facility in Poland? On a U.S. naval vessel in the Indian Ocean?

Did *Al Maqaleh* put too much weight on functionalism and too little on habeas as a limit on executive power? *See* Marc D. Falkoff & Robert Knowles, *Bagram, Boumediene, and Limited Government,* 59 DePaul L. Rev. 851, 898 (2010) (arguing that *Boumediene*'s central principle "lies beyond pragmatism: indefinite detention without any court review is fundamentally inconsistent with any exercise of government power under the U.S. Constitution."); Stephen I. Vladeck, *The Suspension Clause as a Structural Right*, 62 U. Miami L. Rev. 275, 278 (2008) (viewing the Suspension Clause as "'a structural right' . . . creating no rights whatsoever, but merely empowering Congress to do away with the writ of habeas corpus only when exigency demands.").

6. *Constitutional Rights to Be Vindicated by Habeas?* The writ of habeas corpus is merely a means to an end: the end of making the government justify the detention of its prisoner. But recall that the Court of Appeals in *Eisentrager* had reasoned from rights to a habeas remedy: that the prisoners had constitutional rights that they could only vindicate if they had access to habeas. What answer did the Supreme Court give in that case? *See also United States v. Verdugo-Urquidez*, 494 U.S. 259 (1990) (*supra* p. 712) (holding that the Fourth Amendment does not protect an alien without substantial connections to the United States). Did *Rasul* (*supra* p. 784 n.15) change that answer? What about *Boumediene?*

Rasul was released from Guantánamo Bay in 2004. In the following case, he sued for damages, asserting in part that the defendants had violated his Fifth Amendment right to due process and his Eighth Amendment protection against cruel and unusual treatment in detention.

Rasul v. Myers

United States Court of Appeals for the D.C. Circuit, 2010
563 F.3d 527

Before: HENDERSON and BROWN, Circuit Judges, and RANDOLPH, Senior Circuit Judge.

PER CURIAM: . . . The main question in *Boumediene* was whether a provision in the Military Commissions Act, Pub. L. No. 109-366, 120 Stat. 2600 (2006) (codified in part at 28 U.S.C. §2241 & note), depriving federal courts of habeas corpus jurisdiction over petitions filed by Guantánamo detainees, violated the clause of the Constitution governing suspension of the writ, Art. 1, §9, cl. 2. 128 S. Ct. at 2237. . . . The Court acknowledged that it had never before determined that the Constitution protected aliens detained abroad, *id.* at 2262, and explicitly confined its constitutional holding "only" to the extraterritorial reach of the Suspension Clause, *id.* at 2275. The Court stressed that its decision "does not address the *content of the law* that governs petitioners' detention." *Id.* at 2277 (emphasis added). With those words, the Court in *Boumediene* disclaimed any intention to disturb existing law governing the extraterritorial reach of any constitutional provisions, other than the Suspension Clause. *See, e.g., Johnson v. Eisentrager*, 339 U.S. 763 (1950) (holding that aliens detained on a U.S. military base outside sovereign U.S. territory have no due process rights); *United States v. Verdugo-Urquidez*, 494 U.S. 259 (1990) (holding that the Fourth Amendment does not protect nonresident aliens against unreasonable searches or seizures conducted outside sovereign U.S. territory).

Plaintiffs nevertheless maintain that *Boumediene* has eroded the precedential force of *Eisentrager* and its progeny. Whether that is so is not for us to determine; the Court has reminded the lower federal courts that it alone retains the authority to overrule its precedents. . . .

There is another reason why we should not decide whether *Boumediene* portends application of the Due Process Clause and the Cruel and Unusual Punishment Clause to Guantánamo detainees—and it is on this ground we will rest our decision on remand. The doctrine of qualified immunity shields government officials from civil liability to the extent their alleged misconduct "does not violate clearly established statutory or constitutional rights of which a reasonable person would have known." *Harlow v. Fitzgerald*, 457 U.S. 800, 818 (1982)....

...No reasonable government official would have been on notice that plaintiffs had any Fifth Amendment or Eighth Amendment rights. At the time of their detention,[2] neither the Supreme Court nor this court had ever held that aliens captured on foreign soil and detained beyond sovereign U.S. territory had any constitutional rights—under the Fifth Amendment, the Eighth Amendment, or otherwise. The Court in *Boumediene* recognized just that: "It is true that before today the Court has never held that noncitizens detained by our Government in territory over which another country maintains *de jure* sovereignty have any rights under our Constitution." 128 S. Ct. at 2262.

Eisentrager and *Verdugo-Urquidez* were thought to be the controlling Supreme Court cases on the Constitution's application to aliens abroad. *Eisentrager* rejected a habeas petition brought by German nationals imprisoned at a United States military base in Germany. 339 U.S. at 778. The Court held that these alien prisoners, who "at no relevant time were within any territory over which the United States is sovereign," were not entitled to invoke the protection of the writ or the Fifth Amendment. *Id.* The Court referred nine times to the decisive fact that the alien prisoners were, at all relevant times, outside sovereign U.S. territory. *See id.* at 777-78.

"[E]mphatic" is how the Court later described its rejection of the claim that aliens outside the sovereign territory of the United States are entitled to due process rights. *Verdugo-Urquidez*, 494 U.S. at 269 (citing *Eisentrager*, 339 U.S. at 770). Following *Eisentrager*, the Court in *Verdugo-Urquidez* concluded that the Fourth Amendment did not protect nonresident aliens against unreasonable searches or seizures conducted outside the sovereign territory of the United States. *Id.* at 274-75. The majority noted that although American citizens abroad can invoke some constitutional protections, *id.* at 270 (citing *Reid v. Covert*, 354 U.S. 1 (1957) (plurality opinion)), aliens abroad are in an altogether different situation. *Id.* at 271. The long line of cases dealing with constitutional rights of both lawful resident aliens and illegal aliens establishes "only that aliens receive constitutional protections when they have come within the territory of the United States and developed substantial connections with this country." *Id.* (citing *Plyler v. Doe*, 457 U.S. 202, 212 (1982) (The provisions of the Fourteenth Amendment "are universal in their application, *to all persons within the territorial jurisdiction....*") (emphasis added in *Verdugo-Urquidez*); *Kwong Hai Chew v. Colding*, 344 U.S. 590, 596 n.5 (1953) ("The Bill of Rights is a futile authority for the alien seeking admission for the first time to these shores. But *once an alien lawfully enters and resides in this country* he becomes invested with the rights guaranteed by the Constitution to all people within our borders.") (emphasis added in *Verdugo-Urquidez*)). Those cases could not help an alien who, like *Verdugo-Urquidez* and plaintiffs in this case, had at no relevant time been in the country and had "no previous significant voluntary connection with the United States," *id....*

---

2. All four plaintiffs were released more than four years before the Supreme Court decided Boumediene, and months before the Court held even that statutory habeas corpus jurisdiction extended to Guantanamo. See Rasul v. Bush, 542 U.S. 466, 483-84 (2004). We do not require government employees to anticipate future developments in constitutional law.

In short, there was no authority for — and ample authority against — plaintiffs' asserted rights at the time of the alleged misconduct. The defendants are therefore entitled to qualified immunity against plaintiffs' *Bivens* claims. For the foregoing reasons, we affirm the district court's dismissal of [the claims based on petitioners' asserted constitutional rights.]

So ordered.

[Concurring opinion of Circuit Judge BROWN omitted.]

NOTES AND QUESTIONS

1. *Distinguishing Eisentrager and Verdugo-Urquidez?* The Court of Appeals treats the Supreme Court's decisions in *Eisentrager* and *Verdugo-Urquidez* as dispositive on the question of Rasul's constitutional rights, other than the right to habeas. But did the *Myers* court accurately characterize the holdings in those cases? If so, is there any way to distinguish between the *Eisentrager* prisoners and Rasul that could justify the recognition of Fifth Amendment rights for the latter? Is there any difference between Verdugo-Urquidez (a Mexican national who had no connections with the United States when his property was searched by U.S. agents in Mexico) and Rasul that could justify the recognition of Fourth Amendment rights in Rasul?

2. *Habeas for What? Myers* was *not* a habeas case, but its conclusions about Rasul's constitutional rights presumably apply to all current noncitizen detainees who lack any connection to the United States. Does it make sense to find a right to constitutional habeas and then conclude that the petitioner has no constitutional rights? Even if a detainee/petitioner has no *constitutional rights*, are there other rights he could assert? Or is it wrong to frame the questions as one of rights at all, given the limited historical scope of habeas to test the jailor's authority to detain? *See* Jared A. Goldstein, *Habeas Without Rights*, 2007 Wis. L. Rev. 1165, 1169 ("Habeas did not protect rights . . . for a simple reason: habeas predates rights.").

Military Detention
Before 9/11

In Chapter 26 we explored justifications for preventive detention by civilian authorities of suspected terrorists or persons with information about terrorism. In Chapters 27 and 28 we learned that suspension of the writ of habeas corpus does not by itself provide authority for detention; it merely cuts off the right of a detainee to make the government justify its detention in a court of law.

In this chapter we turn to legal theories for detention by military authorities of persons deemed threats to national security before 9/11. In Part A, we consider authority for the detention of noncombatants during a declared war or invasion. In Part B, we analyze traditional law-of-war authority for detention of enemy combatants in armed conflict. In the following chapter, we explore how the same authority has been used to detain U.S. citizens and resident aliens as combatants after 9/11.

A. MILITARY DETENTION OF NONCOMBATANTS BEFORE 9/11

Alien Enemy Act
50 U.S.C. §21 (2006)

Whenever there is a declared war between the United States and any foreign nation or government, or any invasion or predatory incursion is perpetrated, attempted, or threatened against the territory of the United States by any foreign nation or government, and the President makes public proclamation of the event, all natives, citizens, denizens, or subjects of the hostile nation or government, being of the age of fourteen years and upward, who shall be within the United States and not actually naturalized, shall be liable to be apprehended, restrained, secured, and removed as alien enemies. The President is authorized in any such event, by his proclamation thereof, or other public act, to direct the conduct to be observed, on the part of the United States, toward the aliens who become so liable; the manner and degree of the restraint to which they shall be subject and in what cases, and upon what security their residence shall be permitted, and to provide for the removal of those who, not being permitted to reside within the United States, refuse or neglect to depart therefrom; and to establish any other regulations which are found necessary in the premises and for the public safety.

Korematsu v. United States
United States Supreme Court, 1944
323 U.S. 214

Mr. Justice BLACK delivered the opinion of the Court. The petitioner, an American citizen of Japanese descent, was convicted in a federal district court for remaining in San Leandro, California, a "Military Area," contrary to Civilian Exclusion Order No. 34 of the Commanding General of the Western Command, U.S. Army, which directed that after May 9, 1942, all persons of Japanese ancestry should be excluded from that area. No question was raised as to petitioner's loyalty to the United States. The Circuit Court of Appeals affirmed, and the importance of the constitutional question involved caused us to grant certiorari.

It should be noted, to begin with, that all legal restrictions which curtail the civil rights of a single racial group are immediately suspect. That is not to say that all such restrictions are unconstitutional. It is to say that courts must subject them to the most rigid scrutiny. Pressing public necessity may sometimes justify the existence of such restrictions; racial antagonism never can.

In the instant case prosecution of the petitioner was begun by information charging violation of an Act of Congress, of March 21, 1942, 56 Stat. 173, which provides that

> . . . whoever shall enter, remain in, leave, or commit any act in any military area or military zone prescribed, under the authority of an Executive order of the President, by the Secretary of War, or by any military commander designated by the Secretary of War, contrary to the restrictions applicable to any such area or zone or contrary to the order of the Secretary of War or any such military commander, shall, if it appears that he knew or should have known of the existence and extent of the restrictions or order and that his act was in violation thereof, be guilty of a misdemeanor and upon conviction shall be liable to a fine of not to exceed $5,000 or to imprisonment for not more than one year, or both, for each offense.

Exclusion Order No. 34, which the petitioner knowingly and admittedly violated, was one of a number of military orders and proclamations, all of which were substantially based upon Executive Order No. 9066, 7 Fed. Reg. 1407. That order, issued after we were at war with Japan, declared that "the successful prosecution of the war requires every possible protection against espionage and against sabotage to national-defense material, national-defense premises, and national-defense utilities. . . . " [The order also authorized the designation of "military areas . . . from which any and all persons may be excluded."]

One of the series of orders and proclamations, a curfew order, which like the exclusion order here was promulgated pursuant to Executive Order 9066, subjected all persons of Japanese ancestry in prescribed West Coast military areas to remain in their residences from 8 P.M. to 6 A.M. As is the case with the exclusion order here, that prior curfew order was designed as a "protection against espionage and against sabotage." In *Hirabayashi v. United States*, 320 U.S. 81, we sustained a conviction obtained for violation of the curfew order. The Hirabayashi conviction and this one thus rest on the same 1942 Congressional Act and the same basic executive and military orders, all of which orders were aimed at the twin dangers of espionage and sabotage.

The 1942 Act was attacked in the *Hirabayashi* case as an unconstitutional delegation of power; it was contended that the curfew order and other orders on which it rested were beyond the war powers of the Congress, the military authorities and of the President, as Commander in Chief of the Army; and finally that to apply the curfew order against none but citizens of Japanese ancestry amounted to a constitutionally prohibited discrimination solely on account of race. To these questions, we gave the consideration which their importance justified. We upheld the curfew order as an exercise of the power of the government to take steps necessary to prevent espionage and sabotage in an area threatened by Japanese attack.

In the light of the principles we announced in the *Hirabayashi* case, we are unable to conclude that it was beyond the war power of Congress and the Executive to exclude those of Japanese ancestry from the West Coast war area at the time they did. True, exclusion from the area in which one's home is located is a far greater deprivation than constant confinement to the home from 8 P.M. to 6 A.M. Nothing short of apprehension by the proper military authorities of the gravest imminent danger to the public safety can constitutionally justify either. But exclusion from a threatened area, no less than curfew, has a definite and close relationship to the prevention of espionage and sabotage. . . .

Here, as in the *Hirabayashi* case, *supra*, at p. 99, ". . . we cannot reject as unfounded the judgment of the military authorities and of Congress that there were disloyal members of that population, whose number and strength could not be precisely and quickly ascertained. We cannot say that the war-making branches of the Government did not have ground for believing that in a critical hour such persons could not readily be isolated and separately dealt with, and constituted a menace to the national defense and safety, which demanded that prompt and adequate measures be taken to guard against it." . . .

We uphold the exclusion order as of the time it was made and when the petitioner violated it. In doing so, we are not unmindful of the hardships imposed by it upon a large group of American citizens. But hardships are part of war, and war is an aggregation of hardships. All citizens alike, both in and out of uniform, feel the impact of war in greater or lesser measure. Citizenship has its responsibilities as well as its privileges, and in time of war the burden is always heavier. Compulsory exclusion of large groups of citizens from their homes, except under circumstances of direst emergency and peril, is inconsistent with our basic governmental institutions. But when under conditions of modern warfare our shores are threatened by hostile forces, the power to protect must be commensurate with the threatened danger. . . .

It is said that we are dealing here with the case of imprisonment of a citizen in a concentration camp solely because of his ancestry, without evidence or inquiry concerning his loyalty and good disposition towards the United States. Our task would be simple, our duty clear, were this a case involving the imprisonment of a loyal citizen in a concentration camp because of racial prejudice. Regardless of the true nature of the assembly and relocation centers — and we deem it unjustifiable to call them concentration camps with all the ugly connotations that term implies — we are dealing specifically with nothing but an exclusion order. To cast this case into outlines of racial prejudice, without reference to the real military dangers which were presented, merely confuses the issue. Korematsu was not excluded from the Military Area because of hostility to him or his race. He *was* excluded because we are at war with the Japanese Empire, because the properly constituted military authorities feared an invasion of our West Coast and felt constrained to take proper security measures, because they decided that the military urgency of the situation demanded that all citizens of Japanese ancestry be segregated from the West Coast temporarily, and finally, because Congress, reposing its confidence in this time of war in our military leaders—as inevitably it must—determined that they should have the power to do just this. There was evidence of disloyalty on the part of some, the military authorities considered that the need for action was great, and time was short. We cannot—by availing ourselves of the calm perspective of hindsight—now say that at that time these actions were unjustified.

Affirmed.

Japanese-American heads of families line up for relocation, San Francisco, 1942.

Photo courtesy The National Archives.

Mr. Justice FRANKFURTER, concurring.... The provisions of the Constitution which confer on the Congress and the President powers to enable this country to wage war are as much part of the Constitution as provisions looking to a nation at peace. And we have had recent occasion to quote approvingly the statement of former Chief Justice Hughes that the war power of the Government is "the power to wage war successfully." *Hirabayashi v. United States,* supra at 93; and see *Home Bldg. & L. Assn. v. Blaisdell,* 290 U.S. 398, 426. Therefore, the validity of action under the war power must be judged wholly in the context of war. That action is not to be stigmatized as lawless because like action in times of peace would be lawless. To talk about a military order that expresses an allowable judgment of war needs by those entrusted with the duty of conducting war as "an unconstitutional order" is to suffuse a part of the Constitution with an atmosphere of unconstitutionality. The respective spheres of action of military authorities and of judges are of course very different. But within their sphere, military authorities are no more outside the bounds of obedience to the Constitution than are judges within theirs. "The war power of the United States, like its other powers...is subject to applicable constitutional limitations," *Hamilton v. Kentucky Distilleries Co.*, 251 U.S. 146, 156. To recognize that military orders are "reasonably expedient military precautions" in time of war and yet to deny them constitutional legitimacy makes of the Constitution an instrument for dialectic subtleties not reasonably to be attributed to the hard-headed Framers, of whom a majority had had actual participation in war....

Mr. Justice MURPHY, dissenting. This exclusion of "all persons of Japanese ancestry, both alien and non-alien," from the Pacific Coast area on a plea of military necessity in the absence of martial law ought not to be approved. Such exclusion goes over "the very brink of constitutional power" and falls into the ugly abyss of racism.

In dealing with matters relating to the prosecution and progress of a war, we must accord great respect and consideration to the judgments of the military authorities who are on the scene and who have full knowledge of the military facts. The scope of their discretion must, as a matter of necessity and common sense, be wide. And their judgments ought not to be overruled lightly by those whose training and duties ill-equip them to deal intelligently with matters so vital to the physical security of the nation.

At the same time, however, it is essential that there be definite limits to military discretion, especially where martial law has not been declared. Individuals must not be left impoverished of their constitutional rights on a plea of military necessity that has neither substance nor support. Thus, like other claims conflicting with the asserted constitutional rights of the individual, the military claim must subject itself to the judicial process of having its reasonableness determined and its conflicts with other interests reconciled. "What are the allowable limits of military discretion, and whether or not they have been overstepped in a particular case, are judicial questions." *Sterling v. Constantin*, 287 U.S. 378, 401.

The judicial test of whether the Government, on a plea of military necessity, can validly deprive an individual of any of his constitutional rights is whether the deprivation is reasonably related to a public danger that is so "immediate, imminent, and impending" as not to admit of delay and not to permit the intervention of ordinary constitutional processes to alleviate the danger. *United States v. Russell*, 13 Wall. 623, 627-628; *Mitchell v. Harmony*, 13 How. 115, 134-135; *Raymond v. Thomas*, 91 U.S. 712, 716. Civilian Exclusion Order No. 34, banishing from a prescribed area of the Pacific Coast "all persons of Japanese ancestry, both alien and non-alien," clearly does not meet that test. Being an obvious racial discrimination, the order deprives all those within its scope of the equal protection of the laws as guaranteed by the Fifth Amendment. It further deprives these individuals of their constitutional rights to live and work where they will, to establish a home where they choose and to move about freely. In excommunicating them without benefit of hearings, this order also deprives them of all their constitutional rights to procedural due process. Yet no reasonable relation to an "immediate, imminent, and impending" public danger is evident to support this racial restriction which is one of the most sweeping and complete deprivations of constitutional rights in the history of this nation in the absence of martial law....

Mr. Justice JACKSON, dissenting.... [T]he "law" which this prisoner is convicted of disregarding is not found in an act of Congress, but in a military order. Neither the Act of Congress nor the Executive Order of the President, nor both together, would afford a basis for this conviction. It rests on the orders of General DeWitt. And it is said that if the military commander had reasonable military grounds for promulgating the orders, they are constitutional and become law, and the Court is required to enforce them. There are several reasons why I cannot subscribe to this doctrine.

It would be impracticable and dangerous idealism to expect or insist that each specific military command in an area of probable operations will conform to conventional tests of constitutionality. When an area is so beset that it must be put under military control at all, the paramount consideration is that its measures be successful, rather than legal. The armed services must protect a society, not merely its Constitution. The very essence of the military job is to marshall physical force, to remove every obstacle to its effectiveness, to give it every strategic advantage. Defense measures will not, and often should not, be held within the limits that bind civil authority in peace. No court can require such a commander in such circumstances to act as a reasonable man; he may be unreasonably cautious and exacting. Perhaps he should be. But a commander in temporarily focusing the life of a community on defense is carrying out a military program; he is not making law in the sense that the courts know the term. He issues orders, and they may have a certain authority as military commands, although they may be very bad as constitutional law.

But if we cannot confine military expedients by the Constitution, neither would I distort the Constitution to approve all that the military may deem expedient. That is what the Court appears to be doing, whether consciously or not. I cannot say, from any evidence before me, that the orders of General DeWitt were not reasonably expedient military precautions, nor could I say that they were. But even if they were permissible military procedures, I deny that it follows that they are constitutional. If, as the Court holds, it does follow, then we may as well say that any military order will be constitutional and have done with it.

The limitation under which courts always will labor in examining the necessity for a military order [is] illustrated by this case. How does the Court know that these orders have a reasonable basis in necessity? No evidence whatever on that subject has been taken by this or any other court. . . .

In the very nature of things, military decisions are not susceptible of intelligent judicial appraisal. They do not pretend to rest on evidence, but are made on information that often would not be admissible and on assumptions that could not be proved. Information in support of an order could not be disclosed to courts without danger that it would reach the enemy. Neither can courts act on communications made in confidence. Hence courts can never have any real alternative to accepting the mere declaration of the authority that issued the order that it was reasonably necessary from a military viewpoint.

Much is said of the danger to liberty from the Army program for deporting and detaining these citizens of Japanese extraction. But a judicial construction of the due process clause that will sustain this order is a far more subtle blow to liberty than the promulgation of the order itself. A military order, however unconstitutional, is not apt to last longer than the military emergency. Even during that period a succeeding commander may revoke it all. But once a judicial opinion rationalizes such an order to show that it conforms to the Constitution, or rather rationalizes the Constitution to show that the Constitution sanctions such an order, the Court for all time has validated the principle of racial discrimination in criminal procedure and of transplanting American citizens. The principle then lies about like a loaded weapon ready for the hand of any authority that can bring forward a plausible claim of an urgent need.

Every repetition imbeds that principle more deeply in our law and thinking and expands it to new purposes. . . .

I should hold that a civil court cannot be made to enforce an order which violates constitutional limitations even if it is a reasonable exercise of military authority. The courts can exercise only the judicial power, can apply only law, and must abide by the Constitution, or they cease to be civil courts and become instruments of military policy.

Of course the existence of a military power resting on force, so vagrant, so centralized, so necessarily heedless of the individual, is an inherent threat to liberty. But I would not lead people to rely on this Court for a review that seems to me wholly delusive. The military reasonableness of these orders can only be determined by military superiors. If the people ever let command of the war power fall into irresponsible and unscrupulous hands, the courts wield no power equal to its restraint. The chief restraint upon those who command the physical forces of the country, in the future as in the past, must be their responsibility to the political judgments of their contemporaries and to the moral judgments of history.

My duties as a justice as I see them do not require me to make a military judgment as to whether General DeWitt's evacuation and detention program was a reasonable military necessity. I do not suggest that the courts should have attempted to interfere with the Army in carrying out its task. But I do not think they may be asked to execute a military expedient that has no place in law under the Constitution. I would reverse the judgment and discharge the prisoner.

[The opinion of Justice ROBERTS, dissenting, is omitted.]

NOTES AND QUESTIONS

1. *Alien Enemies?* Why did the government not invoke the Alien Enemy Act to confine Korematsu and his fellow internees? Could the government have invoked it to justify the PENTTBOM (referring to the 9/11 investigation) detentions of immigrants described *supra* p. 739? If so, has Congress occupied the field of alien detention during war or invasion with the Alien Enemy Act?

2. *Constitutionality of Emergency Actions in Wartime.* Attorney General Francis Biddle wrote about the decision to create the internments,

> I do not think [President Roosevelt] was much concerned with the gravity or implications of this step. . . . Nor do I think the constitutional difficulty plagued him. The Constitution has not greatly bothered any wartime President. That was a question of law, which ultimately the Supreme Court must decide. And meanwhile — probably a long meanwhile — we must get on with the war. [Francis Biddle, *In Brief Authority* 219 (1962).]

Whatever the President's regard for fidelity to the Constitution, what is the significance of the Court's and Justice Frankfurter's constitutionalization of actions that in times of peace would be lawless? Consider Justice Jackson's warning on this point in his dissenting opinion. Professor Lobel indicates that throughout the twentieth century, but especially since World War II, the expanding U.S. role in global affairs and a nearly constant state of national crisis have promoted the development of a "relativistic" theory that finds emergency powers within the framework of the Constitution: the Commander in Chief and Executive Clauses, the President's inherent power in foreign affairs, and the presumed power of Congress to make laws anticipating every emergency. Jules Lobel, *Emergency Powers and the Decline of Liberalism*, 98 Yale L.J. 1385, 1399-1409 (1989).

If the Court is to review the constitutionality of emergency actions, what standards are to be applied? Are they found in the Constitution itself, or elsewhere?

These questions and others are considered in the classic contemporaneous criticisms of the principal case: Nanete Dembitz, *Racial Discrimination and the Military Judgment: The Supreme Court's Korematsu and Endo Decisions*, 45 Colum. L. Rev. 175 (1945); and Eugene Rostow, *The Japanese American Cases — A Disaster*, 54 Yale L.J. 489 (1945). *See also* Lobel, *supra*, at 1399-1412.

3. *Possible Significance of Citizenship and Loyalty.* In *Ex parte Endo*, 323 U.S. 283 (1944), decided the same day as *Korematsu*, the Court found that a Japanese-American citizen whose loyalty to the United States was conceded by the government could not be detained in a relocation center. The Court noted that

> [t]he Constitution when it committed to the Executive and to Congress the exercise of the war power necessarily gave them wider scope for the exercise of judgment and discretion so that war might be waged effectively and successfully [citing *Hirabayashi*]. At the same time, however, the Constitution is as specific in its enumeration of many of the civil rights of the individual as it is in the enumeration of the powers of his government. . . .
>
> . . . In interpreting a wartime measure we must assume that Congress' purpose was to allow for the greatest possible accommodation between civil liberties and the exigencies of war. [*Id.* at 298-300.]

So saying, the Court refused to find in either the 1942 congressional act or Executive Order No. 9066 any implied authority to detain an admittedly loyal citizen where none was expressly given. Should we infer from the Court's holding that internment based on race or ethnic background might be permissible if it were approved either by an act of Congress or by a clear presidential directive? Or does *Endo* stand for the proposition that an admittedly loyal American may not be locked up, even in time of war? If the latter, how could loyalty be established if it is not admitted, and who has the burden of proving its presence or absence?

A small number of German-Americans were interned during the war after individual loyalty hearings. Why were Japanese-Americans not given the same hearings before internment? After the war, one interned German-American sought compensation from the government. His claim was rejected. The court noted that after "three years of testimony from hundreds of witnesses, Congress concluded that Japanese Americans were detained en masse because of racial prejudice and demagoguery, while German Americans were detained in small numbers, and only after individual hearings about their loyalty." *Jacobs v. Barr*, 959 F.2d 313, 314 (D.C. Cir. 1992).

4. *Standard of Review.* One commentator argues that careful judicial scrutiny is appropriate, if not essential, in cases like *Hirabayashi* and *Korematsu*, "'where there is the most at stake in terms of personal freedom and the political branches are most likely to over-react' — when the government deems it necessary to restrict the most cherished liberties of American citizens to guard the nation's security." Eric R. Yamamoto, *Korematsu Revisited — Correcting the Injustice of Extraordinary Government Excess and Lax Judicial Review*, 26 Santa Clara L. Rev. 1, 48 (1986) (citation omitted). Heightened judicial

scrutiny is especially important in such cases, he suggests, because "it addresses the inherent weakness in the system of majority rule." *Id.* at 48-49.

How is this proposed standard of review different from the one set forth in the second paragraph of the *Korematsu* opinion? What standard of review was actually applied by the *Korematsu* Court? *See Adarand Constructors, Inc. v. Pena,* 515 U.S. 200, 214 (1995) (calling the *Korematsu* Court's application of its "most rigid scrutiny" standard "inexplicab[le]"). How do you think *Korematsu* would be decided today under modern equal protection law? For a description of that law, see *supra* p. 703.

5. *Belated Disclosure of Government Misconduct.* The *Korematsu* Court's extremely deferential review of the government's claim of military necessity enabled a stunning act of official fraud that was not revealed until nearly 40 years later. In 1982, Professor Peter Irons of the University of California at San Diego initiated a Freedom of Information Act request to obtain access to Justice Department records from its prosecution of the *Korematsu* case in 1944. His discoveries encouraged Fred Korematsu to file a petition for a writ of *coram nobis* in the court where he was tried 40 years earlier to vacate his conviction on grounds of government misconduct. Setting aside Korematsu's conviction, the court found that

> the government knowingly withheld information from the courts when they were considering the critical question of military necessity in this case. A series of correspondence regarding what information should be included in the government's brief before the Supreme Court culminated in two different versions of a footnote that was to be used to specify the factual data upon which the government relied for its military necessity justification. The first version read as follows:
>
>> The Final Report of General DeWitt (which is dated June 5, 1943, but which was not made public until January 1944) is relied on in this brief for statistics and other details concerning the actual evacuation and the events that took place subsequent thereto. *The recital of the circumstances justifying the evacuation as a matter of military necessity, however, is in several respects,* particularly with reference to the use of illegal radio transmitters and to shore-to-ship signalling by persons of Japanese ancestry, *in conflict with information in the possession of the Department of Justice. In view of the contrariety of the reports on this matter we do not ask the Court to take judicial notice of the recital of those facts contained in the Report.* Petitioner's Exhibit AA, Memorandum of John L. Burling to Assistant Attorney General Herbert Wechsler, September 11, 1944 [emphasis added]. . . .
>
> The footnote that appeared in the final version of the brief merely read as follows:
>
>> The Final Report of General DeWitt (which is dated June 5, 1943, but which was not made public until January 1944), hereinafter cited as Final Report, is relied on in this brief for statistics and other details concerning the actual evacuation and the events that took place subsequent thereto. *We have specifically recited in this brief the facts relating to the justification for the evacuation, of which we ask the Court to take judicial notice, and we rely upon the Final Report only to the extent that it relates to such facts.*
>
> Brief for the United States, *Korematsu v. United States,* October Term, 1944, No. 22, at 11. The final version made no mention of the contradictory reports. The record is replete with protestations of various Justice Department officials that the government had the obligation to advise the courts of the contrary facts and opinions. In fact, several Department of Justice officials pointed out to their superiors and others the "wilful historical inaccuracies and intentional falsehoods" contained in the DeWitt Report. . . .

> ...Omitted from the reports presented to the courts was information possessed by the Federal Communications Commission, the Department of the Navy, and the Justice Department which directly contradicted General DeWitt's statements. Thus, the court had before it a selective record. [*Korematsu v. United States*, 584 F. Supp. 1406, 1417-1419 (N.D. Cal. 1984).]

The circumstances leading up to the 1984 decision are described in Peter Irons, *Justice at War: The Story of the Japanese American Internment Cases* (1983).

In the first *Korematsu* case, the Supreme Court relied heavily on its earlier decision in *Hirabayashi v. United States*, 320 U.S. 81 (1943). Gordon Hirabayashi's conviction for violating a curfew based on Executive Order No. 9066 was also vacated in a later *coram nobis* proceeding. *Hirabayashi v. United States*, 828 F.2d 591 (9th Cir. 1987). Documents and commentary on the later proceedings may be found in *Justice Delayed: The Record of the Japanese American Internment Cases* (Peter Irons ed., 1989).

Aside from the government briefs to the Supreme Court in *Hirabayashi* and *Korematsu*, the Acting Solicitor General in 2011 suggested that those cases might have been decided differently if the Solicitor General at the time, Charles Fahy, had been candid in his oral arguments before the Court about the lack of any evidence of military necessity. Neal Katyal, *Confession of Error: The Solicitor General's Mistakes During the Japanese-American Internment Cases*, The Justice Blog (May 20, 2011), *at* http://blogs.usdoj.gov/blog/archives/1346. The oral arguments are described in Irons, *Justice at War, supra*, at 235-236, 316-317.

6. *The Role of Government Lawyers in Korematsu.* Why do you think the government lawyers behaved the way they did, both initially in approving the executive order, and later in deliberately misleading the Supreme Court? Some possible reasons are set forth in Peter Irons, *Politics and Principle: An Assessment of the Roosevelt Record on Civil Rights and Liberties*, 59 Wash. L. Rev. 693, 716-720 (1984).

7. *Military Necessity or Racism?* In 1980, Congress established the Commission on Wartime Relocation and Internment of Civilians to review the facts and circumstances surrounding Executive Order No. 9066 and its impact on American citizens and permanent resident aliens. Pub. L. No. 96-317, 94 Stat. 964. In its report, entitled *Personal Justice Denied* (1982), the Commission found that some 120,000 people were held without judicial review, "despite the fact that not a single documented act of espionage, sabotage, or fifth column activity was committed by an American citizen of Japanese ancestry or by a resident Japanese alien on the West Coast.... [T]here was no justification in military necessity for the exclusion,...there was no basis for the detention." *Id.* at 3, 10.

How, then, could this monstrous injustice have occurred? Part of the answer surely lies in the fear and anger that gripped the country in the wake of the attack on Pearl Harbor. But another part can be found in the longstanding hostility of California farmers, businesses, and labor unions toward Japanese immigrants. Within weeks, voices of racism, tribalism, and economic opportunism began calling for the evacuation of all ethnic Japanese, aliens and citizens alike, from the West Coast. For example, columnist Walter Lippmann wrote, "The Pacific Coast is in imminent danger of a combined attack from within and from without.... [S]ome part of it may at any moment be a battlefield. Nobody's constitutional rights include the right to reside and do business on a battlefield." *Quoted in* Jacobus tenBroek, Edward N. Barnhart & Floyd W. Matson, *Prejudice, War and the Constitution* 85 n.45 (1970). Another journalist added, "and to hell with habeas corpus." Westbrook Pegler, *quoted in* Biddle, *supra* p. 817, at 218. The clamor was joined by groups like the Native Sons and Daughters of the Golden West, the American Legion, the California Farm Bureau Federation, and the Grower-Shipper Vegetable Association, who reportedly were able to exert significant influence on General DeWitt and, importantly, President Roosevelt. *See generally* Irons, *Justice at War, supra.*

The military also bears some of the responsibility. But why was the Army involved in the internments, when troops were urgently needed elsewhere to fight the war? It was certainly not because civilian authorities were incapable of rounding up even this large group and imprisoning its members. The West Coast was not a battlefield, the courts remained open, and local governments continued to function. Furthermore, the internees were remarkably cooperative, albeit deeply resentful: there was little resistance to the internments and few reported efforts to escape from the camps. In other words, the Army's unique ability to exert massive force simply was not needed. Moreover, any threats to national security from individual saboteurs and spies were addressed by the FBI in the early weeks of the war, and prosecuted in the criminal justice system.

The Justice and War Departments were intimately involved in the internment decision, as was President Roosevelt. Congress and the courts also played important enabling roles. But do you think the internments could have been carried out without the military's involvement? If not, did the military usurp the authority of civilian government to accomplish what would otherwise have been impossible? Or did the civilian government utilize the military to do what it otherwise could not have? Can you describe a legal regime to reduce the risk of military control of the government, or to make it more difficult for civilian authorities to misuse military power? The domestic role of the military is addressed in depth in Chapter 38.

8. *Apology and Payment.* In 1948, Congress passed the American-Japanese Evacuation Claims Act, 50 U.S.C. App. §§1981-1987 (2006), authorizing payment of up to $100,000 to each internee for loss of real or personal property occasioned by the evacuation. On February 19, 1976, President Gerald Ford rescinded Executive Order No. 9066, 34 years to the day after its issuance. Proclamation No. 4417, 41 Fed. Reg. 7741 (Feb. 20, 1976).

Forty years later, after protracted debate, Congress voted to give $20,000 and an apology to each of 60,000 surviving internees. The measure was signed into law by President Reagan in 1988. 50 U.S.C. App. §§1989 to 1989c-8 (2006). Acceptance of the $20,000 payment "shall be in full satisfaction of all claims" against the government for damages. *Id.* §1989b-4(a)(6). *See* Chris K. Iijima, *Reparations and the "Model Minority" Ideology of Acquiescence: The Necessity to Refuse the Return to Original Humiliation,* 40 B.C. L. Rev. 385 (1998) (warning that reparations must not be used to excuse the racism that caused the internments); Sarah L. Brew, *Making Amends for History: Legislative Reparations for Japanese Americans and Other Minority Groups,* 8 Law & Inequality 179 (1989).

9. *Could It Happen Again?* On the fiftieth anniversary of the internments, Fred Korematsu remarked, "The constitutional violations that were committed have been

cleared. This will never happen again." Katherine Bishop, *Japanese-Americans Treat Pain of Internment in World War II*, N.Y. Times, Feb. 19, 1992. Do you think he was right?

It is suggested that General Dewitt was the evil genius whose singleminded racism was responsible for this sorry turn of events. *See, e.g., Hirabayashi*, 828 F.2d at 599-600. But should General Dewitt be asked to shoulder all or even a major part of the blame? Judge Marilyn Patel concluded her 1984 decision overturning Fred Korematsu's conviction with this warning about the Supreme Court's 1944 decision:

> *Korematsu* remains on the pages of our legal and political history. As a legal precedent it is now recognized as having very limited application. As historical precedent it stands as a constant caution that in times of war or declared military necessity our institutions must be vigilant in protecting constitutional guarantees. It stands as a caution that in times of distress the shield of military necessity and national security must not be used to protect governmental actions from close scrutiny and accountability. It stands as a caution that in times of international hostility and antagonisms our institutions, legislative, executive and judicial, must be prepared to exercise their authority to protect all citizens from the petty fears and prejudices that are so easily aroused. [584 F. Supp. at 1420.]

Taking her admonition to heart, can you describe some legal mechanism that would make us less likely to repeat our mistake? If you think some broader strategy will be required, can you say what it is? *See generally* Aya Gruber, *Raising the Red Flag: The Continued Relevance of the Japanese Internment in the Post-Hamdi World*, 54 U. Kan. L. Rev. 307 (2006).

For a fascinating account of *Korematsu*'s use as precedent since 1944, as well as the use and misuse of narrative in deciding the case, *see* Dean Masaru Hashimoto, *The Legacy of Korematsu v. United States: A Dangerous Narrative Retold*, 4 UCLA Asian Pac. Am. L.J. 72 (1996).

B.   MILITARY DETENTION OF COMBATANTS BEFORE 9/11

Both of the following opinions treat the law-of-war authority for the military *trial* of alleged enemy combatants during an armed insurrection or declared war, a topic which we take up in detail in Chapter 36. But the trial of these individuals presupposes their *detention*, and the opinions therefore also, by necessary implication, address authority for wartime detention.

Ex parte Milligan
United States Supreme Court, 1866
71 U.S. (4 Wall.) 2

[The opinion is set forth *supra* p. 767.]

Ex parte Quirin

United States Supreme Court, 1942
317 U.S. 1

[After war was declared between the United States and Germany, seven German nationals, and Herbert Hans Haupt, a dual U.S.-German national, were trained at a German sabotage school near Berlin. German submarines then carried the saboteurs with a supply of explosives to the United States. They landed on U.S. beaches wearing German Marine Infantry uniforms, which they immediately buried. Before they could engage in any act of sabotage, however, they were betrayed to the FBI by one of their number.

After their arrest, President Roosevelt issued an order declaring that nationals of enemy states or those who acted under their direction, who were charged with sabotage, espionage, or "violations of the law of war," were subject to the jurisdiction of military tribunals. Proclamation No. 2561, 7 Fed. Reg. 5101 (July 7, 1942). A military commission then conducted a secret 18-day trial of the saboteurs. Toward the end of the trial, the Supreme Court decided in an extraordinary expedited summer session to hear argument on the saboteurs' appeal from refusal of the lower courts to entertain their petitions for writs of habeas corpus. Less than 24 hours after argument, it ruled *per curiam* that the military commission was lawfully constituted and authorized to try the saboteurs, promising a full opinion later. Six of the saboteurs were executed eight days after the Supreme Court's *per curiam* ruling (Roosevelt commuted the sentences of the others to imprisonment). The Court issued its full opinion three months later.]

Mr. Chief Justice STONE delivered the opinion of the Court.... We are not here concerned with any question of the guilt or innocence of petitioners. Constitutional safeguards for the protection of all who are charged with offenses are not to be disregarded in order to inflict merited punishment on some who are guilty. *Ex parte Milligan*, [71 U.S. (4 Wall.) 2 (1866)]. But the detention and trial of petitioners — ordered by the President in the declared exercise of his powers as Commander in Chief of the Army in time of war and of grave public danger — are not to be set aside by the courts without the clear conviction that they are in conflict with the Constitution or laws of Congress constitutionally enacted.

Congress and the President, like the courts, possess no power not derived from the Constitution. But one of the objects of the Constitution, as declared by its preamble, is to "provide for the common defence."...

[The Court then catalogued first Congress's, then the President's, national security authorities under the Constitution.]

The Constitution thus invests the President as Commander in Chief with the power to wage war which Congress has declared, and to carry into effect all laws passed by Congress for the conduct of war and for the government and regulation of the Armed Forces, and all laws defining and punishing offences against the law of nations, including those which pertain to the conduct of war.

By the Articles of War, 10 U.S.C. §§1471-1593, Congress has provided rules for the government of the Army.... But the Articles also recognize the "military commission" appointed by military command as an appropriate tribunal for the trial and punishment of offenses against the law of war not ordinarily tried by court martial.

See Arts. 12, 15. Articles 38 and 46 authorize the President, with certain limitations, to prescribe the procedure for military commissions. Articles 81 and 82 authorize trial, either by court martial or military commission, of those charged with relieving, harboring or corresponding with the enemy and those charged with spying. And Article 15 declares that "the provisions of these articles conferring jurisdiction upon courts-martial shall not be construed as depriving military commissions . . . or other military tribunals of concurrent jurisdiction in respect of offenders or offenses that by statute or by the law of war may be triable by such military commissions . . . or other military tribunals." . . .

From the very beginning of its history this Court has recognized and applied the law of war as including that part of the law of nations which prescribes, for the conduct of war, the status, rights and duties of enemy nations as well as of enemy individuals. By the Articles of War, and especially Article 15, Congress has explicitly provided, so far as it may constitutionally do so, that military tribunals shall have jurisdiction to try offenders or offenses against the law of war in appropriate cases. . . .

An important incident to the conduct of war is the adoption of measures by the military command not only to repel and defeat the enemy, but to seize and subject to disciplinary measures those enemies who in their attempt to thwart or impede our military effort have violated the law of war. It is unnecessary for present purposes to determine to what extent the President as Commander in Chief has constitutional power to create military commissions without the support of Congressional legislation. For here Congress has authorized trial of offenses against the law of war before such commissions. . . . We may assume that there are acts regarded in other countries, or by some writers on international law, as offenses against the law of war which would not be triable by military tribunal here, either because they are not recognized by our courts as violations of the law of war or because they are of that class of offenses constitutionally triable only by a jury. It was upon such grounds that the Court denied the right to proceed by military tribunal in *Ex parte Milligan, supra.* But as we shall show, these petitioners were charged with an offense against the law of war which the Constitution does not require to be tried by jury. . . .

. . . [B]y the reference in the 15th Article of War to "offenders or offenses that . . . by the law of war may be triable by such military commissions," Congress has incorporated by reference, as within the jurisdiction of military commissions, all offenses which are defined as such by the law of war, and which may constitutionally be included within that jurisdiction. Congress had the choice of crystallizing in permanent form and in minute detail every offense against the law of war, or of adopting the system of common law applied by military tribunals so far as it should be recognized and deemed applicable by the courts. It chose the latter course.

By universal agreement and practice the law of war draws a distinction between the armed forces and the peaceful populations of belligerent nations and also between those who are lawful and unlawful combatants. Lawful combatants are subject to capture and detention as prisoners of war by opposing military forces. Unlawful combatants are likewise subject to capture and detention, but in addition they are subject to trial and punishment by military tribunals for acts which render their belligerency unlawful. The spy who secretly and without uniform passes the military lines of a belligerent in time of war, seeking to gather military information and communicate it to the enemy, or an enemy combatant who without uniform comes secretly through the lines for the purpose of waging war by destruction of life or property, are familiar examples of belligerents who are generally deemed not to be entitled to the status of prisoners of war, but to be offenders against the law of war subject to trial and punishment by military tribunals. . . .

Specification 1 states that petitioners "being enemies of the United States and acting for . . . the German Reich, a belligerent enemy nation, secretly and covertly passed, in civilian dress, contrary to the law of war, through the military and naval lines and defenses of the United States . . . and went behind such lines, contrary to the law of war, in civilian dress . . . for the purpose of committing . . . hostile acts, and, in particular, to destroy certain war industries, war utilities and war materials within the United States."

This specification . . . plainly alleges violation of the law of war. . . .

Citizenship in the United States of an enemy belligerent does not relieve him from the consequences of a belligerency which is unlawful because in violation of the law of war. Citizens who associate themselves with the military arm of the enemy government, and with its aid, guidance and direction enter this country bent on hostile acts are enemy belligerents within the meaning of the Hague Convention and the law of war. It is as an enemy belligerent that petitioner Haupt is charged with entering the United States, and unlawful belligerency is the gravamen of the offense of which he is accused. . . .

But petitioners insist that even if the offenses with which they are charged are offenses against the law of war, their trial is subject to the requirement of the Fifth Amendment that no person shall be held to answer for a capital or otherwise infamous crime unless on a presentment or indictment of a grand jury, and that such trials by Article III, §2, and the Sixth Amendment must be by jury in a civil court. . . .

Presentment by a grand jury and trial by a jury of the vicinage where the crime was committed were at the time of the adoption of the Constitution familiar parts of the machinery for criminal trials in the civil courts. But they were procedures unknown to military tribunals, which are not courts in the sense of the Judiciary Article, and which in the natural course of events are usually called upon to function under conditions precluding resort to such procedures. . . .

. . . [W]e must conclude that §2 of Article III and the Fifth and Sixth Amendments cannot be taken to have extended the right to demand a jury to trials by military commission, or to have required that offenses against the law of war not triable by jury at common law be tried only in the civil courts. . . .

Petitioners, and especially petitioner Haupt, stress the pronouncement of this Court in the *Milligan* case that the law of war "can never be applied to citizens in states which have upheld the authority of the government, and where the courts are open and their process unobstructed." Elsewhere in its opinion, the Court was at pains to point out that Milligan, a citizen twenty years resident in Indiana, who had never been a resident of any of the states in rebellion, was not an enemy belligerent either entitled to the status of a prisoner of war or subject to the penalties imposed upon unlawful belligerents. We construe the Court's statement as to the inapplicability of the law of war to Milligan's case as having particular reference to the facts before it. From them the Court concluded that Milligan, not being a part of or associated with the armed forces of the enemy, was a non-belligerent, not subject to the law of war save as — in circumstances found not there to be present and not involved here — martial law might be constitutionally established.

The Court's opinion is inapplicable to the case presented by the present record. We have no occasion now to define with meticulous care the ultimate boundaries of the jurisdiction of military tribunals to try persons according to the law of war. It is enough that petitioners here, upon the conceded facts, were plainly within those boundaries, and were held in good faith for trial by military commission, charged with being enemies who, with the purpose of destroying war materials and utilities, entered or after entry remained in our territory without uniform—an offense against the law of war. We hold only that those particular acts constitute an offense against the law of war which the Constitution authorizes to be tried by military commission. . . .

It follows that the orders of the District Court should be affirmed, and that leave to file petitions for habeas corpus in this Court should be denied.

Justice MURPHY took no part in the consideration or decision of these cases.

NOTES AND QUESTIONS

1. *The Overarching Constitution and Historical Understandings. Milligan* seems to stand for the proposition that the Constitution controls in war as in peace, at least where U.S. citizens are concerned. But some argued that it was, in fact, a departure from the historical understanding, one that prevailed through much of the Civil War.

> [Charles] Sumner and others articulated a "dual" theory of the conflict and of the U.S. government's powers: when responding to war-like attacks by its own citizens, the United States had the discretion to choose how to respond: either as a "sovereign" or a "belligerent." The "rebels in arms" were "criminals" because they were committing treason and also "enemies because their combination has assumed the front and proportions of war." The U.S. government, it was argued, may choose "to proceed against them in either character, according to controlling considerations of policy." Then here is the rub: "If we treat them as criminals, then we are under the restraints of the Constitution; if we treat them as enemies, then we have all the latitude sanctioned by the rights of war;" indeed, "the rights against enemies, founded on war . . . are absolutely without constitutional limitation." The choice of means was discretionary; the applicable legal regime flowed from the choice of means made by the U.S. government.

Andrew Kent, *The Constitution and the Laws of War During the Civil War*, 85 Notre Dame L. Rev. 1839, 1851 (2010) (quoting Senator Sumner). Even if the "dual theory" was widely held during the Civil War, did it survive *Milligan*? When, if ever, may U.S. citizens be detained and tried by the military, according to *Milligan*? Does the government have a choice about how to treat them?

2. *Military Necessity.* In *Reid v. Covert*, 354 U.S. 1, 21 (1957), *supra* p. 709, the Court emphasized that

> the jurisdiction of military tribunals is a very limited and extraordinary jurisdiction derived from the cryptic language of Art. I, §8, and, at most, was intended to be only a narrow exception to the normal and preferred method of trial in courts of law. Every extension of military jurisdiction is an encroachment on the jurisdiction of the civil courts, and, more important, acts as a deprivation of the right to jury trial and of other treasured constitutional protections.

At the same time, the *Reid* Court found that the "exigencies which have required military rule on the battlefront are not present . . . where no conflict exists. Military trial of civilians 'in the field' is an extraordinary jurisdiction and it should not be expanded at the expense of the Bill of Rights." *Id.* at 35.

What "exigencies" require military *detention*? Are they geographically limited? Did they apply to the military detention of Milligan? Did the existence of an exigency depend on whether there were reasonable alternatives to his military detention? Were there?

3. *Statutory Authority?* *Quirin* suggests that there was statutory authority for the commission that tried the German saboteurs. Indeed, Articles 81 and 82 of the Articles of War, which it cites, seemed to authorize the trial of spies, at least, by military commission. But the decision places chief reliance on Article 15, which it quotes *supra* p. 824. Does Article 15, which is now 10 U.S.C. §821 (2006), authorize military commissions or is it merely a savings clause? If the latter, what authority does it save? In another World War II case involving military commissions, *In re Yamashita*, 327 U.S. 1 (1946), the Supreme Court explained that "[b]y thus recognizing military commissions in order to preserve their traditional jurisdiction over enemy combatants unimpaired by the Articles, Congress gave sanction, as we held in *Ex parte Quirin*, to any use of the military commission contemplated by the *common law of war.*" *Id.* at 20 (emphasis added).

Presumably the law of war also authorizes the military detention of enemy combatants. If so, is §821 or any statute necessary to authorize military detention as long as we are at war? *See Hamdan v. Rumsfeld*, 548 U.S. 557, 592 (2006), *infra* p. 1075 (refraining from deciding analogous question). Could Congress by statute regulate or prohibit such detentions? On what specific constitutional authority would Congress rely for such a statute? *See id.*

4. *Declared State of War?* If military detention is authorized by the common law of war, must war be declared for the Commander in Chief to detain? War had, of course, been declared before *Quirin* and *Yamashita* were decided. One advantage of requiring a declared war to authorize military detention or trial is that the authority then has a temporal limit; it lasts "so long as a state of war exists from its declaration until peace is proclaimed." *Yamashita*, 327 U.S. at 11-12. "A declaration of war draws clear lines. It defines (or at least has traditionally done so) who the enemy is: another state, and all the nationals of that state. It marks a clear beginning, and (again traditionally) an end, with some act or instrument marking its conclusion." A.B.A. Task Force on Terrorism and the Law, *Report and Recommendations on Military Commissions* 5 (Jan. 4, 2002) (*ABA Task Force Report*).

But we have seen that Congress can authorize "imperfect" war without a formal declaration. Writing of one such war (the Quasi-War with France) in *Talbot v. Seeman*, 5 U.S. 1 (1801), Chief Justice Marshall observed that "congress may authorize general hostilities, in which case the general laws of war apply to our situation; or partial hostilities, in which case the laws of war, so far as they actually apply to our situation, must be noticed." Military detention and trials by military commissions were also common in the field and in occupied Confederate states during the undeclared Civil War.

Yet even those states of war each had a defined and discernible end. Does a war on terrorists have a discernible end? If a state of war triggers common law of war authority, did the Authorization for Use of Military Force (AUMF), Pub. L. No. 107-40, 115 Stat. 224 (2001), *supra* p. 97, approving the use of force against the perpetrators of the September 11 attacks, authorize a state of war permitting the President to direct military detention and to use military commissions? *See Hamdan v. Rumsfeld, supra,* 548 U.S. at 593-594 (yes, as to military commissions, but it does not expand the President's existing authority to convene such commissions). War against whom? Is the power to detain coextensive with the state of war authorized by the AUMF? How long is that? Might it continue longer? *See Hamdi v. Rumsfeld,* 542 U.S. 547 (2004), *infra* p. 831.

5. *Violations of the Law of War.* Were the September 11 attacks acts of war, and did they violate the law of war? Traditionally, states carry out acts of war, and a state's deliberate attack on noncombatant civilians would clearly violate the laws of war. *See, e.g.,* Convention Relative to the Protection of Civilian Persons in Time of War (1949 Geneva Convention IV), Aug. 12, 1949, 6 U.S.T. 3516, 75 U.N.T.S. 287, *supra* p. 239. Some have argued that "war crimes" must by definition either be committed during an international armed conflict between *states* or in an internal armed conflict, and that the war conducted by terrorists is neither. *See, e.g.,* Joan Fitzpatrick, *Jurisdiction of Military Commissions and the Ambiguous War on Terrorism,* 96 Am. J. Int'l L. 345 (2002).

But the law of war applies also to some nonstate actors, such as insurgents. *ABA Task Force Report, supra,* at 7. It also presumably applies to terrorists with state sponsors. But does one also violate the law of war by conspiring with or aiding and abetting al Qaeda? *See* Association of the Bar of the City of New York, Comm. on Military Aff. & Justice, *Inter Arma Silent Leges: In Times of Armed Conflict, Should the Laws Be Silent?* 16 (Dec. 2001) (*N.Y. City Bar Report*) (no). In *Hamdan v. Rumsfeld, supra,* a plurality of the Supreme Court found that conspiracy was not a crime traditionally triable under the law of war. 548 U.S. at 600. Congress responded by purportedly codifying "offenses that have traditionally been triable by military commissions," but then including not only "conspiracy," but also "providing material support for terrorism." Military Commissions Act of 2006, Pub. L. No. 109-366, §3(a), 120 Stat. 2600, 2630.

6. *Reconciling Milligan and Quirin.* Although Attorney General Biddle at first asked the Court in *Quirin* to overrule *Milligan,* he later backed off from this demand in his oral argument and asserted that the Court could uphold the use of the military commission to try the saboteurs "without touching a hair of the *Milligan* case." George Lardner Jr., *Nazi Saboteurs Captured!,* Wash. Post, Jan. 13, 2002, Magazine, at 23. How *did* the Court distinguish *Milligan*? Did it distinguish the defendants by their citizenship? *See Mudd v. Caldera,* 134 F. Supp. 2d 138 (D.D.C. 2001) (citizens and noncitizens alike may be subject to the jurisdiction of a military commission for violating the laws of war). By their acts? (Recall that Milligan was charged with "Violation of the laws of war.") If *Milligan* survived *Quirin,* as the later opinion suggests, how much of it is left?

The *Quirin* Court suggested that *Milligan* should be limited to its facts. On the other hand, Justice Black wrote to the other Justices in *Quirin* that "[i]n this case I want to go no further than to declare that these particular defendants are subject to the jurisdiction of a military tribunal because of the circumstances." *See* Evan P. Schultz, *Now and Later,* Legal Times, Dec. 24, 2001, at 54. Accordingly, the opinion for the Court stated, "We hold only that these particular facts constitute an offense against the law of nations which the Constitution authorizes to be tried by military commission." *Quirin,* 317 U.S. at 20. Do "these particular facts" include the fact of declared war with its attendant limits (including identification of enemy combatants)?

If *Quirin* is limited to *its* facts, and applicable to military detention (not just trial), could the military constitutionally detain a suspected terrorist apprehended in the United States while civilian courts are open? In view of the Court's characterization of the military commission as a "narrow exception to the normal and preferred method of trial in courts of law," should we read *Quirin* for all that its language may be worth, or as narrowly as possible? *Cf. ABA Task Force Report, supra,* at 16 (recommending that "any use of military commissions should be limited to narrow circumstances in which compelling security interests justify their use," and that they not be used against persons lawfully present in the United States or unconnected with the September 11 attacks absent additional specific authority from Congress); *N.Y. City Bar Report, supra,* at 8 (arguing that *Quirin* should be limited to declared war).

Military Detention
After 9/11

In late 2001, President George W. Bush issued a military order authorizing the detention of "[a]ny individual subject to this order...at an appropriate location designated by the Secretary of Defense outside or within the United States." Military Order of Nov. 13, 2001, *Detention, Treatment, and Trial of Certain Non-Citizens in the War Against Terrorism*, 66 Fed. Reg. 57,833, §3(a) (Nov. 13, 2001) (reproduced in full *infra* p. 1071). It provided that:

> The term "individual subject to this order" shall mean any individual who is not a United States citizen with respect to whom I determine from time to time in writing that:
>   (1) there is reason to believe that such individual, at the relevant times,
>   (i) is or was a member of the organization known as al Qaida;
>   (ii) has engaged in, aided or abetted, or conspired to commit, acts of international terrorism, or acts in preparation therefor, that have caused, threaten to cause, or have as their aim to cause, injury to or adverse effects on the United States, its citizens, national security, foreign policy, or economy; or
>   (iii) has knowingly harbored one or more individuals described in subparagraphs (i) or (ii) of subsection 2(a)(1) of this order; and
>   (2) it is in the interest of the United States that such individual be subject to this order. [*Id.* §2(a).]

Pursuant to the order, hundreds of noncitizens captured in Afghanistan or Pakistan were detained at the Guantánamo Bay Naval Station and in other locations abroad. A report by a multi-agency task force asserted that 779 individuals had been detained at Guantánamo, of whom 242 remained in detention as of January 2010. *Final Report: Guantánamo Review Task Force*, Jan. 22, 2010 ("Guantánamo Review"), *available at* http://www.justice.gov/ag/guantanamo-review-final-report.pdf. A year later the number had declined to 172. *See* Cheryl Pellerin, *Military Commission Panel Sentences Guantanamo Detainee*, Am. Forces Press Serv., Feb. 18, 2011.

One of them, however, Yasir Esam Hamdi, turned out to have been born in the United States. When this was discovered, he was transferred to the United States, but still detained in military custody as an "enemy combatant." Another U.S. citizen, Jose Padilla, was arrested as a material witness as he stepped off the plane at O'Hare International Airport in Chicago, and then also transferred into military custody in the United States. Subsequently, a lawfully resident noncitizen, Ali Saleh Kahlah al-Marri, was arrested at his home in Peoria, Illinois, as a material witness and later indicted for credit card fraud and making false statements to the FBI. The government then moved *ex parte* to dismiss the indictment based on an order signed by President Bush the same day, determining al-Marri to be an "enemy combatant" and ordering his detention as such in military custody in the United States.

This chapter explores the authority for what the Obama Administration has called "law-of-war detention," a term we also use in this chapter to refer to laws of war that are recognized by our law or incorporated into our law by the 2001 Authorization for the Use of Military Force. We start in Part A with the Supreme Court's decision in *Hamdi v. Rumsfeld*, 542 U.S. 507 (2004). In Part B, we consider whether authority to detain Hamdi and other battlefield captives extends to the detention of persons like Padilla and al-Marri, who were captured in the United States and not on the battlefield abroad. In Part C, we examine the still-evolving case law about detention authority that is being generated by noncitizen habeas petitions in the D.C. federal courts, prompted by the Supreme Court's decision in *Boumediene v. Bush*, 553 U.S. 723 (2008) (*supra* p. 787). Finally, in Part D we review the Obama administration's efforts to close the Guantánamo Bay Detention Center, and Congress's responses.

A. MILITARY DETENTION OF BATTLEFIELD CAPTIVES

Hamdi v. Rumsfeld

United States Supreme Court, 2004
542 U.S. 507

Justice O'CONNOR announced the judgment of the Court and delivered an opinion, in which THE CHIEF JUSTICE, Justice KENNEDY, and Justice BREYER join. . . .

[During the U.S. military operations in Afghanistan that followed the 9/11 terrorist attacks, petitioner Hamdi was captured by Afghan Northern Alliance forces. He was subsequently transferred to U.S. military custody in Afghanistan and sent to Guantánamo. When it was discovered that he had been born in Louisiana, making him a U.S. citizen, he was transferred to the United States as an enemy combatant and detained at a Navy brig in Charleston, South Carolina. Hamdi's father filed a habeas petition on behalf of his son under 28 U.S.C. §2241, alleging that the government held him in violation of the Fifth and Fourteenth Amendments. In the ensuing proceeding, the government filed an affidavit by Department of Defense official Michael Mobbs, setting forth the foregoing facts based on hearsay.]

II

The threshold question before us is whether the Executive has the authority to detain citizens who qualify as "enemy combatants." There is some debate as to the proper scope of this term, and the Government has never provided any court with the full criteria that it uses in classifying individuals as such. It has made clear, however, that, for purposes of this case, the "enemy combatant" that it is seeking to detain is an individual who, it alleges, was "part of or supporting forces hostile to the United States or coalition partners" in Afghanistan and who "engaged in an armed conflict against the United States" there. We therefore answer only the narrow question before us: whether the detention of citizens falling within that definition is authorized.

The Government maintains that no explicit congressional authorization is required, because the Executive possesses plenary authority to detain pursuant to Article II of the Constitution. We do not reach the question whether Article II provides such authority, however, because we agree with the Government's alternative position, that Congress has in fact authorized Hamdi's detention, through the AUMF [*supra* p. 97].

Associate Justice Sandra Day O'Connor.

Photo by Dane Penland. Collection of the Supreme Court of the United States.

Our analysis on that point, set forth below, substantially overlaps with our analysis of Hamdi's principal argument for the illegality of his detention. He posits that his detention is forbidden by 18 U.S.C. §4001(a). Section 4001(a) states that "[n]o citizen shall be imprisoned or otherwise detained by the United States except pursuant to an Act of Congress." Congress passed §4001(a) in 1971 as part of a bill to repeal the Emergency Detention Act of 1950, 50 U.S.C. §811 *et seq.*, which provided procedures for executive detention, during times of emergency, of individuals deemed likely to engage in espionage or sabotage. Congress was particularly concerned about the possibility that the Act could be used to reprise the Japanese internment camps of World War II. The Government again presses two alternative positions. First, it argues that §4001(a), in light of its legislative history and its location in Title 18, applies only to "the control of civilian prisons and related detentions," not to military detentions. Second, it maintains that §4001(a) is satisfied, because Hamdi is being detained "pursuant to an Act of Congress" — the AUMF. Again, because we conclude that the Government's second assertion is correct, we do not address the first. In other words, for the reasons that follow, we conclude that the AUMF is explicit congressional authorization for the detention of individuals in the narrow category we describe (assuming, without deciding, that such authorization is required), and that the AUMF satisfied §4001(a)'s requirement that a detention be "pursuant to an Act of Congress" (assuming, without deciding, that §4001(a) applies to military detentions).

The AUMF authorizes the President to use "all necessary and appropriate force" against "nations, organizations, or persons" associated with the September 11, 2001, terrorist attacks. 115 Stat. 224. There can be no doubt that individuals who fought against the United States in Afghanistan as part of the Taliban, an organization known to have supported the al Qaeda terrorist network responsible for those attacks, are individuals Congress sought to target in passing the AUMF. We conclude that detention of individuals falling into the limited category we are considering, for the duration of the particular conflict in which they were captured, is so fundamental and accepted an incident to war as to be an exercise of the "necessary and appropriate force" Congress has authorized the President to use.

The capture and detention of lawful combatants and the capture, detention, and trial of unlawful combatants, by "universal agreement and practice," are "important incident[s] of war." *Ex parte Quirin*, 317 U.S. [1 (1942)], at 28. The purpose of detention is to prevent captured individuals from returning to the field of battle and taking up arms once again.

There is no bar to this Nation's holding one of its own citizens as an enemy combatant. In *Quirin*, one of the detainees, Haupt, alleged that he was a naturalized United States citizen. 317 U.S., at 20. We held that "[c]itizens who associate themselves with the military arm of the enemy government, and with its aid, guidance and direction enter this country bent on hostile acts, are enemy belligerents within the meaning of . . . the law of war." *Id.*, at 37-38. While Haupt was tried for violations of the law of war, nothing in *Quirin* suggests that his citizenship would have precluded his mere detention for the duration of the relevant hostilities. See *id.*, at 30-31. Nor can we see any reason for drawing such a line here. A citizen, no less than an alien, can be "part of or supporting forces hostile to the United States or coalition partners" and "engaged in an armed conflict against the United States"; such a citizen, if released, would pose the same threat of returning to the front during the ongoing conflict.

In light of these principles, it is of no moment that the AUMF does not use specific language of detention. Because detention to prevent a combatant's return to the battlefield is a fundamental incident of waging war, in permitting the use of "necessary and appropriate force," Congress has clearly and unmistakably authorized detention in the narrow circumstances considered here. . . .

Hamdi contends that the AUMF does not authorize indefinite or perpetual detention. Certainly, we agree that indefinite detention for the purpose of interrogation is not authorized. Further, we understand Congress' grant of authority for the use of "necessary and appropriate force" to include the authority to detain for the duration of the relevant conflict, and our understanding is based on longstanding law-of-war principles. If the practical circumstances of a given conflict are entirely unlike those of the conflicts that informed the development of the law of war, that understanding may unravel. But that is not the situation we face as of this date. Active combat operations against Taliban fighters apparently are ongoing in Afghanistan. The United States may detain, for the duration of these hostilities, individuals legitimately determined to be Taliban combatants who "engaged in an armed conflict against the United States." If the record establishes that United States troops are still involved in active combat in Afghanistan, those detentions are part of the exercise of "necessary and appropriate force," and therefore are authorized by the AUMF.

Ex parte Milligan, [71 U.S. (4 Wall.) 2 (1866)], does not undermine our holding about the Government's authority to seize enemy combatants, as we define that term today. In that case, the Court made repeated reference to the fact that its inquiry into whether the military tribunal had jurisdiction to try and punish Milligan turned in large part on the fact that Milligan was not a prisoner of war, but a resident of Indiana arrested while at home there. *Id.*, at 118, 131. That fact was central to its conclusion. Had Milligan been captured while he was assisting Confederate soldiers by carrying a rifle against Union troops on a Confederate battlefield, the holding of the Court might well have been different. The Court's repeated explanations that Milligan was not a prisoner of war suggest that had these different circumstances been present he could have been detained under military authority for the duration of the conflict, whether or not he was a citizen. . . .

III

Even in cases in which the detention of enemy combatants is legally authorized, there remains the question of what process is constitutionally due to a citizen who disputes his enemy-combatant status....

A

Though they reach radically different conclusions on the process that ought to attend the present proceeding, the parties begin on common ground. All agree that, absent suspension, the writ of habeas corpus remains available to every individual detained within the United States. U.S. Const., Art. I, §9, cl. 2 ("The Privilege of the Writ of Habeas Corpus shall not be suspended, unless when in Cases of Rebellion or Invasion the public Safety may require it"). Only in the rarest of circumstances has Congress seen fit to suspend the writ.... All agree suspension of the writ has not occurred here. Thus, it is undisputed that Hamdi was properly before an Article III court to challenge his detention under 28 U.S.C. §2241. Further, all agree that §2241 and its companion provisions provide at least a skeletal outline of the procedures to be afforded a petitioner in federal habeas review. Most notably, §2243 provides that "the person detained may, under oath, deny any of the facts set forth in the return or allege any other material facts," and §2246 allows the taking of evidence in habeas proceedings by deposition, affidavit, or interrogatories.

The simple outline of §2241 makes clear both that Congress envisioned that habeas petitioners would have some opportunity to present and rebut facts and that courts in cases like this retain some ability to vary the ways in which they do so as mandated by due process. The Government recognizes the basic procedural protections required by the habeas statute, but asks us to hold that, given both the flexibility of the habeas mechanism and the circumstances presented in this case, the presentation of the Mobbs Declaration to the habeas court completed the required factual development. It suggests two separate reasons for its position that no further process is due.

B

First, the Government urges the adoption of the Fourth Circuit's holding below—that because it is "undisputed" that Hamdi's seizure took place in a combat zone, the habeas determination can be made purely as a matter of law, with no further hearing or factfinding necessary. This argument is easily rejected. As the dissenters from the denial of rehearing en banc noted, the circumstances surrounding Hamdi's seizure cannot in any way be characterized as "undisputed," as "those circumstances are neither conceded in fact, nor susceptible to concession in law, because Hamdi has not been permitted to speak for himself or even through counsel as to those circumstances." 337 F.3d 335, 357 (Luttig, J., dissenting from denial of rehearing en banc). Further, the "facts" that constitute the alleged concession are insufficient to support Hamdi's detention. Under the definition of enemy combatant that we accept today as falling within the scope of Congress' authorization, Hamdi would need to be "part of or supporting forces hostile to the United States or coalition partners" and "engaged in an armed conflict against the United States" to justify his detention in the United States for the duration of the relevant conflict. The habeas petition states only that "[w]hen seized by the United States Government, Mr. Hamdi resided in Afghanistan." An assertion that one *resided* in a country in which combat operations are taking place is not a concession that one was "*captured* in a zone of active combat operations in a foreign theater of war," 316 F.3d, at 459 (emphasis added), and certainly is not a concession that one was "part of or supporting forces hostile to the United States or coalition partners" and "engaged in an armed conflict against the United States." Accordingly, we reject any argument that Hamdi has made concessions that eliminate any right to further process.

C

The Government's second argument requires closer consideration. This is the argument that further factual exploration is unwarranted and inappropriate in light of the extraordinary constitutional interests at stake. Under the Government's most extreme rendition of this argument, "[r]espect for separation of powers and the limited institutional capabilities of courts in matters of military decision-making in connection with an ongoing conflict" ought to eliminate entirely any individual process, restricting the courts to investigating only whether legal authorization exists for the broader detention scheme. At most, the Government argues, courts should review its determination that a citizen is an enemy combatant under a very deferential "some evidence" standard. [Brief for Respondents] 34 ("Under the some evidence standard, the focus is exclusively on the factual basis supplied by the Executive to support its own determination" (citing *Superintendent, Mass. Correctional Institution at Walpole v. Hill*, 472 U.S. 445, 455-457 (1985) (explaining that the some evidence standard "does not require" a "weighing of the evidence," but rather calls for assessing "whether there is any evidence in the record that could support the conclusion")). Under this review, a court would assume the accuracy of the Government's articulated basis for Hamdi's detention, as set forth in the Mobbs Declaration, and assess only whether that articulated basis was a legitimate one. In response, Hamdi emphasizes that this Court consistently has recognized that an individual challenging his detention may not be held at the will of the Executive without recourse to some proceeding before a neutral tribunal to determine whether the Executive's asserted justifications for that detention have basis in fact and warrant in law. *See, e.g., Zadvydas v. Davis*, 533 U.S. 678, 690 (2001). . . .

. . . The ordinary mechanism that we use for balancing such serious competing interests, and for determining the procedures that are necessary to ensure that a citizen is not "deprived of life, liberty, or property, without due process of law," U.S. Const., Amdt. 5, is the test that we articulated in *Mathews v. Eldridge*, 424 U.S. 319 (1976). *Mathews* dictates that the process due in any given instance is determined by weighing "the private interest that will be affected by the official action" against the Government's asserted interest, "including the function involved" and the burdens the Government would face in providing greater process. 424 U.S., at 335. The *Mathews* calculus then contemplates a judicious balancing of these concerns, through an analysis of "the risk of an erroneous deprivation" of the private interest if the process were reduced and the "probable value, if any, of additional or substitute safeguards." *Ibid.* We take each of these steps in turn.

1

It is beyond question that substantial interests lie on both sides of the scale in this case. Hamdi's "private interest . . . affected by the official action," *ibid.*, is the most elemental of liberty interests — the interest in being free from physical detention by one's own government. "In our society liberty is the norm," and detention without trial "is the carefully limited exception." [*United States v. Salerno*, 481 U.S. 739 (1987),] at 755. . . .

Nor is the weight on this side of the *Mathews* scale offset by the circumstances of war or the accusation of treasonous behavior, for "[i]t is clear that commitment for *any* purpose constitutes a significant deprivation of liberty that requires due process protection," *Jones v. United States*, 463 U.S. 354, 361 (1983) (emphasis added; internal quotation marks omitted), and at this stage in the *Mathews* calculus, we consider the interest of the *erroneously* detained individual. Indeed, as *amicus* briefs from media and relief organizations emphasize, the risk of erroneous deprivation of a citizen's liberty in the absence of sufficient process here is very real. See Brief for AmeriCares et al. as *Amici Curiae* 13-22 (noting ways in which "[t]he nature of humanitarian relief work and journalism present a significant risk of mistaken military detentions"). Moreover, as critical as the Government's interest may be in detaining those who actually pose an immediate threat to the national security of the United States during ongoing international conflict, history and common sense teach us that an unchecked system of detention carries the potential to become a means for oppression and abuse of others who do not present that sort of threat. . . .

2

On the other side of the scale are the weighty and sensitive governmental interests in ensuring that those who have in fact fought with the enemy during a war do not return to battle against the United States. As discussed above, the law of war and the realities of combat may render such detentions both necessary and appropriate, and our due process analysis need not blink at those realities. Without doubt, our Constitution recognizes that core strategic matters of warmaking belong in the hands of those who are best positioned and most politically accountable for making them. *Department of Navy v. Egan*, 484 U.S. 518, 530 (1988) (noting the reluctance of the courts "to intrude upon the authority of the Executive in military and national security affairs"); *Youngstown Sheet & Tube Co. v. Sawyer*, 343 U.S. 579, 587 (1952) (acknowledging "broad powers in military commanders engaged in day-to-day fighting in a theater of war").

The Government also argues at some length that its interests in reducing the process available to alleged enemy combatants are heightened by the practical difficulties that would accompany a system of trial-like process. In its view, military officers who are engaged in the serious work of waging battle would be unnecessarily and dangerously distracted by litigation half a world away, and discovery into military operations would both intrude on the sensitive secrets of national defense and result in a futile search for evidence buried under the rubble of war. To the extent that these burdens are triggered by heightened procedures, they are properly taken into account in our due process analysis.

3

Striking the proper constitutional balance here is of great importance to the Nation during this period of ongoing combat. But it is equally vital that our calculus not give short shrift to the values that this country holds dear or to the privilege that is American citizenship. It is during our most challenging and uncertain moments that our Nation's commitment to due process is most severely tested; and it is in those times that we must preserve our commitment at home to the principles for which we fight abroad.

With due recognition of these competing concerns, we believe that neither the process proposed by the Government nor the process apparently envisioned by the District Court below strikes the proper constitutional balance when a United States citizen is detained in the United States as an enemy combatant. That is, "the risk of erroneous deprivation" of a detainee's liberty interest is unacceptably high under the Government's proposed rule, while some of the "additional or substitute procedural safeguards" suggested by the District Court are unwarranted in light of their limited "probable value" and the burdens they may impose on the military in such cases. *Mathews*, 424 U.S., at 335.

We therefore hold that a citizen-detainee seeking to challenge his classification as an enemy combatant must receive notice of the factual basis for his classification, and a fair opportunity to rebut the Government's factual assertions before a neutral decisionmaker. "For more than a century the central meaning of procedural due process has been clear: 'Parties whose rights are to be affected are entitled to be heard; and in order that they may enjoy that right they must first be notified.' It is equally fundamental that the right to notice and an opportunity to be heard 'must be granted at a meaningful time and in a meaningful manner.'" *Fuentes v. Shevin*, 407 U.S. 67, 80 (1972). These essential constitutional promises may not be eroded.

At the same time, the exigencies of the circumstances may demand that, aside from these core elements, enemy combatant proceedings may be tailored to alleviate their uncommon potential to burden the Executive at a time of ongoing military conflict. Hearsay, for example, may need to be accepted as the most reliable available evidence from the Government in such a proceeding. Likewise, the Constitution would not be offended by a presumption in favor of the Government's evidence, so long as that presumption remained a rebuttable one and fair opportunity for rebuttal were provided. Thus, once the Government puts forth credible evidence that the habeas petitioner meets the enemy-combatant criteria, the onus could shift to the petitioner to rebut that evidence with more persuasive evidence that he falls outside the criteria. A burden-shifting scheme of this sort would meet the goal of ensuring that the errant tourist, embedded journalist, or local aid worker has a chance to prove military error while giving due regard to the Executive once it has put forth meaningful support for its conclusion that the detainee is in fact an enemy combatant. In the words of *Mathews*, process of this sort would sufficiently address the "risk of erroneous deprivation" of a detainee's liberty interest while eliminating certain procedures that have questionable additional value in light of the burden on the Government. 424 U.S., at 335.

We think it unlikely that this basic process will have the dire impact on the central functions of warmaking that the Government forecasts. The parties agree that initial captures on the battlefield need not receive the process we have discussed here; that process is due only when the determination is made to *continue* to hold those who have been seized. The Government has made clear in its briefing that documentation regarding battlefield detainees already is kept in the ordinary course of military affairs. Any factfinding imposition created by requiring a knowledgeable affiant to summarize these records to an independent tribunal is a minimal one. Likewise, arguments that military officers ought not have to wage war under the threat of litigation lose much of their steam when factual disputes at enemy-combatant hearings are limited to the alleged combatant's acts. This focus meddles little, if at all, in the strategy or conduct of war, inquiring only into the appropriateness of continuing to detain an individual claimed to have taken up arms against the United States. While we accord the greatest respect and consideration to the judgments of military authorities in matters relating to the actual prosecution of a war, and recognize that the scope of that discretion necessarily is wide, it does not infringe on the core role of the military for the courts to exercise their own time-honored and constitutionally mandated roles of reviewing and resolving claims like those presented here. Cf. *Korematsu v. United States*, 323 U.S. 214, 233-234 (1944) (Murphy, J., dissenting) ("[L]ike other claims conflicting with the asserted constitutional rights of the individual, the military claim must subject itself to the judicial process of having its reasonableness determined and its conflicts with other interests reconciled"); *Sterling v. Constantin*, 287 U.S. 378, 401 (1932) ("What are the allowable limits of military discretion, and whether or not they have been overstepped in a particular case, are judicial questions").

In sum, while the full protections that accompany challenges to detentions in other settings may prove unworkable and inappropriate in the enemy-combatant setting, the threats to military operations posed by a basic system of independent review are not so weighty as to trump a citizen's core rights to challenge meaningfully the Government's case and to be heard by an impartial adjudicator.

D

In so holding, we necessarily reject the Government's assertion that separation of powers principles mandate a heavily circumscribed role for the courts in such circumstances. Indeed, the position that the courts must forgo any examination of the individual case and focus exclusively on the legality of the broader detention scheme cannot be mandated by any reasonable view of separation of powers, as this approach serves only to *condense* power into a single branch of government. We have long since made clear that a state of war is not a blank check for the President when it comes to the rights of the Nation's citizens. *Youngstown Sheet & Tube*, 343 U.S., at 587. Whatever power the United States Constitution envisions for the Executive in its exchanges with other nations or with enemy organizations in times of conflict, it most assuredly envisions a role for all three branches when individual liberties are at stake. *Mistretta v. United States*, 488 U.S. 361, 380 (1989) (it was "the central judgment of the Framers of the Constitution that, within our political scheme, the separation of governmental powers into three coordinate Branches is essential to the preservation of liberty"); *Home Building & Loan Assn. v. Blaisdell*, 290 U.S. 398, 426 (1934) (The war power "is a power to wage war successfully, and thus it permits the harnessing of the entire energies of the people in a supreme cooperative effort to preserve the nation. But even the war power does not remove constitutional limitations safeguarding essential liberties"). Likewise, we have made clear that, unless Congress acts to suspend it, the Great Writ of habeas corpus allows the Judicial Branch to play a necessary role in maintaining this delicate balance of governance, serving as an important judicial check on the Executive's discretion in the realm of detentions. See *INS v. St. Cyr*, 533 U.S. 289, 301 (2001) ("At its historical core, the writ of habeas corpus has served as a means of reviewing the legality of Executive detention, and it is in that context that its protections have been strongest"). Thus, while we do not question that our due process assessment must pay keen attention to the particular burdens faced by the Executive in the context of military action, it would turn our system of checks and balances on its head to suggest that a citizen could not make his way to court with a challenge to the factual basis for his detention by his government, simply because the Executive opposes making available such a challenge. Absent suspension of the writ by Congress, a citizen detained as an enemy combatant is entitled to this process.

Because we conclude that due process demands some system for a citizen detainee to refute his classification, the proposed "some evidence" standard is inadequate. Any process in which the Executive's factual assertions go wholly unchallenged or are simply presumed correct without any opportunity for the alleged combatant to demonstrate otherwise falls constitutionally short. As the Government itself has recognized, we have utilized the "some evidence" standard in the past as a standard of review, not as a standard of proof. That is, it primarily has been employed by courts in examining an administrative record developed after an adversarial proceeding — one with process at least of the sort that we today hold is constitutionally mandated in the citizen enemy-combatant setting. This standard therefore is ill suited to the situation in which a habeas petitioner has received no prior proceedings before any tribunal and had no prior opportunity to rebut the Executive's factual assertions before a neutral decisionmaker.

Today we are faced only with such a case. Aside from unspecified "screening" processes, and military interrogations in which the Government suggests Hamdi could have contested his classification, Hamdi has received no process. An interrogation by one's captor, however effective an intelligence-gathering tool, hardly constitutes a constitutionally adequate factfinding before a neutral decisionmaker. Compare Brief for Respondents 42-43 (discussing the "secure interrogation environment," and noting that military interrogations require a controlled "interrogation dynamic" and "a relationship of trust and dependency" and are "a critical source" of "timely and effective intelligence") with *Concrete Pipe* [*and Products of California, Inc. v. Construction Laborers Pension Trust*], 508 U.S. 602, 617-618 (1993) ("one is entitled as a matter of due process of law to an adjudicator who is not in a situation which would offer a possible temptation to the average man as a judge . . . which might lead him not to hold the balance nice, clear and true" (internal quotation marks omitted)). That even purportedly fair adjudicators "are disqualified by their interest in the controversy to be decided is, of course, the general rule." *Tumey v. Ohio*, 273 U.S. 510, 522 (1927). Plainly, the "process" Hamdi has received is not that to which he is entitled under the Due Process Clause.

There remains the possibility that the standards we have articulated could be met by an appropriately authorized and properly constituted military tribunal. Indeed, it is notable that military regulations already provide for such process in related instances, dictating that tribunals be made available to determine the status of enemy detainees who assert prisoner-of-war status under the Geneva Convention. See Enemy Prisoners of War, Retained Personnel, Civilian Internees and Other Detainees, Army Regulation 190-8, §1-6 (1997). In the absence of such process, however, a court that receives a petition for a writ of habeas corpus from an alleged enemy combatant must itself ensure that the minimum requirements of due process are achieved. . . . As we have discussed, a habeas court in a case such as this may accept affidavit evidence like that contained in the Mobbs Declaration, so long as it also permits the alleged combatant to present his own factual case to rebut the Government's return. We anticipate that a District Court would proceed with the caution that we have indicated is necessary in this setting, engaging in a factfinding process that is both prudent and incremental. We have no reason to doubt that courts faced with these sensitive matters will pay proper heed both to the matters of national security that might arise in an individual case and to the constitutional limitations safeguarding essential liberties that remain vibrant even in times of security concerns.

IV

Hamdi asks us to hold that the Fourth Circuit also erred by denying him immediate access to counsel upon his detention and by disposing of the case without permitting him to meet with an attorney. Since our grant of certiorari in this case, Hamdi has been appointed counsel, with whom he has met for consultation purposes on several occasions, and with whom he is now being granted unmonitored meetings. He unquestionably has the right to access to counsel in connection with the proceedings on remand. No further consideration of this issue is necessary at this stage of the case. . . .

The judgment of the United States Court of Appeals for the Fourth Circuit is vacated, and the case is remanded for further proceedings.

It is so ordered.

Justice SOUTER, with whom Justice GINSBURG joins, concurring in part, dissenting in part, and concurring in the judgment. . . . The plurality rejects [the government's "some evidence"] limit on the exercise of habeas jurisdiction and so far I agree with its opinion. The plurality does, however, accept the Government's position that if Hamdi's designation as an enemy combatant is correct, his detention (at least as to some period) is authorized by an Act of Congress as required by §4001(a), that is, by the Authorization for Use of Military Force, 115 Stat. 224 (hereinafter Force Resolution). Here, I disagree and respectfully dissent. . . .

II

The threshold issue is how broadly or narrowly to read the Non-Detention Act, the tone of which is severe: "No citizen shall be imprisoned or otherwise detained by the United States except pursuant to an Act of Congress." . . . For a number of reasons, the prohibition within §4001(a) has to be read broadly to accord the statute a long reach and to impose a burden of justification on the Government.

First, the circumstances in which the Act was adopted point the way to this interpretation. The provision superseded a cold-war statute, the Emergency Detention Act of 1950, which had authorized the Attorney General, in time of emergency, to detain anyone reasonably thought likely to engage in espionage or sabotage. That statute was repealed in 1971 out of fear that it could authorize a repetition of the World War II internment of citizens of Japanese ancestry; Congress meant to preclude another episode like the one described in *Korematsu v. United States*, 323 U.S. 214 (1944) . . .

. . . To appreciate what is most significant, one must only recall that the internments of the 1940's were accomplished by Executive action. Although an Act of

Congress ratified and confirmed an Executive order authorizing the military to exclude individuals from defined areas and to accommodate those it might remove, see *Ex parte Endo*, 323 U.S. 283, 285-288 (1944), the statute said nothing whatever about the detention of those who might be removed; internment camps were creatures of the Executive, and confinement in them rested on assertion of Executive authority. When, therefore, Congress repealed the 1950 Act and adopted §4001(a) for the purpose of avoiding another *Korematsu*, it intended to preclude reliance on vague congressional authority (for example, providing "accommodations" for those subject to removal) as authority for detention or imprisonment at the discretion of the Executive (maintaining detention camps of American citizens, for example). In requiring that any Executive detention be "pursuant to an Act of Congress," then, Congress necessarily meant to require a congressional enactment that clearly authorized detention or imprisonment.

Second, when Congress passed §4001(a) it was acting in light of an interpretive regime that subjected enactments limiting liberty in wartime to the requirement of a clear statement and it presumably intended §4001(a) to be read accordingly. This need for clarity was unmistakably expressed in *Ex parte Endo, supra*, decided the same day as *Korematsu*.... The petitioner was held entitled to habeas relief in an opinion that set out this principle for scrutinizing wartime statutes in derogation of customary liberty:

> "In interpreting a wartime measure we must assume that [its] purpose was to allow for the greatest possible accommodation between . . . liberties and the exigencies of war. We must assume, when asked to find implied powers in a grant of legislative or executive authority, that the law makers intended to place no greater restraint on the citizen than was clearly and unmistakably indicated by the language they used." *Id.*, at 300.

Congress's understanding of the need for clear authority before citizens are kept detained is itself therefore clear, and §4001(a) must be read to have teeth in its demand for congressional authorization.

Finally, even if history had spared us the cautionary example of the internments in World War II, even if there had been no *Korematsu*, and *Endo* had set out no principle of statutory interpretation, there would be a compelling reason to read §4001(a) to demand manifest authority to detain before detention is authorized. The defining character of American constitutional government is its constant tension between security and liberty, serving both by partial helpings of each. In a government of separated powers, deciding finally on what is a reasonable degree of guaranteed liberty whether in peace or war (or some condition in between) is not well entrusted to the Executive Branch of Government, whose particular responsibility is to maintain security. For reasons of inescapable human nature, the branch of the Government asked to counter a serious threat is not the branch on which to rest the Nation's entire reliance in striking the balance between the will to win and the cost in liberty on the way to victory; the responsibility for security will naturally amplify the claim that security legitimately raises. A reasonable balance is more likely to be reached on the judgment of a different branch, just as Madison said in remarking that "the constant aim is to divide and arrange the several offices in such a manner as that each may be a check on the other — that the private interest of every individual may be a sentinel over the public rights." The Federalist No. 51, p. 349 (J. Cooke ed. 1961). Hence the need for an assessment by Congress before citizens are subject to lockup, and likewise the need for a clearly expressed congressional resolution of the competing claims.

III

Under this principle of reading §4001(a) robustly to require a clear statement of authorization to detain, none of the Government's arguments suffices to justify Hamdi's detention.

A

First, there is the argument that §4001(a) does not even apply to wartime military detentions, a position resting on the placement of §4001(a) in Title 18 of the United States Code, the gathering of federal criminal law. . . . [The] legislative history indicates that Congress was aware that §4001(a) would limit the Executive's power to detain citizens in wartime to protect national security, and it is fair to say that the prohibition was thus intended to extend not only to the exercise of power to vindicate the interests underlying domestic criminal law, but to statutorily unauthorized detention by the Executive for reasons of security in wartime, just as Hamdi claims.[2]

B

Next, there is the Government's claim, accepted by the Court, that the terms of the Force Resolution are adequate to authorize detention of an enemy combatant under the circumstances described,[3] a claim the Government fails to support sufficiently to satisfy §4001(a) as read to require a clear statement of authority to detain. Since the Force Resolution was adopted one week after the attacks of September 11, 2001, it naturally speaks with some generality, but its focus is clear, and that is on the use of military power. It is fairly read to authorize the use of armies and weapons, whether against other armies or individual terrorists. But, like the statute discussed in *Endo*, it never so much as uses the word detention, and there is no reason to think Congress might have perceived any need to augment Executive power to deal with dangerous citizens within the United States, given the well-stocked statutory arsenal of defined criminal offenses covering the gamut of actions that a citizen sympathetic to terrorists might commit. See, *e.g.*, 18 U.S.C. §2339A (material support for various

---

2. Nor is it possible to distinguish between civilian and military authority to detain based on the congressional object of avoiding another *Korematsu v. United States*, 323 U.S. 214 (1944). Although a civilian agency authorized by Executive order ran the detention camps, the relocation and detention of American citizens was ordered by the military under authority of the President as Commander in Chief. See *Ex parte Endo*, 323 U.S. 283, 285-288 (1944). The World War II internment was thus ordered under the same Presidential power invoked here and the intent to bar a repetition goes to the action taken and authority claimed here.

3. . . . [T]he Government argues that a required Act of Congress is to be found in a statutory authorization to spend money appropriated for the care of prisoners of war and of other, similar prisoners, 10 U.S.C. §956(5). It is enough to say that this statute is an authorization to spend money if there are prisoners, not an authorization to imprison anyone to provide the occasion for spending money.

terrorist acts); §2339B (material support to a foreign terrorist organization); §2332a (use of a weapon of mass destruction, including conspiracy and attempt); §2332b(a)(1) (acts of terrorism "transcending national boundaries," including threats, conspiracy, and attempt); 18 U.S.C.A. §2339C (financing of certain terrorist acts); see also 18 U.S.C. §3142(e) (pretrial detention).

C

Even so, there is one argument for treating the Force Resolution as sufficiently clear to authorize detention of a citizen consistently with §4001(a). Assuming the argument to be sound, however, the Government is in no position to claim its advantage.

Because the Force Resolution authorizes the use of military force in acts of war by the United States, the argument goes, it is reasonably clear that the military and its Commander in Chief are authorized to deal with enemy belligerents according to the treaties and customs known collectively as the laws of war. Accordingly, the United States may detain captured enemies, and *Ex parte Quirin*, 317 U.S. 1 (1942), may perhaps be claimed for the proposition that the American citizenship of such a captive does not as such limit the Government's power to deal with him under the usages of war. Thus, the Government here repeatedly argues that Hamdi's detention amounts to nothing more than customary detention of a captive taken on the field of battle: if the usages of war are fairly authorized by the Force Resolution, Hamdi's detention is authorized for purposes of §4001(a)....

By holding him incommunicado, however, the Government obviously has not been treating him as a prisoner of war, and in fact the Government claims that no Taliban detainee is entitled to prisoner of war status. This treatment appears to be a violation of the Geneva Convention provision that even in cases of doubt, captives are entitled to be treated as prisoners of war "until such time as their status has been determined by a competent tribunal." Art. 5, 6 U.S.T., at 3324....

Whether, or to what degree, the Government is in fact violating the Geneva Convention and is thus acting outside the customary usages of war are not matters I can resolve at this point. What I can say, though, is that the Government has not made out its claim that in detaining Hamdi in the manner described, it is acting in accord with the laws of war authorized to be applied against citizens by the Force Resolution. I conclude accordingly that the Government has failed to support the position that the Force Resolution authorizes the described detention of Hamdi for purposes of §4001(a).

It is worth adding a further reason for requiring the Government to bear the burden of clearly justifying its claim to be exercising recognized war powers before declaring §4001(a) satisfied. Thirty-eight days after adopting the Force Resolution, Congress passed the statute entitled Uniting and Strengthening America by Providing Appropriate Tools Required to Intercept and Obstruct Terrorism Act of 2001 (USA PATRIOT ACT), 115 Stat. 272; that Act authorized the detention of alien terrorists for no more than seven days in the absence of criminal charges or deportation proceedings, 8 U.S.C. §1226a(a)(5) (2000 ed., Supp. I). It is very difficult to believe that the same Congress that carefully circumscribed Executive power over alien terrorists on home soil would not have meant to require the Government to justify clearly its detention of an American citizen held on home soil incommunicado.

D

Since the Government has given no reason either to deflect the application of §4001(a) or to hold it to be satisfied, I need to go no further; the Government hints of a constitutional challenge to the statute, but it presents none here. I will, however, stray across the line between statutory and constitutional territory just far enough to note the weakness of the Government's mixed claim of inherent, extrastatutory authority under a combination of Article II of the Constitution and the usages of war. It is in fact in this connection that the Government developed its argument that the exercise of war powers justifies the detention, and what I have just said about its inadequacy applies here as well. Beyond that, it is instructive to recall Justice Jackson's observation that the President is not Commander in Chief of the country, only of the military. *Youngstown Sheet & Tube Co. v. Sawyer*, 343 U.S. 579, 643-644 (1952) (concurring opinion); see also *id.*, at 637-638 (Presidential authority is "at its lowest ebb" where the President acts contrary to congressional will).

There may be room for one qualification to Justice Jackson's statement, however: in a moment of genuine emergency, when the Government must act with no time for deliberation, the Executive may be able to detain a citizen if there is reason to fear he is an imminent threat to the safety of the Nation and its people (though I doubt there is any want of statutory authority). This case, however, does not present that question, because an emergency power of necessity must at least be limited by the emergency; Hamdi has been locked up for over two years. Cf. *Ex parte Milligan*, 4 Wall. 2, 127 (1866) (martial law justified only by "actual and present" necessity as in a genuine invasion that closes civilian courts)....

IV...

It should go without saying that in joining with the plurality to produce a judgment, I do not adopt the plurality's resolution of constitutional issues that I would not reach. It is not that I could disagree with the plurality's determinations (given the plurality's view of the Force Resolution) that someone in Hamdi's position is entitled at a minimum to notice of the Government's claimed factual basis for holding him, and to a fair chance to rebut it before a neutral decision maker; nor, of course, could I disagree with the plurality's affirmation of Hamdi's right to counsel. On the other hand, I do not mean to imply agreement that the Government could claim an evidentiary presumption casting the burden of rebuttal on Hamdi, or that an opportunity to litigate before a military tribunal might obviate or truncate enquiry by a court on habeas.

Subject to these qualifications, I join with the plurality in a judgment of the Court vacating the Fourth Circuit's judgment and remanding the case.

Justice SCALIA, with whom Justice STEVENS joins, dissenting.... Where the Government accuses a citizen of waging war against it, our constitutional tradition has been to prosecute him in federal court for treason or some other crime. Where the exigencies of war prevent that, the Constitution's Suspension Clause, Art. I, §9, cl. 2, allows Congress to relax the usual protections temporarily. Absent suspension, however, the Executive's assertion of military exigency has not been thought sufficient to permit detention without charge. No one contends that the congressional Authorization for Use of Military Force, on which the Government relies to justify its actions here, is an implementation of the Suspension Clause. Accordingly, I would reverse the decision below.

I

The very core of liberty secured by our Anglo-Saxon system of separated powers has been freedom from indefinite imprisonment at the will of the Executive. Blackstone stated this principle clearly:

> "Of great importance to the public is the preservation of this personal liberty: for if once it were left in the power of any, the highest, magistrate to imprison arbitrarily whomever he or his officers thought proper...there would soon be an end of all other rights and immunities.... To bereave a man of life, or by violence to confiscate his estate, without accusation or trial, would be so gross and notorious an act of despotism, as must at once convey the alarm of tyranny throughout the whole kingdom. But confinement of the person, by secretly hurrying him to gaol, where his sufferings are unknown or forgotten; is a less public, a less striking, and therefore a more dangerous engine of arbitrary government....
> "To make imprisonment lawful, it must either be, by process from the courts of judicature, or by warrant from some legal officer, having authority to commit to prison; which warrant must be in writing, under the hand and seal of the magistrate, and express the causes of the commitment, in order to be examined into (if necessary) upon a *habeas corpus*. If there be no cause expressed, the gaoler is not bound to detain the prisoner. For the law judges in this respect,...that it is unreasonable to send a prisoner, and not to signify withal the crimes alleged against him." 1 W. Blackstone, Commentaries on the Laws of England 132-133 (1765) (hereinafter Blackstone).

These words were well known to the Founders. Hamilton quoted from this very passage in The Federalist No. 84, p. 444 (G. Carey & J. McClellan eds., 2001). The two ideas central to Blackstone's understanding—due process as the right secured, and habeas corpus as the instrument by which due process could be insisted upon by a citizen illegally imprisoned—found expression in the Constitution's Due Process and Suspension Clauses. See Amdt. 5; Art. I, §9, cl. 2.

The gist of the Due Process Clause, as understood at the founding and since, was to force the Government to follow those common-law procedures traditionally deemed necessary before depriving a person of life, liberty, or property. When a citizen was deprived of liberty because of alleged criminal conduct, those procedures typically required committal by a magistrate followed by indictment and trial....

II

The allegations here, of course, are no ordinary accusations of criminal activity. Yaser Esam Hamdi has been imprisoned because the Government believes he participated in the waging of war against the United States. The relevant question, then, is whether there is a different, special procedure for imprisonment of a citizen accused of wrongdoing *by aiding the enemy in wartime.*

A

Justice O'Connor, writing for a plurality of this Court, asserts that captured enemy combatants (other than those suspected of war crimes) have traditionally been detained until the cessation of hostilities and then released. That is probably an accurate description of wartime practice with respect to enemy *aliens*. The tradition with respect to American citizens, however, has been quite different. Citizens aiding the enemy have been treated as traitors subject to the criminal process....

The modern treason statute is 18 U.S.C. §2381; it basically tracks the language of the constitutional provision. Other provisions of Title 18 criminalize various acts of warmaking and adherence to the enemy. The only citizen other than Hamdi known to be imprisoned in connection with military hostilities in Afghanistan against the United States *was* subjected to criminal process and convicted upon a guilty plea. See *United States v. Lindh*, 212 F. Supp. 2d 541 (E.D. Va. 2002) (denying motions for dismissal).

B

There are times when military exigency renders resort to the traditional criminal process impracticable. English law accommodated such exigencies by allowing legislative suspension of the writ of habeas corpus for brief periods. Blackstone explained:

> "And yet sometimes, when the state is in real danger, even this [*i.e.,* executive detention] may be a necessary measure. But the happiness of our constitution is, that it is not left to the executive power to determine when the danger of the state is so great, as to render this measure expedient. For the parliament only, or legislative power, whenever it seems proper, can authorize the crown, by suspending the *habeas corpus* act for a short and limited time, to imprison suspected persons without giving any reason for so doing.... In like manner this experiment ought only to be tried in case of extreme emergency; and in these the nation parts with it[s] liberty for a while, in order to preserve it for ever." 1 Blackstone 132....

Our Federal Constitution contains a provision explicitly permitting suspension, but limiting the situations in which it may be invoked: "The privilege of the Writ of Habeas Corpus shall not be suspended, unless when in Cases of Rebellion or Invasion the public Safety may require it." Art. I, §9, cl. 2. Although this provision does not state that suspension must be effected by, or authorized by, a legislative act, it has been so understood, consistent with English practice and the Clause's placement in Article I.

The Suspension Clause was by design a safety valve, the Constitution's only "express provision for exercise of extraordinary authority because of a crisis," *Youngstown Sheet & Tube Co. v. Sawyer*, 343 U.S. 579, 650 (1952) (Jackson, J., concurring)....

III ...

Writings from the founding generation also suggest that, without exception, the only constitutional alternatives are to charge the crime or suspend the writ. In 1788, Thomas Jefferson wrote to James Madison questioning the need for a Suspension Clause in cases of rebellion in the proposed Constitution. His letter illustrates the constraints under which the Founders understood themselves to operate:

> "Why suspend the Hab. corp. in insurrections and rebellions? The parties who may be arrested may be charged instantly with a well defined crime. Of course the judge will remand them. If the publick safety requires that the government should have a man

imprisoned on less probable testimony in those than in other emergencies; let him be taken and tried, retaken and retried, while the necessity continues, only giving him redress against the government for damages." 13 Papers of Thomas Jefferson 442 (July 31, 1788) (J. Boyd ed. 1956)....

Further evidence comes from this Court's decision in *Ex parte Milligan*, [71 U.S. (4 Wall.) 2] (1866). There, the Court issued the writ to an American citizen who had been tried by military commission for offenses that included conspiring to overthrow the Government, seize munitions, and liberate prisoners of war. The Court rejected in no uncertain terms the Government's assertion that military jurisdiction was proper "under the 'laws and usages of war,'" *id.*, at 121:

> "It can serve no useful purpose to inquire what those laws and usages are, whence they originated, where found, and on whom they operate; they can never be applied to citizens in states which have upheld the authority of the government, and where the courts are open and their process unobstructed." *Ibid.*[1]

Milligan is not exactly this case, of course, since the petitioner was threatened with death, not merely imprisonment. But the reasoning and conclusion of *Milligan* logically cover the present case. The Government justifies imprisonment of Hamdi on principles of the law of war and admits that, absent the war, it would have no such authority. But if the law of war cannot be applied to citizens where courts are open, then Hamdi's imprisonment without criminal trial is no less unlawful than Milligan's trial by military tribunal.

Milligan responded to the argument, repeated by the Government in this case, that it is dangerous to leave suspected traitors at large in time of war:

> "If it was dangerous, in the distracted condition of affairs, to leave Milligan unrestrained of his liberty, because he 'conspired against the government, afforded aid and comfort to rebels, and incited the people to insurrection,' the *law* said arrest him, confine him closely, render him powerless to do further mischief; and then present his case to the grand jury of the district, with proofs of his guilt, and, if indicted, try him according to the course of the common law. If this had been done, the Constitution would have been vindicated, the law of 1863 enforced, and the securities for personal liberty preserved and defended." *Id.*, at 122.

Thus, criminal process was viewed as the primary means — and the only means absent congressional action suspending the writ — not only to punish traitors, but to incapacitate them.

The proposition that the Executive lacks indefinite wartime detention authority over citizens is consistent with the Founders' general mistrust of military power permanently at the Executive's disposal. In the Founders' view, the "blessings of liberty" were threatened by "those military establishments which must gradually poison its very fountain." The Federalist No. 45, p. 238 (J. Madison). No fewer than 10 issues of the Federalist were devoted in whole or part to allaying fears of oppression from the proposed Constitution's authorization of standing armies in peacetime. Many

---

1. As I shall discuss presently, the Court purported to limit this language in *Ex parte Quirin*, 317 U.S. 1, 45 (1942). Whatever *Quirin*'s effect on *Milligan*'s precedential value, however, it cannot undermine its value as an indicator of original meaning. Cf. *Reid v. Covert*, 354 U.S. 1, 30 (1957) (plurality opinion) (*Milligan* remains "one of the great landmarks in this Court's history").

safeguards in the Constitution reflect these concerns. Congress's authority "[t]o raise and support Armies" was hedged with the proviso that "no Appropriation of Money to that Use shall be for a longer Term than two Years." U.S. Const., Art. 1, §8, cl. 12. Except for the actual command of military forces, all authorization for their maintenance and all explicit authorization for their use is placed in the control of Congress under Article I, rather than the President under Article II. . . . A view of the Constitution that gives the Executive authority to use military force rather than the force of law against citizens on American soil flies in the face of the mistrust that engendered these provisions.

IV

The Government argues that our more recent jurisprudence ratifies its indefinite imprisonment of a citizen within the territorial jurisdiction of federal courts. It places primary reliance upon *Ex parte Quirin*, 317 U.S. 1 (1942), a World War II case upholding the trial by military commission of eight German saboteurs, one of whom, Hans Haupt, was a U.S. citizen. The case was not this Court's finest hour. The Court upheld the commission and denied relief in a brief *per curiam* issued the day after oral argument concluded; a week later the Government carried out the commission's death sentence upon six saboteurs, including Haupt. The Court eventually explained its reasoning in a written opinion issued several months later.

Only three paragraphs of the Court's lengthy opinion dealt with the particular circumstances of Haupt's case. The Government argued that Haupt, like the other petitioners, could be tried by military commission under the laws of war. In agreeing with that contention, *Quirin* purported to interpret the language of *Milligan* quoted above (the law of war "can never be applied to citizens in states which have upheld the authority of the government, and where the courts are open and their process unobstructed") in the following manner:

> "Elsewhere in its opinion . . . the Court was at pains to point out that Milligan, a citizen twenty years resident in Indiana, who had never been a resident of any of the states in rebellion, was not an enemy belligerent either entitled to the status of a prisoner of war or subject to the penalties imposed upon unlawful belligerents. We construe the Court's statement as to the inapplicability of the law of war to Milligan's case as having particular reference to the facts before it. From them the Court concluded that Milligan, not being a part of or associated with the armed forces of the enemy, was a nonbelligerent, not subject to the law of war. . . ." 317 U.S., at 45.

In my view this seeks to revise *Milligan* rather than describe it. *Milligan* had involved (among other issues) two separate questions: (1) whether the military trial of Milligan was justified by the laws of war, and if not (2) whether the President's suspension of the writ, pursuant to congressional authorization, prevented the issuance of habeas corpus. The Court's categorical language about the law of war's inapplicability to citizens where the courts are open (with no exception mentioned for citizens who were prisoners of war) was contained in its discussion of the first point. See 4 Wall., at 121. The factors pertaining to whether Milligan could reasonably be considered a belligerent and prisoner of war, while mentioned earlier in the opinion, were made relevant and brought to bear in the Court's later discussion of whether Milligan came within the statutory provision that effectively made an exception to Congress's authorized suspension of the writ for (as the Court described it) "all parties, not prisoners of war, resident in their respective jurisdictions, . . . who were citizens of states in which the administration of the laws in the Federal tribunals was unimpaired," *id.* at 116. *Milligan* thus understood was in accord with the traditional law of habeas corpus I have described: Though treason often occurred in wartime, there was, absent provision for special treatment in a congressional suspension of the writ, no exception to the right to trial by jury for citizens who could be called "belligerents" or "prisoners of war."

But even if *Quirin* gave a correct description of *Milligan,* or made an irrevocable revision of it, *Quirin* would still not justify denial of the writ here. In *Quirin* it was uncontested that the petitioners were members of enemy forces. They were "*admitted* enemy invaders," 317 U.S., at 47 (emphasis added), and it was "undisputed" that they had landed in the United States in service of German forces, *id.,* at 20. The specific holding of the Court was only that, "upon the *conceded* facts," the petitioners were "plainly within [the] boundaries" of military jurisdiction, *id.,* at 46 (emphasis added). But where those jurisdictional facts are *not* conceded — where the petitioner insists that he is *not* a belligerent — *Quirin* left the pre-existing law in place: Absent suspension of the writ, a citizen held where the courts are open is entitled either to criminal trial or to a judicial decree requiring his release.

V

It follows from what I have said that Hamdi is entitled to a habeas decree requiring his release unless (1) criminal proceedings are promptly brought, or (2) Congress has suspended the writ of habeas corpus. A suspension of the writ could, of course, lay down conditions for continued detention, similar to those that today's opinion prescribes under the Due Process Clause. But there is a world of difference between the people's representatives' determining the need for that suspension (and prescribing the conditions for it), and this Court's doing so.

The plurality finds justification for Hamdi's imprisonment in the Authorization for Use of Military Force, 115 Stat. 224. . . . This is not remotely a congressional suspension of the writ, and no one claims that it is. Contrary to the plurality's view, I do not think this statute even authorizes detention of a citizen with the clarity necessary to satisfy the interpretive canon that statutes should be construed so as to avoid grave constitutional concerns; with the clarity necessary to comport with cases such as *Ex parte Endo,* 323 U.S. 283, 300 (1944), and *Duncan v. Kahanamoku,* 327 U.S. 304, 314-316, 324 (1946); or with the clarity necessary to overcome the statutory prescription that "[n]o citizen shall be imprisoned or otherwise detained by the United States except pursuant to an Act of Congress." 18 U.S.C. §4001(a).[5] But even if it did, I would not permit it to overcome Hamdi's entitlement to habeas corpus relief. The Suspension Clause of the Constitution, which carefully circumscribes the

___

5. The plurality rejects any need for "specific language of detention" on the ground that detention of alleged combatants is a "fundamental incident of waging war." Its authorities do not support that holding in the context of the present case. Some are irrelevant because they do not address the detention of *American citizens.* The plurality's assertion that detentions of citizen and alien combatants are equally authorized has no basis in law or common sense. Citizens and noncitizens, even if equally dangerous, are not similarly situated. *See, e.g., Milligan, supra; Johnson v. Eisentrager,* 339 U.S. 763 (1950); Rev. Stat. 4067, 50 U.S.C. §21 (Alien Enemy Act). That captivity may be consistent with the principles of international law does not prove that it also complies with the restrictions that the Constitution places on the American Government's treatment of its own citizens. . . .

conditions under which the writ can be withheld, would be a sham if it could be evaded by congressional prescription of requirements *other than the common-law require-ment of committal for criminal prosecution* that render the writ, though available, unavailing. If the Suspension Clause does not guarantee the citizen that he will either be tried or released, unless the conditions for suspending the writ exist and the grave action of suspending the writ has been taken; if it merely guarantees the citizen that he will not be detained unless Congress by ordinary legislation says he can be detained; it guarantees him very little indeed.

It should not be thought, however, that the plurality's evisceration of the Suspension Clause augments, principally, the power of Congress. As usual, the major effect of its constitutional improvisation is to increase the power of the Court. Having found a congressional authorization for detention of citizens where none clearly exists; and having discarded the categorical procedural protection of the Suspension Clause; the plurality then proceeds, under the guise of the Due Process Clause, to prescribe what procedural protections *it* thinks appropriate. . . .

. . . This judicial remediation of executive default is unheard of. The role of habeas corpus is to determine the legality of executive detention, not to supply the omitted process necessary to make it legal. . . .

There is a certain harmony of approach in the plurality's making up for Congress's failure to invoke the Suspension Clause and its making up for the Executive's failure to apply what it says are needed procedures — an approach that reflects what might be called a Mr. Fix-it Mentality. The plurality seems to view it as its mission to Make Everything Come Out Right, rather than merely to decree the consequences, as far as individual rights are concerned, of the other two branches' actions and omissions. Has the Legislature failed to suspend the writ in the current dire emergency? Well, we will remedy that failure by prescribing the reasonable conditions that a suspension should have included. And has the Executive failed to live up to those reasonable conditions? Well, we will ourselves make that failure good, so that this dangerous fellow (if he is dangerous) need not be set free. The problem with this approach is not only that it steps out of the courts' modest and limited role in a democratic society; but that by repeatedly doing what it thinks the political branches ought to do it encourages their lassitude and saps the vitality of government by the people.

VI

Several limitations give my views in this matter a relatively narrow compass. They apply only to citizens, accused of being enemy combatants, who are detained within the territorial jurisdiction of a federal court. This is not likely to be a numerous group; currently we know of only two, Hamdi and Jose Padilla. Where the citizen is captured outside and held outside the United States, the constitutional requirements may be different. Cf. *Johnson v. Eisentrager*, 339 U.S. 763, 769-771 (1950); *Reid v. Covert*, 354 U.S. 1, 74-75 (1957) (Harlan, J., concurring in result); *Rasul v. Bush*, [542 U.S. 466 (2004)] (Scalia, J., dissenting). Moreover, even within the United States, the accused citizen-enemy combatant may lawfully be detained once prosecution is in progress or in contemplation . . .

. . . If the situation demands it, the Executive can ask Congress to authorize suspension of the writ — which can be made subject to whatever conditions Congress deems appropriate, including even the procedural novelties invented by the plurality today. To be sure, suspension is limited by the Constitution to cases of rebellion or invasion. But whether the attacks of September 11, 2001, constitute an "invasion," and whether those attacks still justify suspension several years later, are questions for Congress rather than this Court. . . .

Justice THOMAS, dissenting. The Executive Branch, acting pursuant to the powers vested in the President by the Constitution and with explicit congressional approval, has determined that Yaser Hamdi is an enemy combatant and should be detained. This detention falls squarely within the Federal Government's war powers, and we lack the expertise and capacity to second-guess that decision. As such, petitioners' habeas challenge should fail, and there is no reason to remand the case. . . . I do not think that the Federal Government's war powers can be balanced away by this Court. Arguably, Congress could provide for additional procedural protections, but until it does, we have no right to insist upon them. But even if I were to agree with the general approach the plurality takes, I could not accept the particulars. The plurality utterly fails to account for the Government's compelling interests and for our own institutional inability to weigh competing concerns correctly. I respectfully dissent. . . .

NOTES AND QUESTIONS

1. *The AUMF.* The AUMF (see *supra* p. 97) authorizes the President to use "all necessary and appropriate force," but is completely silent about detention authority. Why does the Supreme Court find that it authorizes detention at all? Even if it does, the use of military force to detain would presumably itself have to be "necessary and appropriate." By what standards or principles does the Court measure necessity and appropriateness?

In 2011, the House Armed Services Committee approved a measure entitled *Affirmation of Armed Conflict with Al-Qaeda, the Taliban, and Associated Forces,* providing:

Congress affirms that —
 (1) the United States is engaged in an armed conflict with al-Qaeda, the Taliban, and associated forces and that those entities continue to pose a threat to the United States and its citizens, both domestically and abroad;
 (2) the President has the authority to use all necessary and appropriate force during the current armed conflict with al-Qaeda, the Taliban, and associated forces pursuant to the Authorization for Use of Military Force (Public Law 107-40; 50 U.S.C. 1541 note);
 (3) the current armed conflict includes nations, organization, and persons who —
  (A) are part of, or are substantially supporting, al-Qaeda, the Taliban, or associated forces that are engaged in hostilities against the United States or its coalition partners; or
  (B) have engaged in hostilities or have directly supported hostilities in aid of a nation, organization, or person described in subparagraph (A); and
 (4) the President's authority pursuant to the Authorization for Use of Military Force. (Public Law 107-40; 50 U.S.C. 1541 note) includes the authority to detain belligerents, including persons described in paragraph (3), until the termination of hostilities.
[National Defense Authorization Act for 2012, H.R. 1540, 112th Cong. §1034 (2011).]

Would this bill clarify or confuse the President's authority to detain under the "affirmed" AUMF?

2. *Necessity for Military Detention in Hamdi.* Authority to detain under the law of war is based on military necessity, a premise echoed in the AUMF authorization for use of "*necessary* and appropriate force." *See* §2(a), *supra* p. 97 (emphasis supplied).

According to Justice O'Connor, "The purpose of detention is to prevent captured individuals from returning to the field of battle and taking up arms once again." They are detained, in other words, both to enable U.S. forces to carry out their mission and to provide force protection. In addition, such individuals are detained to obtain operational intelligence by interrogation. Moreover, the conditions of detention may be important, because the isolation of detainees and their consequent dependence on their captors may induce them to talk. Bringing such persons immediately before a judge, or even holding some kind of hearing, may be impracticable in the midst of hostilities, while the bullets are flying. Moving detainees back from the front lines may not be a cure, because it is often still impractical to withdraw troops from the front to give testimony or to preserve evidence during the fighting. *Cf. Odah v. United States*, 321 F.3d 1134, 1150 (D.C. Cir. 2003) (Randolph, J., concurring) (asserting with respect to military detainees at Camp X-Ray in Guantánamo Naval Base, Cuba, that "[t]he historical meaning of 'in the field' was not restricted to the field of battle. It applied as well to 'organized camps stationed in remote places where civil courts did not exist.'"), *rev'd and remanded by Rasul v. Bush*, 542 U.S. 466 (2004).

Do you agree with the *Hamdi* Court's assessment of military necessity? Would it make a difference whether Hamdi—a U.S. citizen allegedly fighting alongside the enemy—was one of a kind or one of a thousand?

3. *"Longstanding Law-of-War Principles."* The *Hamdi* plurality appeals to "longstanding law-of-war principles." What, exactly, are those principles, and where can they be found? See Chapter 9. How are they relevant here?

The assertion of law-of-war principles presents several thorny questions. First, if their application presupposes a war or armed conflict, must U.S. involvement in that conflict be expressly authorized by Congress? If so, what is its scope, both geographical and temporal? If law-of-war principles apply, do all of the President's war powers apply, as well, or just some of them? *See Hamdan v. Rumsfeld*, 548 U.S. 557, 594 (2006) (declaring that "there is nothing in the text or legislative history of the AUMF even hinting that Congress intended to expand or alter" the President's existing authority to convene a military commission). Note that a use-of-force authorization apparently would not trigger the Alien Enemy Act, *supra* p. 811. Does the AUMF override the Alien Enemy Act? If not, does this mean that the President has law-of-war authority under the AUMF to detain U.S. citizen combatants but not aliens in the United States?

Second, how should we define "enemy combatants"—persons subject to military detention under the law of war? How does the *Hamdi* Court define them? Recall the differences in the status of Milligan and of Quirin. Is Hamdi more like Milligan or like Quirin? In this regard, note that the saboteurs in *Quirin*, unlike Hamdi, did not contest their status as enemy soldiers. What definition of "enemy combatant" would you construct from *Milligan*, *Quirin*, and *Hamdi*?

Or are we looking in the wrong place? If war is authorized by declaration or by a use-of-force statute, should we not look to the congressional authorization for a definition of the enemy, rather than the law of war? Suppose Congress had not authorized the use of force against terrorist organizations like Al Qaeda, but the President had gone ahead anyway on the theory of repelling attack. Would military detention of combatants in that war be authorized? How would they be defined? What about persons detained as terrorists generally in an undeclared "war on terrorism"?

Third, even if the AUMF suffices to authorize military detention in the field, does it apply in the United States? Unlike Afghanistan, where Hamdi was captured, in the United States civilian courts are open and the criminal process is available. Should this make a difference?

Fourth, the principles of the law of war may be "longstanding," but will they be long-lasting? Under what changed circumstances could the majority's understanding of these principles "unravel," as the plurality opinion warns?

4. *The Greater Includes the Lesser?* In *Hamdi*, the court assumed that Supreme Court precedents concerning trial by military commission, especially *Quirin*, were apposite to the legality of military detention. *Quirin* did say that both lawful and unlawful combatants "are subject to capture and *detention*," and that unlawful combatants are additionally subject to military trial and punishment. See *supra* p. 824 (emphasis supplied). A lower court in a separate detention case understood this to reflect the Supreme Court's belief that "detention alone . . . [is] certainly the lesser of the consequences an unlawful combatant could face." *Padilla ex rel. Newman v. Bush*, 233 F. Supp. 2d 564, 595 (S.D.N.Y. 2002), *rev'd sub nom. Rumsfeld v. Padilla*, 352 F.3d 685 (2d Cir. 2003), *rev'd and remanded*, 542 U.S. 426 (2004).

But is that always true? The unlawful combatant who is tried at least will see a resolution of his status. *See Rasul v. Bush*, 542 U.S. 466, 488 (2004) (Kennedy, J., concurring in the judgment) (distinguishing *Eisentrager*, which involved aliens detained after conviction a by military commission, from *Rasul*, involving aliens "being held indefinitely, and without benefit of any legal proceeding to determine their status"). Applying the reasoning in *Hamdi*, might a combatant not be detained by the military indefinitely without trial or even charges, or until the political branches determine that the war is over? If detention is not the "lesser" consequence for such a combatant, is case law establishing the legality of a military *trial* really apposite to the legality of *detention*?

5. *"Plenary" Military Authority.* In *Hamdi*, the government also argued that the Executive has plenary authority under Article II to detain enemy combatants, presumably a "war power" of the Commander in Chief. Though the plurality did not reach this claim, it agreed that the capture and military detention of combatants are "important incident[s] of war," quoting *Quirin*, and Justice Thomas dissented on the ground that Hamdi's "detention falls squarely within the Federal Government's war powers" vested in the executive branch. Does this mean that the President did not need the delegated authority of the AUMF? How would YOU describe the limits on the President's non-statutory power to detain?

6. *Justice Scalia's Dissent.* Justice Scalia, joined by Justice Stevens, relied on the Suspension Clause to find the detention of Hamdi unlawful. What theory of detention did he draw from the Clause? By that theory, what are the government's options

in detaining someone like Hamdi? Does the theory apply to detention of those held at Guantánamo Bay?

7. *The Process Point: Determining the Combatant Status of U.S. Citizens.* The plurality in *Hamdi* employed a due process balancing to describe procedures required for determining the detainee's status. To test your understanding of the Court's conclusion, consider the alternatives.

First, why was combatant status not an issue in *Quirin*? The answer is that the German saboteurs admitted their status. If there is no factual dispute, then even a due process balancing presumably does not require any procedure to decide that status. Why did the Court reject the government's argument that Hamdi's status was undisputed?

If the detainee's combatant status *is* disputed and he is entitled to petition for a writ of habeas corpus, then the habeas corpus statute, 28 U.S.C. §2243, *supra* p. 765, itself suggests some evidentiary proceeding. Can you see why from examining the statute?

But what evidence and what kind of proceeding? The government suggested that "some evidence" would suffice. The government therefore argued that a court's role in a habeas corpus proceeding was only to decide whether the evidence stated in the Mobbs Declaration was sufficient standing alone. Is that argument consistent with the habeas corpus statute? Or with due process?

The Court rejected the "some evidence" standard partly on the grounds that "it primarily has been employed by courts in examining an administrative record developed after an adversarial proceeding. . . ." *Hamdi*, 542 U.S. at 537. But the government asserted that it *had* developed an administrative record after an elaborate internal process for determining combatant status of U.S. citizens, incorporating information developed by the Department of Defense, the Central Intelligence Agency, and the Department of Justice; written assessments by the same agencies; a formal legal opinion by the Office of Legal Counsel; recommendations by the Attorney General and the Secretary of Defense; and a final recommendation to and briefing for the President by the White House Counsel.[1] If such procedures were actually used to designate Hamdi as an enemy combatant and to generate the factual predicates for his military detention, why was the "some evidence" standard not sufficient?

Finally, consider the procedures that the plurality in *Hamdi* found were required by a due process balancing. Are these procedures sufficient to reduce the risk of inaccuracy in light of the interests at stake? What more would Justices Souter and Ginsburg require if they found that Congress had authorized military detention? What would you find necessary if you performed the balancing? In light of the foregoing, are Justices Scalia and Stevens right — is this a job for Congress? If so, what procedures would you recommend that Congress require?

8. *Hamdi After Remand.* After the Supreme Court remanded, Hamdi and the government negotiated an agreement for his release to his family in Saudi Arabia. The government asserted that he no longer had any intelligence value and posed no

---

1. Alberto R. Gonzales, Counsel to the President, Remarks at the American Bar Ass'n Standing Comm. on Law and Nat'l Security, Feb. 24, 2004, transcript *available at* http://www.fas.org/irp/news/2004/02/gonzales.pdf (asserting also, however, that neither these procedures nor any other specific procedures were required by law, but were adopted only by administrative grace).

threat. Under the agreement, Hamdi gave up his U.S. citizenship, renounced terrorism, waived any civil claim he had for his detention, and accepted certain travel restrictions, including a ten-year ban on returning to the United States. *See* Motion to Stay Proceedings, *Hamdi v. Rumsfeld*, No. 2:02CV439 (E.D. Va. Sept. 24, 2004), *available at* http://notablecases.vaed.uscourts.gov/2:02-cv-00439/docs/70223/0.pdf.

B. MILITARY DETENTION OF PERSONS CAPTURED IN THE UNITED STATES

1. José Padilla

Al Qaeda operatives recruited Jose Padilla, a United States citizen, to train for jihad in Afghanistan in February 2000, while Padilla was on a religious pilgrimage to Saudi Arabia. Subsequently, Padilla met with al Qaeda operatives in Afghanistan, received explosives training in an al Qaeda-affiliated camp, and served as an armed guard at what he understood to be a Taliban outpost. When United States military operations began in Afghanistan, Padilla and other al Qaeda operatives moved from safehouse to safehouse to evade bombing or capture. Padilla was, on the facts with which we are presented, "armed and present in a combat zone during armed conflict between al Qaeda/Taliban forces and the armed forces of the United States." Padilla eventually escaped to Pakistan, armed with an assault rifle. Once in Pakistan, Padilla met with Khalid Sheikh Mohammad, a senior al Qaeda operations planner, who directed Padilla to travel to the United States for the purpose of blowing up apartment buildings, in continued prosecution of al Qaeda's war of terror against the United States. After receiving further training, as well as cash, travel documents, and communication devices, Padilla flew to the United States in order to carry out his accepted assignment. [*Padilla v. Hanft*, 423 F.3d 386, 389-390 (4th Cir. 2005) (describing facts that were stipulated for purposes of summary judgment motion).]

Padilla was arrested as a material witness when he stepped off the plane at O'Hare International Airport in Chicago. He was then moved to a civilian correctional facility in New York City, where a grand jury had been convened. While he was there, however, President George W. Bush declared Padilla "an enemy combatant" and ordered the Secretary of Defense to detain him "consistent with U.S. law and the laws of war . . . ." Order by President George W. Bush to the Secretary of Defense (June 9, 2002), *reproduced in Padilla v. Rumsfeld*, 352 F.3d 695, 724-725 app. A (2d Cir. 2003). He was then transferred to military custody in South Carolina.

Initially, Padilla challenged his detention by filing a habeas petition in the Southern District of New York. After the district court held that the government was authorized to detain him if it could adduce "some evidence" that he was an enemy combatant, *Padilla ex rel. Newman v. Bush*, 233 F. Supp. 2d 564 (S.D.N.Y. 2002), the Second Circuit Court of Appeals reversed on the merits. *Padilla v. Rumsfeld*, 352 F.3d 695 (2d Cir. 2003). The Supreme Court, however, then reversed the Second Circuit on jurisdictional grounds, finding that Padilla had petitioned for habeas in the wrong court. *Rumsfeld v. Padilla*, 542 U.S. 426 (2004).

Padilla then refiled his habeas petition in a federal district court in South Carolina, where he was being held in military custody. That court granted the petition. *Padilla v. Hanft*, 389 F. Supp. 2d 678, 691-692 (D.S.C. 2005) (quoting amici curiae in *Rumsfeld v. Padilla, supra*). The Fourth Circuit Court of Appeals reversed.

423 F.3d 386 (4th Cir. 2005), *cert. denied*, 547 U.S. 1062 (2006). Before the Supreme Court could decide Padilla's petition for certiorari, however, the government announced that it was transferring Padilla back to law enforcement custody for criminal prosecution. He was then ultimately convicted of criminal conspiracy to commit murder and providing material support to terrorists, and sentenced to 17 years in prison.

Padilla's saga thus generated dueling appellate opinions concerning the authority for his law-of-war detention, but without any Supreme Court resolution of the conflict. The key differences are shown in the following table.

Padilla v. Rumsfeld, 352 F.3d 695 (2d Cir. 2003)	*Padilla v. Hanft*, 423 F.3d 386 (4th Cir. 2005)
While it may be possible to infer a power of detention from the Joint Resolution in the battlefield context where detentions are necessary to carry out the war, there is no reason to suspect from the language of the Joint Resolution that Congress believed it would be authorizing the detention of an American citizen already held in a federal correctional institution and not "arrayed against our troops" in the field of battle." 352 F.3d at 723.	[*Hamdi*'s] reasoning simply does not admit of a distinction between an enemy combatant captured abroad and detained in the United States, such as Hamdi, and an enemy combatant who escaped capture abroad but was ultimately captured domestically and detained in the United States, such as Padilla. 423 F.3d at 393.
[T]he *Quirin* Court's decision to uphold military jurisdiction rested on express congressional authorization of the use of military tribunals to try combatants who violated the laws of war. . . . Accordingly, *Quirin* does not speak to whether, or to what degree, the President may impose military authority upon United States citizens domestically without clear congressional authorization. 352 F.3d at 715-716.	[I]n no place in *Quirin* did the Court even purport to establish a clear statement rule. . . . In fact, to the extent that Quirin can be understood to have addressed the need for a clear statement of authority from Congress at all, the rule would appear the opposite: [T]he detention and trial of petitioners — ordered by the President in the declared exercise of his powers as Commander in Chief of the Army in time of war and of grave public danger — are not to be set aside by the courts without the clear conviction that they are in conflict with the Constitution or laws of Congress constitutionally enacted. 423 F.3d at 396 (citing *Quirin*, 317 U.S. at 25.)
The plain language of the Joint Resolution contains nothing authorizing the detention of American citizens captured on United States soil, much less the express authorization required by section 4001(a) and the "clear," "unmistakable" language required by *Endo*. 352 F.3d at 723 (referring to *Ex parte Endo*, 323 U.S. 283 (1944)).	[E]ven were a clear statement by Congress required, the AUMF constitutes such a clear statement according to the Supreme Court. In *Hamdi*, stating that "it [was] of no moment that the AUMF does not use specific language of detention," the plurality held that the AUMF "clearly and unmistakably authorized" Hamdi's detention. 423 F.3d at 396 (citing *Hamdi v. Rumsfeld*, 542 U.S. 507, 593 (2004)).

[T]he petitioners in *Quirin* admitted that they were soldiers in the armed forces of a nation against whom the United States had formally declared war. The *Quirin* Court deemed it unnecessary to consider the dispositive issue here — the boundaries of the Executive's military jurisdiction — because the *Quirin* petitioners "upon the conceded facts, were plainly within those boundaries." Padilla makes no such concession.... Moreover,... when *Quirin* was decided in 1942, section 4001(a) had not yet been enacted.... 352 F.3d at 716 (citing *Quirin*, 317 U.S. at 46).	As the Court in *Quirin* explained, the *Milligan* Court's reasoning had "particular reference to the facts before it," namely, that Milligan was not "a part of or associated with the armed forces of the enemy." ... Thus confined, *Milligan* is inapposite here because Padilla, unlike Milligan, associated with, and has taken up arms against the forces of the United States on behalf of, an enemy of the United States. 423 F.3d at 396-397 (citing *Quirin*, 317 U.S. at 45.)

The Fourth Circuit, unlike the Second Circuit, had the benefit of the Supreme Court's decision in *Hamdi*. Ultimately, the Fourth Circuit's decision rested on the court's inability to see any distinction between Padilla and Hamdi.

As the AUMF authorized Hamdi's detention by the President, so also does it authorize Padilla's detention. Under the facts as presented here, Padilla unquestionably qualifies as an "enemy combatant" as that term was defined for purposes of the controlling opinion in *Hamdi*. Indeed, under the definition of "enemy combatant" employed in *Hamdi*, we can discern no difference in principle between Hamdi and Padilla. Like Hamdi, Padilla associated with forces hostile to the United States in Afghanistan. And, like Hamdi, Padilla took up arms against United States forces in that country in the same way and to the same extent as did Hamdi. Because, like Hamdi, Padilla is an enemy combatant, and because his detention is no less necessary than was Hamdi's in order to prevent his return to the battlefield, the President is authorized by the AUMF to detain Padilla as a fundamental incident to the conduct of war. [423 F.3d at 391-392.]

---

2. Ali Saleh Kahlah al-Marri

Al-Marri was a lawful resident alien arrested in Peoria, Illinois, as a material witness, then was indicted for credit card fraud and lying to the FBI. When he moved to suppress certain evidence in civil court, the government moved *ex parte* to dismiss the indictment based on an order signed by the President, declaring al-Marri an enemy combatant and ordering him transferred to military custody. Al-Marri petitioned for a writ of habeas corpus, to which the government filed a declaration ("the Rapp Declaration") asserting that:

al-Marri: (1) is "closely associated with al Qaeda, an international terrorist organization with which the United States is at war"; (2) trained at an al Qaeda terrorist training camp in Afghanistan sometime between 1996 and 1998; (3) in the summer of 2001, was introduced to Osama Bin Laden by Khalid Shaykh Muhammed; (4) at that time, volunteered for a "martyr mission" on behalf of al Qaeda; (5) was ordered to enter the United States sometime before September 11, 2001, to serve as a "sleeper agent" to facilitate terrorist activities and explore disrupting this country's financial system through computer hacking; (6) in the summer of 2001, met with terrorist financier Mustafa Ahmed al-Hawsawi, who gave al-Marri money, including funds to buy a laptop; (7) gathered technical information about poisonous chemicals on his laptop; (8) undertook efforts to obtain false identification, credit cards, and banking information, including stolen credit card numbers; (9) communicated with known terrorists, including Khalid Shaykh Muhammed and al-Hawsawi, by phone and e-mail; and (10) saved information about jihad, the September 11th attacks, and Bin Laden on his laptop computer. [*Al-Marri v. Pucciarelli*, 534 F.3d 213, 220 (4th Cir. 2008) (en banc), *vacated and remanded sub nom. Al-Marri v. Spagone*, 129 S. Ct. 1545 (2009).]

The district court denied relief, and al-Marri appealed. A divided panel of the Fourth Circuit reversed, and al-Marri petitioned for rehearing *en banc*. The sharply divided *en banc* court produced multiple concurring and dissenting opinions. Judge Motz first opined that the Executive lacked authority for the military detention of al-Marri, but only three other judges joined her on this question. Thus, a bare majority of the court upheld the military detention authority. Judge Traxler then abandoned that majority to form a different majority for the proposition that the process afforded al-Marri to challenge his designation did not meet due process standards. These five votes sufficed to send the case back to the district court.

Al-Marri v. Pucciarelli

United States Court of Appeals, Fourth Circuit (en banc), 2008
534 F.3d 213
vacated and remanded sub nom. Al-Marri v. Spagone,
129 S. Ct. 1545 (2009)

PER CURIAM: . . . Having considered the briefs and arguments of the parties, the *en banc* court now holds: (1) by a 5 to 4 vote (Chief Judge Williams and Judges Wilkinson, Niemeyer, Traxler, and Duncan voting in the affirmative; Judges Michael, Motz, King, and Gregory voting in the negative), that, if the Government's allegations about al-Marri are true, Congress has empowered the President to detain him as an enemy combatant; and (2) by a 5 to 4 vote (Judges Michael, Motz, Traxler, King, and Gregory voting in the affirmative; Chief Judge Williams and Judges Wilkinson, Niemeyer, and Duncan voting in the negative), that, assuming Congress has empowered the President to detain al-Marri as an enemy combatant provided the Government's allegations against him are true, al-Marri has not been afforded sufficient process to challenge his designation as an enemy combatant.

Accordingly, the judgment of the district court is reversed and remanded for further proceedings consistent with the opinions that follow.

Reversed and remanded.

DIANA GRIBBON MOTZ, Circuit Judge, concurring in the judgment: . . .

I. . . .

The Rapp Declaration does *not* assert that al-Marri: (1) is a citizen, or affiliate of the armed forces, of any nation at war with the United States; (2) was seized on, near, or having escaped from a battlefield on which the armed forces of the United States or its allies were engaged in combat; (3) was ever in Afghanistan during the armed conflict between the United States and the Taliban there; or (4) directly participated in any hostilities against United States or allied armed forces. . . .

II. . . .

A. . . .

[Judge Motz found that as a lawfully admitted alien with a substantial connection to the United States, al-Marri was entitled to due process before he could be deprived of his liberty. But she also acknowledged that in *Hamdi v. Rumsfeld*, 542 U.S. 507 (2004), the Supreme Court found that Congress had constitutionally authorized the President to order the military detention, without the criminal process ordinarily required by the Due Process Clause, of persons who qualify as "enemy combatants."]

B.

The Government's primary argument is that the AUMF, as construed by precedent and considered against "the legal background against which [it] was enacted," i.e., constitutional and law-of-war principles, empowers the President to order the military to seize and detain al-Marri as an enemy combatant. . . .

1.

Tellingly, the Deputy Solicitor General conceded at oral argument before the *en banc* court that the AUMF only authorizes detention of enemy combatants. Thus, the Government does *not* argue that the broad language of the AUMF authorizes the President to subject to indefinite military detention anyone he believes to have aided any "nation[ ], organization [ ], or person[ ]" related to the September 11th attacks. *See* §2(a), 115 Stat. 224. Such an interpretation would lead to absurd results that Congress could not have intended.

Under that reading of the AUMF, the President would be able to subject to indefinite military detention anyone, including an American citizen, whom the President believed was associated with any organization that the President believed in some way "planned, authorized, committed, or aided" the September 11th attacks, so long as the President believed this to be "necessary and appropriate" to prevent future acts of terrorism.

Under such an interpretation of the AUMF, if some money from a nonprofit charity that feeds Afghan orphans made its way to al Qaeda, the President could subject to indefinite military detention any donor to that charity. Similarly, this interpretation of the AUMF would allow the President to detain indefinitely any employee or shareholder of an American corporation that built equipment used by the

September 11th terrorists; or allow the President to order the military seizure and detention of an American-citizen physician who treated a member of al Qaeda....

2.

... [T]he Government wisely limits its argument. It relies only on the scope of the AUMF as construed by precedent and considered in light of "the legal background against which [it] was enacted." Specifically, the Government contends that "[t]he Supreme Court's and this Court's prior construction of the AUMF govern[s] this case and compel[s] the conclusion that the President is authorized to detain al-Marri as an enemy combatant."

i.

The precedent interpreting the AUMF on which the Government relies for this argument consists of two cases: the Supreme Court's opinion in *Hamdi*, 542 U.S. 507, and our opinion in *Padilla v. Hanft*, 423 F.3d 386 (4th Cir. 2005). The "legal background" for the AUMF, which the Government cites, consists of two cases from earlier conflicts, *Ex Parte Quirin*, 317 U.S. 1 (1942) (World War II), and *Ex Parte Milligan*, 71 U.S. (4 Wall.) 2 (1866) (U.S. Civil War), as well as constitutional and law-of-war principles.

With respect to the latter, we note that American courts have often been reluctant to follow international law in resolving domestic disputes. In the present context, however, they, like the Government here, have relied on the law of war-treaty obligations including the Hague and Geneva Conventions and customary principles developed alongside them. The law of war provides clear rules for determining an individual's status during an international armed conflict, distinguishing between "combatants" (members of a nation's military, militia, or other armed forces, and those who fight alongside them) and "civilians" (all other persons).[11] *See, e.g.*, Geneva Convention Relative to the Treatment of Prisoners of War (Third Geneva Convention) arts. 2, 4, 5, Aug. 12, 1949, 6 U.S.T. 3316, 75 U.N.T.S. 135; Geneva Convention Relative to the Protection of Civilian Persons in Time of War (Fourth Geneva Convention) art. 4, Aug. 12, 1949, 6 U.S.T. 3516, 75 U.N.T.S. 287. American courts have repeatedly looked to these careful distinctions made in the law of war in identifying which individuals fit within the "legal category" of "enemy combatant" under our Constitution. *See, e.g.*, *Hamdi*, 542 U.S. at 518; *Quirin*, 317 U.S. at 30-31 & n.7; *Milligan*, 71 U.S. at 121-22; *Padilla*, 423 F.3d at 391....

Quirin, *Hamdi*, and *Padilla* all emphasize that *Milligan*'s teaching — that our Constitution does not permit the Government to subject *civilians* within the United States

---

11. Thus, "civilian" is a term of art in the law of war, not signifying an innocent person, but rather someone in a certain legal category who is *not* subject to *military* seizure or detention. So, too, a "combatant" is by no means always a wrongdoer, but rather a member of a different "legal category" who is subject to *military* seizure and detention. *Hamdi*, 542 U.S. at 522 n.1. For example, our brave soldiers fighting in Germany during World War II were "combatants" under the law of war, and viewed from Germany's perspective they were "enemy combatants." While civilians are subject to trial and punishment in civilian courts for all crimes committed during wartime in the country in which they are captured and held, combatant status protects an individual from trial and punishment by the capturing nation, unless the combatant has violated the law of war. *See id.* at 518; *Quirin*, 317 U.S. at 28-31. Nations in international conflicts can summarily remove the adversary's "combatants," i.e., the "enemy combatants," from the battlefield and detain them for the duration of such conflicts, but no such provision is made for "civilians." *Hamdi*, 542 U.S. at 518; *Quirin*, 317 U.S. at 28-31.

to military jurisdiction — remains good law. The *Quirin* Court explained that while the petitioners before it were affiliated with the armed forces of an enemy nation and so were enemy belligerents, Milligan was a "non-belligerent" and so "not subject to the law of war." 317 U.S. at 45. The *Hamdi* plurality similarly took care to note that *Milligan* "turned in large part on the fact that Milligan was not a prisoner of war" (i.e., combatant) and suggested that "[h]ad Milligan been captured while he was assisting Confederate soldiers by carrying a rifle against Union troops on a Confederate battle-field, the holding of the Court might well have been different." 542 U.S. at 522. And in *Padilla*, we reaffirmed that "*Milligan* does not extend to enemy combatants" and so "is inapposite here because Padilla, unlike Milligan, associated with, and has taken up arms against the forces of the United States on behalf of, an enemy of the United States." 423 F.3d at 396-97. Thus, although *Hamdi*, *Quirin*, and *Padilla* distinguish *Milligan*, they recognize that its core holding remains the law of the land. That is, civilians within this country (even "dangerous enemies" like Milligan who perpetrate "enormous crime[s]" on behalf of "secret" enemy organizations bent on "overthrowing the Government" of this country) may not be subjected to military control and deprived of constitutional rights.

In sum, the holdings of *Hamdi* and *Padilla* share two characteristics: (1) they look to law-of-war principles to determine who fits within the "legal category" of enemy combatant; and (2) following the law of war, they rest enemy combatant status on affiliation with the military arm of an enemy nation.

ii.

In view of the holdings in *Hamdi* and *Padilla*, we find it remarkable that the Government contends that they "compel the conclusion" that the President may detain al-Marri as an enemy combatant. For unlike Hamdi and Padilla, al-Marri is not alleged to have been part of a Taliban unit, not alleged to have stood alongside the Taliban or the armed forces of any other enemy nation, not alleged to have been on the battlefield during the war in Afghanistan, not alleged to have even been in Afghanistan during the armed conflict there, and not alleged to have engaged in combat with United States forces anywhere in the world. *See* Rapp Declaration (alleging none of these facts, but instead that "[a]l-Marri engaged in conduct in preparation for acts of international terrorism intended to cause injury or adverse effects on the United States"). Indeed, unlike Hamdi and Padilla, al-Marri had been imprisoned in the United States by civil authorities on criminal charges for more than a year before being seized by the military and indefinitely confined in a Navy brig as an enemy combatant.

In place of the "classic wartime detention" that the Government argued justified Hamdi's detention as an enemy combatant, or the "classic battlefield" detention it maintained justified Padilla's, here the Government argues that al-Marri's seizure and indefinite detention by the military in this country are justified "because he engaged in, and continues to pose a very real threat of carrying out, . . . acts of international terrorism." And instead of seeking judicial deference to decisions of "military officers who are engaged in the serious work of waging battle," *Hamdi*, 542 U.S. at 531-32, the Government asks us to defer to the "multi-agency evaluation process" of government bureaucrats in Washington made eighteen months after al-Marri was taken into custody. Neither the holding in *Hamdi* nor that in *Padilla* supports the Government's contentions here. . . .

... Instead, the *Hamdi* plurality emphasized the narrowness of its holding, and the "limited category" of individuals controlled by that holding. In *Padilla*, we similarly saw no need to embrace a broader construction of the AUMF than that adopted by the Supreme Court in *Hamdi*. Indeed, the Government itself *principally* argued that Padilla was an enemy combatant because he, like Hamdi, "engaged in armed conflict" alongside the Taliban "against our forces in Afghanistan." ...

... *Hamdi* and *Padilla* evidence no sympathy for the view that the AUMF permits indefinite military detention beyond the "limited category" of people covered by the "narrow circumstances" of those cases. ...

3. ...

i.

... [T]he Supreme Court's most recent terrorism cases — *Hamdan* [*v. Rumsfeld*, 548 U.S. 557 (2006)] and *Boumediene* — provide no support for the dissenters' position. In *Hamdan*, the Court held that because the conflict between the United States and al Qaeda in Afghanistan is not "between nations," it is a "'conflict not of an international character'" — and so is governed by Common Article 3 of the Geneva Conventions.

Common Article 3 and other Geneva Convention provisions applying to non-international conflicts (in contrast to those applying to international conflicts) simply do *not* recognize the "legal category" of enemy combatant. *See* Third Geneva Convention, art. 3, 6 U.S.T. at 3318. As the International Committee of the Red Cross — the official codifier of the Geneva Conventions — explains, "an 'enemy combatant' is a person who, either lawfully or unlawfully, engages in hostilities for the opposing side in an *international* armed conflict;" in contrast, "[i]n non-international armed conflict combatant status *does not exist*." Int'l Comm. of the Red Cross, Official Statement: The Relevance of IHL in the Context of Terrorism, at 1, 3 (Feb. 21, 2005), http://www.icrc.org/Web/Eng/siteeng0.nsf/htmlall/terrorismihl-210705 (emphasis added).

Perhaps for this reason, our dissenting colleagues and the Government ignore *Hamdan*'s holding that the conflict with al Qaeda in Afghanistan is a non-international conflict and ignore the fact that, in such conflicts, the legal category of enemy combatant does not exist. ...

... Furthermore, in *Boumediene*, the Court demonstrated no more sympathy for the Government's position than it had in any of the other recent terrorism cases. Rather, the Court expressly held that persons designated by the Executive "as enemy combatants" and held by United States forces at Guantánamo Bay must be afforded "the fundamental procedural protections of habeas corpus" guaranteed by our Constitution, even though they were foreign nationals who had been seized in foreign lands. The Court explained that "[t]he laws and Constitution are designed to survive, and remain in force, in extraordinary times."

... Because the legal status of enemy combatant does not exist in non-international conflicts, the law of war leaves the detention of persons in such conflicts to the applicable law of the detaining country. In al-Marri's case, the applicable law is our Constitution. Under our Constitution, even if the Supreme Court should hold that the Government may detain indefinitely Boumediene, Hamdan, and others like them, who were captured *outside* the United States and lack substantial and voluntary connections to this country, that holding would provide no support for approving al-Marri's military detention. For not only was al-Marri seized and detained *within* the United States, he also has substantial connections to the United States and so plainly is protected by the Due Process Clause.

ii. . . .

We recognize the understandable instincts of those who wish to treat domestic terrorists as "combatants" in a "global war on terror." Allegations of criminal activity in association with a terrorist organization, however, do not permit the Government to transform a civilian into an enemy combatant subject to indefinite military detention, just as allegations of murder in association with others while in military service do not permit the Government to transform a civilian into a soldier subject to trial by court martial. *See United States ex rel. Toth v. Quarles*, 350 U.S. 11, 23 (1955) (holding that ex-servicemen, "like other civilians, are entitled to have the benefit of safeguards afforded those tried in the regular courts authorized by Article III of the Constitution").

To be sure, enemy combatants may commit crimes just as civilians may. When an enemy combatant violates the law of war, that conduct will render the person an "unlawful" enemy combatant, subject not only to detention but also to military trial and punishment. *Quirin*, 317 U.S. at 31. But merely engaging in unlawful behavior does not make one an enemy combatant. *Quirin* illustrates these distinctions well. The *Quirin* petitioners were first enemy combatants — associating themselves with the military arm of the German government with which the United States was at war. They became *unlawful* enemy combatants when they violated the law of war by "without uniform com[ing] secretly through the lines for the purpose of waging war." *Id.* By doing so, in addition to being subject to military detention for the duration of the conflict as enemy combatants, they also became "subject to trial and punishment by military tribunals for acts which render their belligerency illegal." *Id.* Had the *Quirin* petitioners never "secretly and without uniform" passed our "military lines," *id.*, they still would have been enemy combatants, subject to military detention, but would not have been *unlawful* enemy combatants subject to military trial and punishment.

Neither *Quirin* nor any other precedent even suggests, as our dissenting colleagues seem to believe, that individuals with constitutional rights, unaffiliated with the military arm of any enemy government, can be subjected to military jurisdiction and deprived of those rights solely on the basis of their conduct on behalf of a terrorist organization. In fact, *Milligan* rejected the Government's attempt to do just this. There, the Court acknowledged that Milligan's conduct — "joining and aiding" a "secret political organization, armed to oppose the laws, and seek[ing] by stealthy means to introduce the enemies of the country into peaceful communities, there to . . . overthrow the power of the United States" — made him and his co-conspirators "dangerous enemies to their country." 71 U.S. at 6, 130. But the Government did not allege that Milligan took orders from any enemy government or took up arms against this country on the battlefield. And so the Court held that the Government could not subject Milligan to trial by military tribunal or treat him as an enemy combatant subject to military detention as a prisoner of war. Milligan was an "enem[y] of the country" and associated with an organization seeking to "overthrow[ ] the Government" of this country, but he was still a civilian and had to be treated as one. *Id.* . . .

iii. . . .

. . . [B]ecause the AUMF contains only a broad grant of war powers and lacks any specific language authorizing detention, the *Hamdi* plurality explained that its opinion "only finds legislative authority to detain under the AUMF once it is sufficiently clear that the individual *is*, in fact, an enemy combatant." 542 U.S. at 523 (emphasis added). Although the military detention of enemy combatants like Hamdi is certainly "a fundamental incident of waging war," *id.* at 519, the military detention of civilians like al-Marri just as certainly is not.

Even assuming the Constitution permitted Congress to grant the President such an awesome and unprecedented power, if Congress intended to grant this authority, it could and would have said so explicitly. The AUMF lacks the particularly clear statement from Congress that would, at a minimum, be necessary to authorize the indefinite military detention of *civilians* as enemy combatants. *See, e.g., Greene v. McElroy,* 360 U.S. 474, 508 (1959) (rejecting Government argument that executive orders and statutes permitted deprivation of liberty rights absent "explicit authorization"); *Duncan v. Kahanamoku,* 327 U.S. 304, 324 (1946) (rejecting Government argument that statute authorized trial of civilians by military tribunals because Congress could not have intended "to exceed the boundaries between military and civilian power, in which our people have always believed"); *Ex Parte Endo,* 323 U.S. 283, 300 (1944) (rejecting Government argument that a "wartime" executive order and statute permitted detention of citizen of Japanese heritage when neither "use[d] the language of detention"); *Brown v. United States,* 12 U.S. (8 Cranch) 110, 128-29 (1814) (rejecting Government argument that declaration of war authorized confiscation of enemy property because it did not clearly "declare[]" the legislature's "will"). We are exceedingly reluctant to infer a grant of authority that is so far afield from anything recognized by precedent or law-of-war principles, especially given the serious constitutional concerns it would raise. . . .

C.

Thus, we turn to the Government's final contention. The Government summarily argues that even if the AUMF does not authorize al-Marri's seizure and indefinite detention as an enemy combatant, the President has "inherent constitutional authority" to order the military to seize and detain al-Marri. According to the Government, the President's "war-making powers" afford him "inherent" authority to subject persons legally residing in this country and protected by our Constitution to military arrest and detention, without the benefit of any criminal process, if the President believes these individuals have "engaged in conduct in preparation for acts of international terrorism." *See* Rapp Declaration. Given that the Government has now acknowledged that aliens lawfully residing in the United States have the same due process rights as United States citizens, this is a breathtaking claim—and one that no member of the court embraces. . . .

1.

In contrast to the AUMF, which is silent on the detention of asserted alien terrorists captured and held within the United States, in the Patriot Act, enacted shortly after the AUMF, Congress carefully stated how it wished the Government to handle aliens believed to be terrorists who were seized and held within the United States. The Patriot Act provides the Executive with broad powers to deal with "terrorist aliens," but it *explicitly prohibits* their indefinite detention.

Section 412 of the Patriot Act, entitled "Mandatory Detention of Suspected Terrorists," permits the short-term "[d]etention of [t]errorist [a]liens." Patriot Act §412(a). The statute authorizes the Attorney General to detain any alien whom he "has reasonable grounds to believe": (1) "seeks to enter the United States" to "violate any law of the United States relating to espionage or sabotage" or to use "force, violence, or other unlawful means" in opposition to the government of the United States; (2) "has engaged in a terrorist activity"; or (3) is "likely to engage after entry in any terrorist activity," has "incited terrorist activity," is a "representative" or "member" of a "terrorist organization," is a "representative" of a "group that endorses or espouses terrorist activity," or "has received military-type training" from a terrorist organization. *Id.*; 8 U.S.C.A. §1182(a)(3)(A)-(B) (West 2007); *see also* 8 U.S.C.A. §1227(a)(4)(A)(i), (a)(4)(A)(iii), (a)(4)(B) (West 2007). In addition, the Patriot Act authorizes the Attorney General to detain any other alien who "is engaged in any other activity that endangers the national security of the United States." Patriot Act §412(a). In particular, the Patriot Act permits the Attorney General to "take into custody" any "terrorist aliens" based only on the Attorney General's "belie[fs]" as to the aliens' threat, with *no* process or evidentiary hearing, and judicial review available only through petition for habeas corpus. *Id.*

Recognizing the breadth of this grant of power, however, Congress also imposed strict limits in the Patriot Act on the duration of the detention of such "terrorist aliens" within the United States. Thus, the Patriot Act expressly prohibits unlimited "indefinite detention"; instead it requires the Attorney General either to begin "removal proceedings" or to "charge the alien with a criminal offense" "not later than 7 days after the commencement of such detention." *Id.* If a terrorist alien's removal "is unlikely for the reasonably foreseeable future," he "may be detained for additional periods of up to six months" if his release "will threaten the national security of the United States." *Id.* But no provision of the Patriot Act allows for unlimited indefinite detention. Moreover, the Attorney General must provide the legislature with reports on the use of this detention authority every six months, which must include the number of aliens detained, the grounds for their detention, and the length of the detention. *Id.* §412(c).

Therefore, the Patriot Act establishes a specific method for the Government to detain aliens affiliated with terrorist organizations who the Government believes have come to the United States to endanger our national security, conduct espionage and sabotage, use force and violence to overthrow the government, engage in terrorist activity, or are likely to engage in any terrorist activity. Congress could not have better described the Government's allegations against al-Marri — *and* Congress decreed that individuals so described are *not* to be detained indefinitely, but only for a limited time, and only by civilian authorities, prior to deportation or criminal prosecution.

In sum, Congress has carefully prescribed the process by which it wishes to permit detention of "terrorist aliens" within the United States, and it has expressly prohibited the indefinite detention the President seeks here. The Government's argument that the President may indefinitely detain al-Marri is thus contrary to Congress's expressed will. "When the President takes measures incompatible with the expressed or implied will of Congress, his power is at its lowest ebb, for then he can rely only upon his own constitutional powers minus any constitutional powers of Congress over the matter." *Youngstown* [*Sheet & Tube Co. v. Sawyer*, 343 U.S. 579 (1952),] at 637 (Jackson, J., concurring). As the Supreme Court has recently explained, "[w]hether or not the President has independent power . . . he may not disregard limitations that Congress has, in proper exercise of its own war powers, placed on his powers." *Hamdan*, 126 S. Ct. at 2774 n.23 (citing *Youngstown*, 343 U.S. at 637 (Jackson, J., concurring)). In such cases, "Presidential claim[s]" to power "must be scrutinized with caution, for what is at stake is the equilibrium established by our constitutional system." *Youngstown*, 343 U.S. at 638 (Jackson, J., concurring). . . .

3.

In light of al-Marri's due process rights under our Constitution and Congress's express prohibition in the Patriot Act on the indefinite detention of those civilians arrested as "terrorist aliens" within this country, we can only conclude that, in the case at hand, the President claims power that far exceeds that granted him by the Constitution.

We do not question the President's wartime authority over enemy combatants, but absent suspension of the writ of habeas corpus, the Constitution simply does not provide the President the power to exercise military authority over civilians within the United States. *See Toth*, 350 U.S. at 14 ("[A]ssertion of military authority over civilians cannot rest on the President's power as commander-in-chief."). The President cannot eliminate constitutional protections with the stroke of a pen by proclaiming a civilian, even a criminal civilian, an enemy combatant subject to indefinite military detention. Put simply, the Constitution does not empower the President to order the military to seize civilians residing within the United States and detain them indefinitely without criminal process, and this is so even if he calls them "enemy combatants."

A "well-established purpose of the Founders" was "to keep the military strictly within its proper sphere, subordinate to civil authority." *Reid* [*v. Covert*, 354 U.S. 1, 30 (1957)]. In the Declaration of Independence, our forefathers lodged the complaint that the King of Great Britain had "affected to render the Military independent of and superior to the Civil power" and objected that the King had "depriv[ed] us in many cases, of the benefits of Trial by Jury." *The Declaration of Independence* paras. 14, 20 (U.S. 1776). Thus, a resolute conviction that civilian authority should govern the military animated the framing of the Constitution. As Alexander Hamilton, no foe of executive power, observed, the President's Commander-in-Chief powers "amount to nothing more than the supreme command and direction of the military and naval forces." The Federalist No. 69, at 386 (Alexander Hamilton) (Clinton Rossiter ed., 1961). "That military powers of the Commander in Chief were not to supersede representative government of *internal affairs* seems obvious from the Constitution and from elementary American history." *Youngstown*, 343 U.S. at 644 (Jackson, J., concurring) (emphasis added). For this reason, in *Youngstown*, the Supreme Court rejected the President's claim to "inherent power" to use the military even to seize property within the United States, despite the Government's argument that the refusal would "endanger the well-being and safety of the Nation." *Id.* at 584 (majority opinion). . . .

To sanction such presidential authority to order the military to seize and indefinitely detain civilians, even if the President calls them "enemy combatants," would have disastrous consequences for the Constitution — and the country. For a court to uphold a claim to such extraordinary power would do more than render lifeless the Suspension Clause, the Due Process Clause, and the rights to criminal process in the

Fourth, Fifth, Sixth, and Eighth Amendments; it would effectively undermine all of the freedoms guaranteed by the Constitution. It is that power—were a court to recognize it—that could lead all our laws "to go unexecuted, and the government itself to go to pieces." We refuse to recognize a claim to power that would so alter the constitutional foundations of our Republic.

III. . . .

. . . We believe that it is unnecessary to litigate whether al-Marri is an enemy combatant, but joining in remand for the evidentiary proceedings outlined by Judge Traxler will at least place the burden on the Government to make an initial showing that normal due process protections are unduly burdensome and that the Rapp declaration is "the most reliable available evidence," supporting the Government's allegations before it may order al-Marri's military detention. Therefore, we concur in the per curiam opinion reversing and remanding for evidentiary proceedings to determine whether al-Marri actually is an enemy combatant subject to military detention.

Judges Michael, King, and Gregory have authorized me to indicate that they join in this opinion.

TRAXLER, Circuit Judge, concurring in the judgment: . . . I agree with my colleagues who hold that the [AUMF] . . . grants the President the power to detain enemy combatants in the war against al Qaeda, including belligerents who enter our country for the purpose of committing hostile and war-like acts such as those carried out by the al Qaeda operatives on 9/11. And, I agree that the allegations made by the government against al-Marri, if true, would place him within this category and permit the President to militarily detain him.

However, I depart from my dissenting colleagues on the issue of whether al-Marri has been afforded a fair opportunity to challenge the factual basis for his designation as an enemy combatant. Because the process afforded al-Marri by the district court to challenge the factual basis for his designation as an enemy combatant did not meet the minimal requirements of due process guaranteed by the Fifth Amendment, I would reverse the district court's dismissal of al-Marri's habeas petition and remand for further evidentiary proceedings on the issue of whether al-Marri is, in fact, an enemy combatant subject to military detention. . . .

II. THE AUTHORITY TO DETAIN. . . .

B. . . .

1. . . .

In my opinion . . . there is no doubt that individuals who are dispatched here by al Qaeda, the organization known to have carried out the 9/11 attacks upon our country, as sleeper agents and terrorist operatives charged with the task of committing additional attacks upon our homeland "are [also] individuals Congress sought to target in passing the AUMF." *Hamdi*, 542 U.S. at 518. Citing the right of the United States "to protect United States citizens *both at home and abroad*," the AUMF authorized the President's use of "all necessary and appropriate force against" the nations *and organizations* that "planned, authorized, committed, or aided" the 9/11 attacks, "or harbored such organizations or persons, in order to prevent any future acts of international terrorism against the United States." 115 Stat. 224. Clearly, Congress was not merely authorizing military retaliation against a reigning foreign government known to have *supported* the enemy force that attacked us in our homeland, but was also authorizing military action against al Qaeda operatives who, like the 9/11 hijackers, were sent by the al Qaeda organization to the United States to conduct additional terror operations here.

As persuasively pointed out by the government, it was the 9/11 attacks which triggered the passage of the AUMF. The al Qaeda operatives who successfully carried out those attacks entered this country under false pretenses for the purpose of carrying out al Qaeda orders and, while finalizing the preparations for these attacks, maintained a facade of peaceful residence until the very moment they boarded the commercial airliners that they used as weapons. The hijackers never engaged in combat operations against our forces on a foreign battlefield. Yet al-Marri would have us rule that when Congress authorized the President to deal militarily with those responsible for the 9/11 attacks upon our country, it did not intend to authorize the President to deal militarily with al Qaeda operatives identically situated to the 9/11 hijackers. There is nothing in the language of the AUMF that suggests that Congress intended to limit the military response or the presidential authorization to acts occurring in foreign territories, and it strains reason to believe that Congress, in enacting the AUMF in the wake of those attacks, did *not* intend for it to encompass al Qaeda operatives standing in the exact position as the attackers who brought about its enactment. Furthermore, Congress has not revised or revoked the AUMF since its enactment or since the Supreme Court decided *Hamdi.*

I am also unpersuaded by the claim that because al Qaeda itself is an international terrorist organization instead of a "nation state" or "enemy government," the AUMF cannot apply, consistent with the laws of war and our constitutional guarantees, to such persons. The premise of that claim seems to be that because al Qaeda is not technically in control of an enemy nation or its government, it cannot be considered as anything other than a criminal organization whose members are entitled to all the protections and procedures granted by our constitution. I disagree.

In my view, al Qaeda is much more and much worse than a criminal organization. And while it may be an unconventional enemy force in a historical context, it is an enemy force nonetheless. The fact that it allied itself with an enemy government of a foreign nation only underscores this point, rendering attempts to distinguish its soldiers or operatives as something meaningfully different from military soldiers in service to the Taliban government (or al Qaeda operatives such as Hamdi and Padilla, who fought beside them) equally strained. The President attacked the Taliban in Afghanistan as *retaliation* for al Qaeda's strike upon our nation *because* al Qaeda was centralized there and allied with the Taliban, and it also strains credulity to assert that while we are legitimately at war with the Taliban government, we cannot be at war with al Qaeda....

2.

If the allegations of the Rapp Declaration are true, I am also of the view that al-Marri would fall within the category of persons who may be lawfully detained pursuant to the authority granted by the AUMF....

III. DUE PROCESS

While I agree with my colleagues who would hold that the President has the legal authority under the AUMF to detain al-Marri as an enemy combatant for the duration of the hostilities, we part company on the issue of whether the process afforded al-Marri to challenge his detention was sufficient to meet the minimum requirements of due process of law. In my opinion, due process demands more procedural safeguards than those provided to al-Marri in the habeas proceedings below....

C. . . .

. . . [I]n my opinion, the district court erred in the initial step of accepting the hearsay affidavit of Rapp "as the most reliable available evidence from the [g]overnment," *id.* at 534, without any inquiry into whether the provision of nonhearsay evidence would unduly burden the government, and erred in failing to then weigh the competing interests of the litigants in light of the factual allegations and burdens placed before it for consideration.

1. . . .

Although I do not rule out the possibility that hearsay evidence might ultimately prove to be the most reliable available evidence from the government in this case, *Hamdi* does not support such a categorical relaxation of the protections due persons who are detained within our borders.... The *Hamdi* plurality's acceptance of hearsay evidence from the government in such settings . . . clearly arose from the context of a battlefield detainee, the "exigencies of [such] circumstances," and the "uncommon potential to burden the Executive at a time of ongoing military conflict." *Id.* at 533. The relaxed evidentiary standard was accepted in the balance as appropriate in light of the facts of that case — a person initially detained abroad by our allies on a battlefield in Afghanistan.... [W]hile the plurality refused to categorically prohibit hearsay declarations, neither did it categorically approve the use of such hearsay declarations in all enemy-combatant proceedings. Hearsay declarations *may* be accepted upon a weighing of the burdens in time of warfare of "providing greater process" against the detainee's liberty interests. *Id.* at 529. But to decide whether a hearsay declaration is acceptable, the court must first take into account "the risk of erroneous deprivation" of the detainee's liberty interest, "the probable value, if any, of any additional or substitute procedural safeguards," and the availability of additional or substitute evidence which might serve the interests of both litigants....

2.

In this case al-Marri's "private interest affected by the official action" is the same as that of Hamdi, *i.e.*, the liberty interest in being free from unlawful seizure and detention. *Hamdi,* 542 U.S. at 529. The risk of an erroneous deprivation of al-Marri's liberty interest, however, is not identical to the risk that was present in *Hamdi.* Al-Marri was not captured on the battlefields of Afghanistan or Iraq, nor even apprehended in a neighboring country where al Qaeda trains its soldiers. He was arrested by civilian federal authorities while residing in Illinois. I am acutely aware of the dangers of detention and imprisonment without compliance with criminal process safeguards, dangers that are even greater when the military detains persons inside the borders of the United States. In my view, the risk of erroneously detaining a civilian or citizen in this country as an enemy combatant is much greater inside the United States than in the very different context addressed by the Supreme Court in *Hamdi*, *i.e.*, a conventional battlefield within the borders of a foreign country in which we are fighting our enemies.

On the other hand, we must consider the government's interest "in detaining those who actually pose an immediate threat to the national security of the United States during ongoing international conflict," *Hamdi*, 542 U.S. at 530, and in "ensuring that those who have in fact fought with the enemy during a war do not return to battle against the United States," *id.* at 531, as well as "the burdens the [g]overnment would face in providing greater process," *id.* at 529.

Here, the government asserts that the Rapp Declaration, which summarizes the intelligence gathered on al-Marri's activities as an al Qaeda operative, is sufficient to meet its initial burden of proving that al-Marri was properly designated an enemy combatant. However, unlike in *Hamdi*, the government has presented *only* the Rapp Declaration. It has made no attempt to show that this hearsay evidence "need[s] to be accepted as the most reliable available evidence from the [g]overnment," *id.* at 533-34, or that additional protections to ensure that the innocent are not detained by our military would be "unworkable and inappropriate in th[is] enemy-combatant setting," *id.* at 535. Nor has there been any consideration of the "probable value, if any, of additional or substitute procedural safeguards" or the availability of more reliable evidence that might be presented by substitute methods which account for the government's weighty interests. *Id.* at 529.

... [A]l-Marri argued below that he believed the discovery [he] sought would be primarily from civilian agencies that could produce it without interfering with the war powers and war operations of this government. At a minimum, I believe the government should be required to demonstrate to the district court why this is not the case and why, in balancing the liberty interest of the detainee and the heightened risk of erroneous deprivation, the Rapp Declaration should be accepted as the most reliable available evidence the government can produce without undue burden or serious jeopardy to either its war efforts or its efforts to ensure the national security of this nation. . . .

GREGORY, Circuit Judge, concurring in the judgment [omitted].

WILLIAMS, Chief Judge, concurring in part and dissenting in part: . . .

I.

A. . . .

A distillation of [the *Milligan*, *Quirin*, and *Hamdi*] precedents, I believe, yields a definition of an enemy combatant subject to detention pursuant to Congressional authorizations as an individual who meets two criteria: (1) he attempts or engages in belligerent acts against the United States, either domestically or in a foreign combat zone; (2) on behalf of an enemy force.

Given the specific allegations against al-Marri, I have little difficulty concluding that he satisfies the first criterion. First, the allegations set forth in the Rapp

Declaration, if true, clearly show that al-Marri was on United States soil to commit acts of belligerency against the United States. *See Quirin*, 317 U.S. at 31 (stating that unlawful combatants include those who commit "hostile acts involving destruction of life or property" on United States soil).

According to the Rapp Declaration, al-Marri also meets what I view as the second requirement of an enemy combatant: that the belligerent acts be carried out on behalf of an enemy force. Unlike the plurality, I cannot accept al-Marri's contention that because he allegedly has ties only to al Qaeda, a terrorist organization that does not control any nation, he does not meet this portion of the definition of enemy combatant.

The plurality opinion may very well be correct that, under the traditional "law of war," persons not affiliated with the military of a *nation-state* may not be considered enemy combatants. And I recognize the respect domestic courts have long afforded the "law of nations." *See Murray v. Schooner Charming Betsy*, 6 U.S. (2 Cranch) 64, 118 (1804) ("[A]n act of Congress ought never to be construed to violate the law of nations if any other possible construction remains."). Here, however, Congress has, through the AUMF, addressed precisely this question by clearly authorizing the President to use force against "organizations," as well as against nation-states. *See Padilla v. Hanft*, 423 F.3d 386, 395-96 (4th Cir. 2005) (noting "the AUMF constitutes...a clear statement" in favor of detention). As a specific and targeted congressional directive, the AUMF controls the question of who may be detained, for purposes of domestic law — at least with respect to those individuals that fall within its scope....

I wish to emphasize that by permitting the President to militarily detain al-Marri pursuant to the AUMF I am not being expansive; in al-Marri we are dealing with someone *squarely* within the purposes of the AUMF, which was passed to target organizations, like al Qaeda, responsible for the September 11 attacks and to prevent future terrorist attacks. This case does not present what to me are more difficult issues regarding enemy combatants and the scope of AUMF, such as the status of an individual who joined al Qaeda after September 11, 2001, or an individual who is part of a designated foreign terrorist organization, that played no role in the September 11 attacks. Instead, al-Marri is clearly an "individual[ ] Congress sought to target in passing the AUMF." *Hamdi*, 542 U.S. at 518. In addition, while "indefinite detention" of enemy combatants is not permitted, *see generally Hamdi*, 542 U.S. at 519-20, we remain engaged against the forces of al Qaeda in the border regions of Afghanistan to this day....

B. ...

...I view section 412 of the Patriot Act to refer to the President's power, under Article II §3, to "take Care that the Laws be faithfully executed." U.S. Const., art. II, §3. The statute refers to the Attorney General, the President's agent in implementing the Take Care Clause, and it is found nestled within the immigration code. Fairly read, the Patriot Act does not therefore purport to limit the President's separate Commander-in-Chief power. But the authorization granted in the AUMF, with its explicit reference to military force, relates to the Commander-in-Chief power. Whatever limitations are present in the Patriot Act, therefore, do not restrict the separate and distinct grant of power effected by the AUMF....

II.

I do not agree, however, with Judge Traxler's separate concurrence, which concludes that a remand is necessary to permit al-Marri to further challenge his detention....

B....

...I see nothing in *Hamdi* that forbids a sworn statement—like the Rapp Declaration—from providing sufficient "notice" of the allegations against al-Marri. Moreover...the magistrate judge required the Government to provide al-Marri the declaration in response to his request....

Finally, and most importantly, *Hamdi* stressed the need for a "prudent" and "incremental" process....By failing to participate, Al-Marri simply short-circuited the entire "incremental" process....

Judge Duncan has authorized me to indicate that she joins in this opinion.

Wilkinson, Circuit Judge, concurring in part and dissenting in part:...

III. THE DETENTION OF AL-MARRI IS CONSISTENT WITH THE LIMITS ESTABLISHED BY OUR CONSTITUTION ON THE MILITARY DETENTION OF THOSE LAWFULLY ON AMERICAN SOIL....

D....

...[A]n "enemy" is any individual who is (1) a member of (2) an organization or nation against whom Congress has declared war or authorized the use of military force. Taken together, these two criteria closely track traditional law of war concepts that distinguish enemies from non-enemies. At the same time, they recognize that modern military threats include those posed by non-state actors.

I first address the criterion of membership. While the traditional requirement of residency or other affiliation with an enemy nation still applies, the advent of enemy organizations requires a functional equivalent to residency for this new stateless actor. This is achieved by the requirement of membership in the enemy organization. Because membership may be considered more amorphous than residency or citizenship, it is important that there be identifiable facts that indicate such affiliation with the enemy organization. Such indicia of membership may include: self-identification with the organization through verbal or written statements; participation in the group's hierarchy or command structure; or knowingly taking overt steps to aid or participate in the organization's activities. Thus, for example, someone who sends money to "a nonprofit charity that feeds Afghan orphans" that unknowingly makes "its way to al Qaeda" would not be a member of the al Qaeda organization, and it is beyond hyperbole for the plurality to suggest otherwise. Furthermore, the membership requirement is important because it aids in distinguishing those who are the enemy from those who merely sympathize with the enemy.

The second criterion—congressional authorization—recognizes that Congress may authorize the use of military force against non-state actors, such as terrorist organizations, as it has already with the AUMF. By contemplating such authorization, this second criterion appropriately excludes from the category of "enemy" those persons or groups against whom Congress has not authorized the use of military force. Thus, the notion that any individual affiliated with an organization engaged in purported terrorist activities — such as the "environmental group" mentioned by the plurality — could be considered an enemy combatant is completely unfounded. For certain, there are many individuals and organizations engaged in unlawful conduct, and even terrorism. But most of these individuals and organizations have nothing to do with al Qaeda, its affiliates, or the September 11 attacks. Under this criterion, such persons would not be eligible for military detention under the AUMF. This is both consistent with our traditional conception of who should and should not be eligible for detention and appropriate in light of the constitutional imperative that military detention be the exception and not the rule. Indeed, not to require congressional authorization for such detentions in this country splits the ground beneath the war powers right in two.

If the first two criteria address who in modern warfare is the enemy, the third criterion addresses who is the combatant. Historically, this distinction has separated those with military aims from those who do not present a threat to opposing forces. Though yesterday's soldier has been replaced, at least in part, by those who eschew the conventions of lawful warfare, the purpose underlying this distinction remains unchanged. In light of today's realities, a "combatant" is a person who knowingly plans or engages in conduct that harms or aims to harm persons or property for the purpose of furthering the military goals of an enemy nation or organization. Like the first two criteria, this requirement closely tracks the relevant traditional law of war rules.

Under this criterion, those who use military-like force against American soldiers or civilians obviously qualify as combatants. Similarly, members of an enemy sleeper terrorist cell that have taken steps, even if preliminary in nature, toward an act of destruction are also considered combatants. Conversely, persons traditionally considered civilians, such as members of the enemy organization who do not possess hostile or military designs, are non-combatants and may not be detained by the military. This includes persons who would clearly be non-combatants, such as a "physician who treated a member of al Qaeda," because they intend no harm to persons or property. Such persons would not be subject to military detention.

Two further examples may help illustrate the scope of this framework. First is a person who joins a terrorist organization after Congress has authorized the use of military force against the respective group. In the present conflict, this would include new recruits to al Qaeda or its affiliates after 9/11. Under the above criteria, such persons are clearly part of the "enemy," even if they were not members of the targeted organization at the time Congress initially acted. This is because it was the organization and its affiliates, and not just the then-members of such groups, against whom Congress authorized the use of force. *See* AUMF, 115 Stat. 224 (authorizing the use of "all necessary and appropriate force against those . . . organizations [that] . . . committed" the 9/11 attacks, "in order to prevent any future acts of international terrorism"). Thus, in the current conflict, any "individual can become part of a covered 'organization' by joining it after the September 11 attacks." As a result, such a person, if also a combatant, would be eligible for military detention.

Second is a person who commits, or plans to commit, a terrorist act but is not otherwise affiliated with an organization or country covered by a congressional proclamation. Timothy McVeigh is one example that comes to mind. Because such a person is not a member of an enemy organization, he may not be detained as an enemy combatant under the above criteria. Indeed, Congress has never declared war against a single individual or even a discrete conspiracy (unless the Barbary pirates qualify), and it is difficult to envision a scenario in which it would. This is unsurprising, in part because prosecutions of individual terrorists do not ordinarily present the same sort of logistical, informational, and evidentiary problems as large scale terrorist networks or nations. . . .

. . . [U]nder these criteria, there are at least three significant limitations on the executive's ability to militarily detain persons lawfully residing in the United States.

First, there is the significant political check of congressional authorization. Specifically, absent some limited inherent authority needed during times of emergency, the executive may only detain those persons against whom Congress has authorized the use of force. If history is any indicator, Congress does not take such a decision lightly. Indeed, it was the dire events of September 11th that gave rise to the use of military force in the present instance, and it is likely that only emergencies of similar magnitude will trigger a similar response.

Second, even if Congress were to authorize the use of military force against a particular group, it would not be authorizing the executive to make a sweep on the basis of mere membership. This is because membership, without more, is not enough to qualify as an enemy combatant under my proposed criteria. Rather, the person in question must have taken steps to further the military goals of the organization. Thus, McCarthy-like accusations of mere group membership would not suffice as a basis for detention.

Third, persons subject to military detention are afforded the opportunity to challenge the accuracy of their detention before a neutral decisionmaker in accordance with the framework articulated in *Hamdi*. This ensures that the government possesses sufficient evidence to justify a measure as serious as military detention. . . .

[The opinion of NIEMEYER, Circuit Judge, concurring in the judgment in part and dissenting in part, is omitted].

[The opinion of DUNCAN, Circuit Judge, concurring in part and dissenting in part, is omitted].

NOTES AND QUESTIONS

1. *The Non-Detention Act — Section 4001(a).* The plurality in *Hamdi* assumed, but did not decide, that §4001(a) applies to military detentions, then found that it was satisfied by the AUMF. If §4001(a) does apply and the AUMF is invoked as a statutory exception within its contemplation, should we apply the clear statement requirement to the AUMF, as Justices Souter and Ginsburg insisted in *Hamdi*, and the Second Circuit did in *Padilla*? Even without insisting on a clear statement, does a natural reading of the AUMF embrace uses of force (and, by implication, military detention) *within* the United States, or just in Afghanistan or wherever else the armed forces are deployed in combat abroad? See Stephen I. Vladeck, Comment, *A Small Problem of Precedent: 18 U.S.C. §4001(a) and the Detention of U.S. Citizen "Enemy Combatants,"* 112 Yale L.J. 961, 967 (2003) (arguing that the AUMF fails to satisfy §4001(a)).

2. *Necessity for Military Detention in Padilla and Al-Marri.* If the arguments of necessity applied to Hamdi, did they also apply to Padilla and al-Marri? What if the government believes someone like Padilla to be an imminent threat to set off a dirty bomb, but lacks probable cause to arrest him? What response does Justice Souter suggest for such an emergency? Here is the District Court's answer, after Padilla refiled his habeas petition on remand from the Supreme Court:

> Simply stated, this is a law enforcement matter, not a military matter.... At the time that [Padilla] was arrested pursuant to the material arrest warrant, any alleged terrorist plans that he harbored were thwarted. From then on, he was available to be questioned — and was indeed questioned —just like any citizen accused of criminal conduct....
>
> There can be no debate that this country's laws amply provide for the investigation, detention and prosecution of citizen and non-citizen terrorists alike....
>
> ... The difference between invocation of the criminal process and the power claimed by the President here, however, is one of accountability. The criminal justice system requires that defendants and witnesses be afforded access to counsel, imposes judicial supervision over government action, and places congressionally imposed limits on incarceration.

[*Padilla v. Hanft*, 389 F. Supp. 2d 678, 691-692 (D.S.C. 2005), *rev'd*, 423 F.3d 387 (4th Cir. 2005), *cert. denied*, 547 U.S. 1062 (2006) (quoting *amici curiae* in *Rumsfeld v. Padilla*, 542 U.S. 426 (2004)).]

Although the Fourth Circuit panel disagreed, Padilla *was* eventually transferred back to law enforcement custody and convicted of a crime.

After the *en banc* decision, Al-Marri promptly petitioned the Supreme Court for *certiorari*. The government then transferred him, as it had Padilla in similar circumstances, back to law enforcement custody, and the Supreme Court therefore vacated the *en banc* opinion and remanded with instructions to dismiss the appeal as moot. Al-Marri was indicted on two counts of providing material support to a foreign terrorist organization (see *infra* p. 990) and pleaded guilty to a single count. He was sentenced to eight years in prison and has a projected release date of 2015.

How would you reframe the authority for military detention to confine it strictly to situations of bona fide military necessity? Does the length of the detention affect the necessity, and, if so, how would you reflect this consideration in your specification of detention authority? Should military necessity be judged in light of the availability and practicality of the ordinary criminal process to detain?

Do the outcomes in *Hamdi, Padilla,* and *Al-Marri* cast any doubt on the propriety of judicial deference to executive claims of military necessity for military detention? (Consider also the aftermath of *Korematsu v. United States*, 323 U.S. 214 (1944), discussed in Chapter 29.) If so, how should courts view such claims?

3. *Defining Enemy Combatant.* All of the judges in *Al-Marri* seem agreed that the President's detention authority extends to enemy combatants, but they disagreed about who is an enemy combatant. We have now reviewed the circumstances of Milligan, Quirin, Hamdi, Padilla, and al-Marri. Can you say who among them are enemy combatants and who are not? Does your analysis suggest any comprehensive definition? Judge Williams remarked that al-Marri was "someone *squarely* within the purposes of the AUMF ...." *Al-Marri*, 534 F.3d at 286. Suppose al-Marri had never left

the United States, but affiliated with al Qaeda through the Internet because he agreed with its aims. Would he still fall squarely within the AUMF?

One factor that seems *not* to figure in the definition is U.S. citizenship. One of the German saboteurs in *Quirin* a citizen, and as a lawfully resident alien al-Marri arguably enjoyed the constitutional rights of a citizen. If he could lawfully be detained, then arguably so could a U.S. citizen in similar circumstances.

4. *"Affirming" the AUMF?* Proposed legislation in 2011 "affirming" the AUMF is set forth *supra* p. 97. Would this measure cover someone like Padilla? Al-Marri? A Saudi who paid for al-Marri's tuition, believing that al-Marri was a "jihadist"? If you find the provision ambiguous, what language would you substitute to clarify the President's detention authority?

5. *The USA Patriot Act.* The Patriot Act provided limited detention authority for persons Judge Motz called "terrorist aliens." In fact, its provision seems tailor-made for someone like al-Marri. Why did the Patriot Act not occupy the field, in the same way that the Labor Management Relations Act occupied the field in *Steel Seizure* or that the statute authorizing interception of ships going to French ports occupied the field in *Little v. Barreme?* Did the judges who upheld detention authority in *al-Marri* find that Congress cannot occupy the field of law-of-war detention, or that it had not? What constitutional authority, if any, does Congress have to occupy this particular field? *See generally* Ingrid Wuerth, *The Captures Clause*, 76 U. Chi. L. Rev. 1683 (2009).

C.   MILITARY DETENTION: EVOLVING LAW OF THE HABEAS CASES

While *Hamdi* involved a U.S. citizen, it set out a broader principle of law-of-war detention. Once the Supreme Court opened the door to habeas petitions from the Guantánamo detainees in *Boumediene v. Bush*, 553 U.S. 723 (2008), that principle was developed in the resulting habeas cases heard in the federal courts of the District of Columbia. As different district courts grappled with both substantive and procedural issues of detention, their opinions inevitably diverged. *See, e.g.*, Nathaniel H. Nesbitt, *Meeting Boumediene's Challenge: The Emergence of an Effective Habeas Jurisprudence and Obsolescence of New Detention Legislation*, 95 Minn. L. Rev. 244 (2010); Robert M. Chesney, *Who May Be Held? Military Detention Through the Habeas Lens*, 52 B.C. L. Rev. 769 (2011); Benjamin Wittes, Robert M. Chesney & Larkin Reynolds, *The Emerging Law of Detention 2.0: The Guantánamo Habeas Cases as Lawmaking* (updated May 12, 2011), *at* http://www.brookings.edu/papers/2011/05_guantanamo_wittes.aspx (analyzing emerging differences).

Substantively, the district courts have reached varying conclusions about whether law-of-war detention authority extends to supporters of Al Qaeda or the Taliban, "substantial" supporters, the Al Qaeda "command structure," or mere members, and whether the scope of such authority is informed or limited by the laws of war in light of the Administration's reliance strictly on the AUMF. Procedurally, the courts have also disagreed about whether (and how far) the government's evidentiary bar moves with the length of detention, an issue related to the substantive question whether detention status is permanent or might change over time. The courts have diverged less sharply on the quality of admissible hearsay and other evidentiary issues that *Hamdi* left to them.

The following decision by the D.C. Circuit Court of Appeals resolved some of these conflicts among the district court opinions, but left others.

Al-Bihani v. Obama

United States Court of Appeals, District of Columbia Circuit, 2010
590 F.3d 866, *rehearing denied en banc*, 619 F.3d 1 (D.C. Cir. 2010)

BROWN, Circuit Judge: . . .

[Ghaleb Nassar Al-Bihani is a Yemeni citizen who traveled to Afghanistan to defend the Taliban's Islamic state against the Northern Alliance. The government alleged that he stayed at Al Qaeda-affiliated guesthouses and may also have received instruction at Al Qaeda terrorist training camps. Al-Bihani did not dispute that he eventually accompanied and served as a cook for a paramilitary group allied with the Taliban, known as the 55th Arab Brigade, which included Al Qaeda members within its command structure and which fought on the front lines against the Northern Alliance. He carried a brigade-issued weapon, but never fired it in combat. Al-Bihani and the rest of the brigade eventually surrendered, under orders, to Northern Alliance forces, which kept him in custody until his handover to U.S. Coalition forces in early 2002. The U.S. military sent Al-Bihani to Guantánamo for detention and interrogation. Al-Bihani unsuccessfully petitioned for a writ of habeas corpus, then brought this appeal.]

II

Al-Bihani's many arguments present this court with two overarching questions regarding the detainees at the Guantánamo Bay naval base. The first concerns whom the President can lawfully detain pursuant to statutes passed by Congress. The second asks what procedure is due to detainees challenging their detention in habeas corpus proceedings. The Supreme Court has provided scant guidance on these questions, consciously leaving the contours of the substantive and procedural law of detention open for lower courts to shape in a common law fashion. In this decision, we aim to narrow the legal uncertainty that clouds military detention.

A

Al-Bihani challenges the statutory legitimacy of his detention by advancing a number of arguments based upon the international laws of war. He first argues that relying on "support," or even "substantial support" of Al Qaeda or the Taliban as an independent basis for detention violates international law. As a result, such a standard should not be read into the ambiguous provisions of the Authorization for Use of Military Force (AUMF), Pub. L. No. 107-40, §2(a), 115 Stat. 224, 224 (2001), the Act empowering the President to respond to the attacks of September 11, 2001. Al-Bihani interprets international law to mean anyone not belonging to an official state military is a civilian, and civilians, he says, must commit a direct hostile act, such as firing a weapon in combat, before they can be lawfully detained. Because Al-Bihani did not commit such an act, he reasons his detention is unlawful. Next, he argues the members of the 55th Arab Brigade were not subject to attack or detention by U.S. Coalition forces under the laws of co-belligerency because the 55th, although allied with the Taliban against the Northern Alliance, did not have the required opportunity to declare its neutrality in the fight against the United States. His third argument is that the conflict in which he was detained, an international war between the United States and Taliban-controlled Afghanistan, officially ended when the Taliban lost control of the Afghan government. Thus, absent a determination of future danger-ousness, he must be released. *See* Geneva Convention Relative to the Treatment of Prisoners of War (Third Geneva Convention) art. 118, Aug. 12, 1949, 6 U.S.T. 3316, 75 U.N.T.S. 135. Lastly, Al-Bihani posits a type of "clean hands" theory by which any authority the government has to detain him is undermined by its failure to accord him the prisoner-of-war status to which he believes he is entitled by international law.

Before considering these arguments in detail, we note that all of them rely heavily on the premise that the war powers granted by the AUMF and other statutes are limited by the international laws of war. This premise is mistaken. There is no indica-tion in the AUMF, the Detainee Treatment Act of 2005 [DTA], Pub. L. No. 109-148, div. A, tit. X, 119 Stat. 2739, 2741-43, or the MCA of 2006 or 2009 [Military Commis-sions Act of 2006, Pub. L. No. 109-366, 120 Stat. 2600; Military Commissions Act of 2009, Pub. L. No. 111-84, 123 Stat. 2190], that Congress intended the international laws of war to act as extra-textual limiting principles for the President's war powers under the AUMF. The international laws of war as a whole have not been imple-mented domestically by Congress and are therefore not a source of authority for U.S. courts. *See* Restatement (Third) of Foreign Relations Law of the United States §111(3)-(4) (1987). Even assuming Congress had at some earlier point implemented the laws of war as domestic law through appropriate legislation, Congress had the power to authorize the President in the AUMF and other later statutes to exceed those bounds. *See id.* §115(1)(a). Further weakening their relevance to this case, the inter-national laws of war are not a fixed code. Their dictates and application to actual events are by nature contestable and fluid. *See id.* §102 cmts. b & c (stating there is "no precise formula" to identify a practice as custom and that "[i]t is often difficult to determine when [a custom's] transformation into law has taken place"). Therefore, while the international laws of war are helpful to courts when identifying the general set of war powers to which the AUMF speaks, *see Hamdi,* 542 U.S. at 520, their lack of controlling legal force and firm definition render their use both inapposite and inadvisable when courts seek to determine the limits of the President's war powers.

Therefore, putting aside that we find Al-Bihani's reading of international law to be unpersuasive, we have no occasion here to quibble over the intricate application of vague treaty provisions and amorphous customary principles. The sources we look to for resolution of Al-Bihani's case are the sources courts always look to: the text of relevant statutes and controlling domestic case law.

Under those sources, Al-Bihani is lawfully detained . . . . The statutes authorizing the use of force and detention not only grant the government the power to craft a workable legal standard to identify individuals it can detain, but also cabin the appli-cation of these definitions. The AUMF authorizes the President to "use all necessary

and appropriate force against those nations, organizations, or persons he determines planned, authorized, committed, or aided the terrorist attacks that occurred
on September 11, 2001, or harbored such organizations or persons." AUMF §2(a).
The Supreme Court in *Hamdi* ruled that "necessary and appropriate force"
includes the power to detain combatants subject to such force. 542 U.S. at 519.
Congress, in the 2006 MCA, provided guidance on the class of persons subject to
detention under the AUMF by defining "unlawful enemy combatants" who can be
tried by military commission. 2006 MCA sec. 3, §948a(1). The 2006 MCA authorized the trial of an individual who "engaged in hostilities or who has purposefully
and materially supported hostilities against the United States or its co-belligerents
who is not a lawful enemy combatant (including a person who is part of the
Taliban, al Qaeda, or associated forces)." *Id.* §948a(1)(A)(i). In 2009, Congress
enacted a new version of the MCA with a new definition that authorized the trial of
"unprivileged enemy belligerents," a class of persons that includes those who
"purposefully and materially supported hostilities against the United States or
its coalition partners." Military Commissions Act of 2009 sec. 1802, §§948a(7),
948b(a), 948c, 123 Stat. 2575-76. The provisions of the 2006 and 2009 MCAs are
illuminating in this case because the government's detention authority logically
covers a category of persons no narrower than is covered by its military commission
authority. Detention authority in fact sweeps wider, also extending at least to
traditional P.O.W.s, *see id.* §948a(6), and arguably to other categories of persons.
But for this case, it is enough to recognize that any person subject to a military
commission trial is also subject to detention, and that category of persons includes
those who are part of forces associated with Al Qaeda or the Taliban or those who
purposefully and materially support such forces in hostilities against U.S. Coalition
partners.

   In light of these provisions of the 2006 and 2009 MCAs, the facts that were both
found by the district court and offered by Al-Bihani ... place Al-Bihani within the
"part of" and "support" prongs of the relevant statutory definition.... His acknowledged actions—accompanying the brigade on the battlefield, carrying a brigade-
issued weapon, cooking for the unit, and retreating and surrendering under brigade
orders—strongly suggest, in the absence of an official membership card, that he was
part of the 55th. Even assuming, as he argues, that he was a civilian "contractor"
rendering services, those services render Al-Bihani detainable under the "purposefully and materially supported" language of both versions of the MCA. That language
constitutes a standard whose outer bounds are not readily identifiable. But wherever
the outer bounds may lie, they clearly include traditional food operations essential to
a fighting force and the carrying of arms. Viewed in full, the facts show Al-Bihani was
part of and supported a group—prior to and after September 11—that was affiliated
with Al Qaeda and Taliban forces and engaged in hostilities against a U.S. Coalition
partner. Al-Bihani, therefore, falls squarely within the scope of the President's statutory detention powers.[2]

   2. In reaching this conclusion, we need not rely on the evidence suggesting that Al-Bihani attended
Al Qaeda training camps in Afghanistan and visited Al Qaeda guesthouses. We do note, however, that
evidence supporting the military's reasonable belief of either of those two facts with respect to a noncitizen seized abroad during the ongoing war on terror would seem to overwhelmingly, if not definitively,
justify the government's detention of such a non-citizen. Cf. Nat'l Comm'n on Terrorist Attacks upon the
United States, the 9/11 Commission Report 66-67.

The government can also draw statutory authority to detain Al-Bihani directly from the language of the AUMF. The AUMF authorizes force against those who "harbored . . . organizations or persons" the President determines "planned, authorized, committed, or aided the terrorist attacks of September 11, 2001." AUMF §2(a). It is not in dispute that Al Qaeda is the organization responsible for September 11 or that it was harbored by the Taliban in Afghanistan. It is also not in dispute that the 55th Arab Brigade defended the Taliban against the Northern Alliance's efforts to oust the regime from power. Drawing from these facts, it cannot be disputed that the actual and foreseeable result of the 55th's defense of the Taliban was the maintenance of Al Qaeda's safe haven in Afghanistan. This result places the 55th within the AUMF's wide ambit as an organization that harbored Al Qaeda, making it subject to U.S. military force and its members and supporters — including Al-Bihani — eligible for detention. . . .

With the government's detention authority established as an initial matter, we turn to the argument that Al-Bihani must now be released according to longstanding law of war principles because the conflict with the Taliban has allegedly ended. *See Hamdi*, 542 U.S. at 521. Al-Bihani offers the court a choice of numerous event dates — the day Afghans established a post-Taliban interim authority, the day the United States recognized that authority, the day Hamid Karzai was elected President — to mark the official end of the conflict. No matter which is chosen, each would dictate the release of Al-Bihani if we follow his reasoning. His argument fails on factual and practical grounds. First, it is not clear if Al-Bihani was captured in the conflict with the Taliban or with Al Qaeda; he does not argue that the conflict with Al Qaeda is over. Second, there are currently 34,800 U.S. troops and a total of 71,030 Coalition troops in Afghanistan, with tens of thousands more to be added soon. The principle Al-Bihani espouses — were it accurate — would make each successful campaign of a long war but a Pyrrhic prelude to defeat. The initial success of the United States and its Coalition partners in ousting the Taliban from the seat of government and establishing a young democracy would trigger an obligation to release Taliban fighters captured in earlier clashes. Thus, the victors would be commanded to constantly refresh the ranks of the fledgling democracy's most likely saboteurs. . . .

Even so, we do not rest our resolution of this issue on international law or mere common sense. The determination of when hostilities have ceased is a political decision, and we defer to the Executive's opinion on the matter, at least in the absence of an authoritative congressional declaration purporting to terminate the war. *See Ludecke v. Watkins*, 335 U.S. 160, 168-70 & n.13 (1948) ("[T]ermination [of a state of war] is a political act."). . . . In the absence of a determination by the political branches that hostilities in Afghanistan have ceased, Al-Bihani's continued detention is justified.

Al-Bihani also argues he should be released because the government's failure to accord him P.O.W. status violated international law and undermined its otherwise lawful authority to detain him. Even assuming Al-Bihani is entitled to P.O.W. status, we find no controlling authority for this "clean hands" theory in statute or in caselaw. The AUMF, DTA, and MCA of 2006 and 2009 do not hinge the government's detention authority on proper identification of P.O.W.s or compliance with international law in general. In fact, the MCA of 2006, in a provision not altered by the MCA of 2009, explicitly precludes detainees from claiming the Geneva conventions — which include criteria to determine who is entitled to P.O.W. status — as a source of rights. *See* 2006 MCA sec. 5(a)....

B ...

Drawing upon *Boumediene*'s holding, Al-Bihani challenges numerous aspects of the habeas procedure devised by the district court....

Al-Bihani's argument clearly demonstrates error, but that error is his own. Habeas review for Guantánamo detainees need not match the procedures developed by Congress and the courts specifically for habeas challenges to criminal convictions. *Boumediene*'s holding explicitly stated that habeas procedures for detainees "need not resemble a criminal trial," 128 S. Ct. at 2269. It instead invited "innovation" of habeas procedure by lower courts, granting leeway for "[c]ertain accommodations [to] be made to reduce the burden habeas corpus proceedings will place on the military." *Id.* at 2276....

... Al-Bihani is a non-citizen who was seized in a foreign country. Requiring highly protective procedures at the tail end of the detention process for detainees like Al-Bihani would have systemic effects on the military's entire approach to war. From the moment a shot is fired, to battlefield capture, up to a detainee's day in court, military operations would be compromised as the government strove to satisfy evidentiary standards in anticipation of habeas litigation....

With Al-Bihani's limited procedural entitlement established as a general matter, we turn to the specific procedural claims warranting serious consideration. The question of what standard of proof is due in a habeas proceeding like Al-Bihani's has not been answered by the Supreme Court. *See Boumediene*, 128 S. Ct. at 2271 ("The extent of the showing required of the Government in these cases is a matter to be determined."). Attempting to fill this void, Al-Bihani argues the prospect of indefinite detention in this unconventional war augurs for a reasonable doubt standard or, in the alternative, at least a clear and convincing standard....

... [But] [i]n addition to the *Hamdi* plurality's approving treatment of military tribunal procedure, it also described as constitutionally adequate — even for the detention of U.S. citizens — a "burden-shifting scheme" in which the government need only present "credible evidence that the habeas petitioner meets the enemy-combatant criteria" before "the onus could shift to the petitioner to rebut that evidence with more persuasive evidence that he falls outside the criteria." *Hamdi*, 542 U.S. at 533-34. That description mirrors a preponderance standard....

... [T]raditional habeas review did not entail review of factual findings, particularly in the military context. *See In re Yamashita*, 327 U.S. 1, 8 (1946) ("If the military tribunals have lawful authority to hear, decide and condemn, their action is not subject to judicial review merely because they have made a wrong decision on disputed facts."). Where factual review has been authorized, the burden in some domestic circumstances has been placed *on the petitioner* to prove his case under a clear and convincing standard. *See* 28 U.S.C. §2254(e)(1) (regulating federal review of state court factual findings). If it is constitutionally permissible to place that higher burden on a citizen petitioner in a routine case, it follows a priori that placing a lower burden on the government defending a wartime detention — where national security interests are at their zenith and the rights of the alien petitioner at their nadir — is also permissible.

We find Al-Bihani's hearsay challenges to be similarly unavailing. Al-Bihani claims that government reports of his interrogation answers — which made up the majority, if not all, of the evidence on which the district court relied — and other informational documents were hearsay improperly admitted absent an examination of reliability and necessity. He contends, in fact, that government reports of his interrogation answers were "*double* hearsay" because his answers were first translated by an interpreter and then written down by an interrogator. We first note that Al-Bihani's interrogation answers themselves were not hearsay; they were instead party-opponent admissions that would have been admitted in any U.S. court. *See* Fed. R. Evid. 801(d)(2)(A). That they were translated does not affect their status. *See United States v. Da Silva*, 725 F.2d 828, 831-32 (2d Cir. 1983). However, that the otherwise admissible answers were relayed through an interrogator's account does introduce a level of technical hearsay because the interrogator is a third party unavailable for cross examination. Other information, such as a diagram of Al Qaeda's leadership structure, was also hearsay.

But that such evidence was hearsay does not automatically invalidate its admission — it only begins our inquiry. . . .

. . . [T]he question a habeas court must ask when presented with hearsay is not whether it is admissible — it is always admissible — but what probative weight to ascribe to whatever indicia of reliability it exhibits. . . .

In Al-Bihani's case, the district court clearly reserved that authority in its process and assessed the hearsay evidence's reliability as required by the Supreme Court. First, the district court retained the authority to assess the weight of the evidence. Second, the district court had ample contextual information about evidence in the government's factual return to determine what weight to give various pieces of evidence. Third, the district court afforded Al-Bihani the opportunity . . . to rebut the evidence and to attack its credibility. Further, Al-Bihani did not contest the truth of the majority of his admissions upon which the district court relied, enhancing the reliability of those reports. We therefore find that the district court did not improperly admit hearsay evidence. . . .

III

Al-Bihani's detention is authorized by statute and there was no constitutional defect in the district court's habeas procedure that would have affected the outcome of the proceeding. For these reasons, the order of the district court denying Al-Bihani's petition for a writ of habeas corpus is

Affirmed.

BROWN, Circuit Judge, concurring: The Supreme Court in *Boumediene* and *Hamdi* charged this court and others with the unprecedented task of developing rules to review the propriety of military actions during a time of war, relying on common law tools. We are fortunate this case does not require us to demarcate the law's full substantive and procedural dimensions. But as other more difficult cases arise, it is important to ask whether a court-driven process is best suited to protecting both the rights of petitioners and the safety of our nation. The common law process depends on incrementalism and eventual correction, and it is most effective where there are a significant number of cases brought before a large set of courts, which in turn enjoy the luxury of time to work the doctrine supple. None of those factors exist in the Guantánamo context. The number of Guantánamo detainees is limited and the circumstances of their confinement are unique. The petitions they file, as the *Boumediene* Court counseled, are funneled through one federal district court and one appellate court. And, in the midst of an ongoing war, time to entertain a process of literal trial and error is not a luxury we have.

While the common law process presents these difficulties, it is important to note that the Supreme Court has not foreclosed Congress from establishing new habeas standards in line with its *Boumediene* opinion. . . . [T]he circumstances that frustrate the judicial process are the same ones that make this situation particularly ripe for Congress to intervene pursuant to its policy expertise, democratic legitimacy, and oath to uphold and defend the Constitution. These cases present hard questions and hard choices, ones best faced directly. Judicial review, however, is just that: *re*-view, an indirect and necessarily backward looking process. And looking backward may not be enough in this new war. The saying that generals always fight the last war is familiar, but familiarity does not dull the maxim's sober warning. In identifying the shape of the law in response to the challenge of the current war, it is incumbent on the President, Congress, and the courts to realize that the saying's principle applies to us as well. Both the rule of law and the nation's safety will benefit from an honest assessment of the new challenges we face, one that will produce an appropriately calibrated response. . . .

WILLIAMS, Senior Circuit Judge, concurring in part and concurring in the judgment: . . . The petitioner's detention is legally permissible by virtue of facts that he himself has conceded. . . .

Within the portion of the opinion addressing the petitioner's substantive argument that his activities in Afghanistan do not put him in the class of people whom the President may detain pursuant to the AUMF, the majority unnecessarily addresses a number of other points. Most notable is the paragraph that begins, "Before considering these arguments in detail," and that reaches the conclusion that "the premise that the war powers granted by the AUMF and other statutes are limited by the international laws of war . . . is mistaken." The paragraph appears hard to square with the approach that the Supreme Court took in *Hamdi*. See 542 U.S. at 521 (O'Connor, J.) (plurality opinion) ("[W]e understand Congress' grant of authority for the use of "necessary and appropriate force" to include the authority to detain for the duration of the relevant conflict, and our understanding is based on longstanding law-of-war principles."); *id.* at 548-49 (Souter, J., opinion concurring in part and dissenting in part) (advocating a more substantial role for the laws of war in interpretations of the President's authority under the AUMF). In any event, there is no need for the court's pronouncements, divorced from application to any particular argument. Curiously, the majority's dictum goes well beyond what even the *government* has argued in this case.

Because the petitioner's detention is lawful by virtue of facts that he has conceded — a conclusion that the majority seems not to dispute — the majority's analysis of the constitutionality of the *procedures* the district court used is unnecessary. . . .

[Portions of the decision denying rehearing *en banc* in this case, 619 F.3d 1 (D.C. Cir. 2010), are reproduced *supra* p. 200.]

NOTES AND QUESTIONS

1. *The Common Law Process of Lawmaking.* While some observers may despair of the divergent cases emerging from the D.C. District courts, the process is familiar. Common law is made incrementally when trial courts need to decide issues in the cases that come before them, and courts of appeals periodically—and with some lag—then resolve some of the differences in opinions that serve as binding precedent for later trial court decisions. *See generally Habeas Works: Federal Courts' Proven Capacity to Handle Guantánamo Cases: A Report from Retired Federal Judges* (Human Rights First and the Constitution Project, June 2010). (In addition to *Al-Bihani, see Bensayah v. Obama*, 610 F.3d 718 (D.C. Cir. 2010); *Barhoumi v. Obama*, 609 F.3d 416 (D.C. Cir. 2010); *Awad v. Obama*, 608 F.3d 1 (D.C. Cir. 2010).) The common law process, however, comes at the cost of at least temporarily fragmented law and disparate outcomes, and, some have argued, at the cost of creating a shaky foundation for a preventive detention regime. *See, e.g.*, Sophia Brill, *The National Security Court We Already Have*, 28 Yale L. & Pol'y Rev. 525 (2010).

2. *Law-of-War Limits?* Two judges in the *Al-Bihani* panel went out of their way to reject Al-Bihani's argument that any detention authority conferred by the AUMF was subject to or incorporated the limits set by the law of war. In other words, they considered detention authority to be exclusively a question of domestic law. The third member of the panel disassociated himself from what he described as *dicta* that went well beyond any argument that even the government had made. In denying *en banc* review, the full court agreed, asserting that determining "the role of international law-of-war principles in interpreting the AUMF . . . is not necessary to the disposition of the merits." *Al-Bihani v. Obama*, 619 F.3d 1, 1 (D.C. Cir 2010).

So what is the role of international law-of-war principles? One view is that Congress was oblivious to law of war when it enacted the AUMF, and that the scope of the AUMF is be found entirely in its plain words (and perhaps, legislative intent). While "necessary and appropriate" is hardly helpful in describing the kinds of force the AUMF authorizes, its identification of the targets of force at least permits some group identification. It is left then to courts to determine individual identification—what degree of association to a targeted group is necessary to justify "AUMF detention."

But they do not do this in a vacuum. If the plain words and legislative history are not dispositive, courts interpret statutes against shared background understandings, often those reflected by like cases. There is a broad background understanding of law enforcement detention in U.S. law, driven or under the shadow of the Fourth Amendment, but the understanding concerning wartime detention is reflected chiefly in *Milligan* and *Quirin*. Ironically, each discusses the law of war. In *Quirin*, the Court said that "[f]rom the very beginning of its history this Court has recognized and applied the law of war as including that part of the law of nations which prescribes, for the conduct of war, the status, rights and duties of enemy nations as well as of enemy individuals." *Ex parte Quirin*, 317 U.S. 1, 27 (1942). Our armed services have also long followed the law of war, dating back at least to the Lieber code. Is that law not therefore part of the background understanding for interpreting the AUMF?

Alternately, is it unreasonable to assume that when Congress legislates about the use of force abroad, it does so against a background of international law that should be taken into account in interpreting its legislation? We have seen that courts construe statutes to avoid conflicts with international law where possible (see *supra*

p. 181); should we assume that Congress, too, has legislated to avoid conflict, unless it clearly overrides international law? Is there anything in the AUMF that clearly overrides law-of-war principles?

Finally, is it possible to construe "appropriate" in the AUMF to *incorporate* relevant law-of-war principles? Congress clearly has the constitutional power to incorporate under the Define and Punish Clause, and in fact has done so; it acted under that clause when it passed the Articles of War, which were cited in *Quirin* as authority for trial by military commission. 317 U.S. at 28.

3. *What Law of War?* Judge Brown eschews law-of-war principles partly because they are "not a fixed code" and lack "firm definition." Assuming that they are relevant to interpreting the AUMF, what do they provide with respect to Al-Bihani? There clearly was an armed conflict in Afghanistan when he was captured. As we saw in Chapter 9, this conflict has been characterized as one not of an international character, making most of the Geneva Conventions inapplicable to it. However, Common Article 3 would still apply, as would Article 75 of AP I. Neither specifies who may be detained, although both address conditions of detention, and Article 75 requires prompt release as soon as the circumstances justifying detention have ceased to exist.

4. *Status.* The AUMF targets organizations and persons who "planned, authorized, committed, or aided" the 9/11 attacks, or harbored such organizations or persons. In habeas litigation, the Administration proposed the following standard for detention under the AUMF:

> The President has the authority to detain persons that the President determines planned, authorized, committed, or aided the terrorist attacks that occurred on September 11, 2001, and persons who harbored those responsible for those attacks. The President also has the authority to detain persons who were part of, or substantially supported, Taliban or al Qaida forces or associated forces that are engaged in hostilities against the United States or its coalition partners, including any person who has committed a belligerent act, or has directly supported hostilities, in aid of such enemy armed forces. [*Hamlily v. Obama*, 616 F. Supp. 2d 63, 67 (D.D.C. 2009) (quoting government brief).]

The government has since explained that this standard is based on the AUMF and "draws on international laws of war to inform our interpretation of the statutory detention authority conferred by Congress in the AUMF." Remarks of Assistant Attorney General Tony West at the ABA Standing Comm. on Law and Nat'l Security Breakfast, Feb. 18, 2011, *available at* http://www.americanbar.org/content/dam/aba/multimedia/migrated/natsecurity/audio/national_security'matters.authcheckdam.mp3.

Al-Bihani was a brigade cook; the government made no claim that he was involved in the 9/11 attacks. Does he meet the Administration standard? If that standard is different from the AUMF standard, does he meet the latter? The court deemed cooking for a Taliban combat unit sufficient. But is that because he was present in the field with the brigade, because it had Al Qaeda members in its command structure, or because he carried a weapon (though he says he never fired it)? Suppose he was not in the field, but purchased food for the brigade in a Pakistani marketplace? Suppose he only donated money for that purpose? *See* Charlie Savage, *Obama Team Is Divided on Anti-Terror Tactics*, N.Y. Times, Mar. 28, 2010 (reporting that

Department of Justice's Office of Legal Counsel "found no precedents justifying detention of mere supporters of Al Qaeda who were picked up far away from enemy forces, [but] it was not prepared to state any definitive conclusion"). Suppose he quit as cook and left the brigade because he was unhappy with the pay? Suppose he was trained in an Al Qaeda camp, but as a cook, not a terrorist? *See* p. 879 n.2. Suppose he received weapons training in a camp in Pakistan, but the camp was neither Al Qaeda nor Taliban, but instead something like the local boy scouts? Can you see why the habeas courts might diverge in deciding who can be detained?

A recent district court habeas decision concluded, (quoting from habeas opinions):

> "[T]here are no settled criteria," for determining who is "part of" the Taliban, al-Qaida, or an associated force. "That determination must be made on a case-by-case basis by using a functional rather than formal approach and by focusing on the actions of the individual in relation to the organization." The Court must consider the totality of the evidence to assess the individual's relationship with the organization. But being "part of['] the Taliban, al-Qaida, or an associated force requires "some level of knowledge or intent." *See also Bensayah*, 610 F.3d at 725 ("purely independent conduct of a freelancer is not enough" to demonstrate an individual was "part of an organization.). [*Khan v. Obama*, 741 F. Supp. 2d 1, 5 (D.D.C. 2010) (omitting internal citations to habeas decisions).]

5. *Spillover" Effects?* The diverging habeas opinions may affect not just the petitioners. One scholar notes that the opinions overhang other detention operations regardless of whether such operations are subject to judicial review, because military authorities are unlikely to ignore judicial opinions about detention authority. They may also affect targeting decisions, because such decisions also pose difficult problems of group and individual identification. Chesney, *supra* p. 876, 52 B.C. L. Rev. at 773-774. The habeas courts "have become, for better or worse, the central U.S. government institution engaged in the critical — and ultimately unavoidable — task of tailoring the laws governing military activity to suit the increasingly important scenario in which states classify clandestine non-state actors as strategic threats requiring a military response." *Id. See generally id.* at 776-781 (identifying possible "detention predicates" and "constraint criteria"). In short, they have reluctantly, and by congressional default, taken the lead in crafting new principles for asymmetric warfare. *See also* Geoffrey S. Corn, *The Role of the Courts in the War on Terror: The Intersection of Hyperbole, Military Necessity, and Judicial Review*, 43 New Eng. L. Rev. 17, 36 (2008) (asserting, approvingly, that "the government might finally be forced by [*Boumediene*] and continuing judicial oversight to clearly articulate and defend the rationale for the expansive application of the term "enemy combatant" that is at the heart of the concept of a "Global War on Terror").

6. *Lawmaking Competency.* It is possible to craft guidance by analogy from 1949 Geneva Convention III, *supra* p. 236, or from customary law-of-war provisions for identifying lawful targets, *see* Chesney, *supra*, 52 B.C. L. Rev. at 793-797, but the project of law-interpreting then morphs quickly into a process of lawmaking. Do you agree with Judge Brown that this is a project for which Congress is better suited than the courts? *But see Habeas Works, supra* p. 884, at 13-16 (asserting that habeas courts have successfully engaged in traditional interpretation and application of detention

standard established by Congress); Nesbitt, *supra*, 95 Minn. L. Rev. at 247-248 (arguing that "while new detention legislation would have made sense during the first eighteen months of habeas litigation, the maturation of the jurisprudence has rendered this option unnecessary at best and counterproductive at worst. Habeas works. Congress should stand back and allow the courts to proceed.").

If this is a project for Congress, what detention standard should it adopt? *See, e.g.*, Chesney, *supra*, 52 B.C. L. Rev. at 857-858; Benjamin Wittes & Colleen A. Peppard, *Designing Detention: A Model Law for Terrorist Incapacitation* 3-4 (Brookings Inst. 2009), *available at* http://www.brookings.edu/papers/2009/0626_detention_wittes.aspx; Madeline Morris *et al.*, *After Guantánamo: War, Crime, and Detention*, Harv. L. & Pol'y Rev. Online (July 14, 2009), http:// www.hlpronline.com/Morris_HLPR_071409.pdf (appending draft of proposed legislation).

D. CLOSING GUANTÁNAMO AND CHOOSING CRIMINAL PROCESS[2]

On May 21, 2009, President Barack Obama ordered "the closing of the prison camp at Guantánamo Bay." Remarks by President Barack Obama, *Protecting Our Security and Our Values*, National Archives, Washington, D.C., May 21, 2009. Asserting that "Guantánamo set back the moral authority that is America's strongest currency in the world," the President explained that the Administration would review the cases of the remaining detainees to decide who should be prosecuted in U.S. civil courts, who should be tried by improved military commissions, who should be transferred to another country, who could neither be prosecuted nor released because they pose a continuing clear danger to the American people, and "those we have been ordered [to] release[] by the courts." *Id.*

Congress, however, erected an obstacle to closing Guantánamo by blocking funding for the transfer of any non-citizen detainee from Guantánamo to the United States, unless the Administration prepared a detailed plan for each proposed transferee. Each plan had to include, "at a minimum — (1) an assessment of the risk that the individual . . . poses to the national security of the United States, its territories, or possessions; (2) a proposal for the disposition of each such individual; (3) the measures to be taken to mitigate any risks [posed by the transfer]; (4) the location or locations at which the individual will be held under the proposal for disposition . . . ; (5) the costs associated with executing the plan, including technical and financial assistance required to be provided to State and local law enforcement agencies, if necessary, to carry out the plan; (6) a summary of the consultation required [with state and local authorities of the transferee location in the United States] . . . ; and (7) a certification by the Attorney General that under the plan the individual poses little or no security risk to the United States, its territories, or Possessions. National Defense Authorization Act for Fiscal Year 2010, Pub. L. No. 111-84, §1041, 123 Stat. 2190, 2454-2455 (2009). The appropriations limitation, as a practical matter, made transfers from Guantánamo to the United States impossible.

---

2. *See generally* Michael John Garcia et al., *Closing the Guantánamo Detention Center: Legal Issues* (Cong. Res. Serv. RL40139), Feb. 11, 2011.

The initial review process ordered by the President was completed in January 2010. It approved 36 detainees for criminal prosecution in federal court (including alleged 9/11 mastermind, Khalid Sheikh Mohammed), 126 detainees for transfer to foreign custody (including 30 approved for "conditional" detention based on the security conditions in Yemen, the country to which they could eventually be transferred), and 48 for continued detention under the AUMF. *Guantánamo Review Task Force, supra* p. 830, at ii. Detainees were designated for continued detention based on their playing a "significant organizational role" within al-Qaeda, the Taliban, or associated forces, advanced training or combat experience, expressed recidivist intent, or "a history of associations with extremist activity." *Id.* at 24.

Congress, however, acted again to block the proposed criminal prosecutions. It included the following limitation in the defense authorization for fiscal year 2011:

> None of the funds authorized to be appropriated by this Act for fiscal year 2011 may be used to transfer, release, or assist in the transfer or release to or within the United States, its territories, or possessions of Khalid Sheikh Mohammed or any other detainee who (1) is not a United States citizen or a member of the Armed Forces of the United States; and (2) is or was held on or after January 20, 2009, at United States Naval Station, Guantánamo Bay, Cuba, by the Department of Defense.

Ike Skelton National Defense Authorization Act for Fiscal Year 2011, Pub. L. No. 111-383, §1032, 124 Stat. 4137, 4351 (2011). Not content with this restriction, Congress also prohibited any use of the authorized appropriation to modify or construct new detention facilities in the United States for Guantánamo detainees. *Id.* §1034(a), 124 Stat. 4353.

The President reluctantly signed the Authorization Act, stating:

> Section 1032 represents a dangerous and unprecedented challenge to critical executive branch authority to determine when and where to prosecute Guantánamo detainees, based on the facts and the circumstances of each case and our national security interests. The prosecution of terrorists in Federal court is a powerful tool in our efforts to protect the Nation and must be among the options available to us. Any attempt to deprive the executive branch of that tool undermines our Nation's counterterrorism efforts and has the potential to harm our national security.
>
> With respect to section 1033, the restrictions on the transfer of detainees to the custody or effective control of foreign countries interfere with the authority of the executive branch to make important and consequential foreign policy and national security determinations regarding whether and under what circumstances such transfers should occur in the context of an ongoing armed conflict. We must have the ability to act swiftly and to have broad flexibility in conducting our negotiations with foreign countries. [Statement by the President on H.R. 6523 (Jan. 7, 2011).]

If the Act's limitation is constitutional, it effectively prevents the President from shutting down Guantánamo as long as the administration believes that any detainee now held there cannot be tried by a military commission for whatever reason but is too dangerous to release. It does not apply, however, to persons not detained at Guantánamo. Nor does it bar or condition the criminal prosecution of persons arrested in the United States for terrorist or related crimes.

Shortly after the report on the review process, Attorney General Eric Holder announced a decision to prosecute the man who tried to bomb a Northwest Airlines flight (popularly known as the "the underwear bomber"), following what he characterized as a long-standing "practice . . . to arrest and detain under federal criminal law all terrorist suspects who are apprehended inside the United States." Letter from Attorney General Eric Holder to Senator Mitch McConnell Regarding Umar Farouk Abdulmutallab, Feb. 3, 2010, *available at* http://www.justice.gov/cjs/docs/ag-letter-2-3-10.pdf. He noted that the initial transfers of both Jose Padilla and Ali Saleh Kahlah al-Marri into "law of war custody raised serious statutory and constitutional questions in the courts concerning the lawfulness of the government's actions and spawned lengthy litigation" that was only ended by their return to "law enforcement custody" and eventual criminal prosecution and imprisonment. *Id.* at 3.

In March, 2011, the White House issued a new policy on the Guantánamo detainees, back-pedaling from the President's 2009 pledge to close the facility.

White House, Office of the Press Secretary, Fact Sheet: New Actions on Guantánamo and Detainee Policy

Mar. 7, 2011

In a speech nearly two years ago at the National Archives, the President advanced a four-part approach to closing the detention facility at Guantánamo Bay, keeping our country safe, and upholding the law: (1) to bring detainees to justice in prosecutions in either federal civilian courts or in reformed military commissions, (2) to comply with court-ordered releases of detainees, (3) to transfer detainees from Guantánamo whenever it is possible to do so safely and humanely, and (4) when neither prosecution nor other legal options are available, to hold these individuals in lawful military detention. He affirmed that "whenever feasible, we will try those who have violated American criminal laws in federal courts."

The Administration remains committed to closing the detention facility at Guantánamo Bay, and to maintain a lawful, sustainable and principled regime for the handling of detainees there, consistent with the full range of U.S. national security interests. In keeping with the strategy we laid out, we are proceeding today with the following actions:

Resumption of Military Commissions

The Secretary of Defense will issue an order rescinding his prior suspension on the swearing and referring of new charges in the military commissions. New charges in military commissions have been suspended since the President announced his review of detainee policy, shortly after taking office.

The Administration, working on a bipartisan basis with members of Congress, has successfully enacted key reforms, such as a ban on the use of statements taken as a result of cruel, inhuman or degrading treatment, and a better system for handling classified information. With these and other reforms, military commissions, along with prosecutions of suspected terrorists in civilian courts, are an available and important tool in combating international terrorists that fall within their jurisdiction while upholding the rule of law.

Executive Order on Periodic Review

In the Archives speech, the President recognized there are certain Guantánamo detainees who have not been charged, convicted, or designated for transfer, but must continue to be detained because they "in effect, remain at war with the United States." For this category of detainees, the President stated: "We must have a thorough process of periodic review, so that any prolonged detention is carefully evaluated and justified."

Today, the President issued an Executive Order establishing such a process for these detainees. . . .

. . . If a final determination is made that a detainee no longer constitutes a significant threat to our security, the Executive Order provides that the Secretaries of State and Defense are to identify a suitable transfer location outside the United States, consistent with the national security and foreign policy interests of the United States and applicable law. As the President has stated before, no Guantánamo detainee will be released into the United States. . . .

Continued Commitment to Article III Trials

Pursuant to the President's order to close Guantánamo, this Administration instituted the most thorough review process ever applied to the detainees held there. Among other things, for the first time, we consolidated all information available to the federal government about these individuals. That information was carefully examined by some of our government's most experienced prosecutors, a process that resulted in the referral of 36 individuals for potential prosecution. Since the time of those referrals, the Departments of Justice and Defense, with the advice of career military and civilian prosecutors, have been working to bring these defendants to justice, securing convictions in a number of cases and evaluating others to determine which system — military or civilian — is most appropriate based on the nature of the evidence and traditional principles of prosecution.

In recent months, some in Congress have sought to undermine this process. In December, Congress enacted restrictions on the prosecution of Guantánamo detainees in Federal courts. The Administration opposes these restrictions as a dangerous and unprecedented challenge to Executive authority to select the most effective means available to bring terrorists to justice and safeguard our security. The Executive Branch possesses the information and expertise necessary to make the best judgment about where a particular prosecution should proceed, and Congress's intrusion upon this function is inconsistent with the long-standing and appropriate allocation of authority between the Executive and Legislative branches. . . .

Military commissions should proceed in cases where it has been determined appropriate to do so. Because there are situations, however, in which our federal courts are a more appropriate forum for trying particular individuals, we will seek repeal of the restrictions imposed by Congress, so that we can move forward in the forum that is, in our judgment, most in line with our national security interests and the interests of justice.

We will continue to vigorously defend the authority of the Executive to make these well-informed prosecution decisions, both with respect to those detainees in our custody at Guantánamo and those we may apprehend in the future. A one-size-fits-all policy for the prosecution of suspected terrorists, whether for past or future cases, undermines our Nation's counterterrorism efforts and harms our national security.

Support for a Strong International Legal Framework

Because of the vital importance of the rule of law to the effectiveness and legitimacy of our national security policy, the Administration is announcing our support for two important components of the international legal framework that covers armed conflicts: Additional Protocol II and Article 75 of Additional Protocol I to the 1949 Geneva Conventions.

Additional Protocol II, which contains detailed humane treatment standards and fair trial guarantees that apply in the context of non-international armed conflicts, was originally submitted to the Senate for approval by President Reagan in 1987. The Administration urges the

Senate to act as soon as practicable on this Protocol, to which 165 States are a party. An extensive interagency review concluded that United States military practice is already consistent with the Protocol's provisions. . . .

Article 75 of Additional Protocol I, which sets forth fundamental guarantees for persons in the hands of opposing forces in an international armed conflict, is similarly important to the international legal framework. Although the Administration continues to have significant concerns with Additional Protocol I, Article 75 is a provision of the treaty that is consistent with our current policies and practice and is one that the United States has historically supported. Our adherence to these principles is also an important safeguard against the mistreatment of captured U.S. military personnel. The U.S. Government will therefore choose out of a sense of legal obligation to treat the principles set forth in Article 75 as applicable to any individual it detains in an international armed conflict, and expects all other nations to adhere to these principles as well.

NOTES AND QUESTIONS

1. *Constitutionality of Limitations.* The President "shall take Care that the Laws be faithfully executed," U.S. Const. art. II, §3. The Ike Skelton Act effectively prohibits execution of the criminal laws against Guantánamo detainees by criminal prosecution in a federal court, as there is no such court in Guantánamo. Is it unconstitutional? The Act also conditions any transfer of a detainee to foreign custody on a burdensome certification, not here reproduced. Is such a condition constitutional?

2. *The Choices Left.* If the Ike Skelton Act's limitations are constitutional, what choices are left for dealing with the remaining Guantánamo detainees? One is to prosecute them by military commission. See Chapter 36. Another is to continue their detention in Guantánamo, effectively leaving their future to the habeas process and the newly adopted process for periodic review. A third is to transfer them to foreign custody, if the arduous certification process imposed by the bill is satisfied. A recent bill would zero out appropriations for even such transfers. *See* Benjamin Wittes, *House GOP to Supreme Court: Bring Gitmo Detainees Here*, Lawfare, Feb. 23, 2011, *available at* http://www.lawfareblog.com/2011/02/a-house-gop-gift-to-habeas.

What choices are left for dealing with future captives? The Act's limitations only apply to Guantánamo detainees, so future captives presumably could be detained and/or criminally prosecuted in the United States. But given the Administration's professed desire still to close the Guantánamo Detention Center, and the political controversy that has attended efforts to try foreign terrorists in the United States, there may be a strong incentive to "outsource" their detention to allies in Afghanistan or Iraq. Alternatively, the detention quandary could be avoided altogether if military operations invariably kill rather than capture. *See* Chesney, *supra* p. 876, 52 B.C. L. Rev. at 804 (asserting, on this view, that the dramatic uptick in targeted killing during the Obama administration "is no surprise").

3. *Presumption for (Or Against) Criminal Prosecution?* The White House Fact Statement asserts that although "[m]ilitary commissions should proceed in cases where it has been determined appropriate to do so, . . . there are situations . . . in which our federal courts are a more appropriate forum for trying particular individuals." The federal courts are open and have gained ever-increasing experience trying terrorism cases since 9/11, and the government has enjoyed a virtually unblemished record of victories in terrorism cases. Why should there not be a presumption in favor of criminal prosecution of terror suspects and criminal imprisonment of terror convicts?

VI
Interrogating Terrorist Suspects

Interrogating Terrorist Suspects

The next three chapters are about the use of torture to extract intelligence information from detainees who will not willingly talk. Reliance on torture to extract confessions is at least as old as Ancient Greece. Before and during the Inquisition, trial by ordeal employed torture to supplement circumstantial evidence in a criminal case. If the accused confessed during torture, he could be convicted. John H. Langbein, *The Legal History of Torture*, in *Torture: A Collection* 93-95 (Sanford Levinson ed., 2004).

In intelligence investigations, especially those that take place during war or in the aftermath of a terrorist attack, investigators do not know in advance what the detainee knows that may be of value. Possible answers range from nothing to something significant. How should legal rules guide this uncertain quest for information? If the human tendency is to extract information by any means necessary, is abusive interrogation an inevitable result of any regime short of an absolute ban on abuse? *See* Joseph Margulies, *Guantanamo and the Abuse of Presidential Power* 29 (2006) (so arguing).

When grotesque photographs of detainees being abused by U.S. personnel at the Abu Ghraib detention facility in Iraq became prime time news in 2004, our nation's leaders engaged in an often vituperative debate about whether gathering intelligence through torture is effective — whether the gain is worth the pain. For example, two former U.S. military commanders wrote in 2007:

> ...These assertions that "torture works" may reassure a fearful public, but it is a false security...and any "flexibility" about torture at the top drops down the chain of command like a stone....If we forfeit our values by signaling that they are negotiable in situations of grave or imminent danger, we drive those undecideds into the arms of the enemy. [Charles C. Krulak & Joseph P. Hoar, *It's Our Cage, Too*, Wash. Post, May 17, 2007.]

This chapter has two objectives. In Part A, we ask you first to review the report of a court-martial at the beginning of the twentieth century and the government's own account of "enhanced interrogation" techniques in the war on terror, then consider where you would draw the line between permissible interrogation and torture. In Part B, a judicial decision and Notes and Questions explore the legal landscape that governs interrogation for intelligence purposes.

In Chapter 32, we ask you to apply this legal framework to a case study of coercive interrogation during the war on terror. In Chapter 33, we consider whether sending suspects to foreign states for coercive interrogation (and detention without trial) avoids or changes that framework.

A.   WHEN IS INTERROGATION TORTURE?

Part of the Spanish-American War was fought in the Philippines, where the U.S. defeat of the Spanish in Manila in 1898 was instrumental in affirming the independence of the Philippines from Spain. U.S. annexation of the Philippines after the war with Spain ended provoked a three-year insurgency by Philippine revolutionary forces. *See* Brian M. Linn, *The Philippine War: 1899-1902* (2000). During the insurrection, several U.S. military officers were court-martialed for war crimes. The report by the Judge Advocate General on the trial of one Army officer follows.

Court-Martial of Major Edwin F. Glenn[1]
Samar, Philippine Islands, April 1902
S. Doc. No. 213, 57th Cong. 20-28

War Department
Office of the Judge-Advocate-General
Washington July 18, 1902

THE SECRETARY OF WAR.

SIR: I beg leave to submit the following report upon the record of trial in the case of Maj. Edwin F. Glenn, Fifth U.S. Infantry.

The court-martial was appointed by the President in an Executive order dated April 30, 1902, and met at Catbalogan, in the island of Samar, on the 23d of May. . . .

Major Glenn was tried on the following charge and specification.

CHARGE

Conduct to the prejudice of good order and military discipline, in violation of the sixty-second article of war.

SPECIFICATION

In that Maj. Edwin F. Glenn, Fifth U.S. Infantry . . . being on duty commanding the United States troops while at the pueblo of Igbarras, province of Iloilo, island of Panay, Philippine Islands, and having in his charge one Tobeniano Ealdama, presidente of the town on Igbarras aforesaid, did unlawfully order, direct, and, by his presence and authority, cause an officer and soldiers, subject to his the said Glenn's

[1. The report may be viewed in its entirety *at* http://web.lexis-nexis.com.lawezproxy.syr.edu/congcomp/document?_m=9c232820280cc08cf2cfdb65e96d8a09&_docnum=1&wchp=dGLbVlb-zSkSA&_md5=cd1516627794a8a5c487192fa20b3f30. — Eds.]

command, to execute upon him, the said Tobeniano Ealdama, a method of punishment commonly known in the Philippine Islands as the "water cure;" that is, did cause water to be introduced into the mouth and stomach of the said Ealdama against his will.

This at Igbarras, Panay, on or about the 27th day of November, 1900.

The accused pleads "Not guilty" to the charge and specification, but submitted the following statement, in the nature of an admission of fact, in connection with his arraignment: . . .

> I would like to state to the court, in explanation of this plea, the facts and circumstances that brought it about. . . . [A] short time since the commanding general of the Division of the Philippines called me into his office and said that he had just received a cablegram from the United States informing him that two enlisted men, now citizens, but formerly of the Twenty-sixth U.S. Volunteer Infantry, had testified before the United States Senate committee that I, while in command at Igbaras, Panay, of a detachment of United States troops had caused the water cure, so called, to be given to the presidente of that town. And the general added that his orders were to prefer charges against me and bring me to trial. . . .
>
> Subsequently this question came up between myself and the judge-advocate, and it was insisted that I should admit the word "water cure," and I have admitted it. My only reason for objection was that the word "water cure" is not a fixed term in its meaning. . . .

Tobeniano Ealdama, the native who was subjected to the water cure by Major Glenn's order, was called as a witness for the prosecution and testified (in Spanish) that . . . Major Glenn arrived at Igbarras in command of a detachment of United States troops, established his headquarters at the convent, and sent for witness (Ealdama). The witness was asked where General Delgado was, and replied that he was not in the town of Igbarras. He was then asked:

Q: What did they do to you then?

A: They told me if I did not tell I would be punished. They told me to take my shirt off, and they tied my arms. The captain and doctor and lieutenant sat at the table and there were some soldiers in the hallway. They laid me on my back and had some water with a faucet, and held my arms tight and proceeded to open my mouth. After they gave me some water for a little while the doctor told them to stop, and then asked me the whereabouts of General Delgado. I told them that I did not know where the general was, and they proceeded again with the water. They gave me water, some through the nose and some through the mouth. I had shortness of breath and pain in the stomach.

Q: Did it have any other effect on you?

A: My throat also hurt me on account of so much water put through it.

Q: How much water did you take in?

A: Four bottles, about four bottles, as best I know.

Q: What effect did that have upon you?

A: I had some pain in my throat.

Q: Did you retain this water on your stomach?

A: I kept it in my stomach.

Q: Did any come off of it?

A: Yes, sir; I did vomit some.

Q: What did they do with you then?

A: They asked me quite a number of questions and I did not know the answer to them, and the Major said, "All right, let him up."

Q: What did they do to you then?

A: I went to the table and sat down and waited, and they administered water to the school-teacher while I was waiting.

Q: Where did you go then?
A: I went downstairs.
Q: What did they do to you there?
A: They asked me if I was in communication with the insurrectos. I said that I was not.
Q: What did they do to you then?
A: They said, "You are a liar. Take off your clothes."
Q: Well, go on.
A: Then I was sleeping. (The interpreter said that he thought the witness meant that he was in a recumbent position.) They brought a kind of syringe.
Q: What did they do with it?
A: Open my mouth and put water in my mouth.
Q: What kind?
A: Salty.
Q: How much did they put in?
A: About one bottle.
Q: What effect did that have?
A: It was very bitter.
Q: Did it have any other effect?
A: My stomach and throat pained me, and also the nose where they passed the salt water through . . .

. . . [S]ubsequent to the occurrences above testified to, the witness (Tobeniano Ealdama) was tried by a military commission at Isiolo between June 7 and 14, 1901, under the charge of "being a war traitor," the specification alleging holding intercourse with the enemy by means of letters, contributing money, and food to the insurrectionary forces, and directing others, members of said forces, to collect contributions. He was also charged with "violating the laws of war" by joining and becoming a captain in the insurrectionary forces and recruiting and swearing into the Insurgent service the members of the local police force of Igbarras. He was found guilty of the offenses charged and sentenced to confinement at hard labor for ten years. He was released from confinement to enable him to testify as a witness in this case.

The accused admitted the facts in connection with the administration of the water cure, but undertook to show, in defense, that his act was not unlawful; that is, it was justified by military necessity and was warranted as a legitimate exercise of force by the laws of war.

In support of this defense it was attempted to show that Ealdama was a war traitor; that he acted as an officer of the insurgent forces; that he organized the native police of Igbarras as a part of such insurgent forces, and he collected contributions of money and supplies for the insurrectionary cause and transmitted them to their destination. The order announcing the result of Ealdama's trial by military commissions, which has already been mentioned, was introduced in support of this contention. . . .

. . . [The] resort to torture is attempted to be justified, not as an exceptional occurrence, but as the habitual method of obtaining information from individual insurgents. The accused took considerable pains to establish the fact that torture was the usual practice of the Spaniards; that it was practiced by the insurgents; and that when a native was punished by the Americans for refusing to assist them in their operations against the insurgents he was not subsequently punished by the insurrectionary leaders for giving such assistance. If this be admitted, the accused was attempting to justify his conduct, not as an act dictated by military necessity, but as a method of conducting operations.

When looked at from this point of view the defense falls completely, inasmuch as it is attempted to establish the principle that a belligerent who is at war with a savage or semicivilized enemy may conduct his operations in violation of the rules of civilized war. This no modern State will admit for an instant; nor was it the rule in the Philippine Islands. It is proper to observe that the several general officers who have exercised chief command in the Philippine Islands have, all of them, expressly forbidden practices like that of which the accused is here charged. Their principal subordinates have given similar instructions forbidding a resort to cruelty in the most positive terms. . . .

The rules respecting the treatment of guerrillas contemplate the existence of large armies which are annoyed in their operations by the presence of small guerrilla bands — that is, by the acts of small bodies of the enemy who are not a part of his combatant forces and who conduct their operations in violation of the rules of war. This was not the case in the Philippine Islands generally, where there were no large armies operating against each other as organized bodies. The troops were operating in detachments against isolated bands or bodies of insurgents, all of which were acting as guerrillas and were conducting their operations in flagrant disregard of the rules of civilized war. The situation thus presented was difficult and to the last degree exasperating, but it did not relieve the officers and men of the occupying forces of their obligation to adhere to the rules of war in the efforts put forth by them with a view to suppress the insurrection and restore public order. . . .

The accused was found guilty upon both charge and specification, and the following sentence was imposed:

> To be suspended from command for the period of one month, and to forfeit the sum of $50 for the same period. The court is thus lenient on account of the circumstances as shown in evidence.

Although the accused was tried for but a single administration of the water-cure — not for habitually resorting to it in the conduct of operations against the insurrectionary forces — the sentence imposed, in my opinion, was inadequate to the offense established by the testimony of the witnesses and the admission of the accused. The sympathy of the court seems to have been with the accused throughout the trial; the feeling of the [jury] members in that respect is also indicated by qualifying words which are added to the sentence, and by the unanimous recommendation to clemency which is appended to the record.

I . . . recommended that the sentence be confirmed and carried into effect.

Very respectfully,

George B. Davis
Judge-Advocate General

On April 16, 2009, the following memorandum, signed by Principal Deputy Assistant Attorney General Stephen G. Bradbury, was released pursuant to a Freedom of Information Act (FOIA) request. Apparently, the General Counsel of the CIA had sought the advice of the Office of Legal Counsel, Department of Justice, concerning the legality of a series of "enhanced interrogation techniques" that were employed by the CIA between 2002 and 2005 in Afghanistan (and perhaps elsewhere). Assistant

AG Bradbury first described the techniques, as he understood them, in the part of the memorandum reproduced here. He quoted an internal CIA document as his source, *Background Paper on CIA's Combined Use of Interrogation Techniques* (Dec. 30, 2004), also released following a FOIA request, and *available at* http://www.aclu.org/torturefoia/released/082409/olcremand/2004olc97.pdf.

Application of 18 U.S.C. §§2340-2340A to the Combined Use of Certain Techniques in the Interrogation of High Value al Qaeda Detainees

Office of Legal Counsel, U.S. Department of Justice (May 10, 2005)
http://www.fas.org/irp/agency/doj/olc/combined.pdf

Memorandum for: John A. Rizzo, Senior Deputy General Counsel,
                Central Intelligence Agency

From: Stephen G. Bradbury, Principal Deputy Assistant Attorney General

Phases of the Interrogation Process

The first phase of the interrogation process, "Initial Conditions," does not involve interrogation techniques.... The "Initial Conditions" nonetheless set the stage for use of the interrogation techniques, which come later.

. . . [B]efore being flown to the site of interrogation, a detainee is given a medical examination. He then is "securely shackled and is deprived of sight and sound through the use of blindfolds, earmuffs, and hoods" during the flight. An onboard medical officer monitors his condition. Security personnel also monitor the detainee for signs of distress. Upon arrival at the site, the detainee "finds himself in complete control of Americans" and is subjected to "precise, quiet, and almost clinical" procedures designed to underscore "the enormity and suddenness of the change in environment, the uncertainty about what will happen next, and the potential dread [a detainee] may have of US custody." His head and face are shaved; his physical condition is documented through photographs taken while he is nude; and he is given medical and psychological interviews to assess his condition and to make sure there are no contraindications to the use of any particular interrogation techniques.

The detainee then enters the next phase, the "Transition to Interrogation." The interrogators conduct an initial interview, "in a relatively benign environment," to ascertain whether the detainee is willing to cooperate. The detainee is "normally clothed but seated and shackled for security purposes." The interrogators take "an open, non-threatening approach," but the detainee "would have to provide information on actionable threats and location information on High-Value targets at large — not lower-level information — for interrogators to continue with [this] neutral approach." If the detainee does not meet this "very high" standard, the interrogators submit a detailed interrogation plan to CIA headquarters for approval. If the medical and psychological assessments find no contraindications to the proposed plan, and if senior CIA officers at headquarters approve some or all of the plan through a cable transmitted to the site of the interrogation, the interrogation moves to the next phase.

Three interrogation techniques are typically used to bring the detainee to "a baseline, dependent state," "demonstrat[ing] to the [detainee] that he has no control over basic human needs" and helping to make him "perceive and value his personal welfare, comfort, and immediate needs more than the information he is protecting." The three techniques used to establish this "baseline" are nudity, sleep deprivation (with shackling and, at least at times, with use of a diaper), and dietary manipulation. These techniques . . . "require little to no physical interaction between the detainees and interrogator."

Other techniques, which "require physical interaction between the interrogator and detainee," are characterized as "corrective" and "are used principally to correct, startle, or achieve another enabling objective with the detainee." These techniques "are not used simultaneously but are often used interchangeably during an individual interrogation session." The insult slap is used "periodically throughout the interrogation process when the interrogator needs to immediately correct the detainee or provide a consequence to a detainee's response or non-response." The insult slap "can be used in combination with water dousing or kneeling stress positions"—techniques that are not characterized as "corrective." Another corrective technique, the abdominal slap, "is similar to the insult slap in application and desired result" and "provides the variation necessary to keep a high level of unpredictability in the interrogation process." The abdominal slap may be simultaneously combined with water dousing, stress positions, and wall standing. A third corrective technique, the facial hold, "is used sparingly throughout interrogation." It is not painful, but "demonstrates the interrogator's control over the [detainee]." It too may be simultaneously combined with water dousing, stress positions, and wall standing. Finally, the attention grasp "may be used several times in the same interrogation" and may be simultaneously combined with water dousing or kneeling stress positions.

Some techniques are characterized as "coercive." These techniques "place the detainee in more physical and psychological stress." Coercive techniques "are typically not used in combination, although some combined use is possible." Walling "[where a detainee is slammed against a false wall, and the loud sound of the impact creates the impression of a powerful impact] is one of the most effective interrogation techniques because it wears down the [detainee] physically, heightens uncertainty in the detainee about what the interrogator may do to him, and creates a sense of dread when the [detainee] knows he is about to be walled again." A detainee "may be walled one time (one impact with the wall) to make a point or twenty to thirty times consecutively when the interrogator requires a more significant response to a question," and "will be walled multiple times" during a session designed to be intense. Walling cannot practically be used at the same time as other interrogation techniques.

Water temperature and other considerations of safety established by OMS [Office of Medical Services] limit the use of another coercive technique, water dousing. The technique "may be used frequently within those guidelines." As suggested above, interrogators may combine water dousing with other techniques, such as stress positions, wall standing, the insult slap, or the abdominal slap.

The use of stress positions is "usually self-limiting in that temporary muscle fatigue usually leads to the [detainee's] being unable to maintain the stress position after a period of time." Depending on the particular position, stress positions may be combined with water dousing, the insult slap, the facial hold, and the attention grasp. Another coercive technique, wall standing, is "usually self-limiting" in the same way as stress positions. It may be combined with water dousing and the abdominal slap. OMS guidelines limit the technique of cramped confinement to no more than eight hours at a time and 18 hours a day, and confinement in the "small box" is limited to two hours. Cramped confinement cannot be used in simultaneous combination with corrective or other coercive techniques.

We understand that the CIA's use of all these interrogation techniques is subject to ongoing monitoring by interrogation team members who will direct that techniques be discontinued if there is a deviation from prescribed procedures and by medical and psychological personnel from OMS who will direct that any or all techniques be discontinued if in their professional judgment the detainee may otherwise suffer severe physical or mental pain or suffering.

A Prototypical Interrogation

In a "prototypical interrogation," the detainee begins his first interrogation session stripped of his clothes, shackled, and hooded, with the walling collar over his head and around his neck. The interrogators remove the hood and explain that the detainee can improve his situation by cooperating and may say that the interrogators "will do what it takes to get important information." As soon as the detainee does anything inconsistent with the interrogators' instructions, the interrogators use an insult slap or abdominal slap. They employ walling if it becomes clear that the detainee is not cooperating in the interrogation. This sequence "may continue for several more iterations as the interrogators continue to measure the [detainee's] resistance posture and apply a negative consequence to [his] resistance efforts." The interrogators and security officers then put the detainee into position for standing sleep deprivation, begin dietary manipulation through a liquid diet, and keep the detainee nude (except for a diaper). The first interrogation session, which could have lasted from 30 minutes to several hours, would then be at an end.

If the interrogation team determines there is a need to continue, and if the medical and psychological personnel advise that there are no contraindications, a second session may begin. The interval between sessions could be as short as an hour or as long as 24 hours. At the start of the second session, the detainee is released from the position for standing sleep deprivation, is hooded, and is positioned against the walling wall, with the walling collar over his head and around his neck. Even before removing the hood, the interrogators use the attention grasp to startle the detainee. The interrogators take off the hood and begin questioning. If the detainee does not give appropriate answers to the first questions, the interrogators use an insult slap or abdominal slap. They employ walling if they determine that the detainee "is intent on maintaining his resistance posture." This sequence "may continue for multiple iterations as the interrogators continue to measure the [detainee's] resistance posture." The interrogators then increase the pressure on the detainee by using a hose to douse the detainee with water for several minutes. They stop and start the dousing as they continue the interrogation. They then end the session by placing the detainee into the same circumstances as at the end of the first session: the detainee is in the standing position for sleep deprivation, is nude (except for a diaper), and is subjected to dietary manipulation. Once again, the session could have lasted from 30 minutes to several hours.

Again, if the interrogation team determines there is a need to continue, and if the medical and psychological personnel find no contraindications, a third session may follow. The session begins with the detainee positioned as at the beginning of the second. If the detainee continues to resist, the interrogators continue to use walling and water dousing. The corrective techniques — the insult slap, the abdominal slap, the facial hold, the attention grasp — "may be used several times during this session based on the responses and actions of the [detainee]." The interrogators integrate stress positions and wall standing into the session. Furthermore, "[i]ntense questioning and walling would be repeated multiple times." Interrogators "use one technique to support another." For example, they threaten the use of walling unless the detainee holds a stress position, thus inducing the detainee to remain in the position longer than he otherwise would. At the end of the session, the interrogators and security personnel place the detainee into the same circumstances as at the end of the first two sessions, with the detainee subject to sleep deprivation, nudity, and dietary manipulation.

In later sessions, the interrogators use those techniques that are proving most effective and drop the others. Sleep deprivation "may continue to the 70 to 120 hour range, or possibly beyond for the hardest resisters, but in no case exceed the 180-hour time limit." If the medical or psychological personnel find contraindications, sleep deprivation will end earlier. While continuing the use of sleep deprivation, nudity, and dietary manipulation, the interrogators may add cramped confinement. As the detainee begins to cooperate, the interrogators "begin gradually to decrease the use of interrogation techniques." They may permit the detainee to sit, supply clothes, and provide more appetizing food.

The entire process in this "prototypical interrogation" may last 30 days. If additional time is required and a new approval is obtained from headquarters, interrogation may go longer than 30 days. Nevertheless, "[o]n average, the actual use of interrogation techniques covers a period of three to seven days, but can vary upwards to fifteen days based on the resilience of the [detainee]." . . .

NOTES AND QUESTIONS

1. *Definitions: Do You Know It When You See It?* The ban on torture is widely said to be *jus cogens* — a universal norm. *See, e.g., Filartiga v. Peña-Irala*, 630 F.2d 876, 884 (2d Cir. 1980) (finding that "official torture is now prohibited by the law of nations"); *Tel-Oren v. Libyan Arab Republic*, 726 F.2d 774, 781, 791 n.20 (D.C. Cir. 1984) (Edwards, J., concurring), *cert. denied*, 470 U.S. 1003 (1985) (asserting that "commentators have begun to identify a handful of heinous actions — each of which violates definable, universal and obligatory norms," including, at a minimum, bans on governmental "torture").

We consider the attempted legal definitions of torture in the next part of this chapter, but if the ban on torture is *jus cogens*, do we need a legal definition? Should we simply know torture when we see it? Which, if any, of the techniques described above do you consider torture? Why? Does it matter to you that we have court-martialed our own soldiers for using such techniques? Would you give the same answer in any set of circumstances? Can a technique not be torture if applied alone, but constitute torture when combined with other techniques? That is, can a whole interrogation procedure amount to torture even if its parts, standing alone, do not?

Even if you are unclear whether a technique — or battery of techniques — is torture, you might well conclude that it is inhumane and offensive to human dignity.

For example, after objections to Israeli mistreatment of detainees during the Palestinian Intifada, the Israeli Supreme Court ruled that certain interrogation methods approved for use by Israel's security services — hooding, shaking, forced crouch on toes, painful handcuffing, seating detainees on low and inclined stools, sleep deprivation, and prolonged extremely loud music — violated the detainees' constitutional protections to a right of dignity, based on Israeli domestic law. *Public Committee Against Torture in Israel v. State of Israel*, HC, 5100/94 (1999). How would you characterize the techniques described in the court-martial report and the OLC memo set out above?

Would a universal definition of torture or inhumane treatment be a good idea? Would it matter? *See* Oren Gross, *Are Torture Warrants Warranted? Pragmatic Absolutism and Official Disobedience*, 88 Minn. L. Rev. 1481, 1487 (2004) ("preventive interrogational torture is far too complex to be addressed by definitional juggling"); Jeremy Waldron, *Torture and Positive Law: Jurisprudence for the White House*, 105 Colum. L. Rev. 1681, 1699 (2005) (a precise definition of torture is advisable, because "if the terms [are] . . . indeterminate, the person to whom the prohibition is addressed may not know exactly what is required of him"). *Compare* John T. Parry, *"Just For Fun": Understanding Torture and Understanding Abu Ghraib*, 1 J. Nat'l Security L. & Pol'y 253, 262-270 (2005) (asserting that the United States and other nations play a "definitional game" where governments parse language and deny responsibility for conduct that goes too far).

2. *Waterboarding.* The interrogation technique described in the *Glenn* court-martial — the "water cure," or more recently waterboarding — pre-dates the Inquisition and owes its longevity and apparent appeal to the fact that it causes extreme physical and mental suffering, but leaves no marks on the body. Eric Weiner, *Waterboarding: A Tortured History* (National Pub. Radio, Nov. 3, 2007), *available at http://www.npr.org/templates/story/story.php?storyId=15886834.* For another description of waterboarding, from another memo prepared for the CIA, *see Memorandum for John Rizzo, Acting General Counsel of the Central Intelligence Agency, from U.S. Department of Justice, Office of Legal Counsel Re: Interrogation of Al Qaeda Operative* 3-4 (Aug. 1, 2002). *See* Joby Warrick, *CIA Tactics Endorsed in Secret Memos*, Wash. Post, Oct. 15, 2008.

Does waterboarding constitute torture? Federal courts in the United States have punished law enforcement personnel for waterboarding, including local sheriffs and Philippine government agents. *See United States v. Lee*, 744 F.2d 1124 (5th Cir. 1984); *In re Estate of Ferdinand E. Marcos, Human Rights Litig.*, 910 F. Supp. 1460, 1463 (D. Haw. 1995). Can you draft language for a law that would forbid use of waterboarding? Would a ban on "torture" accomplish the objective?

3. *The CIA and Torture.* The 2005 Memorandum, written for the CIA, concludes that none of the "enhanced interrogation techniques" described there, alone or in combination, necessarily constitutes torture. Do you agree? What legal standards should be used to measure the CIA practices? Can you think of any reason why CIA rules for coercive interrogation should differ from those followed by the military? By civilian law enforcement personnel?

4. *Who Decides What Interrogation Conduct Is Unlawful?* The official policy of the United States is to condemn and prohibit torture. *See generally* U.S. Dep't of State, *Initial Report of the United States of America to the UN Committee Against Torture*

(Oct. 15, 1999), *available at* http://www.state.gov/www/global/human_rights/ torture_intro.html ("Torture is prohibited by law throughout the United States. It is categorically denounced as a matter of policy and as a tool of state authority."); *Second Periodic Report of the United States of America to the Committee Against Torture* (May 6, 2005), *available at* http://www.state.gov/g/drl/rls/45738.htm ("United States is unequivocally opposed to the use and practice of torture.... No circumstance whatsoever... may be invoked as a justification for or defense to committing torture."). Who decides how to translate the policy into enforceable rules?

5. *The Ticking Bomb: Utilitarianism vs. Morality?* Is it *ever* justifiable to torture a detainee? One perspective emphasizes a range of practical problems that seriously limit the value of information obtained through torture, most importantly the fact that the person being interrogated can be expected to say whatever he thinks the interrogator wants to hear—in order to make the pain stop. Thus, the information is inherently unreliable. *See* Jeannine Bell, *"Behind This Mortal Bone": The (In)effectiveness of Torture*, 83 Ind. L.J. 339 (2008); *see also* J. M. Arrigo, *A Utilitarian Argument Against Torture Interrogation of Terrorists*, 10 Sci. & Eng'g Ethics 543 (2004). But the Bush administration consistently maintained that its harsh interrogation techniques produced intelligence that helped prevent terrorist attacks. For example, officials claimed that Khalid Sheikh Mohammed, the mastermind of the 9/11 attacks, provided detailed intelligence about the Al Qaeda network after being subjected to waterboarding, and that Abu Zubaydah, a top Al Qaeda strategist, implicated Jose Padilla in a dirty-bomb plot after coercive interrogation. Stephen Grey, *Ghost Plane: The True Story of the CIA Torture Program* 242-243 (2006). If this true, does it legitimate torture in some circumstances?

The mere possibility that coercive interrogation could save many lives creates an undoubted and morally complex tension between the need to obtain information and the condoning of torture. Assume, for example, that authorities have in custody someone whom they feel certain has placed an especially destructive explosive device somewhere in a large shopping mall. The explosive may go off at any time, and there may not be enough time to evacuate the mall. If the bomb detonates, thousands will die. The detainee is believed to be the only person with knowledge of the bomb, and he will not talk. Should the interrogators torture the detainee in hopes of learning the location of the bomb before it is too late? *Compare* Alan M. Dershowitz, *Why Terrorism Works* 142-149 (2002) (torture techniques may be morally and legally justified in some circumstances), *with* Association of the Bar of the City of New York, Comm. on Int'l Human Rights, Comm. on Military Affairs & Justice, *Human Rights Standards Applicable to the United States' Interrogation of Detainees* 8-9 (Apr. 30, 2004), *available at* http://www.abcny.org/pdf/HUMANRIGHTS.pdf ("Condoning torture under any circumstances erodes one of the most basic principles of international law and human rights and contradicts our values as a democratic state"), *and* David Luban, *Liberalism, Torture, and the Ticking Bomb*, 91 Va. L. Rev. 1425 (2005) (ticking-bomb scenarios may be used to rationalize institutionalized practices and procedures of torture). *See also* Kim Lane Scheppele, *Hypothetical Torture in the "War on Terrorism,"* 1 J. Nat'l Security L. & Pol'y 285 (2005) (taking a "hard line" against torture on sociological grounds). The Convention Against Torture, to which the United States is a party, says torture can never be justified. *See infra* p. 915. Professor Jeremy Waldron would not allow the authorization of torture even in the ticking-bomb scenario. Waldron argues that a line on what techniques are permitted has to be drawn "somewhere, and I say we should draw it where the law requires it, and where the human rights tradition has insisted that it should be drawn." Waldron, *supra*, at 1715.

How should we respond to the assertion that sometimes torture *works* — that it produces intelligence that exposes terrorist plots? Prominent examples include French claims that coercion exposed terrorist operations in Algeria, Adam Shatz, *The Torture of Algiers*, N.Y. Rev. of Books, Nov. 21, 2002, and U.S. claims that torturing suspects in the Philippines uncovered a plot to crash 11 commercial airliners into the Pacific in 1995. *See* Dershowitz, *supra*, at 137.

6. *Torture Warrants?* Professor Dershowitz would recognize a qualified prohibi- tion on torture. He suggests a form of judicial "torture warrant" before permitting torture of suspected terrorists in interrogations. Dershowitz, *supra* at 148-149, 158-163. What might be the criteria for issuing such warrants? Should a judge, for example, try to balance the credibility or gravity of a threat against the suffering or injury to be inflicted on the recalcitrant detainee? Can you articulate a process that would be helpful to the court in doing that?

Another approach advocates an "emergency exception" to a ban on torture based on a written finding by the President of "an urgent and extraordinary need" reported "within a reasonable period" to appropriate congressional committees. The report would state the reason to believe that the information is known by the person to be interrogated, that it "concerns a specific plan that threatens U.S. lives," and that there are "no reasonable alternatives to save the lives in question." Philip B. Hey- mann & Juliette N. Kayyem, *Long-Term Legal Strategy Project for Preserving Security and Democratic Freedoms in the War on Terrorism* 25-26 (2004). Is this "findings" approach preferable to a torture warrant in the ticking-bomb case?

Alternatively, should we expect government officials confronted with the ticking- bomb case to engage in a form of official disobedience, hoping for ratification of the disobedient conduct after the fact? *See* Gross, *supra*, at 107. *Could* ratification by Con- gress or the President after the fact make lawful torture that was undertaken in dis- obedience of the law?

Which of these approaches is best? If you think torture might be permissible in some circumstances, can you think of other methods for keeping its "qualified" use in check?

B. THE LEGAL STANDARDS AND THEIR APPLICATION

On March 30, 2006, Charles Emmanuel, also known as Chuckie Taylor, Charles Taylor Jr., and Roy Belfast, son of the infamous president of Liberia, Charles Taylor, was arrested when he attempted to enter the United States with a passport obtained through false statements on his passport application. After he pleaded guilty to the passport fraud charge and was sentenced to 11 months in prison in December 2007, a 2008 Justice Department indictment charged Em- manuel with participating in torture in Liberia between 1999 and 2003. The opin- ion below, issued in response to a pretrial motion to dismiss an indictment, is the first judicial interpretation of a federal statute that criminalizes acts of torture committed outside the United States if the offender is a U.S. national or, regard- less of nationality, is present in the United States.

United States v. Charles Emmanuel

United States District Court, Southern District of Florida, 2007
2007 WL 2002452

CECILIA M. ALTONAGA, United States District Judge. This cause is before the Court on Defendant, Charles Emmanuel's Motion to Dismiss the Indictment Based on the Unconstitutionality of 18 U.S.C. §2340A. . . .

I. BACKGROUND

A. International and National Prohibitions of Torture

International prohibition against torture is a *jus cogens* norm of international law. *See Nuru v. Gonzales*, 404 F.3d 1207, 1222-23 (9th Cir. 2005) ("torture is illegal under the law of virtually every country in the world and under the international law of human rights") (internal footnotes omitted). The Universal Declaration of Human Rights, adopted by the United Nations in 1948, states that "no one shall be subjected to torture or to cruel, inhuman or degrading treatment or punishment." Universal Decl. of Human Rights, Dec. 10, 1948, U.N. Doc. A/810, art. 5. The International Covenant on Civil and Political Rights, Dec. 16, 1966, art. 7, 999 U.N.T.S. 171, 6 I.L.M. 368, states that "[n]o one shall be subjected to torture or to cruel, inhuman or degrading treatment or punishment."

On December 10, 1984, the United Nations General Assembly unanimously adopted the Convention Against Torture and Other Cruel, Inhuman or Degrading Treatment or Punishment ("Convention Against Torture" or "Convention"). G.A. Res. 39/46, U.N. GAOR, 39th Sess., Supp. No. 51 at 197, U.N. Doc. A/RES/39/46, S. Treaty Doc. No. 100-20, 1465 U.N.T.S. 85 (Dec. 10, 1984). It was adopted "with the stated purpose to 'make more effective the struggle against torture and other cruel, inhuman or degrading treatment or punishment throughout the world.'" *Auguste v. Ridge*, 395 F.3d 123, 130 (3d Cir. 2005) (quoting the Preamble to the Convention, S. Treaty Doc. No. 100-20, 1465 U.N.T.S. 85)). The Convention entered into force on June 26, 1987. *See id.* It has been described as the "most important U.N. treaty for controlling, regulating, and prohibiting torture and related practices." Winston Nagan & Lucie Atkins, *The International Law of Torture: From Universal Proscription to Effective Application and Enforcement*, 14 Harv. Hum. Rts. J. 87, 97 (2001).

On April 18, 1988, President Ronald Reagan signed the Convention, with the caveat that the United States reserved the right to communicate such reservations, interpretive understandings, or declarations as were deemed necessary. *See Auguste*, 395 F.3d at 130 (citations omitted). President Reagan submitted the Convention Against Torture to the Senate for advice and consent to ratification on May 20, 1988, with seventeen proposed conditions (four reservations, nine understandings, and four declarations). *Id.* at 131 (citing S. Exec. Rep. 101-30, at 2, 7 (1990)).

In January 1990, President George H.W. Bush submitted a revised and reduced list of proposed conditions. *See Auguste*, 395 F.3d at 131. One of the proposed conditions was that in order to constitute torture, the "act must be specifically intended to inflict severe physical or mental pain or suffering." *Id.* (quoting S. Exec. Rep. 101-30 at 9, 36). On January 30, 1990, the Senate Foreign Relations Committee held a hearing and thereafter, on August 30, 1990, issued a report recommending that the Senate give its advice and consent to ratification of the Convention Against Torture, subject to reservations, understandings and declarations.[2] S. Exec. Rep. 101-30 (1990). The full Senate gave its advice and consent to ratification, again, subject to several reservations, understandings and declarations. *See* S17, Cong. Rec. 486, S17491-92 (daily ed. 1990).

On October 21, 1994 and pursuant to Article 26 of the Convention, when President William Clinton deposited the instrument for ratification with the United Nations, *see Xuncax v. Gramajo*, 886 F. Supp. 162, 176 n.12 (D. Mass. 1995), the United States became a party to the Convention. Notably, the President included the Senate understandings in the instrument of ratification." *Auguste*, 395 F.3d at 132 (citing 1830 U.N.T.S. 320, 321, 322 (1994)); Declarations and Reservations made upon Ratification, accession, or Succession (visited Nov. 24, 2004) (http://untreaty.un.org/ENGLISH/bible/englishinternetbible/partI/chapterIV/treaty14.asp)).

In consenting to ratification of the Convention Against Torture, the Senate acknowledged that existing U.S. federal and state criminal statutes prohibited acts of torture occurring within the United States. *See Summary and Analysis of the Convention Against Torture and Other Cruel, Inhuman or Degrading Treatment*, S. Treaty Doc. 100-20, 9-10 (1988). The Senate recognized that in order for the United States to comply with its obligations under the treaty, it would need to enact a criminal statute prohibiting acts of torture by the defendants specified in Article 5 of the Convention, committed outside the United States. *Id.*

There are 144 parties to the Convention Against Torture, representing approximately 75% of the member states of the United Nations, including the United States and Liberia. The Convention defines "torture" as

> any act by which severe pain or suffering, whether physical or mental, is intentionally inflicted on a person for such purposes as obtaining from him or a third person information or a confession, punishing him for an act he or a third person has committed or is suspected of having committed, or intimidating or coercing him or a third person, or for any reason based on discrimination of any kind, when such pain or suffering is inflicted by or at the instigation of or with the consent or acquiescence of a public official or other person acting in an official capacity.

Convention, Article 1(1).

Article 2(1) of the Convention requires each State Party to "take effective legislative, administrative, judicial or other measures to prevent acts of torture in any territory under its jurisdiction." Article 4 requires each State Party to "ensure that all acts of torture are offences under its criminal law. The same shall apply to any attempt to commit torture and to any act by any person which constitutes complicity or participation in torture." Article 5(1) requires each State Party to "take such measures as may be necessary to establish its jurisdiction over the offences . . . (b) When the alleged offender is a national of that State," and "2. . . . where the alleged offender is present in any territory under its jurisdiction and it does not extradite him. . . ."

---

2. The Senate gave advice and consent subject to the reservation that the term "cruel, inhuman or degrading treatment or punishment" is to have a meaning as prohibited by the Fifth, Eighth, and/or Fourteenth Amendments to the U.S. Constitution, and subject to additional understandings, including that the provisions of the Convention are not self-executing. For a complete listing of the reservations, understandings and declarations of the United States Senate, see http://www.unhchr.ch/html/menu2/6/cat/treaties/convention-reserv.htm.

The Convention . . . was not intended to be self-executing. *See Reyes-Sanchez v. United States Attorney Gen.*, 369 F.3d 1239, 1240 n.1 (11th Cir. 2004); *Calderon v. Reno*, 39 F. Supp. 2d 943, 956 (N.D. Ill. 1998); *White v. Paulsen*, 997 F. Supp. 1380, 1383 (E.D. Wash. 1998). . . . The United States therefore enacted 18 U.S.C. §§2340-2340A of the United States Criminal Code pursuant to Articles 4 and 5 of the Convention. The Torture Convention Implementation Act ("Torture Act"), 18 U.S.C. §§2340 and 2340A, contains a definitional section, section 2340, and a section listing proscriptive elements and jurisdictional requirements, section 2340A.

The Torture Act states that "[w]hoever outside the United States commits or attempts to commit torture shall be fined . . . or imprisoned not more than 20 years, or both, and if death results . . . shall be punished by death or imprisoned for any term of years or for life." Federal courts have jurisdiction if "the alleged offender is a national of the United States; or the alleged offender is present in the United States, irrespective of the nationality of the victim or alleged offender." 18 U.S.C. §2340A(b). A person who conspires to commit an offense under the Act is subject to the same penalties prescribed for the offense under section 2340A(c).

Under the Torture Act, torture is defined in a slightly different manner from its definition in the Convention. Torture is defined in the Torture Act as "an act committed by a person acting under the color of law specifically intended to inflict severe physical or mental pain or suffering (other than pain or suffering incidental to lawful sanctions) upon another person within his custody or physical control." 18 U.S.C. §2340(1). "Severe mental pain or suffering" is

the prolonged mental harm caused by or resulting from—
   (A) the intentional infliction or threatened infliction of severe physical pain or suffering;
   (B) the administration or application, or threatened administration or application, of mind-altering substances or other procedures calculated to disrupt profoundly the senses or the personality;
   (C) the threat of imminent death; or
   (D) the threat that another person will imminently be subjected to death, severe physical pain or suffering, or the administration or application of mind-altering substances or other procedures calculated to disrupt profoundly the senses or personality.

U.S.C. §2340(2).
   . . . Pursuant to Article 27 of the Convention, the Torture Act entered into force for the United States on November 20, 1994, thirty days after it was deposited for ratification with the United Nations. *See Xuncax*, 886 F. Supp. at 176 n.12. The conspiracy offense was added in the 2001 amendments. . . .

B. This Prosecution

On December 6, 2006, the Grand Jury returned an Indictment against Defendant, Charles Emmanuel, charging Defendant with conspiracy to commit, and the commission of acts of torture upon an unidentified person ("victim") in the country of Liberia. The Indictment alleges that Defendant was born in Boston, Massachusetts, was present in the United States as a result of his arrival at Miami International

Airport, and at relevant times, was present in the country of Liberia, located in West Africa. Because his father, Charles McArthur Taylor, was president of Liberia, Defendant allegedly had authority to command members of the Liberian Antiterrorist Unit and participated in activities of the Liberian security forces, including the Antiterrorist Unit, a Special Security Service, and the Liberian National Police. During 2002, Liberia had non-violent groups and armed rebel groups opposed to the presidency of Defendant's father.

Count One of the Indictment charges Defendant with knowingly conspiring with others to commit torture by conspiring with others to commit acts, under the color of law, with the specific intent to inflict severe physical pain and suffering upon a person within their custody and control. The object of the conspiracy was to obtain information from the alleged victim about actual, perceived, or potential opponents of the Taylor presidency by, *inter alia*, committing torture, in violation of Title 18, United States Code, §§2340A and 2340(1). The interrogation and torture are alleged to have taken place in various locations in Liberia, on or about July 24, 2002. Among other things, Defendant allegedly made the victim hold scalding water in his hands and repeatedly shocked the victim's genitalia and other body parts, and a co-conspirator poured scalding water on other locations of the victim's body, applied a hot iron to the victim's flesh, and rubbed salt into the victim's open wounds. All acts are alleged to violate 18 U.S.C. §2340A(c).

Count Two alleges that Defendant and others, while intending to inflict severe physical pain and suffering, committed and attempted to commit torture, while acting under color of law, by committing [the acts described above], in violation of 18 U.S.C. §§2340A and 2340(1), and 18 U.S.C. §2. . . .

Defendant's Motion to Dismiss challenges the Indictment on several constitutional grounds. The "core problem with this case," according to Defendant, is that "the government seeks to oversee, through the open-ended terms of federal criminal law—the internal and wholly domestic actions of a foreign government." The essence of the challenge to the prosecution is the constitutional infirmity of 18 U.S.C. §2340A, a law that has been in place for over a decade, and under which Defendant is the first person to be prosecuted. . . .

II. ANALYSIS

A. Congress' Power to Enact the Torture Act

To paraphrase Defendant, he argues that the Torture Act does not implement the Convention Against Torture, but rather, creates a different crime from the act of torture defined in the Convention. According to Defendant, the Torture Act has an expansive statutory prohibition of torture, where pain and suffering need not be inflicted for purposes of intimidation, coercion, or for obtaining a confession. That definition is at odds with the limited treaty terms, which define torture as an act by which severe pain or suffering is intentionally inflicted for such purposes as obtaining information or a confession when inflicted by a public official in an official capacity. Because the definition of torture in the Torture Act, in essence, a definition amounting to aggravated battery, does not track the treaty language, the definition varies sharply from the international understanding of torture as set forth in the Convention, and the statute thus cannot be said to effectuate, or be necessary to or proper for, compliance with the treaty.

Defendant's argument fails to persuade that Congress lacked authorization, under the Necessary and Proper Clause or the Offences Clause of Article I of the Constitution, to enact the Torture Act.

1. Necessary and Proper Clause and the Treaty Power

... Congress certainly had the authority to pass the Torture Act under the Necessary and Proper Clause of Article I, as an adjunct to the Executive's authority under Article II to enter into treaties, with the advice and consent of the Senate....

In determining the intended meaning of the parties, a court should look to a treaty's negotiating and drafting history, as well as the subsequent practice of the parties in their application of the treaty. *See Elcock v. United States*, 80 F. Supp. 2d 70, 78-79 (E.D.N.Y. 2000) (citations omitted). Also, because a treaty implicates questions of foreign policy, the construction given by the Executive Branch, although not binding on the court, is entitled to great weight. *See Factor v. Laubenheimer*, 290 U.S. 276, 295 (1933). Furthermore, "if a treaty fairly admits of two constructions, one restricting the rights that may be claimed under it, and the other enlarging it, the more liberal construction is to be preferred." *Id.* at 293-94. Lastly, a court is under a duty to interpret a statute in a manner consonant with treaty obligations, because "an act of Congress ought never to be construed to violate the law of nations, if any other possible construction remains...." *United States v. PLO*, 695 F. Supp. 1456, 1465 (S.D.N.Y. 1988) (quoting *Murray v. The Charming Betsy*, 6 U.S. (2 Cranch) 64, 118 (1804)).

When the Convention was ratified by the United States, it was explicitly ratified subject to certain understandings and restrictions. Those understandings and limitations were subsequently incorporated into the legislative scheme that effectuated it, including the statutory definition of torture. Defendant cites to no case that compels a finding that where legislation that implements a treaty varies from the language or scope of the treaty, it is constitutionally infirm, or is less necessary and proper to carry out the powers exercised by the Executive under Article II than legislation that mirrors verbatim the language used in the treaty....

Here, the definition of torture in the Torture Act admittedly does not "track the language of the Convention in all material respects." The statutory definition of torture does, however, parallel the definition found in the Convention, in that both texts define torture to include the intentional infliction of severe pain or suffering by a public official or person acting under color of law. The element missing from the statutory definition, that is, that the torture be inflicted for the purposes of obtaining a confession, for punishment, or for intimidation or coercion, does not take the Torture Act outside the authorization given Congress in the Necessary and Proper Clause. Indeed, the more expansive statutory definition, which captures more acts of torture than does the definition contained in the Convention, is consistent with the international community's near universal condemnation of torture and cruel, inhuman or degrading treatment, and is consistent with repeated calls for the international community to be more "effective [in] the struggle against torture." *Convention Preamble; see also Aldana v. Del Monte Fresh Produce, N.A., Inc.*, 416 F.3d 1242, 1247 (11th Cir. 2005) ("State-sponsored torture, unlike torture by private actors, likely violates international law....") (citation omitted)....

... [T]he Torture Act plainly bears a rational relationship to the stated objectives of the Convention, and thus passes constitutional muster under the Necessary and Proper Clause.

2. Offenses Clause

Alternatively, assuming Defendant was correct, and Congress' more expansive definition of torture took the Torture Act outside the realm of the Necessary and Proper Clause, one additional source of constitutional authority for the Torture Act may be found in Article I, §8, cl.10 of the Constitution, that is the "offences against the Law of Nations" Clause. That clause gives Congress the power "[t]o define and punish Piracies and Felonies on the high Seas, and Offences against the Law of Nations." *Id.* Because of the way the clause is written, and contrary to Defendant's proposed interpretation of it, Congress has the power to define and punish offenses against the law of nations, independent of any piracies or felonies that occur on the high seas. . . .

The prohibition against official torture has attained the status of a *jus cogens* norm, not merely the status of customary international law. *See* [*Siderman de Blake v. Republic of Argentina,* 965 F.2d 699, 714, 717 (9th Cir. 1992)] (collecting authorities). In reaching the not surprising conclusion that prohibition of official torture was a *jus cogens* norm, the Ninth Circuit explained:

> [W]e conclude that the right to be free from official torture is fundamental and universal, a right deserving of the highest status under international law, a norm of *jus cogens.* The crack of the whip, the clamp of the thumb screw, the crush of the iron maiden, and, in these more efficient modern times, the shock of the electric cattle prod are forms of torture that the international order will not tolerate. To subject a person to such horrors is to commit one of the most egregious violations of the personal security and dignity of a human being. That states engage in official torture cannot be doubted, but all states believe it is wrong, all that engage in torture deny it, and no state claims a sovereign right to torture its own citizens.

Id. at 717 (citations omitted).

It is beyond peradventure that torture and acts that constitute cruel, inhuman or degrading punishment, acts prohibited by *jus cogens,* are similarly abhorred by the law of nations. *See, e.g., Sosa v. Alvarez-Machain,* 542 U.S. 692, 732 (2004) ("'[F]or purposes of civil liability, the torturer has become — like the pirate and slave trader before him — *hostis humani generis,* an enemy of all mankind.'") (quoting *Filartiga v. Pena-Irala,* 630 F.2d 876, 890 (2d Cir. 1980)). Certainly the numerous international treaties and agreements, and several domestic statutes that contain varying proscriptions against torture, addressing both civil and criminal reparation, demonstrate the law of nations' repudiation of torture.

Over a century ago, the Supreme Court stated that "if the thing made punishable is one which the United States are required by their international obligations to use due diligence to prevent, it is an offense against the law of nations." *United States v. Arjona,* 120 U.S. 479, 488 (1887). In the present international community, it cannot be said that the Torture Act, legislation that criminalizes acts of torture by U.S. nationals or persons present in the United States, committed outside the United States, does not address an act made punishable by the Government's international obligations under the Convention, and which the Government is required to use due diligence to prevent. Thus, the Torture Act also finds constitutional protection as a law enacted by Congress to punish offences against the law of nations....

D. Whether Sections 2340-2340A are Unconstitutionally Vague

Defendant argues that the Torture Act, 18 U.S.C. §§2340-2340A, does not give fair warning of what is outlawed, is void for vagueness, and therefore violates the Due Process Clause of the Fifth Amendment. Specifically, Defendant maintains that the definitions of "torture" and "severe mental pain or suffering," and the various terms used in those definitions, such as "acting under the color of law," and "incidental to lawful sanction," included in the Torture Act, 18 U.S.C. §2340, do "not provide the kind of notice that will allow ordinary people to understand what conduct is prohibited." Defendant also argues that because the statute is vague, a prosecutor may use it as a tool of foreign affairs, and it may consequently authorize or encourage arbitrary and discriminatory enforcement. Defendant challenges the Torture Act as vague on its face and as applied, and as additional support for his position regarding vagueness, Defendant submits with his Reply memorandum two Justice Department memoranda which offer varying interpretations of torture as defined in the Torture Act.[8]

... "Vagueness may invalidate a criminal statute if it either (1) fails 'to provide the kind of notice that will enable ordinary people to understand what conduct it prohibits' or (2) authorizes or encourages 'arbitrary and discriminatory enforcement.'" *United States v. Eckhardt*, 466 F.3d 938, 944 (11th Cir. 2006) (quoting *City of Chicago v. Morales*, 527 U.S. 41, 56 (1999) (citation omitted)); *see also* [*United States v. Hasner*, 340 F.3d 1261 (11th Cir.2003)] at 1269 ("A statute is unconstitutionally vague if it fails to 'define the criminal offense with sufficient definiteness that ordinary people can understand what conduct is prohibited and in a manner that does not encourage arbitrary and discriminatory enforcement.'") (quoting *Kolender v. Lawson*, 461 U.S. 352, 357 (1983)). "[T]he presence of culpable intent as a necessary element of the offense does much to destroy any force in the argument" that a statute is unconstitutionally vague. *Boyce Motor Lines v. United States*, 342 U.S. 337, 342 (1952).

The Torture Statute contains specific intent as one of its elements, as it defines "torture" to be "an act committed by a person acting under the color of law specifically intended to inflict severe physical or mental pain or suffering...." The Indictment informs Defendant that he and his coconspirators, acting under color of law and with the specific intent to inflict severe physical pain and suffering, burned the alleged victim's flesh with a hot iron, forced the alleged victim at gunpoint to hold scalding water in his hands, burned parts of the victim's body with scalding water, repeatedly shocked the genitalia and other parts of the body with an electrical device, and rubbed salt into the alleged victim's wounds. Such allegations, coupled with the statutory language contained in the Torture Statute, certainly advise the ordinary person of prohibited conduct with sufficient definiteness. The Torture Statute,

---

8. An August 1, 2002 memorandum from Assistant Attorney General Jay S. Bybee to Alberto R. Gonzales, then Counsel to the President, states, for example, that "certain acts may be cruel, inhuman, or degrading, but still not produce pain and suffering of the requisite intensity to fall within Section 2340A's proscription against torture." The memorandum goes on to examine possible defenses that would negate a claim that interrogation methods violate the statute. A December 30, 2004 Justice Department memorandum "supercedes" the August 2002 memorandum "in its entirety," because the discussion contained within the latter was "unnecessary."

enacted to fulfill the United States' treaty obligations with most of the countries of the world, certainly put the Defendant, a person born in the United States, on notice of conduct prohibited not only in this country, but in much of the civilized world. . . .

[The Court also held that, because the defendant is a U.S. citizen by birth, extraterritorial application of the Torture Statute does not violate Fifth Amendment Due Process Clause rights. Nor were his Sixth Amendment speedy trial or venue rights violated because, although his alleged crimes occurred years earlier in Liberia, the indictment was only months old and he had not shown that he would be unable to mount a constitutionally adequate defense in Miami.]

NOTES AND QUESTIONS

a. The Convention Against Torture

1. *Interpreting the Convention Against Torture (CAT).* The torture ban in the CAT is explicit. Is the meaning of the prohibition clear? Note that the ban is unconditional: "No exceptional circumstances whatsoever, whether a state of war or a threat of war, internal political instability or any other public emergency, may be invoked as a justification of torture." CAT art. 2(2). Surely the CAT drafters were aware of the so-called "ticking bomb" scenario, in which torture is justified on grounds of saving lives in a crisis. Why do you suppose the CAT did not preserve an exception for the ticking bomb?

2. *Comparing the Definitions of Torture.* As noted in the *Charles Emmanuel* case, when the U.S. Senate gave its consent to the CAT in 1990, it attached a variety of reservations, declarations, and understandings. Included was an understanding about the meaning of the term "torture":

> . . . in order to constitute torture, an act must be specifically intended to inflict severe physical or mental pain or suffering and that mental pain or suffering refers to prolonged mental harm caused by or resulting from (1) the intentional infliction or threatened infliction of severe physical pain or suffering; (2) the administration or application, or threatened administration or application, of mind altering substances or other procedures calculated to disrupt profoundly the senses or the personality; (3) the threat of imminent death; or (4) the threat that another person will imminently be subjected to death, severe physical pain or suffering, or the administration or application of mind altering substances or other procedures calculated to disrupt profoundly the senses or personality.

Later, in its Initial Report to the U.N. Committee against Torture in 1999 (CAT/C/28/Add.5), the United States declared: "In 1994, Congress enacted a new federal law to implement the requirements of the Convention against Torture relating to acts of torture committed outside United States territory. . . . The statute adopts the Convention's definition of torture, consistent with the terms of United States ratification." *Id.* ¶47.

Compare the definitions of torture in the CAT, without the U.S. understanding, with the definition in the Torture Act, which is based on that understanding:

Convention Against Torture – Article 1(1)

For the purposes of this Convention, the term "torture" means any act by which severe pain or suffering, whether physical or mental, is intentionally inflicted on a person for such purposes as obtaining from him or a third person information or a confession, punishing him for an act he or a third person has committed or is suspected of having committed, or intimidating or coercing him or a third person, or for any reason based on discrimination of any kind, when such pain or suffering is inflicted by or at the instigation of or with the consent or acquiescence of a public official acting in an official capacity. It does not include pain or suffering arising only from, inherent in or incidental to lawful sanctions.

Torture Act. 18 U.S.C. §2340

As used in this chapter—

(1) "torture" means an act committed by a person acting under the color of law specifically intended to inflict severe physical or mental pain or suffering (other than pain or suffering incidental to lawful sanctions) upon another person within his custody or physical control;

(2) "severe mental pain or suffering" means the prolonged mental harm caused by or resulting from—

(A) the intentional infliction or threatened infliction of severe physical pain or suffering;

(B) the administration or application, or threatened administration or application, of mind-altering substances or other procedures calculated to disrupt profoundly the senses or the personality;

(C) the threat of imminent death; or

(D) the threat that another person will imminently be subjected to death, severe physical pain or suffering, or the administration or application of mind-altering substances or other procedures calculated to disrupt profoundly the senses or personality....

How do the two authorities differ in their definitions of torture? How does the meaning of mental suffering differ?

Why would the Senate, in approving the CAT, and later Congress, in passing the Torture Act, have added a specific intent requirement to the definition? If causing pain is a purposeful means to the end of obtaining desired intelligence, is there a meaningful distinction between specific intent and knowledge of the consequences? Does an intention to gather intelligence (a legitimate purpose) somehow trump what would otherwise constitute specific intent to torture? If the interrogator specifically intends to cause suffering, does it matter legally why the interrogator causes the pain?

Can you say what interrogation techniques are permitted under the U.S. understanding about the definition of torture? Sleep deprivation? Starvation? Sensory deprivation or bombardment? Which of these, if any, would otherwise be forbidden by the CAT?

Would the Torture Act be improved by defining "the infliction of severe pain and suffering" as "the application of any physical stressors to detainees that are not applied to the detaining nation's own trainees in a nonpunitive setting"? *See* Michael W. Lewis, *A Dark Descent into Reality: Making the Case for an Objective Definition of Torture,* 67 Wash. & Lee L. Rev. 77, 119 (2010) (so arguing).

3. *The CAT and "Cruel, Inhuman, or Degrading Treatment."* Article 16 of the CAT requires that states "undertake to prevent . . . other acts of cruel, inhuman or degrading treatment or punishment which do not amount to torture." How does this requirement differ from the Convention's ban on torture?

One of the reservations attached to the CAT by the U.S. Senate provides that "the United States considers itself bound by the obligation under Article 16 to prevent 'cruel, inhuman or degrading treatment or punishment,' only insofar as [that term] means the cruel, unusual and inhumane treatment or punishment prohibited by the Fifth, Eighth, and/or Fourteenth Amendments to the Constitution of the United States." Resolution of Advice and Consent to the Ratification of the Convention Against Torture and Other Forms of Cruel, Inhuman or Degrading Treatment or Punishment ¶I(2), 136 Cong. Rec. S17491 (Oct. 27, 1990). Why might the Senate have insisted on (and the President have supported) this reservation?

Why do you suppose that Congress failed to include criminal sanctions for cruel, inhuman, or degrading (CID) treatment in the Torture Act? How did this failure affect the U.S. obligation under the Torture Convention not to engage in such treatment?

4. *Deportation and the CAT.* Article 3 of the CAT explicitly prohibits any individual from being deported to a country where there are "substantial grounds for believing" that the individual would be in danger of being tortured. In *Khouzam v. Ashcroft,* 361 F.3d 161 (2d Cir. 2004), the Court overturned a Board of Immigration Appeals (BIA) decision that the abuse that Coptic Christian Khouzam would likely face from Egyptian police if deported to stand trial for an alleged murder does not amount to torture, because the police would not be acting with the consent or approval of government officials. The court acknowledged that the CAT excludes from the torture definition "suffering arising only from, inherent in or incidental to lawful sanctions," but the CAT also lists pain or suffering inflicted for the purpose of "obtaining a confession" as an example of torture. *Id.* The BIA apparently reasoned that cruel acts directed against Khouzam would not constitute torture because the abuse would be part of a lawful sanction. The court stated that it "would totally eviscerate the CAT to hold that once someone is accused of a crime it is a legal impossibility for any abuse inflicted on that person to constitute torture." *Id.* at 169. The court concluded that "torture requires only that government officials know of or remain willfully blind to an act and thereafter breach their legal responsibility to prevent it." *Id.* at 171.

5. *Aliens Held Abroad.* For the purposes of compliance with the CAT, would it matter where the mistreatment of a prisoner by U.S. officials took place? Suppose the CIA beats an alien abroad to force him to reveal the details of an anticipated terrorist attack. Would such CIA conduct violate the CAT? If the measures of compliance with the CAT prohibition against "cruel, inhuman, or degrading treatment" are the Fifth,

Eighth, and Fourteenth Amendments, as stated in the U.S. reservation upon ratification, do aliens held by the United States overseas have any protection from such treatment by U.S. officials under the CAT? *See United States v. Verdugo-Urquidez*, 494 U.S. 259 (1990) (holding Fourth Amendment inapplicable to the search abroad of an alien who lacks substantial connections to the United States); *Johnson v. Eisentrager*, 339 U.S. 763 (1950) (suggesting that the Fifth Amendment has no extraterroritorial application to aliens).

b. Incorporating the Geneva Conventions

1. *The War Crimes Act and Grave Breaches of the Geneva Conventions.* The four Geneva Conventions for the Protection of Victims of War, Aug. 12, 1949, *available at* http://www.icrc.org/Web/Eng/siteeng0.nsf/html/genevaconventions, regulate the treatment of noncombatants during armed conflict, including prisoners of war (POWs), the injured and sick, and civilians. See Chapter 9. The War Crimes Act (WCA), 18 U.S.C. §2441 (2006), provides criminal sanctions for, *inter alia*, "grave breaches" of the Geneva Conventions:

War Crimes Act
18 U.S.C. §2441 (2006)

(a) Offense. — Whoever, whether inside or outside the United States, commits a war crime, in any of the circumstances described in subsection (b), shall be fined under this title or imprisoned for life or any term of years, or both, and if death results to the victim, shall also be subject to the penalty of death.

(b) Circumstances. — The circumstances referred to in subsection (a) are that the person committing such war crime or the victim of such war crime is a member of the Armed Forces of the United States or a national of the United States....

(c) Definition. — As used in this section the term "war crime" means any conduct —

(1) defined as a grave breach in any of the international conventions signed at Geneva 12 August 1949, or any protocol to such convention to which the United States is a party... [or]

(3) which constitutes a violation of common Article 3 of the international conventions signed at Geneva, 12 August 1949, or any protocol to such convention to which the United States is a party and which deals with non-international armed conflict....

Article 130 of Geneva Convention III on POWs defines a grave breach as

willful killing, torture or inhuman treatment, including biological experiments, willfully causing great suffering or serious injury to body or health, compelling a prisoner of war to serve in the forces of the hostile Power, or willfully depriving a prisoner of war of the rights of fair and regular trial prescribed in this Convention.

War Crimes Act §2441(c)(3) also defines as a war crime conduct that "constitutes a violation of common Article 3" of the Geneva Conventions. Common Article 3 reads in relevant part as follows:

Common Article 3, Geneva Conventions for the Protection of Victims of War

In the case of armed conflict not of an international character occurring in the territory of one of the High Contracting Parties, each Party to the conflict shall be bound to apply, as a minimum, the following provisions:

(1) Persons taking no active part in the hostilities, including members of armed forces who have laid down their arms and those placed *hors de combat* by sickness, wounds, detention, or any other cause, shall in all circumstances, be treated humanely, without any adverse distinction founded on race, color, religion or faith, sex, birth or wealth, or any other similar criteria.

To this end, the following acts are and shall remain prohibited at any time and in any place whatsoever with respect to the above-mentioned persons:

(a) violence to life and person, in particular murder of all kinds, mutilation, cruel treatment and torture; . . .

(c) outrages upon personal dignity, in particular humiliating and degrading treatment

(d) the passing of sentences and the carrying out of executions without previous judgment pronounced by a regularly constituted court, affording all the judicial guarantees which are recognized as indispensable by civilized peoples. . . . .

Applying the language of the Geneva Conventions, as incorporated through the WCA, what threshold determinations must be made, and by whom?

a. *What Conduct Is Covered?* If not just "torture," however defined, but also "cruel treatment, . . . [and] outrages upon personal dignity, in particular humiliating and degrading treatment" are grave breaches under the Geneva Conventions, does it make sense to engage in hairsplitting definitional debates about permissible interrogation? For POWs, Article 17 of Geneva Convention III provides that "no physical or mental torture, nor any other form of coercion, may be inflicted on prisoners of war to secure from them information of any kind whatever." For protected civilians, Article 31 of Geneva Convention IV provides that "[n]o physical or moral coercion shall be exercised against [them], in particular to obtain information from them or from third parties." What interrogation techniques would be proscribed by these rules? *See* Jennifer K. Elsea, *Lawfulness of Interrogation Techniques Under the Geneva Conventions* 23-35 (Cong. Res. Serv. RL32567), Sept. 8, 2004.

b. *Are the Conventions Judicially Enforceable?* In *Hamdan v. Rumsfeld*, 548 U.S. 557 (2006), the Supreme Court held that Common Article 3 is applicable to the conflict with Al Qaeda in Afghanistan. Even though its protections fall "short of full protection under the Conventions," *id.* at 630, the Court ruled that Hamdan had to be tried by a "'regularly constituted court affording all the judicial guarantees which are recognized as indispensable by civilized peoples.'" *Id.* at 630, quoting from Common

Article 3(1)(d). Does it follow that the other provisions of Common Article 3 also apply to the conflict in Afghanistan?

In the next chapter, a case study of coercive interrogation in the war on terror provides an opportunity to apply the Geneva Conventions and WCA to actions of interrogators and their superiors in a range of settings.

2. *The International Covenant on Civil and Political Rights (ICCPR).* The ICCPR, like the CAT, forbids torture and cruel, inhuman, and degrading conduct, and was approved as a treaty by the Senate. The ICCPR is non-self-executing, and lower federal courts have found that the ICCPR creates no privately enforceable rights in U.S. courts. *See Buell v. Mitchell,* 274 F.3d 337 (6th Cir. 2001). However, some courts cite the ICCPR as evidence that customary international law prohibits arbitrary arrest, prolonged detention, and torture. See Elsea, *supra,* at 12-13 (United States "has not officially proclaimed an emergency or named measures that would derogate from the ICCPR.").

3. *The Role of Customary International Law and Jus Cogens.* The substantive content of customary international law on the subject of torture is embodied in the CAT and ICCPR, among other instruments. The torture prohibition is also part of *jus cogens* and is so recognized by U.S. courts. *See Restatement (Third) of Foreign Relations Law of the United States* §702 (1986). It remains unclear, however, whether the prohibition against cruel, inhuman, or degrading treatment is also part of *jus cogens.*

c. Domestic Law on Torture

1. *A Domestic Baseline: How We Treat Our Own?* The U.S. reservation to Article 16 of the CAT limits "cruel, inhuman or degrading conduct" to that which violates that Fifth, Eighth, and/or Fourteenth Amendments. What is the content of those constitutional protections? For contrasting views, *see* Seth F. Kreimer, *Too Close to the Rack and the Screw: Constitutional Constraints on Torture in the War on Terror,* 6 U. Pa. J. Const. L. 278 (2003); and John T. Parry, *What Is Torture, Are We Doing It, and What If We Are?,* 64 U. Pitt. L. Rev. 237 (2003). It was not until 1936 that the Supreme Court barred the use in a state criminal trial of a confession obtained by brutally beating the suspects. In *Brown v. Mississippi,* 297 U.S. 278 (1936), the confessions were thrown out on the grounds that interrogation is part of the state machinery for obtaining convictions and is thus subject to the requirements of the Due Process Clause. In *Rogers v. Richmond,* 365 U.S. 534 (1961), the Court extended the Due Process Clause ban to abusive police conduct even where the reliability of a confession was not at issue.

In *Chavez v. Martinez,* 538 U.S. 760 (2003), a badly fractured Supreme Court ruled on claims of liability asserted by a plaintiff who had been subjected to persistent police questioning while he was in the hospital incapacitated by extreme pain. Five Justices voted to remand the question of whether the plaintiff could pursue a claim for violation of his substantive due process rights, but the Court could not agree about the scope and applicability of those rights or the related right against self-incrimination.

Three Justices joined in part of an opinion by Justice Thomas asserting that the interrogation was not egregious or conscience-shocking enough to violate the plaintiff's substantive due process rights. They reasoned that "freedom from unwanted police questioning is [not] a right so fundamental that it cannot be abridged absent a 'compelling state interest.'" *Id.* at 776. For them, it was enough that the questioning was justified by *some* government interest — here, the need to preserve critical evidence concerning a shooting by a police officer — and that it was not "conduct intended to injure in some way unjustifiable by any government interest." *Id.* at 775. Justice Stevens concluded that "the interrogation of respondent was the functional equivalent of an attempt to obtain an involuntary confession from a prisoner by torturous methods," which is "a classic example of a violation of a constitutional right 'implicit in the concept of ordered liberty.'" *Id.* at 788 (Stevens, J., concurring in part, dissenting in part).

Justice Kennedy (joined on this point by Justices Stevens and Ginsburg) agreed that the use of investigatory torture violates a person's fundamental right to liberty but noted that interrogating suspects who are in pain or anguish is not necessarily torture when the police have "legitimate reasons, borne of exigency... [such as] [l]ocating the victim of a kidnapping, ascertaining the whereabouts of a dangerous assailant or accomplice, or determining whether there is a rogue police officer." *Id.* at 796 (Kennedy, J., concurring in part, dissenting in part). On the other hand, he added, the police may not prolong or increase the suspect's suffering or threaten to do so to elicit a statement. The test for a constitutional violation, in Justice Kennedy's view, was whether the police "exploited" the suspect's pain to secure his statement. He found that they had done so in *Chavez.*

Under any of the tests in *Chavez* would torture in the United States of a suspected terrorist to obtain information about a possibly imminent terrorist attack violate substantive due process? How about practices such as hooding and sleep deprivation? Do military or civilian investigators in the war on terrorism have broader authority than the police do to use coercive interrogation techniques because of their different goals in an interrogation? *See* Marcy Strauss, *Torture,* 48 N.Y.L. Sch. L. Rev. 201, 251 (2003) (maintaining that it is unclear whether torture used to gain information violates the Fifth Amendment privilege against self-incrimination if the information is not used in a criminal prosecution; if so used, the right is violated).

Does the Eighth Amendment ban on "cruel and unusual punishment" supply an interpretive standard in the coercive interrogation context? If no judicially imposed punishment is contemplated by the interrogators, does the Eighth Amendment even apply? *See Ingraham v. Wright,* 430 U.S. 651, 671 n.40 (1977) ("[T]he State does not acquire the power to punish with which the Eighth Amendment is concerned until after it has secured a formal adjudication of guilt in accordance with due process of law.").

2. *A Congressional Prohibition.* In 2005, over the strenuous objection of the Bush administration, Congress enacted the Detainee Treatment Act, which provides in part:

Detainee Treatment Act

Pub. L. No. 109-148, §§1001-1006, 119 Stat. 2680, 2739-2744 (2005)

§1003. PROHIBITION ON CRUEL, INHUMAN, OR DEGRADING TREATMENT OR PUNISHMENT OF PERSONS UNDER CUSTODY OR CONTROL OF THE UNITED STATES GOVERNMENT.

(a) In General. — No individual in the custody or under the physical control of the United States Government, regardless of nationality or physical location, shall be subject to cruel, inhuman, or degrading treatment or punishment.

(b) Construction. — Nothing in this section shall be construed to impose any geographical limitation on the applicability of the prohibition against cruel, inhuman, or degrading treatment or punishment under this section.

(c) Limitation on Supersedure. — The provisions of this section shall not be superseded, except by a provision of law enacted after the date of the enactment of this Act which specifically repeals, modifies, or supersedes the provisions of this section.

(d) Cruel, Inhuman, or Degrading Treatment or Punishment Defined. — In this section, the term "cruel, inhuman, or degrading treatment or punishment" means the cruel, unusual, and inhumane treatment or punishment prohibited by the Fifth, Eighth, and Fourteenth Amendments to the Constitution of the United States, as defined in the United States Reservations, Declarations and Understandings to the United Nations Convention Against Torture and Other Forms of Cruel, Inhuman or Degrading Treatment or Punishment done at New York, December 10, 1984.

The same language appears in Pub. L. No. 109-163, §§1401-1406, 119 Stat. 3136, 3474-3480 (2006).

How important is the "regardless of nationality or physical location" language in determining the scope of the government's investigative authority and the rights of the detainee? The definition of "cruel, inhuman, or degrading treatment" mirrors that stated in the U.S. reservation to Article 16 of the CAT and covers only acts prohibited by the Fifth, Eighth, and Fourteenth Amendments. Does the Detainee Treatment Act thus require that persons (including aliens) in U.S. custody or control abroad not be subjected to treatment that would be unconstitutional if it occurred in the United States? If the meaning of the constitutional protections changes over time, the treatment forbidden by the Act presumably will change as well. How would you advise those responsible for supervising interrogations to keep abreast of their responsibilities?

3. *The Army Field Manual.* The Detainee Treatment Act also forbids exposure of persons in the custody or under the effective control of the Department of Defense (DOD) to any interrogation techniques not listed in the U.S. Army's field manual, *Intelligence Interrogation* (FM 34-52, Sept. 28, 1992). Pub. L. No. 109-148, §1002(a), 119 Stat. 2739; Pub. L. No. 109-163, §1402(a), 119 Stat. 3475. In September 2006, the Army replaced its 1992 manual with *Human Intelligence Collection Operations* (FM 2-22.3). The new field manual states that the only interrogation techniques permitted

are those it authorizes. The manual prohibits "any inhumane treatment—including abusive practices, torture, or cruel, inhuman, or degrading treatment or punishment"—and it asserts that "these unlawful and unauthorized forms of treatment are unproductive because they may yield unreliable results, damage subsequent collection efforts, and result in extremely negative consequences at national and international levels." *Id.* app. M-5. It also calls on non-DOD agencies that interrogate military detainees to follow its rules. FM 2-22.3 is considered again in a case study presented in the next chapter.

What is the legal significance of limiting DOD interrogators to techniques in an Army field manual? Why do you suppose that non-DOD interrogators are not subject to the same or some similar restrictions?

4. *The Military Commissions Act (MCA).* In late 2006 Congress enacted the Military Commissions Act (MCA), Pub. L. No. 109-366, 120 Stat. 2600, and there stated that the War Crimes Act satisfies the U.S. obligation to punish grave breaches of Common Article 3 and authorized the President to interpret the meaning and application of the Geneva Conventions. The MCA also narrowed the scope of the WCA by listing specific "grave breaches" to include "cruel and inhuman treatment," defined as conduct "intended to inflict severe or serious physical or mental pain or suffering." Physical pain is limited to "extreme" pain or injury, and mental pain is limited to aggravated acts, such as death threats. *Id.* §6(a)(2), (a)(3)(a). The MCA did not criminalize degrading treatment. Nor did it specifically prohibit techniques such as waterboarding. The flexibility afforded by the MCA permitted President Bush to restore discretion for the CIA to undertake "enhanced" interrogation techniques, through an executive order.

5. *The CIA.* On July 20, 2007, President Bush signed Executive Order 13,340, *Interpretation of the Geneva Conventions Common Article 3 as Applied to a Program of Detention and Interrogation Operated by the Central Intelligence Agency,* 72 Fed. Reg. 40,707. The executive order did not authorize the use of any particular interrogation techniques. Instead, it barred the CIA from certain practices, including those forbidden by the Torture Act, the DTA, and the MCA. However, the order did not proscribe techniques expressly prohibited from being used by the military under the 2006 Army Field Manual—such as waterboarding, hooding, sleep deprivation, or forced standing for long periods. President Obama revoked the Bush order in 2009:

Executive Order No. 13,491, Ensuring Lawful Interrogations
74 Fed. Reg. 4893 (Jan. 22, 2009)

By the authority vested in me by the Constitution and the laws of the United States of America, in order to improve the effectiveness of human intelligence-gathering, to promote the safe, lawful, and humane treatment of individuals in United States custody and of United States personnel who are detained in armed conflicts, to ensure compliance with the treaty obligations of the United States, including the Geneva Conventions, and to take care that the laws of the United States are faithfully executed, I hereby order as follows:

Section 1. Revocation.

Executive Order 13440 of July 20, 2007, is revoked. All executive directives, orders, and regulations inconsistent with this order, including but not limited to those issued to or by the Central Intelligence Agency (CIA) from September 11, 2001, to January 20, 2009, concerning detention or the interrogation of detained individuals, are revoked to the extent of their inconsistency with this order....

Sec. 3. Standards and Practices for Interrogation of Individuals in the Custody or Control of the United States in Armed Conflicts.

(a) Common Article 3 Standards as a Minimum Baseline. Consistent with the requirements of the Federal torture statute, 18 U.S.C. 2340-2340A, section 1003 of the Detainee Treatment Act of 2005, 42 U.S.C. 2000dd, the Convention Against Torture, Common Article 3, and other laws regulating the treatment and interrogation of individuals detained in any armed conflict, such persons shall in all circumstances be treated humanely and shall not be subjected to violence to life and person (including murder of all kinds, mutilation, cruel treatment, and torture), nor to outrages upon personal dignity (including humiliating and degrading treatment), whenever such individuals are in the custody or under the effective control of an officer, employee, or other agent of the United States Government or detained within a facility owned, operated, or controlled by a department or agency of the United States.

(b) Interrogation Techniques and Interrogation-Related Treatment. Effective immediately, an individual in the custody or under the effective control of an officer, employee, or other agent of the United States Government, or detained within a facility owned, operated, or controlled by a department or agency of the United States, in any armed conflict, shall not be subjected to any interrogation technique or approach, or any treatment related to interrogation, that is not authorized by and listed in Army Field Manual 2-22.3 (Manual). Interrogation techniques, approaches, and treatments described in the Manual shall be implemented strictly in accord with the principles, processes, conditions, and limitations the Manual prescribes. Where processes required by the Manual, such as a requirement of approval by specified Department of Defense officials, are inapposite to a department or an agency other than the Department of Defense, such a department or agency shall use processes that are substantially equivalent to the processes the Manual prescribes for the Department of Defense....

(c) Interpretations of Common Article 3 and the Army Field Manual. From this day forward, unless the Attorney General with appropriate consultation provides further guidance, officers, employees, and other agents of the United States Government may, in conducting interrogations, act in reliance upon Army Field Manual 2-22.3, but may not, in conducting interrogations, rely upon any interpretation of the law governing interrogation...issued by the Department of Justice between September 11, 2001, and January 20, 2009.

Sec. 4. Prohibition of Certain Detention Facilities, and Red Cross Access to Detained Individuals.

(a) CIA Detention. The CIA shall close as expeditiously as possible any detention facilities that it currently operates and shall not operate any such detention facility in the future.

(b) International Committee of the Red Cross Access to Detained Individuals. All departments and agencies of the Federal Government shall provide the International Committee of the Red Cross with notification of, and timely access to, any individual detained in any armed conflict in the custody or under the effective control of an officer, employee, or other agent of the United States Government or detained within a facility owned, operated, or controlled by a department or agency of the United States Government, consistent with Department of Defense regulations and policies. . . .

Sec. 6. Construction with Other Laws.

Nothing in this order shall be construed to affect the obligations of officers, employees, and other agents of the United States Government to comply with all pertinent laws and treaties of the United States governing detention and interrogation, including but not limited to: the Fifth and Eighth Amendments to the United States Constitution; the Federal torture statute, 18 U.S.C. 2340-2340A; the War Crimes Act, 18 U.S.C. 2441; the Federal assault statute, 18 U.S.C. 113; the Federal maiming statute, 18 U.S.C. 114; the Federal "stalking" statute, 18 U.S.C. 2261A; articles 93, 124, 128, and 134 of the Uniform Code of Military Justice, 10 U.S.C. 893, 924, 928, and 934; section 1003 of the Detainee Treatment Act of 2005, 42 U.S.C. 2000dd; section 6(c) of the Military Commissions Act of 2006, Public Law 109-366; the Geneva Conventions; and the Convention Against Torture. Nothing in this order shall be construed to diminish any rights that any individual may have under these or other laws and treaties. This order is not intended to, and does not, create any right or benefit, substantive or procedural, enforceable at law or in equity against the United States, its departments, agencies, or other entities, its officers or employees, or any other person.

In what respects does the Obama executive order change the law concerning interrogations for intelligence purposes? Is there any question of his constitutional authority to change the law, to the extent that he has? Are torture and cruel, inhuman, and degrading treatment now unlawful if carried out by any person working on behalf of the United States? How durable are the rules contained in the executive order? Should Congress codify them?

6. *Criminal Sanctions.* Why do you suppose Congress has not enacted a statute specifically outlawing torture within the United States?

The Uniform Code of Military Justice (UCMJ) provides for courts-martial to prosecute torture or inhumane acts committed within or outside the United States by members of the military and certain accompanying civilians. 10 U.S.C. §805 (UCMJ applies worldwide); *id.* §802 (to any service member); *id.* §802(a)(10) (to certain accompanying civilians); *id.* §818 (for an offense against the laws of war); *id.* §855 (torture or cruel or unusual punishment); *id.* §934 ("disorders and neglects to the prejudice of good order and discipline in the armed forces"). The admissibility in courts-martial of evidence concerning abusive interrogations is reviewed in Chapter 32.

7. *Criminal and Civil Defenses to Torture Actions.* One part of the Detainee Treatment Act, *supra* p. 921, provides a legal defense for U.S. personnel in any criminal or

civil action brought against them based on their involvement in an authorized interrogation of suspected foreign terrorists. The defense exists when the U.S. interrogator "did not know that the [interrogation] practices were unlawful and a person of ordinary sense and understanding would not know the practices were unlawful." Pub. L. No. 109-148, §1004(a), 119 Stat. 2740; Pub. L. No. 109-163, §1404, 119 Stat. 3475-3476. A good faith reliance on the advice of counsel may be "an important factor" in measuring the accused's culpability. *Id.* Could a claim of reliance on the memorandum from Stephen G. Bradbury, set out *supra* p. 900, thus immunize an interrogator from any liability?

8. *Civil Sanctions.* The Foreign Claims Act (FCA), 10 U.S.C. §2734(a) (2006), permits recovery of up to $100,000 from the United States for a claim brought by a resident of a foreign country where the injury occurred outside the United States "and is caused by, or is otherwise incident to [the] noncombat activities of" the U.S. military. *Id.* "Noncombat activity" is defined to include any "activity, other than combat, war or armed conflict, that is particularly military in character and has little parallel in the civilian community." 32 C.F.R. §842.41(c) (2010). Under the Act, claims commissions, consisting of commissioned officers, are established for each service branch and are in place wherever the military has a significant presence. However, experience with the FCA in Iraq and Afghanistan suggests that complex procedures and stringent policies have prevented most injured Afghans and Iraqis from obtaining compensation for their injuries. Scott Borrowman, *Sosa v. Alvarez-Machain and Abu Ghraib — Civil Remedies for Victims of Extraterritorial Torts by U.S. Military Personnel and Civilian Contractors*, 2005 BYU L. Rev. 371, 376; Lisa Magarrell & Lorna Peterson, *After Torture: U.S. Accountability and the Right to Redress* 14-15 (International Ctr. for Transitional Justice, Aug. 2010).

The Alien Tort Claims Act (ATCA), 28 U.S.C. §1350 (2006), confers jurisdiction on federal district courts over tort suits by aliens where a violation of the law of nations or a treaty of the United States is alleged. In *Sosa v. Alvarez-Machain*, 542 U.S. 692 (2004), *supra* p. 189, the Supreme Court rejected the ATCA as a basis for jurisdiction in the federal courts over a tort claim related to the abduction of one Mexican national by another who acted with the approval of the Drug Enforcement Administration (DEA). The Court reasoned that the ATCA was intended to create jurisdiction to hear suits based on current international norms, but only those whose "content and acceptance among civilized nations" is no less definite than the small number of "historical paradigms" familiar when the statute was passed in 1789. *Id.* at 718. In the course of its opinion, however, the Court cited with evident approval the decision in *Filartiga v. Peña-Irala*, 630 F.2d 876 (2d Cir. 1980), which applied the ATCA in a torture case.

The Torture Victim Protection Act (TVPA), Pub. L. No. 102-256, 106 Stat. 73 (1992), codified at 28 U.S.C. §1350 note (2006), provides a civil remedy in the federal courts for individuals, including U.S. persons, who have been victims of torture or extrajudicial killing. The TVPA thus may offer relief for U.S. persons that would be unavailable under the ATCA. However, the TVPA only provides a cause of action for torture or extrajudicial killing "under color of law, of any foreign nation." *Id.* §2a. Do you think that the TVPA would support an action for improper removal by U.S. officials of an individual who might be subjected to torture abroad? Would it apply where U.S. officials allegedly direct foreign officials to carry out acts of torture against a non-U.S. citizen? *See Arar v. Ashcroft, infra* p. 953.

Case Study: Coercive Interrogation by U.S. Forces After 9/11

As early as December 2002, U.S. military and civilian interrogators are reported to have abused individuals captured and detained in the war on terrorism by beating them and subjecting them to prolonged sleep and sensory deprivation, as well as to sexual humiliation. The abuse began in Afghanistan, then spread to Guantánamo Bay, Cuba, and other offshore U.S. interrogation centers, and later to Iraq. Several investigations of these abuses revealed that serious injuries and deaths occurred among the detainees.

Our objective in Part A of this chapter is to tell the interrogation story from September 11 through the Abu Ghraib scandal in 2004, with pertinent updates to the present. Next, in Part B, we apply laws reviewed in the previous chapter to the interrogation of persons in U.S. custody after 9/11. We also try to determine whether the President enjoys constitutional or other powers that would excuse him from compliance with the rules.

A. THE EVOLVING HISTORY OF INTERROGATION OF SUSPECTED TERRORISTS[1]

In October 1996, Secretary of Defense William Perry spoke at a meeting of Western Hemisphere defense ministers in Argentina. Responding to criticisms of so-called "torture manuals" used to train Latin American intelligence officers at the U.S. Army School of the Americas in the 1980s and to a 1996 Intelligence Oversight Board report describing intelligence activities in Latin America, Perry said he was shocked when he found out about the manuals. He also declared that the Defense

---

1. Several collections of documents relating to U.S. interrogation of its detainees may be found online. Among the most extensive are New York Times, *A Guide to the Memos on Torture* (n.d.), *at* http://www.nytimes.com/ref/international/24MEMO-GUIDE.html; National Sec. Archive, *Torturing Democracy* (2008), *available at* http://www.gwu.edu/~nsarchiv/torturingdemocracy/timelines/index2.html; and American Civil Liberties Union, National Security Project, *Torture Report* (updated regularly), *at* http://www.thetorturereport.org/node/1. The Department of Defense Web site also provides links to DOD reports, independent panel and inspector general reports, briefing transcripts, and news releases and articles, *at* http://www.defense.gov/news/detainee_investigations.html. Many of the key documents are collected in Mark Danner, *Torture and Truth: America, Abu Ghraib, and the War on Terror* (2004); and *The Torture Papers: The Road to Abu Ghraib* (Karen J. Greenberg & Joshua L. Dratel eds., 2005).

Department would never again advocate torture or other inhumane treatment in its training programs.[2]

Secretary Perry's assertion could not have taken into account September 11 and the war on terrorism that followed. Vice President Dick Cheney appeared on *Meet the Press* on the Sunday immediately after the attacks. Asked how the Administration planned to respond to the continuing threat of terrorism, the Vice President said that the United States would "have to work on the dark side . . . [and] use any means at our disposal."[3] According to Cofer Black, former director of the Central Intelligence Agency's (CIA's) counterterrorism unit, "after 9/11, the gloves came off."[4]

Beginning with the capture in Afghanistan of senior Al Qaeda operatives, the Bush administration had to determine how best to extract intelligence information from individuals detained by U.S. forces. "Setting" the methods and parameters of interrogation thus became an integral part of counterterrorism planning. Should Al Qaeda figures be questioned by the FBI, using traditional methods? By military interrogators, following service branch rules? By the CIA, perhaps using harsher techniques in secret locations?

Answering these questions became intensely political and legally contentious inside the Bush administration. Interrogations were conducted by both military and CIA personnel. At times the two sets of interrogators operated separately, at other times they were co-located, and military personnel often had responsibility for capturing and holding the suspects who were later subject to CIA interrogation. As a result, the two intelligence-gathering efforts tended to overlap if not merge. Meanwhile, the Administration's early legal guidance on interrogation was prepared for the CIA, but DOD then relied on some of the analysis in those memoranda to develop guidance for its own military interrogators. When abusive interrogations by U.S. officials began to be revealed, Congress adopted reforms that covered the military, but apparently not the CIA. Thus, as you review this narrative and questions that follow, recall that CIA and DOD interrogators were sometimes subject to different legal regimes, but that their practices were part of an overlapping and evolving legal picture that remained murky for years.

The Bush administration decided early on to detain indefinitely a number of persons seized in Afghanistan and elsewhere and to create a new detention facility at the U.S. Navy base at Guantánamo Bay to hold at least some of them. The first detainees taken there in January 2002 were designated "unlawful combatants" by President Bush.

Meanwhile, the President directed the CIA to detain and interrogate certain "high value" terrorism suspects. Because of statutory authorities said to enable the CIA to operate in secret (*see supra* Chapter 16), the Administration apparently believed it could hold detainees in secret prisons where no one would know who was being held or what the CIA was doing to them while detained. On September 17, 2001, President Bush authorized the CIA to rely on paramilitary forces to capture, detain, and interrogate suspected terrorists.[5] Yet the directive did not provide guidance on detention or interrogation, and because the CIA had little interrogation

---

2. Linda D. Kozaryn, *Perry Bans U.S. Training in Inhumane Techniques,* American Forces Information Serv., Oct. 9, 1996, *available at* http://osd.dtic.mil/news/Oct1996/n10091996_9610095.html.
   3. Jane Mayer, *The Dark Side: The Inside Story of How the War on Terror Turned into a War on American Ideals* 9-10 (2008).
   4. John Barry, Michael Hirsh & Michael Isikoff, *The Roots of Torture,* Newsweek, May 24, 2004, at 26.
   5. David Johnston, *At a Secret Interrogation, Dispute Flared over Tactics,* N.Y. Times, Sept. 10, 2006.

experience,[6] the Agency sought guidance from decades-old manuals describing a "survive, evade, resist, escape" (SERE) program used in training U.S. service personnel to withstand the effects of torture.[7]

As U.S. forces began to detain fighters in Afghanistan in late 2001, those not held by the military and sent to Guantánamo, the so called "high-value" detainees, were held by the CIA. In early 2002, senior Al Qaeda operative Abu Zubaydah was captured in a firefight and flown to a secret CIA facility in Thailand. After the Federal Bureau of Investigation (FBI) interrogated Zubaydah in a non-coercive manner and learned that Khalid Sheikh Mohammed (KSM) was the apparent mastermind of the September 11 attacks, Zubaydah began to resist interrogation. The CIA then took over interrogation and subjected Zubaydah to waterboarding, reportedly ending his resistance. Eventually Zubaydah was moved to another CIA site in Poland and then to Guantánamo.[8] KSM was captured in March 2003 in Pakistan, then transported to Afghanistan and subsequently to the CIA site in Poland, where he was waterboarded and otherwise subjected to harsh interrogation techniques.[9] The CIA Inspector General later found that the CIA waterboarded Zubaydah 83 times in August 2002, and employed the same technique with KSM 183 times in March 2003.[10]

The President announced in a February 7, 2002, order, *Humane Treatment of Al Qaeda and Taliban Detainees,*[11] that the United States would voluntarily extend the protections of the Third Geneva Convention to captured Taliban fighters, although such fighters were not regarded as unlawful combatants entitled to prisoner-of-war (POW) status. Captured members of Al Qaeda would be treated "humanely," even though the Geneva Conventions were said not to apply to Al Qaeda members at all. This followed advice in a January 9, 2002, memorandum from the Justice Department Office of Legal Counsel (OLC) to the Defense Department, *Application of Treaties and Laws to Al Qaeda and Taliban Detainees,*[12] written by John Yoo and Robert Delahunty, concluding that the President had constitutional authority to suspend application of the Geneva Conventions in Afghanistan, or to decide that the Conventions did not apply to captured Al Qaeda and Taliban detainees. The "humane treatment" order applied only to the armed forces, however, not the CIA, which presumably was free to continue utilizing interrogation techniques described above and in the previous chapter.

In the summer of 2002, the Justice Department was asked to advise what interrogation techniques would violate U.S. or international law. In August, the OLC opined that

> for an act to constitute torture as defined in [the Torture Act], it must inflict pain that is difficult to endure. Physical pain amounting to torture must be equivalent in intensity to the pain accompanying serious physical injury, such as organ failure, impairment of

---

6. Mayer, *supra,* at 144-145.

7. Scott Shane, David Johnston & James Risen, *Secret U.S. Endorsement of Severe Interrogations,* N.Y. Times, Oct. 4, 2007.

8. Johnston, *supra* n.4; Scott Shane, *Inside a 9/11 Mastermind's Interrogation,* N.Y. Times, June 22, 2008.

9. Mayer, *supra* n.3, at 270-274.

10. *See* Office of Inspector Gen., Central Intelligence Agency, *Special Review: Counterterrorism Detention and Interrogation Activities (September 2001-October 2003)* 12-23, 44-45 (May 7, 2004), *at* http://luxmedia.com.edgesuite.net/aclu/IG_Report.pdf.

11. *Reprinted in The Torture Papers, supra* n.1, at 134.

12. *Reprinted id.* at 38.

bodily function, or even death. For purely mental pain or suffering to amount to torture . . . it must result in significant psychological harm of significant duration, e.g., lasting for months or even years. We conclude that the mental harm also must result from one of the predicate acts listed in the statute, namely: threats of imminent death; threats of the infliction of the kind of pain that would amount to physical torture; infliction of such physical pain as a means of psychological torture; use of drugs or other procedures designed to deeply disrupt the senses, or fundamentally alter an individual's personality; or threatening to do any of these things to a third party.[13]

The memorandum suggested that a one-time kick to a prisoner's stomach with military boots while forcing him into a kneeling position would not amount to "torture" that would be subject to prosecution. The OLC memorandum even concluded that torture might be justified in some circumstances, and that the statutory prohibition on torture would not apply to actions taken by the President as Commander in Chief. *Id.* at 33-39.

By the summer of 2002, there were about 600 detainees at Guantánamo. Military interrogators there knew from the President's order that the Geneva Convention POW protections did not apply, and that detainees should be treated "humanely," but they had no clear guidance on the limits of their interrogations other than the statutes reviewed in the last chapter. Reacting to what was characterized as "tenacious resistance by some detainees to existing interrogation methods,"[14] in October 2002 the commander at Guantánamo Bay sought permission to use new interrogation techniques that were more coercive than those authorized in the Army Field Manual, including the "use of stress positions (like standing), for a maximum of four hours"; isolation for up to 30 days; "deprivation of light and auditory stimuli"; hooding; removal of clothing; "forced grooming (shaving of facial hair, etc.)"; and using "fear of dogs . . . to induce stress."[15] A separate legal opinion by Army Lieutenant Colonel Diane Beaver evaluated a range of even more aggressive techniques — from exposure to cold weather or water to threats of death or severe pain to inducing the "misperception of asphyxiation" and "mild noninjurious physical contact."[16] Lieutenant Colonel Beaver found that these techniques were consistent with existing legal standards if they could "plausibly have been thought necessary . . . to achieve a legitimate governmental objective" and the force was applied "in a good faith effort and not maliciously or sadistically for the very purpose of causing harm."[17]

By December 2002, the media began reporting that so-called "stress and duress" tactics or "high pressure methods" were being used in secret detention centers overseas by Defense Department and CIA interrogators in pursuit of "actionable intelligence." Those methods included forcing detainees to stand or kneel for hours in

13. Office of Legal Counsel, U.S. Dep't of Justice, *Memorandum for Alberto R. Gonzales, Counsel to the President, Re: Standards of Conduct for Interrogation Under 18 U.S.C. §§2340-2340A*, at 1 (Aug. 1, 2002) (commonly referred to as the Bybee Memo, for Assistant Attorney General Jay S. Bybee, who signed it), *available at* http://www.gwu.edu/~nsarchiv/NSAEBB/NSAEBB127/02.08.01.pdf. The "organ failure" passage relies on public health statutes of questionable applicability to the interrogation setting.

14. *Final Report of the Independent Panel to Review DoD Detention Operations* 35 (Aug. 24, 2004) (hereinafter *Schlesinger Report*), *at* http://www.defense.gov/news/Aug2004/d20040824finalreport.pdf.

15. Memorandum for Chairman of the Joint Chiefs of Staff from James T. Hill, General, U.S. Army, *Counter-Resistance Techniques* (Oct. 25, 2002), *available at* http://www.gwu.edu/~nsarchiv/NSAEBB/NSAEBB127/02.10.25.pdf.

16. Diane E. Beaver, Joint Task Force 170, Department of Def., *Legal Brief on Proposed Counter-Resistance Strategies* (Oct. 11, 2002), *available at* http://www.gwu.edu/~nsarchiv/NSAEBB/NSAEBB127/02.10.11.pdf.

17. *Id.*

black hoods or spray-painted goggles, bombarding the detainees with lights 24 hours a day, withholding painkillers from wounded detainees, confining them in tiny rooms or binding them in painful positions, subjecting them to loud noises, and depriving them of sleep.[18] A special interrogation plan was authorized for high-value detainee Mohammed al-Qahtani, known then as the "twentieth hijacker" because he sought entry to the United States shortly before 9/11 after communicating with the hijackers. Apparently feeling unconstrained by Geneva Convention limits, interrogators went even further with Qahtani. They isolated him and interrogated him for up to 20 hours per day, threatened him with dogs, and subjected him to sexual humiliation.[19] A June 2004 statement from the Department of Defense confirmed that similarly harsh interrogation techniques were approved by Secretary Donald Rumsfeld on December 2, 2002, for general use in Guantánamo but were rescinded on January 15, 2003.[20] An August 2004 Army report found that interrogators in Afghanistan employed similar techniques beginning in December 2002.[21]

By early 2003, the apparent failure to obtain useful information from certain detainees at Guantánamo led Defense Secretary Rumsfeld to charge an "Interrogation Working Group" of senior Defense Department lawyers to develop guidance on parameters for interrogation. In April 2003, the Working Group, echoing the earlier Bybee Memo, advised that the President as Commander in Chief could authorize torture despite legal prohibitions. Secretary Rumsfeld's response to the Working Group's report is set forth below. The designation "(U)" means unclassified.

Counter-Resistance Techniques in the War on Terrorism
April 16, 2003
http://www.defense.gov/news/Jun2004/d20040622doc9.pdf

Memorandum for: Commander, US Southern Command

From: Donald Rumsfeld, Secretary of Defense

(U) I have considered the report of the Working Group that I directed be established on January 15, 2003.

(U) I approve the use of specified counter-resistance techniques, subject to the following:

(U) a. The techniques I authorize are those lettered A-X, set out at Tab A.

(U) b. These techniques must be used with all the safeguards described at Tab B.

(U) c. Use of these techniques is limited to interrogations of unlawful combatants held at Guantanamo Bay, Cuba.

---

18. *See* Dana Priest & Barton Gellman, *U.S. Decries Abuse But Defends Interrogations*, Wash. Post, Dec. 26, 2002.

19. *Army Regulation 15-6 Final Report: Investigation of FBI Allegations of Detainee Abuse at Guantanamo Bay, Cuba Detention Facility*, amended June 9, 2005, *reprinted in Administration of Torture: A Documentary Record from Washington to Abu Ghraib and Beyond* A-98, A-110-A-118 (Jameel Jaffer & Amrit Singh eds., 2007).

20. Department of Def. News Release, *DoD Provides Details on Interrogation Process* (June 22, 2004), *available at* http://www.defense.gov/releases/release.aspx?releaseid=7487.

21. Maj. Gen. George R. Fay, *AR 15-6 Investigation of the Abu Ghraib Prison and 205th Military Intelligence Brigade* 29 (Aug. 25, 2004) (hereinafter *Fay Report*), *at* http://www.dod.gov/news/Aug2004/d20040825fay.pdf.

(U) d. Prior to the use of these techniques, the Chairman of the Working Group on Detainee Interrogations in the Global War on Terrorism must brief you and your staff.

(U) I reiterate that US Armed Forces shall continue to treat detainees humanely and, to the extent appropriate and consistent with military necessity, in a manner consistent with the principles of the Geneva Conventions. In addition, if you intend to use techniques B, I, O, or X, you must specifically determine that military necessity requires its use and notify me in advance.

(U) If, in your view, you require additional interrogation techniques for a particular detainee, you should provide me, via the Chairman of the Joint Chiefs of Staff, a written request describing the proposed technique, recommended safeguards, and the rationale for applying it with an identified detainee.

(U) Nothing in this memorandum in any way restricts your existing authority to maintain good order and discipline among detainees.

TAB A. INTERROGATION TECHNIQUES

(U) The use of techniques A-X is subject to the general safeguards as provided below as well as specific implementation guidelines to be provided by the appropriate authority. Specific implementation guidance with respect to techniques A-Q is provided in Army Field Manual 34-52. Further implementation guidance with respect to techniques R-X will need to be developed by the appropriate authority.

(U) Of the techniques set forth below, the policy aspects of certain techniques should be considered to the extent those policy aspects reflect the views of other major U.S. partner nations. Where applicable, the description of the technique is annotated to include a summary of the policy issues that should be considered before application of the technique.

A. (U) Direct: Asking straightforward questions.

B. (U) Incentive/Removal of Incentive: Providing a reward or removing a privilege, above and beyond those that are required by the Geneva Convention, from detainees. (Caution: Other nations that believe that detainees are entitled to POW protections may consider that provision and retention of religious items (e.g., the Koran) are protected under international law (see, Geneva III, Article 34). Although the provisions of the Geneva Convention are not applicable to the interrogation of unlawful combatants, consideration should be given to these views prior to the application of the technique.)

C. (U) Emotional Love: Playing on the love a detainee has for an individual or group.

D. (U) Emotional Hate: Playing on the hatred a detainee has for an individual or group.

E. (U) Fear Up Harsh: Significantly increasing the fear level in a detainee.

F. (U) Fear Up Mild: Moderately increasing the fear level in a detainee.

G. (U) Reduced Fear: Reducing the fear level in a detainee.

H. (U) Pride and Ego Up: Boosting the ego of a detainee.

I. (U) Pride and Ego Down: Attacking or insulting the ego of a detainee, not beyond the limits that would apply to a POW. (Caution: Article 17 of the Geneva III provides, "Prisoners of war who refuse to answer may not be threatened, insulted, or exposed to any unpleasant or disadvantageous treatment of any kind." Other nations that believe that detainees are entitled to POW protections may consider this technique inconsistent with the provisions of Geneva. Although the provisions of Geneva are not applicable to the interrogation of unlawful combatants, consideration should be given to these views prior to application of the technique.)

J. (U) Futility: Invoking the feeling of futility of a detainee.

K. (U) We Know All: Convincing the detainee that the interrogator knows the answer to questions he asks the detainee.

L. (U) Establish Your Identity: Convincing the detainee that the interrogator has mistaken the detainee for someone else.

M. (U) Repetition Approach: Continuously repeating the same question to the detainee within interrogation periods of normal duration.

N. (U) File and Dossier: Convincing the detainee that the interrogator has a damning and inaccurate file, which must be fixed.

O. (U) Mutt and Jeff: A team consisting of a friendly and harsh interrogator. The harsh interrogator might employ the Pride and Ego Down technique. (Caution: Other nations that believe that POW protections apply to detainees may view this technique as inconsistent with the Geneva III, Article 13 which provides that POWs must be protected against acts of intimidation. Although the provisions of Geneva are not applicable to the interrogation of unlawful combatants, consideration should be given to these views prior to application of the technique.)

P. (U) Rapid Fire: Questioning in rapid succession without allowing detainee to answer.

Q. (U) Silence: Staring at the detainee to encourage discomfort.

R. (U) Change of Scenery Up: Removing the detainee from the standard interrogation setting (generally to a location more pleasant, but no worse).

S. (U) Change of Scenery Down: Removing the detainee from the standard interrogation setting and placing him in a setting that may be less comfortable; would not constitute a substantial change in environmental quality.

T. (U) Dietary Manipulation: Changing the diet of a detainee; no intended deprivation of food or water; no adverse medical or cultural effect and without intent to deprive subject of food or water, e.g., hot rations to MREs.

U. (U) Environmental Manipulation: Altering the environment to create moderate discomfort (e.g., adjusting temperature or introducing an unpleasant smell). Conditions would not be such that they would injure the detainee. Detainee would be accompanied by interrogator at all times. (Caution: Based on court cases in other countries, some nations may view application of this technique in certain circumstances to be inhumane. Consideration of these views should be given prior to use of this technique.)

V. (U) Sleep Adjustment: Adjusting the sleeping times of the detainee (e.g., reversing sleep cycles from night to day.) This technique is NOT sleep deprivation.

W. (U) False Flag: Convincing the detainee that individuals from a country other than the United States are interrogating him.

X. (U) Isolation: Isolating the detainee from other detainees while still complying with basic standards of treatment. (Caution: The use of isolation as an interrogation technique requires detailed implementation instructions, including specific guidelines regarding the length of isolation, medical and psychological review, and approval for extensions of the length of isolation by the appropriate level in the chain of command. This technique is not known to have been generally used for interrogation purposes for longer than 30 days. Those nations that believe detainees are subject to POW protections may view use of this technique as inconsistent with the requirements of Geneva III, Article 13 which provides that POWs must be protected against acts of intimidation; Article 14 which provides that POWs are entitled to respect for their person; Article 34 which prohibits coercion and Article 126 which ensures access and basic standards of treatment. Although the provisions of Geneva are not applicable to the interrogation of unlawful combatants, consideration should be given to these views prior to application of the technique.)

TAB B. GENERAL SAFEGUARDS

(U) Application of these interrogation techniques is subject to the following general safeguards: (i) limited to use only at strategic interrogation facilities; (ii) there is a good basis to believe that the detainee possesses critical intelligence; (iii) the detainee is medically and operationally evaluated as suitable (considering all techniques to be used in combination); (iv) interrogators are specifically trained for the technique(s); (v) a specific interrogation plan (including reasonable safeguards, limits on duration, intervals between applications, termination criteria and the presence or availability of qualified medical personnel) has been developed; (vi) there is appropriate supervision; and (vii) there is appropriate specified senior approval for use with any specific detainee (after considering the foregoing and receiving legal advice)....

After the United States and its allies invaded Iraq in March 2003, there reportedly was widespread confusion about permissible techniques for interrogating prisoners there. The Geneva Conventions clearly applied in Iraq to captured Iraqis, but the detention facilities also included members of Al Qaeda and other foreign fighters whose status was unclear, based on Administration determinations concerning those held at Guantanamo. A March 14, 2003, OLC opinion written by John Yoo, *Military Interrogation of Alien Unlawful Combatants Held Outside the United States*,[22] contains extensive analysis of supposed broad authorities of the President to make rules for interrogation that fail to comply with either the CAT or the Geneva Conventions. The opinion also suggested defenses that the President would have available if any executive official were charged with abusive interrogation. The opinion failed, however, to take into account application of the Uniform Code of Military Justice (UCMJ) or the Army Field Manual.

The U.S. military command authority initially ordered that standard Field Manual 34-52 rules be followed. In August 2003, however, Defense Secretary Rumsfeld sent the military overseer of interrogation at Guantánamo, Major General Geoffrey Miller, to Iraq to "rapidly exploit internees for actionable intelligence."[23] General Miller brought with him the list of techniques approved by Secretary Rumsfeld for Guantánamo, some of which exceeded the limits of the Army

---

22. *Available at* http://www.justice.gov/olc/docs/memo-combatantsoutsideunitedstates.pdf.
23. General Antonio M. Taguba, *Article 15-6 Investigation of the 800th Military Police Brigade* 7 (Jan. 31, 2004) (hereinafter *Taguba Report*), *available at* http://news.findlaw.com/hdocs/docs/iraq/tagubarpt.html.

Field Manual, although he noted that the Geneva Conventions were supposed to apply in Iraq. In September, the military commander in Iraq approved a policy on interrogation that included portions of the Guantánamo policy and elements of policies then used by special forces.[24] Central Command disapproved the September policy, however, and in October approved rules that mirrored an outdated version of Field Manual 34-52, which permitted interrogators to control "lighting and heating, as well as food, clothing, and shelter given to detainees."[25] The policy on interrogation in Iraq changed again later in October, the third amendment in less than 30 days.[26]

In January 2004, following public reports of detainee abuse, Lieutenant General Ricardo S. Sanchez, Commander of Combined Joint Task Force Seven in Iraq, requested an investigation of the operations of the 800th Military Police Brigade, the unit in charge of Abu Ghraib prison near Baghdad. Major General Antonio M. Taguba, who was appointed to conduct the investigation, found "numerous incidents of sadistic, blatant, wanton criminal abuses" at the prison, "intentionally perpetrated by several members of the military police guard force." The abuses included "punching, slapping, and kicking detainees," a litany of sexual and vulgar insults and attacks, and threats with loaded weapons.[27] In February 2004, the International Committee of the Red Cross (ICRC) issued a report detailing a number of serious human rights abuses by coalition forces in Iraq between March and November 2003.[28] A March 2004 classified report by the CIA Inspector General concluded that some of the interrogation techniques approved for CIA use by the Department of Justice in 2002 might violate the prohibition on "cruel, inhuman, or degrading" treatment in the Convention Against Torture.[29] Finally, in May 2004, public attention focused on Abu Ghraib after graphic photos of prisoner abuse were exposed by the media.[30]

In June 2004, the OLC memos were leaked. In August 2004, the American Bar Association condemned "any use of torture or other cruel, inhuman, or degrading treatment or punishment upon persons within the custody or under the physical control of the United States government [and] any endorsement or authorization of such measures by government lawyers."[31]

Two months after the public disclosure of abuses at Abu Ghraib, the August 2002 Bybee Memo, *supra* n.13, was withdrawn by OLC head Jack Goldsmith because he thought it was "sloppily reasoned, overbroad, and incautious in asserting

---

24. Subsequent investigators described a migration to Iraq of Guantánamo techniques—such as the use of dogs and forced nudity—to intimidate and dehumanize detainees. *See Schlesinger Report, supra* n.13, at 36; *Fay Report, supra* n.21, at 10.

25. *Schlesinger Report, supra* n.14, at 37-38; *see* Department of the Army, *Intelligence Interrogation* (FM 34-52) ch. 3 (Sept. 28, 1992).

26. *Fay Report, supra* n.21, at 28.

27. *Taguba Report, supra* n.23.

28. *Report of the International Committee of the Red Cross (ICRC) on the Treatment by the Coalition Forces of Prisoners of War and Other Protected Persons by the Geneva Conventions in Iraq During Arrest, Internment and Interrogation* (Feb. 2004), *available at* http://www.informationclearinghouse.info/pdf/icrc_iraq.pdf.

29. Douglas Jehl, *Report Warned on CIA's Tactics in Interrogation,* N.Y. Times, Nov. 9, 2005.

30. The Abu Ghraib photos are collected at http://www.salon.com/news/abu_ghraib/2006/03/14/introduction. In November 2009, Secretary of Defense Robert Gates blocked the release of 2,000 additional photos depicting detainee abuse in Iraq and Afghanistan. Gates acted on the basis of authority granted in a Department of Homeland Security Appropriations Act. *Gates Blocks Detainee Abuse Photos* (CBS News, Nov. 14, 2009), *at* http://www.cbc.ca/news/world/story/2009/11/14/prisoner-abuse-photos014.html.

31. ABA House of Delegates, *Resolution 10-B* (Aug. 9, 2004).

extraordinary constitutional authorities on behalf of the President."[32] A new opinion superseding the Bybee Memo was delivered on December 30, 2004.[33] The new memorandum questioned "the appropriateness and relevance of the non-statutory discussion . . . and various aspects of the statutory analysis" in the earlier memo — namely, the assertion that torture required organ failure, impaired bodily function, or death.[34] However, the new memorandum did not disagree with any substantive conclusions offered by the 2002 memorandum. Moreover, it continued to maintain that it was unlikely that a person who "acted in good faith, and only after reasonable investigation establishing that his conduct would not inflict severe physical or mental pain or suffering," would possess the specific intent required to violate the torture statute.[35]

A March 2006 news story described the existence of a temporary, top-secret detention site at Camp Nana, near Baghdad, that since early 2004 included a "Black Room" where placards posted by soldiers stated, "No blood, no foul."[36] Detainee abuse attributed to the Special Operations unit at Camp Nana reflected "confusion over and, in some cases, disregard for" interrogation rules and standards for treatment of detainees.[37]

Since 2006, *WikiLeaks*, an international nonprofit whistle-blowing Web site, has published nearly 400,000 secret U.S. Army field reports. The reports indicate that U.S. authorities failed to investigate hundreds of reports of abuse, rape, and even murder by Iraqi police and U.S. soldiers. These reports, often supported by medical evidence, describe prisoners shackled, blindfolded, hung by wrists or ankles, and subjected to whipping, punching, kicking, or electric shocks. Six reports end with a detainee's apparent death.[38]

A February 2006 United Nations report on the Guantánamo Bay detentions, compiled by U.N. envoys who interviewed former detainees, their families, and their lawyers, along with U.S. officials, concluded that U.S. treatment of detainees there violated the detainees' rights to physical and mental health and, in some cases, constituted torture. United Nations Comm'n on Human Rights, *Situation of Detainees at Guantanamo Bay* (Feb. 15, 2006), *available at* http://www.usawatch.org/docs/E.CN.4.2006.120_.pdf. The United States replied to the U.N. report with a factual and legal defense, *Reply of the Government of the United States of America to the Report of the Five UNCHR Special Rapporteurs on Detainees in Guantanamo Bay, Cuba* (Mar. 10, 2006), *available at* http://www.asil.org/pdfs/ilib0603212.pdf.

In 2008, the Senate Armed Services Committee completed another investigation of detainee treatment:

32. Jack Goldsmith, *The Terror Presidency* 10 (2007).

33. Memorandum for James B. Comey, Deputy Attorney General, from Daniel Levin, Acting Assistant Attorney General, *Legal Standards Applicable Under 18 U.S.C. 2340-2340A* (Dec. 30, 2004), *at* http://www.justice.gov/olc/18usc23402340a2.htm.

34. *Id.* at 1-2.

35. *Id.* at 17.

36. Eric Schmitt & Carolyn Marshall, *In Secret Unit's "Black Room," A Grim Portrait of U.S. Abuse*, N.Y. Times, Mar. 19, 2006.

37. *Id.*

38. Nick Davies, Jonathan Steel & David Leigh, *Iraq War Logs: Secret Files Show How US Ignored Torture*, Guardian, Oct. 22, 2010.

Senate Armed Services Committee Inquiry into the Treatment of Detainees in U.S. Custody

Dec. 11, 2008

http://levin.senate.gov/newsroom/supporting/2008/Detainees.121108.pdf

EXECUTIVE SUMMARY...

(U) The collection of timely and accurate intelligence is critical to the safety of U.S. personnel deployed abroad and to the security of the American people here at home. The methods by which we elicit intelligence information from detainees in our custody affect not only the reliability of that information, but our broader efforts to win hearts and minds and attract allies to our side.

(U) Al Qaeda and Taliban terrorists are taught to expect Americans to abuse them. They are recruited based on false propaganda that says the United States is out to destroy Islam. Treating detainees harshly only reinforces that distorted view, increases resistance to cooperation, and creates new enemies. In fact, the April 2006 National Intelligence Estimate "Trends in Global Terrorism: Implications for the United States" cited "pervasive anti U.S. sentiment among most Muslims" as an underlying factor fueling the spread of the global jihadist movement. Former Navy General Counsel Alberto Mora testified to the Senate Armed Services Committee in June 2008 that "there are serving U.S. flag-rank officers who maintain that the first and second identifiable causes of U.S. combat deaths in Iraq — as judged by their effectiveness in recruiting insurgent fighters into combat — are, respectively the symbols of Abu Ghraib and Guantanamo."

(U) The abuse of detainees in U.S. custody cannot simply be attributed to the actions of "a few bad apples" acting on their own. The fact is that senior officials in the United States government solicited information on how to use aggressive techniques, redefined the law to create the appearance of their legality, and authorized their use against detainees. Those efforts damaged our ability to collect accurate intelligence that could save lives, strengthened the hand of our enemies, and compromised our moral authority. This report is a product of the Committee's inquiry into how those unfortunate results came about....

SENATE ARMED SERVICES COMMITTEE CONCLUSIONS

Conclusion 1: On February 7, 2002, President George W. Bush made a written determination that Common Article 3 of the Geneva Conventions, which would have afforded minimum standards for humane treatment, did not apply to al Qaeda or Taliban detainees. Following the President's determination, techniques such as waterboarding, nudity, and stress positions, used in SERE [Survival Evasion Resistance and Escape] training to simulate tactics used by enemies that refuse to follow the Geneva Conventions, were authorized for use in interrogations of detainees in U.S. custody.

Conclusion 2: Members of the President's Cabinet and other senior officials participated in meetings inside the White House in 2002 and 2003 where specific interrogation techniques were discussed. National Security Council Principals reviewed the CIA's interrogation program during that period.

Conclusions on SERE Training Techniques and Interrogations

Conclusion 3: The use of techniques similar to those used in SERE resistance training — such as stripping students of their clothing, placing them in stress positions, putting hoods over their heads, and treating them like animals — was at odds with the commitment to humane treatment of detainees in U.S. custody. Using those techniques for interrogating detainees was also inconsistent with the goal of collecting accurate intelligence information, as the purpose of SERE resistance training is to increase the ability of U.S. personnel to resist abusive interrogations and the techniques used were based, in part, on Chinese Communist techniques used during the Korean War to elicit false confessions.

Conclusion 4: The use of techniques in interrogations derived from SERE resistance training created a serious risk of physical and psychological harm to detainees. The SERE schools employ strict controls to reduce the risk of physical and psychological harm to students during training. Those controls include medical and psychological screening for students, interventions by trained psychologists during training, and code words to ensure that students can stop the application of a technique at any time should the need arise. Those same controls are not present in real world interrogations.

Conclusions on Senior Official Consideration of SERE Techniques for Interrogations

Conclusion 5: In July 2002, the Office of the Secretary of Defense General Counsel solicited information from the Joint Personnel Recovery Agency (JPRA) [an agency expert in training U.S. personnel to withstand interrogation techniques considered unlawful under the Geneva Conventions] on SERE techniques for use during interrogations. That solicitation, prompted by requests from Department of Defense General Counsel William J. Haynes II, reflected the view that abusive tactics similar to those used by our enemies should be considered for use against detainees in U.S. custody.

Conclusion 6: The Central Intelligence Agency's (CIA) interrogation program included at least one SERE training technique, waterboarding. Senior Administration lawyers, including Alberto Gonzales, Counsel to the President, and David Addington, Counsel to the Vice President, were consulted on the development of legal analysis of CIA interrogation techniques. Legal opinions subsequently issued by the Department of Justice's Office of Legal Counsel (OLC) interpreted legal obligations under U.S. anti-torture laws and determined the legality of CIA interrogation techniques. Those OLC opinions distorted the meaning and intent of anti-torture laws, rationalized the abuse of detainees in U.S. custody and influenced Department of Defense determinations as to what interrogation techniques were legal for use during interrogations conducted by U.S. military personnel.

Conclusions on JPRA Offensive Activities

Conclusion 7: Joint Personnel Recovery Agency (JPRA) efforts in support of "offensive" interrogation operations went beyond the agency's knowledge and expertise. JPRA's support to U.S. government interrogation efforts contributed to detainee abuse. JPRA's offensive support also influenced the development of policies that authorized abusive interrogation techniques for use against detainees in U.S. custody.

Conclusion 8: Detainee abuse occurred during JPRA's support to Special Mission Unit (SMU) Task Force (TF) interrogation operations in Iraq in September 2003. JPRA Commander Colonel Randy Moulton's authorization of SERE instructors, who had no experience in detainee interrogations, to actively participate in Task Force interrogations using SERE resistance training techniques was a serious failure in judgment. The Special Mission Unit Task Force Commander's failure to order that SERE resistance training techniques not be used in detainee interrogations was a serious failure in leadership that led to the abuse of detainees in Task Force custody. Iraq is a Geneva Convention theater and techniques used in SERE school are inconsistent with the obligations of U.S. personnel under the Geneva Conventions. . . .

Conclusions on GTMO's Request for Aggressive Techniques

Conclusion 10: Interrogation techniques in Guantanamo Bay's (GTMO) October 11, 2002 request for authority submitted by Major General Michael Dunlavey, were influenced by JPRA training for GTMO interrogation personnel and included techniques similar to those used in SERE training to teach U.S. personnel to resist abusive enemy interrogations. GTMO Staff Judge Advocate Lieutenant Colonel Diane Beaver's legal review justifying the October 11, 2002 GTMO request was profoundly in error and legally insufficient. Leaders at GTMO, including Major General Dunlavey's successor, Major General Geoffrey Miller, ignored warnings from DoD's Criminal Investigative Task Force and the Federal Bureau of Investigation that the techniques were potentially unlawful and that their use would strengthen detainee resistance. . . .

Conclusion 13: Secretary of Defense Donald Rumsfeld's authorization of aggressive interrogation techniques for use at Guantanamo Bay was a direct cause of detainee abuse there. Secretary Rumsfeld's December 2, 2002 approval of Mr. Haynes's recommendation that most of the techniques contained in GTMO's October 11, 2002 request be authorized, influenced and contributed to the use of abusive techniques, including military working dogs, forced nudity, and stress positions, in Afghanistan and Iraq.

Conclusion 14: Department of Defense General Counsel William J. Haynes II's direction to the Department of Defense's Detainee Working Group in early 2003 to consider a legal memo from John Yoo of the Department of Justice's OLC as authoritative, blocked the Working Group from conducting a fair and complete legal analysis and resulted in a report that, in the words of then Department of the Navy General Counsel Alberto Mora contained "profound mistakes in its legal analysis." Reliance on the OLC memo resulted in a final Working Group report that recommended approval of several aggressive techniques, including removal of clothing, sleep deprivation, and slapping, similar to those used in SERE training to teach U.S. personnel to resist abusive interrogations.

Conclusions on Interrogations in Iraq and Afghanistan

Conclusion 15: Special Mission Unit (SMU) Task Force (TF) interrogation policies were influenced by the Secretary of Defense's December 2, 2002 approval of aggressive interrogation techniques for use at GTMO. SMU TF interrogation policies in Iraq included the use of aggressive interrogation techniques such as military working dogs and stress positions. SMU TF policies were a direct cause of detainee abuse and influenced interrogation policies at Abu Ghraib and elsewhere in Iraq.

Conclusion 16: During his assessment visit to Iraq in August and September 2003, GTMO Commander Major General Geoffrey Miller encouraged a view that interrogators should be more aggressive during detainee interrogations.

Conclusion 17: Interrogation policies approved by Lieutenant General Ricardo Sanchez, which included the use of military working dogs and stress positions, were a direct cause of detainee abuse in Iraq. Lieutenant General Sanchez's decision to issue his September 14, 2003 policy with the knowledge that there were ongoing discussions as to the legality of some techniques in it was a serious error in judgment. The September policy was superseded on October 12, 2003 as a result of legal concerns raised by U.S. Central Command. That superseding policy, however, contained ambiguities and contributed to confusion about whether aggressive techniques, such as military working dogs, were authorized for use during interrogations.

Conclusion 18: U.S. Central Command (CENTCOM) failed to conduct proper oversight of Special Mission Unit Task Force interrogation policies. Though aggressive interrogation techniques were removed from Combined Joint Task Force 7 interrogation policies after CENTCOM raised legal concerns about their inclusion in the September 14, 2003 policy issued by Lieutenant General Sanchez, SMU TF interrogation policies authorized some of those same techniques, including stress positions and military working dogs.

Conclusion 19: The abuse of detainees at Abu Ghraib in late 2003 was not simply the result of a few soldiers acting on their own. Interrogation techniques such as stripping detainees of their clothes, placing them in stress positions, and using military working dogs to intimidate them appeared in Iraq only after they had been approved for use in Afghanistan and at GTMO. Secretary of Defense Donald Rumsfeld's December 2, 2002 authorization of aggressive interrogation techniques and subsequent interrogation policies and plans approved by senior military and civilian officials conveyed the message that physical pressures and degradation were appropriate treatment for detainees in U.S. military custody. What followed was an erosion in standards dictating that detainees be treated humanely.

B. APPLYING THE INTERROGATION LAWS

On April 16, 2009, President Obama authorized the release of four previously undisclosed OLC memos describing interrogation techniques used by the CIA between 2002 and 2005. One, quoted *supra* p. 928 and signed by Jay S. Bybee in 2002, purported to give the CIA legal approval for waterboarding and other harsh treatment, including forced nudity, slamming detainees into walls, and prolonged sleep deprivation. Three others, signed by Stephen G. Bradbury in May 2005, also concluded that the harsh techniques were lawful, even when multiple methods were used in combination. The memos are *available at* http://www.fas.org/irp/agency/doj/olc/index.html.

NOTES AND QUESTIONS

a. **Legality Under International Law**

1. *The Convention Against Torture.* Do any of the techniques in Defense Secretary Rumsfeld's April 16, 2003, memo on Guantánamo exceed the limits set out in

the Torture Convention or the U.S. understandings? See *supra* p. 914. Which techniques? Would the same methods be lawful in Iraq? At some undisclosed offshore location?

Do any of the techniques in Rumsfeld's memo exceed the limits of the Torture Act, 18 U.S.C. §§2340-2340B, *supra* p. 915. Recall that in August 2002 the Justice Department's OLC offered a very narrow definition of "torture," see *supra* p. 928, and argued that in any case the President could authorize torture. It also indicated that interrogation activities "may be cruel, inhuman, or degrading, but still not produce pain and suffering of the requisite intensity" to violate §2340. Bybee Memo, *supra* p. 929 n.13, at 1. The memorandum also asserted that a specific intent to torture is required to violate the torture statute. *Id.* at 4. How would you rate this definition of the key terms against those set out in the Torture Convention, the Torture Act, and the U.S. understanding? *See* Seth F. Kreimer, *"Torture Lite," "Full Bodied" Torture, and the Insulation of Legal Conscience*, 1 J. Nat'l Security L. & Pol'y 187 (2005); Duncan Campbell, *U.S. Interrogators Turn to "Torture Lite,"* Guardian, Jan. 25, 2003. Could the Bybee Memo effectively exempt the CIA from complying with the CAT and the Torture Act?

2. *Applying the Geneva Conventions.* Recall from our consideration of the Geneva Conventions in Chapters 9 and 31 that each one requires nations to criminalize "grave breaches," including acts of "torture or inhuman treatment." Each Convention also calls on nations to "take measures necessary for the suppression of all acts contrary to the provisions of the present Convention other than the grave breaches." One such provision important here is Common Article 3, which requires detainees of every description to be treated humanely, and which forbids "cruel treatment and torture," as well as "outrages on personal dignity, in particular, humiliating and degrading treatment." See *supra* p. 918. The War Crimes Act, *supra* p. 917, was supposed to satisfy U.S. obligations under the Geneva Conventions in this regard by criminalizing grave breaches as well as violations of Common Article 3.

The Bush administration took the position in early 2002 that Al Qaeda and Taliban prisoners were "unlawful combatants" not protected by the Geneva Convention Relative to the Treatment of Prisoners of War (Geneva III), the one most clearly relevant here. Because Geneva III was inapplicable, it argued, the War Crimes Act incorporating it by reference necessarily did not apply to U.S. officials interrogating such prisoners. The White House, President George W. Bush, *Memorandum for the Vice President et al.: Humane Treatment of al Qaeda and Taliban Detainees* (Feb. 7, 2002), *available at* http://www.aclu.org/files/assets/CIA.pdf. The Administration's arguments are reviewed in the following paragraphs.

a. *Terrorists as Protected Belligerents?* The Bush administration first argued that the Geneva Conventions did not apply to members of Al Qaeda, because Al Qaeda is not a High Contracting Party to the Conventions. On the other hand, members of the Taliban, as a group representing the de facto government of Afghanistan, a High Contracting Party, were said to be covered by the Conventions.

As a practical matter, of course, Al Qaeda depended heavily on Taliban support—bordering on sponsorship—in order to carry out its terrorist attacks against the United States. At the same time, the Taliban appear to have been heavily influenced by Al Qaeda. See *supra* p. 340. Under the circumstances, does it make sense to apply the Conventions differently to members of the two enemy groups?

b. *Character of the Conflict.* The Administration maintained that neither Al Qaeda nor Taliban members were entitled to the protection of Common Article 3, however, because the conflict was, at least initially, international, not one described as "not of an international character." Is this argument consistent with the contention that the Taliban were covered by the Conventions generally because the Taliban were the de facto government of Afghanistan? Can you say how the applicability of Common Article 3 to the Taliban might have changed after the election of the Karzai government in Afghanistan in June 2002, when the conflict became internal and foreign forces remained in the country at the invitation of the new government? Should it have changed?

c. *Location of the Fighting?* In *Hamdan v. Rumsfeld,* 548 U.S. 557 (2006), the Supreme Court found that Common Article 3 affords some protection to persons who are not associated with a signatory or nonsignatory "Power" but who are involved in a conflict "in the territory of" a signatory. The Court construed the phrase "not of an international character" literally to distinguish conflicts between nations. Do you think it is consistent with the purposes of the Geneva Conventions to make their application dependent upon where a prisoner is captured?

d. *Status as POWs?* The Administration also insisted that the Taliban were not entitled to protections afforded prisoners of war under Geneva III. Article 4 of the Convention defines POWs as combatants who have a "fixed distinctive sign recognizable at a distance," carry arms openly, and conduct operations in accordance with the laws and customs of war. It was supported in this argument in *United States v. Lindh,* 212 F. Supp. 2d 541 (E.D. Va. 2002). The requirements in question are designed to enable belligerents on one side to distinguish those on the other from noncombatants, who must not be attacked.

A POW must be "humanely treated," and he may not be required to divulge more than his name, rank, serial number, and age. Moreover,

> [n]o physical or mental torture, nor any other form of coercion, may be inflicted on prisoners of war to secure from them information of any kind whatever. Prisoners of war who refuse to answer may not be threatened, insulted, or exposed to unpleasant or disadvantageous treatment of any kind. [Geneva III, art. 17.]

POW status also brings other privileges, including the right to retain personal belongings, to quartering under conditions as favorable as those of the custodian, and to communicate with family members.

Once a prisoner of any sort is in custody, should his failure to fit the definition of a POW expose him to torture or inhumane treatment? Note that Common Article 3 applies to all prisoners, regardless of their status.

e. *Determination of Status.* Article 5 of Geneva Convention III entitles detainees to a determination of whether they are POWs or not by a "competent tribunal." The OLC asserted in its January 22, 2002, memorandum, however, that there can be no doubt about the POW status of any individual affiliated with the Taliban, because the organization was found not to meet the requirements of Article 4. Memorandum for Alberto R. Gonzales, Counsel to the President, and William J. Haynes II, General Counsel, Department of Defense, from Jay S. Bybee, Office of Legal Counsel,

Re: Application of Treaties and Laws to Al Qaeda and Taliban Detainees (Jan. 22, 2002), *available at* http://www.justice.gov/olc/docs/memo-laws-taliban-detainees.pdf. This position appeared to be at variance with U.S. practice in other settings. *See* Jennifer Elsea, *Treatment of "Battlefield Detainees" in the War on Terrorism* 36 (Cong. Res. Serv. RL31367), Jan. 23, 2007 (noting that the United States has in the past required an individualized assessment of detainee status before denying POW status). In the view of one observer, it is "discouraging . . . to see American lawyers arguing for the inapplicability of the Conventions on grounds that are strikingly similar . . . to those invoked by Germany" during World War II. Waldron, *supra*, at 1695.

Can you say what constitutes a "competent tribunal" for purposes of Article 5? Can the President be a "competent tribunal"? Did the U.S. refusal, at least initially, to employ such a tribunal to determine the status of each detainee constitute a violation of the Article 5? If so, would that violation provide an enemy with an argument for arbitrarily denying captured U.S. soldiers the protections of POW status?

f. *Prohibition of Torture as a Customary Norm?* Recall that the United States has recognized Article 75 of Geneva Protocol I as customary international law. See *supra* p. 247. It forbids "torture of all kinds, whether physical or mental," as well as "outrages upon personal dignity, in particular humiliating and degrading treatment, . . . any form of indecent assault, . . . and threats to commit any of the foregoing acts." Protocol I, art. 75(2). Technically, Protocol I applies only to conflicts of an international character. But as customary law, does Article 75 set a baseline for *all* "persons who are in the power of a Party"?

g. *Treatment of Noncombatants?* In remarks about the detention facility at Guantánamo Bay in early 2002, Defense Secretary Rumsfeld declared that "[s]ometimes when you capture a big, large group there will be someone who just happened to be in there that didn't belong in there." *Secretary Rumsfeld Media Availability En Route to Camp X-Ray,* Jan. 27, 2002, *available at* http://www.defense.gov/transcripts/transcript.aspx?transcriptid=2338. What rights do such innocent bystanders have, once detained?

3. *The New Paradigm?* In 2002, White House Counsel Alberto R. Gonzales argued in a memorandum to President Bush that the "nature of the new war" and the "new paradigm render[] obsolete Geneva's strict limitations" on questioning and make other Geneva provisions "quaint." *Decision Re Application of the Geneva Convention on Prisoners of War to the Conflict with Al Qaeda and the Taliban* (Jan. 25, 2002), *available at* http://www.slate.com/features/whatistorture/LegalMemos.html. How would you rebut Gonzales's interpretation? Do Gonzales's arguments apply with equal force in Afghanistan and in Iraq? To detainees captured elsewhere? *See* Derek Jinks & David Sloss, *Is the President Bound by the Geneva Conventions?*, 90 Cornell L. Rev. 97 (2004) (concluding that the President is bound by the Geneva Conventions).

Review the provisions of the Detainee Treatment Act and Executive Order No. 13,491, *supra* pp. 921, 922. If these laws had been in place beginning in October 2001, in what respects, if at all, would the lawfulness of U.S. interrogation practices have been different? Do you think U.S. interrogations would have been conducted differently?

4. *Outsourcing and Hiding Torture?* Article 49 of the Fourth Geneva Convention prohibits "deportations of protected persons from occupied territory." Such a deportation or transfer or unlawful confinement of a protected person is a "grave breach"

of the convention. Geneva IV art. 147. On March 19, 2004, the OLC drafted a memo indicating that the CIA could transfer detainees out of Iraq for interrogation, despite the Geneva Convention, by construing the ban not to apply to illegal aliens who have no legal right to remain in Iraq. The memo concluded that the temporary relocation of persons not charged with a crime to face interrogation at another location outside Iraq is not akin to the wartime practices the Geneva Convention was designed to forbid. Draft Memorandum from Jack Goldsmith, Assistant Attorney General, to Alberto R. Gonzales, Counsel to the President, *Permissibility of Relocating Certain "Protected Persons" from Occupied Iraq* (Mar. 19, 2004), *available at* http://www.washingtonpost.com/wp-srv/nation/documents/doj_memo031904.pdf. The CIA then transported as many as a dozen detainees from Iraq to other countries between March and October of 2004. *See* Dana Priest, *Memo Lets CIA Take Detainees Out of Iraq,* Wash. Post, Oct. 24, 2004. (The practice of "extraordinary rendition" is addressed in Chapter 33.)

The CIA also reportedly held dozens, perhaps up to 100, persons in Iraq as "ghost detainees." In June or July 2003, for example, Hiwa Abdul Rahman Rashul, a suspected member of the Iraqi Al-Ansar terrorist group who was nicknamed "Triple X" by CIA and military officials, was captured by Kurdish fighters. He was turned over to the CIA, which rendered him to Afghanistan for interrogation, then brought him back to Iraq. Then-Director of Central Intelligence (DCI) George Tenet asked Defense Secretary Rumsfeld not to give Rashul a prisoner number and to hide him from the Red Cross. Rashul was then lost in the Iraqi prison system for seven months. When asked about the legal basis for hiding Rashul, Rumsfeld replied, "We know from our knowledge that [Tenet] has authority to do this." *Id.*; Eric Schmitt & Thom Shanker, *Rumsfeld Issued an Order to Hide Detainee in Iraq,* N.Y. Times, June 17, 2004. In late 2005, Human Rights Watch provided a list of 26 "ghost detainees" believed to be in U.S. custody. *U.S. Holding at Least Twenty-Six "Ghost Detainees"* (Dec. 1, 2005). One secret CIA prison was reportedly code-named Bright Light, where the most important Al Qaeda detainees were held in an undisclosed location. James Risen, *State of War: The Secret History of the CIA and the Bush Administration* 31 (2006).

What could be wrong with hiding a detainee in this fashion? How would you respond to the OLC's legal justification for rendering "ghost detainees"?

In a 2006 televised speech, President Bush stated that some individuals captured by the United States

> pose a significant threat, or may have intelligence that we and our allies need . . . and they withhold information that could save American lives. In these cases, it has been necessary to move these individuals to an environment where they can be held secretly, questioned by experts . . . . And so the CIA used an alternative set of procedures. [The White House, *President Discusses Creation of Military Commissions to Try Suspected Terrorists,* Sept. 6, 2006, *available at* http://georgewbush-whitehouse.archives.gov/news/releases/2006/09/20060906-3.html.]

On the basis of what authority would the President have ordered such an "alternative set of procedures"?

b. Responsibility for Abuse

1. *Assigning Responsibility.* Guidance for interrogations at Abu Ghraib prison came from three different sources at different times — from Army field manuals, from personnel who had worked earlier in Afghanistan, and from Guantánamo.

Craig Gordon, *High-Pressure Tactics: Critics Say Bush Policies—Post 9/11—Gave Interrogators Leeway to Push Beyond Normal Limits*, Newsday, May 23, 2004. General Taguba found that operating procedures and copies of the Geneva Conventions were not distributed to the guards handling the prisoners. To complicate matters, senior military commanders called for interrogators to isolate and manipulate detainees who might have "significant intelligence value." R. Jeffrey Smith, *Memo Gave Intelligence Bigger Role: Increased Pressure Sought on Prisoners*, Wash. Post, May 21, 2004.

The overall detention and interrogation picture that has emerged from official statements and documents reveals "a trail of fitful ad hoc policymaking" where interrogation techniques were authorized, then rescinded or modified, at times leading to decisions made in the field or at the Pentagon on a case-by-case basis. Dana Priest & Bradley Graham, *U.S. Struggled Over How Far to Push Tactics*, Wash. Post, June 24, 2004. Unlike CIA requests for expanded interrogation authority that were reviewed by the Department of Justice and the National Security Council, Defense Department interrogation policy decisions were not subjected to outside review. *Id.*

2. *Investigating Interrogation Abuses.* An investigation led by former Secretary of Defense James Schlesinger found 300 allegations of abuse and 66 substantiated cases of confirmed or possible abuse in Iraq.[39] An Army investigation determined that the abuses "resulted from the failure of individuals to follow known standards of discipline and Army values and, in some cases, the failure of a few leaders to enforce those standards of discipline."[40] The Army decided not to charge any of those leaders with wrongdoing, however, finding some senior officers "responsible" but not "culpable."[41] By contrast, the Schlesinger investigation found that the abuses were "more than the failure of a few leaders to enforce proper discipline. There is both institutional and personal responsibility at higher levels."[42]

On March 22, 2006, an Army spokesman reported more than 600 accusations of detainee abuse in Iraq and Afghanistan since October 2001 and disciplinary actions against 251 soldiers.[43]

c.   Criminal Liability

1. *Prosecuting Abuses.* Seven Military Police and two military intelligence soldiers were convicted under the UCMJ of abusing detainees at Abu Ghraib, while 251 other soldiers and officers were punished in some way for detainee abuse in Iraq and Afghanistan.[44] Three of the five officers investigated by the Army for their role in the Abu Ghraib abuses were cleared; Colonel Thomas Pappas, commander of Abu Ghraib prison, was reprimanded and fined, while Brigadier General Janis Karpinski, another commander of Abu Ghraib, was demoted to the rank of colonel.[45] Although

---

39. *Schlesinger Report, supra* n.14, at 5.
40. U.S. Army News Release, *Army Releases Findings in Detainee-Abuse Investigations* (May 5, 2005), *at* http://news.findlaw.com/wash/s/20050506/20050506145910.html.
41. Josh White & Thomas E. Ricks, *Officers Won't Be Charged in Prison Scandal*, Wash. Post, Aug. 27, 2004.
42. *Schlesinger Report, supra* n.14, at 5.
43. Eric Schmitt, *Iraq Abuse Trial Is Again Limited to Lower Ranks*, N.Y. Times, Mar. 23, 2006.
44. *Id.*; Eric Schmitt, *Army Dog Handler Is Convicted in Detainee Abuse at Abu Ghraib*, N.Y. Times, Mar. 22, 2006.
45. U.S. Army News Release, *Army Releases Findings in Detainee-Abuse Investigations* (May 5, 2005), *at* http://news.findlaw.com/wash/s/20050506/20050506145910.html; Frontline, *The Torture Question: Frequently Asked Questions* (PBS, Oct. 18, 2005), *at* http://www.pbs.org/wgbh/pages/frontline/torture/etc/faqs.html#8.

Lieutenant Colonel Steven Jordan, director of the interrogation center at Abu Ghraib, was convicted for disobeying an order when he spoke with others about the Abu Ghraib investigation, his commanding general dismissed the charge and removed the conviction from Jordan's record.[46] Only one person connected to the post-9/11 interrogations has been criminally prosecuted in U.S. civilian courts for detainee abuse. David Passaro, a former CIA contractor, was convicted of assault for beating an Afghan detainee who later died.[47]

In June 2005 the Defense Department promoted or nominated for promotion the former deputy commander of U.S. forces in Iraq and the senior military lawyer for the U.S. command in Baghdad, both involved in overseeing or advising detention and interrogation operations during the Abu Ghraib scandal. The top intelligence officer in Iraq at that time was promoted earlier in the year. Eric Schmitt, *Army Moves to Advance 2 Linked to Abu Ghraib*, N.Y. Times, June 29, 2005. The *Schlesinger Report*, *supra* p. 929 n.14, had found those officers to be among those responsible for the abuses at Abu Ghraib, and the Fay Report, *supra* p. 930 n.21, faulted the commanders for issuing and revising the interrogation rules three times in 30 days, and faulted their legal staffs for giving bad advice — not warning that practices permitted at Guantánamo and in Afghanistan might not be lawful in Iraq. Nevertheless, the Army Inspector General cleared them of any wrongdoing. Inspector Gen., Department of the Army, *Detainee Operations Inspection* (July 21, 2004), *at* http://www.washingtonpost.com/wp-srv/world/iraq/abughraib/detaineereport.pdf.

Only low-level interrogators and handlers were disciplined for interrogation abuses in Afghanistan and at Guantánamo. A review by Air Force Lieutenant General Randall M. Schmidt of three years' practice and more than 24,000 interrogations at Guantánamo led to a recommendation of reprimand for Army Major General Geoffrey C. Miller, commander of the Guantánamo facility in 2002 and 2003, for failing to oversee the interrogation of a high-value detainee who was subjected to abusive treatment. *Army Regulation 15-6: Final Report, Investigation into FBI Allegations of Detainee Abuse at Guantanamo Bay, Cuba Detention Facility* (Apr. 1, 2005, amended June 9, 2005). Nevertheless, the Army's Inspector General decided that Miller had not violated the law or Defense Department policy. David S. Cloud, *Guantanamo Reprimand Was Sought, An Aide Says*, N.Y. Times, July 13, 2005. One suggested reason for the failure to hold senior officials accountable is the lack of an independent prosecutor inside the military, equivalent to a district attorney, who would have command authority to investigate up the chain of command. Eric Schmitt, *Iraq Abuse Trial Is Again Limited to Lower Ranks*, N.Y. Times, Mar. 23, 2006.

At a news conference called in response to the Abu Ghraib publicity in June 2004, White House Counsel Alberto Gonzales denied that "the president . . . authorized, ordered or directed" violations of "the standards of the torture conventions or the torture statute." *Transcript of Press Briefing by Alberto Gonzales* (June 22, 2004). What legal wiggle room does the Gonzales statement leave for the President? Does it mean that President Bush was not responsible for the reported abuses? What do the findings of the Senate Armed Services Committee suggest about the responsibility of the President and other high-ranking Administration officials for the abuses described in their report?

---

46. Josh White, *Army Officer Is Cleared in Abu Ghraib Scandal*, Wash. Post, Jan. 10, 2008.
47. Elizabeth Dunbar, *Ex-CIA Contractor Sentenced to Prison*, Wash. Post, Feb. 13, 2007.

Who do you think is responsible for the abuses at Guantánamo, Abu Ghraib, and Camp Nana?

2. *Possible Defenses to Torture Charges.*

a. *Necessity and Self-Defense.* The criminal law doctrine of self-defense permits the use of force to prevent harm to another person:

Model Penal Code §3.02. Justification Generally: Choice of Evils.

(1) Conduct that the actor believes to be necessary to avoid a harm or evil to himself or to another is justifiable, provided that:

(a) the harm or evil sought to be avoided by such conduct is greater than that sought to be prevented by the law defining the offense charged; and

(b) neither the Code nor other law defining the offense provides exceptions or defenses dealing with the specific situation involved; and

(c) a legislative purpose to exclude the justification claimed does not otherwise plainly appear. . . .

Does that doctrine apply in this setting to excuse otherwise unlawful torture or inhumane treatment by an interrogator of a prisoner? Must the information sought by interrogators be available by no other means than torture? Is an individual claim of self-defense portable to the entire executive branch in the war on terrorism? Would a necessity defense be available even where Congress clearly proscribed the conduct so defended, as it did in the Torture Act? *See* Wayne R. LaFave & Austin W. Scott, 1 *Substantive Criminal Law* §5.4, at 629 (1986). Might such a defense be available to someone charged with carrying out even a specious legal authorization of torture? *See Public Comm. Against Torture in Israel v. State of Israel*, H.C. 5100/94, 53(4) P.D. 817 (1999) (necessity defense available for conduct necessary to save a life from substantial danger of serious harm, absent alternative means for neutralizing the harm).

Does the presence of an arguable defense to an act of torture nullify the requirement that the torture be legally authorized? *See* William C. Banks & Peter Raven-Hansen, *Targeted Killing and Assassination: The U.S. Legal Framework*, 37 U. Rich. L. Rev. 667, 668 (2003) (basic rule of law requires positive legal authority for government actions).

b. *Reasonable Reliance on Official Advice?* The criminal law also provides a defense for ignorance or mistake in some limited circumstances:

Model Penal Code §2.04. Ignorance or Mistake.

(1) Ignorance or mistake as to a matter of fact or law is a defense if:

(a) the ignorance or mistake negatives the purpose, knowledge, belief, recklessness or negligence required to establish a material element of the offense . . . .

(3) A belief that conduct does not legally constitute an offense is a defense to a prosecution for that offense based upon such conduct when:

(a) the statute or other enactment defining the offense is not known to the actor and has not been published or otherwise reasonably made available prior to the conduct alleged; or

(b) he acts in reasonable reliance upon an official statement of the law, afterward determined to be invalid or erroneous, contained in . . .

(iii) an administrative order or grant of permission; or

(iv) an official interpretation of the public officer or body charged by law with responsibility for the interpretation, administration or enforcement of the law defining the offense.

Is the President's order "an administrative order" that could set up this defense? (Recall that White House Counsel Gonzales denied that the President "authorized, ordered or directed" violations of the standards of CAT or the Torture Act.) Is a legal opinion of the Office of Legal Counsel an "official interpretation"? Could any government interrogator "reasonably" rely upon either a presidential order or an OLC opinion to conduct the most coercive forms of interrogation? *See United States v. Barker*, 546 F.2d 940 (D.C. Cir. 1976) (split panel affirming availability of mistake defense to Watergate burglar, but on different rationales). How is this defense different from the "Nuremberg defense" — "I was only following orders" — "a notion from which our criminal justice system, one based on individual accountability and responsibility, has historically recoiled"? *United States v. North*, 910 F.2d 843, 881 (D.C. Cir. 1990).

c. *Article II as a Trump Card?* The January 2002 OLC memo, *supra* p. 928, at 36, 39, asserted that "Congress can no more interfere with the President's conduct of the interrogation of enemy combatants than it can dictate strategic or tactical decisions on the battlefield." In what particular settings is the Article II argument most persuasive? *See* Michael D. Ramsey, *Torturing Executive Power*, 93 Geo. L.J. 1213 (2005). Unlike the Bybee Memo, *supra* p. 929 n.13, the December 30, 2004, OLC memo, *supra* p. 934, made no mention of the constitutional authority of the President to disregard statutory or treaty obligations regarding torture. Of what significance is the revision?

Compare detention and on-the-spot interrogations of those seized on the battlefield during combat with long-term detentions in remote locations away from the battle. Al Qaeda reportedly continues to plan and carry out terrorist acts that threaten national security. Does that ongoing threat give the Commander in Chief a tactical choice to capture and interrogate Al Qaeda operatives using torture?

If you agree that there is a constitutional limit to the authority of Congress to regulate interrogation, can you construe the laws reviewed in this section to avoid the potential constitutional problem? Is the constitutional authority of the President relevant to the international legality of the abusive conduct? *See* W. Michael Reisman, Editorial Comment, *Holding the Center of the Law of Armed Conflict*, 100 Am. J. Int'l L. 852, 854 (2006) (no).

3. *Prosecuting Civilian Contractors?* In June 2004 a federal grand jury in North Carolina indicted a contractor employed by the CIA on assault charges for allegedly beating a detainee in Afghanistan over two days in 2003. The detainee died the next day. The former contractor was found guilty of assault and sentenced to eight years and four months in prison. Elizabeth Dunbar, *Ex-CIA Contractor Sentenced to Prison*,

Wash. Post, Feb. 13, 2007. How might the War Crimes Act, 18 U.S.C. §2441, *supra* pp. 917, apply to the accused in this case?

Generally, the UCMJ has not been used to criminally prosecute civilians accompanying military units in peacetime. *See, e.g., Willenburg v. Neurauter,* 48 M.J. 152, 157 (C.A.A.F. 1998). The Military Extraterritorial Jurisdiction Act of 2000 (MEJA), however, provides for federal jurisdiction over crimes committed abroad by civilians who are "accompanying or employed by" the U.S. military. 18 U.S.C. §§3261-3267 (2006). MEJA creates no new substantive crimes but incorporates a range of existing offenses, such as murder, assault, sexual abuse, and deprivation of rights under color of law. Still, after the 2004 *Taguba Report, supra* p. 933 n.23, named the contracting firms Titan Corporation and CACI International, Inc. as having provided translators and interrogators accused of engaging in detainee abuse at the Abu Ghraib prison, it appeared that the jurisdictional provisions of the MEJA would not reach the contractors that employed the accused individuals, because they were not "accompanying or employed by the military." Moreover, CACI's contract was with the Department of the Interior rather than the Department of Defense (DOD). Scott Shane, *Some U.S. Prison Contractors May Avoid Charges,* Balt. Sun, May 24, 2004.

In response to this jurisdictional gap, the 2005 Defense Authorization Act broadened the range of potential defendants under MEJA to include civilian employees, contractors or subcontractors, and their employees, of DOD or "any other Federal agency, or any provisional authority, to the extent such employment relates to supporting the mission of the Department of Defense overseas." Pub. L. No. 108-375, §1088, 118 Stat. 1811, 2066-2067 (2004). Do these amendments to MEJA plug all the holes? Would they reach State Department or FBI contractors? CIA contractors? *See* Frederick A. Stein, *Have We Closed the Barn Door Yet? A Look at the Current Loopholes in the Military Extraterritorial Jurisdiction Act,* 27 Hous. J. Int'l L. 579 (2005).

Some observers suggest that doubts about the criminal liability of civilian contractors who engage in interrogational torture also point to broader questions about the wisdom of privatizing a range of national security activities normally undertaken by the government. How might these questions be addressed? *See* Jon D. Michaels, *Beyond Accountability: The Constitutional, Democratic, and Strategic Problems with Privatizing War,* 82 Wash. U. L.Q. 1001 (2004).

The National Defense Authorization Act for Fiscal Year 2010, Pub. L. No. 111-84, §1038, 123 Stat. 2190, 2451 (2009), prohibits contractor personnel from interrogating detainees under the control of the Department of Defense, unless the Secretary waives the ban for up to 60 days after he determines that the waiver is "vital to the national security interests of the United States." *Id.* §1038(d) The Secretary must provide written notice to Congress after issuance of a waiver. *Id.* The same provision expressly permits contractors to serve as linguists, interpreters, report writers, information technology technicians, and trainers and advisers to the interrogators, so long as the contractors are subject to the same laws and policies as the government interrogators and are overseen by Defense Department personnel. *Id.* §1038(b). The Defense Department has issued rules implementing the contractor restrictions. 48 C.F.R. §237.173, 75 Fed. Reg. 67,633 (Nov. 3, 2010). Do these provisions provide adequate controls on contract personnel?

4. *Lawyers and Their Role.* Many of the legal opinions in the Justice Department and Defense Department memoranda described and quoted above are highly controversial. Some commentators argued that the memoranda were designed primarily

to protect potentially culpable officials from prosecution for interrogation abuses. *See Lawyers' Statement on Bush Administration's Torture Memos* (Aug. 4, 2004), *at* http://www.sfcityattorney.org/Modules/ShowDocument.aspx?documentid=507 (letter signed by about 130 prominent lawyers); *Letter Sent to the United States Congress Regarding Recent Human Rights Issues in Iraq* (June 16, 2004), *at* http://www.lawprofessorblogs.com/taxprof/linkdocs/harvardimpeach.pdf (letter signed by more than 500 university professors). Others, including Defense Department investigators of detention and interrogation practices, found that the confusion and ambiguity fostered by these memoranda may have contributed to the abusive practices or to a "permissive climate in which abuses were more likely." Richard B. Bilder & Detlev F. Vagts, *Speaking Law to Power: Lawyers and Torture*, 98 Am. J. Int'l L. 689, 691 (2004) (citing, e.g., John Barry, Michael Hirsh & Michael Isikoff, *The Roots of Torture*, Newsweek, May 24, 2004, at 28). What are the legal and ethical responsibilities of government lawyers in the war on terror? *See* Bilder & Vagts, *supra*, at 691-695; *Symposium: Lawyers' Roles and the War on Terror*, 1 J. Nat'l Security L. & Poly. 357 (2005).

The *Schlesinger Report, supra* p. 929 n.14, found that in the development of Defense Department detention and interrogation policies in 2002 and 2003 "the legal resources of the Services' Judge Advocate General and General Counsels were not utilized to their full potential. Had the Secretary of Defense had a wider range of legal opinions and more robust debate regarding detainee policies and operations," the frequent policy changes between December 2002 and April 2003 might have been avoided. *Id.* at 8. Why would the Secretary not have sought more advice from JAG lawyers and General Counsels? What would have been gained by their perspectives?

At a Senate hearing in July 2005, the judge advocates general for the Army, Air Force, and Marines stated that they complained about the Justice Department's definition of "torture" and how it would be applied in the Working Group process early in 2003. Their objections apparently were overruled by the Defense Department General Counsel's office. Neil A. Lewis, *Military's Opposition to Harsh Interrogation Is Outlined*, N.Y. Times, July 28, 2005; Josh White, *Military Lawyers Fought Policy on Interrogations, JAGs Recount Objections to Definition of Torture*, Wash. Post, July 15, 2005. Why do you think the Secretary failed to heed the advice that was offered?

The Senate Armed Services Committee report, *supra* p. 936, also blamed senior Administration lawyers and the authors of the OLC opinions for enabling the abuses documented above. The Office of Professional Responsibility of the Department of Justice completed an investigation of OLC lawyers John Yoo and Keith Bybee in 2009, concluding that they engaged in "professional misconduct" by authorizing enhanced interrogation techniques. Office of Professional Responsibility, Department of Justice, *Report* 260 (2009), *available at* http://judiciary.house.gov/hearings/pdf/OPRFinalReport090729.pdf. A second report from the Associate Deputy Attorney General, David Margolis, said only that the two lawyers exercised "poor judgment," but that he would not recommend referring them for discipline because they did not, in his view, knowingly provide false advice. Memorandum to the Attorney General from David Margolis, Associate Deputy Attorney General (Jan. 5, 2010), *available at* http://judiciary.house.gov/hearings/pdf/DAGMargolisMemo100105.pdf. *See also* David D. Cole, *The Sacrificial Yoo: Accounting for Torture in the OPR Report*, 4 J. Nat'l Security L. & Pol'y 455 (2010).

The latter conclusion thus excused what might otherwise have been an obligation by the Department of Justice to refer Yoo and Bybee to state bar associations for disciplinary proceedings. President Obama also stated that he would not advocate prosecuting the OLC lawyers. *See* Press Release, The White House Office of the Press Sec'y, Statement of President Barack Obama on Release of the OLC Memos (Apr. 16, 2009), *available at* http://www.whitehouse.gov/the-press-office/statement-president-barack-obama-release-olc-memos ("[N]othing will be gained by spending our time and energy laying blame for the past."). Do you believe that these lawyers and/or their highest ranking superiors broke the law? Which laws? Do you agree that nothing would be gained by a prosecution? *See* Jordan J. Paust, *Criminal Responsibility of Bush Administration Officials with Respect to Unlawful Interrogation Tactics and the Facilitating Conduct of Lawyers*, in *The United States and Torture: Interrogation, Incarceration, and Abuse* 281 (Marjorie Kohn ed., 2011).

A Senate Judiciary Subcommittee hearing in 2009 focused on the role of the OLC in authorizing coercive interrogation methods. *See What Went Wrong: Torture and the Office of Legal Counsel in the Bush Administration: Hearing Before the Subcomm. on Administrative Oversight and the Courts of the S. Comm. on the Judiciary*, 111th Cong. (May 13, 2009), *available at* http://www.fas.org/irp/congress/2009_hr/wrong.html.

d.   Civil Liability

1. *Civil Liability for U.S. Government Interrogators?* The memoranda quoted and described above expose an underlying tension in setting the interrogation policy — providing maximum flexibility to pressure detainees to talk while ensuring immunity from criminal sanctions for interrogators if they cross lawful boundaries. This tension is most readily apparent in the January 9, 2002, OLC memorandum from John Yoo and Robert Delahunty, *supra* p. 928, arguing that the Geneva Conventions do not apply to captured Al Qaeda and Taliban detainees. Potential criminal liability is addressed *supra* p. 944.

In February 2006, a federal district court dismissed most of a civil suit for damages brought by Guantánamo Bay detainees who alleged that they were tortured in violation of the Geneva Conventions, the law of nations, and the Constitution. *Rasul v. Rumsfeld*, 414 F. Supp. 2d 26 (D.D.C. 2006). The court held that sovereign immunity barred the law of nations and Geneva Conventions claims, and that qualified immunity of individual government officials required dismissal of the constitutional claims because the rights at stake were not "clearly established." For sovereign immunity to apply to the international law claims, however, the court had to find that the defendants were acting within their scope of employment. How could U.S. officials act within their scope of employment when they torture detainees? The Court of Appeals voted to dismiss all the claims, *Rasul v. Myers*, 512 F.3d 644 (D.C. Cir. 2008), but the Supreme Court reversed and remanded to reconsider the constitutional claims in light of its 2008 decision in *Boumediene v. Bush*, 553 U.S. 723 (2008) (reproduced *supra* p. 787). 129 S. Ct. 763 (2008). On remand, the Court of Appeals again dismissed all the detainees' claims after concluding that the alien detainees lacked clearly established constitutional rights under the Fifth or Eighth Amendments, inasmuch as the Supreme Court has yet to squarely overrule the part of *Johnson v. Eisentrager*, 339 U.S. 763 (1950), suggesting that aliens abroad do not have Fifth Amendment rights). *Rasul v. Myers*, 563 F.3d 527 (D.C. Cir.), *cert. denied*, 130 S. Ct. 1013 (2009).

2. *Civil Liability for Lawyers?* In 2009, a federal district court refused to dismiss most parts of a civil suit by convicted terrorist Jose Padilla against former OLC lawyer

John Yoo. *Padilla v. Yoo*, 633 F. Supp. 2d 1005 (N.D. Cal. 2009). Padilla alleged that he was abused during his confinement at a military brig in South Carolina during his three-year, eight-month detention based on the orders of high-ranking government officials and the legal and policy justifications for abusive interrogation provided by Yoo. The court noted that Yoo is unlikely to be held accountable for his actions in any other forum, and that a reasonable lawyer in Yoo's position should have known that he was authorizing a violation of Padilla's constitutional rights. *Id.* A decision by the Ninth Circuit Court of Appeals on appeal by Yoo was pending at this writing.

     3. *Civil Liability of Contractors?* Relying on the Alien Tort Statute (ATS), 28 U.S.C. §1350 (2006), in 2004 the Center for Constitutional Rights sued two prime security contractors operating for the United States in Iraq — CACI International, Inc. and Titan Corp. — on behalf of Iraqi prisoners, alleging that the contractors conspired with government officials to abuse the detainees and failed adequately to supervise their employees. *See* Renae Merle, *CACI and Titan Sued Over Iraq Operations*, Wash. Post, June 10, 2004. The suit sought damages and an injunction to prevent the contractors from obtaining new government contracts. The Court of Appeals granted summary judgment in favor of both defendants because the contractors were conducting operations under military authority, and, like the military, contractors whose work is fully integrated in the military mission are exempt from the ATS because of the sovereign immunity of the U.S. government. State law tort claims were found to be similarly preempted by the federal interest in protecting military activities. *See Saleh v. Titan Corp.*, 436 F. Supp. 2d 55 (D.D.C. 2006), *aff'd in part and rev'd in part*, 580 F.3d 1 (D.C. Cir. 2009), *cert. denied*, 2011 WL 2518834 (June 27, 2011). In another lawsuit, *Al Shimari v. CACI Premier Technology, Inc.*, 657 F. Supp. 2d 700, 720-725 (E.D. Va. 2009), the court refused to find federal preemption of a state law tort claim based on abusive interrogation by a contractor, because the court concluded that interrogation was not a combat activity.

     If the first decision is correct, is there any other basis for imposing civil liability on contractors for interrogational torture? If not, and if civil suits against the government and government officials are also barred, as suggested above, will the prospect of criminal prosecution provide an adequate deterrence to official torture? Is your answer influenced by the official responses to reports of torture and abusive interrogation set forth in this chapter and the last one?

     If the *Al Shimari* decision is correct, are you prepared to say what is and is not "combat activity" in the ongoing struggle against the threat to national security posed by international terrorists? Should civil liability turn on such a distinction?

Extraordinary Rendition

Rendition is generally understood to be the surrender of a person from one state to another state that has requested him, typically pursuant to an agreement or extradition treaty, for the purpose of criminal prosecution. In the mid-1990s, however, the United States began capturing suspected terrorist operatives and transferring them to foreign countries as part of a CIA program designed to disrupt and dismantle Al Qaeda terrorist operations. Michael Scheuer, *A Fine Rendition*, N.Y. Times, Mar. 11, 2005. The practice is commonly called "extraordinary rendition," because it involves no treaty or formal agreement and is attended by no judicial process.

The first such renditions were set up by senior officials working in the CIA's Islamic-militant unit and involved informal arrangements with the government of Egypt. As it happened, a few of the top Al Qaeda operatives were Egyptians who had been convicted in absentia of offenses in Egypt. The United States captured some of these and rendered them to Egypt, even though abusive interrogations by Egyptian interrogators, including torture, had long been documented by the State Department. *See* Bureau of Democracy, Human Rights & Labor, U.S. Dep't of State, *Egypt: Country Reports on Human Rights Practices* (Feb. 23, 2001), *at* http://www.state.gov/g/drl/rls/hrrpt/2000/nea/784.htm. The arrangement between U.S. and Egyptian intelligence services was such that the Americans could give questions to Egyptian interrogators they wanted put to detainees in the morning and get answers that same day. Scheuer, *supra*.

After September 11, extraordinary renditions expanded. Receiving nations included Syria, Jordan, Morocco, and Uzbekistan, as well as Egypt. The renditions were not limited to individuals wanted by third countries, but included transfers to third countries solely for the purpose of interrogation — to extract intelligence, as quickly as possible. Stephen Grey, *Ghost Plane: The True Story of the CIA Torture Program* 148-152 (2006). The legal bases for extraordinary rendition and potential judicial remedies for its abuses are addressed in the following decision and in notes and questions that follow it.

Arar v. Ashcroft

United States Court of Appeals, Second Circuit (en banc), 2009
585 F.3d 559, *cert. denied*, 130 S. Ct. 3409 (2010)

DENNIS JACOBS, Chief Judge: Maher Arar appeals from a judgment of the United States District Court for the Eastern District of New York (Trager, J.) dismissing his complaint against the Attorney General of the United States, the Secretary of Homeland Security, the Director of the Federal Bureau of Investigation, and others, including senior immigration officials. Arar alleges that he was detained while changing planes at Kennedy Airport in New York (based on a warning from Canadian authorities that he was a member of Al Qaeda), mistreated for twelve days while in United States custody, and then removed to Syria via Jordan pursuant to an intergovernmental understanding that he would be detained and interrogated under torture by Syrian officials. The complaint alleges a violation of the Torture Victim Protection Act ("TVPA") and of his Fifth Amendment substantive due process rights arising from the conditions of his detention in the United States, the denial of his access to counsel and to the courts while in the United States, and his detention and torture in Syria.

The district court dismissed the complaint (with leave to re-plead only as to the conditions of detention in the United States and his access to counsel and the courts during that period) and Arar timely appealed (without undertaking to amend). *Arar v. Ashcroft*, 414 F. Supp. 2d 250 (E.D.N.Y. 2006). A three-judge panel of this Court unanimously held that: (1) the District Court had personal jurisdiction over Thompson, Ashcroft, and Mueller; (2) Arar failed to state a claim under the TVPA; and (3) Arar failed to establish subject matter jurisdiction over his request for a declaratory judgment. *Arar v. Ashcroft*, 532 F.3d 157 (2d Cir. 2008). A majority of the panel also dismissed Arar's *Bivens* claims, with one member of the panel dissenting. *Id.* The Court voted to rehear the appeal *in banc*. We now affirm.

We have no trouble affirming the district court's conclusions that Arar sufficiently alleged personal jurisdiction over the defendants who challenged it, and that Arar lacks standing to seek declaratory relief. We do not reach issues of qualified immunity or the state secrets privilege. As to the TVPA, we agree with the unanimous position of the panel that Arar insufficiently pleaded that the alleged conduct of United States officials was done under color of foreign law. We agree with the district court that Arar insufficiently pleaded his claim regarding detention in the United States, a ruling that has been reinforced by the subsequent authority of *Bell Atlantic Corp. v. Twombly*, 550 U.S. 544, 570 (2007). Our attention is therefore focused on whether Arar's claims for detention and torture in Syria can be asserted under *Bivens v. Six Unknown Named Agents of Federal Bureau of Narcotics*, 403 U.S. 388 (1971) ("*Bivens*").

To decide the *Bivens* issue, we must determine whether Arar's claims invoke *Bivens* in a new context; and, if so, whether an alternative remedial scheme was available to Arar, or whether (in the absence of affirmative action by Congress) " 'special factors counsel[ ] hesitation.' " *See Wilkie v. Robbins*, 551 U.S. 537, 550 (2007) (quoting *Bush v. Lucas*, 462 U.S. 367, 378 (1983)). This opinion holds that "extraordinary rendition" is a context new to *Bivens* claims, but avoids any categorical ruling on alternative remedies—because the dominant holding of this opinion is that, in the context of extraordinary rendition, hesitation is warranted by special factors. We therefore affirm. . . .

Our ruling does not preclude judicial review and oversight in this context. But if a civil remedy in damages is to be created for harms suffered in the context of extraordinary rendition, it must be created by Congress, which alone has the institutional competence to set parameters, delineate safe harbors, and specify relief. If Congress chooses to legislate on this subject, then judicial review of such legislation would be available.

Applying our understanding of Supreme Court precedent, we decline to create, on our own, a new cause of action against officers and employees of the federal government. Rather, we conclude that, when a case presents the intractable "special factors" apparent here, it is for the Executive in the first instance to decide how to implement extraordinary rendition, and for the elected members of Congress — and not for us as judges — to decide whether an individual may seek compensation from government officers and employees directly, or from the government, for a constitutional violation. Administrations past and present have reserved the right to employ rendition, *see* David Johnston, *U.S. Says Rendition to Continue, but with More Oversight*, N.Y. Times, Aug. 24, 2009, and not withstanding prolonged public debate, Congress has not prohibited the practice, imposed limits on its use, or created a cause of action for those who allege they have suffered constitutional injury as a consequence.

I

Arar's complaint sets forth the following factual allegations.

Arar is a dual citizen of Syria, where he was born and raised, and of Canada, to which his family immigrated when he was 17.

While on vacation in Tunisia in September 2002, Arar was called back to work in Montreal. His itinerary called for stops in Zurich and New York.

Arar landed at Kennedy Airport around noon on September 26. Between planes, Arar presented his Canadian passport to an immigration official who, after checking Arar's credentials, asked Arar to wait nearby. About two hours later, Arar was fingerprinted and his bags searched. Between 4 p.m. and 9 p.m., Arar was interviewed by an agent from the Federal Bureau of Investigation ("FBI"), who asked (*inter alia*) about his relationships with certain individuals who were suspected of terrorist ties. Arar admitted knowing at least one of them, but denied being a member of a terrorist group. Following the FBI interview, Arar was questioned by an official from the Immigration and Nationalization Service ("INS") for three more hours; he continued to deny terrorist affiliations.

Arar spent the night alone in a room at the airport. The next morning (September 27) he was questioned by FBI agents from approximately 9 a.m. until 2 p.m.; the agents asked him about Osama Bin Laden, Iraq, Palestine, and other things. That evening, Arar was given an opportunity to return voluntarily to Syria. He refused, citing a fear of torture, and asked instead to go to Canada or Switzerland. Later that evening, he was transferred to the Metropolitan Detention Center ("MDC") in Brooklyn, where he remained until October 8.

On October 1, the INS initiated removal proceedings, and served Arar with a document stating that he was inadmissible because he belonged to a terrorist organization. Later that day, he called his mother-in-law in Ottawa — his prior requests to place calls and speak to a lawyer having been denied or ignored.

His family retained a lawyer to represent him and contacted the Canadian Consulate in New York.

A Canadian consular official visited Arar on October 3. The next day, immigration officers asked Arar to designate in writing the country to which he would want to be removed. He designated Canada. On the evening of October 5, Arar met with his attorney. The following evening, a Sunday, Arar was again questioned by INS officials. The INS District Director in New York left a voicemail message on the office phone of Arar's attorney that the interview would take place, but the attorney did not receive the message in time to attend. Arar was told that she chose not to attend. In days following, the attorney was given false information about Arar's whereabouts.

On October 8, 2002, Arar learned that the INS had: (1) ordered his removal to Syria, (2) made a (required) finding that such removal would be consistent with Article 3 of the Convention Against Torture ("CAT"), and (3) barred him from re-entering the United States for five years. He was found inadmissible to the United States on the basis of 8 U.S.C. §1182(a)(3)(B)(i)(V), which provides that any alien who "is a member of a terrorist organization" is inadmissible to the United States. The finding was based on Arar's association with a suspected terrorist and other (classified) information. Thereafter, Defendant J. Scott Blackman, an INS Regional Director, made a determination that Arar was clearly and unequivocally a member of Al Qaeda and inadmissible to the United States. A "Final Notice of Inadmissibility," dated October 8, and signed by Defendant Deputy Attorney General Larry Thompson, stated that Arar's removal to Syria would be consistent with the CAT, notwithstanding Arar's articulated fear of torture.

Later that day, Arar was taken to New Jersey, whence he flew in a small jet to Washington, D.C., and then to Amman, Jordan. When he arrived in Amman on October 9, he was handed over to Jordanian authorities who treated him roughly and then delivered him to the custody of Syrian officials, who detained him at a Syrian Military Intelligence facility. Arar was in Syria for a year, the first ten months in an underground cell six feet by three, and seven feet high. He was interrogated for twelve days on his arrival in Syria, and in that period was beaten on his palms, hips, and lower back with a two-inch-thick electric cable and with bare hands. Arar alleges that United States officials conspired to send him to Syria for the purpose of interrogation under torture, and directed the interrogations from abroad by providing Syria with Arar's dossier, dictating questions for the Syrians to ask him, and receiving intelligence learned from the interviews.

On October 20, 2002, Canadian Embassy officials inquired of Syria as to Arar's whereabouts. The next day, Syria confirmed to Canada that Arar was in its custody; that same day, interrogation ceased. Arar remained in Syria, however, receiving visits from Canadian consular officials. On August 14, 2003, Arar defied his captors by telling the Canadians that he had been tortured and was confined to a small underground cell. Five days later, after signing a confession that he had trained as a terrorist in Afghanistan, Arar was moved to various locations. On October 5, 2003, Arar was released to the custody of a Canadian embassy official in Damascus, and was flown to Ottawa the next day.

II

On January 22, 2004, Arar filed a four-count complaint in the Eastern District of New York seeking damages from federal officials for harms suffered as a result of his detention and confinement in the United States and his detention and interrogation in Syria. Count One of Arar's complaint seeks relief under the Torture Victim Protection Act ("TVPA"), 28 U.S.C. §1350 note (a)(1) (the "TVPA claim"). Counts Two and Three seek relief under the Fifth Amendment for Arar's alleged torture in Syria (Count Two) and his detention there (Count Three). Count Four seeks relief under the Fifth Amendment for Arar's detention in the United States prior to his removal to Syria. Arar also seeks a declaratory judgment that defendants' conduct violated his "constitutional, civil, and human rights." . . .

III . . .

At the outset, we conclude (as the panel concluded unanimously) that Arar: (1) sufficiently alleged personal jurisdiction over the defendants, and (2) has no standing to seek declaratory relief; in addition, because we dismiss the action for the reasons set forth below, we need not (and do not) reach the issues of qualified immunity or the state secrets privilege. . . .

IV

The TVPA creates a cause of action for damages against any "individual who, under actual or apparent authority, or color of law, of any foreign nation . . . subjects an individual to torture." 28 U.S.C. §1350 note (a)(1). Count One of Arar's complaint alleges that the defendants conspired with Jordanian and Syrian officials to have Arar tortured in direct violation of the TVPA.

Any allegation arising under the TVPA requires a demonstration that the defendants acted under color of foreign law, or under its authority. *Kadic v. Karadzic*, 70 F.3d 232, 245 (2d Cir. 1995). "In construing the term[ ] . . . 'color of law,' courts are instructed to look . . . to jurisprudence under 42 U.S.C. §1983. . . ." *Id.* (citing H.R. Rep. No. 367, 102d Cong., 2d Sess., at 5 (1991) *reprinted in* 1992 U.S.C.C.A.N. 84, 87). Under section 1983, "[t]he traditional definition of acting under color of state law requires that the defendant . . . have exercised power 'possessed by virtue of state law and made possible only because the wrongdoer is clothed with the authority of state law.' " *West v. Atkins*, 487 U.S. 42, 49 (1988) (quoting *United States v. Classic*, 313 U.S. 299, 326 (1941)). The determination as to whether a non-state party acts under color of state law requires an intensely fact-specific judgment unaided by rigid criteria as to whether particular conduct may be fairly attributed to the state. . . .

Accordingly, to state a claim under the TVPA, Arar must adequately allege that the defendants possessed power under Syrian law, and that the offending actions (*i.e.*, Arar's removal to Syria and subsequent torture) derived from an exercise of that power, or that defendants could not have undertaken their culpable actions absent such power. The complaint contains no such allegation. Arar has argued that his allegation of conspiracy cures any deficiency under the TVPA. But the conspiracy allegation is that United States officials encouraged and facilitated the exercise of power by Syrians in Syria, not that the United States officials had or exercised power or authority under Syrian law. The defendants are alleged to have acted under color of federal, not Syrian, law, and to have acted in accordance with alleged federal policies and in pursuit of the aims of the federal government in the international context. At most, it is alleged that the defendants encouraged or solicited certain conduct by foreign officials. Such conduct is insufficient to establish that the defendants were in some way clothed with the authority of Syrian law or that their conduct may otherwise be fairly attributable to Syria. *See, e.g., Harbury v. Hayden*, 444 F. Supp. 2d 19, 42-43 (D.D.C. 2006), *aff'd on other grounds*, 522 F.3d 413 (D.C. Cir. 2008). We therefore agree with the unanimous holding of the panel and affirm the District Court's dismissal of the TVPA claim.

V

Count Four of the complaint alleges that the conditions of confinement in the United States (prior to Arar's removal to Syria), and the denial of access to courts during that detention, violated Arar's substantive due process rights under the Fifth Amendment. The District Court dismissed this claim — without prejudice — as insufficiently pleaded, and invited Arar to re-plead the claim in order to "articulate more precisely the judicial relief he was denied" and to "name those defendants that were personally involved in the alleged unconstitutional treatment." *Arar*, 414 F. Supp. 2d at 286, 287. Arar elected (in his counsel's words) to "stand on the allegations of his original complaint."

On a motion to dismiss, courts require "enough facts to state a claim to relief that is plausible on its face." *Twombly*, 550 U.S. at 570; *see also Ashcroft v. Iqbal*, — U.S. —, 129 S. Ct. 1937, 1949-50 (2009). "Factual allegations must be enough to raise a right to relief above the speculative level. . . ." *Twombly*, 550 U.S. at 555. Broad allegations of conspiracy are insufficient; the plaintiff "must provide some factual basis supporting a meeting of the minds, such that defendants entered into an agreement, express or tacit, to achieve the unlawful end." *Webb v. Goord*, 340 F.3d 105, 110 (2d Cir. 2003) (internal quotation marks omitted) (addressing conspiracy claims under 42 U.S.C. §1985). Furthermore, a plaintiff in a *Bivens* action is required to allege facts indicating that the defendants were personally involved in the claimed constitutional violation. *See Ellis v. Blum*, 643 F.2d 68, 85 (2d Cir. 1981).

Arar alleges that "Defendants' — undifferentiated — 'denied Mr. Arar effective access to consular assistance, the courts, his lawyers, and family members" in order to effectuate his removal to Syria. But he fails to specify any culpable action taken by any single defendant, and does not allege the "meeting of the minds" that a plausible conspiracy claim requires. He alleges (in passive voice) that his requests to make phone calls "were ignored," and that "he was told" that he was not entitled to a lawyer, but he fails to link these denials to any defendant, named or unnamed. Given this omission, and in view of Arar's rejection of an opportunity to re-plead, we agree with the District Court and the panel majority that this Count of the complaint must be dismissed.

We express no view as to the sufficiency of the pleading otherwise, that is, whether the conduct alleged (if plausibly attributable to defendants) would violate a constitutionally protected interest. To the extent that this claim may be deemed to be a *Bivens*-type action, it may raise some of the special factors considered later in this opinion.

VI

Arar's remaining claims seek relief on the basis of torture and detention in Syria, and are cast as violations of substantive due process. At the outset, Defendants argue that the jurisdictional bar of the INA deprived the District Court of subject-matter jurisdiction over these counts because Arar's removal was conducted pursuant to a decision that was "at the discretion" of the Attorney General....

... [W]e need not decide the ... question of whether the INA bar defeats jurisdiction of Arar's substantive due process claims, because we conclude below that the case must be dismissed at the threshold for other reasons.

VII

In *Bivens*, the Supreme Court "recognized for the first time an implied private action for damages against federal officers alleged to have violated a citizen's constitutional rights." *Corr. Servs. Corp. v. Malesko*, 534 U.S. 61, 66 (2001). The plaintiff in *Bivens* had been subjected to an unlawful, warrantless search which resulted in his arrest. The Supreme Court allowed him to state a cause of action for money damages directly under the Fourth Amendment, thereby giving rise to a judicially-created remedy stemming directly from the Constitution itself.

The purpose of the *Bivens* remedy "is to deter individual federal officers from committing constitutional violations." *Malesko*, 534 U.S. at 70. So a *Bivens* action is brought against individuals, and any damages are payable by the offending officers. *Carlson v. Green*, 446 U.S. 14, 21 (1980). Notwithstanding the potential breadth of claims that would serve that objective, the Supreme Court has warned that the *Bivens* remedy is an extraordinary thing that should rarely if ever be applied in "new contexts." *See Malesko*, 534 U.S. at 69 (internal quotation marks omitted). In the 38 years since *Bivens*, the Supreme Court has extended it twice only: in the context of an employment discrimination claim in violation of the Due Process Clause, *Davis v. Passman*, 442 U.S. 228 (1979); and in the context of an Eighth Amendment violation by prison officials, *Carlson*, 446 U.S. 14. Since *Carlson* in 1980, the Supreme Court has declined to extend the *Bivens* remedy in any new direction at all. Among the rejected contexts are: violations of federal employees' First Amendment rights by their employers, *Bush v. Lucas*, 462 U.S. 367 (1983); harms suffered incident to military service, *United States v. Stanley*, 483 U.S. 669 (1987); denials of Social Security benefits, *Schweiker* [*v. Chilicky*, 487 U.S. 412 (1988),] at 412; claims against federal agencies, *FDIC v. Meyer*, 510 U.S. 471 (1994); claims against private corporations operating under federal contracts, *Malesko*, 534 U.S. 61 (2001); and claims of retaliation by federal officials against private landowners, *Wilkie* [*v. Robbins*, 551 U.S. 537 (2007),] at 562.

This case requires us to examine whether allowing this *Bivens* action to proceed would extend *Bivens* to a new "context," and if so, whether such an extension is advisable.

"Context" is not defined in the case law. At a sufficiently high level of generality, any claim can be analogized to some other claim for which a *Bivens* action is afforded, just as at a sufficiently high level of particularity, every case has points of distinction. We construe the word "context" as it is commonly used in law: to reflect a potentially recurring scenario that has similar legal and factual components.

The context of this case is international rendition, specifically, "extraordinary rendition." Extraordinary rendition is treated as a distinct phenomenon in international law. Indeed, law review articles that affirmatively advocate the creation of a remedy in cases like Arar's recognize "extraordinary rendition" as the context. *See, e.g.*, Peter Johnston, Note, *Leaving the Invisible Universe: Why All Victims of Extraordinary Rendition Need a Cause of Action Against the United States*, 16 J.L. & Pol'y 357, 363 (2007).

More particularly, the context of extraordinary rendition in Arar's case is the complicity or cooperation of United States government officials in the delivery of a noncitizen to a foreign country for torture (or with the expectation that torture will take place). This is a "new context": no court has previously afforded a *Bivens* remedy for extraordinary rendition.

Once we have identified the context as "new," we must decide whether to recognize a *Bivens* remedy in that environment of fact and law. The Supreme Court tells us that this is a two-part inquiry. In order to determine whether to recognize a *Bivens* remedy in a new context, we must consider: whether there is an alternative remedial scheme available to the plaintiff; and whether " 'special factors counsel[ ] hesitation' " in creating a *Bivens* remedy. *Wilkie*, 551 U.S. at 550 (quoting *Bush*, 462 U.S. at 378).

VIII ...

... [W]e need not decide whether an alternative remedial scheme was available because, "even in the absence of an alternative [remedial scheme], a *Bivens* remedy is a subject of judgment ... [in which] courts must ... pay particular heed ... to any special factors counselling hesitation before authorizing a new kind of federal litigation." *Wilkie*, 551 U.S. at 550. Such special factors are clearly present in the new context of this case, and they sternly counsel hesitation.

IX

When the *Bivens* cause of action was created in 1971, the Supreme Court explained that such a remedy could be afforded because that "case involve[d] no special factors counselling hesitation in the absence of affirmative action by Congress." *Bivens*, 403 U.S. at 396. This prudential limitation was expressly weighed by the Court in *Davis*, 442 U.S. at 245-46, and *Carlson*, 446 U.S. at 18-19, and such hesitation has defeated numerous *Bivens* initiatives, *see, e.g., Stanley*, 483 U.S. at 683-84; [*Chappell v. Wallace*, 462 U.S. 296 (1983)] at 304; *Wilkie*, 551 U.S. at 554-55; [*Dotson v. Griesa*, 398 F.3d 156 (2d Cir. 2005)] at 166-67. Among the "special factors" that have "counsel[ed] hesitation" and thereby foreclosed a *Bivens* remedy are: military concerns, *Stanley*, 483 U.S. at 683-84; *Chappell*, 462 U.S. at 304; separation of powers, *United States v. City of Philadelphia*, 644 F.2d 187, 200 (3d Cir. 1980); the comprehensiveness of available statutory schemes, *Dotson*, 398 F.3d at 166; national security concerns, *Beattie v. Boeing Co.*, 43 F.3d 559, 563 (10th Cir. 1994); and foreign policy considerations, *United States v. Verdugo-Urquidez*, 494 U.S. 259, 274 (1990).

Two principles emerge from this review of case law:

— "Special factors" is an embracing category, not easily defined; but it is limited in terms to factors that provoke "hesitation." While special factors should be substantial enough to justify the absence of a damages remedy for a wrong, no account is taken of countervailing factors that might counsel alacrity or activism, and none has ever been cited by the Supreme Court as a reason for affording a *Bivens* remedy where it would not otherwise exist.

— The only relevant threshold — that a factor "counsels hesitation" — is remarkably low. It is at the opposite end of the continuum from the unflagging duty to exercise jurisdiction. Hesitation is a pause, not a full stop, or an abstention; and to counsel is not to require. "Hesitation" is "counseled" whenever thoughtful discretion would pause even to consider.

With these principles in mind, we adduce, one by one, special factors that bear upon the recognition of a *Bivens* remedy for rendition.

X

Although this action is cast in terms of a claim for money damages against the defendants in their individual capacities, it operates as a constitutional challenge to policies promulgated by the executive. Our federal system of checks and balances provides means to consider allegedly unconstitutional executive policy, but a private action for money damages against individual policymakers is not one of them. A *Bivens* action is sometimes analogized to an action pursuant to 42 U.S.C. §1983, but it does not reach so far as to create the federal counterpart to an action under *Monell v. Department of Social Services*, 436 U.S. 658 (1978). Here, we need not decide categorically whether a *Bivens* action can lie against policymakers because in the context of extraordinary rendition, such an action would have the natural tendency to affect diplomacy, foreign policy, and the security of the nation, and that fact counsels hesitation. Our holding need be no broader.

A. Security and Foreign Policy

The Executive has practiced rendition since at least 1995. *See* Extraordinary Rendition in U.S. Counterterrorism Policy: The Impact on Transatlantic Relations: Joint Hearing Before the Subcomm. on International Organizations, Human Rights, and Oversight and the Subcomm. on Europe of the H. Comm. on Foreign Affairs, 110th Cong. 15 (2007) (statement of Michael F. Scheuer, Former Chief, Bin Laden Unit, CIA). Arar gives "the mid-1990s" as the date for the inception of the policy under which he was sent to Syria for torture. A suit seeking a damages remedy against senior officials who implement such a policy is in critical respects a suit against the government as to which the government has not waived sovereign immunity. Such a suit unavoidably influences government policy, probes government secrets, invades government interests, enmeshes government lawyers, and thereby elicits government funds for settlement. (Canada has already paid Arar $10 million.)

It is a substantial understatement to say that one must hesitate before extending *Bivens* into such a context. A suit seeking a damages remedy against senior officials who implement an extraordinary rendition policy would enmesh the courts ineluctably in an assessment of the validity and rationale of that policy and its implementation in this particular case, matters that directly affect significant diplomatic and national security concerns. It is clear from the face of the complaint that Arar explicitly targets the "policy" of extraordinary rendition; he cites the policy twice in his complaint, and submits documents and media reports concerning the practice. His claim cannot proceed without inquiry into the perceived need for the policy, the threats to which it responds, the substance and sources of the intelligence used to formulate it, and the propriety of adopting specific responses to particular threats in light of apparent geopolitical circumstances and our relations with foreign countries.

The Supreme Court has expressly counseled that matters touching upon foreign policy and national security fall within "an area of executive action 'in which courts have long been *hesitant* to intrude' " absent congressional authorization. *Lincoln v. Vigil*, 508 U.S. 182, 192 (1993) (emphasis added) (*quoting Franklin v. Massachusetts*, 505 U.S. 788, 819 (1992) (Stevens, J., concurring in part and concurring in the judgment)). It "has recognized 'the generally accepted view that foreign policy was the province and responsibility of the Executive.'... Thus, unless Congress specifically has provided otherwise, courts traditionally have been *reluctant* to intrude upon the authority of the Executive in military and national security affairs." *Dep't of Navy v. Egan*, 484 U.S. 518, 529-30 (1988) (emphasis added) (*quoting Haig v. Agee*, 453 U.S. 280, 293-94 (1981)). This "hesita[tion]" and "reluctan[ce]" is counseled by:

— the constitutional separation of powers among the branches of government, *see United States v. Curtiss-Wright Exp. Co.*, 299 U.S. 304, 320-22 (1936)....

— the limited institutional competence of the judiciary, *see Boumediene v. Bush*, — U.S. ——, 128 S. Ct. 2229, 2276-77 (2008) ("Unlike the President and some designated Members of Congress, neither the Members of this Court nor most federal judges begin the day with briefings that may describe new and serious threats to our Nation and its people. The law must accord the Executive substantial authority to apprehend and detain those who pose a real danger to our security.")....

B. Classified Information

The extraordinary rendition context involves exchanges among the ministries and agencies of foreign countries on diplomatic, security, and intelligence issues. The sensitivities of such classified material are "too obvious to call for enlarged discussion." *Dep't of Navy*, 484 U.S. at 529 (internal quotation marks omitted). Even the probing of these matters entails the risk that other countries will become less willing to cooperate with the United States in sharing intelligence resources to counter terrorism. "At its core," as the panel opinion observed, "this suit arises from the Executive Branch's alleged determination that (a) Arar was affiliated with Al Qaeda, and therefore a threat to national security, and (b) his removal to Syria was appropriate in light of U.S. diplomatic and national security interests." *Arar*, 532 F.3d at 181. To determine the basis for Arar's alleged designation as an Al Qaeda member and his subsequent removal to Syria, the district court would have to consider what was done by the national security apparatus of at least three foreign countries, as well as that of the United States. Indeed, the Canadian government—which appears to have provided the intelligence that United States officials were acting upon when they detained Arar—paid Arar compensation for its role in the events surrounding this lawsuit, but has *also* asserted the need for Canada itself to maintain the confidentiality of certain classified materials related to Arar's claims.

C. Open Courts

Allegations of conspiracy among government agencies that must often work in secret inevitably implicate a lot of classified material that cannot be introduced into the public record. Allowing Arar's claims to proceed would very likely mean that some documents or information sought by Arar would be redacted, reviewed *in camera*, and otherwise concealed from the public. Concealment does not bespeak wrongdoing: in such matters, it is just as important to conceal what has *not* been done. Nevertheless, these measures would excite suspicion and speculation as to the true nature and depth of the supposed conspiracy, and as to the scope and depth of judicial oversight. Indeed, after an inquiry at oral argument as to whether classified materials relating to Arar's claims could be made available for review *in camera*, Arar objected to the supplementation of the record with material he could not see. *See* Letter from David Cole, Counsel for Maher Arar (Dec. 23, 2008). After pointing out that such materials are unnecessary to the adjudication of a motion on the pleadings (where the allegations of the complaint must be accepted as true), Arar protested that any materials submitted *ex parte* and *in camera* would not be subject to adversarial testing and that consideration of such documents would be "presumptively unconstitutional" since they would result in a decision "on the basis of secret information available to only one side of the dispute."

The court's reliance on information that cannot be introduced into the public record is likely to be a common feature of any *Bivens* actions arising in the context of alleged extraordinary rendition. This should provoke hesitation, given the strong preference in the Anglo-American legal tradition for open court proceedings, a value incorporated into modern First and Sixth Amendment law. . . .

XI

A government report states that this case involves assurances received from other governments in connection with the determination that Arar's removal to Syria would be consistent with Article 3 of the CAT. Office of Inspector General, Dep't of Homeland Sec., (Unclassified) *The Removal of a Canadian Citizen to Syria* 5, 22, 26-27 (2008). This case is not unique in that respect. Cases in the context of extraordinary rendition are very likely to present serious questions relating to private diplomatic assurances from foreign countries received by federal officials, and this feature of such claims opens the door to graymail.

A. Assurances

The regulations promulgated pursuant to the [Foreign Affairs Reform and Restructuring Act of 1998 ("FARRA"), 8 U.S.C. §1231 note] explicitly authorize the removal of an alien to a foreign country following receipt from that country of sufficiently reliable assurances that the alien will not be tortured. *See* 8 C.F.R. §208.18(c). Should we decide to extend *Bivens* into the extraordinary rendition context, resolution of these actions will require us to determine whether any such assurances were received from the country of rendition and whether the relevant defendants relied upon them in good faith in removing the alien at issue.

Any analysis of these questions would necessarily involve us in an inquiry into the work of foreign governments and several federal agencies, the nature of certain classified information, and the extent of secret diplomatic relationships. An investigation into the existence and content of such assurances would potentially embarrass our government through inadvertent or deliberate disclosure of information harmful to our own and other states. Given the general allocation of authority over foreign relations to the political branches and the decidedly limited experience and knowledge of the federal judiciary regarding such matters, such an investigation would also implicate grave concerns about the separation of powers and our institutional competence. These considerations strongly counsel hesitation in acknowledging a *Bivens* remedy in this context.

B. Graymail

... [T]here is further reason to hesitate where, as in this case, the challenged government policies are the subject of classified communications: a possibility that such suits will make the government "vulnerable to 'graymail,' *i.e.*, individual lawsuits brought to induce the [government] to settle a case (or prevent its filing) out of fear that any effort to litigate the action would reveal classified information that may undermine ongoing covert operations," or otherwise compromise foreign policy efforts. *Tenet v. Doe*, 544 U.S. 1, 11 (2005). We cast no aspersions on Arar, or his lawyers; this dynamic inheres in any case where there is a risk that a defendant might "disclose classified information in the course of a trial." *United States v. Pappas*, 94 F.3d 795, 799 (2d Cir. 1996). This is an endemic risk in cases (however few) which involve a claim like Arar's.

The risk of graymail is itself a special factor which counsels hesitation in creating a *Bivens* remedy. There would be hesitation enough in an ordinary graymail case, *i.e.*, where the tactic is employed against the *government*, which can trade settlement cash (or the dismissal of criminal charges) for secrecy. *See Tenet*, 544 U.S. at 11; *Pappas*, 94 F.3d at 799. But the graymail risk in a *Bivens* rendition case is uniquely troublesome. The interest in protecting military, diplomatic, and intelligence secrets is located (as always) in the *government*; yet a *Bivens* claim, by definition, is never pleaded against the government. *See, e.g., Malesko*, 534 U.S. at 70. So in a *Bivens* case, there is a dissociation between the holder of the non-disclosure interest (the government, which cannot be sued directly under *Bivens*) and the person with the incentive to disclose (the defendant, who cannot waive, but will be liable for any damages assessed). In a rendition case, the *Bivens* plaintiff could in effect pressure the individual defendants until the *government* cries uncle. Thus any *Bivens* action involving extraordinary rendition would inevitably suck the government into the case to protect its considerable interests, and—if disclosure is ordered—to appeal, or to suffer the disclosure, or to pay....

In the end, a *Bivens* action based on rendition is—in all but name—a claim against the government. It is not for nothing that Canada (the government, not an individual officer of it) paid Arar $10 million dollars.

XII

In the small number of contexts in which courts have implied a *Bivens* remedy, it has often been easy to identify both the line between constitutional and unconstitutional conduct, and the alternative course which officers should have pursued. The guard who beat a prisoner should not have beaten him; the agent who searched without a warrant should have gotten one; and the immigration officer who subjected an alien to multiple strip searches without cause should have left the alien in his clothes. This distinction may or may not amount to a special factor counseling hesitation in the implication of a *Bivens* remedy. But it is surely remarkable that the context of extraordinary rendition is so different, involving as it does a complex and rapidly changing legal framework beset with critical legal judgments that have not yet been made, as well as policy choices that are by no means easily reached.

Consider: should the officers here have let Arar go on his way and board his flight to Montreal? Canada was evidently unwilling to receive him; it was, after all, Canadian authorities who identified Arar as a terrorist (or did something that led their government to apologize publicly to Arar and pay him $10 million).

Should a person identified as a terrorist by his own country be allowed to board his plane and go on to his destination? Surely, that would raise questions as to what duty is owed to the other passengers and the crew.

Or should a suspected terrorist en route to Canada have been released on the Canadian border — over which he could re-enter the United States virtually at will? Or should he have been sent back whence his plane came, or to some third country? Should those governments be told that Canada thinks he is a terrorist? If so, what country would take him?

Or should the suspected terrorist have been sent to Guantanamo Bay or — if no other country would take him — kept in the United States with the prospect of release into the general population? *See Zadvydas v. Davis*, 533 U.S. 678, 699-700 (2001).

None of this is to say that extraordinary rendition is or should be a favored policy choice. At the same time, the officials required to decide these vexed issues are "subject to the pull of competing obligations." *Lombardi v. Whitman*, 485 F.3d 73, 83 (2d Cir. 2007). Many viable actions they might consider "clash with other equally important governmental responsibilities." *Pena v. DePrisco*, 432 F.3d 98, 114 (2d Cir. 2005) (internal quotation marks omitted). Given the ample reasons for pause already discussed, we need not and do not rely on this consideration in concluding that it is inappropriate to extend *Bivens* to this context. Still, Congress is the appropriate branch of government to decide under what circumstances (if any) these kinds of policy decisions — which are directly related to the security of the population and the foreign affairs of the country — should be subjected to the influence of litigation brought by aliens.

XIII

All of these special factors notwithstanding, we cannot ignore that, as the panel dissent put it, "there is a long history of judicial review of Executive and Legislative decisions related to the conduct of foreign relations and national security." *Arar*, 532 F.3d at 213 (Sack, J., concurring in part and dissenting in part). Where does that leave us? We recognize our limited competence, authority, and jurisdiction to make rules or set parameters to govern the practice called rendition. By the same token, we can easily locate that competence, expertise, and responsibility elsewhere: in Congress. Congress may be content for the Executive Branch to exercise these powers without judicial check. But if Congress wishes to create a remedy for individuals like Arar, it can enact legislation that includes enumerated eligibility parameters, delineated safe harbors, defined review processes, and specific relief to be afforded. Once Congress has performed this task, *then* the courts in a proper case will be able to review the statute and provide judicial oversight to the "Executive and Legislative decisions [which have been made with regard] to the conduct of foreign relations and national security." *Id.* . . .

SACK, Circuit Judge, joined by Judges CALABRESI, POOLER, and PARKER, concurring in part and dissenting in part. . . . We disagree . . . with the majority's continued insistence that Arar cannot employ a *Bivens* remedy to seek compensation for his injuries at the hands of government agents. The majority reaches that conclusion by artificially dividing the complaint into a domestic claim that does not involve torture—viz., "[Arar's] claim regarding detention in the United States,"—and a foreign claim that does—viz., "[Arar's] claims for detention and torture in Syria." The majority then dismisses the domestic claim as inadequately pleaded and the foreign claim as one that cannot "be asserted under *Bivens*" in light of the opinion's "dominant holding" that "in the context of involuntary rendition, hesitation is warranted by special factors." . . .

As we will explain, . . . the complaint's allegations cannot properly be divided into claims for mistreatment in the United States and "claims for detention and torture in Syria." Arar's complaint of mistreatment sweeps more broadly than that, encompassing a chain of events that began with his interception and detention at New York's John F. Kennedy Airport ("JFK") and continued with his being sent abroad in shackles by government agents with the knowledge that he would likely be tortured as a result. Viewed in this light, we conclude that Arar's allegations do not present a "new context" for a *Bivens* action.

And even were it a new context, we disagree with what appears to be the *en banc* majority's test for whether a new *Bivens* action should be made available: the existence *vel non* of "special factors counselling hesitation." First, we think heeding "special factors" relating to secrecy and security is a form of double counting inasmuch as those interests are fully protected by the state-secrets privilege. Second, in our view the applicable test is not whether "special factors" exist, but whether after "paying particular heed to" them, a *Bivens* remedy should be recognized with respect to at least some allegations in the complaint. Applying that test, we think a *Bivens* remedy is available. . . .

Our overriding concern, however, is with the majority's apparent determination to go to whatever length necessary to reach what it calls its "dominant holding": that a *Bivens* remedy is unavailable. Such a holding is unnecessary inasmuch as the government assures us that this case could likely be resolved quickly and expeditiously in the district court by application of the state-secrets privilege. . . .

II. THE DISMISSAL OF THE FOURTH CLAIM FOR RELIEF . . .

A. Specification of Defendants' Acts and Conspiracy Allegations . . .

Arar should not have been required to "name those defendants [who] were personally involved in the alleged unconstitutional treatment." *Arar*, 414 F. Supp. 2d at 287. In actions pursuant to 42 U.S.C. §1983, which are "analog[s]" of the less-common *Bivens* action, *Ashcroft v. Iqbal*, —— U.S. ——, ——, 129 S. Ct. 1937, 1948 (2009) (citation omitted), we allow plaintiffs to "maintain[ ] supervisory personnel as defendants . . . until [they have] been afforded an opportunity through at least brief discovery to identify the subordinate officials who have personal liability." *Davis v. Kelly*, 160 F.3d 917, 921 (2d Cir. 1998) (citing Second Circuit authority).

> Similarly, courts have rejected the dismissal of suits against unnamed defendants described by roles . . . until the plaintiff has had some opportunity for discovery to learn the identities of responsible officials. Once the supervisory officer has inquired within the institution and identified the actual decision-makers of the challenged action, those officials may then submit affidavits based on their personal knowledge of the circumstances.

Id. (citations omitted). . . .

To be sure, the Supreme Court has recently set a strict pleading standard for supervisory liability claims under *Bivens* against a former Attorney General of the United States and the Director of the FBI. *See Iqbal, supra.* We do not think, however, that the Court has thereby permitted governmental actors who are unnamed in a complaint automatically to escape personal civil rights liability. A plaintiff must, after all, have some way to identify a defendant who anonymously violates his civil rights. We doubt that *Iqbal* requires a plaintiff to obtain his abusers' business cards in order to state a civil rights claim. Put conversely, we do not think that *Iqbal* implies that federal government miscreants may avoid *Bivens* liability altogether through the simple expedient of wearing hoods while inflicting injury. Some manner of proceeding must be made available for the reasons we recognized in *Davis.*

Whether or not there is a mechanism available to identify the "Doe" defendants, moreover, Arar's complaint *does* sufficiently name some individual defendants who personally took part in the alleged violation of his civil rights. The role of defendant J. Scott Blackman, formerly Director of the Regional Office of INS, for example, is, as reflected in the district court's explication of the facts, *see Arar*, 414 F. Supp. 2d at 252-54, set forth in reasonable detail in the complaint. So are at least some of the acts of the defendant Edward J. McElroy, District Director of the INS....

C. Sufficient Pleading under *Iqbal*

More generally, we think the district court's extended recitation of the allegations in the complaint makes clear that the facts of Arar's mistreatment while within the United States — including the alleged denial of his access to courts and counsel and his alleged mistreatment while in federal detention in the United States — were pleaded meticulously and in copious detail. The assertion of relevant places, times, and events — and names when known — is lengthy and specific. Even measured in light of Supreme Court case law post-dating the district court's dismissal of the fourth claim, which instituted a more stringent standard of review for pleadings, the complaint here passes muster. It does not "offer[ ] 'labels and conclusions' or 'formulaic recitation of the elements of a cause of action.' " *Iqbal*, 129 S. Ct. at 1949 (quoting *Bell Atl. Corp. v. Twombly*, 550 U.S. 544, 555 (2007)). Nor does it "tender[ ] 'naked assertion[s]' devoid of 'further factual enhancement.' " *Id.* (quoting *Twombly*, 550 U.S. at 557). Its allegations of a constitutional violation are " 'plausible on [their] face.' " *Id.* (quoting *Twombly*, 550 U.S. at 555). And, as we have explained, Arar has pled "factual content that allows the court to draw the reasonable inference that the defendant[s] [are] liable for the misconduct alleged." *Id.* (quoting *Twombly*, 550 U.S. at 556). We would therefore vacate the district court's dismissal of the Fourth Claim for Relief....

IV. THE "CONTEXT" IN WHICH A *BIVENS* REMEDY IS SOUGHT

The majority's artificial interpretation of the complaint permits it to characterize the "context" of Arar's *Bivens* action as entirely one of "international rendition, specifically, 'extraordinary rendition.' " This permits the majority to focus on the part of the complaint that presents a "new context" for *Bivens* purposes. But when the complaint is considered in light of all of Arar's allegations, his due process claim for relief from his apprehension, detention, interrogation, and denial of access to counsel and courts in the United States, as well as his expulsion to Syria for further interrogation likely under torture, is not at all "new." ...

C. The New Context Test...

If the alleged facts of Arar's complaint were limited to his claim of "extraordinary rendition" to, and torture in, Syria—that is, limited to his allegations that he was transported by the United States government to Syria via Jordan pursuant to a conspiracy or other arrangement among the countries or their agents and mistreated in Syria as a result—as the majority would have it, then we might well agree that we are dealing with a "new context." But ... the complaint is not so limited. Incarceration in the United States without cause, mistreatment while so incarcerated, denial of access to counsel and the courts while so incarcerated, and the facilitation of torture by others, considered as possible violations of a plaintiff's procedural and substantive due process rights, are hardly novel claims, nor do they present us with a "new context" in any legally significant sense.

We have recognized implied *Bivens* rights of action pursuant to the Due Process Clause, so Arar's claims for relief are not new actions under *Bivens* in that sense.... In *Iqbal*, for example, we considered a *Bivens* action brought on, *inter alia*, a Fifth Amendment substantive due process theory. The plaintiff alleged physical mistreatment and humiliation, as a Muslim prisoner, by federal prison officials, while he was detained at the MDC. After concluding, on interlocutory appeal, that the defendants were not entitled to qualified immunity, we returned the matter to the district court for further proceedings. We did not so much as hint either that a *Bivens* remedy was unavailable or that its availability would constitute an unwarranted extension of the *Bivens* doctrine. *Iqbal*, 490 F.3d at 177-78....

Indeed, even the most "international" of Arar's domestic allegations—that the defendants, acting within the United States, sent Arar to Syria with the intent that he be tortured—present no new context for *Bivens* purposes. Principles of substantive due process apply to a narrow band of extreme misbehavior by government agents acting under color of law: mistreatment that is "so egregious, so outrageous, that it may fairly be said to shock the contemporary conscience." *Lombardi v. Whitman*, 485 F.3d 73, 79 (2d Cir. 2007) (internal quotation marks omitted). Sending Arar from the United States with the intent or understanding that he will be tortured in Syria easily exceeds the level of outrageousness needed to make out a substantive due process claim....

To be sure, Arar alleges not that the defendants themselves tortured him; he says that they "outsourced" it. But we do not think that the question whether the defendants violated Arar's substantive due process rights turns on whom they selected to do the torturing, or that such "outsourcing" somehow changes the essential character of the acts within the United States to which Arar seeks to hold the defendants accountable....

V. DEVISING A NEW *BIVENS* DAMAGES ACTION ...

B. The Special Factors Identified by the Majority...

...After *Iqbal*, it would be difficult to argue that Arar's complaint can survive as against defendants who are alleged to have been supervisors with, at most, "knowledge" of Arar's mistreatment. *See Iqbal*, 129 S. Ct. at 1949; *see also id.* at 1955 (Souter, J., dissenting). And to the extent that the United States remains a defendant, perhaps it should be dismissed for want of possible liability under *Bivens* too. But that does not dispose of the case against the lower-level defendants, such as Blackman, McElroy, and the Doe defendants, who are alleged to have personally undertaken purposeful unconstitutional actions against Arar.

It also may be that to the extent actions against "policymakers" can be equated with lawsuits against policies, they may not survive *Iqbal* either. But while those championing Arar's case may in fact wish to challenge extraordinary rendition policy writ large, the relief Arar himself seeks is principally compensation for an unconstitutional implementation of that policy. That is what *Bivens* actions are for. . . .

. . . The other "special factors" cited by the majority focus our attention on the ability of the executive to conduct the business of diplomacy and government in secret as necessary and to protect public and private security. It is beyond dispute that the judiciary must protect that concern. *See, e.g., Doe v. CIA*, 576 F.3d 95 (2d Cir. 2009). But inasmuch as there are established procedures for doing just that, we think treating that need as giving rise to "special factors counseling hesitation" is an unfortunate form of double counting. The problem can be, should be, and customarily is, dealt with case by case by employing the established procedures of the state-secrets doctrine, rather than by barring all such plaintiffs at the courtroom door without further inquiry.

C. Factors Weighing in Favor of a *Bivens* Action

At least some factors weigh in favor of permitting a *Bivens* action in this case. We assume, as we are required to, that Arar suffered a grievous infringement of his constitutional rights by one or more of the defendants, from his interception and detention while changing planes at an international airport to the time two weeks later when he was sent off in the expectation — perhaps the intent and expectation — that he would be tortured, all in order to obtain information from him. Breach of a constitutional or legal duty would appear to counsel in favor of some sort of opportunity for the victim to obtain a remedy for it. . . .

VI. THE STATE-SECRETS PRIVILEGE

[The dissenters argue that the state-secrets privilege is well suited to provide for a ruling on the merits of Arar's claims.] . . .

BARRINGTON D. PARKER, Circuit Judge, joined by Judges CALABRESI, POOLER, and SACK, dissenting: . . . My point of departure from the majority is the text of the Convention Against Torture, which provides that "[n]o exceptional circumstances whatsoever, whether a state of war or a threat of war, internal political instability or any other public emergency, may be invoked as a justification of torture." United Nations Convention Against Torture and Other Cruel, Inhuman, or Degrading Treatment or Punishment Art. 2, cl. 2, December 10, 1984, S. Treaty Doc. No. 100-20, 1465 U.N.T.S. 85 ("Convention Against Torture"). Because the majority has neglected this basic commitment and a good deal more, I respectfully dissent.

Maher Arar credibly alleges that United States officials conspired to ship him from American soil, where the Constitution and our laws apply, to Syria, where they do not, so that Syrian agents could torture him at federal officials' direction and behest. He also credibly alleges that, to accomplish this unlawful objective, agents of our government actively obstructed his access to this very Court and the protections established by Congress. *See* 8 U.S.C. §1252(a)(2)(D) (providing for judicial review of constitutional claims or questions of law raised by an order of removal).

While I broadly concur with my colleagues who dissent, I write separately to underscore the miscarriage of justice that leaves Arar without a remedy in our courts. The majority would immunize official misconduct by invoking the separation of powers and the executive's responsibility for foreign affairs and national security. Its approach distorts the system of checks and balances essential to the rule of law, and it trivializes the judiciary's role in these arenas. To my mind, the most depressing aspect of the majority's opinion is its sincerity. . . .

Notably, the majority opinion does not appear to dispute the notion that Arar has stated an injury under the Fifth Amendment of the Constitution. That is heartening, because, by any measure, the notion that federal officials conspired to send a man to Syria to be tortured "shocks the conscience." *Rochin v. California*, 342 U.S. 165, 172 (1952). What is profoundly disturbing, however, is the Court's pronouncement that it can offer Arar no opportunity to prove his case and no possibility of relief. This conclusion is at odds with the Court's responsibility to enforce the Constitution's protections and cannot, in my view, be reconciled with *Bivens*. The majority is at odds, too, with our own State Department, which has repeatedly taken the position before the world community that this exact remedy is available to torture victims like Arar. If the Constitution ever implied a damages remedy, this is such a case — where executive officials allegedly blocked access to the remedies chosen by Congress in order to deliver a man to known torturers.

The Court's hesitation today immunizes official conduct directly at odds with the express will of Congress and the most basic guarantees of liberty contained in the Constitution. By doing so, the majority risks a government that can interpret the law to suits its own ends, without scrutiny. . . .

I . . .

When presented with an appropriate case or controversy, courts are entitled — indeed obliged — to act, even in instances where government officials seek to shield their conduct behind invocations of "national security" and "foreign policy." *See, e.g., Hamdan v. Rumsfeld*, 548 U.S. 557 (2006); *Reid v. Covert*, 354 U.S. 1, 23-30 (1957); *Youngstown* [*Sheet & Tube Co. v. Sawyer*, 343 U.S. 579 (1952)]. *Compare Ex parte Quirin*, 317 U.S. 1, 19 (1942) (observing the "duty which rests on the courts, in time of war as well as in time of peace, to preserve unimpaired the constitutional safeguards of civil liberty"), *with* Maj. Op. at 42 (suggesting that Arar's allegations do not trigger the Court's "unflagging duty to exercise [its] jurisdiction"). This authority derives directly from the Constitution and goes hand in hand with the responsibility of the courts to adjudicate all manner of cases put before them. . . .

II . . .

. . . [C]ontrary to the majority's suggestion, the courts require no invitation from Congress before considering claims that touch upon foreign policy or national security. In fact, the Supreme Court has demonstrated its willingness to enter this arena against the express wishes of Congress. In *Boumediene v. Bush*, — U.S. ——, 128 S. Ct. 2229 (2008), the Supreme Court rebuffed legislative efforts to strip the courts of jurisdiction over detainees held at Guantanamo Bay. It held that the writ of habeas corpus extended to the naval base, and that neither Congress nor the executive branch could displace the courts without formally suspending the writ. Importantly, it did so despite the fact that this exercise of judicial power plainly affected the executive's detention of hundreds of enemy combatants and a centerpiece of the war on terror. The Court recognized that habeas proceedings "may divert the attention of military personnel from other pressing tasks" but refused to find these concerns "dispositive." *Id.* at 2261. . . .

POOLER, Circuit Judge, joined by Judges CALABRESI, SACK, and PARKER, dissenting. . . .

II. TVPA . . .

. . . In the Section 1983 context, the Supreme Court has held that private individuals may be liable for joint activities with state actors even where those private individuals had no official power under state law. *Dennis v. Sparks*, 449 U.S. 24, 27-28 (1980). In *Sparks*, the private individuals conspired with a state judge to enjoin the plaintiff's mining operation. The Court held:

> [T]o act "under color of" state law for §1983 purposes does not require that the defendant be an officer of the State. It is enough that he is a willful participant in joint action with the State or its agents. Private persons, jointly engaged with state officials in the challenged action, are acting "under color" of law for purposes of §1983 actions.

Id.; see also Khulumani v. Barclay Nat. Bank Ltd., 504 F.3d 254, 315 (2d Cir. 2007) (Korman, J., concurring in part). Arar alleges that U.S. officials, recognizing that Syrian law was more permissive of torture tha[n] U.S. law, contacted an agent in Syria to arrange to have Arar tortured under the authority of Syrian law. Specifically, Arar alleges that U.S. officials sent the Syrians a dossier containing questions, identical to those questions he was asked while detained in the U.S., including one about his relationship with a particular individual wanted for terrorism. He also alleges the Syrian officials supplied U.S. officials with information they extracted from him, citing a public statement by a Syrian official. Assuming the truth of these allegations, defendants' wrongdoing was only possible due to the latitude permitted under Syrian law and their joint action with Syrian authorities. The torture may fairly be attributed to Syria. . . .

Under Section 1983, non-state actors who willfully participate in joint action with state officials, acting under state law, themselves act under color of state law. By analogy, under the TVPA, non-Syrian actors who willfully participate in joint action with Syrian officials, acting under Syrian law, themselves act under color of Syrian law. In *Aldana v. Del Monte Fresh Produce*, 416 F.3d 1242, 1249, 1265 (11th Cir. 2005), the Eleventh Circuit sustained a TVPA claim where plaintiffs alleged that a U.S. corporation "hir[ed] and direct[ed] its employees and/or agents," including a Guatemalan mayor, "to torture the Plaintiffs and threaten them with death." 416 F.3d at 1265. The allegation that the corporation participated in joint action with the Guatemalan official was sufficient. I see no principled reason to apply different rules to the TVPA context than the Section 1983 context, to federal agent defendants than corporate defendants, or to actors in the United States than actors on foreign soil. Arar alleges that defendants, acting in concert with Syrian officials, interrogated him through torture under color of Syrian law, which they could not have accomplished under color of U.S. law alone. . . .

CALABRESI, Circuit Judge, joined by Judges POOLER, SACK, and PARKER, dissenting. . . . In its utter subservience to the executive branch, its distortion of *Bivens* doctrine, its unrealistic pleading standards, its misunderstanding of the TVPA and of §1983, as well as in its persistent choice of broad dicta where narrow analysis would have sufficed, the majority opinion goes seriously astray. It does so, moreover, with the result that a person—whom we must assume (a) was totally innocent and (b) was made to suffer excruciatingly (c) through the misguided deeds of individuals acting under color of federal law—is effectively left without a U.S. remedy. . . .

All this, as the other dissenters have powerfully demonstrated, is surely bad enough. I write to discuss one last failing, an unsoundness that, although it may not be the most significant to Arar himself, is of signal importance to us as federal judges: the majority's unwavering willfulness. It has engaged in what properly can be described as extraordinary judicial activism. It has violated long-standing canons of restraint that properly must guide courts when they face complex and searing questions that involve potentially fundamental constitutional rights. It has reached out to decide an issue that should not have been resolved at this stage of Arar's case. Moreover, in doing this, the court has justified its holding with side comments (as to other fields of law such as torts) that are both sweeping and wrong. That the majority—made up of colleagues I greatly respect—has done all this with the best of intentions, and in the belief that its holding is necessary in a time of crisis, I do not doubt. But this does not alter my conviction that in calmer times, wise people will ask themselves: how could such able and worthy judges have done that? . . .

NOTES AND QUESTIONS

a. The Rendition Program

1. *Scope of the Operations.* No one knows for sure how many extraordinary renditions have occurred. Some estimate that more than 100 persons have been thus rendered by the United States since the September 11 attacks. Dana Priest, *CIA's Assurances on Transferred Suspects Doubted*, Wash. Post, Mar. 17, 2005.

In June 2005, Italian police officials issued arrest warrants for 22 alleged U.S. intelligence operatives in connection with the rendering of an Islamic cleric, Osama Nasr (also known as Abu Omar) from Italy to Egypt without the approval of the Italian government. Although some reported that Italian authorities knew of and consented to the rendition, the Italian government denied those reports. Craig Whitlock, *Italy Denies Complicity in Alleged CIA Action*, Wash. Post, July 1, 2005. The Italian justice minister nevertheless declined to forward a prosecutor's extradition request to Washington for the 22 accused CIA officers. Peter Kiefer, *Italian Minister Declines to Seek Extradition of C.I.A. Operatives*, N.Y. Times, Apr. 13, 2006. Eventually, however, nine Italians and 26 Americans were indicted, and in November 2009, 22 suspected CIA agents and their aides and two Italian secret service officials were convicted (most in absentia) for an illegal abduction and rendition to Egypt. Rachel Donadio, *Italy Convicts 23 Americans for CIA Renditions*, N.Y. Times, Nov. 4, 2009.

2. *Why Do It?* Why would the United States sponsor or participate in extraordinary renditions? One unnamed official with experience in so rendering detainees explained: "We don't kick the [expletive] out of them. We send them to other countries so they can kick the [expletive] out of them." Dana Priest & Barton Gellman, *U.S. Decries Abuse but Defends Interrogations; "Stress and Duress" Tactics Used on Terrorism Suspects Held in Secret Overseas Facilities*, Wash. Post, Dec. 26, 2002.

3. *The Byproducts of Rendition.* Transfer of a prisoner to the custody of a third country for interrogation always involves the risk that the information derived, whether or not by abusive methods, will be unreliable. Indeed, unless U.S. agents are present during the interrogation, information divulged by the prisoner may be misinterpreted or even misrepresented by his interrogators. Consider the case of Ibn Al-Libi, an Al Qaeda operative, who was captured in Afghanistan in 2002, questioned by FBI agents at Bagram airbase, but then removed from their custody and flown by CIA agents to Egypt. Al-Libi was forced to confess to numerous offenses while in Egyptian custody, and his confessions became the source of false information linking Iraq and Al Qaeda. *See* Gray, *supra*, at 43. See *supra* p. 364.

4. *CIA Charter Flights.* An apparently private charter company, Aero Contractors, is actually a domestic centerpiece of the CIA's secret air service, which conducted flights to render suspects abroad. *See* Scott Shane, *CIA Expanding Terror Battle Under Guise of Charter Flights*, N.Y. Times, May 31, 2005. One 2005 analysis of 26 planes operated by CIA companies showed 307 flights in Europe since September 2001. Ian Fisher, *Reports of Secret U.S. Prisons in Europe Draw Ire and Otherwise Red Faces*, N.Y. Times, Dec. 1, 2005. Assuming that the President's September 2001 finding that authorized the rendition program (*supra* p. 927) complied with the National Security Act, *supra* p. 444, were the renditions lawful? Does it matter legally whether Congress was not notified about individual cases?

Binyam Mohamed, an Ethiopian national and British resident, was detained in Pakistan in 2002 and, for two years, was moved between "black sites" in Pakistan, Morocco, and Afghanistan, and then to Guantánamo, where he remained until he was released to Britain in 2009. Before his release, lawyers for Mohamed sued in Britain to obtain disclosure of any information in the possession of the U.K. government that would support Mohamed's claims that he had been tortured by the United States. Eventually, the U.K. courts ordered the release of limited summaries that confirm that Mohamed was subjected to cruel, inhuman, and degrading treatment by U.S. authorities. Richard Norton-Taylor, *Binyam Mohamed Torture Evidence Must Be Revealed*, Guardian, Feb. 10, 2010. Mohamed and other victims of CIA extraordinary rendition then brought suit under the Alien Tort Statute (ATS) against Jeppesen Dataplan, a company allegedly involved in providing flight services that enabled the CIA to carry out the renditions of Mohamed and his co-plaintiffs. *Mohamed v. Jeppesen Dataplan, Inc.*, 579 F.3d 943 (9th Cir. 2009) (en banc) (*supra* p. 142). During a corporate meeting, Jeppesen executive Bob Overby stated to his colleagues, "We do all of the extraordinary rendition flights — you know, the torture flights." Jane Mayer, *Outsourcing Torture: The Secret History of America's "Extraordinary Rendition" Program*, New Yorker, Feb. 14, 2005. If the state secrets privilege had not effectively ended the lawsuit against Jeppesen Dataplan, how should the court have ruled on Mohamed's claims on the merits?

5. *"Black Sites" and the Use of Contractors.* Although not publicly admitted, presumably the CIA used the services of private contractors to maintain the "black sites" and also to provide logistics and air travel for extraordinary renditions. What laws constrain the use of contractors in these settings, and what regulations would guide their actions? Would a suspect tortured by a contractor in a "black site" have legal remedies in a U.S. court?

6. *Official Policy?* Officials denied that renditions have occurred for the purpose of torture. R. Jeffrey Smith, *Gonzales Defends Transfer of Detainees*, Wash. Post, Mar. 8, 2005 (quoting Attorney General Gonzales as stating that it is not U.S. policy to send persons "to countries where we believe or we know that they're going to be tortured"); Joel Brinkley, *U.S. Interrogations Are Saving European Lives, Rice Says*, N.Y. Times, Dec. 6, 2005 (quoting Secretary of State Condoleezza Rice as stating that "[t]he United States does not transport and has not transported detainees from one country to another for the purpose of interrogation using torture."). How much legal wiggle room do these statements preserve for the Administration? How, if at all, should these statements of U.S. policy affect Arar's likelihood of gaining relief in his lawsuit?

b. Judicial Remedies for Extraordinary Rendition

1. *The Availability of Judicial Remedies.* The Second Circuit ruled that the TVPA does not support a claim where U.S. officials allegedly direct foreign officials to torture a non-U.S. citizen. Does the fact that U.S. officials were alleged to be acting under color of federal, not Syrian, law necessarily mean that those officials did not violate the TVPA? Of what value, then, is the TVPA to victims of torture directed by U.S. agents? Are you persuaded by the dissenters' analogy of the TVPA to Section 1983 suits involving joint action by non-state actors (in this case non-Syrian) and state actors?

2. *Bivens.* Why did the court decline to decide Arar's claim for damages arising out of alleged due process violations? Do you understand the legal basis for the exception to the *Bivens* doctrine, where "special factors counseling hesitation" that include foreign policy, military, and national security concerns bar the tort remedy for violation of Arar's constitutional rights? What sensitive issues of national security between the United States and Syria could justify declining to decide the tort claim?

Other courts have been similarly unwilling to extend *Bivens* liability. A claim by foreign nationals who alleged that they had been tortured by U.S. military personnel was dismissed after finding "special factors counseling hesitation" similar to those relied upon in *Arar* in *In re Iraq & Afghanistan Detainees*, 479 F. Supp. 2d 85 (D.D.C. 2007). The same result was reached in *Lebron v. Rumsfeld*, 764 F. Supp. 2d 787 (D.S.C. 2011) where the court found that "special factors" justified dismissal of a claim that Jose Padilla's constitutional rights were violated when he was allegedly mistreated while in military detention. *See supra* p. 855. Two district courts have allowed similar *Bivens* claims to survive motions to dismiss. *Padilla v. Yoo*, 633 F. Supp. 2d 1005 (N.D. Cal. 2009); *Vance v. Rumsfeld*, 694 F. Supp. 2d 957 (N.D. Ill. 2010). Decisions on appeal in the three most recent cases were pending at this writing.

3. *Assessing the Outcome in Arar.* Do the "what if" circumstances offered in part XII of the majority opinion persuade you that U.S. officials treated Arar reasonably

and lawfully under the circumstances? Were there only two options available — let Arar go on to his destination or render him to Syria? If not, what should U.S. officials have done with Arar when he entered U.S. customs in New York City? For an argument that courts should reject the "categorical deference" to government officials shown in *Arar* "if the government did not show that it had used a less intrusive alternative to extraordinary rendition in a similar case," *see* Peter Marguiles, *Judging Myopia in Hindsight: Bivens Actions, National Security Decisions, and the Rule of Law,* 96 Iowa L. Rev. 195, 243 (2010).

Do you agree with the majority that it is more appropriate for Congress than the courts to fashion a remedy for someone like Arar?

Why did the plausibility-pleading rule justify dismissing Arar's claims concerning the conduct of U.S. officials inside the United States? If senior government officials were involved in the diplomatic communications that led to Arar's removal, is it reasonable to surmise that those officials authorized the steps taken inside the United States to enable his rendition to Syria? *See* Marguiles, *supra,* 96 Iowa L. Rev. at 225 (yes).

4. *Extraterritorial Reach of the Constitution.* The apparent legal assumption of the lawyers who advised those creating the "black sites" and extraordinary rendition program was that if the abusive interrogations occurred outside the United States and the persons seized and interrogated were not U.S. citizens, the resulting abuses could not be challenged as violating the constitutional rights of the victim. Is the assumption correct? How, if at all, is your answer influenced by the decisions in *Reid v. Covert, supra* p. 709; *Verdugo-Urquidez v. United States, supra* p. 712; *Johnson v. Eisentrager,* noted *supra* p. 775; and *Boumediene v. Bush, supra* p. 787?

5. *Availability of Habeas Corpus.* In *Abu Ali v. Ashcroft,* 350 F. Supp. 2d 28 (D.D.C. 2004), U.S. citizen Omar Abu Ali challenged his ongoing detention in a prison in Saudi Arabia allegedly at the direction and with the ongoing supervision of the United States. When Abu Ali's parents sought habeas corpus for their son, the United States argued that the suit must be dismissed for lack of jurisdiction, "no matter how extensive a role the United States might have played and continues to play" in Abu Ali's detention, "for the sole reason that he is presently in a foreign prison." *Id.* at 40. The court held that the United States may not avoid habeas corpus jurisdiction by enlisting a foreign nation to detain an American citizen:

> This position is as striking as it is sweeping. The full contours of the position would permit the United States, at its discretion and without judicial review, to arrest a citizen of the United States and transfer her to the custody of allies overseas in order to avoid constitutional scrutiny; to arrest a citizen of the United States through the intermediary of a foreign ally and ask the ally to hold the citizen at a foreign location indefinitely at the direction of the United States; or even to deliver American citizens to foreign governments to obtain information through the use of torture. In short, the United States is in effect arguing for nothing less than the unreviewable power to separate an American citizen from the most fundamental of his constitutional rights merely by choosing where he will be detained or who will detain him. [*Id.*]

How, if at all, does the court's answer to the government affect those in a situation similar to Arar's?

c.   International Law Limits on Extraordinary Rendition

1. *The CAT and Implementing Legislation.* Review the discussion of the Convention Against Torture and its implementing legislation, *supra* p. 914. CAT Article 3 provides that "[n]o State Party shall expel, return ('refouler') or extradite a person to another State where there are substantial grounds for believing that he would be in danger of being subjected to torture." An understanding attached to the Convention by the Senate upon its advice and consent states that the requirement in Article 3 would apply when it is "more likely than not" that torture would follow such a rendition. S. Exec. Rep. No. 101-30, Resolution of Advice and Consent to Ratification (1990), ¶II(2). What information should lawyers take into account when asked to advise on a "more likely than not" determination? The CAT lacks a parallel provision regarding cruel, inhuman, or degrading treatment following rendition. What is the legal significance of this omission? *See* Michael John Garcia, *Renditions: Constraints Imposed by Laws on Torture* 7 (Cong. Res. Serv. RL32890), Sept. 8, 2009.

In 1998, Congress approved legislation purporting to implement Article 3 of the CAT. Pub. L. No. 105-277, §2242, 112 Stat. 2681, 2681-822 to -823. The measure states that it is

> the policy of the United States not to . . . effect the involuntary return of any person to a country in which there are substantial grounds for believing the person would be in danger of being subjected to torture, regardless of whether the person is physically present in the United States. *Id.* §2242(a).

The Act requires relevant federal agencies to adopt regulations to implement the policy. But it provides no penalties for violation. Article 4(1) of the CAT requires each state party to "ensure that all acts of torture are offenses under its criminal law. The same shall apply to an attempt to commit torture and to an act by any person which constitutes complicity or participation in torture." Does the 1998 legislation satisfy the U.S. obligation under Article 4(1)? How about current Department of Homeland Security regulations that prohibit the removal of all persons to states where they "more likely than not" would be tortured? 8 C.F.R. §§208.16-18, 1208.16-18 (2010). (CIA regulations concerning renditions, if any, are not publicly available.) *See* Garcia, *supra*, at 9.

The Torture Act, 18 U.S.C. §§2340, 2340A (2006), *supra* p. 915, expressly criminalizes acts of torture and attempts to commit torture outside the United States. *Id.* §2340A(a). It also provides punishment for conspiracy to do either of those things. *Id.* §2340A(c). It defines torture as an act "specifically intended to inflict severe physical or mental pain or suffering (other than pain or suffering incidental to lawful sanctions) upon another person within his custody or physical control." *Id.* §2340(1). What facts would have to be proven in order to hold a CIA official criminally liable under the statute who arranged for an extraordinary rendition that resulted in torture? Recall Attorney General Gonzales's comment, *supra* p. 942. Would a mere belief that a suspect might be tortured in the destination state be sufficient to make the CIA official criminally responsible for any torture that occurs there? Does this statute satisfy the U.S. obligation under CAT Article 4(1)?

A March 2002 memorandum to the General Counsel of the Defense Department, signed by Jay S. Bybee of the Office of Legal Counsel, asserted that "the United States is free from any constraints imposed by the Torture Convention in deciding whether to transfer detainees that it is holding abroad to third countries." *Memorandum for William J. Haynes from Jay Bybee, Re: The President's Power as Commander in Chief to Transfer Captured Terrorists to the Control and Custody of Foreign Nations* (Mar. 13, 2002), *available at* http://www.fas.org/irp/agency/doj/olc/index.html (maintaining that the treaty does not apply extraterritorially). Recall that the Bush administration also decided early in 2002 that the Geneva Conventions do not apply to captured Al Qaeda or Taliban detainees. Were these positions legally defensible in 2002? Are they defensible now?

2. *Assurances.* Regulations implementing the CAT provide that any transfers of a captive to another country must be accompanied by "sufficiently reliable" diplomatic assurances from the receiving country to the U.S. Secretary of State that it will not torture the suspect. 8 C.F.R. §208.18(c). CIA officials have stated that Agency guidelines require a receiving country to give assurances that a rendered prisoner will be treated humanely, and require that U.S. personnel monitor compliance with the assurances. Douglas Jehl & David Johnston, *Rule Change Lets CIA Freely Send Suspects Abroad to Jails*, N.Y. Times, Mar. 6, 2005. What capacity does the United States have to enforce promises that detainees are treated humanely? What was the *Arar* court's justification for not inquiring about any assurances regarding Arar's treatment? If courts do not review compliance with the policy expressed in the 1998 legislation excerpted in the previous Note, how can that policy be enforced?

3. *Geneva Convention Limits on Rendition.* An involuntary transfer of "protected persons" to another state is forbidden by Geneva Convention IV, Article 49. A violation constitutes a "grave breach" and is thus a war crime. *Id.* art. 147. Recall the Bush administration's arguments concerning the applicability of the Geneva Conventions in the post–September 11 campaign, *supra* p. 940. Which persons in what places are protected from rendition under the Geneva Conventions? Might these provisions have been helpful to Arar in his lawsuit?

Do the protections of Common Article 3, *supra* p. 918, apply to renditions of persons to countries where they may be tortured? *See* Garcia, *supra*, at 20 (probably not). Would the War Crimes Act, *supra* p. 917, prohibit renditions where torture is likely? *See id.* at 21 (yes, if U.S. personnel conspire with foreign officials and intend to so harm the victim).

4. *Customary International Law.* The *Restatement of the Foreign Relations Law of the United States* declares that "causing the disappearance of individuals" is absolutely prohibited under international law, that it violates the human rights of the victim, and that it constitutes a violation of a peremptory norm or *jus cogens. Id.* §702c cmts. a, c, n. *See* Jordan J. Paust, *Beyond the Law: The Bush Administration's Unlawful Responses in the "War" on Terror* 36-38 (2007).

5. *Effect of the Bush and Obama Executive Orders.* Executive Order No. 13,400, promulgated by President Bush on July 20, 2007, construed Common Article 3 of the Geneva Conventions as not applicable to members of Al Qaeda, the Taliban, or associated forces. The President also reasserted his authority as Commander in Chief to interpret the meaning of Common Article 3, while he stated that the CIA would follow guidelines not to engage in torture, or cruel and inhuman treatment, or to humiliate or degrade prisoners in a manner beyond the bounds of human

decency. *See supra* p. 922. Could extraordinary renditions have been carried out lawfully on the basis of this executive order? President Obama repealed the Bush executive order when he issued Executive Order No. 13,491, 74 Fed. Reg. 4893 (Jan. 22, 2009), *supra* p. 922. Does the Obama order end U.S. participation in extraordinary rendition operations?

d.   Reforms

1. *Effect of the Detainee Treatment Act.* Review the language of the Detainee Treatment Act, *supra* p. 921. If this provision had been in effect when Arar was rendered to Syria, would the Act have been violated?

2. *Further Reforms?* The Obama executive order established the Special Task Force on Interrogation and Transfer Policies. On August 24, 2009, the Task Force issued recommendations to the President, including stronger procedures for obtaining and evaluating diplomatic assurances from a receiving country; a monitoring mechanism to ensure consistent access to transferred persons, with minimal notice to the detaining government; and annual, coordinated reports from the Inspectors General of the Departments of State, Defense, and Homeland Security on transfers that were made on the basis of assurances. Department of Justice, *Special Task Force on Interrogations and Transfer Policies Issues Its Recommendations to the President* (Aug. 24, 2009), *at* http://www.usdooj.gov/opa/pr/2009/August/09-ag-835.html. Do you think these reforms, if implemented, will put a stop to extraordinary renditions? If not, will they ensure that rendered prisoners will not be subjected to abusive interrogation? What other changes in law would you recommend in reforming the practice of extraordinary rendition? *See* Louis Fisher, *Extraordinary Rendition: The Price of Secrecy,* 57 Am. U. L. Rev. 1405 (2008).

VII

Prosecuting Threats to National Security

34

Criminalizing Terrorism and Material Support

Generally, First Amendment protections for freedom of speech, assembly, and association pose no obstacle to prosecution of terrorists for committing terrorist acts. Murder and maiming enjoy no constitutional protection. But the prosecution of such primary offenders — if they survive the terrorist attack and are successfully hunted down — comes too late to prevent the harm. Nor is such prosecution likely to deter others who are religiously or politically motivated to commit terrorist attacks. Counterterrorist criminal law therefore necessarily searches up the chain of causation to secondary defendants who aid and abet, conspire, harbor, or otherwise assist the terrorists. And prosecution of either primary or secondary defendants is complicated when their conduct takes place abroad, given the normal presumption against extraterritorial application of U.S. law.

In Part A of this chapter, we consider a case that suggests that the hoary criminal laws of treason and sedition may be a poor fit for such prosecutions. In the 1990s, Congress therefore criminalized providing "material support" to terrorists or designated "foreign terrorist organizations." In Part B, we consider these laws and the issues they raise about criminalizing advocacy and association as well as personal guilt. Finally, in Part C, we consider the extraterritorial application of U.S. counterterrorism laws.

A. TREASON AND SEDITION

United States v. Rahman

United States Court of Appeals, Second Circuit, 1999
189 F.3d 88

PER CURIAM: These are appeals by ten defendants convicted of seditious conspiracy and other offenses arising out of a wide-ranging plot to conduct a campaign of urban terrorism. Among the activities of some or all of the defendants were rendering assistance to those who bombed the World Trade Center, planning to bomb bridges and tunnels in New York City, murdering Rabbi Meir Kahane, and planning to murder the President of Egypt. We affirm the convictions of all the defendants. . . .

The Government adduced evidence at trial showing the following: Abdel Rahman, a blind Islamic scholar and cleric, was the leader of the seditious conspiracy, the purpose of which was *"jihad,"* in the sense of a struggle against the enemies of Islam. Indicative of this purpose, in a speech to his followers Abdel Rahman instructed that they were to "do *jihad* with the sword, with the cannon, with the grenades, with the missile . . . against God's enemies." Abdel Rahman's role in the conspiracy was generally limited to overall supervision and direction of the membership, as he made efforts to remain a level above the details of individual operations. However, as a cleric and the group's leader, Abdel Rahman was entitled to dispense *"fatwas,"* religious opinions on the holiness of an act, to members of the group sanctioning proposed courses of conduct and advising them whether the acts would be in furtherance of *jihad*.

According to his speeches and writings, Abdel Rahman perceives the United States as the primary oppressor of Muslims worldwide, active in assisting Israel to gain power in the Middle East, and largely under the control of the Jewish lobby. Abdel Rahman also considers the secular Egyptian government of Mubarak to be an oppressor because it has abided Jewish migration to Israel while seeking to decrease Muslim births. Holding these views, Abdel Rahman believes that *jihad* against Egypt and the United States is mandated by the Qur'an. Formation of a *jihad* army made up of small "divisions" and "battalions" to carry out this *jihad* was therefore necessary, according to Abdel Rahman, in order to beat back these oppressors of Islam including the United States. . . .

I. CONSTITUTIONAL CHALLENGES

A. Seditious Conspiracy Statute and the Treason Clause

Defendant Nosair (joined by other defendants) contends that his conviction for seditious conspiracy, in violation of 18 U.S.C. §2384, was illegal because it failed to satisfy the requirements of the Treason Clause of the U.S. Constitution, Art. III, §3.

Article III, Section 3 provides, in relevant part:

> Treason against the United States, shall consist only in levying War against them, or in adhering to their Enemies, giving them Aid and Comfort. No Person shall be convicted of Treason unless on the Testimony of two Witnesses to the same overt Act, or on Confession in open Court.

The seditious conspiracy statute provides:

> If two or more persons in any State or Territory, or in any place subject to the jurisdiction of the United States, conspire to overthrow, put down or to destroy by force the Government of the United States, or to levy war against them, or to oppose by force the authority thereof, or by force to prevent, hinder or delay the execution of any law of the United States, or by force to seize, take, or possess any property of the United States contrary to the authority thereof, they shall each be fined under this title or imprisoned not more than twenty years, or both.

18 U.S.C. §2384.

Nosair contends that because the seditious conspiracy statute punishes conspiracy to "levy war" against the United States without a conforming two-witness requirement, the statute is unconstitutional. He further claims that because his conviction for conspiracy to levy war against the United States was not based on the testimony of two witnesses to the same overt act, the conviction violates constitutional standards.

It is undisputed that Nosair's conviction was not supported by two witnesses to the same overt act. Accordingly the conviction must be overturned if the requirement of the Treason Clause applies to this prosecution for seditious conspiracy.

The plain answer is that the Treason Clause does not apply to the prosecution. The provisions of Article III, Section 3 apply to prosecutions for "treason." Nosair and his co-appellants were not charged with treason. Their offense of conviction, seditious conspiracy under Section 2384, differs from treason not only in name and associated stigma, but also in its essential elements and punishment. . . .

Seditious conspiracy by levying war includes no requirement that the defendant owe allegiance to the United States, an element necessary to conviction of treason. *See* 18 U.S.C. §2381 (defining "allegiance to United States" as an element of treason). . . .

. . . The reference to treason in the constitutional clause necessarily incorporates the elements of allegiance and betrayal that are essential to the concept of treason. . . . Nosair was thus tried for a different, and lesser, offense than treason. We therefore see no reasonable basis to maintain that the requirements of the Treason Clause should apply to Nosair's prosecution.

B. Seditious Conspiracy Statute and the First Amendment

Abdel Rahman, joined by the other appellants, contends that the seditious conspiracy statute, 18 U.S.C. §2384, is an unconstitutional burden on free speech and the free exercise of religion in violation of the First Amendment. First, Abdel Rahman argues that the statute is facially invalid because it criminalizes protected expression and that it is overbroad and unconstitutionally vague. Second, Abdel Rahman contends that his conviction violated the First Amendment because it rested solely on his political views and religious practices.

1. Facial Challenge

a. *Restraint on Speech.* . . . As Section 2384 proscribes "speech" only when it constitutes an agreement to use force against the United States, Abdel Rahman's generalized First Amendment challenge to the statute is without merit. Our court has previously considered and rejected a First Amendment challenge to Section 2384. *See United States v. Lebron*, 222 F.2d 531, 536 (2d Cir. 1955). Although *Lebron*'s analysis of the First Amendment issues posed by Section 2384 was brief, the panel found the question was squarely controlled by the Supreme Court's then-recent decision in *Dennis v. United States*, 341 U.S. 494 (1951). In *Dennis*, the Court upheld the constitutionality of the Smith Act, which made it a crime to advocate, or to conspire to advocate, the overthrow of the United States government by force or violence. *See* 18 U.S.C. §2385; *Dennis*, 341 U.S. at 494. The *Dennis* Court concluded that, while the "element of speech" inherent in Smith Act convictions required that the Act be given close First Amendment scrutiny, the Act did not impermissibly burden the expression of protected speech, as it was properly "directed at advocacy [of overthrow of the government by force], not discussion." *See id.* at 502.

After *Dennis*, the Court broadened the scope of First Amendment restrictions on laws that criminalize subversive advocacy. It remains fundamental that while the state may not criminalize the expression of views — even including the view that violent overthrow of the government is desirable — it may nonetheless outlaw encouragement, inducement, or conspiracy to take violent action. Thus, in *Yates v. United States*, 354 U.S. 298, 318 (1957), overruled in part on other grounds, *Burks v. United States*, 437 U.S. 1, 7 (1978), the Court interpreted the Smith Act to prohibit only the advocacy of concrete violent action, but not "advocacy and teaching of forcible overthrow as an abstract principle, divorced from any effort to instigate action to that end." And in *Brandenburg v. Ohio*, 395 U.S. 444, 447 (1969) (per curiam), the Court held that a state may proscribe subversive advocacy only when such advocacy is directed towards, and is likely to result in, "imminent lawless action."

The prohibitions of the seditious conspiracy statute are much further removed from the realm of constitutionally protected speech than those at issue in *Dennis* and its progeny. To be convicted under Section 2384, one must conspire to *use* force, not just to *advocate* the use of force. We have no doubt that this passes the test of constitutionality. . . .

b. *Vagueness and Overbreadth.* Abdel Rahman also contends that Section 2384 is overbroad and void for vagueness.

(i) *Overbreadth.* A law is overbroad, and hence void, if it "does not aim specifically at evils within the allowable area of State control, but, on the contrary, sweeps within its ambit other activities that . . . constitute an exercise of freedom of speech or of the press." *Thornhill v. Alabama*, 310 U.S. 88, 97 (1940). . . .

We recognize that laws targeting "sedition" must be scrutinized with care to assure that the threat of prosecution will not deter expression of unpopular viewpoints by persons ideologically opposed to the government. But Section 2384 is drawn sufficiently narrowly that we perceive no unacceptable risk of such abuse.

Abdel Rahman argues that Section 2384 is overbroad because Congress could have achieved its public safety aims "without chilling First Amendment rights" by punishing only "substantive acts involving bombs, weapons, or other violent acts." One of the beneficial purposes of the conspiracy law is to permit arrest and prosecution before the substantive crime has been accomplished. The Government, possessed of evidence of conspiratorial planning, need not wait until buildings and tunnels have been bombed and people killed before arresting the conspirators. Accordingly, it is well established that the Government may criminalize certain preparatory steps towards criminal action, even when the crime consists of the use of conspiratorial or exhortatory words. Because Section 2384 prohibits only conspiratorial agreement, we are satisfied that the statute is not constitutionally overbroad.

(ii) *Vagueness.* Abdel Rahman also challenges the statute for vagueness. A criminal statute, particularly one regulating speech, must "define the criminal offense with sufficient definiteness that ordinary people can understand what conduct is prohibited and in a manner that does not encourage arbitrary and discriminatory enforcement." *Kolender v. Lawson*, 461 U.S. 352, 357 (1983). Abdel Rahman argues that Section 2384 does not provide "fair warning" about what acts are unlawful, leaving constitutionally protected speech vulnerable to criminal prosecution.

There is indeed authority suggesting that the word "seditious" does not sufficiently convey what conduct it forbids to serve as an essential element of a crime. *See Keyishian v. Board of Regents*, 385 U.S. 589, 598 (1967) (noting that "dangers fatal to First Amendment freedoms inhere in the word 'seditious,'"and invalidating law that provided, *inter alia*, that state employees who utter "seditious words" may be discharged). But the word "seditious" does not appear in the prohibitory text of the statute; it appears only in the caption. The terms of the statute are far more precise. The portions charged against Abdel Rahman and his co-defendants — conspiracy to levy war against the United States and to oppose by force the authority thereof — do not involve terms of such vague meaning. Furthermore, they unquestionably specify that agreement *to use force* is an essential element of the crime. Abdel Rahman therefore cannot prevail on the claim that the portions of Section 2384 charged against him criminalize mere expressions of opinion, or are unduly vague.

2. Application of Section 2384 to Abdel Rahman's Case

Abdel Rahman also argues that he was convicted not for entering into any conspiratorial agreement that Congress may properly forbid, but "solely for his religious words and deeds" which, he contends, are protected by the First Amendment. In support of this claim, Abdel Rahman cites the Government's use in evidence of his speeches and writings.

There are two answers to Abdel Rahman's contention. The first is that freedom of speech and of religion do not extend so far as to bar prosecution of one who uses a public speech or a religious ministry to commit crimes. Numerous crimes under the federal criminal code are, or can be, committed by speech alone. As examples: Section 2 makes it an offense to "counsel[ ]," "command[ ]," "induce[ ]" or "procure[ ]" the commission of an offense against the United States. 18 U.S.C. §2(a). Section 371 makes it a crime to "conspire . . . to commit any offense against the United States." 18 U.S.C. §371. Section 373, with which Abdel Rahman was charged, makes it a crime to "solicit[ ], command[ ], induce[ ], or otherwise endeavor[ ] to persuade" another person to commit a crime of violence. 18 U.S.C. §373(a). Various other statutes, like Section 2384, criminalize conspiracies of specified objectives, *see, e.g.,* 18 U.S.C. §1751(d) (conspiracy to kidnap); 18 U.S.C. §1951 (conspiracy to interfere with commerce through robbery, extortion, or violence); 21 U.S.C. §846 (conspiracy to violate drug laws). All of these offenses are characteristically committed through speech. Notwithstanding that political speech and religious exercise are among the activities most jealously guarded by the First Amendment, one is not immunized from prosecution for such speech-based offenses merely because one commits them through the medium of political speech or religious preaching. Of course, courts must be vigilant to insure that prosecutions are not improperly based on the mere expression of unpopular ideas. But if the evidence shows that the speeches crossed the line into criminal solicitation, procurement of criminal activity, or conspiracy to violate the laws, the prosecution is permissible.

The evidence justifying Abdel Rahman's conviction for conspiracy and solicitation showed beyond a reasonable doubt that he crossed this line. His speeches were not simply the expression of ideas; in some instances they constituted the crime of conspiracy to wage war on the United States under Section 2384 and solicitation of attack on the United States military installations, as well as of the murder of Egyptian President Hosni Mubarak under Section 373.

For example: Abdel Rahman told Salem he "should make up with God . . . by turning his rifle's barrel to President Mubarak's chest, and kill[ing] him." Tr. 4633.

On another occasion, speaking to Abdo Mohammed Haggag about murdering President Mubarak during his visit to the United States, Abdel Rahman told Haggag, "Depend on God. Carry out this operation. It does not require a fatwa. . . . You are ready in training, but do it. Go ahead." Tr. 10108.

The evidence further showed that Siddig Ali consulted with Abdel Rahman about the bombing of the United Nations Headquarters, and Abdel Rahman told him, "Yes, it's a must, it's a duty." Tr. 5527-5529.

On another occasion, when Abdel Rahman was asked by Salem about bombing the United Nations, he counseled against it on the ground that it would be "bad for Muslims," Tr. 6029, but added that Salem should "find a plan to destroy or to bomb or to . . . inflict damage to the American Army." Tr. 6029-6030.

Words of this nature — ones that instruct, solicit, or persuade others to commit crimes of violence — violate the law and may be properly prosecuted regardless of whether they are uttered in private, or in a public speech, or in administering the duties of a religious ministry. The fact that his speech or conduct was "religious" does not immunize him from prosecution under generally-applicable criminal statutes.

Abdel Rahman also protests the Government's use in evidence of his speeches, writings, and preachings that did not in themselves constitute the crimes of solicitation or conspiracy. He is correct that the Government placed in evidence many instances of Abdel Rahman's writings and speeches in which Abdel Rahman expressed his opinions within the protection of the First Amendment. However, while the First Amendment fully protects Abdel Rahman's right to express hostility against the United States, and he may not be prosecuted for so speaking, it does not prevent the use of such speeches or writings in evidence when relevant to prove a pertinent fact in a criminal prosecution. The Government was free to demonstrate Abdel Rahman's resentment and hostility toward the United States in order to show his motive for soliciting and procuring illegal attacks against the United States and against President Mubarak of Egypt.

Furthermore, Judge Mukasey properly protected against the danger that Abdel Rahman might be convicted because of his unpopular religious beliefs that were hostile to the United States. He explained to the jury the limited use it was entitled to make of the material received as evidence of motive. He instructed that a defendant could not be convicted on the basis of his beliefs or the expression of them — even if those beliefs favored violence. He properly instructed the jury that it could find a defendant guilty only if the evidence proved he committed a crime charged in the indictment.

We reject Abdel Rahman's claim that his conviction violated his rights under the First Amendment. . . .

NOTES AND QUESTIONS

1. *Treason.* "Treason" is the only crime expressly identified in the Constitution, which states that "Treason against the United States, shall consist only in levying War against them, or in adhering to their Enemies, giving them Aid and Comfort." U.S. Const. art. III, §3. Furthermore, the text supplies a special evidentiary rule for treason prosecutions: "No Person shall be convicted of Treason unless on the Testimony of two Witnesses to the same overt Act, or on Confession in open Court." *Id.* Why did the Framers single out treason for special mention and write an evidentiary rule for treason prosecutions directly into the Constitution, while leaving other crimes to legislative definition and evidentiary rules to the courts through the medium of the common law?

The restrictive nature of the constitutional rule of evidence suggests an answer: the Framers feared that the state would use treason prosecutions to suppress dissent.

> The treason clause is a product of the awareness of the Framers of the "numerous and dangerous excrescences" which had disfigured the English law of treason and was therefore intended to put it beyond the power of Congress to "extend the crime and punishment of treason." The debate in the Convention, remarks in the ratifying conventions, and contemporaneous public comment make clear that a restrictive concept of the crime was imposed and that ordinary partisan divisions within political society were not to be escalated by the stronger into capital charges of treason, as so often had happened in England. [S. Doc. No. 92-82, Congressional Research Service, *The Constitution of the United States of America: Analysis and Interpretation* (1973) (citations omitted), *updated version available at* http://www.law.cornell.edu/anncon/authorship.html.]

Indeed, the Framers provided additional protections for such partisan divisions by prohibiting Congress from enacting any law abridging freedom of speech, the press, assembly, petition, and (by judicial implication) association. U.S. Const. amend. I. *See* Ronald D. Rotunda & John E. Nowak, *Treatise on Constitutional Law* §20.41 (3d ed. Pocket Part 2005) (describing case law regarding freedom of association). Are the Framers' concerns about the crime of treason still valid? *See* Kristen Eichensehr, *Treason in an Age of Terrorism: An Explanation and Evaluation of Treason's Return in Democratic States*, 42 Vand. J. Transnat'l L. 1443 (2009).

Why did Abdel Rahman argue that he was effectively convicted of treason? Did the court's answer to his claim bypass the protections that the Framers built into the Treason Clause?

Should he have been prosecuted for treason? *See* Carlton F.W. Larson, *The Forgotten Constitutional Law of Treason and the Enemy Combatant*, 154 U. Pa. L. Rev. 863 (2006) (arguing that conspiracy to levy war is not seditious conspiracy, not treason, but urging revival of treason prosecutions for enemy combatants instead of military trial).

2. *Inciting Imminent Harm.* The *Rahman* court's synopsis of the constitutional law governing advocacy of lawless action makes it sound more consistent than it is. *See, e.g.,* Christina E. Wells, *Fear and Loathing in Constitutional Decision-Making*, 2005 Wis. L. Rev. 115. In a World War I case under the 1918 Sedition Act, the Supreme Court declared that the government could constitutionally criminalize the utterance of "words . . . used in such circumstances . . . as to create a clear and present danger that they will bring about the substantive evils that Congress has a right to prevent." *Schenck v. United States*, 249 U.S. 47, 52 (1919). The Court seemed to relax the clear-and-present-danger test in *Dennis v. United States*, 341 U.S. 494 (1951), by finding that the harm from an overthrow of the government would be so grave that the government need not show its imminence or probability in order to punish advocacy of the overthrow. Dennis and his co-defendants were convicted and sentenced to long prison terms for violating the Smith Act, which made it unlawful "to knowingly or willfully advocate, abet, advise, or teach the duty, necessity, desirability, or propriety of overthrowing or destroying any government in the United States by force or violence. . . ." Act of June 28, 1940, 54 Stat. 670, 671 (1940). What were their criminal

acts? Apparently, according to the evidence adduced by the government, assembling to discuss and plan future teaching of books by Stalin, Marx and Engels, and Lenin. Finally, without disavowing these chilling precedents, the Court reversed a conviction for "criminal syndicalism" in *Brandenberg v. Ohio*, 395 U.S. 444 (1969). There, the defendant had given a racist and anti-Semitic speech at a Ku Klux Klan rally. The Court held that a State could not criminalize "advocacy of the use of force or of law violation except where such advocacy is directed to inciting or producing imminent lawless action *and* is *likely* to incite or produce such action." *Id.* at 447 (emphasis added).

How does Section 2384 fare under these tests? Did the *Rahman* court apply them correctly? *See* John Alan Cohan, *Seditious Conspiracy, the Smith Act, and Prosecution for Religious Speech Advocating the Violent Overthrow of Government*, 17 St. John's J. Legal Comment. 199 (2003).

3. *Expression as Evidence.* Are not Rahman's religious expressions, quoted in the case, quintessentially protected speech? Why was it constitutional to base his criminal prosecution in part on them? *See generally* Cohan, *supra.*

B.   MATERIAL SUPPORT CRIMES

Congress has criminalized a range of terrorist activities—from using weapons of mass destruction to bombing public places or government facilities. *See* 18 U.S.C. §§2331-2339D (2006 & Supp. III 2009). But because terrorists often evade capture or die in the attack, and their supporters are easier to locate and prosecute, prosecutors have more often turned to laws criminalizing material support for terrorism. These make it a crime not only to provide support in preparation for or carrying out terrorist acts, but also to provide support to an organization that the Secretary of State has designated a "foreign terrorist organization" (FTO). 8 U.S.C. §1189(a)(1) (2006).

The Secretary may designate a foreign organization as an FTO if she finds that it engages in "terrorism," defined as "premeditated, politically motivated violence perpetrated against noncombatant targets by subnational groups or clandestine agents," 22 U.S.C.§2656f(d)(2) (2006), or "terrorist activity," defined as

> any activity which is unlawful under the laws of the place where it is committed (or which, if it had been committed in the United States, would be unlawful under the laws of the United States or any State) and which involves any of the following:
>
>   (I) The highjacking or sabotage of any conveyance (including an aircraft, vessel, or vehicle).
>
>   (II) The seizing or detaining, and threatening to kill, injure, or continue to detain, another individual in order to compel a third person (including a governmental organization) to do or abstain from doing any act as an explicit or implicit condition for the release of the individual seized or detained.
>
>   (III) A violent attack upon an internationally protected person (as defined in section 1116(b)(4) of Title 18) or upon the liberty of such a person.
>
>   (IV) An assassination.
>
>   (V) The use of any—
>   (a) biological agent, chemical agent, or nuclear weapon or device, or

(b) explosive, firearm, or other weapon or dangerous device (other than for mere personal monetary gain),

with intent to endanger, directly or indirectly, the safety of one or more individuals or to cause substantial damage to property.

(VI) A threat, attempt, or conspiracy to do any of the foregoing.

[8 U.S.C. §1182(a)(3)(B)(iii) (2006).]

The courts have held that an organization with a U.S. presence is entitled to notice and an opportunity to be heard before it is designated as an FTO, but they have been deferential to the Secretary in making the determination and have rejected claims that she must reveal classified information that forms part of the basis for the designation. *See, e.g., People's Mojahedin Org. of Iran v. Department of State*, 327 F.3d 1238 (D.C. Cir. 2003). *See generally* Sahar Aziz, *The Laws on Providing Material Support to Terrorist Organizations: Erosion of Constitutional Rights or a Legitimate Tool for Preventing Terrorism?*, 9 Tex. J. C.L. & C.R. 45 (2003). The Secretary had designated 48 FTOs as of May 2011, including Hamas (Islamic Resistance Movement), Hizballah (Party of God), Kongra-Gel (KGK, formerly Kurdistan Workers' Party, PKK, KADEK), Liberation Tigers of Tamil Eelam (LTTE), Al Qaeda (AQ), Real IRA (RIRA), and the Revolutionary Armed Forces of Colombia (FARC). Office of the Coordinator for Counterterrorism, U.S. Dep't of State, *Foreign Terrorist Organizations* (May 19, 2011), *available at* http://www.state.gov/s/ct/rls/other/des/123085.htm.

The material support statutes are excerpted below, followed by a Supreme Court decision rejecting a constitutional challenge to 18 U.S.C. §2339B, criminalizing material support for an FTO.

---

18 U.S.C. §2339A. Providing material support to terrorists

(a) Offense. — Whoever provides material support or resources or conceals or disguises the nature, location, source, or ownership of material support or resources, knowing or intending that they are to be used in preparation for, or in carrying out, a violation of [various specific terrorist crimes] or in preparation for, or in carrying out, the concealment of an escape from the commission of any such violation, or attempts or conspires to do such an act, shall be fined under this title, imprisoned not more than 15 years, or both, and, if the death of any person results, shall be imprisoned for any term of years or for life. A violation of this section may be prosecuted in any Federal judicial district in which the underlying offense was committed, or in any other Federal judicial district as provided by law.

(b) Definitions. — As used in this section —

(1) the term "material support or resources" means any property, tangible or intangible, or service, including currency or monetary instruments or financial securities, financial services, lodging, training, expert advice or assistance, safehouses, false documentation or identification, communications equipment, facilities, weapons, lethal substances, explosives, personnel (1 or more individuals who may be or include oneself), and transportation, except medicine or religious materials.

(2) the term "training" means instruction or teaching designed to impart a specific skill, as opposed to general knowledge; and

(3) the term "expert advice or assistance" means advice or assistance derived from scientific, technical or other specialized knowledge.

18 U.S.C. §2339B. Providing material support or resources to designated foreign terrorist organizations

(a)(1) Unlawful conduct. — Whoever knowingly provides material support or resources to a foreign terrorist organization, or attempts or conspires to do so, shall be fined under this title or imprisoned not more than 15 years, or both, and, if the death of any person results, shall be imprisoned for any term of years or for life. To violate this paragraph, a person must have knowledge that the organization is a designated terrorist organization . . . , that the organization has engaged or engages in terrorist activity . . . , or that the organization has engaged or engages in terrorism. . . .

(g) Definitions. — As used in this section — . . .

(4) the term "material support or resources" has the same meaning given that term in section 2339A. . . .

(h) Provision of personnel. — No person may be prosecuted under this section in connection with the term "personnel" unless that person has knowingly provided, attempted to provide, or conspired to provide a foreign terrorist organization with 1 or more individuals (who may be or include himself) to work under that terrorist organization's direction or control or to organize, manage, supervise, or otherwise direct the operation of that organization. Individuals who act entirely independently of the foreign terrorist organization to advance its goals or objectives shall not be considered to be working under the foreign terrorist organization's direction and control.

(i) Rule of construction. — Nothing in this section shall be construed or applied so as to abridge the exercise of rights guaranteed under the First Amendment to the Constitution of the United States. . . .

18 U.S.C. §2339C. Prohibitions against the financing of terrorism

(a) Offenses. —

(1) In general. — Whoever, in a circumstance described in subsection (b) [prescribing jurisdictional attributes of crime], by any means, directly or indirectly, unlawfully and willfully provides or collects funds with the intention that such funds be used, or with the knowledge that such funds are to be used, in full or in part, in order to carry out — . . .

(B) any . . . act intended to cause death or serious bodily injury to a civilian, or to any other person not taking an active part in the hostilities in a situation of armed conflict, when the purpose of such act, by its nature or context, is to intimidate a population, or to compel a government or an international organization to do or to abstain from doing any act, shall be punished as prescribed in subsection (d)(1). . . .

Holder v. Humanitarian Law Project

United States Supreme Court, 2010
130 S. Ct. 2705

Chief Justice ROBERTS delivered the opinion of the Court. . . . [The plaintiffs are two U.S. citizens, the Humanitarian Law Project (HLP) (a human rights organization with consultative status to the United Nations), Ralph Fertig (the HLP's president), and others who want to provide support to the Kurdistan Workers' Party (PKK) (founded to establish an independent Kurdish state in southeastern Turkey), and the Liberation Tigers of Tamil Eelam (LTTE) (founded to create an independent Tamil state in Sri Lanka). The PKK and LTTE were each designated a foreign terrorist organization by the United States based on evidence that they committed numerous terrorist attacks, some of which harmed U.S. citizens. Plaintiffs claimed, however, that they want to support only the lawful humanitarian and political activities of the PKK and LTTE with monetary contributions, other tangible aid, legal training, and political advocacy.]

II

. . . Plaintiffs challenge §2339B's prohibition on four types of material support — "training," "expert advice or assistance," "service," and "personnel." They raise three constitutional claims. First, plaintiffs claim that §2339B violates the Due Process Clause of the Fifth Amendment because these four statutory terms are impermissibly vague. Second, plaintiffs claim that §2339B violates their freedom of speech under the First Amendment. Third, plaintiffs claim that §2339B violates their First Amendment freedom of association.

Plaintiffs do not challenge the above statutory terms in all their applications. Rather, plaintiffs claim that §2339B is invalid to the extent it prohibits them from engaging in certain specified activities. With respect to the HLP and Judge Fertig, those activities are: (1) "train[ing] members of [the] PKK on how to use humanitarian and international law to peacefully resolve disputes"; (2) "engag[ing] in political advocacy on behalf of Kurds who live in Turkey"; and (3) "teach[ing] PKK members how to petition various representative bodies such as the United Nations for relief." With respect to the other plaintiffs, those activities are: (1) "train[ing] members of [the] LTTE to present claims for tsunami-related aid to mediators and international bodies"; (2) "offer[ing] their legal expertise in negotiating peace agreements between the LTTE and the Sri Lankan government"; and (3) "engag[ing] in political advocacy on behalf of Tamils who live in Sri Lanka." . . .

III

Plaintiffs claim, as a threshold matter, that we should affirm the Court of Appeals without reaching any issues of constitutional law. They contend that we should interpret the material-support statute, when applied to speech, to require proof that a defendant intended to further a foreign terrorist organization's illegal activities. That interpretation, they say, would end the litigation because plaintiffs' proposed activities consist of speech, but plaintiffs do not intend to further unlawful conduct by the PKK or the LTTE.

We reject plaintiffs' interpretation of §2339B because it is inconsistent with the text of the statute. Section 2339B(a)(1) prohibits "knowingly" providing material support. It then specifically describes the type of knowledge that is required: "To violate this paragraph, a person must have knowledge that the organization is a designated terrorist organization . . . , that the organization has engaged or engages in terrorist activity . . . , or that the organization has engaged or engages in terrorism. . . ." *Ibid.* Congress plainly spoke to the necessary mental state for a violation of §2339B, and it chose knowledge about the organization's connection to terrorism, not specific intent to further the organization's terrorist activities.

Plaintiffs' interpretation is also untenable in light of the sections immediately surrounding §2339B, both of which do refer to intent to further terrorist activity. See §2339A(a) (establishing criminal penalties for one who "provides material support or resources . . . knowing or intending that they are to be used in preparation for, or in carrying out, a violation of" statutes prohibiting violent terrorist acts); §2339C(a)(1) (setting criminal penalties for one who "unlawfully and willfully provides or collects funds with the intention that such funds be used, or with the knowledge that such funds are to be used, in full or in part, in order to carry out" other unlawful acts). Congress enacted §2339A in 1994 and §2339C in 2002. See §120005(a), 108 Stat. 2022 (§2339A); §202(a), 116 Stat. 724 (§2339C). Yet Congress did not import the intent language of those provisions into §2339B, either when it enacted §2339B in 1996, or when it clarified §2339B's knowledge requirement in 2004.

Finally, plaintiffs give the game away when they argue that a specific intent requirement should apply only when the material-support statute applies to speech. There is no basis whatever in the text of §2339B to read the same provisions in that statute as requiring intent in some circumstances but not others. It is therefore clear that plaintiffs are asking us not to interpret §2339B, but to revise it. "Although this Court will often strain to construe legislation so as to save it against constitutional attack, it must not and will not carry this to the point of perverting the purpose of a statute." *Scales v. United States*, 367 U.S. 203, 211 (1961).

Scales is the case on which plaintiffs most heavily rely, but it is readily distinguishable. That case involved the Smith Act, which prohibited membership in a group advocating the violent overthrow of the government. The Court held that a person could not be convicted under the statute unless he had knowledge of the group's illegal advocacy and a specific intent to bring about violent overthrow. *Id.,* at 220-222, 229. This action is different: Section 2339B does not criminalize mere membership in a designated foreign terrorist organization. It instead prohibits providing "material support" to such a group. Nothing about *Scales* suggests the need for a specific intent requirement in such a case. The Court in *Scales,* moreover, relied on both statutory text and precedent that had interpreted closely related provisions of the Smith Act to require specific intent. Plaintiffs point to nothing similar here.

We cannot avoid the constitutional issues in this litigation through plaintiffs' proposed interpretation of §2339B.

IV

We turn to the question whether the material-support statute, as applied to plaintiffs, is impermissibly vague under the Due Process Clause of the Fifth Amendment. "A conviction fails to comport with due process if the statute under which it is obtained fails to provide a person of ordinary intelligence fair notice of what is prohibited, or is so standardless that it authorizes or encourages seriously discriminatory enforcement." *United States v. Williams*, 553 U.S. 285, 304 (2008). We consider whether a statute is vague as applied to the particular facts at issue, for "[a] plaintiff who engages in some conduct that is clearly proscribed cannot complain of the vagueness of the law as applied to the conduct of others." *Hoffman Estates v. Flipside,*

Hoffman Estates, Inc., 455 U.S. 489, 495 (1982). We have said that when a statute "interferes with the right of free speech or of association, a more stringent vagueness test should apply." *Id.*, at 499. "But 'perfect clarity and precise guidance have never been required even of regulations that restrict expressive activity.'" *Williams, supra,* at 304 (quoting *Ward v. Rock Against Racism*, 491 U.S. 781, 794 (1989))....

... [Cases establish the] rule that "[a] plaintiff who engages in some conduct that is clearly proscribed cannot complain of the vagueness of the law as applied to the conduct of others." *Hoffman Estates, supra,* at 495. That rule makes no exception for conduct in the form of speech. Thus, even to the extent a heightened vagueness standard applies, a plaintiff whose speech is clearly proscribed cannot raise a successful vagueness claim under the Due Process Clause of the Fifth Amendment for lack of notice. And he certainly cannot do so based on the speech of others. Such a plaintiff may have a valid overbreadth claim under the First Amendment, but our precedents make clear that a Fifth Amendment vagueness challenge does not turn on whether a law applies to a substantial amount of protected expression. Otherwise the doctrines would be substantially redundant.

Under a proper analysis, plaintiffs' claims of vagueness lack merit. Plaintiffs do not argue that the material-support statute grants too much enforcement discretion to the Government. We therefore address only whether the statute "provide[s] a person of ordinary intelligence fair notice of what is prohibited." *Williams*, 553 U.S., at 304.

As a general matter, the statutory terms at issue here are quite different from the sorts of terms that we have previously declared to be vague. We have in the past "struck down statutes that tied criminal culpability to whether the defendant's conduct was 'annoying' or 'indecent'—wholly subjective judgments without statutory definitions, narrowing context, or settled legal meanings." *Id.*, at 306; see also *Papachristou v. Jacksonville*, 405 U.S. 156, n.1 (1972) (holding vague an ordinance that punished "vagrants," defined to include "rogues and vagabonds," "persons who use juggling," and "common night walkers" (internal quotation marks omitted)). Applying the statutory terms in this action—"training," "expert advice or assistance," "service," and "personnel"—does not require similarly untethered, subjective judgments.

Congress also took care to add narrowing definitions to the material-support statute over time. These definitions increased the clarity of the statute's terms. See §2339A(b)(2) ("'training' means instruction or teaching designed to impart a specific skill, as opposed to general knowledge"); §2339A(b)(3) ("'expert advice or assistance' means advice or assistance derived from scientific, technical or other specialized knowledge"); §2339B(h) (clarifying the scope of "personnel"). And the knowledge requirement of the statute further reduces any potential for vagueness, as we have held with respect to other statutes containing a similar requirement.

Of course, the scope of the material-support statute may not be clear in every application. But the dispositive point here is that the statutory terms are clear in their application to plaintiffs' proposed conduct, which means that plaintiffs' vagueness challenge must fail. Even assuming that a heightened standard applies because the material-support statute potentially implicates speech, the statutory terms are not vague as applied to plaintiffs.

Most of the activities in which plaintiffs seek to engage readily fall within the scope of the terms "training" and "expert advice or assistance." Plaintiffs want to "train members of [the] PKK on how to use humanitarian and international law to peacefully resolve disputes," and "teach PKK members how to petition various representative bodies such as the United Nations for relief." 552 F.3d at 921 n.1. A person of ordinary intelligence would understand that instruction on resolving disputes through international law falls within the statute's definition of "training" because it imparts a "specific skill," not "general knowledge." §2339A(b)(2). Plaintiffs' activities also fall comfortably within the scope of "expert advice or assistance": A reasonable person would recognize that teaching the PKK how to petition for humanitarian relief before the United Nations involves advice derived from, as the statute puts it, "specialized knowledge." §2339A(b)(3). In fact, plaintiffs themselves have repeatedly used the terms "training" and "expert advice" throughout this litigation to describe their own proposed activities, demonstrating that these common terms readily and naturally cover plaintiffs' conduct.

Plaintiffs respond by pointing to hypothetical situations designed to test the limits of "training" and "expert advice or assistance." They argue that the statutory definitions of these terms use words of degree — like "specific," "general," and "specialized" — and that it is difficult to apply those definitions in particular cases. . . .

Whatever force these arguments might have in the abstract, they are beside the point here. Plaintiffs do not propose to teach a course on geography, and cannot seek refuge in imaginary cases that straddle the boundary between "specific skills" and "general knowledge." We emphasized this point in *Scales*, holding that even if there might be theoretical doubts regarding the distinction between "active" and "nominal" membership in an organization — also terms of degree — the defendant's vagueness challenge failed because his "case present[ed] no such problem." 367 U.S. at 223. . . .

Plaintiffs also contend that they want to engage in "political advocacy" on behalf of Kurds living in Turkey and Tamils living in Sri Lanka. They are concerned that such advocacy might be regarded as "material support" in the form of providing "personnel" or "service[s]," and assert that the statute is unconstitutionally vague because they cannot tell.

As for "personnel," Congress enacted a limiting definition in IRTPA that answers plaintiffs' vagueness concerns. Providing material support that constitutes "personnel" is defined as knowingly providing a person "to work under that terrorist organization's direction or control or to organize, manage, supervise, or otherwise direct the operation of that organization." §2339B(h). The statute makes clear that "personnel" does not cover *independent* advocacy: "Individuals who act entirely independently of the foreign terrorist organization to advance its goals or objectives shall not be considered to be working under the foreign terrorist organization's direction and control." *Ibid.*

"[S]ervice" similarly refers to concerted activity, not independent advocacy. See Webster's Third New International Dictionary 2075 (1993) (defining "service" to mean "the performance of work commanded or paid for by another: a servant's duty: attendance on a superior"; or "an act done for the benefit or at the command of another"). Context confirms that ordinary meaning here. The statute prohibits providing a service "*to* a foreign terrorist organization." §2339B(a)(1) (emphasis added). The use of the word "to" indicates a connection between the service and the foreign group. We think a person of ordinary intelligence would understand that independently advocating for a cause is different from providing a service to a group that is advocating for that cause. . . .

V

A

We next consider whether the material-support statute, as applied to plaintiffs, violates the freedom of speech guaranteed by the First Amendment. Both plaintiffs and the Government take extreme positions on this question. Plaintiffs claim that Congress has banned their "pure political speech." It has not. Under the material-support statute, plaintiffs may say anything they wish on any topic. They may speak and write freely about the PKK and LTTE, the governments of Turkey and Sri Lanka, human rights, and international law. They may advocate before the United Nations. As the Government states: "The statute does not prohibit independent advocacy or expression of any kind." Brief for Government 13. Section 2339B also "does not prevent [plaintiffs] from becoming members of the PKK and LTTE or impose any sanction on them for doing so." *Id.*, at 60. Congress has not, therefore, sought to suppress ideas or opinions in the form of "pure political speech." Rather, Congress has prohibited "material support," which most often does not take the form of speech at all. And when it does, the statute is carefully drawn to cover only a narrow category of speech to, under the direction of, or in coordination with foreign groups that the speaker knows to be terrorist organizations. . . .

[But] [t]he Government is wrong that the only thing actually at issue in this litigation is conduct. . . .[Section] 2339B regulates speech on the basis of its content. Plaintiffs want to speak to the PKK and the LTTE, and whether they may do so under §2339B depends on what they say. If plaintiffs' speech to those groups imparts a "specific skill" or communicates advice derived from "specialized knowledge" — for example, training on the use of international law or advice on petitioning the United Nations — then it is barred. On the other hand, plaintiffs' speech is not barred if it imparts only general or unspecialized knowledge. . . .

B

The First Amendment issue before us is more refined than either plaintiffs or the Government would have it. It is not whether the Government may prohibit pure political speech, or may prohibit material support in the form of conduct. It is instead whether the Government may prohibit what plaintiffs want to do — provide material support to the PKK and LTTE in the form of speech.

Everyone agrees that the Government's interest in combating terrorism is an urgent objective of the highest order. Plaintiffs' complaint is that the ban on material support, applied to what they wish to do, is not "necessary to further that interest." The objective of combating terrorism does not justify prohibiting their speech, plaintiffs argue, because their support will advance only the legitimate activities of the designated terrorist organizations, not their terrorism.

Whether foreign terrorist organizations meaningfully segregate support of their legitimate activities from support of terrorism is an empirical question. When it enacted §2339B in 1996, Congress made specific findings regarding the serious threat posed by international terrorism. See AEDPA §§301(a)(1)-(7), 110 Stat. 1247, note following 18 U.S.C. §2339B (Findings and Purpose). One of those findings explicitly rejects plaintiffs' contention that their support would not further the terrorist activities of the PKK and LTTE: "[F]oreign organizations that engage in terrorist activity are so tainted by their criminal conduct that *any contribution to such an organization* facilitates that conduct." §301(a)(7) (emphasis added).

Plaintiffs argue that the reference to "any contribution" in this finding meant only monetary support. There is no reason to read the finding to be so limited, particularly because Congress expressly prohibited so much more than monetary support in §2339B. Congress's use of the term "contribution" is best read to reflect a determination that any form of material support furnished "to" a foreign terrorist organization should be barred, which is precisely what the material-support statute does. Indeed, when Congress enacted §2339B, Congress simultaneously removed an exception that had existed in §2339A(a) (1994 ed.) for the provision of material support in the form of "humanitarian assistance to persons not directly involved in" terrorist activity. AEDPA §323, 110 Stat. 1255. That repeal demonstrates that Congress considered and rejected the view that ostensibly peaceful aid would have no harmful effects.

We are convinced that Congress was justified in rejecting that view. The PKK and the LTTE are deadly groups. "The PKK's insurgency has claimed more than 22,000 lives." Declaration of Kenneth R. McKune, App. 128, ¶5. The LTTE has engaged in extensive suicide bombings and political assassinations, including killings of the Sri Lankan President, Security Minister, and Deputy Defense Minister. *Id.*, at 130-132; Brief for Government 6-7. "On January 31, 1996, the LTTE exploded a truck bomb filled with an estimated 1,000 pounds of explosives at the Central Bank in Colombo, killing 100 people and injuring more than 1,400. This bombing was the most deadly terrorist incident in the world in 1996." McKune Affidavit, App. 131, ¶6.h. It is not difficult to conclude as Congress did that the "tain[t]" of such violent activities is so great that working in coordination with or at the command of the PKK and LTTE serves to legitimize and further their terrorist means. AEDPA §301(a)(7), 110 Stat. 1247.

Material support meant to "promot[e] peaceable, lawful conduct," Brief for Plaintiffs 51, can further terrorism by foreign groups in multiple ways. "Material support" is a valuable resource by definition. Such support frees up other resources within the organization that may be put to violent ends. It also importantly helps lend legitimacy to foreign terrorist groups—legitimacy that makes it easier for those groups to persist, to recruit members, and to raise funds—all of which facilitate more terrorist attacks. "Terrorist organizations do not maintain *organizational* "firewalls' that would prevent or deter...sharing and commingling of support and benefits." McKune Affidavit, App. 135, ¶11. "[I]nvestigators have revealed how terrorist groups systematically conceal their activities behind charitable, social, and political fronts." M. Levitt, Hamas: Politics, Charity, and Terrorism in the Service of Jihad 2-3 (2006). "Indeed, some designated foreign terrorist organizations use social and political components to recruit personnel to carry out terrorist operations, and to provide support to criminal terrorists and their families in aid of such operations." McKune Affidavit, App. 135, ¶11; Levitt, *supra*, at 2 ("Muddying the waters between its political activism, good works, and terrorist attacks, Hamas is able to use its overt political and charitable organizations as a financial and logistical support network for its terrorist operations").

Money is fungible, and "[w]hen foreign terrorist organizations that have a dual structure raise funds, they highlight the civilian and humanitarian ends to which such moneys could be put." McKune Affidavit, App. 134, ¶9. But "there is reason to believe that foreign terrorist organizations do not maintain legitimate *financial* firewalls between those funds raised for civil, nonviolent activities, and those ultimately used to support violent, terrorist operations." *Id.,* at 135, ¶12. Thus, "[f]unds raised ostensibly for charitable purposes have in the past been redirected by some terrorist groups to fund the purchase of arms and explosives." *Id.,* at 134, ¶10. See also Brief for Anti-Defamation League as *Amicus Curiae* 19-29 (describing fundraising activities by the PKK, LTTE, and Hamas); *Regan v. Wald*, 468 U.S. 222, 243 (1984) (upholding President's decision to impose travel ban to Cuba "to curtail the flow of hard currency to Cuba — currency that could then be used in support of Cuban adventurism"). There is evidence that the PKK and the LTTE, in particular, have not "respected the line between humanitarian and violent activities." McKune Affidavit, App. 135, ¶13 (discussing PKK); see *id.,* at 134 (LTTE).

The dissent argues that there is "no natural stopping place" for the proposition that aiding a foreign terrorist organization's lawful activity promotes the terrorist organization as a whole. But Congress has settled on just such a natural stopping place: The statute reaches only material support coordinated with or under the direction of a designated foreign terrorist organization. . . .

C

In analyzing whether it is possible in practice to distinguish material support for a foreign terrorist group's violent activities and its nonviolent activities, we do not rely exclusively on our own inferences drawn from the record evidence. We have before us an affidavit stating the Executive Branch's conclusion on that question. The State Department informs us that "[t]he experience and analysis of the U.S. government agencies charged with combating terrorism strongly suppor[t]" Congress's finding that all contributions to foreign terrorist organizations further their terrorism. McKune Affidavit, App. 133, ¶8. See *Winter v. Natural Resources Defense Council, Inc.,* 129 S. Ct. 365, 376-377 (2008) (looking to similar affidavits to support according weight to national security claims). In the Executive's view: "Given the purposes, organizational structure, and clandestine nature of foreign terrorist organizations, it is highly likely that any material support to these organizations will ultimately inure to the benefit of their criminal, terrorist functions — regardless of whether such support was ostensibly intended to support non-violent, non-terrorist activities." McKune Affidavit, App. 133, ¶8.

That evaluation of the facts by the Executive, like Congress's assessment, is entitled to deference. This litigation implicates sensitive and weighty interests of national security and foreign affairs. The PKK and the LTTE have committed terrorist acts against American citizens abroad, and the material-support statute addresses acute foreign policy concerns involving relationships with our Nation's allies. See *id.,* at 128-133, 137. We have noted that "neither the Members of this Court nor most federal judges begin the day with briefings that may describe new and serious threats to our Nation and its people." *Boumediene v. Bush*, 553 U.S. 723, 797 (2008). It is vital in this context "not to substitute . . . our own evaluation of evidence for a reasonable evaluation by the Legislative Branch." *Rostker v. Goldberg*, 453 U.S. 57, 68 (1981).

Our precedents, old and new, make clear that concerns of national security and foreign relations do not warrant abdication of the judicial role. We do not defer to the

Government's reading of the First Amendment, even when such interests are at stake. We are one with the dissent that the Government's "authority and expertise in these matters do not automatically trump the Court's own obligation to secure the protection that the Constitution grants to individuals." But when it comes to collecting evidence and drawing factual inferences in this area, "the lack of competence on the part of the courts is marked," *Rostker, supra*, at 65, and respect for the Government's conclusions is appropriate.

One reason for that respect is that national security and foreign policy concerns arise in connection with efforts to confront evolving threats in an area where information can be difficult to obtain and the impact of certain conduct difficult to assess. The dissent slights these real constraints in demanding hard proof—with "detail," "specific facts," and "specific evidence"—that plaintiffs' proposed activities will support terrorist attacks. That would be a dangerous requirement. In this context, conclusions must often be based on informed judgment rather than concrete evidence, and that reality affects what we may reasonably insist on from the Government. The material-support statute is, on its face, a preventive measure—it criminalizes not terrorist attacks themselves, but aid that makes the attacks more likely to occur. The Government, when seeking to prevent imminent harms in the context of international affairs and national security, is not required to conclusively link all the pieces in the puzzle before we grant weight to its empirical conclusions. See *Zemel v. Rusk*, 381 U.S., at 17 ("[B]ecause of the changeable and explosive nature of contemporary international relations, . . . Congress . . . must of necessity paint with a brush broader than that it customarily wields in domestic areas"). . . .

We also find it significant that Congress has been conscious of its own responsibility to consider how its actions may implicate constitutional concerns. First, §2339B only applies to designated foreign terrorist organizations. There is, and always has been, a limited number of those organizations designated by the Executive Branch, see, *e.g.*, 74 Fed. Reg. 29742 (2009); 62 Fed. Reg. 52650 (1997), and any groups so designated may seek judicial review of the designation. Second, in response to the lower courts' holdings in this litigation, Congress added clarity to the statute by providing narrowing definitions of the terms "training," "personnel," and "expert advice or assistance," as well as an explanation of the knowledge required to violate §2339B. Third, in effectuating its stated intent not to abridge First Amendment rights, see §2339B(i), Congress has also displayed a careful balancing of interests in creating limited exceptions to the ban on material support. The definition of material support, for example, excludes medicine and religious materials. See §2339A(b)(1). In this area perhaps more than any other, the Legislature's superior capacity for weighing competing interests means that "we must be particularly careful not to substitute our judgment of what is desirable for that of Congress." *Rostker, supra*, at 68. Finally, and most importantly, Congress has avoided any restriction on independent advocacy, or indeed any activities not directed to, coordinated with, or controlled by foreign terrorist groups.

At bottom, plaintiffs simply disagree with the considered judgment of Congress and the Executive that providing material support to a designated foreign terrorist organization—even seemingly benign support—bolsters the terrorist activities of that organization. That judgment, however, is entitled to significant weight, and we have persuasive evidence before us to sustain it. Given the sensitive interests in national security and foreign affairs at stake, the political branches have adequately substantiated their determination that, to serve the Government's interest in preventing terrorism, it was necessary to prohibit providing material support in the form of training, expert advice, personnel, and services to foreign terrorist groups, even if the supporters meant to promote only the groups' nonviolent ends.

We turn to the particular speech plaintiffs propose to undertake. First, plaintiffs propose to "train members of [the] PKK on how to use humanitarian and international law to peacefully resolve disputes." 552 F.3d at 92 n.1. Congress can, consistent with the First Amendment, prohibit this direct training. It is wholly foreseeable that the PKK could use the "specific skill[s]" that plaintiffs propose to impart, §2339A(b)(2), as part of a broader strategy to promote terrorism. The PKK could, for example, pursue peaceful negotiation as a means of buying time to recover from short-term setbacks, lulling opponents into complacency, and ultimately preparing for renewed attacks. See generally A. Marcus, Blood and Belief: The PKK and the Kurdish Fight for Independence 286-295 (2007) (describing the PKK's suspension of armed struggle and subsequent return to violence). A foreign terrorist organization introduced to the structures of the international legal system might use the information to threaten, manipulate, and disrupt. This possibility is real, not remote.

Second, plaintiffs propose to "teach PKK members how to petition various representative bodies such as the United Nations for relief." 552 F.3d at 921 n.1. The Government acts within First Amendment strictures in banning this proposed speech because it teaches the organization how to acquire "relief," which plaintiffs never define with any specificity, and which could readily include monetary aid. Indeed, earlier in this litigation, plaintiffs sought to teach the LTTE "to present claims for tsunami-related aid to mediators and international bodies," 552 F.3d at 921 n.1, which naturally included monetary relief. Money is fungible, and Congress logically concluded that money a terrorist group such as the PKK obtains using the techniques plaintiffs propose to teach could be redirected to funding the group's violent activities.

Finally, plaintiffs propose to "engage in political advocacy on behalf of Kurds who live in Turkey," and "engage in political advocacy on behalf of Tamils who live in Sri Lanka." 552 F.3d at 921 n.1. As explained above, plaintiffs do not specify their expected level of coordination with the PKK or LTTE or suggest what exactly their "advocacy" would consist of. Plaintiffs' proposals are phrased at such a high level of generality that they cannot prevail in this preenforcement challenge. See [*Washington State Grange v. Washington State Republican Party*, 552 U.S. 442, 454 (2008)]; *Zemel*, 381 U.S., at 20. . . .

All this is not to say that any future applications of the material-support statute to speech or advocacy will survive First Amendment scrutiny. It is also not to say that any other statute relating to speech and terrorism would satisfy the First Amendment. In particular, we in no way suggest that a regulation of independent speech would pass constitutional muster, even if the Government were to show that such speech benefits foreign terrorist organizations. We also do not suggest that Congress could extend the same prohibition on material support at issue here to domestic organizations. We simply hold that, in prohibiting the particular forms of support that plaintiffs seek to provide to foreign terrorist groups, §2339B does not violate the freedom of speech.

VI

Plaintiffs' final claim is that the material-support statute violates their freedom of association under the First Amendment. Plaintiffs argue that the statute criminalizes the mere fact of their associating with the PKK and the LTTE, thereby running afoul of [prior] decisions ... and cases in which we have overturned sanctions for joining the Communist Party.

The Court of Appeals correctly rejected this claim because the statute does not penalize mere association with a foreign terrorist organization. As the Ninth Circuit put it: "The statute does not prohibit being a member of one of the designated groups or vigorously promoting and supporting the political goals of the group.... What [§2339B] prohibits is the act of giving material support...." 205 F.3d at 1133. Plaintiffs want to do the latter. Our decisions scrutinizing penalties on simple association or assembly are therefore inapposite. *See, e.g., Robel, supra,* at 262 ("It is precisely because th[e] statute sweeps indiscriminately across all types of association with Communist-action groups, without regard to the quality and degree of membership, that it runs afoul of the First Amendment")....

* * *

The Preamble to the Constitution proclaims that the people of the United States ordained and established that charter of government in part to "provide for the common defence." As Madison explained, "[s]ecurity against foreign danger is ... an avowed and essential object of the American Union." The Federalist No. 41, p. 269 (J. Cooke ed. 1961). We hold that, in regulating the particular forms of support that plaintiffs seek to provide to foreign terrorist organizations, Congress has pursued that objective consistent with the limitations of the First and Fifth Amendments.

The judgment of the United States Court of Appeals for the Ninth Circuit is affirmed in part and reversed in part, and the cases are remanded for further proceedings consistent with this opinion.

It is so ordered.

Justice BREYER, with whom Justices GINSBURG and SOTOMAYOR join, dissenting. Like the Court, and substantially for the reasons it gives, I do not think this statute is unconstitutionally vague. But I cannot agree with the Court's conclusion that the Constitution permits the Government to prosecute the plaintiffs criminally for engaging in coordinated teaching and advocacy furthering the designated organizations' lawful political objectives. In my view, the Government has not met its burden of showing that an interpretation of the statute that would prohibit this speech- and association-related activity serves the Government's compelling interest in combating terrorism. And I would interpret the statute as normally placing activity of this kind outside its scope.

I. ...

"Coordination" with a group that engages in unlawful activity also does not deprive the plaintiffs of the First Amendment's protection under any traditional "categorical" exception to its protection. The plaintiffs do not propose to solicit a crime. They will not engage in fraud or defamation or circulate obscenity. Cf. *United States v. Stevens,* 130 S. Ct. 1577, 1585 (2010) (describing "categories" of unprotected speech). And the First Amendment protects advocacy even of *unlawful* action so long as that advocacy is not "directed to inciting or producing *imminent lawless action* and . . . *likely to incite or produce* such action." *Brandenburg v. Ohio*, 395 U.S. 444, 447 (1969) (*per curiam*) (emphasis added). Here the plaintiffs seek to advocate peaceful, *lawful* action to secure *political* ends; and they seek to teach others how to do the same. No one contends that the plaintiffs' speech to these organizations can be prohibited as incitement under *Brandenburg*.

Moreover, the Court has previously held that a person who associates with a group that uses unlawful means to achieve its ends does not thereby necessarily forfeit the First Amendment's protection for freedom of association. See *Scales v. United States*, 367 U.S. 203, 229 (1961) ("[Q]uasi-political parties or other groups that may embrace both legal and illegal aims differ from a technical conspiracy, which is defined by its criminal purpose"); see also [*NAACP v. Claiborne Hardware Co.*, 458 U.S. 886, 908 (1982)] ("The right to associate does not lose all constitutional protection merely because some members of the group may have participated in conduct or advocated doctrine that itself is not protected"). Rather, the Court has pointed out in respect to associating with a group advocating overthrow of the Government through force and violence: "If the persons assembling have committed crimes elsewhere . . . , they may be prosecuted for their . . . violation of valid laws. But it is a different matter when the State, instead of prosecuting them for such offenses, seizes upon mere participation in a peaceable assembly and a lawful public discussion as the basis for a criminal charge." [*De Jonge v. Oregon*, 299 U.S. 353, 365 (1937)] (striking down conviction for attending and assisting at Communist Party meeting because "[n]otwithstanding [the party's] objectives, the defendant still enjoyed his personal right of free speech and to take part in peaceable assembly having a lawful purpose"). . . .

Not even the "serious and deadly problem" of international terrorism can require *automatic* forfeiture of First Amendment rights. §301(a)(1), 110 Stat. 1247, note following 18 U.S.C. §2339B. Cf. §2339B(i) (instructing courts not to "constru[e] or appl[y the statute] so as to abridge the exercise of rights guaranteed under the First Amendment"). After all, this Court has recognized that not "'[e]ven the war power . . . remove[s] constitutional limitations safeguarding essential liberties.'" *United States v. Robel*, 389 U.S. 258, 264 (1967) (quoting *Home Building & Loan Assn. v. Blaisdell*, 290 U.S. 398, 426 (1934)). See also *Abrams v. United States*, 250 U.S. 616, 628 (1919) (Holmes, J., dissenting) ("[A]s against dangers peculiar to war, as against others, the principle of the right to free speech is always the same"). Thus, there is no general First Amendment exception that applies here. If the statute is constitutional in this context, it would have to come with a strong justification attached. . . .

The Government does identify a compelling countervailing interest, namely, the interest in protecting the security of the United States and its nationals from the threats that foreign terrorist organizations pose by denying those organizations financial and other fungible resources. I do not dispute the importance of this interest. But I do dispute whether the interest can justify the statute's criminal prohibition. To put the matter more specifically, precisely how does application of the statute to the protected activities before us *help achieve* that important security-related end?

The Government makes two efforts to answer this question. *First*, the Government says that the plaintiffs' support for these organizations is "fungible" in the same sense as other forms of banned support. Being fungible, the plaintiffs' support could, for example, free up other resources, which the organization might put to terrorist ends.

The proposition that the two very different kinds of "support" are "fungible," however, is not *obviously* true. There is no *obvious* way in which undertaking advocacy for political change through peaceful means or teaching the PKK and LTTE, say, how to petition the United Nations for political change is fungible with other resources that might be put to more sinister ends in the way that donations of money, food, or computer training are fungible. It is far from obvious that these advocacy activities can themselves be redirected, or will free other resources that can be directed, towards terrorist ends. Thus, we must determine whether the Government has come forward with evidence to support its claim.

The Government has provided us with no empirical information that might convincingly support this claim. . . .

Second, the Government says that the plaintiffs' proposed activities will "bolste[r] a terrorist organization's efficacy and strength in a community" and "undermin[e] this nation's efforts to *delegitimize and weaken* those groups." Government Brief 56 (emphasis added). In the Court's view, too, the Constitution permits application of the statute to activities of the kind at issue in part because those activities could provide a group that engages in terrorism with "legitimacy." The Court suggests that, armed with this greater "legitimacy," these organizations will more readily be able to obtain material support of the kinds Congress plainly intended to ban — money, arms, lodging, and the like. . . .

But this "legitimacy" justification cannot by itself warrant suppression of political speech, advocacy, and association. Speech, association, and related activities on behalf of a group will often, perhaps always, help to legitimate that group. Thus, were the law to accept a "legitimating" effect, in and of itself and without qualification, as providing sufficient grounds for imposing such a ban, the First Amendment battle would be lost in untold instances where it should be won. Once one accepts this argument, there is no natural stopping place. The argument applies as strongly to "independent" as to "coordinated" advocacy. That fact is reflected in part in the Government's claim that the ban here, so supported, prohibits a lawyer hired by a designated group from filing on behalf of that group an *amicus* brief before the United Nations or even before this Court. . . .

Regardless, the "legitimacy" justification itself is inconsistent with critically important First Amendment case law. Consider the cases involving the protection the First Amendment offered those who joined the Communist Party intending only to further its peaceful activities. In those cases, this Court took account of congressional findings that the Communist Party not only advocated theoretically but also sought to put into practice the overthrow of our Government through force and violence. The Court had previously accepted Congress' determinations that the American Communist Party was a "Communist action organization" which (1) acted under the "control, direction, and discipline" of the world Communist movement, a movement that sought to employ "espionage, sabotage, terrorism, and any other means deemed necessary, to establish a Communist totalitarian dictatorship," and (2) "endeavor[ed]" to bring about "the overthrow of existing governments by . . . force if necessary." *Communist Party of United States v. Subversive Activities Control Bd.*, 367 U.S. 1, 5-6 (1961) (internal quotation marks omitted).

Nonetheless, the Court held that the First Amendment protected an American's right to belong to that party — despite whatever "legitimating" effect membership might have had — as long as the person did not share the party's unlawful purposes. . . . The Government's "legitimating" theory would seem to apply to these cases with equal justifying force; and, if recognized, it would have led this Court to conclusions other than those it reached. . . .

II

For the reasons I have set forth, I believe application of the statute as the Government interprets it would gravely and without adequate justification injure interests of the kind the First Amendment protects. Thus, there is "a serious doubt" as to the statute's constitutionality. [*Crowell v. Benson*, 285 U.S. 22, 62 (1932)]. And where that is so, we must "ascertain whether a construction of the statute is fairly possible by which the question may be avoided." *Ibid.*

I believe that a construction that would avoid the constitutional problem is "fairly possible." In particular, I would read the statute as criminalizing First-Amendment-protected pure speech and association only when the defendant knows or intends that those activities will assist the organization's unlawful terrorist actions. Under this reading, the Government would have to show, at a minimum, that such defendants provided support that they knew was significantly likely to help the organization pursue its unlawful terrorist aims.

A person acts with the requisite knowledge if he is aware of (or willfully blinds himself to) a significant likelihood that his or her conduct will materially support the organization's terrorist ends. On the other hand, for the reasons I have set out, knowledge or intent that this assistance (aimed at lawful activities) could or would help further terrorism simply by helping to legitimate the organization is not sufficient. . . .

Thus, textually speaking, a statutory requirement that the defendant *knew* the support was material can be read to require the Government to show that the defendant knew that the consequences of his acts had a significant likelihood of furthering the organization's terrorist, not just its lawful, aims.

I need not decide whether this is the only possible reading of the statute in cases where "material support" takes the form of "currency," "property," "monetary instruments," "financial securities," "financial services," "lodging," "safehouses," "false documentation or identification," "weapons," "lethal substances," or "explosives," and the like. §2339A(b)(1). Those kinds of aid are inherently more likely to help an organization's terrorist activities, either directly or because they are fungible in nature. Thus, to show that an individual has provided support of those kinds will normally prove sufficient for conviction (assuming the statute's other requirements are met). But where support consists of pure speech or association, I would indulge in no such presumption. Rather, the Government would have to prove that the defendant knew he was providing support significantly likely to help the organization pursue its unlawful terrorist aims (or, alternatively, that the defendant intended the support to be so used). . . .

III

Having interpreted the statute to impose the *mens rea* requirement just described, I would remand the cases so that the lower courts could consider more specifically the precise activities in which the plaintiffs still wish to engage and determine whether and to what extent a grant of declaratory and injunctive relief were [*sic*] warranted. . . .

NOTES AND QUESTIONS

1. *The Anti-Terrorist Prosecutor's Weapon of Choice?* As we noted above, the apparent expansion of the suicide terrorist threat in the 1990s, and the difficulty of identifying

and arresting would-be suicide terrorists in time, has caused the government to begin searching more vigorously up the chain of causation not only for those who plan, but also for those who support, acts of terrorism. Abdel Rahman's prosecution was a way station in this shift in prosecutorial focus to "precursor crimes," because he was prosecuted for "overall supervision and direction of the membership," as the *Rahman* court put it, not for involvement in "individual operations." Yet the "seditious conspiracy" crime that the government there charged was anachronistic, notwithstanding the eventual success of the prosecution. *But see* Carlton F.W. Larson, *The Forgotten Constitutional Law of Treason and the Enemy Combatant Problem*, 154 U. Pa. L. Rev. 863 (2006) (urging prosecution of enemy combatants for treason and noting the historical applicability of the offense not just to citizens, but to anyone within the United States). Prosecutors needed a tool better suited to interdicting material support and, thereby, suicide terrorism.

When Congress responded by enacting the material support provision of AEDPA in 1996 and expanding material support liability in subsequent legislation, prosecutors used their new weapon enthusiastically. The material support charge is increasingly the government's weapon of choice against suspected terrorists. Data through September 2010 indicate that material support offenses ranked first in charges and convictions in the war on terrorism. Center on Law & Sec., *Terrorist Trial Report Card: September 11, 2001-September 11, 2010*, at 12-13 (2010), *available at* http://www.lawandsecurity.org/Portals/0/documents/01_TTRC2010Final1.pdf. *See generally* Norman Abrams, *The Material Support Terrorism Offenses: Perspectives Derived from the (Early) Model Penal Code*, 1 J. Nat'l Security L. & Pol'y 5 (2005); Robert M. Chesney, *The Sleeper Scenario: Terrorism-Support Laws and the Demands of Prevention*, 42 Harv. J. Legis. 3 (2005); Wayne McCormack, *Inchoate Terrorism: Liberalism Clashes with Fundamentalism*, 37 Geo. J. Int'l L. 1 (2005).

2. *Knowledge or Specific Intent?* The plaintiffs argued that §2339B required proof that a defendant intended to further an FTO's terrorist activities. What does the statute say? How do its scienter (state of mind) requirements compare to its companion material support statutes §§2339A and 2339C?

If the statute does not require specific intent, why is it not unconstitutional? In the Smith Act, Congress criminalized knowing membership in any organization that advocates the overthrow of the government by force or violence. 18 U.S.C. §2385 (2006). The Act came before the Supreme Court in *Scales v. United States*, 367 U.S. 203 (1961), in which the Court upheld a conviction for membership only on proof of *knowing* membership or affiliation *and specific intent* to further the group's unlawful goals. The Court explained its insistence on these elements of proof by rejecting the concept of guilt by association:

> In our jurisprudence guilt is personal, and when the imposition of punishment on a status or on conduct can only be justified by reference to the relationship of that status or conduct to other concededly criminal activity (here advocacy of violent overthrow), that relationship must be sufficiently substantial to satisfy the concept of personal guilt in order to withstand attack under the Due Process Clause of the Fifth Amendment. [*Id.* at 224-225.]

Specific intent implements the requirement of personal guilt by "tying the imposition of guilt to an individually culpable act." David Cole, *Hanging with the Wrong*

Crowd: Of Gangs, Terrorists, and the Right of Association, 1999 Sup. Ct. Rev. 203, 217. In First Amendment terms, the specific intent requirement "identifies the only narrowly tailored way to punish individuals for group wrongdoing (essentially by requiring evidence of individual wrongdoing), just as the *Brandenburg* test [*supra* p. 988] sets forth the narrowly tailored way to respond to advocacy of illegal conduct." Cole, *supra,* 1999 Sup. Ct. Rev. at 218. How does the Court distinguish *Scales*? Does §2339B make it a crime to be a member of an FTO?

3. *The Logic of Criminalizing Mere Knowing Support.* Some FTOs, such as Hamas, are dual-purpose organizations; they engage in terrorism, but they also provide social services. *Cf.* Michael Whidden, Note, *Unequal Justice: Arabs in America and United States Antiterrorism in Legislation,* 69 Fordham L. Rev. 2825, 2873 (2001) (asserting that FTOs Hamas and Hezbollah operate orphanages, hospitals, schools, and medical clinics for indigent Palestinians in addition to conducting terrorist activities). Some supporters want only to support the non-terrorist purposes of the FTO. Did Congress in §2339B make it a crime to write a check to Hamas to support its social services? If so, why? Why does the majority in *Holder* not reject Congress's reasoning? Why does the dissent? Did the majority defer too much to congressional "fact" finding? *See* Robert M. Chesney, *National Security Fact Deference,* 95 Va. L. Rev. 1361, 1362 (2009) ("'[N]ational security fact deference' is freighted with constitutional significance. On one hand, it may undermine the capacity of courts to guard against unlawful executive branch actions (in terms of both unjustified assertions of power and violations of individual rights). On the other hand, it may prevent the judicial power from encroaching inappropriately upon executive responsibilities relating to national security, while simultaneously helping to preserve the judiciary's institutional legitimacy. National security fact deference claims, in short, implicate competing values of great magnitude").

4. *Vagueness.* A law is unconstitutionally vague if a reasonable person cannot tell what expression is prohibited and what is permitted. "Material support," as used in §2339B, is defined in §2339A(b). Is the statute vague as applied to the provision of explosives or safehouses to a terrorist or FTO? What about the donation of money to an FTO? If these applications don't seem unconstitutionally vague, what about providing personnel, training, or expert advice? Why did the majority reject the vagueness challenge to the latter terms?

Did the Court rule that there are no applications of these terms that would be unconstitutionally vague? Consider the case of a lawyer for a convicted terrorist who meets periodically with her client in prison and secretly conveys messages between him and his associates (including members of an FTO) outside prison. Is the term "personnel" unconstitutionally vague as applied to prosecute that lawyer for providing *herself* as "personnel" to a terrorist or FTO? *See United States v. Sattar,* 272 F. Supp. 2d 348 (S.D.N.Y. 2003) (*Sattar I*) (yes; government's assertion in oral argument that "you know it when you see it" is an "insufficient guide by which a person can predict the legality of that person's conduct," whatever merit it may have as a way to identify obscenity). Is it too vague for prosecuting the lawyer for supplying *her client* as "personnel" to the FTO, by making him "available" through communications that she conveys? *See United States v. Sattar,* 314 F. Supp. 2d 279, 300 (S.D.N.Y. 2004), *cert. denied,* 130 S. Ct. 1924 (2010), (*Sattar II*) (no; "the 'provision' of 'personnel' — in this case, by making the imprisoned

Sheik Abdel Rahman available as a co-conspirator in a conspiracy to kill and kidnap persons in a foreign country—is conduct that plainly is prohibited by the statute" with sufficient definiteness). How about a U.S. citizen who joins the Taliban to fight alongside Al Qaeda fighters against U.S. armed forces in Afghanistan? *See United States v. Lindh*, 212 F. Supp. 2d 541, 574 (E.D. Va. 2002) (no; "personnel" is not unconstitutionally vague as applied to "employees" or "employee-like operatives" who were under the "direction and control" of an FTO). *See* James P. Fantetti, Comment, *John Walker Lindh, Terrorist? Or Merely a Citizen Exercising His Constitutional Freedom: The Limits of the Freedom of Association in the Aftermath of September Eleventh*, 71 U. Cinn. L. Rev. 1373 (2003).

Suppose a cab driver drives a person he knows to be a member of an FTO to the airport. Can he constitutionally be prosecuted for providing "transportation" to an FTO?

5. *Protected Expression.* Donating money is not membership, but it is also unlike donating weapons, safe houses, or transportation. "The right to join together 'for the advancement of beliefs and ideas' is diluted," the Supreme Court explained, "if it does not include the right to pool money through contributions, for funds are often essential if 'advocacy' is to be truly or optimally 'effective.'" *Buckley v. Valeo*, 424 U.S. 1, 65-66 (1974) (quoting *NAACP v. Alabama ex rel. Patterson*, 357 U.S. 449, 460 (1958)). Why is donating money to an FTO not protected political expression?

One answer is that it *is* protected expression, but that the protection is not absolute. What degree of scrutiny should a court then give to its regulation? *See* Cole, *supra*, 1999 Sup. Ct. Rev. at 237-238 (urging strict scrutiny—requiring a close relationship to a compelling government interest—when government's purpose is to regulate association as such). *See generally* Nina J. Crimm, *High Alert: The Government's War on the Financing of Terrorism and Implications for Donors, Domestic Charitable Organizations, and Global Philanthropy*, 45 Wm. & Mary L. Rev. 1341 (2004); David Cole, *The New McCarthyism: Repeating History in the War on Terrorism*, 38 Harv. C.R.-C.L. L. Rev. 1, 11 (2003).

In *Holder*, however, the plaintiffs were not making financial contributions to the FTOs; nor were they engaged simply in "pure political speech." Instead, they wanted to provide material support to FTOs "in the form of speech" — by providing training lectures and advice. How did prohibiting such support in the form of speech have a close relationship to the concededly compelling interest of preventing or making more difficult terrorist acts by FTOs? Does *Holder* "open[] the door for prohibiting any speech related to a terrorist organization, no matter how peaceful it is, as long as it is expressed in coordination with or under the direction of a terrorist organization"? Daphne Barak-Enez & David Scharia, *Freedom of Speech, Support for Terrorism, and the Challenge of Global Constitutional Law*, 2 Harv. Nat'l Security J. 1, 19 (2011).

The dissent in *Humanitarian Law Project v. Holder* had serious doubts that the prohibition bore the necessary relationship to the counterterrorism interest. How did it avoid the resulting constitutional issue? Does its solution interpret §2339B or rewrite it? Should Congress amend §2339B to require specific intent for support in the form of speech? *See* The Constitution Project, *Reforming the Material Support Laws: Constitutional Concerns Presented by Prohibitions on Material Support to "Terrorist Organizations"* (Nov. 17, 2009) (so arguing).

C. THE LONG ARM OF THE LAW: EXTRATERRITORIAL CRIMINAL JURISDICTION

Congress has enacted a variety of statutes aimed at international terrorism. *See, e.g.,* 18 U.S.C. §§31-32 (2006) (hijacking or sabotaging aircraft); *id.* §§175-178 (developing or possessing biological or toxin weapons); 18 U.S.C. §§2331-2332 (2006 & Supp. III 2009) (killing or injuring U.S. citizens abroad); *id.* §2332a (directing weapons of mass destruction against Americans abroad or against anyone within the United States); *id.* §2339A (providing material support to terrorists); and 49 U.S.C. §§46,501-46,507 (2006) (committing air piracy). Most of these are now expressly extraterritorial in application. But some older criminal statutes are not. The following case discusses the interpretative principles governing extraterritorial application of U.S. criminal laws.

United States v. Bin Laden

United States District Court, Southern District of New York, 2000
92 F. Supp. 2d 189

SAND, District Judge. The sixth superseding indictment in this case ("the Indictment") charges fifteen defendants with conspiracy to murder United States nationals, to use weapons of mass destruction against United States nationals, to destroy United States buildings and property, and to destroy United States defense utilities. The Indictment also charges defendants Mohamed Sadeek Odeh, Mohamed Rashed Daoud al-'Owhali, and Khalfan Khamis Mohamed, among others, with numerous crimes in connection with the August 1998 bombings of the United States Embassies in Nairobi, Kenya, and Dar es Salaam, Tanzania, including 223 counts of murder. . . .

I. EXTRATERRITORIAL APPLICATION

Odeh argues that Counts 5-8, 11-237, and 240-244 must be dismissed because (a) they concern acts allegedly performed by Odeh and his co-defendants outside United States territory, yet (b) are based on statutes that were not intended by Congress to regulate conduct outside United States territory. More specifically, Odeh argues that "the statutes that form the basis for the indictment fail clearly and unequivocally to regulate the conduct of foreign nationals for conduct outside the territorial boundaries of the United States." . . .

A. General Principles of Extraterritorial Application

It is well-established that Congress has the power to regulate conduct performed outside United States territory. It is equally well-established, however, that courts are to presume that Congress has not exercised this power — i.e., that statutes apply only to acts performed within United States territory — unless Congress manifests an intent to reach acts performed outside United States territory. This "clear manifestation" requirement does not require that extraterritorial coverage should be found only if the statute itself explicitly provides for extraterritorial application. Rather, courts should consider "all available evidence about the meaning" of the statute, e.g., its text, structure, and legislative history.

Furthermore, the Supreme Court has established a limited exception to this standard approach for "criminal statutes which are, as a class, not logically dependent on their locality for the Government's jurisdiction, but are enacted because of the right of the Government to defend itself against obstruction, or fraud wherever perpetrated, especially if committed by its own citizens, officers, or agents." *United States v. Bowman*, 260 U.S. 94, 98 (1922). As regards statutes of this type, courts may infer the requisite intent "from the nature of the offense" described in the statute, and thus need not examine its legislative history.[3] *Id.* The Court further observed that "to limit the [] locus [of such a statute] to the strictly territorial jurisdiction [of the United States] would be greatly to curtail the scope and usefulness of the statute and leave open a large immunity for frauds as easily committed by citizens on the high seas and in foreign countries as at home. . . ."

Odeh argues that *Bowman* is "not controlling precedent" because it "involved the application of [a] penal statute[] to United States citizens," i.e., not to foreign nationals such as himself. This argument is unavailing. . . .

. . . Under international law, the primary basis of jurisdiction is the "subjective territorial principle," under which "a state has jurisdiction to prescribe law with respect to . . . conduct that, wholly or in substantial part, takes place within its territory." *Restatement (Third) of the Foreign Relations Law of the United States* §402(1)(a) (1987). International law recognizes five other principles of jurisdiction by which a state may reach conduct *outside* its territory: (1) the objective territorial principle; (2) the protective principle; (3) the nationality principle; (4) the passive personality principle; and (5) the universality principle. The objective territoriality principle provides that a state has jurisdiction to prescribe law with respect to "conduct outside its territory that has or is intended to have substantial effect within its territory." *Restatement* §402(1)(c). The protective principle provides that a state has jurisdiction to prescribe law with respect to "certain conduct outside its territory by *persons not its nationals* that is directed against *the security of the state* or against a limited class of other state interests." *Id.* §402(3) (emphasis added). The nationality principle provides that a state has jurisdiction to prescribe law with respect to "the activities, interests, status, or relations of its nationals outside as well as within its territory." *Id.* §402(2). The passive personality principle provides that "a state may apply law — particularly criminal law — to an act committed outside its territory by a person not its national where the victim of the act was its national." *Id.* §402, cmt. g. The universality principle provides that, "[a] state has jurisdiction to define and prescribe punishment for certain offenses recognized by the community of nations as of universal concern, such as piracy, slave trade, attacks on or hijacking of aircraft, genocide, war crimes, and perhaps *certain acts of terrorism*," regardless of the locus of their occurrence. *Id.* §404 (emphasis added). Because Congress has the power to override international law if it so chooses, *Restatement* §402, cmt. I., none of these five principles places ultimate limits on Congress's power to reach extraterritorial conduct. At the same time, however, "[i]n determining whether a statute applies extraterritorially, [courts] presume that Congress does not intend to violate principles of international

---

3. This is not necessarily to say, however, that legislative history is entirely irrelevant under the *Bowman* exception to the standard approach. Given that the *Bowman* rule is ultimately concerned with congressional intent, if the legislative history clearly indicates that Congress intended the statute in question to apply only within the United States, it would be inconsistent with *Bowman* to ignore this evidence, and conclude — in reliance on *Bowman* — that Congress intended the statute to apply extraterritorially. . . .

law . . . [and] in the absence of an explicit Congressional directive, courts do not give extraterritorial effect to any statute that violates principles of international law." *United States v. Vasquez-Velasco*, 15 F.3d 833, 839 (9th Cir. 1994) (citing *McCulloch v. Sociedad Nacional de Marineros de Honduras*, 372 U.S. 10, 21-22 (1963)). Hence, courts that find that a given statute applies extraterritorially typically pause to note that this finding is consistent with one or more of the five principles of extraterritorial jurisdiction under international law.

The *Bowman* rule would appear to be most directly related to the protective principle, which, as noted, explicitly authorizes a state's exercise of jurisdiction over "conduct outside its territory *by persons not its nationals.*" *Restatement* §402(3). Hence, an application of the *Bowman* rule that results in the extraterritorial application of a statute to the conduct of foreign nationals is consistent with international law. . . .

B. 18 U.S.C. §§844, 924, 930, 1114, and 2155

In light of the preceding general principles, we find that Congress intended each of the following statutory provisions to reach conduct by foreign nationals on foreign soil. . . .

1. 18 U.S.C. §844(f), (h), and (n)

The Indictment predicates Count 5 on 18 U.S.C. §§844(f). . . . Subsection 844(f)(1) provides:

> Whoever maliciously damages or destroys, or attempts to damage or destroy, by means of fire or an explosive, any building, vehicle, or other personal or real property in whole or in part owned or possessed by, or leased to, the United States, or any department or agency thereof, shall be imprisoned for not less than 5 years and not more than 20 years, fined under this title, or both. [18 U.S.C. §844(f)(1).]
>
> Given (i) that this provision is explicitly intended to protect United States property, (ii) that a significant amount of United States property is located outside the United States, and (iii) that, accordingly, foreign nationals are in at least as good a position as are United States nationals to damage such property, we find, under *Bowman*, that Congress intended Section 844(f)(1) to apply extraterritorially — irrespective of the nationality of the perpetrator. . . .

III. CONSTITUTIONAL AUTHORITY

Odeh argues that the Counts based on 18 U.S.C. §§2332 and 2332a must be dismissed because these statutes are unconstitutional in that they exceed Congress's authority to legislate under the Constitution. As noted above, Subsection 2332(b) provides in relevant part that "[w]hoever outside the United States . . . engages in a conspiracy to kill[] a national of the United States shall [be punished as further provided]," 18 U.S.C. §2332(b); and Section 2332a(a) provides in relevant part that, "[a] person who . . . uses, threatens, or attempts or conspires to use, a weapon of mass destruction . . . (1) against a national of the United States while such national is outside of the United States; . . . or (3) against any property that is owned, leased or used by the United States . . . , whether the property is within or outside of the United States, shall [be punished as further provided]." 18 U.S.C. §2332a(a).

Odeh suggests that there is but one constitutional grant of authority to legislate that could support these two statutory provisions: Article I, Section 8, Clause 10. Clause 10 grants Congress the authority "[t]o define and punish Piracies and Felonies committed on the high Seas, and Offenses against the Law of Nations." U.S. Const. art. I, §8, cl. 10. Odeh argues that, as "[t]he acts described in these two statutes . . . are not widely regarded as offenses 'against the law of nations,'" these statutes exceed Congress's authority under Clause 10.

There are two problems with this argument. First, even assuming that the acts described in Sections 2332 and 2332a are not *widely* regarded as violations of international law, it does not necessarily follow that these provisions exceed Congress's authority under Clause 10. Clause 10 does not merely give Congress the authority to punish offenses against the law of nations; it also gives Congress the power to "define" such offenses. Hence, provided that the acts in question are recognized by at least some members of the international community as being offenses against the law of nations, Congress arguably has the power to criminalize these acts pursuant to its power *to define* offenses against the law of nations. *See United States v. Smith*, 18 U.S. (5 Wheat.) 153, 159 (1820) (Story, J.) ("Offenses . . . against the law of nations, cannot, with any accuracy, be said to be completely ascertained and defined in any public code recognized by the common consent of nations. . . . [T]herefore . . . , there is a peculiar fitness in giving the power to define as well as to punish.").

Second, and more important, it is not the case that Clause 10 provides the only basis for Sections 2332 and 2332a. The Supreme Court has recognized that, with regard to foreign affairs legislation, "investment of the federal Government with the powers of external sovereignty did not depend upon the affirmative grants of the Constitution." *United States v. Curtiss-Wright Export Corp.*, 299 U.S. 304, 318 (1936). Rather, Congress's authority to regulate foreign affairs "exist[s] as inherently inseparable from the conception of nationality." *Id.* (citations omitted). More specifically, this "concept of essential sovereignty of a free nation clearly requires the existence and recognition of an inherent power in the state to protect itself from destruction." *United States v. Rodriguez*, 182 F. Supp. 479, 491 (S.D. Cal. 1960), *aff'd in part sub nom. Rocha v. United States*, 288 F.2d 545 (9th Cir.), *cert. denied*, 366 U.S. 948 (1961).

In penalizing extraterritorial conspiracies to kill nationals of the United States, Section 2332(b) is clearly designed to protect a vital United States interest. And, indeed, Congress expressly identified this protective function as the chief purpose of Section 2332. Therefore, we conclude, under *Curtiss-Wright*, that Congress acted within its authority in enacting these provisions. . . .

V. APPLICATION OF 18 U.S.C. §930(c) TO FOREIGN VICTIMS

Odeh argues that interpreting Section 930(c)[1] to reach "the deaths of Kenyan and Tanzanian citizens [as opposed to United States citizens] would be contrary to established principles of international law." More specifically, Odeh advances the following two arguments. First, given (i) that "[u]nder 18 U.S.C. §930(c), the only arguable basis for jurisdiction over the deaths of foreign citizens is the principle of

---

[1. 18 U.S.C. §930(c) provides that "[a] person who kills or attempts to kill any person in the course of a violation of subsection (a) or (b) [involving knowing possession of firearms or other dangerous weapons in a federal facility], or in the course of an attack on a Federal facility involving the use of a firearm or other dangerous weapon, shall be punished [as further provided]." — Eds.]

universality," (ii) that "[u]niversal jurisdiction results where there is *universal* condemnation of an offense, and a general interest in cooperating to suppress them, as reflected in *widely accepted* international agreements," and (iii) that "the universality principle does not encompass terrorist actions resulting in the deaths of individuals who are not diplomatic personnel," it follows that applying Section 930(c) to the deaths of "ordinary" foreign nationals on foreign soil would constitute a violation of international law.

There are two problems with this argument. First, because "universal jurisdiction is increasingly accepted for certain acts of terrorism, such as . . . indiscriminate violent assaults on people at large," Restatement §404, cmt. a, a plausible case could be made that extraterritorial application of Section 930(c) in this case *is* supported by the universality principle.

Second, it is not the case that the universality principle is the "only arguable basis for jurisdiction over the deaths of foreign citizens." As indicated by our conclusion . . . that Section 930(c) is designed to *protect* vital United States interests, the protective principle is also an "arguable basis" for the extraterritorial application of Section 930(c). . . . In providing for the death penalty where death results in the course of an attack on a Federal facility, Section 930(c) is clearly designed to deter attacks on Federal facilities. Given the likelihood that foreign nationals will be in or near Federal facilities located in foreign nations, this deterrent effect would be significantly diminished if Section 930(c) were limited to the deaths of United States nationals. . . .

Odeh argues, second, that, even if the universality principle (or one of the four other principles) did authorize the application of Section 930(c) to the deaths of ordinary foreign nationals on foreign soil, such application would violate international law nevertheless, because (i) "[e]ven where one of the principles authorizes jurisdiction, a nation is nevertheless precluded from exercising jurisdiction where jurisdiction would be 'unreasonable,'" and (ii) application of Section 930(c) to the deaths of ordinary foreign nationals on foreign soil would be unreasonable. *Id.* (citations omitted).

According to the Restatement, the following factors are to be taken into account for the purpose of determining whether exercise of extraterritorial jurisdiction is reasonable:

> (a) the link of the activity to the territory of the regulating state, i.e., the extent to which the activity takes place within the territory, or has substantial, direct, and foreseeable effect upon or in the territory;
> (b) the connections, such as nationality, residence, or economic activity, between the regulating state and the person principally responsible for the activity to be regulated, or between that state and those whom the regulation is designed to protect;
> (c) the character of the activity to be regulated, the importance of regulation to the regulating state, the extent to which other states regulate such activities, and the degree to which the desirability of such regulation is generally accepted;
> (d) the existence of justified expectations that might be protected or hurt by the regulation;
> (e) the importance of the regulation to the international political, legal, or economic system;
> (f) the extent to which the regulation is consistent with the traditions of the international system;

(g) the extent to which another state may have an interest in regulating the activity; and
(h) the likelihood of conflict with regulation by another state.

Restatement §403(2). Given that factor (a) alludes to the subjective territorial principle and the objective territorial principle, it is not especially relevant to a statute, such as Section 930(c), based primarily on the protective principle. Much the same can be said of factor (b), as it alludes to the nationality principle, the subjective territorial principle, and the objective territorial principle. Factor (c), in contrast, is highly relevant to Section 930(c). It is important both to the United States and other nations to prevent the destruction of their facilities — regardless of their location; and such regulation is accordingly widely accepted among the nations of the world. As for factor (d), Section 930(c) protects the expectation of foreign nationals that they will be free of harm while on the premises of United States facilities. We can think of no "justified" expectation, however, that would be hurt by the extraterritorial application of Section 930(c). As for factor (e), in light of the prominent role played by the United States in "the international political, legal, and economic systems," the protection of United States facilities — regardless of their location — is highly important to the stability of these systems. Turning to factor (f), as indicated by the preceding discussion of factor (c), most, if not all, nations are concerned about protecting their facilities, both at home and abroad. Hence, Section 930(c) is highly consistent "with the traditions of the international system." As for (g), it must be acknowledged that when the United States facility is on foreign soil, and when the victims of the attack are nationals of the host nation, the host nation "has a keen interest in regulating and punishing [the] offenders." This is not to say, however, that the host nation has a greater interest than does the United States. Furthermore, even if it were the case that the host nation had a greater interest than the United States, this single factor would be insufficient to support the conclusion that application of Section 930(c) to the bombings of the two Embassies is unreasonable. Coming, finally, to factor (h), Odeh does not argue that application of Section 930(c) to the bombings would conflict with Kenyan and/or Tanzanian law, nor are we otherwise aware of such conflict. On the contrary, the Government informs the Court that "[t]he Kenyan Government voluntarily rendered Odeh (and [co-defendant] al-'Owhali) to the United States, and neither the Kenyan nor the Tanzanian Government has asserted any objection to the United States' exercise of jurisdiction in this case." Factor (h) thus counts in favor of the reasonableness of applying Section 930(c) to the bombings....

NOTES AND QUESTIONS

1. *Extraterritoriality and the Constitution.* No one questions a sovereign state's authority to prescribe laws for its own territory, and the Constitution quite clearly vests limited authority to do so in Congress. But can Congress constitutionally make laws that apply abroad? The Constitution is silent on this question, but Article III states that when a crime is "not committed within any State," trial for the crime shall be conducted where Congress directs. U.S. Const. art. III, §2, cl. 3. Thus, the Framers clearly contemplated criminal sanctions against acts committed outside any state of the union. Moreover, they vested Congress with the authority to define and punish "Offenses against the Law of Nations." *Id.* art. I, §8, cl. 10. See *supra*

pp. 182-184. Because such offenses may be committed abroad, this provision gives Congress extraterritorial lawmaking authority. On what basis does Odeh argue that 18 U.S.C. §§2332 and 2332a exceed Congress's lawmaking authority? Is the court's response consistent with a federal government of limited lawmaking authority?

Assuming that Congress can enact laws with extraterritorial effect, does the Constitution place any limit on extraterritoriality? Civil procedure students may suspect that some "minimum contact" by the defendant or her acts with the United States might be required as a matter of due process. Beyond that, however, customary international law principles of prescriptive jurisdiction might also establish limits as a part of our federal common law. See *supra* p. 185. Indeed, one commentator asserts that "[i]t is arguable that the Constitution permits Congress to make acts committed abroad crimes under United States law only to the extent permitted by international law." Andreas Lowenfeld, *U.S. Law Enforcement Abroad: The Constitution and International Law*, 83 Am. J. Int'l L. 880, 881 (1989). How does the *Bin Laden* court regard this assertion?

If international law does not limit extraterritorial lawmaking by Congress, what role, if any, does it play, according to the court? What rule of statutory construction is implicated by applicable international laws?

2. *Presumption Against Extraterritoriality.* Why should the courts presume that a statute applies locally only, unless Congress clearly manifests an intent to reach acts performed abroad? Sometimes such an intent is manifested by the plain language of the statute. The statute that makes it a crime to develop, produce, stockpile, transfer, acquire, retain, or possess any biological agent, toxin, or delivery system for use as a weapon, for example, expressly provides that "[t]here is extraterritorial Federal jurisdiction over an offense under this section committed by or against a national of the United States." 18 U.S.C. §175 (2006). Similarly, 18 U.S.C. §2332(b) (2006), expressly makes it a crime to engage in a conspiracy "outside the United States" to kill U.S. nationals. *Bowman* created an exception to the presumption against extraterritoriality. Why?

3. *The Territoriality and Nationality Principles of Extraterritorial Jurisdiction.* The court in *Bin Laden* catalogued principles of jurisdiction under customary international law, but such principles are not equally accepted by all nations, and they may not be helpful for other reasons. *See generally* Christopher L. Blakesley, *Extraterritorial Jurisdiction*, in 2 *International Criminal Law* 33 (M. Cherif Bassiouni ed., 2d ed. 1999). The territorial principle, for example, applies both to actors within a sovereign's territory ("subjective territoriality") and to effects in such territory resulting from acts abroad ("objective territoriality"), and it is reflected in *Restatement* §402(1). But while it is the most common and widely accepted principle of jurisdiction, it often will be unavailable for terrorist or other criminal acts performed abroad, including inchoate acts intended ultimately to cause injury in the United States. The nationality principle — allowing a sovereign to exercise jurisdiction over its nationals for their acts performed abroad — is also accepted by the practice of nations. Roman Boed, *United States Legislative Approach to Extraterritorial Jurisdiction in Connection with Terrorism*, in 2 *International Criminal Law*, *supra*, at 147. But international terrorists may not be U.S. nationals, just as most of the *Bin Laden* defendants were not.

4. *The Protective Principle of Extraterritorial Jurisdiction.* The protective principle is more likely to apply to acts of international terrorism, but it is limited to offenses

against the security of the state or acts that threaten the integrity of government functions. *Restatement* §402(3) & cmt. f. (1981). It thus is easily applied to the embassy bombings. Would it apply to terrorist acts committed against private U.S. nationals abroad? "The lack of definition of the range of conduct encompassed by the protective principle and the principle's malleability," Professor Boed worries, "could lead to the principle's justification of a wide-ranging exercise of extraterritorial jurisdiction." Boed, *supra*, at 148.

5. *The Passive Personality Principle of Extraterritorial Jurisdiction.* Even if the protective principle does not apply to terrorist acts against private U.S. nationals, such acts would clearly fall under the passive personality principle. But this principle has not traditionally found wide support in the practice of states, Boed, *supra*, at 149, and it was squarely rejected by the United States until recently. *See* Blakesley, *supra*, at 69-70 ("The passive-personality theory traditionally has been anathema to U.S. law and practice.").

In the Omnibus Diplomatic Security and Antiterrorism Act of 1986, however, Congress made it a crime to kill or conspire to kill or cause physical violence to a U.S. national while such national is outside the United States. Pub. L. No. 99-399, §1202, 100 Stat. 853, 896, now codified at 18 U.S.C. §2332 (2006). The *Bin Laden* defendants were charged with this crime, and it would apply as well to acts of homicide or physical violence against private U.S. nationals traveling abroad. Does that mean that the United States could prosecute an Italian pickpocket for pushing a U.S. tourist in Rome as he extracted the tourist's wallet? Even Congress had doubts about reaching so far, so it added a limitation forbidding any prosecution except upon written certification by the Attorney General or his Deputy that "such offense was intended to coerce, intimidate, or retaliate against a government or a civilian population." 18 U.S.C. §2332(d). Here Congress attempted to narrow the offenses to terrorist offenses without defining them and thus to avoid extending the statute to barroom brawls or ordinary street crimes. But what new problem does this provision arguably create? Who creates jurisdiction under this law, and when is it created? *See* Lowenfeld, *supra*, at 891 (opining that the statute is unconstitutional).

Congress came back to passive personality jurisdiction in the Antiterrorism and Effective Death Penalty Act of 1996. Pub. L. No. 104-132, 110 Stat. 1214 (1996). In a section of that Act entitled "Clarification and Extension of Criminal Jurisdiction Over Certain Terrorism Offenses Overseas," Congress systematically amended multiple sections of the criminal code to supply the "clear manifestation" of extraterritoriality that is needed to overcome the presumption against extraterritoriality. *Id.* §721. These sections address aircraft piracy, destruction of aircraft, violence at international airports, murder of foreign officials and other persons, protection of the same, threats and extortion against the same, kidnaping of internationally protected persons, and developing or possessing biological weapons. *See* Boed, *supra*, at 159-173.

6. *The Universality Principle of Extraterritorial Jurisdiction.* Universality is perhaps the most controversial of the principles of extraterritorial jurisdiction, because it could theoretically result in a state's prosecuting a non-national for acts performed abroad against other non-nationals. *See* Kenneth C. Randall, *Universal Jurisdiction Under International Law*, 66 Tex. L. Rev. 785 (1988). It rests on the assumption that there are some crimes so widely regarded as heinous that their perpetrators are enemies of

mankind, subject to prosecution the world over. The prosecuting nation acts for all nations to protect their collective interest. See *supra* p. 199 (discussing *jus cogens*).

To which crimes does this principle apply, according to the *Bin Laden* court? Do they include terrorism? In 1984, Judge Edwards of the D.C. Circuit Court of Appeals asserted that he was unable to conclude "that the law of nations . . . outlaws politically motivated terrorism, no matter how repugnant it might be to our legal system." *Tel-Oren v. Libyan Arab Republic*, 726 F.2d 774, 796 (D.C. Cir. 1984), *cert. denied*, 470 U.S. 1003 (1985). Why do you suppose that the law of nations might not subject terrorism to universal jurisdiction? On the other hand, the law of nations is not static. *Restatement* §404 (quoted in *Bin Laden, supra* p. 1008) would include "*perhaps* certain acts of terrorism" (emphasis supplied). Professor Blakesley argues that the law of nations has *already* condemned individual offenses (such as air piracy and hostage-taking) for which "terrorism" is merely a composite term. Blakesley, *supra*, at 72. What was the *Bin Laden* court's conclusion in 2000?

7. *The Rule of Reasonableness.* The *Restatement* suggests that traditional principles of extraterritoriality are not to be mechanically applied; a court must always consider whether exercising jurisdiction in the particular circumstances would be reasonable. Indeed, the malleability and overlap of the traditional principles of extraterritorial jurisdiction under international law have caused some to suggest that reasonableness is today the overriding principle, under which the availability or nonavailability of the traditional principles is just a factor in the equation. Blakesley, *supra*, at 41. Is extraterritorial jurisdiction in *Bin Laden* reasonable? Why or why not?

8. *"Substantial Nexus."* We suggested that the civil procedure student might speculate whether the Due Process Clause imposes a "minimum contacts" requirement for extraterritorial jurisdiction. In fact, a few cases have spoken of the need for a substantial nexus between the defendant or his acts and the state exercising extraterritorial jurisdiction. *See, e.g., United States v. Davis*, 905 F.2d 245 (9th Cir. 1990), *cert. denied*, 498 U.S. 1047 (1991). Most courts, however (including the *Bin Laden* court in a portion of the opinion not reproduced here), have concluded that if extraterritorial jurisdiction is justified by the international principles of extraterritorial jurisdiction, due process is satisfied. *Davis*, 905 F.2d at 249. This seems persuasive when jurisdiction is supported by the territoriality, nationality, or protective principle, because each presumes "contact." Can you explain how? But does it work for jurisdiction supported only by the passive personality or universality principle?

Prosecuting Accused Terrorists and Their Supporters in Criminal Courts

It is not just the crimes that pose legal problems in prosecuting accused terrorists and their supporters, but also the evidence. In 1996, Congress for the first time authorized the intelligence community, "upon the request of a United States law enforcement agency, [to] collect information outside the United States about individuals who are not United States persons...notwithstanding that the law enforcement agency intends to use the information collected for purposes of a law enforcement investigation or counterintelligence investigation." 50 U.S.C. §403-5a(a) (2006). Moreover, after 9/11, Congress expressly authorized and encouraged more sharing of information among intelligence and law enforcement agencies. See *supra* p. 549. When intelligence agencies are tasked with information collection for law enforcement and those agencies share their information, the information collected may be used or sought in criminal prosecutions against alleged terrorists or their supporters. *See generally* Note, *Secret Evidence in the War on Terror*, 118 Harv. L. Rev. 1962 (2005).

However, such use or access may compromise the security of the information itself, as well as intelligence sources or methods used to collect it. Moreover, as we saw in Chapters 31 and 32, some evidence may have been obtained by coercive interrogation. Such evidence poses issues of due process and confrontation, and it may not be trustworthy. Judge Wilkinson explained some of these problems in his opinion in *Al-Marri v. Pucciarelli*, 534 F.3d 213 (4th Cir. 2008) (*en banc*), *vacated and remanded sub nom. Al-Marri v. Spagone*, 129 S. Ct. 1545 (2009).

The problems presented by the criminal prosecution of terrorists are even more pronounced at trial....

First, while a showcase of American values, an open and public criminal trial may also serve as a platform for suspected terrorists. Terror suspects may use the bully pulpit of a criminal trial in an attempt to recruit others to their cause. Likewise, terror suspects may take advantage of the opportunity to interact with others during trial to pass critical intelligence to their allies....

Second, and relatedly, the prosecution of some terrorists could present security concerns of a different sort: witnesses and jurors may be subjected to threats of violence or become the targets of attack....

Third, and finally, the plurality also neglects to discuss another serious concern: traditional criminal proceedings, especially public trials, may not be responsive to the executive's legitimate need to protect sensitive information. . . .

However, the government's desire to protect such sensitive intelligence may conflict with a defendant's confrontation and compulsory process rights. By employing those rights, a terror suspect like al-Marri may, in a tactic commonly referred to as "graymail," request highly sensitive materials. Such a request leaves the government facing a Hobson's Choice. The government can withdraw all or part of its case to protect its information, or proceed and surrender its sensitive intelligence and possibly its source. And even if the government is able to suppress the defendant's request, defense counsel will be able to insinuate that the government is hiding information that is favorable to the defendant. . . .

. . . Congress may certainly take [such concerns] into account in deciding that the criminal justice system is not the sole permissible means of dealing with suspected terrorists. . . . [*Al-Marri*, 534 F.3d at 307-308 (Wilkinson, J., concurring in part and dissenting in part.)]

This chapter is about how Congress, the courts, and the Executive have taken such problems into account in criminal prosecutions against accused terrorists and their supporters. First, in criminal cases, a defendant may invoke her constitutional, statutory, and rule-based rights of discovery to gain access to classified information in government hands that she says she needs to defend herself. Alternatively, she may already possess classified information as a current or former government employee, and she may threaten to use that information at trial to rebut or explain the charged conduct. To deal with the discovery and use of classified information in criminal cases, Congress enacted the Classified Information Procedures Act (CIPA) in 1980. We consider CIPA in Part A.

Second, the government may want to use information obtained from classified intelligence sources and methods as evidence against a suspected terrorist or other criminal. It may have to decide whether to proceed and disclose such evidence in open court, or to offer the evidence by methods that keep it from either the public or the defendant, or both. Such efforts are discussed in Part B of this chapter.

Third, criminal defendants may demand access to classified exculpatory evidence. In Part C, we explore the issues raised by such a demand in the criminal prosecution of Zacarias Moussaoui, who was accused of involvement in the 9/11 terrorist attacks.[1]

Fourth, some of the evidence the government seeks to offer at the trial of a terror suspect may have been coerced from the defendant or derived from a witness who was coerced, either by U.S. interrogators or by others. Part D addresses issues surrounding the use of such coerced evidence in a criminal prosecution.

Some commentators—including former federal judge and Attorney General Michael B. Mukasey—have argued that Article III courts are not up to the task of dealing with problems like these, and that the record of criminal prosecutions of terror suspects to date prove it. They have therefore proposed that Congress create a new National Security Court to try terror suspects. In Part E, we consider that proposal.

---

1. We defer until Chapter 41 the related issue of the public's right of access to adjudicative proceedings and the government's desire to close them in order to protect national security information.

A.   THE CLASSIFIED INFORMATION PROCEDURES ACT

Classified Information Procedures Act

18 U.S.C. app. 3 §§1-16 (2006 & Supp. III 2009)

§4. DISCOVERY OF CLASSIFIED INFORMATION BY DEFENDANTS

The court, upon a sufficient showing, may authorize the United States to delete specified items of classified information from documents to be made available to the defendant through discovery under the Federal Rules of Criminal Procedure, to substitute a summary of the information for such classified documents, or to substitute a statement admitting relevant facts that the classified information would tend to prove. The court may permit the United States to make a request for such authorization in the form of a written statement to be inspected by the court alone. . . .

§5. NOTICE OF DEFENDANT'S INTENTION TO DISCLOSE CLASSIFIED INFORMATION

(a) Notice by defendant. If a defendant reasonably expects to disclose or to cause the disclosure of classified information in any manner in connection with any trial or pretrial proceeding involving the criminal prosecution of such defendant, the defendant shall, within the time specified by the court or, where no time is specified, within thirty days prior to trial, notify the attorney for the United States and the court in writing. Such notice shall include a brief description of the classified information. Whenever a defendant learns of additional classified information he reasonably expects to disclose at any such proceeding, he shall notify the attorney for the United States and the court in writing as soon as possible thereafter and shall include a brief description of the classified information. . . .

§6. PROCEDURE FOR CASES INVOLVING CLASSIFIED INFORMATION

(a) Motion for hearing. Within the time specified by the court for the filing of a motion under this section, the United States may request the court to conduct a hearing to make all determinations concerning the use, relevance, or admissibility of classified information that would otherwise be made during the trial or pretrial proceeding. Upon such a request, the court shall conduct such a hearing. Any hearing held pursuant to this subsection (or any portion of such hearing specified in the request of the Attorney General) shall be held in camera if the Attorney General certifies to the court in such petition that a public proceeding may result in the disclosure of classified information. As to each item of classified information, the court shall set forth in writing the basis for its determination. Where the United States' motion under this subsection is filed prior to the trial or pretrial proceeding, the court shall rule prior to the commencement of the relevant proceeding.

(b) Notice.

(1) Before any hearing is conducted pursuant to a request by the United States under subsection (a), the United States shall provide the defendant with notice of the classified information that is at issue. Such notice shall identify the specific classified information at issue whenever that information previously has been made

available to the defendant by the United States. When the United States has not previously made the information available to the defendant in connection with the case, the information may be described by generic category, in such form as the court may approve, rather than by identification of the specific information of concern to the United States.

(2) Whenever the United States requests a hearing under subsection (a), the court, upon request of the defendant, may order the United States to provide the defendant, prior to trial, such details as to the portion of the indictment or information at issue in the hearing as are needed to give the defendant fair notice to prepare for the hearing.

(c) Alternative procedure for disclosure of classified information

(1) Upon any determination by the court authorizing the disclosure of specific classified information under the procedures established by this section, the United States may move that, in lieu of the disclosure of such specific classified information, the court order —

(A) the substitution for such classified information of a statement admitting relevant facts that the specific classified information would tend to prove; or

(B) the substitution for such classified information of a summary of the specific classified information.

The court shall grant such a motion of the United States if it finds that the statement or summary will provide the defendant with substantially the same ability to make his defense as would disclosure of the specific classified information. The court shall hold a hearing on any motion under this section. Any such hearing shall be held in camera at the request of the Attorney General.

(2) The United States may, in connection with a motion under paragraph (1), submit to the court an affidavit of the Attorney General certifying that disclosure of classified information would cause identifiable damage to the national security of the United States and explaining the basis for the classification of such information. If so requested by the United States, the court shall examine such affidavit in camera and ex parte. . . .

(e) Prohibition on disclosure of classified information by defendant, relief for defendant when United States opposes disclosure

(1) Whenever the court denies a motion by the United States that it issue an order under subsection (c) and the United States files with the court an affidavit of the Attorney General objecting to disclosure of the classified information at issue, the court shall order that the defendant not disclose or cause the disclosure of such information.

(2) Whenever a defendant is prevented by an order under paragraph (1) from disclosing or causing the disclosure of classified information, the court shall dismiss the indictment or information; except that, when the court determines that the interests of justice would not be served by dismissal of the indictment or information, the court shall order such other action, in lieu of dismissing the indictment or information, as the court determines is appropriate. Such action may include, but need not be limited to —

(A) dismissing specified counts of the indictment or information;

(B) finding against the United States on any issue as to which the excluded classified information relates; or

(C) striking or precluding all or part of the testimony of a witness. . . .

United States v. Lee

United States District Court, District of New Mexico, 2000
90 F. Supp. 2d 1324

CONWAY, Chief Judge. This matter came on for consideration of the Motion of Dr. Wen Ho Lee for a Declaration that Sections 5 and 6 of the Classified Information Procedures Act (CIPA) are Unconstitutional as Applied.... [Wen Ho Lee was being prosecuted on charges of espionage and mishandling of classified information at the Los Alamos National Laboratory.]

I. CIPA FRAMEWORK

The Classified Information Procedures Act (CIPA), 18 U.S.C. app. III §§1-16 (1988), provides for pretrial procedures to resolve questions of admissibility of classified information in advance of its use in open court.[1] Under CIPA procedures, the defense must file a notice briefly describing any classified information that it "reasonably expects to disclose or to cause the disclosure of" at trial. 18 U.S.C. app. III §5(a). Thereafter, the prosecution may request an *in camera* hearing for a determination of the "use, relevance and admissibility" of the proposed defense evidence. *Id.* at §6(a). If the Court finds the evidence admissible, the government may move for, and the Court may authorize, the substitution of unclassified facts or a summary of the information in the form of an admission by the government.[2] *See id.* at §6(c)(1). Such a motion may be granted if the Court finds that the statement or summary will provide the defendant with "substantially the same ability to make his defense as would disclosure of the specific classified information." *Id.* If the Court does not authorize the substitution, the government can require that the defendant not disclose classified information. *See id.* at §6(e). However, under §6(e)(2), if the government prevents a defendant from disclosing classified information at trial, the court may: (A) dismiss the entire indictment or specific counts, (B) find against the prosecution on any issue to which the excluded information relates, or (C) strike or preclude the testimony of particular government witnesses. *See* 18 U.S.C. app. III §6(e)(2). Finally, CIPA requires that the government provide the defendant with any evidence it will use to rebut the defendant's revealed classified information evidence. *See id.* at §6(f).

II. CONSTITUTIONALITY OF CIPA

Defendant Lee contends that, as applied to him, the notice and hearing requirements of §5 and §6 of CIPA are unconstitutional.... Although I find Defendant's claims unjustified, I will nevertheless address them in turn.[3]...

---

1. Classified information is defined as including "information and material" subject to classification or otherwise requiring protection from public disclosure. *See* 18 U.S.C. app. III §1. Thus, CIPA applies to classified testimony as well as to classified documents.
2. If the court finds that the evidence is not admissible at trial, CIPA is no longer implicated. When determining the use, relevance and admissibility of the proposed evidence, the court may not take into account that the evidence is classified; relevance of classified information in a given case is governed solely by the standards set forth in the Federal Rules of Evidence.
3. Other courts that have considered the constitutionality of CIPA are in accord.

A. Defendant's Privilege Against Self-incrimination

Defendant Lee's first contention is that the notice and hearing requirements of §5 and §6 violate his Fifth Amendment privilege against self-incrimination because they force him to reveal classified aspects of his own trial testimony. Defendant argues that by forcing him to reveal portions of his potential testimony, CIPA unconstitutionally infringes upon his right to remain silent until and unless he decides to testify. Similarly, Defendant argues that if he chooses not to comply with the notice requirements, under the penalty of not being able to offer such testimony at trial, CIPA unconstitutionally denies him the right to testify on his own behalf. In either case, Defendant contends that CIPA forces him to pay a price in the form of a costly pretrial decision in order to preserve his constitutional rights at trial.

CIPA does not require that a defendant specify whether or not he will testify or what he will testify about. Instead, CIPA requires "merely a general disclosure as to what classified information the defense expects to use at trial, regardless of the witness or the document through which that information is to be revealed." *United States v. Poindexter*, 725 F. Supp. 13, 33 (D.D.C. 1989). Defendant's argument that if he discloses the classified information his right to remain silent has been compromised (or in the alternative that if he refuses to disclose the classified information his right to testify has been compromised) is misplaced. Despite CIPA's requirements, Defendant still has the option of not testifying. Similarly, if the defense does not disclose classified information as required by CIPA, the defendant retains the option of testifying, albeit with the preclusion of any classified information.

In addition, the pretrial disclosure of certain aspects of a criminal defense is hardly a novel concept. Examples of such requirements include Fed. R. Crim. P. 12.1 (alibi defense); Fed. R. Crim. P. 12.2 (insanity defense); Fed. R. Crim. P. 12.3 (public authority defense); and Fed. R. Crim. P. 16 (medical and scientific tests, and tangible objects and certain documents). Such provisions have consistently been held constitutional.... CIPA merely provides a mechanism for determining the admissibility of classified information so that classified information is not inadvertently disclosed during open proceedings. Defendant still has the choice of presenting the evidence during trial or not, after it has been deemed admissible. "That the defendant faces...a dilemma demanding a choice between complete silence and presenting a defense has never been thought an invasion of the privilege against compelled self-incrimination." *Williams v. Florida*, 399 U.S. 78, 84 (1970).

Defendant also argues that the burdens placed upon him by CIPA unconstitutionally violate his Fifth Amendment rights in that they do not advance any interests related to the fairness and accuracy of the criminal trial. However, Defendant's argument is unconvincing. CIPA is designed to "assure the fairness and reliability of the criminal trial" while permitting the government to "ascertain the potential damage to national security of proceeding with a given prosecution before trial." *See United States v. Ivy*, 1993 WL 316215 at *4 (citations omitted). As the Supreme Court has noted, "it is obvious and unarguable that no governmental interest is more compelling than the security of the Nation." *Poindexter*, 725 F. Supp. at 34 (quoting *Haig v. Agee*, 453 U.S. 280, 307 (1981)). CIPA serves that interest "by providing a mechanism for protecting both the unnecessary disclosure of sensitive national security information and by helping to ensure that those with significant access to such information will not escape the sanctions of the law applicable to others by use of the greymail route."[5] *Id.* at 34. Accordingly, I find that CIPA does not violate Defendant's privilege against self-incrimination by infringing upon either his right to remain silent or his right to testify on his own behalf.

B. Defendant's Right to Confront and Cross-examine Witnesses

Defendant Lee next argues that §5 and §6 of CIPA violate his Sixth Amendment right to confront and cross-examine government witnesses by forcing him to notify the government pretrial (and explain the significance) of all the classified information he reasonably expects to elicit from prosecution witnesses on cross-examination and all such information that will be contained in defense counsel's questions to those witnesses.[6]

Defendant contends that under CIPA, the "prosecution can shape its case-in-chief to blunt the force of the defense cross examination" and that the advance notice under CIPA "will impede effective defense cross-examination." However, the Confrontation Clause does not guarantee the right to undiminished surprise with respect to cross-examination of prosecutorial witnesses....

CIPA does not require that the defense reveal its plan of cross-examination to the government. CIPA also does not require that the defendant reveal what questions his counsel will ask, in which order, and to which witnesses. Likewise, the defendant need not attribute the information to any particular witness. CIPA merely requires that the defendant identify the classified information he reasonably intends to use. Because the only cited tactical disadvantage that may accrue, minimization of surprise, is slight, defendant has failed to demonstrate that the requirements under CIPA render his opportunity for cross-examination ineffective.

C. Defendant's Right to Due Process

Defendant's due process argument is based on the contention that CIPA's disclosure requirements violate the Due Process Clause by imposing a one-sided burden on the defense, without imposing a mandatory reciprocal duty on the prosecution. However, due process is only denied where the balance of discovery is tipped against the defendant and in favor of the government....

Here, the CIPA burdens are not one-sided. First, the government has already agreed to allow Defendant and his counsel access to all classified files at issue in the indictment. Second, the government must produce all discoverable materials before the defense is required to file a §5(a) notice. Third, before a §6 hearing is conducted, the government must reveal details of its case so as to give the defense fair notice to prepare for the hearing. *See* 18 U.S.C. app. III §6(b)(2). Specifically, the government must provide the defense with any portions of any material it may use to establish the

---

5. Greymail refers to a tactic employed by a defendant who threatens to disclose classified information with the hopes that the prosecution will choose not to prosecute in order to keep the information protected.

6. Under the Sixth Amendment, a criminal defendant "shall enjoy the right ... to be confronted with the witnesses against him." U.S. Const. amend. VI. Pursuant to the right to confront the witnesses against him, a criminal defendant has the "fundamental right" to cross examine witnesses for the prosecution.

"national defense" element of any charges against Lee. Fourth, under §6(f), the government is required to provide notice of any evidence it will use to rebut classified information that the court permits the defense to use at trial. Finally, in addition to the discovery obligations under §6 of CIPA, the government must also comply with the Federal Rules of Criminal Procedure and *Brady v. Maryland,* 373 U.S. 83 (1963).

Despite the fact that the government's reciprocal duties under CIPA are not triggered until it decides to request a §6 hearing, the overall balance of discovery is not tipped against Lee. . . .

III. CONCLUSION

In summary, Defendant Lee has failed to show that the carefully balanced framework for determining the use of classified information by the defense set forth in CIPA violates his Fifth Amendment privilege against self-incrimination, his Fifth Amendment right to remain silent or his Fifth and Sixth Amendment rights to testify on his own behalf. Defendant has also failed to demonstrate that CIPA violates his Fifth Amendment right to due process of law or his Sixth Amendment right to confront and cross-examine witnesses.

NOTES AND QUESTIONS

1. *The Decision to Prosecute.* When the government decides whether to mount a criminal prosecution or initiate an immigration proceeding against an alleged terrorist, it must assess the risk that going forward will expose state secrets or classified information. Consequently, the Attorney General has instructed federal prosecutors, in deciding whether to prosecute, to weigh (a) the likelihood of such exposure, (b) the resulting damage to national security, (c) the likelihood of success if the case is brought, and (d) the nature and importance of other federal interests that prosecution would promote. U.S. Dep't of Justice, *Attorney General's Guidelines for Prosecutions Involving Classified Information* 4-6 (1981). Sometimes this weighing will dictate not prosecuting. How, if at all, would the enactment of CIPA have affected this process? The decision to prosecute and the government's conduct of the trial of Wen Ho Lee are dealt with extensively in Dan Stober & Ian Hoffman, *A Convenient Spy: Wen Ho Lee and the Politics of Nuclear Espionage* (2001).

2. *Is It Classified?* How did the *Lee* court decide whether CIPA was applicable — that is, whether the information Wen Ho Lee was planning to use was "classified"? Must the court simply defer to the government's classification stamp? If so, "the government could make CIPA applicable whenever it suited its purpose simply by rubber-stamping documents that have no relevance to the national security." 26 Charles Alan Wright *et al., Federal Practice and Procedure* §5672 (1992, updated online 2011). Rules for classifying information are examined in Chapter 39.

3. *Graymail.* In *United States v. Reynolds,* 345 U.S. 1, 12 (1953), the Supreme Court said that "it is unconscionable to allow [the government] to undertake prosecution and then invoke its governmental privileges to deprive the accused of anything which might be material to his defense." Rejected Federal Rule of Evidence 509 therefore

provided that when the state secrets privilege is sustained and a party is thereby deprived of material evidence, the court should make whatever orders "the interests of justice require, including striking the testimony of a witness, declaring a mistrial, finding against the government upon an issue as to which the evidence is relevant, or dismissing the action." 26 Wright & Graham, *supra*, at 417. *See generally* Louis Fisher, *In the Name of National Security: Unchecked Presidential Power and the Reynolds Case* (2006) (reviewing the history of the rule).

Can you see how these principles from civil litigation help set the stage for graymail in criminal trials? How does it work? Is it an unfair tactic by unscrupulous defendants or lawyers? Former Assistant Attorney General Philip Heymann has noted that "[i]t would be a mistake . . . to view the 'greymail' problem as limited to instances of unscrupulous or questionable conduct by defendants since wholly proper defense attempts to obtain or disclose classified information may present the government with the same 'disclose or dismiss' dilemma." S. Rep. No. 96-823, at 3 (1980), *reprinted in* 1980 U.S.C.C.A.N. 4294, 4296-4297. Into which category would the disclose-or-dismiss dilemma in the Wen Ho Lee case fall? *See* Bob Drogin, *Nuke Secrets Deemed Vital to Scientist's Case*, L.A. Times, June 16, 2000 (reporting that a member of Lee's legal team characterized as "graymailing the government" his request for complete computer records and 400,000 pages of classified data for nearly every U.S. nuclear weapon). Has the enactment of CIPA eliminated the possibility of graymail?

4. *Defendant's Discovery in Criminal Cases.* In criminal cases, defendants have certain limited rights to discovery. The Supreme Court has held that the prosecution must disclose evidence that is favorable to the defendant and "is material either to guilt or to punishment." *Brady v. Maryland*, 373 U.S. 83, 87 (1963). Specific defense requests thus require the prosecution to turn over all exculpatory evidence, which may include classified information in national security prosecutions. *See United States v. Rezaq*, 156 F.R.D. 514, 516-517 (D.D.C. 1994). In addition, the Jencks Act, 18 U.S.C. §3500 (2006), requires the prosecution to produce statements in its possession by witnesses who have testified on direct examination at trial in order to facilitate cross-examination by the defense. Such statements could include ones made by secret intelligence assets. For example, in the case that prompted enactment of the Act, the statements were confidential reports by paid government informants who were members of the Communist Party. *Jencks v. United States*, 353 U.S. 657 (1957). Finally, Federal Rule of Criminal Procedure 16(a)(1)(A)-(B) permits criminal defendants to discover their own statements, as well as documents and tangible objects in the possession, custody, or control of the government that are material to the defendant's defense, are intended for use by government as evidence, or were obtained from or belong to the defendant. Here again, the documents or tangible objects might include classified information, or their disclosure might reveal intelligence sources and methods. *See generally* Jonathan M. Fredman, *Intelligence Agencies, Law Enforcement, and the Prosecution Team*, 16 Yale L. & Pol'y Rev. 331 (1998).

Of course, intelligence agencies may hold back classified information or sources and methods and provide only unclassified information to the prosecution. Could the prosecution then argue that it had only the latter in its possession, custody, or control, thus avoiding discovery of classified information by the defense? The cases are neither clear nor consistent, but in general they hold that "federal discovery obligations extend to those government agencies that are so closely 'aligned' with the prosecution of a specific matter that justice requires their records be subject to the respective discovery obligations." *Id.* at 347. The *United States Attorneys' Manual* states that "an investigative or prosecutive agency becomes aligned with the government prosecutor when it becomes actively involved in the investigation or the prosecution of a particular case." *United States Attorneys' Manual* tit. 9, *Criminal Resource Manual* §2052(B)(1) (1997).

Does the tasking of an intelligence agency by the FBI under the 1996 law (quoted *supra* p. 1016) constitute sufficient "active involvement" to align it with the prosecution? *See* Fredman, *supra* at 364 (opining that "a court could well [so] conclude"). Suppose the intelligence community on its own initiative forwards to the FBI foreign surveillance information suggesting criminal wrongdoing. Has it thereby aligned itself with the prosecutors if a criminal prosecution results? *Id.* (probably not). Here the *United States Attorneys' Manual* suggests that its role must first "exceed[] the role of providing mere tips or leads based on information generated independently of the criminal case." *Criminal Resource Manual, supra,* §2052(B)(1).

5. *CIPA and Discovery.* CIPA permits the government to argue ex parte against the discovery of classified information, 18 U.S.C. app. 3 §4, but it does not purport to change discovery standards. Nevertheless, some courts and commentators have read CIPA to narrow a defendant's rights or balance them against governmental interests. *See* 26 Wright *et al., supra* p. 1023, §5672. In *United States v. Yunis,* 867 F.2d 617 (D.C. Cir. 1989), for example, the court arguably crafted a new relevancy standard for discovery of classified information by holding that "mere . . . theoretical relevance" was not enough; the defendant was obliged to show that the information is "at least 'helpful to the defense of [the] accused.' " *Id.* at 623 (quoting *Roviaro v. United States,* 353 U.S. 53, 60-61 (1957) (involving informer's privilege)).

When a court in a §4 proceeding *does* find that classified information is discoverable, the government is afforded the option of substituting a summary or a statement admitting relevant facts that the classified information would tend to prove. The courts have also inferred authority from CIPA to order defense counsel to obtain security clearances as a condition of seeing classified information or participating in hearings at which it may be disclosed. *See United States v. Bin Laden,* 58 F. Supp. 2d 113 (S.D.N.Y. 1999) (rejecting the claim that this requirement unconstitutionally interferes with defendant's choice of counsel).

6. *CIPA Notice and the Admissibility Hearing.* A defendant who wishes to disclose classified information in the case must give specific prior notice to the government pursuant to §5, on penalty of having the court exclude any classified information omitted from the notice. 18 U.S.C. app. 3 §5. Why is it not unconstitutional to thus require a defendant to tip his hand, according to *Lee?*

Following a §5 notice, the government may request a hearing concerning the use, relevancy, or admissibility of the identified information. 18 U.S.C. app. 3 §6. This hearing is usually held in camera. CIPA's legislative history is quite clear that it was not intended to change existing rules of evidence applicable in this hearing. *See* 26 Wright *et al., supra,* §5672 (discussing history). Some courts have taken this history to heart and even stated that they must disregard the classified nature of the information in ruling on its relevancy and admissibility. Others — notably the Fourth Circuit — have found that CIPA established "a more strict rule of admissibility" for classified information. *United States v. Smith*, 780 F.2d 1102, 1105 (4th Cir. 1985). *See* Note, *United States v. Smith: Construing the Classified Information Procedures Act as Restricting the Admissibility of Evidence*, 44 Wash. & Lee L. Rev. 720 (1987). Moreover, other courts have obtained the same results as *Smith* by narrowly construing defenses, such as reliance on CIA authority (*see United States v. Lopez-Lima*, 738 F. Supp. 1404 (S.D. Fla. 1990)), in order to rule the classified information irrelevant. *See* 26 Wright *et al.*, *supra*, §5672.

7. *CIPA Substitution*. Courts may find classified information to be relevant and material. CIPA §6 then affords the government the option of moving to substitute an unclassified statement of admissions or an unclassified summary for the classified information. The court must grant that motion "if it finds that the statement or summary will provide the defendant with substantially the same ability to make his defense as would disclosure." 18 U.S.C. app. 3 §6(c)(1).

8. *CIPA: Disclose or Dismiss*. If, on the other hand, the court denies the motion, then the Attorney General must decide whether to disclose the information. *Id.* §6(e)(1). If she decides against disclosure, the court may dismiss all or part of the indictment, find against the government on an issue to which the withheld information relates, or strike testimony. *Id.* §6(e)(2). In deciding among these alternatives, the court is not supposed to balance interests, but instead to take whatever action is necessary "to make the defendant whole again." S. Rep. No. 96-823, at 9 (1980). For example, in *United States v. Fernandez*, 913 F.2d 148 (4th Cir. 1990), a prosecution of the CIA station chief in Costa Rica growing out of the Iran-Contra Affair, the defendant sought to introduce classified documents purporting to show the truth of statements he had made concerning the CIA's role in the resupply of the Contras. Using CIPA procedures, the Independent Counsel proposed that an unclassified summary of evidence be used in substitution for the documents, but the court found that the summary would not provide Fernandez with substantially the same ability to make his defense as would disclosure of the classified information. When the Attorney General refused to declassify the information, the court dismissed the indictment over the strenuous objections of the Independent Counsel. The government also ended the Wen Ho Lee prosecution by accepting his plea to a single count of the multi-count indictment, partly, it is reported, because senior Energy Department officials feared that the judge would order disclosure of classified information to Lee for use in his defense. *See* Bob Drogin, *How FBI's Flawed Case Against Lee Unraveled*, L.A. Times, Sept. 13, 2000.

9. *Another Option: Lying?* In 1983, a former CIA officer named Edwin P. Wilson was tried and convicted for illegally exporting explosives to Libya. He claimed that he was still working for the Agency and acting on its authority. During Wilson's trial, the government introduced an affidavit from a high-ranking CIA official denying Wilson's continued employment. The affidavit was a deliberate falsehood. Before Wilson was sentenced, attorneys at the CIA and the Justice Department learned of the fabrication, yet they failed to inform either the trial court or the appellate court. When the truth came to light 20 years later, Wilson's conviction was vacated. *United States v. Wilson*, 289 F. Supp. 2d 801 (S.D. Tex. 2003). A clearly incensed judge wrote, "Honesty comes hard to the government." *Id.* at 809.

B. USING "SILENT" WITNESSES AND SECRET EVIDENCE

United States v. Abu Ali

United States Court of Appeals, Fourth Circuit, 2008
528 F.3d 210

WILKINSON, MOTZ, and TRAXLER, Circuit Judges: [Ahmed Omar Abu Ali was born in the United States and sent to Saudi Arabia for college. While attending school there, he became affiliated with an Al Qaeda cell. In the course of meetings with Al Qaeda operatives in Saudi Arabia, Abu Ali suggested "assassinations or kidnappings of members of the U.S. Senate, the U.S. Army, and the Bush administration, a plan to rescue the prisoners at Guantánamo Bay, and plans to blow up American warplanes on U.S. bases and at U.S. ports, similar to the USS Cole operation." The cell began his training to reenter the United States as a "sleeper," for purposes of conducting later terrorist acts.

However, the Saudi counterterrorist agency Mabahith arrested Abu Ali before his training was completed and interrogated him. It also notified the FBI, which suggested questions for the interrogation. Eventually, the Saudi authorities surrendered Abu Ali to the United States, where he was tried for providing material support to a foreign terrorist organization, among several counts, partly on the basis of statements he made during the Saudi interrogation.]

Ahmed Omar Abu Ali was convicted by a jury of nine criminal counts arising from his affiliation with an al-Qaeda terrorist cell located in Medina, Saudi Arabia, and its plans to carry out a number of terrorist acts in this country. He was sentenced by the district court to 360 months imprisonment and 360 months of supervised release following imprisonment. Abu Ali appeals his convictions and the government cross-appeals his sentence. For the following reasons, we affirm the conviction, but we vacate and remand for purposes of resentencing.

Unlike some others suspected of terrorist acts and designs upon the United States, Abu Ali was formally charged and tried according to the customary processes of the criminal justice system. Persons of good will may disagree over the precise extent to which the formal criminal justice process must be utilized when those suspected of participation in terrorist cells and networks are involved. There should be no disagreement, however, that the criminal justice system does retain an important place in the ongoing effort to deter and punish terrorist acts without the sacrifice of American constitutional norms and bedrock values. As will be apparent herein, the criminal justice system is not without those attributes of adaptation that will permit it to function in the post-9/11 world. These adaptations, however, need not and must not come at the expense of the requirement that an accused receive a fundamentally fair trial. In this case, we are satisfied that Abu Ali received a fair trial, though not a perfect one, and that the criminal justice system performed those functions which the Constitution envisioned for it....

VI.

Abu Ali ... challenges the district court's handling of certain classified information under the provisions of the Classified Information Procedures Act ("CIPA"), 18

U.S.C. App. 3, §§1-16 (West 2000 & Supp. 2007).[13] Abu Ali's primary contention is that the district court violated his Sixth Amendment Confrontation Clause rights by admitting as evidence unredacted versions of two classified documents that Abu Ali had only been permitted to view in a redacted form, and by refusing to allow Abu Ali and his lead trial counsel to attend and participate in the hearings conducted under CIPA to discuss the classified evidence. . . .

A.

The Sixth Amendment guarantees that "[i]n all criminal prosecutions, the accused shall enjoy . . . the right to be confronted with the witnesses against him." U.S. Const. amend. VI. Its "main and essential purpose . . . is to secure for the opponent the opportunity of cross-examination." *Delaware v. Van Arsdall*, 475 U.S. 673, 678 (1986). However, the right "means more than being allowed to confront the witness physically." *Id.* "[T]he principal evil at which the Confrontation Clause was directed was the civil-law mode of criminal procedure, and particularly its use of *ex parte* examinations as evidence against the accused." *Crawford v. Washington*, 541 U.S. 36, 54 (2004). Thus, while this is not the ordinary case, we think the criminal defendant's right to confront witnesses necessarily encompasses his right to also see any documentary evidence that such witnesses offer at trial as evidence to support a conviction. *Cf. Abourezk v. Reagan,* 785 F.2d 1043, 1060 (D.C. Cir.1986) ("It is a hallmark of our adversary system that we safeguard party access to evidence tendered in support of a requested court judgment. The openness of judicial proceedings serves to preserve both the appearance and the reality of fairness in the adjudications of United States courts. It is therefore the firmly held main rule that a court may not dispose of the merits of a case on the basis of *ex parte, in camera* submissions.").

A defendant's right to see the evidence that is tendered against him *during* trial, however, does not necessarily equate to a right to have classified information disclosed to him *prior* to trial. Evidentiary privileges may serve as valid bases to block the disclosure of certain types of evidence, and the validity of such privileges may be tested by in camera and ex parte proceedings before the court "for the limited purpose of determining whether the asserted privilege is genuinely applicable." *Id.* As a general rule, "[i]f the court finds that the claimed privilege does not apply, then the other side must be given access to the information." *Id.* If the court finds that the privilege does apply, then it may preclude access to the information. But neither scenario results in the conviction of a defendant "based upon evidence he was never permitted to see and to rebut." *Id.*

In the area of national security and the government's privilege to protect classified information from public disclosure, we look to CIPA for appropriate procedures. . . .

C.

With these principles in mind, we turn first to Abu Ali's Confrontation Clause challenge to the government's introduction at trial of two unredacted, classified documents that memorialized communications between Sultan Jubran [an Al

---

13. These issues were separately raised via classified briefs and argued in closed proceedings before this panel.

Qaeda operative] and Abu Ali in the days following the May 2003 safe house raids conducted by the Saudi officials in Medina, as well as to his exclusion from the CIPA proceedings in which these communications were discussed.

1. . . .

[Only one of Abu Ali's lawyers obtained a security clearance. The government disclosed to the security-cleared lawyer unredacted copies of evidence it intended to declassify and introduce at trial, but explained that it would take some precautions to prevent public disclosure of the unredacted documents. It afforded Abu Ali's uncleared lawyers access only to redacted versions of the same documents.]

. . . The first declassified document was dated May 27, 2003, and read as follows:

> Peace, How are you and how is your family? I hope they are good. I heard the news about the children's sickness. I wish them a speedy recovery, God willing. Anyway, please keep in touch. Greetings to the group, Hani.

The government intended to demonstrate that "Hani" was a known alias of Abu Ali and that "news about the children's sickness" was a coded reference to the raids conducted by the Mabahith and the arrest of the Medina cell members. The second declassified document was dated June 6, 2003, and read as follows:

> To my brother, Peace to you with God's mercy and blessings. Thank God, I am fine. I was saved from the accident by a great miracle. I ask God that I would be thankful to Him. I have no idea about the others. However, according to what one doctor mentioned, Adil was not with them, thank God. The important thing is to get yourself ready for the medical checkup because you may have an appointment soon. Therefore, you must keep yourself ready by refraining from eating high fat meals and otherwise.

With regard to this communication, the government intended to demonstrate that the term "accident" was also a coded reference to the safe house raids. According to the government's theory, Sultan Jubran was advising Abu Ali that he did not know which cell members had escaped and which were captured, but that he and al-Faq'asi (a/k/a "Adil"), had escaped, and warning that Abu Ali might also be at risk.

A comparison of the classified and unclassified documents reveals that the declassified versions provided the dates, the opening salutations, the entire substance of the communications, and the closings, and had only been lightly redacted to omit certain identifying and forensic information.

On October 19, 2005, the government filed an in camera, ex parte motion pursuant to §4 of CIPA, seeking a protective order prohibiting testimony and lines of questioning that would lead to the disclosure of the classified information during the trial. *See* 18 U.S.C. App. 3 §4. The government advised that the classified portions of the communications could not be provided to Abu Ali and his uncleared counsel because they contained highly sensitive information which, if confirmed in a public setting, would divulge information detrimental to national security interests. The district court granted the government's motion by in camera, ex parte, sealed order. However, the district court ruled that the United States could use the "silent witness rule" to disclose the classified information to the jury at trial.[18] ...

3.

Having carefully considered the circumstances and evidence below, we conclude that the district court's determination that the redacted classified information need not be disclosed to the defendant, his uncleared counsel, and the public was not an abuse of discretion. Nor do we think that the district court's exclusion of Abu Ali and his uncleared counsel from the CIPA proceedings ran afoul of the Confrontation Clause. The district court's admission of the classified versions of the documents as evidence for consideration by the jury without disclosing the same versions to Abu Ali, however, was clearly contrary to the rights guaranteed to Abu Ali by the Confrontation Clause.

We begin with the district court's exclusion of Abu Ali and his uncleared counsel from the CIPA proceedings. The district court was presented with a §4 motion by the government to protect the classified information and a §5 motion, made at a later date, by Abu Ali that he be allowed to disclose that information. Initially, the district court found the redacted, unclassified version of the communications to be adequate to meet the defendant's need for information. CIPA expressly provides for such redactions of classified information from documents sought or required to be produced to the defendant, and the determination may be based upon an ex parte showing that the disclosure would jeopardize national security interests. The district court appropriately balanced the interests and made a reasonable determination that disclosure of the redacted information was not necessary to a fair trial.

There was likewise no abuse of discretion in the district court's decision to preclude Abu Ali's uncleared counsel from cross-examining the government's witnesses about the redacted information, which would have effectively disclosed the classified information that the court had already ruled need not be disclosed. A defendant and his counsel, if lacking in the requisite security clearance, must be excluded from hearings that determine what classified information is material and whether substitutions crafted by the government suffice to provide the defendant adequate means of presenting a defense and obtaining a fair trial. Thus, the mere exclusion of Abu Ali and his uncleared counsel from the CIPA hearings did not run afoul of CIPA or Abu Ali's Confrontation Clause rights.

We also conclude that the district court struck an appropriate balance between the government's national security interests and the defendant's right to explore the manner in which the communications were obtained and handled. Abu Ali and his uncleared counsel were provided with the substance of the communications, the

---

18. The "silent witness" rule was described in *United States v. Zettl*, 835 F.2d 1059, 1063 (4th Cir. 1987), as follows.

> [T]he witness would not disclose the information from the classified document in open court. Instead, the witness would have a copy of the classified document before him. The court, counsel and the jury would also have copies of the classified document. The witness would refer to specific places in the document in response to questioning. The jury would then refer to the particular part of the document as the witness answered. By this method, the classified information would not be made public at trial but the defense would be able to present that classified information to the jury.

Id.

dates, and the parties involved, and CIPA-cleared defense counsel was provided with the classified versions and afforded unfettered opportunity to cross-examine the government's witnesses concerning these matters. At the conclusion of the examinations, defense counsel pointed to no specific problem with the issues explored. The district court also expressly considered Abu Ali's rights under the Confrontation Clause and determined that public examination of these witnesses was not necessary to prevent infringement of them. Having fully considered the record and the classified information ourselves, we agree. Uncleared defense counsel were not entitled to disclose the classified information via their questioning of the witnesses about their roles in extracting, sharing, transferring, and handling the communications, and Abu Ali, who was ably represented by counsel at the hearing on this issue, was not deprived of his right to confrontation or to a fair trial merely because he and his uncleared counsel were not also allowed to attend.

The error in the case, which appears to have originated in the October 2005 CIPA proceeding, was that CIPA was taken one step too far. The district court did not abuse its discretion in protecting the classified information from disclosure to Abu Ali and his uncleared counsel, in approving a suitable substitute, or in determining that Abu Ali would receive a fair trial in the absence of such disclosure. But, for reasons that remain somewhat unclear to us, the district court granted the government's request that the complete, unredacted classified document could be presented to the jury via the "silent witness" procedure. The end result, therefore, was that the jury was privy to the information that was withheld from Abu Ali.

As noted above, CIPA contemplates and authorizes district courts to prevent the disclosure of classified information, as was done in this case, so long as it does not deprive the defendant of a fair trial. CIPA also authorizes restrictions upon the questioning of the witnesses to ensure that classified information remains classified. Indeed, even the "silent witness" procedure contemplates situations in which the jury is provided classified information that is withheld from the public, but not from the defendant. In addition, CIPA provides district courts wide discretion to evaluate and approve suitable substitutions to be presented to the jury. CIPA does not, however, authorize courts to provide classified documents to the jury when only such substitutions are provided to the defendant. Nor could it. There is a stark difference between ex parte submissions from prosecutors which protect the disclosure of irrelevant, nonexculpatory, or privileged information, and situations in which the government seeks to use *ex parte* information in court as evidence to obtain a conviction. And, the notion that such "safeguards against wide-ranging discovery . . . would be sufficient to justify a conviction on secret evidence is patently absurd." [*United States v. Claudio*, 44 F.3d 10, 14 (1st Cir. 1995).]; *see also United States v. Innamorati*, 996 F.2d 456, 488 (1st Cir. 1993) (finding no error in prosecutor's ex parte submission of information for consideration as to whether it must be disclosed to the defendant, but noting that "there [was] no question . . . of convictions based upon secret evidence furnished to the factfinder but withheld from the defendants").

The same can be said for the evidence here. If classified information is to be relied upon as evidence of guilt, the district court may consider steps to protect some or all of the information from unnecessary public disclosure in the interest of national security and in accordance with CIPA, which specifically contemplates such methods as redactions and substitutions so long as these alternatives do not deprive the defendant of a fair trial. However, the government must at a minimum provide the same version of the evidence to the defendant that is submitted to the jury. We do not balance a criminal defendant's right to see the evidence which will be used to convict him against the government's interest in protecting that evidence from public disclosure. If the government does not want the defendant to be privy to information that is classified, it may either declassify the document, seek approval of an effective substitute, or forego its use altogether. What the government cannot do is hide the evidence from the defendant, but give it to the jury. Such plainly violates the Confrontation Clause.

D.

Having determined that submission of the classified documents to the jury ran afoul of Abu Ali's Confrontation Clause rights, we turn now to consider whether that error was harmless. We conclude that it was. . . .

VIII. . . .

For the foregoing reasons, the judgment is affirmed in part, reversed in part, and remanded for further proceedings consistent with this decision.

Affirmed in part, reversed in part, and remanded.

[Dissenting opinion of DIANA GRIBBON MOTZ, Circuit Judge (regarding sentencing), omitted.]

United States v. Rosen

United States District Court, Eastern District of Virginia, 2007
487 F. Supp. 2d 703

ELLIS, District Judge. This Espionage Act (18 U.S.C. §793) prosecution involves a substantial amount of classified information the government contends is information relating to the national defense ("NDI")[1] and for this reason the government seeks to avoid public disclosure of this material in the course of the trial. To this end, the government, by motion pursuant to §6 of the Classified Information Procedures Act ("CIPA"),[2] has proposed utilizing a procedure at trial whereby substantial quantities of classified information would be disclosed to the Court, the jury, and counsel, but withheld from the public. This novel proposal, if allowed, would effectively close a substantial portion of the trial. Accordingly, defendants challenge this proposed procedure on the grounds that it is neither authorized by CIPA nor constitutionally permissible.

---

1. It is important to recognize that NDI and classified material may not be coextensive sets. . . . While classified status may be probative of information's NDI status, it is not conclusive.
2. 18 U.S.C. App. 3.

I.

Both defendants are charged with conspiracy to communicate NDI to persons not authorized to receive it, in violation of 18 U.S.C. §793(g), (e). Rosen is additionally charged with aiding and abetting alleged co-conspirator Lawrence Franklin's unauthorized communication of NDI to persons not authorized to receive it, in violation of 18 U.S.C. §§793(d) and 2. The superceding indictment generally alleges that over a course of several years, defendants cultivated various sources of information within the United States government, obtained NDI from those sources, and then disseminated that NDI to others not authorized to receive it, including co-workers, journalists, and foreign government officials. . . .

III.

[After defendants proposed to offer classified information in their defense at trial and objected to the government's proposed substitutions pursuant to CIPA], "[t]he government . . . proposed a procedure for handling this material at trial and it is this proposal that is at issue here. The government's proposal is novel; no published opinion has been found or cited in which the precise procedure proposed here was judicially approved or used. Simply put, the government proposes that while the jury, the Court, and counsel will, for the most part, have access to the unredacted classified material, the public will not. Instead, the public, in the course of the trial, will see and hear only the substitutions that have passed through the CIPA §6(c) process. In other words, and putting to one side the not insubstantial practical problems inherent in conducting a trial pursuant to the government's proposed procedure, its use would surely exclude the public from substantial and critical parts of the trial. This result is evident from a more detailed description of the proposed procedure.

The government's proposal is, in effect, a variant and a substantial expansion of the so-called "silent witness rule," a rule that has been used and judicially approved in certain, but not all circumstances. . . . As noted, the effect of using the procedure in this case would be the exclusion of the public from substantial portions of the trial.

The proposed procedure would work as follows: for each classified document discussed at trial, the Court, the witness, counsel, and the jurors would have the unredacted classified document in front of them, either in paper form or via computer screens viewable only by those persons. The public, however, would see only a redacted version. When counsel or a witness wishes to direct the jury to a classified portion of the document, counsel and the witness would refer to the page, paragraph and line numbers, with the Court, opposing counsel, and the jury following along, but members of the public could not follow along because they would be unaware of the specific information referenced by counsel or the witness. And, the witness answering the questions about the document would not be permitted to refer to specific language or information in the document, except by use of certain codes. For example, to rebut the government's contention that certain material is NDI, defendants will likely wish to call witnesses to compare various public source documents with the alleged NDI. To do so effectively may well require the witness to refer to specific language or contents of both the public source document and the alleged NDI. Anticipating this, the government proposes that the witness would not speak the names of certain specific countries, foreign persons, etc., but would instead use a code (e.g., "Country A," "Report X," "Foreign Person Y," "Foreign Person Z," etc.)

provided also to counsel, the Court, and the jury. Moreover, this code would change with respect to different alleged overt acts, presumably to prevent the public from inferring the meaning of the generic designations or otherwise breaking the code. For example, if a witness discussing a particular alleged disclosure is instructed to refer to Monaco as Country A, a different witness (or even the same witness) discussing another alleged disclosure might use Country B or C to refer to Monaco.

Likewise, when recordings discussing classified information are played, the government proposes that the Court, counsel, witness, and jury listen on special headphones to the entire recording. The public, however, would not hear the full recording; instead, the recorded conversations would be played aloud in the courtroom, but where classified information is discussed in the recording, the public version would revert to static. Also, the public would receive only a redacted transcript of the conversations.

In sum, the novel and distinctive feature of the government's proposed procedure is that the public is walled off from seeing and hearing everything the jury, the Court, the attorneys and the witnesses see and hear. What the public does not see or hear is the heart of the case, namely the classified material the government claims is the NDI that the defendants allegedly received and distributed without authorization. A further, related novel and distinctive feature of the government's proposal relates to the jury. Although jurors will see and hear classified material, they, of course, will not have received security clearances for this purpose. Nor has this ever been otherwise in cases involving classified material, for a variety of reasons including the substantial time and effort typically required for such clearances to be completed and the substantial question whether it is constitutionally permissible to exclude jurors because they could not pass a security clearance investigation. The government's remedy for this anomaly is simply to have the jurors instructed that they cannot disclose to anyone the classified material they will see and hear during the trial.

With this description in mind, the analysis now proceeds to address the following questions:

> (i) Whether the government's proposed procedure is explicitly or implicitly authorized by CIPA.
> (ii) Whether the government's proposed procedure violates the right to a public trial, guaranteed to defendants by the Sixth Amendment and to the public by the First Amendment.

IV.

A.

The government urges that the use of the silent witness rule, codes, and redacted recordings are "substitutions" authorized by CIPA. Defendants disagree, noting the government's proposed procedure is nowhere authorized by CIPA, either explicitly or implicitly. Defendants are correct, a conclusion that follows from CIPA's plain language, but also from the fact that the government's proposed procedure simply cannot fit within CIPA's confines even assuming the statute's plain language would not otherwise preclude it.

Analysis of this statutory argument properly focuses on CIPA §6(c) and §8(b) . . . . As noted, CIPA §6(c) allows the government to move that in lieu of disclosing classified information at trial, a "substitution" be used, which could take the form of a summary of the information or a presumably sanitized statement of facts the classified statement would tend to prove. Importantly, no substitutions can be used unless there is a judicial finding that the substitution provides defendants with "substantially the same ability to make his defense as would disclosure of the specific classified information." Consistent with this, CIPA §8(b) also permits introduction and use at trial of redacted versions of classified materials unless "the whole ought in fairness to be considered."

Significantly, neither §6(c) nor §8(b) explicitly authorize[s] or state[s] that "substitutions" may be made available to the public and the jury on different terms. CIPA is at best silent on this issue. Yet, this silence should not be construed as implicitly authorizing the government's proposal. To the contrary, it seems clear that CIPA envisions that "substitutions," if not unfair to defendants, will be used at a public trial in identical form for both the jury and the public. While it is true, as reflected in CIPA's legislative history, that "Congress expected trial judges to fashion creative solutions in the interests of justice for classified information problems,"[9] there is no evidence that Congress expected this creativity to extend to adopting procedures that effectively close the trial to the public. Indeed, given the strong presumption in the law that trials will be open and that evidence will be fully aired in public, CIPA's silence about whether "substitutions" and "excisions" can be made available to the public and jury on different terms should be interpreted as a prohibition on doing so. Closing a trial, even partially, is a highly unusual result disfavored by the law. A statute, even one regulating the use of classified information, should not be construed as authorizing a trial closure based on Congress' mere silence or use of ambiguous language. Rather, because a trial closure implicates important constitutional rights, CIPA should not be read to authorize closure absent a clear and explicit statement by Congress in the statutory language.

In short, CIPA only authorizes the use of substitutions to avoid disclosure of classified information *to the public and the jury*, provided defendant's right to present a defense is not impaired; this authority is not the authority to close a trial to the public.

B.

Even assuming, *arguendo*, that the CIPA provision allowing "substitutions" might be stretched to encompass the government's proposed procedure, there is no doubt that the procedure would not pass muster under CIPA's fairness requirements. Where, as here, a central issue in the case is whether the government's alleged NDI is indeed genuinely NDI, and the proposed procedure would amount to a wholesale use of the silent witness rule to cover all of the alleged NDI, it cannot be said that the procedure affords defendants "substantially the same ability to make [their] defense as would disclosure of the specific classified information." CIPA §6(c). A few examples vividly illustrate this point.

As noted, the government in this case has the burden of proving beyond a reasonable doubt that the alleged NDI is indeed NDI. To this end, the government will likely invite witnesses to compare the substance of certain of defendants' emails, telephone

---

9. *United States v. North*, 713 F. Supp. 1452 (D.D.C. 1989) (citing H. Rep. No. 96-1436, 1980 U.S.C.C.A.N. 4294).

conversations, or faxes with certain alleged NDI to show that defendants had obtained NDI and were disseminating it without authorization. Defendants, of course, may wish to show, and indeed to emphasize, the dissimilarities between the alleged NDI and the information they obtained. Plainly, they would be significantly hobbled in doing so by use of the government's proposed procedure, inasmuch as the specific information could not be used in open court. The silent comparison of paragraphs or sentences, even where supplemented by codes, would effectively preclude defense counsel from driving home important points to the jury.

Similarly, it is apparent that defendants intend at trial to rebut the government's claim that certain material is NDI by having witnesses compare the alleged NDI to contemporaneous public domain material. Once again, the proposed procedure would unfairly impact defendants' ability to establish this defense. In this context, the silent witness rule, applied across the board as the government proposes here, essentially robs defendants of the chance to make vivid and drive home to the jury their view that the alleged NDI is no such thing, as essentially similar material was abundant in the public domain. Importantly in this respect, it is hard to see how defendants could effectively show, via the silent witness rule, that the details of differences between public source material and the alleged NDI are neither minor nor trivial. . . .

. . . In short, the use of codes would render virtually impossible an effective line of cross-examination vital to the defense. . . .

Yet another fatal defect in the fairness of the proposed procedure is apparent from the way in which it would hamper defendants should they choose to testify. Clearly, the proposed procedure would unfairly hinder defendants in their effort to explain why they believed any information they sought to obtain, the information they received, and the information they disclosed to others was not NDI. In this regard, defendants must be able to explain precisely what they knew and when, and from whom or what they learned it, and why they did not believe the material was NDI they were not authorized to have, or otherwise lacked the requisite *mens rea*. Yet, the proposed procedure would unfairly hinder defendants from doing so. For example, statements like "I heard from Foreign Person C the fact about Country X, reflected at Exhibit A page 3 paragraph 4 line 2 — well, except for the last clause — and so when I asked Franklin for confirmation of that fact, I thought I was asking for a matter of public record," may provide some exculpatory description of defendants' state of mind, assuming the jury could decode the statement quickly enough to follow the questioning. Yet, it would be difficult, if not impossible, for defendants to explain fully why they believed the information they sought or had was in the public domain without revealing details about the information, the identity and reliability of Person C, etc. Because the proposed procedure shackles defendants in this way, it cannot pass muster under CIPA.

Finally, it must be noted that the government's proposed frequently-changing system of coded references not only invites juror confusion, but virtually guarantees it. Given the sheer number of substitutions and the proliferation of coded phrases, varying from witness to witness and overt act to overt act, the likelihood of juror confusion would be a sufficient ground, by itself, for rejecting the wholesale proposed substitutions under CIPA §6(c). . . .

V.

Defendants' challenge to the government's proposed procedure rests on constitutional as well as statutory grounds. Specifically, defendants argue that even if

CIPA's language can be stretched to cover the government's proposed procedure, that procedure nonetheless fails as a violation of defendants' Sixth Amendment right to a public trial and the public's First Amendment right to a trial open to public scrutiny. Thus, even if the procedure passed muster under CIPA, constitutional analysis is nonetheless required. This follows, defendants argue, because the proposed procedure effectively excludes the public from essential portions of the trial.[20]

Nor is there any doubt that the portions of the trial that would be closed to the public are critical portions of the trial. It is clear that the government's proposal precludes the public from hearing and evaluating the evidence on a crucial and contested element of the case, namely, whether the information at issue is NDI and whether defendants knew it to be such. Moreover, the quality and quantity of material the government proposes to exclude from public view is significant. Testimony about the putative NDI at issue in seven of the alleged nine disclosures would be partially closed to the public, as would the recordings and documents corresponding to this NDI. Notably, the government's proposed procedure would treat even certain related public domain documents, including news reports, as if they were classified documents. In short, in the circumstances of this case, the government's proposal is clearly equivalent to sealing essential aspects of the trial.

The analysis of defendants' constitutional argument properly begins with the recognition that defendants and the public have a fundamental right to a trial open to the public. The right to a public trial contributes to just adjudication, stimulates public confidence in the judicial system, and ensures that the public is fairly apprised of the proceedings in cases of public concern. A public trial contributes to just adjudication in several ways: (i) requiring witness[es]' testimony to be public deters perjury; (ii) requiring a judge's rulings to be made in public deters partiality and bias; and (iii) requiring prosecutors to present their charges and evidence publicly deters prosecutorial vindictiveness and abuse of power. In these ways, the presence of the public encourages accurate factfinding and wise use of judicial and prosecutorial discretion, thereby contributing to public confidence that justice has prevailed at trial. In short, justice must not only be done, it must be seen to be done.

Given the important interests at stake, it is now well-settled that defendants in criminal cases and the public both have a right to a trial open to public scrutiny. *See Press-Enterprise Co. v. Superior Court of California*, 464 U.S. 501, 510 (1984) (public's First Amendment right); *Waller v. Georgia*, 467 U.S. 39, 44-45 (1984) (defendant's Sixth Amendment right). It is also well-settled that the standard governing whether the public trial right has been infringed is the same whether the right is asserted by the press under the First Amendment or by a defendant under the Sixth Amendment. *Waller*, 467 U.S. at 46-47. Under this constitutional standard, a trial is presumptively

---

20. It is noteworthy in this respect that the government sensibly appears to have abandoned its original position that the proposed use of the silent witness rule, coded testimony, and redacted recordings does not close the trial because the public would be present in the courtroom. This argument, if credited, leads to the absurd result that a trial unintelligible to the public is still "open" to the public simply because the public is physically present to see and hear what they cannot understand. The public's physical presence, by itself, does not guarantee that a trial is public; it is also necessary that the trial be reasonably comprehensible to the physically present public.

open, and may be closed only if certain criteria are met. These criteria are set forth in *Press-Enterprise* and its progeny, as follows:

> (1) an "overriding interest" must exist to close the trial,
> (2) the closure is no broader than necessary to protect that interest,
> (3) the court considers reasonable alternatives to closure, and
> (4) the court makes specific findings on the record concerning the existence of the overriding interest, the breadth of the closure, and the unavailability of alternatives to facilitate appellate review.

Press-Enterprise, 464 U.S. at 510. As the proponent of closing the proceedings, the government bears a "weighty" burden to establish that closure is permissible. *Press-Enterprise*, 464 U.S. at 509-10. Decisions to close trials must be made on a case by case basis, with attention to the facts and circumstances of each case; statutes *per se* requiring closure in certain circumstances are impermissible. *Globe Newspaper Co. v. Superior Court*, 457 U.S. 596, 611 n.27 (1982). Finally, before trials may be closed, the public must be given notice and an opportunity to be heard. *In re Knight Publishing Co.*, 743 F.2d 231, 234-35 (4th Cir. 1984). An erroneous denial of a public trial is a structural error not amenable to harmless error analysis. *Bell*, 236 F.3d at 165 (citing cases).

Each of the four *Press-Enterprise* elements is separately considered.

1. Overriding Interest

The government claims that its interest in protecting classified information is a compelling and overriding one, and has cited numerous cases in support of this claim. While it is true, as an abstract proposition, that the government's interest in protecting classified information can be a qualifying compelling and overriding interest, it is also true that the government must make a specific showing of harm to national security in specific cases to carry its burden in this regard. The government's *ipse dixit* that information is damaging to national security is not sufficient to close the courtroom doors nor to obtain the functional equivalent, namely trial by code. *Press-Enterprise* and *In re Washington Post* require more; they require a judicial inquiry into the legitimacy of the asserted national security interest, and specific findings, sealed if necessary, about the harm to national security that would ensue if the request to close the trial is not granted. *See Press-Enterprise*, 464 U.S. at 510; *In re Washington Post*, 807 F.2d 383, 391-92 (4th Cir. 1986) (rejecting the government's argument that courts should defer to Executive Branch assertions that trial closures are necessary for national security reasons, and stating that a proceeding cannot be closed merely because the case implicated CIPA at an earlier stage). Moreover, the government's *ipse dixit* is insufficient whether it appears by way of classified status, or the bald assertion of counsel that information is damaging to national security. Thus, granting that national security concerns can justify appropriately tailored trial closures, the government nonetheless bears the burden of demonstrating, as a factual matter, that harm to national security would result from failing to close the trial.

Here, the government has not met its burden; instead, it has done no more than to invoke "national security" broadly and in a conclusory fashion, as to all the classified information in the case. Of course, classification decisions are for the Executive Branch, and the information's classified status must inform an assessment of the government's asserted interests under *Press-Enterprise*. But ultimately, trial judges must make their own judgment about whether the government's asserted interest in partially closing the trial is compelling or overriding. As noted, a generalized assertion of "national security interests," whether by virtue of the information's classified status or upon representation of counsel, is not alone sufficient to overcome the presumption in favor of open trials. Here, the government has not proffered any evidence about danger to national security from airing the evidence publicly, let alone an item-by-item description of the harm to national security that will result from disclosure at trial of each specific piece of information as to which closure is sought, as required by *Press-Enterprise.*

Moreover, quite aside from the government's failure to provide any evidence of harm to national security from an open trial, the government's assertion of an overriding interest justifying a trial closure is undermined by the substance of the proposed procedure, to wit, that the jury and uncleared witnesses will be permitted to receive unredacted classified information. Given that the government appears willing to trust its confidential information to jurors, alternates, and uncleared witnesses, including (potentially) defendants, it is difficult to credit fully the government's claim that the classified information at issue is deserving of rigorous protection.

The government urges that this proposed disclosure to the jury does not reflect any inconsistency on its part, because the jurors could be instructed never to disclose the classified information they received at trial. Yet such an instruction appears patently unfair here, because it would suggest to the jury that the information at issue is NDI. Nor is this a minor consideration given that the status of the information as NDI is a central issue in the case, and indeed an element of the charged crime as to which the government bears the burden of proof beyond a reasonable doubt. An instruction that the jurors must treat the information they receive as a closely-held government secret is not easily reconciled with the instruction that the jury is the sole judge of the facts of the case and that it alone determines whether the information at issue is NDI, *i.e.,* whether it is closely held and potentially damaging to national security if revealed. While the two instructions are not flatly contradictory, they would be beyond the capacity of most jurors to reconcile . . . .

In short, the government's asserted overriding interest is not treated as such by the government itself, given that the putative NDI will be disclosed to uncleared jurors and witnesses. And while the government's cited cases support the notion that national security interests *can be* sufficiently compelling to justify a partial closure of the trial, they also require that the government satisfy *Press-Enterprise* by adequately supporting its motion with a description of the specific harm to national security that would ensue from disclosure. The government has not done so here. Accordingly, its motion fails under the first prong of *Press-Enterprise.*

2. Narrowly Tailored

For the same reasons, there is no basis to conclude that the government's proposal is narrowly tailored to protect any national security interests. Since the government has not identified with specificity which of the classified information to be kept from public view would harm national security if disclosed to the broader public, or how the national security would be affected, it is impossible to evaluate whether the proposed closure is as narrowly tailored as possible to protect that asserted interest.

3. Alternatives

Likewise, assuming that an overriding interest exists here because disclosure of some or all of the classified information at issue would damage national security, it is evident that reasonable alternatives to closure exist here. To wit, the government could propose conventional CIPA §6(c) substitutions that would be given to the jury and the public in the same form. Whether these substitutions would pass CIPA §6(c) fairness standards is another question not here presented.

4. Findings

Although the conclusions concerning the other *Press-Enterprise* factors obviate the need for factual findings, the absence of any affidavit describing the ensuing harms to national security should the trial not be closed is noteworthy. A highly detailed explanation of the ensuing harms to national security is especially necessary to make the thorough factual findings required for a closure when, as here, much of the classified information at issue is not self-evidently damaging to national security. . . .

VI.

To summarize, the wholesale use of the silent witness rule, coded testimony, and redacted recordings effectively closes the trial. This procedure is not a "substitution" authorized by CIPA, and even if it were, it would not afford defendants substantially the same opportunity to present their defense as the specific classified information. Moreover, even if the procedure passed muster under CIPA, it nonetheless would have to satisfy the *Press-Enterprise* test because it effectively closes portions of the trial. The proposed procedure does not; the government's showing of an overriding interest in protecting sensitive national security information has been insufficient to this point, and the government's claim that the information at issue is damaging to the national security if publicly disclosed is belied by its own proposal to release the information to uncleared persons. This opinion does not foreclose the government from proposing specific §6(c) substitutions that pass CIPA muster. Nor does this opinion foreclose consideration of or narrowly limited use of the silent witness rule where the government provides a specific factual basis for a claim that public disclosure would damage the national security.

For these reasons, defendants' motion to strike must be granted, and the government's motion to close the trial, styled a CIPA §6(c) motion, must be denied. At the government's request and with no objection from defendants, entry of an appropriate Order will be delayed to afford the government time to consider how to proceed with respect to the CIPA process.

NOTES AND QUESTIONS

1. *Excluding the Defendant and His Lawyers from the CIPA Hearing.* A court may hold a CIPA hearing to decide the relevance and admissibility of classified information. But courts also sometimes exclude a party and its lawyer from in camera hearings to

decide claims of privilege. Such exclusions are pretrial and said to be justified to protect the confidentiality of the putatively privileged information until the court can rule on the claim of privilege. How is the CIPA hearing different?

The court of appeals in *Abu Ali* said it is not different. Moreover, according to the court, defendant's security-cleared lawyer actually attended the CIPA hearing and "ably represented" Abu Ali, and the trial court carefully balanced the national security interests in deciding that providing only the redacted version to him and his uncleared lawyers would permit a sufficient defense. Do you agree with the court's analysis?

2. *Prosecutor's Use of Secret Evidence?* Look closely at the CIPA provisions. Do they permit the prosecutor to use classified information to *make the government's case* against the defendant, either secretly or in substituted or summarized form? If you are not sure, how should we resolve any ambiguity? *See Greene v. McElroy*, 360 U.S. 474 (1959), *supra* p. 102.

After approving the district court's conduct of the pretrial CIPA hearing, the court of appeals in *Abu Ali* still found a fatal flaw in the decision below. The district court not only excluded Abu Ali from the CIPA hearing, it also would have prevented him from seeing the redacted part of the two documents it proposed to use to prove his guilt *at trial.* "There is a stark difference between ex parte submissions from prosecutors which protect the disclosure of irrelevant, nonexculpatory, or privileged information, and situations in which the government seeks to use *ex parte* information in court as evidence to obtain a conviction." 528 F.3d at 255. Indeed, the appeals court agreed with the First Circuit that it is "patently absurd" to think that limitations in discovery could be used to justify a conviction based on evidence kept secret from the defendant. *Id.*

What is the constitutional basis for the court's insistence that Abu Ali be entitled to see the evidence against him? In *Greene*, 360 U.S. at 496-497, the Supreme Court said:

> Certain principles have remained relatively immutable in our jurisprudence. One of these is that where governmental action seriously injures an individual, and the reasonableness of the action depends on fact findings, the evidence used to prove the Government's case must be disclosed to the individual so that he has an opportunity to show that it is untrue. While this is important in the case of documentary evidence, it is even more important where the evidence consists of the testimony of individuals whose memory might be faulty or who, in fact, might be perjurers or persons motivated by malice, vindictiveness, intolerance, prejudice, or jealousy. We have formalized these protections in the requirements of confrontation and cross-examination. They have ancient roots. They find expression in the Sixth Amendment which provides that in all criminal cases the accused shall enjoy the right "to be confronted with the witnesses against him."

In a case involving an immigration proceeding, not a criminal prosecution, the Ninth Circuit Court of Appeals cited the Due Process Clause of the Fifth Amendment to find unlawful the government's use of undisclosed classified information against the immigrants. It applied the balancing test of *Mathews v. Eldridge*, 424 U.S. 319 (1976), in which the Supreme Court held that the process constitutionally due before the government takes a person's life, liberty, or property is determined by balancing (1) the private interest affected by the government action, (2) the risk of erroneous deprivation through the procedures the government has used as well as the value of additional or substitute procedures, and (3) the government's interest in the action and in avoiding additional procedures. *American-Arab Anti-Discrimination Comm. v. Reno*, 70 F.3d 1045 (9th Cir. 1995). It stressed "an exceptionally high risk of erroneous deprivation when undisclosed information is used to determine the merits...." *Id.* at 1069.

3. *The Risk of Inaccuracy in Using Secret Evidence.* In *Jay v. Boyd*, 351 U.S. 345 (1956), decided before *Greene*, the Supreme Court found statutory authority for the government to use "confidential information" in an immigration proceeding over the vigorous dissent of Chief Justice Warren, and Justices Black, Frankfurter, and Douglas. Justice Black asked:

> What is meant by "confidential information"? According to officers of the Immigration Service it may be "merely information we received off the street"; or "what might be termed as hearsay evidence, which could not be gotten into the record..."; or "information from persons who were in a position to give us the information that might be detrimental to the interests of the Service to disclose that person's name..." or "such things, perhaps, as income-tax returns, or maybe a witness who didn't want to be disclosed, or where it might endanger their life, or something of that kind...." No nation can remain true to the ideal of liberty under law and at the same time permit people to have their homes destroyed and their lives blasted by the slurs of unseen and unsworn informers. There is no possible way to contest the truthfulness of anonymous accusations. The supposed accuser can neither be identified nor interrogated. He may be the most worthless and irresponsible character in the community. What he said may be wholly malicious, untrue, unreliable, or inaccurately reported. In a court of law the triers of fact could not even listen to such gossip, much less decide the most trifling issue on it. [*Id.* at 365.]

Illustrating these points, a former Director of Central Intelligence, representing a group of detained Iraqis, found "serious errors" in previously secret evidence used against his clients, including mistranslations, ethnic and religious stereotyping, and rumors derived from inter-group rivalry. *See* Susan M. Akram, *Scheherezade Meets Kafka: Two Dozen Sordid Tales of Ideological Exclusion*, 14 Geo. Immigr. L.J. 51, 87-88 (1999).

The risk of inaccuracy from using secret evidence also may be illustrated by a case described as "the only criminal case since the Sept. 11 attacks in which secret evidence was presented against the defendant." *See* Dale Russakoff, *N.J. Judge Unseals Transcript in Controversial Terror Case*, Wash. Post, June 25, 2003. Reportedly, local (nonfederal) prosecutors convinced a state judge during a bail hearing that evidence against a defendant whom they alleged had ties to terrorists was so sensitive that the defendant could not be allowed to see it. Months later, an appellate judge ruled that prosecutors had not shown the defendant to be a security risk, and the trial judge then unsealed the bail hearing transcript. *Id.*; Robert Hanley & Jonathan Miller, *4 Transcripts Are Released in Case Tied to 9/11 Hijackers*, N.Y. Times, June 25, 2003; Jennifer V. Hughes, *Supposed Links to Terrorism Revealed*, The Record (Bergen Cty., N.J.), June 25, 2003. Most of the evidence consisted of testimony by a detective about what he had heard from FBI agents regarding the defendant. Federal authorities, however, contradicted or denied knowledge of some of this information after release of the transcripts, and the defendant's attorney dismissed it as "slanderous, hearsay, double- and triple-hearsay, evidence which he claimed he could have rebutted if only he and the defendant had been allowed to see it." Russakoff, *supra*. "To think that they kept me in jail on this," the defendant said, after being held for six months as a suspected terrorist. *Id.* The state dropped all but one of 25 counts of selling fraudulent documents to Hispanic immigrants (none tied to terrorism).

What risk of inaccuracy was presented in *Abu Ali*, when Abu Ali's cleared counsel had seen the unredacted classified information?

4. *The Silent Witness Rule.* Suppose that the district court in *Abu Ali* had permitted Abu Ali and his uncleared counsel to see the unredacted evidence. The court would still be concerned about the disclosure of such evidence to the public in open court. (Abu Ali's ability to relay it to his confederates could presumably be controlled as long as he was in custody). The silent witness rule seemed to supply a solution, by having witnesses refer to specific parts of a classified document which was also shown to the jury so it could follow the testimony, without reading from the document in open court. Why did the court of appeals approve that procedure, while the district court in *Rosen* did not? Does CIPA authorize such a procedure? Is there any constitutional limitation on its use? See Chapter 41 for a further discussion of the public's right of access to criminal trials.

C. ACCESS TO SECRET EXCULPATORY TESTIMONY

United States v. Moussaoui

United States Court of Appeals, Fourth Circuit, 2004
365 F.3d 292, *amended on reh'g*, 382 F.3d 453,
cert. denied, 544 U.S. 931 (2005)

[Zacarias Moussaoui was arrested before the 9/11 attacks, then later indicted for acts in connection with those attacks. The government sought the death penalty on several of these charges. Subsequently, Witness **** (asterisks are used by the court to indicate redacted material), a suspected member of al Qaeda, was captured by the United States. Moussaoui moved for access to Witness ****, asserting that the witness would be an important part of his defense. Ultimately, he sought access from two additional witnesses in U.S. custody. The government opposed these requests.

The District Court found that the requested witnesses were material witnesses who might support Moussaoui's claim that he was not involved in the 9/11 attacks and that he should not receive the death penalty if convicted. It ordered their deposition by remote video, but the government appealed. The Court of Appeals remanded for the District Court to determine whether any substitution existed that would place Moussaoui in substantially the same position as would a deposition. The District Court rejected the government's proposed substitutions and again ordered deposition of the witnesses. When the government refused to comply with this order, the District Court dismissed the death notice and prohibited the government "from making any argument, or offering any evidence, suggesting that the defendant had any involvement in, or knowledge of, the September 11 attacks." This appeal followed.]

WILLIAM W. WILKINS, Chief Judge: . . .

III. . . .

A. Process Power

The Sixth Amendment guarantees that "[i]n all criminal prosecutions, the accused shall enjoy the right . . . to have compulsory process for obtaining witnesses in his favor." U.S. Const. amend. VI. The compulsory process right is circumscribed, however, by the ability of the district court to obtain the presence of a witness through service of process. The Government maintains that because the enemy combatant witnesses are foreign nationals outside the boundaries of the United States, they are beyond the process power of the district court and, hence, unavailable to Moussaoui. . . .

The Government's argument overlooks the critical fact that the enemy combatant witnesses are in the custody of an official of the United States Government. Therefore, we are concerned not with the ability of the district court to issue a subpoena to the witnesses, but rather with its power to issue a writ of habeas corpus *ad testificandum* ("testimonial writ") to the witnesses' custodian. . . .

[The court found that Secretary Rumsfeld was the proper custodian and that he was within the process power of the district court.]

IV.

The Government next argues that even if the district court would otherwise have the power to order the production of the witnesses, the January 30 and August 29 orders are improper because they infringe on the Executive's warmaking authority, in violation of separation of powers principles. . . .

B. Governing Principles . . .

This is not a case involving arrogation of the powers or duties of another branch. The district court orders requiring production of the enemy combatant witnesses involved the resolution of questions properly—indeed, exclusively—reserved to the judiciary. Therefore, if there is a separation of powers problem at all, it arises only from the burden the actions of the district court place on the Executive's performance of its duties.

The Supreme Court has explained on several occasions that determining whether a judicial act places impermissible burdens on another branch of government requires balancing the competing interests. *See, e.g., Nixon v. Admin'r of Gen. Servs.*, 433 U.S. 425, 443 (1977). . . .

C. Balancing

1. The Burden on the Government

The Constitution charges the Congress and the Executive with the making and conduct of war. It is not an exaggeration to state that the effective performance of these duties is essential to our continued existence as a sovereign nation. Indeed, "no governmental interest is more compelling than the security of the Nation." *Haig v. Agee*, 453 U.S. 280, 307 (1981). . . .

The Government alleges—and we accept as true—that **** the enemy combatant witnesses is critical to the ongoing effort to combat terrorism by al Qaeda. The witnesses are al Qaeda operatives **** Their value as intelligence sources can hardly be overstated. And, we must defer to the Government's assertion that interruption **** will have devastating effects on the ability to gather information from them. ****, it is not unreasonable to suppose that interruption **** could result in the loss of information that might prevent future terrorist attacks.

The Government also asserts that production of the witnesses would burden the Executive's ability to conduct foreign relations. The Government claims that if the Executive's assurances of confidentiality can be abrogated by the judiciary, the vital ability to obtain the cooperation of other governments will be devastated.

The Government also reminds us of the bolstering effect production of the witnesses might have on our enemies. . . . For example, al Qaeda operatives are trained to disrupt the legal process in whatever manner possible; indications that such techniques may be successful will only cause a redoubling of their efforts.

In summary, the burdens that would arise from production of the enemy combatant witnesses are substantial.

2. Moussaoui's Interest

The importance of the Sixth Amendment right to compulsory process is not subject to question—it is integral to our adversarial criminal justice system:

> The need to develop all relevant facts in the adversary system is both fundamental and comprehensive. The ends of criminal justice would be defeated if judgments were to be founded on a partial or speculative presentation of the facts. The very integrity of the judicial system and public confidence in the system depend on full disclosure of all the facts, within the framework of the rules of evidence. To ensure that justice is done, it is imperative to the function of the courts that compulsory process be available for the production of evidence needed either by the prosecution or by the defense.

United States v. Nixon, 418 U.S. 683, 709 (1974).

The compulsory process right does not attach to any witness the defendant wishes to call, however. Rather, a defendant must demonstrate that the witness he desires to have produced would testify "in his favor." Thus, in order to assess Moussaoui's interest, we must determine whether the enemy combatant witnesses could provide testimony material to Moussaoui's defense.

In the CIPA context,[12] we have adopted the standard articulated by the Supreme Court in *Roviaro v. United States*, 353 U.S. 53 (1957), for determining whether the government's privilege in classified information must give way. Under that standard, a defendant becomes entitled to disclosure of classified information upon a showing that the information " 'is relevant and helpful to the defense . . . or is essential to a fair

---

12. We adhere to our prior ruling that CIPA does not apply because the January 30 and August 29 orders of the district court are not covered by either of the potentially relevant provisions of CIPA: §4 (concerning deletion of classified information from *documents* to be turned over to the defendant during discovery) or §6 (concerning the disclosure of classified information by the defense during pretrial or trial proceedings). *See Moussaoui I*, 333 F.3d [509, 514-515 (4th Cir. 2003).] Like the district court, however, we believe that CIPA provides a useful framework for considering the questions raised by Moussaoui's request for access to the enemy combatant witnesses.

determination of a cause.' " [*United States v. Smith*, 780 F.2d 1102 (4th Cir. 1985)], at 1107 (quoting *Roviaro*, 353 U.S. at 60-61).

Because Moussaoui has not had — and will not receive — direct access to any of the witnesses, he cannot be required to show materiality with the degree of specificity that applies in the ordinary case. Rather, it is sufficient if Moussaoui can make a "plausible showing" of materiality. However, in determining whether Moussaoui has made a plausible showing, we must bear in mind that Moussaoui *does* have access to the **** summaries. . . .

. . . [T]he Government argues that even if the witnesses' testimony would tend to exonerate Moussaoui of involvement in the September 11 attacks, such testimony would not be material because the conspiracies with which Moussaoui is charged are broader than September 11. Thus, the Government argues, Moussaoui can be convicted even if he lacked any prior knowledge of September 11. This argument ignores the principle that the scope of an alleged conspiracy is a jury question, and the possibility that Moussaoui may assert that the conspiracy culminating in the September 11 attacks was distinct from any conspiracy in which he was involved. Moreover, even if the jury accepts the Government's claims regarding the scope of the charged conspiracy, testimony regarding Moussaoui's non-involvement in September 11 is critical to the penalty phase. If Moussaoui had no involvement in or knowledge of September 11, it is entirely possible that he would not be found eligible for the death penalty.

We now consider the rulings of the district court regarding the ability of each witness to provide material testimony in Moussaoui's favor.

The district court did not err in concluding that Witness **** could offer material evidence on Moussaoui's behalf. **** Several statements by Witness **** tend to exculpate Moussaoui. For example, the **** summaries state that **** This statement tends to undermine the theory (which the Government may or may not intend to advance at trial) that Moussaoui was to pilot a fifth plane into the White House. Witness **** has also **** This statement is significant in light of other evidence **** indicating that Moussaoui had no contact with any of the hijackers. **** This is consistent with Moussaoui's claim that he was to be part of a post-September 11 operation. . . .

. . . Moussaoui has made a sufficient showing that evidence from Witness **** would be more helpful than hurtful, or at least that we cannot have confidence in the outcome of the trial without Witness **** evidence. . . .

3. Balancing

Having considered the burden alleged by the Government and the right claimed by Moussaoui, we now turn to the question of whether the district court should have refrained from acting in light of the national security interests asserted by the Government. The question is not unique; the Supreme Court has addressed similar matters on numerous occasions. In all cases of this type — cases falling into "what might loosely be called the area of constitutionally guaranteed access to evidence," *Arizona v. Youngblood*, 488 U.S. 51, 55 (1988) (internal quotation marks omitted) — the Supreme Court has held that the defendant's right to a trial that comports with the Fifth and Sixth Amendments prevails over the governmental privilege. Ultimately, as these cases make clear, the appropriate procedure is for the district court to order production of the evidence or witness and leave to the Government the choice of whether to comply with that order. If the government refuses to produce the information at issue — as it may properly do — the result is ordinarily dismissal. . . .

In addition to the pronouncements of the Supreme Court in this area, we are also mindful of Congress' judgment, expressed in CIPA, that the Executive's interest in protecting classified information does not overcome a defendant's right to present his case. Under CIPA, once the district court determines that an item of classified information is relevant and material, that item must be admitted unless the government provides an adequate substitution. If no adequate substitution can be found, the government must decide whether it will prohibit the disclosure of the classified information; if it does so, the district court must impose a sanction, which is presumptively dismissal of the indictment.

In view of these authorities, it is clear that when an evidentiary privilege — even one that involves national security — is asserted by the Government in the context of its prosecution of a criminal offense, the "balancing" we must conduct is primarily, if not solely, an examination of whether the district court correctly determined that the information the Government seeks to withhold is material to the defense. We have determined that the enemy combatant witnesses can offer material testimony that is essential to Moussaoui's defense, and we therefore affirm the January 30 and August 29 orders. Thus, the choice is the Government's whether to comply with those orders or suffer a sanction.

V.

As noted previously, the Government has stated that it will not produce the enemy combatant witnesses for depositions (or, we presume, for any other purpose related to this litigation). We are thus left in the following situation: the district court has the power to order production of the enemy combatant witnesses and has properly determined that they could offer material testimony on Moussaoui's behalf, but the Government has refused to produce the witnesses. Under such circumstances, dismissal of the indictment is the usual course. Like the district court, however, we believe that a more measured approach is required. Additionally, we emphasize that no punitive sanction is warranted here because the Government has rightfully exercised its prerogative to protect national security interests by refusing to produce the witnesses.

Although, as explained above, this is not a CIPA case, that act nevertheless provides useful guidance in determining the nature of the remedies that may be available. Under CIPA, dismissal of an indictment is authorized only if the government has failed to produce an adequate substitute for the classified information, and the interests of justice would not be served by imposition of a lesser sanction. CIPA thus enjoins district courts to seek a solution that neither disadvantages the defendant nor penalizes the government (and the public) for protecting classified information that may be vital to national security.

A similar approach is appropriate here. Under such an approach, the first question is whether there is any appropriate substitution for the witnesses' testimony. Because we conclude, for the reasons set forth below, that appropriate substitutions are available, we need not consider any other remedy. . . .

C. Instructions

. . . [W]e conclude that the district court erred in ruling that any substitution for the witnesses' testimony is inherently inadequate to the extent it is derived from the **** reports. To the contrary, we hold that the **** summaries (which, as the district court determined, accurately recapitulate the **** reports) provide an adequate basis for the creation of written statements that may be submitted to the jury in lieu of the witnesses' deposition testimony.

The crafting of substitutions is a task best suited to the district court, given its greater familiarity with the facts of the case and its authority to manage the presentation of evidence. Nevertheless, we think it is appropriate to provide some guidance to the court and the parties.

First, the circumstances of this case — most notably, the fact that the substitutions may very well support Moussaoui's defense — dictate that the crafting of substitutions be an interactive process among the parties and the district court. Second, we think that accuracy and fairness are best achieved by crafting substitutions that use the exact language of the **** summaries to the greatest extent possible. We believe that the best means of achieving both of these objectives is for defense counsel to identify particular portions of the **** summaries that Moussaoui may want to admit into evidence at trial. The Government may then argue that additional portions must be included in the interest of completeness . . . . If the substitutions are to be admitted at all (we leave open the possibility that Moussaoui may decide not to use the substitutions in his defense), they may be admitted only by Moussaoui. Based on defense counsel's submissions and the Government's objections, the district court could then create an appropriate set of substitutions. . . .

As previously indicated, the jury must be provided with certain information regarding the substitutions. While we leave the particulars of the instructions to the district court, the jury must be informed, at a minimum, that the substitutions are what the witnesses would say if called to testify; that the substitutions are derived from statements obtained under conditions that provide circumstantial guarantees of reliability; that the substitutions contain statements obtained **** ; and that neither the parties nor the district court has ever had access to the witnesses. . . .

Affirmed in part, vacated in part, and remanded.

[The opinions of WILLIAMS, Circuit Judge, and GREGORY, Circuit Judge, each concurring in part and dissenting in part, are omitted.]

NOTES AND QUESTIONS

1. *Deciding a Clash Between Branches: Formalism or Balancing?* The court concluded that the appropriate separation of powers analysis required by Moussaoui's insistence on access to **** is balancing, as prescribed by *Nixon v. Administrator of General Services*, 433 U.S. 425, 443 (1977) (stating that "the proper inquiry focuses on the extent to which [the judicial act of ordering access, in this instance] prevents the Executive Branch from accomplishing its constitutionally assigned functions, . . . [and whether] that impact is justified by an overriding need to promote objectives within the constitutional authority of [the court]"). See *supra* p. 48. But in *Public Citizen v. United States Department of Justice*, 491 U.S. 440, 485 (1989), noted *supra* p. 46, Justice Kennedy indicated that there is "a line of cases of equal weight and authority, . . . where the Constitution by explicit text commits the power at issue to the exclusive control of the President, . . . [and the Court has] refused to tolerate *any* intrusion by

[the courts]." Why is *Moussaoui* not controlled by the latter line of cases? Doesn't the Commander in Chief Clause of Article II commit command of the armed forces in war to the President, and isn't the interrogation of enemy combatants in war part of that command? Does *Hamdi, supra* p. 831, or *Padilla, supra* p. 855, suggest any answers to these questions?

What other cases would you rely on in making the formalist argument for the government, or, by a balancing analysis, in arguing the extent to which court-ordered access to ****. would prevent the President from conducting the war? In this regard, consider *Keith, supra* p. 559, *Korematsu, supra* p. 812, and *Zadvydas, supra* p. 736, Note 1. If the *Moussaoui* jury had been the target of serious threats of harm, how would you balance his Sixth Amendment right to trial by jury against the government's interest in protecting jurors by empaneling them secretly in a secure location to hear the trial by video?

2. *CIPA by Analogy.* In deciding the alternatives, the court determined that CIPA (see *supra* p. 1018) did not apply but relied on it anyway for a "useful framework." *See also United States v. Paracha,* No. 03 CR. 1197(SHS), 2006 WL 12768 (S.D.N.Y. Jan. 3, 2006) (using CIPA by analogy to impose *Moussaoui*-type solution to terror defendant's demand for access to witnesses in U.S. custody in Afghanistan), *aff'd,* 313 Fed. App'x 347 (2d Cir. 2008). Why did CIPA not apply? By what authority did the court undertake the relevance and balancing inquiries and order access to the summaries? Did the court, in effect, create a "wartime exception" to the Sixth Amendment after all? Is this another example of what Justice Scalia condemned as the "Mr. Fix-It Mentality" of courts? If CIPA is to be amended to cover the *Moussaoui* problem, why not leave that job to Congress?

3. *Switching Forums?* The district court invited the government to "reconsider whether the civilian criminal courts are the appropriate fora" for trying someone like Moussaoui. *United States v. Moussaoui,* No. Cr-01-455-A, 2003 WL 21263699, at *6 (E.D. Va. Mar. 10, 2003). The alternative is trial by military commission, which we explore in Chapter 36. Indeed, even Moussaoui's standby counsel appears to have invited this alternative, gratuitously conceding that the government's authority to try enemy combatants by military commission is "settled," and implying that the government can simply dismiss the criminal prosecution and proceed instead by a military commission to resolve the tension between Moussaoui's Sixth Amendment rights and the war powers. Brief of the Appellee at 3-4, *United States v. Moussaoui,* No. 03-4162 (4th Cir. May 13, 2003).

After you read the materials on military commissions, you can decide for yourself whether this was a wise concession. Do you agree with the apparent assumption upon which that concession and the District Court's invitation rested — that the government can switch forums in midstream? Even assuming that the government could lawfully have tried Moussaoui by military commission *ab initio,* does it necessarily follow that the government may start in a civilian court and then dismiss in favor of a military commission when it is unhappy with the civilian court's rulings? Would it matter how far the criminal prosecution had progressed beyond the indictment? If such a switch survived constitutional challenges, would it nevertheless violate the spirit of the law?

The government did, in fact, make a switch — actually a triple switch — in *Al-Marri v. Hanft,* 378 F. Supp. 2d 673 (D.S.C. 2005), noted *supra* p. 858. After al-Marri lawfully entered the United States with his family to obtain a master's degree, he was initially arrested as a material witness in the 9/11 investigation. In the first switch, he was then rearrested and indicted for making false statements and for credit card fraud. More than two years later, President Bush interrupted the course of normal criminal proceedings (trial had not yet begun) by designating al-Marri an enemy combatant, after which he was transferred to military detention in South Carolina in the government's second switch. The government then successfully moved to drop the criminal indictment with prejudice.

Al-Marri argued that his criminal detention was sufficient to thwart any terrorist acts and that there was no necessity for military detention. The district court rejected his argument in part on the reasoning from case law asserting that when a federal investigation of criminal charges pending in state court reveals a federal crime, the state charges can be dismissed and the matter can be transferred to federal jurisdiction. *Id.* at 681. Is the analogy sound?

Al-Marri also protested that while he might have been acquitted of the criminal charges, he had no opportunity to prove his innocence in military detention. The court rejected this claim as well, reasoning that the purpose of military detention is preventive.

> This Court recognizes the natural response to this reasoning that, when a defendant is acquitted of criminal charges, society should not assume that he ever did nor that he will, in the future, engage in the activities for which he was charged. In this case, however, Petitioner was not charged with crimes of terrorism, and thus, an acquittal of various fraud charges does not lead to the conclusion that he will not, in the future, engage in acts of terrorism as alleged by the government.

Id. at 681 n.8.

As we saw in Chapter 30, after the Court of Appeals later divided sharply on the legality of al-Marri's detention as an enemy combatant and the adequacy of the procedure afforded him in deciding his status, the government switched forums for the third time, indicting al-Marri again. This time al-Marri entered a guilty plea to one count of conspiracy to provide material support to a foreign terrorist organization.

4. *Guilty Plea and Sentence.* On April 22, 2005, Moussaoui surprised everyone by pleading guilty to the key charges against him, while at the same time denying having any intention to commit mass murder. *See Moussaoui Pleads Guilty to Terror Charges* (CNN.com, Apr. 23, 2005), *at* http://www.cnn.com/2005/LAW/04/22/moussaoui/index.html. He was subsequently sentenced to life in prison. *United States v. Moussaoui*, No. 1:01CR00455-001, Judgment in a Criminal Case at 2 (E.D. Va. May 14, 2006).

5. *A Military Brig—the Better Forum?* The following assessment was written before the conclusion of the Moussaoui trial.

> The United States should drop all criminal charges against Zacarias Moussaoui, not because he is innocent, but because he is a foreign citizen who is (or was) a terrorist bent on killing innocent Americans, destroying American property, and disrupting American society. For less than a nanosecond, Moussaoui should be a free man again....
>
> Before the nanosecond of Moussaoui's freedom ends, he should be transferred to the custody of the United States Department of Defense. After that, based on

recommendations coordinated by the National Security Council (NSC) for the President, the Executive Branch should implement a well-conceived decision about Moussaoui's next address. The NSC, rather than a particular United States agency, such as the Justice Department or the Defense Department, is the appropriate forum to vet such policies because they transcend the boundaries between domestic and international spheres, going beyond law enforcement and military issues. . . . The President, in making this decision on Moussaoui's next address, should consider our relations with foreign countries and the safety of our homeland. But whatever happens to Moussaoui, he did not — and does not — belong in criminal custody. [John Radsan, *The Moussaoui Case: The Mess from Minnesota*, 31 Wm. Mitchell L. Rev. 1417, 1417-1419 (2005).]

Do you agree? Did the system work? Or was the system distorted to accommodate national security? Do you think accused terrorists like Moussaoui and al-Marri should be tried by military commissions (a subject to which we turn in the next chapter)?

D. COERCED EVIDENCE

United States v. Ghailani

United States District Court, Southern District of New York, 2010
751 F. Supp. 2d 502

LEWIS A. KAPLAN, District Judge. Ahmed Khalfan Ghailani, an alleged member of Al Qaeda, was indicted in this Court in 1998 and charged with conspiring with Usama Bin Laden and others to kill Americans abroad by, among other means, bombing the United States Embassies in Nairobi, Kenya, and Dar es Salaam, Tanzania, bombings in which 224 people reportedly were killed. Years later, he was captured abroad by a foreign state and subsequently turned over to the Central Intelligence Agency ("CIA"). He was held and interrogated by the CIA at one or more secret locations outside the United States for a substantial period. He then was shifted to a secure facility at the United States naval base at Guantanamo where he remained until June 2009, at which time he was produced in this Court for prosecution on the indictment. Ghailani now moves to dismiss the indictment on the ground that he was tortured by the CIA in violation of his rights under the Due Process Clause of the Constitution.

I . . .

In this case, Ghailani has not identified explicitly the component of his due process rights that allegedly was violated. But he argues that both the CIA's use of "enhanced interrogation techniques" — in his word, torture — to question him and the fact that use of those techniques was authorized by "the highest levels of our government" are "'so fundamentally unfair,' 'shocking to our traditional sense of justice,' and 'outrageous'" that due process requires the indictment to be dismissed. He thereby invokes substantive rather than procedural due process.

The government does not here respond to Ghailani's assertions as to what was done to him while in CIA custody. Nor does it join issue on the question whether those assertions, if true, violated Ghailani's right to due process of law. Rather, it argues that Ghailani's allegations of pretrial custodial abuse are immaterial to this motion because dismissal of the indictment would not be a proper remedy for the government's alleged misconduct. In other words, the government argues that there is no legally significant connection between the alleged torture and any deprivation of the defendant's liberty that might result from this criminal prosecution.

If the government is correct in contending that Ghailani would not be entitled to dismissal of this criminal prosecution on due process grounds even if he was tortured in violation of his constitutional rights, it would be unnecessary for this Court to address the details of Ghailani's alleged treatment while in CIA custody. Nor in that event would it be appropriate to express any opinion as to whether that treatment violated his right to due process of law. The Court therefore passes directly to consideration of the government's argument.

II

The Due Process Clause, so far as is relevant here, protects against deprivations of liberty absent due process of law. The deprivation of liberty that Ghailani claims may occur if this case goes forward is his imprisonment in the event of conviction. In seeking dismissal of the indictment, however, he does not deny that he is being afforded every protection guaranteed to all in the defense of criminal prosecutions. Rather, Ghailani in effect argues that the case should be dismissed to punish the government for its mistreatment of him before he was presented in this Court to face the pending indictment.

For a due process violation to result in consequences adverse to the government in a criminal case—for example, the suppression of evidence or the dismissal of an indictment—there must be a causal connection between the violation and the deprivation of the defendant's life or liberty threatened by the prosecution. That is to say, relief against the government in a criminal case is appropriate if, and only if, a conviction otherwise would be a product of the government misconduct that violated the Due Process Clause. For only in such circumstances may it be said that the deprivation of life or liberty that follows from a criminal conviction flows from the denial of due process. This conclusion thus rests directly on the text of the Due Process Clause itself.

This point finds support also in the Supreme Court's consistent holdings that illegality in arresting or obtaining custody of a defendant does not strip a court of jurisdiction to try that defendant. "An illegal arrest, without more, has never been viewed as a bar to subsequent prosecution, nor as a defense to a valid conviction."

This doctrine, better known as the *Ker-Frisbie* rule,[14] dates back well over a century and "rests on the sound basis that due process of law is satisfied when one present in court is convicted of a crime after being fairly apprized of the charges against him and after a fair trial in accordance with constitutional procedural safeguards."[15] The Court repeatedly has reaffirmed this doctrine even as the concept of substantive due process has expanded. Moreover, the Court explicitly has refused to adopt an exclusionary rule that would operate on the defendant's person:

"Our numerous precedents ordering the exclusion of such illegally obtained evidence assume implicitly that the remedy does not extend to barring the prosecution altogether. So drastic a step might advance marginally some of the ends served by exclusionary rules,

---

14. *See Ker v. Illinois,* 119 U.S. 436 (1886); *Frisbie v. Collins,* 342 U.S. 519 (1952).
15. *Frisbie,* 342 U.S. at 522.

but it would also increase to an intolerable degree interference with the public interest in having the guilty brought to book."[17]

"[A defendant] is not himself a suppressible "fruit," and the illegality of his detention cannot deprive the Government of the opportunity to prove his guilt through the introduction of evidence wholly untainted by the police misconduct."[18] Rather, the proper remedy is money damages or criminal prosecution of the offending officers.

This case follows *a fortiori* from the rationale of the *Ker-Frisbie* rule. Ghailani is charged here with complicity in the murder of 224 people. The government here has stated that it will not use anything that Ghailani said while in CIA custody, or the fruits of any such statement, in this prosecution. In consequence, any deprivation of liberty that Ghailani might suffer as a result of a conviction in this case would be entirely unconnected to the alleged due process violation. Even if Ghailani was mistreated while in CIA custody and even if that mistreatment violated the Due Process Clause, there would be no connection between such mistreatment and this prosecution. If, as *Ker-Frisbie* holds, the illegal arrest of a defendant is not sufficiently related to a prosecution to warrant its dismissal, it necessarily follows that mistreatment of a defendant is not sufficient to justify dismissal where, as here, the connection between the alleged misconduct and the prosecution is non-existent or, at least, even more remote. Certainly the government should not be deprived here "of the opportunity to prove his guilt through the introduction of evidence wholly untainted by [any government] misconduct."[21] Any remedy for any such violation must be found outside the confines of this criminal case.

United States v. Toscanino[22] is not to the contrary. The defendant in that case allegedly was brought before the trial court as a result of being abducted and tortured by government agents, conduct that he claimed violated his right to due process of law. Upon conviction, he appealed on the ground that the agents' actions violated his right to due process and that the district court's jurisdiction over him was a product of that violation. The Second Circuit reversed the conviction and remanded to enable the defendant to attempt to prove that the agents' conduct was sufficiently outrageous to have violated the Due Process Clause. But *Toscanino* does not support Ghailani here.

As an initial matter, *Toscanino* was concerned with "denying the government the fruits of its exploitation of any deliberate and unnecessary lawlessness on its part." To whatever extent it is authoritative, a subject discussed below, the case is limited to situations in which the alleged outrageous government conduct brought the defendant within the court's jurisdiction, and thus was a but-for cause of any resulting conviction, and compromised the fairness and integrity of the criminal proceedings. There is no similar connection between Ghailani's alleged mistreatment while in CIA custody and this prosecution. Hence, to whatever extent that *Toscanino* remains viable, it does not apply here.

Second, as suggested already, it is doubtful that *Toscanino* remains authoritative. Several circuits have expressed doubt as to its continued viability in light of subsequent Supreme Court decisions. Moreover, the Second Circuit itself subsequently has

---

17. *United States v. Blue*, 384 U.S. 251, 255 (1966).
18. *United States v. Crews*, 445 U.S. 463, 474 (1980).
21. *Crews*, 445 U.S. at 474.
22. 500 F.2d 267 (2d Cir. 1974).

relied heavily on the *Ker-Frisbie* rule in deciding a case very similar to the one currently before this Court.

In *Brown v. Doe*,[27] a defendant convicted of felony murder and robbery in state court sought federal habeas corpus relief on the ground, *inter alia,* that his substantive due process rights had been violated by repeated brutal beatings by police following his arrest. He alleged that this pretrial custodial abuse "was so outrageous and so offensive to due process of law that it bar[red] his prosecution and require[d] dismissal of the indictment."[29]

In affirming the district court's denial of relief, the Second Circuit held that the Due Process Clause was the appropriate source of constitutional protection against the alleged pretrial abuse, but it concluded that the requested remedy was inappropriate. In light of the *Ker-Frisbie* line of cases, the court reasoned that "if there is no authority for barring the prosecution of a defendant who was illegally taken into custody, we are in no position to strip New York State of its power to try a defendant...who was lawfully arrested and convicted on untainted evidence."[30] Moreover, "the wrong committed by the police has its own remedies. It is unnecessary to remedy that wrong by absolving [petitioner] of his own crime, and there is no interest of justice served by a result in which the community suffers two unpunished wrongs."[31] The court concluded that "[t]he remedy of dismissal is not required to vindicate [petitioner's] due process rights. Other and more appropriate remedies are available," potentially including civil remedies under 42 U.S.C. §1983 and criminal prosecution of the police who assaulted him.[32]

Brown confirms this Court's view that *Toscanino,* if it retains any force, does so only where the defendant's presence before the trial court is procured by methods that offend the Due Process Clause. Dismissal of the indictment in the absence of a constitutional violation affecting the fairness of the criminal adjudication itself is unwarranted.

CONCLUSION

If, as Ghailani claims, he was tortured in violation of the Due Process Clause, he may have remedies. For the reasons set forth above, however, those remedies do not include dismissal of the indictment. The defendant's motion to dismiss the indictment on the grounds of allegedly outrageous government conduct in violation of his Fifth Amendment due process right is denied.

So ordered.

---

27. 2 F.3d 1236 (2d Cir. 1993).
29. *Id.* at 1242.
30. *Id.* at 1243.
31. *Id.*
32. *Id.*

United States v. Ghailani

United States District Court, Southern District of New York, 2010
743 F. Supp. 2d 261

LEWIS A. KAPLAN, District Judge. The question presented by this motion is whether the government may use in this criminal trial the testimony of a witness whom the government obtained only through information it allegedly extracted by physical and psychological abuse of the defendant. The government has elected not to litigate the details of what was done to the defendant. Instead, it has asked the Court to assume for purposes of the motion that everything the defendant said was coerced in violation of the Fifth Amendment. Accordingly, this decision, at the government's behest, proceeds on that premise. . . .

Ghailani eventually was apprehended in 2004 and turned over to the CIA. The CIA put him in a secret prison outside the United States and subjected him to so-called enhanced interrogation methods and other allegedly abusive treatment. It interrogated him in the secret prison for [REDACTED] Over time, Ghailani gave the CIA the information that led the government directly to Hussein Abebe "[REDACTED]

The government now proposes to call Abebe as a witness against Ghailani. Ghailani moves to preclude the government from doing so. He argues that the government's identification of Abebe and his procurement as a witness flowed directly from statements that he made under duress and that the receipt of Abebe's testimony would violate the Constitution.

The Fifth Amendment states that "[n]o person shall be compelled in any criminal case to be a witness against himself." But it does more. "When an incriminating statement has been obtained through coercion, the Fifth Amendment prohibits use of the statement or its 'fruits'"[2] — that is to say, evidence derived from any statement coerced from the defendant — unless the evidence "has been come at . . . instead by means sufficiently distinguishable to be purged of the primary taint."[3] The government nevertheless argues that Abebe's testimony should be received because it is "attenuated" from the coercion to which Ghailani was subjected. It maintains that Abebe is willing to testify against Ghailani of his own free will, that Ghailani's coerced statements to the CIA played no part in securing Abebe's cooperation, and that the CIA was not motivated in its interrogation of Ghailani by any desire to obtain evidence for use against him in a criminal case. The Court finds that the government has not sustained its burden.

The temptation to allow our revulsion at these bombings, the human instinct for vengeance, and fear of terrorist attacks to overcome principles upon which our nation rests — principles that, although not always observed, are ideals to which we aspire — is powerful. If our nation is to continue as a bastion of liberty, however, we must remain true to our principles and overcome that temptation.

Among those principles is that which has been traced to Deuteronomy, that grew gradually through the long history of English law and in the American colonies, and that then was embodied in the Self Incrimination Clause in the Fifth Amendment. While the connection between fruits of a coerced statement — that is to say, evidence derived from a statement coerced from a defendant — may be so remote, so attenuated, from the coerced statement that the use of that derivative evidence does not

---

2. *Pillsbury Co. v. Conboy*, 459 U.S. 248, 278 (1983).
3. *Wong Sun v. United States*, 371 U.S. 471, 488 (1963).

violate the Fifth Amendment, the burden of proving attenuation is on the government.

In this case, the link between the CIA's coercion of Ghailani and Abebe's testimony is direct and close. Based on an extensive record, the Court's assessment of the credibility of witnesses the government called at the suppression hearing, and the lack of credible evidence to support key aspects of the government's argument, the government has not carried its burden of proving that Abebe's testimony would be so attenuated from Ghailani's coerced statements to permit its use. The motion to preclude Abebe's testimony is granted. . . .

[Substantial parts of the court's account of the facts are redacted with this note in the published opinion: "Text and associated footnote references redacted by government authorities in accordance with the Classified Information Procedures Act."]

II. THE EARLIER RULING . . .

To recapitulate briefly, illegally obtained evidence — including statements made by a defendant under government coercion — and the fruits of such evidence generally are not admissible against the defendant in a criminal trial. Nevertheless, the fruits of illegally obtained evidence are admissible where, insofar as remains relevant here, the government proves that the connection between the illegal government action and the evidence offered at trial — here, Abebe's testimony — is "so attenuated as to dissipate the taint." The ultimate question now before this Court therefore is whether the government has established that the connection between Abebe's testimony and Ghailani's unlawfully coerced statements is so remote as to permit Abebe to testify. . . .

III. ATTENUATION . . .

C. The Balance . . .

The government's strongest argument remains that related to deterrence. It initially contended that the CIA was motivated entirely by intelligence objectives and that exclusion here consequently would serve no deterrent purpose. Put another way, the suggestion was that the CIA would have done exactly the same thing irrespective of any law enforcement interest in prosecuting Ghailani.

The Court accepts that [REDACTED] Whether that means that absolutely no deterrent purpose would be served by suppression of Abebe's testimony here, however, is another matter in light of [REDACTED] And regardless of whether that is the case, deterrence is but one of the pertinent considerations.

In the last analysis, this Court concludes that exclusion of Abebe's testimony would be required here even if the government had identified and found him in otherwise comparable circumstances as a result of an illegal search or seizure, this notwithstanding the relative lack of deterrence of exclusion in these circumstances. If this were a search and seizure case, the relationship between the unlawful conduct and the identification and location would be just as close. Abebe's reluctance to testify and the fear of the authorities that nevertheless moves him to testify would be just as palpable. The government's failure to prove that the illegally seized evidence played no role in securing his cooperation would be just as glaring as [it is] here. These considerations would overcome the facts that the illegal search or seizure would have been a completed historical event and that the deterrent effect of exclusion, if any, would be considerably less than a certainty. But, it bears emphasis, this is not a Fourth Amendment search and seizure case. Hence, two factors make the case for exclusion here much stronger than if it were.

First, as this is a Fifth Amendment case, the receipt in evidence of Abebe's testimony itself would constitute a violation of the self-executing exclusionary rule inherent in the Constitution, not a matter of compliance with a purely utilitarian judge-made rule that was created in the twentieth century only to deter illegal searches and seizures.

Second, the deterrence analysis, which for reasons previously explained is of less importance here than in a Fourth Amendment case, is somewhat different. The CIA, acting upon the highest authority, used coercive methods to gain intelligence. This Court has declined to this point to express an opinion on the constitutionality of such methods, considered in and of themselves. It declines to do so now because that issue is not before it. What is before it, however, is the question whether the Fifth Amendment — which provides that "[n]o person . . . shall be compelled in any criminal case to be a witness against himself" — is violated if a Court receives in a criminal trial evidence that is the fruit of statements coerced from the defendant, at least where the relationship between the coerced statements and the evidence is [as] close as it is here. . . .

IV. CONCLUSION

In all the circumstances, this Court holds that the receipt in evidence of Abebe's testimony would violate the Fifth Amendment.[182] If the government is going to coerce a detainee to provide information to our intelligence agencies, it may not use that evidence — or fruits of that evidence that are tied as closely related to the coerced statements as Abebe's testimony would be here — to prosecute the detainee for a criminal offense. On these facts, the public interest in "making available to the trier of fact all concededly relevant and trustworthy evidence" is outweighed by the public and private interests protected by exclusion. The motion to preclude Abebe as a witness in this case is granted.

As the Court noted in its summary order dated October 5, 2010, it has not reached this conclusion lightly. It is acutely aware of the perilous world in which we live. But we must adhere to the basic principles that govern our nation not only when it is convenient to do so, but when perceived expediency tempts some to pursue a different course. The government may continue its prosecution of Ghailani without using this evidence. It probably may detain him as an enemy combatant as long as the present hostilities continue. What it cannot do is to use Abebe's testimony in its otherwise perfectly appropriate prosecution to convict him of the crimes with which he is charged.

The defendant's motion to preclude Hussein Abebe from testifying at trial is granted. The foregoing as well as the Court's previous opinion on this motion are the Court's findings of fact and conclusions of law.

So ordered.

---

182. It is very far from clear that Abebe's testimony would be admissible if Ghailani were being tried by military commission, even without regard to the question whether the Fifth Amendment would invalidate any more forgiving provisions of the rules of evidence otherwise applicable in such a proceeding. [These rules] . . . preclude or restrict the use of "statements obtained by torture or cruel, inhuman, or degrading treatment," and evidence derived therefrom, and could require exclusion of Abebe's testimony. Even if they did not, the Constitution might do so, even in a military commission proceeding.

NOTES AND QUESTIONS

1. *The Ker-Frisbie Doctrine.* As the court notes, the Supreme Court has declared that how a criminal defendant is brought to the court does not affect the court's jurisdiction over him. The *Ker-Frisbie* doctrine opened the door to abductions of suspects abroad (by a process sometimes called "informal rendition" — the converse of "extraordinary rendition" discussed in Chapter 33).

But *Toscanino* seemed to limit the *Ker-Frisbie* doctrine by refusing to exercise jurisdiction over a defendant who had been abducted by force that "shocked the conscience." See *supra* p. 1053. How does the court in *Ghailani* distinguish *Toscanino*?

2. *Using Ghailani's Coerced Testimony Directly.* Suppose Ghailani confessed during his alleged torture. Would his coerced confession be admissible against him? The courts have traditionally excluded involuntary confessions for two reasons. First,

> because the methods used to extract them offend an underlying principle in the enforcement of our criminal law: that ours is an accusatorial and not an inquisitorial system — a system in which the State must establish guilt by evidence independently and freely secured and may not by coercion prove its charge against an accused out of his own mouth. "A coerced confession is offensive to basic standards of justice, not because the victim has a legal grievance against the police, but because declarations procured by torture are not premises from which a civilized forum will infer guilt." *Lyons* [*v. Okla-homa*], 322 U.S. [596, 605 (1944)]. [*United States v. Karake*, 443 F. Supp. 2d 8, 50 (D.D.C. 2006).]

Second, involuntary confessions may be untrue. "[W]hile a confession obtained by means of torture may be excluded on due process grounds as '[in]consistent with the fundamental principles of liberty and justice which lie at the base of all our civil and political institutions,' *Brown v. Mississippi*, 297 U.S. 278, 286 (1936), another legitimate reason to suppress it is the 'likelihood that the confession is untrue.' *Linkletter v. Walker*, 381 U.S. 618, 638 (1965) (quoting *Blackburn v. Alabama*, 361 U.S. 199, 207 (1960))." *Karake*, 443 F. Supp. 2d at 50-51.

3. *Using Ghailani's Coerced Testimony Indirectly: Fruit of the Poisonous Tree.* The government did not try to use Ghailani's confession, however. Instead it wanted to offer Abebe's testimony, which was allegedly voluntary. Because Abebe had been identified as a witness by Ghailani, Ghailani argued that Abebe's testimony was derived from and therefore tainted by Ghailani's own coercive interrogation — the fruit of the poisonous tree. Why did the court exclude Abebe's testimony?

Some of the evidence against detainees at Guantánamo Bay is derived from their own statements to interrogators, and some is from fellow detainees. Can you see problems these latter evidentiary sources could create for criminal prosecutions like Ghailani's? What is the solution? *Should* the *Ghailani* court have taken into account "the perilous world in which we live" in applying the relevant legal principles? These principles were, after all, chiefly developed in domestic cases involving police abuse of suspects (often with racist overtones). Are criminal prosecutions of accused terrorists who have been interrogated by military and CIA interrogators different?

4. *Ghailani's Conviction: Victory or Defeat?* After a jury trial from which Abebe's testimony was excluded, the jury convicted Ghailani on one count of conspiring to commit murder and acquitted him on 280 others. Charlie Savage, *Terror Verdict Tests Obama's Strategy on Trials*, N.Y. Times, Nov. 18, 2010. The court sentenced Ghailani to life in prison.

Representative Peter King called the outcome a "total miscarriage of justice," Editorial, *The Ghailani Verdict*, N.Y. Times, Nov. 19, 2010, and a "tragic wake-up call to the Obama administration to immediately abandon its ill-advised plan to try Guantanamo terrorists" in civilian courts, and he urged the Administration to try them in military commissions instead. Charlie Savage, *Ghailani Verdict Reignites Debate Over the Proper Court for Terrorism Trials*, N.Y. Times, Nov. 19, 2010. Justice Department spokespersons, on the other hand, declared it a victory, noting that the judge excluded key evidence (in the excerpted opinion) because of Ghailani's treatment during the prior Administration. *Id.* Others pointed out that neither costly security, public grandstanding by Ghailani, nor disclosures or leaks of classified information had resulted from the prosecution, contrary to critics' predictions. *Id.*

Was the mixed verdict a victory for the criminal justice option for dealing with accused terrorists or a defeat? Regarding Representative King's advice to the Administration, consider footnote 182. Had the jury found Ghailani not guilty on all counts, what would the Administration have done in light of Abebe's excluded testimony?

E. DO WE NEED A NATIONAL SECURITY COURT?

The mixed verdict in *Ghailani* renewed an acrimonious debate about the ability of the criminal process to handle terrorist cases. In addition to the problems of secret and coerced evidence discussed above, terror prosecutions potentially pose the following problems:

- whether the right to speedy trial has been violated by lengthy detention as an enemy combatant;
- whether the accused terrorist was entitled to *Miranda* warnings ("you have a right to remain silent. . . .") when he was arrested and detained abroad;
- whether the security of the jury and the judge requires special measures, including shackling the defendant or concealing the identity of jurors;
- whether tensions between the accused terrorist and his court-appointed lawyers render the assistance of counsel ineffective or threaten the conduct of the trial;
- whether the criminal justice system can afford the often lengthy, appeal-interrupted, pretrial motion practice and trial of accused terrorists.

See, e.g., ABA Comm. on Law & Nat'l Security, *Trying Terrorists in Article III Courts* (July 2009) (*Trying Terrorists*); Richard B. Zabel & James J. Benjamin Jr., *In Pursuit of Justice* (Human Rights First, May 2008); Robert Timothy Reagan, *National Security Case Studies: Special Case-Management Challenges* (Federal Judicial Ctr., Feb. 22, 2010); Robert Timothy Reagan, *Terrorism-Related Cases: Special Case-Management Challenges: Problems and Solutions* (Federal Judicial Ctr., Mar. 26, 2008).

Former federal judge and Attorney General Michael B. Mukasey cites Jose Padilla's saga as evidence that "current institutions and statutes are not well suited to even the limited task of supplementing . . . a military effort to combat Islamic terrorism."

Michael B. Mukasey, Op-Ed., *Jose Padilla Makes Bad Law*, Wall St. J., Aug. 22, 2007. He noted that Padilla's criminal case took three months to try, and that criminal cases involving the 1993 World Trade Center bombing, 1996 attacks on Khobar Towers, 1998 attacks on U.S. embassies in Africa, and the 2000 bombing of the *USS Cole* "have strained the financial resources and security resources of the federal courts near to the limit." *Id.* He also asserted that such prosecutions risk disclosing methods and sources of intelligence, and, when the courts relax evidentiary rules or criminal procedures, also can distort the rules applicable to ordinary criminal cases. *Id.*

Judge Mukasey therefore urged Congress to consider a proposal for the creation of a new Article III "national security court" to deal with national security prosecutions, including terrorism cases. *Id.* One such proposal would model the new court on the Foreign Intelligence Surveillance Court (or even "subsume the FISA court and its obligations within a new National Security Court") and staff it with Article III judges. Andrew C. McCarthy & Alykhan Velshi, *Outsourcing American Law: We Need a National Security Court* 24 & n.61 (American Enter. Inst. Working Paper No. 156, 2009), *available at* http://www.aei.org/docLib/20090820-Chapter6.pdf. Such a court would have concurrent jurisdiction with military commissions to try "alleged offenders . . . if those offenders qualify as alien enemy combatants . . . ." *Id.* at 26. Its priority would be "not justice for the individual but security of the American people," and it would therefore need "clear procedural rules which underscore that the overriding mission — into which the judicial function is being imported for very limited purposes — remains executive and military." *Id.* at 30. The proponents of this proposal are not specific about those rules, but they would apparently include a "credible and convincing evidence" standard of proof, a systemic "preference . . . that defendants be convicted and harshly sentenced," and strict limits on "judicial excess," to be enforced by a right of interlocutory appeal by the government to challenge any order "by which the court deviates from the procedural rules." *Id.* at 31-32. Finally, the court would be instructed by Congress to apply a much-narrowed *Brady* exculpatory evidence doctrine. *Id.* at 35. In short, they sum up, "[National Security Court] trials would add the Article III judges to the existing military commission format." *Id.* at 32.

Other proposals for a National Security Court would lengthen the speedy trial limitation, ease the government's burden to show a need for closing a trial to the public, require a two-thirds vote to find proof of guilt beyond a reasonable doubt, relax the hearsay and authentication rules of evidence, and, possibly, permit coerced statements into evidence in some circumstances (although this is unclear). *See* Kevin E. Lunday & Harvey Rishikof, *Due Process Is a Strategic Choice: Legitimacy and the Establishment of an Article III National Security Court*, 39 Cal. W. Int'l L.J. 87 (2008).

NOTES AND QUESTIONS

1. *A National Security Court for Detention Decisions.* A National Security Court has been proposed both to review detention cases and to try terrorism cases. *See, e.g.,* McCarthy & Velshi, *supra,* at 23-27; Lunday & Rishikof, *supra,* 39 Cal. W. Int'l L.J. at 113-118. Such a court would relieve the habeas courts of their burden of reviewing wartime detention and could also be given jurisdiction to authorize or review preventive detention under a new statute. Several scholars assert that the courts in the District of Columbia Circuit already are National Security Courts by default, because of their handling of habeas petitions by Guantánamo detainees. *See, e.g.,* Sophia M.

Brill, *The National Security Court We Already Have*, 28 Yale L. & Pol'y Rev. 525 (2010); Jack Goldsmith, *Long-Term Terrorist Detention and Our National Security Court* 6-8 (Series on Counterterrorism and American Statutory Law, Working Paper No. 5, 2009), *available at* http://www.brookings.edu/papers/2009/0209_detention_goldsmith.aspx.

2. *Need?* Proponents of a National Security Court cite the aforementioned problems, the length of terrorism trials, and the mixed verdict of *Ghailani* as evidence of the need for a new trial court, but is the anecdotal evidence compelling? Opponents note, first, that convictions were obtained in all of the cited cases. Although some scholars have criticized Department of Justice statistics for being over-inclusive and pointed to the surprisingly short *average* sentences handed out in cases that Justice has classified as terrorism-related, more nuanced evaluation of the statistics suggests that the government has obtained lengthy sentences for cases actually based on terrorism and material support charges. *See* Robert M. Chesney, *Federal Prosecution of Terrorism-Related Offenses: Conviction and Sentencing Data in Light of the "Soft-Sentence" and "Data-Reliability" Critiques*, 11 Lewis & Clark L. Rev. 851 (2007). In addition, a detailed study by former prosecutors of more than 100 international terrorism cases concluded that, "contrary to the views of some critics, the court system is generally well-equipped to handle most terrorism cases," Zabel & Benjamin, *supra*, at 5, a conclusion echoed in part by a workshop of judges, prosecutors, and defense attorneys in terrorism cases. *See Trying Terrorists*, *supra*, at 8 ("Many of the *ad hoc* procedures developed by the courts to manage terrorism trials have been effective," although there can be a steep learning curve). Recall, too, that the court of appeals in *Abu Ali* emphasized that "the criminal justice system is not without those attributes of adaptation that will permit it to function in the post-9/11 world." *Abu Ali*, 528 F.3d at 221.

How much stress on the criminal justice system would suffice to justify creation of a National Security Court? On whom should the burden of proof fall, the proponents of such a court or their opponents? The current criminal justice system assumes that protection of the innocent is worth the cost of letting some guilty defendants go free. Does the same assumption apply to accused terrorists?

3. *Changing the Rules or Changing the Court?* Proposals for a National Security Court assume that evidentiary rules and standards of proof can be relaxed. But if this is true, could those rules and standards not be relaxed for ordinary criminal courts without any need to create a controversial new court? *See* Stephen I. Vladeck, *The Case Against National Security Courts*, 45 Willamette L. Rev. 505 (2009). If the answer is no because of constitutional limitations, would the same limitations not apply to the new Article III court?

> Either Congress can amend the Federal Rules of Evidence [or CIPA] to allow for the introduction [or the exclusion] of particular forms of evidence in particular cases, or the Constitution prohibits Congress from so acting. The former would suggest that a move to a national security court would be akin to using a bazooka to kill an ant; the latter would suggest that national security courts *couldn't* have a lesser evidentiary burden. [*Id.* at 519-520 (emphasis in original).]

In fact, the workshop mentioned above also concluded that "[s]ome of the challenges associated with terrorism trials are posed by constitutionally mandated safeguards, and thus, the use of an alternative forum to regulate Article III courts (such as a national security court) may not alleviate some of the challenges." *Trying Terrorists, supra*, at 8.

4. *Blowback*. Even if some of the challenges facing terrorist prosecutions could constitutionally be alleviated by simple rule changes, are they changes we would want to the ordinary criminal justice system? Judge Mukasey expressed concern that "if conventional legal rules are adapted to deal with a terrorist threat, whether by relaxed standards for conviction, searches, the admissibility of evidence or otherwise, those adaptions will infect and change the standards in ordinary cases with ordinary defendants in ordinary courts of law." Mukasey, *supra*. If such rule changes are confined to terrorism cases, then they could effectively convert the criminal court into a "National Security Court" anyway for purposes of terrorism cases. Historically, one protection against unfair rules has always been the fact that rules apply the same way to everyone, sometimes expressed in the aphorism that we are measured by how we treat our enemies. On the other hand, some of the innovations that judges have employed in terrorism cases were borrowed from drug or gang cases. Is concern about the "relaxation" or adaptation of rules in terrorism cases overblown?

5. *Legitimacy*. As *Rosen* stressed, an important attribute of American criminal justice is its transparency. Secret "Star Chamber" courts are contrary to our tradition, and some feel (perhaps unfairly) that the legitimacy of the Foreign Intelligence Surveillance Court is undercut by its closed hearings. Moreover, the United States has traditionally been critical of "special" security courts and military courts used in non-democratic states to stifle opponents and dissidents, as well as to try security risks. "Legitimacy remains a vital strategic weapon against terrorism." Lunday & Rishikof, *supra*, 39 Cal. W. Int'l L.J. at 131. Does not the legitimacy of the state's courts therefore also matter? Would a National Security Court have the same legitimacy as ordinary Article III courts have acquired over time? Should we be concerned not only about its legitimacy to Americans, but also about its legitimacy to our foreign allies and enemies?

Trial by Military Commission —36

Before deploying "necessary and appropriate force" against Al Qaeda and the Taliban in Afghanistan in November 2001, the Bush administration had to decide what it would do with those whom U.S. forces and their allies captured in the fight.

Apart from simply detaining them, one possibility was trying them in U.S. criminal courts. But the problems of secret evidence, which we explored in the previous chapter, not to mention concerns about security and efficiency, given the sheer numbers of anticipated captives, made this option impractical.

A second option was trying them before some ad hoc international tribunal. The surrender of control that this would entail, coupled with the Administration's repudiation of the International Criminal Court, made this option unappealing.

A third option was trying them by court-martial, using the same rules applicable to U.S. service personnel. This option would have used fair and time-tested procedures at the same time that it conformed with the laws of war. But the very fairness of the procedures may have been a strike against them; they may have seemed too fair and, partly as a result, too cumbersome for terrorists charged with horrific war crimes against civilians. *See* Jane Mayer, *The Hidden Power*, New Yorker, May 3, 2006, at 44 (quoting Vice President Dick Cheney on military commissions: "We think it guarantees that we'll have the kind of treatment of these individuals that we believe they deserve."). Their conformity with the laws of war could have been another strike against them, as long as the Administration insisted that such laws did not apply to terrorists. See Chapter 32.

Whatever the precise reasons, the Administration chose a fourth option: to try selected captives by "military commission" under procedures devised for the occasion. Military commissions are tribunals of military officers who sit as judge and jury. Historically, they have been used in the field to try spies, saboteurs, and others who violate the laws of war, and in occupied territories to try common crimes as well. In Chapter 29, we considered two pre-9/11 cases in reviewing the legal authority for *detention* by the military. In Part A of this chapter, we revisit these cases in exploring the legal authority for *trial* by military commission. In Part B, we examine the Military Order of November 13, 2001, which adopted the military commission option and the procedures implementing it, and the Supreme Court's 2006 decision in *Hamdan v. Rumsfeld* about the legal authority for military commissions. In Part C, we consider

Congress's responses to *Hamdan* and the use of military commissions pursuant to military commission legislation enacted after *Hamdan*.

A.   TRIAL BY MILITARY COMMISSION
BEFORE 9/11

Ex parte Milligan

United States Supreme Court, 1866
71 U.S. (4 Wall.) 2

[The opinion is set forth *supra* p. 767.]

Ex parte Quirin

United States Supreme Court, 1942
317 U.S. 1

[The opinion is set forth *supra* p. 823.]

NOTES AND QUESTIONS

[The notes and questions are set forth *supra* p. 826.]

B.   TRIAL BY MILITARY COMMISSION
AFTER 9/11: THE FIRST PHASE

Before the Bush administration turned to the fourth option — trying enemy combatants by military commission — it tasked the Office of Legal Counsel with advising the President on the legality of using military commissions for this purpose. It provided him with an opinion on November 6, 2001, which is excerpted below. A week later, President Bush issued a Military Order authorizing trial by military commissions of persons he designated, which is also reproduced below. The Order delegated to the Secretary of Defense the task of promulgating procedures for such trials. Defense Secretary Donald Rumsfeld and the Department of Defense subsequently issued a host of implementing orders and instructions, many of which were repeatedly revised. *See, e.g.,* Department of Def., *Military Commission Order No. 1* (Mar. 21, 2002); Department of Def., *Military Commissions Instructions Nos. 1-10* (various dates).

Pursuant to the Order issued by President Bush, military commissions were instituted in November 2004 against four persons, including Salim Ahmed Hamdan, a Yemeni national captured during fighting in Afghanistan. Before they got under way, Hamdan challenged the legality of using the military commission to try him as an enemy combatant in a case that resulted in a seminal Supreme Court decision excerpted below. The decision effectively brought to a close what we call the first phase of post-9/11 military commissions, leading to statutory reforms.

Legality of the Use of Military Commissions to Try Terrorists

U.S. Department of Justice, Office of Legal Counsel
Nov. 6, 2001
2001 WL 36175681 (O.L.C.)

The President possesses inherent authority under the Constitution, as Chief Executive and Commander in Chief of the Armed Forces of the United States, to establish military commissions to try and punish terrorists captured in connection with the attacks of September 11 or in connection with U.S. military operations in response to those attacks.

Memorandum Opinion for: Counsel to the President

From: Patrick F. Philbin, Deputy Ass't Attorney General

You have asked us to consider whether terrorists captured in connection with the attacks of September 11 or in connection with ongoing U.S. operations in response to those attacks could be subject to trial before a military court. The Uniform Code of Military Justice ("UCMJ"), 10 U.S.C. §§801-946, authorizes military commissions to try "offenders or offenses that by statute or by the law of war may be tried by military commissions." 10 U.S.C. §821 (2000). The Supreme Court has interpreted identical language (then included in Article 15 of the Articles of War in effect during World War II) to incorporate customary practice and to authorize trial by military commission of any person subject to the laws of war for any offense under the laws of war. *See Ex parte Quirin*, 317 U.S. 1, 30 (1942).

We conclude that under 10 U.S.C. §821 and his inherent powers as Commander in Chief, the President may establish military commissions to try and punish terrorists apprehended as part of the investigation into, or the military and intelligence operations in response to, the September 11 attacks....

BACKGROUND

A military commission is a form of military tribunal typically used in three scenarios: (i) to try individuals (usually members of enemy forces) for violations of the laws of war; (ii) as a general court administering justice in occupied territory; and (iii) as a general court in an area where martial law has been declared and the civil courts are closed. *See generally* William Winthrop, *Military Law and Precedents* 836-40 (2d ed. 1920). The commission is convened by order of a commanding officer and consists of a board of officers who sit as adjudicators without a jury. *See id.* at 835. The commission's decision is subject to review by the convening authority and is not subject to direct judicial review.

Military commissions have been used throughout U.S. history to prosecute violators of the laws of war. "Since our nation's earliest days, such commissions have been constitutionally recognized agencies for meeting many urgent governmental responsibilities related to war. They have been called our common law war courts." *Madsen v. Kinsella*, 343 U.S. 341, 346-47 (1952). Military commissions have tried offenders drawn from the ranks of aliens and citizens alike charged with war crimes arising as early as the Revolutionary War, the Mexican-American War, and the Civil War, and as recently as World War II. *See Quirin*, 317 U.S. at 32 n.10, 42 n.14. President Lincoln's assassins and their accomplices were imprisoned and even executed pursuant to convictions rendered by military commissions. Their offenses were characterized not as criminal matters but rather as acts of rebellion against the government itself. *See Military Commissions*, 11 Op. Att'y Gen. 297 (1865); *Ex parte Mudd*, 17 F. Cas. 954 (S.D. Fla. 1868) (No. 9899). Such use of military commissions has been repeatedly endorsed by federal courts, including as recently as this year. *See Mudd v. Caldera*, 134 F. Supp. 2d 138 (D.D.C. 2001).

Military commissions are not courts within Article III of the Constitution, nor are they subject to the jury trial requirements of the Fifth and Sixth Amendments of the Constitution. *See Quirin*, 317 U.S. at 40. Unlike Article III courts, the powers of military commissions are derived not from statute, but from the laws of war. *See Ex parte Vallandigham*, 68 U.S. (1 Wall.) 243, 249-53 (1863). That is, their authority derives from the Constitution's vesting of the power of Commander in Chief in the President. "Neither their procedure nor their jurisdiction has been prescribed by statute. [Instead,] [i]t has been adapted in each instance to the need that called it forth." *Madsen*, 343 U.S. at 347-48. "In general" [Congress] has left it to the President, and the military commanders representing him, to employ the commission, as occasion may require, for the investigation and punishment of violations of the laws of war." *Id.* at 346 n.9 (quoting Winthrop, *supra* at 831).

I. MILITARY COMMISSIONS MAY BE USED TO TRY ALL OFFENSES AGAINST THE LAWS OF WAR. . . .

A. Congress Has Sanctioned the Broad Jurisdiction of Military Commissions To Try All Offenses Against the Laws of War.

The UCMJ addresses the jurisdiction of military commissions in article 21, which is section 821 of title 10 of the United States Code. Section 821 is phrased somewhat unusually, because it does not *create* military commissions and define their functions and jurisdiction. Instead, it refers to military commissions primarily to acknowledge their existence and to *preserve* their existing jurisdiction. As explained more fully below, military commissions had been created under the authority of the President as Commander in Chief and used to try offenses against the laws of war before there was any explicit statutory sanction for their use. Section 821, which is entitled "Jurisdiction of courts-martial not exclusive," thus states that "[t]he provisions of this chapter conferring jurisdiction upon courts-martial do not *deprive* military commissions...of concurrent jurisdiction with respect to offenders or offenses that by statute or by the law of war may be tried by military commissions." 10 U.S.C. §821 (emphasis added). The jurisdictional provision for courts-martial that is cross-referenced is 10 U.S.C. §818 (2000), which defines the jurisdiction of general courts-martial to include "jurisdiction to try any person who by the law of war is subject to trial by a military tribunal." By its terms, section 821 takes the existence of military commissions as a given and clarifies that the establishment of broad jurisdiction in courts-martial will not curtail the powers of military commissions.

By expressly preserving the jurisdiction of military commissions, section 821 necessarily provides a congressional authorization and sanction for their use. Indeed, the Supreme Court has concluded that identical language in the predecessor provision to section 821 — article 15 of the Articles of War — "*authorized* trial of offenses against the laws of war before such commissions." *Quirin*, 317 U.S. at 29 (emphasis added). . . .

Indeed, if section 821 were read as restricting the use of military commissions and prohibiting practices traditionally followed, it would infringe on the President's express constitutional powers as Commander in Chief. *Cf. Quirin*, 317 U.S. at 47 (declining to "inquire whether Congress may restrict the power of the Commander in Chief to deal with enemy belligerents" by restricting use of military commissions); *id.* (declining also to "consider the question whether the President is compelled by the Articles of War to afford unlawful enemy belligerents a trial before subjecting them to disciplinary measures"). A clear statement of congressional intent would be required before a statute could be read to effect such an infringement on core executive powers. *See, e.g., Public Citizen v. Department of Justice*, 491 U.S. 440, 466 (1989).

The congressional sanction for the use of military commissions is a permissible exercise of Congress's powers under the Constitution. Congress has authority not only to "declare War," but also to "raise and support Armies," and "make Rules for the Government and Regulation of the land and naval Forces." U.S. Const. art. I, §8, cl. 11, 12, 14. To the extent military commissions are used for enforcing discipline within the armed forces of the United States, Congress has authority to sanction their use. In addition, Congress has authority to "define and punish . . . Offences against the Law of Nations." *Id.* art. I, §8, cl. 10. Authorizing the use of military commissions to enforce the laws of war — which are considered a part of the "Law of Nations" — is certainly a permissible exercise of these authorities. Or, to be more precise, it is permissible at least so long as any congressional regulations do not interfere with the President's authority as Commander in Chief. *Cf. Quirin*, 317 U.S. at 47 (declining to address "whether Congress may restrict the power of the Commander in Chief to deal with enemy belligerents" through regulations on military commissions); *cf. also Hamilton v. Dillin*, 88 U.S. (21 Wall.) 73, 87 (1874) (stating that the "President alone" is "constitutionally invested with the entire charge of hostile operations"). . . .

B. Even if Congress Had Not Authorized Creation of Military Commissions, the President Would Have Authority as Commander in Chief To Convene Them. . . .

The Commander in Chief Clause, U.S. Const. art. II, §2, cl. 1, vests in the President the full powers necessary to prosecute successfully a military campaign. It has long been understood that the Constitution provides the federal government all powers necessary for the execution of the duties the Constitution describes. As the Supreme Court explained in *Johnson v. Eisentrager*, "[t]he first of the enumerated powers of the President is that he shall be Commander-in-Chief of the Army and Navy of the United States. And, of course, grant of war power includes all that is necessary and proper for carrying these powers into execution." 339 U.S. 763, 788 (1950) (citation omitted); *see also Lichter v. United States*, 334 U.S. 742, 780 (1948)

1068 Chapter 36. Trial by Military Commission

("The powers of Congress and the President are only those which are to be derived from the Constitution but . . . the primary implication of a war power is that it shall be an effective power to wage the war successfully."); *Home Building & Loan Ass'n v. Blaisdell*, 290 U.S. 398, 426 (1934) (stating that "the war power of the federal government" is "a power to wage war successfully"). One of the necessary incidents of authority over the conduct of military operations in war is the power to punish enemy belligerents for violations of the laws of war. The laws of war exist in part to ensure that the brutality inherent in war is confined within some limits. It is essential for the conduct of a war, therefore, that an army have the ability to enforce the laws of war by punishing transgressions by the enemy. . . .

C. The Use of Military Commissions to Inflict Punishments Without the Procedures Provided for Criminal Trials under Article III, Section 2 and the Fifth and Sixth Amendments Is Constitutionally Permissible. . . .

At the time of the Founding, it was well settled that offenses under the laws of war were a distinct category of offense, unlike criminal offenses against the civil law, and were subject to trial in military tribunals without the benefits of the procedures of the common law enshrined in the Constitution. . . . Thus, under the settled understanding that the rights to jury trial and grand jury indictment do not extend beyond the cases where they were available at common law, those rights simply do not extend to trials before military tribunals for offenses against the laws of war. Such trials never included indictment or jury trial at the time of the Founding. . . .

The primary support for constitutional arguments to *restrict* the use of military commissions would be based on the Supreme Court's decision in *Ex parte Milligan*, 71 U.S. (4 Wall.) 2 (1866). . . .

We believe that the broad pronouncements in *Milligan* do not accurately reflect the requirements of the Constitution and that the case has properly been severely limited by the later decision in *Quirin*. . . .

Thus, the line that the Court ultimately drew in *Quirin* to distinguish *Milligan* may be read to suggest that a citizen (not in the U.S. military) can be tried by military commission *when he acts as a belligerent. See* 317 U.S. at 37. That condition was most clearly met where citizens "associate themselves with the military arm of the enemy government." *Id.* The distinction suggests that *Milligan* can be explained on the basis that the actions charged in *Milligan* did not amount to acts of belligerency. Even under this approach to *Quirin*, we conclude that in the context of the current conflict, any actions by U.S. citizens that amount to hostile acts against the United States or its citizens (and certainly participation in biological attacks, the attacks of September 11, or similar attacks) would make a person a "belligerent" subject to trial by military commission under *Quirin*.

We caution, however, that applying this standard may raise some ambiguities. The *Milligan* decision holds out at least the possibility that some charges that may be articulated under the law of war (such as the charge of giving aid and comfort to the enemy used in *Milligan*) may not, in some circumstances, amount to acts of belligerency triable by military commission. Exactly which acts place a person in the category of an "enemy belligerent" under *Quirin* thus may be a subject of litigation. In addition, it might be argued that *Quirin* should be read as imposing a brighter-line test under which citizens are triable by military commission when they "associate themselves with the military arm of the enemy government." 317 U.S. at 37. That standard, it could be claimed, is difficult to apply here because there are no organized armed forces of another belligerent nation facing the United States. For the reasons outlined above, we conclude that such an approach does not reflect the proper constitutional analysis and is not the proper reading of *Quirin*. Nonetheless, it raises a potential source of litigation risk. . . .

2. Enemy aliens seized in the United States

Even if *Milligan* might raise litigation risks for the use of military commissions to try citizens, it should not raise the same difficulties for trying *aliens* charged with violations of the law of war. . . .

II. THE PRESIDENT MAY CONCLUDE THAT THE LAWS OF ARMED CONFLICT APPLY TO THE TERRORIST ATTACKS.

As explained above, 10 U.S.C. §821 sanctions the full uses of the military commission established by custom and Executive practice in the United States military. That practice, as noted above, has permitted military commissions to try all offenses against the laws of war. The critical question for determining whether military commissions can properly be used here, therefore, is whether the terrorist attacks have created a situation to which the laws of war apply. That is, are the terrorist acts subject to the laws of war at all, or are they solely criminal matters to be treated under the municipal criminal law of the United States or a particular State?

As outlined below, it would be difficult — or impossible — to articulate any precise multi-pronged legal "test" for determining whether a particular attack or set of circumstances constitutes "war" justifying application of the laws of war — or to use the modern terminology, whether it is an "armed conflict" justifying use of the "laws of armed conflict." As the Supreme Court recognized long ago, determining whether a "war" exists depends largely on pragmatic considerations. As the Court put it in evaluating whether President Lincoln could properly invoke the laws of war by imposing a blockade on the southern states at the beginning of the Civil War, a conflict "becomes [a war] by its accidents — the number, power, and organization of the persons who originate and carry it on." *The Prize Cases*, 67 U.S. (2 Black) 635, 666 (1862). Precisely because it is a question that rests on pragmatic judgments that critically affect the national defense and vital matters of foreign policy, it is a determination that is properly left to the political branches, and particularly to the President. We explain in Part A below that the courts should defer to a Presidential determination that the laws of armed conflict apply. In Part B, we outline more specific principles that can be derived from precedents to demonstrate that the present attacks have created a set of circumstances that properly merit invocation of the laws of war. The scale of these attacks, the number of deaths they have caused, and the massive military response they have demanded makes it virtually self-evident that the present situation can be treated as an armed conflict subject to the laws of armed conflict.

A. Determining Whether War Exists Is a Question for the Political Branches. . . .

By making the President Commander in Chief of the armed forces, the Constitution must be understood to grant him the full authorities required for him to effectively defend the Nation in the event of an armed attack. Necessarily included among those powers must be the ability to determine whether persons responsible for an attack should be subject to punishment under the laws of war. We outlined above our conclusion that the President's powers as Commander in Chief must include the authority to convene military commissions to enforce the laws of war. For largely the same reasons, the Commander in Chief's power should include authority to determine when the armed forces are engaged in a conflict that merits application of the laws of war. Use of the laws of war, after all, can be a key component in a strategy for conducting and regulating a military campaign. The ability to apply the laws of war means the ability to punish transgressions by an enemy against those laws, and thereby to compel an enemy to abide by certain standards of conduct. There can be no basis for withdrawing from the Commander in Chief the authority to determine when the Nation has been subjected to such an attack as warrants the use of the laws of war to deal with the enemy.

B. The Terrorist Attacks Have Created a Situation that Can Properly Be Considered War.

Although the determination whether the current situation merits application of the laws of war is properly committed to the discretion of the President as Commander in Chief, there are some standards that the President could take into account. Under principles that can be gleaned both from American precedents and sources addressing the international laws of armed conflict, these factors indicate that the laws of armed conflict are properly applicable here. As the Supreme Court put it in evaluating whether President Lincoln could properly invoke the laws of war by imposing a blockade on the southern states at the beginning of the Civil War, a conflict "becomes [a war] by its accidents—the number, power, and organization of the persons who originate and carry it on." *The Prize Cases*, 67 U.S. at 666. Where an organized force is carrying on a campaign of violence that reaches a sufficient level of intensity, it may be deemed an "armed conflict" by the President, thereby justifying application of the laws of armed conflict, including trials for the violation of those laws. . . .

The critical question for determining whether the laws of armed conflict apply here, therefore, is whether the terrorist attacks were a sufficiently organized and systematic set of violent actions that they crossed a sufficient level of intensity to be considered "armed conflict." There can be no doubt that, whatever the "level of intensity" required to create an armed conflict, the gravity and scale of the violence inflicted on the United States on September 11 crossed that threshold. . . .

III. UNDER THE LAWS OF WAR, THE TERRORISTS ARE UNLAWFUL COMBATANTS SUBJECT TO TRIAL AND PUNISHMENT FOR VIOLATIONS OF THE LAWS OF WAR. . . .

As noted above, the terrorists involved in the attacks did not meet even the minimal conditions required to be recognized as lawful combatants. It is open to some doubt whether persons acting without authorization of a state could *ever* undertake hostile acts without violating the laws of war. But we need not reach that theory to conclude that the terrorists did not meet even the most basic requirements for complying with the laws of war as lawful combatants. They were not bearing arms openly and wearing fixed insignia. Thus, all of their hostile acts can be treated as violations of the laws of war. It is settled that any violation of the laws of war may be prosecuted as a "war crime." The U.S. Army Field Manual, *The Law of Land Warfare*, provides that "[a]ny person, whether a member of the armed forces or a civilian, who commits an act which constitutes a crime under international law is responsible therefor and liable to punishment." FM 27-10 ch. 8, par. 498. "The term 'war crime' is the technical expression for a violation of the law of war by any person or persons, military or civilian. Every violation of the laws of war is a war crime." *Id.* ch. 8, par. 499. Specific offenses here could include violations of the rule prohibiting "[u]se of civilian clothing by troops to conceal their military character," *id.* ch. 8, par. 504(g), the rule prohibiting "[f]iring on localities which are undefended and without military significance," *id.* ch. 8, par. 504(d), and the rule prohibiting deliberate targeting of civilian populations.

In addition, individuals can be prosecuted under the laws of armed conflict using standard theories of aiding and abetting and conspiracy. The U.S. Army Field Manual provides that "[c]onspiracy, direct incitement, and attempts to commit, as well as complicity in the commission of, crimes against peace, crimes against humanity, and war crimes are punishable." *Id.* ch. 8, par. 500. Commanders can also be held responsible for war crimes committed either under their orders or by those under their command.

Military Order of November 13, 2001 Detention, Treatment, and Trial of Certain Non-Citizens in the War Against Terrorism

66 Fed. Reg. 57,833 (Nov. 13, 2001)

By the authority vested in me as President and as Commander in Chief of the Armed Forces of the United States by the Constitution and the laws of the United States of America, including the Authorization for Use of Military Force Joint Resolution (Public Law 107-40, 115 Stat. 224) and sections 821 and 836 of title 10, United States Code, it is hereby ordered as follows:

SECTION 1. *FINDINGS.*

(a) International terrorists, including members of al Qaeda, have carried out attacks on United States diplomatic and military personnel and activities abroad and on citizens and property within the United States on a scale that has created a state of armed conflict that requires the use of the United States Armed Forces.

(b) In light of grave acts of terrorism and threats of terrorism, including the terrorist attacks on Sept. 11, 2001, on the headquarters of the United States Department of Defense in the national capital region, on the World Trade Center in New York, and on civilian aircraft such as in Pennsylvania, I proclaimed a national emergency on Sept. 14, 2001 (Proclamation 7463, Declaration of National Emergency by Reason of Certain Terrorist Attacks).

(c) Individuals acting alone and in concert involved in international terrorism possess both the capability and the intention to undertake further terrorist attacks against the United States that, if not detected and prevented, will cause mass deaths, mass injuries, and massive destruction of property, and may place at risk the continuity of the operations of the United States government.

(d) The ability of the United States to protect the United States and its citizens, and to help its allies and other cooperating nations protect their nations and their citizens, from such further terrorist attacks depends in significant part upon using the United States Armed Forces to identify terrorists and those who support them, to disrupt their activities, and to eliminate their ability to conduct or support such attacks.

(e) To protect the United States and its citizens, and for the effective conduct of military operations and prevention of terrorist attacks, it is necessary for individuals subject to this order pursuant to section 2 hereof to be detained, and, when tried, to be tried for violations of the laws of war and other applicable laws by military tribunals.

(f) Given the danger to the safety of the United States and the nature of international terrorism, and to the extent provided by and under this order, I find consistent with section 836 of title 10, United States Code, that it is not practicable to apply in military commissions under this order the principles of law and the rules of evidence generally recognized in the trial of criminal cases in the United States district courts.

(g) Having fully considered the magnitude of the potential deaths, injuries, and property destruction that would result from potential acts of terrorism against the United States, and the probability that such acts will occur, I have determined that an extraordinary emergency exists for national defense purposes, that this emergency constitutes an urgent and compelling government interest, and that issuance of this order is necessary to meet the emergency.

SECTION 2.   *DEFINITION AND POLICY.*

(a) The term "individual subject to this order" shall mean any individual who is not a United States citizen with respect to whom I determine from time to time in writing that:

    (1) there is reason to believe that such individual, at the relevant times,

        (i) is or was a member of the organization known as al Qaeda;

        (ii) has engaged in, aided or abetted, or conspired to commit, acts of international terrorism, or acts in preparation therefor, that have caused, threaten to cause, or have as their aim to cause, injury to or adverse effects on the United States, its citizens, national security, foreign policy, or economy; or

        (iii) has knowingly harbored one or more individuals described in subparagraphs (i) or (ii) of subsection 2(a)(1) of this order; and

    (2) it is in the interest of the United States that such individual be subject to this order.

(b) It is the policy of the United States that the secretary of defense shall take all necessary measures to ensure that any individual subject to this order is detained in accordance with section 3, and, if the individual is to be tried, that such individual is tried only in accordance with section 4.

(c) It is further the policy of the United States that any individual subject to this order who is not already under the control of the Secretary of Defense but who is under the control of any other officer or agent of the United States or any state shall, upon delivery of a copy of such written determination to such officer or agent, forthwith be placed under the control of the Secretary of Defense.

SECTION 3.   *DETENTION AUTHORITY OF THE SECRETARY OF DEFENSE.*

Any individual subject to this order shall be —

(a) detained at an appropriate location designated by the Secretary of Defense outside or within the United States;

(b) treated humanely, without any adverse distinction based on race, color, religion, gender, birth, wealth, or any similar criteria;

(c) afforded adequate food, drinking water, shelter, clothing, and medical treatment;

(d) allowed the free exercise of religion consistent with the requirements of such detention; and

(e) detained in accordance with such other conditions as the Secretary of Defense may prescribe.

SECTION 4.   *AUTHORITY OF THE SECRETARY OF DEFENSE REGARDING TRIALS OF INDIVIDUALS SUBJECT TO THIS ORDER.*

(a) Any individual subject to this order shall, when tried, be tried by military commission for any and all offenses triable by military commission that such individual is alleged to have committed, and may be punished in accordance with the penalties provided under applicable law, including life imprisonment or death.

(b) As a military function and in light of the findings in section 1, including subsection (f) thereof, the Secretary of Defense shall issue such orders and regulations, including orders for the appointment of one or more military commissions, as may be necessary to carry out subsection (a) of this section.

(c) Orders and regulations issued under subsection (b) of this section shall include, but not be limited to, rules for the conduct of the proceedings of military commissions, including pretrial, trial, and post-trial procedures, modes of proof, issuance of process, and qualifications of attorneys, which shall at a minimum provide for —

(1) military commissions to sit at any time and any place, consistent with such guidance regarding time and place as the Secretary of Defense may provide;

(2) a full and fair trial, with the military commission sitting as the triers of both fact and law;

(3) admission of such evidence as would, in the opinion of the presiding officer of the military commission (or instead, if any other member of the commission so requests at the time the presiding officer renders that opinion, the opinion of the commission rendered at that time by a majority of the commission), have probative value to a reasonable person;

(4) in a manner consistent with the protection of information classified or classifiable under Executive Order 12958 of April 17, 1995, as amended, or any successor Executive Order, protected by statute or rule from unauthorized disclosure, or otherwise protected by law, (A) the handling of, admission into evidence of, and access to materials and information, and (B) the conduct, closure of, and access to proceedings;

(5) conduct of the prosecution by one or more attorneys designated by the Secretary of Defense and conduct of the defense by attorneys for the individual subject to this order;

(6) conviction only upon the concurrence of two-thirds of the members of the commission present at the time of the vote, a majority being present;

(7) sentencing only upon the concurrence of two-thirds of the members of the commission present at the time of the vote, a majority being present; and

(8) submission of the record of the trial, including any conviction or sentence, for review and final decision by me or by the Secretary of Defense if so designated by me for that purpose.

SECTION 5.   *OBLIGATION OF OTHER AGENCIES TO ASSIST THE SECRETARY OF DEFENSE.*

Departments, agencies, entities, and officers of the United States shall, to the maximum extent permitted by law, provide to the Secretary of Defense such assistance as he may request to implement this order.

SECTION 6.   *ADDITIONAL AUTHORITIES OF THE SECRETARY OF DEFENSE.*

(a) As a military function and in light of the findings in section 1, the Secretary of Defense shall issue such orders and regulations as may be necessary to carry out any of the provisions of this order.

(b) The Secretary of Defense may perform any of his functions or duties, and may exercise any of the powers provided to him under this order (other than under section 4(c)(8) hereof) in accordance with section 113(d) of title 10, United States Code.

SECTION 7.   *RELATIONSHIP TO OTHER LAW AND FORUMS.*

(a) Nothing in this order shall be construed to—

(1) authorize the disclosure of state secrets to any person not otherwise authorized to have access to them;

(2) limit the authority of the President as Commander in Chief of the Armed Forces or the power of the President to grant reprieves and pardons; or

(3) limit the lawful authority of the Secretary of Defense, any military commander, or any other officer or agent of the United States or of any State to detain or try any person who is not an individual subject to this order.

(b) With respect to any individual subject to this order—

(1) military tribunals shall have exclusive jurisdiction with respect to offenses by the individual; and

(2) the individual shall not be privileged to seek any remedy or maintain any proceeding, directly or indirectly, or to have any such remedy or proceeding sought on the individual's behalf, in

(i) any court of the United States, or any State thereof,

(ii) any court of any foreign nation, or

(iii) any international tribunal.

(c) This order is not intended to and does not create any right, benefit, or privilege, substantive or procedural, enforceable at law or equity by any party, against the United States, its departments, agencies, or other entities, its officers or employees, or any other person.

(d) For purposes of this order, the term "state" includes any State, district, territory, or possession of the United States.

(e) I reserve the authority to direct the Secretary of Defense, at any time hereafter, to transfer to a governmental authority control of any individual subject to this order. Nothing in this order shall be construed to limit the authority of any such governmental authority to prosecute any individual for whom control is transferred.

SECTION 8.   *PUBLICATION.*

This order shall be published in the *Federal Register*.

George W. Bush

Hamdan v. Rumsfeld

United States Supreme Court, 2006
548 U.S. 557

[Salim Ahmed Hamdan, a Yemeni national, was captured in November 2001 by militia forces in Afghanistan and turned over to the U.S. military. In June 2002, he was transported to the military prison at Guantánamo Bay, Cuba. On July 3, 2003, President Bush determined that Hamdan (and five other detainees at Guantánamo Bay) were subject to the Military Order of November 13, 2001, and therefore triable by military commission. Military counsel was appointed for him, and his counsel promptly filed demands for charges and for a speedy trial pursuant to the Uniform Code of Military Justice (UCMJ), 10 U.S.C. §§801-946 (2006 & Supp. IV 2010). The demands were denied by a military official on the ground that Hamdan was not entitled to any of the protections of the UCMJ. On July 13, 2004, Hamdan was charged with conspiring with members of Al Qaeda to commit the offenses of "attacking civilians; attacking civilian objects; murder by an unprivileged belligerent; and terrorism." Among the overt acts listed in the charges was the claim that Hamdan acted as Osama bin Laden's "bodyguard and personal driver."

Before his trial could begin, Hamdan challenged the legality of the commission by habeas and mandamus petitions. The district court granted his petition for a writ of habeas corpus, but the Court of Appeals, in an opinion by then Judge Roberts, reversed. The Supreme Court granted certiorari and issued the following opinion.]

Justice STEVENS announced the judgment of the Court and delivered the opinion of the Court with respect to Parts I through IV, Parts VI through VI-D-iii, Part VI-D-v, and Part VII, and an opinion with respect to Parts V and VI-D-iv, in which Justice SOUTER, Justice GINSBURG, and Justice BREYER join.... [Hamdan] concedes that a court-martial constituted in accordance with the Uniform Code of Military Justice (UCMJ) would have authority to try him. His objection is that the military commission the President has convened lacks such authority, for two principal reasons: First, neither congressional Act nor the common law of war supports trial by this commission for the crime of conspiracy—an offense that, Hamdan says, is not a violation of the law of war. Second, Hamdan contends, the procedures that the President has adopted to try him violate the most basic tenets of military and international law, including the principle that a defendant must be permitted to see and hear the evidence against him. . . .

For the reasons that follow, we conclude that the military commission convened to try Hamdan lacks power to proceed because its structure and procedures violate both the UCMJ and the Geneva Conventions. Four of us also conclude, see Part V, *infra*, that the offense with which Hamdan has been charged is not an "offens[e] that by . . . the law of war may be tried by military commissions." 10 U.S.C. §821. . . .

II

[The Court found that the Detainee Treatment Act, *supra* p. 786, did not preclude review.]

III

[The Court refused to abstain pending completion of the military commission proceedings against Hamdan, noting that the comity considerations favoring abstention in *Schlesinger v. Councilman*, 420 U.S. 738 (1975), did not apply to Hamdan's case.] . . .

. . . First, Hamdan is not a member of our Nation's Armed Forces, so concerns about military discipline do not apply. Second, the tribunal convened to try Hamdan is not part of the integrated system of military courts, complete with independent review panels, that Congress has established. Unlike the officer in *Councilman*, Hamdan has no right to appeal any conviction to the civilian judges of the Court of Military Appeals (now called the United States Court of Appeals for the Armed Forces, see Pub. L. 103-337, 108 Stat. 2831). Instead, under Dept. of Defense Military Commission Order No. 1 (Commission Order No. 1), which was issued by the President on March 21, 2002, and amended most recently on August 31, 2005, and which governs the procedures for Hamdan's commission, any conviction would be reviewed by a panel consisting of three military officers designated by the Secretary of Defense. Commission Order No. 1 §6(H)(4). Commission Order No. 1 provides that appeal of a review panel's decision may be had only to the Secretary of Defense himself, §6(H)(5), and then, finally, to the President, §6(H)(6).

We have no doubt that the various individuals assigned review power under Commission Order No. 1 would strive to act impartially and ensure that Hamdan receive all protections to which he is entitled. Nonetheless, these review bodies clearly lack the structural insulation from military influence that characterizes the Court of Appeals for the Armed Forces, and thus bear insufficient conceptual similarity to state courts to warrant invocation of abstention principles. . . .

IV

The military commission, a tribunal neither mentioned in the Constitution nor created by statute, was born of military necessity. See W. Winthrop, Military Law and Precedents 831 (rev. 2d ed. 1920) (hereinafter Winthrop). . . .

. . . As further discussed below, each aspect of that seemingly broad [military commission] jurisdiction was in fact supported by a separate military exigency.

Generally, though, the need for military commissions during this period — as during the Mexican War — was driven largely by the then very limited jurisdiction of courts-martial: "The *occasion* for the military commission arises principally from the fact that the jurisdiction of the court-martial proper, in our law, is restricted by statute almost exclusively to members of the military force and to certain specific offences defined in a written code." *Id.,* at 831 (emphasis in original).

Exigency alone, of course, will not justify the establishment and use of penal tribunals not contemplated by Article I, §8 and Article III, §1 of the Constitution unless some other part of that document authorizes a response to the felt need. See *Ex parte Milligan,* [71 U.S.] 4 Wall. 2, 121 (1866) ("Certainly no part of the judicial power of the country was conferred on [military commissions.]"). And that authority, if it exists, can derive only from the powers granted jointly to the President and Congress in time of war. See *In re Yamashita,* 327 U.S. 1, 11 (1946).

The Constitution makes the President the "Commander in Chief" of the Armed Forces, Art. II, §2, cl. 1, but vests in Congress the powers to "declare War . . . and make Rules concerning Captures on Land and Water," Art. I, §8, cl. 11, to "raise and support Armies," *id.,* cl. 12, to "define and punish . . . Offences against the Law of Nations," *id.,* cl. 10, and "To make Rules for the Government and Regulation of the land and naval Forces," *id.,* cl. 14. The interplay between these powers was described by Chief Justice Chase in the seminal case of *Ex parte Milligan*:

> "The power to make the necessary laws is in Congress; the power to execute in the President. Both powers imply many subordinate and auxiliary powers. Each includes all authorities essential to its due exercise. But neither can the President, in war more than in peace, intrude upon the proper authority of Congress, nor Congress upon the proper authority of the President. . . . Congress cannot direct the conduct of campaigns, nor can the President, or any commander under him, without the sanction of Congress, institute tribunals for the trial and punishment of offences, either of soldiers or civilians, unless in cases of a controlling necessity, which justifies what it compels, or at least insures acts of indemnity from the justice of the legislature." 4 Wall., at 139-140.

Whether Chief Justice Chase was correct in suggesting that the President may constitutionally convene military commissions "without the sanction of Congress" in cases of "controlling necessity" is a question this Court has not answered definitively, and need not answer today. For we held in [*Ex parte Quirin,* 317 U.S. 1 (1942), *supra* p. 823] that Congress had, through Article of War 15, sanctioned the use of military commissions in such circumstances. 317 U.S., at 28 ("By the Articles of War, and especially Article 15, Congress has explicitly provided, so far as it may constitutionally do so, that military tribunals shall have jurisdiction to try offenders or offenses against the law of war in appropriate cases"). Article 21 of the UCMJ, the language of which is substantially identical to the old Article 15 and was preserved by Congress after World War II, reads as follows:

> "Jurisdiction of courts-martial not exclusive."
> "The provisions of this code conferring jurisdiction upon courts-martial shall not be construed as depriving military commissions, provost courts, or other military tribunals of concurrent jurisdiction in respect of offenders or offenses that by statute or by the law of war may be tried by such military commissions, provost courts, or other military tribunals." 64 Stat. 115.

We have no occasion to revisit *Quirin*'s controversial characterization of Article of War 15 as congressional authorization for military commissions. Contrary to the Government's assertion, however, even *Quirin* did not view the authorization as a sweeping mandate for the President to "invoke military commissions when he deems them necessary." Rather, the *Quirin* Court recognized that Congress had simply preserved what power, under the Constitution and the common law of war, the President had had before 1916 to convene military commissions — with the express condition that the President and those under his command comply with the law of war. See 317 U.S., at 28-29.[23] That much is evidenced by the Court's inquiry, *following* its conclusion that Congress had authorized military commissions, into whether the law of war had indeed been complied with in that case.

The Government would have us dispense with the inquiry that the *Quirin* Court undertook and find in either the AUMF [Authorization for Use of Military Force, Pub. L. No. 107-40, 115 Stat. 224 (2001), *supra* p. 97] or the DTA [Detainee Treatment Act of 2005, Pub. L. 109-148, 119 Stat. 2739, *supra* p. 786] specific, overriding authorization for the very commission that has been convened to try Hamdan. Neither of these congressional Acts, however, expands the President's authority to convene military commissions. First, while we assume that the AUMF activated the President's war powers, see *Hamdi v. Rumsfeld*, 542 U.S. 507 (2004) (plurality opinion), and that those powers include the authority to convene military commissions in appropriate circumstances, there is nothing in the text or legislative history of the AUMF even hinting that Congress intended to expand or alter the authorization set forth in Article 21 of the UCMJ.[24]

Likewise, the DTA cannot be read to authorize this commission. Although the DTA, unlike either Article 21 or the AUMF, was enacted after the President had convened Hamdan's commission, it contains no language authorizing that tribunal or any other at Guantanamo Bay. The DTA obviously "recognize[s]" the existence of the Guantanamo Bay commissions in the weakest sense because it references some of the military orders governing them and creates limited judicial review of their "final decision[s]," DTA §1005(e)(3), 119 Stat. 2743. But the statute also pointedly reserves judgment on whether "the Constitution and laws of the United States are applicable" in reviewing such decisions and whether, if they are, the "standards and procedures" used to try Hamdan and other detainees actually violate the "Constitution and laws."

Together, the UCMJ, the AUMF, and the DTA at most acknowledge a general Presidential authority to convene military commissions in circumstances where justified under the "Constitution and laws," including the law of war. Absent a more specific congressional authorization, the task of this Court is, as it was in *Quirin*, to decide whether Hamdan's military commission is so justified. It is to that inquiry we now turn.

23. Whether or not the President has independent power, absent congressional authorization, to convene military commissions, he may not disregard limitations that Congress has, in proper exercise of its own war powers, placed on his powers. See *Youngstown Sheet & Tube Co. v. Sawyer*, 343 U.S. 579, 637 (1952) (Jackson, J., concurring). The Government does not argue otherwise.

24. On this point, it is noteworthy that the Court in *Ex parte Quirin*, 317 U.S. 1 (1942), looked beyond Congress' declaration of war and accompanying authorization for use of force during World War II, and relied instead on Article of War 15 to find that Congress had authorized the use of military commissions in some circumstances. Justice Thomas' assertion that we commit "error" in reading Article 21 of the UCMJ to place limitations upon the President's use of military commissions ignores the reasoning in *Quirin*.

V

The common law governing military commissions may be gleaned from past practice and what sparse legal precedent exists. Commissions historically have been used in three situations. First, they have substituted for civilian courts at times and in places where martial law has been declared. Their use in these circumstances has raised constitutional questions, see *Duncan v. Kahanamoku*, 327 U.S. 304 (1946); *Milligan*, 4 Wall., at 121-122, but is well recognized. Second, commissions have been established to try civilians "as part of a temporary military government over occupied enemy territory or territory regained from an enemy where civilian government cannot and does not function." *Duncan*, 327 U.S., at 314; see *Milligan*, 4 Wall., at 141-142 (Chase, C.J., concurring in judgment) (distinguishing "martial law proper" from "military government" in occupied territory)....

The third type of commission, convened as an "incident to the conduct of war" when there is a need "to seize and subject to disciplinary measures those enemies who in their attempt to thwart or impede our military effort have violated the law of war," *Quirin*, 317 U.S., at 28-29, has been described as "utterly different" from the other two. Not only is its jurisdiction limited to offenses cognizable during time of war, but its role is primarily a factfinding one — to determine, typically on the battlefield itself, whether the defendant has violated the law of war. The last time the U.S. Armed Forces used the law-of-war military commission was during World War II. In *Quirin*, this Court sanctioned President Roosevelt's use of such a tribunal to try Nazi saboteurs captured on American soil during the War. 317 U.S. 1. And in *Yamashita*, we held that a military commission had jurisdiction to try a Japanese commander for failing to prevent troops under his command from committing atrocities in the Philippines. 327 U.S. 1.

Quirin is the model the Government invokes most frequently to defend the commission convened to try Hamdan. That is both appropriate and unsurprising. Since Guantanamo Bay is neither enemy-occupied territory nor under martial law, the law-of-war commission is the only model available. At the same time, no more robust model of executive power exists; *Quirin* represents the high-water mark of military power to try enemy combatants for war crimes.

The classic treatise penned by Colonel William Winthrop, whom we have called "the 'Blackstone of Military Law,'" *Reid v. Covert*, 354 U.S. 1, 19, n.38 (1957) (plurality opinion), describes at least four preconditions for exercise of jurisdiction by a tribunal of the type convened to try Hamdan. First, "[a] military commission, (except where otherwise authorized by statute), can legally assume jurisdiction only of offenses committed within the field of the command of the convening commander." Winthrop 836. The "field of command" in these circumstances means the "theatre of war." *Ibid.* Second, the offense charged "must have been committed within the period of the war." *Id.*, at 837. No jurisdiction exists to try offenses "committed either before or after the war." *Ibid.* Third, a military commission not established pursuant to martial law or an occupation may try only "[i]ndividuals of the enemy's army who have been guilty of illegitimate warfare or other offences in violation of the laws of war" and members of one's own army "who, in time of war, become chargeable with crimes or offences not cognizable, or triable, by the criminal courts or under the Articles of war." *Id.*, at 838. Finally, a law-of-war commission has jurisdiction to try only two kinds of offense: "Violations of the laws and usages of war cognizable by military tribunals only," and "[b]reaches of military orders or regulations for which offenders are not legally triable by court-martial under the Articles of war." *Id.*, at 839.

. . . The question is whether the preconditions designed to ensure that a military necessity exists to justify the use of this extraordinary tribunal have been satisfied here.

The charge against Hamdan . . . alleges a conspiracy extending over a number of years, from 1996 to November 2001.[30] All but two months of that more than 5-year-long period preceded the attacks of September 11, 2001, and the enactment of the AUMF — the Act of Congress on which the Government relies for exercise of its war powers and thus for its authority to convene military commissions.[31] Neither the purported agreement with Osama bin Laden and others to commit war crimes, nor a single overt act, is alleged to have occurred in a theater of war or on any specified date after September 11, 2001. None of the overt acts that Hamdan is alleged to have committed violates the law of war.

These facts alone cast doubt on the legality of the charge and, hence, the commission; as Winthrop makes plain, the offense alleged must have been committed both in a theater of war and *during*, not before, the relevant conflict. But the deficiencies in the time and place allegations also underscore — indeed are symptomatic of — the most serious defect of this charge: The offense it alleges is not triable by law-of-war military commission.

There is no suggestion that Congress has, in exercise of its constitutional authority to "define and punish . . . Offences against the Law of Nations," U.S. Const., Art. I, §8, cl. 10, positively identified "conspiracy" as a war crime. As we explained in *Quirin*, that is not necessarily fatal to the Government's claim of authority to try the alleged offense by military commission;Congress, through Article 21 of the UCMJ, has "incorporated by reference" the common law of war, which may render triable by military commission certain offenses not defined by statute. 317 U.S., at 30. When, however, neither the elements of the offense nor the range of permissible punishments is defined by statute or treaty, the precedent must be plain and unambiguous. To demand any less would be to risk concentrating in military hands a degree of adjudicative and punitive power in excess of that contemplated either by statute or by the Constitution. . . .

At a minimum, the Government must make a substantial showing that the crime for which it seeks to try a defendant by military commission is acknowledged to be an offense against the law of war. That burden is far from satisfied here. The crime of "conspiracy" has rarely if ever been tried as such in this country by any law-of-war military commission not exercising some other form of jurisdiction, and does not

---

30. The elements of this conspiracy charge have been defined not by Congress but by the President. See Military Commission Instruction No. 2, 32 C.F.R. §11.6 (2005).

31. Justice Thomas would treat Osama bin Laden's 1996 declaration of jihad against Americans as the inception of the war. But even the Government does not go so far; although the United States had for some time prior to the attacks of September 11, 2001, been aggressively pursuing al Qaeda, neither in the charging document nor in submissions before this Court has the Government asserted that the President's *war powers* were activated prior to September 11, 2001. Justice Thomas' further argument that the AUMF is "backward looking" and therefore authorizes *trial by military commission* of crimes that occurred prior to the inception of war is insupportable. If nothing else, Article 21 of the UCMJ requires that the President comply with the law of war in his use of military commissions. As explained in the text, the law of war permits trial only of offenses "committed within the period of the war." Winthrop 837; see also *Quirin*, 317 U.S., at 28-29 (observing that law-of-war military commissions may be used to try "those enemies *who in their attempt to thwart or impede our military effort* have violated the law of war" (emphasis added)). . . .

appear in either the Geneva Conventions or the Hague Conventions — the major treaties on the law of war. . . .

. . . [T]he only "conspiracy" crimes that have been recognized by international war crimes tribunals (whose jurisdiction often extends beyond war crimes proper to crimes against humanity and crimes against the peace) are conspiracy to commit genocide and common plan to wage aggressive war, which is a crime against the peace and requires for its commission actual participation in a "concrete plan to wage war." 1 Trial of the Major War Criminals Before the International Military Tribunal: Nuremberg, 14 November 1945-1 October 1946, p. 225 (1947). . . .

In sum, the sources that the Government and Justice Thomas rely upon to show that conspiracy to violate the law of war is itself a violation of the law of war in fact demonstrate quite the opposite. Far from making the requisite substantial showing, the Government has failed even to offer a "merely colorable" case for inclusion of conspiracy among those offenses cognizable by law-of-war military commission. Cf. *Quirin*, 317 U.S., at 36. Because the charge does not support the commission's jurisdiction, the commission lacks authority to try Hamdan.

The charge's shortcomings are not merely formal, but are indicative of a broader inability on the Executive's part here to satisfy the most basic precondition — at least in the absence of specific congressional authorization — for establishment of military commissions: military necessity. Hamdan's tribunal was appointed not by a military commander in the field of battle, but by a retired major general stationed away from any active hostilities. Cf. *Rasul v. Bush*, 542 U.S., at 487 (Kennedy, J., concurring in judgment) (observing that "Guantanamo Bay is . . . far removed from any hostilities"). Hamdan is charged not with an overt act for which he was caught redhanded in a theater of war and which military efficiency demands be tried expeditiously, but with an *agreement* the inception of which long predated the attacks of September 11, 2001 and the AUMF. That may well be a crime,[41] but it is not an offense that "by the law of war may be tried by military commissio[n]." 10 U.S.C. §821. None of the overt acts alleged to have been committed in furtherance of the agreement is itself a war crime, or even necessarily occurred during time of, or in a theater of, war. Any urgent need for imposition or execution of judgment is utterly belied by the record; Hamdan was arrested in November 2001 and he was not charged until mid-2004. These simply are not the circumstances in which, by any stretch of the historical evidence or this Court's precedents, a military commission established by Executive Order under the authority of Article 21 of the UCMJ may lawfully try a person and subject him to punishment.

VI

Whether or not the Government has charged Hamdan with an offense against the law of war cognizable by military commission, the commission lacks power to proceed. The UCMJ conditions the President's use of military commissions on compliance not only with the American common law of war, but also with the rest of the UCMJ itself, insofar as applicable, and with the "rules and precepts of the law of

---

41. Justice Thomas' suggestion that our conclusion precludes the Government from bringing to justice those who conspire to commit acts of terrorism is therefore wide of the mark. That conspiracy is not a violation of the law of war triable by military commission does not mean the Government may not, for example, prosecute by court-martial or in federal court those caught "plotting terrorist atrocities like the bombing of the Khobar Towers."

nations," *Quirin*, 317 U.S., at 28—including, *inter alia*, the four Geneva Conventions signed in 1949. The procedures that the Government has decreed will govern Hamdan's trial by commission violate these laws.

A

The commission's procedures are set forth in Commission Order No. 1, which was amended most recently on August 31, 2005—after Hamdan's trial had already begun. Every commission established pursuant to Commission Order No. 1 must have a presiding officer and at least three other members, all of whom must be commissioned officers. §4(A)(1). The presiding officer's job is to rule on questions of law and other evidentiary and interlocutory issues; the other members make findings and, if applicable, sentencing decisions. §4(A)(5). The accused is entitled to appointed military counsel and may hire civilian counsel at his own expense so long as such counsel is a U.S. citizen with security clearance "at the level SECRET or higher." §§4(C)(2)-(3).

The accused also is entitled to a copy of the charge(s) against him, both in English and his own language (if different), to a presumption of innocence, and to certain other rights typically afforded criminal defendants in civilian courts and courts-martial. See §§5(A)-(P). These rights are subject, however, to one glaring condition: The accused and his civilian counsel may be excluded from, and precluded from ever learning what evidence was presented during, any part of the proceeding that either the Appointing Authority or the presiding officer decides to "close." Grounds for such closure "include the protection of information classified or classifiable . . . ; information protected by law or rule from unauthorized disclosure; the physical safety of participants in Commission proceedings, including prospective witnesses; intelligence and law enforcement sources, methods, or activities; and other national security interests." §6(B)(3). Appointed military defense counsel must be privy to these closed sessions, but may, at the presiding officer's discretion, be forbidden to reveal to his or her client what took place therein. *Ibid.*

Another striking feature of the rules governing Hamdan's commission is that they permit the admission of *any* evidence that, in the opinion of the presiding officer, "would have probative value to a reasonable person." §6(D)(1). Under this test, not only is testimonial hearsay and evidence obtained through coercion fully admissible, but neither live testimony nor witnesses' written statements need be sworn. See §§6(D)(2)(b), (3). Moreover, the accused and his civilian counsel may be denied access to evidence in the form of "protected information" (which includes classified information as well as "information protected by law or rule from unauthorized disclosure" and "information concerning other national security interests," §§6(B)(3), 6(D)(5)(a)(v)), so long as the presiding officer concludes that the evidence is "probative" under §6(D)(1) and that its admission without the accused's knowledge would not "result in the denial of a full and fair trial." §6(D)(5)(b).[43] Finally, a presiding officer's determination that evidence "would not have probative

---

43. As the District Court observed, this section apparently permits reception of testimony from a confidential informant in circumstances where "Hamdan will not be permitted to hear the testimony, see the witness's face, or learn his name. If the government has information developed by interrogation of witnesses in Afghanistan or elsewhere, it can offer such evidence in transcript form, or even as summaries of transcripts." 344 F. Supp. 2d 152, 168 (D.D.C. 2004).

value to a reasonable person" may be overridden by a majority of the other commission members. §6(D)(1).

Once all the evidence is in, the commission members (not including the presiding officer) must vote on the accused's guilt. A two-thirds vote will suffice for both a verdict of guilty and for imposition of any sentence not including death (the imposition of which requires a unanimous vote). §6(F). Any appeal is taken to a three-member review panel composed of military officers and designated by the Secretary of Defense, only one member of which need have experience as a judge. §6(H)(4). The review panel is directed to "disregard any variance from procedures specified in this Order or elsewhere that would not materially have affected the outcome of the trial before the Commission." *Ibid.* Once the panel makes its recommendation to the Secretary of Defense, the Secretary can either remand for further proceedings or forward the record to the President with his recommendation as to final disposition. §6(H)(5). The President then, unless he has delegated the task to the Secretary, makes the "final decision." §6(H)(6). He may change the commission's findings or sentence only in a manner favorable to the accused. *Ibid.* . . .

C

In part because the difference between military commissions and courts-martial originally was a difference of jurisdiction alone, and in part to protect against abuse and ensure evenhandedness under the pressures of war, the procedures governing trials by military commission historically have been the same as those governing courts-martial. . . .

The uniformity principle is not an inflexible one; it does not preclude all departures from the procedures dictated for use by courts-martial. But any departure must be tailored to the exigency that necessitates it. See Winthrop 835, n.81. That understanding is reflected in Article 36 of the UCMJ, which provides:

> "(a) The procedure, including modes of proof, in cases before courts-martial, courts of inquiry, military commissions, and other military tribunals may be prescribed by the President by regulations which shall, so far as he considers practicable, apply the principles of law and the rules of evidence generally recognized in the trial of criminal cases in the United States district courts, but which may not be contrary to or inconsistent with this chapter.
>
> "(b) All rules and regulations made under this article shall be uniform insofar as practicable and shall be reported to Congress." 70A Stat. 50.

Article 36 places two restrictions on the President's power to promulgate rules of procedure for courts-martial and military commissions alike. First, no procedural rule he adopts may be "contrary to or inconsistent with" the UCMJ—however practical it may seem. Second, the rules adopted must be "uniform insofar as practicable." That is, the rules applied to military commissions must be the same as those applied to courts-martial unless such uniformity proves impracticable. . . .

. . . Without reaching the question whether any provision of Commission Order No. 1 is strictly "contrary to or inconsistent with" other provisions of the UCMJ, we conclude that the "practicability" determination the President has made is insufficient to justify variances from the procedures governing courts-martial. Subsection (b) of Article 36 was added after World War II, and requires a different showing of impracticability from the one required by subsection (a). Subsection (a) requires that the rules the President promulgates for courts-martial, provost courts, and military commissions alike conform to those that govern procedures in *Article III courts*, "so far as *he considers* practicable." 10 U.S.C. §836(a) (emphasis added). Subsection (b), by contrast, demands that the rules applied in courts-martial, provost courts, and military commissions — whether or not they conform with the Federal Rules of Evidence — be "uniform *insofar as practicable*." §836(b) (emphasis added). Under the latter provision, then, the rules set forth in the Manual for Courts-Martial must apply to military commissions unless impracticable.

The President here has determined, pursuant to subsection (a), that it is impracticable to apply the rules and principles of law that govern "the trial of criminal cases in the United States district courts," §836(a), to Hamdan's commission. We assume that complete deference is owed that determination. The President has not, however, made a similar official determination that it is impracticable to apply the rules for courts-martial. And even if subsection (b)'s requirements may be satisfied without such an official determination, the requirements of that subsection are not satisfied here.

Nothing in the record before us demonstrates that it would be impracticable to apply court-martial rules in this case. There is no suggestion, for example, of any logistical difficulty in securing properly sworn and authenticated evidence or in applying the usual principles of relevance and admissibility. Assuming *arguendo* that the reasons articulated in the President's Article 36(a) determination ought to be considered in evaluating the impracticability of applying court-martial rules, the only reason offered in support of that determination is the danger posed by international terrorism. Without for one moment underestimating that danger, it is not evident to us why it should require, in the case of Hamdan's trial, any variance from the rules that govern courts-martial.

The absence of any showing of impracticability is particularly disturbing when considered in light of the clear and admitted failure to apply one of the most fundamental protections afforded not just by the Manual for Courts-Martial but also by the UCMJ itself: the right to be present. See 10 U.S.C.A. §839(c) (Supp. 2006). Whether or not that departure technically is "contrary to or inconsistent with" the terms of the UCMJ, 10 U.S.C. §836(a), the jettisoning of so basic a right cannot lightly be excused as "practicable."

Under the circumstances, then, the rules applicable in courts-martial must apply. Since it is undisputed that Commission Order No. 1 deviates in many significant respects from those rules, it necessarily violates Article 36(b).

The Government's objection that requiring compliance with the court-martial rules imposes an undue burden both ignores the plain meaning of Article 36(b) and misunderstands the purpose and the history of military commissions. The military commission was not born of a desire to dispense a more summary form of justice than is afforded by courts-martial; it developed, rather, as a tribunal of necessity to be employed when courts-martial lacked jurisdiction over either the accused or the subject matter. See Winthrop 831. Exigency lent the commission its legitimacy, but did not further justify the wholesale jettisoning of procedural protections. That history explains why the military commission's procedures typically have been the ones used by courts-martial. That the jurisdiction of the two tribunals today may sometimes overlap does not detract from the force of this history. Article 21 did not transform the military commission from a tribunal of true exigency into a more convenient adjudicatory tool. Article 36, confirming as much, strikes a careful balance between uniform procedure and the need to accommodate exigencies that may sometimes arise in a theater of war. That Article not having been complied with here, the rules specified for Hamdan's trial are illegal.

D

The procedures adopted to try Hamdan also violate the Geneva Conventions. The Court of Appeals dismissed Hamdan's Geneva Convention challenge on three independent grounds: (1) the Geneva Conventions are not judicially enforceable; (2) Hamdan in any event is not entitled to their protections; and (3) even if he is entitled to their protections, . . . abstention is appropriate. . . .

i . . .

. . . We may assume that "the obvious scheme" of the 1949 Conventions is identical in all relevant respects to that of the 1929 Convention,[57] and even that scheme would, absent some other provision of law, preclude Hamdan's invocation of the Convention's provisions as an independent source of law binding the Government's actions and furnishing petitioner with any enforceable right. For, regardless of the nature of the rights conferred on Hamdan, cf. *United States v. Rauscher*, 119 U.S. 407 (1886), they are, as the Government does not dispute, part of the law of war. And compliance with the law of war is the condition upon which the authority set forth in Article 21 is granted.

ii . . .

The conflict with al Qaeda is not, according to the Government, a conflict to which the full protections afforded detainees under the 1949 Geneva Conventions apply because Article 2 of those Conventions (which appears in all four Conventions) renders the full protections applicable only to "all cases of declared war or of any other armed conflict which may arise between two or more of the High Contracting Parties." 6 U.S.T., at 3318. Since Hamdan was captured and detained incident to the conflict with al Qaeda and not the conflict with the Taliban, and since al Qaeda, unlike Afghanistan, is not a "High Contracting Party" — *i.e.*, a signatory of the Conventions, the protections of those Conventions are not, it is argued, applicable to Hamdan.[60]

We need not decide the merits of this argument because there is at least one provision of the Geneva Conventions that applies here even if the relevant conflict is not one between signatories. Article 3, often referred to as Common Article 3 because, like Article 2, it appears in all four Geneva Conventions, provides that in a "conflict not of an international character occurring in the territory of one of the

---

57. But see, *e.g.*, 4 Int'l Comm. of Red Cross, Commentary: Geneva Convention Relative to the Protection of Civilian Persons in Time of War 21 (1958) (hereinafter GCIV Commentary) (the 1949 Geneva Conventions were written "first and foremost to protect individuals, and not to serve State interests"); GCIII Commentary 91 ("It was not . . . until the Conventions of 1949 . . . that the existence of 'rights' conferred in prisoners of war was affirmed").

60. The President has stated that the conflict with the Taliban is a conflict to which the Geneva Conventions apply.

High Contracting Parties, each Party to the conflict shall be bound to apply, as a minimum," certain provisions protecting "[p]ersons taking no active part in the hostilities, including members of armed forces who have laid down their arms and those placed *hors de combat* by . . . detention." *Id.,* at 3318. One such provision prohibits "the passing of sentences and the carrying out of executions without previous judgment pronounced by a regularly constituted court affording all the judicial guarantees which are recognized as indispensable by civilized peoples." *Ibid.*

The Court of Appeals thought, and the Government asserts, that Common Article 3 does not apply to Hamdan because the conflict with al Qaeda, being "'international in scope,'" does not qualify as a "'conflict not of an international character.'" That reasoning is erroneous. The term "conflict not of an international character" is used here in contradistinction to a conflict between nations. So much is demonstrated by the "fundamental logic [of] the Convention's provisions on its application." [415 F.3d 33, 44 (D.C. Cir. 2005) (Williams, J., concurring).] Common Article 2 provides that "the present Convention shall apply to all cases of declared war or of any other armed conflict which may arise between two or more of the High Contracting Parties." 6 U.S.T., at 3318 (Art. 2, ¶1). High Contracting Parties (signatories) also must abide by all terms of the Conventions vis-à-vis one another even if one party to the conflict is a nonsignatory "Power," and must so abide vis-à-vis the nonsignatory if "the latter accepts and applies" those terms. *Ibid.* (Art. 2, ¶3). Common Article 3, by contrast, affords some minimal protection, falling short of full protection under the Conventions, to individuals associated with neither a signatory nor even a nonsignatory "Power" who are involved in a conflict "in the territory of" a signatory. The latter kind of conflict is distinguishable from the conflict described in Common Article 2 chiefly because it does not involve a clash between nations (whether signatories or not). In context, then, the phrase "not of an international character" bears its literal meaning. See, *e.g.,* J. Bentham, Introduction to the Principles of Morals and Legislation 6, 296 (J. Burns & H. Hart eds. 1970) (using the term "international law" as a "new though not inexpressive appellation" meaning "betwixt nation and nation"; defining "international" to include "mutual transactions between sovereigns as such"). . . .

iii

Common Article 3, then, is applicable here and, as indicated above, requires that Hamdan be tried by a "regularly constituted court affording all the judicial guarantees which are recognized as indispensable by civilized peoples." 6 U.S.T., at 3320 (Art. 3, ¶1(d)). While the term "regularly constituted court" is not specifically defined in either Common Article 3 or its accompanying commentary, other sources disclose its core meaning. The commentary accompanying a provision of the Fourth Geneva Convention, for example, defines "'regularly constituted'" tribunals to include "ordinary military courts" and "definitely exclud[e] all special tribunals." GCIV Commentary 340 (defining the term "properly constituted" in Article 66, which the commentary treats as identical to "regularly constituted"). . . .

The Government offers only a cursory defense of Hamdan's military commission in light of Common Article 3. As Justice Kennedy explains, that defense fails because "[t]he regular military courts in our system are the courts-martial established by congressional statutes." At a minimum, a military commission "can be 'regularly constituted' by the standards of our military justice system only if some practical need explains deviations from court-martial practice." As we have explained, see Part VI-C, *supra,* no such need has been demonstrated here.

iv

Inextricably intertwined with the question of regular constitution is the evaluation of the procedures governing the tribunal and whether they afford "all the judicial guarantees which are recognized as indispensable by civilized peoples." 6 U.S.T., at 3320 (Art. 3, ¶1(d)). Like the phrase "regularly constituted court," this phrase is not defined in the text of the Geneva Conventions. But it must be understood to incorporate at least the barest of those trial protections that have been recognized by customary international law. . . .

We agree with Justice Kennedy that the procedures adopted to try Hamdan deviate from those governing courts-martial in ways not justified by any "evident practical need," and for that reason, at least, fail to afford the requisite guarantees. We add only that, as noted in Part VI-A, *supra,* various provisions of Commission Order No. 1 dispense with the principles, articulated in Article 75 [of Protocol I to the Geneva Conventions of 1949, June 8, 1977, 1125 U.N.T.S. 3, 16 I.L.M. 1391] and indisputably part of the customary international law, that an accused must, absent disruptive conduct or consent, be present for his trial and must be privy to the evidence against him. See §§6(B)(3), (D). That the Government has a compelling interest in denying Hamdan access to certain sensitive information is not doubted. But, at least absent express statutory provision to the contrary, information used to convict a person of a crime must be disclosed to him. . . .

VII

We have assumed, as we must, that the allegations made in the Government's charge against Hamdan are true. We have assumed, moreover, the truth of the message implicit in that charge — viz., that Hamdan is a dangerous individual whose beliefs, if acted upon, would cause great harm and even death to innocent civilians, and who would act upon those beliefs if given the opportunity. It bears emphasizing that Hamdan does not challenge, and we do not today address, the Government's power to detain him for the duration of active hostilities in order to prevent such harm. But in undertaking to try Hamdan and subject him to criminal punishment, the Executive is bound to comply with the Rule of Law that prevails in this jurisdiction.

The judgment of the Court of Appeals is reversed, and the case is remanded for further proceedings.

It is so ordered.

The CHIEF JUSTICE took no part in the consideration or decision of this case.

Justice BREYER, with whom Justice KENNEDY, Justice SOUTER, and Justice GINSBURG join, concurring. The dissenters say that today's decision would "sorely hamper the President's ability to confront and defeat a new and deadly enemy." They suggest that it undermines our Nation's ability to "preven[t] future attacks" of the grievous sort that we have already suffered. That claim leads me to state briefly what I believe the majority sets forth both explicitly and implicitly at greater length. The Court's conclusion ultimately rests upon a single ground: Congress has not issued the Executive a "blank check." Cf. *Hamdi v. Rumsfeld*, 542 U.S. 507, 536 (2004) (plurality opinion). Indeed, Congress has denied the President the legislative authority to create military commissions of the kind at issue here. Nothing prevents the President from returning to Congress to seek the authority he believes necessary.

Where, as here, no emergency prevents consultation with Congress, judicial insistence upon that consultation does not weaken our Nation's ability to deal with danger. To the contrary, that insistence strengthens the Nation's ability to determine — through democratic means — how best to do so. The Constitution places its faith in those democratic means. Our Court today simply does the same.

Justice KENNEDY, with whom Justice SOUTER, Justice GINSBURG, and Justice BREYER join as to Parts I and II, concurring in part. Military Commission Order No. 1, which governs the military commission established to try petitioner Salim Hamdan for war crimes, exceeds limits that certain statutes, duly enacted by Congress, have placed on the President's authority to convene military courts. This is not a case, then, where the Executive can assert some unilateral authority to fill a void left by congressional inaction. It is a case where Congress, in the proper exercise of its powers as an independent branch of government, and as part of a long tradition of legislative involvement in matters of military justice, has considered the subject of military tribunals and set limits on the President's authority. Where a statute provides the conditions for the exercise of governmental power, its requirements are the result of a deliberative and reflective process engaging both of the political branches. Respect for laws derived from the customary operation of the Executive and Legislative Branches gives some assurance of stability in time of crisis. The Constitution is best preserved by reliance on standards tested over time and insulated from the pressures of the moment. . . .

I join the Court's opinion, save Parts V and VI-D-iv. To state my reasons for this reservation, and to show my agreement with the remainder of the Court's analysis by identifying particular deficiencies in the military commissions at issue, this separate opinion seems appropriate.

I

Trial by military commission raises separation-of-powers concerns of the highest order. Located within a single branch, these courts carry the risk that offenses will be defined, prosecuted, and adjudicated by executive officials without independent review. Concentration of power puts personal liberty in peril of arbitrary action by officials, an incursion the Constitution's three-part system is designed to avoid. It is imperative, then, that when military tribunals are established, full and proper authority exists for the Presidential directive. . . .

II . . .

These structural differences between the military commissions and courts-martial — the concentration of functions, including legal decisionmaking, in a single executive official; the less rigorous standards for composition of the tribunal; and the creation of special review procedures in place of institutions created and regulated by Congress — remove safeguards that are important to the fairness of the proceedings and the independence of the court. Congress has prescribed these guarantees for courts-martial; and no evident practical need explains the departures here. For these reasons the commission cannot be considered regularly constituted under United States law and thus does not satisfy Congress' requirement that military commissions conform to the law of war.

Apart from these structural issues, moreover, the basic procedures for the commissions deviate from procedures for courts-martial, in violation of §836(b). As the Court explains, the Military Commission Order abandons the detailed Military Rules of Evidence, which are modeled on the Federal Rules of Evidence in conformity with §836(a)'s requirement of presumptive compliance with district-court rules....

In sum, as presently structured, Hamdan's military commission exceeds the bounds Congress has placed on the President's authority in §§836 and 821 of the UCMJ. Because Congress has prescribed these limits, Congress can change them, requiring a new analysis consistent with the Constitution and other governing laws. At this time, however, we must apply the standards Congress has provided. By those standards the military commission is deficient.

III

In light of the conclusion that the military commission here is unauthorized under the UCMJ, I see no need to consider several further issues addressed in the plurality opinion by Justice Stevens and the dissent by Justice Thomas....

Justice SCALIA, with whom Justice THOMAS and Justice ALITO join, dissenting.... [Justice Scalia found that the DTA deprived the Court of jurisdiction to hear Hamdan's case at this time. He then considered, assuming that the Court had jurisdiction, whether it should abstain from exercising it.]

... The principal opinion on the merits makes clear that it does not believe that the trials by military commission involve any "military necessity" *at all*: "The charge's shortcomings... are indicative of a broader inability on the Executive's part here to satisfy the most basic precondition... for establishment of military commissions: military necessity." This is quite at odds with the views on this subject expressed by our political branches. Because of "military necessity," a joint session of Congress authorized the President to "use all necessary and appropriate force," including military commissions, "against those nations, organizations, or persons [such as petitioner] he determines planned, authorized, committed, or aided the terrorist attacks that occurred on September 11, 2001." Authorization for Use of Military Force, §2(a), 115 Stat. 224, note following 50 U.S.C. §1541 (2000 ed., Supp. III). In keeping with this authority, the President has determined that "[t]o protect the United States and its citizens, and for the effective conduct of military operations and prevention of terrorist attacks, it is necessary for individuals subject to this order... to be detained, and, when tried, to be tried for violations of the laws of war and other applicable laws by military tribunals." Military Order of Nov. 13, 2001, 3 C.F.R. §918(e) (2002). It is not clear where the Court derives the authority — or the audacity — to contradict this determination. If "military necessities" relating to "duty" and "discipline" required abstention in *Councilman, supra,* at 757, military necessities relating to the disabling, deterrence, and punishment of the mass-murdering terrorists of September 11 require abstention all the more here.

The Court further seeks to distinguish *Councilman* on the ground that "the tribunal convened to try Hamdan is not part of the integrated system of military courts, complete with independent review panels, that Congress has established." . . .

Even if we were to accept the Court's extraordinary assumption that the President "lack[s] the structural insulation from military influence that characterizes the Court of Appeals for the Armed Forces,"[8] the Court's description of the review scheme here is anachronistic. As of December 30, 2005, the "fina[l]" review of decisions by military commissions is now conducted by the D.C. Circuit pursuant to §1005(e)(3) of the DTA, and by this Court under 28 U.S.C. §1254(1). This provision for review by Article III courts creates, if anything, a review scheme *more* insulated from Executive control than that in *Councilman*. . . .

Moreover, a third consideration counsels strongly in favor of abstention in this case. . . . Here, apparently for the first time in history, a District Court enjoined ongoing military commission proceedings, which had been deemed "necessary" by the President "[t]o protect the United States and its citizens, and for the effective conduct of military operations and prevention of terrorist attacks." Military Order of Nov. 13, 3 C.F.R. §918(e). Such an order brings the Judicial Branch into direct conflict with the Executive in an area where the Executive's competence is maximal and ours is virtually nonexistent. We should exercise our equitable discretion to *avoid* such conflict. Instead, the Court rushes headlong to meet it. . . .

I would abstain from exercising our equity jurisdiction, as the Government requests. . . .

Justice THOMAS, with whom Justice SCALIA joins, and with whom Justice ALITO joins in all but parts I, II-C-1, and III-B-2, dissenting. . . .

I. . . .

. . . [T]he President's decision to try Hamdan before a military commission for his involvement with al Qaeda is entitled to a heavy measure of deference. In the present conflict, Congress has authorized the President "to use all necessary and appropriate force against those nations, organizations, or persons *he determines* planned, authorized, committed, or aided the terrorist attacks that occurred on September 11, 2001 . . . in order to prevent any future acts of international terrorism against the United States by such nations, organizations or persons." Authorization for Use of Military Force (AUMF), 115 Stat. 224, note following 50 U.S.C. §1541 (2000 ed., Supp. III) (emphasis added). As a plurality of the Court observed in *Hamdi*, the "capture, detention, and *trial* of unlawful combatants, by 'universal agreement and practice,' are 'important incident[s] of war,'" *Hamdi*, 542 U.S., at 518 (quoting *Quirin, supra*, at 28, 30; emphasis added), and are therefore "an exercise of the 'necessary and appropriate force' Congress has authorized the President to use." *Hamdi*, 542 U.S., at 518; *id.*, at 587 (Thomas, J., dissenting). *Hamdi*'s observation that military commissions are included within the AUMF's authorization is supported by this Court's previous recognition that "[a]n important incident to the conduct of war is the adoption of

---

8. The very purpose of Article II's creation of a *civilian* Commander in Chief in the President of the United States was to generate "structural insulation from military influence." See The Federalist No. 28 (A. Hamilton); *id.*, No. 69 (same). We do not live under a military junta. It is a disservice to both those in the Armed Forces and the President to suggest that the President is subject to the undue control of the military.

measures by the military commander, not only to repel and defeat the enemy, but to seize and subject to disciplinary measures those enemies who, in their attempt to thwart or impede our military effort, have violated the law of war." *In re Yamashita*, 327 U.S. 1, 11 (1946)....

...Nothing in the language of Article 21...suggests that it outlines the entire reach of congressional authorization of military commissions in all conflicts—quite the contrary, the language of Article 21 presupposes the existence of military commissions under an independent basis of authorization. Indeed, consistent with *Hamdi*'s conclusion that the AUMF itself authorizes the trial of unlawful combatants, the original sanction for military commissions historically derived from congressional authorization of "the initiation of war" with its attendant authorization of "the employment of all necessary and proper agencies for its due prosecution." W. Winthrop, Military Law and Precedents 831 (2d ed. 1920) (hereinafter Winthrop). Accordingly, congressional authorization for military commissions pertaining to the instant conflict derives not only from Article 21 of the UCMJ, but also from the more recent, and broader, authorization contained in the AUMF.[2] ...

II...

A

... [A] law-of-war military commission may only assume jurisdiction of "offences committed within the field of the command of the convening commander," and...such offenses "must have been committed within the period of the war." See *id.*, at 836, 837. Here, as evidenced by Hamdan's charging document, the Executive has determined that the theater of the present conflict includes "Afghanistan, Pakistan and other countries" where al Qaeda has established training camps, and that the duration of that conflict dates back (at least) to Usama bin Laden's August 1996 "*Declaration of Jihad Against the Americans.*" Under the Executive's description of the conflict, then, every aspect of the charge, which alleges overt acts in "Afghanistan, Pakistan, Yemen and other countries" taking place from 1996 to 2001, satisfies the temporal and geographic prerequisites for the exercise of law-of-war military commission jurisdiction. And these judgments pertaining to the scope of the theater and duration of the present conflict are committed solely to the President in the exercise of his commander-in-chief authority. See [*The Prize Cases*, 67 U.S. (2 Black) 635, 670 (1863), *supra* p. 68] (concluding that the President's commander-in-chief judgment about the nature of a particular conflict was "a question to be decided *by him*, and this Court must be governed by the decisions and acts of the political department of the Government to which this power was entrusted")....

...The starting point of the present conflict (or indeed any conflict) is not determined by congressional enactment, but rather by the initiation of hostilities. See *Prize Cases*, *supra*, at 668 (recognizing that war may be initiated by "invasion of a foreign nation," and that such initiation, and the President's response, usually *precedes* congressional action). Thus, Congress' enactment of the AUMF did not mark the

2. Although the President very well may have inherent authority to try unlawful combatants for violations of the law of war before military commissions, we need not decide that question because Congress has authorized the President to do so. Cf. *Hamdi v. Rumsfeld*, 542 U.S. 507, 587 (2004) (Thomas, J., dissenting) (same conclusion respecting detention of unlawful combatants)....

beginning of this Nation's conflict with al Qaeda, but instead authorized the President to use force in the midst of an ongoing conflict. Moreover, while the President's "war powers" may not have been activated until the AUMF was passed, the date of such activation has never been used to determine the scope of a military commission's jurisdiction.[3] . . .

C

[Justice Thomas also concluded that, under the law of war, Hamdan could properly be charged with membership in a war-criminal enterprise and with conspiracy to commit war crimes.]

3

Ultimately, the plurality's determination that Hamdan has not been charged with an offense triable before a military commission rests not upon any historical example or authority, but upon the plurality's raw judgment of the "inability on the Executive's part here to satisfy the most basic precondition . . . for establishment of military commissions: military necessity." This judgment starkly confirms that the plurality has appointed itself the ultimate arbiter of what is quintessentially a policy and military judgment, namely, the appropriate military measures to take against those who "aided the terrorist attacks that occurred on September 11, 2001." AUMF §2(a), 115 Stat. 224. The plurality's suggestion that Hamdan's commission is illegitimate because it is not dispensing swift justice on the battlefield is unsupportable. Even a cursory review of the authorities confirms that law-of-war military commissions have wide-ranging jurisdiction to try offenses against the law of war in exigent and nonexigent circumstances alike. Traditionally, retributive justice for heinous war crimes is as much a "military necessity" as the "demands" of "military efficiency" touted by the plurality, and swift military retribution is precisely what Congress authorized the President to impose on the September 11 attackers in the AUMF.

Today a plurality of this Court would hold that conspiracy to massacre innocent civilians does not violate the laws of war. This determination is unsustainable. The judgment of the political branches that Hamdan, and others like him, must be held accountable before military commissions for their involvement with and membership in an unlawful organization dedicated to inflicting massive civilian casualties is supported by virtually every relevant authority, including all of the authorities invoked by the plurality today. It is also supported by the nature of the present conflict. We are not engaged in a traditional battle with a nation-state, but with a worldwide, hydra-

---

3. Even if the formal declaration of war were generally the determinative act in ascertaining the temporal reach of the jurisdiction of a military commission, the AUMF itself is inconsistent with the plurality's suggestion that such a rule is appropriate in this case. The text of the AUMF is backward looking, authorizing the use of "all necessary and appropriate force against those nations, organizations, or persons he determines planned, authorized, committed, or aided the terrorist attacks that occurred on September 11, 2001." Thus, the President's decision to try Hamdan by military commission — a use of force authorized by the AUMF — for Hamdan's involvement with al Qaeda prior to September 11, 2001, fits comfortably within the framework of the AUMF. In fact, bringing the September 11 conspirators to justice is the *primary point* of the AUMF. By contrast, on the plurality's logic, the AUMF would not grant the President the authority to try Usama bin Laden himself for his involvement in the events of September 11, 2001.

headed enemy, who lurks in the shadows conspiring to reproduce the atrocities of September 11, 2001, and who has boasted of sending suicide bombers into civilian gatherings, has proudly distributed videotapes of beheadings of civilian workers, and has tortured and dismembered captured American soldiers. But according to the plurality, when our Armed Forces capture those who are plotting terrorist atrocities like the bombing of the Khobar Towers, the bombing of the U.S.S. *Cole*, and the attacks of September 11 — even if their plots are advanced to the very brink of fulfillment — our military cannot charge those criminals with any offense against the laws of war. Instead, our troops must catch the terrorists "redhanded" in the midst of *the attack itself*, in order to bring them to justice. Not only is this conclusion fundamentally inconsistent with the cardinal principle of the law of war, namely protecting non-combatants, but it would sorely hamper the President's ability to confront and defeat a new and deadly enemy....

III

[Justice Thomas concluded that the Court should defer to the President's determination that court-martial procedures are not "practicable" for military commissions and therefore reject any requirement for uniformity of procedures. He also concluded that Common Article 3 was not judicially enforceable; that, if it were, the Court should defer to the President's "reasonable" interpretation of Common Article 3 as inapplicable to the "international" conflict with Al Qaeda; and, finally, that any claim Hamdan might have under Common Article 3 was not ripe.]

For these reasons, I would affirm the judgment of the Court of Appeals.

Justice ALITO, with whom Justices SCALIA and THOMAS join in parts I-III, dissenting. For the reasons set out in Justice Scalia's dissent, which I join, I would hold that we lack jurisdiction. On the merits, I join Justice Thomas' dissent with the exception of Parts I, II-C-1, and III-B-2, which concern matters that I find unnecessary to reach....

I...

In order to determine whether a court has been properly appointed, set up, or established, it is necessary to refer to a body of law that governs such matters. I interpret Common Article 3 as looking to the domestic law of the appointing country because I am not aware of any international law standard regarding the way in which such a court must be appointed, set up, or established, and because different countries with different government structures handle this matter differently. Accordingly, "a regularly constituted court" is a court that has been appointed, set up, or established in accordance with the domestic law of the appointing country....

III...

A...

In sum, I believe that Common Article 3 is satisfied here because the military commissions (1) qualify as courts, (2) that were appointed and established in accordance with domestic law, and (3) any procedural improprieties that might occur in particular cases can be reviewed in those cases.

B

The commentary on Common Article 3 supports this interpretation. The commentary on Common Article 3, ¶1(d) . . . states: ". . . *We must be very clear about one point: it is only 'summary' justice which it is intended to prohibit. . . .*" GCIV Commentary 39 (emphasis added).

It seems clear that the commissions at issue here meet this standard. Whatever else may be said about the system that was created by Military Commission Order No. 1 and augmented by the Detainee Treatment Act, §1005(e)(1), 119 Stat. 2742, this system — which features formal trial procedures, multiple levels of administrative review, and the opportunity for review by a United States Court of Appeals and by this Court — does not dispense "summary justice."

For these reasons, I respectfully dissent.

NOTES AND QUESTIONS

1. *Holding?* What, precisely, did *Hamdan* hold? Note that Justice Kennedy's vote was necessary to form a majority. Which parts of the decision are those of the plurality alone? Note also that the Chief Justice — who wrote the opinion for the Court of Appeals in *Hamdan* — did not participate. Is *Hamdan*'s holding unprecedented? *See* Stephen I. Vladeck, *Congress, the Commander-in-Chief, and the Separation of Powers After Hamdan*, 16 Transnat'l L. & Contemp. Probs. 933, 935-936 (2007) (no, citing *Little v. Barreme, supra* p. 78).

2. *Military Necessity Redux.* We saw in Chapter 29 that the military commission exception to the "preferred" method of civilian trial is justified by necessity. What is the necessity that the majority identified in *Hamdan*? Is it limited by time or place? Is it limited to acts for which a person is "caught redhanded in a theater of war and which military efficiency demands be tried expeditiously," as the plurality suggests? *See supra* p. 1081. If so, is necessity a wasting justification? If necessity for trying Hamdan by military commission is no longer present, is there any necessity for continuing to detain him? What does the Court say and why? *See supra* p. 1087.

Reread section 1 of the Military Order, especially section 1(e), *supra* p. 1072. Has not the President already found military commissions necessary? Why does the Court not defer to his finding, as it did to the finding of military necessity in *Korematsu, supra* p. 1084? Reread the AUMF, *supra* p. 97. Hasn't Congress found necessity and authorized the President to use all "necessary and appropriate force," as he determines? Why does the Court not defer to Congress? Which branch is best equipped to decide necessity?

When there is a "controlling necessity," does the President *need* any statutory authority to use military commissions? That is, does he have inherent authority to establish them? What does the majority say? What does Justice Thomas say? If so, is there any limit on that authority?

3. *Statutory Authority.* The Court does not reach the question of inherent presidential authority for military commissions, because it found that Article 21 preserved or incorporated the common law of war authority for military commissions.

Recall that the Court found that the AUMF authorized the military detention of Yaser Hamdi. *See Hamdi v. Rumsfeld*, 542 U.S. 507 (2004), *supra* p. 831. Why does it not also authorize trial of Hamdan by military commission, especially since the AUMF was enacted after Article 21? Alternatively, why does the DTA not authorize such a trial?

4. *Law-of-War Limits on Military Commissions.* Article 21 is a two-headed coin: if it incorporates the common law of war and thus authorizes military commissions, it also incorporates any jurisdictional and procedural limits set by that law. What are those limits? By what constitutional authority may Congress directly, or by implication, impose any limits on the President's use of military commissions?

One law-of-war limit is temporal — military commission jurisdiction is only for charges committed within the period of war. When did that period commence? If it commenced by attack, was it the attack on 9/11 or the earliest attack by Al Qaeda against U.S. persons or property? Is Justice Thomas correct in arguing that *The Prize Cases* commits this decision to the President's conclusive discretion? If Congress took a different view by enacting the AUMF and referring to the 9/11 attacks, which branch prevails? *See generally* Barbara Salazar Torreon, *Periods of War* (Cong. Res. Serv. RS21405), May 1, 2006.

5. *The UCMJ and the Uniformity Principle.* Article 36 of the UCMJ authorizes the President to prescribe procedures for military commissions. *See generally* Jennifer Elsea, *The Department of Defense Rules for Military Commissions: Analysis of Procedural Rules and Comparison with Proposed Legislation and the Uniform Code of Military Justice* (Cong. Res. Serv. RL31600), Jan. 18, 2005. What two restrictions does it place on the President's procedural power? Why were these restrictions not met by sections 1(f) and 1(g) of the Military Order of November 13, 2001? See *supra* p. 1072. If the President had simply added "or the procedures of courts-martial recognized by the UCMJ" at the end of section 2(f), would that have satisfied the restriction? If not, what else would he have to find?

6. *The Geneva Conventions.* International treaties also impose procedural law-of-war limitations on military commissions. The majority in *Hamdan* held that Common Article 3 of the Geneva Conventions of 1949 applied to the conflict with Al Qaeda. It required trial by a tribunal that is "regularly constituted . . . ." See *supra* p. 237. Why did the majority think that a military commission established by the President's military order and operating under procedures promulgated with his authority was not such a court? How are courts "regularly constituted" in the United States? Could a military commission ever be "regularly constituted"? What was Justice Alito's answer to these questions? Did the Court sufficiently defer to the President in interpreting international law? *See* Julian Ku & John C. Yoo, *Hamdan v. Rumsfeld: The Functional Case for Foreign Affairs Deference to the Executive Branch*, 23 Const. Comment. 179 (2006) (no).

Common Article 3 also forbids "cruel treatment and torture," as well as "outrages upon personal dignity, in particular humiliating and degrading treatment." See *supra* p. 237. Does Common Article 3 now clearly govern investigatory torture of persons captured in the conflict against Al Qaeda, or can you distinguish *Hamdan*?

7. *Military Commission Procedures and Due Process.* In *In re Yamashita*, 327 U.S. 1 (1946), a military commission gave General Yamashita less than three weeks to

prepare for a massive trial that ultimately heard more than 200 witnesses; the commission permitted the government to add 59 new specifications to the 64 pending specifications just two days before trial, then denied his defense any extra time to meet them; it denied Yamashita access to the Army's investigative reports, which might have contained exculpatory materials; it admitted the rankest hearsay; and it even cut back cross-examination "as a means of saving time." *See* Stephen B. Ives Jr., *Vengeance Did Not Deliver Justice*, Wash. Post, Dec. 30, 2001. Most observers concluded that Yamashita did not receive a fair trial, but the Supreme Court refused to review the commission's rulings on the evidence or its conduct of the proceedings and therefore found it "unnecessary to consider what, in other situations, the Fifth Amendment might require." *Yamashita*, 327 U.S. at 23.

Justice Murphy dissented vehemently:

> The immutable rights of the individual, including those secured by the due process clause of the Fifth Amendment, belong not alone to the members of those nations that excel on the battlefield or that subscribe to the democratic ideology. They belong to every person in the world, victor or vanquished, whatever may be his race, color or beliefs. They rise above any status of belligerency or outlawry. They survive any popular passion or frenzy of the moment. No court or legislature or executive, not even the mightiest army in the world, can destroy them. . . .
>
> The failure of the military commission to obey the dictates of the due process requirements of the Fifth Amendment is apparent in this case. . . . No military necessity or other emergency demanded the suspension of the safeguards of due process. Yet petitioner was rushed to trial under an improper charge, given insufficient time to prepare an adequate defense, deprived of the benefits of some of the most elementary rules of evidence, and summarily sentenced to be hanged. [*Id.* at 26-28.]

Justice Rutledge agreed with Justice Murphy in dissent.

Does the Fifth Amendment apply to trial by military commission? Does it depend on where the defendant is captured or whether the military commission sits here or abroad? *See Rasul v. Bush*, 542 U.S. 466, 483 n.15 (2004); *Zadvydas v. Davis*, 533 U.S. 678, 693 (2001) ("[T]he Due Process Clause applies to all 'persons' within the United States, including aliens, whether their presence here is lawful, temporary, or permanent."); *cf. United States v. Verdugo-Urquidez*, 494 U.S. 259 (1990), *supra* p. 712.

The district court found it unnecessary to reach the question whether Hamdan had any constitutional rights, although it noted that the Supreme Court's decision in *Rasul* "may contain some hint that non-citizens held at Guantánamo Bay have some Constitutional protection." 344 F. Supp. 2d 152, 173 n.19 (D.D.C. 2004), *rev'd*, 415 F.3d 33 (D.C. Cir. 2005), *rev'd and remanded*, 126 S. Ct. 2749 (2006). The question of Hamdan's right to due process, if any, was therefore not before the Supreme Court.

C.   MILITARY COMMISSIONS AFTER *HAMDAN*[1]

Congress initially responded to *Hamdan* by enacting the Military Commissions Act of 2006, Pub. L. No. 109-366, 120 Stat. 2600. The Act delegated authority to the

---

1. *See generally* Jennifer K. Elsea, *The Military Commissions Act of 2009: Overview and Legal Issues* (Cong. Res. Serv. RL41163), Apr. 6, 2010; Jennifer K. Elsea, *Comparison of Rights in Military Commission Trials and Trials in Federal Criminal Court* (Cong. Res. Serv. R40932), Jan. 26, 2010, from which the facts in the

President to establish military commissions to try unlawful enemy combatants, and it defined offenses triable by such commissions. It also amended the UCMJ to establish procedures and rules of evidence for trial by military commissions. While the Act provided limited post-trial administrative review and more limited subsequent review by the federal courts, it also stripped all courts of habeas jurisdiction for petitions brought by enemy combatant detainees.

The government proceeded to try Hamdan, David Hicks (an Australian alleged to have fought alongside the Taliban in Afghanistan), and Ali Hamza Ahman Suliman al Bahlul (alleged to have served as Al Qaeda's propaganda chief) by military commission. Although Hicks pleaded guilty to providing material support to terrorism, and the other defendants were convicted, their prosecutions exposed many issues about military commission jurisdiction and procedures.

Upon taking office in 2009, President Obama halted military commissions in order to review their procedures and the detention program. In May 2009, the Administration announced that it was considering restarting the military commission system with upgraded procedures. Congress then incorporated some of these procedural changes and added others in the Military Commissions Act (MCA) of 2009, 10 U.S.C. §§948a-950t (Supp. III 2009).

In November 2009, Attorney General Holder announced plans to try five detainees by military commission, including Omar Khadr, a Canadian captured by U.S. forces at age 15 after a four-hour firefight in Afghanistan in July 2002, during which he is alleged to have thrown a hand grenade that fatally injured a U.S. soldier (the so-called "Child Terrorist"), and whose trial had actually begun in 2007. Holder also announced a plan to transfer five "high value detainees" to New York for trial in federal court. The latter plan was abandoned when it met with strong resistance from Congress, and the Administration said it would try these detainees in military commissions instead. *Statement of the Attorney General on the Prosecution of the 9/11 Conspirators*, Apr. 4, 2011, *available at* http://www.justice.gov/iso/opa/ag/speeches/2011/ag-speech-110404.html; Department of Def., *DOD Announces Charges Sworn Against Five Detainees Allegedly Responsible for 9/11 Attacks* (Mar. 31, 2011), *available at* http://www.defense.gov/releases/release.aspx?releaseid=14532.

The following materials identify selected issues of trial by military commission, with references to the completed trials of Hamdan and Khadr.

1. Personal Jurisdiction

A threshold jurisdictional question of military commission authority is jurisdiction over the person of the defendant. This question implicates the same thorny issues of status in armed conflicts that have sometimes divided the habeas courts. See Chapter 29. The Military Order of November 13, 2001, applied to persons whom the President designated in writing as falling within §2 of that order. The MCA of 2006 subsequently authorized the trial by military commission of an "alien unlawful enemy combatant," defined as a person who engaged in hostilities "or purposefully and materially supported hostilities against the United States or its

---

introduction are chiefly drawn. U.S. Military Commission rulings are collected in the *Military Commission Reporter*, *available at* http://www.wcl.american.edu/nimj/military_commission_law.cfm, and are also provided on a Department of Defense Web site, http://www.defense.gov/news/commissions.html.

co-belligerents who is not a lawful enemy combatant (including a person who is part of the Taliban, Al Qaeda, or associated forces)," or who was determined to be an unlawful enemy combatant by a Combatant Status Review Tribunal (CSRT) "or another competent tribunal established under the authority of the President or the Secretary of Defense." Pub. L. No. 109-366, §3, 120 Stat. 2601. The Act, however, expressly barred military commission jurisdiction over "lawful enemy combatants." *Id.*

NOTES AND QUESTIONS

1. *Personal Jurisdiction Under the Military Order.* If the Order was intended simply to exercise preexisting law-of-war authority, is the statement in §2 of what is, in effect, personal jurisdiction over prospective defendants within such authority? Reflecting concerns raised by the OLC memorandum, *supra* pp. 1068-1069, the Order did not apply to U.S. citizens. But aliens in the United States have been held to enjoy the same rights as citizens. Did the Order apply to them?

2. *Personal Jurisdiction Under MCA of 2006: Who Decides?* The MCA of 2006 gave military commissions jurisdiction over a person "determined to be an unlawful enemy combatant by a Combatant Status Review Tribunal [CSRT]." Pub. L. No. 109-366, §3, 120 Stat. 2601. CSRTs, however, were charged with deciding only whether a detainee was an enemy combatant, not whether he was lawful or unlawful. The military judge in the "Child Terrorist" case found:

> Without any determination of lawful or unlawful status, classification as an "enemy combatant" is sufficient to justify a detaining power's continuing detention of an individual captured in battle or taken into custody in the course of ongoing hostilities. However, under the well recognized body of customary international law relating to armed conflict, and specific provisions of GPW III, lawful combatants enjoy "combatant immunity" for their pre-capture acts of warfare, including the targeting, wounding, or killing of other human beings, provided those actions were performed in the context of ongoing hostilities against lawful military targets, and were not in violation of the law of war. *See Johnson v. Eisentrager,* 339 U.S. 763, 793 (1950) (Black, J. dissenting) ("Legitimate 'acts of warfare,' however murderous, do not justify criminal conviction.... It is no 'crime' to be a soldier....") (citing *Ex parte Quirin,* 317 U.S. 1, 30-31 (1942) ("Mere membership in the armed forces could not under any circumstances create criminal liability....")). Lawful enemy combatants enjoy all the privileges afforded soldiers under the law of war, including combatant immunity and the protections of the Geneva Conventions if wounded or sick, and while being held as prisoners of war (POWs). Additionally, lawful enemy combatants facing judicial proceedings for any of their actions in warfare that violate the law of war, or for post-capture offenses committed while they are POWs, are entitled to be tried by the same courts, and in accordance with the same procedures, that the detaining power would utilize to try members of its own armed forces (i.e., by court-martial for lawful enemy combatants held by the United States). See Arts. 84, 87 and 102, GPW III. [*United States v. Khadr,* CMCR 07-001, Opinion of the Court and Action on Appeal by the United States Filed Pursuant to 10 U.S.C. §950d (U.S. Mil. Comm'n Sept. 24, 2007).]

Defense lawyers for Hamdan and Khadr therefore challenged the military commissions' personal jurisdiction over these defendants, arguing they had not been found "*unlawful* enemy combatants" by CSRTs, and that the commission had no authority to make the jurisdictional finding itself. The military judge in Hamdan's case agreed, finding that the CSRT determination had been made by a different standard than the MCA of 2006, for the different purpose of "determining whether or not [Hamdan] was properly detained and not for the purpose of determining whether he was subject to trial by military commission." *United States v. Hamdan*, Decision and Order — Motion to Dismiss for Lack of Jurisdiction (U.S. Mil. Comm'n June 4, 2007). The judge also found that the President's determination applied to members of Al Qaeda as a group, "and did not represent an individualized determination" about the accused. On the same day, the military judge in Khadr's case reached the same conclusion, adding that nothing in the MCA of 2006 anticipated that the military commission itself would conduct a "mini-trial" to make the findings of fact necessary to assert jurisdiction. *United States v. Khadr*, Hearing Transcript at 17-22 (U.S. Mil. Comm'n June 4, 2007). Both judges dismissed the charges against the defendants.

The MCA of 2006 established and permitted an appeal to the U.S. Court of Military Commission Review. On the government's appeal of dismissal of the charges against Khadr, the Court of Military Commission Review reversed. It agreed that the CSRT designation did not establish jurisdiction. *United States v. Khadr*, 717 F. Supp. 2d 1215 (Ct. Mil. Comm'n Rev. 2007), *appeal dismissed for lack of jurisdiction*, 529 F.3d 1112 (D.C. Cir. 2008). But it held that the military commission could decide for itself whether a defendant was an unlawful enemy combatant and take evidence on that question. *Id.* at 1232. It therefore returned the case to the military commission. The military judge in *Hamdan* ruled that Hamdan qualified as an unlawful enemy combatant because he had taken a direct part in hostilities by driving "a vehicle to and towards the battlefield, containing missiles that could only be used against the United States and its co-belligerents," and he did not fit any of the Geneva Convention definitions of lawful combatants, as he was neither part of regular forces nor of a militia or volunteer forming part of such forces. *United States v. Hamdan*, On Reconsideration Ruling on

Motion to Dismiss for Lack of Jurisdiction (U.S. Mil. Comm'n Dec. 19, 2007).

3. *Personal Jurisdiction and the MCA of 2009.* The MCA of 2009 now provides:

10 U.S.C. §948a. Definitions. . . .

(6) PRIVILEGED BELLIGERENT. — The term "privileged belligerent" means an individual belonging to one of the eight categories enumerated in Article 4 of the Geneva Convention Relative to the Treatment of Prisoners of War.

(7) UNPRIVILEGED ENEMY BELLIGERENT. — The term "unprivileged enemy belligerent" means an individual (other than a privileged belligerent) who —

(A) has engaged in hostilities against the United States or its coalition partners;

(B) has purposefully and materially supported hostilities against the United States or its coalition partners; or

(C) was a part of al Qaeda at the time of the alleged offense under this chapter.

10 U.S.C. §948c. Persons subject to military commissions

Any alien unprivileged enemy belligerent is subject to trial by military commission as set forth in this chapter.

10 U.S.C. §948d. Jurisdiction of military commissions

A military commission under this chapter shall have jurisdiction to try persons subject to this chapter for any offense made punishable by this chapter, sections 904 and 906 of this title (articles 104 and 106 of the Uniform Code of Military Justice), or the law of war, whether such offense was committed before, on, or after September 11, 2001, and may, under such limitations as the President may prescribe, adjudge any punishment not forbidden by this chapter, including the penalty of death when specifically authorized under this chapter. A military commission is a competent tribunal to make a finding sufficient for jurisdiction.

Does this solve the personal jurisdiction problem?

2.   Subject Matter Jurisdiction

Section 1(e) of the Military Order of November 13, 2001, found that it was "necessary for individuals subject to this order . . . when tried, to be tried for violations of the laws of war and other applicable laws by military tribunals." Section 4(a) referred to trial "for any and all offenses triable by military commission," begging the question of what those offenses were. The Order seemed to place law-of-war offenses within a military commission's jurisdiction, but left open the possibility of trial for violations of other, unidentified "applicable laws." If the Order extended subject matter jurisdiction beyond traditional law-of-war offenses, was it lawful?

The MCA of 2006 adopted a list of offenses that DOD had authorized for trial by military commission. The list was substantially retained in the MCA of 2009:

§950t. Crimes triable by military commission

The following offenses shall be triable by military commission under this chapter at any time without limitation:

(1) MURDER OF PROTECTED PERSONS. — Any person subject to this chapter who intentionally kills one or more protected persons shall be punished by death or such other punishment as a military commission under this chapter may direct.

(2) ATTACKING CIVILIANS. — Any person subject to this chapter who intentionally engages in an attack upon a civilian population as such, or individual civilians not taking active part in hostilities, shall be punished, if death results to one or more of the victims, by death or such other punishment as a military commission under this chapter may direct, and, if death does not result to any of the victims, by such punishment, other than death, as a military commission under this chapter may direct. . . .

(7) TAKING HOSTAGES. — Any person subject to this chapter who, having knowingly seized or detained one or more persons, threatens to kill, injure, or continue to detain such person or persons with the intent of compelling any nation, person other than the hostage, or group of persons to act or refrain from acting as an explicit or implicit condition for the safety or release of such person or persons, shall be punished, if death results to one or more of the victims, by death or such other punishment as a military commission under this chapter may direct, and, if death does not result to any of the victims, by such punishment, other than death, as a military commission under this chapter may direct. . . .

(9) USING PROTECTED PERSONS AS A SHIELD. — Any person subject to this chapter who positions, or otherwise takes advantage of, a protected person with the

intent to shield a military objective from attack or to shield, favor, or impede military operations, shall be punished, if death results to one or more of the victims, by death or such other punishment as a military commission under this chapter may direct, and, if death does not result to any of the victims, by such punishment, other than death, as a military commission under this chapter may direct.

(10) USING PROTECTED PROPERTY AS A SHIELD. — Any person subject to this chapter who positions, or otherwise takes advantage of the location of, protected property with the intent to shield a military objective from attack, or to shield, favor, or impede military operations, shall be punished as a military commission under this chapter may direct. . . .

(15) MURDER IN VIOLATION OF THE LAW OF WAR. — Any person subject to this chapter who intentionally kills one or more persons, including privileged belligerents, in violation of the law of war shall be punished by death or such other punishment as a military commission under this chapter may direct. . . .

(23) HIJACKING OR HAZARDING A VESSEL OR AIRCRAFT. — Any person subject to this chapter who intentionally seizes, exercises unauthorized control over, or endangers the safe navigation of a vessel or aircraft that is not a legitimate military objective shall be punished, if death results to one or more of the victims, by death or such other punishment as a military commission under this chapter may direct, and, if death does not result to any of the victims, by such punishment, other than death, as a military commission under this chapter may direct.

(24) TERRORISM. — Any person subject to this chapter who intentionally kills or inflicts great bodily harm on one or more protected persons, or intentionally engages in an act that evinces a wanton disregard for human life, in a manner calculated to influence or affect the conduct of government or civilian population by intimidation or coercion, or to retaliate against government conduct, shall be punished, if death results to one or more of the victims, by death or such other punishment as a military commission under this chapter may direct, and, if death does not result to any of the victims, by such punishment, other than death, as a military commission under this chapter may direct.

(25) PROVIDING MATERIAL SUPPORT FOR TERRORISM. —

(A) OFFENSE. — Any person subject to this chapter who provides material support or resources, knowing or intending that they are to be used in preparation for, or in carrying out, an act of terrorism (as set forth in paragraph (24) of this section), or who intentionally provides material support or resources to an international terrorist organization engaged in hostilities against the United States, knowing that such organization has engaged or engages in terrorism (as so set forth), shall be punished as a military commission under this chapter may direct.

(B) MATERIAL SUPPORT OR RESOURCES DEFINED. — In this paragraph, the term "material support or resources" has the meaning given that term in section 2339A(b) of title 18.

(26) WRONGFULLY AIDING THE ENEMY. — Any person subject to this chapter who, in breach of an allegiance or duty to the United States, knowingly and intentionally aids an enemy of the United States, or one of the co-belligerents of the enemy, shall be punished as a military commission under this chapter may direct. . . .

(29) CONSPIRACY. — Any person subject to this chapter who conspires to commit one or more substantive offenses triable by military commission under this subchapter, and who knowingly does any overt act to effect the object of the conspiracy, shall be punished, if death results to one or more of the victims, by death or such other punishment as a military commission under this chapter may direct, and, if death does not result to any of the victims, by such punishment, other than death, as a military commission under this chapter may direct. . . .

NOTES AND QUESTIONS

1. *Murder in Violation of the Law of War.* As the Court of Military Commission Review declared in *Khadr*, "lawful combatants enjoy 'combatant immunity' for their pre-capture acts of warfare, including the killing of other human beings, provided those actions were performed in the context of ongoing hostilities against lawful military targets, and were not in violation of the law of war." *Khadr, supra,* 717 F. Supp. 2d at 1221. While a civilian who kills a lawful combatant can be tried in civilian courts for murder, it is not clear that such a murder constitutes a violation of the law of war, or that the same principles govern in armed conflict not of an international character, where combatant immunity does not apply. *See* Elsea, *The Military Commissions Act of 2009, supra* p. 1096 n.1, at 11 and authorities cited there. Murder of *protected persons* has been held a war crime, *id.,* but that crime is already covered under a distinct part of the MCA of 2009. *See* 10 U.S.C. §950t(1) (Supp. III 2009). *See generally* David Glazier, *A Court Without Jurisdiction: A Critical Assessment of the Military Charges Against Omar Khadr* 9-18 (Aug. 31, 2010), *available at* http://ssrn.com/abstract=1669946.

Khadr was charged with murder in violation of the law of war for allegedly throwing a grenade at U.S. soldiers during a firefight in which he was himself shot twice in the back and lost an eye. One scholar argues that this charge

> has the practical effect of converting this armed conflict into a human shooting season: the government asserts U.S. combatants had the right to shoot Khadr on sight (he was shot twice in the back based on his being a "hostile" rather than because he posed any particular threat at the time) yet criminally prosecuted him for fighting back. [Glazier, *supra,* at 15-16.]

Leaving aside the question whether a participant in an active firefight is a "particular threat" during the shooting, does this criticism require that Khadr be tried as a civilian in a criminal court, if he is to be tried for murder at all?

A military judge in *United States v. Jawad,* D-007, Ruling on Defense Motion to Dismiss — Lack of Subject Matter Jurisdiction (U.S. Mil. Comm'n Sept. 24, 2008), ruled that it was not enough for the government to show that the defendant was an unlawful enemy combatant who had committed a murder. "[T]hat the Accused might fail to qualify as a lawful combatant does not automatically lead to the conclusion that his conduct violated the law of war, and the propriety of the charges in this case must be based on the nature of the act, not simply on the status of the accused." *Id.* at 3. The government therefore also had to prove "that the method, manner or circumstances used violated the law of war." *Id.* at 2.

2. *Conspiracy?* A plurality in *Hamdan* found that conspiracy was not a recognized violation of the common law of war. But it also emphasized that "[t]here is no suggestion that Congress has, in exercise of its constitutional authority to 'define and punish . . . Offences against the Law of Nations,' U.S. Const., Art. I, §8, cl. 10, positively identified 'conspiracy' as a war crime." Now it has, in the MCA of 2009. Could Hamdan therefore be tried on remand pursuant to the MCA of 2009? Does its enactment cure the problem identified by the plurality?

3. *Material Support?* "Providing material support for terrorism" appears to be another new crime. This provision of the MCA of 2009 is borrowed from the domestic criminal laws that have been deployed so aggressively and successfully by U.S. prosecutors in federal courts. See Chapter 34. But does it run afoul of the common law of war for the same reasons as the conspiracy charges against Hamdan, or is it now lawful? The military judge in *Hamdan* concluded that it was, in fact, consistent with the common law of war, because military commissions tried defendants for cooperating with guerillas or "guerilla-marauders" in the Civil War. *See United States v. Hamdan*, D-012, Ruling on Motion to Dismiss (Ex Post Facto) (U.S. Mil. Comm'n July 14, 2008). Others have argued that the Civil War precedents were called into question by *Milligan* and that some of them appear to have involved distinguishable violations of martial law or occupation law rather than the law of war. Elsea, *The Military Commissions Act of 2009, supra*, at 13.

The Obama administration itself admitted doubt that material support crimes were offenses under the law of war.

[T]here are serious questions as to whether material support for terrorism or terrorist groups is a traditional violation of the law of war. The President has made clear that military commissions are to be used only to prosecute law of war offenses.... [O]ur experts believe that there is a significant risk that appellate courts will ultimately conclude that material support for terrorism is not a traditional law of war offense, thereby reversing hard-won convictions and leading to questions about the system's legitimacy. [*Legal Issues Regarding Military Commissions and the Trial of Detainees for Violations of the Law of War: Hearing Before the S. Comm. on Armed Servs.*, 111th Cong. 12 (2009) (submitted statement of David Kris, Assistant Attorney General).]

Congress included the material support crime in the MCA of 2009 in spite of the Administration's expressed reservation.

4. *Ex Post Facto Law?* The United States has recognized Article 75(4)(c) of 1977 Geneva Additional Protocol I as customary international law. It provides, in part, that "no one shall be accused or convicted of a criminal offence on account of any act or omission which did not constitute a criminal offence under the national or international law to which he was subject at the time when it was committed." Essentially the same rule applies to conflicts not of an international character. Glazier, *supra*, at 6. If Congress created new crimes in the MCA of 2009 (or 2006), would it violate Article 75 to charge defendants for acts that preceded enactment of the statute? Congress gave the following answer in the MCA of 2009:

The provisions of this subchapter codify offenses that have traditionally been triable by military commission. This chapter does not establish new crimes that did not exist before the date of the enactment of this subchapter, as amended [on October 28, 2009], but rather codifies those crimes for trial by military commission. Because the provisions of this subchapter codify offenses that have traditionally been triable under the law of war or otherwise triable by military commission, this subchapter does not preclude trial for offenses that occurred before the date of the enactment of this subchapter, as so amended. [10 U.S.C. §950p(d) (Supp. III 2009).]

Is it up to Congress, or may the courts independently decide such questions regarding their jurisdiction? Glazier, *supra* (arguing the latter).

5. *"Define and Punish" Authority?* The Constitution expressly vests Congress with the power to "define and punish offenses against the law of nations." U.S. Const. art. I, §8, cl. 10. Why does this power not provide a sufficient answer to the questions of subject matter jurisdiction raised by the foregoing notes? Can Congress not "define" as it sees fit? Or is this power "itself logically constrained in [']against the law of nations[']"? Glazier, *supra*, at 8. Did the Framers intend Congress simply to act as a scribe, or was it vested with a more creative task? *See id.* (arguing that "the purpose for including the clause . . . was to allow Congress to put Americans on notice as to the precise conduct that would constitute a crime where there might otherwise be ambiguity"). *See generally* Stephen I. Vladeck, *The Laws of War as a Constitutional Limit on Military Jurisdiction*, 4 J. Nat'l Security L. & Pol'y 295 (2010).

6. *Last in Time?* Does legislative authority rest *just* on the Define and Punish Clause? Why not on the clauses vesting power to make "rules concerning capture" or "rules for the government and regulation of the land and naval forces," or even just to make "all laws which shall be necessary and proper for carrying into execution" the power vested in the President as Commander in Chief for conducting armed conflict? U.S. Const. art. I, §8, cls. 11, 14, and 18, respectively. Does the international law of war restrict these legislative powers? In the event of a conflict between that body of law and the MCA of 2009, which prevails?

3.   Evidence Obtained by Coercion

The Military Order of November 13, 2001, permitted admission of such evidence as the presiding officer of the military commission found would "have probative value to a reasonable person." This rule would have permitted evidence obtained by torture or other coercion, if it had such probative value, as well as hearsay evidence that met the same standard. It thus seemingly tolerated evidence that would be inadmissible in a federal criminal court. The MCA of 2006 prohibited evidence obtained by torture, but allowed evidence obtained by coercion that does not amount to torture committed prior to the 2005 Detainee Treatment Act (*supra*, p. 786) if the "totality of the circumstances" showed that it had probative value and the interests of justice would be served. Pub. L. No. 109-366, §3, 120 Stat. 2607 .

The MCA of 2009 is more restrictive:

10 U.S.C. §948r. Exclusion of statements obtained by torture or cruel, inhuman, or degrading treatment; prohibition of self-incrimination; admission of other statements of the accused

(a) EXCLUSION OF STATEMENTS OBTAIN[ED] BY TORTURE OR CRUEL, INHUMAN, OR DEGRADING TREATMENT.—No statement obtained by the use of torture or by cruel, inhuman, or degrading treatment (as defined by section 1003 of the Detainee Treatment Act of 2005 (42 U.S.C. 2000dd)), whether or not under color of law, shall be admissible in a military commission under this chapter, except against a person accused of torture or such treatment as evidence that the statement was made.

(b) SELF-INCRIMINATION PROHIBITED. — No person shall be required to testify against himself or herself at a proceeding of a military commission under this chapter.

(c) OTHER STATEMENTS OF THE ACCUSED. — A statement of the accused may be admitted in evidence in a military commission under this chapter only if the military judge finds —

(1) that the totality of the circumstances renders the statement reliable and possessing sufficient probative value; and

(2) that —

(A) the statement was made incident to lawful conduct during military operations at the point of capture or during closely related active combat engagement, and the interests of justice would best be served by admission of the statement into evidence; or

(B) the statement was voluntarily given.

(d) DETERMINATION OF VOLUNTARINESS. — In determining for purposes of subsection (c)(2)(B) whether a statement was voluntarily given, the military judge shall consider the totality of the circumstances, including, as appropriate, the following:

(1) The details of the taking of the statement, accounting for the circumstances of the conduct of military and intelligence operations during hostilities.

(2) The characteristics of the accused, such as military training, age, and education level.

(3) The lapse of time, change of place, or change in identity of the questioners between the statement sought to be admitted and any prior questioning of the accused. . . .

In each of the following two cases, the defense cited this provision in support of a motion to suppress statements made by the defendant.

United States of America v. Mohammed Jawad

United States Military Commission, Sept. 24, 2008
D-008, Ruling on Defense Motion to Dismiss — Torture of Detainee

1. The defense asserts the Accused was subjected to an intentional sleep deprivation program and other abusive treatment while detained in U.S. custody which constitutes torture in violation of the law of war, U.S. law and DOD regulations and policy[1] and moves to dismiss the Charge and specifications with prejudice. The government opposes the motion, submitting that, even if the allegations are true, dismissal of charges is not the appropriate remedy, if one exists at all.

2. On or about December 17, 2002, in Kabul, Afghanistan, the Accused allegedly threw a hand grenade into a vehicle in which two American service members and their Afghan interpreter were riding. All suffered serious injuries. The Accused was immediately apprehended by Afghan police and transferred to U.S. custody the next day. He remained in continuous U.S. custody until his transfer to Guantanamo Bay, Cuba on or about February 6, 2003.

3. On December 25, 2003, the accused attempted suicide.

---

1. The President directed in Military Order 1, dated November 13, 2001, that detainees would be treated humanely. A February 7, 2002 White House memo reaffirmed this order and stated further they would be treated, "to the extent appropriate and consistent with military necessity, in a manner consistent with the principles of Geneva."

4. As early as November 2003, Joint Task Force-Guantanamo Bay personnel (JTF-GTMO) used a sleep deprivation measure to disorient selected detainees thought to have important intelligence data, disrupt their sleep cycles and biorhythms, make them more compliant and break down their resistance to interrogation. Pursuant to this technique, euphemistically referred to as the "frequent flyer" program, a detainee would be repeatedly moved from one detention cell to another in quick intervals, usually at night.

5. Shortly after assuming command of JTF-GTMO in March 2004, Major General (MG) Jay Hood ordered the "frequent flyer" program discontinued. Apparently unknown to MG Hood, the accused was subjected to the frequent flyer program and moved from cell to cell 112 times from 7 May 2004 to 20 May 2004, on average of about once every three hours. The accused was shackled and unshackled as he was moved from cell to cell. The Accused was not interrogated and the scheme was calculated to profoundly disrupt his mental senses.

6. While the "frequent flyer" program was intended to create a feeling of hope-lessness and despair in the detainee and set the stage for successful interrogations, by March 2004 the accused was of no intelligence value to any government agency. The infliction of the "frequent flyer" technique upon the Accused thus had no legitimate interrogation purpose.

7. On or about June 2, 2008, the Accused was beaten, kicked, and pepper sprayed for not complying with a guard's instructions. He suffered, among other injuries, a broken nose.

8. The conditions experienced by the Accused while confined at Guantanamo Bay include excessive heat, constant lighting, loud noise, linguistic isolation (separating the accused from other Pashto speakers), and, on at least two separate occasions, 30 days physical isolation.

9. The Accused has not apparently suffered any permanent physical injuries as a result of his detention in U.S. custody. While the long term psychological impact of the Accused's detention is unclear, the Rule for Military Commission (RMC) 706 board concluded the Accused is "not currently suffering from a mental disease or defect," "does have sufficient present ability to consult with his lawyers with a reasonable degree of rational understanding" and "does have sufficient mental capacity to understand the nature of the proceedings against him and cooperate intelligently in his defense." Additionally, the Accused does not require immediate medical or psychological treatment.

10. The Military Commissions Act prohibits both the torture and cruel and inhuman treatment of detainees. Any degrading treatment carries a presumption it was imposed as a punitive not preventative measure.

11. The defense asserts that the government's conduct amounts to torture and violates the principles of due process of such a magnitude that dismissal of the charges is the only acceptable remedy.

12. This Commission finds that, under the circumstances, subjecting this Accused to the "frequent flyer" program from May 7-20, 2004 constitutes abusive conduct and cruel and inhuman treatment. Further, it came at least two months after the JTF-GTMO commander had ordered the program stopped. Its continuation was not simple negligence but flagrant misbehavior. Those responsible should face appropriate disciplinary action, if warranted under the circumstances.

13. That being said, the narrow issue before this Military Commission is whether dismissal of the charges against this Accused is appropriate for the conduct of an apparent few government agents. Answering this question does not require the Military Commission to decide as fact that this Accused was tortured. Assuming, but not deciding, that the government's actions against this Accused produced the pain and suffering of the requisite physical and/or mental intensity and of such duration to rise to the level of "torture," this Military Commission finds that the remedy sought by the defense is not warranted under the circumstances.

14. It is beyond peradventure that a Military Commission may dismiss charges because of abusive treatment of the Accused. However, when other remedies are available to adequately address the wrong, dismissal should be the last of an escalating list of options. Here, the Commission finds other remedies are available to adequately address the wrong inflicted upon the Accused, including, but not limited to, sentence credit towards any approved period of confinement, excluding statements and any evidence derived from the abusive treatment, and prohibiting persons who may have been involved in any improper actions against the Accused from testifying at trial. The Military Commission will rule upon the appropriate application of these, and other proposed remedies, as dictated by developments in this case.

15. Accordingly, the defense motion to dismiss based on torture of the Accused is DENIED.

So ordered this 24th day of September 2008.

Stephen R. Henley
Colonel, US Army
Military Judge

United States of America v. Omar Ahmed Khadr

United States Military Commission, Aug. 17, 2010
Suppression Motions, D-094, D-111, Ruling

1. The Defense moves to suppress certain statements made by the accused as set out in its briefs submitted in support of D094. The Defense alleges such statements are the product of torture, involuntary, unreliable, do not serve the interest of justice, and are fruit of the poisonous tree. Their admission, the defense further alleges, is prohibited under §948r of the Military Commissions Act of 2009 (MCA) and Military Commissions Rule of Evidence (M.C.R.E.) 304. The Defense also moves to suppress the videotape found at the compound where the firefight occurred as set out in its brief submitted in support of D-111. The Defense alleges the videotape was found only as a result of statements obtained improperly from the accused. The Government opposes both motions.

2. The Commission has considered the briefs, the witnesses' testimony, all the other evidence offered during the suppression hearing, and the oral arguments and finds as follows:

a. The accused engaged in a firefight with U.S. forces in Khost, Afghanistan, on 27 July 2002. The accused was severely wounded during the course of the firefight and was captured after the firefight ended. The U.S. forces treated the accused at the scene and transported him to Bagram Airfield, Afghanistan, where U.S. medical personnel operated on the accused and saved his life. The accused received world class medical care from the time he was captured and continues to receive the same world class medical care throughout his detention.

b. The accused was 15 years old at the time of his capture. The accused received limited formal education and received some home schooling prior to his capture; however, the accused speaks several languages, including English. The accused speaks English well enough that he did not need an interpreter to communicate effectively with U.S. forces, U.S. medical personnel, or any other U.S. personnel. At times the accused would volunteer to help translate for U.S. personnel and other detainees. . . .

i. Interrogator #1 was the lead interrogator for the accused while the accused was at the Bagram detention center. He interrogated the accused 20-25 times. He always interrogated the accused in an interrogation room. He never interrogated the accused in the hospital. He used a "fear up" technique as a last resort with the accused. It is a technique used to attempt to raise the fear level of the detainee. He, at times, used a harsh tone of voice with the accused by yelling and cursing at the accused if he caught the accused in what he thought were lies. The accused told him he did not like the cursing and stopped talking to Interrogator #1 at one point because of the cursing. Interrogator #1 one time "got into the accused's face" by yelling at him and flipping a bench so it made a loud noise. The "fear up" technique included the use of stress positions on detainees who were healthy enough to endure that technique. Interrogator #1 never used the stress position technique on the accused. He never inflicted pain on or tried to injure the accused. He never used any dogs while interrogating the accused.

j. During one of the interrogations, Interrogator #1 told the accused a fictitious story about a detainee, an Afghan male, who lied to interrogators and was sent to a US prison for lying. There were "big, black guys" in the prison. The Afghan male was a kid away from home who they could not protect. The Afghan male got hurt when the "big, black guys" raped him in the showers. This fictitious story was unsuccessful in obtaining information from the accused. The "fear up" technique was also not successful in obtaining information from the accused.

k. Interrogator #1 used other types of techniques on the accused, such as a "love of freedom" and "pride/ego down." These were attempts to gather information through appealing to a person's desire to go home or implying that he was not really an important person and attempting to get him to talk about the people who really were important. He also used "fear of incarceration" as a technique. It was used in an attempt to gain cooperation in order to return to a normal life rather than being detained. These techniques did not amount to torture or abuse of the accused.

l. Guards would move detainees, to include the accused, with a hood over their heads. However, Interrogator #1 never interrogated the accused while he had a hood over his head. Interrogator #1 never threw cold water on the accused. He never bound the accused's hands to the ceiling and made him stand. He never made the accused carry heavy water bottles. He never used bright lights with the accused. He never tied a bag over the accused's head. He never pulled or yanked the accused off a stretcher.

m. The accused never told Interrogator #1 that there was a videotape (Appellate Exhibit (AE) 188 remarked as AE 230) in the house where the firefight took place. However, Interrogator #1 eventually obtained a copy of the videotape found in the house where the firefight took place. After he showed the videotape to the accused, the accused appeared somewhat shaken. The accused said that "the Americans know all." There was a dramatic change to the accused's cooperation after he saw the videotape. It was the use of the videotape which was successful in obtaining information from the accused rather than the other techniques used by Interrogator #1. . . .

4. . . .

c. There is no credible evidence the accused was ever tortured as that term in defined under M.C.R.E. 304(b)(3), even using liberal interpretation considering the accused's age. While Interrogator #1 told the accused a story about the rape of an Afghan youth in an America prison, there is no evidence that story caused the accused to make any incriminating statements then or in the future. In fact, the credible evidence is that the accused started to make incriminating statements only after he learned the Americans found the videotape at the compound where the firefight took place which shows the accused and others making improvised explosives and placing them along the roadside at night. No statement offered against the accused was derived from, the product of, or connected to any story Interrogator #1 told to the accused. . . .

e. The Commission concludes that, under the totality of the circumstances, the statements offered against the accused are reliable, possess sufficient probative value, were made voluntarily, are not the product of torture or mistreatment, and whose admission is in the interest of justice.

6. There is no evidence the accused made any statement to anyone about the existence of a videotape found at the scene of the firefight. There is no evidence to support the defense allegation that the commander made a decision to search the compound where the firefight occurred as a result of intelligence information obtained from the accused. The evidence is clear, and the Commission finds, the commander's decision to search the compound where the videotape was found was independent of and not derived from any interrogation of the accused. The videotape is not the "fruit of the poisonous tree" as there is no "poisonous tree."

7. The Commission finds the Government has met its burden to show the admissibility of the statements and videotape by a preponderance of the evidence. See MCRE 304(d)(1).

8. Accordingly, the motions to suppress the accused's statements and the videotape are denied.

So ordered this 17th day of August 2010.

Patrick J. Parish
COL, JA
Military Judge

NOTES AND QUESTIONS

1. *Evidence from "Torture Lite"?* The MCA of 2009 prohibits statements obtained by torture or cruel, inhuman, or degrading treatment, except as evidence of torture by the defendant. The military judge found that use of the "Frequent Flyer" program against Jawad constituted torture that would justify excluding evidence derived by the abusive treatment, although not the dismissal of the charges. Khadr was subject to the "Fear Up" technique instead, while he was recuperating from surgery, and still 15 years old. Why didn't this technique require exclusion of his statements? Should his age or condition make a difference? Khadr claimed that he was hooded, had his hands tied above a door for hours, threatened with dogs, and denied use of the washroom, forcing him to urinate on himself. Multiple government witnesses denied this, as reflected in omitted parts of the ruling, but his chief interrogator later pleaded guilty to abusing detainees to extract confessions after one detainee died in his custody. *See* Michelle Shepard, *Khadr's Military Interrogation Faces Scrutiny*, Toronto Star, Mar. 25, 2008.

Even if you disagree with the military judge in *Khadr*, the MCA ban is only on statements obtained by coercive treatment. The court found that it was after Khadr was shown a videotape seized from the compound where he was found, in which he is seen making and planting roadside bombs, that he started talking, and that his cooperation was fostered by FBI interrogators who treated him more gently. As to these statements, the "totality of the circumstances" arguably supported the finding of voluntariness, unless Khadr was still suffering from prior coercive treatment. *See* Peter Margulies, *The Military Commissions Act, Coerced Confessions, and the Role of the Courts* (Dec. 20, 2006), *available at* http://papers.ssrn.com/sol3/papers.cfm?abstract_id=954415; *cf.* Norman Abrams, *Terrorism Prosecutions in Federal Court: Exceptions to Constitutional Evidence Rules and the Development of a Cabined Exception for Coerced Confessions* (May 19, 2011), *available at* http://papers.ssrn.com/sol3/papers.cfm?abstract_id=1846963 (discussing modified rules for coerced confessions in federal terrorism trials).

2. *Evidence from Torture?* In a different military commission trial, it was revealed that statements were obtained after death threats to the detainee and his family. Do they constitute statements obtained by torture? See *supra* pp. 914-922 (defining torture). Not only were those statements suppressed, but also subsequent statements were suppressed because the circumstances did not sufficiently dissipate the coercive effect of the prior threats. *United States v. Jawad*, D-022, Ruling on Defense Motion to Suppress Out-of-Court Statements of the Accused to Afghan Authorities (U.S. Mil. Comm'n Oct. 28, 2008); *United States v. Jawad*, D-021, Ruling on Defense Motion to Suppress Out-of-Court Statements Made While in U.S. Custody (U.S. Mil. Comm'n Nov. 9, 2008).

Some statements by Khalid Sheikh Mohammed, the alleged mastermind of the 9/11 attacks, were obtained from repeated waterboarding. Scott Shane, *Waterboarding Used 266 Times on 2 Suspects*, N.Y. Times, Apr. 20, 2009. One reason members of Congress objected to the Administration's plan to try him in federal court was the likely inadmissibility of his statements in that forum. Would such statements be admissible in a trial by military commission? If not, can he now be successfully prosecuted before a military commission?

4. Other Evidentiary Rules

The Federal Rules of Evidence have elaborate rules against hearsay, but multiple exceptions as well. Fed. R. Evid. 801-807. There is no general rule against hearsay in formal, on-the-record administrative adjudication, in which "[a]ny oral or documentary evidence may be received, but the agency as a matter of policy shall provide for the exclusion of irrelevant, immaterial, or unduly repetitious evidence." Administrative Procedure Act, 5 U.S.C. §556 (2006).

The MCA of 2009 provides, in relevant part:

10 U.S.C. §949a(b)(3)

In making exceptions in the applicability in trials by military commission under this chapter from the procedures and rules otherwise applicable in general courts-martial, the Secretary of Defense may provide the following:

(A) Evidence seized outside the United States shall not be excluded from trial by military commission on the grounds that the evidence was not seized pursuant to a search warrant or authorization.

(B) A statement of the accused that is otherwise admissible shall not be excluded from trial by military commission on grounds of alleged coercion or compulsory self-incrimination so long as the evidence complies with the provisions of section 948r of this title.

(C) Evidence shall be admitted as authentic so long as —

(i) the military judge of the military commission determines that there is sufficient evidence that the evidence is what it is claimed to be; and

(ii) the military judge instructs the members that they may consider any issue as to authentication or identification of evidence in determining the weight, if any, to be given to the evidence.

(D) Hearsay evidence not otherwise admissible under the rules of evidence applicable in trial by general courts-martial may be admitted in a trial by military commission only if —

(i) the proponent of the evidence makes known to the adverse party, sufficiently in advance to provide the adverse party with a fair opportunity to meet the evidence, the proponent's intention to offer the evidence, and the particulars of the evidence (including information on the circumstances under which the evidence was obtained); and

(ii) the military judge, after taking into account all of the circumstances surrounding the taking of the statement, including the degree to which the statement is corroborated, the indicia of reliability within the statement itself, and whether the will of the declarant was overborne, determines that —

(I) the statement is offered as evidence of a material fact;

(II) the statement is probative on the point for which it is offered;

(III) direct testimony from the witness is not available as a practical matter, taking into consideration the physical location of the witness, the unique circumstances of military and intelligence operations during hostilities, and the adverse impacts on military or intelligence operations that would likely result from the production of the witness; and

(IV) the general purposes of the rules of evidence and the interests of justice will best be served by admission of the statement into evidence....

NOTES AND QUESTIONS

1. *The Necessity for Relaxed Hearsay and Authentication Rules.* In *Hamdi*, the Supreme Court held that rules against hearsay "may need to be accepted as the most reliable available evidence from the Government" in a proceeding to decide enemy combatant status. *Hamdi v. Rumsfeld*, 542 U.S. 507, 533-534 (2004). Why should that be so? Does the same reasoning apply to evidence used to prosecute a detainee for war crimes? Khadr was seized during a firefight that destroyed much of the compound in which he had been found and left many dead and wounded. Do these circumstances affect your view of the evidentiary rules applicable to evidence in his trial by military commission? *See generally* Eun Young Choi, *Veritas, Not Vengeance: An Examination of the Evidentiary Rules for Military Commissions in the War on Terrorism*, 42 Harv. C.R.-C.L. L. Rev. 139 (2007) (written before enactment of the MCA of 2009).

2. *More "Totality of the Circumstances."* Does the MCA rule on hearsay sufficiently assure the reliability of evidence used in military commissions? If not, what rule would be better? Why should we adopt a stronger rule, when the Administrative Procedure Act provides a weaker one for formal administrative adjudications in the United States, such as actions to enforce a civil penalty against a respondent who is charged with violating an agency regulation?

3. *Classified Evidence.* The MCA of 2009 provides for the protection of classified information:

§949p-1. Protection of classified information: applicability of subchapter

(a) PROTECTION OF CLASSIFIED INFORMATION.—Classified information shall be protected and is privileged from disclosure if disclosure would be detrimental to the national security. Under no circumstances may a military judge order the release of classified information to any person not authorized to receive such information.

(b) ACCESS TO EVIDENCE. —Any information admitted into evidence pursuant to any rule, procedure, or order by the military judge shall be provided to the accused.

(c) DECLASSIFICATION. —Trial counsel shall work with the original classification authorities for evidence that may be used at trial to ensure that such evidence is declassified to the maximum extent possible, consistent with the requirements of national security. . . .

Provisions for defendant's access to classified information are partly modeled on the Classified Information Procedures Act (CIPA). In the *Hamdan* case, the defense requested access to "high value" detainees whom it hoped would testify that Hamdan was merely a driver, much as Zacarias Moussaoui requested access to a high-value detainee whom he hoped would testify that he was not operationally involved in the 9/11 attacks. See Chapter 35. The court granted the access subject to supervision by a government security officer, who would review each question and answer, and who would redact or summarize any answer by which he thought the detainee was attempting to communicate a secret message. *United States v. Hamdan*, P-004, On Reconsideration Ruling on Motion for Stay and for Access to High Value Detainees (U.S. Mil. Comm'n Mar. 14, 2008).

5.   Assessment

Prior to the *Hamdan* decision, Justice Scalia, in an unguarded moment, reportedly said of proposals to try enemy combatants in civil courts:

> Give me a break. If he was captured by my army on the battlefield, that is where he belongs. I had a son on that battlefield and they were shooting at my son and I'm not about to give this man who was captured in a war a full jury trial. I mean it's crazy. [*Supreme Court: Detainees' Rights — Justice Scalia Speaks His Mind*, Newsweek, Apr. 3, 2006.]

Do you think it is crazy? In what ways is trial by military commission under the MCA of 2009 now different from a civil trial?

VIII
Homeland Security

Homeland Security 37

Long before the 2001 attacks on the World Trade Center and the Pentagon, the U.S. government had begun to develop extensive plans for a response to asymmetric attacks on the homeland. In Chapters 16-35 we examined the elaborate federal apparatus for detecting and interdicting terrorist threats. Here we consider what to do if those prophylactic efforts fail.

Federal government plans for homeland security have evolved considerably, particularly since September 11. However, the planning documents, organization charts of the important players, and directives telling them what to do and when to do it have proven extremely ephemeral. Instead of tracing any particular plan for responding to a terrorist attack, we approach the problem functionally. To set the stage, in Part A we describe a credible worst-case scenario—an attack on the U.S. homeland using a weapon of mass destruction, and the responses of various government authorities. In Part B, we briefly review current federal government plans and authorities for responding to such an attack, particularly those involving interaction with first responders—local, state, and regional emergency personnel. In Part C, we consider the legal authorities for these first responders, focusing especially on the coordination of their roles. Part D examines federal authorities that may be invoked if a bioterrorist attack requires the compulsion of persons—isolation, quarantine, or vaccination—or commandeering of resources.

A. WORST-CASE SCENARIO: A PLAGUE ON YOUR CITY

Thomas V. Inglesby, Rita Grossman & Tara O'Toole, A Plague on Your City: Observations from TOPOFF

32 Clinical Infectious Diseases 436 (2001)
available at http://www.journals.uchicago.edu/CID/journal/
issues/v32n3/001347/001347.html

May 17: An aerosol of pneumonic plague (*Yersinia pestis*) bacilli is released covertly from a fire extinguisher at a benefit concert in the Denver Performing Arts Center.

1117

May 20: The Colorado Department of Public Health and Environment receives information that increasing numbers of persons began seeking medical attention at Denver area hospitals for cough and fever during the evening of May 19th. By early afternoon on May 20, 500 persons with these symptoms have received medical care, and 25 of those have died.

The Health Department notifies the CDC of the increased volume of sick. Plague is identified first by the state laboratory and subsequently confirmed in a patient specimen by the CDC lab at Ft. Collins. A public health emergency is declared by the State Health Officer, who immediately requests support from DHHS's Office of Emergency Preparedness. The Governor's Emergency Epidemic Response Committee assembles to respond to the unfolding crisis.

Thirty-one CDC staff are sent to Denver. Hospitals and clinics around the Denver area that just a day earlier were dealing with what appeared to be an unusual increase in influenza cases are now recalling staffs, implementing emergency plans, and seeking assistance in determining treatment protocols and protective measures. By late afternoon, hospital staff are beginning to call in sick, and antibiotics and ventilators are becoming more scarce. Some hospital staff have donned respiratory protective equipment.

The CDC and the FBI are notified by Denver police that a dead man has been found with terrorist literature and paraphernalia in his possession; his cause of death is unknown.

The Governor issues an executive order that restricts travel — including bus, rail and air travel — into or out of 14 Denver Metro counties, and commandeers all antibiotics that can be used to prevent or treat plague. At a press conference, the Governor informs the public that there is a plague outbreak in Denver as a result of a terrorist attack, and he announces his executive order. Citizens are instructed to seek treatment at a medical facility if feeling ill or if they have been in contact with a known or suspected case of plague. Those who are well are directed to stay in their homes and avoid public gatherings. The public is told that the disease is spread from person to person only "if you are within 6 feet of someone who is infected and coughing," and told that dust masks are effective at preventing the spread of disease.

Confirmed cases of plague are identified in Colorado locations other than Denver. Patient interviews suggest that most victims were at the Performing Arts Center days earlier. It is announced that the Governor is working with the President of the United States to resolve the crisis and that federal resources are being brought in to support the state agencies. By the end of the day, 783 cases of pneumonic plague have occurred, and 123 persons have died.

May 21: Broadcast media report that a "national crash effort" is underway to move large quantities of antibiotics to the region, as the CDC brings in its "national stockpile," but the quantity of available antibiotics is uncertain. The report explains that early administration of antibiotics is effective in treating plague but that antibiotics must be started within 24 hours of developing symptoms. A news story a few hours later reports that hospitals are running out of antibiotics.

A shipment from the National Pharmaceutical Stockpile (NPS) arrives in Denver, but there are great difficulties moving antibiotics from the airport to the persons who need it for treatment and prophylaxis. Out-of-state cases begin to be reported. The CDC officially notifies bordering states of the epidemic. Cases are reported in England and Japan. Both Japan and the World Health Organization request technical assistance from the CDC.

A number of hospitals in Denver are full to capacity and by the end of the day are unable to see or admit new patients. Thirteen hundred ventilators from the NPS are flown to Colorado. Bodies in hospital morgues are reported to have reached critical levels. The U.S. Surgeon General flies to Colorado to facilitate communications. Many states now are requesting supplies from the NPS. By the end of the day, 1,871 plague cases have been diagnosed throughout the U.S. and abroad. Of these, 389 persons have died.

May 22: Hospitals are under-staffed and have insufficient antibiotics, ventilators, and beds to meet demand. They cannot manage the influx of sick patients into the hospitals. Medical care is "beginning to shut down" in Denver.

Officials from the Health Department and the CDC have determined that a secondary spread of disease is occurring. The population in Denver is encouraged to wear face masks. The CDC advises that Colorado state borders be cordoned off in order to limit further spread of plague throughout the U.S. and other countries. Colorado officials express concern about their ability to get food and supplies into the state. The Governor's executive order is extended to prohibit travel into or out of the state of Colorado. By noon, there are 3,060 U.S. and international cases of pneumonic plague, 795 of whom have died.

The following day, May 23, 2000, this frightening exercise, called TOPOFF, was terminated. It had been organized by the Justice Department to test the ability of top officials at all levels of government to respond to a bioterrorist attack. Among the sobering results was the revelation that local health services — medical personnel, hospitals, and pharmaceutical supplies — were not nearly prepared to treat an outbreak of an infectious disease on such a large scale. Communications among local, state, and federal officials were unreliable. And responses were slowed by cumbersome decision-making processes or by a perception that no one was in charge. Other conclusions are described below.

> The unfolding situation precipitated a series of increasingly stringent containment measures. By the end of the first day, [a travel advisory was issued] . . . that restricted travel in 16 Denver Metro counties. . . . Some people, in fact, were reported to be racing out of the state. As part of the travel advisory, persons were advised to stay home unless they were close contacts of diagnosed cases or were feeling sick; in the case of the latter they were directed to seek medical care. . . . [T]he police and National Guard admitted . . . that they would be unable to keep people at home. . . . [B]y the end of the exercise, "people had been asked to stay in their homes for 72 hours. . . . How were they supposed to get food or medicine?"
>
> Throughout the unfolding epidemic, determining what information the public should be given and how quickly was an important and difficult issue. . . . It was clear that the public message itself would affect the capacity to control the epidemic, in that worried or panicked people might not seek the care they needed or, alternatively, might dangerously crowd health care facilities.
>
> Balancing the rights of the uninfected with the rights of the infected was considered a critical issue. One observer commented that a citizen might be expected to respond to the series of advisories by saying, "You've told me I should just stay in my home, now you have an obligation to give me antibiotics." But there were not enough antibiotics to do this. . . .

Sometime into the exercise, (notional) civil unrest broke out. People had not been allowed to shop. Stores were closed. Food ran out because no trucks were being let into the state. Rioting began to occur. Gridlock occurred around the city, including around health care facilities. The use of snow-plows was proposed as a way of clearing the road of cars. Given the constraints of the exercise, it was not possible to gauge the true extent of social disorder that a bioterrorist attack might evoke, but most observers and participants agreed that serious civil disruption would be a genuine risk in such a crisis.

The wide spectrum of disease containment measures which were considered or implemented illustrated the uncertainty surrounding what measures would, in fact, be feasible and effective. One senior health participant said that sufficient legal powers seemed to exist to carry out the decisions that were being made, and noted that legal authorities were not the problem. The critical issue was having access to the necessary scientific, technical, practical and political expertise, and having sufficient reliable and timely information available (e.g., the number and location of sick persons, etc.) to make sound decisions about how to contain the epidemic....

...Perhaps the most striking observation overall is the recognition that the systems and resources now in place would be hard-pressed to successfully manage a bioweapons attack like that simulated in TOPOFF.... [*Id.*]

NOTES AND QUESTIONS

1. *Assessing the Emergency.* The escalating crisis in the TOPOFF exercise shows the importance of rapid recognition of the nature of an emergency. According to a Department of Homeland Security (DHS) study,

ER physicians, local hospital staff, infectious disease physicians, medical examiners, epidemiologists, and other public health officials should rapidly recognize the seriousness of the incident. Although laboratory methods to suspect preliminary diagnosis of the plague are available at many local public and private laboratories, there may be delayed recognition of the plague since most hospital ER and laboratory personnel in the United States and Canada have limited or no experience in identifying and/or treating plague.

...A rapid onset with large numbers of persons presenting at ERs with pneumonia should create high suspicion of a terrorist incident using the plague. Detection of the plague should also initiate laboratory identification of the plague strain and a determination of the potentiality of known antimicrobial drug resistance.... [Department of Homeland Sec./Homeland Sec. Council, *National Planning Scenarios* 4-5 (Version 21.3 Final Draft, Mar. 2006), *available at* http://info.publicintelligence.net/DHS%20-%20National%20Planning%20Scenarios%20March%202006.pdf.]

The Centers for Disease Control and Prevention (CDC) has developed a standard protocol for reporting possible outbreaks of diseases that might be weaponized by terrorists. *Interim Recommended Notification Procedures for Local and State Public Health Department Leaders in the Event of a Bioterrorist Incident* (Feb. 1, 2001), *at* http://emergency.cdc.gov/eMContact/Protocols.asp. If a local health official suspects that an outbreak of common symptoms might have been caused by a biological weapon, she should inform the state's health department, which will then notify the CDC. If a terrorist source is confirmed or thought by the state health department to be probable, the FBI and other predetermined response partners are to be notified. The CDC reporting protocol is not mandatory, however, and state and local governments have adopted it with some variations. Should it be mandatory?

2. *First Response.* As soon as a bioterrorist attack is detected, a concerted, immediate response will be required to limit the loss of life. What measures would the first responders to such an attack take? A DHS study includes this partial catalog:

> Persons with primary aerosol exposure to plague need to receive antibiotic therapy within 24 hours in order to prevent near certain fatality. The prevention of potential secondary person-to-person spread by fleeing victims will be a challenge. Epidemiological assessments, including contact investigation and notification, will be needed. Actions of incident-site personnel . . . include hazard identification and site control, establishment and operation of the ICS [federal Incident Command System], isolation and treatment of exposed victims, mitigation efforts, obtainment of PPE [personal protective equipment] and prophylaxis for responders, site remediation and monitoring, notification of airlines and other transportation providers, provision of public information, and effective coordination with national and international public health and governmental agencies.
>
> Evacuation and treatment of some victims will be required. Self-quarantine through shelter-in-place may be instituted.
>
> Tens of thousands of people will require treatment or prophylaxis with ventilators and antibiotics. Plague prompts antimicrobial prophylaxis of exposed persons, responders, and pertinent health care workers. Thousands will seek care at hospitals with many needing advanced critical care due to pneumonia caused by plague. Exposed persons will also need to be informed of signs and symptoms suggestive of plague as well as measures to prevent person-to-person spread. PPE (e.g., masks) for responders and health care providers should be available. Mobilization of the SNS [Strategic National Stockpile] for additional critical supplies and antibiotics will be necessary. Public information activities will be needed to promote awareness of potential signs and symptoms of plague. Proper control measures will include the need for rapid treatment; contact tracing; and, potentially, self-quarantine through shelter-in-place or other least restrictive means.
>
> Actions of incident-site personnel tested after the attack include protective action decisions, recognition of the hazard and scope, providing emergency response, communication, protection of special populations, treating victims with additional ventilators at hospitals, providing patient screening clinics, and providing treatment or drug distribution centers for prophylactic antibiotics. Mortuary requirements, animal-based surveillance to monitor potential spread of plague via natural methods, and veterinary services also will need to be considered. Since this is an international incident, the U.S. Department of State will provide appropriate assistance to U.S. citizens traveling or residing abroad, including the timely dissemination of information to allow citizens to make informed plans and decisions. [*Id.* at 4-6 to 4-7.]

Who should be expected to perform all these tasks — state and local personnel, federal officials, or both? What practical and legal problems can you foresee in implementing these measures?

3. *Controlling Public Information.* When word began to spread about the September 11, 2001, attacks on the World Trade Center and the Pentagon, Americans turned immediately to their televisions for news. They were rewarded with days of nonstop pictures, government press releases, and expert speculation about what had happened.

If an attack affects a wider area, as a chemical or radiological weapon might, or involves an infectious biological agent like plague, the public's involvement and cooperation in the response will be critically important. Members of the public cannot be expected to cooperate, of course, unless they receive some information about the nature of the emergency, as well as credible, authoritative instructions about how to respond. What form should that communication take? The CDC has prepared suggested media scripts, including this one:

- This is an urgent health message from the U.S. Department of Health and Human Services (HHS). Please pay careful attention to this message to protect your health and that of others.
- Public health officials believe that the bacteria that cause pneumonic plague may have been deliberately released into the air in the *xxx area*.
- Pneumonic plague is a life-threatening, serious infection of the lungs. It is caused by breathing in the plague bacteria.
- Plague can be spread from person to person. Avoid close and direct contact with people with plague symptoms.
- We have not confirmed the deliberate release of plague and do not know the extent or source of the outbreak. . . .
- Local, state, and federal officials, including HHS, FBI, and Homeland Security, are working together. Updated announcements will be made as soon as officials know more.
- Ill persons should seek care immediately. Symptoms include fever, headache, muscle aches and chills, chest pain, and cough. Some people may cough up blood and have stomach pains. Most people develop symptoms within 1 to 4 days after exposure. . . .
- . . . By staying informed and following instructions from health officials, you can protect yourself, your family, and the community against this public health threat. . . .

     For more information about the plague, visit the HHS Web site at http:www.hhs.gov, the Centers for Disease Control and Prevention's (CDC) plague page at http://www.bt.cdc.gov/agent/plague/, or call the CDC Hotline at 1-800-CDC-INFO for the latest information. [*Communicating in the First Hours, Bioterrorism Agents* (May 14, 2007), *at* http://emergency.cdc.gov/firsthours/.]

How would you react upon hearing this message on the radio or reading it on a smart phone? If your answer is, "I don't know," or "I would panic," how do you think the message could be crafted to evoke a more helpful response? What other steps could be taken that might secure the desired reaction from the public?

     Can you think of reasons that the government might want to regulate media coverage? Do you think it should be able to impose limits on the dissemination of news? If so, can you say under what circumstances? See Chapter 43.

     4. *Civil Unrest.* In the TOPOFF exercise, civil unrest (notionally, but predictably) broke out after a day or two. Can you suggest ways to avoid domestic violence in the wake of a terrorist attack? If such unrest is unavoidable, what government entity should be charged with responsibility for restoring order?

     5. *Secondary Effects.* A WMD attack like the one described in TOPOFF is likely to have widespread ripple effects, including disruptions of the nation's financial infrastructure.

     As the financial world . . . begins to realize the likelihood of an epidemic, a sell-off occurs in the markets. There is a high absentee rate at banks, other financial institutions, and major corporations. Adding to these complications is the fact that bank and other financial customers may be staying home, afraid to venture into public places and trying instead to conduct business on the phone. As a result, the phone systems at financial institutions may become completely tied up, with far fewer transactions than normally occur. [*National Planning Scenarios, supra,* at 4-7.]

How could these kinds of impacts be limited?

6. *Exercising for Disaster.* While the TOPOFF exercise was under way in Denver in May 2000, simulated terrorist attacks involving chemical and radiological weapons were occurring in other cities. Subsequent large-scale exercises organized by DHS were based on notional attacks that also used radiological weapons and cyber warfare. *See generally* R. Eric Petersen et al., *Homeland Emergency Preparedness and the National Exercise Program: Background, Policy Implications, and Issues for Congress* (Cong. Res. Serv. RL34737), Nov. 10, 2008. Congress has ordered DHS to carry out national exercises at least every two years that are designed to be "as realistic as practicable, based on current risk assessments, including credible threats, vulnerabilities, and consequences, and designed to stress the national preparedness system." 6 U.S.C. 748 (2006 & Supp. III 2009). These exercises are part of a National Exercise Program, described in Petersen, *supra,* at 8-24. The Federal Emergency Management Agency (FEMA) has initiated a series of National Level Exercises focused on regional catastrophic response and recovery operations and collaboration between federal, regional, state, local, tribal, and private-sector participants. In 2011, for example, it practiced a response to a major earthquake in the central United States. *See FEMA National Level Exercise 2011: Fact Sheet* (Jan. 28, 2011), *at* http://www.fema.gov/media/fact_sheets/nle2011_fs.shtm.

DHS has also worked with other federal agencies to develop 15 all-hazards scenarios for use in homeland security preparedness activities. *See National Planning Scenarios, supra* p. 1120. The *Scenarios* are marked "For Official Use Only," and DHS has not made them available to the public. Can you make an argument that such planning documents ought to be officially released?

B.   THE FEDERAL RESPONSE ROLE

From 1950, when the Soviet Union tested its first atomic weapon, until the end of the Cold War, the American people lived in constant fear of a nuclear attack. For more than 40 years, the Civil Defense Act of 1950, ch. 1228, 64 Stat. 1245 (1951), as amended, directed the creation of a program to minimize the effects of such an attack on the civilian population and to deal with the resulting emergency conditions. Included in the program were planning for continuity of government, recruitment of emergency personnel, stockpiling of critical materials, and provision of warning systems and shelters. The Act purported to give the President broad powers in a civil defense emergency, for example, to take property "without regard to the limitation of any existing law," *id.* §303(a), 64 Stat. 1252, and to provide the government with immunity from suits for damages to property, personal injury, or death based on its actions during such an emergency. *Id.* §304, 64 Stat. 1253. The civil defense program, administered since 1979 by FEMA, was supposed to convince the American people and the Soviet leadership that the United States could not only survive a nuclear war, but also win one.

1. Stafford Act Authorities

The Civil Defense Act also provided for federal responses to natural disasters, such as floods and hurricanes. It was augmented in 1974 by the Robert T. Stafford Disaster Relief and Emergency Assistance Act (Stafford Act), 42 U.S.C. §§5121-5206 (2006 & Supp. III 2009). That statute provides broadly for federal assistance to states affected by various disasters. In 1994, the Civil Defense Act was repealed, then partially reenacted as an amendment to the Stafford Act. National Defense Authorization Act for Fiscal Year 1995, Pub. L. No. 103-337, §§3411, 3412, 108 Stat. 2663, 3100-3111 (1994). A House Armed Services Committee report declared at the time, ironically, that "the program has lost its defense emphasis. . . . Rather, the chief threats today come from tornadoes, earthquakes, floods, chemical spills, and the like." H.R. Rep. No. 103-499, at 5 (1994), *reprinted in* U.S.C.C.A.N. 2091, 2182-2183.

The Stafford Act may be invoked in the event of a presidentially declared major disaster or emergency, including "any natural catastrophe . . . or, regardless of cause, any fire, flood, or explosion," or on "any occasion for which, in the determination of the President, Federal assistance is needed to supplement State and local efforts and capabilities to save lives and to protect property and public health and safety, or to lessen or avert the threat of a catastrophe." 42 U.S.C. §§5122, 5170, 5191(a). While the President's declaration will usually be based on a state governor's request for help, the President may act without such a request when "the primary responsibility for response rests with the United States." *Id.* §5191(b). Moreover, the President may direct the DOD to perform any emergency work "essential for the preservation of life and property" for up to ten days. *Id.* §5170b(c). President Clinton declared an emergency under the Stafford Act on April 19, 1995, in response to the terrorist bombing that day of the Alfred P. Murrah Federal Building in Oklahoma City, and he ordered FEMA to direct and coordinate responses by other federal agencies and provide needed federal assistance. 60 Fed. Reg. 22,579 (May 8, 1995). *See also* 60 Fed. Reg. 21,819 (May 3, 1995) (declaring a "major disaster" and providing public and individual assistance). The Stafford Act was also invoked on September 11, 2001, when President Bush declared a "major disaster" in the State of New York in order to make available various forms of public and individual assistance, 66 Fed. Reg. 48,682-01, and was invoked on August 31, 2005, for Louisiana, Mississippi, and Alabama following the landfall of Hurricane Katrina. The White House, *The Federal Response to Hurricane Katrina: Lessons Learned* 33 (Feb. 2006).

2. The Homeland Security Act and Related Directives

The Homeland Security Act of 2002, Pub. L. No. 107-296, 116 Stat. 2135 (2002) (codified as amended at 6 U.S.C. §§101-557 (2006) and scattered sections of other titles), directed the Secretary of the new Department of Homeland Security (DHS) to "build a comprehensive national incident management system with Federal, State, and local government personnel, agencies, and authorities, to respond to . . . [terrorist] attacks and disasters." 6 U.S.C. §312(5). The Act required the Secretary to "consolidate existing Federal Government emergency response plans into a single, coordinated national response plan." 6 U.S.C. §312(6). It merged all or portions of 22 federal agencies and 180,000 employees into the DHS. Included were the Coast Guard, Customs Service, Transportation Security Administration, FEMA, Secret

Service, parts of the Immigration and Naturalization Service, and a long list of less well-known federal entities. The Act designated DHS as the lead agency for coordinating disaster and emergency response and recovery assistance with state and local authorities. The startup of this huge new enterprise is traced in Harold C. Relyea, *Homeland Security: Department Organization and Management — Implementation Phase* (Cong. Res. Serv. RL31751), Jan. 3, 2005.

In February 2003, the White House published Homeland Security Presidential Directive/HSPD-5, entitled *Management of Domestic Incidents.* It is meant to "ensure that all levels of the government across the Nation have the capability to work efficiently and effectively together, using a national approach to domestic incident management," *id.* ¶(3), and it declares that the Secretary of Homeland Security is the "principal Federal official for domestic incident management." *Id.* ¶(4). The Secretary of Health and Human Services (HHS) shares responsibility with DHS for biological incidents, Sarah A. Lister, *An Overview of the U.S. Public Health System in the Context of Emergency Preparedness* 22 (Cong. Res. Serv. RL31719), Mar. 17, 2005, while the Attorney General is given lead responsibility for criminal investigations of terrorist threats or acts within the United States, and is directed to "coordinate the activities of other members of the law enforcement community to detect, prevent, preempt, and disrupt terrorist attacks against the United States." HSPD-5 ¶(8). In addition, the Defense Department may provide military support to civil authorities in a domestic incident, but always under the command of the Secretary of Defense. *Id.* ¶(9). While states have the primary role in responding to emergencies, DHS responsibilities are triggered when a federal agency acting under its own authority has requested DHS assistance, when state and local resources are overwhelmed and request federal assistance, when more than one federal agency has become involved in responding to the incident, or when the President directs the Secretary of Homeland Security to assume management of the incident. *Id.* ¶¶(4), (6).

HSPD-5 also orders the creation of a National Incident Management System (NIMS), to provide a flexible national framework within which governments at all levels and private entities can work together to manage domestic "incidents." The NIMS was rolled out a year later. Department of Homeland Sec., *National Incident Management System* (Mar. 1, 2004), *available at* http://www.fema.gov/pdf/emergency/NIMS/NIMS-core.pdf.

3. The National Response Plan

HSPD-5 called for development of a National Response Plan (NRP) to replace existing national emergency response plans. The first NRP was published in January 2005. Like earlier plans, the NRP provided for a coordinated, all-hazards approach to "incident management," spelling out in broad terms the roles of all relevant elements of the national government and calling for communications and operational coordination by offices within DHS. It also set out a framework for federal interaction with state, local, and tribal governments and with the private sector in an emergency.

Weaknesses of the NRP were painfully exposed in the aftermath of Hurricane Katrina in 2005. White House investigators of the flawed federal response to the storm found that, while the NRP is sufficiently "flexible and scalable" to meet any threat or event, "the specific triggers" for the NRP and its components "are unclear." *The Federal Response to Hurricane Katrina, supra,* at 14. DHS Secretary Michael Chertoff declared Katrina to be an incident of national significance (INS) three days after the storm's landfall, on August 30, 2005, when two of the four triggering criteria listed in HSPD-5 ¶(4), noted above, had been met. *Id.* Yet there reportedly was confusion about whether the INS was triggered earlier by the President's emergency declaration under the Stafford Act. And according to the White House report, the NRP failed to articulate what actions should be taken by which agencies once an INS was declared. The lack of clear guidance was blamed for compromising the response. *Id.* at 15.

Congress reacted to these failures by amending the Stafford Act to allow accelerated federal assistance, without a state request, when necessary to save lives, prevent suffering, and mitigate severe damage. 42 U.S.C. §5170(a)(5). This enhanced authority to "push" federal response resources, rather than wait for the "pull" from the states, is limited to situations where the President declares a "major disaster." The same legislation created a National Preparedness System, providing a statutory foundation for intergovernmental and interagency homeland security and emergency management coordination. *See* Department of Homeland Sec., *National Preparedness Guidelines* (Sept. 2007), *at* http://www.dhs.gov/xlibrary/assets/National_Preparedness_Guidelines.pdf.

4.   The National Response Framework

In January 2008 DHS released a reinvented NRP—the National Response Framework (NRF). FEMA is designated overall coordinator of the federal response, and the FEMA administrator is given the responsibility for initiating the federal response to a crisis.

Department of Homeland Security, National Response Framework
pages 7-11, Jan. 2008
http://www.fema.gov/pdf/emergency/nrf/nrf-core.pdf

... The *National Response Framework* is always in effect, and elements can be implemented at any level at any time. The *Framework* is capabilities based, which is to say that local governments, tribes, States, and the Federal Government all develop functional capabilities and identify resources that may be required based on hazard identification and risk assessment, threats, and other potential incidents....

Scope

The *Framework* provides structures for implementing nationwide response policy and operational coordination for all types of domestic incidents. It can be partially or fully implemented in the context of a threat, in anticipation of a significant event, or in response to an incident. Selective implementation allows for a scaled response, delivery of the resources needed, and an appropriate level of coordination....

It is not always obvious at the outset whether a seemingly minor event might be the initial phase of a larger, rapidly growing threat. The *Framework* incorporates standardized organizational structures that promote on-scene initiative, innovation, and sharing of essential resources drawn from all levels of government, NGOs, and the private sector. Response must be quickly scalable, flexible, and adaptable.

The *Framework* is also intended to accelerate the assessment and response to incidents that may require Federal assistance.... [The] coordination of Federal incident assessment and response efforts is intended to occur seamlessly, without the need for any formal trigger mechanism.

This *Framework*, therefore, eliminates the Incident of National Significance declaration....

Response Doctrine

...The overarching objective of response activities centers upon saving lives and protecting property and the environment....

Incidents begin and end locally, and most are wholly managed at the local level. Many incidents require unified response from local agencies, NGOs, and the private sector, and some require additional support from neighboring jurisdictions or the State. A small number require Federal support. National response protocols recognize this and are structured to provide additional, tiered levels of support when there is a need for more resources or capabilities to support and sustain the response and initial recovery. All levels should be prepared to respond, anticipating resources that may be required....

A basic premise of the *Framework* is that incidents are generally handled at the lowest jurisdictional level possible.

Scalable, Flexible, and Adaptable Operational Capabilities

As incidents change in size, scope, and complexity, the response must adapt to meet requirements. The number, type, and sources of resources must be able to expand rapidly to meet needs associated with a given incident. The *Framework*'s disciplined and coordinated process can provide for a rapid surge of resources from all levels of government, appropriately scaled to need....

Unity of Effort Through Unified Command

Effective unified command is indispensable to response activities and requires a clear understanding of the roles and responsibilities of each participating organization. Success requires unity of effort, which respects the chain of command of each participating Federal organization while harnessing seamless coordination across jurisdictions in support of common objectives.

Use of the Incident Command System (ICS) is an important element across multijurisdictional or multiagency incident management activities....

The Department of Defense (DOD) is a full partner in the Federal response to domestic incidents, and its response is fully coordinated through the mechanisms of this *Framework*. Concepts of "command" and "unity of command" have distinct legal and cultural meanings for military forces and military operations. For Federal military forces, command runs from the President to the Secretary of Defense to the Commander of the combatant command to the DOD on-scene commander. Military forces will always remain under the operational and administrative control of the military chain of command, and these forces are subject to redirection or recall at any time. The ICS "unified command" concept is distinct from the military chain of command use of this term. And, as such, military forces do not operate under the command of the Incident Commander or under the unified command structure....

Department of Homeland Security, National Response Framework, Catastrophic Incident Annex

pages 1-7, Nov. 2008
http://www.fema.gov/pdf/emergency/nrf/nrf_CatastrophicIncidentAnnex.pdf

Scope

A catastrophic incident, as defined by the *NRF*, is any natural or manmade incident, including terrorism, that results in extraordinary levels of mass casualties, damage, or disruption severely affecting the population, infrastructure, environment, economy, national morale, and/or government functions. A catastrophic incident could result in sustained nationwide impacts over a prolonged period of time; almost immediately exceeds resources normally available to State, tribal, local, and private-sector authorities in the impacted area; and significantly interrupts governmental operations and emergency services to such an extent that national security could be threatened. These factors drive the urgency for coordinated national planning to ensure accelerated Federal and/or national assistance.

Recognizing that Federal and/or national resources are required to augment overwhelmed State, tribal, and local response efforts, the *NRF-CIA* establishes protocols to preidentify and rapidly deploy key essential resources (e.g., medical teams, search and rescue teams, transportable shelters, medical and equipment caches, etc.) that are expected to be urgently needed/required to save lives and contain incidents.

Upon the occurrence of a catastrophic incident, or in advance if determined by the Secretary of Homeland Security, the Government will deploy Federal resources, organized into incident-specific "packages," in accordance with the *NRF-CIS* [an annual supplement to the *CIA*, published separately] and in coordination with the affected State and incident command structure.

Where State, tribal, or local governments are unable to establish or maintain an effective incident command structure due to catastrophic conditions, the Federal Government, at the direction of the Secretary of Homeland Security, may establish a unified command structure, led by the Unified Coordination Group (UCG), to save lives, protect property, maintain operation of critical infrastructure/key resources (CIKR), contain the event, and protect national security. The Federal Government shall transition to its role of coordinating and supporting the State, tribal, or local government when they are capable of reestablishing their incident command....

Policies

A catastrophic incident will likely trigger a Presidential major disaster declaration and result in the Secretary of Homeland Security or a designee implementing the *NRF-CIA/CIS*.

All deploying Federal resources remain under the control of their respective Federal department or agency during mobilization and deployment. Some Federal departments and agencies have the authority, under their own statutes, to deploy directly to the incident scene.

Federal resources arriving at a National Logistics Staging Area (NLSA) remain there until requested by State/local incident command authorities, when they are integrated into the response effort. . . .

States are encouraged to conduct planning in collaboration with the Federal Government for catastrophic incidents as part of their steady-state preparedness activities.

The Federal Government, in collaboration with States, tribes, local governments, the private sector, and nongovernmental organizations (NGOs), develops proactive plans for activation and implementation of the *NRF-CIA*, to include situations where the need exceeds or challenges the resources and/or capabilities of State and local governments to respond and where the Federal Government may temporarily assume roles typically performed by State, tribal, and local governments.

The occurrence or threat of multiple or successive catastrophic incidents may significantly reduce the size, speed, and depth of the Federal response. If deemed necessary or prudent, the Federal Government may reduce the allocation of finite resources when multiple venues are competing for the same resources.

Situation

The initial response to a catastrophic incident starts on a local level with the local, tribal and/or State responders. However, there may be circumstances that exceed the capabilities of State, local, or tribal authorities in which they are unable to initially establish or maintain a command structure for incident response. In these[] instances, accelerated Federal response may be warranted, and the Department of Homeland Security (DHS)/Federal Emergency Management Agency (FEMA) will coordinate response activities until local, tribal, and/or State authorities are capable or have re-established their incident command structure.

Continuity of Operations (COOP)/Continuity of Government (COG)

Following a catastrophic event, segments of State, tribal, and local governments as well as NGOs and the private sector may be severely compromised. The Federal Government and its national partners must be prepared to fill potential gaps to ensure continuity of government and public- and private-sector operations. The incident may cause significant disruption of the impacted area's CIKR, such as energy, transportation, telecommunications, law enforcement, and public health and health care systems. . . .

Planning Assumptions

A catastrophic incident will result in large numbers of casualties and/or displaced persons, possibly in the tens to hundreds of thousands. During a catastrophic incident response, priority is given to human life-saving operations.

The nature and scope of a catastrophic incident will immediately overwhelm State, tribal, and local response capabilities and require immediate Federal support.

A detailed and credible common operating picture will not be achievable for 24 to 48 hours (or longer) after the incident. As a result, response activities may have to begin without the benefit of a detailed or complete situation and critical needs assessment.

The nature and scope of the catastrophic incident will include major natural or manmade hazards including chemical, biological, radiological, nuclear, or high-yield explosive attacks, and cyber attacks.

A catastrophic incident has unique dimensions/characteristics requiring that response plans/strategies be flexible enough to effectively address emerging needs and requirements.

A catastrophic incident will occur with little or no warning. Some incidents may be well underway before detection.

Multiple incidents will occur simultaneously or sequentially in contiguous and/ or noncontiguous areas. Some incidents, such as a biological WMD attack, may be dispersed over a large geographic area and lack a defined incident site.

A catastrophic incident will produce environmental impacts that severely challenge the ability and capacity of governments and communities to achieve a timely recovery.

Federal resources must be capable of mobilization and deployment before they are requested via normal *NRF* protocols.

Large-scale evacuations, organized or self-directed, may occur.

Existing health care systems in the impacted area are expected to be quickly overwhelmed, requiring evacuation of existing patients from these facilities to accommodate increased patient workload if the facility remains operational. Additionally, those persons with special needs, including residents of nursing homes and extended care facilities, will require special attention during evacuation.

Large numbers of people will be left temporarily or permanently homeless and may require prolonged temporary housing. Some displaced people will require specialized attention, health care assistance, and assistance with activities of daily living based on their special needs....

A catastrophic incident will have significant international dimensions, including impacts on the health and welfare of border community populations, cross-border trade, transit, law enforcement coordination, and others....

Federal Response...

NRF-CIA actions that the Federal Government takes in response to a catastrophic incident include: ...

For no-notice/short-notice catastrophic events when there is little or no time to assess the requirements of the State, tribal, and local governments, Federal departments and agencies initiate actions to mobilize and deploy resources by scenario type as planned for in the *NRF-CIS*. To that end, the Department of Defense (DOD) is prepared to provide capabilities in the following support categories: aviation, communication, defense coordinating officer/defense coordinating element, medical treatment, patient evacuation, decontamination, and logistics.

All Federal departments and agencies and organizations assigned primary or supporting ESF responsibilities immediately begin implementation of those responsibilities, as appropriate or when directed by the President.

Incident-specific resources and capabilities (e.g., medical teams, search and rescue teams, equipment, transportable shelters, preventive and therapeutic pharmaceutical caches, etc.) are activated and prepared for deployment to an NLSA near the incident site....

Regional Federal facilities are activated and prepared to receive and treat casualties from the incident area. Federal facilities are directed to reprioritize services (in some cases possibly reducing or postponing certain customary services) until life-saving activities are concluded....

NOTES AND QUESTIONS

1. *Adequacy of Emergency Response Authority.* As the excerpts above reveal, federal plans for responses to terrorist attacks and other catastrophes are written in very general terms. The NRF urges "[g]overnments at all levels...to develop detailed, robust, all-hazards response plans." National Response Framework, *supra*, at 28, but the Framework itself remains mostly vague and anodyne. The CIA is more detailed, but only in comparison to the NRF.

If you were responsible for implementing the policies outlined in the NRF and CIA, would you know how they required you to respond to a terrorist attack like the release of pneumonic plague? If not, where would you look for guidance to determine the scope of your duties?

2. *National Preparedness.* In 2011, President Obama signed Presidential Policy Directive/PPD-8 (Mar. 30, 2011), *at* http://www.dhs.gov/xlibrary/assets/presidential-policy-directive-8-national-preparedness.pdf. PPD-8 reviews and replaces an earlier directive from President Bush, HSPD-8 (2003), and outlines a vision for strengthening the nation's security and resilience through preparation for threats. The new PPD directs "the development of a national preparedness goal that identifies the core capabilities necessary for preparedness and a national preparedness system to guide activities that will enable the Nation to achieve the goal." *Id.* The national preparedness goal "shall be informed by the risk of specific threats and vulnerabilities — taking into account regional variations — and include concrete, measurable, and prioritized objectives to mitigate the risk." *Id.* Based on this brief description, and considering the provisions of the NRF excerpted above, can you outline the "prioritized objectives" of a national preparedness goal and indicate how to measure our progress in meeting those objectives?

3. *Assigning Agency Responsibilities.* Elimination of the "Incidents of National Significance" designation in the NRF means that the Framework and NIMS are always in effect. Yet the NRF is unclear about most specific operations issues. For example, HSPD-5 (*supra* p. 1125) indicates that DHS should assume overall incident management responsibility when another federal agency requests DHS assistance, when state and local resources are overwhelmed and request federal assistance, when more than one federal agency becomes involved in responding to the incident, or when the President directs the Secretary of Homeland Security to assume management of the incident. These criteria are repeated in the NRF. But what does it mean in practical terms for state and local resources to be "overwhelmed," and which state or local officials must make a request to trigger the federal role?

4. *Coordination with First Responders.* The concept of "unified command" is central to the NRF and NIMS. In contrast to a military-type chain of command, unified command takes into account that there may be multiple agencies and jurisdictions responding to an emergency. Designated leaders of those entities work together to establish a common set of objectives, and they agree upon a single operations plan (SOP) for responding to the event. In operational terms unified command under the NRF and NIMS is facilitated through a Joint Field Office (JFO). What will be required in practical terms to create a viable SOP and to implement it in a crisis?

FEMA also coordinates support through any of the 15 Emergency Support Functions (ESFs) described in the NRF. The ESFs are functionally organized, and are staffed by specialists from federal agencies and the private sector. They integrate capabilities in support of state and local response agencies. Each ESF is headed by a lead federal agency. What is needed to ensure that these functions are carried out as needed?

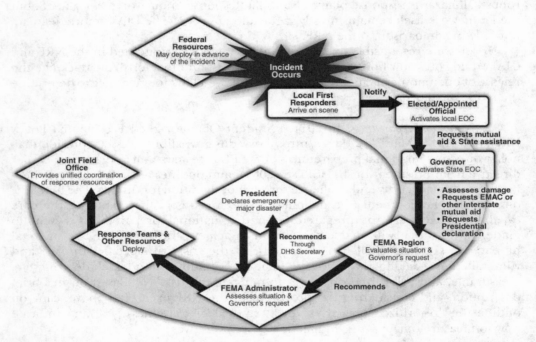

Overview of Stafford Act Support to States.

Department of Homeland Security, *Overview: ESF and Support Annexes Coordinating Federal Assistance in Support of the National Response Framework,* Jan. 2008, at 5.

5. *The Legal Status of the Federal Planning Documents.* Federal agency protocols designed for comprehensive application to government activities are often cast in the form of legislative rules (regulations) and are promulgated following the procedures of the Administrative Procedure Act (APA), 5 U.S.C. §§551-706 (2006).

The Homeland Security Act expressly grants rulemaking authority to DHS and states that the issuance of DHS regulations is generally governed by the APA. 6 U.S.C. §112(e). However, DHS took the position that because the National Response Framework and its associated planning documents were simply guidance documents, intended to create no binding or enforceable norms, it was not required to publish a Notice of Proposed Rulemaking or to invite public comments, as the APA normally requires for binding legislative regulations. Might a more transparent and participatory process produce better plans?

6. *A Military Role?* Each state's National Guard has elements trained and equipped to assist, under the direction of the state governor, in the response to a terrorist attack or a large natural disaster. See *infra* p. 1169. At the federal level, the Stafford Act, the NRF, NRF/CIA, and other planning documents assign the Defense Department a supporting role in responding to a terrorist attack, including one involving a weapon of mass destruction. Should the military be given a larger role, or even lead agency responsibility? Consideration was given to such proposals in the wake of the flawed response to Hurricane Katrina. *See* David E. Sanger, *Bush Wants to Consider Broadening of Military's Powers During Natural Disasters*, N.Y. Times, Sept. 27, 2005. Do you think either state or federal governments could mount a fully effective response to such a calamity without the assistance of military forces? These questions are explored in Chapter 38.

7. *Regional Cooperation.* All 50 states, U.S. territories, and the District of Columbia have entered into a congressionally approved compact of mutual assistance, including help with evacuations. Emergency Management Assistance Compact, Pub. L. No. 104-321, 110 Stat. 3877 (1996). *See EMAC* (n.d.), *at* http://www.emacweb.org/?9. Regional mechanisms for response to disasters, or the lack thereof, were also the focus of reports assessing the 2005 response to Hurricane Katrina. *See The Federal Response to Hurricane Katrina, supra* p. 1125; H. Select Bipartisan Comm. to Investigate the Preparation for and Response to Hurricane Katrina, *A Failure of Initiative* (2006), *available at* www.gpoaccess.gov/katrinareport/fullreport.pdf.

What advantages do regional response structures offer? What legal obstacles can you see to either the creation or implementation of these regional arrangements? Can one locality order its personnel or resources to help outside the locality? If such personnel are injured, who is liable? Who pays their salaries? Can the cost of lost or damaged equipment be recovered? How should such questions be answered?

8. *Viability of Plans?* Any response plans need to promise some predictability about the future. They should provide reasonable assurance that if all our defenses fail and we suffer another catastrophic terrorist attack, basic government structures will nevertheless survive, citizens will be protected from further harm, and normal life will eventually be substantially restored. Furthermore, both the existence of the plans and their viability must be made widely known. If the worst happens, members of the public must be convinced that it is in their best interests to cooperate in the implementation of the plan. The President should be convinced that even in a great crisis the rule of law can provide needed security—that she need not, for example, declare martial law. And potential terrorists should be deterred by the knowledge that if they attack, the American people will not lose faith in their government.

Do plans developed by DHS and other agencies provide these assurances? Any thoughtful answer must recognize the staggering complexity of the task, as well as the remarkable progress made since 9/11. Yet much remains to be done. One study at the end of the Bush administration offered this assessment:

America is not ready for the next catastrophe. . . . There are still no detailed, government-wide plans to respond to a catastrophe. There is still considerable confusion over who will be in charge during a disaster. There are still almost no dedicated military forces on rapid alert to respond to a crisis here at home. There are still no guidelines to determine and assess the capabilities that states, cities, and towns should have to ensure they are prepared for the worst. [Christine E. Wormuth & Anne Witkowsky, *Managing the Next Domestic Catastrophe: Ready (Or Not)?* at vi (Center for Strategic & Int'l Studies, June 2008)]

See also David Heyman & James Jay Carafano, *Homeland Security 3.0: Building a National Enterprise to Keep America Safe, Free, and Prosperous* 1 (Heritage Found. & Center for Strategic & Int'l Studies, Sept. 18, 2008) (urging DHS to "foster better decision making in Congress and in the interagency process, support the development of a new generation of professionals, and facilitate information sharing throughout all elements of the enterprise[] . . . [and to] empower individuals and communities and extend international cooperation").

If you were named Homeland Security Secretary, what first steps would you take to prepare the nation for the next terrorist attack?

C.   FIRST RESPONDERS: THE STATE AND LOCAL RESPONSE

1.   State Law

Even if federal plans provide an overarching blueprint for emergency response, and the allure of federal funds entices states to adopt the NIMS mechanisms and complete the training and exercises that DHS and FEMA supply, the adage that "all incidents are local" has a close connection to reality, both practically and legally. State and local officials are always the first responders. The authority of these officials to act in anticipation of or in response to an emergency is part of a state's police powers. James G. Hodge, *The Role of New Federalism and Public Health Law*, 12 J.L. & Health 309 (1998). Those powers are at the core of state sovereignty and are derived from state constitutions and common law "police powers," and they are part of the reserved powers recognized by the Tenth Amendment to the U.S. Constitution. *See In re World Trade Ctr. Disaster Site Litig.*, 456 F. Supp. 2d 520, 550 (S.D.N.Y. 2006), *aff'd in part and dismissed in part*, 521 F.3d 169 (2d Cir. 2008) ("when an emergent disaster threatens society as a whole, the [common law] doctrine of *salus populi supreme lex* (the welfare of the people is the highest law) . . . encourage[s] immediate action to preserve society").

State constitutions and statutes typically give governors and public health officials broad discretion to act to protect public health and safety, and in an emergency to suspend laws and administrative rules, order evacuations and quarantines, commandeer resources, and control property. In the event of an attack with biological weapons, for example, these officials may prevent infected persons from spreading the disease to others. Healthy but exposed persons may be vaccinated or given medicine or have their movements restricted. *See* Edward A. Fallone, *Preserving the Public Health: A Proposal to Quarantine Recalcitrant AIDS Carriers*, 68 B.U. L. Rev. 441, 460-461 (1988). The federal government additionally has interstate and foreign quarantine authority, assessed *infra* pp. 1141-1145.

NOTES AND QUESTIONS

1. *Quarantine Authority.* The Supreme Court has long recognized the authority of the government to erect quarantines, both to confine persons and to exclude them, in order to prevent the spread of contagious or infectious diseases. In *Gibbons v. Ogden*, 22 U.S. 1, 25 (1824), the Supreme Court referred to a state's authority to quarantine, noting that even though quarantine laws affect commerce, their objective is to protect public health and they are thus within the authority of state and local governments. In recent times the Court approved the confinement of a sexually violent predator, declaring that

> we have never held that the Constitution prevents a State from civilly detaining those for whom no treatment is available, but who nevertheless pose a danger to others. A State could hardly be seen as furthering a "punitive" purpose by involuntarily confining persons afflicted with an untreatable, highly contagious disease. [*Kansas v. Hendricks*, 521 U.S. 346, 366 (1997).]

See also Jacobson v. Massachusetts, 197 U.S. 11 (1905) (upholding mandatory vaccinations following a smallpox outbreak); *Compagnie Francaise de Navigation a Vapeur v. Louisiana Bd. of Health,* 186 U.S. 380 (1902) (upholding a quarantine in New Orleans following a yellow fever outbreak). And while the Supreme Court has called the constitutional right to travel from one state to another "firmly imbedded in our jurisprudence," *Saenz v. Roe,* 526 U.S. 489, 498 (1999), other courts have held that the right may be curtailed in an emergency. *See, e.g., Smith v. Avino,* 91 F.3d 105 (11th Cir. 1996) (upholding a curfew in South Florida in wake of Hurricane Andrew). *See generally* Kathleen S. Swendiman & Jennifer K. Elsea, *Federal and State Quarantine and Isolation Authority* (Cong. Res. Serv. RL33201), Jan. 23, 2007.

According to one analysis, in the event of a bioterrorist attack, "[a]lmost certainly, a clash would occur between public health and legal officials at the local, state, and national levels about the measures necessary and the entity with jurisdiction to act." Smithson & Levy, *supra*, at 269. If state or local response efforts did come directly into conflict with federal measures, the former presumably would have to give way under the Supremacy Clause. Can you describe limits to the federal government's preemptive power to respond to a bioterrorist attack, aside from individual rights protections in the Bill of Rights that constrain all government actions? How about an attack using a chemical or radiological weapon? How could potential conflicts between federal and state or local response efforts be minimized?

2. *Erring on the Side of Caution?* How widely may government officials establish a cordon around an area suspected of containing infected persons or hazardous chemicals? How should doubts be resolved about the possible exposure of individuals to a contagion? In *Empire Kosher Poultry, Inc. v. Hallowell*, 816 F.2d 907 (3d Cir. 1987), a due process case involving a quarantine of poultry to combat avian influenza, the court

said that evidence of disease need not be shown before a quarantine is erected, since tests might not immediately reveal the existence of infection. Moreover, said the court, a broad buffer zone could be established to prevent the inadvertent movement of infected poultry out of the quarantine area.

3. *Enforcing a Quarantine.* One analysis of a 2000 federal TOPOFF exercise described above calls the quarantine of large groups of people "impractical," citing concern about the level of force needed for enforcement:

> Not only were local officials uncertain about their statutory authority to proceed with a quarantine, they believed that the public would probably not cooperate with compulsory orders to commandeer property, restrict movement of people, or forcibly remove them to designated locations. Traditionally, governments have counted upon the public to comply with public health orders on the basis that the good of the community overrides the rights of the individual. These days, however, citizens get angry at forced evacuations for such visible calamities as hurricanes, floods, and wildfires, not to mention a stay-at-home order for a microscopic killer that they may doubt is in their midst. Police also questioned whether their colleagues would recognize the authority of the public health officer to declare a quarantine or would even stick around to enforce the order. Finally, some wondered whether there were enough local and state police to quarantine a large metropolitan area in the first place. [Amy E. Smithson & Leslie-Anne Levy, *Ataxia: The Chemical and Biological Terrorism Threat and the U.S. Response* 269 (Henry L. Stimson Ctr. 2000).]

According to one police captain, "If police officers knew that a biological agent had been released, 99 percent of the cops would not be here. They would grab their families and leave." *Id.* at 270 n.225. Do these practical problems have legal solutions?

How would you describe the authority of law enforcement personnel who remained on duty? Could they, for example, shoot persons trying to escape the quarantine?

4. *Other Constraints on Individual Liberties.* In addition to quarantines, involuntary evacuations, and forced inoculations, government responses to a terrorist attack might include compulsory physical examinations to determine whether individuals are infected with a contagious disease, inspections of private property, and reviews of personal medical records. The Court has held that "regulatory" or "special needs" searches of individuals for noncriminal regulatory purposes (that is, not for the purpose of obtaining criminal evidence) do not offend the Fourth Amendment if the state's interest in the result is sufficiently compelling and the search is reasonable in the circumstances. *See, e.g., Vernonia Sch. Dist. 47J v. Acton,* 515 U.S. 646, 653 (1995) (upholding random drug tests of student athletes when "special needs, beyond the normal need for law enforcement, make the warrant and probable-cause requirement impracticable"); *National Treasury Employees Union v. Von Raab,* 489 U.S. 656 (1989) (approving drug tests of Customs Service employees); *cf. Ferguson v. City of Charleston,* 532 U.S. 67 (2001) (rejecting nonconsensual drug testing of obstetrics patients when results were to be given to police). In *Camara v. Municipal Court of San Francisco,* 387 U.S. 523, 539 (1967), the Court observed that warrantless inspections are "traditionally upheld in emergency situations." (Recall our consideration of these same exceptions to the Fourth Amendment's warrant requirement in connection with efforts to prevent terrorist attacks by surveillance, in Chapter 20, and screening for access to

public places and transportation systems, in Chapter 24.) In the wake of a bioterrorist attack, the government's interest in examining individuals and their property would be strong and immediate. Do you think it would outweigh individual privacy interests? *See* Barry Kellman, *Biological Terrorism: Legal Measures for Preventing Catastrophe*, 24 Harv. J.L. & Pub. Pol'y 417, 478-485 (2001).

Of course, state public health laws, including extreme measures such as quarantine, are also subject to constitutional due process constraints. Freedom from physical restraint is a classic "liberty" interest protected by the Fourteenth Amendment. *Kansas v. Hendricks, supra*, 521 U.S. at 356. How would you describe due process limits on state powers to respond to a terrorist attack? (Recall here our discussion in Chapter 26 of due process considerations in the imprisonment of terrorist suspects.)

2. The Model State Emergency Health Powers Act (MSEHPA)

State quarantine and vaccination laws, many of them decades old, do not reflect current disease or treatment science, and they are often targeted at particular diseases. *See* Lawrence O. Gostin, *The Law and the Public's Health: A Study of Infectious Disease Law in the United States*, 99 Colum. L. Rev. 59, 102-106 (1999).

Spurred by the 9/11 and anthrax attacks in 2001, states and cities began to reconsider a range of emergency response issues, including quarantine and isolation authorities. The Model State Emergency Health Powers Act (MSEHPA) (draft Dec. 21, 2001), *at* http://www.publichealthlaw.net/MSEHPA/MSEHPA.pdf, was drawn up in 2001 by public health experts at Georgetown and Johns Hopkins Universities. *See* Center for Law & the Public's Health, *Model State Public Health Laws* (n.d.), *at* http://www.publichealthlaw.net/ModelLaws/MSEHPA.php.

The MSEHPA borrows from various state laws and provides a template for sweeping state authorities that may be invoked in a public health emergency. It authorizes governors to declare a "public health emergency" after consulting with public health authorities or, in the absence of such consultation, "when the situation calls for prompt and timely action." MSEHPA §401. A "public health emergency" is defined as "an occurrence or imminent threat" of illness that is "believed to be caused" by bioterrorism or other disasters and poses "a high probability" of a large number of deaths, serious or long-term disabilities, or widespread exposure "that poses a significant risk of substantial harm to a large number of people in the affected population." *Id.* §104(m). During a public health emergency, a governor may suspend any statute concerning state government procedures or any agency rule or orders "to the extent that strict compliance with the same would prevent, hinder, or delay necessary action" in response to the public health emergency. *Id.* §403(a)(1). The public health emergency "shall" be terminated by a governor by executive order "upon finding that the occurrence of an illness or health condition that caused the emergency no longer poses a high probability of a large number of deaths in the affected population . . . or a significant risk of substantial future harm to a large number of people in the affected population." *Id.* §405(a). Otherwise, a public health emergency will terminate automatically after 30 days unless renewed by the governor or terminated earlier by majority vote of both chambers of a state legislature. *Id.* §405(b), (c).

In addition, during a public health emergency the MSEHPA authorizes state officials to close, evacuate, or decontaminate "any facility" or decontaminate or destroy "any material" where "there is a reasonable cause to believe that it may endanger the public health." *Id.* §501. Public health authorities are also given power to condemn or assume control over private property, control and manage health care facilities, and control routes and modes of transportation "if such action is reasonable and necessary to respond to the public health emergency." *Id.* §502.

The MSEHPA also includes these provisions concerning vaccination, treatment, isolation, and quarantine:

Model State Emergency Health Powers Act

draft Dec. 21, 2001
at http://www.publichealthlaw.net/MSEHPA/MSEHPA.pdf

ARTICLE VI.   SPECIAL POWERS DURING A STATE OF PUBLIC HEALTH EMERGENCY: PROTECTION OF PERSONS

Section 603. Vaccination and treatment.

During a state of public health emergency the public health authority may exercise the following emergency powers over persons as necessary to address the public health emergency—

(a) Vaccination. To vaccinate persons as protection against infectious disease and to prevent the spread of contagious or possibly contagious disease.

(1) Vaccination may be performed by any qualified person authorized to do so by the public health authority.

(2) A vaccine to be administered must not be such as is reasonably likely to lead to serious harm to the affected individual.

(3) To prevent the spread of contagious or possibly contagious disease the public health authority may isolate or quarantine, pursuant to Section 604, persons who are unable or unwilling for reasons of health, religion, or conscience to undergo vaccination pursuant to this Section.

(b) Treatment. To treat persons exposed to or infected with disease.

(1) Treatment may be administered by any qualified person authorized to do so by the public health authority.

(2) Treatment must not be such as is reasonably likely to lead to serious harm to the affected individual.

(3) To prevent the spread of contagious or possibly contagious disease the public health authority may isolate or quarantine, pursuant to Section 604, persons who are unable or unwilling for reasons of health, religion, or conscience to undergo treatment pursuant to this Section.

Section 604. Isolation and quarantine.

(a) Authorization. During the public health emergency, the public health authority may isolate ... or quarantine ... an individual or groups of individuals. ... The public health authority may also establish and maintain places of isolation and quarantine, and set rules and make orders. Failure to obey these rules, orders, or provisions shall constitute a misdemeanor.

(b) Conditions and principles. The public health authority shall adhere to the following conditions and principles when isolating or quarantining individuals or groups of individuals:

(1) Isolation and quarantine must be by the least restrictive means necessary to prevent the spread of a contagious or possibly contagious disease to others and may include, but are not limited to, confinement to private homes or other private and public premises.

(2) Isolated individuals must be confined separately from quarantined individuals.

(3) The health status of isolated and quarantined individuals must be monitored regularly to determine if they require isolation or quarantine.

(4) If a quarantined individual subsequently becomes infected or is reasonably believed to have become infected with a contagious or possibly contagious disease he or she must promptly be removed to isolation.

(5) Isolated and quarantined individuals must be immediately released when they pose no substantial risk of transmitting a contagious or possibly contagious disease to others.

(6) The needs of persons isolated and quarantined shall be addressed in a systematic and competent fashion, including, but not limited to, providing adequate food, clothing, shelter, means of communication with those in isolation or quarantine and outside these settings, medication, and competent medical care.

(7) Premises used for isolation and quarantine shall be maintained in a safe and hygienic manner and be designed to minimize the likelihood of further transmission of infection or other harms to persons isolated and quarantined.

(8) To the extent possible, cultural and religious beliefs should be considered in addressing the needs of individuals, and establishing and maintaining isolation and quarantine premises. . . .

Section 605.   Procedures for isolation and quarantine.

During a public health emergency, the isolation and quarantine of an individual or groups of individuals shall be undertaken in accordance with the following procedures.

(a) Temporary isolation and quarantine without notice.

(1) Authorization. The public health authority may temporarily isolate or quarantine an individual or groups of individuals through a written directive if delay in imposing the isolation or quarantine would significantly jeopardize the public health authority's ability to prevent or limit the transmission of a contagious or possibly contagious disease to others. . . .

(4) Petition for continued isolation or quarantine. Within ten (10) days after issuing the written directive, the public health authority shall file a petition pursuant to Section 605(b) for a court order authorizing the continued isolation or quarantine of the isolated or quarantined individual or groups of individuals.

[Section 605(b) permits the public health authority to petition for isolation or quarantine with notice to affected individuals and a hearing within five days, with a ten-day extension possible in "extraordinary circumstances." The court will grant the state's petition if a preponderance of the evidence shows that isolation or quarantine is "reasonably necessary to prevent or limit the transmission of a contagious or possibly contagious disease to others."]

NOTES AND QUESTIONS

1. *Status of State Legislation.* According to the Center for Law and the Public's Health, as of July 2009, 38 states and the District of Columbia have enacted legislation that includes provisions from or closely related to the MSEHPA. A table documenting state legislative activity is available at http://www. publichealthlaw.net/Resources/ Modellaws.php. State representatives and various public health experts collaborated in 2003 to produce an alternative model that borrows some provisions from the MSEHPA, and provides a more comprehensive model for public health regulation. *See* State of Alaska, Health & Human Servs., *The Turning Point Model State Public Health Act* (June 21, 2004), *at* http://www.hss.state.ak.us/dph/improving/turningpoint/ MSPHA.htm.

2. *Constitutional?* Would the portions of the Model Act set out above survive a challenge to their constitutionality?

3. *Commandeering Resources.* Article V of the MSEHPA provides sweeping powers for a state public health authority to commandeer private resources during a public health emergency. In addition to the authority to close, evacuate, or decontaminate facilities or materials, and to gain access to and control of facilities, private property, and transportation modes, state officials would be given control over the procurement, rationing, and distribution of health care supplies. MSEHPA §§501-505. The Model Act anticipates that "just compensation" would be paid to any owner for property lawfully taken during the public health emergency. *Id.* §506. Under what circumstances would the provisions of Title V be implemented? If enacted, would these provisions be constitutional? Wise? How would you advise a state legislature interested in providing for these contingencies to ensure against the abuse of such powers?

4. *Compulsion of People.* Review the provisions of Article VI of the MSEHPA above. What is the difference between isolation and quarantine? What practical difference does it make whether a person is subject to an isolation or quarantine order? How useful are the conditions and principles set forth in §604(b) in deciding whether to impose isolation or quarantine? Are the public health needs and rights of affected individuals and other persons adequately served? Are the proposed procedures constitutional? Finally, who would actually enforce the quarantine, and how?

5. *Dealing with a Medical Surge.* Among the biggest challenges facing public health officials and other state and local decision makers in a crisis is the prospect of a medical surge—a demand for services and protection that far outstrips existing capacities. Under triage conditions criteria must be developed to strictly ration care. It may be important to waive licensing and certification requirements for care givers to permit the widespread use of volunteers, and to provide waivers of liability for those volunteers. Neither MSEHPA nor most existing state and local

laws provide expressly for such a medical surge. Federal law requires hospitals with emergency departments to provide medical screening and stabilization for every patient who arrives for care. 42 U.S.C. §1395dd (2006). How would you advise state decision makers to plan for a surge in patient demand that outstrips available resources?

6. *A Needed Set of Correctives?* Should state legislatures enact some version of the MSEHPA? What provisions would you say are most controversial, and why? Some scholars have claimed that the Model Act is unnecessary and is an overreaction to the need for incremental public health law reform. *See* LSU Program in Law, Sci. & Pub. Health, *White Paper #2: Review of the Model State Emergency Health Powers Act; Legislative Alternatives to the Model State Emergency Health Powers Act (MSEHPA)* (Apr. 2003), *available at* http://www.biotech.law.lsu.edu/blaw/bt/MSEHPA-review.htm; Erin M. Page, *Balancing Individual Rights and Public Health Safety During Quarantine: the U.S. and Canada*, 38 Case W. Res. J. Int'l L. 517 (2006-2007).

D. THE FEDERAL ROLE IN RESPONDING TO BIOTERRORIST ATTACKS

The federal responsibility for biological incidents is shared by several agencies, as noted earlier. Overall coordination is supposed to be provided by DHS. HHS, acting through the CDC, will play a leading role based on its specialized experience and expertise. Some of the statutory and regulatory authorities relevant to that role are set out below.

Public Health Service Act
42 U.S.C. §§201-300bbb (2006 & Supp. IV 2010)

§243. General Grant of Authority for Cooperation. . . .

(c) Development of plan to control epidemics and meet emergencies or problems resulting from disasters; . . .
(1) The Secretary [of Health and Human Services (the "Service")] is authorized to develop (and may take such action as may be necessary to implement) a plan under which personnel, equipment, medical supplies, and other resources of the Service and other agencies under the jurisdiction of the Secretary may be effectively used to control epidemics of any disease or condition and to meet other health emergencies or problems. . . .

§264. Regulations to Control Communicable Diseases

(a) Promulgation and Enforcement by Surgeon General. The Surgeon General, with the approval of the Secretary, is authorized to make and enforce such regulations as in his judgment are necessary to prevent the introduction, transmission, or spread of communicable diseases from foreign countries into the States or possessions, or from one State or possession into any other State or possession. For purposes of carrying out and enforcing such regulations, the Surgeon General may provide for such inspection, fumigation, disinfection . . . and other measures, as in his judgment may be necessary.

(b) Apprehension, detention, or conditional release of individuals. Regulations prescribed under this section shall not provide for the apprehension, detention, or conditional release of individuals except for the purpose of preventing the introduction, transmission, or spread of such communicable diseases as may be specified from time to time in Executive orders of the President upon the recommendation of the Secretary, in consultation with the Surgeon General. . . .

(d) (1) Apprehension and examination of persons reasonably believed to be infected. Regulations prescribed under this section may provide for the apprehension and examination of any individual reasonably believed to be infected with a communicable disease in a qualifying stage and (A) to be moving or about to move from a State to another State; or (B) to be a probable source of infection to individuals who, while infected with such disease in a qualifying stage, will be moving from a State to another State. Such regulations may provide that if upon examination any such individual is found to be infected, he may be detained for such time and in such manner as may be reasonably necessary. . . .

HHS has adopted the following regulations to implement this statutory authority:

Interstate Quarantine Regulations
42 C.F.R. pt. 70 (2010)

§70.2 Measures in the Event of Inadequate Local Control.

Whenever the Director of the Centers for Disease Control and Prevention determines that the measures taken by health authorities of any State or possession (including political subdivisions thereof) are insufficient to prevent the spread of any of the communicable diseases from such State or possession to any other State or possession, he/she may take such measures to prevent such spread of the diseases as he/she deems reasonably necessary, including inspection. . . .

§70.5 Certain Communicable Diseases; Special Requirements.

The following provisions are applicable with respect to any person who is in the communicable period of cholera, plague, smallpox, typhus or yellow fever, or who, having been exposed to any such disease, is in the incubation period thereof:

(a) Requirements relating to travelers.

(1) No such person shall travel from one State or possession to another, or on a conveyance engaged in interstate traffic, without a written permit of the Surgeon General or his/her authorized representative. . . .

§70.6 Apprehension and Detention of Persons with Specific Diseases.

Regulations prescribed in this part authorize the detention, isolation, quarantine, or conditional release of individuals, for the purpose of preventing the introduction, transmission, and spread of the communicable diseases listed in an Executive Order setting out a list of quarantinable communicable diseases, as provided under section 361(b) of the Public Health Service Act. Executive Order 13295, of April 4, 2003, contains the current revised list of quarantinable communicable diseases, and may be obtained at http://www.cdc.gov, or at http://www.archives.gov/federal_register/. If this Order is amended, HHS will enforce that amended order immediately and update this reference.

NOTES AND QUESTIONS

1. *Who's in Charge?* Can you tell from the authorities we have examined who will be responsible for coordinating and implementing all these federal, state, and local laws in a great crisis? In a portion of the federal statute not quoted above, the federal government may assist with or take over management of an intrastate incident if requested by a state or if the federal government determines that local efforts are not sufficient. 42 U.S.C. §264(e).

2. *Responding to Listed Pathogens.* The HHS regulations set out above have been amended several times since September 11, 2001, to expand the list of infectious agents for which the CDC may erect quarantines or detain persons. The executive order incorporated by reference in §70.6 lists cholera, diphtheria, infectious tuberculosis, plague, smallpox, yellow fever, and viral hemorrhagic fevers (including Lassa, Marburg, and Ebola). It also lists severe acute respiratory syndrome (SARS). Not listed are tularemia, botulism, and other contagions that could be weaponized and used by terrorists. Nor are there federal regulations authorizing the imposition of quarantine following an attack by chemical, radiological, or nuclear weapons, although federal authority may exist to prevent the transmission of disease that could occur as secondary effects of the contamination. An order aimed at halting the spread of bird flu adds "influenza caused by novel or reemergent influenza viruses that are causing, or have the potential to cause, a pandemic." Exec. Order No. 13,375 (Apr. 1, 2005). How should government authorities respond to the terrorist release of an infectious agent not listed or not immediately identifiable?

In May 2006, the Homeland Security Council issued its *Pandemic Influenza Implementation Plan, available at* http://www.pandemicflu.gov/professional/federal/pandemic-influenza-implementation.pdf. At 233 pages, it sets out fairly elaborate guidance for U.S. planning in areas of primary federal responsibility, international efforts, controls of borders and transportation, protection of human and animal health, and public safety, emphasizing the roles of state and local governments wherever possible. Because a bird flu pandemic would present many of the legal and practical problems posed by a terrorist attack using plague or some other contagious disease, the *Implementation Plan* probably reflects the latest government thinking about large-scale, integrated planning for both kinds of catastrophe. Periodic updates of the *Implementation Plan* may be found at FLU.gov, *Federal Government* (n.d.), *at* http://www.flu.gov/professional/federal. *See generally* Sarah A. Lister, *Public Health and Medical Emergency Management: Issues in the 112th Congress* (Cong. Res. Serv. R41646), Feb. 18, 2011.

3. *Responding to Anthrax.* What measures need to be undertaken by federal officials to address the threat posed by terrorists sending anthrax spores through the mail, as happened in the aftermath of the September 11, 2001, attacks? Anthrax is extremely dangerous but not communicable. Can you explain how various federal agencies might cooperate in this effort? Do HHS and the CDC have the authority they need to be helpful? A Defense Department–sponsored report concluded that the anthrax letter attacks "revealed weaknesses in almost every aspect of U.S. biopreparedness and response." David Heyman, *Lessons from the Anthrax Attacks: Implications for U.S. Bioterrorism Preparedness* at viii (Apr. 2002), *available at* http://www.fas.org/irp/threat/cbw/dtra02.pdf. *See also* Keith Rhodes, *Diffuse Security Threats: Information on U.S. Domestic Anthrax Attacks* (GAO-03-0323T), Dec. 10, 2002, *available at* pp. 808-822 of another report found at http://www.fas.org/irp/congress/2002_rpt/911rept.pdf; General Accounting Office, *Bioterrorism: Public Health Responses to Anthrax Incidents of 2001* (GAO-04-152), Oct. 2003.

4. *Responding to Smallpox.* Reflecting growing fears that remaining supplies of smallpox virus might fall into the hands of terrorists, the CDC has published a plan for responding to an outbreak of a disease thought to have been eradicated in the 1970s. *See CDC Smallpox Response Plan and Guidelines (Version 3.0)* (June 23, 2004, with updates), *at* http://www.bt.cdc.gov/agent/smallpox/response-plan. The plan calls for employment of a "ring" strategy to isolate confirmed and suspected smallpox cases, vaccinate persons who may have come into contact with them, and keep all possible contacts under close surveillance. The size of a ring is to be determined by state and federal health officials.

5. *Federal Authority to Constrain Persons?* HHS's enabling legislation states that an "individual believed to be infected with a communicable disease in a communicable stage" may be "apprehended and examined." 42 U.S.C. §264(d). If found to be infected, the individual may then be "detained for such time and in such manner as may be reasonably necessary." *Id.* Do you think this language is meant to give the CDC authority to quarantine an entire city? Or to require vaccinations? What is the relationship between the HHS/CDC authorities and state law, whether or not a state has adopted something like the MSEHPA?

Do you think that principles of federalism and constitutional limits on the exercise of federal regulatory authority permit a federal quarantine within a single state? The Supreme Court has stated that Congress may "regulate those activities having a substantial relation to interstate commerce," *United States v. Lopez*, 514 U.S. 549, 555 (1995), but it has also ruled that Congress may not regulate non-economic activities within a state solely on the basis of the effect of those activities on interstate commerce. *United States v. Morrison*, 529 U.S. 598 (2000). A 2009 memorandum from the Attorney General to the Secretaries of HHS and DHS and other federal officials concluded that the authority to implement a federal quarantine intrastate is unclear. Memorandum for the President from the Attorney General, *Summary of Legal Authorities for Use in Response to an Outbreak of Pandemic Influenza* (Apr. 25, 2009), *available at* http://www.ncsl.org/IssuesResearch/Health/H1N1FluSwineFluPublicHealthAlert/tabid/17089/Default.aspx. Statutory and constitutional bases and limits for both state and federal public health regulations dealing with bioterrorism threats are briefed extensively in proposed CDC regulations. Department of Health & Human Servs., *Control of Communicable Diseases*, 70 Fed. Reg. 71,892-01, 71,893-71,896 (Nov. 30, 2005).

6. *Enforcing a Quarantine.* HHS and the CDC have no police force of their own to enforce a federal quarantine. Do you think such a quarantine could be enforced without the use of military forces? See *infra* pp. 1169-1174.

7. *Triage and Surge Control Redux.* The CDC maintains the Strategic National Stockpile (SNS) program. Within 12 hours of a terrorist attack, the Stockpile can deliver "push packages" containing needed pharmaceuticals and other medical supplies anywhere in the country. *See* CDC, *Strategic National Stockpile* (Apr. 14, 2005), *at* http://www.cdc.gov/phpr/stockpile.htm. Inventories are nevertheless limited, and they might not be adequate to treat every person affected by an outbreak of some diseases. Who do you think should receive such limited supplies first? Who should be empowered to choose among potential recipients? Would it be a good idea to decide such questions in advance of a terrorist attack or pandemic? If so, how?

Federal law also authorizes the waiver of various regulatory requirements in the event of a public health emergency. For example, the Food and Drug Administration (FDA) may permit the use of an unapproved drug or device in an emergency involving a biological, chemical, radiological, or nuclear agent. 21 U.S.C. §§360bbb-3(a) (2006).

The Military's Domestic Role

38

Until recently the Defense Department had organized itself almost exclusively to fight a conventional war far from America's shores. In part this reflected the absence of the sort of domestic threats that have emerged in the last decade or so. It also demonstrated the public's antipathy toward any sort of military involvement in domestic life. During the Vietnam War, the Supreme Court noted "a traditional and strong resistance of Americans to any military intrusion into civilian affairs." *Laird v. Tatum,* 408 U.S. 1, 15 (1972). *See* W. Kent Davis, *Swords into Plowshares: The Dangerous Politicization of the Military in the Post-Cold War Era,* 33 Val. U. L. Rev. 61, 64-77 (1998). Thus, for most of our history the military's domestic role has consisted primarily of preparations for foreign wars and of occasional support for civilian authorities in curbing civil unrest and fighting the "war on drugs."

On September 11, 2001, however, the military's role, like so much else in this country, began to change. The following day the President described the terrorist attacks as "acts of war." The battlefield in this war obviously extends to the U.S. homeland. We saw in Chapters 29, 30, and 36 that the military may be used to detain and try suspected terrorists. Should troops be deployed even more broadly on this new front? If so, should their Rules of Engagement (ROE) be different from those that guide military operations abroad? What legal authorities exist or would have to be created to accommodate these needed changes?

In Part A of this chapter we address the deep-seated American tradition of avoiding entanglement of the military in civilian life, as reflected in laws designed to limit that entanglement. Part B concerns the domestic intelligence role of the military. Finally, in Part C, we examine the military's role in responding to a terrorist attack on the homeland.

A. THE TRADITIONAL ROLE OF THE MILITARY IN AMERICAN SOCIETY

The domestic use of troops has been a fact of life and a matter of controversy at least since President Washington called out the militia to put down the Whiskey Rebellion in 1794. Many other Presidents have deployed federal military forces to help keep the peace, to aid local governments in natural disasters, and to enforce federal and state laws. State governors have called out their militias even more often, especially in the first three decades of the twentieth century. From the earliest days of the Republic, however, Americans have resisted any involvement by military forces in domestic matters.

1. The Posse Comitatus Act as a Background Principle

Could the President deploy troops to enforce a quarantine in the event of a bioterrorist attack like the one outlined in the plague scenario, *supra* p. 1117? Could the troops detain looters? Could they shoot people trying to break out of the quarantine? The following decision may provide some guidance.

Bissonette v. Haig

United States Court of Appeals, Eighth Circuit, 1985
776 F.2d 1384, *aff'd*, 800 F.2d 812 (8th Cir. 1986) (en banc),
aff'd, 485 U.S. 264 (1988)

ARNOLD, J. This is an action for damages caused by defendants' alleged violations of the Constitution of the United States. . . .

This case arises out of the occupation of the village of Wounded Knee, South Dakota, on the Pine Ridge Reservation by an armed group of Indians on February 27, 1973. On the evening when the occupation began, members of the Federal Bureau of Investigation, the United States Marshals Service, and the Bureau of Indian Affairs Police sealed off the village by establishing roadblocks at all major entry and exit roads. The standoff between the Indians and the law enforcement authorities ended about ten weeks later with the surrender of the Indians occupying the village. . . .

In their amended complaint, plaintiffs allege . . . that they were unreasonably seized and confined in the village of Wounded Knee contrary to the Fourth Amendment and their rights to free movement and travel. Second, they claim that they were unreasonably searched by ground and aerial surveillance. In both cases, plaintiffs assert that the seizures and searches were unreasonable because "Defendants accomplished or caused to be accomplished those actions by means of the unconstitutional and felonious use of parts of the United States Army or Air Force. . . ." . . . This case comes to us on appeal from a dismissal for failure to state a claim, and we therefore accept for present purposes the factual allegations of the complaint.

These allegations must be viewed against the background of the Posse Comitatus Act of 1878, 18 U.S.C. §1385, which plaintiffs claim was violated here. The statute provides:

§1385. Use of Army and Air Force as Posse Comitatus[1]

Whoever, except in cases and under circumstances expressly authorized by the Constitution or Act of Congress, willfully uses any part of the Army or the Air Force as a posse

[1. The Latin term posse comitatus means, literally, "power or authority of the county," but it connotes a body of persons summoned by a sheriff to assist in preserving the peace or enforcing the law. The persons summoned to assist the sheriff might, of course, be either civilian or military. — Eds.]

comitatus or otherwise to execute the laws shall be fined not more than $10,000 or imprisoned not more than two years, or both.

A

The first two sets of claims raise the question whether a search or seizure, otherwise permissible, can be rendered unreasonable under the Fourth Amendment because military personnel or equipment were used to accomplish those actions. We believe that the Constitution, certain Acts of Congress, and the decisions of the Supreme Court embody certain limitations on the use of military personnel in enforcing the civil law, and that searches and seizures in circumstances which exceed those limits are unreasonable under the Fourth Amendment.

... Reasonableness is determined by balancing the interests for and against the seizure. Usually, the interests arrayed against a seizure are those of the individual in privacy, freedom of movement, or, in the case of a seizure by deadly force, life. Here, however, the opposing interests are more societal and governmental than strictly individual in character. They concern the special threats to constitutional government inherent in military enforcement of civilian law. That these governmental interests should weigh in the Fourth Amendment balance is neither novel nor surprising. In the typical Fourth Amendment case, the interests of the individual are balanced against those of the government. That some of those governmental interests are on the other side of the Fourth Amendment balance does not make them any less relevant or important.

Civilian rule is basic to our system of government. The use of military forces to seize civilians can expose civilian government to the threat of military rule and the suspension of constitutional liberties. On a lesser scale, military enforcement of the civil law leaves the protection of vital Fourth and Fifth Amendment rights in the hands of persons who are not trained to uphold these rights. It may also chill the exercise of fundamental rights, such as the rights to speak freely and to vote, and create the atmosphere of fear and hostility which exists in territories occupied by enemy forces.

The interest in limiting military involvement in civilian affairs has a long tradition beginning with the Declaration of Independence and continued in the Constitution, certain Acts of Congress, and decisions of the Supreme Court. The Declaration of Independence states among the grounds for severing ties with Great Britain that the King "has kept among us, in times of peace, Standing Armies without Consent of our Legislature ... [and] has affected to render the Military independent of and superior to the Civil power." These concerns were later raised at the Constitutional Convention. Luther Martin of Maryland said, "when a government wishes to deprive its citizens of freedom, and reduce them to slavery, it generally makes use of a standing army."

The Constitution itself limits the role of the military in civilian affairs: it makes the President, the highest civilian official in the Executive Branch, Commander in Chief of the armed services (Art. II, §2); it limits the appropriations for armed forces to two years and grants to the Congress the power to make rules to govern the armed forces (Art. I, §8, cl. 14); and it forbids the involuntary quartering of soldiers in any house in time of peace (Third Amendment).

Congress has passed several statutes limiting the use of the military in enforcing the civil law [including the Posse Comitatus Act and the Insurrection Act, both addressed *infra*]....

The Supreme Court has also recognized the constitutional limitations placed on military involvement in civilian affairs. A leading case is *Ex parte Milligan*, 71 U.S. 2, 124 (1866).... More recently, in *Laird v. Tatum*, 408 U.S. 1, 15-16 (1972), statements the Court made in dicta reaffirm these limitations....

The governmental interests favoring military assistance to civilian law enforcement are primarily twofold: first, to maintain order in times of domestic violence or rebellion; and second, to improve the efficiency of civilian law enforcement by giving it the benefit of military technologies, equipment, information, and training personnel. These interests can and have been accommodated by Acts of Congress to the overriding interest of preserving civilian government and law enforcement. At the time of the Wounded Knee occupation, Congress had prohibited the use of the military to execute the civilian laws, except when expressly authorized. 18 U.S.C. §1385. And it had placed specific limits on the President's power to use the national guard and military in emergency situations. 10 U.S.C. §§331-335. For example, under 10 U.S.C. §332, the President may call upon the military only after having determined that domestic unrest makes it "impracticable to enforce the laws of the United States by the ordinary course of judicial proceedings," and under 10 U.S.C. §334, he may do so only after having issued a proclamation ordering the insurgents to disperse. Those steps were not taken here.

We believe that the limits established by Congress on the use of the military for civilian law enforcement provide a reliable guidepost by which to evaluate the reasonableness for Fourth Amendment purposes of the seizures and searches in question here. Congress has acted to establish reasonable limits on the President's use of military forces in emergency situations, and in doing so has circumscribed whatever, if any, inherent power the President may have had absent such legislation. This is the teaching of *Youngstown Sheet & Tube Co. v. Sawyer*, 343 U.S. 579 (1952)....

B

... [T]he use of military force for domestic law-enforcement purposes is in a special category, and ... both the courts and Congress have been alert to keep it there. In short, if the use of military personnel is both unauthorized by any statute, and contrary to a specific criminal prohibition, and if citizens are seized or searched by military means in such a case, we have no hesitation in declaring that such searches and seizures are constitutionally "unreasonable." We do not mean to say that every search or seizure that violates a statute of any kind is necessarily a violation of the Fourth Amendment. But the statute prohibiting (if the allegations in the complaint can be proved) the conduct engaged in by defendants here is, as we have attempted to explain, not just any Act of Congress. It is the embodiment of a long tradition of suspicion and hostility towards the use of military force for domestic purposes.

Plaintiffs' Fourth Amendment case, therefore, must stand or fall on the proposition that military activity in connection with the occupation of Wounded Knee violated the Posse Comitatus Act.

In *United States v. Casper*, 541 F.2d 1275 (8th Cir. 1976) (per curiam), *cert. denied*, 430 U.S. 970 (1977), ... the District Court had found on a stipulated record that the following activities did not violate the Act: the use of Air Force personnel, planes, and cameras to fly surveillance; the advice of military officers in dealing with the disorder; and the furnishing of equipment and supplies. We affirmed "on the basis of the trial court's thorough and well-reasoned opinion." 541 F.2d at 1276.

... Therefore, unless plaintiffs now allege that the defendants took actions that went beyond those alleged in the *Casper* case, the actions alleged in the complaint now before us cannot violate the Act.

In *Casper*, quoting from Judge VanSickle's opinion for the District Court, 419 F. Supp. at 194, we approved the following standard for determining whether a violation of the Posse Comitatus Act had occurred:

> Were Army or Air Force personnel used by the civilian law enforcement officers at Wounded Knee in such a manner that the military personnel subjected the citizens to the exercise of military power which was regulatory, proscriptive, or compulsory in nature, either presently or prospectively?

541 F.2d at 1278. . . .

When this concept is transplanted into the present legal context, we take it to mean that military involvement, even when not expressly authorized by the Constitution or a statute, does not violate the Posse Comitatus Act unless it actually regulates, forbids, or compels some conduct on the part of those claiming relief. A mere threat of some future injury would be insufficient. . . .

. . . We of course have no way of knowing what plaintiffs would be able to prove if this case goes to trial, but the complaint, considered simply as a pleading, goes well beyond an allegation that defendants simply furnished supplies, aerial surveillance, and advice. It specifically charges that "the several Defendants maintained or caused to be maintained roadblocks and armed patrols constituting an armed perimeter around the village of Wounded Knee. . . ." Defendants' actions, it is charged, "seized, confined, and made prisoners (of plaintiffs) against their will. . . ." These allegations amount to a claim that defendants' activities, allegedly in violation of the Posse Comitatus Act, were "regulatory, proscriptive, or compulsory," in the sense that these activities directly restrained plaintiffs' freedom of movement. No more is required to survive a motion to dismiss. . . .

As to the second set of claims, . . . plaintiffs charge that they were searched and subjected to surveillance against their will by aerial photographic and visual search and surveillance. As we have already noted, *Casper* holds that this sort of activity does not violate the Posse Comitatus Act. It is therefore not "unreasonable" for Fourth Amendment purposes. . . .

NOTES AND QUESTIONS

1. *Origins of the Posse Comitatus Act.* Early acts of Congress authorized the use of the militia to aid in law enforcement, although such use was never so extensive as it was after the Civil War. Reconstruction era abuses, culminating in the use of federal troops to police polling stations in Southern states (some say to influence the outcome of the presidential election of 1876), led to passage of the Posse Comitatus Act in 1878. The history is set forth in David E. Engdahl, *The New Civil Disturbances Regulations: The Threat of Military Intervention*, 49 Ind. L.J. 581, 597-603 (1974); and University of Colo. Law Revision Ctr., *A Comprehensive Study of the Use of Military Troops in Civil Disorders with Proposals for Legislative Reform*, 43 U. Colo. L. Rev. 399, 402-412 (1972). The Act is described generally in Jennifer Elsea, *The Posse Comitatus Act and Related Matters: A Sketch* (Cong. Res. Serv. RS20590), June 6, 2005; Matthew Carlton Hammond, Note, *The Posse Comitatus Act: A Principle in Need of Renewal*, 75 Wash. U.

L.Q. 953 (1997); and Sean J. Kealy, *Reexamining the Posse Comitatus Act: Toward a Right to Civil Law Enforcement*, 21 Yale L. & Pol'y Rev. 383 (2003).

2. *Elements of a Posse Comitatus Act Violation.* What exactly constitutes use of the armed forces "as a posse comitatus or otherwise to execute the laws"? To the "regulatory, proscriptive, or compulsory" standard set forth in *Bissonette*, we may add criteria from other cases growing out of the Wounded Knee incident: whether there was "direct, active" use of the military in civil law enforcement, *United States v. Red Feather*, 392 F. Supp. 916, 923 (D.S.D. 1975), or whether the use of the Army or the Air Force "pervaded the activities" of the civil law enforcement officers, *United States v. Jaramillo*, 380 F. Supp. 1375, 1379 (D. Neb. 1974), *appeal dismissed*, 510 F.2d 808 (8th Cir. 1975).

The Posse Comitatus Act may be inapplicable when the primary purpose of armed forces involvement is to enforce the Uniform Code of Military Justice or to achieve some distinctly military goal, and the benefits to civilian authorities are merely incidental — the so-called "military purpose" doctrine. *See Applewhite v. United States Air Force*, 995 F.2d 997, 1001 (10th Cir. 1993); *United States v. Thompson*, 33 M.J. 218 (C.M.A. 1991), *cert. denied*, 502 U.S. 1074 (1992).

Are you now prepared to say what particular military activities in aid of law enforcement are forbidden? Do you think the Posse Comitatus Act should be amended to make it easier to predict when the Act would apply? If so, how?

3. *Judicial Remedies for Violations.* There apparently never has been a criminal prosecution of anyone for violation of the Posse Comitatus Act. *See* Paul Jackson Rice, *New Laws and Insights Encircle the Posse Comitatus Act*, 104 Mil. L. Rev. 109, 111 (1984). Violations of the Posse Comitatus Act have, however, often been asserted as a defense to charges under other criminal statutes. For example, in *Red Feather* and *Jaramillo*, *supra*, American Indians at Wounded Knee were charged with interfering with a "law enforcement officer lawfully engaged in the lawful performance of his official duties." *See* 18 U.S.C. §231(a)(3) (2006). The defendants argued that the federal marshals and FBI agents were not performing their duties lawfully, within the meaning of the statute, because they enlisted military forces as a posse comitatus. *See also United States v. Mendoza-Cecelia*, 963 F.2d 1467, 1478 n.9 (11th Cir.), *cert. denied*, 506 U.S. 964 (1992).

Others apprehended by the military while attempting to smuggle drugs into the United States have argued that the evidence obtained in their arrests was inadmissible at trial. However, the federal courts have consistently refused to exclude such evidence in the absence of widespread and repeated Posse Comitatus Act violations. *See, e.g., Hayes v. Hawes*, 921 F.2d 100, 104 (7th Cir. 1990); *see also* Timothy J. Saviano, Note, *The Exclusionary Rule's Applicability to Violations of the Posse Comitatus Act*, Army Law., July 1995, at 61.

In *Bissonette v. Haig*, the appellants sought damages for infringement of their constitutional rights resulting from Posse Comitatus Act violations. Do such statutory violations give rise to a private cause of action separate and apart from any possible constitutional injury? *See Robinson v. Overseas Military Sales Corp.*, 21 F.3d 502 (2d Cir. 1994); *Lamont v. Haig*, 539 F. Supp. 552 (W.D.S.D. 1982) (no legislative intent to create a private right of action).

4. *Which Military Services Are Covered?* The Posse Comitatus Act expressly refers only to the Army and Air Force, and several cases have found that the Act does not restrict Navy law enforcement efforts. *See, e.g., Mendoza-Cecelia, supra*, 963 F.2d at 1477-1478; *but cf. United States v. Chon*, 210 F.3d 990 (9th Cir. 2000). Nevertheless, Navy

regulations have long prohibited the use of the Navy and Marine Corps as a posse comitatus, with certain exceptions, as a matter of Defense Department policy. *See* SECNAVINST 5820.7C (Jan. 26, 2006), *available at* http://www.hqmc.usmc.mil/PP&O/PS/psl/corrections/References/5820.7C.pdf.

Note that the Coast Guard presumably is not covered by the Posse Comitatus Act when, acting as a service of the Department of Homeland Security (DHS), it has a broad range of statutory law enforcement responsibilities. 14 U.S.C. §2. Otherwise, it is "a military service and a branch of the armed forces of the United States at all times" — specifically, a "service in the Navy." 14 U.S.C. §1. It assumes a military role "[u]pon the declaration of war or when the President directs." 14 U.S.C. §3.

In the event of a major terrorist attack or natural disaster, it is likely that unfederalized state National Guard troops will be dispatched to the scene before federal troops are considered or deployed. Several courts have held that until such forces are federalized they are not subject to the strictures of the Posse Comitatus Act. *See, e.g., United States v. Gilbert,* 165 F.3d 470 (6th Cir. 1999). Moreover, Congress has explicitly approved the states' use of the militia for "drug interdiction and counter-drug activities," so long as they remain under state control. 32 U.S.C. §112 (2006).

5. *Contemporary Vitality of the Posse Comitatus Act.* One might suspect that in our post-9/11 society, no one would likely object or even pay much attention to military involvement in civilian law enforcement, especially if it concerned a terrorist threat. But as the following case study suggests, strict compliance with the Posse Comitatus Act today could help avert the very problems that provoked passage of the Act in 1878.

CASE STUDY: RAID ON THE BRANCH DAVIDIANS[2]

After local law enforcement officials near Waco, Texas, reported to the Bureau of Alcohol, Tobacco, and Firearms (ATF) in May 1992 that the Branch Davidians, an obscure religious group, were stockpiling large quantities of firearms and black powder, officials worried that the sect's leader, known to his followers as David Koresh, was creating a military-type compound. An ATF investigation gathered enough evidence of illegal weapons activity to obtain search warrants for the compound. Although ATF had its own highly trained response team, agency officials determined that executing the warrants would require military support. Because ATF did not want to foot the bill for military support, however, agency staff essentially imagined a drug connection to the Branch Davidians, so that military expertise could be supplied without cost to the agency. Air surveillance of the compound revealed no drug activity, but ATF reported the possible presence of a methamphetamine laboratory on the grounds. Although ATF offered no proof of a drug connection, Department of Defense (DOD) drug enforcement officers furnished training facilities and equipment, including seven Bradley fighting vehicles. ATF also requested that Special Forces soldiers assist, including the conduct of "room clearing discriminate fire operations," the military equivalent of "close-quarter combat."

Command officers and their lawyers at Army Special Forces Command and the Judge Advocate General (JAG) office at Fort Bragg, North Carolina, soon grew

---

2. *See* Department of the Treasury, *Report of the Department of the Treasury on the Bureau of Alcohol, Tobacco, and Firearms Investigation of Vernon Wayne Howell also known as David Koresh* (1993), *available at* http://www.archive.org/details/reportofdepartme00unit; *Investigation into the Activities of Federal Law Enforcement Agencies Toward the Branch Davidians,* H.R. Rep. No. 104-749 (1996); Thomas R. Lujan, *Legal Aspects of Domestic Employment of the Army,* Parameters 82 (1997).

suspicious. After a review of plans for the operation — construction of a practice site, the ATF assault, provision of on-site medical services during the raid — the lawyers concluded that the military would be providing forbidden "active" participation in what amounted to law enforcement. Army personnel might find themselves treating injured civilians and searching arrested persons. If there was a drug lab at the site, soldiers could be involved in collecting evidence for prosecutions.

When military officers in Texas learned of the command officers' doubts, they argued that headquarters was an "unwarranted obstacle to mission success." Only after the command lawyers delivered a memorandum for the record to the Office of the Secretary of Defense did the local military officials conduct a more thorough review of the facts and the law. Soon thereafter, the military scaled back its offer of assistance to ATF to include safety, communications, and medical evaluation training. No soldiers would accompany ATF personnel to the compound.

When the raid was executed on February 28, 1993, the resulting firefight killed four agents and wounded more than 20; there were six deaths and four injuries among cult members. Then, after a 51-day siege, a fire swept through the compound, killing 74 Davidians. As tragic as they were, the raid, siege, and eventual fire might have been much worse in the public eye if Army Special Forces had been seen guiding ATF agents in an attack on a religious compound. In the end, the Posse Comitatus Act gave strength to the legal misgivings of headquarters JAG lawyers, and their resistance saved the Army from embarrassment and a backlash from an angry citizenry.

2. Exceptions to the Posse Comitatus Act

Recall that the Posse Comitatus Act prohibition applies "except in cases and under circumstances expressly authorized by the Constitution or Act of Congress." 18 U.S.C. §1850 (2006). The most important exception to the Act is a set of five statutes, referred to collectively as the Insurrection Act. It provides, in part:

Insurrection Act
10 U.S.C. §§331-335 (2006 & Supp. III 2009)

§332. Use of Militia and Armed Forces to Enforce Federal Authority

Whenever the President considers that unlawful obstructions, combinations, or assemblages, or rebellion against the authority of the United States, make it impracticable to enforce the laws of the United States in any State or Territory by the ordinary course of judicial proceedings, he may call into Federal service such of the militia of any State, and use such of the armed forces, as he considers necessary to enforce those laws or to suppress the rebellion.

§333. Major public emergencies; interference with State and Federal law

The President, by using the militia or the armed forces, or both, or by any other means, shall take such measures as he considers necessary to suppress, in a State, any insurrection, domestic violence, unlawful combination, or conspiracy, if it . . .

(2) opposes or obstructs the execution of the laws of the United States or impedes the course of justice under those laws. . . .

§334. Proclamation to Disperse

Whenever the President considers it necessary to use the militia or the armed forces under this chapter, he shall, by proclamation, immediately order the insurgents or those obstructing the enforcement of the laws to disperse and retire peaceably to their abodes within a limited time.[3]

Military Cooperation with Law Enforcement Officials Act

10 U.S.C. §§371-382 (2006 & Supp. III 2009), as amended by
Pub. L. No. 111-383, §1075(b)(10)(A), (B), 124 Stat. 4137, 4369 (2011)

§371. Use of information collected during military operations

(a) The Secretary of Defense may, in accordance with other applicable law, provide to Federal, State, or local civilian law enforcement officials any information collected during the normal course of military training or operations that may be relevant to a violation of any Federal or State law within the jurisdiction of such officials.

(b) The needs of civilian law enforcement officials for information shall, to the maximum extent practicable, be taken into account in the planning and execution of military training or operations.

(c) The Secretary of Defense shall ensure, to the extent consistent with national security, that intelligence information held by the Department of Defense and relevant to drug interdiction or other civilian law enforcement matters is provided promptly to appropriate civilian law enforcement officials. . . .

§375. Restriction on direct participation by military personnel

The Secretary of Defense shall prescribe such regulations as may be necessary to ensure that any activity (including the provision of any equipment or facility or the assignment or detail of any personnel) under this chapter does not include or permit direct participation by a member of the Army, Navy, Air Force, or Marine Corps in a search, seizure, arrest, or other similar activity unless participation in such activity by such member is otherwise authorized by law. . . .

§382. Emergency situations involving chemical or biological weapons of mass destruction

(a) In general. — The Secretary of Defense, upon the request of the Attorney General, may provide assistance in support of Department of Justice activities relating to the enforcement of section 175, 229, or 2332c of title 18 during an emergency situation involving a biological or chemical weapon of mass destruction. Department

---

[3. Section 331 provides for federal military assistance in putting down an insurrection against a state government. Section 335 makes the statutes applicable to Guam and the Virgin Islands. — Eds.]

of Defense resources, including personnel of the Department of Defense, may be used to provide such assistance if—

(1) the Secretary of Defense and the Attorney General jointly determine that an emergency situation exists; and

(2) the Secretary of Defense determines that the provision of such assistance will not adversely affect the military preparedness of the United States.

(b) Emergency situations covered. — In this section, the term "emergency situation involving a biological or chemical weapon of mass destruction" means a circumstance involving a biological or chemical weapon of mass destruction—

(1) that poses a serious threat to the interests of the United States; and

(2) in which—

(A) civilian expertise and capabilities are not readily available to provide the required assistance to counter the threat immediately posed by the weapon involved;

(B) special capabilities and expertise of the Department of Defense are necessary and critical to counter the threat posed by the weapon involved; and

(C) enforcement of section 175, 229, or 2332c of title 18 would be seriously impaired if the Department of Defense assistance were not provided.

(c) Forms of assistance. — The assistance referred to in subsection (a) includes the operation of equipment . . . to monitor, contain, disable, or dispose of the weapon involved or elements of the weapon.

(d) Regulations. —

(1) The Secretary of Defense and the Attorney General shall jointly prescribe regulations concerning the types of assistance that may be provided under this section. Such regulations shall also describe the actions that Department of Defense personnel may take in circumstances incident to the provision of assistance under this section.

(2) (A) Except as provided in subparagraph (B), the regulations may not authorize the following actions:

(i) Arrest.

(ii) Any direct participation in conducting a search for or seizure of evidence related to a violation of section 175, 229, or 2332c of title 18.

(iii) Any direct participation in the collection of intelligence for law enforcement purposes.

(B) The regulations may authorize an action described in subparagraph (A) to be taken under the following conditions:

(i) The action is considered necessary for the immediate protection of human life, and civilian law enforcement officials are not capable of taking the action.

(ii) The action is otherwise authorized under subsection (c) or under otherwise applicable law. . . . [4]

[4. Other sections of the 1981 Act, as amended, deal variously with the use of military equipment and facilities, training and advising civilian law enforcement officials, maintenance and operation of equipment, reimbursement, the use of Coast Guard personnel for law enforcement, and impacts on military preparedness. References to sections 175 and 229 (which has replaced §2332c) of title 18 concern prohibitions on the possession or use of biological or chemical weapons, respectively. — Eds.]

Additional exceptions to the Posse Comitatus Act are considered in the following Notes and Questions.

NOTES AND QUESTIONS

1. *The Insurrection Act.* The Insurrection Act had its origin in a 1792 law invoked by President Washington in suppressing the Whiskey Rebellion. The history of its component parts is traced in Stephen I. Vladeck, Note, *Emergency Power and the Militia Acts*, 114 Yale L.J. 149, 159-167 (2004); William C. Banks, *Providing "Supplemental Security"—The Insurrection Act and the Military Role in Responding to Domestic Crises*, 3 J. Nat'l Security L. & Pol'y 39, 56-72 (2009). In 1827 the Supreme Court indicated that the President had broad discretion in determining when to use these statutes in calling forth the militia, and that his determination was not subject to judicial review. *Martin v. Mott*, 25 U.S. (12 Wheat.) 19, 29-32 (1827). *See also Luther v. Borden*, 48 U.S. (7 How.) 1, 43-45 (1849); *The Prize Cases*, 67 U.S. (2 Black) 635, 668 (1863).

Since that time the Insurrection Act has been invoked for a variety of purposes, including the breaking of the Pullman Strike in 1894. More recently, it has been used to help integrate public schools and universities, to control racial unrest, to collect intelligence about citizens, and to enforce a variety of state and federal laws. It was invoked in 1992 to send federalized California National Guard troops, as well as active-duty soldiers from Fort Ord and Marines from Camp Pendleton, to Los Angeles to help control rioting in the wake of the Rodney King trial verdict. Exec. Order No. 12,804, 57 Fed. Reg. 19,361 (May 1, 1992); Proclamation No. 6427, 57 Fed. Reg. 19,359 (May 1, 1992).

2. *Insurrection Act as a Challenge to State Authority?* Section 333 of U.S.C. title 10 was first enacted in 1956 in the form set out above. A half-century later a great natural disaster prompted its amendment. The original language was then restored two years later.

When Hurricane Katrina hit New Orleans in 2005, local police and other first responders were overwhelmed. The Governor of Louisiana immediately asked the White House for 40,000 soldiers to help in the recovery effort. The White House delayed sending any active-duty military forces for five days, however, and then it deployed only 7,200 troops. Apparently it was felt that the President would have had to federalize Louisiana National Guard forces and invoke the Insurrection Act, then maintain federal control of Guard troops to perform law enforcement duties there—to stop looting and other lawlessness. While the Justice Department's Office of Legal Counsel advised that federal military forces could be sent in, even over the objections of local officials, the President reportedly wanted to avoid the perception that he was seizing command from a female Southern governor of another party. *See* Eric Lipton, Eric Schmitt & Thom Shanker, *Political Issues Snarled Plans for Troop Aid*, N.Y. Times, Sept. 5, 2005. The eventual deployment of military forces, said to be the largest in this country since the Civil War, is described in useful detail in *Failure of Initiative: Final Report of the [House] Bipartisan Committee to Investigate the Preparation for and Response to Hurricane Katrina* 201-238 (Feb. 15, 2006) [hereinafter *Failure of Initiative*].

Paradoxically, the President almost immediately suggested a need for expanded authority for the use of federal troops in such an emergency. Asked whether DOD should play a larger role, the President responded, "Clearly, in the case of a terrorist attack that would be the case, but is there a natural disaster which—of a certain size

82nd Airborne troops patrol New Orleans after Hurricane Katrina.

U.S. Army photo by Daren Reehl.

that would then enable the Defense Department to become a lead agency in coordinating and leading the response effort? That's going to be a very important consideration for Congress to think about." *President's Remarks During Hurricane Rita Briefing
in Texas*, Sept. 25, 2005. A follow-on study, *The Federal Response to Hurricane Katrina:
Lessons Learned* (Feb. 2006), declared that "DOD capabilities must be better identified
and integrated into the Nation's response plans." *Id.* at 54. Moreover, it suggested, in
"extraordinary circumstances" it will be "appropriate for the Department of Defense
to lead the Federal response." *Id.* at 94. DOD and DHS were directed to revise the
National Response Plan to reflect this expanded role. *Id.*

At the Bush administration's urging, 10 U.S.C. §333 was amended in late 2006,
reportedly because of a desire to "clarify" the President's authority. As amended,
§333 provided in significant part:

(a) Use of Armed Forces in Major Public Emergencies —
(1) The President may employ the armed forces, including the National Guard in
Federal service, to —
(A) restore public order and enforce the laws of the United States when, as a
result of a natural disaster, epidemic, or other serious public health emergency,
terrorist attack or incident, or other condition in any State or possession of the
United States, the President determines that —
(i) domestic violence has occurred to such an extent that the constituted
authorities of the State or possession are incapable of maintaining public order; and
(ii) such violence results in a condition described in paragraph (2); or
(B) suppress, in a State, any insurrection, domestic violence, unlawful combination, or conspiracy if such insurrection, violation, combination, or conspiracy
results in a condition described in paragraph (2).

(2) A condition described in this paragraph is a condition that —

(A) so hinders the execution of the laws of a State or possession, as applicable, and of the United States within that State or possession, that any part or class of its people is deprived of a right, privilege, immunity, or protection named in the Constitution and secured by law, and the constituted authorities of that State or possession are unable, fail, or refuse to protect that right, privilege, or immunity, or to give that protection; or

(B) opposes or obstructs the execution of the laws of the United States or impedes the course of justice under those laws. . . .

(b) Notice to Congress — The President shall notify Congress of the determination to exercise the authority in subsection (a)(1)(A) as soon as practicable after the determination and every 14 days thereafter during the duration of the exercise of that authority.

[Pub. L. No. 109-364, §1076, 120 Stat. 2083, 2404-2405 (2006).]

After the 2006 mid-term elections, the National Governors Association persuaded Congress that the amended law could in fact cause confusion and uncertainty about whether a governor or the President is primarily responsible in the event of an emergency, and Congress restored the earlier language. Banks, *supra*, 3 J. Nat'l Security L. & Pol'y at 76. Which version do you think makes it clearer when the President can employ troops domestically to help enforce the law? Might the "constructive ambiguity" of the original and now restored language encourage deliberation between state and federal officials? *See id.*

Did the 2006 amendment to §333 expand or restrict the President's authority? Can you think of any domestic emergency that could not be addressed by the President's using troops if one of the provisions of the Insurrection Act were invoked? Would the unwillingness of a state governor to ask for assistance ever be a bar to such use? Could troops so deployed make searches and arrests, direct traffic, enforce quarantines?

3. *The Military Cooperation with Law Enforcement Officials Act.* A dramatic surge in illicit drug traffic and related criminal activity during the 1970s and 1980s led President Reagan to declare a "war on drugs." *See* Christopher Simpson, *National Security Directives of the Reagan and Bush Administrations* 640-641 (1995). Congress responded in 1981 by enacting the Military Cooperation with Law Enforcement Officials Act, excerpted above, allowing the military to furnish equipment, facilities, and training to civilian law enforcement agencies, and to share relevant intelligence. 10 U.S.C. §§371-373. The Act also authorizes military personnel to operate equipment to intercept vessels or aircraft for law enforcement purposes. *Id.* §374. But it expressly forbids "direct participation by a member of the Army, Navy, Air Force, or Marine Corps in a search, seizure, arrest, or other similar activity unless . . . otherwise authorized by law." *Id.* §375. In separate legislation, the Defense Department was designated lead agency for the detection and monitoring of aerial and maritime shipments of illicit drugs into the United States. 10 U.S.C. §124 (2006). And in 1998 Congress expanded the permitted uses of military personnel to operate loaned equipment to include enforcement of terrorism laws. Pub. L. No. 105-277, §201, 112 Stat. 2681, 2681-567 (1998) (amending 10 U.S.C. §374).

Do you think this legislation added to powers already enjoyed by the President under the Insurrection Act? If not, why did Congress bother to pass it?

4. *Other Statutory Exceptions.* Another exception to the Posse Comitatus Act is found in H.R.J. Res. 1292, Pub. L. No. 90-331, 82 Stat. 170 (1968), which directs federal agencies (including the Department of Defense) to assist the Secret Service in the performance of its protective duties. This authority was used by President Johnson to deploy troops in Chicago during the Democratic National Convention in 1968 and by President Nixon to control antiwar demonstrations on several occasions. Congress has also approved emergency military assistance in enforcing a prohibition on the unauthorized possession or use of nuclear material. 18 U.S.C. §831(d), (e) (2006).

5. *Constitutional Exceptions.* The Posse Comitatus Act includes an exception for "circumstances expressly authorized by the Constitution." See *supra* p. 1153. One possible express constitutional exception may be found in Article IV, section 4, which provides, "The United States shall guarantee to every State in this Union a Republican Form of Government, and shall protect each of them against invasion; and on Application of the Legislature, or of the Executive (when the Legislature cannot be convened) against domestic Violence." Can you describe the limits of the President's power to use troops for law enforcement under this provision? Do these clauses or the Article I Calling Forth Clause, alone or together, provide adequate authority to sustain the Insurrection Act, before or after the 2006 amendment? *See* Banks, *supra,* at 79-86 (no).

Defense Department regulations entitled "Employment of Military Resources in the Event of Civil Disturbances" refer to two "constitutional exceptions" to the Posse Comitatus Act "based upon the inherent legal right of the U.S. Government—a sovereign national entity under the Federal Constitution — to insure the preservation of public order and the carrying out of governmental operations within its territorial limits, by force if necessary." 32 C.F.R. §215.4(c)(1) (2010). One exception is described as emergency authority to take

> prompt and vigorous Federal action, including use of military forces, to prevent loss of life or wanton destruction of property and to restore governmental functioning and public order when sudden and unexpected civil disturbances, disasters, or calamities seriously endanger life and property and disrupt normal governmental functions to such an extent that duly constituted local authorities are unable to control the situations. [*Id.* §215.4(c)(1)(i).]

The other is for "protection of Federal property and functions." *Id.* §215.4(c)(1)(ii). *See also* DOD Dir. 5525.5, *DoD Cooperation with Civilian Law Enforcement Officials* (Dec. 20, 1989), at Encl. 4 §E4.1.2.3. President Johnson apparently believed that he was exercising such inherent powers when he ordered the military to suppress rioting in Washington, D.C., following the assassination of Dr. Martin Luther King Jr. in 1968. *See* Proclamation No. 3840, 33 Fed. Reg. 5495 (Apr. 9, 1968). This regulatory authority closely resembles one for "Immediate Responses," 32 C.F.R. §185.4(e) (2010), noted *infra* p. 1171. The powers claimed in the regulations are not "expressly" set out in the constitutional text, of course.

Has Congress "occupied the field" by its enactment of the Posse Comitatus Act and its exceptions, precluding inconsistent exercise by the President of his inherent constitutional powers? Could Congress do so?

6. *Law Enforcement or War Fighting?* José Padilla was confined in a military brig for more than three years as an "enemy combatant" before finally being charged with criminal offenses related to terrorism. See *supra* p. 885. In responding to his petition for a writ of habeas corpus, one court remarked:

> Padilla argues also that his detention by the military violates the Posse Comitatus Act . . . . First, it is questionable whether that statute is enforceable in a habeas corpus proceeding to secure release from custody. *Cf. Robinson v. Overseas Military Sales Corp.*, 21 F.3d 502, 511 (2d Cir. 1994) (no private right of action to enforce Posse Comitatus Act). Moreover, the statute bars use of the military in civilian law enforcement. Padilla is not being detained by the military in order to execute a civilian law or for violating a civilian law, notwithstanding that his alleged conduct may in fact violate one or more such laws. He is being detained in order to interrogate him about the unlawful organization with which he is said to be affiliated and with which the military is in active combat, and to prevent him from becoming reaffiliated with that organization. Therefore, his detention by the military does not violate the Posse Comitatus Act. [*Padilla v. Bush*, 233 F. Supp. 2d 564, 588 n.9 (S.D.N.Y. 2002), *rev'd in part sub nom. Padilla v. Rumsfeld*, 352 F.3d 695 (2d Cir. 2003).]

Do you think the military can avoid application of the Posse Comitatus Act simply by characterizing a person it suspects of criminal activity as an "enemy combatant"? If you think the designation of enemy combatants might be subject to abuse, can you suggest some realistic process for distinguishing between law enforcement and war fighting, at least for this purpose? Or can you articulate some other principled basis for limiting the military's role in activities that involve both law enforcement and war fighting? What are the implications of the Military Commissions Act of 2009, *supra* p. 1097, in answering these questions?

B.   THE MILITARY'S INTELLIGENCE ROLE IN HOMELAND SECURITY

Since the earliest days of the Republic, military intelligence units have supported domestic uses of military force. Chief Justice Marshall reportedly said of George Washington, "A general must be governed by his intelligence and must regulate his measures by his information. It is his duty to obtain correct information . . . ." *Quoted in Tatum v. Laird*, 444 F.2d 947, 952-953 (D.C. Cir. 1971), *rev'd*, 408 U.S. 1 (1972). In principle, domestic intelligence collection for force protection or as part of DOD's homeland defense mission has never been controversial.

But military intelligence personnel have also been used at times to collect personal information about Americans who pose no real threat to national security. In this part of the chapter we look first at military intelligence activities at home during the Vietnam War, then turn to recent developments ostensibly related to the war on terrorism.

1.   Military Domestic Surveillance During the Vietnam War

Domestic military intelligence activity reached a peak in the late 1960s, when the Pentagon compiled data on more than 100,000 politically active Americans, in an effort to quell civil rights and anti–Vietnam War demonstrations and to discredit protestors. The Army deployed 1,500 plainclothes agents to watch demonstrators, infiltrate organizations, and circulate blacklists. Military officials claimed that they were preparing for the use of troops to put down insurrections. *See* Christopher H. Pyle, *Military Surveillance of Civilian Politics, 1961-1971* (1986). In 1976, the Church Committee, looking into a variety of intelligence community abuses, called the Army program "the worst intrusion that military intelligence has ever made into the civilian community." S. Select Comm. to Study Governmental Operations with Respect to Intelligence Activities, *Improper Surveillance of Private Citizens by the Military (Church Committee Report)*, S. Rep. No. 94-755, bk. III, at 792 (1976). Public disclosure of this activity precipitated the following case.

Laird v. Tatum

United States Supreme Court, 1972
408 U.S. 1

Mr. Chief Justice BURGER delivered the opinion of the Court. Respondents brought this class action in the District Court seeking declaratory and injunctive relief on their claim that their rights were being invaded by the Department of the Army's alleged "surveillance of lawful and peaceful civilian political activity." The petitioners in response describe the activity as "gathering by lawful means . . . (and) maintaining and using in their intelligence activities . . . information relating to potential or actual civil disturbances (or) street demonstrations." . . .

The President is authorized by 10 U.S.C. §331[2] to make use of the armed forces to quell insurrection and other domestic violence if and when the conditions described in that section obtain within one of the States. Pursuant to those provisions, President Johnson ordered federal troops to assist local authorities at the time of the civil disorders in Detroit, Michigan, in the summer of 1967 and during the disturbances that followed the assassination of Dr. Martin Luther King. Prior to the Detroit disorders, the Army had a general contingency plan for providing such assistance to local authorities, but the 1967 experience led Army authorities to believe that more attention should be given to such preparatory planning. The data-gathering system here involved is said to have been established in connection with the development of more detailed and specific contingency planning designed to permit the Army, when called upon to assist local authorities, to be able to respond effectively with a minimum of force. As the Court of Appeals observed,

> In performing this type function the Army is essentially a police force or the back-up of a local police force. To quell disturbances or to prevent further disturbances the Army needs the same tools and, most importantly, the same information to which local police forces have access. Since the Army is sent into territory almost invariably unfamiliar to most soldiers and their commanders, their need for information is likely to be greater than that of the hometown policeman.

---

2. "Whenever there is an insurrection in any State against its government, the President may, upon the request of its legislature or of its governor if the legislature cannot be convened, call into Federal service such of the militia of the other States, in the number requested by that State, and use such of the armed forces, as he considers necessary to suppress the insurrection." . . .

No logical argument can be made for compelling the military to use blind force. When force is employed it should be intelligently directed, and this depends upon having reliable information — in time . . . . So we take it as undeniable that the military, *i.e.*, the Army, need a certain amount of information in order to perform their constitutional and statutory missions. 444 F.2d at 952-953 (footnotes omitted).

The system put into operation as a result of the Army's 1967 experience consisted essentially of the collection of information about public activities that were thought to have at least some potential for civil disorder, the reporting of that information to Army Intelligence headquarters at Fort Holabird, Maryland, the dissemination of these reports from headquarters to major Army posts around the country, and the storage of the reported information in a computer data bank located at Fort Hola- bird. The information itself was collected by a variety of means, but it is significant that the principal sources of information were the news media and publications in general circulation. Some of the information came from Army Intelligence agents who attended meetings that were open to the public and who wrote field reports describ- ing the meetings, giving such data as the name of the sponsoring organization, the identity of speakers, the approximate number of persons in attendance, and an indication of whether any disorder occurred. And still other information was pro- vided to the Army by civilian law enforcement agencies. . . .

Our examination of the record satisfies us that the Court of Appeals properly identified the issue presented, namely, whether the jurisdiction of a federal court may be invoked by a complainant who alleges that the exercise of his First Amendment rights is being chilled by the mere existence, without more, of a governmental inves- tigative and data-gathering activity that is alleged to be broader in scope than is reasonably necessary for the accomplishment of a valid governmental purpose. We conclude, however, that, having properly identified the issue, the Court of Appeals decided that issue incorrectly.

In recent years this Court has found in a number of cases that constitutional violations may arise from the deterrent, or "chilling," effect of governmental regula- tions that fall short of a direct prohibition against the exercise of First Amendment rights. In none of these cases, however, did the chilling effect arise merely from the individual's knowledge that a governmental agency was engaged in certain activities or from the individual's concomitant fear that, armed with the fruits of those activi- ties, the agency might in the future take some other and additional action detrimen- tal to that individual. Rather, in each of these cases, the challenged exercise of governmental power was regulatory, proscriptive, or compulsory in nature, and the complainant was either presently or prospectively subject to the regulations, proscrip- tions, or compulsions that he was challenging. . . .

The decisions in these cases fully recognize that governmental action may be subject to constitutional challenge even though it has only an indirect effect on the exercise of First Amendment rights. At the same time, however, these decisions have in no way eroded the "established principle that to entitle a private individual to invoke the judicial power to determine the validity of executive or legislative action he must show that he has sustained, or is immediately in danger of sustaining, a direct injury as the result of that action . . . ." *Ex parte Levitt*, 302 U.S. 633 (1937).

The respondents do not meet this test; their claim, simply stated, is that they disagree with the judgments made by the Executive Branch with respect to the type and amount of information the Army needs and that the very existence of the Army's data-gathering system produces a constitutionally impermissible chilling effect upon the exercise of their First Amendment rights. That alleged "chilling" effect may perhaps be seen as arising from respondents' very perception of the system as inappropriate to the Army's role under our form of government, or as arising from respondents' beliefs that it is inherently dangerous for the military to be concerned with activities in the civilian sector, or as arising from respondents' less generalized yet speculative apprehensiveness that the Army may at some future date misuse the information in some way that would cause direct harm to respondents. Allegations of a subjective "chill" are not an adequate substitute for a claim of specific present objective harm or a threat of specific future harm....

... [Plaintiffs] would have the federal courts as virtually continuing monitors of the wisdom and soundness of Executive action; such a role is appropriate for the Congress acting through its committees and the "power of the purse"; it is not the role of the judiciary, absent actual present or immediately threatened injury resulting from unlawful governmental action....

The concerns of the Executive and Legislative Branches in response to disclosure of the Army surveillance activities — and indeed the claims alleged in the complaint — reflect a traditional and strong resistance of Americans to any military intrusion into civilian affairs. That tradition has deep roots in our history and found early expression, for example, in the Third Amendment's explicit prohibition against quartering soldiers in private homes without consent and in the constitutional provisions for civilian control of the military. Those prohibitions are not directly presented by this case, but their philosophical underpinnings explain our traditional insistence on limitations on military operations in peacetime. Indeed, when presented with claims of judicially cognizable injury resulting from military intrusion into the civilian sector, federal courts are fully empowered to consider claims of those asserting such injury; there is nothing in our Nation's history or in this Court's decided cases, including our holding today, that can properly be seen as giving any indication that actual or threatened injury by reason of unlawful activities of the military would go unnoticed or unremedied.

Reversed.

Mr. Justice DOUGLAS, with whom Mr. Justice MARSHALL concurs, dissenting.

I

If Congress had passed a law authorizing the armed services to establish surveillance over the civilian population, a most serious constitutional problem would be presented. There is, however, no law authorizing surveillance over civilians, which in this case the Pentagon concededly had undertaken. The question is whether such authority may be implied. One can search the Constitution in vain for any such authority....

... [W]e have until today consistently adhered to the belief that "[i]t is an unbending rule of law, that the exercise of military power, where the rights of the citizen are concerned, shall never be pushed beyond what the exigency requires." *Raymond v. Thomas*, 91 U.S. 712, 716.

It was in that tradition that *Youngstown Sheet & Tube Co. v. Sawyer*, 343 U.S. 579, was decided, in which President Truman's seizure of the steel mills in the so-called Korean War was held unconstitutional. As stated by Justice Black:

> The order cannot properly be sustained as an exercise of the President's military power as Commander in Chief of the Armed Forces. The Government attempts to do so by citing a number of cases upholding broad powers in military commanders engaged in day-to-day fighting in a theater of war. Such cases need not concern us here. Even though "theater of war" be an expanding concept, we cannot with faithfulness to our constitutional system hold that the Commander in Chief of the Armed Forces has the ultimate power as such to take possession of private property in order to keep labor disputes from stopping production. This is a job for the Nation's lawmakers, not for its military authorities. *Id.* at 587. . . .

The act of turning the military loose on civilians even if sanctioned by an Act of Congress, which it has not been, would raise serious and profound constitutional questions. Standing as it does only on brute power and Pentagon policy, it must be repudiated as a usurpation dangerous to the civil liberties on which free men are dependent. For, as Senator Sam Ervin has said, "this claim of an inherent executive branch power of investigation and surveillance on the basis of people's beliefs and attitudes may be more of a threat to our internal security than any enemies beyond our borders." Privacy and Government Investigations, 1971 U. Ill. L.F. 137, 153.

II

The claim that respondents have no standing to challenge the Army's surveillance of them and the other members of the class they seek to represent is too transparent for serious argument. The surveillance of the Army over the civilian sector—a part of society hitherto immune from its control—is a serious charge. It is alleged that the Army maintains files on the membership, ideology, programs, and practices of virtually every activist political group in the country, including groups such as the Southern Christian Leadership Conference, Clergy and Laymen United Against the War in Vietnam, the American Civil Liberties Union, Women's Strike for Peace, and the National Association for the Advancement of Colored People. The Army uses undercover agents to infiltrate these civilian groups and to reach into confidential files of students and other groups. The Army moves as a secret group among civilian audiences, using cameras and electronic ears for surveillance. The data it collects are distributed to civilian officials in state, federal, and local governments and to each military intelligence unit and troop command under the Army's jurisdiction (both here and abroad); and these data are stored in one or more data banks.

Those are the allegations; and the charge is that the purpose and effect of the system of surveillance is to harass and intimidate the respondents and to deter them from exercising their rights of political expression, protest, and dissent "by invading their privacy, damaging their reputations, adversely affecting their employment and their opportunities for employment, and in other ways." Their fear is that "permanent reports of their activities will be maintained in the Army's data bank, and their 'profiles' will appear in the so-called 'Blacklist' and that all of this information will be released to numerous federal and state agencies upon request."

Judge Wilkey, speaking for the Court of Appeals, properly inferred that this Army surveillance "exercises a present inhibiting effect on their full expression and utilization of their First Amendment rights." 444 F.2d 947, 954. That is the test. The "deterrent effect" on First Amendment rights by government oversight marks an unconstitutional intrusion, *Lamont v. Postmaster General*, 381 U.S. 301, 307. Or, as stated by Mr. Justice Brennan, "inhibition as well as prohibition against the exercise of precious First Amendment rights is a power denied to government." *Id.* at 309. . . .

The present controversy is not a remote, imaginary conflict. Respondents were targets of the Army's surveillance. First, the surveillance was not casual but massive and comprehensive. Second, the intelligence reports were regularly and widely circulated and were exchanged with reports of the FBI, state and municipal police departments, and the CIA. Third, the Army's surveillance was not collecting material in public records but staking out teams of agents, infiltrating undercover agents, creating command posts inside meetings, posing as press photographers and newsmen, posing as TV newsmen, posing as students, and shadowing public figures.

Finally, we know from the hearings conducted by Senator Ervin that the Army has misused or abused its reporting functions. Thus, Senator Ervin concluded that reports of the Army have been "taken from the Intelligence Command's highly inaccurate civil disturbance teletype and filed in Army dossiers on persons who have held, or were being considered for, security clearances, thus contaminating what are supposed to be investigative reports with unverified gossip and rumor. This practice directly jeopardized the employment and employment opportunities of persons seeking sensitive positions with the federal government or defense industry."[10]

Surveillance of civilians is none of the Army's constitutional business and Congress has not undertaken to entrust it with any such function. . . .

[Dissenting opinion of Mr. Justice BRENNAN, with whom Mr. Justice STEWART and Mr. Justice MARSHALL join, omitted.]

NOTES AND QUESTIONS

1. *Military vs. Non-Military Intelligence.* Does the domestic collection of intelligence by the military differ in any constitutionally significant way from collection by, say, the FBI? Can you say how?

2. *Standing to Sue.* The *Laird* Court decided that the plaintiffs' claim was nonjusticiable, because they could not demonstrate standing to sue, which would have required a showing of "actual present or immediately threatened injury." What kind of injury did they claim to have suffered? Do you think Vietnam War protesters' fears of reprisal by government agencies were justified?

The *Laird* Court denied standing based on the plaintiffs' complaints about "the very existence of the Army's data-gathering system" and their "[a]llegation of a subjective 'chill' are not an adequate substitute for a claim of specific present objective harm or a threat of specific future harm." 408 U.S. at 13-14. In other words, the

---

10. Hearings on Federal Data Banks, Computers and The Bill of Rights, before the Subcommittee on Constitutional Rights of the Senate Committee on the Judiciary, 92d Cong., 1st Sess. (1971).

Laird plaintiffs did not allege any injuries. Instead they claimed that they *might* be injured if information collected by the military in the future were misused in some way. In *Amnesty International USA v. Clapper*, 638 F.3d 118 (2d Cir. 2011), plaintiffs who believed that they had been subject to surveillance authorized by Congress in the FISA Amendments Act of 2008 (*supra* p. 619) were found to have standing to challenge the constitutionality of the statute based on their assertions of concrete reasons to believe that they are likely to be overheard because their activities bring them into contact with the likely targets of the authorized surveillance. Based on the *Amnesty* and *Laird* decisions, can you predict whether future plaintiffs will be able to get a court to rule on the merits of a challenge to domestic surveillance activities by the military?

3. *Relevance of the Posse Comitatus Act?* According to the *Laird* majority, the Army was "essentially a police force" when it collected domestic intelligence, ostensibly in planning for a response to civil unrest. Did the Army's surveillance program therefore run afoul of the Posse Comitatus Act? Why do you suppose the Court did not refer to the Act? If it had, do you think its constitutional analysis would more nearly have resembled that of the *Bissonnette* court?

4. *Effect of the Insurrection Act?* The *Laird* Court cites 10 U.S.C. §331, one provision of the Insurrection Act (see *supra* p. 1154), as authority for the deployment of military forces to help control rioting in several American cities in 1967 and 1968. It did not point to that same authority for the Army's surveillance program, which extended over a number of years. Could it have done so?

5. *Post-Vietnam Reforms.* In 1976, the Church Committee responded to the abuses outlined in *Laird* by proposing a "precisely drawn legislative charter" that would, *inter alia,* "limit military investigations to activities in the civilian community which are necessary and pertinent to the military mission, and which cannot feasibly be accomplished by civilian agencies." *Church Committee Report, supra,* bk. II, at 310-311. The Committee apparently believed that military intelligence units could make no unique contributions to the domestic security efforts of the FBI, local law enforcement, and other civilian agencies. Its proposal also may have reflected concern about conducting domestic intelligence collection under a military chain of command, whose priority is completion of its military mission, rather than under the Attorney General, whose priority is law enforcement.

Congress did not enact the charter suggested by the Church Committee, but it did pass the Privacy Act in 1974, 5 U.S.C. §552a (2006), as amended by Pub. L. No. 111-148, §6402(b)(2), 124 Stat. 119, 756 (2010), and Pub. L. No. 111-203, §1082, 124 Stat. 1376, 2080 (2010); and the Foreign Intelligence Surveillance Act (FISA), 50 U.S.C. §§1801-1881g (2006 & Supp. III 2009), as amended by Pub. L. No. 111-259, §801, 124 Stat. 2654, 2746 (2010). See *supra* pp. 581-632. Both measures limit the collection, retention, and sharing of information about how individuals exercise rights guaranteed by the First Amendment, as well as information not relevant to the mission of an agency. But serious doubts exist about the efficacy of these laws in safeguarding personal privacy. *See, e.g.,* William C. Banks, *Programmatic Surveillance and FISA: Of Needles and Haystacks,* 88 Tex. L. Rev. 1633 (2010); Orin S. Kerr, *Updating the Foreign Intelligence Surveillance Act,* 75 U. Chi. L. Rev. 225 (2008); Technology & Privacy Advisory Comm., *Safeguarding Privacy in the Fight Against Terrorism (TAPAC Report)* 25-26 (Mar. 2004).

The Defense Department's own rules now limit the domestic collection and use of personal information. For example, DOD Dir. 5200.27, *Acquisition of Information Concerning Persons and Organizations Not Affiliated with the Department of Defense* (Jan. 7, 1980), includes the following restrictions:

> 5.2. No information shall be acquired about a person or organization solely because of lawful advocacy of measures in opposition to Government policy....
>
> 5.5. There shall be no covert or otherwise deceptive surveillance or penetration of civilian organizations unless specifically authorized by the Secretary of Defense, or his designee....
>
> 5.7. No computerized data banks shall be maintained relating to individuals or organizations not affiliated with the Department of Defense, unless authorized by the Secretary of Defense, or his designee....
>
> 6.3. Access to information obtained under the provisions of this Directive shall be restricted to Governmental Agencies that require such information in the execution of their duties....

See also DOD Dir. 5240.1-R, *Procedures Governing the Activities of DoD Intelligence Components That Affect United States Persons* (Dec. 1982); Army Reg. 381-10, *U.S. Army Intelligence Activities* (Nov. 22, 2005), *available at* http://www.fas.org/irp/doddir/army/ar381-10.pdf.

Do these limitations on domestic intelligence collection address the concerns expressed by the Church Committee and by the dissenters in *Laird*? Are additional reforms needed?

2. Domestic Use of Military Intelligence Today

Several developments in the wake of 9/11 point to an expanding domestic role for the military intelligence agencies, which include the Defense Intelligence Agency and intelligence operations within each of the service branches. *See generally* Stephen Dycus, *The Role of Military Intelligence in Homeland Security*, 64 La. L. Rev. 779 (2004). DHS's Office of Intelligence & Analysis (I&A) receives, analyzes, and disseminates data about possible domestic terrorist threats from government and private sources, including the military's intelligence components. *See* Department of Homeland Sec., *Office of Intelligence and Analysis* (Mar. 2, 2011), *at* http://www.dhs.gov/xabout/structure/gc_1220886590914.shtm. The National Counterterrorism Center (NCTC), *supra* p. 551, performs many of the same functions. Military intelligence personnel work in both of these agencies, where they become both suppliers and recipients of personal information, some of which may have no clear relevance to the Pentagon's homeland defense mission. Congress has also approved the creation of an Under Secretary of Defense for Intelligence, 10 U.S.C. §137 (2006), who is supposed to provide "more coordinated, better focused intelligence support for pressing national concerns like homeland security." Department of Def., *Report to Congress on the Role of the Department of Defense in Supporting Homeland Security* 3 (Sept. 2003).

In 2002, DOD created the Northern Command (NORTHCOM), based in Colorado, to assist in homeland defense. *See generally* United States Northern Command, *Defending Our Homeland* (n.d.), *at* http://www.northcom.mil. Like DHS I&A and NCTC, NORTHCOM receives and "fuses" intelligence and law enforcement information from various sources, then redistributes it widely to federal, state, and local agencies. Unlike the two civilian agencies, however, NORTHCOM also collects domestic data directly from a Defense Intelligence Agency (DIA) Defense Counterintelligence and Human Intelligence Center (DCHC), established in August 2008. *See* Department of Defense News Release, *DOD Activates Defense Counterintelligence and Human Intelligence Center* (Aug. 4, 2008), *at* http://www.defense.gov/releases/ release.aspx?releaseid=12106. While disclaiming any law enforcement activity or functions, DCHC develops "offensive counterintelligence operations" for DOD, potentially including efforts to penetrate, "deceive and disable foreign intelligence activities" directed against U.S. forces. Memorandum from the Deputy Secretary of Defense, *Establishment of the Defense Counterintelligence and Human Intelligence Center* (July 22, 2008), *available at* http://www.fas.org/irp/doddir/dod/dchc.pdf.

In June 2005, the Defense Department published *Strategy for Homeland Defense and Civil Support,* *available at* http://www.defense.gov/news/Jun2005/d20050630home land.pdf, declaring that DOD expected to "reorient its intelligence capabilities" to enable it to, *inter alia,* "[c]ollect homeland defense threat information from relevant private and public sector sources, consistent with US constitutional authorities and privacy law," and to "[d]evelop automated tools to improve data fusion, analysis, and management, to track systematically large amounts of data, and to detect, fuse, and analyze aberrant patterns of activity, consistent with US privacy protections." *Id.* at 21. The document pledges that DOD will work to "diminish existing cultural, techno-logical, and bureaucratic obstacles to information sharing" among federal agencies, with state, local, and tribal governments, with private entities, and with "key foreign partners." *Id.* at 23.

Further evidence of DOD's expanding domestic intelligence role can be seen in the Pentagon's use of "noncompulsory" national security letters to collect banking and credit information about hundreds of Americans and others from U.S. financial institutions. *See* Eric Lichtblau & Mark Mazzetti, *Military Expands Intelligence Role in U.S.,* N.Y. Times, Jan. 14, 2007; DOD Instr. 5400.15, *Guidance on Obtaining Information from Financial Institutions* (Dec. 7, 2004), at Encl. 5. (The use of national security letters by the FBI is described *supra* pp. 649-671.)

NOTES AND QUESTIONS

1. *Legal Limits.* Do you think that current domestic intelligence activities out-lined here, including the role of military personnel in DHS's I&A Directorate and in the NCTC, fall within the limits imposed by the Posse Comitatus Act? Do they con-form to DOD's own rules?

If the Posse Comitatus Act is implicated, do any of its constitutional or statutory exceptions apply? Consider in this regard 10 U.S.C. §371, *supra* p. 1154. It directs DOD to give "civilian law enforcement officials any information collected during the normal course of military training or operations that may be relevant to a violation of any Federal or State law," and it declares that the "needs of civilian law enforcement officials for information shall, to the maximum extent practicable, be taken into account in the planning and execution of military training or operations." *Id.* §371(a), (b). In light of this provision, are there any meaningful constraints on military intelligence collection?

2. *Implications for Civil Liberties.* As the military plays a larger domestic intelligence role, how would you weigh possible enhancements in security against possible losses in privacy and related liberties? What civil liberties safeguards apply to civilian intelligence activities that do not apply to the military? Are your answers affected by the availability of new data-mining technology described *supra* p. 671?

C. THE MILITARY'S ROLE IN RESPONDING TO DOMESTIC TERRORIST ATTACKS

Even before September 11, it was assumed that, for practical reasons, the military would be prominently involved in responding to a substantial terrorist attack at home. Several qualities recommend it for such a role. No other agency of government has as much equipment, training, and experience in the use of force as the Defense Department does (although some worry that such force may not be sufficiently refined for use at home). No other agency has such a durable communications system. And no other agency, especially if the National Guard is counted among its forces, is so widely dispersed around the country in places where its services may be urgently needed.

1. Leading or Supporting Role?

Thus far, government planners have prescribed a supporting role for the military. *Homeland Security Presidential Directive/HSPD-5* (Feb. 28, 2003) names the Secretary of Homeland Security as "principal Federal official for domestic incident management," and assigns "lead responsibility for criminal investigations of terrorist acts" to the Attorney General. Current plans generally call for use of the armed forces only when they could be uniquely helpful in responding to a serious emergency:

> The primary mission of the Department of Defense (DOD) and its components is national defense. Because of this critical role, resources are committed after approval by the Secretary of Defense or at the direction of the President. Many DOD components and agencies are authorized to respond to save lives, protect property and the environment, and mitigate human suffering under imminently serious conditions, as well as to provide support under their separate established authorities, as appropriate. The provision of defense support is evaluated by its legality, lethality, risk, cost, appropriateness, and impact on readiness. When Federal military and civilian personnel and resources are authorized to support civil authorities, command of those forces will remain with the Secretary of Defense. DOD elements in the incident area of operations and National Guard forces under the command of a Governor will coordinate closely with response organizations at all levels. [Federal Emergency Mgmt. Agency, *National Response Framework* 27 (Jan. 2008).]

The Defense Department's own regulations have long described its powers in the midst of a great domestic emergency as subordinate. For example, DOD Dir. 3025.1, *Military Support to Civil Authorities* §4.4.4.2 (Jan. 15, 1993), provides that "DOD resources are provided only when response or recovery requirements are beyond the capabilities of civil authorities (as determined by FEMA or another lead Federal agency for emergency response)." *See generally* Department of the Army, *Stability*

Operations and Support Operations (FM 3-07) (Feb. 20, 2003); DOD Dir. 3025.15, *Military Assistance to Civil Authorities* (Feb. 18, 1997).

In mid-2005, a DOD policy document appeared that may signal a significantly more expansive domestic role. Department of Def., *Strategy for Homeland Defense and Civil Support* (June 2005), *supra.* "Our adversaries consider US territory an integral part of a global theater of combat," it declares. "We must therefore have a strategy that applies to the domestic context the key principles that are driving the transformation of US power projection and joint expeditionary warfare." *Id.* at 1. The new policy envisions an "active, layered" defense that could deal with "simultaneous, mass casualty attacks." *Id.* at 7, 10. It also calls for significantly expanded domestic intelligence capabilities. *Id.* at 21-23. Finally, while recognizing that "[d]omestic security is primarily a civilian law enforcement function," the strategy declares that when "directed by the President, the Department will execute land-based military operations to detect, deter, and defeat foreign terrorist attacks within the United States." *Id.* at 26. Still, the Pentagon is careful to distinguish between "homeland defense (HD)," such as domestic air defense, for which DOD is the lead agency, and "homeland security." Jt. Pub. 3-26, *Homeland Security* at v-vi (Aug. 2, 2005), *available at* http://www.acq.osd.mil/ncbdp/nm/nmbook/references/DoD/2.40%20JP%203-26%20Homeland%20Security.pdf. "Except for HD missions," it says, "DOD will serve in a supporting role for domestic incident management." *Id.* at viii.

2.   Controlling Authorities

A "sense of Congress" provision in the Homeland Security Act of 2002 notes that existing laws, including the Insurrection Act and the Stafford Act, "grant the President broad powers that may be invoked in the event of domestic emergencies, including an attack against the Nation using weapons of mass destruction, and these laws specifically authorize the President to use the Armed Forces to help restore public order." 6 U.S.C. §466(a)(5) (2006).

The Stafford Act, 42 U.S.C.A. §§5121-5207 (West 2009), as amended by Pub. L. No. 111-351, §§3, 4, 124 Stat. 3863, 3864 (2011), gives the President authority to use any federal agency, including the Defense Department, to assist state governments in disaster relief operations, *id.* §5192, or specifically to use the armed forces to perform work "essential for the preservation of life and property." *Id.* §5170b(c). It has not been construed to permit the use of those forces to maintain law and order, however. *See* Jennifer K. Elsea & R. Chuck Mason, *The Use of Federal Troops for Disaster Assistance: Legal Issues* 7 (Cong. Res. Serv. RS22266), Nov. 28, 2008.

Several statutory exceptions to the Posse Comitatus Act, especially the Insurrection Act, 10 U.S.C. §§331-335, *supra* p. 1153, give the President wide latitude to use troops for a variety of purposes, including law enforcement, in the aftermath of a terrorist attack or natural disaster. The military may turn over to law enforcement officials any information collected during "the normal course of . . . military operations," and in fact it must take law enforcement needs into account in planning and executing its operations. 10 U.S.C. §371. Treating any attack site as a crime scene, this measure could allow troops to assist in gathering evidence for a criminal prosecution, although a related provision bars any "direct participation" by military personnel in a "search, seizure, arrest, or other similar activity" unless otherwise authorized by law. 10 U.S.C. §375. And during an "emergency situation involving a biological or chemical weapon of mass destruction," military personnel may assist the Department of Justice in the collection of intelligence or in searches or seizures, if it is "necessary for the immediate protection of human life," and civilian law enforcement officials cannot do it. 10 U.S.C. §382. *See also* 18 U.S.C. §831(e) (emergency situation involving nuclear materials). *See generally* Charles Doyle & Jennifer Elsea, *Terrorism: Some Legal Restrictions on Military Assistance to Domestic Authorities Following a Terrorist Attack* (Cong. Res. Serv. RS21012), May 27, 2005.

Without reference to any specific enabling legislation, DOD regulations describing "immediate response authority" say that local military commanders may act in an emergency to "save lives, prevent human suffering, or mitigate great property damage." 32 C.F.R. §185.4(e) (2010). *See also id.* §215.4(c)(1), noted *supra* p. 1159, and *id.* §501.2(a). This authority was cited when the military furnished medivac aircraft, ambulances, bomb detection dog teams, and various personnel to assist civilian officials following the Oklahoma City bombing in 1995. The regulations would also permit evacuation, restoration of essential public services, and traffic control. *See* Jim Winthrop, *The Oklahoma City Bombing: Immediate Response Authority and Other Military Assistance to Civil Authority (MACA)*, Army Law., July 1997, at 3. Do you think this authority should be spelled out in legislation?

3. Organizing for a Response

In 2002, NORTHCOM assumed responsibility for DOD's homeland defense efforts and for provision of military support to civil authorities. *See* William Knight & Steve Bowman, *Homeland Security: Evolving Roles and Missions for United States Northern Command* (Cong. Res. Serv. RS21322), Oct. 11, 2007. It manages military responses to all kinds of threats, from terrorism to hurricanes, working closely with DHS and directing the activities of the Joint Task Force-Civil Support. *See* United States Northern Command, *Joint Task Force Civil Support* (n.d.), *at* http://www.jtfcs.northcom.mil/JTFCS.aspx.

In October 2008, the first ever infantry combat brigade was assigned to NORTHCOM to help in responding to terrorist attacks, natural disasters, and civil unrest. Labeled the CBRNE Consequence Management Response Force, the unit is to receive special training in crowd and traffic control and the use of non-lethal weapons. *See* Gina Cavallaro, *Brigade Homeland Tours Start Oct. 1*, Army Times, Sept. 30, 2008, *available at* http://www.armytimes.com/news/2008/ 09/army_homeland_090708w/.

Regarding coordination between federal and state response efforts, the GAO reported in April 2008 that NORTHCOM was unfamiliar with state emergency response plans, and that a failure of NORTHCOM and the National Guard Bureau to define their respective response roles had resulted in confusion, duplication, and waste. Government Accountability Office, *Homeland Defense: Steps Have Been Taken to Improve U.S. Northern Command's Coordination with States and the National Guard Bureau, but Gaps Remain* (GAO-08-252), Apr. 2008.

The National Guard, with some 450,000 personnel, has a special role to play in the response to a terrorist attack. The nearly 5,000 Army and Air National Guard units scattered across the country have essentially the same relevant training and equipment as active-duty military elements, and they have extensive experience in firefighting, rescue, evacuation, and cleanup after storms and floods. The importance of the

Guard's role and the need for close coordination of the Guard's activities with those of active-duty military forces are spelled out in *Failure of Initiative, supra* p. 1156, at 218-224, 228-231. Unless and until they are federalized by the President's order, however, Guard forces operate under the command of state governors. In this posture, as we have seen, *supra* p. 1147, the Posse Comitatus Act does not apply. Thus, there may be an incentive to delay placing these forces under federal command in order to preserve the maximum flexibility in their use. *See generally* National Guard Bureau home page *at* http://www.ngb.army.mil/; William C. Banks, *The Normalization of Homeland Security After September 11: The Role of the Military in Counterterrorism Preparedness and Response*, 64 La. L. Rev. 735, 762-768 (2004).

The Pentagon has directed Guard forces to provide training and equipment for at least 70 specialized Weapons of Mass Destruction Civil Support Teams of 22 persons each who would be ready on a moment's notice for deployment to the scene of a chemical or biological weapons attack. *See* Department of the Army, *Weapons of Mass Destruction — Civil Support Team Operations, FM 3-11.22* (Mar. 31, 2009), *available at* http://www.fas.org/irp/doddir/army/fm3-11-22.pdf. *See also* GlobalSecurity.org, *Weapons of Mass Destruction Civil Support Teams* (Jan. 12, 2010), *at* http://www.globalsecurity.org/military/agency/army/wmd-cst.htm. Equipped with a mobile analytical laboratory and reliable communications gear, a team would assist state and local personnel in identifying dangerous agents, evacuating victims, and controlling access to affected areas. *See* GlobalSecurity.org, *Weapons of Mass Destruction Civil Support Teams* (n.d.), *at* http://www.globalsecurity.org/military/agency/army/wmd-cst.htm; 10 U.S.C. §12,310(c) (2006 & Supp. III 2009).

4.   New Rules After 9/11?

Six weeks after the terrorist attacks of 9/11, a 37-page Office of Legal Counsel (OLC) opinion described the domestic role of the military in these very expansive terms:

> [T]he President has ample constitutional and statutory authority to deploy the military against international or foreign terrorists operating within the United States. We further believe that the use of such military force generally is consistent with constitutional standards, and that it need not follow the exact procedures that govern law enforcement operations. [Memorandum for Alberto R. Gonzales, Counsel to the President, and William J. Haynes II, General Counsel, Department of Defense, from John C. Yoo, Deputy Assistant Attorney General, and Robert J. Delahunty, Special Counsel, Office of Legal Counsel, *Re: Authority for Use of Military Force to Combat Terrorist Activities Within the United States* (Oct. 23, 2001), *available at* http://www.usdoj.gov/opa/documents/memomilitaryforcecombatus10232001.pdf.]

The opinion was not released to the public when it was written, and the extent of its influence on military planning and policy is unknown.

Seven years later, the Yoo/Delahunty memorandum was repudiated in substantial part by another OLC opinion. Memorandum for the Files from Steven G. Bradbury, Principal Deputy Assistant Attorney General, *October 23, 2001 OLC Opinion Addressing the Domestic Use of Military Force to Combat Terrorist Activities* (Oct. 6, 2008), *available at* http://www.fas.org/irp/agency/doj/olc/caution.pdf. The new opinion urged "caution" in relying on the earlier one, describing several of its provisions as "either incorrect or highly questionable":

> The [2001] memorandum concludes...that the Fourth Amendment would not apply to domestic military operations, designed to deter and prevent further terrorist attacks. This conclusion does not reflect the current views of this Office. The Fourth Amendment is fully applicable to domestic military operations, though the application of the Fourth Amendment's essential "reasonableness" requirement to particular circumstances will be sensitive to the exigencies of military actions....
>
> ...[T]he memorandum also contains certain broad statements...suggesting that First Amendment speech and press rights and other guarantees of individual liberty under the Constitution would potentially be subordinated to overriding military necessities. These statements, too, were unnecessary to the opinion, are overbroad and general, and are not sufficiently grounded in the particular circumstances of a concrete scenario, and therefore cannot be viewed as authoritative.
>
> The memorandum concludes...that the domestic deployment of the Armed Forces by the President to prevent and deter terrorism would fundamentally serve a military purpose rather than a law enforcement purpose, and therefore the Posse Comitatus Act, 18 U.S.C. §1385 (2000), would not apply to such operations. Although the "military purpose" doctrine is a well-established limitation on the applicability of the Posse Comitatus Act, the broad conclusion...is far too general and divorced from specific facts and circumstances to be useful as an authoritative precedent of OLC.
>
> The memorandum treats the Authorization for Use of Military Force ("AUMF"), enacted by Congress in the immediate wake of 9/11, Pub. L. No. 107-40, 115 Stat. 224 (Sept. 18, 2001) [*supra* p. 97], as a statutory exception to the Posse Comitatus Act's restriction on the use of the military for domestic law enforcement. The better view, however, is that a reasonable and necessary use of military force taken under the authority of the AUMF would be a military action, potentially subject to the established "military purpose" doctrine, rather than a law enforcement action.
>
> The memorandum reasons...that in the aftermath of the 9/11 attacks, the Insurrection Act, 10 U.S.C. §333 (2000), would provide general authority for the President to deploy the military domestically to prevent and deter future terrorist attacks; whereas, consistent with the longstanding interpretation of the Executive Branch, any particular application of the Insurrection Act to authorize the use of the military for law enforcement purposes would require the presence of an actual obstruction of the execution of federal law or a breakdown in the ability of state authorities to protect federal rights. [*Id.* at 1-2.]

Neither the Yoo/Delahunty nor the Bradbury memorandum was made public until March 2, 2009, after the Obama administration took office.

NOTES AND QUESTIONS

1. *How the Military Can Help.* Review carefully the plague scenario set forth *supra* p. 1117. What useful role could military forces have played in responding to the notional bioterrorist attack?

Do you agree that we should try to use other agencies whenever possible? If military forces are deployed in such an emergency, who should make the decisions about when and how to use them? What lessons can be learned from the federal response to Hurricane Katrina?

2.   *Need for New Rules?* One study suggests that "[t]here are currently adequate laws and structures in place to facilitate the use of the military in relief efforts in the event of a major catastrophe of whatever kind." ABA Standing Comm. on Law & Nat'l Sec. et al., *Hurricane Katrina Task Force Subcommittee Report* 23 (Feb. 2006). The 2001 Yoo/Delahunty OLC opinion described above apparently did not agree. Who was right?

Suppose the Yoo/Delahunty OLC opinion accurately stated the law after 9/11 — that domestic military counterterrorism operations would not be constrained by the First and Fourth Amendments, and that the AUMF could be read as a statutory exception to the Posse Comitatus Act. (Note that the 2008 Bradbury memo does not altogether dismiss this possibility.) What, if any, limits would then exist on the domestic employment of military forces?

3.   *Cooperation Between DOD and Other Agencies.* Based on the brief description of authorities and plans set out above, how would you rate the chances for a strong, efficient collaboration between the Departments of Defense and Justice in responding to a terrorist attack? What about DOD and FEMA? When the Principal Deputy Assistant Secretary of Defense (Homeland Defense) was asked in August 2005 whether he knew of a document issued by DHS that would help DOD determine the requirements for military assistance to civilian authorities, he replied, "To my knowledge, no such document exists." *See Failure of Initiative, supra* p. 1156, at 203. What would you recommend to improve the chances of collaboration? *See generally* Jeffrey D. Brake, *Terrorism and the Military's Role in Domestic Crisis Management: Background and Issues for Congress* (Cong. Res. Serv. RL30938), Jan. 27, 2003.

4.   *The National Guard's Role.* Is the use of unfederalized National Guard forces in law enforcement consistent with the policies underlying the Posse Comitatus Act?

What advantages or disadvantages can you see to utilizing Guard forces under the control of state governors, rather than federalizing them, to respond to a terrorist attack? How, if at all, is your answer affected by the fact that Guard personnel in every state receive the same training and equipment prescribed by the Pentagon?

D.   MARTIAL LAW: WHEN PLANNING FAILS

If, in the event of an actual or threatened terrorist attack, or a large natural disaster, the execution of federal emergency plans fails to restore order, or if such plans are perceived as inadequate, martial law might be invoked as the option of last resort. Such a drastic step might seem advisable because of the military's extensive, coherent organization, its tradition of discipline, its robust communications systems, and its training in the use of force. Martial law could be declared by the President as Commander in Chief of U.S. armed forces, by a state governor as head of an unfederalized National Guard, or by a military officer in the field. Without specific guidance from higher authority, military leaders would then be governed only by rules fashioned by them to fit the situation. The content of the rules and the duration of their enforcement would, by definition, be impossible to predict. So, necessarily, would be the effect on Americans' civil liberties.

In the middle of the eighteenth century, Blackstone described martial law as

> temporary excrescences bred out of the distemper of the state, and not any part of the permanent and perpetual laws of the kingdom. For martial law, which is built upon no settled principles, but is entirely arbitrary in its decisions, is . . . in truth and reality no law, but something indulged rather than allowed as a law. [2 William Blackstone, *Commentaries* *413.]

A century later, in a Civil War era case, the Supreme Court, in dictum, described the circumstances under which martial law might be invoked.

Ex parte Milligan

United States Supreme Court, 1866
71 U.S. (4 Wall.) 2

[The opinion is set forth *supra* p. 767.]

NOTES AND QUESTIONS

1. *The Necessity for Martial Law.* In an earlier case growing out of a rebellion in Rhode Island, the Court indicated that "a State may use its military power to put down an armed insurrection, too strong to be controlled by the civil authority. The power is essential to the existence of every government, essential to the preservation of order and free institutions, and is as necessary to the States of this Union as to any other government." *Luther v. Borden*, 48 U.S. (7 How.) 1, 44-45 (1849). In litigation arising in New Orleans, after that city had been captured by the Union Army in 1862 and placed under martial law, the Court declared that "[m]artial law is the law of military necessity in the actual presence of war." *United States v. Diekelman*, 92 U.S. (2 Otto) 520, 526 (1876). And in his concurring opinion in *Youngstown Sheet & Tube Co. v. Sawyer* (*Steel Seizure Case*), 343 U.S. 579, 650 n.19 (1952), Justice Jackson was careful to exclude from his discussion of emergency powers based on necessity, "as in a very limited category by itself, the establishment of martial law."

The governor of Hawaii declared martial law immediately after the Japanese attack on Pearl Harbor, as he was authorized to do by the Hawaii Organic Act §67, ch. 339, 31 Stat. 141, 153 (1900). Testing a military tribunal's power to try civilians for ordinary criminal offenses, the Court observed that "the term 'martial law' carries no precise meaning. The Constitution does not refer to 'martial law' at all and no Act of Congress had defined the term. It has been employed in various ways by different people and at different times." *Duncan v. Kahanamoku*, 327 U.S. 304, 315 (1946). Then, struggling to avoid describing the limits of executive or legislative power, the Court found that in using the term "martial law" Congress had not intended to authorize the supplanting of courts by military tribunals. The story is retold in fascinating detail in Harry N. Scheiber & Jane L. Scheiber, *Bayonets in Paradise: A Half-Century Retrospect on Martial Law in Hawai'i, 1941–1946*, 19 Haw. L. Rev. 477 (1997).

2. *Standby Martial Law?* In June 1955, the government conducted a massive civil defense exercise to simulate responses to a nuclear attack. To almost everyone's

surprise, President Eisenhower hypothetically declared nationwide martial law, suspended the writ of habeas corpus, and authorized military commanders to stop the functioning of local courts. His action was widely criticized as unnecessary and improper. *See, e.g.,* Robert S. Rankin & Winfried R. Dallmayr, *Freedom and Emergency Powers in the Cold War* 56-60 (1964). Nevertheless, throughout much of the Cold War the government had in place a comprehensive secret plan, called "Plan D," for responding to the threat of a nuclear attack. One element of that plan, Presidential Emergency Action Directive No. 21, apparently included a draft executive order declaring martial law.

In 1987, the *Miami Herald* reported that Lieutenant Colonel Oliver North and FEMA had drafted a new emergency plan calling for suspension of the Constitution, imposition of martial law, appointment of military commanders to run state and local governments, and detention of dissidents and Central American refugees. Miami Herald, July 5, 1987. *See* Jules Lobel, *Emergency Power and the Decline of Liberalism,* 98 Yale L.J. 1385, 1420 (1989) (noting that Lieutenant Colonel North denied drawing up such a plan).

Do you think the President should carry a draft order declaring martial law with her at all times? If so, do you think the terms of the order and criteria for its execution, or at least the fact of its existence, should be publicized?

3. *Conditions for Martial Law.* One scholar argues that the Insurrection statutes, 10 U.S.C. §§331-335, delegate to the President the power to impose martial law. Vladeck, *supra* p. 1156, at 152-153. If Congress has so conferred this power on the President, it has done no more to clarify the circumstances under which the power might be exercised. The Defense Department, on the other hand, has adopted regulations to cover such an eventuality:

> Martial law depends for its justification upon public necessity. Necessity gives rise to its creation; necessity justifies its exercise; and necessity limits its duration. The extent of the military force used and the actual measures taken, consequently, will depend upon the actual threat to order and public safety which exists at the time. In most instances the decision to impose martial law is made by the President.... However, the decision to impose martial law may be made by the local commander on the spot, if the circumstances demand immediate action, and time and available communications facilities do not permit obtaining prior approval from higher authority. [32 C.F.R. §501.4 (2010).]

How do these regulatory criteria for invocation of martial law compare with those articulated by the Supreme Court in *Ex parte Milligan*? Would it be possible, or wise, to try to develop more specific guidelines? Could you draft the guidelines? Is there any way to challenge the legitimacy of the DOD regulations before they can be used — or even afterward?

4. *Planning to Avoid Martial Law.* As a practical matter, do you think any statutory or regulatory prescriptions could deter the President or military officials from declaring martial law in the wake of a terrorist attack involving a weapon of mass destruction, or in the aftermath of a great natural disaster? Can you think of any way to limit the resort to martial law in such a crisis?

IX

Obtaining and Protecting National Security Information

39

Regulating Access to National Security Information

If a nation expects to be ignorant and free, in a state of civilization, it expects what never was and never will be.

Thomas Jefferson
Letter to Col. Charles Yancey
January 6, 1816

Knowledge will forever govern ignorance, and a people who mean to be their own governors, must arm themselves with the power knowledge gives. A popular government without popular information or the means of acquiring it, is but a prologue to a farce or a tragedy or perhaps both.

James Madison
Letter to W. T. Barry
August 4, 1822

Yes, but the whole point of the doomsday machine is lost if you keep it a secret! Why didn't you tell the whole world, eh?

Dr. Strangelove
from the film *Dr. Strangelove, Or:*
How I Learned to Stop Worrying
and Love the Bomb (1964)

It is no less true today than it was two centuries ago that as citizens we can only make rational decisions about our destinies, indeed can only hope to be in control of our own futures, if we have access to information about the government to which we collectively submit. In 1966, authors of the Freedom of Information Act (FOIA) observed that "[a] democratic society requires an informed, intelligent electorate, and the intelligence of the electorate varies as the quantity and quality of its information varies." H.R. Rep. No. 89-1497, at 12 (1966), *reprinted in* 1966 U.S.C.C.A.N. 2418, 2429.

Of course, there are circumstances when it is in the public interest not to disclose some activities of the government. Among the most compelling are those involving national security and foreign relations. In this democracy we have struck a bargain with ourselves to surrender some knowledge — and with it the power that knowledge gives — to our elected representatives, with the understanding that they will use that knowledge to keep us safe.

Yet the terms of that bargain have always been controversial and are the subject of constant renegotiation. Sissela Bok has observed that

> [t]he contradictions and tensions of secrecy are never stronger than in the military stance of nations. On the one hand, every state requires a measure of secrecy in order to defend itself against enemy forces. . . . But on the other hand, secrecy is as often a weapon in the hands of the aggressors and an aid in every scheme of oppression. . . . As Thomas Jefferson pointed out, citizens do assume they have a right to full information about the possibility of war: "It is their sweat which is to earn all the expenses of the war, and their blood which is to flow in expiation of the causes of it." [Sissela Bok, *Secrets: On the Ethics of Concealment and Revelation* 191 (1983).]

This last section of the casebook addresses our bargain to balance secrecy and knowledge, security and self-determination. In Part A of this chapter we examine aspects of that dynamic bargain. In Part B we review basic guidelines for withholding government information from public view when the national security is implicated, as set forth in the current executive order on classification. In Chapter 40, we consider several statutes — especially the Freedom of Information Act — that make public access to government records and meetings dependent upon the terms of that order. Chapter 41 addresses public and press rights of access grounded in the common law and the Constitution, and the right of Congress to information held by the executive branch. In Chapter 42, we examine contractual controls on access to classified information, as well as government responses to leaks. Special attention is given to enforcement of the security clearance system through Espionage Act prosecutions. Finally, in Chapter 43, we review government efforts to prevent the dissemination of information after it has gotten into the hands of the press.

A. BALANCING SECRECY, SECURITY, AND SELF-DETERMINATION

1. Elements of the Bargain

Arvin S. Quist, Security Classification of Information
pages 1-1, 6-1 to 6-3 (Oak Ridge National Laboratory, 2002)
available at http://www.fas.org/sgp/library/quist/

A government is responsible for the survival of the nation and its people. To ensure that survival, a government must sometimes stringently control certain information that (1) gives the nation a significant advantage over adversaries or (2) prevents adversaries from having an advantage that could significantly damage the nation. Governments protect that special information by classifying it; that is, by giving it a special designation, such as "Secret," and then restricting access to it (e.g., by need-to-know requirements and physical security measures).

This right of a government to keep certain information concerning national security (secrets) from most of the nation's citizens is nearly universally accepted. . . .

. . . However, one of our nation's fundamental principles is the right of its citizens to be informed. We place a high value on open, informed discussion about governmental matters. Therefore, when the U.S. Government keeps secrets from its citizens, that action conflicts with a basic, constitutional right of citizens to be informed of their government's actions so that they can intelligently participate in governmental processes. A democracy's requirement for openness in government is in conflict with a government's need to keep some information secret for reasons of national security. . . .

The conflict between secrecy and openness in our government is sharpest when citizens want to have informed influence on governmental decisions that concern national security matters and that have important, long-term implications. It is frequently too easy for government officials (usually in the executive branch of government) to claim special, inside knowledge about a matter and, for alleged national security reasons, not to share that knowledge with all citizens (or even with most members of Congress). Then, citizens (or Congress) are put into a position of having to accept the decision of the governmental official who has the knowledge, the insider's rationale being that, if others knew what the insider knows, they would agree with the insider's judgment. . . .

Problems of secrecy even affect enforcement of federal laws. Criminal charges are sometimes not brought against alleged lawbreakers because our legal system requires an open trial, and in prosecutions concerning national security matters, the prosecutor may need to rely on classified information as evidence. [See Chapter 35.] . . .

Another important aspect of classification is the effect of governmental secrecy on our national character. Congressman Moss, one of the congressional leaders who spearheaded the effort to establish the Freedom of Information Act (FOIA), stated in 1967, "The strength of our nation is not derived from any policy negative in character." . . .

There are other adverse impacts of classification. Economic costs associated with classification of information include salaries of personnel who classify and declassify information, documents, and materials; costs for physical security and personnel clearance investigations; extra costs of preparing classified documents and manufacturing classified hardware in secure areas; costs of classified procurements; and storage and inventorying costs for classified documents and material. Costs are incurred when wrong decisions are made because pertinent information was kept secret from decision makers, either because of need-to-know restrictions or clearance requirements. . . .

Classification also creates barriers to the accessibility of knowledge, to friend as well as to foe, and thereby slows down the advance of civilization. . . .

The First Amendment to the Constitution established the principle of an informed public. When information is classified, the public's knowledge of the government's activities is reduced, thereby impeding an informed public evaluation of governmental policies and government officials. Thus, the national security advantages gained by the classification of information are *always* counterbalanced, to some extent, by the infringement upon our constitutional right to be informed of our government's activities. . . .

2. Categories of Secrets

One expert identifies three distinct categories of government secrecy:

> The first, "genuine national security secrecy," works to protect information that would pose an identifiable threat to the security of the nation by compromising its defense or the conduct of its foreign relations. Such information could include design details of weapons of mass destruction and other advanced military or intelligence technologies, current

military operational plans, identities of intelligence sources, confidential diplomatic initiatives, and similarly sensitive matters. Protection of such information is not controversial. . . .

A second category that often masks itself as genuine national security secrecy, however, is actually something quite different. . . . It reflects that natural tendency of
bureaucracies . . . to hoard information. Whether out of convenience or a dim suspicion
that disclosure is intrinsically riskier than non-disclosure, government agencies always seem
to err on the side of secrecy even when there is no obvious advantage to doing so. . . .

The third category of secrecy, "political secrecy," uses classification authority for
political advantage. . . . It exploits the generally accepted legitimacy of genuine national
security interests in order to advance a self-serving agenda, to evade controversy, or to
thwart accountability. In extreme cases, political secrecy conceals violations of law and
threatens the integrity of the political process itself. [Steven Aftergood, *Reducing Government Secrecy: Finding What Works*, 27 Yale L. & Pol'y Rev. 399, 402-403 (2009).]

Aftergood's first category of "genuine" secrets needs no explanation. A similar list of
intrinsically sensitive information appears in §1.4 of President Obama's executive
order on classified information, set forth below. The second category is no less
obvious or predictable. Given the natural difficulty of predicting whether or how a
given bit of information might be helpful to our enemies, as well as the possibly
dreadful consequences of a mistake, one can hardly blame a classifying authority
for erring on the side of secrecy. The result is withholding of many millions of documents whose release would not threaten national security. The third category, what
Aftergood calls "political" secrets, is much more sinister. An example is the CIA's
destruction of videotapes of interrogations of terrorist suspects, possibly to avoid
criminal liability. *See* Mark Mazzetti & Charlie Savage, *No Criminal Charges Sought
Over C.I.A. Tapes*, N.Y. Times, Nov. 10, 2010. This kind of concealment strikes at
the very heart of representative government.

Another commentator suggests a possible fourth category: information held by
officials who conceal from outsiders the fact that they are concealing something —
deep secrets. David E. Pozen, *Deep Secrecy*, 62 Stan. L. Rev. 257 (2010). According to
Pozen, this category is revealed in an oft-quoted remark by former Defense Secretary
Donald Rumsfeld: "[A]s we know, there are known knowns; there are things we know
we know. We also know there are known unknowns; that is to say we know there are
some things we do not know. But there are also unknown unknowns — the ones we
don't know we don't know." *Id.* at 257, *quoting from* Department of Defense News
Briefing (Feb. 12, 2002), *available at* http://www.defenselink.mil/transcripts/
transcript.aspx?transcriptid=2636. A clear example is the Bush administration's warrantless monitoring of electronic communications — the so-called Terrorist Surveillance Program — whose very existence was for several years unknown to all but a
handful of executive branch officials. See *supra* p. 609. Such secrets might, in Pozen's
view, pose an even greater threat to democracy.

3.   Greater Security with Fewer Secrets?

A study ordered by Congress concluded that a shift toward greater openness in
government might actually make us more secure.

Even as billions of dollars are spent each year on government secrecy, the classification
and personnel security systems have not always succeeded at their core task of protecting
those secrets most critical to the national security. The classification system, for example,

is used too often to deny the public an understanding of the policymaking process, rather than for the necessary protection of intelligence activities and other highly sensitive matters. . . .

The best way to ensure that secrecy is respected and that the most important secrets *remain* secret, is for secrecy to be returned to its limited but necessary role. Secrets can be protected more effectively if secrecy is reduced overall. . . .

Greater openness permits more public understanding of the Government's actions and also makes it possible for the Government to respond to criticism and justify those actions. . . . In addition, by allowing for a fuller understanding of the past, it provides opportunities to learn lessons from what has gone before — making it easier to resolve issues concerning the Government's past actions and helping prepare for the future. [Commission on Protecting and Reducing Government Secrecy (Moynihan Comm'n), *Secrecy* at xxi (1997).]

See also Daniel Patrick Moynihan, *Secrecy: The American Experience* (1998); *Access Denied: Freedom of Information in the Information Age* (Charles N. Davis & Sigman L. Splichal eds., 2000); Sydney A. Shapiro & Rena I. Steinzor, *The People's Agent: Executive Branch Secrecy and Accountability in an Age of Terrorism*, 69 Law & Contemp. Probs. 99 (2006).

A different, yet related, reason for greater transparency is the growing difficulty of keeping secrets in the electronic age. This problem was demonstrated spectacularly by the release on the Internet of hundreds of thousands of classified U.S. government documents in 2010 and 2011 by *WikiLeaks.org*. The materials included battlefield reports from Afghanistan and Iraq, a quarter-million State Department cables, and extensive prisoner records from Guantánamo. Disclosure of some of the information undoubtedly caused serious injury to national security. See *infra* p. 1298. Nevertheless, according to one observer, "WikiLeaks isn't the problem. It's reams of unnecessarily classified documents that remain hidden from the public eye by overzealous intelligence officials. . . . Secrecy in matters of national security is easily mistaken for security itself. But they are not the same thing, and sometimes they are opposites." Steven Aftergood, *Telling Secrets*, Foreign Pol'y, Oct. 18, 2010. A recent ABA workshop pointed to a possible solution:

[T]he government, as well as the private sector and individuals, confront an enormous challenge in trying to learn how to prevail in an increasingly transparent world. . . . Government must learn what businesses already understand: those who figure out how to operate with fewer secrets will gain a significant advantage over those who continue to cling to traditional notions of indefinite information monopoly. [ABA Standing Comm. on Law & Nat'l Sec., Office of the National Counterintelligence Executive & National Strategy Forum, *No More Secrets: National Security Strategies for a Transparent World* 14 (Jan. 2010).]

None of this is to suggest that there are not many secrets worth keeping. A frightening example may be found among the State Department cables posted on the Internet by *WikiLeaks* in 2010. One cable listed overseas installations "whose loss could critically impact the public health, economic security, and/or national and homeland security of the United States," including dams, bridges, and mines. State Department spokesman P.J. Crowley called this "tantamount to giving a group like al-Qaeda a targeting list." *See* Anthony Faiola, *WikiLeaks Founder Assange in Talks with British Officials to Come Out of Hiding*, Wash. Post, Dec. 6, 2010.

Reflecting a lack of agreement about the proper balance between transparency in government and secrecy, there has been a recurring shift back and forth between the two, as one presidential administration has succeeded another. These shifts may be a reaction to world events as much as a reflection of differing political ideologies. Early in the twenty-first century, for example, one Bush administration official wrote,

> [S]ince the horrific events of September 11 . . . and the possibilities for further terrorist activity in their aftermath, federal agencies are concerned with the need to protect critical systems, facilities, stockpiles, and other assets from security breaches and harm. . . . Such protection efforts, of course, must at the same time include the protection of any agency information that could enable someone to succeed in causing the feared harm. [Memorandum for Heads of All Federal Departments and Agencies from John Ashcroft, Attorney General, *The Freedom of Information Act* (Oct. 15, 2001), *available at* http://www. usdoj.gov/oip/foiapost/2001foiapost19.htm.]

More recently, President Obama declared,

> My Administration is committed to creating an unprecedented level of openness in Government. We will work together to ensure the public trust and establish a system of transparency, public participation, and collaboration. Openness will strengthen our democracy and promote efficiency and effectiveness in Government. [Memorandum from Barack Obama for Heads of Executive Departments and Agencies, *Transparency and Open Government* (Jan. 21, 2009).]

The Obama administration subsequently issued an Open Government Directive, providing more detailed guidance and ordering each department and agency to create an "open government plan" to "improve transparency and integrate public participation and collaboration into its activities." Executive Office of the President, Office of Mgmt. & Budget, *Memorandum for the Heads of Executive: Open Government Directive* (Dec. 8, 2009), *available at* http://www.whitehouse.gov/omb/assets/memoranda_2010/m10-06.pdf. *See generally* Wendy R. Ginsberg, *The Obama Administration's Open Government Initiative: Issues for Congress* (Cong. Res. Serv. R41361), Jan. 28, 2011.

4.   The Cost of Secrecy

Classification of government information is, as Arvin Quist indicates, a large, costly enterprise, although as this text is written, the enterprise appears to be shrinking. In fiscal year 2010, federal agencies reported that they made 224,734 original classification decisions — new secrets. They made more than 77 million derivative classification decisions — those utilizing information already originally classified. These large numbers include Web pages, blogs, wikis, bulletin boards, instant messages, and some e-mail. Agencies also reviewed some 53 million pages of classified documents and declassified about 29 million of them. *See* Information Sec. Oversight Office [ISOO], *2010 Report to the President* (Apr. 15, 2011). In FY 2009 such activities cost almost $9 billion, not counting expenditures by intelligence agencies. *See* OpenTheGovernment .Org, *Secrecy Report Card 2010: Indicators of Secrecy in the Federal Government* (n.d.), at 17.

NOTES AND QUESTIONS

1. *Negotiating for Democracy.* Arvin Quist, the author of the study excerpted above, was responsible for safeguarding some of the most sensitive U.S. nuclear weapons

secrets. Would you call his view of the balance between secrecy and self-determination realistic or romantic? What additional factors need to be considered? How would you describe a proper balance?

Recognizing that the balance is necessarily subject to constant renegotiation, do you think it would be a good idea to codify the bargaining process? What should that process look like? Who should have a say in the negotiation? Should the bargaining always be open and public? Should the process itself be fixed, or subject to review and alteration?

2. *Open Government in an Age of Terrorism.* Does the ongoing fight against international terrorism justify increased secrecy in government? In what particular respects should the balance between secrecy and self-determination be adjusted? Who should be entrusted with making the adjustment? When, if ever, do you suppose the earlier balance might be restored?

B. CLASSIFICATION OF NATIONAL SECURITY INFORMATION

Executive Order No. 13,526, Classified National Security Information

75 Fed. Reg. 707 (Dec. 29, 2009)

This order prescribes a uniform system for classifying, safeguarding, and declassifying national security information, including information relating to defense against transnational terrorism. Our democratic principles require that the American people be informed of the activities of their Government. Also, our Nation's progress depends on the free flow of information both within the Government and to the American people. Nevertheless, throughout our history, the national defense has required that certain information be maintained in confidence in order to protect our citizens, our democratic institutions, our homeland security, and our interactions with foreign nations. Protecting information critical to our Nation's security and demonstrating our commitment to open Government through accurate and accountable application of classification standards and routine, secure, and effective declassification are equally important priorities.

NOW, THEREFORE, I, Barack Obama, by the authority vested in me as President by the Constitution and the laws of the United States of America, [hereby order] as follows:

PART 1 — ORIGINAL CLASSIFICATION

Section 1.1. Classification Standards.

(a) Information may be originally classified under the terms of this order only if all of the following conditions are met:

(1) an original classification authority is classifying the information;

(2) the information is owned by, produced by or for, or is under the control of the United States Government;

(3) the information falls within one or more of the categories of information listed in section 1.4 of this order; and

(4) the original classification authority determines that the unauthorized disclosure of the information reasonably could be expected to result in damage to the national security, which includes defense against transnational terrorism, and the original classification authority is able to identify or describe the damage.

(b) If there is significant doubt about the need to classify information, it shall not be classified. This provision does not:

(1) amplify or modify the substantive criteria or procedures for classification; or

(2) create any substantive or procedural rights subject to judicial review.

(c) Classified information shall not be declassified automatically as a result of any unauthorized disclosure of identical or similar information.

(d) The unauthorized disclosure of foreign government information is presumed to cause damage to the national security.

Sec. 1.2. Classification Levels.

(a) Information may be classified at one of the following three levels:

(1) "Top Secret" shall be applied to information, the unauthorized disclosure of which reasonably could be expected to cause exceptionally grave damage to the national security that the original classification authority is able to identify or describe.

(2) "Secret" shall be applied to information, the unauthorized disclosure of which reasonably could be expected to cause serious damage to the national security that the original classification authority is able to identify or describe.

(3) "Confidential" shall be applied to information, the unauthorized disclosure of which reasonably could be expected to cause damage to the national security that the original classification authority is able to identify or describe.

(b) Except as otherwise provided by statute, no other terms shall be used to identify United States classified information.

(c) If there is significant doubt about the appropriate level of classification, it shall be classified at the lower level.

Sec. 1.3. Classification Authority.

(a) The authority to classify information originally may be exercised only by:

(1) the President and the Vice President;

(2) agency heads and officials designated by the President; and

(3) United States Government officials delegated this authority....

Sec. 1.4. Classification Categories.

Information shall not be considered for classification unless its unauthorized disclosure could reasonably be expected to cause identifiable or describable damage to the national security in accordance with section 1.2 of this order, and it pertains to one or more of the following:

(a) military plans, weapons systems, or operations;

(b) foreign government information;

(c) intelligence activities (including covert action), intelligence sources or methods, or cryptology;

(d) foreign relations or foreign activities of the United States, including confidential sources;

(e) scientific, technological, or economic matters relating to the national security;

(f) United States Government programs for safeguarding nuclear materials or facilities;

(g) vulnerabilities or capabilities of systems, installations, infrastructures, projects, plans, or protection services relating to the national security; or

(h) the development, production, or use of weapons of mass destruction.

Sec. 1.5. Duration of Classification.

(a) At the time of original classification, the original classification authority shall establish a specific date or event for declassification based on the duration of the national security sensitivity of the information. Upon reaching the date or event, the information shall be automatically declassified. Except for information that should clearly and demonstrably be expected to reveal the identity of a confidential human source or a human intelligence source or key design concepts of weapons of mass destruction, the date or event shall not exceed the time frame established in paragraph (b) of this section.

(b) If the original classification authority cannot determine an earlier specific date or event for declassification, information shall be marked for declassification 10 years from the date of the original decision, unless the original classification authority otherwise determines that the sensitivity of the information requires that it be marked for declassification for up to 25 years from the date of the original decision. . . .

(d) No information may remain classified indefinitely. Information marked for an indefinite duration of classification under predecessor orders, for example, marked as "Originating Agency's Determination Required," or classified information that contains incomplete declassification instructions or lacks declassification instructions shall be declassified in accordance with part 3 of this order.

Sec. 1.6. Identification and Markings.

(a) At the time of original classification, the following shall be indicated in a manner that is immediately apparent:

(1) one of the three classification levels defined in section 1.2 of this order;

(2) the identity, by name and position, or by personal identifier, of the original classification authority;

(3) the agency and office of origin, if not otherwise evident;

(4) declassification instructions . . . ; and

(5) a concise reason for classification that, at a minimum, cites the applicable classification categories in section 1.4 of this order. . . .

(c) With respect to each classified document, the agency originating the document shall, by marking or other means, indicate which portions are classified, with the applicable classification level, and which portions are unclassified. . . .

Sec. 1.7. Classification Prohibitions and Limitations.

(a) In no case shall information be classified, continue to be maintained as classified, or fail to be declassified in order to:

(1) conceal violations of law, inefficiency, or administrative error;

(2) prevent embarrassment to a person, organization, or agency; . . . .

(b) Basic scientific research information not clearly related to the national security shall not be classified.

(c) Information may not be reclassified after declassification and release to the public under proper authority unless:

(1) the reclassification is personally approved in writing by the agency head based on a document-by-document determination by the agency that reclassification is required to prevent significant and demonstrable damage to the national security;

(2) the information may be reasonably recovered without bringing undue attention to the information; . . . .

(d) Information that has not previously been disclosed to the public under proper authority may be classified or reclassified after an agency has received a request for it under the Freedom of Information Act (5 U.S.C. 552), the Presidential Records Act, 44 U.S.C. 2204(c)(1), the Privacy Act of 1974 (5 U.S.C. 552a), or the mandatory review provisions of section 3.5 of this order . . . .

Sec. 1.8. Classification Challenges. . . .

(b) . . . [A]n agency head or senior agency official shall establish procedures under which authorized holders of information, including authorized holders outside the classifying agency, are encouraged and expected to challenge the classification of information that they believe is improperly classified or unclassified. These procedures shall ensure that:

(1) individuals are not subject to retribution for bringing such actions;

(2) an opportunity is provided for review by an impartial official or panel; and

(3) individuals are advised of their right to appeal agency decisions to the Interagency Security Classification Appeals Panel (Panel) established by section 5.3 of this order. . . .

Sec. 1.9. Fundamental Classification Guidance Review.

(a) Agency heads shall complete on a periodic basis a comprehensive review of the agency's classification guidance, particularly classification guides, to ensure the guidance reflects current circumstances and to identify classified information that no longer requires protection and can be declassified. . . .

PART 3 — DECLASSIFICATION AND DOWNGRADING

Sec. 3.1. Authority for Declassification.

(a) Information shall be declassified as soon as it no longer meets the standards for classification under this order. . . .

(d) It is presumed that information that continues to meet the classification requirements under this order requires continued protection. In some exceptional cases, however, the need to protect such information may be outweighed by the public interest in disclosure of the information, and in these cases the information should be declassified. . . .

(g) No information may be excluded from declassification under section 3.3 of this order based solely on the type of document or record in which it is found. Rather, the classified information must be considered on the basis of its content. . . .

Sec. 3.3. Automatic Declassification.

(a) Subject to paragraphs (b)-(d) and (g)-(j) of this section, all classified records that (1) are more than 25 years old and (2) have been determined to have permanent historical value under title 44, United States Code, shall be automatically declassified whether or not the records have been reviewed. . . .

(b) An agency head may exempt from automatic declassification under paragraph (a) of this section specific information, the release of which should clearly and demonstrably be expected to:

(1) reveal the identity of a confidential human source, a human intelligence source, a relationship with an intelligence or security service of a foreign government or international organization, or a nonhuman intelligence source; or impair the effectiveness of an intelligence method currently in use, available for use, or under development;

(2) reveal information that would assist in the development, production, or use of weapons of mass destruction;

(3) reveal information that would impair U.S. cryptologic systems or activities;

(4) reveal information that would impair the application of state-of-the-art technology within a U.S. weapon system;

(5) reveal formally named or numbered U.S. military war plans that remain in effect, or reveal operational or tactical elements of prior plans that are contained in such active plans;

(6) reveal information, including foreign government information, that would cause serious harm to relations between the United States and a foreign government, or to ongoing diplomatic activities of the United States;

(7) reveal information that would impair the current ability of United States Government officials to protect the President, Vice President, and other protectees for whom protection services, in the interest of the national security, are authorized;

(8) reveal information that would seriously impair current national security emergency preparedness plans or reveal current vulnerabilities of systems, installations, or infrastructures relating to the national security; or

(9) violate a statute, treaty, or international agreement that does not permit the automatic or unilateral declassification of information at 25 years. . . .

Sec. 3.4. Systematic Declassification Review.

(a) Each agency that has originated classified information under this order or its predecessors shall establish and conduct a program for systematic declassification review for records of permanent historical value exempted from automatic declassification under section 3.3 of this order. . . .

Sec. 3.5. Mandatory Declassification Review.

(a) Except as provided in paragraph (b) of this section, all information classified under this order or predecessor orders shall be subject to a review for declassification by the originating agency if:

(1) the request for a review describes the document or material containing the information with sufficient specificity to enable the agency to locate it with a reasonable amount of effort;

(2) the document or material containing the information responsive to the request is not contained within an operational file exempted from search and review, publication, and disclosure under 5 U.S.C. 552 in accordance with law; and

(3) the information is not the subject of pending litigation.

(b) Information originated by the incumbent President or the incumbent Vice President; the incumbent President's White House Staff or the incumbent Vice President's Staff; committees, commissions, or boards appointed by the incumbent President; or other entities within the Executive Office of the President that solely advise and assist the incumbent President is exempted from the provisions of paragraph (a) of this section. . . .

(c) Agencies conducting a mandatory review for declassification shall declassify information that no longer meets the standards for classification under this order. They shall release this information unless withholding is otherwise authorized and warranted under applicable law. . . .

(e) . . . [A]gency heads shall . . . provide a means for administratively appealing a denial of a mandatory review request, and for notifying the requester of the right to appeal a final agency decision to the Panel. . . .

Sec. 3.6. Processing Requests and Reviews.

. . . [I]n response to a request for information under the Freedom of Information Act, the Presidential Records Act, the Privacy Act of 1974, or the mandatory review provisions of this order:

(a) An agency may refuse to confirm or deny the existence or nonexistence of requested records whenever the fact of their existence or nonexistence is itself classified under this order or its predecessors. . . .

Sec. 3.7. National Declassification Center

(a) There is established within the National Archives a National Declassification Center to streamline declassification processes, facilitate quality-assurance measures, and implement standardized training regarding the declassification of records determined to have permanent historical value. . . .

PART 4 — SAFEGUARDING

Sec. 4.1. General Restrictions on Access.

(a) A person may have access to classified information provided that:

(1) a favorable determination of eligibility for access has been made by an agency head or the agency head's designee;

(2) the person has signed an approved nondisclosure agreement; and

(3) the person has a need-to-know the information....

(g) Consistent with law, executive orders, directives, and regulations, each agency head or senior agency official, or with respect to the Intelligence Community, the Director of National Intelligence, shall establish controls to ensure that classified information is used, processed, stored, reproduced, transmitted, and destroyed under conditions that provide adequate protection and prevent access by unauthorized persons....

PART 6 — GENERAL PROVISIONS

Sec. 6.1. Definitions.

For purposes of this order:...

(l) "Damage to the national security" means harm to the national defense or foreign relations of the United States from the unauthorized disclosure of information, taking into consideration such aspects of the information as the sensitivity, value, utility, and provenance of that information....

NOTES AND QUESTIONS

1. *The Shifting Balance Between Secrecy and Openness.* Before 1982, there was a discernible trend toward less, rather than more, secrecy in government record keeping.

> During the past thirty years, succeeding presidential classification orders have narrowed the bases and discretion for assigning official secrecy to agency records. However, E.O. 12356... clearly reverses this trend by expanding the conditions for classification, requiring the application of official secrecy whenever possible, and maintaining agency records under security protection in perpetuity. [Richard C. Ehlke & Harold C. Relyea, *The Reagan Administration Order on Security Classification: A Critical Assessment*, 30 Fed. Bar News & J. 91 (1983).]

Executive Order No. 12,356, 47 Fed. Reg. 14,874 (Apr. 2, 1982), was promulgated by President Reagan. A possible reason for this change in direction is suggested by an official in the Reagan Justice Department:

> We live in a dangerous world. We face adversaries who have military power greater than any enemy this country has ever faced in a time of war. We live with the ever present threat of a nuclear war, which can destroy the world as we know it. We live with the even more insidious threat of international terrorism which because of its very irrationality is so hard for us to comprehend and deal with. These are very serious problems [that] can only be addressed through the careful execution of national security policy by our government; through military preparedness, diplomatic initiative, and perhaps as the foundation of both of those, an effective intelligence system. In order to execute national security policy we simply must have secrecy as to some matters. [Remarks of Richard Willard, in ABA Standing Comm. on Law & Nat'l Sec., *National Security and the First Amendment* 9 (1983).]

A 1995 executive order promulgated by President Clinton relaxed many of the strictures of the Reagan order. Exec. Order No. 12,958, 60 Fed. Reg. 19,825 (Apr. 17, 1995). For example, it included an instruction to resolve doubts about the need to classify against classification. *Id.* §1.2(b). It also provided for time limits on classification, automatic declassification, and protection for whistleblowers. *Id.* §§1.6, 1.9, and 3.4.

In 2003, President Bush amended the Clinton order. Exec. Order No. 13,292, 68 Fed. Reg. 15,315 (Mar. 25, 2003). The Bush order added to the categories of information that could be classified "transnational terrorism," *id.* §§1.1(a)(4), 1.4(e), "vulnerabilities or capabilities of . . . infrastructures," *id.* §1.4(f), and "weapons of mass destruction." *Id.* §1.4(h). In addition, information that had been declassified could be reclassified under certain conditions. *Id.* §1.7(c). The presumption against classification in the earlier order was removed.

The Obama executive order on classification set out above represents yet another swing of the secrecy pendulum, restoring some but not all of the provisions of the Clinton order. *See generally* Kevin R. Kosar, *Classified Information Policy and Executive Order 13526* (Cong. Res. Serv. R41528), Dec. 10, 2010. The Obama administration also sought to increase the openness and transparency of the executive branch when it issued *Open Government Directive, supra* p. 1184. The OGD, as it is called, orders each agency to take steps to promptly publish more government information online, improve the quality of information available to the public, create and institutionalize a culture of open government, and create an enabling policy framework for open government. *See* Ginsberg, *supra* p. 1184, at 12-32.

As you read through the remaining chapters in the casebook, try to decide whether you think these latest efforts to create greater transparency and accountability in government are ill-timed or long past due.

2. *Sources of Presidential Secrecy Power.* Executive Order No. 10,290, 16 Fed. Reg. 9795 (Sept. 24, 1951), was the first to indicate that the President was relying not upon any specific statutory provision, but rather upon "the authority vested in me by the Constitution and statutes, and as President of the United States." Such reliance upon implied constitutional powers seemed to strengthen the President's discretion to make official secrecy policy by intertwining his responsibility as Commander in Chief with the obligation to "take Care that the Laws be faithfully executed." Ehlke & Relyea, *supra,* at 92.

Does the Commander in Chief Clause of Article II support the President's claim of secrecy authority? See *supra* p. 67. In *Department of the Navy v. Egan,* 484 U.S. 518, 527 (1988), the Supreme Court suggested in a widely quoted dictum that the President's "authority to classify and control access to information bearing on national security . . . flows primarily from this constitutional investment of power in the President and exists quite apart from any explicit congressional grant." If the authority mentioned is not found in the Constitution's text, is it nevertheless a fair or even necessary inference?

Is the President authorized to ignore a congressional mandate to release information to the public if she believes that doing so could jeopardize national security? In another part of the *Egan* decision, the Court observed that "*unless Congress specifically has provided otherwise,* courts traditionally have been reluctant to intrude upon the authority of the Executive in military and national security affairs." *Id.* at 530 (emphasis added).

A supplemental defense appropriations measure for FY 2002 provided that the Defense Department should not adopt new restrictions on access to classified national security information without first giving 30 days' notice to congressional defense committees. Pub. L. No. 107-117, §8007, 115 Stat. 2230, 2248 (2002). But in his signing statement President Bush declared that "situations may arise, especially in wartime, in which the President must promptly establish special access controls on classified national security information under his constitutional grants of the executive power and authority as Commander in Chief of the Armed Forces," and that he would act "in a manner consistent with" that authority. *See* Office of the Press Secretary, The White House, *Defense Bill Signing Statement* (Jan. 10, 2002). Can you think of any way for Congress to enforce its mandate?

3. *Who Can Classify?* According to the Obama executive order, information may be classified only by an original classification authority, Exec. Order No. 13,526 §1.1(a)(1), including the President and Vice President, department heads and others designated by the President, and "officials delegated this authority." *Id.* §1.3(a). At the end of FY 2010, there were 2,378 original classification authorities, 7 percent fewer than the year before. ISOO, *supra* p. 1184, at 1, 4-5. Delegations must be in writing, and all original classification authorities must undergo annual training in proper classification and declassification. Exec. Order No. 13,526 §1.3(c), (d). Who do you think should be authorized — or is needed — to create new government secrets? What should be their qualifications? Should contractors be given this authority?

4. *Applying the Executive Order.* The Obama order, like the Clinton and Bush orders before it, states that information "may" be classified when its unauthorized disclosure "reasonably could be expected to result in damage to the national security . . . and the original classification authority is able to identify or describe the damage." Exec. Order No. 13,526 §1.1(a)(4). "Damage to the national security" is defined in §6(*l*). If you were an agency official with original classification authority, would the executive order provide enough guidance to enable you to determine when information should be classified? Could a federal judge apply these criteria with confidence in any case, or is deference to agency professionals a practical necessity? Can you suggest alternative language or additional instructions that would be more helpful? Should Congress supply additional guidance?

5. *Weighing the Public Interest.* Section 3.1(d) of the Obama order provides that in "some exceptional cases" the need to protect classified information "may be outweighed by the public interest in disclosure of the information, and in these cases the information should be declassified." The same instruction appeared in the Bush, Clinton, and Carter (but not Reagan) orders. In a case decided under the Carter order, one judge remarked:

> It would of course be extremely difficult for judges to "balance" the public's right to know against an acknowledged national security risk, and I do not believe we are currently authorized to do so. However, it seems important in view of recent revelations about past indiscretions in the name of national security, for some government institution, if not the classification system itself, to conduct such a balance. As Emerson explained, "history give[s] value to the present hour and its duty." By not weighing the value to the public of knowing about particularly relevant episodes in the intelligence

agency's history, we may undermine the public's ability to assess the government's performance of its duty. [*McGehee v. Casey*, 718 F.2d 1137, 1150 (D.C. Cir. 1983) (separate
statement of Wald, J.).]

But what government institution is better equipped than the courts to do the balancing?
See U.S. Dep't of Justice v. Reporters Comm. for Freedom of the Press, 489 U.S. 749, 773 (1989).

6. *Challenging Secrecy Within the Executive Branch.* How can executive branch officials be compelled to comply with the standards and procedures set out in the executive order? How can a decision to classify or refusal to declassify information be
challenged?

Section 1.8 of both the Bush and Obama executive orders allows agency personnel with knowledge of classified information to challenge what they believe are erroneous classification decisions. In FY 2010, 722 such challenges were reported. ISOO,
supra, at 13. Why would a bureaucrat seek such a review? Why would she need protection from retribution, and from whom?

Another way to provoke a review of the classification of a document is to request a
mandatory declassification review (MDR) under §3.5 of the Obama executive order.
Anyone may make such a request. When a document is known to be classified and can
be precisely described, an MDR may be the simplest, quickest way to get it. *See* Nate
Jones, *FOIA Tip No. 8— Mandatory Declassification Review* (Jan. 12, 2010, *at* http://
nsarchive.wordpress.com/2010/01/12/foia-tip-8%E2%80%94mandatory-declassifi-
cation-review/; *A FOIA Alternative: Mandatory Declassification Review*, in Reporters
Comm. for Freedom of the Press, *Federal Open Government Guide* (10th ed. 2009),
at http://www.rcfp.org/fogg/index.php?i=sideb.

Still another way to gain access to classified information is to make a request for it
under the Freedom of Information Act (FOIA) or one of its statutory analogues, then
pursue an administrative or judicial appeal if release of the information is denied. We
examine the FOIA process in some detail in the next chapter.

7. *Challenging the Executive Order in Court.* Can you think of any way to test the
propriety of the terms of the executive order? In *Afshar v. Department of State*, 702 F.2d
1125, 1137 (D.C. Cir. 1983), the court remarked, "This court will not, in the absence
of any evidence of illegitimate discrimination, and perhaps not even then, question
the President's determination that the national security requires increased secrecy."
But in *American Federal Government Employees, AFL-CIO v. Reagan*, 870 F.2d 723 (D.C.
Cir. 1989), the court found that an executive order purportedly exerting a statutorily
conferred power was entitled only to a rebuttable presumption of regularity.

8. *Controlled Unclassified Information.* In early 2002, the White House Chief of Staff
ordered all federal agencies to identify records that were sensitive, although not
classified, and protect them from "inappropriate disclosure." Memorandum for
the Heads of Executive Departments and Agencies from Andrew H. Card Jr., *Action
to Safeguard Information Regarding Weapons of Mass Destruction and Other Sensitive Documents Relating to Homeland Security* (Mar. 19, 2002). Later the same year, the Homeland
Security Act directed the President to develop procedures to "identify and safeguard
homeland security information that is sensitive but unclassified." Pub. L. No. 107-296,
§892(a)(1)(B), 116 Stat. 2135, 2253 (2002). Neither the Chief of Staff nor Congress,

however, defined the term "sensitive" or indicated how access to such information might be restricted.

Reliance on the "sensitive but unclassified" (SBU) designation (and others, such as "sensitive security information," and "for official use only") to withhold records from the public expanded rapidly during the Bush administration. Such reliance was widely criticized: agencies had more than a hundred different labels for this kind of information; there were no uniform standards for any such designations, no limits on personnel entitled to affix the labels, and no time limits; and there was no statutory authority for avoiding the disclosure requirements in the Freedom of Information Act and Privacy Act. *See* Genevieve Knezo, *"Sensitive but Unclassified" Information and Other Controls: Policy and Options for Scientific and Technical Information* (Cong. Res. Serv. RL33303), Dec. 29, 2006.

After halting efforts late in the Bush administration to standardize this practice, President Obama issued a new order for safeguarding records bearing the single label "controlled unclassified information (CUI)." Exec. Order No. 13,556, *Controlled Unclassified Information*, 75 Fed. Reg. 68,675 (Nov. 4, 2010). Use of the CUI designation is to be "consistent with:

> (1) applicable law, including protections of confidentiality and privacy rights;
> (2) the statutory authority of the heads of agencies, including authorities related to the protection of information provided by the private sector to the Federal Government; and
> (3) applicable Government-wide standards and guidelines issued by the National Institute of Standards and Technology, and applicable policies established by the Office of Management and Budget. [*Id.* §6(a).]

Implementation of the order is to be supervised by the National Archives and Records Administration, with many details remaining, at this writing, to be worked out. Can you outline a program for managing this kind of information?

9. *Cleaning Out Old Secret Files.* According to the Obama order, "[n]o information may remain classified indefinitely." Exec. Order No. 13,526 §1.5(d). Each document classified must be marked with a date for its automatic declassification not more than 25 years hence, unless its disclosure would "clearly and demonstrably be expected to reveal the identity of a confidential human source or a human intelligence source or key design concepts of weapons of mass destruction." *Id.* §1.5(a). The order also requires the automatic declassification of records determined to have "permanent historical value" after 25 years, although an agency head may exempt such records from release if they present any of the risks described in §3.3(b). Exempted records are subject to systematic declassification review. *Id.* §3.4. In exceptional circumstances, however, they may be withheld for more than 75 years! *Id.* §3.3(h)(3). In one remarkable case the FBI was able to deny a history professor access to files on Gerhard Eisler and Clinton Jencks, suspected Communists investigated by the Bureau in 1947 and 1953, respectively. *See Schrecker v. U.S. Dep't of Justice,* 349 F.3d 657 (D.C. Cir. 2003).

Section 3.7 of the Obama order establishes a National Declassification Center (NDC) to aid in the review process. The NDC is supposed to speed declassification of some 400 million pages of materials at least 25 years old currently held in the National Archives, plus an estimated 1.2 billion more over the next quarter-century. It is to do this by setting priorities for review, assisting in referrals to multiple agencies interested in a given document, and providing training for reviewers. *See* National Archives & Records Admin., *NARA and Declassification: Frequently Asked Questions About the National Declassification Center* (n.d.), *at* http://www.archives.gov/declassification/faqs.html.

Out of some 53 million pages of materials reviewed for declassification in FY 2010, roughly 45 million pages were part of the automatic declassification process, and more than half of those were declassified. ISOO, *supra*, at 16. Of 5.8 million pages subjected to systematic review, 4.6 million were declassified. *Id.* at 17. Is there any way to compel agency compliance with the rules for automatic declassification?

Statutory Access to National Security Information

In the last chapter we examined the bargain that we have struck with ourselves to balance secrecy and knowledge, security and self-determination. Congress has played a key role in implementing that bargain by passing legislation that makes some information about national security available to the public. In Part A we review the structure and operation of the Freedom of Information Act (FOIA), which grants access to agency records. Part B then addresses several other open government laws. As in earlier chapters, we examine closely the interpretation and enforcement of these laws by the courts.

A. THE FREEDOM OF INFORMATION ACT

It would be difficult to overstate the importance of the Freedom of Information Act and its statutory analogues. The Justice Department calls FOIA "a vital part of our democracy." FOIA.gov, *What Is FOIA?* (updated Mar. 2011), *at* http:// www.foia.gov/. Passed in 1966, it opened a window into the operation of the executive branch, transformed the way the government conducts its business, and gave the American people a renewed sense of self-determination. It has special relevance in the national security field, about which information has always been most closely held. In fact, much of the information in this book was obtained through FOIA requests.

A Citizen's Guide on Using the Freedom of Information Act and the Privacy Act of 1974 to Request Government Records

House Committee on Government Reform,
H.R. Rep. No. 109-226, at 3 (2005)

The Freedom of Information Act (FOIA) establishes a presumption that records in the possession of agencies and departments of the executive branch of the U.S. Government are accessible to the people. This was not always the approach to Federal information disclosure policy. Before enactment of the FOIA in 1966, the burden was on the individual to establish a right to examine these government records. There were no statutory guidelines or procedures to help a person seeking information. There were no judicial remedies for those denied access.

With the passage of the FOIA, the burden of proof shifted from the individual to the government. Those seeking information are no longer required to show a need for information. Instead, the "need to know" standard has been replaced by a "right to know" doctrine. The government now has to justify the need for secrecy.

The FOIA sets standards for determining which records must be disclosed and which records may be withheld. The law also provides administrative and judicial remedies for those denied access to records. Above all, the statute requires Federal agencies to provide the fullest possible disclosure of information to the public.

1.　The Statutory Text

Freedom of Information Act

5 U.S.C. §552 (2006 & Supp. III 2009)

§552.　PUBLIC INFORMATION; AGENCY RULES, OPINIONS, ORDERS, RECORDS, AND PROCEEDINGS

(a) Each agency shall make available to the public information as follows:...

(2) Each agency, in accordance with published rules, shall make available for public inspection and copying—

(A) final opinions, including concurring and dissenting opinions, as well as orders, made in the adjudication of cases;

(B) those statements of policy and interpretations which have been adopted by the agency and are not published in the Federal Register;

(C) administrative staff manuals and instructions to staff that affect a member of the public;

(D) copies of all records, regardless of form or format, which have been released to any person under paragraph (3) and which, because of the nature of their subject matter, the agency determines have become or are likely to become the subject of subsequent requests for substantially the same records; and

(E) a general index of the records referred to under subparagraph (D); unless the materials are promptly published and copies offered for sale.... Each agency shall also maintain and make available for public inspection and copying current indexes providing identifying information for the public as to any matter issued, adopted, or promulgated after July 4, 1967, and required by this paragraph to be made available or published.... Each agency shall make the index referred to in subparagraph (E) available by computer telecommunications....

(3)(A) Except with respect to the records made available under paragraphs (1) and (2) of this subsection ... each agency, upon any request for records which (i) reasonably describes such records and (ii) is made in accordance with published rules stating the time, place, fees (if any), and procedures to be followed, shall make the records promptly available to any person.

(B) In making any record available to a person under this paragraph, an agency shall provide the record in any form or format requested by the person if the record is readily reproducible by the agency in that form or format. Each agency shall make reasonable efforts to maintain its records in forms or formats that are reproducible for purposes of this section.

(C) In responding under this paragraph to a request for records, an agency shall make reasonable efforts to search for the records in electronic form or format....

(E) An agency, or part of an agency, that is an element of the intelligence community (as that term is defined in section 3(4) of the National Security Act of 1947 (50 U.S.C. 401a(4))) shall not make any record available under this paragraph to—

(i) any government entity, other than a State, territory, commonwealth, or district of the United States, or any subdivision thereof; or

(ii) a representative of a government entity described in clause (i).

(4)(A)(i) In order to carry out the provisions of this section, each agency shall promulgate regulations, pursuant to notice and receipt of public comment, specifying the schedule of fees applicable to the processing of requests under this section and establishing procedures and guidelines for determining when such fees should be waived or reduced....

(iii) Documents shall be furnished without any charge or at a charge reduced ... if disclosure of the information is in the public interest because it is likely to contribute significantly to public understanding of the operations or activities of the government and is not primarily in the commercial interest of the requester....

(B) On complaint, the district court of the United States in the district in which the complainant resides, or has his principal place of business, or in which the agency records are situated, or in the District of Columbia, has jurisdiction to enjoin the agency from withholding agency records and to order the production of any agency records improperly withheld from the complainant. In such a case the court shall determine the matter de novo, and may examine the contents of such agency records in camera to determine whether such records or any part thereof shall be withheld under any of the exemptions set forth in subsection (b) of this section, and the burden is on the agency to sustain its action....

(E)(i) The court may assess against the United States reasonable attorney fees and other litigation costs reasonably incurred in any case under this section in which the complainant has substantially prevailed.

(ii) For purposes of this subparagraph, a complainant has substantially prevailed if the complainant has obtained relief through either—

(I) a judicial order, or an enforceable written agreement or consent decree; or

(II) a voluntary or unilateral change in position by the agency, if the complainant's claim is not insubstantial.

(F)(i) Whenever the court orders the production of any agency records improperly withheld from the complainant and assesses against the United States reasonable attorney fees and other litigation costs, and the court additionally issues a written finding that the circumstances surrounding the withholding raise questions whether agency personnel acted arbitrarily or capriciously with respect to the withholding, the Special Counsel shall promptly initiate a proceeding to determine whether disciplinary action is warranted against the officer or employee who was primarily responsible for the withholding....

(6) (A) Each agency, upon any request for records...shall—

(i) determine within 20 days...after the receipt of any such request whether to comply with such request and shall immediately notify the person making such request of such determination and the reasons therefor, and of the right of such person to appeal to the head of the agency any adverse determination; and

(ii) make a determination with respect to any appeal within twenty days....

(B) (i) In unusual circumstances...the time limits...may be extended....

(iii) As used in this subparagraph, "unusual circumstances" means...

(I) the need to search for and collect the requested records from field facilities or other establishments that are separate from the office processing the request;

(II) the need to search for, collect, and appropriately examine a voluminous amount of separate and distinct records which are demanded in a single request; or

(III) the need for consultation, which shall be conducted with all practicable speed, with another agency having a substantial interest in the determination of the request....

(7) Each agency shall—

(A) establish a system to assign an individualized tracking number for each request received that will take longer than ten days to process and provide to each person making a request the tracking number assigned to the request; and

(B) establish a telephone line or Internet service that provides information about the status of a request to the person making the request using the assigned tracking number....

(b) This section does not apply to matters that are—

(1) (A) specifically authorized under criteria established by an Executive order to be kept secret in the interest of national defense or foreign policy and (B) are in fact properly classified pursuant to such Executive order;

(2) related solely to the internal personnel rules and practices of an agency;

(3) specifically exempted from disclosure by statute (other than section 552b of this title), if that statute—

(A) (i) requires that the matters be withheld from the public in such a manner as to leave no discretion on the issue; or

(ii) establishes particular criteria for withholding or refers to particular types of matters to be withheld; and

(B) if enacted after the date of enactment of the OPEN FOIA Act of 2009, specifically cites to this paragraph;

(4) trade secrets and commercial or financial information...;

(5) inter-agency or intra-agency memorandums or letters which would not be available by law to a party other than an agency in litigation with the agency;

(6) personnel and medical files...;

(7) records or information compiled for law enforcement purposes, but only to the extent that the production of such law enforcement records or information (A) could reasonably be expected to interfere with enforcement proceedings, (B) would deprive a person of a right to a fair trial or an impartial adjudication, (C) could reasonably be expected to constitute an unwarranted invasion of

personal privacy, (D) could reasonably be expected to disclose the identity of a confidential source,...and, in the case of a record or information compiled by...an agency conducting a lawful national security intelligence investigation, information furnished by a confidential source,...or (F) could reasonably be expected to endanger the life or physical safety of any individual;

    (8)...related to...financial institutions; or

    (9) geological and geophysical information....

Any reasonably segregable portion of a record shall be provided to any person requesting such record after deletion of the portions which are exempt under this subsection. The amount of information deleted, and the exemption under which the deletion is made, shall be indicated on the released portion of the record, unless including that indication would harm an interest protected by the exemption in this subsection under which the deletion is made....

    (c)...(3) Whenever a request is made which involves access to records maintained by the Federal Bureau of Investigation pertaining to foreign intelligence or counterintelligence, or international terrorism, and the existence of the records is classified information as provided in subsection (b)(1), the Bureau may, as long as the existence of the records remains classified information, treat the records as not subject to the requirements of this section.

    (d) This section does not authorize withholding of information or limit the availability of records to the public, except as specifically stated in this section. This section is not authority to withhold information from Congress....

    (f) For purposes of this section, the term —

    (1) "agency" as defined in section 551(1) of this title includes any executive department, military department, Government corporation, Government controlled corporation, or other establishment in the executive branch of the Government (including the Executive Office of the President), or any independent regulatory agency; and

    (2) "record" and any other term used in this section in reference to information includes —

        (A) any information that would be an agency record subject to the requirements of this section when maintained by an agency in any format, including an electronic format; and

        (B) any information described under subparagraph (A) that is maintained for an agency by an entity under Government contract, for the purposes of records management.

    (g) The head of each agency shall prepare and make publicly available upon request, reference material or a guide for requesting records or information from the agency, subject to the exemptions in subsection (b), including —

    (1) an index of all major information systems of the agency;

    (2) a description of major information and record locator systems maintained by the agency; and

    (3) a handbook for obtaining various types and categories of public information from the agency....

NOTES AND QUESTIONS

1. *Codifying the Balance.* Do you think FOIA achieves a proper balance between public participation in government and legitimate needs for government secrecy? Does it strike the right balance between the political branches concerning control over sensitive information? Should Congress provide the Executive with greater flexibility to deal with emerging threats and changes in technology? If so, how could it do that?

The practical effect of the statutory balance depends, of course, on how the statute is implemented. In the wake of the terrorist attacks on September 11, 2001, Attorney General John Ashcroft issued a new statement of policy directing federal agencies to be much more aggressive in protecting information than in the past, instructing them that when they "carefully consider FOIA requests and decide to withhold records, in whole or in part, you can be assured that the Department of Justice will defend your decisions unless they lack a sound legal basis." *Memorandum from John Ashcroft to Heads of All Federal Departments and Agencies* (Oct. 12, 2001). That directive was rescinded by Attorney General Eric Holder, who quoted President Obama: "The Freedom of Information Act should be administered with a clear presumption: In the face of doubt, openness prevails." *Memorandum from the Attorney General for Heads of Executive Departments and Agencies* (Mar. 19, 2009), *available at* http://www.justice.gov/ag/foia-memo-march2009.pdf. Can you guess how implementation of the new policy might have shifted the balance between openness and secrecy? Do you think the shift was justified by a change in threats to the nation? Can you think of any way to challenge the President's interpretation of his statutory obligation?

2. *Balancing Costs and Benefits.* Can you say how exposure of agency records to public view, or at least the prospect of such exposure, might affect the way the government conducts its business? If your answer is that it makes the government process more costly in some ways, do you think the benefits from a better informed electorate outweigh the increased expense? By one estimate, the federal government spends roughly the same amount processing FOIA requests that it does on military bands. Charles H. Wichmann III, Note, *Ridding FOIA of Those "Unanticipated Consequences": Repaving a Necessary Road to Freedom,* 47 Duke L.J. 1213, 1255 (1998).

3. *Usability.* Do you believe that a layperson, unassisted by an attorney, is likely to be able to get the information she seeks from a government agency by utilizing FOIA? Should FOIA be amended to make information more nearly accessible without such assistance? If so, how? A 1996 amendment to the Act requires each agency to "prepare and make publicly available upon request, reference material or a guide for requesting records or information from the agency." 5 U.S.C. §552(g). Instructions for making a FOIA request are set out for each agency in the Code of Federal Regulations. *See, e.g.,* 32 C.F.R. pt. 1900 (2010) (Central Intelligence Agency). In 2010 the Justice Department launched a Web site containing plain-language instructions and addresses for FOIA requests, plus instructional videos. *See* FOIA.gov, *What Is FOIA?* (updated Mar. 2011), *at* http://www.foia.gov/index.html. *See also* Kristin Adair & Catherine Nielsen, National Security Archive, *Effective FOIA Requesting for Everyone* (Jan. 29, 2009), *at* http://www.gwu.edu/~nsarchiv/nsa/foia/foia_guide.html; Reporters Comm. for Freedom of the Press, *Federal Open Government Guide* (10th ed. 2009), *at* http://www.rcfp.org/fogg/index.php?i=intro.

4. *"Any Request."* Although §552(a)(3) provides that an agency must respond to "any request," it was suggested early on that a requester should demonstrate some good reason for wanting particular information. It now seems well settled in principle that it is not necessary for a requester to make any showing of purpose or relevancy. *United States Dep't of Justice v. Reporters Comm. for Freedom of the Press*, 489 U.S. 749, 771 (1989). There is evidence, however, that a court might be influenced by a requester's motives. For example, in his dissent in *Department of the Air Force v. Rose*, 425 U.S. 352 (1976), a case involving information about a cheating scandal at the Air Force Academy, Chief Justice Burger remarked that it was "difficult to attribute to Congress a willingness to subject an individual citizen to the risk of possible severe damage to his reputation simply to permit law students... to prepare a law journal article." *Id.* at 384. Do you suppose that a court might be more reluctant to order release of records if it knew that the requester's intention was to compromise U.S. foreign policy? Should it matter that the release most likely would not have the intended effect? How would you incorporate any concern you have about motive into the statute?

FOIA was amended in 2002 to bar requests from foreign governments, international governmental organizations, or their representatives for records held by elements of the intelligence community. 5 U.S.C. §552(a)(3)(E). This change was reportedly intended to prevent access to intelligence agency records by states that support terrorism. *See* H.R. Rep. No. 107-592, at 27 (2002). Can you think of any other reasons to adopt such a restriction?

5. *Economic Barriers.* In general, FOIA requesters may be charged for direct costs to search for and review requested records, plus duplication costs. Under FOIA §552(a)(4)(A)(iii), however, the requester's motivation may be taken into account by an agency in deciding whether to reduce or waive its standard charges "if disclosure is in the public interest because it is likely to contribute significantly to public understanding of the operations or activities of the government and is not primarily in the commercial interest of the requester." *See generally* Office of Mgmt. & Budget, *Uniform Freedom of Information Act Fee Schedule and Guidelines*, 52 Fed. Reg. 10,012 (Mar. 27, 1987). In *McClellan Ecological Seepage Situation v. Carlucci*, 835 F.2d 1282, 1285-1286 (9th Cir. 1987), the court found that no fee waiver was required because the public interest requester failed to show how it could use the information to contribute to public understanding of the government. But in *National Security Archive v. United States Department of Defense*, 880 F.2d 1381, 1387-1388 (D.C. Cir. 1989), the court rejected, as "contrary to the manifest purpose of [FOIA]...and common sense," DOD's effort to charge "commercial" fees to a not-for-profit organization that compiles government data for scholars, news media, and government researchers. *See also National Security Archive v. CIA*, 584 F. Supp. 2d 144 (D.D.C. 2008) (reduced fees based on requester's news media status). A 2007 amendment to FOIA clarifies the definition of news media entitled to reduced fees. OPEN Government Act of 2007, Pub. L. No. 110-175, §3, 121 Stat. 2524, 2525 (amending §552(a)(4)(A)(ii)).

Search and duplication charges may, of course, be an effective bar to obtaining requested information, and they are occasionally used by an agency to try to intimidate a requester. But an agency's denial of a waiver is not supposed to be arbitrary or capricious. *National Treasury Employees Union v. Griffin*, 811 F.2d 644, 646-650 (D.C. Cir. 1987).

The requester's purpose may also affect the decision to award attorney's fees and costs, under FOIA §552(a)(4)(E), when a requester has "substantially prevailed." In *Kuzma v. Internal Revenue Service*, 821 F.2d 930, 933 (2d Cir. 1987), the court remarked that Congress meant to encourage citizens to act as "private attorneys general" pursuant to "a national policy of disclosure of government information." The OPEN Government Act of 2007 provides that a requester "substantially prevails" if she obtains relief through a judicial order, an enforceable agreement, a consent decree, or a voluntary or unilateral change in position by the agency. Pub. L. No. 110-175, §4, 121 Stat. 2524, 2525 (adding §552(a)(4)(E)(ii)). Will the prospect of a fee award affect the behavior of either agencies or requesters?

6. *"Agency."* What is an "agency" for FOIA purposes? *See* FOIA §552(f)(1). In *Rushforth v. Council of Economic Advisers*, 762 F.2d 1038, 1040-1043 (D.C. Cir. 1985), the court held that records of a government entity lacking "independent authority" to take "direct action," and whose "sole function is to advise and assist the President," need not be disclosed under FOIA. *See also Meyer v. Bush*, 981 F.2d 1288 (D.C. Cir. 1993); *Citizens for Responsibility & Ethics in Washington v. Office of Admin.*, 566 F.3d 219 (D.C. Cir. 2009); Matthew J. Matule, Note, *Congress, the Courts, and Regulatory Oversight After Meyer v. Bush*, 18 Vt. L. Rev. 823 (1994). Can you square this judicial definition with the statutory one?

In *Armstrong v. Executive Office of the President*, 90 F.3d 553 (D.C. Cir. 1996), the court determined that the National Security Council (NSC) is not an "agency" within the meaning of FOIA because the NSC staff exercises "no substantial authority either to make or to implement policy" and no "significant non-advisory function." *Id.* at 561, 565. Can you reconcile what the *Armstrong* court said about the NSC with what you read in Chapter 17 concerning its involvement in the Iran-Contra Affair or with the description of its duties in Executive Order No. 12,333, *supra* p. 451? *See* R. Kevin Bailey, Note, *"Did I Miss Anything?": Excising the National Security Council from FOIA Coverage*, 46 Duke L.J. 1475 (1997).

7. *"Agency Records."* Do you understand what is included in the term "agency records"? In the words of one court, "For requested materials to qualify as 'agency records,' two requirements must be satisfied: (i) an agency must 'either create or obtain' the requested materials, and (ii) the agency must be in control of the requested materials at the time the FOIA request is made." *Grand Central P'ship, Inc. v. Cuomo*, 166 F.3d 473, 479 (2d Cir. 1999) (citations omitted). Thus, materials in agency files have been ruled exempt on grounds that they were not covered by FOIA when created, *Kissinger v. Reporters Comm. for Freedom of the Press*, 445 U.S. 136 (1980) (exempting notes in State Department files of the Secretary's telephone conversations while he was National Security Adviser), or because Congress (which is not an "agency" for FOIA purposes) had not given up control of the materials, *Goland v. CIA*, 607 F.2d 339 (D.C. Cir. 1978) (exempting transcript of secret congressional hearing in CIA files). *Compare Paisley v. CIA*, 712 F.2d 686 (D.C. Cir. 1983) (investigative report created by the CIA for a Senate committee is an agency record). Information collected by an agency illegally has been held not subject to a FOIA request. *Marzen v. United States Dep't of Health & Human Servs.*, 632 F. Supp. 785 (N.D. Ill. 1986), *aff'd*, 825 F.2d 1148 (7th Cir. 1987). Nor must records be disclosed that have been improperly disposed of by an agency. *Kissinger, supra*, 445 U.S. at 146-155.

8. *"Reasonably" Described.* FOIA §552(a)(3) requires an agency to make available records "reasonably" described by the requester. A description is sufficient if it enables a professional employee of the agency who is familiar with the subject area of the request to locate the record with a reasonable amount of effort. H.R. Rep. No. 93-876, at 5-6 (1974), *reprinted in* 1974 U.S.C.C.A.N. 6271. *See Goland v. CIA*, 607 F.2d 339, 353 (D.C. Cir. 1978). Nevertheless, the court in *Kowalczyk v. Department of Justice*, 73 F.3d 386, 389 (D.C. Cir. 1996), declared that the agency is "not obliged to look beyond the four corners of the request for leads to the location of responsive documents." Since a requester usually will not have seen any responsive documents (or even know whether they exist) and will have no way to guess their location, what can she do to improve her chances of getting what she wants?

9. *E-FOIA and E-Government.* In 1996 Congress amended FOIA to reflect increasing reliance on electronic media for both recordkeeping and communication, to make more information available to the public, and to make that information easier to obtain. Electronic Freedom of Information Act Amendments of 1996 (E-FOIA), Pub. L. No. 104-231, 110 Stat. 3048. By requiring agencies to search electronic databases and to furnish requested records in electronic form, Congress hoped that requests could be processed much more quickly. Equally important, by requiring that frequently requested materials be posted in electronic "reading rooms," Congress thought that the volume of requests might be dramatically reduced. *See generally* Joaquin Ferrao, *E-FOIA Law Increases Access for the Public and Brings Challenges to Agencies*, LLRX, Nov. 15, 1999, *at* http://www.llrx.com/features/e-foia.htm. The CIA's electronic reading room may be found at http://www.foia.cia.gov/default.asp.

The E-Government Act of 2002, Pub. L. No. 107-347, 116 Stat. 2899 (2002), furthers the goals of E-FOIA by pushing agencies to make better use of the Internet to provide information and services to citizens. It requires regulatory agencies to conduct rulemaking online, for example, and to post everything on their Web sites that they publish in the Federal Register. It also calls for creation of an online directory of all government Web sites, so that a searcher can locate information on a given topic without having to know which agency holds it. A decade after enactment of the E-FOIA law, however, an independent study found only about one-fifth of federal agencies in full compliance. National Sec. Archive, *File Not Found: Ten Years After E-FOIA, Most Federal Agencies Are Delinquent* (Mar. 12, 2007), *at* http://www.gwu.edu/~nsarchiv/NSAEBB/NSAEBB216/index.htm. *See also* Robert Ratish, *Democracy's Backlog: The Electronic Freedom of Information Act Ten Years Later*, 34 Rutgers Computer & Tech. L.J. 211 (2007). Agency performance aside, can you think of other ways to use advances in technology to improve public access to agency records?

10. *Other Statutes Requiring Secrecy.* FOIA *permits withholding* of classified data when it is requested. Other acts *require withholding* of data from public view — for example, the Atomic Energy Act of 1954, 42 U.S.C. §2162 (2006) (protecting the secrecy of "restricted" nuclear weapons data unless disclosure would not create an unreasonable risk to the common defense and security of the United States), or *criminalize disclosure* of certain information — for example, Intelligence Identities Protection Act of 1982, 50 U.S.C. §421 (2006), as amended by Pub. L. No. 111-259, §363(a), 124 Stat. 2654, 2701 (2010) (disclosure of classified information that identifies a covert agent is punishable by fine or imprisonment).

2.   Statutory Exemptions and Judicial Review

The following cases reveal some of the history of FOIA and describe the application of two exemptions bearing on national security. In particular, they address the role of courts in deciding whether to withhold sensitive data from the public.

Ray v. Turner

United States Court of Appeals, District of Columbia Circuit, 1978
587 F.2d 1187

PER CURIAM: This appeal presents the question whether the district court erred in dismissing a lawsuit under the Freedom of Information Act (FOIA) upon the basis of affidavits supplied by an official of the Central Intelligence Agency (CIA). We find there was error and remand.

I. PROCEDURAL BACKGROUND OF LITIGATION

Plaintiffs (appellants) Ellen Ray and William Schaap sent identical letters to the CIA requesting "a copy of any file you may have on me." The CIA replied that while it did not have files on plaintiffs, there were documents in CIA files that referred to plaintiffs. The CIA refused to release those documents, and after administrative appeals were exhausted, plaintiffs brought this action under the FOIA. The CIA subsequently released portions of the withheld documents, and the government then moved for summary judgment, relying principally on affidavits of one Eloise Page . . . [purporting] to describe the documents at issue and the grounds for the government's claims of exemption.

The district court granted the government's motion for summary judgment and denied plaintiffs' motion for *in camera* inspection. . . . It found that the withheld documents were exempt from disclosure under the FOIA on the basis of Exemption 1 alone, Exemption 3 alone, or the two exemptions coupled together. As to Exemption 1, 5 U.S.C. §552(b)(1), the court found that the affidavit showed that the documents were properly classified under Executive Order 11,652, 3 C.F.R. 339 (1974). As to Exemption 3, 5 U.S.C. §552(b)(3), the court found that the affidavits stated that the release of the information could reasonably be expected to reveal intelligence sources and methods as well as organizational data, and that 50 U.S.C. §§403(d)(3), 403g justified the CIA invocation of Exemption 3. . . .

II. RELEVANT CONSIDERATIONS IN FOIA CASES INVOLVING
NATIONAL SECURITY ISSUES

The FOIA was passed in 1966, as an amendment to the Administrative Procedure Act, in order to increase disclosure of government information to the American people. Agencies were required to disclose all records that did not come within one of nine explicit exemptions specified by Congress. In the event of agency nondisclosure, the Act provided for court review. In any such case, "the court shall determine the matter de novo . . . and the burden is on the agency to sustain its action."[7]

A. Judicial Interpretations and Legislative Modifications

In *EPA v. Mink*, 410 U.S. 73, 81-84 (1973), the Court considered Exemption 1, which at that time covered matters "specifically required by Executive order to be kept secret in the interest of the national defense or foreign policy." 5 U.S.C. §552(b)(1) (1970). It held that a court should not review the substantive propriety of the classification or go behind an agency affidavit stating that the requested documents had been duly classified pursuant to Executive order.[8] The Court said that "Congress chose to follow the Executive's determination in these matters," and *in camera* inspection to test the propriety of the classification was not authorized. 410 U.S. at 81.

In 1974 Congress overrode a presidential veto and amended the FOIA for the express purpose of changing this aspect of the *Mink* case. Exemption 1 was modified to exempt only matters that are "(A) specifically authorized under criteria established by an Executive order to be kept secret in the interest of national defense or foreign policy and (B) are in fact properly classified pursuant to such Executive order." 5 U.S.C. §552(b)(1) (1976).

Furthermore, the 1974 revision changed the FOIA language describing the role of a reviewing court considering *any* claim of exemption. It provided that "the court shall determine the matter de novo, and may examine the contents of such agency records in camera to determine whether such records or any part thereof shall be withheld under any of the exemptions set forth in subsection (b) of this section, and the burden is on the agency to sustain its action." 5 U.S.C. §552(a)(4)(B) (1976). The Conference Report accompanying the amendments explained that "[w]hile *in camera* examination need not be automatic, in many situations it will plainly be necessary and appropriate." S. Rep. No. 93-1200, 93d Cong., 2d Sess. 9 (1974), U.S. Code Cong. & Admin. News 1974, p. 6287.

Exemption 3 originally exempted matters "specifically exempted from disclosure by statute." 5 U.S.C. §552(b)(3) (1970). In *FAA Administrator v. Robertson*, 422 U.S. 255 (1975), the Court held that a statute could "specifically exempt" matters from disclosure even if the statute gave an agency broad discretion to determine whether the information should be withheld. Concerned about excessive agency discretion, Congress in 1976 passed an amendment to change the result reached in *Robertson*. Exemption 3 now authorizes nondisclosure of matters "specifically exempted from disclosure by statute . . . provided that such statute (A) requires that the matters be withheld from the public in such a manner as to leave no

---

7. 5 U.S.C. §552(a)(3) (1976). Courts were given authority to review de novo any denial of access "in order that the ultimate decision as to the propriety of the agency's action is made by the court and [to] prevent [review] from becoming meaningless judicial sanctioning of agency discretion." S. Rep. No. 813, 89th Cong., 1st Sess. 8 (1965).

8. *Mink* involved a request for documents prepared by various government officials for the President in connection with a scheduled nuclear test. The documents were withheld under Exemptions 1 and 5. Those seeking the information had not disputed the government's claim that proper classification procedures had been followed, 410 U.S. at 84, and the Court held that the substantive propriety of the classification had been committed by Congress to Executive discretion. The Court therefore reversed the order of the court of appeals that the district court examine the documents *in camera* and release any segregable nonsecret portions. . . .

discretion on the issue, or (B) establishes particular criteria for withholding or refers to particular types of matters to be withheld." 5 U.S.C. §552(b)(3) (1976).

B. The Nature of De Novo Review

Procedures to Be Observed

In *Vaughn v. Rosen*, 484 F.2d 820 ([D.C. Cir.] 1973), *cert. denied*, 415 U.S. 977 (1974), this court sought to cope with the difficulty of providing de novo review of exemptions claimed by the government. It initiated procedures designed to mitigate the administrative burden on the courts and ensure that the burden of justifying claimed exemptions would in fact be borne by the agencies to whom it had been assigned by Congress.

The court took its cue from a portion of the Supreme Court's *Mink* opinion that was not overruled by Congress — the portion discussing how a court should proceed when there is a factual dispute concerning the nature of the materials being withheld.[11] "Expanding" on the Supreme Court's "outline," the court established the following procedures: (1) A requirement that the agency submit a "relatively detailed analysis [of the material withheld] in manageable segments." "[C]onclusory and generalized allegations of exemptions" would no longer be accepted by reviewing courts. 484 F.2d at 826. (2) "[A]n indexing system [that] would subdivide the document under consideration into manageable parts cross-referenced to the relevant portion of the Government's justification." 484 F.2d at 827. This index would allow the district court and opposing counsel to locate specific areas of dispute for further examination and would be an indispensable aid to the court of appeals reviewing the district court's decision. (3) "[A]dequate adversary testing" would be ensured by opposing counsel's access to the information included in the agency's detailed and indexed justification and by *in camera* inspection, guided by the detailed affidavit and using special masters appointed by the court whenever the burden proved to be especially onerous. 484 F.2d at 828.[12]

In proposing the 1974 amendments, the Senate Committee outlined the ruling in *Vaughn* and added, "The committee supports this approach...."[13]

The Judicial Function as Emphasized by 1974 Amendments

In some of the decisions involving national security issues, there has been confusion about the nature of the evidentiary burdens and the scope of the district judge's discretion. This uncertainty is due to a misunderstanding of the legislative history of the 1974 amendments. There were differences in 1974 between the Senate Committee and the House, between the Senate and its Committee, and between the Legislative and Executive Branches. For an authoritative exposition of the purpose

---

11. See *EPA v. Mink*, 410 U.S. at 92-94....

12. A remaining problem noted by the court in *Vaughn* — the failure of the district court's opinion to reveal the court's reasoning — was dealt with in *Schwartz v. IRS*, 511 F.2d 1303, 1307 (1975). *Schwartz* held that the district court had abused its discretion by not granting a plaintiff/appellant's request for a clarification of the legal grounds of its opinion affirming the agency's refusal to disclose information sought under the FOIA....

13. S. Rep. No. 93-854, 93d Cong., 2d Sess. 15 (1974).

and effect of the 1974 amendments, it suffices for present purposes to quote a few key paragraphs of the Conference Committee report:[15]

> The conference substitute follows the Senate amendment, providing that in determining *de novo* whether agency records have been properly withheld, the court may examine records *in camera* in making its determination under any of the nine categories of exemptions under section 552(b) of the law. In *Environmental Protection Agency v. Mink, et al.*, 410 U.S. 73 (1973), the Supreme Court ruled that *in camera* inspection of documents withheld under section 552(b)(1) of the law, authorizing the withholding of classified information, would ordinarily be precluded in Freedom of Information cases, unless Congress directed otherwise. H.R. 12471 amends the present law to permit such *in camera* examination at the discretion of the court. While *in camera* examination need not be automatic, in many situations it will plainly be necessary and appropriate. Before the court orders *in camera* inspection, the Government should be given the opportunity to establish by means of testimony or detailed affidavits that the documents are clearly exempt from disclosure. The burden remains on the Government under this law. . . .
>
> When linked with the authority conferred upon the Federal courts in this conference substitute for *in camera* examination of contested records as part of their *de novo* determination in Freedom of Information cases, this clarifies Congressional intent to override the Supreme Court's holding in the case of *E.P.A. v. Mink, et al.*, supra, with respect to *in camera* review of classified documents.
>
> However, the conferees recognize that the Executive departments responsible for national defense and foreign policy matters have unique insights into what adverse effects might occur as a result of public disclosure of a particular classified record. Accordingly, the conferees expect that Federal courts, in making *de novo* determinations in section 552(b)(1) cases under the Freedom of Information law, will accord substantial weight to an agency's affidavit concerning the details of the classified status of the disputed record.

The legislative history underscores that the intent of Congress regarding de novo review stood in contrast to, and was a rejection of, the alternative suggestion proposed by the Administration and supported by some Senators: that in the national security context the court should be limited to determining whether there was a reasonable basis for the decision by the appropriate official to withhold the document.[16] In proposing a "reasonable basis" standard, the Administration and supporting legislators argued that de novo responsibility and *in camera* inspection could not properly be assigned to judges, in part because of logistical problems, and in part because of their

---

15. S. Rep. No. 93-1200, 93d Cong., 2d Sess. 9, 12 (1974), U.S. Code Cong. & Admin. News 1974, pp. 6267, 6287, 6290.

16. See, e.g., Message from President Gerald R. Ford Vetoing H.R. 12471, H. Doc. No. 93-383, 93d Cong., 2d Sess. (1974):

> As the legislation now stands, a determination by the Secretary of Defense that disclosure of a document would endanger our national security would, even though reasonable, have to be overturned by a district judge who thought the plaintiff's position just as reasonable. Such a provision would violate constitutional principles, and give less weight before the courts to an executive determination involving the protection of our most vital national defense interests than is accorded determinations involving routine regulatory matters.
>
> I propose, therefore, that where classified documents are requested the courts could review the classification, but would have to uphold the classification if there is reasonable basis to support it. In determining the reasonableness of the classification, the courts would consider all attendant evidence prior to resorting to an *in camera* examination of the document.

lack of relevant experience and meaningful appreciation of the implications of the material involved. Those who prevailed in the legislature both resisted the Administration proposal on first consideration and voted to override President Ford's veto of the bill containing the provision for de novo review and *in camera* inspection. They stressed the need for an objective, independent judicial determination, and insisted that judges could be trusted to approach the national security determinations with common sense, and without jeopardy to national security.[18] They emphasized that in reaching a de novo determination the judge would accord substantial weight to detailed agency affidavits and take into account that the executive had "unique insights into what adverse affects might occur as a result of public disclosure of a particular classified record."[19]

The salient characteristics of de novo review in the national security context can be summarized as follows: (1) The government has the burden of establishing an exemption. (2) The court must make a de novo determination. (3) In doing this, it must first "accord substantial weight to an agency's affidavit concerning the details of the classified status of the disputed record."[20] (4) Whether and how to conduct an *in camera* examination of the documents rests in the sound discretion of the court, in national security cases as in all other cases.[21]

To these observations should be added an excerpt from our opinion in *Weissman* (as revised): "If exemption is claimed on the basis of national security the District Court must, of course, be satisfied that proper procedures have been followed, and

18. See 120 Cong. Rec. 36,870 (1974) (Sen. Muskie):

As a practical matter, I cannot imagine that any Federal judge would throw open the gates of the Nation's classified secrets, or that they would substitute their judgment for that of an agency head without carefully weighing all the evidence in the arguments presented by both sides.

On the contrary, if we constrict the manner in which courts perform this vital review function, we make the classifiers themselves privileged officials, immune from the accountability necessary for Government to function smoothly.

Id. at 17,030 (Sen. Ervin):

The court ought not be required to find anything except that the matter affects or does not affect national security. If a judge does not have enough sense to make that kind of decision, he ought not to be a judge. We ought not to leave that decision to be made by the CIA or any other branch of the Government.

Id. at 17,028 (Sen. Chiles):

If, as the Senator from Mississippi said, there is a reason, why are judges going to be so unreasonable? We say that four-star generals or admirals will be reasonable but a Federal district judge is going to be unreasonable. I cannot buy that argument, especially when I see that general or that admiral has participated in covering up a mistake, and the Federal judge sits there without a bias one way or another. I want him to be able to decide without blinders or having to go in one direction.

19. S. Rep. No. 93-1200, 93d Cong., 2d Sess. 12 (1974), U.S. Code Cong. & Admin. News 1974, p. 6290.

20. Id.

21. The Senate Committee Report on the 1974 amendments emphasizes the procedural flexibility available to a district judge.

In making this [exemption] determination, the court must *first* attempt to resolve the matter "on the basis of affidavits and other information submitted by the parties." If it does decide to examine the contested records in camera, the court may consider further argument by both parties, may take further expert testimony, and may in some cases of a particularly sensitive nature decide to entertain an ex parte showing by the government.

S. Rep. No. 93-854, 93d Cong., 2d Sess. 15-16 (1974) (emphasis added)....

that by its sufficient description the contested document logically falls into the category of the exemption indicated."[22]

In part, the foregoing considerations were developed for Exemption 1. They also apply to Exemption 3 when the statute providing criteria for withholding is in furtherance of national security interests.

In Camera Inspection

In the case at bar, the district court observed: "With respect to documents withheld under exemption 3, in camera inspection is seldom, if ever, necessary or appropriate." The legislative history does not support that conclusion. Congress left the matter of *in camera* inspection to the discretion of the district court, without any indication of the extent of its proper use. The ultimate criterion is simply this: Whether the district judge believes that *in camera* inspection is needed in order to make a responsible de novo determination on the claims of exemption.

In camera inspection requires effort and resources and therefore a court should not resort to it routinely on the theory that "it can't hurt." When an agency affidavit or other showing is specific, there may be no need for *in camera* inspection.

On the other hand, when the district judge is concerned that he is not prepared to make a responsible de novo determination in the absence of *in camera* inspection, he may proceed *in camera* without anxiety that the law interposes an extraordinary hurdle to such inspection. The government would presumably prefer *in camera* inspection to a ruling that the case stands in doubt or equipoise and hence must be resolved by a ruling that the government has not sustained its burden.

The issue of bad faith merits a word. The memorandum of the district court noted that there was no evidence of bad faith on the part of the Agency's officials. Where the record contains a showing of bad faith, the district court would likely require *in camera* inspection. But the government's burden does not mean that all assertions in a government affidavit must routinely be verified by audit. Reasonable specificity in affidavits connotes a quality of reliability. When an affidavit or showing is reasonably specific and demonstrates, if accepted, that the documents are exempt, these exemptions are not to be undercut by mere assertion of claims of bad faith or misrepresentation.

In camera inspection does not depend on a finding or even tentative finding of bad faith. A judge has discretion to order *in camera* inspection on the basis of an uneasiness, on a doubt he wants satisfied before he takes responsibility for a de novo determination. Government officials who would not stoop to misrepresentation may reflect an inherent tendency to resist disclosure, and judges may take this natural inclination into account.

III. RULINGS FOR THE CASE AT BAR

Two affidavits were executed by Eloise Page, Chief, Operations Staff of the Directorate of Operations of the CIA. The first is a general statement about the dangers at large of disclosure, background and local color rather than any attempt to link these concerns with specific documents. It is of little aid in the task of deciding whether the nine specific documents now sought come within the claimed exemptions. . . .

---

22. *Weissman v. CIA*, 565 F.2d 692, 697 ([D.C. Cir.] 1977). Whether there is a "sufficient description" to establish the exemptions is, of course, a key issue.

Page's second affidavit . . . purports to link specific exemptions to specific documents. A glaring defect is that it lumps the exemptions together and fails to identify whether different exemptions are claimed as to different parts of each document. The statement for document 2 reads:

> This document is a three-page memorandum the subject of which is "Rennie Davis and Friends." It is essentially the debriefing report of a sensitive intelligence source. The majority of the information concerns individuals other than the plaintiffs.
>
> This document has been denied in its entirety, primarily to protect intelligence sources and methods since the release of any meaningful portion would disclose the identity of the source, and further, to protect cryptonyms, names of CIA personnel and CIA organizational data. Thus exemptions (b)(1), (b)(3) and (b)(6) apply.

The statement for documents 3, 4 and 5 reads:

> These documents are one-page cables from an overseas CIA installation which advise Headquarters of the receipt of documents and information from a foreign intelligence service and which concern the plaintiffs and other individuals. They are denied in their entirety pursuant to Freedom of Information Act exemptions (b)(1), (b)(3) and (b)(6).

In reviewing the judgment on documents 2-6, we encounter a complex of difficulties. Exemption 3 permits a withholding under the provisions of 50 U.S.C. §403g (1970), which specifies that "in order further to implement the proviso of section 403(d)(3) of this title that the Director of Central Intelligence shall be responsible for protecting intelligence sources and methods from unauthorized disclosure, the Agency shall be exempted from . . . the provisions of any . . . law which require the publication or disclosure of the organization, functions, names, official titles, salaries, or numbers of personnel employed by the Agency. . . ." *Goland v. CIA*, [607 F.2d 339, 349 (D.C. Cir. 1978)]; cf. *Weissman v. CIA*, 565 F.2d 692, 694 ([D.C. Cir.] 1977). However, in *Goland*, the affidavit demonstrated "in nonconclusory and detailed fashion" (slip op. at 21), that the deleted material disclosed intelligence sources and methods. The CIA's affidavit as to documents 2-6 is not a specific presentation such as that in *Goland*. The statement that the release of any meaningful portion of document 2 would disclose the identity of a "sensitive intelligence source" has some particularity, but it runs into a failure to address specifically whether the disclosure of substantive information may be possible without the disclosure of source, and if not why not.

As to Exemption 1, the information that document 2 relates to "Rennie Davis and Friends," might be some indication that it was reasonable for the official involved to have classified it in the first instance. But that mere reference is not enough information to permit a judge to make an independent ruling that the classification was proper. . . .

Overall, we have a critical problem of segregability, that some portion of the document(s) may be exempt, but that the FOIA might contemplate disclosure in part. The difficulty arises from the CIA's proffer of multiple exemptions for each withheld document, and is maintained by the district court's conclusory rulings.

The reviewing court should not be required to speculate on the precise relationship between each exemption claim and the contents of the specific document. The district judge is not called upon to take on the role of censor — going through a line-by-line analysis for each document and removing particular words. If, however, the problematic material appears in a particular place or places that can be manageably identified, indexing is not to be bypassed because it is something of a chore....

... [T]he CIA ... has not been responsive to the requirement that it provide specific affidavits that segregate each of its claims. The "exemption by document" approach has been rejected by our opinions, notably *Vaughn,* 484 F.2d at 825-826, and *Mead Data Central, Inc. v. Dept. of the Air Force,* 566 F.2d 242, 259-262 ([D.C. Cir.] 1977). The agency may not rely on that approach even in a national security context. The agency must provide a reasonable segregation as to the portions of the document that are involved in each of its claims for exemption. As indicated in *Mead,* it is important that the affidavit indicate the extent to which each document would be claimed as exempt under each of the exemptions. The courts cannot meaningfully exercise their responsibility under the FOIA unless the government affidavits are as specific as possible....

We remand for reconsideration of the CIA's exemption claims in light of clarification of the affidavits and for further proceedings not inconsistent with this opinion.

[The concurring opinion of WRIGHT, C.J., is omitted.]

American Civil Liberties Union v. United States Department of Defense

United States Court of Appeals, District of Columbia Circuit, 2011
628 F.3d 612

SENTELLE, Chief Judge: Appellants, the American Civil Liberties Union and the American Civil Liberties Foundation (jointly "ACLU"), submitted Freedom of Information Act ("FOIA") requests to the Department of Defense and the Central Intelligence Agency ("CIA") seeking documents related to fourteen "high value" detainees held at the U.S. Naval Base in Guantanamo Bay, Cuba. In response, the government released redacted versions of the requested documents, from which specific information relating to the capture, detention, and interrogation of the detainees had been withheld. The government defended the redactions as justified by FOIA exemptions 1 and 3, which permit the government to withhold information related to "intelligence sources and methods." ...

I. BACKGROUND

Since January of 2002, the United States has operated a detention facility at the United States Naval Base at Guantanamo Bay, Cuba, for detainees captured in the war on terror. In a September 2006 speech, President Bush revealed that fourteen "suspected terrorist leaders and operatives" had been held and questioned outside of the United States in a separate program operated by the CIA. Remarks on the War on Terror, 42 Weekly Comp. Pres. Doc. 1569, 1570 (Sept. 6, 2006). In his speech, the President announced that this program had been discontinued and that the fourteen detainees were being transferred to Guantanamo Bay. *Id.* at 1573-74. After their transfer, these so-called "high value" detainees received hearings before Combatant Status Review Tribunals ("CSRTs") [described *supra* p. 785.].

Although the Department of Defense had publicly posted redacted transcripts of the detainees' CSRT proceedings, the ACLU submitted Freedom of Information Act requests to the Department seeking full CSRT transcripts of the 14 detainees and all records provided to the CSRTs by or on behalf of the detainees. In response to the request, the government identified and released [eight unclassified CSRT transcripts, six redacted CSRT transcripts, and unclassified or redacted statements of several detainees]. From the redacted documents, the CIA withheld all information relating to the capture, detention, and interrogation of the "high value" detainees.

The ACLU filed the present action in the district court challenging the government's withholdings. The government stood by its withholdings and filed affidavits in support of its position. The government principally relied on the affidavit of Wendy Hilton, the Associate Information Review Officer of the National Clandestine Service of the CIA, to justify the redactions as information protected by FOIA exemptions 1 and 3....

The government moved for summary judgment to dispose of the ACLU's lawsuit....

... The district court granted the government's motion, *A.C.L.U. v. Dep't of Defense*, 664 F. Supp. 2d 72, 79 (D.D.C. 2009), and the ACLU appealed.

II. FOIA EXEMPTIONS 1 AND 3

... [E]xemption 1 permits the government to withhold information "specifically authorized under criteria established by an Executive order to be kept secret in the interest of national defense or foreign policy" if that information has been "properly classified pursuant to such Executive order." 5 U.S.C. §552(b)(1). In this case, the government argues that the redacted information was properly classified under Executive Order 12,958, which "prescribes a uniform system for classifying, safeguarding, and declassifying national security information." Exec. Order No. 12,958.[1] Specifically, the government asserts that the information it withheld was classified as "intelligence sources or methods" pursuant to section 1.4(c) of Executive Order 12,958.

... The government relies on the National Security Act of 1947 to justify withholding the redacted information under exemption 3. We have previously held that the National Security Act, which also authorizes the Executive to withhold "intelligence sources and methods" from public disclosure, 50 U.S.C. §403-1(i)(1), qualifies as an exemption statute under exemption 3. *Larson v. Dep't of State*, 565 F.3d 857, 865 (D.C. Cir. 2009); *Fitzgibbon v. C.I.A.*, 911 F.2d 755, 761 (D.C. Cir. 1990).

An agency withholding responsive documents from a FOIA release bears the burden of proving the applicability of claimed exemptions. Typically it does so by affidavit. We review the district court's decision on the adequacy of the agency's showing *de novo*. *Larson*, 565 F.3d at 862; *Wolf v. C.I.A.*, 473 F.3d 370, 374 (D.C. Cir. 2007). Because courts "lack the expertise necessary to second-guess such agency opinions in the typical national security FOIA case," *Krikorian v. Dep't of State*, 984 F.2d 461, 464 (D.C. Cir. 1993), we "must accord substantial weight to an agency's affidavit concerning the details of the classified status of the disputed record." *Wolf*, 473 F.3d at 374 (quotations omitted). If an agency's affidavit describes the justifications for withholding the information with specific detail, demonstrates that the information withheld logically falls within the claimed exemption, and is not contradicted by contrary evidence in the record or by evidence of the agency's bad faith, then summary judgment is warranted on the basis of the affidavit alone. *Larson*, 565 F.3d at 862; *Wolf*, 473 F.3d at 374.

---

1. Executive Order 12,598 and all amendments thereto have since been superseded by Executive Order 13,526, 75 Fed. Reg. 707 (Dec. 29, 2009) [*supra* p. 1185].

Moreover, a reviewing court "must take into account ... that any affidavit or other agency statement of threatened harm to national security will always be speculative to some extent, in the sense that it describes a potential future harm." *Wolf,* 473 F.3d at 374. "Ultimately, an agency's justification for invoking a FOIA exemption is sufficient if it appears 'logical' or 'plausible.'" *Larson,* 565 F.3d at 862 (quoting *Wolf,* 473 F.3d at 374-75).

A.

The ACLU first claims that the withheld information is not exempt from FOIA because it has already been declassified and is available to the public. The ACLU points to three sets of declassified and released government documents that the ACLU believes contain the same information that the CIA has withheld from the requested CSRT documents: the OLC memoranda [see *supra* p. 933], the CIA Inspector General's report [see *supra* p. 928 n.10], and a CIA "Background Paper" released with the CIA Inspector General's report. The ACLU also argues that a fourth document, the leaked Red Cross report [see *supra* p. 934 n.28], although not an official government disclosure, contains the same information and is available to the public.

In its affidavit, the CIA asserts that despite the declassification and disclosure of some government documents, the specific operational details of the capture, detention, and interrogation of the "high value" detainees remain classified. Hilton Aff. ¶55, Aug. 28, 2009. The affidavit states that the declassified documents contain "descriptions of the enhanced interrogation techniques *in the abstract*" that are "of a qualitatively different nature than the conditions of confinement and interrogation techniques *as applied* described in the CSRT transcripts and detainee written statements." *Id.* at ¶70 (emphasis in original). The affidavit also asserts that the documents "... do not reveal the level of detail described in the [CSRT] transcripts and statements." *Id.* at ¶¶70, 71 (emphasis in original). The CIA also argues that under our opinion in *Fitzgibbon,* the leaked Red Cross report is irrelevant because it does not qualify as an official and documented disclosure by the government. *See* 911 F.2d at 765.

If the government has officially acknowledged information, a FOIA plaintiff may compel disclosure of that information even over an agency's otherwise valid exemption claim. *Wolf,* 473 F.3d at 378. For information to qualify as "officially acknowledged," it must satisfy three criteria: (1) the information requested must be as specific as the information previously released; (2) the information requested must match the information previously disclosed; and (3) the information requested must already have been made public through an official and documented disclosure. *Wolf,* 473 F.3d at 378. As we further explained in *Wolf,* "[p]rior disclosure of similar information does not suffice; instead, the *specific* information sought by the plaintiff must already be in the public domain by official disclosure. This insistence on exactitude recognizes the Government's vital interest in information relating to national security and foreign affairs." 473 F.3d at 378 (citations and quotation omitted).

... According the agency's affidavit the substantial weight it is due regarding the details of the classified status of the disputed record, *see Wolf,* 473 F.3d at 374, we agree with the district court's conclusion that the information withheld by the government "is specific and particular to each detainee and would reveal far more about the CIA's interrogation process than the previously released records." *A.C.L.U.,* 664 F. Supp. 2d at 77.

As the ACLU readily admits, the Red Cross report was not released pursuant to a government declassification process, but was instead leaked to a journalist. We note at the outset that the Red Cross report is not a government document, and we are hard pressed to understand the ACLU's contention that the release of a nongovernment document by a nonofficial source can constitute a disclosure affecting the applicability of the FOIA exemptions. . . .

Neither the official government disclosures of the OLC memoranda and CIA reports nor the unofficial publication of the Red Cross report are sufficient to qualify the information withheld from the CSRT documents as "officially acknowledged." Therefore, despite the ACLU's claim that the information is already widely available to the public, we conclude that FOIA exemptions 1 and 3 validly apply.

B.

The ACLU also argues that the redacted information is not exempt from FOIA because the interrogation techniques and conditions of confinement withheld from the requested documents have been prohibited by the President. Relying on the Supreme Court's ruling in *C.I.A. v. Sims* [471 U.S. 159 (1985)], the ACLU argues that because the President banned the future use of the interrogation techniques and confinement conditions formerly authorized for use on the "high value" detainees, those techniques and conditions are no longer within the "Agency's mandate to conduct foreign intelligence," and therefore not protectable "intelligence sources and methods." *See* 471 U.S. at 169-70.

Sims, the only case offered by the ACLU in support of this proposition, does not remotely support such a claim. The *Sims* decision does in fact discuss the breadth of the protection offered by exemption 3, but says nothing suggesting that the change in the specific techniques of intelligence gathering by the CIA renders unprotected sources and methods previously used. As the *Sims* Court stated, "[t]he 'plain meaning' of section 102(d)(3) may not be squared with any limiting definition that goes beyond the requirement that the information fall within the agency's mandate to conduct foreign intelligence." 471 U.S. at 169. In short, the *Sims* decision refutes rather than supports the ACLU's claim.

To the extent that the ACLU's claim rests on the ACLU's belief that the enhanced interrogation techniques were illegal, there is no legal support for the conclusion that illegal activities cannot produce classified documents. In fact, history teaches the opposite. Documents concerning surveillance activities later deemed illegal may still produce information that may be properly withheld under exemption 1. *See Lesar v. Dep't of Justice*, 636 F.2d 472, 483 (D.C. Cir. 1980). . . .

D.

Finally, in addition to arguing that the information withheld from the requested documents does not qualify for FOIA exemptions 1 and 3 as "intelligence sources or methods," the ACLU also argues the government cannot withhold the information under exemption 1 because public release of the information would not damage national security.[3] . . .

---

3. . . . [T]he government need prevail on only one exemption; it need not satisfy both.

... Executive Order 12,958, which authorizes the classification of "intelligence sources or methods," requires as a prerequisite to classification that disclosure of the information to be classified "reasonably could be expected to result in damage to the national security" and that the government must be "able to identify or describe the damage." Exec. Order No. 12,958 §1.1(a)(4). Thus, the "intelligence sources or methods" withheld by the government are properly classified under Executive Order 12,958, and therefore exempt from disclosure under exemption 1, only if the CIA can establish that public disclosure of the withheld information will harm national security. *See* 5 U.S.C. §552(a)(4)(B) (placing the burden on the agency to sustain its action under FOIA).

Because "[t]he assessment of harm to intelligence sources, methods and operations is entrusted to the Director of Central Intelligence, not to the courts," *Fitzgibbon*, 911 F.2d at 766, the government's burden is a light one. "[I]n the FOIA context, we have consistently deferred to executive affidavits predicting harm to national security, and have found it unwise to undertake searching judicial review." *Ctr. for Nat'l Sec. Studies v. U.S. Dep't of Justice*, 331 F.3d 918, 927 (D.C. Cir. 2003). The CIA's arguments need only be both "plausible" and "logical" to justify the invocation of a FOIA exemption in the national security context. *See Wolf*, 473 F.3d at 374-75.

In this case the CIA identified five reasons why the disclosure of the withheld information might harm national security. Specifically, the CIA affidavit asserted that public release of the information would potentially damage national security by: (1) revealing the CIA's needs, priorities, and capabilities, Hilton Aff. ¶¶50-51; (2) degrading the CIA's ability to effectively question terrorist detainees, *id.* at ¶¶58-59; (3) providing terrorists with insight into the CIA's interrogation techniques, strategies, and methods, *id.* at ¶¶60-64; (4) damaging the CIA's relations with foreign governments, *id.* at ¶¶65-69; and (5) providing al Qaeda with material for propaganda, *id.* at ¶72. ...

... According substantial weight and deference to the CIA's affidavit, *see Wolf*, 473 F.3d at 374, we conclude that it is both plausible and logical that the disclosure of information regarding the capture, detention, and interrogation of detainees would degrade the CIA's ability to carry out its mission. Having concluded that the CIA's arguments are both "plausible" and "logical," and finding no evidence in the record to support the opposite conclusion, no further investigation is required.

... Because the release of the information withheld by the CIA "reasonably could be expected to result in damage to the national security," we conclude that the information may be withheld under FOIA exemption 1.

E.

... The CIA affidavit described, in general terms but on a document-by-document basis, the information withheld from each responsive document. Hilton Aff. ¶¶27-34. ...

In the CIA affidavit, Hilton declared that she had personally reviewed the redacted information and affirmed that it was currently and properly classified. *Id.* at ¶48. ...

Based on the strength of the CIA affidavit, we hold that the government properly invoked FOIA exemptions 1 and 3. The CIA explained with sufficient detail why the withheld information qualifies as "intelligence sources or methods" and adequately described the potential harm to national security that could result from the information's public disclosure. Nothing in the CIA's affidavit is contradicted by the record and we find no evidence of bad faith by the government. We conclude that summary judgment was warranted on the basis of the CIA's affidavit alone.

III. *IN CAMERA* REVIEW

Finally, we consider the ACLU's argument that the district court erred by failing to perform *in camera* review of the redacted information. This court reviews a district court's decision whether to conduct *in camera* review of FOIA documents for abuse of discretion. *Larson*, 565 F.3d at 869. Although Congress provided district courts the option to conduct *in camera* review under FOIA, the statute does not compel the exercise of that option. *Larson*, 565 F.3d at 869. "Congress intended to impose no mandates upon the trial court, but instead leave the decision of whether to conduct *in camera* inspection to the broad discretion of the trial judge." *Center for Auto Safety v. E.P.A.*, 731 F.2d 16, 20 (D.C. Cir. 1984). "If the agency's affidavits 'provide specific information sufficient to place the documents within the exemption category, if this information is not contradicted in the record, and if there is no evidence in the record of agency bad faith, then summary judgment is appropriate without *in camera* review of the documents.'" *Larson*, 565 F.3d at 870 (quoting *Hayden v. N.S.A.*, 608 F.2d 1381, 1387 (D.C. Cir. 1979)). "When the agency meets its burden by means of affidavits, *in camera* review is neither necessary nor appropriate." *Hayden*, 608 F.2d at 1387. *In camera* inspection is particularly a last resort in national security situations like this case — a court should not resort to it routinely on the theory that "it can't hurt." *Larson*, 565 F.3d at 870.

The ACLU claims that *in camera* review of the withheld information is appropriate in this case because there is evidence of bad faith by the CIA. *See Spirko v. U.S. Postal Service*, 147 F.3d 992, 996 (D.C. Cir. 1998) (stating that "*in camera* inspection may be particularly appropriate when ... there is evidence of bad faith on the part of the agency")....

The ACLU's claim that the government acted in bad faith is meritless. None of the information originally redacted but later disclosed after the documents were reprocessed demonstrates that the CIA improperly withheld information.... The government's later decision to declassify [certain records] does not prove that they were originally improperly withheld or that the government acted in bad faith. To the contrary, we find that the government demonstrated good faith by voluntarily reprocessing the documents after the President declassified the OLC memoranda and the CIA Inspector General's report. As in previous FOIA cases, we decline to penalize a government agency for voluntarily reevaluating and revising its FOIA withholdings.

... The district court did not abuse its discretion by granting the government's motion for summary judgment without conducting *in camera* review.

IV. CONCLUSION

We affirm the district court's grant of summary judgment for the Department of Defense and CIA. We agree that the specific details of the "high value" detainees' capture, detention, and interrogation are exempt from FOIA disclosure under exemptions 1 and 3. The district court acted within its broad discretion when it declined to perform *in camera* review.

So ordered.

NOTES AND QUESTIONS

1. *Standards for Reviewing Exemption 1 Claims.* The 1974 amendments to FOIA represent a mid-course legislative correction in response to the holding in the Supreme Court's decision in *EPA v. Mink*, 410 U.S. 73 (1973), as the *Ray* court noted. *See* H. Comm. on Gov't Operations & S. Comm. on the Judiciary, *Freedom of Information Act and Amendments of 1974*, 94th Cong. (Jt. Comm. Print 1975). Section 552(a)(4)(B) clearly aimed to withdraw significant authority from the executive branch and place it in the hands of the courts. In light of the broad delegation of authority to the President in Exemption 1, however, and the expansively drawn standards of Executive Order No. 13,526, reviewed in the last chapter, did the 1974 amendment really diminish the power of the Executive? Put another way, will a court ever be in a position to refute an agency determination that release of certain information "reasonably could be expected to result in damage to the national security"?

Despite the declaration of House and Senate conferees that a reviewing federal court should "accord substantial weight to an agency's affidavit," *Ray v. Turner*, 587 F.2d at 1193, there is a strong tendency among courts today to apply the "reasonable basis" standard of review rejected by Congress in 1974. The very deferential treatment of government claims in *American Civil Liberties Union v. United States Department of Defense* is much more typical in this respect. There are notable exceptions, however. *See, e.g., Center for Int'l Envtl. Law v. Office of the United States Trade Representative*, No. 01–498 (RWR), 2011 WL 1379823, at *5 (D.D.C. Apr. 12, 2011) ("Although a court must defer to agency affidavits predicting harm to the national security, '[d]eference…does not mean acquiescence.'" (citation omitted)).

Can you guess why there is a tendency toward greater judicial deference to executive secrecy claims? Could Exemption 1 be more clearly drawn to eliminate any confusion about this point? Can you suggest amending language? For an argument that courts should be more aggressive in assessing government secrecy claims, see Meredith Fuchs, *Judging Secrets: The Role Courts Should Play in Preventing Unnecessary Secrecy*, 58 Admin. L. Rev. 131 (2006).

2. *In Camera Inspection.* The district court in *Ray v. Turner* abused its discretion by *not* conducting an in camera inspection of the requested documents. In *American Civil Liberties Union v. United States Department of Defense* the district court was found not to have done so. What circumstances led to these different outcomes?

3. *Vaughn Affidavit.* The *Vaughn* affidavit procedure is supposed to represent a practical alternative to the particular burden that courts face in inspecting numerous or voluminous contested documents. It is also designed to give the requester some idea about what is contained in the withheld record so that there will be "adequate adversary testing" of agency exemption claims, as the court put it in *Ray v. Turner. See Halpern v. FBI*, 181 F.3d 279, 285 (2d Cir. 1999) (rejecting as inadequate a *Vaughn* affidavit purporting to justify withholding of files on surveillance of the meat-packing industry: although affiant "wrote much, she said little"). Can you find in the court's opinion in *American Civil Liberties Union v. United States Department of Defense* a test for how much the government must reveal?

Courts are sometimes asked to rely on ex parte government affidavits, *Hayden v. National Sec. Agency/Cent. Sec. Serv.*, 608 F.2d 1381 (D.C. Cir. 1979), or even secret testimony from government witnesses, *Pollard v. FBI*, 705 F.2d 1151 (9th Cir. 1983). If they do so, is any meaningful adversary testing possible? In the absence of requester's counsel, must the court play "devil's advocate" and rehearse the arguments for the requester? In *Arieff v. United States Department of the Navy*, 712 F.2d 1462, 1470-1471 (D.C. Cir. 1983), the court said government affidavits should be considered ex parte and in camera only "where absolutely necessary."

4. *The "Glomar" Principle.* Some agency records are so sensitive that disclosure of their very existence could injure national security. Executive Order No. 13,526 repeats this caution in §3.6(a). The *Glomar* principle is named for the *Hughes Glomar Explorer*, a ship used by the CIA secretly in 1974 to raise a stricken Soviet submarine from the deep ocean floor. *See Phillippi v. CIA*, 546 F.2d 1009 (D.C. Cir. 1976) (upholding refusal to confirm or deny existence of relevant records). In *Hudson River Sloop Clearwater v. Department of the Navy*, 891 F.2d 414 (2d Cir. 1989), the principle allowed the Navy to conceal from a FOIA requester the possible presence of nuclear weapons on ships based in New York Harbor. And in *Minier v. CIA*, 88 F.3d 796 (9th Cir. 1996), the CIA invoked the principle when asked to confirm that it had employed a man who claimed involvement in President Kennedy's assassination. More recently, the CIA successfully invoked the *Glomar* principle in refusing to confirm or deny the existence of documents concerning the rendition of detainees to the Bagram Theater Internment Facility in Afghanistan and their interrogation and treatment there, *American Civil Liberties Union v. Department of Def.*, 752 F. Supp. 2d 361 (S.D.N.Y. 2010). In another case it was invoked when attorneys representing Guantánamo detainees sought National Security Agency (NSA) or Department of Justice (DOJ) records of their communications relating to that representation. *Wilner v. National Security Agency*, 592 F.3d 60 (2d Cir. 2009).

The *Glomar* principle is related to the "mosaic" theory, which has seen increasing use since 9/11. It is invoked in a variety of contexts to withhold bits and pieces of unclassified information that might, according to the theory, be aggregated by an enemy to reveal some important secret. For example, in *Center for National Security Studies v. United States Department of Justice*, 331 F.3d 918, 928 (D.C. Cir. 2003), the court declared that "[a] complete list of names informing terrorists of every suspect detained by the government at any point during the September 11 investigation" could "allow terrorists to better evade the ongoing investigation and more easily formulate or revise counter-efforts." Can you see a potential for abuse with this theory? *See* Christina E. Wells, *CIA v. Sims: Mosaic Theory and Government Attitude*, 58 Admin. L. Rev. 845, 847 (2006) ("mosaic theory too often is a crude tool that results in excessive secrecy by demanding extreme deference from judges when national security is involved"); David E. Pozen, Note, *The Mosaic Theory, National Security, and the Freedom of Information Act*, 115 Yale L.J. 628 (2005).

5. *Classification Procedure.* Exemption 1 permits withholding of materials that "are in fact properly classified" under the relevant executive order. *Ray v. Turner* makes it clear that this requirement has substantive as well as procedural content. But since, according to *American Civil Liberties Union v. United States Department of Defense,* an agency can classify a record or correct an error in the classification

procedure at any time, even after receipt of a FOIA request, does the procedural part of the requirement have any practical significance?

6. *Exemption 3.* What is the purpose of Exemption 3? Does it provide any protection for national security secrets not already afforded by Exemption 1?

In *CIA v. Sims*, 471 U.S. 159 (1985), the Supreme Court applied FOIA Exemption 3 to permit withholding of information under §102(d)(3) of the National Security Act of 1947, currently codified at 50 U.S.C. §403-1(i)(1), which states that the Director of National Intelligence shall "protect intelligence sources and methods from unauthorized disclosure." Based on its reading of "the express intention of Congress [and] the practical necessities of modern intelligence gathering," 471 U.S. at 169, the Court found plenary power in the Director to protect *all* intelligence sources from disclosure, not merely those "who supplied the Agency with information unattainable without guaranteeing confidentiality." *Id.* at 174. Said the Court:

> If potentially valuable intelligence sources come to think that the Agency will be unable to maintain the confidentiality of its relationship to them, many could well refuse to supply information to the Agency in the first place....
>
> We seriously doubt whether a potential intelligence source will rest assured knowing that judges, who have little or no background in the delicate business of intelligence gathering, will order his identity revealed only after examining the facts of the case to determine whether the Agency actually needed to promise confidentiality in order to obtain the information.... Moreover, a court's decision whether an intelligence source will be harmed if his identity is revealed will often require complex political, historical, and psychological judgments. There is no reason for a potential intelligence source, whose welfare and safety may be at stake, to have great confidence in the ability of judges to make those judgments correctly. [*Id.* at 175-176.]

In a separate opinion, Justice Marshall worried that there might be no limit to the information thus shielded from disclosure. "It is difficult to conceive of anything the Central Intelligence Agency might have within its many files that might not disclose or enable an observer to discover something about where the Agency gathers information." *Id.* at 191 (Marshall, J., concurring). Can the Supreme Court's reading of Exemption 3 be squared with the 1976 amendment to FOIA described in *Ray v. Turner*? In an effort to avoid confusion, Congress provided in 2009 that Exemption 3 could only be invoked for future statutes that expressly refer to it. OPEN FOIA Act of 2009, Pub. L. No. 111-83, §564(b), 123 Stat. 2142, 2184 (codified at 5 U.S.C. §552(b)(3)(B)). *See generally* Gina Stevens, *The Freedom of Information Act and Nondisclosure Provisions in Other Federal Laws* (Cong. Res. Serv. R41406), Sept. 24, 2010.

7. *Exemption of Particular Classes of Records.* In 1984, Congress passed the CIA Information Act, 50 U.S.C. §431 (2006), as amended by Pub. L. No. 111-259, §804(6), 124 Stat. 2654, 2747 (2010), exempting most of the CIA's "operational" files, those that describe foreign intelligence and counterintelligence activities, from the search and review requirements of FOIA. Proponents of the measure, including the American Civil Liberties Union, argued that by exempting the agency from searching for files that are almost invariably exempt from disclosure under Exemption 1 or 3 anyway, long delays in answering other requests would be reduced. Judicial review is

available for complaints that records were improperly placed in exempt operational files, but only based on the requester's "personal knowledge or other admissible evidence." *Id.* §431(f)(3). *See* Karen A. Winchester & James W. Zirkle, *Freedom of Information and the CIA Information Act*, 21 U. Rich. L. Rev. 231 (1987).

Congress has also amended FOIA to provide that the FBI need not reveal the existence of classified records pertaining to "foreign intelligence or counterintelligence, or international terrorism." 5 U.S.C. §552(c)(3). Other exemptions apply to operational files of the National Geospatial-Intelligence Agency, NSA, and National Reconnaissance Office. *See An Operational Files Exemption for DIA*, Secrecy News, Jan. 5, 2006.

Do you see any potential for abuse in any of these specific exemptions? If so, can you suggest any way to reduce that potential?

8. *Exemption 5.* FOIA Exemption 5 does not, by its terms, address issues of national security. However, requests for information about national defense and foreign policy are often frustrated by its application. The Supreme Court has interpreted this "somewhat Delphic provision" as "incorporat[ing] the privileges which the Government enjoys under the relevant statutory and case law in the pretrial discovery context." *United States Dep't of Justice v. Julian*, 486 U.S. 1, 11 (1988). The general purpose of Exemption 5 is to withhold "from a member of the public documents which a private party could not discover in litigation with the agency." *National Labor Relations Bd. v. Sears, Roebuck & Co.*, 421 U.S. 132, 148 (1975).

The most important of these discovery privileges for our purposes is the "executive privilege," one aspect of which prevents releases of predecisional communications that would be injurious to the consultative functions of government. For example, in *Russell v. Department of the Air Force*, 682 F.2d 1045 (D.C. Cir. 1982), the court decided that portions of a draft Air Force historical study of the use of the herbicide Agent Orange in Vietnam need not be disclosed to a veterans' organization or a college student writing an honors thesis.

> Exemption (b)(5) shields from the mandatory disclosure requirements of the FOIA the deliberative process that precedes most decisions of government agencies. *Jordan v. United States Dept. of Justice*, 591 F.2d 753, 773 (D.C. Cir. 1978). Thus, the exemption protects not only communications which are themselves deliberative in nature, but all communications which, if revealed, would expose to public view the deliberative process of an agency.... In *Jordan*, Judge Wilkey articulates well the policies behind Exemption (b)(5)'s protection of the deliberative process. He states:
>
>> There are essentially three policy bases for this privilege. First, it protects creative debate and candid consideration of alternatives within an agency, and, thereby, improves the quality of agency policy decisions. Second, it protects the public from the confusion that would result from premature exposure to discussions occurring before the policies affecting it had actually been settled upon. And third, it protects the integrity of the decision-making process itself by confirming that "officials should be judged by what they decided[,] not for matters they considered before making up their minds."

[*Russell*, 682 F.2d at 1047-1048.]

The *Russell* court suggested that any record may, in a sense, be deemed "antecedent to future...decisions." *Id.* at 1049 n.1. If it is true, as Antonio maintained in Shakespeare's play *The Tempest*, that what's past is also prologue, will a requester ever succeed in obtaining a historical report if the agency chooses not to release it? The elements and application of Exemption 5 are described generally in *National Council of La Raza v. Department of Justice*, 411 F.3d 350 (2d Cir. 2005); *Grand Central P'ship, Inc. v. Cuomo*, 166 F.3d 473, 481-482 (2d Cir. 1999).

Concerning the characterization of a communication as "inter-agency or intra-agency," the Supreme Court has ruled that a document prepared for an agency by a truly independent outside consultant may be protected by the exemption, but that advice from an outside entity that has some interest in the agency's decision will not be. *Department of the Interior & Bureau of Indian Affairs v. Klamath Water Users Protective Ass'n*, 532 U.S. 1 (2001). The decision could affect the availability of information about agency contacts with, say, defense contractors or public interest groups.

9. *Exemption 7.* FOIA Exemption 7 is designed to protect certain "records or information compiled for law enforcement purposes." *Center for National Security Studies v. United States Department of Justice*, 331 F.3d 918 (D.C. Cir. 2003), for example, concerned a request for information about persons detained and questioned after 9/11 — more than 700 for immigration law violations, 134 on criminal charges, and others as material witnesses. See Chapter 26. The FOIA plaintiffs sought the names of the detainees and their attorneys, dates of their arrest and release, and reasons for their detention. The court agreed with the government that this was "law enforcement" information, the production of which "could reasonably be expected to interfere with enforcement proceedings," within the meaning of Exemption 7(A). The terrorism investigation, said the court, concerned "a heinous violation of federal law as well as a breach of this nation's security." *Id.* at 926. The court also declared that "the judiciary is in an extremely poor position to second-guess the executive's judgment in this area of national security." *Id.* at 928.

Subsection (D) of Exemption 7 is often invoked in national security or foreign policy cases to prevent disclosure of confidential sources or information furnished by those sources. The importance of secret informants to the conduct of our government can hardly be overstated. Recall the Supreme Court's declaration to this effect in *Central Intelligence Agency v. Sims*, noted above. A "confidential" source need not be a paid informer; it may be anyone given an express or implied assurance of confidentiality by the agency. *Pope v. United States*, 599 F.2d 1383, 1386-1387 (5th Cir. 1979). However, in *United States Department of Justice v. Landano*, 508 U.S. 165 (1993), the Supreme Court rejected a presumption that all sources supplying information to the FBI in a criminal investigation are confidential sources under Exemption 7(D).

10. *Bad Faith.* Agencies do sometimes seem to act in bad faith. In *McGehee v. CIA*, 697 F.2d 1095 (D.C. Cir. 1983), for example, the agency immediately conducted a search that revealed materials relevant to a FOIA request, then waited two and a half years to respond to the requester, after suit was filed in federal court. The agency also searched for records on only one narrow topic requested ("People's Temple") and ignored others ("Jonestown" and "Jim Jones") that were obviously related and relevant to the request. *Id.* at 1098-1100. On rehearing the court decided that the agency nevertheless had not acted in bad faith. 711 F.2d 1076 (D.C. Cir. 1983).

As the *Ray* decision indicates, evidence of agency bad faith may trigger a more thorough judicial review of the requester's complaint. *See Meeropol v. Meese*, 790 F.2d 942, 958 (D.C. Cir. 1986). FOIA §552(a)(4)(F) also requires consideration of disciplinary action against agency personnel who act arbitrarily or capriciously in withholding information. *See* Paul M. Winters, Note, *Revitalizing the Sanctions Provision of the Freedom of Information Act Amendments of 1976*, 84 Geo. L.J. 617 (1996). Is this provision likely to deter misbehavior by agency officials?

11. *Fruits of FOIA.* Is FOIA of any real value in obtaining information about national security or foreign policy matters? District court orders to turn over classified material have rarely been upheld on appeal. Yet the prospect of having to justify its actions before a reviewing court has undoubtedly persuaded some agencies to disclose information that otherwise would not have been made available. For example, in *Miller v. United States Department of State*, 779 F.2d 1378, 1388 (8th Cir. 1985), the requester initially received only seven documents from the agency. Another 56 were released when he filed suit, 72 more when he demanded a pretrial conference, and a total of 232 additional documents before the district court's decision in the case, even though the agency repeatedly insisted that it had already sent all responsive records.

This photographic record of an historic 1970 meeting in the White House was obtained through a FOIA request by the National Security Archive from the National Archives and Records Administration. See http//www.gwu.edu/ nsarchiv/nsa/elvis/elnix.html.

In 1985, former *Washington Post* reporter Scott Armstrong and others founded the National Security Archive in Washington, D.C. Funded by grants, the Archive uses FOIA to collect materials from various agencies, index them, and make them available to the public and Congress. Many of these materials are available online *at* http:// www.gwu.edu/~nsarchiv/. Records relating to national security that were obtained from FOIA requests may also be found on the Web sites of the Federation of American Scientists, http://www.fas.org/; Electronic Frontier Foundation, http://www.fas.org; and a growing number of other online sources.

12. *Other Sources.* In addition to sources cited elsewhere in these notes, the following general references will be helpful to the reader: *Litigation Under the Federal Open Government Laws* (Harry A. Hammitt et al. eds., 25th ed. 2010); James T. O'Reilly, *Federal Information Disclosure* (3d ed. 2000, with updates); National Security Archive, *Effective FOIA Requesting for Everyone: A National Security Archive Guide* (Jan. 2009), *at* http://www.gwu.edu/~nsarchiv/nsa/foia/foia_guide.html; *A Citizen's Guide on Using the Freedom of Information Act and the Privacy Act of 1974 to Request Government Records,* H.R. Rep. No. 109-226 (2005); and various materials found at Department of Justice, *FOIA Resources* (n.d.), *at* http://www.justice.gov/oip/foia-resources.html.

B.   OTHER OPEN GOVERNMENT LAWS

1.   Presidential Records Act

The Presidential Records Act of 1978, 44 U.S.C. §§2201-2207 (2006), requires the President to "assure that the activities, deliberations, decisions, and policies that reflect the performance of his constitutional, statutory, or other official or ceremonial duties are adequately documented" and maintained. *Id.* §2203(a). At the end of the President's term the documents are to be turned over to the Archivist of the United States, who is to make them "available to the public as rapidly and completely as possible consistent with the provisions of this Act." *Id.* §2203(f)(1). However, the outgoing President may require that documents falling into categories roughly paralleling the FOIA exemptions be withheld for up to 12 years. *Id.* §2204(a). Thereafter, public access is controlled by FOIA, except that Exemption 5 is not applicable. *Id.* §2204(c)(1).

Litigation growing out of the Iran-Contra Affair tested the limits of the Act. On January 19, 1989, the final day of the Reagan presidency, the National Security Archive filed FOIA requests for all the material stored on White House electronic communications systems. Simultaneously, the Archive and other plaintiffs filed suit to enjoin the destruction of documents contained in those systems on grounds that they were entitled to protection under the Presidential Records Act and the Federal Records Act, 44 U.S.C. §§2101-2118, 2501-2506, 2901-2910, 3101-3107, 3301-3324 (2006 & Supp. III 2009), the latter setting out requirements for the preservation and disposal of "agency" records. The court held that the Presidential Records Act impliedly precludes judicial review of the President's creation, management, and disposal of records covered by that Act. *Armstrong v. Bush*, 924 F.2d 282, 288-291 (D.C. Cir. 1991). In a subsequent appeal, the same court ruled that the National Security Council, whose records were particularly at issue, is not an "agency" within the meaning of FOIA, *Armstrong v. Executive Office of the President*, 90 F.3d 553 (D.C. Cir. 1996) (see *supra* p. 1204), thus consigning NSC records to administration under the Presidential Records Act and delaying public scrutiny of them. Some of the electronic records at issue in the *Armstrong* case are reproduced in National Security Archive, *White House e-mail* (1995). The lengthy litigation is analyzed in Philip G. Schrag, *Working Papers as Federal Records: The Need for New Legislation to Preserve the History of Federal Policy*, 46 Admin. L. Rev. 95 (1994); James D. Lewis, Note, *White House Electronic Mail and Federal Recordkeeping Law: Press "D" to Delete History*, 93 Mich. L. Rev. 794 (1995).

In the wake of the Watergate scandal, just as in *Armstrong*, concern arose that President Nixon or members of his staff might seek to destroy important historical records that could prove embarrassing or even indicate criminal conduct. Of special interest were Oval Office tape recordings of conversations and telephone calls spanning more than five years. In late 1974, Congress passed the Presidential Recordings and Materials Preservation Act, 44 U.S.C. §2111 note (2006), directing the Archivist to take charge of all materials relating to the Nixon presidency and adopt regulations for public access to them, taking into account, among other factors, "the need to provide the public with the full truth, at the earliest reasonable date, of the abuses of governmental power popularly identified under the generic term 'Watergate.'" *Id.* §104(a)(1). In *Nixon v. Administrator of General Services*, 433 U.S. 425 (1977), the Supreme Court balanced the intrusion into presidential prerogatives against Congress's desire to preserve the materials and make them available to the public, upholding the validity of the Act against charges that it violated the separation of powers, the executive privilege, and the former President's First Amendment rights, as well as the Bill of Attainder Clause, Article I, section 9. *See also Nixon v. Freeman*, 670 F.2d 346 (D.C. Cir.), *cert. denied*, 459 U.S. 1035 (1982) (Act did not violate presidential privilege of confidentiality, right to political association, or Fourth Amendment privacy rights).

Again, on January 19, 1993, just hours before President Clinton's inauguration, outgoing President Bush signed a secret agreement with then-Archivist Don W. Wilson (soon to become head of the George Bush Presidential Studies Center at Texas A&M University) to take charge of thousands of tapes and disks containing White House electronic communications. Presidential information in the materials was to be disposed of only in accordance with instructions from George Bush or his designee. The agreement was struck down as violative of the Presidential Records Act procedure for handling of such materials at the conclusion of a President's term. *American Historical Ass'n v. Peterson*, 876 F. Supp. 1300 (D.D.C. 1995).

Twelve years after President Ronald Reagan left office, when the National Archives and Records Administration announced the impending release of some 68,000 pages of previously undisclosed "confidential communications" of the Reagan presidency, President George W. Bush ordered the release delayed to give him time to decide whether to invoke "a constitutionally based privilege or take other appropriate action." *See* George Lardner Jr., *Bush Clamping Down on Presidential Papers*, Wash. Post., Nov. 1, 2001. The Presidential Records Act provides that "[n]othing in this Act shall be construed to confirm, limit, or expand any constitutionally-based privilege which may be available to an incumbent or former President." 44 U.S.C. §2204(c)(2). Critics accused Bush of seeking to withhold information that might prove embarrassing to his father, who served as Reagan's Vice President, or to several members of his own administration who also held important positions under President Reagan.

President Bush then issued an order invoking various presidential privileges, including the state secrets privilege, see *supra* p. 142, and barring release of any presidential records over the objection of either the incumbent President or the one whose papers are sought. Executive Order No. 13,233, 66 Fed. Reg. 56,025 (Nov. 1, 2001). A coalition of historians and organizations filed suit to compel the release of withheld documents, none of which was subject to withholding under any FOIA exemption. After extended litigation, the court found that the executive order was contrary to the terms of the Presidential Records Act and lacked a valid constitutional basis. *American Historical Ass'n v. National Archives & Records Admin.*, 516 F. Supp. 2d 90 (D.D.C. 2007). Executive Order No. 13,233 was then revoked by President Obama. Exec. Order No. 13,489, *Presidential Records*, 74 Fed. Reg. 4669 (Jan. 21, 2009). *See* Laurent Sacharoff, *Former Presidents and Executive Privilege*, 88 Tex. L. Rev. 301 (2009) (former Presidents should retain no right to assert executive privilege).

2. Privacy Act

The Privacy Act of 1974, 5 U.S.C. §552a (2006), as amended by Pub. L. No. 111-148, §6402(b)(2), 124 Stat. 119, 756 (2010), and Pub. L. No. 111-203, §1082, 124 Stat. 1376, 2080 (2010), was adopted in the wake of revelations that the government compiled secret dossiers on thousands of Americans during the Vietnam War. See *supra* p. 1160. Its purpose is

> to promote governmental respect for the privacy of citizens by requiring all departments and agencies of the executive branch and their employees to observe certain constitutional rules in the computerization, use, and disclosure of personal information about individuals. . . . It is designed to prevent the kind of illegal, unwise, overbroad investigation and record surveillance of law-abiding citizens produced in recent years from actions of some over-zealous investigators, and the curiosity of some government administrators, or the wrongful disclosure and use, in some cases, of personal files held by Federal agencies. . . . It is to prevent the secret gathering of information on people or the creation of secret information systems or data banks on Americans. . . . [S. Rep. No. 93-1183 (1974), *reprinted in* 1974 U.S.C.C.A.N. 6916-6917.]

The Act accomplishes this purpose in five basic ways:

> It requires agencies to publicly report the existence of all systems of records maintained on individuals. It requires that the information contained in these record systems be accurate, complete, relevant, and up-to-date. It provides procedures whereby individuals can inspect and correct inaccuracies in almost all Federal files about themselves. It specifies that information about an individual gathered for one purpose not be used for another without the individual's consent. And, finally, it requires agencies to keep an accurate accounting of the disclosure of records and, with certain exceptions, to make these disclosures available to the subject of the record. In addition, the [Act] provides sanctions to enforce these provisions. [H. Comm. on Government Operations, *A Citizen's Guide on How to Use the Freedom of Information Act and the Privacy Act in Requesting Government Documents*, H.R. Rep. No. 95-793, at 16 (1977).]

An individual may utilize the Privacy Act or FOIA or both to seek access to information about herself in agency records, and she is entitled to the cumulative total of access rights under the two Acts. *Martin v. Office of Special Counsel*, 819 F.2d 1181, 1184 (D.C. Cir. 1987). *See* Thomas M. Susman, *The Privacy Act and the Freedom of Information Act: Conflict and Resolution*, 21 J. Marshall L. Rev. 703 (1988).

By giving access to information about the requester, the Privacy Act may also furnish an alternate route to disclosure of national security information. Privacy Act provisions for access to agency records and for judicial relief generally follow the pattern established in FOIA. Thus, agencies may withhold information that would be subject to FOIA Exemption 1, 5 U.S.C. §552a(k)(1), or that comprises investigatory material for law enforcement purposes. *Id.* §552a(k)(2). Other Privacy Act exemptions generally parallel those in FOIA. Unlike FOIA, however, the Privacy Act enables the CIA and law enforcement agencies to deny access to any "system of records" (e.g., all wiretap transcripts maintained at the FBI indexed by the names of the investigative targets). 5 U.S.C. §552a(j). Can you see why these agencies, which may have the greatest potential for the abuses at which the Act is aimed, are given special protection under the Act? For a suggestion that these "general" exemptions may be so broadly drawn that they threaten constitutional due process rights, see Note, *The Privacy Act of 1974: An Overview*, 1976 Duke L.J. 301, 318-320.

3. Open Meetings Laws

The Government in the Sunshine Act, 5 U.S.C. §552b (2006), and the Federal Advisory Committee Act (FACA), 5 U.S.C. App. 2 §§1-16 (2006), as amended by Pub. L. 111-259, §410(a), 124 Stat. 2654, 2724 (2010), are designed to open up the government decision-making process by giving members of the public an opportunity to attend and perhaps participate in the meetings of deliberative bodies. Each Act contains exemptions analogous to those found in FOIA, permitting meetings to be closed or their transcripts to be withheld. Public access to such meetings may improve the quality of decision making or may stifle creative debate about grave matters of state, depending on one's point of view. *See* Anessa Abrams, *The First Lady: Federal Employee or Citizen-Representative Under FACA?*, 62 Geo. Wash. L. Rev. 855 (1994); Note, *The Government in the Sunshine Act—An Overview*, 1977 Duke L.J. 565, 571-572.

A case involving FACA came before the Supreme Court in 2004. *Cheney v. United States Dist. Court*, 542 U.S. 367 (2004). Public interest groups sought various records of the Vice President's energy policy task force, appointed by President Bush early in his administration. Suing under the Mandamus Act, 28 U.S.C. §1361, and the Administrative Procedure Act, 5 U.S.C. §706, to enforce the disclosure provisions of FACA, the plaintiffs asserted that individuals in the private sector worked so closely with the task force that they became de facto members of it, thereby making it an advisory committee subject to FACA's requirements. To establish this factual predicate, the plaintiffs sought discovery that the Court called "overly broad," since the request covered more information than FACA itself would require to be disclosed. 542 U.S. at 377. On remand, the Court of Appeals reasoned that the alleged de facto private-sector members of the Vice President's energy policy group were not members of an advisory committee covered by FACA, because they had no vote or veto over committee decisions, and the internal communications of the task force could therefore remain confidential. *In re Cheney*, 406 F.3d 723, 728 (D.C. Cir. 2005) (en banc). What, if any, are the implications of the *Cheney* litigation for government decision making that affects national security? *See* Benjamin W. Cramer, *The Power of Secrecy and the Secrecy of Power: FACA and the National Energy Policy Development Group*, 13 Comm. L. & Pol'y 183 (2008). *See generally* Wendy R. Ginsberg, *Federal Advisory Committees: An Overview* (Cong. Res. Serv. R40520), Apr. 16, 2009.

Other Grounds for Access to National Security Information

41

The Freedom of Information Act (FOIA) and its statutory analogues are supposed to enable almost anyone to obtain information about the workings of government for any purpose whatsoever. Nonetheless, exemptions in each statute make many agency records inaccessible. Moreover, none of the open government laws provides for access to government records held by the judicial or legislative branches, or even by some parts of the executive branch.

In this chapter we examine other avenues for obtaining government information relating to national security. In Part A, we consider a right of public access grounded in the common law. Then, in Part B, we address a First Amendment–based "right to know." Finally, in Part C, we analyze the right of Congress to demand national security information from the executive branch.

A. COMMON LAW RIGHT TO KNOW

Schwartz v. United States Department of Justice

United States District Court, District of Columbia, 1977
435 F. Supp. 1203, *aff'd*, 595 F.2d 888 (D.C. Cir. 1979)

PRATT, J. This is an action in which plaintiff seeks certain records from the Department of Justice and Peter A. Rodino, Jr., Chairman of the Committee on the Judiciary of the United States House of Representatives, on the investigation of one Peter R. Schlam. The Department of Justice is sued under the Freedom of Information Act. Mr. Rodino is sued under the common law right of access to public records. The matter is now before the Court on Mr. Rodino's motion to dismiss. Mr. Rodino claims that Congress is not subject to the common law rule which gives citizens a right of access to public records.

The historic common law right to inspect and copy public records is recognized in this jurisdiction. *United States v. Mitchell*, 551 F.2d 1252, 1257 ([D.C. Cir.] 1976). The general rule is that all three branches of government, legislative, executive, and judicial, are subject to the common law right. *Courier-Journal & Louisville Times Co. v. Curtis*, 335 S.W.2d 934, 936 (Ky. 1959), *cert. denied*, 364 U.S. 910 (1960).

Defendant Rodino has set forth no persuasive reason why Congress should be exempted from the common law rule. It is true that Congress has exempted itself from the requirements of the Freedom of Information Act, 5 U.S.C. §552, by 5 U.S.C. §551(1)(A). That Act, however, is not coextensive with the common law rule under discussion. It applies to *all* matters in Government files; the common law rule applies only to "public records." Moreover, we can find no inconsistency or conflict between the Freedom of Information Act and the common law rule. Even if there were an inconsistency or conflict, the Act would have to be construed narrowly, favoring application of the common law, because the Freedom of Information Act is in derogation of the common law.

Accordingly, we hold that Congress is subject to the common law rule which guarantees the public a right to inspect and copy public records. Absent a showing that the matters sought by plaintiff are not "public records" within the meaning of the common law rule or that plaintiff does not possess any "interest" required by the rule, we cannot grant defendant Rodino's motion for dismissal.

If Congress wishes to exempt itself from the common law rule or to impose standards for its application, it has the means to do so readily at its disposal. It has, however, not done so and therefore remains subject to the common law rule.

An order will issue accordingly.

NOTES AND QUESTIONS

1. *FOIA and Common Law Right Compared.* FOIA provides public access to records of "agencies" as that word is defined in 5 U.S.C. §552(f) (2006). The common law right gives access to information in government hands that is broader in one sense but narrower in another. Can you say how?

Do you think Congress intended for FOIA to provide the exclusive means for access to agency records? In *Center for National Security Studies v. United States Department of Justice*, 331 F.3d 918 (D.C. Cir. 2003), plaintiffs asserted a common law right to information about more than 700 post–September 11 detainees held inside the United States. (See Chapter 26.) The government argued that the common law right is limited to judicial records and that, even if that right might otherwise apply to executive records, FOIA has displaced it. The court rejected the government's first argument but accepted the second one:

> FOIA provides an extensive statutory regime for plaintiffs to request the information they seek. Not only is it uncontested that the requested information meets the general category of information for which FOIA mandates disclosure, but for the reasons set forth above, we have concluded that it falls within an express statutory exemption as well. It would make no sense for Congress to have enacted the balanced scheme of disclosure and exemption, and for the court to carefully apply that statutory scheme, and then to turn and determine that the statute had no effect on a preexisting common law right of access. Congress has provided a carefully calibrated statutory scheme, balancing the benefits and harms of disclosure. That scheme preempts any preexisting common law right. . . . [331 F.3d at 936-937.]

Can you reconcile the court's conclusion with the statement in *Schwartz* that "we can find no inconsistency or conflict between the Freedom of Information Act and the common law rule"?

2. *Presumption Favoring Public Access. Nixon v. Warner Communications*, 435 U.S. 589 (1978), involved a broadcaster's assertion of the common law right to obtain from a federal district court copies of Oval Office tape recordings used earlier in the Watergate criminal trials. The Supreme Court found that the plaintiff did not need to demonstrate a proprietary interest in the tapes: "The interest necessary to support the issuance of a writ compelling access has been found, for example, in the citizen's desire to keep a watchful eye on the workings of public agencies, and in a newspaper publisher's intention to publish information concerning the operation of government." *Id.* at 597-598. On the other hand, said the Court, while there is a presumption in favor of public access to judicial records, the right of access is not absolute. A court has discretion to balance that right against proprietary, privacy, and privilege interests of parties resisting release. The Supreme Court decided that the balance was tipped against release because, in its view, Congress intended that the Presidential Recordings and Materials Preservation Act, 44 U.S.C. §2111 note (2006), provide the exclusive means for access to materials of the Nixon presidency. See *supra* p. 1226. Lower courts are divided on the strength of the presumption. *Compare United States v. Myers*, 635 F.2d 945, 952 (2d Cir. 1980) ("only the most compelling circumstances should prevent . . . public access"), *with United States v. McDougal*, 103 F.3d 651 (8th Cir. 1996) (rejecting the strong presumption standard).

3. *"Public Record."* Do you know what a "public record" is? One court calls it "a government document created and kept for the purpose of memorializing or recording an official action, decision, statement, or other matter of legal significance, broadly conceived." *Washington Legal Found. v. United States Sentencing Comm'n*, 89 F.3d 897, 905 (D.C. Cir. 1996). The common law right has been invoked a number of times in federal courts to gain access to evidence in criminal cases. *See, e.g., United States v. Amodeo*, 71 F.3d 1044 (2d Cir. 1995). Also subject to the common law right are records in civil cases, *see, e.g., Hagestad v. Tragesser*, 49 F.3d 1430 (9th Cir. 1995), and nonjudicial records, *see, e.g., Washington Legal Found., supra.* As to whether a report of a congressional investigation is a "public record," compare *Schwartz* with *Pentagen Technologies v. Committee on Appropriations*, 20 F. Supp. 2d 41 (D.D.C. 1998) (reports prepared by staff of House subcommittee protected from compulsory disclosure by the Speech or Debate Clause).

Do you think the "public record" requirement will present an obstacle to disclosure of records addressing national security issues? In *In re Motion for Release of Court Records*, 526 F. Supp. 2d 484 (FISA Ct. 2007), the Foreign Intelligence Surveillance Court (FISC) (described *supra* pp. 583-584) refused to release to the American Civil Liberties Union (ACLU) court orders and government pleadings regarding a top-secret National Security Agency (NSA) program of surveillance of suspected international terrorists. (The so-called Terrorist Surveillance Program is analyzed *supra* p. 609.)

> In the FISA context, there is an unquestioned tradition of secrecy, based on the vitally important need to protect national security. See *Haig v. Agee*, 453 U.S. 280, 307 (1981) (there is no governmental interest more compelling than the security of the nation). The requested records are being maintained under a comprehensive statutory scheme designed to protect FISC records from routine public disclosure. Thus, the statute [FISA], and the Security Procedures adopted thereunder, "occupy this field and would supercede the common law right [of access] even if one existed." *United*

States v. Gonzales, 150 F.3d 1246, 1263 (10th Cir.1998). [*In re Motion for Release of Court Records*, 526 F. Supp. 2d at 490-491.]

In other cases the analysis of national security implications has been more nuanced. Concerning the release of records of FBI investigations into terrorist acts, for example, compare *In re Four Search Warrants*, 945 F. Supp. 1563 (N.D. Ga. 1996) (balancing governmental and public interests and ordering partial release of search warrant affidavits in connection with the Atlanta Olympic Park bombing), with *United States v. McVeigh*, 119 F.3d 806 (10th Cir. 1997) (acknowledging presumption of public availability, but sealing FBI reports and other materials related to bombing of Oklahoma City Murrah Federal Building out of concern for prejudicial pretrial publicity, the danger of impairing law enforcement or judicial efficiency, and privacy interests of third parties).

B.   CONSTITUTIONAL RIGHT TO KNOW

The First Amendment to the U.S. Constitution provides, "Congress shall make no law . . . abridging the freedom of speech, or of the press. . . ." While neither a public nor a press right of access to government information is apparent in this language, Professor Emerson argued that

> [t]he public, as sovereign, must have all information available in order to instruct its servants, the government. As a general proposition, if democracy is to work, there can be no holding back of information; otherwise, ultimate decisionmaking by the people, to whom that function is committed, becomes impossible. Whether or not such a guarantee of the right to know is the sole purpose of the first amendment, it is surely a main element of that provision and should be recognized as such. [Thomas I. Emerson, *Legal Foundations of the Right to Know*, 1976 Wash. U. L.Q. 1, 14.]

Yet the Supreme Court declared in a 1978 jail access case that "[n]either the First Amendment nor the Fourteenth Amendment mandates a right of access to government information or sources of information within the government's control." *Houchins v. KQED, Inc.*, 438 U.S. 1, 15 (1978). Concerning the media in particular, the Court remarked earlier that "the First Amendment does not guarantee the press a constitutional right of special access to information not available to the public generally." *Branzburg v. Hayes*, 408 U.S. 665, 684 (1972).

In 1980, however, the Court recognized a press right to attend criminal trials. *Richmond Newspapers v. Virginia*, 448 U.S. 555 (1980). In a similar case two years later, the Court observed that "the First Amendment serves to ensure that the individual citizen can effectively participate in and contribute to our republican system of self-government." *Globe Newspapers v. Superior Court*, 457 U.S. 596, 604 (1982). Then, in a case involving records of a criminal proceeding, the Supreme Court explained that public access to "governmental processes" will be granted (1) when "there is a tradition of accessibility" — that is, when "the place and process have historically been open to the press and general public," (2) when "public access plays a significant positive role in the functioning of the particular process," and (3) when there is no showing that "closure is essential to preserve higher values and is narrowly tailored to serve that interest." *Press-Enterprise Co. v. Superior Court*, 478 U.S. 1, 8, 9 (1986).

See Eugene Cerruti, *"Dancing in the Courthouse": The First Amendment Right of Access Opens a New Round,* 29 U. Rich. L. Rev. 237 (1995). *See also* Timothy B. Dyk, *Newsgathering, Press Access, and the First Amendment,* 44 Stan. L. Rev. 927 (1992) (arguing that the press should enjoy greater access to government information than the public). These same factors were applied in a recent Espionage Act case to decide the legality of a government proposal for "silent witness" testimony. *United States v. Rosen,* 487 F. Supp. 2d 703 (E.D. Va. 2007), *supra* p. 1032.

Despite the broad language in *Press-Enterprise,* there is considerable uncertainty about the scope of the First Amendment right of access, and the Supreme Court has not addressed the issue again. *Compare WPIX, Inc. v. League of Women Voters,* 595 F. Supp. 1484, 1489 (S.D.N.Y. 1984) ("Under the first amendment, press organizations have a limited right of access to newsworthy events"), *with Foto USA, Inc. v. Board of Regents,* 141 F.3d 1032, 1035 (11th Cir. 1998) ("There is no First Amendment right of access to public information."). Some courts have expressed doubt about the existence of a broader right of access but applied the *Press-Enterprise* criteria anyway. *See, e.g., Capital Cities Media v. Chester,* 797 F.2d 1164 (3d Cir. 1986) (finding no tradition of public access to agency records).

Against this background, lower courts have addressed the scope and applicability of a First Amendment right of access in several cases implicating national security.

North Jersey Media Group, Inc. v. Ashcroft

United States Court of Appeals, Third Circuit, 2002
308 F.3d 198, *cert. denied,* 538 U.S. 1056 (2003)

BECKER, Chief Judge. This civil action was brought in the District Court for the District of New Jersey by a consortium of media groups seeking access to "special interest" deportation hearings involving persons whom the Attorney General has determined might have connections to or knowledge of the September 11, 2001 terrorist attacks. This category was created by a directive issued by Michael Creppy, the Chief United States Immigration Judge, outlining additional security measures to be applied in this class of cases, including closing hearings to the public and the press. Named as defendants in the suit were Attorney General John Ashcroft and Chief Judge Creppy....

As we will now explain in detail, we find that the application of the *Richmond Newspapers* [*Richmond Newspapers, Inc. v. Virginia,* 448 U.S. 555 (1980)] experience and logic tests does not compel us to declare the Creppy Directive unconstitutional....

III. UNDER *RICHMOND NEWSPAPERS,* IS THERE A FIRST AMENDMENT RIGHT TO ATTEND DEPORTATION HEARINGS? ...

A. The "Experience" Test

1. Is there an historical right of access to government proceedings generally?

In *Richmond Newspapers,* 448 U.S. at 575, the Supreme Court acknowledged the State's argument that the Constitution nowhere explicitly guarantees the public's right to attend criminal trials, but it found that right implicit because the Framers drafted the Constitution against a backdrop of longstanding popular access to criminal trials.... Likewise, in *Publicker* [*Industries, Inc. v. Cohen*, 733 F.2d 1059 (3d Cir. 1984),] at 1059, we found a First Amendment right of access to civil trials because at common law, such access had been "beyond dispute."

The history of access to political branch proceedings is quite different. The Government correctly notes that the Framers themselves rejected any unqualified right of access to the political branches for, as we explained in *Capital Cities Media* [*Inc. v. Chester*, 797 F.2d 1164 (3d Cir. 1986)], at 1168-1171, the evidence on this point is extensive and compelling....

This tradition of closing sensitive proceedings extends to many hearings before administrative agencies. For example, although hearings on Social Security disability claims profoundly affect hundreds of thousands of people annually, and have great impact on expenditure of government funds, they are open only to "the parties and to other persons the administrative law judge considers necessary and proper." 20 C.F.R. §404.944. Likewise, administrative disbarment hearings are often presumptively closed....

Faced with this litany of administrative hearings that are closed to the public, the Newspapers... submit that, despite frequent closures throughout the administrative realm, deportation proceedings in particular boast a history of openness sufficient to meet the *Richmond Newspapers* requirement....

2.   Is the history of open deportation proceedings sufficient to satisfy the *Richmond Newspapers* "experience" prong?

For a First Amendment right of access to vest under *Richmond Newspapers*, we must consider whether "the place and process have historically been open to the press and general public," because such a "tradition of accessibility implies the favorable judgment of experience." [*Press-Enterprise Co. v. Superior Court (Press-Enterprise II)*, 478 U.S. 1 (1986)], at 8. Noting preliminarily that the question whether a proceeding has been "historically open" is only arguably an objective inquiry, we nonetheless find that based on both Supreme Court and Third Circuit precedents, the tradition of open deportation hearings is too recent and inconsistent to support a First Amendment right of access.

The strongest historical evidence of open deportation proceedings is that since the 1890s, when Congress first codified deportation procedures, "[t]he governing statutes have always expressly closed *exclusion* hearings, but have *never* closed deportation hearings." (Newspapers' Br. at 30-31.) In 1893, the Executive promulgated the first set of immigration regulations, which expressly stated that exclusion proceedings shall be conducted "separate from the public." *See* Treasury Dept., *Immigration Laws and Regulations* 4 (Washington D.C., Gov't Printing Office 1893). Congress codified those regulations in 1903 and, since that time, it has repeatedly reenacted provisions closing exclusion hearings. In contrast, although Congress codified the regulations governing deportation proceedings in 1904 and has reenacted them many times since, it has never authorized the general closure that has long existed in the exclusion context....

But there is also evidence that, in practice, deportation hearings have frequently been closed to the general public. From the early 1900s, the government has often conducted deportation hearings in prisons, hospitals, or private homes, places where there is no general right of public access. Even in recent times, the government has continued to hold thousands of deportation hearings each year in federal and state prisons. Moreover, hearings involving abused alien children are closed by regulation no matter where they are held, and those involving abused alien spouses are closed presumptively. *See* 8 C.F.R. §3.27(c).

We ultimately do not believe that deportation hearings boast a tradition of openness sufficient to satisfy *Richmond Newspapers*. . . .

IV. DOES THE *RICHMOND NEWSPAPERS* "LOGIC" PRONG, PROPERLY APPLIED, SUPPORT A RIGHT OF ACCESS?

Even if we could find a right of access under the *Richmond Newspapers* logic prong, absent a strong showing of openness under the experience prong, a proposition we do not embrace, we would find no such right here. The logic test compels us to consider "whether public access plays a significant positive role in the functioning of the particular process in question." *Press-Enterprise II*, 478 U.S. at 8. . . .

. . . Under the reported cases, whenever a court has found that openness serves community values, it has concluded that openness plays a "significant positive role" in that proceeding. But that cannot be the story's end, for to gauge accurately whether a role is positive, the calculus must perforce take account of the flip side — the extent to which openness impairs the public good. We note in this respect that, were the logic prong only to determine whether openness serves some good, it is difficult to conceive of a government proceeding to which the public would not have a First Amendment right of access. For example, public access to *any* government affair, even internal CIA deliberations, would "promote informed discussion" among the citizenry. It is unlikely the Supreme Court intended this result.

In this case the Government presented substantial evidence that open deportation hearings would threaten national security. . . .

The Government's security evidence is contained in the declaration of Dale Watson, the FBI's Executive Assistant Director for Counterterrorism and Counterintelligence. Watson presents a range of potential dangers, the most pressing of which we [d]escribe here.

First, public hearings would necessarily reveal sources and methods of investigation. That is information which, "when assimilated with other information the United States may or may not have in hand, allows a terrorist organization to build a picture of the investigation." (Watson Dec. at 4.) Even minor pieces of evidence that might appear innocuous to us would provide valuable clues to a person within the terrorist network, clues that may allow them to thwart the government's efforts to investigate and prevent future acts of violence. *Id.*

Second, "information about how any given individual entered the country (from where, when, and how) may not divulge significant information that would reveal sources and methods of investigation. However, putting entry information into the public realm regarding all 'special interest cases' would allow the terrorist organization to see patterns of entry, what works and what doesn't." *Id.* That information would allow it to tailor future entries to exploit weaknesses in the United States immigration system.

Third, "[i]nformation about what evidence the United States has against members of a particular cell collectively will inform the terrorist organization as to what cells to use and which not to use for further plots and attacks." *Id.* A related concern is that open hearings would reveal what evidence the government lacks. For example, the United States may disclose in a public hearing certain evidence it possesses about a member of a terrorist organization. If that detainee is actually involved in planning an attack, opening the hearing might allow the organization to know that the United States is not yet aware of the attack based on the evidence it presents at the open hearing. *Id.*

Fourth, if a terrorist organization discovers that a particular member is detained, or that information about a plot is known, it may accelerate the timing of a planned attack, thus reducing the amount of time the government has to detect and prevent it. If acceleration is impossible, it may still be able to shift the planned activity to a yet-undiscovered cell. *Id.* at 7.

Fifth, a public hearing involving evidence about terrorist links could allow terrorist organizations to interfere with the pending proceedings by creating false or misleading evidence. Even more likely, a terrorist might destroy existing evidence or make it more difficult to obtain, such as by threatening or tampering with potential witnesses. Should potential informants not feel secure in coming forward, that would greatly impair the ongoing investigation. *Id.* . . .

Finally, Watson represents that "the government cannot proceed to close hearings on a case-by-case basis, as the identification of certain cases for closure, and the introduction of evidence to support that closure, could itself expose critical information about which activities and patterns of behavior merit such closure." (Watson Dec. at 8-9.) Moreover, he explains, given judges' relative lack of expertise regarding national security and their inability to see the mosaic, we should not entrust to them the decision whether an isolated fact is sensitive enough to warrant closure.

The Newspapers are undoubtedly correct that the representations of the Watson Declaration are to some degree speculative, at least insofar as there is no concrete evidence that closed deportation hearings have prevented, or will prevent, terrorist attacks. But the *Richmond Newspapers* logic prong is unavoidably speculative, for it is impossible to weigh objectively, for example, the community benefit of emotional catharsis against the security risk of disclosing the United States' methods of investigation and the extent of its knowledge. We are quite hesitant to conduct a judicial inquiry into the credibility of these security concerns, as national security is an area where courts have traditionally extended great deference to Executive expertise. *See, e.g., Zadvydas v. Davis*, 533 U.S. 678, 696 (2001) (noting that "terrorism or other special circumstances" might warrant "heightened deference to the judgments of the political branches with respect to matters of national security"). *See also Dep't of the Navy v. Egan*, 484 U.S. 518, 530 (1988) (noting that "courts traditionally have been reluctant to intrude upon the authority of the Executive in military and national security affairs"). The assessments before us have been made by senior government officials responsible for investigating the events of September 11th and for preventing future attacks. These officials believe that closure of special interest hearings is necessary to advance these goals, and their concerns, as expressed in the Watson Declaration, have gone unrebutted. To the extent that the Attorney General's national security concerns seem credible, we will not lightly second-guess them.

We are keenly aware of the dangers presented by deference to the executive branch when constitutional liberties are at stake, especially in times of national crisis, when those liberties are likely in greatest jeopardy. On balance, however, we are unable to conclude that openness plays a positive role in special interest deportation hearings at a time when our nation is faced with threats of such profound and unknown dimension.

V. CONCLUSION...

Because we find that open deportation hearings do not pass the two-part *Richmond Newspapers* test, we hold that the press and public possess no First Amendment right of access. . . .

[The opinion of SCIRICA, Circuit Judge, dissenting, is omitted.]

NOTES AND QUESTIONS

1. *Closing the Door on Democracy?* In another case on identical facts that was decided at almost the same moment, a Sixth Circuit Court of Appeals panel reached a dramatically different result. *Detroit Free Press v. Ashcroft*, 303 F.3d 681 (6th Cir. 2002). Concerning the "experience" prong of the *Richmond Newspapers* test, the court found that deportation hearings have historically been open. Moreover, said the court,

> to paraphrase the Supreme Court, deportation hearings "walk, talk, and squawk" very much like a judicial proceeding. Substantively, we look to other proceedings that have the same effect as deportation. Here, the only other federal court that can enter an order of removal is a United States District Court during sentencing in a criminal trial. *See* 8 U.S.C.A. §1228(c) (2002). At common law, beginning with the Transportation Act of 1718, the English criminal courts could enter an order of transportation or banishment as a sentence in a criminal trial. As *Richmond Newspapers* discussed in great length, these types of criminal proceedings have historically been open. *Richmond Newspapers*, 448 U.S. at 564-74. [303 F.3d at 702.]

As for the "logic" prong, the Sixth Circuit panel declared that public access "undoubtedly enhances the quality of deportation proceedings." *Id.* at 703.

> First, public access acts as a check on the actions of the Executive by assuring us that proceedings are conducted fairly and properly. In an area such as immigration, where the government has nearly unlimited authority, the press and the public serve as perhaps the only check on abusive government practices.
>
> Second, openness ensures that government does its job properly; that it does not make mistakes. . . .
>
> Third, after the devastation of September 11 and the massive investigation that followed, the cathartic effect of open deportations cannot be overstated. They serve a "therapeutic" purpose as outlets for "community concern, hostility, and emotions." . . .
>
> Fourth, openness enhances the perception of integrity and fairness. "The value of openness lies in the fact that people not actually attending trials can have confidence that standards of fairness are being observed . . . ." . . .
>
> Fifth, public access helps ensure that "the individual citizen can effectively participate in and contribute to our republican system of self-government." *Globe Newspaper*, 457 U.S. at 604. "[A] major purpose of [the First Amendment] was to protect the free discussion of governmental affairs." *Id.* Public access to deportation proceedings helps inform the public of the affairs of the government. Direct knowledge of how their government is operating enhances the public's ability to affirm or protest government's efforts. When government selectively chooses what information it allows the public to see, it can become a powerful tool for deception. . . . [303 F.3d at 703-705.]

Finding a First Amendment right of access, the Sixth Circuit panel then decided that "the Creppy directive is neither narrowly tailored, nor does it require particularized findings [in individual cases]. Therefore, it impermissibly infringes on the Newspaper Plaintiffs' First Amendment right of access." *Id.* at 705. The court punctuated its ruling with this widely quoted passage:

In our democracy, based on checks and balances, neither the Bill of Rights nor the judiciary can second-guess government's choices. The only safeguard on this extraordinary governmental power is the public, deputizing the press as the guardians of their liberty. "An informed public is the most potent of all restraints upon misgovernment[.]" *Grosjean v. Am. Press Co.*, 297 U.S. 233, 250 (1936). "[They] alone can here protect the values of democratic government." *New York Times v. United States*, 403 U.S. 713, 728 (1971) (per curiam) (Stewart, J., concurring).

Today, the Executive Branch seeks to take this safeguard away from the public by placing its actions beyond public scrutiny. Against non-citizens, it seeks the power to secretly deport a class if it unilaterally calls them "special interest" cases. The Executive Branch seeks to uproot people's lives, outside the public eye, and behind a closed door. Democracies die behind closed doors. The First Amendment, through a free press, protects the people's right to know that their government acts fairly, lawfully, and accurately in deportation proceedings. When government begins closing doors, it selectively controls information rightfully belonging to the people. Selective information is misinformation. The Framers of the First Amendment "did not trust any government to separate the true from the false for us." *Kleindienst v. Mandel*, 408 U.S. 753, 773 (1972) (quoting *Thomas v. Collins*, 323 U.S. 516, 545 (Jackson, J., concurring)). They protected the people against secret government. [303 F.3d at 683.]

Because of the importance of these two cases, as well as the sharp split between the circuits, many were surprised by the Supreme Court's decision to deny certiorari in the *North Jersey Media* case. What, if anything, do you think this portends for First Amendment–based access to government activities and information in the future?

2. *Relationship of the First Amendment Right to National Security.* How would you compare the general attitudes of the Third and Sixth Circuit courts about their roles in cases implicating the national security? In its analysis of the *Richmond Newspapers* logic prong, the *North Jersey Media* court accepted government arguments that disclosure would not serve the public good, because it would reveal sources and methods of investigation, and other information that might be helpful to terrorists. "To the extent that the Attorney General's national security concerns seem credible," the court observed, "we will not lightly second-guess them." 308 F.3d at 219. Do you think the court should have been so deferential? How would you try to persuade this court that a First Amendment right existed to information about national security?

In *In re Motion for Release of Court Records*, 526 F. Supp. 2d 484 (FISA Ct. 2007), the FISC held that there was no First Amendment right of access to court records concerning the NSA's warrantless electronic surveillance program — the Terrorist Surveillance Program (TSP). The FISC, whose proceedings are never open to the public, and which had published only three opinions in nearly three decades, noted that it has no tradition of openness, as required by *Press-Enterprise II*, and that it fails the "logic" test because "[t]he identification of targets and methods of surveillance would permit adversaries to evade surveillance, conceal their activities, and possibly mislead investigators through false information," among other security concerns.

In weighing the public interest, should the court have considered the possibility that the surveillance program in question was illegal? The TSP is examined *supra* p. 609.

3. *The Detainees Redux.* In a suit seeking information about more than 700 persons detained inside the United States in the wake of the September 11 attacks, see Chapter 26, the court considered and rejected First Amendment grounds for releasing the names of the detainees. *Center for Nat'l Sec. Studies v. United States Dep't of Justice,* 331 F.3d 918 (D.C. Cir. 2003).

> The narrow First Amendment right of access to information recognized in *Richmond Newspapers* does not extend to non-judicial documents that are not part of a criminal trial, such as the investigatory documents at issue here. . . .
>
> We will not convert the First Amendment right of access to criminal judicial proceedings into a requirement that the government disclose information compiled during the exercise of a quintessential executive power — the investigation and prevention of terrorism. . . . To be sure, the Sixth Circuit recently held that the public has a constitutional right of access to INS deportation hearings involving the same INS detainees at issue in this case. *See Detroit Free Press; but see North Jersey Media Group* (finding no right of access). However, the Sixth Circuit applied *Richmond Newspapers* only after extensively examining the similarity between deportation proceedings and criminal trials, *Detroit Free Press,* 303 F.3d at 696-99, and noting the crucial distinction between "*investigatory* information" and "access to information relating to a governmental *adjudicative* process," *Id.* at 699. Inasmuch as plaintiffs here request investigatory — not adjudicative — information, we find *Detroit Free Press* distinguishable. We therefore will not expand the First Amendment right of public access to require disclosure of information compiled during the government's investigation of terrorist acts. [331 F.3d at 933-934.]

In a more recent case involving the detainees, however, the court found both a First Amendment and common law right of public access in habeas cases, which are civil proceedings, to unclassified factual returns (containing information about the identity of detainees and what they were accused of doing). *In re Guantanamo Bay Detainee Litig.,* 624 F. Supp. 2d 27 (D.D.C. 2009).

Given the history of litigation described here, can courts be counted on generally to recognize a First Amendment right of access to national security information? *See* Mary-Rose Papandrea, *Under Attack: The Public's Right to Know and the War on Terror,* 25 B.C. Third World L.J. 35, 79-80 (2005) ("[S]ince the terrorist attacks of September 11 . . . courts now appear overtly hostile to the very existence of a right of access during a time of crisis.").

4. *Media Access to Terrorism Trials.* During the criminal prosecution of Zacarias Moussaoui for his alleged involvement in the September 11 terrorist attacks, see *supra* p. 1043, a consortium of media companies asserted common law and First Amendment rights of access to sealed records of pleadings, discovery materials, and oral arguments that included some information classified as top secret. The court rejected the government's argument that the Classified Information Procedures Act (CIPA), 18 U.S.C. App. 3 §§1-16 (2006 & Supp. III 2009), analyzed in Chapter 35, could alone override a constitutional right of access. *United States v. Moussaoui,* 65 Fed. Appx. 881, 887-888 (4th Cir. 2003). Instead, the court determined that the "interest of the public in the flow of information is protected by our exercising independent judgment concerning redactions" of materials from the records. *Id.* at 888. As for access to

appellate proceedings, the court ordered bifurcated hearings. Arguments not involving the discussion of classified information would be open to the public, while others would be conducted in a sealed courtroom, followed by the prompt release of a redacted transcript. *Id.* at 890. The litigation is analyzed in Cameron Stracher, *Eyes Tied Shut: Litigating for Access Under CIPA in the Government's "War on Terror,"* 48 N.Y.L. Sch. L. Rev. 173 (2003).

Media access to military commission proceedings at the Guantánamo Bay Naval Base has been uneven and very controversial. *See* National Inst. of Military Justice, *Public Trials* 2 (n.d.), *at* http://www.wcl.american.edu/nimj/documents/19_publictrials_final.pdf?rd=1 ("the actual practice of the military commissions has been to err on the side of caution by making heavy presumptions in favor of exclusion," but noting several rulings that have balanced interests to allow public access). Equally controversial is a provision of the Military Commissions Act of 2009 that gives a military judge authority to close military commission proceedings to the public (and the press) when she finds it necessary to "protect information the disclosure of which could reasonably be expected to cause damage to the national security." 10 U.S.C. §949d(c) (Supp. III 2009). *See Public Trials, supra.* Do you think such a closure would survive a First Amendment challenge from a representative of the media?

5. *Media Access to the Battlefield.* For more than two centuries the press enjoyed virtually unrestricted access to America's battlefields, although there were some constraints on reporting, with no apparent breaches of security. *See* Michael D. Steger, *Slicing the Gordian Knot: A Proposal to Reform Military Regulation of Media Coverage of Combat Operations,* 28 U.S.F. L. Rev. 957, 960-967 (1994); C. Robert Zelnick, *Military Secrets and First Amendment Values,* 1 J. Nat'l Security L. 21, 23-26 (1997). Television coverage of the Vietnam War, however, was blamed (or credited) for turning public opinion against U.S. military involvement in Southeast Asia, especially after the Tet offensive in 1968.

That all changed with the U.S. invasion of Grenada in 1983, when reporters were barred from that small Caribbean island until the fighting was long over. Press access was severely restricted during the 1990-1991 Persian Gulf conflict out of concern, the Pentagon declared, that with satellite uplink TV broadcasts and instant Internet news, "news media [are] able to broadcast reports instantaneously to the world, including the enemy." Department of Def., *Conduct of the Persian Gulf War: Final Report to Congress* (PB92-163674) at S-2 (Apr. 1992). "[R]eporters might not realize the sensitivity of certain information and might inadvertently divulge details of military plans, capabilities, operations, or vulnerabilities that would jeopardize the outcome of an operation or the safety of U.S. or other Coalition forces." *Id.* at S-4. A severely limited number of media representatives were allowed into Kuwait, but they had to be accompanied at all times by military escorts, whom reporters viewed as attempting to control rather than facilitate news coverage. Many news stories dispatched from the front were delayed — sometimes for days — at the military press center in Dhahran. Meanwhile, the Pentagon conducted its own carefully orchestrated public relations campaign, with daily press briefings and film footage of precision bombing raids. *See* John R. MacArthur, *Second Front: Censorship and Propaganda in the Gulf War* (1992); Marianne D. Short & Jodene Pope, *History and Scope of the Press' Right of Access to Foreign Battlefields,* 41 Naval L. Rev. 1, 8 (1993). The restrictions on media access were challenged on First Amendment grounds. The court, ruling after a cease-fire had been signed with Saddam Hussein, declined to grant declaratory relief, calling the issue "highly abstract," and leaving a decision until another conflict when "a full record is available." *Nation Magazine v. United States Dep't of Def.*, 762 F. Supp. 1558, 1572 (S.D.N.Y. 1991).

Media coverage of U.S. military operations in Afghanistan after 9/11 was said to be even more restricted than in the Persian Gulf War. *See* Carol Morello, *Tight Control Marks Coverage of Afghan War*, Wash. Post, Dec. 7, 2001. Defense Secretary Donald Rumsfeld said he was "committed to the principle that the media should have access to both the good and the bad in this effort." *Id.* But reporters in a small group allowed into Afghanistan were

> not permitted to accompany troops..., were prohibited from reporting much of what they saw, were diverted toward feature stories such as church services and promotion ceremonies, were not allowed to speak to [most] senior commanders, and were barred from reporting details even after they were leaked—and announced—by the Pentagon. [*Id.*]

See Flynt v. Rumsfeld, 355 F.3d 697 (D.C. Cir.), *cert. denied*, 543 U.S. 925 (2004) (upholding restrictions). The Pentagon also commissioned secret profiles on the work of journalists reporting from Afghanistan, and those profiles reportedly were used to deny disfavored reporters access to some fighting units. Leo Shane III, *Army Used Profiles to Reject Reporters*, Stars & Stripes, Aug. 29, 2009.

The Pentagon dramatically revised its rules for press access to the battlefield during the 2003 invasion of Iraq. It "embedded" some 775 print and broadcast journalists into a number of military units, although only about 50 or 60 had "front row seats" for combat. *See Public Affairs Guidance on Embedding Media* (Feb. 10, 2003) (*Guidelines*), *at* http://www.defenselink.mil/news/Feb2003/d20030228pag.pdf. In return for access, reporters had to follow broad guidelines about what could be covered and what could not. Unit commanders could "impose temporary restrictions on electronic transmissions for operational security reasons," and reporters had to "seek approval to use electronic devices in a combat/hostile environment." *Id.* ¶2.C.4. Disputes about coverage of particular events were left to be worked out between reporters and unit commanders. *Id.* ¶6. Commanders were to "ensure that media are provided with every opportunity to observe actual combat operations," but reporters could be given "escorts." *Id.* ¶¶3.F., 3.G. There was no general review process for media products, as there was during the 1991 Persian Gulf War, but embargoes could be imposed "to protect operational security." *Id.* ¶¶3.R., 4.E. *See generally* Alicia C. Shepard, *Narrowing the Gap: Military, Media, and the Iraq War* (McCormick Tribune Found., 2004); Elana J. Zeide, *In Bed with the Military: First Amendment Implications of Embedded Journalism*, 80 N.Y.U. L. Rev. 1309 (2005).

Do you think it is important for the public (and Congress) to be able to receive current information about military operations from nongovernment sources? If you believe that there is a First Amendment–based right of battlefield access, do Pentagon restrictions (in the form of conditions for access) impermissibly infringe that right? *See* David A. Anderson, *Freedom of the Press in Wartime*, 77 U. Colo. L. Rev. 49 (2006) (Press Clause should be read as imposing limits on the government's ability to manipulate public opinion by restricting war coverage); Christiaan Highsmith, Note, *The Liberty-Speech Framework: Resolving the Tension Between Foreign Affairs Power and First Amendment Freedoms*, 88 B.U. L. Rev. 745 (2008) (linking First Amendment press right to Fifth Amendment right to travel to gather news).

6. *The Case That Didn't Exist.* In what may (or may not) be a common occurrence, a federal district court and court of appeals conducted secret hearings and issued secret rulings in a habeas corpus case that appeared on no public record. *M.K.B. v. Warden,* 540 U.S. 1213 (2004), concerned an Algerian waiter in south Florida who was detained by immigration authorities and questioned by the FBI. The case was discovered by a reporter only because of an appeals court clerk's docketing error. Despite arguments by news organizations that the First Amendment and common law right of access required unsealing the records, the Supreme Court refused, without comment, to grant certiorari, following submission of a sealed brief by the Solicitor General. Thus, the government's theory of the case, like the fate of the detainee, is completely unknown, although we might assume that it included the arguments made earlier in *North Jersey Media.* The story is reported in Linda Greenhouse, *News Groups Seek to Open Secret Case,* N.Y. Times, Jan. 5, 2004; Dan Christensen, *Plea for Openness,* Miami Daily Bus. Rev., Nov. 5, 2003. Other cases totally or partially "off the record" are described in *"Sealed v. Sealed": How Courts Confront State Secrets,* Secrecy News, June 29, 2006; Julia Preston, *Judge Issues Secret Ruling in Case of 2 at Mosque,* N.Y. Times, Mar. 11, 2006. *See* Meliah Thomas, *The First Amendment Right of Access to Docket Sheets,* 94 Cal. L. Rev. 1537 (2006).

C.   CONGRESS'S RIGHT OF ACCESS TO NATIONAL SECURITY INFORMATION

It is hardly surprising that the two political branches of government sometimes compete with each other. That competition is nowhere keener than in the quest for—or the protection of—information about national security. Recall that President Washington resisted efforts by the House of Representatives to learn details about the negotiation of the Jay Treaty of 1795. See *supra* p. 57. Two centuries later, Congress was seeking to carve out a larger role for itself in intelligence collection and covert actions, long considered executive prerogatives. See Chapters 16 and 17. Here we explore constitutional, statutory, and practical dimensions of this competition for information, noting carefully the part that courts play as referee.

McGrain v. Daugherty
United States Supreme Court, 1927
273 U.S. 135

[In the course of investigating the administration of the Department of Justice, a select Senate committee issued a subpoena to compel the testimony of a private witness. When the witness refused to comply, the committee ordered his arrest. After his arrest, he brought a petition for habeas corpus, challenging, *inter alia,* the Senate's constitutional authority to investigate. The lower court granted his petition and this appeal followed.]

Mr. Justice VAN DEVANTER delivered the opinion of the court.... The first of the principal questions—the one which the witness particularly presses on our attention—is, as before shown, whether the Senate—or the House of Representatives—both being on the same plane in this regard—has power, through its own process, to compel a private individual to appear before it or one of its committees and give testimony needed to enable it efficiently to exercise a legislative function belonging to it under the Constitution.

The Constitution provides for a Congress consisting of a Senate and House of Representatives and invests it with "all legislative powers" granted to the United States, and with power "to make all laws which shall be necessary and proper" for carrying into execution these powers and "all other powers" vested by the Constitution in the United States or in any department or officer thereof. Article 1, §§1, 8. Other provisions show that, while bills can become laws only after being considered and passed by both houses of Congress, each house is to be distinct from the other, to have its own officers and rules, and to exercise its legislative function independently. Article 1, §§2, 3, 5, 7. But there is no provision expressly investing either house with power to make investigations and exact testimony, to the end that it may exercise its legislative function advisedly and effectively. So the question arises whether this power is so far incidental to the legislative function as to be implied.

In actual legislative practice, power to secure needed information by such means has long been treated as an attribute of the power to legislate. It was so regarded in the British Parliament and in the Colonial legislatures before the American Revolution; and a like view has prevailed and been carried into effect in both houses of Congress and in most of the state Legislatures.

This power was both asserted and exerted by the House of Representatives in 1792, when it appointed a select committee to inquire into the St. Clair expedition and authorized the committee to send for necessary persons, papers and records. Mr. Madison, who had taken an important part in framing the Constitution only five years before, and four of his associates in that work, were members of the House of Representatives at the time, and all voted for the inquiry. 3 Cong. Ann. 494. Other exertions of the power by the House of Representatives, as also by the Senate, are shown in the citations already made. Among those by the Senate, the inquiry ordered in 1859 respecting the raid by John Brown and his adherents on the armory and arsenal of the United States at Harper's Ferry is of special significance. The resolution directing the inquiry authorized the committee to send for persons and papers, to inquire into the facts pertaining to the raid and the means by which it was organized and supported, and to report what legislation, if any, was necessary to preserve the peace of the country and protect the public property. . . .

We are of opinion that the power of inquiry — with process to enforce it — is an essential and appropriate auxiliary to the legislative function. It was so regarded and employed in American Legislatures before the Constitution was framed and ratified. Both houses of Congress took this view of it early in their history — the House of Representatives with the approving votes of Mr. Madison and other members whose service in the convention which framed the Constitution gives special significance to their action — and both houses have employed the power accordingly up to the present time. The acts of 1798 and 1857, judged by their comprehensive terms, were intended to recognize the existence of this power in both houses and to enable them to employ it "more effectually" than before. So, when their practice in the matter is appraised according to the circumstances in which it was begun and to those in which it has been continued, it falls nothing short of a practical construction, long continued, of the constitutional provisions respecting their powers, and therefore should be taken as fixing the meaning of those provisions, if otherwise doubtful.

We are further of opinion that the provisions are not of doubtful meaning, but, as was held by this Court in the cases we have reviewed, are intended to be effectively exercised, and therefore to carry with them such auxiliary powers as are necessary and appropriate to that end. While the power to exact information in aid of the legislative function was not involved in those cases, the rule of interpretation applied there is applicable here. A legislative body cannot legislate wisely or effectively in the absence of information respecting the conditions which the legislation is intended to affect or change; and where the legislative body does not itself possess the requisite information — which not infrequently is true — recourse must be had to others who do possess it. Experience has taught that mere requests for such information often are unavailing, and also that information which is volunteered is not always accurate or complete; so some means of compulsion are essential to obtain what is needed. All this was true before and when the Constitution was framed and adopted. In that period the power of inquiry — with enforcing process — was regarded and employed as a necessary and appropriate attribute of the power to legislate — indeed, was treated as inhering in it. Thus there is ample warrant for thinking, as we do, that the constitutional provisions which commit the legislative function to the two houses are intended to include this attribute to the end that the function may be effectively exercised.

The contention is earnestly made on behalf of the witness that this power of inquiry, if sustained, may be abusively and oppressively exerted. If this be so, it affords no ground for denying the power. The same contention might be directed against the power to legislate, and of course would be unavailing. We must assume, for present purposes, that neither house will be disposed to exert the power beyond its proper bounds, or without due regard to the rights of witnesses. But if, contrary to this assumption, controlling limitations or restrictions are disregarded, the decisions in *Kilbourn v. Thompson* [103 U.S. 168 (1881)] and *Marshall v. Gordon* [243 U.S. 521 (1917)] point to admissible measures of relief. And it is a necessary deduction from the decisions in *Kilbourn v. Thompson* and *In re Chapman* [166 U.S. 661 (1897)] that a witness rightfully may refuse to answer where the bounds of the power are exceeded or the questions are not pertinent to the matter under inquiry.

We come now to the question whether it sufficiently appears that the purpose for which the witness's testimony was sought was to obtain information in aid of the legislative function. The court below answered the question in the negative and put its decision largely on this ground. . . .

It is quite true that the resolution directing the investigation does not in terms avow that it is intended to be in aid of legislation; but it does show that the subject to be investigated was the administration of the Department of Justice — whether its functions were being properly discharged or were being neglected or misdirected, and particularly whether the Attorney General and his assistants were performing or neglecting their duties in respect of the institution and prosecution of proceedings to punish crimes and enforce appropriate remedies against the wrongdoers — specific instances of alleged neglect being recited. Plainly the subject was one on which legislation could be had and would be materially aided by the information which the investigation was calculated to elicit. This becomes manifest when it is reflected that the functions of the Department of Justice, the powers and duties of the Attorney General and the duties of his assistants are all subject to regulation by congressional legislation, and that the department is maintained and its activities are carried on under such appropriations as in the judgment of Congress are needed from year to year.

The only legitimate object the Senate could have in ordering the investigation was to aid it in legislating; and we think the subject-matter was such that the presumption should be indulged that this was the real object. An express avoval of the object would have been better; but in view of the particular subject-matter was not indispensable. . . .

We conclude that the investigation was ordered for a legitimate object; that the witness wrongfully refused to appear and testify before the committee and was lawfully attached; that the Senate is entitled to have him give testimony pertinent to the inquiry, either at its bar or before the committee; and that the district court erred in discharging him from custody under the attachment. . . .

Mr. Justice STONE did not participate in the consideration or decision of the case.

NOTES AND QUESTIONS

1. *Constitutional Basis for Investigation and Oversight.* What constitutional theories support Congress's power of investigation? According to one expert, "Congress's oversight authority derives from its 'implied' powers in the Constitution, public laws, and House and Senate rules. It is an integral part of the American system of checks and balances." Frederick M. Kaiser, *Congressional Oversight* 1 (Cong. Res. Serv. 97-936 GOV), Jan. 3, 2006. In a more recent case involving the Navy, a court of appeals asserted that "[t]here is no doubt that Congress constitutionally can act, without recourse to the full legislative procedure of bicameral passage and presentment, to investigate the conduct of executive officials and others outside the legislative branch; . . . and to influence the executive through the 'illuminating power of investigation.'" *Lear Siegler, Inc. Energy Prods. Div. v. Lehman,* 842 F.2d 1102, 1109 (9th Cir. 1988) (dictum) (quoting *Ameron, Inc. v. United States Army Corps of Eng'rs,* 809 F.2d 979, 992 (3d Cir. 1986)). In addition to the theories discussed in *McGrain, see United States v. American Telephone & Telegraph Co.,* 551 F.2d 384, 394 (D.C. Cir. 1976) (suggesting in dictum that "Congress's power to monitor executive actions is implicit in the appropriations power"). Does *McGrain* suggest any limitations or conditions on this power? *See generally* Heidi Kitrosser, *Congressional Oversight of National Security Activities: Improving Information Funnels,* 29 Cardozo L. Rev. 1049 (2008).

The congressional oversight process is described extensively in Frederick M. Kaiser, Walter J. Oleszek & Todd B. Tatelman, *Congressional Oversight Manual* (Cong. Res. Serv. RL30240), May 19, 2011.

2. *House Resolutions of Inquiry.* Although *McGrain* involved a subpoena to a private witness, an alternative procedure in the House is a *resolution of inquiry,* "a simple resolution making a direct request or demand of the President or the head of an executive department to furnish the House of Representatives with specific factual information in the possession of the executive branch." Louis Fisher, *House Resolutions of Inquiry* 1 (Cong. Res. Serv. RL31909), May 12, 2003 (quoting *Deschler's Precedents,* H.R. Doc. No. 94-661, vol. 7, ch. 24, §8 (1977)). *See also* Louis Fisher, *Congressional Access to Information: Using Legislative Will and Leverage,* 52 Duke L.J. 323 (2002). However, such resolutions have left broad discretion in the executive concerning what information it must produce. In 1952, for example, the House passed a resolution of inquiry directing the Secretary of State to transmit "full and

complete information" regarding any agreements entered into by President Truman and Prime Minister Winston Churchill regarding the deployment of U.S. armed forces beyond the continental limits of the United States or in armed conflict on foreign soil. Fisher, *House Resolutions, supra,* at 9. But even its sponsors said in debate, "We cannot by this resolution make the Executive answer. . . . All we can do, if we pass this resolution, is to say to the Secretary of State and the Department of State: 'Please try again. That answer you sent down was not very good.' " *Id.* (quoting 98 Stat. 1205, 1208 (1952)). Nevertheless, such resolutions were sought often during the Vietnam War to request copies of the Pentagon Papers, information about U.S. covert operations in Laos, and information on military operations in Cambodia, among other matters. *Id.* at 17-20. Even when such resolutions fail, "a substantial amount of information is usually released to Congress." *Id.* at 25. In fact, arguments that the Administration has complied with a resolution are frequently the reason for reporting a resolution adversely and tabling it." *Id.*

3. *Executive Privilege.* "Executive privilege" refers to a group of executive branch justifications for resisting disclosure of information to the public or the other branches. One justification is that the information is a state secret, disclosure of which would jeopardize the nation's security. See *supra* pp. 142-159. Another justification is that the information consists of intrabranch deliberative communications, disclosure of which would chill the candor and usefulness of such communications. A third is designed similarly to preserve the confidentiality of presidential communications. *See United States v. Nixon,* 418 U.S. 683, 705 (1974) ("Human experience teaches that those who expect public dissemination of their remarks may well temper candor with a concern for appearances and for their own interest to the detriment of the decision making process."). *See generally* Mark J. Rozell, *Executive Privilege: The Dilemma of Secrecy and Democratic Accountability* (1994).

Executive privilege was invoked in 2007 to resist compliance with subpoenas from Senate and House committees investigating what some believed were politically motivated firings of a number of U.S. Attorneys. *See* Letter from Fred F. Fielding, Counsel to the President, to Senator Patrick J. Leahy and Representative John Conyers (Aug. 20, 2007). The White House also denied that the information sought was "critically important to any legislative initiatives that you may be pursuing or intending to pursue." *Id. See also* Letter from Paul D. Clement, Solicitor General and Acting Attorney General, to the President (June 27, 2007) (containing a legal analysis of the claim).

But when the Senate Judiciary Committee issued subpoenas for documents relating to the secret NSA warrantless electronic surveillance program — the Terrorist Surveillance Program — the White House simply refused to comply, declaring that the documents requested were "potentially subject to claims of executive privilege." Letter from Fred F. Fielding, Counsel to the President, to Senator Patrick Leahy (Aug. 20, 2007). The conflict was defused when Congress enacted amendments to FISA that apparently approved the secret program. See *supra* p. 619.

4. *Congress's Power to Compel.* Usually, conflicts between Congress and the executive branch about information are resolved by negotiation. *See* Louis Fisher, *Invoking Executive Privilege: Navigating Ticklish Political Waters,* 8 Wm. & Mary Bill Rts. J. 583 (2000); Neal Devins, *Congressional-Executive Information Access Disputes: A Modest Proposal — Do Nothing,* 48 Admin. L. Rev. 109 (1996); Peter M. Shane, *Legal*

Disagreement and Negotiation in a Government of Laws: The Case of Executive Privilege Claims Against Congress, 71 Minn. L. Rev. 462 (1987); 13 Op. O.L.C. 190-193 (1989). *But see* Randall K. Miller, *Congressional Inquests: Suffocating the Constitutional Prerogative of Executive Privilege*, 81 Minn. L. Rev. 631 (1997) (advocating earlier judicial resolution in order to provide full protection to the privilege). Why do you think this is so?

What options are open to Congress when an agreement with the executive branch cannot be reached? Any person—private citizen or government official—who refuses to comply with a congressional subpoena for testimony or documents may be liable for contempt of Congress. Congress has made contempt a misdemeanor. The House or Senate may certify a citation for contempt to the U.S. Attorney, who is ordinarily expected to bring the matter before a grand jury. 2 U.S.C. §192 (2006). What problems can you imagine in using this statute to enforce information demands against the executive branch? *See generally* Morton Rosenberg & Todd B. Tatelman, *Congress's Contempt Power: Law, History, Practice, and Procedure* (Cong. Res. Serv. RL34097), Apr. 15, 2008 (examining the source of contempt power, historical development, statutory and common law basis, and procedures for each type of contempt proceeding).

In 1982, after Environmental Protection Agency Administrator Ann Gorsuch was cited for contempt by the House for her refusal to comply with a congressional subpoena, the Justice Department not only refused to go before the grand jury but sued the House, seeking a declaratory judgment that she need not comply. The suit was dismissed as premature, because claims of executive privilege could be raised as a defense to a contempt trial, which would be necessary only if the branches could not strike a deal. *United States v. United States House of Representatives*, 556 F. Supp. 150 (D.D.C. 1983). *See generally* Todd L. Peterson, *Prosecuting Executive Branch Officials for Contempt of Congress*, 66 N.Y.U. L. Rev. 563 (1991); Ronald L. Claveloux, Note, *The Conflict Between Executive Privilege and Congressional Oversight: The Gorsuch Controversy*, 1983 Duke L.J. 1333. The very title of the case suggests why courts are loath to adjudicate interbranch information disputes and why the political branches typically negotiate a compromise. *See* Joel D. Bush, Note, *Congressional-Executive Access Disputes: Legal Standards and Political Settlements*, 9 J.L. & Pol. 719 (1993); Peter M. Shane, *Legal Disagreement and Negotiation in a Government of Laws: The Case of Executive Privilege Claims Against Congress*, 71 Minn. L. Rev. 462 (1987). *But see* Randall K. Miller, *Congressional Inquests: Suffocating the Constitutional Prerogative of Executive Privilege*, 81 Minn. L. Rev. 631 (1997) (urging earlier judicial resolution). In fact, they reached a compromise in the Gorsuch controversy after the court declined to decide it.

In a more recent case, the House Committee on the Judiciary won a declaratory judgment ordering a former White House Counsel, Harriet Miers, and White House Chief of Staff, Joshua Bolton, to comply with a subpoena to testify and deliver documents, respectively, about the forced resignations of nine U.S. Attorneys. *Committee on Judiciary, U.S. House of Representatives v. Miers*, 558 F. Supp. 2d 53 (D.D.C. 2008). In a lengthy opinion, the court found that the claim of "absolute immunity from compelled congressional process for senior presidential aides is without any support in the case law." *Id.* at 56. Noting that the case was one "of potentially great significance for the balance of power between the Legislative and Executive Branches," however, a D.C. Circuit panel ordered a stay of the proceedings on the ground that before the case could be resolved on the merits, the 110th Congress would expire, as would the subpoenas. *Committee on Judiciary of U.S. House of Representatives v. Miers*, 542 F.3d 909 (D.C. Cir. 2008). The case was then dismissed after the new Congress convened,

No. 08-5357, 2009 WL 3568649 (D.C. Cir. Oct 14, 2009), and the contested subpoenas were sent to the National Archives and Records Administration for handling under the Presidential Records Act (see *supra* p. 1225). No. CIVA 108CV00409 JDB, 2009 WL 86674 (D.D.C. Jan. 13, 2009).

5. *The Role of Courts.* If the political branches cannot reach a compromise, how can a court be expected to decide between a congressional demand for national security information and a claim of executive privilege? The answer appears to be: reluctantly, if at all.

In the *American Telephone & Telegraph* case, *supra*, 551 F.2d 384, a congressional subcommittee subpoenaed FBI requests to the telephone company for warrantless national security wiretaps. The District Court ordered the phone company not to comply. The Court of Appeals, however, was more hesitant about deciding the dispute between the political branches:

> A court seeking to balance the legislative and executive interests asserted here would face severe problems in formulating and applying standards. Granted that the subpoenas are clearly within the proper legislative investigatory sphere, it is difficult to "weigh" Congress's need for the request letters. . . .
>
> As to the danger to national security, a court would have to consider the Subcommittee's track record for security, the likelihood of a leak if other members of the House sought access to the material. In addition to this delicate and possible unseemly determination, the court would have to weigh the effect of a leak on intelligence activities and diplomatic relations. Finally, the court would have to consider the reasonableness of the alternatives offered by the parties and decide which would better reconcile the competing constitutional interests.
>
> Before moving on to a decision of such nerve-center constitutional questions, we pause to allow for further efforts at a settlement. [*Id.* at 394.]

The court then remanded the case to the District Court with instructions to seek a settlement. When this effort failed and a second appeal ensued, the Court of Appeals reiterated its reluctance. Although the court declined to invoke the political question doctrine, it decided against deciding as long as any possibility of a compromise remained. The court then suggested procedures for reaching a compromise. 567 F.2d 121 (D.C. Cir. 1977). This time its efforts bore fruit, and the branches reached an agreement, ending the litigation.

6. *Congress's Last Resort.* If the Justice Department will not prosecute a contempt of Congress citation against an executive branch official, or if a court will not order the Executive to turn over subpoenaed material, what recourse does Congress have? *See* Peterson, *supra*, at 625-631; H.R. Rep. No. 93-1305, at 4 (1974) (recommending an article of impeachment against Richard Nixon for his failure to comply with subpoenas issued by the House Committee on the Judiciary as part of its impeachment inquiry).

7. *Protecting Secrets in Congress.* May the President refuse to provide national security information to Congress on the ground that the information is classified? Currently there is no requirement that any member of Congress obtain a security clearance as a condition of gaining access to classified information. *See* Frederick M. Kaiser, *Protection of Classified Information by Congress: Practices and Proposals* 5

(Cong. Res. Serv. RS20748), Jan. 27, 2010. (Neither the President, Vice President, nor the Justices of the Supreme Court are required to have such clearances, either.) Who might impose such a requirement? Who would make the clearance decision? Could members of Congress be forced, for example, to undergo a polygraph examination? *See* Kaiser, *supra,* at 6.

Congress has various internal protections for sensitive data. For example, intelligence oversight legislation requires the Executive to provide notice of covert operations to the Intelligence Committees but permits the President to limit such notice to eight designated congressional leaders in some cases, or to delay notice for some period in others. See *supra* p. 504. House rules require all its members and staff to take a secrecy oath of nondisclosure of "any classified information received in the course of my service with the House of Representatives, except as authorized by the House of Representatives or in accordance with its Rules." House Rule XXIII, cl.13, 111th Cong. The Senate has nothing comparable. The House and Senate Ethics Committees are authorized to investigate breaches of security by members of the chamber or their staff. Kaiser, *supra,* at 3. But with all these precautions, can Congress keep a secret?

42

Restraining Unauthorized Disclosures of National Security Information

Every contemporary presidential administration has worried about unauthorized "leaks"—intentional disclosures of government secrets to the media by present or past employees—or about the publication of such secrets by past employees. The concern is that such disclosures may chill the candor of executive branch communications, warp the development of sound policies by exposing them prematurely, undermine the discipline of good decision making, interfere with political strategies to keep the Administration "on message," and, sometimes, injure the national security by compromising classified information.

Some leaks of classified information to the media are in fact authorized. Three decades ago, a court pointed to examples in

> [the] disclosure of this country's development of Multiple Independently Targeted Reentry Vehicles and the release of information about North Vietnamese forces operating in South Vietnam, including the identity of units, their strength and the routes they took to reach their operating areas. These . . . were the result of high level executive decisions that disclosure was in the public interest, to counter popular and congressional pressure for more missiles, in the first instance, and, in the second instance, to bolster domestic support for our own military effort in South Vietnam. They are instances of declassification by official public disclosure. [*Alfred A. Knopf, Inc. v. Colby*, 509 F.2d 1362, 1369 (4th Cir. 1975).]

More recently, President Bush approved the clandestine disclosure of portions of the then-classified 2002 National Intelligence Estimate in an effort to shore up support for Administration claims that Iraq was trying to obtain nuclear weapons. *See* David Johnston & David E. Sanger, *Cheney's Aide Says President Approved Leak*, N.Y. Times, Apr. 7, 2006.

One way to control unauthorized leaks is to screen persons to whom secrets are entrusted. Every administration conducts some form of political screening, or vetting, for its high-level appointees. In addition, as a condition of access to classified information (and therefore employment), many government employees and defense contractor personnel must obtain security clearances based on background investigations that vary in intensity depending on the classification level of the information to which they will have access. A security breach, such as a leak, can lead to revocation of a security clearance and attendant loss of employment.

The threat of a job loss alone has not proven adequate, however, to stanch the steady flow of national security information to the media. The government has therefore looked to the courts and to Congress for help. The courts have applied contract theories to prevent past employees from publishing putative national security secrets or, at least, from profiting from such publication. Part A of this chapter examines those contract theories, as well as the secrecy and prepublication review agreements upon which they rest. The government mounted an Espionage Act prosecution against one former government employee who sold information to the press, using federal criminal laws that more traditionally have been invoked against spies in the service of foreign states. More recently it has brought and subsequently dismissed Espionage Act charges against individuals who were neither government employees nor spies. In Part B of this chapter we examine these prosecutions, and we look at recurring efforts to criminalize unauthorized leaks more directly. At the end of the chapter we review an extremely controversial case involving authorized leaks.

A.   RESTRAINING LEAKS BY CONTRACT

1.   The CIA Precedents

United States v. Marchetti

United States Court of Appeals, Fourth Circuit, 1972
466 F.2d 1309, *cert. denied*, 409 U.S. 1063 (1972)

[Victor Marchetti, a former employee of the Central Intelligence Agency (Agency or CIA), signed a secrecy agreement promising not to reveal classified information or information relating to intelligence matters when he joined the Agency, and he signed a similar secrecy oath when he resigned.]

HAYNSWORTH, C.J.... After his resignation, Marchetti published a novel, entitled *The Rope Dancer*, concerning an agency called the "National Intelligence Agency." [He] also published an article in the April 3, 1972 issue of...The Nation [magazine]...criticiz[ing] some policies and practices of the Agency. In March, 1972, Marchetti submitted to Esquire magazine and to six other publishers an article in which he reports some of his experiences as an agent. According to the United States, this article contains classified information concerning intelligence sources, methods and operations.... He has submitted to a publishing house an outline of a book he proposes to write about his intelligence experiences....

[Relying on Marchetti's earlier agreements, the District Court ordered him not to release to any person or corporation any writing, fictional or nonfictional, relating to the Agency or to intelligence without prior authorization from the CIA. Marchetti was also ordered to return any writings or other property of the United States he had acquired while employed at the Agency.]

We readily agreed with Marchetti that the First Amendment limits the extent to which the United States, contractually or otherwise, may impose secrecy requirements upon its employees and enforce them with a system of prior censorship. It precludes such restraints with respect to information which is unclassified or officially disclosed, but we are here concerned with secret information touching upon the national defense and the conduct of foreign affairs, acquired by Marchetti while in a position of trust and confidence and contractually bound to respect it. . . .

Gathering intelligence information and the other activities of the Agency, including clandestine affairs against other nations, are all within the President's constitutional responsibility for the security of the Nation as the Chief Executive and as Commander in Chief of our Armed Forces. Const., art. II, §2. Citizens have the right to criticize the conduct of our foreign affairs, but the Government also has the right and the duty to strive for internal secrecy about the conduct of governmental affairs in areas in which disclosure may reasonably be thought to be inconsistent with the national interest.

The Supreme Court recognized the need for secrecy in government in *United States v. Curtiss-Wright Export Corp.*, 229 U.S. 304, 320 where it said that the President

> has his confidential sources of information. He has his agents in the form of diplomatic, consular and other officials. Secrecy in respect of information gathered by them may be highly necessary, and the premature disclosure of it productive of harmful results. . . .

Congress has imposed on the Director of Central Intelligence the responsibility for protecting intelligence sources and methods. 50 U.S.C. §403(d)(3) [*see* 50 U.S.C. §403-1(i)(1), *supra* p. 446, now imposing the same duty on the Director of National Intelligence]. In attempting to comply with this duty, the Agency requires its employees as a condition of employment to sign a secrecy agreement, and such agreements are entirely appropriate to a program in implementation of the congressional direction of secrecy. . . .

. . . One may speculate that ordinary criminal sanctions might suffice to prevent unauthorized disclosure of such information, but the risk of harm from disclosure is so great and maintenance of the confidentiality of the information so necessary that greater and more positive assurance is warranted. Some prior restraints in some circumstances are approvable of course. See *Freedman v. Maryland*, 380 U.S. 51.

. . . Marchetti by accepting employment with the CIA and by signing a secrecy agreement did not surrender his First Amendment right of free speech. The agreement is enforceable only because it is not a violation of those rights. We would decline enforcement of the secrecy oath signed when he left the employment of the CIA to the extent that it purports to prevent disclosure of unclassified information, for, to that extent, the oath would be in contravention of his First Amendment rights. . . .

Because we are dealing with a prior restraint upon speech, we think that the CIA must act promptly to approve or disapprove any material which may be submitted to it by Marchetti. Undue delay would impair the reasonableness of the restraint. . . . We should think that, in all events, the maximum period for responding after the submission of material for approval should not exceed thirty days.

Furthermore, since First Amendment rights are involved, we think Marchetti would be entitled to judicial review of any action by the CIA disapproving publication of the material. . . . See *Freedman v. Maryland*, 380 U.S. 51. Because of the sensitivity of the area and confidentiality of the relationship in which the information was obtained, however, we find no reason to impose the burden of obtaining judicial review upon the CIA. It ought to be on Marchetti.

Indeed, in most instances, there ought to be no practical reason for judicial review since, because of its limited nature, there would be only narrow areas for possible disagreement.

. . . The CIA is one of the executive agencies whose activities are closely related to the conduct of foreign affairs and to the national defense. . . . If in the conduct of its operations the need for secrecy requires a system of classification of documents and information, the process of classification is part of the executive function beyond the scope of judicial review. See *Oetjen v. Central Leather Co.*, 246 U.S. 297; *United States v. Belmont*, 301 U.S. 324; *Zemel v. Rusk*, 381 U.S. 1.

There is a practical reason for avoidance of judicial review of secrecy classifications. The significance of one item of information may frequently depend upon knowledge of many other items of information. . . . The courts . . . are ill-equipped to become sufficiently steeped in foreign intelligence matters to serve effectively in the review of secrecy classifications in that area.

Information, though classified, may have been publicly disclosed. If it has been, Marchetti should have as much right as anyone else to republish it. Rumor and speculation are not the equivalent of prior disclosure, however, and the presence of that kind of surmise should be no reason for avoidance of restraints upon confirmation from one in a position to know officially. . . .

Generally, therefore, we approve the injunctive order issued by the District Court. The case will be remanded, however, for the purpose of revising the order to limit its reach to classified information and for the conduct of such further proceedings as may be necessary if Marchetti contends that the CIA wrongfully withheld approval of the publication of any information under the standards we have laid down. . . .

CRAVEN, J. (concurring). . . . I concur in the opinion of the court except for the statement that the classification of documents and information by the executive is not subject to judicial review. Because the national security may be involved and because of the expertise of the executive, I would resolve any doubt about the reasonableness of a classification in favor of the government. If the burden were put upon one who assails the classification, and surely it ought to be, much of the difficulty envisioned in the court's opinion would presumably disappear. Indeed, I would not object to a presumption of reasonableness, and a requirement that the assailant demonstrate by clear and convincing evidence that a classification is arbitrary and capricious before it may be invalidated. . . .

Snepp v. United States

United States Supreme Court, 1980
444 U.S. 507

PER CURIAM. . . . Based on his experiences as a CIA agent, Snepp published a book about certain CIA activities in South Vietnam. Snepp published the account without submitting it to the Agency for prepublication review. As an express condition of his employment with the CIA in 1968, however, Snepp had executed an agreement promising that he would "not . . . publish . . . any information or material relating to the Agency, its activities or intelligence activities generally, either during or after the term of [his] employment . . . without specific prior approval by the Agency." . . . Thus, Snepp had pledged not to divulge *classified* information and not to publish *any* information without prepublication clearance. The Government brought this suit to enforce Snepp's agreement. . . .

The District Court found that Snepp had "wilfully, deliberately and surreptitiously breached his position of trust with the CIA and the [1968] secrecy agreement". . . . The court also found that Snepp deliberately misled CIA officials into believing that he would submit the book for prepublication clearance. Finally, the court determined as a fact that publication of the book had "caused the United States irreparable harm and loss." The District Court therefore enjoined future breaches of Snepp's agreement and imposed a constructive trust on Snepp's profits.

The Court of Appeals accepted the findings of the District Court and agreed that Snepp had breached a valid contract.[3] . . . The court, however, concluded that the record did not support imposition of a constructive trust. The conclusion rested on the court's perception that Snepp had a First Amendment right to publish unclassified information and the Government's concession — for the purposes of this litigation — that Snepp's book divulged no classified intelligence. . . .

Whether Snepp violated his trust does not depend upon whether his book actually contained classified information. The Government does not deny — as a general principle — Snepp's right to publish unclassified information. . . . The Government simply claims that, in light of the special trust reposed in him and the agreement that he signed, Snepp should have given the CIA an opportunity to determine whether the material he proposed to publish would compromise classified information or sources. Neither of the Government's concessions undercuts its claim that Snepp's failure to submit to prepublication review was a breach of his trust.

Both the District Court and the Court of Appeals found that a former intelligence agent's publication of unreviewed material relating to intelligence activities can be detrimental to vital national interests even if the published information is unclassified. When a former agent relies on his own judgment about what information is detrimental, he may reveal information that the CIA — with its broader understanding of what may expose classified information and confidential sources — could have identified as harmful. . . .

Undisputed evidence in this case shows that a CIA agent's violation of his obligation to submit writings about the Agency for prepublication review impairs the CIA's ability to perform its statutory duties. Admiral Turner, Director of CIA, testified without contradiction that Snepp's book and others like it have seriously impaired the effectiveness of American intelligence operations. He said:

> Over the last six to nine months, we have had a number of sources discontinue work with us. We have had more sources tell us they are very nervous about continuing work with us. . . .

---

3. . . . He does not claim that he executed this agreement under duress. . . . Moreover, this Court's cases make clear that — even in the absence of an express agreement — the CIA could have acted to protect substantial government interests by imposing reasonable restrictions on employee activities that in other contexts might be protected by the First Amendment. The Government has a compelling interest in protecting both the secrecy of information important to our national security and the appearance of confidentiality so essential to the effective operation of our foreign intelligence service. The agreement that Snepp signed is a reasonable means for protecting this vital interest.

In view of this and other evidence in the record, both the District Court and the Court of Appeals recognized that Snepp's breach of his explicit obligation to submit his material—classified or not—for prepublication clearance has irreparably harmed the United States Government....

The Government could not pursue the only remedy that the Court of Appeals left it without losing the benefit of the bargain it seeks to enforce. Proof of the tortious conduct necessary to sustain an award of punitive damages might force the Government to disclose some of the very confidences that Snepp promised to protect. The trial of such a suit, before a jury if the defendant so elects, would subject the CIA and its officials to probing discovery into the Agency's highly confidential affairs. Rarely would the Government run this risk. In a letter introduced at Snepp's trial, former CIA Director Colby noted the analogous problem in criminal cases. Existing law, he stated, "requires the revelation in open court of confirming or additional information of such a nature that the potential damage to the national security precludes prosecution."... [1]

A constructive trust, on the other hand, protects both the Government and the former agent from unwarranted risks.... If the agent publishes unreviewed material in violation of his fiduciary and contractual obligation, the trust remedy simply requires him to disgorge the benefits of his faithlessness. Since the remedy is swift and sure, it is tailored to deter those who would place sensitive information at risk. And since the remedy reaches only funds attributable to the breach, it cannot saddle the former agent with exemplary damages out of all proportion to his gain.... We therefore reverse the judgment of the Court of Appeals insofar as it refused to impose a constructive trust on Snepp's profits....

Mr. Justice STEVENS, with whom Mr. Justice BRENNAN and Mr. Justice MARSHALL join, dissenting.... In this case Snepp admittedly breached his duty to submit the manuscript of his book, Decent Interval, to the CIA for prepublication review. However, the Government has conceded that the book contains no classified, nonpublic material. Thus, by definition, the interest in confidentiality that Snepp's contract was designed to protect has not been compromised. Nevertheless, the Court today grants the Government unprecedented and drastic relief in the form of a constructive trust....

The rule of law the Court announces today is not supported by statute, by the contract, or by the common law. Although Congress has enacted a number of criminal statutes punishing the unauthorized dissemination of certain types of classified information, it has not seen fit to authorize the constructive trust remedy the Court creates today. Nor does either of the contracts Snepp signed with the Agency provide for any such remedy in the event of a breach. The Court's per curiam opinion seems to suggest that its result is supported by a blend of the law of trusts and the law of contracts. But neither of these branches of the common law supports the imposition of a constructive trust under the circumstances of this case....

... Snepp did not breach his duty to protect confidential information. Rather, he breached a contractual duty, imposed in aid of the basic duty to maintain confidentiality, to obtain prepublication clearance. In order to justify the imposition of a constructive trust, the majority attempts to equate this contractual duty with Snepp's duty

[1. After *Snepp* was decided, Congress addressed this problem by enacting the Classified Information Procedures Act. 18 U.S.C. App. §§1-16 (2006 & Supp. III 2009). See Chapter 34.—Eds.]

not to disclose, labeling them both as "fiduciary." I find nothing in the common law to support such an approach.

Employment agreements often contain covenants designed to ensure in various ways that an employee fully complies with his duty not to disclose or misuse confidential information. One of the most common is a covenant not to compete. Contrary to the majority's approach in this case, the courts have not construed such covenants broadly simply because they support a basic fiduciary duty; nor have they granted sweeping remedies to enforce them. On the contrary, because such covenants are agreements in restraint of an individual's freedom of trade, they are enforceable only if they can survive scrutiny under the "rule of reason." That rule, originally laid down in the seminal case of *Mitchel v. Reynolds*, 1 P. Wms. 181, 24 Eng. Rep. 347 (1711), requires that the covenant be reasonably necessary to protect a legitimate interest of the employer (such as an interest in confidentiality), that the employer's interest not be outweighed by the public interest, and that the covenant not be of any longer duration or wider geographical scope than necessary to protect the employer's interest.

The Court has not persuaded me that a rule of reason analysis should not be applied to Snepp's covenant. . . . Like an ordinary employer, the CIA has a vital interest in protecting certain types of information; at the same time, the CIA employee has a countervailing interest in preserving a wide range of work opportunities (including work as an author) and in protecting his First Amendment rights. The public interest lies in a proper accommodation that will preserve the intelligence mission of the Agency while not abridging the free flow of unclassified information. When the Government seeks to enforce a harsh restriction on the employee's freedom, despite its admission that the interest the agreement was designed to protect — the confidentiality of classified information — has not been compromised, an equity court might well be persuaded that the case is not one in which the covenant should be enforced.

. . . If an employee has used his employer's confidential information for his own personal profit, a constructive trust . . . is obviously an appropriate remedy because the profits are the direct result of the breach. But Snepp admittedly did not use confidential information in his book; nor were the profits from his book in any sense a product of his failure to submit the book for prepublication review. For, even if Snepp had submitted the book to the Agency for prepublication review, the Government's censorship authority would surely have been limited to the excision of classified material. In this case, then, it would have been obliged to clear the book for publication in precisely the same form as it now stands.[11] . . . Thus, Snepp has not gained any profits as a result of his breach; the Government, rather than Snepp, will be unjustly enriched if he is required to disgorge profits attributable entirely to his own legitimate activity.

. . . I do not believe . . . that the Agency has any authority to censor its employees' publication of unclassified information on the basis of its opinion that publication may be "detrimental to vital national interests" or otherwise "identified as harmful." The CIA never attempted to assert such power over Snepp in either of the contracts he signed; rather, the Agency itself limited its censorship power to preventing the

---

11. . . . [D]espite its reference in footnote 3 . . . to the Government's so-called compelling interest in protecting "the appearance of confidentiality" . . . and despite some ambiguity in the Court's reference to "detrimental" and "harmful" as opposed to "classified," . . . I do not understand the Court to imply that the Government could obtain an injunction against the publication of unclassified information.

disclosure of "classified" information. Moreover, even if such a wide-ranging prior restraint would be good national security policy, I would have great difficulty reconciling it with the demands of the First Amendment. . . .

. . . [T]he Court seems unaware of the fact that its drastic new remedy has been fashioned to enforce a species of prior restraint on a citizen's right to criticize his government.[17] Inherent in this prior restraint is the risk that the reviewing agency will misuse its authority to delay the publication of a critical work or to persuade an author to modify the contents of his work beyond the demands of secrecy. The character of the covenant as a prior restraint on free speech surely imposes an especially heavy burden on the censor to justify the remedy it seeks. It would take more than the Court has written to persuade me that that burden has been met. . . .

NOTES AND QUESTIONS

1. *Comparing the Cases.* Which case is a greater inroad on freedom of expression and freedom of the press, *Marchetti* or *Snepp*? How would you compare the two cases on the basis of the kinds of information protected? How would you compare the remedies?

2. *Restraining the Publishers?* Notwithstanding the discussion of Marchetti's constitutional freedom of expression, the court in his case determined that by his confidential employment relationship and his secrecy agreement, Marchetti had effectively relinquished his First Amendment rights. Should the injunction against Marchetti have affected his publisher's press freedom? After the decision set out above, Marchetti and a former State Department employee named John Marks prepared a manuscript for a book, entitled *The C.I.A. and the Cult of Intelligence*, from which the CIA insisted on deleting a number of items. The same court barred publication of classified information that the authors obtained during their government employment, even though that information was already in the publisher's hands. *Alfred A. Knopf, Inc. v. Colby*, 509 F.2d 1362, 1370 (4th Cir. 1975). Could the profits of Snepp's publishers be applied to the trust declared in *Snepp*?

After the *Marchetti* and *Snepp* rulings, are publishers likely to shy away from national security exposés? Or will they instead pressure the author of such an exposé to make any cuts the government demands? Suppose a television producer wants to do a TV miniseries on some CIA intelligence failure or past covert operation, like the ill-fated invasion at the Bay of Pigs in Cuba. If the producer relies partly on a former CIA official for technical advice, would she have to submit the miniseries for prepublication review?

17. The mere fact that the Agency has the authority to review the text of a critical book in search of classified information before it is published is bound to have an inhibiting effect on the author's writing. Moreover, the right to delay publication until the review is completed is itself a form of prior restraint that would not be tolerated in other contexts. See, e.g., *New York Times Co. v. United States*, 403 U.S. 713; *Nebraska Press Assn. v. Stuart*, 427 U.S. 539. In view of the national interest in maintaining an effective intelligence service, I am not prepared to say that the restraint is necessarily intolerable in this context. I am, however, prepared to say that, certiorari having been granted, the issue surely should not be resolved in the absence of full briefing and argument.

3. *Reviewing Prepublication Review.* In its decision in *Alfred A. Knopf, supra,* the Fourth Circuit panel claimed to back away from its earlier view that "executive decisions respecting the classifying of information are not subject to judicial review." 509 F.2d at 1367. Citing the 1974 amendments to FOIA, 5 U.S.C. §552(a)(4)(B), *supra* p. 1199, it acknowledged that deletions could be sustained only if they were found to be both classified and classifiable. 509 F.2d at 1367. The court proceeded to rob this statement of its meaning, however, by indulging the general "presumption of regularity in the performance by a public official of his public duty." *Id.* at 1368. Thus, "the government was required to show no more than that each deletion item disclosed information which was required to be classified in any degree and which was contained in a document bearing a classification stamp." *Id.* Whether the classifier had ever focused on the relevant item's classifiability was considered irrelevant.

The court also found that previous but unofficial public disclosure of classified information would not bear on the efficacy of the censorship. The court reasoned that to allow Marchetti to use such material, as long as he originally had access to it when he was an agent, would enhance the credence of information that might otherwise have only the present force of conjecture or speculation. Thus, Marchetti could not republish material that everyone else might have. In response to this decision, Anthony Lewis noted that Marchetti became "the only person in the history of the United States who has been subjected to a licensing system like that of Tudor and Stuart England." *In the Censor's Grip,* N.Y. Times, Nov. 10, 1977.

4. *Should Motive Matter?* If the motive for revealing the activities of the CIA is personal gain, it is easy to see why the constructive trust remedy strikes some as apt. What if the individual expects no financial reward and simply believes it is in the public interest to divulge the information? Should contract or agency principles be applied either to bar or to punish the disclosure? *Cf. New York Times v. Sullivan,* 376 U.S. 254 (1964), where the Court established the principle that libel law doctrine must yield to constitutional law standards where criticism of government officials is involved.

2. Nondisclosure Agreements and Lifetime Prepublication Review

The force of the CIA precedents was not lost on the Reagan administration. In 1983, President Reagan issued National Security Decision Directive 84 (NSDD 84), directing executive agencies that handle classified information to require all persons with access to it to sign nondisclosure agreements, and those with access to Sensitive Compartmented Information (SCI) to sign prepublication agreements as well. NSDD 84, *Safeguarding National Security Information, reprinted in Hearing Before the S. Comm. on Governmental Affairs,* 98th Cong., at 85-86 (1983). By 1987, 2.5 million current and former employees had signed nondisclosure agreements, and 453,000 (in addition to an undisclosed number of CIA and National Security Agency (NSA) employees) had signed prepublication review agreements. Excerpts of the original agreements follow.

Classified Information Nondisclosure Agreement (SF 189)[2]
Information Security Oversight Office

An Agreement Between _____ and the United States
   (*Name — Printed or Typed*)

1. Intending to be legally bound, I hereby accept the obligations contained in this Agreement in consideration of my being granted access to classified information. As used [herein,] classified information is information that is either classified or classifiable under the standards of Executive Order 12356, or under any other Executive order or statute that prohibits the unauthorized disclosure of information in the interest of national security. . . .

3. I have been advised . . . that direct or indirect unauthorized disclosure, unauthorized retention, or negligent handling of classified information by me could cause irreparable injury to the United States or could be used to advantage by a foreign nation. . . .

4. I have been advised . . . that any breach of this Agreement may result in the termination of any security clearances I hold; removal from any position of special confidence and trust requiring such clearances; and the termination of my employment. . . . In addition, I have been advised . . . that any unauthorized disclosure of classified information by me may constitute a violation or violations of United States criminal laws. . . .

5. I hereby assign to the United States Government all royalties, remunerations, and emoluments that have resulted, will result or may result from any disclosure, publication, or revelation not consistent with the terms of this Agreement.

6. I understand that the United States Government may seek any remedy available to it to enforce this Agreement including, but not limited to, application for a court order prohibiting disclosure of information in breach of this Agreement.

7. I understand that all information to which I may obtain access by signing this Agreement is now and will forever remain the property of the United States Government. I do not now, nor will I ever, possess any right, interest, title, or claim whatsoever to such information. . . .

8. Unless and until I am released in writing by an authorized representative of the United States Government, I understand that all conditions and obligations imposed upon me by this Agreement apply during the time I am granted access to classified information, and at all times thereafter. . . .

10. I have read this Agreement carefully and my questions, if any, have been answered to my satisfaction. I acknowledge that the briefing officer has made available to me Sections 641, 793, 794, 798 and 952 of Title 18, United States Code, Section

[2. SF 189 has been superseded by SF 312, which is substantially identical, except for the deletion of the reference to "classifiable" information from the definition of "classified" in paragraph 1. *See* Information Sec. Oversight Office, National Archives & Records Admin., *Classified Information Nondisclosure Agreement (Standard Form 312) — Briefing Booklet* (2001), *at* http://www.archives.gov/isoo/training/standard-form-312.pdf. — Eds.]

783(b) of Title 50, United States Code, the Intelligence Identities Protection Act of 1982, and Executive Order 12356, so that I may read them at this time, if I so choose.

11. I make this Agreement without mental reservation or purpose of evasion. . . .

Sensitive Compartmented Information Nondisclosure Agreement (SF 4193)[3]
Information Security Oversight Office

4. In consideration of being granted access to [Sensitive Compartmented Information (SCI)] . . . I hereby agree to submit for security review . . . all information or materials, including works of fiction, which contain or purport to contain any [SCI] or description of activities that produce or relate to [SCI] or that I have reason to believe are derived from [SCI], that I contemplate disclosing to any person not authorized to have access to [SCI] or that I have prepared for public disclosure. I understand and agree that my obligation to submit such information and materials for review applies during the course of my access to [SCI] and at all times thereafter. . . .

5. I understand that the purpose of the review described in paragraph 4 is to give the United States a reasonable opportunity to determine whether the information or materials submitted . . . sets forth any [SCI]. . . . [T]he Department or Agency to which I have made a submission will act upon it, coordinating with the Intelligence Community when appropriate, and make a response to me within a reasonable time, not to exceed 30 working days from date of receipt.

NOTES AND QUESTIONS

1. *Authority for Agreements.* The CIA secrecy agreements upheld in *Marchetti* and *Snepp* were explicitly tied to "the CIA Director's statutory mandate to 'protec[t] intelligence sources and methods from unauthorized disclosure,' 50 U.S.C. §403(d)(3)." *Snepp*, 444 U.S. at 509 n.3. Can you identify the source of the President's authority to promulgate NSDD 84 to cover federal officials and employees other than CIA and NSA personnel? What about civilian contract employees?

Should the President be able to control the speech or publications of persons after they leave government employment? If so, should there be any time limit on such control? Not even Justice Holmes's acerbic remark that "Petitioner may have a constitutional right to talk politics, but he has no constitutional right to be a policeman," *McAuliffe v. Mayor of New Bedford*, 155 Mass. 216, 220, 29 N.E. 517 (1892), is as far-reaching as NSDD 84. At least the policeman could quit and then talk.

2. *Waiving First Amendment Rights.* Can First Amendment rights be waived just as, for example, an accused may waive a right to a jury trial? Applying cost-benefit analysis

[3. SF 4193 was identical to SF 189, except for the two additional paragraphs set forth here. SF 4193 has since been replaced by SF 4414, which is similar. *See* Sensitive Compartmented Information Nondisclosure Agreement (SF 4414), *at* http://www.usgs.gov/usgs-manual/handbook/hb/440-7-h/440-7-h-figure5-2.pdf. — Eds.]

to *Snepp*, one commentator concluded that since Snepp entered into his agreement without fraud or coercion, he had made a judgment that he was better off with the agreement than without it. "[One] value of a right . . . is that it can be sold and both parties to the bargain made better off." Frank H. Easterbrook, *Insider Trading, Secret Agents, Evidentiary Privileges, and the Production of Information,* 1981 Sup. Ct. Rev. 309, 347. Does *any* First Amendment right exist with respect to sensitive information that would not have been gained but for the employment? *See* Jonathan C. Medow, *The First Amendment and the Secrecy State: Snepp v. United States,* 130 U. Pa. L. Rev. 775, 811 (1982).

3. *Impacts on an Informed Electorate?* The nondisclosure agreements may be thought to pose a particular threat to public debate of government matters, since their ban on expression is absolute. By contrast, the prepublication requirements contain some procedural safeguards. For example, Department of Justice guidelines require a substantive response to a review request within 30 working days, with priority for material that the author wishes to publish on an expedited basis, such as speeches or newspaper articles. Administrative appeals must be processed within 15 working days. Authors who are dissatisfied with the administrative decision may seek judicial relief or, upon 30 days' notice, may seek an injunction against the government. 28 C.F.R. §17.18(i) (2010).

Unfortunately, agencies sometimes fail to abide by their own timetables. After an employee of the Los Alamos National Laboratory, Danny Stillman, submitted his manuscript, *Inside China's Nuclear Weapons Program,* to the Department of Energy and other agencies for prepublication review, he waited 18 months for an answer. Finally, he sued to dislodge the manuscript, only to learn in discovery that almost a year earlier DOD had concluded, without telling him, that no excisions could correct the "problems" of the manuscript. *See* William J. Broad, *Author to Sue U.S. Over Book on China's Nuclear Advances,* N.Y. Times, June 18, 2001. Two weeks after suit was filed, the government released 85 percent of the manuscript.

4. *Timing the Release of Information.* Professor Scot Powe noted that the prepublication review process, "beyond getting lots of speech within the net," shifted "the timing of speech . . . from the speaker to the censor." *Review of the President's NSDD 84 and the Proposed Department of Defense Directive on Polygraph Use: Hearing Before a Subcomm. of H. Comm. on Gov't Operations,* 98th Cong., at 132 (1983) (*Brooks Hearing*) (testimony of L.A. Scot Powe Jr.). He recalled that a 1983 Senate vote on application of the War Powers Resolution in Lebanon came just 31 days after the first two U.S. Marines were killed in Beirut. An official who had relevant information to contribute to the Senate debate still might have been waiting for his 30-working-day clearance by the time the critical vote was taken. *Id.* at 141. Is there a solution to the problem of delayed responses by agency reviewers?

5. *Scope of Prepublication Review.* Prepublication review guidelines cover everything from newspaper columns and letters to the editor, to works of fiction. *See, e.g.,* 28 C.F.R. §17.18(f) (2010) (Department of Justice). They may also address the special risk of inadvertent oral disclosures.

Oral statements are also within the scope of a prepublication review requirement when based upon written materials, such as an outline of the statements to be made. There is no requirement to prepare written materials for review, however, unless there is reason to believe in advance that oral statements may contain Sensitive Compartmented Information [SCI] or other information required to be submitted for review under the terms of the nondisclosure agreement. Thus, a person may participate in an oral presentation where there is no opportunity for prior presentation (e.g., news interview, panel discussion) without violating the provisions of this paragraph. [28 C.F.R. §17.18(g) (2010).]

If you were a Justice Department lawyer to whom this regulation applied, do you understand when you could or could not accept a speaking invitation without DOJ approval?

6. *Statutory Restrictions on Nondisclosure Agreements.* SF 189 forbade employees from disclosing classified or "classifiable" information. Read literally, the agreement prohibited disclosure not only to unauthorized persons outside the government, but also to Congress. Congress responded with an appropriations rider prohibiting the use of certain funds to enforce either SF 189 or SF 4193 insofar as they (1) contained the term "classifiable," (2) concerned information other than that specifically marked as classified or known by the employee to be in the process of a classification determination, or (3) interfered in any way with the right of an employee to petition or communicate with Congress or the right of Congress "to obtain executive branch information in a secure manner" under its rules. Omnibus Continuing Resolution for Fiscal Year 1988, Pub. L. No. 100-202, §630, 101 Stat. 1329, 1329-432 (1987). Federal employees thereafter sued to enforce the rider and declare enforcement of the agreements unconstitutional. *See National Fed'n of Fed. Employees v. United States (NFFE I),* 688 F. Supp. 671 (D.D.C. 1988), *vacated sub nom. American Foreign Serv. Ass'n v. Garfinkel,* 490 U.S. 153 (1989). Citing *Curtiss-Wright, supra* p. 53, the District Court found that the rider "impermissibly restricts the President's power to fulfill obligations imposed upon him by his express constitutional powers and the role of the Executive in foreign relations." 688 F. Supp. at 685. Professor Glennon called *NFFE I* "the only decision in American case law in which a court has invalidated an exercise of Congress' power over the purse as an unconstitutional encroachment on executive power," describing it as "an ill considered exercise of judicial activism" that "disregards time honored doctrines of Anglo-American jurisprudence." H. Comm. on Gov't Operations, *Legislation Needed to Curb Secrecy Contracts,* H.R. Rep. No. 100-991, at 15 (1988). *See* Peter Raven-Hansen & William C. Banks, *Pulling the Purse Strings of the Commander in Chief,* 80 Va. L. Rev. 833, 923-942 (1994).

B.   RESTRAINING LEAKS BY ESPIONAGE PROSECUTIONS

Espionage and Censorship
18 U.S.C. §§793-798 (2006)

§793.   GATHERING, TRANSMITTING, OR LOSING DEFENSE INFORMATION

(a) Whoever, for the purpose of obtaining information respecting the national defense with intent or reason to believe that the information is to be used to the injury of the United States, or to the advantage of any foreign nation, goes upon, enters, flies over, or otherwise obtains information concerning [any defense facility or property]; or

(b) Whoever, for the purpose aforesaid, and with like intent or reason to believe, copies, takes, makes, or obtains, or attempts to copy, take, make, or obtain, any sketch, photograph, photographic negative, blueprint, plan, map, model, instrument, appliance, document, writing, or note of anything connected with the national defense; or

(c) Whoever, for the purpose aforesaid, receives or obtains or agrees or attempts to receive or obtain from any person, or from any source whatever, any document [or tangible thing, such as a code book] connected with the national defense, knowing or having reason to believe, at the time he receives or obtains, or agrees or attempts to receive or obtain it, that it has been or will be obtained, taken, made, or disposed of by any person contrary to the provisions of this chapter; or

(d) Whoever, lawfully having possession of, access to, control over, or being entrusted with any document [or tangible thing] or information relating to the national defense which information the possessor has reason to believe could be used to the injury of the United States or to the advantage of any foreign nation, willfully communicates, delivers, transmits or causes to be communicated, delivered, or transmitted or attempts to communicate, deliver, transmit or cause to be communicated, delivered or transmitted the same to any person not entitled to receive it, or willfully retains the same and fails to deliver it on demand to the officer or employee of the United States entitled to receive it; . . .

(e) [Substantially identical to §793(d), except that it provides punishment for one having "unauthorized" possession of sensitive materials.]

(f) [Punishes the loss of such materials through gross negligence or the failure to report their loss, theft, or destruction.]

Shall be fined under this title or imprisoned not more than ten years, or both.

(g) If two or more persons conspire to violate any of the foregoing provisions of this section, and one or more of such persons do any act to effect the object of the conspiracy, each of the parties to such conspiracy shall be subject to the punishment provided for the offense which is the object of such conspiracy. . . .

§794.   GATHERING OR DELIVERING DEFENSE INFORMATION TO AID FOREIGN GOVERNMENT

(a) Whoever, with intent or reason to believe that it is to be used to the injury of the United States or to the advantage of a foreign nation, communicates, delivers, or transmits, or attempts to communicate, deliver, or transmit, to any foreign government, or to any faction or party or military or naval force within a foreign country . . . or to any representative, officer, agent, employee, subject, or citizen thereof, either directly or indirectly, any document, writing, code book, signal book, sketch, photograph, photographic negative, blueprint, plan, map, model, note, instrument, appliance, or information relating to the national defense, shall be punished. . . .

[Sections 795-797 criminalize the disclosure of several specific categories of national security information, including photographs or sketches of defense installations.]

§798.   DISCLOSURE OF CLASSIFIED INFORMATION

(a) Whoever knowingly and willfully communicates, furnishes, transmits, or otherwise makes available to an unauthorized person, or publishes, or uses in any manner prejudicial to the safety or interest of the United States or for the benefit of any foreign government to the detriment of the United States any classified information —

(1) concerning the nature, preparation, or use of any code, cipher, or cryptographic system of the United States or any foreign government; or

(2) concerning the design, construction, use, maintenance, or repair of any device, apparatus, or appliance used or prepared or planned for use by the United States or any foreign government for cryptographic or communication intelligence purposes; or

(3) concerning the communication intelligence activities of the United States or any foreign government; or

(4) obtained by the processes of communication intelligence from the communications of any foreign government, knowing the same to have been obtained by such processes —

shall be fined under this title or imprisoned. . . .

(b) As used in subsection (a) of this section — . . . .

The term "communication intelligence" means all procedures and methods used in the interception of communications and the obtaining of information from such communications by other than the intended recipients; . . .

Public Money, Property or Records

18 U.S.C. §641 (2006)

Whoever embezzles, steals, purloins, or knowingly converts to his use or the use of another, or without authority, sells, conveys or disposes of any record, voucher, money, or thing of value of the United States or of any department or agency thereof . . . ; or

Whoever receives, conceals, or retains the same with intent to convert it to his use or gain, knowing it to have been embezzled, stolen, purloined or converted — shall be fined under this title or imprisoned. . . .

United States v. Rosen

United States District Court, Eastern District of Virginia, 2006
445 F. Supp. 2d 602, *as amended*, 2006 WL 5049154

ELLIS, District Judge. In this Espionage Act prosecution, defendants Steven Rosen and Keith Weissman have been charged in Count I of a superseding indictment with conspiring to transmit information relating to the national defense[1] to those not entitled to receive it, in violation of 18 U.S.C. §793(g) [providing criminal liability for co-conspirators]. Defendants, by pretrial motion, attack the constitutionality of

---

1. The phrase "information relating to the national defense" will sometimes be referred to herein as NDI.

§793 in three ways. First, they argue that the statute, as applied to them, is unconstitutionally vague in violation of the Due Process Clause of the Fifth Amendment. Second, they argue that the statute, as applied to them, abridges their First Amendment right to free speech and their First Amendment right to petition the government. Third, defendants assert the First Amendment rights of others by attacking the statute as facially overbroad. In the alternative, defendants urge the Court to avoid these constitutional issues by interpreting the statute as applying only to the transmission of tangible items, *i.e.*, documents, tapes, discs, maps and the like. . . .

I.

During the period of the conspiracy alleged in Count I, defendants Rosen and Weissman were employed by the American Israel Public Affairs Committee (AIPAC) in Washington, D.C. AIPAC is a pro-Israel organization that lobbies the United States executive and legislative branches on issues of interest to Israel, especially U.S. foreign policy with respect to the Middle East. Rosen was AIPAC's Director of Foreign Policy Issues . . . . Rosen did not have a security clearance during the period of the alleged conspiracy. . . . Defendant Weissman was AIPAC's Senior Middle East Analyst. . . . Alleged co-conspirator Lawrence Franklin worked on the Iran desk in the Office of the Secretary of the Department of Defense (DOD) and held a top secret security clearance during the alleged conspiracy.[3]

In general, the superseding indictment alleges that in furtherance of their lobbying activities, defendants (i) cultivated relationships with government officials with access to sensitive U.S. government information, including NDI, (ii) obtained the information from these officials, and (iii) transmitted the information to persons not otherwise entitled to receive it, including members of the media, foreign policy analysts, and officials of a foreign government.

The government's recitation of the acts constituting the conspiracy begins on April 13, 1999, when Rosen told an unnamed foreign official (FO-1) that he had "picked up an extremely sensitive piece of intelligence" which he described as "code-word protected intelligence." Rosen proceeded to relate this piece of intelligence, which concerned terrorist activities in Central Asia, to the foreign official. . . . The superseding indictment alleges further that Weissman's role in the conspiracy became apparent on June 11, 1999, when Weissman told the same foreign official that he had learned of a "secret FBI, classified FBI report" relating to the Khobar Towers bombing from three different sources, including an official of the United States government. Later that day, Weissman told FO-1 that he had interested a member of the media in the report.

According to the superseding indictment, roughly eighteen months later, on December 12, 2000, Rosen and Weissman met with a United States government official (USGO-1) who had access to classified information relating to U.S. strategy pertaining to a certain Middle East country. Following this meeting, Rosen allegedly had a conversation with a member of the media in which he communicated classified

---

3. On October 5, 2005, Franklin pled guilty to one count of conspiracy to communicate national defense information to one not entitled to receive it, in violation of 18 U.S.C. §§793(d) and (g), and to one count of conspiracy to communicate classified information to an agent of a foreign government in violation of 50 U.S.C. §783 and 18 U.S.C. §371.

information relating to the U.S. government's deliberations on its strategy towards that particular Middle Eastern country....

In August 2002, Rosen was introduced to Franklin through a contact at the DOD. Rosen, Weissman, Franklin and another DOD employee finally met nearly six months later, on February 12, 2003. At this meeting, Franklin disclosed to Rosen and Weissman information relating to a classified draft internal United States government policy document concerning a certain Middle Eastern country....Rosen met with FO-2 and discussed the same draft internal policy document that Franklin had discussed with Rosen and Weissman....

[The court goes on to describe in some detail a number of other instances in which Rosen and Weissman allegedly knowingly received classified information and passed it on to other AIPAC employees, foreign officials, and journalists.]

II.

The operative statute at issue in defendant's constitutional challenge is codified at 18 U.S.C. §793 [set forth *supra* pp. 1262-1263.]...A brief history of this statute provides necessary context and helps illuminate the analysis of the questions presented....

[After a lengthy discussion, the court ruled that §793 applies to information transmitted in oral, as well as tangible, form.]

Defendants' first constitutional challenge to the statute is based on the principle that the Due Process clause of the Fifth Amendment prohibits punishment pursuant to a statute so vague that "men of common intelligence must necessarily guess at its meaning and differ as to its application." *United States v. Lanier*, 520 U.S. 259, 266 (1997) (quoting *Connally v. General Constr. Co.*, 269 U.S. 385, 391 (1926))....

IV....

C.

...[A]ny inherent vagueness in the terms "relating to the national defense" or "entitled to receive" as used in §§793(d) and (e) is cured through the judicial glosses that have been added to these phrases. To the extent that oral transmission of information relating to the national defense makes it more difficult for defendants to know whether they are violating the statute, the statute is not thereby rendered unconstitutionally vague because the statute permits conviction only of those who "willfully" commit the prohibited acts and do so with bad faith. So construed, both phrases pass Fifth Amendment muster; they are not unconstitutionally vague as applied to these defendants.

D.

Seeking to avoid this conclusion, defendants argue that notwithstanding the clarity of the statute's language, the application of the statute to these defendants is so novel and unprecedented that it violates the fair warning prong of the vagueness doctrine. As explained *supra*, the constitutionally required clarity of a statute may be provided through the gloss of judicial interpretation, and it is precisely the judicial glosses on §793 that save the statute from defendants' vagueness challenge. The corollary of this principle is that "due process bars courts from applying a novel construction of a criminal statute to conduct that neither the statute nor any prior judicial decision has fairly disclosed to be within its scope." *Lanier,* 520 U.S. at 266. . . . [T]he test . . . is whether the language and application of the statute has provided defendants adequate warning that their conduct was proscribed. Section 793, as applied here, meets this test; its language and history provided adequate warning to these defendants that the statute proscribed the alleged conduct.

Defendants argue that the present prosecution represents a novel construction of the statute which they could not have anticipated because "leaks" of classified information by non-governmental persons have never been prosecuted under this statute. The statute's plain language rebuts this argument.[38] It is clear from this plain language that defendants' conduct, as alleged in the superseding indictment is within the sweep of the statute. . . . [T]he defendants here cannot argue persuasively that the result reached here amounts to an unforeseeable judicial enlargement of §793.

And, it is useful in this regard to address defendants' frequent use of the term "leak" in advancing their argument that there was not constitutionally adequate notice that the statute reached the alleged conduct. The term "leak," at bottom, connotes in this context, an unpermitted or unauthorized transmission or transfer of information, which of course, is an act plainly within §793, assuming all the other requirements are met. So, labeling an event a "leak" does not remove the event from the statute's scope. . . .

Also unsuccessful is defendants' claim that past applications of the statute fail to provide fair warning that the statute could be applied to the facts alleged in the superseding indictment. [*United States v. Morison,* 844 F.2d 1057 (4th Cir. 1988)] itself rebuts this claim. Notably, in *Morison* the Fourth Circuit considered the very similar argument that the statute was intended to apply only to classic espionage cases and therefore did not apply to Morison's "leak" to a news publication. In rejecting this argument, the Fourth Circuit noted the rarity of prosecutions under §793(e), but stated

> that the rarity of prosecution under the statutes does not indicate that the statutes were not to be enforced as written. We think in any event, the rarity of use of the statute as a basis for prosecution is at best a questionable basis for nullifying the clear language of the statute, and we think the revision of 1950 and its reenactment of section 793(d) demonstrate that Congress did not consider such statute meaningless or intend that the statute and its prohibitions were to be abandoned.

Morison, 844 F.2d at 1067. The Fourth Circuit's reasoning in rejecting Morison's challenge is equally applicable to the defendants here, and therefore, for the same reasons, defendants' vagueness challenge based on the novelty of this prosecution fails as well.

V.

The defendants' next constitutional challenge rests on the First Amendment's guarantees of free speech and the right to petition the government for

---

38. In amending the statute in 1950, Congress made it quite clear that the statute was intended to apply to the transmission of national defense information by non-government employees by adding subsection (e). . . .

grievances. . . . Defendants' First Amendment challenge exposes the inherent tension between the government transparency so essential to a democratic society and the government's equally compelling need to protect from disclosure information that could be used by those who wish this nation harm. In addressing this tension, it is important to bear in mind that the question to be resolved here is not whether §793 is the optimal resolution of this tension, but whether Congress, in passing this statute, has struck a balance between these competing interests that falls within the range of constitutionally permissible outcomes.

As an initial matter, it is necessary to confront the government's proposed categorical rule that espionage statutes cannot implicate the First Amendment. This contention overreaches. In the broadest terms, the conduct at issue — collecting information about United States' foreign policy and discussing that information with government officials (both United States and foreign), journalists, and other participants in the foreign policy establishment — is at the core of the First Amendment's guarantees. *See Mills v. Alabama,* 384 U.S. 214, 218 (1966) ("[T]here is practically universal agreement that a major purpose of [the First] Amendment was to protect the free discussion of governmental affairs."). And, even under a more precise description of the conduct — the passing of government secrets relating to the national defense to those not entitled to receive them in an attempt to influence United States foreign policy — the application of §793 to the defendants is unquestionably still deserving of First Amendment scrutiny. . . .

Given that the application of the statute to these defendants warrants First Amendment scrutiny, the question then becomes whether Congress may nonetheless penalize the conduct alleged in the superseding indictment, for while the invocation of "national security" does not free Congress from the restraints of the First Amendment, it is equally well established that the invocation of the First Amendment does not "provide immunity for every possible use of language," *Frohwerk v. U.S.,* 249 U.S. 204, 206 (1919), and that "the societal value of speech must, on occasion, be subordinated to other values and considerations." *Dennis v. United States,* 341 U.S. 494, 503 (1951). As Justice Frankfurter aptly put it in *Dennis:*

> The demands of free speech in a democratic society as well as the interest in national security are better served by a candid and informed weighing of the competing interests, within the confines of the judicial process, than by announcing dogmas too inflexible for the non-Euclidian problems to be solved.

Dennis, 341 U.S. at 524-25 (Frankfurter, J., concurring). Thus, to determine, on any given occasion, whether the government's interest prevails over the First Amendment, courts must begin with "an assessment of the competing societal interests" at stake, *Morison,* 844 F.2d at 1082, and proceed to the "delicate and difficult task" of weighing those interests "to determine whether the resulting restriction on freedom can be tolerated." *United States v. Robel,* 389 U.S. 258, 264 (1967).

As already noted, the defendants' First Amendment interests at stake in this prosecution, and those of the third parties raised by defendants, are significant and implicate the core values the First Amendment was designed to protect. The collection and discussion of information about the conduct of government by defendants and others in the body politic is indispensable to the healthy functioning of a representative government, for "[a]s James Madison put it in 1822: 'A popular Government, without popular information, or a means of acquiring it, is but a Prologue to a Farce or a Tragedy; or, perhaps both.'" *Morison,* 844 F.2d at 1081 (Wilkinson, J., concurring) (quoting 9 Writings of James Madison 103 (G. Hunt ed., 1910)). This is especially so in the context of foreign policy because, as Justice Stewart observed in the Pentagon Papers case:

> In the absence of the government checks and balances present in other areas of our national life, the only effective restraint upon executive policy and power in the areas of national defense and international affairs may lie in an enlightened citizenry — in an informed and critical public opinion which alone can here protect the values of democratic government.

New York Times v. United States, 403 U.S. 713, 728 (1971) (Stewart J., concurring)....

But importantly, the defendants here are not accused merely of disclosing government secrets, they are accused of disclosing NDI, *i.e.,* government secrets the disclosure of which could threaten the security of the nation. And, however vital an informed public may be, it is well established that disclosure of certain information may be restricted in service of the nation's security, for "[i]t is 'obvious and unarguable' that no governmental interest is more compelling than the security of the Nation." *Haig v. Agee,* 453 U.S. 280, 307 (1981). And, as the Supreme Court has repeatedly noted, one aspect of the government's paramount interest in protecting the nation's security is the government's "compelling interest in protecting both the secrecy of information important to our national security and the appearance of confidentiality so essential to the effective operation of our foreign intelligence service." [*Snepp v. United States,* 444 U.S. 507 (1980),] at 509 n.3. Thus, the right to free speech and the value of an informed citizenry is not absolute and must yield to the government's legitimate efforts to ensure "the environment of physical security which a functioning democracy requires." *Morison,* 844 F.2d at 1082. This point is best expressed in the Supreme Court's pithy phrase that "while the Constitution protects against the invasion of individual rights, it is not a suicide pact." [*Aptheker v. Secretary of State,* 378 U.S. 500 (1964),] at 509.

Of course, the abstract proposition that the rights protected by the First Amendment must at times yield to the need for national security does not address the concrete issue of whether the §793, as applied here, violates the First Amendment. This determination depends on whether §793 is narrowly drawn to apply only to those instances in which the government's need for secrecy is legitimate, or whether it is too indiscriminate in its sweep, seeking in effect, to excise the cancer of espionage with a chainsaw instead of a scalpel. In this respect, the first clause of §793(e) implicates only the defendants' right to disclose, willfully, information the government has sought to keep confidential due to the potential harm its disclosure poses to the national security in situations in which the defendants have reason to believe that such disclosure could be used to injure the United States or aid a foreign government. Likewise, §793(d), which defendants are charged with conspiring to violate, implicates the same interests, but is limited to those people — generally government employees or contractors — with authorized possession of the information. Thus, it seems fair to say that §793, taken together with its judicial glosses, is more the result of a legislative scalpel and not a chainsaw. This, however, does not end the analysis.

As defendants correctly argue, the analysis of the First Amendment interests implicated by §§793(d) and (e) depends on the relationship to the government of the person whose First Amendment rights are implicated. In this respect, there are two classes of people roughly correlating to those subject to prosecution under §793(d) and those subject to prosecution under §793(e). The first class consists of persons who have access to the information by virtue of their official position. These people are most often government employees or military personnel with access to classified information, or defense contractors with access to classified information, and are often bound by contractual agreements whereby they agree not to disclose classified information. As such, they are in a position of trust with the government. The second class of persons are those who have no employment or contractual relationship with the government, and therefore have not exploited a relationship of trust to obtain the national defense information they are charged with disclosing, but instead generally obtained the information from one who has violated such a trust.

There can be little doubt, as defendants readily concede, that the Constitution permits the government to prosecute the first class of persons for the disclosure of information relating to the national defense when that person knew that the information is the type which could be used to threaten the nation's security, and that person acted in bad faith, *i.e.*, with reason to believe the disclosure could harm the United States or aid a foreign government. Indeed, the relevant precedent teaches that the Constitution permits even more drastic restraints on the free speech rights of this class of persons. . . .

. . . For this reason, the government may constitutionally punish government employees like Franklin for the willful disclosure of national defense information, and if the government proves the defendants conspired with Franklin in his commission of that offense, they may be subject to prosecution, as well. 18 U.S.C. §793(g).

But the analysis must go beyond this because the defendants are also charged with conspiring to violate §793(e) for their own disclosures of NDI to those not entitled to receive it. In this regard, they belong in the second class of those subject to prosecution under §793 — namely, those who have not violated a position of trust with the government to obtain and disclose information, but have obtained the information from one who has. The defendants argue that unlike Morison, Marchetti or Snepp, they did not agree to restrain their speech as part of their employment, and accordingly their First Amendment interests are more robust. . . .

One possible implication . . . is that a special relationship with the government is necessary before the government may constitutionally punish the disclosure of information relating to the national defense. Seizing upon this possible implication, defendants here contend that the First Amendment bars Congress from punishing those persons, like defendants, without a special relationship to the government for the disclosure of NDI. In essence, their position is that once a government secret has been leaked to the general public and the first line of defense thereby breached, the government has no recourse but to sit back and watch as the threat to the national security caused by the first disclosure multiplies with every subsequent disclosure. This position cannot be sustained. Although the question whether the government's interest in preserving its national defense secrets is sufficient to trump the First Amendment rights of those not in a position of trust with the government is a more difficult question, and although the authority addressing this issue is sparse, both common sense and the relevant precedent point persuasively to the conclusion that the government can punish those outside of the government for the unauthorized receipt and deliberate retransmission of information relating to the national defense.

Of course, in some instances the government's interest is so compelling, and the defendant's purpose so patently unrelated to the values of the First Amendment, that a constitutional challenge is easily dismissed. The obvious example is the unauthorized disclosure of troop movements or military technology to hostile foreign powers by nongovernmental persons, conduct typically prosecuted under §794. But this is not such a case; the government has not charged the defendants under §794(a), and therefore the most relevant precedent, although it dealt with the freedom of press, is the Supreme Court's decision in *New York Times Co. v. United States*, 403 U.S. 713 (1971) (per curiam)…. [A] close reading of [the concurring] opinions indicates that the result may have been different had the government sought to prosecute the newspapers under §793(e) subsequent to the publication of the Pentagon Papers. [Here the court analyzed these opinions. See *infra* pp. 1280-1300.] While the Supreme Court's discussion of the application of §793(e) to the newspapers is clearly *dicta*, lower courts "are bound by the Supreme Court's considered *dicta* almost as firmly as by the Court's outright holdings, particularly when, as here, a *dictum* is of recent vintage and not enfeebled by any subsequent statement." *McCoy v. Massachusetts Institute of Technology*, 950 F.2d 13, 19 (1st Cir. 1991). In sum, Congress's attempt to provide for the nation's security by extending punishment for the disclosure of national security secrets beyond the first category of persons within its trust to the general populace is a reasonable, and therefore constitutional[,] exercise of its power….

    … [E]ven when a person is charged with the transmission of intangible "information" the person had "reason to believe could be used to the injury of the United States," the application of the statute without the requirement that disclosure of the information be potentially harmful to the United States would subject nongovernmental employees to prosecution for the innocent, albeit negligent, disclosure of information relating to the national defense. Punishing defendants engaged in public debate for unwittingly harming a legitimate government interest is inconsistent with the Supreme Court's First Amendment jurisprudence. Limiting the set of information relating to the national defense to that information which the defendant *knows,* if disclosed, is potentially harmful to the United States, by virtue of the statute's willfulness requirement, avoids this problem. Thus, for these reasons, information relating to the national defense, whether tangible or intangible, must necessarily be information which if disclosed, is potentially harmful to the United States, and the defendant must know that disclosure of the information is potentially harmful to the United States. The alternative construction simply is not sustainable. So limited, the statute does not violate the defendants' First Amendment guarantee of free speech.

    For essentially the same reasons, §793, as applied to these defendants, does not violate the defendants' First Amendment right to petition the government for grievances. The Supreme Court has stated that "[t]he right to petition is cut from the same cloth as the other guarantees of [the First] Amendment, and is an assurance of a particular expression of freedom." *McDonald v. Smith*, 472 U.S. 479, 482 (1985). Indeed, "this right is implicit in 'the very idea of government, republican in form.'" *Id.* … For this reason, defendants contend that §793 cannot constitutionally be applied to their alleged conduct.

    This argument suffers the same fatal flaws as defendants' argument under the First Amendment's free speech guarantee. Like the First Amendment's guarantee of free speech, the right to petition the government for grievances is not absolute, and may be validly regulated. *See California Motor Transport v. Trucking Unlimited*, 404 U.S. 508, 514-15 (1972) ("First Amendment rights may not be used as the means or pretext for achieving 'substantive evils'")….

[The court then rejected the defendants' challenge based on the overbreadth doctrine.]

VII.

In the end, it must be said that this is a hard case, and not solely because the parties' positions and arguments are both substantial and complex. It is also a hard case because it requires an evaluation of whether Congress has violated our Constitution's most sacred values, enshrined in the First and the Fifth Amendment, when it passed legislation in furtherance of our nation's security. The conclusion here is that the balance struck by §793 between these competing interests is constitutionally permissible because (1) it limits the breadth of the term "related to the national defense" to matters closely held by the government for the legitimate reason that their disclosure could threaten our collective security; and (2) it imposes rigorous scienter requirements as a condition for finding criminal liability.

The conclusion that the statute is constitutionally permissible does not reflect a judgment about whether Congress could strike a more appropriate balance between these competing interests, or whether a more carefully drawn statute could better serve both the national security and the value of public debate. Indeed, the basic terms and structure of this statute have remained largely unchanged since the administration of William Howard Taft. The intervening years have witnessed dramatic changes in the position of the United States in world affairs and the nature of threats to our national security. The increasing importance of the United States in world affairs has caused a significant increase in the size and complexity of the United States' military and foreign policy establishments, and in the importance of our nation's foreign policy decision making. Finally, in the nearly one hundred years since the passage of the Defense Secrets Act mankind has made great technological advances affecting not only the nature and potential devastation of modern warfare, but also the very nature of information and communication. These changes should suggest to even the most casual observer that the time is ripe for Congress to engage in a thorough review and revision of these provisions to ensure that they reflect both these changes, and contemporary views about the appropriate balance between our nation's security and our citizens' ability to engage in public debate about the United States' conduct in the society of nations.

An appropriate Order will issue.

NOTES AND QUESTIONS

1. *Espionage Act Prosecutions of Non-Spies.* The decision in *Rosen* draws heavily from an earlier one in *United States v. Morison*, 604 F. Supp. 655 (D. Md.), *appeal dismissed*, 774 F.2d 1156 (4th Cir.), *aff'd*, 844 F.2d 1057 (4th Cir. 1985), *cert. denied*, 488 U.S. 908 (1988). *Morison* marked the first successful prosecution under the Espionage Act of a person not accused of being a spy. Samuel Loring Morison was a Navy intelligence analyst who sold classified satellite photographs of a Soviet nuclear-powered aircraft carrier under construction to *Jane's Defence Weekly,* and who was apprehended with other classified materials. He raised, unsuccessfully, the same defenses of vagueness and overbreadth that the defendants in *Rosen* did. His case was widely viewed as a warning to government employees that unauthorized leaks, regardless of motive,

would be vigorously prosecuted. Whether or to what extent it has had a chilling effect on individuals who might have used classified documents to inform the public generally, to air what they regarded as unwise policy choices, or even to publicize government misbehavior or mismanagement is unknown.

Unauthorized leaks have in fact continued, and leakers have occasionally been identified, fired, and even criminally prosecuted. One recent case involved a former NSA senior executive named Thomas Drake, who leaked information, first to the Defense Department's Inspector General and to Congress, and then to a journalist, about financial waste, bureaucratic dysfunction, and possible illegal activities at the agency. *See* Jane Mayer, *The Secret Sharer*, New Yorker, May 23, 2011. Charges of illegally possessing classified information, obstructing an investigation, and lying to the FBI were dropped when Drake pleaded guilty to one misdemeanor count of misusing a computer. *See Ex-Official for N.S.A. Accepts Deal in Leak Case*, N.Y. Times, June 11, 2011.

The government has gone to considerable lengths to learn the identities of leakers or at least to deter additional leaks by bringing journalists before grand juries under threat of contempt to force the revelation of sources. In one recent case, described *infra* p. 1308, a reporter was jailed for 85 days for refusing to cooperate. *See* Don Van Natta Jr., Adam Liptak & Clifford J. Levy, *The Miller Case: A Notebook, a Cause, a Jail Cell and a Deal*, N.Y. Times, Oct. 16, 2005.

What really got the attention of the media in the *Rosen* case was the fact that the defendants were neither spies nor government employees; in this sense the prosecution was unprecedented. While the *Rosen* defendants were not members of the media, as recipients of unauthorized leaks they stood in the same position as a newspaper or TV network or its reporters. If they could be convicted of violating the Espionage Act, so could any member of the press who depends on unnamed government sources. The threat to the media's ability to inform the American electorate about government activities, and to the ability of citizens to hold government accountable, was clear.

Reportedly because of pretrial rulings by the *Rosen* court on the admissibility of classified evidence or the requirement of proof that the defendants knew that their distribution of information would harm the United States, but also perhaps in part because of the implications for representative democracy, or because of the intense public interest in the case, the government dropped all charges in 2009, ending this dramatic chapter in the history of Espionage Act prosecutions. *See* Neil A. Lewis & David Johnston, *U.S. Moves to End Secrets Case Against Israel Lobbyists*, N.Y. Times, May 2, 2009.

2. *Adequate Warning to Potential Leakers?* Responding to defendants' claim that §793 is void for vagueness, in violation of the Due Process Clause of the Fifth Amendment, the *Rosen* court concluded that "its language and history provided adequate warning to these defendants that the statute proscribed the alleged conduct." Do you agree? Do you think the defendants fairly claimed surprise because, with the single exception of *Morison*, the Espionage Act had never been applied except in "classic espionage cases"? If you had done what the *Rosen* defendants allegedly did, would you have been concerned about potential criminal liability?

3. *"National Defense Information."* The *Rosen* court attached particular importance to the fact that the information delivered to the defendants was NDI. Are you clear on the meaning of that term? In *United States v. Heine*, 151 F.2d 813, 815 (2d Cir. 1945), Judge Learned Hand, referring to the term "national defense" in an earlier version of the Espionage Act, wrote, "It seems plain that the section cannot cover information

about all those activities which become tributary to 'the national defense' in time of war; for in modern war there are none which do not." Indeed, what information, secret or not, fails to qualify as NDI? Should the *Rosen* court have been more skeptical about the true national security implications of information that is described as NDI or classified? How might such skepticism have affected the court's analysis?

Might any doubts about the meaning of the term NDI be resolved by reference to the statutory language that leaked data "could be used to the injury of the United States or to the advantage or any foreign country"? Suppose a U.S. government employee of Pakistani background learns through secret intelligence sources, to which he has gained access in his work, that India is contemplating a preemptive strike against a Pakistan nuclear facility. With the motive of warning Pakistan, he publishes a letter in the *Karachi Times* disclosing the information. Would he be guilty of violating §793(d)? Would your answer be the same if he had secretly sent the information to his cousin in the Pakistani embassy in Washington? This hypothetical is loosely based on an alleged "leak." *See Report of the Congressional Committees Investigating the Iran-Contra Affair,* H.R. Rep. No. 100-433, S. Rep. No. 100-216, at 577 (1987) (*Minority Report*).

4. *Was It a Crime to Violate Classification Restrictions?* In *Morison,* as in *Rosen,* the defendant argued that the phrase "not entitled to receive" was vague and overbroad when applied to a case not involving a "subversive purpose." The *Morison* court concluded that "authorization to possess documents and entitlement to receive them may be determined by reference to the classification system...." 604 F. Supp. at 661. Congress has, however, consistently refused to provide criminal sanctions for general violations of the classification restrictions, and there is evidence that Congress never intended under the Espionage Act to reach leaks to the press. The Espionage Act was passed in the midst of war fever in 1917. Several bills that would have given the President full power to restrict the divulgence of government secrets were proposed that year. Harold Edgar & Benno L. Schmidt Jr., *The Espionage Statutes and Publication of Defense Information,* 73 Colum. L. Rev. 929, 946 (1973). A provision enabling the President to issue and enforce regulations on publication of defense information received particularly vigorous debate. Despite President Wilson's support, however, all of the bills were rejected. *Id. See also* James A. Goldston et al., Comment, *A Nation Less Secure: Diminished Public Access to Information,* 21 Harv. C.R.-C.L. L. Rev. 409, 422 n.70 (1986); David M. Rabban, *The Emergence of Modern First Amendment Doctrine,* 50 U. Chi. L. Rev. 1205, 1217-1227 (1983).

A 1950 amendment to §793 provided that "nothing in this Act shall be construed . . . to limit or infringe upon freedom of the press." 64 Stat. 987 (1950). *See* Edgar & Schmidt, *supra,* at 1026-1028.

On the occasions when Congress did adopt prohibitions against disclosure of classified information, it always opted for narrow restrictions. For example, a proposed section of 18 U.S.C. §798 would have prohibited the disclosure of any classified information. *See* S. 805, 79th Cong., 91 Cong. Rec. 3196 (1945). As finally adopted, the statute proscribes only the knowing and willful disclosure of any classified information regarding "communication intelligence" — a relatively small category of classified matter. *See Enhancing Security: Report of the House Judiciary Comm.,* H.R. Rep. No. 81-1895, at 2 (1950); Goldston et al., *supra,* at 423 n.76. Implicit in the passage of such special purpose legislation is the assumption that the general provisions of §793 did not cover such disclosures. *See* Edgar & Schmidt, *supra,* at 1020, 1066, 1072.

One provision of the law does prohibit the disclosure of *any* classified material, whether or not it is "related to the national defense," *id.* at 1074, and whether or not classification is substantively proper. *See Scarbeck v. United States,* 317 F.2d 546, 558 (D.C. Cir.), *cert. denied,* 374 U.S. 856 (1963). That provision is 50 U.S.C. §783(a) (2006), which in pertinent part states:

> It shall be unlawful for any... employee of the United States... to communicate in any manner or by any means, to any other person whom such... employee knows or has reason to believe to be an agent... of any foreign government... any information of a kind which shall have been classified by the President [or by the President's delegates] as affecting the security of the United States, knowing or having reason to know that such information has been so classified....

This statute was passed along with §793(d) and (e) as part of the Internal Security Act of 1950, 64 Stat. 991 (1950). *See* Edgar & Schmidt, *supra,* at 1073-1074.

In 1957 a commission on government security proposed to make it a crime "for any person willfully to disclose without proper authorization, for any purpose whatever, information classified 'secret' or 'top secret,' knowing... such information to have been so classified." *Report of Commission on Government Security* 619-620 (1957). The proposal was "abandoned by the Executive as politically untenable." Edgar & Schmidt, *supra,* at 1056. *See also Espionage Laws and Leaks: Hearings Before the Subcomm. on Legislation of the H. Permanent Select Comm. on Intelligence,* 96th Cong., at 22 (1979).

Given this history, do you think it likely that Congress intended for §793 to criminalize all disclosures of classified information? *See generally* Jennifer K. Elsea, *Criminal Prohibitions on the Publication of Classified Defense Information* (Cong. Res. Serv. R41404), Dec. 6, 2010.

5. *First Amendment "Core Values."* The *Rosen* court undertook the "delicate and difficult task" of weighing First Amendment rights of free expression and association—and the associated right of the public to gain information about the workings of government—against the need to prevent the disclosure of some information in the interest of national security. In this case, the answer turned, the court said, on "whether §793 is narrowly drawn to apply only to those instances in which the government's need for secrecy is legitimate, or whether it is too indiscriminate in its sweep, seeking in effect, to excise the cancer of espionage with a chainsaw instead of a scalpel." Do you agree with the court's finding about Congress's choice of tools?

6. *Insiders vs. Outsiders.* Samual Loring Morison, the Navy analyst, was prosecuted under §793(d), which applies to persons "lawfully having possession" of a document or information. The *Rosen* defendants could only be prosecuted under §793(e), which is applicable to persons having "unauthorized" possession of sensitive materials, unless they could be shown to have conspired with Lawrence Franklin, the DOD employee, to remove the materials, exposing them to §793(g). Does it matter which of these provisions is used in a prosecution? The court declined to decide whether the First Amendment might apply differently to persons "without a special relationship to the government." Does it?

In the end, the *Rosen* court decided that "both common sense and the relevant precedent point persuasively to the conclusion that the government can punish those outside of the government for the unauthorized receipt and deliberate retransmission of information relating to the national defense." 445 F. Supp. 2d at 637. Are you persuaded by the court's reasoning? Can you imagine how this expansive language might be cited as precedent in future cases? What are the broad implications for representative democracy?

7. *Does Motive Matter?* Are motives really irrelevant? Morison claimed he had disclosed the information in order to reveal the progress of a Soviet naval buildup. The government charged that his motives were more selfish — money and ambition. 844 F.2d at 1062. The motive of the *Rosen* defendants was to further the goals of their employer, AIPAC. Should the fact that none of these defendants apparently had either intent or desire to (nor perhaps knowledge that their activities might) injure the United States affect the government's decision to prosecute? What practical problems can you imagine in determining motive? Can you describe a procedure for distinguishing between laudable motives and evil ones?

8. *Is Leaking Theft?* Might 18 U.S.C. §641, *supra* p. 1264, a statute adopted to make remedies for the common law crimes of larceny, embezzlement, and conversion applicable to the theft of government property, be equally applicable to the unauthorized dissemination of information? The *Morison* court apparently thought so, holding that "information" fit within the meaning of the statutory term "a thing of value," which value could be measured by the payment Morison received. But the absence of the language "intent to injure the United States" or some similar culpability standard led one federal judge to question whether §641 could be constitutionally applied to the unauthorized release of classified information. *See United States v. Truong Dinh Hung*, 629 F.2d 908, 924-925 (4th Cir. 1980), *cert. denied*, 454 U.S. 1144 (1982) (dissenting opinion of Judge Winter; the case was decided on other grounds). *See also United States v. Tobias*, 836 F.2d 449, 451 (9th Cir. 1988) (stating that §641 does not apply to intangible goods like classified information).

The theft statute was used to prosecute Daniel Ellsberg for his disclosure of the *Pentagon Papers* to the press. *See infra* p. 1280. Ironically, the prosecution was dismissed when it was learned during the Watergate investigation that the government had itself tried to steal files from Ellsberg's psychiatrist's office in an effort to discredit Ellsberg. *See United States v. Russo*, No. 9373-(WMB)-CD (C.D. Cal. filed Dec. 29, 1971), *dismissed* (C.D. Cal. May 11, 1973). *See* Morton H. Halperin & Daniel Hoffman, *Freedom vs. National Security* 242-248 (1977); Melville B. Nimmer, *National Security Secrets vs. Free Speech: The Issues Left Undecided in the Ellsberg Case*, 26 Stan. L. Rev. 311 (1974).

NOTE ON "AUTHORIZED" LEAKS: THE VALERIE PLAME AFFAIR

The executive branch engages in clandestine leaking of otherwise classified information for its own presumably benign purposes, as we observed at the beginning of this chapter. Members of Congress leak, too. But these unofficial disclosures may not always be entirely harmless. A former Director of Central Intelligence noted:

> [T]he White House staff tends to leak when doing so may help the President politically. The Pentagon leaks, primarily to sell its programs to the Congress and the public. The State Department leaks when it's being forced into a policy move that its people dislike. The CIA leaks when some of its people want to influence policy but know that's a role

they're not allowed to play openly. The Congress is most likely to leak when the issue has political ramifications domestically. [Stansfield Turner, *Secrecy and Democracy* 149 (1985).]

See also Martin Linsky, *Impact: How the Press Affects Federal Policymaking* 172, 238-239 (1986). Some writers go even further, worrying not only about the government's ability to manage and control information through selective leaks, but also about "plants" of deliberate disinformation. *See* I.F. Stone, *Schorr Case: The Real Dangers*, N.Y. Rev. of Books, Apr. 1976, at 6.

Not long after the beginning of the war in Iraq, former ambassador Joseph C. Wilson IV wrote an op-ed piece for the *New York Times* reporting that he had been dispatched to Niger by the CIA in early 2002 to investigate claims that Iraq was seeking to purchase nuclear weapons materials there. *What I Didn't Find in Africa*, N.Y. Times, July 6, 2003. He said that he found the claims "highly doubtful," and that he reported his findings to the CIA. Because his report questioned one of the central rationales for the war, the President and Vice President allegedly instructed the Vice President's Chief of Staff, I. Lewis "Scooter" Libby, to counter it by covertly releasing portions of the then-classified 2002 *National Intelligence Estimate*, which contained language supporting this rationale. *See* David Johnston & David E. Sanger, *Cheney's Aide Says President Approved Leak*, N.Y. Times, Apr. 7, 2006. Libby reportedly was advised that the President's instruction "amounted to declassification of the document," and he did as he was told. *Id.*

At about the same moment, Libby also disclosed to reporters for *Newsweek*, the *New York Times*, and perhaps others that Wilson was married to an undercover CIA operative named Valerie Plame. This leak allegedly was intended to discredit Wilson's account by suggesting that his trip to Niger was a junket arranged by his wife that resulted from nepotism. Libby reportedly was given this information by Vice President Cheney, among others. *See* Murray Waas, *Bush Directed Cheney to Counter War Critic*, Nat'l J., July 3, 2006. The story revealing Plame's identity was broken on July 14, 2003, by syndicated columnist Robert D. Novak, who allegedly got the information from Karl Rove, the President's deputy chief of staff, and others. *See* David Johnston, *Novak Told Prosecutors His Sources in Leak Case*, N.Y. Times, July 12, 2006.

Disclosure of the name of a CIA operative can be a felony under certain circumstances. The Intelligence Identities Protection Act, 50 U.S.C. §§421-426 (2006), provides in part:

> Whoever, having or having had authorized access to classified information that identifies a covert agent, intentionally discloses any information identifying such covert agent to any individual not authorized to receive classified information, knowing that the information disclosed so identifies such covert agent and that the United States is taking affirmative measures to conceal such covert agent's intelligence relationship to the United States, shall be fined . . . or imprisoned. . . . [*Id.* §421(a).]

Subsections 421(b) and (c) punish, respectively, knowing disclosure by a person with authorized access who *learns* the identity of a covert agent and discloses it, and knowing disclosure pursuant to a *pattern of activities* intended to expose covert agents. *See generally* Jennifer K. Elsea, *Intelligence Identities Protection Act* (Cong. Res. Serv. RS21636), Jan. 28, 2011.

After the publication of Plame's name, a special prosecutor was named to look into the case. Two years later, Libby was indicted by a federal grand jury, not for violation of the Intelligence Identities Protection Act, but on five felony counts of making false statements, perjury, and obstruction of justice. *See* David Johnston & Richard W. Stevenson, *Cheney Aide Charged with Lying in Leak Case*, N.Y. Times, Oct. 29, 2005. Can you guess why Libby was charged this way? Why do you suppose Libby allegedly was so circumspect with investigators about how he learned of Plame's identity, and with whom he shared this information? *See* Waas, *supra*.

Should the Intelligence Identities Protection Act be amended to make it easier to use in cases like this one? If so, how? Should journalists who publish the names also be subject to prosecution? Could the President or Vice President lawfully release the name of a covert CIA agent?

43

Restraints on Publication of National Security Information

> You were satisfied to serve the power of your nation
> and we dreamed of giving ours her truth.
>
> Albert Camus, *Letters to a German Friend*[1]

In the previous four chapters we have considered various ways to try to strike a difficult and always contentious balance: between public access to government information that an informed electorate needs in a representative democracy, on the one hand, and protection of some such information when its disclosure would imperil national security, on the other. In this final chapter we extend that inquiry, exploring the power of the federal government, especially the executive branch, to suppress information to which members of the public, most particularly the press, have already gained access. This question relates to the central role of the press in our society — to keep the public informed — and in turn to a more fundamental question: whether ultimate sovereignty in our democracy resides in the executive, the Congress, or the people.

In Part A of this chapter we establish a broad outline for our analysis by reviewing the iconic *Pentagon Papers Case* — a remarkable dispute between the government and two of the nation's leading newspapers over publication of a classified history of the Vietnam War. In the process, we consider the legal and practical implications of the recent publication on the Internet by *WikiLeaks.org* of hundreds of thousands of U.S. government documents relating to national security. In Part B, we push this analysis to its extreme, exploring the power of government to stop the presses when the very survival of the nation may be at stake. In Part C, we examine the use of criminal sanctions as a tactic for controlling journalists and the media. Finally, in Part D, we look briefly at several very recent efforts by government to halt the dissemination of information that might be helpful to our enemies.

---

1. Translated and republished in *Resistance, Rebellion, and Death* 13 (Justin O'Brien trans., 1961).

A. FUNDAMENTALS OF CENSORSHIP: THE *PENTAGON PAPERS* LITIGATION[2]

1. The Roles of Lawyers and Journalists

In 1971, a former Defense Department employee named Daniel Ellsberg surreptitiously provided members of the press with unauthorized copies of a Defense Department study entitled *United States-Vietnam Relations 1945-1967*. Each of the 7,000 pages of analysis and documents was stamped Secret, Top Secret, or Top Secret-Sensitive. The decision to publish the *Pentagon Papers*, as they came to be called, and thus to precipitate the most important modern case involving government censorship, was heralded on the front page of the Sunday *New York Times* on June 13, 1971. Neil Sheehan, *Vietnam Archive: Pentagon Study Traces 3 Decades of Growing U.S. Involvement*. There it was revealed that American involvement in the Vietnam War did not begin with an attack on American ships in the Gulf of Tonkin, as the government had led the public to believe, but as far back as 1950, with large-scale shipments of military equipment to the French by the Truman and Eisenhower administrations. In 1954, U.S. personnel began engaging in sabotage and terror warfare against North Vietnam. The study also reported on U.S. complicity in the overthrow and perhaps in the assassination of South Vietnamese President Ngo Dinh Diem in 1963, on planning for a wider war in the months before the Tonkin Gulf incident in August 1964, and on the careful cultivation of public opinion for support of an expanded conflict. What was particularly provocative about the study was the revelation that the government had deliberately misled the public for several years about the nature and extent of U.S. involvement in Southeast Asia. Other details of the history are set out *supra* pp. 270-276.[3]

It is difficult to assess, let alone impart, the full significance and impact of the publication of these documents. There is, however, little doubt that it had a profound effect on the growing antiwar movement. The disclosures in the detailed study undermined the credibility of the government, and the Nixon administration's effort to suppress the record did nothing to restore public confidence. Indeed, it is arguable that the *Pentagon Papers*, together with subsequent press accounts of the events we now refer to as "Watergate," irreversibly changed the relationship between citizens and government—from one of trust to one of skepticism, if not distrust.[4]

---

2. Much of the information in this study is drawn from Daniel Ellsberg, *Secrets: A Memoir of Vietnam and the Pentagon Papers* (2002); Anthony Lewis, *The Constitution and the Press* (1974) (unpublished course materials, Harvard Law School); David Rudenstine, *The Day the Presses Stopped: A History of the Pentagon Papers Case* (1996); *Inside the Pentagon Papers* (John Prados & Margaret Pratt Porter eds., 2004); Sanford Ungar, *The Papers & The Papers: An Account of the Legal and Political Battle Over the Pentagon Papers* (1989); and John Cary Sims, *Triangulating the Boundaries of Pentagon Papers*, 2 Wm. & Mary Bill Rts. J. 341 (1993). *See also* Floyd Abrams, *Speaking Freely: Trials of the First Amendment* (2005); Anthony Lewis, *More Than Fit to Print*, N.Y. Rev. Books, Apr. 7, 2005, at 8.

3. The unabridged *Times* series was republished in book form: Neil Sheehan, Hedrick Smith, E.W. Kenworthy & Fox Butterfield, *The Pentagon Papers* (1971). More nearly complete versions of the Pentagon study may be found in *The Senator Gravel Edition—The Pentagon Papers: The Defense Department History of United States Decisionmaking in Vietnam* (1971); and *United States-Vietnam Relations, 1945-67: Study Prepared by the Department of Defense* (U.S. Gov't Printing Office 1971).

4. The burglary in June 1972 of the Democratic National Committee headquarters in the Watergate complex in Washington, D.C., by former CIA operatives working for the Republican Committee for the

Journalists thought it was extremely important to print portions of the study and to resist government pressure to desist from publication. It offered, one wrote, "the first good look since the end of World War II at the inner workings of the machinery of the Executive Branch that has grown up under the American Presidency." Sheehan et al., *supra* n.3, at xii. The study showed that the White House manipulated releases of information and appealed to patriotic stereotypes, and regarded "Congress, the news media, the citizenry, even international opinion as a whole...as elements to be influenced." *Id.* at xiii. It also revealed an "absence of emotional anguish or moral questioning" by policymakers. *Id.* at xv.

Excerpts from the study, along with analyses by several *New York Times* reporters, were published in a series of daily installments. Following the second installment, the government sought an injunction against further publication. During the pendency of restraining orders imposed while the courts reviewed the matter, the *Times* editorialized that "Congress and the American people were kept in the dark about fundamental policy decisions affecting the very life of this democracy during the most critical period of the war." *The Pentagon Papers* (June 21, 1971), *reprinted in* Sheehan et al., *supra* n.3, at 646. Moreover, the editorial observed, almost no one inside the government seemed to question the assumption that control of South Vietnam by the Saigon regime justified such a massive U.S. military commitment. A full and open debate in Congress and elsewhere about the reasons for that commitment might, according to the *Times*, have moved the country in a different direction. What the study demonstrated, it said, was "an arrogant disregard for the Congress, for the public, and for the inherent obligation of the responsibilities of leadership in a democratic society." *Id.*

From the beginning, the decision to publish or not to publish was recognized as a truly momentous one, both politically and legally. The journalists, nevertheless, felt very certain about the overriding duty to publish. At the early stages the only lawyer involved in the decision making was James Goodale, general counsel of the *Times*. He, too, apparently was convinced from the outset that the *Times* had a constitutional right, if not a duty, to publish the papers, and he remained a strong voice for that course.

Chief Justice Burger, dissenting in the case that arose out of these facts, said:

> To me it is hardly believable that a newspaper long regarded as a great institution in American life would fail to perform one of the basic and simple duties of every citizen with respect to the discovery or possession of stolen property or secret government documents. That duty, I had thought — perhaps naively — was to report forthwith, to responsible public officers. This duty rests on taxi drivers, Justices, and the *New York Times*. [*New York Times Co. v. United States*, 403 U.S. 713, 751 (1971) (Burger, C.J., dissenting).]

Re-election of President Nixon provided the name "Watergate" for the process that ultimately led to the only "forced" resignation of an American President.

The unauthorized release of the *Pentagon Papers* apparently became an obsession with the Nixon administration. One of the crimes of the so-called White House plumbers, who were supposed to detect and prevent such "leaks," revealed in the course of the Watergate investigation, was a break-in at the office of Daniel Ellsberg's psychiatrist. See *supra* pp. 569, 1276.

What would you have done if you had been an editor of the *Times*? Would you have returned the government documents unread? Or would you have read them before making your decision? Perhaps out of a journalist's natural curiosity, or arrogance, the *Times* editors did not react in the fashion suggested by the Chief Justice. In fact, even before the question of what to do with the documents was formally considered at the editorial level, Neil Sheehan, the reporter who had originally received the papers, holed up in a Washington hotel and pored over them for weeks. Only then, as the decision to publish approached, and the legal ramifications, including fines, imprisonment, and injunctions, loomed larger, did the editors apprise the publisher of the project and seek the advice of outside counsel.

> [The] lawyers...came to a meeting at the *Times* and angrily told Sulzberger [the publisher] and his colleagues that it would be a criminal offense to publish any of the material or stories based on it. Indeed, they said, possession of the papers was a crime at that moment. They refused to look at the documents themselves because, they said, they would then be committing an offense.... They advised the *Times* to return the documents and cancel the project. [Lewis, *The Constitution and the Press*, *supra*, at 34.]

For an extensive description of government deliberations about how to proceed against the *Times*, see Rudenstine, *supra* p. 1280, at 77-95. As it turned out, the advice of the newspaper's law firm, Lord, Day & Lord, headed by former Attorney General Herbert Brownell, was correct—at least as far as then-Attorney General John Mitchell was concerned. After the first two installments of the *Pentagon Papers* were published, the *Times* received a telegram (reproduced on the following page) from Mitchell containing a thinly veiled threat of prosecution under the Espionage Act.[5] Both the telegram and the advice of counsel were based on the premise that the publication of *any* classified material was a *per se* violation of the criminal law no matter what the reports actually contained. As far as the lawyers on both sides were concerned, whether the material was properly classified or, if properly classified, whether the public interest in the information overrode the need for secrecy, were irrelevant questions.

NOTES AND QUESTIONS

1. *Role of the Media Lawyer.* Is it ever appropriate for an attorney to refuse to examine any material relevant to the case against her client? Should it matter that the client asks the attorney to make such an examination? Of course, lawyers must understand their clients and to some degree empathize with them. As outside counsel for generations to the nation's leading newspaper, should the firm of Lord, Day & Lord have been influenced in its advice by broader considerations of the role of the press in American society?

---

5. This copy of the original telegram was furnished by Floyd Abrams, Esq., of Cahill, Gordon & Reindel.

NY K TIMES NY

X

NY K TIMES NY

ARTHUR OCHSSULZBERGER

PRESIDENT AND PUBLISHER

THE NEW YORK TIMES

NEW YORK, NEW YORK

   I HAVE BEEN ADVISED BYTHE SECRETARYOF DEFENSE THAT THE
MATERIAL PUBLISHED IN THE NEW YORK TIMES ON JUNE L3, 14, 1971

CAPTIONED "KEY TEXTS FROM PENTAGON'S VIETNAM STUDY" CONTAINS
INFORMATION RELATING TO THE NATIONAL DEFENSE OF THE UNITED
STATES AND BEARS A TOP SECRET CLASSIFICATION.

   AS, SUCH, PUBLICATION OF THIS INFORMATION IS DIRECTLY
PROHIBITED BY THE PROVISIONS OF THE ESPIONAGE LAW, TITLE
18, UNITED STATES CODE, SECTION 793.

   MOREOVER, FURTHER PUBLICATION OF INFORMATION OF THIS
CHARACTER WILL CAUSEIREXXX IRREPARABLE INJURY TO THE DEFENSE
INTERESTS OF THE UNITED STATES.

   ACCORDINGLY, I RESPECTFULLY REQUEST THAT YOU PUBLISH NO
FURTHER INFORMATION OF THIS CHARACTER AND ADVISE ME THAT
YOU HAVE MADE ARRANGEMENTS FOR THE RETURN OF THESE
DOCUMENTS TO THE DEPARTMENT OF DEFENSE.

                              JOHN N. MITCHELL
                              ATTORNEY GENERAL

1971 JUN 14 PM 8: 34

2. *Institutional Role of the Press.* Consider the following observations of Justice Potter Stewart in 1974:

[The Court] has uniformly reflected its understanding that the Free Press guarantee is, in essence, a *structural* provision of the Constitution. Most of the other provisions in the Bill of Rights protect specific liberties or . . . rights. . . . In contrast, the Free Press Clause extends protection to an institution. The publishing business is, in short, the only organized private business that is given explicit constitutional protection. . . .

. . . If the Free Press guarantee meant no more than freedom of expression, it would be a constitutional redundancy. . . . [M]any of the state constitutions contained clauses protecting freedom of the press while at the same time recognizing no general freedom of speech. By including both guarantees in the First Amendment, the Founders quite clearly recognized the distinction between the two.

It is also a mistake to suppose that the only purpose of the constitutional guarantee of a free press is to insure that a newspaper will serve as a neutral forum for debate, a "market place for ideas". . . . A related theory sees the press as a neutral conduit of information between the people and their elected leaders. These theories, in my view, again give insufficient weight to the institutional autonomy of the press. . . .

In setting up the three branches of . . . Government, the Founders deliberately created an internally competitive system. . . .

The primary purpose of the constitutional guarantee of a free press was a similar one: to create a fourth institution outside the Government as an additional check on the three official branches. . . .

. . . [The] autonomy cuts both ways. The press is free to do battle against secrecy and deception. . . . But the press cannot expect from the Constitution any guarantee that it will succeed. . . . The Constitution itself is neither a Freedom of Information Act nor an Official Secrets Act.

The Constitution, in other words, establishes the contest, not its resolution. Congress may provide a resolution, at least in some instances, through carefully drawn legislation. For the rest, we must rely, as so often in our system we must, on the tug and pull of the political forces in American society. [Potter Stewart, *Or of the Press*, 26 Hastings L.J. 631, 633-636 (1975).]

Chief Justice Burger did not agree with Justice Stewart's view of the "institutional press." Concurring in *First National Bank v. Bellotti*, 435 U.S. 765, 797 (1978), the Chief Justice contended that there was no historical or precedential basis for conferring "special and extraordinary privileges or status on the 'institutional press.'" The commentators are similarly divided. *Compare* David Lange, *The Speech and Press Clauses*, 23 UCLA L. Rev. 77 (1975), *and* Anthony Lewis, *A Preferred Position for Journalism?*, 7 Hofstra L. Rev. 595 (1979), *with* Melville B. Nimmer, *Speech and Press: A Brief Reply*, 23 UCLA L. Rev. 120 (1975), Randall P. Bezanson, *The New Free Press Guarantee*, 63 Va. L. Rev. 731 (1977), *and* Floyd Abrams, *The Press Is Different: Reflections on Justice Stewart and the Autonomous Press*, 7 Hofstra L. Rev. 563 (1979). One commentator lifts the idea of the "checking function" to the level of a general First Amendment theory. *See* Vincent Blasi, *The Checking Value in First Amendment Theory*, 1977 Am. B. Found. Res. J. 523.

3. *A Symbiotic Relationship Between Press and Government.* Is the Stewart view of the relationship between press and government accurate or realistic? Is the relationship perhaps more symbiotic than antagonistic, or sometimes even mutually exploitive? Consider the following excerpt from an affidavit filed by Max Frankel, then-Washington Bureau Chief of the *New York Times*, in the *Pentagon Papers Case*:

The Government's unprecedented challenge to *The Times*...cannot be understood, or decided, without an appreciation of the manner in which a small and specialized corps of reporters and a few hundred American officials regularly make use of so-called classified, secret, and top secret information and documentation. It is a cooperative, competitive, antagonistic and arcane relationship. . . .

Without the use of "secrets" . . . there could be no adequate diplomatic, military and political reporting of the kind our people take for granted, either abroad or in Washington, and there could be no mature system of communication between the Government and the people. That is one reason why the sudden complaint by one party to these regular dealings strikes us as monstrous and hypocritical.[6]

Are you comfortable with an arrangement for guarding the nation's secrets that depends so heavily on the sound judgment of professional journalists and government officials acting covertly? Should it matter whether the leaks are authorized or unauthorized? In this regard recall two authorized leaks in 2003: one revealing the identity of a CIA intelligence operative, another of a hitherto classified *National Intelligence Estimate*. See *supra* pp. 1276-1278. Is it important that information in media stories based on leaks is usually attributed to "unnamed sources" or "government officials who spoke on condition of anonymity"?

What effect, if any, should this secret but pervasive relationship have had on the outcome of the government's case for injunctive relief in the instant case?

4. *Press Self-Censorship.* Anthony Lewis recounts the following history from a 1966 speech by Clifton Daniel, then the *Times*'s managing editor.

The Times had a story for the paper of April 7, 1961, saying that the United States was training an army of Cuban exiles to attack Fidel Castro and that an invasion was imminent. The publisher then, Orvil Dryfoos, was "gravely troubled by the security implications. He could envision failure for the invasion, and he could see *The New York Times* being blamed for a bloody fiasco." After discussion, the story was given less prominent play and mention of the imminence of the invasion deleted. The Bay of Pigs invasion occurred 10 days later. Despite the downplaying of that story, President Kennedy scolded *The Times*. At one newspaper association meeting he suggested that editors, in addition to asking whether a story was news, start asking: "Is it in the interest of national security?" But privately he told a *Times* editor, "If you had printed more about the operation you would have saved us from a colossal mistake." On Sept. 13, 1962, in a conversation with Orvil Dryfoos at the White House, Kennedy remarked, "I wish you had run everything on Cuba." [Lewis, *The Constitution and the Press, supra* p. 1280, at 41.]

In the case of the *Pentagon Papers*, the *New York Times* opted not to print portions of the history that were identified in an off-the-record briefing and in in camera court proceedings as most potentially damaging. Whitney North Seymour Jr., *Press Paranoia — Delusions of Persecution in the Pentagon Papers Case,* 66 N.Y. St. B.J. 10, 11 (1994).

Other examples of media self-censorship — decisions by editors not to publish, or to withhold parts of a story, or to delay publication — abound. The *New York Times* was excoriated by officials in the Bush administration for publishing a story about a long-running, top-secret, warrantless electronic surveillance program, the precise

---

6. The affidavit was supplied by Floyd Abrams, Esq., of Cahill, Gordon & Reindel.

character and scope of which are still not publicly known. James Risen & Eric Licht-blau, *Bush Lets U.S. Spy on Callers Without Courts*, N.Y. Times, Dec. 16, 2005. The *Times* revealed, however, that it had delayed publication of the story for more than a year, to give the government an opportunity to demonstrate that public release of the information would harm national security. *Id.*

In 2006 several newspapers published stories about secret government monitoring of international banking transfers. Following scathing criticism from officials, editors of the *Los Angeles Times* and *New York Times* described an elaborate process for deciding whether to air such a story. There is "no magic formula, no neat metric," they wrote, for measuring either the public interest in a story or the danger its publication might pose to the nation. But, they insisted, the responsibility to decide is "not one we can surrender to the government." Dean Baquet & Bill Keller, Op-Ed., *When Do We Publish a Secret?*, N.Y. Times, July 1, 2006.

What is the effect of a self-imposed delay in publication on the ability of citizens to hold government officials accountable for their actions? How, if at all, should the perhaps uneven tradition of self-regulation by the media affect the judiciary's willingness to impose its own prior or subsequent review of a decision to publish?

2.   An Inherent Power of the Executive to Censor?

With some trepidation the *Times* made the following telegraphic response to the Attorney General's demand that it halt publication:

> We have received the telegram from the Attorney General asking the *Times* to cease further publication of the Pentagon's Vietnam study. The *Times* must respectfully decline the request of the Attorney General, believing that it is in the interest of the people of this country to be informed of the material contained in the series of articles. We have also been informed of the Attorney General's intention to seek an injunction against further publication. We believe that it is properly a matter for the courts to decide. The *Times* will oppose any request for an injunction for the same reason that led us to publish the articles in the first place. We will of course abide by the final decision of the court. [Lewis, *The Constitution and the Press, supra* p. 1280, at 62.]

The next morning, June 15, 1971, the *Times*, represented by Professor Alexander Bickel, who was brought in at the last minute when the *Times*'s regular counsel declined to appear on behalf of its client, appeared in federal court to defend the newspaper's right to continue publication of one of the most significant news stories of the Vietnam period. The request for a temporary restraining order was supported solely by an affidavit from an assistant attorney general declaring that he had "reviewed" the 47-volume study, that the study was classified "top secret-sensitive," and that its publication would prejudice the defense interests of the United States and result in "irreparable injury" to the national defense.

At the hearing the government stressed that a delay in publication was required to give the government and the court time to review the documents. Professor Bickel resisted pressure from the court to agree to a voluntary suspension of publication, arguing that to do so would be to yield to a classic form of censorship. Judge Murray Gurfein granted the restraining order on the ground that he needed a more thorough briefing than there had been opportunity to provide. He added that any temporary harm to the *Times* was far outweighed by the "irreparable harm" that could be done to the interests of the United States. It is worth noting that this was the very first case heard by Judge Gurfein following his appointment to the federal bench. James L. Oakes, *Judge Gurfein and the Pentagon Papers,* 2 Cardozo L. Rev. 5, 14 (1980).

Judge Gurfein's concern was understandable, for he had no way of knowing what the documents contained. The reaction of *Times* editor James Reston was equally understandable: "The fate of this institution is at stake." Lewis, *supra,* at 72. If the government could dictate what the nation's leading newspaper could publish, then the paper's independence was destroyed.

A hearing on the government's motion for a preliminary injunction was set for three days later, Friday, June 18, in order to give the government time to document its claim that publication threatened the national security. At the hearing the government shifted its legal posture. Possible violation of Espionage Act §793(e), described earlier as justifying an injunction, was now cited merely as implicitly supporting the primary argument that the government has "inherent power" to "protect the public interest 'in matters...entrusted to the care of the Nation.'" Lewis, *supra,* at 74. For this proposition the U.S. Attorney for the Southern District of New York, Whitney North Seymour Jr., relied on the old and controversial case of *In re Debs,* 158 U.S. 564, 586 (1895). In that case the Court had upheld the contempt conviction of socialist leader Eugene Debs for violating an injunction against the Chicago Pullman strike. The *Debs* Court recognized an inherent executive power to seek equitable relief in federal court to forestall interference with interstate commerce and the federal mails. In the same vein, the government argued on June 18 that the mere fact of classification raised a presumption that the document's release would injure national security, and that the court should intervene to stop it. (The threat of criminal liability for publication is examined in detail in Part C, below.)

Judge Gurfein rejected the presumption argument and put the government to its proof. In open court the government offered only conclusory generalities about the risk of harm to the nation. The judge then agreed, over the objection of the *Times*'s counsel, to proceed in camera. Even so, government witnesses failed to satisfy the judge's repeated requests for specificity. The U.S. Attorney later explained in a memoir, "Impossible as it may be to believe, the Defense and State Department representatives simply would not explain to the Government lawyers which of the documents in the 47 volumes of the *Pentagon Papers* presented specific risks to national security although they were absolutely positive that such documents existed." Whitney North Seymour Jr., *United States Attorney* 199-200 (1975). Defense Department counsel reportedly forbade the government witnesses to testify in those terms—for security reasons—unless everyone but the judge left the courtroom. Lewis, *supra,* at 85.

On Saturday, June 19, after working through the night, Judge Gurfein wrote an opinion denying the preliminary injunction and dissolving the restraining order, subject to continuation "until such time during the day as the Government may seek a stay from a Judge of the Court of Appeals." *United States v. New York Times,* 328 F. Supp. at 331.

When the Wednesday, June 16, issue of the *Times* appeared without the *Pentagon Papers* continuation, Daniel Ellsberg was very upset. He was afraid that Judge Gurfein's stay was only the beginning of interminable legal delays. After being rebuffed by the national television networks, Ellsberg turned to the *Washington Post.* He supplied the *Post* with substantial portions of the *Papers.* Following a pitched battle between its journalists and its lawyers, the *Post* picked up on Friday, June 18, where the *Times* had left off. Ungar, *supra* p. 1280, at 127-147.

The government moved with more alacrity against the *Post*, possibly to counter the argument by the *Times*'s lawyers that it would be unfair to enjoin it while other newspapers were publishing. By 5:15 that afternoon the *Post* was in federal district court before Judge Gerhard A. Gesell. Within a few hours Judge Gesell denied a temporary restraining order. The government immediately appealed to a three-judge panel of the District of Columbia Circuit Court, and at 1:20 A.M. Saturday morning, by a vote of 2-1, Judge J. Skelly Wright dissenting, the panel reversed Judge Gesell. *United States v. Washington Post Co.*, 446 F.2d 1322 (D.C. Cir. 1971). The decision reflected an element of compromise. Though it called for "an opportunity for the Government to substantiate its claims at [an evidentiary] hearing on its request for a preliminary injunction," the appeals court directed Judge Gesell to hold a hearing and reach a decision by 5:00 P.M. Monday. *Id.* at 1325.

Later that Saturday in New York, the government obtained an extension of the stay of Judge Gurfein's order in favor of the *Times* until a panel of the Second Circuit Court of Appeals could review the district court's ruling, at noon on Monday, June 21. In other words, both newspapers now had received favorable trial court rulings, but both still were restrained from publication.

On Monday Judge Gesell began the hearing promptly at 8:00 A.M. He reluctantly granted a secret hearing but refused to bar *Post* reporters who had expertise in the area of national security. At 4:30 P.M. he ruled for the newspaper in an oral opinion in which he found that the government had failed to show

> that there will be a definite break in diplomatic relations, that there will be an armed attack on the United States, that there will be an armed attack on an ally, that there will be a war, that there will be a compromise of military or defense plans, a compromise of intelligence operations, or a compromise of scientific and technological materials. [Ungar, *supra*, at 173.]

The cases before the two circuit courts of appeal proceeded pretty much in tandem. The D.C. Circuit ruled 7-2 in favor of the *Post*, finding that "the government's proof, judged by the standard suggested in *Near v. Minnesota* . . . does not justify an injunction." 446 F.2d at 1328. The most often quoted dictum in *Near*, 283 U.S. 697 (1931), is

> limitation [on publication] has been recognized only in exceptional cases. "When a nation is at war many things that might be said in time of peace are such a hindrance to its effort that their utterance will not be endured so long as men fight and that no court could regard them as protected by any constitutional right." *Schenck v. United States*, 249 U.S. 47, 52. No one would question but that a government might prevent actual obstruction to its recruiting service or the publication of the sailing dates of transports or the number and location of troops. [283 U.S. at 716.]

In the Second Circuit a 4-4 tie was narrowly averted when a compromise was hammered out, apparently in response to a controversial tactic by U.S. Attorney Seymour. He submitted new affidavits from "defense agencies" to buttress the government's case, and he attached to his brief a "special appendix" that highlighted certain testimony from the secret proceedings and listed specific pages of the *Pentagon Papers* that he said created "particularly grave" risks. The appendix, alleging damaging revelations in the study about, *inter alia*, U.S. intelligence estimates, SEATO contingency war plans, encryption, and the Tonkin Gulf Affair, is reproduced in National Security Archive, *Special Appendix for the Second Circuit, at* http://www.gwu.edu/~nsarchiv/NSAEBB/NSAEBB48/appendix.html. The court ruled that the government's "special appendix," and any additional material the Justice Department claimed was especially dangerous to national security, should be remanded for further secret hearings before Judge Gurfein. *United States v. New York Times Co.*, 444 F.2d 544 (2d Cir. 1971).

On Thursday, June 24, the *New York Times* sought a writ of certiorari from the Supreme Court, and the government sought Supreme Court review of the D.C. Circuit Court judgment. On June 25, five Justices voted to grant review in the consolidated cases on an expedited basis. These five also voted to extend restraint pending the Supreme Court resolution, at least as to all material in the "Special Appendix" and additionally specified "especially sensitive" items. That was to be the last of a long chain of restraining orders the newspapers had to face in connection with publication of the *Pentagon Papers.* The case was set for oral argument the very next day, June 26, and the Supreme Court issued the following decision four days later, on June 30, 1971.

New York Times Co. v. United States
United States Supreme Court, 1971
403 U.S. 713

PER CURIAM. We granted certiorari in these cases in which the United States seeks to enjoin the New York Times and the Washington Post from publishing the contents of a classified study entitled "History of U.S. Decision-Making Process on Vietnam Policy." . . .

"Any system of prior restraints of expression comes to this Court bearing a heavy presumption against its constitutional validity." *Bantam Books, Inc. v. Sullivan*, 372 U.S. 58, 70 (1963); see also *Near v. Minnesota*, 283 U.S. 697 (1931). The Government "thus carries a heavy burden of showing justification for the imposition of such a restraint." *Organization for a Better Austin v. Keefe*, 402 U.S. 415, 419 (1971). The District Court for the Southern District of New York in the *New York Times* case and the District Court for the District of Columbia and the Court of Appeals for the District of Columbia Circuit in the *Washington Post* case held that the Government had not met that burden. We agree.

The judgment of the Court of Appeals for the District of Columbia Circuit is therefore affirmed. The order of the Court of Appeals for the Second Circuit is reversed. . . . The stays entered June 25, 1971, by the Court are vacated. The judgments shall issue forthwith. So ordered.

Mr. Justice BLACK, with whom Mr. Justice DOUGLAS joins, concurring. . . . [E]very moment's continuance of the injunctions against these newspapers amounts to a flagrant, indefensible, and continuing violation of the First Amendment. . . .

In the First Amendment the Founding Fathers gave the free press the protection it must have to fulfill its essential role in our democracy. The press was to serve the governed, not the governors. The Government's power to censor the press was abolished so that the press would remain forever free to censure the Government. The press was protected so that it could bare the secrets of government and inform the people. Only a free and unrestrained press can effectively expose deception in government. And paramount among the responsibilities of a free press is the duty to prevent any part of the government from deceiving the people and sending them off to distant lands to die of foreign fevers and foreign shot and shell. In my view, far from deserving condemnation for their courageous reporting, the New York Times, the Washington Post, and other newspapers should be commended for serving the purpose that the Founding Fathers saw so clearly. In revealing the workings of government that led to the Vietnam war, the newspapers nobly did precisely that which the Founders hoped and trusted they would do.

The Government's case here is based on premises entirely different from those that guided the Framers of the First Amendment.... And the Government argues in its brief that in spite of the First Amendment, "[t]he authority of the Executive Department to protect the nation against publication of information whose disclosure would endanger the national security stems from two interrelated sources: the constitutional power of the President over the conduct of foreign affairs and his authority as Commander-in-Chief."

... To find that the President has "inherent power" to halt the publication of news by resort to the courts would wipe out the First Amendment and destroy the fundamental liberty and security of the very people the Government hopes to make "secure."...

The word "security" is a broad, vague generality whose contours should not be invoked to abrogate the fundamental law embodied in the First Amendment. The guarding of military and diplomatic secrets at the expense of informed representative government provides no real security for our Republic. The Framers of the First Amendment, fully aware of both the need to defend a new nation and the abuses of the English and Colonial governments, sought to give this new society strength and security by providing that freedom of speech, press, religion, and assembly should not be abridged....

Mr. Justice DOUGLAS, with whom Mr. Justice BLACK joins, concurring.... The power to wage war is "the power to wage war successfully." See *Hirabayashi v. United States*, 320 U.S. 81, 93. But the war power stems from a declaration of war.... Nowhere are presidential wars authorized. We need not decide therefore what leveling effect the war power of Congress might have....

... It is common knowledge that the First Amendment was adopted against the widespread use of the common law of seditious libel to punish the dissemination of material that is embarrassing to the powers-that-be.... The present cases will, I think, go down in history as the most dramatic illustration of that principle. A debate of large proportions goes on in the Nation over our posture in Vietnam. That debate antedated the disclosure of the contents of the present documents. The latter are highly relevant to the debate in progress.

Secrecy in government is fundamentally anti-democratic....

Mr. Justice BRENNAN, concurring.... The relative novelty of the questions presented, the necessary haste with which decisions were reached, the magnitude of the interests asserted, and the fact that all the parties have concentrated their arguments upon the question whether permanent restraints were proper may have justified at least some of the restraints heretofore imposed in these cases. Certainly it is difficult to fault the several courts below for seeking to assure that the issues here involved were preserved for ultimate review by this Court. But even if it be assumed that some of the interim restraints were proper in the two cases before us, that assumption has no bearing upon the propriety of similar judicial action in the future.... [T]he First Amendment stands as an absolute bar to the imposition of judicial restraints in circumstances of the kind presented by these cases.

... [T]he First Amendment tolerates absolutely no prior judicial restraints of the press predicated upon surmise or conjecture that untoward consequences may result.* Our cases, it is true, have indicated that there is a single, extremely narrow class of cases in which the First Amendment's ban on prior judicial restraint may be overridden. Our cases have thus far indicated that such cases may arise only when the Nation "is at war," *Schenck v. United States,* 249 U.S. 47, 52 (1919), during which times "[n]o one would question but that a government might prevent actual obstruction to its recruiting service or the publication of the sailing dates of transports or the number and location of troops." *Near v. Minnesota,* 283 U.S. 697, 716 (1931). Even if the present world situation were assumed to be tantamount to a time of war, or if the power of presently available armaments would justify even in peacetime the suppression of information that would set in motion a nuclear holocaust, in neither of these actions has the Government presented or even alleged that publication of items from or based upon the material at issue would cause the happening of an event of that nature.... [O]nly governmental allegation and proof that publication must inevitably, directly, and immediately cause the occurrence of an event kindred to imperiling the safety of a transport already at sea can support even the issuance of an interim restraining order. In no event may mere conclusions be sufficient: for if the Executive Branch seeks judicial aid in preventing publication, it must inevitably submit the basis upon which that aid is sought to scrutiny by the judiciary. And therefore, every restraint issued in this case, whatever its form, has violated the First Amendment — and not less so because that restraint was justified as necessary to afford the courts an opportunity to examine the claim more thoroughly. Unless and until the Government has clearly made out its case, the First Amendment commands that no injunction may issue.

Mr. Justice STEWART, with whom Mr. Justice WHITE joins, concurring. In the governmental structure created by our Constitution, the Executive is endowed with enormous power in the two related areas of national defense and international relations. This power, largely unchecked by the Legislative and Judicial branches, has been pressed to the very hilt since the advent of the nuclear missile age....

In the absence of the governmental checks and balances present in other areas of our national life, the only effective restraint upon executive policy and power in the areas of national defense and international affairs may lie in an enlightened citizenry.... For this reason, it is perhaps here that a press that is alert, aware, and free most vitally serves the basic purpose of the First Amendment. For without an informed and free press there cannot be an enlightened people.

Yet it is elementary that the successful conduct of international diplomacy and the maintenance of an effective national defense require both confidentiality and secrecy. Other nations can hardly deal with this Nation in an atmosphere of mutual trust unless they can be assured that their confidences will be kept. And within our own executive departments, the development of considered and intelligent international policies would be impossible if those charged with their formulation could not

---

* *Freedman v. Maryland,* 380 U.S. 51 (1965), and similar cases regarding temporary restraints of allegedly obscene materials are not in point. For those cases rest upon the proposition that "obscenity is not protected by the freedoms of speech and press." *Roth v. United States,* 354 U.S. 476, 481 (1957). Here there is no question but that the material sought to be suppressed is within the protection of the First Amendment....

communicate with each other freely, frankly, and in confidence. In the area of basic national defense the frequent need for absolute secrecy is, of course, self-evident.

I think there can be but one answer to this dilemma if dilemma it be. The responsibility must be where the power is. If the Constitution gives the Executive a large degree of unshared power in the conduct of foreign affairs and the maintenance of our national defense, then under the Constitution the Executive must have the largely unshared duty to determine and preserve the degree of internal security necessary to exercise that power successfully. It is an awesome responsibility, requiring judgment and wisdom of a high order. I should suppose that moral, political, and practical considerations would dictate that a very first principle of that wisdom would be an insistence upon avoiding secrecy for its own sake. For when everything is classified, then nothing is classified, and the system becomes one to be disregarded by the cynical or the careless, and to be manipulated by those intent on self-protection or self-promotion. . . .

This is not to say that Congress and the courts have no role to play. Undoubtedly Congress has the power to enact specific and appropriate criminal laws to protect government property and preserve government secrets. Congress has passed such laws, and several of them are of very colorable relevance to the apparent circumstances of these cases. And if a criminal prosecution is instituted, it will be the responsibility of the courts to decide the applicability of the criminal law under which the charge is brought. Moreover, if Congress should pass a specific law authorizing civil proceedings in this field, the courts would likewise have the duty to decide the constitutionality of such a law as well as its applicability to the facts proved.

But in the cases before us we are asked neither to construe specific regulations nor to apply specific laws. . . . I am convinced that the Executive is correct with respect to some of the documents involved. But I cannot say that disclosure of any of them will surely result in direct, immediate, and irreparable damage to our Nation or its people. . . .

Mr. Justice WHITE, with whom Mr. Justice STEWART joins, concurring. . . . I do not say that in no circumstances would the First Amendment permit an injunction against publishing information about government plans or operations. Nor, after examining the materials the Government characterizes as the most sensitive and destructive, can I deny that revelation of these documents will do substantial damage to public interests. Indeed, I am confident that their disclosure will have that result. But I nevertheless agree that the United States has not satisfied the very heavy burden that it must meet to warrant an injunction against publication in these cases, at least in the absence of express and appropriately limited congressional authorization for prior restraints in circumstances such as these.

The Government's position is simply stated: The responsibility of the Executive for the conduct of the foreign affairs and for the security of the Nation is so basic that the President is entitled to an injunction against publication of a newspaper story whenever he can convince a court that the information to be revealed threatens "grave and irreparable" injury to the public interest; and the injunction should issue whether or not the material to be published is classified, whether or not publication would be lawful under relevant criminal statutes enacted by Congress, and regardless of the circumstances by which the newspaper came into possession of the information.

At least in the absence of legislation by Congress, based on its own investigations and findings, I am quite unable to agree that the inherent powers of the Executive and the courts reach so far as to authorize remedies having such sweeping potential for inhibiting publications by the press. Much of the difficulty inheres in the "grave and irreparable danger" standard suggested by the United States. If the United States were to have judgment under such a standard in these cases, our decision would be of little guidance to other courts in other cases, for the material at issue here would not be available from the Court's opinion or from public records, nor would it be published by the press. Indeed, even today where we hold that the United States has not met its burden, the material remains sealed in court records and it is properly not discussed in today's opinions....

The Criminal Code contains numerous provisions potentially relevant to these cases.... [Justice White devotes five pages to a discussion of the criminal provisions.]

... I am not, of course, saying that either of these newspapers has yet committed a crime or that either would commit a crime if it published all the material now in its possession. That matter must await resolution in the context of a criminal proceeding if one is instituted by the United States. In that event, the issue of guilt or innocence would be determined by procedures and standards quite different from those that have purported to govern these injunctive proceedings.

Mr. Justice MARSHALL, concurring.... In these cases there is no problem concerning the President's power to classify information as "secret" or "top secret." Congress has specifically recognized Presidential authority, which has been formally exercised in Exec. Order 10501 (1953), to classify documents and information....

The problem here is whether in these particular cases the Executive Branch has authority to invoke the equity jurisdiction of the courts to protect what it believes to be the national interest. See *In re Debs*, 158 U.S. 564, 584 (1895)....

... [The Constitution] did not provide for government by injunction in which the courts and the Executive Branch can "make law" without regard to the action of Congress. It may be more convenient for the Executive Branch if it need only convince a judge to prohibit conduct rather than ask the Congress to pass a law, and it may be more convenient to enforce a contempt order than to seek a criminal conviction in a jury trial. Moreover, it may be considered politically wise to get a court to share the responsibility.... But convenience and political considerations of the moment do not justify a basic departure from the principles of our system of government....

... It is a traditional axiom of equity that a court of equity will not do a useless thing just as it is a traditional axiom that equity will not enjoin the commission of a crime. Here there has been no attempt to make such a showing. The Solicitor General does not even mention in his brief whether the Government considers that there is probable cause to believe a crime has been committed or whether there is a conspiracy to commit future crimes.

If the Government had attempted to show that there was no effective remedy under traditional criminal law, it would have had to show that there is no arguably applicable statute....

On at least two occasions Congress has refused to enact legislation that would have made the conduct engaged in here unlawful and given the President the power that he seeks in this case. In 1917 during the debate over the original Espionage Act, still the basic provisions of 793, Congress rejected a proposal to give the President in time of war or threat of war authority to directly prohibit by proclamation the publication of information relating to national defense that might be useful to the enemy....

In 1957 the United States Commission on Government Security found that "[a]irplane journals, scientific periodicals, and even the daily newspaper have featured articles containing information and other data which should have been deleted in whole or in part for security reasons." In response to this problem the Commission proposed that "Congress enact legislation making it a crime for any person willfully to disclose without proper authorization, for any purpose whatever, information classified 'secret' or 'top secret,' knowing, or having reasonable grounds to believe, such information to have been so classified." Report of Commission on Government Security 619-620 (1957). After substantial floor discussion on the proposal, it was rejected. . . .

Mr. Chief Justice BURGER, dissenting. . . . The newspapers make a derivative claim under the First Amendment; they denominate this right as the public "right to know"; by implication, the Times asserts a sole trusteeship of that right by virtue of its journalistic "scoop." The right is asserted as an absolute. Of course, the First Amendment right itself is not an absolute, as Justice Holmes so long ago pointed out in his aphorism concerning the right to shout "fire" in a crowded theater if there was no fire. There are other exceptions, some of which Chief Justice Hughes mentioned by way of example in *Near v. Minnesota.* . . . Conceivably such exceptions may be lurking in these cases and would have been flushed had they been properly considered in the trial courts, free from unwarranted deadlines and frenetic pressures. An issue of this importance should be tried and heard in a judicial atmosphere conducive to thoughtful, reflective deliberation. . . .

It is not disputed that the Times has had unauthorized possession of the documents for three to four months. . . . After these months of deferral, the alleged "right to know" has somehow and suddenly become a right that must be vindicated instanter.

Would it have been unreasonable, since the newspaper could anticipate the Government's objections to release of secret material, to give the Government an opportunity to review the entire collection and determine whether agreement could be reached on publication? Stolen or not, if security was not in fact jeopardized, much of the material could no doubt have been declassified, since it spans a period ending in 1968. With such an approach — one that great newspapers have in the past practiced and stated editorially to be the duty of an honorable press — the newspapers and Government might well have narrowed the area of disagreement as to what was and was not publishable, leaving the remainder to be resolved in orderly litigation, if necessary. . . .

I agree generally with Mr. Justice Harlan and Mr. Justice Blackmun but I am not prepared to reach the merits. . . .

Mr. Justice HARLAN, with whom The Chief Justice and Mr. Justice BLACKMUN join, dissenting. . . . Due regard for the extraordinarily important and difficult questions involved in these litigations should have led the Court to shun such a precipitate timetable. . . .

Forced as I am to reach the merits of these cases, I dissent from the opinion and judgments of the Court. . . .

. . . It is plain to me that the scope of the judicial function in passing upon the activities of the Executive Branch of the Government in the field of foreign affairs is very narrowly restricted. This view is, I think, dictated by the concept of separation of powers upon which our constitutional system rests. . . .

The power to evaluate the "pernicious influence" of premature disclosure is not, however, lodged in the Executive alone. I agree that, in performance of its duty to protect the values of the First Amendment against political pressures, the judiciary must review the initial Executive determination to the point of satisfying itself that the subject matter of the dispute does lie within the proper compass of the President's foreign relations power. Constitutional considerations forbid "a complete abandonment of judicial control." Cf. *United States v. Reynolds*, 345 U.S. 1, 8 (1953). Moreover, the judiciary may properly insist that the determination that disclosure of the subject matter would irreparably impair the national security be made by the head of the Executive Department concerned — here the Secretary of State or the Secretary of Defense — after actual personal consideration by that officer. This safeguard is required in the analogous area of executive claims of privilege for secrets of state.

But in my judgment the judiciary may not properly go beyond these two inquiries and redetermine for itself the probable impact of disclosure on the national security. . . .

Even if there is some room for the judiciary to override the executive determination, it is plain that the scope of review must be exceedingly narrow. I can see no indication in the opinions of either the District Court or the Court of Appeals in the *Post* litigation that the conclusions of the Executive were given even the deference owing to an administrative agency, much less that owing to a co-equal branch of the Government operating within the field of its constitutional prerogative. . . .

Pending further hearings in each case conducted under the appropriate ground rules, I would continue the restraints on publication. I cannot believe that the doctrine prohibiting prior restraints reaches to the point of preventing courts from maintaining the status quo long enough to act responsibly in matters of such national importance as those involved here.

Mr. Justice BLACKMUN, dissenting. . . . [I] would remand these cases to be developed expeditiously, of course, but on a schedule permitting the orderly presentation of evidence from both sides, with the use of discovery, if necessary, as authorized by the rules, and with the preparation of briefs, oral argument, and court opinions of a quality better than has been seen to this point. . . .

I strongly urge, and sincerely hope, that these two newspapers will be fully aware of their ultimate responsibilities to the United States of America. Judge Wilkey, dissenting in the District of Columbia case, after a review of only the affidavits before his court (the basic papers had not then been made available by either party), concluded that there were a number of examples of documents that . . . "could clearly result in great harm to the nation," and he defined "harm" to mean "the death of soldiers, the destruction of alliances, the greatly increased difficulty of negotiation with our enemies, the inability of our diplomats to negotiate. . . ." I, for one, have now been able to give at least some cursory study not only to the affidavits, but to the material itself. I regret to say that from this examination I fear that Judge Wilkey's statements have possible foundation. I therefore share his concern. I hope that damage has not already been done. If, however, damage has been done, and if, with the Court's action today, these newspapers proceed to publish the critical documents and there results therefrom [the aforementioned harm] to which list I might add the factors of prolongation of the war and of further delay in the freeing of United States prisoners, then the Nation's people will know where the responsibility for these sad consequences rests.

NOTES AND QUESTIONS

1. *Who Really Won?* One of the ultimate questions always asked about the *Pentagon Papers Case* was whether the press *really* won. Some think the press's lawyers yielded too much ground and actually emerged with a balancing test where previously there had been an absolute rule against prior restraint. *See* Don R. Pember, *The "Pentagon Papers" Decision: More Questions Than Answers*, 48 Journalism Q. 403 (1971). For a defense of the strategies they pursued, see Alexander M. Bickel, *The Morality of Consent* 79-88 (1976); Stanley Godofsky (a *Post* lawyer), *Protection of the Press from Prior Restraint and Harassment Under Libel Laws*, 29 U. Miami L. Rev. 462, 471-472 (1975). Bickel himself recognized that something had been lost:

> [L]aw can never make us as secure as we are when we do not need it. Those freedoms which are neither challenged nor defined are the most secure. . . . Before June 15, 1971, through the troubles of 1798, through one civil and two world wars, . . . there had never been an effort by the federal government to censor a newspaper. . . . That spell was broken, and in a sense freedom was thus diminished. . . .
>   . . . We extend the legal reality of freedom at some cost in its limitless appearance. [Alexander M. Bickel, *The "Uninhibited, Robust, and Wide-Open" First Amendment*, 54 Comment. 60, 61 (Nov. 1972).]

See also Erwin N. Griswold, *Teaching Alone Is Not Enough*, 25 J. Leg. Educ. 251, 258 (1973), for a claim of victory for the government.

2. *The Holding.* The per curiam decision is spare: prior restraint of expression bears a heavy presumption of unconstitutionality. The government did not discharge the burden of overcoming it.

The decision was reached within six days from the date of filing and four days after arguments were heard. There simply was too little time to circulate opinions in order to form majority and minority positions. Instead, each Justice wrote an opinion, and except for a concurrence here and there, no single opinion mustered the support of enough Justices to become the majority opinion. Six Justices, however, could agree on the common denominator expressed in the per curiam opinion, so that opinion became the opinion for the Court. One important question this poses is: what is the precedential value of this case? *See* Louis Henkin, *The Right to Know and the Duty to Withhold: The Case of the Pentagon Papers*, 120 U. Pa. L. Rev. 271, 272 (1971).

After the remand by the three-judge D.C. Circuit panel, Judge Gesell complained that he was uncomfortable in the role of censor, particularly without standards to guide him. *See* Ungar, *supra* p. 1280, at 173. Drawing from the different opinions, can you compile a list of the sort of matters that might be enjoined?

More recently, the Supreme Court was asked to apply a federal wiretap law that provides penalties for the knowing disclosure of an illegally recorded communication. *Bartnicki v. Vopper*, 532 U.S. 514 (2001). The case arose when a radio broadcaster aired a taped cell phone conversation between labor union officials. The Court ruled that because of the public importance of the content of the tape and because the broadcaster had not participated in the illegal intercept, the broadcast was protected by the First Amendment. How might the application of these criteria have affected the outcome in the *Pentagon Papers Case*? How might they apply to a future case involving a restraint on publication?

3. *The Secret Pleadings.* The opinions reveal almost nothing about the contents of the *Pentagon Papers* or about the government's efforts to discharge its "heavy burden of showing justification" for a prior restraint. We know that none of the judges or Justices reviewed all of the 7,000-page history. Following Judge Gurfein's continuation of his temporary restraining order, Defense Department and intelligence officials identified what they thought were the most sensitive parts of the document. Those portions were then described in classified appendices to pleadings in the courts of appeal and in a secret brief in the Supreme Court; they have only recently been made available to researchers. The secret pleadings, along with streaming audio and transcripts of taped White House conversations between Nixon and his advisors about the *Papers,* arguments in the Supreme Court, and a trove of related materials, may be found in National Security Archive, *The Pentagon Papers: Secrets, Lies and Audiotapes* (n.d.), *at* http://www.gwu.edu/~nsarchiv/NSAEBB/NSAEBB48/briefs.html. *See also* Sims, *supra* p. 1280. By revealing the justifications for a continuing restraint that were rejected by the Court, these materials may help us to predict the standard that would apply in a future case.

The government, the Court, and, apparently, the *New York Times* were all unaware that Daniel Ellsberg had withheld from the *Times* four volumes of the study devoted to ongoing diplomatic negotiations. Those four volumes headed the list of items the release of which the government felt would injure national interests. They were later published separately. *The Secret Diplomacy of the Vietnam War: The Negotiating Volumes of the Pentagon Papers* (George C. Herring ed., 1983). How, if at all, should this failure of knowledge have affected the government's burden of proof? Should it affect our reliance on a newspaper's independent determination of what information can be safely released to the public?

The government's pleadings also warned about disclosure of the U.S. role in the overthrow of President Ngo Dinh Diem, plans for bombing North Vietnam and for fighting elsewhere in Southeast Asia and China, estimates of Soviet involvement, planning for covert operations, intelligence gathering, and U.S. encryption techniques. The study was also said to contain information embarrassing to our allies, especially South Korea, Thailand, and South Vietnam. Yet no specific examples of threatened injuries were provided. And there was no assertion that publication would "inevitably" result in harm, as Justice Brennan would have required.

According to Professor Sims, the government probably established that the nature and magnitude of the threatened injury were constitutionally adequate to justify a prior restraint, and that the injury would likely result from disclosure. But it failed to show that the feared harm would be a "direct" and "immediate" consequence of publication. Sims, *supra,* 2 Wm. & Mary Bill Rts. J. at 404-415. The Solicitor General who argued the case for the government later declared, "I have never seen any trace of a threat to the national security from the publication." Erwin N. Griswold, *Secrets Not Worth Keeping: The Courts and Classified Information,* Wash. Post, Feb. 15, 1989.

4. *Justiciability.* Has the Court implicitly determined what the public needs to know in order to make a reasoned expression of its political will? Or has the Court confined its inquiry to whether the dissemination of certain information is likely to imperil the national security? Are the two questions related? Is any court properly equipped to deal with either question? *See* Henkin, *supra,* 120 U. Pa. L. Rev. at 278-279 (suggesting no). Is the judiciary entitled under the Constitution to make such a determination?

5. *Balancing Freedom and Death.* During oral argument, Justice Stewart addressed this question to *New York Times* counsel Alexander Bickel:

> Let us assume that when the members of the Court go back and open up this sealed record we find something there that absolutely convinces us that its disclosure would result in the sentencing to death of a hundred young men whose only offense had been that they were 19 years old and had low draft numbers. What should we do?

Professor Bickel reluctantly conceded that such material should not be published. William R. Glendon, lawyer for the *Washington Post,* tried to brush the question aside by responding that the hypothetical was not the case before the Court. William R. Glendon, *Fifteen Days in June That Shook the First Amendment: A First Person Account of the Pentagon Papers Case,* 65 N.Y. St. B.J. 24, 26 (1993). How would you have answered? How do you suppose Justice Black would have responded to Justice Stewart?

6. *Reading the Pentagon Papers Today.* On June 13, 2011, forty years to the day after they were first published, the full text of the *Pentagon Papers* was officially declassified—all but 11 words. *See Eleven Words in Pentagon Papers to Remain Classified,* Secrecy News, May 27, 2011. Why it should have taken so long to do this, and why portions of the history still need to be withheld, have not been explained.

CASE STUDY — WIKILEAKS: THE NEW NEW YORK TIMES?[7]

Early in the twenty-first century, members of the public have begun to rely ever more heavily on Internet sources for news, rather than on traditional print media. This change offers advantages, but also risks. Information can travel around the world instantaneously, portraying events almost as they happen. Such information is becoming better organized and easier to access. The benefits to representative democracy are obvious. At the same time, however, the new electronic media provide an unprecedented opportunity to quickly and irretrievably distribute information that could be harmful to national security.

A spectacular example came in 2010, when *WikiLeaks.org* posted on its Web site some 75,000 classified U.S. military reports, comprising six years of incident reports and intelligence documents about U.S. combat activities in Afghanistan. *See* C.J. Chivers et al., *The War Logs; The Afghan Struggle: A Secret Archive,* N.Y. Times, July 26, 2010. *WikiLeaks* reportedly made no attempt to have the materials vetted by the Defense Department before releasing them. Secretary of Defense Robert Gates remarked that the consequences of the posting were "potentially severe and dangerous for our troops, our allies and Afghan partners, and may well damage our relationships and reputation in that key part of the world." Afghans named in the releases were exposed to retribution for assisting the United States, he indicated, intelligence sources and methods, as well as military tactics, were revealed, and allies would be more reluctant to confide in U.S. officials. *See* Charlie Savage, *Gates Assails WikiLeaks*

---

7. Information in this study was drawn from contemporary news accounts.

Over Release of Reports, N.Y. Times, July 30, 2010. Three months later *WikiLeaks* posted some 400,000 government documents relating to the war in Iraq. *See The Iraq Archive: The Strands of a War*, N.Y. Times, Oct. 23, 2010. In this instance *WikiLeaks* apparently redacted the names of some informants. Then in November *WikiLeaks* began to release portions of a quarter-million confidential U.S. diplomatic cables, to the great consternation of the State Department and officials of other governments around the world. *See* Scott Shane & Andrew W. Lehren, *Leaked Cables Offer a Raw Look Inside U.S. Diplomacy* (Nov. 29, 2010). Secretary of State Hillary Clinton called this release "not just an attack on America's foreign policy interests. It is an attack on the international community — the alliances and partnerships, the conversations and negotiations, that safeguard global security and advance economic prosperity." Hillary Rodham Clinton, *Remarks to the Press on the Release of Confidential Documents*, Washington, D.C., Nov. 29, 2010.

All the released materials are believed to have been provided to *WikiLeaks* by a low-level Army intelligence analyst who gained access to them because of a security loophole. The analyst, Private First Class Bradley Manning, was charged under the Uniform Code of Military Justice with aiding the enemy, a capital offense under UCMJ art. 104; violation of Espionage Act §793(e); violation of Army regulations that forbid downloading classified materials onto a personal computer; computer fraud under 18 U.S.C. §1030; theft of government property under 18 U.S.C. §641; and other offenses. *See Army Adds 22 Charges Against Intelligence Analyst*, Am. Forces Press Serv., Mar. 2, 2011, *at* http://www.defense.gov/News/NewsArticle.aspx?ID=63002.

NOTES AND QUESTIONS

1. *Stopping the WikiLeaks Leaks? WikiLeaks.org* has no official headquarters, and its computer servers are located around the world. Its founder and director, Julian Assange, is an Australian citizen. U.S. government information held by *WikiLeaks* and not yet posted to its Web site apparently is held by an unknown number of individuals in several countries. These facts present both practical and legal obstacles to efforts at barring further releases that might be harmful to U.S. national security. Can you point to other legally significant facts that distinguish the controversy surrounding the *WikiLeaks* releases from the controversy over publication of the *Pentagon Papers* in 1971? Ignoring for the moment questions about extraterritorial jurisdiction and enforcement, and without knowing more about the contents of documents yet to be released, can you say whether a U.S. court would be likely to enjoin such releases based on the precedent set in the *Pentagon Papers Case?*

2. *Applying the First Amendment to WikiLeaks. WikiLeaks* declares on its home page: "We are of assistance to peoples of all countries who wish to reveal unethical behavior in their governments and institutions. We aim for maximum political impact." *WikiLeaks, at* http://mirror.wikileaks.info/. Does it qualify as "press" for purposes of the First Amendment? If not, would its First Amendment protections, if any, be fewer?

Does the First Amendment afford any protections for the press abroad, or for that matter for anyone outside the United States seeking freedom of expression? If so, does it apply the same way abroad that it does domestically? Does it matter for this purpose that neither *WikiLeaks* nor Assange is a U.S. citizen or organization? See generally Chapter 25. Should the answer be affected by the fact that data released by *WikiLeaks* anywhere in the world are instantly available in the United States, as well as worldwide?

3. *Complicity for the New York Times?* The *New York Times* and other newspapers published many of the documents posted by *WikiLeaks* on the Internet. A number of them were classified. Why do you suppose the *Times* wanted to reproduce materials that had already been publicly released? Regarding the diplomatic cables, the *Times* answered:

> [T]he cables tell the unvarnished story of how the government makes its biggest decisions, the decisions that cost the country most heavily in lives and money. They shed light on the motivations—and, in some cases, duplicity—of allies on the receiving end of American courtship and foreign aid. They illuminate the diplomacy surrounding two current wars and several countries, like Pakistan and Yemen, where American military involvement is growing. As daunting as it is to publish such material over official objections, it would be presumptuous to conclude that Americans have no right to know what is being done in their name. [*A Note to Readers: The Decision to Publish Diplomatic Documents*, N.Y. Times, Nov. 29, 2010.]

Whatever you concluded about the right of the *Times* to make its own decision whether to publish the *Pentagon Papers*, do you think this case is different? If so, why?

B. THE EXTREME CASE: *THE PROGRESSIVE*[8]

Eight years after Justice Brennan's opinion in the *Pentagon Papers Case*, the government, believing it faced "the *Near* exception in the nuclear age," moved to enjoin publication in *The Progressive* magazine of an article by Howard Morland entitled *The H-Bomb Secret: How We Got It, Why We're Telling It*. The secret, according to Morland,

> is in the coupling mechanism that enables an ordinary fission bomb ... to trigger ... the energy of hydrogen fusion. The physical pressure and heat generated by x- and gamma radiation, moving outward from the trigger at the speed of light, bounces against the weapon's inner wall and is reflected with enormous force into the sides of a carrot-shaped "pencil" which contains the fusion fuel.

A number of additional details, along with illustrations, were included in the article.

The Energy Department concluded that the Morland piece contained "restricted data," as defined by the Atomic Energy Act of 1946, 42 U.S.C. §§2011-2297g-4 (2006), to mean "all data concerning (1) design, manufacture, or utilization of atomic weapons; (2) the production of special nuclear material; or (3) the use of special nuclear material in the production of energy [except data declassified pursuant to section 2162]." *Id.* §2014(y). The government then sought an injunction against the magazine, asserting that publication of the article would violate two provisions of the Act:

---

8. This account draws extensively from the May and November 1979 issues of *The Progressive*. *See also* Symposium, *Weapons of Mass Destruction, National Security, and a Free Press: Seminal Issues as Viewed Through the Lens of the Progressive Case*, 26 Cardozo L. Rev. 1323 (2005); Erwin Knoll, *National Security: The Ultimate Threat to the First Amendment*, 66 Minn. L. Rev. 161 (1981).

§2274. Whoever, lawfully or unlawfully, having possession of . . . information involving or incorporating Restricted Data . . . (b) communicates, transmits, or discloses the same to any . . . person . . . with reason to believe such data will be utilized to injure the United States or to secure an advantage to any foreign nation, shall . . . be punished. . . .

§2280. Whenever in the judgment of the [Secretary of Energy] any person has engaged or is about to engage in any acts . . . which [do] or will constitute a violation of any provision of this chapter . . . the Attorney General . . . upon a showing [thereof by the Secretary may seek in an appropriate court] a permanent or temporary injunction. . . .

The government distinguished the *Pentagon Papers Case* on the very grounds cited by several opinions in that case: here was both a relevant criminal proscription and statutory authority to enforce the prohibition by injunctive relief.

In *United States v. Progressive, Inc.*, 467 F. Supp. 990 (W.D. Wis. 1979), Judge Warren issued what he believed to be "the first . . . prior restraint against a publication in this fashion in the history of this country," and ruefully added that "[s]uch notoriety is not to be sought." *Id.* at 996. He apparently felt that the gravity of the risk of harm outweighed the First Amendment interests at stake:

What is involved here is information dealing with the most destructive weapon in the history of mankind, information of sufficient destructive potential to nullify the right to free speech and to endanger the right to life itself. . . .

The Secretary of State states that publication will increase thermonuclear proliferation and that this would "irreparably impair the national security of the United States." The Secretary of Defense says that dissemination of the Morland paper will mean a substantial increase in the risk of thermonuclear proliferation and lead to use or threats that would "adversely affect the national security of the United States." . . .

A mistake in ruling against The Progressive will seriously infringe cherished First Amendment rights. . . . It will curtail defendants' First Amendment rights in a drastic and substantial fashion. It will infringe upon our right to know and to be informed as well.

A mistake in ruling against the United States could pave the way for thermonuclear annihilation for us all. In that event, our right to life is extinguished and the right to publish becomes moot.

In the *Near* case, the Supreme Court recognized that publication of troop movements in time of war would threaten national security and could therefore be restrained. Times have changed significantly since 1931 when *Near* was decided. Now war by foot soldiers has been replaced in large part by war by machines and bombs. No longer need there be any advance warning or any preparation time before a nuclear war could be commenced.

In light of these factors, this Court concludes that publication of the technical information on the hydrogen bomb contained in the article is analogous to publication of troop movements or locations in time of war and falls within the extremely narrow exception to the rule against prior restraint.

Because of this "disparity of risk," because the government has met its heavy burden of showing justification for the imposition of a prior restraint . . . and because the Court is unconvinced that suppression of the objected-to technical portions of the Morland article would in any plausible fashion impede the defendants in their laudable crusade to stimulate public knowledge of nuclear armament and bring about enlightened debate on national policy questions, the Court finds that the objected-to portions of the article fall within the narrow area recognized by the Court in *Near v. Minnesota* in which a prior restraint on publication is appropriate.

The government has met its burden under section 2274 of The Atomic Energy Act. In the Court's opinion, it has also met the test enunciated by two Justices in the *New York Times* case, namely grave, direct, immediate and irreparable harm to the United States. [467 F. Supp. at 995-996.]

In an opinion that was initially published secretly, the court subsequently refused to vacate its preliminary injunction. *United States v. Progressive, Inc.*, 486 F. Supp. 5 (W.D. Wis. 1979).

A writ of mandamus for expedited appeal was denied sub nom. *Morland v. Sprecher*, 443 U.S. 709 (1979). The government withdrew from a subsequent appeal to the Seventh Circuit Court of Appeals, however, when similar information appeared in another publication, and the case was dismissed. *United States v. Progressive, Inc.*, 610 F.2d 819 (7th Cir. 1979). The article was then published in *The Progressive*, Nov. 1979, at 14.

NOTES AND QUESTIONS

1. *Balancing Openness Against Possible Annihilation.* One can commiserate with the judge who faces a decision entailing such awesome potential consequences. It is fairly clear from the excerpt of the *Progressive* case, above, that the court applied a balancing test, but it is less clear that the *Pentagon Papers Case*, the ruling law, furnished that test. Even if, counting the dissenters, one concludes that a majority of the *Pentagon Papers* Court supported a balancing approach, on what basis can a court draw the balance justly? Commenting on the *Progressive* decision, one observer noted:

> Experts on nuclear proliferation agree that the obstacles preventing production of a nuclear weapon are not informational. Rather, they lie in acquiring the cadre of skilled scientists needed to reduce the information to application, building the sophisticated and expensive facilities needed for production, and obtaining the necessary plutonium or weapons grade uranium. If this is true, then describing the theory of the H-bomb can not be the equivalent of providing an H-bomb nor will it lead directly and immediately to providing one. . . .
>
> Although acknowledging that *New York Times* governed, the trial court in fact succumbed to the danger that the *New York Times* test was designed to prevent. Instead of requiring that the government meet its heavy burden of proof with clear and convincing evidence, the court weighed the interests on both sides. It balanced the gravity of the risk, posited to be death from nuclear annihilation, against the importance to the public of knowing the specific details of hydrogen bomb manufacture. With the issue thus presented, the result was a foregone conclusion. [Mary M. Cheh, *The Progressive Case and the Atomic Energy Act: Waking to the Dangers of Government Information Controls*, 48 Geo. Wash. L. Rev. 163, 199-200 (1980).]

2. *Security Through Openness?* Six years before the *Progressive* case, Edward Teller, the so-called father of the H-bomb, wrote to the *New York Times*:

> I urge the United States to move . . . toward unilaterally abandoning all forms of scientific and technical secrecy. . . . I advocate this in the enlightened self-interest of the United States. . . . First [because] in science there are very few real secrets. . . . Second [because of] the long term [adverse] effect of secrecy on scientific progress, especially in the United States. [Letter of May 27, 1973, *as republished in* The Progressive, May 1979, at 33.]

Howard Morland and *The Progressive* justified the alleged disclosure of the H-bomb secret on similar grounds. By proving that the secret was discoverable, they said, they sought to demonstrate that reliance on such weapons of mass destruction was a false form of security, and that dispelling the "mystique of secrecy" was essential for an open policy debate about the dangers these weapons posed. The *Washington Post* disagreed, calling the case "John Mitchell's dream case — the one the Nixon administration was never lucky enough to get: a real First Amendment loser." Do you agree? Should the author's or publisher's motives, assuming they could be ascertained, have played a role in the court's decision?

C. PUBLICATION AS A CRIME?

Recall that in his June 14, 1971, telegram to the *New York Times, supra* p. 1283, Attorney General Mitchell asserted that publication of the Pentagon study was "directly prohibited by the provisions of the Espionage Law." On June 15, 1971, following publication of the second installment of the *Pentagon Papers* in the *Times*, the government filed a petition in the federal district court seeking an injunction against further publication, in part to prevent a violation of §793(e) of the Espionage and Censorship Act.

Espionage and Censorship Act
18 U.S.C. §§793-798 (2006)

§793. Gathering, transmitting or losing defense information ...

(e) Whoever having unauthorized possession of, access to, or control over any document, writing, code book, signal book, sketch, photograph, photographic negative, blueprint, plan, map, model, instrument, appliance, or note relating to the national defense, or information relating to the national defense which information the possessor has reason to believe could be used to the injury of the United States or to the advantage of any foreign nation, willfully communicates, delivers, transmits or causes to be communicated, delivered, or transmitted, or attempts to communicate, deliver, transmit or cause to be communicated, delivered, or transmitted the same to any person not entitled to receive it, or willfully retains the same and fails to deliver it to the officer or employee of the United States entitled to receive it . . .
Shall be fined under this title or imprisoned not more than ten years, or both.

Federal District Court Judge Gurfein responded to that particular claim in the following way:

Assuming the right of the United States and, indeed, its duty in this case to attempt to restrain the further publication of these documents, the Government claims and the *Times* denies that there is any statute which *proscribes* such publication. . . . The Government relies [on §793(e)].

... It will be noted that the word "publication" does not appear in this section. The Government contends that the word "communicates" covers the publication by a newspaper of the material interdicted by the subsection. A careful reading of the section would indicate that this is truly an espionage section where what is prohibited is the secret or clandestine communication to a person not entitled to receive it where the possessor has reason to believe that it may be used to the injury of the United States or the advantage of any foreign nation. This conclusion is fortified by the circumstance that in other sections of [the Act] there is specific reference to publication. The distinction is sharply made in Section 794 entitled "Gathering or delivering defense information to aid foreign government." Subsection (a) deals with peace-time communication of documents, writings, code books, etc. relating to national defense. It does not use the word "publication." Subsection (b) on the other hand which deals with "in time of war" does punish anyone who "publishes" specific information "with respect to the movement, numbers, description, condition, or disposition of any of the Armed Forces, ships, [etc.]. ..."

Similarly, in Section 797 one who publishes photographs, sketches, etc. of vital military and naval installations or equipment is subject to punishment. ... [F]inally, in Section 798 which deals with "Disclosure of Classified Information" there is a specific prohibition against one who "publishes" any classified information. This classified information is limited to the nature, preparation, or use of any code, cipher, or cryptographic system ... for ... communications intelligence purposes. ...

... The Government does not contend, nor do the facts indicate, that the publication of the documents in question would disclose the types of classified information specifically prohibited by the Congress. Aside from the internal evidence of the language of the various sections as indicating that newspapers were not intended by Congress to come within the purview of Section 793, there is Congressional history to support the conclusion. Section 793 derives from the original espionage act of 1917 (Act of June 15, 1917, Chap. 30, Title I, Sections 1, 2, 4, 6, 40 Stat. 217, 218, 219). At that time there was proposed in H.R. 291 a provision that "(d)uring any national emergency resulting from a war to which the United States is a party or from threat of such a war, the President may, by proclamation, prohibit the publishing or communicating of, or the attempting to publish or communicate any information relating to the national defense, which in his judgment is of such character that it is or might be useful to the enemy." This provision for prior restraint on publication for security reasons limited to war time or threat of war was voted down by the Congress. [*United States v. New York Times*, 328 F. Supp. 324, 328-329 (S.D.N.Y. 1971).]

No reported case has been found of an Espionage Act prosecution of either a journalist or a media outlet. *See generally* Jennifer K. Elsea, *Criminal Prohibitions on the Publication of Classified Defense Information* (Cong. Res. Serv. R41404), Dec. 6, 2010. One very controversial recent case, however, suggested that possibility. It involved the prosecution of two lobbyists who received classified information from a DOD employee and passed it on to others outside the government. *United States v. Rosen*, 445 F. Supp. 2d 602 (E.D. Va. 2006). Although the case was ultimately dismissed, the court upheld the indictment of the lobbyists for aiding and abetting a violation of §793(d), *supra* p. 1263, which differs significantly from §793(e) only in its application to persons "lawfully having possession" of sensitive information:

Although the question whether the government's interest in preserving its national defense secrets is sufficient to trump the First Amendment rights of those not in a position of trust with the government is a ... difficult question, and although the authority addressing this issue is sparse, both common sense and the relevant precedent point persuasively to the conclusion that the government can punish those outside of the government for the unauthorized receipt and deliberate retransmission of information relating to the national defense. [*Id.* at 637.]

The lobbyists were not journalists, and the organization that employed them was not, strictly speaking, the press. But they had in common with members of the media the facts that they had no apparent intent to harm the United States or aid its enemies, that they had received and were in possession of national security information, and that they apparently conspired with someone in lawful possession of the information to transfer it to them in violation of the Espionage Act. The threat of this ruling to the media was clear. Indeed, the *Rosen* court indicated that it felt bound by the concurring opinions in the *Pentagon Papers Case*, noted above, which suggested that the result in that case might have been different had the government sought to prosecute the newspapers under §793(e). *Id.* at 638-639.

The posting of hundreds of thousands of sensitive U.S. government documents on the *WikiLeaks* Web site in 2010, see *supra* p. 1298, provoked many calls for criminal sanctions. *See, e.g.*, Ellen Nakashima & Jerry Markon, *WikiLeaks Founder Could Face Charges*, Wash. Post, Nov. 30, 2010. As of this writing, however, no decision had been made to prosecute either the *WikiLeaks* organization or its outspoken founder, Julian Assange.

NOTES AND QUESTIONS

1. *Lawyer as Advisor.* After reviewing the various provisions of the Espionage Act excerpted and paraphrased *supra* p. 1262, and described in Judge Gurfein's opinion above, what do you think of the advice counsel offered the *Times*, *supra* p. 1282, respecting the criminality of retaining and studying, or publishing, the papers? Could you answer this question without also reviewing the contents of the *Pentagon Papers* in the context of the ongoing national debate over the Vietnam War?

2. *More Legislative History.* When the *Pentagon Papers Case* reached the Supreme Court, Justice Douglas commended Judge Gurfein's statutory interpretation as "pre-eminently sound." *New York Times Co. v. United States*, 403 U.S. 713, 722 (1971) (concurring opinion). Indeed, Justice Douglas supplemented the district judge's analysis of the history of §793 by recalling that the Internal Security Act of 1950, Pub. L. No. 81-831, 64 Stat. 987, which amended and recodified §793, declared, "Nothing in this Act shall be construed to authorize, require, or establish military or civilian censorship or in any way to limit or infringe upon freedom of the press or of speech as guaranteed by the Constitution and no regulation shall be promulgated hereunder having that effect." 403 U.S. at 722 (Douglas, J., concurring). In light of this history, was there any justification for the charge respecting §793 made by the Attorney General in his telegram? A more extensive history of efforts to criminalize publication of all classified information may be found in Jennifer K. Elsea, *Protection of National Security Information* 15-23 (Cong. Res. Serv. RL33502), June 30, 2006.

3. *Criminal State of Mind.* In the leading precedent construing §793, the Court said:

The obvious delimiting words in the statute are those requiring "intent or reason to believe that the information to be obtained *is* to be used to the injury of the United

> States, or to the advantage of any foreign nation." This requires those prosecuted to have acted in bad faith. The sanctions apply only when scienter is established. [*Gorin v. United States*, 312 U.S. 19, 27-28 (1941) (emphasis added). Gorin was a Soviet national who obtained defense information from a Naval Intelligence investigator and relayed it to the Soviet Union.]

The *Gorin* case involved the violation of that section of the 1917 Espionage Act, later incorporated into §793(a) and (b), which explicitly requires proof of a culpable state of mind, namely "intent" or "reason to believe." See *supra* p. 1263. Section 793(e) does not expressly include the same scienter (criminal state of mind) or culpability requirement, but instead concerns "national defense information which information the possessor has reason to believe *could* be used to the injury of the United States" (emphasis added). Can you imagine that the *New York Times*, its editors, or its reporters *intended* to injure the United States? Do you think they had reason to believe that published excerpts of the *Pentagon Papers would* be used to injure the United States? That those excerpts *could* be so used? How could the government establish the scienter elements of a crime under each statutory provision?

In an exhaustive and authoritative analysis of the legislative history of the espionage laws, two commentators opined that courts should hold that §793(d) and (e) "are not applicable to communication or retention activities incidental to the non-culpable revelations of defense information." Harold Edgar & Benno C. Schmidt Jr., *The Espionage Statutes and the Publication of Defense Information*, 73 Colum. L. Rev. 930, 1058 (1973). What are the practical implications of their argument?

In the wake of publication by the *New York Times* and other papers of stories about warrantless electronic surveillance and secret monitoring of international banking transfers, see *supra* p. 609, there were calls for criminal prosecution of the *Times* and its staff. *See, e.g.,* Peter Baker, *Surveillance Disclosure Denounced*, Wash. Post, June 27, 2006; Gabriel Schoenfeld, *Has the New York Times Violated the Espionage Act?*, Commentary, Mar. 2006. *See also* Adam Liptak, *Gonzales Says Prosecutions of Journalists Are Possible*, N.Y. Times, May 22, 2006 (reporting a statement by Attorney General Gonzales that prosecution of journalists "is a possibility"); Scott Sherman, *Chilling the Press*, Nation, July 17, 2006. Would either §793(d) or §793(e) support a conviction? Would they support a conviction of *WikiLeaks*, which insists that its purpose in releasing sensitive documents is to "to reveal 'unethical behavior' by governments and corporations"? *See* Eric Schmitt, *In Disclosing Secret Documents, WikiLeaks Seeks "Transparency,"* N.Y. Times, July 26, 2010. The current indeterminacy of the law is examined in Stephen I. Vladeck, *Inchoate Liability and the Espionage Act: The Statutory Framework and the Freedom of the Press*, 1 Harv. L. & Pol'y Rev. 219 (2007).

If you think none of the Espionage Act provisions reviewed so far quite fits the *New York Times* or *WikiLeaks*, consider 18 U.S.C. §793(g), which declares:

> If two or more persons conspire to violate any of the foregoing provisions of this section, and one or more of such persons do any act to effect the object of the conspiracy, each of the parties to such conspiracy shall be subject to the punishment provided for the offense which is the object of such conspiracy.

Similar language appears in §794(c). Would a prosecutor have to show that a reporter or newspaper had the same criminal state of mind as its government source to secure a conviction under this provision? Would it matter for this purpose whether the classified information was spontaneously delivered to the paper by a Daniel Ellsberg or was solicited by the paper? *See* Justin Elliott, *Assange Prosecution Would Be "Extremely Dangerous,"* Salon.com, Nov. 30, 2010 (suggesting vulnerability of *WikiLeaks* if it actively solicited leaked diplomatic cables).

4. *Statutes That Expressly Criminalize Publication.* A number of other provisions of the federal criminal code expressly criminalize publication of specific, identified kinds of classified information. *See* Elsea, *supra* Note 2, at 2-11. In his concurring opinion in the *Pentagon Papers Case*, Justice White cited some of these — for example, 18 U.S.C. §797 (2006), which prohibits publication of photographs or other graphic representations of military installations, and 18 U.S.C. §798 (2006), *supra* p. 1264, which prohibits publication of "any classified information . . . concerning the communication intelligence activities of the United States" (including codes) or information obtained from such activities. The Intelligence Identities Protection Act, 50 U.S.C. §§421-426 (2006), as amended by Pub. L. No. 111-259, §363, 124 Stat. 2654, 2701-2702 (2010), criminalizes the intentional *disclosure* of information identifying a covert agent. It was suggested in the district court hearing in the *Pentagon Papers Case* that some of the material in the 47 volumes could have revealed information about the U.S. intelligence system or codes. If you were counsel for the *Times*, how would you have responded to such suggestions?

According to one court, "Under section 798, the propriety of the classification is irrelevant. The fact of classification of a document . . . is enough to satisfy the classification element of the offense." *United States v. Boyce*, 594 F.2d 1246, 1251 (9th Cir. 1979). Do you think that holding is consistent with the purpose of the Espionage Act? What are its implications for a defendant?

Justice White, concurring in the *Pentagon Papers Case*, also said that 18 U.S.C. §794(b) (2006), the statute under which Julius and Ethel Rosenberg were convicted of spying for the Soviet Union, *United States v. Rosenberg*, 195 F.2d 583 (2d Cir. 1952), might be relevant:

> Subsection (b) thereof forbids in time of war the collection or publication, with intent that it shall be communicated to the enemy, of any information with respect to the movements of military forces, "or with respect to the plans or conduct . . . of any . . . military operation . . . or any other information relating to the public defense, which might be useful to the enemy. . . ." [403 U.S. at 740 n.10.]

Was he right, in light of the fact that the *Pentagon Papers* were published in 1971, during the Vietnam War? Many of the documents released by *WikiLeaks* in 2010 included descriptions of U.S. combat activities in Afghanistan. Does that fact suggest liability under §794(b)? How do you think the government could prove the requisite "intent that [the information] shall be communicated to the enemy" in either case? Would sensitive information be less helpful to an enemy because it was communicated openly, rather than clandestinely?

Recall the *New York Times* story in late 2005 of the secret National Security Agency (NSA) warrantless electronic surveillance program, *supra* p. 609. Would the *Times* and its reporters be criminally liable under §798? How about §794(b)?

Why do you suppose Congress forbade the disclosure of certain specified kinds of information in some sections of the Espionage Act, while in other sections it described protected information in more general terms?

5. *The Decision Not to Prosecute.* While disclaiming any intimation that the *Times* had "committed a crime, or that [it] would commit a crime if it published the material in its possession," Justice White gave the strong impression that if the government had proceeded by way of criminal prosecution, instead of seeking injunctive relief, he would have found against the newspaper. *See* 403 U.S. at 737-740, particularly n.9. At least two other Justices, Burger and Marshall, recognized force in Justice White's statutory analysis. Why do you suppose the government did not undertake a criminal prosecution of the *Times*? Why did it not prosecute the paper for its 2005 story about the NSA's warrantless surveillance program? Why might it decide not to seek criminal sanctions against *Wikileaks* or its director, Julian Assange? How would such a prosecution, successful or not, affect press freedoms?

6. *Shooting the Messenger's Messenger?* Threatening criminal prosecution of a newspaper and its reporters is only one way to discourage publication of information that the government wants to keep secret. Another is to cut off the flow of that information by unmasking and prosecuting the reporters' sources. *See Branzburg v. Hayes*, 408 U.S. 665, 679-680 (1972). For example, when a *Washington Post* reporter wrote that the CIA operated a covert network of prisons for terrorism suspects in Eastern Europe and elsewhere, Dana Priest, *CIA Holds Terror Suspects in Secret Prisons*, Wash. Post, Nov. 2, 2005 (a story for which she was awarded a Pulitzer prize), the CIA asked the Justice Department to open a criminal investigation to determine the reporter's sources. David Johnston & Carl Hulse, *C.I.A. Asks Criminal Inquiry Over Secret-Prison Article*, N.Y. Times, Nov. 9, 2005. And when *New York Times* reporter Judith Miller refused to disclose to a grand jury her source of information about another leak, she was jailed for contempt for 85 days. *See* Don Van Natta Jr., Adam Liptak & Clifford J. Levy, *The Miller Case: A Notebook, a Cause, a Jail Cell and a Deal*, N.Y. Times, Oct. 16, 2005. The First Amendment, however, generally affords no protection to journalists who want to keep their sources confidential, at least from a grand jury. *Branzburg, supra.*

Because, in practical terms, such government responses threaten freedom of the press as surely as prior restraints on publication, there have been repeated efforts to enact federal "shield" legislation that would provide such protection. *See generally* Kathleen Ann Ruane, *Journalists' Privilege: Overview of the Law and Legislation in Recent Congresses* (Cong. Res. Serv. RL34193), Jan. 19, 2011. For example, the Free Flow of Information Act of 2009, H.R. 985, 111th Cong. (2010), passed by the House but not the Senate, would have created a privilege for any "person who regularly gathers, prepares, collects, photographs, records, writes, edits, reports, or publishes news or information that concerns local, national, or international events or other matters of public interest for dissemination to the public" commercially. Such a person could not have been forced by courts or executive agencies to furnish information that could reasonably have been expected to reveal the identity of a source, unless

 (A) disclosure of the identity of such a source is necessary to prevent, or to identify any perpetrator of, an act of terrorism against the United States or its allies or other significant and specified harm to national security with the objective to prevent such harm;

 (B) disclosure of the identity of such a source is necessary to prevent imminent death or significant bodily harm with the objective to prevent such death or harm, respectively; . . .

 (D)(i) disclosure of the identity of such a source is essential to identify in a criminal investigation or prosecution a person who without authorization disclosed

> properly classified information and who at the time of such disclosure had authorized access to such information; and
>
> (ii) such unauthorized disclosure has caused or will cause significant and articulable harm to the national security. [*Id.* §2(a)(3).]

Would this measure have prevented the jailing of Judith Miller? Do you think it struck the right balance between national security and the right of the press to keep the public informed? Why do you suppose even so modest a protection for journalists has been so difficult to enact?

Not everyone thinks a shield law is a good idea. *See, e.g.,* William H. Freivogel, *Publishing National Security Secrets: The Case for "Benign Indeterminacy,"* 3 J. Nat'l Security L. & Pol'y 95, 97 (2009) (arguing that "the press — and by extension the public — is better served by a continuation of the state of uncertainty than by brightline rules").

7. *Criminal Liability Based on Risk?* If the Morland article described *supra* p. 1300 had been published before the government learned of it, do you think *The Progressive* could have been successfully prosecuted for a violation of §2274 of the Atomic Energy Act, *supra* p. 1300? The defendants argued that there was no violation of §2274 because evidence that publication would "injure the United States or secure an advantage to any foreign nation" was merely speculative, and because the criminal intent required by §2274 could not be established.

But was the risk of harm to the nation even relevant? The language preceding the term "information" in §2274 is "having possession of, access to, control over, or being entrusted with any document, writing, sketch, photograph, plan, model, instrument, appliance, note, or information. . . ." Does the statutory context of the term "information" affect your answer?

8. *Ongoing Efforts to Criminalize Publication.* Recall from our discussion in the previous chapter that Congress has repeatedly refused to criminalize all unauthorized disclosures of classified information. See *supra* p. 1274. There have also been persistent efforts to adopt criminal penalties for publishing sensitive information. One recent example is the Securing Human Intelligence and Enforcing Law Dissemination Act, S. 315, 112th Cong. (2011), ironically dubbed the "SHIELD Act." It would extend the reach of Espionage Act §798, which already forbids publication of certain types of classified information, to cover human intelligence activities and the identities of intelligence sources or informants. Do you think it should be easier for the government to impose criminal penalties on journalists and the media for publishing information about national security? If so, can you suggest some corresponding ways to avoid prosecutions intended to prevent embarrassment or exposure of government wrongdoing, rather than to protect the nation?

D. INNOVATIONS IN CENSORSHIP

With increasing reliance on electronic media for the dissemination of information, one way to stanch the flow of sensitive data to the public may be to disable an electronic medium before it can release the data. When *WikiLeaks* posted hundreds of thousands of classified U.S. government documents on its Web site in 2010, that Web site immediately came under a concerted cyber attack seeking to shut it down. A Pentagon official claimed to have no knowledge of any DOD responsibility for the attack. *See* Jim Michaels, *WikiLeaks Actions: An Act of Cyberwar?*, USA Today, Dec. 14, 2010. Elements of the Defense Department are nevertheless believed to be able to launch such attacks, which arguably are illegal under the Computer Fraud and Abuse Act, 18 U.S.C. §1030 (2006 & Supp. III 2009), and which are almost impossible to trace to their sources. Can you think of any way to regulate the government's use of cyber weaponry to halt what might otherwise be publication protected by the First Amendment? Can government officials at least be made accountable for such use?

In one apparently unprecedented case the government issued a subpoena in connection with a grand jury investigation requiring the return of "any and all copies" of a classified document leaked to the American Civil Liberties Union (ACLU), asserting authority under the Espionage Act. *Government Subpoenas ACLU to Recover Classified Document*, Secrecy News, Dec. 14, 2006. When the ACLU moved to quash, the Justice Department determined that the document had in fact been declassified, and it withdrew the subpoena. *Government Withdraws Subpoena Against ACLU*, Secrecy News, Dec. 19, 2006.

More recently, a court issued a subpoena under seal for the Web site Twitter to turn over records of alleged *WikiLeaks* supporters, including subscriber and user names, mailing and e-mail addresses, times and durations of uses, length of service, network address, and means and sources of payment for the service. *See* Electronic Frontier Found., *Government Demands for Twitter Records of Birgitta Jonsdottir* (n.d.), *at* https://www.eff.org/cases/government-demands-twitter-records (with links to supporting documents). Should such an effort to ferret out a possible leak source be conducted secretly? Should we be concerned that the data sought are so wide-ranging and personal? Is the approval of a judge adequate protection against a possibly groundless government fishing expedition? What are the First Amendment implications of such a collection?

A more familiar response to unauthorized publication of sensitive information is to seek to punish the author or publisher, either criminally, see *supra* p. 1262, or civilly, as we saw in the government's suit against Frank Snepp, *supra* p. 1253 — in order to discourage others from publishing without government approval. For example, the CIA recently sued a former clandestine services officer for breach of his nondisclosure agreement, when he published *The Human Factor: Inside the CIA's Dysfunctional Intelligence Culture. CIA Sues Author in Prepublication Review Dispute*, Secrecy News, Oct. 19, 2010.

Government officials employed a different tactic in a case in which a former Defense Intelligence Agency (DIA) analyst, Anthony Shaffer, published an Afghan war memoir, *Operation Dark Heart*, that they said disclosed classified information. Although the manuscript for the book was initially cleared by Army reviewers, a subsequent vetting by the DIA raised concerns about its content, but not in time to try to stop the printing of the book or early distribution of some copies. The Defense Department purchased and destroyed what was left of the entire first printing of 10,000 copies, then negotiated an agreement with the author to publish subsequent editions with the allegedly classified passages blacked out. *See* Scott Shane,

Pentagon Plan: Buying Books to Keep Secrets, N.Y. Times, Sept. 10, 2010; Scott Shane, *Afghanistan: Copies of War Memoir Are Destroyed*, N.Y. Times, Sept. 24, 2010. If the publisher, St. Martin's Press, had refused to sell the books to the Pentagon, could the government have compelled the sale? Should the government be allowed to use its overwhelming economic power in the marketplace to stop the publication of information over which it has otherwise lost control? If your answer is that in extreme cases it should, can you describe a regulatory mechanism that would prevent abuses of this power?

Appendix

Constitution of the United States

We the People of the United States, in Order to form a more perfect Union, establish Justice, insure domestic Tranquility, provide for the common defence, promote the general Welfare, and secure the Blessings of Liberty to ourselves and our Posterity, do ordain and establish this Constitution for the United States of America.

Article I

Section 1. All legislative Powers herein granted shall be vested in a Congress of the United States, which shall consist of a Senate and House of Representatives.

Section 2. The House of Representatives shall be composed of Members chosen every second Year by the People of the several States, and the Electors in each State shall have the Qualifications requisite for Electors of the most numerous Branch of the State Legislature....

The House of Representatives shall chuse their Speaker and other Officers; and shall have the sole Power of Impeachment.

Section 3. The Senate of the United States shall be composed of two Senators from each State, [chosen by the Legislature thereof,][1] for six Years; and each Senator shall have one Vote....

The Senate shall have the sole Power to try all Impeachments. When sitting for that Purpose, they shall be on Oath or Affirmation. When the President of the United States is tried, the Chief Justice shall preside: And no Person shall be convicted without the Concurrence of two thirds of the Members present.

Judgment in Cases of Impeachment shall not extend further than to removal from Office, and disqualification to hold and enjoy any Office of honor, Trust or Profit under the United States: but the Party convicted shall nevertheless be liable and subject to Indictment, Trial, Judgment and Punishment, according to Law.

Section 4. The Times, Places and Manner of holding Elections for Senators and Representatives, shall be prescribed in each State by the Legislature thereof; but the

---

1. Changed by the Seventeenth Amendment to read "elected by the people thereof."

Congress may at any time by Law make or alter such Regulations, except as to the Places of chusing Senators.

The Congress shall assemble at least once in every Year, and such Meeting shall [be on the first Monday in December,]² unless they shall by Law appoint a different Day.

Section 5. . . . Each House shall keep a Journal of its Proceedings, and from time to time publish the same, excepting such Parts as may in their Judgment require Secrecy; and the Yeas and Nays of the Members of either House on any question shall, at the Desire of one fifth of those Present, be entered on the Journal. . . .

Section 6. The Senators and Representatives shall receive a Compensation for their Services, to be ascertained by Law, and paid out of the Treasury of the United States. They shall in all Cases, except Treason, Felony and Breach of the Peace, be privileged from Arrest during their Attendance at the Session of their respective Houses, and in going to and returning from the same; and for any Speech or Debate in either House, they shall not be questioned in any other Place.

. . . [N]o Person holding any Office under the United States, shall be a Member of either House during his Continuance in Office.

Section 7. All Bills for raising Revenue shall originate in the House of Representatives; but the Senate may propose or concur with amendments as on other Bills.

Every Bill which shall have passed the House of Representatives and the Senate, shall, before it becomes a Law, be presented to the President of the United States; If he approve he shall sign it, but if not he shall return it, with his Objections to that House in which it shall have originated, who shall enter the Objections at large on their Journal, and proceed to reconsider it. If after such Reconsideration two thirds of that House shall agree to pass the Bill, it shall be sent, together with the Objections, to the other House, by which it shall likewise be reconsidered, and if approved by two thirds of that House, it shall become a Law. . . . If any Bill shall not be returned by the President within ten Days (Sundays excepted) after it shall have been presented to him, the Same shall be a Law, in like Manner as if he had signed it, unless the Congress by their Adjournment prevent its Return, in which Case it shall not be a Law.

Every Order, Resolution, or Vote to which the Concurrence of the Senate and House of Representatives may be necessary (except on a question of Adjournment) shall be presented to the President of the United States; and before the Same shall take Effect, shall be approved by him, or being disapproved by him, shall be repassed by two thirds of the Senate and House of Representatives, according to the Rules and Limitations prescribed in the Case of a Bill.

Section 8. [1] The Congress shall have Power To lay and collect Taxes, Duties, Imposts and Excises, to pay the Debts and provide for the common Defence and general Welfare of the United States; but all Duties, Imposts and Excises shall be uniform throughout the United States;

---

2. Changed by section 2 of the Twentieth Amendment to read "begin at noon on the 3d day of January."

[2] To borrow Money on the credit of the United States;

[3] To regulate Commerce with foreign Nations, and among the several States, and with the Indian Tribes;

[4] To establish an uniform Rule of Naturalization . . . ;

[9] To constitute Tribunals inferior to the supreme Court;

[10] To define and punish Piracies and Felonies committed on the high Seas, and Offences against the Law of Nations;

[11] To declare War, grant Letters of Marque and Reprisal, and make Rules concerning Captures on Land and Water;

[12] To raise and support Armies, but no Appropriation of Money to that Use shall be for a longer Term than two Years;

[13] To provide and maintain a Navy;

[14] To make Rules for the Government and Regulation of the land and naval Forces;

[15] To provide for calling forth the Militia to execute the Laws of the Union, suppress Insurrections and repel Invasions;

[16] To provide for organizing, arming, and disciplining, the Militia, and for governing such Part of them as may be employed in the Service of the United States, reserving to the States respectively, the Appointment of the Officers, and the Authority of training the Militia according to the discipline prescribed by Congress; . . .

[18] To make all Laws which shall be necessary and proper for carrying into Execution the foregoing Powers, and all other Powers vested by this Constitution in the Government of the United States, or in any Department or Officer thereof.

Section 9. . . . [2] The Privilege of the Writ of Habeas Corpus shall not be suspended, unless when in Cases of Rebellion or Invasion the public Safety may require it.

[3] No Bill of Attainder or ex post facto Law shall be passed. . . .

[7] No Money shall be drawn from the Treasury, but in Consequence of Appropriations made by Law; and a regular Statement and Account of the Receipts and Expenditures of all public Money shall be published from time to time.

[8] No Title of Nobility shall be granted by the United States: And no Person holding any Office of Profit or Trust under them, shall, without the Consent of the Congress, accept of any present, Emolument, Office, or Title, of any kind whatever, from any King, Prince, or foreign State.

Section 10. [1] No State shall enter into any Treaty, Alliance, or Confederation; grant Letters of Marque and Reprisal; coin Money; emit Bills of Credit; make any Thing but gold and silver Coin a Tender in Payment of Debts; pass any Bill of Attainder, ex post facto Law, or Law impairing the Obligation of Contracts, or grant any Title of Nobility. . . .

[3] No State shall, without the Consent of Congress, lay any Duty of Tonnage, keep Troops, or Ships of War in time of Peace, enter into any Agreement or Compact with another State, or with a foreign Power, or engage in War, unless actually invaded, or in such imminent Danger as will not admit of delay.

Article II

Section 1. The executive Power shall be vested in a President of the United States of America. He shall hold his Office during the Term of four Years, and, together with the Vice President, chosen for the same Term, be elected, as follows . . .

Before he enter on the Execution of his Office, he shall take the following Oath or Affirmation: — "I do solemnly swear (or affirm) that I will faithfully execute the Office of President of the United States, and will to the best of my Ability, preserve, protect and defend the Constitution of the United States."

Section 2. The President shall be Commander in Chief of the Army and Navy of the United States, and of the Militia of the several States, when called into the actual Service of the United States; he may require the Opinion, in writing, of the principal Officer in each of the executive Departments, upon any Subject relating to the Duties of their respective Offices, and he shall have Power to grant Reprieves and Pardons for Offences against the United States, except in Cases of Impeachment.

He shall have Power, by and with the Advice and Consent of the Senate, to make Treaties, provided two thirds of the Senators present concur; and he shall nominate, and by and with the Advice and Consent of the Senate, shall appoint Ambassadors, other public Ministers and Consuls, Judges of the supreme Court, and all other Officers of the United States, whose Appointments are not herein otherwise provided for, and which shall be established by Law: but the Congress may by Law vest the Appointment of such inferior Officers, as they think proper, in the President alone, in the Courts of Law, or in the Heads of Departments. . . .

Section 3. He shall from time to time give to the Congress Information of the State of the Union, and recommend to their Consideration such Measures as he shall judge necessary and expedient; he may, on extraordinary Occasions, convene both Houses, or either of them, and in Case of Disagreement between them, with Respect to the Time of Adjournment, he may adjourn them to such Time as he shall think proper; he shall receive Ambassadors and other public Ministers; he shall take Care that the Laws be faithfully executed, and shall Commission all the Officers of the United States.

Section 4. The President, Vice President and all civil Officers of the United States, shall be removed from Office on Impeachment for, and Conviction of, Treason, Bribery, or other high Crimes and Misdemeanors.

Article III

Section 1. The judicial Power of the United States, shall be vested in one supreme Court, and in such inferior Courts as the Congress may from time to time ordain and establish. The Judges, both of the supreme and inferior Courts, shall hold their Offices during good Behaviour, and shall, at stated Times, receive for their Services, a Compensation, which shall not be diminished during their Continuance in Office.

Section 2. The judicial Power shall extend to all Cases, in Law and Equity, arising under this Constitution, the Laws of the United States, and Treaties made, or which shall be made, under their Authority;— to all Cases affecting Ambassadors, other public Ministers and Consuls;— to all Cases of admiralty and maritime Jurisdiction;— to Controversies to which the United States shall be a Party;— to Controversies between two or more States;— [between a State and Citizens of another State;—] between Citizens of different States,— between Citizens of the same State claiming Lands under Grants of different States, [and between a State, or the Citizens thereof, and foreign States, Citizens or Subjects.][3]

In all Cases affecting Ambassadors, other public Ministers and Consuls, and those in which a State shall be Party, the supreme Court shall have original Jurisdiction. In all the other Cases before mentioned, the supreme Court shall have appellate Jurisdiction, both as to Law and Fact, with such Exceptions, and under such Regulations as the Congress shall make. . . .

Section 3. Treason against the United States, shall consist only in levying War against them, or in adhering to their Enemies, giving them Aid and Comfort. No Person shall be convicted of Treason unless on the Testimony of two Witnesses to the same overt Act, or on Confession in open Court.

The Congress shall have Power to declare the Punishment of Treason, but no Attainder of Treason shall work Corruption of Blood, or Forfeiture except during the Life of the Person attainted.

Article IV . . .

Section 4. The United States shall guarantee to every State in this Union a Republican Form of Government, and shall protect each of them against Invasion; and on Application of the Legislature, or of the Executive (when the Legislature cannot be convened) against domestic Violence. . . .

Article VI . . .

This Constitution, and the Laws of the United States which shall be made in Pursuance thereof; and all Treaties made, or which shall be made, under the Authority of the United States, shall be the supreme Law of the Land; and the Judges in every State shall be bound thereby, any Thing in the Constitution or Laws of any State to the Contrary notwithstanding.

The Senators and Representatives before mentioned, and the Members of the several State Legislatures, and all executive and judicial Officers, both of the United States and of the several States, shall be bound by Oath or Affirmation, to support this Constitution; . . . .

---

3. The bracketed material in this section is changed by the Eleventh Amendment.

AMENDMENTS TO THE CONSTITUTION OF THE UNITED STATES OF AMERICA

Amendment I

Congress shall make no law respecting an establishment of religion, or prohibiting the free exercise thereof; or abridging the freedom of speech, or of the press, or the right of the people peaceably to assemble, and to petition the Government for a redress of grievances.

Amendment II

A well regulated Militia, being necessary to the security of a free State, the right of the people to keep and bear Arms, shall not be infringed.

Amendment III

No Soldier shall, in time of peace be quartered in any house, without the consent of the Owner, nor in time of war, but in a manner to be prescribed by law.

Amendment IV

The right of the people to be secure in their persons, houses, papers, and effects, against unreasonable searches and seizures, shall not be violated, and no Warrants shall issue, but upon probable cause, supported by Oath or affirmation, and particularly describing the place to be searched, and the persons or things to be seized.

Amendment V

No person shall be held to answer for a capital, or otherwise infamous crime, unless on a presentment or indictment of a Grand Jury, except in cases arising in the land or naval forces, or in the Militia, when in actual service in time of War or public danger; nor shall any person be subject for the same offence to be twice put in jeopardy of life or limb, nor shall be compelled in any criminal case to be a witness against himself, nor be deprived of life, liberty, or property, without due process of law; nor shall private property be taken for public use without just compensation.

Amendment VI

In all criminal prosecutions, the accused shall enjoy the right to a speedy and public trial, by an impartial jury of the State and district wherein the crime shall have been committed; which district shall have been previously ascertained by law, and to be informed of the nature and cause of the accusation; to be confronted with the witnesses against him; to have compulsory process for obtaining witnesses in his favor, and to have the assistance of counsel for his defence. . . .

Amendment VIII

Excessive bail shall not be required, nor excessive fines imposed, nor cruel and unusual punishments inflicted.

Amendment IX

The enumeration in the Constitution of certain rights shall not be construed to deny or disparage others retained by the people.

Amendment X

The powers not delegated to the United States by the Constitution, nor prohibited by it to the States, are reserved to the States respectively, or to the people. . . .

Amendment XIV

Section 1. All persons born or naturalized in the United States and subject to the jurisdiction thereof, are citizens of the United States and of the State wherein they reside. No State shall make or enforce any law which shall abridge the privileges or immunities of citizens of the United States; nor shall any State deprive any person of life, liberty, or property, without due process of law; nor deny to any person within its jurisdiction the equal protection of the laws. . . .

Table of Cases

Principal cases are set in italics. Cases cited in the authors' text, notes, and questions are set in Roman type.

Index